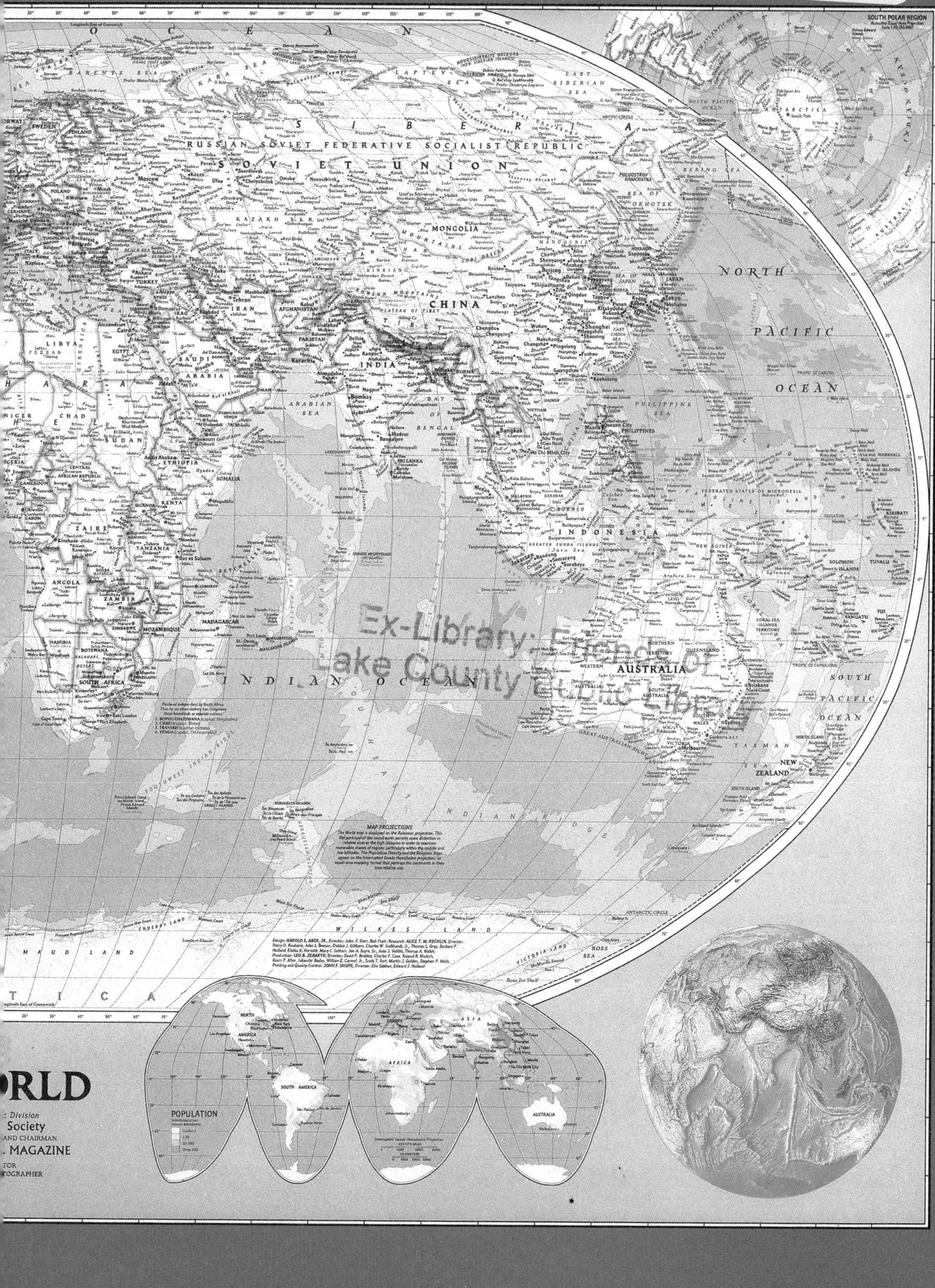
SOUTH POLAR REGION
RUSSIAN SOVIET FEDERATIVE SOCIALIST REPUBLIC
SOVIET UNION
SIBERIA
MONGOLIA
CHINA
INDIA
NORTH PACIFIC OCEAN
PHILIPPINES
INDONESIA
AUSTRALIA
NEW ZEALAND
SOUTH PACIFIC OCEAN
INDIAN OCEAN
ARABIAN SEA
BAY OF BENGAL
SUDAN
ETHIOPIA
ZAIRE
ANGOLA
ZAMBIA
NAMIBIA
BOTSWANA
SOUTH AFRICA
MADAGASCAR
WILKES LAND
ROSS SEA
MAP PROJECTIONS
The World map is displayed on the Robinson projection. This flat portrayal of the round earth permits some distortion in relative sizes at the high latitudes in order to maintain reasonable shapes of regions particularly within the middle and low latitudes. The Population Density and the Religions maps appear on the Interrupted Goode Homolosine projection, an equal-area mapping format that portrays the continents in their true relative size.
Design: HAROLD E. ABER, JR., Director; John. F. Dorr, Bob Pratt; Research: ALICE T. M. RECHLIN, Director; Harry D. Kauhane, John L. Beeson, Debbie J. Gibbons, Charles W. Gotthardt, Jr., Thomas L. Gray, Barbara P. Holland, Eteika K. Horvath, Mary C. Latham, Jon A. Sayre, Sr., Juan J. Valdés, Thomas A. Walsh; Production: LEO B. ZEBARTH, Director; David P. Beddoe, Charles F. Case, Roland R. Nichols, Kevin P. Allen, Iskandar Baday, William E. Carmel, Jr., Scott T. Fort, Martin J. Golden, Stephen P. Wells, Printing and Quality Control: JOHN F. SHUPE, Director; Elie Sabban, Edward J. Holland
POPULATION
NORTH AMERICA
SOUTH AMERICA
EUROPE
AFRICA
ASIA
AUSTRALIA
Interrupted Goode Homolosine Projection
ORLD
c Division
Society
AND CHAIRMAN
L MAGAZINE
TOR
TOGRAPHER

Witness to a Century

*"When we embark on the great ocean of discovery, the horizon
of the unknown advances with us and surrounds us wherever we go.
The more we know, the greater we find is our ignorance."*

GARDINER GREENE HUBBARD
President, National Geographic Society, 1888

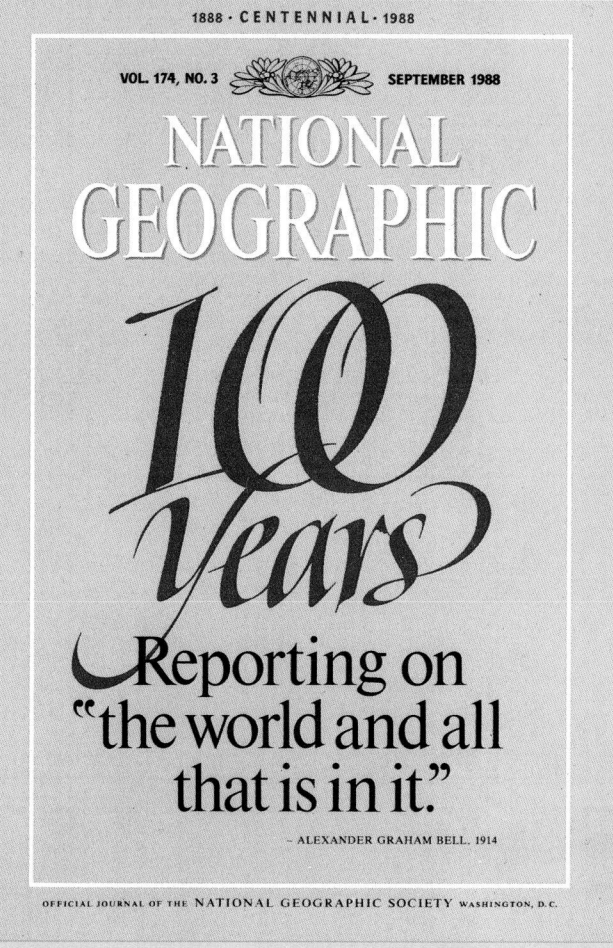

1888 · CENTENNIAL · 1988

VOL. 174, NO. 3   SEPTEMBER 1988

NATIONAL
GEOGRAPHIC
100
Years
Reporting on
"the world and all
that is in it."

– ALEXANDER GRAHAM BELL, 1914

OFFICIAL JOURNAL OF THE NATIONAL GEOGRAPHIC SOCIETY WASHINGTON, D.C.

Wonders of the ancient world, Egypt's Sphinx and Great Pyramid of Khufu, seen here in 1918, have intrigued the imagination for centuries.
DONALD McLEISH

Convulsions of an ever changing earth light the night on the Soviet Union's Kamchatka Peninsula, site of some 20 active volcanoes.
VADIM GIPPENREITER

A torrent of wildebeests plunges over a precipice to cross a river in Tanzania's Serengeti National Park, a premier wildlife refuge.
MITSUAKI IWAGO

Haunted look of famine in their eyes, refugees in Ethiopia gather at a feeding center run by the International Committee of the Red Cross.
STEVE RAYMER, NGS

INDEX
1888-1988

In 1963 a member of the first American expedition to ascend Mount Everest struggles to reach the summit, earth's highest point. BARRY C. BISHOP, NGS

THE NATIONAL GEOGRAPHIC SOCIETY 1989

A publication of the
NATIONAL GEOGRAPHIC SOCIETY

GILBERT M. GROSVENOR, *President and Chairman*
OWEN R. ANDERSON, *Executive Vice President*
WILBUR E. GARRETT, *Editor,* NATIONAL GEOGRAPHIC
ROBERT L. BREEDEN, *Senior Vice President, Publications*

STAFF FOR THIS BOOK:

EDITOR: Wilbur E. Garrett
MANAGING EDITOR: Thomas R. Smith
INDEX EDITOR: Jolene M. Blozis
DESIGN: Gerard A. Valerio
ILLUSTRATIONS EDITOR: Declan Haun
TEXT EDITOR: David Jeffery
LEGENDS EDITOR: Elizabeth A. Moize
ASSISTANT MANAGING EDITORS:
Carolyn H. Anderson, Barbara W. McConnell
INDEXING: George I. Burneston, Diane Coleman, James B. Enzinna,
Dianne L. Hardy, Lisa S. Jenkins, Bryan K. Knedler, Dian Levy,
Anne K. McCain, Elisabeth MacRae-Bobynskyj, Lucinda L. Smith,
Sarah Trott, Maureen Walsh, Michael G. Young, Susan G. Zenel
PICTURE EDITORS: Stephanie F. Lane, Lanng Tamura
EDITORIAL: *Consultant,* Andrew H. Brown; *Legends,* Jennifer Davidson,
John L. Eliot, Peter Miller, Cathy Newman, Peter Porteous, Cliff Tarpy,
Jane Vessels, A. R. Williams
DESIGN AND PRODUCTION: Betty Clayman-DeAtley, Shelley A. Bowen
RESEARCH: Lesley B. Rogers, Michaeline A. Sweeney; Nancy J. Boyd,
Catherine C. Fox, Ann B. Henry, Jan Holderness, Anne A. Jamison,
Amy E. Kezerian, Kathy B. Maher, Elizabeth Roessel Manierre,
Jean B. McConville, Miriam R. Miller, Patricia Penfield, Jeanne E. Peters,
Holly Reckord, Shelley L. Sperry, Abigail A. Tipton, Cheryl Ann Weissman,
Margaret Zackowitz
PHOTOGRAPHY: Sisse Brimberg, Joseph D. Lavenburg; *Photographic Services,*
NGS Custom Photographic Laboratory
ILLUSTRATIONS LIBRARY: Dori Babyak, Bill Bonner, Flora Davis,
Vickie Donovan, Robert A. Henry, April Howard, Scott Sroka,
H. Paul Walker, Catherine Weeks
ADMINISTRATION: *Assistant to the Managing Editor,* Elaine R. Ames;
Tracey L. Blanton, Paul J. Dillon, Victoria Ducheneaux, Karla Harris,
Liisa Maurer
TYPOGRAPHY: Bernard G. Quarrick; Kenneth G. Florence; Mark K. Allen,
Owen N. Banks, Jr., Richard A. Bredeck, Dennis J. Collins,
Patricia C. Goslee, Geza Istvan, Jr., Dennis R. Leonard, Phillip E. Plude,
John R. Reap, Kane A. Scarlett, Robert A. Thompson, Julie A. Tuason,
Robert M. Turner, Robert H. Weck, Jr., Martha A. Young
MANUFACTURING AND QUALITY MANAGEMENT: *Director,* George V. White;
Manager, Vincent P. Ryan; *Production Manager,* David V. Showers;
Production Assistants, Carol R. Curtis, Kevin P. Heubusch

14

Living face and countenance of stone share the strength of a common heritage. The forceful cast of their features bespeaks the Asian forebears of all American Indians. At Copán in Honduras, a bearded ruler might once flushed red with paint that once covered his stela, erected in 742. Leaders man have held the allegiance of their people by granting prestigious ceremonial tasks. A vision of installing religious duties prevails today in the highlands, home of this stone-haired Guatemalan elder of San Juan Atitán (above). Men win honor by doing voluntary service.

Lasting Value From Constant Change

By WILBUR E. GARRETT EDITOR

WHEN THE FIRST NATIONAL GEOGRAPHIC magazine appeared in 1888, the United States of America totaled only 38 states, Turks of the Ottoman Empire occupied the Holy Land, and Tsar Alexander III ruled Russia—though revolution was brewing. Scarcely a hundred years old, the U.S. was a serious young country convinced of its "manifest destiny." Serious men in Washington, D.C., felt the country needed a new geographic society so that "we may all know more of the world upon which we live" and founded one. Within a year they published the first issue of a magazine as their new society's principal means for the "increase and diffusion of geographic knowledge."

Now, some 7,000 magazine articles later, we bring you an index to the first century of that unending quest—a sort of field guide to a fabulous century that has packed within it a millennium's worth of social and political evolutions and revolutions and a mind-numbing cornucopia of scientific discoveries.

As a nation we've come from stampeding west and conquering the wilderness to voicing serious concern about saving what's left. As a magazine we've come from articles stressing the contributions of immigrant labor in a growing industrial complex to a 1988 report on the alarming surge of world population and overconsumption of natural resources by wealthy nations. The latter, as author Paul R. Ehrlich put it, "tends to undermine the life-support capacity of the entire planet."

This index attests that we as the Society and magazine have survived both as witnesses and players in a century that, like a runaway carousel, has seemed to move faster and faster. Yet we ride into our second century with a grip as strong as ever by heeding the editorial policies Gilbert H. Grosvenor developed and followed for more than 50 years. Late in life the "Chief" wrote about those pole stars of his career: "One principle was absolute accuracy. Others required that each article be of permanent value and avoid partisanship and controversy."

The last can no longer be avoided, nor is it always desirable or even responsible to do so. Ironically, absolute accuracy—still a goal—often makes controversy unavoidable. It is, however, possible and absolutely necessary to avoid partisanship.

As with the magazine's articles, we hope this volume itself will prove of lasting value—and not just as an index to a century of reporting. We hope that each essay, entry, page, and illustration will serve as a cue card for your memory and thereby better equip you to deal with a hard-charging future. The past is indeed prologue, but useful only if you know it.

Twice the subject of David Alan Harvey's photography, an elder from the Guatemalan highlands appears little changed in the 13 years since his 1975 appearance in a magazine article on the Maya.

Going again and again to the far corners of the world has been the essential job of NATIONAL GEOGRAPHIC writers and photographers for a century. The purpose is, of course, firsthand reporting. And sometimes after arduous journeying to such out-of-the-way places a staffer may encounter in a village a headman who exclaims, "Oh, the GEOGRAPHIC. Give my regards to Luis Marden."

DAVID ALAN HARVEY

"Let the World Hear From You"

The inventor, the architect, and the spiritual leader

By CHARLES McCARRY   EDITOR-AT-LARGE

O
N MAY 8, 1902, the volcano Pelée erupted on the Caribbean island of Martinique, releasing a pall of superheated ash and steam that killed nearly every man, woman, and child in the French colonial city of St. Pierre. A convict who happened to be confined in a dungeon and two or three others survived, but at least 30,000 lives were lost.

When news of the disaster reached Washington, Gilbert Hovey Grosvenor, the youthful Managing Editor of the monthly magazine of the National Geographic Society, telegraphed the Society's President, who was vacationing in Nova Scotia, to ask if he would approve spending $1,000 to send a two-man scientific expedition to the scene of the eruption. Grosvenor received the following reply:

Go yourself to Martinique in interests of Magazine and I will pay your expenses. . . . This is the opportunity of a lifetime— seize it. Start within 24 hours and let the world hear from you as our representative. Leave Science to . . . others and give us details of living interest beautifully illustrated by photographs.

— ALEXANDER GRAHAM BELL

Bell's telegram was the first true charter of this magazine, and every Editor since Grosvenor has been guided by Bell's masterly instructions to be decisive and quick in sending people and cameras all over the world to bring back "details of living interest beautifully illustrated by photographs."

When Bell became the second President of the National Geographic Society in January 1898, it had only about a thousand members, most of them in the District of Columbia, and debts of nearly $2,000. Bell did not want the job. He was not a geographer, and he was occupied with his inventions—among innumerable other projects, he was attempting to invent the airplane through experiments with tetrahedral kites.

As he later wrote in his diary, he became President of the Society only "in order to save it." Family feeling was involved also: The Society's first President, who died in 1897, was Bell's father-in-law, the lawyer and entrepreneur Gardiner Greene Hubbard.

Bell saw THE NATIONAL GEOGRAPHIC MAGAZINE as the means of

Editing took no holiday for Gilbert H. Grosvenor who bent to the task under a tent at the family's Nova Scotia summer place in about 1910. Giving counsel is his inventor father-in-law, and second National Geographic Society President, Alexander Graham Bell. Leaning on his chair is son Melville (who became Editor in 1957), while daughter Gertrude sits in front.

By 1910 Grosvenor, with Bell's encouragement, had taken a magazine begun as a drab scientific journal (below) and given it a popular style, including the first printing of photographs in color.

J.A.D. McCURDY

OCTOBER 1888

This text appeared in substantially the same form as "Three Men Who Made the Magazine," *National Geographic,* September 1988.

building a great organization that would permit anyone who was interested in the world to participate, as a member of the Society, in its exploration and discovery. Hitherto the privilege of supporting the great private expeditions that fascinated the 19th-century public with reports of strange peoples, inaccessible places, and great ordeals had belonged to a few scientists and men of wealth.

But Bell understood, as Gilbert Grosvenor remarked many years later, that "the simplest man takes pride in supporting research." This idea, more than any other, has been the basis for the growth of the Society and for the popularity of its magazine.

Bell himself loved reading encyclopedias—"articles not too long, constant change in the subjects of thought, always learning something I have not known before." Though he may not have thought of his plan in exactly this way, he set out to turn the magazine into the perpetual encyclopedia that it has since become.

Other members of the Board of Managers strenuously opposed opening membership to men and women who had no qualification for it other than an intelligent interest in the world and all that was in it, but Bell prevailed.

"I can well remember . . . how the idea was laughed at that we should ever reach a membership of ten thousand," Bell said at the National Geographic banquet in 1912. "Why, it was ridiculous!"

Yet by 1912 the Society had increased its membership more than a hundredfold, to 107,000. Prudent management of the Society's funds was providing an annual surplus of $43,000 to be devoted to the promotion of geographic science.

All this, Bell said, was primarily due to one man, Gilbert Grosvenor, who in less than 13 years had transformed the NATIONAL

Guiding lights of a fledgling enterprise, Alexander Graham Bell, right, and his son-in-law, Gilbert H. Grosvenor, walk arm in arm.

On the threshold of America's entry into World War I, 150 Geographic employees follow their young Editor, his wife, Elsie, and the Society's Assistant Secretary George W. Hutchison down Pennsylvania Avenue in Washington, D.C., during the Preparedness Parade, June 14, 1916. Led by President Woodrow Wilson, some 60,000 Washingtonians turned out that day to support the war overseas. Spurred by interest in the Society's new map of Europe, membership in 1916 reached a half million.

THE BETTMANN ARCHIVE (ABOVE); GRACE ADAMS

GEOGRAPHIC into "the greatest educational journal of the world."

Grosvenor was an unlikely candidate for such striking success. When Bell hired him on April Fools' Day, 1899, he was a slender, energetic 23-year-old preparatory-school teacher who had made an outstanding academic record and been a famous tennis player at Amherst College in Massachusetts but had not a single day of experience in the magazine business.

Bell had offered the opportunity to apply for the job to Grosvenor and his identical twin brother. Edwin, the younger twin by about an hour, planned a career as a lawyer, but Bert was deeply interested in Bell's offer.

He was already in love with the Bells' comely young daughter, Elsie May, whom he had gotten to know when her parents invited the twins to visit them in Nova Scotia in the summer of 1897. It was Elsie Bell who had suggested to her father that Bert might be the promising young man he had been looking for.

The NATIONAL GEOGRAPHIC MAGAZINE

Vol. XVI DECEMBER, 1905 No. 12

CONTENTS

	PAGE
The Parsees and the Towers of Silence at Bombay, India. By William Thomas Fee, U.S. Consul General, Bombay	529
China and the United States. By Sir Chentung Liang-Cheng, K.C.M.G., Envoy Extraordinary and Minister Plenipotentiary from China to the United States	554
What Has Been Accomplished by the United States Toward Building the Panama Canal. By Theodore P. Shonts, Chairman of the Isthmian Canal Commission	558
Russia in Recent Literature. By General A. W. Greely, Chief Signal Officer U. S. A.	562

Published by the National Geographic Society
Hubbard Memorial Hall
Washington, D. C.

$2.50 a Year 25 Cents a Number

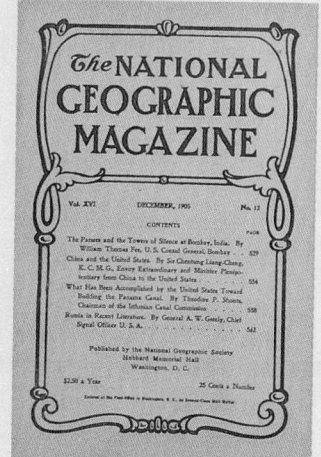

DECEMBER 1905

BELL HIRED Grosvenor at $100 a month, giving him the title of Assistant Editor and the mission of breathing new life into the GEOGRAPHIC. He also offered to put up $87,000 in capital—the same amount Bell and Gardiner Greene Hubbard had lost in an unsuccessful effort to popularize another magazine, *Science,* before selling their interest for $25.

Grosvenor refused, protesting that he lacked the experience to handle such a vast sum (the equivalent of more than one million dollars in today's currency). He said that he believed that new ideas and hard work, rather than an infusion of money, were the answers to the magazine's problems.

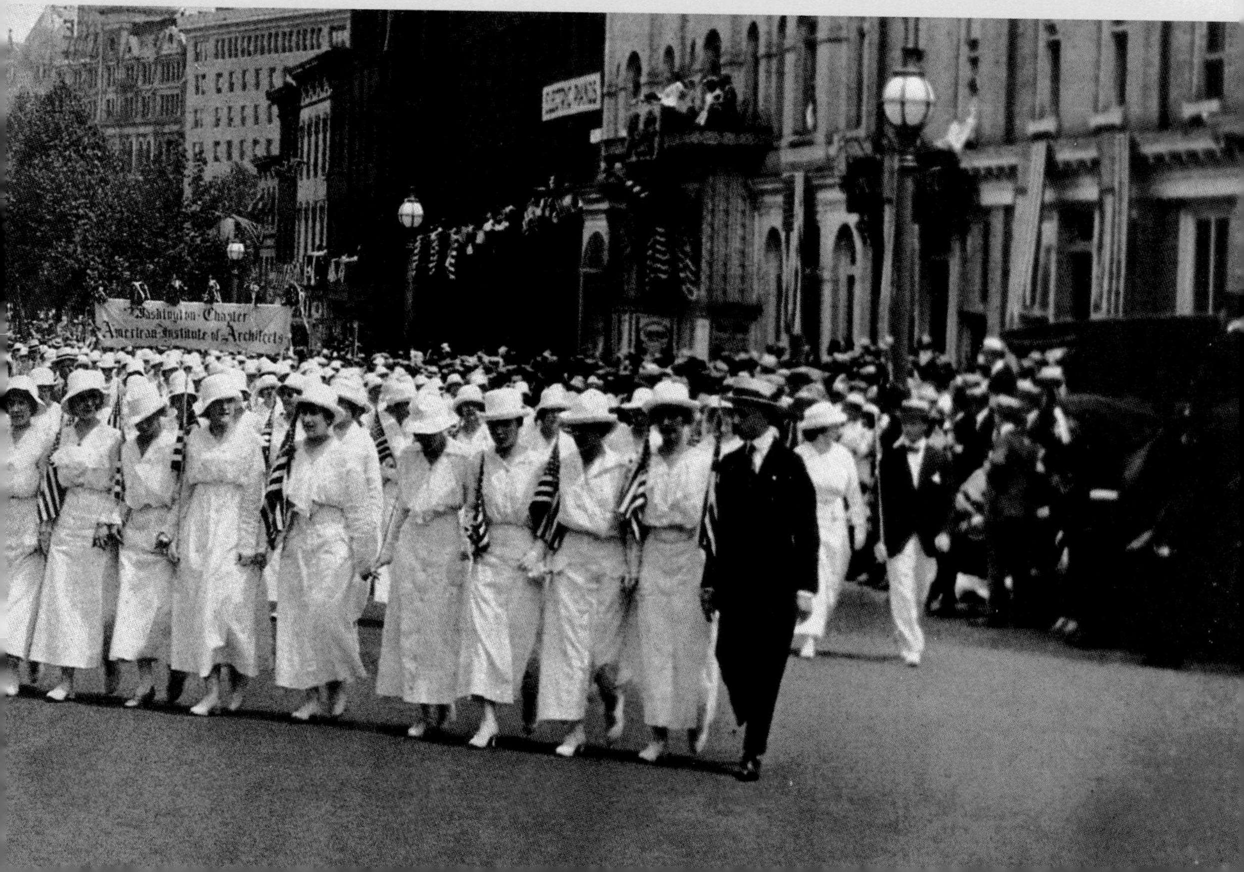

A Native American by the name of Two Whistles, a Crow Indian, achieved a measure of immortality in a photogravure by Edward S. Curtis. Concerned that future generations would never know the richness and diversity of what he considered a "vanishing race," Curtis photographed more than 80 tribes west of the Mississippi between 1900 and 1927. The 20 volumes of photographs and text that resulted are among the most thorough documents of North American Indian life ever produced. The National Geographic, which published a collection of his photographs in July 1907, boasts a complete set of his published volumes in its rare book collection.

EDWARD S. CURTIS

The unpaid Editor was English-born John Hyde, a Department of Agriculture statistician. Grosvenor believed that Hyde and a staff of 12 associate editors, also unpaid, were producing a magazine filled with "cold geographic fact, expressed in hieroglyphic terms which the layman could not understand." In fact, Hyde's magazine contained some colorful, even controversial writing. Hyde was no fainthearted editor where photographs were concerned, either. He published in November 1896 the first photograph of a bare-breasted woman to appear in the magazine.

Despite Bell's plan to change the style of the magazine, Grosvenor had no authority to do so. Nonetheless he went at his new job with a will, nominating his father, his twin brother, and his older brother, Asa, for membership, and pestering his father, Bell, and other eminent men to nominate their friends. The annual membership fee was then two dollars (worth about $28 in today's money), and by November 1899 he had signed up 750 new members.

In his efforts to brighten the magazine's pages, Grosvenor importuned his father to approach his old friend Gen. Lew Wallace, the author of *Ben Hur,* to contribute an article.

THEN AS LATER, Bert seemed to act on the principle that any problem could be solved by a combination of hard work, frank conversation, and good connections. In January 1904 Bell cabled Bert from Gibraltar asking that he arrange a "national reception" for the remains of James Smithson, which Bell was bringing from Genoa for reburial. The 28-year-old Grosvenor asked President Theodore Roosevelt for an American warship to transport Smithson's remains from New York to Washington. Roosevelt detailed the U.S.S. *Dolphin* for this mission. Grosvenor then persuaded the War Department to provide a military escort to accompany the casket of the benefactor of the Smithsonian Institution through the streets of Washington.

Inevitably Bert Grosvenor's youthful brashness and energy brought him into conflict with the anti-Bell faction—some of whom, Bert noted, had "long white beards."

"I do not intend to get out of their way, as they plainly hint they want me to," he wrote to Bell on August 6, 1900. A week earlier he had written these words to his father: "Mr. Hyde is bent on remaining editor and knows that if I stay in, he will go out. . . . Outwardly I am very respectful and submissive, though it makes me boil."

It was a hot summer in Washington, with more than 50 days when the temperature went up to 90 degrees. Grosvenor sought relief from the heat by going out onto the fire escape of the Corcoran Building, where the Society's two-room headquarters was located, and listening to the jolly tunes of a hurdy-gurdy playing in 15th Street below. He found surcease from his battles with Hyde and the whitebeards by describing them in heartfelt letters to Elsie Bell, who was traveling in Europe with her parents.

His tales of intrigue, treachery, and insult had effect. On August 30, 1900, Grosvenor received a letter from Elsie in which she promised to marry him. "I've got her at last and she won't get away—and won't try to, either," a triumphant Bert wrote his mother.

"I doubt whether Elsie would have been as sure of her own mind," Mrs. Bell wrote to Mrs. Grosvenor, "if all her love and sympathy had not been aroused by her indignation at the attacks upon him." The turning point came when Bert was threatened with dismissal. Bell returned posthaste from Europe "to see what I can do for my boy." The Board of Managers gave Grosvenor an $800 raise and the title of Managing Editor.

The infighting that marked this situation left a lasting residue of resentment. Sixty-two years later, in an interview with Assistant Editor Allan C. Fisher, Jr., Grosvenor described his opponents as "real stinkers."

S. S. McClure, the famous editor of *McClure's Magazine,* had recommended that the NATIONAL GEOGRAPHIC change its name, move to New York, abandon the membership idea in favor of newsstand sales, and avoid all mention of the National Geographic Society on grounds that geography was an uninteresting subject. Grosvenor had opposed all these ideas.

When he and Elsie returned from their honeymoon, they learned that the Executive Committee had arranged to have the magazine printed in New York.

Grosvenor canceled the printing contract on his authority as Managing Editor without consulting anyone and brought the magazine home to Washington, where he had it printed at half the cost.

This resolute action completed the rout of the opposition. In February 1903 Grosvenor was made the Editor of the magazine and Director of the Society. At the age of 27, Bert Grosvenor was in charge of everything.

Thereafter very few people outside the family, and almost no one at the Geographic, ever called him "Bert."

Dr. Melvin M. Payne, who came to the Geographic as a secretary in 1932 and rose to be Chairman of the Board of Trustees, says that he never heard anyone but Rear Adm. Richard E. Byrd and John Oliver La Gorce, the first member of the staff hired by Grosvenor, address him by his nickname. "Oh, he was it, the boss in every respect, no questions about that," says Dr. Payne.

E VERY EDITOR who came after Grosvenor has been, as he was and believed the Editor must be, an absolute monarch whose opinions, judgment, and word are final in everything having to do with the magazine.

Although Bell retired as President in 1903, the year after Hubbard Memorial Hall was donated by the family of Gardiner Greene Hubbard as the Society's first real headquarters, his interest in the magazine did not flag. Bell frequently sent his son-in-law story ideas, as well as packages of photographs, clippings, and advice on the technique of editing. Grosvenor did not always find Bell's suggestions practical. "Mr. Bell was always anxious to be an editor," he dryly observed to Allan Fisher in 1962.

Bell kept on urging Grosvenor to travel for the magazine. "Alec won't be content until Bert goes somewhere," Mrs. Bell wrote in 1902. "[This time] it is to the wilds of Newfoundland to ascertain the truth . . . of a mysterious valley shut in among mountains with a

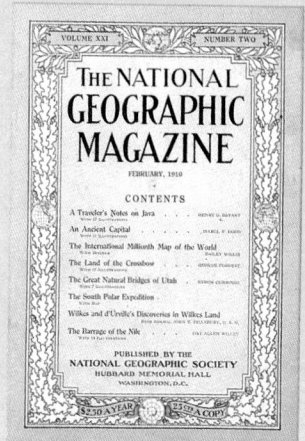

FEBRUARY 1910

A daring groundbreaker in its time, this picture of a Zulu man and his bride appeared in the November 1896 issue of the GEOGRAPHIC. It marked the beginning of the policy to show the peoples of the world as they are—a decision that, over the years, has sparked many a joke and cartoon. The accompanying article, "The Witwatersrand and the Revolt of the Uitlanders," was an ethnocentric description of an armed rebellion by British and other mining entrepreneurs against the Boer government during the early history of South Africa's gold industry.

still more mysterious river that disappears into the face of a perpendicular cliff 1,500 ft. high and goes—no one knows whither."

In 1907, responding to a request from Elsie Bell Grosvenor for his thoughts on the magazine, Bell wrote, "The features of most interest are the illustrations. . . . The disappointing feature of the Magazine is that there is so little in the text about the pictures. . . . It seems to me that one notable line for improvement would be either to adapt the pictures to the text *or the text to the pictures.* Why not the latter?"

In these four sentences, Bell predicted, if he did not invent, the whole future development of the GEOGRAPHIC. With his brilliant gift for perceiving the obvious, he saw that the photograph could be turned into a narrative device that was, for journalistic purposes, more dramatic, more enticing, and more interesting than words.

Grosvenor was a writer by necessity (as a young man he sold articles to other publications as a means of supplementing his earnings in addition to writing or rewriting most of the contents of the GEOGRAPHIC), and in the early years he spoke of improving the GEOGRAPHIC almost exclusively in terms of creating a more readable text. Yet he steadily guided the magazine in the direction Bell indicated. This may well have been because Grosvenor had already perceived that if he wished to make something new, he must use what was new—photography. He had published 11 pages of photographs of Lhasa, Tibet, from the Imperial Russian Geographical Society in the January 1905 issue, an editorial decision so unprecedented—and so expensive—that he expected to be fired for it. Instead readers stopped him in the street to congratulate him.

Grosvenor had printed the Lhasa pictures primarily to fill up empty pages, but when he saw the stir they created, he repeated the experiment, running 32 consecutive pages of photographs of the Philippines in April 1905.

No editor, as he often said, had ever before printed so many pictures (138) on one subject in a single issue, and he regarded this feature as a turning point in the life of the magazine.

Membership grew in 1905 from 3,400 to more than 11,000, and increased revenues permitted the Society to relieve Bell, after nearly six years, of the necessity of paying the first $1,200 of Grosvenor's annual salary out of his own pocket.

Thereafter Grosvenor was continually on the lookout for beautiful and unusual pictures, and by 1908 more than half the magazine's pages were devoted to photographs.

I N A LETTER FROM KYOTO, JAPAN, in 1912 Eliza R. Scidmore, an adventurous writer and photographer who may have been the first American professional geographer of her sex and was certainly the first woman to be elected to the Society's Board of Managers, gently tweaked Grosvenor's nose over his enthusiasm for photographs.

"Herewith 31 pictures of [Japanese] 'Women and Children,' mostly children, as you see," Miss Scidmore wrote. "I have had them made uniform in size and strongly colored, so that you can cover yourself all over with glory with another number in color and thereby catch a few thousand more subscribers."

This was a reference to Grosvenor's triumph in printing, in the November 1910 issue, 24 pages of hand-tinted photographs of scenes in Korea and China. These were black-and-white photographs that had been colored by a Japanese artist according to the instructions of the photographer, William W. Chapin.

The response was so overwhelming that Grosvenor inserted a color feature in every subsequent November issue of the magazine. "November," he explained, "is the big renewal number."

When true color photography was being perfected, he crowded the magazine with images captured by each new process.

Some thought that he overdid it, or did it with too little method. In Grosvenor's time modern ideas of page design had scarcely been thought about. Although GEOGRAPHIC editors provided layouts to show the printer where the words and pictures should go, photographs often appeared in the middle of articles that bore no relation to them whatever.

"It is not against color that my soul rebels. It is against the artificial massing of color, the lily-painting," wrote bluff Maynard Owen Williams later. Williams, the far-ranging Chief of the Foreign Editorial Staff who contributed 70 articles and more than 2,200 photographs to the magazine, described himself as "a rough-neck and a camera-coolie."

From an elephant hunt in Siam to icy Glacier Bay in Alaska, writer and photographer Eliza Ruhamah Scidmore reported on Asia and the North American frontier at the turn of the century. An associate editor, she became the first woman on the Society's Board of Managers, in 1892. To meet the new rage for color images, she exquisitely hand tinted her photographs of Japanese children taken about 1910. Though this one (facing page) was not published, others from the set illustrated her article "Young Japan," in July 1914, the issue containing GEOGRAPHIC's first color-film photograph—a Lumière Autochrome of a Belgium flower show.

ELIZA R. SCIDMORE (OPPOSITE);
MARTIN LUTHER KING LIBRARY

Grosvenor pressed on. He had, wrote Frank Luther Mott in *A History of American Magazines,* "transformed the GEOGRAPHIC into a kind of periodical never before known."

Although it was clear very early that pictures were responsible for this success, Grosvenor continued to take pride in the progress of GEOGRAPHIC writing toward his goal of realistic reportage and simple, clear exposition, and with some reason.

Joseph F. Rock, the most famous and probably the most eccentric of the free-lance explorer-photographer-writers, distilled the style that made the GEOGRAPHIC into this paragraph:

"All was quiet and hushed, as I lay on my camp cot facing the tomb of the buddha whose room I occupied. Outside, the glacier stream roared, the thunder rolled, and Dordjelutru staged an electrical display in this weird canyon. I shivered. Here, all alone, in the presence of a sacred mummy in a hoary lamasery, I listened to the tempest breaking over the icy peak of Minya Konka. . . . Had time been set back a thousand years? Did I dream, or was it all reality?"

Rock and the others traveled by steamship across the oceans and by camel, mule, and litter across the land. Threatened by Chinese bandits, Rock and his coolies escaped with his trunks of cameras and film across a river on inflated goatskins. Correspondents sometimes vanished for a year or two at a time, returning with half a dozen stories and a motion picture.

Grosvenor did not restrict subject matter. "When I hear of a story that will interest our members," he said, "I do not ask if it is about geography." The excavation and mapping of the lost Inca city, Machu Picchu, by Hiram Bingham in 1912, was essentially archaeological—so much so that Grosvenor told Bingham at first that the work might not be "sufficiently geographic" to justify a grant of money. Bingham's findings, supported in part by a $10,000 Geographic grant, produced 186 pages of photographs, text, drawings, and maps for the April 1913 issue of the magazine. The lesson was a valuable one, and after that the Society covered every sort of expedition, flight, voyage, and excavation that promised to produce new knowledge—and good copy.

Honed by two decades of seeking "the last great geographical prize," Comdr. Robert E. Peary claimed victory at the North Pole on April 6, 1909. A staunch supporter, the Geographic contributed $1,000—an early research grant—to his final expedition and upheld Peary's navigational evidence when his discovery was challenged. In 1984 the magazine asked modern Arctic explorer Wally Herbert to evaluate Peary's record. He concluded in the September centennial issue that Peary may have missed the Pole by 30 to 60 miles.

ROBERT E. PEARY COLLECTION, NGS

GROSVENOR was keenly interested in what interested people. He studied other magazines for ideas, and at National Geographic lectures, which commonly attracted 3,000 people in the afternoon and another 3,000 in the evening, he watched both screen and audience to determine which pictures the people liked the most. He found that even well-brought-up young ladies preferred the dramatic ones and were not shocked by the most explicit material.

The result was a dazzling, and sometimes dizzying, array of stories about everything from backyard insects (Grosvenor's brother-in-law, David Fairchild, built a camera 12 feet long, making novel images of grasshoppers, flies, and ants many times larger than the creatures themselves) to royal tombs in Egypt to "The Acorn, a Possibly Neglected Source of Food" to the magnificently illustrated "Fifty Common Birds of Farm and Orchard."

Grosvenor let his writers describe things as they saw them, and they sometimes expressed opinions that would make a modern editor blanch. ("From the sounds [that blind street musicians in China] produced on their strange, discordant instruments," wrote Chapin in 1910, "we thought it would be much to their own advantage to be deaf also.")

Grosvenor tried to turn his writers into photographers, providing them with the best cameras available and all the film they needed.

Some resisted. Grosvenor explained the principle to Maynard Owen Williams: "The illustration made the National Geographic Magazine and the magazine's life depends on getting better and better pictures. The professional writer always *patronizes* the photographer. All right, let him, but pay no attention to him, but go ahead and *get pictures.*"

He continually warned Franklin L. Fisher, the conscientious Chief of the Illustrations Division, against penny-pinching. "Please note that I do not care whether he gets $50 or $100 or $200 worth more photographic material than he can use," he wrote in regard to Rock, a profligate user of film. *"The point to insure is that he get material to work on."*

As Williams told Assistant Editor Jesse R. Hildebrand, "Nothing lies as badly as a photograph that is not up-to-date."

More and more, Grosvenor came to regard text stories as an opportunity for photography. Often he would buy a manuscript, file it away, and wait for years for the photographs that might make it publishable. "There was quite a store of articles to be pulled out in case the subjects became newsworthy," recalls Frederick G. (Ted) Vosburgh, a professional journalist who in 1967 became the only word man to be appointed Editor of the magazine. "That meant you had to update an article that had been lying in the files for maybe ten years.

"Travel funds went mainly to the double threats, fellows like Maynard Owen Williams and that other great field man, Bob Moore, who could bring back the story in words and pictures," says Vosburgh. "Most of us had to write on our own time on subjects close to home to get stories into the magazine."

Grosvenor made himself into a first-rate photographer, and he was a student and teacher of the craft. Some of his pictures, particularly the luminously affectionate candid portraits that he made of his wife and children in the company of the Bells and other relations at their summer place at Baddeck, Nova Scotia, rank among the best ever taken by a GEOGRAPHIC photographer.

Grosvenor, the descendant of seven generations of New England gentry (the first Grosvenor to come to America was killed in 1691 by the blow of an Indian's tomahawk at Roxbury, Massachusetts), was a formal man who called his colleagues and most other people Mr. or Mrs. or Miss; the staff referred to him as "Chief."

There is a certain endearing stiffness to the many photographs of the solemn Grosvenor that were published in the magazine over the years, as if his affectionate wife had placed his aviator's cap on his head or propped him up against a redwood just before the photographer exposed the film.

Yet he was a gregarious man—he loved big ceremonial occasions

"Machu Picchu might prove to be the largest and most important ruin discovered in South America since the days of the Spanish conquest." Hiram Bingham confirmed his hunch a year after he hiked into the legendary Inca outpost in 1911. Backed in part by the Society's first archaeological research grant— $10,000—the Yale University history professor returned to the Andes leading the Peruvian expedition of 1912. Although the project was considered "archaeologic and not sufficiently geographic" at first, the results of Bingham's remarkable excavations in Peru filled the entire April 1913 issue and introduced the "lost city" to the world (following pages).

HARRY WARD FOOTE;
HIRAM BINGHAM (FOLLOWING PAGES)

and was never so happy as on an outing with his wife and children—who seems to have understood the value of humor.

"Father never minded all the jokes about the GEOGRAPHIC," says his daughter Dr. Mabel Grosvenor, a pediatrician. "He said they made people sit up and think about the GEOGRAPHIC."

Grosvenor had a keen sense of public relations. Remembering a dinner that he had inveigled his second cousin, William Howard Taft, who became the 27th President and the tenth Chief Justice of the United States, into attending, he said, "Mr. Taft came, and we got a lot of publicity for the magazine we needed."

Other Presidents, including Calvin Coolidge, who had played handball with Grosvenor at Amherst, visited the Geographic, especially to award the Society's Hubbard Medal to such noted explorers as Richard E. Byrd and Charles A. Lindbergh.

V OLKMAR K. WENTZEL, a member of the Foreign Editorial Staff, was reprimanded by the business office for spending $400 to buy a surplus army ambulance on assignment in India and emblazoning it with the American and Society flags and the legend *National Geographic Photo Survey of India*.

"I was so depressed I was ready to jump into the Ganges," Wentzel recalls. "However, a couple of days later I got a telegram from Dr. Grosvenor saying, 'Congratulations acquisition National Geographic Photo Survey Car.' He understood, you see."

When the *New Yorker* magazine ran a three-part profile of Grosvenor in 1943, some believed that the author, Geoffrey T. Hellman, had had a bit too much fun with the Chief's eccentricities, especially his passion for bird-watching and for inserting pictures of birds in the magazine at every opportunity. But Grosvenor liked

Among the first to make closeup photographs of wildlife in natural environments, George Shiras 3d pioneered techniques of night photography, which he shared in the GEOGRAPHIC of July 1906. He often worked from a skiff's bow, there mounting a jacklight and two cameras of different focal lengths. Hand-holding a pan of magnesium flash powder, Shiras pursued his quarry "at a time when the hunter ordinarily is sound asleep."

His 58-page article pleased readers but offended two Society board members who resigned, huffing that the Editor had turned "the magazine into a picture book."

GEORGE SHIRAS 3D

and was never so happy as on an outing with his wife and children—who seems to have understood the value of humor.

"Father never minded all the jokes about the GEOGRAPHIC," says his daughter Dr. Mabel Grosvenor, a pediatrician. "He said they made people sit up and think about the GEOGRAPHIC."

Grosvenor had a keen sense of public relations. Remembering a dinner that he had inveigled his second cousin, William Howard Taft, who became the 27th President and the tenth Chief Justice of the United States, into attending, he said, "Mr. Taft came, and we got a lot of publicity for the magazine we needed."

Other Presidents, including Calvin Coolidge, who had played handball with Grosvenor at Amherst, visited the Geographic, especially to award the Society's Hubbard Medal to such noted explorers as Richard E. Byrd and Charles A. Lindbergh.

VOLKMAR K. WENTZEL, a member of the Foreign Editorial Staff, was reprimanded by the business office for spending $400 to buy a surplus army ambulance on assignment in India and emblazoning it with the American and Society flags and the legend *National Geographic Photo Survey of India*.

"I was so depressed I was ready to jump into the Ganges," Wentzel recalls. "However, a couple of days later I got a telegram from Dr. Grosvenor saying, 'Congratulations acquisition National Geographic Photo Survey Car.' He understood, you see."

When the *New Yorker* magazine ran a three-part profile of Grosvenor in 1943, some believed that the author, Geoffrey T. Hellman, had had a bit too much fun with the Chief's eccentricities, especially his passion for bird-watching and for inserting pictures of birds in the magazine at every opportunity. But Grosvenor liked

the portrait, admired Hellman's writing and reporting, and wrote *New Yorker* Editor Harold Ross a courtly letter of thanks for "the honor you have done me and the National Geographic Magazine."

A somewhat stunned Ross wrote back: "The National Geographic was my father's favorite magazine. . . . If he were alive, I'd show him your letter and impress him as I never was able to impress him during his lifetime."

Grosvenor's patrician manner probably encouraged the legend that the GEOGRAPHIC was a sort of gentlemen's club, but in fact Grosvenor often was one of the few certifiable gentlemen on the premises. He hired people for what he thought they could do for the magazine, not for their social or educational credentials.

Many belonged to that class of self-taught American go-getters that flourished in the 19th and early 20th centuries. Charles Martin, the inventive head of the photo lab, had been an Army enlisted man whom Dean Worcester, then a government official, had borrowed to make photographs for the article on the Philippines. Joseph Rock was the son of an Austrian manservant. John Oliver La Gorce, Grosvenor's right-hand man for half a century and the third Editor of the magazine, was a charming and gregarious person who made friends with some of the most famous people in the world, but he had only a high-school education.

Some were newspapermen or footloose youths who simply walked in off the street and captured Grosvenor's fancy. Luis Marden, a photographer, writer, and Renaissance man who discovered the wreck of the *Bounty* among many other feats and became one of the greatest stars in the history of the magazine, overheard another man on an elevator saying that the GEOGRAPHIC was looking for an unmarried man to work as a photographer. He applied for the job and, somewhat to his own surprise, got it.

The place became so militantly unpatrician, in fact, that Grosvenor felt that he must warn Franklin Fisher. "I wish you would rid yourself of your grudge against Boston Harvard men," he wrote in 1934. "Our job on the National Geographic Magazine is to get the best material, regardless of whether we like or dislike the speech or manners of the man who has it."

Grosvenor was proud of having been among the first employers in Washington to hire female secretaries and clerks and thought that they were far better than men at such work. His longtime Director of Personnel, Mabel Strider, is still remembered as one of the most powerful figures in the annals of the Society. It is clear from Grosvenor's correspondence with Eliza Scidmore and many others that he liked women and wrote to them in the same tone that he used to address male correspondents. In the 1930s and 1940s he urged his editors to find more female writers, noting in 1938 that many best-sellers of that year were written by women.

"I am sure there must be some hidden talent," he wrote to Hildebrand in 1949. "Men are more forward . . . perhaps that is one reason why the ladies . . . have not received as many assignments."

Yet he insisted that male and female employees eat in separate dining rooms. Exuberant Carolyn Bennett Patterson, who succeeded the crusty Mason (Monty) Sutherland to become Senior

With a lynx shot in a flash of blazing magnesium, Shiras bagged another trophy in Canada. One of his purposes in hunting by camera rather than gun was "to show that the time has come when it is not necessary to convert the wilderness into an untenanted and silent waste." In the process, he invented a whole new category of photographic record and art.

GEORGE SHIRAS 3D

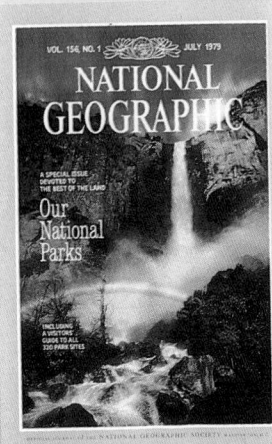

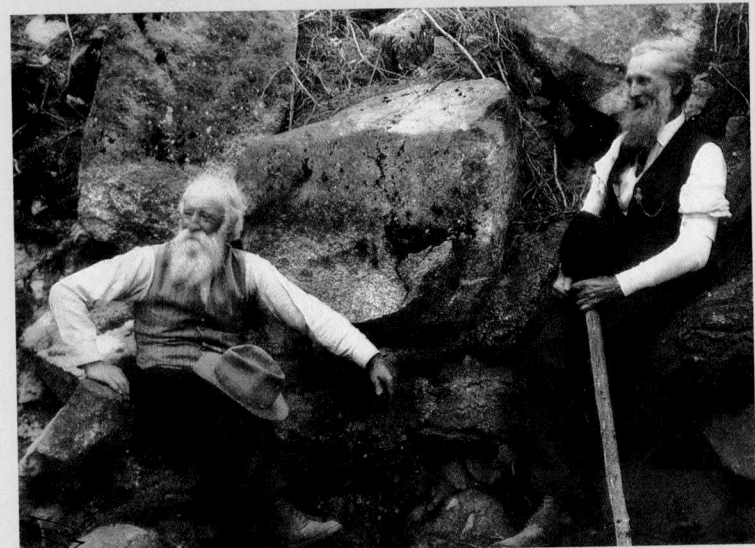

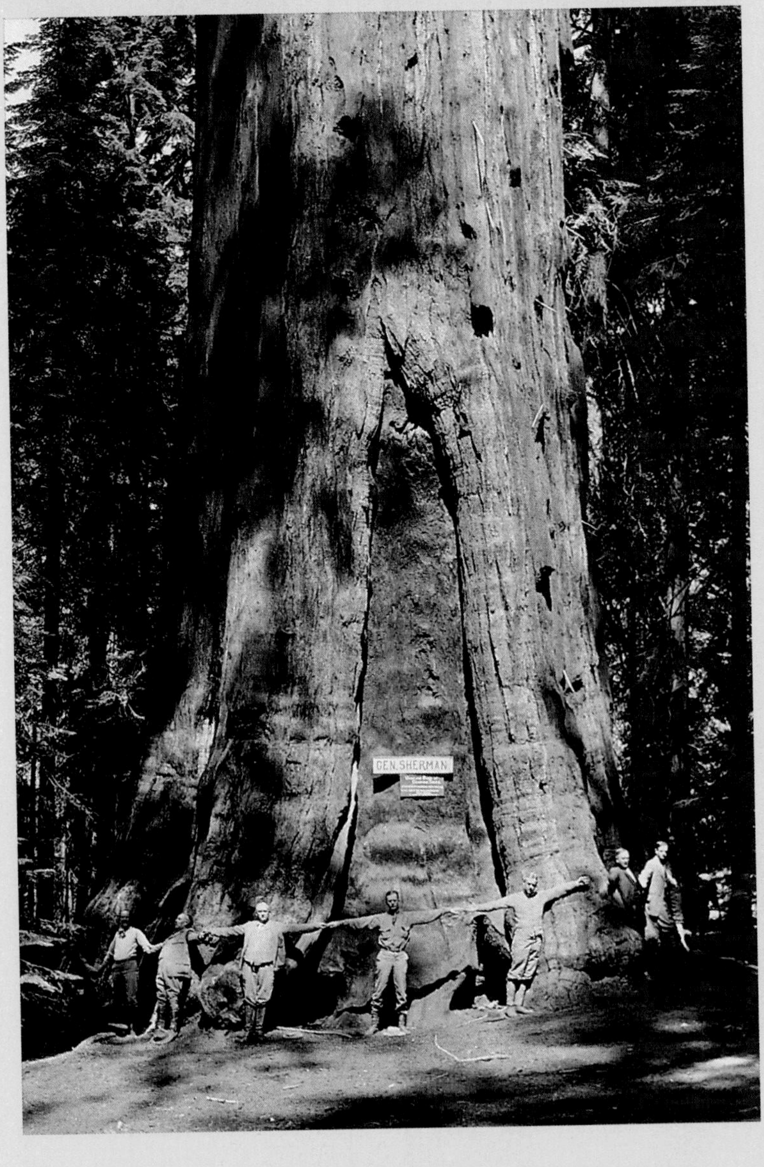

A desire to preserve nature's wonders has prompted the magazine many times to report on national parks—an entire issue was devoted to the glories of and threats to the system in July 1979 (above).

When logging threatened the existence of a grove of giant sequoias in California in 1915, Editor Gilbert H. Grosvenor joined a group of eminent Americans in a visit to the site. The photograph he took of 20 men joining hands to encircle the General Sherman Tree (right) dramatized the size of the huge conifers. Later the Society and its members donated $100,000 for additions to Sequoia National Park.

A 1973 article reviewed the life of John Muir and his role in the establishment of six national parks, including Yosemite. Muir (above right, at right) visited the park with fellow naturalist John Burroughs in 1909. Yosemite's Bridalveil Fall (facing page) charmed readers in 1916.

FRED PAYNE CLATWORTHY (ABOVE RIGHT); GILBERT H. GROSVENOR, NGS (RIGHT); FRANKLIN PRICE KNOTT (FAR RIGHT)

Assistant Editor in charge of the caption writers, recalls that she was scolded by Miss Strider for "walking too fast down the hall."

The practice of printing photographs of women in what a GEOGRAPHIC caption writer described as "true native dress" may seem questionable. While it can hardly be denied that these pictures played a role in the dramatic growth of membership, Grosvenor regarded the decision to publish them as a victory over prudery.

"That sort of picture at that time was quite novel—why, people were afraid to print anything showing a woman's breasts," he told Allan Fisher. Then, breaking off to examine an illustration dating from 1910, he exclaimed, "There you see a suckling child [and its mother]. They're beautiful!"

O N THE OTHER HAND he instructed his first Director of Advertising, John Oliver La Gorce, never to accept advertisements for alcohol, tobacco, or patent medicines. Grosvenor reported in his article on Russia in 1914 that the tsar's wartime ban on vodka had proved so popular with the people that they wished their sovereign to make prohibition permanent.

Grosvenor was overjoyed in his earliest days when someone overheard two workingmen discussing the GEOGRAPHIC. Those were the readers he wanted in their millions.

"Please remember always to make your text as simple and natural as you can—so simple that a child of ten can understand it," he wrote to Williams, a former missionary who sometimes wrote like an ecstatic preacher.

Grosvenor could be brusque with a subordinate who displeased him or who strayed from the principles of accuracy, fairness, and high-quality production that he had laid down. After detecting an error in a story about Chicago, he blistered long-suffering, and in this case quite innocent, Assistant Editor William Joseph Showalter: "The cornerstone of the success of the National Geographic is fidelity to truth; once lose our reputation for accuracy, and the GEOGRAPHIC is doomed." At the bottom of this memo he scrawled, "Please do not talk to me about this matter."

Yet when Luis Marden, then a junior member of the staff, was married, Grosvenor heard about the event and sent him a two-volume bird guide and a touching note of congratulations. "Now that you are married," he wrote, "you will realize what unfortunate people bachelors are."

In 1926 Grosvenor sent this terse memorandum to Assistant Editor Ralph Graves: "Never accept anything from Magoffin. His ways are not our ways." What exactly the ways of Magoffin might have been and why they alienated Grosvenor are not recorded in the files.

Gradually the staff and Gilbert Grosvenor grew old together. Joseph Rock, the friend of the King of Muli (who dined in the same room with the gilded mummy of his royal uncle, and whose body wastes were "molded into pills, gilded, and dispensed among the peasants to prevent illness"), continued to send back his marvelous photographs and his long, convoluted manuscripts from the remotest parts of Asia. In 1948, after 29 years of service, Maynard Owen

Mobile vantage point, the vehicle of writer-photographer Volkmar Wentzel allows him a view of the crowd at the city gates of Bundi in southeastern Rajasthan. For his pictorial survey of India in the late 1940s, Wentzel outfitted a former U.S. Army ambulance bought at an Indian salvage yard after promising membership in the Society to the officer in charge. Improvisation has long marked field coverage by GEOGRAPHIC photographers and writers.

VOLKMAR WENTZEL, NGS

A legend among colleagues and readers alike during his 42 years on the staff, Luis Marden explored the remote and romantic, including the Maya city of Chichén Itzá in 1936. A pioneer underwater photographer and discoverer of the remains of Bounty off Pitcairn Island in the Pacific, Marden has contributed as a free lance since retiring in 1976.

LUIS MARDEN, NGS

Prologue to adventure found Associate Editor (later Editor) John Oliver La Gorce, at far left, displaying the Society's flag prior to the 1930 commencement of a survey by seaplane of the east coast of South America. To La Gorce's left stood staff photographer Jacob Gayer and Assistant Editor Frederick Simpich, the most prolific writer in the magazine's history. Altitude-champion parachutist and aerial photographer Capt. Albert W. Stevens posed below Simpich, whose article on the expedition was published in January 1931.

RICHARD H. STEWART, NGS

PREVIOUS PAGES:
On the plains of Gaba in southern China an expedition led by Joseph F. Rock in 1928 pauses in a valley near Lijiang in Yunnan. Outlaw escorts granted safe passage to the adventuresome journalist on this four-month journey to Gongga Shan at the request of their king, who had seen the magazine showing Rock's travels in Tibet. On rugged expeditions early explorers such as Rock produced glimpses of far-flung corners of the world rarely, if ever, seen by outsiders.

JOSEPH F. ROCK

Williams wrote to Grosvenor: "Never grieve for me if it is my good fortune to die with my boots on. That's what I most hope for."

The magazine settled into a long afternoon, repeating the successes of an earlier day, living by methods of an earlier time. After decades on the job, Grosvenor's staff knew, perhaps too well, what the Chief wanted, and they kept giving it to him.

In the late 1930s the guard began to change. Andrew H. Brown, a fluent young writer who greatly pleased Grosvenor with the popularity of his articles, was hired in 1936. After World War II Beverley Bowie, a former intelligence officer and Harvard man, introduced a note of poetry into the text before dying young of cancer in 1958. The double-threat man-and-wife team of Franc and Jean Shor invested stories with an atmosphere of breezy sophistication.

George W. Long, the only GEOGRAPHIC staffer ever to lose his life in the line of duty (his aircraft vanished over the Atlantic in 1958), and a skillful editor named Robert Conly began handling the copy of the veterans. John Scofield, a future Associate Editor, joined the staff in 1953, after his free-lance articles impressed Ted Vosburgh.

New men, such as forthright Baltimore newsman Nat Kenney, sometimes found older ones out-of-date and chafed under a system that kept editorial experimentation to a minimum.

"Nothing I can do in the name of God, grammar, or friendship will prevail upon Williams to write a simple declarative sentence," wrote Hildebrand to Grosvenor. "I am going home," Williams retorted in a countermemo. "(Declarative sentence.)"

GILBERT HOVEY GROSVENOR remained on the job for 55 years, and when he retired in 1954 at the age of 78, the Society's membership exceeded two million. He had outlived 65 of the 88 persons who had served on the board during his tenure.

In his letter of resignation as Editor, Grosvenor referred to "the presence of a strong son beside me" that he had enjoyed for 30 years, but he recommended John Oliver La Gorce as his successor.

The son, Melville Bell Grosvenor, who had been waiting quietly for his opportunity since 1924, became Associate Editor and Vice President. Melville, born in 1901, was the first of Gilbert and Elsie Grosvenor's two sons and five daughters and is remembered by nearly everyone who ever knew him for his joyful nature, his goodhearted impulsiveness, and his love of life.

"He had the enthusiasm of several 12-year-olds," recalls Melvin Payne. "I don't often use this word, but there was a certain sweetness about Melville. It was unusual in a man as big and strong as he was. But it was there."

Apparently it was there from the beginning. "You never saw such a fascinating baby," wrote Melville's Grandmother Bell in 1902. "I don't know how I live without him from day to day."

Melville and Grandfather Bell were all but inseparable. "My first conscious memory was sitting on the lap of a jolly man with a snow-white Santa Claus beard and sparkling black eyes," Melville wrote after he grew up. "[He'd say,] 'Pull my nose, Melville.' I'd reach up and tweak his nose and he'd go 'bow-wow-wow. . . .' 'Now my beard.' Then he'd bellow an awful growl."

Melville rode on the back of Bell's beautiful coach horse, Champ (and later learned to ride standing up on the back of a galloping horse of his own), did his homework in his grandfather's study while the inventor did his own work, made a toy steamboat with an egg and a candle under the old gentleman's direction, went to the movies with him—and stopped on the way home at the bakeshop at Wisconsin Avenue and P Street for apple pie. Sweets were forbidden to Bell, a diabetic, and he would warn, "Don't you say a word to your grandmother."

Grandfather and grandson spent a whole winter planning a Robinson Crusoe experiment in Nova Scotia, and when summer came, roughed it together in Bell's beached houseboat in an uninhabited cove of Bras d'Or Lake with the idea of living off berries and roots. "They lasted about a day," Dr. Mabel Grosvenor recalls.

"My brother Mel was very like my Grandfather Bell," says Dr. Mabel. "I don't know whether he inherited it or not, but he had the same enthusiasm and curiosity. They were very, very much alike. Mel was much more like Grampy than like Father."

Melville graduated from the United States Naval Academy in 1923. He resigned his commission and joined the staff of NATIONAL GEOGRAPHIC the following year, beginning a wait for leadership that, in its length and in the patience of the heir apparent, rivaled that of Queen Victoria's son, Edward VII, who was 59 when he became King of Great Britain and Ireland. Melville was almost 56 when at last he was appointed Editor and President in January 1957. He had risen through the ranks, performing nearly every job on the masthead dealing with words and pictures.

He was a fine picture editor and an excellent judge of text, even though he was a miserable speller (his father advised him to write faster and look up troublesome words in a 50-cent dictionary afterward). He was such an impatient reader that Senior Assistant Editor Bart McDowell, who ghosted many of the articles that Melville signed, once suggested that manuscripts should be lopped off at the point where the Editor stopped reading, since his attention span was perfectly calibrated to that of the average reader.

T HE MAGAZINE'S distinctive first-person style has been an uncomfortable one for many writers. When Melville's son Gilbert M. Grosvenor and Allan Fisher proposed a poll of the members to see if they would accept a change, Melville told them to go ahead, but predicted that 80 percent would want GEOGRAPHIC writers to continue using "I" and "me."

"He was off by 2 percentage points," says Fisher. "Eighty-two percent of those polled favored keeping the old familiar first person." But Melville's greatest quality, by common consent, was his talent for leadership. He recognized good people when he found them, and when he found them, he hired them.

Few remember him by any but his given name, and few would differ with Senior Assistant Editor Howard E. Paine, who says, six years after his old chief's death and 21 years after his retirement as Editor, "I miss Melville every day."

Like his Grandfather Bell, Melville retained the boundless

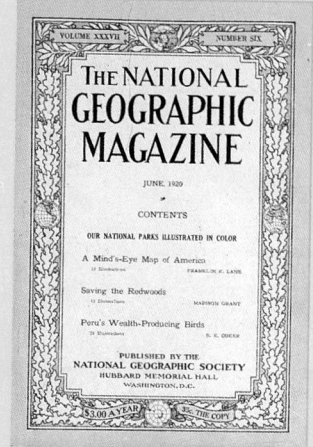

JUNE 1920

The quintessential field man, and one of the first photojournalists, Maynard Owen Williams joined the magazine in 1919. In 1945 he awaited an audience with the King of Saudi Arabia, who had provided him with headdress and robe. But Williams reported that while trying to photograph the king:

"My head shawl got in the way of my sweaty glasses, and I tramped on the corner of my robe. My gold-wound crown slipped over my eyes at a bacchanalian angle. Even my Contax slumped forward on its tiny tripod in an unscheduled curtsy.

"Was this impromptu comedy a howling success? Far from it."

MAYNARD OWEN WILLIAMS, NGS

curiosity of boyhood well into old age. "Oh, boy, this is going to be wonderful!" he would cry, setting out for a sail on Bras d'Or Lake, waters he had navigated thousands of times before. Once under way he would be captain, guide, storyteller, and chief cook all in one, making pancakes in the shape of letters of the alphabet to match the names of any youngsters who happened to be aboard. His style as Editor was not so very different.

This miraculous capacity to be interested in everything brought him through his long apprenticeship with his spirits not only intact but also glowing in anticipation of the fun that lay before him. Although it is likely that Melville's gift for enthusiasm was a factor in the length of that apprenticeship, his father was pleased by the results his son achieved as Editor.

"Melville realizes, as I have tried to, that as the years pass, a different . . . method of expression is necessary," Gilbert Grosvenor said, five years after the changeover.

Even before he took the helm, Melville was working toward methods that would break down the orthodoxy that had settled onto the magazine as the staff grew older and more set in its ways. There had been signs of rigidity for many years. When Maynard Owen Williams tried out a Rolleiflex camera in the 1930s, he was told to "junk it" because the pictures he sent back were square, whereas only rectangular pictures, vertical or horizontal, were permitted in NATIONAL GEOGRAPHIC layouts.

Although the Rolleiflex eventually became standard equipment, a prejudice against candid cameras ran deep and lasted long. Even after the smaller cameras were adopted, they were often used to make the same static pictures produced by older cameras mounted on tripods. By the time Melville took over in 1957, of course, the magazine was half-filled with the slightly overbright, nervous hues of Kodachrome, a film that made it possible, in conjunction with new cameras and lenses, to photograph fast-moving objects in color and to make enlargements of any size that would be absolutely faithful to the colors of the tiny original.

T HE FLEXIBILITY and artistic license that this new technology bestowed on photographers and picture editors opened up the possibility of a magazine as new, in its way, as the one that Melville's father had created.

New technology made possible an expansion, both in circulation and in the horizons of coverage, that the elder Grosvenor could only dream about—although La Gorce had foreseen the need for new printing methods if the magazine was to grow. By the early 1960s Melville had, with the support of Thomas W. McKnew, Executive Vice President, moved the printing of the magazine to Chicago, where the high-speed presses of R. R. Donnelley & Sons made it possible not only to print many times the 2.3 million copies that could be produced on the old presses in Washington but also to print every illustration in color.

Melville wanted a staff that would understand this opportunity and one with the talent and daring to take advantage of it. Even before La Gorce retired, he started hiring. In this, as in everything

Bound for the stratosphere, **Explorer II** *prepares to lift off on November 11, 1935. The historic flight, sponsored by the Geographic and the U.S. Army Air Corps, reached a record altitude of 13.71 miles. On board were Capts. Orvil A. Anderson and Albert W. Stevens. A year earlier Stevens had needed assistance to escape the plummeting gondola of* **Explorer I** *(below).*

Air collected during the 1935 flight was presented for testing and chemical comparison 53 years later. Accepting (above, at center) was Joseph O. Fletcher of the National Oceanic and Atmospheric Administration. Presenting were two Chairman Emeritus of the Society, Thomas W. McKnew, left, and Melvin M. Payne. Both had actively assisted in the balloon project.

MAJ. H. LEE WELL, JR. (OPPOSITE); BILL BALLENBERG

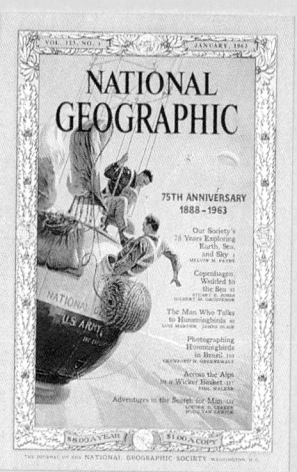

JANUARY 1963

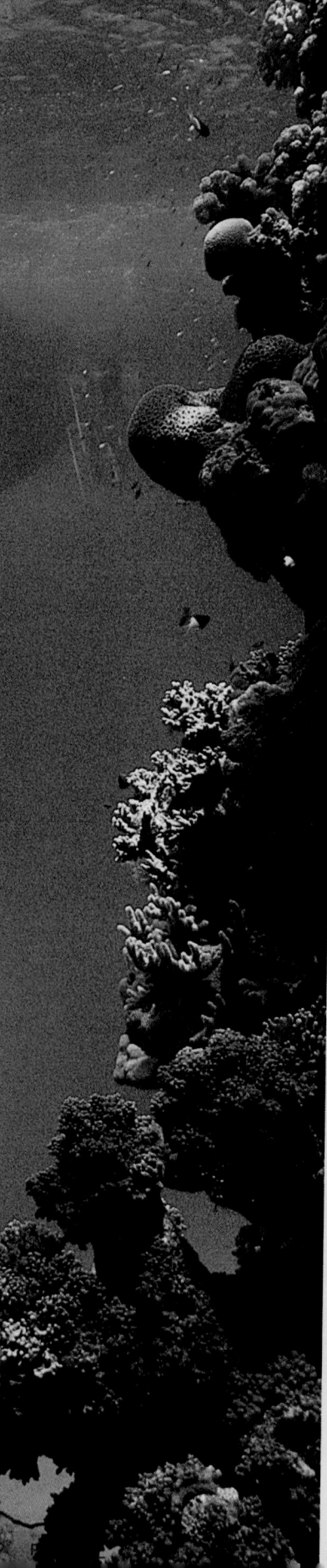

Probing the deep for more than five decades, Capt. Jacques-Yves Cousteau (left) has added immeasurably to man's knowledge of the oceans and life in the sea, often in partnership with the Geographic. Co-inventor of the Aqua-Lung, he also developed experimental undersea human habitats. In 1963 one such project off the coast of Sudan, dubbed Conshelf Two, included a domed "garage" (far left) to house yet another Cousteau first—the diving saucer.

Supporting ocean exploration has long been a hallmark of the Society. One particularly notable undertaking was the 1934 record-breaking 3,028-foot descent—and safe return—of the bathysphere (below) manned by William Beebe.

ROBERT B. GOODMAN (LEFT); BATES LITTLEHALES, NGS (TOP); DAVID KNUDSEN

43

else, he acted decisively on instinct, offering jobs to virtual strangers on the basis of brief interviews. Behind his seeming impulsiveness lay a clear purpose and a firm plan.

Senior Assistant Editor Mary Griswold Smith, one of the first new people brought aboard by Melville, was hired as a picture editor in June 1956. She was 21 years old. "I had very little education, and my only qualifications were that Melville had been introduced to my father and I was crazy about photographs," Mrs. Smith says. "Melville hired me on the spot. He said, 'I'm going to be Editor and I need young people around me.' "

Earlier he had hired an erudite young Columbia University graduate, editor, and former U.S. Army bandleader named Merle Severy, and not long afterward told him to create a new division to publish National Geographic books. Howard Paine, who had been working in an advertising agency in Springfield, Massachusetts, was employed to help Severy with layout and design.

Ted Vosburgh, Melville's Associate Editor, describes Paine as "that art director with the incredibly fertile mind who helped Melville steal the acorns."

Paine, who says that Melville put him "in charge of white space," introduced the principles, possibly even the idea, of modern design to the GEOGRAPHIC, a process that included the gradual elimination, over a period of years, of acorns and oak leaves that framed the famous yellow border of the magazine.

In the spring of 1954 Gilbert Grosvenor had visited the University of Missouri School of Journalism to accept an award for Distinguished Service in Journalism. It proved to be a fateful conjunction. There he met a talkative 24-year-old Navy veteran and Missouri senior, Wilbur E. (Bill) Garrett. He, too, was crazy about photographs and possessed stores of enthusiasm, curiosity, and impulsiveness that may have reminded Grosvenor of his own son. In a memorandum he instructed Melville to hire Garrett. When, 26 years later, Garrett became the seventh Editor of NATIONAL GEOGRAPHIC, Melville presented him with the memo.

Many guessed from the first that the hardworking, outspoken Garrett would end up in the Editor's chair. "Bill was insufferable in those days, but his talent was obvious to everyone," says Mary Smith. "We thought it was black magic." Howard Paine remembers going with Garrett to the Naval Observatory in Washington at 5 a.m. with the idea of photographing Sputnik, the Soviet satellite that was the first man-made object orbiting in space. "Sputnik went right through the bowl of the Big Dipper and Garrett went 'click' and made what may have been the first photograph of Sputnik in orbit," Paine says. "Bill always said that the secret of photography was '*f*/8 and *be* there.' But the luck that guy has!"

At about the same time La Gorce, who had also hired Melville, hired Gilbert Melville Grosvenor, just out of Yale University. He had been a premedical student with no particular thought of a career at the GEOGRAPHIC before being captivated by the camera during a vacation. Gil Grosvenor, son of Melville and grandson of the original Gilbert Grosvenor, was to rise through the masthead like his father and become Editor, President, and Board Chairman.

Elegantly attired, Editor Melville Bell Grosvenor, right, and his wife, Anne, attended the 1967 coronation of the King of Tonga with writer and photographer Luis Marden. In parkas, wet suits, or top hats and tails, GEOGRAPHIC representatives dress to fit the assignment. Grosvenor continued a tradition of widely traveled editors, at home in the field as well as behind a desk.

EDWIN STUART GROSVENOR

W ITHIN TWO YEARS after taking control, Melville had hired the nucleus of the staff that would carry the magazine into the 21st century. In 1964 he moved them out of the dim and crowded precincts of the old headquarters into a light-filled modern building next door.

Foremost among the newcomers—many of whom were recommended by Garrett—was a critical mass of graduates of the University of Missouri School of Journalism, including Robert L. Breeden, now Senior Vice President in charge of Educational Services of the Society, and Associate Editor Thomas R. Smith. In 1959 Minnesotan Thomas J. Abercrombie, whose realistic photographic style marked a turning point in the way the magazine made and selected pictures, became the first of 12 GEOGRAPHIC photographers to be named Magazine Photographer of the Year. Garrett was the fourth, in 1969.

Most of the others were hired by James M. Godbold or Robert E. Gilka, who came to the magazine from midwestern newspapers in 1958. Melville made Godbold the first Director of Photography in 1959, thereby placing the work and well-being of photographers, a breed subject to uncommon stress, in the hands of a single strong executive. This was a momentous departure, and it was the key element in the creation by Godbold, and especially by Gilka, of a corps of photographers and a body of photography unique to the magazine.

Gilka, who succeeded Godbold in 1963, was on the job for 22 years, earning an unusual degree of affection and respect. His methods were much like Melville's. Says Assistant Vice President Carl M. Shrader, who served under Gilka as head of the photo lab, "Bob Gilka never told me what I could *not* do."

In writing, Melville wanted a more journalistic approach, one that would let the people in GEOGRAPHIC stories speak to members of the Society in their own voices. Precise, level-headed Ted Vosburgh acted as a moderating force in this and other enterprises. In Garrett's words, "Ted was the man who held onto the tether of Melville's magnificent airship."

One after the other, Melville hired a stable of new writers who had been seasoned by experience in the world of commercial news-gathering, including Senior Assistant Editor William Graves, a son of Ralph Graves, and several members of the staff of an expiring Washington news magazine called *Town Journal*. These included Bowie, Conly, McDowell, Edward J. Linehan (later the Articles Editor), and a raucous ex-Marine from New Jersey named Howard La Fay, who looked liked one of the Medici, talked like a taxi driver, and wrote like an angel.

In 1965 Joseph Judge, then a civil servant looking for greener pastures but who had been with *Life* magazine and a Washington television station, was asked by Allan Fisher and James Cerruti, the tough-minded editor in charge of free-lance writers, to write a small piece on Monticello to see what he could do.

The magazine bought the article and offered Judge a job. His father had been a star first baseman for the old Washington Senators. "Joe," Melville said to him, "you're going to be as good for

Clamoring to have their picture taken, children of Quemoy in 1959 swarm around Wilbur E. Garrett— photographer and illustrations editor who was named Editor of the magazine in 1980. Joining him to cover this Nationalist Chinese stronghold, shelled by mainland Communist Chinese forces in the late 1950s, was Senior Assistant Editor Franc Shor—who greeted youngsters in Chinese. During his 21 years on the staff, Shor circled the globe many times.

FRANC SHOR (ABOVE); WILBUR E. GARRETT, BOTH NGS

Turning over the helm after ten years as Editor and Society President, Melville Bell Grosvenor, second from right, consults with new Editor Frederick G. Vosburgh at a 1967 meeting in the Control Center. Associate Editor Gilbert M. Grosvenor, standing, created the center to keep track of articles from inception to publication.

The senior Grosvenor, who served the Society for 58 years, expanded grants to research and exploration, created the book divisions, inaugurated TV specials, and introduced the first all-color magazines. "Our quintessential reader. He had perfect pitch so far as what the reader wanted," an associate recalls.

this magazine as your father was for the Senators. I used to sneak out of work to watch him play. I think my aunt 'died' ten times the year they won the pennant!"

Judge became one of the aces of the staff and, upon the premature death of Franc Shor, followed La Gorce, Vosburgh, and Scofield into the second highest post on the magazine.

"Melville transformed the Geographic from a Victorian to a 20th-century organization," says Tom Smith. Like most others of his generation who worked with Melville, Smith remembers the experience as the happiest and most fulfilling of his life. "He was like a father to us—a wonderfully unorthodox father, and that was very stimulating to young people," Smith says. "When you'd done something he liked, he'd put that big paw of a hand on your shoulder, and with a huge smile he'd let you know that he liked you and liked your work. You treasured those moments."

Assistant Editor Peter White remembers returning from Laos to find that deep changes had been made in one of his stories. He stormed into the Editor's office, so upset over the violence that had been done to his prose that he actually shouted at Melville.

"Peter, you're not well!" Melville cried in shocked tones. "You have worms. Somebody else came back from a trip and talked to me like this, and *he* had worms." After calling Garrett into the room to calm White, who by now was misty-eyed with loyal affection, Melville picked up the telephone and dialed a number. "I'm going to send you over to my own doctor right this minute!" he said.

Severy and Paine took the dummy of a 436-page book about ships to the Editor's home on a Saturday morning, expecting to spend about an hour going over the material. "We stayed for lunch, dinner, and many mint juleps—somebody had sent Melville 23 kinds of mint," Paine recalls. "When he saw the dummy, it was 'Wow! The ship book! I've been waiting for this!' So we crawled around on the floor of Melville's study until ten that night, changing the layout around. Time flew."

Predictably, this sort of management released creativity. The whole aspect of the magazine changed; the staff felt itself involved as members of a family. It was impossible to lose interest because the head of the family insisted on living in an atmosphere of new ideas and boundless optimism.

O LD CONSTRICTIONS fell away. Gone were the acorns, the rigid rules about the size of pictures and the way in which pictures might be trimmed, cropped, and laid out on the page. Photographers, exposing thousands of frames of Kodachrome in order to capture the one instant in the life of an image that would speak directly to the reader, achieved pictures the like of which had never before been seen.

Writers roamed the world as freely as photographers in search of equally telling words. The magazine was, as it had been in Gilbert Grosvenor's heyday, wholly at ease with its times. By the time Melville Grosvenor retired as President and Editor in 1967, membership had more than doubled, to 5.6 million.

Melville Bell Grosvenor was Editor of NATIONAL GEOGRAPHIC for only ten years. In that time he built the new headquarters building in downtown Washington and an even larger building in Gaithersburg, Maryland, to house membership services, started Book Service, instituted National Geographic Television Specials, issued the first Geographic atlases and the first globes, modernized the printing of the magazine, opened a new Explorers Hall, greatly expanded the research activities of the Society, and left many other monuments to his time at the head of the Society's affairs.

In a sense, because the young people he chose and inspired more than 30 years ago are now producing the magazine he re-created, Melville is still the spiritual Editor of NATIONAL GEOGRAPHIC, just as Alexander Graham Bell remains its inventor and Gilbert Hovey Grosvenor its architect.

Their GEOGRAPHIC was born out of change, and it has continually reinvented itself in order to keep up with the changing world that is its inexhaustible subject matter. Yet at the end of its first century the magazine remains unmistakably its original self, constant to the principle of accuracy, fairness, optimism, and experimentation on which it was founded.

It is, in short, a monument to the three singular men who made it—and to their truly revolutionary idea that this journal belongs to the millions who read it, not as mere subscribers, but as members of an unending expedition to explore the earth and everything that exists upon it and beyond it.

Viewing the ruins of Angkor Wat, Melville Grosvenor keeps camera at hand in this 1959 photograph in Cambodia. He learned photography at the knee of his father, Gilbert H. Grosvenor. Following his death, the elder Grosvenor was eulogized in the October 1966 issue. Shown bird-watching (below), he spent a lifetime enthralled with every aspect of geography.

W. ROBERT MOORE, NGS

Keeping pace gracefully, Society headquarters in Washington, D.C., has grown from two-story Hubbard Hall (above, far left) to include the tiered building dedicated in 1984. Explorers Hall draws some 350,000 visitors annually to Edward Durell Stone's marble landmark, right. At groundbreaking in 1961 Melville Bell Grosvenor manned a power shovel, while then Chief Justice of the U.S. and Society trustee Earl Warren, standing, at left, consulted with the architect.

The Membership Center's tranquil setting (left) near Gaithersburg, Maryland, belies the busy pace within: Here 400 million pieces of mail are processed each year.

SISSE BRIMBERG (ABOVE); JAMES STANFIELD, NGS (LEFT); J. BAYLOR ROBERTS, NGS

49

Taking Up the Great Global Issues

The magazine in the past two decades

By JOSEPH JUDGE SENIOR ASSOCIATE EDITOR

ARRAYED ON YOUR BOOKSHELF, our magazines seem immutable, impervious to change. The newest number takes its place smartly like a recruit joining the ranks of a renowned and ancient regiment. This is illusion; within its yellow uniform the magazine has changed continuously over the past two decades. From 1970 changes were worked on it by the very act of reporting on a world that was passing through profound social, economic, and political disturbances. Those were the years of Vietnam, of oil price hikes, of terrorism; of acid rain, Chernobyl, and population explosion; of brushfire wars, starvation in the Sahel, and AIDS; and of the continuing collapse of order in what had been the old colonial world.

It was an era of a global economy turned upside down, of power risen from the dust and ashes of Japan and Germany. People in developed nations were asking if the price of progress must be fouled water, impure air, and poisoned land—while those in the poor nations were asking for the chance to have such problems.

Had the GEOGRAPHIC been guided in that turbulent period by the same codes of journalism that had prevailed in earlier years, it would simply have become irrelevant. But under Editors Gilbert M. Grosvenor and Wilbur E. Garrett the magazine took up, in its own distinctive way, the great global issues. It met the tests of relevance, and it flourished.

In many ways the last magazine to appear under Frederick G. (Ted) Vosburgh, a landmark number dealing with the threat of world pollution, was also the first for Gil Grosvenor, since it epitomized one of the enduring interests of his editorship. Gil and the editorial staff who had assembled that issue under Ted helped to set precedents that would mark the next decade as one in which the realities of the world were looked at straight on.

Those realities were marked by the United States' embittered departure from Vietnam and the continuing agony in Asia. They included a seemingly endless Cold War playing out its hot conflicts in Africa and Afghanistan, and a Central America festering from old inequalities of wealth and power. We could not pretend that such a world did not exist, nor could we go at it in the same old way. No longer could the man or woman from the GEOGRAPHIC arrive with 18 Halliburton cases and be greeted more as a celebrity than as a journalist. It was to be the era of the anonymous suitcase, the duffel bag, and the low profile.

Environmental degradation, stewardship of natural resources, the dilemmas of the oil economy and nuclear energy—facing hard issues became a hallmark of the editorship of Gilbert M. Grosvenor, announced in the December 1970 GEOGRAPHIC. After a decade Grosvenor succeeded Robert E. Doyle as President of the Society.

Wilbur E. Garrett was named Editor, a Geographic veteran with firsthand knowledge of the world's hot spots as symbolized by his 1973 photograph of Hmong women in Laos. For years Hmong fought in the war in Southeast Asia for the U.S. Later many emigrated to the United States; others got no farther than a refugee camp.

A constant evolution keeping pace with a constantly changing world has been the story of two decades under two Editors.

WILBUR E. GARRETT, NGS

One of the traditions of the magazine had been a straightforward approach to geographic places. We had often covered cities, states, and countries—*Here's Belgium!*—on the basis of internal inventory rather than on any notion of contemporary interest. To break from that pattern, Gil made new use of an old instrument, a planning council of senior editors; they began to select places for coverage that had a direct bearing on world events or peoples' lives.

H ASH MARKS ON THE SOULS of staff writers from this period depict the trend: La Fay in Uganda, Syria, Leningrad; Ellis in Bangladesh, Cairo, Istanbul, Japan; Jordan in Sri Lanka, Somalia, Turkey; White in South Korea, Poland, Tanzania, Calcutta, Quebec. Jim Cerruti, a gruff but brilliant editor, set about bringing talented free-lance writers to the magazine—names like John McPhee, Charles McCarry, Douglas Chadwick, Peter Benchley, Tom Wolfe, Robert Laxalt, Paul Theroux, François Leydet, and Griffin Smith.

Essential to the GEOGRAPHIC's enduring popularity was the universally admired quality of its photography. Yet it too was undergoing a metamorphosis. Under the direction of Robert Gilka, the young photographic staff brought back images that went to the heart of the new realism typifying the magazine's direction. Jim Stanfield, Jim Blair, Bruce Dale, Gordon Gahan, Dave Harvey, Emory Kristof, Win Parks, Steve Raymer, Jodi Cobb, and others. They and outstanding free-lancers such as David Doubilet, Cary Wolinsky, Jonathan Blair, Bill Allard, Steve McCurry, Sam Abell, Jim Brandenburg were able not only to produce the traditional coverage of people and places but also to do so in sudden and illuminating moments that could make you catch your breath and seemed to look into the heart of things. Coverage was becoming reportage.

The test of reportage was Content with a capital C—that combination of lucid text, distinctive cartography, informative and elegant art, and brilliant photography splendidly printed; each facet complementing and supplementing the others. In a world given to special pleading and contentious haggling, the whole was verified—double- and triple-checked by a research staff second to none.

This was the new GEOGRAPHIC. Not only the moment recorded by the daily press but also the other moments, ones that mattered—thousands of wistful, sad, angry, anxious, hopeful, triumphant moments in human lives that unfolded and gave readers in millions of homes around the world insight into their times and far places.

The deployment of such gifted photographic and writing talent was not haphazard. For instance, the magazine examined American public policy in regard to its natural resources in a series that covered the wilderness system (1974), wild and scenic rivers (1977), national wildlife refuges (1979), national parks (1979)—a series completed in 1982 with the national forests. We had not forgotten the beauty and soul-renewing powers of our natural heritage, forever relevant but not forever unless we looked to its preservation.

This was the age of the supertanker superspill and other environmental crises. The oil embargo had pushed Americans to some hard choices. On the North Slope of Alaska, for example, the

Triggered by revolution in Iran, a gasoline shortage in 1979 spurred the magazine to take a hard look at our nation's spendthrift ways with nonrenewable energy resources. The result was a special 13th issue, published in February 1981. The social and environmental costs of industrialization are now common themes as the Society promotes geographic knowledge in an increasingly interdependent world.

bottom line seemed to be oil now, tundra later. But the range of our concern was wide—from the Everglades and the Serengeti, to Yellowstone and our salt marshes, from the Great Lakes and the Cooper's hawk, to Big Cypress and the world's whales, from the wolf and the Grand Canyon to the last of the tallgrass prairie. It seemed we led articles on such subjects with a question—can we save it?

T HE CONSERVATION MOVEMENT was coming to maturity with the consent of the American people, and legislation was moving forward to protect our air and water and to better manage the parks and forests and wilderness areas. Inevitably a few articles stand out from an effort like this and speak for all others. I think of Tom Canby's and Steve Raymer's "Can the World Feed Its People?" and Allen Boraiko's and Fred Ward's "The Pesticide Dilemma." The magazine was confronting issues crucial to society's progress in a world of growing want, land abuse, and poisoning of the earth in the name of abundance. This brought us to confrontation with powerful lobbies that pleaded expediency on the environment in the name of employment and profit.

The path to confrontation was also being laid by articles on Cuba, a divided Canada, Harlem, the Philippines under Marcos, and South Africa—all "bad news" stories for those Board members who remembered the world in palmier days and thought that perhaps our reporting on those troubled places helped make the trouble. A long-standing part of the magazine's tradition had always been its avoidance of controversy, but here we were awash in it.

Glowing streams of molten waste spill from train-borne ladles onto a slag heap, the dumping ground for a smelter at the Canadian mining town of Copper Cliff, near Sudbury. This area of Ontario supplies much of the free world's nickel and is an important source of copper.

Mankind the producer is also mankind the disposer, a theme addressed in articles covering such topics as radioactive and other hazardous wastes, acid rain, trash, pesticides, oil spills, and air and water pollution.

WINFIELD PARKS, NGS

TAKING UP THE GREAT GLOBAL ISSUES

Masked volunteer undergoing a
test of smog's eye-irritating effects
illustrated the bellwether December 1970 issue, which featured a
major article and a supplement
map on how humankind pollutes
the environment.

In that article the Cuyahoga
River in the Cleveland factory
district (upper right) seemed a
modern-day Styx, so polluted with
oil and debris that it had caught
fire the year before. Raw petroleum
gushed from a drilling platform off
Louisiana (right) after a fire that
burned out of control for a month
in 1970.

Visual pollution assaults our
eyes and sensibilities. Cars stripped
by vandals added to the seediness of
the Sunset Park area of Brooklyn,
a neighborhood since renovated
through a joint initiative of business and government. Near the
foot of the Great Pyramid of
Khufu, pieces of litter sit as rude
testimony to thoughtlessness.

ROBERT W. MADDEN, NGS (RIGHT CENTER);
LOUIE PSIHOYOS (FAR RIGHT); JAMES P. BLAIR, NGS

TAKING UP THE GREAT GLOBAL ISSUES

Our first brush with it came when the American Jewish community reacted sharply to our description of conditions for Jews in the Syrian capital of Damascus. The need to explain our position led to the first Editor's column, which has become a standard feature.

In the mid-1970s certain distressed Board members proposed an editorial oversight committee. It never materialized; no journal can survive with a committee watching over the shoulder of an editor. In its stead, a "Reaffirmation of Editorial Policy" was agreed upon, stressing the slow evolution of change. It was printed on the January 1978 contents page, and we went on with our work.

Actually, the magazine was doing nothing that it had not always done—first-person narrative reporting. The facts stood by themselves beyond our power to affect. The French Canadians were talking of separation from Canada. South Africa, alone among nations, was enforcing racially-based apartheid as a matter of national policy. The family and friends of Marcos were running a nation like a personal corporation. In Cuba Fidel Castro had made dramatic strides in literacy and medical care. We could say no different.

In the Italian industrial city of Milan, a centuries-old Madonna (above) is obliterated by acid formed from rainwater and sulfur deposits left by air pollution. As the environment emerged as a major theme of the GEOGRAPHIC, its spotlight turned to examples of man's carelessness and destructiveness, such as tree-killing emissions from smokestacks and automobiles, pesticides harmful to wildlife, and radiation released from Chernobyl.

Overgrazing by flocks of goats was blamed in part for expanding the wasteland of the African Sahel, where nomads were compelled to settle in shantytowns (facing page) like this one on the edge of Nouakchott, Mauritania.

JAMES P. BLAIR, NGS (ABOVE); GEORG GERSTER

A NEW EXUBERANCE came to the magazine through William Graves's "Expeditions" department. A sign in his office proclaims that "Adventure is a sign of incompetence," and during the past few years a number of unforgettable "incompetents" have trekked through our pages—Tim Severin crossing the Atlantic in a skin boat in the wake of the Irish abbot St. Brendan; Robyn Davidson crossing the Australian outback on a camel; Naomi Uemura making it solo to the North Pole; Ed Yost just failing, then Ben Abruzzo, Maxie Anderson, and Larry Newman succeeding in making the first transatlantic balloon flight. And two figures with that special kind of GEOGRAPHIC magic—Peter and Barbara Jenkins, walking across America and into fame by participating in the life of the unreported people of the back roads.

It was just such people who found themselves in predawn lines for gasoline when the oil embargo and skyrocketing oil prices hit the world and the United States and Western Europe and Japan suddenly realized their vulnerability in providing for their own energy futures. It was a subject in which Gil and his staff had been interested from the beginning. Ken Weaver's "Search for Tomorrow's Power" in 1972 had opened a continuing series of articles on oil resources, coal, wind power, geothermal and solar energy, natural gas. We visited "The Arab World, Inc." and rode the supertankers across the world's oceans. We went where the energy play was—Alaska's North Slope, Canada's tar sands, Oman, Saudi Arabia, Kuwait, the North Sea, and the Atlantic continental shelf.

Then, in 1979, came a decisive moment. In April, within days of publication of our article on "The Promise and Peril of Nuclear Energy," a reactor at Three Mile Island melted down. What the magazine had called "the friendly atom" in 1954 and "the obedient atom" in 1958 suddenly proved to be neither. The extent of the difficulties and dangers in using nuclear fuel as a commercial power source was revealed; the agencies and corporations involved in that development had told less than the whole truth about the depths

Fear and the future's uncertainty
haunt the face of an Afghan girl
(right), eloquently photographed by
Steve McCurry in a refugee camp
in Pakistan. On the cover of a 1985
GEOGRAPHIC, she brought home
the terror of war in a realm where
poorly armed freedom fighters
faced more than 100,000 Soviet
troops. To chronicle global violence
and repression, and dispassionately
explain its roots, magazine writers
and photographers went—often at
great risk—to places making newspaper headlines.

At the funeral of compatriots
killed during a foray into Lebanon,
Israeli soldiers (above) mourn atop
the grave of an earlier battle's casualty. South Africa's unyielding policy of apartheid is epitomized in the
black township of Soweto as a
mother and children stroll toward
an armored vehicle (left).

Robert Caputo's poignant April
1988 article on Uganda reported on
the vicious tribal wars that slaugh-
tered perhaps 800,000—including
the wife of this Baganda farmer—
and the virulent AIDS epidemic.
His report drew kudos from World
Health Organization officials
attempting to stem the disease.

TAKING UP THE GREAT GLOBAL ISSUES

Armed conflicts change borders, governments, and societies—and the NATIONAL GEOGRAPHIC has reported on them since 1900 and the Boxer Rebellion. Both World Wars, Korea, and Vietnam were covered by the magazine.

We sent a team to Pakistan's border with Afghanistan in 1985, seven years into the Soviet Union's ten-year effort to control that country and the mujahidin—freedom fighters. Photographer Steve McCurry found that the business of war kept Afghan refugee arms merchant Haji Baz Gul close to his two telephones and his assorted deadly weapons in Darra, Pakistan. Before him lay coveted AK-47 Kalashnikov assault rifles, priced at $1,200 each.

STEVE McCURRY

of the problems. Where to turn for energy? Some of the best oil resources were controlled by nations of uncertain stability and vulnerability. Burning coal seemed a dirty alternative. Synthetic fuels had promise but were a long way from commercial viability.

Gil decided on a major departure and directed publication of a 13th issue of the magazine in 1981, a special report devoted to a single topic—energy. It appeared in February and was one of the pinnacles of his career as Editor, even though he had become President of the Society by the time it was published. Another was the opening of long-closed doors: In 1971 the magazine published an exclusive report by Audrey Topping, one of the first Western journalists to travel widely in China after the Cultural Revolution. In 1973 Ed Kim squeezed his way into North Korea via Moscow, the first Western photojournalist to visit the country in 30 years. Three years later Fred Ward was able to travel freely inside Cuba, and in 1980 we unlocked the last closed door when Mehmet Biber managed to get into hermetic Albania—altogether a good bag of firsts for any decade of reporting. An ironic footnote is that as of 1988 among the few nations in which we had no members were North Korea and Albania.

Not that in those days we had many in Syria or Egypt, countries we reported on when the Soviet presence was paramount and few American reporters were allowed on the premises. We wanted those stories because Gil stressed the need for balance, for a diverse mix, in every issue. One of his guiding principles was that every member had to find at least one article in every issue that he or she found of interest. Those interested in the dramatic turns of the Middle Eastern world during the 1970s would find them, generally in an issue that featured horses of entirely different colors.

In 1972 Tom Abercrombie's "The Sword and the Sermon" had expounded, for the first time in a major American magazine, the history of Islam and divisions between Shiite and Sunni Muslims, terms the American people would come to know during the Iranian hostage crisis eight years later. Much in history helped to explain the present. Loren McIntyre's piece on the Inca; Howard La Fay's and David Alan Harvey's article on the Maya; Merle Severy's and James Blair's still definitive work on the Celts; and the story I did with Gordon Gahan on the Minoans and Mycenaeans illuminated entire historical epochs and cultures whose tendrils reach into the present. They established a genre that only the GEOGRAPHIC is equipped to do so well.

DRIVEN BY THE SOCIAL CONCERNS of the 1960s and '70s, people turned to the past with relief. But they were also fascinated by glimpses of a future being born out of basic and applied science. The magazine made a permanent record of America's reach into space, documenting Mercury, Gemini, and Apollo flights, culminating in the first and subsequent lunar landings. In 1976 Viking got to Mars and gave us unforgettable images from the red planet. That same year we published "The New Biology," our voyage into the human cell. Samuel Matthews reported on plate tectonics and the new geology and also global climate change. We also went with young scientists like Robert Ballard down to the Galápagos Rift and found there new life forms in the cold abyss of the deep sea. We were a mirror of whatever time we were in. We changed, we reflected, we held up the light, and I cannot but think that people who read the magazine in this turbulent period had a better grip on reality as a result.

A S THE EDITOR'S BATON WAS PASSED to Wilbur E. Garrett in August 1980, a great story bridged past and future. Rowe Findley's masterly account of the cataclysm at Mount St. Helens became at once, and has since remained, the single most memorable article in the magazine's century of publication. The article presaged many things about the Bill Garrett editorship—chief among them the instinct for the big story. We had a peerless first-person account; what we needed were photographs of the colossal event. Under the direction of Tom Smith, chief of illustrations, Bruce McElfresh left no stone unturned in the search. The cover photograph was taken by an amateur, as were many inside pictures. The entire effort was a triumph of collection and editing.

The most recent years of the magazine's history will need a chronicler from the future, for we are still in medias res. But this much can be said without fear of retrospective change—no years have been more creative or innovative. Big and important and different stories became the rule rather than the exception, and the

"Help my baby—please!" For a Vietnamese mother, the desperation of war became almost unbearable when she could find no doctor for her sick infant. When a U.S. Navy patrol boat stopped her vessel for inspection, she thrust her child toward an interpreter with the urgent plea. The sailors gave her all the medical aid they could before moving on. That was in 1968, and it would be 1973 before a truce ended the United States' 12-year combat involvement. The GEOGRAPHIC published a dozen articles on the Southeast Asia conflict that took more than a million lives, including armed forces of both sides but mostly civilians— many of them children.

WILBUR E. GARRETT, NGS

Cataclysm and catastrophe not
only alter the shape of the planet
but also take a continuing toll on
humanity. Behind the headlines
of disasters the GEOGRAPHIC has
always tried to provide both human
and scientific insights. In 1986 a
lake in Cameroon suddenly
expelled a mammoth hiccup of
deadly carbon dioxide that suffo-
cated 1,700 villagers (below).
A mother in Bangladesh mourned
her dead baby in 1975 (right),
victim of famine that recurs in
that overpopulated land. In India's
Rajasthan women were driven to
the scant shelter of a tree by
gritty winds (top center), ominous
prelude to the seasonal monsoon,

whose welcome rain sometimes
means deluge and death.
    In 1980 a National Guard heli-
copter crew found a truck holding
two of the 61 people killed in the
volcanic explosion of Mount
St. Helens (right). For Assistant
Editor Rowe Findley, who wit-
nessed the aftermath of the violent
eruption and reported on it in the
January 1981 GEOGRAPHIC, it
demonstrated the peril "for all of
us living on a planetary crust so
fragilely afloat atop such terrible
heats and pressures. Never again
. . . would I regain my complacency
about this world we live on."

HELIMISSION (ABOVE); STEVE RAYMER, NGS (TOP LEFT);
RALPH PERRY, BLACK STAR (RIGHT); STEVE McCURRY

VOL. 159, NO. 1   JANUARY 1981

NATIONAL
GEOGRAPHIC

MOUNT ST. HELENS
MOUNTAIN WITH A
DEADLY BREATH 3
ON THE PATH OF
DESTRUCTION 35
THE DAY THE
SKY FELL 50

PARABLE OF PREHISTORIC
ANIMALS IN TANZANIA 44

STILL THE MECHANICAL
THE AIRPLANE 36

POLAND'S PROUD
MOUNTAIN PEOPLE 104

THE INVALUABLE
CUCUMBER 130

SEE 'ETOSHA: PLACE OF DRY WATER' WEDNESDAY, JANUARY 7, ON PBS TV

JANUARY 1981

GEOGRAPHIC emerged as a voice of importance and consequence.

Staff writers and photographers felt that Bill Garrett's style was akin to Melville Grosvenor's instinctive journalism: *There's the story, right there; let's go get it!* Often Bill went and got it himself. The old field maxim—you don't know if you don't go—became an operating imperative in the Editor's office. He, for instance, wrangled permission to go to Angkor Wat, closed to the outside world since 1975 when Pol Pot took over Cambodia, now called Kampuchea. He took Peter White and Dave Harvey with him, and they brought out a second story, the living nightmare of Kampuchea, where Pol Pot's revolution had resulted in the death of more than a million of his own people.

With the increase in terrorism and political exploitation of human tragedy in places like Ethiopia, the Sahel, Haiti, and Nicaragua, the stress points seemed to run deeper, and the writing and photography from those places were graver than any we had published. We looked into Khomeini's Iran, and, more hopefully, into a quickly changing China.

We looked as well into the abyss. With "The Poppy," Peter White's and Steve Raymer's brilliant reportage began with a flower. From its seed capsule comes opium, which can be refined into morphine to block severe pain, and heroin, a drug so abused that it affects every aspect of world culture, economy, and politics.

Again, the magazine was changing yet staying the same. New features like Members Forum, On Assignment, and Geographica were added. The most striking innovation, however, was the use of holograms on the cover—the first three ever attempted by a large-circulation magazine. These publishing firsts attracted a lot of public attention, as did Bob Ballard's discovery of *Titanic* and my own article on the landfall of Columbus at Samana Cay in the Bahamas.

As the centennial of the Society drew near, Bill Garrett was once again thinking big—not one centennial issue but four to close the year. Those issues were monuments, containing 130 extra pages and examining Society history and the overriding questions of humanity's past on earth, achievements in exploration, and the future of the planet under the stress of human population and development—great themes played out on a large scale in articles of enduring interest and importance. Two map supplements—a world map using a more realistic projection and an extraordinary view of the Himalaya—were published.

Always the wheel of time and change is turning in human affairs, presenting to the magazine the possibility of new discovery, new exploration, and the unexpected big story that makes the presses rattle. Some who served on the final years of this hundred-year voyage are gone, and this index is their epitaph: Shor, Conly, MacLeish, La Fay, Gahan, Parks, Aikman—staff writers, photographers, and editors who lived interesting lives and brought to you interesting stories from far places.

They were among that particular and peculiar legion of talented journalists upon whose days and nights in the field this particular and peculiar edifice always has and always will rest.

Mountain music springs from the fiddle of Carolyn Tolley (facing page), who plays for a young listener at a festival near Pipestem, West Virginia. Searching for the essence of a place, GEOGRAPHIC stories on states, cities, and nations strive to convey the texture of everyday life.

JODI COBB, NGS

Threatened native: A young jaguar gets a pat from Editor Wilbur E. Garrett in Guatemala. A hotel manager adopted the orphaned cat; its parents probably were killed for their skins, the sale of which is illegal. The owner hopes to breed the cat and free the cubs in the wild.

Long a student of both wildlife and Mesoamerica, Garrett has promoted creation of Central American wildlife sanctuaries. GEOGRAPHIC articles trace the worsening problem of endangered species in the face of shrinking habitats and the illegal international wildlife market.

DAVID ALAN HARVEY

Adventures in search of history and geography have long intrigued GEO-GRAPHIC readers. Using medieval documents, modern-day explorer-historian Tim Severin built a replica of a leather boat (far left) that, legend says, the sixth-century A.D. Irish monk and explorer St. Brendan may have sailed to the New World. Severin successfully sailed the wood-and-oxhide vessel from Ireland to Newfoundland in 1976.

Alone in the outback (left) Australian Robyn Davidson, her four camels, and dog, Diggity, endure a drenching rain on a 1,700-mile trek across Australia's forbidding western desert.

Triumphant hug (below) unites climbers Annie Whitehouse and

Christy Tews after their all-woman team reached the Himalayan summit of 26,504-foot Annapurna I.

Afloat on Arctic ice (left), dogs and crew of the Steger International Polar Expedition struggle on their thousand-mile trip from Canada's Ellesmere Island to the North Pole. They were the first to cover the distance by dogsled without resupply since Robert E. Peary attempted the journey in 1909.

NATHAN BENN (TOP LEFT); RICK SMOLAN, CONTACT PRESS IMAGES (TOP RIGHT); WILL STEGER (LEFT); ARLENE BLUM

Wrecks ancient and modern tell tales with their remains. On her maiden voyage the doomed luxury liner R.M.S. **Titanic** slid beneath the waves on April 14, 1912, after collision with an iceberg 400 miles southeast of Newfoundland. The disaster claimed 1,522 lives.

Seventy-three years later, with National Geographic support, undersea geologist-explorer Robert D. Ballard located **Titanic** two and a half miles beneath the sea and explored her with a combination of manned submersible and a remotely controlled deepsea robot nicknamed **Jason Jr.** (right).

Brandishing porcelain dishes (top), underwater archaeologist Robert Sténuit emerges from a dive on the Dutch East Indiaman **Witte Leeuw (White Lion)** off the remote South Atlantic island of St. Helena. The ship, sunk by Portuguese carracks in 1613, yielded a rich collection of Chinese Ming dynasty porcelain and nautical artifacts from the ship itself.

BATES LITTLEHALES, NGS (TOP);
PAINTING BY WILLIAM H. BOND, NGS;
WOODS HOLE OCEANOGRAPHIC INSTITUTION

Thousands of priceless artifacts from the Late Bronze Age were recovered from a 3,400-year-old wreck off the Turkish coast. When divers (right) tried to lift a clay storage jar, Cypriot pottery packed inside tumbled out. A pile of huge four-handled copper ingots litters the seafloor. George F. Bass, with National Geographic Society support, led the excavation of the wreck, which also yielded weapons, exotic woods, and aromatic resins, as well as terra-cotta jugs, a cup, and bowl, all of Mycenaean workmanship (below right).

BILL CURTSINGER

The sea is a wondrous place that mankind has yet to completely explore. And we continue to find powerful statements in the oceans and their myriad inhabitants. A gentle leviathan (left) cruises the waters off Península Valdés on Argentina's Patagonian coast. This southern right whale, returning to its breeding grounds, senses no danger from a diver.

A southern elephant seal pokes its head through a kelp bed to growl at an intruder (above) in the Kerguélen Islands, part of the French Southern and Antarctic Territories in the Indian Ocean.

Anemone-like zoanthids cushion a dozing California swell shark (bottom, far left), which can inflate itself by gulping water or air.

Off southern Australia a leafy sea dragon sports a beautiful but tough exoskeleton (left).

MITSUAKI IWAGO (ABOVE); DAVID DOUBILET (LEFT); FLIP NICKLIN

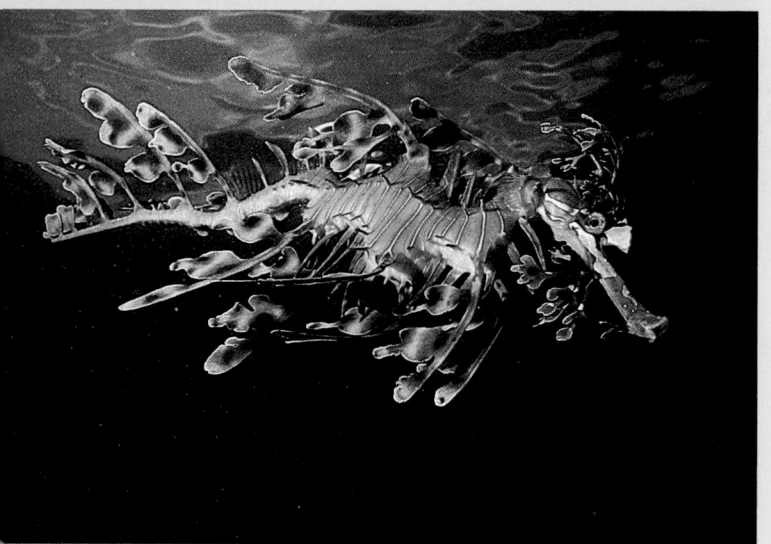

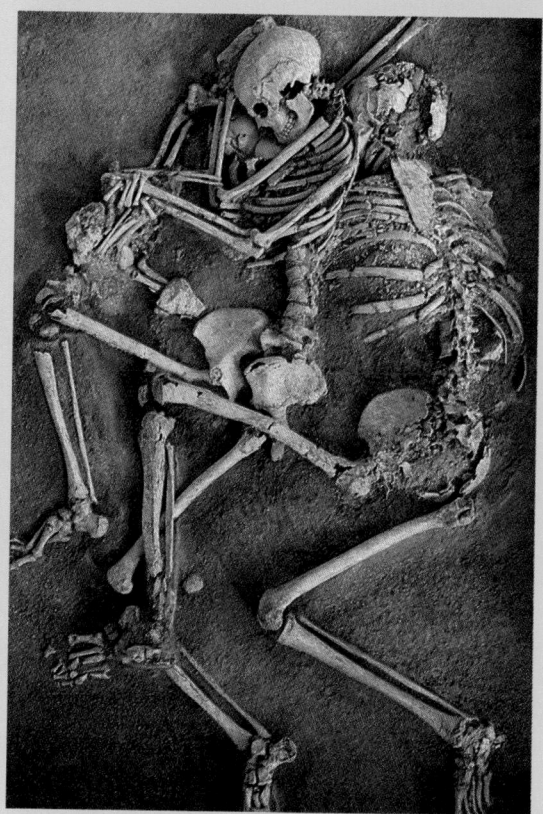

Ancient civilizations tell their tales as archaeologists report on the findings of Society-sponsored expeditions. One of the most spectacular sites, the 1,500-year-old tomb of a warrior-priest (facing page) who ruled the Moche people of Peru's north coast, is watched over by silhouetted guards alert for looters. The grave yielded fabulous gold artifacts. Recitals once echoed through a small marble concert hall called an odeum at Aphrodisias, an ancient Greco-Roman city excavated in Turkey (top). Poignant testimony to disaster, a man, young woman, and small child were crushed during an earthquake in the city of Kourion on Cyprus (left). In Mexico, nine-foot-tall Maya figures stand in the late seventh-century A.D. Palace of Palenque.

BILL BALLENBERG (FACING PAGE); DAVID L. BRILL (TOP);
MARTHA COOPER (LEFT); DAVID ALAN HARVEY

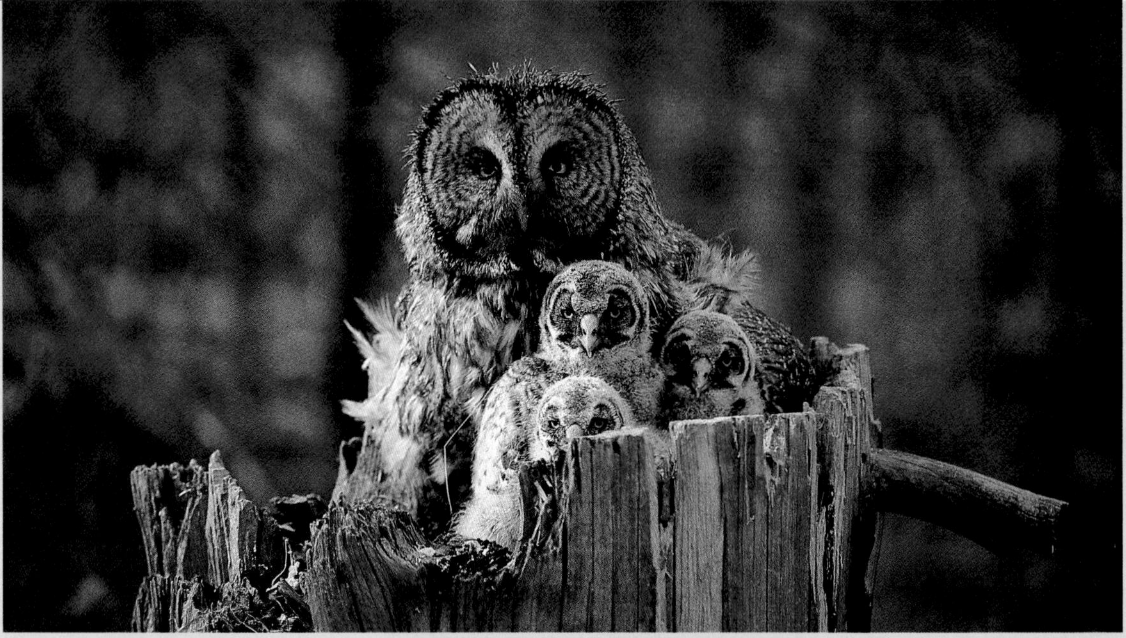

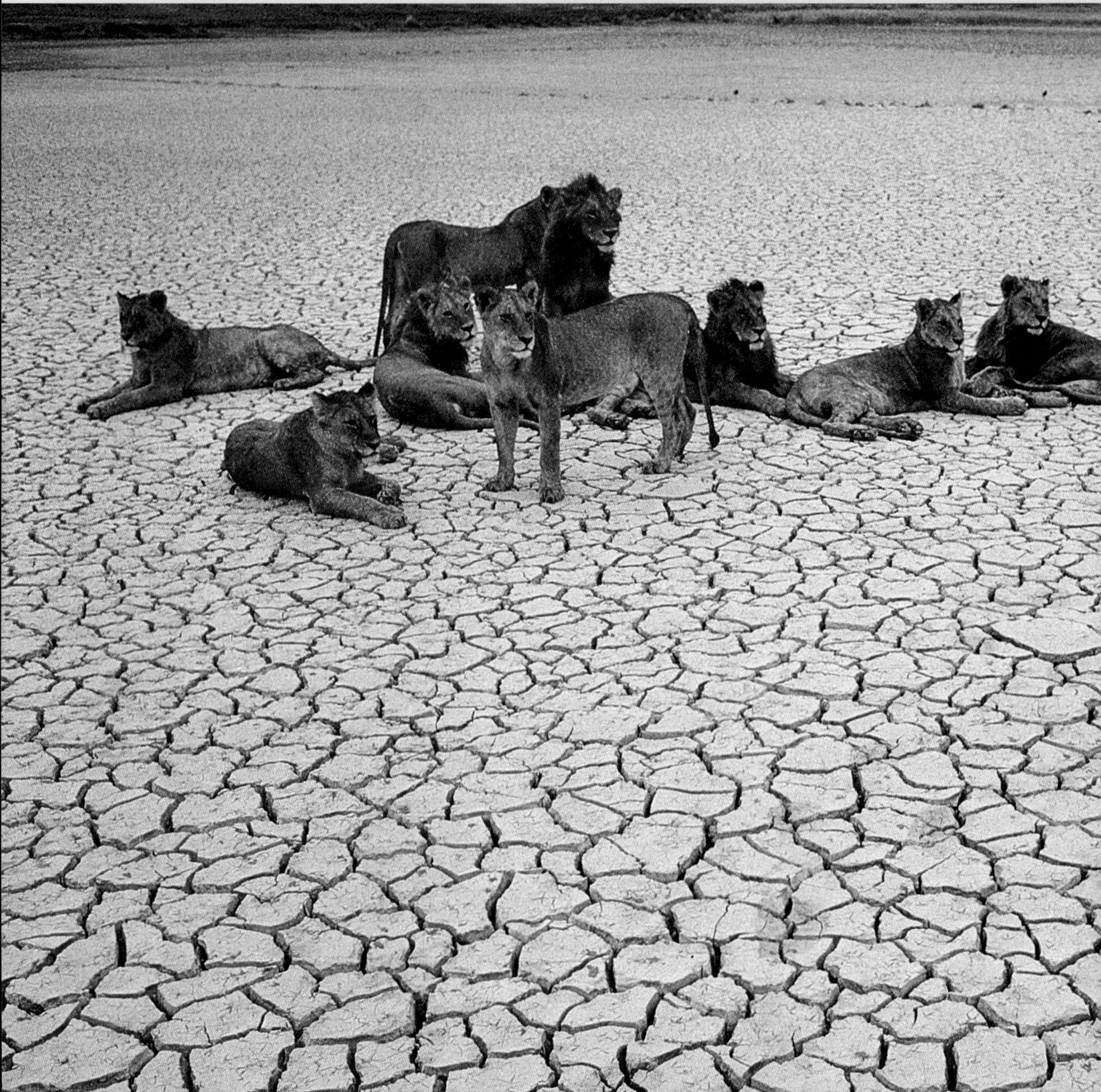

Creatures great and small, fascinating and often imperiled, challenge our stewardship of the planet: from bluebirds to blue whales, marauder ants to muskoxen. In Tanzania's Ngorongoro Crater and nearby Serengeti National Park, black rhinoceroses (right) that numbered in the hundreds in the 1970s have plummeted to only about 20 today due to poaching. Ngorongoro's lions have fared better. Youngsters lounge on a parched lake bed during the dry season (below). In Island Park, Idaho, a great gray owl shelters her owlets after a night's rain (left). Embodying all the raw power of the wild, a brown bear tears into a sockeye salmon in Alaska's Katmai National Park.

Observing the great apes up close—something many scientists once believed was impossible—has yielded a wealth of data about humankind's closest relatives. Supported in part by Society research grants, three scientists have achieved unprecedented field studies of primates. The first, Jane Goodall (right) began in 1960 at remote Gombe National Park in present-day Tanzania, making the chimpanzees' home her home. After earning the trust of the wary animals, she studied their hunting behavior and discovered their tool-making capabilities. Evolutionary biologist Stephen Jay Gould calls her work "one of the Western world's great scientific achievements."

Likewise, Dian Fossey (opposite) pursued studies of the endangered mountain gorilla in the highlands of Rwanda, mapping family relationships and interactions. One of her favorite subjects, Digit (above), was killed by poachers; Dian herself was murdered by an unknown assailant in 1985.

Biruté M. F. Galdikas (right) has accomplished pioneering observations of elusive arboreal orangutans in Kalimantan (Borneo), Indonesia. She also raised orphans confiscated from pet owners for release into the wild.

DEREK BRYCESON (TOP); DIAN FOSSEY (ABOVE); ROD BRINDAMOUR (RIGHT); ROBERT M. CAMPBELL

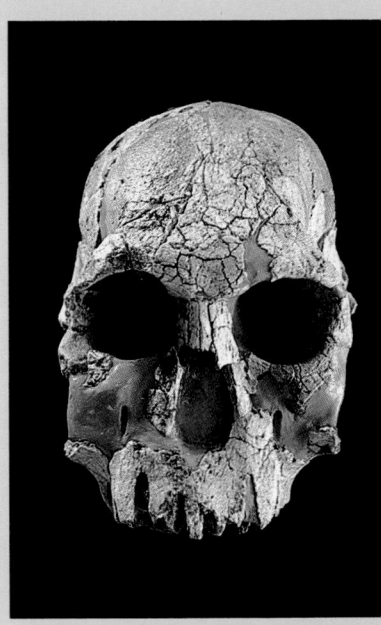

Bringing to light the extraordinary saga of early human species, Louis S. B. Leakey and his son Richard (far left) examine fossils beside Lake Rudolf, Kenya. In this area Richard's team in 1972 located a 2.8-million-year-old skull, designated 1470 (left), earliest evidence yet of the genus Homo. *Louis's wife, Mary, found footprints made by bipedal individuals in damp volcanic ash; this re-creation (below) suggests how the prints were made about 3.7 million years ago.*

In 1974 Donald C. Johanson found the most complete early skeleton to date in northeastern Ethiopia. Nicknamed Lucy, the female—since designated Australopithecus afarensis—*walked upright some three million years ago.*

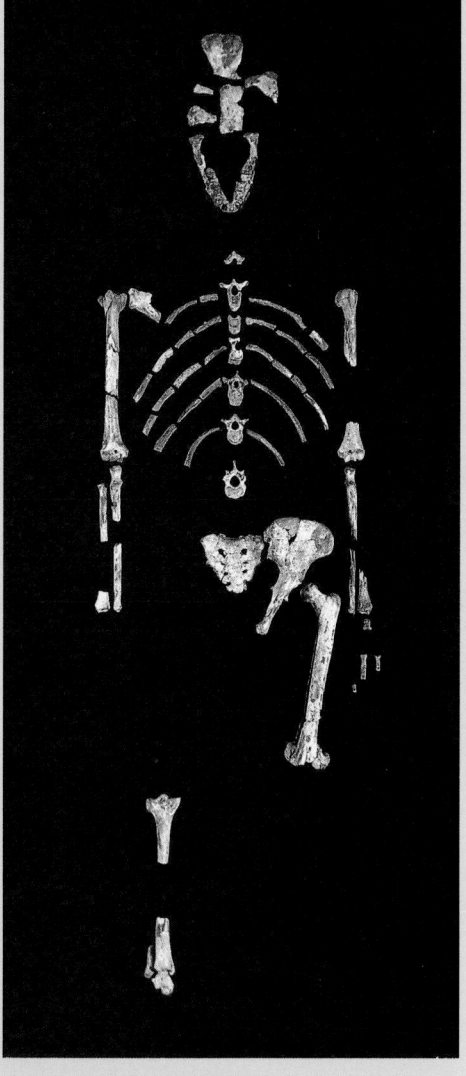

GORDON W. GAHAN (TOP LEFT); ROBERT M. CAMPBELL (TOP CENTER); PAINTING BY JAY H. MATTERNESS; DAVID L. BRILL

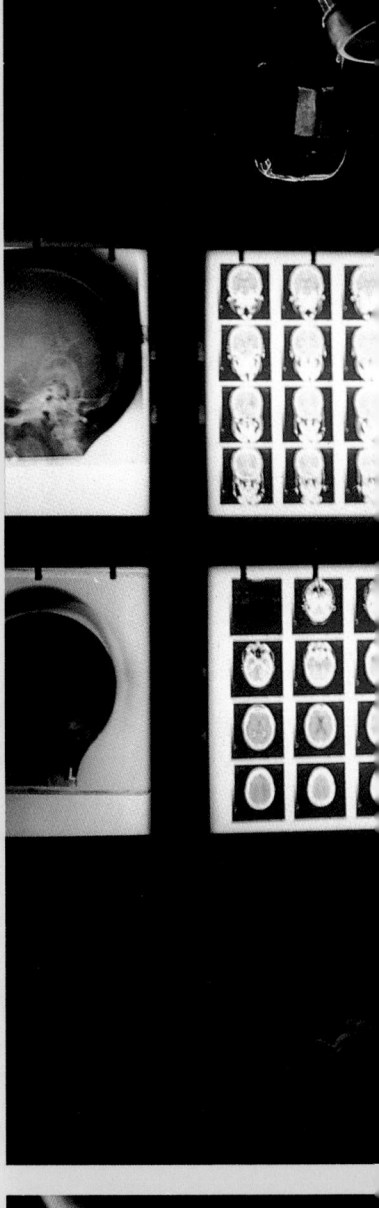

The worlds and wars within our bodies come vividly alive in several GEOGRAPHIC articles dealing with breakthroughs in medical science. In our June 1986 look at the human immune system, a young cancer patient (above) uses a video game to visualize his defense system's T cells. Spotlighting a number of diseases caused by immune disorders, including AIDS, the article was richly illustrated with pictures of human defense cells, like the blood-cleaning macrophage (right center). Lennart Nilsson, the Swedish master of photomicroscopy who captured those images, was a major contributor to the Society's 1986 book **The Incredible Machine**,

which included his remarkable views of prenatal life (right).

In the January 1987 magazine, photojournalist Howard Sochurek reported on state-of-the-art medical technologies, like magnetic resonance imaging (MRI). Able to view tissue through bone (far right), MRI is but one of many new diagnostic tools that are revolutionizing procedures in operating rooms (upper right) around the world.

From the labs of theoretical physics other breakthroughs were reported on in our May 1985 article on the atom. By beaming subatomic particles at cancer cells, neutron therapy (top) performs the equivalent of conventional surgery.

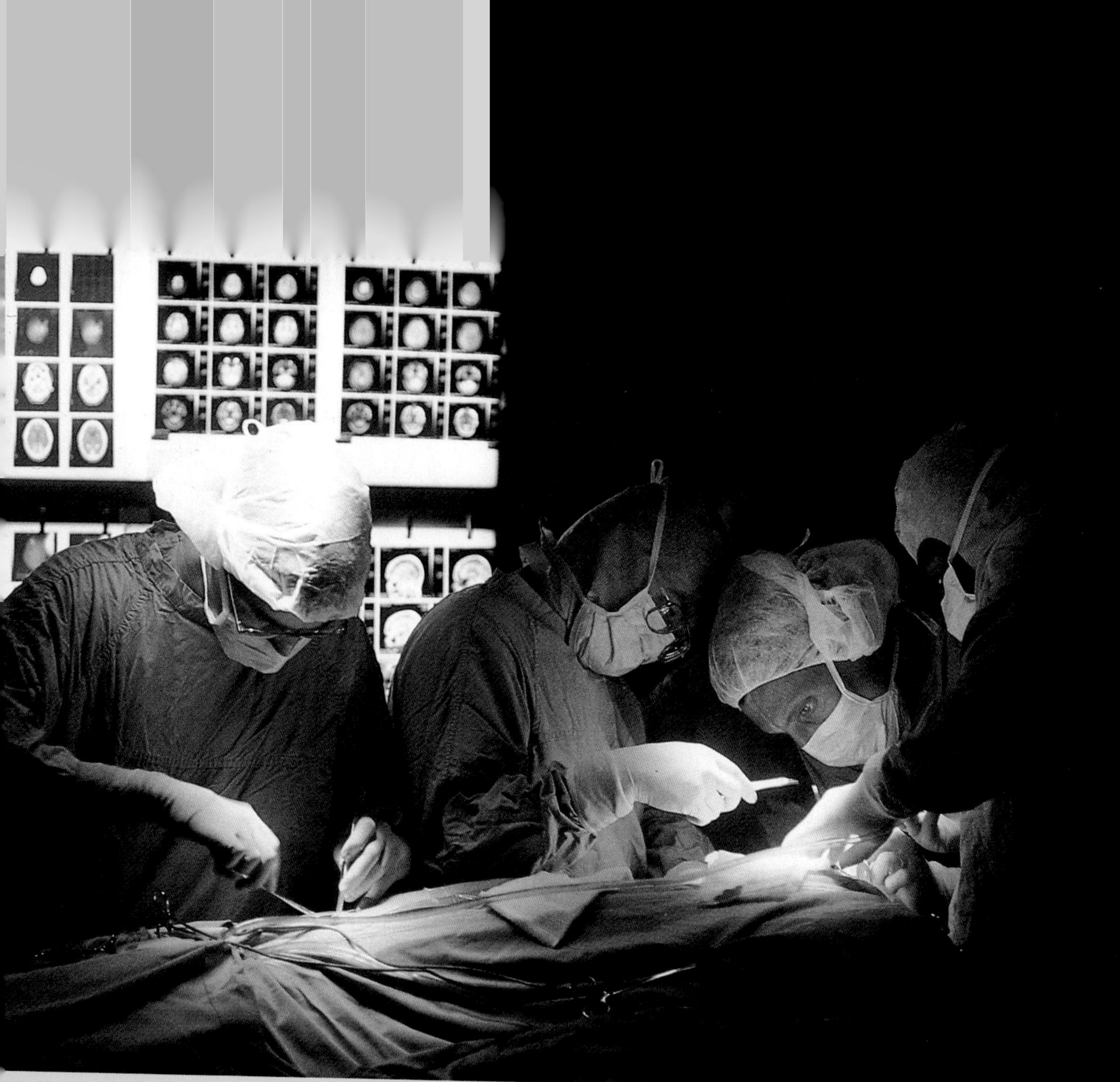

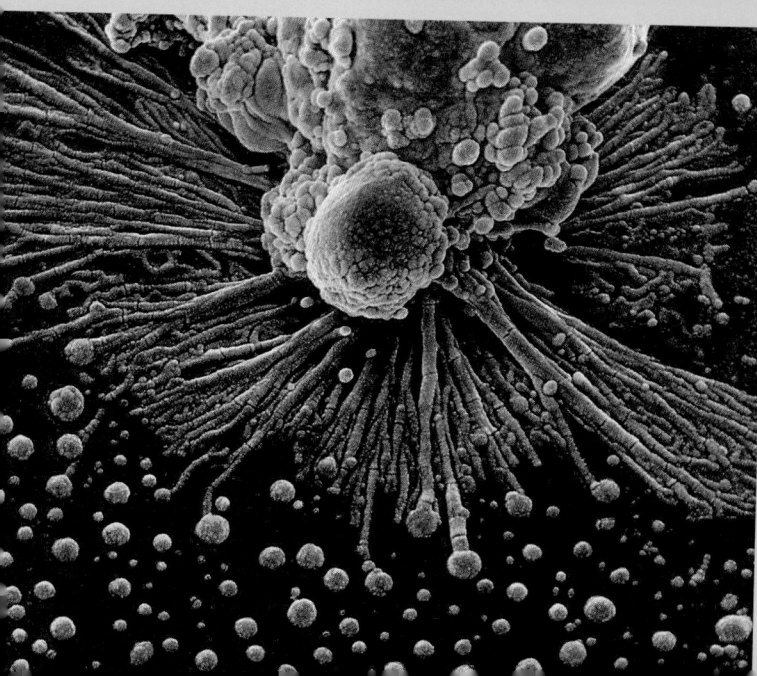

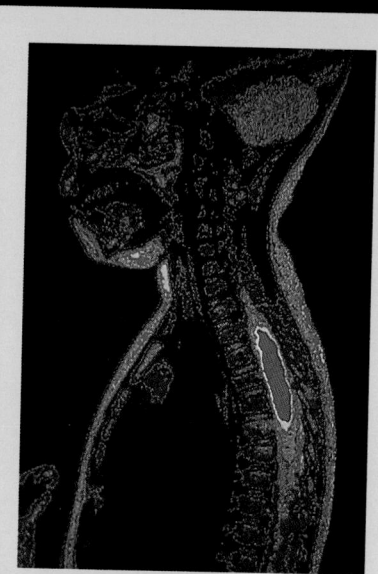

81

Heralding the high-tech 1980s, our October 1982 article on the chip was followed in March 1984 by a survey on lasers and the technology of holograms. On the cover of that issue appeared our first hologram, to be followed by another in November 1985. In celebration of our centennial year, the entire front and back cover of the December 1988 issue consisted of holographic images. At American Bank Note Holographics, Inc., in Elmsford, New York, images of a crystal

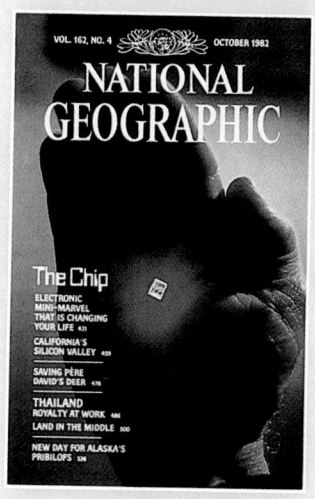

globe were replicated on polyethylene sheets (left). One step in a yearlong process, the images were then metallized, laminated on cover stock, and tinted gold before the binding of 10.9 million copies.

Unimaginable without chip technology, computer-generated images—like the one portraying temperatures on the space shuttle **Columbia** in our November 1982 issue (right)—have appeared in many of our pages. With the aid of computers, scientists are also delving into the domain of the ultrasmall. In our May 1985 article "Worlds Within the Atom" (top right) the tracks of colliding subatomic particles are plotted.

SISSE BRIMBERG (LEFT); KEVIN FLEMING (TOP RIGHT); INFRAMETRICS, INC., FROM NASA VIDEOTAPE BY DOUG NELSON

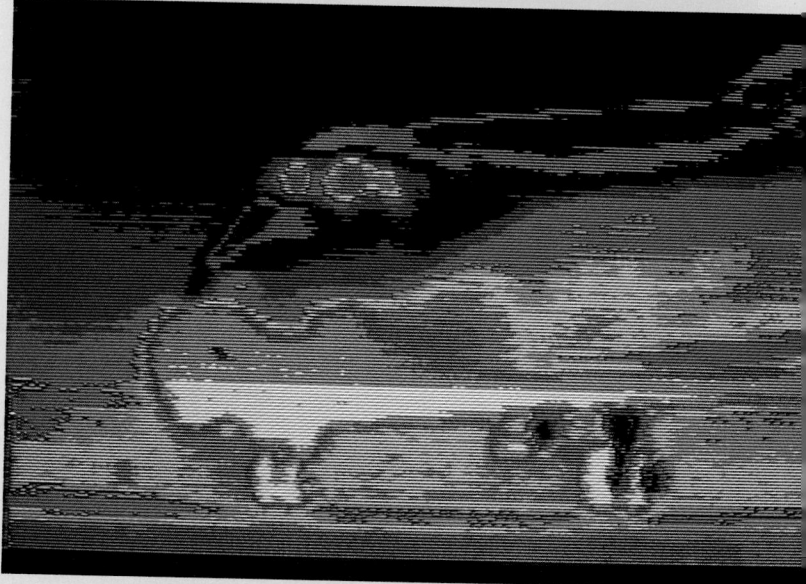

Space is home turf to readers of the GEOGRAPHIC, which has chronicled events from Sputnik to the shuttle. Four years before man first planted his foot on the moon (below), astronaut Frank Borman (above right) commanded the 1965 flight of Gemini 7 on a mission that saw the first rendezvous of two craft in space. Here he performs a vision test—part of early efforts to gauge the effects of weightlessness on the senses. Borman now serves as a member of the Society's Board of Trustees.

At work in space, astronauts James D. A. "Ox" van Hoften and William F. Fisher spacewalk outside the shuttle Discovery in 1985. The crew retrieved, repaired, and relaunched a communications satellite. Earth's limb arcs 220 miles below.

Three years before disaster, Challenger (opposite) poses for the first ship-to-ship photograph of a shuttle in space, taken by a West German satellite that had been put into orbit. The open cargo bay reveals another satellite ready for launch. Challenger blew up 73 seconds after launch in January 1986.

On a tour of Jupiter and Saturn, Voyager 1 sent back this true-color image of the moon Io orbiting Jupiter's bulging girth. ALL BY NASA

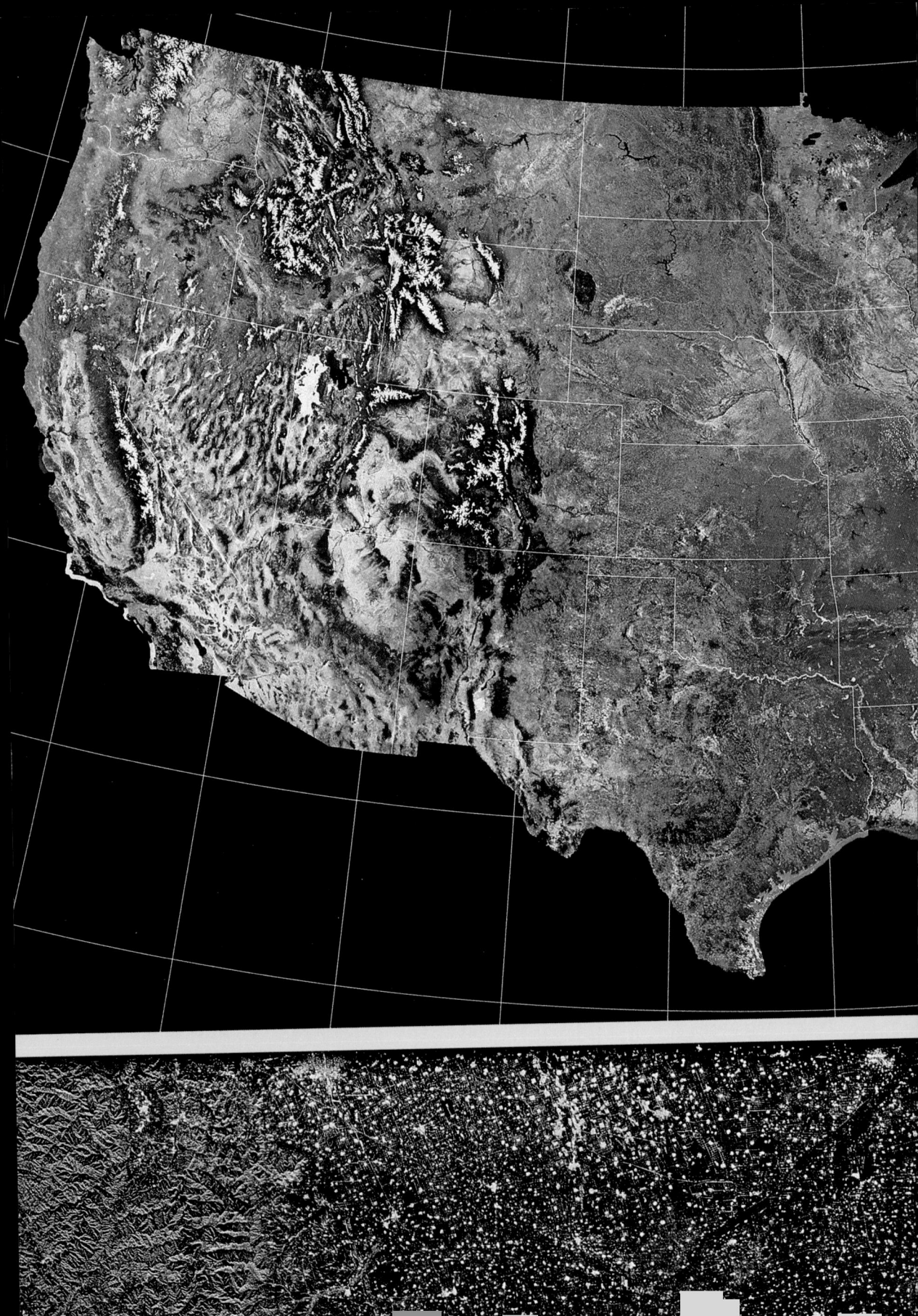

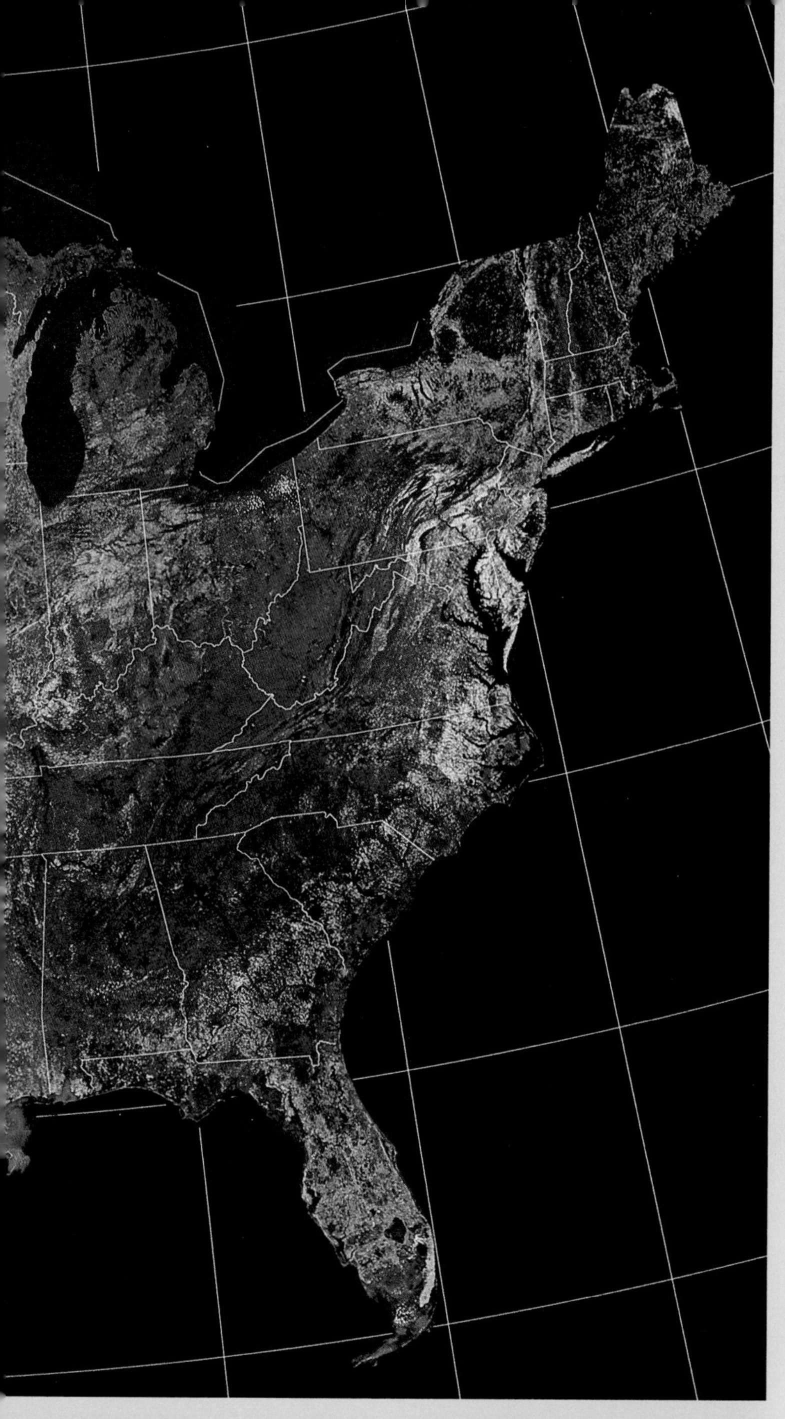

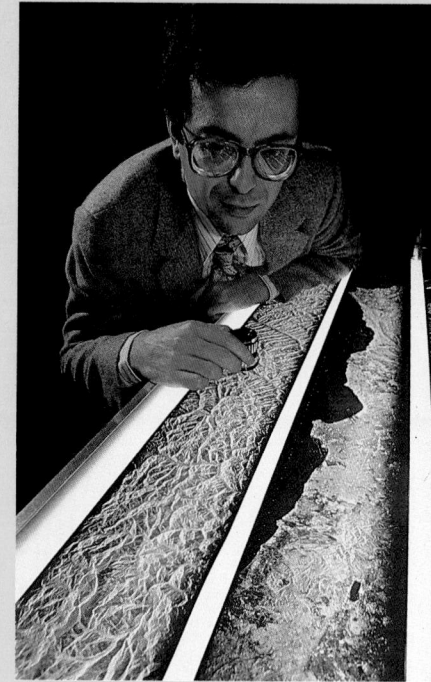

The contiguous 48 states appear virtually cloud free in a mosaic of 15 images taken by the National Oceanic and Atmospheric Administration satellites. Vegetation shows as red. A computerized geometric process, developed by the U.S. Geological Survey's EROS Data Center at Sioux Falls, South Dakota, gives the images a high degree of accuracy.

Space-borne radar from the shuttle **Columbia** in 1981 imaged a swath of China 50 kilometers wide. The pass extended from the Great Wall to the Yellow Sea (inset map). Here in eastern China the clustered villages appear as stars; grid pattern shows field boundaries (bottom left). An earlier pass over the desert to the west proved radar could penetrate sand, revealing ancient drainage patterns of potential value to hydrologists, climatologists, and geologists.

Longer strips of the radar pass undergo inspection at the Jet Propulsion Laboratory in Pasadena, California (above). Physicist Charles Elachi served as principal investigator of the JPL team that developed the radar.

CHUCK O'REAR (TOP); NASA, JET PROPULSION LABORATORY (LEFT); U.S. GEOLOGICAL SURVEY'S EROS DATA CENTER (UPPER LEFT); NGS CARTOGRAPHIC DIVISION

ROBINSON

VAN DER GRINTEN

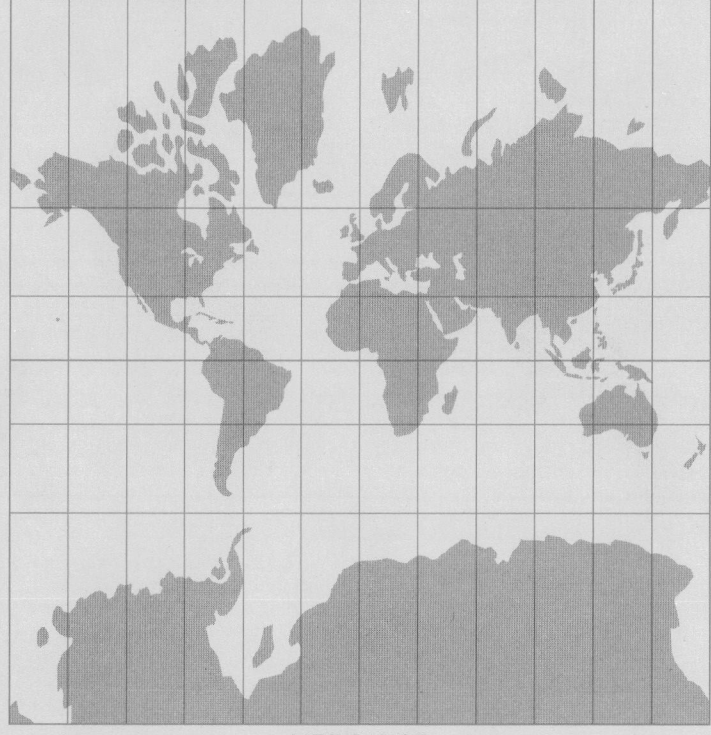

MERCATOR

Which of the three maps at left portrays the earth as it really is? The answer is none, since it is impossible to accurately put the round earth on flat paper—but the Robinson projection comes close.

For centuries mapmakers have grappled with the question of how to map the round earth on flat paper. The Mercator projection, for instance, introduced in 1569 as an aid to navigation, vastly distorts landmasses in the high latitudes—Greenland is 16 times as large as it should be.

Shortly after 1915, when the Cartographic Division was established, the National Geographic Society adopted the projection of Alphons van der Grinten of Chicago, which gave a more realistic view but still greatly enlarged such northern countries as Canada and the U.S.S.R. With an aim toward minimizing distortion, the new world map issued for the Society's 1988 centennial uses a projection devised by Arthur H. Robinson at the University of Wisconsin-Madison.

In addition to mapping the world, the Cartographic Division produces map supplements, such as the 17-map Making of America

series, page maps illustrating magazine stories, atlases, mural maps, and globes. Meticulous research (facing page) and artistic design as well as precise name placement (above) are but three of the steps in the preparation of these products that help our members find their way around the world.

BRETON LITTLEHALES (OPPOSITE AND ABOVE); NGS CARTOGRAPHIC DIVISION

The Future Is an Unbroken Trail

Scouting alternatives for a trek into our second century

By GILBERT M. GROSVENOR   PRESIDENT AND CHAIRMAN OF THE BOARD

"NO ONE EVER THROWS IT AWAY. . . ." The rate at which copies of our Society's yellow-bordered official journal accumulate has become part of American folklore.

We've been told that all those copies would stretch to the moon and back, that all those pages could cover Connecticut (poor Connecticut!), that the weight of growing stacks of them might affect the balance of earth's rotation on its axis. One enterprising writer even investigated the insulation value of GEOGRAPHICS spread over an attic floor. Conclusion: The high-quality paper that makes for sharp images and long storage life turns out to be a poor retainer of heat.

That's as it may be, but the only insulating role we ever intended for our magazine and Society was to ward off the chill of ignorance.

This index gives entries for all the articles that have appeared in a hundred years of NATIONAL GEOGRAPHIC. It also lists the scores of books the Society has published, except those for the very youngest readers. The index includes titles of our Television Specials and video programs. In a separate section it also lists all the thousands of financial grants we have made to explorers, scientists, and other researchers since 1890.

All those entries show a huge growth of information over the past century, the incredible rate of increase in the production of that information, and the fast-multiplying technologies employed to deliver it. The entries also suggest that no listing, however complete, can draw borders around the Society's present activities, much less its future. For make no mistake, change in the Society, as in the larger world, is not only continuing, it is accelerating.

To imagine what lies ahead, let us consider for a moment the Society's founders and the future they faced a century ago. They too lived in an era of technological change. Labor-saving machines were becoming available, even in the home. On the farm reapers, tractors, and threshers increased efficiency and cut the work load. Some farm laborers left for factory work in cities. There giant steam engines were breathing new life into industry, but the world was already moving from the steam age into one of electricity. Edison's electric light, though new, was increasingly driving back the night, and telephone lines were spiderwebbing city streets. The

To put geography back on the map in U.S. classrooms, the Society launched the Geography Education Program in 1985. Its goals: teacher training and support, innovative educational technologies, public-awareness activities. Taking his message to students, Society President Gilbert M. Grosvenor spoke at Wilkinson Foreign Language Experience School in St. Louis, Missouri, where students were given inflatable globes. "Without geography," he said, "we're nowhere."

SISSE BRIMBERG

Society's founders were among the most highly trained and foresighted people of their time, yet could one blame them if they asked themselves in wonder: "What's next?"

What indeed? The first American automobile had not yet appeared, nor had humans yet left the ground in powered flight. The Kodak box camera was introduced in 1888, the same year that the National Geographic Society was born—a propitious coincidence—but wireless radio broadcasts, much less television, were still decades away. How easy for us now to take for granted changes the founders couldn't anticipate. The past is a road paved with hindsight, while the future is an unbroken trail.

We too ask in wonder: "What's next?" Ours is an era of genetic engineering and microchips, an era when lasers and superconductivity hold promise comparable to electricity and the gasoline engine of a century ago. Yet we do not know the answer to "What's next?" any more than did the founders in their time.

W E DO KNOW that this Society has endured because of a willingness from the start to adopt new attitudes and new technologies. We pioneered in the printing of color photography, amid warnings that it would lead to financial ruin. Our television productions became leaders in a new genre of informative programming. We are now in the forefront of developing laser videodiscs that guide junior high and high school students through interactive learning experiences.

Youngsters are also participating in nationwide scientific experiments through a computer network that the Society has begun. Students all over the the country share their findings with other students, often hundreds of miles away, in order that all may contribute to common solutions.

We have always addressed education—in our publications, films, filmstrips, and videos—but never so directly as now. Our centennial gift to the nation has been the creation of the National Geographic Society Education Foundation, with our initial funding of 20 million dollars and the pledge to match an additional 20 million dollars contributed by others. Through the foundation we hope to encourage a renewed emphasis on teaching—and learning—geography. Nationwide surveys funded by the Society have shown the unmistakable need. An appalling geographic illiteracy permeates every age level but is especially acute among the young.

We've set an ambitious goal—erasing that illiteracy from the blackboard by the turn of the 21st century. We're bringing teachers to our headquarters in the nation's capital for intensive month-long geography institutes to improve their knowledge and teaching skills. The program is free to the teachers and their school systems, but we do require one payment. When they go back home, the teacher-graduates must share their new insights and skills with colleagues as well as students. They then become agents of change for better geographic education.

At this writing 27 states have joined with us in organizing

geographic alliances—partnerships of educators, business leaders, and public policymakers dedicated to expanding geographic literacy. We have been instrumental in the creation of those regional alliances, and we continue to assist their growth while promoting the founding of new ones.

I N THIS NEW WAY we are following in the footsteps of the Society's founders: by institutionalizing the importance of geographic knowledge. Such knowledge has always been important but perhaps never more so than now.

Advances in communications are shrinking our world to the point that there are no longer truly remote peoples or isolated problems. Through television, wars in Afghanistan and Angola or unrest in Seoul and South Africa resounds in our living rooms. A starving child on camera in Africa reaches out a bony hand, and millions in the developed world are confronted by that misery and the conditions that cause it. The stock market shudders in New York, and the effects ripple to Tokyo, Hong Kong, Singapore, Paris, and London within a few hours.

Other markets are affected as well. It's no secret that the United States has lost an edge to other countries in trade. I think that says many things—none of them good—about our ignorance of geography. It's an old axiom that you've got to know your territory to make sales, and Society surveys show convincingly that most Americans don't know the global territory. When some years ago the balance of trade began favoring such nations as Japan and West Germany, there arose a cry for more foreign purchase of American goods.

Complaints came back from potential customers: American business representatives knew little of the customs in countries where they hoped to make sales. Look, in contrast, at what the Japanese accomplished by studying the American auto market and then making inroads with fuel-efficient, dependable, and stylish cars at reasonable prices. It is a success story based in part on knowledge of trends and tastes in a nation—the United States—a third of the way around the globe.

Just as Japanese auto—and electronics—makers adopted American manufacturing and marketing techniques to crack the American market, learning more about the world can make us more competitive. It took an American born in the Netherlands to notice that the eels swimming in the Potomac River had more potential than ending up as inexpensive crab bait. Soon he was flying eels across the Atlantic to help satisfy the demand of European gourmets.

To compete in world markets, producers cannot rely on the odd chance that they may have specialized knowledge. Suppose farmers on the Delmarva Peninsula tried to compete effectively in the international market for fresh produce. Do Saudi Arabians like asparagus? Fresh? Do they already grow it? Would they pay a premium for it? Such questions apply in manufacturing and services markets as well as in agriculture.

Geographic knowlege is practical knowledge, and a listing of

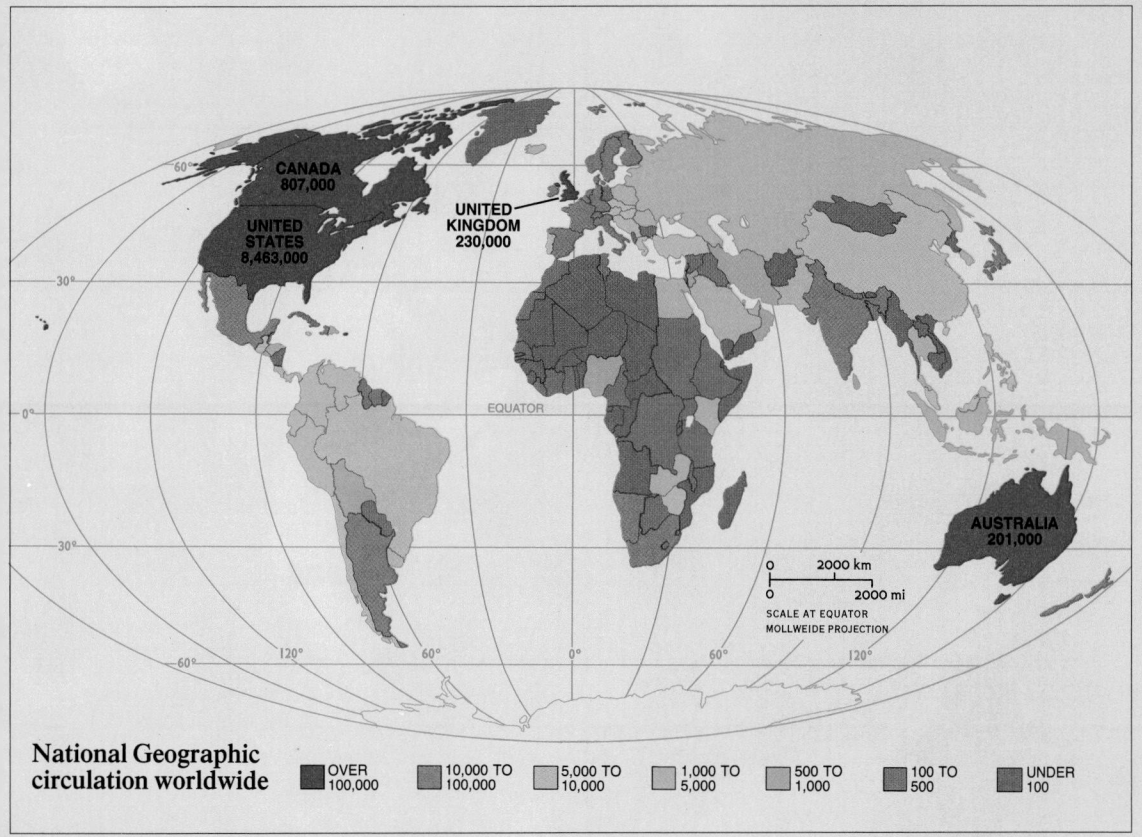

National Geographic circulation worldwide

CANADA 807,000
UNITED STATES 8,463,000
UNITED KINGDOM 230,000
AUSTRALIA 201,000

EQUATOR

0   2000 km
0   2000 mi
SCALE AT EQUATOR
MOLLWEIDE PROJECTION

OVER 100,000 | 10,000 TO 100,000 | 5,000 TO 10,000 | 1,000 TO 5,000 | 500 TO 1,000 | 100 TO 500 | UNDER 100

a region's cultural practices can be just as important in a computer-maintained data base as a list of shipping rates and banking regulations. In the new era of "What's next?" for the Society, I see nothing inherently wrong with our branching out into providing information related to economic geography.

There are, of course, far more serious matters to address than outlets for products. We on planet earth face sobering environmental problems that our Society's founders could not have imagined. While some among them were concerned about the loss of American forests to timber cutting, they could hardly have credited the importance we now attach to the world's fast-disappearing tropical rain forests.

T HE FOUNDERS' TIME was one of reclaiming land by draining swamps; ours is a time of realizing the value of wetlands even as their numbers and extent decline. Theirs was a time of great improvements in city water and sanitation systems; ours is a time of hazardous wastes and air pollution reaching even the most isolated locations in the world.

Theirs was a time when the far reaches of the globe seemed remote. Ours is a time when many of the most serious problems related to geography proclaim: *There are no distant places.* What could be more basic to geography than trying to understand the alteration

Spread across the globe (above), the Society's 10.5 million members share a curiosity about one another and the world in which we live. This curiosity is answered by the Society's four magazines, books, television films, maps, and educational materials, which entertain and inform from childhood through old age. Through agreements with foreign publishers, a growing number of these products are also being translated into such languages as Italian, Swedish, Chinese, and Japanese.

NGS CARTOGRAPHIC DIVISION

THE FUTURE IS AN UNBROKEN TRAIL

of climate by the greenhouse gases—or the depletion of the ozone layer that protects life from the sun's most dangerous ultraviolet rays? Both problems are caused by the release of gases from human activity. Both require massive changes in the materials we use and the fuels we burn to avert eventual disaster.

As you will discover in this index, the Society and its magazine have tried to stay on top of environmental crises for generations. You can find a listing for an article called "Saving the Forests," published in 1907. Another on pollution of the Potomac River is dated 1897. The possibility of future petroleum shortages was first addressed in the February 1920 issue.

We will have to do even more in the future in all our Society's programs and media. The depredations to our planet are not going to disappear easily or soon. Whole patterns of consumption may have to change. What will happen in this age of information when the people of Africa and Asia fully realize that the developed world controls 80 percent of earth's resources—though it contains about a quarter of the population?

That question cannot now be answered. But it is within the mission of the National Geographic Society to raise such questions, so that we can all think about alternative futures before a time without choice is upon us.

It is not within the scope of this Society's charter to become an advocate of one course or another. But we are going to report information as the facts warrant and through whatever media are the most appropriate. Sometimes the information will be disturbing, but as it affects all of us and our world, we call such reporting the responsible diffusion of geographic information.

I expect an index like this one will, a hundred years hence, be rife with stories about how the world dealt with environmental problems and social inequities. Those concerns will doubtless change over time, and such an index, or its bicentennial equivalent, may itself be vastly different.

From the crocodiles of Ethiopia to the Baka Pygmies of Cameroon, the cameras of the Society's Television Division cover it all. Our one-hour Specials, appearing since 1965, are among the most honored documentaries ever broadcast. Since the 1985 debut of National Geographic EXPLORER, a weekly two-hour, magazine-format program on cable, the Society has increased its programming to a hundred hours a year. Films from both EXPLORER and the Specials have also been released as videos.

TECHNOLOGY RUSHES ON. Instantaneous transmission of photographic images from the field to our headquarters is already very near. Film itself may soon become largely a matter of antiquarian interest. Our presses run faster all the time, even as printing quality improves. Yet someday the presses may stop. Direct transfer by laser of images to pages is on the horizon, and no one knows what is over that horizon.

Future Society members may receive an electronic module that they can insert into a device to display still or moving images, to hear sounds of human and other voices, and to display text or retrieve it in some new equivalent of printing.

We recognize that, like those who went before us, we must adjust to changing times and developing technologies. We welcome the next "What's next?" We will do what is necessary to assure that our mission and message will be renewed down the decades of the Society's second century.

NATIONAL GEOGRAPHIC VIDEO

THE EXPLORERS
A CENTURY OF DISCOVERY

One hundred years of spectacular history-making expeditions.

THE FUTURE IS AN UNBROKEN TRAIL

In the Waiting Room

In Worcester, Massachusetts,
I went with Aunt Consuelo
to keep her dentist's appointment
and sat and waited for her
in the dentist's waiting room.
It was winter. It got dark
early. The waiting room
was full of grown-up people,
arctics and overcoats,
lamps and magazines.
My aunt was inside
what seemed like a long time
and while I waited I read
the *National Geographic*
(I could read) and carefully
studied the photographs:
The inside of a volcano,
black, and full of ashes;
then it was spilling over
in rivulets of fire.
Osa and Martin Johnson
dressed in riding breeches,
laced boots, and pith helmets.
A dead man slung on a pole
—"Long Pig," the caption said.
Babies with pointed heads
wound round and round with string;
black, naked women with necks
wound round and round with wire
like the necks of light bulbs.
Their breasts were horrifying.
I read it right straight through.
I was too shy to stop.
And then I looked at the cover:
the yellow margins, the date.

Suddenly, from inside,
came an *oh!* of pain
—Aunt Consuelo's voice—
not very loud or long.
I wasn't at all surprised;
even then I knew she was
a foolish, timid woman.
I might have been embarrassed,
but wasn't. What took me
completely by surprise
was that it was *me:*
my voice, in my mouth.
Without thinking at all
I was my foolish aunt,
I—we—were falling, falling,
our eyes glued to the cover
of the *National Geographic,*
February, 1918.

I said to myself: three days
and you'll be seven years old.
I was saying it to stop
the sensation of falling off
the round, turning world
into cold, blue-black space.
But I felt: you are an *I,*
you are an *Elizabeth,*
you are one of *them.*
Why should you be one, too?
I scarcely dared to look
to see what it was I was.
I gave a sidelong glance
—I couldn't look any higher—
at shadowy gray knees,
trousers and skirts and boots
and different pairs of hands
lying under the lamps.
I knew that nothing stranger
had ever happened, that nothing
stranger could ever happen.

Why should I be my aunt,
or me, or anyone?
What similarities—
boots, hands, the family voice
I felt in my throat, or even
the *National Geographic*
and those awful hanging breasts—
held us all together
or made us all just one?
How—I didn't know any
word for it—how "unlikely"...
How had I come to be here,
like them, and overhear
a cry of pain that could have
got loud and worse but hadn't?

The waiting room was bright
and too hot. It was sliding
beneath a big black wave,
another, and another.

Then I was back in it.
The War was on. Outside,
in Worcester, Massachusetts,
were night and slush and cold,
and it was still the fifth
of February, 1918.

From *The Complete Poems
1927-1979* by Elizabeth Bishop;
© 1979, 1983 by Alice Helen
Methfessel. Reprinted by
permission of Farrar, Straus
and Giroux, Inc.

PAINTING BY JAMES M. GURNEY

Milestones of the National Geographic Society

January 13, 1888
Thirty-three founders—scientists, scholars, military men—meet at the Cosmos Club, then on Lafayette Square in Washington, D.C., to create "a society for the increase and diffusion of geographic knowledge."

October 1888
The first issue of NATIONAL GEOGRAPHIC magazine is sent to 165 charter members.

October 1889
The magazine publishes its first map supplement, showing the Asheville, North Carolina, area.

1890-91
The first National Geographic Society-sponsored expedition maps the Mount St. Elias region, in Alaska, and discovers Canada's highest peak, which the team names Mount Logan.

January 7, 1898
Alexander Graham Bell assumes National Geographic Society's presidency.

April 1, 1899
Gilbert Hovey Grosvenor joins the staff as Assistant Editor.

February 1903
Gilbert H. Grosvenor is appointed Editor of NATIONAL GEOGRAPHIC.

Fall 1903
The National Geographic Society moves to a new headquarters in Washington, D.C., built with donations given by the family of first Society President, Gardiner Greene Hubbard.

January 1905
Gilbert H. Grosvenor fills 11 pages of the magazine with photographs of Lhasa in Tibet. Expecting to be fired, he is instead congratulated by Society members.

July 1906
Grosvenor publishes George Shiras 3d's pioneering flash photographs of animals at night. Two Society board members resign, claiming the magazine is turning into a "picture book."

April 1909
Leader of a Society-supported expedition, Robert E. Peary claims to be the first to reach the North Pole.

February 1910
The magazine adopts a cover design whose border is adorned with oak and laurel leaves, acorns, and four hemispheres.

November 1910
The GEOGRAPHIC publishes 24 pages of hand-tinted photographs, William W. Chapin's "Scenes in Korea and China," far more than any other magazine had published.

1912-15
Society-supported expeditions in the Peruvian Andes led by Hiram Bingham clear and excavate Machu Picchu, lost mountaintop city of the Inca.

1915
The Cartographic Division is established to increase production of maps under direct Society control.

1916
In a Society-sponsored expedition Robert F. Griggs discovers, names, and explores the Valley of Ten Thousand Smokes in a volcanic region near Mount Katmai, Alaska. Within two years a million acres is set aside as Katmai National Monument.

May 1918
"Map of the Western Theatre of War" is published, a tour de force of detailed cartography.

1919
National Geographic *School Bulletin* begins publication.

1920
Gilbert H. Grosvenor becomes President of the Society, a post he is to hold for 34 years.

January 1927
The magazine publishes the first natural-color underwater photographs, taken by staff photographer Charles Martin and scientist W. H. Longley.

November 29, 1929
Richard E. Byrd is the first to fly over the South Pole; he photographs 160,000 square miles of Antarctica from the air.

1930
Melville Bell Grosvenor makes the first natural-color aerial photographs to be published.

April 1931-February 1932
Staff writer-photographer Maynard Owen Williams joins the Citroën-Haardt expedition across Asia from the Mediterranean to the Yellow Sea.

August 15, 1934
In a Society-sponsored investigation, William Beebe and Otis Barton descend in a bathysphere to a record depth of 3,028 feet in the sea off Bermuda.

November 11, 1935
Backed by the Society, U.S. Army Air Corps Capts. Albert W. Stevens and Orvil A. Anderson ascend in the stratospheric balloon *Explorer II* to a record 72,395 feet.

1938-1946
Matthew W. Stirling leads Society-sponsored expeditions that uncover thousand-year-old La Venta, an Olmec site in southern Mexico.

1941
The Society opens its storehouse of photographs, maps, and other cartographic data to President Roosevelt and the U.S. armed forces to aid war efforts.

July 1942
The first cover illustration appears, a U.S. flag.

October 1952
The magazine publishes the first of many articles on undersea exploration by Jacques-Yves Cousteau.

May 1954
John Oliver La Gorce is elected President and Editor.

May 1956
Monumental National Geographic Society-Palomar Observatory Sky Survey is completed—and remains an important basic resource of astronomers.

January 1957
Melville Bell Grosvenor becomes President and Editor.

Luis Marden of the foreign editorial staff finds the 167-year-old remains of the British armed merchant vessel *Bounty* off Pitcairn Island.

The Society's modern Book Service is inaugurated with *The World in Your Garden.*

September 1959
Color photographs begin to appear regularly on the GEOGRAPHIC's cover.

September 1960
The Society reports on fossil remains of a hominid that lived in Africa more than 1.75 million years ago. Called *Zinjanthropus* by discoverers Louis and Mary Leakey, the find opens a new era in paleoanthropology.

1961
A National Geographic Society grant assists Jane Goodall in her study of chimpanzees in Tanzania's Gombe National Park.

May 1961
The Society's first political globe is introduced.

June 1962
John Glenn carries a National Geographic Society flag on the first manned U.S. orbital space flight.
The Society publishes the official White House guidebook, first in a series of public-service books.

May 1963
First Americans attain the summit of Mount Everest in a Society-supported expedition.

June 1963
The first bound *Atlas of the World* is published.

Summer 1963
A National Park Service study to save redwoods is funded by a Society grant. The survey aids establishment of Redwood National Park in California.
Society-sponsored investigation finds evidence in Newfoundland of Norse settlement in North America five centuries before Columbus.

January 18, 1964
New ten-story headquarters building in Washington, D.C., is dedicated by President Lyndon B. Johnson.

July 1965
The Special Publications Division is established.

September 10, 1965
"Americans on Everest" inaugurates a series of hour-long National Geographic Television Specials, first shown on CBS.

1967
Dian Fossey begins a Society-funded study of mountain gorillas in Rwanda.
Frederick G. Vosburgh named Editor.
Ocean-floor relief-map series is instituted.

1968
Society membership exceeds six million, having increased nearly threefold in a decade.

January 1968
First Society-produced filmstrips offered as educational tools for schools.

October 1968
More than a thousand employees move into a new Membership Center Building in Gaithersburg, Maryland.

February 1969
The Cartographic Division produces the first map to show the entire lunar surface on a single sheet.

July 1969
Apollo 11 astronauts carry National Geographic Society flag to the moon.

June 1970
Gilbert M. Grosvenor is elected Editor.
Traveler's map supplements begun.

March 1971
First ethnic magazine supplement map, "The Peoples of Mainland Southeast Asia," launches political and cultural map series.

September 1975
National Geographic WORLD replaces the *School Bulletin* as the magazine for young people. Circulation reaches 1.3 million by 1976.

October 28, 1975
The Society begins a series of Specials on public television with "The Incredible Machine," about the human body. It becomes the most widely watched program ever shown on PBS.

Fall 1975
In anticipation of the nation's Bicentennial, the Book Service publishes *We Americans*. By early 1989 more than 1.2 million copies of the Society's all-time best-selling book had been printed.

Summer 1977
Magazine printing changes to gravure presses in Mississippi.

April 1979
Mary Leakey reports discovery of 3.6-million-year-old footprints in the volcanic ash of a riverbed in Tanzania. They are from upright-walking ancestors of modern humans.

August 1980
Wilbur E. Garrett becomes the magazine's Editor, succeeding Gilbert M. Grosvenor, who becomes President.

February 1981
A Special Report on Energy is published as a 13th issue of the magazine and sent without cost to Society members.

December 1982
The magazine details discovery of skeletons unearthed at Herculaneum, a Roman town buried with Pompeii in the A.D. 79 eruption of Mount Vesuvius.

1984
Undersea archaeological pioneer George F. Bass, supported by the Society, discovers in a 3,400-year-old wrecked ship off the coast of southern Turkey the most extensive collection of Bronze Age trade goods yet found.

March 1984
A holographic image of an eagle appears on NATIONAL GEOGRAPHIC's cover, pioneering the use of holograms in large-circulation magazines.
NATIONAL GEOGRAPHIC TRAVELER, a magazine devoted to educational and practical aspects of travel, is launched.

June 19, 1984
A seven-story addition to the Society's headquarters complex is dedicated by President Ronald Reagan.

Winter 1985
A quarterly scholarly journal, NATIONAL GEOGRAPHIC RESEARCH, is begun to convey findings of Society-sponsored and other research projects.

April 7, 1985
The EXPLORER series has its premier on cable television; it becomes a two-hour weekly feature on SuperStation TBS in 1986.

April 1985
The Geography Education Program is initiated to emphasize the importance of geography's role in the modern world and to improve its instruction, especially in public schools.

September 11, 1985
Details of the discovery of R.M.S. *Titanic* announced at Society headquarters by Robert D. Ballard.

May 1, 1986
Six members of the Steger International Polar Expedition—including one woman—are the first to reach the North Pole by dogsled without resupply since Peary's attempt.

October 1986
Senior Associate Editor Joseph Judge reports that six lines of evidence point to Samana Cay in the Bahamas as the first landfall of Christopher Columbus in the New World.

October 1987
Results of a smell test—largest scientific survey of its kind, which appeared in the September 1986 NATIONAL GEOGRAPHIC—are published.
The magazine is sent to 10.5 million members.

January 1988
The National Geographic Society Education Foundation is established to raise funds and provide grants for geography education. Initial funding is 20 million dollars with another 20 million dollars available to match contributions from other sources.

April 1988
The magazine reports discovery and publishes photographs of a 4,600-year-old boat entombed in a pit beside the Great Pyramid of Khufu in Giza, Egypt.

October 1988
New monthly Geographica section, illustrated with photographs and maps, is launched in the magazine; it includes geographic news briefs and updates of previous stories.

Fall 1988
The magazine celebrates the centennial of the Society with four special issues highlighting its history, the peopling of the earth, exploration, and the environment.
The December cover is made up entirely of holographic images.

A
B

Maneuvering on skis, two adventurers press on during their trek around Alaska's Mount McKinley.

NED GILLETTE

AAFTTC. *See* Army Air Forces Training Command

ABACO (Island), Bahama Islands:
The Loyalists. By Kent Britt. Photos by Ted Spiegel. 510-539, *Apr. 1975*

ABAIANG (Atoll), Gilbert Islands:
Gilbert Islands in the Wake of Battle. By W. Robert Moore. 129-162, *Feb. 1945*

ABALONE:
Goggle Fishing in California Waters. By David Hellyer. Photos by Lamar Boren. 615-632, *May 1949*

ABBE, CLEVELAND:
Board of Managers. 165, Apr. 1889; 270, July 1889; 68, *Apr. 1890*

ABBEY, EDWARD: *Author*
Guadalupe's Trails in Summer (Guadalupe Mountains National Park, Texas). 135-141, *July 1979*

ABBOT, C. G.: *Author*
Hunting an Observatory: A Successful Search for a Dry Mountain on Which to Establish the National Geographic Society's Solar Radiation Station. 503-518, *Oct. 1926*
Measuring the Sun's Heat and Forecasting the Weather: The National Geographic Society to Maintain a Solar Station in a Remote Part of the World to Coöperate with Smithsonian Institution Stations in California and Chile. 111-126, *Jan. 1926*
Do Volcanic Explosions Affect Our Climate? 181-198, *Feb. 1913*

ABBOT, J. LLOYD, Jr.: *Author*
Flight Into Antarctic Darkness. Photos by David S. Boyer. 732-738, *Nov. 1967*

ABBOT, JOHN M.: *Author*
The Buried City of Ceylon. 613-622, *Nov. 1906*

ABBOTSBURY SWANNERY,
England:
The Swans of Abbotsbury. By Michael Moynihan. Photos by Barnet Saidman. 563-570, *Oct. 1959*

ABBOTT RANCH, Cherry County, Nebraska:
Land of Long Sunsets: Nebraska's Sand Hills. By John Madson. Photos by Jodi Cobb. 493-517, *Oct. 1978*

ABDUL AZIZ AL SAUD (King of Saudi Arabia). *See* Al Saud, Abdul Aziz

ABDUL GHAFUR:
Author-Photographer
From America to Mecca on Airborne Pilgrimage. 1-60, *July 1953*

ABDUL-RAUF, MUHAMMAD:
Author
Pilgrimage to Mecca. Photos by Mehmet Biber. 581-607, *Nov. 1978*

ABELL, GEORGE O.: *Author*
Exploring the Farthest Reaches of Space. 782-790, *Dec. 1956*

ABELL, PAUL:
Nomination Page. In Ethiopia. *Sept. 1968*

ABELL, SAM: *Photographer*
■ *Mountain Adventure: Exploring the Appalachian Trail.* By Ron Fisher. 200 pages. *1988*
James Madison, Architect of the Constitution. By Alice J. Hall. 340-369, *Sept. 1987*
A Tunnel Through Time: The Appalachian Trail. By Noel Grove. 216-243, *Feb. 1987*
The World of Tolstoy. By Peter T. White. 758-791, *June 1986*
C. M. Russell, Cowboy Artist. By Bart McDowell. 60-95, *Jan. 1986*
Hagi: Where Japan's Revolution Began. By N. Taylor Gregg. Paintings by Kinuko Y. Craft. 751-773, *June 1984*
The Olympic Peninsula. By Bill Richards. Included: Maps showing wildlife refuges, Indian reservations, and annual precipitation. 644-673, *May 1984*
Herbs for All Seasons. By Lonnelle Aikman. Picture portfolio text by Larry Kohl. 386-409, *Mar. 1983*
The Bonanza Bean—Coffee. By Ethel A. Starbird. 388-405, *Mar. 1981*
Long Island's Quiet Side (East End). By Jane Snow. 662-685, *May 1980*
Ontario, Canada's Keystone. By David S. Boyer. Photos by Sam Abell and the author. 760-795, *Dec. 1978*
Our Wild and Scenic Rivers: The Noatak. By John M. Kauffmann. 52-59, *July 1977*
■ *Still Waters, White Waters: Exploring America's Rivers and Lakes.* By Ron Fisher. Touring by canoe. 199 pages. *1977*
■ *The Pacific Crest Trail.* By William R. Gray. 199 pages. *1975*
Newfoundland Trusts in the Sea. By Gary Jennings. 112-141, *Jan. 1974*
Yellowstone at 100: A Walk Through the Wilderness. By Karen and Derek Craighead. 579-603, *May 1972*

ABEMAMA (Atoll), Gilbert Islands:
Gilbert Islands in the Wake of Battle. By W. Robert Moore. 129-162, *Feb. 1945*

ABERCROMBIE, LYNN:
Nomination Page. In Oman. *July 1981*
Photographer
Arabia's Frankincense Trail. By Thomas J. Abercrombie. 474-513, *Oct. 1985*
Oman: Guardian of the Gulf. By Thomas J. Abercrombie. Photos by the author and Lynn Abercrombie. 344-377, *Sept. 1981*

ABERCROMBIE, THOMAS J.:
On Assignment in Sharjah, United Arab Emirates. *May 1988*
Nomination Page. In Oman. *July 1981*
Editorial. By Gilbert M. Grosvenor. 291, *Mar. 1977*
Nomination Page. In Saudi Arabia. *July 1972*
Nomination Page. In Yemen. *Feb. 1964*

Nomination Page. In Venezuela. *Feb. 1963*
Nomination Page. On Easter Island. *Oct. 1961*
National Geographic Photographers Win Top Magazine Awards. 830-831, *June 1959*
Nomination Page. At the South Pole. *Mar. 1958*
Author
When the Moors Ruled Spain. Photos by Bruno Barbey. 86-119, *July 1988*
The Persian Gulf–Living in Harm's Way. Photos by Steve Raymer. Included: Iraq, Iran, Saudi Arabia, Kuwait, Bahrain, Qatar, United Arab Emirates, Oman. 648-671, *May 1988*
Arabia's Frankincense Trail. Photos by Lynn Abercrombie. 474-513, *Oct. 1985*
Jordan: Kingdom in the Middle. Photos by Jodi Cobb. 236-268, *Feb. 1984*
Perth–Fair Winds and Full Sails. Photos by Cary Wolinsky. 638-667, *May 1982*
Minneapolis and St. Paul. Photos by Annie Griffiths. 665-691, *Nov. 1980*
Islam's Heartland, Up in Arms. 335-345, *Sept. 1980*
Bahrain: Hub of the Persian Gulf. Photos by Steve Raymer. 300-329, *Sept. 1979*
Author-Photographer
Oman: Guardian of the Gulf. Photos by the author and Lynn Abercrombie. 344-377, *Sept. 1981*
Ladakh–The Last Shangri-la. 332-359, *Mar. 1978*
Egypt: Change Comes to a Changeless Land. 312-343, *Mar. 1977*
Algeria: Learning to Live With Independence. 200-233, *Aug. 1973*
The Sword and the Sermon. 3-45, *July 1972*
Morocco, Land of the Farthest West. 834-865, *June 1971*
Kansai, Japan's Historic Heartland. 295-339, *Mar. 1970*
Switzerland, Europe's High-rise Republic. 68-113, *July 1969*
Nomad in Alaska's Outback. 540-567, *Apr. 1969*
Afghanistan: Crossroad of Conquerors. 297-345, *Sept. 1968*
Saudi Arabia: Beyond the Sands of Mecca. 1-53, *Jan. 1966*
Cambodia: Indochina's "Neutral" Corner. 514-551, *Oct. 1964*
Behind the Veil of Troubled Yemen. 403-445, *Mar. 1964*
Venezuela Builds on Oil. 344-387, *Mar. 1963*
Ice Fishing's Frigid Charms. 861-872, *Dec. 1958*
Young-old Lebanon Lives by Trade. 479-523, *Apr. 1958*
Photographer
Underwater Archeology: Key to History's Warehouse. By George F. Bass. Photos by Thomas J. Abercrombie and Robert B. Goodman. 138-156, *July 1963*
The Mighty *Enterprise*. By Nathaniel T. Kenney. 431-448, *Mar. 1963*
Easter Island and Its Mysterious Monuments. By Howard La Fay. 90-117, *Jan. 1962*

At one with his environment, Aborigine Nipper Kapirigi rests in Australia's Kakadu National Park. BELINDA WRIGHT

Enchantress! By Theodore H. Reed. 628-641, *May 1961*

Old-New Iran, Next Door to Russia. By Edward J. Linehan. 44-85, *Jan. 1961*

Man's Deepest Dive. By Jacques Piccard. 224-239, *Aug. 1960*

Brasília, Metropolis Made to Order. By Hernane Tavares de Sá. 704-724, *May 1960*

Alaska Proudly Joins the Union. By Ernest Gruening. 43-83, *July 1959*

You and the Obedient Atom. By Allan C. Fisher, Jr. Photos by B. Anthony Stewart and Thomas J. Abercrombie. 303-353, *Sept. 1958*

Man's First Winter at the South Pole. By Paul A. Siple. 439-478, *Apr. 1958*

Captain Smith of Jamestown. By Bradford Smith. 581-620, *May 1957*

The **ABERRATION** of Sound as Illustrated by the Berkeley Powder Explosion. By Robert H. Chapman. 246-249, *July 1896*

ABIDJAN, Ivory Coast:

The Ivory Coast–African Success Story. By Michael and Aubine Kirtley. 94-125, *July 1982*

ABKHAZIAN A.S.S.R., U.S.S.R.:

"Every Day Is a Gift When You Are Over 100." By Alexander Leaf. Photos by John Launois. 93-119, *Jan. 1973*

ABOARD a Blimp Hunting U-boats: A Day above the Atlantic Reveals Navy Talk and Navy Ways, Creeping Con-

voys, and Torpedoed Wrecks. By Mason Sutherland. 79-96, *July 1943*

ABOARD the N. S. *Savannah:* World's First Nuclear Merchantman. By Alan Villiers. Photos by John E. Fletcher. 280-298, *Aug. 1962*

ABOLITIONISTS:

The Underground Railroad. By Charles L. Blockson. Photos by Louie Psihoyos. 3-39, *July 1984*

"ABOMINABLE SNOWMAN":

Wintering on the Roof of the World. By Barry C. Bishop. 503-547, *Oct. 1962*

ABORIGINAL PEOPLE OF AUSTRALIA:

The First Australians. By Stanley Breeden. Photos by Belinda Wright. 266-289, *Feb. 1988*

The First Australians: Living in Two Worlds. By Belinda Wright and Stanley Breeden. 291-294, *Feb. 1988*

The Tea and Sugar Lifeline in Australia's Outback. By Erla Zwingle. Photos by William Albert Allard. 737-757, *June 1986*

Queensland, Broad Shoulder of Australia. By William S. Ellis. Photos by David Robert Austen. Included: Queensland Fossils Expand Australia's Prehistoric Menagerie. 2-39, *Jan. 1986*

Perth–Fair Winds and Full Sails. By Thomas J. Abercrombie. Photos by Cary Wolinsky. 638-667, *May 1982*

Arnhem Land Aboriginals Cling to Dreamtime. By Clive Scollay. Photos by Penny Tweedie. 644-663, *Nov. 1980*

The Journey of Burke and Wills. By Joseph Judge. Photos by Joseph J. Scherschel. 152-191, *Feb. 1979*

Western Australia, the Big Country. By Kenneth MacLeish. Photos by James L. Stanfield. 150-187, *Feb. 1975*

Rock Paintings of the Aborigines. By Kay and Stanley Breeden. 174-187, *Feb. 1973*

The Top End of Down Under. By Kenneth MacLeish. Photos by Thomas Nebbia. 145-174, *Feb. 1973*

Queensland: Young Titan of Australia's Tropic North. By Kenneth MacLeish. Photos by Winfield Parks. 593-639, *Nov. 1968*

"The Alice" in Australia's Wonderland. By Alan Villiers. Photos by Jeff Carter and David Moore. 230-257, *Feb. 1966*

Australia. By Alan Villiers. 309-385. I. The West and the South. 309-345; II. The Settled East, the Barrier Reef, the Center. 347-385, *Sept. 1963*

Expedition to the Land of the Tiwi (Melville Island). By Charles P. Mountford. 417-440, *Mar. 1956*

From Spear to Hoe on Groote Eylandt. By Howell Walker. 131-142, *Jan. 1953*

Exploring Stone Age Arnhem Land. By Charles P. Mountford. Photos by Howell Walker. NGS research grant. 745-782, *Dec. 1949*

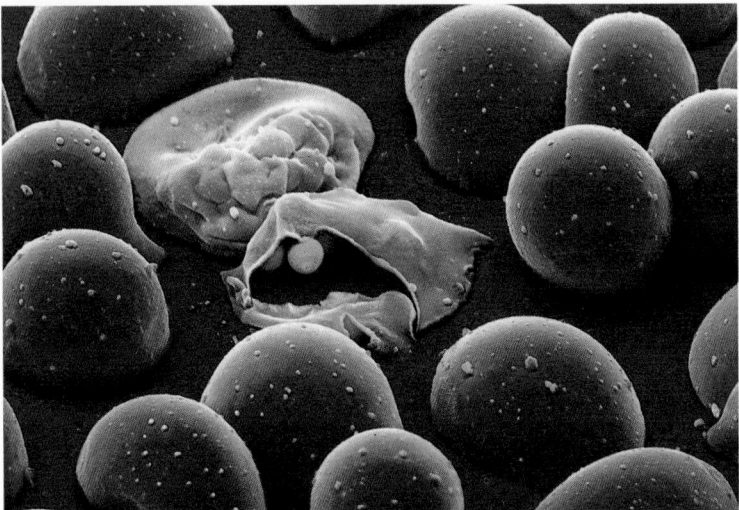

Malaria protozoans burst from red blood cells. Such parasites are lethal to those with immune deficiencies. © LENNART NILSSON

Railroad, and Filanzana. By Charles F. Swingle. 179-211, *Aug. 1929*

ACROSS Nicaragua with Transit and Machéte. By R. E. Peary. 315-335, *Oct. 1889*

ACROSS the Alps in a Wicker Basket. By Phil Walker. 117-131, *Jan. 1963*

ACROSS the Equator with the American Navy. By Herbert Corey. 571-624, *June 1921*

ACROSS the Frozen Desert to Byrd Station. By Paul W. Frazier. Photos by Calvin L. Larsen. 383-398, *Sept. 1957*

ACROSS the Gulf by Rail to Key West. By Jefferson B. Browne. 203-207, *June 1896*

ACROSS the Midi in a Canoe: Two Americans Paddle Along the Canals of Southern France from the Atlantic to the Mediterranean. By Melville Chater. 127-167, *Aug. 1927*

ACROSS the Pacific by Balloon: The Flight of *Double Eagle V*. By Ben L. Abruzzo. 513-521, *Apr. 1982*

ACROSS the Potomac From Washington. By Albert W. Atwood. 1-33, *Jan. 1953*

ACROSS the Ridgepole of the Alps. By Walter Meayers Edwards. 410-419, *Sept. 1960*

ACROSS Tibet from India to China. By Ilia Tolstoy. 169-222, *Aug. 1946*

ACROSS Widest Africa. By A. Henry Savage Landor. 694-737, *Oct. 1908*

ACTS of Faith in Chile. By Allen A. Boraiko. Photos by David Alan Harvey. 54-85, *July 1988*

ADAK (Island), Aleutian Islands:

A Navy Artist Paints the Aleutians. By Mason Sutherland. Paintings by William F. Draper. 157-176, *Aug. 1943*

ADALIA, Turkey:

Historic Islands and Shores of the Aegean Sea. By Ernest Lloyd Harris. 231-261, *Sept. 1915*

ADAM, TASSILO: *Photographer*

Java, Queen of the East Indies. 335-358, *Sept. 1929*

ADAMS, ABIGAIL:

Patriots in Petticoats. By Lonnelle Aikman. Paintings by Louis S. Glanzman. 475-493, *Oct. 1975*

ADAMS, CLIFTON: *Photographer*

The State of Sky-Blue Water and Verdure (Minnesota). Photos by Clifton Adams and Edwin L. Wisherd. 289-296, *Mar. 1935*

A Sunshine Land of Fruits, Flowers, Movies, and Sport (California). Photos by Clifton Adams and Fred Payne Clatworthy. 545-592, *Nov. 1934*

Gay Colors in the Land of Black Majesty (Haiti). 445-452, *Oct. 1934*

Color Highlights of the Empire State (New York). 529-576, *Nov. 1933*

Sunset Hues in the Pacific Northwest (Washington). 155-162, *Feb. 1933*

Where the Last of the West Was Won (Washington). 179-186, *Feb. 1933*

Colorful Corners of the City of Homes (Philadelphia). Photos by Clifton Adams and Edwin L. Wisherd. 675-682, *Dec. 1932*

Nooks and Bays of Storied England. 83-190, *Feb. 1932*

Our Colorful City of Magnificent Distances (Washington, D. C.). 531-610, *Nov. 1931*

New England's Wonderland of Mountain, Lake, and Seascape. 263-270, *Sept. 1931*

Coasting Through the Bay State (Massachusetts). 287-294, *Sept. 1931*

Sauntering Through the Land of Roger Williams (Rhode Island). 311-318, *Sept. 1931*

The Most Famous Battle Field in America (Gettysburg). 66-75, *July 1931*

Rambles Through the Prairie State (Illinois). 545-552, *May 1931*

Chicago, Titan of the Middle West. 585-592, *May 1931*

Cradles of English History. 269-276, *Mar. 1931*

Tempo and Color of a Great City. Photos by Clifton Adams and Edwin L. Wisherd (New York). 539-578, *Nov. 1930*

Secrets of Washington's Lure (Washington, D. C.). 377-384, *Mar. 1930*

High Lights in the Sunshine State (Florida). 27-82, *Jan. 1930*

Highlights of London Town. 569-576, *May 1929*

Lakeland, Home of England's Nature Poets. 593-600, *May 1929*

From Stratford to the North Sea. 617-624, *May 1929*

Scenes and Shrines of the Cavalier Country (Virginia). 425-432, *Apr. 1929*

Unique Gifts of Washington to the Nation (Washington, D. C.). 473-480, *Apr. 1929*

Adventures in Arizona Color Photography. 29-36, *Jan. 1929*

The Home of the First Farmer of America (Mount Vernon). 605-620, *May 1928*

Michigan, Mistress of the Lakes. By Melville Chater. 269-325, *Mar. 1928*

Outside her hogan in Arizona's Painted Desert a Navajo proudly displays a beautiful blanket she has woven for traders. CLIFTON ADAMS, NGS

The Hills and Dales of Erin (Ireland). 317-326, *Mar. 1927*
The Green Mountain State (Vermont). 327-332, *Mar. 1927*
In the Land of the Montezumas. 265-280, *Mar. 1923*
Sardinian Smiles. 31-46, *Jan. 1923*

ADAMS, CYRUS C.: *Author*
"The United States–Land and Waters." 171-185, *May 1903*

ADAMS, HARRIET CHALMERS: *Author*
European Outpost: The Azores. 35-66, *Jan. 1935*
Madeira the Florescent. 81-106, *July 1934*
River-Encircled Paraguay. 385-416, *Apr. 1933*
Madrid Out-of-Doors. 225-256, *Aug. 1931*
Cirenaica, Eastern Wing of Italian Libia. 689-726, *June 1930*
Barcelona, Pride of the Catalans. 373-402, *Mar. 1929*
An Altitudinal Journey Through Portugal: Rugged Scenic Beauty, Colorful Costumes, and Ancient Castles Abound in Tiny Nation That Once Ruled a Vast Empire. 567-610, *Nov. 1927*
Across French and Spanish Morocco. 327-356, *Mar. 1925*
Adventurous Sons of Cádiz (Spain). 153-204, *Aug. 1924*
A Longitudinal Journey Through Chile. 219-273, *Sept. 1922*
Volcano-Girded Salvador: A Prosperous Central American State with the Densest Rural Population in the Western World. 189-200, *Feb. 1922*
The Grand Canyon Bridge. 645-650, *June 1921*
Rio de Janeiro, in the Land of Lure. 165-210, *Sept. 1920*
In French Lorraine: That Part of France Where the First American Soldiers Have Fallen. 499-518, *Nov.-Dec. 1917*
The First Transandine Railroad from Buenos Aires to Valparaiso. 397-417, *May 1910*
Kaleidoscopic La Paz: The City of the Clouds. 119-141, *Feb. 1909*
Cuzco, America's Ancient Mecca. 669-689, *Oct. 1908*
Some Wonderful Sights in the Andean Highlands: The Oldest City in America. Sailing on the Lake of the Clouds: The Yosemite of Peru. 597-618, *Sept. 1908*
Along the Old Inca Highway (Peru). 231-250, *Apr. 1908*
The East Indians in the New World (Trinidad). 485-491, *July 1907*
Picturesque Paramaribo (Surinam). 365-373, *June 1907*

ADAMS, JOHN:
Patriots in Petticoats. By Lonnelle Aikman. Paintings by Louis S. Glanzman. 475-493, *Oct. 1975*
The Living White House. By Lonnelle Aikman. 593-643, *Nov. 1966*
Profiles of the Presidents: I. The Presi-

dency and How It Grew. By Frank Freidel. 642-687, *Nov. 1964*

ADAMS, JOHN QUINCY:
The Living White House. By Lonnelle Aikman. 593-643, *Nov. 1966*
Profiles of the Presidents: I. The Presidency and How It Grew. By Frank Freidel. 642-687, *Nov. 1964*

ADAMS, M. P. GREENWOOD: *Author*
Australia's Wild Wonderland. 329-356, *Mar. 1924*

ADAMS, RICHARD E. W.:
Editorial. By Wilbur E. Garrett. 561, *May 1987*
Author
Río Azul, Lost City of the Maya. Photos by George F. Mobley. Included: Realm of the Maya (map). NGS research grant. 420-451, *Apr. 1986*

ADAMS, SAMUEL:
Firebrands of the Revolution. By Eric F. Goldman. Photos by George F. Mobley. 2-27, *July 1974*

ADAMS, Mount, Washington:
The Altitude of Mount Adams, Washington. 151-153, *Apr. 1896*

ADAMS (Schooner):
Capturing Giant Turtles in the Caribbean. By David D. Duncan. 177-190, *Aug. 1943*

ADAMS FAMILY:
Literary Landmarks of Massachusetts. By William H. Nicholas. Photos by B. Anthony Stewart and John E. Fletcher. 279-310, *Mar. 1950*

ADAM'S Second Eden (Ceylon). By Eliza Ruhamah Scidmore. 105-173, 206, *Feb. 1912*

ADDAX:
Preserving the Addax. Geographica. *Oct. 1988*

ADDIS ABABA, Ethiopia:
Ethiopia: Revolution in an Ancient Empire. By Robert Caputo. 614-645, *May 1983*
Ethiopian Adventure. By Nathaniel T. Kenney. Photos by James P. Blair. 548-582, *Apr. 1965*
Present Day Scenes in the World's Oldest Empire. Photos by W. Robert Moore. 691-722, *June 1931*
Coronation Days in Addis Ababa. By W. Robert Moore. 738-746, *June 1931*

ADELAIDE, Australia:
South Australia, Gateway to the Great Outback. By Howell Walker. Photos by Joseph J. Scherschel. 441-481, *Apr. 1970*
Capital Cities of Australia. By W. Robert Moore. 667-722, *Dec. 1935*
Lonely Australia: The Unique Continent. By Herbert E. Gregory. 473-568, *Dec. 1916*

ADELAIDE UNIVERSITY:
Expeditions:
Earth's Most Primitive People: A Journey with the Aborigines of Central

Australia. By Charles P. Mountford. 89-112, *Jan. 1946*

ADÉLIE PENGUINS:
Antarctica's Most Interesting Citizen: The Comical Penguin Is Both Romantic and Bellicose. By Worth E. Shoults. 251-260, *Feb. 1932*

ADEN PROTECTORATE:
Along the Storied Incense Roads of Aden. By Hermann F. Eilts. Photos by Brian Brake. 230-254, *Feb. 1957*
Sailing with Sindbad's Sons. By Alan Villiers. 675-688, *Nov. 1948*
The Rock of Aden: The Volcanic Mountain Fortress, on the Sea Route from Suez to India, Assumes New Importance. By H.G.C. Swayne. 723-742, *Dec. 1935*
"The Flower of Paradise": The Part Which Khat Plays in the Life of the Yemen Arab. By Charles Moser. 173-186, *Aug. 1917*

ADENA CULTURE:
Who Were the "Mound Builders"? By George E. Stuart. 783-801, *Dec. 1972*
"Pyramids" of the New World. By Neil Merton Judd. 105-128, *Jan. 1948*

ADIRONDACK MOUNTAINS, New York:
My Backyard, the Adirondacks. By Anne LaBastille. Photos by David Alan Harvey. 616-639, *May 1975*
New York State's Air-Conditioned Roof. By Frederick G. Vosburgh. Included: Adirondack Idylls. Photos by Harrison Howell Walker. 715-748, *June 1938*

ADKINS, JAN:
On Assignment. *June 1983*

ADMIRAL Byrd Receives New Honor From The Society. 228-238, *Aug. 1930*

ADMIRAL of the Ends of the Earth. By Melville Bell Grosvenor. 36-48, *July 1957*

ADMIRAL R. W. Meade, U.S.N. (Obituary). 142, *May 1897*

ADOBE New Mexico. By Mason Sutherland. Photos by Justin Locke. 783-830, *Dec. 1949*

ADOLPHUS FREDERICK, DUKE OF MECKLENBURG: *Author*
A Land of Giants and Pygmies (Ruanda). 369-388, *Apr. 1912*

"THE ADORATION OF THE MAGI," painting supplement. *Jan. 1952*

ADRIATIC REGION. See Trieste; Venice; Yugoslavia

ADRIFT on a Raft of Sargassum. Photos by Robert F. Sisson. 188-199, *Feb. 1976*

ADVANCES in Geographic Knowledge During the Nineteenth Century. By A. W. Greely. 143-152, *Apr. 1901*

ADVENTURE (Ship):
The Columbus of the Pacific: Captain

A Minoan priest offers a rare human sacrifice in vain as an earthquake buries a temple on Crete 3,700 years ago. PAINTING BY LOUIS GLANZMAN

Canards in their noses keep Burt Rutan's aircraft from stalling, a major aerodynamic innovation. JAMES A. SUGAR, BLACK STAR

Crewmen leap from the gondola of Explorer I *as the gas bag above them disintegrates during a 1934 probe of the stratosphere. They parachuted to safety.* PAINTING BY TOM LOVELL

Crew of **America,** *led by Richard E. Byrd, second from left, flew their three-engine plane nonstop to France in 1927.* UNDERWOOD & UNDERWOOD/THE BETTMANN ARCHIVE

VOL. 167, NO. 6 — JUNE 1985

NATIONAL GEOGRAPHIC

GREAT SALT LAKE: THE FLOODING DESERT 694

U.S.–MEXICAN BORDER: LIFE ON THE LINE 720

JAVA'S WILDLIFE RETURNS 750

Along Afghanistan's War-torn Frontier 772

Haunted eyes tell of an Afghan refugee's fears

FAIR SKIES FOR THE CAYMAN ISLANDS 798

SEE NATIONAL GEOGRAPHIC EXPLORER EVERY SUNDAY ON NICKELODEON CABLE TV

Porters prepare to carry off a 1909 kill of two zebras in the Great Rift Valley of German East Africa, now Tanzania. UNDERWOOD & UNDERWOOD/THE BETTMANN ARCHIVE

Zebras thread a river of wildebeests, seeking safety during their annual migration across Tanzania's Serengeti Plain. MITSUAKI IWAGO

Liberia; Libya; Mali; Madagascar; Morocco; Mozambique; Namibia; Niger; Nigeria; Nile; Rhodesia; Río Muni; Ruanda; Sahara; Senegambia; Sierra Leone; Sinai, Mount; Sinai Peninsula; Somalia; South Africa; South-West Africa; Sudan; Suez Canal; Tanganyika; Tanzania; Tunisia; Uganda; Upper Volta; Zaire; Zanzibar; Zimbabwe; *and* African Wildlife; Diamonds; Phoenicians; Plate Tectonics

AFRICAN WILDLIFE:

African Odyssey. cover, *Jan. 1988*

The "Gang" Moves to a Strange New Land. By Shirley C. Strum. Note: The baboons of the "Pumphouse Gang" are translocated in Kenya. NGS research grant. 676-690, *Nov. 1987*

Lions of the African Night. President's Page. By Gilbert M. Grosvenor. Jan. 1987; Cover. *Jan. 1987*

Editorial. By Wilbur E. Garrett. 559, *May 1986*

The Serengeti. 560-601. I. A Photographic Portfolio. Photos by Mitsuaki Iwago. Text by John Eliot. 563-585; II. The Glory of Life. By Shana Alexander. 585-601, *May 1986*

Gentle Fliers of the African Night. By Merlin D. Tuttle. Contents: Bats. NGS research grant. 540-558, *Apr. 1986*

They're Killing Off the Rhino. By Esmond Bradley Martin. Photos by Jim Brandenburg. 404-422, *Mar. 1984*

The Living Sands of the Namib. By William J. Hamilton III. Photos by Carol and David Hughes. 364-377, *Sept. 1983*

Editorial. By Wilbur E. Garrett. 287, *Mar. 1983*

Etosha: Namibia's Kingdom of Animals. By Douglas H. Chadwick. Photos by Des and Jen Bartlett. 344-385, *Mar. 1983*

Family Life of Lions. By Des and Jen Bartlett. Included: Lions, Wildebeests, Zebras. 800-819, *Dec. 1982*

Namibia: Nearly a Nation? By Bryan Hodgson. Photos by Jim Brandenburg. 755-797, *June 1982*

Safari! By Gene S. Stuart. Photos by George F. Mobley. Juvenile. 104 pages. *1982*

The Imperiled Mountain Gorilla. By Dian Fossey. Included: Death of Marchessa. Photos by Peter G. Veit. NGS research grant. 501-523, *Apr. 1981*

Etosha: Place of Dry Water. 703, *Dec. 1980*

Gorilla. 703, *Dec. 1980*

Jackals of the Serengeti. By Patricia D. Moehlman. NGS research grant. 840-850, *Dec. 1980*

Africa's Elephants: Can They Survive? By Oria Douglas-Hamilton. Photos by Oria and Iain Douglas-Hamilton. 568-603, *Nov. 1980*

Life and Death at Gombe (Chimpanzees). By Jane Goodall. NGS research grant. 592-621, *May 1979*

Last Stand in Eden. 1, *Jan. 1979*

The Living Sands of Namib. 439, Oct. 1977; cover, Mar. 1978; 1, *Jan. 1979*

African Termites, Dwellers in the Dark. By Glenn D. Prestwich. 532-547, *Apr. 1978*

A Bad Time to Be a Crocodile. By Rick Gore. Photos by Jonathan Blair. 90-115, *Jan. 1978*

Africa's Gentle Giants (Giraffes). By Bristol Foster. Photos by Bob Campbell and Thomas Nebbia. 402-417, *Sept. 1977*

Rescuing the Rothschild. By Carolyn Bennett Patterson. 419-421, *Sept. 1977*

Search for the Great Apes. cover, *Jan. 1976*

Tanzania Marches to Its Own Drum. By Peter T. White. Photos by Emory Kristof. 474-509, *Apr. 1975*

African Wildlife: Man's Threatened Legacy. By Allan C. Fisher, Jr. Photos by Thomas Nebbia. Included: A Continent's Living Treasure. Paintings by Ned Seidler. 147-187, *Feb. 1972*

More Years With Mountain Gorillas. By Dian Fossey. Photos by Robert M. Campbell. NGS research grant. 574-585, *Oct. 1971*

Mzima, Kenya's Spring of Life. By Joan and Alan Root. 350-373, *Sept. 1971*

Making Friends With Mountain Gorillas. By Dian Fossey. Photos by Robert M. Campbell. NGS research grant. 48-67, *Jan. 1970*

Locusts: "Teeth of the Wind." By Robert A. M. Conley. Photos by Gianni Tortoli. 202-227, *Aug. 1969*

Life With the King of Beasts. By George B. Schaller. 494-519, *Apr. 1969*

The Wild Realm: Animals of East Africa. By Louis S. B. Leakey. 199 pages. *1969*

In Quest of the World's Largest Frog. By Paul A. Zahl. 146-152, *July 1967*

"Snowflake," the World's First White Gorilla. By Arthur J. Riopelle. Pho-

tos by Paul A. Zahl. NGS research grant. 443-448, *Mar. 1967*

My Friends the Wild Chimpanzees. By Jane Goodall. Photos by Baron Hugo van Lawick. 204 pages. *1967*

New Discoveries Among Africa's Chimpanzees. By Baroness Jane van Lawick-Goodall. Photos by Baron Hugo van Lawick. NGS research grant. 802-831, *Dec. 1965*

Miss Goodall and the Wild Chimpanzees. 831A-831B, *Dec. 1965*

My Life Among Wild Chimpanzees. By Jane Goodall. Photos by Baron Hugo van Lawick and author. NGS research grant. 272-308, *Aug. 1963*

Orphans of the Wild (Animal Orphanage, Uganda). By Bruce G. Kinloch. 683-699, *Nov. 1962*

Hunting Africa's Smallest Game (Insects). By Edward S. Ross. NGS research grant. 406-419, *Mar. 1961*

Where Elephants Have Right of Way. By George and Jinx Rodger. Included: Buffaloes; Giraffes; Hippopotamuses; Lyrehorned ankoles; Rhinoceroses. 363-389, *Sept. 1960*

The Last Great Animal Kingdom. 390-409, *Sept. 1960*

Face to Face With Gorillas in Central Africa. By Paul A. Zahl. 114-137, *Jan. 1960*

A New Look at Kenya's "Treetops." By Quentin Keynes. 536-541, *Oct. 1956*

Stalking Central Africa's Wildlife. By T. Donald Carter. Paintings by Walter A. Weber. NGS research grant. 264-286, *Aug. 1956*

Safari from Congo to Cairo. By Elsie May Bell Grosvenor. Photos by Gilbert Grosvenor. 721-771, *Dec. 1954*

Spearing Lions with Africa's Masai. By Edgar Monsanto Queeny. 487-517, *Oct. 1954*

Safari Through Changing Africa. By Elsie May Bell Grosvenor. Photos by Gilbert Grosvenor. 145-198, *Aug. 1953*

Africa's Uncaged Elephants. Photos by Quentin Keynes. 371-382, *Mar. 1951*

Roaming Africa's Unfenced Zoos. By W. Robert Moore. 353-380, *Mar. 1950*

Wings Over Nature's Zoo in Africa. Photos by Reginald A. Bourlay. 527-542, *Oct. 1939*

Nature's Most Amazing Mammal: Elephants, Unique Among Animals, Have Many Human Qualities When Wild That Make Them Foremost Citizens of Zoo and Circus. By Edmund Heller. 729-759, *June 1934*

Elephant Hunting in Equatorial Africa with Rifle and Camera. By Carl E. Akeley. 779-810, *Aug. 1912*

Mr. Roosevelt's "African Game Trails." 953-962, *Nov. 1910*

Africa the Largest Game Preserve in the World. By John B. Torbert. 445-448, *Nov. 1900*

See also Baboons; Black Eagles; Cattle Egret; Cheetahs; Egyptian Vulture; Flamingos; Honey-Guide; Hornbills; Hyenas; Lemurs

AFRICANIZED HONEYBEES:

Those Fiery Brazilian Bees. By Rick

Gore. Photos by Bianca Lavies. 491-501, *Apr. 1976*

The **AFRIKANERS.** By André Brink. Photos by David Turnley. 556-585, *Oct. 1988*

AFTER an Empire...Portugal. By William Graves. Photos by Bruno Barbey. 804-831, *Dec. 1980*

AFTER Rhodesia, a Nation Named Zimbabwe. By Charles E. Cobb, Jr. Photos by James L. Stanfield and LeRoy Woodson, Jr. 616-651, *Nov. 1981*

AFTER 2,000 Years of Silence: The Dead Do Tell Tales at Vesuvius. By Rick Gore. Photos by O. Louis Mazzatenta. NGS research grant. 557-613, *May 1984*

AGA KHAN:

Weighing the Aga Khan in Diamonds. Photos by David J. Carnegie. 317-324, *Mar. 1947*

AGAIN–the Olympic Challenge. By Alan J. Gould. 488-513, *Oct. 1964*

AGAVE. *See* Henequen

The AGE of Chivalry. 378 pages. 1969; ▪▪rev. ed. *1978*

The **AGE** of Sail Lives On at Mystic. By Alan Villiers. Photos by Weston Kemp. 220-239, *Aug. 1968*

AGELESS Luster of Greece and Rhodes. Photos by Arnold Genthe. 477-492, *Apr. 1938*

AGELESS Splendors of Our Oldest Park: Yellowstone at 100. 604-615, *May 1972*

AGETON, ARTHUR A.: *Author*

Annapolis, Cradle of the Navy. 789-800, *June 1936*

AGNEW, DONALD H.: *Author*

American Wings Soar Around the World: Epic Story of the Air Transport Command of the U. S. Army Is a Saga of Yankee Daring and Doing. By Donald H. Agnew and William A. Kinney. 57-78, *July 1943*

AGNEW, SPIRO T.:

First Moon Explorers (Apollo 11) Receive the Society's Hubbard Medal. Included: Vice President Agnew's presentation of medal to Apollo 8 astronauts. 859-861, *June 1970*

AGOGINO, GEORGE: *Author*

Wyoming Muck Tells of Battle: Ice Age Man vs. Mammoth. By Cynthia Irwin, Henry Irwin, and George Agogino. 828-837, *June 1962*

AGRA, India:

Through the Heart of Hindustan: A Teeming Highway Extending for Fifteen Hundred Miles, from the Khyber Pass to Calcutta. By Maynard Owen Williams. 433-467, *Nov. 1921* *See also* Taj Mahal

AGRICULTURAL AND BOTANICAL EXPLORERS:

A Hunter of Plants. By David Fairchild. 57-77, *July 1919*

AGRICULTURAL Capacity of Alaska: What Population Can the Territory Support? By C. C. Georgeson. 676-679, *July 1909*

AGRICULTURAL Possibilities in Tropical Mexico. By Pehr Olsson-Seffer. 1021-1040, *Dec. 1910*

AGRICULTURE:

Beyond Supermouse: Changing Life's Genetic Blueprint. By Robert F. Weaver. Photos by Ted Spiegel. Included: Engineering of crops and livestock. 818-847, *Dec. 1984*

Pollen: Breath of Life and Sneezes. By Cathy Newman. Photos by Martha Cooper. 490-521, *Oct. 1984*

The Okies–Beyond the Dust Bowl. By William Howarth. Photos by Chris Johns. 322-349, *Sept. 1984*

Do We Treat Our Soil Like Dirt? By Boyd Gibbons. Photos by Steven C. Wilson. 350-389, *Sept. 1984*

Patterns of Plenty: The Art in Farming. Photo essay by Georg Gerster. 391-399, *Sept. 1984*

Tropical Rain Forests: Nature's Dwindling Treasures. By Peter T. White. Photos by James P. Blair. Paintings by Barron Storey. Included: Slash-and-burn farming, Tree plantations, Soil-management project. 2-47, *Jan. 1983*

Rediscovering America's Forgotten Crops. By Noel D. Vietmeyer. Photos by Burgess Blevins. Paintings by Paul M. Breeden. 702-712, *May 1981*

Our Most Precious Resource: Water. By Thomas Y. Canby. Photos by Ted Spiegel. 144-179, *Aug. 1980*

The Year the Weather Went Wild. By Thomas Y. Canby. Included: The severe drought in the northern plains and the western United States. 799-829, *Dec. 1977*

What's Happening to Our Climate? By Samuel W. Matthews. Included: The relationship between climatic change and cultivation. 576-615, *Nov. 1976*

This Land of Ours–How Are We Using It? By Peter T. White. Photos by Emory Kristof. 20-67, *July 1976*

Farmland as art: Patterns made on a Texas cotton field by an implement called a sand fighter swirl around a water-filled depression. GEORG GERSTER

Mule-powered combine kicks up a cloud of dust as it harvests wheat in hills southeast of Lake Chelan, Washington. © ASAHEL CURTIS

in cooperation with the United States Capitol Historical Society. 143 pages. 1963; rev. ed. *1985*

Herbs for All Seasons. Photos by Sam Abell. Picture portfolio text by Larry Kohl. 386-409, *Mar. 1983*

■ *Nature's Healing Arts: From Folk Medicine to Modern Drugs.* Photos by Nathan Benn and Ira Block. 199 pages. *1977*

Patriots in Petticoats. Paintings by Louis S. Glanzman. 475-493, *Oct. 1975*

Nature's Gifts to Medicine. Paintings by Lloyd K. Townsend and Don Crowley. 420-440, *Sept. 1974*

■ *George Washington–Man and Monument.* By Frank Freidel and Lonnelle Aikman. Published in cooperation with the Washington National Monument Association. 69 pages. 1965; rev. ed. *1973*

The Lights Are Up at Ford's Theatre. 392-401, *Mar. 1970*

The Living White House. 593-643, *Nov. 1966*

Under the Dome of Freedom: The United States Capitol. Photos by George F. Mobley. 4-59, *Jan. 1964*

Inside the White House. Photos by B. Anthony Stewart and Thomas Nebbia. 3-43, *Jan. 1961*

Census 1960: Profile of the Nation. By Albert W. Atwood and Lonnelle Aikman. 697-714, *Nov. 1959*

New Stars for Old Glory. 86-121, *July 1959*

Mount Vernon Lives On. 651-682, *Nov. 1953*

U. S. Capitol, Citadel of Democracy. 143-192, *Aug. 1952*

The DAR Story. Photos by B. Anthony Stewart and John E. Fletcher. 565-598, *Nov. 1951*

Perfume, the Business of Illusion. 531-550, *Apr. 1951*

Bizarre Battleground–the Lonely Aleutians. 316-317, *Sept. 1942*

Platinum in the World's Work. 345-360, *Sept. 1937*

AILINGLAPALAP (Atoll), Marshall Islands:

Our New Military Wards, the Marshalls. By W. Robert Moore. 325-360, *Sept. 1945*

AINU:

Hokkaido, Japan's Last Frontier. By Douglas Lee. Photos by Michael S. Yamashita. 62-93, *Jan. 1980*

Japan's "Sky People," the Vanishing Ainu. By Mary Inez Hilger. Photos by Eiji Miyazawa. NGS research grant. 268-296, *Feb. 1967*

AÏR (Region), Niger:

The Inadan: Artisans of the Sahara. By Michael and Aubine Kirtley. 282-298, *Aug. 1979*

AIR Adventures in Peru: Cruising Among Andean Peaks, Pilots and Cameramen Discover Wondrous Works of an Ancient People. By Robert Shippee. 81-120, *Jan. 1933*

AIR Age Brings Life to Canton Island. By Howell Walker. 117-132, *Jan. 1955*

AIR AND SPACE MUSEUM, Smithsonian Institution, Washington, D. C.:

Of Air and Space. By Michael Collins. Included: Picture Portfolio by Nathan Benn, Robert S. Oakes, and Joseph D. Lavenburg, with text by Michael E. Long. 819-837, *June 1978*

AIR BASES:

Crosscurrents Sweep the Indian Ocean. By Bart McDowell. Photos by Steve Raymer. 422-457, *Oct. 1981*

Of Planes and Men. By Kenneth F. Weaver. Photos by Emory Kristof and Albert Moldvay. 298-349, *Sept. 1965*

Four-ocean Navy in the Nuclear Age. By Thomas W. McKnew. 145-187, *Feb. 1965*

Artists Roam the World of the U. S. Air Force. By Curtis E. LeMay. 650-673, *May 1960*

Alaska's Warmer Side. By Elsie May Bell Grosvenor. Included: Eielson Air Force Base, Ladd Air Force Base. 737-775, *June 1956*

Our Navy in the Far East. By Arthur W. Radford. Photos by J. Baylor Roberts. 537-577, *Oct. 1953*

Here Come the Marines. By Frederick Simpich. Included: Anacostia Naval Air Station, Washington, D. C.; Cherry Point Air Station, North Carolina; El Toro Air Station, California. 647-672, *Nov. 1950*

Flying in the "Blowtorch" Era. By Frederick G. Vosburgh. Contents: Andrews Air Force Base, Maryland; Carswell Air Force Base, Texas; Edwards Air Force Base, California; Eglin Air Force Base, Florida; Langley Air Force Base, Virginia; Larson Air Force Base, Washington; March Air Force Base, California; Moffett Naval Air Station, California; Wil-

The National Air and Space Museum displays the command ship of the first manned lunar landing.   JIM MENDENHALL

liams Air Force Base, Arizona; Wright-Patterson Air Force Base, Ohio. 281-322, *Sept. 1950*

Okinawa, Pacific Outpost. 538-552, *Apr. 1950*

Americans Stand Guard in Greenland. By Andrew H. Brown. 457-500, *Oct. 1946*

Servicing Arctic Airbases. By Robert A. Bartlett. 602-616, *May 1946*

Air Power for Peace. By H. H. Arnold. 137-193, *Feb. 1946*

China's Hand-built Air Bases. 231-236, *Aug. 1945*

See also Canton Island; Edwards Air Force Base; Stead Air Force Base; Thule Air Base

AIR Bridge to Siberia. By Wilbur E. Garrett. Photos by Steve Raymer. 504-509, *Oct. 1988*

AIR CARRIER CONTRACT PERSONNEL:

Heroes of Wartime Science and Mercy. By Elizabeth W. King. 715-740, *Dec. 1943*

AIR COMMANDO FORCE. See U. S. First Air Commando Force

AIR Conquest: From the Early Days of Giant Kites and Birdlike Gliders, the National Geographic Society Has Aided and Encouraged the Growth of Aviation. 233-242, *Aug. 1927*

AIR Cruising Through New Brazil: A National Geographic Reporter Spots Vast Resources Which the Republic's War Declaration Adds to Strength of United Nations. By Henry Albert Phillips. 503-536, *Oct. 1942*

AIR FORCE. See U. S. Air Force; U. S. Army Air Forces

AIR MAIL:

Flying. By Gilbert Grosvenor. 585-630, *May 1933*

Flying the "Hump" of the Andes. By Albert W. Stevens. 595-636, *May 1931*

Flying the World's Longest Air-Mail Route: From Montevideo, Uruguay, Over the Andes, Up the Pacific Coast, Across Central America and the Caribbean to Miami, Florida, in 67 Thrilling Flying Hours. By Junius B. Wood. 261-325, *Mar. 1930*

On the Trail of the Air Mail: A Narrative of the Experiences of the Flying Couriers Who Relay the Mail Across America at a Speed of More than 2,000 Miles a Day. By J. Parker Van Zandt. 1-61, *Jan. 1926*

AIR PLANTS. See Bromeliads; Orchids

AIR POLLUTION:

The Great Lakes' Troubled Waters. By Charles E. Cobb, Jr. Photos by Bob Sacha and Richard Olsenius. Note: Airborne toxics threaten the health of the Great Lakes. 2-31, *July 1987*

Editorial. By Wilbur E. Garrett. 421, *Apr. 1987*

Air: An Atmosphere of Uncertainty. By Noel Grove. Photos by Ted Spiegel. Paintings by William H. Bond. Included: A deadly soup (a list of

One of 14 aircraft carriers of the Pacific Fleet at the end of the 1950s, the three-block-long U.S.S. **Ranger** *leaves Pearl Harbor, Hawaii.*   WILBUR E. GARRETT, NGS

Crossing the Traleika divide, mountaineers make a circuit of Mount McKinley, North America's highest peak. ALLAN BARD

Previously uncharted features were surveyed by the 1935 National Geographic Society Yukon expedition, led by Bradford Washburn. · DRAWN BY RALPH E. McALEER

An ivory-faced Eskimo doll, crafted by parents from a Yukon River village, wears Western trappings. SISSE BRIMBERG

Amid the warmth of family ties, Eskimos fashion goods of ivory and reindeer hide in the early 1900s for life in the Arctic. GEORGE R. KING

ALASKA KING CRAB:

The Crab That Shakes Hands. By Clarence P. Idyll. Photos by Robert F. Sisson. 254-271, *Feb. 1971*

ALASKA MILITARY HIGHWAY:

Alaskan Highway an Engineering Epic: Mosquitoes, Mud, and Muskeg Minor Obstacles of 1,671-mile Race to Throw the Alcan Life Line Through Thick Forests and Uninhabited Wilderness. By Froelich Rainey. 143-168, *Feb. 1943*

ALASKA RANGE, Alaska:

New Mount McKinley Challenge– Trekking Around the Continent's Highest Peak. By Ned Gillette. 66-79, *July 1979*

Mount McKinley Conquered by New Route. By Bradford Washburn. 219-248, *Aug. 1953*

Wildlife of Mount McKinley National Park. By Adolph Murie. Paintings by Walter A. Weber. 249-270, *Aug. 1953*

ALASKAN AIR COMMAND, U. S. Air Force:

Three Months on an Arctic Ice Island. By Joseph O. Fletcher. 489-504, *Apr. 1953*

The **ALASKAN** Boundary. By John W. Foster. 425-456, *Nov. 1899*

ALASKAN Boundary Decision. 423, *Nov. 1903*

ALASKAN Boundary Dispute. 79, *Feb. 1903*

The **ALASKAN** Boundary Survey. I–Introduction. By T. C. Mendenhall. II–

The Boundary South of Fort Yukon. By J. E. McGrath. III–The Boundary North of Fort Yukon. By J. Henry Turner. 177-197, *Feb. 8, 1893*

The **ALASKAN** Boundary Tribunal. By John W. Foster. 1-12, *Jan. 1904*

The **ALASKAN** Brown Bear. By Wilfred H. Osgood. 332-333, *Apr. 1909*

ALASKAN–CANADIAN MILITARY HIGHWAY:

Alaskan Highway an Engineering Epic: Mosquitoes, Mud, and Muskeg Minor Obstacles of 1,671-mile Race to Throw the Alcan Life Line Through Thick Forests and Uninhabited Wilderness. By Froelich Rainey. 143-168, *Feb. 1943*

ALASKAN MOOSE:

Giants of the Wilderness: Alaskan Moose. By Victor Van Ballenberghe. Photos by Michio Hoshino. 260-280, *Aug. 1987*

ALASKAN PIPELINE:

Oil in the Wilderness: An Arctic Dilemma. By Douglas Lee. Photos by James P. Blair. 858-871, *Dec. 1988*

The Pipeline: Alaska's Troubled Colossus. By Bryan Hodgson. Photos by Steve Raymer. Included: Diagram, Anatomy of the pipeline; map showing potential and producing oil and gas areas. 684-717, *Nov. 1976*

Alaska: Rising Northern Star. By Joseph Judge. Photos by Bruce Dale. 730-767, *June 1975*

Oil, the Dwindling Treasure. By Noel

Grove. Photos by Emory Kristof. 792-825, *June 1974*

Will Oil and Tundra Mix? Alaska's North Slope Hangs in the Balance. By William S. Ellis. Photos by Emory Kristof. 485-517, *Oct. 1971*

ALASKA'S New Railway. 567-589, *Dec. 1915*

ALBANIA:

Albania, Alone Against the World. By Mehmet Biber. 530-557, *Oct. 1980*

Europe's Newest Kingdom: After Centuries of Struggle, Albania at Last Enjoys an Era of Peace and Stability. By Melville Chater. 131-190, *Feb. 1931*

The Races of Europe. By Edwin A. Grosvenor. 441-534, *Dec. 1918*

Recent Observations in Albania. By George P. Scriven. 90-114, *Aug. 1918*

The Changing Map in the Balkans. By Frederick Moore. 199-226, *Feb. 1913*

The Albanians. By Theron J. Damon. 1090-1103, *Nov. 1912*

The Young Turk. By Colby M. Chester. 43-89, *Jan. 1912*

ALBANY, New York:

Henry Hudson's River. By Willard Price. Photos by Wayne Miller. 364-403, *Mar. 1962*

The Mighty Hudson. By Albert W. Atwood. Photos by B. Anthony Stewart. 1-36, *July 1948*

ALBATROSS (Ship):

Deep-Sea Exploring Expedition of the Steamer "Albatross." By Hugh M. Smith. 291-296, *Aug. 1899*

Antlers down, Alaskan bull moose charge into a fall battle over the right to breed with a nearby group of cows. MICHIO HOSHINO

ALBATROSSES:

Penguins and Their Neighbors. By Roger Tory Peterson. Photos by Des and Jen Bartlett. 237-255, *Aug. 1977*

The Gooney Birds of Midway. By John W. Aldrich. 839-851, *June 1964*

Birds of the High Seas: Albatrosses and Petrels; Gannets, Man-o'-war-birds, and Tropic-birds. By Robert Cushman Murphy. Paintings by Allan Brooks. 226-251, *Aug. 1938*

South Georgia, an Outpost of the Antarctic. By Robert Cushman Murphy. 409-444, *Apr. 1922*

A Bird City (Laysan Island, Hawaii). 494-498, *Dec. 1904*

ALBEE, RUTH: *Author*

Family Afoot in Yukon Wilds: Two Young Children and Their Parents Live Off the Country in the Northwest Canada Wilderness Now To Be Traversed by the Alaska Highway. By William Hamilton Albee, with Ruth Albee. 589-616, *May 1942*

ALBEE, WILLIAM HAMILTON:
Author

Family Afoot in Yukon Wilds: Two Young Children and Their Parents Live Off the Country in the Northwest Canada Wilderness Now To Be Traversed by the Alaska Highway. By William Hamilton Albee, with Ruth Albee. 589-616, *May 1942*

ALBEMARLE COUNTY, Virginia:

Mr. Jefferson's Charlottesville. By Anne Revis. 553-592, *May 1950*

Albemarle in Revolutionary Days. By G. Brown Goode. 271-281, *Aug. 1896*

See also Monticello

ALBERTA (Province), Canada:

Waterton-Glacier International Peace Park: Pride of Two Nations. By David S. Boyer. Photos by Lowell Georgia. 796-823, *June 1987*

Calgary: Canada's Not-So-Wild West. By David S. Boyer. Photos by Ottmar Bierwagen. 378-403, *Mar. 1984*

Heart of the Canadian Rockies. By Elizabeth A. Moize. Photos by Jim Brandenburg. 757-779, *June 1980*

⊕ *Close-up, Canada: British Columbia, Alberta, Yukon Territory.* Text on reverse. *Apr. 1978*

Canada's "Now" Frontier. By Robert Paul Jordan. Photos by Lowell Georgia. 480-511, *Oct. 1976*

Oil, the Dwindling Treasure. By Noel Grove. Photos by Emory Kristof. 792-825, *June 1974*

Canada's Heartland, the Prairie Provinces. By W. E. Garrett. 443-489, *Oct. 1970*

Canadian Rockies, Lords of a Beckoning Land. By Alan Phillips. Photos by James L. Stanfield. 353-393, *Sept. 1966*

From Sun-clad Sea to Shining Mountains. By Ralph Gray. Photos by James P. Blair. 542-589, *Apr. 1964*

Alberta Unearths Her Buried Treasures. By David S. Boyer. 90-119, *July 1960*

On the Ridgepole of the Rockies. By

Walter Meayers Edwards. Included: Canada's Rocky Mountain Playground. 745-780, *June 1947*

Peaks and Parks of Western Canada. Photos by W. J. Oliver. 516-526, *Oct. 1941*

The Columbia (River) Turns on the Power. By Maynard Owen Williams. 749-792, *June 1941*

Peaks and Trails in the Canadian Alps. Photos by Byron Harmon and Clifford White. 627-642, *May 1934*

The Mother of Rivers: An Account of a Photographic Expedition to the Great Columbia Ice Field of the Canadian Rockies. By Lewis R. Freeman. 377-446, *Apr. 1925*

Hunting Big Game of Other Days: A Boating Expedition in Search of Fossils in Alberta, Canada. By Barnum Brown. 407-429, *May 1919*

The Monarch of the Canadian Rockies: The Robson Peak District of British Columbia and Alberta. By Charles D. Walcott. Included: The Monarch of the Canadian Rockies–Robson Peak (panorama). 626-639, *May 1913*

Landslides and Rock Avalanches. By Guy Elliott Mitchell. 277-287, *Apr. 1910*

Recent Exploration in the Canadian Rockies. By Walter D. Wilcox. 151-168, May 1902; Part II, 185-200, *June 1902*

Exploration in the Canadian Rockies. 135-136, *Apr. 1899*

See also Bikepacking; Great Divide Trail; Waterton-Glacier International Peace Park

ALBERTS, ARTHUR S.:
Author-Photographer

Hunting Musical Game in West Africa. 262-282, *Aug. 1951*

ALBINO ANIMALS:

Growing Up With Snowflake (Gorilla). By Arthur J. Riopelle. Photos by Michael Kuh. NGS research grant. 491-503, *Oct. 1970*

White Tiger in My House. By Elizabeth C. Reed. Photos by Donna K. Grosvenor. 482-491, *Apr. 1970*

"Snowflake," the World's First White Gorilla. By Arthur J. Riopelle. Photos by Paul A. Zahl. NGS research grant. 443-448, *Mar. 1967*

Enchantress! (Tigress). By Theodore H. Reed. Photos by Thomas J. Abercrombie. 628-641, *May 1961*

ALBRECHT, FLORENCE CRAIG:
Author

The Splendor of Rome. 593-626, *June 1922*

London. 263-294, *Sept. 1915*

Channel Ports–And Some Others. 1-55, *July 1915*

Frontier Cities of Italy. 533-586, *June 1915*

Austro–Italian Mountain Frontiers. 321-376, *Apr. 1915*

The Town of Many Gables (Münster, Germany). 107-140, *Feb. 1915*

The City of Jacqueline (Ter Goes, Netherlands). 29-56, *Jan. 1915*

ALBUQUERQUE, New Mexico:

New Mexico: The Golden Land. By Robert Laxalt. Photos by Adam Woolfitt. 299-345, *Sept. 1970*

"ALCAN" HIGHWAY. See Alaskan-Canadian Military Highway

ALCOCK, LESLIE:

Nomination Page. In Wales. *May 1971*

ALCOTT, LOUISA MAY:

Literary Landmarks of Massachusetts. By William H. Nicholas. Photos by B. Anthony Stewart and John E. Fletcher. 279-310, *Mar. 1950*

ALDANA E., GUILLERMO:

On Assignment in Mexico City. *Oct. 1984*

On Assignment in Mexico. *Nov. 1982*

Author-Photographer

Mesa del Nayar's Strange Holy Week. 780-795, *June 1971*

Photographer

What's Killing the Palm Trees? By Randolph E. McCoy. 120-130, *July 1988*

Earthquake in Mexico. By Allen A. Boraiko. Photos by James L. Stanfield and Guillermo Aldana E. Included: The rise and fall of buildings–a primer for survival in quake city. 654-675, *May 1986*

Following Cortés: Path to Conquest. By S. Jeffrey K. Wilkerson. Paintings by Ned Seidler and Rosalie Seidler. 420-459, *Oct. 1984*

The Disaster of El Chichón. By Boris Weintraub. Photos by Guillermo Aldana E. and Kenneth Garrett. Included: Volcanic Cloud May Alter Earth's Climate. By Robert I. Tilling. 654-684, *Nov. 1982*

The Huichols, Mexico's People of Myth and Magic. By James Norman. 832-853, *June 1977*

ALDEN, CARROLL STORRS: *Author*

Megaspelæon, the Oldest Monastery in Greece. 310-323, *Mar. 1913*

ALDERNEY (Island), Channel Islands:

Britain's "French" Channel Islands. By James Cerruti. Photos by James L. Amos. 710-740, *May 1971*

The Channel Islands. By Edith Carey. 143-164, *Aug. 1920*

ALDO LEOPOLD: "A Durable Scale of Values." By Boyd Gibbons. Photos by Jim Brandenburg. 682-708, *Nov. 1981*

ALDRICH, JOHN W.: *Author*

The Gooney Birds of Midway. 839-851, *June 1964*

ALDRIN, EDWIN E., Jr.:

First Moon Explorers (Apollo 11) Receive the Society's Hubbard Medal. 859-861, *June 1970*

First Explorers on the Moon: The Incredible Story of Apollo 11. 735-797. I. Man Walks on Another World. By Neil A. Armstrong, Edwin E. Aldrin, Jr., and Michael Collins. 738-749; II. Sounds of the Space Age, From Sputnik to Lunar Landing. A record narrated by Frank Borman. 750-751; III. The Flight of Apollo 11: "One giant leap for mankind." By Kenneth F. Weaver. 752-787, *Dec. 1969*

ALEKSIUK, MICHAEL: *Author*

Manitoba's Fantastic Snake Pits. Photos by Bianca Lavies. 715-723, *Nov. 1975*

ALEPPO, Syria:

Syria and Lebanon Taste Freedom. By Maynard Owen Williams. 729-763, *Dec. 1946*

Impressions of Asiatic Turkey. By Stephen van Rensselaer Trowbridge. 598-609, *Dec. 1914*

From Jerusalem to Aleppo. By John D. Whiting. 71-113, *Jan. 1913*

ALERT Anatolia. 481-492, *Apr. 1944*

ALEUTIAN ISLANDS, Alaska:

The Aleutians: Alaska's Far-out Islands. By Lael Morgan. Photos by Steven C. Wilson. Note: 95 percent of the islands are claimed by the federal government as wildlife refuges and military sites. 336-363, *Sept. 1983*

Operation Eclipse: 1948. By William A. Kinney. NGS research grant. 325-372, *Mar. 1949*

Exploring Aleutian Volcanoes. By G. D. Robinson. 509-528, *Oct. 1948*

A Navy Artist Paints the Aleutians. By Mason Sutherland. Paintings by William F. Draper. 157-176, *Aug. 1943*

Riddle of the Aleutians: A Botanist Explores the Origin of Plants on Ever-misty Islands Now Enshrouded in the Fog of War. By Isobel Wylie Hutchison. 769-792, *Dec. 1942*

Bizarre Battleground–the Lonely Aleutians. By Lonnelle Davison. 316-317, *Sept. 1942*

A Jack in the Box: An Account of the Strange Performances of the Most Wonderful Island in the World (Bogoslof Volcano). By F. M. Munger. 194-199, *Feb. 1909*

See also Atka; Unimak

ALEUTIAN RANGE, Alaska:

Lonely Wonders of Katmai (National Monument). By Ernest Gruening. Photos by Winfield Parks. 800-831, *June 1963*

ALEUTS:

The Aleutians: Alaska's Far-out Islands. By Lael Morgan. Photos by Steven C. Wilson. 336-363, *Sept. 1983*

Peoples of the Arctic. Introduction by Joseph Judge. 144-149, *Feb. 1983*

⊕ *Peoples of the Arctic; Arctic Ocean. Feb. 1983*

New Day for Alaska's Pribilof Islanders. By Susan Hackley Johnson. Photos by Tim Thompson. 536-552, *Oct. 1982*

Atka, Rugged Home of My Aleut Friends. By Lael Morgan. 572-583, *Oct. 1974*

The Fur Seal Herd Comes of Age. By Victor B. Scheffer and Karl W. Kenyon. 491-512, *Apr. 1952*

Indians of Our North Pacific Coast. By Matthew W. Stirling. Paintings by W. Langdon Kihn. 25-52, *Jan. 1945*

ALEXANDER THE GREAT:

In the Footsteps of Alexander the Great. By Helen and Frank Schreider. Paintings by Tom Lovell. 1-65, *Jan. 1968*

ALEXANDER, HOPE: *Photographer*

Friend of the Wind: The Common Tern. By Ian Nisbet. 234-247, *Aug. 1973*

ALEXANDER, SHANA: *Author*

The Serengeti: The Glory of Life. 585-601, *May 1986*

ALEXANDER ARCHIPELAGO, Alaska:

Alaska's Southeast: A Place Apart. By Bill Richards. 50-87, *Jan. 1984*

An Incredible Feasting of Whales. By Al Giddings. 88-93, *Jan. 1984*

ALEXANDER GRAHAM BELL. By Robert V. Bruce. Photos by Ira Block. 358-385, *Sept. 1988*

ALEXANDER GRAHAM BELL MUSEUM, Baddeck, Nova Scotia:

Bell Museum, Baddeck, Nova Scotia. 358-359, 361, 362, *Mar. 1975*

Down East to Nova Scotia. By Winfield Parks. 853-879, *June 1964*

Bell Museum, Baddeck, Nova Scotia. 256, 257, 259, 261, *Aug. 1959*

Alexander Graham Bell Museum: Tribute to Genius. By Jean Lesage. 227-256, *Aug. 1956*

ALEXANDRIA, Virginia:

Across the Potomac From Washington. By Albert W. Atwood. 1-33, *Jan. 1953*

ALFRED THE GREAT:

The British Way. By Sir Evelyn Wrench. 421-541, *Apr. 1949*

ALGAE:

Undersea World of a Kelp Forest. By Sylvia A. Earle. Photos by Al Giddings. 411-426, *Sept. 1980*

Those Marvelous, Myriad Diatoms. By

Richard B. Hoover. 871-878, *June 1979*

Life Springs From Death in Truk Lagoon. By Sylvia A. Earle. Photos by Al Giddings. Included: More than a hundred species of green, red, and brown algae, including 15 previously unknown in Micronesia. 578-613, *May 1976*

Adrift on a Raft of Sargassum. Photos by Robert F. Sisson. 188-199, *Feb. 1976*

Algae: the Life-givers. By Paul A. Zahl. 361-377, *Mar. 1974*

Giant Kelp, Sequoias of the Sea. By Wheeler J. North. Photos by Bates Littlehales. 251-269, *Aug. 1972*

Can We Save Our Salt Marshes? By Stephen W. Hitchcock. Photos by William R. Curtsinger. 729-765, *June 1972*

Teeming Life of a Pond. By William H. Amos. 274-298, *Aug. 1970*

ALGÅRD, GÖRAN: *Photographer*

Iceland Tapestry. By Deena Clark. 599-630, *Nov. 1951*

Lapland's Reindeer Roundup. 109-116, *July 1949*

ALGERIA:

Oasis of Art in the Sahara. By Henri Lhote. Photos by Kazuyoshi Nomachi. Contents: Rock paintings of Tassili-n-Ajjer, Algeria. 180-191, *Aug. 1987*

Algeria: Learning to Live With Independence. By Thomas J. Abercrombie. 200-233, *Aug. 1973*

Dry-land Fleet Sails the Sahara. By Jean du Boucher. Photos by Jonathan S. Blair. 696-725, *Nov. 1967*

France's Stepchild, Problem and Promise. By Howard LaFay. Photos by Robert F. Sisson. 768-795, *June 1960*

Sand in My Eyes (Motor Trip). By Jinx Rodger. 664-705, *May 1958*

Oasis-hopping in the Sahara. By Maynard Owen Williams. 209-236, *Feb. 1949*

Americans on the Barbary Coast. By Willard Price. 1-31, *July 1943*

Eastward from Gibraltar: Overland Route Across North Africa to Tunisia and Libia. By Cyrus French Wicker. 115-142, *Jan. 1943*

Trans-Africa Safari: A Motor Caravan Rolls Across Sahara and Jungle Through Realms of Dusky Potentates and the Land of Big-Lipped Women. By Lawrence Copley Thaw and Margaret Stout Thaw. 327-364, *Sept. 1938*

On the Fringe of the Great Desert. Photos by Gervais Courtellemont. 207-222, *Feb. 1928*

The Conquest of the Sahara by the Automobile. 87-93, *Jan. 1924*

Here and There in Northern Africa. By Frank Edward Johnson. 1-132, *Jan. 1914*

The Country of the Ant Men. By Thomas H. Kearney. Included: panorama. 367-382, *Apr. 1911*

The Date Gardens of the Jerid. By Thomas H. Kearney. 543-567, *July 1910*

A woman swathed in blue belongs to the nomadic Reguibat tribe of the Sahara, people of Arab and Berber stock. JONATHAN BLAIR

In Civilized French Africa. By James F. J. Archibald. 303-311, *Mar. 1909*

Biskra, the Ziban Queen. By Mrs. George C. Bosson, Jr. 563-593, *Aug. 1908*

The American Eclipse Expedition. By Colby M. Chester. 589-612, *Nov. 1906*

See also Algiers

ALGIERS, Algeria:

Eastward from Gibraltar: Overland Route Across North Africa to Tunisia and Libia. By Cyrus French Wicker. 115-142, *Jan. 1943*

The White City of Algiers. By Gordon Casserly. 206-232, *Feb. 1928*

ALGONQUIAN INDIANS:

Indian Life Before the Colonists Came. By Stuart E. Jones. Engravings by Theodore de Bry, 1590. 351-368, *Sept. 1947*

America's First Settlers, the Indians. By Matthew W. Stirling. Paintings by W. Langdon Kihn. 535-596, *Nov. 1937*

ALGONQUIAN LINGUISTIC STOCK:

Nomads of the Far North. By Matthew W. Stirling. Included: Hearty Folk Defy Arctic Storms. Paintings by W. Langdon Kihn. 471-504, *Oct. 1949*

ALGUÉ, JOSÉ: *Author*

The Manila Observatory. 427-438, *Nov. 1900*

ALHAMBRA (Fortress-Palace), Granada, Spain:

Andalusia, the Spirit of Spain. By Howard La Fay. Photos by Joseph J. Scherschel. 833-857, *June 1975*

The Changing Face of Old Spain. By Bart McDowell. Photos by Albert Moldvay. 291-339, *Mar. 1965*

Speaking of Spain. By Luis Marden. 415-456, *Apr. 1950*

ALI Goes to the Clinic. By Herndon

and Mary Hudson. 764-766, *Dec. 1946*

ALICE (Yacht):

Southward Ho! In the "Alice." By Henry Howard. 265-312, *Mar. 1938*

ALICE DEAL JUNIOR HIGH SCHOOL, Washington, D. C.:

President's Page. By Gilbert M. Grosvenor. *July 1986*

ALICE SPRINGS, Australia:

"The Alice" in Australia's Wonderland. By Alan Villiers. Photos by Jeff Carter and David Moore. 230-257, *Feb. 1966*

ALIKULUF INDIANS:

Inside Cape Horn. By Amos Burg. 743-783, *Dec. 1937*

The Indian Tribes of Southern Patagonia, Tierra del Fuego, and the Adjoining Islands. By J. B. Hatcher. 12-22, *Jan. 1901*

ALIREZA, MARIANNE:

On Assignment in Saudi Arabia. *Oct. 1987*

Author

Women of Saudi Arabia. Photos by Jodi Cobb. 423-453, *Oct. 1987*

ALKMAAR, Netherlands:

A North Holland Cheese Market. By Hugh M. Smith. 1051-1066, *Dec. 1910*

ALL-AMERICA ROSE SELECTION (AARS). *See* Portrait Rose

ALL Around the Bay of Passamaquoddy. By Albert S. Gatschet. 16-24, *Jan. 1897*

ALL-GIRL Team Tests the Habitat (Tektite II). By Sylvia A. Earle. Paintings by Pierre Mion. 291-296, *Aug. 1971*

ALL-OUT Assault on Antarctica. By Richard E. Byrd. 141-180, *Aug. 1956*

ALLAGASH COUNTRY, Maine:

In the Allagash Country. By Kenneth Fuller Lee. 505-520, *Apr. 1929*

ALLAGASH WILDERNESS WATERWAY, Maine:

Autumn Flames Along the Allagash. By François Leydet. Photos by Farrell Grehan. 177-187, *Feb. 1974*

ALLAHABAD, India:

Through the Heart of Hindustan: A Teeming Highway Extending for Fifteen Hundred Miles from the Khyber Pass to Calcutta. By Maynard Owen Williams. 433-467, *Nov. 1921*

ALLARD, WILLIAM ALBERT:

Nomination Page. At Machu Picchu, Peru. *Mar. 1982*

Nomination Page. *July 1966*

Author-Photographer

Chief Joseph. 409-434, *Mar. 1977*

Chinatown, the Gilded Ghetto (San Francisco). 627-643, *Nov. 1975*

Cowpunching on the Padlock Ranch. 478-499, *Oct. 1973*

Bryan Allen pedals **Gossamer Albatross** *on the first man-powered flight across the English Channel.* OTIS IMBODEN, NGS

ALLEN, LESLIE: *Author*

■■ *Liberty: The Statue and the American Dream.* The official book for the Centennial of the Statue of Liberty published by the Statue of Liberty–Ellis Island Foundation, Inc. Prepared and produced as a public service by NGS. 304 pages. *1985*

ALLEN, ROBERT PORTER: *Author*

Our Only Native Stork, the Wood Ibis. Photos by Frederick Kent Truslow. 294-306, *Feb. 1964*

Roseate Spoonbills, Radiant Birds of the Gulf Coast. Photos by Frederick Kent Truslow. 274-288, *Feb. 1962*

Whooping Cranes Fight for Survival. Photos by Frederick Kent Truslow. 650-669, *Nov. 1959*

ALLEN, THOMAS B.: *Author*

Time Catches Up With Mongolia. Photos by Dean Conger. 242-269, *Feb. 1985*

■■ *Vanishing Wildlife of North America.* 207 pages. *1974*

ALLEN-WARNER VALLEY ENERGY SYSTEM, Utah: Proposed:

Coal vs. Parklands. By François Leydet. Photos by Dewitt Jones. 776-803, *Dec. 1980*

ALLENBY, EDMUND HENRY HYNMAN:

Old Jewel in the Proper Setting: An Eyewitness's Account of the Reconquest of the Holy Land by Twentieth Century Crusaders. By Charles W. Whitehair. 325-344, *Oct. 1918*

ALLERGIES:

Pollen: Breath of Life and Sneezes. By Cathy Newman. Photos by Martha Cooper. Included: Anatomy of a Sneeze; Yellow Rain; A Misery Index. 490-521, *Oct. 1984*

ALLIED MILITARY GOVERNMENT:

Europe's Looted Art. By John Walker. 39-52, *Jan. 1946*

Americans Help Liberated Europe Live Again. By Frederick Simpich, Jr. 747-768, *June 1945*

See also American Military Government

ALLIGATOR REEF, Florida:

Marvels of a Coral Realm. By Walter A. Starck II. NGS research grant. 710-738, *Nov. 1966*

Photographing the Night Creatures of Alligator Reef. By Robert E. Schroeder. Photos by author and Walter A. Starck II. NGS research grant. 128-154, *Jan. 1964*

ALLIGATORS:

■ Realm of the Alligator. President's Page. By Gilbert M. Grosvenor. Jan. 1986; Cover. *Apr. 1986*

A Bad Time to Be a Crocodile. By Rick Gore. Photos by Jonathan Blair. Included: American and Chinese alligators. 90-115, *Jan. 1978*

Twilight Hope for Big Cypress. By Rick Gore. Photos by Patricia Caulfield. 251-273, *Aug. 1976*

Alligators: Dragons in Distress. By Ar-

chie Carr. Photos by Treat Davidson and Laymond Hardy. 133-148, *Jan. 1967*

See also Caimans; *and* Everglades (Region)

ALLMON, CHARLES:

Author-Photographer

Happy-go-lucky Trinidad and Tobago. 35-75, *Jan. 1953*

Barbados, Outrider of the Antilles. 363-392, *Mar. 1952*

Shores and Sails in the South Seas (Marquesas Islands). 73-104, *Jan. 1950*

Photographer

Martinique: A Tropical Bit of France. By Gwen Drayton Allmon. 255-283, *Feb. 1959*

Virgin Islands: Tropical Playland, U.S.A. By John Scofield. 201-232, *Feb. 1956*

Spectacular Rio de Janeiro. By Hernane Tavares de Sá. 289-328, *Mar. 1955*

Bermuda, Cradled in Warm Seas. By Beverley M. Bowie. 203-238, *Feb. 1954*

The *Yankee*'s Wander-world. By Irving and Electa Johnson. 1-50, *Jan. 1949*

Rubber-cushioned Liberia. By Henry S. Villard. 201-228, *Feb. 1948*

ALLMON, GWEN DRAYTON: *Author*

Martinique: A Tropical Bit of France. Photos by Charles Allmon. 255-283, *Feb. 1959*

ALLYN, RUBE: *Author*

Cruising Florida's Western Waterways. Photos by Bates Littlehales. 49-76, *Jan. 1955*

ALMADA, Lisbon, Portugal:

Lisbon, the City of the Friendly Bay. By Clifford Albion Tinker. 505-552, *Nov. 1922*

ALMASY, PAUL: *Author*

Madagascar: Mystery Island: Japan's Push into the Indian Ocean Swings the Searchlight of World Attention to This Huge French Sentinel off the African Coast. 797-830, *June 1942*

ALONE Across the Outback. By Robyn Davidson. Photos by Rick Smolan. 581-611, *May 1978*

ALONE to Antarctica. By David Lewis. Drawings by Noel Sickles. 808-821, *Dec. 1973*

ALONG London's Coronation Route. By Maynard Owen Williams. 609-632, *May 1937*

ALONG Our Side of the Mexican Border. By Frederick Simpich. 61-80, *July 1920*

ALONG the Banks of the Colorful Nile. Photos by Gervais Courtellemont. 323-338, *Sept. 1926*

ALONG the Great Divide. By Mike Edwards. Photos by Nicholas deVore III. 483-515, *Oct. 1979*

ALONG the Nile, Through Egypt and the Sudan. By Frederick Simpich. 379-410, *Oct. 1922*

ALONG the Old Inca Highway. By Harriet Chalmers Adams. 231-250, *Apr. 1908*

ALONG the Old Mandarin Road of Indo-China. By W. Robert Moore. 157-199, *Aug. 1931*

ALONG the Old Silk Routes: A Motor Caravan with Air-conditioned Trailer Retraces Ancient Roads from Paris across Europe and Half of Asia to Delhi. By Lawrence Copley Thaw and Margaret S. Thaw. 453-486, *Oct. 1940*

ALONG the Old Spanish Road in Mexico: Life Among the People of Nayarit and Jalisco, Two of the Richest States of the Southern Republic. By Herbert Corey. 225-281, *Mar. 1923*

ALONG the Post Road Today. Photos by B. Anthony Stewart. 206-233, *Aug. 1962*

ALONG the Storied Incense Roads of Aden. By Hermann F. Eilts. Photos by Brian Brake. 230-254, *Feb. 1957*

ALONG the Way of the Magi. Photos by American Colony Photographers. 709-716, *Dec. 1929*

ALONG the Yangtze, Main Street of China. By W. Robert Moore. 325-356, *Mar. 1948*

ALONG the Yukon Trail. By Amos Burg. 395-416, *Sept. 1953*

ALPACAS:

Camels of the Clouds. By W. H. Hodge. 641-656, *May 1946*

ALPHABETS:

Secrets from Syrian Hills: Explorations Reveal World's Earliest Known Alphabet, Deciphered from Schoolboy Slates and Dictionaries of 3,000 Years Ago. By Claude F. A. Schaeffer. 97-126, *July 1933*

A New Alphabet of the Ancients Is Unearthed: An Inconspicuous Mound in

A student scribed rows of cuneiform writing on a tablet found in Syria dating from 1400 B.C.   CLAUDE F. A. SCHAEFFER

A daring rock climber bridges a gap between towering peaks in the Italian Dolomites, an area of the Alps where erosion carved exotic formations.

AL SAUD, ABDUL AZIZ, King (Saudi Arabia):

Guest in Saudi Arabia. By Maynard Owen Williams. 463-487, *Oct. 1945*

ALSOP, JOSEPH: *Author*

Warriors From a Watery Grave (Bronze Sculptures). 821-827, *June 1983*
Joseph Alsop: A Historical Perspective (on Minoan Human Sacrifice). 223, *Feb. 1981*

ALTAI MOUNTAINS, Outer Mongolia-Sinkiang:

Western Siberia and the Altai Mountains: With Some Speculations on the Future of Siberia. By James Bryce. 469-507, *May 1921*

ALTAÏR (Ship):

Sailing Forbidden Coasts (Africa). By Ida Treat. 357-386, *Sept. 1931*

The **ALTITUDE** of Mount Adams, Washington. By Edgar McClure. 151-153, *Apr. 1896*

ALTITUDES:

The Highest Point in Each State. 539-541, *June 1909*
The World's Highest Altitudes and First Ascents. By Charles E. Fay. 493-530, *June 1909*

An **ALTITUDINAL** Journey Through Portugal: Rugged Scenic Beauty, Colorful Costumes, and Ancient Castles Abound in Tiny Nation That Once Ruled a Vast Empire. By Harriet Chalmers Adams. 567-610, *Nov. 1927*

ALUMINUM:

Aluminum, the Magic Metal. By Thomas Y. Canby. Photos by James L. Amos. 186-211, *Aug. 1978*
Kitimat–Canada's Aluminum Titan. By David S. Boyer. 376-398, *Sept. 1956*

AL 'UQAYR, Saudi Arabia. *See* Gerrha

ALVA, WALTER: *Author*

Discovering the New World's Richest Unlooted Tomb. Photos by Bill Ballenberg. Included: Into the Tomb of a Moche Lord. Paintings by Ned Seidler; Iconography of the Moche: Unraveling the Mystery of the Warrior-Priest. By Christopher B. Donnan. NGS research grant. 510-555, *Oct. 1988*

ALVAREZ, LUIS W.:

Nomination Page. *Oct. 1969*

ALVIN (Research Submersible):

Epilogue for *Titanic*. By Robert D. Ballard. 454-463, *Oct. 1987*
A Long Last Look at *Titanic*. By Robert D. Ballard. Included: High-tech partners plumb new depths; Poignant relics of a disaster. Illustrations text by Cliff Tarpy. 698-727, *Dec. 1986*
Incredible World of the Deep-sea Rifts. 680-705. I. Strange World Without Sun. The Editor. 680-688; II. Return to Oases of the Deep. By Robert D. Ballard and J. Frederick Grassle. 689-705, *Nov. 1979*
Oases of Life in the Cold Abyss (Galapagos Rift). By John B. Corliss and Robert D. Ballard. 441-453, *Oct. 1977*

Window on Earth's Interior. By Robert D. Ballard. Photos by Emory Kristof. 228-249, *Aug. 1976*
Project FAMOUS. 586-614. I. Where the Earth Turns Inside Out. By J. R. Heirtzler. Photos by Emory Kristof. 586-603; II. Dive Into the Great Rift. By Robert D. Ballard. Photos by Emory Kristof. 604-615, *May 1975*

AMA, Sea Nymphs of Japan. By Luis Marden. 122-135, *July 1971*

AMA DABLAM (Mountain), Nepal:

Wintering on the Roof of the World. By Barry C. Bishop. 503-547, *Oct. 1962*

AMADEO, LUIGI, Prince of Savoy. *See* Abruzzi, Duke of the

AMALFI, Italy's Divine Coast. By Luis Marden. 472-509, *Oct. 1959*

AMAMI O SHIMA (Island), Ryukyu Retto:

Peacetime Rambles in the Ryukyus. By William Leonard Schwartz. 543-561, *May 1945*

AMANA COLONIES, Iowa:

Iowa's Enduring Amana Colonies. By Laura Longley Babb. Photos by Steve Raymer. 863-878, *Dec. 1975*

AMARANTH:

Rediscovering America's Forgotten Crops. By Noel D. Vietmeyer. Photos by Burgess Blevins. Paintings by Paul M. Breeden. 702-712, *May 1981*

AMARNATH CAVE, Kashmir:

Himalayan Pilgrimage. By Christopher Rand. 520-535, *Oct. 1956*

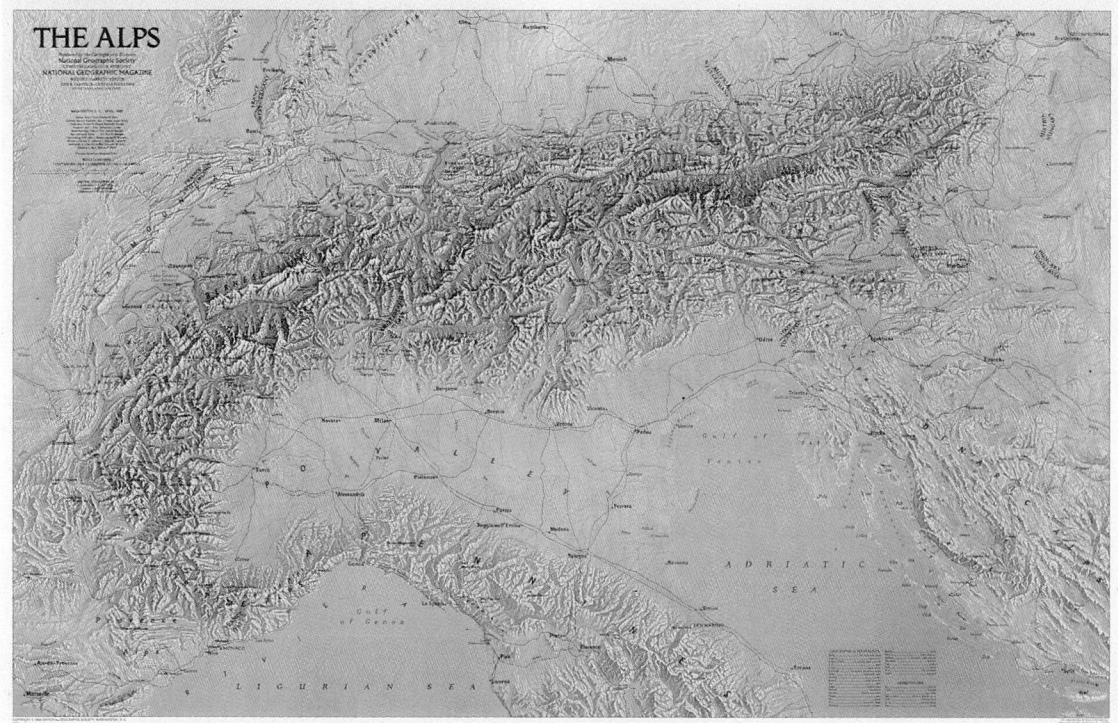

THE ALPS

A double map supplement of the Alps appeared with the April 1985 GEOGRAPHIC.

A Pilgrimage to Amernath, Himalayan Shrine of the Hindu Faith. By Louise Ahl Jessop. 513-542, *Nov. 1921*

AMATEUR Gardener Creates a New Rose. By Elizabeth A. Moize. Photos by Farrell Grehan. 286-294, *Aug. 1972*

AMAZING Animals of Australia. Juvenile. 104 pages. *1984*

AMAZING Animals of the Sea. Included: Pinnipeds, sea otters, manatees, and whales. Juvenile. 104 pages. *1981*

The **AMAZING** Frog-Eating Bat. By Merlin D. Tuttle. 78-91, *Jan. 1982*

AMAZING Mysteries of the World. By Catherine O'Neill. Contents: Mystifying phenomena such as auroras, black holes, Bigfoot, the Bermuda Triangle, and UFOs. Juvenile. 104 pages. *1983*

AMAZON BASIN, South America:

Rondônia: Brazil's Imperiled Rain Forest. By William S. Ellis. Photos by William Albert Allard and Loren McIntyre. 772-779, *Dec. 1988*

Kayaking the Amazon. By Piotr Chmielinski. Photos by Zbigniew Bzdak. 461-473, *Apr. 1987*

Brazil: Moment of Promise and Pain. By Priit J. Vesilind. Photos by Stephanie Maze. 348-385, *Mar. 1987*

Tropical Rain Forests: Nature's Dwindling Treasures. By Peter T. White. Photos by James P. Blair. Paintings by Barron Storey. 2-47, *Jan. 1983*

Jari: A Billion-dollar Gamble. By Loren McIntyre. Contents: Daniel K. Ludwig's paper-pulp and food-production enterprise in Brazil's Amazon basin. 686-711, *May 1980*

Brazil's Wild Frontier. By Loren McIntyre. 684-719, *Nov. 1977*

The Amazon. Photos by Loren McIntyre. 445-455, *Oct. 1972*

Amazon–The River Sea. By Loren McIntyre. 456-495, *Oct. 1972*

Exploring the Amazon. Written and photographed by Helen and Frank Schreider. 207 pages. *1970*

Amazon. 295A-295B, *Feb. 1968*

Giant Insects of the Amazon. By Paul A. Zahl. 632-669, *May 1959*

Jungle Jaunt on Amazon Headwaters. By Bernice M. Goetz. 371-388, *Sept. 1952*

Sea Fever. By John E. Schultz. 237-268, *Feb. 1949*

A Journey by Jungle Rivers to the Home of the Cock-of-the-rock: Naturalists Enter the Amazon, Voyage Through the Heart of Tropical South America, and Emerge at the Mouth of the Orinoco. By Ernest G. Holt. 585-630, *Nov. 1933*

Exploring the Valley of the Amazon in a Hydroplane: Twelve Thousand Miles of Flying Over the World's Greatest River and Greatest Forest to Chart the Unknown Parima River from the Sky. By Albert W. Stevens. 353-420, *Apr. 1926*

The Amazon, Father of Waters: The Earth's Mightiest River Drains a Basin of More Than 2,700,000 Square Miles, from Which Came Originally the World's Finest Rubber. By W. L. Schurz. 445-463, *Apr. 1926*

Fishing and Hunting Tales from Brazil. By Dewey Austin Cobb. 917-920, *Oct. 1909*

A New Peruvian Route to the Plain of the Amazon. By Solon I. Bailey. 432-448, *Aug. 1906*

South America. Annual Address by the President, Gardiner G. Hubbard. 1-29, *Mar. 28, 1891*

See also Brazil; Colombia; Ecuador

AMAZON BASIN INDIANS:

"Last Days of Eden," Rondônia's Urueu-Wau-Wau Indians. By Loren McIntyre. Photos by W. Jesco von Puttkamer. 800-817, *Dec. 1988*

Brazil: Moment of Promise and Pain. By Priit J. Vesilind. Photos by Stephanie Maze. 348-385, *Mar. 1987*

What Future for the Wayana Indians? By Carole Devillers. 66-83, *Jan. 1983*

Man in the Amazon: Stone Age Present Meets Stone Age Past. By W. Jesco von Puttkamer. Included: Paleo-Indians; Wasúsus of the Nambicuara confederation. NGS research grant. 60-83, *Jan. 1979*

Brazil's Wild Frontier. By Loren McIntyre. Included: Mato Grosso tribes: Érigpactsã, Kabano Iáras and Kabano Pomons of the Cintas Largas, Xingu. 684-719, *Nov. 1977*

Amazon–The River Sea. By Loren McIntyre. 456-495, *Oct. 1972*

Indians of the Amazon Darkness. By Harald Schultz. NGS research grant. 737-758, *May 1964*

See also Cinta Larga Indians; Erigbaagtsa Indians; Kayapo Indians; Kraho Indians; Kreen-Akarore Indians; Machiguenga Indians; Suyá Indians; Tchikao Indians; Tukuna Indians; Txukahamei Indians; Waurá Indians

AMBASSADORS of Good Will: Annual Messengers from Our Neighbor Republics to the South Bring Cheer and Add Interest to the Out-of-Doors (Birds). By Arthur A. Allen. 786-796, *June 1942*

AMBASSADORS of Good Will: The Peace Corps. By Sargent Shriver and Peace Corps Volunteers. 297-345, *Sept. 1964*

AMBER:

Golden Window on the Past. Photos by Paul A. Zahl. Text by Thomas J. O'Neill. 423-435, *Sept. 1977*

Exploring the World of Gems. By W. F. Foshag. 779-810, *Dec. 1950*

AMBERGRIS:

The Islands of Bermuda: A British Colony with a Unique Record in Popular Government. By William Howard Taft. 1-26, *Jan. 1922*

AMCHITKA (Island), Aleutian Islands:

A Navy Artist Paints the Aleutians. By Mason Sutherland. Paintings by William F. Draper. 157-176, *Aug. 1943*

AMERASIAN Children. Editorial by Wilbur E. Garrett. 141, *Feb. 1982*

AMERICA. *See* The Americas

AMERICA (Airplane):

Our Transatlantic Flight. By Richard Evelyn Byrd. 347-368, *Sept. 1927*

AMERICA Enters the Modern Era. By Frank Freidel. 537-577, *Oct. 1965*

AMERICA Fights on the Farms. 33-48, *July 1944*

AMERICA from the Air: No Such Series of Airplane Views Has Ever Before Been Printed. Photos by Albert W. Stevens. 85-92, *July 1924*

AMERICA Goes to the Fair. By Samuel W. Matthews. 293-333, *Sept. 1954*

AMERICA in 1888. "Tell me if your civilization is interesting": Those Electrifying Eighteen Eighties When the

Daring the rain-swollen Amazon River, a jaguar puts a lethal hold on a caiman and earns a meal.   LOREN McINTYRE

A towering refinery distills crude oil into 100-octane gasoline to power U.S. aircraft during World War II. PAINTING BY THORNTON OAKLEY

An **AMERICAN** Floating Exposition. 204-205, *May 1901*

AMERICAN FORESTRY ASSOCIATION:

Summer Meeting of the American Forestry Association. 352-358, *Sept. 1902*

An **AMERICAN** 4-H Exchange: Down on the Farm in the U.S.S.R. By John Garaventa. Photos by James Tobin and Carol Schmidt. 768-797, *June 1979*

AMERICAN Game Birds. By Henry Wetherbee Henshaw. Paintings by Louis Agassiz Fuertes. 105-158, *Aug. 1915*

AMERICAN Geographic Education. By W J McGee. 305-307, *July 1898*

The **AMERICAN** Giant Comes of Age. By Frank Freidel. 660-711, *May 1965*

An **AMERICAN** Gibraltar: Notes on the Danish West Indies. 89-96, *July 1916*

An **AMERICAN** Girl Cycles Across Romania: Two-wheel Pilgrim Pedals the Land of Castles and Gypsies, Where Roman Empire Traces Mingle With Remnants of Oriental Migration. By Dorothy Hosmer. 557-588, *Nov. 1938*

AMERICAN Goods in China. 173-175, *Mar. 1906*

An **AMERICAN** in Russia's Capital. By Thomas T. Hammond. Photos by Dean Conger. 297-351, *Mar. 1966*

An **AMERICAN** Indian's View: This Land of Ours. By N. Scott Momaday. 13-19, *July 1976*

AMERICAN Industries Geared for War. By Thornton Oakley. Paintings by author. 716-734, *Dec. 1942*

The **AMERICAN** Lobster, Delectable Cannibal. By Luis Marden. Photos by David Doubilet. 462-487, *Apr. 1973*

AMERICAN Masters in the National Gallery. By John Walker. 295-324, *Sept. 1948*

AMERICAN Military Government: Sunset in the East (Japan). By Blair A. Walliser. 797-812, *June 1946*

An **AMERICAN** Moslem Explores the Arab Past: The Sword and the Sermon. By Thomas J. Abercrombie. 3-45, *July 1972*

AMERICAN MOUNT EVEREST EXPEDITION:

Americans on Everest. 448-452, Sept. 1965; 575, *Nov. 1976*
America's First Everest Expedition. 460-515. I. Six to the Summit. By Norman G. Dyhrenfurth. Photos by Barry C. Bishop. 460-473; II. How We Climbed Everest. By Barry C. Bishop. 477-507; III. The First Traverse. By Thomas F. Hornbein and William F. Unsoeld. 509-513; IV. President Kennedy Presents the

Hubbard Medal. 514-515. NGS research grant. 460-515, *Oct. 1963*
American and Geographic Flags Top Everest. By Melvin M. Payne. Photos by Barry C. Bishop. 157-157C, *Aug. 1963*
Mount Rainier: Testing Ground for Everest. By Barry C. Bishop. NGS research grant. 688-711, *May 1963*

AMERICAN Mountain People. Photos by Bruce Dale. 199 pages. *1973*

AMERICAN MUSEUM OF NATURAL HISTORY, New York:

Expeditions
Dinosaur expedition to Texas. 710, 715, 717, *May 1954*
Unknown New Guinea: Circumnavigating the World in a Flying Boat, American Scientists Discover a Valley of 60,000 People Never Before Seen by White Men. By Richard Archbold. 315-344, *Mar. 1941*
Fighting Giants of the Humboldt. By David D. Duncan. 373-400, *Mar. 1941*
On the Bottom of a South Sea Pearl Lagoon. By Roy Waldo Miner. 365-390, *Sept. 1938*
See also American Museum-Armand Denis Expedition; Edgar M. Queeny-American Museum of Natural History Expedition; Gilliard Expeditions; Weeks Expedition

Museum
Behind New York's Window on Nature: The American Museum of Natural History. By James A. Oliver. Photos by Robert F. Sisson. 220-259, *Feb. 1963*
Dinosaur Hall: *Brontosaurus*. 707, 719, 721, 722, *May 1954*
Gem collection. 786, 797, 799, 801, *Dec. 1950*

Study Grant
Western Grebes. 626, *May 1982*
See also Lerner Marine Laboratory

AMERICAN MUSEUM-ARMAND DENIS EXPEDITION:

New Guinea's Rare Birds and Stone Age Men. By E. Thomas Gilliard. 421-488, *Apr. 1953*

AMERICAN Pathfinders in the Pacific. By William H. Nicholas. 617-640, *May 1946*

The **AMERICAN** People Must Become Ship-Minded. By Edward N. Hurley. 201-211, *Sept. 1918*

AMERICAN POINT ISLAND, Minnesota:

Men, Moose, and Mink of Northwest Angle. By William H. Nicholas. 265-284, *Aug. 1947*

AMERICAN Potash for America. By Guy Elliott Mitchell. 399-405, *Apr. 1911*

AMERICAN PRIMITIVE ART. *See* Garbisch Collection

AMERICAN Processional: History on Canvas. By John and Blanche Leeper. 173-212, *Feb. 1951*

AMERICAN Progress in Cuba. 76, *Feb. 1902*

AMERICAN Progress in Habana. 97-108, *Mar. 1902*

AMERICAN RED CROSS:

The American Red Cross: A Century of Service. By Louise Levathes. Photos by Annie Griffiths. 777-791, *June 1981*
Scenes of Postwar Finland. By La Verne Bradley. Photos by Jerry Waller. 233-264, *Aug. 1947*

Doing their part for the doughboys, American Red Cross volunteers prepare to serve World War I soldiers in a Paris canteen.

Red Cross Girl Overseas. By Margaret Cotter. 745-768, *Dec. 1944*

Heroes of Wartime Science and Mercy. By Elizabeth W. King. 715-740, *Dec. 1943*

The Great Mississippi Flood of 1927: Since White Man's Discovery This Mighty River Has Served Him Well, Yet It Has Brought Widespread Devastation Along Its Lower Reaches. By Frederick Simpich. 243-289, *Sept. 1927*

The Healer of Humanity's Wounds. 308-324, *Oct. 1918*

The Symbol of Service to Mankind. By Stockton Axson. 375-390, *Apr. 1918*

Help Our Red Cross. By Woodrow Wilson. 422, *May 1917*

Our Armies of Mercy. By Henry P. Davison. 423-427, *May 1917*

Bind the Wounds of France. By Herbert C. Hoover. 439-444, *May 1917*

America's Duty. By Newton D. Baker. 453-457, *May 1917*

Stand by the Soldier. By John J. Pershing. 457-459, *May 1917*

A Poisoned World. By William Howard Taft. 459-467, *May 1917*

The Red Cross Spirit. By Eliot Wadsworth. 467-474, *May 1917*

The National Geographic Society. Speech by Mabel Boardman. 272-298, *Mar. 1912*

The American Red Cross in Italy. By Mabel Boardman. 396-397, *Apr. 1909*

Honors to the American Navy. National Geographic Society Banquet Speech by Mabel Boardman. 77-95, *Jan. 1909*

An **AMERICAN** Retraces "Travels With a Donkey." By Carolyn Bennett Patterson. Photos by Cotton Coulson. 535-561, *Oct. 1978*

AMERICAN REVOLUTION:

Yorktown Shipwreck. By John D. Broadwater. Photos by Bates Littlehales. 804-823, *June 1988*

George Washington: The Man Behind the Myths. By Howard La Fay. Photos by Ted Spiegel. 90-111, *July 1976*

Thomas Jefferson: Architect of Freedom. By Mike W. Edwards. Photos by Linda Bartlett. 231-259, *Feb. 1976*

Patriots in Petticoats. By Lonnelle Aikman. Paintings by Louis S. Glanzman. Contents: Abigail Adams, Sarah Franklin Bache, Anne Bailey, Kate Moore Barry, Martha Bell, Margaret Cochran Corbin, Lydia Darragh, Mary Katherine Goddard, Elizabeth Hager, Nancy Hart, Elizabeth Hutchinson Jackson, Dicey Langston, Sybil Ludington, Rebecca Motte, Molly Pitcher (Mary Hays), Esther Reed, Deborah Sampson, Jane Thomas, Mercy Otis Warren, Martha Washington, Phillis Wheatley, Elizabeth Zane. 475-493, *Oct. 1975*

Benjamin Franklin, Philosopher of Dissent. By Alice J. Hall. Photos by Linda Bartlett. 93-123, *July 1975*

The Loyalists. By Kent Britt. Photos by Ted Spiegel. 510-539, *Apr. 1975*

Firebrands of the Revolution. By Eric

Thomas Jefferson: architect of the Declaration of Independence, philosopher, scientist, and President.

PAINTING BY REMBRANDT PEALE, COURTESY NEW YORK HISTORICAL SOCIETY

F. Goldman. Photos by George F. Mobley. 2-27, *July 1974*

North Through History Aboard *White Mist.* By Melville Bell Grosvenor. Photos by Edwin Stuart Grosvenor. 1-55, *July 1970*

From Sword to Scythe in Champlain Country. By Ethel A. Starbird. Photos by B. Anthony Stewart and Emory Kristof. 153-201, *Aug. 1967*

▪▪ *The Revolutionary War: America's Fight for Freedom.* By Bart McDowell. 199 pages. *1967*

Massachusetts Builds for Tomorrow. By Robert de Roos. Photos by B. Anthony Stewart. 790-843, *Dec. 1966*

Profiles of the Presidents: I. The Presidency and How It Grew. By Frank Freidel. 642-687, *Nov. 1964*

Philadelphia Houses a Proud Past. By Harold Donaldson Eberlein. Photos by Thomas Nebbia. 151-191, *Aug. 1960*

I'm From New Jersey. By John T. Cunningham. Photos by Volkmar Wentzel. 1-45, *Jan. 1960*

New Stars for Old Glory. By Lonnelle Aikman. 86-121, *July 1959*

History and Beauty Blend in a Concord Iris Garden. By Robert T. Cochran, Jr. Photos by M. Woodbridge Williams. 705-719, *May 1959*

Washington Lives Again at Valley Forge. By Howell Walker. 197-202, *Feb. 1954*

U. S. Capitol, Citadel of Democracy. By Lonnelle Aikman. Included: Paintings and frescoes of the Revolution by John Trumbull and Constantino Brumidi. 143-192, *Aug. 1952*

Our First Alliance (France). By J. J. Jusserand. 518-548, *June 1917*

Albemarle in Revolutionary Days. By G. Brown Goode. 271-281, *Aug. 1896*

See also Boston Post Roads; Daughters of the American Revolution

AMERICAN SAMOA (Islands), Pacific Ocean:

The Two Samoas, Still Coming of Age. By Robert Booth. Photos by Melinda Berge. 452-473, *Oct. 1985*

Problems in Paradise. By Mary and Laurance S. Rockefeller. Photos by Thomas Nebbia. 782-793, *Dec. 1974*

The **AMERICAN** Scene. Contents: Winning photos in the Sixth Annual Newspaper National Snapshot Awards, with explanatory note. 220-246, *Feb. 1941*

AMERICAN Skiers Find Adventure in Western China. By Ned Gillette. Photos by the author and Galen Rowell. Included: Skiing From the Summit of China's Ice Mountain. 174-199, *Feb. 1981*

AMERICAN Soldier in Reykjavik. By Luther M. Chovan. 536-568, *Nov. 1945*

AMERICAN South Polar Expedition. 885-888, *Dec. 1908*

AMERICAN Special Forces in Action in Viet Nam. By Howard Sochurek. 38-65, *Jan. 1965*

AMERICAN TELEPHONE AND TELEGRAPH COMPANY: Research. *See* Telstar

AMERICAN Transportation Vital to Victory. By Thornton Oakley. Paintings by author. 671-688, *Dec. 1943*

AMERICAN UNIVERSITY AT CAIRO, Egypt:

American Alma Maters in the Near East. By Maynard Owen Williams. 237-256, *Aug. 1945*

AMERICAN UNIVERSITY OF BEIRUT, Lebanon:

American Alma Maters in the Near East. By Maynard Owen Williams. 237-256, *Aug. 1945*

The **AMERICAN** Virgins (Virgin Islands): After Dark Days, These Adopted Daughters of the United States Are Finding a New Place in the Caribbean Sun. By DuBose Heyward and Daisy Reck. 273-308, *Sept. 1940*

AMERICAN Wild Flower Odyssey. By P. L. Ricker. 603-634, *May 1953*

AMERICAN Wild Flowers. Paintings by Mary E. Eaton. 507-517, *May 1915*

AMERICAN Wings Soar Around the World: Epic Story of the Air Transport Command of the U. S. Army Is a Saga of Yankee Daring and Doing. By Donald H. Agnew and William A. Kinney. 57-78, *July 1943*

AMERICANA. Contents: Winning photos in the Seventh Annual Newspaper National Snapshot Awards. 657-666, *May 1942*

AMERICANIZATION:

New York–The Metropolis of Mankind. By William Joseph Showalter. 1-49, *July 1918*

What Is It To Be an American? By

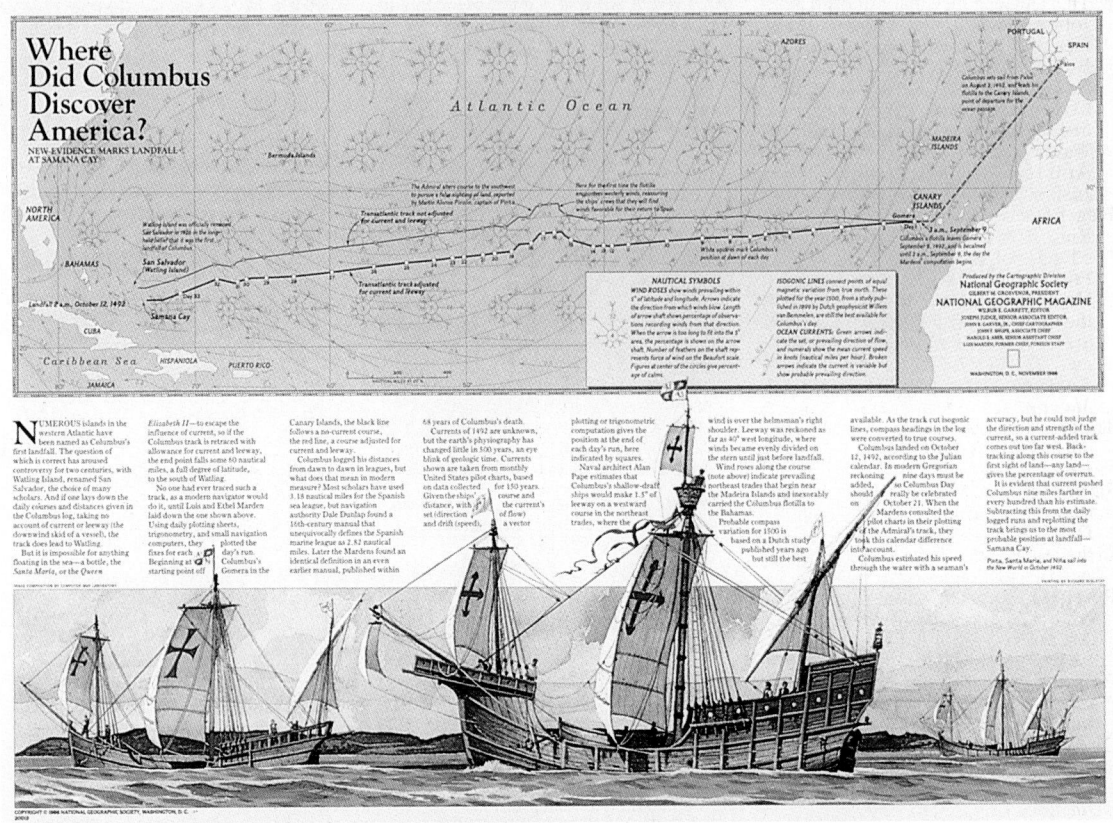

A supplement map in the November 1986 GEOGRAPHIC retraces the first voyage of Columbus, pinpointing his landfall at Samana Cay.

The Thirteen Original States.–Capt.
John Smith's Map of Virginia.–The
Opening of the American West:
Burr's 1840 Map.–Captain Smith's
New England.–The Pilgrims' Cape
Cod.–Alaska, Seward's Icebox, Be-
came a Treasure Chest.–George
Washington's Travels, Traced on the
Arrowsmith Map. 757-769,
June 1953

Flags of the Americas. By Elizabeth W.
King. Contents: The Flag of the Unit-
ed States and the Jack; Flags of the
President, the Vice President, and
Heads of Executive Departments of
the United States; Flags of the United
States Armed Forces and Govern-
ment Agencies; Flags of the Latin-
American Republics. 633-657,
May 1949

The First Landfall of Columbus. By Jacques W. Redway. 179-192,
Dec. 29, 1894

Sir Francis Drake's Anchorage. By Edward L. Berthoud. 208-214,
Dec. 29, 1894

In the Wake of Columbus. By Frederick
A. Ober. 187-196, *Jan. 31, 1894*

Recent Disclosures Concerning Pre-Co-
lumbian Voyages to America in the
Archives of the Vatican. By William
Eleroy Curtis. 197-234, *Jan. 31, 1894*

Early Voyages on the Northwestern
Coast of America. By George Davidson. 235-256, *Jan. 31, 1894*

Discoverers of America. Annual Ad-
dress by the President, Gardiner G.
Hubbard. 1-20, *Apr. 7, 1893*
⊕ *Juan de la Cosa Map, 1500.*
Apr. 7, 1893
⊕ *Ruysch Map, 1508. Apr. 7, 1893*

Discovery of America: Fourth Centennial Anniversary: International Literary Contest (Madrid, Spain). 273-
276, *July 1889*

See also Central America; Colonial
America; North America; South
America

AMERICA'S Amazing Railway Traffic.
By William Joseph Showalter. 353-
404, *Apr. 1923*

AMERICA'S Ancient Cities. By Gene S.
▦ Stuart. Photos by Richard Alexander
Cooke III. Art by H. Tom Hall. 199
pages. *1988*

AMERICA'S Atlantic Isles. By H. Rob-
▦ ert Morrison and Christine Eckstrom
Lee. Photos by David Alan Harvey.
199 pages. *1981*

AMERICA'S Auto Mania. By David
Jeffery. Photos by Bruce Dale. 24-31,
Special Report on Energy.
(Feb. 1981)

AMERICA'S Debt to the Hen. By Harry R. Lewis. 453-467, *Apr. 1927*

AMERICA'S Duty. By Newton D. Baker. 453-457, *May 1917*

AMERICA'S First Painters: Indians. By
Dorothy Dunn. 349-377, *Mar. 1955*

AMERICA'S First Settlers, the Indians.
By Matthew W. Stirling. Paintings by
W. Langdon Kihn. 535-596,
Nov. 1937

AMERICA'S First Undersea Park. By
Charles M. Brookfield. Photos by
Jerry Greenberg. 58-69, *Jan. 1962*

AMERICA'S Forgotten Crops. By Noel
D. Vietmeyer. Photos by Burgess
Blevins. Paintings by Paul M. Bree-
den. 702-712, *May 1981*

AMERICA'S Great Hideaways. Con-
▦ tents: Arizona, Baja California, California, Canadian Rockies, Finger
Lakes, Kauai, Martha's Vineyard
and Nantucket, Minnesota, Montana, Oregon, Suwannee River, Virgin Islands, and West Virginia. 199
pages. *1986*

AMERICA'S Hidden Corners: Places
▦ *Off the Beaten Path.* Contents: Bad-
lands, Chesapeake Bay, Four Cor-
ners, Great Basin, Gulf Coast,
Michigan's Upper Peninsula, and
Ozarks. 199 pages. *1983*

AMERICA'S Hidden Wilderness: Lands
▦ *of Seclusion.* Contents: Arctic re-
gions; Baxter State Park, Maine;
l'Eau Claire wilderness, Quebec;
Grand Gulch Primitive Area, Utah;
Great Burn wilderness area, Idaho-
Montana; Lacandon Forest, Mexico;
Mojave Desert. 200 pages. *1988*

AMERICA'S Historylands, Touring Our
▦ *Landmarks of Liberty.* Companion
volume to *America's Wonderlands.*
575 pages. 1962; rev. ed. *1967*

AMERICA'S Inland Waterway: Explor-
▦ *ing the Atlantic Seaboard.* By Allan
C. Fisher, Jr. Photos by James L.
Amos. 207 pages. *1973*

AMERICA'S Little Mainstream. By
Harvey Arden. Photos by Matt Bradley. 344-359, *Mar. 1977*

AMERICA'S Magnificent Mountains.
▦ 207 pages. *1980*

AMERICA'S Majestic Canyons. 207
▦ pages. *1979*

AMERICA'S "Meat on the Hoof." By
William H. Nicholas. 33-72,
Jan. 1952

AMERICA'S Most Valuable Fishes. By
Hugh M. Smith. 494-514, *May 1912*

AMERICA'S New Crescent of Defense
(Air and Naval Bases). 621-628,
Nov. 1940

AMERICA'S New Soldier Cities: The
Geographical and Historical Envi-
ronment of the National Army Can-
tonments and National Guard
Camps. By William Joseph
Showalter. 439-476, *Nov.-Dec. 1917*

AMERICA'S Outdoor Wonders: State
▦ *Parks and Sanctuaries.* 199 pages.
1987

AMERICA'S Part in the Allies' Mastery
of the Air. By Joseph Tulasne. 1-5,
Jan. 1918

AMERICA'S Seashore Wonderlands.
▦ 199 pages. *1985*

AMERICA'S 6,000-mile Walk in Space.
440-447, *Sept. 1965*

AMERICA'S South Sea Soldiers
(American Samoa). By Lorena Mac-
Intyre Quinn. 267-274, *Sept. 1919*

AMERICA'S Spectacular Northwest.
▦ Photos by Robert W. Madden. 199
pages. *1982*

AMERICA'S Sunset Coast. By Merrill
▦ Windsor. Photos by James A. Sugar.
211 pages. *1978*

AMERICA'S Surpassing Fisheries:
Their Present Condition and Future
Prospects, and How the Federal Gov-
ernment Fosters Them. By Hugh M.
Smith. 546-583, *June 1916*

AMERICA'S Wild and Scenic Rivers.
▦ 199 pages. *1983*

AMERICA'S Wild Woodlands. 199
▦ pages. *1985*

AMERICA'S Wilderness: How Much
Can We Save? By Gilbert M. Grosvenor, François Leydet, and Joseph
Judge. Photos by Farrell Grehan.
151-205, *Feb. 1974*

AMERICA'S Wonderlands: The Scenic
▦ *National Parks and Monuments of the*
United States. 552 pages. 1959; rev.
ed. *1980*

AMERNATH (Cave), India. *See*
Amarnath

AMHARA TRIBESPEOPLE:

Ethiopia: Revolution in an Ancient Empire. By Robert Caputo. 614-645,
May 1983

AMHERST, Massachusetts:

Literary Landmarks of Massachusetts.
By William H. Nicholas. Photos by
B. Anthony Stewart and John E.
Fletcher. 279-310, *Mar. 1950*

AMIABLE Amsterdam. By William
Davenport. Photos by Adam Woolfitt. 683-705, *May 1974*

AMID the Mighty Walls of Zion. By
Lewis F. Clark. 37-70, *Jan. 1954*

AMID the Snow Peaks of the Equator:
A Naturalist's Explorations Around
Ruwenzori, with an Excursion to the
Congo State, and an Account of the
Terrible Scourge of Sleeping Sick-
ness. By A.F.R. Wollaston. 256-277,
Mar. 1909

AMID the Snows and Swamps of Tropical Africa. Photos by Vittorio Sella
and others. 163-178, *Feb. 1925*

AMID the Snows of Switzerland. Photos
by Albert Steiner. 277-292,
Mar. 1922

AMIDST the Templed Hills of Greece.
Photos by Maynard Owen Williams.
665-672, *Dec. 1930*

AMIENS, France:

The Beauties of France. By Arthur
Stanley Riggs. 391-491, *Nov. 1915*

AMISH (Sect):

The Plain People of Pennsylvania. Photo essay by Jerry Irwin. Text by
Douglas Lee. Included: Amish

Amish boy pets a guinea pig raised on his family's farm in Lancaster County, Pennsylvania. WILLIAM ALBERT ALLARD

AMMAN, Jordan:

AMNE MACHIN SHAN (Mountain Range), Qinghai Province, China:

AMOCO CADIZ (Oil Tanker):

AMOS, JAMES L.:

AMOS, WILLIAM H.:

AMPHIBIANS:

AMPHIBIOUS FORCE, U. S. Navy:

AMPHIBIOUS TRAINING BASE,
Solomons Island, Maryland:
Landing Craft for Invasion. By Melville Bell Grosvenor. 1-30, *July 1944*

AMPHITRITE (Inflatable Ship):
Inflatable Ship Opens Era of Airborne Undersea Expeditions. By Jacques-Yves Cousteau. NGS research grant. 142-148, *July 1961*

AMRITSAR, India:
Through the Heart of Hindustan: A Teeming Highway Extending for Fifteen Hundred Miles, from the Khyber Pass to Calcutta. By Maynard Owen Williams. 433-467, *Nov. 1921*

AMSTERDAM, The Netherlands:
Amiable Amsterdam. By William Davenport. Photos by Adam Woolfitt. 683-705, *May 1974*
The Netherlands: Nation at War With the Sea. By Alan Villiers. Photos by Adam Woolfitt. 530-571, *Apr. 1968*
Mid-century Holland Builds Her Future. By Sydney Clark. 747-778, *Dec. 1950*
Holland Rises from War and Water. By Thomas R. Henry. 237-260, *Feb. 1946*
Behind Netherlands Sea Ramparts: Dikes and Pumps Keep Ocean and Rivers at Bay While a Busy People Carries on Peacetime Work. By McFall Kerbey. 255-290, *Feb. 1940*
Glimpses of Holland. By William Wisner Chapin. 1-29, *Jan. 1915*

AMU DARYA (Oxus River), U.S.S.R.:
Surveying Through Khoresm: A Journey into Parts of Asiatic Russia Which Have Been Closed to Western Travelers Since the World War. By Lyman D. Wilbur. 753-780, *June 1932*

AMUNDSEN, ROALD:
The First Meeting of the Poles (Photograph of the first meeting of Robert E. Peary, discoverer of the North Pole, and Roald Amundsen, discoverer of the South Pole, at the National Geographic Society, January 11, 1913). 114, Jan. 1913; 126, *Jan. 1936*
Admiral Robert E. Peary presents the Special Gold Medal to Amundsen. 127, 149, *Jan. 1936*
Hubbard Medal presented to Amundsen by the Vice-President of the United States, Charles W. Fairbanks. 149, *Jan. 1936*
Navigating the "Norge" from Rome to the North Pole and Beyond: The Designer and Pilot of the First Dirigible to Fly Over the Top of the World Describes a Thrilling Voyage of More Than 8,000 Miles. By Umberto Nobile. 177-215, *Aug. 1927*
Honors to Amundsen and Peary (Presentation of Special Gold Medal). 113-130, *Jan. 1913*
Honors to Amundsen and Peary (Special Gold Medal Presented to Amundsen by Peary). 120, 129, *Jan. 1913*
Amundsen's Attainment of the South Pole. 205-208, *Feb. 1912*

Honors for Amundsen (Presentation of Hubbard Gold Medal by Charles W. Fairbanks). 55-76, *Jan. 1908*
Election of Roald Amundsen as Honorary Member of the Society. 51, *Jan. 1907*
A Modern Viking. 38-41, *Jan. 1906*
Norwegian Expedition to the Magnetic North Pole by Roald Amundsen. 293-294, *July 1903*

AMUSEMENT PARKS. *See* Disneyland; Tivoli; Walt Disney World

AN LAC, Viet Nam:
Viet Nam's Montagnards. By Howard Sochurek. 443-487, *Apr. 1968*

ANABAPTIST GROUPS. *See* Amish; Hutterites; Mennonites

ANABLEPS. *See* Four-eyed Fish

ANASAZI CULTURE:
The Anasazi–Riddles in the Ruins. By Thomas Y. Canby. Photos by Dewitt Jones and David Brill. Paintings by Roy Andersen. 554-592, *Nov. 1982*
Pueblo Pottery–2,000 Years of Artistry. By David L. Arnold. 593-605, *Nov. 1982*
🌐 *The Southwest,* The Making of America series. *Nov. 1982*
Solving the Riddles of Wetherill Mesa. By Douglas Osborne. Paintings by Peter V. Bianchi. 155-195, *Feb. 1964*
Searching for Cliff Dwellers' Secrets. By Carroll A. Burroughs. 619-625, *Nov. 1959*
Your Society to Seek New Light on the Cliff Dwellers. 154-156, *Jan. 1959*

First explorer to reach the South Pole, Roald Amundsen is awarded the Society's Special Gold Medal by Robert E. Peary.   HARRIS AND EWING

Ancient Cliff Dwellers of Mesa Verde. By Don Watson. Photos by Willard R. Culver. 349-376, *Sept. 1948*

ANATOLIA (Region), Turkey:

Ancient Aphrodisias Lives Through Its Art. By Kenan T. Erim. Photos by David Brill. NGS research grant. 527-551, *Oct. 1981*

Aphrodisias, Awakened City of Ancient Art. By Kenan T. Erim. Photos by Jonathan Blair. NGS research grant. 766-791, *June 1972*

Keeping House in a Cappadocian Cave. By Jonathan S. Blair. 127-146, *July 1970*

Ancient Aphrodisias and Its Marble Treasures. By Kenan T. Erim. Photos by Jonathan S. Blair. NGS research grant. 280-294, *Aug. 1967*

Peasants of Anatolia. By Alfred Marchionini. 57-72, *July 1948*

The Turkish Republic Comes of Age. By Maynard Owen Williams. 581-616, *May 1945*

Alert Anatolia. 481-492, *Apr. 1944*

Turkey, Where Earthquakes Followed Timur's Trail. Photos by Maynard Owen Williams. 395-406, *Mar. 1940*

East of Constantinople: Glimpses of Village Life in Anatolia, the Battleground of East and West, Where the Turks Reorganized Their Forces After the World War. By Melville Chater. 509-534, *May 1923*

ANATOMY of a Burmese Beauty Secret. By John M. Keshishian. 798-801, *June 1979*

ANCESTOR of the British Navy: England's Oldest Known War Vessel Is Unearthed, Laden with Remarkable Treasures of an Anglo-Saxon Ruler. By C. W. Phillips. 247-268, *Feb. 1941*

ANCHORAGE, Alaska:

Hello Anchorage, Good-Bye Dream.

Dancer in stone, a celestial apsara survives in the temple of Angkor Wat in Kampuchea. DAVID ALAN HARVEY

By Larry L. King. Photos by Chris Johns. 364-389, *Mar. 1988*

Earthquake! By William P. E. Graves. 112-139, *July 1964*

An Alaskan Family's Night of Terror (Earthquake). By Tay Pryor Thomas. 142-156, *July 1964*

ANCIENT Aphrodisias and Its Marble Treasures. By Kenan T. Erim. Photos by Jonathan S. Blair. 280-294, *Aug. 1967*

ANCIENT Aphrodisias Lives Through Its Art. By Kenan T. Erim. Photos by David Brill. 527-551, *Oct. 1981*

ANCIENT Ashfall Creates a Pompeii of Prehistoric Animals. By Michael R. Voorhies. Photos by Annie Griffiths. Paintings by Jay Matternes. 66-75, *Jan. 1981*

ANCIENT Bulgaria's Golden Treasures. By Colin Renfrew. Photos by James L. Stanfield. Paintings by Jean-Leon Huens. 112-129, *July 1980*

An **ANCIENT** Capital (Boghaz Keoy, Turkey). By Isabel F. Dodd. 111-124, *Feb. 1910*

ANCIENT Carthage in the Light of Modern Excavation. By Count Byron Khun de Prorok. 391-423, *Apr. 1924*

ANCIENT CIVILIZATIONS. *See* Early Civilizations

ANCIENT Cliff Dwellers of Mesa Verde. By Don Watson. Photos by Willard R. Culver. 349-376, *Sept. 1948*

ANCIENT Ebla Opens a New Chapter of History. By Howard La Fay. Photos by James L. Stanfield. Paintings by Louis S. Glanzman. 730-759, *Dec. 1978*

ANCIENT Egypt: Discovering its Splendors. 256 pages. *1978*

ANCIENT Europe Is Older Than We Thought. By Colin Renfrew. Photos by Adam Woolfitt. 615-623, *Nov. 1977*

ANCIENT Glory in Stone (Angkor). By Peter T. White. Photos by Wilbur E. Garrett. 552-589, *May 1982*

ANCIENT Iceland, New Pawn of War. 75-90, *July 1941*

ANCIENT Mesopotamia: A Light That Did Not Fail. By E. A. Speiser. Paintings by H. M. Herget. 41-105, *Jan. 1951*

ANCIENT Rome Brought to Life. By Rhys Carpenter. Paintings by H. M. Herget. 567-633, *Nov. 1946*

ANCIENT Shipwreck Yields New Facts–and a Strange Cargo. By Peter Throckmorton. Photos by Kim Hart and Joseph J. Scherschel. 282-300, *Feb. 1969*

ANCIENT "Skyscrapers" of the Yemen. Photos by Richard H. Sanger. 645-668, *Nov. 1947*

ANCIENT Temples and Modern Guns in Thailand. Photos by Maynard

Owen Williams and others. 653-660, *Nov. 1941*

AND Now to Touch the Moon's Forbidding Face. By Kenneth F. Weaver. 633-635, *May 1969*

ANDALUSIA (Region), Spain:

Andalusia, the Spirit of Spain. By Howard La Fay. Photos by Joseph J. Scherschel. 833-857, *June 1975*

The Changing Face of Old Spain. By Bart McDowell. Photos by Albert Moldvay. 291-339, *Mar. 1965*

Gypsy Cave Dwellers of Andalusia. 572-582, *Oct. 1957*

Holy Week and the Fair in Sevilla. By Luis Marden. 499-530, *Apr. 1951*

Speaking of Spain. By Luis Marden. 415-456, *Apr. 1950*

In Andalusia, Home of Song and Sunshine. Photos by Gervais Courtellemont. 301-308, *Mar. 1929*

ANDAMAN ISLANDS, India:

The Last Andaman Islanders. By Raghubir Singh. 66-91, *July 1975*

ANDEAN CONDORS:

The Condor, Soaring Spirit of the Andes. By Jerry McGahan. Photos by Libby McGahan. 684-709, *May 1971*

ANDEREGG, FRED: *Photographer*

Mount Sinai's Holy Treasures (St. Catherine's Monastery). By Kurt Weitzmann. 109-127, *Jan. 1964*

ANDERS, WILLIAM A.:

Hubbard Medal recipient. 861, *June 1970*

"A Most Fantastic Voyage": The Story of Apollo 8's Rendezvous With the Moon. By Sam C. Phillips. 593-631, *May 1969*

ANDERSEN, HANS CHRISTIAN:

The Magic World of Hans Christian Andersen. By Harvey Arden. Photos by Sisse Brimberg. 825-849, *Dec. 1979*

ANDERSEN, MAGNUS: *Author*

Norway and the Vikings. 132-136, *Jan. 31, 1894*

ANDERSEN, ROY: *Artist*

Mission to Mars. By Michael Collins. Photos by Roger H. Ressmeyer. Paintings by Pierre Mion and Roy Andersen. 733-764, *Nov. 1988*

Children of the First Fleet. By John Everingham. 233-245, *Feb. 1988*

The Anasazi–Riddles in the Ruins. By Thomas Y. Canby. Photos by Dewitt Jones and David Brill. 554-592, *Nov. 1982*

The Search for the First Americans. By Thomas Y. Canby. Photos by Kerby Smith. 330-363, *Sept. 1979*

"Australia, Land of Living Fossils," painting supplement. Map on reverse. *Feb. 1979*

A New Look at Dinosaurs. By John H. Ostrom. 152-185, *Aug. 1978*

ANDERSON, CAROLYN H.:

Nomination Page. In Iceland. *July 1973*

ANDERSON, GEORGE E.: *Author*

The Wonderful Canals of China. 68-69, *Feb. 1905*

ANDERSON, GEORGE W., Jr.:
Author
Our Nuclear Navy. 449-450, *Mar. 1963*

ANDERSON, KRISTIAN: *Author*
Kitty Hawk Floats Across North America. By Maxie and Kristian Anderson. 260-271, *Aug. 1980*

ANDERSON, MAXIE:
Editorial. By Wilbur E. Garrett. 707, *Dec. 1983*
A Wild, Ill-fated Balloon Race. 778-797. I. Wild Launch. 778-787; II. The Fantastic Flight of *Cote d'Or*. By Cynthia Shields. 789-793; III. Last Ascent of a Heroic Team (Maxie Anderson and Don Ida). 794-797, *Dec. 1983*
Author
Kitty Hawk Floats Across North America. By Maxie and Kristian Anderson. 260-271, *Aug. 1980*
Double Eagle II Has Landed! Crossing the Atlantic by Balloon. By Ben L. Abruzzo, with Maxie L. Anderson and Larry Newman. 858-882, *Dec. 1978*

ANDERSON, NIKE: *Author*
October Holiday on the Outer Banks. Photos by J. Baylor Roberts. 501-529, *Oct. 1955*

ANDERSON, ORVIL A.:
Hubbard Medals Awarded to Stratosphere Explorers: Presentation by General Pershing. 712-714, *May 1936*
Man's Farthest Aloft: Rising to 13.71 Miles, the National Geographic Society-U. S. Army Stratosphere Expedition Gathers Scientific Data at Record Altitude. By Albert W. Stevens. 59-94, *Jan. 1936*
Exploring the Stratosphere. By Albert W. Stevens. 397-434, *Oct. 1934*

ANDERSON, RON J.: *Author*
The Kiwi, New Zealand's Wonder Bird. 395-398, *Sept. 1955*

ANDERSON, SALLY: *Author*
Norway's Reindeer Lapps. Photos by Erik Borg. 364-379, *Sept. 1977*

ANDERSON, STEWART:
Author-Photographer
The West Through Boston Eyes. 733-776, *June 1949*

ANDERSON, WILLIAM R.:
Submarine Through the North Pole. By William G. Lalor, Jr. Photos by John J. Krawczyk. 1-20, *Jan. 1959*
Author
The Arctic as a Sea Route of the Future. 21-24, *Jan. 1959*

ANDES (Mountains), South America:
The High Andes: South America's Islands in the Sky. By Loren McIntyre. 422-459, *Apr. 1987*
Eruption in Colombia. By Bart McDowell. Photos by Steve Raymer. 640-653, *May 1986*
When the Earth Moves. The Editor. 638-639, *May 1986*

Mountain air has chapped the cheeks of a young Bolivian, who wears a hat that identifies her home as the village of Calcha. LOREN McINTYRE

Peru's Pilgrimage to the Sky. By Robert Randall. Photos by Loren McIntyre and Ira Block. 60-69, *July 1982*
The Incredible Potato. By Robert E. Rhoades. Photos by Martin Rogers. Included: The International Potato Center in Lima, Peru; The World Potato Collection in a research station at Huancayo, Peru; Cultivation and worship of potatoes by early Peruvian Indians. 668-694, *May 1982*
The Two Souls of Peru. By Harvey Arden. Photos by William Albert Allard. 284-321, *Mar. 1982*
⊕ Indians of South America; Archaeology of South America. Mar. 1982
To Torre Egger's Icy Summit. By Jim Donini. 813-823, *Dec. 1976*
Parks, Plans, and People: How South America Guards Her Green Legacy.

By Mary and Laurance Rockefeller. Photos by George F. Mobley. Included: Christ of the Andes; Lake District; Moreno Glacier; Mount Aconcagua; Nahuel Huapí National Park. 74-119, *Jan. 1967*
Avalanche! (Peru). By Bart McDowell. Photos by John E. Fletcher. 855-880, *June 1962*
In Quest of the Rarest Flamingo. By William G. Conway. Photos by Bates Littlehales. 91-105, *July 1961*
At Home in the High Andes. By Harry Tschopik, Jr. 133-146, *Jan. 1955*
Peru, Homeland of the Warlike Inca. By Kip Ross. 421-462, *Oct. 1950*
Puya, the Pineapple's Andean Ancestor. By Mulford B. Foster. 463-480, *Oct. 1950*
Sky-high Bolivia. 481-496, *Oct. 1950*

El Sangay, Fire-breathing Giant of the Andes. By G. Edward Lewis. 117-138, *Jan. 1950*

Bolivia–Tin Roof of the Andes. By Henry Albert Phillips. 309-332, *Mar. 1943*

Chile's Land of Fire and Water: Smoking Volcanoes and Ice-hooded Peaks Stand Sentinel Over Limpid Lakes in the Far Southern Andes. By W. Robert Moore. 91-110, *July 1941*

Stone Idols of the Andes Reveal a Vanished People: Remarkable Relics of One of the Oldest Aboriginal Cultures of America are Unearthed in Colombia's San Agustín Region. By Hermann von Walde-Waldegg. 627-647, *May 1940*

A Forgotten Valley of Peru: Conquered by Incas, Scourged by Famine, Plagues, and Earthquakes, Colca Valley Shelters the Last Fragment of an Ancient Andean Tribe. By Robert Shippee. 111-132, *Jan. 1934*

Air Adventures in Peru: Cruising Among Andean Peaks, Pilots and Cameramen Discover Wondrous Works of an Ancient People. By Robert Shippee. 81-120, *Jan. 1933*

Flying the "Hump" of the Andes. By Albert W. Stevens. 595-636, *May 1931*

The World's Highest International Telephone Cable. 722-731, *Dec. 1930*

The Lure of Lima, City of the Kings. By William Joseph Showalter. 727-784, *June 1930*

Flying the World's Longest Air-Mail Route: From Montevideo, Uruguay, Over the Andes, Up the Pacific Coast, Across Central America and the Caribbean to Miami, Florida, in 67 Thrilling Flying Hours. By Junius B. Wood. 261-325, *Mar. 1930*

The Volcanoes of Ecuador, Guideposts in Crossing South America. By G. M. Dyott. 49-93, *Jan. 1929*

How Latin America Looks from the Air: U. S. Army Airplanes Hurdle the High Andes, Brave Brazil Jungles, and Follow Smoking Volcanoes to Map New Sky Paths Around South America. By Herbert A. Dargue. 451-502, *Oct. 1927*

The Heart of Aymará Land: A Visit to Tiahuanaco, Perhaps the Oldest City of the New World, Lost Beneath the Drifting Sand of Centuries in the Bolivian Highlands. By Stewart E. McMillin. 213-256, *Feb. 1927*

A Longitudinal Journey Through Chile. By Harriet Chalmers Adams. 219-273, *Sept. 1922*

Over the Andes to Bogotá. By Frank M. Chapman. 353-373, *Oct. 1921*

The First Transandine Railroad from Buenos Aires to Valparaiso. By Harriet Chalmers Adams. 397-417, *May 1910*

The World's Highest Altitudes and First Ascents. By Charles E. Fay. 493-530, *June 1909*

Some Wonderful Sights in the Andean Highlands: The Oldest City in America. Sailing on the Lake of the Clouds: The Yosemite of Peru. By

Steam billows above snowy slopes of Ecuador's Sangay, the most active volcano in the Andes. LOREN McINTYRE

Harriet Chalmers Adams. 597-618, *Sept. 1908*

A New Peruvian Route to the Plain of the Amazon. By Solon I. Bailey. 432-448, *Aug. 1906*

ANDORRA:

The Enduring Pyrenees. By Robert Laxalt. Photos by Edwin Stuart Grosvenor. 794-819, *Dec. 1974*

Incredible Andorra. By Lawrence L. Klingman. Photos by B. Anthony Stewart. 262-290, *Aug. 1949*

Andorra–Mountain Museum of Feudal Europe. By Lawrence A. Fernsworth. 493-512, *Oct. 1933*

A Unique Republic, Where Smuggling Is an Industry. By Herbert Corey. 279-299, *Mar. 1918*

ANDRE, DENA:

On Assignment. *Sept. 1988*

ANDREANOF ISLANDS, Aleutians. *See* Adak

ANDRÉE, SALOMON AUGUST:

No Man's Land–Spitzbergen. 455-458, *July 1907*

Geographic Notes (No News of Andrée). 177, *May 1902*

An Interesting Rumor Concerning Andrée. By John Hyde. 102-103, *Mar. 1898*

Some Recent Geographic Events. By John Hyde. 359-362, *Dec. 1897*

ANDREWS, C. L.: *Author*

Muir Glacier (Alaska). 441-444, *Dec. 1903*

ANDREWS, E. WYLLYS:

Nomination Page. At Tulane University, New Orleans. *June 1971*

Author

Dzibilchaltun: Lost City of the Maya. 91-109, *Jan. 1959*

ANDREWS, ROY CHAPMAN:

Hubbard Medal winner. 792, *June 1934*

Author

Explorations in the Gobi Desert. 653-716, *June 1933*

Exploring Unknown Corners of the "Hermit Kingdom" (Korea). 25-48, *July 1919*

Shore-Whaling: A World Industry. 411-442, *May 1911*

ANDRONICOS, MANOLIS: *Author*

Regal Treasures From a Macedonian Tomb. Photos by Spyros Tsavdaroglou. 55-77, *July 1978*

ANDROS ISLAND, Bahama Islands:

Probing the Deep Reefs' Hidden Realm. By Walter A. Starck II and Jo D. Starck. 867-886, *Dec. 1972*

Flamingos' Last Stand on Andros Island. By Paul A. Zahl. 635-652, *May 1951*

Coral Castle Builders of Tropic Seas. By Roy Waldo Miner. Paintings by Else Bostelmann. 703-728, *June 1934*

See also Blue Holes

ANDRUS, CECIL D.: *Author*

Sharing Alaska: How Much for Parks? Opposing views by Jay S. Hammond and Cecil D. Andrus. 60-65, *July 1979*

ANEMOSPILIA (Area), Crete:

Drama of Death in a Minoan Temple. By Yannis Sakellarakis and Efi Sapouna-Sakellaraki. Photos by Otis Imboden and Spyros Tsavdaroglou. 205-222, *Feb. 1981*

ANGAUR (Island), Palau Islands, Carolines:

South from Saipan. By W. Robert Moore. 441-474, *Apr. 1945*

ANGEL FALLS, Venezuela:

Jungle Journey to the World's Highest Waterfall. By Ruth Robertson. 655-690, *Nov. 1949*

ANGERS, France:

The Beauties of France. By Arthur Stanley Riggs. 391-491, *Nov. 1915*

ANGKOR, Kampuchea:

The Temples of Angkor. 548-589. I. Will They Survive? Introduction by Wilbur E. Garrett. 548-551; II. Ancient Glory in Stone. By Peter T. White. Photos by Wilbur E. Garrett. 552-589, *May 1982*

Cambodia: Indochina's "Neutral" Corner. By Thomas J. Abercrombie. 514-551, *Oct. 1964*

Angkor, Jewel of the Jungle. By W. Robert Moore. Paintings by Maurice Fiévet. 517-569, *Apr. 1960*

Portrait of Indochina. By W. Robert Moore and Maynard Owen Williams. Paintings by Jean Despujols. 461-490, *Apr. 1951*

Four Faces of Siva: The Mystery of Angkor. By Robert J. Casey. 303-332, *Sept. 1928*

The Forgotten Ruins of Indo-China. By Jacob E. Conner. 209-272, *Mar. 1912*

ANGLER (Fish):

Fishes That Carry Lanterns. 453-456, *May 1910*

The Purple Veil: A Romance of the Sea. By H. A. Largelamb (Alexander Graham Bell). 337-341, *July 1905*

The **ANGLO-AMERICAN** Polar Expedition. By E. de K. Leffingwell. 796, *Dec. 1907*

ANGLO-EGYPTIAN SUDAN:

An Unbeliever Joins the Hadj: On the Age-Old Pilgrimage to Mecca, Babies Are Born, Elders Die, and Families May Halt a Year to Earn Funds in Distant Lands. By Owen Tweedy. 761-789, *June 1934*

Two Fighting Tribes of the Sudan. By Merian C. Cooper. Photos by Ernest B. Schoedsack. 465-486, *Oct. 1929*

Crossing the Untraversed Libyan Desert: The Record of a 2,200-Mile Journey of Exploration Which Resulted in the Discovery of Two Oases of Strategic Importance on the Southwestern Frontier of Egypt. By A. M. Hassanein Bey. 233-277, *Sept. 1924*

Adventures Among the "Lost Tribes of Islam" in Eastern Darfur: A Personal Narrative of Exploring, Mapping, and Setting Up a Government in the Anglo-Egyptian Sudan Borderland. By Edward Keith-Roach. 41-73, *Jan. 1924*

Along the Nile, Through Egypt and the Sudan. By Frederick Simpich. 379-410, *Oct. 1922*

The New British Empire of the Sudan. By Herbert L. Bridgman. 241-267, *May 1906*

See also present name, Sudan

ANGLO-JAPANESE ALLIANCE:

The Purpose of the Anglo-Japanese Alliance. By Eki Hioki. 333-337, *July 1905*

The **ANGLO-VENEZUELAN** Boundary Dispute. By Marcus Baker. 129-144, *Apr. 1900*

ANGMAGSSALIK, Greenland:

Desolate Greenland, Now an American Outpost. Photos by Willie Knutsen and F. Vogel. 393-406, *Sept. 1941*

ANGOLA:

Angola, Unknown Africa. By Volkmar Wentzel. 347-383, *Sept. 1961*

Angola, the Last Foothold of Slavery. 625-630, *July 1910*

ANGRA DO HEROISMO, Terceira (Island), Azores:

American Airmen in the Azores. 177-184, *Feb. 1946*

ANIAKCHAK CRATER, Alaska:

A World Inside a Mountain: Aniakchak, the New Volcanic Wonderland of the Alaska Peninsula Is Explored. By Bernard R. Hubbard. 319-345, *Sept. 1931*

ANIMAL Architects. Structures built by different animals. Juvenile. 104 pages. *1987*

ANIMAL BEHAVIOR. *See* Animals

ANIMAL EYES:

Nature's Alert Eyes. By Constance P. Warner. 558-569, *Apr. 1959*

See also Four-eyed Fish; *Photoblepharon*

ANIMAL INTRODUCTION:

Florida, Noah's Ark for Exotic Newcomers. By Rick Gore. Photos by David Doubilet. 538-559, *Oct. 1976*

New Tricks Outwit Our Insect Enemies. By Hal Higdon. Photos by Robert F. Sisson and Emory Kristof. 380-399, *Sept. 1972*

See also Africanized Honeybees; Cattle Egret; Fig Wasps; Orioles; Walking Catfish

ANIMAL ORPHANAGE, Entebbe, Uganda:

Orphans of the Wild. By Bruce G. Kinloch. 683-699, *Nov. 1962*

ANIMAL-PRODUCT TRADE:

Wild Cargo: the Business of Smuggling Animals. By Noel Grove. Photos by Steve Raymer. 287-315, *Mar. 1981*

ANIMAL SACRIFICE:

Inside the Sacred Hopi Homeland. By Jake Page. Photos by Susanne Page. Included: Golden eagle sacrifice ceremony. 607-629, *Nov. 1982*

The Last Israelitish Blood Sacrifice: How the Vanishing Samaritans Celebrate the Passover on Sacred Mount

Serene faces of stone smile on two saffron-robed Buddhist monks peering from a temple in Angkor Thom.   WILBUR E. GARRETT, NGS

Wild Animals of North America

Gerizim. By John D. Whiting. 1-46, *Jan. 1920*

ANIMAL SAFARI to British Guiana. By David Attenborough. Photos by Charles Lagus and author. 851-874, *June 1957*

ANIMALS:

Animal Architects. Structures built by different animals. Juvenile. 104 pages. *1987*

Wild Animals of North America. 406 pages. 1979; rev. ed. *1987*

Wildlife: Making a Comeback. By Judith E. Rinard. Juvenile. 104 pages. *1987*

The Intimate Sense of Smell. By Boyd Gibbons. Photos by Louie Psihoyos. Included: Pheromone communication in insect colonies; odor imprinting among fishes; territorial marking by mammals; the role of scent in mating and parental bonding; sniffer dogs in criminal investigation. 324-361, *Sept. 1986*

The Secret World of Animals. Animal habitats. Juvenile. 104 pages. *1986*

Your World of Pets. By Susan McGrath. Art by Barbara L. Gibson. Juvenile. 104 pages. *1985*

Amazing Animals of Australia. Juvenile. 104 pages. *1984*

How Animals Behave: A New Look at Wildlife. Juvenile. 104 pages. *1984*

Teeming Life of a Rain Forest. By Carol and David Hughes. 49-65, *Jan. 1983*

Giants from the Past: The Age of Mammals. By Joseph H. Bailey. Juvenile. 104 pages. *1983*

Secrets of Animal Survival. Juvenile. 104 pages. *1983*

The Animals Nobody Loved. Cover, *Feb. 1976*

Safari! By Gene S. Stuart. Photos by George F. Mobley. Juvenile. 104 pages. *1982*

The Marvels of Animal Behavior. 422 pages. *1972*

The Mystery of Animal Behavior. 592A-592B, *Oct. 1969*

The Wild Realm: Animals of East Africa. By Louis S. B. Leakey. 199 pages. *1969*

Animals Were Allies, Too. 75-88, *Jan. 1946*

Animal Wealth of the United States. By Francis E. Warren. 511-524, *Sept. 1906*

Doe and Twin Fawns. Photo by George Shiras, 3d. *July 1913*

Laws of Temperature Control of the Geographic Distribution of Terrestrial Animals and Plants. Annual Address by Vice-President, C. Hart Merriam. 229-238, *Dec. 29, 1894*

See also Albino Animals; Amphibians; Animal Introduction; Animal Orphanage; Animal-product Trade; Animal Sacrifice; Animal Safari; Arthropods; Birds; Camouflage; Cephalopods; Circuses; Communication, Animal; Corals and Coral Reefs; Crustaceans; Endangered and Threatened Species; Evolution; Extinct Species; Fishes; Frogs; Galápagos Islands, Pacific Ocean; Game Preserves; Insects; Madagascar; Mammals; Mammals, Prehistoric; Marine Biology; Microorganisms; Migration; Mollusks; Primates; Reptiles; Scorpions; Spiders; Tool-using Animals; Wildlife; Wildlife Refuges; Worms; Zoos

ANIMATION:

The Magic Worlds of Walt Disney. By Robert de Roos. Photos by Thomas Nebbia. Included: Animation: Mickey Mouse Explains the Art to Mr. G. O. Graphic. 159-207, *Aug. 1963*

ANIMISM:

Living Theater in New Guinea's Highlands. By Gillian Gillison. Photos by David Gillison. 147-169, *Aug. 1983*

Where Magic Ruled: Art of the Bering Sea. By William W. Fitzhugh and Susan A. Kaplan. Photos by Sisse Brimberg. 198-205, *Feb. 1983*

Inside the Sacred Hopi Homeland. By Jake Page. Photos by Susanne Page. Included: Kachinas; Golden eagle sacrifice. 607-629, *Nov. 1982*

The Ivory Coast–African Success Story. By Michael and Aubine Kirtley. 94-125, *July 1982*

Trek to Nepal's Sacred Crystal Mountain. By Joel F. Ziskin. 500-517, *Apr. 1977*

Rock Paintings of the Aborigines. By Kay and Stanley Breeden. 174-187, *Feb. 1973*

Spirits of Change Capture the Karens. By Peter Kunstadter. 267-285, *Feb. 1972*

Taboos and Magic Rule Namba Lives. By Kal Muller. 57-83, *Jan. 1972*

Foxes Foretell the Future in Mali's Dogon Country. By Pamela Johnson Meyer. 431-448, *Mar. 1969*

Beyond the Bight of Benin. By Jeannette and Maurice Fiévet. Included: Cameroon and Nigerian tribal rites. 221-253, *Aug. 1959*

Kachinas: Masked Dancers of the Southwest. By Paul Coze. 219-236, *Aug. 1957*

See also Shamanism; Sorcery; Voodoo

ANKARA, Turkey:

When the President Goes Abroad (Ei-

senhower Tour). By Gilbert M. Grosvenor. 588-649, *May 1960*

Turkey Paves the Path of Progress. By Maynard Owen Williams. 141-186, *Aug. 1951*

The Turkish Republic Comes of Age. By Maynard Owen Williams. 581-616, *May 1945*

Alert Anatolia. 481-492, *Apr. 1944*

The Transformation of Turkey: New Hats and New Alphabet are the Surface Symbols of the Swiftest National Changes in Modern Times. By Douglas Chandler. 1-50, *Jan. 1939*

ANN, Cape, Massachusetts:

Windjamming Around New England. By Tom Horgan. Photos by Robert F. Sisson. 141-169, *Aug. 1950*

ANNALS of Life Written in Rock: Fossils. Photos by James L. Amos. Text by David Jeffery. 182-191, *Aug. 1985*

ANNAM (State), French Indo-China:

Along the Old Mandarin Road of Indo-China. By W. Robert Moore. 157-199, *Aug. 1931*

ANNAPOLIS, Maryland:

Annapolis: Camelot on the Bay. By Larry Kohl. Photos by Kevin Fleming. 162-189, *Aug. 1988*

Maryland on the Half Shell. By Stuart E. Jones. Photos by Robert W. Madden. 188-229, *Feb. 1972*

Old Line State Cyclorama. Photos by W. Robert Moore, B. Anthony Stewart. 409-432, *Apr. 1941*

Annapolis, Cradle of the Navy. By Arthur A. Ageton. 789-800, *June 1936*

ANNAPURNA I (Mountain), Nepal:

Triumph and Tragedy on Annapurna. By Arlene Blum. Included: On the Summit. By Irene Miller, with Vera Komarkova. 295-313, *Mar. 1979*

ANNA'S HUMMINGBIRDS:

Hummingbirds: The Nectar Connection. By Paul W. Ewald. Photos by Robert A. Tyrrell. 223-227, *Feb. 1982*

ANNETTE ISLAND, Alaska:

The Metlakatla Mission in Danger. By Wm. H. Dall. 187-189, *Apr. 1898*

The **ANNEXATION** Fever. By Henry Gannett. 354-358, *Dec. 1897*

ANNOUNCEMENT. (Organization of the National Geographic Society and Publication of the Magazine). i-ii, *Oct. 1888*

ANNOUNCEMENT of the Seventh Annual Excursion and Field Meeting (Fredericksburg, Va.), Saturday, May 4, 1895. *Apr. 20, 1895*

ANNOUNCING a New National Geographic Society Foundation. By Lloyd H. Elliott. Contents: Geographic Education Foundation. 329A-329D, *Mar. 1988*

ANNUAL Report of the Superintendent of the United States Coast and Geodetic Survey. 186-188, *May 1896*

Robert Swan confronts 900 miles without dog team or radio in a successful bid to retrace Robert Falcon Scott's trek across Antarctica to the Pole. ROGER MEAR

Bottom up, an Antarctic iceberg shows features smoothed by seawater before it became unbalanced and rolled over.   HARRY KEYS

Waterbuck, Wildebeest (Gnu). 353-380, *Mar. 1950*
See also Pronghorns

ANTHONY, A. W.: *Author*

A Cruise Among Desert Islands (Baja California). By G. Dallas Hanna and A. W. Anthony. 71-99, *July 1923*

ANTHONY, H. E.: *Author*

Over Trail and Through Jungle in Ecuador: Indian Head-Hunters of the Interior, an Interesting Study in the South American Republic. 327-352, *Oct. 1921*

ANTHROPOLOGY, Cultural. *See* Ethnology

ANTHROPOLOGY, Physical:

The Search for Modern Humans. By John J. Putman. Photos by Sisse Brimberg and Ira Block. Paintings by Jack Unruh. 439-477, *Oct. 1988*
Sealed in Time–Ice Entombs an Eskimo Family for Five Centuries. By Albert A. Dekin, Jr. Photos by Victor R. Boswell, Jr., and Scott Rutherford. Paintings by James M. Gurney. 824-836, *June 1987*
Mysteries of the Bog. By Louise E. Levathes. Photos by Fred Bavendam. Included: Peat holds clues to early American life. 397-420, *Mar. 1987*
Editorial. By Wilbur E. Garrett. Skull of a 1.6-million-year-old hominid, found near Lake Turkana, Kenya. 419, *Oct. 1986*
The Search for Our Ancestors. By Kenneth F. Weaver. Photos by David L. Brill. Paintings by Jay H. Matternes. 560-623, *Nov. 1985*
Homo Erectus Unearthed: A Fossil Skeleton 1,600,000 Years Old. By Richard Leakey and Alan Walker. Photos by David L. Brill. NGS research grant. 624-629, *Nov. 1985*
The Dead Do Tell Tales at Vesuvius. By Rick Gore. Photos by O. Louis Mazzatenta. NGS research grant. 557-613, *May 1984*
The Search for the First Americans. By Thomas Y. Canby. Photos by Kerby Smith. Paintings by Roy Andersen. 330-363, *Sept. 1979*
Footprints in the Ashes of Time. By Mary D. Leakey. NGS research grant. 446-457, *Apr. 1979*
 The Legacy of L.S.B. Leakey. 439, Oct. 1977; cover, *Jan. 1978*
Ethiopia Yields First "Family" of Early Man. By Donald C. Johanson. Photos by David Brill. NGS research grant. 790-811, *Dec. 1976*
A Bold New Look at Our Past. The Editor. NGS research grant. 62-63, *Jan. 1975*
Exploring the Mind of Ice Age Man. By Alexander Marshack. NGS research grant. 64-89, *Jan. 1975*
Skull 1470. By Richard E. Leakey. Photos by Bob Campbell. NGS research grant. 819-829, *June 1973*
The Leakey Tradition Lives On. By Melvin M. Payne. NGS research grant. 143-144, *Jan. 1973*
Primitive Worlds: People Lost in Time. Contents: Mbotgate, Somba,

Tarahumara, Tifalmin, Turkana, and Yanomamo. 211 pages. *1973*
Nomads of the World. 199 pages. *1971*
In Search of Man's Past at Lake Rudolf. By Richard E. Leakey. Photos by Gordon W. Gahan. NGS research grant. 712-734, *May 1970*
Mexico's Window on the Past (National Museum). By Bart McDowell. Photos by B. Anthony Stewart. 492-519, *Oct. 1968*
Vanishing Peoples of the Earth. 207 pages. *1968*
Dr. Leakey and the Dawn of Man. 703A-703B, *Nov. 1966*
Preserving the Treasures of Olduvai Gorge. By Melvin M. Payne. Photos by Joseph J. Scherschel. Included: *Homo erectus, Homo habilis, Kenyapithecus, Zinjanthropus.* NGS research grant. 701-709, *Nov. 1966*
The Leakeys of Africa: Family in Search of Prehistoric Man. By Melvin M. Payne. Included: *Homo habilis, Kenyapithecus, Proconsul, Zinjanthropus.* NGS research grant. 194-231, *Feb. 1965*
Adventures in the Search for Man. By Louis S. B. Leakey. Photos by Hugo van Lawick. NGS research grant. 132-152, *Jan. 1963*
Wyoming Muck Tells of Battle: Ice Age Man vs. Mammoth. By Cynthia Irwin, Henry Irwin, and George Agogino. 828-837, *June 1962*
Exploring 1,750,000 Years Into Man's Past. By L.S.B. Leakey. Photos by Robert F. Sisson. NGS research grant. 564-589, *Oct. 1961*
Finding the World's Earliest Man *(Zinjanthropus boisei).* By L.S.B. Leakey. Photos by Des Bartlett. NGS research grant. 420-435, *Sept. 1960*
Vanished Mystery Men of Hudson Bay. By Henry B. Collins. Included: Dor-

set Eskimos, Sadlermiuts. 669-687, *Nov. 1956*
Ice Age Man, the First American. By Thomas R. Henry. Paintings by Andre Durenceau. 781-806, *Dec. 1955*
Twelve National Geographic Society Scientific Projects Under Way. NGS research grant. 869-870, *June 1954*
Lifelike Man Preserved 2,000 Years in Peat. By P. V. Glob. 419-430, *Mar. 1954*
Mountain Tribes of Iran and Iraq. By Harold Lamb. 385-408, *Mar. 1946*
New Guinea's Mountain and Swampland Dwellers. By Ray T. Elsmore. 671-694, *Dec. 1945*
Indians of Our Western Plains. By Matthew W. Stirling. Paintings by W. Langdon Kihn. 73-108, *July 1944*
Discovering Alaska's Oldest Arctic Town (Ipiutak): A Scientist Finds Ivory-eyed Skeletons of a Mysterious People and Joins Modern Eskimos in the Dangerous Spring Whale Hunt. By Froelich G. Rainey. 319-336, *Sept. 1942*
Parade of Life Through the Ages: Records in Rocks Reveal a Strange Procession of Prehistoric Creatures, from Jellyfish to Dinosaurs, Giant Sloths, Saber-toothed Tigers, and Primitive Man. By Charles R. Knight. Paintings by author. 141-184, *Feb. 1942*
Indian Tribes of Pueblo Land. By Matthew W. Stirling. Paintings by W. Langdon Kihn. 549-596, *Nov. 1940*
America's First Settlers, the Indians. By Matthew W. Stirling. Paintings by W. Langdon Kihn. 535-596, *Nov. 1937*
In the Empire of the Aztecs: Mexico City Is Rich in Relics of a People Who Practiced Human Sacrifice, Yet Loved Flowers, Education, and Art. By Frank H. H. Roberts, Jr. Paintings by H. M. Herget. 725-750, *June 1937*
Strange Tribes in the Shan States of Burma. Photos by W. Robert Moore. Contents: Kang, Kaw, Khun, Lahu Na, Lahu Shi, Shan. 247-254, *Aug. 1930*
The Battle-Line of Languages in Western Europe: A Problem in Human Geography More Perplexing Than That of International Boundaries. By A. L. Guerard. Contents: Chins, Kachins, Karens, Kaws, Padaungs, Shans. 145-180, *Feb. 1923*
Who Shall Inherit Long Life? On the Existence of a Natural Process at Work Among Beings Tending to Improve the Vigor and Vitality of Succeeding Generations. By Alexander Graham Bell. 505-514, *June 1919*
The Races of Europe. By Edwin A. Grosvenor. 441-534, *Dec. 1918*
How Old Is Man? By Theodore Roosevelt. 111-127, *Feb. 1916*
The Cradle of Civilization: The Historic Lands Along the Euphrates and Tigris Rivers Where Briton Is Fighting Turk. By James Baikie. 127-162, *Feb. 1916*
The Origin of Stefansson's Blond Eskimo. By A. W. Greely. 1225-1238, *Dec. 1912*

Gold rings and bracelets adorned a woman entombed at Herculaneum by the eruption of Mount Vesuvius.   O. LOUIS MAZZATENTA, NGS

Our Immigration Laws from the Viewpoint of National Eugenics. By Robert De C. Ward. 38-41, *Jan. 1912*

A Few Thoughts Concerning Eugenics. By Alexander Graham Bell. 119-123, *Feb. 1908*

The Supposed Birthplace of Civilizations. 499-504, *Nov. 1905*

The Sex, Nativity, and Color of the People of the United States. By G. H. Grosvenor. 381-389, *Nov. 1901*

Work of the Bureau of American Ethnology. By W J McGee. 369-372, *Oct. 1901*

National Growth and National Character. By W J McGee. 185-206, *June 1899*

The Enchanted Mesa (New Mexico). By F. W. Hodge. 273-284, *Oct. 1897*

The Effects of Geographic Environment in the Development of Civilization in Primitive Man. By Gardiner G. Hubbard. 161-176, *June 1897*

Explorations by the Bureau of American Ethnology in 1895. By W J McGee. 77-80, *Feb. 1896*

See also Archaeology; Archeomagnetism Dating; Potassium-Argon Dating; Radiocarbon Dating

ANTICOSTI ISLAND, Canada:

Anticosti Island, Nugget of the North. By Eugene E. Wilson. 121-140, *Jan. 1942*

ANTIGUA, Guatemala:

Guatemala, Maya and Modern. By Louis de la Haba. Photos by Joseph J. Scherschel. 661-689, *Nov. 1974*

Easter Week in Indian Guatemala. By John Scofield. 406-417, *Mar. 1960*

To Market in Guatemala. By Luis Marden. Photos by Giles Greville Healey and Charles S. Pineo. 87-104, *July 1945*

Guatemala, the Country of the Future. By Edine Frances Tisdel. 596-624, *July 1910*

ANTIGUA (Island), West Indies:

A Fresh Breeze Stirs the Leewards. By Carleton Mitchell. Photos by Winfield Parks. 488-537, *Oct. 1966*

Americans in the Caribbean. By Luis Marden. 723-758, *June 1942*

British West Indian Interlude. By Anne Rainey Langley. 1-46, *Jan. 1941*

ANTILLES, Greater. *See* Cuba; Dominican Republic; Haiti; Jamaica; Puerto Rico

ANTILLES, Lesser. *See* Antigua; Aruba; Barbados; Bonaire; Curaçao; Dominica; Guadeloupe; Leeward Islands; Martinique; Netherlands Antilles; Saba; St. Kitts; St. Lucia; St. Vincent; Trinidad; Tobago; Virgin Islands; Windward Islands (Martinique; St. Lucia; St. Vincent)

ANTIOCH the Glorious. By William H. Hall. 81-103, *Aug. 1920*

ANTIOCHUS I, King (Commagene):

Throne Above the Euphrates. By Theresa Goell. 390-405, *Mar. 1961*

ANTIQUITIES:

The Roman Way. By Edith Hamilton. 545-565, *Nov. 1946*

The Greek Way. By Edith Hamilton. 257-271, *Mar. 1944*

See also Archaeology; *and* names of ancient cities and countries

ANTLERED Majesties of Many Lands (Deer). Paintings by Walter A. Weber. 479-510, *Oct. 1939*

ANTOFAGASTA, Chile:

A Longitudinal Journey Through Chile. By Harriet Chalmers Adams. 219-273, *Sept. 1922*

ANTS:

Marauders of the Jungle Floor. By Mark W. Moffett. NGS research grant. 273-286, *Aug. 1986*

The Ant and Her World. Introduction by Caryl P. Haskins. 774-777, *June 1984*

Ways of the Ant. By Bert Hölldobler. Paintings by John D. Dawson. Illustrations text by Alice J. Hall. Included: Amazon ants; army ants; common black ants; European wood

Sculptured pendentives once supported the dome of the Antigua, Guatemala, cathedral, shattered by a 1773 earthquake.   LUIS MARDEN, NGS

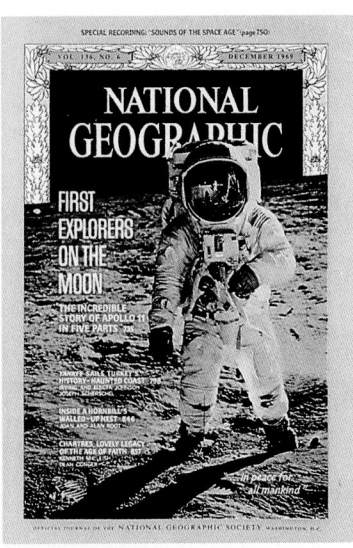

APOLLO-SOYUZ MISSION:

Apollo-Soyuz: Handclasp in Space. By Thomas Y. Canby. 183-187, *Feb. 1976*

APPALACHIA (Region), U. S.:

Wrestlin' for a Livin' With King Coal. By Michael E. Long. Photos by Michael O'Brien. 793-819, *June 1983*

Chattooga River Country: Wild Water, Proud People. By Don Belt. Photos by Steve Wall. 458-477, *Apr. 1983*

The People of Cumberland Gap. By John Fetterman. Photos by Bruce Dale. 591-621, *Nov. 1971*

My Neighbors Hold to Mountain Ways. By Malcolm Ross. Photos by Flip Schulke. 856-880, *June 1958*

See also Cades Cove; *and* West Virginia

APPALACHIAN MOUNTAINS, U. S.:

Wrestlin' for a Livin' With King Coal. By Michael E. Long. Photos by Michael O'Brien. 793-819, *June 1983*

Geomorphology of the Southern Appalachians. By Charles Willard Hayes and Marius R. Campbell. 63-126, *May 23, 1894*

See also Adirondack Mountains; Berkshires; Blue Ridge Mountains; Cumberland Valley; Great Smoky Mountains; Great Smoky Mountains National Park; Green Mountains; White Mountains, New Hampshire

APPALACHIAN TRAIL, U. S.:

■■ *Mountain Adventure: Exploring the Appalachian Trail.* By Ron Fisher. Photos by Sam Abell. 200 pages. *1988*

A Tunnel Through Time: The Appalachian Trail. By Noel Grove. Photos by Sam Abell. 216-243, *Feb. 1987*

■■ *The Appalachian Trail.* By Ronald M. Fisher. Photos by Dick Durrance II. 199 pages. *1972*

Pack Trip Through the Smokies. By Val Hart. Photos by Robert F. Sisson. 473-502, *Oct. 1952*

Skyline Trail from Maine to Georgia. By Andrew H. Brown. Photos by Robert F. Sisson. 219-251, *Aug. 1949*

An **APPEAL** to Members of the National Geographic Society (Food Conservation). 347-348, *Apr. 1918*

APPEL, FREDRIC C.: *Author*

The Coming Revolution in Transportation. Photos by Dean Conger. 301-341, *Sept. 1969*

APPENNINES (Mountains), Italy:

Carrara Marble: Touchstone of Eternity. By Cathy Newman. Photos by Pierre Boulat. 42-59, *July 1982*

APPERCEPTION in Geography. By M. E. Kelton. 192-199, *May 1900*

APPIAN WAY, Italy:

Down the Ancient Appian Way. By James Cerruti. Photos by O. Louis Mazzatenta. 714-747, *June 1981*

APPLE GROWING:

Washington's Yakima Valley. By Mark Miller. Photos by Sisse Brimberg. 609-631, *Nov. 1978*

APPLE TREE:

The World of My Apple Tree. By Robert F. Sisson. 836-847, *June 1972*

APPLEBY FAIR, Appleby, England:

When Gypsies Gather at Appleby Fair. Photos by Bruce Dale. 848-869, *June 1972*

APPLIED PHYSICS LABORATORY, Johns Hopkins University. *See* DODGE Satellite

APPLIED Physiography in South Carolina. By L. C. Glenn. 152-154, *May 1897*

APPOMATTOX COURT HOUSE, Virginia:

Appomattox: Where Grant and Lee Made Peace With Honor a Century Ago. By Ulysses S. Grant 3rd. Photos by Bruce Dale. 435-469, *Apr. 1965*

APPROACH to Peiping. By John W. Thomason, Jr. 275-308, *Feb. 1936*

APPROACHING Washington by Tidewater Potomac. By Paul Wilstach. 372-392, *Mar. 1930*

APUAN ALPS, Italy:

Carrara Marble: Touchstone of Eternity. By Cathy Newman. Photos by Pierre Boulat. 42-59, *July 1982*

AQABA, Gulf of, Red Sea:

Scorpionfish: Danger in Disguise. By David Doubilet. 634-643, *Nov. 1987*

The Red Sea's Sharkproof Fish. By Eugenie Clark. Photos by David Doubilet. 718-727, *Nov. 1974*

The Red Sea's Gardens of Eels. By Eugenie Clark. Photos by James L. Stanfield and David Doubilet. 724-735, *Nov. 1972*

The Other Side of Jordan. By Luis Marden. 790-825, *Dec. 1964*

'AQABA, Trans-Jordan (now Jordan):

On the Trail of King Solomon's Mines:

Light seems to suspend maple leaves resting on a mossy boulder on Mount Washington, New Hampshire. SAM ABELL

The Bible, in Addition to Its Spiritual Values, Continues to Prove a Rich Geography and Guide to Exploration of the Holy Land. By Nelson Glueck. 233-256, *Feb. 1944*

AQUACULTURE:

Plight of the Bluefin Tuna. By Michael J. A. Butler. Photos by David Doubilet. Paintings by Stanley Meltzoff. 220-239, *Aug. 1982*

Giant Kelp, Sequoias of the Sea. By Wheeler J. North. Photos by Bates Littlehales. 251-269, *Aug. 1972*

Shrimp Nursery: Science Explores New Ways to Farm the Sea. By Clarence P. Idyll. Photos by Robert F. Sisson. NGS research grant. 636-659, *May 1965*

AQUALUNG:

Fish Men Discover a 2,200-year-old Greek Ship. By Jacques-Yves Cousteau. 1-36, *Jan. 1954*

Fish Men Explore a New World Undersea. By Jacques-Yves Cousteau. 431-472, *Oct. 1952*

See also Divers and Diving

AQUARIUMS. *See* Marineland (Florida)

AQUARIUMS, Home:

In the Wilds of a City Parlor. By Paul A. Zahl. 645-672, *Nov. 1954*

Net Results from Oceania: Collecting Aquarium Specimens in Tropical Pacific Waters. By Walter H. Chute. 347-372, *Mar. 1941*

Tropical Fish Immigrants Reveal New Nature Wonders. By Walter H. Chute. 93-109, *Jan. 1934*

Tropical Toy Fishes: More Than 600 Varieties of Aquarium Pygmies Afford a Fascinating Field of Zoölogical Study in the Home. By Ida Mellen. Paintings by Hashime Murayama. 287-317, *Mar. 1931*

Treasure-House of the Gulf Stream: The Completion and Opening of the New Aquarium and Biological Laboratory at Miami, Florida. By John Oliver La Gorce. Paintings by Hashime Murayama. 53-68, *Jan. 1921*

See also Goldfish

AQUASCOPE:

One Hundred Hours Beneath the Chesapeake. By Gilbert C. Klingel. Photos by Willard R. Culver. NGS research grant. 681-696, *May 1955*

AQUEDUCTS:

New York–The Metropolis of Mankind. By William Joseph Showalter. 1-49, *July 1918*

Staircase Farms of the Ancients: Astounding Farming Skill of Ancient Peruvians, Who Were Among the Most Industrious and Highly Organized People in History. By O. F. Cook. 474-534, *May 1916*

Carrying Water Through a Desert. By Burt A. Heinly. 568-596, *July 1910*

The Washington Aqueduct and Cabin John Bridge. By D. D. Gaillard. 337-344, *Dec. 1897*

See also Los Angeles Aqueduct

*Travelers from Jordan's desert warm themselves before a Nabataean temple or tomb at
the ancient city of Petra.* THOMAS J. ABERCROMBIE, NGS

ARABIAN GULF. *See* Persian Gulf

THE ARABIAN NIGHTS ENTER-
TAINMENTS *(The Thousand and*
One Nights):

In the Wake of Sindbad. By Tim Severin. Photos by Richard Greenhill. 2-41, *July 1982*

ARABIAN PENINSULA:

The Persian Gulf–Living in Harm's Way. By Thomas J. Abercrombie. Photos by Steve Raymer. Included: Iraq, Iran, Saudi Arabia, Kuwait, Bahrain, Qatar, United Arab Emirates, Oman. 648-671, *May 1988*

Arabia's Frankincense Trail. By Thomas J. Abercrombie. Photos by Lynn Abercrombie. 474-513, *Oct. 1985*

✢ *Africa and the Arabian Peninsula. Mar. 1950*

In Search of Arabia's Past. By Peter Bruce Cornwall. 493-522, *Apr. 1948*

An Unbeliever Joins the Hadj: On the Age-Old Pilgrimage to Mecca, Babies Are Born, Elders Die, and Families May Halt a Year to Earn Funds in Distant Lands. By Owen Tweedy. 761-789, *June 1934*

Into Burning Hadhramaut: The Arab Land of Frankincense and Myrrh, Ever a Lodestone of Western Exploration. By D. van der Meulen. 387-429, *Oct. 1932*

A Visit to Three Arab Kingdoms: Transjordania, Iraq, and the Hedjaz Present Many Problems to European Powers. By Junius B. Wood. 535-568, *May 1923*

The Rise of the New Arab Nation. By Frederick Simpich. 369-393, *Nov. 1919*

Mecca the Mystic: A New Kingdom Within Arabia (Hejaz). By S. M. Zwemer. 157-172, *Aug. 1917*

"The Flower of Paradise": The Part Which Khat Plays in the Life of the Yemen Arab. By Charles Moser. 173-186, *Aug. 1917*

Notes on Oman. By S. M. Zwemer. 89-98, *Jan. 1911*

Arabia, the Desert of the Sea. By Archibald Forder. 1039-1062, 1117, *Dec. 1909*

One Thousand Miles of Railway Built for Pilgrims and Not for Dividends (Damascus to Mecca). By F. R. Maunsell. 156-172, *Feb. 1909*

Travels in Arabia and Along the Persian Gulf. By David G. Fairchild. 139-151, *Apr. 1904*

Damascus and Mecca Railway. 408, *Nov. 1901*

Sheik Said. By Ernest de Sasseville. 155-156, *May 1897*

Geographic Progress of Civilization. Annual Address by the President, Gardiner G. Hubbard. 1-22, *Feb. 14, 1894*

See also Aden Protectorate; Bahrain; Kuwait; Oman; Saudi Arabia; United Arab Emirates; Yemen Arab Republic

ARABS:

Ali Goes to the Clinic. By Herndon and Mary Hudson. 764-766, *Dec. 1946*

Palestine Today. By Francis Chase, Jr. 501-516, *Oct. 1946*

Guest in Saudi Arabia. By Maynard Owen Williams. 463-487, *Oct. 1945*

On the Trail of King Solomon's Mines: The Bible, in Addition to Its Spiritual Values, Continues to Prove a Rich Geography and Guide to Exploration of the Holy Land. By Nelson Glueck. 233-256, *Feb. 1944*

Forty Years Among the Arabs. By John Van Ess. 385-420, *Sept. 1942*

Pearl Fishing in the Red Sea. By Henri de Monfreid. 597-626, *Nov. 1937*

Pilgrims' Progress to Mecca. Photos by Oscar Marcus. 627-642, *Nov. 1937*

Bedouin Life in Bible Lands: The Nomads of the "Houses of Hair" Offer Unstinted Hospitality to an American. By John D. Whiting. 59-83, *Jan. 1937*

Cirenaica, Eastern Wing of Italian Libia. By Harriet Chalmers Adams. 689-726, *June 1930*

New Light on Ancient Ur: Excavations at the Site of the City of Abraham Reveal Geographical Evidence of the Biblical Story of the Flood. By M.E.L. Mallowan. 95-130, *Jan. 1930*

Archeology, the Mirror of the Ages: Our Debt to the Humble Delvers in the Ruins at Carchemish and at Ur. By C. Leonard Woolley. 207-226, *Aug. 1928*

The White City of Algiers. By Gordon Casserly. 206-232, *Feb. 1928*

Among the Bethlehem Shepherds: A Visit to the Valley Which David

Storm-driven pack ice entombed an Eskimo family living on the coast of the Arctic Ocean nearly 500 years ago.   PAINTING BY JAMES M. GURNEY

Relics from the 1923 excavation of a Chuska Mountain cave span centuries of prehistory in northeastern Arizona. EARL H. MORRIS

A diver lifts a timber from the stern of a 16th-century Basque whaling vessel found off Labrador, Canada. BILL CURTSINGER

Reconstructing Egypt's History. By Wallace N. Stearns. 1021-1042, *Sept. 1913*

The Sacred Ibis Cemetery and Jackal Catacombs at Abydos. By Camden M. Cobern. 1042-1056, *Sept. 1913*

In the Wonderland of Peru. By Hiram Bingham. Included: The Ruins of an Ancient Inca Capital, Machu Picchu (panorama). 387-574, *Apr. 1913*

Excavations at Quirigua, Guatemala. By Sylvanus Griswold Morley. 339-361, *Mar. 1913*

Mysterious Temples of the Jungle: The Prehistoric Ruins of Guatemala. By W. F. Sands. 325-338, *Mar. 1913*

From Jerusalem to Aleppo. By John D. Whiting. 71-113, *Jan. 1913*

China's Treasures. By Frederick Mc-Cormick. 996-1040, *Oct. 1912*

Explorations in Peru. 417-422, *Apr. 1912*

The Forgotten Ruins of Indo-China. By Jacob E. Conner. 209-272, *Mar. 1912*

Adam's Second Eden (Ceylon). By Eliza Ruhamah Scidmore. 105-173, 206, *Feb. 1912*

The Sea-Kings of Crete. By James Baikie. 1-25, *Jan. 1912*

The Greek Bronzes of Tunisia. By Frank Edward Johnson. 89-103, *Jan. 1912*

The Greek Bronzes. Contents: Requests for photographs of bronzes. 104, *Jan. 1912*

The Mole Men: An Account of the Troglodytes of Southern Tunisia. By Frank Edward Johnson. 787-846, *Sept. 1911*

Hewers of Stone (Mitla, Mexico). By Jeremiah Zimmerman. 1002-1020, *Dec. 1910*

An Interesting Visit to the Ancient Pyramids of San Juan Teotihuacan. By A. C. Galloway. 1041-1050, *Dec. 1910*

Guatemala, the Country of the Future. By Edine Frances Tisdel. 596-624, *July 1910*

An Ancient Capital (Boghaz Keoy, Turkey). By Isabel F. Dodd. 111-124, *Feb. 1910*

Explorations in Crete. By Edith H. Hall. 778-787, *Sept. 1909*

The Prehistoric Ruins of Tsankawi (New Mexico). By George L. Beam. 807-822, *Sept. 1909*

The Buried Cities of Asia Minor. By Ernest L. Harris. 1-18, *Jan. 1909*

The Ruins at Selinus (Sicily). By Marion Crawford. 117, *Jan. 1909*

Some Ruined Cities of Asia Minor. By Ernest L. Harris. 833-858, *Dec. 1908*

The Ruined Cities of Asia Minor. By Ernest L. Harris. 741-760, *Nov. 1908*

Some Wonderful Sights in the Andean Highlands: The Oldest City in America. Sailing on the Lake of the Clouds: The Yosemite of Peru. By Harriet Chalmers Adams. 597-618, *Sept. 1908*

American Discoveries in Egypt. 801-806, *Dec. 1907*

The Rock City of Petra. By Franklin E. Hoskins. 283-291, *May 1907*

Archæology in the Air. By Eliza R. Scidmore. 151-163, *Mar. 1907*

The Buried City of Ceylon. By John M. Abbot. 613-622, *Nov. 1906*

The Supposed Birthplace of Civilizations. 499-504, *Nov. 1905*

Excavations at Abydos. By W. M. Flinders Petrie. 358-359, *Sept. 1903*

Recent Discoveries in Egypt. 396-397, *Nov. 1901*

Excavations of M. de Morgan at Susa. 315, *Aug. 1901*

The Indian Village of Baum (Ohio). By H. C. Brown. 272-274, *July 1901*

Excavations at Nippur (Iraq). 392, *Oct. 1900*

Mesa Verde. By F. H. Newell. 431-434, *Oct. 1898*

Dwellings of the Saga-Time in Iceland, Greenland, and Vineland. By Cornelia Horsford. 73-84, *Mar. 1898*

Three Weeks in Hubbard Bay, West Greenland. By Robert Stein. 1-11, *Jan. 1898*

See also Antiquities; Aztecs; Chan Chan; Easter Island; Glass; Gravel Pictographs; Incas; Lascaux Cave; La Venta, Mexico; Machu Picchu, Peru; Maya; Mesa Verde National Park, Colorado; Mesopotamia; Moche Culture; Olmec Culture; Petra, Jordan; Roman Empire; Scilly, Isles of; Temple Caves; Toltec Culture; Zimbabwe (Ruins); *and* Anthropology, Physical; Archaeology, Underwater; Potassium-Argon Dating; Radiocarbon Dating; Tree-ring Dating

ARCHAEOLOGY, Underwater:

Yorktown Shipwreck. By John D. Broadwater. Photos by Bates Littlehales. 804-823, *June 1988*

◼◼ *Hidden Treasures of the Sea.* Juvenile. 104 pages. *1988*

Oldest Known Shipwreck Reveals Splendors of the Bronze Age. By George F. Bass. Photos by William R. Curtsinger. Included: Bronze Age Trade, The Cosmopolitan World of the Late Bronze Age, The Painstaking Art of Marine Archaeology. NGS research grant. 693-733, *Dec. 1987*

Epilogue for *Titanic*. By Robert D. Ballard. 454-463, *Oct. 1987*

President's Page. By Gilbert M. Grosvenor. Dec. 1985; *July 1987*

Caesarea Maritima. By Robert L. Hohlfelder. Photos by J. Robert Teringo. NGS research grant. 261-279, *Feb. 1987*

A Long Last Look at *Titanic*. By Robert D. Ballard. Included: High-tech partners plumb new depths; Poignant relics of a disaster. Illustrations text by Cliff Tarpy. 698-727, *Dec. 1986*

Editorial. By Wilbur E. Garrett. 695, *Dec. 1985*

How We Found *Titanic*. By Robert D. Ballard in association with Jean-Louis Michel. 696-719, *Dec. 1985*

Editorial. By Wilbur E. Garrett. 421, *Oct. 1985*

Wreck of H.M.S. *Pandora*. By Luis Marden. 423-451, *Oct. 1985*

16th-Century Basque Whalers in America. Photos by Bill Curtsinger. Paintings by Richard Schlecht. 40-71. I. Discovery in Labrador: A 16th-Century Basque Whaling Port and Its Sunken Fleet. 40-49; II. Unearthing Red Bay's Whaling History. By James A. Tuck. 50-57; III. Excavating a 400-year-old Basque Galleon. By Robert Grenier. 58-67; IV. The Indomitable Basques. By Robert Laxalt. 69-71, *July 1985*

Editorial. By Wilbur E. Garrett. 1-2, *Jan. 1985*

Bronze Age Shipwreck. By Wilbur E. Garrett and George F. Bass. NGS research grant. 1-3, *Jan. 1985*

Exploring a 140-year-old Ship Under Arctic Ice (*Breadalbane*). By Joseph B. MacInnis. Photos by Emory Kristof. 104A-104D, *July 1983*

Warriors From a Watery Grave (Bronze Sculptures). By Joseph Alsop. 821-827, *June 1983*

On a 1986 visit re-created by an artist, a research submarine inspects **Titanic***'s rusted bow where it settled in the North Atlantic on April 15, 1912.* PAINTING BY PIERRE MION

French doctor Jean-Louis Etienne pulls his sled across the frozen Arctic on a 64-day solo trek in 1986 to the North Pole. JIM BRANDENBURG

ARCTIC INSTITUTE OF NORTH AMERICA: Expedition. *See* Curlews

ARCTIC NATIONAL WILDLIFE REFUGE, Alaska:

ARCTIC OCEAN:

ARCTIC REGIONS:

Sails at rest, explorers' ships move cautiously through Baffin Bay, waters well-known to Inuit and commercial whalers. UNDERWOOD & UNDERWOOD/THE BETTMANN ARCHIVE

The Mummies of Qilakitsoq. By Jens P. Hart Hansen, Jørgen Meldgaard, and Jørgen Nordqvist. 191-207, *Feb. 1985*

Narwhal Hunters of Greenland. By Ivars Silis. 520-539, *Apr. 1984*

Circling Earth From Pole to Pole. By Sir Ranulph Fiennes. 464-481, *Oct. 1983*

Arctic Odyssey. By John Bockstoce. Photos by Jonathan Wright. Paintings by Jack Unruh. 100-127, *July 1983*

Exploring a 140-year-old Ship Under Arctic Ice *(Breadalbane)*. By Joseph B. MacInnis. Photos by Emory Kristof. 104A-104D, *July 1983*

Peoples of the Arctic. 144-223. I. Introduction by Joseph Judge. 144-149; II. Hunters of the Lost Spirit: Alaskans, Canadians, Greenlanders, Lapps. By Priit J. Vesilind. Photos by David Alan Harvey, Ivars Silis, and Sisse Brimberg. 150-197; III. Where Magic Ruled: Art of the Bering Sea. By William W. Fitzhugh and Susan A. Kaplan. Photos by Sisse Brimberg. 198-205; IV. People of the Long Spring (Chukchis). By Yuri Rytkheu. Photos by Dean Conger. 206-223, *Feb. 1983*

⊕ *Peoples of the Arctic; Arctic Ocean. Feb. 1983*

Eskimo and Viking Finds in the High Arctic: Ellesmere Island. By Peter Schledermann. Photos by Sisse Brimberg. 575-601, *May 1981*

Our Wildest Wilderness: Alaska's Arctic National Wildlife Range. By Douglas H. Chadwick. Photos by Lowell Georgia. 737-769, *Dec. 1979*

Learning the Ways of the Walrus. By G. Carleton Ray. Photos by Bill Curtsinger. 565-580, *Oct. 1979*

Solo to the Pole. By Naomi Uemura. Photos by the author and Ira Block. 298-325, *Sept. 1978*

Norway's Strategic Arctic Islands (Svalbard). By Gordon Young. Photos by Martin Rogers. 267-283, *Aug. 1978*

Still Eskimo, Still Free: The Inuit of Umingmaktok. By Yva Momatiuk and John Eastcott. 624-647, *Nov. 1977*

Trek Across Arctic America. By Colin Irwin. 295-321, *Mar. 1974*

■ Journey to the High Arctic. 590A-590B, *Apr. 1971*

Polar Bear: Lonely Nomad of the North. By Thor Larsen. 574-590, *Apr. 1971*

I Live With the Eskimos (Canadian). By Guy Mary-Rousseliere. 188-217, *Feb. 1971*

Domesticating the Wild and Woolly Musk Ox. By John J. Teal, Jr. Photos by Robert W. Madden. 862-879, *June 1970*

North for Oil: *Manhattan* Makes the Historic Northwest Passage. By Bern Keating. Photos by Tomas Sennett. 374-391, *Mar. 1970*

First Woman Across Greenland's Ice. By Myrtle Simpson. Photos by Hugh Simpson. 264-279, *Aug. 1967*

⊕ *Top of the World*, Atlas series. *Nov. 1965*

North Toward the Pole on Skis. By

Bjørn O. Staib. NGS research grant. 254-281, *Feb. 1965*

Banks Island: Eskimo Life on the Polar Sea. By William O. Douglas. Photos by Clyde Hare. 703-735, *May 1964*

Friendly Flight to Northern Europe. By Lyndon B. Johnson. Photos by Volkmar Wentzel. 268-293, *Feb. 1964*

DEW Line, Sentry of the Far North. By Howard La Fay. 128-146, *July 1958*

Admiral of the Ends of the Earth (Richard E. Byrd). By Melville Bell Grosvenor. 36-48, *July 1957*

A Visit to the Living Ice Age. By Rutherford Platt. 525-545, *Apr. 1957*

Weather From the White North. By Andrew H. Brown. Photos by John E. Fletcher. 543-572, *Apr. 1955*

The Peary Flag Comes to Rest. By Marie Peary Stafford. 519-532, *Oct. 1954*

The Society's Hubbard Medal Awarded to Commander MacMillan. 563-564, *Apr. 1953*

We Followed Peary to the Pole. By Gilbert Grosvenor and Thomas W. McKnew. 469-484, *Oct. 1953*

Far North with "Captain Mac." By Miriam MacMillan. 465-513, *Oct. 1951*

Milestones in My Arctic Journeys. By Willie Knutsen. 543-570, *Oct. 1949*

Nomads of the Far North. By Matthew W. Stirling. Included: Hearty Folk Defy Arctic Storms. Paintings by W. Langdon Kihn. 471-504, *Oct. 1949*

⊕ *The Top of the World. Oct. 1949*

⊕ *Canada, Alaska, and Greenland. June 1947*

Servicing Arctic Airbases. By Robert A. Bartlett. 602-616, *May 1946*

⊕ *Northern Hemisphere. Feb. 1946*

Coast Guard Patrol in Greenland. Photos by Thomas S. La Farge. 565-572, *May 1943*

⊕ *Northern and Southern Hemispheres. Apr. 1943*

Discovering Alaska's Oldest Arctic Town: A Scientist Finds Ivory-eyed Skeletons of a Mysterious People and Joins Modern Eskimos in the Dangerous Spring Whale Hunt. By Froelich G. Rainey. 319-336, *Sept. 1942*

Greenland Turns to America. By James K. Penfield. 369-383, *Sept. 1942*

Desolate Greenland, Now an American Outpost. Photos by Willie Knutsen and F. Vogel. 393-406, *Sept. 1941*

Greenland from 1898 to Now: "Captain Bob," Who Went North with Peary, Tells of 42 Years of Exploration in the Orphan Island of New Aerial and Naval Interest. By Robert A. Bartlett. 111-140, *July 1940*

The Nomads of Arctic Lapland: Mysterious Little People of a Land of the Midnight Sun Live Off the Country Above the Arctic Circle. By Clyde Fisher. 641-676, *Nov. 1939*

Our Search for the Lost Aviators: An Arctic Area Larger Than Montana First Explored in Hunt for Missing Russians. By Sir Hubert Wilkins. 141-172, *Aug. 1938*

Flights from Arctic to Equator: Conquering the Alps, the Ice Peaks of Spitsbergen, of Persia, and Africa's

Mountains of the Moon. By Walter Mittelholzer. 445-498, *Apr. 1932*

A Woman's Winter on Spitsbergen. By Martha Phillips Gilson. 227-246, *Aug. 1928*

Commander Byrd at the North Pole. Reproduction in color of the painting by N. C. Wyeth, National Geographic Society, Washington, D. C. *May 1928*

Navigating the "Norge" (Airship) from Rome to the North Pole and Beyond: The Designer and Pilot of the First Dirigible to Fly Over the Top of the World Describes a Thrilling Voyage of More Than 8,000 Miles. By Umberto Nobile. 177-215, *Aug. 1927*

The First Flight to the North Pole. By Richard Evelyn Byrd. 357-376, *Sept. 1926*

Commander Byrd Receives the Hubbard Gold Medal: The First Explorer to Reach the North Pole by Air Receives Coveted Honor at Brillant National Geographic Society Reception. 377-388, *Sept. 1926*

A Naturalist with MacMillan in the Arctic. By Walter N. Koelz. 299-318, *Mar. 1926*

Flying Over the Arctic. By Richard E. Byrd. 519-532, *Nov. 1925*

The MacMillan Arctic Expedition Returns: U. S. Navy Planes Make First Series of Overland Flights in the Arctic and National Geographic Society Staff Obtains Valuable Data and Specimens for Scientific Study. By Donald B. MacMillan. 477-518, *Nov. 1925*

⊕ *The Arctic Regions. Nov. 1925*

MacMillan in the Field. 473-476, *Oct. 1925*

Scientific Aspects of the MacMillan Arctic Expedition. 349-354, *Sept. 1925*

The MacMillan Arctic Expedition Sails. 225-226, *Aug. 1925*

To Seek the Unknown in the Arctic: United States Navy Fliers to Aid MacMillan Expedition Under the Auspices of the National Geographic Society in Exploring Vast Area. 673-675, *June 1925*

The "Bowdoin" (Ship) in North Greenland: Arctic Explorers Place Tablet to Commemorate Sacrifices of the Lady Franklin Bay Expedition. By Donald B. MacMillan. 677-722, *June 1925*

With an Exile in Arctic Siberia: The Narrative of a Russian Who Was Compelled to Turn Polar Explorer for Two Years. By Vladimir M. Zenzinov. 695-718, *Dec. 1924*

Sailing the Seven Seas in the Interest of Science: Adventures Through 157,000 Miles of Storm and Calm, from Arctic to Antarctic and Around the World, in the Non-magnetic Yacht "Carnegie." By J. P. Ault. 631-690, *Dec. 1922*

The Arctic as an Air Route of the Future. By Vilhjalmur Stefansson. 205-218, *Aug. 1922*

Peary as a Leader: Incidents from the Life of the Discoverer of the North Pole Told by One of His Lieutenants

On top of its world a lone arctic wolf surveys Ellesmere Island from an iceberg. JIM BRANDENBURG

ARCTIC SMALL TOOL CULTURE:

ARCTIC WOLVES:

ARDASTRA GARDENS, Nassau, Bahamas:

ARDEN, HARVEY:

AREA and Drainage Basin of Lake Superior.

ARECUNA INDIANS:

ARGAEUS, Mount, Turkey:

ARGENTINA:

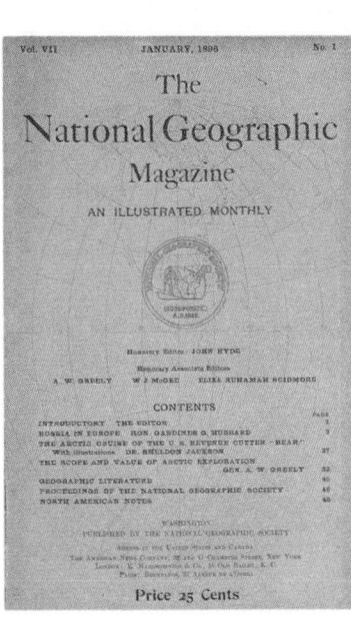

Tough as the land he lives on, 72-year-old Henry Gray has run cattle along the U.S.-Mexico border in Arizona's Sonoran Desert for half a century. WILLIAM ALBERT ALLARD

A jack-in-the-box fright reflex propels an alarmed armadillo three feet into the air during a night's forage. BIANCA LAVIES

Unbridled exuberance characterizes "Smoking Up," a sculpture by Western artist Charles Russell once owned by Theodore Roosevelt. SIEGEL STUDIO, PHOENIX, FROM THE FREDERIC G. RENNER COLLECTION

Norbert Casteret. Photos by Maynard Owen Williams. Contents: La Baume Ladrone, La Henne Morte, La Mouthe, Lascaux, Montespan, Niaux, Trois Frères, Tuc D'Audoubert, in France; and Altamira in Spain. 771-794, *Dec. 1948*

Arctic

Where Magic Ruled: Art of the Bering Sea. By William W. Fitzhugh and Susan A. Kaplan. Photos by Sisse Brimberg. 198-205, *Feb. 1983*

Eskimo and Viking Finds in the High Arctic: Ellesmere Island. By Peter Schledermann. Photos by Sisse Brimberg. 575-601, *May 1981*

Asian

Focus on India: Festivals Across U. S. Celebrate a Diverse Culture. By John J. Putman. 460-461, *Apr. 1985*

Indonesia Rescues Ancient Borobudur. By W. Brown Morton III. Photos by Dean Conger. 126-142, *Jan. 1983*

The Temples of Angkor. 548-589. I. Ancient Glory in Stone. By Peter T. White. Photos by Wilbur E. Garrett. 552-589; II. Will They Survive? Introduction by Wilbur E. Garrett. 548-551. *May 1982*

Pagan, on the Road to Mandalay. By W. E. Garrett. 343-365, *Mar. 1971*

Angkor, Jewel of the Jungle. By W. Robert Moore. Paintings by Maurice Fiévet. 517-569, *Apr. 1960*

See also Byzantine; Chinese; Islamic; Japanese; Middle Eastern, *following*

Byzantine

The Byzantine Empire. 709-777. I. Rome of the East. By Merle Severy. Photos by James L. Stanfield. 709-767; II. Mount Athos. 739-745; III. Eternal Easter in a Greek Village. By Maria Nicolaidis-Karanikolas. Photos by James L. Stanfield. 768-777, *Dec. 1983*

Island of Faith in the Sinai Wilderness (St. Catherine's Monastery). By George H. Forsyth. Photos by Robert F. Sisson. 82-106, *Jan. 1964*

Mount Sinai's Holy Treasures (St. Catherine's Monastery). By Kurt Weitzmann. Photos by Fred Anderegg. 109-127, *Jan. 1964*

A New Look at Medieval Europe. By Kenneth M. Setton. Paintings by André Durenceau and Birney Lettick. 799-859, *Dec. 1962*

Ivory head was preserved at the bottom of a well in Assyrian king Ashurnasirpal II's palace in Nimrud, Iraq. STEVE MCCURRY

Athens to Istanbul. By Jean and Franc Shor. 37-76, *Jan. 1956*

Chinese

China's Incredible Find. By Audrey Topping. Paintings by Yang Hsien-min. Included: The first emperor's burial mound, with guardian army of terra-cotta men and horses. 440-459, *Apr. 1978*

China Unveils Her Newest Treasures. Photos by Robert W. Madden. 848-857, *Dec. 1974*

A Lady From China's Past. Photos from *China Pictorial.* Text by Alice J. Hall. Included: Treasures from a noblewoman's tomb. 660-681, *May 1974*

Mukden, the Manchu Home, and Its Great Art Museum. By Eliza R. Scidmore. 289-320, *Apr. 1910*

Egyptian

Lost Outpost of the Egyptian Empire. By Trude Dothan. Photos by Sisse Brimberg. Paintings by Lloyd K. Townsend. NGS research grant. 739-769, *Dec. 1982*

Egypt: Legacy of a Dazzling Past. By Alice J. Hall. 293-311, *Mar. 1977*

Computer Helps Scholars Re-create an Egyptian Temple. By Ray Winfield

Smith. Photos by Emory Kristof. NGS research grant. 634-655, *Nov. 1970*

Abu Simbel's Ancient Temples Reborn. By Georg Gerster. 724-744, *May 1969*

Saving the Ancient Temples at Abu Simbel. By Georg Gerster. Paintings by Robert W. Nicholson. 694-742, *May 1966*

Yankee Cruises the Storied Nile. By Irving and Electa Johnson. Photos by Winfield Parks. 583-633, *May 1965*

Threatened Treasures of the Nile. By Georg Gerster. 587-621, *Oct. 1963*

Tutankhamun's Golden Trove. By Christiane Desroches Noblecourt. Photos by F. L. Kenett. 625-646, *Oct. 1963*

Fresh Treasures from Egypt's Ancient Sands. By Jefferson Caffery. Photos by David S. Boyer. 611-650, *Nov. 1955*

Life, Culture, and History of the Egyptians. Paintings by H. M. Herget. 436-514, *Oct. 1941*

European

Treasures of the Vatican. Photos by James L. Stanfield and Victor R. Boswell, Jr. 764-775, *Dec. 1985*

The Great Good Places: English Country Houses. By Mark Girouard. Photos by Fred J. Maroon. 658-694, *Nov. 1985*

The Dead Do Tell Tales at Vesuvius. By Rick Gore. Photos by O. Louis Mazzatenta. NGS research grant. 557-613, *May 1984*

Toledo–El Greco's Spain Lives On. By Louise E. Levathes. Photos by James P. Blair. Included: The Genius of El Greco. Introduction by J. Carter Brown. 726-753, *June 1982*

Belgium: One Nation Divisible. By James Cerruti. Photos by Martin Rogers. Included: Flemish oil-painting techniques. 314-341, *Mar. 1979*

The Louvre, France's Palace of the Arts. By Hereward Lester Cooke, Jr. 796-831, *June 1971*

The National Gallery After a Quarter Century. By John Walker. 348-371, *Mar. 1967*

The Kress Collection: A Gift to the Nation. By Guy Emerson. 823-865, *Dec. 1961*

Unrolled by photography, a painting on a tomb vase depicts a Maya ruler peering into an obsidian mirror. DUMBARTON OAKS

Greek

Impressionist

Islamic

Art lovers in the Louvre pass in a blur before "Venus de Milo," one of the Paris museum's masterpieces. BRUCE DALE, NGS

Japanese

Medieval

Middle Eastern

Modern

Pre-Columbian

Photos by B. Anthony Stewart. 492-519, *Oct. 1968*

Giant Effigies of the Southwest. By George C. Marshall. 389, *Sept. 1952*

Mexico's Booming Capital. By Mason Sutherland. Photos by Justin Locke. 785-824, *Dec. 1951*

Indian Life Before the Colonists Came. By Stuart E. Jones. Engravings by Theodore de Bry, 1590. 351-368, *Sept. 1947*

Finding the Tomb of a Warrior-God. By William Duncan Strong. Photos by Clifford Evans, Jr. 453-482, *Apr. 1947*

On the Trail of La Venta Man. By Matthew W. Stirling. Photos by Richard H. Stewart. Included: Hunting Mexico's Buried Temples. 145-168. NGS research grant. 137-172, *Feb. 1947*

Renaissance

Restoration Reveals the "Last Supper." By Carlo Bertelli. Photos by Victor R. Boswell, Jr. 664-685, *Nov. 1983*

Carrara Marble: Touchstone of Eternity. By Cathy Newman. Photos by Pierre Boulat. 42-59, *July 1982*

Leonardo da Vinci: A Man for All Ages. By Kenneth MacLeish. Photos by James L. Amos. 296-329, *Sept. 1977*

The Renaissance Lives On in Tuscany. By Luis Marden. Photos by Albert Moldvay. 626-659, *Nov. 1974*

Venice Fights for Life. By Joseph Judge. Photos by Albert Moldvay. 591-631, *Nov. 1972*

When in Rome.... By Stuart E. Jones. Photos by Winfield Parks. 741-789, *June 1970*

■■ *The Renaissance: Maker of Modern Man.* 402 pages. *1970*

Florence Rises From the Flood. By Joseph Judge. 1-43, *July 1967*

Escorting Mona Lisa to America. By Edward T. Folliard. 838-847, *June 1963*

"The Adoration of the Magi," painting supplement, *Jan. 1952*

Roman

Ancient Aphrodisias Lives Through Its Art. By Kenan T. Erim. Photos by David Brill. NGS research grant. 527-551, *Oct. 1981*

Down the Ancient Appian Way. By James Cerruti. Photos by O. Louis Mazzatenta. 714-747, *June 1981*

Aphrodisias, Awakened City of Ancient Art. By Kenan T. Erim. Photos by Jonathan Blair. NGS research grant. 766-791, *June 1972*

Ancient Aphrodisias and Its Marble Treasures. By Kenan T. Erim. Photos by Jonathan S. Blair. NGS research grant. 280-294, *Aug. 1967*

Last Moments of the Pompeians. By Amedeo Maiuri. Photos by Lee E. Battaglia. Paintings by Peter V. Bianchi. 651-669, *Nov. 1961*

Roman Life in 1,600-year-old Color Pictures. By Gino Vinicio Gentili. Photos by Duncan Edwards. 211-229, *Feb. 1957*

Ancient Rome Brought to Life. Paintings by H. M. Herget. 570-633, *Nov. 1946*

See also Animation; Architecture; *listing under* Art Galleries; Cave Art; Ceramics; Crafts; Folk Art; Glass; Metalwork; Mosaics; Painting; Pottery; Rock Art; Sculpture

ART GALLERIES. *See* Corcoran Gallery of Art; Dresden Treasures; Hermitage; Huntington; Kunsthistorisches Museum; Louvre; National Gallery of Art; National Museum of Anthropology, Mexico City; Vizcaya; *and* Vatican City

The **ART** of Photography At National Geographic. By Jane Livingston. 322-351, *Sept. 1988*

The **ART** in Farming. Photo essay by Georg Gerster. 391-399, *Sept. 1984*

ART RESTORATION:

Vatican City. By James Fallows. Photos by James L. Stanfield and Victor R. Boswell, Jr. Included: Treasures of the Vatican; Restoration of Sistine frescoes; Reconstruction of Michelangelo's "Pietà." 723-775, *Dec. 1985*

Restoration Reveals the "Last Supper." By Carlo Bertelli. Photos by Victor R. Boswell, Jr. 664-685, *Nov. 1983*

Warriors From a Watery Grave (Bronze Sculptures). By Joseph Alsop. 821-827, *June 1983*

Venice Fights for Life. By Joseph Judge. Photos by Albert Moldvay. Included: Venice's Golden Legacy. Photos by Victor R. Boswell, Jr. 591-631, *Nov. 1972*

Thera, Key to the Riddle of Minos. By Spyridon Marinatos. Photos by Otis Imboden. 702-726, *May 1972*

Florence Rises From the Flood. By Joseph Judge. 1-43, *July 1967*

ART SUPPLEMENTS. *See* Pictorial Supplements: Enlargements and Panoramas

ARTESIAN Water Predictions. 361-363, *Apr. 1910*

ARTHROPODS. *See* Crustaceans; Insects; Scorpions; Spiders

ARTHUR, CHESTER A.:

Profiles of the Presidents: III. The American Giant Comes of Age. By Frank Freidel. 660-711, *May 1965*

Inside the White House. By Lonnelle Aikman. Photos by B. Anthony Stewart and Thomas Nebbia. 3-43, *Jan. 1961*

The only statue Michelangelo signed, the "Pietà," restored after a 1972 attack, now rests behind bulletproof glass in St. Peter's Basilica, Vatican City. VICTOR R. BOSWELL, JR., NGS

ARTISANS. *See* Crafts; Folk Art

ARTIST Adventures on the Island of Bali. By Franklin Price Knott. 326-347, *Mar. 1928*

ARTISTS:

Remington, the Man and the Myth. By Louise E. Levathes. Photos by Chris Johns. 200-231, *Aug. 1988*

C. M. Russell, Cowboy Artist. By Bart McDowell. Photos by Sam Abell. 60-95, *Jan. 1986*

Restoration Reveals the "Last Supper." By Carlo Bertelli. Photos by Victor R. Boswell, Jr. 664-685, *Nov. 1983*

Toledo–El Greco's Spain Lives On. By Louise E. Levathes. Photos by James P. Blair. Included: The Genius of El Greco. Introduction by J. Carter Brown. 726-753, *June 1982*

Goal at the End of the Trail: Santa Fe. By William S. Ellis. Photos by Gordon W. Gahan and Otis Imboden. 323-345, *Mar. 1982*

Belgium: One Nation Divisible. By James Cerruti. Photos by Martin Rogers. Included: How the Flemings brought depth to painting. 314-341, *Mar. 1979*

Leonardo da Vinci: A Man for All Ages. By Kenneth MacLeish. Photos by James L. Amos. 296-329, *Sept. 1977*

Audubon "On the Wing." By David Jeffery. Photos by Bates Littlehales. 149-177, *Feb. 1977*

Venice Fights for Life. By Joseph Judge. Photos by Albert Moldvay. Included: Venice's Golden Legacy: Giovanni Bellini, Giorgione, Giuseppe Heintz, Jacopo Tintoretto, Titian, Paolo Veronese, Andrea del Verrocchio, Leonardo da Vinci. Photos by Victor R. Boswell, Jr. 591-631, *Nov. 1972*

Chelsea, London's Haven of Individualists. By James Cerruti. Photos by Adam Woolfitt. Included: Sir Jacob Epstein, Anthony Gray, Walter Greaves, Edward Halliday, Augustus John, Guy Roddon, Dante Gabriel Rossetti, John Singer Sargent, William Thomson, Joseph Mallord William Turner, James McNeill Whistler. 28-55, *Jan. 1972*

The Louvre, France's Palace of the Arts. By Hereward Lester Cooke, Jr. Included: P. Cézanne, J. Chardin, J. Clouet, H. Daumier, J. David, E. Delacroix, Jan van Eyck, C. Le Brun, É. Manet, A. Mantegna, G. Metsu, Michelangelo, F. Perrier, Rembrandt, H. Rigaud, G. Seurat, Leonardo da Vinci, J. A. Watteau, James A. McNeill Whistler. 796-831, *June 1971*

The National Gallery After a Quarter Century. By John Walker. 348-371, *Mar. 1967*

In Quest of Beauty. By Paul Mellon. Contents: Frédéric Bazille, Pierre Bonnard, Mary Cassatt, Paul Cézanne, Edgar Degas, Paul Gauguin, Vincent van Gogh, Édouard Manet, Claude Monet, Berthe Morisot, Pablo Picasso, Auguste Renoir, Henri Rousseau, Georges Seurat, Henri de Toulouse-Lautrec. 372-385, *Mar. 1967*

Under the Dome of Freedom: The United States Capitol. By Lonnelle Aikman. Photos by George F. Mobley. 4-59, *Jan. 1964*

Early America Through the Eyes of Her Native Artists. By Hereward Lester Cooke, Jr. Contents: Francis Alexander, Winthrop Chandler, James Evans, George A. Hayes, Edward Hicks, Joseph H. Hidley, H. Knight, Hyacinthe Laclotte, Linton Park, H.M.T. Powell, Charles S. Raleigh, A. Tapy, John Toole, Benjamin West, J. Wiess. 356-389, *Sept. 1962*

The Kress Collection: A Gift to the Nation. By Guy Emerson. Contents: Giovanni Bellini, Bernardo Bellotto, Abraham Van Beyeren, Paris Bordone, Canaletto (Antonio Canale), Bernardino Fungai, El Greco, Francesco Guardi, Frans Hals, Pieter de Hooch, Lorenzo Lotto, Master of the Braunschweig Diptych, The Montaione Master, Neroccio de' Landi, Piero di Cosimo, Rembrandt Van Rijn, Jusepe de Ribera, Cosimo Rosselli, Peter Paul Rubens, Jan Steen, Bernardo Strozzi, Giovanni Battista Tiepolo, Jacopo Tintoretto, Titian, Sir Anthony Van Dyck, Domenico Veneziano, Paolo Veronese, Elisabeth Vigée-Lebrun, Simon Vouet. 823-865, *Dec. 1961*

Great Masters of a Brave Era in Art (Impressionist). By Hereward Lester Cooke, Jr. Contents: Eugene Boudin, Mary Cassatt, Paul Cézanne, Jean-Baptiste-Camille Corot, Honoré Daumier, Edgar Degas, Eugène Delacroix, Henri Fantin-Latour, Paul Gauguin, Vincent van Gogh, Édouard Manet, Claude Monet, Berthe Morisot, Camille Pissarro, Auguste Renoir, Henri Rousseau, Henri de Toulouse-Lautrec. 661-697, *May 1961*

The Nation's Newest Old Masters (National Gallery of Art). By John Walker. Paintings from Kress Collection. Contents: Nicolò dell' Abate and Denys Calvaert, Albrecht Altdorfer, Sandro Botticelli, Cima da Conegliano, François Clouet, Jacques-Louis David, Juan de Flandes, Jean-Honoré Fragonard, Orazio Gentileschi, El Greco, Lucas Van-Leyden, Hans Memling, Pieter Jansz. Saenredam, St. Bartholomew Master, Jacopo Tintoretto, Titian, Juan van der Hamen y Leon, Sir Anthony Van Dyck, Paolo Veronese, Leonardo da Vinci. 619-657, *Nov. 1956*

America's First Painters: Indians. By Dorothy Dunn. 349-377, *Mar. 1955*

U. S. Capitol, Citadel of Democracy. By Lonnelle Aikman. 143-192, *Aug. 1952*

Your National Gallery of Art After 10 Years. By John Walker. Paintings from Kress Collection. Contents: Pieter Bruegel the Elder, Canaletto, Philippe de Champagne, Jean Baptiste Siméon Chardin, Albrecht Dürer, Benozzo Gozzoli, Jean Auguste Dominique Ingres, Giovanni Battista Piazzetta, Hubert Robert, Girolamo Romanino, Master of St. Gilles, Sebastiano del Piombo, Luca Signorelli, Sodoma, Bernardo Strozzi, Titian, Sir Anthony Van Dyck. 73-103, *Jan. 1952*

American Processional: History on Canvas. By John and Blanche Leeper. Contents: John and Victor Audubon, George Caleb Bingham, David G. Blythe, James E. Butterworth, James H. Cafferty, Conrad Wise Chapman, John Singleton Copley, Robert Dudley, Thomas Eakins, J. G. Evans, Ambroise Louis Garneray, Henry Gilder, William Hahn, George Peter Alexander Healy, Winslow Homer, Thomas Hovenden, Frederick Kemmelmeyer, Edward Moran, Linton Park, Charles Willson Peale, Adrian Persac, Frederick Remington, C. Riess, Charles G. Rosenberg, John Searle, Dominique Serres, John Stevens, Louis Comfort Tiffany, John Trumbull, Charles F. Ulrich, Benjamin West. 173-212, *Feb. 1951*

The Vienna Treasures and Their Collectors. By John Walker. Contents: Michelangelo Merisi da Caravaggio, Domenico Feti, Albrecht Dürer, Francesco Guardi, Jacob Jordaens, Lorenzo Lotto, Jusepe de Ribera, Peter Paul Rubens, Jan Steen, Tintoretto, Titian, Sir Anthony Van Dyck, Diego Rodriguez de Silva y Velázquez, Jan Vermeer, Paolo Veronese. 737-776, *June 1950*

The British Way. By Sir Evelyn Wrench. Included: William Hogarth, Hans Holbein, Sir Edwin Landseer, Sir Joshua Reynolds, Benjamin West. 421-541, *Apr. 1949*

Our Search for British Paintings. By Franklin L. Fisher. 543-550, *Apr. 1949*

Masterpieces on Tour. By Harry A. McBride. Contents: Hans Baldung, Alessandro Botticelli, Pieter Bruegel the Elder, Andrea del Castagno, Jean Baptiste Siméon Chardin, Albrecht Dürer, Jan Van Eyck, Frans Hals, Meindert Hobbema, Hans Holbein the Younger, Georges de La Tour, Lucas Van Leyden, Édouard Manet, Raphael, Rembrandt, Peter Paul Rubens, Jan Steen, Bernardo Strozzi, Gerard Ter Borch, Titian, Jan Vermeer, Antoine Watteau, Rogier Van der Weyden. 717-750, *Dec. 1948*

American Masters in the National Gallery. By John Walker. Contents: George Bellows, Mary Cassatt, William Merritt Chase, John Singleton Copley, Thomas Eakins, Chester Harding, Childe Hassam, Winslow Homer, George Inness, Rembrandt Peale, John Quidor, Edward Savage, Christian Schussele, Gilbert Stuart, Thomas Sully, James Abbott McNeill Whistler. 295-324, *Sept. 1948*

Artists Look at Pennsylvania. By John Oliver La Gorce. Contents: Aaron Bohrod, Adolf Dehn, Ernest Fiene,

Armed with pastel crayons, Alexandre Iacovleff captures the intensity of nomadic horsemen wearing shakos of dyed sheepskin in Herat, Afghanistan.   MAYNARD OWEN WILLIAMS, NGS

World. By Priit J. Vesilind. Photos by Steve McCurry. 712-747, *Dec. 1984*

❀ *South Asia, with Afghanistan and Burma; Peoples of South Asia. Dec. 1984*

They're Killing Off the Rhino. By Esmond Bradley Martin. Photos by Jim Brandenburg. 404-422, *Mar. 1984*

Islam's Heartland, Up in Arms. By Thomas J. Abercrombie. Included: Afghanistan, Iraq, Israel, Jerusalem, Lebanon, Saudi Arabia, Soviet Central Asia. 335-345, *Sept. 1980*

The Desert: An Age-old Challenge Grows. By Rick Gore. Photos by Georg Gerster and Bruce Dale. Included: The Arabian Desert; Gobi Desert, China-Mongolia; Iranian Desert, Iran-Afghanistan-Pakistan; Negev Desert, Israel; Takla Makan Desert, China; Thar (Great Indian Desert), India-Pakistan; and the Turkestan Desert, U.S.S.R. 586-639, *Nov. 1979*

The Search for the First Americans. By Thomas Y. Canby. Photos by Kerby Smith. Paintings by Roy Andersen. Included: Cultural and racial links between Paleo-Indians and Asians. 330-363, *Sept. 1979*

The Proud Armenians. By Robert Paul Jordan. Photos by Harry N. Naltchayan. Included: Armenian S.S.R., Lebanon, Turkey. 846-873, *June 1978*

A Bad Time to Be a Crocodile. By Rick Gore. Photos by Jonathan Blair. Included: The critically endangered Chinese alligator; the false gharial of Malaysia; the long-nosed gharial, or gavial, of the Indian subcontinent; India's mugger crocodile; and the Siamese crocodile. 90-115, *Jan. 1978*

The Rat, Lapdog of the Devil. By Thomas Y. Canby. Photos by James L. Stanfield. Included: Burma, India, Pakistan, Philippines. 60-87, *July 1977*

The Lands and Peoples of Southeast Asia. 295-365. I. Mosaic of Cultures. By Peter T. White. Photos by W. E. Garrett. 296-329; II. New Light on a Forgotten Past. By Wilhelm G. Solheim II. 330-339; III. Pagan, on the Road to Mandalay. By W. E. Garrett. 343-365, *Mar. 1971*

❀ *Asia; The Peoples of Mainland Southeast Asia. Mar. 1971*

❀ *Southeast Asia. Dec. 1968*

In the Footsteps of Alexander the Great. By Helen and Frank Schreider. Paintings by Tom Lovell. 1-65, *Jan. 1968*

❀ *Viet Nam, Cambodia, Laos, and Thailand. Feb. 1967*

Asian Insects in Disguise. By Edward S. Ross. 433-439, *Sept. 1965*

❀ *Viet Nam, Cambodia, Laos, and Eastern Thailand. Text on reverse. Jan. 1965*

Ambassadors of Good Will: The Peace Corps. By Sargent Shriver and Peace Corps Volunteers. Included: Sarawak, Turkey. 297-345, *Sept. 1964*

YWCA: International Success Story. By Mary French Rockefeller. Photos by Otis Imboden. 904-933, *Dec. 1963*

❀ *Southwest Asia, Atlas series. May 1963*

Round the World School (ISA). By Paul Antze. Photos by William Eppridge. Included: Hong Kong, India, Japan, Thailand. 96-127, *July 1962*

❀ *Southeast Asia, Atlas series. May 1961*

When the President Goes Abroad (Eisenhower Tour). By Gilbert M. Grosvenor. Included: Afghanistan, India, Iran, Pakistan, Turkey. 588-649, *May 1960*

Sky Road East (Southwest Asia). By Tay and Lowell Thomas, Jr. 71-112, *Jan. 1960*

Around the World and the Calendar with the Geographic: The President's Annual Message. By Melville Bell Grosvenor. Included: Cambodia, Hong Kong, India, Japan, Pakistan, Thailand, Viet Nam. 832-866, *Dec. 1959*

❀ *Asia and Adjacent Areas, Atlas series. Dec. 1959*

New Guinea to Bali in *Yankee*. By Irving and Electa Johnson. Included: Cambodia, Indonesia, Laos, Thailand. 767-815, *Dec. 1959*

Station Wagon Odyssey: Baghdad to Istanbul. By William O. Douglas. 48-87, *Jan. 1959*

West from the Khyber Pass. By William O. Douglas. Photos by Mercedes H. Douglas and author. 1-44, *July 1958*

Flight to Adventure. By Tay and Lowell Thomas, Jr. 49-112, *July 1957*

❀ *Southeast Asia. Sept. 1955*

Our Navy in the Far East. By Arthur W. Radford. Photos by J. Baylor Roberts. 537-577, *Oct. 1953*

❀ *The Far East. Sept. 1952*

❀ *Southwest Asia, including India, Pakistan, and Northeast Africa. June 1952*

"Around the World in Eighty Days." By Newman Bumstead. Included: China, India, Iraq, Japan, Pakistan, Thailand, Turkey. 705-750, *Dec. 1951*

How Fruit Came to America. By J. R. Magness. Paintings by Else Bostelmann. Included: Two Stone Fruits from the Orient (Apricots, Japanese Plums); Plums and Prunes from Europe and West Asia. 325-377, *Sept. 1951*

❀ *Asia and Adjacent Areas. Mar. 1951*

Our Vegetable Travelers. By Victor R. Boswell. Paintings by Else Bostelmann. Included: Native vegetables from India and the Orient. 145-217, *Aug. 1949*

Cane Bridges of Asia. Photos from Paul Popper. 243-250, *Aug. 1948*

The World in Your Garden (Flowers). By W. H. Camp. Paintings by Else Bostelmann. Included: Native flower species from Southeastern Asia, China, and Japan. 1-65, *July 1947*

New Road to Asia (U.S.S.R.). By Owen Lattimore. 641-676, *Dec. 1944*

❀ *Southeast Asia and Pacific Islands from the Indies and the Philippines to the Solomons. Oct. 1944*

❀ *Japan and Adjacent Regions of Asia and the Pacific Ocean. Apr. 1944*

❀ *Asia and Adjacent Areas. Dec. 1942*

❀ *Theater of War in Europe, Africa, and Western Asia. July 1942*

❀ *Indian Ocean, including Australia, New Zealand and Malaysia. Mar. 1941*

Along the Old Silk Routes: A Motor Caravan with Air-conditioned Trailer Retraces Ancient Roads from Paris across Europe and Half of Asia to Delhi. By Lawrence Copley Thaw and Margaret S. Thaw. 453-486, *Oct. 1940*

With the Nomads of Central Asia: A Summer's Sojourn in the Tekes Valley, Plateau Paradise of Mongol and Turkic Tribes. By Edward Murray. Paintings and drawings by Alexandre Iacovleff. 1-57, *Jan. 1936*

❀ *Asia and Adjacent Regions. Dec. 1933*

From the Mediterranean to the Yellow Sea by Motor: The Citroën-Haardt Expedition Successfully Completes Its Dramatic Journey. By Maynard Owen Williams. 513-580, *Nov. 1932*

First Over the Roof of the World by Motor: The Trans-Asiatic Expedition Sets New Records for Wheeled Transport in Scaling Passes of the Himalayas. By Maynard Owen Williams. 321-363, *Mar. 1932*

The Citroën Trans-Asiatic Expedition Reaches Kashmir: Scientific Party Led by Georges-Marie Haardt Successfully Crosses Syria, Iraq, Persia, and Afghanistan to Arrive at the Pamir. By Maynard Owen Williams. 387-443, *Oct. 1931*

The Trans-Asiatic Expedition Starts. By Georges-Marie Haardt. 776-782, *June 1931*

On the World's Highest Plateaus: Through an Asiatic No Man's Land to the Desert of Ancient Cathay. By Hellmut de Terra. 319-367, *Mar. 1931*

❀ *Europe and the Near East. Dec. 1929*

The Desert Road to Turkestan: Twentieth Century Travel Through

Innermost Asia, Along Caravan Trails Over Which Oriental Commerce Was Once Borne from China to the Medieval Western World. By Owen Lattimore. 661-702, *June 1929*

The World's Greatest Overland Explorer: How Marco Polo Penetrated Farthest Asia, "Discovered" Many Lands Unknown to Europe, and Added Numerous Minerals, Animals, Birds, and Plants to Man's Knowledge. By J. R. Hildebrand. 505-568, *Nov. 1928*

Seeing the World from the Air. By Sir Alan J. Cobham. 349-384, *Mar. 1928*

By Coolie and Caravan Across Central Asia: Narrative of a 7,900-Mile Journey of Exploration and Research Over "the Roof of the World," from the Indian Ocean to the Yellow Sea. By William J. Morden. 369-431, *Oct. 1927*

From England to India by Automobile: An 8,527-mile Trip Through Ten Countries, from London to Quetta, Requires Five and a Half Months. By F.A.C. Forbes-Leith. 191-223, *Aug. 1925*

Adventures with a Camera in Many Lands. By Maynard Owen Williams. 87-112, *July 1921*

⊕ *Map of Asia and Adjoining Europe with a Portion of Africa. May 1921*

From London to Australia by Aëroplane: A Personal Narrative of the First Aërial Voyage Half Around the World. By Sir Ross Smith. 229-339, *Mar. 1921*

The Flags of Europe, Asia, and Africa. By Byron McCandless and Gilbert Grosvenor. 372-378, *Oct. 1917*

Prejudice in the Far East. By Melville E. Stone. 973-985, *Dec. 1910*

Commercial Prize of the Orient. By O. P. Austin. 399-423, *Sept. 1905*

⊕ *Kirin, Harbin, Vladivostok. June 1905*

Geographical Pivot of History (Steppes of Central Asia). By H. J. Mackinder. 331-335, *Aug. 1904*

Place Names in Eastern Asia. 136, *Mar. 1904*

Sven Hedin's Explorations in Central Asia. 393-395, *Nov. 1901*

Asia, the Cradle of Humanity. By W J McGee. 281-290, *Aug. 1901*

The Link Relations of Southwestern Asia. By Talcott Williams. 291-299, *Aug. 1901*

The Link Relations of Southwestern Asia. By Talcott Williams. 249-265, *July 1901*

⊕ *The Philippine Islands as the Geographical Center of the Far East. Jan. 1900*

The Great Unmapped Areas on the Earth's Surface Awaiting the Explorer and Geographer. By J. Scott Keltie. 251-266, *Sept. 1897*

Geographic Progress of Civilization. Annual Address by the President, Gardiner G. Hubbard. Included: Arabia; China; India; Mesopotamia; Persia; Syria. 1-22, *Feb. 14, 1894*

See also Afghanistan; Arabian Peninsula; Bahrain; Bali; Bangladesh; People's Republic of; Burma; China,

People's Republic of; Hong Kong; India; Indian Ocean; Indonesia; Iran; Iraq; Israel; Japan; Jordan; Kampuchea; Korea; Ladakh; Laos; Lebanon; Malaysia; Middle East; Mongolia; Nepal; Oman; Pakistan; Philippines; Saudi Arabia; Siberia; Sinai Peninsula; Singapore; Soviet Central Asia; Sri Lanka; Syria; Taiwan; Thailand; Tibet; Turkey; Union of Soviet Socialist Republics; Vietnam War; Yemen Arab Republic; *and* Himalaya; Holy Land; Karakoram Range; Mekong; Pacific Fleet, U. S.; Red Sea

ASIA MINOR:

Our Vegetable Travelers. By Victor R. Boswell. Paintings by Else Bostelmann. 145-217, *Aug. 1949*

Alert Anatolia. 481-492, *Apr. 1944*

Turkey, Where Earthquakes Followed Timur's Trail. Photos by Maynard Owen Williams. 395-406, *Mar. 1940*

Crossing Asia Minor, the Country of the New Turkish Republic. By Robert Whitney Imbrie. 445-472, *Oct. 1924*

East of Constantinople: Glimpses of Village Life in Anatolia, the Battleground of East and West, Where the Turks Reorganized Their Forces After the World War. By Melville Chater. 509-534, *May 1923*

A Sketch of the Geographical History of Asia Minor. By Sir William Ramsay. 553-570, *Nov. 1922*

Asia Minor in the Time of the Seven Wise Men. By Mary Mills Patrick. 47-67, *Jan. 1920*

The Cone-Dwellers of Asia Minor: A Primitive People Who Live in Nature-Made Apartment Houses, Fashioned by Volcanic Violence and Trickling Streams. By J. R. Sitlington Sterrett. 281-331, *Apr. 1919*

Peculiar Caves of Asia Minor. By Elizabeth H. Brewer. 870-875, *Sept. 1911*

The Fringe of Verdure Around Asia Minor. By Ellsworth Huntington. 761-775, *Sept. 1910*

Scenes in Asia Minor. 173-193, *Feb. 1909*

The Buried Cities of Asia Minor. By Ernest L. Harris. 1-18, *Jan. 1909*

Some Ruined Cities of Asia Minor. By Ernest L. Harris. 833-858, *Dec. 1908*

The Ruined Cities of Asia Minor. By Ernest L. Harris. 741-760, *Nov. 1908*

See also Turkey

ASIMOV, ISAAC: *Author*

Five Noted Thinkers Explore the Future. 72-73, *July 1976*

The Next Frontier? Paintings by Pierre Mion. 76-89, *July 1976*

ASKOLE, Pakistan:

Baltistan–The 20th Century Comes to Shangri-la. By Galen Rowell. Photos by the author and Barbara Cushman Rowell. Included: War among the peaks. 526-550, *Oct. 1987*

ASMAT TRIBESPEOPLE:

The Asmat of New Guinea, Headhunters in Today's World. By Malcolm S. Kirk. 376-409, *Mar. 1972*

Netherlands New Guinea: Bone of Contention in the South Pacific. By John Scofield. 584-603, *May 1962*

ASPEN, Colorado:

A Town...a Mountain...a Way of Life. By Jill Durrance and Dick Durrance II. 788-807, *Dec. 1973*

Colorado, the Rockies' Pot of Gold. By Edward J. Linehan. Photos by James L. Amos. 157-201, *Aug. 1969*

ASPHALT:

Happy-go-lucky Trinidad and Tobago. By Charles Allmon. 35-75, *Jan. 1953*

A proud grocer in Yerevan, capital of Soviet Armenia, sells pomegranates grown on small, private plots. HARRY N. NALTCHAYAN

ASQUITH, HERBERT HENRY:
Author
A Tribute to America. 295-296,
Apr. 1917

ASSAM (State), India:
Long Journey of the Brahmaputra. By
Jere Van Dyk. Photos by Raghubir
Singh and Galen Rowell. Included: A
Rare Visit to a World Unto Itself. By
Raghubir Singh. 672-711, *Nov. 1988*
Stalking the Great Indian Rhino. By
Lee Merriam Talbot. 389-398,
Mar. 1957
Caught in the Assam-Tibet Earthquake.
By F. Kingdon-Ward. 403-416,
Mar. 1952
Cane Bridges of Asia. Photos from Paul
Popper. 243-250, *Aug. 1948*
Stilwell Road–Land Route to China. By
Nelson Grant Tayman. 681-698,
June 1945
See also Naga Hills

ASSATEAGUE ISLAND, Maryland-
Virginia:
Chincoteague: Watermen's Island
Home. By Nathaniel T. Kenney.
Photos by James L. Amos. 810-829,
June 1980

ASSISI, Italy:
Inexhaustible Italy. By Arthur Stanley
Riggs. 273-368, *Oct. 1916*

An **ASSUMED** Inconstancy in the Level
of Lake Nicaragua; A Question of
Permanency of the Nicaragua Canal.
By C. Willard Hayes. 156-161,
Apr. 1900

ASSUMPTION ISLAND, Indian
Ocean:
Camera Under the Sea. By Luis Mar-
den. 162-200, *Feb. 1956*

ASSYRIA (Ancient Empire):
Ancient Mesopotamia: A Light That
Did Not Fail. By E. A. Speiser.
Paintings by H. M. Herget. 41-105,
Jan. 1951
The Cradle of Civilization: The Historic
Land Along the Euphrates and Tigris
Rivers Where Briton Is Fighting
Turk. By James Baikie. 127-162,
Feb. 1916
Pushing Back History's Horizon: How

the Pick and Shovel Are Revealing
Civilizations That Were Ancient
When Israel Was Young. By Albert
T. Clay. 162-216, *Feb. 1916*

ASTEROIDS:
Meteorites–Invaders From Space. By
Kenneth F. Weaver. Photos by Jona-
than Blair. 390-418, *Sept. 1986*
Voyage to the Planets. By Kenneth F.
Weaver. Paintings by Ludek Pesek.
147-193, *Aug. 1970*
Our Universe Unfolds New Wonders.
By Albert G. Wilson. 245-260,
Feb. 1952

ASTON, WILLIAM J.: *Author*
Midshipmen's Cruise. By William J. Aston and Alexander G. B. Grosvenor.
711-754, *June 1948*

The **ASTONISHING** Armadillo. By Eleanor E. Storrs. Photos by Bianca
Lavies. 820-830, *June 1982*

ASTRONAUTS:
Spacelab 1: *Columbia.* By Michael E.
Long. Included: John W. Young,
Brewster H. Shaw, Jr., Owen K.
Garriott, Robert A. R. Parker, By-
ron K. Lichtenberg, and Ulf Mer-
bold. 301-307, *Sept. 1983*
Columbia's Astronauts' Own Story:
Our Phenomenal First Flight. By
John W. Young and Robert L. Crip-
pen. Paintings by Ken Dallison. Con-
tents: The first flight in space shuttle
Columbia by John W. Young and
Robert L. Crippen; also included are
astronauts Joe H. Engle and Richard
H. Truly who will test *Columbia's*
second flight. 478-503, *Oct. 1981*

*Feeling right at home, the nine members
of Skylab's three crews gather in a train-
ing simulator of America's first space
station, launched in 1973. From left,
they are Capt. Alan L. Bean, USN; Maj.
Jack R. Lousma, USMC; Capt. Charles
Conrad, Jr., USN; Comdr. Paul J. Weitz,
USN; Comdr. Joseph P. Kerwin, M.D.,
USN; Lt. Col. Gerald P. Carr, USMC;
Edward G. Gibson, Ph.D.; Col. William
R. Pogue, USAF; and Owen K. Garriott,
Ph.D.*   MICHAEL LAWTON

Columbia's Landing Closes a Circle. By
Tom Wolfe. Contents: John W.
Young and Robert L. Crippen return
the first space shuttle to Edwards Air
Force Base in California. 474-477,
Oct. 1981
When the Space Shuttle Finally Flies.
By Rick Gore. Photos by Jon Schnee-
berger. Paintings by Ken Dallison.
Included: Vance Brand, Dan Bran-
denstein, Robert L. Crippen, Anna
Fisher, Gordon Fullerton, Michael
Lampton, Byron Lichtenberg, Shan-
non Lucid, Judith Resnik, Sally Ride,
Rhea Seddon, Donald K. "Deke"
Slayton, Kathryn Sullivan, Richard
H. Truly, John W. Young, and Euro-
peans Wubbo Ockels, Ulf Merbold,
and Claude Nicollier. 317-347,
Mar. 1981
Apollo-Soyuz: Handclasp in Space. By
Thomas Y. Canby. Included: Ameri-
can astronauts Thomas P. Stafford,
Vance D. Brand, and Donald K.
"Deke" Slayton and Soviet cosmo-
nauts Aleksey A. Leonov and Va-
leriy Kubasov. 183-187, *Feb. 1976*
■ *Man's Conquest of Space.* By William
R. Shelton. 199 pages. 1968; rev. ed.
1975
Skylab. Photos by the nine mission as-
tronauts. Contents: The flights of
three Skylab crews: Charles "Pete"
Conrad, Jr., Joseph P. Kerwin, and
Paul J. Weitz; Alan L. Bean, Owen
K. Garriott, and Jack R. Lousma;
Gerald P. Carr, Edward G. Gibson,
and William R. Pogue. 441-503. I.
Outpost in Space. By Thomas Y.
Canby. 441-469; II. Its View of
Earth. 471-493; III. The Sun Un-
veiled. By Edward G. Gibson. 494-
503, *Oct. 1974*
Exploring Taurus-Littrow. By Harrison
H. Schmitt. Photos by the crew of
Apollo 17. Contents: Harrison H.
Schmitt and Eugene A. Cernan land-
ed on the moon in *Challenger*, while
Ronald E. Evans orbited in com-
mand module *America.* 290-307,
Sept. 1973
What Is It Like to Walk on the Moon?
By David R. Scott. Included: David
R. Scott, James B. Irwin, Harrison
H. Schmitt, and Eugene A. Cernan.
326-331, *Sept. 1973*

ASTRONOMY:

ASTRONOMY, Ancient:

ASTROPHYSICS:

After splashdown of the first U.S. manned space flight on May 5, 1961, the aircraft carrier **Lake Champlain** *picks up pilot Alan B. Shepard and* **Freedom 7.** DEAN CONGER, NGS

Its tail streaming, comet Morehouse streaks through the heavens in 1908. During observation the tail broke into fragments several times .   YERKES OBSERVATORY

Visitors to Atlantic City around 1920 stroll along the Boardwalk and crowd the beach of the New Jersey resort.   WILLIAM H. RAU

Tim Kollman gets a warm welcome home in Charleston, South Carolina, a major Atlantic coast naval base. ANNIE GRIFFITHS BELT

I Sailed with Portugal's Captains Courageous. By Alan Villiers. 565-596, *May 1952*

Midshipmen's Cruise. By William J. Aston and Alexander G. B. Grosvenor. 711-754, *June 1948*

Our Transatlantic Flight. By Richard Evelyn Byrd. 347-368, *Sept. 1927*

ATLANTIC SALMON:

Atlantic Salmon: The "Leaper" Struggles to Survive. By Art Lee. Photos by Bianca Lavies. 600-615, *Nov. 1981*

ATLANTIS I (Submersible):

Down the Cayman Wall. By Eugenie Clark. Included: Zones of Life. NGS research grant. 712-731, *Nov. 1988*

ATLAS MOUNTAINS, North Africa:

Beyond the Grand Atlas: Where the French Tricolor Flies Beside the Flag of the Sultan of Morocco. By V. C. Scott O'Connor. 261-319, *Mar. 1932*
See also High Atlas

An **ATLAS** of Energy Resources. Contents: Maps locating major resources of oil, natural gas, coal, geothermal energy, uranium, and solar energy in North America. 58-69, *Special Report on Energy. (Feb. 1981)*

ATLASES, NGS:

North America
▦ *Atlas of North America: Space Age Portrait of a Continent.* 264 pages. *1985*

United States
▦ *Historical Atlas of the United States.* 289 pages. *1988*
▦ *The Story of America: A National Geographic Picture Atlas.* By John Anthony Scott. Juvenile. 324 pages. *1984*
▦ *National Geographic Picture Atlas of Our Fifty States.* Included: Pertinent information about the geography, climate, and population of each state. Juvenile. 304 pages. *1978*

The Geologic Atlas of the United States. By W J McGee. 339-342, *July 1898*

The Topographic Atlas of the United States. By W J McGee. 343-344, *July 1898*

Universe
▦ *National Geographic Picture Atlas of Our Universe.* By Roy A. Gallant. Juvenile. 284 pages. 1980; rev. ed. *1986*

World
▦ *Peoples and Places of the Past: The National Geographic Illustrated Cultural Atlas of the Ancient World.* 424 pages. *1983*
▦ *Atlas of the World.* 383 pages. 1963; fifth ed. *1981*
▦ *National Geographic Picture Atlas of Our World.* Juvenile. 312 pages. *1979*
Microfilmed copy placed in Time Capsule, New York World's Fair, 1964-65. 525, *Apr. 1965*

ATMOSPHERE:

Air: An Atmosphere of Uncertainty. By Noel Grove. Photos by Ted Spiegel. Paintings by William H. Bond. Included: A Deadly soup (a list of harmful chemicals), Careless neighbors, A global greenhouse, The ozone enigma, Getting the lead out, The enemy within. 502-537, *Apr. 1987*

ATOCHA (Galleon):

Treasure From the Ghost Galleon: *Santa Margarita.* By Eugene Lyon. Photos by Don Kincaid. 228-243, *Feb. 1982*
▨ Treasure! 575, Nov. 1976; cover, *Dec. 1976*
Atocha, Tragic Treasure Galleon of the Florida Keys. By Eugene Lyon. 787-809, *June 1976*

ATOM:

Worlds Within the Atom. By John Boslough. Photos by Kevin Fleming. Illustrations text by David Jeffery. Included: A Particle Factory: Tevatron; Search for the Atom. Paintings by Barron Storey; Inside the Atom: An Outbreak of Quarks; A Unification of Forces; Applications for the Future. 634-663, *May 1985*

You and the Obedient Atom. By Allan C. Fisher, Jr. 303-353, *Sept. 1958*

Man's New Servant, the Friendly Atom. By F. Barrows Colton. Photos by Volkmar Wentzel. 71-90, *Jan. 1954*
See also Cosmic Rays

The **ATOMIC** Age: Its Problems and Promises. By Frank Freidel. 66-119, *Jan. 1966*

ATOMIC BOMB TESTS:

Bikini–A Way of Life Lost. By William S. Ellis. Photos by James P. Blair. 813-834, *June 1986*

Nevada Learns to Live with the Atom. By Samuel W. Matthews. 839-850, *June 1953*

Operation Crossroads. Photos by Joint Task Force I. Paintings by Charles Bittinger. 519-530, *Apr. 1947*

Farewell to Bikini. By Carl Markwith. 97-116, *July 1946*

Air Power for Peace. By H. H. Arnold. 137-193, *Feb. 1946*

ATOMIC ENERGY. *See* Nuclear Energy

ATREVIDA GLACIER, Alaska:

The National Geographic Society's Alaskan Expedition of 1909. By Ralph S. Tarr and Lawrence Martin. 1-54, *Jan. 1910*

ATTA ANTS:

Color Glows in the Guianas, French and Dutch. By Nicol Smith. 459-480, *Apr. 1943*

ATTAR OF ROSES:

Bulgaria's Valley of Roses. Photos by Wilhelm Tobien and Georg Paskoff. 187-194, *Aug. 1932*

ATTENBOROUGH, DAVID:
Author-Photographer

Animal Safari to British Guiana. Photos by Charles Lagus and author. 851-874, *June 1957*

ATWOOD, ALBERT W.: *Author*

Census 1960: Profile of the Nation. By Albert W. Atwood and Lonnelle Aikman. 697-714, *Nov. 1959*

Immigrants Still Flock to Liberty's Land. 708-724, *Nov. 1955*

Stately Homes of Old Virginia. 787-802, *June 1953*

Across the Potomac from Washington. 1-33, *Jan. 1953*

Today on the Delaware, Penn's Glorious River. Photos by Robert F. Sisson. 1-40, *July 1952*

The Eternal Flame. 540-564, *Oct. 1951*

The Merrimack: River of Industry and Romance. Photos by B. Anthony Stewart. 106-140, *Jan. 1951*

The Nation's Library (Library of Congress). 663-684, *May 1950*

Leather boat named for St. Brendan took explorer Timothy Severin from Ireland to Newfoundland in 1976-77, proving that the Irish saint could have done the same. NATHAN BENN

Atom bomb blasts Nagasaki, Japan, on August 9, 1945, signaling the end of World War II. U.S. ARMY AIR FORCES, OFFICIAL

Gilbert Grosvenor's Golden Jubilee. 253-261, *Aug. 1949*

Pittsburgh: Workshop of the Titans. 117-144, *July 1949*

The Fire of Heaven: Electricity Revolutionizes the Modern World. 655-674, *Nov. 1948*

The Mighty Hudson. Photos by B. Anthony Stewart. 1-36, *July 1948*

Washington: Home of the Nation's Great. 699-738, *June 1947*

Steel: Master of Them All. Photos by Willard R. Culver. 415-452, *Apr. 1947*

Northeast of Boston. 257-292, *Sept. 1945*

Potomac, River of Destiny. 33-70, *July 1945*

Coal: Prodigious Worker for Man. 569-592, *May 1944*

The Healing Arts in Global War: As Weapons Grow Deadlier, Scientific Medicine Pits Its Ever-rising Skill Against Them. 599-618, *Nov. 1943*

Revealing Earth's Mightiest Ocean (Pacific). 291-306, *Sept. 1943*

The Long River of New England: In War and Peace, from Mountain Wilderness to the Sea, Flows the Connecticut River, Through a Valley Abounding in History, Scenery, Inventive Genius, and Industry. 401-434, *Apr. 1943*

The Miracle of War Production: For Victory the United States Transforms Its Complex Industry into the Biggest Factory and Mightiest Arsenal the World Has Ever Known. Paintings by Thornton Oakley. 693-715, *Dec. 1942*

Tidewater Virginia, Where History Lives. 617-656, *May 1942*

Washington–Storehouse of Knowledge. 325-359, *Mar. 1942*

ATWOOD, WALLACE W., Jr.: *Author*

Crater Lake and Yosemite Through the Ages. Paintings by Eugene Kingman. 327-343, *Mar. 1937*

AUCKLAND, New Zealand:

New Zealand: the Last Utopia? By Robert Paul Jordan. Photos by Kevin Fleming. 654-681, *May 1987*

New Zealand: Gift of the Sea. By Maurice Shadbolt. Photos by Brian Brake. 465-511, *Apr. 1962*

New Zealand, Pocket Wonder World. By Howell Walker. 419-460, *Apr. 1952*

AUDUBON, JOHN JAMES:

Audubon "On the Wing." By David Jeffery. Photos by Bates Littlehales. 149-177, *Feb. 1977*

Blizzard of Birds: The Tortugas Terns. By Alexander Sprunt, Jr. 213-230, *Feb. 1947*

An **AUGUST** First in Gruyères (Switzerland). By Melville Bell Grosvenor. 137-168, *Aug. 1936*

AUGUSTA NATURAL BRIDGE, Utah:

Colossal Natural Bridges of Utah. 367-369, *Sept. 1904*

AUGUSTUS–Emperor and Architect: Two Thousand Years Ago Was Born the Physically Frail But Spiritually Great Roman Who Became the Master of His World. By W. Coleman Nevils. 535-556, *Oct. 1938*

AUJOULAT, NORBERT: *Photographer*

Art Treasures from the Ice Age: Lascaux Cave. By Jean-Philippe Rigaud. Photos by Sisse Brimberg and Norbert Aujoulat. 482-499, *Oct. 1988*

AUKLETS:

Birds of the Northern Seas. By Alexander Wetmore. Paintings by Allan Brooks. Included: Auks and Their Northland Neighbors. 95-122, *Jan. 1936*

AUKS:

Birds of the Northern Seas. By Alexander Wetmore. Paintings by Allan Brooks. Included: Auks and Their Northland Neighbors. 95-122, *Jan. 1936*

AULT, J. P.: *Author*

Sailing the Seven Seas in the Interest of Science: Adventures Through 157,000 Miles of Storm and Calm, from Arctic to Antarctic and Around the World, in the Non-magnetic Yacht "Carnegie." 631-690, *Dec. 1922*

AURANGZEB:

When the Moguls Ruled India. By Mike Edwards. Photos by Roland Michaud. 463-493, *Apr. 1985*

AURIFEROUS SANDS:

Report on Auriferous Sands from Yakutat Bay (Alaska). By J. Stanley-Brown. 196-198, *May 29, 1891*

AURNESS, CRAIG: *Photographer*

California Desert, A Worldly Wilderness. By Barry Lopez. 42-77, *Jan. 1987*

Colorado Dreaming. By Mike Edwards. 186-219, *Aug. 1984*

East of Eden–California's Mid-coast. By Harvey Arden. 424-461, *Apr. 1984*

The Troubled Waters of Mono Lake. By Gordon Young. 504-519, *Oct. 1981*

Iowa, America's Middle Earth. By Harvey Arden. 603-629, *May 1981*

The Pony Express. By Rowe Findley. 45-71, *July 1980*

The People Who Made Saskatchewan. By Ethel A. Starbird. 651-679, *May 1979*

New Mexico's Mountains of Mystery. By Robert Laxalt. 416-436, *Sept. 1978*

AURORA BOREALIS:

Unlocking Secrets of the Northern Lights. By Carl W. Gartlein. Paintings by William Crowder. Included: Descriptions and photos of twelve forms of auroras. NGS research grant. 673-704, *Nov. 1947*

Aurora Borealis: Research under the auspices of the National Geographic Society and Cornell University. 580, May 1941; 640, Nov. 1944; 387, *Sept. 1946*

The Mystery of Auroras: National Geographic Society and Cornell University Study Spectacular Displays in the Heavens. 689-690, *May 1939*

The Northern Lights. By Alice Rollins Crane. 69, *Feb. 1901*

AUSLANDER, MARC:

On Assignment. *Nov. 1986*

AUSTEN, DAVID ROBERT:

On Assignment in Australia. *Feb. 1988*

On Assignment in Australia. *Jan. 1986*

On Assignment in Papua New Guinea. *Aug. 1982*

Photographer

Australia at 200. By Ross Terrill. 181-211, *Feb. 1988*

Queensland, Broad Shoulder of Australia. By William S. Ellis. Included: Queensland Fossils Expand Australia's Prehistoric Menagerie. 2-39, *Jan. 1986*

The Land Where the Murray Flows. By Louise E. Levathes. 252-278, *Aug. 1985*

Across Australia by Sunpower. By Hans Tholstrup and Larry Perkins. 600-607, *Nov. 1983*

Papua New Guinea. By Robert J. Gordon and François Leydet. 143-171, *Aug. 1982*

AUSTIN, BARBARA: *Author*

A Paradise Called the Palouse. Photos by Phil Schofield. Included: The farmland hill country of Idaho and Washington. 798-819, *June 1982*

AUSTIN, O. P.:

Reports by. 87, Feb. 1905; 88-89, Jan. 1910; 211, 214, Feb. 1911; 255, *Feb. 1913*

National Geographic Society (O. P. Austin Elected Secretary). 425, *Nov. 1903*

Author

The Remarkable Growth of Europe During 40 Years of Peace. 272-274, *Sept. 1914*

The Probable Effect of the Panama Canal on the Commercial Geography of the World. 245-248, *Feb. 1914*

Progress of the National Geographic Society. 251-256, *Feb. 1913*

Queer Methods of Travel in Curious Corners of the World. 687-715, *Nov. 1907*

Commercial Prize of the Orient. 399-423, *Sept. 1905*

The United States: Her Industries. 301-320, *Aug. 1903*

Problems of the Pacific–The Commerce of the Great Ocean. 303-318, *Aug. 1902*

Commerce of Mexico and the United States. 25-26, *Jan. 1902*

An Around-the-World American Exposition. 49-53, *Feb. 1901*

Our New Possessions and the Interest They Are Exciting. 32-33, *Jan. 1900*

The Commercial Development of Japan. 329-337, *Sept. 1899*

The Commercial Importance of Samoa. 218-220, *June 1899*

Colonial Systems of the World. 21-26, *Jan. 1899*

AUSTRALASIA:

Treasure Islands of Australasia: New Guinea, New Caledonia, and Fiji Trace across the South Pacific a Fertile Crescent Incredibly Rich in Minerals and Foods. By Douglas L. Oliver. 691-722, *June 1942*

See also Australia; New Guinea; New Zealand; *and* adjacent islands

AUSTRALIA:

Australia. 155-294. Editorial. 156; Portraits of the Land. 157-169; Child of Gondwana. By Joseph Judge. 170-177; Australia at 200. By Ross Terrill. Photos by David Robert Austen. 181-211; Australians. Photos by Michael O'Brien. Picture text by Elizabeth A. Moize. Text by Joseph Judge. 213-231; Children of the First Fleet. By John Everingham. Painting by Roy Andersen. 233-245; Sydney's Changing Face. Photos by Mary Ellen Mark. Introduction by Elizabeth A. Moize. 246-265; The First Australians. By Stanley Breeden. Photos by Belinda Wright. 266-289; The First Australians: Living in Two Worlds. By Belinda Wright and Stanley Breeden. 291-294, *Feb. 1988*

⊕ *A Traveler's Look at Australia; Australia's Continental Odyssey. Feb. 1988*

▨ Twilight of the Dreamtime. 270, cover, *Feb. 1988*

On Assignment. *Feb. 1988*

Australia's Southern Seas. By Richard Ellis. Photos by David Doubilet. 286-319, *Mar. 1987*

The Royal Spoonbill. By M. Philip Kahl. NGS research grant. 281-284, *Feb. 1987*

The Tea and Sugar Lifeline in Australia's Outback. By Erla Zwingle. Photos by William Albert Allard. 737-757, *June 1986*

Queensland, Broad Shoulder of Australia. By William S. Ellis. Photos by David Robert Austen. Included: Queensland Fossils Expand Australia's Prehistoric Menagerie. 2-39, *Jan. 1986*

On Assignment. *Jan. 1986*

Wreck of H.M.S. *Pandora*. By Luis Marden. 423-451, *Oct. 1985*

The Land Where the Murray Flows. By Louise E. Levathes. Photos by David Robert Austen. 252-278, *Aug. 1985*

Monsoons: Life Breath of Half the World. By Priit J. Vesilind. Photos by Steve McCurry. 712-747, *Dec. 1984*

El Niño's Ill Wind. By Thomas Y. Canby. Included: Drought, dust storms, bushfires, and floods caused by El Niño current. 144-183, *Feb. 1984*

Exploring a Sunken Realm in Australia. By Hillary Hauser. Photos by David Doubilet. 129-142, *Jan. 1984*

▥▥ *Amazing Animals of Australia.* Juvenile. 104 pages. *1984*

Across Australia by Sunpower. By Hans Tholstrup and Larry Perkins. Photos by David Austen. 600-607, *Nov. 1983*

▨ Australia's Animal Mysteries. 824, Dec. 1982; cover, *Feb. 1983*

Australia's Great Barrier Reef. 630-663. I. A Marine Park Is Born. By Soames Summerhays. Photos by Ron and Valerie Taylor. 630-635; II. Paradise Beneath the Sea. By Ron and Valerie Taylor. 636-663, *May 1981*

A Jawbreaker for Sharks. By Valerie Taylor. 664-667, *May 1981*

The Desert: An Age-old Challenge Grows. By Rick Gore. Photos by

Georg Gerster and Bruce Dale. 586-639, *Nov. 1979*

Skylab's Fiery Finish. By Tom Riggert. 581-584, *Oct. 1979*

The Journey of Burke and Wills. By Joseph Judge. Photos by Joseph J. Scherschel. 152-191, *Feb. 1979*

Those Kangaroos! They're a Marvelous Mob. By Geoffrey B. Sharman. Photos by Des and Jen Bartlett. 192-209, *Feb. 1979*

Sydney: Big, Breezy, and a Bloomin' Good Show. By Ethel A. Starbird. Photos by Robert W. Madden. 211-235, *Feb. 1979*

⊕ *Australia; Land of Living Fossils. Feb. 1979*

Alone Across the Outback. By Robyn Davidson. Photos by Rick Smolan. 581-611, *May 1978*

A Bad Time to Be a Crocodile. By Rick Gore. Photos by Jonathan Blair. 90-115, *Jan. 1978*

The Satin Bowerbird, Australia's Feathered Playboy. By Philip Green. 865-872, *Dec. 1977*

Australia's Bizarre Wild Flowers. By Paul A. Zahl. 858-868, *Dec. 1976*

Captain Cook: The Man Who Mapped the Pacific. By Alan Villiers. Photos by Gordon W. Gahan. 297-349, *Sept. 1971*

In the Wake of Darwin's *Beagle*. By Alan Villiers. Photos by James L. Stanfield. 449-495, *Oct. 1969*

▨ Australia: The Timeless Land. 300A-300B, *Feb. 1969*

▥▥ *Australia.* 219 pages. *1968*

Australia. By Alan Villiers. 309-385. I. The West and the South. 309-345; II. The Settled East, the Barrier Reef, the Center. 347-385, *Sept. 1963*

Strange Animals of Australia. By David Fleay. Photos by Stanley Breeden. 388-411, *Sept. 1963*

⊕ *Australia,* Atlas series. *Sept. 1963*

Australia's Amazing Bowerbirds. By Norman Chaffer. 866-873, *Dec. 1961*

Flight of the Platypuses. By David Fleay. 512-525, *Oct. 1958*

Off the Beaten Track of Empire (Prince Philip's Tour). By Beverley M. Bowie. Photos by Michael Parker. 584-626, *Nov. 1957*

Expedition to the Land of the Tiwi. By Charles P. Mountford. NGS research grant. 417-440, *Mar. 1956*

The Making of a New Australia. By Howell Walker. 233-259, *Feb. 1956*

Arnhem Land Expedition of 1948. NGS research grant. 430, *Mar. 1948*

⊕ *Australia. Mar. 1948*

The World in Your Garden (Flowers). By W. H. Camp. Paintings by Else Bostelmann. Included: Australian Plants and Geography (Eucalyptus or Gum-tree, Bottle-brush, Strawflower, Swan River Daisy, Blue laceflower). 1-65, *July 1947*

Earth's Most Primitive People: A Journey with the Aborigines of Central Australia. By Charles P. Mountford. Included: Australia's Stone Age Men. 89-112, *Jan. 1946*

The Fairy Wrens of Australia: The Little Longtailed "Blue Birds of Happiness" Rank High Among the Island

With four camels and a dog, Robyn Davidson traverses 1,700 miles of Australia's wild outback. RICK SMOLAN

AUSTRALIANS. Photos by Michael O'Brien. Picture text by Elizabeth A. Moize. Text by Joseph Judge. 213-231, *Feb. 1988*

Standing outside the house she has lived in for 60 years, Maude Trenaman watches the sky over Meekatharra, Western Australia. MICHAEL O'BRIEN

*An **Australopithecus africanus** female, who lived perhaps 2.5 to 3 million years ago, digs tubers for a meal; a male pulls edible ant galls from a thorn.* PAINTING BY © JAY H. MATTERNES

Autumn foliage adorns the outdoor living room of campers in Great Smoky Mountains National Park, visited by about 12 million people each year. DAVID ALAN HARVEY

Crippen. Paintings by Ken Dallison. 478-503, *Oct. 1981*

When the Space Shuttle Finally Flies. By Rick Gore. Photos by Jon Schneeberger. Paintings by Ken Dallison. Contents: The space shuttle *Columbia* will be joined by *Challenger, Discovery,* and *Atlantis.* 317-347, *Mar. 1981*

They're Redesigning the Airplane. By Michael E. Long. Photos by James A. Sugar. 76-103, *Jan. 1981*

Of Air and Space (National Air and Space Museum). By Michael Collins. Included: Picture portfolio by Nathan Benn, Robert S. Oakes, and Joseph D. Lavenburg, with text by Michael E. Long. 819-837, *June 1978*

The Air-Safety Challenge. By Michael E. Long. Photos by Bruce Dale. 209-235, *Aug. 1977*

Happy Birthday, Otto Lilienthal! By Russell Hawkes. Photos by James Collison. 286-292, *Feb. 1972*

World War I Aircraft Fly Again in Rhinebeck's Rickety Rendezvous. By Harvey Arden. Photos by Howard Sochurek. 578-587, *Oct. 1970*

The Coming Revolution in Transportation. By Fredric C. Appel. Photos by Dean Conger. 301-341, *Sept. 1969*

National Geographic Society Honors Air Pioneer Juan Trippe. 584-586, *Apr. 1968*

Sailors of the Sky. By Gordon Young. Photos by Emory Kristof and Jack Fields. Paintings by Davis Meltzer. 49-73, *Jan. 1967*

Of Planes and Men. By Kenneth F. Weaver. Photos by Emory Kristof and Albert Moldvay. 298-349, *Sept. 1965*

The Gooney Birds of Midway. By John W. Aldrich. 839-851, *June 1964*

First Flight Across the Bottom of the World. By James R. Reedy. Photos by Otis Imboden. 454-464, *Mar. 1964*

I Fly the X-15. By Joseph A. Walker. Photos by Dean Conger. 428-450, *Sept. 1962*

Sailors in the Sky: Fifty Years of Naval Aviation. By Patrick N. L. Bellinger. 276-296, *Aug. 1961*

You and the Obedient Atom. By Allan C. Fisher, Jr. Photos by B. Anthony Stewart and Thomas J. Abercrombie. Included: Nuclear aircraft. 303-353, *Sept. 1958*

MATS: America's Long Arm of the Air. By Beverley M. Bowie. Photos by Robert F. Sisson. 283-317, *Mar. 1957*

Charting Our Sea and Air Lanes (U. S. Coast and Geodetic Survey). By Stuart E. Jones. Photos by J. Baylor Roberts. 189-209, *Feb. 1957*

Alexander Graham Bell Museum: Tribute to Genius. By Jean Lesage. 227-256, *Aug. 1956*

Aviation Looks Ahead on Its 50th Birthday. By Emory S. Land. 721-739, *Dec. 1953*

Fact Finding for Tomorrow's Planes. By Hugh L. Dryden. Photos by Luis Marden. 757-780, *Dec. 1953*

Fifty Years of Flight. 740-756, *Dec. 1953*

Flying in the "Blowtorch" Era. By Frederick G. Vosburgh. 281-322, *Sept. 1950*

Skyway Below the Clouds. By Carl R. Markwith. Photos by Ernest J. Cottrell. 85-108, *July 1949*

Our Air Age Speeds Ahead. By F. Barrows Colton. 249-272, *Feb. 1948*

Aviation in Commerce and Defense. By F. Barrows Colton. 685-726, *Dec. 1940*

See also Aeronautics; Aircraft Carriers; Balloons; Civil Air Patrol; Experimental Aircraft; Helicopters; Parachute Jumps; Parachute Rigger School; Recreational Aircraft; Space Shuttles; Ultralight Aircraft; U. S. Air Force

AVIATION CADETS, U. S. Navy:

Pocket Carriers Fight the Submarines. U. S. Navy official photos. 521-544, *Nov. 1943*

AVIATION MEDICINE:

Aviation Medicine on the Threshold of Space. By Allan C. Fisher, Jr. Photos by Luis Marden. 241-278, *Aug. 1955*

Our Air Age Speeds Ahead. By F. Barrows Colton. 249-272, *Feb. 1948*

New Frontier in the Sky. By F. Barrows Colton. 379-408, *Sept. 1946*

Flying Our Wounded Veterans Home. By Catherine Bell Palmer. 363-384, *Sept. 1945*

The Healing Arts in Global War: As Weapons Grow Deadlier, Scientific Medicine Pits Its Ever-rising Skill Against Them. By Albert W. Atwood. 599-618, *Nov. 1943*

See also Military Air Transport Service; Space Medicine; *Strato-Lab*

AVIATORS. *See* Aeronautics

AVOCET (Ship):

Eclipse Adventures on a Desert Isle (Canton). By J. F. Hellweg. 377-394, *Sept. 1937*

Flensers cut apart a sperm whale in the Azores, where islanders still hunt whales with hand harpoons. O. LOUIS MAZZATENTA, NGS

AVON (River), England:

Through the Heart of England in a Canadian Canoe. By R. J. Evans. 473-497, *May 1922*

An **AWAKENED** Continent to the South of Us. By Elihu Root. 61-72, *Jan. 1907*

The **AWAKENING** of Argentina and Chile: Progress in the Lands That Lie Below Capricorn. By Bailey Willis. 121-142, *Aug. 1916*

AWASH in Change: North Carolina's Outer Banks. By Charles E. Cobb, Jr. Photos by David Alan Harvey. Included: Impressions of an early visitor (1580s); Sea currents shape the Outer Banks. 484-513, *Oct. 1987*

The **AWE-INSPIRING** Spectacle of the Valley of Ten Thousand Smokes, Discovered and Explored by National Geographic Society Expeditions. Panorama. *Feb. 1918*

AWESOME Views of the Forbidding Moonscape. 233-239, *Feb. 1969*

The **AWESOME** Worlds Within a Cell. By Rick Gore. Photos by Bruce Dale. Paintings by Davis Meltzer. 355-395, *Sept. 1976*

AXSON, STOCKTON: *Author*

The Symbol of Service to Mankind (American National Red Cross). 375-390, *Apr. 1918*

AYATOLLAH KHOMEINI:

Iran Under the Ayatollah. By Michael Coyne. 108-135, *July 1985*

AYERS ROCK, Australia:

Earth's Most Primitive People: A Journey with the Aborigines of Central Australia. By Charles P. Mountford. 89-112, *Jan. 1946*

AYMARÁS:

The Lost Empire of the Incas. By Loren McIntyre. Art by Ned and Rosalie Seidler. 729-787, *Dec. 1973*

Titicaca, Abode of the Sun. By Luis Marden. Photos by Flip Schulke. 272-294, *Feb. 1971*

Flamboyant Is the Word for Bolivia. By Loren McIntyre. 153-195, *Feb. 1966*

At Home in the High Andes. By Harry Tschopik, Jr. 133-146, *Jan. 1955*

Puya, the Pineapple's Andean Ancestor. By Mulford B. Foster. 463-480, *Oct. 1950*

The Heart of Aymará Land: A Visit to Tiahuanacu, Perhaps the Oldest City of the New World, Lost Beneath the Drifting Sand of Centuries in the Bolivian Highlands. By Stewart E. McMillin. 213-256, *Feb. 1927*

AZALEAS:

Nautical Norfolk Turns to Azaleas. By William H. Nicholas. Photos by B. Anthony Stewart. 606-614, *May 1947*

AZERBAIJAN S.S.R., U.S.S.R.:

Russia's Orphan Races: Picturesque Peoples Who Cluster on the Southeastern Borderland of the Vast Slav Dominions. By Maynard Owen Williams. 245-278, *Oct. 1918*

Boatman punts past agricultural islands, called **chinampas,** *in the floating gardens of Xochimilco outside Mexico City.* DAVID HISER

Olive baboons that range grassland and scrubland near Gilgil, Kenya, inspect an equally curious domestic feline. TIMOTHY W. RANSOM

B-17 (Flying Fortress Bomber):
8th Air Force in England. U. S. Army Air Forces official photos. 297-304, *Mar. 1945*
American Bombers Attacking from Australia. By Howell Walker. 49-70, *Jan. 1943*

B-24 (Liberator Bomber):
8th Air Force in England. Photos from U. S. Army Air Forces. 297-304, *Mar. 1945*

B-26 (Marauder Bomber):
Return to Florence. By Benjamin C. McCartney. 257-296, *Mar. 1945*

B-36 (Jet Bomber):
Flying in the "Blowtorch" Era. By Frederick G. Vosburgh. 281-322, *Sept. 1950*

B-50 (Superfortress Bomber):
Flying in the "Blowtorch" Era. By Frederick G. Vosburgh. 281-322, *Sept. 1950*
Operation Eclipse: 1948. By William A. Kinney. NGS research grant. 325-372, *Mar. 1949*

BB (Boat):
Experimental boat of Dr. Alexander Graham Bell, driven by aërial propellers. 671, *Oct. 1907*

BAALBEK, Lebanon:
Journey Into the Great Rift: the Northern Half. By Helen and Frank Schreider. 254-290, *Aug. 1965*
Young-old Lebanon Lives by Trade. By

Thomas J. Abercrombie. 479-523, *Apr. 1958*
From Jerusalem to Aleppo. By John D. Whiting. 71-113, *Jan. 1913*

BABB, CYRUS C.:
Secretary. ii, xvii, May 5, 1894; ii, *Oct. 31, 1895*
Report. xx-xxi, *May 5, 1894*
Author
A Relic of the Lewis and Clarke Expedition. 100-101, *Mar. 1898*
Geographic Notes. Included: The Antarctic Continent; Magnetic Observations in Iceland, Jan Mayen and Spitzbergen in 1892; A New Light on the Discovery of America; Monographs of the National Geographic Society; Important Announcement Concerning Essays. 217-228, *Dec. 29, 1894*

BABB, LAURA LONGLEY: *Author*
Iowa's Enduring Amana Colonies. Photos by Steve Raymer. 863-878, *Dec. 1975*

BABBLERS (Birds). *See* Spiny Babbler

BABCOCK, RICHARD F.: *Author*
Five Noted Thinkers Explore the Future. 70-71, *July 1976*

"BABES in the Wood." Pictorial supplement of bears, *Aug. 1917*

BABOONS:
The "Gang" Moves to a Strange New Land. By Shirley C. Strum. Note: The baboons of the "Pumphouse

Gang" are translocated in Kenya. NGS research grant. 676-690, *Nov. 1987*
Life with the "Pumphouse Gang": New Insights Into Baboon Behavior. By Shirley C. Strum. Photos by Timothy W. Ransom. 672-691, *May 1975*

BABUR:
When the Moguls Ruled India. By Mike Edwards. Photos by Roland Michaud. 463-493, *Apr. 1985*

BABYLONIA:
Ancient Mesopotamia: A Light That Did Not Fail. By E. A. Speiser. Paintings by H. M. Herget. 41-105, *Jan. 1951*
New Light on Ancient Ur: Excavations at the Site of the City of Abraham Reveal Geographical Evidence of the Biblical Story of the Flood. By M.E.L. Mallowan. 95-130, *Jan. 1930*
The Cradle of Civilization: The Historic Lands Along the Euphrates and Tigris Rivers Where Briton Is Fighting Turk. By James Baikie. 127-162, *Feb. 1916*
Pushing Back History's Horizon: How the Pick and Shovel Are Revealing Civilizations That Were Ancient When Israel Was Young. By Albert T. Clay. 162-216, *Feb. 1916*
Where Adam and Eve Lived. By Frederick and Margaret Simpich. 546-588, *Dec. 1914*
The Most Historic Lands on Earth. 615, *Dec. 1914*
Excavations at Nippur. 392, *Oct. 1900*

BACK to Afghanistan. By Maynard Owen Williams. 517-544, *Oct. 1946*

BACK to the Historic Black Hills. By Leland D. Case. Photos by Bates Littlehales. 479-509, *Oct. 1956*

BACK-YARD Monsters in Color. By Paul A. Zahl. 235-260, *Aug. 1952*

BACKER, OLE FRIELE:
Author-Photographer
Seal Hunting Off Jan Mayen. 57-72, *Jan. 1948*
Photographer
Norway Cracks Her Mountain Shell. By Sydney Clark. Photos by Gilbert Grosvenor and Ole Friele Backer. 171-211, *Aug. 1948*

BACKER, WILLIAM SLADE: *Author*
Down the Danube by Canoe. Photos by Richard S. Durrance and Christopher G. Knight. 34-79, *July 1965*

BACKPACKING. See Hiking Trips

BACKWOODS Japan During American Occupation. By M. A. Huberman. 491-518, *Apr. 1947*

BACON, EDMUND N.: *Author*
Five Noted Thinkers Explore the Future. 74, *July 1976*

BACTERIA:
The Wild World of Compost. By Cecil E. Johnson. Photos by Bianca Lavies. Included: Actinomycetes; Aerobic bacteria. 273-284, *Aug. 1980*

BAD Days for the Brown Pelican. By Ralph W. Schreiber. Photos by William R. Curtsinger and author. 111-123, *Jan. 1975*

BAD GODESBERG, West Germany:
War's Wake in the Rhineland. By Thomas R. Henry. 1-32, *July 1945*

A BAD Time to Be a Crocodile. By Rick Gore. Photos by Jonathan Blair. 90-115, *Jan. 1978*

BADDECK, Nova Scotia, Canada:
Down East to Nova Scotia. By Winfield Parks. 853-879, *June 1964*
Canada's Winged Victory: the *Silver Dart*. By Gilbert M. Grosvenor. 254-267, *Aug. 1959*
Miracle Men of the Telephone. By F. Barrows Colton. Included: Photographs of Dr. Alexander Graham Bell and members of his family at their home in Baddeck. 273-316, *Mar. 1947*
Salty Nova Scotia: In Friendly New Scotland Gaelic Songs Still Answer the Skirling Bagpipes. By Andrew H. Brown. 575-624, *May 1940*
The Charm of Cape Breton Island: The Most Picturesque Portion of Canada's Maritime Provinces–A Land Rich in Historic Associations, Natural Resources, and Geographic Appeal. By Catherine Dunlop Mackenzie. 34-60, *July 1920*
See also Bell Museum

BADEN (State), West Germany:
Wandering Through the Black Forest.

Photos by Hans Hildenbrand. 659-666, *Dec. 1928*

BADEN-WÜRTTEMBERG (State), West Germany:
Treasure From a Celtic Tomb. By Jörg Biel. Photos by Volkmar Wentzel. 428-438, *Mar. 1980*

BADGES, Military:
Decorations, Medals, Service Ribbons, Badges and Women's Insignia. 414-444, *Oct. 1943*

BADLANDS:
South Dakota's Badlands: Castles in Clay. By John Madson. Photos by Jim Brandenburg. 524-539, *Apr. 1981*
North Dakota Comes into Its Own. By Leo A. Borah. Photos by J. Baylor Roberts. 283-322, *Sept. 1951*
The West Through Boston Eyes. By Stewart Anderson. 733-776, *June 1949*
South Dakota Keeps Its West Wild. By Frederick Simpich. 555-588, *May 1947*
Big Game Hunting (Paleontology) in the Land of Long Ago. By Joseph P. Connolly and James D. Bump. NGS research grant. 589-605, *May 1947*
The Bad Lands of South Dakota. By N. H. Darton. 339-343, *Sept. 1899*

BAEKELAND, G. BROOKS:
Nomination Page. In Manhattan and the Peruvian Andes. *Aug. 1964*
Author-Photographer
By Parachute Into Peru's Lost World. Photos by author and Peter R. Gimbel. 268-296, *Aug. 1964*

BAFFIN ISLAND, Northwest Territories, Canada:
I Live With the Eskimos. By Guy Mary-Rousseliere. 188-217, *Feb. 1971*
Far North with "Captain Mac." By Miriam MacMillan. Included: Brevoort Island; Pond Inlet. 465-513, *Oct. 1951*
Milestones in My Arctic Journeys. By Willie Knutsen. Included: Airfield at Frobisher Bay and the activities of the Arctic Search and Rescue section of the Air Force. 543-570, *Oct. 1949*
Servicing Arctic Airbases. By Robert A. Bartlett. 602-616, *May 1946*
Dr. Bell's Survey in Baffinland. By W J McGee. 113, *Mar. 1902*

A BAG of Bird Portraits. Photos by Arthur A. Allen. 697-712, *June 1944*

BAGANDA TRIBESPEOPLE:
Return to Uganda. By Jerry and Sarah Kambites. Photos by Sarah Leen. 73-89, *July 1980*

BAGG, ETHEL MATHER:
Letters from the Italian Front. By Marchesa Louise de Rosales to Ethel Mather Bagg. 47-67, *July 1917*

BAGGARA TRIBESPEOPLE:
With the Nuba Hillmen of Kordofan. By Robin Strachan. 249-278, *Feb. 1951*

BAGHDAD, Iraq:
The New Face of Baghdad. By William S. Ellis. Photos by Steve McCurry. Included: Iraq at war; Treasures from Iraq's past. 80-109, *Jan. 1985*
Station Wagon Odyssey: Baghdad to İstanbul. By William O. Douglas. 48-87, *Jan. 1959*
Iraq–Where Oil and Water Mix. By Jean and Franc Shor. 443-489, *Oct. 1958*
"Around the World in Eighty Days." By Newman Bumstead. 705-750, *Dec. 1951*
Where Adam and Eve Lived. By Frederick and Margaret Simpich. 546-588, *Dec. 1914*
Travels in Arabia and Along the Persian Gulf. By David G. Fairchild. 139-151, *Apr. 1904*

BAHAMAS:
Where Columbus Found the New World. By Joseph Judge. Photos by James L. Stanfield. 566-599, *Nov. 1986*
⊕ *Where Did Columbus Discover America? New Evidence Marks Landfall at Samana Cay.* Included: Threading the Islands: Which Track Fits? Samana Cay and the Columbus Log. *Nov. 1986*
The Bahamas: Boom Times and Buccaneering. By Peter Benchley. Photos by Bruce Dale. 364-395, *Sept. 1982*
Blue-water Plankton: Ghosts of the Gulf Stream. By William M. Hamner. NGS research grant. 530-545, *Oct. 1974*
Diving Into the Blue Holes of the Bahamas. 347-363, *Sept. 1970*
More of Sea Than of Land: The Bahamas. By Carleton Mitchell. Photos by James L. Stanfield. 218-267, *Feb. 1967*
Cape Canaveral's 6,000-mile Shooting Gallery. By Allan C. Fisher, Jr. Photos by Luis Marden and Thomas Nebbia. 421-471, *Oct. 1959*
The Bahamas, Isles of the Blue-green Sea. By Carleton Mitchell. Photos by B. Anthony Stewart. 147-203, *Feb. 1958*
Bahama Holiday. By Frederick Simpich. 219-245, *Feb. 1958*
Coral Castle Builders of Tropic Seas. By Roy Waldo Miner. Paintings by Else Bostelmann. 703-728, *June 1934*
Devil-Fishing in the Gulf Stream. By John Oliver La Gorce. 476-488, *June 1919*
The First Landfall of Columbus. By Jacques W. Redway. Included: Mariguana (Mayaguana); Samaná; Watling (San Salvador). 179-192, *Dec. 29, 1894*
See also Abaco; Andros Island; Bimini Islands; Great Bahama Bank; Great Inagua; Nassau

BAHIA, Brazil. See Salvador

BAHRAIN:
The Persian Gulf–Living in Harm's Way. By Thomas J. Abercrombie. Photos by Steve Raymer. 648-671, *May 1988*
Bahrain: Hub of the Persian Gulf. By

Thomas J. Abercrombie. Photos by Steve Raymer. 300-329, *Sept. 1979*

Troubled Waters East of Suez. By Ernest M. Eller. 483-522, *Apr. 1954*

In Search of Arabia's Past. By Peter Bruce Cornwall. 493-522, *Apr. 1948*

Bahrein: Port of Pearls and Petroleum. By Maynard Owen Williams. 195-210, *Feb. 1946*

The Rise of the New Arab Nation. By Frederick Simpich. 369-393, *Nov. 1919*

BAIKAL, Lake, U.S.S.R. *See* Baykal

BAIKIE, JAMES: *Author*

The Cradle of Civilization: The Historic Lands Along the Euphrates and Tigris Rivers Where Briton Is Fighting Turk. 127-162, *Feb. 1916*

The Resurrection of Ancient Egypt. 957-1020, *Sept. 1913*

The Sea-Kings of Crete. 1-25, *Jan. 1912*

BAILEY, ALFRED M.:

Author-Photographer

Desert River Through Navajo Land. Photos by author and Fred G. Brandenburg. 149-172, *Aug. 1947*

High Country of Colorado. Photos by author, Robert J. Niedrach, and F. G. Brandenburg. 43-72, *July 1946*

Cruise of the *Kinkajou:* Among Desert Islands of Mexico Voyagers Find Outdoor Laboratories for the Naturalist and Ideal Fishing Grounds for the Sportsman. Included: Birds and Beasts of Mexico's Desert Islands. Photos by Ed N. Harrison, Robert J. Niedrach, and author. 339-366, *Sept. 1941*

Photographer

Nature and Man in Ethiopia. By Wilfred H. Osgood. Note: Photos by author and Alfred M. Bailey, a member of the Abyssinian Expedition of 1926-1927. 121-176, *Aug. 1928*

BAILEY, JOSEPH H.: *Author*

■■ *Giants from the Past: The Age of Mammals.* Juvenile. 104 pages. *1983*

Photographer

■■ *We, The People: The Story of the United States Capitol, Its Past and Its Promise.* By Lonnelle Aikman. Photos by George F. Mobley and Joseph H. Bailey. Published in cooperation with the United States Capitol Historical Society. 143 pages. 1963; rev. ed. *1985*

■■ *Small Inventions That Make a Big Difference.* Art by John Huehnergarth. Juvenile. 104 pages. *1984*

BAILEY, SOLON I.: *Author*

A New Peruvian Route to the Plain of the Amazon. 432-448, *Aug. 1906*

BAILEY, TRUMAN: *Photographer*

Samoa–South Sea Outpost of the U. S. Navy. 615-630, *May 1941*

BAILEY, VERNON: *Author*

Bats of the Carlsbad Cavern (New Mexico). 321-330, *Sept. 1925*

BAINBRIDGE, OLIVER: *Author*

The Chinese Jews. 621-632, *Oct. 1907*

BAIT:

The Worm Turns. By Samuel Sandrof. 775-786, *June 1946*

BAJA CALIFORNIA (Peninsula), Mexico:

Baja's Murals of Mystery. By Harry Crosby. Photos by Charles O'Rear. 692-702, *Nov. 1980*

Baja California's Rugged Outback. By Michael E. Long. 543-567, *Oct. 1972*

Rocks, Ruts, and Sand: Driving the Mexican 1000. By Michael E. Long. 569-575, *Oct. 1972*

Hunting the Heartbeat of a Whale. By Paul Dudley White and Samuel W. Matthews. 49-64, *July 1956*

Baja California Wakes Up. By Frederick Simpich. 253-275, *Aug. 1942*

Cruise of the *Kinkajou:* Among Desert Islands of Mexico Voyagers Find Outdoor Laboratories for the Naturalist and Ideal Fishing Grounds for the Sportsman. By Alfred M. Bailey. 339-366, *Sept. 1941*

A Cruise Among Desert Islands. By G. Dallas Hanna and A. W. Anthony. 71-99, *July 1923*

Adventuring Down the West Coast of Mexico. By Herbert Corey. 449-503, *Nov. 1922*

A Mexican Land of Canaan: Marvelous Riches of The Wonderful West Coast of Our Neighbor Republic. By Frederick Simpich. 307-330, *Oct. 1919*

A Land of Drought and Desert–Lower California: Two Thousand Miles on Horseback Through the Most Extraordinary Cacti Forests in the World. By E. W. Nelson. 443-474, *May 1911*

Seriland. By W J McGee and Willard D. Johnson. 125-133, *Apr. 1896*

See also Raza, Isla; Scammon Lagoon; Seri Indians

BAJAUS:

Sea Gypsies of the Philippines. By Anne de Henning Singh. Photos by Raghubir Singh. 659-677, *May 1976*

BAKER, BETTY HAYNES: *Artist*

Flags of the United Nations. By Elizabeth W. King. 213-238, *Feb. 1951*

Flags of the Americas. By Elizabeth W. King. 633-657, *May 1949*

BAKER, BRUCE A.:

Nomination Page. *May 1970*

BAKER, JOHN H.: *Author*

Saving Man's Wildlife Heritage. Photos by Robert F. Sisson. 581-620, *Nov. 1954*

BAKER, MARCUS:

Marcus Baker Memorial Address by Wm. H. Dall. 40-43, *Jan. 1904*

Appreciation by Board of Managers. 40-43, *Jan. 1904*

Portrait. 41, *Jan. 1904*

Board of Managers. 165, Apr. 1889; 270, July 1889; 68, Apr. 1890; 294, 297; xii, Feb. 19, 1892; xix, Feb. 20, 1893; xix, 1894; 191, *June 1897*

Vice President. 216, *June 1896*

Reports. 296-298, Apr. 1891; vii-ix, *Feb. 20, 1893*

Secretary. 289, *Apr. 1891*

Author

Sarichef's Atlas, 1826. 86-92, *Mar. 1902*

The Lost Boundary of Texas. 430-432, *Dec. 1901*

Kodiak Not Kadiak. 397-398, *Nov. 1901*

The National Geographic Society's Eclipse Expedition to Norfolk, Va. 320, *Aug. 1900*

The Anglo-Venezuelan Boundary Dispute. 129-144, *Apr. 1900*

The Historical Development of the National Capital. 323-329, *July 1898*

Geographical Research in the United States. By Gardiner G. Hubbard and Marcus Baker. 285-293, *Oct. 1897*

Geographic Literature. 232, *July-Aug. 1897*

The Venezuelan Boundary Commission and Its Work. 193-201, *July-Aug. 1897*

Surveys and Maps of the District of Columbia. Included: List of Maps of Washington and the District of Columbia. 149-178, *Nov. 1, 1894*

An Undiscovered Island Off the Northern Coast of Alaska. 76-78, *July 10, 1893*

Geographic Nomenclature. Remarks by Herbert G. Ogden, Gustave Herrle, Marcus Baker, and A. H. Thompson. 261-278, *Aug. 1890*

On the Alleged Observation of a Lunar Eclipse by Bering in 1728-9. 167-169, *May 1890*

BAKER, NEWTON D.: *Author*

America's Duty. 453-457, *May 1917*

BAKER, ROY W.: *Author*

The Balearics, Island Sisters of the Mediterranean. 177-206, *Aug. 1928*

BAKHTIARI TRIBESPEOPLE:

I Become a Bakhtiari. By Paul Edward Case. 325-358, *Mar. 1947*

Mountain Tribes of Iran and Iraq. By Harold Lamb. 385-408, *Mar. 1946*

BAKLUZAN DERE TRIBESPEOPLE:

The Cone-Dwellers of Asia Minor: A Primitive People Who Live in Nature-Made Apartment Houses, Fashioned by Volcanic Violence and Trickling Streams. By J. R. Sitlington Sterrett. 281-331, *Apr. 1919*

BAKU, Azerbaijan S.S.R., U.S.S.R.:

Russia's Orphan Races: Picturesque Peoples Who Cluster on the Southeastern Borderland of the Vast Slav Dominions. By Maynard Owen Williams. 245-278, *Oct. 1918*

The British Take Baku. 163-164, *Aug. 1918*

BALATON, Lake, Hungary:

Hungary, a Kingdom Without a King: A Tour from Central Europe's Largest Lake to the Fertile Plains of the Danube and the Tisza. By Elizabeth P. Jacobi. 691-728, *June 1932*

BALCH, EDWIN SWIFT: *Author*

Highest Camps and Climbs. 713, *Dec. 1906*

Some Recent English Statements About the Antarctic. 266, *June 1904*

Termination Land (Antarctica). 220-221, *May 1904*

American Claims in the Antarctic. 77-78, *Feb. 1903*

BALD EAGLES, American:

Editorial. By Wilbur E. Garrett. 695, *June 1982*

Our Bald Eagle: Freedom's Symbol Survives. By Thomas C. Dunstan. Photos by Jeff Foott. NGS research grant. 186-199, *Feb. 1978*

Eye to Eye With Eagles. By Frederick Kent Truslow. 123-148, *Jan. 1961*

The Eagle in Action: An Intimate Study of the Eyrie Life of America's National Bird. By Francis H. Herrick. 635-660, *May 1929*

BALDWIN, EVELYN B.:

Portrait. 118, *Mar. 1901*

Author

The Baldwin-Ziegler Arctic Expedition. 358-359, *Sept. 1902*

The Meteorological Observations of the Second Wellman Expedition. 512-516, *Dec. 1899*

BALEARIC ISLANDS, Spain:

Spain's Sun-blest Pleasure Isles. By Ethel A. Starbird. Photos by James A. Sugar. 679-701, *May 1976*

The Balearics Are Booming. By Jean and Franc Shor. 621-660, *May 1957*

The Balearics, Island Sisters of the Mediterranean. By Roy W. Baker. 177-206, *Aug. 1928*

Keeping House in Majorca. By Phoebe Binney Harnden. 425-440, *Apr. 1924*

BALFOUR, ARTHUR J.:

The Oldest Free Assemblies: Address of Right Hon. Arthur J. Balfour, in the United States House of Representatives, May 5, 1917. 368-371, *Apr. 1917*

BALI (Island), Indonesia:

Bali Celebrates a Festival of Faith. By Peter Miller. Photos by Fred and Margaret Eiseman. 416-427, *Mar. 1980*

Bali by the Back Roads. By Donna K. and Gilbert M. Grosvenor. 657-697, *Nov. 1969*

Bali's Sacred Mountain Blows Its Top. Photos by Robert F. Sisson. 436-458. I. Disaster in Paradise. By Windsor P. Booth. 436-447; II. Devastated Land and Homeless People. By Samuel W. Matthews. 447-458, *Sept. 1963*

Indonesia, the Young and Troubled Island Nation. By Helen and Frank Schreider. 579-625, *May 1961*

New Guinea to Bali in *Yankee.* By Irving and Electa Johnson. 767-815, *Dec. 1959*

This Young Giant, Indonesia. By Beverley M. Bowie. Photos by J. Baylor Roberts. 351-392, *Sept. 1955*

Yankee Roams the Orient. By Irving and Electa Johnson. 327-370, *Mar. 1951*

Republican Indonesia Tries Its Wings. By W. Robert Moore. 1-40, *Jan. 1951*

Bali and Points East: Crowded, Happy

Isles of the Flores Sea Blend Rice Terraces, Dance Festivals, and Amazing Music in Their Pattern of Living. By Maynard Owen Williams. Included: Bali, Gem of the Netherlands Indies. Photos by Maynard Owen Williams. 313-352, *Mar. 1939*

Artist Adventures on the Island of Bali. By Franklin Price Knott. 326-347, *Mar. 1928*

BALIM (River), Netherlands New Guinea (now Irian Jaya, Indonesia):

"Shangri-la" in Panorama. Photos by Ray T. Elsmore. 681-688, *Dec. 1945*

The **BALKANS:**

⊕ *The Balkans,* Atlas series. *Feb. 1962*

⊕ *Central Europe, including the Balkan States. Sept. 1951*

The Danube, Highway of Races: From the Black Forest to the Black Sea, Europe's Most Important River Has Borne the Traffic of Centuries. By Melville Chater. 643-697, *Dec. 1929*

The New Map of Europe: Showing the Boundaries Established by the Peace Conference at Paris and by Subsequent Decisions of the Supreme Council of the Allied and Associated Powers. By Ralph A. Graves. 157-177, *Feb. 1921*

The Whirlpool of the Balkans. By George Higgins Moses. 179-197, *Feb. 1921*

The Races of Europe. By Edwin A. Grosvenor. 441-534, *Dec. 1918*

⊕ *Map of the New Balkan States and Central Europe. Aug. 1914*

The Changing Map in the Balkans. By Frederick Moore. 199-226, *Feb. 1913*

Two Possible Solutions for the Eastern Problem. By James Bryce. 1149-1157, *Nov. 1912*

The Great Turk and His Lost Provinces. By William E. Curtis. 45-61, *Feb. 1903*

See also Albania; Bulgaria; Greece; Romania; Turkey; Yugoslavia

BALL, ALBERT:

Tales of the British Air Service. By William A. Bishop. 27-37, *Jan. 1918*

BALL, J. H.: *Photographer*

Surf-Boarders Capture California. 355-362, *Sept. 1944*

BALL, SIR ROBERT: *Author*

The Eruption of Krakatoa. 200-204, *June 1902*

BALLANTINE, JOSEPH W.: *Author*

I Lived on Formosa. 1-24, *Jan. 1945*

BALLARD, ROBERT D.:

Recipient of the National Geographic Society Centennial Award. President's Page. By Gilbert M. Grosvenor. *Dec. 1988*

Editorial. By Wilbur E. Garrett. 697, *Dec. 1986*

Tectonics to *Titanic.* President's Page. By Gilbert M. Grosvenor. *Dec. 1985*

On Assignment in the North Atlantic. *Apr. 1985*

Author

Epilogue for *Titanic.* 454-463, *Oct. 1987*

A Long Last Look at *Titanic.* Included: High-tech partners plumb new depths; Poignant relics of a disaster. Illustrations text by Cliff Tarpy. 698-727, *Dec. 1986*

How We Found *Titanic.* By Robert D. Ballard in association with Jean-Louis Michel. 696-719, *Dec. 1985*

NR-1, the Navy's Inner-Space Shuttle. Photos by Emory Kristof. 450-459, *Apr. 1985*

Mysterious figures in headdresses adorn a Baja California cave where Indians in an unknown time created North America's largest rock-art murals. CHARLES O'REAR, WEST LIGHT

■■ *Exploring Our Living Planet.* 366 pages. *1983*

Incredible World of the Deep-sea Rifts. 680-705. I. Strange World Without Sun. The Editor. 680-688; II. Return to Oases of the Deep. By Robert D. Ballard and J. Frederick Grassle. 689-705, *Nov. 1979*

Oases of Life in the Cold Abyss (Galapagos Rift). By John B. Corliss and Robert D. Ballard. 441-453, *Oct. 1977*

Window on Earth's Interior. Photos by Emory Kristof. 228-249, *Aug. 1976*

Dive Into the Great Rift (Project FAMOUS). Photos by Emory Kristof. 604-615, *May 1975*

BALLARD, WALTER J.: *Author*

Australia's Future. 570-571, *Dec. 1905*

The Population of Japan. 482, *Oct. 1905*

European Populations. 432, *Sept. 1905*

BALLENBERG, BILL: *Photographer*

Discovering the New World's Richest Unlooted Tomb. By Walter Alva. Included: Into the Tomb of a Moche Lord. Paintings by Ned Seidler; Iconography of the Moche: Unraveling the Mystery of the Warrior-Priest. By Christopher B. Donnan. NGS research grant. 510-555, *Oct. 1988*

Exploring Our Forgotten Century: Between Columbus and Jamestown. By Joseph Judge. Paintings by John Berkey. 330-363, *Mar. 1988*

Searching for Columbus's Lost Colony: La Navidad. By Kathleen A. Deagan. 672-675, *Nov. 1987*

BALLERINAS in Pink. By Carleton Mitchell. Photos by B. Anthony Stewart. 553-571, *Oct. 1957*

BALLESTAS (Islands), Peru:

Peru's Wealth-Producing Birds: Vast Riches in the Guano Deposits of Cormorants, Pelicans, and Petrels which Nest on Her Barren, Rainless Coast. By R. E. Coker. 537-566, *June 1920*

BALLOON RACES:

A Wild, Ill-fated Balloon Race. 778-797. I. Wild Launch. 778-787; II. The Fantastic Flight of *Cote d'Or.* By Cynthia Shields. 789-793; III. Last Ascent of a Heroic Team (Maxie Anderson and Don Ida). 794-797, *Dec. 1983*

BALLOONS:

President's Page, on *Explorer II* and *Rodney the Jazz Bird.* By Gilbert M. Grosvenor. *Mar. 1986*

The Long, Lonely Flight. By Joe W. Kittinger, Jr. Contents: Transatlantic solo flight by balloon. 270-276, *Feb. 1985*

A Wild, Ill-fated Balloon Race. 778-797. I. Wild Launch. 778-787; II. The Fantastic Flight of *Cote d'Or.* By Cynthia Shields. 789-793; III. Last Ascent of a Heroic Team (Maxie Anderson and Don Ida). 794-797, *Dec. 1983*

First Across the Pacific: The Flight of *Double Eagle V.* By Ben L. Abruzzo. 513-521, *Apr. 1982*

The balloon Silver Fox *set new transatlantic records but touched down short of the European coast.* OTIS IMBODEN, NGS

Kitty Hawk Floats Across North America. By Maxie and Kristian Anderson. 260-271, *Aug. 1980*

Double Eagle II Has Landed! Crossing the Atlantic by Balloon. By Ben L. Abruzzo, with Maxie L. Anderson and Larry Newman. 858-882, *Dec. 1978*

The Longest Manned Balloon Flight *(Silver Fox).* By Ed Yost. 208-217, *Feb. 1977*

Laboratory in a Dirty Sky. By Rudolf J. Engelmann and Vera Simons. Contents: Project Da Vinci's manned research balloon. NGS research grant. 616-621, *Nov. 1976*

Hot-air Balloons Race on Silent Winds. By William R. Berry. Photos by Don W. Jones. 392-407, *Mar. 1966*

Across the Alps in a Wicker Basket *(Bernina).* By Phil Walker. 117-131, *Jan. 1963*

We Saw the World From the Edge of Space. By Malcolm D. Ross. Photos by Walter Meayers Edwards. Contents: U. S. Navy's Project Strato-Lab High 5. 671-685, *Nov. 1961*

The Long, Lonely Leap. By Joseph W. Kittinger, Jr. Photos by Volkmar Wentzel. Contents: Project Excelsior. 854-873, *Dec. 1960*

Braving the Atlantic by Balloon *(Small World).* By Arnold Eiloart. 123-146, *July 1959*

Rockets Explore the Air Above Us. By Newman Bumstead. Contents: Rockoons, rocket-and-balloon research tools. 562-580, *Apr. 1957*

To 76,000 Feet by *Strato-Lab* Balloon. By Malcolm D. Ross and M. Lee Lewis. 269-282, *Feb. 1957*

Trailing Cosmic Rays in Canada's North. By Martin A. Pomerantz. Included: Balloon-borne Geiger counters. NGS research grant. 99-115, *Jan. 1953*

National Geographic Society-U. S. Army Air Corps Stratosphere Flight of 1935 in Balloon *Explorer II* (Contributed Technical Papers, *Stratosphere Series No. 2*). 340, Mar. 1937; 802, *June 1937*

First natural-color photograph taken in the stratosphere. By Albert W. Stevens. Included: *Explorer II.* 340, *Mar. 1937*

The Scientific Results of the World-Record Stratosphere Flight. By Albert W. Stevens. 693-712, *May 1936*

The First Photograph Ever Made Showing the Division Between the Troposphere and Stratosphere and also the Actual Curvature of the Earth. Aerial photo by Albert W. Stevens. Supplement. *May 1936*

Man's Farthest Aloft: Rising to 13.71 Miles, the National Geographic Society-U. S. Army Stratosphere Expedition Gathers Scientific Data at Record Altitude. By Albert W. Stevens. Included: *Explorer II's* perfect landing. 59-94, *Jan. 1936*

A Report of the Second Stratosphere Expedition. Contents: *Explorer II.* 535-536, *Oct. 1935*

Studies Planned for New Stratosphere Flight with Helium. Contents: *Explorer II.* 795-800, *June 1935*

The Society Announces New Flight into the Stratosphere. By Gilbert Grosvenor. Included: An account of the explosion of *Explorer* I and announcement of new flight. 265-272, *Feb. 1935*

■■ *The National Geographic Society-U. S. Army Air Corps Stratosphere Flight of 1934 in the Balloon* Explorer. Contributed technical papers. 122 pages. *1935*

Exploring the Stratosphere. By Albert W. Stevens. Contents: *Explorer* I. 397-434, *Oct. 1934*

World's Largest Free Balloon to Explore Stratosphere. Contents: *Explorer* I. 107-110, *July 1934*

Your Society Sponsors an Expedition to Explore the Stratosphere. Contents: *Explorer* I. 528-530, *Apr. 1934*

Ballooning in the Stratosphere: Two Balloon Ascents to Ten-Mile Altitudes Presage New Mode of Aërial Travel. By Auguste Piccard. Contents: *F.N.R.S.* and *Explorer* I. 353-384, *Mar. 1933*

Helium, the New Balloon Gas. By G. Sherburne Rogers. 441-456, *May 1919*

No Man's Land–Spitzbergen. Included: The balloon flight of S. A. Andrée. 455-458, *July 1907*

BALMAT, JACQUES:

The Ascent of Mont Blanc. By Walter Woodburn Hyde. 861-942, *Aug. 1913*

Tribute to American Topographers. By A. H. Barnes. 358, *July 1905*

BALOGH, RUDOLF: *Photographer*

Yugoslavia: Where Oriental Hues Splash Europe. Photos by Konstantin J. Kostich and Rudolf Balogh. 699-738, *June 1939*

Rural Hungarian Rhapsody. Photos by

Rudolf Balogh and Hans Hildenbrand. 17-48, *Jan. 1938*

BALSAS, Río, Mexico:

Down Mexico's Río Balsas. By John W. Webber. Photos by author, Kenneth Segerstrom, and Jack Breed. 253-272, *Aug. 1946*

BALTIC SEA REGION, Europe:

Viking Trail East. By Robert Paul Jordan. Photos by Jim Brandenburg. Paintings by Michael A. Hampshire. 278-317, *Mar. 1985*
Amber: Golden Window on the Past. Photos by Paul A. Zahl. Text by Thomas J. O'Neill. 423-435, *Sept. 1977*
Baltic Cruise of the *Caribbee.* By Carleton Mitchell. 605-646, *Nov. 1950*
Flying Around the Baltic. By Douglas Chandler. 767-806, *June 1938*

BALTIC STATES. *See* Estonia; Latvia; Lithuania

BALTIMORE, Maryland:

Baltimore: The Hidden City. By Fred Kline. Photos by Martin Rogers. 188-215, *Feb. 1975*
Maryland on the Half Shell. By Stuart E. Jones. Photos by Robert W. Madden. 188-229, *Feb. 1972*
Chesapeake Country. By Nathaniel T. Kenney. Photos by Bates Littlehales. 370-411, *Sept. 1964*
Spices, the Essence of Geography. By Stuart E. Jones. Included: McCormick and Company. 401-420, *Mar. 1949*
Maryland Presents–. By W. Robert Moore. 401-448, *Apr. 1941*
Colossal Work in Baltimore. By Calvin W. Hendrick. 365-373, *Apr. 1909*
See also Sherwood Gardens; Sparrows Point

BALTISTAN (District), Pakistan:

Baltistan–The 20th Century Comes to Shangri-la. By Galen Rowell. Photos by the author and Barbara Cushman Rowell. Included: War among the peaks. 526-550, *Oct. 1987*
Trek to Lofty Hunza–and Beyond. By Sabrina and Roland Michaud. 644-669, *Nov. 1975*
Among the Great Himalayan Glaciers. 405-406, *Nov. 1902*

BALUCHISTAN:

Pakistan, New Nation in an Old Land. By Jean and Franc Shor. 637-678, *Nov. 1952*
Flying the World: In a Homemade Airplane the Author and Her Husband Enjoy 16,000 Miles of Adventurous Flight Across Europe, Asia, and America. By Gladys M. Day. 655-690, *June 1932*
Adventures With a Camera in Many Lands. By Maynard Owen Williams. 87-112, *July 1921*

BAMBALA TRIBESPEOPLE:

Curious and Characteristic Customs of Central African Tribes (Belgian Congo). By E. Torday. 342-368, *Oct. 1919*

BAMBOO:

Secrets of the Wild Panda. By George B. Schaller. Included: Saving the panda. 284-309, *Mar. 1986*
Bamboo, the Giant Grass. By Luis Marden. Photos by Jim Brandenburg. 502-529, *Oct. 1980*
New Plant Immigrants. By David Fairchild. 879-907, *Oct. 1911*
Lessons from Japan. 221-225, *May 1904*

BAMIAN (Region), Afghanistan:

Back to Afghanistan. By Maynard Owen Williams. 517-544, *Oct. 1946*

BAMPTON, England:

England's Wild Moorland Ponies. 129-136, *Jan. 1946*

BANANAS:

Land of the Painted Oxcarts (Costa Rica). By Luis Marden. 409-456, *Oct. 1946*
Costa Rica, Land of the Banana. By Paul B. Popenoe. 201-220, *Feb. 1922*
How the World Is Fed. By William Joseph Showalter. 1-110, *Jan. 1916*
Where Our Bananas Come From (Costa Rica). By Edwin R. Fraser. 713-730, *July 1912*

BANARAS, India:

Banaras: India's City of Light. By Santha Rama Rau. Photos by Tony Heiderer. 214-251, *Feb. 1986*
The Ganges, River of Faith. By John J. Putman. Photos by Raghubir Singh. 445-483, *Oct. 1971*
Through the Heart of Hindustan: A Teeming Highway Extending for Fifteen Hundred Miles, from the Khyber Pass to Calcutta. By Maynard Owen Williams. 433-467, *Nov. 1921*
The Bathing and Burning Ghats at Benares. By Eliza R. Scidmore. 118-128, *Feb. 1907*

A Nepalese boy scales bamboo, the fast-growing and versatile tree grass used as scaffolding in Asia. JIM BRANDENBURG

BANCROFT, ANN:

Editorial. By Wilbur E. Garrett. 287, *Sept. 1986*
North to the Pole. By Will Steger. Photos by the author and Jim Brandenburg. Note: Ann Bancroft is the first woman to have walked to the North Pole. 289-317, *Sept. 1986*

BAND, GEORGE: *Photographer*

Triumph on Everest. 1-63. I. Siege and Assault. By Sir John Hunt. 1-43; II. The Conquest of the Summit. By Sir Edmund Hillary. 45-63, *July 1954*

BANDAI-SAN (Mountain), Japan:

Do Volcanic Explosions Affect Our Climate? By C. G. Abbot. 181-198, *Feb. 1913*

BANDELIER NATIONAL MONUMENT, New Mexico:

Adobe New Mexico. By Mason Sutherland. Photos by Justin Locke. 783-830, *Dec. 1949*

BANDING, Bird:

Tireless Voyager, the Whistling Swan. By William J. L. Sladen. Photos by Bianca Lavies. NGS research grant. 134-147, *July 1975*

BANFF NATIONAL PARK, Alberta, Canada:

Heart of the Canadian Rockies. By Elizabeth A. Moize. Photos by Jim Brandenburg. 757-779, *June 1980*
Hiking the Backbone of the Rockies: Canada's Great Divide Trail. By Mike W. Edwards. Photos by Lowell Georgia. 795-817, *June 1973*
Canadian Rockies, Lords of a Beckoning Land. By Alan Phillips. Photos by James L. Stanfield. 353-393, *Sept. 1966*
On the Ridgepole of the Rockies. By Walter Meayers Edwards. 745-780, *June 1947*

BANGKOK, Thailand:

Thailand's Working Royalty. Photos by John Everingham. 486-499, *Oct. 1982*
Thailand: Luck of a Land in the Middle. By Bart McDowell. Photos by Steve Raymer. 500-535, *Oct. 1982*
Bangkok, City of Angels. By William Graves. Photos by John Launois. 96-129, *July 1973*
Hopes and Fears in Booming Thailand. By Peter T. White. Photos by Dean Conger. 76-125, *July 1967*
Thailand Bolsters Its Freedom. By W. Robert Moore. 811-849, *June 1961*
"Around the World in Eighty Days." By Newman Bumstead. 705-750, *Dec. 1951*
Yankee Roams the Orient. By Irving and Electa Johnson. 327-370, *Mar. 1951*
Operation Eclipse: 1948. By William A. Kinney. NGS research grant. 325-372, *Mar. 1949*
Scintillating Siam. By W. Robert Moore. 173-200, *Feb. 1947*
Ancient Temples and Modern Guns in Thailand. Photos by Maynard Owen Williams. 653-660, *Nov. 1941*

Wealthy Muslims in Dhaka, Bangladesh, examine the wedding finery of a bride who has traded the tradition of arranged marriage for a match of her own making. DICK DURRANCE II

"Land of the Free" in Asia: Siam Has Blended New With Old in Her Progressive March to Modern Statehood in the Family of Nations. By W. Robert Moore. 531-576, *May 1934*

Hunting the Chaulmoogra Tree. By Joseph F. Rock. 243-276, *Mar. 1922*

The Coronation of His Majesty King Maha-Vajiravudh of Siam. By Lea Febiger. 389-416, *Apr. 1912*

BANGLADESH, People's Republic of:

Long Journey of the Brahmaputra. By Jere Van Dyk. Photos by Raghubir Singh and Galen Rowell. Included: A Rare Visit to a World Unto Itself. By Raghubir Singh. 672-711, *Nov. 1988*

They Stopped the Sea. By Hans van Duivendijk. Photos by Pablo Bartholomew. 92-101, *July 1987*

By Rail Across the Indian Subcontinent. By Paul Theroux. Photos by Steve McCurry. 696-743, *June 1984*

Bangladesh: The Nightmare of Famine. Photos by Steve Raymer. 33-39, *July 1975*

The Peaceful Mrus of Bangladesh. By

Claus-Dieter Brauns. 267-286, *Feb. 1973*

Bangladesh: Hope Nourishes a New Nation. By William S. Ellis. Photos by Dick Durrance II. 295-333, *Sept. 1972*

See also former name, East Pakistan

BANISHING the Devil of Disease Among the Nashi: Weird Ceremonies Performed by an Aboriginal Tribe in the Heart of Yünnan Province, China. By Joseph F. Rock. 473-499, *Nov. 1924*

BANKOFF, H. ARTHUR:

Nomination Page. *Mar. 1979*

BANKS ISLAND, Northwest Territories, Canada:

Banks Island: Eskimo Life on the Polar Sea. By William O. Douglas. Photos by Clyde Hare. 703-735, *May 1964*

BANNINGA, JOHN J.: *Author*

The Marriage of the Gods (Religious Festival). 1314-1330, *Dec. 1913*

The Indian Census of 1911. 633-638, *July 1911*

BANTU TRIBESPEOPLE:

My Life With Africa's Little People. By Anne Eisner Putnam. 278-302, *Feb. 1960*

BARBADOS:

Robin Sails Home. By Robin Lee Graham. 504-545, *Oct. 1970*

Barbados, Outrider of the Antilles. By Charles Allmon. 363-392, *Mar. 1952*

British West Indian Interlude. By Anne Rainey Langley. 1-46, *Jan. 1941*

BARBEY, BRUNO: *Photographer*

When the Moors Ruled Spain. By Thomas J. Abercrombie. 86-119, *July 1988*

Morocco's Ancient City of Fez. By Harvey Arden. 330-353, *Mar. 1986*

⊕ The Face and Faith of Poland, map, photo and essay supplement. By Peter Miller. Essay by Czesław Miłosz. *Apr. 1982*

After an Empire...Portugal. By William Graves. 804-831, *Dec. 1980*

Fátima: Beacon for Portugal's Faithful. By Jane Vessels. 832-839, *Dec. 1980*

Nigeria Struggles With Boom Times. By Noel Grove. 413-444, *Mar. 1979*

BARBOUR, THOMAS: *Author*

Notes on Burma. 841-866, *Oct. 1909*

Further Notes on Dutch New Guinea. 527-545, *Aug. 1908*

Notes on a Zoological Collecting Trip to Dutch New Guinea. 469-484, *July 1908*

BARBOUR, WILLIAM R.: *Author*

Buenos Aires and Its River of Silver: A Journey Up the Paraná and Paraguay to the Chaco Cattle Country. 393-432, *Oct. 1921*

BARCELONA, Spain:

Catalonia: Spain's Country Within a Country. By Randall Peffer. Photos by Stephanie Maze. 95-127, *Jan. 1984*

Montserrat, Spain's Mountain Shrine. By E. John Long. 121-130, *Jan. 1933*

Barcelona, Pride of the Catalans. By Harriet Chalmers Adams. 373-402, *Mar. 1929*

BARCELONA ZOO, Barcelona, Spain:

Growing Up With Snowflake (White Gorilla). By Arthur J. Riopelle. Photos by Michael Kuh. NGS research grant. 491-503, *Oct. 1970*

BARE Feet and Burros of Haiti. By Oliver P. Newman. 307-328, *Sept. 1944*

BAREHANDED Battle to Cleanse the Bay. By Peter T. White. Photos by Jonathan S. Blair. 866-881, *June 1971*

BARGES:

The Civilizing Seine. By Charles McCarry. Photos by David L. Arnold. 478-511, *Apr. 1982*

The Danube: River of Many Nations, Many Names. By Mike Edwards. Photos by Winfield Parks. 455-485, *Oct. 1977*

That Dammed Missouri River. By Gordon Young. Photos by David Hiser. 374-413, *Sept. 1971*

St. Louis: New Spirit Soars in Mid-America's Proud Old City. By Robert Paul Jordan. Photos by Bruce Dale. Included: Mississippi River barge traffic. 605-641, *Nov. 1965*

Inside Europe Aboard *Yankee*. By Irving and Electa Johnson. Photos by Joseph J. Scherschel. 157-195, *Aug. 1964*

Paris to Antwerp with the Water Gypsies. By David S. Boyer. 530-559, *Oct. 1955*

See also Intracoastal Waterways; Ohio (River); Rhine (River)

BARK (Ship). *See Breadalbane*

BARLETT, JOE M.:

On Assignment. *Mar. 1988*

BARNACLES:

Friendless Squatters of the Sea. By Ethel A. Starbird. Photos by Robert F. Sisson. 623-633, *Nov. 1973*

BARNES, A. H.: *Author-Photographer*

Beauty Spots in the United States. 406-409, *Apr. 1916*

Photographer

The Great White Monarch of the Pacific Northwest (Mount Rainier). 593-626, *June 1912*

BARNUM & BAILEY CIRCUS. *See* Ringling Bros. and Barnum & Bailey Circus

BARRA, FRANCISCO LEON DE LA:

In Honor of the Army and Aviation (Speech by Senor de la Barra). 267-284, *Mar. 1911*

BARRA (Island), Scotland:

Isles on the Edge of the Sea: Scotland's Outer Hebrides. By Kenneth MacLeish. Photos by Thomas Nebbia. Included: The Thrush on the Island of Barra. By Archibald MacLeish. 676-711, *May 1970*

Scotland From Her Lovely Lochs and Seas. By Alan Villiers. Photos by Robert F. Sisson. 492-541, *Apr. 1961*

From Barra to Butt in the Hebrides. By Isobel Wylie Hutchison. 559-580, *Oct. 1954*

Hunting Folk Songs in the Hebrides. By Margaret Shaw Campbell. 249-272, *Feb. 1947*

The **BARRAGE** of the Nile. By Day Allen Willey. 175-184, *Feb. 1910*

BARRETT, CHARLES: *Author*

The Great Barrier Reef and Its Isles: The Wonder and Mystery of Australia's World-Famous Geographical Feature. 355-384, *Sept. 1930*

BARRETT, JOHN:

The Discovery of the North Pole (Speech by John Barrett). 63-82, *Jan. 1910*

Author

Latin America and Colombia. 692-709, *Dec. 1906*

China: Her History and Development. 209-218, June 1901; 266-272, *July 1901*

The Philippine Islands and Their Environment. 1-14, *Jan. 1900*

BARRETT, O. W.: *Author*

Impressions and Scenes of Mozambique. 807-830, *Oct. 1910*

BARRO COLORADO ISLAND, Panama:

The Amazing Frog-Eating Bat. By Merlin D. Tuttle. NGS research grant. 78-91, *Jan. 1982*

Who Treads Our Trails? A Camera Trapper Describes His Experiences on an Island in the Canal Zone, a Natural-History Laboratory in the American Tropics. By Frank M. Chapman. 331-345, *Sept. 1927*

BARROW, Alaska:

Sealed in Time–Ice Entombs an Eskimo Family for Five Centuries. By Albert A. Dekin, Jr. Photos by Victor R. Boswell, Jr., and Scott Rutherford.

Paintings by James M. Gurney. 824-836, *June 1987*

Peoples of the Arctic. 144-223. I. Introduction by Joseph Judge. 144-149; II. Hunters of the Lost Spirit: Alaskans. By Priit J. Vesilind. Photos by David Alan Harvey. 150-173, *Feb. 1983*

Will Oil and Tundra Mix? Alaska's North Slope Hangs in the Balance. By William S. Ellis. Photos by Emory Kristof. 485-517, *Oct. 1971*

BARROWS, DAVID P.: *Author*

The Colorado Desert. 337-351, *Sept. 1900*

BARTHOLDI, FRÉDÉRIC AUGUSTE:

Liberty Lifts Her Lamp Once More. By Alice J. Hall. 2-19, *July 1986*

■■ *Liberty: The Statue and the American Dream.* By Leslie Allen. 304 pages. *1985*

Oil and coal barges ply the Danube as it enters Austria, one of eight countries united—and divided—by the historic, romantic river. WINFIELD PARKS, NGS

Jute sack caps one of 15,000 Bangladeshis who dammed the Feni River in 1985 to control floods. PABLO BARTHOLOMEW,GAMMA-LIAISON

BARTHOLOMEW, PABLO:
Photographer
They Stopped the Sea. By Hans van Duivendijk. 92-101, *July 1987*

BARTIMEUS (Pseudonym):
Malta Invicta. By Bartimeus (A Captain in the Royal Navy). 375-400, *Mar. 1943*

BARTKO, BOHDAN:
Precious Corals, Hawaii's Deep-sea Jewels. By Richard W. Grigg. Photos by David Doubilet. 719-732, *May 1979*

BARTLETT, CHARLES H.: *Author*
Untoured Burma. 835-853, *July 1913*

BARTLETT, DES:
On Assignment in Namibia. *Mar. 1983*
Nomination Page. *Jan. 1979*
Nomination Page. *Feb. 1976*
Nomination Page. *Aug. 1973*
Author-Photographer
Family Life of Lions. By Des and Jen Bartlett. 800-819, *Dec. 1982*
Beavers, Nature's Aquatic Engineers. By Des and Jen Bartlett. 716-732, *May 1974*
Beyond the North Wind With the Snow Goose. By Des and Jen Bartlett. Included: ...And Then There was Fred.... 822-843, *Dec. 1973*
Photographer
Etosha: Namibia's Kingdom of Animals. By Douglas H. Chadwick. 344-385, *Mar. 1983*
Those Kangaroos! They're a Marvelous Mob. By Geoffrey B. Sharman. 192-209, *Feb. 1979*
Penguins and Their Neighbors. By Roger Tory Peterson. 237-255, *Aug. 1977*
Patagonia. 290-339. I. Argentina Protects Its Wildlife Treasures. By

William G. Conway. 290-297; II. Where Two Worlds Meet. 298-321; III. At Home With Right Whales. By Roger Payne. 322-339, *Mar. 1976*
Finding the World's Earliest Man. By L.S.B. Leakey. 420-435, *Sept. 1960*

BARTLETT, JEN:
On Assignment in Namibia. *Mar. 1983*
Nomination Page. *Jan. 1979*
Nomination Page. *Feb. 1976*
Nomination Page. *Aug. 1973*
Author-Photographer
Family Life of Lions. By Des and Jen Bartlett. 800-819, *Dec. 1982*
Beavers, Nature's Aquatic Engineers. By Des and Jen Bartlett. 716-732, *May 1974*
Beyond the North Wind With the Snow Goose. By Des and Jen Bartlett. Included: ...And Then There was Fred.... 822-847, *Dec. 1973*
Photographer
Etosha: Namibia's Kingdom of Animals. By Douglas H. Chadwick. 344-385, *Mar. 1983*
Those Kangaroos! They're a Marvelous Mob. By Geoffrey B. Sharman. 192-209, *Feb. 1979*
Penguins and Their Neighbors. By Roger Tory Peterson. 237-255, *Aug. 1977*
Patagonia. 290-339. I. Argentina Protects Its Wildlife Treasures. By William G. Conway. 290-297; II. Where Two Worlds Meet. 298-321; III. At Home With Right Whales. By Roger Payne. 322-339, *Mar. 1976*

BARTLETT, JOHN R.:
Vice-President. 165, *Apr. 1889*; 270, *July 1889*; 134, *Jan. 1936*

BARTLETT, LINDA: *Photographer*
Montenegro: Yugoslavia's "Black Mountain." By Bryan Hodgson. 663-683, *Nov. 1977*
Irish Ways Live On in Dingle. By Bryan Hodgson. 551-576, *Apr. 1976*
Thomas Jefferson: Architect of Freedom. By Mike W. Edwards. 231-259, *Feb. 1976*
Benjamin Franklin, Philosopher of Dissent. By Alice J. Hall. 93-123, *July 1975*
Exploring England's Canals. By Bryan Hodgson. 76-111, *July 1974*
Mountain Voices, Mountain Days (West Virginia). By Bryan Hodgson. 118-146, *July 1972*

BARTLETT, ROBERT A.:
Newfoundland, Canada's New Province. By Andrew H. Brown. Photos by author and Robert F. Sisson. 777-812, *June 1949*
"Captain Bob" Bartlett awarded the Hubbard Medal. 609, *May 1946*
The Discovery of the North Pole (Presentation of Hubbard Gold Medal to Captain Bartlett). 63-82, *Jan. 1910*
Resolution awarding medal to Captain Bartlett. 1009, *Nov. 1909*
Author
Servicing Arctic Airbases. 602-616, *May 1946*
Greenland from 1898 to Now: "Captain Bob," Who Went North with Peary, Tells of 42 Years of Exploration in

the Orphan Island of New Aerial and Naval Interest. 111-140, *July 1940*
The Sealing Saga of Newfoundland. 91-130, *July 1929*

BARTON, CLARA:
The American Red Cross: A Century of Service. By Louise Levathes. Photos by Annie Griffiths. 777-791, *June 1981*

BARTON, OTIS:
A Half Mile Down: Strange Creatures, Beautiful and Grotesque as Figments of Fancy, Reveal Themselves at Windows of the Bathysphere. By William Beebe. Paintings by Else Bostelmann, Helen D. Tee-Van, E. J. Geske. 661-704, *Dec. 1934*

BARUNTSE (Peak), Himalaya:
Beyond Everest. By Sir Edmund Hillary. 579-610, *Nov. 1955*

BASEL, Switzerland:
The Rhine: Europe's River of Legend. By William Graves. Photos by Bruce Dale. 449-499, *Apr. 1967*

BASILIQUE DE LA SAINTE MARIE MADELEINE, Vézelay, France:
Vézelay, Hill of the Pilgrims. By Melvin Hall. 229-247, *Feb. 1953*

BASIN AND RANGE GEOLOGICAL PROVINCE, U. S.:
The Rising Great Salt Lake: No Way to Run a Desert. By Rick Gore. Photos by Jim Richardson. 694-719, *June 1985*

BASIN REGION, Utah-Nevada. *See* Great Basin

BASKET MAKER CULTURE:
20th-century Indians Preserve Customs of the Cliff Dwellers. Photos by William Belknap, Jr. NGS research grant. 196-211, *Feb. 1964*
Ancient Cliff Dwellers of Mesa Verde. By Don Watson. Photos by Willard R. Culver. 349-376, *Sept. 1948*

BASQUES:
16th-Century Basque Whalers in America. Photos by Bill Curtsinger. Paintings by Richard Schlecht. 40-71. I. Discovery in Labrador: A 16th-Century Basque Whaling Port and Its Sunken Fleet. 40-49; II. Unearthing Red Bay's Whaling History. By James A. Tuck. 50-57; III. Excavating a 400-year-old Basque Galleon. By Robert Grenier. 58-67; IV. The Indomitable Basques. By Robert Laxalt. 69-71, *July 1985*
The Enduring Pyrenees. By Robert Laxalt. Photos by Edwin Stuart Grosvenor. 794-819, *Dec. 1974*
Land of the Ancient Basques. By Robert Laxalt. Photos by William Albert Allard. 240-277, *Aug. 1968*
Lonely Sentinels of the American West: Basque Sheepherders. By Robert Laxalt. Photos by William Belknap, Jr. 870-888, *June 1966*
Life in the Land of the Basques. By John E. H. Nolan. Photos by Justin Locke. 147-186, *Feb. 1954*
Pigeon Netting–Sport of Basques.

Photos by Irene Burdette-Scougall. 405-416, *Sept. 1949*

The Land of the Basques: Home of a Thrifty, Picturesque People, Who Take Pride in the Sobriquet, "The Yankees of Spain." By Harry A. McBride. 63-87, *Jan. 1922*

The Races of Europe. By Edwin A. Grosvenor. 441-534, *Dec. 1918*

BASRA, Iraq:

From London to Australia by Aëroplane: A Personal Narrative of the First Aërial Voyage Half Around the World. By Sir Ross Smith. 229-339, *Mar. 1921*

BASS, GEORGE F.:

Recipient of the National Geographic Society Centennial Award. President's Page. By Gilbert M. Grosvenor. *Dec. 1988*

On Assignment in Ulu Burun, Turkey. *Dec. 1987*

Nomination Page. *Feb. 1977*
Nomination Page. *July 1968*
Nomination Page. *June 1963*
Nomination Page. *Aug. 1962*

Author

Oldest Known Shipwreck Reveals Splendors of the Bronze Age. Photos by William R. Curtsinger. Included: Bronze Age Trade, The Cosmopolitan World of the Late Bronze Age, The Painstaking Art of Marine Archaeology. NGS research grant. 693-733, *Dec. 1987*

Bronze Age Shipwreck. By Wilbur E. Garrett and George F. Bass. NGS research grant. 1-3, *Jan. 1985*

Glass Treasure From the Aegean. Photos by Jonathan Blair. 768-793, *June 1978*

After diving in a bathysphere off Bermuda to 3,028 feet in 1934, William Beebe, right, and Otis Barton return. JOHN TEE-VAN

New Tools for Undersea Archeology. Photos by Charles R. Nicklin, Jr. 403-423, *Sept. 1968*

Underwater Archeology: Key to History's Warehouse. Photos by Thomas J. Abercrombie and Robert B. Goodman. 138-156, *July 1963*

BASS ISLANDS, Ohio:

Yesterday Lingers on Lake Erie's Bass Islands. By Terry and Lyntha Eiler. 86-101, *July 1978*

BASSARI TRIBESPEOPLE:

Dusky Tribesmen of French West Africa. Photos by Enzo de Chetelat. 639-662, *May 1941*

BASTAR (Region), India:

New Life for India's Villagers. By Anthony and Georgette Dickey Chapelle. 572-588, *Apr. 1956*

BASTOGNE, Belgium:

Belgium Comes Back. By Harvey Klemmer. Photos by Maynard Owen Williams. 575-614, *May 1948*

BATAK HIGHLANDS, Sumatra (Island), Indonesia:

By Motor Through the East Coast and Batak Highlands of Sumatra. By Melvin A. Hall. 69-102, *Jan. 1920*

BATAVIA, Java (Island), Indonesia:

Postwar Journey Through Java. By Ronald Stuart Kain. 675-700, *May 1948*

Java Assignment. By Dee Bredin. 89-119, *Jan. 1942*

A Traveler's Notes on Java. By Henry G. Bryant. 91-111, *Feb. 1910*

See also present name, Djakarta

BATCHELDER, A. G.: *Author*

The Immediate Necessity for Military Highways. 477-499, *Nov.-Dec. 1917*

BATCHELDER, R. N.:

Vice-President. xix, *Feb. 20, 1893*

BATES, MARSTON:

Author-Photographer

Ifalik, Lonely Paradise of the South Seas. 547-571, *Apr. 1956*

Photographer

Keeping House for a Biologist in Colombia. By Nancy Bell Fairchild Bates. 251-274, *Aug. 1948*

BATES, NANCY BELL FAIRCHILD:

Author

Keeping House for a Biologist in Colombia. Photos by Marston Bates. 251-274, *Aug. 1948*

The **BATHING** and Burning Ghats at Benares. By Eliza R. Scidmore. 118-128, *Feb. 1907*

BATHYMETRICAL Survey of the Fresh-water Lakes of England. 408, *Nov. 1901*

BATHYSCAPHS:

Down to *Thresher* by Bathyscaph. By Donald L. Keach. 764-777, *June 1964*

Man's Deepest Dive (*Trieste*). By Jacques Piccard. Photos by Thomas J. Abercrombie. 224-239, *Aug. 1960*

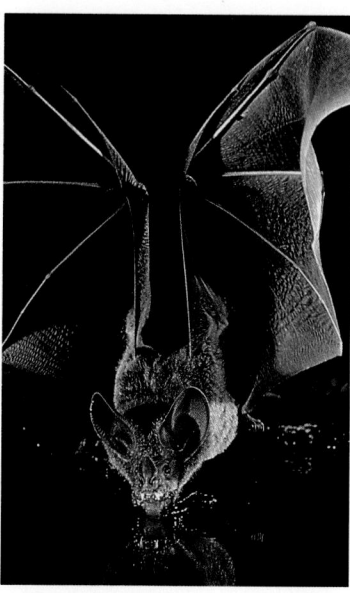

Native to forests from Mexico to southern Brazil, the frog-eating bat drinks on the wing to avoid predators. MERLIN D. TUTTLE

Deep Diving off Japan. By Georges S. Houot. NGS research grant. 138-150, *Jan. 1960*

Four Years of Diving to the Bottom of the Sea. By Georges S. Houot. NGS research grant. 715-731, *May 1958*

Diving Through an Undersea Avalanche. By Jacques-Yves Cousteau. NGS research grant. 538-542, *Apr. 1955*

Photographing the Sea's Dark Underworld. By Harold E. Edgerton. NGS research grant. 523-537, *Apr. 1955*

To the Depths of the Sea by Bathyscaphe. By Jacques-Yves Cousteau. NGS research grant. 67-79, *July 1954*

Two and a Half Miles Down. By Georges S. Houot. NGS research grant. 80-86, *July 1954*

See also Archimède

BATHYSPHERE:

A Half Mile Down: Strange Creatures, Beautiful and Grotesque as Figments of Fancy, Reveal Themselves at Windows of the Bathysphere. By William Beebe. Paintings by Else Bostelmann, Helen D. Tee-Van, E. J. Geske. 661-704, *Dec. 1934*

A Round Trip to Davy Jones's Locker. By William Beebe. Paintings by E. Bostelmann. 653-678, *June 1931*

BATS:

President's Page. By Gilbert M. Grosvenor. *Feb. 1987*. Included: Bat houses.

Gentle Fliers of the African Night. By Merlin D. Tuttle. NGS research grant. 540-558, *Apr. 1986*

The Amazing Frog-Eating Bat. By Merlin D. Tuttle. NGS research grant. 78-91, *Jan. 1982*

Bats Aren't All Bad. By Alvin Novick.

Photos by Bruce Dale. 615-637, *May 1973*

How Bats Hunt With Sound. By J.J.G. McCue. 571-578, *Apr. 1961*

Mystery Mammals of the Twilight. By Donald R. Griffin. 117-134, *July 1946*

Bats of the Carlsbad Cavern (New Mexico). By Vernon Bailey. 321-330, *Sept. 1925*

A Mexican Land of Canaan: Marvelous Riches of the Wonderful West Coast of Our Neighbor Republic. By Frederick Simpich. 307-330, *Oct. 1919*

Nature's Transformation at Panama: The Remarkable Changes in Faunal and Physical Conditions in the Gatun Lake Region. By George Shiras, 3d. 159-194, *Aug. 1915*

BATTAGLIA, LEE E.:

Nomination Page. *Oct. 1963*

Author-Photographer
Wedding of Two Worlds (Sikkim). 708-727, *Nov. 1963*

Photographer
History Revealed in Ancient Glass. By Ray Winfield Smith. Photos by B. Anthony Stewart and Lee E. Battaglia. 346-369, *Sept. 1964*

Last Moments of the Pompeians. By Amedeo Maiuri. Paintings by Peter V. Bianchi. 651-669, *Nov. 1961*

BATTLE For a Bigger Bob. By Mike Edwards. Photos by Dewitt Jones. 690-692, *May 1985*

BATTLE GLACIER, British Columbia, Canada:

Some Tramps Across the Glaciers and Snowfields of British Columbia. By Howard Palmer. 457-487, *June 1910*

The **BATTLE-LINE** of Languages in Western Europe: A Problem in Human Geography More Perplexing Than That of International Boundaries. By A. L. Guerard. 145-180, *Feb. 1923*

BATTLE MONUMENTS. *See* War Memorials

BATTLE OF THE BULGE:

Luxembourg, the Quiet Fortress. By Robert Leslie Conly. Photos by Ted H. Funk. 69-97, *July 1970*

Luxembourg, Survivor of Invasions. By Sydney Clark. Photos by Maynard Owen Williams. 791-810, *June 1948*

Belgium Comes Back. By Harvey Klemmer. Photos by Maynard Owen Williams. 575-614, *May 1948*

The **BATTLE** of the Forest. By B. E. Fernow. 127-148, *June 22, 1894*

BATTLEFIELDS:

Gettysburg and Vicksburg: the Battle Towns Today. By Robert Paul Jordan. Map notes by Carolyn Bennett Patterson. Included: Annotated maps charting course of battles. 4-57, *July 1963*

⊕ *Battlefields of the Civil War.* Atlas series. *Apr. 1961*

Our National War Memorials in Europe. By John J. Pershing. 1-36, *Jan. 1934*

The Most Famous Battle Field in America (Gettysburg). Photos by Clifton Adams and Orren R. Louden. 66-75, *July 1931*

Armistice Day and the American Battle Fields. By J. J. Jusserand. Included: The Battle Fields of France Eleven Years After. Photos by Gervais Courtellemont. 509-554, *Nov. 1929*

See also names of battles and wars, *as:* American Revolution; Hastings, Battle of

BATTLE-GROUND of Nature: The Atlantic Seaboard. By John Oliver La Gorce. 511-546, *June 1918*

BATTLESHIPS:

Henry VIII's Lost Warship: *Mary Rose.* By Margaret Rule. Introduction and picture text by Peter Miller. Paintings by Richard Schlecht. 646-675, *May 1983*

Midshipmen's Cruise. By William J. Aston and Alexander G. B. Grosvenor. Included: *New Jersey; Wisconsin.* 711-754, *June 1948*

Your Navy as Peace Insurance. By Chester W. Nimitz. 681-736, *June 1946*

Victory's Portrait in the Marianas. By William Franklin Draper. Paintings by author. 599-616, *Nov. 1945*

Battleship *Missouri* Comes of Age. Photos from U. S. Navy. 353-360, *Mar. 1945*

BATTLING the Juggernaut: Avalanche! By David Cupp. 290-305, *Sept. 1982*

BATTLING with the Panama Slides. By William Joseph Showalter. 133-153, *Feb. 1914*

BAUER, L. A.: *Author*

Most Curious Craft Afloat: The Compass in Navigation and the Work of the Non-Magnetic Yacht "Carnegie." 223-245, *Mar. 1910*

The Magnetic Survey of Africa. 291-297, *Mar. 1909*

The Work in the Pacific Ocean of the Magnetic Survey Yacht "Galilee." 601-611, *Sept. 1907*

The San Francisco Earthquake of April 18, 1906, as Recorded by the Coast and Geodetic Survey Magnetic Observatories. By L. A. Bauer and J. E. Burbank. 298-300, *May 1906*

Magnetic Survey of the Pacific Ocean. 237, *Apr. 1906*

Magnetic Survey of the United States. 92-95, *Mar. 1902*

Magnetic Work of the Coast and Geodetic Survey. 288-289, *Aug. 1899*

BAUER, SIEGBERT: *Photographer*

Behind the Scenes in the Home of the Passion Play (Oberammergau, Germany). 753-760, *Dec. 1935*

BAUM, Ohio:

The Indian Village of Baum. By H. C. Brown. 272-274, *July 1901*

BAUMANN, J. BRUCE: *Photographer*

A Most Uncommon Town: Columbus, Indiana. By David Jeffery. 383-397, *Sept. 1978*

An Eye for an Eye: Pakistan's Wild Frontier. By Mike W. Edwards. 111-139, *Jan. 1977*

Indiana's Self-reliant Uplanders. By James Alexander Thom. 341-363, *Mar. 1976*

The Other Nevada. By Robert Laxalt. 733-761, *June 1974*

Heart of the Bluegrass. By Charles McCarry. 634-659, *May 1974*

BAUXITE:

Aluminum, the Magic Metal. By Thomas Y. Canby. Photos by James L. Amos. 186-211, *Aug. 1978*

BAVARIA (State), West Germany:

Bavaria: Mod, Medieval–and Bewitching. By Gary Jennings. Photos by George F. Mobley. 409-431, *Mar. 1974*

From Chalet to Palace in Bavaria. Photos by Hans Hildenbrand. 683-690, *Dec. 1928*

The Beauty of the Bavarian Alps. By Fitzhugh Lee Minnigerode. 632-649, *June 1926*

The Races of Europe. By Edwin A. Grosvenor. 441-534, *Dec. 1918*

See also Berchtesgaden; Dinkelsbühl; Nördlingen; Oberammergau; Rothenburg

BAVENDAM, FRED: *Photographer*

Mysteries of the Bog. By Louise E. Levathes. Included: Peat holds clues to early American life. 397-420, *Mar. 1987*

Man and Manatee: Can We Live Together? By Alice J. Hall. Included: Man Can Save the Manatee. By Jesse R. White. 400-418, *Sept. 1984*

"BAY OF FIRE." *See* Phosphorescent Bay

BAYEUX TAPESTRY:

900 Years Ago: the Norman Conquest. By Kenneth M. Setton. Photos by George F. Mobley. The complete Bayeux Tapestry photographed by Milton A. Ford and Victor R. Boswell, Jr. 206-251, *Aug. 1966*

The Beauties of France. By Arthur Stanley Riggs. 391-491, *Nov. 1915*

BAYKAL, Lake, U.S.S.R.:

Siberia: Russia's Frozen Frontier. By Dean Conger. 297-345, *Mar. 1967*

Western Siberia and the Altai Mountains: With Some Speculations on the Future of Siberia. By James Bryce. 469-507, *May 1921*

BAYNES, ERNEST HAROLD: *Author*

Mankind's Best Friend (Dog): Companion of His Solitude, Advance Guard in the Hunt, and Ally of the Trenches. 185-201, *Mar. 1919*

Our Common Dogs. By Louis Agassiz Fuertes and Ernest Harold Baynes. Paintings by Louis Agassiz Fuertes. 201-253, index 280, *Mar. 1919*

BAZAARS:

Peiping's Happy New Year: Lunar Celebration Attracts Throngs to Temple Fairs, Motley Bazaars, and Age-old Festivities. By George Kin Leung. 749-792, *Dec. 1936*

Muzzle scarred from past battles, a grizzly in Alaska's Denali National Park and Preserve feeds on a yearling bear he killed after chasing off its mother. TOM MANGELSEN

"BE Ye Men of Valour." By Howard La Fay. 159-197, *Aug. 1965*

BEACH, EDWARD L.:
Nomination Page. *Nov. 1960*
Author
Triton Follows Magellan's Wake. Photos by J. Baylor Roberts. 585-615, *Nov. 1960*

BEACHES and Bathers of the Jersey Shore. Photos by Edwin L. Wisherd. 535-542, *May 1933*

BEACONS of the Sea. By George R. Putnam. 1-53, *Jan. 1913*

BEACONSFIELD, England:
Bekonscot, England's Toy-Size Town. By Andrew H. Brown and B. Anthony Stewart. 649-661, *May 1937*

BEAGLE, H.M.S.:
In the Wake of Darwin's *Beagle*. By Alan Villiers. Photos by James L. Stanfield. 449-495, *Oct. 1969*

BEAM, GEORGE L.:
Author-Photographer
The Prehistoric Ruin of Tsankawi (New Mexico). 807-822, *Sept. 1909*

BEAN, ALAN L.:
Skylab, Outpost on the Frontier of Space. By Thomas Y. Canby. Photos by the nine mission astronauts. 441-469, *Oct. 1974*

BEAR (Revenue Cutter):
The Arctic Cruise of the United States Revenue Cutter "Bear." By Sheldon Jackson. 27-31, *Jan. 1896*

BEAR MOUNTAIN, New York:
Skyline Trail (Appalachian Trail) from Maine to Georgia. By Andrew H. Brown. Photos by Robert F. Sisson. 219-251, *Aug. 1949*

BEAR RIVER MIGRATORY BIRD REFUGE, Utah:
Island, Prairie, Marsh, and Shore. By Charlton Ogburn. Photos by Bates Littlehales. 350-381, *Mar. 1979*
The Dauntless Little Stilt. By Frederick Kent Truslow. 241-245, *Aug. 1960*

BEARD, DANIEL B.: *Author*
Wildlife of Everglades National Park. Paintings by Walter A. Weber. 83-116, *Jan. 1949*

BEARING of Physiography Upon

Suess' Theories. By Wm. M. Davis. 430, *Oct. 1904*

BEARS:
■ The Grizzlies. President's Page. By Gilbert M. Grosvenor. Jan. 1987; cover, *Mar. 1987*
"Grizz"–Of Men and the Great Bear. By Douglas H. Chadwick. 182-213, *Feb. 1986*
Studying Grizzly Habitat by Satellite. By John Craighead. NGS research grant. 148-158, *July 1976*
Among Alaska's Brown Bears. By Allan L. Egbert and Michael H. Luque. NGS research grant. 428-442, *Sept. 1975*
Studying Wildlife by Satellite. By Frank Craighead, Jr., and John Craighead. NGS research grant. 120-123, *Jan. 1973*
■ Grizzly! 639A-639B, *Nov. 1967*
Trailing Yellowstone's Grizzlies by Radio. By Frank Craighead, Jr., and John Craighead. NGS research grant. 252-267, *Aug. 1966*
Knocking Out Grizzly Bears For Their Own Good. By Frank and John Craighead. NGS research grant. 276-291, *Aug. 1960*
When Giant Bears Go Fishing. By Cecil E. Rhode. Contents: Brown bears. 195-205, *Aug. 1954*
Once in a Lifetime: Black Bears Rarely Have Quadruplets, But Goofy Did–and the Camera Caught Her Nursing Her Remarkable Family. By Paul B. Kinney. 249-258, *Aug. 1941*
Lords of the Rockies: Photographing Big Game Animals in Their Primeval Surroundings, from Arizona to Canada, Brings Adventure to Two Wilderness Wanderers. By Wendell and Lucie Chapman. 87-128, *July 1939*
"Babes in the Wood." Supplement, *Aug. 1917*
The Larger North American Mammals. By E. W. Nelson. Paintings by Louis Agassiz Fuertes. Included: The Largest Carnivorous Animal Extant: The Alaska Brown Bear (Pictorial supplement). 385-472, *Nov. 1916*
The Big Game of Alaska. By Wilfred H. Osgood. 624-636, *July 1909*
Hunting Bears on Horseback (Wyoming). By Alan D. Wilson. 350-356, *May 1908*
The Bear Hunt. 222, *Mar. 1908*
A Bear Hunt in Montana. By Arthur Alvord Stiles. 149-154, *Feb. 1908*
See also Polar Bears

BEAUFORT SEA:
Arctic Odyssey. By John Bockstoce. Photos by Jonathan Wright. Paintings by Jack Unruh. 100-127, *July 1983*

BEAUHARNAIS, JOSÉPHINE DE. *See* Joséphine, Empress (France)

BEAUMONT, ARTHUR: *Author-Artist*
Painting the Army on Maneuvers. Included: U. S. Army. 577-602, *Nov. 1942*
Ships of Our Navy. 329-336, *Sept. 1941*

The **BEAUTIES** of France. By Arthur Stanley Riggs. 391-491, *Nov. 1915*

BEAUTIES of Our Common Grasses. Paintings by E. J. Geske. 627-634, *June 1921*

The **BEAUTIES** of the Severn Valley. By Frank Wakeman. 417-452, *Apr. 1933*

BEAUTIFUL Belgium, Restored by Peace. Photos by Paul G. Guillumette and A. Buyssens. 555-562, *Nov. 1929*

BEAUTIFUL Ecuador. By Joseph Lee. 81-91, *Feb. 1907*

BEAUTY and Bounty of Southern State Trees. By William A. Dayton. Paintings by Walter A. Weber. 508-552, *Oct. 1957*

BEAUTY, History, and Romance Enrich the Château Country (France). Photos by Gervais Courtellemont. 467-474, *Oct. 1930*

The **BEAUTY** of the Bavarian Alps. By Fitzhugh Lee Minnigerode. 632-649, *June 1926*

BEAVERS:

Beavers, Nature's Aquatic Engineers. By Des and Jen Bartlett. 716-732, *May 1974*

Arizona's Operation Beaver Lift. By Willis Peterson. 666-680, *May 1955*

The Romance of American Furs. By Wanda Burnett. 379-402, *Mar. 1948*

Mickey the Beaver: An Animal Engineer Performs for the Camera as a Star in the Activities of His Species. By James MacGillivray. 741-756, *Dec. 1928*

The Wild Life of Lake Superior, Past and Present: The Habits of Deer, Moose, Wolves, Beavers, Muskrats, Trout, and Feathered Wood-Folk Studied with Camera and Flashlight. By George Shiras, 3d. 113-204, *Aug. 1921*

Wild Animals That Took Their Own Pictures by Day and by Night. By George Shiras, 3d. 763-834, *July 1913*

BECAUSE It Rains on Hawaii. By Frederick Simpich, Jr. 571-610, *Nov. 1949*

BECK, CHARLES W., Jr.: *Author*

Rothenburg, the City Time Forgot. 184-194, *Feb. 1926*

BECK, FRANCIS:

California Trapdoor Spider Performs Engineering Marvels. By Lee Passmore. 195-211, *Aug. 1933*

BECK, ROLLO H.: *Photographer*

Iridescent Isles of the South Seas. 403-418, *Oct. 1925*

BECKER, JIM: *Author*

Look What's Happened to Honolulu! Photos by Bates Littlehales. 500-531, *Oct. 1969*

BECKER, GEORGE F.: *Author*

The Witwatersrand and the Revolt of the Uitlanders. 349-367, *Nov. 1896*

BECKET, THOMAS À:

Canterbury Cathedral. By Kenneth

MacLeish. Photos by Thomas Nebbia. 364-379, *Mar. 1976*

BECKWITH, CAROL:

On Assignment in Niger. *Oct. 1983*

Author-Photographer

Niger's Wodaabe: "People of the Taboo." 483-509, *Oct. 1983*

BEDI, NARESH: *Photographer*

The Cobra, India's "Good Snake." By Harry Miller. 393-409, *Sept. 1970*

BEDI, RAJESH: *Photographer*

India Struggles to Save Her Wildlife. By John J. Putman. 299-343, *Sept. 1976*

The Cobra, India's "Good Snake." By Harry Miller. 393-409, *Sept. 1970*

BEDOUIN:

Eternal Sinai. By Harvey Arden. Photos by David Doubilet and Kevin Fleming. 420-461. Included: Egyptian Sector. Photos by Kevin Fleming. 430-443; Israeli Sector. Photos by David Doubilet. 444-461, *Apr. 1982*

In Search of Moses. By Harvey Arden. Photos by Nathan Benn. 2-37, *Jan. 1976*

The Sword and the Sermon (Islam). By Thomas J. Abercrombie. 3-45, *July 1972*

Morocco, Land of the Farthest West. By Thomas J. Abercrombie. 834-865, *June 1971*

Abraham, the Friend of God. By Kenneth MacLeish. Photos by Dean Conger. 739-789, *Dec. 1966*

Saudi Arabia: Beyond the Sands of Mecca. By Thomas J. Abercrombie. 1-53, *Jan. 1966*

Holy Land, My Country. By His Majesty King Hussein of Jordan. 784-789, *Dec. 1964*

The Other Side of Jordan. By Luis Marden. 790-825, *Dec. 1964*

Jerusalem, My Home. By Bertha Spafford Vester. 826-847, *Dec. 1964*

In a nocturnal self-portrait, a beaver trips a string to ignite flash powder, a revolutionary technique in 1921. GEORGE SHIRAS, 3D

Report from the Locust Wars. By Tony and Dickey Chapelle. 545-562, *Apr. 1953*

Arab Land Beyond the Jordan. Photos by Frank Hurley. 753-768, *Dec. 1947*

Ali Goes to the Clinic. By Herndon and Mary Hudson. 764-766, *Dec. 1946*

On the Trail of King Solomon's Mines: The Bible, in Addition to Its Spiritual Values, Continues to Prove a Rich Geography and Guide to Exploration of the Holy Land. By Nelson Glueck. 233-256, *Feb. 1944*

Forty Years Among the Arabs. By John Van Ess. 385-420, *Sept. 1942*

Bedouin Life in Bible Lands: The Nomads of the "Houses of Hair" Offer Unstinted Hospitality to an American. By John D. Whiting. 59-83, *Jan. 1937*

Cirenaica, Eastern Wing of Italian Libia. By Harriet Chalmers Adams. 689-726, *June 1930*

Among the Bethlehem Shepherds: A Visit to the Valley Which David Probably Recalled When He Wrote the Twenty-third Psalm. By John D. Whiting. 729-753, *Dec. 1926*

Where Adam and Eve Lived. By Frederick and Margaret Simpich. 546-588, *Dec. 1914*

Arabia, the Desert of the Sea. By Archibald Forder. 1039-1062, 1117, *Dec. 1909*

BEEBE, HENRY:

Nomination Page. In the Virgin Islands. *Feb. 1958*

BEEBE, WILLIAM: *Author*

The High World of the Rain Forest. Paintings by Guy Neale. 838-855, *June 1958*

A Half Mile Down: Strange Creatures, Beautiful and Grotesque as Figments of Fancy, Reveal Themselves at Windows of the Bathysphere. Paintings by Else Bostelmann, Helen D. Tee-Van, E. J. Geske. 661-704, *Dec. 1934*

The Society Takes Part in Three Geographic Expeditions. 625-626, *May 1934*

A Wonderer Under Sea. Paintings by E. Bostelmann. 741-758, *Dec. 1932*

The Depths of the Sea: Strange Life Forms a Mile Below the Surface. Paintings by E. Bostelmann. 65-88, *Jan. 1932*

A Round Trip to Davy Jones's Locker: Peering into Mysteries a Quarter Mile Down in the Open Sea, by Means of the Bathysphere. Paintings by E. Bostelmann. 653-678, *June 1931*

"BEEBE PROJECT":

Sharks at 2,000 Feet. By Eugenie Clark and Emory Kristof as reported to Douglas Lee. NGS research grant. 681-691, *Nov. 1986*

BEECH, JOSEPH: *Author*

The Eden of the Flowery Republic (Szechuan, China). 355-390, *Nov. 1920*

BEECHEY ISLAND, Northwest Territories, Canada:

Exploring a 140-year-old Ship Under

Refugees again, Shiite Muslims linger in Beirut's Normandy Hotel after an Israeli shelling in 1982. STEVE McCURRY

Spirited sons of the Tutsi dance the "bow and arrow combat" in Ruanda (today's Rwanda). FRANZ STOEDTNER

Where Exploration Is Needed (Africa). 163-164, *Apr. 1900*

Lloyd's Journey Across the Great Pygmy Forest. 26-30, *Jan. 1899*

See also Congo, Democratic Republic of the; *and* present name, Zaire

BELGIUM:

Belgium: One Nation Divisible. By James Cerruti. Photos by Martin Rogers. 314-341, *Mar. 1979*

Inside Europe Aboard *Yankee.* By Irving and Electa Johnson. Photos by Joseph J. Scherschel. 157-195, *Aug. 1964*

⊕ *France, Belgium, and the Netherlands,* Atlas series. *June 1960*

Belgium Welcomes the World (1958 World's Fair). By Howell Walker. 795-837, *June 1958*

Paris to Antwerp with the Water Gypsies. By David S. Boyer. 530-559, *Oct. 1955*

Thumbs Up Round the North Sea's Rim. By Frances James. Photos by Erica Koch. 685-704, *May 1952*

Belgium Comes Back. By Harvey Klemmer. Photos by Maynard Owen Williams. 575-614, *May 1948*

Low Countries Await Liberation. 221-228, *Aug. 1944*

Belgium–Europe in Miniature. By Douglas Chandler. Included: Belgian Portraits. Photos by B. Anthony Stewart. 397-450, *Apr. 1938*

Beautiful Belgium, Restored by Peace. Photos by Paul G. Guillumette and A. Buyssens. 555-562, *Nov. 1929*

Through the Back Doors of Belgium: Artist and Author Paddle for Three Weeks Along 200 Miles of Low-Countries Canals in a Canadian Canoe. By Melville Chater. 499-540, *May 1925*

The Singing Towers of Holland and Belgium. By William Gorham Rice. 357-376, *Mar. 1925*

The New Map of Europe: Showing the Boundaries Established by the Peace Conference at Paris and by Subsequent Decisions of the Supreme Council of Allied and Associated Powers. By Ralph A. Graves. 157-177, *Feb. 1921*

The Races of Europe. By Edwin A. Grosvenor. 441-534, *Dec. 1918*

⊕ *Map of the Western Theatre of War.* Inset: France and Belgium. *May 1918*

Belgium's Plight. By John H. Gade. 433-439, *May 1917*

Belgium: The Innocent Bystander. By William Joseph Showalter. 223-264, *Sept. 1914*

See also Bruges

BELGRADE, Yugoslavia:

Yugoslavia: Six Republics in One. By Robert Paul Jordan. Photos by James P. Blair. 589-633, *May 1970*

Yugoslavia, Between East and West. By George W. Long. Photos by Volkmar Wentzel. 141-172, *Feb. 1951*

BELIZE:

Unearthing the Oldest Known Maya. By Norman Hammond. Photos by

Lowell Georgia and Martha Cooper. 126-140, *July 1982*

Troubled Times for Central America. By Wilbur E. Garrett, Editor. 58-61, *July 1981*

Belize, the Awakening Land. By Louis de la Haba. Photos by Michael E. Long. Included: Belize City; Belmopan. 124-146, *Jan. 1972*

See also former name, British Honduras

BELKNAP, WILLIAM, Jr.:

Author-Photographer

Shooting Rapids in Reverse! Jet Boats Climb the Colorado's Torrent Through the Grand Canyon. 552-565, *Apr. 1962*

Man on the Moon in Idaho (Craters of the Moon National Monument). 505-525, *Oct. 1960*

Nature Carves Fantasies in Bryce Canyon. 490-511, *Oct. 1958*

New Mexico's Great White Sands. 113-137, *July 1957*

Photographer

Lonely Sentinels of the American West: Basque Sheepherders. By Robert Laxalt. 870-888, *June 1966*

20th-century Indians Preserve Customs of the Cliff Dwellers. 196-211, *Feb. 1964*

Where Falcons Wear Air Force Blue, United States Air Force Academy. By Nathaniel T. Kenney. 845-873, *June 1959*

BELKNAP, REGINALD R.: *Author*

The North Sea Mine Barrage. By Reginald R. Belknap. 85-110, *Feb. 1919*

BELL, ALEXANDER GRAHAM:

Alexander Graham Bell. By Robert V. Bruce. Photos by Ira Block. 358-385, *Sept. 1988*

Three Men Who Made the Magazine. By Charles McCarry. 287-316, *Sept. 1988*

President of NGS (1898-1903). 273, Mar. 1947; 270, 272, 273, *Aug. 1982*

To Gilbert Grosvenor: a Monthly Monument 25 Miles High. By Frederick G. Vosburgh and the staff of the National Geographic Society. 445-487, *Oct. 1966*

1898: The Bells on Sable. Photos by Arthur W. McCurdy. 408-409, 416-417, *Sept. 1965*

The Romance of the Geographic: National Geographic Magazine Observes Its Diamond Anniversary. By Gilbert Hovey Grosvenor. 516-585, *Oct. 1963*

Canada's Winged Victory: the *Silver Dart.* By Gilbert M. Grosvenor. 254-267, *Aug. 1959*

Alexander Graham Bell Museum: Tribute to Genius. By Jean Lesage. 227-256, *Aug. 1956*

Clarke School for the Deaf, Northampton, Massachusetts: Active for 51 years as teacher, consultant, researcher, and president of the board. 379, 385, *Mar. 1955*

Washington's Historic Georgetown. By William A. Kinney. 513-544, *Apr. 1953*

Miracle Men of the Telephone. By F. Barrows Colton. 273-316, *Mar. 1947*

Alexander Graham Bell (Announcement of the Death of Alexander Graham Bell). 302, *Sept. 1922*

Portraits. Frontispiece, 104, Mar. 1898; 353, Oct. 1901; 302, *Sept. 1922*

The Charm of Cape Breton Island: The Most Picturesque Portion of Canada's Maritime Provinces–A Land Rich in Historic Associations, Natural Resources, and Geographic Appeal (Dr. Bell's Laboratories and Home). By Catherine Dunlop Mackenzie. 34-60, *July 1920*

Future of the Airplane (Dr. Bell's Support of Aviation). By Robert E. Peary. 107-113, *Jan. 1918*

Society President Alexander Graham Bell (left) and Editor Gilbert H. Grosvenor (beside him) vacation with their families in 1903 in Nova Scotia. GILBERT H. GROSVENOR COLLECTION

Life's Tempo on Nantucket. Photos by James L. Stanfield. 810-839, *June 1970*

The **BENDS** (Caisson Disease):

At Home in the Sea. By Jacques-Yves Cousteau. 465-507, *Apr. 1964*
Underwater Archeology: Key to History's Warehouse. By George F. Bass. Photos by Thomas J. Abercrombie and Robert B. Goodman. 138-156, *July 1963*
Dzibilchaltun: Up from the Well of Time. By Luis Marden. 110-129, *Jan. 1959*
Fish Men Explore a New World Undersea. By Jacques-Yves Cousteau. 431-472, *Oct. 1952*

BENEATH Colombia's Azure Skies. Photos by Luis Marden. 513-536, *Oct. 1940*

BENEDICTINES:

Mont Saint Michel. By Kenneth MacLeish. Photos by Cotton Coulson. 820-831, *June 1977*

BENELUX NATIONS. *See* Belgium; Luxembourg; Netherlands

BENGAL, Bay of:

✦ *Pacific Ocean and the Bay of Bengal. Sept. 1943*

BENGASI, Libya:

Red Cross Girl Overseas. By Margaret Cotter. 745-768, *Dec. 1944*

BENGUET–The Garden of the Philippines. 203-210, *May 1903*

BENIER, ANDRE: *Photographer*

Avalanche! "I'm OK, I'm Alive!" By David Cupp. Photos by Lanny Johnson and Andre Benier. 282-289, *Sept. 1982*

BENJAMIN, GEORGE J.: *Author-Photographer*

Diving Into the Blue Holes of the Bahamas. 347-363, *Sept. 1970*

BENJAMIN, MARCUS:

Gardiner Greene Hubbard: Memorial Meeting. Address by Marcus Benjamin. 53-57, *Feb. 1898*

BENJAMIN BOWRING (Research Ship):

Circling Earth From Pole to Pole. By Sir Ranulph Fiennes. 464-481, *Oct. 1983*

BENJAMIN FRANKLIN, Philosopher of Dissent. By Alice J. Hall. Photos by Linda Bartlett. 93-123, *July 1975*

BENN, NATHAN: *Photographer*

The South Koreans. By Boyd Gibbons. 232-257, *Aug. 1988*
Shakespeare Lives at the Folger. By Merle Severy. 244-259, *Feb. 1987*
The Dutch Touch. By Bart McDowell. Photos by Nathan Benn and Farrell Grehan. 501-525, *Oct. 1986*
Florida–A Time for Reckoning. By William S. Ellis. Photos by Nathan Benn and Kevin Fleming. 172-219, *Aug. 1982*
Massachusetts' North Shore: Harboring

Packed with 144 optical fibers, a telephone cable keeps messages flowing on beams of infrared light. FRED WARD, BLACK STAR

Old Ways. By Randall S. Peffer. 568-590, *Apr. 1979*
Old Prague in Winter. By Peter T. White. 546-567, *Apr. 1979*
Of Air and Space (National Air and Space Museum). By Michael Collins. Included: Picture portfolio by Nathan Benn, Robert S. Oakes, and Joseph D. Lavenburg, with text by Michael E. Long. 819-837, *June 1978*
The Living Dead Sea. By Harvey Arden. 225-245, *Feb. 1978*
New York's Land of Dreamers and Doers (Finger Lakes Region). By Ethel A. Starbird. 702-724, *May 1977*
◼◼ *Nature's Healing Arts: From Folk Medicine to Modern Drugs.* By Lonnelle Aikman. Photos by Nathan Benn and Ira Block. 199 pages. *1977*
In Search of Moses. By Harvey Arden. 2-37, *Jan. 1976*
The Pious Ones (Brooklyn's Hasidic Jews). By Harvey Arden. 276-298, *Aug. 1975*
Vermont–a State of Mind and Mountains. By Ethel A. Starbird. 28-61, *July 1974*
Cuba's Exiles Bring New Life to Miami. By Edward J. Linehan. 68-95, *July 1973*

BENNETT, FLOYD:

Floyd Bennett awarded Gold Medal; presentation by President Coolidge. 868, *Dec. 1957*
Awarded Gold Medal. 238, *Aug. 1927*
Commander Byrd Receives the Hubbard Gold Medal: The First Explorer to Reach the North Pole by Air Receives Coveted Honor at Brilliant National Geographic Society Reception (Also Presentation of Gold Medal to Floyd Bennett). 377-388, *Sept. 1926*

BENTLEY, WILSON A.: *Author*

The Magic Beauty of Snow and Dew. 103-112, *Jan. 1923*

Photographer
Snow Crystals. 30-37, *Jan. 1904*

BERBER TRIBESPEOPLE:

Berber Brides' Fair. By Carla Hunt. Photos by Nik Wheeler. 119-129, *Jan. 1980*
Trek by Mule Among Morocco's Berbers. By Victor Englebert. 850-875, *June 1968*
Morocco, "The Land of the Extreme West" and the Story of My Captivity. By Ion Perdicaris. 117-157, *Mar. 1906*

BERCHTESGADEN, West Germany:

This Was Austria. Included: German border towns. 71-86, *July 1945*

BERGE, MELINDA: *Photographer*

In the Far Pacific: At the Birth of Nations. By Carolyn Bennett Patterson. Photos by David Hiser and Melinda Berge. Included: Kosrae, Mariana Islands, Marshall Islands, Pohnpei, Truk, Yap, Palau. 460-499, *Oct. 1986*
The Two Samoas, Still Coming of Age. By Robert Booth. 452-473, *Oct. 1985*
Pitcairn and Norfolk–The Saga of *Bounty*'s Children. By Ed Howard. Photos by David Hiser and Melinda Berge. 510-541. Included: Pitcairn Island. 512-529; Norfolk Island. 530-541, *Oct. 1983*
A Walk and Ride on the Wild Side: Tasmania. By Carolyn Bennett Patterson. Photos by David Hiser and Melinda Berge. 676-693, *May 1983*

BERGEN, Norway:

Norway, Land of the Generous Sea. By Edward J. Linehan. Photos by George F. Mobley. 1-43, *July 1971*
Stop-and-Go Sail Around South Norway. By Edmond J. Moran. Photos by Randi Kjekstad Bull and Andrew H. Brown. 153-192, *Aug. 1954*
Norway Cracks Her Mountain Shell. By Sydney Clark. Photos by Gilbert Grosvenor and Ole Friele Backer. 171-211, *Aug. 1948*
The White War in Norway. By Thomas R. Henry. 617-640, *Nov. 1945*

BERGMAN, CHARLES A.: *Author*

The Triumphant Trumpeter. Photos by Art Wolfe. 544-558, *Oct. 1985*

BERING, VITUS:

The Cartography and Observations of Bering's First Voyage. By A. W. Greely. 205-230, *Jan. 28, 1892; Feb. 19, 1892*
A Critical Review of Bering's First Expedition, 1725-30, Together with a Translation of His Original Report Upon It. By Wm. H. Dall. 111-169, *May 1890*

BERING SEA PEOPLE. *See* Old Bering Sea People

BERING SEA REGION:

Celebrating Peoples of the Bering Strait. Geographica. *Nov. 1988*
Air Bridge to Siberia. By Wilbur E. Garrett. Photos by Steve Raymer. 504-509, *Oct. 1988*
Eskimo Hunters of the Bering Sea. By

Brad Reynolds. Photos by Don Doll. 814-834, *June 1984*

The Aleutians: Alaska's Far-out Islands. By Lael Morgan. Photos by Steven C. Wilson. 336-363, *Sept. 1983*

🔷 *Peoples of the Arctic; Arctic Ocean. Feb. 1983*

Where Magic Ruled: Art of the Bering Sea. By William W. Fitzhugh and Susan A. Kaplan. Photos by Sisse Brimberg. 198-205, *Feb. 1983*

New Day for Alaska's Pribilof Islanders. By Susan Hackley Johnson. Photos by Tim Thompson. 536-552, *Oct. 1982*

Learning the Ways of the Walrus. By G. Carleton Ray. Photos by Bill Curtsinger. 565-580, *Oct. 1979*

The Search for the First Americans. By Thomas Y. Canby. Photos by Kerby Smith. Paintings by Roy Andersen. 330-363, *Sept. 1979*

Editorial. By Gilbert M. Grosvenor. 147, *Aug. 1977*

Ice Age Man, the First American. By Thomas R. Henry. Paintings by Andre Durenceau. 781-806, *Dec. 1955*

Alaska's Russian Frontier: Little Diomede. Photos by Audrey and Frank Morgan. 551-562, *Apr. 1951*

The Arctic Cruise of the U.S.S. Thetis in the Summer and Autumn of 1889. By Charles H. Stockton. 171-198, *July 1890*

See also King Island; Pribilof Islands

BERKELEY, California:

The Aberration of Sound as Illustrated by the Berkeley Powder Explosion. By Robert H. Chapman. 246-249, *July 1896*

BERKEY, JOHN: *Artist*

Exploring Our Forgotten Century: Between Columbus and Jamestown. By Joseph Judge. Photos by Bill Ballenberg. 330-363, *Mar. 1988*

BERKSHIRES (Mountains), Massachusetts:

Home to the Enduring Berkshires. By Charles McCarry. Photos by Jonathan S. Blair. 196-221, *Aug. 1970*

Massachusetts Builds for Tomorrow. By Robert de Roos. Photos by B. Anthony Stewart. 790-843, *Dec. 1966*

Mountains Top Off New England. By F. Barrows Colton. Photos by Robert F. Sisson. 563-602, *May 1951*

BERLIN, Germany:

Berlin, on Both Sides of the Wall. By Howard Sochurek. 1-47, *Jan. 1970*

Modern Miracle, Made in Germany. By Robert Leslie Conly. Photos by Erich Lessing. 735-791, *June 1959*

Berlin, Island in a Soviet Sea. By Frederick G. Vosburgh. Photos by Volkmar Wentzel. 689-704, *Nov. 1951*

Airlift to Berlin. 595-614, *May 1949*

What I Saw Across the Rhine. By J. Frank Dobie. 57-86, *Jan. 1947*

Changing Berlin. By Douglas Chandler. 131-177, *Feb. 1937*

Renascent Germany. By Lincoln Eyre. 689-717, *Dec. 1928*

Yupik Eskimos in western Alaska will share emperor geese, bagged by one girl's father, with neighbors. DON DOLL

BERLIN, East, East Germany:

Two Berlins–A Generation Apart. By Priit J. Vesilind. Photos by Cotton Coulson. 2-51, *Jan. 1982*

East Germany: The Struggle to Succeed. By John J. Putman. Photos by Gordon W. Gahan. 295-329, *Sept. 1974*

BERLIN, West:

Two Berlins–A Generation Apart. By Priit J. Vesilind. Photos by Cotton Coulson. 2-51, *Jan. 1982*

Life in Walled-off West Berlin. By Nathaniel T. Kenney and Volkmar Wentzel. Photos by Thomas Nebbia. 735-767, *Dec. 1961*

BERLIN WALL:

Two Berlins–A Generation Apart. By Priit J. Vesilind. Photos by Cotton Coulson. 2-51, *Jan. 1982*

BERMUDA (Islands), Atlantic Ocean:

Sharks at 2,000 Feet. By Eugenie Clark and Emory Kristof as reported to Douglas Lee. NGS research grant. 681-691, *Nov. 1986*

Reach for the New World. By Mendel Peterson. Photos by David L. Arnold. Paintings by Richard Schlecht. Included: Salvaged shipwreck treasure. 724-767, *Dec. 1977*

By Square-rigger from Baltic to Bicentennial. By Kenneth Garrett. Included: Collision of tall ships in Bermuda waters. 824-857, *Dec. 1976*

Bermuda–Balmy, British, and Beautiful. By Peter Benchley. Photos by Emory Kristof. 93-121, *July 1971*

To Europe with a Racing Start. By Carleton Mitchell. 758-791, *June 1958*

Bermuda, Cradled in Warm Seas. By

Beverley M. Bowie. Photos by Charles Allmon. 203-238, *Feb. 1954*

Americans in the Caribbean. By Luis Marden. 723-758, *June 1942*

Happy Landing in Bermuda. By E. John Long. 213-238, *Feb. 1939*

A Half Mile Down: Strange Creatures, Beautiful and Grotesque as Figments of Fancy, Reveal Themselves at Windows of the Bathysphere. By William Beebe. Paintings by Else Bostelmann, Helen D. Tee-Van, E. J. Geske. 661-704, *Dec. 1934*

The Depths of the Sea: Strange Life Forms a Mile Below the Surface. By William Beebe. Paintings by E. Bostelmann. 65-88, *Jan. 1932*

A Round Trip to Davy Jones's Locker: Peering into Mysteries a Quarter Mile Down in the Open Sea, by Means of the Bathysphere. By William Beebe. Paintings by E. Bostelmann. 653-678, *June 1931*

The Islands of Bermuda: A British Colony with a Unique Record in Popular Government. By William Howard Taft. 1-26, *Jan. 1922*

BERN, Switzerland:

Switzerland, Europe's High-rise Republic. By Thomas J. Abercrombie. 68-113, *July 1969*

Surprising Switzerland. By Jean and Franc Shor. 427-478, *Oct. 1956*

Switzerland Guards the Roof of Europe. By William H. Nicholas. Photos by Willard R. Culver. 205-246, *Aug. 1950*

BERNADOU, J. B.: *Author*

Korea and the Koreans. 231-242, *Aug. 1890*

BERNHEIMER, CHARLES L.: *Author*

Encircling Navajo Mountain (Utah) with a Pack-Train: An Expedition to a Hitherto Untraversed Region of Our Southwest Discovers a New Route to Rainbow Natural Bridge. 197-224, *Feb. 1923*

BERNINA (Balloon):

Across the Alps in a Wicker Basket. By Phil Walker. 117-131, *Jan. 1963*

BERNSTORFF, JOHANN HEINRICH, COUNT VON:

Honors to Colonel Goethals: The Presentation, by President Woodrow Wilson, of the National Geographic Society Special Gold Medal, and Addresses by Secretary of State Bryan, the French Ambassador, the German Ambassador, and Congressman James R. Mann. 677-690, *June 1914*

In Honor of the Army and Aviation (Address by Count von Bernstorff). 267-284, *Mar. 1911*

BERRIES:

How Fruit Came to America. By J. R. Magness. Paintings by Else Bostelmann. 325-377, *Sept. 1951*

American Berries of Hill, Dale, and Wayside. Paintings by Mary E. Eaton. Contents: American Bittersweet, American Cranberry, American Holly, American Mountain Ash, Bayberry, Black Alder,

Black Gum, Blue Cohosh, Blueleaf Greenbriar, Bunchberry, Chokeberries, Coral Berry, Early Highbush Blueberry, Highbush Blueberry, Highbush Cranberry, Longspine Thorn, Mapleleaf Arrowwood, Roundleaf Greenbriar, Shadbush, Silky Cornel, Smooth Sumac, Snowberry, Spicebush, Sweet Cherry, Sweet Elder, Wild Black Cherry, Wintergreen. 168-184, *Feb. 1919*

The Wild Blueberry Tamed: The New Industry of the Pine Barrens of New Jersey. By Frederick V. Coville. 535-546, *June 1916*

Taming the Wild Blueberry. By Frederick V. Coville. 137-147, *Feb. 1911*
See also Cranberries; Kiwifruit

BERROETA, ANDRÉ DE: *Author*
Flying in France. 9-26, *Jan. 1918*

BERRY, WILLIAM R.: *Author*
Hot-air Balloons Race on Silent Winds. Photos by Don W. Jones. 392-407, *Mar. 1966*

BERTELLI, CARLO: *Author*
Restoration Reveals the "Last Supper." Photos by Victor R. Boswell, Jr. 664-685, *Nov. 1983*

BERTHOUD, EDWARD L.: *Author*
Sir Francis Drake's Anchorage. 208-214, *Dec. 29, 1894*

BERYL:
India's Treasures Helped the Allies. By John Fischer. 501-522, *Apr. 1946*

BESIDE the Bosporus, Divider of Continents. Photos by Maynard Owen Williams. 493-500, *Oct. 1929*

BESIDE the Persian Gulf. Photos by

Maynard Owen Williams. 341-356, *Mar. 1947*

BESSARABIA (Division), Romania:
Roumania and Its Rubicon. By John Oliver La Gorce. 185-202, *Sept. 1916*

BEST, EMORY F.: *Author*
The Utilization of the Vacant Public Lands. 49-57, *Feb. 1897*

The **BEST** of Our Land (National Parks). By Gilbert M. Grosvenor. 1-2, *July 1979*

BETELGEUSE (Ketch):
Chesapeake Country. By Nathaniel T. Kenney. Photos by Bates Littlehales. 370-411, *Sept. 1964*

BETHELL, UNION NOBLE:
Voice Voyages by the National Geographic Society: A Tribute to the Geographic Achievements of the Telephone (Address by Union Noble Bethell). 296-326, *Mar. 1916*

BETHLEHEM, West Bank:
Pilgrims Follow the Christmas Star. By Maynard Owen Williams. 831-840, *Dec. 1952*
Hashemite Jordan, Arab Heartland. By John Scofield. 841-856, *Dec. 1952*
Bethlehem and the Christmas Story. By John D. Whiting. 699-735, *Dec. 1929*

BETIO ISLAND, Tarawa, Gilbert Islands (now Kiribati):
Gilbert Islands in the Wake of Battle. By W. Robert Moore. 129-162, *Feb. 1945*

BETTER Days for the Navajos. By Jack Breed. Photos by Charles W. Herbert. 809-847, *Dec. 1958*

BETWEEN Massacres in Van (Armenian Capital). By Maynard Owen Williams. 181-184, *Aug. 1919*

BETWEEN the Heather and the North Sea: Bold English Headlands Once Sheltered Sea Robbers, Later Were Ports of Wooden Ships, Centers of the Jet and Alum Trades, To-day Are Havens of Adventurous Fishing Fleets. By Leo Walmsley. 197-232, *Feb. 1933*

BEUKEMA, HERMAN: *Author*
West Point and the Grey-Clad Corps. 777-788, *June 1936*

BEVAN, BERNARD: *Author*
Travels with a Donkey in Mexico: Three Adventurers Trudge from Oaxaca to Acapulco, 400 Miles, Through Back Country, Their Equipment Carried by Burros. 757-788, *Dec. 1934*

BEYOND Australia's Cities. By W. Robert Moore. 709-747, *Dec. 1936*

BEYOND Everest. By Sir Edmund Hillary. 579-610, *Nov. 1955*

BEYOND Supermouse: Changing Life's Genetic Blueprint. By Robert F. Weaver. Photos by Ted Spiegel. 818-847, *Dec. 1984*

BEYOND the Bight of Benin. By Jeannette and Maurice Fiévet. 221-253, *Aug. 1959*

BEYOND the Clay Hills: An Account of the National Geographic Society's Reconnaissance of a Previously Unexplored Section in Utah. By Neil M. Judd. 275-302, *Mar. 1924*

BEYOND the Dust Bowl. By William Howarth. Photos by Chris Johns. 322-349, *Sept. 1984*

BEYOND the Grand Atlas: Where the French Tricolor Flies Beside the Flag of the Sultan of Morocco. By V. C. Scott O'Connor. 261-319, *Mar. 1932*

BEYOND the North Wind With the Snow Goose. By Des and Jen Bartlett. 822-843, *Dec. 1973*

BEYROUTH, Lebanon. *See* Beirut

BHAKTAPUR, Nepal:
At the Crossroads of Kathmandu. By Douglas H. Chadwick. Photos by William Thompson. 32-65, *July 1987*

BHATGAON, Nepal:
Nepal: A Little-Known Kingdom. By John Claude White. 245-283, *Oct. 1920*

BHAVNANI, ENAKSHI: *Author*
A Journey to "Little Tibet." Photos by Volkmar Wentzel. 603-634, *May 1951*

BHOTIA TRIBESPEOPLE:
High Adventure in the Himalayas. By Thomas Weir. 193-234, *Aug. 1952*

BHUMIBOL ADULYADEJ, King (Thailand):
Thailand's Working Royalty. Photos by John Everingham. 486-499, *Oct. 1982*

In East Berlin, half of the city that symbolizes a divided Europe, guards march past U.S. troops at the Memorial to the Victims of Fascism and Militarism. COTTON COULSON

A palace weaver patterns cloth in Thimbu, capital of the Himalayan nation of Bhutan.   DESMOND DOIG

BINGHAM, HIRAM:

Nomination Page. In Peru. *Mar. 1982*
Peru, Homeland of the Warlike Inca.
By Kip Ross. 421-462, *Oct. 1950*
Awarded Jane M. Smith Life Membership. 342 (footnote), *Apr. 1920*
Honors to Amundsen and Peary
(Speech by Hiram Bingham). 113-130, *Jan. 1913*

Author

Building America's Air Army. 48-86, *Jan. 1918*
Further Explorations in the Land of the Incas: The Peruvian Expedition of 1915 of the National Geographic Society and Yale University. Included: The Greatest Achievement of Ancient Man in America (Fortress of Sacsahuaman, Peru). Panorama from photo by author. 431-473, *May 1916*
The Story of Machu Picchu: The Peruvian Expeditions of the National Geographic Society and Yale University. 172-217, *Feb. 1915*
In the Wonderland of Peru. Included: The Ruins of an Ancient Inca Capital, Machu Picchu. Panorama from photo by author. 387-573, *Apr. 1913*
Explorations in Peru. 417-422, *Apr. 1912*

BIOCHEMICAL RESEARCH:

Our Immune System: The Wars Within. By Peter Jaret. Photos by Lennart Nilsson. Illustrations text by Larry Kohl. 702-735, *June 1986*
Beyond Supermouse: Changing Life's Genetic Blueprint. By Robert F. Weaver. Photos by Ted Spiegel. 818-847, *Dec. 1984*

BIOCHEMISTRY:

The Wild World of Compost. By Cecil

E. Johnson. Photos by Bianca Lavies. 273-284, *Aug. 1980*
The Awesome Worlds Within a Cell. By Rick Gore. Photos by Bruce Dale. Paintings by Davis Meltzer. 355-395, *Sept. 1976*
See also Bioluminescence

BIOGRAPHIES. *See* Abraham; Alex-

ander the Great; Andersen, Hans Christian; Audubon, John James; Bell, Alexander Graham; Boone, Daniel; Burke, Robert; Byrd, Richard E.; Cather, Willa; Churchill, Winston; Clark, William; Cody, William (Buffalo Bill); Columbus, Christopher; Cook, James; Cortés, Hernán; Custer, George Armstrong; Dickens, Charles; Disney, Walt; Drake, Sir Francis; Edgerton, Harold E.; Eisenhower, Dwight D.; Elizabeth I; Elizabeth II; Franklin, Benjamin; Franklin, John; Frost, Robert; El Greco; Grosvenor, Elsie May Bell; Grosvenor, Gilbert H.; Grosvenor, Melville Bell; Henry, Prince; Houston, Samuel; Humboldt, Alexander von; Jefferson, Thomas; Jesus; Joseph, Chief; Kamehameha the Great; Leakey Family; Leopold, Aldo; Lewis, Meriwether; Lilienthal, Otto; Lincoln, Abraham; Luther, Martin; Madison, James; Magellan, Ferdinand; Marshall, Bob; Moses; Muir, John; Napoleon I; Paul, St.; Remington, Frederic; Roosevelt, Theodore; Russell, Charles Marion; Shakespeare, William; Smith, John; Süleyman the Magnificent; Thoreau, Henry D.; Tolstoy, Leo Nikolayevich; Twain, Mark; Vinci, Leonardo da; Washington, George; Wills, William; Yoshida Shoin; *and* Mogul Emperors

BIOLOGY:

Editorial. By Gilbert M. Grosvenor. 297, *Sept. 1976*
The New Biology. 355-407. I. The Awesome Worlds Within a Cell. By Rick Gore. Photos by Bruce Dale. Paintings by Davis Meltzer. 355-395; II. The Cancer Puzzle. By Robert F. Weaver. 396-399; III. Seven Giants Who Led the Way. Paintings by Ned Seidler. Text by Rick Gore. Contents: Francis Crick, Charles Darwin, Anton van Leeuwenhoek, Gregor Mendel, Thomas Hunt Morgan, Louis Pasteur, James D. Watson. 401-407, *Sept. 1976*
Algae: the Life-givers. By Paul A. Zahl. 361-377, *Mar. 1974*
Antarctica's Nearer Side. By Samuel W. Matthews. Photos by William R. Curtsinger. Included: Laboratory studies of Antarctic land and marine life. 622-655, *Nov. 1971*
Life in a "Dead" Sea–Great Salt Lake. By Paul A. Zahl. 252-263, *Aug. 1967*
Report–Geography of Life. By C. Hart Merriam. 160-162, *Apr. 1889*
See also Birds; Ecosystems; Insects; Mammals; Marine Biology; Molecular Biology; Plants; Scorpions; Spiders; U. S. Bureau of Biological Survey

BIOLUMINESCENCE:

Nature's Night Lights: Probing the Secrets of Bioluminescence. By Paul A. Zahl. 45-69, *July 1971*
Sailing a Sea of Fire (Phosphorescent Bay). By Paul A. Zahl. 120-129, *July 1960*
Fishing in the Whirlpool of Charybdis. By Paul A. Zahl. 579-618, *Nov. 1953*
See also Fireflies; Hatchetfish; *Photoblepharon;* Railroad Worm

Hiram Bingham paddles across Peru's Apurímac River in 1912, a year after his finds at the Inca ruins of Machu Picchu. PAUL BESTOR

BIOMES. *See* Ecosystems

BIORHYTHM RESEARCH:

Six Months Alone in a Cave. By Michel
Siffre. 426-435, *Mar. 1975*

BIOTECHNOLOGY:

Our Immune System: The Wars Within.
By Peter Jaret. Photos by Lennart
Nilsson. Illustrations text by Larry
Kohl. 702-735, *June 1986*
Beyond Supermouse: Changing Life's
Genetic Blueprint. By Robert F.
Weaver. Photos by Ted Spiegel. 818-
847, *Dec. 1984*

BIRA, Sulawesi (Island), Indonesia:

Seafarers of South Celebes. By G.E.P.
Collins. 53-78, *Jan. 1945*

BIRD, F. L.: *Author*

Modern Persia and Its Capital: And an
Account of an Ascent of Mount
Demavend, the Persian Olympus.
353-400, *Apr. 1921*

BIRD, ROLAND T.: *Author*

We Captured a 'Live' Brontosaur. 707-
722, *May 1954*

BIRD ANTING:

The Enigma of Bird Anting. By Hance
Roy Ivor. 105-119, *July 1956*

BIRD Banding, the Telltale of Migratory Flight: A Modern Method of
Learning the Flight-Ways and Habits
of Birds. By E. W. Nelson. 91-131,
Jan. 1928

BIRD DOGS:

Born Hunters, the Bird Dogs. By Roland Kilbon. Paintings by Walter A.
Weber. 369-398, *Sept. 1947*

The **BIRD** Men. By Luis Marden. Photos by Charles O'Rear. 198-217,
Aug. 1983

BIRD ROCK, Santa Catalina Island,
California:

Undersea World of a Kelp Forest. By
Sylvia A. Earle. Photos by Al Giddings. 411-426, *Sept. 1980*

**BIRD SANCTUARIES AND
ROOKERIES:**

The Triumphant Trumpeter. By
Charles A. Bergman. Photos by Art
Wolfe. Included: Kenai N.W.R.,
Alaska; Red Rocks Lakes N.W.R.,
Montana. 544-558, *Oct. 1985*
North American Waterfowl: Troubles
and Triumphs. By John Madson. 562-
599, *Nov. 1984*
Lord of the Shallows–The Great Blue
Heron. By Richard J. Dolesh. Photos
by Cameron Davidson. Included:
Maryland heronries at Black Swamp
Creek and Nanjemoy Creek. 540-
554, *Apr. 1984*
The Japanese Crane, Bird of Happi-
ness. By Tsuneo Hayashida. Includ-
ed: Kushiro marshland refuge. 542-
556, *Oct. 1983*
Roosevelt Country: T. R.'s Wilderness
Legacy. By John L. Eliot. Photos by
Farrell Grehan. 340-363, *Sept. 1982*
⊕ *America's Federal Lands; The United
States. Sept. 1982*

*A migratory bird overflies the stylized sources of its mysterious homing prowess—from
star patterns to magnetic fields.*   PAINTING BY BARRON STOREY

Where Oil and Wildlife Mix. By Steven
C. Wilson and Karen C. Hayden. In-
cluded: Aransas National Wildlife
Refuge, Texas; Padre Island Nation-
al Seashore, Texas. 145-173,
Feb. 1981
Island, Prairie, Marsh, and Shore. By
Charlton Ogburn. Photos by Bates
Littlehales. Contents: Bear River Mi-
gratory Bird Refuge, Utah; Farallon
Islands Refuge, California;
Lostwood Wildlife Refuge, North
Dakota; Merritt Island National
Wildlife Refuge, Florida. 350-381,
Mar. 1979
Hawaii's Far-flung Wildlife Paradise.
By John L. Eliot. Photos By Jona-
than Blair. Contents: Hawaiian Na-
tional Wildlife Refuge. 670-691,
May 1978
Tireless Voyager, the Whistling Swan.
By William J. L. Sladen. Photos by
Bianca Lavies. Included: Back Bay,
Virginia; Blackwater, Maryland;
Eastern Neck, Maryland; Mattamus-
keet, North Carolina; Pungo, North
Carolina; Upper Mississippi River
Wild Life and Fish Refuge, Minneso-
ta. 134-147, *July 1975*
Beyond the North Wind With the Snow
Goose. By Des and Jen Bartlett. In-
cluded: De Soto, Missouri River;
Sand Lake, South Dakota; Squaw
Creek, Missouri. 822-843, *Dec. 1973*
New Scarlet Bird in Florida Skies. By
Paul A. Zahl. Included: Caroni
Swamp Sanctuary, Trinidad;

Greynolds Park Rookery, North Mi-
ami Beach. 874-882, *Dec. 1967*
Our Only Native Stork, the Wood Ibis.
By Robert Porter Allen. Photos by
Frederick Kent Truslow. Included:
Bear Island Rookery; Corkscrew
Swamp Rookery; Cuthbert Lake
Rookery. 294-306, *Feb. 1964*
Saving Man's Wildlife Heritage. By
John H. Baker. Photos by Robert F.
Sisson. Included: The National Au-
dubon Society's sanctuaries in Texas,
Florida, and Louisiana. 581-620,
Nov. 1954
Duck Hunting with a Color Camera. By
Arthur A. Allen. Included: Bear
River Marshes, Utah; Bombay
Hook, Delaware; Cayuga Lake, New
York; Horseshoe Lake Island, Illi-
nois; Lower Souris, North Dakota;
Roaches Run, Virginia. 514-539,
Oct. 1951
Sea Birds of Isla Raza. By Lewis Wayne
Walker. 239-248, *Feb. 1951*
The Pink Birds of Texas. By Paul A.
Zahl. Contents: Roseate spoonbills
and the National Audubon Society's
sanctuary system on the Texas bird is-
lands along the Gulf of Mexico. 641-
654, *Nov. 1949*
Wildlife of Everglades National Park.
By Daniel B. Beard. Paintings by
Walter A. Weber. Included: Cuth-
bert Lake Rookery; East River
Rookery. 83-116, *Jan. 1949*
Sea Bird Cities Off Audubon's Labra-
dor. By Arthur A. Allen. Contents:

BIRDS:

■■*Stalking Birds with Color Camera.* By Arthur A. Allen. 328 pages. *1951*

An Artist's Glimpses of Our Roadside Wildlife. Paintings by Walter A. Weber. Included: Avocets, Bald eagles, Blue-winged teals, Coots, Evening grosbeaks, Fish hawks (Ospreys), Gadwalls, Holboell's grebes, Kingbirds, Magpies, Marsh hawks, Mountain chickadees, Oregon juncos, Pine grosbeaks, Prairie falcons, Pygmy owls, Ravens, Red-breasted nuthatches, Redhead ducks, Red-tailed hawks, Ring-necked pheasants, Scissor-tailed flycatchers, Shovelers, Townsend warblers, Trumpeter swans, Vermilion flycatchers. 16-32, *July 1950*

Wildlife In and Near the Valley of the Moon. By H. H. Arnold. Photos by Paul J. Fair. 401-414, *Mar. 1950*

Peerless Nepal–A Naturalist's Paradise. By S. Dillon Ripley. Photos by Volkmar Wentzel. Included: National Geographic Society-Yale University-Smithsonian Institution Expedition's rediscovery of the Spiny babbler and unsuccessful search for the Mountain quail; other birds noted and collected: Bush larks, Darjeeling woodpeckers, Flycatchers, Hedge sparrows, Hill partridges, Mergansers, Rose finches, Rufous-chinned laughing thrushes, Slaty-headed parakeets, Warblers, White-throated laughing thrushes, Yellow-billed blue magpies. 1-40, *Jan. 1950*

Exploring Stone Age Arnhem Land. By Charles P. Mountford. Photos by Howell Walker. 745-782, *Dec. 1949*

Wildlife of Everglades National Park. By Daniel B. Beard. Paintings by Walter A. Weber. 83-116, *Jan. 1949*

The Curlew's Secret. By Arthur A. Allen. Included: Alaska longspur, Alaska yellow wagtail, Baird's sandpiper, Black-bellied plover, Bristle-thighed curlew, Cackling goose, Cranes, Ducks, Emperor goose, Frigate bird, Geese, Golden plover, Hoary redpoll, Hudsonian curlew, Little brown crane, Northern phalarope, Oldsquaw, Pacific godwit, Parasitic jaeger, Pectoral sandpiper, Ruddy turnstone, Sabine's gull, Savannah sparrow, Snow bunting, Spectacled eider, Tree sparrow, Varied thrush, Western sandpiper, Whistling swan, White-fronted goose, Wilson's snipe. 751-770, *Dec. 1948*

Seeking Mindanao's Strangest Creatures. By Charles Heizer Wharton. Included: Crested serpent eagle, Hornbill, Monkey-eating eagle. 389-408, *Sept. 1948*

A New Light Dawns on Bird Photography. By Arthur A. Allen. Included: Dynamics of bird flight. 774-790, *June 1948*

Sea Bird Cities Off Audubon's Labrador. By Arthur A. Allen. NGS research grant. 755-774, *June 1948*

Lundy, Treasure Island of Birds. By P. T. Etherton. Photos by J. Allan Cash. 675-698, *May 1947*

Birds of Timberline and Tundra. By Arthur A. Allen. Contents: Arctic Loons, Arctic Terns, Black-poll Warblers, Bonaparte's Gulls, Dowitchers, Golden Plovers, Harris's Sparrows, Herring Gulls, Horned Grebes, Hoyt's Horned Larks, Hudsonian Curlews, Lapland Longspurs, Least Sandpipers, Lesser Yellowlegs, Northern Phalaropes, Northern Shrikes, Parasitic Jaeger, Pintail Ducks, Pipits, Red-backed Sandpipers, Semipalmated Plovers, Semipalmated Sandpipers, Snow Buntings, Starlings, Stilt Sandpipers, Tree Sparrows, White-crowned Sparrows, Wild Geese, Willow Ptarmigans, Yellow Warblers. 313-339, *Sept. 1946*

High Country of Colorado. By Alfred M. Bailey. Photos by author, Robert J. Niedrach, and F. G. Brandenburg. Contents: Bluebirds, Flickers, Golden Eagles, Goshawks, Hawks, Hummingbirds, Juncos, Owls, Pine Grosbeaks, Ptarmigans, Robins, Sage Grouse, Sap-suckers, Sparrows, Vireos, Warblers, Woodpeckers. 43-72, *July 1946*

Sights and Sounds of the Winged World: Study of Birds to Make National Geographic Color Photographs Yields Rich Scientific Knowledge of Their Habits and Behavior. By Arthur A. Allen. Contents: Albino Rose-breasted Grosbeak, Baltimore Oriole, Bank Swallow, Black-billed Cuckoo, Black-capped Chickadee, Bronzed Grackle, Chestnut-sided Warbler, Crested Flycatcher, Forster's Tern, Hairy Woodpecker, Kingbird, Long-billed Marsh Wren, Marsh Hawk, Orchard Oriole, Pectoral Sandpiper, Pileated Woodpecker, Prairie Chicken, Redpoll,

Dressed in courting plumage, a common egret eyes nesting grounds on the Vingtune Islands of Texas. FREDERICK KENT TRUSLOW

With talons poised in silent flight, a five-week-old long-eared owlet swoops through the night toward its prey. ART WOLFE

Rotating its wings in reverse, a bald eagle places its head down and tail up while bracing its feet for a landing on a perch in the Florida Everglades. FREDERICK KENT TRUSLOW

BISHOP, WILLIAM A.: *Author*
Tales of the British Air Service. 27-37, *Jan. 1918*

BISITUN, Mount, Iran:
Darius Carved History on Ageless Rock. By George G. Cameron. 825-844, *Dec. 1950*

BISKRA, the Ziban Queen. By Mrs. George C. Bosson, Jr. 563-593, *Aug. 1908*

BISMARCK ARCHIPELAGO. *See* New Britain

BISMARCK SEA:
Ghosts of War in the South Pacific. By Peter Benchley. Photos by David Doubilet. 424-457, *Apr. 1988*

BISON, American:
Buffalo Bill and the Enduring West. By Alice J. Hall. Photos by James L. Amos. 76-103, *July 1981*
Bison Kill By Ice Age Hunters. By Dennis Stanford. NGS research grant. 114-121, *Jan. 1979*
Yellowstone Wildlife in Winter. By William Albert Allard. 637-661, *Nov. 1967*
The Wichitas: Land of the Living Prairie. By M. Woodbridge Williams. 661-697, *May 1957*
Springtime Comes to Yellowstone National Park. By Paul A. Zahl. 761-779, *Dec. 1956*
Hays, Kansas, at the Nation's Heart. By Margaret M. Detwiler. Photos by John E. Fletcher. 461-490, *Apr. 1952*
Lords of the Rockies: Photographing Big Game Animals in Their Primeval Surroundings, from Arizona to Canada, Brings Adventure to Two Wilderness Wanderers. By Wendell and Lucie Chapman. 87-128, *July 1939*

A **BIT** of Elizabethan England in America: Fisher Folk of the Islands Off North Carolina Conserved the Speech and Customs of Sir Walter Raleigh's Colonists. By Blanch Nettleton Epler. 695-730, *Dec. 1933*

A **BIT** of Old Russia Takes Root in Alaska: Nikolaevsk. By Jim Rearden. Photos by Charles O'Rear. 401-425, *Sept. 1972*

BITTER ROOT FOREST RESERVE, Idaho-Montana:
Bitter Root Forest Reserve. By Richard U. Goode. 387-400, *Sept. 1898*

BITTERNS (Birds):
The Large Wading Birds: Long Legs and Remarkable Beaks, as Well as Size, Form, and Color, Distinguish the Herons, Ibises, and Flamingos. By T. Gilbert Pearson. Paintings by Allan Brooks. 441-469, *Oct. 1932*

The **BITTERSWEET** Waters of the Lower Colorado. By Rowe Findley. Photos by Charles O'Rear. 540-569, *Oct. 1973*

BITTINGER, CHARLES: *Artist*
Operation Crossroads. Photos by Joint Task Force I. 519-530, *Apr. 1947*

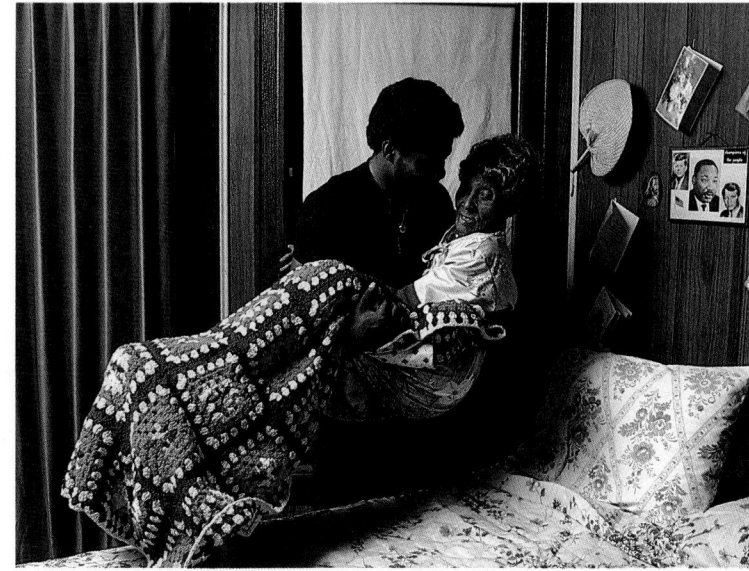

Born a slave in 1861, Mary Duckworth counted some 300 descendants, including great-great-grandson Michael David Thompson, before her death in 1983. LOUIE PSIHOYOS

Solar System's Eternal Show. 16-24, *July 1939*
Unfurling Old Glory on Canton Island. Note: Painting of the eclipse by Charles Bittinger. 753-760, *June 1938*

BIZARRE Battleground–the Lonely Aleutians. By Lonnelle Davison. 316-317, *Sept. 1942*

BIZARRE Dragons of the Sea. Photos by Paul A. Zahl. 838-845, *June 1978*

BIZARRE World of the Fungi. By Paul A. Zahl. 502-527, *Oct. 1965*

BIZERTE, Tunisia:
Eastward from Gibraltar: Overland Route Across North Africa to Tunisia and Libia. By Cyrus French Wicker. 115-142, *Jan. 1943*

BLACK Acres (Mucklands of New York): A Thrilling Sketch in the Vast Volume of Who's Who Among the Peoples That Make America. By Dorothea D. and Fred Everett. 631-652, *Nov. 1941*

BLACK AMERICANS:
Sea Change in the Sea Islands. By Charles L. Blockson. Photos by Karen Kasmauski. Included: Gullah, an African-influenced creole that shapes and defines the black culture of the Sea Islands. 735-763, *Dec. 1987*
The Hidden Tenn-Tom: Bypassed But Still Striving. Photos by Sandy Felsenthal. Text by Alice J. Hall. 384-387, *Mar. 1986*
The Underground Railroad. By Charles L. Blockson. Photos by Louie Psihoyos. 3-39, *July 1984*
Savannah to Charleston–A Good Life in the Low Country. By John J. Putman. Photos by Annie Griffiths. 798-829, *Dec. 1983*

Brooklyn: The Other Side of the Bridge. By Alice J. Hall. Photos by Robert W. Madden. 580-613, *May 1983*
Washington, D. C.: Hometown Behind the Monuments. By Henry Mitchell. Photos by Adam Woolfitt. 84-125, *Jan. 1983*
To Live in Harlem.... By Frank Hercules. Photos by LeRoy Woodson, Jr. 178-207, *Feb. 1977*

BLACK-BACKED JACKALS:
Jackals of the Serengeti. By Patricia D. Moehlman. 840-850, *Dec. 1980*

BLACK BEARS:
Studying Wildlife by Satellite. By Frank Craighead, Jr., and John Craighead. NGS research grant. 120-123, *Jan. 1973*
Once in a Lifetime: Black Bears Rarely Have Quadruplets, But Goofy Did–and the Camera Caught Her Nursing Her Remarkable Family. By Paul B. Kinney. 249-258, *Aug. 1941*

BLACK Day for Brittany. Photos by Martin Rogers. Text by Noel Grove. 124-135, *July 1978*

BLACK DEATH (Epidemic):
Fleas: The Lethal Leapers. By Nicole Duplaix. 672-694, *May 1988*
Fearful Famines of the Past: History Will Repeat Itself Unless the American People Conserve Their Resources. By Ralph A. Graves. 69-90, *July 1917*
The Conquest of Bubonic Plague in the Philippines. 185-195, *May 1903*
Geographic Miscellanea. 248, *June 1900*
The History and Geographic Distribution of Bubonic Plague. By George M. Sternberg. 97-113, *Mar. 1900*

Ghost ships ride out winter on a marsh near Wellfleet, a village beside Massachusetts' Cape Cod Bay. JAMES P. BLAIR, NGS

By Gordon Young. 738-781, *Dec. 1970*

Orissa, Past and Promise in an Indian State. By Bart McDowell. 546-577, *Oct. 1970*

Yugoslavia: Six Republics in One. By Robert Paul Jordan. 589-633, *May 1970*

The Revolution in American Agriculture. By Jules B. Billard. 147-185, *Feb. 1970*

Wild Elephant Roundup in India. By Harry Miller. Photos by author and James P. Blair. 372-385, *Mar. 1969*

Crystals, Magical Servants of the Space Age. By Kenneth F. Weaver. 278-296, *Aug. 1968*

New National Park Proposed: The Spectacular North Cascades. By Nathaniel T. Kenney. 642-667, *May 1968*

Czechoslovakia: The Dream and the Reality. By Edward J. Linehan. 151-193, *Feb. 1968*

New Grandeur for Flowering Washington. By Joseph Judge. 500-539, *Apr. 1967*

Freedom Speaks French in Ouagadougou. By John Scofield. 153-203, *Aug. 1966*

One Man's London. By Allan C. Fisher, Jr. 743-791, *June 1966*

California, the Golden Magnet: II. Nature's North. By William Graves. Photos by James P. Blair and Jonathan S. Blair. 641-679, *May 1966*

The Fair Reopens (New York World's Fair, 1964-1965). Text by Carolyn Bennett Patterson. 505-529, *Apr. 1965*

Ethiopian Adventure. By Nathaniel T. Kenney. 548-582, *Apr. 1965*

Ambassadors of Good Will: The Peace Corps. By Sargent Shriver and Peace Corps Volunteers. 297-345, *Sept. 1964*

From Sun-clad Sea to Shining Mountains. By Ralph Gray. 542-589, *Apr. 1964*

Florida Rides a Space-age Boom. By Benedict Thielen. Photos by Winfield Parks and James P. Blair. 858-903, *Dec. 1963*

Gettysburg and Vicksburg: the Battle Towns Today. By Robert Paul Jordan. Map notes by Carolyn Bennett Patterson. 4-57, *July 1963*

The Man Who Talks to Hummingbirds. By Luis Marden. 80-99, *Jan. 1963*

In the Crusaders' Footsteps. By Franc Shor. Photos by Thomas Nebbia and James P. Blair. 731-789, *June 1962*

Martha's Vineyard. By William P. E. Graves. 778-809, *June 1961*

Rotterdam–Reborn From Ruins. By Helen Hill Miller. 526-553, *Oct. 1960*

BLAIR, JONATHAN:

Nomination Page. In Florida. *Jan. 1978*

Author-Photographer

Keeping House in a Cappadocian Cave. 127-146, *July 1970*

Photographer

Meteorites–Invaders From Space. By Kenneth F. Weaver. 390-418, *Sept. 1986*

Yosemite–Forever? By David S. Boyer. 52-79, *Jan. 1985*

A Buried Roman Town Gives Up Its Dead (Herculaneum). By Joseph Judge. 687-693, *Dec. 1982*

The Mediterranean–Sea of Man's Fate. By Rick Gore. 694-737, *Dec. 1982*

Synfuels: Fill 'er Up! With What? By Thomas Y. Canby. 74-95, *Special Report on Energy. (Feb. 1981)*

Graveyard of the Quicksilver Galleons. By Mendel Peterson. 850-876, *Dec. 1979*

Mysteries of Bird Migration. By Allan C. Fisher, Jr. 154-193, *Aug. 1979*

Glass Treasure From the Aegean. By George F. Bass. 768-793, *June 1978*

Hawaii's Far-flung Wildlife Paradise. By John L. Eliot. 670-691, *May 1978*

A Bad Time to Be a Crocodile. By Rick Gore. 90-115, *Jan. 1978*

Riding the Outlaw Trail. By Robert Redford. 622-657, *Nov. 1976*

Sicily, Where All the Songs Are Sad. By Howard La Fay. 407-436, *Mar. 1976*

Stockholm, Where "Kvalitet" Is a Way of Life. By James Cerruti. Photos by Albert Moldvay and Jonathan Blair. 43-69, *Jan. 1976*

New Life for the Troubled Suez Canal. By William Graves. 792-817, *June 1975*

Florida's Booming–and Beleaguered– Heartland. By Joseph Judge. 585-621, *Nov. 1973*

Madeira, Like Its Wine, Improves With Age. By Veronica Thomas. 488-513, *Apr. 1973*

Cyprus Under Four Flags: A Struggle for Unity. By Kenneth MacLeish. 356-383, *Mar. 1973*

Aphrodisias, Awakened City of Ancient Art. By Kenan T. Erim. 766-791, *June 1972*

Yellowstone at 100: The Pitfalls of Success. By William S. Ellis. 616-631, *May 1972*

On the Road With an Old-time Circus. By John Fetterman. 410-434, *Mar. 1972*

Barehanded Battle to Cleanse the Bay. By Peter T. White. 866-881, *June 1971*

Home to the Enduring Berkshires. By Charles McCarry. 196-221, *Aug. 1970*

Dry-land Fleet Sails the Sahara. By Jean du Boucher. 696-725, *Nov. 1967*

Ancient Aphrodisias and Its Marble Treasures. By Kenan T. Erim. 280-294, *Aug. 1967*

California, the Golden Magnet: II. Nature's North. By William Graves. Photos by James P. Blair and Jonathan S. Blair. 641-679, *May 1966*

BLAKE, THOMAS EDWARD: *Photographer*

Waves and Thrills at Waikiki (Honolulu). 597-604, *May 1935*

BLAKELY, R. L.: *Author*

Miniature Horses. Photos by Thomas Nebbia. 384-393, *Mar. 1985*

BLANC, Mont, France:

The Ascent of Mont Blanc. By Walter Woodburn Hyde. 861-942, *Aug. 1913*

A Woman's Climbs in the High Alps. By Dora Keen. 643-675, *July 1911*

BLANCHARD, C. J.: *Author*

The Spirit of the West (U. S.): The Wonderful Agricultural Development Since the Dawn of Irrigation. 333-360, *Apr. 1910*

The Call of the West. 403-437, *May 1909*

Home-Making by the Government: An Account of the Eleven Immense Irrigating Projects to be Opened in 1908. 250-287, *Apr. 1908*

Millions for Moisture: An Account of the Work of the U. S. Reclamation Service. 217-243, *Apr. 1907*

Winning the West. 82-98, *Feb. 1906*

BLANCHARD, FRIEDA COBB: *Author*

Tuatara: "Living Fossils" Walk on Well-Nigh Inaccessible Rocky Islands off the Coast of New Zealand. 649-662, *May 1935*

BLAYNEY, THOMAS LINDSEY: *Author*

A Journey in Morocco: "The Land of the Moors." 750-775, *Aug. 1911*

BLEDSOE, MARGARET:

Nomination Page. *Nov. 1958*

BLESSING OF THE FLEET:

Gloucester Blesses Its Portuguese Fleet. By Luis Marden. 75-84, *July 1953*

BLEVINS, BURGESS: *Photographer*

Rediscovering America's Forgotten Crops. By Noel D. Vietmeyer. Paintings by Paul M. Breeden. 702-712, *May 1981*

BLIGH, WILLIAM:

Pitcairn and Norfolk–The Saga of *Bounty*'s Children. By Ed Howard. Photos by David Hiser and Melinda Berge. 510-541. Included: Pitcairn Island. 512-529; Norfolk Island. 530-541, *Oct. 1983*

Tahiti, "Finest Island in the World." By Luis Marden. 1-47, *July 1962*

Huzza for Otaheite! By Luis Marden. 435-459, *Apr. 1962*

I Found the Bones of the *Bounty*. By Luis Marden. 725-789, *Dec. 1957*

BLIMPS:

Aboard a Blimp Hunting U-boats: A Day above the Atlantic Reveals Navy Talk and Navy Ways, Creeping Convoys, and Torpedoed Wrecks. By Mason Sutherland. 79-96, *July 1943*

BLISS, HOWARD S.: *Author*

Sunshine in Turkey. 66-76, *Jan. 1909*

BLITHE Birds of Dooryard, Bush, and Brake. Paintings by Allan Brooks. 579-594, *May 1934*

BLIZZARD of Birds: The Tortugas Terns. By Alexander Sprunt, Jr. 213-230, *Feb. 1947*

BLIZZARD OF 1888:

The Great Storm of March 11-14, 1888. By A. W. Greely. 37-39, *Oct. 1888*

The Great Storm Off the Atlantic Coast of the United States, March 11th-

14th, 1888. By Everett Hayden. 40-58, *Oct. 1888*

BLOCH, SARA: *Author*

Sheep Dog Trials in Llangollen: Trained Collies Perform Marvels of Herding in the Cambrian Stakes, Open to the World. 559-574, *Apr. 1940*

BLOCK, IRA: *Photographer*

The Search for Modern Humans. By John J. Putman. Photos by Sisse Brimberg and Ira Block. Paintings by Jack Unruh. 439-477, *Oct. 1988*

An Ice Age Ancestor? By Alexander Marshack. Photos by the author and Ira Block. 478-481, *Oct. 1988*

Alexander Graham Bell. By Robert V. Bruce. 358-385, *Sept. 1988*

Peru's Pilgrimage to the Sky. By Robert Randall. Photos by Loren McIntyre and Ira Block. 60-69, *July 1982*

New Clues to an Old Mystery (Virginia's Wolstenholme Towne). By Ivor Noël Hume. Paintings by Richard Schlecht. 53-77, *Jan. 1982*

■■ *Back Roads America: A Portfolio of Her People.* By Thomas O'Neill. 199 pages. *1980*

First Look at a Lost Virginia Settlement (Martin's Hundred). By Ivor Noël Hume. Paintings by Richard Schlecht. 735-767, *June 1979*

Solo to the Pole. By Naomi Uemura. Photos by the author and Ira Block. 298-325, *Sept. 1978*

The Continental Shelf: Man's New Frontier. By Luis Marden. 495-531, *Apr. 1978*

■■ *Nature's Healing Arts: From Folk Medicine to Modern Drugs.* By Lonnelle Aikman. Photos by Nathan Benn and Ira Block. 199 pages. *1977*

BLOCKSON, CHARLES L.:

On Assignment in Pennsylvania. *July 1984*

Author

Sea Change in the Sea Islands. Photos by Karen Kasmauski. 735-763, *Dec. 1987*

The Underground Railroad. Photos by Louie Psihoyos. 3-39, *July 1984*

BLODGETT, JAMES H.: *Author*

Geographic Literature. 478-480, *Nov. 1898*

"Free Burghs" in the United States. 116-122, *Mar. 1896*

BLOOD, NED: *Photographer*

Sheep Airlift in New Guinea. 831-844, *Dec. 1949*

"BLOOD, Toil, Tears, and Sweat": An American Tells the Story of Britain's War Effort, Summed up in Prime Minister Churchill's Unflinching Words. By Harvey Klemmer. 141-166, *Aug. 1942*

BLOOD SERVICES:

The American Red Cross: A Century of Service. By Louise Levathes. Photos by Annie Griffiths. 777-791, *June 1981*

BLOODWORMS:

The Worm Turns. By Samuel Sandrof. 775-786, *June 1946*

BLOSSOM (Ship):

Sindbads of Science: Narrative of a Windjammer's Specimen-Collecting Voyage to the Sargasso Sea, to Senegambian Africa and Among Islands of High Adventure in the South Atlantic. By George Finlay Simmons. 1-75, *July 1927*

BLOSSOMS That Defy the Seasons. By Geneal Condon. Photos by David S. Boyer. 420-427, *Sept. 1958*

BLOUNT, HENRY F.:

Resolution in memory of Henry F. Blount. 371, *Apr. 1918*

Board of Managers. xii, Feb. 19, 1892; xix, Feb. 20, 1893; xix, May 5, 1894; 191, June 1897; 88, *Jan. 1910*

BLOUNT, ROY, Jr.: *Author*

Spoofing the Geographic. 353-357, *Sept. 1988*

BLOWFISH. *See* Puffer Fish

BLOWGUN Hunters of the South Pacific. By Jane C. Goodale. Photos by Ann Chowning. 793-817, *June 1966*

BLUE, RUPERT: *Author*

Conserving the Nation's Man-Power: Disease Weakens Armies, Cripples Industry, Reduces Production. How the Government is Sanitating the Civil Zones Around Cantonment Areas. A Nation-wide Campaign for Health. 255-278, *Sept. 1917*

BLUE CRABS:

This Is My Island, Tangier (Virginia). By Harold G. Wheatley. Photos by David Alan Harvey. 700-725, *Nov. 1973*

Can We Save Our Salt Marshes? By Stephen W. Hitchcock. Photos by William R. Curtsinger. 729-765, *June 1972*

The Blue Crab. 46, *Jan. 1906*

BLUE-EYED Indian: A City Boy's Sojourn with Primitive Tribesmen in Central Brazil. By Harald Schultz. 65-89, *July 1961*

BLUE HOLES, Great Bahama Bank:

Diving Into the Blue Holes of the Bahamas. By George J. Benjamin. 347-363, *Sept. 1970*

BLUE Horizons: Paradise Isles of the
■■ *Pacific.* Includes the Cook Islands, Fiji, French Polynesia, Hawaii, the Samoa Islands, and Tonga. 199 pages. *1985*

BLUE MOUNTAIN, Maryland:

The Geologist at Blue Mountain, Maryland. By Charles D. Walcott. 84-88, *July 10, 1893*

BLUE RIDGE (Mountains), U. S.:

Wrestlin' for a Livin' With King Coal. By Michael E. Long. Photos by Michael O'Brien. 793-819, *June 1983*

Chattooga River Country: Wild Water,

Proud People. By Don Belt. Photos by Steve Wall. 458-477, *Apr. 1983*

The Virginians. By Mike W. Edwards. Photos by David Alan Harvey. 588-617, *Nov. 1974*

Shenandoah, I Long to Hear You. By Mike W. Edwards. Photos by Thomas Anthony DeFeo. 554-588, *Apr. 1970*

My Neighbors Hold to Mountain Ways. By Malcolm Ross. Photos by Flip Schulke. 856-880, *June 1958*

Skyline Trail from Maine to Georgia. By Andrew H. Brown. Photos by Robert F. Sisson. 219-251, *Aug. 1949*

Appalachian Valley Pilgrimage. By Catherine Bell Palmer. Photos by Justin Locke. 1-32, *July 1949*

Spottswood's Expedition of 1716. By William M. Thornton. 265-269, *Aug. 1896*

BLUE Seas and Brilliant Costumes Along the Brittany Coast. Photos by Gervais Courtellemont. 143-174, *Aug. 1929*

BLUE-WATER Life by Night. By Kenneth Brower. Photos by William R. Curtsinger and Chris Newbert. 834-847, *Dec. 1981*

BLUE-WATER Plankton: Ghosts of the Gulf Stream. By William M. Hamner. 530-545, *Oct. 1974*

BLUE WHALES:

Rare Look At Sperm and Blue Whales, The Unknown Giants. By Hal Whitehead. Photos by Flip Nicklin. 774-789, *Dec. 1984*

Killer Whale Attack! Text by Cliff Tarpy. Contents: Blue whale attacked by thirty killer whales. 542-545, *Apr. 1979*

BLUEBERRIES:

The Wild Blueberry Tamed: The New Industry of the Pine Barrens of New Jersey. By Frederick V. Coville. 535-546, *June 1916*

Taming the Wild Blueberry. By Frederick V. Coville. 137-147, *Feb. 1911*

BLUEBIRDS:

Song of Hope for the Bluebird. By Lawrence Zeleny. Photos by Michael L. Smith. 855-865, *June 1977*

Seeing Birds as Real Personalities. By Hance Roy Ivor. Included: Bluebirds on the Wing in Color. Photos by Bernard Corby and author. 523-530, *Apr. 1954*

BLUEFIN TUNA:

Plight of the Bluefin Tuna. By Michael J. A. Butler. Photos by David Doubilet. Paintings by Stanley Meltzoff. 220-239, *Aug. 1982*

BLUEGRASS REGION, Kentucky:

Heart of the Bluegrass. By Charles McCarry. Photos by J. Bruce Baumann. 634-659, *May 1974*

BLUM, ARLENE: *Author*

Triumph and Tragedy on Annapurna. 295-311, *Mar. 1979*

This boatload of Haitian refugees sailed to Florida in 1981, fleeing poverty and oppression in their homeland. NATHAN BENN

BOARDMAN, MABEL:

The National Geographic Society (Address by Mabel Boardman at Annual Banquet). 288-290, *Mar. 1912*

Honors to the American Navy (Address by Mabel Boardman at NGS Banquet). 84-86, *Jan. 1909*

Author

The American Red Cross in Italy. 396-397, *Apr. 1909*

BOAT PEOPLE:

Florida–A Time for Reckoning. By William S. Ellis. Photos by Nathan Benn and Kevin Fleming. Included: Refugees from the 1980 Cuban boatlift and from Haiti. 172-219, *Aug. 1982*

Troubled Odyssey of Vietnamese Fishermen. By Harvey Arden. Photos by Steve Wall. 378-395, *Sept. 1981*

Hong Kong's Refugee Dilemma. By William S. Ellis. Photos by William Albert Allard. 709-732, *Nov. 1979*

BOAT RACES:

The Thames: That Noble River. By Ethel A. Starbird. Photos by O. Louis Mazzatenta. Included: Cambridge vs. Oxford; Henley Royal Regatta. 750-791, *June 1983*

By Square-rigger from Baltic to Bicentennial. By Kenneth Garrett. 824-857, *Dec. 1976*

Down East to Nova Scotia. By Winfield Parks. Included: Marblehead-Halifax race; Bras d'Or Lakes 15-mile race for the McCurdy Cup; Jones Trophy for Canadian yachts. 853-879, *June 1964*

To Europe with a Racing Start. By Carleton Mitchell. Included: Newport-to-Bermuda race. 758-791, *June 1958*

See also Yachting

BOATS:

The Thames: That Noble River. By Ethel A. Starbird. Photos by O. Louis Mazzatenta. 750-791, *June 1983*

Massachusetts' North Shore: Harboring Old Ways. By Randall S. Peffer. Photos by Nathan Benn. Included: Fishing boats, boatbuilding, and sailmaking. 568-590, *Apr. 1979*

California's Surprising Inland Delta. By Judith and Neil Morgan. Photos by Charles O'Rear. 409-430, *Sept. 1976*

Ships Through the Ages: A Saga of the Sea. By Alan Villiers. Included: Small craft, precursors of the ship. 494-545, *Apr. 1963*

Shooting Rapids in Reverse! Jet Boats Climb the Colorado's Torrent Through the Grand Canyon. By William Belknap, Jr. 552-565, *Apr. 1962*

Inflatable Ship *(Amphitrite)* Opens Era of Airborne Undersea Expeditions. By Jacques-Yves Cousteau. 142-148, *July 1961*

The Lower Mississippi. By Willard Price. Photos by W. D. Vaughn. 681-725, *Nov. 1960*

The Upper Mississippi. By Willard Price. 651-699, *Nov. 1958*

The Thames Mirrors England's Varied Life. By Willard Price. Photos by Robert F. Sisson. 45-93, *July 1958*

Here's New York Harbor. By Stuart E.

Jones. Photos by Robert F. Sisson and David S. Boyer. 773-813, *Dec. 1954*

On the Winds of the Dodecanese. By Jean and Franc Shor. 351-390, *Mar. 1953*

"Delmarva," Gift of the Sea. By Catherine Bell Palmer. Included: Chesapeake Bay boats: Bugeyes, Hampton-class sloops, Log canoes, Skipjacks. 367-399, *Sept. 1950*

Windjamming Around New England. By Tom Horgan. Photos by Robert F. Sisson. Contents: "Brutal Beasts," Cape Cod Baby Knockabouts, Dinghies, International 210-class sloops, Lightning-class sloops. 141-169, *Aug. 1950*

Trawling the China Seas. Photos by J. Charles Thompson. Contents: Junks, Sampans. 381-395, *Mar. 1950*

Pirate-Fighters of the South China Sea. By Robert Cardwell. 787-796, *June 1946*

Landing Craft for Invasion. By Melville Bell Grosvenor. 1-30, *July 1944*

The Tuna Harvest of the Sea: A Littleknown Epic of the Ocean Is the Story of Southern California's Far-ranging Tuna Fleet. By John Degelman. 393-408, *Sept. 1940*

Ships, from Dugouts to Dreadnoughts. By Dudley W. Knox. 57-98, *Jan. 1938*

China's Teeming Life on the Rivers and Sea. Photos by Paul De Gaston and W. Robert Moore. 625-640, *Nov. 1934*

Cosmopolitan Shanghai, Key Seaport of

Restored English barges and smaller smacks carry partygoers rather than heavy cargo during a nostalgic race on the lower Thames River. O. LOUIS MAZZATENTA, NGS

Flamboyant Is the Word for Bolivia. By Loren McIntyre. 153-195, *Feb. 1966*

Ambassadors of Good Will: The Peace Corps. By Sargent Shriver and Peace Corps Volunteers. Included: Bolivia. By Edward S. Dennison. 297-345, *Sept. 1964*

In Quest of the Rarest Flamingo. By William G. Conway. Photos by Bates Littlehales. 91-105, *July 1961*

Puya, the Pineapple's Andean Ancestor. By Mulford B. Foster. 463-480, *Oct. 1950*

Sky-high Bolivia. 481-496, *Oct. 1950*

Bolivia–Tin Roof of the Andes. By Henry Albert Phillips. 309-332, *Mar. 1943*

Tin, the Cinderella Metal. By Alicia O'Reardon Overbeck. 659-684, *Nov. 1940*

Bolivia, Land of Fiestas. By Alicia O'Reardon Overbeck. 645-660, *Nov. 1934*

Buenos Aires to Washington by Horse: A Solitary Journey of Two and a Half Years, Through Eleven American Republics, Covers 9,600 Miles of Mountain and Plain, Desert and Jungle. By A. F. Tschiffely. 135-196, *Feb. 1929*

The Heart of Aymará Land: A Visit to Tiahuanacu, Perhaps the Oldest City of the New World, Lost Beneath the Drifting Sand of Centuries in the Bolivian Highlands. By Stewart E. McMillin. 213-256, *Feb. 1927*

Kaleidoscopic La Paz: The City of the Clouds. By Harriet Chalmers Adams. 119-141, *Feb. 1909*

Some Wonderful Sights in the Andean Highlands: The Oldest City in America. Sailing on the Lake of the Clouds: The Yosemite of Peru. By Harriet Chalmers Adams. 597-618, *Sept. 1908*

Bolivia–A Country Without a Debt. By Y. Calderon. 573-586, *Sept. 1907*

From Panama to Patagonia. By Charles M. Pepper. 449-452, *Aug. 1906*

What the Latin American Republics Think of the Pan-American Conferences. 474-479, *Aug. 1906*

The Road to Bolivia (Part II). By William E. Curtis. 264-280, *July 1900*

The Road to Bolivia (Part I). By William E. Curtis. 209-224, *June 1900*

See also Titicaca, Lake

BOLL WEEVILS:

The Pesticide Dilemma. By Allen A. Boraiko. Photos by Fred Ward. 145-183, *Feb. 1980*

The Red Ant Versus the Boll Weevil. 262-264, *June 1904*

BOMBAY, India:

Bombay, the Other India. By John Scofield. Photos by Raghubir Singh. 104-129, *July 1981*

The Parsees and the Towers of Silence at Bombay, India. By William Thomas Fee. 529-554, *Dec. 1905*

BOMBERS:

Flying in the "Blowtorch" Era. By Frederick G. Vosburgh. 281-322, *Sept. 1950*

Our Air Age Speeds Ahead. By F. Barrows Colton. 249-272, *Feb. 1948*

Fun Helped Them Fight. By Stuart E. Jones. 95-104, *Jan. 1948*

Air Power for Peace. By H. H. Arnold. 137-193, *Feb. 1946*

Saga of the Carrier *Princeton*. By William H. Buracker. 189-218, *Aug. 1945*

Return to Florence (Italy). By Benjamin C. McCartney. 257-296, *Mar. 1945*

8th Air Force in England. Photos from U. S. Army Air Forces. 297-304, *Mar. 1945*

Painting History in the Pacific. Paintings by William F. Draper. 408-424, *Oct. 1944*

Navy Wings over the Pacific. Photos from U. S. Navy. 241-248, *Aug. 1944*

Cruise on an Escort Carrier. By Melville Bell Grosvenor. 513-546, *Nov. 1943*

American Bombers Attacking from Australia. By Howell Walker. 49-70, *Jan. 1943*

The New Queen of the Seas. By Melville Bell Grosvenor. 1-30, *July 1942*

BOMBS:

Air Power for Peace. By H. H. Arnold. 137-193, *Feb. 1946*

London Wins the Battle. By Marquis W. Childs. 129-152, *Aug. 1945*

Bombs over Bible Lands. By Frederick Simpich and W. Robert Moore. 141-180, *Aug. 1941*

See also Atomic Bomb Tests

BONAIRE (Island), Netherlands Antilles:

The Netherlands Antilles: Holland in the Caribbean. By James Cerruti. Photos by Emory Kristof. 115-146, *Jan. 1970*

Curaçao and Aruba on Guard. By W. Robert Moore. 169-192, *Feb. 1943*

A Waurá wrestler awaits his bout during a ceremonial competition among tribes along the Amazon River.   LOREN MCINTYRE

The **BONANZA** Bean–Coffee. By Ethel A. Starbird. Photos by Sam Abell. 388-405, *Mar. 1981*

BONAPARTE, CHARLES J.:

Honors to Peary (Address by Charles J. Bonaparte). 49-60, *Jan. 1907*

BONAPARTE, NAPOLEON. *See* Napoleon I

BOND, WILLIAM H.:

On Assignment. *Nov. 1983*

Nomination Page. *Aug. 1980*

Artist

Air: An Atmosphere of Uncertainty. By Noel Grove. Photos by Ted Spiegel. Included: A deadly soup (a list of harmful chemicals), Careless neighbors, A global greenhouse, The ozone enigma, Getting the lead out, The enemy within. 502-537, *Apr. 1987*

Have We Solved the Mysteries of the Moon? By Kenneth F. Weaver. 309-325, *Mar. 1973*

⊕ "How Man Pollutes His World," painting supplement. Text notes by Gordon Young. World map on reverse. *Dec. 1970*

BONDA TRIBESPEOPLE:

Orissa, Past and Promise in an Indian State. By Bart McDowell. Photos by James P. Blair. 546-577, *Oct. 1970*

BONDS Between the Americas. By Frederick Simpich. 785-808, *Dec. 1937*

BONE WORKING:

The Search for the First Americans. By Thomas Y. Canby. Photos by Kerby Smith. Paintings by Roy Andersen. 330-363, *Sept. 1979*

BONIN ISLANDS, North Pacific Ocean:

The Bonins and Iwo Jima Go Back to Japan. By Paul Sampson. Photos by Joe Munroe. 128-144, *July 1968*

American Pathfinders in the Pacific. By William H. Nicholas. 617-640, *May 1946*

Springboards to Tokyo. By Willard Price. 385-407, *Oct. 1944*

Hidden Key to the Pacific: Piercing the Web of Secrecy Which Long Has Veiled Japanese Bases in the Mandated Islands. By Willard Price. 759-785, *June 1942*

BONITA (Yawl):

Cruising to Crete: Four French Girls Set Sail in a Breton Yawl for the Island of the Legendary Minotaur. By Marthe Oulié and Mariel Jean-Brunhes. 249-272, *Feb. 1929*

BONIVARD, FRANÇOIS DE:

The Millennial City: The Romance of Geneva, Capital of the League of Nations. By Ralph A. Graves. 457-476, *June 1919*

BONN, West Germany:

War's Wake in the Rhineland. By Thomas H. Henry. 1-32, *July 1945*

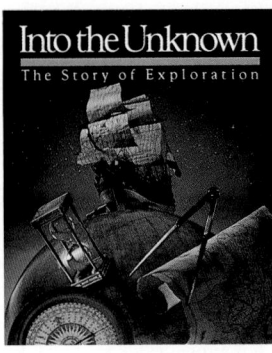

BONNEVILLE, Lake (Pleistocene Lake), Utah:

The Rising Great Salt Lake: No Way to Run a Desert. By Rick Gore. Photos by Jim Richardson. 694-719, *June 1985*

BONNIE Scotland, Postwar Style. By Isobel Wylie Hutchison. 545-601, *May 1946*

BONPLAND, AIMÉ:

Humboldt's Way. By Loren McIntyre. Note: French naturalist Bonpland was Humboldt's expedition botanist. 318-351, *Sept. 1985*

BOOBIES:

Peru Profits from Sea Fowl. By Robert Cushman Murphy. Photos by author and Grace E. Barstow Murphy. 395-413, *Mar. 1959*

BOOK, NGS Centennial:

▪▪ *The National Geographic Society: 100 Years of Adventure and Discovery.* By C.D.B. Bryan. Published by Harry N. Abrams, Inc. 484 pages. *1987*

BOOKS, NGS:

President's Page. By Gilbert M. Grosvenor. *Sept. 1988*
America's Ancient Cities. By Gene S. Stuart. Photos by Richard Alexander Cooke III. Art by H. Tom Hall. 199 pages. *1988*
America's Hidden Wilderness: Lands of Seclusion. Contents: Arctic regions; Baxter State Park, Maine; l'Eau Claire wilderness, Quebec; Grand Gulch Primitive Area, Utah; Great Burn wilderness area, Idaho-Montana; Lacandon Forest, Mexico; Mojave Desert. 200 pages. *1988*
Excursion to Enchantment: A Journey to the World's Most Beautiful Places. Included: East Africa, Loire Valley, Bhutan, Chile-Argentina Lake District, Inside Passage, and the Caribbean. 200 pages. *1988*
Inventors and Discoverers: Changing Our World. 320 pages. *1988*
Living on the Earth. Contents: How various peoples have adapted to the world's environments. 320 pages. *1988*
Mountain Adventure: Exploring the Appalachian Trail. By Ron Fisher. Photos by Sam Abell. 200 pages. *1988*
Mountain Worlds. 320 pages. *1988*

America's Outdoor Wonders: State Parks and Sanctuaries. 199 pages. *1987*
Into the Unknown: The Story of Exploration. 336 pages. *1987*
Majestic Island Worlds. Contents: Bali, Galapagos, Ireland, Japan, New Zealand, and Seychelles. 199 pages. *1987*
Our World's Heritage. Contents: UNESCO-designated World Heritage Sites. 312 pages. *1987*
Traveling the Trans-Canada: From Newfoundland to British Columbia. By William Howarth. Photos by George F. Mobley. 199 pages. *1987*
Wild Animals of North America. 406 pages. 1979; rev. ed. *1987*
Window on America. Contents: America's scenic treasures. 199 pages. *1987*
America's Great Hideaways. Contents: Arizona, Baja California, California, Canadian Rockies, Finger Lakes, Kauai, Martha's Vineyard and Nantucket, Minnesota, Montana, Oregon, Suwannee River, Virgin Islands, and West Virginia. 199 pages. *1986*
Builders of the Ancient World: Marvels of Engineering. Contents: Greece and Rome, Mesoamerica, South America, India and Southeast Asia, and China. 199 pages. *1986*
The Incredible Machine. Contents: The human body. 384 pages. *1986*
Nature on the Rampage: Our Violent Earth. 199 pages. *1986*
Our Awesome Earth: Its Mysteries and Its Splendors. 199 pages. *1986*
The Adventure of Archaeology. By Brian M. Fagan. 368 pages. *1985*
America's Seashore Wonderlands. 199 pages. *1985*
America's Wild Woodlands. 199 pages. *1985*
Atlas of North America: Space Age Portrait of a Continent. 264 pages. *1985*
Blue Horizons: Paradise Isles of the Pacific. Contents: Cook Islands, Fiji, French Polynesia, Hawaii, Samoa Islands, and Tonga. 199 pages. *1985*
Discovering Britain & Ireland. 448 pages. *1985*
Exploring America's Scenic Highways. 199 pages. *1985*
Alaska's Magnificent Parklands. 199 pages. *1984*
Exploring America's Valleys: From the Shenandoah to the Rio Grande. 199 pages. *1984*

Great Rivers of the World. 448 pages. *1984*
Lakes, Peaks, and Prairies: Discovering the United States-Canadian Border. By Thomas O'Neill. Photos by Michael S. Yamashita. 199 pages. *1984*
Our Threatened Inheritance: Natural Treasures of the United States. By Ron Fisher. Photos by James P. Blair. 400 pages. *1984*
A Guide to Our Federal Lands. 227 pages. *1984*
Wild Lands for Wildlife: America's National Refuges. By Noel Grove. Photos by Bates Littlehales. 207 pages. *1984*
America's Hidden Corners: Places Off the Beaten Path. Contents: Badlands, Chesapeake Bay, Four Corners, Great Basin, Gulf Coast, Michigan's Upper Peninsula, and Ozarks. 199 pages. *1983*
America's Wild and Scenic Rivers. 199 pages. *1983*
Exploring Our Living Planet. By Robert D. Ballard. 366 pages. *1983*
Field Guide to the Birds of North America. 464 pages. *1983*
Nature's World of Wonders. 199 pages. *1983*
Peoples and Places of the Past: The National Geographic Illustrated Cultural Atlas of the Ancient World. 424 pages. *1983*
Preserving America's Past. 199 pages. *1983*
The Wonder of Birds. Included: *Guide to Birds* recording and *Field Guide to the Birds of North America.* 280 pages. *1983*
America's Spectacular Northwest. Photos by Robert W. Madden. 199 pages. *1982*
Canada's Wilderness Lands. 199 pages. *1982*
The Desert Realm: Lands of Majesty and Mystery. 304 pages. *1982*
Journey Into China. 518 pages. *1982*
Lost Empires, Living Tribes. 402 pages. *1982*
On the Brink of Tomorrow: Frontiers of Science. Photos by Mark Godfrey. Art by Susan Sanford. 199 pages. *1982*
Secret Corners of the World. Contents: Northern Afghanistan, the Alpujarras, the Santa Martas, the Marquesas, Tierra Del Fuego, and the Ruwenzori. 199 pages. *1982*

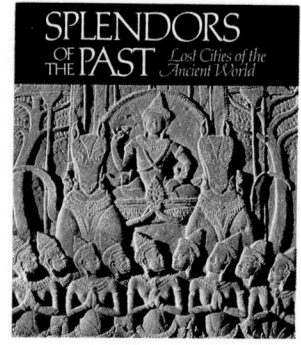 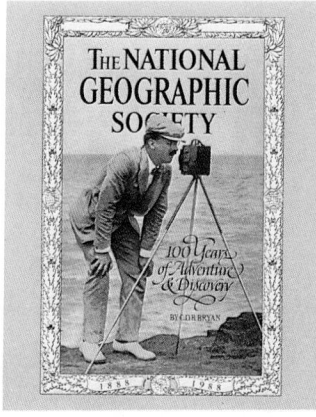 

America's Atlantic Isles. By H. Robert Morrison and Christine Eckstrom Lee. Photos by David Alan Harvey. 199 pages. *1981*

Atlas of the World. 383 pages. 1963; fifth ed. *1981*

High Country Trail: Along the Continental Divide. By Michael Robbins. Photos by Paul Chesley. 199 pages. *1981*

Images of the World: Photography at the National Geographic. 396 pages. *1981*

The Mighty Aztecs. By Gene S. Stuart. Photos by Mark Godfrey. Art by Louis S. Glanzman. 199 pages. *1981*

National Geographic Photographer's Field Guide. By Albert Moldvay. 120 pages. *1981*

Our Country's Presidents. By Frank Freidel. 279 pages. 1966; rev. ed. *1981*

Romance of the Sea. Contents: Maritime history. 312 pages. *1981*

Splendors of the Past: Lost Cities of the Ancient World. Included: Angkor; Kush; Middle East; Pompeii; Sinhalese Kingdoms. 295 pages. *1981*

Voyages to Paradise: Exploring in the Wake of Captain Cook. By William R. Gray. Photos by Gordon W. Gahan. 215 pages. *1981*

We Americans. 456 pages. 1975; rev. ed. *1981*

America's Magnificent Mountains. 207 pages. *1980*

America's Wonderlands: The Scenic National Parks and Monuments of the United States. 552 pages. 1959; rev. ed. *1980*

Back Roads America: A Portfolio of Her People. By Thomas O'Neill. Photos by Ira Block. 199 pages. *1980*

Exploring the Deep Frontier: The Adventure of Man in the Sea. By Sylvia A. Earle and Al Giddings. 246 pages. *1980*

The Great Southwest. By Charles McCarry. Photos by George F. Mobley. 199 pages. *1980*

Isles of the Caribbean. 215 pages. *1980*

America's Majestic Canyons. 207 pages. *1979*

Exploring America's Backcountry. 215 pages. *1979*

Mysteries of the Ancient World. Contents: Ancient Indian cities, Easter Island, Egyptian pyramids, Etruscans, European megaliths, Ice Age

cave art, Jericho, Minoans, and Mycenaeans. 223 pages. *1979*

Trails West. 207 pages. *1979*

The Age of Chivalry. 378 pages. 1969; rev. ed. *1978*

America's Sunset Coast. By Merrill Windsor. Photos by James A. Sugar. 211 pages. *1978*

Ancient Egypt: Discovering its Splendors. 256 pages. *1978*

Into the Wilderness. Photos by Lowell Georgia. Art by H. Tom Hall. Contents: Seven famous historic explorations and trails. 207 pages. *1978*

The Ocean Realm. 199 pages. *1978*

Powers of Nature. 199 pages. *1978*

Everyday Life in Bible Times. 448 pages. 1967; rev. ed. *1977*

Journey Across Russia: The Soviet Union Today. By Bart McDowell. Photos by Dean Conger. 367 pages. *1977*

The Mysterious Maya. By George E. and Gene S. Stuart. Photos by David Alan Harvey and Otis Imboden. 199 pages. *1977*

Nature's Healing Arts: From Folk Medicine to Modern Drugs. By Lonnelle Aikman. Photos by Nathan Benn and Ira Block. 199 pages. *1977*

Railroads: The Great American Adventure. By Charlton Ogburn. Photos by James A. Sugar. 203 pages. *1977*

Still Waters, White Waters: Exploring America's Rivers and Lakes. By Ron Fisher. Photos by Sam Abell. Contents: Touring by canoe. 199 pages. *1977*

Visiting Our Past: America's Historylands. Included: Companion directory, *Visiting Our Past: A Supplemental Guide to Selected Sites.* 400 pages. *1977*

Alaska: High Roads to Adventure. Photos by George F. Mobley. 199 pages. *1976*

Clues to America's Past. Contents: Examination of significant archaeological projects. 199 pages. *1976*

John Muir's Wild America. By Tom Melham. Photos by Farrell Grehan. Art by H. Tom Hall. 199 pages. *1976*

The Majestic Rocky Mountains. By William S. Ellis. Photos by Dick Durrance II. 199 pages. *1976*

Our Continent: A Natural History of North America. 398 pages. *1976*

The Amazing Universe. By Herbert Friedman. Contents: Revelations

and theories of astronomy. 199 pages. *1975*

The Craftsman in America. 199 pages. *1975*

The Incredible Incas and Their Timeless Land. Written and photographed by Loren McIntyre. Art by Louis S. Glanzman. 199 pages. *1975*

Man's Conquest of Space. By William R. Shelton. 199 pages. 1968; rev. ed. *1975*

The New America's Wonderlands: Our National Parks. 464 pages. 1959; rev. ed. *1975*

The Pacific Crest Trail. By William R. Gray. Photos by Sam Abell. 199 pages. *1975*

Life in Rural America. 207 pages. *1974*

Undersea Treasures. 199 pages. *1974*

Vanishing Wildlife of North America. By Thomas B. Allen. 207 pages. *1974*

The Wild Shores: America's Beginnings. By Tee Loftin Snell. Photos by Walter Meayers Edwards. Art by Louis S. Glanzman. 203 pages. *1974*

The World of the American Indian. 399 pages. *1974*

The Alps. 207 pages. *1973*

American Mountain People. Photos by Bruce Dale. 199 pages. *1973*

America's Inland Waterway: Exploring the Atlantic Seaboard. By Allan C. Fisher, Jr. Photos by James L. Amos. 207 pages. *1973*

Men, Ships, and the Sea. By Alan Villiers and other adventurers on the sea. Contents: Maritime history. 436 pages. 1962; rev. ed. *1973*

Primitive Worlds: People Lost in Time. Contents: Mbotgate, Somba, Tarahumara, Tifalmin, Turkana, and Yanomamo. 211 pages. *1973*

Wilderness U.S.A. 344 pages. *1973*

The American Cowboy in Life and Legend. By Bart McDowell. Photos by William Albert Allard. 211 pages. *1972*

The Appalachian Trail. By Ronald M. Fisher. Photos by Dick Durrance II. 199 pages. *1972*

Great American Deserts. By Rowe Findley. Photos by Walter Meayers Edwards. 207 pages. *1972*

The Marvels of Animal Behavior. 422 pages. *1972*

The Vikings. By Howard La Fay. Photos by Ted Spiegel. Art by Louis S. Glanzman. 207 pages. *1972*

Alaska. By Bern Keating. Photos by

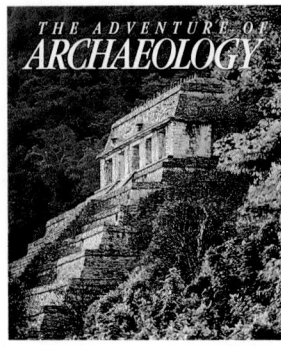

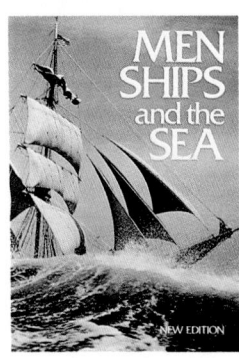
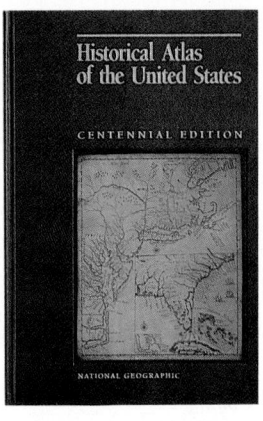

George F. Mobley. 207 pages. 1969; rev. ed. *1971*

As We Live and Breathe: The Challenge of Our Environment. 239 pages. *1971*

Great Religions of the World. Contents: Buddhism, Christianity, Hinduism, Islam, and Judaism. 420 pages. *1971*

The Mighty Mississippi. By Bern Keating. Photos by James L. Stanfield. 199 pages. *1971*

Nomads of the World. 199 pages. *1971*

Those Inventive Americans. 231 pages. *1971*

Exploring the Amazon. Written and photographed by Helen and Frank Schreider. 207 pages. *1970*

Gypsies: Wanderers of the World. By Bart McDowell. Photos by Bruce Dale. 215 pages. *1970*

Hawaii. By William Graves. Photos by James L. Amos. 203 pages. *1970*

In the Footsteps of Lewis and Clark. By Gerald S. Snyder. Photos by Dick Durrance II. Paintings by Richard Schlecht. 215 pages. *1970*

The Renaissance: Maker of Modern Man. 402 pages. *1970*

Vacationland U.S.A. 424 pages. *1970*

The Civil War. By Robert Paul Jordan. 215 pages. *1969*

Discovering Man's Past in the Americas. By George E. and Gene S. Stuart. 211 pages. *1969*

The Wild Realm: Animals of East Africa. By Louis S. B. Leakey. 199 pages. *1969*

Wondrous World of Fishes. 373 pages. 1965; rev. ed. *1969*

Australia. 219 pages. *1968*

Greece and Rome: Builders of Our World. 448 pages. *1968*

Isles of the South Pacific. By Maurice Shadbolt and Olaf Ruhen. 211 pages. *1968*

Vanishing Peoples of the Earth. 207 pages. *1968*

America's Historylands, Touring Our Landmarks of Liberty. Companion volume to *America's Wonderlands.* 575 pages. 1962; rev. ed. *1967*

Exploring Canada from Sea to Sea. 208 pages. *1967*

My Friends the Wild Chimpanzees. By Jane Goodall. Photos by Baron Hugo van Lawick. 204 pages. *1967*

The Revolutionary War: America's Fight for Freedom. By Bart McDowell. 199 pages. *1967*

World Beneath the Sea. 204 pages. *1967*

The Book of Dogs. Note: The title of the 1966 edition is *Man's Best Friend.* 429 pages. 1958; rev. ed. *1966*

Isles of the Caribbees. By Carleton Mitchell. 208 pages. *1966*

Man's Best Friend. Note: Originally published as *The Book of Dogs.* 430 pages. 1958; rev. ed. *1966*

The River Nile. By Bruce Brander. 207 pages. *1966*

This England. 440 pages. *1966*

Water, Prey, and Game Birds of North America. 464 pages. *1965*

Song and Garden Birds of North America. 400 pages. *1964*

Great Adventures With National Geographic: Exploring Land, Sea, and Sky. 504 pages. *1963*

The Book of Fishes. 339 pages. 1952, rev. ed. *1961*

Everyday Life in Ancient Times. Contents: Egypt, Greece, Mesopotamia, and Rome. 368 pages. 1951; rev. ed. *1961*

Indians of the Americas. 431 pages. 1955; rev. ed. *1961*

Wild Animals of North America. 400 pages. *1960*

The World in Your Garden. Art by Else Bostelmann. 231 pages. *1957*

Our Insect Friends and Foes and Spiders: A Series of Fascinating Stories of Bee, Ant, Beetle, Bug, Fly, Butterfly, Moth, and Spider Life. 252 pages. *1955*

Stalking Birds with Color Camera. By Arthur A. Allen. 328 pages. *1951*

The National Geographic Society and Its Magazine. By Gilbert Grosvenor. Reprint of the Foreword to the Cumulative Index to the National Geographic Magazine, 1899 to 1946. 116 pages. 1936; rev. ed. *1948*

The Round Earth on Flat Paper: Map Projections Used By Cartographers. By Wellman Chamberlin. Art by Charles E. Riddiford. 126 pages. *1947*

Insignia and Decorations of the U. S. Armed Forces. Reprint of June 1943 NGM. 208 pages. 1943; rev. ed. *1944*

The Book of Birds: The First Work Presenting in Full Color All the Major Species of the United States and Canada. Art by Allan Brooks. 2 volumes: I, 355 pages; II, 374 pages. 1932; rev. ed. *1937*

Hunting Wild Life With Camera And Flashlight: A Record of Sixty-five

Years' Visits to the Woods and Waters of North America. Written and photographed by George Shiras 3d. 2 volumes: I, 450 pages; II, 454 pages. 1898; rev. ed. *1936*

The National Geographic Society-U. S. Army Air Corps Stratosphere Flight of 1934 in the Balloon Explorer. Contributed technical papers. 122 pages. *1935*

The Book of Wild Flowers: An Introduction to the Ways of Plant Life, Together with Biographies of 250 Representative Species and Chapters on Our State Flowers and Familiar Grasses. 243 pages. 1924; rev. ed. *1933*

The Cattle of the World: Their Place in the Human Scheme–Wild Types and Modern Breeds in Many Lands. By Alvin Howard Sanders. Art by Edward Herbert Miner. 142 pages. 1925; rev. ed. *1926*

The Capital of Our Country. 154 pages. *1923*

The Horses of the World: The Development of Man's Companion in War Camp, on Farm, in the Marts of Trade, and in the Field of Sports. By William Harding Carter. Art by Edward Herbert Miner. 118 pages. *1923*

The Valley of Ten Thousand Smokes. By Robert F. Griggs. 341 pages. 1912; rev. ed. *1922*

The Book of Birds: Common Birds of Town and Country and American Game Birds. By Henry W. Henshaw. Art by Louis Agassiz Fuertes. 195 pages. 1914; rev. ed. *1918*

Scenes From Every Land: Picturing the People, Natural Phenomena, and Animal Life in All Parts of the World (Fourth Series). 216 pages. *1918*

Wild Animals of North America: Intimate Studies of Big and Little Creatures of the Mammal Kingdom. By Edward W. Nelson. Paintings by Louis Agassiz Fuertes. Sketches by Ernest Thompson Seton. 612 pages. *1918*

Flags of the World. By Byron McCandless and Gilbert Grosvenor. Reprint of Oct. 1917 NGM. 139 pages. *1917*

Henry Gannett, President of the National Geographic Society 1910-1914. By S.N.D. North. 34 pages. *1915*

Washington, The Nation's Capital. By William Howard Taft and James Bryce. Reprint of two articles:

"Washington: Its Beginning, Its Growth, and Its Future" by William Howard Taft; and "The Nation's Capital" by James Bryce. 101 pages. 1913; rev. ed. *1915*

Alaskan Glacier Studies of the National Geographic Society in the Yakutat Bay, Prince William Sound and Lower Copper River Regions. By Ralph Stockman Tarr and Lawrence Martin. 498 pages. *1914*

Book of Monsters: Portraits and Biographies of a Few of the Inhabitants of Woodland and Meadow. By David and Marion Fairchild. Reprint. 266 pages. *1914*

Common Birds of Town and Country. Contains four reprints from NGM. 1911; rev. ed. *1914*

Young Russia: The Land of Unlimited Possibilities. By Gilbert H. Grosvenor. Reprint of Nov. 1914 NGM. 28 pages. *1914*

Fifty Common Birds of Farm and Orchard. By Henry W. Henshaw. Art by Louis Agassiz Fuertes. Originally prepared as Bulletin 513 of the U. S. Department of Agriculture. Reprint of June 1913 article by special permission of the Secretary of Agriculture. 29 pages. *1913*

Scenes From Every Land: Picturing the People, Natural Phenomena, and Animal Life in All Parts of the World (Third Series). Edited by Gilbert H. Grosvenor. 216 pages. *1912*

Scenes From Every Land: Illustrations Picturing the People, Natural Phenomena, and Animal Life in All Parts of the World (Second Series). Edited by Gilbert H. Grosvenor. 223 pages. *1909*

Scenes From Every Land: A Collection of Illustrations From NGM Picturing the People, Natural Phenomena, and Animal Life in All Parts of the World. 224 pages. *1907*

See also Atlases, NGS; Indexes, NGM; Research Reports

Children's Books

Dogs on Duty. By Catherine O'Neill. 104 pages. *1988*

Geo-Whiz! By Susan Mondshein Tejada. Art by Laurie Hamilton. Contents: Startling and fascinating geographical, geological, and cultural facts from around the world. 104 pages. *1988*

Hidden Treasures of the Sea. 104 pages. *1988*

Why on Earth? Contents: Questions and answers on a variety of subjects. 96 pages. *1988*

Animal Architects. Contents: Structures built by different animals. 104 pages. *1987*

Wildlife: Making a Comeback. By Judith E. Rinard. 104 pages. *1987*

You Won't Believe Your Eyes. Contents: Optical illusions. 104 pages. *1987*

Dolphins: Our Friends in the Sea. By Judith E. Rinard. 104 pages. *1986*

Fun With Physics. By Susan McGrath. 104 pages. *1986*

National Geographic Picture Atlas of Our Universe. By Roy A. Gallant. 284 pages. 1980; rev. ed. *1986*

The Secret World of Animals. Contents: Animal habitats. 104 pages. *1986*

A World of Things To Do. Contents: Crafts, activities, games, puzzles, and recipes to be done alone or with others. 104 pages. *1986*

Computers: Those Amazing Machines. By Catherine O'Neill. 104 pages. *1985*

Science: It's Changing Your World. Contents: Fuel and food, industry, medicine, transportation, and space. 104 pages. *1985*

Why in the World? Contents: Questions and answers on a variety of subjects. 104 pages. *1985*

Your World of Pets. By Susan McGrath. Art by Barbara L. Gibson. 104 pages. *1985*

Amazing Animals of Australia. 104 pages. *1984*

How Animals Behave: A New Look at Wildlife. 104 pages. *1984*

Messengers to the Brain: Our Fantastic Five Senses. By Paul D. Martin. 104 pages. *1984*

Natural Wonders of North America. By Catherine O'Neill. 104 pages. *1984*

Small Inventions That Make a Big Difference. Photos by Joseph H. Bailey. Art by John Huehnergarth. 104 pages. *1984*

The Story of America: A National Geographic Picture Atlas. By John Anthony Scott. 324 pages. *1984*

Amazing Mysteries of the World. By Catherine O'Neill. Contents: Mystifying phenomena such as auroras, black holes, Bigfoot, the Bermuda Triangle, and UFOs. 104 pages. *1983*

Giants from the Past: The Age of Mammals. By Joseph H. Bailey. 104 pages. *1983*

How Things Work. 104 pages. *1983*

Secrets of Animal Survival. 104 pages. *1983*

More Far-Out Facts. 104 pages. *1982*

Our Violent Earth. 104 pages. *1982*

Safari! By Gene S. Stuart. Photos by George F. Mobley. 104 pages. *1982*

Your Wonderful Body. 104 pages. *1982*

Amazing Animals of the Sea. Included: Pinnipeds, sea otters, manatees, and whales. 104 pages. *1981*

Book of Mammals. 2 volumes. Vol. I, A-J; vol. II, K-Z. 608 pages. *1981*

Hidden Worlds. Contents: Vision, light, and magnification. 104 pages. *1981*

How Things Are Made. 104 pages. *1981*

Zoos Without Cages. By Judith E. Rinard. 104 pages. *1981*

Far-Out Facts. 104 pages. *1980*

The Mysterious Undersea World. By Jan Leslie Cooke. 104 pages. *1980*

Wilderness Challenge. Included: Backpacking, camping, mountain climbing, and river trips. 104 pages. *1980*

Wildlife Alert! The Struggle to Survive. By Gene S. Stuart. 104 pages. *1980*

National Geographic Picture Atlas of Our World. 312 pages. *1979*

Secrets From the Past. By Gene S. Stuart. 104 pages. *1979*

National Geographic Picture Atlas of Our Fifty States. Included: Pertinent information about the geography, climate, and population of each state. 304 pages. *1978*

Public Service Books

Equal Justice Under the Law: The Supreme Court in American Life. By Mary Ann Harrell. Published in cooperation with The Foundation of the Federal Bar Association. 151 pages. 1965; rev. ed. *1988*

The Living White House. By Lonnelle Aikman. Published in cooperation with the White House Historical Association. 151 pages. 1966; rev. ed. *1987*

The President's House: A History. By William Seale. Published in cooperation with the White House Historical Association. 2 volumes, 1224 pages. *1986*

A polar bear makes a meal of a ribbon seal, an uncommon species with a range that includes the Alaska coast south of the Yukon Delta. PAINTING BY LOUIS AGASSIZ FUERTES

BORAIKO, ALLEN A.:
On Assignment in Chile. *July 1988*
On Assignment in Ohio. *Mar. 1985*
On Assignment. *Oct. 1982*
Nomination Page. *June 1982*
Author
Chile: Acts of Faith. Photos by David
Alan Harvey. 54-85, *July 1988*
Earthquake in Mexico. Photos by James
L. Stanfield and Guillermo Aldana
E. Included: The rise and fall of
buildings–a primer for survival in
quake city. 654-675, *May 1986*
Hazardous Waste...Storing Up Trou-
ble. Photos by Fred Ward. 318-351,
Mar. 1985
Lasers–"A Splendid Light." Photos by
Charles O'Rear. 335-363, *Mar. 1984*
The Chip: Electronic Mini-marvel. Pho-
tos by Charles O'Rear. 421-457,
Oct. 1982
Silver: A Mineral of Excellent Nature.
Photos by Fred Ward. 280-313,
Sept. 1981
The Indomitable Cockroach. Photos by
Bates Littlehales. 130-142, *Jan. 1981*
The Pesticide Dilemma. Photos by Fred
Ward. 145-183, *Feb. 1980*
Fiber Optics: Harnessing Light by a
Thread. Photos by Fred Ward. 516-
535, *Oct. 1979*

BORCHGREVINK, C. E.:
The National Geographic Society Expedition to Martinique and St. Vincent.
183-184, *June 1902*
The National Geographic Society Expedition in the West Indies. 209-213,
June 1902

BORDEAUX (Region), France:
Bordeaux: Fine Wines and Fiery Gascons. By William Davenport. Photos
by Adam Woolfitt. 233-259,
Aug. 1980

BORDER DISPUTES:
Editorial. By Wilbur E. Garrett. 711,
Dec. 1984

BOREN, LAMAR: *Photographer*
Goggle Fishing in California Waters. By
David Hellyer. 615-632, *May 1949*

BORG, ERIK: *Photographer*
Norway's Reindeer Lapps. By Sally Anderson. 364-379, *Sept. 1977*

BORMAN, FRANK:
Hubbard Medal recipient. 861,
June 1970
Sounds of the Space Age, from Sputnik
to Lunar Landing. Record narrated
by Frank Borman. 750-751,
Dec. 1969
"A Most Fantastic Voyage": The Story
of Apollo 8's Rendezvous With the
Moon. By Sam C. Phillips. 593-631,
May 1969
Space Rendezvous, Milestone on the
Way to the Moon. By Kenneth F.
Weaver. 539-553, *Apr. 1966*

BORN Hunters, the Bird Dogs. By Roland Kilbon. Paintings by Walter A.
Weber. 369-398, *Sept. 1947*

BORNEO (Island), Indonesia-
Malaysia-Brunei:
Keeping House in Borneo. By Virginia
Hamilton. 293-324, *Sept. 1945*
Sarawak: The Land of the White Ra-
jahs. By Harrison W. Smith. 110-167,
Feb. 1919
Notes on the Sea Dyaks of Borneo. By
Edwin H. Gomes. 695-723,
Aug. 1911
Colonial Government in Borneo. By
James M. Hubbard. 359-363,
Sept. 1900
See also Brunei; Sabah (North Borneo);
Sarawak; Tanjung Puting Reserve

BORNHOLM (Island), Denmark:
Baltic Cruise of the *Caribbee*. By Carle-
ton Mitchell. 605-646, *Nov. 1950*
2,000 Miles Through Europe's Oldest
Kingdom. By Isobel Wylie Hutchi-
son. Photos by Maynard Owen Wil-
liams. 141-180, *Feb. 1949*
Bornholm–Denmark in a Nutshell. By
Mason Sutherland. 239-256,
Feb. 1945

BOROBUDUR (Temple), Java,
Indonesia:

Indonesia Rescues Ancient Borobudur.
By W. Brown Morton III. Photos by
Dean Conger. 126-142, *Jan. 1983*

BORTON, NAN and JAMES W.:
Authors
Ambassadors of Good Will: The Peace
Corps. By Sargent Shriver and Peace
Corps Volunteers. Included: Turkey.
297-345, *Sept. 1964*

BOSLOUGH, JOHN: *Author*
Worlds Within the Atom. Photos by
Kevin Fleming. Illustrations text by
David Jeffery. 634-663, *May 1985*

BOSNIA (Region), Yugoslavia:
East of the Adriatic: Notes on Dalma-
tia, Montenegro, Bosnia, and Herze-
govina. By Kenneth McKenzie. 1159-
1187, 1284, *Dec. 1912*
Where East Meets West: Visit to Pictur-
esque Dalmatia, Montenegro and
Bosnia. By Marian Cruger Coffin.
309-344, *May 1908*
The Great Turk and His Lost Provinces.
By William E. Curtis. 45-61,
Feb. 1903

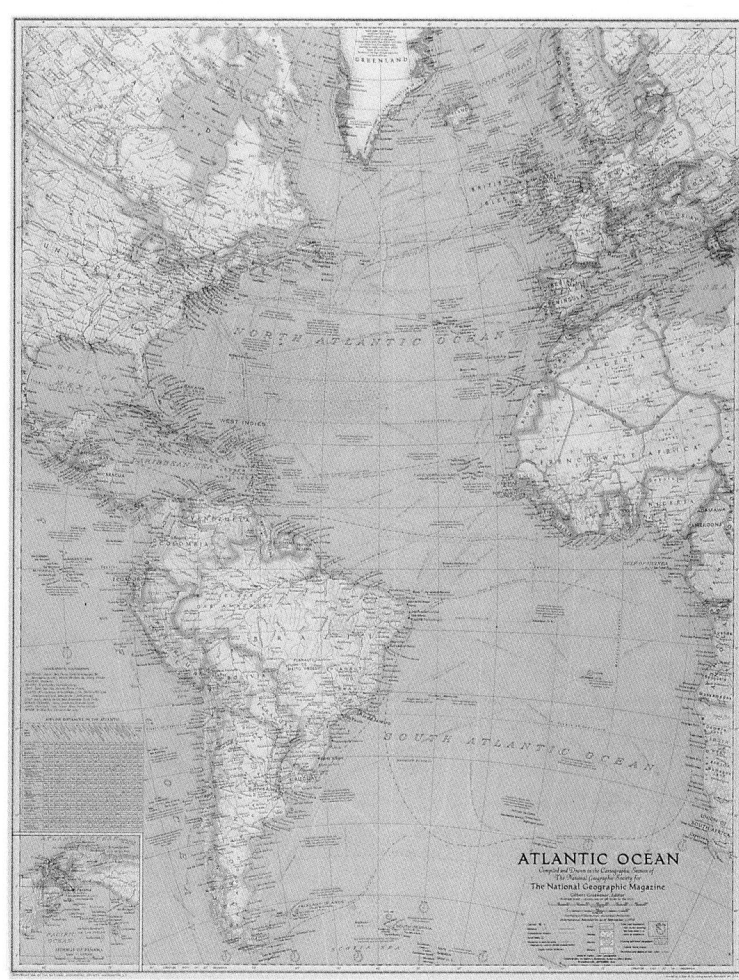

Map of the Atlantic ran with a September 1941 article on the ocean's strategic strongholds,
co-authored by GEOGRAPHIC staff members Leo A. Borah and Wellman Chamberlin.

BOSNIA-HERCEGOVINA (Republic), Yugoslavia:

Yugoslavia: Six Republics in One. By Robert Paul Jordan. Photos by James P. Blair. 589-633, *May 1970*

BOSPORUS (Strait):

Summer Holidays on the Bosporus. By Maynard Owen Williams. 457-508, *Oct. 1929*

Seeing 3,000 Years of History in Four Hours: A Panorama of Ancient, Medieval, and Modern Events Against a Background of Mythology Unfolds During an Airplane Journey from Constantinople to Athens. By Maynard Owen Williams. 719-739, *Dec. 1928*

The Gates to the Black Sea: The Dardanelles, the Bosphorus, and the Sea of Marmora. By Harry Griswold Dwight. 435-459, *May 1915*

Constantinople and Sancta Sophia. By Edwin A. Grosvenor. 459-482, *May 1915*

BOSQUE, FERNANDO DEL:

Expedition into Texas of Fernando del Bosque, Standard-Bearer of the King, Don Carlos II, in the Year 1675. Translated from an Old, Unpublished Spanish Manuscript. By Betty B. Brewster. 339-348, *Sept. 1903*

BOSSHARD, W.: *Photographer*

Life on the Steppes and Oases of Chinese Turkestan. 333-356, *Mar. 1931*

BOSSON, MRS. GEORGE C., Jr.: *Author*

Notes on Normandy. 775-782, *Sept. 1910*

Sicily, the Battle-Field of Nations and of Nature. 97-118, *Jan. 1909*

Biskra, the Ziban Queen. 563-593, *Aug. 1908*

BOSTELMANN, ELSE: *Artist*

■■ *The World in Your Garden.* 231 pages. *1957*

How Fruit Came to America. By J. R. Magness. 325-377, *Sept. 1951*

Our Vegetable Travelers. By Victor R. Boswell. 145-217, *Aug. 1949*

The World in Your Garden (Flowers). By W. H. Camp. 1-65, *July 1947*

Whales, Porpoises, and Dolphins. Included: A complete set of color pictures. 41-80, *Jan. 1940*

Sea Floor Aquarelles from Tongareva. Paintings by Else Bostelmann under direction Roy W. Miner. 383-390, *Sept. 1938*

Strange Creatures of Sunny Seas (Mollusks, Crustaceans, etc.). Paintings by Else Bostelmann under direction Roy W. Miner. 211-218, *Feb. 1937*

Undersea Gardens of the North Atlantic Coast. Paintings by Else Bostelmann under direction Roy W. Miner. 217-224, *Aug. 1936*

Monster and Midget Squid and Octopuses. Paintings by Else Bostelmann under direction Roy W. Miner. 193-200, *Aug. 1935*

Flashes From Ocean Deeps. Paintings by Else Bostelmann and Helen D. Tee-Van. 677-684, *Dec. 1934*

Carnivores of a Lightless World (Fishes). Paintings by Else Bostelmann and E. J. Geske. 693-700, *Dec. 1934*

Multi-Hued Marvels of a Coral Reef. 719-726, *June 1934*

Exploring Neptune's Hidden World of Vivid Color. 747-754, *Dec. 1932*

Fantastic Sea Life from Abyssal Depths. 71-78, *Jan. 1932*

Luminous Life in the Depths of the Sea. 667-674, *June 1931*

BOSTON, England:

The Original Boston: St. Botolph's Town. By Veronica Thomas. Photos by James L. Amos. 382-389, *Sept. 1974*

BOSTON, Massachusetts:

Benjamin Franklin, Philosopher of Dissent. By Alice J. Hall. Photos by Linda Bartlett. 93-123, *July 1975*

Those Proper and Other Bostonians. By Joseph Judge. Photos by Ted Spiegel. 352-381, *Sept. 1974*

Firebrands of the Revolution. By Eric F. Goldman. Photos by George F. Mobley. 2-27, *July 1974*

Massachusetts Builds for Tomorrow. By Robert de Roos. Photos by B. Anthony Stewart. 790-843, *Dec. 1966*

The Post Road Today. Photos by B. Anthony Stewart. 206-233, *Aug. 1962*

Literary Landmarks of Massachusetts. By William H. Nicholas. Photos by B. Anthony Stewart and John E. Fletcher. 279-310, *Mar. 1950*

The Wonder City That Moves by Night (Circus). By Francis Beverly Kelley. 289-324, *Mar. 1948*

Boston Through Midwest Eyes. By Frederick Simpich. 37-82, *July 1936*

◍ *A Map of the Travels of George Washington.* Included: Inset of Boston and vicinity. *Jan. 1932*

BOSTON POST ROADS:

The Old Boston Post Roads. By Donald Barr Chidsey. 189-205, *Aug. 1962*

The Post Road Today. Photos by B. Anthony Stewart. 206-233, *Aug. 1962*

BOSWELL, VICTOR R.: *Author*

Our Vegetable Travelers. Paintings by Else Bostelmann. 145-217, *Aug. 1949*

BOSWELL, VICTOR R., Jr.:

On Assignment in Rome. *Dec. 1985*

Nomination Page. *Aug. 1966*

Photographer

Riddle of the Pyramid Boats. By Peter Miller. 534-550, *Apr. 1988*

Sealed in Time–Ice Entombs an Eskimo Family for Five Centuries. By Albert A. Dekin, Jr. Photos by Victor R. Boswell, Jr., and Scott Rutherford. Paintings by James M. Gurney. 824-836, *June 1987*

Treasures of the Vatican. Photos by James L. Stanfield and Victor R. Boswell, Jr. 764-775, *Dec. 1985*

Restoration Reveals the "Last Supper." By Carlo Bertelli. 664-685, *Nov. 1983*

Treasures of Dresden. By John L. Eliot. 702-717, *Nov. 1978*

Venice's Golden Legacy. 609-619, *Nov. 1972*

The Magic Lure of Sea Shells. By Paul A. Zahl. Photos by Victor R. Boswell, Jr., and author. 386-429, *Mar. 1969*

900 Years Ago: the Norman Conquest. By Kenneth M. Setton. Photos by George F. Mobley. The complete Bayeux Tapestry photographed by Milton A. Ford and Victor R. Boswell, Jr. 206-251, *Aug. 1966*

BOSWORTH, ABBIE L.: *Author*

Life in a Norway Valley: An American Girl Is Welcomed into the Homemaking and Haying of Happy Hallingdal. 627-648, *May 1935*

BOTANICAL EXPLORERS. *See* Agricultural and Botanical Explorers

BOTANICAL GARDENS:

Herbs for All Seasons. By Lonnelle Aikman. Photos by Sam Abell. Picture portfolio text by Larry Kohl. Included: Caprilands, Chelsea Physic Garden, colonial gardens, Hampton Court Palace Gardens, Huntington Botanical Gardens, Jacqueline Kennedy Garden, National Herb Garden, New York Botanical Garden, Oxford University Garden, Royal Botanical Gardens at Kew, Shakespeare Elizabethan Garden, Taylor's Herb Garden, Williamsburg gardens, Willow Oak Flower and Herb Farm. 386-409, *Mar. 1983*

See also Longwood Gardens; Royal Botanic Gardens

BOTANY. *See* Agricultural and Botanical Explorers; *and* Flowers; Plants; Trees

BOTFLIES (Insects):

Life Story of the Mosquito. By Graham Fairchild. 180-195, *Feb. 1944*

BOTSWANA:

El Niño's Ill Wind. By Thomas Y. Canby. Included: Drought caused by the current. 144-183, *Feb. 1984*

BOTTLENOSE DOLPHINS:

The Trouble With Dolphins. By Edward J. Linehan. Photos by Bill Curtsinger. 506-541, *Apr. 1979*

BOTTOM SCRATCHERS CLUB:

Goggle Fishing in California Waters. By David Hellyer. Photos by Lamar Boren. 615-632, *May 1949*

BOUCHAGE, LUC: *Author*

Mysore Celebrates the Death of a Demon. Photos by Ylla. 706-711, *May 1958*

BOUCHER, JEAN DU: *Author*

Dry-land Fleet Sails the Sahara. Photos by Jonathan S. Blair. 696-725, *Nov. 1967*

BOUGAINVILLE (Island), Solomon Islands:

Fiji Patrol on Bougainville. By David D. Duncan. 87-104, *Jan. 1945*

A quartet of bottlenose dolphins abandon their customary shyness to investigate the photographer in the rich waters of Australia's southern seas.   DAVID DOUBILET

Jungle War: Bougainville and New Caledonia. Paintings by William F. Draper. 417-432, *Apr. 1944*

A Woman's Experiences among Stone Age Solomon Islanders: Primitive Life Remains Unchanged in Tropical Jungleland Where United States Forces Now Are Fighting. By Eleanor Schirmer Oliver. 818-836, *Dec. 1942*

BOULAT, PIERRE: *Photographer*

Carrara Marble: Touchstone of Eternity. By Cathy Newman. 42-59, *July 1982*

BOULTON, LAURA C.: *Author*

Timbuktu and Beyond: Desert City of Romantic Savor and Salt Emerges into World Life Again as Trading Post of France's Vast African Empire. 631-670, *May 1941*

BOUNDARIES:

Editorial. By Wilbur E. Garrett. 711, *Dec. 1984*

The Geographic's New Map of Germany and Its Approaches: With a Review of The Society's Maps of Europe. By Gilbert Grosvenor. Included: Boundary changes in Europe (1912-1940). 66-72, *July 1944*

How the United States Grew. By McFall Kerbey. 631-649, *May 1933*

The Battle-Line of Languages in Western Europe: A Problem in Human Geography More Perplexing Than That of International Boundaries. By A. L. Guerard. 145-180, *Feb. 1923*

New Map of Europe: Showing the Boundaries Established by the Peace Conference at Paris and by Subsequent Decisions of the Supreme Council of the Allied and Associated Powers. By Ralph A. Graves. 157-177, *Feb. 1921*

Along Our Side of the Mexican Border. By Frederick Simpich. 61-80, *July 1920*

Wandering Islands in the Rio Grande. By Mrs. Albert S. Burleson. 381-386, *Mar. 1913*

Surveying the 141st Meridian (Boundary Line Between Canada and Alaska). By Thomas Riggs, Jr. 685-718, *July 1912*

Marking the Alaskan Boundary. By Thomas Riggs, Jr. 593-607, *July 1909*

Charting a Coast-Line of 26,000 Miles (Alaska). 608-609, *July 1909*

The Original Boundary Stones of the District of Columbia. By Ernest A. Shuster, Jr. 356-359, *Apr. 1909*

Marking the Alaskan Boundary. 176-189, *Mar. 1908*

The Alaskan Boundary Tribunal. By John W. Foster. 1-12, *Jan. 1904*

Decision of the Alaskan Boundary Tribunal. 12-14, *Jan. 1904*

Alaskan Boundary Decision. 423, *Nov. 1903*

The Canadian Boundary. By John W. Foster. 85-90, *Mar. 1903*

Argentina-Chile Boundary Award. 115-116, *Mar. 1903*

Alaskan Boundary Dispute. 79, *Feb. 1903*

Chile-Argentina Boundary Dispute. 220, *June 1902*

Argentina-Chile Boundary. 117, *Mar. 1902*

Argentine-Chile Boundary Dispute. 27-28, *Jan. 1902*

The Lost Boundary of Texas. By Marcus Baker. 430-432, *Dec. 1901*

Boundaries of Territorial Acquisitions. 373-377, *Oct. 1901*

Brazil-French Guiana Boundary Decision. 83, *Feb. 1901*

Location of the Boundary Between Nicaragua and Costa Rica. By Arthur P. Davis. 22-28, *Jan. 1901*

The Anglo-Venezuelan Boundary Dispute. By Marcus Baker. 129-144, *Apr. 1900*

The Idaho and Montana Boundary Line. By Richard U. Goode. 23-29, *Jan. 1900*

The Alaskan Boundary. By John W. Foster. 425-456, *Nov. 1899*

The California and Nevada Boundary. By C. H. Sinclair. 416-417, *Oct. 1899*

The Venezuelan Boundary Commission and Its Work. By Marcus Baker. 193-201, *July-Aug. 1897*

Venezuela: Her Government, People, and Boundary. By William E. Curtis. 49-58, *Feb. 1896*

Oregon: Its History, Geography, and Resources. By John H. Mitchell. 239-284, *Apr. 20, 1895*

Surveys and Maps of the District of Columbia. By Marcus Baker. Included: List of Maps of Washington and the District of Columbia. 149-178, *Nov. 1, 1894*

The Alaskan Boundary Survey. I–Introduction. By T. C. Mendenhall. II–The Boundary South of Fort Yukon. By J. E. McGrath. III–The Boundary North of Fort Yukon. By J. Henry Turner. 177-197, *Feb. 8, 1893*

BOUNTY (Vessel):

Wreck of H.M.S. *Pandora*. By Luis Marden. 423-451, *Oct. 1985*

Pitcairn and Norfolk–The Saga of *Bounty*'s Children. By Ed Howard. Photos by David Hiser and Melinda Berge. 510-541. Included: Pitcairn Island. 512-529; Norfolk Island. 530-541, *Oct. 1983*

Huzza for Otaheite! By Luis Marden. 435-459, *Apr. 1962*

Bounty Descendants Live on Remote Norfolk Island. By T. C. Roughley. Photos by J. Baylor Roberts. 559-584, *Oct. 1960*

I Found the Bones of the *Bounty*. By Luis Marden. 725-789, *Dec. 1957*

BOUNTY (Replica):

Tahiti, "Finest Island in the World." By Luis Marden. 1-47, *July 1962*

Huzza for Otaheite! By Luis Marden. 435-459, *Apr. 1962*

BOURCHIER, JAMES D.: *Author*

The Rise of Bulgaria. 1105-1118, *Nov. 1912*

BOURDILLON, TOM:

Triumph on Everest. 1-63. I. Siege and Assault. By Sir John Hunt. 1-43; II. The Conquest of the Summit. By Sir Edmund Hillary. 45-63, *July 1954*

BOURGES, France:

The Beauties of France. By Arthur Stanley Riggs. 391-491, *Nov. 1915*

BOURLAY, REGINALD A.: *Author*

Wings Over Nature's Zoo in Africa. 527-542, *Oct. 1939*

BOUTWELL, WILLIAM DOW: *Author-Photographer*

Old World Charm in Modern Quebec. 507-514, *Apr. 1930*

Quebec, Capital of French Canada. 515-522, *Apr. 1930*

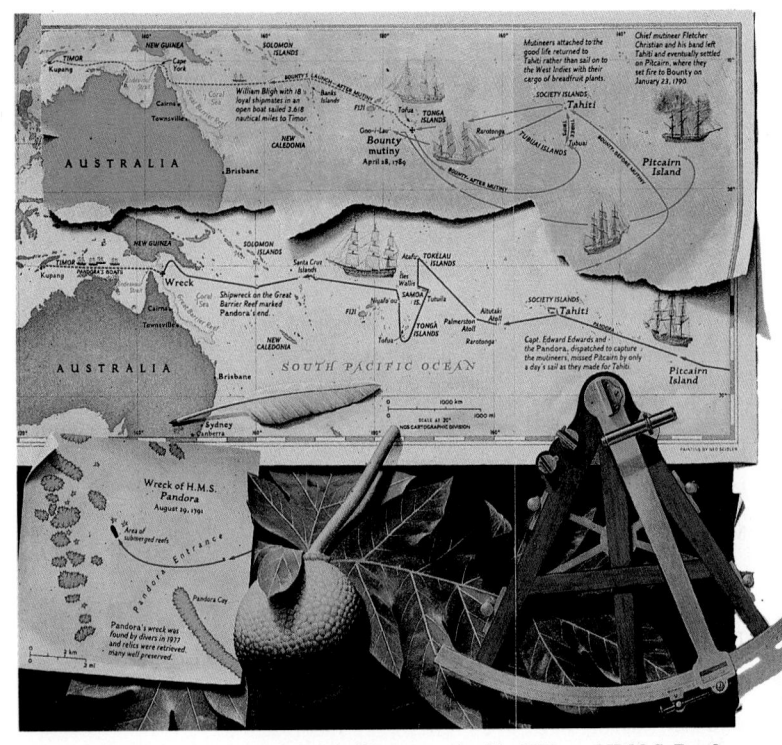

Charts trace His Majesty's Armed Vessel **Bounty**, *seized in 1789, and H.M.S.* **Pandora**, *which sank off Australia after capturing 14* **Bounty** *mutineers.* PAINTING BY NED SEIDLER, NGS

Columbia's Lifeline. Photos by Chris Johns. 44-75, *July 1986*
Yosemite–Forever? Photos by Jonathan Blair. 52-79, *Jan. 1985*
Calgary: Canada's Not-So-Wild West. Photos by Ottmar Bierwagen. 378-403, *Mar. 1984*
Golden Gate–Of City, Ships, and Surf (Golden Gate National Recreation Area, California). 98-105, *July 1979*
Micronesia: The Americanization of Eden. 702-744, *May 1967*
Portugal's Gem of the Ocean: Madeira. 364-394, *Mar. 1959*

Author-Photographer
Warm Springs Indians Carve Out a Future. 494-505, *Apr. 1979*
Ontario, Canada's Keystone. Photos by Sam Abell and the author. 760-795, *Dec. 1978*
Our Wild and Scenic Rivers: The St. Croix. 30-37, *July 1977*
Our Wild and Scenic Rivers: The Skagit. 38-45, *July 1977*
Minnesota, Where Water Is the Magic Word. Photos by author and David Brill. 200-229, *Feb. 1976*
Powerhouse of the Northwest (Columbia River). 821-847, *Dec. 1974*
The Glittering World of Rockhounds. 276-294, *Feb. 1974*
The Canadian North: Emerging Giant. 1-43, *July 1968*
Wyoming: High, Wide, and Windy. 554-594, *Apr. 1966*
Over and Under Chesapeake Bay. 593-612, *Apr. 1964*
Alberta Unearths Her Buried Treasures. 90-119, *July 1960*
Geographical Twins (Holy Land and Utah) a World Apart. 848-859, *Dec. 1958*
British Columbia: Life Begins at 100. 147-189, *Aug. 1958*
Huntington Library, California Treasure House. 251-276, *Feb. 1958*

Year of Discovery Opens in Antarctica. 339-381, *Sept. 1957*
Jerusalem to Rome in the Path of St. Paul. 707-759, *Dec. 1956*
Kitimat–Canada's Aluminum Titan. 376-398, *Sept. 1956*
Petra, Rose-red Citadel of Biblical Edom. 853-870, *Dec. 1955*
Paris to Antwerp with the Water Gypsies. 530-559, *Oct. 1955*
Rhododendron Glories of Southwest Scotland. Photos by B. Anthony Stewart and author. 641-664, *May 1954*

Photographer
Flight Into Antarctic Darkness. By J. Lloyd Abbot, Jr. 732-738, *Nov. 1967*
Ambassadors of Good Will: The Peace Corps. By Sargent Shriver and Peace Corps Volunteers. 297-345, *Sept. 1964*
Relics from the Rapids. By Sigurd F. Olson. 413-435, *Sept. 1963*
Canada, My Country. By Alan Phillips. Photos by David S. Boyer and Walter Meayers Edwards. 769-819, *Dec. 1961*
Blossoms That Defy the Seasons (Flower Preservation). By Geneal Condon. 420-427, *Sept. 1958*
We Are Living at the South Pole. By Paul A. Siple. 5-35, *July 1957*
Boom on San Francisco Bay. By Franc Shor. 181-226, *Aug. 1956*
A Stroll to John o'Groat's. By Isobel Wylie Hutchison. 1-48, *July 1956*
Lake District, Poets' Corner of England. By H. V. Morton. 511-545, *Apr. 1956*
Fresh Treasures from Egypt's Ancient Sands. By Jefferson Caffery. 611-650, *Nov. 1955*
Crusader Lands Revisited. By Harold Lamb. 815-852, *Dec. 1954*
Here's New York Harbor. By Stuart E. Jones. Photos by Robert F. Sisson

and David S. Boyer. 773-813, *Dec. 1954*
Eastman of Rochester: Photographic Pioneer. By Allan C. Fisher, Jr. 423-438, *Sept. 1954*
In the London of the New Queen. By H. V. Morton. 291-342, *Sept. 1953*
London's Zoo of Zoos. By Thomas Garner James. 771-786, *June 1953*
Our Navy's Long Submarine Arm. By Allan C. Fisher, Jr. Photos by David S. Boyer and author. 613-636, *Nov. 1952*

BOYHOOD of Sir Walter Raleigh. Painting by Sir John Millais, Tate Gallery, London. 596, *May 1926*

BOYLE, ROBERT:
The British Way. By Sir Evelyn Wrench. 421-541, *Apr. 1949*

BOYS' and Girls' Agricultural Clubs. 639-641, *July 1911*

BRACQ, JEAN C.: *Author*
The Colonial Expansion of France. By Jean C. Bracq. 225-238, *June 1900*

BRADFORD, ERNLE: *Author*
The Faeroes, Isles of Maybe. Photos by Adam Woolfitt. 410-442, *Sept. 1970*
Democracy's Fortress: Unsinkable Malta. Photos by Ted H. Funk. 852-879, *June 1969*

BRADLEY, LA VERNE: *Author*
Scenes of Postwar Finland. Photos by Jerry Waller. 233-264, *Aug. 1947*
Women at Work. 193-220, *Aug. 1944*
Women in Uniform. 445-458, *Oct. 1943*
San Francisco: Gibraltar of the West Coast. 279-308, *Mar. 1943*

BRADLEY, MATT: *Photographer*
Nahanni: Canada's Wilderness Park. By Douglas H. Chadwick. 396-420, *Sept. 1981*
Easygoing, Hardworking Arkansas. By Boyd Gibbons. 396-427, *Mar. 1978*
America's Little Mainstream (Buffalo National River). By Harvey Arden. 344-359, *Mar. 1977*

BRADLEY, WALTER W.: *Author*
Some Mexican Transportation Scenes. 985-991, *Dec. 1910*

BRADSTREET, ANNE:
Literary Landmarks of Massachusetts. By William H. Nicholas. Photos by B. Anthony Stewart and John E. Fletcher. 279-310, *Mar. 1950*

BRAEMAR, Scotland:
Clans in Kilt and Plaidie Gather at Braemar. Photos by Maynard Owen Williams. 153-160, *Aug. 1935*

BRAGG, JOHN: *Photographer*
To Torre Egger's Icy Summit. By Jim Donini. 813-823, *Dec. 1976*

BRAHMAPUTRA (River), Tibet-India-Bangladesh:
Long Journey of the Brahmaputra. By Jere Van Dyk. Photos by Raghubir Singh and Galen Rowell. Included: A Rare Visit to a World Unto Itself. By Raghubir Singh. 672-711, *Nov. 1988*

Anchor fluke from the **Bounty** *points from the seafloor off Pitcairn Island in the Pacific Ocean.* LUIS MARDEN, NGS

The Tsangpo. By James Mascarene Hubbard. 32-35, *Jan. 1901*

BRAHUI TRIBESPEOPLE:

Pakistan, New Nation in an Old Land. By Jean and Franc Shor. 637-678, *Nov. 1952*

BRAILLE EDITION OF NATIONAL GEOGRAPHIC MAGAZINE:

Editorial. By Wilbur E. Garrett. 145, *Aug. 1986*

BRAIN:

■■ *Messengers to the Brain: Our Fantastic Five Senses.* By Paul D. Martin. Juvenile. 104 pages. *1984*

BRAINTREE, England. *See* New Mills

BRAKE, BRIAN: *Photographer*

Maoris: Treasures of the Tradition. By Douglas Newton. 542-553, *Oct. 1984*
New Zealand: Gift of the Sea. By Maurice Shadbolt. 465-511, *Apr. 1962*
Peking: a Pictorial Record. 194-197, 199-223, *Aug. 1960*
Jerusalem, the Divided City. By John Scofield. 492-531, *Apr. 1959*
The Emperor's Private Garden: Kashmir. By Nigel Cameron. 606-647, *Nov. 1958*
Along the Storied Incense Roads of Aden. By Hermann F. Eilts. 230-254, *Feb. 1957*
Progress and Pageantry in Changing Nigeria. By W. Robert Moore. 325-365, *Sept. 1956*

BRAND, VANCE D.:

Apollo-Soyuz: Handclasp in Space. By Thomas Y. Canby. 183-187, *Feb. 1976*

BRANDENBURG, FRED G.: *Photographer*

Desert River (San Juan) Through Navajo Land. By Alfred M. Bailey. Photos by author and Fred G. Brandenburg. 149-172, *Aug. 1947*

BRANDENBURG, JIM:

On Assignment in Kiev, U.S.S.R. *Mar. 1985*
On Assignment in Namibia. *June 1982*

Photographer

Ellesmere Island–Life in the High Arctic. By L. David Mech. 750-767, *June 1988*
At Home with the Arctic Wolf. By L. David Mech. 562-593, *May 1987*
The Captivating Kiwifruit. By Noel D. Vietmeyer. 683-688, *May 1987*
Red Deer and Man. By T. H. Clutton-Brock. 538-555, *Oct. 1986*
North to the Pole. By Will Steger. Photos by the author and Jim Brandenburg. 289-317, *Sept. 1986*
Viking Trail East. By Robert Paul Jordan. Paintings by Michael A. Hampshire. 278-317, *Mar. 1985*
They're Killing Off the Rhino. By Esmond Bradley Martin. 404-422, *Mar. 1984*
Namibia: Nearly a Nation? By Bryan Hodgson. 755-797, *June 1982*
Aldo Leopold: "A Durable Scale of Values." By Boyd Gibbons. 682-708, *Nov. 1981*

Largest South American monkey, the **muriqui** *lives only in a forest region along Brazil's Atlantic coast.* ANDREW L. YOUNG

South Dakota's Badlands: Castles in Clay. By John Madson. 524-539, *Apr. 1981*
Bamboo, the Giant Grass. By Luis Marden. 502-529, *Oct. 1980*
Heart of the Canadian Rockies. By Elizabeth A. Moize. 757-779, *June 1980*
The Tallgrass Prairie: Can It Be Saved? By Dennis Farney. 37-61, *Jan. 1980*

BRANDER, BRUCE: *Author*

■■ *The River Nile.* 207 pages. *1966*

BRANDES, E. W.: *Author*

Into Primeval Papua by Seaplane: Seeking Disease-resisting Sugar Cane, Scientists Find Neolithic Man in Unmapped Nooks of Sorcery and Cannibalism. 253-332, *Sept. 1929*

BRANDING:

Cowpunching on the Padlock Ranch. By William Albert Allard. 478-499, *Oct. 1973*

BRANNER, J. C.: *Author*

The Recent Ascent of Itambé (Brazil). 183, *May 1899*

BRAS D'OR LAKES, Nova Scotia, Canada:

Nova Scotia, the Magnificent Anchorage. By Charles McCarry. Photos by Gordon W. Gahan. 334-363, *Mar. 1975*
Down East to Nova Scotia. By Winfield Parks. 853-879, *June 1964*
Canada's Winged Victory: the *Silver Dart.* By Gilbert M. Grosvenor. 254-267, *Aug. 1959*

BRASÍLIA, Brazil:

Brazil, Ôba! By Peter T. White. Photos by Winfield Parks. 299-353, *Sept. 1962*

Brasília, Metropolis Made to Order. By Hernane Tavares de Sá. Photos by Thomas J. Abercrombie. 704-724, *May 1960*

BRAUNS, CLAUS-DIETER:

Nomination Page. In Bangladesh. *Feb. 1973*

Author-Photographer
The Peaceful Mrus of Bangladesh. 267-286, *Feb. 1973*

BRAVING the Atlantic by Balloon. By Arnold Eiloart. 123-146, *July 1959*

BRAVO (Malamute-Husky):

Antarctic Scientist Honored by The Society. Note: Bravo is proclaimed a VID (Very Important Dog) and is given an honorable discharge from the U. S. Navy. 792-793, *June 1958*
Man's First Winter at the South Pole. By Paul A. Siple. 439-478, *Apr. 1958*

BRAVO (Weather Patrol), North Atlantic:

Rugged Is the Word for Bravo. By Philip M. Swatek. 829-843, *Dec. 1955*

BRAZIL:

Rondônia: Brazil's Imperiled Rain Forest. By William S. Ellis. Photos by William Albert Allard and Loren McIntyre. 772-779, *Dec. 1988*
"Last Days of Eden," Rondônia's Urueu-Wau-Wau Indians. By Loren McIntyre. Photos by W. Jesco von Puttkamer. 800-817, *Dec. 1988*
Brazil: Flight to the Cities. By Paul R. and Anne H. Ehrlich. Photos by Mary Ellen Mark. 934-937, *Dec. 1988*
Brazil: Moment of Promise and Pain. By Priit J. Vesilind. Photos by Stephanie Maze. 348-385, *Mar. 1987*
Monkey in Peril: Rescuing Brazil's Muriqui. By Russell A. Mittermeier. Photos by Andrew L. Young. 387-395, *Mar. 1987*
Brazil's Kayapo Indians, Beset by a Golden Curse. By Vanessa Lea. Photos by Miguel Rio Branco. 675-694, *May 1984*
Tropical Rain Forests: Nature's Dwindling Treasures. By Peter T. White. Photos by James P. Blair. Paintings by Barron Storey. 2-47, *Jan. 1983*
The Bonanza Bean–Coffee. By Ethel A. Starbird. Photos by Sam Abell. 388-405, *Mar. 1981*
The Gauchos, Last of a Breed. By Robert Laxalt. Photos by O. Louis Mazzatenta. 478-501, *Oct. 1980*
Jari: A Billion-dollar Gamble. By Loren McIntyre. Contents: Daniel K. Ludwig's paper-pulp and food-production enterprise in Brazil's Amazon basin. 686-711, *May 1980*
Man in the Amazon: Stone Age Present Meets Stone Age Past. By W. Jesco von Puttkamer. NGS research grant. 60-83, *Jan. 1979*
Brazil's Golden Beachhead. By Bart McDowell. Photos by Nicholas deVore III. 246-277, *Feb. 1978*
Brazil's Wild Frontier. By Loren McIntyre. 684-719, *Nov. 1977*
Those Fiery Brazilian Bees. By Rick

Still living off the land in Brazilian Amazonia, a Tukuna woman in a settlement near the Peruvian border balances a cayman destined to become a meal. STEPHANIE MAZE

Mighty Niagara, Wonderful Victoria, and Picturesque Iguazu. By Theodore W. Noyes. 29-59, *July 1926*

Exploring the Valley of the Amazon in a Hydroplane: Twelve Thousand Miles of Flying Over the World's Greatest River and Greatest Forest to Chart the Unknown Parima River from the Sky. By Albert W. Stevens. 353-420, *Apr. 1926*

The Amazon, Father of Waters: The Earth's Mightiest River Drains a Basin of More Than 2,700,000 Square Miles, from Which Came Originally the World's Finest Rubber. By W. L. Schurz. 445-463, *Apr. 1926*

A Visit to the Brazilian Coffee Country. By Robert De C. Ward. 908-931, *Oct. 1911*

Fishing and Hunting Tales from Brazil. By Dewey Austin Cobb. 917-920, *Oct. 1909*

South America Fifty Years Hence. By Charles M. Pepper. 427-432, *Aug. 1906*

The Falls of Iguazu. By Marie Robinson Wright. 456-460, *Aug. 1906*

Brazil and Peru. 203-204, *Apr. 1906*

Brazil-French Guiana Boundary Decision. 83, *Feb. 1901*

The Recent Ascent of Itambé. By J. C. Branner. 183, *May 1899*

The Peak of Itambé. 476, *Nov. 1898*

South America. Annual Address by the President, Gardiner G. Hubbard. 1-29, *Mar. 28, 1891*

See also Rio de Janeiro; Santos; São Paulo

BRAZILIAN BEES:

Those Fiery Brazilian Bees. By Rick Gore. Photos by Bianca Lavies. 491-501, *Apr. 1976*

BRAZILIAN OTTERS:

Giant Otters: "Big Water Dogs" in Peril. By Nicole Duplaix. Photos by the author and Bates Littlehales. NGS research grant. 130-142, *July 1980*

BREAD MAKING:

How the World Is Fed. By William Joseph Showalter. 1-110, *Jan. 1916*

Bread Making in Many Lands. 165-179, *Mar. 1908*

BREADALBANE (British Bark):

Exploring a 140-year-old Ship Under Arctic Ice. By Joseph B. MacInnis. Photos by Emory Kristof. 104A-104D, *July 1983*

BREADFRUIT:

Tahiti, "Finest Island in the World." By Luis Marden. 1-47, *July 1962*

Huzza for Otaheite! By Luis Marden. 435-459, *Apr. 1962*

The **"BREAKING** Up" of the Yukon. By George S. Gibbs. 268-272, *May 1906*

BREAKTHROUGH in Wildlife Studies. By John Craighead. NGS research grant. 148-158, *July 1976*

BREASTED, CHARLES: *Author*

Exploring the Secrets of Persepolis. 381-420, *Oct. 1933*

BRECKENFELD, GURNEY:
Photographer

Sierra High Trip. By David R. Brower. 844-868, *June 1954*

BREDIN, DEE: *Author*

Java Assignment. 89-119, *Jan. 1942*

BREED, AUSTIN A.: *Photographer*

Spain and Morocco. 257-270, *Mar. 1917*

BREED, JACK: *Author*

Better Days for the Navajos. Photos by Charles W. Herbert. 809-847, *Dec. 1958*

Author-Photographer

Shooting Rapids in Dinosaur Country. Photos by author and Justin Locke. 363-390, *Mar. 1954*

Roaming the West's Fantastic Four Corners. 705-742, *June 1952*

First Motor Sortie into Escalante Land. 369-404, *Sept. 1949*

Land of the Havasupai. 655-674, *May 1948*

Utah's Arches of Stone. 173-192, *Aug. 1947*

Flaming Cliffs of Monument Valley. Photos by author and Warren T. Mithoff. 452-461, *Oct. 1945*

Photographer

Colorado's Friendly Topland (Rocky Mountains). By Robert M. Ormes. 187-214, *Aug. 1951*

Windjamming Around New England. By Tom Horgan. 141-169, *Aug. 1950*

BREEDEN, KAY:
Author-Photographer

Rock Paintings of the Aborigines. By Kay and Stanley Breeden. 174-187, *Feb. 1973*

Eden in the Outback. By Kay and Stanley Breeden. 189-203, *Feb. 1973*

BREEDEN, PAUL M.: *Artist*

Rediscovering America's Forgotten Crops. By Noel D. Vietmeyer. Photos by Burgess Blevins. 702-712, *May 1981*

BREEDEN, STANLEY:

On Assignment in Australia. *Feb. 1988*

Nomination Page. *Sept. 1976*

Author

The First Australians. Photos by Belinda Wright. 266-289, *Feb. 1988*

Tiger! Lord of the Indian Jungle. Photos by Belinda Wright. 748-773, *Dec. 1984*

Author-Photographer

The First Australians: Living in Two Worlds. By Belinda Wright and Stanley Breeden. 291-294, *Feb. 1988*

Rock Paintings of the Aborigines. By Kay and Stanley Breeden. 174-187, *Feb. 1973*

Eden in the Outback. By Kay and Stanley Breeden. 189-203, *Feb. 1973*

Photographer

India Struggles to Save Her Wildlife. By John J. Putman. 299-343, *Sept. 1976*

Strange Animals of Australia. By David Fleay. 388-411, *Sept. 1963*

BREEDER REACTORS:

The Promise and Peril of Nuclear Energy. By Kenneth F. Weaver. Photos by Emory Kristof. 459-493, *Apr. 1979*

BRENDAN, Saint:

Who Discovered America? A New Look at an Old Question. The Editor. 769, *Dec. 1977*

The Voyage of *Brendan*. By Timothy Severin. Photos by Cotton Coulson. 770-797, *Dec. 1977*

BRENDAN (Leather-hulled Sailboat):

Who Discovered America? A New Look at an Old Question. The Editor. 769, *Dec. 1977*

The Voyage of *Brendan*. By Timothy Severin. Photos by Cotton Coulson. 770-797, *Dec. 1977*

BR'ER Possum, Hermit of the Lowlands. By Agnes Akin Atkinson. Photos by Charles Philip Fox. 405-418, *Mar. 1953*

BREWER, ELIZABETH A.: *Author*

Peculiar Caves of Asia Minor. 870-875, *Sept. 1911*

BREWER, NADINE: *Author*

Home to the Heart of Kentucky. Photos by William Strode. 522-546, *Apr. 1982*

BREWERIES:

Milwaukee: More Than Beer. By Louise Levathes. Photos by Michael Mauney. 180-201, *Aug. 1980*

BREWSTER, BETTY B.: *Author*

Expedition into Texas of Fernando del Bosque, Standard-Bearer of the King, Don Carlos II, in the Year 1675. Translated from an Old, Unpublished Spanish Manuscript. 339-348, *Sept. 1908*

BRIDES' FAIR:

Berber Brides' Fair. By Carla Hunt. Photos by Nik Wheeler. 119-129, *Jan. 1980*

BRIDGE CONSTRUCTION:

A Century Old, the Wonderful Brooklyn Bridge. By John G. Morris. Photos by Donal F. Holway. 565-579, *May 1983*

BRIDGES:

A Century Old, the Wonderful Brooklyn Bridge. By John G. Morris. Photos by Donal F. Holway. 565-579, *May 1983*
Over and Under Chesapeake Bay. By David S. Boyer. Contents: The Chesapeake Bay Bridge-Tunnel. 593-612, *Apr. 1964*
Cane Bridges of Asia. Photos from Paul Popper. 243-250, *Aug. 1948*
California's Coastal Redwood Realm: Along a Belt of Tall Trees a Giant Bridge Speeds the Winning of Our Westernmost Frontier. By J. R. Hildebrand. 133-184, *Feb. 1939*
Bridges, from Grapevine to Steel. By Frederick Simpich. 391-406, *Mar. 1936*
The Washington Aqueduct and Cabin John Bridge. By D. D. Gaillard. 337-344, *Dec. 1897*
See also Delaware (River), for Delaware Memorial Bridge; Languedoc (Region), France, for Pont du Gard; San Francisco (City and Bay), California, for Golden Gate Bridge

BRIDGES, Natural:

Bursts of Color in Sculptured Utah. 593-616, *May 1936*
Encircling Navajo Mountain (Utah) with a Pack-Train: An Expedition to a Hitherto Untraversed Region of Our Southwest Discovers a New Route to Rainbow Natural Bridge. By Charles L. Bernheimer. 197-224, *Feb. 1923*
The Great Rainbow Natural Bridge of Southern Utah. By Joseph E. Pogue. 1048-1056, *Nov. 1911*
The Great Natural Bridges of Utah. By Byron Cummings. 157-167, *Feb. 1910*
The Great Natural Bridges of Utah. 199-204, *Mar. 1907*
Colossal Natural Bridges of Utah. 367-369, *Sept. 1904*
The Natural Bridge of Virginia. By Charles D. Walcott. 59-62, *July 10, 1893*
See also Arches National Park; Canyonlands National Park; Escalante Canyon; Natural Bridges National Monument; Rainbow Bridge National Monument; Zion National Park

BRIDGMAN, HERBERT L.: *Author*

Ten Years of the Peary Arctic Club. 661-668, *Sept. 1908*
The New British Empire of the Sudan. 241-267, *May 1906*
Peary's Work and Prospects. 414-415, *Oct. 1899*

A **BRIEF** Account of the Geographic Work of the U. S. Coast and Geodetic Survey. By T. C. Mendenhall and Otto H. Tittmann. 294-299, *Oct. 1897*

BRIGANTINE. *See Yankee*

BRIGGS, LYMAN J.:

Nomination Page. *June 1958*
Eclipse Hunting in Brazil's Ranchland. By F. Barrows Colton. Photos by Richard H. Stewart and Guy W. Starling. NGS research grant. 285-324, *Sept. 1947*
Author
When Mt. Mazama Lost Its Top: The Birth of Crater Lake. 128-133, *July 1962*
How Old Is It? (Radiocarbon Dating). By Lyman J. Briggs and Kenneth F. Weaver. 234-255, *Aug. 1958*
Uncle Sam's House of 1,000 Wonders (National Bureau of Standards). By Lyman J. Briggs and F. Barrows Colton. 755-784, *Dec. 1951*

BRIGHAM, ALBERT PERRY: *Author*

An Introduction to Physical Geography. By Grove Karl Gilbert and Albert Perry Brigham. 21-26, *Jan. 1903*

BRIGHT ANGEL TRAIL, Arizona:

Experiences in the Grand Canyon. By Ellsworth and Emery Kolb. 99-184, *Aug. 1914*

BRIGHT Bits in Poland's Mountainous South. Photos by Hans Hildenbrand. 353-360, *Mar. 1935*

BRIGHT Corners of Time-Mellowed Germany. Photos by Hans Hildenbrand and Wilhelm Tobien. 223-230, *Aug. 1933*

BRIGHT Dyes Reveal Secrets of Canada Geese. By John and Frank Craighead. 817-832, *Dec. 1957*

BRIGHT Facets of Brazil. Photos by W. Robert Moore. 49-72, *Jan. 1944*

BRIGHT Facets of Italy's Grandeur. Photos by B. Anthony Stewart. 355-362, *Mar. 1940*

BRIGHT Flashes from Pacific Corals (Fishes). Photos by Walter H. Chute. 349-372, *Mar. 1941*

BRIGHT-HUED Pets of Cage and Aviary. Paintings by Allan Brooks. 783-790, *Dec. 1938*

BRIGHT Pages from an Asiatic Travel Log. Photos by Maynard Owen Williams. 545-552, *Nov. 1932*

BRIGHT Patterns of Long Island Life. Photos by Willard R. Culver. 429-460, *Apr. 1939*

BRILL, DAVID: *Photographer*

The Search for Our Ancestors. By Kenneth F. Weaver. Paintings by Jay H. Matternes. 560-623, *Nov. 1985*
Homo Erectus Unearthed: A Fossil Skeleton 1,600,000 Years Old. By Richard Leakey and Alan Walker. NGS research grant. 624-629, *Nov. 1985*
The Anasazi–Riddles in the Ruins. By Thomas Y. Canby. Photos by Dewitt Jones and David Brill. Paintings by Roy Andersen. 554-592, *Nov. 1982*
Ancient Aphrodisias Lives Through Its Art. By Kenan T. Erim. 527-551, *Oct. 1981*
Ethiopia Yields First "Family" of Early

Man. By Donald C. Johanson. 790-811, *Dec. 1976*
Minnesota, Where Water Is the Magic Word. By David S. Boyer. Photos by author and David Brill. 200-229, *Feb. 1976*
Chan Chan, Peru's Ancient City of Kings. By Michael E. Moseley and Carol J. Mackey. 318-345, *Mar. 1973*

BRIMBERG, SISSE:

On Assignment in Israel. *Dec. 1982*
Photographer
The Search for Modern Humans. By John J. Putman. Photos by Sisse Brimberg and Ira Block. Paintings by Jack Unruh. 439-477, *Oct. 1988*
Art Treasures from the Ice Age: Lascaux Cave. By Jean-Philippe Rigaud. Photos by Sisse Brimberg and Norbert Aujoulat. 482-499, *Oct. 1988*
Chocolate: Food of the Gods. By Gordon Young. Photos by James L. Stanfield and Sisse Brimberg. 664-687, *Nov. 1984*
Hunters of the Lost Spirit: Lapps. By Priit J. Vesilind. 194-197, *Feb. 1983*
Where Magic Ruled: Art of the Bering Sea. By William W. Fitzhugh and Susan A. Kaplan. 198-205, *Feb. 1983*
Lost Outpost of the Egyptian Empire. By Trude Dothan. Paintings by Lloyd K. Townsend. 739-769, *Dec. 1982*
Eskimo and Viking Finds in the High Arctic: Ellesmere Island. By Peter Schledermann. Included: Artifacts of the Norse, the Dorset, the Thule. 575-601, *May 1981*
Washington Cathedral: "House of Prayer for All People." By Robert Paul Jordan. 552-573, *Apr. 1980*
The Magic World of Hans Christian Andersen. By Harvey Arden. 825-849, *Dec. 1979*
Washington's Yakima Valley. By Mark Miller. 609-631, *Nov. 1978*

BRINDAMOUR, ROD: *Photographer*

Living with the Great Orange Apes: Indonesia's Orangutans. By Biruté M. F. Galdikas. 830-853, *June 1980*
Orangutans, Indonesia's "People of the Forest." By Biruté Galdikas-Brindamour. 444-473, *Oct. 1975*

BRINGING Old Testament Times to Life. By G. Ernest Wright. Paintings by Henry J. Soulen. 833-864, *Dec. 1957*

BRINGING the World to Our Foreign Language Soldiers: How a Military Training Camp is Solving a Seemingly Unsurmountable Problem by Using the Geographic. By Christina Krysto. 81-90, *Aug. 1918*

BRINK, ANDRÉ: *Author*

The Afrikaners. Photos by David Turnley. 556-585, *Oct. 1988*

BRINKLEY, DAVID:

Nomination Page. *Aug. 1965*

BRIQUETS (Fuel):

An Ideal Fuel Manufactured Out of Waste Products: The American Coal Briquetting Industry. By Guy Elliott Mitchell. 1067-1074, *Dec. 1910*

Young Donny Edenshaw of British Columbia's Queen Charlotte Islands poses beside a paddle decorated in the tradition of his Haida ancestors. DEWITT JONES

Rockies (Part II). By Walter D. Wilcox. 185-200, *June 1902*

Recent Exploration in the Canadian Rockies (Part I). By Walter D. Wilcox. 151-168, *May 1902*

Life on a Yukon Trail. By Alfred Pearce Dennis. 377-391, Oct. 1899; 457-466, *Nov. 1899*

Exploration in the Canadian Rockies. 135-136, *Apr. 1899*

The Stikine River in 1898. By Eliza Ruhamah Scidmore. 1-15, *Jan. 1899*

Overland Routes to the Klondike. By Hamlin Garland. 113-116, *Apr. 1898*

The Future of the Yukon Goldfields. By William H. Dall. 117-120, *Apr. 1898*

An Interesting Rumor Concerning Andrée. By John Hyde. 102-103, *Mar. 1898*

An Expedition through the Yukon District. By Charles Willard Hayes. 117-159, *May 15, 1892*

See also Columbia River and Basin; Great Divide Trail; Kitimat; Vancouver; *and* Bikepacking

BRITISH COMMONWEALTH OF NATIONS:

H.R.H. The Prince Philip, Duke of Edinburgh, Introduces to Members the Narrative of His Round-the-world Tour. 583-584, *Nov. 1957*

Off the Beaten Track of Empire (Prince Philip's Tour). By Beverley M. Bowie. Photos by Michael Parker. 584-626, *Nov. 1957*

Yanks at Westminster. By Leonard David Gammans. 223-252, *Aug. 1946*

The United States and the British Empire. By Leonard David Gammans. 562-564, *May 1945*

The British Commonwealth of Nations: "Organized Freedom" Around the World. By Eric Underwood. 485-524, *Apr. 1943*

The Flags of the British Empire. By Byron McCandless and Gilbert Grosvenor. 378-385, *Oct. 1917*

Great Britain's Bread Upon the Waters: Canada and Her Other Daughters. By William Howard Taft. 217-272, *Mar. 1916*

The Expansion of England. By Edwin D. Mead. 249-263, *July 1900*

See also Great Britain; Northern Ireland; *and* names of former dominions and colonies

BRITISH COMMONWEALTH TRANS-ANTARCTIC EXPEDITION:

Society Honors the Conquerors of Antarctica. 589-590, *Apr. 1959*

The Crossing of Antarctica. By Sir Vivian Fuchs. Photos by George Lowe. 25-47, *Jan. 1959*

Man's First Winter at the South Pole. By Paul A. Siple. 439-478, *Apr. 1958*

BRITISH Dominions Scenes. 233-248, *Mar. 1916*

BRITISH EAST AFRICA:

The British Commonwealth of Nations: "Organized Freedom" Around the World. By Eric Underwood. 485-524, *Apr. 1943*

Uganda, "Land of Something New": Equatorial African Area Reveals

Snow-crowned Peaks, Crater Lakes, Jungle-story Beasts, Human Giants, and Forest Pygmies. By Jay Marston. 109-130, *Jan. 1937*

When a Drought Blights Africa: Hippos and Elephants Are Driven Insane by Suffering, in the Lorian Swamp, Kenya Colony. By A. T. Curle. 521-528, *Apr. 1929*

Elephant Hunting in Equatorial Africa with Rifle and Camera. By Carl E. Akeley. 779-810, *Aug. 1912*

Zanzibar. By Mrs. Harris R. Childs. 810-824, *Aug. 1912*

Wild Man and Wild Beast in Africa. By Theodore Roosevelt. 1-33, *Jan. 1911*

Where Roosevelt Will Hunt. By Sir Harry Johnston. 207-256, *Mar. 1909*

Amid the Snow Peaks of the Equator: A Naturalist's Exploration Around Ruwenzori, with an Excursion to the Congo State, and an Account of the Terrible Scourge of Sleeping Sickness. By A.F.R. Wollaston. 256-277, *Mar. 1909*

A Great African Lake (Victoria). By Sir Henry M. Stanley. 169-172, *May 1902*

See also present names, Kenya; Tanzania; Uganda

BRITISH EMPIRE. *See* British Commonwealth of Nations

BRITISH GUIANA (now Guyana):

Strange Little World of the Hoatzin. By J. Lear Grimmer. Photos by M. Woodbridge Williams. NGS research grant. 391-401, *Sept. 1962*

Strange Courtship of the (Golden) Cock-of-the-Rock. By E. Thomas Gilliard. NGS research grant. 134-140, *Jan. 1962*

Animal Safari to British Guiana. By David Attenborough. Photos by Charles Lagus and author. 851-874, *June 1957*

Life Among the Wai Wai Indians. By

Clifford Evans and Betty J. Meggers. 329-346, *Mar. 1955*

A New World to Explore. Contents: British Guiana. By R.W.G. Hingston. 617-642, *Nov. 1932*

Kaieteur and Roraima: The Great Falls and the Great Mountain of the Guianas. By Henry Edward Crampton. 227-244, *Sept. 1920*

The World's Greatest Waterfall: The Kaieteur Fall, in British Guiana. By Leonard Kennedy. 846-859, *Sept. 1911*

Notes from a Naturalist's Experiences in British Guiana. By C. H. Eigenmann. 859-870, *Sept. 1911*

An Impression of the Guiana Wilderness. By Angelo Heilprin. 373-381, *June 1907*

The Anglo-Venezuelan Boundary Dispute. By Marcus Baker. 129-144, *Apr. 1900*

The Venezuelan Boundary Commission and Its Work. By Marcus Baker. 193-201, *July-Aug. 1897*

South America. Address by Gardiner G. Hubbard. 1-29, *Mar. 28, 1891*

BRITISH HONDURAS (now Belize):

Notes on Central America. 272-279, *Apr. 1907*

BRITISH ISLES:

✦ *British Isles; Medieval England. Oct. 1979*

✦ *A Traveler's Map of the British Isles. Text on reverse. Apr. 1974*

✦ *British Isles, Atlas series. July 1958*

✦ *The British Isles. Apr. 1949*

A Modern Pilgrim's Map of the British Isles. By Andrew H. Brown. 795-802, *June 1937*

✦ *A Modern Pilgrim's Map of the British Isles or More Precisely the Kingdom of Great Britain and Northern Ireland and the Irish Free State. June 1937*

British Isles. 551-566, *Dec. 1915*

Lounging on lush grass in 1909, a Burchell's zebra surveys the Athi plains of British East Africa, today's Kenya. C. E. AKELEY

A Geographical Description of the British Islands. By W. M. Davis. 208-211, *June 1896*

See also Arran, Island of; Caldy; Channel Islands; Great Britain; Hebrides; Ireland; Lundy; Man, Isle of; Orkney Islands; St. Michael's Mount; Scilly, Isles of; Shetland Islands; Skokholm; Skomer; Wight, Isle of; *and* The Renaissance; Vikings

BRITISH MALAYA:

The British Commonwealth of Nations: "Organized Freedom" Around the World. By Eric Underwood. 485-524, *Apr. 1943*

See also present name, Malaysia; *and* Singapore

BRITISH MOUNT EVEREST EXPEDITION:

Triumph on Everest. 1-64. I. Siege and Assault. By Sir John Hunt. 1-43; II. The Conquest of the Summit. By Sir Edmund Hillary. 45-63; III. President Eisenhower Presents the Hubbard Medal to Everest's Conquerors. 64, *July 1954*

BRITISH NEW GUINEA. *See* Papua New Guinea

BRITISH Pacific Cable. 78, *Feb. 1901*

BRITISH SOUTH AFRICA. *See* South Africa

BRITISH South Africa and the Transvaal. By F. F. Hilder. 81-96, *Mar. 1900*

The **BRITISH** South Polar Expedition. 210-212, *May 1903*

The **BRITISH** Take Baku. 163-164, *Aug. 1918*

BRITISH TRANSGLOBE EXPEDITION:

Circling Earth From Pole to Pole. By Sir Ranulph Fiennes. 464-481, *Oct. 1983*

The **BRITISH** Way: Great Britain's Major Gifts to Freedom, Democratic Government, Science, and Society. By Sir Evelyn Wrench. Paintings from British and American artists. 421-541, *Apr. 1949*

BRITISH WEST AFRICA:

The British Commonwealth of Nations: "Organized Freedom" Around the World. By Eric Underwood. 485-524, *Apr. 1943*

Three-Wheeling Through Africa: Two Adventurers Cross the So-called Dark Continent North of Lake Chad on Motorcycles with Side Cars. By James C. Wilson. 37-92, *Jan. 1934*

Notes on the Ekoi. By P. A. Talbot. 33-38, *Jan. 1912*

See also Gold Coast (Ghana); Nigeria

BRITISH WEST INDIES:

The British Commonwealth of Nations: "Organized Freedom" Around the World. By Eric Underwood. 485-524, *Apr. 1943*

Americans in the Caribbean. By Luis Marden. 723-758, *June 1942*

British West Indian Interlude. By Anne Rainey Langley. 1-46, *Jan. 1941*

Bringing home the bread, a French schoolboy carries two baguettes in Quimperlé, Brittany. HOWELL WALKER, NGS

See also Bahamas; Barbados; Cayman Islands; Jamaica; Leeward Islands; St. Vincent; Trinidad; Windward Islands

BRITISH Yukon Telegraph. 164, *Apr. 1901*

BRITT, KENT: *Author*

Costa Rica Steers the Middle Course. 32-57, *July 1981*

The Joy of Pigs. Photos by George F. Mobley. 398-415, *Sept. 1978*

The Loyalists. Photos by Ted Spiegel. 510-539, *Apr. 1975*

Pennsylvania's Old-time Dutch Treat. Photos by H. Edward Kim. 564-578, *Apr. 1973*

BRITTANY (Region), France:

Superspill: Black Day for Brittany. Photos by Martin Rogers. Text by Noel Grove. 124-135, *July 1978*

France Meets the Sea in Brittany. By Howell Walker. 470-503, *Apr. 1965*

Here Rest in Honored Glory...The United States Dedicates Six New Battle Monuments in Europe to Americans Who Gave Their Lives During World War II. Included: Brittany American Cemetery and Memorial. By Howell Walker. 739-768, *June 1957*

The Coasts of Normandy and Brittany. By W. Robert Moore. 205-232, *Aug. 1943*

Where Bretons Wrest a Living from the Sea. Photos by F. W. Goro. 751-766, *June 1937*

St. Malo, Ancient City of Corsairs: An Old Brittany Seaport Whose Past Bristles with Cannons and Cutlasses. By Junius B. Wood. 131-177, *Aug. 1929*

Through the Back Doors of France: A Seven Weeks' Voyage in a Canadian Canoe from St. Malo, Through Brittany and the Château Country, to Paris. By Melville Chater. 1-51, *July 1923*

The Mysterious Prehistoric Monuments of Brittany. By Charles Buxton Going. 53-69, *July 1923*

Scenes from France. 29-44, *July 1921*

The Beauties of France. By Arthur Stanley Riggs. 391-491, *Nov. 1915*

The France of Today. By A. W. Greely. 193-222, *Sept. 1914*

Brittany: The Land of the Sardine. By Hugh M. Smith. 541-573, *June 1909*

See also Celts

BRITTON, WRIGHT: *Author*

Sailing Iceland's Rugged Coasts. Photos by James A. Sugar. 228-265, *Aug. 1969*

BROAD, PHILIP: *Author*

Within the Halls of Cambridge (University). 333-349, *Sept. 1936*

BROAD Shoulder of Australia: Queensland. By William S. Ellis. Photos by David Robert Austen. Included: Queensland Fossils Expand Australia's Prehistoric Menagerie. 2-39, *Jan. 1986*

BROADBILL. *See* Swordfish

BROADSTAIRS, England:

The England of Charles Dickens. By Richard W. Long. Photos by Adam Woolfitt. Included: Dickens Festival; "Bleak House," Dickens's summer home. 443-483, *Apr. 1974*

BROADWATER, JOHN D.: *Author*

Yorktown Shipwreck. Photos by Bates Littlehales. 804-823, *June 1988*

BROMELIADS:

Hidden Worlds in the Heart of a Plant. By Paul A. Zahl. 389-397, *Mar. 1975*

Puya, the Pineapple's Andean Ancestor. By Mulford B. Foster. 463-480, *Oct. 1950*

BRONTOSAURS:

We Captured a 'Live' Brontosaur. By Roland T. Bird. 707-722, *May 1954*

BRONX ZOO, Bronx, New York:

President's Page. By Gilbert M. Grosvenor. *June 1986*

See also New York Zoological Park

BRONZE AGE:

Oldest Known Shipwreck Reveals Splendors of the Bronze Age. By George F. Bass. Photos by William R. Curtsinger. Included: Bronze Age Trade, The Cosmopolitan World of the Late Bronze Age, The Painstaking Art of Marine Archaeology. NGS research grant. 693-733, *Dec. 1987*

Mysteries of the Bog. By Louise E. Levathes. Photos by Fred Bavendam. Contents: Bronze Age executions and bog burials. 397-420, *Mar. 1987*

Lost Outpost of the Egyptian Empire. By Trude Dothan. Photos by Sisse Brimberg. Paintings by Lloyd K.

Townsend. NGS research grant. 739-769, *Dec. 1982*

Drama of Death in a Minoan Temple. By Yannis Sakellarakis and Efi Sapouna-Sakellaraki. Photos by Otis Imboden and Spyros Tsavdaroglou. 205-222, *Feb. 1981*

Ebla: Splendor of an Unknown Empire. By Howard La Fay. Photos by James L. Stanfield. Paintings by Louis S. Glanzman. 730-759, *Dec. 1978*

Minoans and Mycenaeans: Greece's Brilliant Bronze Age. By Joseph Judge. Photos by Gordon W. Gahan. Paintings by Lloyd K. Townsend. 142-185, *Feb. 1978*

Oldest Known Shipwreck Yields Bronze Age Cargo. By Peter Throckmorton. NGS research grant. 697-711, *May 1962*

Thirty-three Centuries Under the Sea (Shipwreck). By Peter Throckmorton. 682-703, *May 1960*

See also Hoabinhian Culture; Minoan Civilization

BRONZE AGE SHIPS:

Oldest Known Shipwreck Reveals Splendors of the Bronze Age. By George F. Bass. Photos by William R. Curtsinger. Included: Bronze Age Trade, The Cosmopolitan World of the Late Bronze Age, The Painstaking Art of Marine Archaeology. NGS research grant. 693-733, *Dec. 1987*

The Quest for Ulysses. By Tim Severin. Photos by Kevin Fleming. 197-225, *Aug. 1986*

Jason's Voyage: In Search of the Golden Fleece. By Tim Severin. Photos by John Egan and Seth Mortimer. 406-420, *Sept. 1985*

Bronze Age Shipwreck. By Wilbur E. Garrett and George F. Bass. Contents: Turkish discovery. NGS research grant. 1-3, *Jan. 1985*

BRONZES:

Warriors From a Watery Grave (Bronze Sculptures). By Joseph Alsop. 821-827, *June 1983*

China Unveils Her Newest Treasures. Photos by Robert W. Madden. 848-857, *Dec. 1974*

Mosaic of Cultures (Southeast Asia). By Peter T. White. Photos by W. E. Garrett. 296-329, *Mar. 1971*

See also Dreyfus Collection

BROOK LIFE:

Unseen Life of a Mountain Stream. By William H. Amos. 562-580, *Apr. 1977*

BROOKFIELD, CHARLES M.: *Author*

Key Largo Coral Reef: America's First Undersea Park. Photos by Jerry Greenberg. 58-69, *Jan. 1962*

An Exotic New Oriole Settles in Florida. By Charles M. Brookfield and Oliver Griswold. 261-264, *Feb. 1956*

Cannon on Florida Reefs Solve Mystery of Sunken Ship. 807-824, *Dec. 1941*

BROOKLYN (Borough), New York, N. Y.:

Brooklyn: The Other Side of the Bridge. By Alice J. Hall. Photos by

Robert W. Madden. 580-613, *May 1983*

The Pious Ones (Brooklyn's Hasidic Jews). By Harvey Arden. Photos by Nathan Benn. 276-298, *Aug. 1975*

Long Island Outgrows the Country. By Howell Walker. Photos by B. Anthony Stewart. 279-326, *Mar. 1951*

Spin Your Globe to Long Island: Only Six States Have More People than the Insular Empire that Ranges from a World's Fair Through Potato Patches, Princely Estates, and Historic Shrines. By Frederick Simpich. 413-460, *Apr. 1939*

BROOKLYN BRIDGE, New York, N. Y.:

Editorial. By Wilbur E. Garrett. 563, *May 1983*

A Century Old, the Wonderful Brooklyn Bridge. By John G. Morris. Photos by Donal F. Holway. 565-579, *May 1983*

BROOKS, ALFRED H.:

Awarded Jane M. Smith Life Membership. 342 (footnote), *Apr. 1920*

Board of Managers. 87, *Feb. 1905*

The Brooks Alaskan Expedition. 389, *Oct. 1902*

Author

Railway Routes in Alaska. By Alfred H. Brooks. 165-190, *Mar. 1907*

How Much Is Known of Alaska. By Alfred H. Brooks. 112-114, *Feb. 1906*

Tribute to American Topographers. By A. H. Brooks. 358, *July 1905*

The Geography of Alaska. By Alfred H. Brooks. 213-219, *May 1904*

Plan for Climbing Mt. McKinley. By Alfred H. Brooks and D. L. Reaburn. 30-35, *Jan. 1903*

Proposed Surveys in Alaska in 1902. By Alfred H. Brooks. 133-135, *Apr. 1902*

Ice Cliffs on White River, Yukon Terri-

tory. By C. Willard Hayes and Alfred H. Brooks. 199-201, *May 1900*

BROOKS, ALLAN: *Artist*

Sparrows, Towhees, and Longspurs. Paintings by Allan Brooks and Walter A. Weber. 361-375, *Mar. 1939*

Bright-hued Pets of Cage and Aviary. 788-790, *Dec. 1938*

Wings Over the Bounding Main (Ocean Birds). 237-251, *Aug. 1938*

Feathered Foragers of Swamp and Shore. 191-222, *Aug. 1937*

■■ *The Book of Birds: The First Work Presenting in Full Color All the Major Species of the United States and Canada.* 2 volumes: I, 355 pages; II, 374 pages. 1932; rev. ed. *1937*

Hunted Birds of Field and Wild. Contents: Chacalacas, Doves, Grouse, Partridges, Pheasants, Pigeons, Prairie Chickens, Ptarmigans, Quails, Turkeys. 469-500, *Oct. 1936*

Flycatchers and Other Friends in Feathers. Contents: Anis, Cuckoos, Flycatchers, Kingbirds, Kingfishers, Parakeets, Parrots, Pewees, Phoebes, Trogons. 807-822, *June 1936*

Some Songsters and Flyers of Wide Repute. Contents: Swallows, Thrashers, Thrushes. 529-544, *Apr. 1936*

Auks and Their Northland Neighbors. Contents: Auklets, Auks, Dovekies, Guillemots, Murrelets, Murres, Puffins. 101-116, *Jan. 1936*

Bird Beauties of the Tanager and Finch Families. 513-528, *Apr. 1935*

Silent-Winged Owls of North America. 225-240, *Feb. 1935*

Birds in Glossy Black and Vivid Color. Contents: Blackbirds, Bobolinks, Cowbirds, Flycatchers, Grackles, Meadowlarks, Orioles, Shrikes, Vireos, Waxwings. 113-128, *July 1934*

Blithe Birds of Dooryard, Bush, and Brake. Contents: Chickadees, Creepers, Dippers, Gnatcatchers, Kinglets, Nuthatches, Titmice, Wren-tits, Wrens. 579-594, *May 1934*

Birds of Lake and Lagoon, Marsh and Seacoast. Contents: Cormorants, Grebes, Loons, Pelicans, Water Turkeys. 313-328, *Mar. 1934*

Eagles, Hawks, and Vultures. 65-94, *July 1933*

North American Woodpeckers. 465-478, *Apr. 1933*

Crows, Magpies, and Jays. 65-79, *Jan. 1933*

Ibises, Herons, and Flamingos. 455-468, *Oct. 1932*

Humming Birds, Swifts and Goatsuckers. 75-88, *July 1932*

Author-Artist

Far-Flying Wild Fowl and Their Foes. Included: Wild Geese, Ducks, and Swans. 487-528, *Oct. 1934*

BROOKS, RHODA and EARLE:

Authors

Ambassadors of Good Will: The Peace Corps. By Sargent Shriver and Peace Corps Volunteers. Included: Ecuador. 297-345, *Sept. 1964*

Blessing his bread as he slices it, a Hasidic Jew follows tradition in Brooklyn's Williamsburg enclave. NATHAN BENN

BROOKS, SYDNEY: *Author*

What Great Britain Is Doing (The British War Effort). 193-210, *Mar. 1917*

BROOKS RANGE, Alaska:

Our Wildest Wilderness: Alaska's Arctic National Wildlife Range. By Douglas H. Chadwick. Photos by Lowell Georgia. 737-769, *Dec. 1979*

BROUGHTON, VERA, LADY: *Author*

A Modern Dragon Hunt on Komodo: An English Yachting Party Traps and Photographs the Huge and Carnivorous Dragon Lizard of the Lesser Sundas. 321-331, *Sept. 1936*

BROWER, DAVID R.: *Author*

Sierra High Trip. 844-868, *June 1954*

BROWER, KENNETH: *Author*

In Hawaii's Crystal Sea, A Galaxy of Life Fills the Night. Photos by William R. Curtsinger and Chris Newbert. 834-847, *Dec. 1981*

BROWER, WARD, Jr.:

Easter Egg Chickens. By Frederick G. Vosburgh. Photos by B. Anthony Stewart. 377-387, *Sept. 1948*

BROWN, ANDREW H.: *Author*

Sweden, Quiet Workshop for the World. 451-491, *Apr. 1963*
New St. Lawrence Seaway Opens the Great Lakes to the World. 299-339, *Mar. 1959*
Weather from the White North. Photos by John E. Fletcher. 543-572, *Apr. 1955*
Ontario, Pivot of Canada's Power. Photos by B. Anthony Stewart and Bates Littlehales. 823-852, *Dec. 1953*
Versatile Wood Waits on Man. 109-140, *July 1951*
Men Against the Hurricane. 537-560, *Oct. 1950*
Sno-Cats Mechanize Oregon Snow Survey. Photos by John E. Fletcher. 691-710, *Nov. 1949*
Quebec's Forests, Farms, and Frontiers. 431-470, *Oct. 1949*
Skyline Trail from Maine to Georgia. Photos by Robert F. Sisson. 219-251, *Aug. 1949*
Newfoundland, Canada's New Province. Photos by Robert F. Sisson. 777-812, *June 1949*
Americans Stand Guard in Greenland. 457-500, *Oct. 1946*
Salty Nova Scotia. 575-624, *May 1940*
A Modern Pilgrim's Map of the British Isles. 795-802, *June 1937*
Bekonscot, England's Toy-Size Town. By Andrew H. Brown and B. Anthony Stewart. 649-661, *May 1937*

Author-Photographer

Norway's Fjords Pit Men Against Mountains. 96-122, *Jan. 1957*
Philmont Scout Ranch Helps Boys Grow Up. 399-416, *Sept. 1956*
Work-hard, Play-hard Michigan. 279-320, *Mar. 1952*
Labrador Canoe Adventure. By Andrew Brown and Ralph Gray. 65-99, *July 1951*
Saving Earth's Oldest Living Things (Sequoias). Photos by Raymond Moulin and author. 679-695, *May 1951*
Haunting Heart of the Everglades.

Photos by author and Willard R. Culver. 145-173, *Feb. 1948*

Photographer

All-out Assault on Antarctica. By Richard E. Byrd. 141-180, *Aug. 1956*
Stop-and-Go Sail Around South Norway. By Edmond J. Moran. Photos by Randi Kjekstad Bull and Andrew H. Brown. 153-192, *Aug. 1954*
Native's Return to Norway. By Arnvid Nygaard. 683-691, *Nov. 1953*

BROWN, BARNUM: *Author*

Hunting Big Game of Other Days: A Boating Expedition in Search of Fossils in Alberta, Canada. 407-429, *May 1919*

BROWN, G.M.L.: *Author*

Three Old Ports on the Spanish Main. 622-638, *Nov. 1906*

BROWN, H. C.: *Author*

The Indian Village of Baum (Ohio). 272-274, *July 1901*

BROWN, J. CARTER: *Author*

The Genius of El Greco. 736-744, *June 1982*
The National Gallery's New Masterwork on the Mall. Photos by James A. Sugar. 680-701, *Nov. 1978*

BROWN, J. STANLEY. *See* Stanley-Brown, Joseph

BROWN, JOHN:

History Awakens at Harpers Ferry. By Volkmar Wentzel. 399-416, *Mar. 1957*

BROWN, JOSEPHINE A.: *Author*

6,000 Miles over the Roads of Free China. 355-384, *Mar. 1944*

BROWN, ROBERT MARSHALL: *Author*

A Simple Method of Proving That the Earth Is Round. 771-774, *Dec. 1907*

BROWN, ROLAND W.: *Author*

Fossils Lift the Veil of Time. By Harry S. Ladd and Roland W. Brown. 363-386, *Mar. 1956*

BROWN, WILLIAM S.:

On Assignment in New York. *July 1987*

Author

Hidden Life of the Timber Rattler. Photos by Bianca Lavies. NGS research grant. 128-138, *July 1987*

BROWN BEARS:

"Grizz"–Of Men and the Great Bear. By Douglas H. Chadwick. 182-213, *Feb. 1986*
Among Alaska's Brown Bears. By Allan L. Egbert and Michael H. Luque. NGS research grant. 428-442, *Sept. 1975*
When Giant Bears Go Fishing. By Cecil E. Rhode. 195-205, *Aug. 1954*

BROWN PELICANS:

Bad Days for the Brown Pelican. By Ralph W. Schreiber. Photos by William R. Curtsinger and author. 111-123, *Jan. 1975*

BROWNE, JEFFERSON B.: *Author*

Across the Gulf by Rail to Key West (Florida). 203-207, *June 1896*

BROWNSVILLE, Texas:

The Texas Delta of an American Nile: Orchards and Gardens Replace Thorny Jungle in the Southmost Tip of the Lone Star State. By McFall Kerbey. 51-96, *Jan. 1939*

BRUCE, AILSA MELLON: Art Collection:

In Quest of Beauty. Text by Paul Mellon. 372-385, *Mar. 1967*

BRUCE, ROBERT V.: *Author*

Alexander Graham Bell. Photos by Ira Block. 358-385, *Sept. 1988*

BRUGES, Belgium:

Belgium Welcomes the World (1958 World's Fair). By Howell Walker. 795-837, *June 1958*
Bruges, the City the Sea Forgot. By Luis Marden. 631-665, *May 1955*
Belgium Comes Back. By Harvey Klemmer. Photos by Maynard Owen Williams. 575-614, *May 1948*

BRUKKAROS, Mount, Namibia:

Keeping House for the "Shepherds of the Sun." By Mrs. William H. Hoover. 483-506, *Apr. 1930*
Hunting an Observatory: A Successful Search for a Dry Mountain on Which to Establish the National Geographic Society's Solar Radiation Station. By C. G. Abbot. 503-518, *Oct. 1926*

BRUNEI:

Magellan: First Voyage Around the World. By Alan Villiers. Photos by Bruce Dale. 721-753, *June 1976*
Brunei, Borneo's Abode of Peace. By Joseph Judge. Photos by Dean Conger. 207-225, *Feb. 1974*
In Storied Lands of Malaysia. By Maurice Shadbolt. Photos by Winfield Parks. 734-783, *Nov. 1963*

BRUSSELS, Belgium:

Belgium: One Nation Divisible. By James Cerruti. Photos by Martin Rogers. 314-341, *Mar. 1979*
Belgium Welcomes the World (1958 World's Fair). By Howell Walker. 795-837, *June 1958*
Belgium Comes Back. By Harvey Klemmer. Photos by Maynard Owen Williams. 575-614, *May 1948*
Belgium–Europe in Miniature. By Douglas Chandler. 397-450, *Apr. 1938*

BRY, THEODORE DE:

Indian Life Before the Colonists Came. By Stuart E. Jones. Contents: Engravings by Theodore de Bry (1590). 351-368, *Sept. 1947*

BRYAN, C.D.B.:

President's Page. By Gilbert M. Grosvenor. *Sept. 1987*
■■ *The National Geographic Society: 100 Years of Adventure and Discovery.* By C.D.B. Bryan. Published by Harry N. Abrams, Inc. 484 pages. *1987*

As if seeking protection, a Nepalese in Kathmandu sits at the feet of an image of a wrestler. WILLIAM THOMPSON

BRYAN, WILLIAM JENNINGS:
Honors to Colonel Goethals: The Presentation, by President Woodrow Wilson, of the National Geographic Society Special Gold Medal, and Addresses by Secretary of State Bryan, the French Ambassador, the German Ambassador, and Congressman James R. Mann. 677-690, *June 1914*

BRYANT, HENRY G.: *Author*
A Traveler's Notes on Java. 91-111, *Feb. 1910*

BRYANT, WILLIAM CULLEN:
Literary Landmarks of Massachusetts. By William H. Nicholas. Photos by B. Anthony Stewart and John E. Fletcher. 279-310, *Mar. 1950*

BRYCE, JAMES:
Honors to Amundsen and Peary (Address by James Bryce). 113-130, *Jan. 1913*
The National Geographic Society (Announcing the Election of James Bryce, British Ambassador, as an Honorary Member of the Society). 272-298, *Mar. 1912*
In Honor of the Army and Aviation (Address by James Bryce). 267-284, *Mar. 1911*
The Discovery of the North Pole (Address by James Bryce). 63-82, *Jan. 1910*
Honors for Amundsen (Address by James Bryce). 55-76, *Jan. 1908*
Author
The Scenery of North America. 339-389, *Apr. 1922*
Western Siberia and the Altai Mountains: With Some Speculations on the Future of Siberia. 469-507, *May 1921*
Impressions of Palestine. 293-317, *Mar. 1915*
■■ *Washington, The Nation's Capital.* By William Howard Taft and James

Bryce. Reprint of two articles: "Washington: Its Beginning, Its Growth, and Its Future" by William Howard Taft; and "The Nation's Capital" by James Bryce. 101 pages. 1913; rev. ed. *1915*
The Nation's Capital (Washington, D. C.). 717-750, *June 1913*
Two Possible Solutions for the Eastern Problem. 1149-1157, *Nov. 1912*

BRYCE CANYON NATIONAL PARK, Utah:
Nature Carves Fantasies in Bryce Canyon. By William Belknap, Jr. 490-511, *Oct. 1958*
The West Through Boston Eyes. By Stewart Anderson. 733-776, *June 1949*
Bursts of Color in Sculptured Utah. 593-616, *May 1936*
Photographing the Marvels of the West in Colors. By Fred Payne Clatworthy. 694-719, *June 1928*

BUBONIC PLAGUE:
Fleas: The Lethal Leapers. By Nicole Duplaix. 672-694, *May 1988*
Fearful Famines of the Past: History Will Repeat Itself Unless the American People Conserve Their Resources. By Ralph A. Graves. 69-90, *July 1917*
The Conquest of Bubonic Plague in the Philippines. 185-195, *May 1903*
Geographic Miscellanea. 248, *June 1900*
The History and Geographic Distribution of Bubonic Plague. By George M. Sternberg. 97-113, *Mar. 1900*
See also Rats

BUCHAN, SUSAN CHARLOTTE (Lady Tweedsmuir): *Author*
Tweedsmuir Park: The Diary of a Pilgrimage. 451-476, *Apr. 1938*

BUCHANAN, JAMES:
The Living White House. By Lonnelle Aikman. 593-643, *Nov. 1966*
Profiles of the Presidents: II. A Restless Nation Moves West. By Frank Freidel. 80-121, *Jan. 1965*

BUCHANAN, TODD: *Photographer*
On Canada's Hood River: Clues to a Tragic Trek. By John W. Lentz. 128-140, *Jan. 1986*

BUCHAREST, Romania:
Roumania and Its Rubicon. By John Oliver La Gorce. 185-202, *Sept. 1916*
Roumania, the Pivotal State. By James Howard Gore. 360-390, *Oct. 1915*

BUCK ISLAND REEF NATIONAL MONUMENT, St. Croix, Virgin Islands:
Buck Island–Underwater Jewel. By Jerry and Idaz Greenberg. 677-683, *May 1971*

A **BUCKAROO** Stew of Fact and Legend: The Pony Express. By Rowe Findley. Photos by Craig Aurness. 45-71, *July 1980*

BUCKLE, H. T.:
The Geologic Atlas of the United States. By W J McGee. 339-342, *July 1898*

BUDAPEST, Hungary:
Hungary's New Way: A Different Communism. By John J. Putman. Photos by Bill Weems. 225-261, *Feb. 1983*
The Danube: River of Many Nations, Many Names. By Mike Edwards. Photos by Winfield Parks. 455-485, *Oct. 1977*
Hungary: Changing Homeland of a Tough, Romantic People. By Bart McDowell. Photos by Albert Moldvay and Joseph J. Scherschel. 443-483, *Apr. 1971*
A Tale of Three Cities. By Thomas R. Henry. 641-669, *Dec. 1945*
Budapest, Twin City of the Danube. By J. R. Hildebrand. 729-742, *June 1932*
Hungary: A Land of Shepherd Kings. By C. Townley-Fullam. 311-393, *Oct. 1914*
Saint Stephen's Fete in Budapest. By De Witt Clinton Falls. 548-558, *Aug. 1907*

BUDDHISM:
At the Crossroads of Kathmandu. By Douglas H. Chadwick. Photos by William Thompson. 32-65, *July 1987*
Time and Again in Burma. By Bryan Hodgson. Photos by James L. Stanfield. 90-121, *July 1984*
Indonesia Rescues Ancient Borobudur. By W. Brown Morton III. Photos by Dean Conger. Contents: World's largest Buddhist monument. 126-142, *Jan. 1983*
The Temples of Angkor. 548-589. I. Will They Survive? Introduction by Wilbur E. Garrett. 548-551; II. Ancient Glory in Stone. By Peter T. White. Photos by Wilbur E. Garrett. 552-589, *May 1982*
Nomads of China's West. By Galen Rowell. Photos by the author and

Shipka Memorial Church raises gilded domes above the Valley of Roses in Bulgaria. JAMES L. STANFIELD, NGS

Arden. Photos by Matt Bradley. Note: In 1972, Congress created the Buffalo National River, a unique administrative unit. 344-359, *Mar. 1977*

BUILDERS *of the Ancient World:* ■■ *Marvels of Engineering.* Contents: Greece and Rome, Mesoamerica, South America, India and Southeast Asia, and China. 199 pages. *1986*

BUILDING a New Austria. By Beverley M. Bowie. Photos by Volkmar Wentzel. 172-213, *Feb. 1959*

BUILDING America's Air Army. By Hiram Bingham. 48-86, *Jan. 1918*

The **BUILDING** of Tenochtitlan. By Augusto F. Molina Montes. Paintings by Felipe Dávalos. 753-765, *Dec. 1980*

BUILDING the Alaskan Telegraph System. By William Mitchell. 357-361, *Sept. 1904*

BUILDINGS. See Architecture

BUKHARA, Uzbek S.S.R., U.S.S.R.:

The Land of Lambskins: An Expedition to Bokhara, Russian Central Asia, to Study the Karakul Sheep Industry. By Robert K. Nabours. 77-88, *July 1919*
Russia's Orphan Races: Picturesque Peoples Who Cluster on the Southeastern Borderland of the Vast Slav Dominions. By Maynard Owen Williams. 245-278, *Oct. 1918*

BULAWAYO, Southern Rhodesia (now Zimbabwe):

Rhodesia, Hobby and Hope of Cecil Rhodes. By W. Robert Moore. 281-306, *Sept. 1944*

BULGARIA:

Ancient Bulgaria's Golden Treasures. By Colin Renfrew. Photos by James L. Stanfield. Paintings by Jean-Leon Huens. 112-129, *July 1980*
The Bulgarians. By Boyd Gibbons. Photos by James L. Stanfield. 91-111, *July 1980*
The Danube: River of Many Nations, Many Names. By Mike Edwards. Photos by Winfield Parks. 455-485, *Oct. 1977*
Down the Danube by Canoe. By William Slade Backer. Photos by Richard S. Durrance and Christopher G. Knight. 34-79, *July 1965*
Bulgaria, Farm Land Without a Farmhouse: A Nation of Villagers Faces the Challenge of Modern Machinery and Urban Life. By Maynard Owen Williams. Included: Bulgaria's Valley of Roses. Photos by Wilhelm Tobien and Georg Paskoff. 185-218, *Aug. 1932*
The Whirlpool of the Balkans. By George Higgins Moses. 179-197, *Feb. 1921*
The Races of Europe. By Edwin A. Grosvenor. 441-534, *Dec. 1918*
Flags of Austria-Hungary, Bulgaria, Germany, and Turkey. By Byron McCandless and Gilbert Grosvenor. 386-388, *Oct. 1917*

Bulgaria and Its Women. By Hester Donaldson Jenkins. 377-400, *Apr. 1915*
The Changing Map in the Balkans. By Frederick Moore. 199-226, *Feb. 1913*
The Rise of Bulgaria. By James D. Bourchier. 1105-1118, *Nov. 1912*
Bulgaria, the Peasant State. 760-778, *Nov. 1908*
Tirnova, the City of Hanging Gardens. By Felix J. Koch. 632-640, *Oct. 1907*
The Great Turk and His Lost Provinces. By William E. Curtis. 45-61, *Feb. 1903*

BULGE, Battle of the:

Luxembourg, the Quiet Fortress. By Robert Leslie Conly. Photos by Ted H. Funk. 69-97, *July 1970*
Luxembourg, Survivor of Invasions. By Sydney Clark. Photos by Maynard Owen Williams. 791-810, *June 1948*
Belgium Comes Back. By Harvey Klemmer. Photos by Maynard Owen Williams. 575-614, *May 1948*

BULHAK, JAN: *Photographer*
Wilno, Stepchild of the Polish Frontier. 777-784, *June 1938*

BULL, RANDI KJEKSTAD: *Photographer*
Stop-and-Go Sail Around South Norway. By Edmond J. Moran. Photos by Randi Kjekstad Bull and Andrew H. Brown. 153-192, *Aug. 1954*

BULL DERBY, Madura (Island), Indonesia:

Postwar Journey Through Java. By Ronald Stuart Kain. 675-700, *May 1948*

BULLDOG ANTS:

At Home With the Bulldog Ant. By Robert F. Sisson. Included: Face-to-Face with a World of Ants. 62-75, *July 1974*

Bulgaria preserves a Greek-style bronze helmet from the late sixth century B.C.
JAMES L. STANFIELD, NGS

BULLFIGHTS:

Camargue, the Cowboy Country of Southern France. By André Vialles. 1-34, *July 1922*
See also Andalusia (Region), Spain; Camargue (Region), France; Mexico City; Portugal at the Crossroads; Tijuana, Mexico

BULLFROG Ballet Filmed in Flight. By Treat Davidson. 791-799, *June 1963*

BUMP, JAMES D.: *Author*
Big Game Hunting in the Land of Long Ago. By Joseph P. Connolly and James D. Bump. 589-605, *May 1947*

BUMSTEAD, ALBERT H.:
Appointed Chief Cartographer. 130, *Jan. 1936*
Inventor of the sun-compass, used by Richard E. Byrd on polar flights. 523, 520, *Nov. 1925*; 367, 381, 378, *Sept. 1926*; 238, 242, *Aug. 1927*; 233, *Aug. 1930*; 130, *Jan. 1936*

BUMSTEAD, NEWMAN:
Nomination Page. *Jan. 1961*
Developed further the photo-composing machine invented by his father, Albert H. Bumstead. 419, *Mar. 1953*
Author
Rockets Explore the Air Above Us. 562-580, *Apr. 1957*
Children's Art Around the World. 365-387, *Mar. 1957*
Atlantic Odyssey: Iceland to Antarctica. Photos by Volkmar Wentzel. 725-780, *Dec. 1955*
"Around the World in Eighty Days." 705-750, *Dec. 1951*
A Map Maker Looks at the United States. 705-748, *June 1951*

BUNDI, India:
Feudal Splendor Lingers in Rajputana. By Volkmar Wentzel. 411-458, *Oct. 1948*

BUNDY, CARTER:
New Scarlet Bird in Florida Skies. By Paul A. Zahl. 874-882, *Dec. 1967*

BUNLAP, Pentecost Island:
Land Diving With the Pentecost Islanders. By Kal Muller. 799-817, *Dec. 1970*

BURACKER, WILLIAM H.: *Author*
Saga of the Carrier *Princeton.* 189-218, *Aug. 1945*

BURBANK, J. E.: *Author*
The San Francisco Earthquake of April 18, 1906, as Recorded by the Coast and Geodetic Survey Magnetic Observatories. By L. A. Bauer and J. E. Burbank. 298-300, *May 1906*

BURDEKIN, H. B.: *Photographer*
Shadowy London by Night. 177-184, *Aug. 1935*

BURDEN, DAN: *Author-Photographer*
Bikepacking Across Alaska and Canada. 682-695, *May 1973*

BURDEN, W. DOUGLAS: *Author*
Stalking the Dragon Lizard on the Island of Komodo. 216-232, *Aug. 1927*

Hanged and laid to rest 2,000 years ago, Tollund man was preserved in a peat bog in Denmark. LENNART LARSEN

The **BURDEN** France Has Borne. By Granville Fortescue. 323-344, *Apr. 1917*

BURDETT-SCOUGALL, IRENE: *Photographer*

Pigeon Netting–Sport of Basques. 405-416, *Sept. 1949*

BURDSALL, RICHARD L.: *Author*

Climbing Mighty Minya Konka: Americans First Scaled Mountain That Now Is Landmark of China's New Skyway. By Richard L. Burdsall and Terris Moore. 625-650, *May 1943*

The **BUREAU** of Fisheries: How the Rich Fisheries of the United States Are Protected and New Fishing Grounds Discovered or Created. By Barton Warren Evermann. 191-212, *May 1904*

BUREAU OF STANDARDS. See National Bureau of Standards

BURG, AMOS: *Author*

Endeavour Sails the Inside Passage. 801-828, *June 1947*

Author-Photographer

Along the Yukon Trail. 395-416, *Sept. 1953*

North Star Cruises Alaska's Wild West. 57-86, *July 1952*

Cruising Colombia's "Ol' Man River." 615-660, *May 1947*

Britain Just Before the Storm: A Canadian Canoe Threads Old English Waterways Athrob with the Midlands' Industrial Life. Included: Canals and Pageants of Peacetime England. 185-212, *Aug. 1940*

Inside Cape Horn. Included: Land of

the Horn, America's Tiptoe. 743-783, *Dec. 1937*

A Native Son's Rambles in Oregon. Included: Scenes and Round-Ups of the Beaver State. 173-234, *Feb. 1934*

Photographer

Alaska–Our Northwestern Outpost. Photos by Ernest H. Gruening, Amos Burg, and Froelich Rainey. 297-308, *Sept. 1942*

Color Glimpses of the Changing South Seas. 281-288, *Mar. 1934*

On Mackenzie's Trail to the Polar Sea. 127-156, *Aug. 1931*

To-day on "The Yukon Trail of 1898." 85-126, *July 1930*

BURGUNDY (Region), France:

Living the Good Life in Burgundy. By William Davenport. Photos by Robert Freson. 794-817, *June 1978*

BURIAL CUSTOMS:

Discovering the New World's Richest Unlooted Tomb. By Walter Alva. Photos by Bill Ballenberg. Contents: The tomb of a Moche lord. NGS research grant. 510-549, *Oct. 1988*

The Eternal Etruscans. By Rick Gore. Photos by O. Louis Mazzatenta. Paintings by James M. Gurney. 696-743, *June 1988*

Mysteries of the Bog. By Louise E. Levathes. Photos by Fred Bavendam. Included: Peat holds clues to early American life. 397-420, *Mar. 1987*

The Mummies of Qilakitsoq. By Jens P. Hart Hansen, Jørgen Meldgaard, and Jørgen Nordqvist. 191-207, *Feb. 1985*

China Unveils Her Newest Treasures. Photos by Robert W. Madden. 848-857, *Dec. 1974*

A Lady From China's Past. Photos from *China Pictorial*. Text by Alice J. Hall. 660-681, *May 1974*

Life and Death in Tana Toradja. By Pamela and Alfred Meyer. 793-815, *June 1972*

Tutankhamun's Golden Trove. By Christiane Desroches Noblecourt. Photos by F. L. Kenett. 625-646, *Oct. 1963*

Periscope on the Etruscan Past. By Carlo M. Lerici. 337-350, *Sept. 1959*

Fresh Treasures from Egypt's Ancient Sands. By Jefferson Caffery. Photos by David S. Boyer. 611-650, *Nov. 1955*

Lifelike Man Preserved 2,000 Years in Peat. By P. V. Glob. 419-430, *Mar. 1954*

Ancient Mesopotamia: A Light That Did Not Fail. By E. A. Speiser. Paintings by H. M. Herget. 41-105, *Jan. 1951*

See also Funerals

BURIAL MOUNDS. See Bahrain; Ch'angsha; Indian Mounds; Mound Builders; Tombs; Ur

BURIAL SHIPS:

Finding a Pharaoh's Funeral Bark. By Farouk El-Baz. Photos by James P. Blair and Claude E. Petrone. Included: The world's oldest ship. 513-533, *Apr. 1988*

Ancestor of the British Navy: England's

Oldest Known War Vessel Is Unearthed, Laden with Remarkable Treasures of an Anglo-Saxon Ruler. By C. W. Phillips. 247-268, *Feb. 1941*

The **BURIED** Cities of Asia Minor. By Ernest L. Harris. 1-18, *Jan. 1909*

The **BURIED** City of Ceylon. By John M. Abbot. 613-622, *Nov. 1906*

A **BURIED** Roman Town Gives Up Its Dead (Herculaneum). By Joseph Judge. Photos by Jonathan Blair. NGS research grant. 687-693, *Dec. 1982*

BURKE, ARLEIGH A.:

Hubbard Medal recipient. 589-590, *Apr. 1959*

BURKE, ERIC KEAST: *Photographer*

Modern Life in the Cradle of Civilization (Iraq). 390-407, *Apr. 1922*

BURKE, ROBERT O'HARA:

The Journey of Burke and Wills: First Across Australia. By Joseph Judge. Photos by Joseph J. Scherschel. 152-191, *Feb. 1979*

BURKE, WALTER: *Author*

Hurdle Racing in Canoes: A Thrilling and Spectacular Sport Among the Maoris of New Zealand. 440-444, *May 1920*

BURKINA FASO. See former name, Upper Volta

BURLESON, MRS. ALBERT S.: *Author*

Wandering Islands in the Rio Grande. 381-386, *Mar. 1913*

BURMA:

The Poppy. By Peter T. White. Photos by Steve Raymer. 143-189, *Feb. 1985*

🌏 *South Asia, with Afghanistan and Burma; Peoples of South Asia. Dec. 1984*

Editorial. By Wilbur E. Garrett. 1, *July 1984*

Time and Again in Burma. By Bryan Hodgson. Photos by James L. Stanfield. 90-121, *July 1984*

Anatomy of a Burmese Beauty Secret. By John M. Keshishian. 798-801, *June 1979*

Burma's Leg Rowers and Floating Farms. Photos by W. E. Garrett. Text by David Jeffery. 826-845, *June 1974*

The Lands and Peoples of Southeast Asia. 295-365. I. Mosaic of Cultures. By Peter T. White. Photos by W. E. Garrett. 296-329; II. New Light on a Forgotten Past. By Wilhelm G. Solheim II. 330-339; III. Pagan, on the Road to Mandalay. By W. E. Garrett. 343-365, *Mar. 1971*

Burma, Gentle Neighbor of India and Red China. By W. Robert Moore. 153-199, *Feb. 1963*

Operation Eclipse: 1948. By William A. Kinney. NGS research grant. 325-372, *Mar. 1949*

Cane Bridges of Asia. Photos from Paul Popper. 243-250, *Aug. 1948*

🌏 *India and Burma. Apr. 1946*

Yank Meets Native. By Wanda Burnett. 105-128, *July 1945*

Stilwell Road–Land Route to China. By Nelson Grant Tayman. 681-698, *June 1945*

The Aerial Invasion of Burma. By H. H. Arnold. 129-148, *Aug. 1944*

Burma: Where India and China Meet: In the Massive Mountains of Southeast Asia, Swarming Road Builders Wage the "War of the Highways" for Free China and Her Allies. By John LeRoy Christian. 489-512, *Oct. 1943*

The British Commonwealth of Nations: "Organized Freedom" Around the World. By Eric Underwood. 485-524, *Apr. 1943*

Burma Road, Back Door to China: Like the Great Wall of Ancient Times, This Mighty Mountain Highway Has Been Built by Myriad Chinese to Help Defend Their Homeland. By Frank Outram and G. E. Fane. 629-658, *Nov. 1940*

The Five Thousand Temples of Pagān: Burma's Sacred City Is a Place of Enchantment in the Midst of Ruins. By William H. Roberts. 445-454, *Oct. 1931*

Shan Tribes Make Burma's Hills Flash with Color. Photos by W. Robert Moore. 455-462, *Oct. 1931*

Working Teak in the Burma Forests: The Sagacious Elephant Is Man's Ablest Ally in the Logging Industry of the Far East. By A. W. Smith. 239-256, *Aug. 1930*

Hunting the Chaulmoogra Tree. By Joseph F. Rock. 243-276, *Mar. 1922*

Among the Hill Tribes of Burma–An Ethnological Thicket. By Sir George Scott. 293-321, *Mar. 1922*

Untoured Burma. By Charles H. Bartlett. 835-853, *July 1913*

Notes on Burma. By Thomas Barbour. 841-866, *Oct. 1909*

BURMA ROAD:

Stilwell Road–Land Route to China. By Nelson Grant Tayman. 681-698, *June 1945*

Burma: Where India and China Meet: In the Massive Mountains of Southeast Asia, Swarming Road Builders Wage the "War of the Highways" for Free China and Her Allies. By John LeRoy Christian. 489-512, *Oct. 1943*

China Opens Her Wild West: In the Mountain-girt Heart of a Continent a New China Has Been Created During the Years of War. By Owen Lattimore. 337-367, *Sept. 1942*

Burma Road, Back Door to China: Like the Great Wall of Ancient Times, This Mighty Mountain Highway Has Been Built by Myriad Chinese to Help Defend Their Homeland. By Frank Outram and G. E. Fane. 629-658, *Nov. 1940*

BURNETT, DAVID: *Photographer*

Jamaica: Hard Times, High Hopes. By Charles E. Cobb, Jr. 114-140, *Jan. 1985*

BURNETT, WANDA: *Author*

The Romance of American Furs. 379-402, *Mar. 1948*

Cape Cod People and Places. 737-774, *June 1946*

Yank Meets Native. 105-128, *July 1945*

What the Fighting Yanks See. 451-476, *Oct. 1944*

BURNING the Roads. 583-586, *Oct. 1906*

BURNS, ROBERT:

Poets' Voices Linger in Scottish Shrines. By Isobel Wylie Hutchison. Photos by Kathleen Revis. 437-488, *Oct. 1957*

BURNS, ROBERT K., Jr.: *Author-Photographer*

Saint Véran, France's Highest Village. 571-588, *Apr. 1959*

BURPEE, LAWRENCE J.: *Author*

New Brunswick Down by the Sea. 595-614, *May 1941*

Canada's Awakening North. 749-768, *June 1936*

BURR, FRANKLIN L.:

Franklin L. Burr Prize established under the bequest of the late Mary C. Burr, in memory of her father, awarded to Albert W. Stevens. 626, *May 1934*

BURR, MARY C.:

Fund bequeathed by Mary C. Burr. 626, *May 1934*

BURR, WILLIAM H.: *Author*

The Republic of Panama. 57-73, *Feb. 1904*

BURR PRIZE (Franklin L. Burr Prize):

Burr Prizes Awarded to Dr. Edgerton and Dr. Van Biesbroeck. 705-706, May 1953; 523, *Apr. 1955*

BURRALL, JESSIE L.: *Author*

Sight-Seeing in School: Taking Twenty Million Children on a Picture Tour of the World. 489-503, *June 1919*

A teak masterpiece graces Shwe Nandaw Monastery, once part of the Royal Palace in Mandalay, Burma. JAMES L. STANFIELD, NGS

Byzantine mosaic adorns a wall at Sant'Apollinare Nuovo in Ravenna, Italy. JAMES L. STANFIELD, VICTOR R. BOSWELL, JR., AND LARRY D. KINNEY, ALL NGS

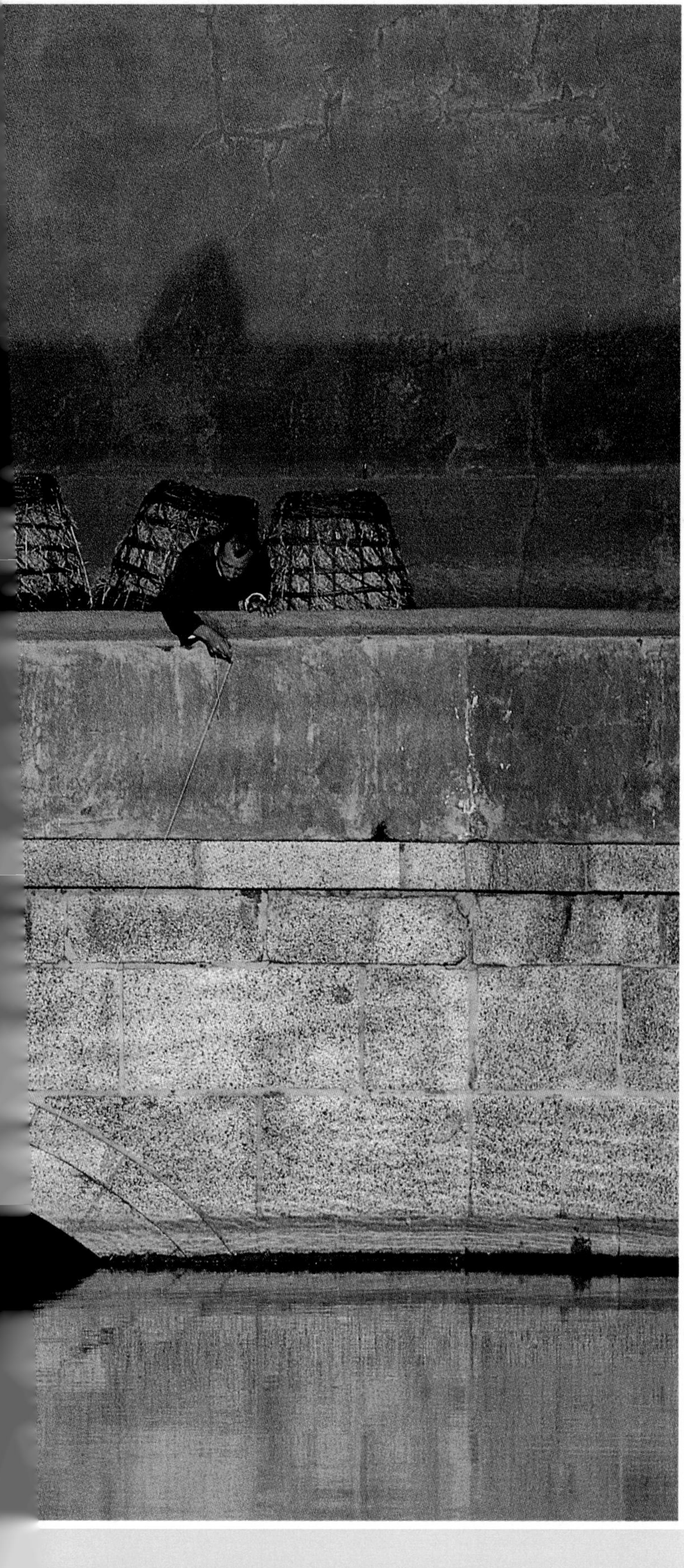

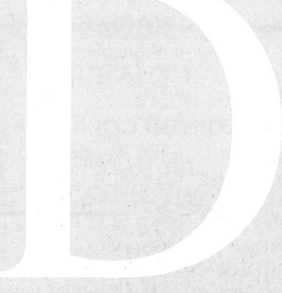

C D

CAIRO
CALIFORNIA
CAMBODIA
CAMOUFLAGE
CANADA
CAPE COD
CARNIVOROUS PLANTS
CARTOGRAPHY
CHEROKEE INDIANS
CHIMPANZEES
CHINA
CIVIL WAR
CLIMATE
COLONIAL AMERICA
CHRISTOPHER COLUMBUS
COMPUTER TECHNOLOGY
CONSERVATION
CORALS AND CORAL REEFS
CRUISES AND VOYAGES
DANUBE
CHARLES DARWIN
DEATH VALLEY
DEFORESTATION
DESERTS
DIAMONDS
EMILY DICKINSON
DINOSAURS
DISEASE
WALT DISNEY
DIVERS AND DIVING
DOGS
DOLPHINS
SIR FRANCIS DRAKE
DROUGHT
DRUG ABUSE
DUBLIN
DUCKS
DZIBILCHALTÚN

An angler tests his line as he fishes the 57-yard-wide moat in China's Forbidden City.

JIM BRANDENBURG

C & O CANAL. *See* Chesapeake and Ohio Canal

CG-4As (Cargo Gliders):
Gliders–Silent Weapons of the Sky. By William H. Nicholas. 149-160, *Aug. 1944*

C. M. RUSSELL, Cowboy Artist. By Bart McDowell. Photos by Sam Abell. 60-95, *Jan. 1986*

CT (Computed Tomography):
Medicine's New Vision. By Howard Sochurek. Paintings by Davis Meltzer. Illustrations text by Peter Miller. 2-41, *Jan. 1987*

CABIN JOHN, Maryland:
The Washington Aqueduct and Cabin John Bridge. By D. D. Gaillard. 337-344, *Dec. 1897*

CABLE CONSTRUCTION (Wire):
A Century Old, the Wonderful Brooklyn Bridge. By John G. Morris. Photos by Donal F. Holway. 565-579, *May 1983*

CABLE TELEVISION PROGRAMMING:
President's Page. By Gilbert M. Grosvenor. Mar. 1985; *Jan. 1987*
Secrets of the *Titanic.* President's Page. By Gilbert M. Grosvenor. *Jan. 1987*
National Geographic Explorer–A New Series on Cable TV. President's Page. By Gilbert M. Grosvenor. *Apr. 1985*
See also Television Films: Explorer

CABLES:
The World's Highest International Telephone Cable. 722-731, *Dec. 1930*
⊕ *Chart of the World on Mercator's Projection, showing Submarine Cables and Connections, and also Tracks for full-powered Steam Vessels. Feb. 1905*
The United States Government Telegraph and Cable Lines. 490-494, *Dec. 1904*
Girdling the Globe. 236, *May 1904*
The completion of the cable between Canada and Australia. 410, *Nov. 1902*
⊕ *The Philippines.* Progress Map of Signal Corps Telegraph Lines and Cables in the Military Division of the Philippines. *Jan. 1902*
New French Ocean Cables. 315-316, *Aug. 1901*
German Submarine Cable System. 163, *Apr. 1901*
British Pacific Cable. 78, *Feb. 1901*
The Influence of Submarine Cables Upon Military and Naval Supremacy. By George O. Squier. 1-12, *Jan. 1901*
The Submarine Cables of the World. By Gustave Herrle. Included: Chart compiled by U. S. Hydrographic Office. 102-107, *Mar. 1896*
Peter Cooper and Submarine Telegraphy. 108-110, *Mar. 1896*
The Russo-American Telegraph Project of 1864-'67. By William H. Dall. 110-111, *Mar. 1896*

A Harris's hawk nests in a saguaro in Arizona's Organ Pipe Cactus National Monument. WALTER MEAYERS EDWARDS, NGS

⊕ *Submarine Cables of the World, with the Principal Connecting Land Lines, also Coaling, Docking, and Repairing Stations. Mar. 1896*

CABLEWAY:
Across the Ridgepole of the Alps. By Walter Meayers Edwards. 410-419, *Sept. 1960*

CABOT, JOHN:
The British Way. By Sir Evelyn Wrench. 421-541, *Apr. 1949*

CABRILLO, JUAN RODRIGUEZ:
Early Voyages on the Northwestern Coast of America. By George Davidson. 235-256, *Jan. 31, 1894*

CACAO:
Chocolate: Food of the Gods. By Gordon Young. Photos by James L. Stanfield and Sisse Brimberg. 664-687, *Nov. 1984*
Happy-go-lucky Trinidad and Tobago. By Charles Allmon. 35-75, *Jan. 1953*
São Tomé, the Chocolate Island. By William Leon Smyser. 657-680, *May 1946*

CACTUS CULT. *See* Huichol Indians

CACTUSES:
Abundant Life in a Desert Land. By Walter Meayers Edwards. 424-436, *Sept. 1973*
American Wild Flower Odyssey. By P. L. Ricker. 603-634, *May 1953*
The Saguaro, Cactus Camel of Arizona. By Forrest Shreve. Included: Saguaro, King of the Arizona Desert. Photos by Esther Henderson, Jack Breed, and Max Kegley. 695-704, *Dec. 1945*
The Saguaro Forest (Arizona). By H. L. Shantz. Included: Arizona Sands, Home of the Cactus King. 515-532, *Apr. 1937*
Canyons and Cacti of the American Southwest. Photos by Edwin L.

Wisherd, Jacob Gayer, and Charles Martin. 275-290, *Sept. 1925*
Fantastic Plants of Our Western Deserts. Photos by Frank M. Campbell. 33-40, *Jan. 1924*
A Land of Drought and Desert–Lower California: Two Thousand Miles on Horseback Through the Most Extraordinary Cacti Forests in the World. By E. W. Nelson. 443-474, *May 1911*
Notes on the Deserts of the United States and Mexico. Extracted from a Publication of Daniel T. MacDougal. 691-714, *Aug. 1910*
Utilizing the Desert. 242-244, *May 1905*

CADES COVE, Tennessee:
The People of Cades Cove. By William O. Douglas. Photos by Thomas Nebbia and Otis Imboden. 60-95, *July 1962*

CADETS. *See* Aviation Cadets, U. S. Navy; U. S. Air Force Academy; U. S. Merchant Marine Academy; West Point

CÁDIZ, Spain:
Adventurous Sons of Cádiz. By Harriet Chalmers Adams. 153-204, *Aug. 1924*

CAERNARVON CASTLE, Caernarvonshire, Wales:
The Investiture of Great Britain's Prince of Wales. By Allan C. Fisher, Jr. Photos by James L. Stanfield and Adam Woolfitt. 698-715, *Nov. 1969*

CAESAREA, Israel:
Caesarea Maritima. By Robert L. Hohlfelder. Photos by Bill Curtsinger. Paintings by J. Robert Teringo. NGS research grant. 261-279, *Feb. 1987*

CAESAREA MARITIMA. By Robert L. Hohlfelder. Photos by Bill Curtsinger. Paintings by J. Robert Teringo. NGS research grant. 261-279, *Feb. 1987*

CAESAR'S City Today (Rome). Photos by Bernard F. Rogers, Jr. and Luigi Pellerano. 285-316, *Mar. 1937*

CAETANI, GELASIO:
Author-Photographer
Redemption of the Pontine Marshes: By Draining the Malarial Wastes Around Rome, Italy Has Created a Promised Land. 201-217, *Aug. 1934*
The Story and the Legends of the Pontine Marshes: After Many Centuries of Fruitless Effort, Italy Is to Inaugurate a Gigantic Enterprise to Drain the Fertile Region Southeast of Rome. 357-374, *Apr. 1924*

CAFFERY, JEFFERSON: *Author*
Fresh Treasures from Egypt's Ancient Sands. Photos by David S. Boyer. 611-650, *Nov. 1955*

CAHALANE, VICTOR H.: *Author*
King of Cats and His Court (Leopards, Lions, and Tigers). Paintings by Walter A. Weber. 217-259, *Feb. 1943*
Deer of the World: As Workers, Pets, and Graceful "Living Statuary" in Parks and Estates, These Versatile

Creatures Have Endeared Themselves to Mankind. Paintings by Walter A. Weber. 463-510, *Oct. 1939*

CAHUILLA, Lake, California:

Lake Cahuilla: The Ancient Lake of the Colorado Desert. 830, *Dec. 1907*

CAIMANS:

In the Wilds of a City Parlor. By Paul A. Zahl. 645-672, *Nov. 1954*

Wonder Island of the Amazon Delta: On Marajó Cowboys Ride Oxen, Tree-dwelling Animals Throng Dense Forests, While Strange Fishes and Birds Help Make a Zoologist's Paradise. By Hugh B. Cott. 635-670, *Nov. 1938*

CAIRNS, ROBERT: *Author*

Sunny Corsica: French Morsel in the Mediterranean. Photos by Joseph J. Scherschel. 401-423, *Sept. 1973*

CAIRO, Egypt:

Cairo, Troubled Capital of the Arab World. By William S. Ellis. Photos by Winfield Parks. 639-667, *May 1972*

Safari from Congo to Cairo. By Elsie May Bell Grosvenor. Photos by Gilbert Grosvenor. 721-771, *Dec. 1954*

"Around the World in Eighty Days." By Newman Bumstead. 705-750, *Dec. 1951*

American Fighters Visit Bible Lands. By Maynard Owen Williams. 311-340, *Mar. 1946*

American Alma Maters in the Near East. By Maynard Owen Williams. 237-256, *Aug. 1945*

Red Cross Girl Overseas. By Margaret Cotter. 745-768, *Dec. 1944*

Cairo to Cape Town, Overland: An Adventurous Journey of 135 Days, Made by an American Man and His Wife, Through the Length of the African Continent. By Felix Shay. 123-260, *Feb. 1925*

See also Akhenaten Temple Project

CAISSON DISEASE. *See* The Bends

CAJUNS:

Trouble in Bayou Country: Louisiana's Atchafalaya. By Jack and Anne Rudloe. Photos by C. C. Lockwood. 377-397, *Sept. 1979*

Cajunland, Louisiana's French-speaking Coast. By Bern Keating. Photos by Charles Harbutt and Franke Keating. 353-391, *Mar. 1966*

CALABRIA (Region), Italy:

Daily Life in Calabria. Photos by A. W. Cutler. 181-196, *Feb. 1923*

A Country Where Going to America Is an Industry (Sicily). By Arthur H. Warner. 1063-1102, *Dec. 1909*

CALAVERAS BIG TREES STATE PARK, California:

Saving Earth's Oldest Living Things. By Andrew H. Brown. Photos by Raymond Moulin and author. 679-695, *May 1951*

CALCULATIONS of Population in June, 1900. By Henry Farquhar. 406-413, *Oct. 1899*

CALCUTTA, India:

Calcutta, India's Maligned Metropolis. By Peter T. White. Photos by Raghubir Singh. 534-563, *Apr. 1973*

The Ganges, River of Faith. By John J. Putman. Photos by Raghubir Singh. 445-483, *Oct. 1971*

From the Hair of Siva. By Helen and Frank Schreider. 445-503, *Oct. 1960*

Through the Heart of Hindustan: A Teeming Highway Extending for Fifteen Hundred Miles, from the Khyber Pass to Calcutta. By Maynard Owen Williams. 433-467, *Nov. 1921*

CALDERON, ALFREDO ALVAREZ: *Author*

Peru–Its Resources, Development, and Future. 311-323, *Aug. 1904*

CALDERON, IGNACIO:

What the Latin American Republics Think of the Pan-American Conferences. Address by Ignacio Calderon. 474-479, *Aug. 1906*

Author

Bolivia–A Country Without a Debt. 573-586, *Sept. 1907*

CALDY, the Monks' Island (Wales). By John E. H. Nolan. 564-578, *Oct. 1955*

CALENDARS:

A Bold New Look at Our Past. The Editor. NGS research grant. 62-63, *Jan. 1975*

Exploring the Mind of Ice Age Man. By Alexander Marshack. NGS research grant. 64-89, *Jan. 1975*

Editorial. By Gilbert M. Grosvenor. 727, *Dec. 1975*

The Maya: Riddle of the Glyphs. By George E. Stuart. Photos by Otis Imboden. 768-791, *Dec. 1975*

CALGARY, Alberta, Canada:

Calgary: Canada's Not-So-Wild West. By David S. Boyer. Photos by Ottmar Bierwagen. 378-403, *Mar. 1984*

Canada's Heartland, the Prairie Provinces. By W. E. Garrett. 443-489, *Oct. 1970*

CALI, Colombia:

Over the Andes to Bogotá. By Frank M. Chapman. 353-373, *Oct. 1921*

CALICUT, India:

The Pathfinder of the East: Setting Sail to Find "Christians and Spices," Vasco da Gama Met Amazing Adventures, Founded an Empire, and Changed the History of Western Europe. By J. R. Hildebrand. Included: Vasco da Gama at the Court of the Zamorin of Calicut. Painting by José Velloso Salgado, Sociedade de Geographia de Lisboa. 503-550, *Nov. 1927*

CALIFORNIA:

California Desert, A Worldly Wilderness. By Barry Lopez. Photos by Craig Aurness. 42-77, *Jan. 1987*

■■ *America's Outdoor Wonders: State Parks and Sanctuaries.* 199 pages. *1987*

Japanese Americans: Home at Last. By Arthur Zich. Photos by Michael S. Yamashita. 512-539, *Apr. 1986*

■■ *Nature on the Rampage: Our Violent Earth.* 199 pages. *1986*

Life on the Line: U. S.-Mexican Border. By Mark Kramer. Photos by Danny Lehman. 720-749, *June 1985*

■■ *Exploring America's Scenic Highways.* 199 pages. *1985*

The Okies–Beyond the Dust Bowl. By William Howarth. Photos by Chris Johns. 322-349, *Sept. 1984*

East of Eden–California's Mid-coast. By Harvey Arden. Photos by Craig Aurness. 424-461, *Apr. 1984*

■■ *Exploring America's Valleys: From the Shenandoah to the Rio Grande.* 199 pages. *1984*

■■ *A Guide to Our Federal Lands.* 227 pages. *1984*

■■ *Our Threatened Inheritance: Natural*

Desert winds whip board sailors across a pond in southern California, an area served by some 4,000 electric-generating wind turbines. CRAIG AURNESS, WEST LIGHT

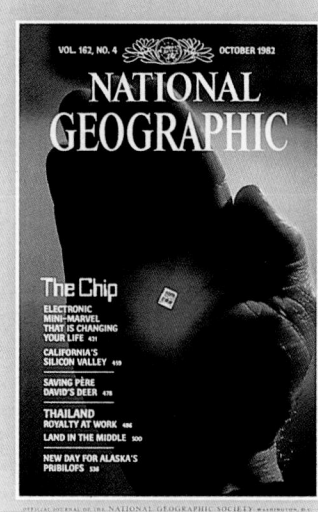

VOL. 162, NO. 4　OCTOBER 1982

NATIONAL GEOGRAPHIC

The Chip

ELECTRONIC MINI-MARVEL THAT IS CHANGING YOUR LIFE 421

CALIFORNIA'S SILICON VALLEY 459

SAVING PÈRE DAVID'S DEER 478

THAILAND ROYALTY AT WORK 486 LAND IN THE MIDDLE 500

NEW DAY FOR ALASKA'S PRIBILOFS 536

A tanker bringing crude oil into San Francisco Bay passes beneath a fog-shrouded span of the Golden Gate Bridge.   JAMES L. STANFIELD, NGS

The Colorado Desert. By David P. Barrows. 337-351, *Sept. 1900*

The California and Nevada Boundary. By C. H. Sinclair. 416-417, *Oct. 1899*

The Redwood Forest of the Pacific Coast. By Henry Gannett. 145-159, *May 1899*

California. By George C. Perkins. 317-327, *Oct. 1896*

Sir Francis Drake's Anchorage. By Edward L. Berthoud. 208-214, *Dec. 29, 1894*

Early Voyages on the Northwestern Coast of America. By George Davidson. 235-256, *Jan. 31, 1894*

Irrigation in California. By William Hammond Hall. 277-290, *Oct. 1889*

See also Berkeley; Colorado Desert; Death Valley National Monument; Edwards Air Force Base; Farallon Islands Refuge; Golden Gate National Recreation Area; Henry E. Huntington Library and Art Gallery; La Jolla; Lompoc Valley; Los Angeles; Mojave Desert; Monterey Peninsula; Newport Beach; Pacific Crest Trail; Pacific Grove; Palm Springs; Palomar Observatory; Sacramento; San Diego; San Francisco; San Francisco Bay; Santa Barbara Islands; Santa Catalina Island; Sierra Nevada; Tournament of Roses; Yosemite National Park

CALIFORNIA, Baja. *See* Baja California

CALIFORNIA, Gulf of:

A Strange Ride in the Deep (on Manta Rays). By Peter Benchley. 200-203, *Feb. 1981*

See also Raza, İsla

CALIFORNIA ACADEMY OF SCIENCES: Expeditions and Research:

Kelp study. 414, *Sept. 1980*

Galapagos Scientific Project. 545, *Apr. 1967*

NGS grant in entomology to Edward S. Ross. 408, Mar. 1961; 15, 16, Jan. 1963; 282, Feb. 1965; 433, 437, *Sept. 1965*

CALIFORNIA DELTA:

San Francisco Bay: The Beauty and the Battles. By Cliff Tarpy. Photos by James A. Sugar. 814-845, *June 1981*

California's Surprising Inland Delta. By Judith and Neil Morgan. Photos by Charles O'Rear. 409-430, *Sept. 1976*

The **CALIFORNIA** Gray Whale Comes Back. By Theodore J. Walker. 394-415, *Mar. 1971*

CALIFORNIA INSTITUTE OF TECHNOLOGY:

Can We Predict Quakes? By Thomas Y. Canby. Included: Seismological Laboratory of CIT. 830-835, *June 1976*

Jet Propulsion Laboratory. *See* Mariner Missions; Ranger Spacecraft; Surveyor Spacecraft; Viking Spacecraft Missions; Voyager

See also Sky Survey

CALIFORNIA STATE HIGHWAY NO. 1:

California's Wonderful One. By Frank

Cameron. Photos by B. Anthony Stewart. 571-617, *Nov. 1959*

CALIFORNIA Trapdoor Spider Performs Engineering Marvels. By Lee Passmore. 195-211, *Aug. 1933*

CALIFORNIA WESTERN RAILROAD:

The Friendly Train Called Skunk. By Dean Jennings. Photos by B. Anthony Stewart. 720-734, *May 1959*

CALIFORNIA'S Coastal Redwood Realm: Along a Belt of Tall Trees a Giant Bridge Speeds the Winning of Our Westernmost Frontier. By J. R. Hildebrand. 133-184, *Feb. 1939*

The **CALL** of the West. By C. J. Blanchard. 403-437, *May 1909*

The **CALL** to the Colors. 345-361, *Apr. 1917*

CALLEROS, CLEOFAS:

Nomination Page. *Mar. 1962*

CALLISTO (Jovian Satellite):

What Voyager Saw: Jupiter's Dazzling Realm. By Rick Gore. Photos by NASA. 2-29, *Jan. 1980*

CALVERT, JAMES F.: *Author*

Up Through the Ice of the North Pole (*Skate*). 1-41, *July 1959*

CALVIN, JACK: *Author-Photographer*

"Nakwasina" Goes North: A Man, a Woman, and a Pup Cruise from Tacoma to Juneau in a 17-Foot Canoe. 1-42, *July 1933*

Before overrunning a Viet Cong sanctuary in 1968, Vietnamese Marines tackle the muck of the Mekong Delta. WILBUR E. GARRETT, NGS

CALVIN, JOHN:

The Millennial City: The Romance of Geneva, Capital of the League of Nations. By Ralph A. Graves. 457-476, *June 1919*

CALVO, JOAQUIN BERNARDO:

What the Latin American Republics Think of the Pan-American Conferences. Address by Joaquin Bernardo Calvo. 474-479, *Aug. 1906*

CALYPSO (Ship):

At Home in the Sea. By Jacques-Yves Cousteau. 465-507, *Apr. 1964*
Calypso Explores an Undersea Canyon (Romanche Trench). By Jacques-Yves Cousteau. Photos by Bates Littlehales. NGS research grant. 373-396, *Mar. 1958*
Camera Under the Sea. By Luis Marden. NGS research grant. 162-200, *Feb. 1956*
Exploring Davy Jones's Locker with *Calypso*. By Jacques-Yves Cousteau. Photos by Luis Marden. NGS research grant. 149-161, *Feb. 1956*
Calypso Explores for Underwater Oil. By Jacques-Yves Cousteau. NGS research grant. 155-184, *Aug. 1955*
Photographing the Sea's Dark Underworld. By Harold E. Edgerton. NGS research grant. 523-537, *Apr. 1955*
Fish Men Discover a 2,200-year-old Greek Ship. By Jacques-Yves Cousteau. NGS research grant. 1-36, *Jan. 1954*
Fish Men Explore a New World Undersea. By Jacques-Yves Cousteau. 431-472, *Oct. 1952*

CAMARACOTO INDIANS:

Jungle Journey to the World's Highest Waterfall. By Ruth Robertson. 655-690, *Nov. 1949*

CAMARGUE (Region), France:

France's Wild, Watery South, the Camargue. By William Davenport. 696-726, *May 1973*
The Camargue, Land of Cowboys and Gypsies. By Eugene L. Kammerman. 667-699, *May 1956*
Camargue, the Cowboy Country of Southern France. By André Vialles. 1-34, *July 1922*

CAMBODIA:

Vietnam Veterans Memorial: America Remembers. Editor's Postscript: Southeast Asia Ten Years Later. 574-575, *May 1985*
The Lands and Peoples of Southeast Asia. 295-365. I. Mosaic of Cultures. By Peter T. White. Photos by W. E. Garrett. 296-329; II. New Light on a Forgotten Past. By Wilhelm G. Solheim II. 330-339, *Mar. 1971*
The Mekong, River of Terror and Hope. By Peter T. White. Photos by W. E. Garrett. 737-787, *Dec. 1968*
🌐 *Viet Nam, Cambodia, Laos, and Thailand. Feb. 1967*
🌐 *Viet Nam, Cambodia, Laos, and Eastern Thailand. Text on reverse. Jan. 1965*
Cambodia: Indochina's "Neutral"

In the Mekong Delta of 1968 the wife of a South Vietnamese soldier peers through barbed wire. WILBUR E. GARRETT, NGS

Corner. By Thomas J. Abercrombie. 514-551, *Oct. 1964*
Angkor, Jewel of the Jungle. By W. Robert Moore. Paintings by Maurice Fiévet. 517-569, *Apr. 1960*
Indochina Faces the Dragon. By George W. Long. Photos by J. Baylor Roberts. 287-328, *Sept. 1952*
Portrait of Indochina. By W. Robert Moore and Maynard Owen Williams. Paintings by Jean Despujols. 461-490, *Apr. 1951*
Strife-torn Indochina. By W. Robert Moore. 499-510, *Oct. 1950*
Along the Old Mandarin Road of Indo-China. By W. Robert Moore. 157-199, *Aug. 1931*
Four Faces of Siva: The Mystery of Angkor. By Robert J. Casey. 303-332, *Sept. 1928*
The Forgotten Ruins of Indo-China. By Jacob E. Conner. 209-272, *Mar. 1912*
See also Kampuchea

CAMBODIAN REFUGEES:

Thailand: Refuge From Terror. By W. E. Garrett. 633-642, *May 1980*

CAMBRIAN STAKES (Sheep Dog Trials):

Sheep Dog Trials in Llangollen: Trained Collies Perform Marvels of Herding in the Cambrian Stakes, Open to the World. By Sara Bloch. 559-574, *Apr. 1940*

CAMBRIDGE, England:

Our War Memorials Abroad: A Faith Kept. By George C. Marshall. Included: Cambridge American Cemetery and Memorial. 731-737, *June 1957*
Here Rest in Honored Glory: The United States Dedicates Six New Battle Monuments in Europe to Americans Who Gave Their Lives During World War II. By Howell Walker. Included:

Cambridge American Cemetery and Memorial. 739-768, *June 1957*

CAMBRIDGE, Massachusetts:

Literary Landmarks of Massachusetts. By William H. Nicholas. Photos by B. Anthony Stewart and John E. Fletcher. 279-310, *Mar. 1950*

CAMBRIDGE UNIVERSITY, England:

A Texan Teaches American History at Cambridge University. By J. Frank Dobie. 409-441, *Apr. 1946*
Within the Halls of Cambridge University. By Philip Broad. 333-349, *Sept. 1936*

The **CAMEL** of the Frozen Desert (Reindeer). By Carl J. Lomen. 539-556, *Dec. 1919*

CAMEL CARAVANS:

Winter Caravan to the Roof of the World. By Sabrina and Roland Michaud. 435-465, *Apr. 1972*
I Joined a Sahara Salt Caravan. By Victor Englebert. 694-711, *Nov. 1965*

CAMELIDS:

Camels of the Clouds (Lamoids). By W. H. Hodge. 641-656, *May 1946*
See also Guanacos; Vicuñas

CAMELOT on the Bay: Annapolis. By Larry Kohl. Photos by Kevin Fleming. 162-189, *Aug. 1988*

CAMELS:

Alone Across the Outback (Australia). By Robyn Davidson. Photos by Rick Smolan. 581-611, *May 1978*
The Camel, Man's Humpy, Grumpy Servant. 393-406, *Sept. 1942*
The Road to Wang Ye Fu: An Account of the Work of the National Geographic Society's Central-China Expedition in the Mongol Kingdom of Ala Shan. By Frederick R. Wulsin. 197-234, *Feb. 1926*
Here and There in Northern Africa. By Frank Edward Johnson. 1-132, *Jan. 1914*

CAMENZIND, FRANZ J.:
Photographer

Last of the Black-footed Ferrets? By Tim W. Clark. Photos by Franz J. Camenzind and the author. 828-838, *June 1983*

CAMERA Adventures in the African Wilds (Book Review). Photos by A. Radclyffe Dugmore. 385-396, *May 1910*

CAMERA Cruising in the Philippines. Photos by J. Baylor Roberts, Fenno Jacobs, and others. 545-552, *Nov. 1944*

CAMERA Pastels in French Canada. Photos by Harrison Howell Walker. 601-624, *May 1939*

CAMERA Under the Sea. By Luis Marden. 162-200, *Feb. 1956*

CAMERAS. *See* Photography

The **CAMERA'S** Color Records of North Africa. Photos by Gervais Courtellemont. 333-340, *Mar. 1925*

CAMERON, FRANK: *Author*
California's Wonderful One (State Highway No. 1). Photos by B. Anthony Stewart. 571-617, *Nov. 1959*

CAMERON, GEORGE G.: *Author-Photographer*
Darius Carved History on Ageless Rock. 825-844, *Dec. 1950*

CAMERON, NIGEL: *Author*
The Emperor's Private Garden: Kashmir. Photos by Brian Brake. 606-647, *Nov. 1958*

CAMEROON:
Silent Death from Cameroon's Killer Lake. By Curt Stager. Photos by Anthony Suau. 404-420, *Sept. 1987*
Afo-A-Kom: A Sacred Symbol Comes Home. By William S. Ellis. Photos by James P. Blair. 141-148, *July 1974*
Freedom Speaks French in Ouagadougou. By John Scofield. 153-203, *Aug. 1966*
Beyond the Bight of Benin. By Jeannette and Maurice Fiévet. 221-253, *Aug. 1959*
Carefree People of the Cameroons. Photos by Pierre Ichac. 233-248, *Feb. 1947*
Trans-Africa Safari: A Motor Caravan Rolls Across Sahara and Jungle Through Realms of Dusky Potentates and the Land of Big-Lipped Women. By Lawrence Copley Thaw and Margaret Stout Thaw. 327-364, *Sept. 1938*
The Mandate of Cameroun: A Vast African Territory Ruled by Petty Sultans Under French Sway. By John W. Vandercook. 225-260, *Feb. 1931*
See also Weeks Expedition

CAMEROON MOUNTAIN, Cameroon:
Timbuktu and Beyond: Desert City of Romantic Savor and Salt Emerges into World Life Again as Trading Post of France's Vast African Empire. By Laura C. Boulton. 631-670, *May 1941*

CAMOUFLAGE:
■■*The Secret World of Animals.* Contents: Animal habitats. Juvenile. 104 pages. *1986*
Mantids, the Praying Predators. By Edward S. Ross. Photos by Dwight Kuhn and the author. 268-280, *Feb. 1984*
Hidden Life of an Undersea Desert. By Eugenie Clark. Photos by David Doubilet. 129-144, *July 1983*
■■*Secrets of Animal Survival.* Juvenile. 104 pages. *1983*
Deception: Formula for Survival. By Robert F. Sisson. Included: Grass shrimp, insects, plants, and sea horses. 394-415, *Mar. 1980*
Asian Insects in Disguise. By Edward S. Ross. NGS research grant. 433-439, *Sept. 1965*
See also Decoy Fish; Sargassum Fish

CAMP, W. H.: *Author*
The World in Your Garden (Flowers). Paintings by Else Bostelmann. 1-65, *July 1947*

CAMP CARSON, Colorado:
School for Survival. By Curtis E. LeMay. 562-602, *May 1953*

CAMP CENTURY, Greenland:
Nuclear Power for the Polar Regions. By George J. Dufek. 712-730, *May 1962*

CAMP DAVID ACCORDS:
Eternal Sinai. By Harvey Arden. Photos by David Doubilet and Kevin Fleming. 420-461. Included: Israeli withdrawal from the Sinai Peninsula by April 25, 1982, as part of the Camp David accords; Egyptian Sector. Photos by Kevin Fleming. 430-443; Israeli Sector. Photos by David Doubilet. 444-461, *Apr. 1982*

CAMP LEJEUNE MARINE BASE, North Carolina:
Here Come the Marines. By Frederick Simpich. 647-672, *Nov. 1950*

CAMP PENDLETON MARINE BASE, California:
Here Come the Marines. By Frederick Simpich. 647-672, *Nov. 1950*

CAMPBELL, ALFRED S.: *Author*
Guernsey, the Friendly Island. 361-396, *Mar. 1938*

CAMPBELL, FRANK M.: *Photographer*
Fantastic Plants of Our Western Deserts. 33-40, *Jan. 1924*

CAMPBELL, MARGARET SHAW: *Author-Photographer*
Hunting Folk Songs in the Hebrides. 249-272, *Feb. 1947*

CAMPBELL, MARIUS R.: *Author*
How Long Will the Coal Reserves of the United States Last? 129-138, *Feb. 1907*
Geomorphology of the Southern Appalachians. By Charles Willard Hayes and Marius R. Campbell. 63-126, *May 23, 1894*

CAMPBELL, MARJORIE WILKINS: *Author*
Canada's Dynamic Heartland, Ontario. Photos by Winfield Parks. 58-97, *July 1963*

CAMPBELL, ROBERT M.: *Photographer*
Africa's Gentle Giants (Giraffes). By Bristol Foster. Photos by Robert M. Campbell and Thomas Nebbia. 402-417, *Sept. 1977*
Skull 1470. By Richard E. Leakey. 819-829, *June 1973*
More Years With Mountain Gorillas. By Dian Fossey. 574-585, *Oct. 1971*
Making Friends With Mountain Gorillas. By Dian Fossey. 48-67, *Jan. 1970*

CAMPBELL, WILLIAM W., III: *Photographer*
The President's Music Men (U. S. Marine Band). By Stuart E. Jones. 752-766, *Dec. 1959*

CAMPHOR:
Formosa the Beautiful. By Alice Ballantine Kirjassoff. 247-292, *Mar. 1920*

CAMPING TRIPS. *See* Bikepacking; Hiking Trips; Mountain Climbing; Pack Trips; Philmont Scout Ranch

CAMPS, Summer:
■■*Wilderness Challenge.* Included: Backpacking, camping, mountain climbing, and river trips. Juvenile. 104 pages. *1980*
In Touch With Nature. Text by Elizabeth A. Moize. Photos by Steve Raymer. Contents: Camps near Eagle River, Wisconsin. 537-543, *Apr. 1974*

CAMPS and Cruises of an Ornithologist. By George Shiras, 3d. 438-463, *May 1909*

CAN Man Save This Fragile Earth? 766-946, *Dec. 1988*

CAN the Atlantic Salmon Survive? By Art Lee. Photos by Bianca Lavies. 600-615, *Nov. 1981*

CAN the Cooper's Hawk Survive? By Noel Snyder. Photos by author and Helen Snyder. 433-442, *Mar. 1974*

CAN the Tallgrass Be Saved? By Dennis Farney. Photos by Jim Brandenburg. 37-61, *Jan. 1980*

CAN the World Feed Its People? By Thomas Y. Canby. Photos by Steve Raymer. 2-31, *July 1975*

CAN We Harness the Wind? By Roger Hamilton. Photos by Emory Kristof. 812-829, *Dec. 1975*

CAN We Live Better on Less? By Rick Gore. 34-57, *Special Report on Energy. (Feb. 1981)*

CAN We Predict Quakes? By Thomas Y. Canby. 830-835, *June 1976*

CAN We Save Our Salt Marshes? By Stephen W. Hitchcock. Photos by William R. Curtsinger. 729-765, *June 1972*

In northern Canada, Pi Kennedy snares fox to sell to a former store of the Hudson's Bay Company. KEVIN FLEMING

CANAAN:

Abraham, the Friend of God. By Kenneth MacLeish. Photos by Dean Conger. 739-789, *Dec. 1966*

CANAANITES. *See* Phoenicians

CANADA:

Caribou: Majestic Wanderers. Photos by Michio Hoshino. 849-857, *Dec. 1988*

Oil in the Wilderness: An Arctic Dilemma. By Douglas Lee. Photos by James P. Blair. 858-871, *Dec. 1988*

■■*America's Hidden Wilderness: Lands of Seclusion.* Contents: Arctic regions; Baxter State Park, Maine; l'Eau Claire wilderness, Quebec; Grand Gulch Primitive Area, Utah; Great Burn wilderness area, Idaho-Montana; Lacandon Forest, Mexico; Mojave Desert. 200 pages. *1988*

Editorial. By Wilbur E. Garrett. 421, *Oct. 1987*

The Hudson's Bay Company: Canada's Fur-Trading Empire. By Peter C. Newman. Photos by Kevin Fleming. 192-229, *Aug. 1987*

■■*Traveling the Trans-Canada: From Newfoundland to British Columbia.* By William Howarth. Photos by George F. Mobley. 199 pages. *1987*

The Untamed Fraser River, British Columbia's Lifeline. By David S. Boyer. Photos by Chris Johns. 44-75, *July 1986*

On Canada's Hood River: Clues to a Tragic Trek. By John W. Lentz. Photos by Todd Buchanan. 128-140, *Jan. 1986*

■■*America's Great Hideaways.* Contents: Arizona, Baja California, California, Canadian Rockies, Finger Lakes, Kauai, Martha's Vineyard and Nantucket, Minnesota, Montana, Oregon, Suwannee River, Virgin Islands, and West Virginia. 199 pages. *1986*

⊕ *Canada; Canada's Vacationlands.* Text and inset maps on reverse. *Nov. 1985*

⊕ *Northern Approaches: Maine and the Maritimes.* The Making of America series. *Feb. 1985*

■■*Lakes, Peaks, and Prairies: Discovering the United States–Canadian Border.* By Thomas O'Neill. Photos by Michael S. Yamashita. 199 pages. *1984*

⊕ *Atlantic Gateways.* The Making of America series. Included: Delaware, Maryland, New Jersey, New York, Pennsylvania, northern Virginia, West Virginia, and in Canada, southern Ontario and southern Quebec. On reverse: Indians and Trade, Nation in the Making, Peopling of the Gateways, Race for the Hinterlands, Growth of Industry, Spreading Urban Corridors. *Mar. 1983*

Ghost Ships of the War of 1812: *Hamilton* and *Scourge.* By Daniel A. Nelson. Photos by Emory Kristof. Paintings by Richard Schlecht. 289-313, *Mar. 1983*

Peoples of the Arctic. 144-223. I. Introduction by Joseph Judge. 144-149; II. Hunters of the Lost Spirit: Canadians. By Priit J. Vesilind. Photos by David Alan Harvey. 174-189, *Feb. 1983*

⊕ *Peoples of the Arctic; Arctic Ocean.* *Feb. 1983*

Avalanche! Battling the Juggernaut. By David Cupp. 290-305, *Sept. 1982*

Western Grebes: The Birds That Walk on Water. By Gary L. Nuechterlein. NGS research grant. 624-637, *May 1982*

Henry Hudson's Changing Bay. By Bill Richards. Photos by David Hiser. 380-405, *Mar. 1982*

Quebec's Northern Dynamo. By Larry Kohl. Photos by Ottmar Bierwagen. 406-418, *Mar. 1982*

■■*Canada's Wilderness Lands.* 199 pages. *1982*

Nahanni: Canada's Wilderness Park. By Douglas H. Chadwick. Photos by Matt Bradley. 396-420, *Sept. 1981*

Heart of the Canadian Rockies. By Elizabeth A. Moize. Photos by Jim Brandenburg. 757-779, *June 1980*

⊕ *Close-up, Canada: Quebec, Newfoundland.* Text on reverse, inset Southern Quebec. *May 1980*

Editorial. By Gilbert M. Grosvenor. 585, *May 1980*

The St. Lawrence River: Canada's Highway to the Sea. By William S. Ellis. Photos by Bruce Dale. 586-623, *May 1980*

⊕ *Close-up, Canada: Saskatchewan, Manitoba, Northwest Territories.* Text on reverse. *May 1979*

⊕ *Close-up, Canada: Ontario.* Text on reverse. *Dec. 1978*

⊕ *Close-up, Canada: British Columbia, Alberta, Yukon Territory.* Text on reverse. *Apr. 1978*

Yukon Fever: Call of the North. By Robert Booth. Photos by George F. Mobley. 548-578, *Apr. 1978*

Song of Hope for the Bluebird. By Lawrence Zeleny. Photos by Michael L.

Smith. Note: Canada boasts the world's longest bluebird nesting-box trail, 2,000 miles in length. 855-865, *June 1977*

Editorial. By Gilbert M. Grosvenor. 435, *Apr. 1977*

One Canada–or Two? By Peter T. White. Photos by Winfield Parks. 436-465, *Apr. 1977*

Canada's "Now" Frontier. By Robert Paul Jordan. Photos by Lowell Georgia. Included: Oil exploration in Alberta and the Northwest Territories. 480-511, *Oct. 1976*

■■*Our Continent: A Natural History of North America.* 398 pages. *1976*

The Changing World of Canada's Crees. By Fred Ward. 541-569, *Apr. 1975*

The Loyalists. By Kent Britt. Photos by Ted Spiegel. 510-539, *Apr. 1975*

⊕ *Close-up: Canada, Maine, with the Maritime Provinces of Canada.* Text on reverse. *Mar. 1975*

Trek Across Arctic America. By Colin Irwin. 295-321, *Mar. 1974*

■■*Vanishing Wildlife of North America.* By Thomas B. Allen. 207 pages. *1974*

Hiking the Backbone of the Rockies: Canada's Great Divide Trail. By Mike W. Edwards. Photos by Lowell Georgia. Contents: Alberta; British Columbia. 795-817, *June 1973*

Bikepacking Across Alaska and Canada. By Dan Burden. Included: Alberta; British Columbia; Yukon Territory. 682-695, *May 1973*

⊕ *Canada.* Text on reverse. *Mar. 1972*

I Live With the Eskimos. By Guy Mary-Rousseliere. 188-217, *Feb. 1971*

■ Journey to the High Arctic. *1971*

Canada's Heartland, the Prairie Provinces. By W. E. Garrett. Contents: Alberta; Manitoba; Saskatchewan. 443-489, *Oct. 1970*

North Through History Aboard *White Mist.* By Melville Bell Grosvenor. Photos by Edwin Stuart Grosvenor. 1-55, *July 1970*

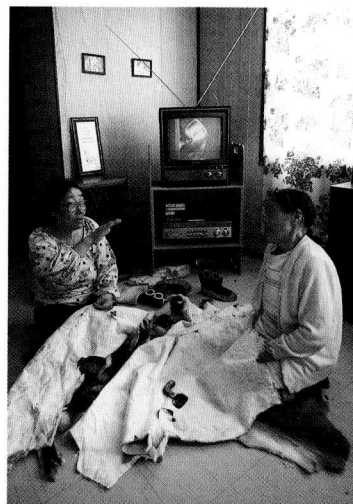

Inuit women prepare caribou skins for traditional outerwear for the villagers of Canada's Hudson Bay. DAVID HISER

A freighter cuts through loose ice on the St. Lawrence River, Canada's commercial highway from the Great Lakes to the Atlantic. BRUCE DALE, NGS

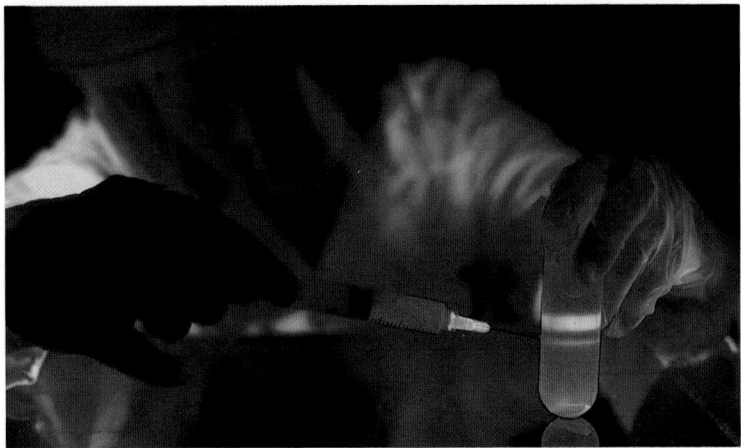

A technician at a biotechnology company in Madison, Wisconsin, extracts fluid containing the genes of a common bean for transplant to another species. TED SPIEGEL, BLACK STAR

Industrial Life. By Amos Burg. Included: Canals and Pageants of Peacetime England. Photos by Amos Burg. 185-212, *Aug. 1940*

By Sail Across Europe. By Merlin Minshall. 533-567, *May 1937*

Grand Canal Panorama (China). By Willard Price. 487-514, *Apr. 1937*

Surveying Through Khoresm: A Journey Into Parts of Asiatic Russia Which Have Been Closed to Western Travelers Since the World War. By Lyman D. Wilbur. 753-780, *June 1932*

An Army Engineer Explores Nicaragua: Mapping a Route for a New Canal Through the Largest of Central American Republics. By Dan I. Sultan. 593-627, *May 1932*

Across the Midi in a Canoe: Two Americans Paddle Along the Canals of Southern France from the Atlantic to the Mediterranean. By Melville Chater. 127-167, *Aug. 1927*

Ho for the Soochow Ho (China). By Mabel Craft Deering. 623-649, *June 1927*

Life Afloat in China: Tens of Thousands of Chinese in Congested Ports Spend Their Entire Existence on Boats. By Robert F. Fitch. 665-686, *June 1927*

Through the Back Doors of Belgium: Artist and Author Paddle for Three Weeks Along 200 Miles of Low-Countries Canals in a Canadian Canoe. By Melville Chater. 499-540, *May 1925*

Through the Back Doors of France: A Seven Weeks' Voyage in a Canadian Canoe from St. Malo, Through Brittany and the Château Country, to Paris. By Melville Chater. 1-51, *July 1923*

Through the Heart of England in a Canadian Canoe. By R. J. Evans. 473-497, *May 1922*

Shantung–China's Holy Land. By Charles K. Edmunds. 231-252, *Sept. 1919*

The Industrial Titan of America: Pennsylvania, Once the Keystone of the Original Thirteen, Now the Keystone

of Forty-eight Sovereign States. By John Oliver La Gorce. 367-406, *May 1919*

The Venice of Mexico (Aztec Lake Country). By Walter Hough. 69-88, *July 1916*

Glimpses of Holland. By William Wisner Chapin. 1-29, *Jan. 1915*

The Cape Cod Canal. By J. W. Miller. 185-190, *Aug. 1914*

The Wonderful Canals of China. By F. H. King. 931-958, *Oct. 1912*

The Deep-Water Route from Chicago to the Gulf. 679-685, *Oct. 1907*

The New Erie Canal. 568-570, *Dec. 1905*

The Great Canals of the World. 475-479, *Oct. 1905*

The Wonderful Canals of China. By George E. Anderson. 68-69, *Feb. 1905*

The Latest Route Proposed for the Isthmian Canal–Mandingo Route. 64-70, *Feb. 1902*

The Isthmian Canal Commission. 161, *Apr. 1900*

A Canal from the Atlantic to the Mediterranean. 122-123, *Mar. 1900*

Nicaragua and the Isthmian Routes. By A. P. Davis. 247-266, *July 1899*

Completion of the La Boca Dock (Panama Canal). 84, *Mar. 1898*

The Evolution of Commerce. Annual Address by the President, Hon. Gardiner G. Hubbard. 1-18, *Mar. 26, 1892*

See also Chesapeake and Ohio Canal; Florida Coast Line Canal; New York State Barge Canal; Nicaragua Canal; Panama Canal; Suez Canal; Sweden (Baltic Cruise), for Göta Canal; *and* Bangkok, Thailand; Bruges, Belgium; Mekong (River); The Netherlands; Venice, Italy

CANARIES:

Canaries and Other Cage-Bird Friends. By Alexander Wetmore. Paintings by Allan Brooks. 775-806, *Dec. 1938*

CANARY ISLANDS, Atlantic Ocean:

Lanzarote, the Strangest Canary. By

Stephanie Dinkins. 117-139, *Jan. 1969*

Spain's "Fortunate Isles," the Canaries. By Jean and Franc Shor. 485-522, *Apr. 1955*

New Map of the Atlantic Ocean: Foremost Sea of Commerce Becomes World's Battleground and Its Peaceful Islands Rise to Strategic Importance. By Leo A. Borah and Wellman Chamberlin. 407-418, *Sept. 1941*

Hunting for Plants in the Canary Islands. By David Fairchild. Included: In the Canary Islands Where Streets Are Carpeted With Flowers. Photos by Wilhelm Tobien. 607-652, *May 1930*

CANAVERAL, Cape, Florida:

Columbia's Astronauts' Own Story: Our Phenomenal First Flight. By John W. Young and Robert L. Crippen. Paintings by Ken Dallison. 478-503, *Oct. 1981*

When the Space Shuttle Finally Flies. By Rick Gore. Photos by Jon Schneeberger. Paintings by Ken Dallison. 317-347, *Mar. 1981*

Cape Canaveral's 6,000-mile Shooting Gallery. By Allan C. Fisher, Jr. Photos by Luis Marden and Thomas Nebbia. 421-471, *Oct. 1959*

CANBERRA, Australian Capital Territory, Australia:

Capital Cities of Australia. By W. Robert Moore. 667-722, *Dec. 1935*

CANBY, THOMAS Y:

On Assignment. *Aug. 1987*

On Assignment in Moscow. *Oct. 1986*

On Assignment in Botswana. *Feb. 1984*

On Assignment in Colorado. *Nov. 1982*

Nomination Page. *July 1977*

Nomination Page. *Aug. 1975*

Nomination Page. *Sept. 1974*

Author

Are the Soviets Ahead in Space? 420-459, *Oct. 1986*

El Niño's Ill Wind. 144-183, *Feb. 1984*

Satellites That Serve Us. 281-335, *Sept. 1983*

The Anasazi–Riddles in the Ruins. Photos by Dewitt Jones and David Brill. Paintings by Roy Andersen. 554-592, *Nov. 1982*

Synfuels: Fill 'er Up! With What? Photos by Jonathan Blair. 74-95, *Special Report on Energy. (Feb. 1981)*

Our Most Precious Resource: Water. Photos by Ted Spiegel. 144-179, *Aug. 1980*

The Search for the First Americans. Photos by Kerby Smith. Paintings by Roy Andersen. 330-363, *Sept. 1979*

Aluminum, the Magic Metal. Photos by James L. Amos. 186-211, *Aug. 1978*

The Year the Weather Went Wild. 799-829, *Dec. 1977*

The Rat, Lapdog of the Devil. Photos by James L. Stanfield. 60-87, *July 1977*

Can We Predict Quakes? 830-835, *June 1976*

Apollo-Soyuz: Handclasp in Space. 183-187, *Feb. 1976*

Can the World Feed Its People? Photos by Steve Raymer. 2-31, *July 1975*

Skylab, Outpost on the Frontier of Space. Photos by the nine mission astronauts. 441-469, *Oct. 1974*

Pioneers in Man's Search for the Universe. Paintings by Jean-Leon Huens. 627-633, *May 1974*

California's San Andreas Fault. Photos by James P. Blair. 38-53, *Jan. 1973*

CANCER RESEARCH:

Our Immune System: The Wars Within. By Peter Jaret. Photos by Lennart Nilsson. Illustrations text by Larry Kohl. 702-735, *June 1986*

Beyond Supermouse: Changing Life's Genetic Blueprint. By Robert F. Weaver. Photos by Ted Spiegel. 818-847, *Dec. 1984*

The Cancer Puzzle. By Robert F. Weaver. 396-399, *Sept. 1976*

You and the Obedient Atom. By Allan C. Fisher, Jr. Photos by B. Anthony Stewart and Thomas J. Abercrombie. 303-353, *Sept. 1958*

The Discovery of Cancer in Plants. 53-70, *Jan. 1913*

CANDEE, HELEN CHURCHILL:
Author

Normandy–Choice of the Vikings. 625-665, *May 1936*

Summering in an English Cottage: Quiet and Loveliness Invite Contemplation in the Extra "Room," the Garden of the Thatched House. 429-456, *Apr. 1935*

Life's Pattern on the Italian Riviera. 67-100, *Jan. 1935*

CANDIA, Crete (Island), Greece:

Crete, Where Sea-Kings Reigned. By Agnes N. Stillwell. 547-568, *Nov. 1943*

CANDY:

Chocolate: Food of the Gods. By Gordon Young. Photos by James L. Stanfield and Sisse Brimberg. 664-687, *Nov. 1984*

CANE BRIDGES of Asia. Photos from Paul Popper. 243-250, *Aug. 1948*

CANEK (Maya Hero):

The Home of a Forgotten Race: Mysterious Chichen Itza, in Yucatan, Mexico. By Edward H. Thompson. 585-648, *June 1914*

CANNIBALISM, Chimpanzee:

Life and Death at Gombe. By Jane Goodall. NGS research grant. 592-621, *May 1979*

CANNIBALISM, Human:

Into Primeval Papua by Seaplane: Seeking Disease-resisting Sugar Cane, Scientists Find Neolithic Man in Unmapped Nooks of Sorcery and Cannibalism. By E. W. Brandes. 253-332, *Sept. 1929*

Curious and Characteristic Customs of Central African Tribes (Belgian Congo). By E. Torday. 342-368, *Oct. 1919*

A Vanishing People of the South Seas: The Tragic Fate of the Marquesan Cannibals, Noted for Their Warlike

Courage and Physical Beauty. By John W. Church. 275-306, *Oct. 1919*

The Luster of Ancient Mexico (Aztecs). By William H. Prescott. 1-31, *July 1916*

Among the Cannibals of Belgian Kongo. Taken from Notes of E. Torday. 969-971, *Nov. 1910*

See also Asmat Tribespeople; Biami Tribespeople; Erigbaagtsa Indians

CANNING:

Forming New Fashions in Food: The Bearing of Taste on One of Our Great Food Economies, the Dried Vegetable, Which Is Developing into a Big War Industry. By David Fairchild. 356-368, *Apr. 1918*

How the World Is Fed. By William Joseph Showalter. 1-110, *Jan. 1916*

CANNON, JOSEPH:

The Discovery of the North Pole. Speech by Joseph Cannon. 63-82, *Jan. 1910*

CANNON:

Pirate-Fighters of the South China Sea. By Robert Cardwell. 787-796, *June 1946*

Cannon on Florida Reefs Solve Mystery of Sunken Ship. By Charles M. Brookfield. 807-824, *Dec. 1941*

The Prevention of Hailstorms by the Use of Cannon. 239-241, *June 1900*

CANOE RACE:

Winter Brings Carnival Time to Quebec. By Kathleen Revis. 69-97, *Jan. 1958*

CANOE TRIPS:

America's Little Mainstream (Buffalo National River). By Harvey Arden. Photos by Matt Bradley. 344-359, *Mar. 1977*

■■*Still Waters, White Waters: Exploring America's Rivers and Lakes.* By Ron Fisher. Photos by Sam Abell. Contents: Touring by canoe. 199 pages. *1977*

■ Voyage of the *Hokule'a.* 575, *Nov. 1976*

Hokule'a Follows the Stars to Tahiti. By David Lewis. Photos by Nicholas deVore III. 512-537, *Oct. 1976*

A Canoe Helps Hawaii Recapture Her Past. By Herb Kawainui Kane. Photos by David Hiser. 468-489, *Apr. 1976*

Isles of the Pacific. 732-793. I. The Coming of the Polynesians. By Kenneth P. Emory. 732-745; II. The Pathfinders. Paintings by Herb Kawainui Kane. 756-769, *Dec. 1974*

Trek Across Arctic America. By Colin Irwin. 295-321, *Mar. 1974*

Autumn Flames Along the Allagash. By François Leydet. Photos by Farrell Grehan. 177-187, *Feb. 1974*

Okefenokee, the Magical Swamp. By François Leydet. Photos by Farrell Grehan. 169-175, *Feb. 1974*

Kayak Odyssey: From the Inland Sea to Tokyo. By Dan Dimancescu. Photos by Christopher G. Knight. 295-337, *Sept. 1967*

Down the Danube by Canoe. By William Slade Backer. Photos by Richard S. Durrance and Christopher G. Knight. 34-79, *July 1965*

Relics from the Rapids. By Sigurd F. Olson. Photos by David S. Boyer. 413-435, *Sept. 1963*

Across Canada by Mackenzie's Track. By Ralph Gray. 191-239, *Aug. 1955*

Kayaks Down the Nile. By John M. Goddard. 697-732, *May 1955*

Jungle Jaunt on Amazon Headwaters. By Bernice M. Goetz. 371-388, *Sept. 1952*

Rich confections spill from a chocolate bag, final forms of a substance that has been made from tropical cacao beans for some 4,000 years. SISSE BRIMBERG

CANOEIRO INDIANS. *See* Erigbaagtsa Indians

CANOVA, ENRIQUE C.: *Author*

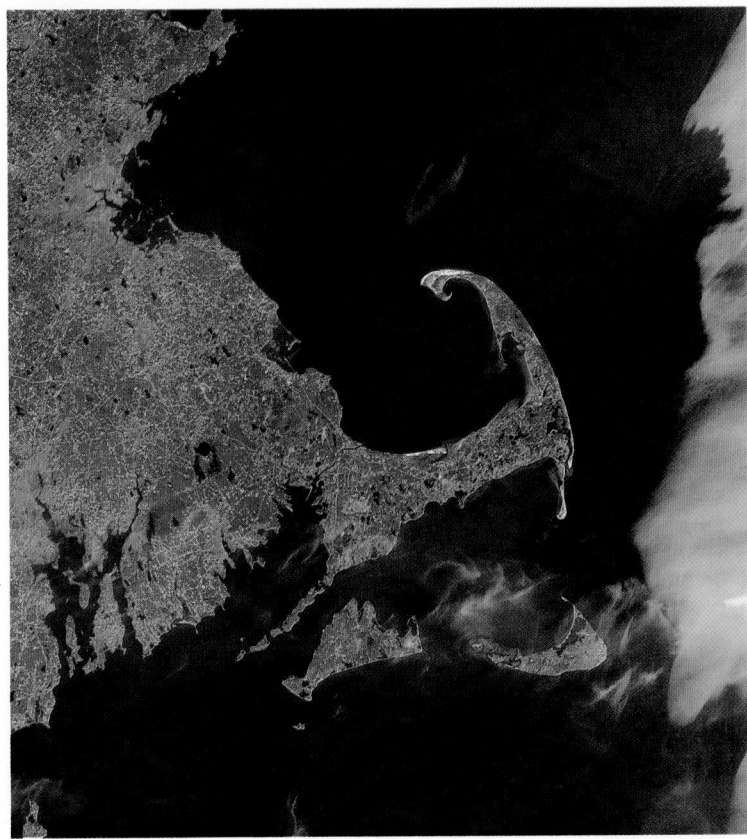

This Landsat view published in the Atlas of North America *shows Cape Cod, Massachusetts, a fishhook of woodland, bog, and beach.* EARTH SATELLITE CORPORATION

CANTERBURY CATHEDRAL, Canterbury, England:

CANTIGNY, France:

CANTON, China. *See* Guangzhou

CANTON ISLAND, Phoenix Islands, Kiribati:

CANTWELL, J. C.: *Author*

CANYON OF DEATH, Arizona:

CANYONLANDS NATIONAL PARK, Utah:

CANYONS:

Utah; Chaco Canyon, New Mexico; Dinosaur National Monument, Colorado-Utah; Escalante Canyon, Utah; Grand Canyon, Arizona; Navajo National Monument, Arizona; Sierra Nevada (Mountains), California (Fabulous Sierra Nevada); Zion National Park, Utah; *and* listing under Gorges

CAODAISM:

Indochina Faces the Dragon. By George W. Long. Photos by J. Baylor Roberts. 287-328, *Sept. 1952*

CAPE BRETON ISLAND, Nova Scotia, Canada:

Nova Scotia, the Magnificent Anchorage. By Charles McCarry. Photos by Gordon W. Gahan. 334-363, *Mar. 1975*

Salty Nova Scotia: In Friendly New Scotland Gaelic Songs Still Answer the Skirling Bagpipes. By Andrew H. Brown. 575-624, *May 1940*

The Charm of Cape Breton Island; The Most Picturesque Portion of Canada's Maritime Provinces–A Land Rich in Historic Associations, Natural Resources, and Geographic Appeal. By Catherine Dunlop Mackenzie. 34-60, *July 1920*

See also Baddeck

CAPE CANAVERAL, Florida. *See* Canaveral, Cape

CAPE COD, Massachusetts:

Cape Cod's Circle of Seasons. By Tom Melham. Photos by James P. Blair. 40-65, *July 1975*

Massachusetts Builds for Tomorrow. By Robert de Roos. Photos by B. Anthony Stewart. 790-843, *Dec. 1966*

Cape Cod, Where Sea Holds Sway Over Man and Land. By Nathaniel T. Kenney. Photos by Dean Conger. 149-187, *Aug. 1962*

Captain Smith's New England... and the Pilgrims' Cape Cod. 764-765, *June 1953*

Windjamming Around New England. By Tom Horgan. Photos by Robert F. Sisson. 141-169, *Aug. 1950*

Cape Cod People and Places. By Wanda Burnett. 737-774, *June 1946*

Collarin' Cape Cod: Experiences on Board a U. S. Navy Destroyer in a Wild Winter Storm. By H. R. Thurber. 427-472, *Oct. 1925*

The Cape Cod Canal. By J. W. Miller. 185-190, *Aug. 1914*

CAPE HATTERAS NATIONAL SEASHORE, North Carolina:

North Carolina's Outer Banks: Awash in Change. By Charles E. Cobb, Jr. Photos by David Alan Harvey. Included: Impressions of an early visitor (1580s); Sea currents shape the Outer Banks. 484-513, *Oct. 1987*

Lonely Cape Hatteras, Besieged by the Sea. By William S. Ellis. Photos by Emory Kristof. 392-421, *Sept. 1969*

CAPE HORN, South America. *See* Horn, Cape

CAPE NOME, Alaska:

Origin of the Name "Cape Nome." By George Davidson. 398, *Nov. 1901*

The Cape Nome Gold District. By F. C. Schrader. 15-23, *Jan. 1900*

CAPE OF GOOD HOPE, Province of, Republic of South Africa:

Safari Through Changing Africa. By Elsie May Bell Grosvenor. Photos by Gilbert Grosvenor. 145-198, *Aug. 1953*

Busy Corner–the Cape of Good Hope: Ships Bound for Faraway Battlegrounds Stream Past Capetown, "Tavern of the Seas," and Other Ports of Virile South Africa. By W. Robert Moore. 197-223, *Aug. 1942*

Cape of Good Hope: The Floral Province. By Melville Chater. 391-430, *Apr. 1931*

See also Cape Town

CAPE-TO-CAIRO RAILWAY:

Transporting a Navy Through the Jungles of Africa in War Time. By Frank J. Magee. 331-362, *Oct. 1922*

CAPE-TO-CAIRO TELEGRAPH:

The Cape to Cairo Telegraph. 76-77, *Feb. 1902*

Cape to Cairo Telegraph. 162-163, *Apr. 1901*

CAPE TOWN, Republic of South Africa:

South Africa Close-up. By Kip Ross. 641-681, *Nov. 1962*

Africa: The Winds of Freedom Stir a Continent. By Nathaniel T. Kenney. Photos by W. D. Vaughn. 303-359, *Sept. 1960*

Safari Through Changing Africa. By Elsie May Bell Grosvenor. Photos by Gilbert Grosvenor. 145-198, *Aug. 1953*

Busy Corner–the Cape of Good Hope: Ships Bound for Faraway Battlegrounds Stream Past Capetown, "Tavern of the Seas," and Other Ports of Virile South Africa. By W. Robert Moore. 197-223, *Aug. 1942*

Under the South African Union. By Melville Chater. 391-512, *Apr. 1931*

Cairo to Cape Town, Overland: An Adventurous Journey of 135 Days, Made by an American Man and His Wife, Through the Length of the African Continent. By Felix Shay. 123-260, *Feb. 1925*

Sailing the Seven Seas in the Interest of Science: Adventures Through 157,000 Miles of Storm and Calm, from Arctic to Antarctic and Around the World, in the Non-magnetic Yacht "Carnegie." By J. P. Ault. 631-690, *Dec. 1922*

CAPE VERDE ISLANDS, Atlantic Ocean:

New Map of the Atlantic Ocean: Foremost Sea of Commerce Becomes World's Battleground and Its Peaceful Islands Rise to Strategic Importance. By Leo A. Borah and Wellman Chamberlin. 407-418, *Sept. 1941*

Sindbads of Science: Narrative of a Windjammer's Specimen-Collecting

Voyage to the Sargasso Sea, to Senegambian Africa and Among Islands of High Adventure in the South Atlantic. By George Finlay Simmons. 1-75, *July 1927*

CAPITAL and Chief Seaport of Chile (Santiago and Valparaíso). By W. Robert Moore. 477-500, *Oct. 1944*

CAPITAL and Country of Old Cathay. 749-764, *June 1933*

CAPITAL Cities of Australia. By W. Robert Moore. 667-722, *Dec. 1935*

*The **CAPITAL** of Our Country.* 154 ▪▪ pages. *1923*

CAPITOL, U. S. *See* U. S. Capitol

CAPITOL REEF NATIONAL PARK, Utah. *See* Escalante Canyon

CAPPADOCIA (Region), Turkey:

Keeping House in a Cappadocian Cave. By Jonathan S. Blair. 127-146, *July 1970*

Cappadocia: Turkey's Country of Cones. Photos by Marc Riboud. 122-146, *Jan. 1958*

The Turkish Republic Comes of Age. By Maynard Owen Williams. 581-616, *May 1945*

Where Early Christians Lived in Cones of Rock: A Journey to Cappadocia in Turkey Where Strange Volcanic Pinnacles Are Honeycombed with Hermit Cells and Monasteries. By John D. Whiting. 763-802, *Dec. 1939*

The Cone-Dwellers of Asia Minor: A Primitive People Who Live in Nature-Made Apartment Houses, Fashioned by Volcanic Violence and Trickling Streams. By J. R. Sitlington Sterrett. 281-331, *Apr. 1919*

Peculiar Caves of Asia Minor. By Elizabeth H. Brewer. 870-875, *Sept. 1911*

CAPPS, STEPHEN R.: *Author*

A Game Country Without Rival in America: The Proposed Mount McKinley National Park. 69-84, *Jan. 1917*

CAPRI (Island), Italy:

Capri, Italy's Enchanted Rock. By Carleton Mitchell. Photos by David F. Cupp. 795-809, *June 1970*

Capri, the Island Retreat of Roman Emperors. Photos by Morgan Heiskell. 627-638, *June 1922*

The Isle of Capri: An Imperial Residence and Probable Wireless Station of Ancient Rome. By John A. Kingman. 213-231, *Sept. 1919*

Inexhaustible Italy. By Arthur Stanley Riggs. 273-368, *Oct. 1916*

CAPRICORNIA REGION, Australia. *See* Heron Island

CAPRON, LOUIS: *Author*

Florida's Emerging Seminoles. Photos by Otis Imboden. 716-734, *Nov. 1969*

Florida's "Wild" Indians, the Seminole. Photos by Willard R. Culver. 819-840, *Dec. 1956*

CAPTAIN Charles D. Sigsbee, U.S.N. By Henry Gannett. 250, *May 1898*

A young woman and a sailor visit on Capri, Italy's island retreat since the days of the Caesars. MORGAN HEISKELL

CAPTAIN COOK: The Man Who Mapped the Pacific. By Alan Villiers. Photos by Gordon W. Gahan. 297-349, *Sept. 1971*

CAPT. John Smith's Map of Virginia. 760-761, *June 1953*

CAPTAIN Smith of Jamestown. By Bradford Smith. 581-620, *May 1957*

CAPTAIN Smith's New England...and the Pilgrims' Cape Cod. 764-765, *June 1953*

The **CAPTIVATING** Kiwifruit. By Noel D. Vietmeyer. Photos by Jim Brandenburg. 683-688, *May 1987*

The **CAPTURE** of Jerusalem. By Franc Shor. Photos by Thomas Nebbia. 839-855, *Dec. 1963*

CAPTURING Giant Turtles in the Caribbean. By David D. Duncan. 177-190, *Aug. 1943*

CAPTURING Strange Creatures in Colombia. By Marte Latham. Photos by Tor Eigeland. 682-693, *May 1966*

CAPUTO, ROBERT:
On Assignment in Sudan. *May 1985*
On Assignment in Sudan. *Mar. 1982*
Author-Photographer
Uganda–Land Beyond Sorrow. 468-491, *Apr. 1988*
Journey Up the Nile. 577-633, *May 1985*
Ethiopia: Revolution in an Ancient Empire. 614-645, *May 1983*
Sudan: Arab-African Giant. 346-379, *Mar. 1982*
Photographer
Kenya: A Population Exploding. By Paul R. and Anne H. Ehrlich. 918-921, *Dec. 1988*

CARACAS, Venezuela:
Venezuela's Crisis of Wealth. By Noel Grove. Photos by Robert W. Madden. 175-209, *Aug. 1976*

Caracas, Cradle of the Liberator: The Spirit of Simón Bolívar, South American George Washington, Lives On in the City of His Birth. By Luis Marden. 477-513, *Apr. 1940*

I Kept House in a Jungle: The Spell of Primeval Tropics in Venezuela, Riotous With Strange Plants, Animals, and Snakes, Enthralls a Young American Woman. By Anne Rainey Langley. 97-132, *Jan. 1939*

CARAVAGGIO, MICHELANGELO MERISI DA:
The Vienna Treasures and Their Collectors. By John Walker. 737-776, *June 1950*

A **CARAVAN** Journey Through Abyssinia: From Addis Ababa Through Lalibela, the Strange Jerusalem of Ethiopia, in Search of New Grains for American Farms. By Harry V. Harlan. 613-663, *June 1925*

CARAVAN ROUTES:
Arabia's Frankincense Trail. By Thomas J. Abercrombie. Photos by Lynn Abercrombie. 474-513, *Oct. 1985*
Silk–The Queen of Textiles. By Nina Hyde. Photos by Cary Wolinsky. Included: Map of Asia's Silk Road. 2-49, *Jan. 1984*

CARAVANS, Camel:
Winter Caravan to the Roof of the World. By Sabrina and Roland Michaud. 435-465, *Apr. 1972*
I Joined a Sahara Salt Caravan. By Victor Englebert. 694-711, *Nov. 1965*

CARAVANS, Trailer:
I See America First. By Lynda Bird Johnson. Photos by William Albert Allard. 874-904, *Dec. 1965*
Through Europe by Trailer Caravan. By Norma Miller. Photos by Ardean R. Miller III. 769-816, *June 1957*

CARAVELS:
The Caravels of Columbus. Painting by N. C. Wyeth, National Geographic Society, Washington, D. C. Supplement, *July 1928*
The Caravels of Columbus. By Victor Maria Concas. 180-186, *Jan. 31, 1894*
See also Niña

CARBON DIOXIDE POISONING:
Silent Death from Cameroon's Killer Lake. By Curt Stager. Photos by Anthony Suau. 404-420, *Sept. 1987*

CARBON 14. *See Radiocarbon Dating*

CARCHEMISH (Ancient City), Turkey:
Archeology, the Mirror of the Ages: Our Debt to the Humble Delvers in the Ruins at Carchemish and at Ur. By C. Leonard Woolley. 207-226, *Aug. 1928*

CARDINALS:
The Bird's Year. By Arthur A. Allen. 791-816, *June 1951*

CARDWELL, ROBERT:
Author-Photographer
Pirate-Fighters of the South China Sea. 787-796, *June 1946*

CAREFREE People of the Cameroons. Photos by Pierre Ichac. 233-248, *Feb. 1947*

CAREY, EDITH: *Author*
The Channel Islands. 143-164, *Aug. 1920*

CARGO CULTS:
Tanna Awaits the Coming of John Frum. By Kal Muller. 706-715, *May 1974*
Change Ripples New Guinea's Sepik River. By Malcolm S. Kirk. 354-381, *Sept. 1973*

CARIA (Ancient Division), Asia Minor. *See Aphrodisias (Ruins), Turkey*

CARIB Cruises the West Indies. By Carleton Mitchell. 1-56, *Jan. 1948*

CARIB INDIANS. *See Wayana Indians*

CARIBBEAN Green Turtle: Imperiled Gift of the Sea. By Archie Carr. Photos by Robert E. Schroeder. 876-890, *June 1967*

CARIBBEAN REGION:
Down the Cayman Wall. By Eugenie Clark. Included: Zones of Life; Exploration by submersibles *Atlantis I, Perry* (PC), and *Pisces II.* NGS research grant. 712-731, *Nov. 1988*
■ *Excursion to Enchantment: A Journey to the World's Most Beautiful Places.* Included: East Africa, Loire Valley, Bhutan, Chile-Argentina Lake District, Inside Passage, and the Caribbean. 200 pages. *1988*
⊕ *West Indies. The Making of America series. On reverse: Spanish Caribbean, Imperial Rivalries, European Sea, American Sea, Forces of Change. Nov. 1987*
The Caribbean: Sun, Sea, and Seething. By Noel Grove. Photos by Steve Raymer. 244-271, *Feb. 1981*
⊕ *Tourist Islands of the West Indies; West Indies and Central America. Feb. 1981*
Hurricane! By Ben Funk. Photos by Robert W. Madden. 346-379. Included: Dominica. By Fred Ward. 357-359; Dynamics of a Hurricane. 370-371; Into the Eye of David. By John L. Eliot. 368-369; Paths of Fury–This Century's Worst American Storms. 360-361, *Sept. 1980*
■ *Isles of the Caribbean.* 215 pages. *1980*
St. Vincent, the Grenadines, and Grenada: Taking It as It Comes. By Ethel A. Starbird. Photos by Cotton Coulson. 399-425, *Sept. 1979*
Reach for the New World. By Mendel Peterson. Photos by David L. Arnold. Paintings by Richard Schlecht. 724-767, *Dec. 1977*
Christopher Columbus and the New World He Found. By John Scofield. Photos by Adam Woolfitt. 584-625, *Nov. 1975*
Robin Sails Home. By Robin Lee Graham. Included: Barbados; Panama; Virgin Islands. 504-545, *Oct. 1970*

Imperiled Gift of the Sea: Caribbean Green Turtle. By Archie Carr. Photos by Robert E. Schroeder. 876-890, *June 1967*

■■ *Isles of the Caribbees.* By Carleton Mitchell. 208 pages. *1966*

Cape Canaveral's 6,000-mile Shooting Gallery. By Allan C. Fisher, Jr. Photos by Luis Marden and Thomas Nebbia. Included: Antigua; Dominican Republic; Mayagüez, Puerto Rico; St. Lucia. 471, *Oct. 1959*

✥ *Countries of the Caribbean, including Mexico, Central America, and the West Indies. Oct. 1947*

Capturing Giant Turtles in the Caribbean. By David D. Duncan. 177-190, *Aug. 1943*

Americans in the Caribbean. By Luis Marden. 723-758, *June 1942*

✥ *Mexico, Central America, and the West Indies. Dec. 1939*

Hunting Useful Plants in the Caribbean. By David Fairchild. 705-737, *Dec. 1934*

✥ *Mexico, Central America, and the West Indies. Dec. 1934*

The Haunts of the Caribbean Corsairs: The West Indies a Geographic Background for the Most Adventurous Episodes in the History of the Western Hemisphere. By Nell Ray Clarke. 147-187, *Feb. 1922*

✥ *The Countries of the Caribbean, Including Mexico, Central America, the West Indies and the Panama Canal. Feb. 1922*

✥ *Map of Central America, Cuba, Porto Rico and the Islands of the Caribbean Sea. Feb. 1913*

Fundamental Geographic Relation of the Three Americas. By Robert T. Hill. 175-181, *May 1896*

See also Cayman Islands; Cayman Trough; Central America; Grenada; Haiti; Jamaica; Venezuela; Virgin Islands; West Indies

CARIBBEE (Yawl):

Baltic Cruise of the *Caribbee*. By Carleton Mitchell. 605-646, *Nov. 1950*

CARIBOU:

Caribou: Majestic Wanderers. Photos by Michio Hoshino. 849-857, *Dec. 1988*

Our Wildest Wilderness: Alaska's Arctic National Wildlife Range. By Douglas H. Chadwick. Photos by Lowell Georgia. 737-769, *Dec. 1979*

Caribou: Hardy Nomads of the North. By Jim Rearden. 858-878, *Dec. 1974*

Trek Across Arctic America. By Colin Irwin. 295-321, *Mar. 1974*

Wildlife of Mount McKinley National Park. By Adolph Murie. Paintings by Walter A. Weber. 249-270, *Aug. 1953*

Canada Counts Its Caribou. 261-268, *Aug. 1952*

A Game Country Without Rival in America: The Proposed Mount McKinley National Park. By Stephen R. Capps. 69-84, *Jan. 1917*

The Big Game of Alaska. By Wilfred H. Osgood. 624-636, *July 1909*

CARIBOU ESKIMOS. *See* Padlermiut

CARILLONS:

The Singing Towers of Holland and Belgium. By William Gorham Rice. 357-376, *Mar. 1925*

CARIOCA Carnival (Rio de Janeiro). Photos by W. Robert Moore. 291-322, *Sept. 1939*

CARLIN GOLD MINE, Nevada:

Nevada's Mountain of Invisible Gold. By Samuel W. Matthews. Photos by David F. Cupp. 668-679, *May 1968*

CARLSBAD CAVERNS, New Mexico:

Carlsbad Caverns in Color. By Mason Sutherland. Photos by E. "Tex" Helm. 433-468, *Oct. 1953*

Bats of the Carlsbad Cavern. By Vernon Bailey. 321-330, *Sept. 1925*

New Discoveries in Carlsbad Cavern: Vast Subterranean Chambers with Spectacular Decorations are Explored, Surveyed, and Photographed. By Willis T. Lee. 301-319, *Sept. 1925*

A Visit to Carlsbad Cavern: Recent Explorations of a Limestone Cave in the Guadalupe Mountains of New Mexico Reveal a Natural Wonder of the First Magnitude. By Willis T. Lee. 1-40, *Jan. 1924*

CARMEL, California:

California's Land Apart–the Monterey Peninsula. By Mike W. Edwards. 682-703, *Nov. 1972*

California's Wonderful One. By Frank Cameron. Photos by B. Anthony Stewart. 571-617, *Nov. 1959*

In summer bands of caribou calve and graze on coastal plains of the Arctic National Wildlife Range in northeastern Alaska, then return south in September. LOWELL GEORGIA

CARMICHAEL, LEONARD:

NGS Committee for Research and Exploration: Chairman. 882, Dec. 1961; 903, Dec. 1962; 9, 136, 146, 150, Jan. 1963; 626, Oct. 1963; 582, Oct. 1967; 230, Aug. 1970; 274, Aug. 1982
Leonard Carmichael: An Appreciation. By Melvin M. Payne. 871-874, *Dec. 1973*
Nomination Page. *July 1970*
Nomination Page. *July 1969*
Nomination Page. *Sept. 1965*
NGS Vice President for Research and Exploration. 525, *Apr. 1965*
Nomination Page. *May 1964*
NGS Board of Trustees. 419, 420, 423, Mar. 1957; 592, May 1957; 834, Dec. 1959; 796-797, June 1960; 881, 883, *Dec. 1960*
Nomination Page. *May 1960*

Author
The Smithsonian, Magnet on the Mall. Photos by Volkmar Wentzel. 796-845, *June 1960*

CARMICHAEL, PETER:
Photographer
Scotland, Ghosts, and Glory. By Rowe Findley. 40-69, *July 1984*

CARNEGIE, ANDREW:
The Discovery of the North Pole. Speech by Andrew Carnegie. 63-82, *Jan. 1910*

CARNEGIE, DAVID J.: *Photographer*
Weighing the Aga Khan in Diamonds. 317-324, *Mar. 1947*

CARNEGIE (Yacht):
Sailing the Seven Seas in the Interest of Science: Adventures Through 157,000 Miles of Storm and Calm, from Arctic to Antarctic and Around the World, in the Non-magnetic Yacht "Carnegie." By J. P. Ault. 631-690, *Dec. 1922*
Most Curious Craft Afloat: The Compass in Navigation and the Work of the Non-Magnetic Yacht "Carnegie." By L. A. Bauer. 223-245, *Mar. 1910*

CARNEGIE INSTITUTION OF WASHINGTON:
The Carnegie Institution. 124, *Feb. 1908*
Geologists in China. 640-644, *Oct. 1907*
Recent Magnetic Work by the Carnegie Institution of Washington. 648, *Nov. 1906*
See also Carnegie (Yacht)

CARNIVAL (Pre-Lenten Festival):
Brazil: Moment of Promise and Pain. By Priit J. Vesilind. Photos by Stephanie Maze. Included: Carnival in Rio de Janeiro. 348-385, *Mar. 1987*
Marking Time in Grenada. By Charles E. Cobb, Jr. Photos by David Alan Harvey. 688-710, *Nov. 1984*
Carnival in Trinidad. By Howard La Fay. Photos by Winfield Parks. 693-701, *Nov. 1971*
Brazil, Ôba! By Peter T. White. Photos by Winfield Parks. 299-353, *Sept. 1962*
Spectacular Rio de Janeiro. By Hernane

Tavares de Sá. Photos by Charles Allmon. 289-328, *Mar. 1955*
Rio Panorama: Breath-taking Is This Fantastic City amid Peaks, Palms, and Sea, and in Carnival Time It Moves to the Rhythm of Music. By W. Robert Moore. Included: Carioca Carnival. 283-324, *Sept. 1939*
Carnival Days on the Riviera. By Maynard Owen Williams. 467-501, *Oct. 1926*
See also Mardi Gras

CARNIVALS. See Fairs; Festivals

CARNIVORES of a Lightless World
(Fishes). Paintings by Else Bostelmann and E. J. Geske. 693-700, *Dec. 1934*

CARNIVOROUS PLANTS:
Malaysia's Giant Flowers and Insect-trapping Plants. By Paul A. Zahl. 680-701, *May 1964*
Plants That Eat Insects. By Paul A. Zahl. 643-659, *May 1961*

CAROLINE ISLANDS, Pacific Ocean:
In the Far Pacific: At the Birth of Nations. By Carolyn Bennett Patterson. Photos by David Hiser and Melinda Berge. Note: The Caroline Islands, stretching 2,000 miles from Palau to Kosrae, are divided politically into the Republic of Palau and the Federated States of Micronesia. 460-499, *Oct. 1986*
Micronesia: The Americanization of Eden. By David S. Boyer. 702-744, *May 1967*
Pacific Wards of Uncle Sam. By W. Robert Moore. 73-104, *July 1948*
American Pathfinders in the Pacific. By William H. Nicholas. 617-640, *May 1946*
South from Saipan. By W. Robert Moore. 441-474, *Apr. 1945*
Hidden Key to the Pacific: Piercing the Web of Secrecy Which Long Has Veiled Japanese Bases in the Mandated Islands. By Willard Price. 759-785, *June 1942*
Yap and Other Pacific Islands under Japanese Mandate. By Junius B. Wood. 591-627, *Dec. 1921*
The Caroline Islands. 227, *June 1899*
See also Ifalik; Kapingamarangi; Palau; Truk Islands; Ulithi; Yap

CARONI SWAMP SANCTUARY, Trinidad:
New Scarlet Bird in Florida Skies. By Paul A. Zahl. 874-882, *Dec. 1967*

CARPATHIAN MOUNTAINS, Europe:
Americans Afoot in Rumania. By Dan Dimancescu. Photos by Dick Durrance II and Christopher G. Knight. 810-845, *June 1969*
See also Tatra Mountains

CARPENTER, FRANK G.:
Awarded Jane M. Smith Life Membership. 342, *Apr. 1920*

CARPENTER, RHYS: *Author*
Ancient Rome Brought to Life. Paintings by H. M. Herget. 567-633, *Nov. 1946*

CARR, ARCHIE: *Author*
Imperiled Gift of the Sea: Caribbean Green Turtle. Photos by Robert E. Schroeder. 876-890, *June 1967*
Alligators: Dragons in Distress. Photos by Treat Davidson and Laymond Hardy. 133-148, *Jan. 1967*

CARR, GERALD P.:
Skylab, Outpost on the Frontier of Space. By Thomas Y. Canby. Photos by the nine mission astronauts. 441-469, *Oct. 1974*

CARRAO, Río, Venezuela:
Jungle Journey to the World's Highest Waterfall. By Ruth Robertson. 655-690, *Nov. 1949*

CARRARA MARBLE:
Carrara Marble: Touchstone of Eternity. By Cathy Newman. Photos by Pierre Boulat. 42-59, *July 1982*

CARRIERS, Airplane. See Aircraft Carriers; Escort Carriers

CARRYING the Color Camera Through Unmapped China. Photos by Joseph F. Rock. 403-434, *Oct. 1930*

CARRYING Water Through a Desert: The Story of the Los Angeles Aqueduct. By Burt A. Heinly. 568-596, *July 1910*

CARROLL, ALLEN:
Graphics Designer
The Smell Survey Results. By Avery N. Gilbert and Charles J. Wysocki. Graphics designed by Allen Carroll and painted by Mark Seidler. 514-525, *Oct. 1987*
The World's Urban Explosion. By Robert W. Fox. 179-185, *Aug. 1984*

CARS. See Automobiles

CARSON, Camp, Colorado:
School for Survival. By Curtis E. LeMay. 565-602, *May 1953*

CARSON CITY, Nevada:
Nevada, Desert Treasure House. By W. Robert Moore. 1-38, *Jan. 1946*

CARTAGO, Costa Rica:
Costa Rica–Vulcan's Smithy. By H. Pittier. 494-525, *June 1910*

CARTER, JEFF: *Photographer*
"The Alice" in Australia's Wonderland. By Alan Villiers. Photos by Jeff Carter and David Moore. 230-257, *Feb. 1966*

CARTER, T. DONALD: *Author*
Stalking Central Africa's Wildlife. Paintings by Walter A. Weber. 264-286, *Aug. 1956*

CARTER, WILLIAM HARDING:
Author
The Story of the Horse: The Development of Man's Companion in War Camp, on Farm, in the Marts of Trade, and in the Field of Sports. Paintings by Edward Herbert Miner. 455-566, *Nov. 1923*
■■ *The Horses of the World: The Development of Man's Companion in War*

One of the National Geographic Society's earliest cartographic supplements, issued in 1907, shows explorers' routes in the North Pole regions.

Camp, on Farm, in the Marts of Trade, and in the Field of Sports. Art by Edward Herbert Miner. 118 pages. *1923*

CARTER'S GROVE, Virginia:

New Clues to an Old Mystery (Virginia's Wolstenholme Towne). By Ivor Noël Hume. Photos by Ira Block. Paintings by Richard Schlecht. 53-77, *Jan. 1982*

First Look at a Lost Virginia Settlement (Martin's Hundred). By Ivor Noël Hume. Photos by Ira Block. Paintings by Richard Schlecht. 735-767, *June 1979*

CARTHAGE (Ancient City), Tunisia:

The Phoenicians, Sea Lords of Antiquity. By Samuel W. Matthews. Photos by Winfield Parks. Paintings by Robert C. Magis. 149-189, *Aug. 1974*

Ancient Carthage in the Light of Modern Excavation. By Count Byron Khun de Prorok. Included: Tunisia, Where Sea and Desert Meet. Photos by Gervais Courtellemont. 391-423, *Apr. 1924*

CARTIER, JACQUES:

North Through History Aboard *White Mist.* By Melville Bell Grosvenor. Photos by Edwin Stuart Grosvenor. 1-55, *July 1970*

CARTOGRAPHERS:

Eight Maps of Discovery. 757-769, *June 1953*

CARTOGRAPHY:

New Perspective on the World. By John B. Garver, Jr. 911-913, *Dec. 1988*

Mount Everest: Surveying the Third Pole. By Bradford Washburn. NGS research grant. 653-659, *Nov. 1988*

President's Page. By Gilbert M. Grosvenor. *May 1984*

Editorial. By Wilbur E. Garrett. 145, *Aug. 1983*

Editorial. By Wilbur E. Garrett. 685, *Dec. 1982*

Editorial. By Gilbert M. Grosvenor. 1, *July 1980*

Editorial. By Gilbert M. Grosvenor. 729, *Dec. 1978*

Landsat Looks at Hometown Earth. By Barry C. Bishop. Contents: How the color photomosaic supplement *Portrait U.S.A.* was made from Landsat imagery. 140-147, *July 1976*

Editorial. By Gilbert M. Grosvenor. 583, *Nov. 1975*

How We Mapped the Moon. By David W. Cook. 240-245, *Feb. 1969*

Remote Sensing: New Eyes to See the World. By Kenneth F. Weaver. 46-73, *Jan. 1969*

Science Explores the Monsoon Sea. By Samuel W. Matthews. Photos by Robert F. Sisson. 554-575, *Oct. 1967*

Mapping the Unknown Universe. By F.

See also Bumstead, Newman; Chamberlin, Wellman; NGS: Cartographic Division

Barrows Colton. NGS research grant. 401-420, *Sept. 1950*

The Round Earth on Flat Paper. By Wellman Chamberlin. 399, *Mar. 1950*

■■ *The Round Earth on Flat Paper: Map Projections Used By Cartographers.* By Wellman Chamberlin. Art by Charles E. Riddiford. 126 pages. *1947*

Charting a World at War. By William H. Nicholas. 617-640, *Nov. 1944*

The Making of Military Maps. By William H. Nicholas. 765-778, *June 1943*

Your Society Aids War Effort. 277-278, *Feb. 1943*

Maps for Victory: National Geographic Society's Charts Used in War on Land, Sea, and in the Air. By Gilbert Grosvenor. 667-690, *May 1942*

The Story of the Map. 759-774, *Dec. 1932*

The Unexplored Philippines from the Air: Map-making over Jungle Lands Never Before Seen By White Men. By George W. Goddard. 311-343, *Sept. 1930*

The International Millionth Map of the World. By Bailey Willis. 125-132, *Feb. 1910*

Topographic Maps Issued by the Geological Survey in 1907. 226-227, *Mar. 1908*

International Flat Globe and Geographical History. 281-282, *Apr. 1907*

Maps Recently Published by the U. S. Geological Survey. 423-427, *Sept. 1905*

Plan of a Map of the World. By Albrecht Penck. 405-408, *Oct. 1904*

The Geography of Alaska: Illustrated by a New Map. By Alfred H. Brooks. 213-219, *May 1904*

The famous Waldseemüller map of 1507. 50, *Jan. 1904*

The Copyright of a Map or Chart. By William Alexander Miller. 437-443, *Dec. 1902*

Sarichef's Atlas, 1826. By Marcus Baker. 86-92, *Mar. 1902*

Two Famous Maps of America. 72, *Feb. 1902*

Bitter Root Forest Reserve. By Richard U. Goode. Included: U. S. Geological Survey's mapping of forest reserves. 387-400, *Sept. 1898*

Gomez and the New York Gulf. By L. D. Scisco. 371-373, *Aug. 1898*

Geographic Work of the General Government. By Henry Gannett. 329-338, *July 1898*

The Geologic Atlas of the United States. By W J McGee. 339-342, *July 1898*

The Topographic Atlas of the United States. By W J McGee. 343-344, *July 1898*

A Geographical Description of the British Islands. By W. M. Davis. 208-211, *June 1896*

The Submarine Cables of the World. By Gustave Herrle. Included: Chart compiled by U. S. Hydrographic Office. 102-107, *Mar. 1896*

The First Landfall of Columbus. By Jacques W. Redway. 179-192, *Dec. 29, 1894*

An artist airbrushes relief onto the most accurate and detailed map of Mount Everest ever prepared. ADAM WOOLFITT

CARTOONS, Animated:

CARTOONS AND COMIC STRIPS:

CARTS, Painted:

CARTY, JOHN J.:

CARVING, Wood. *See* Wood Carving

CARVINGS, Stone. *See* Archaeology; Sculpture; Stone Faces (Monuments)

CASABLANCA, Morocco:

CASASUS, JOAQUIN D.: *Author*

CASCADE RANGE, U. S.-Canada:

See also Rainier, Mount; St. Helens, Mount

CASE, LELAND D.: *Author*

CASE, PAUL EDWARD: *Author*

The **CASE** of the Killer Caterpillars. By Steven L. Montgomery. Photos by Robert F. Sisson. 219-225, *Aug. 1983*

CASEY, ROBERT J.: *Author*

CASH, J. ALLAN: *Photographer*

CASO, ALFONSO: *Author*

CASSAVA (Plant):

CASSERLY, GORDON: *Author*

Using wooden tablets, Moroccan students learn the Koran in the Atlas Mountains village of Aremd. THOMAS J. ABERCROMBIE, NGS

On the Fringe of the Great Desert (Algeria). Photos by Gervais Courtellemont. 206-232, *Feb. 1928*

Tripolitania (Africa), Where Rome Resumes Sway: The Ancient Trans-Mediterranean Empire, on the Fringe of the Libyan Desert, Becomes a Promising Modern Italian Colony. 131-161, *Aug. 1925*

CASSIDY, BUTCH:

Riding the Outlaw Trail. By Robert Redford. Photos by Jonathan Blair. 622-657, *Nov. 1976*

CASSILS, JOHN:

Nomination Page. *Feb. 1977*

CASTAWAYS:

They Survived at Sea. By Samuel F. Harby. 617-640, *May 1945*

CASTE SYSTEM. *See* Hinduism

CASTELROSSO (Island), Aegean Sea: Rhodes, and Italy's Aegean Islands. By Dorothy Hosmer. 449-480, *Apr. 1941*

CASTERET, NORBERT: *Author*

Lascaux Cave, Cradle of World Art. Photos by Maynard Owen Williams. 771-794, *Dec. 1948*

Discovering the Oldest Statues in the World: A Daring Explorer Swims Through a Subterranean River of the Pyrenees and Finds Rock Carvings Made 20,000 Years Ago. 123-152, *Aug. 1924*

Author-Photographer

Probing Ice Caves of the Pyrenees. Included: Casteret Grotto. 391-404, *Mar. 1953*

CASTILLO DE SAN MARCOS, St. Augustine, Florida:

St. Augustine, Nation's Oldest City, Turns 400. By Robert L. Conly. 196-229, *Feb. 1966*

CASTLE, WILLIAM R.: *Author*

Hawaii, Then and Now: Boyhood Recollections and Recent Observations by An American Whose Grandfather Came to the Islands 102 Years Ago. 419-462, *Oct. 1938*

Tokyo To-day. 131-162, *Feb. 1932*

Moonlight and fading sun soften the jagged top of Washington State's Glacier Peak Wilderness, part of the 2,400-mile Pacific Crest Trail. DAVID HISER

CASTLES:

Windsor Castle. By Anthony Holden. Photos by James L. Stanfield. Included: The Grandeur of Windsor. Text by David Jeffery. 604-631, *Nov. 1980*

Hungary: Changing Homeland of a Tough, Romantic People. By Bart McDowell. Photos by Albert Moldvay and Joseph J. Scherschel. Included: Buda, Eger, Eszterházy, Köszeg, Royal Palace, Siklós, Székesféhérvar. 443-483, *Apr. 1971*

Luxembourg, the Quiet Fortress. By Robert Leslie Conly. Photos by Ted H. Funk. Included: Lucilinburhuc on the Bock, Vianden. 69-97, *July 1970*

The Investiture of Great Britain's Prince of Wales. By Allan C. Fisher, Jr. Photos by James L. Stanfield and Adam Woolfitt. Included: Caernarvon Castle. 698-715, *Nov. 1969*

The Rhine: Europe's River of Legend.

By William Graves. Photos by Bruce Dale. Included: "Cat Castle," Gutenberg, Munot, and Schönburg Castles. 449-499, *Apr. 1967*

Fabled Mount of St. Michael. By Alan Villiers. Photos by Bates Littlehales. 880-898, *June 1964*

The Britain That Shakespeare Knew. By Louis B. Wright. Photos by Dean Conger. Included: Baynard's, Berkeley, Cawdor, Glamis, Middleham, Tower of London, Windsor. 613-665, *May 1964*

Tirol, Austria's Province in the Clouds. By Peter T. White. Photos by Volkmar Wentzel. Included: Ambras, Hasegg, Hilltop, Lichtwert, and Weissenstein Castles. 107-141, *July 1961*

Scotland From Her Lovely Lochs and Seas. By Alan Villiers. Photos by Robert F. Sisson. Included: Coll,

Dunvegan, Edinburgh, Inverlochy, Kisimul, Urquhart. 492-541, *Apr. 1961*

California's Wonderful One (State Highway No. 1). By Frank Cameron. Photos by B. Anthony Stewart. Included: Hearst San Simeon Historical Monument. 571-617, *Nov. 1959*

Modern Miracle, Made in Germany. By Robert Leslie Conly. Photos by Erich Lessing. Included: Gutenfels, Heidelberg, Katz, Maus, Sababurg, Schönburg. 735-791, *June 1959*

Building a New Austria. By Beverley M. Bowie. Photos by Volkmar Wentzel. Included: Bernstein, Dürnstein, Forchtenstein, Güssing, Hofburg, Raabs, Riegersburg, Rosenburg, Schönbrunn, Schreckenwald. 172-213, *Feb. 1959*

Poets' Voices Linger in Scottish Shrines. By Isobel Wylie Hutchison.

Photos by Kathleen Revis. Included: Caerlaverock, Duart, Dunnotar, Dunvegan, Edinburgh, Glamis. 437-488, *Oct. 1957*

A Stroll to John o'Groat's. By Isobel Wylie Hutchison. Included: Balmoral, Belmont, Edinburgh, Falkland, Girnigoe, Invercauld, Sinclair Haunt. 1-48, *July 1956*

Crusader Lands Revisited. By Harold Lamb. Photos by David S. Boyer. Included: Krak des Chevaliers, Margat, and Sidon. 815-852, *Dec. 1954*

Rhododendron Glories of Southwest Scotland. By David S. Boyer. Photos by B. Anthony Stewart and author. Included: Castle Kennedy, Culzean, Lochinch. 641-664, *May 1954*

Silkworms in England Spin for the Queen. By John E. H. Nolan. Included: Lullingstone Castle's silk farm. 689-704, *May 1953*

Over the Sea to Scotland's Skye. By Robert J. Reynolds. Included: Dunvegan Castle. 87-112, *July 1952*

Cyprus, Idyllic Island in a Troubled Sea. By Jean and Franc Shor. Included: Castle of Kyrenia, St. Hilarion Castle. 627-664, *May 1952*

Baltic Cruise of the *Caribbee.* By Carleton Mitchell. Included: Bohus, Hammershus, Kalmar Nyckel, Karlsten Fortress, and Stegeborg. 605-646, *Nov. 1950*

British Castles, History in Stone. By Norman Wilkinson. 111-129, *July 1947*

War's Wake in the Rhineland. By Thomas R. Henry. 1-32, *July 1945*

Castles and Progress in Portugal. By W. Robert Moore. 133-188, *Feb. 1938*

How Warwick Was Photographed in Color. By Maynard Owen Williams. 83-93, *July 1936*

Castles, Shrines, and Parks of Japanese Pilgrimage. Photos by W. Robert Moore. 457-464, *Apr. 1936*

Hunting Castles in Italy. By Melville Chater. 329-366, *Sept. 1935*

Country-House Life in Sweden: In Castle and Cottage the Landed Gentry Gallantly Keep the Old Traditions. By Amelie Posse-Brázdová. 1-64, *July 1934*

Palaces and Peasants in Rome's Old Colony (Romania). Photos by Wilhelm Tobien. 439-446, *Apr. 1934*

The Road of the Crusaders: A Historian Follows the Steps of Richard the Lion Heart and Other Knights of the Cross Over the "Via Dei." By Harold Lamb. 645-693, *Dec. 1933*

Beyond the Grand Atlas: Where the French Tricolor Flies Beside the Flag of the Sultan of Morocco. By V. C. Scott O'Connor. 261-319, *Mar. 1932*

Crusader Castles of the Near East. By William H. Hall. 369-390, *Mar. 1931*

Château Land–France's Pageant on the Loire. 466-475, *Oct. 1930*

The Danube, Highway of Races: From the Black Forest to the Black Sea, Europe's Most Important River Has Borne the Traffic of Centuries. By Melville Chater. 643-697, *Dec. 1929*

Transylvania and Its Seven Castles: A Motor Circuit Through Rumania's

New Province of Racial Complexity and Architectural Charm. By J. Theodore Marriner. 319-352, *Mar. 1926*

Through the Back Doors of France: A Seven Weeks' Voyage in a Canadian Canoe from St. Malo, Through Brittany and the Château Country, to Paris. By Melville Chater. 1-51, *July 1923*

Castles in the Air: Experiences and Journeys in Unknown Bhutan. By John Claude White. 365-455, *Apr. 1914*

See also Chateaux; Palaces

CASTRO, FIDEL:

Inside Cuba Today. By Fred Ward. 32-69, *Jan. 1977*

CATALINA ISLAND, California. *See* Santa Catalina

CATALONIA (Autonomous Region), Spain:

Catalonia: Spain's Country Within a Country. By Randall Peffer. Photos by Stephanie Maze. 95-127, *Jan. 1984*

CATALPA (Tree):

The Hardy Catalpa. 348-353, *Sept. 1903*

CATASTROPHE at Kourion. By David Soren. Photos by Martha Cooper. NGS research grant. 30-53, *July 1988*

CATERPILLARS:

The Case of the Killer Caterpillars. By Steven L. Montgomery. Photos by Robert F. Sisson. Contents: Predatory inchworms found only in the Hawaiian Islands. 219-225, *Aug. 1983*

An Insect Community Lives in Flower Heads. By James G. Needham. 340-356, *Sept. 1946*

Strange Habits of Familiar Moths and Butterflies. By William Joseph Showalter. 77-105, *July 1927*

Fighting Insects with Airplanes: An Account of the Successful Use of the Flying-Machine in Dusting Tall Trees Infected with Leaf-Eating Caterpillars

By C. R. Neillie and J. S. Houser. 333-338, *Mar. 1922*

See also Silkworms

CATFISH:

New Florida Resident, the Walking Catfish. By Clarence P. Idyll. Photos by Robert F. Sisson. 847-851, *June 1969*

CATHEDRAL CHURCH OF SAINT PETER AND SAINT PAUL. *See* Washington Cathedral

CATHEDRALS:

Cathedrals of England: An Artist's Pilgrimage to These Majestic Monuments of Man's Genius and Faith. By Norman Wilkinson. Dry-point engravings by author. 741-762, *Dec. 1939*

Cathedrals of the Old and New World. By J. Bernard Walker. 61-114, *July 1922*

The Beauties of France. By Arthur Stanley Riggs. 391-491, *Nov. 1915*

Venice. By Karl Stieler. 587-630, *June 1915*

Glimpses of the Russian Empire. By William Wisner Chapin. 1043-1078, *Nov. 1912*

See also Canterbury Cathedral; Chartres; Notre Dame de Paris; Ste. Cécile; St. Magnus Cathedral; Washington Cathedral; *and* listing under Churches

CATHER, WILLA:

The Country of Willa Cather. By William Howarth. Photos by Farrell Grehan. 71-93, *July 1982*

CATHOLICISM. *See* Roman Catholicism

CATS, Domestic:

Koko's Kitten. Text by Jane Vessels. Photos by Ronald H. Cohn. 110-113, *Jan. 1985*

The Cats in Our Lives. By Adolph Suehsdorf. Photos by Walter Chandoha. 508-541, *Apr. 1964*

The Panther of the Hearth: Lithe Grace and Independence of Spirit Contribute to the Appeal of Cats, "The Only Domestic Animal Man Has Never Conquered." By Frederick B. Eddy. Included: Catdom's Royalty Photographed in Color by Willard R. Culver. 589-634, *Nov. 1938*

CATS, Wild:

■ African Odyssey. cover, *Jan. 1988*

■ Lions of the African Night. President's Page. By Gilbert M. Grosvenor. cover, *Jan. 1987*

Tracking the Elusive Snow Leopard. By Rodney Jackson and Darla Hillard. NGS research grant. 793-809, *June 1986*

■ Land of the Tiger. 754, Dec. 1984; President's Page; cover, *Jan. 1985*

Tiger! Lord of the Indian Jungle. By Stanley Breeden. Photos by Belinda Wright. 748-773, *Dec. 1984*

■ The Big Cats. 442A-442B, *Mar. 1974*

King of Cats and His Court. By Victor H. Cahalane. Paintings by Walter A. Weber. Contents: African Wildcat, Bengal Tiger, Bobcat, Cheetah,

Clouded Leopard, European Wild-cat, Golden Cat, Jaguar, Jaguarundi, Leopard, Lion, Lynx, Marbled Cat, Ocelot, Pallas's Cat, Puma, Serval, Siberian Tiger, Snow Leopard, Tabby, Tiger Cat. 217-259, *Feb. 1943*
See also Cheetahs; Jaguar Hunting; Lions; Mountain Lions; Snow Leopards; Tigers

CATSKILL AQUEDUCT, New York:
New York–The Metropolis of Mankind. By William Joseph Showalter. 1-49, *July 1918*

CATSKINS:
Wild Cargo: the Business of Smuggling Animals. By Noel Grove. Photos by Steve Raymer. 287-315, *Mar. 1981*

CATTLE EGRET:
A New Bird Immigrant Arrives. By Roger Tory Peterson. 281-292, *Aug. 1954*

CATTLE RAISING:
Tsetse–Fly of the Deadly Sleep. By Georg Gerster. Included: Nagana, a disease that kills three million cattle annually in Africa. 814-833, *Dec. 1986*
Buffalo Bill and the Enduring West. By Alice J. Hall. Photos by James L. Amos. 76-103, *July 1981*
The Gauchos, Last of a Breed. By Robert Laxalt. Photos by O. Louis Mazzatenta. 478-501, *Oct. 1980*
Land of Long Sunsets: Nebraska's Sand Hills. By John Madson. Photos by Jodi Cobb. 493-517, *Oct. 1978*
Cowpunching on the Padlock Ranch. By William Albert Allard. 478-499, *Oct. 1973*
The Wichitas: Land of the Living Prairie. By M. Woodbridge Williams. Included: Longhorns. 661-697, *May 1957*
South in the Sudan. By Harry Hoogstraal. Included: Zebu cattle. 249-272, *Feb. 1953*
America's "Meat on the Hoof." By William H. Nicholas. Included: King Ranch, Cattle Empire in Texas. 33-72, *Jan. 1952*
4-H Boys and Girls Grow More Food. By Frederick Simpich. 551-582, *Nov. 1948*
Grass Makes Wyoming Fat. By Frederick Simpich. 153-188, *Aug. 1945*
Nebraska, The Cornhusker State. By Leo A. Borah. 513-542, *May 1945*
Exploring a Grass Wonderland of Wild West China. By Ray G. Johnson. 713-742, *June 1944*
Through Paraguay and Southern Matto Grosso. By Sir Christopher H. Gibson. 459-488, *Oct. 1943*
Wonder Island of the Amazon Delta: On Marajó Cowboys Ride Oxen, Tree-dwelling Animals Throng Dense Forests, While Strange Fishes and Birds Help Make a Zoologist's Paradise. By Hugh B. Cott. 635-670, *Nov. 1938*
Beyond Australia's Cities. By W. Robert Moore. 709-747, *Dec. 1936*
Life on the Argentine Pampa. By Frederick Simpich. 449-491, *Oct. 1933*

■■ *The Cattle of the World: Their Place in the Human Scheme–Wild Types and Modern Breeds in Many Lands.* By Alvin Howard Sanders. Art by Edward Herbert Miner. 142 pages. 1925; rev. ed. *1926*
The Taurine World: Cattle and Their Place in the Human Scheme–Wild Types and Modern Breeds in Many Lands. By Alvin Howard Sanders. Paintings by Edward Herbert Miner. Contents: Aberdeen-Angus, Ayrshire, Banteng, Brahman, Brown Swiss, Devon, Dutch Belted, Gaur, Guernsey, Hereford, Holstein-Friesian, Indian Buffalo, Jersey, Nivernais-Charolais, Red Africander, Red Polls, Shorthorn, Texas Longhorn, West Highlander, Wild White, Yak. 591-710, *Dec. 1925*
Lonely Australia: The Unique Continent. By Herbert E. Gregory. 473-568, *Dec. 1916*
The Sage Plains of Oregon. By Frederick V. Coville. 395-404, *Dec. 1896*

CAUCA (River), Colombia:
Over the Andes to Bogotá. By Frank M. Chapman. 353-373, *Oct. 1921*

CAUCASUS Mountains, U.S.S.R.:
Roaming Russia's Caucasus: Rugged Mountains and Hardy Fighters Guard the Soviet Union's Caucasian Treasury of Manganese and Oil. By Rolf Singer. 91-121, *July 1942*
An Island in the Sea of History: The Highlands of Daghestan. By George Kennan. 1087-1140, *Oct. 1913*

The World's Highest Altitudes and First Ascents. By Charles E. Fay. 493-530, *June 1909*
See also Abkhazian A.S.S.R., U.S.S.R.

CAUGHT in the Assam-Tibet Earthquake. By F. Kingdon-Ward. 403-416, *Mar. 1952*

CAULFIELD, H. JOHN: *Author*
The Wonder of Holography. Photos by Charles O'Rear. 364-377, *Mar. 1984*

CAULFIELD, PATRICIA:
Photographer
The Hard Life of the Prairie Dog. By Tim W. Clark. 270-281, *Aug. 1979*
Twilight Hope for Big Cypress. By Rick Gore. 251-273, *Aug. 1976*

The **CAUSE** of Earthquakes. By Robert F. Griggs. 443-451, *Oct. 1923*

The **CAUSE** of the Earth's Heat. 124-125, *Mar. 1905*

The **CAUSES** That Led Up to the Siege of Pekin. By William Alexander Parsons Martin. 53-63, *Feb. 1901*

CAVE ART:
Art Treasures from the Ice Age: Lascaux Cave. By Jean-Philippe Rigaud. Photos by Sisse Brimberg and Norbert Aujoulat. 482-499, *Oct. 1988*
Maya Art Treasures Discovered in Cave. By George E. Stuart. Photos by Wilbur E. Garrett. 220-235, *Aug. 1981*
Baja's Murals of Mystery. By Harry

Koko, a resident of California's Gorilla Foundation, used sign language to ask for a pet cat. Named All Ball by Koko, the kitten did not fear her 230-pound friend. RONALD H. COHN

The only human in prehistoric drawings in France's Lascaux cave, a stick-figure man with a bird head or mask appears beside an eviscerated bison.   NORBERT AUJOULAT

Warriors march across a panel of the Gundestrup caldron, fashioned in silver by a Celtic craftsman some 2,000 years ago and found in a Danish peat bog in 1891. JAMES P. BLAIR, NGS

Nilsson. Illustrations text by Larry Kohl. 702-735, *June 1986*

■■ *The Incredible Machine.* Contents: The human body. 384 pages. *1986*

Beyond Supermouse: Changing Life's Genetic Blueprint. By Robert F. Weaver. Photos by Ted Spiegel. 818-847, *Dec. 1984*

The Awesome Worlds Within a Cell. By Rick Gore. Photos by Bruce Dale. Paintings by Davis Meltzer. Included: Foldout showing geography of the cell. 355-395, *Sept. 1976*

CELLULOSE:

Versatile Wood Waits on Man. By Andrew H. Brown. 109-140, *July 1951*

CELTS:

Treasure From a Celtic Tomb. By Jörg Biel. Photos by Volkmar Wentzel. 428-438, *Mar. 1980*

The Celts. By Merle Severy. Photos by James P. Blair. Paintings by Robert C. Magis. 582-633, *May 1977*

Editorial. By Gilbert M. Grosvenor. 581, *May 1977*

⊕ *Europe; Celtic Europe. May 1977*

CEMETERIES, Military:

Our National War Memorials in Europe. By John J. Pershing. 1-36, *Jan. 1934*

Armistice Day and the American Battle Fields. By J. J. Jusserand. 509-554, *Nov. 1929*

Fame's Eternal Camping Ground: Beautiful Arlington (Virginia), Burial Place of America's Illustrious Dead. By Enoch A. Chase. 621-638, *Nov. 1928*

"The Glory That Was Greece." By Alexander Wilbourne Weddell. Included: Cerameicus (Cemetery), Athens. 571-630, *Dec. 1922*

Koyasan, the Japanese Valhalla. By Eliza Ruhamah Scidmore. 650-670, *Oct. 1907*

See also Arlington National Cemetery, Virginia; War Memorials

CENOTES. *See* Chichén Itzá; Dzibilchaltun

CENSUS:

Census 1960: Profile of the Nation. By Albert W. Atwood and Lonnelle Aikman. 697-714, *Nov. 1959*

New United States Map Shows Census Changes. 821-824, *Dec. 1940*

The Indian Census of 1911. By John J. Banninga. 633-638, *July 1911*

A Revelation of the Filipinos (Summary of Report of the First Census of the Philippines). By Gilbert H. Grosvenor. 139-192, *Apr. 1905*

The Census of 1900 (U. S.). By F. H. Wines. 34-36, *Jan. 1900*

The Russian Census of 1897. By A. W. Greely. 335-336, *Nov. 1897*

The Mexican Census. 211, *June 1896*

The Great Populous Centers of the World. By A. W. Greely. 89-92, *July 10, 1893*

See also Population; U. S. Bureau of the Census

CENTENARIANS. *See* Oldest People

CENTRAL AFRICAN REPUBLIC:

Freedom Speaks French in Ouagadougou. By John Scofield. 153-203, *Aug. 1966*

CENTRAL AMERICA:

Editorial. By Wilbur E. Garrett. 695, *June 1988*

⊕ *Central America; Central America Past and Present.* Included: Land Use, Ethnic Distribution, Population Density. On reverse: Pre-Columbian Glory, Conquests and Colonies, Time of Independence, Prelude to Change, Upheaval and Uncertainty. *Apr. 1986*

Unearthing the Oldest Known Maya. By Norman Hammond. Photos by Lowell Georgia and Martha Cooper. NGS research grant. 126-140, *July 1982*

Troubled Times for Central America. By Wilbur E. Garrett, Editor. Included: Belize, Costa Rica, El Salvador, Guatemala, Honduras, Nicaragua, Panama. 58-61, *July 1981*

⊕ *Tourist Islands of the West Indies; West Indies and Central America. Feb. 1981*

⊕ *Visitor's Guide to the Aztec World; Mexico and Central America. Dec. 1980*

⊕ *Central America; Mexico. May 1973*

⊕ *West Indies and Central America. Jan. 1970*

The Quetzal, Fabulous Bird of Maya Land. By Anne LaBastille Bowes. Photos by David G. Allen. 141-150, *Jan. 1969*

⊕ *Archeological Map of Middle America, Land of the Feathered Serpent.* Text on reverse. *Oct. 1968*

⊕ *Mexico and Central America.* Atlas series. *Oct. 1961*

⊕ *Mexico and Central America. Mar. 1953*

How Fruit Came to America. By J. R. Magness. Paintings by Else Bostelmann. Included: Banana industry; Native fruits. 325-377, *Sept. 1951*

Our Vegetable Travelers. By Victor R. Boswell. Paintings by Else Bostelmann. Included: Native beans, common and lima. 145-217, *Aug. 1949*

Flags of the Americas. By Elizabeth W. King. 633-657, *May 1949*

⊕ *Countries of the Caribbean, including Mexico, Central America, and the West Indies. Oct. 1947*

⊕ *Mexico, Central America, and the West Indies. Dec. 1939*

⊕ *Mexico, Central America, and the West Indies. Dec. 1934*

Skypaths Through Latin America: Flying From Our Nation's Capital Southward Over Jungles, Remote Islands, and Great Cities on an Aërial Survey of the East Coast of South America. By Frederick Simpich. 1-79, *Jan. 1931*

Flying the World's Longest Air-Mail Route: From Montevideo, Uruguay, Over the Andes, Up the Pacific Coast, Across Central America and the Caribbean to Miami, Florida, in 67 Thrilling Flying Hours. By Junius B. Wood. 261-325, *Mar. 1930*

Buenos Aires to Washington by Horse: A Solitary Journey of Two and a Half Years, Through Eleven American Republics, Covers 9,600 Miles of Mountain and Plain, Desert and Jungle. By A. F. Tschiffely. 135-196, *Feb. 1929*

To Bogotá and Back by Air: The Narrative of a 9,500-Mile Flight from Washington, Over Thirteen Latin-American Countries and Return, in the Single-Seater Airplane "Spirit of St. Louis." By Charles A. Lindbergh. 529-601, *May 1928*

How Latin America Looks from the Air: U. S. Army Airplanes Hurdle the High Andes, Brave Brazil Jungles, and Follow Smoking Volcanoes to Map New Sky Paths Around South America. By Herbert A. Dargue. 451-502, *Oct. 1927*

⊕ *The Countries of the Caribbean, Including Mexico, Central America, the West Indies and the Panama Canal. Feb. 1922*

Shattered Capitals of Central America. By Herbert J. Spinden. 185-212, *Sept. 1919*

The Flags of Pan-America. By Byron

CENTRAL ASIATIC EXPEDITION:

The CENTRAL Great Plains (U. S.).

CENTRAL PARK: Manhattan's Big Outdoors.

CENTRAL VALLEY, California:

"The CENTRE" (Region), Australia:

CENTURY, Camp, Greenland:

A CENTURY Old, the Wonderful Brooklyn Bridge.

CEPHALONIA (Island), Greece:

CEPHALOPODS:

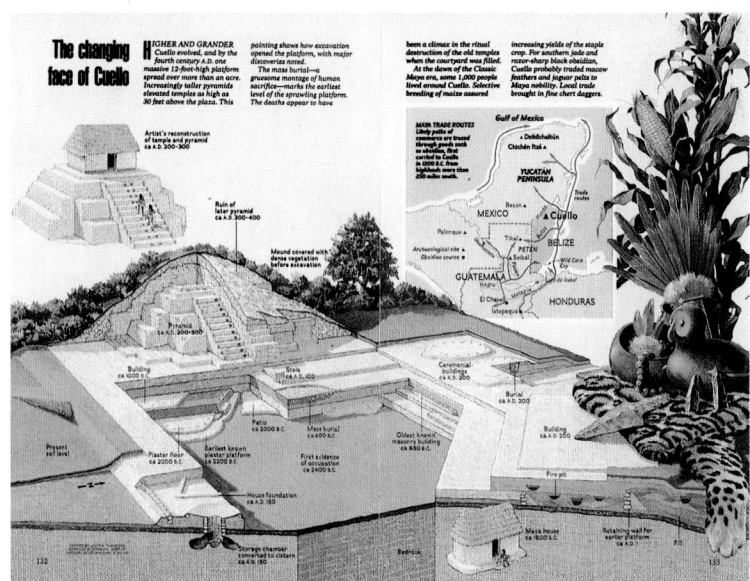

Four seasons of excavation unearthed Cuello, a Maya ceremonial center in Belize that spanned some 26 centuries of Mesoamerican prehistory. PAINTING BY LLOYD K. TOWNSEND

See also Chambered Nautilus; Octopuses; Squids

CERAMICS:

See also Pottery

CERN (Particle Physics Laboratory), Geneva, Switzerland:

CERNAN, EUGENE A.:

CERRITOS, ISLA, Mexico:

CERRO DE LAS MESAS, Mexico:

CERRUTI, JAMES: *Author*

CERTAIN Citizens of the Warm Sea.

CETACEANS. See Dolphins; Porpoises; Whales

CETINJE, Yugoslavia:

The Whirlpool of the Balkans. By George Higgins Moses. 179-197, *Feb. 1921*

Greece and Montenegro. By George Higgins Moses. 281-310, *Mar. 1913*

East of the Adriatic: Notes on Dalmatia, Montenegro, Bosnia, and Herzegovina. By Kenneth McKenzie. 1159-1187, 1284, *Dec. 1912*

CÉVENNES (Mountains), France:

Travels With a Donkey–100 Years Later. By Carolyn Bennett Patterson. Photos by Cotton Coulson. 535-561, *Oct. 1978*

France's Past Lives in Languedoc. By Walter Meayers Edwards. 1-43, *July 1951*

CEYLON:

Ceylon, the Resplendent Land. By Donna K. and Gilbert M. Grosvenor. 447-497, *Apr. 1966*

Troubled Waters East of Suez. By Ernest M. Eller. 483-522, *Apr. 1954*

Ceylon, Island of the "Lion People." By Helen Trybulowski Gilles. 121-136, *July 1948*

Sigiriya, "A Fortress in the Sky." By Wilson K. Norton. 665-680, *Nov. 1946*

The British Commonwealth of Nations: "Organized Freedom" Around the World. By Eric Underwood. 485-524, *Apr. 1943*

The Perahera Processions of Ceylon. By G.H.G. Burroughs. 90-100, *July 1932*

Fishing for Pearls in the Indian Ocean. By Bella Sidney Woolf. 161-183, *Feb. 1926*

Sailing the Seven Seas in the Interest of Science: Adventures Through 157,000 Miles of Storm and Calm, from Arctic to Antarctic and Around the World, in the Non-magnetic Yacht "Carnegie." By J. P. Ault. 631-690, *Dec. 1922*

India and Ceylon. Photos by Helen Messinger Murdoch. 281-288, *Mar. 1921*

Adam's Second Eden. By Eliza Ruhamah Scidmore. 105-173, 206, *Feb. 1912*

The Pearl Fisheries of Ceylon. By Hugh M. Smith. 173-194, *Feb. 1912*

Archæology in the Air. By Eliza Ruhamah Scidmore. 151-163, *Mar. 1907*

The Buried City of Ceylon. By John M. Abbot. 613-622, *Nov. 1906*

See also present name, Sri Lanka

CHACO (Region), Paraguay:

Paraguay, Paradox of South America. By Gordon Young. Photos by O. Louis Mazzatenta. 240-269, *Aug. 1982*

Through Paraguay and Southern Matto Grosso. By Sir Christopher H. Gibson. 459-488, *Oct. 1943*

Buenos Aires and Its Rivers of Silver: A Journey Up the Paraná and Paraguay to the Chaco Cattle Country. By William R. Barbour. 393-432, *Oct. 1921*

CHACO BOREAL (Region), Paraguay:

Through Paraguay and Southern Matto

Grosso. By Sir Christopher H. Gibson. 459-488, *Oct. 1943*

CHACO CANYON, New Mexico:

The Anasazi–Riddles in the Ruins. By Thomas Y. Canby. Photos by Dewitt Jones and David Brill. Paintings by Roy Andersen. 554-592, *Nov. 1982*

Everyday Life in Pueblo Bonito: As Disclosed by the National Geographic Society's Archeologic Explorations in the Chaco Canyon National Monument, New Mexico. By Neil M. Judd. 227-262, *Sept. 1925*

Pueblo Bonito, the Ancient: The National Geographic Society's Third Expedition to the Southwest Seeks to Read in the Rings of Trees the Secret of the Age of Ruins. By Neil M. Judd. 99-108, *July 1923*

The Pueblo Bonito Expedition of the National Geographic Society. By Neil M. Judd. 323-331, *Mar. 1922*

A New National Geographic Society Expedition: Ruins of Chaco Canyon, New Mexico, Nature-Made Treasure-Chest of Aboriginal American History, To Be Excavated and Studied; Work Begins This Month. 637-643, *June 1921*

CHAD:

Africa's Sahel: The Stricken Land. By William S. Ellis. Photos by Steve McCurry. 140-179, *Aug. 1987*

Freedom Speaks French in Ouagadougou. By John Scofield. 153-203, *Aug. 1966*

Three-Wheeling Through Africa: Two Adventurers Cross the So-called Dark Continent North of Lake Chad on Motorcycles with Side Cars. By James C. Wilson. 37-92, *Jan. 1934*

Recent Geographic Advances, Especially in Africa. By A. W. Greely. 383-398, *Apr. 1911*

CHADWICK, DOUGLAS H.: *Author*

At the Crossroads of Kathmandu. Photos by William Thompson. 32-65, *July 1987*

"Grizz"–Of Men and the Great Bear. 182-213, *Feb. 1986*

Etosha: Namibia's Kingdom of Animals. Photos by Des and Jen Bartlett. 344-385, *Mar. 1983*

Using ancient methods and motifs, a potter of New Mexico's Acoma Pueblo crafted this jar in the 1890s. JERRY D. JACKA

Nahanni: Canada's Wilderness Park. Photos by Matt Bradley. 396-420, *Sept. 1981*

Our Wildest Wilderness: Alaska's Arctic National Wildlife Range. Photos by Lowell Georgia. 737-769, *Dec. 1979*

Spring Comes Late to Glacier (Glacier National Park, Montana). 125-133, *July 1979*

Our Wild and Scenic Rivers: The Flathead. Photos by Lowell Georgia. 13-19, *July 1977*

Author-Photographer

Mountain Goats: Daring Guardians of the Heights. 284-296, *Aug. 1978*

CHAFFER, NORMAN:

Author-Photographer

Australia's Amazing Bowerbirds. 866-873, *Dec. 1961*

CHAGNON, NAPOLEON A.:

Nomination Page. *July 1976*

Author-Photographer

Yanomamo, the True People. 211-223, *Aug. 1976*

CHAKRI DYNASTY:

Thailand's Working Royalty. Photos by John Everingham. 486-499, *Oct. 1982*

CHALLACOMBE, J. R.: *Author*

The Fabulous Sierra Nevada. 825-843, *June 1954*

The **CHALLENGE** of Air Safety. By Michael E. Long. Photos by Bruce Dale. 209-235, *Aug. 1977*

CHALLENGER DEEP. *See* Mariana Trench

The **CHAMBERED NAUTILUS,** Exquisite Living Fossil. Photos by Douglas Faulkner. 38-41, *Jan. 1976*

CHAMBERLIN, ROLLIN T.: *Author*

Populous and Beautiful Szechuan: A Visit to the Restless Province of China, in which the Present Revolution Began. 1094-1119, *Dec. 1911*

CHAMBERLIN, T. C.:

Board of Managers. 87, *Feb. 1905*

Author

The Relations of Geology to Physiography in Our Educational System. 154-160, *Jan. 31, 1894*

CHAMBERLIN, WELLMAN:

Grandson of noted explorer, Walter Wellman. 347, *Mar. 1967*

Cartographic innovations. 488, Apr. 1956; 808, Dec. 1957; 49, July 1960; 698, May 1961; 875, Dec. 1961; 897, Dec. 1962; 95, July 1966; 243, *Feb. 1967*

Nomination Page. *Jan. 1965*

Chamberlin Trimetric Projection. 841, June 1947; 431, Mar. 1948; 826, June 1949; 399, Mar. 1950; 417, Mar. 1952; 591, *Apr. 1964*

Nomination Page. *May 1961*

Cartographer, NGS. 431, *Mar. 1948*

Author

■■ *The Round Earth on Flat Paper: Map Projections Used By Cartographers.*

C
D

Pleasure craft bob in the harbor of St. Peter Port, capital of Guernsey in Britain's Channel Islands. JAMES L. AMOS, NGS

Learning the ropes, students climb aloft on the 19th-century square-rigger **Joseph Conrad** *during the Mariner Training Program at Mystic Seaport, Connecticut.* WESTON KEMP

Across the Midi in a Canoe: Two Americans Paddle Along the Canals of Southern France from the Atlantic to the Mediterranean. 127-167, *Aug. 1927*

Skirting the Shores of Sunrise: Seeking and Finding "The Levant" in a Journey by Steamer, Motor-Car, and Train from Constantinople to Port Said. 649-728, *Dec. 1926*

Motor-Coaching Through North Carolina. 475-523, *May 1926*

History's Greatest Trek: Tragedy Stalks Through the Near East as Greece and Turkey Exchange Two Million of Their People. 533-590, *Nov. 1925*

Rediscovering the Rhine: A Trip by Barge from the Sea to the Headwaters of Europe's Storied Stream. 1-43, *July 1925*

Through the Back Doors of Belgium: Artist and Author Paddle for Three Weeks Along 200 Miles of Low-Countries Canals in a Canadian Canoe. 499-540, *May 1925*

Zigzagging Across Sicily. 303-352, *Sept. 1924*

Through the Back Doors of France: A Seven Weeks' Voyage in a Canadian Canoe, from St. Malo, Through Brittany and the Château Country, to Paris. 1-51, *July 1923*

East of Constantinople: Glimpses of Village Life in Anatolia, the Battleground of East and West, Where the Turks Reorganized Their Forces After the World War. 509-534, *May 1923*

The Land of the Stalking Death: A Journey Through Starving Armenia on an American Relief Train. 393-420, *Nov. 1919*

Author-Photographer
Under the South African Union. Included: Faces and Flowers Below the Tropics; Scenes on High Veld and Low; Trekking South Africa with a Color Camera. 391-512, *Apr. 1931*

CHATHAM, Massachusetts:
Cape Cod People and Places. By Wanda Burnett. 737-774, *June 1946*

CHATTANOOGA AREA, Tennessee:
Geomorphology of the Southern Appalachians. By Charles Willard Hayes and Marius R. Campbell. 63-126, *May 23, 1894*

CHATTOOGA (River), Georgia-North Carolina-South Carolina:
Chattooga River Country: Wild Water, Proud People. By Don Belt. Photos by Steve Wall. 458-477, *Apr. 1983*

CHATURVEDI, M. D.: *Author*
The Elephant and I. 489-507, *Oct. 1957*

CHAUCER, GEOFFREY:
The British Way. By Sir Evelyn Wrench. 421-541, *Apr. 1949*

CHAULMOOGRA OIL:
Hunting the Chaulmoogra Tree. By Joseph F. Rock. 243-276, *Mar. 1922*

CHEESE MAKING:
Switzerland, Europe's High-rise

Republic. By Thomas J. Abercrombie. 68-113, *July 1969*

Helping Holland Rebuild Her Land. By Gilbert M. Grosvenor and Charles Neave. 365-413, *Sept. 1954*

The Goats of Thunder Hill. By Elizabeth Nicholds. Photos by Robert F. Sisson. 625-640, *May 1954*

Deep in the Heart of "Swissconsin." By William H. Nicholas. Photos by J. Baylor Roberts. 781-800, *June 1947*

An August First in Gruyères. By Melville Bell Grosvenor. 137-168, *Aug. 1936*

Glimpses of Holland. By William Wisner Chapin. 1-29, *Jan. 1915*

A North Holland Cheese Market. By Hugh M. Smith. 1051-1066, *Dec. 1910*

CHEETAHS: In a Race for Survival. By George W. and Lory Herbison Frame. 712-728, *May 1980*

CHEKIANG PROVINCE, China. *See* Zhejiang

CHELAN, Lake, Washington:
Lake Chelan. By Henry Gannett. 417-428, *Oct. 1898*

CHELAN NATIONAL FOREST, Washington:
Forest Lookout. By Ella E. Clark. 73-96, *July 1946*

CHELLEAN CULTURE:
Exploring 1,750,000 Years Into Man's Past. By L.S.B. Leakey. Photos by Robert F. Sisson. NGS research grant. 564-589, *Oct. 1961*

CHELSEA, London's Haven of Individualists. By James Cerruti. Photos by Adam Woolfitt. 28-55, *Jan. 1972*

CHEMICAL Discussion of Analyses of Volcanic Ejecta from Martinique and St. Vincent. By W. F. Hillebrand. 296-299, *July 1902*

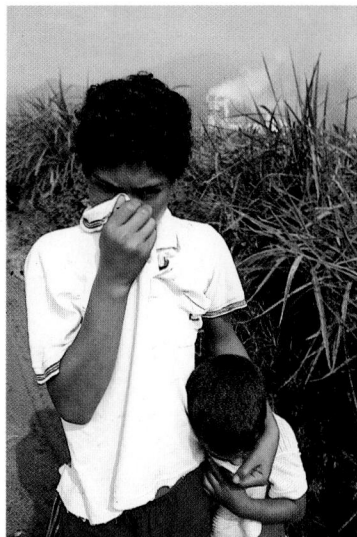
Boys' shirts filter noxious fumes from a fertilizer plant, among scores of polluters in Cubatão, Brazil. TED SPIEGEL, BLACK STAR

CHEMICAL INDUSTRY:
Delaware–Who Needs to Be Big? By Jane Vessels. Photos by Kevin Fleming. 171-197, *Aug. 1983*

Today on the Delaware, Penn's Glorious River. By Albert W. Atwood. Photos by Robert F. Sisson. 1-40, *July 1952*

CHEMICAL POLLUTION:
Editorial. By Wilbur E. Garrett. 1, *July 1987*

The Great Lakes' Troubled Waters. By Charles E. Cobb, Jr. Photos by Bob Sacha and Richard Olsenius. Included: A great meeting of waters; North America's fifth coast. 2-31, *July 1987*

Air: An Atmosphere of Uncertainty. By Noel Grove. Photos by Ted Spiegel. Paintings by William H. Bond. Included: A deadly soup (a list of harmful chemicals), Careless neighbors, A global greenhouse, The ozone enigma, Getting the lead out, The enemy within. 502-537, *Apr. 1987*

Editorial. By Wilbur E. Garrett. 277, *Mar. 1985*

Hazardous Waste…Storing Up Trouble. By Allen A. Boraiko. Photos by Fred Ward. 318-351, *Mar. 1985*

Acid Rain–How Great a Menace? By Anne LaBastille. Photos by Ted Spiegel. 652-681, *Nov. 1981*

The Pesticide Dilemma. By Allen A. Boraiko. Photos by Fred Ward. 145-183, *Feb. 1980*

Quicksilver and Slow Death. By John J. Putman. Photos by Robert W. Madden. 507-527, *Oct. 1972*

Pollution, Threat to Man's Only Home. By Gordon Young. Photos by James P. Blair. 738-781, *Dec. 1970*

CHEMISTRY:
Uncle Sam's House of 1,000 Wonders (National Bureau of Standards). By Lyman J. Briggs and F. Barrows Colton. 755-784, *Dec. 1951*

The British Way. By Sir Evelyn Wrench. 421-541, *Apr. 1949*

The Romance of American Furs. By Wanda Burnett. Included: The plasticizing of furs, developed by Dr. José B. Calva. 379-402, *Mar. 1948*

Chemists Make a New World: Creating Hitherto Unknown Raw Materials, Science Now Disrupts Old Trade Routes and Revamps the World Map of Industry. By Frederick Simpich. Included: From Nature's Hidden Building Blocks. Photos by Willard R. Culver. 601-640, *Nov. 1939*

See also Biochemistry; Perfume

CHEMOSYNTHESIS:
Incredible World of the Deep-sea Rifts. NGS research grant. 680-705. I. Strange World Without Sun. The Editor. 680-688; II. Return to Oases of the Deep. By Robert D. Ballard and J. Frederick Grassle. 689-705, *Nov. 1979*

Oases of Life in the Cold Abyss (Galapagos Rift). By John B. Corliss and Robert D. Ballard. 441-453, *Oct. 1977*

Mask of jade, pyrite, and shell was buried with a Maya nobleman about A.D. 527 at Tikal, Guatemala. VICTOR R. BOSWELL, JR., NGS

After centuries of outside influence families in the Mexican highlands have abandoned ancient Maya ways and adopted European clothing, religion, and language.   DAVID BRILL

A woman pauses for a quiet moment after dressing a Christ figure for an Easter celebration in Chíuchíu, Chile.   DAVID ALAN HARVEY

the Far Southern Andes. By W. Robert Moore. 91-110, *July 1941*

Inside Cape Horn. By Amos Burg. 743-783, *Dec. 1937*

Flying the "Hump" of the Andes. By Albert W. Stevens. 595-636, *May 1931*

Flying the World's Longest Air-Mail Route: From Montevideo, Uruguay, Over the Andes, Up the Pacific Coast, Across Central America and the Caribbean to Miami, Florida, in 67 Thrilling Flying Hours. By Junius B. Wood. 261-325, *Mar. 1930*

Twin Stars of Chile: Valparaiso, the Gateway, and Santiago, the Capital–Key Cities with a Progressive Present and a Romantic Past. By William Joseph Showalter. 197-247, *Feb. 1929*

A Longitudinal Journey Through Chile. By Harriet Chalmers Adams. 219-273, *Sept. 1922*

The Awakening of Argentina and Chile: Progress in the Lands That Lie Below Capricorn. By Bailey Willis. 121-142, *Aug. 1916*

Some Personal Experiences with Earthquakes (Arica). By L. G. Billings. 57-71, *Jan. 1915*

The First Transandine Railroad from Buenos Aires to Valparaiso. By Harriet Chalmers Adams. 397-417, *May 1910*

From Panama to Patagonia. By Charles M. Pepper. 449-452, *Aug. 1906*

Argentina-Chile Boundary Award. 115-116, *Mar. 1903*

Chile-Argentina Boundary Dispute. 220, *June 1902*

Argentina-Chile Boundary. 117, *Mar. 1902*

Argentine-Chile Boundary Dispute. 27-28, *Jan. 1902*

Chile's Disputes with Peru and Bolivia. 401-402, *Nov. 1901*

The Indian Tribes of Southern Patagonia, Tierra del Fuego, and the Adjoining Islands. By J. B. Hatcher. 12-22, *Jan. 1901*

Some Geographic Features of Southern Patagonia, with a Discussion of Their Origin. By J. B. Hatcher. 41-55, *Feb. 1900*

Hatcher's Work in Patagonia. By W J McGee. 319-322, *Nov. 1897*

Patagonia. By J. B. Hatcher. 305-319, *Nov. 1897*

A Winter Voyage Through the Straits of Magellan. By R. W. Meade. 129-141, *May 1897*

See also Easter Island; Juan Fernández Island; Patagonia; Torre Egger; Valparaíso

CHILIN, Kirin Province, China. *See* Jilin

CHILKAT TLINGIT INDIANS:

Indians of Our North Pacific Coast. By Matthew W. Stirling. Paintings by W. Langdon Kihn. 25-52, *Jan. 1945*

CHIMOR EMPIRE:

Chan Chan, Peru's Ancient City of Kings. By Michael E. Moseley and Carol J. Mackey. Photos by David Brill. NGS research grant. 318-345, *Mar. 1973*

Air Adventures in Peru: Cruising Among Andean Peaks, Pilots and Cameramen Discover Wondrous Works of an Ancient People. By Robert Shippee. 81-120, *Jan. 1933*

CHIMPANZEES:

President's Page. By Gilbert M. Grosvenor. *June 1987*

◖ Among the Wild Chimpanzees. cover, *Jan. 1984*

Life and Death at Gombe. By Jane Goodall. NGS research grant. 592-621, *May 1979*

▮▮*My Friends the Wild Chimpanzees.* By Jane Goodall. Photos by Baron Hugo van Lawick. 204 pages. *1967*

◖ Miss Goodall and the Wild Chimpanzees. 831A-831B, *Dec. 1965*

New Discoveries Among Africa's Chimpanzees. By Baroness Jane van Lawick-Goodall. Photos by Baron Hugo van Lawick. NGS research grant. 802-831, *Dec. 1965*

My Life Among Wild Chimpanzees. By Jane Goodall. Photos by Baron Hugo van Lawick and author. NGS research grant. 272-308, *Aug. 1963*

School for Space Monkeys. 725-729, *May 1961*

Man's Closest Counterparts: Heavyweight of Monkeydom Is the "Old Man" Gorilla, by Far the Largest of the Four Great Apes. By William M. Mann. Paintings by Elie Cheverlange. 213-236, *Aug. 1940*

CHIMU CIVILIZATION. *See* Chimor Empire

CH'IN SHIH HUANG TI, Emperor (China):

China's Incredible Find. By Audrey Topping. Paintings by Yang Hsien-min. 440-459, *Apr. 1978*

With a stern gaze the Living Buddha of Guya ruled a Tibetan monastery in 1927 at the tender age of six.   JOSEPH F. ROCK

CHINA (Pre-Revolution):

Our Vegetable Travelers. By Victor R. Boswell. Paintings by Else Bostelmann. Included: Chinese cabbage. 145-217, *Aug. 1949*

Operation Eclipse: 1948. By William A. Kinney. NGS research grant. 325-372, *Mar. 1949*

Along the Yangtze, Main Street of China. By W. Robert Moore. 325-356, *Mar. 1948*

The World in Your Garden (Flowers). By W. H. Camp. Paintings by Else Bostelmann. Included: Chinese Mountainsides Yield Treasures (Regal Lily, Abelia, Peony); More Plants from Age-old China (Camellia, Hollyhock, China Aster, Blackberry-lily, Chrysanthemum, Clematis, Forsythia). 1-65, *July 1947*

In Manchuria Now. By W. Robert Moore. 389-414, *Mar. 1947*

Adventures in Lololand. By Rennold L. Lowy. 105-118, *Jan. 1947*

Pirate-Fighters of the South China Sea. By Robert Cardwell. 787-796, *June 1946*

China's Hand-built Air Bases. 231-236, *Aug. 1945*

China Fights Erosion with U. S. Aid. By Walter C. Lowdermilk. 641-680, *June 1945*

Stilwell Road–Land Route to China. By Nelson Grant Tayman. 681-698, *June 1945*

❁ *China. June 1945*

Today on the China Coast. By John B. Powell. 217-238, *Feb. 1945*

Salt for China's Daily Rice. 329-336, *Sept. 1944*

Exploring a Grass Wonderland of Wild West China. By Ray G. Johnson. 713-742, *June 1944*

6,000 Miles over the Roads of Free China. By Josephine A. Brown. 355-384, *Mar. 1944*

Climbing Mighty Minya Konka: Americans First Scaled Mountain That Now Is Landmark of China's New Skyway. By Richard L. Burdsall and Terris Moore. 625-650, *May 1943*

China Opens Her Wild West (Yünnan): In the Mountain-girt Heart of a Continent a New China Has Been Created During the Years of War. By Owen Lattimore. 337-367, *Sept. 1942*

Taming "Flood Dragons" Along China's Hwang Ho River. By Oliver J. Todd. 205-234, *Feb. 1942*

Burma Road, Back Door to China: Like the Great Wall of Ancient Times, This Mighty Mountain Highway Has Been Built by Myriad Chinese to Help Defend Their Homeland. By Frank Outram and G. E. Fane. 629-658, *Nov. 1940*

Four Thousand Hours Over China. By Hans Koester. 571-598, *May 1938*

China's Great Wall of Sculpture: Man-hewn Caves and Countless Images Form a Colossal Art Wonder of Early Buddhism. By Mary Augusta Mullikin. Paintings by author and Anna M. Hotchkis. 313-348, *Mar. 1938*

Landscaped Kwangsi, China's Province of Pictorial Art. By G. Weidman Groff and T. C. Lau. Photos by

The English side of a Spanish-English newspaper is perused by a man in Shanghai, China, in 1979. BRUCE DALE, NGS

A 1920 river boat at Ichang, China, carries cable to tow the craft through rapids in the Yangtze gorges.   ROBERT F. FITCH

Wrists pinioned, 20-year-old Lau Ying Siu awaits deportation back to China after an unsuccessful attempt to cross the border into Hong Kong. WILLIAM ALBERT ALLARD

By Ross Terrill. Photos by Cary Wolinsky. 280-317, *Sept. 1985*
The Eden of the Flowery Republic. By Joseph Beech. 355-390, *Nov. 1920*

CHONI (Jône), Kansu Province, China:

Life Among the Lamas of Choni: Describing the Mystery Plays and Butter Festival in the Monastery of an Almost Unknown Tibetan Principality in Kansu Province, China. By Joseph F. Rock. 569-619, *Nov. 1928*

CHOQQUEQUIRAU, Peru:

In the Wonderland of Peru. By Hiram Bingham. 387-573, *Apr. 1913*

CHOSEN. *See* Korea

CHOU EN-LAI:

Return to Changing China. By Audrey Topping. 801-833, *Dec. 1971*

CHOVAN, LUTHER M.:
Author-Photographer

American Soldier in Reykjavík. Included: Iceland Defrosted. 536-568, *Nov. 1945*

CHOWNING, ANN: *Photographer*

Blowgun Hunters of the South Pacific. By Jane C. Goodale. 793-817, *June 1966*

CHRIST OF THE ANDES, Argentina-Chile:

The First Transandine Railroad from Buenos Aires to Valparaiso. By Harriet Chalmers Adams. 397-417, *May 1910*

CHRISTCHURCH, New Zealand:

New Zealand's Bountiful South Island.

By Peter Benchley. Photos by James L. Amos. 93-123, *Jan. 1972*
New Zealand, Pocket Wonder World. By Howell Walker. 419-460, *Apr. 1952*

CHRISTIAN, JOHN LEROY: *Author*

Burma: Where India and China Meet: In the Massive Mountains of Southeast Asia, Swarming Road Builders Wage the "War of the Highways" for Free China and Her Allies. 489-512, *Oct. 1943*

CHRISTIANITY:

Vatican City. By James Fallows. Photos by James L. Stanfield. 723-775, *Dec. 1985*
Viking Trail East. By Robert Paul Jordan. Photos by Jim Brandenburg. Paintings by Michael A. Hampshire. Included: Evidence of early Orthodox Christianity; Runic crosses. 278-317, *Mar. 1985*
The World of Martin Luther. By Merle Severy. Photos by James L. Amos. 418-463, *Oct. 1983*
Ethiopia: Revolution in an Ancient Empire. By Robert Caputo. Included: Ethiopian Orthodox Church. 614-645, *May 1983*
This Year in Jerusalem. By Joseph Judge. Photos by Jodi Cobb. 479-515, *Apr. 1983*
The Mystery of the Shroud. By Kenneth F. Weaver. Contents: The Shroud of Turin, believed by some to be Christ's burial cloth. 730-753, *June 1980*
■■ *Great Religions of the World.* Contents: Buddhism, Christianity, Hin-

duism, Islam, and Judaism. 420 pages. *1971*
Searching Out Medieval Churches in Ethiopia's Wilds. By Georg Gerster. 856-884, *Dec. 1970*
✤ *Lands of the Bible Today. Dec. 1967*
Where Jesus Walked. By Howard La Fay. Photos by Charles Harbutt. 739-781, *Dec. 1967*
The Land of Galilee. By Kenneth MacLeish. Photos by B. Anthony Stewart. 832-865, *Dec. 1965*
The Other Side of Jordan. By Luis Marden. 790-825, *Dec. 1964*
✤ *Holy Land Today.* Atlas series. *Dec. 1963*
Jerusalem to Rome in the Path of St. Paul. By David S. Boyer. 707-759, *Dec. 1956*
✤ *Lands of the Bible Today. Dec. 1956*
Vézelay, Hill of the Pilgrims. By Melvin Hall. 229-247, *Feb. 1953*
Hashemite Jordan, Arab Heartland. By John Scofield. Included: The shrines of Bethlehem and Jerusalem; Latrun Monastery. 841-856, *Dec. 1952*
Pilgrims Follow the Christmas Star. By Maynard Owen Williams. 831-840, *Dec. 1952*
The Ghosts of Jericho. By James L. Kelso. 825-844, *Dec. 1951*
The Pageant of Jerusalem: The Capital of the Land of Three Great Faiths Is Still the Holy City for Christian, Moslem, and Jew. By Edward Keith-Roach. 635-681, *Dec. 1927*
Recent Disclosures Concerning Pre-Columbian Voyages to America in the Archives of the Vatican. By William Eleroy Curtis. 197-234, *Jan. 31, 1894*
See also Amish; Eastern Orthodoxy; Mennonites; Protestantism; Roman Catholicism; *and* Voodoo

CHRISTIANSØ (Island), Denmark:

Baltic Cruise of the *Caribbee*. By Carleton Mitchell. 605-646, *Nov. 1950*

CHRISTMAS:

Editorial. By Gilbert M. Grosvenor. 727, *Dec. 1975*
Old Salem, Morning Star of Moravian Faith. By Rowe Findley. Photos by Robert W. Madden. 818-837, *Dec. 1970*
Williamsburg, City for All Seasons. By Joseph Judge. Photos by James L. Amos. 790-823, *Dec. 1968*
Christmas in Cookie Tree Land. By Louise Parker La Gorce. Photos by B. Anthony Stewart. 844-851, *Dec. 1955*
Pilgrims Follow the Christmas Star. By Maynard Owen Williams. 831-840, *Dec. 1952*
"The Adoration of the Magi," painting supplement. *Jan. 1952*
Bethlehem and the Christmas Story. By John D. Whiting. 699-735, *Dec. 1929*
Celebrating Christmas on the Meuse. By Clifton Lisle. 527-537, *Dec. 1919*

CHRISTMAS ISLAND, Indian Ocean:

Red Crabs on the March on Christmas Island. By John W. Hicks. 822-831, *Dec. 1987*
At Home on the Oceans: Whales and Sharks Make Exciting Neighbors for

Prime Minister Winston Churchill, encouraging Britain's war effort, chats with a commando as he inspects the soldier's knife during World War II. BRITISH COMBINE

CHURCHILL, Manitoba, Canada:

Henry Hudson's Changing Bay. By Bill Richards. Photos by David Hiser. 380-405, *Mar. 1982*

■ Polar Bear Alert. 395, cover, *Mar. 1982*

Canada's Heartland, the Prairie Provinces. By W. E. Garrett. 443-489, *Oct. 1970*

Rockets Explore the Air Above Us. By Newman Bumstead. 562-580, *Apr. 1957*

Trailing Cosmic Rays in Canada's North. By Martin A. Pomerantz. NGS research grant. 99-115, *Jan. 1953*

Birds of Timberline and Tundra. By Arthur A. Allen. 313-339, *Sept. 1946*

CHURCHILL DOWNS, Louisville, Kentucky:

Heart of the Bluegrass. By Charles McCarry. Photos by J. Bruce Baumann. 634-659, *May 1974*

CHUTE, WALTER H.:
Author

Net Results from Oceania: Collecting Aquarium Specimens in Tropical Pacific Waters. Included: Bright Flashes from Pacific Corals (Fishes). 347-372, *Mar. 1941*

Tropical Fish Immigrants Reveal New Nature Wonders. 93-109, *Jan. 1934*

CICADAS:

Rip Van Winkle of the Underground (Periodical Cicada). By Kenneth F. Weaver. 133-142, *July 1953*

CINCHONA:

Quinine Hunters in Ecuador. By Froelich Rainey. 341-363, *Mar. 1946*

CINCINNATI, Ohio:

Ohio, the Gateway State. By Melville Chater. 525-591, *May 1932*

CINDER FARMING. *See* Lanzarote

CINTA LARGA INDIANS:

Brazil Protects Her Cinta Larga Indians. By W. Jesco von Puttkamer. 420-444, *Sept. 1971*

CINTRA, Portugal:

The Woods and Gardens of Portugal. By Martin Hume. 883-894, *Oct. 1910*

CIRCLING Earth From Pole to Pole. By Sir Ranulph Fiennes. 464-481, *Oct. 1983*

CIRCUSES:

■ Inside the Soviet Circus. cover, *Mar. 1988*

On the Road With an Old-time Circus. By John Fetterman. Photos by Jonathan Blair. 410-434, *Mar. 1972*

The Wonder City That Moves by Night. By Francis Beverly Kelley. Included: Circus Action in Color. By Harold E. Edgerton. 289-324, *Mar. 1948*

The Land of Sawdust and Spangles–A World in Miniature. By Francis Beverly Kelley. 463-516, *Oct. 1931*

CIRENAICA (District), Libya:

Cirenaica, Eastern Wing of Italian Libia. By Harriet Chalmers Adams.

Included: Cirenaica, On the Edge of the Saharan Sands. Photos by Luigi Pellerano. 689-726, *June 1930*

Crossing the Untraversed Libyan Desert: The Record of a 2,200-Mile Journey of Exploration Which Resulted in the Discovery of Two Oases of Strategic Importance on the Southwestern Frontier of Egypt. By Ahmed Mohammed Hassanein Bey. 233-277, *Sept. 1924*

Tripoli: A Land of Little Promise. By Adolf L. Vischer. 1035-1047, *Nov. 1911*

CITÉ, Île de la, Paris, France:

The More Paris Changes.... By Howell Walker. Photos by Gordon W. Gahan. 64-103, *July 1972*

Île de la Cité, Birthplace of Paris. By Kenneth MacLeish. Photos by Bruce Dale. 680-719, *May 1968*

CITIES Like Worcester Make America. By Howell Walker. 189-214, *Feb. 1955*

CITIES of Stone in Utah's Canyonland. By W. Robert Moore. 653-677, *May 1962*

The **CITIES** That Gold and Diamonds Built: Transvaal Treasures Have Created Bustling Johannesburg and Fostered Pretoria, Administrative Capital of the South African Union. By W. Robert Moore. 735-766, *Dec. 1942*

The **CITIZEN** Army of Holland. By Henrik Willem Van Loon. 609-622, *June 1916*

The **CITIZEN** Army of Switzerland. 503-510, *Nov. 1915*

CITROËN AFRICAN EXPEDITIONS:

Through the Deserts and Jungles of Africa by Motor: Caterpillar Cars Make 15,000-Mile Trip from Algeria to

Putting on a happy face, Italo Fornasari of the Hoxie Bros. Gigantic 3-Ring Circus applies clown makeup. JONATHAN BLAIR

Madagascar in Nine Months. By Georges-Marie Haardt. 651-720, *June 1926*

The Conquest of the Sahara by the Automobile. 87-93, *Jan. 1924*

CITROËN-HAARDT TRANS-ASIATIC EXPEDITION:

From the Mediterranean to the Yellow Sea by Motor: The Citroën-Haardt Expedition Successfully Completes Its Dramatic Journey. By Maynard Owen Williams. 513-580, *Nov. 1932*

First Over the Roof of the World by Motor: The Trans-Asiatic Expedition Sets New Records for Wheeled Transport in Scaling Passes of the Himalayas. By Maynard Owen Williams. 321-363, *Mar. 1932*

The Citroën Trans-Asiatic Expedition Reaches Kashmir: Scientific Party Led by Georges-Marie Haardt Successfully Crosses Syria, Iraq, Persia, and Afghanistan to Arrive at the Pamir. By Maynard Owen Williams. 387-443, *Oct. 1931*

The Trans-Asiatic Expedition Starts. By Georges-Marie Haardt. 776-782, *June 1931*

CITRUS FRUITS:

Florida Rides a Space-age Boom. By Benedict Thielen. Photos by Winfield Parks and James P. Blair. 858-903, *Dec. 1963*

How Fruit Came to America. By J. R. Magness. Paintings by Else Bostelmann. Included: Grapefruit, Lemon, Lime, Orange. 325-377, *Sept. 1951*

"The **CITY**"–London's Storied Square Mile. By Allan C. Fisher, Jr. 735-777, *June 1961*

The **CITY** Around Red Square: Moscow. By John J. Putman. Photos by Gordon W. Gahan. 2-45, *Jan. 1978*

CITY Astride Two Continents: Istanbul. By William S. Ellis. Photos by Winfield Parks. 501-533, *Oct. 1973*

A **CITY** Learns to Smile Again (Nancy, France). By Frederick G. Vosburgh. 361-384, *Mar. 1945*

The **CITY** of Jacqueline (Ter Goes, Netherlands). By Florence Craig Albrecht. 29-56, *Jan. 1915*

A **CITY** of Realized Dreams (San Francisco). By Franklin K. Lane. 169-171, *Feb. 1915*

CITY PLANNING. *See* Brasília; Rotterdam; *and* listing under Urban Renewal

A **CITY** That Refused to Die (Plymouth, England). By Harvey Klemmer. 211-236, *Feb. 1946*

The **CITY** They Call Red China's Showcase. By Franc Shor. 193-223, *Aug. 1960*

CITY UNIVERSITY OF NEW YORK:
Study Grants:

Anthropology: Papua New Guinea. 128, *July 1977*

CIUDAD TRUJILLO, Dominican Republic. *See* Santo Domingo

CIVIL AIR PATROL:

Minutemen of the Civil Air Patrol. By Allan·C. Fisher, Jr. Photos by John E. Fletcher. 637-665, *May 1956*

Heroes of Wartime Science and Mercy. By Elizabeth W. King. 715-740, *Dec. 1943*

The **CIVIL** Government of Alaska. By George C. Perkins. 172-178, *Apr. 1898*

CIVIL WAR, U. S.:

Echoes of Shiloh (Shiloh National Military Park, Tennessee). By Shelby Foote. 106-111, *July 1979*

How We Found the *Monitor*. By John G. Newton. 48-61, *Jan. 1975*

The Virginians. By Mike W. Edwards. Photos by David Alan Harvey. 588-617, *Nov. 1974*

■■ *The Civil War*. By Robert Paul Jordan. 215 pages. *1969*

Appomattox: Where Grant and Lee Made Peace With Honor a Century Ago. By Ulysses S. Grant 3rd. Photos by Bruce Dale. 435-469, *Apr. 1965*

Gettysburg and Vicksburg: the Battle Towns Today. By Robert Paul Jordan. Map notes by Carolyn Bennett Patterson. 4-57, *July 1963*

Just a Hundred Years Ago. By Carl Sandburg. 1-3, *July 1963*

✦ *Battlefields of the Civil War*. Atlas series. *Apr. 1961*

The Civil War. By Ulysses S. Grant 3rd. 437-449, *Apr. 1961*

Witness to a War: British Correspondent Frank Vizetelly. By Robert T. Cochran, Jr. 453-491, *Apr. 1961*

Lincoln, Man of Steel and Velvet. By Carl Sandburg. 239-241, *Feb. 1960*

Our Land Through Lincoln's Eyes. By Carolyn Bennett Patterson. Photos by W. D. Vaughn. 243-277, *Feb. 1960*

The Most Famous Battle Field in America (Gettysburg). Photos by Clifton Adams and Orren R. Louden. 66-75, *July 1931*

Fame's Eternal Camping Ground: Beautiful Arlington (Virginia), Burial Place of America's Illustrious Dead. By Enoch A. Chase. 621-638, *Nov. 1928*

See also American Processional: History on Canvas; Atlanta; Harpers Ferry; Mobile; South Carolina (South Carolina Rediscovered)

CIVILIZATION:

The Effects of Geographic Environment in the Development of Civilization in Primitive Man. By Gardiner G. Hubbard. 161-176, *June 1897*

The National Geographic Society: Synopsis of a Course of Lectures on the Effects of Geographic Environment in Developing the Civilization of the World. By Gardiner G. Hubbard. 29-32, *Jan. 1897*

Geographic Progress of Civilization. Annual Address by the President, Gardiner G. Hubbard. 1-22, *Feb. 14, 1894*

CIVILIZATIONS, Early. *See* Early Civilizations

The **CIVILIZING** Seine. By Charles McCarry. Photos by David L. Arnold. 478-511, *Apr. 1982*

CLANS in Kilt and Plaidie Gather at Braemar (Scotland). Photos by Maynard Owen Williams. 153-160, *Aug. 1935*

CLARK, AUSTIN H.: *Author*

Potent Personalities–Wasps and Hornets: Though Often Painfully Stung, Mankind Profits Immeasurably from the Pest-killing Activities of These Fiery Little Flyers. Paintings by Hashime Murayama. 47-72, *July 1937*

Who's Who Among the Butterflies. Paintings by Hashime Murayama. 679-692, *May 1936*

CLARK, CHARLES UPSON: *Author*

Romantic Spain. 187-215, *Mar. 1910*

CLARK, D. WORTH: *Author*

Idaho Made the Desert Bloom. Photos by Maynard Owen Williams. 641-688, *June 1944*

CLARK, DEENA: *Author*

The Flowers That Say "Aloha." Photos by Robert B. Goodman. 121-131, *Jan. 1967*

La Jolla, a Gem of the California Coast. Photos by J. Baylor Roberts. 755-782, *Dec. 1952*

Iceland Tapestry. 599-630, *Nov. 1951*

Home Life in Paris Today. Photos by Willard R. Culver. 43-72, *July 1950*

CLARK, ELLA E.: *Author*

Forest Lookout. 73-96, *July 1946*

CLARK, EUGENIE:

Nomination Page. *June 1981*

Nomination Page. *Aug. 1974*

Author

Down the Cayman Wall. Included: Zones of Life. NGS research grant. 712-731, *Nov. 1988*

Sharks at 2,000 Feet. By Eugenie Clark and Emory Kristof as reported to Douglas Lee. NGS research grant. 681-691, *Nov. 1986*

Japan's Izu Oceanic Park. Photos by David Doubilet. 465-491, *Apr. 1984*

Hidden Life of an Undersea Desert. Photos by David Doubilet. 129-144, *July 1983*

Sharks: Magnificent and Misunderstood. Photos by David Doubilet. 138-187, *Aug. 1981*

Flashlight Fish of the Red Sea. Photos by David Doubilet. 719-728, *Nov. 1978*

The Strangest Sea. Photos by David Doubilet. 338-343, *Sept. 1975*

Into the Lairs of "Sleeping" Sharks. Photos by David Doubilet. 570-584, *Apr. 1975*

The Red Sea's Sharkproof Fish. Photos by David Doubilet. 718-727, *Nov. 1974*

The Red Sea's Gardens of Eels. Photos by James L. Stanfield and David Doubilet. 724-735, *Nov. 1972*

Rare photograph of a shark attacking a baited cage was made from a submersible down 2,000 feet, on an expedition led by shark expert Dr. Eugenie Clark.   EMORY KRISTOF, NGS

CLARK, HARLAN B.: *Author*
Yemen–Southern Arabia's Mountain Wonderland. 631-672, *Nov. 1947*

CLARK, HUBERT LYMAN: *Author*
The Paradise of the Tasman (Lord Howe Island): A Pacific Island Provides the Palms Which Decorate Hotels, Churches, Steamships, and Homes. 115-136, *July 1935*

CLARK, JAMES L.:
By Coolie and Caravan Across Central Asia: Narrative of a 7,900-Mile Journey of Exploration and Research Over "the Roof of the World," from the Indian Ocean to the Yellow Sea. Contents: Morden-Clark Asiatic Expedition. By William J. Morden. 369-431, *Oct. 1927*

CLARK, JOE:
Home Folk around Historic Cumberland Gap. By Leo A. Borah. 741-768, *Dec. 1943*

CLARK, LEONARD:
Author-Photographer
Among the Big Knot Lois of Hainan: Wild Tribesmen With Topknots Roam the Little-known Interior of This Big and Strategically Important Island in the China Sea. 391-418, *Sept. 1938*

CLARK, LEWIS F.: *Author*
Amid the Mighty Walls of Zion (Zion National Park). 37-70, *Jan. 1954*

CLARK, MILTON J.:
Author-Photographer
How the Kazakhs Fled to Freedom. 621-644, *Nov. 1954*

CLARK, ROBERT:
Nomination Page. *Oct. 1975*
Photographer
Rafting Down the Yukon. By Keith Tryck. 830-861, *Dec. 1975*

CLARK, RONALD W.: *Author*
Liechtenstein Thrives on Stamps. 105-112, *July 1948*

CLARK, SYDNEY: *Author*
Mid-century Holland Builds Her Future. 747-778, *Dec. 1950*
Norway Cracks Her Mountain Shell. Photos by Gilbert Grosvenor and Ole Friele Backer. 171-211, *Aug. 1948*
Luxembourg, Survivor of Invasions. Photos by Maynard Owen Williams. 791-810, *June 1948*

CLARK, TIM W.:
Nomination Page. *Sept. 1977*
Author
The Hard Life of the Prairie Dog. Photos by Patricia Caulfield. 270-281, *Aug. 1979*
Author-Photographer
Last of the Black-footed Ferrets? Photos by Franz J. Camenzind and the author. 828-838, *June 1983*

CLARK, WILLIAM:
Following the Trail of Lewis and Clark. By Ralph Gray. 707-750, *June 1953*

Wit, cynic, and romantic, author Mark Twain wears Oxford University robe.
ALVIN LANGDON COBURN, COURTESY MARK TWAIN MEMORIAL, HARTFORD, CONNECTICUT

CLARK, Lake, Alaska:
Lake Clark, a Little Known Alaskan Lake. By Wilfred H. Osgood. 326-331, *Aug. 1904*

CLARKE, ARTHUR C.: *Author*
Sri Lanka's Wildlife Heritage: A Personal Perspective. 254-255, *Aug. 1983*

CLARKE, FREDERICK J.: *Author*
Ascension Island, an Engineering Victory. 623-640, *May 1944*

CLARKE, NELL RAY: *Author*
The Haunts of the Caribbean Corsairs: The West Indies a Geographic Background for the Most Adventurous Episodes in the History of the Western Hemisphere. 147-187, *Feb. 1922*

CLARKE SCHOOL FOR THE DEAF, Northampton, Massachusetts:
Deaf Children Learn to Talk at Clarke School. By Lilian Grosvenor. Photos by Willard R. Culver. 379-397, *Mar. 1955*

CLASSICAL LANDS:
❋ *Classical Lands of the Mediterranean.* *Dec. 1949*
Ancient Rome Brought to Life. By Rhys Carpenter. Paintings by H. M. Herget. 567-633, *Nov. 1946*
Greece–the Birthplace of Science and Free Speech: Explorations on the Mainland and in Crete and the Aegean Isles Reveal Ancient Life Similar to That of the Present. By Richard Stillwell. Paintings by H. M. Herget. 273-353, *Mar. 1944*
Classic Greece Merges Into 1941 News. Photos by B. Anthony Stewart and Maynard Owen Williams. 93-108, *Jan. 1941*
Italy, From Roman Ruins to Radio: History of Ancient Bridge Building

and Road Making Repeats Itself in Modern Public Works and Engineering Projects. By John Patric. 347-394, *Mar. 1940*
❋ *Classical Lands of the Mediterranean.* *Mar. 1940*
Modern Odyssey in Classic Lands: Troy's Treasures, Athens' Parthenon, and Rome's First "Broad Way" Influence Today's Banks, Costumes, Jewelry, and Railroad Timetables. By Maynard Owen Williams. 291-337, *Mar. 1940*
The Ruins at Selinus, Sicily. By Marion Crawford. 117, *Jan. 1909*
See also Athens; Carthage; Greece; Roman Empire; Troy

The **CLASSIFICATION** of Geographic Forms by Genesis. By W J McGee. 27-36, *Oct. 1888*

CLATWORTHY, FRED PAYNE:
Photographer
A Sunshine Land of Fruits, Flowers, Movies, and Sport. 585-592, *Nov. 1934*
Among the Peaks and Parks of the Rockies. 39-46, *July 1932*
Adventures in Color on Mexico's West Coast. 61-68, *July 1930*
Scenic Glories of Western United States. 223-230, *Aug. 1929*
Photographing the Marvels of the West in Colors. 694-719, *June 1928*
Western Views in the Land of the Best. 405-420, *Apr. 1923*

CLAY, ALBERT T.: *Author*
Pushing Back History's Horizon: How the Pick and Shovel Are Revealing Civilizations That Were Ancient When Israel Was Young. 162-216, *Feb. 1916*

CLAY FIGURES, Chinese. *See* Terracotta Army

CLAY HILLS, Utah:
Beyond the Clay Hills: An Account of the National Geographic Society's Reconnaissance of a Previously Unexplored Section of Utah. By Neil M. Judd. 275-302, *Mar. 1924*

CLAY TABLETS. *See* Cuneiform

CLEARWATER (River), Idaho:
Idaho Loggers Battle a River. 117-130, *July 1951*

CLEAVES, HOWARD H.:
Author-Photographer
Hunting with the Lens (Birds). 1-35, *July 1914*

CLEMENS, SAMUEL LANGHORNE. *See* Twain, Mark

CLEMENTS, EDITH S.: *Author-Artist*
Flower Pageant of the Midwest: From March to November Nature Embroiders an Ever-changing Pattern of Living Color. By Edith S. and Frederic E. Clements. Included: Floral Garlands of Prairie, Plain, and Woodland. 219-271, *Aug. 1939*
Wild Flowers of the West (U. S.). 566-622, *May 1927*

Glittering
cities, lonely
wild lands

Faces and places of the Northeast come alive in this "Close-up: U.S.A." supplement to the January 1978 GEOGRAPHIC. *The reverse shows one in a series of U.S. regional maps.*

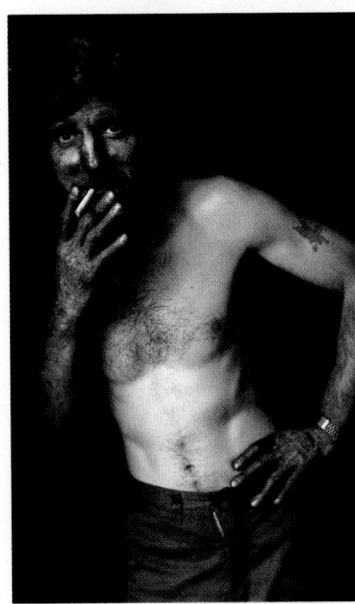

Mine foreman Alfred Wooten relaxes after his shift of digging coal near Beckley, West Virginia. MICHAEL O'BRIEN

Veiled by tradition, a young Bedouin woman in Saudi Arabia wears the covering prescribed by a strict code for female modesty. JODI COBB, NGS

Reaching for red cherries that hold ripe beans, a girl adds to the coffee harvest in Indonesia, a leading exporter. SAM ABELL

I Sailed with Portugal's Captains Courageous. By Alan Villiers. 565-596, *May 1952*

Newfoundland, Canada's New Province. By Andrew H. Brown. Photos by Robert F. Sisson. 777-812, *June 1949*

Fishing in the Lofotens. Photos by Lennart Nilsson. 377-388, *Mar. 1947*

Islands Adrift: St. Pierre and Miquelon: In a Key Position on the North Atlantic Air Route, France's Oldest Colony Rides Out Another Storm. By Frederic K. Arnold. 743-768, *Dec. 1941*

Newfoundland, North Atlantic Rampart: From the "First Base of American Defense" Planes Fly to Britain's Aid over Stout Fishing Schooners of the Grand Banks. By George Whiteley, Jr. 111-140, *July 1941*

Viking Life in the Storm-Cursed Faeroes. By Leo Hansen. 607-648, *Nov. 1930*

Fishes and Fisheries of Our North Atlantic Seaboard. By John Oliver La Gorce. Paintings by Hashime Murayama. 567-634, *Dec. 1923*

CODRAI, RONALD:
Author-Photographer
Desert Sheikdoms of Arabia's Pirate Coast. 65-104, *July 1956*

CODY, WILLIAM F.:
Buffalo Bill and the Enduring West. By Alice J. Hall. Photos by James L. Amos. 76-103, *July 1981*

Hays, Kansas, at the Nation's Heart. By Margaret M. Detwiler. Photos by John E. Fletcher. 461-490, *Apr. 1952*

CODY, Wyoming:
Buffalo Bill and the Enduring West. By Alice J. Hall. Photos by James L. Amos. 76-103, *July 1981*

COE, WILLIAM R.: *Author*
The Maya: Resurrecting the Grandeur of Tikal. 792-798, *Dec. 1975*

COELACANTHS, the Fish That Time Forgot. Article and photos by Hans Fricke. 824-838, *June 1988*

COEN, MARCEL: *Photographer*
Sheep Trek in the French Alps. By Maurice Moyal. 545-564, *Apr. 1952*

COFFEE:
The Bonanza Bean–Coffee. By Ethel A. Starbird. Photos by Sam Abell. 388-405, *Mar. 1981*

Behind the Veil of Troubled Yemen. By Thomas J. Abercrombie. Included: The origin of coffee drinking. 403-445, *Mar. 1964*

Brazil, Ôba! By Peter T. White. Photos by Winfield Parks. 299-353, *Sept. 1962*

Land of the Painted Oxcarts (Costa Rica). By Luis Marden. 409-456, *Oct. 1946*

Coffee Is King in El Salvador. By Luis Marden. 575-616, *Nov. 1944*

As São Paulo Grows: Half the World's Coffee Beans Flavor the Life and Speed the Growth of an Inland Brazil City. By W. Robert Moore. 657-688, *May 1939*

Costa Rica, Land of the Banana. By Paul B. Popenoe. 201-220, *Feb. 1922*

A Visit to the Brazilian Coffee Country. By Robert De C. Ward. 908-931, *Oct. 1911*

Guatemala, the Country of the Future. By Edine Frances Tisdel. 596-624, *July 1910*

See also Colombia; Costa Rica; Guatemala

COFFIN, MARIAN CRUGER:
Author-Photographer
Where East Meets West: Visit to Picturesque Dalmatia, Montenegro and Bosnia. 309-344, *May 1908*

COGNAT, ANDRÉ:
What Future for the Wayana Indians? By Carole Devillers. 66-83, *Jan. 1983*

COHN, RONALD H.:
On Assignment. *Jan. 1985*

Photographer
Koko's Kitten. Text by Jane Vessels. 110-113, *Jan. 1985*

Conversations With a Gorilla. By Francine Patterson. 438-465, *Oct. 1978*

COIMBRA, Portugal:
The Woods and Gardens of Portugal. By Martin Hume. 883-894, *Oct. 1910*

COINS AND COINAGE:
Pieces of Silver. By Frederick Simpich. 253-292, *Sept. 1933*

The Geography of Money. By William Atherton Du Puy. 745-768, *Dec. 1927*

Our Heterogeneous System of Weights and Measures. By Alexander Graham Bell. 158-169, *Mar. 1906*

COKER, ROBERT ERVIN:
Author-Photographer
Peru's Wealth-Producing Birds: Vast Riches in the Guano Deposits of Cormorants, Pelicans, and Petrels which Nest on Her Barren, Rainless Coast. 537-566, *June 1920*

COLBERT, L. O.:
Board of Trustees. 618, 640, *Nov. 1944*
Presents wings to a flying daughter (Women's AirForce Service Pilots). 458, *Oct. 1943*

COLCA VALLEY, Peru:
A Forgotten Valley of Peru: Conquered by Incas, Scourged by Famine, Plagues, and Earthquakes, Colca Valley Shelters the Last Fragment of an Ancient Andean Tribe. By Robert Shippee. 111-132, *Jan. 1934*

COLE, MABEL COOK: *Author*
The Island of Nias, at the Edge of the World. 201-224, *Aug. 1931*

COLIN, THOMAS J.: *Author*
The U. S. Virgin Islands. Photos by William Albert Allard and Cary Wolinsky. 225-243, *Feb. 1981*

COLLARIN' Cape Cod (Massachusetts): Experiences on Board a U. S. Navy Destroyer in a Wild Winter Storm. By H. R. Thurber. 427-472, *Oct. 1925*

COLLECTIVE FARMS:
Down on the Farm, Soviet Style–a 4-H Adventure. By John Garaventa. Photos by James Tobin and Carol Schmidt. 768-797, *June 1979*

Palestine Today. By Francis Chase, Jr. 501-516, *Oct. 1946*

Sunny Siberia. By Owen Lattimore. Included: Ernst Thaelmann Collective Farm. 649-672, *Dec. 1944*

See also Kibbutzim

COLLECTORS OF ANTIQUITIES:
In Defense of the Collector. By Gillett G. Griffin. 462-465, *Apr. 1986*

COLLEGES. *See* Universities and Colleges

COLLIES:
Sheep Dog Trials in Llangollen; Trained Collies Perform Marvels of Herding in the Cambrian Stakes, Open to the World. By Sara Bloch. 559-574, *Apr. 1940*

COLLINS, G.E.P.:
Author-Photographer
Seafarers of South Celebes. 53-78, *Jan. 1945*

COLLINS, G. N.:
Author-Photographer
Notes on Southern Mexico (Agricultural Products). By G. N. Collins and C. B. Doyle. 301-320, *Mar. 1911*

Dumboy, the National Dish of Liberia. 84-88, *Jan. 1911*

Kboo, a Liberian Game. 944-948, *Nov. 1910*

A Primitive Gyroscope in Liberia. 531-535, *June 1910*

COLLINS, HENRY B.: *Author*

Vanished Mystery Men of Hudson Bay. 669-687, *Nov. 1956*

Exploring Frozen Fragments of American History: On the Trail of Early Eskimo Colonists Who Made a 55-Mile Crossing from the Old World to the New. 633-656, *May 1939*

COLLINS, LORENCE G.: *Author-Photographer*

Finding Rare Beauty in Common Rocks. 121-129, *Jan. 1966*

COLLINS, MICHAEL:

First Moon Explorers (Apollo 11) Receive the Society's Hubbard Medal. 859-861, *June 1970*

First Explorers on the Moon: The Incredible Story of Apollo 11. 735-797. I. Man Walks on Another World. By Neil A. Armstrong, Edwin E. Aldrin, Jr., and Michael Collins. 738-749; II. Sounds of the Space Age, From Sputnik to Lunar Landing. A record narrated by Frank Borman. 750-751; III. The Flight of Apollo 11: "One giant leap for mankind." By Kenneth F. Weaver. 752-787, *Dec. 1969*

Author

Mission to Mars. Photos by Roger H. Ressmeyer. Paintings by Pierre Mion and Roy Andersen. 733-764, *Nov. 1988*

Of Air and Space (National Air and Space Museum). 819-837. Picture portfolio by Nathan Benn, Robert S. Oakes, and Joseph D. Lavenburg, with text by Michael E. Long. 825-837, *June 1978*

Man Walks on Another World. By Neil A. Armstrong, Edwin E. Aldrin, Jr.,
and Michael Collins. 738-749, *Dec. 1969*

COLLINSON, SIR RICHARD:

Collinson's Arctic Journey. By A. W. Greely. 198-200, *Feb. 8, 1893*

COLLISON, JAMES: *Photographer*

Happy Birthday, Otto Lilienthal! By Russell Hawkes. 286-292, *Feb. 1972*

COLOGNE, West Germany:

War's Wake in the Rhineland. By Thomas R. Henry. 1-32, *July 1945*

Cologne, Key City of the Rhineland. By Francis Woodworth. 829-848, *June 1936*

COLOMBIA:

When the Earth Moves. The Editor. 638-639, *May 1986*

Eruption in Colombia. By Bart McDowell. Photos by Steve Raymer. 640-653, *May 1986*

Colombia, from Amazon to Spanish Main. By Loren McIntyre. 235-273, *Aug. 1970*

Capturing Strange Creatures in Colombia. By Marte Latham. Photos by Tor Eigeland. 682-693, *May 1966*

Jungle Jaunt on Amazon Headwaters. By Bernice M. Goetz. 371-388, *Sept. 1952*

Keeping House for a Biologist in Colombia. By Nancy Bell Fairchild Bates. Photos by Marston Bates. 251-274, *Aug. 1948*

Cruising Colombia's "Ol' Man River." By Amos Burg. 615-660, *May 1947*

Hail Colombia! By Luis Marden. 505-536, *Oct. 1940*

Stone Idols of the Andes Reveal a Vanished People: Remarkable Relics of One of the Oldest Aboriginal Cultures of America are Unearthed in Colombia's San Agustín Region. By Hermann von Walde-Waldegg. 627-647, *May 1940*

Round About Bogotá: A Hunt for New Fruits and Plants Among the Mountain Forests of Colombia's Unique Capital. By Wilson Popenoe. 127-160, *Feb. 1926*

Over the Andes to Bogotá. By Frank M. Chapman. 353-373, *Oct. 1921*

Latin America and Colombia. By John Barrett. 692-709, *Dec. 1906*

Notes on Panama and Colombia. 458-466, *Dec. 1903*

See also Andean Condors; Gems; Gold; Orchids

COLOMBO, Sri Lanka:

Sri Lanka: Time of Testing For an Ancient Land. By Robert Paul Jordan. Photos by Raghubir Singh. 123-150, *Jan. 1979*

Ceylon, the Resplendent Land. By Donna K. and Gilbert M. Grosvenor. 447-497, *Apr. 1966*

COLONIAL AMERICA:

Exploring Our Forgotten Century: Between Columbus and Jamestown. By Joseph Judge. Photos by Bill Ballenberg. Paintings by John Berkey. 330-363, *Mar. 1988*

⊕ *Deep South.* The Making of America series. Included: Alabama, Florida, Georgia, Louisiana, Mississippi, South Carolina, and parts of Arkansas, North Carolina, and Tennessee. On reverse: Indian Legacy, Imperial Footholds, Three Empires and Three Races, Cotton Kingdom, Postbellum, New Deep South, Subtropical Playground. *Aug. 1983*

Herbs for All Seasons. By Lonnelle Aikman. Photos by Sam Abell. Picture portfolio text by Larry Kohl. 386-409, *Mar. 1983*

They'd Rather Be in Philadelphia. By Ethel A. Starbird. Photos by Ted Spiegel. 314-343, *Mar. 1983*

⊕ *Atlantic Gateways.* The Making of America series. Included: Delaware, Maryland, New Jersey, New York, Pennsylvania, northern Virginia, West Virginia, and in Canada, southern Ontario and southern Quebec. On reverse: Indians and Trade, Nation in the Making, Peopling of the Gateways, Race for the Hinterlands, Growth of Industry, Spreading Urban Corridors. *Mar. 1983*

⊕ *The Southwest.* The Making of America series. Included: Arizona, New Mexico, and parts of California, Colorado, Texas, Utah; and in Mexico: Baja California Norte, Chihuahua, Sonora. On reverse: 12,000 Years of History; Spanish Conquest; Anglo-American Entry and Occupancy. *Nov. 1982*

New Clues to an Old Mystery (Virginia's Wolstenholme Towne). By Ivor Noël Hume. Photos by Ira Block. Paintings by Richard Schlecht. 53-77, *Jan. 1982*

First Look at a Lost Virginia Settlement (Martin's Hundred). By Ivor Noël

Shelled by bombers during the first great Allied air raids of World War II, the bridges and buildings of Cologne, Germany, lie in ruins.   SGT. REG KENNY FROM *YANK*

Hume. Photos by Ira Block. Paintings by Richard Schlecht. 735-767, *June 1979*

Reach for the New World. By Mendel Peterson. Photos by David L. Arnold. Paintings by Richard Schlecht. 724-767, *Dec. 1977*

⊕ *Colonization and Trade in the New World.* Text on reverse. *Dec. 1977*

▓▓*Visiting Our Past: America's Historylands.* Included: Companion directory, *Visiting Our Past: A Supplemental Guide to Selected Sites.* 400 pages. *1977*

Thomas Jefferson: Architect of Freedom. By Mike W. Edwards. Paintings by Linda Bartlett. 231-259, *Feb. 1976*

Benjamin Franklin, Philosopher of Dissent. By Alice J. Hall. Photos by Linda Bartlett. 93-123, *July 1975*

▓▓*The Wild Shores: America's Beginnings.* By Tee Loftin Snell. Photos by Walter Meayers Edwards. Art by Louis S. Glanzman. 203 pages. *1974*

From Sword to Scythe in Champlain Country. By Ethel A. Starbird. Photos by B. Anthony Stewart and Emory Kristof. 153-201, *Aug. 1967*

The St. Lawrence, River Key to Canada. By Howard La Fay. Photos by John Launois. 622-667, *May 1967*

▓▓*America's Historylands, Touring Our Landmarks of Liberty.* Companion volume to *America's Wonderlands.* 575 pages. 1962; rev. ed. *1967*

▓▓ *The Revolutionary War: America's Fight for Freedom.* By Bart McDowell. 199 pages. *1967*

Massachusetts Builds for Tomorrow. By Robert de Roos. Photos by B. Anthony Stewart. Included: Boston, Concord, Duxbury, Plymouth, Sudbury. 790-843, *Dec. 1966*

Roving Maryland's Cavalier Country. By William A. Kinney. 431-470, *Apr. 1954*

Founders of New England. By Sir Evelyn Wrench. Photos by B. Anthony Stewart. 803-838, *June 1953*

Founders of Virginia. By Sir Evelyn Wrench. Photos by B. Anthony Stewart. 433-462, *Apr. 1948*

⊕ *A Map of the Travels of George Washington.* Insets: New York and the lower Hudson, Tidewater Virginia, Philadelphia, Boston, Mount Vernon. *Jan. 1932*

See also Boston Post Roads; Concord, Massachusetts; Deerfield, Massachusetts; Jamestown, Virginia; Maryland (Roving); Philadelphia, Pennsylvania; Roanoke Island, for Lost Colony; St. Augustine, Florida; Williamsburg, Virginia

The **COLONIAL** Expansion of France. By Jean C. Bracq. 225-238, *June 1900*

COLONIAL GOVERNMENT:

The United States and the British Empire. By Leonard David Gammans. 562-564, *May 1945*

The British Commonwealth of Nations: "Organized Freedom" Around the World. By Eric Underwood. 485-524, *Apr. 1943*

Colonial Government in Borneo. By

James M. Hubbard. 359-363, *Sept. 1900*

Colonial Systems of the World. By O. P. Austin. 21-26, *Jan. 1899*

COLONIAL NATIONAL HISTORICAL PARK (Jamestown, Williamsburg, and Yorktown), Virginia:

The Restoration of Colonial Williamsburg. By W.A.R. Goodwin. 402-443, *Apr. 1937*

COLONIZATION:

Editorial. By Gilbert M. Grosvenor. 723, *Dec. 1977*

Reach for the New World. By Mendel Peterson. Photos by David L. Arnold. Paintings by Richard Schlecht. 724-767, *Dec. 1977*

⊕ *Colonization and Trade in the New World.* Text on reverse. *Dec. 1977*

The Vikings. By Howard La Fay. Photos by Ted Spiegel. 492-541, *Apr. 1970*

Mozambique: Land of the Good People. By Volkmar Wentzel. Included: Limpopo Colonato. 197-231, *Aug. 1964*

Capt. John Smith's Map of Virginia. 760-761; Captain Smith's New England...and the Pilgrims' Cape Cod. 764-765, *June 1953*

Founders of New England. By Sir Evelyn Wrench. Photos by B. Anthony Stewart. 803-838, *June 1953*

The British Way. By Sir Evelyn Wrench. 421-541, *Apr. 1949*

Founders of Virginia. By Sir Evelyn Wrench. Photos by B. Anthony Stewart. 433-462, *Apr. 1948*

See also Colonial America; Vinland

COLOPHON (Ancient City), Turkey:

Some Ruined Cities of Asia Minor. By Ernest L. Harris. 833-858, *Dec. 1908*

Indians scalp a colonist at Wolstenholme Towne, Virginia, an attack revealed by archaeology.   PAINTING BY RICHARD SCHLECHT

The **COLOR** and Customs of Sweden's Chateau Country. Photos by Gustav Heurlin. 33-40, *July 1934*

COLOR at Africa's Southern Tip. Photos by W. Robert Moore. 213-220, *Aug. 1942*

COLOR Brightens Rustic Life in Jugoslavia. Photos by Hans Hildenbrand and Wilhelm Tobien. 273-304, *Sept. 1930*

The **COLOR** Camera Explores the Country That Moves by Night (Circus). Photos by Richard H. Stewart, W. Robert Moore, Orren R. Louden, Jacob Gayer. 479-510, *Oct. 1931*

COLOR Camera Records of New Orleans. Photos by Edwin L. Wisherd. 459-466, *Apr. 1930*

The **COLOR** Camera Records Scenes in Eastern Spain. Photos by Gervais Courtellemont. 365-372, *Mar. 1929*

The **COLOR** Camera's First Aërial Success. By Melville Bell Grosvenor. 344-353, *Sept. 1930*

COLOR Close-ups of Europe's Corner Land (Portugal). Photos by W. Robert Moore. 149-180, *Feb. 1938*

COLOR Close-ups of Familiar Birds. Photos by Arthur A. Allen. 779-786, *June 1939*

COLOR Contrasts in Northern Spain. Photos by Gervais Courtellemont. 113-120, *Jan. 1931*

COLOR Cruising in Paraguay. Photos by Fenno Jacobs. 465-472, *Oct. 1943*

COLOR Glimpses of the Changing South Seas. Photos by Amos Burg. 281-288, *Mar. 1934*

COLOR Glows in the Guianas, French and Dutch. By Nicol Smith. 459-480, *Apr. 1943*

COLOR Highlights of the Empire State. Photos by Clifton Adams, James A. G. Davey, and Edwin L. Wisherd. 529-576, *Nov. 1933*

The **COLOR** Palette of the Caribbean (Jamaica). Photos by Jacob Gayer. 45-55, *Jan. 1927*

COLOR Records from the Changing Life of the Holy City (Jerusalem). By Maynard Owen Williams. 682-707, *Dec. 1927*

COLORADO:

Colorado Dreaming. By Mike Edwards. Photos by Craig Aurness. 186-219, *Aug. 1984*

▓▓*America's Magnificent Mountains.* 207 pages. *1980*

Along the Great Divide. By Mike Edwards. Photos by Nicholas deVore III. 483-515, *Oct. 1979*

A Walk Across America: Part II. By Peter and Barbara Jenkins. 194-229, *Aug. 1979*

Bison Kill By Ice Age Hunters. By Dennis Stanford. 114-121, *Jan. 1979*

⊕ *Close-up: U.S.A., The Southwest.* Text on reverse. *Oct. 1977*

Oil, the Dwindling Treasure. By Noel

COLORADO DESERT, California:

Desert-tough Walter Burkhead and son Wesley put down roots in Datil, New Mexico, along the Continental Divide. NICHOLAS DEVORE III

COLORADO PLATEAU, U. S.:

COLORADO RIVER AND BASIN, U. S.-Mexico:

COLORFUL Corners of the City of Homes (Philadelphia). Photos by

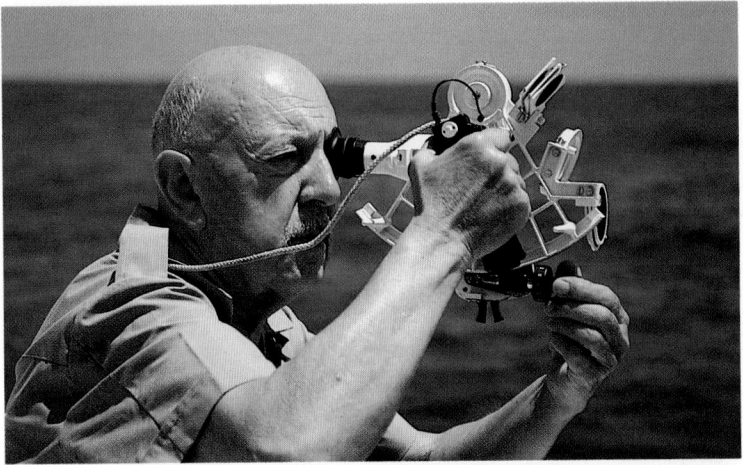

Longtime GEOGRAPHIC writer, photographer, sailor, and navigator, Luis Marden shoots the sun as he tracks Columbus's first voyage to the New World.   WILBUR E. GARRETT, NGS

Study of Peculiar Rodent of Western North America. By William T. Shaw. 587-596, *May 1925*

COLUMBUS, CHRISTOPHER:

Searching for Columbus's Lost Colony: La Navidad. By Kathleen A. Deagan. Photos by Bill Ballenberg. 672-675, *Nov. 1987*

Columbus and the New World. 562A-605. Editorial. By Wilbur E. Garrett. 562A-563; Behaim Globe reproduction. 564-565; Where Columbus Found the New World. By Joseph Judge. Photos by James L. Stanfield. 566-599; The First Landfall of Columbus. By Luis Marden. 572-577; 15th-Century Manuscript Yields First Look at Niña. By Eugene Lyon. 601-605, *Nov. 1986*

On Assignment. *Nov. 1986*

✤ *Where Did Columbus Discover America? New Evidence Marks Landfall at Samana Cay.* Included: Threading the Islands: Which Track Fits?; Samana Cay and the Columbus Log. *Nov. 1986*

Editorial. By Wilbur E. Garrett. 141, *Feb. 1986*

Christopher Columbus and the New World He Found. By John Scofield. Photos by Adam Woolfitt. 584-625, *Nov. 1975*

Genoa, Where Columbus Learned to Love the Sea. By McFall Kerbey. Included: Fate Directs the Faltering Footsteps of Columbus. Painting by Alfred Dehodencq, Paris. Supplement, *Sept. 1928*

The Caravels of Columbus. Painting by N. C. Wyeth, National Geographic Society, Washington, D. C. Supplement, *July 1928*

Jamaica, the Isle of Many Rivers. By John Oliver La Gorce. 1-55, *Jan. 1927*

The Countries of the Caribbean. By William Joseph Showalter. 227-250, *Feb. 1913*

The First Landfall of Columbus. By Jacques W. Redway. 179-192, *Dec. 29, 1894*

The Caravels of Columbus. By Victor Maria Concas. 180-186, *Jan. 31, 1894*

In the Wake of Columbus. By Frederick A. Ober. 187-196, *Jan. 31, 1894*

Discoverers of America. Annual Address by the President, Hon. Gardiner G. Hubbard. 1-20, *Apr. 7, 1893*

COLUMBUS, JOSEPH V.:

Nomination Page. *Nov. 1958*

COLUMBUS, Indiana:

A Most Uncommon Town: Columbus, Indiana. By David Jeffery. Photos by J. Bruce Baumann. 383-397, *Sept. 1978*

COLUMBUS, Ohio:

Ohio, the Gateway State. By Melville Chater. 525-591, *May 1932*

The **COLUMBUS** of the Pacific: Captain James Cook, Foremost British Navigator, Expanded the Great Sea to Correct Proportions and Won for Albion an Insular Empire by Peaceful Exploration and Scientific Study. By J. R. Hildebrand. 85-132, *Jan. 1927*

COMANCHE (Mountain), Bolivia:

Puya, the Pineapple's Andean Ancestor. By Mulford B. Foster. 463-480, *Oct. 1950*

COMANCHE INDIANS:

Big Bend: Jewel in the Texas Desert. By Nathaniel T. Kenney. Photos by James L. Stanfield. 104-133, *Jan. 1968*

COMBINES (Harvesting Machines). *See* Agriculture (The Revolution); Wheat Growing (North With the Wheat Cutters)

COMEBACK in the Caribbean–The Dominican Republic. By James Cerruti. Photos by Martin Rogers. 538-565, *Oct. 1977*

COMETS:

Halley's Comet '86. By Rick Gore. 758-785, *Dec. 1986*

What You Didn't See in Kohoutek. By Kenneth F. Weaver. 214-223, *Aug. 1974*

How to Catch a Passing Comet (Kohoutek). By Kenneth F. Weaver. 148-150, *Jan. 1974*

Giant Comet (Ikeya-Seki) Grazes the Sun. By Kenneth F. Weaver. Included: Halley's comet. 259-261, *Feb. 1966*

COMEX: Expedition Grant:

Underwater Salvage: *Witte Leeuw.* 566, *Oct. 1978*

Samana Cay in the Bahamas was the site of Columbus's New World landfall, according to a GEOGRAPHIC study. JAMES L. STANFIELD, NGS

COMING of Age the Apache Way. By Nita Quintero. Photos by Bill Hess. 262-271, *Feb. 1980*

The COMING of the Polynesians. By Kenneth P. Emory. 732-745, *Dec. 1974*

The COMING Revolution in Transportation. By Fredric C. Appel. Photos by Dean Conger. 301-341, *Sept. 1969*

COMMAGENE (Ancient Country):

Throne Above the Euphrates. By Theresa Goell. 390-405, *Mar. 1961*

COMMANDER Robert E. Peary: Did He Reach the Pole? By Wally Herbert. Introduction by the Editor. 387-413, *Sept. 1988*

COMMANDOS, Air. *See* U. S. First Air Commando Force

COMMERCE. *See* Trade

COMMON American Wild Flowers. Paintings by Mary E. Eaton. 584-609, *June 1916*

COMMON *Birds of Town and Country.* Contains four reprints from NGM. 1911; rev. ed. *1914*

COMMON Mushrooms of the United States. By Louis C. C. Krieger. Paintings by author. 387-439, *May 1920*

COMMON TERNS:

Friend of the Wind: The Common Tern. By Ian Nisbet. Photos by Hope Alexander. 234-247, *Aug. 1973*

COMMONWEALTH BAY, Antarctica:

Voyage to the Antarctic. By David Lewis. 544-562, *Apr. 1983*

COMMONWEALTH OF NATIONS. *See* former name, British Commonwealth of Nations

COMMUNAL LIVING:

Return to Changing China. By Audrey Topping. 801-833, *Dec. 1971*

Worker assembles a blowup of a silicon chip, the tiny circuit that has revolutionized electronics. CHARLES O'REAR, WEST LIGHT

Old Salem, Morning Star of Moravian Faith. By Rowe Findley. Photos by Robert W. Madden. 818-837, *Dec. 1970*

From Spear to Hoe on Groote Eylandt. By Howell Walker. 131-142, *Jan. 1953*

See also Amana Colonies; Hutterites; Kibbutzim; Old Believers; Padanaram; Saint Véran; Shakers; Tasadays

COMMUNICATION, Animal:

Editorial. By Wilbur E. Garrett. 409, *Apr. 1985*

Koko's Kitten. Text by Jane Vessels. Photos by Ronald H. Cohn. Included: Gorilla Foundation address. 110-113, *Jan. 1985*

Rare Look At Sperm and Blue Whales, The Unknown Giants. By Hal Whitehead. Photos by Flip Nicklin. 774-789, *Dec. 1984*

Western Grebes: The Birds That Walk on Water. By Gary L. Nuechterlein. NGS research grant. 624-637, *May 1982*

New Light on the Singing Whales. Introduction by Roger Payne. Photos by Flip Nicklin. NGS research grant. 463-477, *Apr. 1982*

Humpback Whales. NGS research grant. 2-25. I. The Gentle Giants. By Sylvia A. Earle. Photos by Al Giddings. 2-17; II. Their Mysterious Songs. By Roger Payne. Photos by Al Giddings. 18-25; III. Symphony of the Deep: "Songs of the Humpback Whale" (Sound sheet). 24-24B, *Jan. 1979*

Conversations With a Gorilla. By Francine Patterson. Photos by Ronald H. Cohn. NGS research grant. 438-465, *Oct. 1978*

COMMUNICATIONS:

Satellites That Serve Us. By Thomas Y. Canby. 281-335, *Sept. 1983*

Fiber Optics: Harnessing Light by a Thread. By Allen A. Boraiko. Photos by Fred Ward. 516-535, *Oct. 1979*

Telephone a Star: the Story of Communications Satellites. By Rowe Findley. 638-651, *May 1962*

DEW Line, Sentry of the Far North. By Howard La Fay. 128-146, *July 1958*

How Man-made Satellites Can Affect Our Lives. By Joseph Kaplan. 791-810, *Dec. 1957*

New Miracles of the Telephone Age. By Robert Leslie Conly. 87-120, *July 1954*

The Flying Telegraph (Homing Pigeon). By Joseph F. Spears. Official U. S. Army Signal Corps photos. 531-554, *Apr. 1947*

Miracle Men of the Telephone. By F. Barrows Colton. 273-316, *Mar. 1947*

Winged Words–New Weapon of War (Radio). By F. Barrows Colton. 663-692, *Nov. 1942*

Bonds Between the Americas. By Frederick Simpich. 785-808, *Dec. 1937*

The Miracle of Talking by Telephone. By F. Barrows Colton. 395-433, *Oct. 1937*

See also Cables; Radio; Telegraphy; Telephone; Television

COMMUNITY DEVELOPMENT PROGRAMS. *See* Bastar, India; *and* Peace Corps; YWCA

A COMMUNITY of Dwarfs (Insects). Photos by Willard R. Culver. 345-352, *Sept. 1946*

COMO, Lake, Italy:

Lombardy's Lakes, Blue Jewels in Italy's Crown. By Franc Shor. Photos by Joseph J. Scherschel. 58-99, *July 1968*

Frontier Cities of Italy. By Florence Craig Albrecht. 533-586, *June 1915*

Gems of the Italian Lakes. By Arthur Ellis Mayer. 943-956, *Aug. 1913*

COMORO ISLANDS, Indian Ocean:

Coelacanths, the Fish That Time Forgot. Article and photos by Hans Fricke. 824-838, *June 1988*

Crosscurrents Sweep the Indian Ocean. By Bart McDowell. Photos by Steve Raymer. 422-457, *Oct. 1981*

A COMPARISON of Norway and Sweden. 429-431, *Sept. 1905*

A COMPARISON of Our Unprotected with Our Protected Forests. 739-740, *Oct. 1908*

COMPASSES:

Charting a World at War. By William H. Nicholas. 617-640, *Nov. 1944*

The First Flight to the North Pole. By Richard Evelyn Byrd. 357-376, *Sept. 1926*

Most Curious Craft Afloat: The Compass in Navigation and the Work of the Non-Magnetic Yacht "Carnegie." By L. A. Bauer. 223-245, *Mar. 1910*

The Compass in Modern Navigation. By G. W. Littlehales. 266-272, *Sept. 1897*

See also Sun-Compass

COMPIÈGNE, France:

The Maid of France Rides By: Compiègne, Where Joan of Arc Fought Her Last Battle, Celebrates Her Fifth Centenary. By Inez Buffington Ryan. 607-616, *Nov. 1932*

"COMPLEAT ANGLER" Fishes for Fossils. By Imogene Powell. 251-258, *Aug. 1934*

The COMPLETED report of the Isthmian Canal Commission. 441, *Dec. 1901*

The COMPLETION of the cable between Canada and Australia. 410, *Nov. 1902*

COMPLETION of the La Boca Dock (Panama Canal). 84, *Mar. 1898*

COMPOST:

The Wild World of Compost. By Cecil E. Johnson. Photos by Bianca Lavies. 273-284, *Aug. 1980*

COMPUTED TOMOGRAPHY (CT):

Medicine's New Vision. By Howard Sochurek. Paintings by Davis Meltzer. Illustrations text by Peter Miller. 2-41, *Jan. 1987*

COMPUTER APPLICATIONS:

Tornado! By Peter Miller. Photos by Chris Johns. Included: Map of tornado activity, 1950-1985; diagram of tornado dynamics. 690-715, *June 1987*

Medicine's New Vision. By Howard Sochurek. Paintings by Davis Meltzer. Illustrations text by Peter Miller. 2-41, *Jan. 1987*

Editorial. By Wilbur E. Garrett. 701, *June 1986*

■■ *Computers: Those Amazing Machines.* By Catherine O'Neill. Juvenile. 104 pages. *1985*

Editorial. By Wilbur E. Garrett. 281, *Mar. 1984*

Satellites That Serve Us. By Thomas Y. Canby. 281-335. Included: A portfolio, Images of Earth. 316-325; Spacelab 1: *Columbia.* By Michael E. Long. 301-307, *Sept. 1983*

The Once and Future Universe. By Rick Gore. Photos by James A. Sugar. Paintings by Barron Storey. Picture text by David Jeffery. 704-749, *June 1983*

Heat Paints *Columbia*'s Portrait. By Cliff Tarpy. 650-653, *Nov. 1982*

Columbia's Astronauts' Own Story: Our Phenomenal First Flight. By John W. Young and Robert L. Crippen. Paintings by Ken Dallison. 478-503, *Oct. 1981*

Columbia's Landing Closes a Circle. By Tom Wolfe. 474-477, *Oct. 1981*

When the Space Shuttle Finally Flies. By Rick Gore. Photos by Jon Schneeberger. Paintings by Ken Dallison. 317-347, *Mar. 1981*

Eyes of Science. By Rick Gore. Photos by James P. Blair. 360-389, *Mar. 1978*

We're Doing Something About the Weather! By Walter Orr Roberts. 518-555, *Apr. 1972*

Computer Helps Scholars Re-create an Egyptian Temple. By Ray Winfield Smith. Photos by Emory Kristof. 634-655, *Nov. 1970*

The Coming Revolution in Transportation. By Fredric C. Appel. Photos by Dean Conger. 301-341, *Sept. 1969*

See also Landsat; Space Flights and Research

COMPUTER TECHNOLOGY:

■ Miraculous Machines. cover, *Apr. 1985*

■■ *Computers: Those Amazing Machines.* By Catherine O'Neill. Juvenile. 104 pages. *1985*

California's Silicon Valley. By Moira Johnston. Photos by Charles O'Rear. 459-477, *Oct. 1982*

The Chip: Electronic Mini-marvel. By Allen A. Boraiko. Photos by Charles O'Rear. 421-457, *Oct. 1982*

Editorial. By Wilbur E. Garrett. 419, *Oct. 1982*

Behold the Computer Revolution. By Peter T. White. Photos by Bruce Dale and Emory Kristof. 593-633, *Nov. 1970*

Crystals, Magical Servants of the Space Age. By Kenneth F. Weaver. Photos by James P. Blair. 278-296, *Aug. 1968*

In Turkey amid Cappadocia's surreal landscape, a rocky cone holds chapels made by early Christians.   MARC RIBOUD

CONCARNEAU, France:

Brittany: The Land of the Sardine. By Hugh M. Smith. 541-573, *June 1909*

CONCAS, VICTOR MARIA: *Author*

The Caravels of Columbus. 180-186, *Jan. 31, 1894*

A **CONCISE** Guide to National Parks. 111-123, *July 1979*

CONCORD, Massachusetts:

Thoreau, a Different Man. By William Howarth. Photos by Farrell Grehan. 349-387, *Mar. 1981*

History and Beauty Blend in a Concord Iris Garden. By Robert T. Cochran, Jr. Photos by M. Woodbridge Williams. 705-719, *May 1959*

Literary Landmarks of Massachusetts. By William H. Nicholas. Photos by B. Anthony Stewart and John E. Fletcher. 279-310, *Mar. 1950*

Winter Rambles in Thoreau's Country. By Herbert W. Gleason. 165-180, *Feb. 1920*

CONCORD, New Hampshire:

The Merrimack: River of Industry and Romance. By Albert W. Atwood. Photos by B. Anthony Stewart. 106-140, *Jan. 1951*

CONDITIONS in Cuba as Revealed by the Census. By Henry Gannett. 200-202, *Feb. 1909*

CONDITIONS in Liberia. By Roland P. Folkner, George Sale, and Emmett J. Scott. 729-741, *Sept. 1910*

CONDON, GENEAL: *Author*

Blossoms That Defy the Seasons (Flower Preservation). Photos by David S. Boyer. 420-427, *Sept. 1958*

CONDORS:

The Condor, Soaring Spirit of the Andes. By Jerry McGahan. Photos by Libby McGahan. 684-709, *May 1971*

The Eagle, King of Birds, and His Kin. By Alexander Wetmore. Paintings by Allan Brooks. 43-95, *July 1933*

CONDUITS. See Aqueducts

CONE DWELLINGS:

Keeping House in a Cappadocian Cave. By Jonathan S. Blair. 127-146, *July 1970*

Cappadocia: Turkey's Country of Cones. Photos by Marc Riboud. 122-146, *Jan. 1958*

The Turkish Republic Comes of Age. By Maynard Owen Williams. 581-616, *May 1945*

Where Early Christians Lived in Cones of Rock: A Journey to Cappadocia in Turkey Where Strange Volcanic Pinnacles Are Honeycombed With Hermit Cells and Monasteries. By John D. Whiting. 763-802, *Dec. 1939*

The Cone-Dwellers of Asia Minor: A Primitive People Who Live in Nature-Made Apartment Houses, Fashioned by Volcanic Violence and Trickling Streams. By J. R. Sitlington Sterrett. 281-331, *Apr. 1919*

Peculiar Caves of Asia Minor. By Elizabeth H. Brewer. 870-875, *Sept. 1911*

See also Beehive Homes

CONFERENCES. See International Geographic Conference; Pan-American Conferences; Peace Conference

CONFUCIANISM:

The Geography of China: The Influence of Physical Environment on the History and Character of the Chinese People. By Frank Johnson Goodnow. 651-664, *June 1927*

The Descendants of Confucius. By Maynard Owen Williams. 253-265, *Sept. 1919*

Shantung–China's Holy Land. By Charles K. Edmunds. 231-252, *Sept. 1919*

Curious and Characteristic Customs of China. By Kenneth F. Junor. 791-806, *Sept. 1910*

China: Her History and Development. By John Barrett. 209-218, *June 1901*

CONGER, CLEMENT E.:
Author-Photographer

Portugal Is Different. 583-622, *Nov. 1948*

CONGER, DEAN:

Nomination Page. *Sept. 1978*

Nomination Page. In the Philippines. *Aug. 1971*

Nomination Page. In Thailand. *June 1967*

Nomination Page. In Mongolia. *Feb. 1966*

Nomination Page. In Mongolia. *Feb. 1962*

Nomination Page. *Sept. 1961*

Author-Photographer

Five Times to Yakutsk. 256-269, *Aug. 1977*

Siberia: Russia's Frozen Frontier. 297-345, *Mar. 1967*

Everything occupies its own niche in the African rain forest's complex web of life, stretching from the lofty crowns of the tallest trees to the gloomy green at ground level. PAINTING BY BARRON STOREY

The **CONQUEST** of the Sahara by the Automobile. 87-93, *Jan. 1924*

CONQUEST of the Summit: The Forgotten Face of Everest. By James D. Morrissey. 79-89, *July 1984*

CONQUISTADORES:

Following Cortés: Path to Conquest. By S. Jeffrey K. Wilkerson. Photos by Guillermo Aldana E. Paintings by Ned Seidler and Rosalie Seidler. 420-459, *Oct. 1984*

CONRAD, ANNA:

Avalanche! By David Cupp. 280-305. II. "I'm OK, I'm Alive!" Photos by Lanny Johnson and Andre Benier. Note: Anna Conrad was rescued five days after the Alpine Meadows, California, avalanche. 282-289, *Sept. 1982*

CONRAD, CHARLES, Jr.:

Skylab, Outpost on the Frontier of Space. By Thomas Y. Canby. Photos by the nine mission astronauts. 441-469, *Oct. 1974*

CONRAD, JOSEPH: *Author*

Geography and Some Explorers. 239-274, *Mar. 1924*

CONSERVATION:

Earth '88: Will We Mend Our Earth? Introduction by Gilbert M. Grosvenor. 766-771, *Dec. 1988*

Quietly Conserving Nature. By Noel Grove. Photos by Stephen J. Kraseman. 818-845, *Dec. 1988*

Prairie Preservation: Good News, Bad News. Geographica. *Dec. 1988*

The Mighty Himalaya: A Fragile Heritage. By Barry C. Bishop. Photos by William Thompson. 624-631, *Nov. 1988*

Heavy Hands on the Land. By Larry Kohl. Photos by William Thompson and Galen Rowell. 633-651, *Nov. 1988*

Citizens Band Together to Save Their Environment. Geographica. *Nov. 1988*

President's Page. By Gilbert M. Grosvenor. *Feb. 1988*

President's Page. By Gilbert M. Grosvenor. *Nov. 1986*

Editorial. By Wilbur E. Garrett. 283, *Mar. 1986*

Do We Treat Our Soil Like Dirt? By Boyd Gibbons. Photos by Steven C. Wilson. 350-389, *Sept. 1984*

Chesapeake Bay Foundation. President's Page. By Gilbert M. Grosvenor. *July 1984*

■■ *Our Threatened Inheritance: Natural Treasures of the United States.* By Ron Fisher. Photos by James P. Blair. 400 pages. *1984*

A Walk and Ride on the Wild Side: Tasmania. By Carolyn Bennett Patterson. Photos by David Hiser and Melinda Berge. 676-693, *May 1983*

Along the Great Divide. By Mike Edwards. Photos by Nicholas deVore III. 483-515, *Oct. 1979*

CONTINENTAL DRIFT. *See* Plate Tectonics

CONTINENTAL SHELF RESEARCH:

Down the Cayman Wall. By Eugenie Clark. Included: Zones of Life. NGS research grant. 712-731, *Nov. 1988*

The Continental Shelf: Man's New Frontier. By Luis Marden. Photos by Ira Block. 495-531, *Apr. 1978*

The Deepest Days. By Robert Sténuit. NGS research grant. 534-547, *Apr. 1965*

Outpost Under the Ocean. By Edwin A. Link. Photos by Bates Littlehales. NGS research grant. 530-533, *Apr. 1965*

Tomorrow on the Deep Frontier. By Edwin A. Link. NGS research grant. 778-801, *June 1964*

See also Conshelf Bases

A **CONTINENT'S** Living Treasure. Paintings by Ned Seidler. 164-167, *Feb. 1972*

CONTRARY New Hampshire. By Robert Booth. Photos by Sandy Felsenthal. 770-799, *Dec. 1982*

CONTRAS (Nicaraguan Counterrevolutionaries):

Nicaragua: Nation in Conflict. By Mike Edwards. Photos by James Nachtwey. 776-811, *Dec. 1985*

CONTROLLING Sand Dunes in the United States and Europe. By A. S. Hitchcock. 43-47, *Jan. 1904*

CONVERSATIONS With a Gorilla. By Francine Patterson. Photos by Ronald H. Cohn. NGS research grant. 438-465, *Oct. 1978*

The **CONVERSION** of Old Newspapers and Candle Ends into Fuel. 568-570, *June 1917*

CONVOYS to Victory. By Harvey Klemmer. 193-216, *Feb. 1943*

CONWAY, WILLIAM G.:

Nomination Page. At the New York Zoological Park. *Oct. 1960*

Author

Argentina Protects Its Wildlife Treasures. Photos by Des and Jen Bartlett. 290-297, *Mar. 1976*

In Quest of the Rarest Flamingo. Photos by Bates Littlehales. 91-105, *July 1961*

COOBER PEDY, South Australia:

Coober Pedy: Opal Capital of Australia's Outback. By Kenny Moore. Photos by Penny Tweedie. 560-571, *Oct. 1976*

COOK, DAVID W.:

Nomination Page. *Jan. 1969*

COOK, FREDERICK A.:

Commander Robert E. Peary: Did He Reach the Pole? By Wally Herbert. Introduction by the Editor. 387-413, *Sept. 1988*

Committee members appointed by the

Passing instruments laid aside after the parade and band concert she missed, a young girl arrives late for a church service on one of the Cook Islands. WILLIAM ALBERT ALLARD

University of Copenhagen to examine Cook's claims of having reached the North Pole. 86-87, *Jan. 1910*

Honors to Peary. Address by Frederick A. Cook. 49-60, *Jan. 1907*

Portrait. 78, *Feb. 1902*

Author

The North Pole. 921-922, *Nov. 1909*

The Discovery of the Pole: First Report by Dr. Frederick A. Cook, Sept. 1, 1909. 892-916, *Oct. 1909*

COOK, JAMES:

Voyages to Paradise: Exploring in the Wake of Captain Cook. By William R. Gray. Photos by Gordon W. Gahan. 215 pages. *1981*

Captain Cook: The Man Who Mapped the Pacific. By Alan Villiers. Photos by Gordon W. Gahan. 297-349, *Sept. 1971*

Nomination Page. *Sept. 1971*

The British Way. By Sir Evelyn Wrench. 421-541, *Apr. 1949*

Revealing Earth's Mightiest Ocean (Pacific). By Albert W. Atwood. 291-306, *Sept. 1943*

The Columbus of the Pacific: Captain James Cook, Foremost British Navigator, Expanded the Great Sea to Correct Proportions and Won for Albion an Insular Empire by Peaceful Exploration and Scientific Study. By J. R. Hildebrand. 85-132, *Jan. 1927*

COOK, ORATOR FULLER:

Awarded Jane M. Smith Life Membership. 342, *Apr. 1920*

Author

Staircase Farms of the Ancients: Astounding Farming Skill of Ancient Peruvians, Who Were Among the Most Industrious and Highly Organized People in History. 474-534, *May 1916*

COOK ISLANDS, South Pacific Ocean:

Blue Horizons: Paradise Isles of the Pacific. Contents: Cook Islands, Fiji,

French Polynesia, Hawaii, Samoa Islands, and Tonga. 199 pages. *1985*

Isles of the South Pacific. By Maurice Shadbolt and Olaf Ruhen. 211 pages. *1968*

New Zealand's Cook Islands: Paradise in Search of a Future. By Maurice Shadbolt. Photos by William Albert Allard. 203-231, *Aug. 1967*

The Dream Ship: The Story of a Voyage of Adventure More Than Half Around the World in a 47-foot Lifeboat. By Ralph Stock. 1-52, *Jan. 1921*

See also Tongareva

COOKE, HEREWARD LESTER, Jr.:

Author

The Louvre, France's Palace of the Arts. 796-831, *June 1971*

Early America Through the Eyes of Her Native Artists. 356-389, *Sept. 1962*

Great Masters of a Brave Era in Art (Impressionist). 661-697, *May 1961*

COOKE, HOPE:

Wedding of Two Worlds. By Lee E. Battaglia. 708-727, *Nov. 1963*

Nomination Page. *Oct. 1963*

COOKE, JAN LESLIE: *Author*

The Mysterious Undersea World. Juvenile. 104 pages. *1980*

COOKE, RICHARD ALEXANDER, III:

Photographer

America's Ancient Cities. By Gene S. Stuart. Art by H. Tom Hall. 199 pages. *1988*

Molokai—Forgotten Hawaii. By Ethel A. Starbird. 188-219, *Aug. 1981*

COOKE, WELLS W.: *Author*

Saving the Ducks and Geese. 361-380, *Mar. 1913*

Our Greatest Travelers: Birds that Fly from Pole to Pole and Shun the Darkness: Birds that Make 2,500 Miles in a Single Flight. 346-365, *Apr. 1911*

COOKIES:

Christmas in Cookie Tree Land. By Louise Parker La Gorce. Photos by B. Anthony Stewart. 844-851, *Dec. 1955*

COOLIDGE, CALVIN:

The Living White House. By Lonnelle Aikman. 593-643, *Nov. 1966*

Profiles of the Presidents: IV. America Enters the Modern Era. By Frank Freidel. 537-577, *Oct. 1965*

Inside the White House. By Lonnelle Aikman. Photos by B. Anthony Stewart and Thomas Nebbia. 3-43, *Jan. 1961*

Mr. Coolidge Becomes a Member of The Society's Board of Trustees. 750, *June 1929*

President Coolidge Bestows Lindbergh Award: The National Geographic Society's Hubbard Medal Is Presented to Aviator Before the Most Notable Gathering in the History of Washington. Address by President Coolidge. 132-140, *Jan. 1928*

Commander Byrd Receives the Hubbard Gold Medal: The First Explorer to Reach the North Pole by Air Receives Coveted Honor at Brilliant National Geographic Society Reception. Address by President Coolidge. 377-388, *Sept. 1926*

Author

Massachusetts and Its Position in the Life of the Nation. 337-352, *Apr. 1923*

COOLIDGE (Liner):

Wreck of the *Coolidge.* Text and photos by David Doubilet. 458-467, *Apr. 1988*

COONEY, JOHN:

Nomination Page. At the Cleveland Museum of Art. *Mar. 1977*

COOPER, MARTHA: *Photographer*

The Day the World Ended at Kourion. By David Soren. NGS research grant. 30-53, *July 1988*

Pollen: Breath of Life and Sneezes. By Cathy Newman. 490-521, *Oct. 1984*

Unearthing the Oldest Known Maya. By Norman Hammond. Photos by Lowell Georgia and Martha Cooper. 126-140, *July 1982*

COOPER, MERIAN C.: *Author*

Two Fighting Tribes of the Sudan. Photos by Ernest B. Schoedsack. 465-486, *Oct. 1929*

The Warfare of the Jungle Folk: Campaigning Against Tigers, Elephants, and Other Wild Animals in Northern Siam. Photos by Ernest B. Schoedsack. 233-268, *Feb. 1928*

COOPER, PETER:

Peter Cooper and Submarine Telegraphy. 108-110, *Mar. 1896*

COOPER RIVER WATER PROJECT:

South Carolina Rediscovered. By Herbert Ravenel Sass. Photos by Robert F. Sisson. 281-321, *Mar. 1953*

COOPERATIVE FARMS. *See* Amana Colonies; China, People's Republic

A Copenhagen store draped with nearly a thousand overcoats in 1936 drew such a crowd that all were sold. ACME

of (Return to Changing China); Collective Farms; Groote Eylandt (From Spear to Hoe); Hutterites; Kibbutzim; Old Believers; Old Salem; Padanaram; Saint Véran

COOPER'S HAWK:

Can the Cooper's Hawk Survive? By Noel Snyder. Photos by author and Helen Snyder. NGS research grant. 433-442, *Mar. 1974*

COOTIES and Courage. By Herbert Corey. 495-509, *June 1918*

COPENHAGEN, Denmark:

The Magic World of Hans Christian Andersen. By Harvey Arden. Photos by Sisse Brimberg. 825-849, *Dec. 1979*

Denmark, Field of the Danes. By William Graves. Photos by Thomas Nebbia. 245-275, *Feb. 1974*

Friendly Flight to Northern Europe. By Lyndon B. Johnson. Photos by Volkmar Wentzel. 268-293, *Feb. 1964*

Copenhagen, Wedded to the Sea. By Stuart E. Jones. Photos by Gilbert M. Grosvenor. 45-79, *Jan. 1963*

Under Canvas in the Atomic Age. By Alan Villiers. 49-84, *July 1955*

Thumbs Up Round the North Sea's Rim. By Frances James. Photos by Erica Koch. 685-704, *May 1952*

"Around the World in Eighty Days." By Newman Bumstead. 705-750, *Dec. 1951*

Baltic Cruise of the *Caribbee.* By Carleton Mitchell. 605-646, *Nov. 1950*

2,000 Miles Through Europe's Oldest Kingdom. By Isobel Wylie Hutchison. Photos by Maynard Owen Williams. 141-180, *Feb. 1949*

Royal Copenhagen, Capital of a Farming Kingdom: A Fifth of Denmark's Thrifty Population Resides in a Metropolis Famous for Its Porcelains, Its

Silver, and Its Lace. By J. R. Hildebrand. 217-250, *Feb. 1932*

Denmark and the Danes. By Maurice Francis Egan. 115-164, *Aug. 1922*

COPERNICUS, NICOLAUS:

▪ *National Geographic Picture Atlas of Our Universe.* By Roy A. Gallant. 284 pages. 1980; rev. ed. *1986*

▪ *The Amazing Universe.* By Herbert Friedman. Contents: Revelations and theories of astronomy. 199 pages. *1975*

Pioneers in Man's Search for the Universe. Paintings by Jean-Leon Huens. Text by Thomas Y. Canby. 627-633, *May 1974*

COPIAPÓ, Chile:

A Longitudinal Journey Through Chile. By Harriet Chalmers Adams. 219-273, *Sept. 1922*

COPPER:

Alaska, the Big Land. By W. Robert Moore. 776-807, *June 1956*

From Tucson to Tombstone. By Mason Sutherland. 343-384, *Sept. 1953*

Work-hard, Play-hard Michigan. By Andrew H. Brown. Included: Calumet and Hecla Consolidated Copper mines. 279-320, *Mar. 1952*

White Magic in the Belgian Congo. By W. Robert Moore. Included: Copper mines. 321-362, *Mar. 1952*

"Rockhounds" Uncover Earth's Mineral Beauty. By George S. Switzer. Included: Ontonagon copper boulder. 631-660, *Nov. 1951*

Ancient Mesopotamia: A Light That Did Not Fail. By E. A. Speiser. Paintings by H. M. Herget. 41-105, *Jan. 1951*

Montana, Shining Mountain Treasureland. By Leo A. Borah. Included: Anaconda Copper Mining Company. 693-736, *June 1950*

The **COPPER** River Delta, Alaska. By E. D. Preston. 29-31, *Jan. 1900*

COPRA:

Clove-scented Zanzibar. By W. Robert Moore. 261-278, *Feb. 1952*

Copra-ship Voyage to Fiji's Outlying Islands. By Marjory C. Thomas. 121-140, *July 1950*

Shores and Sails in the South Seas. By Charles Allmon. 73-104, *Jan. 1950*

Pacific Wards of Uncle Sam. By W. Robert Moore. 73-104, *July 1948*

The Samoan Cocoanut. By A. W. Greely. 12-24, *Jan. 1898*

The **COPYRIGHT** of a Map or Chart. By William Alexander Miller. 437-443, *Dec. 1902*

CORA INDIANS:

Mesa del Nayar's Strange Holy Week. By Guillermo Aldana E. 780-795, *June 1971*

CORACLES:

Wales, Land of Bards. By Alan Villiers. Photos by Thomas Nebbia. 727-769, *June 1965*

CORALS AND CORAL REEFS:

Ghosts of War in the South Pacific. By

Peter Benchley. Photos by David Doubilet. 424-457, *Apr. 1988*

Strange World of Palau's Salt Lakes. By William M. Hamner. Photos by David Doubilet. 264-282, *Feb. 1982*

Australia's Great Barrier Reef. 630-663. I. A Marine Park Is Born. By Soames Summerhays. Photos by Ron and Valerie Taylor. 630-635; II. Paradise Beneath the Sea. By Ron and Valerie Taylor. 636-663, *May 1981*

Precious Corals, Hawaii's Deep-sea Jewels. By Richard W. Grigg. 719-732, *May 1979*

Dazzling Corals of Palau. By Thomas O'Neill. Photos by Douglas Faulkner. 136-150, *July 1978*

■■ *The Ocean Realm.* 199 pages. *1978*

Life Springs From Death in Truk Lagoon. By Sylvia A. Earle. Photos by Al Giddings. Included: From Graveyard to Garden. 578-613, *May 1976*

Rainbow World Beneath the Red Sea. Photos by David Doubilet. 344-365, *Sept. 1975*

The Strangest Sea (Red Sea). By Eugenie Clark. Photos by David Doubilet. 338-343, *Sept. 1975*

Life Cycle of a Coral. By Robert F. Sisson. 780-793, *June 1973*

Probing the Deep Reefs' Hidden Realm. By Walter A. Starck II and Jo D. Starck. NGS research grant. 867-886, *Dec. 1972*

Tektite II: Part One. Science's Window on the Sea. By John G. VanDerwalker. Photos by Bates Littlehales. 256-289, *Aug. 1971*

Starfish Threaten Pacific Reefs. By James A. Sugar. 340-353, *Mar. 1970*

Photographing the Night Creatures of Alligator Reef. By Robert E. Schroeder. Photos by author and Walter A. Starck II. NGS research grant. 128-154, *Jan. 1964*

Fluorescent Gems from Davy Jones's Locker. By Paul A. Zahl. 260-271, *Aug. 1963*

Unsung Beauties of Hawaii's Coral Reefs (Nudibranchs). By Paul A. Zahl. 510-525, *Oct. 1959*

Fish Men Explore a New World Undersea. By Jacques-Yves Cousteau. 431-472, *Oct. 1952*

Man-of-war Fleet Attacks Bimini. By Paul A. Zahl. 185-212, *Feb. 1952*

Bright Flashes from Pacific Corals. Photos by Walter H. Chute. 349-372, *Mar. 1941*

Net Results from Oceania: Collecting Aquarium Specimens in Tropical Pacific Waters. By Walter H. Chute. 347-372, *Mar. 1941*

Where Nature Runs Riot: On Australia's Great Barrier Reef Marine Animals Grow to Unusual Size, Develop Strange Weapons of Attack and Defense, and Acquire Brilliant Colors. By Theodore Cleveland Roughley. 823-850, *June 1940*

On the Bottom of a South Sea Pearl Lagoon. By Roy Waldo Miner. Paintings by Else Bostelmann. 365-390, *Sept. 1938*

Coral Castle Builders of Tropic Seas. By Roy Waldo Miner. Paintings by Else Bostelmann. 703-728, *June 1934*

The Great Barrier Reef and Its Isles: The Wonder and Mystery of Australia's World-Famous Geographical Feature. By Charles Barrett. 355-384, *Sept. 1930*

The First Autochromes from the Ocean Bottom: Marine Life in Its Natural Habitat Along the Florida Keys Is Successfully Photographed in Colors. Photos by William Harding Longley and Charles Martin. 56-60, *Jan. 1927*

Life on a Coral Reef: The Fertility and Mystery of the Sea Studied Beneath the Waters Surrounding Dry Tortugas. By William Harding Longley. 61-83, *Jan. 1927*

See also Alligator Reef; Buck Island Reef National Monument; Great Barrier Reef, Australia; John Pennekamp Coral Reef State Park; Key Largo Coral Reef; Sha'ab Rūmi (Roman Reef); *and* Aqaba, Gulf of; Bermuda; Fiji Islands; Tuamotu Archipelago

CORBY, BERNARD: *Photographer*

Bluebirds on the Wing in Color. Photos by Bernard Corby and Hance Roy Ivor. 527-530, *Apr. 1954*

CORCA DHUIBHNE. *See* Dingle Peninsula, Ireland

CORCORAN GALLERY OF ART, Washington, D. C.:

Odyssey: The Art of Photography at National Geographic. By Jane Livingston. Note: The exhibition of photographs from National Geographic that will be seen in museums around the world was organized by the Corcoran Gallery. 322-351, *Sept. 1988*

Exhibit of National Geographic photographs. Editorial. By Wilbur E. Garrett. 1, *July 1988*

American Processional: History on Canvas. By John and Blanche Leeper. 173-212, *Feb. 1951*

CORCOVADO NATIONAL PARK, Costa Rica:

Teeming Life of a Rain Forest. By Carol and David Hughes. 49-65, *Jan. 1983*

CORDILLERA ORIENTAL, Andes Mountains. *See* Oriental, Cordillera

CORDILLERA VILCABAMBA, Andes Mountains, Peru. *See* Vilcabamba, Cordillera

CÓRDOBA, Spain:

Andalusia, the Spirit of Spain. By Howard La Fay. Photos by Joseph J. Scherschel. 833-857, *June 1975*

Holy Week and the Fair in Sevilla. By Luis Marden. 499-530, *Apr. 1951*

COREY, CAROL: *Author*

A Day with Our Boys in the Geographic Wards. 69-80, *July 1918*

Plain Tales from the Trenches: As Told Over the Tea Table in Blighty–A Soldier's "Home" in Paris. 300-312, *Mar. 1918*

From the Trenches to Versailles. 535-550, *Nov.-Dec. 1917*

COREY, HERBERT: *Author*

Down Devon Lanes. 529-568, *May 1929*

Among the Zapotecs of Mexico: A Visit to the Indians of Oaxaca, Home State of the Republic's Great Liberator, Juárez, and Its Most Famous Ruler, Diaz. 501-553, *May 1927*

The Green Mountain State (Vermont). 333-369, *Mar. 1927*

London from a Bus Top. 551-596, *May 1926*

A Char-à-Bancs in Cornwall. 653-694, *Dec. 1924*

The Isthmus of Tehuantepec (Mexico). 549-579, *May 1924*

Along the Old Spanish Road in Mexico: Life Among the People of Nayarit and Jalisco, Two of the Richest States of the Southern Republic. 225-281, *Mar. 1923*

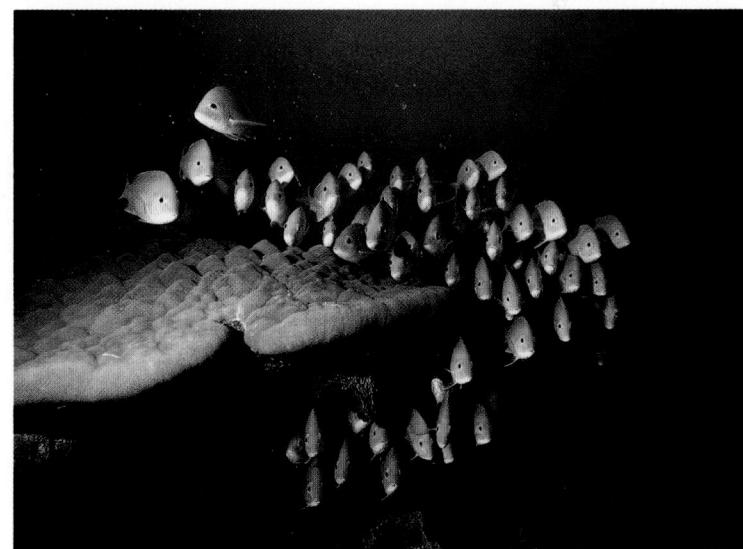

By day yellow-banded hussars find safety in numbers near a coral head on Australia's Great Barrier Reef; by night they will disperse to hunt. RON AND VALERIE TAYLOR

Corn-ear feeder, spelling out the state's name, draws pigeons—and neighbors' consternation—to Vernon Schall's yard in Des Moines, Iowa.   DANA DOWNIE

Queen Elizabeth II's June 1953 coronation parade passes London's Trafalgar Square on its way to Buckingham Palace. © UNITED PRESS

CORONATIONS:

Bhutan Crowns a New Dragon King. Picture story by John Scofield. 546-571, *Oct. 1974*

Coronations a World Apart. By the Editor. 299, *Mar. 1968*

Iran's Shah Crowns Himself and His Empress. By Franc Shor. Photos by James L. Stanfield and Winfield Parks. 301-321, *Mar. 1968*

South Seas' Tonga Hails a King (Taufa'ahau Tupou IV). By Melville Bell Grosvenor. Photos by Edwin Stuart Grosvenor. 322-343, *Mar. 1968*

Coronation in Katmandu (Mahendra, King of Nepal). By E. Thomas Gilliard. Photos by Marc Riboud. 139-152, *July 1957*

In the London of the New Queen (Elizabeth II). By H. V. Morton. 291-342, *Sept. 1953*

Silkworms in England Spin for the Queen. By John E. H. Nolan. 689-704, *May 1953*

Along London's Coronation Route. By Maynard Owen Williams. 609-632, *May 1937*

Present Day Scenes in the World's Oldest Empire (Ethiopia). Photos by W. Robert Moore. 691-722, *June 1931*

Coronation Days in Addis Ababa. By W. Robert Moore. 738-746, *June 1931*

The Coronation of His Majesty King Maha-Vajiravudh of Siam. By Lea Febiger. 389-416, *Apr. 1912*

CORPUS CHRISTI CELEBRATION:

Peru's Pilgrimage to the Sky. By Robert Randall. Photos by Loren McIntyre and Ira Block. 60-69, *July 1982*

Lanzarote, the Strangest Canary. By Stephanie Dinkins. 117-139, *Jan. 1969*

Spain's "Fortunate Isles," the Canaries. By Jean and Franc Shor. 485-522, *Apr. 1955*

In the Canary Islands, Where Streets Are Carpeted With Flowers. Photos by Wilhelm Tobien. 615-622, *May 1930*

The **CORRECT** Display of the Stars and Stripes. By Byron McCandless and Gilbert Grosvenor. 404-413, *Oct. 1917*

CORREGIDOR (Island), Philippines:

Saving the Corregidor World War II Memorial. Geographica. *Oct. 1988*

Corregidor Revisited. By William Graves. Photos by Steve McCurry. 118-131, *July 1986*

CORSICA (Island), Mediterranean Sea:

Sunny Corsica: French Morsel in the Mediterranean. By Robert Cairns. Photos by Joseph J. Scherschel. 401-423, *Sept. 1973*

The Coasts of Corsica: Impressions of a Winter's Stay in the Island Birthplace of Napoleon. By Maynard Owen Williams. Included: Peasant Home in Corsica, pictorial supplement. 221-312, *Sept. 1923*

CORTÉS, HERNÁN:

Following Cortés: Path to Conquest. By S. Jeffrey K. Wilkerson. Photos by Guillermo Aldana E. Paintings by Ned Seidler and Rosalie Seidler. 420-459, *Oct. 1984*

On the Cortés Trail. By Luis Marden. 335-375, *Sept. 1940*

CORTHELL, ELMER L.: *Author*

The Delta of the Mississippi River. 351-354, *Dec. 1897*

The Tehuantepec Ship Railway. 64-72, *Feb. 1896*

COS (Island), Aegean Sea. *See* Kos

COSMIC RAYS:

Trailing Cosmic Rays in Canada's North. By Martin A. Pomerantz. NGS research grant. 99-115, *Jan. 1953*

New Frontier in the Sky. By F. Barrows Colton. 379-408, *Sept. 1946*

Series of flights under auspices of National Geographic Society, U. S. Army Air Forces, and Bartol Research Foundation of the Franklin Institute. 387, 388, *Sept. 1946*

Ballooning in the Stratosphere: Two Balloon Ascents to Ten-Mile Altitudes Presage New Mode of Aërial Travel. By Auguste Piccard. 353-384, *Mar. 1933*

COSMOLOGY:

The Once and Future Universe. By Rick Gore. Photos by James A. Sugar. Paintings by Barron Storey. Picture text by David Jeffery. 704-749, *June 1983*

COSMONAUTS:

Are the Soviets Ahead in Space? By Thomas Y. Canby. 420-459, *Oct. 1986*

Apollo-Soyuz: Handclasp in Space. By Thomas Y. Canby. Contents: The rendezvous in space of cosmonauts Aleksey A. Leonov and Valeriy Kubasov with astronauts Thomas P. Stafford, Vance D. Brand, and Donald K. "Deke" Slayton. 183-187, *Feb. 1976*

COSMOPOLITAN Shanghai, Key Seaport of China. By W. Robert Moore. 311-335, *Sept. 1932*

COSTA, GUIDO: *Author*

The Island of Sardinia and Its People: Traces of Many Civilizations to be Found in the Speech, Customs, and Costumes of This Picturesque Land. 1-75, *Jan. 1923*

COSTA DEL SOL, Spain:

Andalusia, the Spirit of Spain. By Howard La Fay. Photos by Joseph J. Scherschel. 833-857, *June 1975*

A leading Costa Rican export, bananas make this coastal plantation worker smile.

JOHN MASON, COMM PHOTO INTERNATIONAL

COSTA RICA:

Editorial. By Wilbur E. Garrett. 695, *June 1988*

Teeming Life of a Rain Forest. By Carol and David Hughes. 49-65, *Jan. 1983*

■ Rain Forest. 824, *Dec. 1982*

Costa Rica Steers the Middle Course. By Kent Britt. 32-57, *July 1981*

Troubled Times for Central America. By Wilbur E. Garrett, Editor. 58-61, *July 1981*

Nature's Living, Jumping Jewels. By Paul A. Zahl. 130-146, *July 1973*

Costa Rica, Free of the Volcano's Veil. By Robert de Roos. 125-152, *July 1965*

Land of the Painted Oxcarts. By Luis Marden. 409-456, *Oct. 1946*

Costa Rica, Land of the Banana. By Paul B. Popenoe. 201-220, *Feb. 1922*

Shattered Capitals of Central America. By Herbert J. Spinden. 185-212, *Sept. 1919*

The Countries of the Caribbean. By William Joseph Showalter. 227-250, *Feb. 1913*

Where Our Bananas Come From. By Edwin R. Fraser. 713-730, *July 1912*

Costa Rica–Vulcan's Smithy. By H. Pittier. 494-525, *June 1910*

Methods of Obtaining Salt in Costa Rica. 28-34, *Jan. 1908*

Notes on Central America. 272-279, *Apr. 1907*

Location of the Boundary Between Nicaragua and Costa Rica. By Arthur P. Davis. 22-28, *Jan. 1901*

Costa Rica. By Ricardo Villafranca. 143-151, *May 1897*

See also Ostional Beach

COSTUME Pageants in the French Pyrenees. Photos by W. Robert Moore. 435-450, *Oct. 1937*

COSTUMES of Czechoslovakia. Photos by Hans Hildenbrand. 725-740, *June 1927*

COTE D'OR (Balloon):

The Fantastic Flight of *Cote d'Or.* By Cynthia Shields. 789-793, *Dec. 1983*

COTIDAL Lines for the World. By R. A. Harris. 303-309, *June 1906*

COTSWOLD HILLS, England:

The Cotswolds, "Noicest Parrt o'England." By James Cerruti. Photos by Adam Woolfitt. 846-869, *June 1974*

The Thames Mirrors England's Varied Life. By Willard Price. Photos by Robert F. Sisson. 45-93, *July 1958*

By Cotswold Lanes to Wold's End. By Melville Bell Grosvenor. 615-654, *May 1948*

COTT, HUGH B.: *Author*

Wonder Island of the Amazon Delta: On Marajó Cowboys Ride Oxen, Tree-dwelling Animals Throng Dense Forests, While Strange Fishes and Birds Help Make a Zoologist's Paradise. 635-670, *Nov. 1938*

COTTAGE INDUSTRIES:

An Ozark Family Carves a Living and a Way of Life. Picture story by Bruce Dale. 124-133, *July 1975*

Mountain Voices, Mountain Days. By

Bryan Hodgson. Photos by Linda Bartlett. 118-146, *July 1972*

Domesticating the Wild and Woolly Musk Ox. By John J. Teal, Jr. Photos by Robert W. Madden. 862-879, *June 1970*

Isles on the Edge of the Sea: Scotland's Outer Hebrides. By Kenneth MacLeish. Photos by Thomas Nebbia. 676-711, *May 1970*

From Barra to Butt in the Hebrides. By Isobel Wylie Hutchison. 559-580, *Oct. 1954*

COTTER, MARGARET: *Author*

Red Cross Girl Overseas. 745-768, *Dec. 1944*

COTTON:

Alabama, Dixie to a Different Tune. By Howard LaFay. Photos by Dick Durrance II. 534-569, *Oct. 1975*

The Greener Fields of Georgia. By Howell Walker. Photos by author and B. Anthony Stewart. 287-330, *Mar. 1954*

South Carolina Rediscovered. By Herbert Ravenel Sass. Photos by Robert F. Sisson. 281-321, *Mar. 1953*

The Merrimack: River of Industry and Romance. By Albert W. Atwood. Photos by B. Anthony Stewart. 106-140, *Jan. 1951*

Dixie Spins the Wheel of Industry. By William H. Nicholas. Photos by J. Baylor Roberts. 281-324, *Mar. 1949*

Cotton: Foremost Fiber of the World. By J. R. Hildebrand. Included: Golden Fleece of Dixie. Photos by Willard R. Culver. 137-192, *Feb. 1941*

Massachusetts–Beehive of Business. By William Joseph Showalter. 203-245, *Mar. 1920*

The Modern Alchemist (Work of Department of Agriculture). By James Wilson. 781-795, *Dec. 1907*

Paper From Cotton Stalks. 425, *July 1906*

Our Plant Immigrants. By David Fairchild. 179-201, *Apr. 1906*

Cotton and the Chinese Boycott (From an Address by President Roosevelt to the Citizens of Atlanta, October 20, 1905). 516-517, *Nov. 1905*

The Farmers of the United States. 39-46, *Jan. 1905*

Cotton for England. 39, *Jan. 1904*

COTTONSEED OIL:

Cotton: Foremost Fiber of the World. By J. R. Hildebrand. 137-192, *Feb. 1941*

COTTRELL, ERNEST J.: *Photographer*

Skyway Below the Clouds. By Carl R. Markwith. 85-108, *July 1949*

COUGARS. *See* Mountain Lions

COULSON, COTTON: *Photographer*

Switzerland: The Clockwork Country. By John J. Putman. 96-127, *Jan. 1986*

Home to Kansas. By Cliff Tarpy. 352-383, *Sept. 1985*

Surviving, Italian Style. By William S. Ellis. 185-209, *Feb. 1984*

Two Berlins–A Generation Apart. By Priit J. Vesilind. 2-51, *Jan. 1982*

*In her multihued sari, an Indian girl be-
came a compelling subject for an Autochrome portrait.* GERVAIS COURTELLEMONT

Icelandic girl. *Feb. 1987*
Computer image of tumor. *Jan. 1987*
Titanic wreckage and robot submersible. *Dec. 1986*
Columbus discovering the New World (woodcut). *Nov. 1986*
Cosmonaut outside Salyut 7 station. *Oct. 1986*
Arctic explorer Brent Boddy, with ice-encrusted face. *Sept. 1986*
Covered wagons and pioneers, Oregon Trail. *Aug. 1986*
Statue of Liberty. *July 1986*
Snow leopard. *June 1986*
Lioness and cub. *May 1986*
Maya fuchsite funerary mask. *Apr. 1986*
Giant panda peering from tent. *Mar. 1986*
Ndebele woman wearing neck rings, South Africa. *Feb. 1986*
"Bronc to Breakfast," painting by Charles M. Russell. *Jan. 1986*
Titanic starboard rail wreckage. *Dec. 1985*
Hologram of fossil skull. *Nov. 1985*
Painted hand of Yemeni woman. *Oct. 1985*
Chinese couple holding pigs. *Sept. 1985*
Australian cowgirl (jilleroo). *Aug. 1985*
Diver holding Basque galleon timber. *July 1985*
Afghan refugee girl. *June 1985*
Vietnam Veterans Memorial, Washington, D. C. *May 1985*
Sitar player, Pakistan. *Apr. 1985*
Toxic waste cleanup. *Mar. 1985*
Mummified Eskimo infant. *Feb. 1985*
Koko (gorilla) holding a kitten. *Jan. 1985*
Tailor shouldering sewing machine in monsoon floodwaters. *Dec. 1984*
Chocolate Statue of Liberty. *Nov. 1984*
Croquet players wearing Hincherton Hayfever Helmets. *Oct. 1984*
Manatee with diver. *Sept. 1984*
Mexican woman and child. *Aug. 1984*
Harriet Tubman with slaves on the Underground Railroad. *July 1984*
Steam locomotive passing the Taj Mahal, India. *June 1984*
Skeleton with gold jewelry, Herculaneum, Italy. *May 1984*

To celebrate its first century, which began in October 1888, NATIONAL GEOGRAPHIC reprinted its illustrated covers in September 1988 (below).

Sled dog team, Greenland. *Apr. 1984*
Hologram of eagle. *Mar. 1984*
Elephants at dry waterhole, Botswana. *Feb. 1984*
Humpback whale breaching. *Jan. 1984*
"Virgin and Child," Byzantine sacred art. *Dec. 1983*
"Last Supper" restoration. *Nov. 1983*
Wodaabe man, Niger. *Oct. 1983*
Astronauts hovering near space shuttle *Challenger. Sept. 1983*
Ultralight aircraft. *Aug. 1983*
Arctic dive in WASP suit. *July 1983*
Horsehead Nebula. *June 1983*
Brooklyn Bridge construction. *May 1983*
Recycled-trash statue. *Apr. 1983*
Shipwreck's figurehead, Lake Ontario. *Mar. 1983*

Inupiat child in red scarf, Alaska. *Feb. 1983*
Frog sitting in red mushroom. *Jan. 1983*
Lioness carrying cub. *Dec. 1982*
Pueblo pottery. *Nov. 1982*
Silicon microchip. *Oct. 1982*
Woman diving from sailboat, Bahamas. *Sept. 1982*
Tribesman with nose painted red, Papua New Guinea. *Aug. 1982*
Reconstructed Arab merchant ship of Sindbad's era. *July 1982*
Ostrich with hatching chicks. *June 1982*
Stone face, Angkor, Kampuchea. *May 1982*
Uniformed Polish coal miner with photo of the Pope on lapel button. *Apr. 1982*
Mondari woman, smoking pipe, waterpot on head, Sudan. *Mar. 1982*
Camels passing Pyramids of Giza. *Feb. 1982*
Goose-stepping East German guard. *Jan. 1982*
Giant panda. *Dec. 1981*
Deer wading in pond. *Nov. 1981*
Launch of space shuttle *Columbia. Oct. 1981*
Vietnamese refugee girl in red dress, Biloxi, Mississippi. *Sept. 1981*
Maya cave painting of ballplayer. *Aug. 1981*
Saturn (enhanced Voyager 1 image). *July 1981*
Somali refugee boy cradling goat. *June 1981*
Shark attacking chain-mail diving suit. *May 1981*
Stone walls, Inishmore, Aran Islands. *Apr. 1981*
Space shuttle *Columbia* on launchpad. *Mar. 1981*
Whooping crane. *Feb. 1981*
Infrared image of tar-sands plant, Alberta, Canada. *Special Report on Energy. (Feb. 1981)*
Mount St. Helens' volcanic ash cloud. *Jan. 1981*
Aztec obsidian knife. *Dec. 1980*
Windsor Castle in the snow. *Nov. 1980*
Japanese fencers with bamboo swords. *Oct. 1980*
Camel race, Saudi Arabia. *Sept. 1980*

Voladores whirl above Huastec temple, Mexico. *Aug. 1980*
Silver and gold horse artifact, Bulgaria. *July 1980*
Orangutan and boy in bath basin. *June 1980*
Cheetah cubs. *May 1980*
Pink sea anemones. *Apr. 1980*
Bespectacled Chinese man. *Mar. 1980*
Tibetan shepherdess with sling. *Feb. 1980*
Volcanic eruption on Io. *Jan. 1980*
Caribou. *Dec. 1979*
Bella tribesman in white turban and sunglasses. *Nov. 1979*
Chinese children in Guilin. *Oct. 1979*
Ice Age tools in snow. *Sept. 1979*
Hikers with umbrellas. *Aug. 1979*
Rainbow below Yosemite's Bridalveil Fall. *July 1979*
Ukrainian girl dancing. *June 1979*
Mountaineers on K-2. *May 1979*
Diver with dolphin. *Apr. 1979*
Puffin. *Mar. 1979*
Wallabies sparring. *Feb. 1979*
Feet of colossal Buddha, Sri Lanka. *Jan. 1979*
Double Eagle II (helium balloon). *Dec. 1978*
Sacred Mosque, Mecca, Saudi Arabia. *Nov. 1978*
Koko (gorilla) with camera. *Oct. 1978*
Naomi Uemura, Japanese Arctic explorer. *Sept. 1978*
Tyrannosaurus attacking *Anatosaurus*. *Aug. 1978*
Grand Canyon, Arizona. *July 1978*
Leafy sea dragon. *June 1978*
Robyn Davidson feeding camel. *May 1978*
Terra-cotta soldier, China. *Apr. 1978*
Ladakhi woman in turquoise-covered headdress. *Mar. 1978*
Gold death mask, Mycenae. *Feb. 1978*
Ballerina, Bolshoi Theater. *Jan. 1978*
Brendan (leather boat). *Dec. 1977*
Jaguar. *Nov. 1977*
Woman carrying orange daisies. *Oct. 1977*
Lapp boy, Norway. *Sept. 1977*
Lockheed TriStar jet. *Aug. 1977*
Undine Falls, Yellowstone National Park. *July 1977*

Noah's Ark (Huichol yarn artwork). *June 1977*
Frigatebird with chick. *May 1977*
Nepalese man in fur hat. *Apr. 1977*
Tutankhamun's gold funerary mask. *Mar. 1977*
Silver Fox (helium balloon). *Feb. 1977*
Surface of Mars (Viking spacecraft photo). *Jan. 1977*
Tall-ships race. *Dec. 1976*
Cowboy. *Nov. 1976*
Washington, D. C., at night (Capitol, Washington Monument, Lincoln Memorial). *Oct. 1976*
Golden langur (monkey). *Sept. 1976*
Monarch butterflies. *Aug. 1976*
Bald eagle. *July 1976*
Japanese woman in kimono. *June 1976*
Encrusted tank wreckage, Truk Lagoon. *May 1976*
Irish boy. *Apr. 1976*
Right whale breaching. *Mar. 1976*
Siberian woman in winter attire. *Feb. 1976*
Harp seal pup. *Jan. 1976*
Maya calendar symbols carved in limestone. *Dec. 1975*
Cuna Indian woman with gold nose ring. *Nov. 1975*
Biruté Galdikas with orangutans. *Oct. 1975*
Moray eels. *Sept. 1975*
Fulani woman wearing gold earrings and filigree jewelry. *Aug. 1975*
Benjamin Franklin. *July 1975*
Andalusian woman in black hat. *June 1975*
Baboons. *May 1975*
Diver swimming with shark. *Apr. 1975*
Volcanic eruption, Mauna Ulu, Hawaii. *Mar. 1975*
Txukahamei Indian in black face paint and white neck beads. *Feb. 1975*
Ice Age cave painting of a bison. *Jan. 1975*
Polynesian girl. *Dec. 1974*
Guatemalan man spinning thread. *Nov. 1974*
King Jigme Singye Wangchuck (Bhutan). *Oct. 1974*
Kingfisher. *Sept. 1974*
Red-bearded face on Phoenician amulet. *Aug. 1974*

Oxford Canal, England. *July 1974*
Mountaineer scaling Yosemite's Half Dome. *June 1974*
Trifid Nebula. *May 1974*
English boy looking through rain-spattered window. *Apr. 1974*
Explorer and dogsled crossing Arctic ice. *Mar. 1974*
Red fox. *Feb. 1974*
Gold lion artifact, West Africa. *Jan. 1974*
Aymara Indian with llama in reed boat. *Dec. 1973*
Crab nipping boy's finger. *Nov. 1973*
Chilean woman holding flag. *Oct. 1973*
New Guinea tribesman wearing pig tusks and cowrie shells. *Sept. 1973*
Common tern. *Aug. 1973*
Volcanic eruption, Iceland. *July 1973*
Diver, Great Barrier Reef. *June 1973*
Wild horses, Camargue, France. *May 1973*
Bubble-eyed goldfish. *Apr. 1973*
Eskimo whalers in walrus-skin boat. *Mar. 1973*
Australian Aboriginal rock painting. *Feb. 1973*
Elderly Ecuadorean man. *Jan. 1973*
Giant panda, Ling-Ling. *Dec. 1972*
Surf battering Monterey coast, California. *Nov. 1972*
Txukahamei Indian girl in red face paint. *Oct. 1972*
High-wheeler bicycle. *Sept. 1972*
Tasaday boy climbing vine, Philippines. *Aug. 1972*
Saudi Arabian man. *July 1972*
Family rafting on Willamette River, Oregon. *June 1972*
Tourists photographing black bear, Yellowstone National Park. *May 1972*
Kirghiz boy in fur cap. *Apr. 1972*
Lapland longspur. *Mar. 1972*
Leopard. *Feb. 1972*
Namba woman in face paint, New Hebrides (Vanuatu). *Jan. 1972*
Chinese schoolchildren, Beijing. *Dec. 1971*
Penguin with telemetry backpack. *Nov. 1971*
Hindu woman with ink design on face. *Oct. 1971*
Diver stalking python. *Sept. 1971*

Man shoveling wheat. *Aug. 1971*
Astronaut Alan B. Shepard on the moon. *July 1971*
Hikers, Pacific Crest Trail. *June 1971*
Andean condor pecking at handler. *May 1971*
Orchid. *Apr. 1971*
Akha woman in silver-trinketed headdress, Laos. *Mar. 1971*
Eskimo fisherman with spear. *Feb. 1971*
Ra II (reed boat). *Jan. 1971*
Oil-soaked grebe. *Dec. 1970*
Stone profile of Queen Nefertiti. *Nov. 1970*
Schoolboy with slate, India. *Oct. 1970*
Cobra. *Sept. 1970*
Saturn (painting). *Aug. 1970*
Hutterite family. *July 1970*
The Colosseum, Rome, Italy. *June 1970*
Black skimmer. *May 1970*
White tiger cub. *Apr. 1970*
Geisha drummer. *Mar. 1970*
Flamingos. *Feb. 1970*
Dian Fossey with gorillas. *Jan. 1970*
Astronaut Edwin Aldrin on the moon. *Dec. 1969*
Ramayana performance in Bali, Indonesia. *Nov. 1969*
Black eagle diving at woman. *Oct. 1969*
Irish woman in red blouse. *Sept. 1969*
Anglers at Maroon Lake, Colorado. *Aug. 1969*
Diver and cormorant. *July 1969*
Graduate of Eaglebrook School, Deerfield, Massachusetts. *June 1969*
Colossus of Ramesses II reassembled, Abu Simbel, Egypt. *May 1969*
Robin Lee Graham taking a bucket bath aboard *Dove*. *Apr. 1969*
Scallops and starfish. *Mar. 1969*
African elephant. *Feb. 1969*
Rice farmer with water buffalo, Taiwan. *Jan. 1969*
Vietnamese children praying. *Dec. 1968*
Cattle ranchers, Queensland, Australia. *Nov. 1968*
Robin Lee Graham aboard the *Dove*. *Oct. 1968*
Afghan nomad tribeswoman with baby. *Sept. 1968*
Candlelit cemetery, Mexico. *Aug. 1968*
Sailboat, Lake Como, Italy. *July 1968*
Berber girls playing leapfrog. *June 1968*
Mountaineers above Trapper Lake, Washington. *May 1968*
Vietnamese fisherman holding fish in teeth. *Apr. 1968*
Scottish girl under tartan blanket. *Mar. 1968*
Whitetip shark. *Feb. 1968*
Afghan horsemen. *Jan. 1968*
Wayfarers with donkey, Samaria. *Dec. 1967*
Land yachts sailing the Sahara. *Nov. 1967*
Traditional wooden grave marker, Madagascar. *Oct. 1967*
Torii offshore in Inland Sea, Japan. *Sept. 1967*
Marble head, Aphrodisias, Turkey. *Aug. 1967*
Jet boats, Lake Powell, Arizona-Utah. *July 1967*
Chicago skyscrapers at night. *June 1967*
Micronesian girl crowned with red flowers. *May 1967*

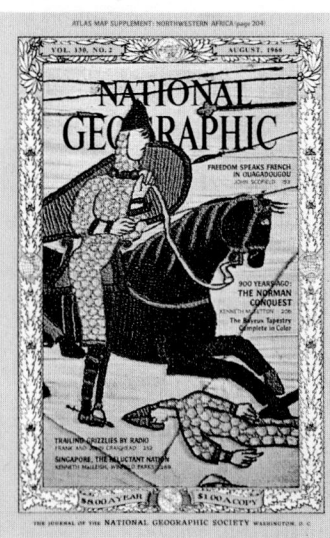

Rhine freighters passing castle ruins. *Apr. 1967*
Snowflake (albino gorilla). *Mar. 1967*
Vietnamese staring out from under hat. *Feb. 1967*
Pakistani girls on swing. *Jan. 1967*
Arab shepherd tending flock, Jordan Valley. *Dec. 1966*
Queen angelfish. *Nov. 1966*
Gilbert H. Grosvenor with binoculars. *Oct. 1966*
Philippine woman playing *bandurria*. *Sept. 1966*
Bayeux Tapestry detail of Norman horseman. *Aug. 1966*
Bather in surf. *July 1966*
Life Guard in plumed helmet, London, England. *June 1966*
Sailboats below Golden Gate Bridge, San Francisco, California. *May 1966*
Divers working on oil rig. *Apr. 1966*
St. Basil's Cathedral, Moscow, U.S.S.R. *Mar. 1966*
Bolivian woman weighing grapes. *Feb. 1966*
Bedouin horseman wielding scimitar. *Jan. 1966*
Jane Goodall with chimpanzee. *Dec. 1965*
Tuareg man in black turban and veil. *Nov. 1965*
Mustangese women and child, Nepal. *Oct. 1965*
Fighter jets over Fujiyama, Japan. *Sept. 1965*
Winston Churchill. *Aug. 1965*
Parliament Building, Budapest, Hungary. *July 1965*
Sphinx moth sipping nectar. *June 1965*
Red-and-white sails of *Yankee* (ketch) pass Colossi of Ramesses II at Abu Simbel. *May 1965*
Ethiopian holy man with Coptic cross. *Apr. 1965*
Flamenco dancer. *Mar. 1965*
Aircraft carrier *Enterprise* and escort. *Feb. 1965*
Green Beret leading Vietnamese. *Jan. 1965*
Pair of white turtledoves. *Dec. 1964*

Peking Opera School actress in jeweled headdress. *Nov. 1964*
Cambodian dancer holding mask of Yeaksa. *Oct. 1964*
Peace Corps volunteer hugging Ecuadorean woman. *Sept. 1964*
Parachutist. *Aug. 1964*
Redwood tree. *July 1964*
Carlsbad Caverns, New Mexico. *June 1964*
President and Mrs. Lyndon B. Johnson in Explorers Hall. *May 1964*
Diver at Conshelf Two in the Red Sea. *Apr. 1964*
Astronaut tethered to Gemini spacecraft. *Mar. 1964*
Peruvian Indian child in red cap. *Feb. 1964*
U. S. Capitol, Washington, D. C. *Jan. 1964*
Byzantine soldiers entering fortress of Nicaea, First Crusade. *Dec. 1963*
Children viewing deer through window. *Nov. 1963*
NGS 75th Anniversary photo composite: Tutankhamun's mask; Mt. Everest climber; first cover. *Oct. 1963*
Rescue boat splashing over ocean surf, Australia. *Sept. 1963*
Girls surrounded by balloons, Disneyland. *Aug. 1963*
Bronze bust of god; Parthenon (Photo composite). *July 1963*
Portofino, on the Italian Riviera. *June 1963*
Rajasthan woman wearing nose ring. *May 1963*
Resolution (warship) on rough seas. *Apr. 1963*
Navajo herdsmen, Monument Valley, Arizona. *Mar. 1963*
Burmese dancer. *Feb. 1963*
Balloonists abandoning *Explorer II*. *Jan. 1963*
El Morro fortress, San Juan Bay, Puerto Rico. *Dec. 1962*
South Vietnamese village afire. *Nov. 1962*
Hollywood Boulevard, Los Angeles, California. *Oct. 1962*
Fishermen on Copacabana Beach, Rio de Janeiro, Brazil. *Sept. 1962*
Illustrated map of Cape Cod, Massachusetts. *Aug. 1962*
Tahitian woman cleaning fish. *July 1962*
Friendship 7 spacecraft reentering atmosphere. *June 1962*
New Guinea chieftain with headdress and nose quills. *May 1962*
Bounty replica. *Apr. 1962*
Mongolians inside tent. *Mar. 1962*
Roseate spoonbill. *Feb. 1962*
Woman diver on Florida coral reef. *Jan. 1962*
"Madonna and Child with Saints and Angels" (Fungai). *Dec. 1961*
Illustrated map of Italy. *Nov. 1961*
Mexican woman carrying bowl on head. *Oct. 1961*
United Nations Secretariat, New York City, New York. *Sept. 1961*
Laotian children eating noodles. *Aug. 1961*
Photos of landscapes framed in outline of United States. *July 1961*
Toddler admiring Grenadier Guard, Tower of London. *June 1961*

Cowboys take a midday break from rounding up cattle in Wyoming's rugged Bighorn country.   WILLIAM ALBERT ALLARD

CRAFT, KINUKO Y.: *Artist*

Hagi: Where Japan's Revolution Began. By N. Taylor Gregg. Photos by Sam Abell. 751-773, *June 1984*

CRAFTS:

Kyoto and Nara: Keepers of Japan's Past. By Charles McCarry. Photos by George F. Mobley. 836-851, *June 1976*

■ *The Craftsman in America.* 199 pages. *1975*

Human Treasures of Japan. By William Graves. Photos by James L. Stanfield. 370-379, *Sept. 1972*

Williamsburg, City for All Seasons. By Joseph Judge. Photos by James L. Amos. 790-823, *Dec. 1968*

The Past Is Present in Greenfield Village. By Beverley M. Bowie. Photos by Neal P. Davis and Willard R. Culver. 96-127, *July 1958*

Williamsburg: Its College and Its Cinderella City. By Beverley M. Bowie. 439-486, *Oct. 1954*

See also Embroidery; Folk Art; Goldsmithing; Model Aircraft; Pottery; Ship Crafting; Weaving; Wood Carving

CRAIGE, JOHN HOUSTON: *Author*

Haitian Vignettes. 435-485, *Oct. 1934*

CRAIGHEAD, CHARLES:

Nomination Page. *Aug. 1967*

Photographer

Sharing the Lives of Wild Golden Eagles. By John Craighead. Photos by Charles and Derek Craighead. 420-439, *Sept. 1967*

CRAIGHEAD, DEREK:

Nomination Page. *Aug. 1967*

Author

Yellowstone at 100: A Walk Through the Wilderness. By Karen and Derek Craighead. Photos by Sam Abell. 579-603, *May 1972*

Photographer

Sharing the Lives of Wild Golden Eagles. By John Craighead. Photos by Charles and Derek Craighead. 420-439, *Sept. 1967*

CRAIGHEAD, FRANK, Jr.:

Recipient of the National Geographic Society Centennial Award. President's Page. By Gilbert M. Grosvenor. *Dec. 1988*

■ Grizzly! 639A-639B, *Nov. 1967*
Nomination Page. *Aug. 1967*
Nomination Page. *Nov. 1959*

Author

We Survive on a Pacific Atoll. 73-94, *Jan. 1948*

Author-Photographer

Studying Wildlife by Satellite. 120-123, *Jan. 1973*

White-water Adventure on Wild Rivers of Idaho. 213-239, *Feb. 1970*

Trailing Yellowstone's Grizzlies by Radio. 252-267, *Aug. 1966*

Knocking Out Grizzly Bears For Their Own Good. 276-291, *Aug. 1960*

Bright Dyes Reveal Secrets of Canada Geese. 817-832, *Dec. 1957*

Inspired by a NATIONAL GEOGRAPHIC *article, twins Frank Jr. (above) and John Craighead took up falconry in the 1930s, training owls as well as hawks.*   JOHN CRAIGHEAD

Wildlife Adventuring in Jackson Hole. 1-36, *Jan. 1956*

Cloud Gardens in the Tetons. 811-830, *June 1948*

Life with an Indian Prince: As Guests of a Maharaja's Brother, Two Young American Naturalists Study Age-old Methods of Hunting with Trained Falcons and Cheetahs and Savor the Pomp of Royal India. By Frank and John Craighead. 235-272, *Feb. 1942*

In Quest of the Golden Eagle: Over Lonely Mountain and Prairie Soars This Rare and Lordly Bird, But Three Youths from the East Catch Up With Him at Last. By Frank and John Craighead. 693-710, *May 1940*

Adventures with Birds of Prey. By Frank and John Craighead. 109-134, *July 1937*

CRAIGHEAD, JOHN:

Recipient of the National Geographic Society Centennial Award. President's Page. By Gilbert M. Grosvenor. *Dec. 1988*

Nomination Page. *Jan. 1970*
■ Grizzly! 639A-639B, *Nov. 1967*
Nomination Page. *Aug. 1967*
Nomination Page. *Nov. 1959*

Author

Studying Grizzly Habitat by Satellite. 148-158, *July 1976*

Sharing the Lives of Wild Golden Eagles. Photos by Charles and Derek Craighead. 420-439, *Sept. 1967*

We Survive on a Pacific Atoll. 73-94, *Jan. 1948*

Author-Photographer

Studying Wildlife by Satellite. 120-123, *Jan. 1973*

White-water Adventure on Wild Rivers of Idaho. 213-239, *Feb. 1970*

Trailing Yellowstone's Grizzlies by Radio. 252-267, *Aug. 1966*

Knocking Out Grizzly Bears For Their Own Good. 276-291, *Aug. 1960*

Bright Dyes Reveal Secrets of Canada Geese. 817-832, *Dec. 1957*

Wildlife Adventuring in Jackson Hole. 1-36, *Jan. 1956*

Cloud Gardens in the Tetons. 811-830, *June 1948*

Life with an Indian Prince: As Guests of a Maharaja's Brother, Two Young American Naturalists Study Age-old Methods of Hunting with Trained Falcons and Cheetahs and Savor the Pomp of Royal India. By Frank and John Craighead. 235-272, *Feb. 1942*

In Quest of the Golden Eagle: Over Lonely Mountain and Prairie Soars This Rare and Lordly Bird, But Three Youths from the East Catch Up With Him at Last. By Frank and John Craighead. 693-710, *May 1940*

Adventures with Birds of Prey. By Frank and John Craighead. 109-134, *July 1937*

CRAIGHEAD, KAREN: *Author*

Yellowstone at 100: A Walk Through the Wilderness. By Karen and Derek Craighead. Photos by Sam Abell. 579-603, *May 1972*

CRAMPTON, HENRY EDWARD:

Author

Kaieteur and Roraima: The Great Falls and the Great Mountain of the Guianas. 227-244, *Sept. 1920*

CRANBERRIES:

The People of New Jersey's Pine Barrens. By John McPhee. Photos by William R. Curtsinger. 52-77, *Jan. 1974*

CRANE, ALICE ROLLINS: *Author*

The Midnight Sun in the Klondike. 66-67, *Feb. 1901*

The Northern Lights. 69, *Feb. 1901*

CRANE, JOCELYN:
Nomination Page. In Trinidad.
Oct. 1959

Author
Keeping House for Tropical Butterflies.
Photos by M. Woodbridge Williams.
193-217, *Aug. 1957*

CRANES (Birds):
The Japanese Crane, Bird of Happi-
ness. By Tsuneo Hayashida. Con-
tents: Red-crowned crane. 542-556,
Oct. 1983
Where Oil and Wildlife Mix. By Steven
C. Wilson and Karen C. Hayden. In-
cluded: Whooping cranes. 145-173,
Feb. 1981
Teamwork Helps the Whooping Crane.
By Roderick C. Drewien, with Ernie
Kuyt. Contents: A U. S.-Canadian
effort to establish a second breeding
flock of wild whoopers among close-
kin sandhill cranes. 680-693,
May 1979
And Then There Was Fred.... Contents:
Sandhill crane. 843-847, *Dec. 1973*
Whooping Cranes Fight for Survival. By
Robert Porter Allen. Photos by Fred-
erick Kent Truslow. 650-669,
Nov. 1959
The Shore Birds, Cranes, and Rails:
Willets, Plovers, Stilts, Phalaropes,
Sandpipers, and Their Relatives De-
serve Protection. By Arthur A. Al-
len. Paintings by Allan Brooks. 183-
222, *Aug. 1937*
See also Whooping Cranes

CRATER LAKE, Oregon:
Crater Lake Summer. By Walter
Meayers Edwards. 134-148,
July 1962
When Mt. Mazama Lost Its Top: The
Birth of Crater Lake. By Lyman J.
Briggs. 128-133, *July 1962*
"Where Rolls the Oregon." Photos by
Ray Atkeson. 689-728, *Dec. 1946*
Crater Lake, Oregon. 221, *June 1902*
Crater Lake, Oregon. By J. S. Diller.
33-48, *Feb. 1897*
The Mazamas. By J. S. Diller. 58-59,
Feb. 1897
Oregon: Its History, Geography, and
Resources. By John H. Mitchell. 239-
284, *Apr. 20, 1895*

CRATER LAKE NATIONAL PARK,
Oregon:
Crater Lake and Yosemite Through the
Ages. By Wallace W. Atwood, Jr.
Paintings by Eugene Kingman. 327-
343, *Mar. 1937*
Our National Parks. By L. F. Schmeck-
ebier. 531-579, *June 1912*

CRATERS:
Meteorites–Invaders From Space. By
Kenneth F. Weaver. Photos by Jona-
than Blair. 390-418, *Sept. 1986*
See also Volcanoes

**CRATERS OF THE MOON
NATIONAL MONUMENT,** Idaho:
Man on the Moon in Idaho. By William
Belknap, Jr. 505-525, *Oct. 1960*
Among the "Craters of the Moon": An
Account of the First Expeditions
Through the Remarkable Volcanic

Lava Beds of Southern Idaho. By
R. W. Limbert. 303-328, *Mar. 1924*

CRAWFISH. *See* Crayfish

CRAWFORD, MARION: *Author*
The Ruins at Selinus (Sicily). 117,
Jan. 1909

CRAWFURD, OSWALD: *Author*
The Greatness of Little Portugal. 867-
883, *Oct. 1910*

CRAYFISH:
Trouble in Bayou Country: Louisiana's
Atchafalaya. By Jack and Anne Rud-
loe. Photos by C. C. Lockwood. 377-
397, *Sept. 1979*
Certain Citizens of the Warm Sea. By
Louis L. Mowbray. Paintings by Ha-
shime Murayama. 27-62, *Jan. 1922*
See also Spiny Lobsters

CREATURES That Deceive to Survive.
By Robert F. Sisson. 394-415,
Mar. 1980

CREE INDIANS:
Quebec's Northern Dynamo. By Larry
Kohl. Photos by Ottmar Bierwagen.
406-418, *Mar. 1982*
The Changing World of Canada's
Crees. By Fred Ward. 541-569,
Apr. 1975
Nomads of the Far North. By Matthew
W. Stirling. Included: Hearty Folk
Defy Arctic Storms. Paintings by W.
Langdon Kihn. 471-504, *Oct. 1949*

CREEK INDIANS:
Indians of the Southeastern United
States. By Matthew W. Stirling.
Paintings by W. Langdon Kihn. 53-
74, *Jan. 1946*
The Five Civilized Tribes and the Sur-
vey of Indian Territory. By C. H.
Fitch. 481-491, *Dec. 1898*

CRESSON, OSBORNE C.:
Photographer
American Family in Afghanistan. By
Rebecca Shannon Cresson. 417-432,
Sept. 1953

CRESSON, REBECCA SHANNON:
Author
We Lived in Turbulent Tehran. 707-
720, *Nov. 1953*
American Family in Afghanistan. Pho-
tos by Osborne C. Cresson. 417-432,
Sept. 1953

CRESSON, WILLIAM PENN: *Author*
Persia: The Awakening East. 356-384,
May 1908

CRETAN CIVILIZATION. *See* Minoan
Civilization

CRETE (Island), Greece:
Drama of Death in a Minoan Temple.
By Yannis Sakellarakis and Efi Sa-
pouna-Sakellaraki. Photos by Otis
Imboden and Spyros Tsavdaroglou.
205-222, *Feb. 1981*
Joseph Alsop: A Historical Perspective
(on Minoan Human Sacrifice). 223,
Feb. 1981
Minoans and Mycenaeans: Greece's
Brilliant Bronze Age. By Joseph
Judge. Photos by Gordon W. Gahan.

Paintings by Lloyd K. Townsend.
142-185, *Feb. 1978*
The Aegean Isles: Poseidon's Play-
ground. By Gilbert M. Grosvenor.
733-781, *Dec. 1958*
Crete, Cradle of Western Civilization.
By Maynard Owen Williams. 693-
706, *Nov. 1953*
War-torn Greece Looks Ahead. By
Maynard Owen Williams. 711-744,
Dec. 1949
Greece–the Birthplace of Science and
Free Speech: Explorations on the
Mainland and in Crete and the Age-
an Isles Reveal Ancient Life Similar
to That of the Present. By Richard
Stillwell. Paintings by H. M. Herget.
273-353, *Mar. 1944*
Crete, Where Sea-Kings Reigned. By
Agnes N. Stillwell. 547-568,
Nov. 1943
Classic Greece Merges Into 1941 News.
Photos by B. Anthony Stewart and
Maynard Owen Williams. 93-108,
Jan. 1941
Cruising to Crete: Four French Girls Set
Sail in a Breton Yawl for the Island of
the Legendary Minotaur. By Marthe
Oulié and Mariel Jean-Brunhes. 249-
272, *Feb. 1929*
The Sea-Kings of Crete. By James Bai-
kie. 1-25, *Jan. 1912*
Explorations in Crete. By Edith H.
Hall. 778-787, *Sept. 1909*

CRICKETS, Nature's Expert Fiddlers.
By Catherine Bell Palmer. 385-394,
Sept. 1953

CRILLON, Mount, Alaska:
The Conquest of Mount Crillon. By
Bradford Washburn. 361-400,
Mar. 1935

CRIME DETECTION:
The FBI: Public Friend Number One.
By Jacob Hay. Photos by Robert F.
Sisson. 860-886, *June 1961*

*Nearly five feet tall, a Japanese crane
leaps high above its lifelong partner during a mating dance.* TSUNEO HAYASHIDA

Queen among gems, the 44.5-carat Hope diamond is in the Smithsonian Institution.

JAMES L. STANFIELD AND VICTOR R. BOSWELL, JR., BOTH NGS

Cruising the Aegean Sea in a replica of a late Bronze Age galley, explorer Timothy Severin seeks Ulysses' triumphant route home after the Trojan War. KEVIN FLEMING

Robin Lee Graham took this self-portrait while showering on the 1968 Atlantic leg of his global solo voyage. ROBIN LEE GRAHAM

Home of the Cock-of-the-rock: Naturalists Enter the Amazon, Voyage Through the Heart of Tropical South America, and Emerge at the Mouth of the Orinoco. By Ernest G. Holt. 585-630, *Nov. 1933*

The Cape Horn Grain-Ship Race: The Gallant "Parma" Leads the Vanishing Fleet of Square-Riggers Through Raging Gales and Irksome Calm 16,000 Miles, from Australia to England. By A. J. Villiers. 1-39, *Jan. 1933*

The Greatest Voyage in the Annals of the Sea (Magellan). By J. R. Hildebrand. 699-739, *Dec. 1932*

A Modern Saga of the Seas: The Narrative of a 17,000-Mile Cruise on a 40-Foot Sloop by the Author, His Wife, and a Baby, Born on the Voyage. By Erling Tambs. 645-688, *Dec. 1931*

Sailing Forbidden Coasts (Africa). By Ida Treat. 357-386, *Sept. 1931*

Rounding the Horn in a Windjammer. By A. J. Villiers. 191-224, *Feb. 1931*

The Danube, Highway of Races: From the Black Forest to the Black Sea, Europe's Most Important River Has Borne the Traffic of Centuries. By Melville Chater. 643-697, *Dec. 1929*

Cruising to Crete: Four French Girls get Sail in a Breton Yawl for the Island of the Legendary Minotaur. By Marthe Oulié and Mariel Jean-Brunhes. 249-272, *Feb. 1929*

A Voyage to the Island Home of Robinson Crusoe. By Waldo L. Schmitt. 353-370, *Sept. 1928*

Around the World in the "Islander": A Narrative of the Adventures of a Solitary Voyager on His Four-Year Cruise in a Thirty-Four-Foot Sailing Craft. By Harry Pidgeon. 141-205, *Feb. 1928*

The Pathfinder of the East: Setting Sail to Find "Christians and Spices," Vasco da Gama Met Amazing Adventures, Founded an Empire, and Changed the History of Western Europe. By J. R. Hildebrand. 503-550, *Nov. 1927*

Sinbads of Science: Narrative of a Windjammer's Specimen-Collecting Voyage to the Sargasso Sea, to Senegambian Africa and Among Islands of High Adventure in the South Atlantic. By George Finlay Simmons. 1-75, *July 1927*

The Columbus of the Pacific: Captain James Cook, Foremost British Navigator, Expanded the Great Sea to Correct Proportions and Won for Albion an Insular Empire by Peaceful Exploration and Scientific Study. By J. R. Hildebrand. 85-132, *Jan. 1927*

Skirting the Shores of Sunrise: Seeking and Finding "The Levant" in a Journey by Steamer, Motor-Car, and Train from Constantinople to Port Said. By Melville Chater. 649-728, *Dec. 1926*

The Romance of Science in Polynesia: An Account of Five Years of Cruising Among the South Sea Islands. By Robert Cushman Murphy. Paintings by Hashime Murayama. 355-426, *Oct. 1925*

Bird Life Among Lava Rock and Coral Sand: The Chronicle of a Scientific Expedition to Little-known Islands of Hawaii. By Alexander Wetmore. 77-108, *July 1925*

Rediscovering the Rhine: A Trip by Barge from the Sea to the Headwaters of Europe's Storied Stream. By Melville Chater. 1-43, *July 1925*

Surveying the Grand Canyon of the Colorado: An Account of the 1923 Boating Expedition of the United States Geological Survey. By Lewis R. Freeman. 471-548, *May 1924*

A Cruise Among Desert Islands (Baja California). By G. Dallas Hanna and A. W. Anthony. 71-99, *July 1923*

Sailing the Seven Seas in the Interest of Science: Adventures Through 157,000 Miles of Storm and Calm, from Arctic to Antarctic and Around the World, in the Non-magnetic Yacht "Carnegie." By J. P. Ault. 631-690, *Dec. 1922*

The Dream Ship: The Story of a Voyage of Adventure More Than Half

Around the World in a 47-foot Lifeboat. By Ralph Stock. 1-52, *Jan. 1921*

Voyaging on the Volga Amid War and Revolution: War-time Sketches on Russia's Great Waterway. By William T. Ellis. 245-265, *Mar. 1918*

Diary of a Voyage from San Francisco to Tahiti and Return, 1901. By S. P. Langley. 413-429, *Dec. 1901*

The Road to Bolivia. By William E. Curtis. 209-224, *June 1900*

Deep-Sea Exploring Expedition of the Steamer "Albatross." By Hugh M. Smith. 291-296, *Aug. 1899*

A Summer Voyage to the Arctic. By G. R. Putnam. 97-110, *Apr. 1897*

The Arctic Cruise of the United States Revenue Cutter "Bear." By Sheldon Jackson. 27-31, *Jan. 1896*

The Antarctic Continent (Geographic Notes). By Cyrus C. Babb. Note: A resumé of the expeditions and discoveries in the Antarctic from 1567 through 1894. 217-223, *Dec. 29, 1894*

Sir Francis Drake's Anchorage. By

A Soviet square-rigged ship cruising the Black Sea greets a replica of the ancient Greek galley Argo *retracing in 1984 Jason's mythological quest for the Golden Fleece.* JOHN EGAN

CRUSADES:

CRUSOE, ROBINSON:

CRUSTACEANS:

CRUZEN, RICHARD H.:

CRYSTAL (River), Florida:

CRYSTAL MOUNTAIN, Nepal:

CRYSTALS:

CUBA:

CUBAN REFUGEES:

To increase man's understanding of earth's magnetic field, the nonmagnetic yacht Carnegie *sailed the world in six journeys between 1909 and 1921.*   J. P. AULT

Man's Mightiest Ally. 423-450, *Apr. 1947*

Birthplace of Telephone Magic. 289-312, *Mar. 1947*

Arkansas Traveler of 1946. 289-312, *Sept. 1946*

A Community of Dwarfs (Insects). 345-352, *Sept. 1946*

George Washington's Historic River (Potomac). Photos by Willard R. Culver and Robert F. Sisson. 41-64, *July 1945*

Dogs in Toyland. 473-480, *Apr. 1944*

From Sand to Seer and Servant of Man (Glassmaking). 17-48, *Jan. 1943*

Flavor and Savor of American Foods. 289-320, *Mar. 1942*

Golden Fleece of Dixie (Cotton). 153-192, *Feb. 1941*

From Trees to Tires and Toys (Rubber). Photos by Willard R. Culver and J. Baylor Roberts. 159-190, *Feb. 1940*

From Nature's Hidden Building Blocks. 609-640, *Nov. 1939*

Bright Patterns of Long Island Life. 429-459, *Apr. 1939*

Catdom's Royalty Photographed in Color. 597-628, *Nov. 1938*

Old and New Blend in Yankeeland (Connecticut). 295-326, *Sept. 1938*

Virginia, Maryland, and Delaware: Tri-State Medley. 33-40, *July 1938*

Washington of Tradition (D. C.) Builds for the Future. 671-694, *June 1937*

Nomads Among the Butterflies. Paintings by Hashime Murayama. 569-584, *May 1937*

Virginia's Colonial Heritage (Williamsburg). 417-440, *Apr. 1937*

Hoosier Haunts and Holidays (Indiana). 283-314, *Sept. 1936*

Winged Jewels from Many Lands (Butterflies). Paintings by Hashime Murayama. 673-688, *May 1936*

CUMANA, Venezuela:

Old Ports on the Spanish Main. By G.M.L. Brown. 622-638, *Nov. 1906*

CUMBERLAND, Maryland:

Potomac, River of Destiny. By Albert W. Atwood. 33-70, *July 1945*

CUMBERLAND GAP, and Region, Kentucky-Tennessee:

The People of Cumberland Gap. By John Fetterman. Photos by Bruce Dale. 591-621, *Nov. 1971*

Home Folk around Historic Cumberland Gap. By Leo A. Borah. 741-768, *Dec. 1943*

CUMBERLAND ISLAND, Georgia:

Cumberland, My Island for a While. By John Pennington. Photos by Jodi Cobb. Note: Designated a national seashore in 1972. 649-661, *Nov. 1977*

Sea Islands: Adventuring Along the South's Surprising Coast. By James Cerruti. Photos by Thomas Nebbia and James L. Amos. 366-393, *Mar. 1971*

CUMBERLAND VALLEY, Pennsylvania:

Appalachian Valley Pilgrimage. By Catherine Bell Palmer. Photos by Justin Locke. 1-32, *July 1949*

CUMMINGS, BYRON: *Author*

Ruins of Cuicuilco May Revolutionize Our History of Ancient America: Lofty Mound Sealed and Preserved by Great Lava Flow for Perhaps Seventy Centuries Is Now Being Excavated in Mexico. 203-220, *Aug. 1923*

The Great Natural Bridges of Utah. 157-167, *Feb. 1910*

CUMMINGS, CLARA E.: *Author*

Cryptogams Collected by Dr. C. Willard Hayes in Alaska, 1891. 160-162, *May 15, 1892*

CUNA INDIANS:

Panama: Ever at the Crossroads. By Charles E. Cobb, Jr. Photos by Danny Lehman. 466-493, *Apr. 1986*

See also San Blas Indians

CUNEIFORM:

Ebla: Splendor of an Unknown Empire. By Howard La Fay. Photos by James L. Stanfield. Paintings by Louis S. Glanzman. 730-759, *Dec. 1978*

Darius Carved History on Ageless Rock. By George G. Cameron. 825-844, *Dec. 1950*

CUNNINGHAM, JOHN T.: *Author*

I'm From New Jersey. Photos by Volkmar Wentzel. 1-45, *Jan. 1960*

Staten Island Ferry, New York's Seagoing Bus. By John T. Cunningham and Jay Johnston. Photos by W. D. Vaughn. 833-843, *June 1959*

CUPP, DAVID:

On Assignment in Alpine Meadows, California. *Sept. 1982*

Nomination Page. At Mount St. Helens, Washington. *Jan. 1981*

Author

Avalanche! 280-305. I. Winter's White Death. 280-281; II. "I'm OK, I'm Alive!" Photos by Lanny Johnson and Andre Benier. 282-289, *Sept. 1982*

Author-Photographer

Avalanche! III. Battling the Juggernaut. 290-305, *Sept. 1982*

Photographer

Our National Forests: Problems in Paradise. By Rowe Findley. 306-339, *Sept. 1982*

Denver, Colorado's Rocky Mountain High. By John J. Putman. 383-411, *Mar. 1979*

Capri, Italy's Enchanted Rock. By Carleton Mitchell. 795-809, *June 1970*

Gail Hammond cheerfully sorts mail for the few families who still live on Cumberland Island, off Georgia's coast. JODI COBB, NGS

Like his pioneer ancestors, Appalachian mountain man Bunt Howard lives and farms near Cumberland Gap, where Kentucky, Virginia, and Tennessee meet. BRUCE DALE, NGS

A rugged canyon near Cuzco, Peru, was explored by Hiram Bingham's 1915 expedition. HIRAM BINGHAM

Possible sacrifice to the sun, an Inca boy was entombed 500 years ago near a shrine in the Chilean Andes. LOREN MCINTYRE

CZECHOSLOVAKIA:

Instant divinity, a Tibetan boy is paraded through Lhasa by monks who identified him as a Living Buddha—the reincarnation of a high-ranking lama.   HEINRICH HARRER

Ambassador of fellowship, Pauline Garey cheers a housebound neighbor in a west Dallas housing project. DAVID ALAN HARVEY

To generate power and irrigate Arizona farmland, the Mormon Flat Dam created Canyon Lake—and a lovely vista—in 1925. GILBERT H. GROSVENOR, NGS

DAMON, THERON J.: *Author*
The Albanians. 1090-1103, *Nov. 1912*

DAMPIER, WILLIAM:
Revealing Earth's Mightiest Ocean (Pacific). By Albert W. Atwood. 291-306, *Sept. 1943*

DAMS:
They Stopped the Sea. By Hans van Duivendijk. Photos by Pablo Bartholomew. 92-101, *July 1987*
Man Against the Sea, the Oosterschelde Barrier. By Larry Kohl. 526-537, *Oct. 1986*
The Tennessee-Tombigbee Waterway: Bounty or Boondoggle? By Carolyn Bennett Patterson. Photos by Sandy Felsenthal. Included: The Hidden Tenn-Tom: Bypassed But Still Striving. By Alice J. Hall. 364-387, *Mar. 1986*
A Dam Against Famine: Aswan. By Farouk El-Baz. 595, *May 1985*
Paraguay, Paradox of South America. By Gordon Young. Photos by O. Louis Mazzatenta. Included: Itaipú Hydroelectric Development. 240-269, *Aug. 1982*
Quebec's Northern Dynamo. By Larry Kohl. Photos by Ottmar Bierwagen. 406-418, *Mar. 1982*
Our Most Precious Resource: Water. By Thomas Y. Canby. Photos by Ted Spiegel. 144-179, *Aug. 1980*
Powerhouse of the Northwest (Columbia River). By David S. Boyer. 821-847, *Dec. 1974*
The Bittersweet Waters of the Lower Colorado. By Rowe Findley. Photos by Charles O'Rear. 540-569, *Oct. 1973*
Whatever Happened to TVA? By Gordon Young. Photos by Emory Kristof. 830-863, *June 1973*
That Dammed Missouri River. By Gordon Young. Photos by David Hiser. 374-413, *Sept. 1971*
The Mekong, River of Terror and Hope. By Peter T. White. Photos by W. E. Garrett. 737-787, *Dec. 1968*
The Canadian North: Emerging Giant. By David S. Boyer. 1-43, *July 1968*
Following the Trail of Lewis and Clark. By Ralph Gray. 707-750, *June 1953*
From Sagebrush to Roses on the Columbia. By Leo A. Borah. Included: Dams completed and dams under construction: Albeni Falls, American Falls, Anderson Ranch, Bonneville, Chief Joseph, The Dalles, Detroit, Grand Coulee, Hungry Horse, Lookout Point, McNary, Minidoka, Palisades, Rock Island. 571-611, *Nov. 1952*
A Map Maker Looks at the United States. By Newman Bumstead. Included: Grand Coulee, Hoover, Jackson Lake, Shasta. 705-748, *June 1951*
Britain Tackles the East African Bush. By W. Robert Moore. Included: Dam for Lake Victoria, just below Owen Falls. 311-352, *Mar. 1950*
Around the "Great Lakes of the South." By Frederick Simpich. Photos by J. Baylor Roberts. Contents: TVA system. 463-491, *Apr. 1948*
Along the Yangtze, Main Street of China. By W. Robert Moore. 325-356, *Mar. 1948*
More Water for California's Great Central Valley. By Frederick Simpich. 645-664, *Nov. 1946*
Taming the Outlaw Missouri River. By Frederick Simpich. 569-598, *Nov. 1945*
The Columbia River Turns on the Power. By Maynard Owen Williams. 749-792, *June 1941*
By Felucca Down the Nile: Giant Dams Rule Egypt's Lifeline River, Yet Village Life Goes On As It Did in the Time of the Pharaohs. By Willard Price. 435-476, *Apr. 1940*
The Marble Dams of Rajputana. By Eleanor Maddock. 469-499, *Nov. 1921*
The Panama Canal. By William L. Sibert. 153-183, *Feb. 1914*
The Highest Dam in the World (Roosevelt Dam). 440-441, *Sept. 1905*
See also Aswân High Dam; St. Lawrence Seaway; *and* Powell, Lake, for Glen Canyon Dam

DANAKIL DEPRESSION, Ethiopia:
The Danakil: Nomads of Ethiopia's Wasteland. By Victor Englebert. 186-211, *Feb. 1970*

DANAKIL TRIBESPEOPLE:
The Danakil: Nomads of Ethiopia's Wasteland. By Victor Englebert. 186-211, *Feb. 1970*
Sailing Forbidden Coasts. By Ida Treat. 357-386, *Sept. 1931*

DA NANG, Vietnam:
Behind the Headlines in Viet Nam. By Peter T. White. Photos by Winfield Parks. 149-189, *Feb. 1967*

DANCES:
Samoa–South Sea Outpost of the U. S. Navy. Photos by Truman Bailey. Included: Siva Dance. 615-630, *May 1941*
Bali and Points East: Crowded, Happy Isles of the Flores Sea Blend Rice Terraces, Dance Festivals, and Amazing Music in Their Pattern of Living. By Maynard Owen Williams. 313-352, *Mar. 1939*
Costume Pageants in the French Pyrenees. Photos by W. Robert Moore. Included: Sword dancing. 435-450, *Oct. 1937*
The Mexican Indian Flying Pole Dance. By Helga Larsen. 387-400, *Mar. 1937*
The Perahera Processions of Ceylon. By G.H.G. Burroughs. Included: Kandyan Dancers. 90-100, *July 1932*
With the Devil Dancers of China and Tibet. Photos by Joseph F. Rock. 19-58, *July 1931*
Java, Queen of the East Indies. Photos by W. Robert Moore and Tassilo Adam. Included: Srimpi and Bedoyo Dances. 335-358, *Sept. 1929*
Life Among the Lamas of Choni: Describing the Mystery Plays and Butter Festival in the Monastery of an Almost Unknown Tibetan Principality in Kansu Province, China. By Joseph F. Rock. Included: The Chamngyonwa (Old Dance). 569-619, *Nov. 1928*
Four Faces of Siva: The Mystery of Angkor (Cambodia). By Robert J. Casey. Included: Ballet Dancers of Cambodia. 303-332, *Sept. 1928*
Artist Adventures on the Island of Bali. By Franklin Price Knott. Included: Bali Dancing Girls; Lion Dance. 326-347, *Mar. 1928*
The Land of the Basques: Home of a Thrifty, Picturesque People, Who Take Pride in the Sobriquet, "The Yankees of Spain." By Harry A. McBride. Included: The Arresku Dance. 63-87, *Jan. 1922*

Here and There in Northern Africa. By Frank Edward Johnson. Included: Dance of the Hair; Dance of the Ouled Naïls. 1-132, *Jan. 1914*

An Island in the Sea of History: The Highlands of Daghestan. By George Kennan. Included: Caucasian Dancing. 1087-1140, *Oct. 1913*

Head-Hunters of Northern Luzon. By Dean C. Worcester. Included: Kalinga War Dance; Ilongot Dances. 833-930, *Sept. 1912*

The Two Great Moorish Religious Dances. By George Edmund Holt. 777-785, *Aug. 1911*

Field Sports Among the Wild Men of Northern Luzon. By Dean C. Worcester. Included: The Bird Dance; Circle Dance; Head Dance. 215-267, *Mar. 1911*

The Snake Dance (Hopi Indians). By Marion L. Oliver. 107-137, *Feb. 1911*

Impressions and Scenes of Mozambique. By O. W. Barrett. Included: Batuque (Lengthy Ceremonial Dance); War Dances of the M'chopi tribe. 807-830, *Oct. 1910*

The Forests and Deserts of Arizona. By Bernhard E. Fernow. Included: Snake Dance. 203-226, *July-Aug. 1897*

DANIEL BOONE, First Hero of the Frontier. By Elizabeth A. Moize. Photos by William Strode. 812-841, *Dec. 1985*

DANIELS, JOSEPHUS:

Voice Voyages by the National Geographic Society: A Tribute to the Geographic Achievements of the Telephone. Address by Josephus Daniels. 296-326, *Mar. 1916*

Author

The Gem of the Ocean: Our American Navy. 313-335, *Apr. 1918*

DANISH WEST INDIES. *See* Virgin Islands

DANUBE (River), Europe:

The Danube: River of Many Nations, Many Names. By Mike Edwards. Photos by Winfield Parks. 455-485, *Oct. 1977*

Down the Danube by Canoe. By William Slade Backer. Photos by Richard S. Durrance and Christopher G. Knight. 34-79, *July 1965*

Budapest, Twin City of the Danube. By J. R. Hildebrand. 729-742, *June 1932*

The Danube, Highway of Races: From the Black Forest to the Black Sea, Europe's Most Important River Has Borne the Traffic of Centuries. By Melville Chater. 643-697, *Dec. 1929*

DANUBE DELTA, Romania:

Caviar Fishermen of Romania: From Vâlcov, "Little Venice" of the Danube Delta, Bearded Russian Exiles Go Down to the Sea. By Dorothy Hosmer. 407-434, *Mar. 1940*

DANZIG, Poland. *See* Gdańsk

DAR ES SALAAM, Tanzania:

Tanzania Marches to Its Own Drum. By Peter T. White. Photos by Emory Kristof. 474-509, *Apr. 1975*

Weighing the Aga Khan in Diamonds. Photos by David J. Carnegie. 317-324, *Mar. 1947*

DAR POMORZA (Training Ship):

By Square-rigger from Baltic to Bicentennial. By Kenneth Garrett. 824-857, *Dec. 1976*

DARDANELLES (Strait), Turkey:

The Gates to the Black Sea: The Dardanelles, the Bosphorus, and the Sea of Marmora. By Harry Griswold Dwight. 435-459, *May 1915*

DARFUR (Region), Sudan:

Adventures Among the "Lost Tribes of Islam" In Eastern Darfur: A Personal Narrative of Exploring, Mapping, and Setting Up a Government in the Anglo-Egyptian Sudan Borderland. By Edward Keith-Roach. 41-73, *Jan. 1924*

DARGUE, HERBERT A.: *Author*

How Latin America Looks from the Air: U. S. Army Airplanes Hurdle the High Andes, Brave Brazil Jungles, and Follow Smoking Volcanoes

"THE WORST MELANCHOLY OF MY LIFE"

DANNIEL BOONE

Frontiersman Daniel Boone visited the grave of his son James, killed by Indians in 1773. Wolves had disturbed the site; a storm deepened the gloom. PAINTING BY JACK UNRUH

to Map New Sky Paths Around South America. 451-502, *Oct. 1927*

DARIÉN (Province), Panama:

A Trip to Panama and Darien. By Richard U. Goode. 301-314, *Oct. 1889*

DARIÉN GAP, Panama:

We Drove Panama's Darién Gap. By Kip Ross. 368-389, *Mar. 1961*

DARIUS THE GREAT, King (Persia):

In the Footsteps of Alexander the Great. By Helen and Frank Schreider. Paintings by Tom Lovell. 1-65, *Jan. 1968*
Darius Carved History on Ageless Rock. By George G. Cameron. 825-844, *Dec. 1950*

DARIUSLEUT (Sect):

The Hutterites, Plain People of the West. By William Albert Allard. 98-125, *July 1970*

DARLEY, JAMES M.:

Chief Cartographer, NGS. 875, Dec. 1961; 897, Dec. 1962; 108, 109, *July 1964*
Nomination Page. *Jan. 1958*
Author
New Atlas Maps Announced by the Society: Expanded Map Program, Marking National Geographic's 70th Year, Will Bring to Members Plates for a Big New Atlas. 66-68, *Jan. 1958*
The Society's New Map of China. 745-746, *June 1945*
The Society Maps Northwestern United States and Neighboring Canadian Provinces. 805-806, *June 1941*
The World That Rims the Narrowing Atlantic: Latest Ten-color Map Supplement Shows Four Continents and New Transatlantic Air Routes Which Make This Ocean Only One Day Wide. 139-142, *July 1939*

DARLING, JAMES D.: *Author*

Whales: An Era of Discovery. Photos by Flip Nicklin. 872-909, *Dec. 1988*

DARLING (River), Australia:

The Land Where the Murray Flows. By Louise E. Levathes. Photos by David Robert Austen. 252-278, *Aug. 1985*

DARTMOUTH OUTING CLUB:

Skiing Over the New Hampshire Hills. By Fred H. Harris. 151-164, *Feb. 1920*

DARTON, N. H.: *Author*

Texas, Our Largest State. 1330-1360, *Dec. 1913*
The Southwest (U. S.): Its Splendid Natural Resources, Agricultural Wealth, and Scenic Beauty. 631-665, *Aug. 1910*
Our Pacific Northwest. 645-663, *July 1909*
Mexico–The Treasure House of the World. 493-519, *Aug. 1907*
Bighorn Mountains. 355-364, *June 1907*
The Bad Lands of South Dakota. 339-343, *Sept. 1899*
Shawangunk Mountain, New York. 23-34, *Mar. 17, 1894*

DARWIN, CHARLES:

Galápagos Wildlife Under Pressure. Photo essay by Dieter and Mary Plage. 122-145, *Jan. 1988*
In the Wake of Darwin's *Beagle.* By Alan Villiers. Photos by James L. Stanfield. 449-495, *Oct. 1969*
The Galapagos, Eerie Cradle of New Species. By Roger Tory Peterson. Photos by Alan and Joan Root. 541-585, *Apr. 1967*
Lost World of the Galapagos. By Irving and Electa Johnson. 681-703, *May 1959*
The British Way. By Sir Evelyn Wrench. 421-541, *Apr. 1949*

DARWIN, Australia:

The Top End of Down Under. By Kenneth MacLeish. Photos by Thomas Nebbia. 145-174, *Feb. 1973*
Life in Dauntless Darwin: A National Geographic Staff Writer Gives a Vivid Description of the Australian Town That Guards the Continent's Northern Door. By Howell Walker. 123-138, *July 1942*

DASARA (Festival):

Mysore Celebrates the Death of a Demon. By Luc Bouchage. Photos by Ylla. 706-711, *May 1958*
India Mosaic. By Peter Muir and Frances Muir. 443-470, *Apr. 1946*

DASHEEN (Vegetable):

In Honor of the Army and Aviation (NGS Banquet). Note: Dasheen, recently introduced into this country, was served at banquet. 267-284, *Mar. 1911*

DASSEN ISLAND, South Africa:

Oil and Penguins Don't Mix. Photos by Mike Holmes. 384-397, *Mar. 1973*

DATA PROCESSING, Electronic:

▪▪*Computers: Those Amazing Machines.* By Catherine O'Neill. Juvenile. 104 pages. *1985*
Behold the Computer Revolution. By Peter T. White. Photos by Bruce Dale and Emory Kristof. 593-633, *Nov. 1970*
Computer Helps Scholars Re-create an Egyptian Temple. By Ray Winfield Smith. Photos by Emory Kristof. NGS research grant. 634-655, *Nov. 1970*
See also Computer Applications; Computer Technology; Computers

DATE LINE: United Nations, New York. By Carolyn Bennett Patterson. Photos by B. Anthony Stewart and John E. Fletcher. 305-331, *Sept. 1961*

DATE PALMS:

The Lure of the Changing Desert (California). 817-824, *June 1954*
Here and There in Northern Africa. By Frank Edward Johnson. 1-132, *Jan. 1914*
The National Geographic Society (NGS Banquet). Included: First American-grown dates ever served at a public function; *and* information about date cultivation in this country. 278, 279, 293, *Mar. 1912*

New Plant Immigrants. By David Fairchild. 879-907, *Oct. 1911*
The Country of the Ant Men (Souf, Algeria). By Thomas H. Kearney. 367-382, *Apr. 1911*
The Date Gardens of the Jerid. By Thomas H. Kearney. 543-567, *July 1910*
Our Plant Immigrants. By David Fairchild. 179-210, *Apr. 1906*

DATING METHODS:

The Anasazi–Riddles in the Ruins. By Thomas Y. Canby. Photos by Dewitt Jones and David Brill. Paintings by Roy Andersen. Included: Archaeomagnetism; radiocarbon dating; tree-ring dating. 554-592, *Nov. 1982*
The Search for the First Americans. By Thomas Y. Canby. Photos by Kerby Smith. Paintings by Roy Andersen. Included: Radiocarbon dating; amino acid racemization; dentition; stratigraphy. 330-363, *Sept. 1979*
Ancient Europe Is Older Than We Thought. By Colin Renfrew. Photos by Adam Woolfitt. Included: Radiocarbon dating; tree-ring dating. 615-623, *Nov. 1977*
What's Happening to Our Climate? By Samuel W. Matthews. Included: Ice-core dating; Sea-core dating; Tree-ring dating. 576-615, *Nov. 1976*
This Changing Earth. By Samuel W. Matthews. Included: Carbon 14 dating; fossil dating; paleomagnetics; potassium-argon dating; radioactive-isotope dating. 1-37, *Jan. 1973*
See also Archeomagnetism; Potassium-Argon Dating; Radiocarbon Dating; Tree-Ring Dating

DAUFUSKIE (Island), South Carolina:

Sea Islands: Adventuring Along the South's Surprising Coast. By James Cerruti. Photos by Thomas Nebbia and James L. Amos. 366-393, *Mar. 1971*

DAUGHTERS OF THE AMERICAN REVOLUTION:

The DAR Story. By Lonnelle Aikman. Photos by B. Anthony Stewart and John E. Fletcher. 565-598, *Nov. 1951*

The **DAUNTLESS** Little Stilt. By Frederick Kent Truslow. 241-245, *Aug. 1960*

DÁVALOS, FELIPE: *Artist*

The Aztecs. By Bart McDowell. Photos by David Hiser. 714-751, *Dec. 1980*
The Building of Tenochtitlan. By Augusto F. Molina Montes. 753-765, *Dec. 1980*

DÁVALOS HURTADO, EUSEBIO: *Author*

Into the Well of Sacrifice. I. Return to the Sacred Cenote. 540-549, *Oct. 1961*

DAVAO, Mindanao (Island), Philippines:

Mindanao, on the Road to Tokyo. By Frederick Simpich. 539-574, *Nov. 1944*

DAVENPORT, WILLIAM: *Author*

Bordeaux: Fine Wines and Fiery

Derelict tugboat rusts in a Staten Island salvage yard behind Charles Mead, who helps cut up part of the scrap metal that New York Harbor exports in bulk. BRUCE DAVIDSON, MAGNUM

Gascons. Photos by Adam Woolfitt. 233-259, *Aug. 1980*

Living the Good Life in Burgundy. Photos by Robert Freson. 794-817, *June 1978*

Provence, Empire of the Sun. Photos by James A. Sugar. 692-715, *May 1975*

Amiable Amsterdam. Photos by Adam Woolfitt. 683-705, *May 1974*

France's Wild, Watery South, the Camargue. 696-726, *May 1973*

DAVIDSON, BRUCE: *Photographer*
New York Harbor–The Golden Door. By Erla Zwingle. 21-43, *July 1986*

DAVIDSON, CAMERON:
Photographer
Lord of the Shallows–The Great Blue Heron. By Richard J. Dolesh. 540-554, *Apr. 1984*

DAVIDSON, GEORGE: *Author*
Origin of the Name "Cape Nome." 398, *Nov. 1901*
Early Voyages on the Northwestern Coast of America. 235-256, *Jan. 31, 1894*

DAVIDSON, ROBYN: *Author*
Alone Across the Outback (Australia). Photos by Rick Smolan. 581-611, *May 1978*

DAVIDSON, TREAT:
Author-Photographer
Tree Snails, Gems of the Everglades. 372-387, *Mar. 1965*
Bullfrog Ballet Filmed in Flight. 791-799, *June 1963*
Rose Aphids. 851-859, *June 1961*
Inside the World of the Honeybee. 188-217, *Aug. 1959*
Freezing the Trout's Lightning Leap. 525-530, *Apr. 1958*
Photographer
Alligators: Dragons in Distress. By Archie Carr. Photos by Treat Davidson

and Laymond Hardy. 133-148, *Jan. 1967*
Moths That Behave Like Hummingbirds. 770-775, *June 1965*

DAVIES, LLEWELLYN JAMES:
Author
The Chinese "Boxers." 281-287, *July 1900*

DA VINCI, Project:
Laboratory in a Dirty Sky. By Rudolf J. Engelmann and Vera Simons. NGS research grant. 616-621, *Nov. 1976*

DAVIS, ARTHUR P.:
Four Prominent Geographers. 425-428, *June 1907*
Author
The New Inland Sea (Salton Sea). 37-49, *Jan. 1907*
Location of the Boundary Between Nicaragua and Costa Rica. 22-28, *Jan. 1901*
The Water Supply for the Nicaragua Canal. 363-365, *Sept. 1900*
Nicaragua and the Isthmian Routes. 247-266, *July 1899*
The Kansas River. 181-184, *May 1896*

DAVIS, MALCOLM: *Author*
Nature's Clown, the Penguin. By David Hellyer and Malcolm Davis. 405-428, *Sept. 1952*

DAVIS, NEAL P.: *Photographer*
The Past Is Present in Greenfield Village. By Beverley M. Bowie. Photos by Neal P. Davis and Willard R. Culver. 96-127, *July 1958*

DAVIS, NOEL: *Author*
The Removal of the North Sea Mine Barrage. 103-133, *Feb. 1920*

DAVIS, WILLIAM MORRIS:
Board of Managers. 87, *Feb. 1905*
Geographic Literature. 184-185, May 1896; 408-409, *Dec. 1896*

Author
Bearing of Physiography Upon Seuss' Theories. 430, *Oct. 1904*
Practical Exercises in Geography. 62-78, *Feb. 1900*
The Rational Element in Geography. 466-473, *Nov. 1899*
The Seine, the Meuse, and the Moselle. Part II. 228-238, *July 1896*
A Geographical Description of the British Islands. 208-211, *June 1896*
The Seine, the Meuse, and the Moselle. Part I. 189-202, *June 1896*
The Improvement of Geographical Teaching. 68-75, *July 10, 1893*
The Rivers of Northern New Jersey, with Notes on the Classification of Rivers in General. 81-110, *May 1890*
The Rivers and Valleys of Pennsylvania. 183-253, *July 1889*
Geographic Methods in Geologic Investigation. 11-26, *Oct. 1888*

DAVIS STRAIT, Canada-Greenland:
I Sailed with Portugal's Captains Courageous. By Alan Villiers. 565-596, *May 1952*

DAVISON, HENRY P.: *Author*
Our Armies of Mercy (American National Red Cross). 423-427, *May 1917*

DAVISON, LONNELLE. See Aikman, Lonnelle Davison

DAVY, SIR HUMPHRY:
The British Way. By Sir Evelyn Wrench. 421-541, *Apr. 1949*

DAWES, CHARLES G.:
Board of Trustees. 793, *June 1934*

DAWSON, GEORGE M.:
George M. Dawson (Biography). By Henry Gannett. 197, *May 1901*

DAWSON, JOHN D.: *Artist*
Ways of the Ant. By Bert Hölldobler. Illustrations text by Alice J. Hall. NGS research grant. 779-813, *June 1984*

DAWSON, Yukon Territory, Canada:
Yukon Fever: Call of the North. By Robert Booth. Photos by George F. Mobley. 548-578, *Apr. 1978*
Along the Yukon Trail. By Amos Burg. 395-416, *Sept. 1953*

DAY, CHARLES HEALY:
Flying the World: In a Homemade Airplane the Author and Her Husband Enjoy 16,000 Miles of Adventurous Flight Across Europe, Asia, and America. By Gladys M. Day. 655-690, *June 1932*

DAY, DAVID T.:
Board of Managers. 216, *June 1896*
Author
The Course of the Retail Coal Trade. 394-398, *Nov. 1902*

DAY, GLADYS M.: *Author*
Flying the World: In a Homemade Airplane the Author and Her Husband Enjoy 16,000 Miles of Adventurous Flight Across Europe, Asia, and America. 655-690, *June 1932*

DAY of the Rice God. Photos by H. Edward Kim. Text by Douglas Lee. 78-85, *July 1978*

The **DAY** the Sky Fell. By Rowe Findley. 50-65, *Jan. 1981*

The **DAY** the World Ended at Kourion. By David Soren. Photos by Martha Cooper. NGS research grant. 30-53, *July 1988*

A **DAY** with Our Boys in the Geographic Wards. By Carol Corey. 69-80, *July 1918*

DAYAKS. *See* Iban

DAYR AZ ZAWR, Syria:
Ali Goes to the Clinic. By Herndon and Mary Hudson. 764-766, *Dec. 1946*

DAYTON, WILLIAM A.: *Author*
Beauty and Bounty of Southern State Trees. Paintings by Walter A. Weber. 508-552, *Oct. 1957*
Wealth and Wonder of Northern State Trees. Paintings by Walter A. Weber. 651-691, *Nov. 1955*

DAZZLING Corals of Palau. By Thomas O'Neill. Photos by Douglas Faulkner. 136-150, *July 1978*

DAZZLING Legacy of an Ancient Quest. By Alice J. Hall. 293-311, *Mar. 1977*

DEAD, Rites for the. *See* Burial Customs; Funerals; Funerary Boats

The **DEAD** Do Tell Tales at Vesuvius. By Rick Gore. Photos by O. Louis Mazzatenta. NGS research grant. 557-613, *May 1984*

DEAD SEA, Israel-Jordan:
The Living Dead Sea. By Harvey Arden. Photos by Nathan Benn. Included: Map showing Israeli-occupied territory, water fluctuations of Dead Sea, diagram comparing Dead Sea water level with sea level. 225-245, *Feb. 1978*
Abraham, the Friend of God. By Kenneth MacLeish. Photos by Dean Conger. 739-789, *Dec. 1966*

Geographical Twins (Holy Land and Utah) a World Apart. By David S. Boyer. 848-859, *Dec. 1958*

DEAD SEA SCROLLS:
The Men Who Hid the Dead Sea Scrolls. By A. Douglas Tushingham. Paintings by Peter V. Bianchi. 785-808, *Dec. 1958*

The **DEADLY** Fisher. By Charles E. Lane. 388-397, *Mar. 1963*

The **DEAF,** Schools for:
Deaf Children Learn to Talk at Clarke School. By Lilian Grosvenor. Photos by Willard R. Culver. 379-397, *Mar. 1955*
Washington's Historic Georgetown. By William A. Kinney. Included: Volta Bureau. 513-544, *Apr. 1953*
President Alexander Graham Bell on Japan. By John Hyde. Included: Dr. Bell's discussion of the deaf and mute in Japan. 509-512, *Dec. 1898*

DEAGAN, KATHLEEN A.: *Author*
Searching for Columbus's Lost Colony: La Navidad. Photos by Bill Ballenberg. 672-675, *Nov. 1987*

DEAL SCHOOL. *See* Alice Deal Junior High School

DEALINGS of the United States with the Nations of the World. 186-187, *Apr. 1904*

DE ALWIS, LYN: *Author*
Sri Lanka's Wildlife: A Nation Rises to the Challenge. Photos by Dieter and Mary Plage. 274-278, *Aug. 1983*

DEARBORN, N.: *Author*
The Pest of English Sparrows. 948-952, *Nov. 1910*

DEARBORN, Michigan. *See* Henry Ford Museum

DEATH of an Island, Tristan da Cunha. By P.J.F. Wheeler. 678-695, *May 1962*

DEATH of a Star. By Robert P.

Kirshner. Photos by Roger H. Ressmeyer. 619-647, *May 1988*

DEATH of G. Brown Goode. By W J McGee. 316, *Sept. 1896*

DEATH of Marchessa. Photos by Peter G. Veit. 508-511, *Apr. 1981*

DEATH VALLEY, California:
Lowest Point in the United States. 824-825, *Dec. 1907*
The Deserts of Nevada and the Death Valley. By Robert H. Chapman. 483-497, *Sept. 1906*

DEATH VALLEY NATIONAL MONUMENT, California:
California Desert, A Worldly Wilderness. By Barry Lopez. Photos by Craig Aurness. 42-77, *Jan. 1987*
■■ *Exploring America's Backcountry.* 215 pages. *1979*
Getting to Know the Wild Burros of Death Valley. By Patricia des Roses Moehlman. Photos by Ira S. Lerner and author. NGS research grant. 502-517, *Apr. 1972*
■ The Great Mojave Desert. 294A-294B, *Feb. 1971*
Death Valley, the Land and the Legend. By Rowe Findley. Photos by David Hiser. 69-103, *Jan. 1970*
See also Los Angeles Aqueduct

DE BEERS CONSOLIDATED MINES, Ltd.:
The Incredible Crystal: Diamonds. By Fred Ward. 85-113, *Jan. 1979*

DE BRY, THEODORE. *See* Bry, Theodore de

A **DECADE** of Innovation, a Lifetime of Service (Melville Bell Grosvenor). By Bart McDowell. 270-278, *Aug. 1982*

DEČANI MONASTERY, Yugoslavia:
The Clock Turns Back in Yugoslavia: The Fortified Monastery of Mountain-girt Dečani Survives Its Six Hundredth Birthday. By Ethel Chamberlain Porter. 493-512, *Apr. 1944*

DECEPTION: Formula for Survival. By Robert F. Sisson. 394-415, *Mar. 1980*

DECEPTION ISLAND, Antarctica:
Antarctica's Nearer Side. By Samuel W. Matthews. Photos by William R. Curtsinger. 622-655, *Nov. 1971*

DE CHÉTELAT, ELEANOR. *See* Chételat, Eleanor de

DE CHÉTELAT, ENZO. *See* Chételat, Enzo de

DECISION of the Alaskan Boundary Tribunal. 12-14, *Jan. 1904*

DECORATIONS, Military:
Insignia and Decorations of the United States Armed Forces. By Gilbert Grosvenor. 185-186, *Feb. 1945*
■■ *Insignia and Decorations of the U. S. Armed Forces.* Reprint of June 1943 NGM. 208 pages. 1943; rev. ed. *1944*
Decorations, Medals, Service Ribbons, Badges, and Women's Insignia. 414-444, *Oct. 1943*

Wide-eyed with fear, a red deer stag flees hounds in England. The species is increasingly domesticated in New Zealand and fostered in the British Isles. MICHAEL HUSKISSON

With a saw imported two generations ago, men cut up a mahogany tree in a Zairian rain forest in 1980. JAMES P. BLAIR, NGS

Chicken king Frank Perdue shoulders a bird in Delaware, where the modern poultry industry began in 1923. KEVIN FLEMING

DEKIN, ALBERT A., Jr.: *Author*

Sealed in Time–Ice Entombs an Eskimo Family for Five Centuries. Photos by Victor R. Boswell, Jr., and Scott Rutherford. Paintings by James M. Gurney. 824-836, *June 1987*

De La HABA, LOUIS: *Author*

Guatemala, Maya and Modern. Photos by Joseph J. Scherschel. 661-689, *Nov. 1974*

Mexico, the City That Founded a Nation. Photos by Albert Moldvay. 638-669, *May 1973*

Belize, the Awakening Land. Photos by Michael E. Long. 124-146, *Jan. 1972*

De La MADRID HURTADO, MIGUEL:

A Scholarly President Looks at Mexico's Future. The Editor. 175, *Aug. 1984*

DELAWARE:

Delaware–Who Needs to Be Big? By Jane Vessels. Photos by Kevin Fleming. 171-197, *Aug. 1983*

Our Changing Atlantic Coastline. By Nathaniel T. Kenney. Photos by B. Anthony Stewart. Included: Dewey Beach; Rehoboth Beach. 860-887, *Dec. 1962*

Today on the Delaware, Penn's Glorious River. By Albert W. Atwood. Photos by Robert F. Sisson. 1-40, *July 1952*

"Delmarva," Gift of the Sea. By Catherine Bell Palmer. 367-399, *Sept. 1950*

Diamond Delaware, Colonial Still: Tradition Rules the "Three Lower Counties" Over Which William Penn and Lord Baltimore Went to Law. By Leo A. Borah. 367-398, *Sept. 1935*

Maryland, Delaware, and District of Columbia. Feb. 1927

See also Henlopen Dunes; Noxontown Pond

DELAWARE (River), U. S.:

Today on the Delaware, Penn's Glorious River. By Albert W. Atwood. Photos by Robert F. Sisson. 1-40, *July 1952*

Atlantic Estuarine Tides. By Mark S. W. Jefferson. 400-409, *Sept. 1898*

The **DELECTABLE** Shrimp: Once a Culinary Stepchild, Today a Gulf Coast Industry. By Harlan Major. 501-512, *Oct. 1944*

DELHI, India:

Delhi, Capital of a New Dominion. By Phillips Talbot. 597-630, *Nov. 1947*

India Mosaic. By Peter Muir and Frances Muir. 443-470, *Apr. 1946*

New Delhi Goes Full Time. By Maynard Owen Williams. Note: Information is also included about "old" Delhi. 465-494, *Oct. 1942*

Through the Heart of Hindustan: A Teeming Highway Extending for Fifteen Hundred Miles, from the Khyber Pass to Calcutta. By Maynard Owen Williams. 433-467, *Nov. 1921*

The Temples of India. Photos by W. M. Zumbro. 922-971, *Nov. 1909*

See also New Delhi

DELI, Sumatra, Indonesia:

By Motor Through the East Coast and Batak Highlands of Sumatra. By Melvin A. Hall. 69-102, *Jan. 1920*

DELIGHT (Yawl):

Sailing Iceland's Rugged Coasts. By Wright Britton. Photos by James A. Sugar. 228-265, *Aug. 1969*

DE'LISLE, GORDON: *Photographer*

Australia. By Alan Villiers. 309-385. Included: The West and the South. 309-345; The Settled East, the Barrier Reef, the Center. 347-385, *Sept. 1963*

DE L'ISLE, J. N.:

The Cartography and Observations of Bering's First Voyage. By A. W. Greely. Note: Map is a reproduction of the original produced by J. N. De l'Isle, Paris, in 1752. 205-230, Jan. 28, 1892; Feb. 19, 1892

DELMARVA PENINSULA (Delaware-Maryland-Virginia):

"Delmarva," Gift of the Sea. By Catherine Bell Palmer. 367-399, *Sept. 1950*

DELOS (Island), Aegean Sea:

The Isles of Greece: Aegean Birthplace of Western Culture. By Melville Bell Grosvenor. Photos by Edwin Stuart Grosvenor and Winfield Parks. 147-193, *Aug. 1972*

Fish Men Discover a 2,200-year-old Greek Ship. By Jacques-Yves Cousteau. NGS research grant. 1-36, *Jan. 1954*

The Isles of Greece. By Richard Stillwell. 593-622, *May 1944*

DELPHI, Greece:

"The Glory That Was Greece." By Alexander Wilbourne Weddell. 571-630, *Dec. 1922*

DELPHIC FESTIVAL:

Festival Days on the Slopes of Mount Parnassus, Greece. Photos by Maynard Owen Williams. 713-720, *Dec. 1930*

DELTA, Inland. *See* California Delta

DELTA MARSH, Manitoba, Canada:

Western Grebes: The Birds That Walk on Water. By Gary L. Nuechterlein. NGS research grant. 624-637, *May 1982*

The **DELTA** of the Mississippi River. By E. L. Corthell. 351-354, *Dec. 1897*

DELTA PROJECT, The Netherlands:

Man Against the Sea, the Oosterschelde Barrier. By Larry Kohl. 526-537, *Oct. 1986*

DELTA WATERFOWL RESEARCH STATION, Manitoba, Canada: Study Grant:

Western Grebes: The Birds That Walk on Water. By Gary L. Nuechterlein. NGS research grant. 624-637, *May 1982*

DEMAVEND, Mount, Iran:

Modern Persia and Its Capital: And an Account of an Ascent of Mount Demavend, the Persian Olympus. By F. L. Bird. 353-400, *Apr. 1921*

DEMOCRACY'S Fortress: Unsinkable Malta. By Ernle Bradford. Photos by Ted H. Funk. 852-879, *June 1969*

DEMOCRACY'S Royal Palace, Westminster. Photos by B. Anthony Stewart. 233-248, *Aug. 1946*

DEMOCRATIC PEOPLE'S REPUBLIC OF KOREA. *See* Korea, North

DEMOLISHING Germany's North Sea Ramparts. By Stuart E. Jones. 635-644, *Nov. 1946*

DEMON DANCERS. *See* Devil Dancers

DEMON-POSSESSED Tibetans and Their Incredible Feats. 479-486, *Oct. 1935*

DENALI NATIONAL PARK AND PRESERVE, Alaska:

Giants of the Wilderness: Alaskan Moose. By Victor Van Ballenberghe. Photos by Michio Hoshino. 260-280, *Aug. 1987*

"Grizz"–Of Men and the Great Bear. By Douglas H. Chadwick. 182-213, *Feb. 1986*

Alaska's Magnificent Parklands. 199 pages. 1984

See also former name, Mount McKinley National Park

DENBY, EDWIN:

A Memorial to Peary: The National Geographic Society Dedicates Monument in Arlington National Cemetery to Discoverer of the North Pole. Address by Edwin Denby. 639-646, *June 1922*

DENE NATION:

Peoples of the Arctic. 144-223. I.

Introduction by Joseph Judge. 144-149; II. Hunters of the Lost Spirit: Canadians. By Priit J. Vesilind. Photos by David Alan Harvey. 174-189, *Feb. 1983*

DENG BAO-LING: *Artist*

China's Wonderland–Yen Tang Shan (Chekiang Province). Photos by Herbert Clarence White and Clarence C. Crisler. Camera paintings by Deng Bao-ling and Hwang Yao-tso. 687-694, *Dec. 1937*

A Peiping Panorama in Vivid Pigments. Photos by Herbert Clarence White and Clarence C. Crisler. Camera paintings by Deng Bao-ling and Hwang Yao-tso. 753-784, *Dec. 1936*

DENIS, ARMAND:

New Guinea's Rare Birds and Stone Age Men. By E. Thomas Gilliard. Note: Armand Denis was the leader of the American Museum-Armand Denis Expedition. NGS research grant. 421-488, *Apr. 1953*

DENISE (Diving Saucer):

Diving Saucer Takes to the Deep. By Jacques-Yves Cousteau. NGS research grant. 571-586, *Apr. 1960*

DENISON, Cape, Antarctica:

Voyage to the Antarctic. By David Lewis. 544-562, *Apr. 1983*

DENIZENS of Our Warm Atlantic Waters (Mollusks and Crustaceans). By Roy Waldo Miner. Paintings by Else Bostelmann. 199-219, *Feb. 1937*

DENKER, DEBRA: *Author*

Along Afghanistan's War-torn Frontier. Photos by Steve McCurry. 772-797, *June 1985*

Pakistan's Kalash: People of Fire and Fervor. Photos by Steve McCurry. 458-473, *Oct. 1981*

DENMARK:

Mysteries of the Bog. By Louise E. Levathes. Photos by Fred Bavendam. 397-420, *Mar. 1987*

The Magic World of Hans Christian Andersen. By Harvey Arden. Photos by Sisse Brimberg. Included: Copenhagen; Odense. 825-849, *Dec. 1979*

Denmark, Field of the Danes. By William Graves. Photos by Thomas Nebbia. 245-275, *Feb. 1974*

The Vikings. By Howard La Fay. Photos by Ted Spiegel. 492-541, *Apr. 1970*

Friendly Flight to Northern Europe. By Lyndon B. Johnson. Photos by Volkmar Wentzel. 268-293, *Feb. 1964*

By Full-rigged Ship to Denmark's Fairyland. By Alan Villiers. Photos by Alexander Taylor and author. 809-828, *Dec. 1955*

Under Canvas in the Atomic Age (U. S. Coast Guard). By Alan Villiers. 49-84, *July 1955*

Lifelike Man Preserved 2,000 Years in Peat. By P. V. Glob. 419-430, *Mar. 1954*

Thumbs Up Round the North Sea's Rim. By Frances James. Photos by Erica Koch. 685-704, *May 1952*

Baltic Cruise of the *Caribbee*. By Carleton Mitchell. 605-646, *Nov. 1950*

2,000 Miles Through Europe's Oldest Kingdom. By Isobel Wylie Hutchison. Photos by Maynard Owen Williams. 141-180, *Feb. 1949*

On Danish By-Lanes: An American Cycles Through the Quaint City of Lace, the Curiosity Town Where Time Stands Still, and Even Finds a Frontier in the Farming Kingdom. By Willis Lindquist. Included: Denmark–Land of Tranquility. 1-34, *Jan. 1940*

Royal Copenhagen, Capital of a Farming Kingdom: A Fifth of Denmark's Thrifty Population Resides in a Metropolis Famous for Its Porcelains, Its Silver, and Its Lace. By J. R. Hildebrand. Included: Denmark, Land of Farms and Fisheries. Photos by Gustav Heurlin. 217-250, *Feb. 1932*

Denmark and the Danes. By Maurice Francis Egan. 115-164, *Aug. 1922*

See also Bornholm (Island); Copenhagen; Faeroe Islands; Greenland

DENNIS, ALFRED PEARCE: *Author*

Norway, A Land of Stern Reality: Where Descendants of the Sea Kings of Old Triumphed Over Nature and Wrought a Nation of Arts and Crafts. 1-44, *July 1930*

The Land of Egypt: A Narrow Green Strip of Fertility Stretching for a Thousand Miles Through Walls of Desert. 271-298, *Mar. 1926*

Life on a Yukon Trail. 377-391, Oct. 1899; 457-466, *Nov. 1899*

DENNISON, EDWARD S.: *Author*

Ambassadors of Good Will: The Peace Corps. By Sargent Shriver and Peace Corps Volunteers. Included: Bolivia. By Edward S. Dennison. 297-345, *Sept. 1964*

Tallest monarch of his day, King Christian X of Denmark celebrated his jubilee in 1937. © INTERNATIONAL NEWS PHOTO

DENT DU REQUIN (Mountain), France:

A Woman's Climbs in the High Alps. By Dora Keen. 643-675, *July 1911*

DENTON, IVAN, Family:

An Ozark Family Carves a Living and a Way of Life. Photos by Bruce Dale. 124-133, *July 1975*

DENVER, Colorado:

Denver, Colorado's Rocky Mountain High. By John J. Putman. Photos by David Cupp. 383-411, *Mar. 1979*

Colorado, the Rockies' Pot of Gold. By Edward J. Linehan. Photos by James L. Amos. 157-201, *Aug. 1969*

Colorado by Car and Campfire. By Kathleen Revis. 207-248, *Aug. 1954*

Colorado, a Barrier That Became a Goal: Where Water Has Transformed Dry Plains Into Verdant Farms, and Highways Have Opened up Mineral and Scenic Wealth. By McFall Kerbey. 1-63, *July 1932*

DEOXYRIBONUCLEIC ACID (DNA):

Beyond Supermouse: Changing Life's Genetic Blueprint. By Robert F. Weaver. Photos by Ted Spiegel. 818-847, *Dec. 1984*

The Awesome Worlds Within a Cell. By Rick Gore. Photos by Bruce Dale. Paintings by Davis Meltzer. Included: "Language of Life" foldout showing the replication of DNA and the manufacture of RNA and proteins. 355-395, *Sept. 1976*

The **DEPTHS** of the Sea: Strange Life Forms a Mile Below the Surface. By William Beebe. Paintings by E. Bostelmann. 65-88, *Jan. 1932*

DE ROOS, ROBERT: *Author*

New England's "Lively Experiment," Rhode Island. Photos by Fred Ward. 370-401, *Sept. 1968*

The Flower Seed Growers: Gardening's Color Merchants. Photos by Jack Fields. 720-738, *May 1968*

Massachusetts Builds for Tomorrow. Photos by B. Anthony Stewart. 790-843, *Dec. 1966*

The Philippines, Freedom's Pacific Frontier. Photos by Ted Spiegel. 301-351, *Sept. 1966*

Costa Rica, Free of the Volcano's Veil. 125-152, *July 1965*

The Magic Worlds of Walt Disney. Photos by Thomas Nebbia. 159-207, *Aug. 1963*

Arizona: Booming Youngster of the West. Photos by Robert F. Sisson. 299-343, *Mar. 1963*

Los Angeles, City of the Angels. Photos by Thomas Nebbia. 451-501, *Oct. 1962*

The **DESCENDANTS** of Confucius (Industries in Shantung). By Maynard Owen Williams. 253-265, *Sept. 1919*

DESCENDANTS of the Expeditions. Photos by Bob Sacha. 414-429. I. The Peary Family. By Edward Peary Stafford. 417-421; II. The Henson Family. By S. Allen Counter. 422-429, *Sept. 1988*

In a heavily rained-on dry lake bed in California's Mojave Desert, a thrill seeker spins his wheels in a four-wheel-drive truck. CRAIG AURNESS, WEST LIGHT

A bird's-eye view of Detroit, Michigan, and environs unfolds from an altitude of 440 miles in this image made by Landsat 4. NASA/ENVIRONMENTAL RESEARCH INSTITUTE OF MICHIGAN

Londoners share a church porch in a scene reminiscent of the rough street life in Charles Dickens's day. ADAM WOOLFITT

DIAMONDS:

Namibia: Nearly a Nation? By Bryan Hodgson. Photos by Jim Brandenburg. 755-797, *June 1982*

The Incredible Crystal: Diamonds. By Fred Ward. 85-113, *Jan. 1979*

Questing for Gems. By George S. Switzer. 835-863, *Dec. 1971*

The Many-sided Diamond. By George S. Switzer. 568-586, *Apr. 1958*

The Jungle Was My Home. By Sasha Siemel. 695-712, *Nov. 1952*

White Magic in the Belgian Congo. By W. Robert Moore. 321-362, *Mar. 1952*

Exploring the World of Gems. By W. F. Foshag. 779-810, *Dec. 1950*

Britain Tackles the East African Bush. By W. Robert Moore. Included: Williamson mine in Tanganyika. 311-352, *Mar. 1950*

Weighing the Aga Khan in Diamonds. Photos by David J. Carnegie. 317-324, *Mar. 1947*

Under the South African Union. By Melville Chater. 391-512, *Apr. 1931*

The Diamond Mines of South Africa. By Gardiner F. Williams. 344-356, *June 1906*

Africa Since 1888, with Special Reference to South Africa and Abyssinia. By Gardiner G. Hubbard. 157-175, *May 1896*

DIANA (Ship):

Peary's Explorations in 1898-1899. 415-416, *Oct. 1899*

The Mission of the "Diana" (Peary Arctic Club). 273, *July 1899*

DIARY of a Voyage from San Francisco to Tahiti and Return, 1901. By S. P. Langley. 413-429, *Dec. 1901*

DIARY of the President's Daughter: I See America First. By Lynda Bird Johnson. Photos by William Albert Allard. 874-904, *Dec. 1965*

DIATOMS:

Those Marvelous, Myriad Diatoms. By Richard B. Hoover. 871-878, *June 1979*

DÍAZ DEL CASTILLO, BERNAL:

Following Cortés: Path to Conquest. By S. Jeffrey K. Wilkerson. Photos by Guillermo Aldana E. Paintings by Ned Seidler and Rosalie Seidler. Included: Excerpts from Díaz's chronicle. 420-459, *Oct. 1984*

DICK SMITH EXPLORER (Schooner):

Icebound in Antarctica. By David Lewis. Photos by Mimi George. 634-663, *Nov. 1984*

Voyage to the Antarctic. By David Lewis. 544-562, *Apr. 1983*

DICKENS, CHARLES:

The England of Charles Dickens. By Richard W. Long. Photos by Adam Woolfitt. 443-483, *Apr. 1974*

The British Way. By Sir Evelyn Wrench. 421-541, *Apr. 1949*

DICKEY, W. A.: *Author*

The Sushitna River, Alaska. 322-327, *Nov. 1897*

Dickey Chapelle was the first American woman correspondent to die in action in South Vietnam, in 1965. DICKEY CHAPELLE

DICKEY CHAPELLE Killed in Action. By W. E. Garrett. 270-271, *Feb. 1966*

DICKINSON, EMILY:

Literary Landmarks of Massachusetts. By William H. Nicholas. Photos by B. Anthony Stewart and John E. Fletcher. 279-310, *Mar. 1950*

DID Peary Reach the Pole? By Wally Herbert. 387-413, *Sept. 1988*

DIEGO GARCIA (Island), Indian Ocean:

Crosscurrents Sweep the Indian Ocean. By Bart McDowell. Photos by Steve Raymer. 422-457, *Oct. 1981*

DIEPPE, France:

Rehearsal at Dieppe. By W. Robert Moore. 495-502, *Oct. 1942*

DIETZ, ROBERT S.: *Author*

The Explosive Birth of Myojin Island. 117-128, *Jan. 1954*

DIFFENDERFER, HOPE A.: *Author*

Okinawa, the Island Rebuilt. 265-288, *Feb. 1955*

A **DIFFERENT** Communism: Hungary's New Way. By John J. Putman. Photos by Bill Weems. 225-261, *Feb. 1983*

The **DIFFIDENT** Truffle, France's Gift to Gourmets. 419-426, *Sept. 1956*

DIGIT FUND:

President's Page. By Gilbert M. Grosvenor. Included: Mailing address. *May 1986*

DIGITAL SUBTRACTION ANGIOGRAPHY (DSA):

Medicine's New Vision. By Howard Sochurek. Paintings by Davis Meltzer. Illustrations text by Peter Miller. 2-41, *Jan. 1987*

DIKES AND LEVEES:

Mississippi Delta: The Land of the River. By Douglas Lee. Photos by C. C. Lockwood. 226-253, *Aug. 1983*

California's Surprising Inland Delta. By Judith and Neil Morgan. Photos by Charles O'Rear. Included: Map showing the 1,100 miles of levees that rim the 55 islands reclaimed from marshland. 409-430, *Sept. 1976*

■ Holland Against the Sea. *1970*

The Lower Mississippi. By Willard Price. Photos by W. D. Vaughn. 681-725, *Nov. 1960*

Helping Holland Rebuild Her Land. By Gilbert M. Grosvenor and Charles Neave. 365-413, *Sept. 1954*

Mending Dikes in the Netherlands. Photos by Lawrence Earl. 791-806, *Dec. 1946*

The Great Mississippi Flood of 1927: Since White Man's Discovery This Mighty River Has Served Him Well, Yet It Has Brought Widespread Devastation Along Its Lower Reaches. By Frederick Simpich. 243-289, *Sept. 1927*

The Dikes of Holland. By Gerard H. Matthes. 219-234, *June 1901*

The Delta of the Mississippi River. By E. L. Corthell. 351-354, *Dec. 1897*

DILEMMA of Independence: South Africa's Ndebele People. Introduction by The Editor. 260-261, *Feb. 1986*

DILLER, J. S.: *Author*

Volcanic Rocks of Martinique and St. Vincent: Collected by Robert T. Hill and Israel C. Russell. 285-296, *July 1902*

Crater Lake, Oregon. 33-48, *Feb. 1897*

The Mazamas. 58-59, *Feb. 1897*

Our Youngest Volcano. 93-96, *July 10, 1893*

DILLON, LUTHER E.:

Nomination Page. *Feb. 1979*

DILLON, RAYMOND A.: *Photographer*

War Finds Its Way to Gilbert Islands: United States Forces Dislodge Japanese from Enchanted Atolls Which Loom Now as Stepping Stones along South Sea Route from Australia to Hawaii. By Sir Arthur Grimble. 71-92, *Jan. 1943*

DILMUN (Ancient Civilization):

Bahrain: Hub of the Persian Gulf. By Thomas J. Abercrombie. Photos by Steve Raymer. 300-329, *Sept. 1979*

DIMANCESCU, DAN: *Author*

Americans Afoot in Rumania. Photos by Dick Durrance II and Christopher G. Knight. 810-845, *June 1969*

Kayak Odyssey: From the Inland Sea to Tokyo. Photos by Christopher G. Knight. 295-337, *Sept. 1967*

DINGLE PENINSULA, Ireland:

Irish Ways Live On in Dingle. By Bryan Hodgson. Photos by Linda Bartlett. 551-576, *Apr. 1976*

DINKA TRIBESPEOPLE:

Across Widest Africa. By A. Henry Savage Landor. 694-737, *Oct. 1908*

Four species of rats live in close association with humans: the Norway rat, roof rat, Polynesian rat, and lesser bandicoot (clockwise from left).   PAINTING BY WILLIAM H. BOND, NGS

The **DISCUS FISH** Yields a Secret. By Gene Wolfsheimer. 675-681, *May 1960*

DISEASE:

Fleas: The Lethal Leapers. By Nicole Duplaix. 672-694, *May 1988*

Medicine's New Vision. By Howard Sochurek. Paintings by Davis Meltzer. Illustrations text by Peter Miller. 2-41, *Jan. 1987*

Tsetse–Fly of the Deadly Sleep. By Georg Gerster. 814-833, *Dec. 1986*

Our Immune System: The Wars Within. By Peter Jaret. Photos by Lennart Nilsson. Illustrations text by Larry Kohl. 702-735, *June 1986*

■■ *The Incredible Machine.* Contents: The human body. 384 pages. *1986*

■■ *Science: It's Changing Your World.* Contents: Fuel and food, industry, medicine, transportation, and space. Juvenile. 104 pages. *1985*

Beyond Supermouse: Changing Life's Genetic Blueprint. By Robert F. Weaver. Photos by Ted Spiegel. 818-847, *Dec. 1984*

Mosquitoes, the Mighty Killers. By Lewis T. Nielsen. Included: Dengue fever, dog heartworm, encephalitis, filariasis, malaria, and yellow fever. 427-440, *Sept. 1979*

The Rat, Lapdog of the Devil. By Thomas Y. Canby. Photos by James L. Stanfield. Included: Map showing plague areas of the Americas, Africa, and Asia; the number of reported cases in 1975. 60-87, *July 1977*

■■ *Nature's Healing Arts: From Folk Medicine to Modern Drugs.* By Lonnelle Aikman. Photos by Nathan Benn and Ira Block. 199 pages. *1977*

Ali Goes to the Clinic. By Herndon and Mary Hudson. 764-766, *Dec. 1946*

Saboteur Mosquitoes. By Harry H. Stage. 165-179, *Feb. 1944*

Life Story of the Mosquito. By Graham Fairchild. 180-195, *Feb. 1944*

Tracking the Columbian Ground-Squirrel to Its Burrow: Loss of Millions to Crops and Danger of the Spread of Spotted Fever Necessitated Study of Peculiar Rodent of Western North America. By William T. Shaw. 587-596, *May 1925*

Map-Changing Medicine. By William Joseph Showalter. 303-330, *Sept. 1922*

Fearful Famines of the Past: History Will Repeat Itself Unless the American People Conserve Their Resources. By Ralph A. Graves. Included: The Black Death. 69-90, *July 1917*

The Rat Pest: The Labor of 200,000 Men in the United States Required to Support Rats, Man's Most Destructive and Dangerous Enemy. By Edward W. Nelson. Included: Bubonic plague. 1-23, *July 1917*

Redeeming the Tropics. By William Joseph Showalter. 344-364, *Mar. 1914*

Our Army Versus a Bacillus. By Alton G. Grinnell. 1146-1152, *Oct. 1913*

The Changing Map in the Balkans. By Frederick Moore. Included: The cholera camps of the Turks. 199-226, *Feb. 1913*

The Discovery of Cancer in Plants. 53-70, *Jan. 1913*

Economic Loss to the People of the United States Through Insects That Carry Disease. By L. O. Howard. 735-749, *Aug. 1909*

Amid the Snow Peaks of the Equator: A Naturalist's Explorations Around Ruwenzori, with an Excursion to the Congo State, and an Account of the Terrible Scourge of Sleeping Sickness. By A.F.R. Wollaston. 256-277, *Mar. 1909*

The Conquest of Bubonic Plague in the Philippines. 185-195, *May 1903*

The History and Geographic Distribution of Bubonic Plague. By George M. Sternberg. 97-113, *Mar. 1900*

Diseases of the Philippines. 123-124, *Mar. 1900*

See also Cancer Research; Hansen's Disease; Sanitation; Smallpox; *and* Medicine and Health

DISMAL Swamp in Legend and History: George Washington Owned Large Tracts in Region Which He Described as a "Glorious Paradise." By John Francis Ariza. 121-130, *July 1932*

DISNEY, WALT:

Walt Disney: Genius of Laughter and Learning. By Melville Bell Grosvenor. 157D, *Aug. 1963*

The Magic Worlds of Walt Disney. By Robert de Roos. Photos by Thomas Nebbia. 159-207, *Aug. 1963*

DISNEY WORLD, Lake Buena Vista, Florida:

Florida's Booming–and Beleaguered–Heartland. By Joseph Judge. Photos by Jonathan Blair. 585-621, *Nov. 1973*

DISNEYLAND, Anaheim, California:

The Magic Worlds of Walt Disney. By

Checking on costumes for a film, Walt Disney called NATIONAL GEOGRAPHIC an "invaluable research tool." THOMAS NEBBIA

Robert de Roos. Photos by Thomas Nebbia. 159-207, *Aug. 1963*

DISPOSITION of the Philippines. By Charles E. Howe. 304, *June 1898*

The **DISPOSSESSED** (Somali Refugees). By Larry Kohl. 756-763, *June 1981*

DISTANT EARLY WARNING LINE. *See* DEW Line

DISTRICT OF COLUMBIA. *See* Washington, D. C.

DITMARS, RAYMOND L.: *Author*

Reptiles of All Lands. 601-633, *July 1911*

DIVE Into the Great Rift. By Robert D. Ballard. Photos by Emory Kristof. 604-615, *May 1975*

DIVERS, Land. *See* Land Divers

DIVERS AND DIVING:

Ghosts of War in the South Pacific. By Peter Benchley. Photos by David Doubilet. 424-457, *Apr. 1988*

Wreck of the *Coolidge*. Text and photos by David Doubilet. 458-467, *Apr. 1988*

■■ *Hidden Treasures of the Sea.* Juvenile. 104 pages. *1988*

Australia's Southern Seas. By Richard Ellis. Photos by David Doubilet. 286-319, *Mar. 1987*

Under Antarctic Ice. By Bill Curtsinger. 497-511, *Apr. 1986*

Sharks: Magnificent and Misunderstood. By Eugenie Clark. Photos by David Doubilet. Included: Antishark cages. NGS research grant. 138-187, *Aug. 1981*

A Jawbreaker for Sharks. By Valerie Taylor. Contents: A chain-mail diving suit. 664-667, *May 1981*

A Walk in the Deep. By Sylvia A. Earle. Photos by Al Giddings and Chuck Nicklin. Included: First open ocean use of diving suit "Jim" for scientific research; deepest solo exploration of its kind yet made. 624-631, *May 1980*

■■ *Exploring the Deep Frontier: The Adventure of Man in the Sea.* By Sylvia A. Earle and Al Giddings. 246 pages. *1980*

■■ *The Mysterious Undersea World.* By Jan Leslie Cooke. Juvenile. 104 pages. *1980*

■■ *The Ocean Realm.* 199 pages. *1978*

■■ *Undersea Treasures.* 199 pages. *1974*

Diving Beneath Arctic Ice. By Joseph B. MacInnis. Photos by William R. Curtsinger. 248-267, *Aug. 1973*

Australia's Great Barrier Reef. Photos by Valerie and Ron Taylor. 728-741, *June 1973*

Tektite II. 256-296. I. Science's Window on the Sea. By John G. VanDerwalker. Photos by Bates Littlehales. 256-289; II. All-girl Team Tests the Habitat. By Sylvia A. Earle. Paintings by Pierre Mion. 291-296, *Aug. 1971*

Ama, Sea Nymphs of Japan. By Luis Marden. 122-135, *July 1971*

A Taxi for the Deep Frontier. By

Kenneth MacLeish. Photos by Bates Littlehales. 139-150, *Jan. 1968*

■■ *World Beneath the Sea.* 204 pages. *1967*

Working for Weeks on the Sea Floor. By Jacques-Yves Cousteau. Photos by Philippe Cousteau and Bates Littlehales. NGS research grant. 498-537, *Apr. 1966*

■ The World of Jacques-Yves Cousteau. 529A-529B, *Apr. 1966*

Stalking Seals Under Antarctic Ice. By Carleton Ray. 54-65, *Jan. 1966*

Outpost Under the Ocean. By Edwin A. Link. Photos by Bates Littlehales. NGS research grant. 530-533, *Apr. 1965*

The Deepest Days. By Robert Sténuit. NGS research grant. 534-547, *Apr. 1965*

Tomorrow on the Deep Frontier. By Edwin A. Link. NGS research grant. 778-801, *June 1964*

At Home in the Sea. By Jacques-Yves Cousteau. 465-507, *Apr. 1964*

Twenty Fathoms Down for Mother-of-Pearl. By Winston Williams. Photos by Bates Littlehales. 512-529, *Apr. 1962*

Diving Saucer Takes to the Deep. By Jacques-Yves Cousteau. NGS research grant. 571-586, *Apr. 1960*

Goggle Fishing in California Waters. By David Hellyer. Photos by Lamar Boren. 615-632, *May 1949*

On the Bottom of a South Sea Pearl Lagoon. By Roy Waldo Miner. Paintings by Else Bostelmann. 365-390, *Sept. 1938*

Wonderer Under Sea. By William Beebe. Paintings by E. Bostelmann. 741-758, *Dec. 1932*

A Round Trip to Davy Jones's Locker: Peering into Mysteries a Quarter Mile Down in the Open Sea, by Means of the Bathysphere. By William Beebe. Paintings by E. Bostelmann. 653-678, *June 1931*

See also Archaeology, Underwater; Diving Cylinder; Diving Saucers; Sponge-Fishing Industry; Underwater Exploration

DIVING BELL (Rescue Compartment):

Our Navy's Long Submarine Arm. By Allan C. Fisher, Jr. 613-636, *Nov. 1952*

DIVING BIRDS:

Western Grebes: The Birds That Walk on Water. By Gary L. Nuechterlein. NGS research grant. 624-637, *May 1982*

DIVING CYLINDER:

Our Man-in-Sea Project. By Edwin A. Link. NGS research grant. 713-717, *May 1963*

The Long, Deep Dive. By Lord Kilbracken. Photos by Bates Littlehales. NGS research grant. 718-731, *May 1963*

DIVING SAUCERS:

Diving Saucer *(Denise)* Takes to the Deep. By Jacques-Yves Cousteau. NGS research grant. 571-586, *Apr. 1960*

See also Cyana; DS-2; Deepstar

DIVING With Sea Snakes. By Kenneth MacLeish. Photos by Ben Cropp. 565-578, *Apr. 1972*

DIXIE Spins the Wheel of Industry. By William H. Nicholas. Photos by J. Baylor Roberts. 281-324, *Mar. 1949*

DIXON, JOSEPH: *Author*

Wild Ducks as Winter Guests in a City Park. 331-342, *Oct. 1919*

DJAKARTA, Java (Island), Indonesia:

Java–Eden in Transition. By Kenneth MacLeish. Photos by Dean Conger. 1-43, *Jan. 1971*

See also former name, Batavia

DJIBOUTI, Republic of:

Djibouti, Tiny New Nation on Africa's Horn. By Marion Kaplan. 518-533, *Oct. 1978*

DJOKJAKARTA, Java, Indonesia:

Postwar Journey Through Java. By Ronald Stuart Kain. 675-700, *May 1948*

See also present name, Jogjakarta

DNIEPER (River), U.S.S.R.:

Viking Trail East. By Robert Paul Jordan. Photos by Jim Brandenburg. Paintings by Michael A. Hampshire. 278-317, *Mar. 1985*

A **DO-IT-YOURSELF** Gardener Creates a New All-America Rose. By Elizabeth A. Moize. Photos by Farrell Grehan. 286-294, *Aug. 1972*

DO Volcanic Explosions Affect Our Climate? By C. G. Abbot. 181-198, *Feb. 1913*

DO We Treat Our Soil Like Dirt? By Boyd Gibbons. Photos by Steven C. Wilson. 350-389, *Sept. 1984*

DO Your Bit for America: A Proclamation by President Wilson to the

American People. 287-293, *Apr. 1917*

DOBIE, J. FRANK: *Author*

What I Saw Across the Rhine. 57-86, *Jan. 1947*

A Texan Teaches American History at Cambridge University. 409-441, *Apr. 1946*

"DOC" Edgerton–The Man Who Made Time Stand Still. By Erla Zwingle. Photos by Harold E. Edgerton and Bruce Dale. 464-483, *Oct. 1987*

DR. BELL'S Man-Lifting Kite. By Gilbert H. Grosvenor. 35-52, *Jan. 1908*

DR. BELL'S Survey in Baffinland. By W J McGee. 113, *Mar. 1902*

DR. BELL'S Tetrahedral Tower. By Gilbert H. Grosvenor. 672-675, *Oct. 1907*

DODD, ISABEL F.: *Author*

An Ancient Capital: Boghaz Keoy, Turkey. 111-124, *Feb. 1910*

DODECANESE ISLANDS, Aegean Sea:

The Isles of Greece: Aegean Birthplace of Western Culture. By Melville Bell Grosvenor. Photos by Edwin Stuart Grosvenor and Winfield Parks. 147-193, *Aug. 1972*

On the Winds of the Dodecanese. By Jean and Franc Shor. 351-390, *Mar. 1953*

Rhodes, and Italy's Aegean Islands. By Dorothy Hosmer. 449-480, *Apr. 1941*

Historic Islands and Shores of the Ægean Sea. By Ernest Lloyd Harris. 231-261, *Sept. 1915*

See also Rhodes (Island)

DODGE, RICHARD E.: *Author*

The Teaching of Physical Geography in Elementary Schools. 470-475, *Dec. 1900*

Borzois, once bred as wolfhounds by crossing an Arabian greyhound with a type of Russian collie, are a handful at a British kennel in the 1930s. © FOX PHOTOS

DODGE SATELLITE:
Historic Color Portrait of Earth From Space. By Kenneth F. Weaver. Photos by DODGE Satellite. 726-731, *Nov. 1967*

DODO (Bird):
Mauritius, Island of the Dodo. By Quentin Keynes. 77-104, *Jan. 1956*

DOE and Twin Fawns. Photo by George Shiras, 3d. Supplement, *July 1913*

DOG SHOWS:
Westminster, World Series of Dogdom. By John W. Cross, Jr. 91-116, *Jan. 1954*
Dog Mart Day in Fredericksburg. By Frederick G. Vosburgh. 817-832, *June 1951*

DOGONS:
Foxes Foretell the Future in Mali's Dogon Country. By Pamela Johnson Meyer. 431-448, *Mar. 1969*

DOGS:
▪▪ *Dogs on Duty.* By Catherine O'Neill. Juvenile. 104 pages. *1988*
▪▪ *Man's Best Friend.* 430 pages. *1966*
Dogs Work for Man. By Edward J. Linehan. Paintings by Edwin Megargee and R. E. Lougheed. 190-233, *Aug. 1958*
▪▪ *The Book of Dogs.* 429 pages. *1958*
Born Hunters, the Bird Dogs. By Roland Kilbon. Paintings by Walter A. Weber. Contents: American Cocker Spaniel, American Water Spaniel, Brittany Spaniel, Chesapeake Bay Retriever, Clumber Spaniel, Curly-coated Retriever, English Cocker Spaniel, English Setter, English Springer Spaniel, Flat-coated Retriever, German Short-haired Pointer, Golden Retriever, Gordon Setter, Irish Setter, Irish Water Spaniel, Labrador Retriever, Pointer, Sussex Spaniel, Weimaraner, Welsh Springer Spaniel, Wire-haired Pointing Griffon. 369-398, *Sept. 1947*
Animals Were Allies, Too. 75-88, *Jan. 1946*
Other Working Dogs and the Wild Species. By Stanley P. Young. Paintings by Walter A. Weber. 363-384, *Sept. 1944*
Toy Dogs, Pets of Kings and Commoners. By Freeman Lloyd. Included: Dogs in Toyland. Photos by Willard R. Culver. 459-480, *Apr. 1944*
Non-sporting Dogs. By Freeman Lloyd. Paintings by Walter A. Weber. Contents: Boston Terrier, Chow, Dalmatian, English Bulldog, French Bulldog, Keeshond, Poodle, Schipperke. 569-588, *Nov. 1943*
Your Dog Joins Up. By Frederick Simpich. 93-113, *Jan. 1943*
Dogs of Duty and Devotion. By Frederick G. Vosburgh. 769-774, *Dec. 1941*
Working Dogs of the World. By Freeman Lloyd. Paintings by Edward Herbert Miner. Contents: Alaskan Malemute, Australian Kelpie, Belgian Sheep Dog, Bouvier de Flandres, Boxer, Briard, Bull Mastiff, Collie, Doberman Pinscher, Eskimo, German Shepherd, Giant

Schnauzer, Great Dane, Great Pyrenees, Kuvasz, Mastiff, Newfoundland, Norwegian Elkhound, Old English Sheep Dog, Rottweiler, St. Bernard, Samoyede, Shetland Sheep Dog, Siberian Husky, Welsh Corgi. 776-806, *Dec. 1941*
Sheep Dog Trials in Llangollen: Trained Collies Perform Marvels of Herding in the Cambrian Stakes, Open to the World. By Sara Bloch. 559-574, *Apr. 1940*
Hark to the Hounds. By Freeman Lloyd. Paintings by Edward Herbert Miner. Contents: Afghan Hound, American Foxhound, Basset Hound, Beagle, Bloodhound, Borzoi, or Russian Wolfhound, Deerhound, English Foxhound, Greyhound, Harrier, Irish Wolfhound, Otterhound, Rampur Hound, Saluki, Welsh Foxhound, Whippet. 453-484, *Oct. 1937*
Field Dogs in Action. By Freeman Lloyd. Paintings by Edward Herbert Miner. Contents: Chesapeake Bay Retriever, Clumber Spaniel, Cocker Spaniel, Curly-coated Retriever, Dachshund, English Setter, English Springer Spaniel, Field Spaniel, Flat-coated Retriever, German Short-haired Pointer, Golden Retriever, Gordon Setter, Irish Red Setter, Irish Water Spaniel, Labrador Retriever, Pointer, Sussex Spaniel, Wire-haired Pointing Griffon. 85-108, *Jan. 1937*
Man's Oldest Ally, the Dog: Since Cave-Dweller Days This Faithful Friend Has Shared the Work, Exploration, and Sport of Humankind. By Freeman Lloyd. Paintings by Edward Herbert Miner. Contents: Airedale Terrier, Bedlington Terrier, Bull Terrier, Cairn Terrier, Dandie Dinmont Terrier, Irish Terrier, Kerry Blue Terrier, Lakeland Terrier, Manchester Terrier, Miniature Schnauzer, Scottish Terrier, Sealyham Terrier, Skye Terrier, Smooth Fox Terrier, Standard Schnauzer, Welsh Terrier, West Highland White

Terrier, Wire-haired Fox Terrier. 247-274, *Feb. 1936*
Mankind's Best Friend: Companion of His Solitude, Advance Guard in the Hunt, and Ally of the Trenches. By Ernest Harold Baynes. 185-201, *Mar. 1919*
Our Common Dogs. By Louis Agassiz Fuertes and Ernest Harold Baynes. Paintings by Louis Agassiz Fuertes. Contents: Basset, Beagle, Belgian Shepherd, Bloodhound, Brussels Griffon, Bulldogs, Chihuahua, Chow, Collies, Dachshund, Dalmatian, English Sheep-Dog, Eskimo, Foxhound, German Shepherd, Great Dane, Greyhound, Irish Wolfhound, Mastiff, Mexican Hairless, Newfoundland, Norwegian Elkhound, Otterhound, Pekingese, Persian Gazelle Hound, Pointer, Pomeranian, Poodles, Pug, Pyrenean Sheep-Dog, Retrievers, Russian Wolfhound, St. Bernard, Samoyed, Schipperke, Scottish Deerhound, Setters, Spaniels, Spitz, Terriers, Whippet; index. ᐧ201-253, *Mar. 1919*
The Sagacity and Courage of Dogs: Instances of the Remarkable Intelligence and Unselfish Devotion of Man's Best Friend Among Dumb Animals. 253-275, *Mar. 1919*
Sheep-Killers–The Pariahs of Dogkind. 275-280, *Mar. 1919*
The Lure of the Frozen Desert: North Polar Regions. Panorama. *Dec. 1912*
See also Bravo (Malamute-Husky); St. Bernard Dogs; Sled Dogs; *and* Dog Shows

DOGSLED RACE. *See* Sled Dog Race

DOIG, DESMOND:
Nomination Page. In Nepal. *Oct. 1966*
Author
Sherpaland, My Shangri-La. 545-577, *Oct. 1966*
Sikkim. 398-429, *Mar. 1963*
Author-Photographer
Bhutan: Mountain Kingdom Between Tibet and India. 384-415, *Sept. 1961*

DOLAN, BROOKE, 2D:
Across Tibet from India to China. By Ilia Tolstoy. 169-222, *Aug. 1946*

DOLESH, RICHARD J.: *Author*
Lord of the Shallows–The Great Blue Heron. Photos by Cameron Davidson. 540-554, *Apr. 1984*

DOLGANS:
People of the Long Spring. By Yuri Rytkheu. Photos by Dean Conger. 206-223, *Feb. 1983*

DOLL, DON: *Photographer*
Eskimo Hunters of the Bering Sea. By Brad Reynolds. 814-834, *June 1984*

DOLLHOUSE:
Royal House for Dolls. By David Jeffery. Photos by James L. Stanfield. 632-643, *Nov. 1980*

DOLLS:
The World in Dolls. By Samuel F. Pryor. Photos by Kathleen Revis. 817-831, *Dec. 1959*

Carolyn Bennett Patterson reenacted Robert Louis Stevenson's sojourn in France's Cévennes. COTTON COULSON

See also Dolls, Miniature; Dzibilchaltun, for Temple of the Seven Dolls; Kachinas

DOLLS, Miniature:

Cuernavaca, the Sun Child of the Sierras (Mexico). By Russell Hastings Millward. Included: Miniature dolls made by Isabel Belaunsaran. 291-301, *Mar. 1911*

DOLOMITES (Mountains), Italy:

A Stroll to Venice. By Isobel Wylie Hutchison. Note: The author walked from Innsbruck, Austria, through the Tyrol and Dolomites, to Venice, Italy. 378-410, *Sept. 1951*

The Land of Contrast: Austria-Hungary. By D. W. and A. S. Iddings. 1188-1217, 1284, *Dec. 1912*

DOLPHINS:

■■ *Dolphins: Our Friends in the Sea.* By Judith E. Rinard. Juvenile. 104 pages. *1986*

■■ *Amazing Animals of the Sea.* Included: Pinnipeds, dolphins, sea otters, manatees, and whales. Juvenile. 104 pages. *1981*

The Trouble With Dolphins. By Edward J. Linehan. Photos by Bill Curtsinger. 506-541, *Apr. 1979*

Whales, Giants of the Sea: Wonder Mammals, Biggest Creatures of All Time, Show Tender Affection for Young, But Can Maim or Swallow Human Hunters. By Remington Kellogg. Paintings by Else Bostelmann. Included: Porpoises and Dolphins. 35-90, *Jan. 1940*

See also Killer Whales; Porpoises

DOLPO (Region), Nepal:

Trek to Nepal's Sacred Crystal Mountain. By Joel F. Ziskin. 500-517, *Apr. 1977*

DOMESDAY BOOK:

The Ordnance Survey of Great Britain—Its History and Object. By Josiah Pierce, Jr. 243-260, *Aug. 1890*

DOMESTIC Fowls of Field, Park, and Farmyard. Paintings by Hashime Murayama. 329-360, *Mar. 1930*

DOMESTICATING the Wild and Woolly Musk Ox. By John J. Teal, Jr. Photos by Robert W. Madden. 862-879, *June 1970*

DOMINGUEZ SANCHEZ, GENARO:
Nomination Page. *July 1980*

DOMINICA (Island), Leeward Islands, West Indies:

Hurricane! By Ben Funk. Photos by Robert W. Madden. Included: Dominica. By Fred Ward; Dynamics of a Hurricane; Into the Eye of David. By John L. Eliot; Paths of Fury—This Century's Worst American Storms. 346-379, *Sept. 1980*

■ *Isles of the Caribbean.* 215 pages. *1980*

■ *Isles of the Caribees.* By Carleton Mitchell. 208 pages. *1966*

Finisterre Sails the Windward Islands. By Carleton Mitchell. Photos by Winfield Parks. 755-801, *Dec. 1965*

British West Indian Interlude. By Anne Rainey Langley. 1-46, *Jan. 1941*

Report by Robert T. Hill on the Volcanic Disturbances in the West Indies. 223-267, *July 1902*

DOMINICAN REPUBLIC:

Graveyard of the Quicksilver Galleons. By Mendel Peterson. Photos by Jonathan Blair. Note: The *Nuestra Señora de Guadalupe* and the *Conde de Tolosa* sank off the coast of the Dominican Republic in 1724 while carrying a cargo of mercury to the New World. 850-876, *Dec. 1979*

The Dominican Republic: Caribbean Comeback. By James Cerruti. Photos by Martin Rogers. 538-565, *Oct. 1977*

Amber: Golden Window on the Past. Photos by Paul A. Zahl. Text by Thomas J. O'Neill. 423-435, *Sept. 1977*

The Land Columbus Loved. By Oliver P. Newman. Included: Dominican Republic, Land of Plenty. Photos by B. Anthony Stewart. 197-224, *Feb. 1944*

Hispaniola Rediscovered. By Jacob Gayer. 80-112, *Jan. 1931*

Haiti, the Home of Twin Republics. By Sir Harry Johnston. 483-496, *Dec. 1920*

Wards of the United States: Notes on What Our Country Is Doing for Santo Domingo, Nicaragua, and Haiti. 143-177, *Aug. 1916*

Arbitration Treaties. By William Howard Taft. 1165-1172, *Dec. 1911*

Haiti: A Degenerating Island. By Colby M. Chester. 200-217, *Mar. 1908*

DONINI, JIM: *Author-Photographer*

To Torre Egger's Icy Summit. 813-823, *Dec. 1976*

DONKEYS:

Travels With a Donkey–100 Years Later. By Carolyn Bennett Patterson. Photos by Cotton Coulson. 535-561, *Oct. 1978*

See also Burros, Wild

DONNAN, CHRISTOPHER B.: *Author*

Iconography of the Moche: Unraveling the Mystery of the Warrior-Priest. 551-555, *Oct. 1988*

DONNELLEY, R. R., & SONS COMPANY, Chicago, Illinois:

Exploring an Epic Year: A Message from Your Society's President and Editor. By Melville Bell Grosvenor. 874-886, *Dec. 1960*

DOOR PENINSULA, Wisconsin:

Wisconsin's Door Peninsula. By William S. Ellis. Photos by Ted Rozumalski. 347-371, *Mar. 1969*

DORDOGNE (Department), France:

Art Treasures from the Ice Age: Lascaux Cave. By Jean-Philippe Rigaud. Photos by Sisse Brimberg and Norbert Aujoulat. 482-499, *Oct. 1988*

Exploring the Mind of Ice Age Man. By Alexander Marshack. Included: The caves of La Roche, Lascaux, Pech-Merle, Rouffignac, and the Blanchard rock shelter. NGS research grant. 64-89, *Jan. 1975*

See also Lascaux Cave

DORIES:

Dory on the Banks: A Day in the Life of a Portuguese Fisherman. By James H. Pickerell. 573-583, *Apr. 1968*

■ The Lonely Dorymen. 579A-579B, *Apr. 1968*

I Sailed With Portugal's Captains Courageous. By Alan Villiers. 565-596, *May 1952*

See also Blessing of the Fleet

DORJUN (Boat):

Inside Cape Horn. By Amos Burg. 743-783, *Dec. 1937*

DORR, GEORGE B.: *Author*

The Unique Island of Mount Desert (Maine). By George B. Dorr, Ernest Howe Forbush, and M. L. Fernald. 75-89, *July 1914*

DORR, JOHN F:
Nomination Page. *May 1977*

DORSET INUIT:

Eskimo and Viking Finds in the High Arctic: Ellesmere Island. By Peter Schledermann. Photos by Sisse Brimberg. 575-601, *May 1981*

Vanished Mystery Men of Hudson Bay. By Henry B. Collins. NGS research grant. 669-687, *Nov. 1956*

DORSETSHIRE, England. *See* Abbotsbury Swannery

DORSETT, J. H.: *Photographer*

Peacetime Plant Hunting About Peiping. By P. H. and J. H. Dorsett. 509-534, *Oct. 1937*

Braving the North Atlantic in their small dories, Portuguese fishermen pursue cod on the Grand Banks. JAMES H. PICKERELL, BLACK STAR

Stanfield and David Doubilet. 724-735, *Nov. 1972*

DOUBLE EAGLE II Has Landed! Crossing the Atlantic by Balloon. By Ben L. Abruzzo, with Maxie L. Anderson and Larry Newman. 858-882, *Dec. 1978*

DOUBLE EAGLE V (Manned Helium Balloon):
First Across the Pacific: The Flight of *Double Eagle V*. By Ben L. Abruzzo. 513-521, *Apr. 1982*

A **DOUBTFUL** Island of the Pacific. By James D. Hague. 478-489, *Dec. 1904*

DOUGLAS, MERCEDES H.:
Nomination Page. *Feb. 1962*
Photographer
Station Wagon Odyssey: Baghdad to Istanbul. By William O. Douglas. Photos by author, Mercedes H. Douglas, and W. Robert Moore. 48-87, *Jan. 1959*
West from the Khyber Pass. By William O. Douglas. Photos by Mercedes H. Douglas and author. 1-44, *July 1958*

DOUGLAS, WILLIAM O.:
Nomination Page. *Feb. 1962*
Author
Banks Island: Eskimo Life on the Polar Sea. Photos by Clyde Hare. 703-735, *May 1964*
The People of Cades Cove. Photos by Thomas Nebbia and Otis Imboden. 60-95, *July 1962*
Journey to Outer Mongolia. Photos by Dean Conger. 289-345, *Mar. 1962*
The Friendly Huts of the White Mountains. Photos by Kathleen Revis. 205-239, *Aug. 1961*
Author-Photographer
Station Wagon Odyssey: Baghdad to Istanbul. Photos by author, Mercedes H. Douglas, and W. Robert Moore. 48-87, *Jan. 1959*
West from the Khyber Pass. Photos by Mercedes H. Douglas and author. 1-44, *July 1958*

DOUGLAS-HAMILTON, IAIN:
Nomination Page. In Africa. *Sept. 1980*
Photographer
Africa's Elephants: Can They Survive? By Oria Douglas-Hamilton. Photos by Oria and Iain Douglas-Hamilton. 568-603, *Nov. 1980*

DOUGLAS-HAMILTON, ORIA:
Nomination Page. In Africa. *Sept. 1980*
Author-Photographer
Africa's Elephants: Can They Survive? Photos by Oria and Iain Douglas-Hamilton. 568-603, *Nov. 1980*

DOUGLASS, ANDREW ELLICOTT:
Author
The Secret of the Southwest Solved by Talkative Tree Rings: Horizons of American History Are Carried Back to A. D. 700 and a Calendar for 1,200 Years Established by National Geographic Society Expeditions. 737-770, *Dec. 1929*

DOUIRAT, Tunisia:
The Mole Men: An Account of the Troglodytes of Southern Tunisia. By Frank Edward Johnson. 787-846, *Sept. 1911*

DOURO (River), Portugal:
Iberia's Vintage River. By Marion Kaplan. Photos by Stephanie Maze. 460-489, *Oct. 1984*

DOUTHITT, WILLIAM T.:
On Assignment on the Susquehanna River. *May 1986*
On Assignment. *June 1983*
Photographer
Susquehanna: America's Small-Town River. By Peter Miller. 352-383, *Mar. 1985*

DOVE (Sloop):
Robin Sails Home. By Robin Lee Graham. 504-545, *Oct. 1970*
World-roaming Teen-ager Sails On. By Robin Lee Graham. 449-493, *Apr. 1969*
A Teen-ager Sails the World Alone. By Robin Lee Graham. 445-491, *Oct. 1968*

DOVEKIES (Birds):
Birds of the Northern Seas. By Alexander Wetmore. Paintings by Allan Brooks. 95-122, *Jan. 1936*

DOVER, England:
Front-line Town of Britain's Siege. By Harvey Klemmer. 105-128, *Jan. 1944*

DOVES:
Game Birds of Prairie, Forest, and Tundra. By Alexander Wetmore. Paintings by Allan Brooks. 461-500, *Oct. 1936*

DOWN Devon Lanes. By Herbert Corey. 529-568, *May 1929*

DOWN East Cruise. By Tom Horgan. Photos by Luis Marden. 329-369, *Sept. 1952*

A triggerfish feasts on a prickly sea urchin in the Red Sea, having overturned it with a well-aimed squirt of water. DAVID DOUBILET

DOWN East to Nova Scotia. By Winfield Parks. 853-879, *June 1964*

DOWN Idaho's River of No Return: Salmon River. By Philip J. Shenon and John C. Reed. 95-136, *July 1936*

DOWN Mark Twain's River on a Raft. By Rex E. Hieronymus. 551-574, *Apr. 1948*

DOWN Mexico's Río Balsas. By John W. Webber. Photos by author, Kenneth Segerstrom, and Jack Breed. 253-272, *Aug. 1946*

DOWN on the Farm, Soviet Style–a 4-H Adventure. By John Garaventa. Photos by James Tobin and Carol Schmidt. 768-797, *June 1979*

DOWN the Ancient Appian Way. By James Cerruti. Photos by O. Louis Mazzatenta. 714-747, *June 1981*

DOWN the Cayman Wall. By Eugenie Clark. Included: Zones of Life. NGS research grant. 712-731, *Nov. 1988*

DOWN the Danube by Canoe. By William Slade Backer. Photos by Richard S. Durrance and Christopher G. Knight. 34-79, *July 1965*

DOWN the Grand Canyon 100 Years After Powell. By Joseph Judge. Photos by Walter Meayers Edwards. 668-713, *May 1969*

DOWN the Potomac by Canoe. By Ralph Gray. Photos by Walter Meayers Edwards. 213-242, *Aug. 1948*

DOWN the Rio Grande: Tracing this Strange, Turbulent Stream on Its Long Course from Colorado to the Gulf of Mexico. By Frederick Simpich. 415-462, *Oct. 1939*

DOWN the Susquehanna by Canoe. By Ralph Gray. Photos by Walter Meayers Edwards. 73-120, *July 1950*

DOWN to *Thresher* by Bathyscaph. By Donald L. Keach. 764-777, *June 1964*

DOYLE, C. B.: *Author*
Notes on Southern Mexico: Agricultural Products. By G. N. Collins and C. B. Doyle. 301-320, *Mar. 1911*

DOYLE, GERALD A.:
Nomination Page. *May 1972*

DOYLE, ROBERT E.:
Memorial tribute. By Wilbur E. Garrett. 695, *June 1984*
President (1976-1980). 159, 224-226, Aug. 1976; 1, Jan. 1978; 427, Oct. 1980; 276, *Aug. 1982*
Board of Trustees, Vice Chairman (1980-1984). 427, *Oct. 1980*
Board of Trustees. 225, *Aug. 1976*
Secretary, Assistant (1951). 225, *Aug. 1976*
Secretary, Associate (1958). 225, *Aug. 1976*
Secretary (1967). 577, 581, 587, 590, *Oct. 1967*
Vice President (1961). 577, 587, *Oct. 1967*

As if tranquilized, a reef shark rests with an entourage of barjacks in a 55-foot-deep cave off Mexico's coast. DAVID DOUBILET

In a dreamlike double exposure, neurobiologist Michel Jouvet presides over his artistically labeled collection of scholarly papers on sleep research. LOUIE PSIHOYOS

The Friendly Irish. By John Scofield. Photos by James A. Sugar. 354-391, *Sept. 1969*

Dublin's Historic Horse Show. By Maynard Owen Williams. 115-132, *July 1953*

I Walked Some Irish Miles. By Dorothea Sheats. 653-678, *May 1951*

DU BOIS, ARTHUR E.: *Author*

The Heraldry of Heroism. 409-413, *Oct. 1943*

The Traditions and Glamour of Insignia. 652-655, *June 1943*

Du BOUCHER, JEAN: *Author*

Dry-land Fleet Sails the Sahara. Photos by Jonathan S. Blair. 696-725, *Nov. 1967*

DUBROVNIK (former name, Ragusa), Yugoslavia:

Yugoslavia's Window on the Adriatic. By Gilbert M. Grosvenor. 219-247, *Feb. 1962*

DU CHAILLU, PAUL:

Paul Du Chaillu (Biography). 282-285, *July 1903*

DUCK RAISING:

Long Island Outgrows the Country. By Howell Walker. Photos by B. Anthony Stewart. 279-326, *Mar. 1951*

DUCKBILLS. *See* Platypuses

DUCKS:

North American Waterfowl: Troubles and Triumphs. By John Madson. 562-599, *Nov. 1984*

Humble Masterpieces: Decoys. By George Reiger. Photos by Kenneth Garrett. 639-663, *Nov. 1983*

Duck Hunting with a Color Camera. By Arthur A. Allen. Contents: Baldpates; Black Ducks; Buffleheads; Canvasbacks; Eiders; Gadwalls; Golden-eyes; Mallards; Mergansers; Muscovy Ducks; Old-squaws; Pintails; Redheads; Ringnecks; Ruddy Ducks; Scaups, Greater and Lesser; Shovellers; Teals, Blue-winged, and Cinnamon; Widgeons, European; Wood Ducks. 514-539, *Oct. 1951*

Far-Flying Wild Fowl and Their Foes. By Allan Brooks. Paintings by author. 487-528, *Oct. 1934*

Wild Life of the Atlantic and Gulf Coasts: A Field Naturalist's Photographic Record of Nearly Half a Century of Fruitful Exploration. By George Shiras, 3d. 261-309, *Sept. 1932*

Fowls of Forest and Stream Tamed by Man. By Morley A. Jull. Paintings by Hashime Murayama. Contents: Aylesbury, Black East India, Blue Swedish, Buff, Cayuga, Crested White, Gray Call, Khaki Campbell, Muscovy, Pekin, Rouen, Runner. 327-371, *Mar. 1930*

Wild Ducks as Winter Guests in a City Park. By Joseph Dixon. 331-342, *Oct. 1919*

American Game Birds. By Henry Wetherbee Henshaw. Paintings by Louis Agassiz Fuertes. 105-158, *Aug. 1915*

Saving the Ducks and Geese. By Wells W. Cooke. 361-380, *Mar. 1913*

See also Duck Raising

DUERO (River), Spain:

Iberia's Vintage River. By Marion Kaplan. Photos by Stephanie Maze. 460-489, *Oct. 1984*

DUFEK, GEORGE J.:

Hubbard Medal recipient. 589-590, *Apr. 1959*; 530, *Oct. 1959*

Author

Nuclear Power for the Polar Regions. 712-730, *May 1962*

What We've Accomplished in Antarctica. 527-557, *Oct. 1959*

DUG-GYE JONG (Fort), Bhutan:

Castles in the Air–Experiences and Journeys in Unknown Bhutan. By John Claude White. 365-455, *Apr. 1914*

DUGMORE, A. RADCLYFFE:

Photographer

Camera Adventures in the African Wilds (Book Review). 385-396, *May 1910*

DUGOUT CANOES:

Jungle Journey to the World's Highest Waterfall. By Ruth Robertson. 655-690, *Nov. 1949*

Sea Fever. By John E. Schultz. 237-268, *Feb. 1949*

DUKE of the Abruzzi in the Himalayas. By A. W. Greely. 245-249, *Mar. 1910*

DULUTH, Minnesota:

Minnesota Makes Ideas Pay. By Frederick G. Vosburgh. Photos by John E. Fletcher and B. Anthony Stewart. 291-336, *Sept. 1949*

DUMAS, FRÉDÉRIC:

Fish Men Explore a New World Undersea. By Jacques-Yves Cousteau. 431-472, *Oct. 1952*

DUMBOY, the National Dish of Liberia. By G. N. Collins. 84-88, *Jan. 1911*

DUMONT D'URVILLE, JULES SÉBASTIEN CÉSAR:

Wilkes' and D'Urville's Discoveries in Wilkes Land. By John E. Pillsbury. 171-173, *Feb. 1910*

DUMPS:

Hazardous Waste...Storing Up Trouble. By Allen A. Boraiko. Photos by Fred Ward. 318-351, *Mar. 1985*

The Fascinating World of Trash. By Peter T. White. Photos by Louie Psihoyos. 424-457, *Apr. 1983*

DUNANT, HENRI:

The Symbol of Service to Mankind. By Stockton Axson. 375-390, *Apr. 1918*

DUNCAN, DAVID D.: *Author*

Fiji Patrol on Bougainville. 87-104, *Jan. 1945*

Capturing Giant Turtles in the Caribbean. 177-190, *Aug. 1943*

Fighting Giants of the Humboldt: Fish and Squid. 373-400, *Mar. 1941*

Author-Photographer

Yap Meets the Yanks. 364-372, *Mar. 1946*

Okinawa, Threshold to Japan. 411-428, *Oct. 1945*

Photographer

Power Comes Back to Peiping. By Nelson T. Johnson and W. Robert Moore. 337-368, *Sept. 1949*

Coffee Is King in El Salvador. By Luis Marden. Photos by author and David D. Duncan. 585-616, *Nov. 1944*

DUNCAN, WILLIAM:

The Metlakatla Mission in Danger. By William H. Dall. Note: The Reverend William Duncan is missionary to the Tsimshian Indians at Metlakatla, Alaska. 187-189, *Apr. 1898*

DUNDEE, Scotland:

Low Road, High Road, Around Dundee. By Maurice P. Dunlap. 547-576, *Apr. 1936*

DUNKIRK, France:

Thumbs Up Round the North Sea's Rim. By Frances James. Photos by Erica Koch. 685-704, *May 1952*

DUNLAP, MAURICE PRATT: *Author*

Low Road, High Road, Around Dundee (Scotland). 547-576, *Apr. 1936*

Outwitting the Water Demons of Kashmir. 499-511, *Nov. 1921*

DUNN, DOROTHY: *Author*

America's First Painters: Indians. 349-377, *Mar. 1955*

DUNSTAN, THOMAS C.: *Author*

Our Bald Eagle: Freedom's Symbol Survives. Photos by Jeff Foott. 186-199, *Feb. 1978*

DUPLAIX, NICOLE:

Nomination Page. In South America. *June 1978*

Author-Photographer

Fleas: The Lethal Leapers. 672-694, *May 1988*

Giant Otters: "Big Water Dogs" in Peril. Photos by the author and Bates Littlehales. 130-142, *July 1980*

DU PONT, PIERRE S.: Estate:

Wonderland in Longwood Gardens. By Edward C. Ferriday, Jr. 45-64, *July 1951*

DU PONT DE NEMOURS, E. I., & COMPANY, Wilmington, Delaware:

Delaware–Who Needs to Be Big? By Jane Vessels. Photos by Kevin Fleming. 171-197, *Aug. 1983*

Gossamer Albatross sponsor. 645, *Nov. 1979*

Villagers of Golah, Liberia, posed in 1911 for an article on **dumboy,** *a national dish made from the cassava plant.* G. N. COLLINS

Today on the Delaware, Penn's Glorious River. By Albert W. Atwood. Photos by Robert F. Sisson. 1-40, *July 1952*

DU PUY, WILLIAM ATHERTON:
Author

The Geography of Money. 745-768, *Dec. 1927*

"A **DURABLE** Scale of Values." By Boyd Gibbons. Photos by Jim Brandenburg. 682-708, *Nov. 1981*

DURBAN, South Africa:

Safari Through Changing Africa. By Elsie May Bell Grosvenor. Photos by Gilbert Grosvenor. 145-198, *Aug. 1953*

Natal: The Garden Province. By Melville Chater. 447-478, *Apr. 1931*

Natal: The Garden Colony. By Russell Hastings Millward. 278-291, *Mar. 1909*

DURBAR GATHERINGS:

Progress and Pageantry in Changing Nigeria. By W. Robert Moore. 325-365, *Sept. 1956*

In the Realms of the Maharajas. By Lawrence Copley Thaw and Margaret S. Thaw. 727-780, *Dec. 1940*

Castles in the Air–Experiences and Journeys in Unknown Bhutan. By John Claude White. 365-455, *Apr. 1914*

DURENCEAU, ANDRE: *Artist*

A New Look at Medieval Europe. By Kenneth M. Setton. Paintings by Andre Durenceau and Birney Lettick. 799-859, *Dec. 1962*

Ice Age Man, the First American. By Thomas R. Henry. 781-806, *Dec. 1955*

DURRANCE, DICK, II:
Author-Photographer

A Town…a Mountain…a Way of Life. By Jill Durrance and Dick Durrance II. 788-807, *Dec. 1973*

Photographer

Striking It Rich in the North Sea. By Rick Gore. 519-549, *Apr. 1977*

■■ *The Majestic Rocky Mountains.* By William S. Ellis. 199 pages. *1976*

Library of Congress: The Nation's Bookcase. By Fred Kline. 671-687, *Nov. 1975*

Alabama, Dixie to a Different Tune. By Howard La Fay. 534-569, *Oct. 1975*

Bangladesh: Hope Nourishes a New Nation. By William S. Ellis. 295-333, *Sept. 1972*

■■ *The Appalachian Trail.* By Ronald M. Fisher. 199 pages. *1972*

The Zulus: Black Nation in a Land of Apartheid. By Joseph Judge. 738-775, *Dec. 1971*

Leningrad, Russia's Window on the West. By Howard La Fay. 636-673, *May 1971*

On the Track of the West's Wild Horses. By Hope Ryden. Photos by author and Dick Durrance II. 94-109, *Jan. 1971*

White-water Adventure on Wild Rivers of Idaho. By Frank Craighead, Jr., and John Craighead. 213-239, *Feb. 1970*

Kay Hampton takes a pensive break from the family business of basket weaving, near Nectar, Alabama. DICK DURRANCE II

■■ *In the Footsteps of Lewis and Clark.* By Gerald S. Snyder. Paintings by Richard Schlecht. 215 pages. *1970*

Americans Afoot in Rumania. By Dan Dimancescu. Photos by Dick Durrance II and Christopher G. Knight. 810-845, *June 1969*

Mr. Jefferson's Monticello. By Joseph Judge. Photos by Dean Conger and Richard S. Durrance. 426-444, *Sept. 1966*

Down the Danube by Canoe. By William Slade Backer. Photos by Richard S. Durrance and Christopher G. Knight. 34-79, *July 1965*

DURRANCE, JILL:
Author-Photographer

A Town…a Mountain…a Way of Life. By Jill Durrance and Dick Durrance II. 788-807, *Dec. 1973*

D'URVILLE, JULES SÉBASTIEN CÉSAR DUMONT. *See* Dumont D'Urville, Jules Sébastien César

DUSKY Tribesmen of French West Africa. Photos by Enzo de Chetelat. 639-662, *May 1941*

DUST BOWL:

The Okies–Beyond the Dust Bowl. By William Howarth. Photos by Chris Johns. 322-349, *Sept. 1984*

DUTCH EAST INDIA COMPANY:
Ships. *See* Slot ter Hooge; Witte Leeuw

DUTCH EAST INDIES. *See* Indonesia

DUTCH GUIANA. *See* Suriname

DUTCH NEW GUINEA. *See* Irian Jaya

The **DUTCH** Touch. By Bart McDowell. Photos by Nathan Benn and Farrell Grehan. 501-525, *Oct. 1986*

DUTCH WEST INDIES. *See* Netherlands Antilles

DWELLERS in the Dark (Termites). By Glenn D. Prestwich. 532-547, *Apr. 1978*

DWELLINGS. *See* Castles; Chateaux; Cliff Dwellers; Cone Dwellings; Estates and Plantations; Houses; Housing; Huts

DWELLINGS of the Saga-Time in Iceland, Greenland, and Vineland. By Cornelia Horsford. 73-84, *Mar. 1898*

DWIGHT, HARRY GRISWOLD:
Author

Saloniki (Greece). 203-232, *Sept. 1916*

The Hoary Monasteries of Mt. Athos (Greece). 249-272, *Sept. 1916*

The Gates to the Black Sea: The Dardanelles, the Bosphorus, and the Sea of Marmora. 435-459, *May 1915*

Life in Constantinople. 521-545, *Dec. 1914*

DYAKS. *See* Iban

DYAR, HARRISON G.:

Where Our Moths and Butterflies Roam. 105-126, *July 1927*

DYER, GEORGE L.:

Vice President. 270, *July 1889*

Author

Report–Geography of the Sea. 136-150, *Apr. 1889*

DYGERT, RUTH E.: *Author*

Ambassadors of Good Will: The Peace Corps. By Sargent Shriver and Peace Corps Volunteers. Included: Tanganyika. By Ruth E. Dygert. 297-345, *Sept. 1964*

DYHRENFURTH, NORMAN G.:

● Americans on Everest. 448-452, Sept. 1965; 575, *Nov. 1976*

America's First Everest Expedition. NGS research grant. 460-515, *Oct. 1963*

American and Geographic Flags Top Everest. By Melvin M. Payne. Photos by Barry C. Bishop. 157-157C, *Aug. 1963*

Mount Rainier: Testing Ground for Everest. By Barry C. Bishop. NGS research grant. 688-711, *May 1963*

Author

Six to the Summit (Everest). Photos by Barry C. Bishop. 460-473, *Oct. 1963*

DYNAMIC Ontario. By Marjorie Wilkins Campbell. Photos by Winfield Parks. 58-97, *July 1963*

DYNAMICS of a Hurricane. 370-371, *Sept. 1980*

DYOTT, G. M.: *Author*

The Volcanoes of Ecuador, Guideposts in Crossing South America. 49-93, *Jan. 1929*

DYSON, ROBERT, Jr.:

Nomination Page. In Iran. *Mar. 1978*

DZIBILCHALTÚN, Yucatán, Mexico:

Dzibilchaltun. NGS research grant. 91-129. I. Lost City of the Maya. By E. Wyllys Andrews. 91-109; II. Up from the Well of Time. By Luis Marden. 110-129, *Jan. 1959*

E
F

A soft, grainy texture lends an Impressionist quality to this 1925 Autochrome of the French countryside.

GERVAIS COURTELLEMONT

361

ECA. *See* Economic Cooperation Administration

EPA. *See* Environmental Protection Agency

EADS SHIP RAILWAY:
The Tehuantepec Ship Railway. By Elmer L. Corthell. 64-72, *Feb. 1896*

EAGLE (Lunar Module):
The Flight of Apollo 11: "One giant leap for mankind." By Kenneth F. Weaver. 752-787, *Dec. 1969*

EAGLE (Training Ship):
By Square-rigger from Baltic to Bicentennial. Included: *Eagle.* By Kenneth Garrett. 824-857, *Dec. 1976*
Under Canvas in the Atomic Age (U. S. Coast Guard Cadets). By Alan Villiers. 49-84, *July 1955*

EAGLES:
The Eagle, King of Birds, and His Kin. By Alexander Wetmore. Paintings by Allan Brooks. Included: Eagles, Hawks, and Vultures. 43-95, *July 1933*

Bald Eagles, American
Editorial. By Wilbur E. Garrett. 695, *June 1982*
Our Bald Eagle: Freedom's Symbol Survives. By Thomas C. Dunstan. Photos by Jeff Foott. NGS research grant. 186-199, *Feb. 1978*
Eye to Eye With Eagles. By Frederick Kent Truslow. 123-148, *Jan. 1961*
The Eagle in Action: An Intimate Study of the Eyrie Life of America's National Bird. By Francis H. Herrick. 635-660, *May 1929*

Black Eagles
Adventures With South Africa's Black Eagles. By Jeanne Cowden. Photos

Fledgling bald eagles await a meal brought by their parents to an aerie in the Florida Everglades. FREDERICK KENT TRUSLOW

by author and Arthur Bowland. 533-543, *Oct. 1969*

Golden Eagles
Inside the Sacred Hopi Homeland. By Jake Page. Photos by Susanne Page. Included: Sacrifice of a golden eagle. 607-629, *Nov. 1982*
Sharing the Lives of Wild Golden Eagles. By John Craighead. Photos by Charles and Derek Craighead. 420-439, *Sept. 1967*
Scotland's Golden Eagles at Home. By C. Eric Palmar. 273-286, *Feb. 1954*
In Quest of the Golden Eagle: Over Lonely Mountain and Prairie Soars This Rare and Lordly Bird, But Three Youths from the East Catch Up With Him at Last. By John and Frank Craighead. 693-710, *May 1940*

Philippine Eagles
Saving the Philippine Eagle. By Robert S. Kennedy. Photos by Alan R. Degen, Neil L. Rettig, and Wolfgang A. Salb. NGS research grant. 847-856, *June 1981*
Seeking Mindanao's Strangest Creatures. By Charles Heizer Wharton. Included: Crested Serpent Eagle, Monkey-eating Eagle. 389-408, *Sept. 1948*

EARHART, AMELIA:
President Hoover presents medal to Amelia Earhart. 134, *Jan. 1936*
The Society's Special Medal Awarded to Amelia Earhart: First Woman to Receive Geographic Distinction at Brilliant Ceremony in the National Capital. Address by Amelia Earhart. 358-367, *Sept. 1932*

Author
My Flight from Hawaii. 593-609, *May 1935*

EARL, LAWRENCE: *Photographer*
Mending Dikes in the Netherlands. 791-806, *Dec. 1946*

EARLE, SYLVIA A.:
Nomination Page. *Oct. 1978*
Nomination Page. *Apr. 1976*
Author
Undersea World of a Kelp Forest. Photos by Al Giddings. 411-426, *Sept. 1980*
A Walk in the Deep. Photos by Al Giddings and Chuck Nicklin. 624-631, *May 1980*
Exploring the Deep Frontier: The Adventure of Man in the Sea. By Sylvia A. Earle and Al Giddings. 246 pages. *1980*
Humpbacks: The Gentle Whales. Photos by Al Giddings. 2-17, *Jan. 1979*
Life Springs From Death in Truk Lagoon. Photos by Al Giddings. 578-603, *May 1976*
All-girl Team Tests the Habitat. Paintings by Pierre Mion. 291-296, *Aug. 1971*

EARLIEST Geographics to Be Reprinted. By Melvin M. Payne. 688-689, *Nov. 1964*

EARLY AMERICA Through the Eyes of Her Native Artists. By Hereward Lester Cooke, Jr. 356-389, *Sept. 1962*

EARLY CIVILIZATIONS:
America's Ancient Cities. By Gene S. Stuart. Photos by Richard Alexander Cooke III. Art by H. Tom Hall. 199 pages. *1988*
Builders of the Ancient World: Marvels of Engineering. Contents: Greece and Rome, Mesoamerica, South America, India and Southeast Asia, and China. 199 pages. *1986*
Amazing Mysteries of the World. By Catherine O'Neill. Included: Ancient cities, earth art, stone circles, stone statues, pyramids, temples, and tombs. Juvenile. 104 pages. *1983*
Peoples and Places of the Past: The National Geographic Illustrated Cultural Atlas of the Ancient World. 424 pages. *1983*
Splendors of the Past: Lost Cities of the Ancient World. 295 pages. *1981*
Mysteries of the Ancient World. Contents: Ancient Indian cities, Easter Island, Egyptian pyramids, Etruscans, European megaliths, Ice Age cave art, Jericho, Minoans, and Mycenaeans. 223 pages. *1979*
Secrets From the Past. By Gene S. Stuart. Juvenile. 104 pages. *1979*
Everyday Life in Ancient Times. Contents: Egypt, Greece, Mesopotamia, and Rome. 368 pages. 1951; rev. ed. *1961*

Africa
Finding West Africa's Oldest City. By Susan and Roderick McIntosh. Photos by Michael and Aubine Kirtley. Contents: Jenne-jeno site in Mali. 396-418, *Sept. 1982*
Ancient Carthage in the Light of Modern Excavation. By Count Byron Khun de Prorok. 391-423, *Apr. 1924*
See also Egypt, Ancient

Asia, Eastern
China's Incredible Find. By Audrey Topping. Paintings by Yang Hsien-min. Included: The first emperor's burial mound, with guardian army of terra-cotta men and horses. 440-459, *Apr. 1978*
China Unveils Her Newest Treasures. Photos by Robert W. Madden. 848-857, *Dec. 1974*
A Lady From China's Past. Photos from *China Pictorial.* Text by Alice J. Hall. 660-681, *May 1974*
The Lands and Peoples of Southeast Asia. 295-365. I. Mosaic of Cultures. By Peter T. White. Photos by W. E. Garrett. 296-329; II. New Light on a Forgotten Past. By Wilhelm G. Solheim II. 330-339; III. Pagan, on the Road to Mandalay. By W. E. Garrett. 343-365, *Mar. 1971*

Europe
Ancient Bulgaria's Golden Treasures. By Colin Renfrew. Photos by James L. Stanfield. Paintings by Jean-Leon Huens. 112-129, *July 1980*
Ancient Europe Is Older Than We Thought. By Colin Renfrew. Photos by Adam Woolfitt. 615-623, *Nov. 1977*
Land of the Ancient Basques. By Robert Laxalt. Photos by William Albert Allard. 240-277, *Aug. 1968*

"There's a beautiful earth out there," commented astronaut Frank Borman in 1968 during man's first orbit of the moon. FRANK BORMAN, NASA

See also Celts; Etruscans; Greece, Ancient

Middle East
Ebla: Splendor of an Unknown Empire. By Howard La Fay. Photos by James L. Stanfield. Paintings by Louis S. Glanzman. Included: Akkad, Babylon, Ebla, Mari, Mesopotamia, Nippur, Sumer, Ugarit. 730-759, *Dec. 1978*
✦ *Middle East, Eastern Mediterranean; Early Civilizations of the Middle East. Sept. 1978*
■■ *Everyday Life in Bible Times.* 448 pages. *1967; rev. ed. 1977*
The Phoenicians, Sea Lords of Antiquity. By Samuel W. Matthews. Photos by Winfield Parks. Paintings by Robert C. Magis. 149-189, *Aug. 1974*
Jericho Gives Up Its Secrets. By Kathleen M. Kenyon and A. Douglas Tushingham. Photos by Nancy Lord. 853-870, *Dec. 1953*
See also Mesopotamia

North America
Man's Eighty Centuries in Veracruz. By S. Jeffrey K. Wilkerson. Photos by David Hiser. Paintings by Richard Schlecht. NGS research grant. 203-231, *Aug. 1980*
■■ *Discovering Man's Past in the Americas.* By George E. and Gene S. Stuart. 211 pages. *1969*
See also Anasazi Culture; Hohokam Culture; Mound Builders; Olmec Culture

South America
Chan Chan, Peru's Ancient City of Kings. By Michael E. Moseley and Carol J. Mackey. Photos by David Brill. NGS research grant. 318-345, *Mar. 1973*
■■ *Discovering Man's Past in the Americas.* By George E. and Gene S. Stuart. 211 pages. *1969*
Finding the Tomb of a Warrior-God. By William Duncan Strong. Photos by Clifford Evans, Jr. 453-482, *Apr. 1947*
Staircase Farms of the Ancients: Astounding Farming Skill of Ancient Peruvians. By O. F. Cook. 474-534, *May 1916*

EARLY MAN. *See* Man, Prehistoric

EARLY Voyages on the Northwestern Coast of America. By George Davidson. 235-256, *Jan. 31, 1894*

EARTH:
Earth '88: Will We Mend Our Earth? Introduction by Gilbert M. Grosvenor. 766-771, *Dec. 1988*
New Perspective on the World. By John B. Garver, Jr. 911-913, *Dec. 1988*
✦ *World; Endangered Earth. Dec. 1988*
Exploring Cradle Earth. By Wilbur E. Garrett. 612, *Nov. 1988*
Meteorites–Invaders From Space. By Kenneth F. Weaver. Photos by Jonathan Blair. 390-418, *Sept. 1986*
■■ *Nature on the Rampage: Our Violent Earth.* 199 pages. *1986*
■■ *Our Awesome Earth: Its Mysteries and Its Splendors.* 199 pages. *1986*
Our Restless Planet Earth. By Rick Gore. Photos by James A. Sugar.

142-181. Included: Continents Adrift; Life's Triumph *and* Origin of Earth and Life. Painting by Ned M. Seidler. Text by Larry Kohl. 146-151, *Aug. 1985*
✦ *Earth's Dynamic Crust. Aug. 1985*
The Planets: Between Fire and Ice. By Rick Gore. 4-51, *Jan. 1985*
Satellites That Serve Us. By Thomas Y. Canby. Included: Images of Earth. 281-335, *Sept. 1983*
■■ *Exploring Our Living Planet.* By Robert D. Ballard. 366 pages. *1983*
■■ *Our Violent Earth.* Juvenile. 104 pages. *1982*
Editorial. By Gilbert M. Grosvenor. 143, *Aug. 1980*
Voyager's Historic View of Earth and Moon. 53, *July 1978*
Geothermal Energy: The Power of Letting Off Steam. By Kenneth F. Weaver. 566-579, *Oct. 1977*
What's Happening to Our Climate? By Samuel W. Matthews. 576-615, *Nov. 1976*
Skylab Looks at Earth. 471-493, *Oct. 1974*
Have We Solved the Mysteries of the Moon? By Kenneth F. Weaver. Paintings by William H. Bond. Included: The moon compared with earth. 309-325, *Sept. 1973*
"The Earth from Space," photo supplement. Apollo astronauts on reverse. *Sept. 1973*
■ The Violent Earth. 286A-286B, *Feb. 1973*
This Changing Earth. By Samuel W. Matthews. 1-37, *Jan. 1973*
Apollo 16 Brings Us Visions From Space. 856-865, *Dec. 1972*
Pollution, Threat to Man's Only Home. By Gordon Young. Photos by James P. Blair. 738-781, *Dec. 1970*
✦ "How Man Pollutes His World," painting supplement. Map of the World on reverse. *Dec. 1970*
Voyage to the Planets. By Kenneth F. Weaver. Paintings by Ludek Pesek. 147-193, *Aug. 1970*
Historic Color Portrait of Earth From Space. By Kenneth F. Weaver. Photos by DODGE Satellite. 726-731, *Nov. 1967*
The Earth From Orbit. By Paul D. Lowman, Jr. 645-671, *Nov. 1966*
Extraordinary Photograph Shows Earth Pole to Pole. Photos by Nimbus I. 190-193, *Feb. 1965*
Scientists Drill at Sea to Pierce Earth's Crust (Project Mohole). By Samuel W. Matthews. Photos by J. Baylor Roberts. 686-697, *Nov. 1961*
Our Earth as a Satellite Sees It. By W. G. Stroud. 293-302, *Aug. 1960*
Our Home-town Planet, Earth. By F. Barrows Colton. 117-139, *Jan. 1952*
Seeing the Earth from 80 Miles Up. By Clyde T. Holliday. 511-528, *Oct. 1950*
The First Photograph Ever Made Showing the Division Between the Troposphere and Stratosphere and also the Actual Curvature of the Earth. Aërial photo by Albert W. Stevens. Photo supplement, *May 1936*
See also Plate Tectonics

■■ BOOKS ✦ MAPS ■ TELEVISION

Mexico City's worst earthquake killed more than 9,000 people on September 19, 1985, including patients and staff in a hospital that collapsed.   HERMAN J. KOKOJAN, BLACK STAR

Earthquake. By Frederick Leslie Ransome. 280-296, *May 1906*

The Record of the Great Earthquake Written in Washington by the Seismograph of the U. S. Weather Bureau. By C. F. Marvin. 296-298, *May 1906*

The San Francisco Earthquake of April 18, 1906, as Recorded by the Coast and Geodetic Survey Magnetic Observatories. By L. A. Bauer and J. E. Burbank. 298-300, *May 1906*

Resolution Adopted by the Eighth International Geographic Congress, September, 1904. 415-418, *Oct. 1904*

The Recent Earthquake Wave on the Coast of Japan. By Eliza Ruhamah Scidmore. 285-289, *Sept. 1896*

EARTH'S Most Primitive People: A Journey with the Aborigines of Central Australia. By Charles P. Mountford. 89-112, *Jan. 1946*

EARTH'S Richest Nation–A Tiny Pacific Islet. By Mike Holmes. 344-353, *Sept. 1976*

EARTHWATCH: Study Grant:

Rhesus monkeys in temples of Nepal. 576, 577, *Apr. 1980*

EARTHWORMS:

Capturing Strange Creatures in Colombia. By Marte Latham. Photos by Tor Eigeland. 682-693, *May 1966*

Biggest Worm Farm Caters to Platypuses. By W. H. Nicholas. 269-280, *Feb. 1949*

EAST, BEN: *Author*

Winter Sky Roads to Isle Royal (Michigan). 759-774, *Dec. 1931*

The **EAST** (Region), U. S.:

A Journey Down Old U. S. 1. By Bruce Dale. 790-817, *Dec. 1984*

The Parks in Your Backyard. By Conrad L. Wirth. Included: The East. 647-707, *Nov. 1963*

See also Atlantic Coast; New England

EAST AFRICA:

■■ *Excursion to Enchantment: A Journey to the World's Most Beautiful Places.* Included: East Africa, Loire Valley, Bhutan, Chile-Argentina Lake District, Alaska's Inside Passage, and the Caribbean. 200 pages. *1988*

The Leakey Tradition Lives On. By Melvin M. Payne. NGS research grant. 143-144, *Jan. 1973*

East Africa's Majestic Flamingos. Photos by M. Philip Kahl. NGS research grant. 276-294, *Feb. 1970*

■■ *The Wild Realm: Animals of East Africa.* By Louis S. B. Leakey. 199 pages. *1969*

See also Ethiopia; Kenya; Tanzania; Uganda

EAST From Bali by Seagoing Jeep to Timor. By Helen and Frank Schreider. 236-279, *Aug. 1962*

EAST GERMANY. *See* Germany, East

EAST INDIA COMPANY, Dutch. *See* Slot ter Hooge; Witte Leeuw

The **EAST** Indians in the New World (Trinidad). By Harriet Chalmers Adams. 485-491, *July 1907*

EAST INDIES. *See* Netherlands East Indies

EAST of Constantinople: Glimpses of Village Life in Anatolia, the Battleground of East and West, Where the Turks Reorganized Their Forces After the World War. By Melville Chater. 509-534, *May 1923*

EAST of Eden–California's Mid-coast. By Harvey Arden. Photos by Craig Aurness. 424-461, *Apr. 1984*

EAST of Suez to the Mount of the Decalogue: Following the Trail Over Which Moses Led the Israelites from the Slave-Pens of Egypt to Sinai. By Maynard Owen Williams. 709-743, *Dec. 1927*

EAST of the Adriatic: Notes on Dalmatia, Montenegro, Bosnia, and Herzegovina. By Kenneth McKenzie. 1159-1187, 1284, *Dec. 1912*

EAST PAKISTAN:

Pakistan: Problems of a Two-part Land. By Bern Keating. Photos by Albert Moldvay. 1-47, *Jan. 1967*

East Pakistan Drives Back the Jungle. By Jean and Franc Shor. 399-426, *Mar. 1955*

See also present name, Bangladesh

EAST PRUSSIA:

Flying Around the Baltic. By Douglas Chandler. 767-806, *June 1938*

EAST RIVER (Strait), New York:

A Century Old, the Wonderful Brooklyn Bridge. By John G. Morris. Photos by Donal F. Holway. 565-579, *May 1983*

EAST ST. LOUIS, Illinois:

"Pyramids" of the New World. By Neil Merton Judd. 105-128, *Jan. 1948*

EASTCOTT, JOHN:
Author-Photographer

Slovakia's Spirit of Survival. By Yva Momatiuk and John Eastcott. 120-146, *Jan. 1987*

Maoris: At Home in Two Worlds. By Yva Momatiuk and John Eastcott. 522-541, *Oct. 1984*

Poland's Mountain People. By Yva Momatiuk and John Eastcott. 104-129, *Jan. 1981*

New Zealand's High Country. By Yva Momatiuk and John Eastcott. 246-265, *Aug. 1978*

Still Eskimo, Still Free: The Inuit of Umingmaktok. By Yva Momatiuk and John Eastcott. 624-647, *Nov. 1977*

Photographer
Newfoundland: The Enduring Rock. By Harry Thurston. Photos by Yva Momatiuk and John Eastcott. 676-700, *May 1986*

EASTER, S. E.: *Author*

Jade. 9-17, *Jan. 1903*

EASTER:

Eternal Easter in a Greek Village. By Maria Nicolaidis-Karanikolas. Photos by James L. Stanfield. 768-777, *Dec. 1983*

Nikolaevsk: A Bit of Old Russia Takes Root in Alaska. By Jim Rearden. Photos by Charles O'Rear. 401-425, *Sept. 1972*

Easter Greetings From the Ukrainians. By Robert Paul Jordan. Photos by James A. Sugar. 556-563, *Apr. 1972*

Easter Week in Indian Guatemala. By John Scofield. 406-417, *Mar. 1960*

See also Holy Week

Stone faces of Easter Island seem to ponder the 1986 arrival of Halley's comet, shown above them in a double exposure. JAMES BALOG

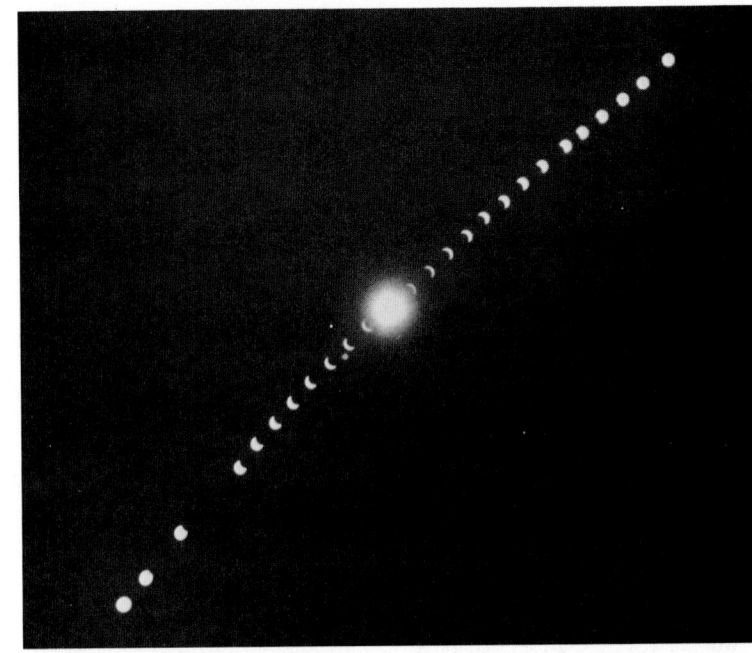

The sun's vanishing act was captured by multiple exposures made five minutes apart during a 1936 solar eclipse viewed from Soviet Central Asia. MERRIEL M. GARDNER

ECHAGÜE, J. ORTIZ: *Photographer*
Flashing Fashions of Old Spain. 413-428, *Mar. 1936*

ECHOES from Yugoslavia. 793-804, *June 1941*

ECHOES of a War: Vietnam Veterans Memorial. By Timothy S. Kolly. 554, *May 1985*

ECHOES of Shiloh (Shiloh National Military Park, Tennessee). By Shelby Foote. 106-111, *July 1979*

ECHOES of the San Francisco Earthquake. By Robert E. C. Stearns. 351-353, *May 1907*

ECHOES of Whaling Days (Nantucket). Photos by B. Anthony Stewart. 449-456, *Apr. 1944*

ECHOLOCATION:
Stalking Seals Under Antarctic Ice. By Carleton Ray. 54-65, *Jan. 1966*
See also Bats; Dolphins; Killer Whales; Oilbirds; Porpoises

ECKENER, HUGO: *Author*
The First Airship Flight Around the World: Dr. Hugo Eckener Tells of an Epochal Geographic Achievement upon the Occasion of the Bestowal of the National Geographic Society's Special Gold Medal. 653-688, *June 1930*

ECLIPSES:
Solar Eclipse, Nature's Super Spectacular. By Donald H. Menzel and Jay M. Pasachoff. NGS research grant. 222-233, *Aug. 1970*
The Sun. By Herbert Friedman. 713-743, *Nov. 1965*
The Solar Eclipse From a Jet. By Wolfgang B. Klemperer. Included: Path of totality of eclipse from Hokkaido, Japan, to beyond Bar Harbor, Maine. NGS research grant. 785-796, *Nov. 1963*
Burr Prizes Awarded to Dr. Edgerton and Dr. Van Biesbroeck. 705-706, May 1953; 523, *Apr. 1955*
South in the Sudan. By Harry Hoogstraal. Included: Khartoum, 1952 eclipse site (total eclipse of the sun, February 25). 249-272, *Feb. 1953*
Operation Eclipse: 1948. By William A. Kinney. Contents: Eclipse observation stations in Burma; Thailand; China; Korea; Japan; Aleutian Islands. NGS research grant. 325-372, *Mar. 1949*
Eclipse Hunting in Brazil's Ranchland. By F. Barrows Colton. Photos by Richard H. Stewart and Guy W. Starling. NGS research grant. 285-324, *Sept. 1947*
Your Society Observes Eclipse in Brazil. NGS research grant. 661, *May 1947*
Unfurling Old Glory on Canton Island. Painting by Charles Bittinger and color photo of the eclipse, showing the corona. 753-760, *June 1938*
Nature's Most Dramatic Spectacle. By S. A. Mitchell. 361-376, *Sept. 1937*
Eclipse Adventures on a Desert Isle

(Canton). By J. F. Hellweg. 377-394, *Sept. 1937*
First natural-color photograph of an eclipse ever reproduced, showing the corona. By Irvine C. Gardner. 178, *Feb. 1937*
Observing an Eclipse in Asiatic Russia. By Irvine C. Gardner. 179-197, *Feb. 1937*
Photographing the Eclipse of 1932 from the Air: From Five Miles Above the Earth's Surface, the National Geographic Society-Army Air Corps Survey Obtains Successful Photographs of the Moon's Shadow. By Albert W. Stevens. 581-596, *Nov. 1932*
Observing a Total Eclipse of the Sun: Dimming Solar Light for a Few Seconds Entails Years of Work for Science and Attracts Throngs to "Nature's Most Magnificent Spectacle." By Paul A. McNally. 597-605, *Nov. 1932*
The American Eclipse Expedition. By Colby M. Chester. 589-612, *Nov. 1906*
To Observe Solar Eclipse. 88, *Feb. 1905*
The National Geographic Society's Eclipse Expedition to Norfolk, Va. By Marcus Baker. 320, *Aug. 1900*
The Scientific Work of the National Geographic Society's Eclipse Expedition to Norfolk, Va. By Simon Newcomb. 321-324, *Aug. 1900*
The Total Eclipse of the Sun, May 28, 1900. By F. H. Bigelow. 33-34, *Jan. 1900*
The Cartography and Observations of Bering's First Voyage. By Adolphus W. Greely. 205-230, Jan. 28, 1892; *Feb. 19, 1892*
On the Alleged Observation of a Lunar Eclipse by Bering in 1728-9. By Marcus Baker. 167-169, *May 1890*

ECOLOGY:
Aldo Leopold: "A Durable Scale of Values." By Boyd Gibbons. Photos

by Jim Brandenburg. 682-708, *Nov. 1981*
Florida, Noah's Ark for Exotic Newcomers. By Rick Gore. Photos by David Doubilet. 538-559, *Oct. 1976*
Last Stand for the Bighorn. By James K. Morgan. 383-399, *Sept. 1973*
Giant Tortoises: Goliaths of the Galapagos. By Craig MacFarland. Photos by author and Jan MacFarland. 632-649, *Nov. 1972*
Giant Kelp, Sequoias of the Sea. By Wheeler J. North. Photos by Bates Littlehales. 251-269, *Aug. 1972*
A River Restored: Oregon's Willamette. By Ethel A. Starbird. Photos by Lowell J. Georgia. 816-835, *June 1972*
African Wildlife: Man's Threatened Legacy. By Allan C. Fisher, Jr. Photos by Thomas Nebbia. Paintings by Ned Seidler. 147-187, *Feb. 1972*
■■ *As We Live and Breathe: The Challenge of Our Environment.* 239 pages. *1971*
Our Ecological Crisis. 737-795. I. Pollution, Threat to Man's Only Home. By Gordon Young. Photos by James P. Blair. 738-781; II. The World and How We Abuse It. 782-783; III. The Fragile Beauty All About Us. Photos by Harry S. C. Yen. 785-795, *Dec. 1970*
✦ *The World; How Man Pollutes His World. Dec. 1970*
The Osprey, Endangered World Citizen. By Roger Tory Peterson. Photos by Frederick Kent Truslow. NGS research grant. 53-67, *July 1969*
New Florida Resident, the Walking Catfish. By Clarence P. Idyll. Photos by Robert F. Sisson. 847-851, *June 1969*
Life with the King of Beasts. By George B. Schaller. 494-519, *Apr. 1969*
See also Ecosystems; Life Zones; and Photosynthesis, for marine ecology

Fragile pasqueflowers spring from the northern prairie country celebrated by naturalist Aldo Leopold, an early champion of the ecologist's ethic. JIM BRANDENBURG

The **ECONOMIC** Aspects of Soil Erosion. (Part I). By Nathaniel S. Shaler. 328-338, *Oct. 1896*

The **ECONOMIC** Aspects of Soil Erosion. (Part II). By Nathaniel S. Shaler. 368-377, *Nov. 1896*

The **ECONOMIC** Condition of the Philippines. By Max L. Tornow. 33-64, *Feb. 1899*

ECONOMIC COOPERATION ADMINISTRATION:

Roaming Korea South of the Iron Curtain. By Enzo de Chetelat. 777-808, *June 1950*

War-torn Greece Looks Ahead. By Maynard Owen Williams. 711-744, *Dec. 1949*

With Uncle Sam and John Bull in Germany. By Frederick Simpich. 117-140, *Jan. 1949*

The **ECONOMIC** Evolution of Alaska. By Adolphus W. Greely. 585-593, *July 1909*

ECONOMIC Loss to the People of the United States Through Insects That Carry Disease. By Leland O. Howard. 735-749, *Aug. 1909*

ECONOMIC ZONES: People's Republic of China:

China's Opening Door. By John J. Putman. Photos by H. Edward Kim. 64-83, *July 1983*

ECONOMICS:

Five Noted Thinkers Explore the Future. Included: Isaac Asimov, Richard F. Babcock, Edmund N. Bacon, Buckminster Fuller, Gerard Piel. 68-75, *July 1976*

ECOSYSTEMS:

Population, Plenty, and Poverty. By Paul R. and Anne H. Ehrlich. Included: Kenya: A Population Exploding. Photos by Robert Caputo; China: Back from the Brink. Photos by Patrick Zachmann; Hungary: A Static Society. Photos by Steve McCurry; India: Life on the Edge. Photos by Raghu Rai; Brazil: Flight to the Cities. Photos by Mary Ellen Mark; United States: Geared to Consumption. Photos by Pam Spaulding. 914-945, *Dec. 1988*

The Great Lakes' Troubled Waters. By Charles E. Cobb, Jr. Photos by Bob Sacha and Richard Olsenius. Included: A great meeting of waters; North America's fifth coast. 2-31, *July 1987*

Mysteries of the Bog. By Louise E. Levathes. Photos by Fred Bavendam. Included: Peat holds clues to early American life. 397-420, *Mar. 1987*

The Serengeti. 560-601. I. A Photographic Portfolio. Photos by Mitsuaki Iwago. Text by John Eliot. 563-585; II. The Glory of Life. By Shana Alexander. 585-601, *May 1986*

Tide Pools: Windows Between Land and Sea. By Robert F. Sisson. 252-259, *Feb. 1986*

A Short Hike With Bob Marshall. By Mike Edwards. Photos by Dewitt Jones. 664-689, *May 1985*

Battle For a Bigger Bob (Bob Marshall Wilderness). By Mike Edwards. Photos by Dewitt Jones. 690-692, *May 1985*

Isle Royale, A North Woods Park Primeval. By John L. Eliot. Photos by Mitch Kezar. 534-550, *Apr. 1985*

The Living Sands of the Namib. By William J. Hamilton III. Photos by Carol and David Hughes. 364-377, *Sept. 1983*

Hidden Life of an Undersea Desert. By Eugenie Clark. Photos by David Doubilet. 129-144, *July 1983*

Etosha: Namibia's Kingdom of Animals. By Douglas H. Chadwick. Photos by Des and Jen Bartlett. 344-385, *Mar. 1983*

Tropical Rain Forests. 2-65. Included: Nature's Dwindling Treasures. By Peter T. White. Photos by James P. Blair. Paintings by Barron Storey. 2-47; Teeming Life of a Rain Forest. By Carol and David Hughes. 49-65, *Jan. 1983*

Strange World of Palau's Salt Lakes. By William M. Hamner. Photos by David Doubilet. 264-282, *Feb. 1982*

In Hawaii's Crystal Sea, A Galaxy of Life Fills the Night. By Kenneth Brower. Photos by William R. Curtsinger and Chris Newbert. 834-847, *Dec. 1981*

The Troubled Waters of Mono Lake. By Gordon Young. Photos by Craig Aurness. NGS research grant. 504-519, *Oct. 1981*

Life on a Rock Ledge. By William H. Amos. 558-566, *Oct. 1980*

The Wild World of Compost. By Cecil E. Johnson. Photos by Bianca Lavies. 273-284, *Aug. 1980*

The Tallgrass Prairie: Can It Be Saved? By Dennis Farney. Photos by Jim Brandenburg. 37-61, *Jan. 1980*

Incredible World of the Deep-sea Rifts. NGS research grant. 680-705. I. Strange World Without Sun. The Editor. 680-688; II. Return to Oases of the Deep. By Robert D. Ballard and J. Frederick Grassle. 689-705, *Nov. 1979*

The Tree Nobody Liked (Red Mangrove). By Rick Gore. Photos by Bianca Lavies. 669-689, *May 1977*

Unseen Life of a Mountain Stream. By William H. Amos. 562-580, *Apr. 1977*

Miracle of the Potholes. By Rowe Findley. Photos by Robert F. Sisson. 570-579, *Oct. 1975*

Hidden Worlds in the Heart of a Plant (Bromeliad). By Paul A. Zahl. 389-397, *Mar. 1975*

Abundant Life in a Desert Land. By Walter Meayers Edwards. 424-436, *Sept. 1973*

Can We Save Our Salt Marshes? By Stephen W. Hitchcock. Photos by William R. Curtsinger. 729-765, *June 1972*

The World of My Apple Tree. By Robert F. Sisson. 836-847, *June 1972*

The Imperiled Everglades. By Fred Ward. 1-27, *Jan. 1972*

Mzima, Kenya's Spring of Life. By Joan and Alan Root. 350-373, *Sept. 1971*

Teeming Life of a Pond. By William H. Amos. 274-298, *Aug. 1970*

Life in a "Dead" Sea–Great Salt Lake. By Paul A. Zahl. 252-263, *Aug. 1967*

The Living Sand. By William H. Amos. 820-833, *June 1965*

See also Corals and Coral Reefs; Kelp Forests; Tundra

ECUADOR:

El Niño's Ill Wind. By Thomas Y. Canby. 144-183, *Feb. 1984*

Ecuador–Low and Lofty Land Astride the Equator. By Loren McIntyre. 259-298, *Feb. 1968*

Ambassadors of Good Will: The Peace Corps. By Sargent Shriver and Peace Corps Volunteers. Included: Ecuador. By Rhoda and Earle Brooks. 297-345, *Sept. 1964*

El Sangay, Fire-breathing Giant of the Andes. By G. Edward Lewis. 117-138, *Jan. 1950*

Sea Fever. By John E. Schultz. 237-268, *Feb. 1949*

Quinine Hunters in Ecuador. By Froelich Rainey. 341-363, *Mar. 1946*

From Sea to Clouds in Ecuador. By W. Robert Moore. 717-740, *Dec. 1941*

Mrs. Robinson Crusoe in Ecuador. By Mrs. Richard C. Gill. 133-172, *Feb. 1934*

The Volcanoes of Ecuador, Guideposts in Crossing South America. By George M. Dyott. 49-93, *Jan. 1929*

Over Trail and Through Jungle in Ecuador: Indian Head-Hunters of the Interior, an Interesting Study in the South American Republic. By H. E. Anthony. 327-352, *Oct. 1921*

Beautiful Ecuador. By Joseph Lee. 81-91, *Feb. 1907*

South American Immigration. 587, *Oct. 1906*

The Road to Bolivia. By William E. Curtis. 209-224, *June 1900*

A Journey in Ecuador. By Mark B. Kerr. 238-245, *July 1896*

See also Galápagos Islands; Vilcabamba

EDAM CHEESE:

A North Holland Cheese Market. By Hugh M. Smith. 1051-1066, *Dec. 1910*

EDDY, FREDERICK B.: *Author*

The Panther of the Hearth: Lithe Grace and Independence of Spirit Contribute to the Appeal of Cats, "The Only Domestic Animal Man Has Never Conquered." 589-634, *Nov. 1938*

EDDY, JOHN A.: *Author*

Probing the Mystery of the Medicine Wheels. Photos by Thomas E. Hooper. 140-146, *Jan. 1977*

EDDY, WILLIAM A.:

Saudi Arabia, Oil Kingdom. Photos by Maynard Owen Williams. 497-512, *Apr. 1948*

EDEN, Garden of:

The Cradle of Civilization: The Historic Lands Along the Euphrates and Tigris Rivers Where Briton Is Fighting Turk. By James Baikie. 127-162, *Feb. 1916*

A 1,900-mile-an-hour bullet is frozen by a stroboscopic light, a technique pioneered by Harold "Doc" Edgerton, the father of high-speed photography. HAROLD E. EDGERTON

Where Adam and Eve Lived. By Frederick and Margaret Simpich. 546-588, *Dec. 1914*

EDEN in the Outback. By Kay and Stanley Breeden. 189-203, *Feb. 1973*

The **EDEN** of the Flowery Republic (Sichuan Province, China). By Joseph Beech. 355-390, *Nov. 1920*

EDGAR M. QUEENY-AMERICAN MUSEUM OF NATURAL HISTORY EXPEDITION:

Spearing Lions with Africa's Masai. By Edgar Monsanto Queeny. 487-517, *Oct. 1954*

EDGEØYA (Island), Svalbard:

Polar Bear: Lonely Nomad of the North. By Thor Larsen. 574-590, *Apr. 1971*

EDGERTON, GLEN E.: *Author*

An Engineer's View of the Suez Canal. 123-140, *Jan. 1957*

EDGERTON, HAROLD E.:

Recipient of the National Geographic Society Centennial Award. President's Page. By Gilbert M. Grosvenor. *Dec. 1988*

"Doc" Edgerton–The Man Who Made Time Stand Still. By Erla Zwingle. Photos by Harold E. Edgerton and Bruce Dale. 464-483, *Oct. 1987*

Burr Prizes Awarded to Dr. Edgerton and Dr. Van Biesbroeck. Note: Electronic flashlight for ultra-high-speed photography invented by Dr. Edgerton. 705-706, May 1953; 523, Apr. 1955; 467, Oct. 1955; 847, *June 1960*

Nomination Page. *Aug. 1959*

Mystery Mammals of the Twilight (Bats). By Donald R. Griffin. Included: Photographs taken by the high-

speed camera developed by Harold E. Edgerton. 117-134, *July 1946*

Author

Stonehenge–New Light on an Old Riddle. Paintings by Brian Hope-Taylor. 846-866, *June 1960*

Circus Action in Color. 305-308, *Mar. 1948*

Author-Photographer

Photographing the Sea's Dark Underworld. NGS research grant. 523-537, *Apr. 1955*

Freezing the Flight of Hummingbirds. By Harold E. Edgerton, R. J. Niedrach, and Walker Van Riper. NGS research grant. 245-261, *Aug. 1951*

Hummingbirds in Action. 221-232, *Aug. 1947*

Photographer

"Doc" Edgerton–The Man Who Made Time Stand Still. By Erla Zwingle. Photos by Harold E. Edgerton and Bruce Dale. 464-483, *Oct. 1987*

Calypso Explores an Undersea Canyon (Romanche Trench). By Jacques-Yves Cousteau. Photos by Bates Littlehales and Harold E. Edgerton. NGS research grant. 373-396, *Mar. 1958*

To the Depths of the Sea by Bathyscaphe. By Jacques-Yves Cousteau. NGS research grant. 67-79, *July 1954*

Fish Men Discover a 2,200-year-old Greek Ship. By Jacques-Yves Cousteau. NGS research grant. 1-36, *Jan. 1954*

The Wonder City That Moves by Night (Circus). By Francis Beverly Kelley. 289-324, *Mar. 1948*

EDINBURGH, Scotland:

Edinburgh: Capital in Search of a Country. By James Cerruti. Photos by Adam Woolfitt. 274-296, *Aug. 1976*

Poets' Voices Linger in Scottish Shrines. By Isobel Wylie Hutchison. Photos by Kathleen Revis. 437-488, *Oct. 1957*

Midshipmen's Cruise. By William J. Aston and Alexander G. B. Grosvenor. 711-754, *June 1948*

Bonnie Scotland, Postwar Style. By Isobel Wylie Hutchison. 545-601, *May 1946*

Scotland in Wartime. By Isobel Wylie Hutchison. 723-743, *June 1943*

Vagabonding in England: A Young American Works His Way Around the British Isles and Sees Sights from an Unusual Point of View. By John McWilliams. 357-398, *Mar. 1934*

Edinburgh, Athens of the North: Romantic History of Cramped Medieval City Vies With Austere Beauty of Newer Wide Streets and Stately Squares. By J. R. Hildebrand. 219-246, *Aug. 1932*

EDISON, THOMAS ALVA:

Laboratory and Buildings. *See* Greenfield Village

EDITOR'S Postscript. By Wilbur E. Garrett. 115, *Special Report on Energy. (Feb. 1981)*

EDMONTON, Alberta, Canada:

Canada's "Now" Frontier. By Robert Paul Jordan. Photos by Lowell Georgia. 480-511, *Oct. 1976*

EDMUNDS, CHARLES K.: *Author*

Shantung–China's Holy Land. 231-252, *Sept. 1919*

EDOM. *See* Jordan

EDSON, JOHN JOY:

Tribute by Gilbert H. Grosvenor. 162, *Jan. 1936*

NGS Treasurer, photograph of. 790, *June 1934*

Reports by. 80, Feb. 1902; 89-90, Jan. 1910; 214, Feb. 1911; 256, *Feb. 1913*

EDUCATING the Filipinos. 46-49, *Jan. 1905*

EDUCATION:

Denmark and the Danes. By Maurice Francis Egan. 115-164, *Aug. 1922*

Sight-Seeing in School: Taking Twenty Million Children on a Picture Tour of the World. By Jessie L. Burrall. 489-503, *June 1919*

Bringing the World to Our Foreign-Language Soldiers: How a Military Training Camp is Solving a Seemingly Unsurmountable Problem by Using the Geographic. By Christina Krysto. 81-90, *Aug. 1918*

New York–The Metropolis of Mankind. By William Joseph Showalter. 1-49, *July 1918*

For Teaching Physiography. 353, *May 1907*

Present Conditions in China. By John W. Foster. 651-672, 709-711, *Dec. 1906*

Educating the Filipinos. 46-49, *Jan. 1905*

President Alexander Graham Bell on Japan. By John Hyde. 509-512, *Dec. 1898*

The Relations of Geology to Physiography in Our Educational System. By Thomas C. Chamberlin. 154-160, *Jan. 31, 1894*
See also Geographic Education; World's Congress of Education

EDUCATION FOUNDATION:

President Grosvenor Announces the National Geographic Society Education Foundation. By Lloyd H. Elliott. 329A-329D, *Mar. 1988*

EDUCATIONAL AIDS. *See* Atlases; Books; Films and Filmstrips; Globes; Map Supplements; NGM: Indexes; Records and Sound Sheets; WORLD

EDWARDS, CLARENCE R.: *Author*

Governing the Philippine Islands. 273-284, *July 1904*
The Work of the Bureau of Insular Affairs. 239-255, *June 1904*

EDWARDS, DUNCAN: *Photographer*

Roman Life in 1,600-year-old Color Pictures (Mosaics). By Gino Vinicio Gentili. 211-229, *Feb. 1957*

EDWARDS, MIKE W.:

On Assignment in Ukraine. *May 1987*
On Assignment in Colorado. *Aug. 1984*
Nomination Page. *June 1980*

Author

Ukraine. Photos by Steve Raymer. 595-631, *May 1987*
Chernobyl–One Year After. Photos by Steve Raymer. Paintings by Pierre Mion. 632-653, *May 1987*
Nicaragua: Nation in Conflict. Photos by James Nachtwey. 776-811, *Dec. 1985*
A Short Hike With Bob Marshall. Photos by Dewitt Jones. 664-689, *May 1985*
Battle For a Bigger Bob (Bob Marshall Wilderness). Photos by Dewitt Jones. 690-692, *May 1985*
When the Moguls Ruled India. Photos by Roland Michaud. 463-493, *Apr. 1985*
Afghanistan's Troubled Capital–Kabul. Photos by Steve Raymer. 494-505, *Apr. 1985*
Colorado Dreaming. Photos by Craig Aurness. 186-219, *Aug. 1984*
Honduras: Eye of the Storm. Photos by David Alan Harvey. 608-637, *Nov. 1983*
Shanghai: Born-again Giant. Photos by Bruce Dale. 2-43, *July 1980*
Tunisia: Sea, Sand, Success. Photos by David Alan Harvey. 184-217, *Feb. 1980*
Along the Great Divide. Photos by Nicholas deVore III. 483-515, *Oct. 1979*
Dream On, Vancouver. Photos by Charles O'Rear. 467-491, *Oct. 1978*
Mexico: "A Very Beautiful Challenge." Photos by Thomas Nebbia. 612-647, *May 1978*
The Danube: River of Many Nations, Many Names. Photos by Winfield Parks. 455-485, *Oct. 1977*
An Eye for an Eye: Pakistan's Wild Frontier. Photos by J. Bruce Baumann. 111-139, *Jan. 1977*

A snowy egret patiently waits for fish in southern Florida's Everglades National Park. FREDERICK KENT TRUSLOW

Should They Build a Fence Around Montana? Photos by Nicholas deVore III. 614-649, *May 1976*
Thomas Jefferson: Architect of Freedom. Photos by Linda Bartlett. 231-259, *Feb. 1976*
The Virginians. Photos by David Alan Harvey. 588-617, *Nov. 1974*
Hiking the Backbone of the Rockies: Canada's Great Divide Trail. Photos by Lowell Georgia. 795-817, *June 1973*
California's Land Apart–the Monterey Peninsula. 682-703, *Nov. 1972*
Mexico to Canada on the Pacific Crest Trail. Photos by David Hiser. 741-779, *June 1971*
Through Ozark Hills and Hollows. Photos by Bruce Dale. 656-689, *Nov. 1970*
Shenandoah, I Long to Hear You. Photos by Thomas Anthony DeFeo. 554-588, *Apr. 1970*

EDWARDS, WALTER MEAYERS:

Nomination Page. *June 1966*

Author-Photographer

Abundant Life in a Desert Land. 424-436, *Sept. 1973*
Lake Powell: Waterway to Desert Wonders. 44-75, *July 1967*
Crater Lake Summer. 134-148, *July 1962*
Across the Ridgepole of the Alps. 410-419, *Sept. 1960*
Eternal France. 725-764, *June 1960*
France's Past Lives in Languedoc. 1-43, *July 1951*
On the Ridgepole of the Rockies. Included: Canada's Rocky Mountain Playground (Banff and Jasper National Parks). 745-780, *June 1947*

Photographer

■■ *The Wild Shores: America's Beginnings.* By Tee Loftin Snell. Art by Louis S. Glanzman. 203 pages. *1974*

■■ *Great American Deserts.* By Rowe Findley. 207 pages. *1972*
Canyonlands, Realm of Rock and the Far Horizon. By Rowe Findley. 71-91, *July 1971*
Retracing John Wesley Powell's Historic Voyage Down the Grand Canyon. By Joseph Judge. 668-713, *May 1969*
Micronesia: The Americanization of Eden. By David S. Boyer. 702-744, *May 1967*
The Alps: Man's Own Mountains. By Ralph Gray. Photos by Walter Meayers Edwards and William Eppridge. 350-395, *Sept. 1965*
Canada, My Country. By Alan Phillips. Photos by David S. Boyer and Walter Meayers Edwards. 769-819, *Dec. 1961*
We Saw the World From the Edge of Space. By Malcolm D. Ross. 671-685, *Nov. 1961*
The Camargue, Land of Cowboys and Gypsies. By Eugene L. Kammerman. 667-699, *May 1956*
Down the Susquehanna by Canoe. By Ralph Gray. 73-120, *July 1950*
Down the Potomac by Canoe. By Ralph Gray. 213-242, *Aug. 1948*
Our Nation's Capital on Parade. Photos by B. Anthony Stewart, Walter M. Edwards, and others. 265-288, *Sept. 1943*
Where the Winding Cam Mirrors Cambridge (University) Spires. Photos by Bernard Wakeman and Walter M. Edwards. 339-346, *Sept. 1936*

EDWARDS AIR FORCE BASE, California:

Columbia's Landing Closes a Circle. By Tom Wolfe. 474-477, *Oct. 1981*
Fact Finding for Tomorrow's Planes. By Hugh L. Dryden. Photos by Luis Marden. 757-780, *Dec. 1953*

EELS:

The Red Sea's Gardens of Eels. By Eugenie Clark. Photos by James L. Stanfield and David Doubilet. NGS research grant. 724-735, *Nov. 1972*
Night Life in the Gulf Stream. By Paul A. Zahl. 391-416, *Mar. 1954*
The Mysterious Life of the Common Eel. By Hugh M. Smith. 1140-1146, *Oct. 1913*

EFATE (Island), New Hebrides:

Palms and Planes in the New Hebrides. By Robert D. Heinl, Jr. 229-256, *Aug. 1944*

The **EFFECTS** of Geographic Environment in the Development of Civilization in Primitive Man. By Gardiner G. Hubbard. 161-176, *June 1897*

EFFIE M. MORRISSEY (Schooner):

Servicing Arctic Airbases. By Robert A. Bartlett. 602-616, *May 1946*

EFFIGIES, Indian. *See* Gravel Pictographs

EFFORTS to Obtain Greater Energy from Coal. 138-140, *Feb. 1907*

EGAN, JOHN: *Photographer*

Jason's Voyage: In Search of the Golden Fleece. By Tim Severin. Photos by

John Egan and Seth Mortimer. 406-420, *Sept. 1985*

EGAN, MAURICE FRANCIS: *Author*

Norway and the Norwegians. 647-696, *June 1924*

Denmark and the Danes. 115-164, *Aug. 1922*

EGBERT, ALLAN L.:
Author-Photographer

Among Alaska's Brown Bears. By Allan L. Egbert and Michael H. Luque. NGS research grant. 428-442, *Sept. 1975*

EGGS:

Easter Greetings From the Ukrainians. By Robert Paul Jordan. Photos by James A. Sugar. 556-563, *Apr. 1972*

Easter Egg Chickens. By Frederick G. Vosburgh. Photos by B. Anthony Stewart. 377-387, *Sept. 1948*

Guillemot Eggs. 386-388, *Oct. 1903*

See also Aepyornis; Cooper's Hawk; Ospreys; Scarlet Ibis

EGRETS:

Saving Man's Wildlife Heritage. By John H. Baker. Photos by Robert F. Sisson. 581-620, *Nov. 1954*

A New Bird Immigrant Arrives. Contents: Cattle egret. By Roger Tory Peterson. 281-292, *Aug. 1954*

Wildlife of Everglades National Park. By Daniel B. Beard. Paintings by Walter A. Weber. 83-116, *Jan. 1949*

The Large Wading Birds: Long Legs and Remarkable Beaks, as Well as Size, Form, and Color, Distinguish the Herons, Ibises, and Flamingos. By T. Gilbert Pearson. Paintings by Allan Brooks. 441-469, *Oct. 1932*

EGYPT:

A Change of Fortunes On the River Nile. Geographica. *Dec. 1988*

Journey Up the Nile. By Robert Caputo. Included: Africa's River of Legend, a foldout map of the Nile; A Dam Against Famine. By Farouk El-Baz. 577-633, *May 1985*

The Mediterranean–Sea of Man's Fate. By Rick Gore. Photos by Jonathan Blair. 694-737, *Dec. 1982*

Eternal Sinai. By Harvey Arden. Photos by David Doubilet and Kevin

Fleming. 420-461. Included: Egyptian control of the Sinai is returned as part of the Camp David accords. Egyptian Sector. Photos by Kevin Fleming. 430-443; Israeli Sector. Photos by David Doubilet. 444-461, *Apr. 1982*

Egypt's Desert of Promise. By Farouk El-Baz. Photos by Georg Gerster. 190-221, *Feb. 1982*

Editorial. By Gilbert M. Grosvenor. 291, *Mar. 1977*

Egypt: Two Perspectives. 293-343. I. Legacy of a Dazzling Past. By Alice J. Hall. 293-311; II. Omens for a Better Tomorrow. By Thomas J. Abercrombie. 312-343, *Mar. 1977*

Eyewitness to War in the Holy Land. By Charles Harbutt. 782-795, *Dec. 1967*

■■ *The River Nile.* By Bruce Brander. 207 pages. *1966*

Journey Into the Great Rift: the Northern Half. By Helen and Frank Schreider. 254-290, *Aug. 1965*

Yankee Cruises the Storied Nile. By Irving and Electa Johnson. Photos by Winfield Parks. 583-633, *May 1965*

Island of Faith in the Sinai Wilderness (St. Catherine's Monastery). By George H. Forsyth. Photos by Robert F. Sisson. 82-106, *Jan. 1964*

Mount Sinai's Holy Treasures (St. Catherine's Monastery). By Kurt Weitzmann. Photos by Fred Anderegg. 109-127, *Jan. 1964*

YWCA: International Success Story. By Mary French Rockefeller. Photos by Otis Imboden. 904-933, *Dec. 1963*

✣ *Africa: Countries of the Nile,* Atlas series supplement. *Oct. 1963*

Round the World School (ISA). By Paul Antze. Photos by William Eppridge. 96-127, *July 1962*

Africa: The Winds of Freedom Stir a Continent. By Nathaniel T. Kenney. Photos by W. D. Vaughn. 303-359, *Sept. 1960*

Kayaks Down the Nile. By John M. Goddard. 697-732, *May 1955*

Safari from Congo to Cairo. By Elsie May Bell Grosvenor. Photos by Gilbert Grosvenor. 721-771, *Dec. 1954*

Troubled Waters East of Suez. By Ernest M. Eller. 483-522, *Apr. 1954*

"Around the World in Eighty Days."

Sunlight floods the Great Temple at Abu Simbel and the 30-foot statues of Egyptian god-king Ramses II. GEORG GERSTER

By Newman Bumstead. Included: Cairo, Giza, Ismailia, Port Said, Suez Canal. 705-750, *Dec. 1951*

Sinai Sheds New Light on the Bible. By Henry Field. Photos by William B. and Gladys Terry. Included: St. Catherine's Monastery. 795-815, *Dec. 1948*

✣ *Bible Lands and the Cradle of Western Civilization.* Insets: Holy Land Today, Holy Land in Biblical Times, Jerusalem, Traditional Route of the Exodus, St. Paul's Travels and the Seven Churches, The Crusades. *Dec. 1946*

American Fighters Visit Bible Lands. By Maynard Owen Williams. 311-340, *Mar. 1946*

American Alma Maters in the Near East. By Maynard Owen Williams. 237-256, *Aug. 1945*

Red Cross Girl Overseas. By Margaret Cotter. 745-768, *Dec. 1944*

The British Commonwealth of Nations: "Organized Freedom" Around the World. By Eric Underwood. 485-524, *Apr. 1943*

War Meets Peace in Egypt. By Grant Parr and G. E. Janssen. 503-526, *Apr. 1942*

Old-New Battle Grounds of Egypt and Libia. By W. Robert Moore. 809-820, *Dec. 1940*

By Felucca Down the Nile: Giant Dams Rule Egypt's Lifeline River, Yet Village Life Goes On As It Did in the Time of the Pharaohs. By Willard Price. 435-476, *Apr. 1940*

Change Comes to Bible Lands. By Frederick Simpich. 695-750, *Dec. 1938*

✣ *Bible Lands and the Cradle of Western Civilization.* Insets: Jerusalem, The Holy Land, Economic Development, Route of the Exodus, St. Paul's Travels and the Seven Churches, The

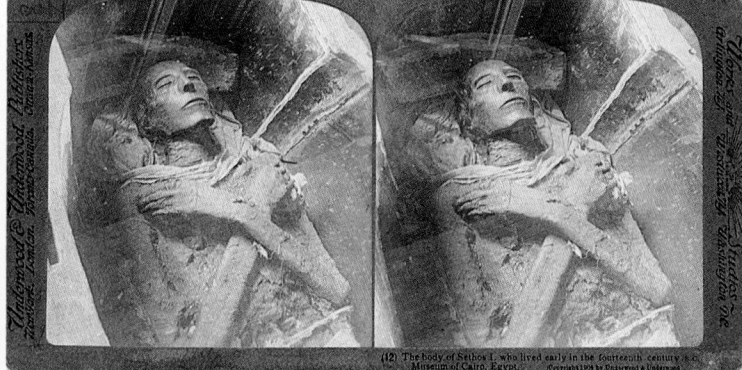

Seen in a stereoscopic view, the perfectly preserved mummy of King Seti I lies in stately repose in a museum in Cairo, Egypt. UNDERWOOD & UNDERWOOD/THE BETTMANN ARCHIVE

In Egypt's Dakhla basin archaeologists excavating the ruins of a town that flourished between 2345 and 2181 B.C. have uncovered a more recent skeleton.   GEORG GERSTER

EGYPTIAN VULTURE:

EHRLICH, ANNE H.: *Author*

EHRLICH, PAUL R.: *Author*

EIGELAND, TOR: *Photographer*

EIGENMANN, CARL H.: *Author*

EIGHTEEN EIGHTIES:

Still steaming after the eruption, a crater gapes at the top of El Chichón in Mexico. Volcanic pressure blew off its jungle-covered dome on April 4, 1982. GUILLERMO ALDANA E.

EIGHTH INTERNATIONAL GEOGRAPHIC CONGRESS. *See* International Geographic Congress

EIGNER, JULIUS: *Author*

EILER, LYNTHA:
Author-Photographer

EILER, TERRY: *Author-Photographer*

Photographer

EILOART, ARNOLD: *Author*

EILTS, HERMANN F.: *Author*

ÉIRE. *See* Ireland, Republic of

EISEMAN, FRED and MARGARET:
Photographers

EISENHOWER, DWIGHT D.:

Inside the White House. By Lonnelle Aikman. Photos by B. Anthony Stewart and Thomas Nebbia. 3-43, *Jan. 1961*

When the President Goes Abroad. By Gilbert M. Grosvenor. 588-649, *May 1960*

President Eisenhower Presents the Society's Hubbard Medal to the Conquerors of Antarctica. 589-590, *Apr. 1959*

President Eisenhower Presents to Prince Philip the National Geographic Society's Medal. 865-868, *Dec. 1957*

President Eisenhower Presents the Hubbard Medal to Everest's Conquerors (British). 64, *July 1954*

Author

The Churchill I Knew. 153-157, *Aug. 1965*

A Message From the President of the United States. 587, *May 1960*

EISENHOWER, MAMIE GENEVA DOUD:

The Eisenhower Story. By Howard La Fay. 1-39, *July 1969*

Author

Introduction to article, "Inside the White House." 1, *Jan. 1961*

EISTEDDFODS:

Wales, Land of Bards. By Alan Villiers. Photos by Thomas Nebbia. 727-769, *June 1965*

EKA DASA RUDRA (Festival):

Bali Celebrates a Festival of Faith. By Peter Miller. Photos by Fred and Margaret Eiseman. 416-427, *Mar. 1980*

EKLINGI (Temple), Rajputana, India:

The Marble Dams of Rajputana. By Eleanor Maddock. 469-499, *Nov. 1921*

EKOI TRIBESPEOPLE:

Notes on the Ekoi (Nigeria). By Percy A. Talbot. 33-38, *Jan. 1912*

EL-BAZ, FAROUK:

On Assignment in Egypt. *Apr. 1988*
On Assignment in Egypt. *Feb. 1982*

Author

Finding a Pharaoh's Funeral Bark. Photos by James P. Blair and Claude E. Petrone. Included: Craft for eternity; The world's oldest ship. 513-533, *Apr. 1988*

A Dam Against Famine: Aswan. 595, *May 1985*

Egypt's Desert of Promise. Photos by Georg Gerster. 190-221, *Feb. 1982*

ELBOWROOM for the Millions. By Louise Levathes. 86-97, *July 1979*

ELBURZ MOUNTAINS, Iran:

Modern Persia and Its Capital: And an Account of an Ascent of Mount Demavend, the Persian Olympus. By F. L. Bird. 353-400, *Apr. 1921*

EL CAPITAN (Monolith), Yosemite National Park, California:

Yosemite–Forever? By David S. Boyer. Photos by Jonathan Blair. 52-79, *Jan. 1985*

EL CHICHÓN (Volcano), Mexico:

When the Earth Moves. The Editor. 638-639, *May 1986*

The Disaster of El Chichón. By Boris Weintraub. Photos by Guillermo Aldana E. and Kenneth Garrett. 654-684. Included: Volcanic Cloud May Alter Earth's Climate. By Robert I. Tilling. 672-675, *Nov. 1982*

ELDFELL (Volcano), Heimaey, Iceland:

Vestmannaeyjar: Up From the Ashes. By Noel Grove. Photos by Robert S. Patton. 690-701, *May 1977*

See also former name, Kirkjufell

ELECTRIC Street Railways (U. S.). By John Hyde. 284, *Oct. 1897*

ELECTRICITY:

Special Report on Energy, an extra issue of NGM. 115 pages. *(Feb. 1981)*

Solar Energy, the Ultimate Powerhouse. By John L. Wilhelm. Photos by Emory Kristof. 381-397, *Mar. 1976*

Can We Harness the Wind? By Roger Hamilton. Photos by Emory Kristof. 812-829, *Dec. 1975*

Whatever Happened to TVA? By Gordon Young. Photos by Emory Kristof. 830-863, *June 1973*

The Search for Tomorrow's Power. By Kenneth F. Weaver. Photos by Emory Kristof. 650-681, *Nov. 1972*

Uncle Sam's House of 1,000 Wonders (National Bureau of Standards). By Lyman J. Briggs and F. Barrows Colton. 755-784, *Dec. 1951*

Lightning in Action. By F. Barrows Colton. 809-828, *June 1950*

The Fire of Heaven. By Albert W. Atwood. 655-674, *Nov. 1948*

See also Geothermal Energy; Hydroelectric Power; Nuclear Energy; Solar Energy

ELECTRON MICROSCOPY:

Our Immune System: The Wars Within. By Peter Jaret. Photos by Lennart Nilsson. Illustrations text by Larry Kohl. 702-735, *June 1986*

▣ The Invisible World. 1, Jan. 1980; cover, *Mar. 1980*

Electronic Voyage Through an Invisible World. By Kenneth F. Weaver. Included: Field ion microscope, scanning electron microscope, transmission electron microscope. 274-290, *Feb. 1977*

At Home With the Bulldog Ant. By Robert F. Sisson. 62-75. Included: Face-to-Face With a World of Ants (Electron Micrographs). 72-75, *July 1974*

ELECTRONIC Mini-marvel That Is Changing Your Life: The Chip. By Allen A. Boraiko. Photos by Charles O'Rear. 421-457, *Oct. 1982*

ELECTRONICS:

New Miracles of the Telephone Age. By Robert Leslie Conly. 87-120, *July 1954*

Your New World of Tomorrow. By F. Barrows Colton. 385-410, *Oct. 1945*

See also Computer Applications;

Computer Technology; DEW Line; Electron Microscopy; Infrared Imagery; Lasers; Microelectronics; Radar; Satellites; Sonar

ELEPHANT BIRDS:

Madagascar: Island at the End of the Earth. By Luis Marden. Photos by Albert Moldvay. 443-487, *Oct. 1967*

Re-creating Madagascar's Giant Extinct Bird. By Alexander Wetmore. 488-493, *Oct. 1967*

ELEPHANT SEALS. *See* Sea Elephants

ELEPHANTS:

Elephant Update. Geographica. *Oct. 1988*

Sri Lanka's Wildlife: A Nation Rises to the Challenge. By Lyn de Alwis. Photos by Dieter and Mary Plage. 274-278, *Aug. 1983*

Etosha: Namibia's Kingdom of Animals. By Douglas H. Chadwick. Photos by Des and Jen Bartlett. 344-385, *Mar. 1983*

Editorial. By Wilbur E. Garrett. 285, *Mar. 1981*

Africa's Elephants: Can They Survive? By Oria Douglas-Hamilton. Photos by Oria and Iain Douglas-Hamilton. 568-603, *Nov. 1980*

▣ Last Stand in Eden. 1, *Jan. 1979*

On the Road With an Old-time Circus. By John Fetterman. Photos by Jonathan Blair. 410-434, *Mar. 1972*

Wild Elephant Roundup in India. By Harry Miller. Photos by author and James P. Blair. 372-385, *Mar. 1969*

Where Elephants Have Right of Way (Africa). By George and Jinx Rodger. Photos by George Rodger. 363-389, *Sept. 1960*

The Elephant and I. By M. D. Chaturvedi. 489-507, *Oct. 1957*

Bhutan, Land of the Thunder Dragon. By Burt Kerr Todd. 713-754, *Dec. 1952*

Africa's Uncaged Elephants. Photos by Quentin Keynes. 371-382, *Mar. 1951*

Wings Over Nature's Zoo in Africa. Photos by Reginald A. Bourlay. 527-542, *Oct. 1939*

Nature's Most Amazing Mammal: Elephants, Unique Among Animals, Have Many Human Qualities When Wild That Make Them Foremost Citizens of Zoo and Circus. By Edmund Heller. 729-759, *June 1934*

The Perahera Processions of Ceylon. By G.H.G. Burroughs. 90-100, *July 1932*

The Land of Sawdust and Spangles–A World in Miniature. By Francis Beverly Kelley. 463-516, *Oct. 1931*

Working Teak in the Burma Forests: The Sagacious Elephant Is Man's Ablest Ally in the Logging Industry of the Far East. By A. W. Smith. 239-256, *Aug. 1930*

When a Drought Blights Africa: Hippos and Elephants Are Driven Insane by Suffering, in the Lorian Swamp, Kenya Colony. By A. T. Curle. 521-528, *Apr. 1929*

The Warfare of the Jungle Folk: Campaigning Against Tigers, Elephants, and Other Wild Animals in Northern

E
F

Elephant cows and calves drink from a water hole at Agab in Namibia's Etosha National Park. DES AND JEN BARTLETT

Siam. By Merian C. Cooper. Photos by Ernest B. Schoedsack. 233-268, *Feb. 1928*

Elephant Hunting in Equatorial Africa with Rifle and Camera. By Carl E. Akeley. 779-810, *Aug. 1912*

Wild Man and Wild Beast in Africa. By Theodore Roosevelt. 1-33, *Jan. 1911*

Where Roosevelt Will Hunt (Africa). By Sir Harry Johnston. 207-256, *Mar. 1909*

The Greatest Hunt in the World. By Eliza Ruhamah Scidmore. 673-692, *Dec. 1906*

See also Mammoth

ELEVENTH Annual Report of the Interstate Commerce Commission. Review by H. T. Newcomb. 29-31, *Jan. 1898*

ELEVENTH International Congress of Orientalists. 303, *Oct. 1897*

EL GRECO:

Toledo–El Greco's Spain Lives On. By Louise E. Levathes. Photos by James P. Blair. Introduction by J. Carter Brown. 726-753, *June 1982*

EL HATILLO CULTURE:

Exploring the Past in Panama. By Matthew W. Stirling. Photos by Richard H. Stewart. NGS research grant. 373-399, *Mar. 1949*

ELIOT, CHARLES W.: *Author*

The Need of Conserving the Beauty and Freedom of Nature in Modern Life. 67-74, *July 1914*

ELIOT, JOHN L.: *Author*

Glaciers on the Move. Photos by Chris Johns. 107-119, *Jan. 1987*

The Serengeti: A Photographic Portfolio. Photos by Mitsuaki Iwago. 563-585, *May 1986*

Isle Royale, A North Woods Park Primeval. Photos by Mitch Kezar. 534-550, *Apr. 1985*

Roosevelt Country: T. R.'s Wilderness Legacy. Photos by Farrell Grehan. 340-363, *Sept. 1982*

Into the Eye of David (Hurricane). 368-369, *Sept. 1980*

Treasures of Dresden. Photos by Victor R. Boswell, Jr. 702-717, *Nov. 1978*

Hawaii's Far-flung Wildlife Paradise. Photos by Jonathan Blair. 670-691, *May 1978*

Japan's Warriors of the Wind. Photos by David Alan Harvey. 551-561, *Apr. 1977*

ELISABETHVILLE, Democratic Republic of the Congo:

White Magic in the Belgian Congo. By W. Robert Moore. 321-362, *Mar. 1952*

ELISOFON, ELIOT: *Photographer*

Yesterday's Congo, Today's Zaire. By John J. Putman. 398-432, *Mar. 1973*

ELIZABETH I, Queen (England):

The World of Elizabeth I. By Louis B. Wright. Photos by Ted Spiegel. 668-709, *Nov. 1968*

The British Way. By Sir Evelyn Wrench. 421-541, *Apr. 1949*

Founders of Virginia. By Sir Evelyn Wrench. Photos by B. Anthony Stewart. 433-462, *Apr. 1948*

ELIZABETH II, Queen (Great Britain and Northern Ireland):

Royal Pomp Before Debate: In Centuries-old Ceremonial, the Queen Opens Parliament. 730-732, *Dec. 1986*

Windsor Castle. By Anthony Holden. Photos by James L. Stanfield. 604-631, *Nov. 1980*

The Investiture of Great Britain's Prince of Wales. By Allan C. Fisher, Jr. Photos by James L. Stanfield and Adam Woolfitt. 698-715, *Nov. 1969*

Queen Elizabeth Opens Parliament. By W. E. Roscher. Photos by Robert B. Goodman. 699-707, *Nov. 1961*

Queen of Canada. By Phyllis Wilson. Photos by Kathleen Revis. 825-829, *June 1959*

An artisan from the Maya city of El Mirador in Guatemala records events on a stone slab. PAINTING BY T. W. RUTLEDGE

Success. Photos by Jonathan Blair. 616-631, *May 1972*

Cairo, Troubled Capital of the Arab World. Photos by Winfield Parks. 639-667, *May 1972*

Will Oil and Tundra Mix? Alaska's North Slope Hangs in the Balance. Photos by Emory Kristof. 485-517, *Oct. 1971*

Lebanon, Little Bible Land in the Crossfire of History. Photos by George F. Mobley. 240-275, *Feb. 1970*

Lonely Cape Hatteras, Besieged by the Sea. Photos by Emory Kristof. 393-421, *Sept. 1969*

Wisconsin's Door Peninsula. Photos by Ted Rozumalski. 347-371, *Mar. 1969*

Atlanta, Pacesetter City of the South. Photos by James L. Amos. 246-281, *Feb. 1969*

Tracking Danger With the Ice Patrol. Photos by James R. Holland. 780-793, *June 1968*

ELLIS, WILLIAM T.: *Author*

Voyaging on the Volga Amid War and Revolution: War-time Sketches on Russia's Great Waterway. 245-265, *Mar. 1918*

ELLISON, NORMAN: *Author*

Shark Fishing–An Australian Industry. 369-386, *Sept. 1932*

ELLSWORTH, LINCOLN:

New Stamps for Antarctic Explorers. Geographica. *Oct. 1988*

Ellsworth Awarded the Hubbard Medal. 36, *July 1936*

Navigating the "Norge" from Rome to the North Pole and Beyond: The Designer and Pilot of the First Dirigible to Fly Over the Top of the World Describes a Thrilling Voyage of More Than 8,000 Miles. By Umberto Nobile. 177-215, *Aug. 1927*

Author

My Four Antarctic Expeditions: Explorations of 1933-39 Have Stricken Vast Areas from the Realm of the Unknown. 129-138, *July 1939*

My Flight Across Antarctica. 1-35, *July 1936*

ELLSWORTH HIGHLAND TRAVERSE:

Exploring Antarctica's Phantom Coast. By Edwin A. McDonald. Photos by W. D. Vaughn. 251-273, *Feb. 1962*

ELLSWORTH MOUNTAINS, Antarctica. *See* Sentinel Range

EL MIRADOR (Maya City), Guatemala:

El Mirador: An Early Maya Metropolis Uncovered. By Ray T. Matheny. Paintings by T. W. Rutledge. NGS research grant. 317-339, *Sept. 1987*

EL MORRO, Story in Stone (New Mexico). By Edwards Park. 237-244, *Aug. 1957*

EL NIÑO (Aberrant Weather Pattern):

El Niño's Ill Wind. By Thomas Y. Canby. Contents: Drought, storms, and flooding around the globe. 144-183, *Feb. 1984*

A brilliant-hued Parson's chameleon makes its home in Madagascar, where many creatures are endangered by growing human populations. FRANS LANTING

EL OUED (Oasis), Algeria:

The Country of the Ant Men. By Thomas H. Kearney. 367-382, *Apr. 1911*

EL PASO, Texas:

Along Our Side of the Mexican Border. By Frederick Simpich. 61-80, *July 1920*

EL SALVADOR:

Troubled Times for Central America. By Wilbur E. Garrett, Editor. 58-61, *July 1981*

Coffee Is King in El Salvador. By Luis Marden. 575-616, *Nov. 1944*

Volcano-Girded Salvador: A Prosperous Central American State with the Densest Rural Population in the Western World. By Harriet Chalmers Adams. 189-200, *Feb. 1922*

Shattered Capitals of Central America. By Herbert J. Spinden. 185-212, *Sept. 1919*

The Countries of the Caribbean. By William Joseph Showalter. 227-250, *Feb. 1913*

Notes on Central America. 272-279, *Apr. 1907*

EL SANGAY, Fire-breathing Giant of the Andes. By G. Edward Lewis. 117-138, *Jan. 1950*

ELSIE (Yawl):

Down East to Nova Scotia. By Winfield Parks. 853-879, *June 1964*

ELSMORE, RAY T.:
Author-Photographer

New Guinea's Mountain and Swampland Dwellers. Included: "Shangri-la" in Panorama. 671-694, *Dec. 1945*

EL TAJÍN (Site), Mexico:

Man's Eighty Centuries in Veracruz. By S. Jeffrey K. Wilkerson. Photos by David Hiser. Paintings by Richard Schlecht. 203-231, *Aug. 1980*

An **ELYSIUM** for the Beauty-Seeking Traveler (Canary Islands). Photos by Wilhelm Tobien. 631-638, *May 1930*

The **EMANCIPATION** of Mohammedan Women. By Mary Mills Patrick. 42-66, *Jan. 1909*

EMBROIDERY:

Madeira, Like Its Wine, Improves With Age. By Veronica Thomas. Photos by Jonathan Blair. 488-513, *Apr. 1973*

EMERALDS:

Questing for Gems. By George S. Switzer. 835-863, *Dec. 1971*

EMERSON, GILBERT: *Artist*

How Man-made Satellites Can Affect Our Lives. By Joseph Kaplan. 791-810, *Dec. 1957*

EMERSON, GUY: *Author*

The Kress Collection: A Gift to the Nation. 823-865, *Dec. 1961*

EMERSON, HARRINGTON: *Author*

Opening of the Alaskan Territory. 99-106, *Mar. 1903*

EMERSON, RALPH WALDO:

Literary Landmarks of Massachusetts. By William H. Nicholas. Photos by B. Anthony Stewart and John E. Fletcher. 279-310, *Mar. 1950*

EMERSON, ROSS:

Nomination Page. *Apr. 1981*

EMIGRATION from Siberia. 32-33, *Jan. 1902*

EMIGRATION to America an Industry (Sicily). By Arthur H. Warner. 1063-1102, *Dec. 1909*

EMMONS, SAMUEL FRANKLIN:
Author

Alaska and Its Mineral Resources. 139-172, *Apr. 1898*

EMORY, JERRY: *Author*
Managing Another Galápagos Species–Man. Photos by Dieter and Mary Plage. 146-154, *Jan. 1988*

EMORY, KENNETH P.: *Author*
The Coming of the Polynesians. 732-745, *Dec. 1974*

EMPEROR WORSHIP:
Behind the Mask of Modern Japan. By Willard Price. 513-535, *Nov. 1945*

The **EMPEROR'S** Private Garden: Kashmir. By Nigel Cameron. Photos by Brian Brake. 606-647, *Nov. 1958*

EMPIRE of Romance–India. 481-496, *Nov. 1921*

The **EMPIRE** of the Risen Sun (Japan). By William Elliot Griffis. 415-443, *Oct. 1923*

EMPIRE State Onions and Pageantry (New York). Photos by J. Baylor Roberts and Volkmar Wentzel. 641-648, *Nov. 1941*

EMU WRENS:
The Fairy Wrens of Australia: The Little Long-tailed "Blue Birds of Happiness" Rank High Among the Island Continent's Remarkable Birds. By Neville W. Cayley. Paintings by author. 488-498, *Oct. 1945*

ENCAMPMENTS of the Dispossessed (Somalis). By Larry Kohl. 756-763, *June 1981*

The **ENCHANTED MESA** (New Mexico). By F. W. Hodge. 273-284, *Oct. 1897*

ENCHANTRESS! (White Tigress). By Theodore H. Reed. Photos by Thomas J. Abercrombie. 628-641, *May 1961*

ENCIRCLING Navajo Mountain (Utah) with a Pack-Train: An Expedition to a Hitherto Untraversed Region of Our Southwest Discovers a New Route to Rainbow Natural Bridge. By Charles L. Bernheimer. 197-224, *Feb. 1923*

ENCOURAGING Birds Around the Home. By Frederick H. Kennard. 315-344, *Mar. 1914*

ENCYCLOPAEDIA BRITANNICA EDUCATIONAL CORPORATION:
The World in Geographic Filmstrips. By Melvin M. Payne. 134-137, *Jan. 1968*

The **END** of Innocence for the Urueu-Wau-Wau Indians. By Loren McIntyre. Photos by W. Jesco von Puttkamer. 800-817, *Dec. 1988*

ENDANGERED AND THREATENED SPECIES:
Quietly Conserving Nature. By Noel Grove. Photos by Stephen J. Kraseman. 818-845, *Dec. 1988*
President's Page. By Gilbert M. Grosvenor. *Feb. 1988*
Galápagos Wildlife Under Pressure. Photo essay by Dieter and Mary Plage. 122-154, *Jan. 1988*

NATIONAL GEOGRAPHIC

A special report in the public interest

ENERGY

Facing up to the problem, getting down to solutions

Madagascar: A World Apart. By Alison Jolly. Photos by Frans Lanting. 148-183, *Feb. 1987*
■ *Wildlife: Making a Comeback.* By Judith E. Rinard. Juvenile. 104 pages. *1987*
Editorial. By Wilbur E. Garrett. 283, *Mar. 1986*
Return of Java's Wildlife. By Dieter and Mary Plage. 750-771, *June 1985*
North American Waterfowl: Troubles and Triumphs. By John Madson. Included: Loons, trumpeter swans, wood ducks. 562-599, *Nov. 1984*
President's Page. By Gilbert M. Grosvenor. *Apr. 1984*
The Japanese Crane, Bird of Happiness. By Tsuneo Hayashida. 542-556, *Oct. 1983*
Editorial. By Wilbur E. Garrett. 703, *June 1983*
Last of the Black-footed Ferrets? By Tim W. Clark. Photos by Franz J. Camenzind and the author. NGS research grant. 828-838, *June 1983*
Tropical Rain Forests. 2-65. Included: Nature's Dwindling Treasures. By Peter T. White. Photos by James P. Blair. Paintings by Barron Storey. 2-47; Teeming Life of a Rain Forest. By Carol and David Hughes. 49-65, *Jan. 1983*
Editorial. By Wilbur E. Garrett. 285, *Mar. 1981*
Wild Cargo: the Business of Smuggling Animals. By Noel Grove. Photos by Steve Raymer. 287-315, *Mar. 1981*
Where Oil and Wildlife Mix. By Steven C. Wilson and Karen C. Hayden. 145-173, *Feb. 1981*
■ *Wildlife Alert! The Struggle to Survive.* By Gene S. Stuart. Juvenile. 104 pages. *1980*
The Tree Nobody Liked (Red Mangrove). By Rick Gore. Photos by Bianca Lavies. Note: Many imperiled tropical birds find sanctuary among Florida's mangroves; and the Key deer has made a comeback. 669-689, *May 1977*

India Struggles to Save Her Wildlife. By John J. Putman. Paintings by Ned Seidler. 299-343, *Sept. 1976*
Editorial. By Gilbert M. Grosvenor. 1, *Jan. 1976*
■ *Vanishing Wildlife of North America.* By Thomas B. Allen. 207 pages. *1974*
African Wildlife: Man's Threatened Legacy. By Allan C. Fisher, Jr. Photos by Thomas Nebbia. Paintings by Ned Seidler. 147-187, *Feb. 1972*
Threatened Glories of Everglades National Park. By Frederick Kent Truslow and Frederick G. Vosburgh. Photos by Frederick Kent Truslow and Otis Imboden. 508-553, *Oct. 1967*
The Last Great Animal Kingdom: A Portfolio of Africa's Vanishing Wildlife. 390-409, *Sept. 1960*
Saving Man's Wildlife Heritage. By John H. Baker. Photos by Robert F. Sisson. 581-620, *Nov. 1954*
Wildlife of Everglades National Park. By Daniel B. Beard. Paintings by Walter A. Weber. 83-116, *Jan. 1949*
See also Andean Condors; Atlantic Salmon; Bald Eagles; Bighorn Sheep; Bluebirds; Bluefin Tuna; Brown Pelicans; Cheetahs; Crocodilians; Elephants; Freshwater Turtles; Giant Brazilian Otters; Giant Pandas; Giant Tortoises; Gorillas; Gray Whales; Grizzly Bears; Harp Seals; Horses, Wild; Humpback Whales; Lemurs; Manatees; Muriquis; Orangutans; Philippine Eagles; Pinnipeds; Polar Bears; Rhinoceroses; Rothschild's Giraffe; Snow Leopards; Tigers; Tree Snails; Trumpeter Swans; Vicuñas; Whales; Whooping Cranes; Wolves; Wood Storks

ENDEAVOUR (Bark):
Captain Cook: The Man Who Mapped the Pacific. By Alan Villiers. Photos by Gordon W. Gahan. 297-349, *Sept. 1971*
The Columbus of the Pacific: Captain James Cook, Foremost British Navigator, Expanded the Great Sea to Correct Proportions and Won for Albion an Insular Empire by Peaceful Exploration and Scientific Study. By Jesse R. Hildebrand. 85-132, *Jan. 1927*

ENDEAVOUR (Cutter):
Endeavor Sails the Inside Passage. By Amos Burg. 801-828, *June 1947*

The **ENDURING** Pyrenees. By Robert Laxalt. Photos by Edwin Stuart Grosvenor. 794-819, *Dec. 1974*

ENERGY:
Editorial. By Wilbur E. Garrett. 143, *Feb. 1981*
Special Report on Energy, an extra issue of NGM. Contents: The Unbalanced World. By NGS President Gilbert M. Grosvenor. 1; Our Energy Predicament. By Kenneth F. Weaver. 2-23; America's Auto Mania. By David Jeffery. Photos by Bruce Dale. 24-31; The Auto: Problem Child With a Promising Future. 32-33; Conservation: Can We Live Better on Less?

A sometimes source of energy, trash by the bargeful heads past the Statue of Liberty on its way to a Staten Island dump. LOUIE PSIHOYOS

ENGINEERING PROJECTS, Ancient:

ENGLAND:

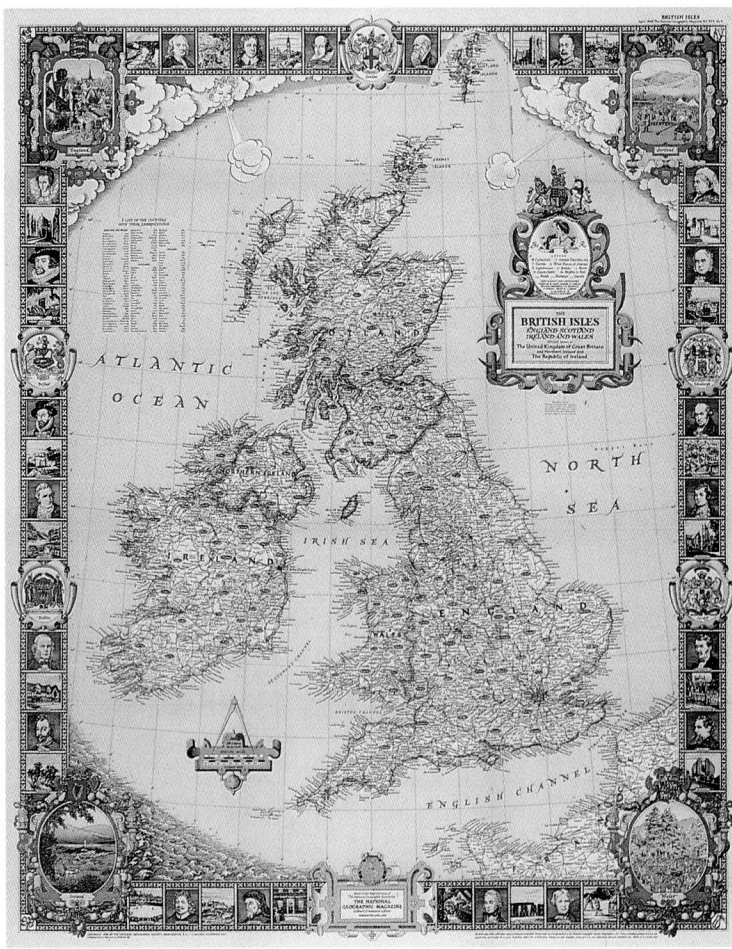

Decorated with a border of famous places and personages, a supplement map of the British Isles accompanied the April 1949 GEOGRAPHIC.

Flags flew at half-staff and guns boomed a somber tribute outside England's St. Paul's Cathedral at the 1965 funeral of statesman Winston Churchill. BATES LITTLEHALES, NGS

The Ties that Bind: Our Natural Sympathy with English Traditions, the French Republic, and the Russian Outburst for Liberty. By John Sharp Williams. 281-286, *Mar. 1917*

One Hundred British Seaports. 84-94, *Jan. 1917*

British Isles. 551-566, *Dec. 1915*

Channel Ports–And Some Others. By Florence Craig Albrecht. 1-55, *July 1915*

Europe's Endangered Fish Supply: The War and the North Sea Fisheries. 141-152, *Feb. 1915*

The Oldest Nation of Europe: Geographical Factors in the Strength of Modern England. By Roland G. Usher. 393-414, *Oct. 1914*

King Herring: An Account of the World's Most Valuable Fish, the Industries It Supports, and the Part It Has Played in History. By Hugh M. Smith. Included: Great Yarmouth; Lowestoft. 701-735, *Aug. 1909*

Transportation in England. 88, *Feb. 1905*

Cotton for England. 39, *Jan. 1904*

Bathymetrical Survey of the Fresh-water Lakes of England. 408, *Nov. 1901*

The Expansion of England. By Edwin D. Mead. 249-263, *July 1900*

A Geographical Description of the British Islands. By W. M. Davis. 208-211, *June 1896*

The Ordnance Survey of Great Britain–Its History and Object. By Josiah Pierce, Jr. 243-260, *Aug. 1890*

See also Abbotsbury Swannery; Appleby Fair; Bampton; Beaconsfield; Cambridge; Canterbury Cathedral; Channel Islands; Cornwall; Cotswold Hills; Devon; Dover; Lake District; London; Lundy (Island); Man, Isle of; Oxford; Plymouth; Portsmouth; St. Michael's Mount; Scilly, Isles of; Southampton; Stonehenge; Warwick; Winchester; Windsor Castle; *and* Elizabethan Age; *Mayflower II*

ENGLEBERT, VICTOR:

Nomination Page. In the Sahara. *Mar. 1974*

Author-Photographer

Drought Threatens the Tuareg World. 544-571, *Apr. 1974*

The Danakil: Nomads of Ethiopia's Wasteland. 186-211, *Feb. 1970*

Trek by Mule Among Morocco's Berbers. 850-875, *June 1968*

I Joined a Sahara Salt Caravan. 694-711, *Nov. 1965*

ENGLISH CHANNEL:

Winged Victory of *Gossamer Albatross.* By Bryan Allen. 640-651, *Nov. 1979*

Channel Cruise to Glorious Devon. By Alan Villiers. Photos by Bates Littlehales. 208-259, *Aug. 1963*

Cowes to Cornwall. By Alan Villiers. Photos by Robert B. Goodman. 149-201, *Aug. 1961*

Oil for Victory Piped under the Sea. 721-726, *Dec. 1945*

Normandy's Made-in-England Harbors. 565-580, *May 1945*

See also Channel Islands; St. Michael's Mount

ENGLISH COUNTRY HOUSES:

The Great Good Places: English Country Houses. By Mark Girouard. Photos by Fred J. Maroon. 658-694, *Nov. 1985*

ENGLISH SETTLERS:

Founders of New England. By Sir Evelyn Wrench. Photos by B. Anthony Stewart. 803-838, *June 1953*

Founders of Virginia. By Sir Evelyn Wrench. Photos by B. Anthony Stewart. 433-462, *Apr. 1948*

See also Roanoke Island, for Lost Colony; Williamsburg, Virginia; Wolstenholme Towne (Site), Virginia; *and* Victoria, Kansas (19th Century)

ENGRAVINGS AND ETCHINGS:

Cathedrals of England: An Artist's

Pilgrimage to These Majestic Monuments of Man's Genius and Faith. By Norman Wilkinson. Engravings by author. 741-762, *Dec. 1939*

Ships of the Centuries. Etchings by Norman Wilkinson. 65-80, *Jan. 1938*

The **ENIGMA** of Bird Anting. By Hance Roy Ivor. 105-119, *July 1956*

The **ENIGMA** of Cambodia. Photos by Gervais Courtellemont. 307-322, *Sept. 1928*

ENIWETOK ATOLL, Marshall Islands. *See* Enewetak

ENTEBBE ANIMAL REFUGE, Uganda:

Orphans of the Wild. By Bruce G. Kinloch. 683-699, *Nov. 1962*

ENTERING the Front Doors of Medieval Towns: The Adventures of an American Woman and Her Daughter in a Folding Boat on Eight Rivers of Germany and Austria. By Cornelia Stratton Parker. 365-394, *Mar. 1932*

ENTERPRISE, H.M.S.:

Collinson's Arctic Journey. By Adolphus W. Greely. 198-200, *Feb. 8, 1893*

ENTERPRISE, U.S.S.:

The Mighty *Enterprise.* By Nathaniel T. Kenney. Photos by Thomas J. Abercrombie. 431-448, *Mar. 1963*

ENTOMOLOGY. *See* Insects

ENTRE RÍOS (Province), Argentina:

Pioneer Gaucho Days. Paintings by Cesáreo Bernaldo de Quirós. 453-460, *Oct. 1933*

ENVIRONMENTAL CONCERNS:

Editorial. By Wilbur E. Garrett. *Dec. 1988*

Earth '88: Will We Mend Our Earth? Introduction by Gilbert M. Grosvenor. 766-771, *Dec. 1988*

Rondônia: Brazil's Imperiled Rain Forest. By William S. Ellis. Photos by William Albert Allard and Loren McIntyre. 772-779, *Dec. 1988*

Quietly Conserving Nature. By Noel Grove. Photos by Stephen J. Kraseman. 818-845, *Dec. 1988*

Population, Plenty, and Poverty. By Paul R. and Anne H. Ehrlich. Included: Kenya: A Population Exploding. Photos by Robert Caputo; China: Back from the Brink. Photos by Patrick Zachmann; Hungary: A Static Society. Photos by Steve McCurry; India: Life on the Edge. Photos by Raghu Rai; Brazil: Flight to the Cities. Photos by Mary Ellen Mark; United States: Geared to Consumption. Photos by Pam Spaulding. 914-945, *Dec. 1988*

✦ *World; Endangered Earth.* Included: Pastures of the Sea; The Continental Garden; Global Carbon Dioxide; Ice Age Vegetation 18,000 Years BP; Greenhouse-Effect Vegetation Zones; Population Explosion; Peru-Ecuador Upwelling; Minnesota's Boreal Forest; Population Projections; Environmental timeline; Growing Threats: Population Pressure, Air

Air raids over England during World War II sent some 150,000 Londoners underground to find shelter on subway platforms and train tracks. ACME

Pollution, Ozone Concerns, Acid Rain, Water Pollution, Species Extinctions, Fisheries Depletion, Deforestation, Desertification. *Dec. 1988*

Citizens Band Together to Save Their Environment. Geographica. *Nov. 1988*

The Mighty Himalaya: A Fragile Heritage. By Barry C. Bishop. Photos by William Thompson. 624-631, *Nov. 1988*

Heavy Hands on the Land. By Larry Kohl. Photos by William Thompson and Galen Rowell. 633-651, *Nov. 1988*

■■ *Our Threatened Inheritance: Natural Treasures of the United States.* By Ron Fisher. Photos by James P. Blair. 400 pages. *1984*

See also Conservation; Desertification; Ecology; Endangered and Threatened Species; Energy; Erosion; Land Use; Pollution; Radioactive Wastes; Rain Forests; Strip Mining; Waste Disposal; Water Resources

ENVIRONMENTAL PROTECTION AGENCY:

The Pesticide Dilemma. By Allen A. Boraiko. Photos by Fred Ward. 145-183, *Feb. 1980*

EPHESUS (Ancient City):

Some Ruined Cities of Asia Minor. By Ernest L. Harris. 833-858, *Dec. 1908*

EPILOGUE for *Titanic.* By Robert D. Ballard. 454-463, *Oct. 1987*

ÉPINAL, France:

Here Rest in Honored Glory...The United States Dedicates Six New Battle Monuments in Europe to Americans Who Gave Their Lives During World War II. By Howell Walker. Included: Épinal American Cemetery and Memorial. 739-768, *June 1957*

EPITAPH for a Killer? By Donald A. Henderson. Photos by Marion Kaplan. 796-805, *Dec. 1978*

EPLER, BLANCH NETTLETON: *Author*

A Bit of Elizabethan England in America: Fisher Folk of the Islands Off North Carolina Conserved the Speech and Customs of Sir Walter Raleigh's Colonists. 695-730, *Dec. 1933*

EPPRIDGE, WILLIAM: *Photographer*

The Alps: Man's Own Mountains. By Ralph Gray. Photos by Walter Meayers Edwards and William Eppridge. 350-395, *Sept. 1965*

Round the World School. By Paul Antze. 96-127, *July 1962*

EQUAL Justice Under the Law: The Su-
■■*preme Court in American Life.* By Mary Ann Harrell. Published in cooperation with The Foundation of the Federal Bar Association. 151 pages. 1965; rev. ed. *1988*

EQUATORIAL AFRICA:

Recent Explorations in Equatorial

An island of earth in Tennessee bears witness to soil erosion, a result of diminished plant cover. STEVEN C. WILSON, ENTHEOS

Africa. By Ernest de Sasseville. 88-91, *Mar. 1897*

See also Central African Republic; Chad; Congo, People's Republic of the; Gabon; Kenya; Uganda; Zaire

EQUATORIAL GUINEA, Republic of. *See* Río Muni

EREBUS, Mount, Antarctica:

The Heart of the Antarctic. By Ernest H. Shackleton. 972-1007, *Nov. 1909*

El **ERG** (Region), Algeria:

The Country of the Ant Men. By Thomas H. Kearney. 367-382, *Apr. 1911*

ERICSSON, LEIF:

Dwellings of the Saga-Time in Iceland, Greenland, and Vineland. By Cornelia Horsford. 73-84, *Mar. 1898*

Discoverers of America. Annual Address by the President, Gardiner G. Hubbard. 1-20, *Apr. 7, 1893*

ERIE, Lake, Canada-U. S.:

The Great Lakes' Troubled Waters. By Charles E. Cobb, Jr. Photos by Bob Sacha and Richard Olsenius. Included: A great meeting of waters; North America's fifth coast. 2-31, *July 1987*

Yesterday Lingers on Lake Erie's Bass Islands. By Terry and Lyntha Eiler. 86-101, *July 1978*

The Great Lakes: Is It Too Late? By Gordon Young. Photos by James L. Amos and Martin Rogers. 147-185, *Aug. 1973*

Rainfall and the Level of Lake Erie. By E. L. Moseley. 327-328, *Aug. 1903*

Testing the Currents of Lake Erie. By E. L. Moseley. 41-42, *Jan. 1903*

Submerged Valleys in Sandusky Bay. By E. L. Moseley. 398-403, *Nov. 1902*

ERIE, Pennsylvania:

The Industrial Titan of America: Pennsylvania, Once the Keystone of the Original Thirteen, Now the Keystone of Forty-eight Sovereign States. By John Oliver La Gorce. 367-406, *May 1919*

ERIE CANAL, New York:

The New Erie Canal. 568-570, *Dec. 1905*

ERIGBAAGTSA INDIANS:

Indians of the Amazon Darkness. By Harald Schultz. NGS research grant. 737-758, *May 1964*

ERIK THE RED:

Dwellings of the Saga-Time in Iceland, Greenland, and Vineland. By Cornelia Horsford. 73-84, *Mar. 1898*

ERIM, KENAN T.:

Recipient of the National Geographic Society Centennial Award. President's Page. By Gilbert M. Grosvenor. *Dec. 1988*

Nomination Page. In Turkey. *Aug. 1981*

Nomination Page. In Turkey. *Apr. 1969*

Author

Ancient Aphrodisias Lives Through Its Art. Photos by David Brill. 527-551, *Oct. 1981*

Aphrodisias, Awakened City of Ancient Art. Photos by Jonathan Blair. 766-791, *June 1972*

Ancient Aphrodisias and Its Marble Treasures. Photos by Jonathan S. Blair. 280-294, *Aug. 1967*

ERITREA (Province), Ethiopia:

Eritrea: Region in Rebellion. By Anthony Suau. 384-405, *Sept. 1985*

With the Italians in Eritrea: Torrid Colony Between the Red Sea and Ethiopia, 2,600 Miles by Sea from Rome, Is Mobilization Place of Fascist Troops and Planes. By Harald P. Lechenperg. 265-295, *Sept. 1935*

ERIVAN, Armenian S.S.R., U.S.S.R.:

The Land of the Stalking Death: A Journey Through Starving Armenia on an American Relief Train. By Melville Chater. 393-420, *Nov. 1919*

The Old Post-Road from Tiflis to Erivan. By Esther Lancraft Hovey. 300-309, *Aug. 1901*

ERNST THAELMANN (Collective Farm), U.S.S.R.:

Sunny Siberia. Photos by Owen Lattimore. 649-672, *Dec. 1944*

ERONGARÍCUARO, Mexico:

Lost Kingdom in Indian Mexico (Tarascan). By Justin Locke. 517-546, *Oct. 1952*

EROSION:

Lonely Rocks Important to Japan. Geographica. *Nov. 1988*

Africa's Sahel: The Stricken Land. By William S. Ellis. Photos by Steve McCurry. 140-179, *Aug. 1987*

The Great Lakes' Troubled Waters. By Charles E. Cobb, Jr. Photos by Bob Sacha and Richard Olsenius. Included:

ERRANT (Airplane):

The **ERRATIC** (Geologic Formation of the United States). By O. A. Ljungstedt. 525-531, *June 1910*

ERTAUD, JACQUES: *Photographer*

ERUPTION in Colombia. By Bart McDowell. Photos by Steve Raymer. 640-653, *May 1986*

The **ERUPTION** of Krakatoa. By Sir Robert Ball. 200-204, *June 1902*

ERUPTION of Mount St. Helens. By Rowe Findley. 3-65. I. Mountain With a Death Wish. 3-33; II. In the Path of Destruction. 35-49; III. The Day the Sky Fell. 50-65, *Jan. 1981*

The **ERUPTION** of Mount Vesuvius, April 7-8, 1906. By Thomas Augustus Jaggar, Jr. 318-325, *June 1906*

The **ERUPTIONS** of La Soufrière, St. Vincent, in May, 1902. By Edmund Otis Hovey. 444-459, *Dec. 1902*

A 500-year-old mummy found in Qilakitsoq, Greenland, remains hauntingly preserved. JOHN LEE, NATIONAL MUSEUM, COPENHAGEN

ERZURUM, Turkey:

ESCALANTE CANYON, Utah:

ESCAPE From Slavery: The Underground Railroad. By Charles L. Blockson. Photos by Louie Psihoyos. 3-39, *July 1984*

ESCORT CARRIERS:

ESCORTING Mona Lisa to America. By Edward T. Folliard. 838-847, *June 1963*

ESDRAELON (Plain), Palestine:

Impressions of Palestine. By James Bryce. 293-317, *Mar. 1915*

ESKIMAUAN LINGUISTIC STOCK:

ESKIMOS:

Included: Inupiat and Nunamiut Eskimos; also Eskimos of Nunapitchuk, Selawik, and Wainwright. 730-767, *June 1975*

Caribou: Hardy Nomads of the North. By Jim Rearden. 858-878, *Dec. 1974*

Trek Across Arctic America. By Colin Irwin. 295-321, *Mar. 1974*

The Last U. S. Whale Hunters. By Emory Kristof. 346-355. Included: "Ocean mammals are to us what the buffalo was to the Plains Indian." By Lael Morgan. 354-355, *Mar. 1973*

❖ *Indians of North America.* Included: Central Eskimos; Copper Eskimos. *Dec. 1972*

Will Oil and Tundra Mix? Alaska's North Slope Hangs in the Balance. By William S. Ellis. Photos by Emory Kristof. 485-517, *Oct. 1971*

I Live With the Eskimos. By Guy Mary-Rousseliere. 188-217, *Feb. 1971*

Domesticating the Wild and Woolly Musk Ox. By John J. Teal, Jr. Photos by Robert W. Madden. 862-879, *June 1970*

Nomad in Alaska's Outback. By Thomas J. Abercrombie. 540-567, *Apr. 1969*

The Canadian North: Emerging Giant. By David S. Boyer. 1-43, *July 1968*

Banks Island: Eskimo Life on the Polar Sea. By William O. Douglas. Photos by Clyde Hare. 703-735, *May 1964*

Alaska Proudly Joins the Union. By Ernest Gruening. Photos by Thomas J. Abercrombie. 43-83, *July 1959*

A Visit to the Living Ice Age. By Rutherford Platt. 525-545, *Apr. 1957*

Vanished Mystery Men of Hudson Bay. By Henry B. Collins. NGS research grant. 669-687, *Nov. 1956*

Weather from the White North. By Andrew H. Brown. Photos by John E. Fletcher. 543-572, *Apr. 1955*

Cliff Dwellers of the Bering Sea. By Juan Muñoz. 129-146, *Jan. 1954*

Canada Counts Its Caribou. 261-268, *Aug. 1952*

North Star Cruises Alaska's Wild West. By Amos Burg. 57-86, *July 1952*

Far North with "Captain Mac." By Miriam MacMillan. Included: Eskimos of Baffin Island, Greenland, Labrador; Polar Eskimos. 465-513, *Oct. 1951*

Alaska's Russian Frontier: Little Diomede. Photos by Audrey and Frank Morgan. 551-562, *Apr. 1951*

Nomads of the Far North. By Matthew W. Stirling. 471-504. Included: Hearty Folk Defy Arctic Storms. Paintings by W. Langdon Kihn. 479-494, *Oct. 1949*

Milestones in My Arctic Journeys. By Willie Knutsen. 543-570, *Oct. 1949*

Canada's Caribou Eskimos. By Donald B. Marsh. 87-104, *Jan. 1947*

Coast Guard Patrol in Greenland. Photos by Thomas S. La Farge. 565-572, *May 1943*

Alaska–Our Northwestern Outpost. Photos by Ernest H. Gruening, Amos Burg, Froelich Rainey. 297-308, *Sept. 1942*

Discovering Alaska's Oldest Arctic Town (Ipiutak): A Scientist Finds

Ivory-eyed Skeletons of a Mysterious People and Joins Modern Eskimos in the Dangerous Spring Whale Hunt. By Froelich G. Rainey. 319-336, *Sept. 1942*

Desolate Greenland, Now an American Outpost. Photos by Willie Knutsen and F. Vogel. 393-406, *Sept. 1941*

Greenland from 1898 to Now: "Captain Bob," Who Went North with Peary, Tells of 42 Years of Exploration in the Orphan Island of New Aerial and Naval Interest. By Robert A. Bartlett. 111-140, *July 1940*

Exploring Frozen Fragments of American History: On the Trail of Early Eskimo Colonists Who Made a 55-Mile Crossing from the Old World to the New. By Henry B. Collins, Jr. 633-656, *May 1939*

The First Natural-Color Photographs from the Arctic. Photos by Jacob Gayer and Maynard Owen Williams. 301-316, *Mar. 1926*

Peary as a Leader: Incidents from the Life of the Discoverer of the North Pole Told by One of His Lieutenants on the Expedition Which Reached the Goal. By Donald B. MacMillan. 293-317, *Apr. 1920*

The Origin of Stefansson's Blond Eskimo. By Adolphus W. Greely. 1225-1238, *Dec. 1912*

On Eskimo Geographic Names Ending in Miut. By John Murdoch. 190, *Apr. 1898*

Two Hundred Miles up the Kuskokwim. By Charles Hallock. 85-92, *Mar. 1898*

Three Weeks in Hubbard Bay, West Greenland. By Robert Stein. 1-11, *Jan. 1898*

A Summer Voyage to the Arctic. By G. R. Putnam. 97-110, *Apr. 1897*

An Undiscovered Island Off the Northern Coast of Alaska. I–By Marcus Baker. II–By Edward Perry Heren-

deen. III–By Adolphus W. Greely. 76-83, *July 10, 1893*

The Arctic Cruise of the U.S.S. Thetis in the Summer and Autumn of 1889. By Charles H. Stockton. 171-198, *July 1890*

ESKIMOS, Canadian. *See* Inuit

ESPIRITU SANTO (Island), New Hebrides (now Vanuatu):

Wreck of the *Coolidge.* Text and photos by David Doubilet. 458-467, *Apr. 1988*

Painting History in the Pacific. Paintings by William F. Draper. 408-424, *Oct. 1944*

ESSAY SUPPLEMENT:

❖ *The Face and Faith of Poland,* map, photo, and essay supplement. By Peter Miller. Essay by Czesław Miłosz. Photos by Bruno Barbey. *Apr. 1982*

The **ESSENCE** of Life–Salt. By Gordon Young. Photos by Volkmar Wentzel and Georg Gerster. 381-401, *Sept. 1977*

ESSENES:

The Men Who Hid the Dead Sea Scrolls. By A. Douglas Tushingham. Paintings by Peter V. Bianchi. 785-808, *Dec. 1958*

ESSICK, PETER: *Photographer*

Model Airplanes: To Dream, to Build …And Then to Fly. By Michael E. Long. Included: New wings for an old reptile. 132-144, *July 1986*

ESTATES AND PLANTATIONS:

Philadelphia Houses a Proud Past. By Harold Donaldson Eberlein. Photos by Thomas Nebbia. 151-191, *Aug. 1960*

California's Wonderful One (State Highway No. 1). By Frank Cameron. Photos by B. Anthony Stewart.

A crowd of visitors reflects upon the palatial grandeur of the indoor pool at William Randolph Hearst's castle near San Simeon, California. CRAIG AURNESS, WEST LIGHT

ESTES, RICHARD D.:

ESTONIA:

ESTUARY TIDES:

ETHERTON, PERCY THOMAS:

ETHIOPIA (Abyssinia):

Victims of famine in Ethiopia, two boys and their grandmother lay near death in 1985 at a field hospital in Eritrea, the country's northernmost province. ANTHONY SUAU, BLACK STAR

ETHNOLOGY:

Child of the Kazak, a seminomadic ethnic minority in China, shows off her finery in the city of Golmud. WONG HOW-MAN

Africa

Asia

Andaman Islands; Bhutan; Hunza; Ladakh; Naga Hills; Tibet; Wakhis

Australia. *See* Aboriginal People of Australia

Europe. *See* Basques; Lapps

Middle East
⊕ *The Peoples of the Middle East.* Text on reverse. *July 1972*

Pacific Islands
Maoris: At Home in Two Worlds. By Yva Momatiuk and John Eastcott. 522-541, *Oct. 1984*

Maoris: Treasures of the Tradition. By Douglas Newton. Photos by Brian Brake. 542-553, *Oct. 1984*
⊕ *Discoverers of the Pacific. Dec. 1974*

Blowgun Hunters of the South Pacific. By Jane C. Goodale. Photos by Ann Chowning. 793-817, *June 1966*

Yap Meets the Yanks. By David D. Duncan. 364-372, *Mar. 1946*

War Finds Its Way to Gilbert Islands: United States Forces Dislodge Japanese from Enchanted Atolls Which Loom Now as Stepping Stones along South Sea Route from Australia to Hawaii. By Sir Arthur Grimble. 71-92, *Jan. 1943*

A Woman's Experiences among Stone Age Solomon Islanders: Primitive Life Remains Unchanged in Tropical Jungleland Where United States Forces Now Are Fighting. By Eleanor Schirmer Oliver. 813-836, *Dec. 1942*

Notes on Some Primitive Philippine Tribes. By Dean C. Worcester. Included: Aëtas, or Negritos; Battaks; Mangyans; Moros; Tagbanuas. 284-301, *June 1898*

See also Iban; Moro Tribespeople; *and* New Britain; New Guinea; New Hebrides

Union of Soviet Socialist Republics
⊕ *Peoples of the Soviet Union. Feb. 1976*

ETIENNE, JEAN-LOUIS:
Editorial. By Wilbur E. Garrett. 287, *Sept. 1986*

Author
Skiing Alone to the Pole. 318-323, *Sept. 1986*

ETOSHA NATIONAL PARK,
Namibia:
Etosha: Namibia's Kingdom of Animals. By Douglas H. Chadwick. Photos by Des and Jen Bartlett. 344-385, *Mar. 1983*

Family Life of Lions. By Des and Jen Bartlett. 800-819, *Dec. 1982*

Namibia: Nearly a Nation? By Bryan Hodgson. Photos by Jim Brandenburg. 755-797, *June 1982*
▣ Etosha: Place of Dry Water. 703, *Dec. 1980*

ETRUSCANS:
The Eternal Etruscans. By Rick Gore. Photos by O. Louis Mazzatenta. Paintings by James M. Gurney. 696-743, *June 1988*

Periscope on the Etruscan Past. By Carlo M. Lerici. 337-350, *Sept. 1959*

Ancient Rome Brought to Life. By

The "Apollo of Veio," probably created by the master sculptor Vulca, adorned an Etruscan temple. O. LOUIS MAZZATENTA, NGS

Rhys Carpenter. Paintings by H. M. Herget. 567-633, *Nov. 1946*

EUCALYPTUS (Tree):
Lonely Australia: The Unique Continent. By Herbert E. Gregory. 473-568, *Dec. 1916*

Notes on the Eucalyptus Tree from the United States Forest Service. 668-673, *July 1909*

The Tallest Tree That Grows. By Edgerton R. Young. 664-667, *July 1909*

EUGENICS:
Who Shall Inherit Long Life? On the Existence of a Natural Process at Work Among Human Beings Tending to Improve the Vigor and Vitality of Succeeding Generations. By Alexander Graham Bell. 505-514, *June 1919*

Our Immigration Laws from the Viewpoint of National Eugenics. By Robert De C. Ward. 38-41, *Jan. 1912*

A Few Thoughts Concerning Eugenics. By Alexander Graham Bell. 119-123, *Feb. 1908*

EUPHRATES (River), Asia:
Throne Above the Euphrates. By Theresa Goell. 390-405, *Mar. 1961*

The Cradle of Civilization: The Historic

Lands Along the Euphrates and Tigris Rivers Where Briton Is Fighting Turk. By James Baikie. 127-162, *Feb. 1916*

Mystic Nedjef, the Shia Mecca. By Frederick Simpich. 589-598, *Dec. 1914*

Where Adam and Eve Lived. By Frederick and Margaret Simpich. 546-588, *Dec. 1914*

The Mountaineers of the Euphrates. By Ellsworth Huntington. 142-156, *Feb. 1909*

EUROPA (Jovian Satellite):
What Voyager Saw: Jupiter's Dazzling Realm. By Rick Gore. Photos by NASA. 2-29, *Jan. 1980*

EUROPE:
The World of Süleyman the Magnificent. By Merle Severy. Photos by James L. Stanfield. 552-601, *Nov. 1987*

The Quest for Ulysses. By Tim Severin. Photos by Kevin Fleming. 197-225, *Aug. 1986*
⊕ *A Traveler's Map of the Alps. Apr. 1985*

Viking Trail East. By Robert Paul Jordan. Photos by Jim Brandenburg. Paintings by Michael A. Hampshire. 278-317, *Mar. 1985*

The Byzantine Empire. 709-777. I. Rome of the East. By Merle Severy. Photos by James L. Stanfield. 709-767; II. Mount Athos. 739-745; III. Eternal Easter in a Greek Village. By Maria Nicolaidis-Karanikolas. Photos by James L. Stanfield. 768-777, *Dec. 1983*

A Wild, Ill-fated Balloon Race. 778-797. I. Wild Launch. 778-787; II. The Fantastic Flight of Cote d'Or. By Cynthia Shields. 789-793; III. Last Ascent of a Heroic Team (Maxie Anderson and Don Ida). 794-797, *Dec. 1983*
⊕ *Europe; Historical Map of Europe. Dec. 1983*

The World of Martin Luther. By Merle Severy. Photos by James L. Amos. 418-463, *Oct. 1983*

The Mediterranean—Sea of Man's Fate. By Rick Gore. Photos by Jonathan Blair. 694-737, *Dec. 1982*
⊕ *The Historic Mediterranean; The Mediterranean Seafloor. Dec. 1982*

The Incredible Potato. By Robert E. Rhoades. Photos by Martin Rogers. 668-694, *May 1982*

Napoleon. By John J. Putman. Photos by Gordon W. Gahan. 142-189, *Feb. 1982*
▮▮ *The Age of Chivalry. 378 pages. 1969; rev. ed. 1978*

Reach for the New World. By Mendel Peterson. Photos by David L. Arnold. Paintings by Richard Schlecht. Included: Trade and colonization by England, France, the Netherlands, Spain. 724-767, *Dec. 1977*

Ancient Europe Is Older Than We Thought. By Colin Renfrew. Photos by Adam Woolfitt. 615-623, *Nov. 1977*

The Danube: River of Many Nations, Many Names. By Mike Edwards.

Both Buda, a city razed in 1526 by Süleyman's Ottoman army, and Pest, the other half of Hungary's modern capital, stand reflected in a window. JAMES L. STANFIELD, NGS

Shadows climb Mount Everest's southwestern face, route for many who have surmounted the Himalayan peak. WILLIAM THOMPSON

EVANS, RONALD E.:

Exploring Taurus-Littrow. By Harrison H. Schmitt. Photos by the crew of Apollo 17. 290-307, *Sept. 1973*

EVANS, WALTER H.: *Author*

Some of the Conditions and Possibilities of Agriculture in Alaska. 178-187, *Apr. 1898*

EVER Changing California, Land of Startling Contrasts. Photos by Charles Martin. 705-744, *June 1929*

EVEREST, Mount, China-Nepal:

Exploring Cradle Earth. By Wilbur E. Garrett. 612, *Nov. 1988*

Roof of the World. Photos by William Thompson. 613-623, *Nov. 1988*

The Mighty Himalaya: A Fragile Heritage. By Barry C. Bishop. Photos by William Thompson. 624-631, *Nov. 1988*

Heavy Hands on the Land. By Larry Kohl. Photos by William Thompson and Galen Rowell. 633-651, *Nov. 1988*

Mount Everest: Surveying the Third Pole. By Bradford Washburn. NGS research grant. 653-659, *Nov. 1988*

⊕ *Mount Everest; High Himalaya. Nov. 1988*

▇ Americans on Everest. 448-452, Sept. 1965; 575, Nov. 1976; President's Page. *Jan. 1985*

The Forgotten Face of Everest. By Andrew Harvard. Photos by Expedition Members. 71-89. Included: Conquest of the Summit. By James D. Morrissey. 79-89, *July 1984*

▇ Return to Everest. Cover. *Mar. 1984*

Park at the Top of the World: Mount Everest National Park. By Rick Ridgeway. Photos by Nicholas deVore III. 704-725. Included: Preserving a Mountain Heritage. By Sir Edmund Hillary. 696-703, *June 1982*

At My Limit–I Climbed Everest Alone. By Reinhold Messner. Photos by the author and Nena Holguín. 552-566, *Oct. 1981*

Six to the Summit. By Norman G. Dyhrenfurth. Photos by Barry C. Bishop. NGS research grant. 460-473, *Oct. 1963*

How We Climbed Everest. By Barry C. Bishop. NGS research grant. 477-507, *Oct. 1963*

The First Traverse. By Thomas F. Hornbein and William F. Unsoeld. NGS research grant. 509-513, *Oct. 1963*

American and Geographic Flags Top Everest. By Melvin M. Payne. Photos by Barry C. Bishop. NGS research grant. 157-157C, *Aug. 1963*

Triumph on Everest. 1-63. I. Siege and Assault. By Sir John Hunt. 1-43; II. The Conquest of the Summit. By Sir Edmund Hillary. 45-63, *July 1954*

The Aërial Conquest of Everest: Flying Over the World's Highest Mountain Realizes the Objective of Many Heroic Explorers. By L.V.S. Blacker. 127-162, *Aug. 1933*

EVERETT, CURTIS T.:

Children of the Sun and Moon (Kraho Indians). By Harald Schultz; translated from German by Curtis T. Everett. 340-363, *Mar. 1959*

EVERETT, DOROTHEA D.: *Author*

Black Acres: A Thrilling Sketch in the Vast Volume of Who's Who Among the Peoples That Make America. By Dorothea D. and Fred Everett. 631-652, *Nov. 1941*

EVERETT, FRED: *Author*

Black Acres: A Thrilling Sketch in the Vast Volume of Who's Who Among the Peoples That Make America. By Dorothea D. and Fred Everett. 631-652, *Nov. 1941*

EVERGLADES (Region), Florida:

The Tree Nobody Liked (Red Mangrove). By Rick Gore. Photos by Bianca Lavies. 669-689, *May 1977*

The Swallow-tailed Kite: Graceful Aerialist of the Everglades. 496-505, *Oct. 1972*

The Imperiled Everglades. By Fred Ward. 1-27, *Jan. 1972*

Businessman in the Bush. By Frederick Kent Truslow. 634-675, *May 1970*

Racing across four million years of evolution, hominids show such changes as smaller jaws and larger brains. PAINTING BY © JAY H. MATTERNES

Florida's Emerging Seminoles. By Louis Capron. Photos by Otis Imboden. Contents: Seminole and Miccosukee reservations and settlements. 716-734, *Nov. 1969*

Threatened Glories of Everglades National Park. By Frederick Kent Truslow and Frederick G. Vosburgh. Photos by Frederick Kent Truslow and Otis Imboden. Included: Drainage from Lake Okeechobee in 1880, 1920, and 1967. 508-553, *Oct. 1967*

When Disaster Struck a Woodpecker's Home. By Frederick Kent Truslow. 882-884, *Dec. 1966*

Shrimp Nursery: Science Explores New Ways to Farm the Sea. By Clarence P. Idyll. Photos by Robert F. Sisson. NGS research grant. 636-659, *May 1965*

Tree Snails, Gems of the Everglades. By Treat Davidson. 372-387, *Mar. 1965*

Our Only Native Stork, the Wood Ibis. By Robert Porter Allen. Photos by Frederick Kent Truslow. 294-306, *Feb. 1964*

Florida Rides a Space-age Boom. By Benedict Thielen. Photos by Winfield Parks and James P. Blair. 858-903, *Dec. 1963*

Eye to Eye With Eagles. By Frederick Kent Truslow. 123-148, *Jan. 1961*

Florida's "Wild" Indians, the Seminole. By Louis Capron. Photos by Willard R. Culver. 819-840, *Dec. 1956*

Saving Man's Wildlife Heritage. By John H. Baker. Photos by Robert F. Sisson. 581-620, *Nov. 1954*

Wildlife of Everglades National Park. By Daniel B. Beard. Paintings by Walter A. Weber. 83-116, *Jan. 1949*

Haunting Heart of the Everglades. By Andrew H. Brown. Photos by author and Willard R. Culver. 145-173, *Feb. 1948*

South Florida's Amazing Everglades: Encircled by Populous Places Is a Seldom-visited Area of Rare Birds, Prairies, Cowboys, and Teeming Wild Life of Big Cypress Swamp. By John O'Reilly. 115-142, *Jan. 1940*

The Geography of the Southern Peninsula of the United States. By John N. MacGonigle. 381-394, *Dec. 1896*

EVERHART, WILLIAM C.: *Author*
So Long, St. Louis, We're Heading West. 643-669, *Nov. 1965*

EVERINGHAM, JOHN:
On Assignment in Australia. *Feb. 1988*
Nomination Page. *May 1980*
Nomination Page. In Laos. *Jan. 1974*
Author
Children of the First Fleet. Painting by Roy Andersen. 233-245, *Feb. 1988*
Author-Photographer
One Family's Odyssey to America. 642-661, *May 1980*
Photographer
Thailand's Working Royalty. 486-499, *Oct. 1982*

EVERINGHAM FAMILY:
Children of the First Fleet. By John Everingham. Painting by Roy Andersen. Included: Descendants of Matthew James Everingham. 233-245, *Feb. 1988*

EVERMANN, BARTON WARREN:
Author
The Bureau of Fisheries. 191-212, *May 1904*

"EVERY Day Is a Gift When You Are Over 100." By Alexander Leaf. Photos by John Launois. 93-119, *Jan. 1973*

EVERY-DAY Life in Afghanistan. By Frederick Simpich and "Haji Mirza Hussein." 85-110, *Jan. 1921*

EVERYDAY Life in Ancient Times.
■ Contents: Egypt, Greece, Mesopotamia, and Rome. 368 pages. 1951; rev. ed. *1961*

EVERYDAY Life in Bible Times. 448
■ pages. 1967; rev. ed. *1977*

EVERYDAY Life in Pueblo Bonito: As Disclosed by the National Geographic Society's Archeologic Explorations in the Chaco Canyon National Monument, New Mexico. By Neil M. Judd. 227-262, *Sept. 1925*

EVERYDAY Life in Wartime England. By Harvey Klemmer. 497-534, *Apr. 1941*

EVERYONE'S Servant, the Post Office. By Allan C. Fisher, Jr. Photos by Volkmar Wentzel. 121-152, *July 1954*

EVIDENCE of Recent Volcanic Action in Southeast Alaska. 173-176, *Mar. 1906*

EVOLUTION:
"Where Did We Come From?" Editorial by Wilbur E. Garrett. Included: Map, The Peopling of the Earth. 434-437, *Oct. 1988*

The Search for Modern Humans. By John J. Putman. Photos by Sisse Brimberg and Ira Block. Paintings by Jack Unruh. 439-477, *Oct. 1988*

Galápagos Wildlife Under Pressure. Photo essay by Dieter and Mary Plage. 122-154, *Jan. 1988*

Madagascar: A World Apart. By Alison Jolly. Photos by Frans Lanting. Note: The island is described as a living laboratory for evolution. 148-183, *Feb. 1987*

Editorial. By Wilbur E. Garrett. 419, *Oct. 1986*

The Search for Our Ancestors. By Kenneth F. Weaver. Photos by David L. Brill. Paintings by Jay H. Matternes. 560-623, *Nov. 1985*

Our Restless Planet Earth. By Rick Gore. Photos by James A. Sugar. 142-181. Included: Continents Adrift; Life's Triumph *and* Origin of Earth and Life. Painting by Ned M. Seidler. Text by Larry Kohl. 146-151, *Aug. 1985*

Editorial. By Gilbert M. Grosvenor. 297, *Sept. 1976*

The New Biology. 355-407. I. The Awesome Worlds Within a Cell. By Rick Gore. Photos by Bruce Dale. Paintings by Davis Meltzer. 355-395; II. The Cancer Puzzle. By Robert F. Weaver. 396-399; III. Seven Giants Who Led the Way. Paintings by Ned Seidler. Text by Rick Gore. 401-407, *Sept. 1976*

In the Wake of Darwin's *Beagle*. By Alan Villiers. Photos by James L. Stanfield. 449-495, *Oct. 1969*

The Galapagos, Eerie Cradle of New Species. By Roger Tory Peterson.

Photos by Alan and Joan Root. 541-585, *Apr. 1967*
See also Paleontology

The **EVOLUTION** of Commerce. Annual Address by the President, Gardiner G. Hubbard. 1-18, *Mar. 26, 1892*

EVOLUTION of Russian Government. By Edwin A. Grosvenor. 309-332, *July 1905*

EWALD, PAUL W.: *Author*

Hummingbirds: The Nectar Connection. Photos by Robert A. Tyrrell. 223-227, *Feb. 1982*

EWENS PONDS, South Australia, Australia:

Exploring a Sunken Realm in Australia. By Hillary Hauser. Photos by David Doubilet. 129-142, *Jan. 1984*

EWING, HENRY E.: *Author*

Afield with the Spiders: Web Hunting in the Marshlands and Woodlands and Along the Lanes. Paintings by Hashime Murayama. 163-194, *Aug. 1933*

EWING, MAURICE: *Author*

New Discoveries on the Mid-Atlantic Ridge. Photos by Robert F. Sisson. 611-640, *Nov. 1949*

Exploring the Mid-Atlantic Ridge. 275-294, *Sept. 1948*

EXCAVATING a 400-year-old Basque Galleon. By Robert Grenier. Photos by Bill Curtsinger. 58-67, *July 1985*

EXCAVATIONS at Abydos. By W. M. Flinders Petrie. 358-359, *Sept. 1903*

EXCAVATIONS at Nippur (Iraq). 392, *Oct. 1900*

EXCAVATIONS at Quirigua, Guatemala. By Sylvanus Griswold Morley. 339-361, *Mar. 1913*; 1056, *Sept. 1913*

EXCAVATIONS of M. de Morgan at Susa. 315, *Aug. 1901*

An **EXCITING** Year of Discovery: President's Report to Members. By Gilbert M. Grosvenor. 820-824, *Dec. 1982*

EXCURSION to Enchantment: A Journey to the World's Most Beautiful Places. Included: East Africa, Loire Valley, Bhutan, Chile-Argentina Lake District, Alaska's Inside Passage, and the Caribbean. 200 pages. *1988*

EXMOOR PONIES:

England's Wild Moorland Ponies. 129-136, *Jan. 1946*

The **EXODUS:**

Lost Outpost of the Egyptian Empire. By Trude Dothan. Photos by Sisse Brimberg. Paintings by Lloyd K. Townsend. 739-769, *Dec. 1982*

Eternal Sinai. By Harvey Arden. Photos by David Doubilet and Kevin Fleming. 420-461, *Apr. 1982*

In Search of Moses. By Harvey Arden. Photos by Nathan Benn. Included: Map of Sinai Peninsula indicating two possible routes. 2-37, *Jan. 1976*

East of Suez to the Mount of the Decalogue: Following the Trail Over Which Moses Led the Israelites from the Slave-Pens of Egypt to Sinai. By Maynard Owen Williams. 709-743, *Dec. 1927*

The Route Over Which Moses Led the Children of Israel Out of Egypt. By Franklin E. Hoskins. 1011-1038, *Dec. 1909*

EXOTIC-BIRD TRADE:

Wild Cargo: the Business of Smuggling Animals. By Noel Grove. Photos by Steve Raymer. 287-315, *Mar. 1981*

EXOTIC Birds in Manhattan's Bowery. By Paul A. Zahl. 77-98, *Jan. 1953*

An **EXOTIC** New Oriole Settles in Florida. By Charles M. Brookfield and Oliver Griswold. 261-264, *Feb. 1956*

The **EXPANSION** of England. By Edwin D. Mead. 249-263, *July 1900*

EXPEDITIONS:

Expedition to the Land of the Tiwi. By Charles P. Mountford. 417-440, *Mar. 1956*

Quinine Hunters in Ecuador. By Froelich Rainey. 341-363, *Mar. 1946*

Earth's Most Primitive People: A Journey with the Aborigines of Central Australia. By Charles P. Mountford. 89-112, *Jan. 1946*

Fit to Fight Anywhere (Quartermaster Corps Expedition). By Frederick Simpich. 233-256, *Aug. 1943*

Climbing Mighty Minya Konka: Americans First Scaled Mountain That Now Is Landmark of China's New Skyway. By Richard L. Burdsall and Terris Moore. 625-650, *May 1943*

Expedition Unearths Buried Masterpieces of Carved Jade (Cerro de las Mesas, Mexico). By Matthew W. Stirling. 277-302, *Sept. 1941*

By Coolie and Caravan Across Central Asia: Narrative of a 7,900-Mile Journey of Exploration and Research Over the "Roof of the World," from the Indian Ocean to the Yellow Sea (Morden-Clark Asiatic Expedition). By William J. Morden. 369-431, *Oct. 1927*

Through the Deserts and Jungles of Africa by Motor: Caterpillar Cars Make 15,000-Mile Trip from Algeria to Madagascar in Nine Months. By Georges-Marie Haardt. 651-720, *June 1926*

The Conquest of the Sahara by the Automobile. 87-93, *Jan. 1924*

The Crosby Expedition to Tibet. 229-231, *May 1904*

Expedition into Texas of Fernando del Bosque, Standard-Bearer of the King, Don Carlos II, in the Year 1675. Translated from an Old, Unpublished Spanish Manuscript. By Betty B. Brewster. 339-348, *Sept. 1903*

Expedition to Turkestan. 215, *May 1903*

Expeditions in the Arctic and Antarctic. 179-180, *May 1902*

A Yukon Pioneer, Mike Lebarge. Note: First trip from headwaters of the Yukon to the sea. 137-139, *Apr. 1898*

The Mt. St. Elias Expedition of Prince Luigi Amadeo of Savoy, 1897. By E. R. Scidmore. 93-96, *Mar. 1898*

Some Recent Geographic Events. By John Hyde. Included: Andrée Balloon Expedition; de Gerlache

Desert police inspect French-built tractors during a pioneering expedition by motor vehicle across the Sahara in 1922. ANDRÉ CITRÖEN

A Greek pilot pedals the experimental **Daedalus**—*68.5 pounds of graphite, plastic, and MIT engineering*—*72 miles into the record books.* CHARLES O'REAR, WEST LIGHT

EXPLORER (NGS Cable Television Programming):

EXPLORER I (Stratosphere Balloon):

EXPLORER II (Stratosphere Balloon):

Moored by soldiers, **Explorer II** *prepares to lift two pilots to a record-shattering 13.71 miles in 1935.* RICHARD H. STEWART, NGS

EXPLORERS (Senior Boy Scouts):

EXPLORERS, DISCOVERERS, AND NAVIGATORS:

Aztec ruler Moctezuma II greets Hernán Cortés and his conquistadores near Tenochtitlan. PAINTING BY NED SEIDLER, NGS, AND ROSALIE SEIDLER

Cobwebs and Aboriginal paintings adorn Howell Walker's temporary office in Arnhem Land, Australia, in 1949. HOWELL WALKER, NGS

Miles of Flying Over the World's Greatest River and Greatest Forest to Chart the Unknown Parima River from the Sky. By Albert W. Stevens. 353-420, *Apr. 1926*

EXPLORING the Wonders of the Insect World. By William Joseph Showalter. Paintings by Hashime Murayama. 1-90, *July 1929*

EXPLORING the World of Gems. By W. F. Foshag. 779-810, *Dec. 1950*

EXPLORING Tibet. 403-404, *Nov. 1901*

EXPLORING Tomorrow With the Space Agency. By Allan C. Fisher, Jr. Photos by Dean Conger. 48-89, *July 1960*

EXPLORING Unknown Corners of the "Hermit Kingdom" (Korea). By Roy Chapman Andrews. 25-48, *July 1919*

EXPLORING Yukon's Glacial Stronghold. By Bradford Washburn. 715-748, *June 1936*

EXPLOSION:

The Aberration of Sound as Illustrated by the Berkeley Powder Explosion. By Robert H. Chapman. 246-249, *July 1896*

The **EXPLOSIVE** Birth of Myojin Island. By Robert S. Dietz. 117-128, *Jan. 1954*

EXPO 67:

Montreal Greets the World. By Jules B. Billard. 600-621, *May 1967*

EXPO '70:

Kansai, Japan's Historic Heartland. By Thomas J. Abercrombie. 295-339, *Mar. 1970*

EXPORTS AND IMPORTS. See Trade; *and name of product*

EXPORTS of Manufactures. 434-437, *Sept. 1905*

EXPOSITIONS:

A City of Realized Dreams (San Francisco). By Franklin K. Lane. 169-171, *Feb. 1915*

An American Floating Exposition. 204-205, *May 1901*

An Austro-Hungarian floating exposition. 164, *Apr. 1901*

The Philippine Exhibit at the Pan-American Exposition. By D. O. Noble Hoffmann. 119-122, *Mar. 1901*

An Around-the-World American Exposition. By O. P. Austin. 49-53, *Feb. 1901*

Proceedings of the International Geographic Conference, held in conjunction with the World's Columbian Exposition, Chicago, May 1-October 30, 1893. 97-256, *Jan. 31, 1894*

See also Fairs; Ibero-American Exposition; World's Fairs

EXQUISITE Living Fossil, the Chambered Nautilus. Photos by Douglas Faulkner. 38-41, *Jan. 1976*

The **EXQUISITE** Orchids. By Luis Marden. 485-513, *Apr. 1971*

EXTINCT SPECIES:

Meteorites–Invaders From Space. By Kenneth F. Weaver. Photos by Jonathan Blair. Included: Theory of cataclysm that caused extinction of most reptiles of Cretaceous period. 390-418, *Sept. 1986*

Queensland, Broad Shoulder of Australia. By William S. Ellis. Photos by David Robert Austen. Included: Queensland Fossils Expand Australia's Prehistoric Menagerie. 2-39, *Jan. 1986*

Editorial. By Wilbur E. Garrett. 703, *June 1983*

■■ *Giants from the Past: The Age of Mammals*. By Joseph H. Bailey. Juvenile. 104 pages. *1983*

Exploring the Mind of Ice Age Man. By Alexander Marshack. NGS research grant. 64-89, *Jan. 1975*

✷ "Ice Age Mammals of the Alaskan Tundra," painting supplement. Map on reverse. *Mar. 1972*

Extinct Reptiles Found in Nodules. By H. A. Largelamb (Alexander Graham Bell). 170-173, *Mar. 1906*

See also Aepyornis; Dinosaurs; Mammals, Prehistoric

EXTRAORDINARY Photograph Shows Earth Pole to Pole. Photos by Nimbus I. 190-193, *Feb. 1965*

EXTRAORDINARY Photographs of Earth Taken by Satellite *Tiros*. By W. G. Stroud. 293-302, *Aug. 1960*

EXUMA CAYS, Bahama Islands:

More of Sea Than of Land: The Bahamas. By Carleton Mitchell. Photos by James L. Stanfield. 218-267, *Feb. 1967*

The Bahamas, Isles of the Blue-green Sea. By Carleton Mitchell. Photos by B. Anthony Stewart. 147-203, *Feb. 1958*

An **EYE** for an Eye: Pakistan's Wild Frontier. By Mike W. Edwards. Photos by J. Bruce Baumann. 111-139, *Jan. 1977*

EYE to Eye With Eagles. By Frederick Kent Truslow. 123-148, *Jan. 1961*

EYES:

Flashlight Fish of the Red Sea. By Eugenie Clark. Photos by David Doubilet. 719-728, *Nov. 1978*

The Four-eyed Fish Sees All. Photos by Paul A. Zahl. Text by Thomas O'Neill. 390-395, *Mar. 1978*

Nature's Alert Eyes. By Constance P. Warner. Included: Owl, Chameleon, Scallop, Grass Spider, Tree Frog, Gecko, Skate, Catfish, Emperor Penguin, Hornbill, Pufferfish, Praying Mantis, Horsefly, and Fish. 558-569, *Apr. 1959*

EYES of Science. By Rick Gore. Photos by James P. Blair. 360-389, *Mar. 1978*

EYES on the China Coast. By George W. Long. 505-512, *Apr. 1953*

EYEWITNESS to War in the Holy Land. By Charles Harbutt. 782-795, *Dec. 1967*

EYRE, EDWARD JOHN:

Edward John Eyre (Biography). 75, *Feb. 1902*

EYRE, LINCOLN: *Author*

Renascent Germany. 639-717, *Dec. 1928*

EZION-GEBER, Jordan:

On the Trail of King Solomon's Mines: The Bible, in Addition to Its Spiritual Values, Continues to Prove a Rich Geography and Guide to Exploration of the Holy Land. By Nelson Glueck. 233-256, *Feb. 1944*

In clear waters off the Exuma Cays, a bow lookout pilots the **Finisterre** *by color: purple-brown of coral heads, yellow of sand, cobalt blue of deep waters.* JAMES L. STANFIELD, NGS

FAO. *See* United Nations Food and Agriculture Organization

The **FBI:** Public Friend Number One. By Jacob Hay. Photos by Robert F. Sisson. 860-886, *June 1961*

F.N.R.S. 3 (Bathyscaph):
Deep Diving off Japan. By Georges S. Houot. NGS research grant. 138-150, *Jan. 1960*
Four Years of Diving to the Bottom of the Sea. By Georges S. Houot. NGS research grant. 715-731, *May 1958*
Photographing the Sea's Dark Underworld. By Harold E. Edgerton. NGS research grant. 523-537, *Apr. 1955*
Diving Through an Undersea Avalanche. By Jacques-Yves Cousteau. NGS research grant. 538-542, *Apr. 1955*
To the Depths of the Sea by Bathyscaphe. By Jacques-Yves Cousteau. NGS research grant. 67-79, *July 1954*
Two and a Half Miles Down. By Georges S. Houot. NGS research grant. 80-86, *July 1954*

FABLED Mount of St. Michael. By Alan Villiers. Photos by Bates Littlehales. 880-898, *June 1964*

FABRIC:
Wool–Fabric of History. By Nina Hyde. Photos by Cary Wolinsky. Included: Living in Wool. 552-591, *May 1988*
Silk–The Queen of Textiles. By Nina Hyde. Photos by Cary Wolinsky. 2-49, *Jan. 1984*
Cotton: Foremost Fiber of the World. By J. R. Hildebrand. 137-192, *Feb. 1941*

The **FABULOUS** Sierra Nevada. By J. R. Challacombe. 825-843, *June 1954*

The **FABULOUS** State of Texas. By Stanley Walker. Photos by B. Anthony Stewart and Thomas Nebbia. 149-195, *Feb. 1961*

FABULOUS Yellowstone. By Frederick G. Vosburgh. 769-794, *June 1940*

The FACE and Faith of Poland, map, ✥ photo, and essay supplement. By Peter Miller. Essay by Czesław Miłosz. Photos by Bruno Barbey. *Apr. 1982*

FACE of Japan. By W. Robert Moore. 753-768, *Dec. 1945*

The **FACE** of the Netherlands Indies. Photos by Maynard Owen Williams and others. 261-276, *Feb. 1946*

FACE to Face With Gorillas in Central Africa. By Paul A. Zahl. 114-137, *Jan. 1960*

FACES, Stone (Monuments). *See* Stone Faces

FACES and Fashions of Asia's Changeless Tribes. Paintings and drawings by Alexandre Iacovleff. 21-36, *Jan. 1936*

FACES and Flowers Below the Tropics (Union of South Africa). Photos by Melville Chater. 453-460, *Apr. 1931*

FACING War's Challenge "Down

Under" (Australia and New Zealand). Photos by Howell Walker. 425-456, *Apr. 1942*

FACT Finding for Tomorrow's Planes. By Hugh L. Dryden. Photos by Luis Marden. 757-780, *Dec. 1953*

FACTORS Which Modify the Climate of Victoria (British Columbia). By Arthur W. McCurdy. 345-348, *May 1907*

FACTS about the Philippines. By Frederick Simpich. 185-202, *Feb. 1942*

FAEROE ISLANDS, North Atlantic Ocean:
▦ The Last Vikings. 434A-434B, *Mar. 1972*
The Faeroes, Isles of Maybe. By Ernle Bradford. Photos by Adam Woolfitt. 410-422, *Sept. 1970*
Viking Life in the Storm-Cursed Faeroes. By Leo Hansen. 607-648, *Nov. 1930*

FAGAN, BRIAN M.: *Author*
▦▦ *The Adventure of Archaeology.* 368 pages. *1985*

FAIR, PAUL J.: *Photographer*
Wildlife In and Near the Valley of the Moon. By H. H. Arnold. 401-414, *Mar. 1950*

FAIR of the Berber Brides. By Carla Hunt. Photos by Nik Wheeler. 119-129, *Jan. 1980*

FAIR Skies for the Cayman Islands. By Peter Benchley. Photos by David Doubilet. 798-824, *June 1985*

FAIR Winds and Full Sails. By Thomas J. Abercrombie. Photos by Cary Wolinsky. 638-667, *May 1982*

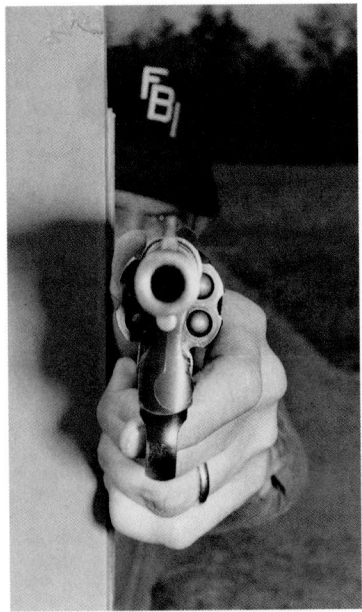

Taking careful aim, a new FBI agent learns to shoot ably with either hand.
ROBERT F. SISSON AND JOHN E. FLETCHER, BOTH NGS

FAIRBANKS, CHARLES W.:
Honors to the American Navy. Address by Charles W. Fairbanks. 77-95, *Jan. 1909*
Honors for Amundsen. Address by Charles W. Fairbanks. 55-76, *Jan. 1908*

FAIRBANKS, Alaska:
Busy Fairbanks Sets Alaska's Pace. By Bruce A. Wilson. 505-523, *Oct. 1949*

FAIRCHILD, DAVID: *Author*
Hunting Useful Plants in the Caribbean. 705-737, *Dec. 1934*
The Jungles of Panama. 131-145, *Feb. 1932*
Hunting for Plants in the Canary Islands. 607-652, *May 1930*
A Hunter of Plants. 57-77, *July 1919*
Forming New Industries in Food: The Bearing of Taste on One of Our Great Food Economies, the Dried Vegetable, Which Is Developing Into a Big War Industry. 356-368, *Apr. 1918*
A Book of Monsters (Insects). By David and Marian Fairchild. Note: Announcement and summary of NGS publication, *A Book of Monsters.* 89-98, *July 1914*
▦▦ *Book of Monsters: Portraits and Biographies of a Few of the Inhabitants of Woodland and Meadow.* By David and Marion Fairchild. 266 pages. *1914*
The Monsters of Our Back Yards. 575-626, *May 1913*
New Plant Immigrants. 879-907, *Oct. 1911*
Madeira, on the Way to Italy. 751-771, *Dec. 1907*
Our Plant Immigrants. 179-201, *Apr. 1906*
Travels in Arabia and Along the Persian Gulf. 139-151, *Apr. 1904*
Sumatra's West Coast. 449-464, *Nov. 1898*

FAIRCHILD, GRAHAM: *Author*
Life Story of the Mosquito. 180-195, *Feb. 1944*

FAIRCHILD, MARIAN: *Author*
A Book of Monsters (Insects). By David and Marian Fairchild. Note: Announcement and summary of NGS publication, *A Book of Monsters.* 89-98, *July 1914*
▦▦ *Book of Monsters: Portraits and Biographies of a Few of the Inhabitants of Woodland and Meadow.* By David and Marian Fairchild. 266 pages. *1914*

FAIRS:
Mississippi's Grand Reunion at the Neshoba County Fair. By Carolyn Bennett Patterson. Photos by C. C. Lockwood. 854-866, *June 1980*
Berber Brides' Fair. By Carla Hunt. Photos by Nik Wheeler. 119-129, *Jan. 1980*
Pennsylvania's Old-time Dutch Treat. By Kent Britt. Contents: Kutztown Folk Festival. Photos by H. Edward Kim. 564-578, *Apr. 1973*
When Gypsies Gather at Appleby Fair.

FAIRY TALES:

FAIRY TERNS:

FAIRY WRENS:

Hans Christian Andersen told his fairy tales to little Ida Thiele, whose great-great-granddaughters, Anja and Katja, wear flowered crowns in her memory. SISSE BRIMBERG

FALCON ISLAND, Tonga Islands:

FALCONRY:

FALCONS:

FALI TRIBESPEOPLE:

FALKLAND ISLANDS, Atlantic Ocean:

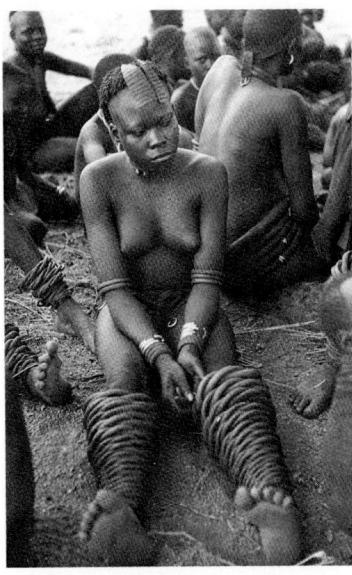

A Fali woman rests after ceremonial dances in the Mandara region, northern Cameroon, in the 1930s. PIERRE ICHAC

FALLING MOUNTAIN, Alaska:

The Valley of Ten Thousand Smokes: An Account of the Discovery and Exploration of the Most Wonderful Volcanic Region in the World. By Robert F. Griggs. 115-169, *Feb. 1918*

FALLOWS, JAMES: *Author*

Vatican City. Photos by James L. Stanfield. 723-775, *Dec. 1985*

FALLS, DE WITT CLINTON: *Author*

Saint Stephen's Fete in Budapest. 548-558, *Aug. 1907*

FALLS. See Waterfalls

The **FALLS** of Iguazu. By Marie Robinson Wright. 456-460, *Aug. 1906*

FALTBOATS. See Foldboats

FAME'S Eternal Camping Ground: Beautiful Arlington (Virginia), Burial Place of America's Illustrious Dead. By Enoch A. Chase. 621-638, *Nov. 1928*

FAMILIAR Grasses and Their Flowers. By E. J. Geske and W. J. Showalter. Paintings by E. J. Geske. 625-636, *June 1921*

FAMILY Afoot in Yukon Wilds: Two Young Children and Their Parents Live Off the Country in the Northwest Canada Wilderness Now To Be Traversed by the Alaska Highway. By William Hamilton Albee, with Ruth Albee. 589-616, *May 1942*

FAMILY FARMS:

The Plain People of Pennsylvania. Photo essay by Jerry Irwin. Text by Douglas Lee. 492-519, *Apr. 1984*
Home to the Heart of Kentucky. By Nadine Brewer. Photos by William Strode. 522-546, *Apr. 1982*
The Family Farm Ain't What It Used To

Be. By James A. Sugar. 391-411, *Sept. 1974*

FAMILY in Search of Prehistoric Man: The Leakeys of Africa. By Melvin M. Payne. 194-231, *Feb. 1965*

FAMILY ISLANDS, Bahamas:

The Bahamas: Boom Times and Buccaneering. By Peter Benchley. Photos by Bruce Dale. 364-395, *Sept. 1982*

FAMILY LIFE:

Home to the Heart of Kentucky. By Nadine Brewer. Photos by William Strode. 522-546, *Apr. 1982*
Growing Up in Montana. Photos by Nicholas deVore III. 650-657, *May 1976*
An Ozark Family Carves a Living and a Way of Life. Photos by Bruce Dale. 124-133, *July 1975*
The Family: a Mormon Shrine. 459-463, *Apr. 1975*

FAMILY Life of Lions. By Des and Jen Bartlett. 800-819, *Dec. 1982*

The **FAMILY** Tree of the Flowers. By Frederic E. Clements and William Joseph Showalter. 555-563, *May 1927*

FAMINE:

Africa's Sahel: The Stricken Land. By William S. Ellis. Photos by Steve McCurry. 140-179, *Aug. 1987*
Eritrea: Region in Rebellion. By Anthony Suau. 384-405, *Sept. 1985*
Somalia's Hour of Need. By Robert Paul Jordan. Photos by Michael S. Yamashita and Kevin Fleming. 748-775. Included: Encampments of the Dispossessed. By Larry Kohl. 756-763, *June 1981*
The Niger: River of Sorrow, River of Hope. By Georg Gerster. 152-189, *Aug. 1975*
Can the World Feed Its People? By Thomas Y. Canby. Photos by Steve Raymer. 2-31, *July 1975*
Bangladesh: The Nightmare of Famine. Photos by Steve Raymer. 33-39, *July 1975*
Drought Threatens the Tuareg World. By Victor Englebert. 544-571, *Apr. 1974*
Drought Bedevils Brazil's Sertão. By John Wilson. Photos by Gordon W. Gahan. 704-723, *Nov. 1972*
Report from the Locust Wars. By Tony and Dickey Chapelle. 545-562, *Apr. 1953*
The Land of the Stalking Death: A Journey Through Starving Armenia on an American Relief Train. By Melville Chater. 393-420, *Nov. 1919*
Forerunners of Famine. By Frederic C. Walcott. 336-347, *Apr. 1918*
Fearful Famines of the Past: History Will Repeat Itself Unless the American People Conserve Their Resources. By Ralph A. Graves. 69-90, *July 1917*

FAMOUS (French-American Mid-Ocean Undersea Study):

Project FAMOUS–Man's First Voyages Down to the Mid-Atlantic Ridge. By J. R. Heirtzler and Robert D.

Ballard. Photos by Emory Kristof. 586-615, *May 1975*

The **FAMOUS** Waldseemüller map of 1507. 50, *Jan. 1904*

FANCH'ENG, Hubei Province, China:

Return to Changing China. By Audrey Topping. 801-833, *Dec. 1971*

FANE, G. E.: *Author*

Burma Road, Back Door to China: Like the Great Wall of Ancient Times, This Mighty Mountain Highway Has Been Built by Myriad Chinese to Help Defend Their Homeland. By Frank Outram and G. E. Fane. 629-658, *Nov. 1940*

FANTASTIC Dwellers in a Coral Fairyland (Great Barrier Reef). Photos by T. C. Roughley. 831-838, *June 1940*

The **FANTASTIC** Flight of *Cote d'Or.* By Cynthia Shields. 789-793, *Dec. 1983*

FANTASTIC Plants of Our Western Deserts. Photos by Frank M. Campbell. 33-40, *Jan. 1924*

FANTASTIC Sea Life From Abyssal Depths. Paintings by Else Bostelmann. 71-78, *Jan. 1932*

FANTI TRIBESPEOPLE:

The Gold Coast, Ashanti, and Kumassi. By George K. French. 1-15, *Jan. 1897*

FAR EAST:

Jade: Stone of Heaven. By Fred Ward. 282-315, *Sept. 1987*
Monsoons: Life Breath of Half the World. By Priit J. Vesilind. Photos by Steve McCurry. 712-747, *Dec. 1984*
Pacific Fleet: Force for Peace. By Franc Shor. Photos by W. E. Garrett. 283-335, *Sept. 1959*
Our Navy in the Far East. By Arthur W. Radford. Photos by J. Baylor Roberts. 537-577, *Oct. 1953*
✤ *The Far East. Sept. 1952*
Yankee Roams the Orient. By Irving and Electa Johnson. 327-370, *Mar. 1951*
✤ *Japan and Adjacent Regions of Asia and the Pacific Ocean. Apr. 1944*
✤ *Indian Ocean, including Australia, New Zealand and Malaysia. Mar. 1941*
✤ *The Philippine Islands as the Geographical Center of the Far East. Jan. 1900*
See also Borneo; China, People's Republic of; French Indo-China; Hong Kong; Japan; Korea; Korea, North; Korea, South; Manchuria; New Guinea; Quemoy; Southeast Asia; Sumatra; Taiwan; Timor

The **FAR** Eastern Republic (U.S.S.R.). By Junius B. Wood. 565-592, *June 1922*

FAR-FLUNG Search for the First Americans. By Thomas Y. Canby. Photos by Kerby Smith. Paintings by Roy Andersen. 330-363, *Sept. 1979*

FAR-FLYING Phalaropes. By Joseph R. Jehl, Jr. 520-525, *Oct. 1981*

FAR-FLYING Wild Fowl and Their Foes. By Allan Brooks. Paintings by author. 487-528, *Oct. 1934*

FAR NORTH with "Captain Mac." By Miriam MacMillan. 465-513, *Oct. 1951*

FAR-OUT FACTS:
■■ *More Far-Out Facts.* Juvenile. 104 pages. *1982*
■■ *Far-Out Facts.* Juvenile. 104 pages. *1980*

FARADAY, MICHAEL:
The British Way. By Sir Evelyn Wrench. 421-541, *Apr. 1949*

FARALLON ISLANDS REFUGE, California:
Island, Prairie, Marsh, and Shore. By Charlton Ogburn. Photos by Bates Littlehales. 350-381, *Mar. 1979*

FAREWELL to Bikini. By Carl Markwith. 97-116, *July 1946*

FARMERS' Friends Among the Wasps and Hornets. Paintings by Hashime Murayama. 57-64, *July 1937*

FARMERS Keep Them Eating. By Frederick Simpich. 435-458, *Apr. 1943*

The **FARMERS** of the United States. 39-46, *Jan. 1905*

FARMERS Since the Days of Noah: China's Remarkable System of Agriculture Has Kept Alive the Densest Population in the World. By Adam Warwick. 469-500, *Apr. 1927*

FARMING. See Agriculture; Aquaculture

FARMING on the Isthmus of Panama. By Dillwyn M. Hazlett. 229-234, *Apr. 1906*

FARMS:
Chattooga River Country: Wild Water, Proud People. By Don Belt. Photos by Steve Wall. 458-477, *Apr. 1983*
Home to the Heart of Kentucky. By Nadine Brewer. Photos by William Strode. 522-546, *Apr. 1982*
Down on the Farm, Soviet Style–a 4-H Adventure. By John Garaventa. Photos by James Tobin and Carol Schmidt. 768-797, *June 1979*
The Family Farm Ain't What It Used To Be. By James A. Sugar. 391-411, *Sept. 1974*
Burma's Leg Rowers and Floating Farms. Photos by W. E. Garrett. Text by David Jeffery. 826-845, *June 1974*
■■ *Life in Rural America.* 207 pages. *1974*
The World of My Apple Tree. By Robert F. Sisson. Included: Harmony Hollow farm, Virginia. 836-847, *June 1972*
The Revolution in American Agriculture. By Jules B. Billard. Photos by James P. Blair. Included: Farm of the future (painting). 147-185, *Feb. 1970*
The Goats of Thunder Hill. By Elizabeth Nicholds. Photos by Robert F.

Sisson. Contents: Goat farm. 625-640, *May 1954*
Sunny Siberia. Photos by Owen Lattimore. Included: Ernst Thaelmann (Collective Farm). 649-672, *Dec. 1944*
America Fights on the Farms. 33-48, *July 1944*
Life's Flavor on a Swedish Farm: From the Rocky Hills of Småland Thousands of Sturdy Citizens Have Emigrated to the United States. By Willis Lindquist. 393-414, *Sept. 1939*
Farms and Workshops of "The Garden State" (New Jersey). Photos by Edwin L. Wisherd. 559-566, *May 1933*
A Northern Crusoe's Island: Life on a Fox Farm Off the Coast of Alaska, Far from Contact with the World Eleven Months a Year. By Margery Pritchard Parker. 313-326, *Sept. 1923*
Staircase Farms of the Ancients: Astounding Farming Skill of Ancient Peruvians, Who Were Among the Most Industrious and Highly Organized People in History. By O. F. Cook. 474-534, *May 1916*
Seed Farms in California. By A. J. Wells. 515-530, *May 1912*
See also Estates and Plantations; Kibbutzim; Ranches

FARNE ISLANDS, England:
Pilgrimage to Holy Island and the Farnes. By John E. H. Nolan. 547-570, *Oct. 1952*

FARNEY, DENNIS: *Author*
The Tallgrass Prairie: Can It Be Saved? Photos by Jim Brandenburg. 37-61, *Jan. 1980*

FAROE ISLANDS. *See* Faeroe Islands

FARQUHAR, HENRY: *Author*
Calculations of Population in June, 1900. 406-413, *Oct. 1899*

FARTHEST North (Peary). 638-644, *Nov. 1906*

The **FARTHEST-NORTH** Republic: Olympic Games and Arctic Flying Bring Sequestered Finland into New Focus of World Attention. By Alma Luise Olson. 499-533, *Oct. 1938*

The **FASCINATING** World of Trash. By Peter T. White. Photos by Louie Psihoyos. 424-457, *Apr. 1983*

"FATE Directs the Faltering Footsteps of Columbus." Painting by Alfred Dehodencq, Paris. Painting supplement, *Sept. 1928*

FÁTIMA, Portugal:
Fátima: Beacon for Portugal's Faithful. By Jane Vessels. Photos by Bruno Barbey. 832-839, *Dec. 1980*

FATU-HIVA (Island), Marquesas Islands:
Turning Back Time in the South Seas. By Thor Heyerdahl. 109-136, *Jan. 1941*

FAULKNER, DOUGLAS:
Author-Photographer
Finned Doctors of the Deep. 867-873, *Dec. 1965*
Photographer
Dazzling Corals of Palau. By Thomas O'Neill. 136-150, *July 1978*

On a broiling summer day Margie Crisp of Highlands, North Carolina, finds relief in a pool of the Chattooga, a wild river threading mountains and farms. STEVE WALL

J. Edgar Hoover, at right, meets with top FBI officials in 1961. The bureau was founded in 1908 to wage war against criminals. ROBERT F. SISSON AND JOHN E. FLETCHER, BOTH NGS

The Chambered Nautilus, Exquisite Living Fossil. 38-41, *Jan. 1976*

FAULTS AND FAULTING:

Our Restless Planet Earth. By Rick Gore. Photos by James A. Sugar. 142-181. Included: Continents Adrift; Life's Triumph *and* Origin of Earth and Life. Painting by Ned M. Seidler. Text by Larry Kohl. 146-151, *Aug. 1985*

⊕ *The Shaping of a Continent: North America's Active West; Earth's Dynamic Crust.* Included: Spreading, Subduction, Collision, Faulting, Accretion, Hot Spots, 90 Million Years of Drift. *Aug. 1985*

Incredible World of the Deep-sea Rifts. NGS research grant. 680-705. I. Strange World Without Sun. The Editor. 680-688; II. Return to Oases of the Deep. By Robert D. Ballard and J. Frederick Grassle. 689-705, *Nov. 1979*

Oases of Life in the Cold Abyss. By John B. Corliss and Robert D. Ballard. 441-453, *Oct. 1977*

This Changing Earth. By Samuel W. Matthews. 1-37, *Jan. 1973*

See also Earthquakes; Ocean Floors; *and* Great Rift Valley; San Andreas Fault; Wasatch Fault

FAY, CHARLES E.: *Author*

The World's Highest Altitudes and First Ascents. 493-530, *June 1909*

FAYAL (Island), Azores:

A New Volcano Bursts From the Atlantic. By John Scofield. Photos by Robert F. Sisson. 735-757, *June 1958*

FAYETTEVILLE, Arkansas:

Arkansas Rolls Up Its Sleeves. By Frederick Simpich. 273-312, *Sept. 1946*

FEARFUL Famines of the Past: History Will Repeat Itself Unless the American People Conserve Their Resources. By Ralph A. Graves. 69-90, *July 1917*

FEAST Day in Kapingamarangi. By W. Robert Moore. 523-537, *Apr. 1950*

FEATHERED Dancers of Little Tobago. By E. Thomas Gilliard. Photos by Frederick Kent Truslow. 428-440, *Sept. 1958*

FEATHERED Foragers of Swamp and Shore. Paintings by Allan Brooks. 191-222, *Aug. 1937*

FEBIGER, LEA: *Author*

The Coronation of His Majesty King Maha-Vajiravudh of Siam. 389-416, *Apr. 1912*

FEDERAL BUREAU OF INVESTIGATION:

The FBI: Public Friend Number One. By Jacob Hay. Photos by Robert F. Sisson. 860-886, *June 1961*

FEDERAL Fish Farming; or, Planting Fish by the Billion. By Hugh M. Smith. 418-446, *May 1910*

FEDERAL LANDS:

▓▓*America's Wild Woodlands.* 199 pages. *1985*

▓▓*Exploring America's Scenic Highways.* 199 pages. *1985*

▓▓*A Guide to Our Federal Lands.* 227 pages. *1984*

▓▓*Our Threatened Inheritance: Natural Treasures of the United States.* By Ron Fisher. Photos by James P. Blair. 400 pages. *1984*

The Aleutians: Alaska's Far-out Islands. By Lael Morgan. Photos by Steven C. Wilson. Note: 95 percent of the islands are claimed by the federal government as wildlife refuges and military sites. 336-363, *Sept. 1983*

Roosevelt Country: T. R.'s Wilderness Legacy. By John L. Eliot. Photos by Farrell Grehan. 340-363, *Sept. 1982*

⊕ *America's Federal Lands; The United States. Sept. 1982*

See also National Forests; National Mil-

itary Parks; National Monuments; National Parks; National Wild and Scenic Rivers System; National Wildlife Refuges; *and listings under* National Recreation Areas; National Scenic Trails; National Seashores

FEDERAL REPUBLIC OF GERMANY. *See* Germany, West

FEE, WILLIAM THOMAS: *Author*

The Parsees and the Towers of Silence at Bombay, India. 529-554, *Dec. 1905*

FEENEY, CORINNE B.: *Author*

Arch-Isolationists, the San Blas Indians: Coconuts Serve as Cash on Islands Off the Panama Coast Where Tribesmen Cling to Their Ancient Ways and Discourage Visitors. 193-220, *Feb. 1941*

FELSENTHAL, SANDY: *Photographer*

Indianapolis: City on the Rebound. By Louise E. Levathes. 230-259, *Aug. 1987*

The Tennessee-Tombigbee Waterway: Bounty or Boondoggle? By Carolyn Bennett Patterson. Included: The Hidden Tenn-Tom: Bypassed But Still Striving. By Alice J. Hall. 364-387, *Mar. 1986*

Contrary New Hampshire. By Robert Booth. 770-799, *Dec. 1982*

FEN DISTRICT, England:

A Tour in the English Fenland. By Christopher Marlowe. 605-634, *May 1929*

FENI (River), Bangladesh-India:

They Stopped the Sea. By Hans van Duivendijk. Photos by Pablo Bartholomew. 92-101, *July 1987*

FERGUSON, ALBERT F.:

Report of the Annual Dinner of the National Geographic Society. 22-23, *Jan. 1906*

FERMI NATIONAL ACCELERATOR LABORATORY, Batavia, Illinois:

Worlds Within the Atom. By John Boslough. Photos by Kevin Fleming. Illustrations text by David Jeffery. 634-663, *May 1985*

FERNALD, MERRITT LYNDON: *Author*

The Unique Island of Mount Desert. By George B. Dorr, Ernest Howe Forbush, and Merritt Lyndon Fernald. 75-89, *July 1914*

FERNOW, BERNHARD E.: *Author*

The Forests and Deserts of Arizona. 203-226, *July-Aug. 1897*

The Battle of the Forest. 127-148, *June 22, 1894*

FERNS:

Ferns as a Hobby. By William R. Maxon. Paintings by E. J. Geske. Contents: Adder's-Tongue, Bracken, Bulblet Bladder, Christmas, Climbing, Common Wood, Dwarf Spleenwort, Eastern Lady, Interrupted, Maidenhair, Marginal, Marsh,

In a country balancing tribal traditions and national unity, women of the Ivory Coast wear the local costumes of a women's association at a festival. MICHAEL AND AUBINE KIRTLEY

Men of the Wodaabe in Niger adorn themselves with makeup for the yaake *dance to charm women.* CAROL BECKWITH

The Ziegler Polar Expedition. Report by Anthony Fiala. 414-417, *Nov. 1903*

Author
Polar Photography. 140-142, *Feb. 1907*

Photographer
The Lure of the Frozen Desert. Photo supplement, *Dec. 1912*

FIBER OPTICS:
Fiber Optics: Harnessing Light by a Thread. By Allen A. Boraiko. Photos by Fred Ward. 516-535, *Oct. 1979*

FIELD, HENRY: *Author*
Sinai Sheds New Light on the Bible. Photos by William B. and Gladys Terry. 795-815, *Dec. 1948*

FIELD Courses in Geology. 250, *May 1905*

FIELD Dogs in Action. By Freeman Lloyd. Paintings by Edward Herbert Miner. Contents: Chesapeake Bay Retriever, Clumber Spaniel, Cocker Spaniel, Curly-coated Retriever, Dachshund, English Setter, English Springer Spaniel, Field Spaniel, Flat-coated Retriever, German Short-haired Pointer, Golden Retriever, Gordon Setter, Irish Red Setter, Irish Water Spaniel, Labrador Retriever, Pointer, Sussex Spaniel, Wire-haired Pointing Griffon. 85-108, *Jan. 1937*

FIELD *Guide to the Birds of North* ■■ *America.* 464 pages. *1983*

FIELD Sports Among the Wild Men of Northern Luzon. By Dean C. Worcester. 215-267, *Mar. 1911*

FIELDS, JACK: *Photographer*
The Flower Seed Growers: Gardening's Color Merchants. By Robert de Roos. 720-738, *May 1968*
Micronesia: The Americanization of Eden. By David S. Boyer. 702-744, *May 1967*
Sailors of the Sky. By Gordon Young. Photos by Emory Kristof and Jack Fields. Paintings by Davis Meltzer. 49-73, *Jan. 1967*

FIELDWORK of the United States Geological Survey for the Season 1902. 322-325, *Aug. 1902*

FIENNES, SIR RANULPH: *Author*
Circling Earth From Pole to Pole. 464-481, *Oct. 1983*

FIESTAS. *See* Festivals

FIÉVET, JEANNETTE:
Author-Illustrator
Beyond the Bight of Benin. By Jeannette and Maurice Fiévet. 221-253, *Aug. 1959*

FIÉVET, MAURICE: *Artist*
Angkor, Jewel of the Jungle. By W. Robert Moore. 517-569, *Apr. 1960*

Author-Illustrator
Beyond the Bight of Benin. By Jeannette and Maurice Fiévet. 221-253, *Aug. 1959*

15TH-CENTURY Manuscript Yields First Look at *Niña*. By Eugene Lyon. 601-605, *Nov. 1986*

15TH-CENTURY Vignettes of Compiègne (France). Photos by Gervais Courtellemont. 609-616, *Nov. 1932*

FIFTH ARMY, U. S.:
Italy Smiles Again. By Edgar Erskine Hume. 693-732, *June 1949*

FIFTY Common Birds of Farm and Orchard. By Henry Wetherbee Henshaw. Paintings by Louis Agassiz Fuertes. 669-697, *June 1913*

FIFTY *Common Birds of Farm and Orchard.* By Henry W. Henshaw. Art ■■ by Louis Agassiz Fuertes. Originally prepared as Bulletin 513 of the U. S. Department of Agriculture. Reprint of June 1913 article by special permission of the Secretary of Agriculture. 29 pages. *1913*

FIFTY Years of Flight. 740-756, *Dec. 1953*

FIG WASPS:
The Wasp That Plays Cupid to a Fig. By Robert F. Sisson. 690-697, *Nov. 1970*

The **FIGHT** Against Forest Fires. By Henry S. Graves. 662-683, *July 1912*

The **FIGHT** at the Timber-Line. By John Oliver La Gorce. 165-196, *Aug. 1922*

FIGHT the Flies. 383-385, 452, *May 1910*

FIGHTING Forest Fires. 328-331, *Sept. 1982*

FIGHTING Giants of the Humboldt (Fish and Squid). By David D. Duncan. 373-400, *Mar. 1941*

FIGHTING Insects with Airplanes: An Account of the Successful Use of the Flying-Machine in Dusting Tall Trees

Dressed for the spear dance, a Fiji Island chief of the 1950s enters his thatched, mat-lined house. LUIS MARDEN, NGS

Infested with Leaf-Eating Caterpillars. By C. R. Neillie and J. S. Houser. 333-338, *Mar. 1922*

FIGHTING the Polar Ice (Book Review). 72-77, *Jan. 1907*

FIGS:
The Wasp That Plays Cupid to a Fig. By Robert F. Sisson. 690-697, *Nov. 1970*

FIJI ISLANDS, Pacific Ocean:
A Teen-ager Sails the World Alone. By Robin Lee Graham. 445-491, *Oct. 1968*
The Islands Called Fiji. By Luis Marden. 526-561, *Oct. 1958*
Copra-ship Voyage to Fiji's Outlying Islands. By Marjory C. Thomas. Included: Kava ceremony and the fire walkers of Mbengga. 121-140, *July 1950*
American Pathfinders in the Pacific. By William H. Nicholas. 617-640, *May 1946*
The British Commonwealth of Nations: "Organized Freedom" Around the World. By Eric Underwood. 485-524, *Apr. 1943*
Treasure Islands of Australasia: New Guinea, New Caledonia, and Fiji Trace across the South Pacific a Fertile Crescent Incredibly Rich in Minerals and Foods. By Douglas L. Oliver. 691-722, *June 1942*
Net Results from Oceania: Collecting Aquarium Specimens in Tropical Pacific Waters. By Walter H. Chute. 347-372, *Mar. 1941*
In the Savage South Seas. By Beatrice Grimshaw. 1-19, *Jan. 1908*

FIJI Patrol on Bougainville. By David D. Duncan. 87-104, *Jan. 1945*

FILLMORE, MILLARD:
Profiles of the Presidents: II. A Restless Nation Moves West. By Frank Freidel. 80-121, *Jan. 1965*

FILMS AND FILMSTRIPS, NGS:
Film-strip service planned. 581, Oct. 1967; 583, *Nov. 1975*
More than 50 films are available covering dozens of subjects in the fields of science and social studies. 583, *Nov. 1975*
The World in Geographic Filmstrips. By Melvin M. Payne. 134-137, *Jan. 1968*
See also Television Films, NGS

The **FINAL** Flight (Exploring Taurus-Littrow). By Harrison H. Schmitt. Photos by the crew of Apollo 17. 290-307, *Sept. 1973*

The **FINAL** Tribute (Churchill Funeral). Text by Carolyn Bennett Patterson. 199-225, *Aug. 1965*

FINANCIAL STATISTICS:
Commercial and Financial Statistics of the Principal Countries of the World. 420-423, *June 1907*

FINCHES:
The Galapagos, Eerie Cradle of New Species. By Roger Tory Peterson. Photos by Alan and Joan Root. 541-585, *Apr. 1967*

Prying a grub from a tree on Ecuador's Galápagos Islands, a woodpecker finch makes a tool of a cactus spine. ALAN ROOT

FINLEY, IRENE: *Photographer*

Successful Shots With a Friendly Camera. Photos by H. T. Bohlman, Irene Finley, and William L. Finley. 165-180, *Aug. 1923*

FINLEY, JOHN H.: *Author*

The Red Cross Spirit Speaks (Poem). 474, *May 1917*

FINLEY, WILLIAM L.: *Author-Photographer*

Hunting Birds With a Camera: A Record of Twenty Years of Adventure in Obtaining Photographs of Feathered Wild Life in America. Included: Successful Shots With a Friendly Camera. Photos by author, H. T. Bohlman, and Irene Finley. 161-201, *Aug. 1923*

FINNED Doctors of the Deep (Wrasses). By Douglas Faulkner. 867-873, *Dec. 1965*

FIRE and Ash, Darkness at Noon: El Chichón. By Boris Weintraub. Photos by Guillermo Aldana E. and Kenneth Garrett. 654-684. Included: Volcanic Cloud May Alter Earth's Climate. By Robert I. Tilling. 672-675, *Nov. 1982*

FIRE ANTS:

The Pesticide Dilemma. By Allen A. Boraiko. Photos by Fred Ward. 145-183, *Feb. 1980*

FIRE FIGHTING:

Fighting Forest Fires. 328-331, *Sept. 1982*
Forest Fire: The Devil's Picnic. By Stuart E. Jones and Jay Johnston. 100-127, *July 1968*
The Fight Against Forest Fires. By Henry S. Graves. 662-683, *July 1912*

The **FIRE** of Heaven: Electricity Revolutionizes the Modern World. By Albert W. Atwood. 655-674, *Nov. 1948*

"The **FIRE** That Never Dies." By Harvey Arden. Photos by Steve Wall. 375-403, *Sept. 1987*

FIRE WALKING:

The Islands Called Fiji. By Luis Marden. 526-561, *Oct. 1958*
Copra-ship Voyage to Fiji's Outlying Islands. By Marjory C. Thomas. 121-140, *July 1950*
The Fire-walking Hindus of Singapore. By L. Elizabeth Lewis. 513-522, *Apr. 1931*

FIREBRANDS of the Revolution. By Eric F. Goldman. Photos by George F. Mobley. 2-27, *July 1974*

FIREFLIES:

Nature's Night Lights: Probing the Secrets of Bioluminescence. By Paul A. Zahl. 45-69, *July 1971*
Wing-borne Lamps of the Summer Night. By Paul A. Zahl. 48-59, *July 1962*
Torchbearers of the Twilight. By Frederick G. Vosburgh. 697-704, *May 1951*

FIRST Across the Pacific: The Flight of *Double Eagle V.* By Ben L. Abruzzo. 513-521, *Apr. 1982*

FIRST AID:

The American Red Cross: A Century of Service. By Louise Levathes. Photos by Annie Griffiths. 777-791, *June 1981*

FIRST AIR COMMANDO FORCE, U. S.:

The Aerial Invasion of Burma. By Henry H. Arnold. 129-148, *Aug. 1944*

The **FIRST** Airship Flight Around the World: Hugo Eckener Tells of an Epochal Geographic Achievement upon the Occasion of the Bestowal of the National Geographic Society's Special Gold Medal. 653-688, *June 1930*

The **FIRST** Alaskan Air Expedition. By St. Clair Streett. 499-552, *May 1922*

FIRST American Ascent of Mount St. Elias. By Maynard M. Miller. 229-248, *Feb. 1948*

The **FIRST** American Census of Porto Rico. 328, *Aug. 1900*

A **FIRST** American Views His Land. By N. Scott Momaday. 13-19, *July 1976*

The **FIRST** Americans. By Thomas Y. Canby. Photos by Kerby Smith. Paintings by Roy Andersen. 330-363, *Sept. 1979*

The **FIRST** Australians. By Stanley Breeden. Photos by Belinda Wright. 266-289, *Feb. 1988*

The **FIRST** Autochromes from the Ocean Bottom: Marine Life in Its Natural Habitat Along the Florida Keys Is Successfully Photographed in Colors. Photographs by William H. Longley and Charles Martin. 56-60, *Jan. 1927*

1ST BATTALION, Fiji Infantry Regiment:

Fiji Patrol on Bougainville. By David D. Duncan. 87-104, *Jan. 1945*

FIRST Colony in Space. By Isaac Asimov. Paintings by Pierre Mion. 76-89, *July 1976*

FIRST Color Photographs on the Moon's Rocky Face. By Homer E. Newell. 578-592, *Oct. 1966*

FIRST Color Portraits of the Heavens. By William C. Miller. 670-679, *May 1959*

FIRST Color Record of the Life Cycle of a Coral. By Robert F. Sisson. 780-793, *June 1973*

FIRST Conquest of Antarctica's Highest Peaks. By Nicholas B. Clinch. 836-863, *June 1967*

FIRST Crossings of the Ends of the Earth. The Editor. 1, *Jan. 1959*

The **FIRST** Emperor's Army: China's Incredible Find. By Audrey Topping. Paintings by Yang Hsien-min. 440-459, *Apr. 1978*

FIRST Expedition of National Geographic Society: Mount St. Elias Expedition, under the leadership of Israel C. Russell. 288, *Apr. 1891*; 39-40, *Apr. 30, 1891*; vii-ix, *Feb. 20, 1893*; 177, *Jan. 31, 1894*

FIRST Explorers on the Moon: The Incredible Story of Apollo 11. 735-797, *Dec. 1969*

FIRST Families of Southeastern America (Indians). Paintings by W. Langdon Kihn. 65-72, *Jan. 1946*

This 1927 Autochrome of a porgy was one of the first published natural-color photographs made beneath the surface of the sea. CHARLES MARTIN, NGS

A pioneer in the exploration of the sea, French oceanographer Jacques-Yves Cousteau eyes a school of fish in the depths of the Indian Ocean. LUIS MARDEN, NGS

FISHER, ANGELA:

FISHER, CLYDE: *Author*

FISHER, FRANKLIN L.:

FISHER, MELVIN A.:

Captive Atlantic salmon in Eastport, Maine, surface for a meal of fish pellets. Nets protect them from attack by swimming or airborne predators. KEVIN FLEMING

FISHER, RON: *Author*

FISHER, WALTER L.:

FISHER TOWERS, Utah:

FISHERIES:

FISHERMEN:

An 18th-century block print by Kitagawa Utamaro depicts ama, *Japan's diving fisherwomen.* MUSEUM OF FINE ARTS, BOSTON

FISHERWOMEN:

FISHES:

A vicious-looking saber-toothed viperfish from the depths of the Mediterranean bares fearsome fangs. PAUL A. ZAHL, NGS

Twenty walleyes, frozen solid, kiss the snow of Mille Lacs, Minnesota. Weighing as much as seven pounds each, they were one family's weekend catch. THOMAS J. ABERCROMBIE, NGS

FISHING (Industry):

A giant Atlantic bluefin tuna falls prey to a killer whale, one of the few creatures this prodigious swimmer cannot outdistance. PAINTING BY STANLEY MELTZOFF

Golden Beaches of Portugal. By Alan Villiers. 673-696, *Nov. 1954*

Gloucester Blesses Its Portuguese Fleet. By Luis Marden. 75-84, *July 1953*

Down East Cruise. By Tom Horgan. Photos by Luis Marden. 329-369, *Sept. 1952*

I Sailed with Portugal's Captains Courageous. By Alan Villiers. 565-596, *May 1952*

"Delmarva," Gift of the Sea. By Catherine Bell Palmer. 367-399, *Sept. 1950*

Trawling the China Seas. Photos by J. Charles Thompson. 381-395, *Mar. 1950*

Menhaden–Uncle Sam's Top Commercial Fish. By Leonard C. Roy. Photos by Robert F. Sisson. 813-823, *June 1949*

Shad in the Shadow of Skyscrapers. By Dudley B. Martin. Photos by Luis Marden. 359-376, *Mar. 1947*

Oregon Finds New Riches. By Leo A. Borah. 681-728, *Dec. 1946*

The Maine American and the American Lobster. By John D. Lucas. 523-543, *Apr. 1946*

Newfoundland, North Atlantic Rampart: From the "First Base of American Defense" Planes Fly to Britain's Aid over Stout Fishing Schooners of the Grand Banks. By George Whiteley, Jr. 111-140, *July 1941*

The Tuna Harvest of the Sea: A Little-known Epic of the Ocean Is the Story of Southern California's Far-ranging Tuna Fleet. By John Degelman. 393-408, *Sept. 1940*

Caviar Fishermen of Romania: From Vâlcov, "Little Venice" of the Danube Delta, Bearded Russian Exiles Go Down to the Sea. By Dorothy Hosmer. 407-434, *Mar. 1940*

Fishing in Pacific Coast Streams. By Leonard P. Schultz. Paintings by Hashime Murayama. 185-212, *Feb. 1939*

Treasures of the Pacific: Marine Fishes and Fisheries Yield Vast Wealth from Alaska to Baja California. By Leonard P. Schultz. Paintings by Hashime Murayama. 463-498, *Oct. 1938*

Where Bretons Wrest a Living from the Sea. Photos by F. W. Goro. 751-766, *June 1937*

When the Herring Fleet Comes to Great Yarmouth. By W. Robert Moore. 233-250, *Aug. 1934*

Between the Heather and the North Sea: Bold English Headlands Once Sheltered Sea Robbers, Later Were Ports of Wooden Ships, To-day Are Havens of Adventurous Fishing Fleets. By Leo Walmsley. 197-232, *Feb. 1933*

Shark Fishing–An Australian Industry. By Norman Ellison. 369-386, *Sept. 1932*

Viking Life in the Storm-Cursed Faeroes. By Leo Hansen. 607-648, *Nov. 1930*

Goldfish and Their Cultivation in America. By Hugh M. Smith. Paintings by Hashime Murayama. 375-400, *Oct. 1924*

Fishes and Fisheries of Our North Atlantic Seaboard. By John Oliver La

Gorce. Paintings by Hashime Murayama. 567-634, *Dec. 1923*

Life on the Grand Banks: An Account of the Sailor-Fishermen Who Harvest the Shoal Waters of North America's Eastern Coasts. By Frederick William Wallace. 1-28, *July 1921*

America's Surpassing Fisheries: Their Present Condition and Future Prospects, and How the Federal Government Fosters Them. By Hugh M. Smith. 546-583, *June 1916*

Europe's Endangered Fish Supply: The War and the North Sea Fisheries. 141-152, *Feb. 1915*

Federal Fish Farming; or, Planting Fish by the Billion. By Hugh M. Smith. 418-446, *May 1910*

King Herring: An Account of the World's Most Valuable Fish, the Industries It Supports, and the Part It Has Played in History. By Hugh M. Smith. 701-735, *Aug. 1909*

Helping the Filipino Fisheries. 795-796, *Dec. 1907*

Planting Fishes in the Ocean. By George M. Bowers. 715-723, *Nov. 1907*

Cultivation of Marine and Fresh-Water Animals in Japan. By K. Mitsukuri. 524-531, *Sept. 1906*

Restocking Our Rivers and Waters with Fish. 424-425, *July 1906*

The Fisheries of Japan (Part II). By Hugh M. Smith. 201-220, *May 1905*

The Fisheries of Japan (Part I). By Hugh M. Smith. 362-364, *Sept. 1904*

The Bureau of Fisheries. By Barton Warren Evermann. 191-212, *May 1904*

See also Cod Fishing; Herring; Salmon; Tuna; *and* Shellfish Industry

FISHING (Sport):

Ice Fishing's Frigid Charms. By Thomas J. Abercrombie. 861-872, *Dec. 1958*

Goggle Fishing in California Waters. By David Hellyer. Photos by Lamar Boren. 615-632, *May 1949*

The Worm Turns. By Samuel Sandrof. Included: Worms for bait. 775-786, *June 1946*

Cruise of the *Kinkajou:* Among Desert Islands of Mexico Voyagers Find Outdoor Laboratories for the Naturalist and Ideal Fishing Grounds for the Sportsman (Fishing for Marlin and Wahoo). By Alfred M. Bailey. 339-366, *Sept. 1941*

Fishing in Pacific Coast Streams. By Leonard P. Schultz. Paintings by Hashime Murayama. 185-212, *Feb. 1939*

Devil-Fishing in the Gulf Stream. By John Oliver La Gorce. 476-488, *June 1919*

Fishing and Hunting Tales from Brazil. By Dewey Austin Cobb. 917-920, *Oct. 1909*

See also Game Fishes

FISHING, Night (Marine Biology Studies):

Night Life in the Gulf Stream. By Paul A. Zahl. 391-418, *Mar. 1954*

FISHING and Hunting Tales from Brazil. By Dewey Austin Cobb. 917-920, *Oct. 1909*

FISHING for Pearls in the Indian Ocean. By Bella Sidney Woolf. 161-183, *Feb. 1926*

FISHING in Pacific Coast Streams. By Leonard P. Schultz. Paintings by Hashime Murayama. 185-212, *Feb. 1939*

FISHING in the Lofotens. Photos by Lennart Nilsson. 377-388, *Mar. 1947*

FISHING in the Whirlpool of Charybdis. By Paul A. Zahl. 579-618, *Nov. 1953*

FISHING VESSELS. *See* Fishing (Industry)

FISSURE LAKE, Alaska:

The Valley of Ten Thousand Smokes: An Account of the Discovery and Exploration of the Most Wonderful Volcanic Region in the World. By Robert F. Griggs. 115-169, *Feb. 1918*

FIT to Fight Anywhere (Army Quartermaster Tests). By Frederick Simpich. 233-256, *Aug. 1943*

FITA-FITAS (Samoan Soldiers):

America's South Sea Soldiers. By Lorena MacIntyre Quinn. 267-274, *Sept. 1919*

FITCH, C. H.: *Author*

The Five Civilized Tribes and the Survey of Indian Territory. 481-491, *Dec. 1898*

FITCH, CLYDE:

Literary Landmarks of Massachusetts. By William H. Nicholas. Photos by B. Anthony Stewart and John E. Fletcher. 279-310, *Mar. 1950*

FITCH, ROBERT F.: *Author-Photographer*

Puto, the Enchanted Island. 373-384, *Mar. 1946*

Life Afloat in China: Tens of Thousands of Chinese in Congested Ports Spend Their Entire Existence on Boats. 665-686, *June 1927*

Photographer

China. 377-389, *Nov. 1920*

FITZ ROY, ROBERT:

In the Wake of Darwin's *Beagle*. By Alan Villiers. Photos by James L. Stanfield. 449-495, *Oct. 1969*

FITZHUGH, WILLIAM W.: *Author*

Where Magic Ruled: Art of the Bering Sea. By William W. Fitzhugh and Susan A. Kaplan. Photos by Sisse Brimberg. 198-205, *Feb. 1983*

The **FIVE** Civilized Tribes and the Survey of Indian Territory. By C. H. Fitch. 481-491, *Dec. 1898*

FIVE NATIONS CONFEDERACY:

"The Fire That Never Dies." By Harvey Arden. Photos by Steve Wall. 375-403, *Sept. 1987*

FIVE Noted Thinkers Explore the Future. 68-75, *July 1976*

The **FIVE** Thousand Temples of Pagän: Burma's Sacred City Is a Place of Enchantment in the Midst of Ruins. By William H. Roberts. 445-454, *Oct. 1931*

The 1915-1920 Society expeditions to Alaska's Valley of Ten Thousand Smokes named many features, such as Fissure Lake. R. F. GRIGGS

Freeing Flamingos From Anklets of Death. By John G. Williams. Photos by Alan Root. 934-944, *Dec. 1963*

In Quest of the Rarest Flamingo (James's Flamingo). By William G. Conway. Photos by Bates Littlehales. 91-105, *July 1961*

Ballerinas in Pink. By Carleton Mitchell. Photos by B. Anthony Stewart. 553-571, *Oct. 1957*

Flamingos' Last Stand on Andros Island. By Paul A. Zahl. 635-652, *May 1951*

Flame-Feathered Flamingos of Florida. By W. A. Watts. Photos by W. F. Gerecke. 56-65, *Jan. 1941*

The Large Wading Birds: Long Legs and Remarkable Beaks, as Well as Size, Form, and Color, Distinguish the Herons, Ibises, and Flamingos. By T. Gilbert Pearson. Paintings by Allan Brooks. 441-469, *Oct. 1932*

Camps and Cruises of an Ornithologist. By George Shiras, 3d. 438-463, *May 1909*

The Story of the Flamingo. 50, *Jan. 1905*

The Remarkable Photograph of Flamingo Nests. 83, *Feb. 1904*

FLANDERS (Region), Belgium:

Belgium: One Nation Divisible. By James Cerruti. Photos by Martin Rogers. 314-341, *Mar. 1979*

FLANDRIN, M.: *Photographer*

Modern Life in Morocco, Western Outpost of Islam. 679-694, *June 1935*

FLASHES from Finland. 239-254, *Feb. 1940*

FLASHES from Ocean Deeps. Paintings by Else Bostelmann and Helen D. Tee-Van. 677-684, *Dec. 1934*

FLASHES of Color in the Fifth Continent (Australia). Photos by W. Robert Moore. 681-704, *Dec. 1935*

FLASHES of Color Throughout France. Photos by Gervais Courtellemont. 529-544, *Nov. 1924*

FLASHING Fashions of Old Spain. Photos by J. Ortiz Echagüe. 413-428, *Mar. 1936*

FLASHLIGHT Fish of the Red Sea. By Eugenie Clark. Photos by David Doubilet. 719-728, *Nov. 1978*

A **FLASHLIGHT** Photo by George Shiras, 3d, of a Doe and Her Twin Fawns Feeding on a Lake in Northern Michigan. Photo supplement, *July 1913*

A **FLASHLIGHT** Story of an Albino Porcupine and of a Cunning but Unfortunate Coon. By George Shiras, 3d. 572-596, *June 1911*

FLASHLIGHTS from the Jungle. 534-548, *Aug. 1907*

FLAT TOP COALFIELD, West Virginia:

Mountain Voices, Mountain Days. By Bryan Hodgson. Photos by Linda Bartlett. 118-146, *July 1972*

FLATHEAD (River), Canada-U. S.:

Our Wild and Scenic Rivers: The Flathead. By Douglas H. Chadwick. Photos by Lowell Georgia. 13-19, *July 1977*

FLAVOR and Savor of American Foods. Photos by J. Baylor Roberts, Willard R. Culver, and others. 289-320, *Mar. 1942*

FLEA MARKET, Paris, France:

Paris Flea Market. By Franc Shor. Photos by Alexander Taylor. 318-326, *Mar. 1957*

FLEAS:

The Lethal Leapers. By Nicole Duplaix. 672-694, *May 1988*

FLEAY, DAVID: *Author*

Strange Animals of Australia. Photos by Stanley Breeden. 388-411, *Sept. 1963*

Author-Photographer

Flight of the Platypuses. 512-525, *Oct. 1958*

FLECKS of Color in the Fertile Fields of Louisiana. Photos by Edwin L. Wisherd. 419-426, *Apr. 1930*

FLEDGLING Wings of the Air Force. By Thomas W. McKnew. 266-271, *Aug. 1957*

FLEISCHMAN, MAX: *Author*

Seventy-Five Days in the Arctics. 439-446, *July 1907*

FLEMING, SIR ALEXANDER:

The British Way. By Sir Evelyn Wrench. 421-541, *Apr. 1949*

FLEMING, KEVIN:

On Assignment in Annapolis, Maryland. *Aug. 1988*

On Assignment in Egypt. *Apr. 1982*

Photographer

Annapolis: Camelot on the Bay. By Larry Kohl. 162-189, *Aug. 1988*

The Hudson's Bay Company: Canada's Fur-Trading Empire. By Peter C. Newman. 192-229, *Aug. 1987*

New Zealand: the Last Utopia? By Robert Paul Jordan. 654-681, *May 1987*

The Quest for Ulysses. By Tim Severin. 197-225, *Aug. 1986*

Worlds Within the Atom. By John Boslough. Illustrations text by David Jeffery. Paintings by Barron Storey. 634-663, *May 1985*

Maine's Working Coast. By David Jeffery. 208-241, *Feb. 1985*

Delaware—Who Needs to Be Big? By Jane Vessels. 171-197, *Aug. 1983*

Florida—A Time for Reckoning. By William S. Ellis. Photos by Nathan Benn and Kevin Fleming. 172-219, *Aug. 1982*

Eternal Sinai. By Harvey Arden. 420-461. Included: Egyptian Sector. Photos by Kevin Fleming. 430-443; Israeli Sector. Photos by David Doubilet. 444-461, *Apr. 1982*

Somalia's Hour of Need. By Robert Paul Jordan. Photos by Michael S. Yamashita and Kevin Fleming. 748-775, *June 1981*

FLEMING, ROBERT V.:

Memorial tribute: Robert V. Fleming, 1890-1967. By Melville Bell Grosvenor. 526-529, *Apr. 1968*

Vice President of NGS. 882, 883, Dec. 1960; 585, Oct. 1963; 672, May 1964; 589, *Oct. 1967*

Treasurer of NGS. 260, 261, Aug. 1949; 64, 65A-65B, 65D, July 1954; 419, 420, 421, 423, *Mar. 1957*

NGS Board of Trustees member. 159, Jan. 1936; 706, May 1953; 81, *Jan. 1957*

Presentation of Hubbard Medal by President Truman to H. H. Arnold. 141, *Feb. 1946*

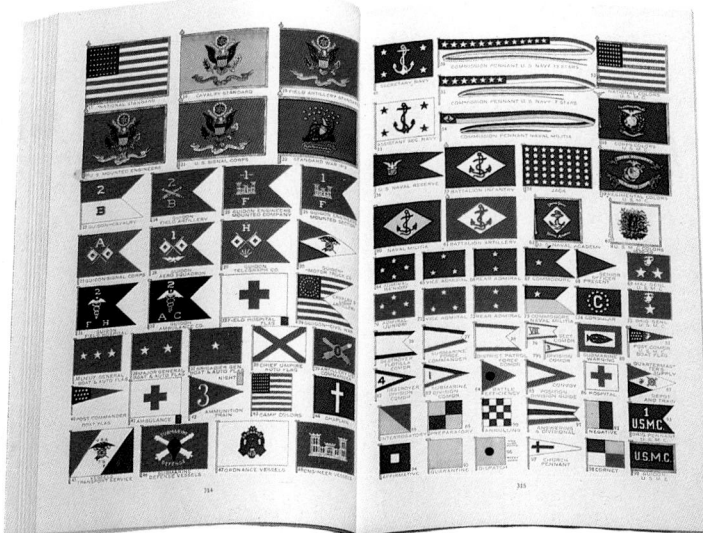

Amid patriotic fervor in 1917, the GEOGRAPHIC *presented a "Flags of the World" October issue with some 1,500 flags and insignia.*

FLEMINGS:

Belgium: One Nation Divisible. By James Cerruti. Photos by Martin Rogers. 314-341, *Mar. 1979*

FLETCHER, JOHN E.:

Nomination Page. In Peru. *June 1962*

Author-Photographer

Graduation by Parachute (Parachute Rigger School). 833-846, *June 1952*

Photographer

Aboard the N. S. *Savannah:* World's First Nuclear Merchantman. By Alan Villiers. 280-298, *Aug. 1962*

Avalanche! (Peru). By Bart McDowell. 855-880, *June 1962*

The United Nations: Capital of the Family of Man. By Adlai E. Stevenson. Photos by B. Anthony Stewart and John E. Fletcher. 297-303, *Sept. 1961*

Date Line: United Nations, New York. By Carolyn Bennett Patterson. Photos by B. Anthony Stewart and John E. Fletcher. 305-331, *Sept. 1961*

Mardi Gras in New Orleans. By Carolyn Bennett Patterson. Photos by Robert F. Sisson and John E. Fletcher. 726-732, *Nov. 1960*

All-out Assault on Antarctica. By Richard E. Byrd. 141-180, *Aug. 1956*

Minutemen of the Civil Air Patrol. By Allan C. Fisher, Jr. 637-665, *May 1956*

Men Who Measure the Earth. By Robert Leslie Conly. 335-362, *Mar. 1956*

Weather From the White North. By Andrew H. Brown. 543-572, *Apr. 1955*

America Goes to the Fair. By Samuel W. Matthews. 293-333, *Sept. 1954*

Mount Vernon Lives On. By Lonnelle Aikman. 651-682, *Nov. 1953*

Beltsville Brings Science to the Farm. By Samuel W. Matthews. 199-218, *Aug. 1953*

Stately Homes of Old Virginia. By Albert W. Atwood. 787-802, *June 1953*

Washington's Historic Georgetown. By William A. Kinney. 513-544, *Apr. 1953*

Hays, Kansas, at the Nation's Heart. By Margaret M. Detwiler. 461-490, *Apr. 1952*

The DAR Story. By Lonnelle Aikman. Photos by B. Anthony Stewart and John E. Fletcher. 565-598, *Nov. 1951*

Folger: Biggest Little Library in the World. By Joseph T. Foster. Photos by B. Anthony Stewart and John E. Fletcher. 411-424, *Sept. 1951*

Dog Mart Day in Fredericksburg. By Frederick G. Vosburgh. 817-832, *June 1951*

The Merrimack: River of Industry and Romance. By Albert W. Atwood. 106-140, *Jan. 1951*

Sea to Lakes on the St. Lawrence. By George W. Long. Photos by B. Anthony Stewart and John E. Fletcher. 323-366, *Sept. 1950*

"Delmarva," Gift of the Sea. By Catherine Bell Palmer. 367-399, *Sept. 1950*

Literary Landmarks of Massachusetts. By William H. Nicholas. Photos by B. Anthony Stewart and John E. Fletcher. 279-310, *Mar. 1950*

Sno-Cats Mechanize Oregon Snow Survey. By Andrew H. Brown. 691-710, *Nov. 1949*

Quebec's Forests, Farms, and Frontiers. By Andrew H. Brown. 431-470, *Oct. 1949*

Minnesota Makes Ideas Pay. By Frederick G. Vosburgh. Photos by John E. Fletcher and B. Anthony Stewart. 291-336, *Sept. 1949*

Pittsburgh: Workshop of the Titans. By Albert W. Atwood. 117-144, *July 1949*

Exploring Ottawa. By Bruce Hutchison. 565-596, *Nov. 1947*

Exploring America's Great Sand Barrier Reef. By Eugene R. Guild. Photos by John E. Fletcher and author. 325-350, *Sept. 1947*

Hillside houses overlook smoke-belching steel mills in Pittsburgh, Pennsylvania, in 1949. JOHN E. FLETCHER AND B. ANTHONY STEWART, BOTH NGS

Across the water from Venice's church of San Giorgio Maggiore, a makeshift walkway carries pedestrians along the flooded banks of the San Marco Canal. ALBERT MOLDVAY

FLORAL EMBLEMS:

Octogenarian Al Kuster pitches in a softball game limited to men 74 and older in St. Petersburg, Florida. KEVIN FLEMING

FLUORESCENT Gems From Davy Jones's Locker. By Paul A. Zahl. 260-271, *Aug. 1963*

FLY of the Deadly Sleep. By Georg Gerster. 814-833, *Dec. 1986*

FLYCATCHERS (Birds):

Birds on the Home Front. By Arthur A. Allen. 32-56, *July 1943*

Parrots, Kingfishers, and Flycatchers: Strange Trogons and Curious Cuckoos are Pictured with these Other Birds of Color, Dash, and Courage. By Alexander Wetmore. Paintings by Allan Brooks. Included: Flycatchers and Other Friends in Feathers. 801-828, *June 1936*

FLYING. By Gilbert Grosvenor. 585-630, *May 1933*

FLYING Around the Baltic. By Douglas Chandler. 767-806, *June 1938*

FLYING Around the North Atlantic. By Anne Morrow Lindbergh. Foreword by Charles A. Lindbergh. 259-337, *Sept. 1934*

Half-hidden by a profusion of blooms, a flower seller plies his trade on the Avenida de las Delicias in Santiago, Chile, in 1921. © PUBLISHERS' PHOTO SERVICE

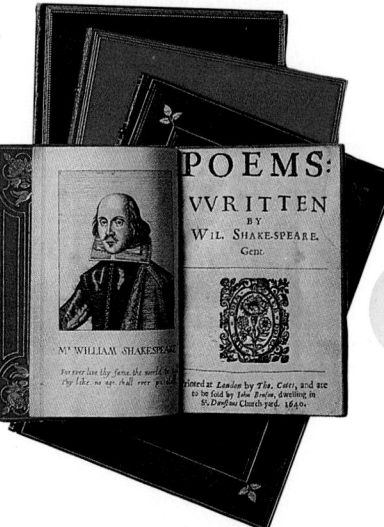

The Folger Shakespeare Library contains this 1640 volume padded with many poems not penned by the Bard. NATHAN BENN

Lacquer artist Gonroku Matsuda, a living treasure in Japan, decorates a tray with conch shells. JAMES L. STANFIELD, NGS

FORAGING. *See* Wild Foods

FORAN, W. ROBERT: *Author*

Tristan da Cunha, Isles of Contentment: On Lonely Sea Spots of Pirate Lore and Shipwrecks Seven Families Live Happily Far from War Rumors and World Changes. 671-694, *Nov. 1938*

FORBES, EDGAR ALLEN: *Author*

Macao, "Land of Sweet Sadness": The Oldest European Settlement in the Far East, Long the Only Haven for Distressed Mariners in the China Sea. 337-357, *Sept. 1932*

Author-Photographer

Notes on the Only American Colony in the World (Liberia). 719-729, *Sept. 1910*

FORBES-LEITH, F.A.C.: *Author*

From England to India by Automobile: An 8,527-mile Trip Through Ten Countries, from London to Quetta, Requires Five and a Half Months. 191-223, *Aug. 1925*

FORBUSH, ERNEST HOWE: *Author*

The Unique Island of Mount Desert. By George B. Dorr, Ernest Howe Forbush, and M. L. Fernald. 75-89, *July 1914*

FORD, HENRY, MUSEUM, Dearborn, Michigan:

The Past Is Present in Greenfield Village. By Beverley M. Bowie. Photos by Neal P. Davis and Willard R. Culver. 96-127, *July 1958*

FORD, JOHN K. B. and DEBORAH:

The Whales Called "Killer." By Erich Hoyt. 220-237, *Aug. 1984*

Authors

Narwhal: Unicorn of the Arctic Seas. Photos by Flip Nicklin. 354-363, *Mar. 1986*

FORD, MILTON A.:

Nomination Page. *Aug. 1966*

Photographer

900 Years Ago: The Norman Conquest. By Kenneth M. Setton. Photos by George F. Mobley. The complete Bayeux Tapestry photographed by Milton A. Ford and Victor R. Boswell, Jr. 206-251, *Aug. 1966*

FORD, RICHARD: *Author*

Seville, More Spanish Than Spain: The City of the Ibero-American Exposition, Which Opens This Spring, Presents a Tapestry of Many Ages and of Nations Old and New. 273-310, *Mar. 1929*

FORDER, ARCHIBALD:

Author-Photographer

Damascus, the Pearl of the Desert. 62-82, *Jan. 1911*

Arabia, the Desert of the Sea. 1039-1062, 1117, *Dec. 1909*

FORD'S THEATRE Reborn in Memory of Lincoln. By Lonnelle Aikman. 392-401, *Mar. 1970*

FORECASTING the Weather. By Alfred J. Henry. 285-292, *July 1904*

FORECASTING the Weather and Storms. By Willis L. Moore. 255-305, *June 1905*

The **FOREIGN-BORN** of the United States. 265-271, *Sept. 1914*

FOREIGN Commerce of the United States in 1903. 359-360, *Sept. 1903*

FOREIGNERS and Foreign Firms in China. 330, *Aug. 1900*

The **FOREMOST** Intellectual Achievement of Ancient America: The Hieroglyphic Inscriptions on the Monuments in the Ruined Cities of Mexico, Guatemala, and Honduras Are Yielding the Secrets of the Maya Civilization. By Sylvanus Griswold Morley. 109-130, *Feb. 1922*

FORERUNNERS of Famine. By Frederic C. Walcott. 336-347, *Apr. 1918*

FOREST DWELLERS. *See* Cinta Larga Indians; Erigbaagtsa Indians; Kreen-Akarore; Tasadays; Tukuna Indians; Txukahamei; Wayana Indians

FOREST FIRES:

Fighting Forest Fires. 328-331, *Sept. 1982*

Forest Fire: The Devil's Picnic. By Stuart E. Jones and Jay Johnston. 100-127, *July 1968*

The Fight Against Forest Fires. By Henry S. Graves. 662-683, *July 1912*

Protecting Our Forests from Fire. By James Wilson. 98-106, *Jan. 1911*

"Forest Fires in the Adirondacks in 1903." By H. M. Suter. 224, *May 1904*

The Relation of Forests and Forest Fires. By Gifford Pinchot. 393-403, *Oct. 1899*

FOREST PRODUCTS:

Tropical Rain Forests: Nature's Dwindling Treasures. By Peter T. White.

Hunger crowds a girl awaiting relief food in Bangladesh, a nation beset by floods and famine. STEVE RAYMER, NGS

Photos by James P. Blair. Paintings by Barron Storey. 2-47, *Jan. 1983*

Brazil's Wild Frontier. By Loren McIntyre. 684-719, *Nov. 1977*

See also Lumber Industry; Paper Pulp Industry

FOREST SERVICE, U. S. Department of Agriculture:

Battle For a Bigger Bob. By Mike Edwards. Photos by Dewitt Jones. 690-692, *May 1985*

A Short Hike With Bob Marshall. By Mike Edwards. Photos by Dewitt Jones. 664-689, *May 1985*

Our National Forests: Problems in Paradise. By Rowe Findley. Photos by David Cupp. 306-339, *Sept. 1982*

Timber: How Much Is Enough? By John J. Putman. Photos by Bruce Dale. 485-511, *Apr. 1974*

Mexico to Canada on the Pacific Crest Trail. By Mike W. Edwards. Photos by David Hiser. 741-779, *June 1971*

Forest Fire: The Devil's Picnic. By Stuart E. Jones and Jay Johnston. Included: Northern regional headquarters, Missoula, Montana; Smokejumper Center; Northern Forest Fire Laboratory. 100-127, *July 1968*

Washington Wilderness, the North Cascades. By Edwards Park. Photos by Kathleen Revis. 335-367, *Mar. 1961*

Our Green Treasury, the National Forests. By Nathaniel T. Kenney. Photos by J. Baylor Roberts. 287-324, *Sept. 1956*

Notes on the Eucalyptus Tree from the United States Forest Service. 668-673, *July 1909*

The Value of the United States Forest Service. 29-41, *Jan. 1909*

Saving the Forests. By Herbert A. Smith. 519-534, *Aug. 1907*

Notes on the Forest Service. 142-145, *Feb. 1907*

Two Great Undertakings (Work of U. S. Bureau of Reclamation and U. S. Forest Service). 645-647, *Nov. 1906*

Government Assistance in Handling Forest Lands. 450-452, *Nov. 1904*

FORESTS:

Citizens Band Together to Save Their Environment. Geographica. *Nov. 1988*

▓ *Living on the Earth.* Contents: How various peoples have adapted to the world's environments. 320 pages. *1988*

▓ *Our Awesome Earth: Its Mysteries and Its Splendors.* 199 pages. *1986*

Battle For a Bigger Bob (Bob Marshall Wilderness). By Mike Edwards. Photos by Dewitt Jones. 690-692, *May 1985*

A Short Hike With Bob Marshall. By Mike Edwards. Photos by Dewitt Jones. 664-689, *May 1985*

▓ *America's Wild Woodlands.* 199 pages. *1985*

Editorial. By Wilbur E. Garrett. 279, *Sept. 1982*

Our National Forests: Problems in Paradise. By Rowe Findley. Photos by David Cupp. 306-339, *Sept. 1982*

Cut to car size, one-half of a California redwood rolls to the mill in 1907. U.S. FOREST SERVICE

Flames in Oregon's Deschutes National Forest blaze behind Kim McKillop, member of a crack crew trained to fight forest fires under the most dangerous conditions. CHRIS JOHNS

FORTY Years Among the Arabs. By John Van Ess. 385-420, *Sept. 1942*

FOSFORESCÉNTE, Bahía, Puerto Rico. *See* Phosphorescent Bay

FOSHAG, WILLIAM F.:

Paricutín, the Cornfield That Grew a Volcano (Mexico). By James A. Green. 129-164, *Feb. 1944*

Author

Exploring the World of Gems. 779-810, *Dec. 1950*

FOSSEY, DIAN:

President's Page. By Gilbert M. Grosvenor. *May 1986*

▪ Gorilla. 703, Dec. 1980; cover, *Apr. 1981*

▪ Search for the Great Apes. cover, *Jan. 1976*

Nomination Page. *Oct. 1971*

Author

The Imperiled Mountain Gorilla. Included: Death of Marchessa. Photos by Peter G. Veit. 508-511. 501-523, *Apr. 1981*

More Years With Mountain Gorillas. Photos by Robert M. Campbell. 574-585, *Oct. 1971*

Making Friends With Mountain Gorillas. Photos by Robert M. Campbell. 48-67, *Jan. 1970*

FOSSIL FUELS. *See* Coal; Natural Gas; Oil

FOSSILS:

Uncovering the Bones in a Mammoth Graveyard. Geographica. *Dec. 1988*

School Field Trip Yields Prehistoric Bone. Geographica. *Nov. 1988*

Queensland, Broad Shoulder of Australia. By William S. Ellis. Photos by David Robert Austen. Included: Queensland Fossils Expand Australia's Prehistoric Menagerie. 2-39, *Jan. 1986*

The Search for Our Ancestors. By Kenneth F. Weaver. Photos by David L. Brill. Paintings by Jay H. Matternes. 560-623, *Nov. 1985*

Homo Erectus Unearthed: A Fossil Skeleton 1,600,000 Years Old. By Richard Leakey and Alan Walker. Photos by David L. Brill. NGS research grant. 624-629, *Nov. 1985*

Fossils: Annals of Life Written in Rock. Photos by James L. Amos. Text by David Jeffery. 182-191, *Aug. 1985*

South Dakota's Badlands: Castles in Clay. By John Madson. Photos by Jim Brandenburg. Included: Oligocene mammal fossils; Fossilized turtles. 524-539, *Apr. 1981*

Ancient Ashfall Creates a Pompeii of Prehistoric Animals. By Michael R. Voorhies. Photos by Annie Griffiths. Paintings by Jay Matternes. NGS research grant. 66-75, *Jan. 1981*

The Search for the First Americans. By Thomas Y. Canby. Photos by Kerby Smith. Paintings by Roy Andersen. 330-363, *Sept. 1979*

Footprints in the Ashes of Time. By Mary D. Leakey. NGS research grant. 446-457, *Apr. 1979*

Bison Kill By Ice Age Hunters. By Dennis Stanford. NGS research grant. 114-121, *Jan. 1979*

A New Look at Dinosaurs. By John H. Ostrom. Paintings by Roy Andersen. NGS research grant. 152-185, *Aug. 1978*

Amber: Golden Window on the Past. Photos by Paul A. Zahl. Text by Thomas J. O'Neill. 423-435, *Sept. 1977*

In the Wake of Darwin's *Beagle*. By Alan Villiers. Photos by James L. Stanfield. Included: Extinct mammal fossils: mastodon, machcrauchenia, megatherium, mylodon, toxodon. 449-495, *Oct. 1969*

Fossils Lift the Veil of Time. By Harry S. Ladd and Roland W. Brown. 363-386, *Mar. 1956*

"Compleat Angler" Fishes for Fossils. By Imogene Powell. 251-258, *Aug. 1934*

Hunting Big Game of Other Days: A Boating Expedition in Search of Fossils in Alberta, Canada. By Barnum Brown. 407-429, *May 1919*

The Wyoming Fossil Fields Expedition of July, 1899. By Wilbur C. Knight. 449-465, *Dec. 1900*

Report on Fossil Plants (Mount St. Elias Expedition). By Lester F. Ward. 199-200, *May 29, 1891*

See also Paleontology

FOSTER, BRISTOL: *Author*

Africa's Gentle Giants (Giraffes). Photos by Bob Campbell and Thomas Nebbia. 402-417, *Sept. 1977*

FOSTER, JOHN W.: *Author*

Present Conditions in China. 651-672, 709-711, *Dec. 1906*

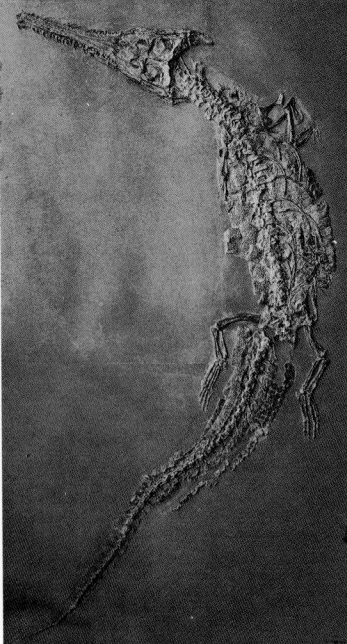

Fossil of a crocodile ancestor, a 13-foot-long **Mystriosaurus bollensis** *was preserved in a Bavarian quarry.* VON HAUFF

China. 463-478, *Dec. 1904*

The Alaskan Boundary Tribunal. 1-12, *Jan. 1904*

The Canadian Boundary. 85-90, *Mar. 1903*

The New Mexico. 1-24, *Jan. 1902*

The Latin-American Constitutions and Revolutions. 169-175, *May 1901*

The Alaskan Boundary. 425-456, *Nov. 1899*

FOSTER, JOSEPH T.: *Author*

Folger: Biggest Little Library in the World. Photos by B. Anthony Stewart and John E. Fletcher. 411-424, *Sept. 1951*

FOSTER, MULFORD B.:

Author-Photographer

Puya, the Pineapple's Andean Ancestor. 463-480, *Oct. 1950*

FOUM TATAHOUINE, Tunisia:

The Mole Men: An Account of the Troglodytes of Southern Tunisia. By Frank Edward Johnson. 787-846, *Sept. 1911*

FOUND–a Lost Virginia Settlement (Martin's Hundred). By Ivor Noël Hume. Photos by Ira Block. Paintings by Richard Schlecht. 735-767, *June 1979*

FOUND at Last: the Monarch's Winter Home. By Fred A. Urquhart. Photos by Bianca Lavies. NGS research grant. 161-173, *Aug. 1976*

FOUNDERS of New England. By Sir Evelyn Wrench. Photos by B. Anthony Stewart. 803-838, *June 1953*

FOUNDERS of Virginia. By Sir Evelyn Wrench. Photos by B. Anthony Stewart. 433-462, *Apr. 1948*

FOUNTAIN of Fire in Hawaii. By Frederick Simpich, Jr. Photos by Robert B. Goodman and Robert Wenkam. 303-327, *Mar. 1960*

4-H CLUBS:

Down on the Farm, Soviet Style–a 4-H Adventure. By John Garaventa. Photos by James Tobin and Carol Schmidt. 768-797, *June 1979*

America Goes to the Fair. By Samuel W. Matthews. 293-333, *Sept. 1954*

4-H Boys and Girls Grow More Food. By Frederick Simpich. 551-582, *Nov. 1948*

FOUR CORNERS COUNTRY (Arizona-Colorado-New Mexico-Utah):

The Anasazi–Riddles in the Ruins. By Thomas Y. Canby. Photos by Dewitt Jones and David Brill. Paintings by Roy Andersen. 554-592, *Nov. 1982*

Pueblo Pottery–2,000 Years of Artistry. By David L. Arnold. 593-605, *Nov. 1982*

Inside the Sacred Hopi Homeland. By Jake Page. Photos by Susanne Page. 607-629, *Nov. 1982*

⊕ *The Southwest*, The Making of America series. Included: Arizona, New Mexico, and parts of California, Colorado, Texas, Utah; and in Mexico: Baja California Norte, Chihuahua, Sonora. On reverse: 12,000 Years of

History; Spanish Conquest; Anglo-American Entry and Occupancy. *Nov. 1982*

Stalking the West's Wild Foods. By Euell Gibbons. Photos by David Hiser. 186-199, *Aug. 1973*

Roaming the West's Fantastic Four Corners. By Jack Breed. 705-742, *June 1952*

See also Mesa Verde National Park; Rainbow Bridge National Monument; *and* Navajo Indians

FOUR-EYED FISH:

The Four-eyed Fish Sees All. Photos by Paul A. Zahl. Text by Thomas O'Neill. 390-395, *Mar. 1978*

Coffee Is King in El Salvador. By Luis Marden. Included: The four-eyed fish, *Anableps dowei*. 575-616, *Nov. 1944*

FOUR Faces of Siva: The Mystery of Angkor (Cambodia). By Robert J. Casey. 303-332, *Sept. 1928*

FOUR-OCEAN Navy in the Nuclear Age. By Thomas W. McKnew. 145-187, *Feb. 1965*

A **FOUR-PART** Look at the Isles of the Pacific. 732-793, *Dec. 1974*

FOUR Prominent Geographers. Contents: Biographies and portraits of the following: Arthur P. Davis, Frederick Haynes Newell, George Otis Smith, and Charles D. Walcott. 425-428, *June 1907*

FOUR Thousand Hours Over China. By Hans Koester. 571-598, *May 1938*

FOUR Years of Diving to the Bottom of the Sea. By Georges S. Houot. 715-731, *May 1958*

"1470 MAN." *See* Skull 1470

A **14TH-CENTURY** Cargo Makes Port at Last. Photos by H. Edward Kim. Introduction by Donald H. Keith. 231-243, *Aug. 1979*

FOWL:

Scientist Studies Japan's Fantastic Long-tailed Fowl. By Frank X. Ogasawara. Photos by Eiji Miyazawa. NGS research grant. 845-855, *Dec. 1970*

Fowls of Forest and Stream Tamed by Man. By Morley A. Jull. Paintings by Hashime Murayama. Contents: Ducks, Geese, Guinea Fowl, Peafowl, Swans, Turkeys. 327-371, *Mar. 1930*

The Races of Domestic Fowl. By M. A. Jull. Paintings by Hashime Murayama. Included: Ancona, Andalusian, Araucana, Bantam, Brahma, Campine, Cochin, Cornish, Dominique, Frizzle, Hamburg, Houdan, Jersey Black Giant, Langshan, Leghorn, Minorca, Plymouth Rock, Polish, Red Jungle Fowl, Rhode Island Red, Silkie, Sussex, Wyandotte, Yokohama. 379-452, *Apr. 1927*

See also Poultry

FOWL, Japanese Long-Tailed:

Scientist Studies Japan's Fantastic Long-tailed Fowl. By Frank X. Oga-

Sewing sheets and clothing, Father André helps sustain the community of monks at Our Lady of the Snows Trappist monastery in southern France. COTTON COULSON

sawara. Photos by Eiji Miyazawa. NGS research grant. 845-855, *Dec. 1970*

FOWLER, FREDERICK HALL: *Author-Photographer*

Week-Ends with the Prairie Falcon: A Commuter Finds Recreation in Scaling Cliffs to Observe the Nest Life and Flying Habits of These Elusive Birds. 611-626, *May 1935*

FOWLIANG, Jiangxi Province, China. *See* Jingdezhen

FOX, CHARLES J.:

Portrait of Gilbert H. Grosvenor. 252, 258, *Aug. 1949*

FOX, CHARLES PHILIP: *Photographer*

Skunks Want Peace–or Else! By Melvin R. Ellis. 279-294, *Aug. 1955*

Br'er Possum, Hermit of the Lowlands. By Agnes Akin Atkinson. 405-418, *Mar. 1953*

FOX, EVELYN:

Nomination Page. *Jan. 1968*

FOX, ROBERT B.:

Nomination Page. In the Philippines. *Sept. 1967*

FOX, ROBERT W.: *Author*

The World's Urban Explosion. Graphics by Allen Carroll. 179-185, *Aug. 1984*

FOX FARMING:

A Northern Crusoe's Island: Life on a Fox Farm Off the Coast of Alaska, Far from Contact with the World Eleven Months a Year. By Margery Pritchard Parker. 313-326, *Sept. 1923*

The Policemen of the Air: An Account of the Biological Survey of the Department of Agriculture. By Henry Wetherbee Henshaw. Included: Fox farming. 79-118, *Feb. 1908*

FOX ISLAND PASSES, Alaska:

Some Notes on the Fox Island Passes, Alaska. By J. J. Gilbert. 427-429, *Sept. 1905*

FOXES:

Foxes Foretell the Future in Mali's Dogon Country. By Pamela Johnson Meyer. 431-448, *Mar. 1969*

The Romance of American Furs. By Wanda Burnett. 379-402, *Mar. 1948*

See also Fox Farming

The **FRAGILE** Beauty All About Us. Photos by Harry S. C. Yen. 785-795, *Dec. 1970*

A **FRAGILE** Heritage: The Mighty Himalaya. By Barry C. Bishop. Photos by William Thompson. 624-631, *Nov. 1988*

FRAGILE Nurseries of the Sea: Can We Save Our Salt Marshes? By Stephen W. Hitchcock. Photos by William R. Curtsinger. 729-765, *June 1972*

FRALIN, FRANCES:

On Assignment. *Sept. 1988*

FRAM (Ship):

The Nansen Polar Expedition. Special Report of Ernest A. Man. 339-344, *Oct. 1896*

The Return of Dr. Nansen. 290, *Sept. 1896*

Nansen's Polar Expedition. By Adolphus W. Greely. 98-101, *Mar. 1896*

FRAME, GEORGE W. and LORY HERBISON: *Author-Photographers*

Cheetahs: In a Race for Survival. 712-728, *May 1980*

FRANCE:

The Incredible Potato. By Robert E. Rhoades. Photos by Martin Rogers. Included: Académie Parmentier,

Would-be toreros, Basques in Bayonne, France, will make themselves moving targets as bulls are set free to roam the streets. JUSTIN LOCKE

FRANCOPHONES, Canada-U. S.:

FRANK, Alberta, Canada:

FRANKENFIELD, H. C.: *Author*

FRANKINCENSE:

FRANKINCENSE TRAIL:

FRANKLIN, ALICELIA: *Author*

FRANKLIN, BENJAMIN:

FRANKLIN, SIR JOHN:

FRANKLIN, WILLIAM: *Author*

FRANKLIN, WILLIAM L.: *Author-Photographer*

FRANKLIN (River), Tasmania:

On the ancient frankincense trail, a Bedouin cradles her newborn baby near Main, Yemen. LYNN ABERCROMBIE

FRANKLIN INSTITUTE:

Series of flights sponsored by National Geographic Society, U. S. Army Air Forces, and Bartol Research Foundation of the Franklin Institute, to study cosmic rays. 387, *Sept. 1946*

FRANKLIN L. BURR PRIZE:

Burr Prizes Awarded to Dr. Edgerton and Dr. Van Biesbroeck. 705-706, *May 1953*

FRANZ JOSEF LAND, Russia:

The Wellman Polar Expedition. By Walter Wellman. 481-505, *Dec. 1899*
Through Franz Josef Land. 362, *Sept. 1899*

FRANZÉN, ANDERS: *Author*

Ghost From the Depths: the Warship *Vasa.* 42-57, *Jan. 1962*

FRASER, EDWIN R.: *Author*

Where Our Bananas Come From (Costa Rica). 713-730, *July 1912*

FRASER, LAURA GARDIN:

Designer of NGS Medals: Grosvenor Medal. 255, 261, Aug. 1949; 422, Mar. 1957; 516, Oct. 1963; Hubbard Medal. 564, Apr. 1953; Special Medal of Honor. 45, *July 1957*

FRASER (River), Canada:

The Untamed Fraser River, British Columbia's Lifeline. By David S. Boyer. Photos by Chris Johns. 44-75, *July 1986*

FRAZER, JOHN E.: *Author*

India's Energetic Sikhs. Photos by James P. Blair. 528-541, *Oct. 1972*
Kuwait, Aladdin's Lamp of the Middle East. Photos by David F. Cupp. 636-667, *May 1969*

FRAZIER, PAUL W.: *Author*

Across the Frozen Desert to Byrd Station. Photos by Calvin L. Larsen. 383-398, *Sept. 1957*

FREDERIC REMINGTON–The Man and the Myth. By Louise E. Levathes. Photos by Chris Johns. 200-231, *Aug. 1988*

FREDERIC W. PUTNAM. By John Hyde. 429-431, *Oct. 1898*

FREDERICK G. VOSBURGH Retires as Editor; Gilbert M. Grosvenor Succeeds Him. By Melvin M. Payne. 838-843, *Dec. 1970*

FREDERICK SOUND, Alaska:

Alaska's Southeast: A Place Apart. By Bill Richards. 50-87, *Jan. 1984*
An Incredible Feasting of Whales. By Al Giddings. 88-93, *Jan. 1984*

FREDERICKSBURG, Virginia:

Dog Mart Day in Fredericksburg. By Frederick G. Vosburgh. 817-832, *June 1951*
Announcement of the Seventh Annual Excursion and Field Meeting, Saturday, May 4, 1895. Foldout, *Apr. 20, 1895*

"FREE BURGHS" in the United States. By James H. Blodgett. 116-122, *Mar. 1896*

Fleeing Soviet tanks that rolled into Budapest in 1956, a Hungarian family in Vienna heads for a train to Munich; ultimately they reached Long Island. ROBERT F. SISSON, NGS

FREEDOM Flight from Hungary. Photos by Robert F. Sisson. 424-436, *Mar. 1957*

FREEDOM 7 (Spacecraft):
The Flight of *Freedom 7*. By Carmault B. Jackson, Jr. 416-431, *Sept. 1961*
The Pilot's Story. By Alan B. Shepard, Jr. Photos by Dean Conger. 432-444, *Sept. 1961*

FREEDOM Speaks French in Ouagadougou. By John Scofield. 153-203, *Aug. 1966*

FREEDOM TRAIN Tours America. 529-542, *Oct. 1949*

FREEDOM'S Progress South of the Sahara. By Howard La Fay. Photos by Joseph J. Scherschel. 603-637, *Nov. 1962*

FREEING Flamingos From Anklets of Death. By John G. Williams. Photos by Alan Root. 934-944, *Dec. 1963*

FREEMAN, LEWIS R.: *Author*

Trailing History Down the Big Muddy: In the Homeward Wake of Lewis and Clark, a Folding Steel Skiff Bears Its Lone Pilot on a 2,000 Mile Cruise on the Yellowstone-Missouri. 73-120, *July 1928*
The Mother of Rivers: An Account of a Photographic Expedition to the Great Columbia Ice Field of the Canadian Rockies. 377-446, *Apr. 1925*
Surveying the Grand Canyon of the Colorado: An Account of the 1923 Boating Expedition of the United States Geological Survey. 471-548, *May 1924*

FREETOWN, Sierra Leone:

The Loyalists. By Kent Britt. Photos by Ted Spiegel. Note: Slaves of Patriot colonists, liberated by the British during the American Revolution, founded Freetown after the war. 510-539, *Apr. 1975*

FREEZING the Flight of Hummingbirds. By Harold E. Edgerton, R. J. Niedrach, and Walker Van Riper. NGS research grant. 245-261, *Aug. 1951*

FREEZING the Trout's Lightning Leap. By Treat Davidson. 525-530, *Apr. 1958*

FREHSEE, RICK: *Photographer*

Strange March of the Spiny Lobster. By William F. Herrnkind. Photos by Rick Frehsee and Bruce Mounier. 819-831, *June 1975*

FREIBURG, West Germany:

Freiburg–Gateway to the Black Forest. By Alicia O'Reardon Overbeck. 213-252, *Aug. 1933*

FREIDEL, FRANK B., Jr.: *Author*

▌▌*Our Country's Presidents.* By Frank Freidel. 279 pages. 1966; rev. ed. *1981*
▌▌*George Washington–Man and Monument.* By Frank Freidel and Lonnelle Aikman. Published in cooperation with the Washington National Monument Association. 69 pages. 1965; rev. ed. *1973*

Profiles of the Presidents
Part V. The Atomic Age: Its Problems and Promises. 66-119, *Jan. 1966*

Part IV. America Enters the Modern Era. 537-577, *Oct. 1965*
Part III. The American Giant Comes of Age. 660-711, *May 1965*
Part II. A Restless Nation Moves West. 80-121, *Jan. 1965*
Part I. The Presidency and How It Grew. 642-687, *Nov. 1964*

FREIGHTERS of Fortune on our Great Lakes. Photos by Maynard Owen Williams. 463-470, *Apr. 1934*

FRENCH, GEORGE K.: *Author*

The Gold Coast, Ashanti, and Kumassi. 1-15, *Jan. 1897*

FRENCH-AMERICAN MID-OCEAN UNDERSEA STUDY. *See* FAMOUS

FRENCH AND INDIAN WAR:

The Travels of George Washington: Dramatic Episodes in His Career as the First Geographer of the United States. By William Joseph Showalter. 1-63, *Jan. 1932*

FRENCH-CANADIAN PROVINCES. *See* New Brunswick; Quebec

FRENCH-CANADIANS:

The Origin of French-Canadians. 96-97, *Mar. 1898*

FRENCH Conquest of the Sahara. By Charles Rabot. 76-80, *Feb. 1905*

FRENCH EQUATORIAL AFRICA:

Freedom Speaks French in Ouagadougou. By John Scofield. Included: Central African Republic; Chad; Gabon. 153-203, *Aug. 1966*
Three-Wheeling Through Africa: Two Adventurers Cross the So-called Dark Continent North of Lake Chad on Motorcycles with Side Cars. By James C. Wilson. 37-92, *Jan. 1934*
Through the Deserts and Jungles of Africa by Motor: Caterpillar Cars Make 15,000-Mile Trip from Algeria to Madagascar in Nine Months. By Georges-Marie Haardt. 651-720, *June 1926*
See also present names, Central African Republic; Chad; Congo, People's Republic of the; Gabon

FRENCH GUIANA:

What Future for the Wayana Indians? By Carole Devillers. 66-83, *Jan. 1983*
Color Glows in the Guianas, French and Dutch. By Nicol Smith. 459-480, *Apr. 1943*
Brazil-French Guiana Boundary Decision. 83, *Feb. 1901*

FRENCH GUINEA:

Dusky Tribesmen of French West Africa. Photos by Enzo de Chetelat. 639-662, *May 1941*
My Domestic Life in French Guinea: An American Woman Accompanies Her Husband, a French Geologist, on His Explorations in a Little-Known Region. By Eleanor de Chételat. 695-730, *June 1935*
See also present name, Guinea

FRENCH IMPRESSIONISTS:

In Quest of Beauty. Text by Paul Mellon. 372-385, *Mar. 1967*

Great Masters of a Brave Era in Art. By Hereward Lester Cooke, Jr. 661-697, *May 1961*

FRENCH INDOCHINA:

By Motor Trail Across French Indo-China. By Maynard Owen Williams. 487-534, *Oct. 1935*
Along the Old Mandarin Road of Indo-China. By W. Robert Moore. 157-199, *Aug. 1931*
Four Faces of Siva: The Mystery of Angkor. By Robert J. Casey. 303-332, *Sept. 1928*
Glimpses of Asia. 553-568, *May 1921*
The Forgotten Ruins of Indo-China. By Jacob E. Conner. 209-272, *Mar. 1912*
See also Cambodia; Laos; Vietnam

FRENCH MOROCCO. *See* Morocco

FRENCH NORTH AFRICA:

Yank Meets Native. By Wanda Burnett. 105-128, *July 1945*
Americans on the Barbary Coast. By Willard Price. 1-31, *July 1943*
Eastward from Gibraltar: Overland Route Across North Africa to Tunisia and Libia. By Cyrus French Wicker. 115-142, *Jan. 1943*
Through the Deserts and Jungles of Africa by Motor: Caterpillar Cars Make 15,000-Mile Trip from Algeria to Madagascar in Nine Months. By Georges-Marie Haardt. 651-720, *June 1926*
In Civilized French Africa. By James F. J. Archibald. 303-311, *Mar. 1909*
See also Algeria; Morocco; Tunisia

FRENCH POLYNESIA. *See* Marquesas Islands; Society Islands; Tuamotu Archipelago

FRENCH RIVIERA: Storied Playground on the Azure Coast. By Carleton Mitchell. Photos by Thomas Nebbia. 798-835, *June 1967*

FRENCH SOMALILAND:

Sailing Forbidden Coasts. By Ida Treat. 357-386, *Sept. 1931*
Across Widest Africa. By A. Henry Savage Landor. 694-737, *Oct. 1908*

FRENCH SUDAN:

Timbuktu and Beyond: Desert City of Romantic Savor and Salt Emerges into World Life Again as Trading Post of France's Vast African Empire. By Laura C. Boulton. 631-670, *May 1941*
Timbuktu, in the Sands of the Sahara. By Cecil D. Priest. 73-85, *Jan. 1924*
See also Mali

FRENCH WEST AFRICA:

Freedom Speaks French in Ouagadougou. By John Scofield. Included: Dahomey; Guinea; Ivory Coast; Mali; Mauritania; Niger; Senegal. 153-203, *Aug. 1966*
French West Africa in Wartime. By Paul M. Atkins. 371-408, *Mar. 1942*
Timbuktu and Beyond: Desert City of Romantic Savor and Salt Emerges into World Life Again as Trading Post of France's Vast African

Empire. By Laura C. Boulton. 631-670, *May 1941*
My Domestic Life in French Guinea: An American Woman Accompanies Her Husband, a French Geologist, on His Explorations in a Little-Known Region. By Eleanor de Chételat. 695-730, *June 1935*
Three-Wheeling Through Africa: Two Adventurers Cross the So-called Dark Continent North of Lake Chad on Motorcycles with Side Cars. By James C. Wilson. 37-92, *Jan. 1934*
Sindbads of Science: Narrative of a Windjammer's Specimen-Collecting Voyage to the Sargasso Sea, to Senegambian Africa and Among Islands of High Adventure in the South Atlantic. By George Finlay Simmons. 1-75, *July 1927*
Through the Deserts and Jungles of Africa by Motor: Caterpillar Cars Make 15,000-Mile Trip from Algeria to Madagascar in Nine Months. By Georges-Marie Haardt. 651-720, *June 1926*
Timbuktu, in the Sands of the Sahara. By Cecil D. Priest. 73-85, *Jan. 1924*
French Conquest of the Sahara. By Charles Rabot. 76-80, *Feb. 1905*
Recent French Explorations in Africa. By Charles Rabot. 119-132, *Apr. 1902*
See also Mali; Mauritania; Niger; Senegal; *and* Tuareg

FRENCH WEST INDIES. *See* Guadeloupe; Martinique

FRESCOES:

Multicolored Cones of Cappadocia. Photos by Eric Matson. 769-800, *Dec. 1939*
See also Cappadocia; Cave Art; Etruscans; Minoan Civilization; Sistine Chapel

A **FRESH** Breeze Stirs the Leewards. By Carleton Mitchell. Photos by Winfield Parks. 488-537, *Oct. 1966*

FRESH Treasures from Egypt's Ancient Sands. By Jefferson Caffery. Photos by David S. Boyer. 611-650, *Nov. 1955*

FRESH-WATER Denizens of the Far West (Salmon, Trout, etc.). Paintings by Hashime Murayama. 193-204, *Feb. 1939*

FRESH-WATER Fishes of the United States. Paintings by Hashime Murayama. 133-148, *Aug. 1923*

FRESHWATER TURTLES:

Freshwater Turtles–Designed for Survival. By Christopher P. White. Photos by Bill Curtsinger. 40-59, *Jan. 1986*

FRESON, ROBERT: *Photographer*

Living the Good Life in Burgundy. By William Davenport. 794-817, *June 1978*

FRIANT DAM, California:

More Water for California's Great Central Valley. By Frederick Simpich. 645-664, *Nov. 1946*

A blur and a splash to the human eye, a frog's leap is fragmented into multiple-exposure images by a high-speed flash at MIT's engineering laboratory.   TREAT DAVIDSON

World. By Sir Ross Smith. 229-339, *Mar. 1921*

FROM Nature's Hidden Building Blocks (Synthetic Products). Photos by Willard R. Culver. 609-640, *Nov. 1939*

FROM Notch to Notch in the White Mountains: Soaring Heights of New Hampshire Attract Multitudes to America's Oldest Mountain Recreation Area. By Leonard Cornell Roy. 73-104, *July 1937*

FROM One Sovereign People to Another. 370-373, *Sept. 1987*

FROM Panama to Patagonia. By Charles M. Pepper. 449-452, *Aug. 1906*

FROM Sagebrush to Roses on the Columbia. By Leo A. Borah. 571-611, *Nov. 1952*

FROM Sand to Seer and Servant of Man (Glassmaking). Photos by Willard R. Culver. 17-48, *Jan. 1943*

FROM Sea to Clouds in Ecuador. By W. Robert Moore. 717-740, *Dec. 1941*

FROM Sea to Sahara in French Morocco. By Jean and Franc Shor. 147-188, *Feb. 1955*

FROM Sea to Shining Sea: A Cross Section of the United States Along Historic Route 40. By Ralph Gray. Photos by Dean Conger and author. 1-61, *July 1961*

FROM Spear to Hoe on Groote

Eylandt. By Howell Walker. 131-142, *Jan. 1953*

FROM Stratford to the North Sea (England). Photos by Clifton Adams. 617-624, *May 1929*

FROM Sun-clad Sea to Shining Mountains. By Ralph Gray. Photos by James P. Blair. 542-589, *Apr. 1964*

FROM Sword to Scythe in Champlain Country. By Ethel A. Starbird. Photos by B. Anthony Stewart and Emory Kristof. 153-201, *Aug. 1967*

FROM the Bahamas to Belize: Probing the Deep Reefs' Hidden Realm. By Walter A. Starck II and Jo D. Starck. 867-886, *Dec. 1972*

FROM the Hair of Siva. By Helen and Frank Schreider. 445-503, *Oct. 1960*

FROM the Halls of Montezuma (Mexico). Photos by Richard H. Stewart and others. 137-164, *Feb. 1944*

FROM the Mediterranean to the Yellow Sea by Motor: The Citroën-Haardt Expedition Successfully Completes Its Dramatic Journey. By Maynard Owen Williams. 513-580, *Nov. 1932*

FROM the Plains of Madras to the Snows of Kashmir. 561-576, *Nov. 1924*

FROM the Trenches to Versailles. By Carol Corey. 535-550, *Nov.-Dec. 1917*

FROM the War-Path to the Plow. By Franklin K. Lane. 73-87, *Jan. 1915*

FROM Tucson to Tombstone. By Mason Sutherland. 343-384, *Sept. 1953*

FRONT-LINE Town of Britain's Siege (Dover). By Harvey Klemmer. 105-128, *Jan. 1944*

FRONTIER, 19th-century U. S.:

Life and Death on the Oregon Trail: The Itch to Move West. By Boyd Gibbons. Photos by James L. Amos. 147-177, *Aug. 1986*

Daniel Boone, First Hero of the Frontier. By Elizabeth A. Moize. Photos by William Strode. 812-841, *Dec. 1985*

⊕ *Central Rockies,* The Making of America series. Included: Fur and Frontier, Mission to Succeed, Mineral Riches, Lure of the Mountains. *Aug. 1984*

Buffalo Bill and the Enduring West. By Alice J. Hall. Photos by James L. Amos. 76-103, *July 1981*

The Pony Express. By Rowe Findley. Photos by Craig Aurness. 45-71, *July 1980*

■■*Trails West.* 207 pages. *1979*

Chief Joseph. By William Albert Allard. 409-434, *Mar. 1977*

Riding the Outlaw Trail. By Robert Redford. Photos by Jonathan Blair. 622-657, *Nov. 1976*

■■*The American Cowboy in Life and Legend.* By Bart McDowell. Photos by William Albert Allard. 211 pages. *1972*

So Long, St. Louis, We're Heading West. By William C. Everhart. 643-669, *Nov. 1965*

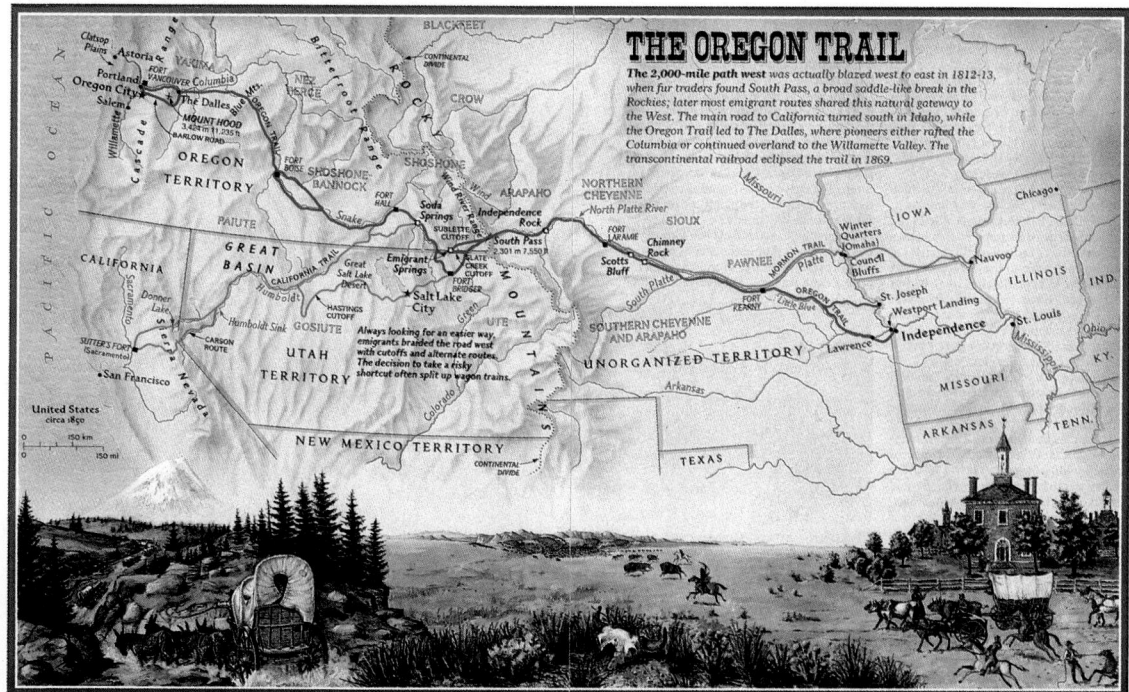

Endured by half a million pioneers, the Oregon Trail led west across the frontier and through the Rockies. NGS CARTOGRAPHIC DIVISION

A Restless Nation Moves West. By Frank Freidel. Paintings from the White House Collection. 80-121, *Jan. 1965*

From Tucson to Tombstone. By Mason Sutherland. 343-384, *Sept. 1953*

Hays, Kansas, at the Nation's Heart. By Margaret M. Detwiler. Photos by John E. Fletcher. 461-490, *Apr. 1952*

See also The West

FRONTIER Cities of Italy. By Florence Craig Albrecht. 533-586, *June 1915*

FROST, ROBERT:

Editorial. By Gilbert M. Grosvenor. 437, *Apr. 1976*

Robert Frost and New England. By Archibald MacLeish. Included: Look of a Land Beloved. Photos by Dewitt Jones. 438-467, *Apr. 1976*

FROST:

Frost, Nature's Icing. By Robert F. Sisson. 398-405, *Mar. 1976*

The Magic Beauty of Snow and Dew. By Wilson A. Bentley. 103-112, *Jan. 1923*

FROZEN FOODS:

Your New World of Tomorrow. By F. Barrows Colton. 385-410, *Oct. 1945*

FROZEN SEA EXPEDITION:

Icebound in Antarctica. By David Lewis. Photos by Mimi George. 634-663, *Nov. 1984*

FRUIT BATS:

Gentle Fliers of the African Night. By Merlin D. Tuttle. NGS research grant. 540-558, *Apr. 1986*

FRUIT GROWING:

Washington's Yakima Valley. By Mark Miller. Photos by Sisse Brimberg. Included: Apple growing. 609-631, *Nov. 1978*

Our Life on a Border Kibbutz. By Carol and Al Abrams. Photos by Al Abrams. 364-391, *Sept. 1970*

Florida Rides a Space-age Boom. By Benedict Thielen. Photos by Winfield Parks and James P. Blair. 858-903, *Dec. 1963*

The Lure of the Changing Desert (California). Included: Date raising. 817-824, *June 1954*

California, Horn of Plenty. By Frederick Simpich. Photos by Willard R. Culver. 553-594, *May 1949*

More Water for California's Great Central Valley. By Frederick Simpich. 645-664, *Nov. 1946*

Fruitful Shores of the Finger Lakes (New York). By Harrison Howell Walker. 559-594, *May 1941*

The Texas Delta of an American Nile: Orchards and Gardens Replace Thorny Jungle in the Southmost Tip of the Lone Star State. By McFall Kerbey. 51-96, *Jan. 1939*

Costa Rica, Land of the Banana. By Paul B. Popenoe. 201-220, *Feb. 1922*

The Wild Blueberry Tamed: The New Industry of the Pine Barrens of New Jersey. By Frederick V. Coville. 535-546, *June 1916*

Where Our Bananas Come From (Costa Rica). By Edwin R. Fraser. 713-

730, *July 1912*

Taming the Wild Blueberry. By Frederick V. Coville. 137-147, *Feb. 1911*

Agricultural Possibilities in Tropical Mexico. By Pehr Olsson-Seffer. 1021-1040, *Dec. 1910*

The Date Gardens of the Jerid (Northern Africa). By Thomas H. Kearney. 543-567, *July 1910*

The United States; Its Soils and Their Products. By H. W. Wiley. 263-279, *July 1903*

See also Grape Culture; Kiwifruit; Pineapple Growing

FRUITFUL Shores of the Finger Lakes (New York). By Harrison Howell Walker. 559-594, *May 1941*

FRUITS:

■▥ *The World in Your Garden.* Art by Else Bostelmann. 231 pages. *1957*

How Fruit Came to America. By J. R. Magness. Paintings by Else Bostelmann. Contents: American Plum, Apple, Apricot, Avocado, Banana, Blackberry, Blueberry, Cherry, Cranberry, Currant, Date, Fig, Gooseberry, Grape, Grapefruit, Japanese Plum, Lemon, Lime, Mango, Olive, Orange, Papaya, Peach, Pear, Persimmon, Pineapple, Plum, Prune, Quince, Raspberry, Strawberry. 325-377, *Sept. 1951*

Our Vegetable Travelers. By Victor R. Boswell. Paintings by Else Bostelmann. Included: Watermelon, Muskmelon. 145-217, *Aug. 1949*

Patent Plants Enrich Our World. By Orville H. Kneen. Photos from U. S. Plant Patents. 357-378, *Mar. 1948*

Flavor and Savor of American Foods. Photos by J. Baylor Roberts, Willard R. Culver, and others. 289-320, *Mar. 1942*

Peacetime Plant Hunting About Peiping. By P. H. and J. H. Dorsett. 509-534, *Oct. 1937*

Round About Bogota: A Hunt for New Fruits and Plants Among the Mountain Forests of Colombia's Unique Capital. By Wilson Popenoe. 127-160, *Feb. 1926*

Reviving a Lost Art (Drying Fruits and Vegetables). 475-481, *June 1917*

New Plant Immigrants. By David Fairchild. 879-907, *Oct. 1911*

See also Bananas; Berries; Citrus Fruits; Figs; Grapes; Kiwifruit; Mangoes; Pineapples

FUCHS, SIR VIVIAN:

Society Honors the Conquerors of Antarctica. 589-590, *Apr. 1959*

Author

The Crossing of Antarctica. Photos by George Lowe. 25-47, *Jan. 1959*

FUEGIAN INDIANS:

In the Wake of Darwin's *Beagle.* By Alan Villiers. Photos by James L. Stanfield. 449-495, *Oct. 1969*

FUEL:

The Conversion of Old Newspapers and Candle Ends into Fuel. 568-570, *June 1917*

An Ideal Fuel Manufactured Out of Waste Products: The American Coal

Briquetting Industry. By Guy Elliott Mitchell. 1067-1074, *Dec. 1910*

Natural-Gas, Oil, and Coal Supply of the United States. 186, *Apr. 1904*

See also Coal; Natural Gas; Oil

FUERST, FRANCIS C.: *Photographer*

Merry Maskers of Imst (Austria). 201-208, *Aug. 1936*

FUERTES, LOUIS AGASSIZ: *Artist*

Smaller Mammals of North America. By E. W. Nelson. 371*-493, *May 1918*

■▥ *The Book of Birds: Common Birds of Town and Country and American Game Birds.* By Henry W. Henshaw. 195 pages. 1914; rev. ed. *1918*

■▥ *Wild Animals of North America: Intimate Studies of Big and Little Creatures of the Mammal Kingdom.* By Edward W. Nelson. Sketches by Ernest Thompson Seton. 612 pages. *1918*

Friends of Our Forests. By Henry Wetherbee Henshaw. Paintings by Louis Agassiz Fuertes. Included: The Warblers of North America. 297-321, *Apr. 1917*

The Larger North American Mammals. By E. W. Nelson. 385-472, *Nov. 1916*

The Alaska Brown Bear: The Largest Carnivorous Animal Extant. Painting supplement. *Nov. 1916*

American Game Birds. By Henry Wetherbee Henshaw. 105-158, *Aug. 1915*

Birds of Town and Country. By Henry Wetherbee Henshaw. 494-531, *May 1914*

Fifty Common Birds of Farm and Orchard. By Henry Wetherbee Henshaw. 669-697, *June 1913*

■▥ *Fifty Common Birds of Farm and Orchard.* By Henry W. Henshaw. Art by Louis Agassiz Fuertes. Originally prepared as Bulletin 513 of the U. S. Department of Agriculture. Reprint of June 1913 article by special permission of the Secretary of Agriculture. 29 pages. *1913*

Author-Artist

Falconry, the Sport of Kings. 429-460, *Dec. 1920*

Our Common Dogs. By Louis Agassiz Fuertes and Ernest Harold Baynes. 201-253, *Mar. 1919*

FUGU:

The Preposterous Puffer. By Noel D. Vietmeyer. Photos by Joseph J. Scherschel. 260-270, *Aug. 1984*

FUJI (Peak), Japan:

The Geography of Japan: With Special Reference to Its Influence on the Character of the Japanese People. By Walter Weston. 45-84, *July 1921*

FULAH TRIBESPEOPLE:

Dusky Tribesmen of French West Africa. Photos by Enzo de Chételat. 639-662, *May 1941*

FULANI TRIBESPEOPLE:

Oursi, Magnet in the Desert. By Carole E. Devillers. 512-525, *Apr. 1980*

The Niger: River of Sorrow, River of Hope. By Georg Gerster. 152-189, *Aug. 1975*

FULLER, BUCKMINSTER: *Author*
Five Noted Thinkers Explore the Future. 72-73, *July 1976*

FULLER, R. STEVEN:
Author-Photographer
Winterkeeping in Yellowstone. 829-857, *Dec. 1978*

FUMAROLES:
Our Greatest National Monument. By Robert F. Griggs. 219-292, *Sept. 1921*
The Valley of Ten Thousand Smokes. By Robert F. Griggs. 115-169, *Feb. 1918*

FUN Helped Them Fight. By Stuart E. Jones. 95-104, *Jan. 1948*

FUN With Physics. By Susan McGrath. ■■Juvenile. 104 pages. *1986*

FUNAI:
Brazil's Kayapo Indians, Beset by a Golden Curse. By Vanessa Lea. Photos by Miguel Rio Branco. Included: Efforts of Brazil's Indian bureau (FUNAI) to keep peace between Kayapo and outsiders. 675-694, *May 1984*
See also listing under National Foundation for the Indian

FUNAN, Kingdom of:
Mosaic of Cultures (Southeast Asia). By Peter T. White. Photos by W. E. Garrett. 296-329, *Mar. 1971*
See also Angkor, for Khmers

FUNCHAL, Madeira:
Madeira, Like Its Wine, Improves With Age. By Veronica Thomas. Photos by Jonathan Blair. 488-513, *Apr. 1973*
Madeira the Florescent. By Harriet Chalmers Adams. 81-106, *July 1934*

FUNDAMENTAL Geographic Relation of the Three Americas. By Robert T. Hill. 175-181, *May 1896*

FUNDY, Bay of, Canada:
The Giant Tides of Fundy. By Paul A. Zahl. 153-192, *Aug. 1957*
Tides in the Bay of Fundy. 71-76, *Feb. 1905*
Atlantic Coast Tides. By Mark S. W. Jefferson. 497-509, *Dec. 1898*

FUNERALS:
Life and Death in Tana Toradja. By Pamela and Alfred Meyer. 793-815, *June 1972*
Taboos and Magic Rule Namba Lives. By Kal Muller. 57-83, *Jan. 1972*
The Ganges, River of Faith. By John J. Putman. Photos by Raghubir Singh. Included: Hindu funeral. 445-483, *Oct. 1971*
New Orleans and Her River. By Joseph Judge. Photos by James L. Stanfield. Included: Jazz funeral. 151-187, *Feb. 1971*
Gangtok, Cloud-wreathed Himalayan Capital. By John Scofield. Included:

An endangered leopard cat from the Thai rain forest snarls in a Bangkok market.
STEVE RAYMER, NGS

Funeral of Princess Sonam Padaun. 698-713, *Nov. 1970*
Expedition to the Land of the Tiwi. By Charles P. Mountford. Note: Australian Aboriginal artistic and social activities are centered on funeral ceremonies. NGS research grant. 417-440, *Mar. 1956*
See also Burial Customs

FUNERALS, State. *See* Churchill, Sir Winston; Eisenhower, Dwight D.; Kennedy, John F.

FUNERARY BOATS:
Finding a Pharaoh's Funeral Bark. By Farouk El-Baz. Photos by James P. Blair and Claude E. Petrone. Included: Craft for eternity; The world's oldest ship. 513-533, *Apr. 1988*
Riddle of the Pyramid Boats. By Peter Miller. Photos by Victor R. Boswell, Jr. 534-550, *Apr. 1988*

FUNGI:
Slime Mold: The Fungus That Walks. By Douglas Lee. Photos by Paul A. Zahl. Note: This protoplasm is not a true fungus. 131-136, *July 1981*
The Wild World of Compost. By Cecil E. Johnson. Photos by Bianca Lavies. 273-284, *Aug. 1980*
Bizarre World of the Fungi. By Paul A. Zahl. 502-527, *Oct. 1965*
Common Mushrooms of the United States. By Louis C. C. Krieger. Paintings by author. 387-439, *May 1920*
See also Truffles

FUNK, BEN: *Author*
Hurricane! By Ben Funk. Photos by Robert W. Madden. 346-379, *Sept. 1980*

FUNK, TED H.: *Photographer*
The Manx and Their Isle of Man. By

Veronica Thomas. 426-444, *Sept. 1972*
Luxembourg, the Quiet Fortress. By Robert Leslie Conly. 69-97, *July 1970*
Democracy's Fortress: Unsinkable Malta. By Ernle Bradford. 852-879, *June 1969*
San Marino, Little Land of Liberty. By Donna Hamilton Shor. 233-251, *Aug. 1967*

FUR SEALS:
New Day for Alaska's Pribilof Islanders. By Susan Hackley Johnson. Photos by Tim Thompson. 536-552, *Oct. 1982*
Making the Fur Seal Abundant. By Hugh M. Smith. 1139-1165, *Dec. 1911*

FUR TRADE:
The Hudson's Bay Company: Canada's Fur-Trading Empire. By Peter C. Newman. Photos by Kevin Fleming. 192-229, *Aug. 1987*

FURS:
New Day for Alaska's Pribilof Islanders. By Susan Hackley Johnson. Photos by Tim Thompson. 536-552, *Oct. 1982*
Wild Cargo: the Business of Smuggling Animals. By Noel Grove. Photos by Steve Raymer. 287-315, *Mar. 1981*
Life or Death for the Harp Seal. By David M. Lavigne. Photos by William R. Curtsinger. 129-142, *Jan. 1976*
The Fur Seal Herd Comes of Age. By Victor B. Scheffer and Karl W. Kenyon. 491-512, *Apr. 1952*
The Romance of American Furs. By Wanda Burnett. 379-402, *Mar. 1948*
Men, Moose, and Mink of Northwest Angle. By William H. Nicholas. Photos by J. Baylor Roberts. 265-284, *Aug. 1947*
See also Fox Farming

FURTHER Explorations in the Land of the Incas: The Peruvian Expedition of 1915 of the National Geographic Society and Yale University. By Hiram Bingham. 431-473, *May 1916*

FURTHER Notes on Dutch New Guinea. By Thomas Barbour. 527-545, *Aug. 1908*

FUSION:
The Fusion Solution. 45, *Special Report on Energy. (Feb. 1981)*

FUTAGAMI JIMA (Island), Japan:
Living in a Japanese Village. By William Graves. Photos by James L. Stanfield. 668-693, *May 1972*

The **FUTURE** of the Airplane. By Robert E. Peary. 107-113, *Jan. 1918*

The **FUTURE** of the Yukon Goldfields. By William H. Dall. 117-120, *Apr. 1898*

FYN (Island), Denmark:
By Full-rigged Ship to Denmark's Fairyland. By Alan Villiers. Photos by Alexander Taylor and author. 809-828, *Dec. 1955*

GAELS
GALÁPAGOS ISLANDS
GALAXIES
GALLEONS
GASPÉ PENINSULA
GENETIC RESEARCH
GEOGRAPHY
GLACIERS
GLYPHS
GOLD
GRAND CANYON
GRAPE CULTURE
GREAT WALL OF CHINA
GREENHOUSE EFFECT
GRIZZLY BEARS
GILBERT H. GROSVENOR
GULF COAST
GYPSIES
HABITAT DESTRUCTION
HANG GLIDERS
HARLEM
HARP SEALS
HAWAII
HEADHUNTERS
HIEROGLYPHS
HIMALAYA
HOLOGRAPHY
HONEYBEES
HONG KONG
HOPI INDIANS
HORSESHOE CRABS
HOSTELS
HOT SPRINGS
HUMMINGBIRDS
HUMPBACK WHALES
HUNGARY
HURRICANES
HYDROELECTRIC POWER

A glowing tower of the Golden Gate Bridge rises above the fog rolling into San Francisco Bay.

JAMES A. SUGAR, BLACK STAR

439

The **GI** and the Kids of Korea. Text and photos by Robert H. Mosier. 635-664, *May 1953*

GABERELL, JEAN: *Photographer*

Skiing in Switzerland's Realm of Winter Sports. 345-352, *Mar. 1933*

GABES, Tunisia:

The Mole Men: An Account of the Troglodytes of Southern Tunisia. By Frank Edward Johnson. 787-846, *Sept. 1911*

GABON:

Ambassadors of Good Will: The Peace Corps. By Sargent Shriver and Peace Corps Volunteers. 297-345. Included: Gabon. By John F. Murphy, Jr. 325-329, *Sept. 1964*

GADE, JOHN H.: *Author*

Belgium's Plight. 433-439, *May 1917*

GAELS:

Scotland's Inner Hebrides: Isles of the Western Sea. By Kenneth MacLeish. Photos by R. Stephen Uzzell III. 690-717, *Nov. 1974*
Isles on the Edge of the Sea: Scotland's Outer Hebrides. By Kenneth MacLeish. Photos by Thomas Nebbia. 676-711, *May 1970*
The Highlands, Stronghold of Scottish Gaeldom. By Kenneth MacLeish. Photos by Winfield Parks. 398-435, *Mar. 1968*
See also Celts

GAHAN, GORDON W.: *Photographer*

Goal at the End of the Trail: Santa Fe. By William S. Ellis. Photos by Gordon W. Gahan and Otis Imboden. 323-345, *Mar. 1982*
Napoleon. By John J. Putman. 142-189, *Feb. 1982*
Voyages to Paradise: Exploring in the Wake of Captain Cook. By William R. Gray. 215 pages. *1981*
Texas! By Howard La Fay. 440-483, *Apr. 1980*
Minoans and Mycenaeans: Greece's Brilliant Bronze Age. By Joseph Judge. Paintings by Lloyd K. Townsend. 142-185, *Feb. 1978*
Moscow: The City Around Red Square. By John J. Putman. 2-45, *Jan. 1978*
Turkey: Cross Fire at an Ancient Crossroads. By Robert Paul Jordan. 88-123, *July 1977*
Nova Scotia, the Magnificent Anchorage. By Charles McCarry. 334-363, *Mar. 1975*
Sir Francis Drake. By Alan Villiers. 216-253, *Feb. 1975*
East Germany: The Struggle to Succeed. By John J. Putman. 295-329, *Sept. 1974*
Israel–The Seventh Day. By Joseph Judge. 816-855, *Dec. 1972*
Drought Bedevils Brazil's Sertão. By John Wilson. 704-723, *Nov. 1972*
The More Paris Changes.... By Howell Walker. 64-103, *July 1972*
Captain Cook: The Man Who Mapped the Pacific. By Alan Villiers. 297-349, *Sept. 1971*
Maui, Where Old Hawaii Still Lives. By

Kenneth F. Weaver. 514-543, *Apr. 1971*
In Search of Man's Past at Lake Rudolf. By Richard E. Leakey. 712-734, *May 1970*

GAILLARD, D. D.: *Author*

The Washington Aqueduct and Cabin John Bridge. 337-344, *Dec. 1897*

GALÁPAGOS ISLANDS, Pacific Ocean:

Galápagos Wildlife Under Pressure. Photo essay by Dieter and Mary Plage. 122-145, *Jan. 1988*
Managing Another Galápagos Species– Man. By Jerry Emory. Photos by Dieter and Mary Plage. 146-154, *Jan. 1988*
Undersea Wonders of the Galapagos. By Gerard Wellington. Photos by David Doubilet. 363-381, *Sept. 1978*
Giant Tortoises: Goliaths of the Galapagos. By Craig MacFarland. Photos by author and Jan MacFarland. Included: Española; Isabela; Pinzón; Santa Cruz. 632-649, *Nov. 1972*
Robin Sails Home. By Robin Lee Graham. 504-545, *Oct. 1970*
In the Wake of Darwin's *Beagle.* By Alan Villiers. Photos by James L. Stanfield. 449-495, *Oct. 1969*
The Galapagos, Eerie Cradle of New Species. By Roger Tory Peterson. Photos by Alan and Joan Root. 541-585, *Apr. 1967*
Lost World of the Galapagos. By Irving and Electa Johnson. 681-703, *May 1959*
The *Yankee*'s Wander-world. By Irving and Electa Johnson. 1-50, *Jan. 1949*
Westward Bound in the *Yankee.* By Irving and Electa Johnson. 1-44, *Jan. 1942*

Seen from below, a marine iguana swims on the surface in Ecuador's Galápagos archipelago. DAVID DOUBILET

At Home on the Oceans: Whales and Sharks Make Exciting Neighbors for a Professor's Wife, Turned Able Seaman, On a Three-year Voyage Around the World. By Edith Bauer Strout. 33-86, *July 1939*
The Dream Ship: The Story of a Voyage of Adventure More Than Half Around the World in a 47-foot Lifeboat. By Ralph Stock. 1-52, *Jan. 1921*

GALÁPAGOS RIFT, Pacific Ocean:

▨ Dive to the Edge of Creation: Galapagos II Expedition. 682, Nov. 1979; 1, cover, *Jan. 1980*
Incredible World of the Deep-sea Rifts. NGS research grant. 680-705. I. Strange World Without Sun. The Editor. 680-688; II. Return to Oases of the Deep. By Robert D. Ballard and J. Frederick Grassle. 689-705, *Nov. 1979*
Oases of Life in the Cold Abyss. By John B. Corliss and Robert D. Ballard. 441-453, *Oct. 1977*

GALAXIES:

The Once and Future Universe. By Rick Gore. Photos by James A. Sugar. Paintings by Barron Storey. Picture text by David Jeffery. 704-749, *June 1983*
⊕ *Journey Into the Universe Through Time and Space; National Geographic-Palomar Sky Survey Charting the Heavens. June 1983*

A **GALAXY** of Life Fills the Night. By Kenneth Brower. Photos by William R. Curtsinger and Chris Newbert. 834-847, *Dec. 1981*

GALDIKAS, BIRUTÉ M. F.:

Nomination Page. In Borneo. *Apr. 1980*
Nomination Page. In Borneo. *Apr. 1973*
Author
Living with the Great Orange Apes: Indonesia's Orangutans. Photos by Rod Brindamour. 830-853, *June 1980*
Orangutans, Indonesia's "People of the Forest." Photos by Rod Brindamour. 444-473, *Oct. 1975*

GALICIA:

Partitioned Poland. By William Joseph Showalter. 88-106, *Jan. 1915*

GALILEE (Region), Israel:

Where Jesus Walked. By Howard La Fay. Photos by Charles Harbutt. 739-781, *Dec. 1967*
The Land of Galilee. By Kenneth MacLeish. Photos by B. Anthony Stewart. 832-865, *Dec. 1965*
The Geography of the Jordan. By Nelson Glueck. 719-744, *Dec. 1944*
Impressions of Palestine. By James Bryce. 293-317, *Mar. 1915*

GALILEE (Ship):

The Work in the Pacific Ocean of the Magnetic Survey Yacht "Galilee." By L. A. Bauer. 601-611, *Sept. 1907*

GALILEO GALILEI:

The Renaissance Lives On in Tuscany.

By Luis Marden. Photos by Albert Moldvay. 626-659, *Nov. 1974*

GALL MIDGES. *See* Midges

GALLANT, ROY A.: *Author*

■■ *National Geographic Picture Atlas of Our Universe.* Juvenile. 284 pages. 1980; rev. ed. *1986*

GALLANT Little Sportsmen of the Terrier Tribe. Paintings by Edward Herbert Miner. 253-268, *Feb. 1936*

GALLATIN COUNTY, Illinois. *See* Shawneetown

GALLEASSES:

Priceless Relics of the Spanish Armada. By Robert Sténuit. Photos by Bates Littlehales. Included: The galleass *Girona.* 745-777, *June 1969*

GALLEONS:

16th-Century Basque Whalers in America. Photos by Bill Curtsinger. Paintings by Richard Schlecht. 40-71. I. Discovery in Labrador: A 16th-Century Basque Whaling Port and Its Sunken Fleet. 40-49; II. Unearthing Red Bay's Whaling History. By James A. Tuck. 50-57; III. Excavating a 400-year-old Basque Galleon. By Robert Grenier. 58-67; IV. The Indomitable Basques. By Robert Laxalt. 69-71, *July 1985*

Treasure From the Ghost Galleon: *Santa Margarita.* By Eugene Lyon. Photos by Don Kincaid. Included: *Atocha; Santa Margarita.* 228-243, *Feb. 1982*

Graveyard of the Quicksilver Galleons. By Mendel Peterson. Photos by Jonathan Blair. Included: *Nuestra Señora de Guadalupe; Conde de Tolosa.* 850-876, *Dec. 1979*

Reach for the New World. By Mendel Peterson. Photos by David L. Arnold. Paintings by Richard Schlecht. 724-767, *Dec. 1977*

⊕ "History Salvaged From the Sea," painting supplement. Map on reverse. Included: Cutaway painting of a galleon. *Dec. 1977*

▨ Treasure! 575, Nov. 1976; cover, *Dec. 1976*

Atocha, Tragic Treasure Galleon of the Florida Keys. By Eugene Lyon. Included: *Santa Margarita* wreck. 787-809, *June 1976*

Drowned Galleons Yield Spanish Gold. By Kip Wagner. Photos by Otis Imboden. 1-37, *Jan. 1965*

GALLEYS, Bronze Age:

Oldest Known Shipwreck Reveals Splendors of the Bronze Age. By George F. Bass. Photos by William R. Curtsinger. Included: Bronze Age Trade, The Cosmopolitan World of the Late Bronze Age, The Painstaking Art of Marine Archaeology. NGS research grant. 693-733, *Dec. 1987*

The Quest for Ulysses. By Tim Severin. Photos by Kevin Fleming. Included: *Argo.* 197-225, *Aug. 1986*

Jason's Voyage: In Search of the Golden Fleece. By Tim Severin. Photos by John Egan and Seth Mortimer. Included: *Argo.* 406-420, *Sept. 1985*

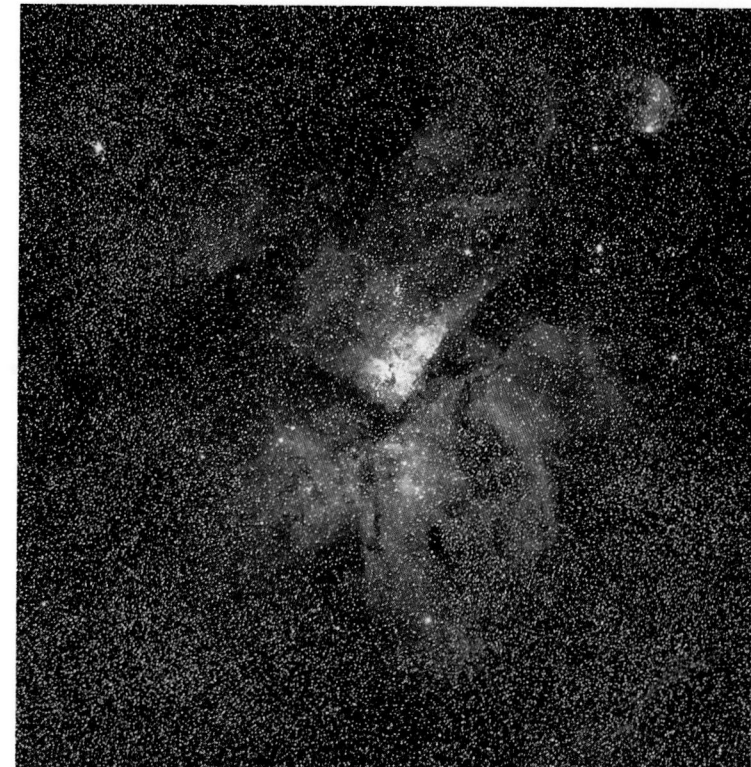

Some 50,000 stars spangle the sky in a small part of the Milky Way, one of the universe's billions of galaxies. CERRO TOLOLO INTER-AMERICAN OBSERVATORY, © AURA, INC.

Bronze Age Shipwreck. By Wilbur E. Garrett and George F. Bass. Contents: Turkish discovery. NGS research grant. 1-3, *Jan. 1985*

GALLINAZO CULTURE:

Finding the Tomb of a Warrior-God. By William Duncan Strong. Photos by Clifford Evans, Jr. 453-482, *Apr. 1947*

GALLOWAY, A. C.: *Author*

An Interesting Visit to the Ancient Pyramids of San Juan Teotihuacan. 1041-1050, *Dec. 1910*

GALVESTON, Texas:

How We Use the Gulf of Mexico. By Frederick Simpich. 1-40, *Jan. 1944*

Texas, Our Largest State. By N. H. Darton. 1330-1360, *Dec. 1913*

The Lessons of Galveston. By W J McGee. 377-383, *Oct. 1900*

GAMA, VASCO DA:

The Pathfinder of the East: Setting Sail to Find "Christians and Spices," Vasco da Gama Met Amazing Adventures, Founded an Empire, and Changed the History of Western Europe. By Jesse R. Hildebrand. 503-550, *Nov. 1927*

Vasco da Gama at the Court of the Zamorin of Calicut. Painting by José Velloso Salgado, Sociedade de Geographia de Lisboa. Supplement. *Nov. 1927*

The GAMBIA:

Senegambia: A Now and Future Nation. By Michael and Aubine Kirtley. 224-251, *Aug. 1985*

Freedom Speaks French in Ouagadougou. By John Scofield. 153-203, *Aug. 1966*

GAME:

Lords of the Rockies: Photographing Big Game Animals in Their Primeval Surroundings, from Arizona to Canada, Brings Adventure to Two Wilderness Wanderers. By Wendell and Lucie Chapman. 87-128, *July 1939*

The Warfare of the Jungle Folk: Campaigning Against Tigers, Elephants, and Other Wild Animals in Northern Siam. By Merian C. Cooper. Photos by Ernest B. Schoedsack. 233-268, *Feb. 1928*

Tiger-Hunting in India. By William Mitchell. 545-598, *Nov. 1924*

A Game Country Without Rival in America: The Proposed Mount McKinley National Park. By Stephen R. Capps. 69-84, *Jan. 1917*

Mr. Roosevelt's "African Game Trails." 953-962, *Nov. 1910*

The Big Game of Alaska. By Wilfred H. Osgood. 624-636, *July 1909*

Where Roosevelt Will Hunt (Africa). By Sir Harry Johnston. 207-256, *Mar. 1909*

One Season's Game-Bag with the Camera. By George Shiras, 3d. 387-446, *June 1908*

Flanked by Masai of eastern Africa, an American game hunter in 1909 celebrates a successful morning. UNDERWOOD & UNDERWOOD/THE BETTMANN ARCHIVE

Kboo, a Liberian Game. By G. N. Collins. 944-948, *Nov. 1910*

A Primitive Gyroscope in Liberia. By G. N. Collins. 531-535, *June 1910*

See also Highland Games; Olympic Games; Sports

GAMMANS, LEONARD DAVID: *Author*

Yanks at Westminster. 223-252, *Aug. 1946*

The United States and the British Empire. 562-564, *May 1945*

GAN SHEMUEL (Collective Farm), Palestine:

Palestine Today. By Francis Chase, Jr. 501-516, *Oct. 1946*

GANDHI, MOHANDAS KARAMCHAND:

Delhi, Capital of a New Dominion. By Phillips Talbot. Photos by Volkmar Wentzel. 597-630, *Nov. 1947*

The "GANG" Moves to a Strange New Land. By Shirley C. Strum. Note: The baboons of the "Pumphouse Gang" are translocated in Kenya. NGS research grant. 676-690, *Nov. 1987*

GANGES (River), India-Bangladesh:

Banaras: India's City of Light. By Santha Rama Rau. Photos by Tony Heiderer. 214-251, *Feb. 1986*

The Ganges, River of Faith. By John J. Putman. Photos by Raghubir Singh. 445-483, *Oct. 1971*

From the Hair of Siva. By Helen and Frank Schreider. 445-503, *Oct. 1960*

GANGTOK, Sikkim:

Gangtok, Cloud-wreathed Himalayan Capital. By John Scofield. 689-713, *Nov. 1970*

Wedding of Two Worlds. By Lee E. Battaglia. 708-727, *Nov. 1963*

Sikkim. By Desmond Doig. 398-429, *Mar. 1963*

GANNETS:

Sea Bird Cities Off Audubon's Labrador. By Arthur A. Allen. NGS research grant. 755-774, *June 1948*

Birds of the High Seas: Albatrosses and Petrels; Gannets, Man-o'-war-birds, and Tropic-birds. By Robert Cushman Murphy. Paintings by Allan Brooks. 226-251, *Aug. 1938*

GANNETT, HENRY:

President of NGS. 88, Jan. 1910; 95, *July 1946*

Naming of Electric Peak, Yellowstone National Park. 794, *June 1940*

Secretary. 165, Apr. 1889; 270, July 1889; 68, Apr. 1890; 297, Apr. 1891; 216, June 1896; 134, *Jan. 1936*

■■ *Henry Gannett, President of the National Geographic Society 1910-1914. By S.N.D. North. 34 pages. 1915*

Biography. 609-613, *Dec. 1914*

Portraits. Frontispiece, Aug. 1896; 195, May 1901; 611, *Dec. 1914*

Death notice. 520, *Nov. 1914*

Honors to Amundsen and Peary. Speech by Henry Gannett. 113-130, *Jan. 1913*

SEE "BORN OF FIRE" WEDNESDAY, APRIL 6, ON PBS TV

Speeches. 267, Mar. 1911; 272, Mar. 1912; 115, *Jan. 1913*

The National Geographic Society. Speech by Henry Gannett. 272-298, *Mar. 1912*

In Honor of the Army and Aviation. Speech by Henry Gannett. 267-284, *Mar. 1911*

Board of Managers. 297, Apr. 1891; xii, Feb. 19, 1892; xix, Feb. 20, 1893; 414, Sept. 1898; 87, Feb. 1905; 211, *Feb. 1911*

Chairman of committee appointed to consider claims of Cook and Peary. 921, 922, 1008, *Nov. 1909*

Chairman of Research Committee. 486, *May 1909*

Geographical Society of Paris, elected member of the 428, *June 1907*

Founder. 23, *Jan. 1906*

Judge of prize essay contest. 32, *Jan. 1899*

Treasurer. 87, Feb. 1905; 416, *Sept. 1898*

The Topographic Atlas of the United States (compiled by Henry Gannett). By W J McGee. 343-344, *July 1898*

Reports by. 164-166, Apr. 1889; 66, *Apr. 1890*

Author

Recent Population Figures. 785-786, *Aug. 1911*

The Population of the United States. 34-48, *Jan. 1911*

The Great Ice Barrier (Antarctica). 173-174, *Feb. 1910*

Conditions in Cuba as Revealed by the Census. 200-202, *Feb. 1909*

Conservation League of America. 737-739, *Oct. 1908*

The Philippine Islands and Their People. 91-112, *Mar. 1904*

Agriculture in Alaska. 112, *Mar. 1902*

The General Geography of Alaska. 180-196, *May 1901*

The Origin of Yosemite Valley. 86-87, *Feb. 1901*

The Harriman Alaska Expedition. 507-512, *Dec. 1899*

Place Names in Canada. 519-520, *Dec. 1899*

The Redwood Forest of the Pacific Coast. 145-159, *May 1899*

Lake Chelan. 417-428, *Oct. 1898*

The Forest Conditions and Standing Timber of the State of Washington. 410-412, *Sept. 1898*

Geographic Work of the General Government. 329-338, *July 1898*

Captain Charles D. Sigsbee, U.S.N. 250, *May 1898*

Geographic Serials. 25-26, Jan. 1897; 61-63, Feb. 1897; 92-94, Mar. 1897; 127-128, Apr. 1897; 158-159, May 1897; 190-191, June 1897; 256, *May 1898*

Geographic Literature. 60-61, Feb. 1897; 230-232, July-Aug. 1897; 365, Dec. 1897; 71-72, *Feb. 1898*

Our Foreign Trade. 27-28, *Jan. 1898*

The Annexation Fever. 354-358, *Dec. 1897*

Miscellanea. 160, *May 1897*

Statistics of Railways in the United States. 406-407, *Dec. 1896*

The Work of the United States Board on Geographic Names. 221-227, *July 1896*

Survey and Subdivision of Indian Territory. 112-115, *Mar. 1896*

The Movements of Our Population. 21-44, *Mar. 20, 1893*

The Mother Maps of the United States. 101-116, *Mar. 31, 1892*

The Survey and Map of Massachusetts. 78-86, *Oct. 1888*

GANNETT, S. S.: *Author*

Recent Triangulation in the Cascades (Washington). 150, *Apr. 1896*

GANSU PROVINCE, China:

The Caves of the Thousand Buddhas. By Franc and Jean Shor. Contents: Ansi; Kiuchuan (Suchow); Yumen; and the Tunhwang Caves. 383-415, *Mar. 1951*

China Fights Erosion with U. S. Aid. By Walter C. Lowdermilk. 641-680, *June 1945*

"Where the Mountains Walked": An Account of the Recent Earthquake in Kansu Province, China, Which Destroyed 100,000 Lives. By Upton Close and Elsie McCormick. 445-464, *May 1922*

See also Choni

GANYMEDE (Jovian Satellite):

What Voyager Saw: Jupiter's Dazzling Realm. By Rick Gore. Photos by NASA. 2-29, *Jan. 1980*

GARAVENTA, JOHN: *Author*

Down on the Farm, Soviet Style–a 4-H Adventure. Photos by James Tobin and Carol Schmidt. 768-797, *June 1979*

GARBAGE:

The Fascinating World of Trash. By Peter T. White. Photos by Louie Psihoyos. 424-457, *Apr. 1983*

GARBISCH COLLECTION:

Early America Through the Eyes of Her Native Artists. By Hereward Lester

Cooke, Jr. Paintings by American primitive artists. 356-389, *Sept. 1962*

GARCIA, MARIO ENRIQUE:
Nomination Page. *May 1976*

GARDENING in Northern Alaska. By Middleton Smith. 355-357, *Sept. 1903*

GARDENING'S Color Merchants: The Flower Seed Growers. By Robert de Roos. Photos by Jack Fields. 720-738, *May 1968*

GARDENS:
Herbs for All Seasons. By Lonnelle Aikman. Photos by Sam Abell. Picture portfolio text by Larry Kohl. Included: National Herb Garden. 386-409, *Mar. 1983*
Rose Aphids. By Treat Davidson. 851-859, *June 1961*
History and Beauty Blend in a Concord Iris Garden. By Robert T. Cochran, Jr. Photos by M. Woodbridge Williams. Included: Buttrick Garden. 705-719, *May 1959*
Ballerinas in Pink (Flamingos). By Carleton Mitchell. Photos by B. Anthony Stewart. Included: Ardastra Gardens. 553-571, *Oct. 1957*
■■ The World in Your Garden. Art by Else Bostelmann. 231 pages. *1957*
Maytime Miracle in Sherwood Gardens. By Nathaniel T. Kenney. 700-709, *May 1956*
Rhododendron Glories of Southwest Scotland. By David S. Boyer. Photos by B. Anthony Stewart and author. 641-664, *May 1954*
South Carolina Rediscovered. By Herbert Ravenel Sass. Included: Cypress Gardens; Magnolia Gardens; Middleton Gardens; Swan Lake Gardens. 281-321, *Mar. 1953*
Tropical Gardens of Key West. By Luis Marden. 116-124, *Jan. 1953*
Wonderland in Longwood Gardens. By Edward C. Ferriday, Jr. 45-64, *July 1951*
Kew: The Commoners' Royal Garden. By Thomas Garner James. Photos by B. Anthony Stewart. 479-506, *Apr. 1950*
Our Vegetable Travelers. By Victor R. Boswell. Paintings by Else Bostelmann. 145-217, *Aug. 1949*
The World in Your Garden (Flowers). By W. H. Camp. Paintings by Else Bostelmann. Contents: Gardens of Africa, Australia, China, Colonial America, Egypt, England, France, Greece, Holland, India, Japan, the Mediterranean region, Mexico, Persia, Rome, South America, Spain; and Alpine meadow gardens; Botanical gardens; Buddhist gardens; Hanging gardens; Informal gardens; Moslem gardens; Renaissance gardens; Rock gardens; Victory gardens. 1-65, *July 1947*
Nautical Norfolk Turns to Azaleas. By William H. Nicholas. Photos by B. Anthony Stewart. 606-614, *May 1947*
Gardens and Shrines of Old Virginia. Photos by B. Anthony Stewart and J. Baylor Roberts. 623-646, *May 1942*
Maytime in the Heart of Maryland

(Sherwood Gardens). Photos by B. Anthony Stewart and Charles Martin. 441-448, *Apr. 1941*
Charleston: Where Mellow Past and Present Meet. By DuBose Heyward. 273-312, *Mar. 1939*
The Garden Isles of Scilly: Geologists May Throw Stones at Legend of Lost Lyonnesse, But Natives Grow Flowers in Glass Houses for London. By W. Robert Moore. 755-774, *Dec. 1938*
Bekonscot, England's Toy-Size Town. By Andrew H. Brown and B. Anthony Stewart. 649-661, *May 1937*
Summering in an English Cottage: Quiet and Loveliness Invite Contemplation in the Extra "Room," the Garden of the Thatched House. By Helen Churchill Candee. 429-456, *Apr. 1935*
England's Island Garden of Rocks and Flowers (Isle of Wight). Photos by W. Robert Moore. 17-24, *Jan. 1935*
The Home of the First Farmer of America (Mount Vernon). By Worth E. Shoults. 603-628, *May 1928*
A Vacation in a Fifteenth Century English Manor House. By George Alden Sanford. 629-636, *May 1928*
The Ashley River and Its Gardens. By E.T.H. Shaffer. 525-550, *May 1926*
The Palace of Versailles, Its Park and the Trianons. By Franklin L. Fisher. 49-62, *Jan. 1925*
The Woods and Gardens of Portugal. By Martin Hume. 883-894, *Oct. 1910*
Tirnova, the City of Hanging Gardens. By Felix J. Koch. 632-640, *Oct. 1907*
The Gardens of the West. 118-123, *Mar. 1905*

GARDIANS (French Cowboys):
France's Wild, Watery South, the Camargue. By William Davenport. 696-726, *May 1973*
The Camargue, Land of Cowboys and Gypsies. By Eugene L. Kammerman. 667-699, *May 1956*

GARDINER GREENE HUBBARD. (Announcement of the Death of Mr. Hubbard). By John Hyde. 345, *Dec. 1897*

GARDINER GREENE HUBBARD: An Address delivered at the Memorial Services held at the Church of the Covenant, Washington, D. C., December 13, 1897. By Teunis S. Hamlin. 33-38, *Feb. 1898*

GARDINER GREENE HUBBARD: Memorial Meeting, held in the City of Washington, January 21, 1898, Alexander Graham Bell, President of the National Geographic Society, presiding. 39-70, *Feb. 1898*

GARDNER, BEATRICE T. and R. ALLEN:
Nomination Page. *Aug. 1972*

GARDNER, IRVINE C.:
Author-Photographer
Crusoes of Canton Island: Life on a Tiny Pacific Atoll That Has Flashed Into World Importance. Included: Natural-color photograph of 1937

eclipse, showing the corona. 749-766, *June 1938*
Observing an Eclipse in Asiatic Russia. Included: First natural-color photograph of an eclipse (1936) ever reproduced, showing the corona. 179-197, *Feb. 1937*

GARDNER, Mount, Antarctica:
First Conquest of Antarctica's Highest Peaks. By Nicholas B. Clinch. NGS research grant. 836-863, *June 1967*

GARFIELD, JAMES A.:
The Living White House. By Lonnelle Aikman. 593-643, *Nov. 1966*
Profiles of the Presidents: III. The American Giant Comes of Age. By Frank Freidel. 660-711, *May 1965*

GARFINKEL, PERRY: *Author*
Madawaska: Down East With a French Accent. Photos by Cary Wolinsky. 380-409, *Sept. 1980*

GARLAND, HAMLIN: *Author*
Overland Routes to the Klondike. 113-116, *Apr. 1898*

GARNER, WILLIAM: *Author*
High Road to "Victory": Soviet and U. S. Climbers Conquer Pik Pobedy. Photos by Medford Taylor. 256-271, *Aug. 1986*

GARRETT, KENNETH:
On Assignment. *Nov. 1983*
Author-Photographer
By Square-rigger from Baltic to Bicentennial. 824-857, *Dec. 1976*
Photographer
George Washington's Patowmack Canal. By Wilbur E. Garrett. 716-753, *June 1987*
Humble Masterpieces: Decoys. By George Reiger. 639-663, *Nov. 1983*
The Disaster of El Chichón. By Boris Weintraub. Photos by Guillermo Aldana E. and Kenneth Garrett. 654-684, *Nov. 1982*

GARRETT, WILBUR E.:
On Assignment in Egypt. *Apr. 1988*
Editor (1980-). 427, Oct. 1980; 567, Nov. 1980; 222, 234, Aug. 1981; 849, 851, Dec. 1981; 585, 589, May 1982; 270, 276, 278, *Aug. 1982*
On Assignment in Southeast Asia. *May 1982*
Nomination Page. *May 1980*
Nomination Page: Photo by. *June 1979*
Nomination Page. *July 1978*
Nomination Page. *June 1976*
Nomination Page. *Jan. 1974*
Nomination Page. *July 1966*
Nomination Page. *May 1963*
Nomination Page. *Oct. 1962*
National Geographic Photographers Win Top Magazine Awards. 830-831, *June 1959*
Author
Air Bridge to Siberia. Photos by Steve Raymer. 504-509, *Oct. 1988*
George Washington's Patowmack Canal. Photos by Kenneth Garrett. 716-753, *June 1987*
When the Earth Moves. 638-639, *May 1986*

Whether coming or going, travelers between Saskatoon, Saskatchewan, and Edmonton, Alberta, find an endless horizon in Canada's Prairie Provinces.   WILBUR E. GARRETT, NGS

Snow geese rise above South Dakota at a refuge along the central flyway. DES AND JEN BARTLETT

GATES, THOMAS S., Jr.:
Secretary of the Navy Thomas S. Gates, Jr., accepts Hubbard Medal for the U. S. Navy Antarctic Expeditions, 1955-1959. 589-590, *Apr. 1959*

GATES AND GATEWAYS:
Sculptured Gates to English Learning (Cambridge University). Photos by B. Anthony Stewart. 417-440, *Apr. 1946*

The **GATES** to the Black Sea: The Dardanelles, the Bosphorus, and the Sea of Marmora. By Harry Griswold Dwight. 435-459, *May 1915*

GATEWAY NATIONAL RECREATION AREA, New Jersey-New York:
Gateway–Elbowroom for the Millions. By Louise Levathes. 86-97, *July 1979*

GATEWAY to Westward Expansion. By William C. Everhart. 643-669, *Nov. 1965*

GATSCHET, ALBERT S.: *Author*
All Around the Bay of Passamaquoddy. 16-24, *Jan. 1897*

GATUN LAKE, Panama:
Nature's Transformation at Panama: Remarkable Changes in Faunal and Physical Conditions in the Gatun Lake Region. By George Shiras, 3d. 159-194, *Aug. 1915*

GATUN LOCKS AND DAM, Panama:
The Panama Canal. By William L. Sibert. 153-183, *Feb. 1914*

GAUCHOS:
The Gauchos, Last of a Breed. By Robert Laxalt. Photos by O. Louis Mazzatenta. 478-501, *Oct. 1980*

Brazil, Oba! By Peter T. White. Photos by Winfield Parks. 299-353, *Sept. 1962*

Argentina: Young Giant of the Far South. By Jean and Franc Shor. 297-352, *Mar. 1958*

The Purple Land of Uruguay. By Luis Marden. 623-654, *Nov. 1948*

Life on the Argentine Pampa. By Frederick Simpich. Paintings by Cesáreo Bernaldo de Quirós. 449-491, *Oct. 1933*

GAULS. *See* Celts

GAVIALS. *See* Gharials

GAY Colors in the Land of Black Majesty (Haiti). Photos by Clifton Adams. 445-452, *Oct. 1934*

GAYER, JACOB:
Author-Photographer
Hispaniola Rediscovered (Dominican Republic). Included: Scenic Resources of the Dominican Republic. 80-112, *Jan. 1931*

Photographer
Springtime Wreathes a Garland for the Nation's Capital. 473-480, *Apr. 1935*
Where the Winning of the West Began (Ohio). 563-570, *May 1932*
Our Colorful City of Magnificent Distances (Washington, D. C.). 531-610, *Nov. 1931*
Among the Snows and Flowers of Peru. 733-764, *June 1930*
Scenes of Beauty in Copper Land (Chile). 199-214, *Feb. 1929*
Among the Highlands of the Equator Republic (Ecuador). 69-76, *Jan. 1929*

The Color Palette of the Caribbean (Jamaica). 45-55, *Jan. 1927*
In the Land of the Quetzal (Guatemala). 611-626, *Nov. 1926*
Exploring the Atlantic Seaboard with a Color Camera. 533-548, *May 1926*
The First Natural-Color Photographs from the Arctic. 301-316, *Mar. 1926*
Canyons and Cacti of the American Southwest. 275-290, *Sept. 1925*

GAZA STRIP, Israeli-occupied Egypt:
Lost Outpost of the Egyptian Empire. By Trude Dothan. Photos by Sisse Brimberg. Paintings by Lloyd K. Townsend. 739-769, *Dec. 1982*

GAZETTEERS:
A Dictionary of Universal Geography. 114, *Feb. 1906*
Gazetteers of the States. 369-370, *Sept. 1904*

GDANSK, Poland:
Historic Danzig: Last of the City-States. By William and Alicelia Franklin. 677-696, *Nov. 1939*
War Clouds Over Danzig and Poland's Port. 551-558, *Oct. 1939*
Flying Around the Baltic. By Douglas Chandler. 767-806, *June 1938*

GDYNIA, Poland:
War Clouds Over Danzig and Poland's Port. 551-558, *Oct. 1939*

GEESE:
North American Waterfowl: Troubles and Triumphs. By John Madson. 562-599, *Nov. 1984*
Beyond the North Wind With the Snow Goose. By Des and Jen Bartlett. 822-843, *Dec. 1973*

Saving the Nene, World's Rarest Goose. By S. Dillon Ripley. Photos by Jerry Chong. 745-754, *Nov. 1965*

Bright Dyes Reveal Secrets of Canada Geese. By John and Frank Craighead. 817-832, *Dec. 1957*

Far-Flying Wild Fowl and Their Foes. By Allan Brooks. Paintings by author. 487-528, *Oct. 1934*

Fowls of Forest and Stream Tamed by Man. By Morley A. Jull. Paintings by Hashime Murayama. Contents: Canadian, Chinese, Egyptian, Embden, Gray African, Sebastopol, Toulouse. 327-371, *Mar. 1930*

American Game Birds. By Henry Wetherbee Henshaw. Paintings by Louis Agassiz Fuertes. 105-158, *Aug. 1915*

Saving the Ducks and Geese. By Wells W. Cooke. 361-380, *Mar. 1913*

GEHMAN, RICHARD: *Author*

Amish Folk: Plainest of Pennsylvania's Plain People. Photos by William Albert Allard. 227-253, *Aug. 1965*

GEHRELS, TOM:

Nomination Page. *Jan. 1975*

GEIKIE GLACIER, British Columbia, Canada:

Some Tramps Across the Glaciers and Snowfields of British Columbia. By Howard Palmer. 457-487, *June 1910*

GEISER, KARL FREDERICK: *Author*

Peasant Life in the Black Forest. 635-649, *Sept. 1908*

GEISHA:

Kansai, Japan's Historic Heartland. By Thomas J. Abercrombie. 295-339, *Mar. 1970*

GEITHMANN, HARRIET: *Author*

Ströbeck, Home of Chess: A Medieval Village in the Harz Mountains of Germany Teaches the Royal Game in Its Public School. 637-652, *May 1931*

GELIDONYA, Cape, Turkey:

Oldest Known Shipwreck Yields Bronze Age Cargo. By Peter Throckmorton. NGS research grant. 697-711, *May 1962*

The **GEM** of the Ocean: Our American Navy. By Josephus Daniels. 313-335, *Apr. 1918*

GEMINI MISSIONS:

The Earth From Orbit. By Paul D. Lowman, Jr. 645-671, *Nov. 1966*

Space Rendezvous, Milestone on the Way to the Moon. By Kenneth F. Weaver. 539-553, *Apr. 1966*

America's 6,000-mile Walk in Space. 440-447, *Sept. 1965*

The Making of an Astronaut. By Robert R. Gilruth. 122-144, *Jan. 1965*

Footprints on the Moon. By Hugh L. Dryden. Paintings by Davis Meltzer and Pierre Mion. 357-401, *Mar. 1964*

GEMS:

Precious Corals, Hawaii's Deep-sea Jewels. By Richard W. Grigg. 719-732, *May 1979*

Imperial Russia's Glittering Legacy. 24-33, *Jan. 1978*

The Glittering World of Rockhounds. By David S. Boyer. 276-294, *Feb. 1974*

Questing for Gems. By George S. Switzer. Included: Gem mining in Africa, Brazil, and Colombia; samplings of the Crown Jewel collections of Great Britain, Iran, and tsarist Russia; the history of the Koh-i-noor, Hope, and Orloff diamonds. 835-863, *Dec. 1971*

Exploring the World of Gems. By W. F. Foshag. 779-810, *Dec. 1950*

The Purple Land of Uruguay. By Luis Marden. Included: Agates, Amethysts, Quartz. 623-654, *Nov. 1948*

Brazil's Land of Minerals. By W. Robert Moore. Contents: Amethyst, Aquamarine, Citrine, Diamond, Emerald, Morganite, Topaz, Tourmaline. 479-508, *Oct. 1948*

The Diamond Mines of South Africa. By Gardiner F. Williams. 344-356, *June 1906*

Precious Stones. 451-458, *Dec. 1903*

See also Amber, a gemlike fossil resin; Diamonds; Jade; Lapidary Work; Opal Mining; Pearls

GEMS from Scotland. 519-534, *Nov.-Dec. 1917*

GEMS of the Italian Lakes. By Arthur Ellis Mayer. 943-956, *Aug. 1913*

GENERAL ELECTRIC COMPANY:

Landsat Looks at Hometown Earth. By

Barry C. Bishop. Note: GE's Photographic Engineering Laboratory's color-mosaic expertise was combined with Landsat imagery to produce Portrait U.S.A., first color photomosaic of the 48 contiguous states. 140-147, *July 1976*

Studying Grizzly Habitat by Satellite. By John Craighead. Included: GE Image 100 computer system, used with Landsat imagery to produce satellite-computer maps of grizzly bear habitat. 148-158, *July 1976*

Drums to Dynamos on the Mohawk. By Frederick G. Vosburgh. Photos by B. Anthony Stewart. 67-110, *July 1947*

See also Tektite II, for undersea equipment

The **GENERAL** Geography of Alaska. By Henry Gannett. 180-196, *May 1901*

GENERAL GRANT NATIONAL PARK, California:

Our National Parks. By L. F. Schmeckebier. 531-579, *June 1912*

GENERAL LAND OFFICE (U. S.):

Geographic Work of the General Government. By Henry Gannett. 329-338, *July 1898*

Geographical Research in the United States. By Gardiner G. Hubbard and Marcus Baker. 285-293, *Oct. 1897*

See also Public Lands

GENERAL MILLS, INC.: Research and Engineering. *See Strato-Lab*

A two-man Gemini capsule nears a historic rendezvous with a second Gemini craft 185 miles above the Pacific Ocean in 1965. THOMAS P. STAFFORD, NASA

GENERAL SHERMAN TREE, Sequoia
National Park, California:
The General Sherman: Earth's Biggest
Living Thing. 605-608, *May 1958*
The Oldest Living Thing. Photo supplement, *Apr. 1916*

A **GENERATION** After Sputnik...Are
the Soviets Ahead in Space? By
Thomas Y. Canby. 420-459,
Oct. 1986

GENERATORS, Wind-driven:
Can We Harness the Wind? By Roger
Hamilton. Photos by Emory Kristof.
812-829, *Dec. 1975*

GENESIS of the Williamsburg Restoration. By John D. Rockefeller, Jr. 401,
Apr. 1937

GENETIC ENGINEERING:
Beyond Supermouse: Changing Life's
Genetic Blueprint. By Robert F.
Weaver. Photos by Ted Spiegel. 818-
847, *Dec. 1984*

GENETIC RESEARCH:
The Incredible Potato. By Robert E.
Rhoades. Photos by Martin Rogers.
Included: The study of fusing two bo-
tanical cousins, the potato and toma-
to, and research in "true seed"
adaptation. 668-694, *May 1982*
The Awesome Worlds Within a Cell. By
Rick Gore. Photos by Bruce Dale.
Paintings by Davis Meltzer. 355-395,
Sept. 1976

GENEVA, Switzerland:
Switzerland, Europe's High-rise Re-
public. By Thomas J. Abercrombie.
68-113, *July 1969*
"Around the World in Eighty Days."
By Newman Bumstead. 705-750,
Dec. 1951
Switzerland Guards the Roof of Eu-
rope. By William H. Nicholas. Pho-
tos by Willard R. Culver. 205-246,
Aug. 1950
The Millennial City: The Romance of

Geneva, Capital of the League of
Nations. By Ralph A. Graves. 457-
476, *June 1919*

GENEVA, Lake, Switzerland-France:
Lake Geneva: Cradle of Conferences.
By F. Barrows Colton. 727-742,
Dec. 1937

The **GENIUS** of El Greco. Introduction
by J. Carter Brown. 736-744,
June 1982

GENOA, Italy:
Italian Riviera, Land That Winter For-
got. By Howell Walker. 743-789,
June 1963
Genoa, Where Columbus Learned to
Love the Sea. By McFall Kerbey. In-
cluded: Painting supplement. 333-
352, *Sept. 1928*
Inexhaustible Italy. By Arthur Stanley
Riggs. 273-368, *Oct. 1916*
Frontier Cities of Italy. By Florence
Craig Albrecht. 533-586, *June 1915*

GENTHE, ARNOLD: *Photographer*
Ageless Luster of Greece and Rhodes.
477-492, *Apr. 1938*

GENTHE, MARTHA KRUG: *Author*
German Geographers and German Geography. 324-337, *Sept. 1901*

GENTILI, GINO VINICIO: *Author*
Roman Life in 1,600-year-old Color Pic-
tures (Mosaics). Photos by Duncan
Edwards. 211-229, *Feb. 1957*

GENTLE Fliers of the African Night.
By Merlin D. Tuttle. Contents: Bats.
NGS research grant. 540-558,
Apr. 1986

GENTLE Folk Settle Stern Saguenay:
On French Canada's Frontier Home-
spun Colonists Keep the Customs of
Old Norman Settlers. By Harrison
Howell Walker. 595-632, *May 1939*

The **GENTLE** Yamis of Orchid Island.
Photos by Chang Shuhua. 98-109,
Jan. 1977

GENTLEMEN Adventurers of the Air:
Many Regions of Canada's Vast Wilderness, Long Hidden Even from Fur
Trappers, Are Now Revealed by Exploring Airmen. By J. A. Wilson.
597-642, *Nov. 1929*

GENTRY, ROGER L.: *Author*
Seals and Their Kin. 475-501, *Apr. 1987*

GEODESY:
Charting a World at War. By William
H. Nicholas. 617-640, *Nov. 1944*
A Simple Method of Proving That the
Earth Is Round. By Robert Marshall
Brown. 771-774, *Dec. 1907*
Recent Contributions to Our Knowl-
edge of the Earth's Shape and Size,
by the United States Coast and Geo-
detic Survey. By C. A. Schott. 36-41,
Jan. 1901

GEODETIC SURVEYS:
Wringing Secrets from Greenland's Ice-
cap. By Paul-Emile Victor. 121-147,
Jan. 1956
See also Inter-American Geodetic Sur-
vey; U. S. Coast and Geodetic Survey

GEODYNAMICS:
This Changing Earth. By Samuel W.
Matthews. 1-37, *Jan. 1973*
Our Home-town Planet, Earth. By F.
Barrows Colton. 117-139, *Jan. 1952*
See also Earthquakes; Faulting; Plate
Tectonics; Volcanoes

GEOGRAPHERS:
Four Prominent Geographers. Con-
tents: Biographies and portraits of
Arthur P. Davis, Frederick Haynes
Newell, George Otis Smith, and
Charles D. Walcott. 425-428,
June 1907
See also names of geographers, NGM
editors, staff members, and
contributors

A **GEOGRAPHIC** Achievement. 667-
668, *June 1913*

GEOGRAPHIC CONFERENCE. *See*
International Geographic
Conference

GEOGRAPHIC CONGRESS. *See* International Geographic Congress

**GEOGRAPHIC DISTRIBUTION OF
LIFE:**
Laws of Temperature Control of the
Geographic Distribution of Terrestri-
al Animals and Plants. Annual Ad-
dress by C. Hart Merriam. 229-238,
Dec. 29, 1894
Geography of Life. By C. Hart Mer-
riam. 160-162, *Apr. 1889*

GEOGRAPHIC EDUCATION:
Gallup Survey of geographic knowl-
edge. President's Page. By Gilbert
M. Grosvenor. Included: Nation's
Report Card program of tests; Geog-
raphy Awareness Week; National
Geography Bee. *Nov. 1988*
President Grosvenor Announces the
NGS Education Foundation. 329A-
329D, *Mar. 1988*
President's Page. By Gilbert M.
Grosvenor. Aug. 1984; Sept. 1984;

*A Genoese got a horse when his pint-size car was further compacted in a 1962 collision
amid the ever increasing traffic in the Italian Riviera's largest city.* ALBERT MOLDVAY

GEOGRAPHIC EDUCATION NATIONAL IMPLEMENTATION PROJECT (GENIP):

GEOGRAPHIC ENVIRONMENT:

GEOGRAPHIC NAMES:

Geographer Alexander von Humboldt made a pioneer study of plant ecology on Ecuadorian volcanoes in the 19th century. ARCHIV FÜR KUNST UND GESCHICHTE, BERLIN

GEOGRAPHIC SOCIETIES:

GEOGRAPHICA:

GEOGRAPHY:

Thirty thousand lives were snuffed out when Mount Pelée erupted in 1902, annihilating Martinique's port of St. Pierre.   MORRIS J. ELSING

The Classification of Geographic Forms by Genesis. By W J McGee. 27-36, *Oct. 1888*

See also Expeditions; Explorers, Discoverers, and Navigators; Geographic Education; Geographic Names; Oceanography; *and* expeditions by subject

GEOGRAPHY AWARENESS WEEK:

November 13-19, 1988. President's Page. By Gilbert M. Grosvenor. *Nov. 1988*

President's Page. By Gilbert M. Grosvenor. *Jan. 1988*

November 15-21, 1987. President's Page. By Gilbert M. Grosvenor. *Nov. 1987*

"GEOGRAPHY DAY":

President's Page. By Gilbert M. Grosvenor. *Feb. 1986; July 1986*

The **GEOGRAPHY** of a Hurricane: A Doughnut-shaped Storm Turned Back Time in New England to Candlelight Days, but Revealed Anew Yankee Courage and Ingenuity. By F. Barrows Colton. 529-552, *Apr. 1939*

The **GEOGRAPHY** of Games: How the Sports of Nations Form a Gazetteer of the Habits and Histories of Their Peoples. By Jesse R. Hildebrand. 89-144, *Aug. 1919*

The **GEOGRAPHY** of Life. By C. Hart Merriam. 160-162, *Apr. 1889*

The **GEOGRAPHY** of Medicines: War's Effect Upon the World's Sources of Supply. By John Foote. 213-238, *Sept. 1917*

The **GEOGRAPHY** of Money. By William Atherton Du Puy. 745-768, *Dec. 1927*

GEOHOUSE:

Modern House, Ancient Architecture. 42-43, *Special Report on Energy. (Feb. 1981)*

GEOLOGY:

Meteorites–Invaders From Space. By Kenneth F. Weaver. Photos by Jonathan Blair. 390-418, *Sept. 1986*

Our Restless Planet Earth. By Rick Gore. Photos by James A. Sugar. 142-181. Included: Continents Adrift; Life's Triumph *and* Origin of Earth and Life. Painting by Ned M. Seidler. Text by Larry Kohl. 146-151, *Aug. 1985*

✤ *The Shaping of a Continent: North America's Active West; Earth's Dynamic Crust.* Included: Spreading, Subduction, Collision, Faulting, Accretion, Hot Spots, 90 Million Years of Drift. *Aug. 1985*

Geothermal Energy: The Power of Letting Off Steam. By Kenneth F. Weaver. 566-579, *Oct. 1977*

Window on Earth's Interior. By Robert D. Ballard. Photos by Emory Kristof. Contents: Cayman Trough. 228-249, *Aug. 1976*

■■ *Our Continent: A Natural History of North America.* 398 pages. *1976*

This Changing Earth. By Samuel W. Matthews. 1-37, *Jan. 1973*

The Earth From Orbit. By Paul D. Lowman, Jr. 645-671, *Nov. 1966*

Afoot in Roadless Nepal (Geological Survey). By Toni Hagen. 361-405, *Mar. 1960*

Roaming the West's Fantastic Four Corners. By Jack Breed. 705-742, *June 1952*

Our Home-town Planet, Earth: Examining the Iron-hearted Globe, Science Gains New Knowledge of Earthquakes, Volcanoes, and Earth's Birth and Future. By F. Barrows Colton. 117-139, *Jan. 1952*

Utah's Arches of Stone. By Jack Breed. 173-192, *Aug. 1947*

Where Early Christians Lived in Cones of Rock: A Journey to Cappadocia in Turkey Where Strange Volcanic Pinnacles Are Honeycombed With Hermit Cells and Monasteries. By John D. Whiting. 763-802, *Dec. 1939*

We Keep House on an Active Volcano: After Flying to Study a Spectacular Eruption in Belgian Congo, a Geologist Settles Down on a Newborn Craterless Vent for Eight Months' Study. By Jean Verhoogen. 511-550, *Oct. 1939*

Crater Lake and Yosemite Through the Ages. By Wallace W. Atwood, Jr. Paintings by Eugene Kingman. 327-343, *Mar. 1937*

A Geologist's Paradise (Canadian Rockies). By Charles D. Walcott. 509-536, *June 1911*

The Erratic. By O. A. Ljungstedt. 525-531, *June 1910*

Landslides and Rock Avalanches. By Guy Elliott Mitchell. 277-287, *Apr. 1910*

Geologists in China. 640-644, *Oct. 1907*

The Central Great Plains (U. S.). 389-397, *Aug. 1905*

Geologic Folios in Schools. 244-247, *May 1905*

Field Courses in Geology. 250, *May 1905*

The Cause of the Earth's Heat. 124-125, *Mar. 1905*

Limiting Width of Meander Belts. By Mark S. W. Jefferson. 373-384, *Oct. 1902*

Report by Robert T. Hill on the Volcanic Disturbances in the West Indies. 223-267, *July 1902*

Volcanic Rocks of Martinique and St. Vincent: Collected by Robert T. Hill and Israel C. Russell. By J. S. Diller. 285-296, *July 1902*

Porto Rico. By Robert T. Hill. 93-112, *Mar. 1899*

Origin of the Physical Features of the United States. By G. K. Gilbert. 308-317, *July 1898*

Geographic Development of the District of Columbia. By W J McGee. 317-323, *July 1898*

The Geologic Atlas of the United States. By W J McGee. 339-342, *July 1898*

Cuba. By Robert T. Hill. 193-242, *May 1898*

Alaska and Its Mineral Resources. By

Samuel Franklin Emmons. 139-172, *Apr. 1898*

Crater Lake, Oregon. By J. S. Diller. 33-48, *Feb. 1897*

Geographic History of the Piedmont Plateau. By W J McGee. 261-265, *Aug. 1896*

Geomorphology of the Southern Appalachians. By Charles Willard Hayes and Marius R. Campbell. 63-126, *May 23, 1894*

Shawangunk Mountain (New York). By N. H. Darton. 23-34, *Mar. 17, 1894*

The Relations of Geology to Physiography in Our Educational System. By T. C. Chamberlin. 154-160, *Jan. 31, 1894*

The Geologist at Blue Mountain, Maryland. By Charles D. Walcott. 84-88, *July 10, 1893*

An Expedition through the Yukon District. By Charles Willard Hayes. 117-159, *May 15, 1892*

Notes on the Geology of the Vicinity of Muir Glacier. By H. P. Cushing. 56-62, *Mar. 21, 1892*

Notes on Some Eruptive Rocks from Alaska. By George H. Williams. 63-74, *Mar. 21, 1892*

An Expedition to Mount St. Elias, Alaska. By Israel C. Russell. 53-191, *May 29, 1891*

The Rivers of Northern New Jersey, with Notes on the Classification of Rivers in General. By William Morris Davis. 81-110, *May 1890*

The Rivers and Valleys of Pennsylvania. By William Morris Davis. 183-253, *July 1889*

Geography of the Land. By Herbert G. Ogden. 125-135, *Apr. 1889*

The Classification of Geographic Forms by Genesis. By W J McGee. 27-36, *Oct. 1888*

Geographic Methods in Geologic Investigation. By W. M. Davis. 11-26, *Oct. 1888*

See also Canyons; Caves; Earthquakes; Erosion; Geology, Space; Geophysical Research; Geysers; Glaciers; Minerals and Metals; Mountains; Ocean Floors; Paleontology; Plate Tectonics; Soil Erosion; Stone Spheres; Volcanoes; *and* Basin and Range Geological Province, U. S.; Mohole, Project; U. S. Geological Survey; White Sands National Monument; Yellowstone National Park; Zion National Park

GEOLOGY, Lunar:

Exploring Taurus-Littrow. By Harrison H. Schmitt. Photos by the crew of Apollo 17. 290-307, *Sept. 1973*

Have We Solved the Mysteries of the Moon? By Kenneth F. Weaver. Paintings by William H. Bond. 309-325, *Sept. 1973*

Apollo 15 Explores the Mountains of the Moon. By Kenneth F. Weaver. Photos from NASA. 233-265, *Feb. 1972*

The Climb Up Cone Crater. By Alice J. Hall. Photos by Edgar D. Mitchell and Alan B. Shepard, Jr. 136-148, *July 1971*

First Explorers on the Moon: The Incredible Story of Apollo 11. 735-797. I. Man Walks on Another World. By Neil A. Armstrong, Edwin E. Aldrin, Jr., and Michael Collins. 738-749; III. The Flight of Apollo 11. By Kenneth F. Weaver. 752-787; IV. What the Moon Rocks Tell Us. By Kenneth F. Weaver. 788-791, *Dec. 1969*

That Orbèd Maiden...the Moon. By Kenneth F. Weaver. 207-230, *Feb. 1969*

Awesome Views of the Forbidding Moonscape. 233-239, *Feb. 1969*

The Moon Close Up. By Eugene M. Shoemaker. Photos by Ranger 7. 690-707, *Nov. 1964*

GEOLOGY, Space:

Mariner Unveils Venus and Mercury (Mariner 10). By Kenneth F. Weaver. 858-869, *June 1975*

See also Geology, Lunar

GEOMAGNETISM:

Charting a World at War. By William H. Nicholas. 617-640, *Nov. 1944*

Sailing the Seven Seas in the Interest of Science: Adventures Through 157,000 Miles of Storm, and Calm, from Arctic to Antarctic and Around the World, in the Non-magnetic Yacht "Carnegie." By J. P. Ault. 631-690, *Dec. 1922*

Our Guardians on the Deep. By William Joseph Showalter. 655-677, *June 1914*

Most Curious Craft Afloat: The Compass in Navigation and the Work of the Non-Magnetic Yacht "Carnegie." By L. A. Bauer. 223-245, *Mar. 1910*

Magnetic Observations in Alaska. By Daniel L. Hazard. 675-676, *July 1909*

The Magnetic Survey of Africa. By L. A. Bauer. 291-297, *Mar. 1909*

Magnetic Survey of the Pacific. 447-448, *June 1908*

Work in the Pacific Ocean of the Magnetic Survey Yacht "Galilee." By L. A. Bauer. 601-611, *Sept. 1907*

Recent Magnetic Work by the Carnegie Institution of Washington. 648, *Nov. 1906*

Magnetic Survey of the Pacific Ocean. By L. A. Bauer. 237, *Apr. 1906*

Magnetic Disturbances Caused by the Explosion of Mont Pelée. 208-209, *June 1902*

Magnetic Survey of the United States. By L. A. Bauer. 92-95, *Mar. 1902*

Magnetic Work of the Coast and Geodetic Survey. By L. A. Bauer. 288-289, *Aug. 1899*

Magnetic Observations in Iceland, Jan Mayen and Spitzbergen in 1892. By Cyrus C. Babb. 223-224, *Dec. 29, 1894*

GEOMORPHOLOGY of the Southern Appalachians. By Charles Willard Hayes and Marius R. Campbell. 63-126, *May 23, 1894*

GEOPHYSICAL RESEARCH:

Ice on the World. By Samuel W. Matthews. 79-103, *Jan. 1987*

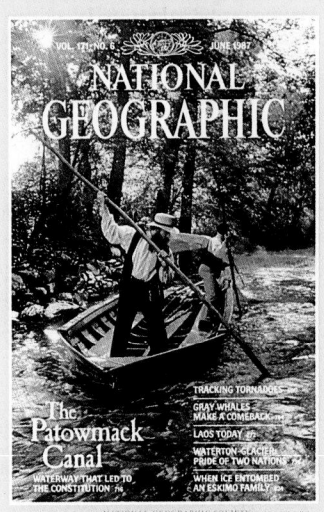

Science Explores the Monsoon Sea. By Samuel W. Matthews. Photos by Robert F. Sisson. 554-575, *Oct. 1967*

Scientists Ride Ice Islands on Arctic Odysseys. By Lowell Thomas, Jr. Photos by Ted Spiegel. 670-691, *Nov. 1965*

How Man-made Satellites Can Affect Our Lives. By Joseph Kaplan. 791-810, *Dec. 1957*

Three Months on an Arctic Ice Island. By Joseph O. Fletcher. 489-504, *Apr. 1953*

See also Geodetic Surveys; International Geophysical Year; listing under Meteorology; Oceanography; Plate Tectonics; Seismology; Volcanoes

GEORG STAGE (School Ship):

By Full-rigged Ship to Denmark's Fairyland. By Alan Villiers. Photos by Alexander Taylor and author. 809-828, *Dec. 1955*

GEORGE, MIMI:

On Assignment in Antarctica. *Nov. 1984*

Photographer

Icebound in Antarctica. By David Lewis. 634-663, *Nov. 1984*

GEORGE, Lake, Alaska:

Alaska's Automatic Lake Drains Itself. 835-844, *June 1951*

GEORGE W. MELVILLE, Engineer-in-chief, U.S.N. By Adolphus W. Greely. 187-190, *June 1897*

GEORGE WASHINGTON–Man and Monument. By Frank Freidel and Lonnelle Aikman. Published in cooperation with the Washington National Monument Association. 69 pages. 1965; rev. ed. *1973*

GEORGE WASHINGTON: The Man Behind the Myths. By Howard La Fay. Photos by Ted Spiegel. 90-111, *July 1976*

GEORGE WASHINGTON'S Historic River (Potomac). Photos by Willard R. Culver and Robert F. Sisson. 41-64, *July 1945*

GEORGE WASHINGTON'S Patowmack Canal. By Wilbur E. Garrett. Photos by Kenneth Garrett. 716-753, *June 1987*

GEORGES POMPIDOU NATIONAL CENTER OF ART AND CULTURE, Paris:

Pompidou Center, Rage of Paris. By Cathy Newman. Photos by Marc Riboud. 469-477, *Oct. 1980*

GEORGESON, C. C.: *Author*

Agricultural Capacity of Alaska: What Population Can the Territory Support? 676-679, *July 1909*

The Possibilities of Alaska. 81-85, *Mar. 1902*

GEORGETOWN, Washington, D. C.:

George Washington's Patowmack Canal. By Wilbur E. Garrett. Photos by Kenneth Garrett. 716-753, *June 1987*

Washington's Historic Georgetown. By William A. Kinney. 513-544, *Apr. 1953*

Washington: Home of the Nation's Great. By Albert W. Atwood. 699-738, *June 1947*

Potomac, River of Destiny. By Albert W. Atwood. 33-70, *July 1945*

GEORGIA, LOWELL: *Photographer*

Waterton-Glacier International Peace Park: Pride of Two Nations. By David S. Boyer. 796-823, *June 1987*

Unearthing the Oldest Known Maya. By Norman Hammond. Photos by Lowell Georgia and Martha Cooper. 126-140, *July 1982*

My Chesapeake–Queen of Bays. By Allan C. Fisher, Jr. 428-467, *Oct. 1980*

Our Wildest Wilderness: Alaska's Arctic National Wildlife Range. By Douglas H. Chadwick. 737-769, *Dec. 1979*

Natural Gas: The Search Goes On. By Bryan Hodgson. 632-651, *Nov. 1978*

Into the Wilderness. Art by H. Tom Hall. Contents: Seven famous historic explorations and trails. 207 pages. *1978*

Our Wild and Scenic Rivers: The Flathead. By Douglas H. Chadwick. 13-19, *July 1977*

Canada's "Now" Frontier. By Robert Paul Jordan. 480-511, *Oct. 1976*

Nebraska...the Good Life. By Robert Paul Jordan. 378-407, *Mar. 1974*

Hiking the Backbone of the Rockies: Canada's Great Divide Trail. By Mike W. Edwards. 795-817, *June 1973*

A River Restored: Oregon's Willamette. By Ethel A. Starbird. 816-835, *June 1972*

GEORGIA:

Sea Change in the Sea Islands. By Charles L. Blockson. Photos by Karen Kasmauski. 735-763, *Dec. 1987*

Savannah to Charleston–A Good Life in the Low Country. By John J.

G
H

Caked with a day's worth of coal dust, a miner in West Germany's Ruhr region doffs his gear and prepares for a shower. ERICH LESSING, MAGNUM

Once an artillery factory for the Third Reich, Germany's Krupp Works in Essen was converted to rolling-stock repair after World War II. ACME

SEE JERUSALEM: WITHIN THESE WALLS WEDNESDAY, MARCH 12, ON PBS TV

Over? By Theodore H. Reed. Photos by Donna K. Grosvenor. 803-815, *Dec. 1972*

GIANT SEQUOIAS Draw Millions to California Parks. By John Michael Kauffmann. Photos by B. Anthony Stewart. 147-187, *Aug. 1959*

The **GIANT** Tides of Fundy. By Paul A. Zahl. 153-192, *Aug. 1957*

GIANT TORTOISES:

Giant Tortoises: Goliaths of the Galapagos. By Craig MacFarland. Photos by author and Jan MacFarland. 632-649, *Nov. 1972*

GIANTS *from the Past: The Age of Mammals.* By Joseph H. Bailey. Juvenile. 104 pages. *1983*

GIANTS of the Wilderness: Alaskan Moose. By Victor Van Ballenberghe. Photos by Michio Hoshino. 260-280, *Aug. 1987*

GIANTS That Move the World's Oil: Superships. By Noel Grove. Photos by Martin Rogers. 102-124, *July 1978*

GIBBONS, A. ST. H.: *Author*

Methods of Exploration in Africa. 408-410, *Oct. 1904*

GIBBONS, BOYD:

On Assignment on the Oregon Trail. *Aug. 1986*

Author

The South Koreans. Photos by Nathan Benn. 232-257, *Aug. 1988*

The Intimate Sense of Smell. Photos by Louie Psihoyos. Included: Smell Survey. 324-361, *Sept. 1986*

Life and Death on the Oregon Trail: The Itch to Move West. Photos by James L. Amos. 147-177, *Aug. 1986*

Do We Treat Our Soil Like Dirt? Photos by Steven C. Wilson. 350-389, *Sept. 1984*

Aldo Leopold: "A Durable Scale of Values." Photos by Jim Brandenburg. 682-708, *Nov. 1981*

The Bulgarians. Photos by James L. Stanfield. 91-111, *July 1980*

Risk and Reward on Alaska's Violent Gulf. Photos by Steve Raymer. 237-267, *Feb. 1979*

Easygoing, Hardworking Arkansas. Photos by Matt Bradley. 396-427, *Mar. 1978*

GIBBONS, EUELL: *Author*

Stalking the West's Wild Foods. Photos by David Hiser. 186-199, *Aug. 1973*

Stalking Wild Foods on a Desert Isle. Photos by David Hiser. 47-63, *July 1972*

GIBBONS:

The Ape With Friends in Washington. By Margaretta Burr Wells. 61-74, *July 1953*

Man's Closest Counterparts: Heavyweight of Monkeydom Is the "Old Man" Gorilla, by Far the Largest of the Four Great Apes. By William M. Mann. Paintings by Elie Cheverlange. 213-236, *Aug. 1940*

GIBBS, GEORGE S.: *Author*

The "Breaking Up" of the Yukon. 268-272, *May 1906*

Transportation Methods in Alaska. 69-82, *Feb. 1906*

GIBRALTAR:

The Mediterranean–Sea of Man's Fate. By Rick Gore. Photos by Jonathan Blair. 694-737, *Dec. 1982*

Gibraltar–Rock of Contention. By Howard La Fay. Photos by Bates Littlehales. 102-121, *July 1966*

The Rock of Gibraltar: Key to the Mediterranean. 376-391, *Sept. 1940*

From Granada to Gibraltar–A Tour of Southern Spain. By Harry A. McBride. 205-232, *Aug. 1924*

The American Eclipse Expedition. By Colby M. Chester. 589-612, *Nov. 1906*

GIBSON, BARBARA L.: *Artist*

Your World of Pets. By Susan McGrath. Juvenile. 104 pages. *1985*

GIBSON, SIR CHRISTOPHER H.: *Author*

Through Paraguay and Southern Matto Grosso. 459-488, *Oct. 1943*

GIBSON, EDWARD G.:

Skylab, Outpost on the Frontier of Space. By Thomas Y. Canby. Photos by the nine mission astronauts. 441-469, *Oct. 1974*

Author

The Sun As Never Seen Before. 494-503, *Oct. 1974*

GIDDINGS, AL:

On Assignment in Alaska. *Jan. 1984*

Author

Exploring the Deep Frontier: The Adventure of Man in the Sea. By Sylvia A. Earle and Al Giddings. 246 pages. *1980*

Author-Photographer

An Incredible Feasting of Whales. 88-93, *Jan. 1984*

Photographer

Undersea World of a Kelp Forest. By Sylvia A. Earle. 411-426, *Sept. 1980*

A Walk in the Deep. By Sylvia A. Earle. Photos by Al Giddings and Chuck Nicklin. 624-631, *May 1980*

Humpback Whales. 2-25. I. The Gentle Giants. By Sylvia A. Earle. 2-17; II. Their Mysterious Songs. By Roger Payne. 18-25, *Jan. 1979*

Life Springs From Death in Truk Lagoon. By Sylvia A. Earle. 578-613. Included: From Graveyard to Garden. 604-613, *May 1976*

GIFFORD, JOHN: *Author*

The Florida Keys. 5-16, *Jan. 1906*

GIFTS for the Jaguar God. By Philip Drucker and Robert F. Heizer. 367-375, *Sept. 1956*

The **GIFTS** of Golden Byzantium. By Merle Severy. Photos by James L. Stanfield. 722-767, *Dec. 1983*

GIGANTIC Brazil and Its Glittering Capital. By Frederick Simpich. 733-778, *Dec. 1930*

GIGNILLIAT, T. HEYWARD: *Author*

The Valley of the Orinoco. 92, *Feb. 1896*

GILBERT, AVERY N.:

On Assignment. *Oct. 1987*

Author

The Smell Survey Results. By Avery N. Gilbert and Charles J. Wysocki. Graphics designed by Allen Carroll and painted by Mark Seidler. 514-525, *Oct. 1987*

GILBERT, GROVE KARL:

The Discovery of the North Pole (Presentation of Hubbard Gold Medal). 63-82, *Jan. 1910*

Eighth International Geographic Congress. Speech of welcome by G. K. Gilbert. 419, *Oct. 1904*

Vice-President. 216, June 1896; 176, *Apr. 1904*

Mr. Ziegler and the National Geographic Society. Included: Letter from G. K. Gilbert recommending types of research to be undertaken by the Ziegler Polar Expedition. 251-254, *June 1903*

Portrait. Frontispiece, *July 1900*

Biography. 289, *July 1900*

Board of Managers. 294, Apr. 1891; xii, Feb. 19, 1892; xix, Feb. 20, 1893; xix, May 5, 1894; 216, June 1896; 520, *Dec. 1898*

Author

The Glaciers of Alaska. 449-450, *Nov. 1904*

An Introduction to Physical Geography. By Grove Karl Gilbert and Albert Perry Brigham. 21-26, *Jan. 1903*

Origin of the Physical Features of the United States. 308-317, *July 1898*

Modification of the Great Lakes by Earth Movement. 233-247, *Sept. 1897*

GILBERT, J. J.: *Author*

Some Notes on the Fox Island Passes, Alaska. 427-429, *Sept. 1905*

GILBERT, SIR WILLIAM:

The British Way. By Sir Evelyn
Wrench. 421-541, *Apr. 1949*

GILBERT GROSVENOR Is Elected
Chairman of the Board, John Oliver
La Gorce Chosen President and Editor of the National Geographic Society. 65, 65A-65H, 66, *July 1954*

GILBERT GROSVENOR'S Golden Jubilee. By Albert W. Atwood. 253-
261, *Aug. 1949*

GILBERT H. GROSVENOR VISITOR
CENTER, Russell Cave, Alabama:

Russell Cave Dedicated; New Visitor
Center Named for Gilbert H.
Grosvenor. NGS research grant. 440-
442, *Sept. 1967*

GILBERT ISLANDS (now Kiribati),
Pacific Ocean:

American Pathfinders in the Pacific. By
William H. Nicholas. 617-640,
May 1946
Gilbert Islands in the Wake of Battle.
By W. Robert Moore. 129-162,
Feb. 1945
War Finds Its Way to Gilbert Islands:
United States Forces Dislodge Japa-
nese from Enchanted Atolls Which
Loom Now as Stepping Stones along
South Sea Route from Australia to
Hawaii. By Sir Arthur Grimble. Pho-
tos by Raymond A. Dillon. 1-92,
Jan. 1943
See also Tarawa

GILDED Domes Against an Azure Sky
(Iran). Photos by Stephen H. Nyman. 339-346, *Sept. 1939*

GILGAMESH, Epic of:

Ancient Mesopotamia: A Light That
Did Not Fail. By E. A. Speiser.
Paintings by H. M. Herget. 41-105,
Jan. 1951

GILGIT, Kashmir:

Pakistan, New Nation in an Old Land.
By Jean and Franc Shor. 637-678,
Nov. 1952

GILKA, ROBERT E.:

On Assignment in Rome. *Dec. 1985*
Photographer
New Zealand's Milford Track: "Walk of
a Lifetime." By Carolyn Bennett Patterson. 117-129, *Jan. 1978*

GILL, RICHARD C.:

Mrs. Robinson Crusoe in Ecuador. By
Mrs. Richard C. Gill. 133-172,
Feb. 1934

GILL, MRS. RICHARD C.: *Author*

Mrs. Robinson Crusoe in Ecuador. 133-
172, *Feb. 1934*

GILL, WILLIAM J.: *Author*

Pittsburgh, Pattern for Progress. Photos
by Clyde Hare. 342-371, *Mar. 1965*

GILLES, HELEN TRYBULOWSKI:
Author

Ceylon, Island of the "Lion People."
121-136, *July 1948*
Nigeria: From the Bight of Benin to Africa's Desert Sands. 537-568,
May 1944

GILLETTE, NED:
Author-Photographer

American Skiers Find Adventure in
Western China. Photos by the author
and Galen Rowell. Included: Skiing
From the Summit of China's Ice
Mountain, the highest ski descent in
history. 174-199, *Feb. 1981*
New Mount McKinley Challenge–
Trekking Around the Continent's
Highest Peak. 66-79, *July 1979*

GILLETTE, Wyoming:

Powder River Basin: New Energy Frontier. By Bill Richards. Photos by
Louie Psihoyos. 96-113, *Special Report on Energy. (Feb. 1981)*

GILLIARD, E. THOMAS:

Nomination Page. In British Guiana
(Guyana). *Aug. 1961*
Nomination Page. *Feb. 1959*
Author
Feathered Dancers of Little Tobago.
Photos by Frederick Kent Truslow.
428-440, *Sept. 1958*
Coronation in Katmandu. Photos by
Marc Riboud. 139-152, *July 1957*
Author-Photographer
Strange Courtship of the Cock-of-the-
Rock. 134-140, *Jan. 1962*
Exploring New Britain's Land of Fire.
. 260-292, *Feb. 1961*
To the Land of the Head-hunters. 437-
486, *Oct. 1955*
New Guinea's Rare Birds and Stone
Age Men. 421-488, *Apr. 1953*
New Guinea's Paradise of Birds. 661-
688, *Nov. 1951*

GILLIARD, MARGARET:

Nomination Page. *Feb. 1959*
Photographer
New Guinea's Rare Birds and Stone
Age Men. By E. Thomas Gilliard.
Photos by E. Thomas and Margaret
Gilliard. 421-488, *Apr. 1953*

*T-shirt of miner Ed Martinez makes a
backhanded advertisement for a coal
boomtown of the late 1970s.* LOUIE PSIHOYOS

GILLIARD EXPEDITIONS:

Exploring New Britain's Land of Fire.
By E. Thomas Gilliard. NGS re-
search grant. 260-292, *Feb. 1961*
Feathered Dancers of Little Tobago. By
E. Thomas Gilliard. Photos by Fred-
erick Kent Truslow. NGS research
grant. 428-440, *Sept. 1958*
To the Land of the Head-hunters. By E.
Thomas Gilliard. 437-486, *Oct. 1955*
New Guinea's Paradise of Birds. By E.
Thomas Gilliard. 661-688, *Nov. 1951*

GILLISON, DAVID:

On Assignment in Papua New Guinea.
Aug. 1983
Nomination Page. *June 1977*
Photographer
Living Theater in New Guinea's High-
lands. By Gillian Gillison. 147-169,
Aug. 1983
Fertility Rites and Sorcery in a New
Guinea Village. By Gillian Gillison.
124-146, *July 1977*

GILLISON, GILLIAN:

On Assignment in Papua New Guinea.
Aug. 1983
Author
Living Theater in New Guinea's High-
lands. Photos by David Gillison. 147-
169, *Aug. 1983*
Fertility Rites and Sorcery in a New
Guinea Village. Photos by David
Gillison. 124-146, *July 1977*

GILMAN, DANIEL C.:

The Late Daniel C. Gilman (Biography). 883, *Dec. 1908*
Gardiner Greene Hubbard: Memorial
Meeting. Address by Daniel C. Gilman. 57-59, *Feb. 1898*

GILMAN, RAE: *Photographer*

Roaming Korea South of the Iron Curtain. By Enzo de Chetelat. 777-808,
June 1950

GILMAN, S. C.: *Author*

The Olympic Country. 133-140,
Apr. 1896

GILMORE, EDDY: *Author*

Crimea Reborn. 487-512, *Apr. 1945*
Liberated Ukraine. 513-536, *May 1944*
I Learn About the Russians. 619-640,
Nov. 1943

GILRUTH, ROBERT R.: *Author*

The Making of an Astronaut. 122-144,
Jan. 1965

GILSON, MARTHA PHILLIPS:
Author

A Woman's Winter on Spitsbergen.
227-246, *Aug. 1928*

GIMBEL, PETER R.:

Nomination Page. In Peru. *Aug. 1964*
Photographer
By Parachute Into Peru's Lost World.
By G. Brooks Baekeland. Photos by
author and Peter R. Gimbel. 268-
296, *Aug. 1964*

GIMBEL BROTHERS:

Artists Look at Pennsylvania. By John
Oliver La Gorce. 37-56, *July 1948*

Prince of Wales Hotel shelters guests in Waterton-Glacier International Peace Park on the U.S.-Canadian border. LOWELL GEORGIA

GIMIS:

Living Theater in New Guinea's Highlands. By Gillian Gillison. Photos by David Gillison. 147-169, *Aug. 1983*

Fertility Rites and Sorcery in a New Guinea Village. By Gillian Gillison. Photos by David Gillison. 124-146, *July 1977*

GIPSON, HENRY CLAY:
Photographer

Peru on Parade. Photos by Henry Clay Gipson and Jack Kuhne. 173-196, *Aug. 1942*

GIRAFFES:

Africa's Gentle Giants. By Bristol Foster. Photos by Bob Campbell and Thomas Nebbia. 402-417, *Sept. 1977*

Rescuing the Rothschild. By Carolyn Bennett Patterson. 419-421, *Sept. 1977*

Where Roosevelt Will Hunt (Africa). By Sir Harry Johnston. 207-256, *Mar. 1909*

GIRDLING the Globe. 236, *May 1904*

GIRL SCOUTS:

Star and Crescent on Parade (Turkey). Photos by Maynard Owen Williams. 585-616, *May 1945*

GIRONA (Armada Galleass):

Priceless Relics of the Spanish Armada. By Robert Sténuit. Photos by Bates Littlehales. 745-777, *June 1969*

GIRONDE (Department), France:

Bordeaux: Fine Wines and Fiery Gascons. By William Davenport. Photos by Adam Woolfitt. 233-259, *Aug. 1980*

GIROUARD, MARK: *Author*

The Great Good Places: English Country Houses. Photos by Fred J. Maroon. 658-694, *Nov. 1985*

GIZA, Pyramids of, Egypt:

Finding a Pharaoh's Funeral Bark. By Farouk El-Baz. Photos by James P. Blair and Claude E. Petrone. Included: Craft for eternity; The world's oldest ship. 513-533, *Apr. 1988*

Egypt: Two Perspectives. 293-343. I: Legacy of a Dazzling Past. By Alice J. Hall. 293-311; II. Omens for a Better Tomorrow. By Thomas J. Abercrombie. 312-343. Included: Great Pyramid of Giza, Pyramid of Meidum near El Faiyum. *Mar. 1977*

Fresh Treasures from Egypt's Ancient Sands. By Jefferson Caffery. Photos by David S. Boyer. 611-650, *Nov. 1955*

Sinai Sheds New Light on the Bible. By Henry Field. Photos by William B. and Gladys Terry. 795-815, *Dec. 1948*

Daily Life in Ancient Egypt (Part I). Daily Life in Ancient Egypt: *The Later Period* (Part II). By William C. Hayes. Paintings by H. M. Herget. 419-515, *Oct. 1941*

The Resurrection of Ancient Egypt. By James Baikie. 957-1020, *Sept. 1913*

GJOA (Ship):

A Modern Viking. 38-41, *Jan. 1906*

GLACIER BAY, Alaska:

Humpbacks: The Gentle Whales. By Sylvia A. Earle. Photos by Al Giddings. NGS research grant. 2-17, *Jan. 1979*

The Recession of the Glaciers of Glacier Bay, Alaska. By Fremont Morse. 76-78, *Jan. 1908*

The Discovery of Glacier Bay, Alaska. By Eliza Ruhamah Scidmore. 140-146, *Apr. 1896*

See also Glacier Bay National Monument

GLACIER BAY NATIONAL MONUMENT, Alaska:

John Muir's Wild America. By Harvey Arden. Photos by Dewitt Jones. 433-461, *Apr. 1973*

GLACIER NATIONAL PARK, Montana:

Waterton-Glacier International Peace Park: Pride of Two Nations. By David S. Boyer. Photos by Lowell Georgia. 796-823, *June 1987*

"Grizz"—Of Men and the Great Bear. By Douglas H. Chadwick. 182-213, *Feb. 1986*

Spring Comes Late to Glacier. By Douglas H. Chadwick. 125-133, *July 1979*

Many-splendored Glacierland. By George W. Long. Photos by Kathleen Revis. 589-636, *May 1956*

Montana, Shining Mountain Treasureland. By Leo A. Borah. 693-736, *June 1950*

The West Through Boston Eyes. By

Stewart Anderson. 733-776, *June 1949*

Our National Parks. By L. F. Schmeckebier. 531-579, *June 1912*

A New National Park. By Guy Elliott Mitchell. 215-223, *Mar. 1910*

GLACIERS:

Ice on the World. By Samuel W. Matthews. 79-103, *Jan. 1987*

Glaciers on the Move. By John L. Eliot. Photos by Chris Johns. Included: Anatomy of a tidewater glacier. 107-119, *Jan. 1987*

On the Trail of Wisconsin's Ice Age. By Anne LaBastille. Photos by Cary Wolinsky. Included: Glacial landforms; map showing Wisconsin's future Ice Age Trail along the terminal moraine. 182-205, *Aug. 1977*

Avalanche! (Peru). By Bart McDowell. Photos by John E. Fletcher. 855-880, *June 1962*

Climbing Our Northwest Glaciers. Photos by Bob and Ira Spring. 103-114, *July 1953*

Far North with "Captain Mac." By Miriam MacMillan. 465-513, *Oct. 1951*

Alaska's Automatic Lake Drains Itself (Lake George). 835-844, *June 1951*

First American Ascent of Mount St. Elias. By Maynard M. Miller. 229-248, *Feb. 1948*

Our Navy Explores Antarctica. By Richard E. Byrd. U. S. Navy official photos. 429-522, *Oct. 1947*

On the Ridgepole of the Rockies. By Walter Meayers Edwards. Included: Canada's Rocky Mountain Playground. 755-770. 745-780, *June 1947*

Crater Lake and Yosemite Through the Ages. By Wallace W. Atwood, Jr. Paintings by Eugene Kingman. 327-343, *Mar. 1937*

The Conquest of Mount Logan: North America's Second Highest Peak Yields to the Intrepid Attack of Canadian Climbers. By H. F. Lambart. 597-631, *June 1926*

■■ *Alaskan Glacier Studies of the National Geographic Society in the Yakutat Bay, Prince William Sound and Lower Copper River Regions.* By Ralph Stockman Tarr and Lawrence Martin. 498 pages. *1914*

The Ascent of Mont Blanc. By Walter Woodburn Hyde. 861-942, *Aug. 1913*

The Monarch of the Canadian Rockies. By Charles D. Walcott. 626-639, *May 1913*

Scenes Among the High Cascades in Central Oregon. By Ira A. Williams. 579-592, *June 1912*

The Great White Monarch of the Pacific Northwest (Mount Rainier). By A. H. Barnes. 593-626, *June 1912*

The Form of Glacier Terminals. 786, *Aug. 1911*

The National Geographic Society Researches in Alaska. By Lawrence Martin. 537-561, *June 1911*

Some Tramps Across the Glaciers and Snowfields of British Columbia. By Howard Palmer. 457-487, *June 1910*

The National Geographic Society's Alaskan Expedition of 1909. By

Ralph S. Tarr and Lawrence Martin. 1-54, *Jan. 1910*

Photography in Glacial Alaska. By O. D. von Engeln. 54-62, *Jan. 1910*

A Wonderland of Glaciers and Snow (Mount Rainier National Park). By Milnor Roberts. 530-537, *June 1909*

Is Our Noblest Volcano Awakening to New Life: A Description of the Glaciers and Evidences of Volcanic Activity of Mount Hood. By A. H. Sylvester. 515-525, *July 1908*

The Recession of the Glaciers of Glacier Bay, Alaska. By Fremont Morse. 76-78, *Jan. 1908*

Note on Glacier Discovery. By W. H. Jackson. 587, *Oct. 1906*

The Glaciers of Alaska. By Grove Karl Gilbert. 449-450, *Nov. 1904*

Muir Glacier. By C. L. Andrews. 441-444, *Dec. 1903*

Among the Great Himalayan Glaciers. 405-406, *Nov. 1902*

The Stikine River in 1898 (British Columbia). By Eliza Ruhamah Scidmore. 1-15, *Jan. 1899*

Lake Chelan. By Henry Gannett. 417-428, *Oct. 1898*

An Expedition through the Yukon District. By Charles Willard Hayes. 117-159, *May 15, 1892*

Studies of Muir Glacier, Alaska. By Harry Fielding Reid. 19-55, *Mar. 21, 1892*

An Expedition to Mount St. Elias, Alaska. By Israel C. Russell. 53-191. Included: Glaciers of the St. Elias Region. 176-188, *May 29, 1891*

See also Alps; Annapurna I; Columbia Ice Field; Everest, Mount; Glacier National Park; Greenland; Himalaya; Ice Ages; Jökulsá á Fjöllum (River), Iceland; K2; Kluane National Park Reserve, Yukon Territory, Canada; McKinley, Mount; Olympic National Park; Ruwenzori

GLACIOLOGY:

Ice on the World. By Samuel W. Matthews. 79-103, *Jan. 1987*

Glaciers on the Move. By John L. Eliot. Photos by Chris Johns. Included: Anatomy of a tidewater glacier. 107-119, *Jan. 1987*

Voyage to the Antarctic. By David Lewis. 544-562, *Apr. 1983*

What's Happening to Our Climate? By Samuel W. Matthews. 576-615, *Nov. 1976*

Antarctica's Nearer Side. By Samuel W. Matthews. Photos by William R. Curtsinger. Included: Glaciological studies of Deception Island. NGS research grant. 622-655, *Nov. 1971*

Alaska's Mighty Rivers of Ice. By Maynard M. Miller. Photos by Christopher G. Knight. NGS research grant. 194-217, *Feb. 1967*

■■ *Alaskan Glacier Studies of the National Geographic Society in the Yakutat Bay, Prince William Sound and Lower Copper River Regions.* By Ralph Stockman Tarr and Lawrence Martin. 498 pages. *1914*

The Form of Glacier Terminals. 786, *Aug. 1911*

The National Geographic Society Researches in Alaska. By Lawrence Martin. 537-561, *June 1911*

The Recession of the Glaciers of Glacier Bay, Alaska. By Fremont Morse. 76-78, *Jan. 1908*

The Glaciers of Alaska. By Grove Karl Gilbert. 449-450, *Nov. 1904*

Muir Glacier. By C. L. Andrews. 441-444, *Dec. 1903*

Among the Great Himalayan Glaciers. 405-406, *Nov. 1902*

Studies of Muir Glacier, Alaska. By Harry Fielding Reid. 19-55, *Mar. 21, 1892*

An Expedition to Mount St. Elias, Alaska. By Israel C. Russell. 53-191. Included: Glaciers of the St. Elias Region. 176-188, *May 29, 1891*

The **GLAMOUR** of Historic Havana. Photos by F. S. Lincoln. 357-364, *Sept. 1933*

The **GLAMOUR** of Mexico–Old and

Field headquarters of Michigan State University's Summer Institute of Glaciological and Arctic Sciences rests above Alaska's Taku Glacier. CHRISTOPHER G. KNIGHT

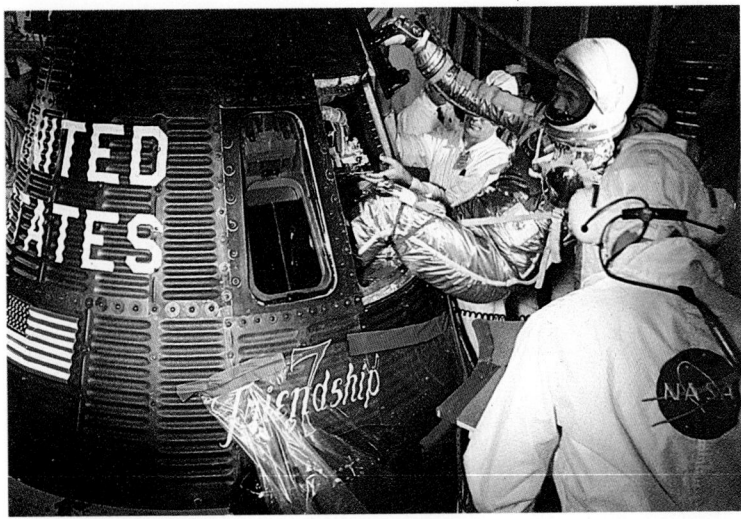

Astronaut John Glenn eases through the hatch into the **Friendship 7** *spacecraft before beginning the United States' first manned orbital space flight.* BILL TAUB, NASA

New. Photos by Pérez Parra. 345-352, *Mar. 1934*

GLANZMAN, LOUIS S.: *Artist*

■■ *The Mighty Aztecs.* By Gene S. Stuart. Photos by Mark Godfrey. 199 pages. *1981*

Ebla: Splendor of an Unknown Empire. By Howard La Fay. Photos by James L. Stanfield. 730-759, *Dec. 1978*

Patriots in Petticoats. By Lonnelle Aikman. 475-493, *Oct. 1975*

■■ *The Incredible Incas and Their Timeless Land.* Written and photographed by Loren McIntyre. 199 pages. *1975*

■■ *The Wild Shores: America's Beginnings.* By Tee Loftin Snell. Photos by Walter Meayers Edwards. 203 pages. *1974*

■■ *The Vikings.* By Howard La Fay. Photos by Ted Spiegel. 207 pages. *1972*

GLASGOW, Scotland:

Bonnie Scotland, Postwar Style. By Isobel Wylie Hutchison. 545-601, *May 1946*

GLASS:

Oldest Known Shipwreck Reveals Splendors of the Bronze Age. By George F. Bass. Photos by William R. Curtsinger. Included: Bronze Age Trade, The Cosmopolitan World of the Late Bronze Age, The Painstaking Art of Marine Archaeology. NGS research grant. 693-733, *Dec. 1987*

Graveyard of the Quicksilver Galleons. By Mendel Peterson. Photos by Jonathan Blair. Included: Glassware recovered from the *Nuestra Señora de Guadalupe* and the *Conde de Tolosa.* 850-876, *Dec. 1979*

Glass Treasure From the Aegean. By George F. Bass. Photos by Jonathan Blair. NGS research grant. 768-793, *June 1978*

History Revealed in Ancient Glass. By Ray Winfield Smith. Photos by B.

Anthony Stewart and Lee E. Battaglia. 346-369, *Sept. 1964*

Glass "Goes to Town." By J. R. Hildebrand. Included: From Sand to Seer and Servant of Man. Photos by Willard R. Culver. 1-48, *Jan. 1943*

The Industrial Titan of America: Pennsylvania, Once the Keystone of the Original Thirteen, Now the Keystone of Forty-eight Sovereign States. By John Oliver La Gorce. 367-406, *May 1919*

The **GLASS-BOTTOM** Boat. By Charles Frederick Holder. 761-778, *Sept. 1909*

GLASS Menageries of the Sea. By Paul A. Zahl. 797-822, *June 1955*

GLASSEY, FRANK P. S.: *Author*

Helsingfors–A Contrast in Light and Shade. 597-612, *May 1925*

GLEAMING Fishes of Pacific Coastal Waters. Paintings by Hashime Murayama. 467-498, *Oct. 1938*

GLEASON, HERBERT W.: *Author*

Winter Rambles in Thoreau's Country. 165-180, *Feb. 1920*

On the Trail of a Horse Thief (British Columbia). 349-358, *Apr. 1919*

GLEN CANYON NATIONAL RECREATION AREA, Arizona-Utah:

Lake Powell: Waterway to Desert Wonders. By Walter Meayers Edwards. 44-75, *July 1967*

Experiences in the Grand Canyon. By Ellsworth and Emery Kolb. 99-184, *Aug. 1914*

GLENDORA, California:

Southern California's Trial by Mud and Water. By Nathaniel T. Kenney. Photos by Bruce Dale. 552-573, *Oct. 1969*

GLENFINNAN, Scotland:

Heather Paints the Highlands. Photos

by B. Anthony Stewart. 561-600, *May 1946*

GLENN, JOHN H., Jr.:

Recipient of the National Geographic Society Centennial Award. President's Page. By Gilbert M. Grosvenor. *Dec. 1988*

John Glenn's Three Orbits in *Friendship 7:* A Minute-by-Minute Account of America's First Orbital Space Flight. By Robert B. Voas. 792-827, *June 1962*

John Glenn Receives the Society's Hubbard Medal. 827, *June 1962*

GLENN, L. C.: *Author*

Applied Physiography in South Carolina. 152-154, *May 1897*

GLENORA, British Columbia, Canada:

The Stikine River in 1898. By Eliza Ruhamah Scidmore. 1-15, *Jan. 1899*

GLIDE BOMBS:

Air Power for Peace. By H. H. Arnold. 137-193, *Feb. 1946*

GLIDERS (Aircraft):

The Aerial Invasion of Burma. By H. H. Arnold. 129-148, *Aug. 1944*

Gliders–Silent Weapons of the Sky. By William H. Nicholas. 149-160, *Aug. 1944*

Men-Birds Soar on Boiling Air. By Frederick Vosburgh. 123-140, *July 1938*

On the Wings of the Wind: In Motorless Planes, Pilots Ride in Flying-Fox Fashion, Cruising on Upward Air Streams and Lifted by the Suction of Moving Clouds. By Howard Siepen. 751-780, *June 1929*

Air Conquest: From the Early Days of Giant Kites and Birdlike Gliders, the National Geographic Society Has Aided and Encouraged the Growth of Aviation. 233-242, *Aug. 1927*

Remarkable Photograph of Lilienthal's Gliding Machine. By R. W. Wood. 596, *Aug. 1908*; 271, *Mar. 1911*; 235, *Aug. 1927*

See also Sailplanes

GLIDING POSSUMS:

Strange Animals of Australia. By David Fleay. Photos by Stanley Breeden. 388-411, *Sept. 1963*

GLIMPSES East and West in America. 531-546, *May 1924*

GLIMPSES of Asia. 553-568, *May 1921*

GLIMPSES of Holland. By William Wisner Chapin. 1-29, *Jan. 1915*

GLIMPSES of Japan. By William W. Chapin. 965-1002, *Nov. 1911*

GLIMPSES of Korea and China. By William W. Chapin. 895-934, *Nov. 1910*

GLIMPSES of Siberia, the Russian "Wild East." By Cody Marsh. 513-536, *Dec. 1920*

GLIMPSES of the Russian Empire. By William Wisner Chapin. 1043-1078, *Nov. 1912*

The **GLITTERING** World of Rock-hounds. By David S. Boyer. 276-294, *Feb. 1974*

GLOB, P. V.: *Author*

Lifelike Man Preserved 2,000 Years in Peat. 419-430, *Mar. 1954*

GLOBAL AIR POLLUTION:

Editorial. By Wilbur E. Garrett. 421, *Apr. 1987*

Air: An Atmosphere of Uncertainty. By Noel Grove. Photos by Ted Spiegel. Paintings by William H. Bond. Included: A deadly soup (a list of harmful chemicals), Careless neighbors, A global greenhouse, The ozone enigma, Getting the lead out, The enemy within. 502-537, *Apr. 1987*

GLOBAL POSITIONING SYSTEM (GPS):

Satellites That Serve Us. By Thomas Y. Canby. By Michael E. Long. 281-335, *Sept. 1983*

GLOBAL Weather Disasters. By Thomas Y. Canby. 144-183, *Feb. 1984*

GLOBEFISH. *See* Puffer Fish

GLOBES:

Hologram of shattering crystal globe. cover, *Dec. 1988*

Behaim Globe reproduction. 563-565, *Nov. 1986*

GLOBES, NGS:

Axis-free globe. 270, *Aug. 1982*

First. 698-701, 716, May 1961; 580, 581, Oct. 1967; 275, *Aug. 1982*

National Geographic Physical Globe announced. 736, *Nov. 1971*

16-inch globe presented to Mrs. Lyndon B. Johnson. 676, 679, May 1964; 584, *Oct. 1967*

16-inch globe and 12-inch globe. 897, *Dec. 1962*

Manufacturer of NGS globes. 874-875, 876-878, *Dec. 1961*

Great Globe: Explorers Hall, NGS:

President's Page. By Gilbert M. Grosvenor. *Oct. 1987*

12-foot globe. 673-675, 677, 679, May 1964; 880, Dec. 1964; 578-579, *Oct. 1967*

GLOMAR CHALLENGER (Deep Sea Drilling Project Ship):

This Changing Earth. By Samuel W. Matthews. 1-37, *Jan. 1973*

The **GLORIES** of the Minya Konka: Magnificent Snow Peaks of the China-Tibetan Border Are Photographed at Close Range by a National Geographic Society Expedition. By Joseph F. Rock. 385-437, *Oct. 1930*

GLORIES Past and Present of Northern Spain. Photos by Gervais Courtellemont. 341-348, *Mar. 1929*

GLORIOUS Bronzes of Ancient Greece: Warriors From a Watery Grave. By Joseph Alsop. 821-827, *June 1983*

The **GLORY** of Life: The Serengeti. By Shana Alexander. 585-601, *May 1986*

"The **GLORY** That Was Greece." By Alexander Wilbourne Weddell. 571-630, *Dec. 1922*

"The **GLORY** That Was Greece." Paintings by H. M. Herget. 290-352, *Mar. 1944*

The **GLORY** That Was Imperial Peking. By W. Robert Moore. 745-780, *June 1933*

GLOUCESTER, Massachusetts:

Gloucester Blesses Its Portuguese Fleet. By Luis Marden. 75-84, *July 1953*

Windjamming Around New England. By Tom Horgan. Photos by Robert F. Sisson. 141-169, *Aug. 1950*

Northeast of Boston. By Albert D. Atwood. 257-292, *Sept. 1945*

GLOWWORMS (Beetle Larvae):

Nature's Night Lights: Probing the Secrets of Bioluminescence. By Paul A. Zahl. 45-69, *July 1971*

GLUECK, NELSON: *Author*

An Archeologist Looks at Palestine. 739-752, *Dec. 1947*

The Geography of the Jordan. 719-744, *Dec. 1944*

On the Trail of King Solomon's Mines: The Bible, in Addition to Its Spiritual Values, Continues to Prove a Rich Geography and Guide to Exploration of the Holy Land. 233-256, *Feb. 1944*

GLYPHS:

El Mirador: An Early Maya Metropolis Uncovered. By Ray T. Matheny. Paintings by T. W. Rutledge. NGS research grant. 317-339, *Sept. 1987*

Editorial. By Wilbur E. Garrett. 561, *May 1987*

Río Azul. Photos by George F. Mobley. NGS research grant. 420-465. I. Lost City of the Maya. By Richard E. W. Adams. Included: Realm of the Maya (map). 420-451; II. Looters Rob Graves and History. By Ian Graham. 452-461; III. In Defense of the

Maya priest in a feathered headdress chants incantations as a noble's tomb is sealed at Río Azul in Guatemala. PAINTING BY ROY ANDERSEN

Collector. By Gillett G. Griffin. 462-465, *Apr. 1986*

Maya Art Treasures Discovered in Cave. By George E. Stuart. Photos by Wilbur E. Garrett. 220-235, *Aug. 1981*

■ *The Mysterious Maya.* By George E. and Gene S. Stuart. Photos by David Alan Harvey and Otis Imboden. 199 pages. *1977*

The Maya. 729-811. I. Children of Time. By Howard La Fay. Photos by David Alan Harvey. 729-767; II. Riddle of the Glyphs. By George E. Stuart. Photos by Otis Imboden. 768-791, *Dec. 1975*

See also Petroglyphs

GNATCATCHERS (Birds):

Winged Denizens of Woodland, Stream, and Marsh. By Alexander Wetmore. Paintings by Allan Brooks. 577-596, *May 1934*

GOAL at the End of the Trail: Santa Fe. By William S. Ellis. Photos by Gordon W. Gahan and Otis Imboden. 323-345, *Mar. 1982*

GOATS:

Mountain Goats: Daring Guardians of the Heights. By Douglas H. Chadwick. 284-296, *Aug. 1978*

The Goats of Thunder Hill. By Elizabeth Nicholds. Photos by Robert F. Sisson. 625-640, *May 1954*

Sheep Trek in the French Alps. By Maurice Moyal. Photos by Marcel Coen. 545-564, *Apr. 1952*

The Milch Goat. 237, *May 1905*

GOATSUCKERS (Birds):

Seeking the Smallest Feathered Creatures: Humming Birds, Peculiar to the New World, Are Found from Canada and Alaska to the Strait of Magellan. Swifts and Goatsuckers, Their Nearest Relatives. By Alexander Wetmore. Paintings by Allan Brooks. 65-89, *July 1932*

GOBI (Desert), Asia:

Journey to Outer Mongolia. By William O. Douglas. Photos by Dean Conger. 289-345, *Mar. 1962*

The Caves of the Thousand Buddhas. By Franc and Jean Shor. 383-415, *Mar. 1951*

Explorations in the Gobi Desert. By Roy Chapman Andrews. 653-716, *June 1933*

The Desert Road to Turkestan: Twentieth Century Travel Through Innermost Asia Along Caravan Trails Over Which Oriental Commerce Was Once Borne from China to the Medieval Western World. By Owen Lattimore. 661-702, *June 1929*

The Lama's Motor-Car. By Ethan C. Le Munyon. 641-670, *May 1913*

GODDARD, GEORGE W.: *Author*

The Unexplored Philippines from the Air: Map-making Over Jungle Lands Never Before Seen By White Men. 311-343, *Sept. 1930*

Photographer

Aerial Color Photography Becomes a

War Weapon. By H. H. Arnold. 757-766, *June 1940*

GODDARD, JOHN M.: *Author*

Kayaks Down the Nile. 697-732, *May 1955*

GODESBERG, Bad, West Germany:

War's Wake in the Rhineland. By Thomas R. Henry. 1-32, *July 1945*

GODFREY, MARK: *Photographer*

■■ *On the Brink of Tomorrow: Frontiers of Science.* Art by Susan Sanford. 199 pages. *1982*

■■ *The Mighty Aztecs.* By Gene S. Stuart. Art by Louis S. Glanzman. 199 pages. *1981*

GODIVA, LADY:

The British Way. By Sir Evelyn Wrench. 421-541, *Apr. 1949*

GODLEY, JOHN, Third Baron Kilbracken. *See* Kilbracken, Lord

GODTHAAB, Greenland:

Greenland Turns to America. By James K. Penfield. 369-383, *Sept. 1942*

GODWIN AUSTEN (Peak), China-Pakistan. *See* K2

GOELL, THERESA:

Nomination Page. In Turkey. *May 1965*

Author-Photographer

Throne Above the Euphrates. 390-405, *Mar. 1961*

GOES, The Netherlands:

The City of Jacqueline. By Florence Craig Albrecht. 29-56, *Jan. 1915*

GOETHALS, GEORGE W.:

NGS Special Gold Medal recipient. 141, *Feb. 1978*

Honors to Colonel Goethals: The Presentation, by President Woodrow Wilson, of the National Geographic Society Special Gold Medal, and Addresses by Secretary of State Bryan, the French Ambassador, the German

Ambassador, and Congressman James R. Mann. 677-690, *June 1914*

Author

The Panama Canal. 148-211, *Feb. 1911*

The Panama Canal. 334-355, *Apr. 1909*

GOETZ, BERNICE M.:

Author-Photographer

Jungle Jaunt on Amazon Headwaters. 371-388, *Sept. 1952*

GOETZMANN, WILLIAM H.:

On Assignment. *Jan. 1988*

Author

"Tell me if your civilization is interesting": Those Electrifying Eighteen Eighties When the National Geographic Society Was Born. Illustrated by Fred Otnes. 8-37, *Jan. 1988*

GOGGLE FISHING in California Waters. By David Hellyer. Photos by Lamar Boren. 615-632, *May 1949*

GOHIER, FRANÇOIS: *Photographer*

Gray Whales of San Ignacio. By Steven L. Swartz and Mary Lou Jones. NGS research grant. 754-771, *June 1987*

GOING, CHARLES BUXTON: *Author*

The Mysterious Prehistoric Monuments of Brittany (France). By Charles Buxton Going. 53-69, *July 1923*

GOLD:

Treasure From the Ghost Galleon: *Santa Margarita*. By Eugene Lyon. Photos by Don Kincaid. 228-243, *Feb. 1982*

Ancient Bulgaria's Golden Treasures. By Colin Renfrew. Photos by James L. Stanfield. Paintings by Jean-Leon Huens. 112-129, *July 1980*

● Gold! 1, *Jan. 1979*

Regal Treasures From a Macedonian Tomb. By Manolis Andronicos. Photos by Spyros Tsavdaroglou. 55-77, *July 1978*

Minoans and Mycenaeans: Greece's Brilliant Bronze Age. By Joseph Judge. Photos by Gordon W. Gahan. Paintings by Lloyd K. Townsend. 142-185. *Feb. 1978*

Imperial Russia's Glittering Legacy. 24-33, *Jan. 1978*

Reach for the New World. By Mendel Peterson. Photos by David L. Arnold. Paintings by Richard Schlecht. Included: Gold artifacts from salvaged cargoes. 724-767, *Dec. 1977*

Atocha, Tragic Treasure Galleon of the Florida Keys. By Eugene Lyon. Included: *Santa Margarita* wreck. 787-809, *June 1976*

Gold, the Eternal Treasure. By Peter T. White. Photos by James L. Stanfield. Included: Golden Masterpieces. 1-51, *Jan. 1974*

Priceless Relics of the Spanish Armada. By Robert Sténuit. Photos by Bates Littlehales. 745-777, *June 1969*

Drowned Galleons Yield Spanish Gold. By Kip Wagner. Photos by Otis Imboden. 1-37, *Jan. 1965*

Men and Gold. By Frederick Simpich. 481-518, *Apr. 1933*

The World's Production of Gold (from an address to the American Bankers'

Convention, by F. A. Vanderlip, October 11, 1905). 571-572, *Dec. 1905*
Report on Auriferous Sands from Yakutat Bay (Alaska). By J. Stanley-Brown. 196-198, *May 29, 1891*
Korea and the Koreans. By J. B. Bernadou. 231-242, *Aug. 1890*
See also Gold Mining; Goldsmithing

GOLD COAST, West Africa:
Hunting Musical Game in West Africa. By Arthur S. Alberts. 262-282, *Aug. 1951*
The Revolt of the Ashantis. 244, *June 1900*
The Gold Coast, Ashanti, and Kumassi. By George K. French. 1-15, *Jan. 1897*
See also present name, Ghana

GOLD MEDAL, NGS. *See* Special Gold Medal

GOLD MEDAL Awarded to Mrs. Robert E. Peary. 148, *Jan. 1956*

GOLD MINING:
Brazil's Kayapo Indians, Beset by a Golden Curse. By Vanessa Lea. Photos by Miguel Rio Branco. 675-694, *May 1984*
Yukon Fever: Call of the North. By Robert Booth. Photos by George F. Mobley. 548-578, *Apr. 1978*
Brazil's Wild Frontier. By Loren McIntyre. 684-719, *Nov. 1977*
Gold, the Eternal Treasure. By Peter T. White. Photos by James L. Stanfield. Included: Golden Masterpieces. 1-51, *Jan. 1974*
Golden Ghosts of the Lost Sierra. By Robert Laxalt. Photos by David Hiser. 332-353, *Sept. 1973*
Nevada's Mountain of Invisible Gold. By Samuel W. Matthews. Photos by David F. Cupp. 668-679, *May 1968*
Along the Yukon Trail. By Amos Burg. 395-416, *Sept. 1953*
Busy Fairbanks Sets Alaska's Pace. By Bruce A. Wilson. Photos by O. C. Sweet. 505-523, *Oct. 1949*
The Cities That Gold and Diamonds Built: Transvaal Treasures Have Created Bustling Johannesburg and Fostered Pretoria, Administrative Capital of the South African Union. By W. Robert Moore. 735-766, *Dec. 1942*
Beyond Australia's Cities. By W. Robert Moore. 709-747, *Dec. 1936*
Men and Gold. By Frederick Simpich. 481-518, *Apr. 1933*
Colorado, a Barrier That Became a Goal: Where Water Has Transformed Dry Plains Into Verdant Farms, and Highways Have Opened up Mineral and Scenic Wealth. By McFall Kerbey. 1-63, *July 1932*
Under the South African Union. By Melville Chater. 391-512, *Apr. 1931*
Lonely Australia: The Unique Continent. By Herbert E. Gregory. 473-568, *Dec. 1916*
The Nome Gold Fields. 384-385, *May 1908*
A Growing Camp in the Tanana Gold Fields, Alaska. By Sidney Paige. 104-111, *Mar. 1905*
The World's Production of Gold (from

an address to the American Bankers' Convention, by F. A. Vanderlip, October 11, 1905). 571-572, *Dec. 1905*
Gold in the Philippines. By F. F. Hilder. 465-470, *Dec. 1900*
The Cape Nome Gold District (Alaska). By F. C. Schrader. 15-23, *Jan. 1900*
The Future of the Yukon Goldfields. By William H. Dall. 117-120, *Apr. 1898*
Alaska and Its Mineral Resources. By Samuel Franklin Emmons. 139-172, *Apr. 1898*
🌐 *The Gold and Coal Fields of Alaska, Together with the Principal Steamer Routes and Trails.* Insets: Trails from Tide Water to the Headwaters of the Yukon River; The Klondike Gold Region, Canada. *Apr. 1898*
The Witwatersrand and the Revolt of the Uitlanders. By George F. Becker. 349-367, *Nov. 1896*
Venezuela: Her Government, People, and Boundary. By William E. Curtis. 49-58, *Feb. 1896*

GOLDEN Beaches of Portugal. By Alan Villiers. 673-696, *Nov. 1954*

GOLDEN COCKS-OF-THE-ROCK:
Cock-of-the-Rock: Jungle Dandy. By Pepper W. Trail. NGS research grant. 831-839, *Dec. 1983*
Strange Courtship of the Cock-of-the-Rock. By E. Thomas Gilliard. NGS research grant. 134-140, *Jan. 1962*

GOLDEN EAGLES:
Inside the Sacred Hopi Homeland. By Jake Page. Photos by Susanne Page. Included: Sacrifice of a golden eagle. 607-629, *Nov. 1982*
Sharing the Lives of Wild Golden Eagles. By John Craighead. Photos by Charles and Derek Craighead. 420-439, *Sept. 1967*
Scotland's Golden Eagles at Home. By C. Eric Palmar. 273-286, *Feb. 1954*

In Quest of the Golden Eagle: Over Lonely Mountain and Prairie Soars This Rare and Lordly Bird, But Three Youths from the East Catch Up with Him at Last. By John and Frank Craighead. 693-710, *May 1940*

GOLDEN FLEECE LEGEND:
Jason's Voyage: In Search of the Golden Fleece. By Tim Severin. Photos by John Egan and Seth Mortimer. 406-420, *Sept. 1985*

GOLDEN Fleece of Dixie (Cotton). By Willard R. Culver. 153-192, *Feb. 1941*

The **GOLDEN** Gate, and Redwood Evergreens (California). Photos by B. Anthony Stewart. 149-160, *Feb. 1939*

GOLDEN GATE NATIONAL RECREATION AREA, California:
Golden Gate—Of City, Ships, and Surf. By David S. Boyer. 98-105, *July 1979*

GOLDEN Ghosts of the Lost Sierra. By Robert Laxalt. Photos by David Hiser. 332-353, *Sept. 1973*

GOLDEN HIND (Sailing Ship):
Sir Francis Drake. By Alan Villiers. Photos by Gordon W. Gahan. 216-253, *Feb. 1975*

The **GOLDEN** Isles of Guale (Sea Islands, Georgia). By W. Robert Moore. 235-264, *Feb. 1934*

GOLDEN JACKALS:
Jackals of the Serengeti. By Patricia D. Moehlman. NGS research grant. 840-850, *Dec. 1980*

GOLDEN JUBILEES:
La Gorce, John Oliver: Golden Jubilee. 422, 423, Mar. 1957; 442, *Mar. 1960*
Gilbert Grosvenor's Golden Jubilee. By Albert W. Atwood. 253-261, *Aug. 1949*

With functional beauty, San Francisco's Golden Gate Bridge connects two sections of the 38,600-acre Golden Gate National Recreation Area. DAVID ALAN HARVEY

GOLDEN TROUT:

Lake Sunapee's Golden Trout. Photos by Robert F. Sisson. 529-536, *Oct. 1950*

The Golden Trout. 424, *July 1906*

GOLDEN Window on the Past. Photos by Paul A. Zahl. Text by Thomas J. O'Neill. 423-435, *Sept. 1977*

GOLDFISH:

Those Outlandish Goldfish! By Paul A. Zahl. 514-533, *Apr. 1973*

Goldfish and Their Cultivation In America. By Hugh M. Smith. Paintings by Hashime Murayama. 375-400, *Oct. 1924*

The Fisheries of Japan. By Hugh M. Smith. 201-220, *May 1905*

GOLDMAN, ERIC F.: *Author*

Firebrands of the Revolution. Photos by George F. Mobley. 2-27, *July 1974*

GOLDSMITHING:

Africa Adorned. By Angela Fisher. 600-633, *Nov. 1984*

Gold, the Eternal Treasure. By Peter T. White. Photos by James L. Stanfield. Included: Golden Masterpieces. 29-39. 1-51, *Jan. 1974*

GOLF:

Scotland, Ghosts, and Glory. By Rowe Findley. Photos by Peter Carmichael. Included: The Old Course at St. Andrews. 40-69, *July 1984*

California's Land Apart–the Monterey Peninsula. By Mike W. Edwards. Included: Cypress Point Golf Links; Monterey Peninsula Country Club; Pacific Grove Municipal Golf Links; Pebble Beach Golf Links; Spyglass Hill Golf Course. 682-703, *Nov. 1972*

Playing 3,000 Golf Courses in Fourteen Lands. By Ralph A. Kennedy. 113-132, *July 1952*

GOLIATH FROGS. *See* Giant Frogs

GOLIATHS of the Galapagos (Giant Tortoises). By Craig MacFarland. Photos by author and Jan MacFarland. 632-649, *Nov. 1972*

Product of selective breeding, a grotesque goldfish called a calico telescope searches nearsightedly for food. PAUL A. ZAHL, NGS

GOLOGS:

Nomads of China's West. By Galen Rowell. Photos by the author and Harold A. Knutson. 244-263, *Feb. 1982*

GOMBE NATIONAL PARK, Tanzania:

Life and Death at Gombe. By Jane Goodall. NGS research grant. 592-621, *May 1979*

◼◼ *My Friends the Wild Chimpanzees.* By Jane Goodall. Photos by Baron Hugo van Lawick. 204 pages. *1967*

New Discoveries Among Africa's Chimpanzees. By Baroness Jane van Lawick-Goodall. Photos by Baron Hugo van Lawick. NGS research grant. 802-831, *Dec. 1965*

My Life Among Wild Chimpanzees. By Jane Goodall. Photos by Baron Hugo van Lawick and author. NGS research grant. 272-308, *Aug. 1963*

GOMES, EDWIN H.: *Author*

Notes on the Sea Dyaks of Borneo. 695-723, *Aug. 1911*

GOMEZ, ESTEVAN:

Gomez and the New York Gull. By L. D. Scisco. 371-373, *Aug. 1898*

GONDS. *See* Muria Gonds

GONDWANA:

Child of Gondwana. By Joseph Judge. 170-177, *Feb. 1988*

GONGGA SHAN. *See* Minya Konka

GOOD-BYE to the Stone Age: Brazil's Txukahameis. Photos by W. Jesco von Puttkamer. 270-283, *Feb. 1975*

GOOD HOPE, Cape of, South Africa:

Yankee Roams the Orient. By Irving and Electa Johnson. 327-370, *Mar. 1951*

Busy Corner–the Cape of Good Hope: Ships Bound for Faraway Battle-grounds Stream Past Capetown, "Tavern of the Seas," and Other Ports of Virile South Africa. By W. Robert Moore. 197-223, *Aug. 1942*

Cape of Good Hope: The Floral Province. By Melville Chater. 391-430, *Apr. 1931*

A **GOOD** Life in the Low Country–Savannah to Charleston. By John J. Putman. Photos by Annie Griffiths. 798-829, *Dec. 1983*

A **GOOD** Life on the Potomac. By James L. Stanfield. 470-479, *Oct. 1976*

GOOD Times and Bad in Appalachia: Wrestlin' for a Livin' With King Coal. By Michael E. Long. Photos by Michael O'Brien. 793-819, *June 1983*

GOOD-WILL Ambassadors of the U. S. Navy Win Friends in the Far East. By Franc Shor. Photos by W. E. Garrett. 283-335, *Sept. 1959*

GOODALE, JANE C.: *Author*

Blowgun Hunters of the South Pacific. Photos by Ann Chowning. 793-817, *June 1966*

Photographer

Expedition to the Land of the Tiwi. By Charles P. Mountford. 417-440, *Mar. 1956*

GOODALL, JANE:

Recipient of the National Geographic Society Centennial Award. President's Page. By Gilbert M. Grosvenor. *Dec. 1988*

President's Page. By Gilbert M. Grosvenor. *June 1987*

Editorial. By Gilbert M. Grosvenor. 591, *May 1979*

Editorial. By Gilbert M. Grosvenor. 437, *Oct. 1978*

◼ Miss Goodall and the Wild Chimpanzees. 831A-831B, *Dec. 1965*

Nomination Page. In Tanzania. *Sept. 1965*

Author

Life and Death at Gombe. 592-621, *May 1979*

Tool-using Bird: The Egyptian Vulture. Photos by Baron Hugo van Lawick. 631-641, *May 1968*

◼◼ *My Friends the Wild Chimpanzees.* Photos by Baron Hugo van Lawick. 204 pages. *1967*

New Discoveries Among Africa's Chimpanzees. Photos by Baron Hugo van Lawick. 802-831, *Dec. 1965*

Author-Photographer

My Life Among Wild Chimpanzees. Photos by Baron Hugo van Lawick and author. 272-308, *Aug. 1963*

GOODALL, RAE NATALIE P.: *Author*

Housewife at the End of the World. Photos by James L. Stanfield. 130-150, *Jan. 1971*

GOODE, G. BROWN:

Death of G. Brown Goode. By W J McGee. 316, *Sept. 1896*

Board of Managers. 165, Apr. 1889; 270, July 1889; 68, Apr. 1890; 294, *Apr. 1891*

Author

Albemarle in Revolutionary Days. 271-281, *Aug. 1896*

GOODE, RICHARD URQUHART:

Portrait. 424, *Nov. 1903*

Richard Urquhart Goode (Biography). 424-425, *Nov. 1903*

Author

The Idaho and Montana Boundary Line. 23-29, *Jan. 1900*

Bitter Root Forest Reserve. 387-400, *Sept. 1898*

The Height of Mt. Rainier. 97-98, *Mar. 1898*

A Trip to Panama and Darien. 301-314, *Oct. 1889*

GOODING, PAUL: *Author*

Tahiti: A Playground of Nature. 301-326, *Oct. 1920*

GOODMAN, ROBERT B.:

Photographer

The Flowers That Say "Aloha." By Deena Clark. 121-131, *Jan. 1967*

Australia. By Alan Villiers. 309-385, *Sept. 1963*

Underwater Archeology: Key to

History's Warehouse. By George F. Bass. Photos by Thomas J. Abercrombie and Robert B. Goodman. 138-156, *July 1963*

Western Samoa, the Pacific's Newest Nation. By Maurice Shadbolt. 573-602, *Oct. 1962*

Queen Elizabeth Opens Parliament. By W. E. Roscher. 699-707, *Nov. 1961*

Cowes to Cornwall (England). By Alan Villiers. 149-201, *Aug. 1961*

Fountain of Fire in Hawaii. By Frederick Simpich, Jr. Photos by Robert B. Goodman and Robert Wenkam. 303-327, *Mar. 1960*

GOODNOW, FRANK JOHNSON: *Author*

The Geography of China: The Influence of Physical Environment on the History and Character of the Chinese People. 651-664, *June 1927*

GOODWIN, W.A.R.: *Author*

The Restoration of Colonial Williamsburg. 402-443, *Apr. 1937*

The **GOONEY BIRDS** of Midway. By John W. Aldrich. 839-851, *June 1964*

GOOSE BAY, Labrador, Newfoundland:

Milestones in My Arctic Journeys. By Willie Knutsen. Included: Activities of the Search and Rescue section of the Air Force. 543-570, *Oct. 1949*

GOOSE FISH:

The Purple Veil: A Romance of the Sea. By H. A. Largelamb (Alexander Graham Bell). 337-341, *July 1905*

GOPHERS:

Into the Land of the Chipmunk. By Ruth Alexander Nichols. 77-98, *July 1931*

GÓRALE:

Poland's Mountain People. By Yva Momatiuk and John Eastcott. 104-129, *Jan. 1981*

GORDON, ROBERT J.: *Author*

Nation in the Making: Papua New Guinea. Photos by David Austen. 143-149, *Aug. 1982*

GORE, JAMES HOWARD:

Board of Managers. 211, *Feb. 1911*
The Discovery of the North Pole. Speech by James Howard Gore. 63-82, *Jan. 1910*
Author
Holland's War with the Sea. 283-325, *Mar. 1923*
Roumania, the Pivotal State. 360-390, *Oct. 1915*
As Seen from a Dutch Window. 619-634, *Sept. 1908*
The Return of Wellman. 348-351, *Sept. 1899*
The Wellman Polar Expedition (Arctic). 267-268, *July 1899*

GORE, LILLIAN: *Author*

In Beautiful Delecarlia (Dalecarlia, Sweden). 464-477, *May 1909*

GORE, RICK:

On Assignment in Italy. *May 1984*

Jane Goodall takes to the trees to study chimpanzees in Tanzania's Gombe National Park. BARON HUGO VAN LAWICK

On Assignment. *June 1983*
Nomination Page. *Apr. 1981*
Nomination Page. In China. *Feb. 1980*
Nomination Page. In Florida. *Jan. 1978*
Author
The Eternal Etruscans. Photos by O. Louis Mazzatenta. Paintings by James M. Gurney. 696-743, *June 1988*
Halley's Comet '86. Included: Research probes. 758-785, *Dec. 1986*
Uranus: Voyager Visits a Dark Planet. Photos by NASA. 179-195, *Aug. 1986*
Our Restless Planet Earth. Photos by James A. Sugar. Included: Continents Adrift; Life's Triumph *and* Origin of Earth and Life. Painting by Ned M. Seidler. 142-181, *Aug. 1985*
The Rising Great Salt Lake: No Way to Run a Desert. Photos by Jim Richardson. 694-719, *June 1985*
The Planets: Between Fire and Ice. 4-51, *Jan. 1985*
The Dead Do Tell Tales at Vesuvius. Photos by O. Louis Mazzatenta. NGS research grant. 557-613, *May 1984*
A Prayer for Pozzuoli. Photos by O. Louis Mazzatenta. 615-625, *May 1984*
The Once and Future Universe. Photos by James A. Sugar. Paintings by Barron Storey. Picture text by David Jeffery. 704-749, *June 1983*
The Mediterranean–Sea of Man's Fate. Photos by Jonathan Blair. 694-737, *Dec. 1982*

Voyager 1 at Saturn: Riddles of the Rings. Photos by NASA. 3-31, *July 1981*
When the Space Shuttle Finally Flies. Photos by Jon Schneeberger. Paintings by Ken Dallison. 317-347, *Mar. 1981*
Conservation: Can We Live Better on Less? 34-57, *Special Report on Energy. (Feb. 1981)*
Journey to China's Far West. Photos by Bruce Dale. 292-331, *Mar. 1980*
What Voyager Saw: Jupiter's Dazzling Realm. Photos by NASA. 2-29, *Jan. 1980*
The Desert: An Age-old Challenge Grows. Photos by Georg Gerster and Bruce Dale. 586-639, *Nov. 1979*
Eyes of Science. Photos by James P. Blair. 360-389, *Mar. 1978*
A Bad Time to Be a Crocodile. Photos by Jonathan Blair. 90-115, *Jan. 1978*
The Tree Nobody Liked (Red Mangrove). Photos by Bianca Lavies. 669-689, *May 1977*
Striking It Rich in the North Sea. Photos by Dick Durrance II. 519-549, *Apr. 1977*
Sifting for Life in the Sands of Mars. 9-31, *Jan. 1977*
Florida, Noah's Ark for Exotic Newcomers. Photos by David Doubilet. 538-559, *Oct. 1976*
The Awesome Worlds Within a Cell. Photos by Bruce Dale. Paintings by Davis Meltzer. 355-395, *Sept. 1976*
Seven Giants Who Led the Way. Paintings by Ned Seidler. 401-407, *Sept. 1976*
Twilight Hope for Big Cypress. Photos by Patricia Caulfield. 251-273, *Aug. 1976*
Those Fiery Brazilian Bees. Photos by Bianca Lavies. 491-501, *Apr. 1976*

GORGES:

Cane Bridges of Asia. Photos from Paul Popper. 243-250, *Aug. 1948*
See also Dinosaur National Monument; Languedoc (Region), France, for Gorges du Tarn; Olduvai Gorge; Yangtze River; *and* Canyons

GORGONIANS (Coral):

The First Autochromes from the Ocean Bottom: Marine Life in Its Natural Habitat Along the Florida Keys Is Successfully Photographed in Colors. Photos by W. H. Longley and Charles Martin. 56-60, *Jan. 1927*
Life on a Coral Reef: The Fertility and Mystery of the Sea Studied Beneath the Waters Surrounding Dry Tortugas. By W. H. Longley. 61-83, *Jan. 1927*

GORILLAS:

Snowflake the Gorilla. Geographica. *Oct. 1988*
President's Page. By Gilbert M. Grosvenor. *May 1986*
Editorial. By Wilbur E. Garrett. 409, *Apr. 1985*
Koko's Kitten. Text by Jane Vessels. Photos by Ronald H. Cohn. Included: Gorilla Foundation address. 110-113, *Jan. 1985*
The Imperiled Mountain Gorilla. By

First white gorilla in captivity, two-year-old Snowflake romps at a collection station in Equatorial Guinea in 1966 before being sent to the Barcelona Zoo. PAUL A. ZAHL, NGS

GRAHAM LAND, Antarctica:

American Discoverers of the Antarctic Continent. By Adolphus W. Greely. 298-312, *Mar. 1912*

GRAN SABANA (Region), Venezuela:

Jungle Journey to the World's Highest Waterfall. By Ruth Robertson. 655-690, *Nov. 1949*

GRANADA, Spain:

Andalusia, the Spirit of Spain. By Howard La Fay. Photos by Joseph J. Scherschel. 833-857, *June 1975*
The Changing Face of Old Spain. By Bart McDowell. Photos by Albert Moldvay. 291-339, *Mar. 1965*
Speaking of Spain. By Luis Marden. 415-456, *Apr. 1950*
From Granada to Gibraltar–A Tour of Southern Spain. By Harry A. McBride. 205-232, *Aug. 1924*

GRAND BANKS, Atlantic Ocean:

Newfoundland Trusts in the Sea. By Gary Jennings. Photos by Sam Abell. 112-141, *Jan. 1974*
Dory on the Banks: A Day in the Life of a Portuguese Fisherman. By James H. Pickerell. 573-583, *Apr. 1968*
■ The Lonely Dorymen. 579A-579B, *Apr. 1968*
I Sailed with Portugal's Captains Courageous. By Alan Villiers. 565-596, *May 1952*
Life on the Grand Banks: An Account of the Sailor-Fishermen Who Harvest the Shoal Waters of North America's Eastern Coasts. By Frederick William Wallace. 1-28, *July 1921*

GRAND CANAL, China:

Grand Canal Panorama. By Willard Price. 487-514, *Apr. 1937*
Shantung–China's Holy Land. By Charles K. Edmunds. 231-252, *Sept. 1919*

GRAND CANYON, Arizona:

Inside the Sacred Hopi Homeland. By Jake Page. Photos by Susanne Page. 607-629, *Nov. 1982*
Grand Canyon. Photos by W. E. Garrett. 2-15, *July 1978*
Grand Canyon: Are We Loving It to Death? By W. E. Garrett. 16-51, *July 1978*
⊕ *The Grand Canyon.* Text on reverse. NGS research grant. *July 1978*
Indian Shangri-La of the Grand Canyon. By Jay Johnston. Photos by Terry Eiler. 355-373, *Mar. 1970*
Retracing John Wesley Powell's Historic Voyage Down the Grand Canyon. By Joseph Judge. Photos by Walter Meayers Edwards. 668-713, *May 1969*
Shooting Rapids in Reverse! Jet Boats Climb the Colorado's Torrent Through the Grand Canyon. By William Belknap, Jr. 552-565, *Apr. 1962*
Grand Canyon: Nature's Story of Creation. By Louis Schellbach. Photos by Justin Locke. 589-629, *May 1955*
Land of the Havasupai. By Jack Breed. 655-674, *May 1948*
Scenic Glories of Western United

States. Photos by Fred Payne Clatworthy. 223-230, *Aug. 1929*
Photographing the Marvels of the West in Colors. By Fred Payne Clatworthy. 694-719, *June 1928*
Surveying the Grand Canyon of the Colorado: An Account of the 1923 Boating Expedition of the United States Geological Survey. By Lewis R. Freeman. 471-548, *May 1924*
The Scenery of North America. By James Bryce. 339-389, *Apr. 1922*
The Grand Canyon Bridge. By Harriet Chalmers Adams. 645-650, *June 1921*
Experiences in the Grand Canyon. By Ellsworth and Emery Kolb. 99-184, *Aug. 1914*
The Southwest: Its Splendid Natural Resources, Agricultural Wealth, and Scenic Beauty. By N. H. Darton. 631-665, *Aug. 1910*
Survey of the Grand Canyon. 162-163, *Apr. 1903*
The Forests and Deserts of Arizona. By Bernhard E. Fernow. 203-226, *July-Aug. 1897*
The North American Deserts. By Johannes Walther. 163-176, *Feb. 8, 1893*

GRAND CANYON NATIONAL PARK, Arizona:

Grand Canyon. Photos by W. E. Garrett. 2-15, *July 1978*
Grand Canyon: Are We Loving It to Death? By W. E. Garrett. 16-51, *July 1978*
⊕ *The Grand Canyon.* Text on reverse. NGS research grant. *July 1978*
Grand Canyon: Nature's Story of Creation. By Louis Schellbach. Photos by Justin Locke. 589-629, *May 1955*
The West Through Boston Eyes. By

Stewart Anderson. 733-776, *June 1949*

GRAND CAYMAN (Island), Caribbean Sea:

Down the Cayman Wall. By Eugenie Clark. Included: Zones of Life. NGS research grant. 712-731, *Nov. 1988*
Fair Skies for the Cayman Islands. By Peter Benchley. Photos by David Doubilet. 798-824, *June 1985*

GRAND CONGLOUÉ (Island), Mediterranean Sea:

Fish Men Discover a 2,200-year-old Greek Ship. By Jacques-Yves Cousteau. NGS research grant. 1-36, *Jan. 1954*

GRAND COULEE DAM, Washington:

Powerhouse of the Northwest. By David S. Boyer. 821-847, *Dec. 1974*
From Sagebrush to Roses on the Columbia. By Leo A. Borah. 571-611, *Nov. 1952*
The Columbia (River) Turns on the Power. By Maynard Owen Williams. 749-792, *June 1941*

The **GRAND** Duchy of Luxemburg. By Maynard Owen Williams. 501-528, *Nov. 1924*

GRAND TETON NATIONAL PARK, Wyoming:

Grand Teton–A Winter's Tale. By François Leydet. 148-152, *July 1979*
Jackson Hole: Good-bye to the Old Days? By François Leydet. Photos by Jonathan Wright. 768-789, *Dec. 1976*
Wyoming: High, Wide, and Windy. By David S. Boyer. 554-594, *Apr. 1966*
I See America First. By Lynda Bird Johnson. Photos by William Albert Allard. 874-904, *Dec. 1965*
Wildlife Adventuring in Jackson Hole.

Nearing the end of his five-year solo journey around the world, Robin Lee Graham uses a sextant in 1970 to find his bearings. ROBIN LEE GRAHAM

By Frank and John Craighead. 1-36, *Jan. 1956*

The West Through Boston Eyes. By Stewart Anderson. 733-776, *June 1949*

Cloud Gardens in the Tetons. By Frank and John Craighead. 811-830, *June 1948*

GRAND UNION CANAL, England:

Britain Just Before the Storm: A Canadian Canoe Threads Old English Waterways Athrob with the Midlands' Industrial Life. By Amos Burg. 185-212, *Aug. 1940*

GRAND VALLEY, Irian Jaya, Indonesia:

New Guinea's Mountain and Swampland Dwellers. By Ray T. Elsmore. 671-694, *Dec. 1945*

Unknown New Guinea: Circumnavigating the World in a Flying Boat, American Scientists Discover a Valley of 60,000 People Never Before Seen by White Men. By Richard Archbold. 315-344, *Mar. 1941*

GRANDE BAIE, Quebec, Canada:

Gentle Folk Settle Stern Saguenay: On French Canada's Frontier Homespun Colonists Keep the Customs of Old Norman Settlers. By Harrison Howell Walker. 595-632, *May 1939*

The **GRANDEST** and Most Mighty Terrestrial Phenomenon: The Gulf Stream. By John Elliott Pillsbury. 767-778, *Aug. 1912*

The **GRANDEUR** of Windsor. By Anthony Holden. Photos by James L. Stanfield. Included: Picture portfolio text by David Jeffery. 604-631, *Nov. 1980*

The **GRANITE** City of the North: Austere Stockholm, Sweden's Prosperous Capital, Presents a Smiling Aspect in Summer. By Ralph A. Graves. 403-424, *Oct. 1928*

GRANT, G. A.: *Photographer*

Western National Parks Invite America Out of Doors. 65-80, *July 1934*

GRANT, MADISON: *Author*

Saving the Redwoods. 519-536, *June 1920*

GRANT, ULYSSES S.:

Profiles of the Presidents: III. The American Giant Comes of Age. By Frank Freidel. 660-711, *May 1965*

Appomattox: Where Grant and Lee Made Peace With Honor a Century Ago. By Ulysses S. Grant 3rd. Photos by Bruce Dale. 435-469, *Apr. 1965*

GRANT, ULYSSES S., 3rd:

Nomination Page. *Apr. 1965*

Author

Appomattox: Where Grant and Lee Made Peace With Honor a Century Ago. Photos by Bruce Dale. 435-469, *Apr. 1965*

The Civil War. 437-449, *Apr. 1961*

GRAPE CULTURE:

Iberia's Vintage River (Douro-Duero).

Luscious grapes dangle from vines in Tulare County, California, in 1936. The state's fertile soil and equable climate produce the choicest European varieties. HAMMOND

By Marion Kaplan. Photos by Stephanie Maze. 460-489, *Oct. 1984*

Bordeaux: Fine Wines and Fiery Gascons. By William Davenport. Photos by Adam Woolfitt. 233-259, *Aug. 1980*

Napa, California's Valley of the Vine. By Moira Johnston. Photos by Charles O'Rear. 695-717, *May 1979*

Living the Good Life in Burgundy. By William Davenport. Photos by Robert Freson. 794-817, *June 1978*

My Life in the Valley of the Moon (California). By H. H. Arnold. Photos by Willard R. Culver. 689-716, *Dec. 1948*

Fruitful Shores of the Finger Lakes (New York). By Harrison Howell Walker. 559-594, *May 1941*

The Grape-Growing Industry in the United States. 445-451, *Dec. 1903*

GRAPES:

How Fruit Came to America. By J. R. Magness. Paintings by Else Bostelmann. 325-377, *Sept. 1951*

GRASS Makes Wyoming Fat. By Frederick Simpich. 153-188, *Aug. 1945*

"GRASS Never Grows Where the Turkish Hoof Has Trod." By Edwin Pears. 1132-1148, *Nov. 1912*

GRASS-SKIRTED Yap. By W. Robert Moore. 805-830, *Dec. 1952*

GRASSE, FRANÇOIS JOSEPH PAUL DE:

Our First Alliance. By J. J. Jusserand. 518-548, *June 1917*

GRASSES:

The Tallgrass Prairie: Can It Be Saved? By Dennis Farney. Photos by Jim Brandenburg. Included: Bluestem, Cordgrass, Indian grass; and aliens,

Fescue, Kentucky bluegrass. 37-61, *Jan. 1980*

Exploring a Grass Wonderland of Wild West China. By Ray G. Johnson. 713-742, *June 1944*

■■ *The Book of Wild Flowers: An Introduction to the Ways of Plant Life, Together with Biographies of 250 Representative Species and Chapters on Our State Flowers and Familiar Grasses.* 243 pages. 1924; rev. ed. 1933

Familiar Grasses and Their Flowers. By E. J. Geske and W. J. Showalter. Paintings by E. J. Geske. Contents: Barnyard Grass, Kentucky Bluegrass, Orchard Grass, Purple-Top, Redtop, Rye-Grass, Timothy, Yellow Foxtail. 625-636, *June 1921*

American Wild Flowers. Paintings by Mary E. Eaton. 483-517, *May 1915*

See also Bamboo

GRASSHOPPERS:

Back-yard Monsters in Color. By Paul A. Zahl. 235-260, *Aug. 1952*

GRASSHOPPERS, Migratory. *See* Locusts

GRASSLANDS:

■ *Our Awesome Earth: Its Mysteries and Its Splendors.* 199 pages. 1986

The Tallgrass Prairie: Can It Be Saved? By Dennis Farney. Photos by Jim Brandenburg. Included: Bluestem, Cordgrass, Indian grass; and aliens, Fescue, Kentucky bluegrass. 37-61, *Jan. 1980*

See also Prairie

GRASSLE, J. FREDERICK: *Author*

Incredible World of the Deep-sea Rifts. 680-705. I. Strange World Without Sun. The Editor. 680-688; II. Return to Oases of the Deep. By Robert D. Ballard and J. Frederick Grassle. 689-705, *Nov. 1979*

GRAVEL PICTOGRAPHS:
Giant Effigies of the Southwest. By George C. Marshall. 389, *Sept. 1952*
Seeking the Secret of the Giants. By Frank M. Setzler. Photos by Richard H. Stewart. Included: Map of Colorado River Basin, showing sites near Blythe, Ripley, Topock; the Hâ-âk lying site near Gila River Indian Reservation. 390-404, *Sept. 1952*

's **GRAVENHAGE** (The Hague), Netherlands:
Mid-century Holland Builds Her Future. By Sydney Clark. 747-778, *Dec. 1950*

GRAVES, HENRY S.: *Author*
The Fight Against Forest Fires. 662-683, *July 1912*

GRAVES, RALPH A.:
Memorial tribute of the Board of Trustees and Officers of the National Geographic Society to Ralph A. Graves, late Senior Assistant Editor of the National Geographic Magazine. 606, *Nov. 1932*

Author
Louisiana, Land of Perpetual Romance. Photos by Edwin L. Wisherd. 393-482, *Apr. 1930*
Through the English Lake District Afoot and Awheel. 577-603, *May 1929*
The Granite City of the North: Austere Stockholm, Sweden's Prosperous Capital, Presents a Smiling Aspect in Summer. 403-424, *Oct. 1928*
Marching Through Georgia Sixty Years After: Multifold Industries and Diversified Agriculture Are Restoring the Prosperity of America's Largest State East of the Mississippi. 259-311, *Sept. 1926*
A Short Visit to Wales: Historic Associations and Scenic Beauties Contend for Interest in the Little Land Behind the Hills. 635-675, *Dec. 1923*
The New Map of Europe: Showing the Boundaries Established by the Peace Conference at Paris and by Subsequent Decisions of the Supreme Council of the Allied and Associated Powers. 157-177, *Feb. 1921*
Human Emotion Recorded by Photography. 284-300, *Oct. 1920*
The Millennial City: The Romance of Geneva, Capital of the League of Nations. 457-476, *June 1919*
Ships for the Seven Seas: The Story of America's Maritime Needs, Her Capabilities and Her Achievements. 165-200, *Sept. 1918*
Helping to Solve Our Allies' Food Problem: America Calls for a Million Young Soldiers of the Commissary to Volunteer for Service in 1918. 170-194, *Feb. 1918*
Fearful Famines of the Past: History Will Repeat Itself Unless the American People Conserve Their Resources. 69-90, *July 1917*

GRAVES, WILLIAM:
On Assignment in the Philippines. *July 1986*
Nomination Page. In Japan. *July 1977*
Author
Tokyo, A Profile of Success. Photos by David Alan Harvey. 606-645, *Nov. 1986*
Corregidor Revisited. Photos by Steve McCurry. 118-131, *July 1986*
After an Empire...Portugal. Photos by Bruno Barbey. 804-831, *Dec. 1980*
Puget Sound, Sea Gate of the Pacific Northwest. Photos by David Alan Harvey. 71-97, *Jan. 1977*
The Imperiled Giants (Whales). 722-751, *Dec. 1976*
New Life for the Troubled Suez Canal. Photos by Jonathan Blair. 792-817, *June 1975*
Iran: Desert Miracle. Photos by James P. Blair. 2-47, *Jan. 1975*
Denmark, Field of the Danes. Photos by Thomas Nebbia. 245-275, *Feb. 1974*
Bangkok, City of Angels. Photos by John Launois. 96-129, *July 1973*
Human Treasures of Japan. Photos by James L. Stanfield. 370-379, *Sept. 1972*
Living in a Japanese Village. Photos by James L. Stanfield. 668-693, *May 1972*
■■ *Hawaii.* Photos by James L. Amos. 203 pages. *1970*
San Francisco Bay, the Westward Gate. Photos by James L. Stanfield. 593-637, *Nov. 1969*
World's Last Salute to a Great American (Dwight D. Eisenhower). By William Graves and other members of the National Geographic staff. 40-51, *July 1969*
Finland: Plucky Neighbor of Soviet

Spikes of Indian grass survive on a remnant of the tallgrass prairie that once covered the U.S. Midwest. JIM BRANDENBURG

Russia. Photos by George F. Mobley. 587-629, *May 1968*
Mobile, Alabama's City in Motion. Photos by Joseph J. Scherschel and Robert W. Madden. 368-397, *Mar. 1968*
The Rhine: Europe's River of Legend. Photos by Bruce Dale. 449-499, *Apr. 1967*
California, the Golden Magnet. 595-679. I. The South. Photos by Thomas Nebbia. 595-639; II. Nature's North. Photos by James P. Blair and Jonathan S. Blair. 641-679, *May 1966*
Washington: The City Freedom Built. Photos by Bruce Dale and Thomas Nebbia. 735-781, *Dec. 1964*
Tokyo, the Peaceful Explosion. Photos by Winfield Parks. 445-487, *Oct. 1964*
Earthquake! (Alaska, 1964). 112-139, *July 1964*
Martha's Vineyard. Photos by James P. Blair. 778-809, *June 1961*
Maine's Lobster Island, Monhegan. Photos by Kosti Ruohomaa. 285-298, *Feb. 1959*

GRAVEYARD of the Quicksilver Galleons. By Mendel Peterson. Photos by Jonathan Blair. 850-876, *Dec. 1979*

GRAVOSA, Yugoslavia:
East of the Adriatic: Notes on Dalmatia, Montenegro, Bosnia, and Herzegovina. By Kenneth McKenzie. 1159-1187, 1284, *Dec. 1912*

GRAY, RALPH:
Nomination Page. *Sept. 1969*
Nomination Page. *Mar. 1964*
Nomination Page. *Sept. 1960*
Author
The Alps: Man's Own Mountains. Photos by Walter Meayers Edwards and William Eppridge. 350-395, *Sept. 1965*
From Sun-clad Sea to Shining Mountains. Photos by James P. Blair. 542-589, *Apr. 1964*
Rhododendron Time on Roan Mountain. 819-828, *June 1957*
Down the Susquehanna by Canoe. Photos by Walter Meayers Edwards. 73-120, *July 1950*
Down the Potomac by Canoe. Photos by Walter Meayers Edwards. 213-242, *Aug. 1948*
Author-Photographer
From Sea to Shining Sea: A Cross Section of the United States Along Historic Route 40. Photos by Dean Conger and author. 1-61, *July 1961*
Three Roads to Rainbow. 547-561, *Apr. 1957*
Across Canada by Mackenzie's Track. 191-239, *Aug. 1955*
Following the Trail of Lewis and Clark. 707-750, *June 1953*
Vacation Tour Through Lincoln Land. 141-184, *Feb. 1952*
Labrador Canoe Adventure. By Andrew Brown and Ralph Gray. 65-99, *July 1951*

GRAY, WILLIAM R.: *Author*
■■ *Voyages to Paradise: Exploring in the*

Wake of Captain Cook. Photos by Gordon W. Gahan. 215 pages. *1981*

■■ *The Pacific Crest Trail.* Photos by Sam Abell. 199 pages. *1975*

GRAY OWLS:

The Great Gray Owl. By Michael S. Quinton. 123-136, *July 1984*

GRAY WHALES:

Gray Whales of San Ignacio. By Steven L. Swartz and Mary Lou Jones. Photos by François Gohier. NGS research grant. 754-771, *June 1987*

The California Gray Whale Comes Back. By Theodore J. Walker. 394-415, *Mar. 1971*

GRAY WOLVES:

Isle Royale, A North Woods Park Primeval. By John L. Eliot. Photos by Mitch Kezar. 534-550, *Apr. 1985*

Where Can the Wolf Survive? By L. David Mech. 518-537, *Oct. 1977*

Wolves Versus Moose on Isle Royale. By Durward L. Allen and L. David Mech. 200-219, *Feb. 1963*

GRAYS LAKE NATIONAL WILD-LIFE REFUGE, Idaho:

Teamwork Helps the Whooping Crane. By Roderick C. Drewien, with Ernie Kuyt. 680-693, *May 1979*

GRAZZINI, ATHOS D.:

Nomination Page. *Jan. 1967*

GREAT Adventures With National Geo- ■■ *graphic: Exploring Land, Sea, and Sky.* 504 pages. *1963*

A **GREAT** African Lake (Victoria). By Sir Henry M. Stanley. 169-172, *May 1902*

GREAT AMERICAN DESERT, Utah:

The Nation's Undeveloped Resources. By Franklin K. Lane. 183-225, *Feb. 1914*

GREAT American Deserts. By Rowe ■■ Findley. Photos by Walter Meayers Edwards. 207 pages. *1972*

GREAT ANDAMANESE (Negrito Tribe):

The Last Andaman Islanders. By Raghubir Singh. 66-91, *July 1975*

GREAT BAHAMA BANK, Bahama Islands:

Strange March of the Spiny Lobster. By William F. Herrnkind. Photos by Rick Frehsee and Bruce Mounier. NGS research grant. 819-831, *June 1975*

Diving Into the Blue Holes of the Bahamas. By George J. Benjamin. 347-363, *Sept. 1970*

GREAT BARRIER REEF, Australia:

Wreck of H.M.S. *Pandora.* By Luis Marden. 423-451, *Oct. 1985*

Australia's Great Barrier Reef. 630-663. I. A Marine Park Is Born. By Soames Summerhays. Photos by Ron and Valerie Taylor. 630-635; II. Paradise Beneath the Sea. By Ron and Valerie Taylor. 636-663, *May 1981*

Australia's Great Barrier Reef. Photos by Valerie and Ron Taylor. 728-741, *June 1973*

Exploring Australia's Coral Jungle. By Kenneth MacLeish. 743-779, *June 1973*

Life Cycle of a Coral. By Robert F. Sisson. 780-793, *June 1973*

Queensland: Young Titan of Australia's

Tropic North. By Kenneth MacLeish. Photos by Winfield Parks. 593-639, *Nov. 1968*

Australia. II. The Settled East, the Barrier Reef, the Center. By Alan Villiers. 347-385, *Sept. 1963*

On Australia's Coral Ramparts. By Paul A. Zahl. 1-48, *Jan. 1957*

Where Nature Runs Riot: On Australia's Great Barrier Reef Marine Animals Grow to Unusual Size, Develop Strange Weapons of Attack and Defense, and Acquire Brilliant Colors. By T. C. Roughley. 823-850, *June 1940*

The Great Barrier Reef and Its Isles: The Wonder and Mystery of Australia's World-Famous Geographical Feature. By Charles Barrett. 355-384, *Sept. 1930*

GREAT BASIN, U. S.:

Indians of the Far West. By Matthew W. Stirling. Paintings by W. Langdon Kihn. 175-200, *Feb. 1948*

See also Basin and Range Geological Province, U. S.; Death Valley National Monument; Great Salt Lake; Mojave Desert

The **GREAT** Blue Heron. By Richard J. Dolesh. Photos by Cameron Davidson. 540-554, *Apr. 1984*

GREAT BRITAIN:

■■ *Discovering Britain & Ireland.* 448 pages. *1985*

Editorial. By Gilbert M. Grosvenor. 441, *Oct. 1979*

✤ *Medieval England; British Isles. Oct. 1979*

■ This Britain. 583, Nov. 1975; cover, *Dec. 1975*

Questing for Gems. By George S. Switzer. Included: The Crown Jewels of Great Britain. 835-863, *Dec. 1971*

The Investiture of Great Britain's Prince of Wales. By Allan C. Fisher, Jr. Photos by James L. Stanfield and Adam Woolfitt. 698-715, *Nov. 1969*

✤ *A Traveler's Map of the British Isles.* Text on reverse. *Apr. 1974*

The Britain That Shakespeare Knew. By Louis B. Wright. Photos by Dean Conger. 613-665, *May 1964*

✤ *Shakespeare's Britain. May 1964*

✤ *British Isles,* Atlas series. *July 1958*

The British Way: Great Britain's Major Gifts to Freedom, Democratic Government, Science, and Society. By Sir Evelyn Wrench. 421-541, *Apr. 1949*

Our Search for British Paintings. By Franklin L. Fisher. 543-550, *Apr. 1949*

✤ *The British Isles. Apr. 1949*

British Castles, History in Stone. By Norman Wilkinson. 111-129, *July 1947*

Britain Fights in the Fields. By Francis A. Flood. 31-65, *July 1944*

Lend-Lease Is a Two-way Benefit: Innovation in Creative Statesmanship Pools Resources of United Nations, and Supplies American Forces Around the World. By Francis Flood. 745-761, *June 1943*

The British Commonwealth of Nations: "Organized Freedom" Around the

A green turtle hatchling has survived gulls and ghost crabs on the beach and now faces predators in the open sea beyond Australia's Great Barrier Reef. RON AND VALERIE TAYLOR

World. By Eric Underwood. 485-524, *Apr. 1943*

A Modern Pilgrim's Map of the British Isles. By Andrew H. Brown. 795-802, *June 1937*

A Modern Pilgrim's Map of the British Isles or More Precisely the Kingdom of Great Britain and Northern Ireland and the Irish Free State. June 1937

Great Britain on Parade. By Maynard Owen Williams. 137-184, *Aug. 1935*

The Races of Europe. By Edwin A. Grosvenor. 441-534, *Dec. 1918*

What the War Has Done for Britain. By Judson C. Welliver. 278-297, *Oct. 1918*

Tales of the British Air Service. By William A. Bishop. 27-37, *Jan. 1918*

The Flags of the British Empire. By Byron McCandless and Gilbert Grosvenor. 378-385, *Oct. 1917*

The Oldest Free Assemblies: Address of Right Hon. Arthur J. Balfour, in the United States House of Representatives, May 5, 1917. 368-371, *Apr. 1917*

What Great Britain Is Doing (The British War Effort). By Sydney Brooks. 193-210, *Mar. 1917*

One Hundred British Seaports. 84-94, *Jan. 1917*

Great Britain's Bread Upon the Waters: Canada and Her Other Daughters. By William Howard Taft. 217-272, *Mar. 1916*

Great Britain in the Yangtze Valley. 163, *Apr. 1901*

Some Significant Facts Concerning the Foreign Trade of Great Britain. 480, *Dec. 1900*

The Ordnance Survey of Great Britain–Its History and Object. By Josiah Pierce, Jr. 243-260, *Aug. 1890*

See also England; Scotland; Wales

GREAT BRITAIN II (Ketch):

By Square-rigger from Baltic to Bicentennial. By Kenneth Garrett. 824-857, *Dec. 1976*

The **GREAT** Canals of the World. 475-479, *Oct. 1905*

GREAT DEPRESSION:

The Okies–Beyond the Dust Bowl. By William Howarth. Photos by Chris Johns. 322-349, *Sept. 1984*

GREAT DIVIDE TRAIL, Alberta-British Columbia, Canada:

Hiking the Backbone of the Rockies: Canada's Great Divide Trail. By Mike W. Edwards. Photos by Lowell Georgia. Included: Banff, Jasper, Kootenay, and Yoho National Parks; Mount Assiniboine, Mount Robson, and Willmore Wilderness Provincial Parks. 795-817, *June 1973*

See also Continental Divide

GREAT FALLS, Potomac River, Maryland-Virginia:

George Washington's Patowmack Canal. By Wilbur E. Garrett. Photos by Kenneth Garrett. 716-753, *June 1987*

Potomac, River of Destiny. By Albert W. Atwood. 33-70, *July 1945*

The Great Falls of the Potomac. By Gilbert Grosvenor. 385-400, *Mar. 1928*

The **GREAT** Good Places: English Country Houses. By Mark Girouard. Photos by Fred J. Maroon. 658-694, *Nov. 1985*

The **GREAT** Gray Owl. By Michael S. Quinton. 123-136, *July 1984*

GREAT ICE BARRIER, Antarctica:

The Great Ice Barrier. By Henry Gannett. 173-174, *Feb. 1910*

An Ice Wrapped Continent. By Gilbert H. Grosvenor. 95-117, *Feb. 1907*

Geography. By Sir W.J.L. Wharton. 483-498, *Nov. 1905*

GREAT INAGUA (Island), Bahamas:

Carib Cruises the West Indies. By Carleton Mitchell. 1-56, *Jan. 1948*

GREAT INDIAN DESERT, India-Pakistan:

The Desert: An Age-old Challenge Grows. By Rick Gore. Photos by Georg Gerster and Bruce Dale. 586-639, *Nov. 1979*

GREAT LAKES, and Region, Canada-U. S.:

Editorial. By Wilbur E. Garrett. 1, *July 1987*

The Great Lakes' Troubled Waters. By Charles E. Cobb, Jr. Photos by Bob Sacha and Richard Olsenius. Included: A great meeting of waters; North America's fifth coast. 2-31, *July 1987*

Great Lakes, The Making of America series. Included: Michigan, Wisconsin. On reverse: Indians, French, British; Creation of a Borderland; Influx of Settlers; Lake-country Lumber; Industrial Powerhouse; Region in Readjustment. *July 1987*

The Great Lakes: Is It Too Late? By Gordon Young. Photos by James L. Amos and Martin Rogers. 147-185, *Aug. 1973*

Close-up: U.S.A., Wisconsin, Michigan, and the Great Lakes. Text on reverse. *Aug. 1973*

Relics from the Rapids (Voyageurs). By Sigurd F. Olson. Photos by David S. Boyer. 413-435, *Sept. 1963*

New Era on the Great Lakes. By Nathaniel T. Kenney. 439-490, *Apr. 1959*

Northeastern United States, including the Great Lakes Region, Atlas series. *Apr. 1959*

New St. Lawrence Seaway Opens the Great Lakes to the World. By Andrew H. Brown. 299-339, *Mar. 1959*

The Great Lakes Region of the United States and Canada. Dec. 1953

J. W. Westcott, Postman for the Great Lakes. By Cy La Tour. 813-824, *Dec. 1950*

Great Lakes and Great Industries. Photos by B. Anthony Stewart, Alfred T. Palmer, Willard R. Culver. 689-712, *Dec. 1944*

By Car and Steamer Around Our Inland Seas. By Maynard Owen Williams. 451-491, *Apr. 1934*

Honors for Amundsen. Address: "The Five Inland Seas," by Harvey Goulder. 55-76, *Jan. 1908*

Rainfall and the Level of Lake Erie. By E. L. Moseley. 327-328, *Aug. 1903*

Testing the Currents of Lake Erie. By E. L. Moseley. 41-42, *Jan. 1903*

Submerged Valleys in Sandusky Bay. By E. L. Moseley. 398-403, *Nov. 1902*

Variations in Lake Levels and Atmospheric Precipitation. By Alfred J. Henry. 403-406, *Oct. 1899*

Modification of the Great Lakes by Earth Movement. By G. K. Gilbert. 233-247, *Sept. 1897*

In full court regalia, Winston Churchill takes an open-air ride from Great Britain's Buckingham Palace on March 2, 1911. RADIO TIMES HULTON PICTURE LIBRARY

Barely keeping above water, Interstate 80 carves a path across Utah's flooded Great Salt Lake in July 1984. JIM RICHARDSON

Area and Drainage Basin of Lake Superior. By Mark W. Harrington. 111-120, *Apr. 1897*

See also Erie, Lake; Ontario, Lake; Superior, Lake; *and* Illinois; Indiana; Michigan; Minnesota; New York; Ohio; Ontario; Wisconsin

GREAT LAMESHUR BAY, St. John (Island), U. S. Virgin Islands. *See* Tektite II

GREAT Masters of a Brave Era in Art. By Hereward Lester Cooke, Jr. 661-697, *May 1961*

The **GREAT** Mississippi Flood of 1927: Since White Man's Discovery This Mighty River Has Served Him Well, Yet It Has Brought Widespread Devastation Along Its Lower Reaches. By Frederick Simpich. 243-289, *Sept. 1927*

The **GREAT** Natural Bridges of Utah. 199-204, *Mar. 1907*

The **GREAT** Natural Bridges of Utah. By Byron Cummings. 157-167, *Feb. 1910*

GREAT PLAINS, U. S. *See* Midwest

The **GREAT** Populous Centers of the World. By Adolphus W. Greely. 89-92, *July 10, 1893*

The **GREAT** Rainbow Natural Bridge of Southern Utah. By Joseph E. Pogue. 1048-1056, *Nov. 1911*

GREAT Religions of the World. Contents: Buddhism, Christianity, Hinduism, Islam, and Judaism. 420 pages. *1971*

GREAT RIFT VALLEY, Africa-Asia:

Journey Into the Great Rift: the Northern Half. By Helen and Frank Schreider. 254-290, *Aug. 1965*

Where Roosevelt Will Hunt (Kenya). By Sir Harry Johnston. 207-256, *Mar. 1909*

See also Aqàba, Gulf of; Danakil Depression, Ethiopia; Dead Sea; Olduvai Gorge, Tanzania; Red Sea; Rudolf, Lake, Kenya

GREAT Rivers of the World. 448 pages. *1984*

The **GREAT** St. Bernard Hospice Today. By George Pickow. 49-62, *Jan. 1957*

GREAT SALT LAKE, Utah:

Utah's Shining Oasis. By Charles McCarry. Photos by James L. Amos. 440-473, *Apr. 1975*

Life in a "Dead" Sea–Great Salt Lake. By Paul A. Zahl. Included: Ancient inland sea, Lake Bonneville. 252-263, *Aug. 1967*

Geographical Twins a World Apart. By David S. Boyer. Included: Great Salt Lake and the Dead Sea. 848-859, *Dec. 1958*

GREAT SALT LAKE BASIN, Utah:

The Rising Great Salt Lake: No Way to Run a Desert. By Rick Gore. Photos by Jim Richardson. 694-719, *June 1985*

GREAT SAND BARRIER REEF, North Carolina-Virginia:

How We Found the *Monitor.* By John G. Newton. NGS research grant. 48-61, *Jan. 1975*

Lonely Cape Hatteras, Besieged by the Sea. By William S. Ellis. Photos by Emory Kristof. 393-421, *Sept. 1969*

Our Changing Atlantic Coastline. By Nathaniel T. Kenney. Photos by B. Anthony Stewart. 860-887, *Dec. 1962*

October Holiday on the Outer Banks. By Nike Anderson. Photos by J. Baylor Roberts. 501-529, *Oct. 1955*

Exploring America's Great Sand Barrier Reef. By Eugene R. Guild. Photos by John E. Fletcher and author. 325-350, *Sept. 1947*

GREAT SMOKY MOUNTAINS, North Carolina-Tennessee:

The People of Cades Cove. By William O. Douglas. Photos by Thomas Nebbia and Otis Imboden. 60-95, *July 1962*

Around the "Great Lakes of the South." By Frederick Simpich. Photos by J. Baylor Roberts. 463-491, *Apr. 1948*

Rambling Around the Roof of Eastern America. By Leonard C. Roy. 243-266, *Aug. 1936*

See also Great Smoky Mountains National Park

GREAT SMOKY MOUNTAINS NATIONAL PARK, North Carolina-Tennessee:

Autumn–Season of the Smokies. By Gordon Young. 142-147, *July 1979*

Great Smokies National Park: Solitude for Millions. By Gordon Young. Photos by James L. Amos. 522-549, *Oct. 1968*

Pack Trip Through the Smokies. By Val Hart. Photos by Robert F. Sisson. 473-502, *Oct. 1952*

Skyline Trail from Maine to Georgia. By Andrew H. Brown. Photos by Robert F. Sisson. 219-251, *Aug. 1949*

The **GREAT** *Southwest.* By Charles McCarry. Photos by George F. Mobley. 199 pages. *1980*

GREAT Stone Faces of Easter Island. 225-232, *Feb. 1944*

GREAT Stone Faces of the Mexican Jungle: Five Colossal Heads and Numerous Other Monuments of Vanished Americans Are Excavated by the Latest National Geographic-Smithsonian Expedition. By Matthew W. Stirling. 309-334, *Sept. 1940*

The **GREAT** Storm of March 11-14, 1888. By A. W. Greely. 37-39, *Oct. 1888*

The **GREAT** Storm Off the Atlantic Coast of the United States, March 11th-14th, 1888. By Everett Hayden. 40-58, *Oct. 1888*

GREAT TEMPLE OF TENOCHTITLAN:

The Aztecs. 704-775. I. The Aztecs. By Bart McDowell. Photos by David Hiser. Paintings by Felipe Dávalos. 714-751; II. The Building of Tenochtitlan. By Augusto F. Molina Montes. Paintings by Felipe Dávalos. 753-765; III. New Finds in the Great Temple. By Eduardo Matos Moctezuma. Photos by David Hiser. 767-775, *Dec. 1980*

Visitor's Guide to the Aztec World; Mexico and Central America. *Dec. 1980*

The **GREAT** Turk and His Lost Provinces. By William E. Curtis. 45-61, *Feb. 1903*

The **GREAT** Unmapped Areas on the Earth's Surface Awaiting the Explorer and Geographer. By J. Scott Keltie. 251-266, *Sept. 1897*

GREAT WALL OF CHINA:

■■*Journey Into China.* 518 pages. *1982*

A Thousand Miles Along the Great Wall of China: The Mightiest Barrier Ever Built by Man Has Stood Guard Over the Land of Chin for Twenty Centuries. By Adam Warwick. Included: The Great Wall of China Near Nankow Pass (panorama). 113-143, *Feb. 1923*

Peking, the City of the Unexpected. By James Arthur Muller. 335-355, *Nov. 1920*

China's Treasures. By Frederick Mc-Cormick. 996-1040, *Oct. 1912*

The Great Wall of China. By James H. Wilson. 372-374, *Sept. 1900*

The **GREAT** White Monarch of the Pacific Northwest (Mount Rainier). By A. H. Barnes. 593-626, *June 1912*

GREAT WHITE SHARK:

Sharks: Magnificent and Misunderstood. By Eugenie Clark. Photos by David Doubilet. NGS research grant. 138-187, *Aug. 1981*

Wolves of the Sea. By Nathaniel T. Kenney. 222-257, *Feb. 1968*

GREAT YARMOUTH, England:

When the Herring Fleet Comes to Great Yarmouth. By W. Robert Moore. 233-250, *Aug. 1934*

King Herring: An Account of the World's Most Valuable Fish, the Industries It Supports, and the Part It Has Played in History. By Hugh M. Smith. 701-735, *Aug. 1909*

GREATER ANTILLES. *See* Cuba; Dominican Republic; Haiti; Jamaica; Puerto Rico

GREATER BIRDS OF PARADISE:

Feathered Dancers of Little Tobago. By E. Thomas Gilliard. Photos by Frederick Kent Truslow. NGS research grant. 428-440, *Sept. 1958*

GREATER New York...Metropolis of Mankind. Aërial photo by Albert W. Stevens. Photo supplement, *Nov. 1933*

GREATER SANDHILL CRANES:

Teamwork Helps the Whooping Crane. By Roderick C. Drewien, with Ernie Kuyt. Contents: A U. S.-Canadian effort to establish a second breeding flock of wild whoopers among close-kin sandhill cranes. 680-693, *May 1979*

GREATER SUNDA ISLANDS. *See* Borneo; Celebes; Java; Sumatra

The **GREATEST** Achievement of Ancient Man in America (Fortress of Sacsahuaman, Peru). Panorama, *May 1916*

The **GREATEST** Hunt in the World (Elephant Hunting). By Eliza Ruhamah Scidmore. 673-692, *Dec. 1906*

"The **GREATEST** Job in the World?" By Joseph Judge. Contents: Recollections of writers and photographers by the Senior Associate Editor. 317-321, *Sept. 1988*

The **GREATEST** Volcanoes of Mexico. By A. Melgareio. 741-760, *Sept. 1910*

The **GREATEST** Voyage in the Annals of the Sea. By J. R. Hildebrand. 699-739, *Dec. 1932*

The **GREATNESS** of Little Portugal. By Oswald Crawfurd. 867-883, *Oct. 1910*

GREBES:

Western Grebes: The Birds That Walk on Water. By Gary L. Nuechterlein. NGS research grant. 624-637, *May 1982*

Birds That Cruise the Coast and Inland Waters. By T. Gilbert Pearson. Paintings by Allan Brooks. 299-328, *Mar. 1934*

El GRECO:

Toledo–El Greco's Spain Lives On. By Louise E. Levathes. Photos by James P. Blair. Included: The Genius of El Greco. Introduction by J. Carter Brown. 736-744. 726-753, *June 1982*

GRECO-ROMAN CULTURE:

The Day the World Ended at Kourion. By David Soren. Photos by Martha Cooper. NGS research grant. 30-53, *July 1988*

Caesarea Maritima. By Robert L. Hohlfelder. Photos by Bill Curtsinger. Paintings by J. Robert Teringo. NGS research grant. 261-279, *Feb. 1987*

■■*Greece and Rome: Builders of Our World.* 448 pages. *1968*

See also Aphrodisias

GREECE:

The Quest for Ulysses. By Tim Severin. Photos by Kevin Fleming. 197-225, *Aug. 1986*

Eternal Easter in a Greek Village. By Maria Nicolaidis-Karanikolas. Photos by James L. Stanfield. 768-777, *Dec. 1983*

Mount Athos. 739-745, *Dec. 1983*

Editorial. By Gilbert M. Grosvenor. 291, *Mar. 1980*

Greece: "To Be Indomitable, To Be Joyous." By Peter T. White. Photos by James P. Blair. 360-393, *Mar. 1980*

Homeward With Ulysses (Ionian Islands). By Melville Bell Grosvenor. Photos by Edwin Stuart Grosvenor. 1-39, *July 1973*

The Isles of Greece: Aegean Birthplace of Western Culture. By Melville Bell Grosvenor. Photos by Edwin Stuart Grosvenor and Winfield Parks. 147-193, *Aug. 1972*

Athens: Her Golden Past Still Lights the World. By Kenneth F. Weaver. Photos by Phillip Harrington. 100-137, *July 1963*

Round the World School (ISA). By Paul Antze. Photos by William Eppridge. 96-127, *July 1962*

The Aegean Isles: Poseidon's Playground. By Gilbert M. Grosvenor. 733-781, *Dec. 1958*

✥ *Greece and the Aegean,* Atlas series. *Dec. 1958*

Athens to Istanbul. By Jean and Franc Shor. 37-76, *Jan. 1956*

Crete, Cradle of Western Civilization. By Maynard Owen Williams. 693-706, *Nov. 1953*

On the Winds of the Dodecanese. By Jean and Franc Shor. 351-390, *Mar. 1953*

"Around the World in Eighty Days." By Newman Bumstead. Included: Athens, Corinth, Gulf of Korinthiakós, Gulf of Patraïkós, Kallithéa, Piraiévs. 705-750, *Dec. 1951*

✥ *Classical Lands of the Mediterranean. Dec. 1949*

Erosion, Trojan Horse of Greece. By F. G. Renner. 793-812, *Dec. 1947*

The Isles of Greece. By Richard Stillwell. 593-622, *May 1944*

The Greek Way. By Edith Hamilton. 257-271, *Mar. 1944*

A pair of western grebes lunges upright to skitter across the surface of the Delta Marsh in Manitoba, Canada, in a courtship ritual known as rushing. GARY L. NUECHTERLEIN

GREECE, Ancient:

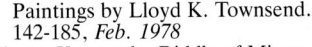

Moods of Greece offer haunting contrast, as when darkly clad women make their rounds through bright sunlight in Anoyia on the island of Crete.   JAMES P. BLAIR, NGS

Maynard Owen Williams. 719-739, *Dec. 1928*

"The Glory That Was Greece." By Alexander Wilbourne Weddell. 571-630, *Dec. 1922*

GREEK ART AND ARCHITECTURE:

Warriors From a Watery Grave (Bronze Sculptures). By Joseph Alsop. 821-827, *June 1983*

The Tower of the Winds. By Derek J. de Solla Price. Paintings by Robert C. Magis. NGS research grant. 587-596, *Apr. 1967*

Athens: Her Golden Past Still Lights the World. By Kenneth F. Weaver. Photos by Phillip Harrington. 100-137, *July 1963*

Athens to Istanbul. By Jean and Franc Shor. 37-76, *Jan. 1956*

Festival Days on the Slopes of Mount Parnassus. Photos by Maynard Owen Williams. 713-720, *Dec. 1930*

The Greek Bronzes of Tunisia. By Frank Edward Johnson. 89-104, *Jan. 1912*

GREEK MYTHOLOGY. *See* Golden Fleece Legend; Ulysses

GREEK ORTHODOX CHURCH:

The Byzantine Empire. 709-777. Included: I. Rome of the East. By Merle Severy. Photos by James L. Stanfield. 709-767; II. Mount Athos. 739-745; III. Eternal Easter in a Greek Village. By Maria Nicolaidis-Karanikolas. Photos by James L. Stanfield. 768-777, *Dec. 1983*

Island of Faith in the Sinai Wilderness (St. Catherine's Monastery). By George H. Forsyth. Photos by Robert F. Sisson. 82-106, *Jan. 1964*

Mount Sinai's Holy Treasures (St. Catherine's Monastery). By Kurt Weitzmann. Photos by Fred Anderegg. 109-127, *Jan. 1964*

On the Winds of the Dodecanese. By Jean and Franc Shor. 351-390, *Mar. 1953*

Hashemite Jordan, Arab Heartland. By John Scofield. 841-856, *Dec. 1952*

Home to the Holy Land. By Maynard Owen Williams. 707-746, *Dec. 1950*

Sinai Sheds New Light on the Bible. By Henry Field. Photos by William B. and Gladys Terry. 795-815, *Dec. 1948*

Sponge Fishermen of Tarpon Springs. By Jennie E. Harris. 119-136, *Jan. 1947*

The **GREEK** Way. By Edith Hamilton. 257-271, *Mar. 1944*

GREEKS:

Cyprus Under Four Flags: A Struggle for Unity. By Kenneth MacLeish. Photos by Jonathan Blair. 356-383, *Mar. 1973*

Sponge Fishermen of Tarpon Springs (Florida). By Jennie E. Harris. 119-136, *Jan. 1947*

GREELY, ADOLPHUS WASHINGTON:

Far North with "Captain Mac." By Miriam MacMillan. Included: Greely

Accessible only by ladder and rope bag in 1909, the Barlaam monastery in Thessaly, Greece, held a remarkable Byzantine library. ELIZABETH PERKINS

Arctic Expedition of 1881-1884. 465-513, *Oct. 1951*

Founder. 23, Jan. 1906; 793, June 1934; 133, *Aug. 1943*

Photograph. 129, *Jan. 1936*

Vice-President. 165, Apr. 1889; 270, July 1889; Apr. 1890; 294, Apr. 1891; xii, Feb. 19, 1892; xix, Feb. 20, 1893; xix, May 5, 1894; 216, June 1896; 134, *Jan. 1936*

The "Bowdoin" (Ship) in North Greenland: Arctic Explorers Place Tablet to Commemorate Sacrifices of the Lady Franklin Bay Expedition. By Donald B. MacMillan. 677-722, *June 1925*

The National Geographic Society's Notable Year. Address by A. W. Greely. 338-345, *Apr. 1920*

In Honor of the Army and Aviation. Address by A. W. Greely. 267-284, *Mar. 1911*

Board of Managers. 414, Sept. 1898; 87, Feb. 1905; 211, *Feb. 1911*

Greely's "Handbook of Alaska." By Gilbert H. Grosvenor. 491-492, *May 1909*

Honors to the American Navy. Address by A. W. Greely. 77-95, *Jan. 1909*

Farthest north reached by General Greely. 50, *Jan. 1907*

National Geographic Society Notes (Election of A. W. Greely as Chairman of the Committee on Eighth International Geographic Congress). 218-219, *June 1902*

Portrait. Frontispiece, June 1896; 355, *Oct. 1901*

Geographic Literature. 191, *Apr. 1898*

Gardiner Greene Hubbard: Memorial Meeting. Address by A. W. Greely. 68-70, *Feb. 1898*

Miscellanea. 64, *Feb. 1897*

Geography of the Air. Annual Address by A. W. Greely. 200-207, *Dec. 29, 1894*

Author

The National Geographic Society in War Time. 369-375, *Apr. 1918*

The France of Today. 193-222, *Sept. 1914*

The Origin of Stefansson's Blond Eskimo. 1225-1238, *Dec. 1912*

The Land of Promise (Siberia). 1078-1090, *Nov. 1912*

American Discoverers of the Antarctic Continent. 298-312, *Mar. 1912*

Recent Geographic Advances, Especially in Africa. 383-398, *Apr. 1911*

Duke of the Abruzzi in the Himalayas. 245-249, *Mar. 1910*

The Economic Evolution of Alaska. 585-593, *July 1909*

Peary's Twenty Years Service in the Arctics. 451-454, *July 1907*

Geographical Exploration: Its Moral and Material Results. 1-5, *Jan. 1906*

Russia in Recent Literature. 564-568, *Dec. 1905*

Advances in Geographic Knowledge During the Nineteenth Century. 143-152, *Apr. 1901*

Hurricanes on the Coast of Texas. 442-445, *Nov. 1900*

Climatic Conditions of Alaska. 132-137, *Apr. 1898*

The Samoan Cocoanut. 12-24, *Jan. 1898*

The Russian Census of 1897. 335-336, *Nov. 1897*

George W. Melville, Engineer-in-chief, U.S.N. 187-190, *June 1897*

The Siberian Transcontinental Railroad. 121-124, *Apr. 1897*

Rubber Forests of Nicaragua and Sierra Leone. 83-88, *Mar. 1897*

Sixth International Geographical Congress. 380, *Nov. 1896*

Charles Francis Hall and Jones Sound. 308-310, *Sept. 1896*

Jefferson as a Geographer. 269-271, *Aug. 1896*

Snug as two bugs in a rug, an Inuit woman and child brave the chill in Angmagssalik, Greenland, in 1941. WILLIE KNUTSEN

neighbors, A global greenhouse, The ozone enigma, Getting the lead out, The enemy within. 502-537, *Apr. 1987*

GREENHOUSES:

The Flower Seed Growers: Gardening's Color Merchants. By Robert de Roos. Photos by Jack Fields. Painting by Ned M. Seidler. 720-738, *May 1968*

See also Kew Gardens; Longwood Gardens; Scilly, Isles of

GREENLAND:

Commander Robert E. Peary: Did He Reach the Pole? By Wally Herbert. Introduction by the Editor. 387-413, *Sept. 1988*

Descendants of the Expeditions. Photos by Bob Sacha. 414-429. I. The Peary Family. By Edward Peary Stafford. 417-421; II. The Henson Family. By S. Allen Counter. 422-429, *Sept. 1988*

The Mummies of Qilakitsoq. By Jens P. Hart Hansen, Jørgen Meldgaard, and Jørgen Nordqvist. 191-207, *Feb. 1985*

Narwhal Hunters of Greenland. By Ivars Silis. 520-539, *Apr. 1984*

Hunters of the Lost Spirit: Greenlanders. By Priit J. Vesilind. Photos by Ivars Silis. 191-193, *Feb. 1983*

⊕ *Peoples of the Arctic; Arctic Ocean. Feb. 1983*

What's Happening to Our Climate? By Samuel W. Matthews. 576-615, *Nov. 1976*

Greenland Feels the Winds of Change. By John J. Putman. Photos by George F. Mobley. 366-393, *Sept. 1975*

Greenland's "Place by the Icebergs." By Mogens Bloch Poulsen. Photos by Thomas Nebbia. 849-869, *Dec. 1973*

Vinland Ruins Prove Vikings Found the New World. By Helge Ingstad. NGS research grant. 708-734, *Nov. 1964*

A Visit to the Living Ice Age. By Rutherford Platt. 525-545, *Apr. 1957*

The Peary Flag Comes to Rest. By Marie Peary Stafford. 519-532, *Oct. 1954*

We Followed Peary to the Pole. By Gilbert Grosvenor and Thomas W. McKnew. 469-484, *Oct. 1953*

I Sailed with Portugal's Captains Courageous. By Alan Villiers. 565-596, *May 1952*

Far North with "Captain Mac." By Miriam MacMillan. Included: Cape Morris Jesup, Cape York, Disko Island, Etah, Godhavn, Godthaab, Holsteinsborg, Jakobshavn, Nugâtsiaq, Qutdligssat, Refuge Harbor, Sioropaluk, Sukkertoppen, Thule. 465-513, *Oct. 1951*

Milestones in My Arctic Journeys. By Willie Knutsen. 543-570, *Oct. 1949*

⊕ *Canada, Alaska, and Greenland. June 1947*

Americans Stand Guard in Greenland. By Andrew H. Brown. 457-500, *Oct. 1946*

Servicing Arctic Airbases. By Robert A. Bartlett. 602-616, *May 1946*

Coast Guard Patrol in Greenland.

Photos by Thomas S. La Farge. 565-572, *May 1943*

Greenland Turns to America. By James K. Penfield. Included: Greenland–U. S. Base in the Arctic. 369-383, *Sept. 1942*

Desolate Greenland, Now an American Outpost. Photos by Willie Knutsen and F. Vogel. 393-406, *Sept. 1941*

Greenland from 1898 to Now: "Captain Bob," Who Went North with Peary, Tells of 42 Years of Exploration in the Orphan Island of New Aerial and Naval Interest. By Robert A. Bartlett. 111-140, *July 1940*

Flying Around the North Atlantic. By Anne Morrow Lindbergh. Foreword by Charles A. Lindbergh. 259-337, *Sept. 1934*

A Naturalist with MacMillan in the Arctic. By Walter N. Koelz. 299-318, *Mar. 1926*

The MacMillan Arctic Expedition Returns: U. S. Navy Planes Make First Series of Overland Flights in the Arctic and National Geographic Society Staff Obtains Valuable Data and Specimens for Scientific Study. By Donald B. MacMillan. 477-518, *Nov. 1925*

Flying Over the Arctic. By Richard E. Byrd. 519-532, *Nov. 1925*

The "Bowdoin" (Ship) in North Greenland: Arctic Explorers Place Tablet to Commemorate Sacrifices of the Lady Franklin Bay Expedition. By Donald B. MacMillan. 677-722, *June 1925*

The Origin of Stefansson's Blond Eskimo. By Adolphus W. Greely. 1225-1238, *Dec. 1912*

Scenes from Greenland. 877-891, *Oct. 1909*

A Hunting Trip to Northern Greenland. By Fullerton Merrill. 118-122, *Mar. 1900*

On Eskimo Geographic Names Ending in Miut. By John Murdoch. 190, *Apr. 1898*

Dwellings of the Saga-Time in Iceland, Greenland, and Vineland. By Cornelia Horsford. 73-84, *Mar. 1898*

Geographic Names in West Greenland. By Ralph S. Tarr. 103-104, *Mar. 1898*

Three Weeks in Hubbard Bay, West Greenland. By Robert Stein. 1-11, *Jan. 1898*

A Summer Voyage to the Arctic. By G. R. Putnam. 97-110, *Apr. 1897*

Recent Disclosures Concerning Pre-Columbian Voyages to America in the Archives of the Vatican. By William Eleroy Curtis. 197-234, *Jan. 31, 1894*

See also Greenland Icecap; Thule Air Base; *and* Vikings

GREENLAND ICECAP:

First Woman Across Greenland's Ice. By Myrtle Simpson. Photos by Hugh Simpson. 264-279, *Aug. 1967*

Nuclear Power for the Polar Regions. By George J. Dufek. 712-730, *May 1962*

Wringing Secrets from Greenland's Icecap. By Paul-Emile Victor. 121-147, *Jan. 1956*

GREENS Grow for GI's on Soilless Ascension. By W. Robert Moore. 219-230, *Aug. 1945*

GREGG, N. TAYLOR:

Nomination Page. *Sept. 1978*
Author
Hagi: Where Japan's Revolution

On a narwhal hunt in early July, dogs pulling a kayak-laden sled battle across a break in the ice at the mouth of Inglefield Fjord in northwestern Greenland. IVARS SILIS

Began. Photos by Sam Abell. Paintings by Kinuko Y. Craft. 751-773, *June 1984*

GRÉGOIRE, ROBERT: *Photographer*
Iceland's Wild Glacier-born River. By Paul Vander-Molen. Photos by Robert Grégoire and Jean-Luc Chéron. 306-321, *Sept. 1984*

GREGORY, ALFRED: *Photographer*
Triumph on Everest. 1-63. I. Siege and Assault. By Sir John Hunt. 1-43; II. The Conquest of the Summit. By Sir Edmund Hillary. 45-63, *July 1954*

GREGORY, HERBERT E.: *Author*
Lonely Australia: The Unique Continent. 473-568, *Dec. 1916*

GREGORY, W. M.: *Author*
Ore-Boat Unloaders. 343-345, *May 1907*

GREHAN, FARRELL: *Photographer*
The Dutch Touch. By Bart McDowell. Photos by Nathan Benn and Farrell Grehan. 501-525, *Oct. 1986*
Wales, the Lyric Land. By Bryan Hodgson. 36-63, *July 1983*
Roosevelt Country: T. R.'s Wilderness Legacy. By John L. Eliot. 340-363, *Sept. 1982*
The Country of Willa Cather. By William Howarth. 71-93, *July 1982*
Thoreau, a Different Man. By William Howarth. 349-387, *Mar. 1981*
Tulips: Holland's Beautiful Business. By Elizabeth A. Moize. 712-728, *May 1978*
■■*John Muir's Wild America.* By Tom Melham. Art by H. Tom Hall. 199 pages. *1976*
The Mazatzal's Harsh but Lovely Land Between. By François Leydet. 161-167, *Feb. 1974*
Okefenokee, the Magical Swamp. By François Leydet. 169-175, *Feb. 1974*
Autumn Flames Along the Allagash. By François Leydet. 177-187, *Feb. 1974*

The Olympics: Northwest Majesty. By François Leydet. 188-197, *Feb. 1974*
Amateur Gardener Creates a New Rose. By Elizabeth A. Moize. 286-294, *Aug. 1972*

GRENADA (Island), West Indies:
Marking Time in Grenada. By Charles E. Cobb, Jr. Photos by David Alan Harvey. 688-710, *Nov. 1984*
St. Vincent, the Grenadines, and Grenada: Taking It as It Comes. By Ethel A. Starbird. Photos by Cotton Coulson. 399-425, *Sept. 1979*
Finisterre Sails the Windward Islands. By Carleton Mitchell. Photos by Winfield Parks. 755-801, *Dec. 1965*
Carib Cruises the West Indies. By Carleton Mitchell. 1-56, *Jan. 1948*
British West Indian Interlude. By Anne Rainey Langley. 1-46, *Jan. 1941*

The **GRENADINES** (Islands), West Indies:
St. Vincent, the Grenadines, and Grenada: Taking It as It Comes. By Ethel A. Starbird. Photos by Cotton Coulson. 399-425, *Sept. 1979*
Finisterre Sails the Windward Islands. By Carleton Mitchell. Photos by Winfield Parks. 755-801, *Dec. 1965*

GRENFELL, SIR WILFRED T.: *Author*
A Land of Eternal Warring (Labrador). Note: Author's name erroneously published as Wilfrid. 665-690, *Aug. 1910*

GRENIER, ROBERT: *Author*
Excavating a 400-year-old Basque Galleon. 58-67, *July 1985*

GREW, JOSEPH C.: *Author*
Japan and the Pacific. 385-414, *Apr. 1944*
Waimangu and the Hot-Spring Country of New Zealand: The World's Greatest Geyser Is One of Many Natural Wonders in a Land of Inferno and Vernal Paradise. 109-130, *Aug. 1925*

GREYNOLDS PARK, North Miami Beach, Florida:
New Scarlet Bird in Florida Skies. By Paul A. Zahl. 874-882, *Dec. 1967*

GRIFFIN, DONALD R.: *Author*
Mystery Mammals of the Twilight (Bats). 117-134, *July 1946*

GRIFFIN, EDWARD I.: *Author*
Making Friends With a Killer Whale. 418-446, *Mar. 1966*

GRIFFIN, GILLETT G.: *Author*
In Defense of the Collector. 462-465, *Apr. 1986*

GRIFFIS, WILLIAM ELLIOT: *Author*
Japan, Child of the World's Old Age: An Empire of Mountainous Islands, Whose Alert People Constantly Conquer Harsh Forces of Land, Sea, and Sky. 257-301, *Mar. 1933*
The Empire of the Risen Sun (Japan). 415-443, *Oct. 1923*

GRIFFITHS, ANNIE: *Photographer*
North Dakota–Tough Times on the Prairie. By Bryan Hodgson. 320-347, *Mar. 1987*
To Scotland Afoot Along the Pennine Way. By David Yeadon. 388-418, *Mar. 1986*
Savannah to Charleston–A Good Life in the Low Country. By John J. Putman. 798-829, *Dec. 1983*
High-Flying Tulsa. By Robert Paul Jordan. 378-403, *Sept. 1983*
The American Red Cross: A Century of Service. By Louise Levathes. 777-791, *June 1981*
Ancient Ashfall Creates a Pompeii of Prehistoric Animals. By Michael R. Voorhies. 66-75, *Jan. 1981*
Minneapolis and St. Paul. By Thomas J. Abercrombie. 665-691, *Nov. 1980*

GRIFFITHS, WILLIAM ARTHUR: *Author*
Malta: The Halting Place of Nations: First Account of Remarkable Prehistoric Tombs and Temples Recently Unearthed on the Island. 445-478, *May 1920*

GRIGG, RICHARD W.: *Author*
Precious Corals, Hawaii's Deep-sea Jewels. Photos by David Doubilet. 719-732, *May 1979*

GRIGGS, ROBERT F.:
Awarded Jane M. Smith Life Membership. 342, *Apr. 1920*
Author
The Cause of Earthquakes. 443-451, *Oct. 1923*
■■*The Valley of Ten Thousand Smokes.* 341 pages. 1912; rev. ed. *1922*
Our Greatest National Monument: The National Geographic Society Completes Its Explorations in the Valley of Ten Thousand Smokes. 219-292, *Sept. 1921*
The Valley of Ten Thousand Smokes: An Account of the Discovery and Exploration of the Most Wonderful Volcanic Region in the World. Included: The Awe-Inspiring Spectacle of the Valley of Ten Thousand Smokes,

A cricket player in Grenada wields his bat by the wall where radicals gunned down some 40 people, including Prime Minister Maurice Bishop, in 1983. DAVID ALAN HARVEY

Discovered and Explored by National Geographic Society Expeditions. Panorama from photo by author. 115-169, *Feb. 1918*

The Valley of Ten Thousand Smokes: National Geographic Society Explorations in the Katmai District of Alaska. 13-68, *Jan. 1917*

A **GRIM** Struggle for Survival: The Imperiled Mountain Gorilla. By Dian Fossey. Included: Death of Marchessa. Photos by Peter G. Veit. 508-511. NGS research grant. 501-523, *Apr. 1981*

GRIMBLE, SIR ARTHUR: *Author*

War Finds Its Way to Gilbert Islands: United States Forces Dislodge Japanese from Enchanted Atolls Which Loom Now as Stepping Stones along South Sea Route from Australia to Hawaii. 71-92, *Jan. 1943*

GRIMES, S. A.: *Photographer*

Birds on the Home Front. Photos by Arthur A. Allen, S. A. Grimes, and others. 33-56, *July 1943*

GRIMMER, J. LEAR:

Nomination Page. In British Guiana (Guyana). *Feb. 1961*

Author

Strange Little World of the Hoatzin. Photos by M. Woodbridge Williams. 391-401, *Sept. 1962*

GRIMM'S Fairyland in Northwestern Germany. Photos by Hans Hildenbrand and Wilhelm Tobien. 641-648, *May 1931*

GRIMSBY, England:

Europe's Endangered Fish Supply: The War and the North Sea Fisheries. 141-152, *Feb. 1915*

GRIMSHAW, BEATRICE: *Author*

In the Savage South Seas. 1-19, *Jan. 1908*

GRINI (Concentration Camp), Norway:

The White War in Norway. By Thomas R. Henry. 617-640, *Nov. 1945*

GRINNELL, ALTON G.: *Author*

Our Army Versus a Bacillus. 1146-1152, *Oct. 1913*

GRISCOM, LLOYD C.:

The Annnal Dinner of the National Geographic Society. Speech by Lloyd C. Griscom. 22-37, *Jan. 1906*

GRISWOLD, OLIVER: *Author*

An Exotic New Oriole Settles in Florida. By Charles M. Brookfield and Oliver Griswold. 261-264, *Feb. 1956*

GRIT and Glory: The Pony Express. By Rowe Findley. Photos by Craig Aurness. 45-71, *July 1980*

GRIZZLY BEARS:

The Grizzlies. President's Page. By Gilbert M. Grosvenor. Jan. 1987; Cover. *Mar. 1987*

"Grizz"–Of Men and the Great Bear. By Douglas H. Chadwick. 182-213, *Feb. 1986*

Tracking grizzly bears in Montana's Scapegoat Wilderness, John Craighead, at left, studies a satellite-computer map of the area. KAREN CRAIGHEAD HAYNAM

Studying Grizzly Habitat by Satellite. By John Craighead. NGS research grant. 148-158, *July 1976*

Grizzly! 639A-639B, *Nov. 1967*

Trailing Yellowstone's Grizzlies by Radio. By Frank Craighead, Jr., and John Craighead. NGS research grant. 252-267, *Aug. 1966*

Knocking Out Grizzly Bears For Their Own Good. By Frank and John Craighead. NGS research grant. 276-291, *Aug. 1960*

GROFF, G. WEIDMAN: *Author*

Landscaped Kwangsi, China's Province of Pictorial Art. By G. Weidman Groff and T. C. Lau. 671-710, *Dec. 1937*

GROOTE EYLANDT (Island), Northern Territory, Australia:

From Spear to Hoe on Groote Eylandt. By Howell Walker. 131-142, *Jan. 1953*

Exploring Stone Age Arnhem Land. By Charles P. Mountford. Photos by Howell Walker. NGS research grant. 745-782, *Dec. 1949*

GROSVENOR, ALEXANDER G. B.: *Author*

Midshipmen's Cruise. By William J. Aston and Alexander G. B. Grosvenor. 711-754, *June 1948*

GROSVENOR, ANNE REVIS. *See* Revis, Anne

GROSVENOR, DONNA KERKAM: *Author-Photographer*

Bali by the Back Roads. By Donna K. and Gilbert M. Grosvenor. 657-697, *Nov. 1969*

Ceylon, the Resplendent Land. By Donna K. and Gilbert M. Grosvenor. 447-497, *Apr. 1966*

Miniature Monaco. By Gilbert M. and Donna Kerkam Grosvenor. 546-573, *Apr. 1963*

Photographer

What's Black and White and Loved All Over? By Theodore H. Reed. 803-815, *Dec. 1972*

White Tiger in My House. By Elizabeth C. Reed. 482-491, *Apr. 1970*

GROSVENOR, EDWIN AUGUSTUS:

Literary Landmarks of Massachusetts. By William H. Nicholas. Photos by B. Anthony Stewart and John E. Fletcher. 279-310, *Mar. 1950*

Lectures. 31-32, Jan. 1897; 5-6, Feb. 1897; 159, May 1897; 32, *Jan. 1898*

Author

The Races of Europe: The Graphic Epitome of a Never-ceasing Human Drama. The Aspirations, Failures, Achievements, and Conflicts of the Polyglot People of the Most Densely Populated Continent. 441-534, *Dec. 1918*

Constantinople and Sancta Sophia. 459-482, *May 1915*

Evolution of Russian Government. 309-332, *July 1905*

Siberia. 317-324, *Sept. 1901*

The Growth of Russia. 169-185, *May 1900*

GROSVENOR, EDWIN STUART: *Photographer*

The Enduring Pyrenees. By Robert Laxalt. 794-819, *Dec. 1974*

Homeward With Ulysses. By Melville Bell Grosvenor. 1-39, *July 1973*

The Isles of Greece: Aegean Birthplace

G
H

of Western Culture. By Melville Bell Grosvenor. Photos by Edwin Stuart Grosvenor and Winfield Parks. 147-193, *Aug. 1972*

North Through History Aboard *White Mist.* By Melville Bell Grosvenor. 1-55, *July 1970*

South Seas' Tonga Hails a King. By Melville Bell Grosvenor. 322-343, *Mar. 1968*

GROSVENOR, ELSIE MAY BELL:

To Gilbert Grosvenor: a Monthly Monument 25 Miles High. By Frederick G. Vosburgh and the staff of the National Geographic Society. 445-487, *Oct. 1966*

First Lady of the National Geographic. By Gilbert Hovey Grosvenor. 101-121, *July 1965*

Flag of the National Geographic Society designed by. 637, May 1949; 145, Aug. 1953; 516, 557, 564, Oct. 1963; 100, 101, 118, *July 1965*

Author

Alaska's Warmer Side. Photos by Gilbert Grosvenor and W. Robert Moore. 737-775, *June 1956*

Safari from Congo to Cairo. Photos by Gilbert Grosvenor. 721-771, *Dec. 1954*

Safari Through Changing Africa. Photos by Gilbert Grosvenor. 145-198, *Aug. 1953*

GROSVENOR, GILBERT HOVEY:

Three Men Who Made the Magazine. By Charles McCarry. 287-316, *Sept. 1988*

Editor (1899-1954). 65, 65B, July 1954; 459, 518, 529, 560, 561, 581, Oct. 1963; 445, 396; 143, Feb. 1980; 848, Dec. 1981; 270, 272, 276, *Aug. 1982*

President of NGS (1920-1954). 65, 65B, July 1954; 270, 276, *Aug. 1982*

Nomination Page. *July 1978*

Russell Cave Dedicated; New Visitor

Center Named for Gilbert H. Grosvenor. 440-442, *Sept. 1967*

Board of Trustees, Chairman (1954-1966). 65, 65B, 65D, July 1954; 445, 464, 485, *Oct. 1966*

To Gilbert Grosvenor: a Monthly Monument 25 Miles High. By Frederick G. Vosburgh and the staff of the National Geographic Society. 445-487, *Oct. 1966*

Geographic sites named for. 370, 371, 373, Sept. 1949; 570, Oct. 1949; 416, 418, Sept. 1955; 737, 753, June 1956; 552, Apr. 1957; 46, July 1957; 578, Apr. 1962; 807, 826-827, June 1963; 447, 450-451, 478, *Oct. 1966*

Grosvenor Medal Presented to Dr. Grosvenor by Charles F. Kettering. 253-255, 260, 261, Aug. 1949; 65G, July 1954; 449, 481, *Oct. 1966*

Gilbert Grosvenor's Golden Jubilee. By Albert W. Atwood. 253-261, *Aug. 1949*

Home, Boyhood. 600, May 1945; 237-238, *Aug. 1945*

Tribute by Admiral Byrd. 106, *July 1937*

*The Book of Birds: The First Work Presenting in Full Color All the Major Species of the United States and Canada.* Edited by Gilbert H. Grosvenor and Alexander Wetmore. Art by Allan Brooks. 2 volumes: I, 355 pages; II, 374 pages. 1932; rev. ed. *1937*

Scientific Advisory Committee member, second stratosphere flight. 272, Feb. 1935; 94, *Jan. 1936*

Alexander Graham Bell's tribute to work of. 274, Mar. 1912; 148, *Jan. 1936*

Married Elsie May Bell. 274, Mar. 1912; 148, *Jan. 1936*

Assistant Editor. 274, Mar. 1912; 123, 136-137, 139, 148, *Jan. 1936*

Growth of Society attributed to; certificate given in recognition. 148, 155, *Jan. 1936*

Radio communications with stratosphere flyers. 85, *Jan. 1936*

Scientific committee to stratosphere flight appointed by. 398, *Oct. 1934*

Mount Grosvenor, China. 409, 415, 428, *Oct. 1930*

Gilbert Grosvenor Trail, Antarctica. 184, 193, 198, 218, *Aug. 1930*

President Herbert Hoover introduced by Dr. Grosvenor to members of the Society on the occasion of the presentation of the Society's Special Gold Medal to Adm. Richard E. Byrd. 229, 231, *Aug. 1930*

Nansen received by Dr. Grosvenor. 22, *July 1930*

Home, Wild Acres, Maryland. 202, Feb. 1927; 592, *May 1930*

Lake Grosvenor, Alaska, named for. 222, 287, 284, 288, Sept. 1921; 89, *July 1926*

J. Howard Gore praises the NGS President for aiding the Allied cause during World War I. 676, *Dec. 1923*

Election of Gilbert Grosvenor as President of the Society. 345, *Apr. 1920*

War work of the Society directed by Gilbert Grosvenor. 375, *Apr. 1918*

*Scenes From Every Land: Picturing the People, Natural Phenomena, and Animal Life in All Parts of the World (Fourth Series).* Edited by Gilbert H. Grosvenor. 216 pages. *1918*

Report. 318-320, *Mar. 1915*

Editorial Policy: the seven guiding principles. 319, *Mar. 1915*

Office of the Editor. 460, *Apr. 1914*

Report. 251-255, *Feb. 1913*

The National Geographic Society (Dr. Grosvenor's Work as Editor of the Magazine). 272-298, *Mar. 1912*

*Scenes From Every Land: Picturing the People, Natural Phenomena, and Animal Life in All Parts of the World (Third Series).* Edited by Gilbert H. Grosvenor. 216 pages. *1912*

Mount Grosvenor, Alaska. 551, *June 1911*

President Taft's appreciation of. 276, *Mar. 1911*

Board of Managers. 87, Feb. 1905; 211, *Feb. 1911*

*Scenes From Every Land: Illustrations Picturing the People, Natural Phenomena, and Animal Life in All Parts of the World (Second Series).* Edited by Gilbert H. Grosvenor. 223 pages. *1909*

Chairman, committee of arrangements for banquet honoring Peary. 58, *Jan. 1907*

*Scenes From Every Land: A Collection of Illustrations From NGM Picturing the People, Natural Phenomena, and Animal Life in All Parts of the World.* Edited by Gilbert H. Grosvenor. 224 pages. *1907*

Cousin of President William Howard Taft. 25, *Jan. 1906*

Editor of report of proceedings of Eighth International Geographic Congress. 199, *Apr. 1905*

Paul Du Chaillu (Dr. Grosvenor's First Guest). 282-285, *July 1903*

Addresses by

Speech on opening of the Society's fifty fifth annual series of lectures in Constitution Hall, Nov. 20, 1942. 277-278, *Feb. 1943*

As Gilbert H. Grosvenor photographs an elaborately decorated building in Kano, Nigeria, in 1952, locals assemble for a group portrait. W. ROBERT MOORE, NGS

Poulter, Thomas C., awarded the Society's Special Gold Medal. 105, *July 1937*

Byrd, Richard E., Tribute to, heard via short-wave broadcast in Guatemala. 436, *Oct. 1936*

Ellsworth, Lincoln, awarded the Hubbard Medal. 36, *July 1936*

Stevens, Albert W., and Anderson, Orvil A., awarded Hubbard Medals. 713, *May 1936*

Byrd, Richard E., honored at reception. 107-108, *July 1935*

The Society Awards Hubbard Medal to Anne Morrow Lindbergh (Address by Gilbert Grosvenor). 791-794, *June 1934*

The Society's Special Medal Awarded to Amelia Earhart: First Woman to Receive Geographic Distinction at Brilliant Ceremony in the National Capital (Address by Gilbert Grosvenor). 358-367, *Sept. 1932*

Admiral Byrd Receives New Honors From The Society (Address by Gilbert Grosvenor). 228-238, *Aug. 1930*

The First Airship Flight Around the World: Dr. Hugo Eckener Tells of an Epochal Geographic Achievement upon the Occasion of the Bestowal of the National Geographic Society's Special Gold Medal (Presentation Address by Gilbert Grosvenor). 653-688, *June 1930*

President Coolidge Bestows Lindbergh Award: The National Geographic Society's Hubbard Medal Is Presented to Aviator Before the Most Notable Gathering in the History of Washington (Address by Gilbert Grosvenor). 132-140, *Jan. 1928*

Commander Byrd Receives the Hubbard Gold Medal: The First Explorer to Reach the North Pole by Air Receives Coveted Honor at Brilliant National Geographic Society Reception (Address by Gilbert Grosvenor). 377-388, *Sept. 1926*

The Hawaiian Islands: America's Strongest Outpost of Defense–The Volca-

nic and Floral Wonderland of the World (Address Delivered before the Society). 115-238, *Feb. 1924*

A Memorial to Peary: The National Geographic Society Dedicates Monument in Arlington National Cemetery to Discoverer of the North Pole (Address by Gilbert Grosvenor). 639-645, *June 1922*

Honors to Colonel Goethals: The Presentation, by President Woodrow Wilson, of the National Geographic Society Special Gold Medal, and Addresses by Secretary of State Bryan, the French Ambassador, the German Ambassador, and Congressman James R. Mann (Address by Gilbert H. Grosvenor). 677-690, *June 1914*

Author

First Lady of the National Geographic (Elsie May Bell Grosvenor). 101-121, *July 1965*

The Romance of the Geographic: National Geographic Magazine Observes Its Diamond Anniversary. 516-585, *Oct. 1963*

Hydrofoil Ferry "Flies" the Strait of Messina. 493-496, *Apr. 1957*

■■ *The National Geographic Society and Its Magazine.* Reprint of the Foreword to the Cumulative Index to the National Geographic Magazine, 1899 to 1946. 116 pages. 1936; rev. ed. *1948*

Insignia and Decorations of the United States Armed Forces. 185-186, *Feb. 1945*

Insignia of the United States Armed Forces. 651, *June 1943*

Your Society Aids War Effort. 277-278, *Feb. 1943*

The Mystery of Auroras: National Geographic Society and Cornell University Study Spectacular Displays in the Heavens. 689-690, *May 1939*

The Society's Special Medal Is Awarded to Dr. Thomas C. Poulter: Admiral Byrd's Second-in-Command and Senior Scientist Is Accorded High Geographic Honor (Presentation by Gilbert Grosvenor). 105-108, *July 1937*

Hubbard Medals Awarded to Stratosphere Explorers: Presentation by General Pershing (Address by Gilbert Grosvenor). 713, *May 1936*

The National Geographic Society and Its Magazine. 123-164, *Jan. 1936*

A Report of the Second Stratosphere Expedition. 535-536, *Oct. 1935*

Studies Planned for New Stratosphere Flight with Helium. 795-800, *June 1935*

The Society Announces New Flight into the Stratosphere. 265-272, *Feb. 1935*

Flags of the World. By Gilbert Grosvenor and William J. Showalter. 339-396, *Sept. 1934*

World's Largest Free Balloon to Explore Stratosphere. 107-110, *July 1934*

The Society Takes Part in Three Geographic Expeditions. 625-626, *May 1934*

Your Society Sponsors an Expedition to Explore the Stratosphere. 528-530, *Apr. 1934*

Flying. 585-630, *May 1933*

Washington Through the Years: On Rolling Wooded Hills and Colonial Tobacco Fields, Where George Washington Dreamed Our Nation's

On his golden anniversary as the GEOGRAPHIC's Editor in 1949 Gilbert H. Grosvenor is congratulated by the District of Columbia. BY CLIFFORD K. BERRYMAN, THE WASHINGTON STAR

GEOGRAPHIC Editor Gilbert H. Grosvenor camps at the foot of a giant sequoia in 1915. HORACE ALBRIGHT

GEOGRAPHIC members got a glimpse of Editor Gilbert H. Grosvenor hard at work in 1914, the 15th year of his tenure.

Alexander Graham Bell plays with grandson Melville Bell Grosvenor.

Elsie Bell Grosvenor, photographed in 1901 by husband Gilbert H. Grosvenor.
GROSVENOR COLLECTION, LIBRARY OF CONGRESS

Grosvenor and Ole Friele Backer. 171-211, *Aug. 1948*

Tai Shan, Sacred Mountain of the East. By Mary Augusta Mullikin. 699-719, *June 1945*

China's Great Wall of Sculpture: Man-hewn Caves and Countless Images Form a Colossal Art Wonder of Early Buddhism. By Mary Augusta Mulli-kin. Paintings by author and Anna M. Hotchkis. 313-348, *Mar. 1938*

The Charm of Cape Breton Island: The Most Picturesque Portion of Cana-da's Maritime Provinces–A Land Rich in Historic Associations, Natu-ral Resources, and Geographic Ap-peal. By Catherine Dunlop Mackenzie. 34-60, *July 1920*

GROSVENOR, MRS. GILBERT HOVEY. See Grosvenor, Elsie May Bell

GROSVENOR, GILBERT M.:

Announcing a New National Geograph-ic Society Foundation. Contents: Education Foundation. By Lloyd H. Elliott. 329A-329D, *Mar. 1988*

Editor (1970-1980). 838-843, Dec. 1970; 226, Aug. 1976; 1, Jan. 1978; 427, Oct. 1980; 567, Nov. 1980; 848, Dec. 1981; 276, 278, *Aug. 1982*

President of NGS (1980-). 427, Oct. 1980; 567, Nov. 1980; 276, 278, *Aug. 1982*

Associate Editor (1967-1970). 576, 583, 584, 586-588, Oct. 1967; 843, Dec. 1970; 226, *Aug. 1976*

Board of Trustees (1966-). 485, Oct. 1966; 584, 588, Oct. 1967; 843, Dec. 1970; 226, *Aug. 1976*

Vice President of NGS (1967-1980). 576, 584, 587, 588, Oct. 1967; 843, *Dec. 1970*

Nomination Page. *Mar. 1966*

Author

Earth '88: Will We Mend Our Earth? 766-771, *Dec. 1988*

New Atlas Unfurls Nation's History. Contents: Announcement of *Histori-cal Atlas of the United States.* 430-432, *Sept. 1988*

Our Society Opens New Doors. 554-560, *Oct. 1984*

President's Report to Members: An Ex-citing Year of Discovery. 820-824, *Dec. 1982*

The Unbalanced World. 1, *Special Re-port on Energy. (Feb. 1981)*

President's Report to Members. It's Been a Banner Year! 848-852, *Dec. 1981*

The Best of Our Land (National Parks). 1-2, *July 1979*

Author-Photographer

Bali by the Back Roads. By Donna K. and Gilbert M. Grosvenor. 657-697, *Nov. 1969*

Ceylon, the Resplendent Land. By Donna K. and Gilbert M. Grosvenor. 447-497, *Apr. 1966*

Miniature Monaco. By Gilbert M. and Donna Kerkam Grosvenor. 546-573, *Apr. 1963*

Yugoslavia's Window on the Adriatic. 219-247, *Feb. 1962*

When the President Goes Abroad (Ei-senhower Tour). 588-649, *May 1960*

Canada's Winged Victory: the *Silver Dart.* 254-267, *Aug. 1959*

The Aegean Isles: Poseidon's Play-ground. 733-781, *Dec. 1958*

Helping Holland Rebuild Her Land. By Gilbert M. Grosvenor and Charles Neave. 365-413, *Sept. 1954*

Photographer

The Leakeys of Africa: Family in Search of Prehistoric Man. By Melvin M. Payne. 194-231, *Feb. 1965*

Italian Riviera, Land That Winter For-got. By Howell Walker. 743-789, *June 1963*

Copenhagen, Wedded to the Sea. By Stuart E. Jones. 45-79, *Jan. 1963*

GROSVENOR, LILIAN: *Author*

Deaf Children Learn to Talk at Clarke School. Photos by Willard R. Culver. 379-397, *Mar. 1955*

GROSVENOR, MELVILLE BELL:

Three Men Who Made the Magazine. By Charles McCarry. 287-316, *Sept. 1988*

Editor (1957-1967). 419-423, Mar. 1957; 270-278, *Aug. 1982*

Melville Bell Grosvenor, A Decade of Innovation, a Lifetime of Service. By Bart McDowell. 270-278, *Aug. 1982*

President of NGS (1957-1967). 419-423, Mar. 1957; 270-278, *Aug. 1982*

Articles by. 275, *Aug. 1982*

Board of Trustees, Chairman Emeritus (1976-1982). 225, 226, *Aug. 1976*

Editor-in-Chief (1967-1977). 576-577, 584, 586, 589, Oct. 1967; 225, 226, *Aug. 1976*

Board of Trustees, Chairman (1967-1976). 576-577, 584-589, Oct. 1967; 442, *Sept. 1970*

Nomination Page. *Sept. 1969*

Board of Trustees, member (1945-1967). 65, 65B, 65D, July 1954; 835, Dec. 1959; 882, 883, Dec. 1960; 583, 584, *Oct. 1967*

Nomination Page. *Nov. 1962*

Author

A Long History of New Beginnings (Na-tional Parks). 18-29, *July 1979*

Homeward With Ulysses. Photos by Ed-win Stuart Grosvenor. 1-39, *July 1973*

The Isles of Greece: Aegean Birthplace of Western Culture. Photos by Edwin Stuart Grosvenor and Winfield Parks. 147-193, *Aug. 1972*

North Through History Aboard *White Mist.* Photos by Edwin Stuart Grosvenor. 1-55, *July 1970*

Robert V. Fleming, 1890-1967. 526-529, *Apr. 1968*

South Seas' Tonga Hails a King. Photos by Edwin Stuart Grosvenor. 322-343, *Mar. 1968*

White Mist Cruises to Wreck-haunted St. Pierre and Miquelon. 378-419, *Sept. 1967*

A Park to Save the Tallest Trees. 62-64, *July 1966*

Safe Landing on Sable, Isle of 500 Ship-wrecks. 398-431, *Sept. 1965*

World's Tallest Tree Discovered. Pho-tos by George F. Mobley. 1-9, *July 1964*

The Last Full Measure (Tribute to Pres-ident Kennedy). 307-355, *Mar. 1964*

Your Society's President Reports: A Year of Widening Horizons. By Mel-ville Bell Grosvenor. 888-906, *Dec. 1962*

The Nation Honors Admiral Richard E. Byrd (Byrd Memorial Dedication). 567-578, *Apr. 1962*

Our Society Welcomes Its 3,000,000th Member. 579-582, *Apr. 1962*

Your Society Takes Giant New Steps: The President's Annual Message to Members. By Melville Bell Grosve-nor. 874-886, *Dec. 1961*

Exploring an Epic Year. By Melville Bell Grosvenor. 874-886, *Dec. 1960*

National Geographic Society Presents Russell Cave to the American Peo-ple. 438, *Mar. 1958*

Admiral of the Ends of the Earth (Rich-ard E. Byrd). 36-48, *July 1957*

Landing Craft for Invasion. 1-30, *July 1944*

Cruise on an Escort Carrier. 513-546, *Nov. 1943*

The Grosvenor Medal has been given to Society officers and employees since 1949 for "exceptional service to geography."

The New Queen of the Seas (Aircraft Carrier). 1-30, *July 1942*

An August First in Gruyères (Switzerland). 137-168, *Aug. 1936*

Styria (Austria), a Favored Vacation Land of Central Europe. 430-439, *Oct. 1932*

Poland, Land of the White Eagle. 435-444, *Apr. 1932*

The Color Camera's First Aërial Success. 344-353, *Sept. 1930*

Author-Photographer

Around the World and the Calendar with the Geographic: The President's Annual Message. 832-866, *Dec. 1959*

Corkscrew Swamp–Florida's Primeval Show Place. 98-113, *Jan. 1958*

By Cotswold Lanes to Wold's End. 615-654, *May 1948*

Cuba–American Sugar Bowl. 1-56, *Jan. 1947*

Photographer

The Leakeys of Africa: Family in Search of Prehistoric Man. By Melvin M. Payne. 194-231, *Feb. 1965*

GROSVENOR, MRS. MELVILLE BELL. *See* Revis, Anne, for article by

GROSVENOR ARCH, Utah. *See* Escalante Canyon

GROSVENOR MEDAL:

Designed by Laura Gardin Fraser. 255, 261, Aug. 1949; 422, Mar. 1957; 516, *Oct. 1963*

Recipients

Grosvenor, Gilbert H.:

First Grosvenor Medal recipient. 253, 254, 255, 260, 261, Aug. 1949; 65G, July 1954; 449, 481, *Oct. 1966*

Gilbert Grosvenor's Golden Jubilee. By Albert W. Atwood. 253-261, *Aug. 1949*

La Gorce, John Oliver:

Presentation of medal by Gilbert H. Grosvenor. 422, 423, 442, Mar. 1960; 449, *Oct. 1966*

John Oliver La Gorce Is Elected Vice-Chairman of the Board, Melville Bell Grosvenor President and Editor of the National Geographic Society. 419-423, *Mar. 1957*

GROTTOES:

Probing Ice Caves of the Pyrenees. By Norbert Casteret. Included: Casteret Grotto. 391-404, *Mar. 1953*

See also Caves

GROUND CREWS, U. S. Army Air Forces:

They Sustain the Wings. By Frederick Simpich. 333-354, *Sept. 1943*

GROUNDNUT SCHEME: East Africa:

Britain Tackles the East African Bush. By W. Robert Moore. 311-352, *Mar. 1950*

GROUNDNUTS:

Rediscovering America's Forgotten Crops. By Noel D. Vietmeyer. Photos by Burgess Blevins. Paintings by Paul M. Breeden. 702-712, *May 1981*

GROUNDWATER. *See* Aquifers

GROUSE (Bird):

Game Birds of Prairie, Forest, and Tundra. By Alexander Wetmore. Paintings by Allan Brooks. 461-500, *Oct. 1936*

The Wild Life of Lake Superior, Past and Present: The Habits of Deer, Moose, Wolves, Beavers, Muskrats, Trout, and Feathered Wood-Folk Studied with Camera and Flashlight. By George Shiras, 3d. 113-204, *Aug. 1921*

See also Sage Grouse

GROVE, NOEL:

On Assignment on the Appalachian Trail. *Feb. 1987*

Nomination Page. In Thailand. *Feb. 1981*

Nomination Page. *Aug. 1979*

Nomination Page. In Iceland. *July 1973*

Author

Quietly Conserving Nature. Photos by Stephen J. Kraseman. 818-845, *Dec. 1988*

Air: An Atmosphere of Uncertainty. Photos by Ted Spiegel. Paintings by William H. Bond. Included: A deadly soup (a list of harmful chemicals), Careless neighbors, A global greenhouse, The ozone enigma, Getting the lead out, The enemy within. 502-537, *Apr. 1987*

A Tunnel Through Time: The Appalachian Trail. Photos by Sam Abell. 216-243, *Feb. 1987*

■■ *Wild Lands for Wildlife: America's National Refuges.* Photos by Bates Littlehales. 207 pages. *1984*

Swing Low, Sweet Chariot! Photos by Bruce Dale. 2-35, *July 1983*

Taiwan Confronts a New Era. Photos by John Chao. 93-119, *Jan. 1982*

Wild Cargo: the Business of Smuggling Animals. Photos by Steve Raymer. 287-315, *Mar. 1981*

The Caribbean: Sun, Sea, and Seething. Photos by Steve Raymer. 244-271, *Feb. 1981*

North Yemen. Photos by Steve Raymer. 244-269, *Aug. 1979*

The Two Worlds of Michigan. Photos by James L. Amos. 802-843, *June 1979*

Nigeria Struggles With Boom Times. Photos by Bruno Barbey. 413-444, *Mar. 1979*

Giants That Move the World's Oil: Superships. Photos by Martin Rogers. 102-124, *July 1978*

Superspill: Black Day for Brittany. Photos by Martin Rogers. 124-135, *July 1978*

Vestmannaeyjar: Up From the Ashes. Photos by Robert S. Patton. 690-701, *May 1977*

Venezuela's Crisis of Wealth. Photos by Robert W. Madden. 175-209, *Aug. 1976*

Mark Twain: Mirror of America. Photos by James L. Stanfield. 300-337, *Sept. 1975*

Oil, the Dwindling Treasure. Photos by Emory Kristof. 792-825, *June 1974*

A Village Fights for Its Life. 40-67, *July 1973*

Bicycles Are Back–and Booming! Photos by Michael Pfleger. 671-681, *May 1973*

North With the Wheat Cutters. Photos by James A. Sugar. 194-217, *Aug. 1972*

GROVES, P.R.C.: *Author*

Flying Over Egypt, Sinai, and Palestine: Looking Down Upon the Holy Land During an Air Journey of Two and a Half Hours from Cairo to Jerusalem. By P.R.C. Groves and J. R. McCrindle. 313-355, *Sept. 1926*

A **GROWING** Camp in the Tanana Gold Fields, Alaska. By Sidney Paige. 104-111, *Mar. 1905*

GROWING Pains Beset Puerto Rico. By William H. Nicholas. Photos by Justin Locke. 419-460, *Apr. 1951*

GROWING Up in Montana. Photos by Nicholas deVore III. 650-657, *May 1976*

GROWING Up With Snowflake (White Gorilla). By Arthur J. Riopelle. Photos by Michael Kuh. NGS research grant. 491-503, *Oct. 1970*

GROWTH of Florida. 424, *July 1906*

GROWTH of Maritime Commerce. By John Hyde. 30-31, *Jan. 1899*

The **GROWTH** of Russia. By Edwin A. Grosvenor. 169-185, *May 1900*

The **GROWTH** of the United States. By W J McGee. 377-386, *Sept. 1898*

GRUENING, ERNEST: *Author*

Lonely Wonders of Katmai. Photos by Winfield Parks. 800-831, *June 1963*

Alaska Proudly Joins the Union. Photos by Thomas J. Abercrombie. 43-83, *July 1959*

Author-Photographer

Strategic Alaska Looks Ahead: Our Vast Territory, Now Being More Closely Linked to Us by Road and Rail, Embodies the American Epic of Freedom, Adventure, and the Pioneer Spirit. Included: Alaska–Our Northwestern Outpost. Photos by author, Amos Burg, Froelich Rainey. 281-315, *Sept. 1942*

GRUNDTVIG, NIKOLAI FREDERIK SEVERIN:

Denmark and the Danes. By Maurice Francis Egan. 115-164, *Aug. 1922*

GRUNION, the Fish That Spawns on Land. By Clarence P. Idyll. Photos by Robert F. Sisson. 714-723, *May 1969*

GRUYÈRES, Switzerland:

An August First in Gruyères. By Melville Bell Grosvenor. 137-168, *Aug. 1936*

GUADALAJARA, Mexico:

The Most Mexican City, Guadalajara. By Bart McDowell. Photos by Volkmar Wentzel. 412-441, *Mar. 1967*

Vignettes of Guadalajara. By Frederick Simpich. 329-356, *Mar. 1934*

On an annual pilgrimage to pray for her health, Julian Rivas Martínez carries his mother to a Catholic festival in Chajul, Guatemala.   JAMES NACHTWEY, MAGNUM

GUADALCANAL (Island), Solomon Islands:

Wreck of the *Coolidge*. Text and photos by David Doubilet. Note: When sunk, the *Coolidge* was bearing reinforcements and supplies for the Allied troops on Guadalcanal. 458-467, *Apr. 1988*

At Ease in the South Seas. By Frederick Simpich, Jr. 79-104, *Jan. 1944*

What the Fighting Yanks See. By Wanda Burnett. 451-476, *Oct. 1944*

GUADALUPE (Island), Mexico:

A Cruise Among Desert Islands. By G. Dallas Hanna and A. W. Anthony. 71-99, *July 1923*

GUADALUPE, NUESTRA SEÑORA DE (Spanish Galleon):

Graveyard of the Quicksilver Galleons. By Mendel Peterson. Photos by Jonathan Blair. 850-876, *Dec. 1979*

GUADALUPE MOUNTAINS, New Mexico-Texas:

A Visit to Carlsbad Cavern: Recent Explorations of a Limestone Cave in the Guadalupe Mountains of New Mexico Reveal a Natural Wonder of the First Magnitude. By Willis T. Lee. 1-40, *Jan. 1924*

GUADALUPE MOUNTAINS NATIONAL PARK, Texas:

Guadalupe's Trails in Summer. By Edward Abbey. 135-141, *July 1979*

GUADELOUPE (Islands), West Indies:

A Fresh Breeze Stirs the Leewards. By Carleton Mitchell. Photos by Winfield Parks. 488-537, *Oct. 1966*

Colorful Paths in Martinique and Guadeloupe. Photos by Edwin L. Wisherd. 281-288, *Mar. 1938*

Report by Robert T. Hill on Volcanic Disturbances in the West Indies. 223-267, *July 1902*

GUALE. *See* Sea Islands, Georgia

GUAM (Island), Pacific Ocean:

Magellan: First Voyage Around the World. By Alan Villiers. Photos by Bruce Dale. 721-753, *June 1976*

Starfish Threaten Pacific Reefs. By James A. Sugar. 340-353, *Mar. 1970*

Victory's Portrait in the Marianas. By William Franklin Draper. 599-616, *Nov. 1945*

Springboards to Tokyo. By Willard Price. 385-407, *Oct. 1944*

Guam–Perch of the China Clippers. By Margaret M. Higgins. 99-122, *July 1938*

Our Smallest Possession–Guam. By William E. Safford. 229-237, *May 1905*

GUANA (Island), Virgin Islands:

Carib Cruises the West Indies. By Carleton Mitchell. 1-56, *Jan. 1948*

GUANACOS:

Guanacos: Wild Camels of South America. By William L. Franklin. NGS research grant. 63-75, *July 1981*

Camels of the Clouds. By W. H. Hodge. 641-656, *May 1946*

GUANAJUATO, Mexico:

Experiment in International Living. By Hugh M. Hamill, Jr. 323-350, *Mar. 1953*

The Treasure Chest of Mercurial Mexico (Silver Mines). By Frank H. Probert. 33-68, *July 1916*

GUAÑAPE CULTURE:

Finding the Tomb of a Warrior-God. By William Duncan Strong. Photos by Clifford Evans, Jr. 453-482, *Apr. 1947*

GUANAYES (Birds):

The Most Valuable Bird in the World. By Robert Cushman Murphy. 279-302, *Sept. 1924*

GUANGDONG PROVINCE, China. *See* Guangzhou

GUANGZHOU (Canton), Guangdong Province, China:

Changing Canton. Photos by Siukee Mack, Alfred T. Palmer, Kinchue Wong. 711-726, *Dec. 1937*

GUANGXI AUTONOMOUS REGION, China:

Landscaped Kwangsi, China's Province of Pictorial Art. By G. Weidman Groff and T. C. Lau. 671-710, *Dec. 1937*
See also Guilin

GUANO INDUSTRY:

Peru Profits from Sea Fowl. By Robert Cushman Murphy. Photos by author and Grace E. Barstow Murphy. 395-413, *Mar. 1959*

The Most Valuable Bird in the World (Guanay). By Robert Cushman Murphy. 279-302, *Sept. 1924*

Peru's Wealth-Producing Birds: Vast Riches in the Guano Deposits of

Cormorants, Pelicans, and Petrels which Nest on Her Barren, Rainless Coast. By R. E. Coker. 537-566, *June 1920*

GUANTÁNAMO, Cuba:

Guantánamo: Keystone in the Caribbean. By Jules B. Billard. Photos by W. E. Garrett and Thomas Nebbia. 420-436, *Mar. 1961*

GUANTÁNAMO BAY, Cuba:

Guantánamo: Keystone in the Caribbean. By Jules B. Billard. Photos by W. E. Garrett and Thomas Nebbia. 420-436, *Mar. 1961*
Across the Equator With the American Navy. By Herbert Corey. 571-624, *June 1921*

GUAREQUI (Plant):

Notes on the Deserts of the United States and Mexico (Extracted from a Publication by Daniel T. MacDougal). 691-714, *Aug. 1910*

GUARDIAN of the Gulf. By Thomas J. Abercrombie. Photos by the author and Lynn Abercrombie. 344-377, *Sept. 1981*

GUATEMALA:

Editorial. By Wilbur E. Garrett. 695, *June 1988*
Guatemala: A Fragile Democracy. By Griffin Smith, Jr. Photos by James Nachtwey. 768-803, *June 1988*
El Mirador: An Early Maya Metropolis Uncovered. By Ray T. Matheny. Paintings by T. W. Rutledge. NGS research grant. 317-339, *Sept. 1987*
Río Azul. Photos by George F. Mobley. NGS research grant. I. Lost City of the Maya. By Richard E. W. Adams. Included: Realm of the Maya (map); II. Looters Rob Graves and History. By Ian Graham; III. In Defense of the Collector. By Gillett G. Griffin. 420-465, *Apr. 1986*
The Usumacinta River: Troubles on a Wild Frontier. By S. Jeffrey K. Wilkerson. Photos by David Hiser. 514-543, *Oct. 1985*

Editorial. By Wilbur E. Garrett. Maya tomb. 137-137B, *Aug. 1984*
Editorial. By Wilbur E. Garrett. 137, *Aug. 1981*
Maya Art Treasures Discovered in Cave. By George E. Stuart. Photos by Wilbur E. Garrett. 220-235, *Aug. 1981*
Troubled Times for Central America. By Wilbur E. Garrett, Editor. 58-61, *July 1981*
■ *The Mysterious Maya.* By George E. and Gene S. Stuart. Photos by David Alan Harvey and Otis Imboden. 199 pages. *1977*
Editorial. By Gilbert M. Grosvenor. 719, *June 1976*
Earthquake in Guatemala. By Bart McDowell. Photos by W. E. Garrett and Robert W. Madden. 810-829, *June 1976*
The Maya. 729-811. I. Children of Time. By Howard La Fay. Photos by David Alan Harvey. 729-767; II. Riddle of the Glyphs. By George E. Stuart. Photos by Otis Imboden. 768-791; III. Resurrecting the Grandeur of Tikal. By William R. Coe. 792-798; IV. A Traveler's Tale of Ancient Tikal. Paintings by Peter Spier. Text by Alice J. Hall. 799-811, *Dec. 1975*
Guatemala, Maya and Modern. By Louis de la Haba. Photos by Joseph J. Scherschel. 661-689, *Nov. 1974*
Who Were the "Mound Builders"? By George E. Stuart. 783-801, *Dec. 1972*
The Quetzal, Fabulous Bird of Maya Land. By Anne LaBastille Bowes. Photos by David G. Allen. 141-150, *Jan. 1969*
Easter Week in Indian Guatemala. By John Scofield. 406-417, *Mar. 1960*
"Pyramids" of the New World. By Neil Merton Judd. Included: Piedras Negras, Tikal. 105-128, *Jan. 1948*
Guatemala Revisited. By Luis Marden. 525-564, *Oct. 1947*
To Market in Guatemala. By Luis Marden. Photos by Giles Greville Healey and Charles S. Pineo. 87-104, *July 1945*

Guatemala Interlude: In the Land of the Quetzal a Modern Capital Contrasts With Primitive Indian Villages and the "Pompeii of America." By E. John Long. 429-460, *Oct. 1936*
Preserving Ancient America's Finest Sculptures. By J. Alden Mason. Paintings by H. M. Herget. 537-570, *Nov. 1935*
Unearthing America's Ancient History: Investigation Suggests That the Maya May Have Designed the First Astronomical Observatory in the New World in Order to Cultivate Corn. By Sylvanus Griswold Morley. 99-126, *July 1931*
Buenos Aires to Washington by Horse: A Solitary Journey of Two and a Half Years, Through Eleven American Republics, Covers 9,600 Miles of Mountain and Plain, Desert and Jungle. By A. F. Tschiffely. 135-196, *Feb. 1929*
Guatemala: Land of Volcanoes and Progress: Cradle of Ancient Mayan Civilization, Redolent With Its Later Spanish and Indian Ways, Now Reaping Prosperity from Bananas and Coffee. By Thomas F. Lee. 599-648, *Nov. 1926*
The Foremost Intellectual Achievement of Ancient America: The Hieroglyphic Inscriptions on the Monuments in the Ruined Cities of Mexico, Guatemala, and Honduras Are Yielding the Secrets of the Maya Civilization. By Sylvanus Griswold Morley. 109-130, *Feb. 1922*
Shattered Capitals of Central America. By Herbert J. Spinden. 185-212, *Sept. 1919*
The Countries of the Caribbean. By William Joseph Showalter. 227-250, *Feb. 1913*
Note on excavations at Quirigua, Guatemala. 1056, *Sept. 1913*
Mysterious Temples of the Jungle: The Prehistoric Ruins of Guatemala. By W. F. Sands. 325-338, *Mar. 1913*
Excavations at Quirigua, Guatemala. 339-361, *Mar. 1913*
Guatemala, the Country of the Future. By Edine Frances Tisdel. 596-624, *July 1910*
Notes on Central America. 272-279, *Apr. 1907*

GUAYAQUIL, Ecuador:

Ecuador–Low and Lofty Land Astride the Equator. By Loren McIntyre. 259-298, *Feb. 1968*
From Sea to Clouds in Ecuador. By W. Robert Moore. 717-740, *Dec. 1941*
Over Trail and Through Jungle in Ecuador: Indian Head-Hunters of the Interior, an Interesting Study in the South American Republic. By H. E. Anthony. 327-352, *Oct. 1921*
Beautiful Ecuador. By Joseph Lee. 81-91, *Feb. 1907*

GUAYMAS, Mexico:

Tracking America's Man in Orbit. By Kenneth F. Weaver. Photos by Robert F. Sisson. 184-217, *Feb. 1962*
Adventuring Down the West Coast of Mexico. By Herbert Corey. 449-503, *Nov. 1922*

In the uplands of Guatemala it takes two to carry and one to play a large marimba made of gourds. The instrument resembles a xylophone but sounds like a harp. JACOB GAYER

A Texas horned lizard prowls for ants and other insects on an abandoned airfield on Matagorda Island. STEVEN C. WILSON, ENTHEOS

GUAYMI INDIANS:

Exploring the Past in Panama. By Matthew W. Stirling. Photos by Richard H. Stewart. NGS research grant. 373-399, *Mar. 1949*

Little-Known Parts of Panama. By Henry Pittier. 627-662, *July 1912*

GUAYULE:

Rediscovering America's Forgotten Crops. By Noel D. Vietmeyer. Photos by Burgess Blevins. Paintings by Paul M. Breeden. Included: Rubber from the guayule. 702-712, *May 1981*

GUELMA, Algeria:

The American Eclipse Expedition. By Colby M. Chester. 589-612, *Nov. 1906*

GUÉRANDE (Peninsula), France:

Where Bretons Wrest a Living from the Sea. Photos by F. W. Goro. 751-766, *June 1937*

GUERARD, A. L.: *Author*

The Battle-Line of Languages in Western Europe: A Problem in Human Geography More Perplexing Than That of International Boundaries. 145-180, *Feb. 1923*

GUERMESSA, Tunisia:

Here and There in Northern Africa. By Frank Edward Johnson. 1-132, *Jan. 1914*

GUERNSEY (Island), English Channel:

Britain's "French" Channel Islands. By James Cerruti. Photos by James L. Amos. 710-740, *May 1971*

Guernsey, the Friendly Island. By Alfred S. Campbell. 361-396, *Mar. 1938*

The Channel Islands. By Edith Carey. 143-164, *Aug. 1920*

GUERRERO (State), Mexico:

Down Mexico's Río Balsas. By John W. Webber. Photos by author, Kenneth Segerstrom, Jack Breed. 253-272, *Aug. 1946*

GUEST in Saudi Arabia. By Maynard Owen Williams. 463-487, *Oct. 1945*

GUIANA, British. *See* British Guiana

GUIANA, Dutch. *See* Surinam

GUIANA, French. *See* French Guiana

GUIANAN COCKS-OF-THE-ROCK:

Cock-of-the-Rock: Jungle Dandy. By Pepper W. Trail. NGS research grant. 831-839, *Dec. 1983*

Strange Courtship of the Cock-of-the-Rock. By E. Thomas Gilliard. NGS research grant. 134-140, *Jan. 1962*

A **GUIDE** *to Our Federal Lands.* 227 ▪▪pages. *1984*

A **GUIDE** to Parklands (United States National Parks System). 111-123, *July 1979*

GUIDED MISSILES:

Cape Canaveral's 6,000-mile Shooting Gallery. By Allan C. Fisher, Jr. Photos by Luis Marden and Thomas Nebbia. 421-471, *Oct. 1959*

Seeing the Earth from 80 Miles Up. By Clyde T. Holliday. 511-528, *Oct. 1950*

Our Air Age Speeds Ahead. By F. Barrows Colton. 249-272, *Feb. 1948*

See also Nike

GUILD, EUGENE R.:

Author-Photographer

Exploring America's Great Sand Barrier Reef. Photos by John E. Fletcher and author. 325-350, *Sept. 1947*

GUILFORD (Suburb), Baltimore. *See* Sherwood Gardens

GUILIN, Guangxi Autonomous Region, China:

Guilin, China's Beauty Spot. By W. E. Garrett. 536-563, *Oct. 1979*

GUILLEMOTS (Birds):

Birds of the Northern Seas. By Alexander Wetmore. Paintings by Allan Brooks. 95-122, *Jan. 1936*

Guillemot Eggs. 386-388, *Oct. 1903*

GUILLUMETTE, PAUL G:

Photographer

Beautiful Belgium, Restored by Peace. 555-562, *Nov. 1929*

GUINEA:

Freedom Speaks French in Ouagadougou. By John Scofield. 153-203, *Aug. 1966*

See also former name, French Guinea

GUINEA, Gulf of:

Calypso Explores an Undersea Canyon. By Jacques-Yves Cousteau. Photos by Bates Littlehales. Included: Islands: Annobón, Príncipe, São Tomé. NGS research grant. 373-396, *Mar. 1958*

GUINEA FOWL:

Fowls of Forest and Stream Tamed by Man. By Morley A. Jull. Paintings by Hashime Murayama. 327-371, *Mar. 1930*

GUINEY, LOUISE IMOGEN:

Literary Landmarks of Massachusetts. By William H. Nicholas. Photos by B. Anthony Stewart and John E. Fletcher. 279-310, *Mar. 1950*

GUIZHOU PROVINCE, China:

Peoples of China's Far Provinces. By Wong How-Man. 283-333, *Mar. 1984*

GULF COAST, U. S.-Mexico:

Troubled Odyssey of Vietnamese Fishermen. By Harvey Arden. Photos by Steve Wall. 378-395, *Sept. 1981*

Where Oil and Wildlife Mix. By Steven C. Wilson and Karen C. Hayden. 145-173, *Feb. 1981*

Hurricane! By Ben Funk. Photos by Robert W. Madden. 346-379, *Sept. 1980*

The Gulf's Workaday Waterway. By Gordon Young. Photos by Charles O'Rear. Included: The Gulf Intracoastal Waterway. 200-223, *Feb. 1978*

Oil, the Dwindling Treasure. By Noel Grove. Photos by Emory Kristof. Included: Plans for superports in Alabama, Louisiana, and Texas. 792-825, *June 1974*

Cajunland, Louisiana's French-speaking Coast. By Bern Keating. Photos by Charles Harbutt and Franke Keating. 353-391, *Mar. 1966*

Roseate Spoonbills, Radiant Birds of the Gulf Coast. By Robert Porter Allen. Photos by Frederick Kent Truslow. 274-288, *Feb. 1962*

The Lower Mississippi. By Willard Price. Photos by W. D. Vaughn. 681-725, *Nov. 1960*

Cruising Florida's Western Waterways. By Rube Allyn. Photos by Bates Littlehales. 49-76, *Jan. 1955*

The Pink Birds of Texas. By Paul A. Zahl. 641-654, *Nov. 1949*

Louisiana Trades with the World. By Frederick Simpich. Photos by J. Baylor Roberts. 705-738, *Dec. 1947*

The Delectable Shrimp: Once a Culinary Stepchild, Today a Gulf Coast Industry. By Harlan Major. 501-512, *Oct. 1944*

How We Use the Gulf of Mexico. By Frederick Simpich. Included: Gulf Coast Towns Get into the Fight. Photos by J. Baylor Roberts. 1-40, *Jan. 1944*

A pony cart makes a morning run into the town of Appleby in northern England to collect groceries for Gypsies camped nearby for the annual June fair.   BRUCE DALE, NGS

See also Houston; Key West; Mississippi Delta; Mobile; New Orleans; Tampa Bay

GULF OF CALIFORNIA. See Raza, Isla

GULF STREAM:

Blue-water Plankton: Ghosts of the Gulf Stream. By William M. Hamner. NGS research grant. 530-545, *Oct. 1974*

Night Life in the Gulf Stream. By Paul A. Zahl. 391-418, *Mar. 1954*

Strange Babies of the Sea (Plankton). By Hilary B. Moore. Paintings by Craig Phillips and Jacqueline Hutton. NGS research grant. 41-56, *July 1952*

Certain Citizens of the Warm Sea. By Louis L. Mowbray. Paintings by Hashime Murayama. 27-62, *Jan. 1922*

Treasure-House of the Gulf Stream: The Completion and Opening of the New Aquarium and Biological Laboratory at Miami, Florida. By John Oliver La Gorce. Paintings by Hashime Murayama. 53-68, *Jan. 1921*

Interesting Citizens of the Gulf Stream. By John T. Nichols. 69-84, *Jan. 1921*

Devil-Fishing in the Gulf Stream. By John Oliver La Gorce. 476-488, *June 1919*

The Grandest and Most Mighty Terrestrial Phenomenon: The Gulf Stream. By John Elliott Pillsbury. 767-778, *Aug. 1912*

Ocean Currents. By James Page. 135-142, *Apr. 1902*

The Relations of the Gulf Stream and the Labrador Current. By William Libbey, Junior. 161-166, *Jan. 31, 1894*

GULL ISLAND, Quebec, Canada:

Sea Bird Cities Off Audubon's Labrador. By Arthur A. Allen. NGS research grant. 755-774, *June 1948*

GULL-BILLED TERNS:

Pelican Profiles. By Lewis Wayne Walker. Included: The Gull-billed Tern of the Salton Sea Area, California. 589-598, *Nov. 1943*

GULLERS, KARL W.: *Photographer*

Viking Festival in the Shetlands. 853-862, *Dec. 1954*

GULLS:

Sea Birds of Isla Raza (Mexico). By Lewis Wayne Walker. Included: Yellow-footed and Heermann's Gulls. NGS research grant. 239-248, *Feb. 1951*

Sea Bird Cities Off Audubon's Labrador. By Arthur A. Allen. Included: Black-backed Gull, Herring Gull, Ring-billed Gull. NGS research grant. 755-774, *June 1948*

Black-Headed Gulls in London. By A. H. Hall. 664-672, *June 1925*

The White Sheep, Giant Moose, and Smaller Game of the Kenai Peninsula, Alaska. By George Shiras, 3d. 423-494, *May 1912*

GUNBOATS, Ironclad:

How We Found the *Monitor*. By John G. Newton. NGS research grant. 48-61, *Jan. 1975*

GUNS. See Cannon

GURKHAS:

Nepal: A Little-Known Kingdom. By John Claude White. 245-283, *Oct. 1920*

GURNEY, JAMES M.: *Artist*

The Eternal Etruscans. By Rick Gore. Photos by O. Louis Mazzatenta. 696-743, *June 1988*

Sealed in Time–Ice Entombs an Eskimo Family for Five Centuries. By Albert A. Dekin, Jr. Photos by Victor R. Boswell, Jr., and Scott Rutherford. 824-836, *June 1987*

GUT, Silkworm:

Spain's Silkworm Gut. By Luis Marden. 100-108, *July 1951*

GUTHRIE, RUSSELL D.: *Author*

Re-creating a Vanished World. 294-301, *Mar. 1972*

GUTMANN, JOHN: *Photographer*

Kunming Pilgrimage. 213-226, *Feb. 1950*

GUYANA. See former name, British Guiana

GUYNEMER, GEORGES:

Aces of the Air. By Jacques De Sieyes. 5-9, *Jan. 1918*

GYANGZÊ (Gyangtse), Tibet, China:

A Woman Paints the Tibetans. By Lafugie. 659-692, *May 1949*

Across Tibet from India to China. By Ilia Tolstoy. 169-222, *Aug. 1946*

GYPSIES:

France's Wild, Watery South, the Camargue. By William Davenport. 696-726, *May 1973*

When Gypsies Gather at Appleby Fair. Photos by Bruce Dale. 848-869, *June 1972*

Hungary: Changing Homeland of a Tough, Romantic People. By Bart McDowell. Photos by Albert Moldvay and Joseph J. Scherschel. 443-483, *Apr. 1971*

■ *Gypsies: Wanderers of the World.* By Bart McDowell. Photos by Bruce Dale. 215 pages. *1970*

Gypsy Cave Dwellers of Andalusia (Spain). 572-582, *Oct. 1957*

The Camargue, Land of Cowboys and Gypsies. By Eugene L. Kammerman. 667-699, *May 1956*

Speaking of Spain. By Luis Marden. 415-456, *Apr. 1950*

An American Girl Cycles Across Romania: Two-wheel Pilgrim Pedals the Land of Castles and Gypsies, Where Roman Empire Traces Mingle With Remnants of Oriental Migration. By Dorothy Hosmer. 557-588, *Nov. 1938*

Camargue, the Cowboy Country of Southern France. By André Vialles. 1-34, *July 1922*

The Races of Europe. By Edwin A. Grosvenor. 441-534, *Dec. 1918*

Hungary: A Land of Shepherd Kings. By C. Townley-Fullam. 311-393, *Oct. 1914*

GYPSUM:

The White Sands of Alamogordo: A Dry Ocean of Granular Gypsum Billows Under Desert Winds in a New National Playground. By Carl P. Russell. 250-264, *Aug. 1935*

GYPSY MOTH:

New Tricks Outwit Our Insect Enemies. By Hal Higdon. Photos by Robert F. Sisson and Emory Kristof. 380-399, *Sept. 1972*

Explorers of a New Kind: Successful Introduction of Beetles and Parasites to Check Ravages of the Gipsy-moth and Brown-tail Moth. By L. O. Howard. 38-67, *July 1914*

Pests and Parasites: Why We Need a National Law to Prevent the Importation of Insect-Infested and Diseased Plants. By Charles Lester Marlatt. 321-346, *Apr. 1911*

The Gypsy Moth. 461-464, *Aug. 1906*

GYROSCOPE:

A Primitive Gyroscope in Liberia. By G. N. Collins. 531-535, *June 1910*

HD-4:

Hydrofoil boat, *HD-4,* designed by Alexander Graham Bell. 493, 495, 496, *Apr. 1957;* 257, 264, *Aug. 1959;* 554-555, *Oct. 1963*

H.R.H. Philip, Prince, Duke of Edinburgh, Introduces to Members the Narrative of His Round-the-World Tour. 583-584, *Nov. 1957*

HA ON (Kibbutz), Israel:

Our Life on a Border Kibbutz. By Carol and Al Abrams. Photos by Al Abrams. 364-391, *Sept. 1970*

HÂ-ÂK VÂ-ÂK (Hâ-âk Lying Site), Arizona:

Seeking the Secret of the Giants. By Frank M. Setzler. Photos by Richard H. Stewart. 390-404, *Sept. 1952*

HAAKON VII, King (Norway):

The White War in Norway. By Thomas R. Henry. 617-640, *Nov. 1945*

HAARDT, GEORGES-MARIE:

From the Mediterranean to the Yellow Sea by Motor: The Citroën-Haardt Expedition Successfully Completes Its Dramatic Journey. By Maynard Owen Williams. 513-580, *Nov. 1932*

First Over the Roof of the World by Motor: The Trans-Asiatic Expedition Sets New Records for Wheeled Transport in Scaling Passes of the Himalayas. By Maynard Owen Williams. 321-363, *Mar. 1932*

The Citroën Trans-Asiatic Expedition Reaches Kashmir: Scientific Party Led by Georges-Marie Haardt Successfully Crosses Syria, Iraq, Persia, and Afghanistan to Arrive at the Pamir. By Maynard Owen Williams. 387-443, *Oct. 1931*

The Trans-Asiatic Expedition Starts. By Georges-Marie Haardt. 776-782, *June 1931*

Through the Deserts and Jungles of Africa by Motor: Caterpillar Cars Make 15,000-Mile Trip from Algeria to Madagascar in Nine Months. By Georges-Marie Haardt. Photos by members of the expedition. 651-720, *June 1926*

Author

The Trans-Asiatic Expedition Starts. 776-782, *June 1931*

Through the Deserts and Jungles of Africa by Motor: Caterpillar Cars Make 15,000-Mile Trip from Algeria to Madagascar in Nine Months. 651-720, *June 1926*

HABACHI, LABIB:

Nomination Page. *Mar. 1977*

HABANA, Cuba. *See* Havana

HABER, HEINZ: *Author*

Space Satellites, Tools of Earth Research. Paintings by William N. Palmstrom. 487-509, *Apr. 1956*

HABITAT DESTRUCTION:

North American Waterfowl: Troubles and Triumphs. By John Madson. Included: Loons, swans, wood ducks. 562-599, *Nov. 1984*

Tropical Rain Forests. 2-65. Included: Nature's Dwindling Treasures. By Peter T. White. Photos by James P. Blair. Paintings by Barron Storey. 2-47; Teeming Life of a Rain Forest. By Carol and David Hughes. 49-65, *Jan. 1983*

▪Rain Forest. 824, *Dec. 1982;* cover, 49, *Jan. 1983*

HABSBURGS (Rulers):

The Vienna Treasures and Their Collectors. By John Walker. Included: Kunsthistorisches Museum. 737-776, *June 1950*

HACIENDAS:

On a Chilean Hacienda. Photos by E. P. Haddon. 489-496, *Oct. 1944*

Mrs. Robinson Crusoe in Ecuador. By Mrs. Richard C. Gill. 133-172, *Feb. 1934*

A Mexican Hacienda. By J. E. Kirkwood. 563-584, *May 1914*

HADAR, Ethiopia:

Ethiopia Yields First "Family" of Early Man. By Donald C. Johanson. Photos by David Brill. NGS research grant. 790-811, *Dec. 1976*

HADDON, E. P.: *Photographer*

On a Chilean Hacienda. 489-496, *Oct. 1944*

HADJ. *See* Hajj

HADRAMAWT REGION, Arabian Peninsula:

Arabia's Frankincense Trail. By Thomas J. Abercrombie. Photos by Lynn Abercrombie. 474-513, *Oct. 1985*

Into Burning Hadhramaut: The Arab Land of Frankincense and Myrrh, Ever a Lodestone of Western Exploration. By D. van der Meulen. 387-429, *Oct. 1932*

See also Aden Protectorate

A tractor balances on a collapsing trail in the Karakoram Range during the first motorized trek across Asia, in the 1930s. MAYNARD OWEN WILLIAMS, NGS

Seeking the favor of bountiful fishing for their village, schoolboys prepare to dance in a Shinto festival in Hagi, Japan. SAM ABELL

From America to Mecca on Airborne Pilgrimage. By Abdul Ghafur. 1-60, *July 1953*

Pilgrims' Progress to Mecca. Photos by Oscar Marcus. 627-642, *Nov. 1937*

An Unbeliever Joins the Hadj: On the Age-Old Pilgrimage to Mecca, Babies Are Born, Elders Die, and Families May Halt a Year to Earn Funds in Distant Lands. By Owen Tweedy. 761-789, *June 1934*

See also Mecca, Saudi Arabia

HAKLUYT, RICHARD:

Founders of Virginia. By Sir Evelyn Wrench. Photos by B. Anthony Stewart. 433-462, *Apr. 1948*

HAL SAFLIENI (Temple), Malta:

Malta: The Halting Place of Nations: First Account of Remarkable Prehistoric Tombs and Temples Recently Unearthed on the Island. By William Arthur Griffiths. 445-478, *May 1920*

HALE, EDWARD E.: *Author*

Philip Nolan and the "Levant." 114-116, *Mar. 1905*

HALE, SARAH JOSEPHA:

Literary Landmarks of Massachusetts. By William H. Nicholas. Photos by B. Anthony Stewart and John E. Fletcher. 279-310, *Mar. 1950*

HALEAKALA NATIONAL PARK, Hawaii:

Maui, Where Old Hawaii Still Lives. By Kenneth F. Weaver. Photos by Gordon W. Gahan. 514-543, *Apr. 1971*

HALF DOME (Massif), Yosemite National Park, California:

Yosemite–Forever? By David S. Boyer. Photos by Jonathan Blair. 52-79, *Jan. 1985*

Climbing Half Dome the Hard Way. By Galen Rowell. 782-791, *June 1974*

A **HALF** Mile Down: Strange Creatures, Beautiful and Grotesque as Figments of Fancy, Reveal Themselves at Windows of the Bathysphere. By William Beebe. Paintings by Else Bostelmann, Helen D. Tee-Van, E. J. Geske. 661-704, *Dec. 1934*

HALIFAX, LORD (Edward Frederick Lindley Wood): *Author*

India–Yesterday, Today, and Tomorrow. 385-408, *Oct. 1943*

HALIFAX RACE (Marblehead-Halifax):

Down East to Nova Scotia. By Winfield Parks. 853-879, *June 1964*

HALL, A. H.: *Author-Photographer*

Black-Headed Gulls in London. Included: Aces of Aviation (Gulls). 664-672, *June 1925*

HALL, ALICE J.: *Author*

James Madison, Architect of the Constitution. Photos by Sam Abell. 340-369, *Sept. 1987*

Liberty Lifts Her Lamp Once More. 2-19, *July 1986*

The Hidden Tenn-Tom: Bypassed But

Still Striving. Photos by Sandy Felsenthal. 384-387, *Mar. 1986*

Man and Manatee: Can We Live Together? Photos by Fred Bavendam. 400-413, *Sept. 1984*

Ways of the Ant. By Bert Hölldobler. Paintings by John D. Dawson. Illustrations text by Alice J. Hall. NGS research grant. 779-813, *June 1984*

Brooklyn: The Other Side of the Bridge. Photos by Robert W. Madden. 580-613, *May 1983*

Buffalo Bill and the Enduring West. Photos by James L. Amos. 76-103, *July 1981*

Georgia, Unlimited. Photos by Bill Weems. 212-245, *Aug. 1978*

The Hudson: "That River's Alive." Photos by Ted Spiegel. 62-89, *Jan. 1978*

Dazzling Legacy of an Ancient Quest (Egypt). 293-311, *Mar. 1977*

A Traveler's Tale of Ancient Tikal. Paintings by Peter Spier. 799-811, *Dec. 1975*

Benjamin Franklin, Philosopher of Dissent. Photos by Linda Bartlett. 93-123, *July 1975*

A Lady From China's Past. Photos from *China Pictorial.* 660-681, *May 1974*

The Climb Up Cone Crater. Photos by Edgar D. Mitchell and Alan B. Shepard, Jr. 136-148, *July 1971*

HALL, CHAPIN: *Author*

California, Our Lady of Flowers. 703-750, *June 1929*

HALL, CHARLES FRANCIS:

Charles Francis Hall and Jones Sound.

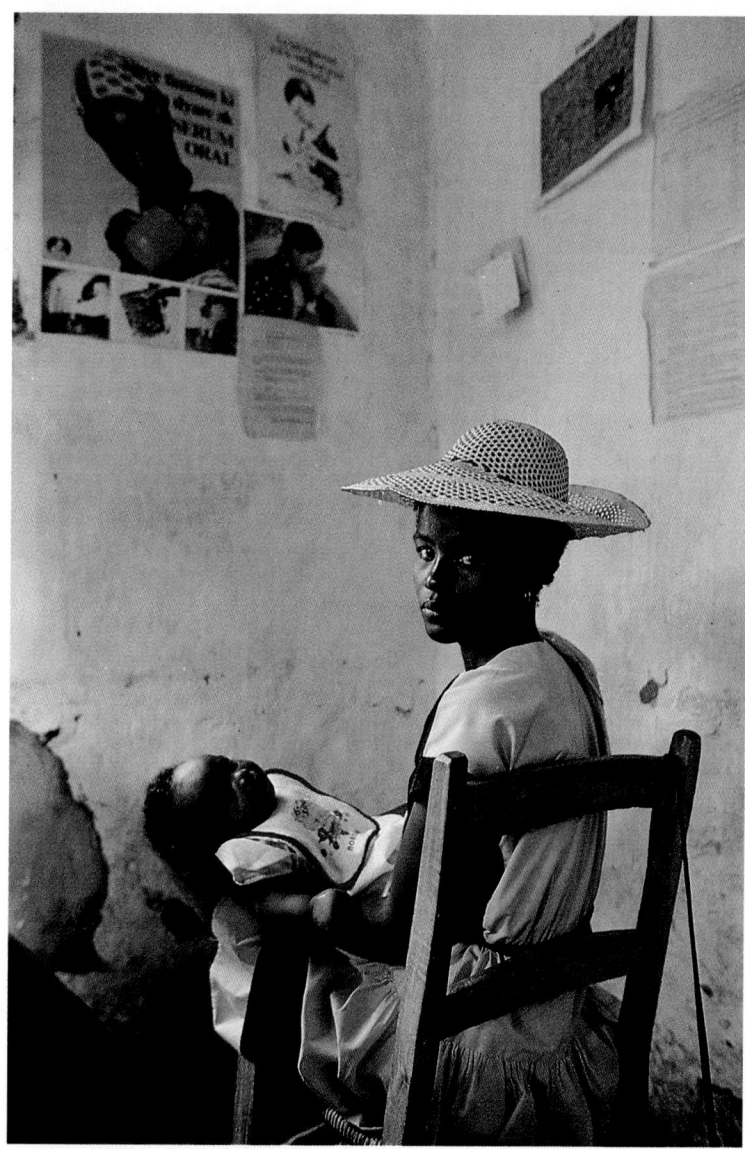

Cradling her sick child, a mother waits for medical treatment at a clinic in poverty-stricken Haiti. JAMES P. BLAIR, NGS

By A. W. Greely. 308-310,
Sept. 1896

HALL, EDITH H.: *Author*
Explorations in Crete. 778-787,
Sept. 1909

HALL, H. TOM: *Artist*
■■*America's Ancient Cities.* By Gene S.
Stuart. Photos by Richard Alexander
Cooke III. 199 pages. *1988*
■■*Into the Wilderness.* Photos by Lowell
Georgia. Contents: Seven famous
historic explorations and trails. 207
pages. *1978*
■■*John Muir's Wild America.* By Tom
Melham. Photos by Farrell Grehan.
199 pages. *1976*

HALL, JOSEF W. *See* Close, Upton

HALL, MELVIN:
Author-Photographer
Vézelay, Hill of the Pilgrims. 229-247,
Feb. 1953

HALL, MELVIN A.:
Author-Photographer
By Motor Through the East Coast and
Batak Highlands of Sumatra. 69-102,
Jan. 1920

HALL, ROSS: *Photographer*
Idaho Loggers Battle a River. 117-130,
July 1951

HALL, WILLIAM H.: *Author*
Crusader Castles of the Near East. 369-
390, *Mar. 1931*
Antioch the Glorious. 81-103,
Aug. 1920
Under the Heel of the Turk: A Land
with a Glorious Past, a Present of
Abused Opportunities, and a Future
of Golden Possibilities. 51-69,
July 1918

HALL, WILLIAM HAMMOND:
Author
Irrigation in California. 277-290,
Oct. 1889

HALLEY'S Comet '86. By Rick Gore.
758-785, *Dec. 1986*

HALLINGDAL (Valley), Norway:
Life in a Norway Valley: An American
Girl Is Welcomed Into the Home-
making and Haying of Happy Hallingdal. By Abbie L. Bosworth. 627-
648, *May 1935*

HALLOCK, CHARLES:
On Eskimo Geographic Names Ending
in Miut. (Commentary by John Murdoch, on Kuskokwim River article
written by Charles Hallock). 190,
Apr. 1898
Author
Two Hundred Miles up the Kuskokwim. 85-92, *Mar. 1898*

The **HALLOWED** Isle, Mont Saint Michel. By Kenneth MacLeish. Photos
by Cotton Coulson. 820-831,
June 1977

HALLSTROM, E.J.L.:
Sheep Airlift in New Guinea. Photos by
Ned Blood. 831-844, *Dec. 1949*

*Celebrating Halley's comet, Solaris
"Buddy" Gregory of Key West, Florida,
dons heavenly paint in 1986.* BOB SACHA

HAMA, Syria:
From Jerusalem to Aleppo. By John D.
Whiting. 71-113, *Jan. 1913*

HAMADA EL HOMRA (Desert),
Libya:
The Mysteries of the Desert. By Hanns
Vischer. 1056-1059, *Nov. 1911*

HAMADSHA (Dance):
The Two Great Moorish Religious
Dances. By George Edmund Holt.
777-785, *Aug. 1911*

HAMAMATSU, Japan:
Japan's Warriors of the Wind. Photos
by David Alan Harvey. Text by John
Eliot. Contents: Annual kite festival.
551-561, *Apr. 1977*

HAMBLETON, JAMES I.: *Author*
Man's Winged Ally, the Busy Honey-
bee: Modern Research Adds a New
Chapter to Usefulness of the Insect
Which Has Symbolized Industry
Since Early Bible Times. Paintings by
Hashime Murayama. 401-428,
Apr. 1935

HAMBURG, West Germany:
Hamburg Speaks with Steam Sirens. By
Frederick Simpich. 717-744,
June 1933

HAMI, Sinkiang:
The Caves of the Thousand Buddhas.
By Franc and Jean Shor. 383-415,
Mar. 1951

HAMILL, HUGH M., Jr.:
Author-Photographer
Experiment in International Living.
323-350, *Mar. 1953*

HAMILTON, EDITH: *Author*
The Roman Way. 545-565, *Nov. 1946*
The Greek Way. 257-271, *Mar. 1944*

HAMILTON, LAURIE: *Artist*
■■*Geo–Whiz!* By Susan Mondshein Tejada. Contents: Startling and fascinating geographical, geological, and
cultural facts from around the world.
Juvenile. 104 pages. *1988*

HAMILTON, ROGER: *Author*
Can We Harness the Wind? Photos by
Emory Kristof. 812-829, *Dec. 1975*

HAMILTON, VIRGINIA: *Author*
Keeping House in Borneo. 293-324,
Sept. 1945

HAMILTON, WILLIAM J., III:
Author
The Living Sands of the Namib. Photos
by Carol and David Hughes. 364-377,
Sept. 1983

HAMILTON (River), Newfoundland,
Canada:
Labrador Canoe Adventure. By An-
drew Brown and Ralph Gray. 65-99,
July 1951

HAMILTON and *Scourge:* Ghost Ships
of the War of 1812. By Daniel A. Nelson. Photos by Emory Kristof. Paintings by Richard Schlecht. 289-313,
Mar. 1983

HAMLIN, TEUNIS S.: *Author*
Gardiner Greene Hubbard: An Address delivered at the Memorial Services held at the Church of the
Covenant, Washington, D. C., December 13, 1897. 33-38, *Feb. 1898*

HAMMARSKJÖLD, DAG:
Author-Photographer
A New Look at Everest. 87-93,
Jan. 1961

HAMMERFEST, Norway:
Sailing the Seven Seas in the Interest of
Science: Adventures Through
157,000 Miles of Storm and Calm,
from Arctic to Antarctic and Around
the World, in the Non-magnetic
Yacht "Carnegie." By J. P. Ault.
631-690, *Dec. 1922*

HAMMOND, JAY S.: *Author*
Sharing Alaska: How Much for Parks?
Opposing views by Jay S. Hammond
and Cecil D. Andrus. 60-65,
July 1979

HAMMOND, MRS. JOHN HAYS:
The National Geographic Society.
Speech by Mrs. John Hays Ham-
mond. 272-298, *Mar. 1912*

HAMMOND, NORMAN: *Author*
Unearthing the Oldest Known Maya.
Photos by Lowell Georgia and Mar-
tha Cooper. 126-140, *July 1982*

HAMMOND, THOMAS T.: *Author*
An American in Russia's Capital. Pho-
tos by Dean Conger. 297-351,
Mar. 1966
Firsthand Look at the Soviet Union.
Photos by Erich Lessing. 352-407,
Sept. 1959

HAMMURAPI, King (Babylon):
Ancient Mesopotamia: A Light That

Did Not Fail. By E. A. Speiser. Paintings by H. M. Herget. 41-105, *Jan. 1951*

HAMMURAPI, Code of:

Pushing Back History's Horizon: How the Pick and Shovel Are Revealing Civilizations That Were Ancient When Israel Was Young. By Albert T. Clay. 162-216, *Feb. 1916*

HAMNER, WILLIAM M.: *Author*

Krill–Untapped Bounty From the Sea? Photos by Flip Nicklin. 626-643, *May 1984*

Strange World of Palau's Salt Lakes. Photos by David Doubilet. 264-282, *Feb. 1982*

Blue-water Plankton: Ghosts of the Gulf Stream. 530-545, *Oct. 1974*

HAMPSHIRE, MICHAEL A.: *Artist*

Viking Trail East. By Robert Paul Jordan. Photos by Jim Brandenburg. 278-317, *Mar. 1985*

HAMPTON, Virginia:

Hampton Roads, Where the Rivers End. By William S. Ellis. Photos by Karen Kasmauski. 72-107, *July 1985*

HAMPTON ROADS, Virginia:

Hampton Roads, Where the Rivers End. By William S. Ellis. Photos by Karen Kasmauski. 72-107, *July 1985*

HAN DYNASTY TOMBS:

China Unveils Her Newest Treasures. Photos by Robert W. Madden. 848-857, *Dec. 1974*

A Lady From China's Past. Photos from *China Pictorial.* Text by Alice J. Hall. 660-681, *May 1974*

HANDCLASP in Space: Apollo-Soyuz. By Thomas Y. Canby. 183-187, *Feb. 1976*

HANDICRAFTS. *See* Crafts; Folk Art

HANDLEY, MARIE LOUISE: *Author*

Siena's Palio, an Italian Inheritance from the Middle Ages. 245-258, *Aug. 1926*

HANG GLIDERS:

Happy Birthday, Otto Lilienthal! By Russell Hawkes. Photos by James Collison. 286-292, *Feb. 1972*

HANGZHOU (Hangchow), Zhejiang Province, China:

Ho for the Soochow Ho. By Mabel Craft Deering. 623-649, *June 1927*

HANKOU (Hankow), Hubei Province, China:

Along the Yangtze, Main Street of China. By W. Robert Moore. 325-356, *Mar. 1948*

HANNA, G. DALLAS:
Author-Photographer

A Cruise Among Desert Islands. By G. Dallas Hanna and A. W. Anthony. 71-99, *July 1923*

HANNIBAL, Missouri:

Mark Twain: Mirror of America. By Noel Grove. Photos by James L. Stanfield. 300-337, *Sept. 1975*

Tom Sawyer's Town. By Jerry Allen. 121-140, *July 1956*

The West Through Boston Eyes. By Stewart Anderson. 733-776, *June 1949*

HANSEN, JENS P. HART: *Author*

The Mummies of Qilakitsoq. By Jens P. Hart Hansen, Jørgen Meldgaard, and Jørgen Nordqvist. 191-207, *Feb. 1985*

HANSEN, LEO: *Author-Photographer*

Viking Life in the Storm-Cursed Faeroes. 607-648, *Nov. 1930*

HANSEN'S DISEASE:

The Astonishing Armadillo. By Eleanor E. Storrs. Photos by Bianca Lavies.

Included: Immunology research with leprosy bacilli cultivated in armadillos. 820-830, *June 1982*

Molokai–Forgotten Hawaii. By Ethel A. Starbird. Photos by Richard A. Cooke III. Included: Kalaupapa lepers' colony. 188-219, *Aug. 1981*

Hunting the Chaulmoogra Tree. By Joseph F. Rock. 243-276, *Mar. 1922*

HANSON, EARL: *Author*

The Island of the Sagas (Iceland). 499-511, *Apr. 1928*

HANSON, GEORGE M.: *Author*

"As the Tuan Had Said." 631-644, *Nov. 1933*

HAPGOOD, FRED: *Author*

The Prodigious Soybean. Photos by Chris Johns. 67-91, *July 1987*

HAPPY Birthday, Otto Lilienthal! By Russell Hawkes. Photos by James Collison. 286-292, *Feb. 1972*

HAPPY-GO-LUCKY Trinidad and Tobago. By Charles Allmon. 35-75, *Jan. 1953*

HAPPY Landing in Bermuda. By E. John Long. 213-238, *Feb. 1939*

HAPSBURGS. *See* Habsburgs

HARARE, Zimbabwe. *See* former name, Salisbury, Rhodesia

HARBERTON, Estancia, Tierra del Fuego, Argentina:

Housewife at the End of the World. By Rae Natalie P. Goodall. Photos by James L. Stanfield. 130-150, *Jan. 1971*

HARBIN, Heilongjiang Province, China:

In Manchuria Now. By W. Robert Moore. 389-414, *Mar. 1947*

Japan Faces Russia in Manchuria. By Willard Price. 603-634, *Nov. 1942*

Here in Manchuria: Many Thousand Lives Were Lost and More Than Half the Crops Destroyed by the Floods of 1932. By Lilian Grosvenor Coville. 233-256, *Feb. 1933*

The Land of Promise. By A. W. Greely. 1078-1090, *Nov. 1912*

Russian Development of Manchuria. By Henry B. Miller. 113-127, *Mar. 1904*

HARBORS AND PORTS:

Normandy's Made-in-England Harbors. 565-580, *May 1945*

Today on the China Coast. By John B. Powell. 217-238, *Feb. 1945*

Marseille, Battle Port of Centuries. By a Staff Correspondent. 425-448, *Oct. 1944*

Charm Spots Along England's Harassed Coast. 237-252, *Aug. 1940*

Between the Heather and the North Sea: Bold English Headlands Once Sheltered Sea Robbers, Later Were Ports of Wooden Ships, Centers of the Jet and Alum Trades, To-day Are Havens of Adventurous Fishing Fleets. By Leo Walmsley. 197-232, *Feb. 1933*

Mark Twain's famous character gets perpetual top billing in his hometown of Hannibal, Missouri. WERNER J. SEVERIN

One Hundred British Seaports. 84-94,
Jan. 1917

Channel Ports–And Some Others. By
Florence Craig Albrecht. 1-55,
July 1915

Three Old Ports on the Spanish Main.
By G.M.L. Brown. 622-638,
Nov. 1906

HARBUTT, CHARLES:
Author-Photographer

Eyewitness to War in the Holy Land.
782-795, *Dec. 1967*

Photographer

Today Along the Natchez Trace, Pathway Through History. By Bern Keating. 641-667, *Nov. 1968*

Where Jesus Walked. By Howard La
Fay. 739-781, *Dec. 1967*

Cajunland, Louisiana's French-speaking Coast. By Bern Keating. Photos
by Charles Harbutt and Franke Keating. 353-391, *Mar. 1966*

HARBY, SAMUEL F.: *Author*

They Survived at Sea. 617-640,
May 1945

The **HARD** Life of the Prairie Dog. By
Tim W. Clark. Photos by Patricia
Caulfield. NGS research grant. 270-
281, *Aug. 1979*

HARDING, WARREN GAMALIEL:

The Living White House. By Lonnelle
Aikman. 593-643, *Nov. 1966*

Profiles of the Presidents: IV. America
Enters the Modern Era. By Frank
Freidel. 537-577, *Oct. 1965*

President Harding present at unveiling
of the Peary Memorial in Arlington
National Cemetery, Apr. 6, 1922.
639-646, *June 1922*

HARDY, LAYMOND: *Photographer*

Alligators: Dragons in Distress. By Archie Carr. Photos by Treat Davidson
and Laymond Hardy. 133-148,
Jan. 1967

The **HARDY** Catalpa. 348-353,
Sept. 1903

HARE, CLYDE: *Photographer*

Pittsburgh, Pattern for Progress. By
William J. Gill. 342-371, *Mar. 1965*

Banks Island: Eskimo Life on the Polar
Sea. By William O. Douglas. 703-
735, *May 1964*

HARGRAVE, LAURENCE:

The Tetrahedral Principle in Kite Structure. By Alexander Graham Bell. Included: Hargrave's experimental
kites. 219-251, *June 1903*

HARGRAVE, THOMAS J.:
Author-Photographer

Photographing a Volcano in Action.
561-563, *Oct. 1955*

HARK! Pictorial supplement of deer.
Flashlight photo by George Shiras,
3d. *Aug. 1921*

HARK to the Hounds. By Freeman
Lloyd. Paintings by Edward Herbert
Miner. 453-484, *Oct. 1937*

HARLAN, HARRY V.: *Author*

A Caravan Journey Through Abyssinia:
From Addis Ababa Through Lalibela, the Strange Jerusalem of Ethiopia, in Search of New Grains for
American Farms. 613-663, *June 1925*

HARLEM, New York, New York:

Editorial. By Gilbert M. Grosvenor.
147, *Feb. 1977*

To Live in Harlem.... By Frank Hercules. Photos by LeRoy Woodson, Jr.
178-207, *Feb. 1977*

HARMON, BYRON: *Photographer*

Peaks and Trails in the Canadian Alps.
627-642, *May 1934*

HARMONY HOLLOW (Farm),
Virginia:

The World of My Apple Tree. By Robert F. Sisson. 836-847, *June 1972*

HARMSWORTH, SIR LEICESTER:
Renaissance Library:

Folger: Biggest Little Library in the

World. By Joseph T. Foster. Photos
by B. Anthony Stewart and John E.
Fletcher. 411-424, *Sept. 1951*

HARNDEN, PHOEBE BINNEY:
Author

Keeping House in Majorca. 425-440,
Apr. 1924

HARNESSING the Wind. 38, *Special
Report on Energy. (Feb. 1981)*

HAROLD II, King (England):

900 Years Ago: the Norman Conquest.
By Kenneth M. Setton. Photos by
George F. Mobley. 206-251,
Aug. 1966

HARP SEALS:

Life or Death for the Harp Seal. By David M. Lavigne. Photos by William
R. Curtsinger. 129-142, *Jan. 1976*

HARPER, FRANCIS:
Author-Photographer

The Okefinokee Wilderness: Exploring
the Mystery Land of the Suwannee
River Reveals Natural Wonders and
Fascinating Folklore. 597-624,
May 1934

HARPERS FERRY, West Virginia:

History Awakens at Harpers Ferry. By
Volkmar Wentzel. 399-416,
Mar. 1957

Potomac, River of Destiny. By Albert
W. Atwood. 33-70, *July 1945*

HARPUT, Turkey:

The Mountaineers of the Euphrates. By
Ellsworth Huntington. 142-156,
Feb. 1909

HARRELL, MARY ANN: *Author*

■■ *Equal Justice Under the Law: The Supreme Court in American Life.* Published in cooperation with The
Foundation of the Federal Bar Association. 151 pages. 1965; rev. ed. *1988*

HARRER, HEINRICH:
Author-Photographer

My Life in Forbidden Lhasa. 1-48,
July 1955

HARRIMAN, Pennsylvania:

Ships for the Seven Seas: The Story of
America's Maritime Needs, Her Ca-
pabilities and Her Achievements. By
Ralph A. Graves. 165-200,
Sept. 1918

The **HARRIMAN** Alaska Expedition.
By Henry Gannett. 507-512,
Dec. 1899

The **HARRIMAN** Alaska Expedition in
Cooperation with the Washington
Academy of Sciences. By G. H.
Grosvenor. 225-227, *June 1899*

HARRINGTON, MARK W.: *Author*

Area and Drainage Basin of Lake Superior. 111-120, *Apr. 1897*

Weather Making, Ancient and Modern.
35-62, *Apr. 25, 1894*

HARRINGTON, PHILLIP:
Photographer

Athens: Her Golden Past Still Lights
the World. By Kenneth F. Weaver.
100-137, *July 1963*

*New York City neighbors gather for checkers in the streets of Harlem, a longtime bastion
of black American art, music, and culture.* LEROY WOODSON, JR.

HARRIS, ERNEST LLOYD: *Author*

Historic Islands and Shores of the Aegean Sea. 231-261, *Sept. 1915*

Notes on Troy. 531-532, *May 1915*

The Buried Cities of Asia Minor. 1-18, *Jan. 1909*

Some Ruined Cities of Asia Minor. 833-858, *Dec. 1908*

The Ruined Cities of Asia Minor. 741-760, *Nov. 1908*

HARRIS, FRED H.: *Author*

Skiing Over the New Hampshire Hills. 151-164, *Feb. 1920*

HARRIS, JENNIE E.: *Author*

Sponge Fishermen of Tarpon Springs. 119-136, *Jan. 1947*

Living Casks of Honey (Ants). 193-199, *Aug. 1934*

HARRIS, R. A.: *Author*

Cotidal Lines for the World. 303-309, *June 1906*

Some Indications of Land in the Vicinity of the North Pole. 255-261, *June 1904*

HARRISON, BENJAMIN:

Profiles of the Presidents: III. The American Giant Comes of Age. By Frank Freidel. 660-711, *May 1965*

HARRISON, ED N.: *Photographer*

Birds and Beasts of Mexico's Desert Islands. Photos by Ed N. Harrison, Alfred M. Bailey, and Robert J. Niedrach. 353-360, *Sept. 1941*

HARRISON, WILLIAM HENRY:

Profiles of the Presidents: II. A Restless Nation Moves West. By Frank Freidel. 80-121, *Jan. 1965*

HARRY FRANK GUGGENHEIM FOUNDATION: Study Grant:

Jackals of the Serengeti. NGS research grant. 840, *Dec. 1980*

HART, ALBERT BUSHNELL:

Judge of NGS prize essay contest. 32, *Jan. 1899*

HART, CATHERINE:

Nomination Page. *Jan. 1965*

HART, KIM: *Photographer*

Ancient Shipwreck Yields New Facts–and a Strange Cargo. By Peter Throckmorton. Photos by Kim Hart and Joseph J. Scherschel. 282-300, *Feb. 1969*

HART, VAL: *Author*

Pack Trip Through the Smokies. Photos by Robert F. Sisson. 473-502, *Oct. 1952*

HART DYKE, ZOË, LADY:

Silkworms in England Spin for the Queen. By John E. H. Nolan. 689-704, *May 1953*

HARTFORD, Connecticut:

Connecticut, Prodigy of Ingenuity: Factories Play a Symphony of Industry Amid Colonial Scenes in the State of Steady Habits. By Leo A. Borah. 279-326, *Sept. 1938*

HARTLEY, FRED L.:

What Six Experts Say. 70-73, *Special Report on Energy. (Feb. 1981)*

HARTMAN, DANIEL S.:

Nomination Page. In Florida. *Aug. 1968*

Author

Florida's Manatees, Mermaids in Peril. Photos by James A. Sugar. 342-353, *Sept. 1969*

HARTZ, JIM: *Author*

New Jersey: A State of Surprise. Photos by Bob Krist and Michael S. Yamashita. 568-599, *Nov. 1981*

HARTZOG, GEORGE B., Jr.: *Author*

The Next 100 Years: A Master Plan for Yellowstone. 632-637, *May 1972*

Parkscape, U.S.A.: Tomorrow in Our National Parks. 48-93, *July 1966*

HARVARD, ANDREW: *Author*

The Forgotten Face of Everest. Photos by Expedition Members. 71-77, *July 1984*

HARVARD UNIVERSITY: Biological Laboratories:

Mystery Mammals of the Twilight (Bats). By Donald R. Griffin. 117-134, *July 1946*

HARVESTING:

North With the Wheat Cutters. By Noel Grove. Photos by James A. Sugar. 194-217, *Aug. 1972*

HARVEY, DAVID ALAN:

On Assignment in Chile. *July 1988*

On Assignment in Alaska. *Feb. 1983*

On Assignment in Southeast Asia. *May 1982*

Nomination Page. *June 1979*

Nomination Page. *Sept. 1978*

Photographer

Chile: Acts of Faith. By Allen A. Boraiko. 54-85, *July 1988*

North Carolina's Outer Banks: Awash in Change. By Charles E. Cobb, Jr. Included: Impressions of an early visitor (1580s); Sea currents shape the Outer Banks. 484-513, *Oct. 1987*

Tokyo, A Profile of Success. By William Graves. 606-645, *Nov. 1986*

Marking Time in Grenada. By Charles E. Cobb, Jr. 688-710, *Nov. 1984*

Dallas! By Griffin Smith, Jr. 272-305, *Sept. 1984*

Honduras: Eye of the Storm. By Mike Edwards. 608-637, *Nov. 1983*

Hunters of the Lost Spirit: Alaskans, Canadians. By Priit J. Vesilind. 150-189, *Feb. 1983*

Kampuchea Wakens From a Nightmare. By Peter T. White. 590-623, *May 1982*

A Sumatran Journey. By Harvey Arden. 406-430, *Mar. 1981*

■■*America's Atlantic Isles.* By H. Robert Morrison and Christine Eckstrom Lee. 199 pages. *1981*

Tunisia: Sea, Sand, Success. By Mike Edwards. 184-217, *Feb. 1980*

Harpers Ferry, West Virginia, stands guard at the confluence of the Shenandoah and rail-spanned Potomac Rivers. SAM ABELL

Our National Parks. 1-152, *July 1979*

Spain: It's a Changed Country. By Peter T. White. 297-331, *Mar. 1978*

Malaysia: Youthful Nation With Growing Pains. By William S. Ellis. 635-667, *May 1977*

Japan's Warriors of the Wind. Text by John Eliot. 551-561, *Apr. 1977*

Puget Sound, Sea Gate of the Pacific Northwest. By William Graves. 71-97, *Jan. 1977*

■■ *The Mysterious Maya.* By George E. and Gene S. Stuart. Photos by David Alan Harvey and Otis Imboden. 199 pages. *1977*

The Maya, Children of Time. By Howard La Fay. 729-767, *Dec. 1975*

My Backyard, the Adirondacks. By Anne LaBastille. 616-639, *May 1975*

The Virginians. By Mike W. Edwards. 588-617, *Nov. 1974*

This Is My Island, Tangier. By Harold G. Wheatley. 700-725, *Nov. 1973*

HARVEY, WILLIAM:

The British Way. By Sir Evelyn Wrench. 421-541, *Apr. 1949*

HASANOĞLAN, Turkey: Village Institutes:

The Turkish Republic Comes of Age. By Maynard Owen Williams. 581-616, *May 1945*

HASHEMITE Jordan, Arab Heartland. By John Scofield. 841-856, *Dec. 1952*

HASIDIC JEWS:

The Pious Ones (Brooklyn's Hasidic Jews). By Harvey Arden. Photos by Nathan Benn. 276-298, *Aug. 1975*

HASKINS, CARYL P.: *Author*

The Ant and Her World. Introduction by Caryl P. Haskins. 774-777, *June 1984*

HASSANEIN BEY, A. M.:
Author-Photographer

Crossing the Untraversed Libyan Desert: The Record of a 2,200-Mile Journey of Exploration Which Resulted in the Discovery of Two Oases of Strategic Importance on the Southwestern Frontier of Egypt. 233-277, *Sept. 1924*

HASTINGS, Battle of:

900 Years Ago: The Norman Conquest. By Kenneth M. Setton. Photos by George F. Mobley. 206-251, *Aug. 1966*

HATAY:

In the Land of Moses and Abraham. Photos by W. Robert Moore. 711-742, *Dec. 1938*

HATCH RIVER EXPEDITIONS:

Shooting Rapids in Dinosaur Country. By Jack Breed. Photos by author and Justin Locke. 363-390, *Mar. 1954*

HATCHER, J. B.:

Hatcher's Work in Patagonia. By W J McGee. 319-322, *Nov. 1897*

Author
The Indian Tribes of Southern Patagonia, Tierra del Fuego, and the Adjoining Islands. 12-22, *Jan. 1901*

A Landsat image depicts North Carolina's Outer Banks, including Cape Hatteras.

EOSAT COMPANY/GENERAL ELECTRIC SPACE SYSTEMS

Some Geographic Features of Southern Patagonia, with a Discussion of Their Origin. 41-55, *Feb. 1900*

Patagonia. 305-319, *Nov. 1897*

HATCHETFISH, Torchbearers of the Deep. By Paul A. Zahl. 713-714, *May 1958*

HATHAWAY, SIBYL (La Dame de Serk): *Author*

The Feudal Isle of Sark: Where Sixteenth-Century Laws Are Still Observed. 101-119, *July 1932*

HATTERAS, Cape, North Carolina:

North Carolina's Outer Banks: Awash in Change. By Charles E. Cobb, Jr. Photos by David Alan Harvey. Included: Impressions of an early visitor (1580s); Sea currents shape the Outer Banks. 484-513, *Oct. 1987*

How We Found the *Monitor.* By John G. Newton. Contents: Search in two expeditions for the wreck of the first ironclad gunboat, lost off Cape Hatteras during the Civil War. NGS research grant. 48-61, *Jan. 1975*

Lonely Cape Hatteras, Besieged by the Sea. By William S. Ellis. Photos by Emory Kristof. 393-421, *Sept. 1969*

October Holiday on the Outer Banks. By Nike Anderson. Photos by J. Baylor Roberts. 501-529, *Oct. 1955*

Exploring America's Great Sand Barrier Reef. By Eugene R. Guild. Photos by John E. Fletcher and author. 325-350, *Sept. 1947*

A Bit of Elizabethan England in America: Fisher Folk of the Islands Off North Carolina Conserved the Speech and Customs of Sir Walter Raleigh's Colonists. By Blanch Nettleton Epler. 695-730, *Dec. 1933*

Where the Wind Does the Work. By Collier Cobb. 310-317, *June 1906*

HATTERIA (Reptile). *See* Tuatara

HAUDENOSAUNEE (People of the Longhouse):

"The Fire That Never Dies." By Harvey Arden. Photos by Steve Wall. 375-403, *Sept. 1987*

HAUN, DECLAN:

On Assignment. *Sept. 1988*

Photographer
Quebec: French City in an Anglo-Saxon World. By Kenneth MacLeish. Photos by James L. Stanfield and Declan Haun. 416-442, *Mar. 1971*

HAUNTING Heart of the Everglades. By Andrew H. Brown. Photos by author and Willard R. Culver. 145-173, *Feb. 1948*

The **HAUNTS** of the Caribbean Corsairs: The West Indies a Geographic Background for the Most Adventurous Episodes in the History of the Western Hemisphere. By Nell Ray Clarke. 147-187, *Feb. 1922*

HAURY, EMIL W.: *Author*

The Hohokam: First Masters of the American Desert. Photos by Helga Teiwes. 670-695, *May 1967*

HAUSER, HILLARY: *Author*

Exploring a Sunken Realm in Australia. Photos by David Doubilet. 129-142, *Jan. 1984*

HAVANA (Habana), Cuba:

Inside Cuba Today. By Fred Ward. 32-69, *Jan. 1977*

Cuba–American Sugar Bowl. By Melville Bell Grosvenor. 1-56, *Jan. 1947*

Cuba–The Isle of Romance. By Enrique C. Canova. 345-380, *Sept. 1933*

Cuba–The Sugar Mill of the Antilles. By William Joseph Showalter. 1-33, *July 1920*

American Progress in Habana. 97-108, *Mar. 1902*

HAVASUPAI INDIANS:

Indian Shangri-La of the Grand Canyon. By Jay Johnston. Photos by Terry Eiler. 355-373, *Mar. 1970*

Land of the Havasupai. By Jack Breed. 655-674, *May 1948*

Indian Tribes of Pueblo Land. By Matthew W. Stirling. Paintings by W. Langdon Kihn. 549-596, *Nov. 1940*

Experiences in the Grand Canyon. By Ellsworth and Emery Kolb. 99-184, *Aug. 1914*

HAVE Excavations on the Island of Thera Solved the Riddle of the Minoans? By Spyridon Marinatos. Photos by Otis Imboden. 702-726, *May 1972*

HAVE We Solved the Mysteries of the Moon? By Kenneth F. Weaver. Paintings by William H. Bond. 309-325, *Sept. 1973*

HAWAII:

Editorial. By Wilbur E. Garrett. 557, *Nov. 1983*

Kamehameha–Hawaii's Warrior King. By Louise E. Levathes. Photos by Steve Raymer. Paintings by Herb Kawainui Kane. 558-599, *Nov. 1983*

G
H

Huge leaves of the ape-ape plant dwarf a man on the Hawaiian island of Maui in 1921. GILBERT H. GROSVENOR, NGS

World. By Gilbert Grosvenor. 115-238, *Feb. 1924*

The Key to the Pacific. By George C. Perkins. 295-298, *Apr. 1908*

Hawaii for Homes. By H. P. Wood. 298-299, *Apr. 1908*

A Bird City. 494-498, *Dec. 1904*

See also Kauai; Maui; Molokai

HAWAII VOLCANOES NATIONAL PARK, Hawaii:

Hawaii, Island of Fire and Flowers. By Gordon Young. Photos by Robert W. Madden. 399-425, *Mar. 1975*

Fountain of Fire in Hawaii (Kilauea Iki Crater). By Frederick Simpich, Jr. Photos by Robert B. Goodman and Robert Wenkam. 303-327, *Mar. 1960*

Volcanic Fires of the 50th State: Hawaii National Park. By Paul A. Zahl. 793-823, *June 1959*

Photographing a Volcano in Action. By Thomas J. Hargrave. 561-563, *Oct. 1955*

HAWAIIAN ISLANDS NATIONAL WILDLIFE REFUGE:

Hawaii's Far-flung Wildlife Paradise. By John L. Eliot. Photos by Jonathan Blair. 670-691, *May 1978*

HAWKE (Cutter):

By Sail Across Europe. By Merlin Minshall. 533-567, *May 1937*

HAWKES, RUSSELL: *Author*

Happy Birthday, Otto Lilienthal! Photos by James Collison. 286-292, *Feb. 1972*

HAWKS:

Can the Cooper's Hawk Survive? By Noel Snyder. Photos by author and Helen Snyder. NGS research grant. 433-442, *Mar. 1974*

A New Light Dawns on Bird Photography. By Arthur A. Allen. Included: Cooper's hawk, Peregrine falcon,

Red-tailed hawk, Sparrow hawk; and Falconry. 774-790, *June 1948*

Life with an Indian Prince: As Guests of a Maharaja's Brother, Two Young American Naturalists Study Age-old Methods of Hunting with Trained Falcons and Cheetahs and Savor the Pomp of Royal India. By John and Frank Craighead. 235-272, *Feb. 1942*

In Quest of the Golden Eagle: Over Lonely Mountain and Prairie Soars This Rare and Lordly Bird, But Three Youths from the East Catch Up With Him at Last. By John and Frank Craighead. 693-710, *May 1940*

Adventures with Birds of Prey. By Frank and John Craighead. 109-134, *July 1937*

The Eagle, King of Birds, and His Kin. By Alexander Wetmore. Paintings by Allan Brooks. 43-95, *July 1933*

Photographing the Nest Life of the Osprey. By C.W.R. Knight. 247-260, *Aug. 1932*

Falconry, the Sport of Kings. By Louis Agassiz Fuertes. Paintings by author. 429-460, *Dec. 1920*

American Birds of Prey–A Review of Their Value. 460-467, *Dec. 1920*

Hunting with the Lens. By Howard H. Cleaves. 1-35, *July 1914*

HAWTHORNE, NATHANIEL:

Literary Landmarks of Massachusetts. By William H. Nicholas. Photos by B. Anthony Stewart and John E. Fletcher. 279-310, *Mar. 1950*

HAY, JACOB: *Author*

The FBI: Public Friend Number One. Photos by Robert F. Sisson. 860-886, *June 1961*

HAY FEVER:

Pollen: Breath of Life and Sneezes. By Cathy Newman. Photos by Martha Cooper. Included: A Misery Index. 490-521, *Oct. 1984*

Examining tissue samples from laboratory rats helps Dow Chemical scientists minimize health hazards of new compounds. FRED WARD, BLACK STAR

HAYASHIDA, TSUNEO: *Author-Photographer*

The Japanese Crane, Bird of Happiness. 542-556, *Oct. 1983*

HAYDEN, CARL: *Author*

The Nation's Capitol Revealed as Never Before. 1-3, *Jan. 1964*

HAYDEN, EVERETT:

Board of Managers. xix, May 5, 1894; 191, June 1897; 520, *Dec. 1898*

Secretary. ii, xxi-xxv, Oct. 31, 1895; 216, June 1896; 70, *Feb. 1898*

Vice President. 68, Apr. 1890; 294, Apr. 1891; xii, Feb. 19, 1892; xix, *Feb. 20, 1893*

Author

Chronometer and Time Service of the U. S. Naval Observatory and the Present Status of Standard Time. 430-431, *Oct. 1904*

The Law of Storms, Considered with Special Reference to the North Atlantic. 199-211, *July 1890*

The Great Storm Off the Atlantic Coast of the United States, March 11th-14th, 1888. 40-58, *Oct. 1888*

HAYDEN, KAREN C.: *Author-Photographer*

Where Oil and Wildlife Mix. By Steven C. Wilson and Karen C. Hayden. 145-173, *Feb. 1981*

HAYDON, Mount, Alaska:

First American Ascent of Mount St. Elias. By Maynard M. Miller. 229-248, *Feb. 1948*

HAYES, ALDEN:

Nomination Page. *July 1960*

HAYES, C. WILLARD:

Cryptogams Collected by Dr. C. Willard Hayes in Alaska, 1891. By Clara E. Cummings. 160-162, *May 15, 1892*

Author

Ice Cliffs on White River, Yukon Territory. By C. Willard Hayes and Alfred H. Brooks. 199-201, *May 1900*

An Assumed Inconstancy in the Level of Lake Nicaragua; A Question of Permanency of the Nicaragua Canal. 156-161, *Apr. 1900*

Physiography of the Nicaragua Canal Route. 233-246, *July 1899*

Geomorphology of the Southern Appalachians. By C. Willard Hayes and Marius R. Campbell. 63-126, *May 23, 1894*

An Expedition Through the Yukon District. 117-159, *May 15, 1892*

HAYES, RUTHERFORD B.:

Profiles of the Presidents: III. The American Giant Comes of Age. By Frank Freidel. 660-711, *May 1965*

HAYES, WILLIAM C.: *Author*

Daily Life in Ancient Egypt (Part I). Daily Life in Ancient Egypt: *The Later Period* (Part II). Paintings by H. M. Herget. 419-515, *Oct. 1941*

HAYNES, C. VANCE:

Nomination Page. *Apr. 1968*

In Washington's Puget Sound, Namu is fed by a diver before yielding the first electrocardiogram of an uninjured, unrestrained killer whale. FLIP SCHULKE

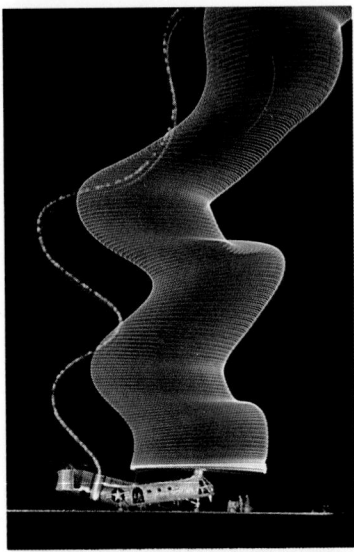

A time exposure of rotor lights reveals the night landing of a Vertol helicopter at San Marcos, Texas. GORDON TENNEY, BLACK STAR

Drawings by Carlotta Gonzales Lahey. Included: Charts, designed by author, showing star positions for each month. 97-128, *July 1943*
See also Universe

HEAVY Hands on the Land. By Larry Kohl. Photos by William Thompson and Galen Rowell. 632-651, *Nov. 1988*

HEBEI PROVINCE, China:
Peacetime Plant Hunting About Peiping. By P. H. and J. H. Dorsett. 509-534, *Oct. 1937*
Grand Canal Panorama. By Willard Price. 487-514, *Apr. 1937*
See also Beijing

HEBREWS:
Abraham, the Friend of God. By Kenneth MacLeish. Photos by Dean Conger. 739-789, *Dec. 1966*
The Last Thousand Years Before Christ. By G. Ernest Wright. Paintings by H. J. Soulen and Peter V. Bianchi. 812-853, *Dec. 1960*
Bringing Old Testament Times to Life. By G. Ernest Wright. Paintings by Henry J. Soulen. 833-864, *Dec. 1957*
See also Moses

HEBRIDES (Islands), Scotland:
Scotland From Her Lovely Lochs and Seas. By Alan Villiers. Photos by Robert F. Sisson. 492-541, *Apr. 1961*
See also Inner Hebrides; Outer Hebrides

HEDIN, SVEN:
Dr. Sven Hedin (Biography). 26-29, *Jan. 1903*
Sven Hedin in Tibet. 96-97, *Mar. 1902*
Sven Hedin's Explorations in Central Asia. 393-395, *Nov. 1901*
Royal Geographical Society's Founders' Medal conferred on Dr. Sven Hedin. 342, *July 1898*

HEDJAZ. See Hejaz

HEIDERER, TONY: *Photographer*
Banaras: India's City of Light. By Santha Rama Rau. 214-251, *Feb. 1986*

HEIGHT and Position of Mount St. Elias. By Israel C. Russell. 231-237, *Feb. 19, 1892*

HEIGHT and Position of Mount St. Elias (Part V, from "An Expedition to Mount St. Elias, Alaska," by Israel C. Russell). 189-191, *May 29, 1891*

The **HEIGHT** of Mt. Rainier. By Richard U. Goode. 97-98, *Mar. 1898*

HEILONGJIANG PROVINCE, China.
See Harbin

HEILPRIN, ANGELO:
Board of Managers. 87, *Feb. 1905*
The National Geographic Society Expedition in the West Indies. 209-213, *June 1902*
Author
An Impression of the Guiana Wilderness. Photos by Harriet C. Adams. 373-381, *June 1907*
The Shattered Obelisk of Mont Pelée. 465-474, *Aug. 1906*
Destruction of Pompeii as Interpreted by the Volcanic Eruptions of Martinique. 431, *Oct. 1904*

HEIMAEY (Island), Westmann Islands, Iceland:
Vestmannaeyjar: Up From the Ashes. By Noel Grove. Photos by Robert S. Patton. 690-701, *May 1977*
A Village Fights for Its Life. By Noel Grove. 40-67, *July 1973*

HEINICKE, ALFRED: *Photographer*
Persia. 401-416, *Apr. 1921*

HEINL, ROBERT D., Jr.: *Author*
Palms and Planes in the New Hebrides. 229-256, *Aug. 1944*

HEINLY, BURT A.: *Author*
Carrying Water Through a Desert: The Story of the Los Angeles Aqueduct. 568-596, *July 1910*

HEIRTZLER, JAMES R.: *Author*
Where the Earth Turns Inside Out. Photos by Emory Kristof. 586-603, *May 1975*

HEISKELL, MORGAN: *Photographer*
Capri, the Island Retreat of Roman Emperors. 627-638, *June 1922*

HEIZER, ROBERT F.: *Author*
Gifts for the Jaguar God. By Philip Drucker and Robert F. Heizer. 367-375, *Sept. 1956*

HEJAZ (Arab Kingdom):
A Visit to Three Arab Kingdoms: Transjordania, Iraq, and the Hedjaz Present Many Problems to European Powers. By Junius B. Wood. 535-568, *May 1923*

HELGOLAND (Island), West Germany:
Demolishing Germany's North Sea Ramparts. By Stuart E. Jones. 635-644, *Nov. 1946*

HELICOPTERS:
Air Rescue Behind Enemy Lines (North Vietnam). By Howard Sochurek. 346-369, *Sept. 1968*
Helicopter War in South Viet Nam. By Dickey Chapelle. 723-754, *Nov. 1962*
The Incredible Helicopter. By Peter T. White. 533-557, *Apr. 1959*
Everyone's Servant, the Post Office. By Allan C. Fisher, Jr. Photos by Volkmar Wentzel. 121-152, *July 1954*
Aviation Looks Ahead on Its 50th Birthday. By Emory S. Land. 721-739, *Dec. 1953*
Flying in the "Blowtorch" Era. By Frederick G. Vosburgh. 281-322, *Sept. 1950*
Exploring Ancient Panama by Helicopter. By Matthew W. Stirling. Photos by Richard H. Stewart. NGS research grant. 227-246, *Feb. 1950*
Our Air Age Speeds Ahead. By F. Barrows Colton. 249-272, *Feb. 1948*

HELIUM:
Studies Planned for New Stratosphere Flight with Helium. 795-800, *June 1935*
Helium, the New Balloon Gas. By G. Sherburne Rogers. 441-456, *May 1919*
Modern Transmutation of the Elements. By Sir William Ramsay. 201-203, *Apr. 1906*

HELL, Norway:
The White War in Norway. By Thomas R. Henry. 617-640, *Nov. 1945*

HELLCATS (Airplanes):
Take-off for Japan. U. S. Navy official photos. 193-208, *Aug. 1945*

HELLER, EDMUND: *Author*
Nature's Most Amazing Mammal: Elephants, Unique Among Animals, Have Many Human Qualities When Wild That Make Them Foremost Citizens of Zoo and Circus. 729-759, *June 1934*

HELLO Anchorage, Good-Bye Dream. By Larry L. King. Photos by Chris Johns. 364-389, *Mar. 1988*

HELLWEG, J. F.: *Author*
Eclipse Adventures on a Desert Isle (Canton). 377-394, *Sept. 1937*

HELLYER, DAVID: *Author*
Nature's Clown, the Penguin. By David Hellyer and Malcolm Davis. 405-428, *Sept. 1952*
Goggle Fishing in California Waters. Photos by Lamar Boren. 615-632, *May 1949*

HELM, ENNIS CREED ("Tex"): *Photographer*
Carlsbad Caverns in Color. By Mason Sutherland. 433-468, *Oct. 1953*

HELP for Philippine Tribes in Trouble. By Kenneth MacLeish. Photos by Dean Conger. 220-255, *Aug. 1971*

HELPING Holland Rebuild Her Land. By Gilbert M. Grosvenor and Charles Neave. 365-413, *Sept. 1954*

G
H

*Deafening sound of mortar fire alarms children in a South Vietnamese village near Binh
Hung in 1962.* DICKEY CHAPELLE

HENRY E. HUNTINGTON LIBRARY AND ART GALLERY, San Marino, California:

Huntington Library, California Treasure House. By David S. Boyer. 251-276, *Feb. 1958*

HENRY FORD MUSEUM, Dearborn, Michigan:

The Past Is Present in Greenfield Village. By Beverley M. Bowie. Photos by Neal P. Davis and Willard R. Culver. 96-127, *July 1958*

HENRY GANNETT, *President of the National Geographic Society 1910–1914.* By S.N.D. North. 34 pages. *1915*

HENRY HUDSON, Magnificent Failure: Just 330 Years Ago He and His Mutinous Crew Found Manhattan Covered With "Goodly Oakes" and Fought Indians in New York Harbor. By Frederick G. Vosburgh. 461-490, *Apr. 1939*

HENRY HUDSON'S Changing Bay. By Bill Richards. Photos by David Hiser. 380-405, *Mar. 1982*

HENRY HUDSON'S River. By Willard Price. Photos by Wayne Miller. 364-403, *Mar. 1962*

HENSHAW, HENRY WETHERBEE: *Author*

■■ *The Book of Birds: Common Birds of Town and Country and American Game Birds.* Art by Louis Agassiz Fuertes. 195 pages. 1914; rev. ed. *1918*

Friends of Our Forests. Paintings by Louis Agassiz Fuertes. 297-321, *Apr. 1917*

American Game Birds. Paintings by Louis Agassiz Fuertes. 105-158, *Aug. 1915*

Birds of Town and Country. Paintings by Louis Agassiz Fuertes. 494-531, *May 1914*

Fifty Common Birds of Farm and Orchard. Paintings by Louis Agassiz Fuertes. 669-697, *June 1913*

■■ *Fifty Common Birds of Farm and Orchard.* Art by Louis Agassiz Fuertes. Originally prepared as Bulletin 513 of the U. S. Department of Agriculture. Reprint of June 1913 article by special permission of the Secretary of Agriculture. 29 pages. *1913*

The Policemen of the Air: An Account of the Biological Survey of the Department of Agriculture. 79-118, *Feb. 1908*

Photographer

Some of Nature's Scenic Gifts to Hawaii. 159-174, *Feb. 1924*

HENSON, MATTHEW A.:

Commander Robert E. Peary: Did He Reach the Pole? By Wally Herbert. Introduction by the Editor. 387-413, *Sept. 1988*

Descendants of the Expeditions. Photos by Bob Sacha. 414-429. I. The Peary Family. By Edward Peary Stafford. 417-421; II. The Henson Family. By S. Allen Counter. 422-429, *Sept. 1988*

Peary as a Leader: Incidents from the Life of the Discoverer of the North Pole Told by One of His Lieutenants on the Expedition Which Reached the Goal. By Donald B. MacMillan. 293-317, *Apr. 1920*

The Discovery of the Pole: First Report by Commander Robert E. Peary, September 6, 1909. 892-916, *Oct. 1909*

HENTSCHEL, FAITH:

On Assignment in Ulu Burun, Turkey. *Dec. 1987*

HĒRÁKLEION, Crete (Island). *See* Candia

HERALDRY. *See* Coats of Arms

The **HERALDRY** of Heroism. By Arthur E. Du Bois. 409-413, *Oct. 1943*

HERBAL MEDICINE:

Herbs for All Seasons. By Lonnelle Aikman. Photos by Sam Abell. Picture portfolio text by Larry Kohl. 386-409, *Mar. 1983*

■■ *Nature's Healing Arts. 1977*

Nature's Gifts to Medicine. By Lonnelle Aikman. Paintings by Lloyd K. Townsend and Don Crowley. 420-440, *Sept. 1974*

The People of Cumberland Gap. By John Fetterman. Photos by Bruce Dale. 591-621, *Nov. 1971*

Karnali, Roadless World of Western Nepal. By Lila M. and Barry C. Bishop. NGS research grant. 656-689, *Nov. 1971*

HERBERT, CHARLES W.:

Author-Photographer

Saba, Crater Treasure of the Indies. Included: Up and Down on Saba. 597-620, *Nov. 1940*

Photographer

Better Days for the Navajos. By Jack Breed. 809-847, *Dec. 1958*

Californians Escape to the Desert. By

Soothing teas made from herbs like chamomile and lemongrass have found a new place on American tables. SAM ABELL

Mason Sutherland. 675-724, *Nov. 1957*

Sonora Is Jumping. By Mason Sutherland. 215-246, *Feb. 1955*

Island Treasures of the Caribbean. Photos by Edwin L. Wisherd and C. W. Herbert. 281-304, *Sept. 1940*

HERBERT, WALLY: *Author*

Commander Robert E. Peary: Did He Reach the Pole? Introduction by the Editor. 387-413, *Sept. 1988*

HERBICIDES:

The Pesticide Dilemma. By Allen A. Boraiko. Photos by Fred Ward. 145-183, *Feb. 1980*

HERBS:

Herbs for All Seasons. By Lonnelle Aikman. Photos by Sam Abell. Picture portfolio text by Larry Kohl. 386-409, *Mar. 1983*

See also Herbal Medicine; *and* Spices

HERCULANEUM (Ancient City), Italy:

■ In the Shadow of Vesuvius. President's Page. By Gilbert M. Grosvenor. Jan. 1987; cover, *Feb. 1987*

The Dead Do Tell Tales at Vesuvius. By Rick Gore. Photos by O. Louis Mazzatenta. NGS research grant. 557-613, *May 1984*

A Buried Roman Town Gives Up Its Dead. By Joseph Judge. Photos by Jonathan Blair. NGS research grant. 687-693, *Dec. 1982*

HERCULES, FRANK: *Author*

To Live in Harlem.... Photos by LeRoy Woodson, Jr. 178-207, *Feb. 1977*

HERE and There in Northern Africa. By Frank Edward Johnson. 1-132, *Jan. 1914*

HERE Come the Marines. By Frederick Simpich. 647-672, *Nov. 1950*

HERE in Manchuria: Many Thousand Lives Were Lost and More Than Half the Crops Destroyed by the Floods of 1932. By Lilian Grosvenor Coville. 233-256, *Feb. 1933*

HERE Rest in Honored Glory... (War Memorials). By Howell Walker. 739-768, *June 1957*

HERENDEEN, EDWARD PERRY: *Author*

An Undiscovered Island Off the Northern Coast of Alaska. 78-80, *July 10, 1893*

HÉRENS, Val d', Switzerland:

Switzerland's Enchanted Val d'Hérens. By Georgia Engelhard Cromwell. 825-848, *June 1955*

HERERO TRIBESPEOPLE:

Namibia: Nearly a Nation? By Bryan Hodgson. Photos by Jim Brandenburg. 755-797, *June 1982*

HERE'S New York Harbor. By Stuart E. Jones. Photos by Robert F. Sisson and David S. Boyer. 773-813, *Dec. 1954*

HERE'S to Milwaukee. By Louise Levathes. Photos by Michael Mauney. 180-201, *Aug. 1980*

HERGET, H. M.: *Artist*

Ancient Mesopotamia: A Light That Did Not Fail. By E. A. Speiser. Included: How the Herget Paintings Were Composed. 41-105, *Jan. 1951*

Ancient Rome Brought to Life. 570-633, *Nov. 1946*

"The Glory That Was Greece." 290-352, *Mar. 1944*

Life, Culture, and History of the Egyptians. 436-514, *Oct. 1941*

In the Realm of the Sons of the Sun. 229-236, *Feb. 1938*

Aztecs Under the War God's Reign. 735-742, *June 1937*

Life and Death in Ancient Maya Land. 623-630, *Nov. 1936*

Portraits of Ancient Mayas, a Peace-Loving People. 553-560, *Nov. 1935*

HERITAGE of Beauty and History. By Conrad L. Wirth. Contents: U. S. National Parks. 587-661, *May 1958*

HERKI TRIBESPEOPLE:

Mountain Tribes of Iran and Iraq. By Harold Lamb. 385-408, *Mar. 1946*

HERM (Island), English Channel:

Britain's "French" Channel Islands. By James Cerruti. Photos by James L. Amos. 710-740, *May 1971*

The Channel Islands. By Edith Carey. 143-164, *Aug. 1920*

HERMES, R. C.: *Photographer*

The Solemn, Sociable Puffins. By R. M. Lockley. 414-422, *Sept. 1954*

HERMITAGE (State Museum), Leningrad, U.S.S.R.:

Leningrad, Russia's Window on the West. By Howard La Fay. Photos by Dick Durrance II. 636-673, *May 1971*

HERO (Research Vessel):

Antarctica's Nearer Side. By Samuel W. Matthews. Photos by William R. Curtsinger. 622-655, *Nov. 1971*

HEROD THE GREAT, King (Judea):

Caesarea Maritima. By Robert L. Hohlfelder. Photos by Bill Curtsinger. Paintings by J. Robert Teringo. NGS research grant. 261-279, *Feb. 1987*

The Ghosts of Jericho. By James L. Kelso. 825-844, *Dec. 1951*

HEROES of Wartime Science and Mercy. By Elizabeth W. King. 715-740, *Dec. 1943*

HEROES' Return. By William H. Nicholas. 333-352, *Mar. 1945*

HEROIC Flags of the Middle Ages. By Byron McCandless and Gilbert Grosvenor. 388-399, *Oct. 1917*

HEROIN:

The Poppy. By Peter T. White. Photos by Steve Raymer. 143-189, *Feb. 1985*

HERON ISLAND, Australia:

Australia's Great Barrier Reef. 630-663. I. A Marine Park Is Born. By Soames Summerhays. Photos by Ron

Bobbing its way from Africa to the West Indies in 1970, **Ra II,** *Thor Heyerdahl's papyrus-reed ship, proves the seaworthiness of such ancient boats.* GEORGES SOURIAL

and Valerie Taylor. 630-635; II. Paradise Beneath the Sea. By Ron and Valerie Taylor. 636-663, *May 1981*

HERONS:

Lord of the Shallows–The Great Blue Heron. By Richard J. Dolesh. Photos by Cameron Davidson. 540-554, *Apr. 1984*

Aha! It Really Works! By Robert F. Sisson. Contents: Green heron that fishes with bait. 143-147, *Jan. 1974*

Wildlife of Everglades National Park. By Daniel B. Beard. Paintings by Walter A. Weber. 83-116, *Jan. 1949*

The Large Wading Birds: Long Legs and Remarkable Beaks, as Well as Size, Form, and Color, Distinguish the Herons, Ibises, and Flamingos. By T. Gilbert Pearson. Paintings by Allan Brooks. 441-469, *Oct. 1932*

HERRICK, FRANCIS H.: *Author*

The Eagle in Action: An Intimate Study of the Eyrie Life of America's National Bird. 635-660, *May 1929*

Microscopical Examination of Wood from the Buried Forest, Muir Inlet, Alaska. 75-78, *Mar. 21, 1892*

HERRING:

Scenes of Postwar Finland. By La Verne Bradley. Photos by Jerry Waller. 233-264, *Aug. 1947*

Bornholm–Denmark in a Nutshell. By Mason Sutherland. 239-256, *Feb. 1945*

When the Herring Fleet Comes to Great Yarmouth. By W. Robert Moore. 233-250, *Aug. 1934*

Fishes and Fisheries of Our North Atlantic Seaboard. By John Oliver La Gorce. Paintings by Hashime Murayama. 567-634, *Dec. 1923*

King Herring: An Account of the World's Most Valuable Fish, the Industries It Supports, and the Part It

Has Played in History. By Hugh M. Smith. 701-735, *Aug. 1909*

See also Menhaden

HERRLE, GUSTAVE:

Geographic Nomenclature. Remarks by Herbert G. Ogden, Gustave Herrle, Marcus Baker, and A. H. Thompson. 261-278, *Aug. 1890*

Author

The Submarine Cables of the World. Included: Chart compiled by U. S. Hydrographic Office. 102-107, *Mar. 1896*

Rules for the Orthography of Geographic Names. 279-285, *Aug. 1890*

HERRNKIND, WILLIAM F.: *Author*

Strange March of the Spiny Lobster. Photos by Rick Frehsee and Bruce Mounier. 819-831, *June 1975*

HERSEY, HENRY E.:

Member of Wellman Polar Expedition. 205, *Apr. 1906*; 712, *Dec. 1906*

HERZ FOUNDATION: Study Grant: Orangutans. 835, *June 1980*

HERZEGOVINA:

East of the Adriatic: Notes on Dalmatia, Montenegro, Bosnia, and Herzegovina. By Kenneth McKenzie. 1159-1187, 1284, *Dec. 1912*

Where East Meets West: Visit to Picturesque Dalmatia, Montenegro and Bosnia. By Marian Cruger Coffin. 309-344, *May 1908*

HERZFELD, ERNST EMIL:

Exploring the Secrets of Persepolis. By Charles Breasted. Note: Herzfeld, field director of the expedition sponsored by the Oriental Institute of the University of Chicago. 381-420, *Oct. 1933*

Truck drivers roar down a Los Angeles highway to pick up 17.5 tons of ripe strawberries due in New York City in less than four days. JAMES A. SUGAR, BLACK STAR

HESS, BILL: *Author-Photographer*
Seeking the Best of Two Worlds. Contents: Apache Indians. 272-290, *Feb. 1980*

Photographer
Coming of Age the Apache Way. By Nita Quintero. 262-271, *Feb. 1980*

HEURLIN, GUSTAV:
Photographer
The Color and Customs of Sweden's Chateau Country. 33-40, *July 1934*
Denmark, Land of Farms and Fisheries. 223-230, *Feb. 1932*
Fjords and Fjells of Viking Land. 13-44, *July 1930*
Types and Costumes of Old Sweden. 425-440, *Oct. 1928*

HEWERS of Stone (Mitla, Mexico). By Jeremiah Zimmerman. 1002-1020, *Dec. 1910*

HEWES, LAURENCE ILSLEY:
Author
Butterflies–Try and Get Them. 667-678, *May 1936*

HEYDEN, FRANCIS J.:
Eclipse Hunting in Brazil's Ranchland. By F. Barrows Colton. Photos by Richard H. Stewart and Guy W. Starling. 285-324, *Sept. 1947*

HEYERDAHL, THOR:
■ The *Tigris* Expedition. 826, Dec. 1978; 1, Jan. 1979; cover, *Apr. 1979*
Author
Tigris Sails Into the Past. Photos by Carlo Mauri and the crew of the *Tigris*. 806-827, *Dec. 1978*
The Voyage of *Ra II*. Photos by Carlo Mauri and Georges Sourial. 44-71, *Jan. 1971*
Turning Back Time in the South Seas (Fatu-Hiva Island). 109-136, *Jan. 1941*

HEYWARD, DuBOSE: *Author*
The American Virgins (Virgin Islands): After Dark Days, These Adopted Daughters of the United States Are Finding a New Place in the Caribbean Sun. By DuBose Heyward and Daisy Reck. 273-308, *Sept. 1940*
Charleston: Where Mellow Past and Present Meet. Photos by B. Anthony Stewart. 273-312, *Mar. 1939*

HIALEAH PARK, Florida:
Flame-Feathered Flamingos of Florida. By W. A. Watts. Photos by W. F. Gerecke. 56-65, *Jan. 1941*

HIBERNATION:
Poorwill Sleeps Away the Winter. By Edmund C. Jaeger. 273-280, *Feb. 1953*
Mystery Mammals of the Twilight. By Donald R. Griffin. 117-134, *July 1946*
See also Grizzly Bears

HICKORY (Salvage Ship):
Graveyard of the Quicksilver Galleons. By Mendel Peterson. Photos by Jonathan Blair. 850-876, *Dec. 1979*

HICKS, JOHN W.:
Author-Photographer
Red Crabs on the March on Christmas Island. 822-831, *Dec. 1987*

HIDDEN GLACIER, Alaska:
The National Geographic Society's Alaska Expedition of 1909. By Ralph S. Tarr and Lawrence Martin. 1-54, *Jan. 1910*

HIDDEN Key to the Pacific: Piercing the Web of Secrecy Which Long Has Veiled Japanese Bases in the Mandated Islands. By Willard Price. 759-785, *June 1942*

HIDDEN Life of an Undersea Desert.

By Eugenie Clark. Photos by David Doubilet. 129-144, *July 1983*

HIDDEN Life of the Timber Rattler. By William S. Brown. Photos by Bianca Lavies. NGS research grant. 128-138, *July 1987*

HIDDEN Perils of the Deep. By G. R. Putnam. 822-837, *Sept. 1909*

The **HIDDEN** Tenn-Tom: Bypassed But Still Striving. By Alice J. Hall. Photos by Sandy Felsenthal. 384-387, *Mar. 1986*

HIDDEN *Treasures of the Sea.* Juvenile. ■■ 104 pages. *1988*

HIDDEN VALLEY, Irian Jaya, Indonesia. *See* Grand Valley

HIDDEN *Worlds.* Contents: Vision, ■■ light, and magnification. Juvenile. 104 pages. *1981*

HIDDEN Worlds in the Heart of a Plant (Bromeliad). By Paul A. Zahl. 389-397, *Mar. 1975*

HIDES AND SKINS:
New Day for Alaska's Pribilof Islanders. By Susan Hackley Johnson. Photos by Tim Thompson. 536-552, Included: Fur seal harvest by Aleuts. *Oct. 1982*
Wild Cargo: the Business of Smuggling Animals. By Noel Grove. Photos by Steve Raymer. 287-315, *Mar. 1981*

HIERAPOLIS (Ancient City), Turkey:
The Ruined Cities of Asia Minor. By Ernest L. Harris. 741-760, *Nov. 1908*

HIEROGLYPHS:
Computer Helps Scholars Re-create an Egyptian Temple. By Ray Winfield Smith. Photos by Emory Kristof. NGS research grant. 634-655, *Nov. 1970*

HIERONYMUS, REX E.: *Author*
Down Mark Twain's River on a Raft. 551-574, *Apr. 1948*

HIGAONON TRIBESPEOPLE:
Help for Philippine Tribes in Trouble. By Kenneth MacLeish. Photos by Dean Conger. 220-255, *Aug. 1971*

HIGDON, HAL: *Author*
New Tricks Outwit Our Insect Enemies. Photos by Robert F. Sisson and Emory Kristof. 380-399, *Sept. 1972*

HIGGINS, MARGARET M.: *Author*
Guam–Perch of the China Clippers. 99-122, *July 1938*

HIGH, Wild World of the Vicuña. By William L. Franklin. 77-91, *Jan. 1973*

HIGH Adventure in the Himalayas. By Thomas Weir. 193-234, *Aug. 1952*

The **HIGH** Andes: South America's Islands in the Sky. By Loren McIntyre. 422-459, *Apr. 1987*

HIGH ATLAS (Mountains), Africa:
Berber Brides' Fair. By Carla Hunt. Photos by Nik Wheeler. 119-129, *Jan. 1980*
Morocco, Land of the Farthest West.

By Thomas J. Abercrombie. 834-865, *June 1971*

Trek by Mule Among Morocco's Berbers. By Victor Englebert. 850-875, *June 1968*

HIGH Country of Colorado. By Alfred M. Bailey. Photos by author, Robert J. Niedrach, F. G. Brandenburg. 43-72, *July 1946*

HIGH Country Trail: Along the Continental Divide. By Michael Robbins. Photos by Paul Chesley. 199 pages. *1981*

HIGH-FLYING Tulsa. By Robert Paul Jordan. Photos by Annie Griffiths. 378-403, *Sept. 1983*

HIGH Road and Low through the Mountain State (West Virginia). Photos by B. Anthony Stewart and Volkmar Wentzel. 157-180, *Aug. 1940*

HIGH Road in the Pyrenees. By H. V. Morton. Photos by Justin Locke. 299-334, *Mar. 1956*

HIGH Road to "Victory": Soviet and U. S. Climbers Conquer Pik Pobedy. By William Garner. Photos by Medford Taylor. 256-271, *Aug. 1986*

HIGH Sierra. 213-214, *Mar. 1907*

HIGH-STEPPING Idaho. By William S. Ellis. Photos by Dean Conger. 290-317, *Mar. 1973*

HIGH Tech, High Risk, and High Life in Silicon Valley. By Moira Johnston. Photos by Charles O'Rear. 459-477, *Oct. 1982*

HIGH-TECH Partners Plumb New Depths. Illustrations text by Cliff Tarpy. 706-727, *Dec. 1986*

HIGH Trail Through the Canadian Rockies. By Mike W. Edwards. Photos by Lowell Georgia. 795-817, *June 1973*

The **HIGH** World of the Rain Forest. By William Beebe. Paintings by Guy Neale. 838-855, *June 1958*

The **HIGHEST** Camp in the World. 647-648, *Nov. 1906*

HIGHEST Camps and Climbs. By Edwin Swift Balch. 713, *Dec. 1906*

The **HIGHEST** Dam in the World (Roosevelt Dam). 440-441, *Sept. 1905*

The **HIGHEST** Point in Each State. 539-541, *June 1909*

HIGHLAND GAMES:

Over the Sea to Scotland's Skye. By Robert J. Reynolds. 87-112, *July 1952*

The **HIGHLANDS,** Stronghold of Scottish Gaeldom. By Kenneth MacLeish. Photos by Winfield Parks. 398-435, *Mar. 1968*

HIGH LIGHTS in the Peruvian and Bolivian Andes. Photos by W. Robert Moore. 219-234, *Feb. 1927*

HIGH LIGHTS in the Sunshine State.

Photos by Clifton Adams and Charles Edward Hagle. 27-82, *Jan. 1930*

HIGHLIGHTS of London Town. Photos by Clifton Adams. 569-576, *May 1929*

HIGHLIGHTS of the Volunteer State: Men and Industry in Tennessee Range from Pioneer Stages to Modern Machine Age. By Leonard Cornell Roy. 553-594, *May 1939*

HIGHWAYS AND ROADS:

Traveling the Trans-Canada: From Newfoundland to British Columbia. By William Howarth. Photos by George F. Mobley. 199 pages. *1987*

Exploring America's Scenic Highways. 199 pages. *1985*

A Journey Down Old U. S. 1. By Bruce Dale. 790-817, *Dec. 1984*

The Okies–Beyond the Dust Bowl. By William Howarth. Photos by Chris Johns. Included: U. S. 66. 322-349, *Sept. 1984*

Back Roads America: A Portfolio of Her People. By Thomas O'Neill. Photos by Ira Block. 199 pages. *1980*

Trucks Race the Clock From Coast to Coast. By James A. Sugar. 226-243, *Feb. 1974*

Our Growing Interstate Highway System. By Robert Paul Jordan. 195-219, *Feb. 1968*

From Sun-clad Sea to Shining Mountains. By Ralph Gray. Photos by James P. Blair. Contents: "International 89": Mexico's West Coast Highway; U. S. 89; Canada's Coleman-Kananaskis Road and Banff-Jasper Highway. 542-589, *Apr. 1964*

The Old Boston Post Roads. By Donald Barr Chidsey. 189-205, *Aug. 1962*

The Post Road Today. Photos by B. Anthony Stewart. 206-233, *Aug. 1962*

From Sea to Shining Sea: A Cross Section of the United States Along

Youngsters from Camp Timberlake of Vermont's Farm and Wilderness Foundation hike the Appalachian Trail. SAM ABELL

Historic Route 40. By Ralph Gray. Photos by Dean Conger and author. 1-61, *July 1961*

California's Wonderful One (State Highway No. 1). By Frank Cameron. Photos by B. Anthony Stewart. 571-617, *Nov. 1959*

Amalfi, Italy's Divine Coast. By Luis Marden. 472-509, *Oct. 1959*

Stilwell Road–Land Route to China. By Nelson Grant Tayman. 681-698, *June 1945*

6,000 Miles over the Roads of Free China. By Josephine A. Brown. 355-384, *Mar. 1944*

Alaskan Highway an Engineering Epic: Mosquitoes, Mud, and Muskeg Minor Obstacles of 1,671-mile Race to Throw the Alcan Life Line Through Thick Forests and Uninhabited Wilderness. By Froelich Rainey. 143-168, *Feb. 1943*

U. S. Roads in War and Peace. By Frederick Simpich. 687-716, *Dec. 1941*

The Land of the Free in Africa. By Harry A. McBride. 411-430, *Oct. 1922*

The Immediate Necessity for Military Highways. By A. G. Batchelder. 477-499, *Nov.-Dec. 1917*

Burning the Roads. 583-586, *Oct. 1906*

The Old Post-Road from Tiflis to Erivan. By Esther Lancraft Hovey. 300-309, *Aug. 1901*

See also Appian Way, Italy; Burma Road; Natchez Trace; New York State Thruway; Pan American Highway; *and* Close-up Map Series

HIKING TRIPS:

Mountain Adventure: Exploring the Appalachian Trail. By Ron Fisher. Photos by Sam Abell. 200 pages. *1988*

A Tunnel Through Time: The Appalachian Trail. By Noel Grove. Photos by Sam Abell. 216-243, *Feb. 1987*

To Scotland Afoot Along the Pennine Way. By David Yeadon. Photos by Annie Griffiths. 388-418, *Mar. 1986*

A Short Hike With Bob Marshall. By Mike Edwards. Photos by Dewitt Jones. 664-689, *May 1985*

Battle For a Bigger Bob (Bob Marshall Wilderness). By Mike Edwards. Photos by Dewitt Jones. 690-692, *May 1985*

A Walk and Ride on the Wild Side: Tasmania. By Carolyn Bennett Patterson. Photos by David Hiser and Melinda Berge. 676-693, *May 1983*

Preserving a Mountain Heritage. By Sir Edmund Hillary. 696-703, *June 1982*

Park at the Top of the World: Mount Everest National Park. By Rick Ridgeway. Photos by Nicholas deVore III. 704-725, *June 1982*

Along the Great Divide. By Mike Edwards. Photos by Nicholas deVore III. 483-515, *Oct. 1979*

A Walk Across America: Part II. By Peter and Barbara Jenkins. 194-229, *Aug. 1979*

New Mount McKinley Challenge–Trekking Around the Continent's Highest Peak. By Ned Gillette. 66-79, *July 1979*

Travels With a Donkey–100 Years Later. By Carolyn Bennett Patterson.

First to conquer Everest, Edmund Hillary, left, and Tenzing Norgay pause shortly before their final assault on May 29, 1953. ALFRED GREGORY, © RGS AND ALPINE CLUB

HILDEBRAND, JESSE RICHARDSON:

HILDENBRAND, HANS:

Photographer

Tyrol, the Happy Mountain Land. 371-378, *Mar. 1932*

Dinkelsbühl, Romantic Vision from the Past. 693-700, *Dec. 1931*

Grimm's Fairyland in Northwestern Germany. 641-648, *May 1931*

Color Brightens Rustic Life in Jugoslavia. 273-304, *Sept. 1930*

Alpine Villagers of Austria. 669-676, *Dec. 1929*

Wandering Through the Black Forest. 659-666, *Dec. 1928*

From Chalet to Palace in Bavaria. 683-690, *Dec. 1928*

Medieval Pageantry in Modern Nördlingen. 707-714, *Dec. 1928*

Man and Nature Paint Italian Scenes in Prodigal Colors. 443-466, *Apr. 1928*

Medieval Glory Haunts the Eastern Adriatic. 65-80, *Jan. 1928*

Costumes of Czechoslovakia. 725-740, *June 1927*

In the Birthplace of Christianity. 697-720, *Dec. 1926*

The France of Sunshine and Flowers. 481-496, *Oct. 1926*

Under Radiant Italian Skies. 249-256, *Aug. 1926*

The Beauty of the Bavarian Alps. 633-648, *June 1926*

Rothenburg, the City Time Forgot. 185-192, *Feb. 1926*

HILDER, FRANK FREDERICK:

Frank Frederick Hilder (Biography). By W J McGee. 85-86, *Feb. 1901*

Author

Gold in the Philippines. 465-470, *Dec. 1900*

British South Africa and the Transvaal. 81-96, *Mar. 1900*

The Philippine Islands. 257-284, *June 1898*

HILGARD, E. W.: *Author*

Geographic Nomenclature. 36-37, *Jan. 1900*

A Hindu rolls through a Nepalese town near Kathmandu to gain merit during Svasthani Vrata festival. WILLIAM THOMPSON

HILGER, MARY INEZ:

Nomination Page. *Sept. 1966*

Author

Japan's "Sky People," the Vanishing Ainu. Photos by Eiji Miyazawa. 268-296, *Feb. 1967*

HILL, DAVID JAYNE: *Author*

Republics–The Ladder to Liberty. 240-254, *Mar. 1917*

The Original Territory of the United States. 73-92, *Mar. 1899*

HILL, EBENEZER J.: *Author*

A Trip Through Siberia. 37-54, *Feb. 1902*

HILL, ROBERT T.:

Volcanic Rocks of Martinique and St. Vincent: Collected by Robert T. Hill and Israel C. Russell. By J. S. Diller. 285-296, *July 1902*

The National Geographic Society Expedition to Martinique and St. Vincent. Included: Portrait of Hill. 183-184, *June 1902*

The National Geographic Society Expedition in the West Indies. 209-213, *June 1902*

Author

Report by Robert T. Hill on the Volcanic Disturbances in the West Indies. 223-267, *July 1902*

Porto Rico or Puerto Rico? 516-517, *Dec. 1899*

Porto Rico. 93-112, *Mar. 1899*

Geographic Literature. 518-519, *Dec. 1898*

Cuba. 193-242, *May 1898*

Descriptive Topographic Terms of Spanish America. 291-302, *Sept. 1896*

Fundamental Geographic Relation of the Three Americas. 175-181, *May 1896*

The Panama Canal Route. 59-64, *Feb. 1896*

HILLARD, DARLA:

Author-Photographer

Tracking the Elusive Snow Leopard. By Rodney Jackson and Darla Hillard. NGS research grant. 793-809, *June 1986*

HILLARY, SIR EDMUND:

Recipient of the National Geographic Society Centennial Award. President's Page. By Gilbert M. Grosvenor. *Dec. 1988*

The Crossing of Antarctica. By Sir Vivian Fuchs. Photos by George Lowe. 25-47, *Jan. 1959*

Triumph on Everest. 1-63, *July 1954*

President Eisenhower Presents the Hubbard Medal to Everest's Conquerors. 64, *July 1954*

Author

Preserving a Mountain Heritage: Contents: Mount Everest National Park. 696-703, *June 1982*

We Build a School for Sherpa Children. 548-551, *Oct. 1962*

Beyond Everest. 579-610, *Nov. 1955*

The Conquest of the Summit. 45-63, *July 1954*

HILLEBRAND, W. F.: *Author*

Chemical Discussion of Analyses of Volcanic Ejecta from Martinique and St. Vincent. 296-299, *July 1902*

The **HILLS** and Dales of Erin. Photos by Clifton Adams. 317-326, *Mar. 1927*

HILO, Hawaii:

Hawaii, Island of Fire and Flowers. By Gordon Young. Photos by Robert W. Madden. 399-425, *Mar. 1975*

HILTON HEAD (Island), South Carolina:

Sea Islands: Adventuring Along the South's Surprising Coast. By James Cerruti. Photos by Thomas Nebbia and James L. Amos. 366-393, *Mar. 1971*

HIMALAYA, Asia:

Exploring Cradle Earth. By Wilbur E. Garrett. 612, *Nov. 1988*

Roof of the World. Photos by William Thompson. 613-623, *Nov. 1988*

The Mighty Himalaya: A Fragile Heritage. By Barry C. Bishop. Photos by William Thompson. 624-631, *Nov. 1988*

Heavy Hands on the Land. By Larry Kohl. Photos by William Thompson and Galen Rowell. 633-651, *Nov. 1988*

Mount Everest: Surveying the Third Pole. By Bradford Washburn. NGS research grant. 653-659, *Nov. 1988*

⊕ *Mount Everest; High Himalaya. Nov. 1988*

Tracking the Elusive Snow Leopard. By Rodney Jackson and Darla Hillard. NGS research grant. 793-809, *June 1986*

Triumph and Tragedy on Annapurna. By Arlene Blum. Included: On the Summit. By Irene Miller, with Vera Komarkova. 295-313, *Mar. 1979*

Wintering on the Roof of the World. By Barry C. Bishop. Included: Death

Threatens Man in the Thin Air. NGS research grant. 503-547, *Oct. 1962*

A New Look at Everest. By Dag Hammarskjöld. 87-93, *Jan. 1961*

Himalayan Pilgrimage. By Christopher Rand. 520-535, *Oct. 1956*

Beyond Everest. By Sir Edmund Hillary. 579-610, *Nov. 1955*

High Adventure in the Himalayas. By Thomas Weir. 193-234, *Aug. 1952*

Caught in the Assam-Tibet Earthquake. By F. Kingdon-Ward. 403-416, *Mar. 1952*

A Woman Paints the Tibetans. By Lafugie. 659-692, *May 1949*

The Aërial Conquest of Everest: Flying Over the World's Highest Mountain Realizes the Objective of Many Heroic Explorers. By L.V.S. Blacker. 127-162, *Aug. 1933*

First Over the Roof of the World by Motor: The Trans-Asiatic Expedition Sets New Records for Wheeled Transport in Scaling Passes of the Himalayas. By Maynard Owen Williams. 321-363, *Mar. 1932*

A Pilgrimage to Amernath, Himalayan Shrine of the Hindu Faith. By Louise Ahl Jessop. 513-542, *Nov. 1921*

Nepal: A Little-Known Kingdom. By John Claude White. 245-283, *Oct. 1920*

Castles in the Air: Experiences and Journeys in Unknown Bhutan. By John Claude White. 365-455, *Apr. 1914*

Duke of the Abruzzi in the Himalayas. By A. W. Greely. 245-249, *Mar. 1910*

The World's Highest Altitudes and First Ascents. By Charles E. Fay. 493-530, *June 1909*

The Highest Camp in the World. 647-648, *Nov. 1906*

Record Ascents in the Himalayas. 420-421, *Nov. 1903*

Among the Great Himalayan Glaciers. 405-406, *Nov. 1902*

See also Bhutan; Everest, Mount; Kashmir; Ladakh; Mustang; Nepal; Sikkim; Tibet

HIMBA TRIBESPEOPLE:

Namibia: Nearly a Nation? By Bryan Hodgson. Photos by Jim Brandenburg. 755-797, *June 1982*

HIMIS MONASTERY, Ladakh District, India:

A Journey to "Little Tibet." By Enakshi Bhavnani. Photos by Volkmar Wentzel. 603-634, *May 1951*

A Woman Paints the Tibetans. By Lafugie. 659-692, *May 1949*

HINDUISM:

At the Crossroads of Kathmandu. By Douglas H. Chadwick. Photos by William Thompson. 32-65, *July 1987*

Banaras: India's City of Light. By Santha Rama Rau. Photos by Tony Heiderer. 214-251, *Feb. 1986*

The Temples of Angkor. 548-589. I. Will They Survive? Introduction by Wilbur E. Garrett. 548-551; II. Ancient Glory in Stone. By Peter T. White. Photos by Wilbur E. Garrett. 552-589, *May 1982*

Bombay, the Other India. By John Scofield. Photos by Raghubir Singh. 104-129, *July 1981*

Kathmandu's Remarkable Newars. By John Scofield. 269-285, *Feb. 1979*

Purdah in India: Life Behind the Veil. By Doranne Wilson Jacobson. Included: Hindu purdah of Nimkhera, India. 270-286, *Aug. 1977*

Bangladesh: Hope Nourishes a New Nation. By William S. Ellis. Photos by Dick Durrance II. 295-333, *Sept. 1972*

Karnali, Roadless World of Western Nepal. By Lila M. and Barry C.

Bishop. NGS research grant. 656-689, *Nov. 1971*

The Ganges, River of Faith. By John J. Putman. Photos by Raghubir Singh. 445-483, *Oct. 1971*

The Lands and Peoples of Southeast Asia. 295-365, *Mar. 1971*

Orissa, Past and Promise in an Indian State. By Bart McDowell. Photos by James P. Blair. 546-577, *Oct. 1970*

The Cobra, India's "Good Snake." By Harry Miller. 393-409, *Sept. 1970*

Royal Wedding at Jaisalmer. By Marilyn Silverstone. 66-79, *Jan. 1965*

India in Crisis. By John Scofield. 599-661, *May 1963*

From the Hair of Siva. By Helen and Frank Schreider. 445-503, *Oct. 1960*

Himalayan Pilgrimage. By Christopher Rand. 520-535, *Oct. 1956*

India's Sculptured Temple Caves. By Volkmar Wentzel. 665-678, *May 1953*

The Idyllic Vale of Kashmir. By Volkmar Wentzel. 523-550, *Apr. 1948*

Delhi, Capital of a New Dominion. By Phillips Talbot. 597-630, *Nov. 1947*

India Mosaic. By Peter Muir and Frances Muir. 443-470, *Apr. 1946*

Yank Meets Native. By Wanda Burnett. 105-128, *July 1945*

India–Yesterday, Today, and Tomorrow. By Lord Halifax. 385-408, *Oct. 1943*

The Fire-Walking Hindus of Singapore. By L. Elizabeth Lewis. 513-522, *Apr. 1931*

A Pilgrimage to Amernath, Himalayan Shrine of the Hindu Faith. By Louise Ahl Jessop. 513-542, *Nov. 1921*

Religious Penances and Punishments Self-Inflicted by the Holy Men of India. By W. M. Zumbro. 1257-1314, *Dec. 1913*

The Marriage of the Gods. By John J. Banninga. Contents: Festival at Madura, India. 1314-1330, *Dec. 1913*

The Bathing and Burning Ghats at Benares. By Eliza R. Scidmore. 118-128, *Feb. 1907*

See also Bali, for Hindu-animist beliefs

HINDUSTAN (Region), Asia:

Through the Heart of Hindustan: A Teeming Highway Extending for Fifteen Hundred Miles, from the Khyber Pass to Calcutta. By Maynard Owen Williams. 443-467, *Nov. 1921*

See also India; Pakistan

HINE, JAMES S.:

The Valley of Ten Thousand Smokes: An Account of the Discovery and Exploration of the Most Wonderful Volcanic Region in the World. By Robert F. Griggs. Note: James S. Hine, zoologist of the Katmai Expedition. 115-169, *Feb. 1918*

HINGSTON, R.W.G.:

Author-Photographer

A New World to Explore: In the Tree-Roof of the British Guiana Forest Flourishes Much Hitherto-Unknown Life. 617-642, *Nov. 1932*

HIOKI, EKI: *Author*

Japan, America, and the Orient. 498-504, *Sept. 1906*

Like great sculptured boulders, hippopotamuses share a mud wallow in South Africa's 7,770-square-mile Kruger National Park. EMIL SCHULTHESS, BLACK STAR

The Purpose of the Anglo-Japanese Alliance. 333-337, *July 1905*
A Chapter from Japanese History. 220-228, *May 1905*

HIPPOPOTAMUSES:
Mzima, Kenya's Spring of Life. Photos by Joan and Alan Root. 350-373, *Sept. 1971*
When a Drought Blights Africa: Hippos and Elephants Are Driven Insane by Suffering, in the Lorian Swamp, Kenya Colony. By A. T. Curle. 521-528, *Apr. 1929*

HIROHITO, Emperor (Japan):
Behind the Mask of Modern Japan. By Willard Price. 513-535, *Nov. 1945*

HISER, DAVID:
On Assignment in Mexico. *Oct. 1985*
On Assignment in Canada. *Mar. 1982*

Photographer
In the Far Pacific: At the Birth of Nations. By Carolyn Bennett Patterson. Photos by David Hiser and Melinda Berge. 460-499, *Oct. 1986*
The Usumacinta River: Troubles on a Wild Frontier. By S. Jeffrey K. Wilkerson. 514-543, *Oct. 1985*
Pitcairn and Norfolk–The Saga of *Bounty*'s Children. By Ed Howard. Photos by David Hiser and Melinda Berge. 510-541, *Oct. 1983*
A Walk and Ride on the Wild Side: Tasmania. By Carolyn Bennett Patterson. Photos by David Hiser and Melinda Berge. 676-693, *May 1983*
Henry Hudson's Changing Bay. By Bill Richards. 380-405, *Mar. 1982*
The Aztecs. By Bart McDowell. Paintings by Felipe Dávalos. 714-751, *Dec. 1980*
New Finds in the Great Temple. By Eduardo Matos Moctezuma. 767-775, *Dec. 1980*
Man's Eighty Centuries in Veracruz. By S. Jeffrey K. Wilkerson. Paintings by Richard Schlecht. 203-231, *Aug. 1980*
Mexican Folk Art. By Fernando Horcasitas. 648-669, *May 1978*
A Way of Life Called Maine. By Ethel A. Starbird. 727-757, *June 1977*
The Tarahumaras: Mexico's Long Distance Runners. By James Norman. 702-718, *May 1976*
A Canoe Helps Hawaii Recapture Her Past. By Herb Kawainui Kane. 468-489, *Apr. 1976*
San Antonio: "Texas, Actin' Kind of Natural." By Fred Kline. 524-549, *Apr. 1976*
The "Lone" Coyote Likes Family Life. By Hope Ryden. Photos by author and David Hiser. 278-294, *Aug. 1974*
Golden Ghosts of the Lost Sierra. By Robert Laxalt. 332-353, *Sept. 1973*
Stalking the West's Wild Foods. By Euell Gibbons. 186-199, *Aug. 1973*
Stalking Wild Foods on a Desert Isle. By Euell Gibbons. 47-63, *July 1972*
That Dammed Missouri River. By Gordon Young. 374-413, *Sept. 1971*
Mexico to Canada on the Pacific Crest Trail. By Mike W. Edwards. 741-779, *June 1971*

An adult and baby hippopotamus adorn a sandstone wall at Tassili-n-Ajjer in Algeria. Such rock art may date from 5000 B.C., when the Sahara was green. KAZUYOSHI NOMACHI

Death Valley, the Land and the Legend. By Rowe Findley. 69-103, *Jan. 1970*

HISPANIC CULTURE:
Editorial. By Wilbur E. Garrett. 141, *Feb. 1986*

HISPANIOLA (Island), West Indies:
Christopher Columbus and the New World He Found. By John Scofield. Photos by Adam Woolfitt. 584-625, *Nov. 1975*
Hispaniola Rediscovered. By Jacob Gayer. 80-112, *Jan. 1931*
See also Dominican Republic; Haiti

HISS, PHILIP HANSON: *Photographer*
Surinam Subjects of Queen Wilhelmina. 465-472, *Apr. 1943*
Curaçao and Aruba, Oil Isles of the Caribbean. Photos by Philip Hanson Hiss and Robert Yarnall Richie. 175-182, *Feb. 1943*

The **HISTORIC** City of Brotherly Love: Philadelphia, Born of Penn and Strengthened by Franklin, a Metropolis of Industries, Homes, and Parks. By John Oliver La Gorce. 643-697, *Dec. 1932*

HISTORIC Color Portrait of Earth From Space. By Kenneth F. Weaver. Photos by DODGE Satellite. 726-731, *Nov. 1967*

HISTORIC Danzig: Last of the City-States. By William and Alicelia Franklin. 677-696, *Nov. 1939*

HISTORIC Islands and Shores of the Aegean Sea. By Ernest Lloyd Harris. 231-261, *Sept. 1915*

HISTORICAL *Atlas of the United States.* 289 pages. *1988*

The **HISTORICAL** Development of the National Capital. By Marcus Baker. 323-329, *July 1898*

HISTORY, African:
Oasis of Art in the Sahara. By Henri Lhote. Photos by Kazuyoshi Nomachi. Contents: Rock paintings of Tassili-n-Ajjer, Algeria. 180-191, *Aug. 1987*
Into the Unknown: The Story of Exploration. 336 pages. *1987*
Editorial. By Wilbur E. Garrett. European colonial history of equatorial Africa. 559, *May 1986*
Finding West Africa's Oldest City. By Susan and Roderick McIntosh. Photos by Michael and Aubine Kirtley. Contents: Jenne-jeno (site), Mali. 396-418, *Sept. 1982*
Two Centuries of Conflict in the Middle East; Mideast in Turmoil. Included: Egypt, Ethiopia, Libya, Somalia, and Sudan; Islam's spread to northern Africa. *Sept. 1980*
Africa; Africa, Its Political Development. Feb. 1980
The Niger: River of Sorrow, River of Hope. By Georg Gerster. 152-189, *Aug. 1975*
The Sword and the Sermon (Islam). By Thomas J. Abercrombie. 3-45, *July 1972*
The Peoples of Africa; The Heritage of Africa. Dec. 1971
Freedom Speaks French in Ouagadougou. By John Scofield. Contents: Cameroon; Chad; Dahomey; Gambia; Guinea; Ivory Coast; Mali; Mauritania; Niger; Senegal; Togo; Upper Volta. 153-203, *Aug. 1966*
Africa's Bushman Art Treasures. By Alfred Friendly. Photos by Alex R. Willcox. 848-865, *June 1963*
Freedom's Progress South of the Sahara. By Howard La Fay. Photos by Joseph J. Scherschel. Contents: Burundi; Congo, Democratic Republic of the; Congo, People's Republic of the; Kenya; Mozambique;

HISTORY, Ancient:

HISTORY, Asian:

Family stalled near Lordsburg, New Mexico, in 1937 joined half a million Americans fleeing the Dust Bowl for work in the West. DOROTHEA LANGE, LIBRARY OF CONGRESS COLLECTION

HISTORY, European:

by Gordon W. Gahan. 142-189, *Feb. 1982*

Ancient Europe Is Older Than We Thought. By Colin Renfrew. Photos by Adam Woolfitt. 615-623, *Nov. 1977*

Geographic Progress of Civilization. Annual Address by the President, Gardiner G. Hubbard. 1-22, *Feb. 14, 1894*

The Evolution of Commerce. Annual Address by the President, Gardiner G. Hubbard (Jan. 15, 1892). 1-18, *Mar. 26, 1892*

See also Celts; History, Ancient; Medieval Europe; The Renaissance

HISTORY, Medieval. *See* Byzantine Empire; Medieval Europe

HISTORY, United States:

"Tell me if your civilization is interesting": Those Electrifying Eighteen Eighties When the National Geographic Society Was Born. By William H. Goetzmann. Illustrated by Fred Otnes. 8-37, *Jan. 1988*

■■ *Historical Atlas of the United States.* 289 pages. *1988*

James Madison, Architect of the Constitution. By Alice J. Hall. Photos by Sam Abell. 340-369, *Sept. 1987*

✦ *The United States; The Territorial Growth of the United States.* Included: Europe Claims North America, A New Nation on Stage, Expanding West of the Mississippi, Coming of Age, Coast To Coast, The Union Holds, The Fifty States Today, 1987; A Broader View. *Sept. 1987*

George Washington's Patowmack Canal. By Wilbur E. Garrett. Photos by Kenneth Garrett. 716-753, *June 1987*

Ghosts on the Little Bighorn. By Robert Paul Jordan. Photos by Scott Rutherford. 787-813, *Dec. 1986*

Life and Death on the Oregon Trail: The Itch to Move West. By Boyd Gibbons. Photos by James L. Amos. 147-177, *Aug. 1986*

Liberty Lifts Her Lamp Once More. By Alice J. Hall. 2-19, *July 1986*

Japanese Americans: Home at Last. By Arthur Zich. Photos by Michael S. Yamashita. 512-539, *Apr. 1986*

Sam Houston: A Man Too Big for Texas. By Bart McDowell. Photos by Charles O'Rear. Included: The Battle of San Jacinto. 311-329, *Mar. 1986*

C. M. Russell, Cowboy Artist. By Bart McDowell. Photos by Sam Abell. 60-95, *Jan. 1986*

Daniel Boone, First Hero of the Frontier. By Elizabeth A. Moize. Photos by William Strode. 812-841, *Dec. 1985*

A Journey Down Old U. S. 1. By Bruce Dale. 790-817, *Dec. 1984*

The Okies–Beyond the Dust Bowl. By William Howarth. Photos by Chris Johns. 322-349, *Sept. 1984*

The Underground Railroad. By Charles L. Blockson. Photos by Louie Psihoyos. 3-39, *July 1984*

■■ *The Story of America: A National Geographic Picture Atlas.* By John

Anthony Scott. Juvenile. 324 pages. *1984*

Buffalo Bill and the Enduring West. By Alice J. Hall. Photos by James L. Amos. 76-103, *July 1981*

Thoreau, a Different Man. By William Howarth. Photos by Farrell Grehan. 349-387, *Mar. 1981*

■■ *We Americans.* 456 pages. 1975; rev. ed. *1981*

The Pony Express. By Rowe Findley. Photos by Craig Aurness. 45-71, *July 1980*

■■ *Trails West.* 207 pages. *1979*

■■ *Into the Wilderness.* Photos by Lowell Georgia. Art by H. Tom Hall. Contents: Seven famous historic explorations and trails. 207 pages. *1978*

Chief Joseph. By William Albert Allard. 409-434, *Mar. 1977*

■■ *Railroads: The Great American Adventure.* By Charlton Ogburn. Photos by James A. Sugar. 203 pages. *1977*

■■ *Visiting Our Past: America's Historylands.* Included: Companion directory *Visiting Our Past: A Supplemental Guide to Selected Sites.* 400 pages. *1977*

Riding the Outlaw Trail. By Robert Redford. Photos by Jonathan Blair. 622-657, *Nov. 1976*

■■ *Clues to America's Past.* Contents: Examination of significant archaeological projects. 199 pages. *1976*

The Virginians. By Mike W. Edwards. Photos by David Alan Harvey. 588-617, *Nov. 1974*

■■ *The Wild Shores: America's Beginnings.* By Tee Loftin Snell. Photos by Walter Meayers Edwards. Art by Louis S. Glanzman. 203 pages. *1974*

North Through History Aboard *White Mist.* By Melville Bell Grosvenor. Photos by Edwin Stuart Grosvenor. 1-55, *July 1970*

■■ *In the Footsteps of Lewis and Clark.* By Gerald S. Snyder. Photos by Dick Durrance II. Paintings by Richard Schlecht. 215 pages. *1970*

■■ *The Civil War.* By Robert Paul Jordan. 215 pages. *1969*

Today Along the Natchez Trace, Pathway Through History. By Bern Keating. Photos by Charles Harbutt. 641-667, *Nov. 1968*

■■ *America's Historylands, Touring Our Landmarks of Liberty.* Companion volume to *America's Wonderlands.* 575 pages. 1962; rev. ed. *1967*

So Long, St. Louis, We're Heading West. By William C. Everhart. 643-669, *Nov. 1965*

Early America Through the Eyes of Her Native Artists. By Hereward Lester Cooke, Jr. 356-389, *Sept. 1962*

From Sea to Shining Sea: A Cross Section of the United States Along Historic Route 40. By Ralph Gray. Photos by Dean Conger and author. 1-61, *July 1961*

New Stars for Old Glory. By Lonnelle Aikman. 86-121, *July 1959*

Following the Trail of Lewis and Clark. By Ralph Gray. 707-750, *June 1953*

Eight Maps of Discovery. 757-769, *June 1953*

✦ *Historical Map of the United States.* *June 1953*

American Processional: History on Canvas. By John and Blanche Leeper. 173-212, *Feb. 1951*

Shrines of Each Patriot's Devotion. By Frederick G. Vosburgh. 51-82, *Jan. 1949*

The Growth of the United States. By W J McGee. 377-386, *Sept. 1898*

The Historical Development of the National Capital. By Marcus Baker. 323-329, *July 1898*

The Evolution of Commerce. Annual Address by the President, Gardiner G. Hubbard (Jan. 15, 1892). 1-18, *Mar. 26, 1892*

See also The Americas; Bicentennial, U. S.; Colonial America; *and* American Revolution; Civil War, U. S.; Frontier; Korean War; The Making of America Map Series; Presidents of the United States; Vietnam War; War of 1812; World War II; *also* U. S. Capitol; White House; *and* the states; *and* historical cities and sites, *as* Boston; Deerfield; Harpers Ferry; Jamestown; Mystic Seaport; Natchez; Philadelphia, Pennsylvania; Roanoke Island; St. Augustine; Washington, D. C.; Williamsburg, Virginia

HISTORY and Beauty Blend in a Concord Iris Garden. By Robert T. Cochran, Jr. Photos by M. Woodbridge Williams. 705-719, *May 1959*

The **HISTORY** and Geographic Distribution of Bubonic Plague. By George M. Sternberg. 97-113, *Mar. 1900*

HISTORY Awakens at Harpers Ferry. By Volkmar Wentzel. 399-416, *Mar. 1957*

HISTORY Keeps House in Virginia. By Howell Walker. 441-484, *Apr. 1956*

HISTORY Repeats in Old Natchez. By William H. Nicholas. Photos by Willard R. Culver. 181-208, *Feb. 1949*

HISTORY Revealed in Ancient Glass. By Ray Winfield Smith. Photos by B. Anthony Stewart and Lee E. Battaglia. 346-369, *Sept. 1964*

HISTORY Written in the Skies (U. S. Air Force). 273-294, *Aug. 1957*

HISTORY'S Greatest Trek: Tragedy Stalks Through the Near East as Greece and Turkey Exchange Two Million of Their People. By Melville Chater. 535-590, *Nov. 1925*

HITCHCOCK, A. S.: *Author*

Controlling Sand Dunes in the United States and Europe. 43-47, *Jan. 1904*

HITCHCOCK, STEPHEN W.: *Author*

Can We Save Our Salt Marshes? Photos by William R. Curtsinger. 729-765, *June 1972*

HITTITES:

A Sketch of the Geographical History of Asia Minor. By Sir William Ramsay. 553-570, *Nov. 1922*

Syria: The Land Link of History's

Chain. By Maynard Owen Williams. 437-462, *Nov. 1919*

An Ancient Capital (Boghaz Keoy, Turkey). By Isabel F. Dodd. 111-124, *Feb. 1910*

HLUHLUWE GAME RESERVE, South Africa:

Safari Through Changing Africa. By Elsie May Bell Grosvenor. Photos by Gilbert Grosvenor. 145-198, *Aug. 1953*

Roaming Africa's Unfenced Zoos. By W. Robert Moore. 353-380, *Mar. 1950*

HMONG:

The Hmong in America: Laotian Refugees in the "Land of the Giants." By Spencer Sherman. Photos by Dick Swanson. 586-610, *Oct. 1988*

Laos Today. By Peter T. White. Photos by Seny Norasingh. 772-795, *June 1987*

The Hmong of Laos: No Place to Run. By W. E. Garrett. 78-111, *Jan. 1974*

HMONG REFUGEES:

The Hmong in America: Laotian Refugees in the "Land of the Giants." By Spencer Sherman. Photos by Dick Swanson. 586-610, *Oct. 1988*

Thailand: Refuge From Terror. By W. E. Garrett. 633-642, *May 1980*

One Family's Odyssey to America. By John Everingham. 642-661, *May 1980*

The Hmong of Laos: No Place to Run. By W. E. Garrett. 78-111, *Jan. 1974*

HO CHI MINH CITY, Vietnam. *See* former name, Saigon

HO for the Soochow Ho (China). By Mabel Craft Deering. 623-649, *June 1927*

HOABINHIAN CULTURE:

New Light on a Forgotten Past. By Wilhelm G. Solheim II. 330-339, *Mar. 1971*

The **HOARY** Monasteries of Mt. Athos. By H. G. Dwight. 249-272, *Sept. 1916*

HOATZIN:

Strange Little World of the Hoatzin. By J. Lear Grimmer. Photos by M. Woodbridge Williams. NGS research grant. 391-401, *Sept. 1962*

HOBART, ALICE TISDALE: *Author*

How Half the World Works. By Alice Tisdale Hobart and Mary A. Nourse. 509-524, *Apr. 1932*

HOBART, Tasmania, Australia:

Capital Cities of Australia. By W. Robert Moore. 667-722, *Dec. 1935*

HOCHDORF, West Germany:

Treasure From a Celtic Tomb. By Jörg Biel. Photos by Volkmar Wentzel. 428-438, *Mar. 1980*

HODEIDA, North Yemen:

Arabia, the Desert of the Sea. By Archibald Forder. 1039-1062, 1117, *Dec. 1909*

HODGE, F. W.: *Author*

The Enchanted Mesa (New Mexico). 273-284, *Oct. 1897*

HODGE, JOHN R.: *Author*

With the U. S. Army in Korea. 829-840, *June 1947*

HODGE, W. H.: *Author*

Camels of the Clouds (Lamoids). 641-656, *May 1946*

HODGSON, BRYAN:

On Assignment in Namibia. *June 1982* Nomination Page. *Oct. 1976*

Author

The Falkland Islands–Life After the War. Photos by Steve Raymer. 390-411, *Mar. 1988*

North Dakota–Tough Times on the Prairie. Photos by Annie Griffiths. 320-347, *Mar. 1987*

Argentina's New Beginning. Photos by James P. Blair. 226-255, *Aug. 1986*

New Delhi: Mirror of India. Photos by Steve Raymer. 506-533, *Apr. 1985*

Time and Again in Burma. Photos by James L. Stanfield. 90-121, *July 1984*

Wales, the Lyric Land. Photos by Farrell Grehan. 36-63, *July 1983*

Namibia: Nearly a Nation? Photos by Jim Brandenburg. 755-797, *June 1982*

War and Peace in Northern Ireland. Photos by Cary Wolinsky. 470-499, *Apr. 1981*

Singapore: Mini-size Superstate. Photos by Dean Conger. 540-561, *Apr. 1981*

Natural Gas: The Search Goes On. Photos by Lowell Georgia. 632-651, *Nov. 1978*

Montenegro: Yugoslavia's "Black Mountain." Photos by Linda Bartlett. 663-683, *Nov. 1977*

The Pipeline: Alaska's Troubled Colossus. Photos by Steve Raymer. 684-717, *Nov. 1976*

Irish Ways Live On in Dingle. Photos by Linda Bartlett. 551-576, *Apr. 1976*

Exploring England's Canals. Photos by Linda Bartlett. 76-111, *July 1974*

Mountain Voices, Mountain Days. Photos by Linda Bartlett. 118-146, *July 1972*

HOFFMANN, D. O. NOBLE: *Author*

The Philippine Exhibit at the Pan-American Exposition. 119-122, *Mar. 1901*

HOFFMEISTER, J. EDWARD: *Author*

Falcon, the Pacific's Newest Island. By J. Edward Hoffmeister and Harry S. Ladd. 757-766, *Dec. 1928*

HOG ISLAND, Pennsylvania:

Ships for the Seven Seas: The Story of America's Maritime Needs, Her Capabilities and Her Achievements. By Ralph A. Graves. 165-200, *Sept. 1918*

HOG RAISING:

The Joy of Pigs. By Kent Britt. Photos by George F. Mobley. 398-415, *Sept. 1978*

The Family Farm Ain't What It Used To Be. By James A. Sugar. 391-411, *Sept. 1974*

The Diffident Truffle, France's Gift to Gourmets. Included: Truffle-hunting sows. 419-426, *Sept. 1956*

America's "Meat on the Hoof." By William H. Nicholas. 33-72, *Jan. 1952*

HÖGAKULL (Farm), Sweden:

Life's Flavor on a Swedish Farm: From the Rocky Hills of Småland Thousands of Sturdy Citizens Have Emigrated to the United States. By Willis Lindquist. 393-414, *Sept. 1939*

HOGARTH, WILLIAM:

The British Way. By Sir Evelyn Wrench. 421-541, *Apr. 1949*

HOGBIN, H. IAN:
Author-Photographer

Coconuts and Coral Islands (Ontong Java). 265-298, *Mar. 1934*

Hmong refugee Bee Kha stiches an appliqué quilt in her new Pennsylvania home. The Hmong were Laotian allies of the U. S. during the Vietnam War. DICK SWANSON

Tomeyo Oba braves February's snows on Hokkaido, northernmost of Japan's major islands. MICHAEL S. YAMASHITA

HOHLFELDER, ROBERT L.: *Author*

Caesarea Maritima. Photos by Bill Curtsinger. Paintings by J. Robert Teringo. NGS research grant. 261-279, *Feb. 1987*

HOHOKAM CULTURE:

Pueblo Pottery–2,000 Years of Artistry. By David L. Arnold. 593-605, *Nov. 1982*
The Hohokam: First Masters of the American Desert. By Emil W. Haury. Photos by Helga Teiwes. 670-695, *May 1967*
Magnetic Clues Help Date the Past. By Kenneth F. Weaver. 696-701, *May 1967*

HOKKAIDO (Island), Japan:

The Japanese Crane, Bird of Happiness. By Tsuneo Hayashida. 542-556, *Oct. 1983*
Hokkaido, Japan's Last Frontier. By Douglas Lee. Photos by Michael S. Yamashita. 62-93, *Jan. 1980*
Snow Festival in Japan's Far North. By Eiji Miyazawa. 824-833, *Dec. 1968*
Japan's "Sky People," the Vanishing Ainu. By Mary Inez Hilger. Photos by Eiji Miyazawa. 268-296, *Feb. 1967*

HOKULE'A (Voyaging Canoe):

■ Voyage of the *Hokule'a.* 575, *Nov. 1976*
Hokule'a Follows the Stars to Tahiti. By David Lewis. Photos by Nicholas deVore III. 512-537, *Oct. 1976*
A Canoe Helps Hawaii Recapture Her Past. By Herb Kawainui Kane. Photos by David Hiser. 468-489, *Apr. 1976*

HOLDEN, ANTHONY: *Author*

Windsor Castle. Photos by James L. Stanfield. 604-631, *Nov. 1980*

HOLDER, CHARLES FREDERICK: *Author*

The Glass-Bottom Boat. 761-778, *Sept. 1909*
Big Things of the West. 279-282, *July 1903*
A Remarkable Salt Deposit. 391-392, *Nov. 1901*

HOLDING, FLORENCE POLK: *Author*

The Salzkammergut, a Playground of Austria. 445-485, *Apr. 1937*

HOLDRIDGE, DESMOND: *Photographer*

Cowboys and Caymans of Marajó (Brazil). 645-652, *Nov. 1938*

HOLGUÍN, NENA: *Photographer*

At My Limit–I Climbed Everest Alone. By Reinhold Messner. Photos by the author and Nena Holguín. 552-566, *Oct. 1981*

HOLIDAYS. *See* Christmas; Easter; Holy Week; Memorial Day Ceremonies; New Year Celebrations; *and* Festivals

HOLIDAYS Among the Hill Towns of Umbria and Tuscany. By Paul Wilstach. 401-442, *Apr. 1928*

HOLIDAYS with Humming Birds. By Margaret L. Bodine. 731-742, *June 1928*

HOLLAND, JAMES R.: *Photographer*

Tracking Danger With the Ice Patrol. By William S. Ellis. 780-793, *June 1968*

HOLLAND. *See* The Netherlands

HOLLAND, Michigan:

Work-hard, Play-hard Michigan. By Andrew H. Brown. 279-320, *Mar. 1952*

HOLLAND in the Caribbean: The Netherlands Antilles. By James Cerruti. Photos by Emory Kristof. 115-146, *Jan. 1970*

HOLLAND Rises from War and Water. By Thomas R. Henry. 237-260, *Feb. 1946*

HOLLAND'S Beautiful Business: Tulips. By Elizabeth A. Moize. Photos by Farrell Grehan. 712-728, *May 1978*

HOLLAND'S War with the Sea. By James Howard Gore. 283-325, *Mar. 1923*

HÖLLDOBLER, BERT: *Author*

Ways of the Ant. Paintings by John D. Dawson. Illustrations text by Alice J. Hall. NGS research grant. 779-813, *June 1984*

HOLLIDAY, CARL: *Author*

Our Friends, the French: An Appraisal of the Traits and Temperament of the Citizens of Our Sister Republic. 345-377, *Nov. 1918*

HOLLIDAY, CLYDE T.: *Author*

Seeing the Earth From 80 Miles Up. 511-528, *Oct. 1950*

HOLMES, CHARLES H.: *Author*

Australia's Patchwork Creature, the Platypus: Man Succeeds in Making Friends with This Duck-billed, Fur-coated Paradox. 273-282, *Aug. 1939*

HOLMES, HENRIETTA ALLEN: *Author*

The Spell of Romania: An American Woman's Narrative of Her Wanderings Among Colorful People and Long-Hidden Shrines. 399-450, *Apr. 1934*

At an Israeli training camp, Sgt. Osnat Abraham, at right, and Lt. Avi Hrbin relax after a rigorous day. Abraham teaches recruits to fire automatic weapons. JAMES L. STANFIELD, NGS

HOLMES, MIKE:
Author-Photographer

Nauru, the World's Richest Nation. 344-353, *Sept. 1976*

Oil and Penguins Don't Mix. 384-397, *Mar. 1973*

HOLMES, WILLIAM H.:
Awarded Jane M. Smith Life Membership. 342, *Apr. 1920*

The HOLOCAUST:
Remnants: The Last Jews of Poland. By Małgorzata Niezabitowska. Photos by Tomasz Tomaszewski. 362-389, *Sept. 1986*

HOLOCENE EPOCH:
Ice on the World. By Samuel W. Matthews. 79-103, *Jan. 1987*

HOLOGRAM COVERS, NGM:
Crystal globe. *Dec. 1988*
Skull. *Nov. 1985*
Eagle. *Mar. 1984*

HOLOGRAPHY:
Editorial. By Wilbur E. Garrett. *Dec. 1988*

Geographica. *Dec. 1988*

Bruce Dale, making hologram of crystal globe. On Assignment. *Dec. 1988*

Editorial. By Wilbur E. Garrett. 281, *Mar. 1984*

The Wonder of Holography. By H. John Caulfield. Photos by Charles O'Rear. Note: NGM was the first major magazine to feature a hologram on its cover. 364-377, *Mar. 1984*

HOLT, ERNEST G.:
Author-Photographer

A Journey by Jungle Rivers to the Home of the Cock-of-the-rock: Naturalists Enter the Amazon, Voyage Through the Heart of Tropical South America, and Emerge at the Mouth of the Orinoco. 585-630, *Nov. 1933*

In Humboldt's Wake: Narrative of a National Geographic Society Expedition Up the Orinoco and Through the Strange Casiquiare Canal to Amazonian Waters. 621-644, *Nov. 1931*

HOLT, GEORGE EDMUND:
Author-Photographer

The Two Great Moorish Religious Dances. 777-785, *Aug. 1911*

HOLWAY, DONAL F.:
On Assignment in New York City. *May 1983*

Photographer

A Century Old, the Wonderful Brooklyn Bridge. By John G. Morris. 565-579, *May 1983*

HOLY ISLAND (Lindisfarne), England:
Pilgrimage to Holy Island and the Farnes. By John E. H. Nolan. 547-570, *Oct. 1952*

HOLY LAND:
◼ Jerusalem: Within These Walls. President's Page. Jan. 1986; cover, *Mar. 1986*

Israel: Searching for the Center. By Priit J. Vesilind. Photos by James L. Stanfield. 2-39, *July 1985*

Jordan: Kingdom in the Middle. By Thomas J. Abercrombie. Photos by Jodi Cobb. 236-268, *Feb. 1984*

The Living Dead Sea. By Harvey Arden. Photos by Nathan Benn. Included: Biblical history of the Dead Sea region; discovery site of the Dead Sea Scrolls. 225-245, *Feb. 1978*

◼◼ *Everyday Life in Bible Times.* 448 pages. 1967; rev. ed. *1977*

In Search of Moses. By Harvey Arden. Photos by Nathan Benn. 2-37, *Jan. 1976*

Where Jesus Walked. By Howard La Fay. Photos by Charles Harbutt. 739-781, *Dec. 1967*

Eyewitness to War in the Holy Land. By Charles Harbutt. 782-795, *Dec. 1967*

⊕ *Lands of the Bible Today. Dec. 1967*

Abraham, the Friend of God. By Kenneth MacLeish. Photos by Dean Conger. 739-789, *Dec. 1966*

The Land of Galilee. By Kenneth MacLeish. Photos by B. Anthony Stewart. 832-865, *Dec. 1965*

Journey Into the Great Rift. By Helen and Frank Schreider. 254-290, *Aug. 1965*

Israel: Land of Promise. By John Scofield. Photos by B. Anthony Stewart. 395-434, *Mar. 1965*

Holy Land, My Country. By His Majesty King Hussein of Jordan. 784-789, *Dec. 1964*

The Other Side of Jordan. By Luis Marden. 790-825, *Dec. 1964*

Crusader Road to Jerusalem. By Franc Shor. Photos by Thomas Nebbia. 797-855. I. Desert Ordeal of the Knights. 797-837; II. Conquest of the Holy City. 839-855, *Dec. 1963*

⊕ *Holy Land Today,* Atlas series. *Dec. 1963*

◼◼ *Everyday Life in Ancient Times.* Contents: Egypt, Greece, Mesopotamia, and Rome. 368 pages. 1951; rev. ed. *1961*

The Last Thousand Years Before Christ. By G. Ernest Wright. Paintings by H. J. Soulen and Peter V. Bianchi. 812-853, *Dec. 1960*

Geographical Twins a World Apart. By David S. Boyer. Contents: Dead Sea, Sea of Galilee, Jordan River, Qumrān caves compared with counterparts in Utah. 848-859, *Dec. 1958*

Bringing Old Testament Times to Life. By G. Ernest Wright. Paintings by Henry J. Soulen. 833-864, *Dec. 1957*

Jerusalem to Rome in the Path of St. Paul. By David S. Boyer. 707-759, *Dec. 1956*

⊕ *Lands of the Bible Today. Dec. 1956*

Crusader Lands Revisited. By Harold Lamb. Photos by David S. Boyer. Contents: Israel; Jordan; Lebanon; Syria; Turkey. 815-852, *Dec. 1954*

Pilgrims Follow the Christmas Star. By Maynard Owen Williams. 831-840, *Dec. 1952*

Home to the Holy Land. By Maynard Owen Williams. 707-746, *Dec. 1950*

Sinai Sheds New Light on the Bible. By Henry Field. Photos by William B. and Gladys Terry. 795-815, *Dec. 1948*

An Archeologist Looks at Palestine. By Nelson Glueck. 739-752, *Dec. 1947*

⊕ *Bible Lands and the Cradle of Western Civilization.* Insets: Holy Land Today, Holy Land in Biblical Times, Jerusalem, Traditional Route of the Exodus, St. Paul's Travels and the Seven Churches, The Crusaders. *Dec. 1946*

American Fighters Visit Bible Lands. By Maynard Owen Williams. 311-340, *Mar. 1946*

American Alma Maters in the Near East. By Maynard Owen Williams. 237-256, *Aug. 1945*

The Geography of the Jordan. By Nelson Glueck. 719-744, *Dec. 1944*

On the Trail of King Solomon's Mines: The Bible, in Addition to Its Spiritual Values, Continues to Prove a Rich Geography and Guide to Exploration

Stranding travelers in midstream, a mountain torrent washes out a section of the main bridge of Tegucigalpa, capital of Honduras, in 1916.   F. J. YOUNGBLOOD

HOLY ROMAN EMPIRE:

HOLY WEEK:

Braving a cliff in central Nepal, 64-year-old Mani Lal scrapes slabs of honeycomb from the hives of the world's largest honeybee. ERIC VALLI AND DIANE SUMMERS

HOMER:

HOMESTEADING:

HOMINIDS:

Photos by Bob Campbell. Contents: *Homo habilis* skull. NGS research grant. 819-829, *June 1973*

Preserving the Treasures of Olduvai Gorge. By Melvin M. Payne. Photos by Joseph J. Scherschel. Included: *Homo erectus, Homo habilis, Kenyapithecus, Zinjanthropus.* NGS research grant. 701-709, *Nov. 1966*

The Leakeys of Africa: Family in Search of Prehistoric Man. By Melvin M. Payne. Included: *Homo habilis, Kenyapithecus, Proconsul, Zinjanthropus.* NGS research grant. 194-231, *Feb. 1965*

See also Australopithecines

HOMRA, Hamada el (Desert), Libya:

The Mysteries of the Desert. By Hanns Vischer. 1056-1059, *Nov. 1911*

HONDURAS:

Honduras: Eye of the Storm. By Mike Edwards. Photos by David Alan Harvey. 608-637, *Nov. 1983*

Troubled Times for Central America. By Wilbur E. Garrett, Editor. 58-61, *July 1981*

"Pyramids" of the New World. By Neil Merton Judd. Included: Copán. 105-128, *Jan. 1948*

Honduran Highlights. Photos by H. C. Lanks. 360-369, *Mar. 1942*

The Foremost Intellectual Achievement of Ancient America: The Hieroglyphic Inscriptions on the Monuments in the Ruined Cities of Mexico, Guatemala, and Honduras are Yielding the Secrets of the Maya Civilization. By Sylvanus Griswold Morley. 109-130, *Feb. 1922*

A Little Journey in Honduras. By F. J. Youngblood. 177-184, *Aug. 1916*

The Countries of the Caribbean. By William Joseph Showalter. 227-250, *Feb. 1913*

Notes on Central America. 272-279, *Apr. 1907*

HONDURAS, British. *See* British Honduras; *and present name,* Belize

HONEY ANTS:

Ways of the Ant. By Bert Hölldobler. Paintings by John D. Dawson. Illustrations text by Alice J. Hall. NGS research grant. 779-813, *June 1984*

Living Honey Jars of the Ant World. By Ross E. Hutchins. 405-411, *Mar. 1962*

Living Casks of Honey. By Jennie E. Harris. 193-199, *Aug. 1934*

HONEY EATERS of Currumbin (Lorikeets). By Paul A. Zahl. 510-519, *Oct. 1956*

HONEY-GUIDE: The Bird That Eats Wax. By Herbert Friedmann. Paintings by Walter A. Weber. 551-560, *Apr. 1954*

HONEY Hunters of Nepal. By Eric Valli and Diane Summers. 660-671, *Nov. 1988*

HONEYBEES:

Honey Hunters of Nepal. By Eric Valli and Diane Summers. 660-671, *Nov. 1988*

A young Hopi Indian's hair is arranged in the traditional style for unmarried women in this 1925 picture taken in Oraibi, Arizona. O. C. HAVENS

Those Fiery Brazilian Bees. By Rick Gore. Photos by Bianca Lavies. 491-501, *Apr. 1976*

Crossroads of the Insect World. By J. W. MacSwain. Photos by Edward S. Ross. 844-857, *Dec. 1966*

Inside the World of the Honeybee. By Treat Davidson. 188-217, *Aug. 1959*

Man's Winged Ally, the Busy Honeybee: Modern Research Adds a New Chapter to Usefulness of the Insect Which Has Symbolized Industry Since Early Bible Times. By James I. Hambleton. Paintings by Hashime Murayama. 401-428, *Apr. 1935*

HONEYCUTT, BROOKS:
Photographer

Life 8,000 Years Ago Uncovered in an Alabama Cave. By Carl F. Miller. 542-558, *Oct. 1956*

HONG KONG:

Hong Kong's Refugee Dilemma. By William S. Ellis. Photos by William Albert Allard. 709-732, *Nov. 1979*

● Hong Kong: A Family Portrait. 1, Jan. 1979; cover, *Feb. 1979*

Those Outlandish Goldfish! By Paul A. Zahl. 514-533, *Apr. 1973*

Hong Kong, Saturday's Child. By Joseph Judge. Photos by Bruce Dale. 541-573, *Oct. 1971*

YWCA: International Success Story. By Mary French Rockefeller. Photos by Otis Imboden. 904-933, *Dec. 1963*

Round the World School. By Paul Antze. Photos by William Eppridge. 96-127, *July 1962*

Hong Kong Has Many Faces. By John Scofield. 1-41, *Jan. 1962*

Hong Kong Hangs On. By George W. Long. Photos by J. Baylor Roberts. 239-272, *Feb. 1954*

Eyes on the China Coast. By George W. Long. 505-512, *Apr. 1953*

Trawling the China Seas. Photos by J. Charles Thompson. 381-395, *Mar. 1950*

Hong Kong Restored. 483-490, *Apr. 1947*

Today on the China Coast. By John B. Powell 217-238, *Feb. 1945*

1940 Paradox in Hong Kong. By Frederick Simpich. 531-558, *Apr. 1940*

Hong Kong–Britain's Far-flung Outpost in China. 349-360, *Mar. 1938*

See also Pacific Fleet, U. S.

HONOLULU, Oahu (Island), Hawaii:

Which Way Oahu? By Gordon Young. Photos by Robert W. Madden. 653-679, *Nov. 1979*

Look What's Happened to Honolulu! By Jim Becker. Photos by Bates Littlehales. 500-531, *Oct. 1969*

Honolulu, Mid-ocean Capital. By Frederick Simpich, Jr. Photos by B. Anthony Stewart. 577-624, *May 1954*

Because It Rains on Hawaii. By Frederick Simpich, Jr. 571-610, *Nov. 1949*

Life on the Hawaii "Front": All-out Defense and Belt Tightening of Pacific Outpost Foreshadow the Things to Come on Mainland. By Frederick Simpich, Jr. 541-560, *Oct. 1942*

Hawaii, Then and Now: Boyhood Recollections and Recent Observations by an American Whose Grandfather Came to the Islands 102 Years Ago. By William R. Castle. 419-462, *Oct. 1938*

Waves and Thrills at Waikiki. Photos by Thomas Edward Blake. 597-604, *May 1935*

HONORS for Amundsen. 55-76, *Jan. 1908*

HONORS to Amundsen and Peary. 113-130 *Jan. 1913*

HONORS to Colonel Goethals: The Presentation by President Woodrow Wilson, of the National Geographic Society Special Gold Medal and Addresses by Secretary of State Bryan, the French Ambassador, the German Ambassador, and Congressman James R. Mann. 677-690, *June 1914*

HONORS to Peary. 49-60, *Jan. 1907*

HONORS to the American Navy. 77-95, *Jan. 1909*

HONSHU (Island), Japan:

The Japan Alps. By Charles McCarry. Photos by George F. Mobley. 238-259, *Aug. 1984*

Hagi: Where Japan's Revolution Began. By N. Taylor Gregg. Photos by Sam Abell. Paintings by Kinuko Y. Craft. 751-773, *June 1984*

⊕ *Japan; Historical Japan.* Included: Scroll of a Nation, Stone Age and Archaic Japan, Birth of a Central State, Age of the Courtiers, Medieval and Feudal Japan, Modern Japan, Imperialist Japan. *June 1984*

Japan's Izu Oceanic Park. By Eugenie Clark. Photos by David Doubilet. Included: World's Largest Crustacean (Giant Spider Crab). 465-491, *Apr. 1984*

Japan's Amazing Inland Sea. By William S. Ellis. Photos by James L. Stanfield. 830-863, *Dec. 1977*

Kayak Odyssey: From the Inland Sea to Tokyo. By Dan Dimancescu. Photos by Christopher G. Knight. 295-337, *Sept. 1967*

Backwoods Japan During American Occupation. By M. A. Huberman. 491-518, *Apr. 1947*

HOOD, Mount, Oregon:

Oregon Finds New Riches. By Leo A. Borah. 681-728, *Dec. 1946*

Is Our Noblest Volcano Awakening to New Life: A Description of the Glaciers and Evidences of Volcanic Activity of Mount Hood. By A. H. Sylvester. 515-525, *July 1908*

HOOD (River), Northwest Territories, Canada:

On Canada's Hood River: Clues to a Tragic Trek. By John W. Lentz. Photos by Todd Buchanan. 128-140, *Jan. 1986*

HOOFED MAMMALS. *See* Ungulates

HOOGSTRAAL, HARRY: *Author*
South in the Sudan. 249-272, *Feb. 1953*
Yemen Opens the Door to Progress. 213-244, *Feb. 1952*

HOOKWORM (Disease):

Map-Changing Medicine. By William Joseph Showalter. 303-330, *Sept. 1922*

Redeeming the Tropics. By William Joseph Showalter. 344-364, *Mar. 1914*

HOOPER, THOMAS E.: *Photographer*
Probing the Mystery of the Medicine Wheels. By John A. Eddy. 140-146, *Jan. 1977*

HOOSIER Haunts and Holidays. Photos by Willard R. Culver. 283-314, *Sept. 1936*

HOOVER, HERBERT:
The Living White House. By Lonnelle Aikman. 593-643, *Nov. 1966*

Profiles of the Presidents: IV. America Enters the Modern Era. By Frank Freidel. 537-577, *Oct. 1965*

The Society's Special Medal Awarded to Amelia Earhart: First Woman to Receive Geographic Distinction at Brilliant Ceremony in the National Capital. Address by Herbert Hoover. 358-367, *Sept. 1932*

Admiral Byrd Receives New Honor From The Society. Address by Herbert Hoover. 228-238, *Aug. 1930*

The Great Mississippi Flood of 1927: Since White Man's Discovery This Mighty River Has Served Him Well, Yet It Has Brought Widespread Devastation Along Its Lower Reaches. By Frederick Simpich. Note: Hoover visits disaster area. 243-289, *Sept. 1927*

Author
Food for Our Allies in 1919. 242-244, *Sept. 1918*

The Food Armies of Liberty. 187-196, *Sept. 1917*

The Weapon of Food. 197-212, *Sept. 1917*

Bind the Wounds of France. 439-444, *May 1917*

HOOVER, MRS. HERBERT:
Member of National Geographic Society since 1902. 231, Aug. 1930; 362, *Sept. 1932*

HOOVER, RICHARD B.:
Author-Photographer
Those Marvelous, Myriad Diatoms. 871-878, *June 1979*

HOOVER, MRS. WILLIAM H.:
Author
Keeping House for the "Shepherds of the Sun." 483-506, *Apr. 1930*

HOPE (Ship):
A Summer Voyage to the Arctic. By G. R. Putnam. 97-110, *Apr. 1897*

HOPE and Danger in the Philippines. By Arthur Zich. Photos by Steve McCurry. 76-117, *July 1986*

HOPE for Big Cypress Swamp. By Rick Gore. Photos by Patricia Caulfield. 251-273, *Aug. 1976*

HOPE for the Bluebird. By Lawrence Zeleny. Photos by Michael L. Smith. 855-865, *June 1977*

The **HOPE** That Never Dies: Poland. By Tad Szulc. Photos by James L. Stanfield. 80-121, *Jan. 1988*

HOPE-TAYLOR, BRIAN: *Artist*
Stonehenge–New Light on an Old Riddle. By Harold E. Edgerton. 846-866, *June 1960*

HOPEH PROVINCE, China. *See* Hebei Province

HOPES and Fears in Booming Thai-

land. By Peter T. White. Photos by Dean Conger. 76-125, *July 1967*

HOPES and Worries Along the Columbia River, Powerhouse of the Northwest. By David S. Boyer. 821-847, *Dec. 1974*

HOPEWELL CULTURE:
Who Were the "Mound Builders"? By George E. Stuart. 783-801, *Dec. 1972*

"Pyramids" of the New World. By Neil Merton Judd. 105-128, *Jan. 1948*

HOPI INDIANS:
Inside the Sacred Hopi Homeland. By Jake Page. Photos by Susanne Page. 607-629, *Nov. 1982*

⊕ *The Southwest,* The Making of America series. Included: Arizona, New Mexico, and parts of California, Colorado, Texas, Utah; and in Mexico: Baja California Norte, Chihuahua, Sonora. On reverse: 12,000 Years of History; Spanish Conquest; Anglo-American Entry and Occupancy. *Nov. 1982*

Kachinas: Masked Dancers of the Southwest. By Paul Coze. 219-236, *Aug. 1957*

Indian Tribes of Pueblo Land. By Matthew W. Stirling. Paintings by W. Langdon Kihn. 549-596, *Nov. 1940*

The Secret of the Southwest Solved by Talkative Tree Rings: Horizons of American History Are Carried Back to A.D. 700 and a Calendar for 1,200 Years Established by National Geographic Society Expeditions. By Andrew Ellicott Douglass. 737-770, *Dec. 1929*

Photographing the Marvels of the West in Colors. By Fred Payne Clatworthy. 694-719, *June 1928*

Everyday Life in Pueblo Bonito: As Disclosed by the National Geographic Society's Archeologic Explorations in the Chaco Canyon National Monument, New Mexico. By Neil M. Judd. 227-262, *Sept. 1925*

Exploring in the Canyon of Death: Remains of a People Who Dwelt in Our Southwest at Least 4,000 Years Ago Are Revealed. By Earl H. Morris. 263-300, *Sept. 1925*

Scenes from America's Southwest. 651-664, *June 1921*

The Land of the Best. By Gilbert H. Grosvenor. Included: Pictorial supplement. 327-430, *Apr. 1916*

The Snake Dance. By Marion L. Oliver. 107-137, *Feb. 1911*

North American Indians. 469-484, *July 1907*

HORACE–Classic Poet of the Countryside. By W. Coleman Nevils. 771-795, *Dec. 1935*

HORCASITAS, FERNANDO: *Author*
Mexican Folk Art. Photos by David Hiser. 648-669, *May 1978*

HORE, E. C.: *Author*
The Heart of Africa. 238-247, *Feb. 19, 1892*

G
H

Thoroughbred yearlings gambol at dawn across a Kentucky pasture in the heart of Bluegrass country. J. BRUCE BAUMANN

Passed down through generations, country houses of Britain's upper class are showcases of art and architecture. FRED J. MAROON

Penn's Land of Modern Miracles. By John Oliver La Gorce. 1-58, *July 1935*

Summering in an English Cottage: Quiet and Loveliness Invite Contemplation in the Extra "Room," the Garden of the Thatched House. By Helen Churchill Candee. 429-456, *Apr. 1935*

England's Island Garden of Rocks and Flowers (Isle of Wight). Photos by W. Robert Moore. 17-24, *Jan. 1935*

Country-House Life in Sweden; In Castle and Cottage the Landed Gentry Gallantly Keep the Old Traditions. By Amelie Posse-Brázdová. 1-64, *July 1934*

The Feudal Isle of Sark: Where Sixteenth-Century Laws Are Still Observed. By Sibyl Hathaway. 101-119, *July 1932*

Ohio, the Gateway State. By Melville Chater. 525-591, *May 1932*

Smoke Over Alabama. By Frederick Simpich. 703-758, *Dec. 1931*

Louisiana, Land of Perpetual Romance. By Ralph A. Graves. 393-482, *Apr. 1930*

The Stone Beehive Homes of the Italian Heel: In Trulli-Land the Native Builds His Dwelling and Makes His Field Arable in the Same Operation. By Paul Wilstach. 229-264, *Feb. 1930*

Virginia–A Commonwealth That Has Come Back. By William Joseph Showalter. 403-472, *Apr. 1929*

Fame's Eternal Camping Ground: Beautiful Arlington, Burial Place of America's Illustrious Dead. By Enoch A. Chase. 621-638, *Nov. 1928*

A Vacation in a Fifteenth Century English Manor House. By George Alden Sanford. 629-636, *May 1928*

Maryland Pilgrimage: Visits to Hallowed Shrines Recall the Major Rôle Played by This Prosperous State in the Development of Popular Government in America. By Gilbert Grosvenor. 133-212, *Feb. 1927*

Marching Through Georgia Sixty Years After: Multifold Industries and Diversified Agriculture Are Restoring the Prosperity of America's Largest State East of the Mississippi. By Ralph A. Graves. 259-311, *Sept. 1926*

The Ashley River and Its Gardens (South Carolina). By E.T.H. Shaffer. Included: Exploring the Atlantic Seaboard with a Color Camera. Photos by Charles Martin and Jacob Gayer. 525-550, *May 1926*

Some Human Habitations. By Collier Cobb. 509-515, *July 1908*

Dwellings of the Saga-Time in Iceland, Greenland, and Vineland. By Cornelia Horsford. 73-84, *Mar. 1898*

See also Castles; Cones and Cone Dwellers; Haciendas; Houseboats; Housing; Palaces; *and* Hearst San Simeon State Historical Monument; Henry E. Huntington Library and Art Gallery; Henry Ford Museum; Monticello; Mount Vernon; White House

HOUSES, Underwater. *See* Conshelf Bases; Link Igloo; SPID; Tektite II

HOUSES OF PARLIAMENT. *See* Parliament, Houses of

HOUSEWIFE at the End of the World. By Rae Natalie P. Goodall. Photos by James L. Stanfield. 130-150, *Jan. 1971*

HOUSING, U. S. Government:
Wartime Washington. By William H. Nicholas. 257-290, *Sept. 1943*

HOUSTON, DAVID F.: *Author*
Soldiers of the Soil: Our Food Crops Must Be Greatly Increased. 273-280, *Mar. 1917*

HOUSTON, SAMUEL:
Sam Houston: A Man Too Big for Texas. By Bart McDowell. Photos by Charles O'Rear. Included: The Battle of San Jacinto. 311-329, *Mar. 1986*

HOUSTON, Texas:
Texas! By Howard La Fay. Photos by Gordon W. Gahan. 440-483, *Apr. 1980*

Houston, Prairie Dynamo. By Stuart E. Jones. Photos by William Albert Allard. 338-377, *Sept. 1967*

HOUSTON-MOUNT EVEREST FLIGHT:
The Aërial Conquest of Everest: Flying over the World's Highest Mountain Realizes the Objective of Many Heroic Explorers. By L.V.S. Blacker. 127-162, *Aug. 1933*

HOVEY, EDMUND OTIS: *Author*
The Eruptions of La Soufrière, St. Vincent, in May 1902. 444-459, *Dec. 1902*

Legendary hostelry for centuries, London's George Inn is mentioned in Charles Dickens's **Little Dorrit.** © BRITISH COUNCIL

HOVEY, ESTHER LANCRAFT: *Author*
The Old Post-Road from Tiflis to Erivan. 300-309, *Aug. 1901*

HOVEY, H. C.: *Author*
The Skeleton in Luray Cave. 425-426, *July 1906*

HOW a 38,000-mile Lifeline Grew (India's Railway). By Michael G. Satow. 744-749, *June 1984*

HOW Animals Behave: A New Look at ■■*Wildlife.* Juvenile. 104 pages. *1984*

HOW Bats Hunt With Sound. By J.J.G. McCue. 571-578, *Apr. 1961*

HOW Canada Went to the Front. By T. B. Macaulay. 297-307, *Oct. 1918*

HOW Earth and Moon Look to a Space Voyager. 53, *July 1978*

HOW Fruit Came to America. By J. R. Magness. Paintings by Else Bostelmann. 325-377, *Sept. 1951*

HOW Half the World Works. By Alice Tisdale Hobart and Mary A. Nourse. 509-524, *Apr. 1932*

HOW Latin America Looks from the Air: U. S. Army Airplanes Hurdle the High Andes, Brave Brazil Jungles, and Follow Smoking Volcanoes to Map New Sky Paths Around South America. By Herbert A. Dargue. 451-502, *Oct. 1927*

HOW Long a Whale May Carry a Harpoon. By Wm. H. Dall. 136-137, *Apr. 1899*

HOW Long Will the Coal Reserves of the United States Last? By Marius R. Campbell. 129-138, *Feb. 1907*

HOW Man-made Satellites Can Affect Our Lives. By Joseph Kaplan. 791-810, *Dec. 1957*

HOW Much is Known of Alaska. By Alfred H. Brooks. 112-114, *Feb. 1906*

HOW Old Is It? By Lyman J. Briggs and Kenneth F. Weaver. 234-255, *Aug. 1958*

HOW Old Is Man? By Theodore Roosevelt. 111-127, *Feb. 1916*

HOW One of the Society's Maps Saved a Precious Cargo. 844, *June 1947*

HOW Soon Will We Measure In Metric? By Kenneth F. Weaver. Drawings by Donald A. Mackay. 287-294, *Aug. 1977*

HOW the Decoy Fish Catches Its Dinner. Photos by Robert J. Shallenberger and William D. Madden. 224-227, *Aug. 1974*

HOW the Earth Telegraphed Its Tokyo Quake to Washington. By Francis A. Tondorf. 453-454, *Oct. 1923*

HOW the Kazakhs Fled to Freedom. By Milton J. Clark. 621-644, *Nov. 1954*

HOW the Sun Gives Life to the Sea. By Paul A. Zahl. 199-225, *Feb. 1961*

HOW the United States Grew. By McFall Kerbey. 631-649, *May 1933*

HOW the World Is Fed. By William Joseph Showalter. 1-110, *Jan. 1916*

HOW the World Is Shod. 649-660, *Sept. 1908*

HOW Things Are Made. Juvenile. 104 ■pages. *1981*

HOW Things Work. Juvenile. 104 ■pages. *1983*

HOW to Catch a Passing Comet. By Kenneth F. Weaver. 148-150, *Jan. 1974*

HOW to End a War: Grant and Lee at Appomattox. By Ulysses S. Grant 3rd. Photos by Bruce Dale. 435-469, *Apr. 1965*

HOW to Use the Star Charts. Star charts designed by Donald H. Menzel. 116-128, *July 1943*

HOW Warwick Was Photographed in Color. By Maynard Owen Williams. Contents: Warwick Castle. 83-93, *July 1936*

HOW We Climbed Everest. By Barry C. Bishop. 477-507, *Oct. 1963*

HOW We Fight with Photographs. By F. Barrows Colton. 257-280, *Sept. 1944*

HOW We Found the *Monitor.* By John G. Newton. 48-61, *Jan. 1975*

HOW We Found *Titanic.* By Robert D. Ballard in association with Jean-Louis Michel. 696-719, *Dec. 1985*

HOW We Plan to Put Men on the Moon. By Hugh L. Dryden. Paintings by Davis Meltzer and Pierre Mion. 357-401, *Mar. 1964*

HOW We Sailed the New *Mayflower* to America. By Alan Villiers. 627-672, *Nov. 1957*

HOW We Use the Gulf of Mexico. By Frederick Simpich. 1-40, *Jan. 1944*

HOWARD, ED: *Author*
Pitcairn and Norfolk–The Saga of

Bounty's Children. Photos by David Hiser and Melinda Berge. 510-541, *Oct. 1983*

HOWARD, HENRY: *Author*
Southward Ho! In the "Alice." 265-312, *Mar. 1938*

HOWARD, L. O.: *Author*
Explorers of a New Kind: Successful Introduction of Beetles and Parasites to Check Ravages of the Gipsy-moth and Brown-tail Moth. 38-67, *July 1914*
Economic Loss to the People of the United States Through Insects That Carry Disease. 735-749, *Aug. 1909*

HOWARTH, WILLIAM: *Author*
■■*Traveling the Trans-Canada: From Newfoundland to British Columbia.* Photos by George F. Mobley. 199 pages. *1987*
The Okies–Beyond the Dust Bowl. Photos by Chris Johns. 322-349, *Sept. 1984*
The Country of Willa Cather. Photos by Farrell Grehan. 71-93, *July 1982*
Thoreau, a Different Man. Photos by Farrell Grehan. 349-387, *Mar. 1981*

HOWE, CHARLES E.: *Author*
The Disposition of the Philippines. 304, *June 1898*

HOWE, JULIA WARD:
Literary Landmarks of Massachusetts. By William H. Nicholas. Photos by B. Anthony Stewart and John E. Fletcher. 279-310, *Mar. 1950*

HOWELL, THOMAS R.: *Author*
What a Place to Lay an Egg! 414-419, *Sept. 1971*

HOWELLS, J. HARVEY: *Author*
Home to Arran, Scotland's Magic Isle. 80-99, *July 1965*

HOXIE BROS. GIGANTIC 3-RING CIRCUS:
On the Road With an Old-time Circus. By John Fetterman. Photos by Jonathan Blair. 410-434, *Mar. 1972*

On the go with old-time Hoxie Bros. Gigantic 3-Ring Circus, a four-ton elephant travels through Kentucky on a 13-state, seven-month itinerary. JONATHAN BLAIR

HOYT, ERICH: *Author*
The Whales Called "Killer." 220-237, *Aug. 1984*

HRDLIČKA, ALEŠ: *Author*
Bohemia and the Czechs. 163-187, *Feb. 1917*

HSINKING, Manchuria. *See* Changchun

HUACA DE LA CRUZ, Virú Valley, Peru:
Finding the Tomb of a Warrior-God. By William Duncan Strong. Photos by Clifford Evans, Jr. 453-482, *Apr. 1947*

HUASCARÁN NEVADO (Peak), Peru:
Avalanche! By Bart McDowell. Photos by John E. Fletcher. 855-880, *June 1962*

HUASTEC INDIANS:
Man's Eighty Centuries in Veracruz. By S. Jeffrey K. Wilkerson. Photos by David Hiser. Paintings by Richard Schlecht. NGS research grant. 203-231, *Aug. 1980*

HUAVE INDIANS:
The Isthmus of Tehuantepec: "The Bridge of the World's Commerce." By Helen Olsson-Seffer. 991-1002, *Dec. 1910*

The HUB City, Cradle of American Liberty. Photos by B. Anthony Stewart and Luis Marden. Contents: Boston, Massachusetts. 49-72, *July 1936*

HUBBARD, BERNARD R.:
The Society Takes Part in Three Geographic Expeditions. 625-626, *May 1934*
Author-Photographer
A World Inside a Mountain: Aniakchak, the New Volcanic Wonderland of the Alaska Peninsula, Is Explored. 319-345, *Sept. 1931*

HUBBARD, GARDINER GREENE:
First President of NGS. 87, Oct. 1888; 165, Apr. 1889; 270, July 1889; 68, Apr. 1890; 294, Apr. 1891; xii, Feb. 19, 1892; xix, Feb. 20, 1893; xix, May 5, 1894; 216, June 1896; 134, Jan. 1936; 273, Mar. 1947; 517, 522, Oct. 1963; 1, 101, 103, 113, July 1965; 456, 458, Oct. 1966; 584, *Apr. 1968*
Founder of the NGS. 23, 24, Jan. 1906; 131, Jan. 1936; 387, Mar. 1955; 3, Jan. 1963; 459, Oct. 1963; 456, *Oct. 1966*
Clarke School for the Deaf. 382, 385, 386, 387, *Mar. 1955*
Seal of the Society, designed under supervision of. 34, pl. 28, *July 1946*
Alaskan glacier named for. 99-100, May 1891; 7, 16, Jan. 1910; 599, June 1926; 725, June 1936; 288, *Sept. 1942*
Mount Hubbard, Alaska, named for. 16, *Jan. 1910*
Toast to the memory of. 24, *Jan. 1906*
Hubbard Memorial Window, Church of the Covenant, Washington, D. C. 174-175, *May 1902*
Contributed generously to the Society. 222-223, *June 1899*

First President of the National Geographic Society, Gardiner Greene Hubbard—here with his wife, Gertrude—helped found the organization in 1888. PETER BISSETT

Gardiner Greene Hubbard: An Address delivered at the Memorial Services held at the Church of the Covenant, Washington, D. C., December 13, 1897. By Teunis S. Hamlin. 33-38, *Feb. 1898*

Gardiner Greene Hubbard: Memorial Meeting, City of Washington, January 21, 1898. 39-70, *Feb. 1898*

Portraits. Frontispiece, May 1896; Frontispiece, *Feb. 1898*

Gardiner Greene Hubbard (Announcement of death). By John Hyde. 345, *Dec. 1897*

Headquarters building named for. *See* Hubbard Memorial Hall, National Geographic Society Headquarters

Addresses

1888: Introductory Address by the President, Mr. Gardiner Greene Hubbard. 2-7, *Jan. 1988*

Russia in Europe (Annual Address). By Gardiner G. Hubbard. 3-26, *Jan. 1896*

Geographic Progress of Civilization. Annual Address by the President, Gardiner G. Hubbard. 1-22, *Feb. 14, 1894*

Discoverers of America. Annual Address by the President, Gardiner G. Hubbard. 1-20, *Apr. 7, 1893*

The Evolution of Commerce. Annual Address by the President, Gardiner G. Hubbard. 1-18, *Mar. 26, 1892*

South America. Annual Address by the President, Gardiner G. Hubbard. 1-29, *Mar. 28, 1891*

Introductory Address. By the President, Mr. Gardiner G. Hubbard. 3-10, *Oct. 1888*

Author

Geographical Research in the United States. By Gardiner G. Hubbard and Marcus Baker. 285-293, *Oct. 1897*

The Effects of Geographic Environment in the Development of Civilization in Primitive Man. 161-176, *June 1897*

The National Geographic Society: Synopsis of a Course of Lectures on the Effects of Geographic Environment in Developing the Civilization of the World. 29-32, *Jan. 1897*

Africa Since 1888, with Special Reference to South Africa and Abyssinia. 157-175, *May 1896*

Relations of Air and Water to Temperature and Life. 112-124, *Jan. 31, 1894*

Africa, Its Past and Future. 99-124, *Apr. 1889*

HUBBARD, MRS. GARDINER GREENE:

Tribute of respect to the memory of Mrs. Gardiner Greene Hubbard, adopted by the Board of Managers of the National Geographic Society at a special meeting held at Hubbard Memorial Hall, October 23, 1909. 1008, *Nov. 1909*

HUBBARD, GERARD: *Author*

Aircraft Insignia, Spirit of Youth. 710-722, *June 1943*

HUBBARD, JAMES MASCARENE: *Author*

Singan–The Present Capital of the Chinese Empire. 63-66, *Feb. 1901*

The Tsangpo. 32-35, *Jan. 1901*

Colonial Government in Borneo. 359-363, *Sept. 1900*

Problems in China. 297-308, *Aug. 1900*

HUBBARD, THOMAS H.:

The Discovery of the North Pole. Speech by Thomas H. Hubbard. 63-82, *Jan. 1910*

HUBBARD BAY, Greenland:

Three Weeks in Hubbard Bay, West Greenland. By Robert Stein. 1-11, *Jan. 1898*

HUBBARD GLACIER, Alaska-Canada:

Glaciers on the Move. By John L. Eliot. Photos by Chris Johns. Included: Anatomy of a tidewater glacier. 107-119, *Jan. 1987*

The National Geographic Society's Alaskan Expedition of 1909. By Ralph S. Tarr and Lawrence Martin. 1-54, *Jan. 1910*

HUBBARD MEDAL:

Medal designed by Laura Gardin Fraser; both sides shown. 564, *Apr. 1953*

Recipients

Astronauts John W. Young and Robert L. Crippen, for the first flight of the Space Shuttle *Columbia*. 852, *Dec. 1981*

Wetmore, Alexander. 151, *Aug. 1975*

Apollo 8 and Apollo 11 astronauts. 859-861, *June 1970*

Arnold, Henry H. 141, Feb. 1946; 868, Dec. 1957; 583, Oct. 1963; 584, *Apr. 1968*

British Mount Everest Expedition: Medal presented to Sir John Hunt, with bronze replicas to Sir John, Sir Edmund Hillary, and Tenzing Norgay (in India). 64, July 1954; 846, June 1955; 867-868, Dec. 1957; 98, Jan. 1966; 584, *Apr. 1968*

Byrd, Richard E. 377-388, Sept. 1926; 238, 239, Aug. 1927; 139, Jan. 1936; 250, Feb. 1948; 65H, July 1954; 38, 39, July 1957; 868, Dec. 1957; 574, 576, Apr. 1962; 556, Oct. 1963; 571, Oct. 1965; 584, *Apr. 1968*

Ellsworth, Lincoln. 36, July 1936; 868, Dec. 1957; 583, Oct. 1963; 689, Nov. 1964; 847, June 1967; 584, *Apr. 1968*

Glenn, John H., Jr. 827, June 1962; 904, 905, 906, Dec. 1962; 29, Jan. 1963; 584, *Apr. 1968*

Lindbergh, Charles A. 233-242, Aug. 1927; 132-140, Jan. 1928; 137, 138, Jan. 1936; 868, Dec. 1957; 563, Oct. 1963; 584, 586, *Apr. 1968*

Peary, Robert E. 49-60, Jan. 1907; 137, 149, Jan. 1936; 867, Dec. 1957; 589, Apr. 1959; 905, Dec. 1962; 514, Oct. 1963; 584, *Apr. 1968*

Trippe, Juan. 584-586, *Apr. 1968*

American Mount Everest Expedition: Medal presented to Norman G. Dyhrenfurth, leader of the expedition, with 21 gold-plated bronze replicas to individual members. 514-515, Oct. 1963; 1B, Jan. 1964; 331, Mar. 1964; 15, *July 1965*

Leakey, Dr. and Mrs. Louis S. B. 903, 905, Dec. 1962; 197, 231, *Feb. 1965*

Lindbergh, Anne Morrow. 791-794, June 1934; 136, 137, Jan. 1936; 562, *Oct. 1963*

U. S. Navy Antarctic Expeditions of 1955-1959: Medal presented to Secretary of the Navy Thomas S. Gates, Jr., with gold duplicates to Adm. Arleigh A. Burke and Rear Adm. George Dufek. 589-590, Apr. 1959; 530, *Oct. 1959*

Comdr. Robert E. Peary was awarded the Society's Hubbard Medal in 1907 for his achievements in Arctic exploration.

The Society's Hubbard Medal is awarded for distinction in exploration, discovery, and research.

HUBBARD MEMORIAL HALL, National Geographic Society Headquarters:

HUBEI PROVINCE, China. *See* Hankou

HUBERMAN, M. A.: *Author*

HUDSON, HENRY:

By Frederick G. Vosburgh. 461-490, *Apr. 1939*

HUDSON, HERNDON and MARY: *Authors*

Ali Goes to the Clinic. By Herndon and Mary Hudson. 764-766, *Dec. 1946*

HUDSON (River), New York:

The Hudson: "That River's Alive." By Alice J. Hall. Photos by Ted Spiegel. 62-89, *Jan. 1978*

North Through History Aboard *White Mist*. By Melville Bell Grosvenor. Photos by Edwin Stuart Grosvenor. 1-55, *July 1970*

Henry Hudson's River. By Willard Price. Photos by Wayne Miller. 364-403, *Mar. 1962*

Here's New York Harbor. By Stuart E. Jones. Photos by Robert F. Sisson and David S. Boyer. 773-813, *Dec. 1954*

The Mighty Hudson. By Albert W. Atwood. Photos by B. Anthony Stewart. 1-36, *July 1948*

Shad in the Shadow of Skyscrapers. By Dudley B. Martin. Photos by Luis Marden. 359-376, *Mar. 1947*

Henry Hudson, Magnificent Failure: Just 330 Years Ago He and His Mutinous Crew Found Manhattan Covered With "Goodly Oakes" and Fought Indians in New York Harbor. By Frederick G. Vosburgh. 461-490, *Apr. 1939*

Atlantic Estuarine Tides. By Mark S. W. Jefferson. 400-409, *Sept. 1898*

HUDSON BAY, and Region, Canada:

Henry Hudson's Changing Bay. By Bill Richards. Photos by David Hiser. 380-405, *Mar. 1982*

◼ Polar Bear Alert. 395, cover, *Mar. 1982*

Vanished Mystery Men of Hudson Bay. By Henry B. Collins. NGS research grant. 669-687, *Nov. 1956*

Trailing Cosmic Rays in Canada's North. By Martin A. Pomerantz. NGS research grant. 99-115, *Jan. 1953*

Birds of Timberline and Tundra. By Arthur A. Allen. 313-339, *Sept. 1946*

See also Igloolik; James Bay; McConnell River Region; Southampton Island

HUDSON'S BAY COMPANY:

The Hudson's Bay Company: Canada's Fur-Trading Empire. By Peter C. Newman. Photos by Kevin Fleming. 192-229, *Aug. 1987*

Henry Hudson's Changing Bay. By Bill Richards. Photos by David Hiser. 380-405, *Mar. 1982*

The Northwest Passes to the Yukon. By Eliza R. Scidmore. 105-112, *Apr. 1898*

Overland Routes to the Klondike. By Hamlin Garland. 113-116, *Apr. 1898*

Oregon: Its History, Geography, and Resources. By John H. Mitchell. 239-284, *Apr. 20, 1895*

HUE, Vietnam:

Behind the Headlines in Viet Nam. By Peter T. White. Photos by Winfield Parks. 149-189, *Feb. 1967*

Drawn by the aroma of frying bacon, a polar bear near Churchill, Manitoba, drops in on a visiting National Geographic Society television documentary crew. DAVID HISER

Portrait of Indochina. By W. Robert Moore and Maynard Owen Williams. Paintings by Jean Despujols. 461-490, *Apr. 1951*

HUEHNERGARTH, JOHN: *Artist*

◼◼ *Small Inventions That Make a Big Difference*. Photos by Joseph H. Bailey. Juvenile. 104 pages. *1984*

HUENS, JEAN-LEON: *Artist*

Ancient Bulgaria's Golden Treasures. By Colin Renfrew. Photos by James L. Stanfield. 112-129, *July 1980*

Sir Francis Drake. By Alan Villiers. Photos by Gordon W. Gahan. 216-253, *Feb. 1975*

Pioneers in Man's Search for the Universe. By Thomas Y. Canby. 627-633, *May 1974*

HUGHES, CAROL and DAVID:

On Assignment in Costa Rica. *Jan. 1983*

Author-Photographers

Teeming Life of a Rain Forest. 49-65, *Jan. 1983*

Photographers

The Living Sands of the Namib. By William J. Hamilton III. 364-377, *Sept. 1983*

HUGHES, CHARLES EVANS:

Board of Trustees. 792, *June 1934*

HUGHO, KIMO:

Nomination Page. *Mar. 1976*

HUICHOL INDIANS:

The Huichols, Mexico's People of Myth and Magic. By James Norman. Photos by Guillermo Aldana E. 832-853, *June 1977*

HUMAN BODY:

Medicine's New Vision. By Howard Sochurek. Paintings by Davis Meltzer. Illustrations text by Peter Miller. Contents: New techniques for imaging internal organs. 2-41, *Jan. 1987*

Our Immune System: The Wars Within. By Peter Jaret. Photos by Lennart Nilsson. Illustrations text by Larry Kohl. 702-735, *June 1986*

◼◼ *The Incredible Machine*. Contents: The human body. 384 pages. *1986*

◼ The Incredible Machine. President's Page. *Jan. 1985*

◼◼ *Your Wonderful Body*. Juvenile. 104 pages. *1982*

◼ Mysteries of the Mind. 1, Jan. 1980; cover, *Feb. 1980*

◼ The Incredible Machine. 299, Sept. 1975; cover, Oct. 1975; 583, Nov. 1975; 575, *Nov. 1976*

See also Medicine and Health

HUMAN Emotions Recorded by Photography. By Ralph A. Graves. 284-300, *Oct. 1920*

HUMAN-POWERED FLIGHT. *See Daedalus; Gossamer Albatross; Gossamer Condor*

HUMAN SACRIFICE:

Mysteries of the Bog. By Louise E. Levathes. Photos by Fred Bavendam. Contents: Bronze Age and Iron Age sacrifices and bog burials. 397-420, *Mar. 1987*

Following Cortés: Path to Conquest. By S. Jeffrey K. Wilkerson. Photos by Guillermo Aldana E. Paintings by Ned Seidler and Rosalie Seidler. 420-459, *Oct. 1984*

Drama of Death in a Minoan Temple. By Yannis Sakellarakis and Efi Sapouna-Sakellaraki. Photos by Otis Imboden and Spyros Tsavdaroglou. 205-222, *Feb. 1981*

Joseph Alsop: A Historical Perspective (on Minoan Human Sacrifice). 223, *Feb. 1981*

The Aztecs. 704-775. I. The Aztecs. By Bart McDowell. Photos by David Hiser. Paintings by Felipe Dávalos. 714-751; II. The Building of Tenochtitlan. By Augusto F. Molina Montes. Paintings by Felipe Dávalos.

An Anna's hummingbird sips on nectar from California fuchsia, simultaneously pollinating the blossoms. ROBERT A. TYRRELL

753-765; III. New Finds in the Great Temple. By Eduardo Matos Moctezuma. Photos by David Hiser. 767-775, *Dec. 1980*

Into the Well of Sacrifice (Chichén Itzá). 540-561. NGS research grant. I. Return to the Sacred Cenote. By Eusebio Dávalos Hurtado. 540-549; II. Treasure Hunt in the Deep Past. By Bates Littlehales. 550-561, *Oct. 1961*

HUMAN Treasures of Japan. By William Graves. Photos by James L. Stanfield. 370-379, *Sept. 1972*

HUMANITY Amid the Horrors of War. By Peter T. White. Photos by Steve Raymer. 647-679, *Nov. 1986*

HUMASON, MILTON L.: *Author*
First Photographs of Planets and Moon Taken with Palomar's 200-inch Telescope. 125-130, *Jan. 1953*

HUMAYUN:
When the Moguls Ruled India. By Mike Edwards. Photos by Roland Michaud. 463-493, *Apr. 1985*

HUMBLE Masterpieces: Decoys. By George Reiger. Photos by Kenneth Garrett. 639-663, *Nov. 1983*

HUMBOLDT, ALEXANDER VON:
Humboldt's Way. By Loren McIntyre. 318-351, *Sept. 1985*

HUMBOLDT CURRENT, Pacific Ocean:
Fighting Giants of the Humboldt (Fish and Squid). By David D. Duncan. 373-400, *Mar. 1941*

HUMBOLDT REDWOODS STATE PARK, California:
World's Tallest Tree Discovered. By Melville Bell Grosvenor. Photos by George F. Mobley. 1-9, *July 1964*

Finding the Mt. Everest of All Living Things. By Paul A. Zahl. 10-51, *July 1964*

HUME, EDGAR ERSKINE: *Author*
The Palio of Siena. 231-244, *Aug. 1951*
Italy Smiles Again. 693-732, *June 1949*

HUME, IVOR NOËL. *See* Noël Hume, Ivor

HUME, MARTIN: *Author*
The Woods and Gardens of Portugal. 883-894, *Oct. 1910*

HUMMINGBIRDS:
Hummingbirds: The Nectar Connection. By Paul W. Ewald. Photos by Robert A. Tyrrell. 223-227, *Feb. 1982*
The Marvelous Hummingbird Rediscovered. By Crawford H. Greenewalt. 98-101, *July 1966*
The Man Who Talks to Hummingbirds (Augusto Ruschi). By Luis Marden. Photos by James Blair. 80-99, *Jan. 1963*
Photographing Hummingbirds in Brazil. By Crawford H. Greenewalt. 100-115, *Jan. 1963*
The Hummingbirds. By Crawford H. Greenewalt. 658-679, *Nov. 1960*
Freezing the Flight of Hummingbirds. By Harold E. Edgerton, R. J. Niedrach, and Walker Van Riper. NGS research grant. 245-261, *Aug. 1951*
Hummingbirds in Action. By Harold E. Edgerton. 221-232, *Aug. 1947*
Seeking the Smallest Feathered Creatures: Humming Birds, Peculiar to the New World, Are Found from Canada and Alaska to the Strait of Magellan. Swifts and Goatsuckers, Their Nearest Relatives. By Alexander Wetmore. Paintings by Allan Brooks. 65-89, *July 1932*
Holidays with Humming Birds. By Margaret L. Bodine. 731-742, *June 1928*

HUMPBACK WHALES:
An Incredible Feasting of Whales. By Al Giddings. 88-93, *Jan. 1984*
New Light on the Singing Whales. Introduction by Roger Payne. Photos by Flip Nicklin. NGS research grant. 463-477, *Apr. 1982*
Humpback Whales. 2-25. NGS research grant. I. The Gentle Giants. By Sylvia A. Earle. Photos by Al Giddings. 2-17; II. Their Mysterious Songs. By Roger Payne. Photos by Al Giddings. 18-25; III. Symphony of the Deep: "Songs of the Humpback Whale" (Sound sheet). 24-24B, *Jan. 1979*

HUNAN PROVINCE, China:
A Lady From China's Past. Photos from *China Pictorial.* Text by Alice J. Hall. 660-681, *May 1974*
Hunan–The Closed Province of China. By William Barclay Parsons. 393-400, *Oct. 1900*

HUNGARIANS:
Freedom Flight from Hungary. Photos by Robert F. Sisson. 424-436, *Mar. 1957*

HUNGARY:
Hungary: A Static Society. By Paul R. and Anne H. Ehrlich. Photos by Steve McCurry. 927-929, *Dec. 1988*
Hungary's New Way: A Different Communism. By John J. Putman. Photos by Bill Weems. 225-261, *Feb. 1983*
The Danube: River of Many Nations, Many Names. By Mike Edwards. Photos by Winfield Parks. 455-485, *Oct. 1977*
Hungary: Changing Homeland of a Tough, Romantic People. By Bart McDowell. Photos by Albert Moldvay and Joseph J. Scherschel. 443-483, *Apr. 1971*

Five little boys in short trousers and aprons smile—and one looks glum—in the Hungarian village of Mikepércs in 1914. A. W. CUTLER

Dazzlingly graceful, a humpback whale arcs through the air above the calm waters of Alaska's Glacier Bay. AL GIDDINGS, SEA FILMS, INC.

In the shadow of the Karakoram peaks farmers and their oxen plow the land in 1953 in the Hunza region of northern Pakistan. JEAN AND FRANC SHOR, NGS

HURLEY, EDWARD N.: *Author*

The American People Must Become Ship-Minded. 201-211, *Sept. 1918*

HURLEY, FRANK: *Photographer*

Arab Land Beyond the Jordan. 753-768, *Dec. 1947*

Pictorial Jaunt Through Papua. 109-124, *Jan. 1927*

HÜRLIMANN, MARTIN: *Photographer*

Remote Nepal, Land of Mystery. 329-336, *Mar. 1935*

HURON, Lake, Canada-U. S.:

The Great Lakes' Troubled Waters. By Charles E. Cobb, Jr. Photos by Bob Sacha and Richard Olsenius. Included: A great meeting of waters; North America's fifth coast. 2-31, *July 1987*

The Great Lakes: Is It Too Late? By Gordon Young. Photos by James L. Amos and Martin Rogers. 147-185, *Aug. 1973*

HURON INDIANS:

America's First Settlers, the Indians. By Matthew W. Stirling. Paintings by W. Langdon Kihn. 535-596, *Nov. 1937*

HURRICANES:

The Lost Fleet of Kublai Khan. By Torao Mozai. Photos by Koji Nakamura. 634-649, *Nov. 1982*

Hurricane! By Ben Funk. Photos by Robert W. Madden. 346-379. Included: Dominica. By Fred Ward. 357-359; Dynamics of a Hurricane. 370-371; Into the Eye of David. By John L. Eliot. 368-369; Paths of Fury–This Century's Worst American Storms. 360-361, *Sept. 1980*

We're Doing Something About the Weather! By Walter Orr Roberts. 518-555, *Apr. 1972*

Cajunland, Louisiana's French-speaking Coast. By Bern Keating. Photos by Charles Harbutt and Franke Keating. Included: Hurricane Audrey (1957); Hurricane Betsy (1965). 353-391, *Mar. 1966*

Men Against the Hurricane. By Andrew H. Brown. 537-560, *Oct. 1950*

Cape Cod People and Places. By Wanda Burnett. 737-774, *June 1946*

Charting a World at War. By William B. Nicholas. 617-640, *Nov. 1944*

The Geography of a Hurricane: A Doughnut-shaped Storm Turned Back Time in New England to Candlelight Days, but Revealed Anew Yankee Courage and Ingenuity. By F. Barrows Colton. 529-552, *Apr. 1939*

The Islands of Bermuda: A British Colony with a Unique Record in Popular Government. By William Howard Taft. 1-26, *Jan. 1922*

Forecasting the Weather and Storms. By Willis L. Moore. 255-306, *June 1905*

Hurricanes on the Coast of Texas. By A. W. Greely. 442-445, *Nov. 1900*

The Lessons of Galveston. By W J McGee. 377-383, *Oct. 1900*

The West Indian Hurricane of September 1-12, 1900. By E. B. Garriott. 384-392, *Oct. 1900*

The West Indian Hurricane of August 7-14, 1899. By E. B. Garriott. 343-348, *Sept. 1899*

The West Indian Hurricane of September 10-11, 1898. By E. B. Garriott. 17-20, *Jan. 1899*

United States Daily Atmospheric Survey. By Willis L. Moore. 299-303, *Oct. 1897*

The Law of Storms, Considered with Special Reference to the North Atlantic. By Everett Hayden. 199-211, *July 1890*

HURTADO, EUSEBIO DÁVALOS. *See* Dávalos Hurtado, Eusebio

HUSSEIN, King (Jordan):

The Other Side of Jordan. By Luis Marden. 790-825, *Dec. 1964*

Author

Holy Land, My Country. 784-789, *Dec. 1964*

HUSSEIN, HAJI MIRZA (Oscar Von Niedermeyer): *Author*

Every-Day Life in Afghanistan. By Frederick Simpich and "Haji Mirza Hussein." 85-110, *Jan. 1921*

HUTCHINS, ROSS E.: *Author-Photographer*

Living Honey Jars of the Ant World. 405-411, *Mar. 1962*

HUTCHINSON, PAUL: *Author*

New China and the Printed Page. 687-722, *June 1927*

HUTCHISON, BRUCE: *Author*

Exploring Ottawa. 565-596, *Nov. 1947*

Canada's War Effort: A Canadian Pictures the Swift and Sweeping Transformation from a Peaceful Dominion to a Nation Geared for War. 553-590, *Nov. 1941*

Hurricane David lashes Miami Beach in 1979 as it passes just offshore, having devastated the Caribbean. J. SCOTT APPLEWHITE, *MIAMI HERALD*

HUTCHISON, GEORGE W.:
Memorial tribute to George W. Hutchison. 720, *June 1945*
Photographs of. 790, June 1934; 157, Jan. 1936; 432, Apr. 1941; 720, *June 1945*
Tribute by Gilbert H. Grosvenor. 154, *Jan. 1936*

HUTCHISON, ISOBEL WYLIE:
Author
Poets' Voices Linger in Scottish Shrines. Photos by Kathleen Revis. 437-488, *Oct. 1957*
A Stroll to John o'Groat's. 1-48, *July 1956*
From Barra to Butt in the Hebrides. 559-580, *Oct. 1954*
Shetland and Orkney, Britain's Far North. 519-536, *Oct. 1953*
A Stroll to Venice. 378-410, *Sept. 1951*
A Stroll to London. Photos by B. Anthony Stewart. 171-204, *Aug. 1950*
2,000 Miles Through Europe's Oldest Kingdom. Photos by Maynard Owen Williams. 141-180, *Feb. 1949*
Bonnie Scotland, Postwar Style. Photos by B. Anthony Stewart. 545-601, *May 1946*
Wales in Wartime. 751-768, *June 1944*
Scotland in Wartime. 723-743, *June 1943*
Riddle of the Aleutians: A Botanist Explores the Origin of Plants on Ever-misty Islands Now Enshrouded in the Fog of War. 769-792, *Dec. 1942*
A Walking Tour Across Iceland. 467-497, *Apr. 1928*

HUTS:
Some Human Habitations. By Collier Cobb. 509-515, *July 1908*

HUTSON, PAT: *Author*
Snow-mantled Stehekin: Where Solitude Is in Season. Photos by Bruce Dale. 572-588, *Apr. 1974*

HUTTERITES:
The Hutterites, Plain People of the West. By William Albert Allard. 98-125, *July 1970*

HUTTON, JACQUELINE: *Artist*
Strange Babies of the Sea. By Hilary B. Moore. Paintings by Craig Phillips and Jacqueline Hutton. 41-56, *July 1952*

HUZZA for Otaheite! By Luis Marden. 435-459, *Apr. 1962*

HWANG HO (Yellow River), China:
Taming "Flood Dragons" Along China's Hwang Ho. By Oliver J. Todd. 205-234, *Feb. 1942*
Raft Life on the Hwang Ho. By W. Robert Moore. 743-752, *June 1932*
Shantung—China's Holy Land. By Charles K. Edmunds. 231-252, *Sept. 1919*

HWANG YAO-TSO: *Artist*
China's Wonderland–Yen Tang Shan (Zhejiang Province). Photos by Herbert Clarence White and Clarence C. Crisler. Camera paintings by Deng Bao-ling and Hwang Yao-tso. 687-694, *Dec. 1937*
A Peiping Panorama in Vivid Pigments. Photos by H. C. and J. H. White. Camera paintings by Deng Bao-ling and Hwang Yao-tso. 753-784, *Dec. 1936*

HYANNIS, Massachusetts:
Cape Cod People and Places. By Wanda Burnett. 737-774, *June 1946*

HYBRIDS:
Those Fiery Brazilian Bees. By Rick Gore. Photos by Bianca Lavies. 491-501, *Apr. 1976*
Amateur Gardener Creates a New Rose. By Elizabeth A. Moize. Photos by Farrell Grehan. 286-294, *Aug. 1972*
The Exquisite Orchids. By Luis Marden. 485-513, *Apr. 1971*

HYDE, JOHN:
Board of Managers. xii, Feb. 19, 1892; xix, Feb. 20, 1893; xix, May 5, 1894; 414, *Sept. 1898*
Author
Puerto Rico, Not Porto Rico. 37-38, *Jan. 1900*
The National Geographic Magazine and the U. S. Board on Geographic Names. 517-519, *Dec. 1899*
The National Geographic Society. Contents: Early history of the Society. 220-223, *June 1899*
Growth of Maritime Commerce. 30-31, *Jan. 1899*
Geographic Literature. 212-214, June 1896; 156-157, May 1897; 192, Apr. 1898; 253, May 1898; 514, *Dec. 1898*
President Alexander Graham Bell on Japan. 509-512, *Dec. 1898*
Frederic W. Putnam. 429-431, *Oct. 1898*
American Association for the Advancement of Science. 412-413, *Sept. 1898*
Wellman Polar Expedition. 373-375, *Aug. 1898*
Commerce of the Philippine Islands. 301-303, *June 1898*
Reception to Captain C. D. Sigsbee, U.S.N. 251-252, *May 1898*
Trade of the United States with Cuba. 247-249, *May 1898*
An Interesting Rumor Concerning Andrée. 102-103, *Mar. 1898*
Gardiner Greene Hubbard. 345, *Dec. 1897*
Sir John Evans and Prof. W J McGee. 358-359, *Dec. 1897*
Some Recent Geographic Events. 359-362, *Dec. 1897*
Electric Street Railways (U. S.). 284, *Oct. 1897*
Geographic Notes. 304, *Oct. 1897*
The Toronto Meeting of the British Association for the Advancement of Science. 247-251, *Sept. 1897*
Mineral Production in the United States. 201-202, *July-Aug. 1897*
Admiral R. W. Meade, U.S.N. (Obituary). 142, *May 1897*
Miscellanea. 64, *Feb. 1897*
The United States Department of Agriculture and Its Biological Survey. 405-406, *Dec. 1896*
A Critical Period in South African History. 377-379, *Nov. 1896*
Introductory: The Editor. 1-2, *Jan. 1896*

HYDE, NINA:
On Assignment in China. *May 1988*
Author
Wool–Fabric of History. Photos by Cary Wolinsky. Included: Living in Wool. 552-591, *May 1988*

On the banks of China's Yellow River in 1938 dike builders drag long ropes of woven willow sticks and packs of kaoliang stalks to the water's edge.   OLIVER J. TODD

As an audience of golden jackals awaits, a pack of fiery-eyed hyenas rips into its prey, a luckless Burchell's zebra. BARON HUGO VAN LAWICK

Silk–The Queen of Textiles. Photos by Cary Wolinsky. 2-49, *Jan. 1984*

HYDE, WALTER WOODBURN:
Author

The Ascent of Mont Blanc. 861-942, *Aug. 1913*

HYDROCARBON FUELS. *See* Coal; Natural Gas; Oil; Synfuels

HYDROELECTRIC POWER:

Paraguay, Paradox of South America. By Gordon Young. Photos by O. Louis Mazzatenta. Included: Itaipú Dam. 240-269, *Aug. 1982*

Quebec's Northern Dynamo. By Larry Kohl. Photos by Ottmar Bierwagen. Note: It is expected that nine power-houses will produce 13,700 mega-watts. 406-418, *Mar. 1982*

Egypt's Desert of Promise. By Farouk El-Baz. Photos by Georg Gerster. Included: The proposed Qattara project. 190-221, *Feb. 1982*

Powerhouse of the Northwest (Columbia River). By David S. Boyer. 821-847, *Dec. 1974*

Niagara Falls, Servant of Good Neighbors. Photos by Walter Meayers Edwards. 574-587, *Apr. 1963*

New St. Lawrence Seaway Opens the Great Lakes to the World. By Andrew H. Brown. 299-339, *Mar. 1959*

Kitimat–Canada's Aluminum Titan. By David S. Boyer. Included: Kemano power development. 376-398, *Sept. 1956*

The Fire of Heaven. By Albert W. Atwood. 655-674, *Nov. 1948*

HYDROFOIL BOATS:

Hydrofoil, *HD-4,* designed by Alexander Graham Bell. 493, 495, 496, Apr. 1957; 257, 264, Aug. 1959; 554-555, *Oct. 1963*

Hydrofoil Ferry "Flies" the Strait of Messina. By Gilbert Grosvenor. Contents: *Arrow of the Sun, HD-4.* 493-496, *Apr. 1957*

HYDROGRAPHY:

Servicing Arctic Airbases. By Robert A. Bartlett. 602-616, *May 1946*

Charting a World at War. By William H. Nicholas. 617-640, *Nov. 1944*

A Battle-Ground of Nature: The Atlantic Seaboard. By John Oliver La Gorce. 511-546, *June 1918*

Warfare on Our Eastern Coast. By John Oliver La Gorce. 195-230, *Sept. 1915*

Our Guardians on the Deep. By William Joseph Showalter. 655-677, *June 1914*

Hidden Perils of the Deep. By O. R. Putnam. 822-837, *Sept. 1909*

Marine Hydrographic Surveys of the Coasts of the World. By George W. Littlehales. 63-67, *Feb. 1905*

The Work of the U. S. Hydrographic Office. By W.H.H. Southerland. 61-75, *Feb. 1903*

Hydrographic Work of the U. S. Geological Survey. 324-325, *Aug. 1900*

Helping Navigation. 162-163, *Apr. 1900*

Captain Charles D. Sigsbee, U.S.N. By Henry Gannett. 250, *May 1898*

Recent Hydrographic Work. By F. H. Newell. 347-348, *Oct. 1896*

Hydrography in the United States. By Frederick H. Newell. 146-150, *Apr. 1896*

See also U. S. Geological Survey; U. S. Hydrographic Office

HYDROPLANES. *See* Seaplanes

HYDROPONICS:

Greens Grow for GI's on Soilless Ascension. By W. Robert Moore. 219-230, *Aug. 1945*

HYDRO-QUÉBEC:

Quebec's Northern Dynamo. By Larry Kohl. Photos by Ottmar Bierwagen. 406-418, *Mar. 1982*

HYDROTHERMAL ENERGY. *See* Geothermal Energy

HYDROTHERMAL VENTS:

Incredible World of the Deep-sea Rifts. 680-705. NGS research grant. I. Strange World Without Sun. The Editor. 680-688; II. Return to Oases of the Deep. By Robert D. Ballard and J. Frederick Grassle. 689-705, *Nov. 1979*

Oases of Life in the Cold Abyss (Galapagos Rift). By John B. Corliss and Robert D. Ballard. 441-453, *Oct. 1977*

See also Geothermal Energy

HYENAS:

The Flamingo Eaters of Ngorongoro. By Richard D. Estes. 535-539, *Oct. 1973*

Hyenas, the Hunters Nobody Knows. By Hans Kruuk. Photos by Baron Hugo van Lawick. 44-57, *July 1968*

I J

*A caravan creeps up a
Himalayan pass in Ladakh, India's
most remote region.*

THOMAS J. ABERCROMBIE, NGS

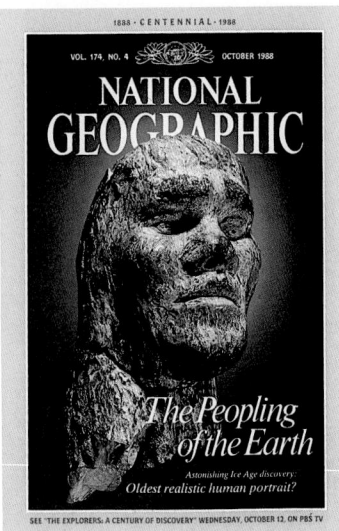

IAGS. *See* Inter-American Geodetic Survey

IC. *See* Integrated Circuits

IGY. *See* International Geophysical Year

ISA. *See* International School of America

I'M From New Jersey. By John T. Cunningham. Photos by Volkmar Wentzel. 1-45, *Jan. 1960*

"I'M OK, I'm Alive!" Avalanche! By David Cupp. Photos by Lanny Johnson and Andre Benier. 282-289, *Sept. 1982*

I BECOME a Bakhtiari. By Paul Edward Case. 325-358, *Mar. 1947*

I CLIMBED Everest Alone. By Reinhold Messner. Photos by the author and Nena Holguín. 552-566, *Oct. 1981*

I FLY the X-15. By Joseph A. Walker. Photos by Dean Conger. 428-450, *Sept. 1962*

I FOUND the Bones of the *Bounty.* By Luis Marden. 725-789, *Dec. 1957*

I JOINED a Sahara Salt Caravan. By Victor Englebert. 694-711, *Nov. 1965*

I KEPT House in a Jungle: The Spell of Primeval Tropics in Venezuela Riotous With Strange Plants, Animals, and Snakes, Enthralls a Young American Woman. By Anne Rainey Langley. 97-132, *Jan. 1939*

I LEARN About the Russians. By Eddy Gilmore. 619-640, *Nov. 1943*

I LIVE With the Eskimos. By Guy Mary-Rousseliere. 188-217, *Feb. 1971*

I LIVED on Formosa. By Joseph W. Ballantine. 1-24, *Jan. 1945*

I SAILED with Portugal's Captains

Courageous. By Alan Villiers. 565-596, *May 1952*

I SEE America First. By Lynda Bird Johnson. Photos by William Albert Allard. 874-904, *Dec. 1965*

I WALKED Some Irish Miles. By Dorothea Sheats. 653-678, *May 1951*

"I WILL Fight No More Forever." By William Albert Allard. 409-434, *Mar. 1977*

IACOVLEFF, ALEXANDRE: *Artist*

Faces and Fashions of Asia's Changeless Tribes. 21-36, *Jan. 1936*

IBAN:

Brunei, Borneo's Abode of Peace. By Joseph Judge. Photos by Dean Conger. 207-225, *Feb. 1974*

In Storied Lands of Malaysia. By Maurice Shadbolt. Photos by Winfield Parks. 734-783, *Nov. 1963*

Jungle Journeys in Sarawak. By Hedda Morrison. 710-736, *May 1956*

IBERIAN PENINSULA:

Iberia's Vintage River (Douro-Duero). By Marion Kaplan. Photos by Stephanie Maze. 460-489, *Oct. 1984*

⊕ *A Traveler's Map of Spain and Portugal. Oct. 1984*

⊕ *Spain and Portugal,* Atlas series. *Mar. 1965*

See also Gibraltar; Portugal; Spain

IBERO-AMERICAN EXPOSITION:

Seville, More Spanish Than Spain: The City of the Ibero-American Exposition, Which Opens This Spring, Presents a Tapestry of Many Ages and of Nations Old and New. By Richard Ford. 273-310, *Mar. 1929*

IBISES:

New Scarlet Bird in Florida Skies. By Paul A. Zahl. 874-882, *Dec. 1967*

Our Only Native Stork, the Wood Ibis.

By Robert Porter Allen. Photos by Frederick Kent Truslow. 294-306, *Feb. 1964*

Search for the Scarlet Ibis in Venezuela. By Paul A. Zahl. NGS research grant. 633-661, *May 1950*

Wildlife of Everglades National Park. By Daniel B. Beard. Paintings by Walter A. Weber. 83-116, *Jan. 1949*

The Large Wading Birds: Long Legs and Remarkable Beaks, as Well as Size, Form, and Color, Distinguish the Herons, Ibises, and Flamingos. By T. Gilbert Pearson. Included: Ibises, Herons, and Flamingos. Paintings by Allan Brooks. 441-469, *Oct. 1932*

The Sacred Ibis Cemetery and Jackal Catacombs at Abydos. By Camden M. Cobern. 1042-1056, *Sept. 1913*

IBIZA (Island), Balearic Islands, Mediterranean Sea:

Spain's Sun-blest Pleasure Isles. By Ethel A. Starbird. Photos by James A. Sugar. 679-701, *May 1976*

IBN SAUD, King (Saudi Arabia). *See* Al Saud, Abdul Aziz

IBU, Bougainville Island, Papua New Guinea:

Fiji Patrol on Bougainville. By David D. Duncan. 87-104, *Jan. 1945*

ICE AGE ANIMALS:

The Search for the First Americans. By Thomas Y. Canby. Photos by Kerby Smith. Paintings by Roy Andersen. 330-363, *Sept. 1979*

Bison Kill By Ice Age Hunters. By Dennis Stanford. NGS research grant. 114-121, *Jan. 1979*

⊕ "Ice Age Mammals of the Alaskan Tundra," painting supplement. Map of Canada. *Mar. 1972*

ICE AGE MAN:

"Where Did We Come From?" Editorial by Wilbur E. Garrett. Included:

At home on Wisconsin wetlands born in the Ice Age, a flock of sandhill cranes roams at the International Crane Foundation near Baraboo. CARY WOLINSKY, STOCK, BOSTON

ICE AGES:

ICE BIRD (Sloop):

ICE CAVES:

ICE-CLIFFS on the Kowak River

ICE CLIFFS on White River, Yukon

ICE-CLIFFS on White River, Yukon

ICE-CORE DATING:

ICE Entombs an Eskimo Family for

ICE FISHING:

Castle in the sea, a massive iceberg, its waterline smoothed and polished by waves, dwarfs an 180-foot-long vessel in the North Atlantic. JAMES R. HOLLAND

ICE ISLANDS:

ICE on the World. By Samuel W. Mat-

ICE PATROL. *See* International

Ice Patrol

ICE SCULPTURE:

An ICE Wrapped Continent. By G. H.

ICEBERGS:

ICEBOUND in Antarctica. By David

ICEBREAKERS:

North for Oil: *Manhattan* Makes the Historic Northwest Passage. By Bern Keating. Photos by Tomas Sennett. 374-391, *Mar. 1970*

Sea to Lakes on the St. Lawrence. By George W. Long. Photos by B. Anthony Stewart and John E. Fletcher. 323-366, *Sept. 1950*

Our Navy Explores Antarctica. By Richard E. Byrd. U. S. Navy official photos. 429-522, *Oct. 1947*

ICELAND:

Iceland: Life Under the Glaciers. By Louise E. Levathes. Photos by Bob Krist. 184-215, *Feb. 1987*

Iceland's Wild Glacier-born River. By Paul Vander-Molen. Photos by Robert Grégoire and Jean-Luc Chéron. 306-321, *Sept. 1984*

Vestmannaeyjar: Up From the Ashes. By Noel Grove. Photos by Robert S. Patton. 690-701, *May 1977*

This Changing Earth. By Samuel W. Matthews. 1-37, *Jan. 1973*

Sailing Iceland's Rugged Coasts. By Wright Britton. Photos by James A. Sugar. 228-265, *Aug. 1969*

Friendly Flight to Northern Europe. By Lyndon B. Johnson. Photos by Volkmar Wentzel. 268-293, *Feb. 1964*

Atlantic Odyssey: Iceland to Antarctica. By Newman Bumstead. Photos by Volkmar Wentzel. 725-780, *Dec. 1955*

"Around the World in Eighty Days." By Newman Bumstead. Included: Hekla Volcano; Reykjavík; Vatna Jökull. 705-750, *Dec. 1951*

Iceland Tapestry. By Deena Clark. 599-630, *Nov. 1951*

American Soldier in Reykjavík. By Luther M. Chovan. Included: Iceland Defrosted. 536-568, *Nov. 1945*

Ancient Iceland, New Pawn of War. 75-90, *July 1941*

A Walking Tour Across Iceland. By Isobel Wylie Hutchison. 467-497, *Apr. 1928*

The Island of the Sagas. By Earl Hanson. 499-511, *Apr. 1928*

Sailing the Seven Seas in the Interest of Science: Adventures Through 157,000 Miles of Storm and Calm, from Arctic to Antarctic and Around the World, in the Non-magnetic Yacht "Carnegie." By J. P. Ault. 631-690, *Dec. 1922*

A Visit to Lonely Iceland. By Perley H. Noyes. 731-741, *Nov. 1907*

The Land of Fire. By Jon Stefansson. 741-744, *Nov. 1907*

Proposed Meteorological Station in Iceland. 228, *June 1899*

Dwellings of the Saga-Time in Iceland, Greenland, and Vineland. By Cornelia Horsford. 73-84, *Mar. 1898*

Magnetic Observations in Iceland, Jan Mayen and Spitzbergen in 1892. By Cyrus C. Babb. 223-224, *Dec. 29, 1894*

See also Heimaey (Island); Surtsey (Island); *and* Vikings

ICHAC, PIERRE: *Photographer*

Carefree People of the Cameroons. 233-248, *Feb. 1947*

About to be tagged for study, a mountain lion retreats in Idaho's Salmon River Mountains. MAURICE G. HORNOCKER

ICONOGRAPHY of the Moche: Unraveling the Mystery of the Warrior-Priest. By Christopher B. Donnan. 551-555, *Oct. 1988*

ICONS:

The Byzantine Empire. 709-777. I. Rome of the East. By Merle Severy. Photos by James L. Stanfield. 709-767; II. Mount Athos. 739-745; III. Eternal Easter in a Greek Village. By Maria Nicolaidis-Karanikolas. Photos by James L. Stanfield. 768-777, *Dec. 1983*

Mount Sinai's Holy Treasures (St. Catherine's Monastery). By Kurt Weitzmann. Photos by Fred Anderegg. 109-127, *Jan. 1964*

ID FESTIVAL:

India at Work and Play. Photos by Peter Upton Muir, Maynard Owen Williams, Frances Muir. 449-464, *Apr. 1946*

IDA, DON:

A Wild, Ill-fated Balloon Race. 778-797. I. Wild Launch. 778-787; II. The Fantastic Flight of *Cote d'Or.* By Cynthia Shields. 789-793; III. Last Ascent of a Heroic Team (Maxie Anderson and Don Ida). 794-797, *Dec. 1983*

IDAHO:

Raptor Nursery Raises Birds for the Wild. Geographica. *Nov. 1988*

The Incredible Potato. By Robert E. Rhoades. Photos by Martin Rogers. Note: The Russet Burbank has allowed Idaho and Washington to surpass Maine's production lead. 668-694, *May 1982*

Along the Great Divide. By Mike Edwards. Photos by Nicholas deVore III. 483-515, *Oct. 1979*

Chief Joseph. By William Albert Allard. 409-434, *Mar. 1977*

High-stepping Idaho. By William S. Ellis. Photos by Dean Conger. 290-317, *Mar. 1973*

White-water Adventure on Wild Rivers of Idaho. By Frank Craighead, Jr., and John Craighead. 213-239, *Feb. 1970*

◼ Wild River. 239A-239B, *Feb. 1970*

Stalking the Mountain Lion–to Save Him. By Maurice G. Hornocker. 638-655, *Nov. 1969*

Forest Fire: The Devil's Picnic. By Stuart E. Jones and Jay Johnston. Included: Blazes in Kaniksu National Forest and Nezperce National Forest. 100-127, *July 1968*

Man on the Moon in Idaho. By William Belknap, Jr. 505-525, *Oct. 1960*

Following the Trail of Lewis and Clark. By Ralph Gray. 707-750, *June 1953*

Idaho Loggers Battle a River. 117-130, *July 1951*

A Map Maker Looks at the United States. By Newman Bumstead. Included: Coeur d'Alene; Lewiston; Pleasant Valley Rapids; Pocatello; Seven Devils country; Snake River; Weiser. 705-748, *June 1951*

Idaho Made the Desert Bloom. By D. Worth Clark. 641-688, *June 1944*

Down Idaho's River of No Return (Salmon River). By Philip J. Shenon and John C. Reed. 95-136, *July 1936*

Among the "Craters of the Moon": An Account of the First Expeditions Through the Remarkable Volcanic Lava Beds of Southern Idaho. By R. W. Limbert. 303-328, *Mar. 1924*

A Mind's-Eye Map of America. By Franklin K. Lane. 479-518, *June 1920*

Prosperous Idaho (An Interview with Governor Gooding, of Idaho, Published in the New York *Sun*, December, 1905). 16-22, *Jan. 1906*

The Idaho and Montana Boundary Line. By Richard U. Goode. 23-29, *Jan. 1900*

Bitter Root Forest Reserve. By Richard U. Goode. 387-400, *Sept. 1898*

See also Grays Lake National Wildlife Refuge; Island Park; Morgan Creek; Palouse Hills

IDDINGS, A. S. and D. W.: *Authors*

The Land of Contrast: Austria-Hungary. 1188-1217, 1284, *Dec. 1912*

An **IDEAL** Fuel Manufactured Out of Waste Products: The American Coal Briquetting Industry. By Guy Elliott Mitchell. 1067-1074, *Dec. 1910*

IDITAROD TRAIL SLED DOG RACE, Alaska:

Thousand-mile Race to Nome: A Woman's Icy Struggle. By Susan Butcher. Photos by Kerby Smith. 411-422, *Mar. 1983*

IDYLL, CLARENCE P.:

Nomination Page. *Mar. 1968*

Author

The Crab That Shakes Hands. Photos by Robert F. Sisson. 254-271, *Feb. 1971*

New Florida Resident, the Walking Catfish. Photos by Robert F. Sisson. 847-851, *June 1969*

Grunion, the Fish That Spawns on Land. Photos by Robert F. Sisson. 714-723, *May 1969*

The Incredible Salmon. Photos by Robert F. Sisson. Paintings by Walter A. Weber. 195-219, *Aug. 1968*

Shrimp Nursery: Science Explores New Ways to Farm the Sea. Photos by Robert F. Sisson. 636-659, *May 1965*

Shrimpers Strike Gold in the Gulf. Photos by Robert F. Sisson. 699-707, *May 1957*

The **IDYLLIC** Vale of Kashmir. By Volkmar Wentzel. 523-550, *Apr. 1948*

IFALIK, Caroline Islands, Pacific Ocean:

Ifalik, Lonely Paradise of the South Seas. By Marston Bates. 547-571, *Apr. 1956*

IFITAMIN, Papua New Guinea:

New Guinea's Mountain and Swampland Dwellers. By Ray T. Elsmore. 671-694, *Dec. 1945*

IGDRASIL (Sloop):

At Home on the Oceans: Whales and Sharks Make Exciting Neighbors for a Professor's Wife, Turned Able Seaman, On a Three-year Voyage Around the World. By Edith Bauer Strout. 33-86, *July 1939*

IGLOOLIK, Northwest Territories, Canada:

Hunters of the Lost Spirit: Canadians. By Priit J. Vesilind. Photos by David Alan Harvey. 174-189, *Feb. 1983*

I Live With the Eskimos. By Guy Mary-Rousseliere. 188-217, *Feb. 1971*

IGUANAS:

Undersea Wonders of the Galapagos. By Gerard Wellington. Photos by David Doubilet. 363-381, *Sept. 1978*

The Galapagos, Eerie Cradle of New Species. By Roger Tory Peterson. Photos by Alan and Joan Root. 541-585, *Apr. 1967*

Lost World of the Galapagos. By Irving and Electa Johnson. 681-703, *May 1959*

In the Wilds of a City Parlor. By Paul A. Zahl. 645-672, *Nov. 1954*

IGUAZU FALLS, Argentina-Brazil:

The World's Great Waterfalls: Visits to Mighty Niagara, Wonderful Victoria, and Picturesque Iguazu. By Theodore W. Noyes. 29-59, *July 1926*

The Falls of Iguazu. By Marie Robinson Wright. 456-460, *Aug. 1906*

IKEYA-SEKI COMET:

Giant Comet Grazes the Sun. By Kenneth F. Weaver. 259-261, *Feb. 1966*

ÎLE DE LA CITÉ, Birthplace of Paris. By Kenneth MacLeish. Photos by Bruce Dale. 680-719, *May 1968*

ILHA NOVA, Azores:

A New Volcano Bursts from the Atlantic. By John Scofield. Photos by Robert F. Sisson. 735-757, *June 1958*

ILIAD (Homer):

The Quest for Ulysses. By Tim Severin. Photos by Kevin Fleming. 197-225, *Aug. 1986*

ILLINOIS:

Prairie Preservation: Good News, Bad News. Geographica. *Dec. 1988*

The Tallgrass Prairie: Can It Be Saved? By Dennis Farney. Photos by Jim Brandenburg. 37-61, *Jan. 1980*

✦ *Close-up: U.S.A., Illinois, Indiana, Ohio, and Kentucky.* Text on reverse. *Feb. 1977*

Who Were the "Mound Builders"? By George E. Stuart. Included: Cahokia; Koster farm site. 783-801, *Dec. 1972*

Illinois: The City and the Plain. By Robert Paul Jordan. Photos by James L. Stanfield and Joseph J. Scherschel. 745-797, *June 1967*

The Upper Mississippi. By Willard Price. 651-699, *Nov. 1958*

Illinois–Healthy Heart of the Nation. By Leo A. Borah. Photos by B. Anthony Stewart and Willard R. Culver. 781-820, *Dec. 1953*

Following the Trail of Lewis and Clark. By Ralph Gray. 707-750, *June 1953*

Vacation Tour Through Lincoln Land. By Ralph Gray. 141-184, *Feb. 1952*

Mapping the Nation's Breadbasket. By Frederick Simpich. 831-849, *June 1948*

"Pyramids" of the New World. By Neil Merton Judd. Included: Cahokia. 105-128, *Jan. 1948*

Illinois, Crossroads of the Continent. By Junius B. Wood. 523-594, *May 1931*

✦ *Illinois. May 1931*

See also Chicago; Shawneetown

ILLINOIS (River), Illinois:

Down Mark Twain's River on a Raft. By Rex E. Hieronymus. Included:

A tree spreads its branches before a checkerboard backdrop of skyscraper windows in Chicago, Illinois. WINFIELD PARKS, NGS

The Illinois and Mississippi rivers. 551-574, *Apr. 1948*

ILLUSTRATED LONDON NEWS:

Witness to a War (U. S. Civil War): British Correspondent Frank Vizetelly. By Robert T. Cochran, Jr. 453-491, *Apr. 1961*

ILULÍSSAT, Greenland. *See* Jakobshavn

IMAGES of the World: Photography at ■■ *the National Geographic.* 396 pages. *1981*

IMAGINATION and Geography. 825, *Dec. 1907*

IMAGING TECHNOLOGY:

Editorial. By Wilbur E. Garrett. 423, *Apr. 1988*

President's Page. By Gilbert M. Grosvenor. *July 1987*

Medicine's New Vision. By Howard Sochurek. Paintings by Davis Meltzer. Illustrations text by Peter Miller. Included: Computed Tomography, Magnetic Resonance Imaging, Sonography, Digital Subtraction Angiography, Radioisotope imaging. 2-41, *Jan. 1987*

Editorial. By Wilbur E. Garrett. 701, *June 1986*

Satellites That Serve Us. By Thomas Y. Canby. 281-335. Included: A portfolio, Images of Earth; Spacelab 1: *Columbia.* By Michael E. Long. 301-307, *Sept. 1983*

The Once and Future Universe. By Rick Gore. Photos by James A. Sugar. Paintings by Barron Storey. Picture text by David Jeffery. 704-749, *June 1983*

The Mystery of the Shroud. By Kenneth F. Weaver. Included: Density scans, stereometric photography, and ultraviolet photography. 730-753, *June 1980*

◼ The Invisible World. 1, *Jan. 1980*; cover, *Mar. 1980*

Editorial. By Gilbert M. Grosvenor. 295, *Mar. 1978*

Eyes of Science. By Rick Gore. Photos by James P. Blair. 360-389, *Mar. 1978*

See also Fiber Optics; Photography; Photography, Infrared; Photography, Underwater; Photomicrography; Thermograms

IMBODEN, OTIS: *Photographer*

Goal at the End of the Trail: Santa Fe. By William S. Ellis. Photos by Gordon W. Gahan and Otis Imboden. 323-345, *Mar. 1982*

Drama of Death in a Minoan Temple. By Yannis Sakellarakis and Efi Sapouna-Sakellaraki. Photos by Otis Imboden and Spyros Tsavdaroglou. 205-222, *Feb. 1981*

The Thousand-mile Glide. By Karl Striedieck. 431-438, *Mar. 1978*

■■ *The Mysterious Maya.* By George E. and Gene S. Stuart. Photos by David Alan Harvey and Otis Imboden. 199 pages. *1977*

The Maya: Riddle of the Glyphs. By George E. Stuart. 768-791, *Dec. 1975*

Thera, Key to the Riddle of Minos. By Spyridon Marinatos. 702-726, *May 1972*

Florida's Emerging Seminoles. By Louis Capron. 716-734, *Nov. 1969*

Threatened Glories of Everglades National Park. By Frederick Kent Truslow and Frederick G. Vosburgh. Photos by Frederick Kent Truslow and Otis Imboden. 508-553, *Oct. 1967*

Drowned Galleons Yield Spanish Gold. By Kip Wagner. 1-37, *Jan. 1965*

First Flight Across the Bottom of the World. By James R. Reedy. 454-464, *Mar. 1964*

YWCA: International Success Story. By Mary French Rockefeller. 904-933, *Dec. 1963*

The People of Cades Cove. By William O. Douglas. Photos by Thomas Nebbia and Otis Imboden. 60-95, *July 1962*

IMBRIE, ROBERT WHITNEY:
Author

Crossing Asia Minor, the Country of the New Turkish Republic. 445-472, *Oct. 1924*

IMILCHIL PLATEAU, Morocco:

Berber Brides' Fair. By Carla Hunt. Photos by Nik Wheeler. 119-129, *Jan. 1980*

The **IMMEDIATE** Necessity for Military Highways. By A. G. Batchelder. 477-499, *Nov.-Dec. 1917*

IMMIGRATION:

Australia
Children of the First Fleet. By John Everingham. Painting by Roy Andersen. 233-245, *Feb. 1988*

Coober Pedy: Opal Capital of Australia's Outback. By Kenny Moore. Photos by Penny Tweedie. 560-571, *Oct. 1976*

South Australia, Gateway to the Great Outback. By Howell Walker. Photos by Joseph J. Scherschel. 441-481, *Apr. 1970*

The Making of a New Australia. By Howell Walker. 233-259, *Feb. 1956*

Canada
Canadian Immigration. 356, *June 1906*

The Origin of French-Canadians. 96-97, *Mar. 1898*

Ecuador
South American Immigration. 587, *Oct. 1906*

Israel
Israel–The Seventh Day. By Joseph Judge. Photos by Gordon W. Gahan. 816-855, *Dec. 1972*

Our Life on a Border Kibbutz. By Carol and Al Abrams. Photos by Al Abrams. 364-391, *Sept. 1970*

United States
Editorial. By Wilbur E. Garrett. 1, *July 1986*

Liberty Lifts Her Lamp Once More. By Alice J. Hall. 2-19, *July 1986*

Japanese Americans: Home at Last. By Arthur Zich. Photos by Michael S. Yamashita. 512-539, *Apr. 1986*

Life on the Line: U. S.-Mexican Border. By Mark Kramer. Photos by Danny Lehman. 720-749, *June 1985*

■■ *Liberty: The Statue and the American Dream.* By Leslie Allen. The official book for the Centennial of the Statue of Liberty published by the Statue of Liberty-Ellis Island Foundation, Inc. Prepared and produced as a public service by NGS. 304 pages. *1985*

Brooklyn: The Other Side of the Bridge. By Alice J. Hall. Photos by Robert W. Madden. Included: Caribbean Blacks, Germans, Hasidim, Hispanics, Irish, Italians, Russian Jews, Sephardim. 580-613, *May 1983*

✦ *Atlantic Gateways,* The Making of America series. On reverse: Indians

and Trade, Nation in the Making, Peopling of the Gateways, Race for the Hinterlands, Growth of Industry, Spreading Urban Corridors. *Mar. 1983*

They'd Rather Be in Philadelphia. By Ethel A. Starbird. Photos by Ted Spiegel. Included: Asians, Germans, Irish, Italians, Jews, Poles. 314-343, *Mar. 1983*

Florida–A Time for Reckoning. By William S. Ellis. Photos by Nathan Benn and Kevin Fleming. Included: Cubans; Haitians; Jamaicans; Jews of European origin; Puerto Ricans. 172-219, *Aug. 1982*

The Incredible Potato. By Robert E. Rhoades. Photos by Martin Rogers. Included: Scotch-Irish. 668-694, *May 1982*

One Family's Odyssey to America. By John Everingham. 642-661, *May 1980*

Chinatown, the Gilded Ghetto. By William Albert Allard. 627-643, *Nov. 1975*

New England's "Little Portugal." By O. Louis Mazzatenta. 90-109, *Jan. 1975*

Cuba's Exiles Bring New Life to Miami. By Edward J. Linehan. Photos by Nathan Benn. 68-95, *July 1973*

Nikolaevsk: A Bit of Old Russia Takes Root in Alaska. By Jim Rearden. Photos by Charles O'Rear. 401-425, *Sept. 1972*

Immigrants Still Flock to Liberty's Land. By Albert W. Atwood. 708-724, *Nov. 1955*

New York–The Metropolis of Mankind. By William Joseph Showalter. 1-49, *July 1918*

Our Foreign-Born Citizens. 95-130, *Feb. 1917*

The Foreign-Born of the United States. 265-271, *Sept. 1914*

Our Immigration Laws from the Viewpoint of National Eugenics. By Robert De C. Ward. 38-41, *Jan. 1912*

Some of Our Immigrants. 317-334, *May 1907*

Immigration to the Southern States. 517-519, *Nov. 1905*

Our Immigration in 1905. 434-435, *Sept. 1905*

The Character of Our Immigration, Past and Present. By Z. F. McSweeny. 1-15, *Jan. 1905*

Our Immigration During 1904. 15-27, *Jan. 1905*

Immigration and Naturalization. 51-52, *Jan. 1905*

The Sex, Nativity, and Color of the People of the United States. By G. H. Grosvenor. 381-389, *Nov. 1901*

The Movements of Our Population. By Henry Gannett. 21-44, *Mar. 20, 1893*

See also German Colonists; Hutterites; Moravians; Refugees; Swiss Colonists; Ukrainians

IMMUNE SYSTEM:

Our Immune System: The Wars Within. By Peter Jaret. Photos by Lennart Nilsson. Illustrations text by Larry Kohl. 702-735, *June 1986*

Beyond Supermouse: Changing Life's Genetic Blueprint. By Robert F.

Subdued at their long journey's end, newly arrived immigrants to the U.S. nervously await official approval at Ellis Island in 1918. PAUL THOMPSON

Weaver. Photos by Ted Spiegel. 818-847, *Dec. 1984*

IMPERIAL Rome Reborn. By John Patric. 269-325, *Mar. 1937*

IMPERIAL Russia's Glittering Legacy. 24-33, *Jan. 1978*

The **IMPERILED** Everglades. By Fred Ward. 1-27, *Jan. 1972*

The **IMPERILED** Giants. By William Graves. 722-751, *Dec. 1976*

IMPERILED Gift of the Sea: Caribbean Green Turtle. By Archie Carr. Photos by Robert E. Schroeder. 876-890, *June 1967*

The **IMPERILED** Mountain Gorilla. By Dian Fossey. 501-523. Included: Death of Marchessa. Photos by Peter G. Veit. 508-511, *Apr. 1981*

IMPERILED Phantom of Asian Peaks: First Photographs of Snow Leopards in the Wild. By George B. Schaller. 702-707, *Nov. 1971*

IMPHAL, India:
Manipur—Where Japan Struck at India. 743-750, *June 1944*

IMPORTANT Announcement Concerning Essays. 227-228, *Dec. 29, 1894*

An **IMPORTANT** New Guide for Shipping: Navassa Light, on a Barren Island in the West Indies, is the First Signal for the Panama Canal. By George R. Putnam. 401-406, *Nov. 1918*

An **IMPRESSION** of the Guiana Wilderness. By Angelo Heilprin. 373-381, *June 1907*

IMPRESSIONIST ART. *See* French Impressionists

IMPRESSIONS and Scenes of Mozambique. By O. W. Barrett. 807-830, *Oct. 1910*

IMPRESSIONS of Asiatic Turkey. By Stephen van Rensselaer Trowbridge. 598-609, *Dec. 1914*

IMPRESSIONS of Palestine. By James Bryce. 293-317, *Mar. 1915*

IMPRINTING. *See* Snow Geese

The **IMPROVEMENT** of Geographical Teaching. By William Morris Davis. 68-75, *July 10, 1893*

IMPROVEMENTS in the City of Manila. 195-197, *May 1903*

IMPROVEMENTS in the Republic of Panama. 441-442, *Sept. 1905*

IMST, Austria:
Merry Maskers of Imst. Photos by Francis C. Fuerst. 201-208, *Aug. 1936*

IN Andalusia, Home of Song and Sunshine. Photos by Gervais Courtellemont. 301-308, *Mar. 1929*

IN Beautiful Delecarlia (Sweden). By Lillian Gore. 464-477, *May 1909*

IN *Bounty*'s Wake: Finding the Wreck

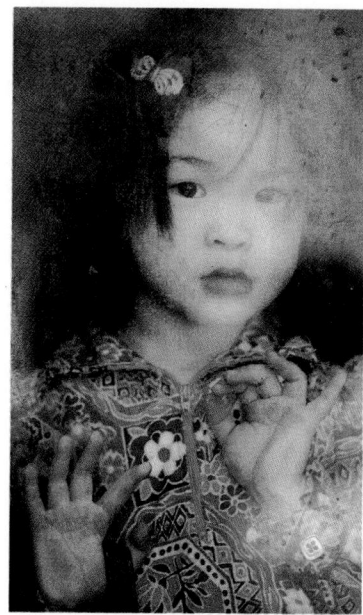

While her seamstress mother works, a child in San Francisco's Chinatown looks out the shop window. WILLIAM ALBERT ALLARD

of H.M.S. *Pandora*. By Luis Marden. 423-451, *Oct. 1985*

IN Civilized French Africa. By James F. J. Archibald. 303-311, *Mar. 1909*

IN Defense of the Collector. By Gillett G. Griffin. 462-465, *Apr. 1986*

IN Field and Hive with the Busy Honeybee. Paintings by Hashime Murayama. 417-424, *Apr. 1935*

IN French Lorraine: That Part of France Where the First American Soldiers Have Fallen. By Harriet Chalmers Adams. 499-518, *Nov.-Dec. 1917*

IN Hawaii's Crystal Sea, A Galaxy of Life Fills the Night. By Kenneth Brower. Photos by William R. Curtsinger and Chris Newbert. 834-847, *Dec. 1981*

IN Honor of the Army and Aviation. 267-284, *Mar. 1911*

IN Humboldt's Wake: Narrative of a National Geographic Society Expedition Up the Orinoco and Through the Strange Casiquiare Canal to Amazonian Waters. By Ernest G. Holt. 621-644, *Nov. 1931*

IN Long-Forbidden Tibet. By Fred Ward. 218-259, *Feb. 1980*

IN Manchuria Now. By W. Robert Moore. 389-414, *Mar. 1947*

IN Montezuma's Painted Land (Mexico). Photos by Luis Marden. 345-368, *Sept. 1940*

IN Quaint, Curious Croatia. By Felix J. Koch. 809-832, *Dec. 1908*

IN Quest of Beauty. Text by Paul Mellon. 372-385, *Mar. 1967*

IN Quest of the Golden Eagle: Over Lonely Mountain and Prairie Soars This Rare and Lordly Bird, But Three Youths from the East Catch Up With Him at Last. By John and Frank Craighead. 693-710, *May 1940*

IN Quest of the Rarest Flamingo. By William G. Conway. Photos by Bates Littlehales. 91-105, *July 1961*

IN Quest of the World's Largest Frog. By Paul A. Zahl. 146-152, *July 1967*

IN Search of Arabia's Past. By Peter Bruce Cornwall. 493-522, *Apr. 1948*

IN Search of Man's Past at Lake Rudolf. By Richard E. Leakey. Photos by Gordon W. Gahan. 712-734, *May 1970*

IN Search of Modern Humans. By John J. Putman. Photos by Sisse Brimberg and Ira Block. Paintings by Jack Unruh. Included: A fragmentary modern skull found in South Africa's Border Cave tentatively dated back to 100,000 BP. 439-477, *Oct. 1988*

IN Search of Moses. By Harvey Arden. Photos by Nathan Benn. 2-37, *Jan. 1976*

IN Smiling Alsace, Where France Has Resumed Sway. Photos by Gervais Courtellemont. 168-176, *Aug. 1927*

IN Storied Lands of Malaysia. By Maurice Shadbolt. Photos by Winfield Parks. 734-783, *Nov. 1963*

IN the Allagash Country (Maine). By Kenneth Fuller Lee. 505-520, *Apr. 1929*

IN the Birthplace of Christianity. Photos by Hans Hildenbrand, Maynard Owen Williams, Gervais Courtellemont. 697-720, *Dec. 1926*

IN the Canary Islands, Where Streets are Carpeted with Flowers. Photos by Wilhelm Tobien. 615-622, *May 1930*

IN the Crusaders' Footsteps. By Franc Shor. Photos by Thomas Nebbia and James P. Blair. 731-789, *June 1962*

IN the Diamond Mountains: Adventures Among the Buddhist Monasteries of Eastern Korea. By the Marquess Curzon of Kedleston. 353-374, *Oct. 1924*

IN the Empire of the Aztecs: Mexico City Is Rich in Relics of a People Who Practiced Human Sacrifice, Yet Loved Flowers, Education, and Art. By Frank H. H. Roberts, Jr. Paintings by H. M. Herget. 725-750, *June 1937*

IN the Far Pacific: At the Birth of Nations. By Carolyn Bennett Patterson. Photos by David Hiser and Melinda Berge. Included: Mariana Islands, Marshall Islands, Kosrae, Pohnpei, Truk, Yap, Palau. 460-499, *Oct. 1986*

IN the Footsteps of Alexander the Great. By Helen and Frank Schreider. Paintings by Tom Lovell. 1-65, *Jan. 1968*

Solemn features of a present-day Andean
reflect the heritage of Peru's fabled Inca.
LOREN MCINTYRE

The **INCREDIBLE** Helicopter. By Peter T. White. 533-557, *Apr. 1959*

*The **INCREDIBLE** Incas and Their* ■■*Timeless Land.* Written and photographed by Loren McIntyre. Art by Louis S. Glanzman. 199 pages. *1975*

The **INCREDIBLE** Kangaroo. By David H. Johnson. 487-500, *Oct. 1955*

*The **INCREDIBLE** Machine.* Contents: ■■The human body. 384 pages. *1986*

INCREDIBLE Photograph Shows Earth From Pole to Pole. Photos by Nimbus I. 190-193, *Feb. 1965*

The **INCREDIBLE** Potato. By Robert E. Rhoades. Photos by Martin Rogers. 668-694, *May 1982*

The **INCREDIBLE** Rat. By Thomas Y. Canby. Photos by James L. Stanfield. 60-87, *July 1977*

The **INCREDIBLE** Salmon. By Clarence P. Idyll. Photos by Robert F. Sisson. Paintings by Walter A. Weber. 195-219, *Aug. 1968*

The **INCREDIBLE** Universe. By Kenneth F. Weaver. Photos by James P. Blair. 589-625, *May 1974*

INCREDIBLE World of the Deep-sea Rifts. 680-705, *Nov. 1979*

*INDEPENDENCE-*class Light Carrier. *See Princeton*

INDIA:

India: Life on the Edge. By Paul R. and Anne H. Ehrlich. Photos by Raghu Rai. 930-933, *Dec. 1988*

Long Journey of the Brahmaputra. By Jere Van Dyk. Photos by Raghubir Singh and Galen Rowell. Included: A Rare Visit to a World Unto Itself. By Raghubir Singh. 672-711, *Nov. 1988*

Focus on India: Festivals Across U. S. Celebrate a Diverse Culture. By John J. Putman. 460-461, *Apr. 1985*

When the Moguls Ruled India. By Mike Edwards. Photos by Roland Michaud. 463-493, *Apr. 1985*

New Delhi: Mirror of India. By Bryan Hodgson. Photos by Steve Raymer. 506-533, *Apr. 1985*

The Poppy. By Peter T. White. Photos by Steve Raymer. 143-189, *Feb. 1985*

■ Land of the Tiger. 754, Dec. 1984; President's Page; cover, *Jan. 1985*

Monsoons: Life Breath of Half the World. By Priit J. Vesilind. Photos by Steve McCurry. 712-747, *Dec. 1984*

Tiger! Lord of the Indian Jungle. By Stanley Breeden. Photos by Belinda Wright. 748-773, *Dec. 1984*

✠ *South Asia, with Afghanistan and Burma; Peoples of South Asia. Dec. 1984*

By Rail Across the Indian Subcontinent. By Paul Theroux. Photos by Steve McCurry. 696-743, *June 1984*

India's Railway Lifeline. By Michael G. Satow. 744-749, *June 1984*

They're Killing Off the Rhino. By

Esmond Bradley Martin. Photos by Jim Brandenburg. 404-422, *Mar. 1984*

Silver: A Mineral of Excellent Nature. By Allen A. Boraiko. Photos by Fred Ward. 280-313, *Sept. 1981*

Bombay, the Other India. By John Scofield. Photos by Raghubir Singh. 104-129, *July 1981*

The Desert: An Age-old Challenge Grows. By Rick Gore. Photos by Georg Gerster and Bruce Dale. 586-639, *Nov. 1979*

A Bad Time to Be a Crocodile. By Rick Gore. Photos by Jonathan Blair. 90-115, *Jan. 1978*

Purdah in India: Life Behind the Veil. By Doranne Wilson Jacobson. 270-286, *Aug. 1977*

The Rat, Lapdog of the Devil. By Thomas Y. Canby. Photos by James L. Stanfield. 60-87, *July 1977*

India Struggles to Save Her Wildlife. By John J. Putman. Paintings by Ned Seidler. 299-343, *Sept. 1976*

Can the World Feed Its People? By Thomas Y. Canby. Photos by Steve Raymer. 2-31, *July 1975*

Nature's Gifts to Medicine. By Lonnelle Aikman. Paintings by Lloyd K. Townsend and Don Crowley. 420-440, *Sept. 1974*

Calcutta, India's Maligned Metropolis. By Peter T. White. Photos by Raghubir Singh. 534-563, *Apr. 1973*

India's Energetic Sikhs. By John E. Frazer. Photos by James P. Blair. 528-541, *Oct. 1972*

The Ganges, River of Faith. By John J.

warms of workers, 125,000 strong, scramble over scaffolding to erect a huge dam in India's Andhra Pradesh state.   JOHN SCOFIELD, NGS

Cloaked in glory, a state elephant of Mysore, India, plays his majestic part in a ceremonial parade in the early 1900s. BARTON & SON

With unwavering hand, a master craftsman in Jaipur, India, adds the finishing touches to an enameled tray depicting hunting scenes. MELVILLE BELL GROSVENOR, NGS

*Gene and George Stuart ponder glyphs
on a doorjamb carved by Maya Indians
at Xcalumkin, one of the archaeological
sites included on a 1968 supplement
map (below).* OTIS IMBODEN, NGS

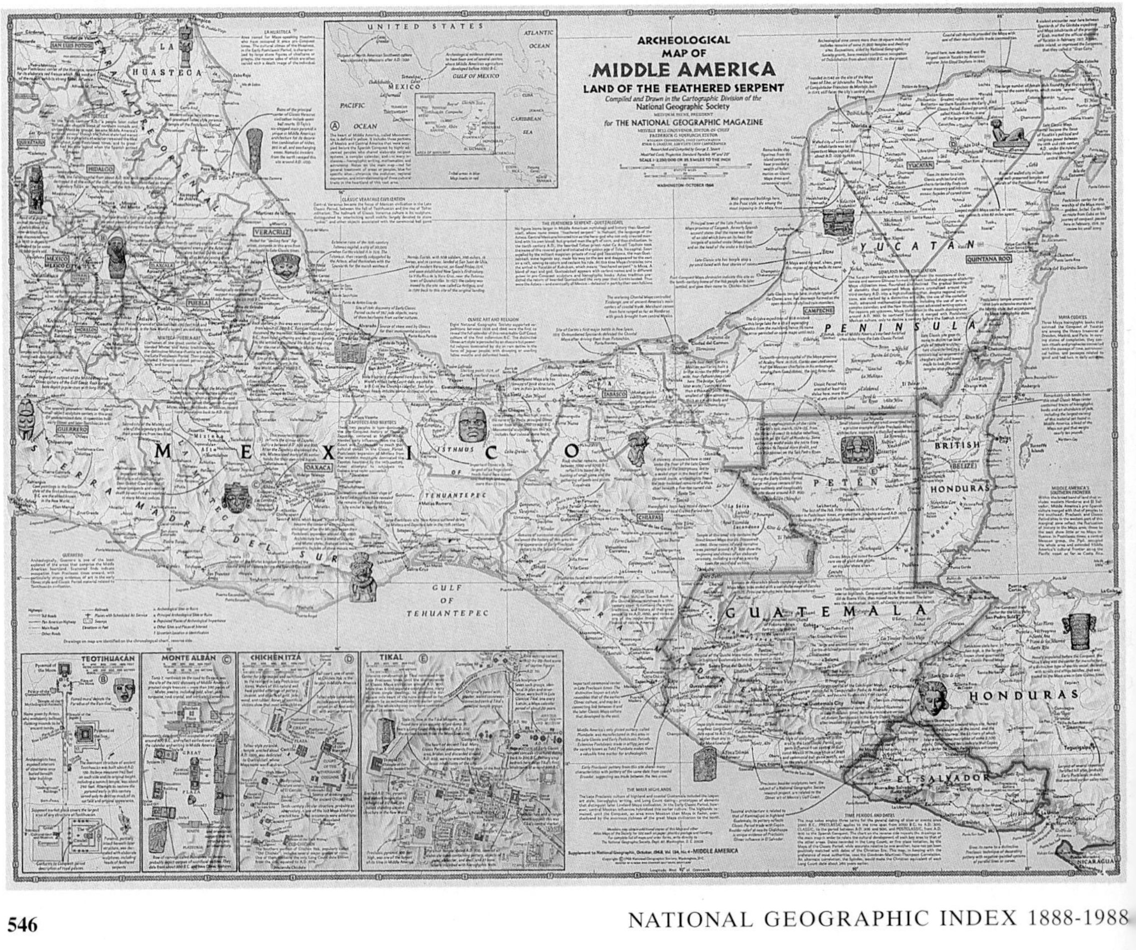

INDIANS OF NORTH AMERICA:

Chief Leon Shenandoah of the Six Nations Iroquois Confederacy leans solemnly on his ceremonial staff. STEVE WALL

Iroquois of the Akwesasne Mohawk longhouse dance to the rhythms of water drum and cow-horn rattle. STEVE WALL

Charles Marion Russell, renowned cowboy artist of the American West, expresses his loyalty to American Indians in this 1914 drawing.

C. M. RUSSELL MUSEUM, GREAT FALLS, MONTANA

This is the only real American
He fought an died for his country
to day he has no vote no country and is not a citizen
but history will not forget him

Ruins of thousand-year-old Mesa Verde in Colorado bear witness to the extraordinary ingenuity of its builders, the Anasazi. DEWITT JONES

INDIANS OF SOUTH AMERICA:

In time-honored tradition, a North American Indian mother in California combines working with caring for her children in 1914.

An Aymara Indian from Lake Titicaca's Island of the Sun paddles a sacrificial llama to an annual ceremony.　LOREN MCINTYRE

An armored car and jeep ford a flooded trail in 1952, as French troops capture Hoa Binh in the part of Indochina that is now Vietnam. FRENCH DEPARTMENT OF INFORMATION

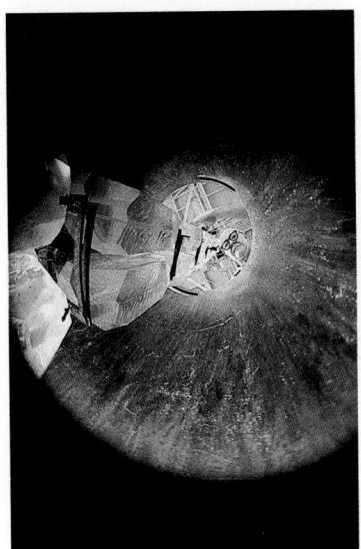

Peering into a device like a pressure cooker, a technician lifts out crystals of synthetic quartz. SAM ABELL

New Guinea to Bali in *Yankee.* By Irving and Electa Johnson. 767-815, *Dec. 1959*
This Young Giant, Indonesia. By Beverley M. Bowie. Photos by J. Baylor Roberts. 351-392, *Sept. 1955*
Republican Indonesia Tries Its Wings. By W. Robert Moore. 1-40, *Jan. 1951*
See also former name, Netherlands East Indies; *and* Bali; Celebes; Irian Jaya (Western New Guinea); Java; Krakatau; Lesser Sunda Islands; Moluccas; *also* Tanjung Puting Reserve

INDONESIAN INSTITUTE OF SCIENCES: Sponsorship:
Orangutans. 835, *June 1980*

INDONESIAN NEW GUINEA. *See* Irian Jaya, Indonesia

INDOOR AIR POLLUTION:
Air: An Atmosphere of Uncertainty. By Noel Grove. Photos by Ted Spiegel. Paintings by William H. Bond. Included: A deadly soup (a list of harmful chemicals), Careless neighbors, A global greenhouse, The ozone enigma, Getting the lead out, The enemy within. 502-537, *Apr. 1987*

INDUSTRIAL MUSEUMS. *See* Corning Museum of Glass; Henry Ford Museum; John Woodman Higgins Armory

The **INDUSTRIAL** Titan of America: Pennsylvania, Once the Keystone of the Original Thirteen, Now the Keystone of Forty-eight Sovereign States. By John Oliver La Gorce. 367-406, *May 1919*

The **INDUSTRIAL** Training of the German People. 111-114, *Mar. 1905*

INDUSTRIAL WASTE:
Air: An Atmosphere of Uncertainty. By Noel Grove. Photos by Ted Spiegel. Paintings by William H. Bond. Included: A deadly soup (a list of harmful chemicals), Careless neighbors, A global greenhouse, The ozone enigma, Getting the lead out, The enemy within. 502-537, *Apr. 1987*
Editorial. By Wilbur E. Garrett. 277, *Mar. 1985*
Hazardous Waste...Storing Up Trouble. By Allen A. Boraiko. Photos by Fred Ward. 318-351, *Mar. 1985*
Acid Rain–How Great a Menace? By Anne LaBastille. Photos by Ted Spiegel. 652-681, *Nov. 1981*
A River Restored: Oregon's Willamette. By Ethel A. Starbird. Photos by Lowell J. Georgia. 816-835, *June 1972*
Barehanded Battle to Cleanse the Bay: San Francisco's Tragic Oil Spill Triggers Spontaneous Cooperation Between Industry and Concerned Citizens. By Peter T. White. Photos by Jonathan S. Blair. 866-881, *June 1971*
Pollution, Threat to Man's Only Home. By Gordon Young. Photos by James P. Blair. 738-781, *Dec. 1970*

INDUSTRY:
Those Successful Japanese. By Bart McDowell. Photos by Fred Ward. 323-359, *Mar. 1974*
Yesterday Lingers Along the Connecticut. By Charles McCarry. Photos by David L. Arnold. 334-369, *Sept. 1972*
Crystals, Magical Servants of the Space Age. By Kenneth F. Weaver. Photos by James P. Blair. 278-296, *Aug. 1968*
Cities Like Worcester Make America. By Howell Walker. 189-214, *Feb. 1955*

Dixie Spins the Wheel of Industry. By William H. Nicholas. Photos by J. Baylor Roberts. 281-324, *Mar. 1949*
"Magnetic City" (Magnitogorsk), Core of Valiant Russia's Industrial Might. By John Scott. 525-556, *May 1943*
Chemists Make a New World: Creating Hitherto Unknown Raw Materials, Science Now Disrupts Old Trade Routes and Revamps the World Map of Industry. By Frederick Simpich. Note: Synthetic products. 601-640, *Nov. 1939*
See also Agriculture; Aluminum; Automotive Industry; Cottage Industries; Cotton; Energy; Fishing (Industry); Hydroelectric Power; Lumber Industry; Meat Industry; Mines and Mining; Motion Picture Industry; Paper Pulp Industry; Platinum; Rugs; Shoe Industry; Steel Industry; Technology; Transportation; War Industries; *and* country and state articles describing local industries

INDUSTRY'S Greatest Asset–Steel. By William Joseph Showalter. 121-156, *Aug. 1917*

INEXHAUSTIBLE Italy. By Arthur Stanley Riggs. 273-368, *Oct. 1916*

INFANTRYMEN–The Fighters of War. By W. H. Wilbur. 513-538, *Nov. 1944*

INFLATABLE Ship Opens Era of Airborne Undersea Expeditions. By Jacques-Yves Cousteau. 142-148, *July 1961*

The **INFLUENCE** of Forestry upon the Lumber Industry of the United States. By Overton W. Price. 381-386, *Oct. 1903*

INFLUENCE of Geographical Conditions on Military Operations in South Africa. By W. A. Simpson. 186-192, *May 1900*

Blast furnaces of the Tennessee Coal, Iron and Railroad Company light the night in 1949 in Ensley, a steelmaking suburb of Birmingham, Alabama. J. BAYLOR ROBERTS, NGS

The **INFLUENCE** of Submarine Cables upon Military and Naval Supremacy. By George O. Squier. 1-12, *Jan. 1901*

INFORMAL Salute to the English Lakes. By Maynard Owen Williams. 511-521, *Apr. 1936*

INFORMATION TRANSMISSION. *See* Chips; Communications

INFRARED IMAGERY:

Heat Paints *Columbia*'s Portrait. By Cliff Tarpy. 650-653, *Nov. 1982*
Our Energy Predicament. By Kenneth F. Weaver. Included: An Infrared Look at Personal Insulation; Heat Loss: A Thief in the Night; Mapping Urban Hot Spots. 2-23, *Special Report on Energy. (Feb. 1981)*
Remote Sensing: New Eyes to See the World. By Kenneth F. Weaver. 46-73, *Jan. 1969*
See also Photography, Infrared

INGALLS, HUNTLEY:
Author-Photographer

We Climbed Utah's Skyscraper Rock. Photos by author and Barry C. Bishop. 705-721, *Nov. 1962*

INGLEFIELD FJORD, Greenland:

Narwhal Hunters of Greenland. By Ivars Silis. 520-539, *Apr. 1984*

INGSTAD, HELGE: *Author*

Vinland Ruins Prove Vikings Found the New World. 708-734, *Nov. 1964*

INISHEER, INISHMAAN, INISH-MORE (Islands), Ireland:

The Arans, Ireland's Invincible Isles. By Veronica Thomas. Photos by Winfield Parks. 545-573, *Apr. 1971*

INLAND SEA, Japan:

Japan's Amazing Inland Sea. By William S. Ellis. Photos by James L. Stanfield. 830-863, *Dec. 1977*
Living in a Japanese Village. By William Graves. Photos by James L. Stanfield. 668-693, *May 1972*
Kayak Odyssey: From the Inland Sea to Tokyo. By Dan Dimancescu. Photos by Christopher G. Knight. 295-337, *Sept. 1967*
Cruising Japan's Inland Sea. By Willard Price. 619-650, *Nov. 1953*

INLAND WATERWAYS. *See* Canals; Inside Passage; Intracoastal Waterways; River Trips; St. Lawrence Seaway

INLE (Lake), Burma:

Burma's Leg Rowers and Floating Farms. Photos by W. E. Garrett. Text by David Jeffery. 826-845, *June 1974*

INNER HEBRIDES (Islands), Scotland:

Scotland's Inner Hebrides: Isles of the Western Sea. By Kenneth MacLeish. Photos by R. Stephen Uzzell III. 690-717, *Nov. 1974*
Scotland From Her Lovely Lochs and Seas. By Alan Villiers. Photos by Robert F. Sisson. 492-541, *Apr. 1961*
Over the Sea to Scotland's Skye. By Robert J. Reynolds. 87-112, *July 1952*

A gorged mosquito escapes with blood from a human finger. Transmitting a grim array of diseases, this insect is the deadliest in the world. DWIGHT R. KUHN

INNSBRUCK, Austria:

Tirol, Austria's Province in the Clouds. By Peter T. White. Photos by Volkmar Wentzel. 107-141, *July 1961*
A Stroll to Venice. By Isobel Wylie Hutchison. 378-410, *Sept. 1951*
Occupied Austria, Outpost of Democracy. By George W. Long. Photos by Volkmar Wentzel. 749-790, *June 1951*

INOCULATING the Ground. 225-228, *May 1904*

INSANITY:

The Geographical Distribution of Insanity in the United States. By William A. White. 361-378, *Oct. 1903*

INSECT CONTROL:

Tstetse–Fly of the Deadly Sleep. By Georg Gerster. 814-833, *Dec. 1986*
The Pesticide Dilemma. By Allen A. Boraiko. Photos by Fred Ward. 145-183, *Feb. 1980*
Mosquitoes, the Mighty Killers. By Lewis T. Nielsen. 427-440, *Sept. 1979*
New Tricks Outwit Our Insect Enemies. By Hal Higdon. Photos by Robert F. Sisson and Emory Kristof. 380-399, *Sept. 1972*
What's So Special About Spiders? By Paul A. Zahl. 190-219, *Aug. 1971*
Pollution, Threat to Man's Only Home. By Gordon Young. Photos by James P. Blair. Included: The use of DDT during World War II against mosquitoes and body lice. 738-781, *Dec. 1970*
Following the Ladybug Home. By Kenneth S. Hagen. Photos by Robert F. Sisson. 543-553, *Apr. 1970*
The Revolution in American Agriculture. By Jules B. Billard. Photos by James P. Blair. 147-185, *Feb. 1970*
Man's New Servant, the Friendly Atom. By F. Barrows Colton. Photos by Volkmar Wentzel. Included: Insects

tagged with radioisotopes, easily identified; sterilizing of screwworm fly; experiments on effectiveness of insect poisons. 71-90, *Jan. 1954*
Beltsville Brings Science to the Farm. By Samuel W. Matthews. 199-218, *Aug. 1953*
Fighting Insects with Airplanes: An Account of the Successful Use of the Flying-Machine in Dusting Tall Trees Infested with Leaf-Eating Caterpillars. By C. R. Neillie and J. S. Houser. 333-338, *Mar. 1922*
Explorers of a New Kind: Successful Introduction of Beetles and Parasites to Check Ravages of the Gipsy-moth and Brown-tail Moth. By L. O. Howard. 38-67, *July 1914*
See also Locusts

INSECT-TRAPPING PLANTS. *See* Carnivorous Plants

INSECTICIDE POLLUTION:

The Pesticide Dilemma. By Allen A. Boraiko. Photos by Fred Ward. Included: The harmful effects on beneficial insects and other forms of life. 145-183, *Feb. 1980*
Pollution, Threat to Man's Only Home. By Gordon Young. Photos by James P. Blair. Included: DDT and the other chlorinated hydrocarbon insecticides are toxic to many forms of animal and marine life. 738-781, *Dec. 1970*

INSECTICIDES. *See* Insect Control

INSECTS:

The Living Sands of the Namib. By William J. Hamilton III. Photos by Carol and David Hughes. 364-377, *Sept. 1983*
Teeming Life of a Rain Forest. By Carol and David Hughes. 49-65, *Jan. 1983*
Life on a Rock Ledge. By William H. Amos. 558-566, *Oct. 1980*

*With a voracious appetite, the short-
horned grasshopper ravages African
croplands.*   PAUL A. ZAHL, NGS

INSIDE the White House. By Lonnelle Aikman. Photos by B. Anthony Stewart and Thomas Nebbia. 3-43, *Jan. 1961*

INSIDE the World of the Honeybee. By Treat Davidson. 188-217, *Aug. 1959*

INSIGNIA:

Seals of Our Nation, States, and Territories. By Elizabeth W. King. Paintings by Carlotta Gonzales Lahey, Irvin E. Alleman, Theodora Price. Contents: Seals of the States and the District of Columbia; Seals of the Territories, Island Possessions, the Canal Zone, and the Philippine Commonwealth; Great Seal of the United States and Other Federal Seals; Seals of the President and of the Government Departments. 1-42, *July 1946*

Insignia and Decorations of the United States Armed Forces. By Gilbert Grosvenor. 185-186, *Feb. 1945*

■■*Insignia and Decorations of the U. S. Armed Forces.* Reprint of June 1943 NGM. 208 pages. 1943; rev. ed. *1944*

Heroes of Wartime Science and Mercy. By Elizabeth W. King. Note: Insignia of the following organizations: Air Carrier Contract Personnel, American Red Cross, Civil Air Patrol, U. S. Army Transportation Corps Vessels, U. S. Coast and Geodetic Survey, U. S. Maritime Service, U. S. Public Health Service. 715-740, *Dec. 1943*

Decorations, Medals, Service Ribbons, Badges, and Women's Insignia. 414-444, *Oct. 1943*

Insignia of the United States Armed Forces. By Gilbert Grosvenor. 651, *June 1943*

The Traditions and Glamour of Insignia. By Arthur E. Du Bois. 652-655, *June 1943*

United States Military Insignia. 656-693, *June 1943*

United States Navy, Marine Corps, and Coast Guard Insignia. 694-709, *June 1943*

Aircraft Insignia, Spirit of Youth. By Gerard Hubbard. 710-722, *June 1943*

The Romance of Military Insignia: How the United States Government Recognizes Deeds of Heroism and Devotion to Duty. By Robert E. Wyllie. 463-501, *Dec. 1919*

American Decorations and Insignia of Honor and Service. By Robert E. Wyllie. 502-526, *Dec. 1919*

Index to Flags and Insignia (Our Flag Number). 285, *Oct. 1917*

The Insignia of the Uniformed Forces of the United States. By Byron McCandless and Gilbert Grosvenor. 413-419, *Oct. 1917*

INSTITUT FRANÇAIS DE RE-CHERCHES POUR L'EXPLOITA-TION DES MERS. *See* Titanic, R.M.S.

INSTITUTE OF NAUTICAL ARCHE-OLOGY, Texas A & M University: Expeditions:

Aegean Sea. 768, 774, *June 1978*
Mediterranean Sea. 694, 702, 708, *Dec. 1987*

INSTITUTE OF NORTHERN AGRI-CULTURAL RESEARCH, Huntington Center, Vermont: Study Grant: Musk Ox. 863, 866, *June 1970*

INTEGRATED CIRCUITS:

The Chip: Electronic Mini-marvel. By Allen A. Boraiko. Photos by Charles O'Rear. 421-457, *Oct. 1982*

California's Silicon Valley. By Moira Johnston. Photos by Charles O'Rear. 459-477, *Oct. 1982*

Crystals, Magical Servants of the Space Age. By Kenneth F. Weaver. Photos by James P. Blair. 278-296, *Aug. 1968*

INTER-AMERICAN GEODETIC SURVEY (IAGS):

Expedition to Amazon source. 445, 459, 460, *Oct. 1972*

Men Who Measure the Earth. By Robert Leslie Conly. Photos by John E. Fletcher. 335-362, *Mar. 1956*

INTER-AMERICAN HIGHWAY. *See* Pan American Highway

INTERESTING Citizens of the Gulf Stream. By John T. Nichols. 69-84, *Jan. 1921*

An **INTERESTING** Rumor Concerning Andrée. By John Hyde. 102-103, *Mar. 1898*

An **INTERESTING** Visit to the Ancient Pyramids of San Juan Teotihuacan. By A. C. Galloway. 1041-1050, *Dec. 1910*

INTERNATIONAL Arbitration and Its Possibilities. 162, *Apr. 1900*

The **INTERNATIONAL** Cloud Work of the Weather Bureau. By Frank H. Bigelow. 351-354, *Sept. 1899*

INTERNATIONAL COMMITTEE OF THE RED CROSS:

A Little Humanity Amid the Horrors of War. By Peter T. White. Photos by Steve Raymer. 647-679, *Nov. 1986*
See also Red Cross

INTERNATIONAL CONGRESS OF ORIENTALISTS:

Eleventh International Congress of Orientalists. 303 (note), *Oct. 1897*

INTERNATIONAL Flat Globe and Geographical History. 281-282, *Apr. 1907*

INTERNATIONAL GEOGRAPHIC CONFERENCE:

Proceedings of the International Geographic Conference in Chicago, July 27-28, 1893. Included: Minutes of the Conference; Memoirs and Addresses. 97-256, *Jan. 31, 1894*

INTERNATIONAL GEOGRAPHIC CONGRESS:

Delegates to Ninth Congress. 385-386, *May 1908*

Ninth International Geographical Congress, Geneva, Switzerland, 1908. 491, *July 1907*

Publication of Proceedings of Eighth Congress. 198-199, *Apr. 1905*

Geographic Congress Abstracts (Eighth). 502-503, *Dec. 1904*

Address by Commander Robert E. Peary, U.S.N., On the Assembling of the Congress in Washington, September 8, 1904. 387-392, *Oct. 1904*

The Special Telegraphic Time Signal from the Naval Observatory. 411-415, *Oct. 1904*

Resolutions Adopted by the Eighth International Geographic Congress, September, 1904. 415-418, *Oct. 1904*

Political prisoners in El Salvador await a visit from their advocate, a delegate from the International Committee of the Red Cross. STEVE RAYMER, NGS

Stimulating a sow in heat with a spray of synthesized boar saliva, a Minnesota farmer prepares to artificially inseminate his subject. LOUIE PSIHOYOS

Ivory harpoon head was unearthed near an Inupiat family entombed in Alaskan ice for 500 years. SCOTT RUTHERFORD

An Iranian rehabilitation center stocked with braces and artificial limbs in 1985 attests the ravages of the nation's war with Iraq. MICHAEL COYNE, THE IMAGE BANK

quering the Alps, the Ice Peaks of Spitsbergen, of Persia, and Africa's Mountains of the Moon. By Walter Mittelholzer. 445-498, *Apr. 1932*

The Citroën Trans-Asiatic Expedition Reaches Kashmir: Scientific Party Led by Georges-Marie Haardt Successfully Crosses Syria, Iraq, Persia, and Afghanistan to Arrive at the Pamir. By Maynard Owen Williams. 387-443, *Oct. 1931*

From England to India by Automobile: An 8,527-mile Trip Through Ten Countries, from London to Quetta, Requires Five and a Half Months. By F.A.C. Forbes-Leith. 191-223, *Aug. 1925*

Modern Persia and Its Capital: And an Account of an Ascent of Mount Demavend, the Persian Olympus. By F. L. Bird. 353-400, *Apr. 1921*

Persian Caravan Sketches: The Land of the Lion and the Sun as Seen on a Summer Caravan Trip. By Harold F. Weston. 417-468, *Apr. 1921*

A Talk About Persia and Its Women. By Ella C. Sykes. 847-866, *Oct. 1910*

The Afghan Borderland. By Ellsworth Huntington. Part II: The Persian Frontier. 866-876, *Oct. 1909*

The Afghan Borderland. By Ellsworth Huntington. Part I: The Russian Frontier. 788-799, *Sept. 1909*

The Mountaineers of the Euphrates. By Ellsworth Huntington. 142-156, *Feb. 1909*

Persia: The Awakening East. By W. P. Cresson. 356-384, *May 1908*

Persia–Past and Present. 91-95, *Feb. 1907*

Travels in Arabia and Along the Persian Gulf. By David G. Fairchild. 139-151, *Apr. 1904*

Excavations of M. de Morgan at Susa. 315, *Aug. 1901*

A German Route to India. By Gilbert H. Grosvenor. 203-204, *May 1900*

Geographic Progress of Civilization. Annual Address by the President, Gardiner G. Hubbard. 1-22, *Feb. 14, 1894*

IRAN-IRAQ WAR:

The Persian Gulf–Living in Harm's Way. By Thomas J. Abercrombie. Photos by Steve Raymer. 648-671, *May 1988*

Iran Under the Ayatollah. By Michael Coyne. 108-135, *July 1985*

The New Face of Baghdad. By William S. Ellis. Photos by Steve McCurry. Included: Iraq at war; Treasures from Iraq's past. 80-109, *Jan. 1985*

IRAQ:

The New Face of Baghdad. By William S. Ellis. Photos by Steve McCurry. Included: Iraq at war; Treasures from Iraq's past. 80-109, *Jan. 1985*

■ The *Tigris* Expedition. 826, Dec. 1978; 1, Jan. 1979; cover, *Apr. 1979*

Tigris Sails Into the Past. By Thor Heyerdahl. Photos by Carlo Mauri and the crew of the *Tigris*. 806-827, *Dec. 1978*

Water Dwellers in a Desert World. By Gavin Young. Photos by Nik Wheeler. 502-523, *Apr. 1976*

The Kurds of Iraq: "We Who Face Death." By LeRoy Woodson, Jr. 364-387, *Mar. 1975*

Abraham, the Friend of God. By Kenneth MacLeish. Photos by Dean Conger. 739-789, *Dec. 1966*

Station Wagon Odyssey: Baghdad to Istanbul. By William O. Douglas. 48-87, *Jan. 1959*

Iraq–Where Oil and Water Mix. By Jean and Franc Shor. 443-489, *Oct. 1958*

West from the Khyber Pass. By William O. Douglas. Photos by Mercedes H. Douglas and author. 1-44, *July 1958*

Marsh Dwellers of Southern Iraq. By Wilfred Thesiger. Photos by Gavin Maxwell. 205-239, *Feb. 1958*

Troubled Waters East of Suez. By Ernest M. Eller. 483-522, *Apr. 1954*

Report from the Locust Wars. By Tony and Dickey Chapelle. 545-562, *Apr. 1953*

"Around the World in Eighty Days." By Newman Bumstead. Included: Baghdad; Basra; Tigris River. 705-750, *Dec. 1951*

Ancient Mesopotamia: A Light That Did Not Fail. By E. A. Speiser. Paintings by H. M. Herget. 41-105, *Jan. 1951*

Beside the Persian Gulf. Photos by Maynard Owen Williams. Included: Port near Basra. 341-356, *Mar. 1947*

Forty Years Among the Arabs. By John Van Ess. 385-420, *Sept. 1942*

Bombs over Bible Lands. By Frederick Simpich and W. Robert Moore. 141-180, *Aug. 1941*

Change Comes to Bible Lands. By Frederick Simpich. 695-750, *Dec. 1938*

New Light on Ancient Ur: Excavations at the Site of the City of Abraham Reveal Geographical Evidence of the

A sheikh's bodyguard, this man belongs to the Madan, marsh dwellers of southern Iraq. WILFRED THESIGER

Biblical Story of the Flood. By M.E.L. Mallowan. 95-130, *Jan. 1930*

Archeology, the Mirror of the Ages: Our Debt to the Humble Delvers in the Ruins at Carchemish and at Ur. By C. Leonard Woolley. 207-226, *Aug. 1928*

From England to India by Automobile: An 8,527-mile Trip Through Ten Countries, from London to Quetta, Requires Five and a Half Months. By F.A.C. Forbes-Leith. 191-223, *Aug. 1925*

A Visit to Three Arab Kingdoms: Transjordania, Iraq, and the Hedjaz Present Many Problems to European Powers. By Junius B. Wood. 535-568, *May 1923*

Modern Life in the Cradle of Civilization. 390-407, *Apr. 1922*

Under the Heel of the Turk: A Land with a Glorious Past, a Present of Abused Opportunities, and a Future of Golden Possibilities. By William H. Hall. 51-69, *July 1918*

The Cradle of Civilization: The Historic Lands Along the Euphrates and Tigris Rivers Where Briton Is Fighting Turk. By James Baikie. 127-162, *Feb. 1916*

Pushing Back History's Horizon: How the Pick and Shovel Are Revealing Civilizations That Were Ancient When Israel Was Young. By Albert T. Clay. 162-216, *Feb. 1916*

Where Adam and Eve Lived. By Frederick and Margaret Simpich. 546-588, *Dec. 1914*

Mystic Nedjef, the Shia Mecca. By Frederick Simpich. 589-598, *Dec. 1914*

The Most Historic Lands on Earth. 614-615, *Dec. 1914*

The Mountaineers of the Euphrates. By Ellsworth Huntington. 142-156, *Feb. 1909*

Travels in Arabia and Along the Persian Gulf. By David G. Fairchild. 139-151, *Apr. 1904*

Excavations at Nippur. 392, *Oct. 1900*

IRAZÚ (Volcano), Costa Rica:

Costa Rica, Free of the Volcano's Veil. By Robert de Roos. 125-152, *July 1965*

IRELAND, Northern:

■■ *Discovering Britain & Ireland.* 448 pages. *1985*

Editorial. By Wilbur E. Garrett. 431, *Apr. 1981*

Ireland. 432-499. I. The Travail of Ireland. By Joseph Judge. Photos by Cotton Coulson. 432-441; II. A New Day for Ireland. By John J. Putman. Photos by Cotton Coulson. 442-469; III. War and Peace in Northern Ireland. By Bryan Hodgson. Photos by Cary Wolinsky. 470-499, *Apr. 1981*

⬡ *Ireland and Northern Ireland: A Visitor's Guide; Historic Ireland* (Pre-Norman, Medieval, Modern), *Apr. 1981*

Ireland's Rugged Coast Yields Priceless Relics of the Spanish Armada. By Robert Sténuit. Photos by Bates Littlehales. 745-777, *June 1969*

Father Patrick Flynn administers confession, Communion, and care to 90-year-old Mary Carroll during monthly visits in Ireland's County Tipperary. COTTON COULSON

Lifelike Man Preserved 2,000 Years in Peat. By P. V. Glob. 419-430, *Mar. 1954*

IROQUOIS CONFEDERACY:

Editorial. By Wilbur E. Garrett. 281, *Sept. 1987*

Living Iroquois Confederacy. 370-403. Included: From One Sovereign People to Another. 370-373; "The Fire That Never Dies." By Harvey Arden. Photos by Steve Wall. 375-403, *Sept. 1987*

America's First Settlers, the Indians. By Matthew W. Stirling. Paintings by W. Langdon Kihn. 535-596, *Nov. 1937*

See also Mohawk Indians

IRRAWADDY (River), Burma:

Untoured Burma. By Charles H. Bartlett. 835-853, *July 1913*

IRRIGATION:

They Stopped the Sea. By Hans van Duivendijk. Photos by Pablo Bartholomew. 92-101, *July 1987*

Do We Treat Our Soil Like Dirt? By Boyd Gibbons. Photos by Steven C. Wilson. 350-389, *Sept. 1984*

The Desert: An Age-old Challenge Grows. By Rick Gore. Photos by Georg Gerster and Bruce Dale. 586-639, *Nov. 1979*

Western Australia, the Big Country. By Kenneth MacLeish. Photos by James L. Stanfield. 150-187, *Feb. 1973*

Two Wheels Along the Mexican Border. By William Albert Allard. 591-635, *May 1971*

The Hohokam: First Masters of the American Desert. By Emil W. Haury. Photos by Helga Teiwes. 670-695, *May 1967*

Behind the Veil of Troubled Yemen. By Thomas J. Abercrombie. 403-445, *Mar. 1964*

Sand in My Eyes. By Jinx Rodger. Photos by George Rodger. 664-705, *May 1958*

Californians Escape to the Desert. By Mason Sutherland. Photos by Charles W. Herbert. 675-724, *Nov. 1957*

From Sagebrush to Roses on the Columbia. By Leo A. Borah. 571-611, *Nov. 1952*

Water for the World's Growing Needs. By Herbert B. Nichols and F. Barrows Colton. 269-286, *Aug. 1952*

North Dakota Comes into Its Own. By Leo A. Borah. Photos by J. Baylor Roberts. 283-322, *Sept. 1951*

Erosion, Trojan Horse of Greece. By F. G. Renner. 793-812, *Dec. 1947*

I Become a Bakhtiari. By Paul Edward Case. 325-358, *Mar. 1947*

More Water for California's Great Central Valley. By Frederick Simpich. 645-664, *Nov. 1946*

China Fights Erosion with U. S. Aid. By Walter C. Lowdermilk. 641-680, *June 1945*

Farmers Since the Days of Noah: China's Remarkable System of Agriculture Has Kept Alive the Densest Population in the World. By Adam Warwick. 469-500, *Apr. 1927*

The Spirit of the West: The Wonderful

Merry faces of Drogheda belie the town's grim history. In one of Ireland's greatest battles, Drogheda fell to Oliver Cromwell's forces in 1649.   CLIFTON ADAMS, NGS

Agricultural Development Since the Dawn of Irrigation. By C. J. Blanchard. 333-360, *Apr. 1910*

The Call of the West. By C. J. Blanchard. 403-437, *May 1909*

Home-Making by the Government: An Account of the Eleven Immense Irrigating Projects to be Opened in 1908. By C. J. Blanchard. 250-287, *Apr. 1908*

The Arid Regions of the United States. By F. H. Newell. 167-172, *Jan. 31, 1894*

The Irrigation Problem in Montana. By H. M. Wilson. 212-229, *July 1890*

Irrigation in California. By Wm. Hammond Hall. 277-290, *Oct. 1889*

See also U. S. Bureau of Reclamation

IRVINE RANCH, California:

Orange, a Most California County. By Judith and Neil Morgan. Photos by Vince Streano. 750-779, *Dec. 1981*

IRVING, WASHINGTON:

Washington Irving's Spain. *1966*

IRWIN, COLIN:

Nomination Page. In the Arctic. *Feb. 1974*

Author-Photographer

Trek Across Arctic America. 295-321, *Mar. 1974*

IRWIN, CYNTHIA and HENRY:

Authors

Wyoming Muck Tells of Battle: Ice Age Man vs. Mammoth. By Cynthia Irwin, Henry Irwin, and George Agogino. 828-837, *June 1962*

IRWIN, JAMES B.:

What Is It Like to Walk on the Moon? By David R. Scott. 326-331, *Sept. 1973*

Apollo 15 Explores the Mountains of the Moon. By Kenneth F. Weaver. Photos from NASA. 233-265, *Feb. 1972*

IRWIN, JERRY:

On Assignment in Pennsylvania. *April 1984*

Photographer

The Plain People of Pennsylvania. Text by Douglas Lee. 492-519, *Apr. 1984*

IS Climatic Aridity Impending on the Pacific Slope? The Testimony of the Forest. By J. B. Leiberg. 160-181, *May 1899*

IS Our Noblest Volcano Awakening to New Life: A Description of the Glaciers and Evidences of Volcanic Activity of Mount Hood. By A. H. Sylvester. 515-525, *July 1908*

IS This the Tomb of Philip of Macedon? By Manolis Andronicos. Photos by Spyros Tsavdaroglou. 55-77, *July 1978*

ISABELA ISLAND, Mexico:

Cruise of the *Kinkajou:* Among Desert Islands of Mexico Voyagers Find Outdoor Laboratories for the Naturalist and Ideal Fishing Grounds for the Sportsman. By Alfred M. Bailey. 339-366, *Sept. 1941*

ISBJORN (Ketch):

Wind, Wave, Star, and Bird. By David Lewis. Photos by Nicholas deVore III. 747-781, *Dec. 1974*

ISCHIA, Island of the Unexpected. By Dorothea and Stuart E. Jones. 531-550, *Apr. 1954*

ISFAHAN, Iran:

Iran in Wartime: Through Fabulous Persia, Hub of the Middle East, Americans, Britons and Iranians Keep Sinews of War Moving to the Embattled Soviet Union. By John N. Greely. 129-156, *Aug. 1943*

Persian Caravan Sketches: The Land of the Lion and the Sun as Seen on a

A shepherd braces himself during a sandstorm on the Tunisian island of Jerba, where a mosque bears witness to the Islamic presence in North Africa. JAMES L. STANFIELD, NGS

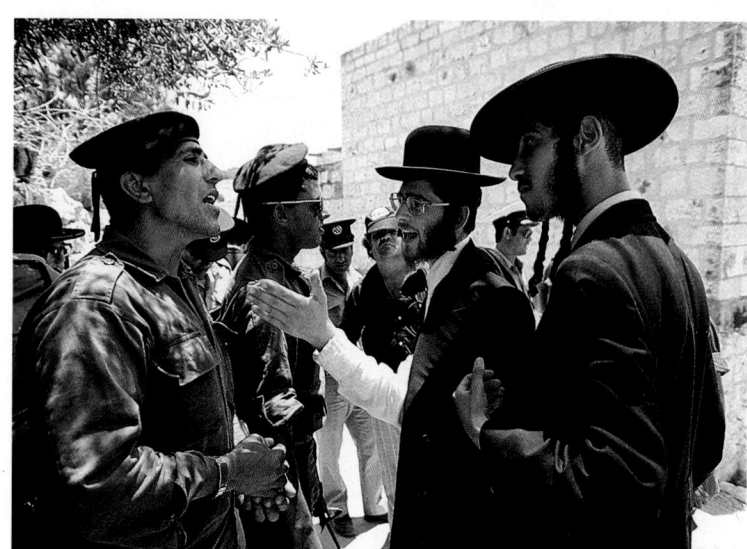

Ultraorthodox Jews confront police at a demonstration against excavations in Jerusalem. The protesters claimed that a medieval cemetery would be disturbed. JODI COBB, NGS

The River Arno rages through Florence, where Renaissance treasures were rescued from the November 4, 1966, flood. GIANNI TORTOLI

Timeless scene in the Spanish quarter of Naples reflects entrenched tradition in Italy's south, where incomes lag despite government efforts at revitalization. COTTON COULSON

■▪ BOOKS ⊕ MAPS ▪ TELEVISION

Austro-Italian Mountain Frontiers. By Florence Craig Albrecht. 321-376, *Apr. 1915*

The Ascent of Mont Blanc. By Walter Woodburn Hyde. 861-942, *Aug. 1913*

Gems of the Italian Lakes. By Arthur Ellis Mayer. 943-956, *Aug. 1913*

The Majesty of the Matterhorn. Pictorial supplement. 514, *May 1912*

Scenes in Italy. 321-332, *Apr. 1910*

The American Red Cross in Italy. By Mabel Boardman. 396-397, *Apr. 1909*

The Eruption of Mount Vesuvius, April 7-8, 1906. By Thomas Augustus Jaggar, Jr. 318-325, *June 1906*

Mount Vesuvius. 272-279, *May 1906*

See also Florence; Genoa; Italian Riviera; Marostica; Nettuno; Pompeii; Pontine Marshes; Rome; Siena; Trieste; Tuscany; Venice; *and* islands: Capri; Ischia; Sardinia; Sicily

ITAMBÉ (Peak), Brazil:

The Recent Ascent of Itambé. By J. C. Branner. 183, *May 1899*

The Peak of Itambé. 476, *Nov. 1898*

The **ITCH** To Move West: Life and Death on the Oregon Trail. By Boyd Gibbons. Photos by James L. Amos. 147-177, *Aug. 1986*

ITHACA (Island), Greece:

Homeward With Ulysses. By Melville Bell Grosvenor. Photos by Edwin Stuart Grosvenor. 1-39, *July 1973*

ITHERA (Oasis), Saudi Arabia:

Arabia, the Desert of the Sea. By Archibald Forder. 1039-1062, 1117, *Dec. 1909*

IT'S a Way of Life: Mexican Folk Art. By Fernando Horcasitas. Photos by David Hiser. 648-669, *May 1978*

IT'S Been a Banner Year! President's Report to Members. By Gilbert M. Grosvenor. 848-852, *Dec. 1981*

ITURI FOREST, Zaire:

My Life With Africa's Little People. By Anne Eisner Putnam. 278-302, *Feb. 1960*

IVAN IV, Csar (Russia):

Young Russia: The Land of Unlimited Possibilities. By Gilbert H. Grosvenor. 421-520, *Nov. 1914*

IVIZA (Island), Balearic Islands. *See* Ibiza

IVOR, HANCE ROY: *Author*

The Enigma of Bird Anting. 105-119, *July 1956*

Author-Photographer

Seeing Birds as Real Personalities. Included: Bluebirds on the Wing in Color. Photos by Bernard Corby and author. 523-530, *Apr. 1954*

IVORY:

An Ice Age Ancestor? By Alexander Marshack. Photos by the author and Ira Block. 478-481, *Oct. 1988*

Where Magic Ruled: Art of the Bering Sea. By William W. Fitzhugh and Susan A. Kaplan. Photos by Sisse Brimberg. Contents: Eskimo art. 198-205, *Feb. 1983*

IVORY COAST:

The Ivory Coast–African Success Story. By Michael and Aubine Kirtley. 94-125, *July 1982*

Freedom Speaks French in Ouagadougou. By John Scofield. 153-203, *Aug. 1966*

IVORY TRADE:

Wild Cargo: the Business of Smuggling Animals. By Noel Grove. Photos by Steve Raymer. Included: Illegal trade in elephant and walrus ivory. 287-315, *Mar. 1981*

Africa's Elephants: Can They Survive? By Oria Douglas-Hamilton. Photos by Oria and Iain Douglas-Hamilton. 568-603, *Nov. 1980*

IWAGO, MITSUAKI: *Photographer*

The Serengeti: A Photographic Portfolio. Text by John Eliot. 563-585, *May 1986*

IWO JIMA (Island), Volcano Islands:

The Bonins and Iwo Jima Go Back to Japan. By Paul Sampson. Photos by Joe Munroe. 128-144, *July 1968*

Adventures with the Survey Navy. By Irving Johnson. 131-148, *July 1947*

IZALCO VOLCANO, El Salvador:

Coffee Is King in El Salvador. By Luis Marden. 575-616, *Nov. 1944*

İZMIR (Smyrna), Turkey:

The Turkish Republic Comes of Age. By Maynard Owen Williams. 581-616, *May 1945*

History's Greatest Trek: Tragedy Stalks Through the Near East as Greece and Turkey Exchange Two Million of Their People. By Melville Chater. 533-590, *Nov. 1925*

Some Ruined Cities of Asia Minor. By Ernest L. Harris. 833-858, *Dec. 1908*

IZU OCEANIC PARK, Japan:

Japan's Izu Oceanic Park. By Eugenie Clark. Photos by David Doubilet. Included: World's Largest Crustacean (Giant Spider Crab). 465-491, *Apr. 1984*

Laundry lines festoon a narrow street in Naples, a city in the shadow of Mount Vesuvius founded by Greek colonists around 600 B.C. FROM MRS. GARDINER G. HUBBARD

J. W. WESTCOTT, Postman for the Great Lakes. By Cy La Tour. 813-824, *Dec. 1950*

A **JACK** in the Box: An Account of the Strange Performances of the Most Wonderful Island in the World (Bogoslof Volcano, Alaska). By F. W. Munger. 194-199, *Feb. 1909*

JACKALS:

Jackals of the Serengeti. By Patricia D. Moehlman. NGS research grant. 840-850, *Dec. 1980*

The Sacred Ibis Cemetery and Jackal Catacombs at Abydos. By Camden M. Cobern. 1042-1056, *Sept. 1913*

JACKSON, ANDREW:

Today Along the Natchez Trace, Pathway Through History. By Bern Keating. Photos by Charles Harbutt. 641-667, *Nov. 1968*

The Living White House. By Lonnelle Aikman. 593-643, *Nov. 1966*

Profiles of the Presidents: II. A Restless Nation Moves West. By Frank Freidel. 80-121, *Jan. 1965*

Inside the White House. By Lonnelle Aikman. Photos by B. Anthony Stewart and Thomas Nebbia. 3-43, *Jan. 1961*

JACKSON, CARMAULT B., Jr.: *Author*

The Flight of *Freedom 7.* 416-431, *Sept. 1961*

JACKSON, RODNEY: *Author-Photographer*

Tracking the Elusive Snow Leopard. By Rodney Jackson and Darla Hillard. NGS research grant. 793-809, *June 1986*

JACKSON, SHELDON:

Introducing Reindeer into Labrador. 686, *Oct. 1907*

Reindeer in Alaska. By Gilbert H. Grosvenor. Note: Jackson's introduction of reindeer into Alaska. 127-149, *Apr. 1903*

Some of the Conditions and Possibilities of Agriculture in Alaska. By Walter H. Evans. 178-187, *Apr. 1898*

Agriculture in the Yukon Valley. 189-190, *Apr. 1898*

Author

The Arctic Cruise of the United States Revenue Cutter "Bear." 27-31, *Jan. 1896*

JACKSON, W. H.: *Author*

Note on Glacier Discovery. 587, *Oct. 1906*

JACKSON, Mississippi:

Machines Come to Mississippi. By J. R. Hildebrand. 263-318, *Sept. 1937*

JACKSON HOLE, Wyoming:

Grand Teton–A Winter's Tale. By François Leydet. 148-152, *July 1979*

Jackson Hole: Good-bye to the Old Days? By François Leydet. Photos by Jonathan Wright. 768-789, *Dec. 1976*

Wyoming: High, Wide, and Windy. By David S. Boyer. 554-594, *Apr. 1966*

I See America First. By Lynda Bird

On Africa's Serengeti Plain a young jackal helps rear his little brother, a common practice. PATRICIA D. MOEHLMAN

Johnson. Photos by William Albert Allard. 874-904, *Dec. 1965*

Wildlife Adventuring in Jackson Hole. By Frank and John Craighead. 1-36, *Jan. 1956*

JACOBI, ELIZABETH P.: *Author*

Hungary, a Kingdom Without a King: A Tour from Central Europe's Largest Lake to the Fertile Plains of the Danube and the Tisza. 691-728, *June 1932*

JACOBINS (Pigeons):

Man's Feathered Friends of Longest Standing: Peoples of Every Clime and Age Have Lavished Care and Affection Upon Lovely Pigeons. By Elisha Hanson. Paintings by Hashime Murayama. 63-110, *Jan. 1926*

JACOBS, FENNO: *Photographer*

Mid-century Holland Builds Her Future. By Sydney Clark. 747-778, *Dec. 1950*

Camera Cruising in the Philippines. Photos by J. Baylor Roberts, Fenno Jacobs, and others. 545-552, *Nov. 1944*

Color Cruising in Paraguay. 465-472, *Oct. 1943*

Bolivia–Tin Roof of the Andes. Photos by Carl S. Bell and Fenno Jacobs. 311-326, *Mar. 1943*

JACOBSON, DORANNE WILSON: *Author-Photographer*

Purdah in India: Life Behind the Veil. 270-286, *Aug. 1977*

JACQUELINE, Countess of Holland:

The City of Jacqueline (Ter Goes, Netherlands). By Florence Craig Albrecht. 29-56, *Jan. 1915*

JACQUES-YVES COUSTEAU

Receives National Geographic Society Medal at White House. 146-147, *July 1961*

JADE:

Jade: Stone of Heaven. By Fred Ward. 282-315, *Sept. 1987*

China Unveils Her Newest Treasures. By Robert W. Madden. 848-857, *Dec. 1974*

Exploring the World of Gems. By W. F. Foshag. 779-810, *Dec. 1950*

La Venta's Green Stone Tigers. By Matthew W. Stirling. 321-332, *Sept. 1943*

Finding Jewels of Jade in a Mexican Swamp (La Venta). By Matthew W. and Marion Stirling. 635-661, *Nov. 1942*

Expedition Unearths Buried Masterpieces of Carved Jade (Cerro de las Mesas, Mexico). By Matthew W. Stirling. 277-302, *Sept. 1941*

Jade. By S. E. Easter. 9-17, *Jan. 1903*

JAEGER, EDMUND C.: *Author*

Poorwill Sleeps Away the Winter. 273-280, *Feb. 1953*

JAFFA, Israel. *See* Tel Aviv-Jaffa

JAGANNATH FESTIVAL:

Orissa, Past and Promise in an Indian State. By Bart McDowell. Photos by James P. Blair. 546-577, *Oct. 1970*

JAGGAR, THOMAS AUGUSTUS: *Author*

Mapping the Home of the Great Brown Bear: Adventures of the National Geographic Society's Pavlof Volcano Expedition to Alaska. Photos by R. H. Stewart. 109-134, *Jan. 1929*

Sakurajima, Japan's Greatest Volcanic Eruption: A Convulsion of Nature Whose Ravages Were Minimized by Scientific Knowledge, Compared with the Terrors and Destruction of the Recent Tokyo Earthquake. 441-470, *Apr. 1924*

The Eruption of Mount Vesuvius, April 7-8, 1906. 318-325, *June 1906*

Author-Photographer

Living on a Volcano: An Unspoiled Patch of Polynesia Is Niuafoō, Nicknamed "Tin Can Island" by Stamp Collectors. 91-106, *July 1935*

JAGUAR GOD:

Gifts for the Jaguar God. By Philip Drucker and Robert F. Heizer. NGS research grant. 367-375, *Sept. 1956*

JAGUAR HUNTING:

The Jungle Was My Home. By Sasha Siemel. 695-712, *Nov. 1952*

JAHAN, SHAH. *See* Shah Jahan

JAHANGIR:

When the Moguls Ruled India. By Mike Edwards. Photos by Roland Michaud. 463-493, *Apr. 1985*

JAINS (Religious Sect):

India's Sculptured Temple Caves. By Volkmar Wentzel. 665-678, *May 1953*

JAIPUR, India:

Feudal Splendor Lingers in Rajputana. By Volkmar Wentzel. 411-458, *Oct. 1948*

The Oriental Pageantry of Northern India. Photos by Franklin Price Knott. 429-460, *Oct. 1929*

JAISALMER, India:

Royal Wedding at Jaisalmer. By Marilyn Silverstone. 66-79, *Jan. 1965*

Feudal Splendor Lingers in Rajputana. By Volkmar Wentzel. 411-458, *Oct. 1948*

JAKARTA, Indonesia. *See* Djakarta

JAKOBSHAVN, Greenland:

Greenland's "Place by the Icebergs." By Mogens Bloch Poulsen. Photos by Thomas Nebbia. 849-869, *Dec. 1973*

JALISCO (State), Mexico:

The Most Mexican City, Guadalajara. By Bart McDowell. Photos by Volkmar Wentzel. 412-441, *Mar. 1967*

Vignettes of Guadalajara. By Frederick Simpich. 329-356, *Mar. 1934*

Along the Old Spanish Road in Mexico: Life Among the People of Nayarit and Jalisco, Two of the Richest States of the Southern Republic. By Herbert Corey. 225-281, *Mar. 1923*

See also Stone Spheres

JAMAICA:

Jamaica: Hard Times, High Hopes. By Charles E. Cobb, Jr. Photos by David Burnett. 114-140, *Jan. 1985*

The Caribbean: Sun, Sea, and Seething. By Noel Grove. Photos by Steve Raymer. 244-271, *Feb. 1981*

Reach for the New World. By Mendel Peterson. Photos by David L. Arnold. Paintings by Richard Schlecht. Included: Port Royal. 724-767, *Dec. 1977*

Jamaica Goes It Alone. By James Cerruti. Photos by Thomas Nebbia. 843-873, *Dec. 1967*

Wing-borne Lamps of the Summer Night (Fireflies). By Paul A. Zahl. 48-59, *July 1962*

Exploring the Drowned City of Port Royal. By Marion Clayton Link. Photos by Luis Marden. NGS research grant. 151-183, *Feb. 1960*

Jamaica–Hub of the Caribbean. By W. Robert Moore. 333-362, *Mar. 1954*

Jamaica, the Isle of Many Rivers. By John Oliver La Gorce. 1-55, *Jan. 1927*

JAMBO–First Gorilla Raised by Its Mother in Captivity. By Ernst M. Lang. Photos by Paul Steinemann. 446-453, *Mar. 1964*

JAMES I, King (Great Britain):

The British Way. By Sir Evelyn Wrench. Included: James I and the translation of the Bible (1611). 421-541, *Apr. 1949*

JAMES, FRANCES: *Author*

Thumbs Up Round the North Sea's Rim. Photos by Erica Koch. 685-704, *May 1952*

Keeping House in London. 769-792, *Dec. 1947*

JAMES, THOMAS GARNER: *Author*

London's Zoo of Zoos. 771-786, *June 1953*

Portsmouth, Britannia's Sally Port. Photos by B. Anthony Stewart. 513-544, *Apr. 1952*

Kew: The Commoners' Royal Garden. Photos by B. Anthony Stewart. 479-506, *Apr. 1950*

JAMES BAY, and Region, Canada:

Quebec's Northern Dynamo. By Larry Kohl. Photos by Ottmar Bierwagen. 406-418, *Mar. 1982*

The Changing World of Canada's Crees. By Fred Ward. 541-569, *Apr. 1975*

JAMES MADISON, Architect of the Constitution. By Alice J. Hall. Photos by Sam Abell. 340-369, *Sept. 1987*

JAMES RIVER, Virginia:

Hampton Roads, Where the Rivers End. By William S. Ellis. Photos by Karen Kasmauski. 72-107, *July 1985*

Stately Homes of Old Virginia. By Albert W. Atwood. 787-802, *June 1953*

JAMESTOWN, Virginia:

Captain Smith of Jamestown. By Bradford Smith. 581-620, *May 1957*

JAMISON, ANNE:

On Assignment in Australia. *Feb. 1988*

JAMMU AND KASHMIR (State), India:

Ladakh–The Last Shangri-la. By Thomas J. Abercrombie. 332-359, *Mar. 1978*

See also former name, Kashmir

JAN MAYEN (Island), Norwegian Sea:

Seal Hunting Off Jan Mayen. By Ole Friele Backer. 57-72, *Jan. 1948*

Magnetic Observations in Iceland, Jan Mayen and Spitzbergen in 1892. By Cyrus C. Babb. 223-224, *Dec. 29, 1894*

JANE AND JUSTIN DART FOUNDATION: Study Grant:

Orangutans. 835, *June 1980*

JANE GOODALL Finds Warfare and Cannibalism Among Gombe's Chimpanzees. By Jane Goodall. 592-621, *May 1979*

JANE M. SMITH AWARD:

Johnson, Lyndon B.: Vice President Johnson Accepts the Society's Jane Smith Award. 906, Dec. 1962; 113, Jan. 1966; 468, *Oct. 1966*

Ingram, Sir Bruce. 474, *Apr. 1961*

JANEL FISHERIES (Tuna Ranch), Canada:

Plight of the Bluefin Tuna. By Michael J. A. Butler. Photos by David Doubilet. Paintings by Stanley Meltzoff. Included: Captive fattening of bluefin tuna for sale to Japanese market. 220-239, *Aug. 1982*

JANITZIO (Island), Lake Pátzcuaro, Mexico. *See* Pátzcuaro (City and Lake)

JANSSEN, G. E.: *Author*

War Meets Peace in Egypt. By Grant Parr and G. E. Janssen. 503-526, *Apr. 1942*

JANSSEN OBSERVATORY, Mont Blanc Summit, France:

The Ascent of Mont Blanc. By Walter Woodburn Hyde. 861-942, *Aug. 1913*

JAP Rule in the Hermit Nation (Korea). By Willard Price. 429-451, *Oct. 1945*

JAPAN:

The Prodigious Soybean. By Fred Hapgood. Photos by Chris Johns. 67-91, *July 1987*

Visitor cools off at Dunn's River Falls, whose waters cascade over stone ledges to the north-coast beach near Ocho Rios, Jamaica. DAVID BURNETT, CONTACT PRESS IMAGES

The rise of Japan from an island world of provincial clans to a world economic power is traced on a June 1984 supplement map.

A Japanese girl's picture is taken on Seven-Five-Three Day, a holdover from days of high child mortality when those ages were considered milestones. DAVID ALAN HARVEY

Photos by George F. Mobley. 238-259, *Aug. 1984*

JAPAN TRENCH, Pacific Ocean:

Deep Diving off Japan. By Georges S. Houot. NGS research grant. 138-150, *Jan. 1960*

JAPANESE Americans: Home at Last. By Arthur Zich. Photos by Michael S. Yamashita. 512-539, *Apr. 1986*

JAPANESE ART:

■ Living Treasures of Japan. 703, *Dec. 1980*

Kyoto and Nara: Keepers of Japan's Past. By Charles McCarry. Photos by George F. Mobley. 836-851, *June 1976*

Human Treasures of Japan. By William Graves. Photos by James L. Stanfield. Included: Ironcasting, Kabuki, Lacquer working, Swordsmithing, Wood sculpture. 370-379, *Sept. 1972*

The **JAPANESE** Crane, Bird of Happiness. By Tsuneo Hayashida. 542-556, *Oct. 1983*

JARAWAS (Negrito Tribespeople):

The Last Andaman Islanders. By Raghubir Singh. 66-91, *July 1975*

JARCHÉ, JAMES: *Photographer*

In the London of the New Queen. By H. V. Morton. 291-342, *Sept. 1953*

JARET, PETER: *Author*

Our Immune System: The Wars Within. Photos by Lennart Nilsson. Illustrations text by Larry Kohl. 702-735, *June 1986*

JARI RIVER REGION, Brazil:

Jari: A Billion-dollar Gamble. By Loren McIntyre. Contents: Daniel K. Ludwig's paper-pulp and food-production enterprise in Brazil's Amazon Basin. 686-711, *May 1980*

Brazil's Wild Frontier. By Loren McIntyre. Included: Daniel K. Ludwig's three-million-acre agricultural and forestry experiment. 684-719, *Nov. 1977*

Amazon–The River Sea. By Loren McIntyre. Included: Daniel K. Ludwig's planned paper pulp and food-production enterprise in Brazil's Amazon Basin. 456-495, *Oct. 1972*

JASON JR. (Submersible Robot):

Epilogue for *Titanic*. By Robert D. Ballard. 454-463, *Oct. 1987*

A Long Last Look at *Titanic*. By Robert D. Ballard. Included: High-tech partners plumb new depths; Poignant relics of a disaster. Illustrations text by Cliff Tarpy. 698-727, *Dec. 1986*

JASON'S Voyage: In Search of the Golden Fleece. By Tim Severin. Photos by John Egan and Seth Mortimer. 406-420, *Sept. 1985*

JASPER NATIONAL PARK, Canada:

Heart of the Canadian Rockies. By Elizabeth A. Moize. Photos by Jim Brandenburg. 757-779, *June 1980*

JAUF (Al Jawf), Saudi Arabia:

Arabia, the Desert of the Sea. By Archibald Forder. 1039-1062, 1117, *Dec. 1909*

JAVA (Island), Indonesia:

Return of Java's Wildlife. By Dieter and Mary Plage. 750-771, *June 1985*

Indonesia Rescues Ancient Borobudur. By W. Brown Morton III. Photos by Dean Conger. 126-142, *Jan. 1983*

Java–Eden in Transition. By Kenneth MacLeish. Photos by Dean Conger. 1-43, *Jan. 1971*

Postwar Journey Through Java. By Ronald Stuart Kain. 675-700, *May 1948*

The Face of the Netherlands Indies. Photos by Maynard Owen Williams and others. 261-276, *Feb. 1946*

Java Assignment. By Dee Bredin. 89-119, *Jan. 1942*

Through Java in Pursuit of Color. By W. Robert Moore. Included: Java, Queen of the East Indies. Photos by author and Tassilo Adam. 333-362, *Sept. 1929*

A Traveler's Notes on Java. By Henry G. Bryant. 91-111, *Feb. 1910*

JAVAHÉ INDIANS:

Blue-eyed Indian: A city boy's sojourn with primitive tribesmen in central Brazil. By Harald Schultz. 65-89, *July 1961*

A **JAWBREAKER** for Sharks. By Valerie Taylor. 664-667, *May 1981*

JAYS:

Crows, Magpies, and Jays: Unusual Intelligence Has Earned a Unique Position for These Birds. By T. Gilbert Pearson. Paintings by Allan Brooks. 51-79, *Jan. 1933*

The White Sheep, Giant Moose, and Smaller Game of the Kenai Peninsula, Alaska. By George Shiras, 3d. 423-494, *May 1912*

JEAN-BRUNHES, MARIEL: *Author*

Cruising to Crete: Four French Girls Set Sail in a Breton Yawl for the Island of the Legendary Minotaur. By Marthe Oulié and Mariel Jean-Brunhes. 249-272, *Feb. 1929*

JEANNETTE (Ship):

The So-called "Jeannette Relics." By William H. Dall. 93-98, *Mar. 1896*

JEEP, Amphibious. *See Tortuga II*

JEFFERSON, MARK S. W.: *Author*

Limiting Width of Meander Belts. 373-385, *Oct. 1902*

Atlantic Coast Tides. 497-509, *Dec. 1898*

What Is the Tide of the Open Atlantic? 465-475, *Nov. 1898*

Atlantic Estuarine Tides. 400-409, *Sept. 1898*

JEFFERSON, THOMAS:

Thomas Jefferson: Architect of Freedom. By Mike W. Edwards. Photos by Linda Bartlett. 231-259, *Feb. 1976*

The Living White House. By Lonnelle Aikman. 593-643, *Nov. 1966*

Mr. Jefferson's Monticello. By Joseph Judge. Photos by Dean Conger and Richard S. Durrance. 426-444, *Sept. 1966*

Profiles of the Presidents: I. The Presidency and How It Grew. By Frank Freidel. 642-687, *Nov. 1964*

Inside the White House. By Lonnelle Aikman. Photos by B. Anthony Stewart and Thomas Nebbia. 3-43, *Jan. 1961*

Mr. Jefferson's Charlottesville. By Anne Revis. 553-592, *May 1950*

Jefferson's Little Mountain: Romance Enfolds Monticello, the Restored Home of the Author of the Declaration of Independence. By Paul Wilstach. 481-503, *Apr. 1929*

Jefferson as a Geographer. By A. W. Greely. 269-271, *Aug. 1896*

JEFFERY, DAVID:

On Assignment. *June 1983*

Nomination Page. *Apr. 1981*

Author

South Africa's Ndebele People. 262-282, *Feb. 1986*

A Japanese peasant transports goods with his own power, reflecting the rarity of draft animals on the nation's farms in the early 20th century.   A. NIELEN

A jellyfish trails its stinging tentacles through summer waters of the Chesapeake Bay. WILLARD R. CULVER, NGS

Fossils: Annals of Life Written in Rock. Photos by James L. Amos. 182-191, *Aug. 1985*

Worlds Within the Atom. By John Boslough. Photos by Kevin Fleming. Illustrations text by David Jeffery. Included: A Particle Factory: Tevatron; Search for the Atom. Paintings by Barron Storey; Inside the Atom; An Outbreak of Quarks; A Unification of Forces; Applications for the Future. 634-663, *May 1985*

Maine's Working Coast. Photos by Kevin Fleming. 208-241, *Feb. 1985*

The Once and Future Universe. By Rick Gore. Photos by James A. Sugar. Paintings by Barron Storey. Picture text by David Jeffery. 704-749, *June 1983*

America's Auto Mania. Photos by Bruce Dale. 24-31, *Special Report on Energy. (Feb. 1981)*

The Grandeur of Windsor (Portfolio). 616-625, *Nov. 1980*

Royal House for Dolls. Photos by James L. Stanfield. 632-643, *Nov. 1980*

A Most Uncommon Town: Columbus, Indiana. Photos by J. Bruce Baumann. 383-397, *Sept. 1978*

Arizona's Suburbs of the Sun. Photos by H. Edward Kim. 486-517, *Oct. 1977*

Audubon "On the Wing." Photos by Bates Littlehales. 149-177, *Feb. 1977*

Preserving America's Last Great Wilderness (Alaska). 769-791, *June 1975*

Burma's Leg Rowers and Floating Farms. Photos by W. E. Garrett. 826-845, *June 1974*

JEH TRIBESPEOPLE:

Viet Nam's Montagnards. By Howard Sochurek. 443-487, *Apr. 1968*

JEHL, JOSEPH R., Jr.:
Author-Photographer

Mono Lake: A Vital Way Station for the Wilson's Phalarope. 520-525, *Oct. 1981*

JEKYLL ISLAND, Georgia:

Sea Islands: Adventuring Along the South's Surprising Coast. By James Cerruti. Photos by Thomas Nebbia and James L. Amos. 366-393, *Mar. 1971*

JELLYFISHES:

Strange World of Palau's Salt Lakes. By William M. Hamner. Photos by David Doubilet. 264-282, *Feb. 1982*

Glass Menageries of the Sea. By Paul A. Zahl. 797-822, *June 1955*

The Life of the Moon-Jelly. By William Crowder. Paintings by author. Included: *Aurelia Aurita, Beroe Cucumis, Cunoctantha Octonaria, Cyanea Capillata, Dactylometra Quinquecirra, Eutima Variabilis, Gonionemus Murbachii, Linerges Mercurius, Mnemiopsis Leidyi, Pelagia Cyanella, Pleurobrachia Rhododactyla, Sarsia Mirabilis, Stomolophus Meleagris, Zygodactyla Groenlandica.* 187-202, *Aug. 1926*

See also Portuguese Man-of-War

JENKINS, BARBARA:
Author-Photographer

A Walk Across America: Part II. By Peter and Barbara Jenkins. 194-229, *Aug. 1979*

JENKINS, FARISH A., Jr.:
Nomination Page. *Jan. 1982*

JENKINS, HESTER DONALDSON:
Author

Armenia and the Armenians. 329-360, *Oct. 1915*

Bulgaria and Its Women. 377-400, *Apr. 1915*

JENKINS, PETER GORTON:
Author-Photographer

A Walk Across America: Part II. By Peter and Barbara Jenkins. 194-229, *Aug. 1979*

A Walk Across America. 466-499, *Apr. 1977*

JENKS, GEORGE ELWOOD:
Author-Photographer

Marvels of Metamorphosis: A Scientific "G-man" Pursues Rare Trapdoor Spider Parasites for Three Years With a Spade and a Candid Camera. 807-828, *Dec. 1938*

JENNE, Mali:

Finding West Africa's Oldest City. By Susan and Roderick McIntosh. Photos by Michael and Aubine Kirtley. Contents: Jenne-jeno (site). 396-418, *Sept. 1982*

JENNER, EDWARD:

The British Way. By Sir Evelyn Wrench. 421-541, *Apr. 1949*

JENNINGS, DEAN: *Author*

The Friendly Train Called Skunk. Photos by B. Anthony Stewart. 720-734, *May 1959*

JENNINGS, GARY: *Author*

Bavaria: Mod, Medieval–and Bewitching. Photos by George F. Mobley. 409-431, *Mar. 1974*

Newfoundland Trusts in the Sea. Photos by Sam Abell. 112-141, *Jan. 1974*

JENSEN, JAMES:
Nomination Page. *Aug. 1978*

JERICHO, West Bank:

Jericho Gives Up Its Secrets. By Kathleen M. Kenyon and A. Douglas Tushingham. Photos by Nancy Lord. 853-870, *Dec. 1953*

Hashemite Jordan, Arab Heartland. By John Scofield. 841-856, *Dec. 1952*

The Ghosts of Jericho. By James L. Kelso. 825-844, *Dec. 1951*

The Geography of the Jordan. By Nelson Glueck. 719-744, *Dec. 1944*

JERID (Region), Algeria-Tunisia:

The Date Gardens of the Jerid. By Thomas H. Kearney. 543-567, *July 1910*

JERSEY (Island), English Channel:

Britain's "French" Channel Islands. By James Cerruti. Photos by James L. Amos. 710-740, *May 1971*

The Channel Islands. By Edith Carey. 143-164, *Aug. 1920*

JERSTAD, LUTHER G.:

American and Geographic Flags Top Everest. By Melvin M. Payne. Photos by Barry C. Bishop. 157-157C, *Aug. 1963*

See also American Mount Everest Expedition

JERUSALEM:

▣ Jerusalem: Within These Walls. President's Page. By Gilbert M. Grosvenor. Jan. 1986; cover, *Mar. 1986*

Editorial. By Wilbur E. Garrett. 423, *Apr. 1983*

This Year in Jerusalem. By Joseph Judge. Photos by Jodi Cobb. 479-515, *Apr. 1983*

Peter and Barbara Jenkins pass through New Mexico in 1977 on Part II of "Walk Across America." JAY DICKMAN

Hurling a rock at Israeli police, a woman vents her rage at the arrest of a Palestinian during a 1982 shopkeepers' strike in troubled East Jerusalem. JODI COBB, NGS

Left for dead by Nazi executioners, Jonasz Stern fled Poland in 1943, later returning to become an artist in Kraków.   TOMASZ TOMASZEWSKI

Earle. Photos by Al Giddings and Chuck Nicklin. 624-631, *May 1980*

JINGDEZHEN (Ching-teh-chen), Jiangxi Province, China:

The World's Ancient Porcelain Center. By Frank B. Lenz. 391-406, *Nov. 1920*

JIVARO INDIANS:

Over Trail and Through Jungle in Ecuador: Indian Head-Hunters of the Interior, an Interesting Study in the South American Republic. By H. E. Anthony. 327-352, *Oct. 1921*

JOAN OF ARC:

The Maid of France Rides By: Compiègne, Where Joan of Arc Fought Her Last Battle, Celebrates Her Fifth Centenary. By Inez Buffington Ryan. 607-616, *Nov. 1932*

JOBOS Harbor (Puerto Rico). By O. H. Tittmann. 206, *June 1899*

JODHPUR, India:

Feudal Splendor Lingers in Rajputana. By Volkmar Wentzel. 411-458, *Oct. 1948*

JOGJAKARTA, Java, Indonesia:

Java–Eden in Transition. By Kenneth Macleish. Photos by Dean Conger. 1-43, *Jan. 1971*
See also former name, Djokjakarta

JOHANNESBURG, South Africa:

The Cities That Gold and Diamonds Built: Transvaal Treasures Have Created Bustling Johannesburg and Fostered Pretoria, Administrative Capital of the South African Union. By W. Robert Moore. 735-766, *Dec. 1942*
Transvaal: The Treasure-House Province. By Melville Chater. 479-512, *Apr. 1931*

Weathered face of a Persian Jew illustrated a 1927 story on diverse Jerusalem residents. MAYNARD OWEN WILLIAMS, NGS

JOHANSEN, FREDERIC H.:

The Nansen Polar Expedition. Special Report of Ernest A. Man. 339-344, *Oct. 1896*

JOHANSON, DONALD C.: *Author*

Ethiopia Yields First "Family" of Early Man. Photos by David Brill. 790-811, *Dec. 1976*

JOHN ELLIOTT PILLSBURY (Research Vessel):

Squids: Jet-powered Torpedoes of the Deep. By Gilbert L. Voss. Photos by Robert F. Sisson. NGS research grant. 386-411, *Mar. 1967*

JOHN F. KENNEDY: The Last Full Measure. By Melville Bell Grosvenor. 307-355, *Mar. 1964*

JOHN FRUM CULT:

Tanna Awaits the Coming of John Frum. By Kal Muller. 706-715, *May 1974*

JOHN G. SHEDD AQUARIUM, Chicago. *See* Shedd Aquarium

JOHN GLENN Receives the Society's Hubbard Medal. 827, *June 1962*

JOHN GLENN'S Three Orbits in *Friendship 7.* By Robert B. Voas. 792-827, *June 1962*

JOHN MUIR'S Wild America. By Harvey Arden. Photos by Dewitt Jones. 433-461, *Apr. 1973*

JOHN MUIR'S *Wild America.* By Tom Melham. Photos by Farrell Grehan. Art by H. Tom Hall. 199 pages. *1976*

JOHN OLIVER LA GORCE Is Elected Vice-Chairman of the Board, Melville Bell Grosvenor President and Editor of the National Geographic Society. 419-423, *Mar. 1957*

JOHN OLIVER LA GORCE MEDAL:

A Geographic Gold Medal Honors Kenyan Fossil Finder (Kamoya Kimeu). President's Page. By Gilbert M. Grosvenor. *Nov. 1985*

JOHN PAUL II, Pope:

The Face and Faith of Poland, map, photo, and essay supplement. By Peter Miller. Essay by Czesław Miłosz. Photos by Bruno Barbey. *Apr. 1982*

JOHN PENNEKAMP CORAL REEF STATE PARK, Florida:

The Lower Keys, Florida's "Out Islands." By John Scofield. Photos by Emory Kristof and Bates Littlehales. 72-93, *Jan. 1971*
Key Largo Coral Reef: America's First Undersea Park. By Charles M. Brookfield. Photos by Jerry Greenberg. 58-69, *Jan. 1962*
Florida's Coral City Beneath the Sea. By Jerry Greenberg. 70-89, *Jan. 1962*

JOHN WOODMAN HIGGINS ARMORY:

Cities Like Worcester Make America. By Howell Walker. 189-214, *Feb. 1955*

JOHNS, CHRIS: *Photographer*

Remington, the Man and the Myth. By Louise E. Levathes. 200-231, *Aug. 1988*
Hello Anchorage, Good-Bye Dream. By Larry L. King. 364-389, *Mar. 1988*
The Prodigious Soybean. By Fred Hapgood. 67-91, *July 1987*
Tornado! By Peter Miller. 690-715, *June 1987*
Glaciers on the Move. By John L. Eliot. 107-119, *Jan. 1987*
The Untamed Fraser River, British Columbia's Lifeline. By David S. Boyer. 44-75, *July 1986*
The Okies–Beyond the Dust Bowl. By William Howarth. 322-349, *Sept. 1984*

JOHNS HOPKINS APPLIED PHYSICS LABORATORY. *See* DODGE Satellite

JOHNS HOPKINS UNIVERSITY, Baltimore, Maryland:

A Maryland Pilgrimage: Visits to Hallowed Shrines Recall the Major Rôle Played by This Prosperous State in the Development of Popular Government in America. By Gilbert Grosvenor. 133-212, *Feb. 1927*

Research
Torchbearers of the Twilight (Fireflies). By Frederick G. Vosburgh. Contents: The experiments of Dr. William D. McElroy with cold light, such as that of fireflies. 697-704, *May 1951*

JOHNS ISLAND, South Carolina:

Sea Islands: Adventuring Along the South's Surprising Coast. By James Cerruti. Photos by Thomas Nebbia and James L. Amos. 366-393, *Mar. 1971*

JOHNSON, ANDREW:

The Living White House. By Lonnelle Aikman. 593-643, *Nov. 1966*
Profiles of the Presidents: III. The

Backed by his crew, Irving Johnson trims a topsail on his schooner Yankee *during a 1939 voyage around the world.* EDMUND ZACHER

American Giant Comes of Age. By Frank Freidel. 660-711, *May 1965*

JOHNSON, CECIL E.: *Author*
The Wild World of Compost. Photos by Bianca Lavies. 273-284, *Aug. 1980*

JOHNSON, DAVID H.: *Author*
The Incredible Kangaroo. 487-500, *Oct. 1955*

JOHNSON, ELECTA:
Saga of a Ship, the *Yankee* (Brigantine). By Luis Marden. 263-269, *Feb. 1966*
Author
Yankee (Ketch) Cruises Turkey's History-haunted Coast. By Irving and Electa Johnson. Photos by Irving Johnson and Joseph J. Scherschel. 798-845, *Dec. 1969*
Yankee (Ketch) Cruises the Storied Nile. By Irving and Electa Johnson. Photos by Winfield Parks. 583-633, *May 1965*
Inside Europe Aboard *Yankee* (Ketch). By Irving and Electa Johnson. Photos by Irving Johnson and Joseph J. Scherschel. 157-195, *Aug. 1964*
New Guinea to Bali in *Yankee* (Brigantine). By Irving and Electa Johnson. 767-815, *Dec. 1959*
Lost World of the Galapagos. By Irving and Electa Johnson. 681-703, *May 1959*
South Seas' Incredible Land Divers (New Hebrides Islanders). By Irving and Electa Johnson. Photos by Arthur Johnson and Irving Johnson. 77-92, *Jan. 1955*
Yankee (Brigantine) Roams the Orient. By Irving and Electa Johnson. 327-370, *Mar. 1951*
The *Yankee*'s (Brigantine) Wanderworld. By Irving and Electa Johnson. 1-50, *Jan. 1949*

Westward Bound in the *Yankee*. By Irving and Electa Johnson. Included: Storied Islands of the South Sea. Photos by Irving Johnson. 1-44, *Jan. 1942*

JOHNSON, EMORY R.: *Author*
The Interoceanic Canal. 311-316, *Aug. 1899*

JOHNSON, FRANK EDWARD:
Author
Here and There in Northern Africa. 1-132, *Jan. 1914*
The Greek Bronzes of Tunisia. 89-103, *Jan. 1912*
The Sacred City of the Sands (Kairouan, Tunisia). 1061-1093, *Dec. 1911*
The Mole Men: An Account of the Troglodytes of Southern Tunisia. 787-846, *Sept. 1911*
Tunis of Today. 723-749, *Aug. 1911*

JOHNSON, IRVING:
Saga of a Ship, the *Yankee* (Brigantine). By Luis Marden. 263-269, *Feb. 1966*
Nomination Page. *Apr. 1959*
Windjamming Around New England. By Tom Horgan. Photos by Robert F. Sisson. 141-169, *Aug. 1950*
Author
Yankee (Ketch) Cruises the Storied Nile. By Irving and Electa Johnson. Photos by Winfield Parks. 583-633, *May 1965*
New Guinea to Bali in *Yankee* (Brigantine). By Irving and Electa Johnson. 767-815, *Dec. 1959*
Lost World of the Galapagos. By Irving and Electa Johnson. 681-703, *May 1959*
Yankee (Brigantine) Roams the Orient. By Irving and Electa Johnson. 327-370, *Mar. 1951*

The *Yankee*'s (Brigantine) Wanderworld. By Irving and Electa Johnson. 1-50, *Jan. 1949*
Adventures with the Survey Navy. By Irving Johnson. 131-148, *July 1947*
Author-Photographer
Yankee (Ketch) Cruises Turkey's History-haunted Coast. By Irving and Electa Johnson. Photos by Irving Johnson and Joseph J. Scherschel. 798-845, *Dec. 1969*
Inside Europe Aboard *Yankee* (Ketch). By Irving and Electa Johnson. Photos by Irving Johnson and Joseph J. Scherschel. 157-195, *Aug. 1964*
South Seas' Incredible Land Divers (New Hebrides Islanders). By Irving and Electa Johnson. Photos by Arthur Johnson and Irving Johnson. 77-92, *Jan. 1955*
Westward Bound in the *Yankee*. By Irving and Electa Johnson. Included: Storied Islands of the South Sea. 1-44, *Jan. 1942*

JOHNSON, LADY BIRD:
President's Page. By Gilbert M. Grosvenor. *Aug. 1988*
Author
Texas in Bloom. 493-499, *Apr. 1988*

JOHNSON, LANNY:
On Assignment in California. *Sept. 1982*
Photographer
Avalanche! "I'm OK, I'm Alive!" Photos by Lanny Johnson and Andre Benier. 282-289, *Sept. 1982*

JOHNSON, LYNDA BIRD: *Author*
I See America First. Photos by William Albert Allard. 874-904, *Dec. 1965*

JOHNSON, LYNDON B.:
The Living White House. By Lonnelle Aikman. 593-643, *Nov. 1966*
Profiles of the Presidents: V. The Atomic Age: Its Problems and Promises. By Frank Freidel. 66-119, *Jan. 1966*
President Johnson Dedicates the Society's New Headquarters. 669-679, *May 1964*
Vice President Johnson Accepts the Society's Jane M. Smith Award. 906, *Dec. 1962*
Vice President Lyndon B. Johnson presents the Hubbard Medal to John H. Glenn, Jr. 827, *June 1962*
Author
Friendly Flight to Northern Europe. Photos by Volkmar Wentzel. 268-293, *Feb. 1964*

JOHNSON, NELSON T.: *Author*
Power Comes Back to Peiping. By Nelson T. Johnson and W. Robert Moore. 337-368, *Sept. 1949*

JOHNSON, RAY G.:
Author-Photographer
Exploring a Grass Wonderland of Wild West China. 713-742, *June 1944*

JOHNSON, SUSAN HACKLEY:
Author
New Day for Alaska's Pribilof Islanders. Photos by Tim Thompson. 536-552, *Oct. 1982*

JOHNSON, WILLARD D.:
Board of Managers. 270, July 1889; 68, Apr. 1890; 294, *Apr. 1891*

Author
Cloud Scenery of the High Plains. 493-496, *Dec. 1898*
Seriland. By W J McGee and Willard D. Johnson. 125-133, *Apr. 1896*

JOHNSTON, DAVID:
Eruption of Mount St. Helens. By Rowe Findley. 3-65. I. Mountain With a Death Wish. 3-33; II. In the Path of Destruction. 35-49; III. The Day the Sky Fell. Note: David Johnston lost his life in the eruption of Mount St. Helens. 50-65, *Jan. 1981*

JOHNSTON, SIR HARRY: *Author*
Haiti, the Home of Twin Republics. 483-496, *Dec. 1920*
Where Roosevelt Will Hunt (Africa). 207-256, *Mar. 1909*
The Black Republic–Liberia. By Sir Harry Johnston and Ernest Lyon. 334-343, *May 1907*

JOHNSTON, JAY:
Nomination Page. In Oregon. *June 1968*

Author
Indian Shangri-La of the Grand Canyon. Photos by Terry Eiler. 355-373, *Mar. 1970*
Forest Fire: The Devil's Picnic. By Stuart E. Jones and Jay Johnston. 100-127, *July 1968*
Waterway to Washington, the C & O Canal. 419-439, *Mar. 1960*
Staten Island Ferry, New York's Seagoing Bus. By John T. Cunningham and Jay Johnston. Photos by W. D. Vaughn. 833-843, *June 1959*

JOHNSTON, MOIRA: *Author*
Canada's Queen Charlotte Islands, Homeland of the Haida. Photos by Dewitt Jones. 102-127, *July 1987*
California's Silicon Valley. Photos by Charles O'Rear. 459-477, *Oct. 1982*
Napa, California's Valley of the Vine. Photos by Charles O'Rear. 695-717, *May 1979*

JOHNSTONE STRAIT, British Columbia, Canada:
The Whales Called "Killer." By Erich Hoyt. 220-237, *Aug. 1984*

JOINT HURRICANE WARNING CENTER, Miami, Florida:
Men Against the Hurricane. By Andrew H. Brown. 537-560, *Oct. 1950*

JOINT OCEANOGRAPHIC INSTITUTIONS FOR DEEP EARTH SAMPLING (JOIDES). *See* Deep Sea Drilling Project

JOINT TASK FORCE I. *See* Operation Crossroads

JOJOBA:
Rediscovering America's Forgotten Crops. By Noel D. Vietmeyer. Photos by Burgess Blevins. Paintings by Paul M. Breeden. Included: Oil from jojoba seeds. 702-712, *May 1981*

JÖKULSÁ Á FJÖLLUM (River), Iceland:
Iceland's Wild Glacier-born River. By Paul Vander-Molen. Photos by Robert Grégoire and Jean-Luc Chéron. 306-321, *Sept. 1984*

JOLLY, ALISON: *Author*
Madagascar's Lemurs: On the Edge of Survival. Photos by Frans Lanting. 132-161, *Aug. 1988*
Madagascar: A World Apart. Photos by Frans Lanting. 148-183, *Feb. 1987*

JONAS, LUCIEN: *Artist*
Three Drawings of the World War. 355-355b, *Apr. 1918*

JONCH CUSPINERA, ANTONIO:
Nomination Page. *Mar. 1967*

JONÊ (Choni), Gansu Province, China:
Life Among the Lamas of Choni: Describing the Mystery Plays and Butter Festival in the Monastery of an Almost Unknown Tibetan Principality in Kansu Province, China. By Joseph F. Rock. 569-619, *Nov. 1928*

JONES, DEWITT:
Editorial. By Gilbert M. Grosvenor. 437, *Apr. 1976*

Photographer
Canada's Queen Charlotte Islands, Homeland of the Haida. By Moira Johnston. 102-127, *July 1987*
A Short Hike With Bob Marshall. By Mike Edwards. 664-689, *May 1985*
Battle For a Bigger Bob (Bob Marshall Wilderness). By Mike Edwards. 690-692, *May 1985*
The Anasazi–Riddles in the Ruins. By Thomas Y. Canby. Photos by Dewitt Jones and David Brill. Paintings by Roy Andersen. 554-592, *Nov. 1982*
Coal vs. Parklands. By François Leydet. 776-803, *Dec. 1980*
Redwoods, Rain, and Lots of Room: California's North Coast. By Judith and Neil Morgan. 330-363, *Sept. 1977*
Look of a Land Beloved (New England). 444-467, *Apr. 1976*
John Muir's Wild America. By Harvey Arden. 433-461, *Apr. 1973*

JONES, DON W.: *Photographer*
Hot-air Balloons Race on Silent Winds. By William R. Berry. 392-407, *Mar. 1966*

JONES, DOROTHEA SHEATS:
Author
Slow Boat to Florida (*Tradewinds*). By Dorothea and Stuart E. Jones. 1-65, *Jan. 1958*
Pennsylvania Avenue, Route of Presidents. By Dorothea and Stuart E. Jones. Photos by Volkmar Wentzel. 63-95, *Jan. 1957*

Author-Photographer
Ischia, Island of the Unexpected. By Dorothea and Stuart E. Jones. 531-550, *Apr. 1954*
See also Sheats, Dorothea

JONES, E. LESTER:
Board of Trustees. 384, Sept. 1926; 640, *Nov. 1944*

JONES, FRANK I.: *Photographer*
Katmai. 271-278, *Sept. 1921*

JONES, LILIAN GROSVENOR. *See* Grosvenor, Lilian

JONES, MARY LOU: *Author*
Gray Whales of San Ignacio. By Steven L. Swartz and Mary Lou Jones. Photos by François Gohier. NGS research grant. 754-771, *June 1987*

JONES, STUART E.:
Nomination Page. In Oregon. *June 1968*

Author
Maryland on the Half Shell. Photos by Robert W. Madden. 188-229, *Feb. 1972*
When in Rome.... Photos by Winfield Parks. 741-789, *June 1970*
Oregon's Many Faces. Photos by Bates Littlehales. 74-115, *Jan. 1969*
Forest Fire: The Devil's Picnic. By Stuart E. Jones and Jay Johnston. 100-127, *July 1968*
Houston, Prairie Dynamo. Photos by William Albert Allard. 338-377, *Sept. 1967*
Copenhagen, Wedded to the Sea. Photos by Gilbert M. Grosvenor. 45-79, *Jan. 1963*
Central Park: Manhattan's Big Outdoors. Photos by Bates Littlehales. 781-811, *Dec. 1960*
The President's Music Men (Marine Band). Photos by William W. Campbell III. 752-766, *Dec. 1959*
Slow Boat to Florida (*Tradewinds*). By Dorothea and Stuart E. Jones. 1-65, *Jan. 1958*
Charting Our Sea and Air Lanes (U. S. Coast and Geodetic Survey). Photos by J. Baylor Roberts. 189-209, *Feb. 1957*
Pennsylvania Avenue, Route of Presidents. By Dorothea and Stuart E. Jones. Photos by Volkmar Wentzel. 63-95, *Jan. 1957*
Here's New York Harbor. Photos by Robert F. Sisson and David S. Boyer. 773-813, *Dec. 1954*
Spices, the Essence of Geography. 401-420, *Mar. 1949*
Fun Helped Them Fight. 95-104, *Jan. 1948*
Indian Life Before the Colonists Came. Engravings by Theodore de Bry, 1590. 351-368, *Sept. 1947*
Demolishing Germany's North Sea Ramparts. 635-644, *Nov. 1946*

Author-Photographer
Ischia, Island of the Unexpected. By Dorothea and Stuart E. Jones. 531-550, *Apr. 1954*

JONES, MRS. STUART E. *See* Jones, Dorothea Sheats

JONES SOUND, Northwest Territories, Canada:
Charles Francis Hall and Jones Sound. By A. W. Greely. 308-310, *Sept. 1896*

JORDAN, ROBERT PAUL:
On Assignment in Kiev, U.S.S.R. *Mar. 1985*

College graduates in Amman, the capital of Jordan, face the future with a common tradition of scholarship and a mix of emotions. JODI COBB, NGS

Arab Land Beyond the Jordan. Photos by Frank Hurley. 753-768, *Dec. 1947*

The Geography of the Jordan. By Nelson Glueck. 719-744, *Dec. 1944*

On the Trail of King Solomon's Mines: The Bible, in Addition to Its Spiritual Values, Continues to Prove a Rich Geography and Guide to Exploration of the Holy Land. By Nelson Glueck. 233-256, *Feb. 1944*

Bedouin Life in Bible Lands: The Nomads of the "Houses of Hair" Offer Unstinted Hospitality to an American. By John D. Whiting. 59-83, *Jan. 1937*

A Visit to Three Arab Kingdoms: Transjordania, Iraq, and the Hedjaz Present Many Problems to European Powers. By Junius B. Wood. 535-568, *May 1923*

One Thousand Miles of Railway Built for Pilgrims and Not for Dividends (Damascus to Mecca). By F. R. Maunsell. 156-172, *Feb. 1909*

See also Jericho; Khirbat Qumrān; Petra

JORDAN (River), Israel-Jordan:

Geographical Twins a World Apart. By David S. Boyer. Included: A comparison of the Jordan River in the Holy Land with the Jordan River in Utah. 848-859, *Dec. 1958*

The Geography of the Jordan. By Nelson Glueck. 719-744, *Dec. 1944*

Canoeing Down the River Jordan: Voyagers in Rubber Boats Find the Bible Stream Little Tamed Today as It Plunges to the Dead Sea Over the Earth's Lowest River Bed. By John D. Whiting. 781-808, *Dec. 1940*

JORDAN (River), Utah:

Geographical Twins a World Apart. By David S. Boyer. Included: A comparison of the Jordan River in the Holy Land with the Jordan River in Utah. 848-859, *Dec. 1958*

JOSEPH, Chief:

Chief Joseph. By William Albert Allard. 409-434, *Mar. 1977*

JOSEPH ALSOP: A Historical Perspective (on Minoan Human Sacrifice). 223, *Feb. 1981*

JOSEPH CONRAD (Training Ship):

The Age of Sail Lives On at Mystic. By Alan Villiers. Photos by Weston Kemp. 220-239, *Aug. 1968*

North About. By Alan J. Villiers. 221-250, *Feb. 1937*

JOSÉPHINE, Empress (France):

Napoleon. By John J. Putman. Photos by Gordon W. Gahan. 142-189, *Feb. 1982*

JOSEPHINE FORD (Airplane):

The First Flight to the North Pole. By Richard Evelyn Byrd. 357-376, *Sept. 1926*

JOURNALISM:

New China and the Printed Page. By Paul Hutchinson. 687-722, *June 1927*

The Making of a Japanese Newspaper. By Thomas E. Green. 327-334, *Oct. 1920*

JOURNEY Across Russia: The Soviet ▮▮ *Union Today.* By Bart McDowell. Photos by Dean Conger. 367 pages. *1977*

A **JOURNEY** by Jungle Rivers to the Home of the Cock-of-the-rock: Naturalists Enter the Amazon, Voyage Through the Heart of Tropical South America, and Emerge at the Mouth of the Orinoco. By Ernest G. Holt. 585-630, *Nov. 1933*

A **JOURNEY** Down Old U. S. 1. By Bruce Dale. 790-817, *Dec. 1984*

A **JOURNEY** in Ecuador. By Mark B. Kerr. 238-245, *July 1896*

A **JOURNEY** in Morocco: "The Land of the Moors." By Thomas Lindsey Blayney. 750-775, *Aug. 1911*

JOURNEY Into China. 518 pages. ▮▮ *1982*

JOURNEY Into Stone Age New Guinea. By Malcolm S. Kirk. 568-592, *Apr. 1969*

JOURNEY Into the Great Rift: the Northern Half. By Helen and Frank Schreider. 254-290, *Aug. 1965*

JOURNEY Into Troubled Iran. By George W. Long. Photos by J. Baylor Roberts. 425-464, *Oct. 1951*

The **JOURNEY** of Burke and Wills: First Across Australia. By Joseph Judge. Photos by Joseph J. Scherschel. 152-191, *Feb. 1979*

A **JOURNEY** Through the Eastern Portion of the Congo State. By P.H.G. Powell-Cotton. 155-163, *Mar. 1908*

A **JOURNEY** Through Tibet. By Sorrel Wilby. 764-785, *Dec. 1987*

JOURNEY Through Time: Papua New Guinea. By François Leydet. Photos by David Austen. 150-171, *Aug. 1982*

JOURNEY to China's Far West. By Rick Gore. Photos by Bruce Dale. 292-331, *Mar. 1980*

A **JOURNEY** to "Little Tibet." By Enakshi Bhavnani. Photos by Volkmar Wentzel. 603-634, *May 1951*

JOURNEY to Mars. By Kenneth F. Weaver. Paintings by Ludek Pesek. 231-263, *Feb. 1973*

JOURNEY to Outer Mongolia. By William O. Douglas. Photos by Dean Conger. 289-345, *Mar. 1962*

A **JOURNEY** Up the Nile. By Robert Caputo. Included: Africa's River of Legend, a foldout map of the Nile; A Dam Against Famine. By Farouk El-Baz. 577-633, *May 1985*

The **JOY** of Pigs. By Kent Britt. Photos by George F. Mobley. 398-415, *Sept. 1978*

JUAN FERNÁNDEZ ISLAND, South Pacific Ocean:

A Voyage to the Island Home of Robinson Crusoe. By Waldo L. Schmitt. 353-370, *Sept. 1928*

JUÁREZ, BENITO:

Among the Zapotecs of Mexico: A Visit to the Indians of Oaxaca, Home State of the Republic's Great Liberator, Juárez, and Its Most Famous Ruler, Diaz. By Herbert Corey. 501-553, *May 1927*

JUBILEES:

La Gorce, John Oliver. Golden Anniversary with the Society. 422, 423, Mar. 1957; 442, *Mar. 1960*

Gilbert Grosvenor's Golden Jubilee. By Albert W. Atwood. 253-261, *Aug. 1949*

See also Diamond Jubilee

JUDAISM:

Remnants: The Last Jews of Poland. By

An Arab family, divided by the 1948 partition of Palestine, shares a tearfully brief reunion outside Jerusalem's Mandelbaum Gate. BRIAN BRAKE

Małgorzata Niezabitowska. Photos by Tomasz Tomaszewski. 362-389, *Sept. 1986*

■ Jerusalem: Within These Walls. President's Page. By Gilbert M. Grosvenor. Jan. 1986; cover, *Mar. 1986*

Israel: Searching for the Center. By Priit J. Vesilind. Photos by James L. Stanfield. 2-39, *July 1985*

This Year in Jerusalem. By Joseph Judge. Photos by Jodi Cobb. 479-515, *Apr. 1983*

In Search of Moses. By Harvey Arden. Photos by Nathan Benn. 2-37, *Jan. 1976*

The Pious Ones (Brooklyn's Hasidic Jews). By Harvey Arden. Photos by Nathan Benn. 276-298, *Aug. 1975*

■■ *Great Religions of the World.* Contents: Buddhism, Christianity, Hinduism, Islam, and Judaism. 420 pages. *1971*

Our Life on a Border Kibbutz. By Carol and Al Abrams. Photos by Al Abrams. 364-391, *Sept. 1970*

✥ *Lands of the Bible Today. Dec. 1967*

Abraham, the Friend of God. By Kenneth MacLeish. Photos by Dean Conger. 739-789, *Dec. 1966*

✥ *Holy Land Today.* Atlas series. *Dec. 1963*

The Last Thousand Years Before Christ. By G. Ernest Wright. Paintings by H. J. Soulen and Peter V. Bianchi. 812-853, *Dec. 1960*

The Men Who Hid the Dead Sea Scrolls. By A. Douglas Tushingham. Paintings by Peter V. Bianchi. 785-808, *Dec. 1958*

Bringing Old Testament Times to Life. By G. Ernest Wright. Paintings by Henry J. Soulen. 833-864, *Dec. 1957*

✥ *Lands of the Bible Today. Dec. 1956*

The Pageant of Jerusalem: The Capital of the Land of Three Great Faiths Is Still the Holy City for Christian, Moslem, and Jew. By Edward Keith-Roach. 635-681, *Dec. 1927*

See also Jews; Samaritans

JUDD, NEIL MERTON: *Author*

"Pyramids" of the New World. 105-128, *Jan. 1948*

Everyday Life in Pueblo Bonito: As Disclosed by the National Geographic Society's Archeologic Explorations in the Chaco Canyon National Monument, New Mexico. 227-262, *Sept. 1925*

Beyond the Clay Hills: An Account of the National Geographic Society's Reconnaissance of a Previously Unexplored Section in Utah. 275-302, *Mar. 1924*

Pueblo Bonito, the Ancient: The National Geographic Society's Third Expedition to the Southwest Seeks to Read in the Rings of Trees the Secret of the Age of Ruins. 99-108, *July 1923*

The Pueblo Bonito Expedition of the National Geographic Society. 323-331, *Mar. 1922*

JUDGE, JOSEPH:

On Assignment in Florida. *Mar. 1988*
Associate Editor. 427, *Oct. 1980*

VOL. 157, NO. 1   JANUARY 1980

NATIONAL GEOGRAPHIC

VOYAGER VIEWS JUPITER'S DAZZLING REALM 2

LONG-EARED OWLS: MASTERS OF THE NIGHT 31

CAN THE TALLGRASS PRAIRIE BE SAVED? 37

HOKKAIDO—JAPAN'S LAST FRONTIER 62

UTAH ROCK ART: WILDERNESS LOUVRE 97

FAIR OF THE BERBER BRIDES 119

LILY-PAD WORLD TEENS WITH LIFE 131

SEE "DIVE TO THE EDGE OF CREATION" MONDAY, JANUARY 7, ON PBS TV

Nomination Page. *Aug. 1973*
Nomination Page. In Italy. *July 1967*

Author

"The Greatest Job in the World?" Contents: Recollections of writers and photographers by the Senior Associate Editor. 317-321, *Sept. 1988*

Exploring Our Forgotten Century: Between Columbus and Jamestown. Photos by Bill Ballenberg. Paintings by John Berkey. 330-363, *Mar. 1988*

Child of Gondwana. 170-177, *Feb. 1988*

Australians. Photos by Michael O'Brien. Picture text by Elizabeth A. Moize. 213-231, *Feb. 1988*

Where Columbus Found the New World. Photos by James L. Stanfield. 566-599, *Nov. 1986*

This Year in Jerusalem. Photos by Jodi Cobb. 479-515, *Apr. 1983*

Peoples of the Arctic. 144-223. I. Introduction by Joseph Judge. 144-149; II. Hunters of the Lost Spirit: Alaskans, Canadians, Greenlanders, Lapps. By Priit J. Vesilind. Photos by David Alan Harvey, Ivars Silis, and Sisse Brimberg. 150-197; III. Where Magic Ruled: Art of the Bering Sea. By William W. Fitzhugh and Susan A. Kaplan. Photos by Sisse Brimberg. 198-205; IV. People of the Long Spring (Chukchis). By Yuri Rytkheu. Photos by Dean Conger. 206-223, *Feb. 1983*

A Buried Roman Town Gives Up Its Dead (Herculaneum). Photos by Jonathan Blair. 687-693, *Dec. 1982*

The Travail of Ireland. Photos by Cotton Coulson. 432-441, *Apr. 1981*

The Journey of Burke and Wills: First Across Australia. Photos by Joseph J. Scherschel. 152-191, *Feb. 1979*

Minoans and Mycenaeans: Greece's Brilliant Bronze Age. Photos by Gordon W. Gahan. Paintings by Lloyd K. Townsend. 142-185, *Feb. 1978*

Alaska: Rising Northern Star. Photos by Bruce Dale. 730-767, *June 1975*

Those Proper and Other Bostonians. Photos by Ted Spiegel. 352-381, *Sept. 1974*

Wind River Range: Many-treasured Splendor. 198-205, *Feb. 1974*

Brunei, Borneo's Abode of Peace. Photos by Dean Conger. 207-225, *Feb. 1974*

Florida's Booming–and Beleaguered–Heartland. Photos by Jonathan Blair. 585-621, *Nov. 1973*

Israel–The Seventh Day. Photos by Gordon W. Gahan. 816-855, *Dec. 1972*

Venice Fights for Life. Photos by Albert Moldvay. 591-631, *Nov. 1972*

The Zulus: Black Nation in a Land of Apartheid. Photos by Dick Durrance II. 738-775, *Dec. 1971*

Hong Kong, Saturday's Child. Photos by Bruce Dale. 541-573, *Oct. 1971*

New Orleans and Her River. Photos by James L. Stanfield. 151-187, *Feb. 1971*

Retracing John Wesley Powell's Historic Voyage Down the Grand Canyon. Photos by Walter Meayers Edwards. 668-713, *May 1969*

Williamsburg, City for All Seasons. Photos by James L. Amos. 790-823, *Dec. 1968*

Florence Rises From the Flood. 1-43, *July 1967*

New Grandeur for Flowering Washington. Photos by James P. Blair. 500-539, *Apr. 1967*

Mr. Jefferson's Monticello. Photos by Dean Conger and Richard S. Durrance. 426-444, *Sept. 1966*

JUDITH RIVER BASIN, Montana. *See* Spring Creek Hutterite Colony

JUGOSLAVIA. *See* Yugoslavia

JUGOSLAVIA–Ten Years After. By Melville Chater. 257-309, *Sept. 1930*

JULL, MORLEY A.: *Author*

Fowls of Forest and Stream Tamed by Man. Paintings by Hashime Murayama. 327-371, *Mar. 1930*

The Races of Domestic Fowl. Paintings by Hashime Murayama. 379-452, *Apr. 1927*

A **JUMPING** Salmon. 124-125, *Feb. 1908*

JUNE Week at Annapolis, Cradle of the Navy. 791-798, *June 1936*

JUNEAU, Alaska:

Avalanche! Battling the Juggernaut. By David Cupp. 290-305, *Sept. 1982*
Endeavour Sails the Inside Passage. By Amos Burg. 801-828, *June 1947*

JUNEAU ICEFIELD, Alaska:

Alaska's Mighty Rivers of Ice. By Maynard M. Miller. Photos by Christopher G. Knight. 194-217, *Feb. 1967*

JUNGE, CARL-JOHAN: *Photographer*

The Shy and Spectacular Kingfisher. Photos by Carl-Johan Junge and Emil Lütken. 413-419, *Sept. 1974*

JUNGFRAU (Peak), Switzerland:

Switzerland Guards the Roof of Europe. By William H. Nicholas. Photos by Willard R. Culver. 205-246, *Aug. 1950*

A silent cannon stands in the Gettysburg battlefield, commemorated in Carl Sandburg's 1963 magazine essay, "Just a Hundred Years Ago."

K
L

KALAHARI BUSHMEN
KANGAROOS
KARAKORAM RANGE
KASHMIR
KATMAI NATIONAL PARK
KAYAKING
KELP FORESTS
KENNEDY SPACE CENTER
KIBBUTZIM
KILAUEA VOLCANO
KILLER WHALES
KING CRABS
KINGS CANYON NATIONAL PARK
KIWIFRUIT
KOALAS
KOKO
KOMODO DRAGONS
KREMLIN
KUBLAI KHAN
LABRADOR
LADYBUGS
LAND YACHTS
LANDFILLS
LANDSAT
LAOTIAN REFUGEES
LAPLAND
LASCAUX CAVE
LASERS
LEAKEY FAMILY
LEMURS
LEONARDO DA VINCI
LEWIS AND CLARK EXPEDITION
LIGHT TECHNOLOGY
LIONS
LITERATURE
LOBSTERS
LONG-NECKED WOMEN
LUNAR RESEARCH

A lioness and her cub
lie in wait in the Serengeti, Africa's
premier wildlife sanctuary.

MITSUAKI IWAGO

585

K2 (Peak), China-Pakistan:

Americans Climb K2. Photos by members of the expedition. 623-649. I. The Ultimate Challenge. By James W. Whittaker. 624-639; II. On to the Summit. By James Wickwire. 641-649, *May 1979*

KNM-WT 15000 (*Homo Erectus* Fossil Skeleton):

Homo Erectus Unearthed: A Fossil Skeleton 1,600,000 Years Old. By Richard Leakey and Alan Walker. Photos by David L. Brill. Note: KNM-WT 15000 is the most complete *Homo erectus* skeleton yet found. NGS research grant. 624-629, *Nov. 1985*

KABUKI:

Human Treasures of Japan. By William Graves. Photos by James L. Stanfield. 370-379, *Sept. 1972*

Kansai, Japan's Historic Heartland. By Thomas J. Abercrombie. 295-339, *Mar. 1970*

KABUL, Afghanistan:

Afghanistan's Troubled Capital–Kabul. By Mike Edwards. Photos by Steve Raymer. 494-505, *Apr. 1985*

Back to Afghanistan. By Maynard Owen Williams. 517-544, *Oct. 1946*

KACHINAS:

Inside the Sacred Hopi Homeland. By Jake Page. Photos by Susanne Page. 607-629, *Nov. 1982*

Kachinas: Masked Dancers of the Southwest. By Paul Coze. 219-236, *Aug. 1957*

KADAYAN:

Brunei, Borneo's Abode of Peace. By Joseph Judge. Photos by Dean Conger. 207-225, *Feb. 1974*

KAF, Saudi Arabia:

Arabia, the Desert of the Sea. By Archibald Forder. 1039-1062, 1117, *Dec. 1909*

KAFIR TRIBESPEOPLE:

In the Footsteps of Alexander the Great. By Helen and Frank Schreider. Paintings by Tom Lovell. 1-65, *Jan. 1968*

Impressions and Scenes of Mozambique. By O. W. Barrett. 807-830, *Oct. 1910*

KAHL, M. PHILIP:
Author-Photographer

The Royal Spoonbill. NGS research grant. 281-284, *Feb. 1987*

East Africa's Majestic Flamingos. 276-294, *Feb. 1970*

KAHN, MIRZA ALI KULI:

The National Geographic Society (Speech by Kahn). 272-298, *Mar. 1912*

KAIETEUR FALLS, Guyana:

Kaieteur and Roraima: The Great Falls and the Great Mountain of the Guianas. By Henry Edward Crampton. 227-244, *Sept. 1920*

The World's Greatest Waterfall: The

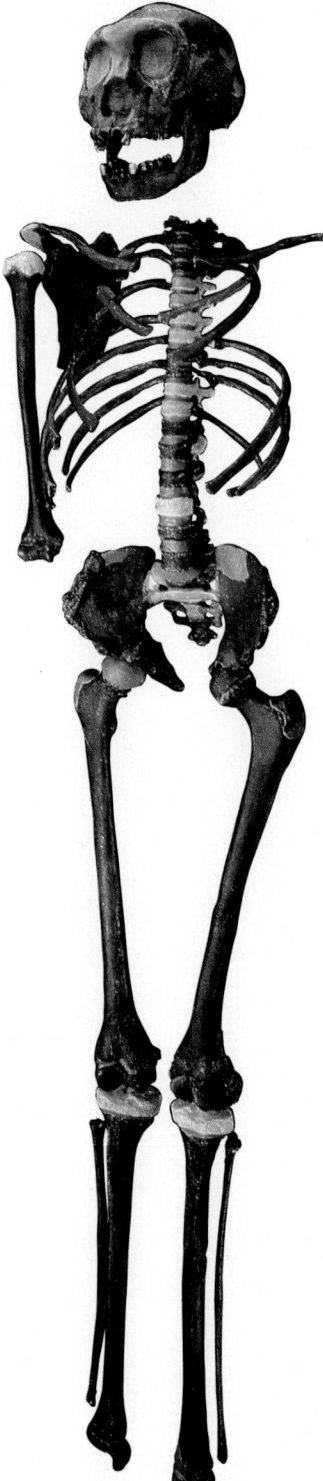

Most complete early human skeleton, of a 1.6-million-year-old boy, was found in Kenya in 1984. DAVID BRILL

Kaieteur Fall, in British Guiana. By Leonard Kennedy. 846-859, *Sept. 1911*

KAIJO (Songdo), Korea:

Chosen–Land of Morning Calm. By Mabel Craft Deering. 421-448, *Oct. 1933*

KAIN, RONALD STUART: *Author*

Postwar Journey Through Java. 675-700, *May 1948*

KAIROUAN, Tunisia:

Eastward from Gibraltar: Overland Route Across North Africa to Tunisia and Libia. By Cyrus French Wicker. 115-142, *Jan. 1943*

The Sacred City of the Sands. By Frank Edward Johnson. 1061-1093, *Dec. 1911*

KAISER WILHELM CANAL, West Germany:

The Great Canals of the World. 475-479, *Oct. 1905*

KALAHARI BUSHMEN:

▇ Bushmen of the Kalahari. 578A-578B, *Apr. 1973*; 732A-732B, *May 1974*

Africa's Bushman Art Treasures. By Alfred Friendly. Photos by Alex R. Willcox. 848-865, *June 1963*

Bushmen of the Kalahari. By Elizabeth Marshall Thomas. 866-888, *June 1963*

KALASH TRIBESPEOPLE:

Pakistan's Kalash: People of Fire and Fervor. By Debra Denker. Photos by Steve McCurry. 458-473, *Oct. 1981*

KALAVRYTA, Greece:

Erosion, Trojan Horse of Greece. By F. G. Renner. 793-812, *Dec. 1947*

KALEIDOSCOPIC Land of Europe's Youngest King: Yugoslavia Holds a Mosaic of Slavs and the City Where Pistol Shots Touched Off the World War. By Douglas Chandler. 691-738, *June 1939*

KALEIDOSCOPIC La Paz: The City of the Clouds. By Harriet Chalmers Adams. 119-141, *Feb. 1909*

KALIMANTAN. *See* Borneo

KALIMNOS (Island), Greece:

The Isles of Greece: Aegean Birthplace of Western Culture. By Melville Bell Grosvenor. Photos by Edwin Stuart Grosvenor and Winfield Parks. 147-193, *Aug. 1972*

KALMBACH, E. R.: *Author*

The Crow, Bird Citizen of Every Land: A Feathered Rogue Who Has Many Fascinating Traits and Many Admirable Qualities Despite His Marauding Propensities. 322-337, *Apr. 1920*

KALMUCK TRIBESPEOPLE:

With the Nomads of Central Asia: A Summer's Sojourn in the Tekes Valley, Plateau Paradise of Mongol and Turkic Tribes. By Edward Murray. Paintings and drawings by Alexandre Iacovleff. 1-57, *Jan. 1936*

Boxing in the tall grass, gray kangaroos grapple in Flinders Chase National Park on Kangaroo Island, South Australia.   MITSUAKI IWAGO

K
L

These Missourians. By Frederick Simpich. 277-310, *Mar. 1946*
Taming the Outlaw Missouri River. By Frederick Simpich. 569-598, *Nov. 1945*

The **KANSAS** River. By Arthur P. Davis. 181-184, *May 1896*

KANSU PROVINCE, China. *See* Gansu Province

KANTON ISLAND, Phoenix Islands, Kiribati. *See* Canton Island

KAPINGAMARANGI (Atoll), Micronesia:
Feast Day in Kapingamarangi. By W. Robert Moore. 523-537, *Apr. 1950*

KAPLAN, JOSEPH: *Author*
How Man-made Satellites Can Affect Our Lives. Paintings by Gilbert Emerson. 791-810, *Dec. 1957*

KAPLAN, MARION: *Author*
Iberia's Vintage River (Douro-Duero). Photos by Stephanie Maze. 460-489, *Oct. 1984*

Author-Photographer
Twilight of the Arab Dhow. 330-351, *Sept. 1974*

Photographer
Smallpox–Epitaph for a Killer? By Donald A. Henderson. 796-805, *Dec. 1978*
Djibouti, Tiny New Nation on Africa's Horn. 518-533, *Oct. 1978*

KAPLAN, SUSAN A.: *Author*
Where Magic Ruled: Art of the Bering Sea. By William W. Fitzhugh and Susan A. Kaplan. Photos by Sisse Brimberg. 198-205, *Feb. 1983*

KAPSIKI TRIBESPEOPLE:
Carefree People of the Cameroons. Photos by Pierre Ichac. 233-248, *Feb. 1947*

KARACHI, Pakistan:
Pakistan Under Pressure. By William S. Ellis. Photos by James L. Stanfield. 668-701, *May 1981*

KARAGANDA, U.S.S.R.:
New Road to Asia. By Owen Lattimore. 641-676, *Dec. 1944*

KARAKORAM RANGE, Central Asia:
Baltistan–The 20th Century Comes to Shangri-la. By Galen Rowell. Photos by the author and Barbara Cushman Rowell. Included: War among the peaks. 526-550, *Oct. 1987*
Americans Climb K2. Photos by members of the expedition. 623-649. I. The Ultimate Challenge. By James W. Whittaker. 624-639. II. On to the Summit. By James Wickwire. 641-649, *May 1979*
See also Hunza

KARAKUL SHEEP:
The Land of Lambskins: An Expedition to Bokhara, Russian Central Asia, to Study the Karakul Sheep Industry. By Robert K. Nabours. 77-88, *July 1919*

Sikh sentries guard a Himalayan pass in India's frigid region of Ladakh in Kashmir. Chinese troops invaded in November 1962, claiming sovereignty. WILBUR E. GARRETT, NGS

KARAMOJONG TRIBESPEOPLE:
Uganda, Africa's Uneasy Heartland. By Howard La Fay. Photos by George F. Mobley. 708-735, *Nov. 1971*

KARBALA, Iraq:
Mystic Nedjef, the Shia Mecca. By Frederick Simpich. 589-598, *Dec. 1914*

KAREN TRIBESPEOPLE:
Spirits of Change Capture the Karens. By Peter Kunstadter. 267-285, *Feb. 1972*
Burma: Where India and China Meet: In the Massive Mountains of Southeast Asia, Swarming Road Builders Wage the "War of the Highways" for Free China and Her Allies. By John LeRoy Christian. 489-512, *Oct. 1943*
Among the Hill Tribes of Burma–An Ethnological Thicket. By Sir George Scott. 293-321, *Mar. 1922*
Notes on Burma. By Thomas Barbour. 841-866, *Oct. 1909*

KARISOKE RESEARCH CENTRE, Rwanda:
The Imperiled Mountain Gorilla. By Dian Fossey. 501-523. Included: Death of Marchessa. Photos by Peter G. Veit. 508-511, *Apr. 1981*

KARNAK, Egypt:
The Resurrection of Ancient Egypt. By James Baikie. 957-1020, *Sept. 1913*
See also Akhenaten Temple Project

KARNALI ZONE, Nepal:
Karnali, Roadless World of Western Nepal. By Lila M. and Barry C. Bishop. NGS research grant. 656-689, *Nov. 1971*
Peerless Nepal–A Naturalist's Paradise. By S. Dillon Ripley. Photos by Volkmar Wentzel. NGS research grant. 1-40, *Jan. 1950*

KARNATKA (State), India. *See* former name, Mysore

KÄRNTEN (State), Austria:
Entering the Front Doors of Medieval Towns: The Adventures of an American Woman and Her Daughter in a Folding Boat on Eight Rivers of Germany and Austria. By Cornelia Stratton Parker. 365-394, *Mar. 1932*

KÁRPATHOS (Island), Greece:
Eternal Easter in a Greek Village. By Maria Nicolaidis-Karanikolas. Photos by James L. Stanfield. 768-777, *Dec. 1983*

KARST FORMATIONS:
Guilin, China's Beauty Spot. By W. E. Garrett. 536-563, *Oct. 1979*

KARYÉS, Greece:
The Hoary Monasteries of Mt. Athos. By H. G. Dwight. 249-272, *Sept. 1916*

KASHGAI TRIBESPEOPLE:
We Dwelt in Kashgai Tents. By Jean and Franc Shor. 805-832, *June 1952*
Journey into Troubled Iran. By George W. Long. Photos by J. Baylor Roberts. 425-464, *Oct. 1951*
Mountain Tribes of Iran and Iraq. By Harold Lamb. 385-408, *Mar. 1946*

KASHI (Kashgar), and Region, China:
American Skiers Find Adventure in Western China. By Ned Gillette. Photos by the author and Galen Rowell. Included: Skiing From the Summit of China's Ice Mountain. 174-199, *Feb. 1981*

KASHMIR:
Mountaintop War in Remote Ladakh. By W. E. Garrett. 664-687, *May 1963*
The Emperor's Private Garden: Kashmir. By Nigel Cameron. Photos by Brian Brake. 606-647, *Nov. 1958*

Fumarole steams in Alaska's Valley of Ten Thousand Smokes, surveyed by eight Geographic expeditions and designated Katmai National Monument in 1918. JASPER D. SAYRE

Hodgson. Photos by Jim Brandenburg. 755-797, *June 1982*

KAW TRIBESPEOPLE:

Burma: Where India and China Meet: In the Massive Mountains of Southeast Asia, Swarming Road Builders Wage the "War of the Highways" for Free China and Her Allies. By John LeRoy Christian. 489-512, *Oct. 1943*

Shan Tribes Make Burma's Hills Flash With Color. Photos by W. Robert Moore. 455-462, *Oct. 1931*

Strange Tribes in the Shan States of Burma. Photos by W. Robert Moore. 247-254, *Aug. 1930*

KAYAKING:

Kayaking the Amazon. By Piotr Chmielinski. Photos by Zbigniew Bzdak. 461-473, *Apr. 1987*

Iceland's Wild Glacier-born River. By Paul Vander-Molen. Photos by Robert Grégoire and Jean-Luc Chéron. 306-321, *Sept. 1984*

White-water Adventure on Wild Rivers of Idaho. By Frank Craighead, Jr., and John Craighead. 213-239, *Feb. 1970*

Kayak Odyssey: From the Inland Sea to Tokyo. By Dan Dimancescu. Photos by Christopher G. Knight. 295-337, *Sept. 1967*

Kayaks Down the Nile. By John M. Goddard. 697-732, *May 1955*

KAYANS:

Sarawak: The Land of the White Rajahs. By Harrison W. Smith. 110-167, *Feb. 1919*

KAYAPO INDIANS:

Brazil's Kayapo Indians, Beset by a Golden Curse. By Vanessa Lea. Photos by Miguel Rio Branco. 675-694, *May 1984*

KAZAKH SOVIET SOCIALIST REPUBLIC, U.S.S.R.:

New Road to Asia. By Owen Lattimore. 641-676, *Dec. 1944*
See also Ak Bulak

KAZAKS:

Journey to China's Far West. By Rick Gore. Photos by Bruce Dale. 292-331, *Mar. 1980*

How the Kazakhs Fled to Freedom. By Milton J. Clark. 621-644, *Nov. 1954*

New Road to Asia. By Owen Lattimore. 641-676, *Dec. 1944*

KAZAN RETTO (Volcano Islands), Pacific Ocean:

Springboards to Tokyo. By Willard Price. 385-407, *Oct. 1944*
See also Iwo Jima

KAZIRANGA WILD LIFE SANCTUARY, Assam, India:

Long Journey of the Brahmaputra. By Jere Van Dyk. Photos by Raghubir Singh and Galen Rowell. Included: A Rare Visit to a World Unto Itself. By Raghubir Singh. 672-711, *Nov. 1988*

Stalking the Great Indian Rhino. By Lee Merriam Talbot. 389-398, *Mar. 1957*

KBOO, a Liberian Game. By G. N. Collins. 944-948, *Nov. 1910*

KEA (Island), Greece:

The Isles of Greece: Aegean Birthplace of Western Culture. By Melville Bell Grosvenor. Photos by Edwin Stuart Grosvenor and Winfield Parks. 147-193, *Aug. 1972*

KEACH, DONALD L.: *Author*

Down to *Thresher* by Bathyscaph. 764-777, *June 1964*

KEARNEY, THOMAS H.: *Author*

The Country of the Ant Men. 367-382, *Apr. 1911*

Author-Photographer

The Date Gardens of the Jerid. 543-567, *July 1910*

KEARNY, Camp, California:

Bringing the World to Our Foreign-Language Soldiers: How a Military Training Camp is Solving a Seemingly Unsurmountable Problem by Using the Geographic. By Christina Krysto. 81-90, *Aug. 1918*

KEATING, BERN: *Author*

■■*Alaska.* Photos by George F. Mobley. 207 pages. 1969; rev. ed. *1971*

■■*The Mighty Mississippi.* Photos by James L. Stanfield. 199 pages. *1971*

North for Oil: *Manhattan* Makes the Historic Northwest Passage. Photos by Tomas Sennett. 374-391, *Mar. 1970*

Today Along the Natchez Trace, Pathway Through History. Photos by Charles Harbutt. 641-667, *Nov. 1968*

Pakistan: Problems of a Two-part Land. Photos by Albert Moldvay. 1-47, *Jan. 1967*

Cajunland, Louisiana's French-speaking Coast. Photos by Charles Harbutt and Franke Keating. 353-391, *Mar. 1966*

KEATING, FRANKE: *Photographer*

Cajunland, Louisiana's French-speaking Coast. By Bern Keating. Photos by Charles Harbutt and Franke Keating. 353-391, *Mar. 1966*

KEBON DJAHE, Sumatra, Indonesia:

By Motor Through the East Coast and Batak Highlands of Sumatra. By Melvin A. Hall. 69-102, *Jan. 1920*

KEELING ISLANDS, Indian Ocean.
See Cocos Islands

KEEN, DORA: *Author-Photographer*

A Woman's Climbs in the High Alps. Photos by author and others. 643-675, *July 1911*

KEEPING House for a Biologist in Colombia. By Nancy Bell Fairchild Bates. Photos by Marston Bates. 251-274, *Aug. 1948*

KEEPING House for the "Shepherds of the Sun." By Mrs. William H. Hoover. 483-506, *Apr. 1930*

KEEPING House for Tropical Butterflies. By Jocelyn Crane. Photos by M. Woodbridge Williams. NGS research grant. 193-217, *Aug. 1957*

KEEPING House in a Cappadocian Cave. By Jonathan S. Blair. 127-146, *July 1970*

KEEPING House in Borneo. By Virginia Hamilton. 293-324, *Sept. 1945*

KEEPING House in London. By Frances James. 769-792, *Dec. 1947*

KEEPING House in Majorca. By Phoebe Binney Harnden. 425-440, *Apr. 1924*

A kayaker startles a Peruvian fisherman during a half-year trip down the 4,000-mile-long Amazon River. ZBIGNIEW BZDAK, © CANOANDES, INC.

KEEPING House on the Congo. By Ruth Q. McBride. 643-670, *Nov. 1937*

KEIJO, South Korea. *See* Seoul

KEITH, DONALD H.: *Author*
Yellow Sea Yields Shipwreck Trove. Photos by H. Edward Kim. 231-243, *Aug. 1979*

KEITH-ROACH, EDWARD: *Author*
Changing Palestine. 493-527, *Apr. 1934*
The Pageant of Jerusalem: The Capital of the Land of Three Great Faiths Is Still the Holy City for Christian, Moslem, and Jew. Photos by Maynard Owen Williams. 635-681, *Dec. 1927*

Author-Photographer
Adventures Among the "Lost Tribes of Islam" in Eastern Darfur: A Personal Narrative of Exploring, Mapping, and Setting Up a Government in the Anglo-Egyptian Sudan Borderland. 41-73, *Jan. 1924*

KÈKAWNGDU TRIBESPEOPLE:
Among the Hill Tribes of Burma–An Ethnological Thicket. By Sir George Scott. 293-321, *Mar. 1922*

KEKOPEY RANCH, Kenya:
The "Gang" Moves to a Strange New Land. By Shirley C. Strum. Note: The baboons of the "Pumphouse Gang" are translocated. NGS research grant. 676-690, *Nov. 1987*
Life With the "Pumphouse Gang": New Insights Into Baboon Behavior. By Shirley C. Strum. Photos by Timothy W. Ransom. 672-691, *May 1975*

KELLEY, FRANCIS BEVERLY:
Author
The Wonder City That Moves by Night. 289-324, *Mar. 1948*
The Land of Sawdust and Spangles–A World in Miniature. 463-516, *Oct. 1931*

KELLOGG, PAT:
On Assignment. *June 1983*

KELLOGG, REMINGTON: *Author*
Whales, Giants of the Sea: Wonder Mammals, Biggest Creatures of All Time, Show Tender Affection for Young, But Can Maim or Swallow Human Hunters. Paintings by Else Bostelmann. 35-90, *Jan. 1940*

KELP FORESTS:
Undersea World of a Kelp Forest. By Sylvia A. Earle. Photos by Al Giddings. 411-426, *Sept. 1980*
Giant Kelp, Sequoias of the Sea. By Wheeler J. North. Photos by Bates Littlehales. 251-269, *Aug. 1972*

KELSO, JAMES L.:
Author-Photographer
The Ghosts of Jericho. 825-844, *Dec. 1951*

KELTIE, J. SCOTT: *Author*
The Great Unmapped Areas on the Earth's Surface Awaiting the Explorer and Geographer. 251-266, *Sept. 1897*

Americans in 1963 mourn slain President John F. Kennedy in the Rotunda of the U.S. Capitol, a televised rite shared by some 175 million citizens. U.S. DEPARTMENT OF DEFENSE

KELTON, M. E.: *Author*
Apperception in Geography. 192-199, *May 1900*

KEMAL ATATÜRK. *See* Mustapha Kemal

KEMANO POWER DEVELOPMENT:
Kitimat–Canada's Aluminum Titan. By David S. Boyer. 376-398, *Sept. 1956*

KEMP, WESTON: *Photographer*
The Age of Sail Lives On at Mystic. By Alan Villiers. 220-239, *Aug. 1968*

KENAI PENINSULA, Alaska:
The White Sheep, Giant Moose, and Smaller Game of the Kenai Peninsula, Alaska. By George Shiras, 3d. 423-494, *May 1912*

KENASTON, C. A.:
Secretary. 294, 296-298, *Apr. 1891*; vii-ix, *Feb. 20, 1893*
Board of Managers. 270, July 1889; 68, *Apr. 1890*

KENETT, F. L.: *Photographer*
Tutankhamun's Golden Trove. By Christiane Desroches Noblecourt. 625-646, *Oct. 1963*

KENNAN, GEORGE:
Secretary. ii, Oct. 1888; 164-166, Apr. 1889; 270, July 1889; 134, *Jan. 1936*
Awarded Jane M. Smith Life Membership. 342, *Apr. 1920*
Author
An Island in the Sea of History: The Highlands of Daghestan. By George Kennan. 1087-1140, *Oct. 1913*

KENNARD, FREDERICK H.: *Author*
Encouraging Birds Around the Home. 315-344, *Mar. 1914*

KENNEBEC (River), Maine:
Atlantic Estuarine Tides. By Mark S. W. Jefferson. 400-409, *Sept. 1898*

KENNEDY, JACQUELINE BOUVIER:
The Living White House. By Lonnelle Aikman. 593-643, *Nov. 1966*
The Last Full Measure. By Melville Bell Grosvenor. 307-355, *Mar. 1964*
■■ *The White House* (guidebook) presented to President and Mrs. John F. Kennedy. 888-889, 892, *Dec. 1962*

KENNEDY, JOHN F.:
The Living White House. By Lonnelle Aikman. 593-643, *Nov. 1966*
Profiles of the Presidents: V. The Atomic Age: Its Problems and Promises. By Frank Freidel. 66-119, *Jan. 1966*
The Last Full Measure. By Melville Bell Grosvenor. 307-355, *Mar. 1964*
To the Memory of Our Beloved President, Friend to All Mankind. 1A-1B, *Jan. 1964*
President Kennedy Presents the Hubbard Medal (American Mount Everest Expedition). 514-515, *Oct. 1963*
■■ *The White House* (guidebook) presented to President and Mrs. John F. Kennedy. 888-889, 892, *Dec. 1962*
White House News Photographers Association's first-place award presented to Robert F. Sisson. 880, *Dec. 1961*
Distinguished Flying Cross awarded posthumously to Victor A. Prather, Jr. 684, 685, *Nov. 1961*
Jacques-Yves Cousteau Receives National Geographic Society Medal at White House. 146-147, *July 1961*

KENNEDY, MRS. JOHN F. *See* Kennedy, Jacqueline Bouvier

KENNEDY, LEONARD: *Author*
The World's Greatest Waterfall: The Kaieteur Fall, in British Guiana. 846-859, *Sept. 1911*

KENNEDY, RALPH A.: *Author*
Playing 3,000 Golf Courses in Fourteen Lands. 113-132, *July 1952*

KENNEDY, ROBERT F.: *Author*
Canada's Mount Kennedy: A Peak Worthy of the President. 5-9, *July 1965*

KENNEDY, ROBERT S.:
Nomination Page. *Mar. 1981*
Author
Saving the Philippine Eagle. Photos by Alan R. Degen, Neil L. Rettig, and Wolfgang A. Salb. 847-856, *June 1981*

KENNEDY, Mount, Canada:
⊕ *The Massif of Mount Hubbard, Mount Alverstone, and Mount Kennedy.* Wall map announced. 736, *Nov. 1968*
Canada's Mount Kennedy: The Discovery. By Bradford Washburn; A Peak Worthy of the President. By Robert F. Kennedy; The First Ascent. By James W. Whittaker. Photos by William Albert Allard. NGS research grant. 1-33, *July 1965*

KENNEDY SPACE CENTER, Cape Canaveral, Florida:
Columbia's Astronauts' Own Story: Our Phenomenal First Flight. By John W. Young and Robert L. Crippen. Paintings by Ken Dallison. 478-503, *Oct. 1981*
"A Most Fantastic Voyage": The Story of Apollo 8's Rendezvous With the Moon. By Sam C. Phillips. 593-631, *May 1969*
Cape Canaveral's 6,000-mile Shooting Gallery. By Allan C. Fisher, Jr. Photos by Luis Marden and Thomas Nebbia. 421-471, *Oct. 1959*
Reaching for the Moon. By Allan C. Fisher, Jr. Photos by Luis Marden. 157-171, *Feb. 1959*

KENNEY, NATHANIEL T.:
Nomination Page. *June 1959*
Author
Chincoteague: Watermen's Island Home. Photos by James L. Amos. 810-829, *June 1980*
Our Wild and Scenic Rivers: The Rio Grande. Photos by Bank Langmore. 46-51, *July 1977*
The Other Yosemite. Photos by Dean Conger. 762-781, *June 1974*
A New Riviera: Mexico's West Coast. Photos by Charles O'Rear. 670-699, *Nov. 1973*
Southern California's Trial by Mud and Water. Photos by Bruce Dale. 552-573, *Oct. 1969*
New National Park Proposed: The Spectacular North Cascades. Photos by James P. Blair. 642-667, *May 1968*
Sharks: Wolves of the Sea. 222-257, *Feb. 1968*
Big Bend: Jewel in the Texas Desert. Photos by James L. Stanfield. 104-133, *Jan. 1968*
Ethiopian Adventure. Photos by James P. Blair. 548-582, *Apr. 1965*
Chesapeake Country. Photos by Bates Littlehales. 370-411, *Sept. 1964*

Photographer William Albert Allard (right) and Senator Robert F. Kennedy stand atop the Canadian peak named for President John F. Kennedy. DEE MOLENAAR

The Mighty *Enterprise*. Photos by Thomas J. Abercrombie. 431-448, *Mar. 1963*
Our Changing Atlantic Coastline. Photos by B. Anthony Stewart. 860-887, *Dec. 1962*
Cape Cod, Where Sea Holds Sway Over Man and Land. Photos by Dean Conger. 149-187, *Aug. 1962*
Life in Walled-off West Berlin. By Nathaniel T. Kenney and Volkmar Wentzel. Photos by Thomas Nebbia. 735-767, *Dec. 1961*
United Italy Marks Its 100th Year. 593-647, *Nov. 1961*
Africa: The Winds of Freedom Stir a Continent. Photos by W. D. Vaughn. 303-359, *Sept. 1960*
Where Falcons Wear Air Force Blue, United States Air Force Academy. Photos by William Belknap, Jr. 845-873, *June 1959*
New Era on the Great Lakes. 439-490, *Apr. 1959*
Our Green Treasury, the National Forests. Photos by J. Baylor Roberts. 287-324, *Sept. 1956*
Maytime Miracle in Sherwood Gardens. 700-709, *May 1956*
Kings Point: Maker of Mariners. Photos by Volkmar Wentzel. 693-706, *Nov. 1955*

KENT (County), England:
Britain Fights in the Fields. By Francis A. Flood. 31-65, *July 1944*
Front-line Town of Britain's Siege (Dover). By Harvey Klemmer. 105-128, *Jan. 1944*
Charm Spots Along England's Harassed Coast. 237-252, *Aug. 1940*

KENTUCKY:
Daniel Boone, First Hero of the Frontier. By Elizabeth A. Moize. Photos

by William Strode. 812-841, *Dec. 1985*
Wrestlin' for a Livin' With King Coal. By Michael E. Long. Photos by Michael O'Brien. 793-819, *June 1983*
Home to the Heart of Kentucky. By Nadine Brewer. Photos by William Strode. 522-546, *Apr. 1982*
The Ohio–River With a Job to Do. By Priit J. Vesilind. Photos by Martin Rogers. 245-273, *Feb. 1977*
⊕ *Close-up: U.S.A., Illinois, Indiana, Ohio, and Kentucky.* Text on reverse. *Feb. 1977*
Heart of the Bluegrass. By Charles McCarry. Photos by J. Bruce Baumann. 634-659, *May 1974*
Whatever Happened to TVA? By Gordon Young. Photos by Emory Kristof. 830-863, *June 1973*
The People of Cumberland Gap. By John Fetterman. Photos by Bruce Dale. 591-621, *Nov. 1971*
Vacation Tour Through Lincoln Land. By Ralph Gray. 141-184, *Feb. 1952*
So Much Happens Along the Ohio River. By Frederick Simpich. Photos by Justin Locke. 177-212, *Feb. 1950*
Around the "Great Lakes of the South." By Frederick Simpich. Photos by J. Baylor Roberts. 463-491, *Apr. 1948*
Home Folk around Historic Cumberland Gap. By Leo A. Borah. 741-768, *Dec. 1943*
Kentucky, Boone's Great Meadow: The Bluegrass State Celebrates Its Sesquicentennial As It Helps the Nation Gird for War. By Leo A. Borah. 57-89, *July 1942*
A Patriotic Pilgrimage to Eastern National Parks: History and Beauty Live Along Paved Roads, Once Indian Trails, Through Virginia, North Carolina, Tennessee, Kentucky, and West Virginia. By Leo A. Borah. 663-702, *June 1934*

KENYA:
Kenya: A Population Exploding. By Paul R. and Anne H. Ehrlich. Photos by Robert Caputo. 918-921, *Dec. 1988*
The Search for Our Ancestors. By Kenneth F. Weaver. Photos by David L. Brill. Paintings by Jay H. Matternes. 560-623, *Nov. 1985*
The Threatened Ways of Kenya's Pokot People. By Elizabeth L. Meyerhoff. Photos by Murray Roberts. NGS research grant. 120-140, *Jan. 1982*
Wild Cargo: the Business of Smuggling Animals. By Noel Grove. Photos by Steve Raymer. 287-315, *Mar. 1981*
Africa's Elephants: Can They Survive? By Oria Douglas-Hamilton. Photos by Oria and Iain Douglas-Hamilton. 568-603, *Nov. 1980*
■ Last Stand in Eden (Elephants). 1, Jan. 1979; cover, *Mar. 1979*
Africa's Gentle Giants (Giraffes). By Bristol Foster. Photos by Bob Campbell and Thomas Nebbia. 402-417, *Sept. 1977*
Rescuing the Rothschild (Giraffe). By Carolyn Bennett Patterson. 419-421, *Sept. 1977*

East Africa's Majestic Flamingos. By
M. Philip Kahl. NGS research grant.
276-294, *Feb. 1970*

Kenya Says *Harambee!* By Allan C.
Fisher, Jr. Photos by Bruce Dale.
151-205, *Feb. 1969*

The Leakeys of Africa: Family in Search
of Prehistoric Man. By Melvin M.
Payne. NGS research grant. 194-231,
Feb. 1965

YWCA: International Success Story.
By Mary French Rockefeller. Photos
by Otis Imboden. 904-933, *Dec. 1963*

Freeing Flamingos From Anklets of
Death (Lake Magadi). By John G.
Williams. Photos by Alan Root. 934-
944, *Dec. 1963*

Adventures in the Search for Man. By
Louis S. B. Leakey. Photos by Hugo
van Lawick. 132-152, *Jan. 1963*

Where Elephants Have Right of Way.
By George and Jinx Rodger. Photos
by George Rodger. 363-389,
Sept. 1960

A New Look at Kenya's "Treetops." By
Quentin Keynes. 536-541, *Oct. 1956*

Spearing Lions with Africa's Masai. By
Edgar Monsanto Queeny. 487-517,
Oct. 1954

Africa's Uncaged Elephants. Photos by
Quentin Keynes. 371-382, *Mar. 1951*

Britain Tackles the East African Bush.
By W. Robert Moore. 311-352,
Mar. 1950

Roaming Africa's Unfenced Zoos. By
W. Robert Moore. Included: "Treetops Hotel," near Mount Kenya. 353-
380, *Mar. 1950*

When a Drought Blights Africa: Hippos
and Elephants Are Driven Insane by
Suffering, in the Lorian Swamp, Kenya Colony. By A. T. Curle. 521-528,
Apr. 1929

Where Roosevelt Will Hunt. By Sir
Harry Johnston. 207-256, *Mar. 1909*

See also Serengeti-Mara Ecosystem,
Kenya-Tanzania; Tsavo National
Park; Turkana, Lake; *and* Baboons

KENYON, KARL W.: *Author*

Return of the Sea Otter. Photos by
James A. Mattison, Jr. 520-539,
Oct. 1971

Author-Photographer

The Fur Seal Herd Comes of Age. By
Victor B. Scheffer and Karl W. Kenyon. 491-512, *Apr. 1952*

KENYON, KATHLEEN M.:

Nomination Page. *July 1963*

Author

Jericho Gives Up Its Secrets. By Kathleen M. Kenyon and A. Douglas Tushingham. Photos by Nancy Lord.
853-870, *Dec. 1953*

KEPNER, WILLIAM E.:

Exploring the Stratosphere. By Albert
W. Stevens. 397-434, *Oct. 1934*

KERALA (State), India:

Kerala, Jewel of India's Malabar Coast.
By Peter Miller. Photos by Raghubir
Singh. 592-617, *May 1988*

KERBELA, Iraq. *See* Karbala

KERBEY, McFALL: *Author*

Behind Netherlands Sea Ramparts:
Dikes and Pumps Keep Ocean and
Rivers at Bay While a Busy People
Carries on Peacetime Work. 255-290,
Feb. 1940

The Texas Delta of an American Nile:
Orchards and Gardens Replace
Thorny Jungle in the Southmost Tip
of the Lone Star State. 51-96,
Jan. 1939

How the United States Grew. 631-649,
May 1933

Colorado, a Barrier That Became a
Goal: Where Water Has Trans-
formed Dry Plains Into Verdant
Farms, and Highways Have Opened
up Mineral and Scenic Wealth. 1-63,
July 1932

Genoa, Where Columbus Learned to
Love the Sea. Included: Pictorial supplement. 333-352, *Sept. 1928*

Toilers of the Sky: Tenuous Clouds Perform the Mighty Task of Shaping the
Earth and Sustaining Terrestrial Life.
163-189, *Aug. 1925*

KERENSKY, ALEXANDER:

Russia from Within: Her War of Yesterday, Today, and Tomorrow. By Stanley Washburn. 91-120, *Aug. 1917*

Russia's Man of the Hour: Alexander
Kerensky's First Speeches and Proclamations. 24-45, *July 1917*

KERN, JAMES A.:
Author-Photographer

Dragon Lizards of Komodo. 872-880,
Dec. 1968

KERNAN, MICHAEL: *Author*

There's More to Nashville than Music.
Photos by Jodi Cobb. 692-711,
May 1978

KERR, MARK B.: *Author*

A Journey in Ecuador. 238-245,
July 1896

Report on Topographic Work (Mount
St. Elias Expedition). 195,
May 29, 1891

KERRY, County, Ireland. *See* Dingle
Peninsula

KERTEZI, Greece:

Erosion, Trojan Horse of Greece. By
F. G. Renner. 793-812, *Dec. 1947*

KERWIN, JOSEPH P.:

Skylab, Outpost on the Frontier of
Space. By Thomas Y. Canby. Photos
by the nine mission astronauts. 441-
469, *Oct. 1974*

KESHISHIAN, JOHN M.: *Author*

Anatomy of a Burmese Beauty Secret.
798-801, *June 1979*

KETCHAM, WALTER E.:
Author-Photographer

Dipo, the Little Desert "Kangaroo."
537-548, *Oct. 1940*

KETCHES. *See* Betelgeuse; Carib;
*Great Britain II; Isbjorn; Nomad;
Tectona; Tradewinds; Yankee*

KETCHIKAN, Alaska:

Ketchikan. 508-509, *Nov. 1905*

KETTERING, CHARLES F.:

Board of Trustees. 703, *Dec. 1944*

KEW GARDENS, London, England:

Kew: The Commoners' Royal Garden.
By Thomas Garner James. Photos by
B. Anthony Stewart. 479-506,
Apr. 1950

KEY LARGO CORAL REEF, Florida:

Key Largo Coral Reef: America's First
Undersea Park. By Charles M.
Brookfield. Photos by Jerry Green-
berg. 58-69, *Jan. 1962*

Florida's Coral City Beneath the Sea.
By Jerry Greenberg. 70-89, *Jan. 1962*

The **KEY** to the Pacific (Hawaii). By

*Facade of weatherboarding preserves an original two-story log cabin built on a home-
stead in the heart of Kentucky around 1800.* WILLIAM STRODE

George C. Perkins. 295-298, *Apr. 1908*

KEY WEST, Florida:

The Lower Keys, Florida's "Out Islands." By John Scofield. Photos by Emory Kristof and Bates Littlehales. 72-93, *Jan. 1971*

Shrimpers Strike Gold in the Gulf. By Clarence P. Idyll. Photos by Robert F. Sisson. 699-707, *May 1957*

Tropical Gardens of Key West. By Luis Marden. 116-124, *Jan. 1953*

Our Navy's Long Submarine Arm. By Allan C. Fisher, Jr. 613-636, *Nov. 1952*

From Indian Canoes to Submarines at Key West. By Frederick Simpich. Photos by J. Baylor Roberts. 41-72, *Jan. 1950*

Capturing Giant Turtles in the Caribbean. By David D. Duncan. 177-190, *Aug. 1943*

Across the Gulf by Rail to Key West. By Jefferson B. Browne. 203-207, *June 1896*

KEYHOE, DONALD E.:
Author-Photographer

Seeing America With Lindbergh: The Record of a Tour of More Than 20,000 Miles by Airplane Through Forty-eight States on Schedule Time. 1-46, *Jan. 1928*

KEYNES, QUENTIN:
Author-Photographer

Seychelles, Tropic Isles of Eden. 670-695, *Nov. 1959*

A New Look at Kenya's "Treetops." 536-541, *Oct. 1956*

Mauritius, Island of the Dodo. 77-104, *Jan. 1956*

St. Helena: the Forgotten Island. 265-280, *Aug. 1950*

Photographer

Africa's Uncaged Elephants. 371-382, *Mar. 1951*

KEZAR, MITCH: *Photographer*

Isle Royale, A North Woods Park Primeval. By John L. Eliot. 534-550, *Apr. 1985*

KHAFRE, King (Egypt):

Nomination Page. *Oct. 1969*

KHARKOV, U.S.S.R.:

Liberated Ukraine. By Eddy Gilmore. 513-536, *May 1944*

Ukraine, Past and Present. By Nevin O. Winter. 114-128, *Aug. 1918*

KHAT (Flower):

"The Flower of Paradise": The Part Which Khat Plays in the Life of the Yemen Arab. By Charles Moser. 173-186, *Aug. 1917*

KHATMANDU, Nepal. *See* Kathmandu

KHIOS (Island), Greece:

Historic Islands and Shores of the Ægean Sea. By Ernest Lloyd Harris. 231-261, *Sept. 1915*

KHIRBAT QUMRĀN, West Bank:

The Men Who Hid the Dead Sea Scrolls. By A. Douglas Tushingham.

Paintings by Peter V. Bianchi. 785-808, *Dec. 1958*

KHMER EMPIRE. *See* Angkor, Kampuchea

KHMER REPUBLIC. *See* Kampuchea

KHMER ROUGE:

The Temples of Angkor. 548-589. I. Will They Survive? Introduction by Wilbur E. Garrett. 548-551. II. Ancient Glory in Stone. By Peter T. White. Photos by Wilbur E. Garrett. 552-589, *May 1982*

Kampuchea Wakens From a Nightmare. By Peter T. White. Photos by David Alan Harvey. 590-623, *May 1982*

KHMERS:

The Temples of Angkor. 548-589. I. Will They Survive? Introduction by Wilbur E. Garrett. 548-551. II. Ancient Glory in Stone. By Peter T. White. Photos by Wilbur E. Garrett. 552-589, *May 1982*

Kampuchea Wakens From a Nightmare. By Peter T. White. Photos by David Alan Harvey. 590-623, *May 1982*

Cambodia: Indochina's "Neutral" Corner. By Thomas J. Abercrombie. 514-551, *Oct. 1964*

Angkor: Jewel of the Jungle. By W. Robert Moore. Paintings by Maurice Fiévet. 517-569, *Apr. 1960*

Portrait of Indochina. By W. Robert Moore and Maynard Owen Williams. Paintings by Jean Despujols. 461-490, *Apr. 1951*

KHOMEINI, RUHOLLAH (Ayatollah):

Iran Under the Ayatollah. By Michael Coyne. 108-135, *July 1985*

KHORESM OBLAST, U.S.S.R.:

Surveying Through Khoresm: A

A Pashtun tribesman reflects the rigors of life in Afghanistan's Khyber Pass in 1920. © R. B. HOLMES AND COMPANY

Journey Into Parts of Asiatic Russia Which Have Been Closed to Western Travelers Since the World War. By Lyman D. Wilbur. 753-780, *June 1932*

KHUFU, King (Egypt):

Finding a Pharaoh's Funeral Bark. By Farouk El-Baz. Photos by James P. Blair and Claude E. Petrone. Included: The world's oldest ship. 513-533, *Apr. 1988*

KHUMBU DISTRICT, Nepal:

Preserving a Mountain Heritage. By Sir Edmund Hillary. 696-703, *June 1982*

Park at the Top of the World: Mount Everest National Park. By Rick Ridgeway. Photos by Nicholas deVore III. 704-725, *June 1982*

KHUN, BYRON, COUNT DE PROROK. *See* Prorok, Byron Khun de

KHUN TRIBESPEOPLE:

Strange Tribes in the Shan States of Burma. Photos by W. Robert Moore. 247-254, *Aug. 1930*

KHYBER PASS, Afghanistan-Pakistan:

Through the Heart of Hindustan: A Teeming Highway Extending for Fifteen Hundred Miles, from the Khyber Pass to Calcutta. By Maynard Owen Williams. 433-467, *Nov. 1921*

KIANGSI PROVINCE, China. *See* Jiangxi Province

KIBBUTZIM:

Our Life on a Border Kibbutz. By Carol and Al Abrams. Photos by Al Abrams. 364-391, *Sept. 1970*

The Land of Galilee. By Kenneth MacLeish. Photos by B. Anthony Stewart. 832-865, *Dec. 1965*

Israel: Land of Promise. By John Scofield. Photos by B. Anthony Stewart. 395-434, *Mar. 1965*

Palestine Today. By Francis Chase, Jr. 501-516, *Oct. 1946*

KIEL CANAL. *See* former name, Kaiser Wilhelm Canal

KIENLUNG, Emperor (China):

Mukden, the Manchu Home and Its Great Art Museum. By Eliza R. Scidmore. 289-320, *Apr. 1910*

KIEV, U.S.S.R.:

Ukraine. By Mike Edwards. Photos by Steve Raymer. 595-631, *May 1987*

Viking Trail East. By Robert Paul Jordan. Photos by Jim Brandenburg. Paintings by Michael A. Hampshire. 278-317, *Mar. 1985*

Liberated Ukraine. By Eddy Gilmore. 513-536, *May 1944*

Ukraine, Past and Present. By Nevin O. Winter. 114-128, *Aug. 1918*

KIHN, W. LANGDON: *Artist*

Hearty Folk Defy Arctic Storms. 479-494, *Oct. 1949*

Indians of the Far West. By Matthew W. Stirling. 175-200, *Feb. 1948*

First Families of Southeastern America (Indians). 65-72, *Jan. 1946*

Blazing fountain and a river of lava pour from a vent of Kilauea on the island of Hawaii. The volcano has erupted frequently since 1960. ROBERT W. MADDEN, NGS

Totem-pole Builders. 33-48, *Jan. 1945*
Indians of Our Western Plains. 81-96, *July 1944*
Red Men of the Southwest. 557-596, *Nov. 1940*
When Red Men Ruled Our Forests. 551-590, *Nov. 1937*
A Palette from Spain. 407-440, *Mar. 1936*

KILAUEA VOLCANO, Hawaii:
Hawaii, Island of Fire and Flowers. By Gordon Young. Photos by Robert W. Madden. 399-425, *Mar. 1975*
Fountain of Fire in Hawaii. By Frederick Simpich, Jr. Photos by Robert B. Goodman and Robert Wenkam. 303-327, *Mar. 1960*
Volcanic Fires of the 50th State: Hawaii National Park. By Paul A. Zahl. 793-823, *June 1959*
Photographing a Volcano in Action. By Thomas J. Hargrave. 561-563, *Oct. 1955*

KILBON, ROLAND: *Author*
Born Hunters, the Bird Dogs. Paintings by Walter A. Weber. 369-398, *Sept. 1947*

KILBRACKEN, LORD (John Godley, Third Baron Kilbracken):
Nomination Page. *Apr. 1963*
Author
The Long, Deep Dive. Photos by Bates Littlehales. 718-731, *May 1963*
KILI ISLAND, Marshall Islands:
Bikini–A Way of Life Lost. By William S. Ellis. Photos by James P. Blair. 813-834, *June 1986*

KILLARNEY, Lakes of, Ireland:
Dublin's Historic Horse Show. By Maynard Owen Williams. 115-132, *July 1953*

KILLDEER (Bird):
Hunting with the Lens. By Howard H. Cleaves. 1-35, *July 1914*

KILLER BEES. *See* Africanized Honeybees

KILLER CATERPILLARS. *See* Inchworms

KILLER WHALES:
The Whales Called "Killer." By Erich Hoyt. 220-237, *Aug. 1984*
Killer Whale Attack! Text by Cliff Tarpy. 542-545, *Apr. 1979*
Where Two Worlds Meet (Patagonia). Photos by Des and Jen Bartlett. 298-321, *Mar. 1976*
Making Friends With a Killer Whale. By Edward I. Griffin. 418-446, *Mar. 1966*

KILLIN, BENTON:
Some of the Conditions and Possibilities of Agriculture in Alaska. By Walter H. Evans. 178-187, *Apr. 1898*

KIM, H. EDWARD:
Nomination Page. *Aug. 1975*
Nomination Page. *July 1974*
Author-Photographer
Seoul: Korean Showcase. 770-797, *Dec. 1979*
Rare Look at North Korea. 252-277, *Aug. 1974*
Photographer
Kyongju, Where Korea Began. By Cathy Newman. 258-268, *Aug. 1988*
China's Opening Door. By John J. Putman. 64-83, *July 1983*
Yellow Sea Yields Shipwreck Trove. Introduction by Donald H. Keith. 231-243, *Aug. 1979*
Day of the Rice God (Festival in Japan). By Douglas Lee. 78-85, *July 1978*
Arizona's Suburbs of the Sun. By David Jeffery. 486-517, *Oct. 1977*
South Korea: What Next? By Peter T. White. 394-427, *Sept. 1975*
Pennsylvania's Old-time Dutch Treat. By Kent Britt. 564-578, *Apr. 1973*

KIMBERLEY (Region), Australia:
Western Australia, the Big Country. By Kenneth MacLeish. Photos by James L. Stanfield. 150-187, *Feb. 1975*

KIMEU, KAMOYA:
A Geographic Gold Medal Honors Kenyan Fossil Finder. President's Page. By Gilbert M. Grosvenor. *Nov. 1985*
Homo Erectus Unearthed: A Fossil Skeleton 1,600,000 Years Old. By Richard Leakey and Alan Walker. Photos by David L. Brill. Included: Discovery by Kimeu. NGS research grant. 624-629, *Nov. 1985*

KINALING, Sumatra, Indonesia:
By Motor Through the East Coast and Batak Highlands of Sumatra. By Melvin A. Hall. 69-102, *Jan. 1920*

KINCAID, DON: *Photographer*
Treasure From the Ghost Galleon: Santa Margarita. By Eugene Lyon. 228-243, *Feb. 1982*

KINDERZECHE (Festival):
Dinkelsbühl (Germany) Rewards Its Children. By Charles Belden. 255-268, *Feb. 1957*

KING, ELIZABETH W.: *Author*
Flags of the United Nations. 213-238, *Feb. 1951*
Flags of the Americas. 633-657, *May 1949*
Seals of Our Nation, States, and Territories. Paintings by Carlotta Gonzales Lahey, Irvin E. Alleman, Theodora Price. 1-42, *July 1946*
Heroes of Wartime Science and Mercy. 715-740, *Dec. 1943*

KING, F. H.:
Awarded Grant Squires Prize. 115, *Jan. 1913*
Author
The Wonderful Canals of China. 931-958, *Oct. 1912*

KING, JOHN:
The Journey of Burke and Wills. By Joseph Judge. Photos by Joseph J. Scherschel. 152-191, *Feb. 1979*

KING, LARRY L.:
On Assignment in Alaska and Texas. *Mar. 1988*
Author
Hello Anchorage, Good-Bye Dream. Photos by Chris Johns. 364-389, *Mar. 1988*

KING, MARIEL:
Nomination Page. *Oct. 1968*

KING CRABS:
The Crab That Shakes Hands. By Clarence P. Idyll. Photos by Robert F. Sisson. 254-271, *Feb. 1971*

KING Herring: An Account of the World's Most Valuable Fish, the Industries It Supports, and the Part It Has Played in History. By Hugh M. Smith. 701-735, *Aug. 1909*

A giant sequoia in California's Kings Canyon National Park area triumphed over fire that left a scar. B. ANTHONY STEWART, NGS

KING ISLAND, Alaska:

Cliff Dwellers of the Bering Sea. By Juan Muñoz. 129-146, *Jan. 1954*
North Star Cruises Alaska's Wild West. By Amos Burg. 57-86, *July 1952*

KING of Cats and His Court (Leopards, Lions, and Tigers). By Victor H. Cahalane. Paintings by Walter A. Weber. 217-259, *Feb. 1943*

KING RANCH, Texas:

America's "Meat on the Hoof." By William H. Nicholas. Included: King Ranch, Cattle Empire in Texas. 33-72, *Jan. 1952*

The **KINGDOM** of Flowers: An Account of the Wealth of Trees and Shrubs of China and of What the Arnold Arboretum, with China's Help, Is Doing to Enrich America. By Ernest H. Wilson. 1003-1035, *Nov. 1911*

A **KINGDOM** of Many Tribes (Afghanistan). Photos by Maynard Owen Williams. 745-752, *Dec. 1933*

The **KINGDOM** of Servia. By William Joseph Showalter. 417-432, *Apr. 1915*

KINGDON-WARD, F.:
Author-Photographer

Caught in the Assam-Tibet Earthquake. 403-416, *Mar. 1952*

KINGFISHERS:

The Shy and Spectacular Kingfisher (European). Photos by Carl-Johan Junge and Emil Lütken. 413-419, *Sept. 1974*
Parrots, Kingfishers, and Flycatchers: Strange Trogons and Curious Cuckoos are Pictured with these Other Birds of Color, Dash, and Courage. By Alexander Wetmore. Paintings by Allan Brooks. 801-828, *June 1936*

KINGLETS (Birds):

Winged Denizens of Woodland, Stream, and Marsh. By Alexander Wetmore. Paintings by Allan Brooks. 577-596, *May 1934*

KINGMAN, EUGENE: *Artist*

Crater Lake and Yosemite Through the Ages. 333-339, *Mar. 1937*

KINGMAN, JOHN A.: *Author*

The Isle of Capri: An Imperial Residence and Probable Wireless Station of Ancient Rome. 213-231, *Sept. 1919*

KINGS CANYON NATIONAL PARK, California:

Giant Sequoias Draw Millions to California Parks. By John Michael Kauffmann. Photos by B. Anthony Stewart. 147-187, *Aug. 1959*

KINGS COUNTY, New York:

Brooklyn: The Other Side of the Bridge. By Alice J. Hall. Photos by Robert W. Madden. 580-613, *May 1983*

KINGS POINT, New York: U. S. Merchant Marine Academy:

Kings Point: Maker of Mariners. By Nathaniel T. Kenney. Photos by Volkmar Wentzel. 693-706, *Nov. 1955*

KINGSFORD-SMITH, CHARLES E.: *Author*

Our Conquest of the Pacific: The Narrative of the 7,400-Mile Flight from San Francisco to Brisbane in Three Ocean Hops. By Charles E. Kingsford-Smith and Charles T. P. Ulm. 371-402, *Oct. 1928*

KINGSTON, Jamaica:

Jamaica, the Isle of Many Rivers. By John Oliver La Gorce. 1-55, *Jan. 1927*

KINGSTON, Massachusetts:

Land of the Pilgrims' Pride. By George W. Long. Photos by Robert F. Sisson. 193-219, *Aug. 1947*

KINGSTON, Ontario, Canada:

Sea to Lakes on the St. Lawrence. By George W. Long. Photos by B. Anthony Stewart and John E. Fletcher. 323-366, *Sept. 1950*

KINGTEHCHEN, China. *See* Jingdezhen

KINKAJOU (Yacht):

Cruise of the *Kinkajou:* Among Desert Islands of Mexico Voyagers Find Outdoor Laboratories for the Naturalist and Ideal Fishing Grounds for the Sportsman. By Alfred M. Bailey. 339-366, *Sept. 1941*

KINLOCH, BRUCE G.:
Author-Photographer

Orphans of the Wild. 683-699, *Nov. 1962*

KINNEY, PAUL B.:
Author-Photographer

Once in a Lifetime: Black Bears Rarely Have Quadruplets, But Goofy Did–and the Camera Caught Her Nursing Her Remarkable Family. 249-258, *Aug. 1941*

KINNEY, WILLIAM A.: *Author*

Roving Maryland's Cavalier Country. 431-470, *Apr. 1954*
Washington's Historic Georgetown. 513-544, *Apr. 1953*
Operation Eclipse: 1948. 325-372, *Mar. 1949*
American Wings Soar Around the World: Epic Story of the Air Transport Command of the U. S. Army Is a Saga of Yankee Daring and Doing. By Donald H. Agnew and William A. Kinney. 57-78, *July 1943*

KIRCHHOFF, C.: *Author*

The United States–Her Mineral Resources. 331-339, *Sept. 1903*

KIRGHIZ:

Winter Caravan to the Roof of the World. By Sabrina and Roland Michaud. 435-465, *Apr. 1972*
We Took the Highroad in Afghanistan. By Jean and Franc Shor. 673-706, *Nov. 1950*
With the Nomads of Central Asia: A Summer's Sojourn in the Tekes Valley, Plateau Paradise of Mongol and Turkic Tribes. By Edward Murray. Paintings and drawings by Alexandre Iacovleff. 1-57, *Jan. 1936*
First Over the Roof of the World by Motor: The Trans-Asiatic Expedition Sets New Records for Wheeled Transport in Scaling Passes of the Himalayas. By Maynard Owen Williams. 321-363, *Mar. 1932*

KIRIBATI. *See* former names, Canton Island, Phoenix Islands; Gilbert Islands

KIRIN (Chilin), China. *See* Jilin

KIRJASSOFF, ALICE BALLANTINE: *Author*

Formosa the Beautiful. 247-292, *Mar. 1920*

KIRK, MALCOLM S.:
Author-Photographer

Change Ripples New Guinea's Sepik River. 354-381, *Sept. 1973*
The Asmat of New Guinea, Headhunters in Today's World. 376-409, *Mar. 1972*
New Guinea Festival of Faces. 148-156, *July 1969*
Journey Into Stone Age New Guinea. 568-592, *Apr. 1969*

KIRKJUFELL (Volcano), Heimaey, Iceland:

A Village Fights for Its Life. By Noel Grove. 40-67, *July 1973*
See also present name, Eldfell

KIRKWOOD, J. E.: *Author*

A Mexican Hacienda. 563-584, *May 1914*

KIRSHNER, ROBERT P.: *Author*

Supernova–Death of a Star. Photos by Roger H. Ressmeyer. 619-647, *May 1988*

KIRTLEY, MICHAEL and AUBINE:

On Assignment in the Ivory Coast. *July 1982*

Author-Photographers
Senegambia: A Now and Future Nation. 224-251, *Aug. 1985*
The Ivory Coast–African Success Story. 94-125, *July 1982*
The Inadan: Artisans of the Sahara. 282-298, *Aug. 1979*

Photographers
Finding West Africa's Oldest City. By Susan and Roderick McIntosh. Contents: Jenne-jeno (site), Mali. 396-418, *Sept. 1982*

KITES:

Japan's Warriors of the Wind. Photos by David Alan Harvey. Text by John Eliot. 551-561, *Apr. 1977*
Alexander Graham Bell Museum: Tribute to Genius. By Jean Lesage. 227-256, *Aug. 1956*
Miracle Men of the Telephone. By F. Barrows Colton. Included: Illustrations of Alexander Graham Bell's multicelled and tetrahedral kites. 273-316, *Mar. 1947*
Air Conquest: From the Early Days of Giant Kites and Birdlike Gliders, the National Geographic Society Has Aided and Encouraged the Growth of Aviation. 233-242, *Aug. 1927*
The Charm of Cape Breton Island: The Most Picturesque Portion of Canada's Maritime Provinces–A Land Rich in Historic Associations, Natural Resources, and Geographic Appeal. By Catherine Dunlop Mackenzie. Included: Alexander Graham Bell's kites. 34-60, *July 1920*
Dr. Bell's Man-Lifting Kite. By Gilbert H. Grosvenor. 35-52, *Jan. 1908*
Aërial Locomotion: With a Few Notes of Progress in the Construction of an Aërodrome. By Alexander Graham Bell. 1-34, *Jan. 1907*
The Tetrahedral Kite. 294, *July 1903*
The Tetrahedral Principle in Kite Structure. By Alexander Graham Bell. 219-251, *June 1903*
Kite Work of the Weather Bureau. By H. C. Frankenfield. 55-62, *Feb. 1900*

KITES (Birds):

The Swallow-tailed Kite: Graceful Aerialist of the Everglades. Photos by Ray O. Green, Jr., Norman D. Reed, and Myron H. Wright, Jr. 496-505, *Oct. 1972*
The Eagle, King of Birds, and His Kin. By Alexander Wetmore. Paintings by Allan Brooks. 43-95, *July 1933*

KITIMAT–Canada's Aluminum Titan. By David S. Boyer. 376-398, *Sept. 1956*

KITTINGER, JOSEPH W., Jr.: *Author*

The Long, Lonely Flight. Contents: Transatlantic solo by balloon. 270-276, *Feb. 1985*
The Long, Lonely Leap. Photos by Volkmar Wentzel. 854-873, *Dec. 1960*

KITTY HAWK Floats Across North America. By Maxie and Kristian Anderson. 260-271, *Aug. 1980*

The **KIWI,** New Zealand's Wonder Bird. By Ron J. Anderson. 395-398, *Sept. 1955*

KIWIFRUIT:

The Captivating Kiwifruit. By Noel D. Vietmeyer. Photos by Jim Brandenburg. 683-688, *May 1987*

The **KIZILBASH** Clans of Kurdistan. By Melville Chater. 485-504, *Oct. 1928*

KLAMATH INDIANS:

Wokas, a Primitive Indian Food. 183-185, *Apr. 1904*

KLAPTHOR, MARGARET BROWN: *Author*

■■ *The First Ladies.* Published in cooperation with the White House Historical Association. 87 pages. 1975; rev. ed. *1983*

KLEMMER, HARVEY: *Author*

Belgium Comes Back. Photos by Maynard Owen Williams. 575-614, *May 1948*
A City That Refused to Die (Plymouth, England). Photos by B. Anthony Stewart. 211-236, *Feb. 1946*
Lend-Lease and the Russian Victory. 499-512, *Oct. 1945*
Michigan Fights. 677-715, *Dec. 1944*
Front-line Town of Britain's Siege (Dover). 105-128, *Jan. 1944*
Convoys to Victory. 193-216, *Feb. 1943*
"Blood, Toil, Tears, and Sweat": An American Tells the Story of Britain's War Effort, Summed up in Prime Minister Churchill's Unflinching Words. 141-166, *Aug. 1942*
Rural Britain Carries On. 527-552, *Oct. 1941*

An ice cave near Mount Logan in Canada's Yukon Territory leads to a frozen underworld in Kluane National Park Reserve. GEORGE F. MOBLEY, NGS

A 3,500-year-old gold mask was found at Mycenae, Greece, home to Bronze Age kings. NATIONAL ARCHAEOLOGICAL MUSEUM, ATHENS

Lisbon–Gateway to Warring Europe. 259-276, *Aug. 1941*

Everyday Life in Wartime England. 497-534, *Apr. 1941*

KLEMPERER, WOLFGANG B.:
Author

The Solar Eclipse From a Jet. 785-796, *Nov. 1963*

KLIMSTRA, W. D:

Nomination Page. *Oct. 1972*

KLINE, FRED: *Author*

San Antonio: "Texas, Actin' Kind of Natural." Photos by David Hiser. 524-549, *Apr. 1976*

Library of Congress: The Nation's Bookcase. Photos by Dick Durrance II. 671-687, *Nov. 1975*

Baltimore: The Hidden City. Photos by Martin Rogers. 188-215, *Feb. 1975*

KLINGEL, GILBERT C.: *Author*

One Hundred Hours Beneath the Chesapeake. Photos by Willard R. Culver. 681-696, *May 1955*

KLINGMAN, LAWRENCE L.: *Author*

Incredible Andorra. Photos by B. Anthony Stewart. 262-290, *Aug. 1949*

KLONDIKE DISTRICT, Canada:

Yukon Fever: Call of the North. By Robert Booth. Photos by George F. Mobley. 548-578, *Apr. 1978*

Overland Routes to the Klondike. By Hamlin Garland. 113-116, *Apr. 1898*

Climatic Conditions of Alaska. By A. W. Greely. Included: Temperature recordings at Dawson and Fort Reliance. 132-137, *Apr. 1898*

✦ *The Gold and Coal Fields of Alaska, Together with the Principal Steamer Routes and Trails.* Insets: Trails from Tide Water to the Headwaters of the Yukon River; The Klondike Gold Region, Canada. *Apr. 1898*

A Winter Weather Record From the Klondike Region. By E. W. Nelson. 327-335, *Nov. 1897*

KLUANE NATIONAL PARK RE-SERVE, Yukon Territory, Canada:

Kluane: Canada's Icy Wilderness Park.

By Douglas Lee. Photos by George F. Mobley. 630-653, *Nov. 1985*

Kluane: A Century of Exploration. By Barry C. Bishop. 654-657, *Nov. 1985*

KNEEN, ORVILLE H.: *Author*

Patent Plants Enrich Our World. 357-378, *Mar. 1948*

KNIGHT, C.W.R.:
Author-Photographer

Photographing the Nest Life of the Osprey. 247-260, *Aug. 1932*

KNIGHT, CHARLES R.: *Author-Artist*

Parade of Life Through the Ages: Records in Rocks Reveal a Strange Procession of Prehistoric Creatures, from Jellyfish to Dinosaurs, Giant Sloths, Saber-toothed Tigers, and Primitive Man. 141-184, *Feb. 1942*

KNIGHT, CHRISTOPHER G.:
Photographer

Americans Afoot in Rumania. By Dan Dimancescu. Photos by Dick Durrance II and Christopher G. Knight. 810-845, *June 1969*

Kayak Odyssey: From the Inland Sea to Tokyo. By Dan Dimancescu. 295-337, *Sept. 1967*

Alaska's Mighty Rivers of Ice. By Maynard M. Miller. 194-217, *Feb. 1967*

Down the Danube by Canoe. By William Slade Backer. Photos by Richard S. Durrance and Christopher G. Knight. 34-79, *July 1965*

KNIGHT, ROYCE:

Nomination Page. *June 1966*

KNIGHT, WILBUR C.: *Author*

The Wyoming Fossil Fields Expedition of July, 1899. 449-465, *Dec. 1900*

"KNIGHTS OF THE GOLDEN HORSESHOE":

Spottswood's Expedition of 1716. By William M. Thornton. 265-269, *Aug. 1896*

KNIK GLACIER AND RIVER, Alaska:

Alaska's Automatic Lake Drains Itself (Lake George). 835-844, *June 1951*

KNOCKING Out Grizzly Bears for Their Own Good. By Frank and John Craighead. NGS research grant. 276-291, *Aug. 1960*

KNOSSOS (Ancient City), Crete:

Minoans and Mycenaeans: Greece's Brilliant Bronze Age. By Joseph Judge. Photos by Gordon W. Gahan. Paintings by Lloyd K. Townsend. 142-185, *Feb. 1978*

Crete, Where Sea-Kings Reigned. By Agnes N. Stillwell. 547-568, *Nov. 1943*

KNOTT, FRANKLIN PRICE:
Author-Photographer

Artist Adventures on the Island of Bali. 326-347, *Mar. 1928*

Photographer

The Oriental Pageantry of Northern India. 429-460, *Oct. 1929*

People and Places. 233-248, *Sept. 1916*

Beauty Spots in the United States. 379-405, *Apr. 1916*

In homage to the gods the head of a bull with gilded horns is readied for royal entombment by Minoans at Knossos on Crete around 1400 B.C. PAINTING BY LLOYD K. TOWNSEND

'**KNOWN** but to God' (Unknown Heroes). By Beverley M. Bowie. 593-605, *Nov. 1958*

KNOX, DUDLEY W.: *Author*
Ships, from Dugouts to Dreadnoughts. 57-98, *Jan. 1938*

KNUD PENINSULA, Ellesmere Island, Canada:
Eskimo and Viking Finds in the High Arctic: Ellesmere Island. By Peter Schledermann. Photos by Sisse Brimberg. Included: Artifacts from Dorset sites. 575-601, *May 1981*

KNUDSEN, DON C.: *Photographer*
Alaska's Automatic Lake Drains Itself (Lake George). 835-844, *June 1951*

KNUTSEN, WILLIE: *Author*
Milestones in My Arctic Journeys. 543-570, *Oct. 1949*
Photographer
Desolate Greenland, Now an American Outpost. Photos by Willie Knutsen and F. Vogel. 393-406, *Sept. 1941*

KNUTSON, HAROLD A.:
Photographer
Nomads of China's West. By Galen Rowell. Photos by the author and Harold A. Knutson. 244-263, *Feb. 1982*

KOALAS:
The Koala, or Australian Teddy Bear. By F. Lewis. 346-355, *Sept. 1931*

KOBLICK, IAN:
Tektite II. 256-296. I. Science's Window on the Sea. By John G. VanDerwalker. Photos by Bates Littlehales. 256-289, *Aug. 1971*

KOCH, ERICA: *Photographer*
Thumbs Up Round the North Sea's Rim. By Frances James. 685-704, *May 1952*

KOCH, FELIX J.: *Author*
Tirnova, the City of Hanging Gardens. 632-640, *Oct. 1907*
Author-Photographer
In Quaint, Curious Croatia. 809-832, *Dec. 1908*

KODIAK (Island), Alaska:
A Navy Artist Paints the Aleutians. By Mason Sutherland. Paintings by William F. Draper. 157-176, *Aug. 1943*
The Valley of Ten Thousand Smokes: National Geographic Society Explorations in the Katmai District of Alaska. By Robert F. Griggs. 13-68, *Jan. 1917*
The Recent Eruption of Katmai Volcano in Alaska. By George C. Martin. 131-181, *Feb. 1913*
Volcanoes of Alaska (Report by K. W. Perry on the Eruption of Mt. Katmai in June 1912). 824-832, *Aug. 1912*
Kodiak Not Kadiak. By Marcus Baker. 397-398, *Nov. 1901*

KOELZ, WALTER N.: *Author*
A Naturalist with MacMillan in the Arctic. 299-318, *Mar. 1926*

Young girl in a working-class district of Seoul, South Korea, waits patiently while her hair is tied back. NATHAN BENN

KOESTER, HANS:
Author-Photographer
Four Thousand Hours Over China. 571-598, *May 1938*

KOFFLER, CAMILLA (Ylla):
Photographer
Mysore Celebrates the Death of a Demon. By Luc Bouchage. 706-711, *May 1958*

KØGE, Denmark:
2,000 Miles Through Europe's Oldest Kingdom. By Isobel Wylie Hutchison. Photos by Maynard Owen Williams. 141-180, *Feb. 1949*

KOH-I-NOOR (Diamond):
Questing for Gems. By George S. Switzer. 835-863, *Dec. 1971*

KOHL, LARRY: *Author*
Heavy Hands on the Land. Photos by William Thompson and Galen Rowell. 633-651, *Nov. 1988*
Annapolis: Camelot on the Bay. Photos by Kevin Fleming. 162-189, *Aug. 1988*
Man Against the Sea, the Oosterschelde Barrier. 526-537, *Oct. 1986*
Our Immune System: The Wars Within. By Peter Jaret. Photos by Lennart Nilsson. Illustrations text by Larry Kohl. 702-735, *June 1986*
Our Restless Planet Earth. By Rick Gore. Photos by James A. Sugar. Included: Continents Adrift; Life's Triumph *and* Origin of Earth and Life. Painting by Ned M. Seidler. Picture text by Larry Kohl. 142-181, *Aug. 1985*
Herbs for All Seasons. By Lonnelle Aikman. Photos by Sam Abell. Picture portfolio text by Larry Kohl. 386-409, *Mar. 1983*
Père David's Deer Saved From

Extinction. Photos by Bates Littlehales. 478-485, *Oct. 1982*
Quebec's Northern Dynamo. Photos by Ottmar Bierwagen. 406-418, *Mar. 1982*
Encampments of the Dispossessed (Somalis). 756-763, *June 1981*
British Columbia's Cold Emerald Sea. Photos by David Doubilet. 526-551, *Apr. 1980*

KOHOUTEK (Comet):
What You Didn't See in Kohoutek. By Kenneth F. Weaver. 214-223, *Aug. 1974*
How to Catch a Passing Comet. By Kenneth F. Weaver. 148-150, *Jan. 1974*

KOKO (Gorilla):
On Assignment. *June 1985*
Editorial. By Wilbur E. Garrett. 409, *Apr. 1985*
Koko's Kitten. Text by Jane Vessels. Photos by Ronald H. Cohn. 110-113, *Jan. 1985*
On Assignment. *Jan. 1985*
Conversations With a Gorilla. By Francine Patterson. Photos by Ronald H. Cohn. NGS research grant. 438-465, *Oct. 1978*

KOKSOAK (Big River), Quebec, Canada:
Servicing Arctic Airbases. By Robert A. Bartlett. 602-616, *May 1946*

KOLB, ELLSWORTH and EMERY:
Author-Photographers
Experiences in the Grand Canyon. 99-184, *Aug. 1914*

KOLD, KRISTEN:
Denmark and the Danes. By Maurice Francis Egan. 115-164, *Aug. 1922*

KOLLM, GEORG: *Author*
The German South Polar Expedition. 377-379, *Oct. 1901*

KOLLY, TIMOTHY S.: *Author*
Echoes of a War. 552-575, *May 1985*

KOM, Kingdom of, Cameroon:
Afo-A-Kom: A Sacred Symbol Comes Home. By William S. Ellis. Photos by James P. Blair. 141-148, *July 1974*

KOMARKOVA, VERA: *Author*
On the Summit (Annapurna). By Irene Miller, with Vera Komarkova. 312-313, *Mar. 1979*

KOMENSKY, JAN AMOS:
Bohemia and the Czechs. By Aleš Hrdlička. 163-187, *Feb. 1917*

KOMODO DRAGONS:
Dragon Lizards of Komodo. By James A. Kern. 872-880, *Dec. 1968*
A Modern Dragon Hunt on Komodo: An English Yachting Party Traps and Photographs the Huge and Carnivorous Dragon Lizard of the Lesser Sundas. By Lady Broughton. 321-331, *Sept. 1936*
Stalking the Dragon Lizard on the Island of Komodo. By W. Douglas Burden. 216-232, *Aug. 1927*

K L

KOMSOMOLSK, U.S.S.R.:
New Road to Asia. By Owen Lattimore. 641-676, *Dec. 1944*

KONDOA (Region), Tanzania:
Tanzania's Stone Age Art. By Mary D. Leakey. Photos by John Reader. 84-99, *July 1983*

KONKA RISUMGONGBA, Holy Mountain of the Outlaws. By Joseph F. Rock. 1-65, *July 1931*

KORDOFAN PROVINCE, Sudan:
With the Nuba Hillmen of Kordofan. By Robin Strachan. 249-278, *Feb. 1951*

KOREA:
⊕ *Japan and Korea,* Atlas series. *Dec. 1960*
⊕ *Japan and Korea.* Insets: Kuril Islands, Pescadores, Karafuto, Ryukyu Islands, Okinawa, Formosa, Tokyo. *Dec. 1945*
Jap Rule in the Hermit Nation. By Willard Price. 429-451, *Oct. 1945*
Chosen–Land of Morning Calm. By Mabel Craft Deering. 421-448, *Oct. 1933*
In the Diamond Mountains: Adventures Among the Buddhist Monasteries of Eastern Korea. By the Marquess Curzon of Kedleston. 353-374, *Oct. 1924*
Exploring the Unknown Corners of the "Hermit Kingdom." By Roy Chapman Andrews. 25-48, *July 1919*
A Hunter of Plants. By David Fairchild. 57-77, *July 1919*
Glimpses of Korea and China. By William W. Chapin. 895-934, *Nov. 1910*
Scenes from the Land Where Everybody Dresses in White. Photos by J. Z. Moore. 871-877, *Dec. 1908*
Notes and Scenes from Korea. 498-508, *July 1908*
The Passing of Korea. 575-581, *Oct. 1906*
⊕ *Map of Korea and Manchuria. Mar. 1904*
Some Facts About Korea. 79, *Feb. 1904*
Korea–The Hermit Nation. By Harrie Webster. 145-155, *Apr. 1900*
Korea and the Koreans. By J. B. Bernadou. 231-242, *Aug. 1890*

KOREA, North:
Rare Look at North Korea. By H. Edward Kim. 252-277, *Aug. 1974*

KOREA, South:
Editorial. By Wilbur E. Garrett. 131, *Aug. 1988*
The South Koreans. By Boyd Gibbons. Photos by Nathan Benn. 232-257, *Aug. 1988*
Kyongju, Where Korea Began. By Cathy Newman. Photos by H. Edward Kim. 258-268, *Aug. 1988*
Seoul: Korean Showcase. By H. Edward Kim. 770-797, *Dec. 1979*
Yellow Sea Yields Shipwreck Trove. Photos by H. Edward Kim. Introduction by Donald H. Keith. 231-243, *Aug. 1979*
South Korea: What Next? By Peter T.

Victorious Korongo wrestler of the Sudan is carried from the arena by a teammate in 1949. GEORGE RODGER, MAGNUM

White. Photos by H. Edward Kim. 394-427, *Sept. 1975*
South Korea: Success Story in Asia. By Howard Sochurek. 301-345, *Mar. 1969*
YWCA: International Success Story. By Mary French Rockefeller. Photos by Otis Imboden. 904-933, *Dec. 1963*
Roaming Korea South of the Iron Curtain. By Enzo de Chetelat. 777-808, *June 1950*
Operation Eclipse: 1948. By William A. Kinney. NGS research grant. 325-372, *Mar. 1949*
With the U. S. Army in Korea. By John R. Hodge. 829-840, *June 1947*

KOREA STRAIT:
The Lost Fleet of Kublai Khan. By Torao Mozai. Photos by Koji Nakamura. Paintings by Issho Yada. 634-649, *Nov. 1982*

KOREAN WAR:
South Korea: Success Story in Asia. By Howard Sochurek. 301-345, *Mar. 1969*
Our Navy in the Far East. By Arthur W. Radford. Photos by J. Baylor Roberts. 537-577, *Oct. 1953*
The GI and the Kids of Korea. By Robert H. Mosier. 635-664, *May 1953*

KORFF, ALLETTA, BARONESS:
Author
Where Women Vote (Finland). 487-493, *June 1910*
Notes on Finland. 493-494, *June 1910*

KORNBLAU, GERALD:
Photographer
The GI and the Kids of Korea. By Robert H. Mosier. 635-664, *May 1953*

KORONGO TRIBESPEOPLE:
With the Nuba Hillmen of Kordofan. By Robin Strachan. Photos by George Rodger. 249-278, *Feb. 1951*

KOS (Island), Greece:
The Isles of Greece: Aegean Birthplace of Western Culture. By Melville Bell Grosvenor. Photos by Edwin Stuart Grosvenor and Winfield Parks. 147-193, *Aug. 1972*
Rhodes, and Italy's Aegean Islands. By Dorothy Hosmer. 449-480, *Apr. 1941*

KOSRAE (Island), Micronesia:
In the Far Pacific: At the Birth of Nations. By Carolyn Bennett Patterson. Photos by David Hiser and Melinda Berge. 460-499, *Oct. 1986*

KOSTICH, KONSTANTIN J.:
Photographer
Yugoslavia: Where Oriental Hues Splash Europe. Photos by Konstantin J. Kostich and Rudolph Balogh. 699-738, *June 1939*
Finland: Land of Sky-Blue Lakes. 515-522, *Oct. 1938*

KOURION, Cyprus:
The Day the World Ended at Kourion. By David Soren. Photos by Martha Cooper. NGS research grant. 30-53, *July 1988*

KOWAK (River), Alaska:
Ice-cliffs on the Kowak River. By J. C. Cantwell. 345-346, *Oct. 1896*

KOYASAN, the Japanese Valhalla. By Eliza R. Scidmore. 650-670, *Oct. 1907*

KPWESI TRIBESPEOPLE:
The Land of the Free in Africa. By Harry A. McBride. 411-430, *Oct. 1922*

KRAHO INDIANS:
Children of the Sun and Moon. By Harald Schultz; translated from German by Curtis T. Everett. 340-363, *Mar. 1959*

KRAKATAU (Island), Indonesia:
Return of Java's Wildlife. By Dieter and Mary Plage. 750-771, *June 1985*
Do Volcanic Explosions Affect Our Climate? By C. G. Abbot. 181-198, *Feb. 1913*
The Eruption of Krakatoa. By Sir Robert Ball. 200-294, *June 1902*

KRAKEL, DEAN, II: *Photographer*
The Untamed Yellowstone. By Bill Richards. 257-278, *Aug. 1981*

KRAKÓW, Poland:
Pedaling Through Poland: An American Girl Free-wheels Alone from Kraków, and Its Medieval Byways, Toward Ukraine's Restive Borderland. By Dorothy Hosmer. 739-775, *June 1939*

Poland, Land of the White Eagle. By Melville Bell Grosvenor. Photos by Hans Hildenbrand. 435-444, *Apr. 1932*

KRAMER, MARK: *Author*

Life on the Line: U. S.-Mexican Border. Photos by Danny Lehman. 720-749, *June 1985*

KRASEMANN, STEPHEN J.: *Photographer*

Quietly Conserving Nature. By Noel Grove. 818-845, *Dec. 1988*

KRAWCZYK, JOHN J.: *Photographer*

Submarine Through the North Pole. By William G. Lalor, Jr. 1-20, *Jan. 1959*

KREEN-AKARORE INDIANS:

Brazil's Kreen-Akarores: Requiem for a Tribe? By W. Jesco von Puttkamer. 254-269, *Feb. 1975*

KREIDER, HERMAN H.: *Photographer*

Looking in on the Everyday Life of New Turkey. 501-508, *Apr. 1932*

KREMLIN, Moscow, U.S.S.R.:

Moscow: The City Around Red Square. By John J. Putman. Photos by Gordon W. Gahan. Included: Imperial Russia's Glittering Legacy. 2-45, *Jan. 1978*

An American in Russia's Capital. By Thomas T. Hammond. Photos by Dean Conger. 297-351, *Mar. 1966*

Russia of the Hour: Giant Battle Ground for Theories of Economy, Society, and Politics, as Observed by an Unbiased Correspondent. By Junius B. Wood. 519-598, *Nov. 1926*

The Rebirth of Religion in Russia: The Church Reorganized While Bolshevik Cannon Spread Destruction in the Nation's Holy of Holies. By Thomas Whittemore. 379-401, *Nov. 1918*

Young Russia: The Land of Unlimited Possibilities. By Gilbert H. Grosvenor. 421-520, *Nov. 1914*

KRESS COLLECTION:

The Kress Collection: A Gift to the Nation. By Guy Emerson. 823-865, *Dec. 1961*

The Nation's Newest Old Masters (National Gallery of Art). By John Walker. 619-657, *Nov. 1956*

Your National Gallery of Art After 10 Years. By John Walker. 73-103, *Jan. 1952*

KRIEGER, LOUIS C. C.: *Author-Artist*

Common Mushrooms of the United States. 387-439, *May 1920*

KRILL:

Krill—Untapped Bounty From the Sea? By William M. Hamner. Photos by Flip Nicklin. 626-643, *May 1984*

KRIST, BOB: *Photographer*

Iceland: Life Under the Glaciers. By Louise E. Levathes. 184-215, *Feb. 1987*

New Jersey: A State of Surprise. By Jim Hartz. Photos by Bob Krist and

Michael S. Yamashita. 568-599, *Nov. 1981*

KRISTOF, EMORY:

President's Page. By Gilbert M. Grosvenor. *July 1987*

On Assignment in the North Atlantic. *Apr. 1985*

Nomination Page. *Aug. 1980*

Nomination Page. *Aug. 1976*

Designed shutterless camera. 492, *Apr. 1975*

Nomination Page. In Iceland. *July 1973*

Author

Sharks at 2,000 Feet. By Eugenie Clark and Emory Kristof as reported to Douglas Lee. NGS research grant. 681-691, *Nov. 1986*

Author-Photographer

The Last U. S. Whale Hunters. 346-353, *Mar. 1973*

Photographer

NR-1, the Navy's Inner-Space Shuttle. By Robert D. Ballard. 450-459, *Apr. 1985*

Exploring a 140-year-old Ship Under Arctic Ice *(Breadalbane).* By Joseph B. MacInnis. 104A-104D, *July 1983*

Ghost Ships of the War of 1812: *Hamilton* and *Scourge.* By Daniel A. Nelson. Paintings by Richard Schlecht. 289-313, *Mar. 1983*

The Promise and Peril of Nuclear Energy. By Kenneth F. Weaver. 459-493, *Apr. 1979*

Loch Ness: The Lake and the Legend. By William S. Ellis. Photos by Emory Kristof and David Doubilet. 759-779, *June 1977*

Window on Earth's Interior. By Robert D. Ballard. 228-249, *Aug. 1976*

This Land of Ours–How Are We Using It? By Peter T. White. 20-67, *July 1976*

Soviet ballerina Alla Mikhalchenko awaits competition in Moscow's Bolshoi Theater. GORDON W. GAHAN

Solar Energy, the Ultimate Powerhouse. By John L. Wilhelm. 381-397, *Mar. 1976*

Can We Harness the Wind? By Roger Hamilton. 812-829, *Dec. 1975*

Project FAMOUS. 586-615. I. Where the Earth Turns Inside Out. By J. R. Heirtzler. 586-603; II. Dive Into the Great Rift. By Robert D. Ballard. 604-615, *May 1975*

Tanzania Marches to Its Own Drum. By Peter T. White. 474-509, *Apr. 1975*

Oil, the Dwindling Treasure. By Noel Grove. 792-825, *June 1974*

Whatever Happened to TVA? By Gordon Young. 830-863, *June 1973*

The Search for Tomorrow's Power. By Kenneth F. Weaver. 650-681, *Nov. 1972*

New Tricks Outwit Our Insect Enemies. By Hal Higdon. Photos by Robert F. Sisson and Emory Kristof. 380-399, *Sept. 1972*

Will Oil and Tundra Mix? Alaska's North Slope Hangs in the Balance. By William S. Ellis. 485-517, *Oct. 1971*

Bermuda–Balmy, British, and Beautiful. By Peter Benchley. 93-121, *July 1971*

The Lower Keys, Florida's "Out Islands." By John Scofield. Photos by Emory Kristof and Bates Littlehales. 72-93, *Jan. 1971*

Behold the Computer Revolution. By Peter T. White. Photos by Bruce Dale and Emory Kristof. 593-633, *Nov. 1970*

Computer Helps Scholars Re-create an Egyptian Temple. By Ray Winfield Smith. 634-655, *Nov. 1970*

The Netherlands Antilles: Holland in the Caribbean. By James Cerruti. 115-146, *Jan. 1970*

Lonely Cape Hatteras, Besieged by the Sea. By William S. Ellis. 393-421, *Sept. 1969*

From Sword to Scythe in Champlain Country. By Ethel A. Starbird. Photos by B. Anthony Stewart and Emory Kristof. 153-201, *Aug. 1967*

Sailors of the Sky. By Gordon Young. Photos by Emory Kristof and Jack Fields. Paintings by Davis Meltzer. 49-73, *Jan. 1967*

Of Planes and Men. By Kenneth F. Weaver. Photos by Emory Kristof and Albert Moldvay. 298-349, *Sept. 1965*

KRU TRIBESPEOPLE:

The Land of the Free in Africa. By Harry A. McBride. 411-430, *Oct. 1922*

KRUGER NATIONAL PARK, South Africa:

Safari Through Changing Africa. By Elsie May Bell Grosvenor. Photos by Gilbert Grosvenor. 145-198, *Aug. 1953*

KRUISINGA, J.C.M.: *Author*

A New Country Awaits Discovery: The Draining of the Zuider Zee Makes Room for the Excess Population of the Netherlands. 293-320, *Sept. 1933*

KRUNG THEP, Thailand. *See* Bangkok

KRUUK, HANS: *Author*
Hyenas, the Hunters Nobody Knows. Photos by Baron Hugo van Lawick. 44-57, *July 1968*

KRYSTO, CHRISTINA: *Author*
Bringing the World to Our Foreign-Language Soldiers: How a Military Training Camp is Solving a Seemingly Unsurmountable Problem by Using the Geographic. 81-90, *Aug. 1918*

KUBASOV, VALERIY:
Apollo-Soyuz: Handclasp in Space. By Thomas Y. Canby. 183-187, *Feb. 1976*

KUBLAI KHAN:
The Lost Fleet of Kublai Khan. By Torao Mozai. Photos by Koji Nakamura. Paintings by Issho Yada. 634-649, *Nov. 1982*
The World's Greatest Overland Explorer: How Marco Polo Penetrated Farthest Asia, "Discovered" Many Lands Unknown to Europe, and Added Numerous Minerals, Animals, Birds, and Plants to Man's Knowledge. By J. R. Hildebrand. 505-568, *Nov. 1928*

KUEILIN, China. *See* Guilin

KUH, MICHAEL: *Photographer*
Growing Up With Snowflake. By Arthur J. Riopelle. 491-503, *Oct. 1970*

KUHN, DELIA: *Author*
Poland Opens Her Doors. By Delia and Ferdinand Kuhn. Photos by Erich Lessing. 354-398, *Sept. 1958*

KUHN, DWIGHT: *Photographer*
Mantids, the Praying Predators. By Edward S. Ross. Photos by Dwight Kuhn and the author. 268-280, *Feb. 1984*

KUHN, FERDINAND: *Author*
Poland Opens Her Doors. By Delia and Ferdinand Kuhn. Photos by Erich Lessing. 354-398, *Sept. 1958*
The Yankee Sailor Who Opened Japan. 85-102, *July 1953*
Where Turk and Russian Meet. 743-766, *June 1952*

KUHNE, JACK: *Photographer*
Peru on Parade. Photos by Henry Clay Gipson and Jack Kuhne. 173-196, *Aug. 1942*
Europe's Northern Nomads (Lapps). 657-664, *Nov. 1939*
Norwegian Fjords and Folkways. 501-524, *Apr. 1939*

KUIBYSHEV, U.S.S.R.:
Mother Volga Defends Her Own. By Maynard Owen Williams. 793-811, *Dec. 1942*

KULUSUK, Greenland:
Uncle Sam's Icebox Outposts. Photos by John E. Schneider and Robert B. Sykes, Jr. 473-496, *Oct. 1946*

KUMASSI:
The Gold Coast, Ashanti, and Kumassi. By George K. French. 1-15, *Jan. 1897*

KUNG BUSHMEN:
Namibia: Nearly a Nation? By Bryan

Hodgson. Photos by Jim Brandenburg. 755-797, *June 1982*
■ Bushmen of the Kalahari. 578A-578B, Apr. 1973; 732A-732B, *May 1974*
Bushmen of the Kalahari. By Elizabeth Marshall Thomas. Photos by Laurence K. Marshall. 866-888, *June 1963*

KUNMING, Yunnan, China:
Letter From Kunming: Two American Teachers in China. By Elisabeth B. Booz. Photos by Thomas Nebbia. 793-813, *June 1981*
Kunming Pilgrimage. Photos by John Gutmann and Joseph Passantino. 213-226, *Feb. 1950*
Kunming, Southwestern Gateway to China. By Joseph E. Passantino. 137-168, *Aug. 1946*

KUNSTADTER, PETER:
Nomination Page. In Thailand. *Feb. 1970*

Author-Photographer
Spirits of Change Capture the Karens. 267-285, *Feb. 1972*
Living With Thailand's Gentle Lua. 122-152, *July 1966*

KUNSTHISTORISCHES MUSEUM, Vienna, Austria:
The Vienna Treasures and Their Collectors. By John Walker. 737-776, *June 1950*

KUNTZ, ROBERT E.: *Photographer*
Yemen Opens the Door to Progress. By Harry Hoogstraal. 213-244, *Feb. 1952*

Crossing a damaged bridge in northern Iraq, Kurds help a companion wounded in their fight for independence. LEROY WOODSON, JR.

KURDISTAN (Region), Asia:

The Kurds of Iraq: "We Who Face Death." By LeRoy Woodson, Jr. 364-387, *Mar. 1975*
See also Tepe Gawra

KURDS:

The Kurds of Iraq: "We Who Face Death." By LeRoy Woodson, Jr. 364-387, *Mar. 1975*
Iraq—Where Oil and Water Mix. By Jean and Franc Shor. 443-489, *Oct. 1958*
Mountain Tribes of Iran and Iraq. By Harold Lamb. 385-408, *Mar. 1946*
The Kizilbash Clans of Kurdistan. By Melville Chater. 485-504, *Oct. 1928*
Persian Caravan Sketches: The Land of the Lion and the Sun as Seen on a Summer Caravan Trip. By Harold F. Weston. 417-468, *Apr. 1921*
The Mountaineers of the Euphrates. By Ellsworth Huntington. 142-156, *Feb. 1909*

KUSAIE (Island), Micronesia:

Hidden Key to the Pacific: Piercing the Web of Secrecy Which Long Has Veiled Japanese Bases in the Mandated Islands. By Willard Price. 759-785, *June 1942*

KUSH, Kingdom of:

Sudan: Arab-African Giant. By Robert Caputo. 346-379, *Mar. 1982*

KUSKOKWIM (River), Alaska:

Two Hundred Miles up the Kuskokwim. By Charles Hallock. 85-92, *Mar. 1898*

KUTZTOWN, Pennsylvania:

Pennsylvania's Old-time Dutch Treat. By Kent Britt. Photos by H. Edward Kim. 564-578, *Apr. 1973*
Pennsylvania Dutch Folk Festival. By Maynard Owen Williams. 503-516, *Oct. 1952*

KUUSAMO, Finland:

Scenes of Postwar Finland. By La Verne

Bradley. Photos by Jerry Waller. 233-264, *Aug. 1947*

KUWAIT:

The Persian Gulf—Living in Harm's Way. By Thomas J. Abercrombie. Photos by Steve Raymer. 648-671, *May 1988*
The Arab World, Inc. By John J. Putman. Photos by Winfield Parks. 494-533, *Oct. 1975*
Oil, the Dwindling Treasure. By Noel Grove. Photos by Emory Kristof. 792-825, *June 1974*
Kuwait, Aladdin's Lamp of the Middle East. By John E. Frazer. Photos by David F. Cupp. 636-667, *May 1969*
Boom Time in Kuwait. By Paul Edward Case. 783-802, *Dec. 1952*

KUYT, ERNIE: *Author*

Teamwork Helps the Whooping Crane. By Roderick C. Drewien, with Ernie Kuyt. 680-693, *May 1979*

KUZZILILAR, Turkey:

The Fringe of Verdure Around Asia Minor. By Ellsworth Huntington. 761-775, *Sept. 1910*

KWAJALEIN (Atoll), Marshall Islands:

We Survive on a Pacific Atoll. By John and Frank Craighead. 73-94, *Jan. 1948*
Adventures with the Survey Navy. By Irving Johnson. 131-148, *July 1947*
Our New Military Wards, the Marshalls. By W. Robert Moore. 325-360, *Sept. 1945*

KWAKIUTL INDIANS:

Canada's Window on the Pacific: The British Columbia Coast. By Jules B. Billard. Photos by Ted Spiegel. 338-375, *Mar. 1972*
Indians of Our North Pacific Coast. By Matthew W. Stirling. Paintings by W. Langdon Kihn. 25-52, *Jan. 1945*

KWANDEBELE HOMELAND, South Africa:

South Africa's Ndebele People. 260-282. Included: Dilemma of Independence. Introduction by The Editor. 260-261; Pioneers in Their Own Land. By David Jeffery. Photos by Peter Magubane. 262-282, *Feb. 1986*

KWANGSI (Autonomous Region), China. *See* Guangxi (Autonomous Region)

KWAZULU (Region), South Africa:

Zulu King Weds a Swazi Princess. By Volkmar Wentzel. 47-61, *Jan. 1978*

KWEILIN, China. *See* Guilin

KYONGJU, South Korea:

Kyongju, Where Korea Began. By Cathy Newman. Photos by H. Edward Kim. 258-268, *Aug. 1988*

KYOTO, Japan:

Kyoto and Nara: Keepers of Japan's Past. By Charles McCarry. Photos by George F. Mobley. 836-851, *June 1976*
Kyoto Says Happy New Year. A picture portfolio by George F. Mobley. 852-859, *June 1976*
Kansai, Japan's Historic Heartland. By Thomas J. Abercrombie. 295-339, *Mar. 1970*
Glimpses of Japan. By William W. Chapin. 965-1002, *Nov. 1911*

KYRENIA SHIP:

Last Harbor for the Oldest Ship. By Susan W. and Michael L. Katzev. NGS research grant. 618-625, *Nov. 1974*
Resurrecting the Oldest Known Greek Ship. By Michael L. Katzev. Photos by Bates Littlehales. NGS research grant. 841-857, *June 1970*

KYUSHU (Island), Japan:

Backwoods Japan During American Occupation. By M. A. Huberman. 491-518, *Apr. 1947*

K
L

After her wedding to the king of the Zulus, a Swazi princess distributes gifts to her new in-laws—all 94 of them—in a South African ceremony. VOLKMAR WENTZEL, NGS

L-5 (Space Colony, A.D. 2026):

The Next Frontier? By Isaac Asimov. Paintings by Pierre Mion. 76-89, *July 1976*

LBJ RANCH, near Austin, Texas:

Texas in Bloom. By Lady Bird Johnson. 493-499, *Apr. 1988*

LCI (Landing Craft, Infantry):

Landing Craft for Invasion. By Melville Bell Grosvenor. 1-30, *July 1944*

LCT (Landing Craft, Tank):

Landing Craft for Invasion. By Melville Bell Grosvenor. 1-30, *July 1944*

LG 2 (Hydroelectric Site), Quebec Province, Canada:

Quebec's Northern Dynamo. By Larry Kohl. Photos by Ottmar Bierwagen. 406-418, *Mar. 1982*

L.S.B. LEAKEY FOUNDATION:

Contributions invited; address given. 144, *Jan. 1973*

Study Grants

Pokot People of Kenya. 122, *Jan. 1982*
Orangutans. 835, *June 1980*

Chimpanzees. 598, *May 1979*
Early-man research in Ethiopia. 805, *Dec. 1976*

LST (Landing Ship, Tank):

Landing Craft for Invasion. By Melville Bell Grosvenor. 1-30, *July 1944*

LaBASTILLE, ANNE: *Author*

Acid Rain–How Great a Menace? Photos by Ted Spiegel. 652-681, *Nov. 1981*
On the Trail of Wisconsin's Ice Age. Photos by Cary Wolinsky. 182-205, *Aug. 1977*
My Backyard, the Adirondacks. Photos by David Alan Harvey. 616-639, *May 1975*
See also Bowes, Anne LaBastille

LA BEAUCE (Plain), France:

Chartres: Legacy From the Age of Faith. By Kenneth MacLeish. Photos by Dean Conger. 857-882, *Dec. 1969*

LA BOCA, Panama:

Completion of the La Boca Dock. 84, *Mar. 1898*

LABORATORY in a Dirty Sky. By

Rudolf J. Engelmann and Vera Simons. NGS research grant. 616-621, *Nov. 1976*

LABRADOR (Peninsula), Canada:

Newfoundland: The Enduring Rock. By Harry Thurston. Photos by Yva Momatiuk and John Eastcott. 676-700, *May 1986*
16th-Century Basque Whalers in America. Photos by Bill Curtsinger. Paintings by Richard Schlecht. 40-71. I. Discovery in Labrador: A 16th-Century Basque Whaling Port and Its Sunken Fleet. 40-49; II. Unearthing Red Bay's Whaling History. By James A. Tuck. 50-57; III. Excavating a 400-year-old Basque Galleon. By Robert Grenier. 58-67; IV. The Indomitable Basques. By Robert Laxalt. 69-71, *July 1985*
School for Survival. By Curtis E. LeMay. 565-602, *May 1953*
Far North with "Captain Mac." By Miriam MacMillan. 465-513, *Oct. 1951*
Labrador Canoe Adventure. By Andrew Brown and Ralph Gray. 65-99, *July 1951*
Milestones in My Arctic Journeys. By Willie Knutsen. Included: Air base at Goose Bay. 543-570, *Oct. 1949*
Newfoundland, Canada's New Province. By Andrew H. Brown. Photos by author and Robert F. Sisson. 777-812, *June 1949*
Sea Bird Cities Off Audubon's Labrador. By Arthur A. Allen. NGS research grant. 755-774, *June 1948*
The MacMillan Arctic Expedition Returns: U. S. Navy Planes Make First Series of Overhead Flights in the Arctic and National Geographic Society Staff Obtains Valuable Data and Specimens for Scientific Study. By Donald B. MacMillan. 477-518, *Nov. 1925*
A Land of Eternal Warring. By Sir Wilfred T. Grenfell. 665-690, *Aug. 1910*
Introducing Reindeer into Labrador. 686, *Oct. 1907*
Origin of "Labrador." 587-588, *Oct. 1906*
Labrador Expedition. 185, *Apr. 1904*

LABRADOR CURRENT:

The Relations of the Gulf Stream and the Labrador Current. By William Libbey, Jr. 161-166, *Jan. 31, 1894*

LACQUER WARE:

A Lady From China's Past. Photos from *China Pictorial*. Text by Alice J. Hall. 660-681, *May 1974*
Human Treasures of Japan. By William Graves. Photos by James L. Stanfield. 370-379, *Sept. 1972*

LA CRAU (Plain), France:

Sheep Trek in the French Alps. By Maurice Moyal. Photos by Marcel Coen. 545-564, *Apr. 1952*

LADAKH (Region), China-India-Pakistan:

Ladakh–The Last Shangri-la. By Thomas J. Abercrombie. 332-359, *Mar. 1978*

Battle-ready U.S. Marines in landing craft prepare to rendezvous before an assault on Japanese-held Bougainville in the Solomon Islands in 1943. U.S. COAST GUARD, OFFICIAL

Mountaintop War in Remote Ladakh. By W. E. Garrett. 664-687, *May 1963*

A Journey to "Little Tibet." By Enakshi Bhavnani. Photos by Volkmar Wentzel. 603-634, *May 1951*

A Woman Paints the Tibetans. By Lafugie. 659-692, *May 1949*

In the World's Highest Plateaus: Through an Asiatic No Man's Land to the Desert of Ancient Cathay. By Hellmut de Terra. 319-367, *Mar. 1931*

See also Baltistan

LADD, HARRY S.: *Author*

Fossils Lift the Veil of Time. By Harry S. Ladd and Roland W. Brown. 363-386, *Mar. 1956*

Falcon, the Pacific's Newest Island. By J. Edward Hoffmeister and Harry S. Ladd. 757-766, *Dec. 1928*

LADY FRANKLIN BAY EXPEDITION:

The "Bowdoin" (Ship) in North Greenland: Arctic Explorers Place Tablet to Commemorate Sacrifices of the Lady Franklin Bay Expedition. By Donald B. MacMillan. 677-722, *June 1925*

A **LADY** From China's Past. Photos from *China Pictorial.* Text by Alice J. Hall. 660-681, *May 1974*

LADYBUGS:

New Tricks Outwit Our Insect Enemies. By Hal Higdon. Photos by Robert F. Sisson and Emory Kristof. 380-399, *Sept. 1972*

Following the Ladybug Home. By Kenneth S. Hagen. Photos by Robert F. Sisson. 543-553, *Apr. 1970*

LAETOLI (Region), Tanzania:

Footprints in the Ashes of Time. By Mary D. Leakey. NGS research grant. 446-457, *Apr. 1979*

LA FARGE, THOMAS S.: *Photographer*

Coast Guard Patrol in Greenland. 565-572, *May 1943*

LA FAY, HOWARD:

Editorial. By Wilbur E. Garrett. 709, *Dec. 1981*

Nomination Page. On Easter Island. *Oct. 1961*

Author

Texas! Photos by Gordon W. Gahan. 440-483, *Apr. 1980*

Ebla: Splendor of an Unknown Empire. Photos by James L. Stanfield. Paintings by Louis S. Glanzman. 730-759, *Dec. 1978*

Syria Tests a New Stability. Photos by James L. Stanfield. 326-361, *Sept. 1978*

George Washington: The Man Behind the Myths. Photos by Ted Spiegel. 90-111, *July 1976*

Sicily, Where All the Songs Are Sad. Photos by Jonathan Blair. 407-436, *Mar. 1976*

The Maya, Children of Time. Photos by David Alan Harvey. 729-767, *Dec. 1975*

Alabama, Dixie to a Different Tune.

A wealthy merchant of Ladakh, a region of India's Kashmir, traveled to Tibet in 1946 to make purchases such as robes and tapestries. VOLKMAR WENTZEL, NGS

Photos by Dick Durrance II. 534-569, *Oct. 1975*

Andalusia, the Spirit of Spain. Photos by Joseph J. Scherschel. 833-857, *June 1975*

■■ *The Vikings.* Photos by Ted Spiegel. Art by Louis S. Glanzman. 207 pages. *1972*

Carnival in Trinidad. Photos by Winfield Parks. 693-701, *Nov. 1971*

Uganda, Africa's Uneasy Heartland. Photos by George F. Mobley. 708-735, *Nov. 1971*

Leningrad, Russia's Window on the West. Photos by Dick Durrance II. 636-673, *May 1971*

The Vikings. Photos by Ted Spiegel. 492-541, *Apr. 1970*

The Eisenhower Story. 1-39, *July 1969*

Where Jesus Walked. Photos by Charles Harbutt. 739-781, *Dec. 1967*

The St. Lawrence, River Key to Canada. Photos by John Launois. 622-667, *May 1967*

Gibraltar–Rock of Contention. Photos

by Bates Littlehales. 102-121, *July 1966*

Portugal at the Crossroads. Photos by Volkmar Wentzel. 453-501, *Oct. 1965*

"Be Ye Men of Valour" (Churchill's Life and Funeral). 159-197, *Aug. 1965*

Freedom's Progress South of the Sahara. Photos by Joseph J. Scherschel. 603-637, *Nov. 1962*

Easter Island and Its Mysterious Monuments. Photos by Thomas J. Abercrombie. 90-117, *Jan. 1962*

Algeria: France's Stepchild, Problem and Promise. Photos by Robert F. Sisson. 768-795, *June 1960*

DEW Line, Sentry of the Far North. 128-146, *July 1958*

LAFAYETTE, MARQUIS DE:

Lafayette's Homeland, Auvergne. By Howell Walker. 419-436, *Sept. 1957*

Our First Alliance. By J. J. Jusserand. 518-548, *June 1917*

LAFAYETTE ESCADRILLE:

Armistice Day and the American Battle Fields. By J. J. Jusserand. 509-554, *Nov. 1929*

The Life Story of an American Airman in France: Extracts from the Letters of Stuart Walcott, Who, Between July and December, 1917, Learned to Fly in French Schools of Aviation, Won Fame at the Front, and Fell Near Saint Souplet. 86-106, *Jan. 1918*

LAFAYETTE NATIONAL PARK, Maine:

The Unique Island of Mount Desert. By George B. Dorr, Ernest Howe Forbush, M. L. Fernald. 75-89, *July 1914*

LAFCADIO Hearn on the Island and People of Martinique. 214-216, *June 1902*

LA FLORIDA:

Exploring Our Forgotten Century: Between Columbus and Jamestown. By Joseph Judge. Photos by Bill Ballenberg. Paintings by John Berkey. 330-363, *Mar. 1988*

LAFUGIE, Madame: *Author-Artist*

A Woman Paints the Tibetans. 659-692, *May 1949*

LA GORCE, GILBERT GROSVENOR:

NGM advertising director. 442, 444, *Mar. 1960*

Author

Marineland, Florida's Giant Fish Bowl. Photos by Luis Marden. 679-694, *Nov. 1952*

LA GORCE, JOHN OLIVER:

Editor (1954-1957). 65, 65D, July 1954; 441, 442, 444, Mar. 1960; 46-47, 67, *July 1967*

Board of Trustees, Vice Chairman. 419-423, Mar. 1957; 98, *Jan. 1966*

Nomination Page. *May 1960*

Colleague of the Golden Years: John Oliver La Gorce (Memorial Tribute). By Gilbert Grosvenor. 440-444, *Mar. 1960*

Editor, Associate. 461, Apr. 1914; 156, Jan. 1936; 65, 65C, July 1954; 418, Mar. 1957; 441, 443, *Mar. 1960*

Golden Anniversary with the Society. 422, 423, Mar. 1957; 442, *Mar. 1960*

President of NGS (1954-1957). 65, 65D, July 1954; 418, 419, 423, Mar. 1957; 440-444, *Mar. 1960*

Vice President of NGS. 255, 260, 261, Aug. 1949; 65, 65C, July 1954; 441, 443, *Mar. 1960*

Grosvenor Medal recipient. 422, 423, *Mar. 1957*

Vice President. 352, Sept. 1925; 230, Aug. 1930; 2, Jan. 1931; 391, Oct. 1931; 366, Sept. 1932; 790, June 1934; 126, 133, 134, 156, 159, Jan. 1936; 336, Sept. 1943; 141, *Feb. 1946*

Employed by National Geographic Society. 152, *Jan. 1936*

Tribute by Gilbert H. Grosvenor. 152-153, *Jan. 1936*

Expedition to the Bahamas led by Doctors Fuertes and La Gorce. 452, *Oct. 1932*

During the heat of war in 1919 Gen. John J. Pershing, commander of the American Expeditionary Forces, chats with an admirer in Soissons, France. U.S. ARMY SIGNAL CORPS

Meteorological station, Antarctica, named for. 184, 193, *Aug. 1930*

Mount La Gorce, Alaska, named for. 222, 287, *Sept. 1921*

Board of Managers. 345, *Apr. 1920*

Author

Artists Look at Pennsylvania. 37-56, *July 1948*

Penn's Land of Modern Miracles. 1-58, *July 1935*

The Historic City of Brotherly Love: Philadelphia, Born of Penn and Strengthened by Franklin, a Metropolis of Industries, Homes, and Parks. 643-697, *Dec. 1932*

Florida–The Fountain of Youth. 1-93, *Jan. 1930*

Jamaica, the Isle of Many Rivers. 1-55, *Jan. 1927*

Pirate Rivers and Their Prizes: The Warfare of Waterways Has Sometimes Changed the Geography of Our Continents. 87-132, *July 1926*

Porto Rico, the Gate of Riches: Amazing Prosperity Has Been the Lot of Ponce de León's Isle Under American Administration. Photos by Charles Martin. 599-651, *Dec. 1924*

Fishes and Fisheries of Our North Atlantic Seaboard. Paintings by Hashime Murayama. 567-634, *Dec. 1923*

The Fight at the Timber-Line. 165-196, *Aug. 1922*

Treasure-House of the Gulf Stream: The Completion and Opening of the New Aquarium and Biological Laboratory at Miami, Florida. Paintings by Hashime Murayama. 53-68, *Jan. 1921*

Devil-Fishing in the Gulf Stream. 476-488, *June 1919*

The Industrial Titan of America: Pennsylvania, Once the Keystone of the Original Thirteen, Now the Keystone of Forty-eight Sovereign States. 367-406, *May 1919*

A Battle-Ground of Nature: The Atlantic Seaboard. 511-546, *June 1918*

Roumania and Its Rubicon. 185-202, *Sept. 1916*

The Warfare on Our Eastern Coast. 195-230, *Sept. 1915*

Photographer

The Argosy of Geography (Sailing Ship). Pictorial supplement. *Jan. 1921*

LA GORCE, LOUISE PARKER:

Author

Christmas in Cookie Tree Land. Photos by B. Anthony Stewart. 844-851, *Dec. 1955*

LA GORCE MEDAL:

A Geographic Gold Medal Honors Kenyan Fossil Finder (Kamoya Kimeu). President's Page. By Gilbert M. Grosvenor. *Nov. 1985*

First La Gorce Medal Honors Antarctic Expedition. Note: Melvin M. Payne guided the design of the medal, which was executed by Peter V. Bianchi and Howard E. Paine. NGS research grant. 864-867, *June 1967*

LAGOS, Nigeria:

Nigeria: From the Bight of Benin to Africa's Desert Sands. By Helen Trybulowski Gilles. 537-568, *May 1944*

La GRANDE (River), Canada:

Quebec's Northern Dynamo. By Larry Kohl. Photos by Ottmar Bierwagen. 406-418, *Mar. 1982*

LA GRANDE COMPLEX (Hydroelectric Sites), Quebec Province, Canada:

Quebec's Northern Dynamo. By Larry Kohl. Photos by Ottmar Bierwagen. 406-418, *Mar. 1982*

LAGUNILLA RIVER VALLEY, Colombia:

Eruption in Colombia. By Bart McDowell. Photos by Steve Raymer. 640-653, *May 1986*

LAGUS, CHARLES: *Photographer*

Animal Safari to British Guiana. By David Attenborough. Photos by Charles Lagus and author. 851-874, *June 1957*

LAHAINA RESTORATION FOUNDATION: Study Grants:

Humpback Whales. 2, Jan. 1979; 466, *Apr. 1982*

LAHARS (Volcanic Mudflows):

Eruption in Colombia. By Bart McDowell. Photos by Steve Raymer. 640-653, *May 1986*

LAHEY, CARLOTTA GONZALES: *Artist*

Flags of the United Nations. By Elizabeth W. King. 213-238, *Feb. 1951*
Flags of the Americas. By Elizabeth W. King. 633-657, *May 1949*
Seals of Our Nation, States, and Territories. Paintings by Carlotta Gonzales Lahey, Irvin E. Alleman, Theodora Price. 17-32, *July 1946*
The Heavens Above: On Land, Sea, and in the Air the Stars Serve Modern Man as Map, Compass, and Clock. By Donald H. Menzel. Included: Charts designed by author. 97-128, *July 1943*

LAHORE, Pakistan:

Through the Heart of Hindustan: A Teeming Highway Extending for Fifteen Hundred Miles, from the Khyber Pass to Calcutta. By Maynard Owen Williams. 433-467, *Nov. 1921*

LAIRD, NORMAN: *Photographer*

Nature's Clown, the Penguin. By David Hellyer and Malcolm Davis. 405-428, *Sept. 1952*

LA JOLLA, California:

La Jolla, a Gem of the California Coast. By Deena Clark. Photos by J. Baylor Roberts. 755-782, *Dec. 1952*
Goggle Fishing in California Waters. By David Hellyer. Photos by Lamar Boren. 615-632, *May 1949*

LAKE Cahuilla: The Ancient Lake of the Colorado Desert. 830, *Dec. 1907*

LAKE CHARLES, Louisiana:

Louisiana Trades With the World. By Frederick Simpich. Photos by J. Baylor Roberts. 705-738, *Dec. 1947*

LAKE Chelan. By Henry Gannett. 417-428, *Oct. 1898*

LAKE Clark, a Little Known Alaskan Lake. By Wilfred H. Osgood. 326-331, *Aug. 1904*

LAKE DISTRICT, Argentina-Chile:

■■ *Excursion to Enchantment: A Journey to the World's Most Beautiful Places.* Included: East Africa, Loire Valley, Bhutan, Chile-Argentina Lake District, Alaska's Inside Passage, and the Caribbean. 200 pages. *1988*
Chile's Land of Fire and Water: Smoking Volcanoes and Ice-hooded Peaks Stand Sentinel Over Limpid Lakes in the Far Southern Andes. By W. Robert Moore. 91-110, *July 1941*

LAKE DISTRICT, England:

Lake District, Poets' Corner of England. By H. V. Morton. Photos by David S. Boyer. 511-545, *Apr. 1956*
Informal Salute to the English Lakes. By Maynard Owen Williams. 511-521, *Apr. 1936*
Through the English Lake District Afoot and Awheel. By Ralph A. Graves. 577-603, *May 1929*

LAKE Erie's Bass Islands. By Terry and Lyntha Eiler. 86-101, *July 1978*

LAKE Geneva: Cradle of Conferences. By F. Barrows Colton. 727-742, *Dec. 1937*

LAKE MANYARA NATIONAL PARK, Tanzania:

Africa's Elephants: Can They Survive? By Oria Douglas-Hamilton. Photos by Oria and Iain Douglas-Hamilton. 568-603, *Nov. 1980*

LAKE OF THE WOODS, Canada-U. S. *See* Woods, Lake of the

LAKE Sunapee's Golden Trout. Photos by Robert F. Sisson. 529-536, *Oct. 1950*

LAKEHURST, New Jersey: U. S. Naval Air Station:

Aboard a Blimp Hunting U-boats: A Day above the Atlantic Reveals Navy Talk and Navy Ways, Creeping Convoys, and Torpedoed Wrecks. By Mason Sutherland. 79-96, *July 1943*
See also Parachute Rigger School

LAKELAND, Home of England's Nature Poets. Photos by Clifton Adams. 593-600, *May 1929*

LAKES:

■■ *Lakes, Peaks, and Prairies: Discovering the United States-Canadian Border.* By Thomas O'Neill. Photos by Michael S. Yamashita. 199 pages. *1984*
■■ *Nature's World of Wonders.* Included: The world's deepest, highest navigable, and largest lakes. 199 pages. *1983*
Strange World of Palau's Salt Lakes. By William M. Hamner. Photos by David Doubilet. 264-282, *Feb. 1982*
■■ *Still Waters, White Waters: Exploring America's Rivers and Lakes.* By Ron Fisher. Photos by Sam Abell. Contents: Touring by canoe. 199 pages. *1977*
Lombardy's Lakes, Blue Jewels in Italy's Crown. By Franc Shor. Photos by Joseph J. Scherschel. Included: Como, Garda, Maggiore. 58-99, *July 1968*
The Night the Mountains Moved. By Samuel W. Matthews. Photos by J. Baylor Roberts. Included: Hebgen Lake, Earthquake Lake. 329-359, *Mar. 1960*
Geographical Twins a World Apart. By David S. Boyer. Contents: Comparisons between the Dead Sea and Great Salt Lake; the Sea of Galilee and Utah Lake. 848-859, *Dec. 1958*
Labrador Canoe Adventure. By Andrew Brown and Ralph Gray. Included: Dyke, Forget-me-not, Gabbro, Grand, Jacopie, Lake E, Lake Melville, Sandgirt, Winokapau. 65-99, *July 1951*
A Map Maker Looks at the United States. By Newman Bumstead. Photos by U. S. Air Force. Included:

A somewhat unconventional carriage bears a bridal party to the church in 1925 during seasonal flooding in the English Fens. STARR AND RIGNALL

Mirrored in dusk's tranquillity, watercraft await tomorrow's passengers at Georgia's Stephen C. Foster State Park on the edge of the Okefenokee Swamp. SAM ABELL

Chelan, Crater, Diamond, Franklin Delano Roosevelt, Jackson, Kachess, Mead, Michigan, Tahoe, Utah. 705-748, *June 1951*

Italy Smiles Again. By Edgar Erskine Hume. Included: Como, Garda, Maggiore. 693-732, *June 1949*

Around the "Great Lakes of the South." By Frederick Simpich. Photos by J. Baylor Roberts. 463-491, *Apr. 1948*

A Land of Lakes and Volcanoes (Nicaragua). By Luis Marden. 161-192, *Aug. 1944*

Bathymetrical Survey of the Freshwater Lakes of England. 408, *Nov. 1901*

Shawangunk Mountain (New York). By N. H. Darton. Included: Lake Awosting; Lake Maratanza; Lake Minnewaska; Lake Mohonk. 23-34, *Mar. 17, 1894*

See also lakes by name

LALIBALA, Ethiopia:

Searching Out Medieval Churches in Ethiopia's Wilds. By Georg Gerster. 856-884, *Dec. 1970*

A Caravan Journey Through Abyssinia: From Addis Ababa Through Lalibela, the Strange Jerusalem of Ethiopia, in Search of New Grains for American Farms. By Harry V. Harlan. 613-663, *June 1925*

LALOR, WILLIAM G., Jr.: *Author*

Submarine Through the North Pole. Photos by John J. Krawczyk. 1-20, *Jan. 1959*

LAMAISM. *See* Tibetan Buddhism

The **LAMA'S** Motor-Car: A Trip Across the Gobi Desert by Motor-Car. By Ethan C. Le Munyon. 641-670, *May 1913*

LAMB, HAROLD: *Author*

Crusader Lands Revisited. Photos by David S. Boyer. 815-852, *Dec. 1954*

Mountain Tribes of Iran and Iraq. 385-408, *Mar. 1946*

The Road of the Crusaders: A Historian Follows the Steps of Richard the Lion Heart and Other Knights of the Cross Over the "Via Dei." 645-693, *Dec. 1933*

LAMBART, H. F.: *Author*

The Conquest of Mount Logan: North America's Second Highest Peak Yields to the Intrepid Attack of Canadian Climbers. 597-631, *June 1926*

LAMMER, ALFRED: *Photographer*

Children's Village in Switzerland, Pestalozzi. 268-282, *Aug. 1959*

Ornate crucifix is cherished by Ethiopian Orthodox Christians in a cavern church near Lalibala. GEORG GERSTER

LAMOIDS:

Guanacos: Wild Camels of South America. By William L. Franklin. NGS research grant. Included: Alpacas, Guanacos, Llamas, Vicuñas. 63-75, *July 1981*

High, Wild World of the Vicuña. By William L. Franklin. 77-91, *Jan. 1973*

Camels of the Clouds. By W. H. Hodge. Included: Alpacas, Guanacas, Llamas, Vicuñas. 641-656, *May 1946*

LAMPREYS. *See* Sea Lampreys

La NAVIDAD (Columbus's Colony), Haiti:

Searching for Columbus's Lost Colony: La Navidad. By Kathleen A. Deagan. Photos by Bill Ballenberg. 672-675, *Nov. 1987*

LANCASTER COUNTY, Pennsylvania:

The Plain People of Pennsylvania. Photo essay by Jerry Irwin. Text by Douglas Lee. 492-519, *Apr. 1984*

Amish Folk: Plainest of Pennsylvania's Plain People. By Richard Gehman. Photos by William Albert Allard. 227-253, *Aug. 1965*

Artists Look at Pennsylvania. By John Oliver La Gorce. 37-56, *July 1948*

Pennsylvania Dutch–In a Land of Milk and Honey. Photos by J. Baylor Roberts. 49-56, *July 1938*

LANCHOU, China. *See* Lanzhou

LAND, EMORY S.: *Author*

Aviation Looks Ahead on Its 50th Birthday. 721-739, *Dec. 1953*

A **LAND** Apart–the Monterey Peninsula. By Mike W. Edwards. 682-703, *Nov. 1972*

LAND CLAIMS, Native-American:

The Aleutians: Alaska's Far-out Islands. By Lael Morgan. Photos by Steven C. Wilson. 336-363, *Sept. 1983*

Peoples of the Arctic. 144-223. I. Introduction by Joseph Judge. 144-149; II. Hunters of the Lost Spirit: Alaskans, Canadians, Greenlanders, Lapps. By Priit J. Vesilind. Photos by David Alan Harvey, Ivars Silis, and Sisse Brimberg. 150-197, *Feb. 1983*

⊕ *Peoples of the Arctic; Arctic Ocean. Feb. 1983*

A First American Views His Land. By N. Scott Momaday. 13-19, *July 1976*

Editorial. By Gilbert M. Grosvenor. 729, *June 1975*

Alaska: Rising Northern Star. By Joseph Judge. Photos by Bruce Dale. Included: Alaska's land-use plan. 730-767, *June 1975*

The **LAND** Columbus Loved. By Oliver P. Newman. 197-224, *Feb. 1944*

LAND DIVERS:

Land Diving With the Pentecost Islanders. By Kal Muller. 799-817, *Dec. 1970*

South Seas' Incredible Land Divers. By Irving and Electa Johnson. 77-92, *Jan. 1955*

LAND in the Middle: Thailand. By Bart

McDowell. Photos by Steve Raymer. 500-535, *Oct. 1982*

LAND of a Million Smiles. By Frederick Simpich. 589-623, *May 1943*

The LAND of Contrast: Austria-Hungary. By D. W. and A. S. Iddings. 1183-1217, 1284, *Dec. 1912*

A LAND of Drought and Desert–Lower California: Two Thousand Miles on Horseback Through the Most Extraordinary Cacti Forests in the World. By E. W. Nelson. 443-474, *May 1911*

The LAND of Egypt: A Narrow Green Strip of Fertility Stretching for a Thousand Miles Through Walls of Desert. By Alfred Pearce Dennis. 271-298, *Mar. 1926*

A LAND of Eternal Warring. By Sir Wilfred T. Grenfell. 665-690, *Aug. 1910*

The LAND of Fire. By Jon Stefansson. 741-744, *Nov. 1907*

The LAND of Galilee. By Kenneth MacLeish. Photos by B. Anthony Stewart. 832-865, *Dec. 1965*

The LAND of Genghis Khan in Its True Colors. Photos by Maynard Owen Williams. 569-576, *Nov. 1932*

A LAND of Giants and Pygmies. By the Duke Adolphus Frederick of Mecklenburg. 369-388, *Apr. 1912*

A LAND of Lakes and Volcanoes. By Luis Marden. 161-192, *Aug. 1944*

The LAND of Lambskins: An Expedition to Bokhara, Russian Central Asia, to Study the Karakul Sheep Industry. By Robert K. Nabours. 77-88, *July 1919*

LAND of Long Sunsets: Nebraska's Sand Hills. By John Madson. Photos by Jodi Cobb. 493-517, *Oct. 1978*

LAND of Louisiana Sugar Kings. By Harnett T. Kane. Photos by Willard R. Culver. 531-567, *Apr. 1958*

The LAND of Promise (Siberia). By A. W. Greely. 1078-1090, *Nov. 1912*

LAND of Sagebrush and Silver. Photos by W. Robert Moore. 9-32, *Jan. 1946*

The LAND of Sawdust and Spangles–A World in Miniature. By Francis Beverly Kelley. 463-516, *Oct. 1931*

LAND of the Ancient Basques. By Robert Laxalt. Photos by William Albert Allard. 240-277, *Aug. 1968*

The LAND of the Basques: Home of a Thrifty, Picturesque People, Who Take Pride in the Sobriquet, "The Yankees of Spain." By Harry A. McBride. 63-87, *Jan. 1922*

The LAND of the Best. By Gilbert H. Grosvenor. Pictorial supplement. 327-430, *Apr. 1916*

The LAND of the Crossbow. By George Forrest. 132-156, *Feb. 1910*

The LAND of the Free in Africa. By Harry A. McBride. 411-430, *Oct. 1922*

"LAND of the Free" in Asia: Siam Has Blended New With Old in Her Progressive March to Modern Statehood in the Family of Nations. By W. Robert Moore. 531-576, *May 1934*

LAND of the Havasupai. By Jack Breed. 655-674, *May 1948*

LAND of the Horn, America's Tiptoe. Photos by Amos Burg. 751-758, *Dec. 1937*

New Hebrides land divers prove their manhood by leaping from a 65-foot tower.

IRVING JOHNSON (LEFT); ROGER BELLINGER

On its last legs, a walking stick in the New Hebrides crawls over a Melanesian boy, who will soon roast and eat it. KAL MULLER

LANGLADE ISLAND (Petite Miquelon). *See* Miquelon

LANGLEY, ANNE RAINEY: *Author*
British West Indian Interlude. 1-46, *Jan. 1941*
I Kept House in a Jungle: The Spell of Primeval Tropics in Venezuela, Riotous With Strange Plants, Animals, and Snakes, Enthralls a Young American Woman. 97-132, *Jan. 1939*

LANGLEY, S. P.:
Aërial Locomotion. By Alexander Graham Bell. 1-34, *Jan. 1907*
Biography of S. P. Langley. 170, *Mar. 1906*
Gardiner Greene Hubbard: Memorial Meeting (Address by Langley). 43, *Feb. 1898*
Author
Diary of a Voyage from San Francisco to Tahiti and Return, 1901. 413-429, *Dec. 1901*

LANGMORE, BANK: *Photographer*
Our Wild and Scenic Rivers: The Rio Grande. By Nathaniel T. Kenney. 46-51, *July 1977*

LANGU GORGE, Nepal:
Tracking the Elusive Snow Leopard. By Rodney Jackson and Darla Hillard. NGS research grant. 793-809, *June 1986*

LANGUAGES:
The World's Words. By William H. Nicholas. 689-700, *Dec. 1943*
Secrets from Syrian Hills: Explorations Reveal World's Earliest Known Alphabet, Deciphered from Schoolboy Slates and Dictionaries of 3,000 Years Ago. By Claude F. A. Schaeffer. 97-126, *July 1933*
A New Alphabet of the Ancients Is Unearthed: An Inconspicuous Mound in Northern Syria Yields Archeological Treasures of Far-reaching Significance. By F. A. Schaeffer. 477-516, *Oct. 1930*
Turkey Goes to School. By Maynard Owen Williams. 95-108, *Jan. 1929*
New China and the Printed Page. By Paul Hutchinson. 687-722, *June 1927*
The Battle-Line of Languages in Western Europe: A Problem in Human Geography More Perplexing Than That of International Boundaries. By A. L. Guerard. 145-180, *Feb. 1923*
The Origin of French-Canadians. 96-97, *Mar. 1898*
See also Geographic Names

LANGUEDOC (Region), France:
France's Past Lives in Languedoc. By Walter Meayers Edwards. 1-43, *July 1951*

LANKA. *See* former name, Ceylon; *and* present name, Sri Lanka

LANKS, H. C.: *Photographer*
Honduran Highlights. Photos by R. C. Lanks. 360-369, *Mar. 1942*

L'ANSE AU MEADOW, Newfoundland, Canada:
Vinland Ruins Prove Vikings Found the New World. By Helge Ingstad. 708-734, *Nov. 1964*

LANSING, ROBERT: *Author*
Prussianism. 546-557, *June 1918*

LANTING, FRANS:
On Assignment in Madagascar. *Feb. 1987*
Photographer
Madagascar's Lemurs: On the Edge of Survival. By Alison Jolly. 132-161, *Aug. 1988*
Falkland Islands Wildlife. 413-422, *Mar. 1988*
Madagascar: A World Apart. By Alison Jolly. 148-183, *Feb. 1987*

LANZAROTE, the Strangest Canary. By Stephanie Dinkins. 117-139, *Jan. 1969*

LANZHOU, Gansu Province, China:
Journey to China's Far West. By Rick Gore. Photos by Bruce Dale. 292-331, *Mar. 1980*

LAODICEA (Ancient City), Turkey:
The Ruined Cities of Asia Minor. By Ernest L. Harris. 741-760, *Nov. 1908*

LAOS:
Laos Today. By Peter T. White. Photos by Seny Norasingh. 772-795, *June 1987*
Missing in Action, 1972–U. S. Plane Found in Laos. By Peter T. White. Photos by Seny Norasingh. 692-696, *Nov. 1986*
The Hmong of Laos: No Place to Run. By W. E. Garrett. 78-111, *Jan. 1974*
The Lands and Peoples of Southeast Asia. 295-365. I. Mosaic of Cultures. By Peter T. White. Photos by W. E. Garrett. 296-329; II. New Light on a

Driven from their homes in Laos during the Vietnam War, Hmong girls cling to each other. WILBUR E. GARRETT, NGS

Forgotten Past. By Wilhelm G. Solheim II. 330-339, *Mar. 1971*
The Mekong, River of Terror and Hope. By Peter T. White. Photos by W. E. Garrett. 737-787, *Dec. 1968*
⊕ Viet Nam, Cambodia, Laos, and Thailand. *Feb. 1967*
⊕ Viet Nam, Cambodia, Laos, and Eastern Thailand. Text on reverse. *Jan. 1965*
Report on Laos. By Peter T. White. Photos by W. E. Garrett. 241-275, *Aug. 1961*
Little Laos, Next Door to Red China. By Elizabeth Perazic. 46-69, *Jan. 1960*
War and Quiet on the Laos Frontier. By W. Robert Moore. 665-680, *May 1954*

LAOTIAN REFUGEES:
The Hmong in America: Laotian Refugees in the "Land of the Giants." By Spencer Sherman. Photos by Dick Swanson. 586-610, *Oct. 1988*
Thailand: Refuge From Terror. By W. E. Garrett. 633-642, *May 1980*
One Family's Odyssey to America. By John Everingham. 642-661, *May 1980*
The Hmong of Laos: No Place to Run. By W. E. Garrett. 78-111, *Jan. 1974*

LA PAZ, Baja California Sur, Mexico:
Baja California's Rugged Outback. By Michael E. Long. 543-567, *Oct. 1972*
Rocks, Ruts, and Sand: Driving the Mexican 1000. By Michael E. Long. 569-575, *Oct. 1972*
Adventuring Down the West Coast of Mexico. By Herbert Corey. 449-503, *Nov. 1922*

LA PAZ, Bolivia:
Flamboyant Is the Word for Bolivia. By Loren McIntyre. 153-195, *Feb. 1965*
Sky-high Bolivia. 481-496, *Oct. 1950*
Bolivia–Tin Roof of the Andes. By Henry Albert Phillips. 309-332, *Mar. 1943*
Kaleidoscopic La Paz: The City of the Clouds. By Harriet Chalmers Adams. 119-141, *Feb. 1909*

LAPIDARY WORK:
The Glittering World of Rockhounds. By David S. Boyer. 276-294, *Feb. 1974*
My Neighbors Hold to Mountain Ways. By Malcolm Ross. Photos by Flip Schulke. 856-880, *June 1958*
"Rockhounds" Uncover Earth's Mineral Beauty. By George S. Switzer. 631-660, *Nov. 1951*

LA PITA, Panama:
Exploring Ancient Panama by Helicopter. By Matthew W. Stirling. Photos by Richard H. Stewart. NGS research grant. 227-246, *Feb. 1950*

LAPLAND:
Hunters of the Lost Spirit: Lapps. By Priit J. Vesilind. Photos by Sisse Brimberg. 194-197, *Feb. 1983*
Norway's Reindeer Lapps. By Sally Anderson. Photos by Erik Borg. 364-379, *Sept. 1977*
Norway, Land of the Generous Sea. By

Edward J. Linehan. Photos by George F. Mobley. 1-43, *July 1971*

Friendly Flight to Northern Europe. By Lyndon B. Johnson. Photos by Volkmar Wentzel. 268-293, *Feb. 1964*

North with Finland's Lapps. By Jean and Franc Shor. 249-280, *Aug. 1954*

Lapland's Reindeer Roundup. 109-116, *July 1949*

The Nomads of Arctic Lapland: Mysterious Little People of a Land of the Midnight Sun Live Off the Country Above the Arctic Circle. By Clyde Fisher. 641-676, *Nov. 1939*

LAPPS:

Hunters of the Lost Spirit: Lapps. By Priit J. Vesilind. Photos by Sisse Brimberg. 194-197, *Feb. 1983*

Norway's Reindeer Lapps. By Sally Anderson. Photos by Erik Borg. 364-379, *Sept. 1977*

North with Finland's Lapps. By Jean and Franc Shor. 249-280, *Aug. 1954*

Lapland's Reindeer Roundup. 109-116, *July 1949*

The Nomads of Arctic Lapland: Mysterious Little People of a Land of the Midnight Sun Live Off the Country Above the Arctic Circle. By Clyde Fisher. 641-676, *Nov. 1939*

LARGE MAGELLANIC CLOUD:

Supernova–Death of a Star. By Robert P. Kirshner. Photos by Roger H. Ressmeyer. 619-647, *May 1988*

The **LARGE** Wading Birds: Long Legs

and Remarkable Beaks, as Well as Size, Form, and Color, Distinguish the Herons, Ibises, and Flamingos. By T. Gilbert Pearson. Paintings by Allan Brooks. 441-469, *Oct. 1932*

LARGELAMB, H. A. (Alexander Graham Bell): *Author*

Notes on the Remarkable Habits of Certain Turtles and Lizards. 413-419, *June 1907*

Extinct Reptiles Found in Nodules. 170-173, *Mar. 1906*

The Purple Veil: A Romance of the Sea. 337-341, *July 1905*

The **LARGER** North American Mammals. By E. W. Nelson. Paintings by Louis Agassiz Fuertes. Pictorial supplement. 385-472, *Nov. 1916*

LARSEN, CALVIN L.: *Photographer*

Across the Frozen Desert to Byrd Station. By Paul W. Frazier. 383-398, *Sept. 1957*

LARSEN, HELGA: *Author*

The Mexican Indian Flying Pole Dance. 387-400, *Mar. 1937*

LARSEN, THOR:
Author-Photographer

Polar Bear: Lonely Nomad of the North. 574-590, *Apr. 1971*

LARUE COUNTY, Kentucky:

Home to the Heart of Kentucky. By Nadine Brewer. Photos by William Strode. 522-546, *Apr. 1982*

LARVAE, Insect:

The Case of the Killer Caterpillars. By Steven L. Montgomery. Photos by Robert F. Sisson. 219-225, *Aug. 1983*

Nature's Night Lights: Probing the Secrets of Bioluminescence. By Paul A. Zahl. 45-69, *July 1971*

Nature's Toy Train, the Railroad Worm. By Darwin L. Tiemann. Photos by Robert F. Sisson. NGS research grant. 56-67, *July 1970*

See also Silkworms

LASCAUX CAVE, Montignac, France:

Art Treasures from the Ice Age: Lascaux Cave. By Jean-Philippe Rigaud. Photos by Sisse Brimberg and Norbert Aujoulat. 482-499, *Oct. 1988*

Lascaux Cave, Cradle of World Art. By Norbert Casteret. Photos by Maynard Owen Williams. 771-794, *Dec. 1948*

LASERS:

Editorial. By Wilbur E. Garrett. 281, *Mar. 1984*

Lasers–"A Splendid Light." By Allen A. Boraiko. Photos by Charles O'Rear. 335-363, *Mar. 1984*

The Wonder of Holography. By H. John Caulfield. Photos by Charles O'Rear. 364-377, *Mar. 1984*

Fiber Optics: Harnessing Light by a Thread. By Allen A. Boraiko. Photos by Fred Ward. 516-535, *Oct. 1979*

The Laser's Bright Magic. By Thomas Meloy. Photos by Howard Sochurek. 858-881, *Dec. 1966*

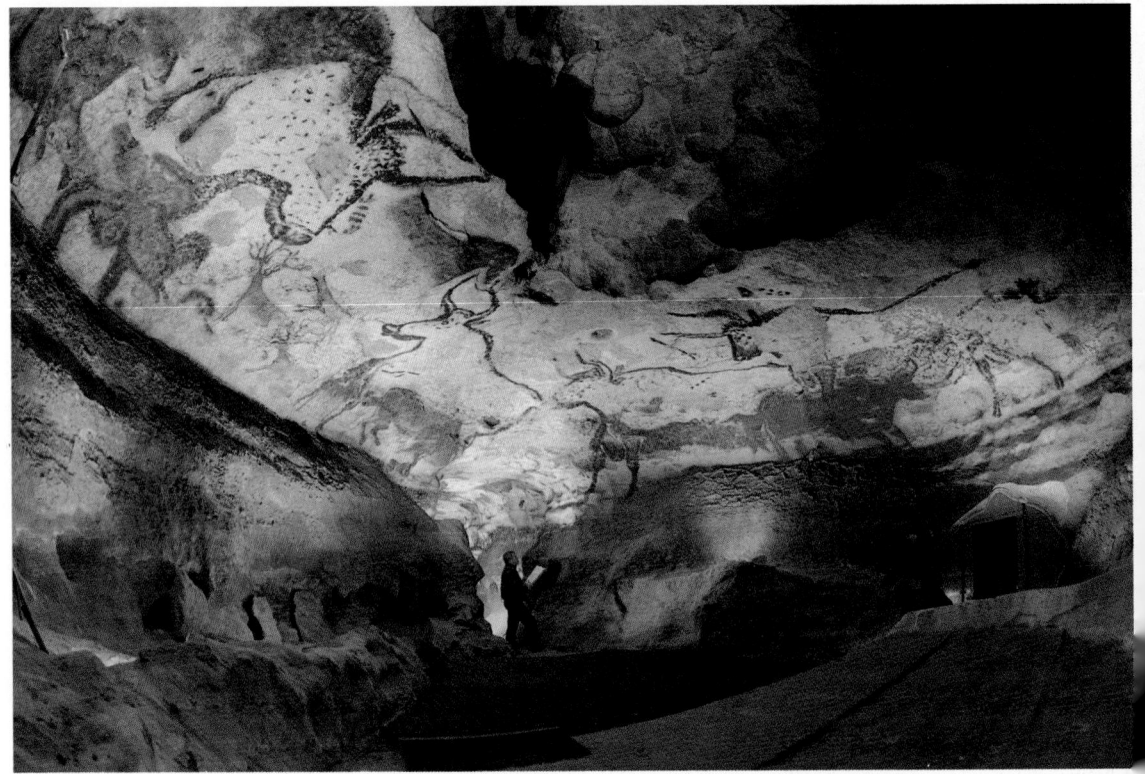

Paleolithic artists painted and engraved hundreds of images in Lascaux cave in southwest France 17,000 years ago. SISSE BRIMBERG

Drucker and Robert F. Heizer. NGS research grant. 367-375, *Sept. 1956*

On the Trail of La Venta Man. By Matthew W. Stirling. Photos by Richard H. Stewart. NGS research grant. Included: Hunting Mexico's Buried Temples. 137-172, *Feb. 1947*

Wildlife of Tabasco and Veracruz. By Walter A. Weber. Paintings by author. 187-216, *Feb. 1945*

La Venta's Green Stone Tigers. By Matthew W. Stirling. 321-332, *Sept. 1943*

Finding Jewels of Jade in a Mexican Swamp. By Matthew W. and Marion Stirling. 635-661, *Nov. 1942*

Great Stone Faces of the Mexican Jungle: Five Colossal Heads and Numerous Other Monuments of Vanished Americans Are Excavated by the Latest National Geographic-Smithsonian Expedition. By Matthew W. Stirling. 309-334, *Sept. 1940*

LAVIES, BIANCA: *Photographer*

Hidden Life of the Timber Rattler. By William S. Brown. NGS research grant. 128-138, *July 1987*

The Astonishing Armadillo. By Eleanor E. Storrs. 820-830, *June 1982*

Atlantic Salmon: The "Leaper" Struggles to Survive. By Art Lee. 600-615, *Nov. 1981*

The Wild World of Compost. By Cecil E. Johnson. 273-284, *Aug. 1980*

Life Around a Lily Pad. Text by Charles R. Miller. 131-142, *Jan. 1980*

The Tree Nobody Liked (Red Mangrove). By Rick Gore. 669-689, *May 1977*

Found at Last: the Monarch's Winter Home. By Fred A. Urquhart. 161-173, *Aug. 1976*

Those Fiery Brazilian Bees. By Rick Gore. 491-501, *Apr. 1976*

Manitoba's Fantastic Snake Pits. By Michael Aleksiuk. 715-723, *Nov. 1975*

Tireless Voyager, the Whistling Swan. By William J. L. Sladen. 134-147, *July 1975*

LAVIGNE, DAVID M.:

Nomination Page. *Jan. 1976*

Author

Life or Death for the Harp Seal. Photos by William R. Curtsinger. 129-142, *Jan. 1976*

LAW:

■■ *Equal Justice Under the Law: The Supreme Court in American Life*. By Mary Ann Harrell. Published in cooperation with The Foundation of the Federal Bar Association. 151 pages. 1965; rev. ed. 1988

Ancient Mesopotamia: A Light That Did Not Fail. By E. A. Speiser. Paintings by H. M. Herget. Included: The Law Protects Zealously the Institution of Marriage.–Justice Catches Up With a Corrupt Magistrate. 41-105, *Jan. 1951*

The British Way. By Sir Evelyn Wrench. Included: Jury System (1066-1086); Magna Carta (1215); The Mother of Parliaments (1295); William Blackstone (1723-1780). 421-541, *Apr. 1949*

Open-Air Law Courts of Ethiopia. Photos by Harald P. Lechenperg. 633-646, *Nov. 1935*

Pushing Back History's Horizon: How the Pick and Shovel Are Revealing Civilizations That Were Ancient When Israel Was Young. Included: Hammurapi's Code. By Albert T. Clay. 162-216, *Feb. 1916*

Our Immigration Laws from the Viewpoint of National Eugenics. By Robert De C. Ward. 38-41, *Jan. 1912*

The Civil Government of Alaska. By George C. Perkins. 172-178, *Apr. 1898*

The Utilization of the Vacant Public Lands. By Emory F. Best. Included: Homestead Act. 49-57, *Feb. 1897*

LAW ENFORCEMENT:

The FBI: Public Friend Number One. By Jacob Hay. Photos by Robert F. Sisson. 860-886, *June 1961*

The **LAW** of Storms, Considered with Special Reference to the North Atlantic. By Everett Hayden. 199-211, *July 1890*

LAWAS. *See* Luas

LAWICK, HUGO VAN: *Photographer*

Hyenas, the Hunters Nobody Knows. By Hans Kruuk. 44-57, *July 1968*

Tool-using Bird: The Egyptian Vulture. By Baroness Jane van Lawick-Goodall. 631-641, *May 1968*

■■ *My Friends the Wild Chimpanzees.* By Jane Goodall. 204 pages. 1967

New Discoveries Among Africa's Chimpanzees. By Baroness Jane van Lawick-Goodall. 802-831, *Dec. 1965*

The Leakeys of Africa: Family in Search of Prehistoric Man. By Melvin M. Payne. 194-231, *Feb. 1965*

My Life Among Wild Chimpanzees. By Jane Goodall. Photos by Baron Hugo van Lawick and author. 272-308, *Aug. 1963*

Flourishing cape and sword, an aspiring bullfighter practices in Spain's Basque country. WILLIAM ALBERT ALLARD

Adventures in the Search for Man. By Louis S. B. Leakey. 132-152, *Jan. 1963*

LAWICK-GOODALL, JANE VAN. *See* Goodall, Jane

LAWRENCE, FREDERICK W.:

Author

The Origin of American State Names. 105-143, *Aug. 1920*

LAWRENCE, Massachusetts:

The Merrimack: River of Industry and Romance. By Albert W. Atwood. Photos by B. Anthony Stewart. 106-140, *Jan. 1951*

LAWS of Temperature Control of the Geographic Distribution of Terrestrial Animals and Plants. Annual Address by Vice-President, C. Hart Merriam. 229-238, *Dec. 29, 1894*

LAXALT, ROBERT:

Nomination Page. *Aug. 1975*

Author

The Indomitable Basques. 69-71, *July 1985*

The Gauchos, Last of a Breed. Photos by O. Louis Mazzatenta. 478-501, *Oct. 1980*

New Mexico's Mountains of Mystery. Photos by Craig Aurness. 416-436, *Sept. 1978*

The Enduring Pyrenees. Photos by Edwin Stuart Grosvenor. 794-819, *Dec. 1974*

The Other Nevada. Photos by J. Bruce Baumann. 733-761, *June 1974*

Golden Ghosts of the Lost Sierra. Photos by David Hiser. 332-353, *Sept. 1973*

New Mexico: The Golden Land. Photos by Adam Woolfitt. 299-345, *Sept. 1970*

Land of the Ancient Basques. Photos by William Albert Allard. 240-277, *Aug. 1968*

Lonely Sentinels of the American West: Basque Sheepherders. Photos by William Belknap, Jr. 870-888, *June 1966*

LAYKAWKEY (Village), Thailand:

Spirits of Change Capture the Karens. By Peter Kunstadter. 267-285, *Feb. 1972*

LAYSAN ISLAND, Leeward Islands, Hawaii:

Hawaii's Far-flung Wildlife Paradise. By John L. Eliot. Photos by Jonathan Blair. 670-691, *May 1978*

Bird Life Among Lava Rock and Coral Sand: The Chronicle of a Scientific Expedition to Little-known Islands of Hawaii. By Alexander Wetmore. 77-108, *July 1925*

A Bird City. 494-498, *Dec. 1904*

LEA, JOHN S.: *Editor*

■■ *Research Reports.* 1976 Projects. 968 pages. *1984*

■■ *Research Reports.* 1975 Projects. 844 pages. *1984*

■■ *Research Reports.* 1971, 1973, or 1974 Projects. 787 pages. *1983*

■■ *Research Reports.* 1973 Projects. 736 pages. *1982*

In search of early humans anthropologist Richard E. Leakey, left, and team explore northern Kenya. GORDON W. GAHAN

An abandoned antiaircraft gun becomes a plaything for Muslim children outside the war-ravaged city of Beirut, Lebanon. STEVE McCURRY

Lebanon, Little Bible Land in the Crossfire of History. By William S. Ellis. Photos by George F. Mobley. 240-275, *Feb. 1970*

Journey Into the Great Rift: The Northern Half. By Helen and Frank Schreider. 254-290, *Aug. 1965*

YWCA: International Success Story. By Mary French Rockefeller. Photos by Otis Imboden. 904-933, *Dec. 1963*

Young-old Lebanon Lives by Trade. By Thomas J. Abercrombie. 479-523, *Apr. 1958*

Troubled Waters East of Suez. By Ernest M. Eller. 483-522, *Apr. 1954*

Syria and Lebanon Taste Freedom. By Maynard Owen Williams. 729-763, *Dec. 1946*

American Alma Maters in the Near East. By Maynard Owen Williams. 237-256, *Aug. 1945*

In the Land of Moses and Abraham. Photos by W. Robert Moore. 711-742, *Dec. 1938*

The Road of the Crusaders: A Historian Follows the Steps of Richard the Lion Heart and Other Knights of the Cross Over the "Via Dei." By Harold Lamb. 645-693, *Dec. 1933*

Crusader Castles of the Near East. By William H. Hall. 369-390, *Mar. 1931*

Skirting the Shores of Sunrise: Seeking and Finding "The Levant" in a Journey by Steamer, Motor-Car, and Train from Constantinople to Port Said. By Melville Chater. 649-728, *Dec. 1926*

Syria: The Land Link of History's Chain. Included: Beirut. By Maynard Owen Williams. 437-462, *Nov. 1919*

From Jerusalem to Aleppo. By John D. Whiting. 71-113, *Jan. 1913*

LEBARGE, MICHEL:
A Yukon Pioneer, Mike Lebarge. By William H. Dall. 137-139, *Apr. 1898*

LECHENPERG, HARALD P.:
Author-Photographer
With the Italians in Eritrea: Torrid Colony Between the Red Sea and Ethiopia, 2,600 Miles by Sea from Rome, Is Mobilization Place of Fascist Troops and Planes. 265-295, *Sept. 1935*
Photographer
Open-Air Law Courts of Ethiopia. 633-646, *Nov. 1935*

LE CONTE, JOSEPH:
Joseph Le Conte (Biography). By W J McGee. 309-311, *Aug. 1901*

LEDO-BURMA ROAD. *See* Stilwell Road

LEE, ART: *Author*
Atlantic Salmon: The "Leaper" Struggles to Survive. Photos by Bianca Lavies. 600-615, *Nov. 1981*

LEE, CHRISTINE ECKSTROM:
Author
▪▪ *America's Atlantic Isles.* By H. Robert Morrison and Christine Eckstrom Lee. Photos by David Alan Harvey. 199 pages. *1981*

LEE, DOUGLAS B.: *Author*
Oil in the Wilderness: An Arctic Dilemma. Photos by James P. Blair. 858-871, *Dec. 1988*

Sharks at 2,000 Feet. By Eugenie Clark and Emory Kristof as reported to Douglas Lee. NGS research grant. 681-691, *Nov. 1986*

Kluane: Canada's Icy Wilderness Park. Photos by George F. Mobley. 630-653, *Nov. 1985*

The Plain People of Pennsylvania. Photo essay by Jerry Irwin. Text by Douglas Lee. 492-519, *Apr. 1984*

Mississippi Delta: The Land of the

River. Photos by C. C. Lockwood. 226-253, *Aug. 1983*

Slime Mold: The Fungus That Walks. Photos by Paul A. Zahl. 131-136, *July 1981*

Hokkaido, Japan's Last Frontier. Photos by Michael S. Yamashita. 62-93, *Jan. 1980*

Day of the Rice God (Festival in Japan). Photos by H. Edward Kim. 78-85, *July 1978*

LEE, J. R.:
Transporting a Navy Through the Jungles of Africa in War Time. By Frank J. Magee. Note: J. R. Lee, originator of the plan. 331-362, *Oct. 1922*

LEE, JOSEPH: *Author*
Beautiful Ecuador. 81-91, *Feb. 1907*

LEE, KENNETH FULLER:
Author-Photographer
In the Allagash Country (Maine). 505-520, *Apr. 1929*

LEE, ROBERT E.:
Appomattox: Where Grant and Lee Made Peace With Honor a Century Ago. By Ulysses S. Grant 3rd. Photos by Bruce Dale. 435-469, *Apr. 1965*

LEE, THOMAS F.: *Author*
Guatemala: Land of Volcanoes and Progress: Cradle of Ancient Mayan Civilization, Redolent With Its Later Spanish and Indian Ways, Now Reaping Prosperity from Bananas and Coffee. 599-648, *Nov. 1926*

LEE, WILLIS T.: *Author*
New Discoveries in Carlsbad Cavern: Vast Subterranean Chambers with Spectacular Decorations Are Explored, Surveyed, and Photographed. 301-319, *Sept. 1925*

A Visit to Carlsbad Cavern: Recent Explorations of a Limestone Cave in the Guadalupe Mountains of New Mexico Reveal a Natural Wonder of the First Magnitude. 1-40, *Jan. 1924*

LEE, Camp, Virginia:
Training the New Armies of Liberty: Camp Lee, Virginia's Home for the National Army. By Granville Fortescue. 421-437, *Nov.-Dec. 1917*

LEEN, SARAH: *Photographer*
Return to Uganda. By Jerry and Sarah Kambites. 73-89, *July 1980*

LEEPER, JOHN and BLANCHE:
Authors
American Processional: History on Canvas. 173-212, *Feb. 1951*

LEEWARD ISLANDS, Hawaii:
Hawaii's Far-flung Wildlife Paradise. By John L. Eliot. Photos by Jonathan Blair. 670-691, *May 1978*

Bird Life Among Lava Rock and Coral Sand: The Chronicle of a Scientific Expedition to Little-known Islands of Hawaii. By Alexander Wetmore. 77-108, *July 1925*

A Bird City. 494-498, *Dec. 1904*

LEEWARD ISLANDS, Lesser Antilles, West Indies:

A Fresh Breeze Stirs the Leewards. By Carleton Mitchell. Photos by Winfield Parks. Included: Antigua; Dominica; Guadeloupe; Îles des Saintes; Nevis; Saba; St. Barthélemy; St. Christopher; St. Eustatius; St. Martín; Virgin Islands. 488-537, *Oct. 1966*
Carib Cruises the West Indies. By Carleton Mitchell. 1-56, *Jan. 1948*
British West Indian Interlude. By Anne Rainey Langley. 1-46, *Jan. 1941*
See also Antigua; Dominica; Guadeloupe; Saba; St. Christopher; Sint Eustatius; Virgin Islands

LEFFINGWELL, E. DE K.: *Author*
The Anglo-American Polar Expedition. 796, *Dec. 1907*

LEGACY From the Age of Faith, Chartres. By Kenneth MacLeish. Photos by Dean Conger. 857-882, *Dec. 1969*

LEGACY From the Deep: Henry VIII's Lost Warship. By Margaret Rule. Introduction and picture text by Peter Miller. Paintings by Richard Schlecht. 646-675, *May 1983*

LEGACY of a Dazzling Past. By Alice J. Hall. 293-311, *Mar. 1977*

LEGACY of Lively Treasures: Sri Lanka's Wildlife. By Dieter and Mary Plage. 256-273, *Aug. 1983*

LEGENDS:

■■ *Amazing Mysteries of the World.* By Catherine O'Neill. Contents: Mystifying phenomena such as auroras, black holes, Bigfoot, the Bermuda Triangle, and UFOs. Juvenile. 104 pages. *1983*
War's Wake in the Rhineland. By Thomas R. Henry. 1-32, *July 1945*
The Story and Legends of the Pontine Marshes: After Many Centuries of Fruitless Effort, Italy Is to Inaugurate a Gigantic Enterprise to Drain the Fertile Region Southeast of Rome. By Don Gelasio Caetani. 357-374, *Apr. 1924*
See also Gilgamesh, Epic of; Golden Fleece Legend; Hâ-âk Vâ-âk; Kamikaze Legend; Loch Ness; Marostica, Italy, for Chess Game (Living Pieces); Messina, Strait of, for Charybdis; St. Michael's Mount; Stonehenge

LEGUMES. *See* Soybeans

LEH, Ladakh (District), Jammu and Kashmir, India:

A Journey to "Little Tibet." By Enakshi Bhavnani. Photos by Volkmar Wentzel. 603-634, *May 1951*
A Woman Paints the Tibetans. By Lafugie. 659-692, *May 1949*

LEHMAN, DANNY: *Photographer*
New Mexico: Between Frontier and Future. By Bart McDowell. 602-633, *Nov. 1987*
Panama: Ever at the Crossroads. By Charles E. Cobb, Jr. 466-493, *Apr. 1986*

Life on the Line: U. S.-Mexican Border. By Mark Kramer. 720-749, *June 1985*

LEIBERG, J. B.: *Author*
Is Climatic Aridity Impending on the Pacific Slope? The Testimony of the Forest. 160-181, *May 1899*

LEIS:
The Flowers That Say "Aloha." By Deena Clark. Photos by Robert B. Goodman. 121-131, *Jan. 1967*
Leis from Aloha Land (Hawaii). Photos by Richard H. Stewart. 435-442, *Oct. 1938*

LEM (Lunar Excursion Module). *See* Apollo Missions

LeMAY, CURTIS E.: *Author*
U. S. Air Force: Power for Peace. 291-297, *Sept. 1965*
Artists Roam the World of the U. S. Air Force. 650-673, *May 1960*
School for Survival. 565-602, *May 1953*

LE MOYNE DE MORGUES, JACQUES:
Indian Life Before the Colonists Came. By Stuart E. Jones. Engravings by Theodore de Bry, 1590. 351-368, *Sept. 1947*

LE MUNYON, ETHAN C.: *Author*
The Lama's Motor-Car. 641-670, *May 1913*

LEMURS:
Madagascar's Lemurs: On the Edge of Survival. By Alison Jolly. Photos by Frans Lanting. 132-161, *Aug. 1988*
Seeking Mindanao's Strangest Creatures. By Charles Heizer Wharton. 389-408, *Sept. 1948*

LEND-LEASE:
Lend-Lease and the Russian Victory. By Harvey Klemmer. 499-512, *Oct. 1945*
Iran in Wartime: Through Fabulous Persia, Hub of the Middle East, Americans, Britons, and Iranians Keep Sinews of War Moving to the Embattled Soviet Union. By John N. Greely. 129-156, *Aug. 1943*
Lend-Lease Is a Two-way Benefit: Innovation in Creative Statesmanship Polls Resources of United Nations, and Supplies American Forces Around the World. By Francis Flood. 745-761, *June 1943*

LENDOMBWEY. *See* Malekula (Island)

LENINGRAD, U.S.S.R.:
Leningrad, Russia's Window on the West. By Howard La Fay. Photos by Dick Durrance II. 636-673, *May 1971*
Young Russia: The Land of Unlimited Possibilities. By Gilbert H. Grosvenor. 421-520, *Nov. 1914*
Glimpses of the Russian Empire. By William Wisner Chapin. 1043-1078, *Nov. 1912*

LENTZ, JOHN W.: *Author*
On Canada's Hood River: Clues to a Tragic Trek. Photos by Todd Buchanan. 128-140, *Jan. 1986*

LENZ, FRANK B.:
Author-Photographer
The World's Ancient Porcelain Center (Kingtehchen). 391-406, *Nov. 1920*

LEONARD CARMICHAEL: An Appreciation. By Melvin M. Payne. 871-874, *Dec. 1973*

A crowned lemur, a Madagascar primate threatened by deforestation, crosses pinnacles of eroded limestone to reach a tree where it can feed on foliage. FRANS LANTING

Prowling stealthily, a snow leopard in the Himalaya takes a self-portrait after activating a concealed camera. RODNEY JACKSON AND DARLA HILLARD

Alphabet, Deciphered from School-boy Slates and Dictionaries of 3,000 Years Ago. By Claude F. A. Schaeffer. 97-126, *July 1933*

Crusader Castles of the Near East. By William H. Hall. 369-390, *Mar. 1931*

A New Alphabet of the Ancients Is Unearthed: An Inconspicuous Mound in Northern Syria Yields Archeological Treasures of Far-reaching Significance. By F. A. Schaeffer. 477-516, *Oct. 1930*

Skirting the Shores of Sunrise: Seeking and Finding "The Levant" in a Journey by Steamer, Motor-Car, and Train from Constantinople to Port Said. By Melville Chater. 649-728, *Dec. 1926*

Under the Heel of the Turk: A Land with a Glorious Past, a Present of Abused Opportunities, and a Future of Golden Possibilities. By William H. Hall. 51-69, *July 1918*

Impressions of Asiatic Turkey. By Stephen van Rensselaer Trowbridge. 598-609, *Dec. 1914*

From Jerusalem to Aleppo. By John D. Whiting. 71-113, *Jan. 1913*

Damascus, the Pearl of the Desert. By A. Forder. 62-82, *Jan. 1911*

One Thousand Miles of Railway Built for Pilgrims and Not for Dividends. By F. R. Maunsell. 156-172, *Feb. 1909*

Scenes in Asia Minor. 173-193, *Feb. 1909*

Damascus and Mecca Railway. 408, *Nov. 1901*

LEVATHES, LOUISE E.: *Author*

Remington, the Man and the Myth. Photos by Chris Johns. 200-231, *Aug. 1988*

Indianapolis: City on the Rebound. Photos by Sandy Felsenthal. 230-259, *Aug. 1987*

Mysteries of the Bog. Photos by Fred Bavendam. Included: Peat holds clues to early American life. 397-420, *Mar. 1987*

Iceland: Life Under the Glaciers. Photos by Bob Krist. 184-215, *Feb. 1987*

The Land Where the Murray Flows. Photos by David Robert Austen. 252-278, *Aug. 1985*

Kamehameha–Hawaii's Warrior King. Photos by Steve Raymer. Paintings by Herb Kawainui Kane. 558-599, *Nov. 1983*

Toledo–El Greco's Spain Lives On. Photos by James P. Blair. 726-753, *June 1982*

The American Red Cross: A Century of Service. Photos by Annie Griffiths. 777-791, *June 1981*

Milwaukee: More Than Beer. Photos by Michael Mauney. 180-201, *Aug. 1980*

Gateway–Elbowroom for the Millions (Gateway National Recreation Area, New Jersey-New York). 86-97, *July 1979*

LEVEES. *See* Dikes and Levees

LEVKAS (Island), Greece:

Homeward With Ulysses. By Melville Bell Grosvenor. Photos by Edwin Stuart Grosvenor. 1-39, *July 1973*

LEWIS, DAVID:

On Assignment in Antarctica. *Nov. 1984*

Editorial. By Gilbert M. Grosvenor. 431, *Oct. 1976*

Nomination Page. *July 1975*

Author

Icebound in Antarctica. Photos by Mimi George. 634-663, *Nov. 1984*

Voyage to the Antarctic. 544-562, *Apr. 1983*

Hokule'a Follows the Stars to Tahiti. Photos by Nicholas deVore III. 512-537, *Oct. 1976*

Wind, Wave, Star, and Bird. Photos by Nicholas deVore III. 747-781, *Dec. 1974*

Alone to Antarctica. Drawings by Noel Sickles. 808-821, *Dec. 1973*

Author-Photographer

Ice Bird Ends Her Lonely Odyssey. 216-233, *Aug. 1975*

LEWIS, F.: *Author-Photographer*

The Koala, or Australian Teddy Bear. 346-355, *Sept. 1931*

LEWIS, G. EDWARD:
Author-Photographer

El Sangay, Fire-breathing Giant of the Andes. 117-138, *Jan. 1950*

LEWIS, HARRY R.: *Author*

America's Debt to the Hen. 453-467, *Apr. 1927*

LEWIS, L. ELIZABETH: *Author*

The Fire-Walking Hindus of Singapore. 513-522, *Apr. 1931*

LEWIS, LEWIS: *Author-Photographer*

New Life for the "Loneliest Isle" (Tristan da Cunha). 105-116, *Jan. 1950*

LEWIS, M. LEE: *Author*

To 76,000 Feet by *Strato-Lab* Balloon. By Malcolm D. Ross and M. Lee Lewis. 269-282, *Feb. 1957*

LEWIS, Isle of, Scotland:

Isles on the Edge of the Sea: Scotland's Outer Hebrides. By Kenneth MacLeish. Photos by Thomas Nebbia. 676-711, *May 1970*

LEWIS AND CLARK EXPEDITION:

■■ *In the Footsteps of Lewis and Clark.* By Gerald S. Snyder. Photos by Dick Durrance II. Paintings by Richard Schlecht. 215 pages. *1970*

So Long, St. Louis, We're Heading West. By William C. Everhart. 643-669, *Nov. 1965*

Following the Trail of Lewis and Clark. By Ralph Gray. 707-750, *June 1953*

Trailing History Down the Big Muddy: In the Homeward Wake of Lewis and Clark, a Folding Steel Skiff Bears Its Lone Pilot on a 2,000-Mile Cruise on the Yellowstone-Missouri. By Lewis R. Freeman. 73-120, *July 1928*

A Relic of the Lewis and Clarke Expedition. By Cyrus C. Babb. 100-101, *Mar. 1898*

Oregon: Its History, Geography, and Resources. By John H. Mitchell. 239-284, *Apr. 20, 1895*

LEXINGTON, Kentucky:

Heart of the Bluegrass. By Charles McCarry. Photos by J. Bruce Baumann. 634-659, *May 1974*

LEYDET, FRANÇOIS: *Author*

Journey Through Time: Papua New Guinea. Photos by David Austen. 150-171, *Aug. 1982*

Coal vs. Parklands. Photos by Dewitt Jones. 776-803, *Dec. 1980*

Grand Teton–A Winter's Tale. 148-152, *July 1979*

Jackson Hole: Good-bye to the Old Days? Photos by Jonathan Wright. 768-789, *Dec. 1976*

The Mazatzal's Harsh but Lovely Land Between. Photos by Farrell Grehan. 161-167, *Feb. 1974*

Okefenokee, the Magical Swamp.

Young women of Liberia, in West Africa, paint their skin with clay and adorn themselves with beads, bangles, and gold and silver coins for a 1922 festival. FROM HARRY A. MCBRIDE

Photos by Farrell Grehan. 169-175, *Feb. 1974*

Autumn Flames Along the Allagash. Photos by Farrell Grehan. 177-187, *Feb. 1974*

The Olympics: Northwest Majesty. Photos by Farrell Grehan. 188-197, *Feb. 1974*

LHASA, Tibet:

Nomads' Land: A Journey Through Tibet. By Sorrel Wilby. 764-785, *Dec. 1987*

Editorial. By Gilbert M. Grosvenor. 143, *Feb. 1980*

In Long-Forbidden Tibet. By Fred Ward. 218-259, *Feb. 1980*

My Life in Forbidden Lhasa. By Heinrich Harrer. 1-48, *July 1955*

Across Tibet from India to China. By Ilia Tolstoy. 169-222, *Aug. 1946*

The World's Strangest Capital. By John Claude White. Included: Lhasa–The Mecca of the Buddhist Faith (panorama). 273-295, *Mar. 1916*

The Most Extraordinary City in the World: Notes on Lhasa–The Mecca of the Buddhist Faith. By Shaoching H. Chuan. 959-995, *Oct. 1912*

Views of Lhasa. 27-38, *Jan. 1905*

Notes on Tibet. 292-294, *July 1904*

Explorations in Tibet. 353-355, *Sept. 1903*

LHOTE, HENRI: *Author*

Oasis of Art in the Sahara. Photos by Kazuyoshi Nomachi. Contents: Rock paintings of Tassili-n-Ajjer, Algeria. 180-191, *Aug. 1987*

LI (River), China:

Guilin, China's Beauty Spot. By W. E. Garrett. 536-563, *Oct. 1979*

LIANG-CHENG, SIR CHENTUNG: *Author*

China and the United States. 554-557, *Dec. 1905*

LIAONING PROVINCE, China. *See* Lüda

LIBBEY, WILLIAM, Jr.: *Author*

The Relations of the Gulf Stream and the Labrador Current. 161-166, *Jan. 31, 1894*

LIBBY, ERNEST L.: *Author-Photographer*

Miracle of the Mermaid's Purse (Skate). 413-420, *Sept. 1957*

LIBERATED Ukraine. By Eddy Gilmore. 513-536, *May 1944*

LIBERATORS (Bombers):

8th Air Force in England. Photos from U. S. Army Air Forces. 297-304, *Mar. 1945*

LIBERIA:

Africa: The Winds of Freedom Stir a Continent. By Nathaniel T. Kenney. Photos by W. D. Vaughn. 303-359, *Sept. 1960*

Rubber-cushioned Liberia. By Henry S. Villard. Photos by Charles W. Allmon. 201-228, *Feb. 1948*

The Land of the Free in Africa. By Harry A. McBride. 411-430, *Oct. 1922*

Dumboy, the National Dish of Liberia. By G. N. Collins. 84-88, *Jan. 1911*

Kboo, a Liberian Game. By G. N. Collins. 944-948, *Nov. 1910*

Notes on the Only American Colony in the World. By Edgar Allen Forbes. 719-729, *Sept. 1910*

Conditions in Liberia. By Roland P. Folkner, George Sale, Emmett J. Scott. 729-741, *Sept. 1910*

A Primitive Gyroscope in Liberia. By G. N. Collins. 531-535, *June 1910*

Scene in Liberia. 298-301, *Mar. 1909*

The Black Republic–Liberia. By Sir Harry Johnston and Ernest Lyon. 334-343, *May 1907*

LIBERIA, Costa Rica:

Land of the Painted Oxcarts. By Luis Marden. 409-456, *Oct. 1946*

LIBERTY: *The Statue and the American* ■■ *Dream.* By Leslie Allen. The official

book for the Centennial of the Statue of Liberty published by the Statue of Liberty-Ellis Island Foundation, Inc. Prepared and produced as a public service by NGS. 304 pages. *1985*

LIBERTY Lifts Her Lamp Once More. By Alice J. Hall. 2-19, *July 1986*

LIBRARIES:

Florence Rises From the Flood. By Joseph Judge. Included: Biblioteca Nazionale Centrale, Gabinetto Vieusseux. 1-43, *July 1967*

The DAR Story. By Lonnelle Aikman. Photos by B. Anthony Stewart and John E. Fletcher. Included: Genealogical Library. 565-598, *Nov. 1951*

Miami's Expanding Horizons. By William H. Nicholas. Included: Brett Memorial Library, Miami Memorial Library, Montgomery Museum and Library, State Library, University of Miami Library. 561-594, *Nov. 1950*

Literary Landmarks of Massachusetts. By William H. Nicholas. Photos by B. Anthony Stewart and John E. Fletcher. Included: Adams Library, The Athenaeum, Boston College Library, Boston Public Library, Converse Memorial Library, Houghton Library, Lamont Library. 279-310, *Mar. 1950*

See also Folger Shakespeare Library; Henry E. Huntington Library and Art Gallery; Library of Congress

LIBRARY OF CONGRESS, Washington, D. C.:

Editorial. By Wilbur E. Garrett. Braille edition and sound recordings of *National Geographic* and National Geographic WORLD. 145, *Aug. 1986*

Library of Congress: The Nation's Bookcase. By Fred Kline. Photos by Dick Durrance II. 671-687, *Nov. 1975*

The Nation's Library. By Albert W. Atwood. 663-684, *May 1950*

Washington–Storehouse of Knowledge.

Part of the U.S. Air Force in Europe, three F-100s thunder across Tripoli, Libya, in 1965 on their way to desert gunnery practice. EMORY KRISTOF, NGS

By Albert W. Atwood. 325-359, *Mar. 1942*

The Color Camera's First Aërial Success. Photos by Melville Bell Grosvenor. Included: Library of Congress. 344-353, *Sept. 1930*

The Transformation of Washington: A Glance at the History and Along the Vista of the Future of the Nation's Capital. By Charles Moore. 569-595, *June 1923*

The Capitol, Wonder Building of the World. By Gilbert Grosvenor. Included: Library of Congress. 603-638, *June 1923*

Washington: Its Beginning, Its Growth, and Its Future. By William Howard Taft. 221-292, *Mar. 1915*

LIBRARY OF CONGRESS–NATIONAL GEOGRAPHIC SOCIETY MAP PRESERVATION PROJECT:

President's Page. By Gilbert M. Grosvenor. *Apr. 1988*

LIBYA:

Red Cross Girl Overseas. By Margaret Cotter. 745-768, *Dec. 1944*

Americans on the Barbary Coast. By Willard Price. 1-31, *July 1943*

Old-New Battle Grounds of Egypt and Libia. By W. Robert Moore. 809-820, *Dec. 1940*

Cirenaica, Eastern Wing of Italian Libia. By Harriet Chalmers Adams. 689-726, *June 1930*

Tripolitania, Where Rome Resumes Sway: The Ancient Trans-Mediterranean Empire, on the Fringe of the Libyan Desert, Becomes a Promising Modern Italian Colony. By Gordon Casserly. 131-161, *Aug. 1925*

Crossing the Untraversed Libyan Desert: The Record of a 2,200-Mile Journey of Exploration Which Resulted in the Discovery of Two Oases of Strategic Importance on the Southwestern Frontier of Egypt. By A. M. Hassanein Bey. 233-277, *Sept. 1924*

Here and There in Northern Africa. By Frank Edward Johnson. 1-132, *Jan. 1914*

Tripoli: A Land of Little Promise. By Adolf L. Vischer. 1035-1047, *Nov. 1911*

The Mysteries of the Desert. By Hanns Vischer. 1056-1059, *Nov. 1911*

LIBYAN DESERT, Africa:

Crossing the Untraversed Libyan Desert: The Record of a 2,200-Mile Journey of Exploration Which Resulted in the Discovery of Two Oases of Strategic Importance on the Southwestern Frontier of Egypt. By A. M. Hassanein Bey. 233-277, *Sept. 1924*
See also Tripolitania

LICE:

Pollution, Threat to Man's Only Home. By Gordon Young. Photos by James P. Blair. Included: The use of DDT during World War II against mosquitoes and body lice. 738-781, *Dec. 1970*

Cooties and Courage. By Herbert Corey. 495-509, *June 1918*

Hospital Heroes Convict the Cootie. 510, *June 1918*

LICHENS:

Life on a Rock Ledge. By William H. Amos. 558-566, *Oct. 1980*

LIECHTENSTEIN:

Liechtenstein: A Modern Fairy Tale. By Robert Booth. Photos by John Launois. 273-284, *Feb. 1981*

Liechtenstein Thrives on Stamps. By Ronald W. Clark. 105-112, *July 1948*

Round About Liechtenstein: A Tiny Principality Which the Visitor May Encompass in a Single View Affords Adventurous Climbs Among Steep Pastures and Quaint Villages. By Maynard Owen Williams. 611-634, *Nov. 1927*

LIFE, Culture, and History of the Egyptians. Paintings by H. M. Herget. 436-514, *Oct. 1941*

LIFE Afloat in China: Tens of Thousands of Chinese in Congested Ports Spend Their Entire Existence on Boats. By Robert F. Fitch. 665-686, *June 1927*

LIFE Along the Central China Coast. Photos by W. Robert Moore. 317-324, *Sept. 1932*

LIFE Among Mountain Gorillas. By Dian Fossey. NGS research grant. 501-523, *Apr. 1981*

LIFE Among the Lamas of Choni: Describing the Mystery Plays and Butter Festival in the Monastery of an Almost Unknown Tibetan Principality in Kansu Province, China. By Joseph F. Rock. 569-619, *Nov. 1928*

LIFE Among the People of Eastern Tibet. By A. L. Shelton. 293-326, *Sept. 1921*

LIFE Among the Wai Wai Indians. By Clifford Evans and Betty J. Meggers. 329-346, *Mar. 1955*

LIFE and Color Under the Rising Sun. Photos by W. Robert Moore and Kiyoshi Sakamoto. 289-296, *Mar. 1933*

LIFE and Death at Gombe. By Jane Goodall. NGS research grant. 592-621, *May 1979*

LIFE and Death in Ancient Maya Land. Paintings by H. M. Herget. 623-630, *Nov. 1936*

LIFE and Death in Tana Toradja. By Pamela and Alfred Meyer. 793-815, *June 1972*

LIFE and Death in Toradjaland. Photos by Maynard Owen Williams and Helene Fischer. 65-80, *July 1940*

LIFE and Death on the Oregon Trail: The Itch to Move West. By Boyd Gibbons. Photos by James L. Amos. 147-177, *Aug. 1986*

LIFE and Luster of Berlin. Photos by Wilhelm Tobien and Hans Hildenbrand. 147-177, *Feb. 1937*

LIFE Around a Lily Pad. Photos by Bianca Lavies. Text by Charles R. Miller. 131-142, *Jan. 1980*

LIFE Ashore Beckons the Sea Gypsies. By Anne de Henning Singh. Photos by Raghubir Singh. 659-677, *May 1976*

LIFE Breath of Half the World: Monsoons By Priit J. Vesilind. Photos by Steve McCurry. 712-747, *Dec. 1984*

LIFE by Night in a Desert Sea. By Kenneth Brower. Photos by William R. Curtsinger and Chris Newbert. 834-847, *Dec. 1981*

LIFE Cycle of a Coral. By Robert F. Sisson. 780-793, *June 1973*

LIFE 8,000 Years Ago Uncovered in an Alabama Cave. By Carl F. Miller. NGS research grant. 542-558, *Oct. 1956*

A makeshift umbrella does little to protect two chilled Javanese girls from Indonesia's fierce monsoon rains, life breath of the region. STEVE McCURRY

Enduring icy conditions in December 1919, the tender **Marigold** *arrives at Raspberry Island Station in Lake Superior to relieve lightkeepers.* U.S. LIGHTHOUSE SERVICE

LIGNITE:
Alaska and Its Mineral Resources. By Samuel Franklin Emmons. 139-172, *Apr. 1898*

LIGUUS FASCIATUS (Snail):
Tree Snails, Gems of the Everglades. By Treat Davidson. 372-387, *Mar. 1965*

LILIENTHAL, OTTO:
Happy Birthday, Otto Lilienthal! By Russell Hawkes. Photos by James Collison. 286-292, *Feb. 1972*
Remarkable Photograph of Lilienthal's Gliding Machine. By R. W. Wood. 596, Aug. 1908; 271, Mar. 1911; 235, *Aug. 1927*
Aërial Locomotion. By Alexander Graham Bell. 1-34, *Jan. 1907*

LILY PADS:
Life Around a Lily Pad. Photos by Bianca Lavies. Text by Charles R. Miller. 131-142, *Jan. 1980*

LIMA, Peru:
The Incredible Potato. By Robert E. Rhoades. Photos by Martin Rogers. 668-694, *May 1982*
The Two Souls of Peru. By Harvey Arden. Photos by William Albert Allard. 284-321, *Mar. 1982*
The Lure of Lima, City of the Kings. By William Joseph Showalter. 727-784, *June 1930*

LIMBERT, R. W.:
Author-Photographer
Among the "Craters of the Moon": An Account of the First Expeditions

Through the Remarkable Volcanic Lava Beds of Southern Idaho. 303-328, *Mar. 1924*

LIMESTONE FORMATIONS:
Guilin, China's Beauty Spot. By W. E. Garrett. 536-563, *Oct. 1979*

LIMESTONE SINKS:
Manitoba's Fantastic Snake Pits. By Michael Aleksiuk. Photos by Bianca Lavies. 715-723, *Nov. 1975*

The **LIMITED** Water Supply of the Arid Region. By Frederick H. Newell. 438-442, *Nov. 1900*

LIMITING Width of Meander Belts. By Mark S. W. Jefferson. 373-384, *Oct. 1902*

LIMNOLOGY. *See* Brook Life; Mzima Springs; Pond Life

LIMÓN, Costa Rica:
Land of the Painted Oxcarts. By Luis Marden. 409-456, *Oct. 1946*

LIMPKIN, the "Crying Bird" That Haunts Florida Swamps. By Frederick Kent Truslow. 114-121, *Jan. 1958*

LIN, MAYA:
Vietnam Veterans Memorial: An interview with Maya Lin, designer. 557, *May 1985*

LINCOLN, ABRAHAM:
The Lights Are Up at Ford's Theatre. By Lonnelle Aikman. 392-401, *Mar. 1970*
The Living White House. By Lonnelle Aikman. 593-643, *Nov. 1966*
Profiles of the Presidents: III. The

American Giant Comes of Age. By Frank Freidel. 660-711, *May 1965*
Inside the White House. By Lonnelle Aikman. Photos by B. Anthony Stewart and Thomas Nebbia. 3-43, *Jan. 1961*
Lincoln, Man of Steel and Velvet. By Carl Sandburg. 239-241, *Feb. 1960*
Our Land Through Lincoln's Eyes. By Carolyn Bennett Patterson. Photos by W. D. Vaughn. 243-277, *Feb. 1960*
Vacation Tour Through Lincoln Land. By Ralph Gray. 141-184, *Feb. 1952*
Washington: Home of the Nation's Great. By Albert W. Atwood. 699-738, *June 1947*

LINCOLN, F. S.: *Photographer*
The Glamour of Historic Havana. 357-364, *Sept. 1933*

LINCOLN, Nebraska:
The West Through Boston Eyes. By Stewart Anderson. 733-776, *June 1949*
Nebraska, the Cornhusker State. By Leo A. Borah. 513-542, *May 1945*

LINCOLN MEMORIAL, Washington, D. C.:
The Lincoln Memorial. By William Howard Taft. 597-602, *June 1923*
▪▪ *The Capital of Our Country.* 154 pages. *1923*
Views of the Lincoln Memorial in Washington. 197-204, *Aug. 1922*

LINDBERG, JAN:
On Assignment. *June 1986*

LINDBERGH, ANNE MORROW:
Hubbard Gold Medal presented to. 136, 137, *Jan. 1936*
The Society Awards Hubbard Medal to Anne Morrow Lindbergh. Included: Acceptance by Mrs. Lindbergh; Basis of award; Design and inscription; Messages of congratulation; Photograph of medal; Presentation by Gilbert H. Grosvenor; Previous recipients; Projection used for map design on medal. 791-794, *June 1934*
Author
Flying Around the North Atlantic. By Anne Morrow Lindbergh. Foreword by Charles A. Lindbergh. 259-337, *Sept. 1934*

LINDBERGH, CHARLES A.:
Hubbard Medal awarded to. 137, 138, *Jan. 1936*
Flying Around the North Atlantic. By Anne Morrow Lindbergh. Foreword by Charles A. Lindbergh. 259-337, *Sept. 1934*
Seeing America with Lindbergh: The Record of a Tour of More Than 20,000 Miles by Airplane Through Forty-eight States on Schedule Time. By Donald E. Keyhoe. 1-46, *Jan. 1928*
President Coolidge Bestows Lindbergh Award: The National Geographic Society's Hubbard Medal Is Presented to Aviator Before the Most Notable Gathering in the History of Washington. Included: Acceptance

by Lindbergh; Inscription; Presentation by President. 132-140, *Jan. 1928*

Air Conquest: From the Early Days of Giant Kites and Birdlike Gliders the National Geographic Society Has Aided and Encouraged the Growth of Aviation (Hubbard Gold Medal Awarded Lindbergh). Included: Basis of award; Inscription; Letter from Gilbert Grosvenor announcing award; Lindbergh notified by Richard E. Byrd; Photograph of medal; Previous recipients. 233-242, *Aug. 1927*

Author

To Bogotá and Back by Air: The Narrative of a 9,500-Mile Flight from Washington, Over Thirteen Latin-American Countries and Return, in the Single-Seater Airplane "Spirit of St. Louis." 529-601, *May 1928*

LINDBERGH, JON:

Outpost Under the Ocean. By Edwin A. Link. Photos by Bates Littlehales. 530-533, *Apr. 1965*

The Deepest Days. By Robert Sténuit. 534-547, *Apr. 1965*

LINDISFARNE (Island), England:

Pilgrimage to Holy Island and the Farnes. By John E. H. Nolan. 547-570, *Oct. 1952*

LINDQUIST, WILLIS: *Author*

On Danish By-Lanes: An American Cycles Through the Quaint City of Lace, the Curiosity Town Where Time Stands Still, and Even Finds a Frontier in the Farming Kingdom. 1-34, *Jan. 1940*

Author-Photographer

Life's Flavor on a Swedish Farm: From the Rocky Hills of Småland Thousands of Sturdy Citizens Have Emigrated to the United States. 393-414, *Sept. 1939*

LINDSAY ISLAND, Antarctic Region:

Sailing the Seven Seas in the Interest of Science: Adventures Through 157,000 Miles of Storm and Calm,

---

from Arctic to Antarctic and Around the World, in the Non-magnetic Yacht "Carnegie." By J. P. Ault. 631-690, *Dec. 1922*

LINE, FRANCIS R.:
Author-Photographer

Arizona Sheep Trek. 457-478, *Apr. 1950*

LINEHAN, EDWARD J.: *Author*

The Trouble With Dolphins. Photos by Bill Curtsinger. 506-541, *Apr. 1979*

Cuba's Exiles Bring New Life to Miami. Photos by Nathan Benn. 68-95, *July 1973*

Norway, Land of the Generous Sea. Photos by George F. Mobley. 1-43, *July 1971*

Colorado, the Rockies' Pot of Gold. Photos by James L. Amos. 157-201, *Aug. 1969*

Czechoslovakia: The Dream and the Reality. Photos by James P. Blair. 151-193, *Feb. 1968*

Old-new Iran, Next Door to Russia. Photos by Thomas J. Abercrombie. 44-85, *Jan. 1961*

Dogs Work for Man. Paintings by Edwin Megargee and R. E. Lougheed. 190-233, *Aug. 1958*

LINGNAN UNIVERSITY, Guangzhou, China: Expedition:

Landscaped Kwangsi, China's Province of Pictorial Art. By G. Weidman Groff and T. C. Lau. 671-710, *Dec. 1937*

LINK, EDWIN A.:

Exploring the Drowned City of Port Royal. By Marion Clayton Link. Photos by Luis Marden. 151-183, *Feb. 1960*

Author

Outpost Under the Ocean. Photos by Bates Littlehales. 530-533, *Apr. 1965*

Tomorrow on the Deep Frontier. 778-801, *June 1964*

Our Man-in-Sea Project. 713-717, *May 1963*

LINK, MARION CLAYTON: *Author*

Exploring the Drowned City of Port Royal. Photos by Luis Marden. 151-183, *Feb. 1960*

LINK IGLOO:

Tomorrow on the Deep Frontier. By Edwin A. Link. NGS research grant. 778-801, *June 1964*

The **LINK** Relations of Southwestern Asia. By Talcott Williams. 249-265, July 1901; 291-299, *Aug. 1901*

LIONS:

■ Lions of the African Night. President's Page. By Gilbert M. Grosvenor. *Jan. 1987*; cover, *Jan. 1987*

Etosha: Namibia's Kingdom of Animals. By Douglas H. Chadwick. Photos by Des and Jen Bartlett. 344-385, *Mar. 1983*

Family Life of Lions. By Des and Jen Bartlett. 800-819, *Dec. 1982*

Life with the King of Beasts. By George B. Schaller. 494-519, *Apr. 1969*

Spearing Lions with Africa's Masai. By

Regally ensconced, Abraham Lincoln surveys a few of the annual millions of visitors to the Lincoln Memorial in Washington, D.C. W. D. VAUGHN AND JOHN E. FLETCHER, NGS

Col. Charles A. Lindbergh prepares for takeoff on his 1927 nonstop flight from Washington, D.C., to Mexico City. U.S. ARMY AIR CORPS

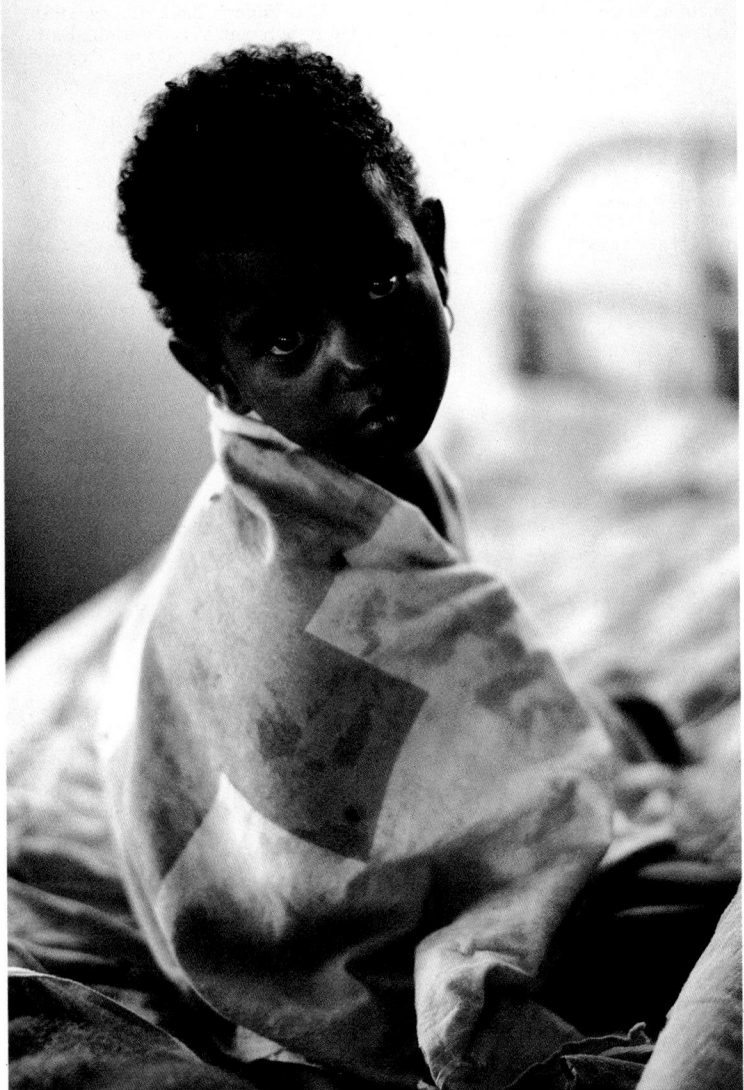

Ethiopian child awaits food at a center run by the International Committee of the Red Cross, which offers "A Little Humanity Amid the Horrors of War." STEVE RAYMER, NGS

Divers in a Florida freshwater spring seem to jump for joy among sand-covered cliffs of dolomite. BATES LITTLEHALES, NGS

Ranches in the Sea. By Earl Warren, Jr. 257-283, *Aug. 1958*

Calypso Explores an Undersea Canyon. By Jacques-Yves Cousteau. 373-396, *Mar. 1958*

Nomad Sails Long Island Sound. By Thomas Horgan. 295-338, *Sept. 1957*

Back to the Historic Black Hills. By Leland D. Case. 479-509, *Oct. 1956*

New England, a Modern Pilgrim's Pride. By Beverley M. Bowie. 733-796, *June 1955*

Ohio Makes Its Own Prosperity. By Leo A. Borah. Photos by B. Anthony Stewart and Bates Littlehales. 435-484, *Apr. 1955*

Cruising Florida's Western Waterways. By Rube Allyn. 49-76, *Jan. 1955*

Ontario, Pivot of Canada's Power. By Andrew H. Brown. Photos by B. Anthony Stewart and Bates Littlehales. 823-852, *Dec. 1953*

LITTLEHALES, GEORGE W.: *Author*

Marine Hydrographic Surveys of the Coasts of the World. 63-67, *Feb. 1905*

The Compass in Modern Navigation. 266-272, *Sept. 1897*

LIVESTOCK:

Beyond Supermouse: Changing Life's Genetic Blueprint. By Robert F. Weaver. Photos by Ted Spiegel. 818-847, *Dec. 1984*

The Family Farm Ain't What It Used To Be. By James A. Sugar. 391-411, *Sept. 1974*

Domesticating the Wild and Woolly Musk Ox. By John J. Teal, Jr. Photos by Robert W. Madden. 862-879, *June 1970*

America Goes to the Fair. By Samuel W. Matthews. 293-333, *Sept. 1954*

Beltsville Brings Science to the Farm. By Samuel W. Matthews. 199-218, *Aug. 1953*

America's "Meat on the Hoof." By William H. Nicholas. 33-72, *Jan. 1952*

4-H Boys and Girls Grow More Food. By Frederick Simpich. 551-582, *Nov. 1948*

Carnival in San Antonio. By Mason Sutherland. Photos by J. Baylor Roberts. 813-844, *Dec. 1947*

Grass Makes Wyoming Fat. By Frederick Simpich. 153-188, *Aug. 1945*

Britain Fights in the Fields. By Francis A. Flood. 31-65, *July 1944*

Exploring a Grass Wonderland of Wild West China. By Ray G. Johnson. 713-742, *June 1944*

See also Cattle Raising; Goats; Hog Raising; Horses; Poultry; Sheep Raising

LIVING Casks of Honey. By Jennie E. Harris. 193-199, *Aug. 1934*

The LIVING Dead Sea. By Harvey Arden. Photos by Nathan Benn. 225-245, *Feb. 1978*

LIVING Honey Jars of the Ant World. By Ross E. Hutchins. 405-411, *Mar. 1962*

LIVING in a Japanese Village. By William Graves. Photos by James L. Stanfield. 668-693, *May 1972*

A giant "parentie," or lace lizard, is captured in central Australia in 1945.

CHARLES P. MOUNTFORD

LIVING in Harm's Way–The Persian Gulf. By Thomas J. Abercrombie. Photos by Steve Raymer. Included: Iraq, Iran, Saudi Arabia, Kuwait, Bahrain, Qatar, United Arab Emirates, Oman. 648-671, *May 1988*

LIVING in Two Worlds: The First Australians. By Belinda Wright and Stanley Breeden. 291-294, *Feb. 1988*

LIVING Iroquois Confederacy: Keepers of the Fire. By Harvey Arden. Photos by Steve Wall. 375-403, *Sept. 1987*

LIVING Jewels of the Sea. By William Crowder. Paintings by author. 290-304, *Sept. 1927*

LIVING on a Volcano: An Unspoiled Patch of Polynesia Is Niuafo'ou, Nicknamed "Tin Can Island" by Stamp Collectors. By Thomas A. Jaggar. 91-106, *July 1935*

LIVING on the Earth. Contents: How various peoples have adapted to the world's environments. 320 pages. *1988*

The LIVING Sand. By William H. Amos. 820-833, *June 1965*

The LIVING Sands of the Namib. By William J. Hamilton III. Photos by Carol and David Hughes. 364-377, *Sept. 1983*

LIVING the Good Life in Burgundy. By William Davenport. Photos by Robert Freson. 794-817, *June 1978*

LIVING Theater in New Guinea's

Highlands. By Gillian Gillison. Photos by David Gillison. 147-169, *Aug. 1983*

The LIVING White House. By Lonnelle Aikman. 593-643, *Nov. 1966*

The LIVING White House. By Lonnelle Aikman. Published in cooperation with the White House Historical Association. 151 pages. 1966; rev. ed. 1987

LIVING With Guanacos. By William L. Franklin. NGS research grant. 63-75, *July 1981*

LIVING With Thailand's Gentle Lua. By Peter Kunstadter. NGS research grant. 122-152, *July 1966*

LIVING With the Great Orange Apes: Indonesia's Orangutans. By Biruté M. F. Galdikas. Photos by Rod Brindamour. NGS research grant. 830-853, *June 1980*

LIVINGSTON, JANE:

On Assignment. *Sept. 1988*

Author

Odyssey: The Art of Photography at National Geographic. 322-351, *Sept. 1988*

LIZARDS:

Reptiles and Amphibians. 875A-875B, *Dec. 1968*

In the Wilds of a City Parlor. By Paul A. Zahl. 645-672, *Nov. 1954*

The Lure of the Changing Desert. 817-824, *June 1954*

Lonely Australia: The Unique Continent. By Herbert E. Gregory. Included: Monitor, Skink, Slow-worm. 473-568, *Dec. 1916*

Reptiles of All Lands. By Raymond L. Ditmars. Included: Black Tegu, Flying Dragon, Gecko, Gila Monster, Horned Lizard, Iguana, Malayan Kabara-Goya, Monitor, Spiny Lizard. 601-633, *July 1911*

Notes on the Remarkable Habits of Certain Turtles and Lizards. By H. A. Largelamb. Included: Glass "Snake," Mexican Horned Lizard, Pacific Horned Lizard, Plated Lizard, Regal Horned Lizard, Two-Footed Worm Lizard. 413-419, *June 1907*

See also Iguanas; Komodo Dragons

LIZARRIETA, Col de, Pyrenees Mountains, Europe:

Pigeon Netting–Sport of Basques. Photos by Irene Burdett-Scougall. 405-416, *Sept. 1949*

LJUNGSTEDT, O. A.: *Author*

The Erratic (Geologic Formation of the United States). 525-531, *June 1910*

LLAMAS:

Camels of the Clouds. By W. H. Hodge. 641-656, *May 1946*

LLANGOLLEN, Wales:

Sheep Dog Trials in Llangollen: Trained Collies Perform Marvels of Herding in the Cambrian Stakes, Open to the World. By Sarah Bloch. 559-574, *Apr. 1940*

LLOYD, ALBERT B.:

Lloyd's Journey Across the Great Pygmy Forest (Belgian Congo). 26-30, *Jan. 1899*

LLOYD, FREEMAN: *Author*

Toy Dogs, Pets of Kings and Commoners. 459-480, *Apr. 1944*

Non-sporting Dogs. Paintings by Walter A. Weber. 569-588, *Nov. 1943*

Working Dogs of the World. Paintings by Edward Herbert Miner. 776-806, *Dec. 1941*

Hark to the Hounds. Paintings by Edward Herbert Miner. 453-484, *Oct. 1937*

Field Dogs in Action. Paintings by Edward Herbert Miner. 85-108, *Jan. 1937*

Man's Oldest Ally, the Dog: Since Cave-Dweller Days This Faithful Friend Has Shared the Work, Exploration, and Sport of Humankind. Paintings by Edward Herbert Miner. 247-274, *Feb. 1936*

LLOYD, HENRY DEMAREST: *Author*

Problems of the Pacific–New Zealand. 342-352, *Sept. 1902*

LLOYD'S Journey Across the Great Pygmy Forest. 26-30, *Jan. 1899*

LOANDA, Angola. *See* Luanda

LOBOS ISLANDS, Peru:

Peru's Wealth-Producing Birds: Vast Riches in the Guano Deposits of Cormorants, Pelicans, and Petrels which Nest on Her Barren, Rainless Coast. By R. E. Coker. 537-566, *June 1920*

LOBSTERS:

Maine's Working Coast. By David Jeffery. Photos by Kevin Fleming. 208-241, *Feb. 1985*

The American Lobster, Delectable Cannibal. By Luis Marden. Photos by David Doubilet. 462-487, *Apr. 1973*

Martha's Vineyard. By William P. E. Graves. Photos by James P. Blair. 778-809, *June 1961*

Maine's Lobster Island, Monhegan. By William P. E. Graves. Photos by Kosti Ruohomaa. 285-298, *Feb. 1959*

The Maine American and the American Lobster. By John D. Lucas. 523-543, *Apr. 1946*

See also Spiny Lobsters

LOCATION of the Boundary Between Nicaragua and Costa Rica. By Arthur P. Davis. 22-28, *Jan. 1901*

LOCH NESS, Scotland:

Loch Ness: The Lake and the Legend. By William S. Ellis. Photos by Emory Kristof and David Doubilet. 759-779, *June 1977*

LOCKE, JUSTIN:

Author-Photographer

Lost Kingdom in Indian Mexico. 517-546, *Oct. 1952*

Photographer

High Road in the Pyrenees. By H. V. Morton. 299-334, *Mar. 1956*

Grand Canyon: Nature's Story of

Creation. By Louis Schellbach. 589-629, *May 1955*

Shooting Rapids in Dinosaur Country. By Jack Breed. Photos by author and Justin Locke. 363-390, *Mar. 1954*

Life in the Land of the Basques. By John E. H. Nolan. 147-186, *Feb. 1954*

Amid the Mighty Walls of Zion. By Lewis F. Clark. 37-70, *Jan. 1954*

New Orleans: Jambalaya on the Levee. By Harnett T. Kane. 143-184, *Feb. 1953*

Paris, Home Town of the World. By Donald William Dresden. 767-804, *June 1952*

Mexico's Booming Capital. By Mason Sutherland. 785-824, *Dec. 1951*

Growing Pains Beset Puerto Rico. By William H. Nicholas. 419-460, *Apr. 1951*

Miami's Expanding Horizons. By William H. Nicholas. 561-594, *Nov. 1950*

Vizcaya: An Italian Palazzo in Miami. By William H. Nicholas. 595-604, *Nov. 1950*

So Much Happens Along the Ohio River. By Frederick Simpich. 177-212, *Feb. 1950*

Adobe New Mexico. By Mason Sutherland. 783-830, *Dec. 1949*

Appalachian Valley Pilgrimage. By Catherine Bell Palmer. 1-32, *July 1949*

The Smithsonian Institution. By Thomas R. Henry. 325-348, *Sept. 1948*

LOCKLEY, R. M.: *Author*

The Solemn, Sociable Puffins. 414-422, *Sept. 1954*

Author-Photographer

We Live Alone, and Like It–On an

Presiding over an annual ritual that dates back several centuries, Britain's Elizabeth II formally opens Parliament in London in November 1985.   ADAM WOOLFITT

■■ **BOOKS** ✦ **MAPS** ■ **TELEVISION**

Island (Skokholm). Photos by author and H. Morrey Salmon. 252-278, *Aug. 1938*

LOCKWOOD, C. C.:
Nomination Page. *Sept. 1979*
Photographer
Mississippi Delta: The Land of the River. By Douglas Lee. 226-253, *Aug. 1983*
Mississippi's Grand Reunion at the Neshoba County Fair. By Carolyn Bennett Patterson. 854-866, *June 1980*
Trouble in Bayou Country: Louisiana's Atchafalaya. By Jack and Anne Rudloe. 377-397, *Sept. 1979*

LOCUSTS:
Locusts: "Teeth of the Wind." By Robert A. M. Conley. Photos by Gianni Tortoli. 202-227, *Aug. 1969*
Report from the Locust Wars. By Tony and Dickey Chapelle. 545-562, *Apr. 1953*
Jerusalem's Locust Plague: Being a Description of the Recent Locust Influx into Palestine, and Comparing Same with Ancient Locust Invasions as Narrated in the Old World's History Book, the Bible. By John D. Whiting. 511-550, *Dec. 1915*
Here and There in Northern Africa. By Frank Edward Johnson. 1-132, *Jan. 1914*
Life in the Great Desert of Central Asia. By Ellsworth Huntington. 749-760, *Aug. 1909*

LOCUSTS, Seventeen-year:
Rip Van Winkle of the Underground (Periodical Cicada). By Kenneth F. Weaver. 133-142, *July 1953*

LODORE CANYON, Colorado:
Experiences in the Grand Canyon. By Ellsworth and Emery Kolb. 99-184, *Aug. 1914*

LOFOTEN (Islands), Norway:
Fishing in the Lofotens. Photos by Lennart Nilsson. 377-388, *Mar. 1947*

LOGAN, Mount, Canada:
The Conquest of Mount Logan: North America's Second Highest Peak Yields to the Intrepid Attack of Canadian Climbers. By H. F. Lambart. 597-631, *June 1926*

LOGGING. *See* Lumber Industry

LOI TRIBESPEOPLE:
Among the Big Knot Lois of Hainan: Wild Tribesmen With Topknots Roam the Little-known Interior of This Big and Strategically Important Island in the China Sea. By Leonard Clark. 391-418, *Sept. 1938*

LOIRE RIVER AND VALLEY, France:
■■*Excursion to Enchantment: A Journey to the World's Most Beautiful Places.* Included: East Africa, Loire Valley, Bhutan, Chile-Argentina Lake District, Alaska's Inside Passage, and the Caribbean. 200 pages. *1988*
River of Counts and Kings: The Loire. By Kenneth MacLeish. Photos by

Dean Conger. 822-869, *June 1966*
Château Land–France's Pageant on the Loire. 466-475, *Oct. 1930*

LOJA, Ecuador:
Over Trail and Through Jungle in Ecuador: Indian Head-Hunters of the Interior, an Interesting Study in the South American Republic. By H. E. Anthony. 327-352, *Oct. 1921*

LOLO TRIBESPEOPLE:
Adventures in Lololand. By Rennold L. Lowy. 105-118, *Jan. 1947*

LOMBARDY (Region), Italy:
Lombardy's Lakes, Blue Jewels in Italy's Crown. By Franc Shor. Photos by Joseph J. Scherschel. 58-99, *July 1968*
Inexhaustible Italy. By Arthur Stanley Riggs. 273-368, *Oct. 1916*

LOMEN, CARL J.: *Author.*
The Camel of the Frozen Desert (Reindeer). Photos by the Lomen brothers. 539-556, *Dec. 1919*

LOMPOC VALLEY, California:
The Flower Seed Growers: Gardening's Color Merchants. By Robert de Roos. Photos by Jack Fields. 720-738, *May 1968*

LONDON, England:
Westminster, the Palace That Became Parliament. By Patrick Cormack. Photos by Adam Woolfitt. Included: Royal Pomp Before Debate: In Centuries-old Ceremonial, the Queen Opens Parliament. 728-757, *Dec. 1986*
The Thames: That Noble River. By Ethel A. Starbird. Photos by O. Louis Mazzatenta. 750-791, *June 1983*
■ The Thames. cover, *Apr. 1982*
Two Englands. By Allan C. Fisher, Jr. Photos by Cary Wolinsky. 442-481, *Oct. 1979*
Benjamin Franklin, Philosopher of Dissent. By Alice J. Hall. Photos by Linda Bartlett. 93-123, *July 1975*
The England of Charles Dickens. By Richard W. Long. Photos by Adam Woolfitt. 443-483, *Apr. 1974*
Chelsea, London's Haven of Individualists. By James Cerruti. Photos by Adam Woolfitt. 28-55, *Jan. 1972*
The World of Elizabeth I. By Louis B. Wright. Photos by Ted Spiegel. 668-709, *Nov. 1968*
One Man's London. By Allan C. Fisher, Jr. Photos by James P. Blair. 743-791, *June 1966*
"Be Ye Men of Valour" (Churchill's Life; Funeral). By Howard La Fay. 159-197, *Aug. 1965*
The Final Tribute. Text by Carolyn Bennett Patterson. Contents: Churchill's funeral. 199-225, *Aug. 1965*
The Britain That Shakespeare Knew. By Louis B. Wright. Photos by Dean Conger. 613-665, *May 1964*
Queen Elizabeth Opens Parliament. By W. E. Roscher. Photos by Robert B. Goodman. 699-707, *Nov. 1961*
"The City"–London's Storied Square Mile. By Allan C. Fisher, Jr. 735-777, *June 1961*

The Thames Mirrors England's Varied Life. By Willard Price. Photos by Robert F. Sisson. 45-93, *July 1958*
Landmarks of Literary England. By Leo A. Borah. Photos by Kathleen Revis. 295-350, *Sept. 1955*
In the London of the New Queen. By H. V. Morton. 291-342, *Sept. 1953*
London's Zoo of Zoos. By Thomas Garner James. 771-786, *June 1953*
Founders of New England. By Sir Evelyn Wrench. Photos by B. Anthony Stewart. 803-838, *June 1953*
"Around the World in Eighty Days." By Newman Bumstead. 705-750, *Dec. 1951*
A Stroll to London. By Isobel Wylie Hutchison. Photos by B. Anthony Stewart. 171-204, *Aug. 1950*
The British Way. By Sir Evelyn Wrench. 421-541, *Apr. 1949*
Founders of Virginia. By Sir Evelyn Wrench. Photos by B. Anthony Stewart. 433-462, *Apr. 1948*
Keeping House in London. By Frances James. 769-792, *Dec. 1947*
Yanks at Westminster. By Leonard David Gaumans. 223-252, *Aug. 1946*
London Wins the Battle. By Marquis W. Childs. 129-152, *Aug. 1945*
When GI Joes Took London. By Frederick Simpich, Jr. 337-354, *Sept. 1944*
Everyday Life in Wartime England. By Harvey Klemmer. 497-534, *Apr. 1941*
Along London's Coronation Route. By Maynard Owen Williams. 609-632, *May 1937*
As London Toils and Spins. By Frederick Simpich. 1-57, *Jan. 1937*
Shadowy London by Night. Photos by H. B. Burdekin. 177-184, *Aug. 1935*
Vagabonding in England: A Young American Works His Way Around the British Isles. By John McWilliams. 357-398, *Mar. 1934*
Some Forgotten Corners of London: Many Places of Beauty and Historic Interest Repay the Search of the Inquiring Visitor. By Harold Donaldson Eberlein. 163-198, *Feb. 1932*
Highlights of London Town. Photos by Clifton Adams. 569-576, *May 1929*
London from a Bus Top. By Herbert Corey. 551-596, *May 1926*
Black-Headed Gulls in London. By A. H. Hall. 664-672, *June 1925*
London. By Florence Craig Albrecht. 263-294, *Sept. 1915*
See also Kew Gardens; Royal Academy of Arts

The **"LONE"** Coyote Likes Family Life. By Hope Ryden. Photos by author and David Hiser. 278-294, *Aug. 1974*

LONE Sailor Completes His Globe-girdling Voyage. By Robin Lee Graham. 504-545, *Oct. 1970*

LONELY Australia: The Unique Continent. By Herbert E. Gregory. 473-568, *Dec. 1916*

LONELY Cape Hatteras, Besieged by the Sea. By William S. Ellis. Photos by Emory Kristof. 393-421, *Sept. 1969*

Stepping out in formation, Grenadier Guards passing St. James's Palace in London inspire a pint-size imitator. STEVE RAYMER, NGS

Abstract expressionist Willem de Kooning finds inspiration on Long Island, haven for many artists and writers.   SAM ABELL

LOOK What's Happened to Honolulu! By Jim Becker. Photos by Bates Littlehales. 500-531, *Oct. 1969*

LOOKING Down on Europe: The Thrills and Advantages of Sight-seeing by Airplane, as Demonstrated on a 6,500-mile Tour Over Commercial Aviation Routes. By J. Parker Van Zandt. 261-326, *Mar. 1925*

LOOKING Down on Europe Again: Crisscrossing Air Tracks Reveal Nature's Scenic Masterpieces and Man's Swift-changing Boundaries and Structures. By J. Parker Van Zandt. 791-822, *June 1939*

LOOKING in on New Turkey. Included: Looking in on the Everyday Life of New Turkey. Photos by Herman H. Kreider, Maynard Owen Williams, Gervais Courtellemont. 499-508, *Apr. 1932*

LOONEY, RALPH: *Author*

The Navajos. Photos by Bruce Dale. 740-781, *Dec. 1972*

LOONS:

Birds of Timberline and Tundra. By Arthur A. Allen. 313-339, *Sept. 1946*

Birds That Cruise the Coast and Inland Waters. By T. Gilbert Pearson. Paintings by Allan Brooks. 299-328, *Mar. 1934*

LOOTERS Rob Graves and History. By Ian Graham. Photos by George F. Mobley. 452-461, *Apr. 1986*

LOP BASIN, Xinjiang Autonomous Region, China:

Medieval Tales of the Lop Basin in Central Asia. By Ellsworth Huntington. 289-295, *Apr. 1908*

LOPEZ, BARRY: *Author*

California Desert, A Worldly Wilderness. Photos by Craig Aurness. 42-77, *Jan. 1987*

LORD, NANCY: *Photographer*

Jericho Gives Up Its Secrets. By Kathleen M. Kenyon and A. Douglas Tushingham. 853-870, *Dec. 1953*

LORD HOWE (Island), Tasman Sea:

The Paradise of the Tasman: A Pacific Island Provides the Palms Which Decorate Hotels, Churches, Steamships, and Homes. By Hubert Lyman Clark. 115-136, *July 1935*

LORD HOWE GROUP. *See* Ontong Java

LORD of the Shallows–The Great Blue Heron. By Richard J. Dolesh. Photos by Cameron Davidson. 540-554, *Apr. 1984*

LORDS of the Rockies: Photographing Big Game Animals in Their Primeval Surroundings, from Arizona to Canada, Brings Adventure to Two Wilderness Wanderers. By Wendell and Lucie Chapman. 87-128, *July 1939*

LORIAN SWAMP, Kenya:

When a Drought Blights Africa: Hippos and Elephants Are Driven Insane by Suffering, in the Lorian Swamp, Kenya Colony. By A. T. Curle. 521-528, *Apr. 1929*

LORIKEETS:

Honey Eaters of Currumbin. By Paul A. Zahl. 510-519, *Oct. 1956*

LORRAINE (Region), France:

A City Learns to Smile Again (Nancy). By Frederick G. Vosburgh. 361-384, *Mar. 1945*

In French Lorraine: That Part of France Where the First American Soldiers Have Fallen. By Harriet Chalmers Adams. 499-518, *Nov.-Dec. 1917*

LOS ALAMOS, New Mexico:

Adobe New Mexico. By Mason Sutherland. Photos by Justin Locke. 783-830, *Dec. 1949*

LOS ALAMOS SCIENTIFIC LABORATORY, New Mexico:

The Search for Tomorrow's Power. By Kenneth F. Weaver. Photos by Emory Kristof. 650-681, *Nov. 1972*

LOS ANGELES, California:

The Mexican Americans: A People on the Move. By Griffin Smith, Jr. Photos by Stephanie Maze. 780-809, *June 1980*

Los Angeles: City in Search of Itself. By William S. Ellis. Photos by Jodi Cobb. 26-59, *Jan. 1979*

Southern California's Trial by Mud and Water. By Nathaniel T. Kenney. Photos by Bruce Dale. 552-573, *Oct. 1969*

California, the Golden Magnet. 595-679. I. The South. By William

Heads-up coaching earns Monty Basgall a playful kiss from Los Angeles catcher Steve Yeager in 1978. JODI COBB, NGS

Graves. Photos by Thomas Nebbia.
595-639, *May 1966*
Los Angeles, City of the Angels. By
Robert de Roos. Photos by Thomas
Nebbia. 451-501, *Oct. 1962*
New Rush to Golden California. By
George W. Long. 723-802, *June 1954*
Southern California at Work. By Frederick Simpich. 529-600, *Nov. 1934*
See also Los Angeles Aqueduct

LOS ANGELES AQUEDUCT:

The Troubled Waters of Mono Lake.
By Gordon Young. Photos by Craig
Aurness. 504-519, *Oct. 1981*
California's Parched Oasis, the Owens
Valley. By Judith and Neil Morgan.
Photos by Jodi Cobb and Galen
Rowell. 98-127, *Jan. 1976*
Carrying Water Through a Desert: The
Story of the Los Angeles Aqueduct.
By Burt A. Heinly. 568-596,
July 1910

LOS ANGELES BASIN, California:

Southern California's Trial by Mud and
Water. By Nathaniel T. Kenney.
Photos by Bruce Dale. 552-573,
Oct. 1969

LOSS of Life by Lightning. 115,
Mar. 1902

LOSS of Property from Lightning. 82,
Feb. 1901

The **LOST** Boundary of Texas. By Marcus Baker. 430-432, *Dec. 1901*

LOST City of the Maya. By Richard
E. W. Adams. Photos by George F.
Mobley. Included: Realm of the
Maya (map). 420-451, *Apr. 1986*

LOST COLONY. *See* Roanoke Island,
North Carolina

The **LOST** Empire of the Incas. By
Loren McIntyre. Art by Ned and Rosalie Seidler. 729-787, *Dec. 1973*

***LOST** Empires, Living Tribes.* 402
▇▇ pages. *1982*

The **LOST** Fleet of Kublai Khan. By
Torao Mozai. Photos by Koji Nakamura. Paintings by Issho Yada. 634-649, *Nov. 1982*

LOST Kingdom in Indian Mexico. By
Justin Locke. 517-546, *Oct. 1952*

LOST Outpost of the Egyptian Empire.
By Trude Dothan. Photos by Sisse
Brimberg. Paintings by Lloyd K.
Townsend. NGS research grant. 739-769, *Dec. 1982*

LOST Ship Waits Under Arctic Ice. By
Joseph B. MacInnis. Photos by
Emory Kristof. 104A-104D,
July 1983

The **LOST SIERRA,** California:

Golden Ghosts of the Lost Sierra. By
Robert Laxalt. Photos by David
Hiser. 332-353, *Sept. 1973*

The **LOST** Wealth of the Kings of Midas. By Ellsworth Huntington. 831-846, *Oct. 1910*

*The elephant-riding army of India's King Porus falls in 326 B.C. at the Jhelum River,
giving Alexander the Great's weary army its last victory.* PAINTING BY TOM LOVELL

LOST World of the Galapagos. By
Irving and Electa Johnson. 681-703,
May 1959

LOSTWOOD WILDLIFE REFUGE,
North Dakota:

Island, Prairie, Marsh, and Shore. By
Charlton Ogburn. Photos by Bates
Littlehales. 350-381, *Mar. 1979*

A **LOT** of Trouble and a Few Triumphs:
North American Waterfowl. By John
Madson. 562-599, *Nov. 1984*

LOTHERS, JOHN:
Nomination Page. *May 1961*

LOTUKA TRIBESPEOPLE:

South in the Sudan. By Harry Hoogstraal. 249-272, *Feb. 1953*

LOUDEN, ORREN R.: *Photographer*

Springtime Wreathes a Garland for the
Nation's Capital. 473-480, *Apr. 1935*
Our Colorful City of Magnificent Distances. 531-610, *Nov. 1931*
The Color Camera Explores the Country That Moves by Night. 479-510,
Oct. 1931
The Most Famous Battle Field in America. 66-75, *July 1931*
Secrets of Washington's Lure. 377-384,
Mar. 1930

LOUDER, MAX:

North With the Wheat Cutters. By Noel
Grove. Photos by James A. Sugar.
194-217, *Aug. 1972*

LOUGHEED, R. E.: *Artist*

Dogs Work for Man. By Edward J.
Linehan. Paintings by Edwin Megargee and R. E. Lougheed. 190-233,
Aug. 1958

LOUISBOURG (Fortress), Nova Scotia, Canada:

Nova Scotia, the Magnificent Anchorage. By Charles McCarry. Photos by
Gordon W. Gahan. 334-363,
Mar. 1975
The St. Lawrence, River Key to Canada. By Howard La Fay. Photos by
John Launois. 622-667, *May 1967*

LOUISE, Lake, Canada:

Canadian Rockies, Lords of a Beckoning Land. By Alan Phillips. Photos by
James L. Stanfield. 353-393,
Sept. 1966

LOUISIADE ARCHIPELAGO, Papua
New Guinea:

Adventures with the Survey Navy. By
Irving Johnson. 131-148, *July 1947*

LOUISIANA:

Trouble in Bayou Country: Louisiana's
Atchafalaya. By Jack and Anne Rudloe. Photos by C. C. Lockwood. 377-397, *Sept. 1979*
A Walk Across America: Part II. By Peter and Barbara Jenkins. 194-229,
Aug. 1979
The Gulf's Workaday Waterway. By

Gordon Young. Photos by Charles O'Rear. 200-223, *Feb. 1978*

New Orleans and Her River. By Joseph Judge. Photos by James L. Stanfield. 151-187, *Feb. 1971*

Cajunland, Louisiana's French-speaking Coast. By Bern Keating. Photos by Charles Harbutt and Franke Keating. 353-391, *Mar. 1966*

The Lower Mississippi. By Willard Price. Photos by W. D. Vaughn. 681-725, *Nov. 1960*

Mardi Gras in New Orleans. By Carolyn Bennett Patterson. Photos by Robert F. Sisson and John E. Fletcher. 726-732, *Nov. 1960*

Land of Louisiana Sugar Kings. By Harnett T. Kane. Photos by Willard R. Culver. 531-567, *Apr. 1958*

New Orleans: Jambalaya on the Levee. By Harnett T. Kane. Photos by Justin Locke. 143-184, *Feb. 1953*

Skyway Below the Clouds. By Carl R. Markwith. Photos by Ernest J. Cottrell. Included: Monroe; Shreveport; Shreveport Municipal Airport. 85-108, *July 1949*

Louisiana Trades with the World. By Frederick Simpich. Photos by J. Baylor Roberts. 705-738, *Dec. 1947*

The Delectable Shrimp: Once a Culinary Stepchild, Today a Gulf Coast Industry. By Harlan Major. 501-512, *Oct. 1944*

How We Use the Gulf of Mexico. By Frederick Simpich. 1-40, *Jan. 1944*

Louisiana, Land of Perpetual Romance. By Ralph A. Graves. 393-482, *Apr. 1930*

⊕ *Louisiana. Apr. 1930*

The Great Mississippi Flood of 1927: Since White Man's Discovery This Mighty River Has Served Him Well, Yet It Has Brought Widespread Devastation Along Its Lower Reaches. By Frederick Simpich. 243-289, *Sept. 1927*

The Delta of the Mississippi River. By E. L. Corthell. 351-354, *Dec. 1897*

See also Mississippi River Delta

LOUISIANA PURCHASE:

Boundaries of Territorial Acquisitions. 373-377, *Oct. 1901*

LOUSMA, JACK R.:

Skylab, Outpost on the Frontier of Space. By Thomas Y. Canby. Photos by the nine mission astronauts. 441-469, *Oct. 1974*

The **LOUVRE,** Paris:

The Louvre, France's Palace of the Arts. By Hereward Lester Cooke, Jr. 796-831, *June 1971*

LOVE TERNS. *See* Fairy Terns

LOVELL, JAMES A., Jr.:

Hubbard Medal recipient. 861, *June 1970*

"A Most Fantastic Voyage": The Story of Apollo 8's Rendezvous With the Moon. By Sam C. Phillips. 593-631, *May 1969*

Space Rendezvous, Milestone on the Way to the Moon. By Kenneth F. Weaver. 539-553, *Apr. 1966*

LOVELL, TOM: *Artist*

In the Footsteps of Alexander the Great. By Helen and Frank Schreider. 1-65, *Jan. 1968*

LOVINS, AMORY B.:

What Six Experts Say. 70-73, *Special Report on Energy. (Feb. 1981)*

LOW COUNTRIES, Europe:

⊕ *France, Belgium, and the Netherlands,* Atlas series. *June 1960*

Low Countries Await Liberation (Belgium and The Netherlands). 221-228, *Aug. 1944*

See also Belgium; Luxembourg; The Netherlands

LOW Road, High Road, Around Dundee. By Maurice P. Dunlap. 547-576, *Apr. 1936*

LOWDERMILK, WALTER C.:
Author-Photographer

China Fights Erosion with U. S. Aid. 641-680, *June 1945*

LOWE, GEORGE: *Photographer*

The Crossing of Antarctica. By Sir Vivian Fuchs. 25-47, *Jan. 1959*

Triumph on Everest. 1-63. I. Siege and Assault. By Sir John Hunt. 1-43; II. The Conquest of the Summit. By Sir Edmund Hillary. 45-63, *July 1954*

LOWELL, JAMES RUSSELL:

Literary Landmarks of Massachusetts. By William H. Nicholas. Photos by B. Anthony Stewart and John E. Fletcher. 279-310, *Mar. 1950*

LOWELL, Massachusetts:

The Merrimack: River of Industry and Romance. By Albert W. Atwood. Photos by B. Anthony Stewart. 106-140, *Jan. 1951*

LOWELL OBSERVATORY, Arizona: Expedition:

New Light on the Changing Face of Mars. By E. C. Slipher. NGS research grant. 427-436, *Sept. 1955*

LOWER CALIFORNIA. *See* Baja California

The **LOWER** Keys, Florida's "Out Islands." By John Scofield. Photos by Emory Kristof and Bates Littlehales. 72-93, *Jan. 1971*

The **LOWER** Mississippi. By Willard Price. Photos by W. D. Vaughn. 681-725, *Nov. 1960*

LOWER SLAUGHTER, England:

By Cotswold Lanes to Wold's End. By Melville Bell Grosvenor. 615-654, *May 1948*

LOWER SOURIS NATIONAL WILDLIFE REFUGE, North Dakota:

Duck Hunting with a Color Camera. By Arthur A. Allen. 514-539, *Oct. 1951*

LOWEST Point in the United States. 824-825, *Dec. 1907*

LOWMAN, PAUL D., Jr.: *Author*

The Earth From Orbit. 645-671, *Nov. 1966*

LOWREY, PERRY:

Jungle Journey to the World's Highest Waterfall. By Ruth Robertson. 655-690, *Nov. 1949*

LOWY, RENNOLD L.:
Author-Photographer

Adventures in Lololand. 105-118, *Jan. 1947*

The **LOYALISTS:** Americans With a Difference. By Kent Britt. Photos by Ted Spiegel. 510-539, *Apr. 1975*

LUALABA (River), Zaire:

Transporting a Navy Through the Jungles of Africa in War Time. By Frank J. Magee. 331-362, *Oct. 1922*

LUANDA, Angola:

Angola, the Last Foothold of Slavery. 625-630, *July 1910*

LUAS:

Living With Thailand's Gentle Lua. By Peter Kunstadter. NGS research grant. 122-152, *July 1966*

LUBUMBASHI, Zaire. *See former* name, Elisabethville, Democratic Republic of the Congo

LUCAS, JOHN D.: *Author*

The Maine American and the American Lobster. Photos by John E. Fletcher. 523-543, *Apr. 1946*

LUCERNE, Switzerland:

Switzerland Guards the Roof of Europe. By William H. Nicholas. Photos by Willard R. Culver. 205-246, *Aug. 1950*

LUCIA GLACIER, Alaska:

The National Geographic Society's Alaskan Expedition of 1909. By Ralph S. Tarr and Lawrence Martin. 1-54, *Jan. 1910*

LÜDA (Dairen), Liaoning Province, China:

Japan Faces Russia in Manchuria. By Willard Price. 603-634, *Nov. 1942*

Mukden, the Manchu Home, and Its Great Art Museum. By Eliza Ruhamah Scidmore. 289-320, *Apr. 1910*

Building of Dalny. 360, *Sept. 1903*

LUDWIG, DANIEL KEITH:

Jari: A Billion-dollar Gamble. By Loren McIntyre. Contents: Daniel K. Ludwig's paper-pulp and food-production enterprise in Brazil's Amazon Basin. 686-711, *May 1980*

Brazil's Wild Frontier. By Loren McIntyre. Included: Daniel K. Ludwig's three-million acre agricultural and forestry enterprise. 684-719, *Nov. 1977*

Amazon–The River Sea. By Loren McIntyre. Included: Daniel K. Ludwig's planned paper-pulp and food-production enterprise in Brazil's Amazon basin. 456-495, *Oct. 1972*

LUGANO, Lake, Italy-Switzerland:

Frontier Cities of Italy. By Florence Craig Albrecht. 533-586, *June 1915*

Gems of the Italian Lakes. By Arthur Ellis Mayer. 943-956, *Aug. 1913*

Free-floating logs are corralled at Coos Bay, Oregon, one of the world's largest ports for forest products. COTTON COULSON

On the Alleged Observation of a Lunar Eclipse by Bering in 1728-9. By Marcus Baker. 167-169, *May 1890*

LUNAR ORBITERS (Satellites):
Awesome Views of the Forbidding Moonscape. Contents: Photos by Lunar Orbiter 2, 4, 5. 233-239, *Feb. 1969*

LUNAR RESEARCH:
What the Moon Rocks Tell Us. By Kenneth F. Weaver. Included: Lunar Receiving Laboratory at the Manned Spacecraft Center in Houston, Texas. 788-791, *Dec. 1969*
And Now to Touch the Moon's Forbidding Face. By Kenneth F. Weaver. 633-635, *May 1969*
Awesome Views of the Forbidding Moonscape. Contents: Photos by Lunar Orbiter 2, 4, 5. 233-239, *Feb. 1969*
See also Apollo Missions; Ranger Spacecraft; Surveyor Spacecraft; *and* Moon

LUNAR ROVER. *See* Rover (Lunar Vehicle)

LUNDY (Island), England:
Lundy, Treasure Island of Birds. By P. T. Etherton. Photos by J. Allan Cash. 675-698, *May 1947*

LUNÉVILLE, France:
In French Lorraine: That Part of France Where the First American Soldiers Have Fallen. By Harriet Chalmers Adams. 499-518, *Nov.-Dec. 1917*

LUPE, RONNIE:
The White Mountain Apache. Included: Coming of Age the Apache Way. By Nita Quintero. Photos by Bill Hess; Seeking the Best of Two Worlds. By Bill Hess. 260-290, *Feb. 1980*
Author
At Peace With the Past, In Step With the Future. 260-261, *Feb. 1980*

LUQUE, MICHAEL H.:
Author-Photographer
Among Alaska's Brown Bears. By Allan L. Egbert and Michael H. Luque. 428-442, *Sept. 1975*

LURAY CAVERNS, Virginia:
The Skeleton in Luray Cave. By H. C. Hovey. 425-426, *July 1906*
The Luray Caverns. 358-362, *June 1906*

The **LURE** of Lima, City of the Kings. By William Joseph Showalter. 727-784, *June 1930*

The **LURE** of the Changing Desert. 817-824, *June 1954*

The **LURE** of the Frozen Desert. Panorama. *Dec. 1912*

The **LURE** of the Land of Ice. 255-270, *Mar. 1924*

LURING Deep-sea Life. By Eugenie Clark and Emory Kristof as reported to Douglas Lee. NGS research grant. 681-691, *Nov. 1986*

LURS:
Mountain Tribes of Iran and Iraq. By Harold Lamb. 385-408, *Mar. 1946*

The **LUSTER** of Ancient Mexico. By William H. Prescott. 1-32, *July 1916*

LUTHER, MARTIN:
The World of Martin Luther. By Merle Severy. Photos by James L. Amos. 418-463, *Oct. 1983*

LÜTKEN, EMIL: *Photographer*
The Shy and Spectacular Kingfisher. Photos by Carl-Johan Junge and Emil Lütken. 413-419, *Sept. 1974*

LUXEMBOURG:
Luxembourg, the Quiet Fortress. By Robert Leslie Conly. Photos by Ted H. Funk. 69-97, *July 1970*
Luxembourg, Survivor of Invasions. By Sydney Clark. Photos by Maynard Owen Williams. 791-810, *June 1948*
The Grand Duchy of Luxemburg: A Miniature Democratic State of Many Charms Against a Feudal Background. By Maynard Owen Williams. 501-528, *Nov. 1924*

LUXOR, Egypt:
The Resurrection of Ancient Egypt. By James Baikie. 957-1020, *Sept. 1913*

LUZ, HORST: *Photographer*
Proud Primitives, the Nuba People. By Oskar Luz. 673-699, *Nov. 1966*

LUZ, OSKAR: *Author*
Proud Primitives, the Nuba People. Photos by Horst Luz. 673-699, *Nov. 1966*

LUZON (Island), Philippines:
What Luzon Means to Uncle Sam. By Frederick Simpich. 305-332, *Mar. 1945*
Camera Cruising in the Philippines. Photos by J. Baylor Roberts, Fenno Jacobs, and others. 545-552, *Nov. 1944*

Logger Charles Charleston rests from wielding ax and saw in a redwood forest in northern California.   DEWITT JONES

The Non-Christian Peoples of the Philippine Islands. By Dean C. Worcester. 1157-1256, *Nov. 1913*
Head-Hunters of Northern Luzon. By Dean C. Worcester. 833-930, *Sept. 1912*
Taal Volcano and Its Recent Destructive Eruption. By Dean C. Worcester. 313-367, *Apr. 1912*
Field Sports Among the Wild Men of Northern Luzon. By Dean C. Worcester. 215-267, *Mar. 1911*

LYNDON B. JOHNSON SPACE CENTER, Houston, Texas. *See* former name, Manned Spacecraft Center

LYON, ERNEST: *Author*
The Black Republic–Liberia. By Sir Harry Johnston and Ernest Lyon. 334-343, *May 1907*

LYON, EUGENE: *Author*
15th-Century Manuscript Yields First Look at *Niña.* 601-605, *Nov. 1986*
Treasure From the Ghost Galleon: *Santa Margarita.* Photos by Don Kincaid. 228-243, *Feb. 1982*
Atocha, Tragic Treasure Galleon of the Florida Keys. 787-809, *June 1976*

LYREBIRD, Australia's Meistersinger. By L. H. Smith. 849-857, *June 1955*

The **LYRIC** Land of Wales. By Bryan Hodgson. Photos by Farrell Grehan. 36-63, *July 1983*

LYTTELTON, New Zealand:
Sailing the Seven Seas in the Interest of Science: Adventures Through 157,000 Miles of Storm and Calm, from Arctic to Antarctic and Around the World, in the Non-magnetic Yacht "Carnegie." By J. P. Ault. 631-690, *Dec. 1922*

M
N

Etta Spencer and great-grandson Chad O'Neal visit in Ocracoke on North Carolina's Outer Banks.

DAVID ALAN HARVEY

A dog tag of missing-in-action Capt. Richard Castillo of the U.S. Air Force was uncovered in Laos in 1986. SENY NORASINGH

MIAs:

Laos Today. By Peter T. White. Photos by Seny Norasingh. Included: Map of plane-crash sites. 772-795, *June 1987*
Missing in Action, 1972–U. S. Plane Found in Laos. By Peter T. White. Photos by Seny Norasingh. 692-696, *Nov. 1986*

MRI (Magnetic Resonance Imaging):

Medicine's New Vision. By Howard Sochurek. Paintings by Davis Meltzer. Illustrations text by Peter Miller. 2-41, *Jan. 1987*

MACAO (Macau):

China's Opening Door. By John J. Putman. Photos by H. Edward Kim. Included: Zhuhai Special Economic Zone, adjoining Macau. 64-83, *July 1983*
Macao Clings to the Bamboo Curtain. By Jules B. Billard. Photos by Joseph J. Scherschel. 521-539, *Apr. 1969*
Macau, a Hole in the Bamboo Curtain. By George W. Long. Photos by J. Baylor Roberts. 679-688, *May 1953*
Eyes on the China Coast. By George W. Long. 505-512, *Apr. 1953*
"Land of Sweet Sadness": The Oldest European Settlement in the Far East, Long the Only Haven for Distressed Mariners in the China Sea. By Edgar Allen Forbes. 337-357, *Sept. 1932*

MacARTHUR, DOUGLAS:

Japan Tries Freedom's Road. By Frederick G. Vosburgh. Photos by J. Baylor Roberts. 593-632, *May 1950*

MacASKILL, W. R.: *Photographer*

Tartan Tints New Scotland (Nova Scotia). Photos by John Mills, Jr., W. R. MacAskill, and others. 591-622, *May 1940*

MACAULAY, T. B.: *Author*

How Canada Went to the Front. 297-307, *Oct. 1918*

McBAIN, DONALD: *Photographer*

The Wild Animals in My Life. By William M. Mann. 497-524, *Apr. 1957*
Williamsburg: Its College and Its Cinderella City. By Beverley M. Bowie. 439-486, *Oct. 1954*
Beltsville Brings Science to the Farm. By Samuel W. Matthews. 199-218, *Aug. 1953*
Stately Homes of Old Virginia. By Albert W. Atwood. 787-802, *June 1953*

MACBETH, JAMES B:

Nomination Page. *Mar. 1963*

McBRIDE, HARRY A.: *Author*

Masterpieces on Tour. 717-750, *Dec. 1948*
Pursuing Spanish Bypaths Northwest of Madrid. 121-130, *Jan. 1931*
On the Bypaths of Spain. 311-364, *Mar. 1929*
From Granada to Gibraltar–A Tour of Southern Spain. 205-232, *Aug. 1924*
The Land of the Free in Africa. 411-430, *Oct. 1922*
The Land of the Basques: Home of a Thrifty, Picturesque People, Who Take Pride in the Sobriquet, "The Yankees of Spain." 63-87, *Jan. 1922*

McBRIDE, RUTH Q.: *Author*

Old Masters in a New National Gallery. 1-50, *July 1940*
Keeping House on the Congo. 643-670, *Nov. 1937*
Turbulent Spain. 397-427, *Oct. 1936*

McCANDLESS, BYRON: *Author*

The Story of the American Flag. By Byron McCandless and Gilbert Grosvenor. 286-303, *Oct. 1917*
The Flags of Our Army, Navy, and Government Departments. By Byron McCandless and Gilbert Grosvenor. 305-322, *Oct. 1917*
Our State Flags. By Byron McCandless and Gilbert Grosvenor. 325-341, *Oct. 1917*
Flags Famous in American History. By Byron McCandless and Gilbert Grosvenor. 341-361, *Oct. 1917*
The Flags of Pan-America. By Byron McCandless and Gilbert Grosvenor. 361-369, *Oct. 1917*
The Naval Flags of the World. By Byron McCandless and Gilbert Grosvenor. 369, *Oct. 1917*
The Flags of Europe, Asia, and Africa. By Byron McCandless and Gilbert Grosvenor. 372-378, *Oct. 1917*
The Flags of the British Empire. By Byron McCandless and Gilbert Grosvenor. 378-385, *Oct. 1917*
Flags of Austria-Hungary, Bulgaria, Germany, and Turkey. By Byron McCandless and Gilbert Grosvenor. 386-388, *Oct. 1917*
Heroic Flags of the Middle Ages. By Byron McCandless and Gilbert Grosvenor. 388-399, *Oct. 1917*
Pennants of Patriotism 200 Years Ago. By Byron McCandless and Gilbert Grosvenor. 399-403, *Oct. 1917*
The Correct Display of the Stars and Stripes. By Byron McCandless and Gilbert Grosvenor. 404-413, *Oct. 1917*
The Insignia of the Uniformed Forces of the United States. By Byron McCandless and Gilbert Grosvenor. 413-419, *Oct. 1917*
■ *Flags of the World.* By Byron McCandless and Gilbert Grosvenor. Reprint of Oct. 1917 NGM. 139 pages. *1917*

McCARRY, CHARLES:

On Assignment in Japan. *Aug. 1984*
Author
Three Men Who Made the Magazine. 287-316, *Sept. 1988*

The Japan Alps. Photos by George F. Mobley. 238-259, *Aug. 1984*
The Civilizing Seine. Photos by David L. Arnold. 478-511, *Apr. 1982*
■■ *The Great Southwest.* Photos by George F. Mobley. 199 pages. *1980*
Kyoto and Nara: Keepers of Japan's Past. Photos by George F. Mobley. 836-851, *June 1976*
Utah's Shining Oasis. Photos by James L. Amos. 440-473, *Apr. 1975*
Nova Scotia, the Magnificent Anchorage. Photos by Gordon W. Gahan. 334-363, *Mar. 1975*
New Zealand's North Island: The Contented Land. Photos by Bates Littlehales. 190-213, *Feb. 1974*
Heart of the Bluegrass. Photos by J. Bruce Baumann. 634-659, *May 1974*
Yesterday Lingers Along the Connecticut. Photos by David L. Arnold. 334-369, *Sept. 1972*
Home to the Enduring Berkshires. Photos by Jonathan S. Blair. 196-221, *Aug. 1970*

McCARTNEY, BENJAMIN C.: *Author-Photographer*

Return to Florence. Included: Northern Italy: Scenic Battleground. Photos by B. Anthony Stewart and author. 257-296, *Mar. 1945*

McCAUSLAND, BILL:

Nomination Page. *Feb. 1979*

McCLELLAN-KERR ARKANSAS RIVER NAVIGATION SYSTEM:

Oklahoma, the Adventurous One. By Robert Paul Jordan. Photos by Robert W. Madden. 149-189, *Aug. 1971*

McCLURE, EDGAR: *Author*

The Altitude of Mount Adams, Washington. 151-153, *Apr. 1896*

McCLURE, HENRY HERBERT: *Author*

Shortening Time Across the Continent. 319-321, *Aug. 1902*

McCONNELL, BARBARA W.:

On Assignment. *June 1983*

McCONNELL RIVER REGION, Canada:

Beyond the North Wind With the Snow Goose. By Des and Jen Bartlett. 822-843. Included: ...And Then There Was Fred.... 843-847, *Dec. 1973*

McCORMICK, ELSIE: *Author*

"Where the Mountains Walked": An Account of the Recent Earthquake in Kansu Province, China, Which Destroyed 100,000 Lives. By Upton Close and Elsie McCormick. 445-464, *May 1922*

McCORMICK, FREDERICK: *Author*

China's Treasures. 996-1040, *Oct. 1912*
Present Conditions in China. 1120-1138, *Dec. 1911*

McCOY, RANDOLPH E.: *Author*

What's Killing the Palm Trees? Photos by Guillermo Aldana E. 120-130, *July 1988*

MacCRACKEN, WILLIAM P.:

President Coolidge Bestows Lindbergh Award: The National Geographic Society's Hubbard Medal Is Presented to Aviator Before the Most Notable Gathering in the History of Washington. Address by Secretary MacCracken. 132-140, *Jan. 1928*

McCRANE, MARION P.: *Author*

Zoo Animals Go to School. Photos by W. E. Garrett. 694-706, *Nov. 1956*

MacCREADY, PAUL B.:

Model Airplanes: To Dream, to Build … And Then to Fly. By Michael E. Long. Photos by Peter Essick. Included: New wings for an old reptile. 132-144, *July 1986*
Winged Victory of *Gossamer Albatross.* By Bryan Allen. 640-651, *Nov. 1979*
The Flight of the *Gossamer Condor.* By Michael E. Long. 130-140, *Jan. 1978*

McCRINDLE, J. R.: *Author*

Flying Over Egypt, Sinai, and Palestine: Looking Down Upon the Holy Land During an Air Journey of Two and a Half Hours from Cairo to Jerusalem. By P.R.C. Groves and J. R. McCrindle. 313-355, *Sept. 1926*

McCUDDEN, JAMES BYFORD:

Aces Among Aces (Aviators). By Laurence La Tourette Driggs. 568-580, *June 1918*

McCUE, J.J.G.: *Author*

How Bats Hunt With Sound. 571-578, *Apr. 1961*

McCURDY, ARTHUR W.: *Author*

Factors Which Modify the Climate of Victoria (British Columbia). 345-348, *May 1907*

Photographer
1898: The Bells on Sable. 408-409, 416-417, *Sept. 1965*

McCURRY, STEVE:

On Assignment. *Aug. 1987*
On Assignment in the Philippines. *July 1986*
On Assignment in Afghanistan. *Aug. 1985*
On Assignment in India and Nepal. *June 1984*

Photographer
Hungary: A Static Society. By Paul R. and Anne H. Ehrlich. 927-929, *Dec. 1988*
Africa's Sahel: The Stricken Land. By William S. Ellis. 140-179, *Aug. 1987*
Corregidor Revisited. By William Graves. 118-131, *July 1986*
Hope and Danger in the Philippines. By Arthur Zich. 76-117, *July 1986*
Along Afghanistan's War-torn Frontier. By Debra Denker. 772-797, *June 1985*
The New Face of Baghdad. By William S. Ellis. 80-109, *Jan. 1985*
Monsoons: Life Breath of Half the World. By Priit J. Vesilind. 712-747, *Dec. 1984*
By Rail Across the Indian Subcontinent. By Paul Theroux. 696-743, *June 1984*
Beirut–Up From the Rubble. By William S. Ellis. 262-286, *Feb. 1983*

Pakistan's Kalash: People of Fire and Fervor. By Debra Denker. 458-473, *Oct. 1981*

McDADE, MATT C.: *Author*

New York State's New Main Street. 567-618, *Nov. 1956*

McDIVITT, JAMES A.:

America's 6,000-mile Walk in Space. 440-447, *Sept. 1965*

McDONALD, EDWIN A.:

In the Antarctic. Nomination Page. *Nov. 1961*

Author
Exploring Antarctica's Phantom Coast. Photos by W. D. Vaughn. 251-273, *Feb. 1962*

McDONALD, EUGENE F., Jr.:

The Society's Hubbard Medal Awarded to Commander MacMillan. Note: Lieutenant Commander McDonald, present at the ceremony, was a member of the 1925 National Geographic Society–United States Navy MacMillan Arctic Expedition. 563-564, *Apr. 1953*

MacDONALD, T. L.:

Board of Managers. 88, *Jan. 1910*

MacDOUGAL, DANIEL T.: *Author*

Notes on the Deserts of the United States and Mexico (from a publication of Daniel T. MacDougal). 691-714, *Aug. 1910*
More Changes of the Colorado River. 52-54, *Jan. 1908*

India's summer monsoon—at once a blessing and a curse—floods a street in Delhi. STEVE McCURRY

McDOWELL, BART:

On the Indian Ocean. Nomination Page. *Sept. 1981*

In Guatemala. Nomination Page. *June 1976*

In Peru. Nomination Page. *June 1962*

Author

New Mexico: Between Frontier and Future. Photos by Danny Lehman. 602-633, *Nov. 1987*

The Dutch Touch. Photos by Nathan Benn and Farrell Grehan. 501-525, *Oct. 1986*

Eruption in Colombia. Photos by Steve Raymer. 640-653, *May 1986*

Sam Houston: A Man Too Big for Texas. Photos by Charles O'Rear. Included: The Battle of San Jacinto. 311-329, *Mar. 1986*

C. M. Russell, Cowboy Artist. Photos by Sam Abell. 60-95, *Jan. 1986*

Mexico City: An Alarming Giant. Photos by Stephanie Maze. 138-175, *Aug. 1984*

Thailand: Luck of a Land in the Middle. Photos by Steve Raymer. 500-535, *Oct. 1982*

Melville Bell Grosvenor, A Decade of Innovation, a Lifetime of Service. 270-278, *Aug. 1982*

Crosscurrents Sweep the Indian Ocean. Photos by Steve Raymer. 422-457, *Oct. 1981*

The Aztecs. Photos by David Hiser. Paintings by Felipe Dávalos. 714-751, *Dec. 1980*

Brazil's Golden Beachhead. Photos by Nicholas deVore III. 246-277, *Feb. 1978*

The Panama Canal Today. Photos by George F. Mobley. 279-294, *Feb. 1978*

▣▣ *Journey Across Russia: The Soviet Union Today.* Photos by Dean Conger. 367 pages. *1977*

Earthquake in Guatemala. Photos by W. E. Garrett and Robert W. Madden. 810-829, *June 1976*

Those Successful Japanese. Photos by Fred Ward. 323-359, *Mar. 1974*

▣▣ *The American Cowboy in Life and Legend.* Photos by William Albert Allard. 211 pages. *1972*

Hungary: Changing Homeland of a Tough, Romantic People. Photos by Albert Moldvay and Joseph J. Scherschel. 443-483, *Apr. 1971*

Orissa, Past and Promise in an Indian State. Photos by James P. Blair. 546-577, *Oct. 1970*

▣▣ *Gypsies: Wanderers of the World.* Photos by Bruce Dale. 215 pages. *1970*

Deerfield Keeps a Truce With Time. Photos by Robert W. Madden. 780-809, *June 1969*

Mexico's Window on the Past. Photos by B. Anthony Stewart. 492-519, *Oct. 1968*

The Most Mexican City, Guadalajara. Photos by Volkmar Wentzel. 412-441, *Mar. 1967*

▣▣ *The Revolutionary War: America's Fight for Freedom.* 199 pages. *1967*

The Changing Face of Old Spain. Photos by Albert Moldvay. 291-339, *Mar. 1965*

Puerto Rico's Seven-league Bootstraps. Photos by B. Anthony Stewart. 755-793, *Dec. 1962*

Avalanche! Photos by John E. Fletcher. 855-880, *June 1962*

Mexico in Motion. Photos by Kip Ross. 490-537, *Oct. 1961*

Theodore Roosevelt: a Centennial Tribute. 572-590, *Oct. 1958*

MACEDON (Ancient Kingdom):

Regal Treasures From a Macedonian Tomb. By Manolis Andronicos. Photos by Spyros Tsavdaroglou. 55-77, *July 1978*

MACEDONIA (Republic), Yugoslavia:

Yugoslavia: Six Republics in One. By Robert Paul Jordan. Photos by James P. Blair. 589-633, *May 1970*

New Greece, the Centenarian, Forges Ahead. By Maynard Owen Williams. 649-721, *Dec. 1930*

The Whirlpool of the Balkans. By George Higgins Moses. 179-197, *Feb. 1921*

On the Monastir Road. By Herbert Corey. 383-412, *May 1917*

Saloniki. By H. G. Dwight. 203-232, *Sept. 1916*

The Hoary Monasteries of Mt. Athos. By H. G. Dwight. 249-272, *Sept. 1916*

The Races and Religions of Macedonia. By Luigi Villari. 1118-1132, *Nov. 1912*

"Grass Never Grows Where the Turkish Hoof Has Trod." By Edwin Pears. 1132-1148, *Nov. 1912*

Notes on Macedonia. 790-802, *Nov. 1908*

The Great Turk and His Lost Provinces. By William E. Curtis. 45-61, *Feb. 1903*

McELFRESH, BRUCE:

On Assignment. *Oct. 1982*

McELROY, WILLIAM D.:

Torchbearers of the Twilight (Fireflies). By Frederick G. Vosburgh. 697-704, *May 1951*

McEWEN, COLIN:

School Field Trip Yields Prehistoric Bone. Geographica. *Dec. 1988*

MacFARLAND, CRAIG:

In the Galápagos Islands. Nomination Page. *Feb. 1971*

Author-Photographer

Giant Tortoises: Goliaths of the Galapagos. Photos by author and Jan MacFarland. 632-649, *Nov. 1972*

MacFARLAND, JAN:

In the Galápagos Islands. Nomination Page. *Feb. 1971*

Photographer

Giant Tortoises: Goliaths of the Galapagos. By Craig MacFarland. Photos by author and Jan MacFarland. 632-649, *Nov. 1972*

McGAHAN, JERRY:

Nomination Page. *June 1969*

Author

The Condor, Soaring Spirit of the Andes. Photos by Libby McGahan. 684-709, *May 1971*

McGAHAN, LIBBY: *Photographer*

The Condor, Soaring Spirit of the Andes. By Jerry McGahan. 684-709, *May 1971*

McGEE, ANITA NEWCOMB:

Judge of NGS prize essay contest. 32, *Jan. 1899*

McGEE, W J:

President. 176, *Apr. 1904*

Chairman of Committee on Eighth International Geographic Congress. 254-255, *June 1903*

Portrait. Plate 38, Dec. 1897; 354, *Oct. 1901*

Board of Managers. 294, Apr. 1891;

From an artillery post in Macedonia in 1916, World War I Allied forces assess Serbian strategy in a distant battle. HERBERT COREY

xii, Feb. 19, 1892; xix, Feb. 20, 1893;
xix, May 5, 1894; 414, *Sept. 1898*
Vice-President. 416, *Sept. 1898*
Sir John Evans and Prof. W J McGee.
By John Hyde. 358-359, *Dec. 1897*

Author
Problems of the Pacific–The Great
Ocean in World Growth. 333-342,
Sept. 1902
Dr. Bell's Survey in Baffinland. 113,
Mar. 1902
Ice Caves and Frozen Wells. 433-434,
Dec. 1901
Work of the Bureau of American Eth-
nology. 369-372, *Oct. 1901*
Asia, the Cradle of Humanity. 281-290,
Aug. 1901
Joseph Le Conte (Biography). 309-311,
Aug. 1901
The Old Yuma Trail. 103-107, Mar.
1901; 129-143, *Apr. 1901*
Frank Frederick Hilder (Biography).
85-86, *Feb. 1901*
The Lessons of Galveston. 377-383,
Oct. 1900
The Isthmian Canal Problem. 363-364,
Sept. 1899
National Growth and National Charac-
ter. 185-206, *June 1899*
Professor O. C. Marsh (Biography).
181-182, *May 1899*
Geographic Literature. 59-60, Feb.
1897; 91-92, Mar. 1897; 124-127,
Apr. 1897; 362-364, Dec. 1897; 477-
478, Nov. 1898; 512-514, 515-518,
Dec. 1898
The Geospheres. 435-447, *Oct. 1898*
The Growth of the United States. 377-
386, *Sept. 1898*
Papagueria. 345-371, *Aug. 1898*
American Geographic Education. 305-
307, *July 1898*
Geographic Development of the Dis-
trict of Columbia. 317-323, *July 1898*
The Geologic Atlas of the United
States. 339-342, *July 1898*
The Topographic Atlas of the United
States. 343-344, *July 1898*
Geographic Work by the Bureau of
American Ethnology. 98-100,
Mar. 1898
The Modern Mississippi Problem. 24-
27, *Jan. 1898*
Hatcher's Work in Patagonia. 319-322,
Nov. 1897
Death of G. Brown Goode. 316,
Sept. 1896
The Work of the National Geographic
Society. 253-259, *Aug. 1896*
Geographic History of the Piedmont
Plateau. 261-265, *Aug. 1896*
Seriland. By W J McGee and Willard D.
Johnson. 125-133, *Apr. 1896*
Explorations by the Bureau of Ameri-
can Ethnology in 1895. 77-80,
Feb. 1896
The Classification of Geographic Forms
by Genesis. 27-36, *Oct. 1888*

MacGILLIVRAY, JAMES: *Author*
Mickey the Beaver: An Animal Engineer Performs for the Camera as a
Star in the Activities of His Species.
741-756, *Dec. 1928*

MacGONIGLE, JOHN N.: *Author*
The Geography of the Southern

Peru's Machu Picchu was found in 1911 by Hiram Bingham, who received funding from National Geographic to explore the ancient Inca city. BATES LITTLEHALES, NGS

Peninsula of the United States.
381-394, *Dec. 1896*

McGRATH, J. E.: *Author*
The Alaskan Boundary Survey. Part II.
The Boundary South of Fort Yukon.
181-188, *Feb. 8, 1893*

McGRATH, SUSAN: *Author*
■■ *Fun With Physics.* Juvenile. 104
pages. *1986*
■■ *Your World of Pets.* Art by Barbara
L. Gibson. Juvenile. 104 pages. *1985*

McGREGOR MOUNTAIN,
Washington:
Forest Lookout. By Ella E. Clark. 73-
96, *July 1946*

McGUIRE, BIRD S.: *Author*
Big Oklahoma. 103-105, *Feb. 1906*

MACHIGUENGA INDIANS:
Amazon–The River Sea. By Loren Mc-
Intyre. 456-495, *Oct. 1972*
By Parachute Into Peru's Lost World.
By G. Brooks Baekeland. Photos by
author and Peter R. Gimbel. 268-
296, *Aug. 1964*

MACHINES Come to Mississippi. By
J. R. Hildebrand. 263-318,
Sept. 1937

MACHU PICCHU, Peru:
The Five Worlds of Peru. By Kenneth
F. Weaver. Photos by Bates Little-
hales. 213-265, *Feb. 1964*
Peru, Homeland of the Warlike Inca.
By Kip Ross. Contents: National
Geographic Society–Yale University
expeditions. 421-462, *Oct. 1950*
The Pith of Peru: A Journey from
Talara to Machu Picchu, with

Memorable Stopovers. By Henry
Albert Phillips. 167-196, *Aug. 1942*
Further Explorations in the Land of the
Incas: The Peruvian Expedition of
1915 of the National Geographic So-
ciety and Yale University. By Hiram
Bingham. 431-473, *May 1916*
Story of Machu Picchu: The Peruvian
Expeditions of the National Geo-
graphic Society and Yale University.
By Hiram Bingham. 172-217,
Feb. 1915
In the Wonderland of Peru. By Hiram
Bingham. Included: Ruins of an An-
cient Inca Capital, Machu Picchu
(Panorama). 387-573, *Apr. 1913*
Honors to Amundsen and Peary. Na-
tional Geographic Society Banquet
Address by Hiram Bingham. 113-
130, *Jan. 1913*

MacINNIS, JOSEPH B.:
In the Arctic. Nomination Page.
Aug. 1973

Author
Exploring a 140-year-old Ship Under
Arctic Ice *(Breadalbane).* Photos by
Emory Kristof. 104A-104D,
July 1983
Diving Beneath Arctic Ice. Photos by
William R. Curtsinger. 248-267,
Aug. 1973

McINTOSH, SUSAN and RODERICK:
Authors
Finding West Africa's Oldest City. Photos by Michael and Aubine Kirtley.
396-418, *Sept. 1982*

McINTYRE, LOREN:
On Assignment in Peru. *Apr. 1987*
Editorial. By Wilbur E. Garrett. 553,
Nov. 1982

Alaskan sunlight gilds 20,320-foot Mount McKinley, North America's premier mountain.   BRADFORD WASHBURN

Mount McKinley Conquered by New Route. By Bradford Washburn. 219-248, *Aug. 1953*

Wildlife of Mount McKinley National Park. By Adolph Murie. Paintings by Walter A. Weber. 249-270, *Aug. 1953*

Fit to Fight Anywhere (Quartermaster Corps Expedition). By Frederick Simpich. 233-256, *Aug. 1943*

Over the Roof of Our Continent. By Bradford Washburn. 78-98, *July 1938*

A Game Country Without Rival in America: The Proposed Mount McKinley National Park. By Stephen R. Capps. 69-84, *Jan. 1917*

Mount Huntington and Mount McKinley. 597-600, *June 1911*

The Monarchs of Alaska. By R. H. Sargent. 610-623, *July 1909*

Plan for Climbing Mt. McKinley. By Alfred H. Brooks and D. L. Reaburn. 30-35, *Jan. 1903*

Mount McKinley. By Robert Muldrow. 312-313, *Aug. 1901*

The Sushitna River, Alaska. By W. A. Dickey. 322-327, *Nov. 1897*

McKNEW, THOMAS W.:

Board of Trustees, Vice Chairman. 579, 582, Apr. 1962; 583, 626, Oct. 1963; 484, Oct. 1966; 274, *Aug. 1982*

Board of Trustees, Advisory Chairman. 576, 579, 588, 590, Oct. 1967; 529, Apr. 1968; 861, June 1970; 227, *Aug. 1976*

Achievements and awards. 582, Apr. 1962; 588, 590, *Oct. 1967*

Board of Trustees, Chairman. 484, Oct. 1966; 588, *Oct. 1967*

Board of Trustees, Life Trustee. 588, *Oct. 1967*

Building Committee, Chairman. 673, May 1964; 588, *Oct. 1967*

National Geographic Society Trustees Elect Key Executives. 576-590, *Oct. 1967*

Secretary. 586, May 1947; 835, 836, Dec. 1959; 588, *Oct. 1967*

Vice President, Executive. 834, 835, 836, Dec. 1959; 882, 883, Dec. 1960; 881, Dec. 1961; 579, 580, 582, Apr. 1962; 588, *Oct. 1967*

Nomination Page. *Jan. 1959*

Vice President. 419, 420, 421, 423, Mar. 1957; 866, 867, Dec. 1957; 793, *June 1958*

Anniversary, twenty-fifth, with the Society: Board of Trustees dinner. 423, *Mar. 1957*

Secretary. 141, Feb. 1946; 39, *July 1946*

Author

Four-ocean Navy in the Nuclear Age. 145-187, *Feb. 1965*

Fledgling Wings of the Air Force. 266-271, *Aug. 1957*

We Followed Peary to the Pole. By Gilbert Grosvenor and Thomas W. McKnew. 469-484, *Oct. 1953*

MacLEISH, ARCHIBALD:

Editorial. By Gilbert M. Grosvenor. 437, *Apr. 1976*

Author

Robert Frost and New England. 438-444, *Apr. 1976*

The Thrush on the Island of Barra. 692-693, *May 1970*

McLEISH, DONALD: *Photographer*

A Vacation in Holland. 367-374, *Sept. 1929*

In the Land of the Vikings. 661-676, *June 1924*

In the Land of Windmills and Wooden Shoes. 297-312, *Mar. 1923*

Italy, France, Switzerland. 439-450, *Nov. 1915*

MacLEISH, KENNETH:

In the Philippines. Nomination Page. *Aug. 1971*

Author

Leonardo da Vinci: A Man for All Ages. Photos by James L. Amos. 296-329, *Sept. 1977*

Mont Saint Michel. Photos by Cotton Coulson. 820-831, *June 1977*

Canterbury Cathedral. Photos by Thomas Nebbia. 364-379, *Mar. 1976*

Western Australia, the Big Country. Photos by James L. Stanfield. 150-187, *Feb. 1975*

Martinique: Liberté, Egalité, and Uncertainty in the Caribbean. Photos by John Launois. 124-148, *Jan. 1975*

Scotland's Inner Hebrides: Isles of the Western Sea. Photos by R. Stephen Uzzell III. 690-717, *Nov. 1974*

Exploring Australia's Coral Jungle. 743-779, *June 1973*

Cyprus Under Four Flags: A Struggle for Unity. Photos by Jonathan Blair. 356-383, *Mar. 1973*

The Top End of Down Under. Photos by Thomas Nebbia. 145-174, *Feb. 1973*

The Tasadays, Stone Age Cavemen of Mindanao. Photos by John Launois. 219-249, *Aug. 1972*

Diving With Sea Snakes. Photos by Ben Cropp. 565-578, *Apr. 1972*

Help for Philippine Tribes in Trouble. Photos by Dean Conger. 220-255, *Aug. 1971*

Quebec: French City in an Anglo-Saxon World. Photos by James L. Stanfield and Declan Haun. 416-442, *Mar. 1971*

Java–Eden in Transition. Photos by Dean Conger. 1-43, *Jan. 1971*

Isles on the Edge of the Sea: Scotland's Outer Hebrides. Photos by Thomas Nebbia. 676-711, *May 1970*

Chartres: Legacy From the Age of Faith. Photos by Dean Conger. 857-882, *Dec. 1969*

Reunited Jerusalem Faces Its Problems. Photos by Ted Spiegel. 835-871, *Dec. 1968*

Queensland: Young Titan of Australia's Tropic North. Photos by Winfield Parks. 593-639, *Nov. 1968*

Île de la Cité, Birthplace of Paris. Photos by Bruce Dale. 680-719, *May 1968*

The Highlands, Stronghold of Scottish Gaeldom. Photos by Winfield Parks. 398-435, *Mar. 1968*

A Taxi for the Deep Frontier. Photos by Bates Littlehales. 139-150, *Jan. 1968*

Abraham, the Friend of God. Photos by Dean Conger. 739-789, *Dec. 1966*

Singapore, Reluctant Nation. Photos by Winfield Parks. 269-300, *Aug. 1966*

River of Counts and Kings: The Loire. Photos by Dean Conger. 822-869, *June 1966*

The Land of Galilee. Photos by B. Anthony Stewart. 832-865, *Dec. 1965*

MacLEOD CLAN:

Over the Sea to Scotland's Skye. By Robert J. Reynolds. 87-112, *July 1952*

McMASTER, JOHN BACH:

Judge of NGS prize essay contest. 32, *Jan. 1899*

MacMILLAN, DONALD BAXTER:

A Visit to the Living Ice Age. By Rutherford Platt. Included: MacMillan's route in the *Bowdoin*. 525-545, *Apr. 1957*

The Society's Hubbard Medal Awarded to Commander MacMillan. 563-564, *Apr. 1953*

Far North with "Captain Mac." By Miriam MacMillan. 465-513, *Oct. 1951*

Author

The MacMillan Arctic Expedition Returns: U. S. Navy Planes Make First Series of Overland Flights in the Arctic and National Geographic Society Staff Obtains Valuable Data and Specimens for Scientific Study. 477-518, *Nov. 1925*

The "Bowdoin" in North Greenland: Arctic Explorers Place Tablet to Commemorate Sacrifices of the Lady Franklin Bay Expedition. Note: The National Geographic Society was the donor of the bronze tablet erected at Cape Sabine, Ellesmere Island, in memory of the brave men of the Lady Franklin Bay Expedition who perished in the spring of 1884. 677-722, *June 1925*

Peary as a Leader: Incidents from the Life of the Discoverer of the North Pole Told by One of His Lieutenants on the Expedition Which Reached the Goal. 293-317, *Apr. 1920*

MacMILLAN, MIRIAM: *Author*

Far North with "Captain Mac." 465-513, *Oct. 1951*

MacMILLAN ARCTIC EXPEDITION:

A Naturalist with MacMillan in the Arctic. By Walter N. Koelz. 299-318, *Mar. 1926*

Flying Over the Arctic. By Richard E. Byrd. 519-532, *Nov. 1925*

The MacMillan Arctic Expedition Returns: U. S. Navy Planes Make First Series of Overland Flights in the Arctic and National Geographic Society Staff Obtains Valuable Data and Specimens for Scientific Study. By Donald B. MacMillan. 477-518, *Nov. 1925*

MacMillan in the Field. 473-476, *Oct. 1925*

Scientific Aspects of the MacMillan Arctic Expedition. 349-354, *Sept. 1925*

The MacMillan Arctic Expedition Sails. 225-226, *Aug. 1925*

To Seek the Unknown in the Arctic:

M
N

United States Navy Flyers to Aid MacMillan Expedition Under the Auspices of the National Geographic Society in Exploring Vast Area. 673-675, *June 1925*

McMILLIN, STEWART E.: *Author*

The Heart of Aymará Land: A Visit to Tiahuanacu, Perhaps the Oldest City of the New World, Lost Beneath the Drifting Sand of Centuries in the Bolivian Highlands. 213-256, *Feb. 1927*

McMURDO SOUND, Antarctica:

Under Antarctic Ice. By Bill Curtsinger. 497-511, *Apr. 1986*

McMURDO STATION, Antarctica:

Antarctica: Icy Testing Ground for Space. By Samuel W. Matthews. Photos by Robert W. Madden. 569-592, *Oct. 1968*

Flight Into Antarctic Darkness. By J. Lloyd Abbot, Jr. Photos by David S. Boyer. 732-738, *Nov. 1967*

First Flight Across the Bottom of the World. By James R. Reedy. Photos by Otis Imboden. 454-464, *Mar. 1964*

What We've Accomplished in Antarctica. By George J. Dufek. 527-557, *Oct. 1959*

McNALLY, PAUL A.: *Author*

Observing a Total Eclipse of the Sun. 597-605, *Nov. 1932*

McNEAL, HERBERT P.:
Photographer

Casablanca Smiles. 17-24, *July 1943*

McNEIL, NORMAN M.:
Photographer

Square-rigger in a Tempest *(Pamir).* 703-710, *May 1948*

McNEIL RIVER STATE GAME SANCTUARY, Alaska:

Among Alaska's Brown Bears. By Allan L. Egbert and Michael H. Luque. 428-442, *Sept. 1975*

McPHEE, JOHN: *Author*

The People of New Jersey's Pine Barrens. Photos by William R. Curtsinger. 52-77, *Jan. 1974*

MACQUARIE ISLAND, South Pacific Ocean:

Nature's Clown, the Penguin. By David Hellyer and Malcolm Davis. 405-428, *Sept. 1952*

McQUESTEN, L. N.:

A Winter Weather Record From the Klondike Region. By E. W. Nelson. 327-335, *Nov. 1897*

MACREADY, JOHN A.: *Author*

Exploring the Earth's Stratosphere: The Holder of the American Altitude Record Describes His Experiences in Reaching the "Ceiling" of His Plane at an Elevation of Nearly Eight Miles. 755-776, *Dec. 1926*

The Non-Stop Flight Across America. Photos by Albert W. Stevens. 1-83, *July 1924*

MacSWAIN, J. W.: *Author*

Crossroads of the Insect World. Photos

Near McMurdo Station, Antarctica, a driller extracts a core of ice that holds clues to past climate. DAVID S. BOYER, NGS

by Edward S. Ross. 844-857, *Dec. 1966*

McSWEENY, Z. F.: *Author*

The Character of Our Immigration, Past and Present. 1-15, *Jan. 1905*

McWILLIAMS, JOHN: *Author*

Vagabonding in England: A Young American Works His Way Around the British Isles and Sees Sights from an Unusual Point of View. 357-398, *Mar. 1934*

MADAGASCAR:

Madagascar's Lemurs: On the Edge of Survival. By Alison Jolly. Photos by Frans Lanting. 132-161, *Aug. 1988*

President's Page. By Gilbert M. Grosvenor. *Dec. 1987*

Madagascar: A World Apart. By Alison Jolly. Photos by Frans Lanting. 148-183, *Feb. 1987*

Crosscurrents Sweep the Indian Ocean. By Bart McDowell. Photos by Steve Raymer. 422-457, *Oct. 1981*

Madagascar: Island at the End of the Earth. By Luis Marden. Photos by Albert Moldvay. 443-487, *Oct. 1967*

Re-creating Madagascar's Giant Extinct Bird. By Alexander Wetmore. 488-493, *Oct. 1967*

The World in Your Garden. By W. H. Camp. Paintings by Else Bostelmann. Included: Plant Marvels of Madagascar (Flamboyant or Royal Poinciana, Crown-of-thorns, Travelers-tree). 1-65, *July 1947*

Madagascar: Mystery Island: Japan's Push into the Indian Ocean Swings the Searchlight of World Attention to This Huge French Sentinel off the

African Coast. By Paul Almasy. 797-830, *June 1942*

Across Madagascar by Boat, Auto, Railroad, and Filanzana. By Charles F. Swingle. 179-211, *Aug. 1929*

Through the Deserts and Jungles of Africa by Motor: Caterpillar Cars Make 15,000-Mile Trip from Algeria to Madagascar in Nine Months (Citroën Central African Expedition). By Georges-Marie Haardt. 651-720, *June 1926*

MA'DAN TRIBESPEOPLE:

Water Dwellers in a Desert World. By Gavin Young. Photos by Nik Wheeler. 502-523, *Apr. 1976*

Marsh Dwellers of Southern Iraq. By Wilfred Thesiger. Photos by Gavin Maxwell. 205-239, *Feb. 1958*

Forty Years Among the Arabs. By John Van Ess. 385-420, *Sept. 1942*

MADAWASKA: Down East With a French Accent. By Perry Garfinkel. Photos by Cary Wolinsky. 380-409, *Sept. 1980*

MADDEN, ROBERT W.:

On Assignment in Brooklyn. *May 1983*
In Guatemala. Nomination Page. *June 1976*

Photographer
Brooklyn: The Other Side of the Bridge. By Alice J. Hall. 580-613, *May 1983*

■ *America's Spectacular Northwest.* 199 pages. *1982*

Hurricane! By Ben Funk. 346-379. Included: Dominica. By Fred Ward. 357-359; Dynamics of a Hurricane. 370-371; Into the Eye of David. By John L. Eliot. 368-369; Paths of Fury–This Century's Worst American Storms. 360-361, *Sept. 1980*

Which Way Oahu? By Gordon Young. 653-679, *Nov. 1979*

Sydney: Big, Breezy, and a Bloomin' Good Show. By Ethel A. Starbird. 211-235, *Feb. 1979*

Kauai, the Island That's Still Hawaii. By Ethel A. Starbird. 584-613, *Nov. 1977*

West Germany: Continuing Miracle. By John J. Putman. 149-181, *Aug. 1977*

Venezuela's Crisis of Wealth. By Noel Grove. 175-209, *Aug. 1976*

Earthquake in Guatemala. By Bart McDowell. Photos by W. E. Garrett and Robert W. Madden. 810-829, *June 1976*

Toronto: Canada's Dowager Learns to Swing. By Ethel A. Starbird. 190-215, *Aug. 1975*

Hawaii, Island of Fire and Flowers. By Gordon Young. 399-425, *Mar. 1975*

China Unveils Her Newest Treasures. 848-857, *Dec. 1974*

Quicksilver and Slow Death. By John J. Putman. 507-527, *Oct. 1972*

Maryland on the Half Shell. By Stuart E. Jones. 188-229, *Feb. 1972*

Oklahoma, the Adventurous One. By Robert Paul Jordan. 149-189, *Aug. 1971*

Old Salem, Morning Star of Moravian Faith. By Rowe Findley. 818-837, *Dec. 1970*

Domesticating the Wild and Woolly Musk Ox. By John J. Teal, Jr. 862-879, *June 1970*

Deerfield Keeps a Truce With Time. By Bart McDowell. 780-809, *June 1969*

Antarctica: Icy Testing Ground for Space. By Samuel W. Matthews. 569-592, *Oct. 1968*

Mobile, Alabama's City in Motion. By William Graves. Photos by Joseph J. Scherschel and Robert W. Madden. 368-397, *Mar. 1968*

MADDEN, WILLIAM D.: *Photographer*

Something's Fishy About That Fin! Photos by Robert J. Shallenberger and William D. Madden. 224-227, *Aug. 1974*

MADDOCK, ELEANOR: *Author*

The Marble Dams of Rajputana. 469-499, *Nov. 1921*

MADEIRA ISLANDS, Atlantic Ocean:

The Treasure of Porto Santo. By Robert Sténuit. Photos by author and William R. Curtsinger. 260-275, *Aug. 1975*

Madeira, Like Its Wine, Improves With Age. By Veronica Thomas. Photos by Jonathan Blair. 488-513, *Apr. 1973*

Portugal's Gem of the Ocean: Madeira. By David S. Boyer. 364-394, *Mar. 1959*

Madeira the Florescent. By Harriet Chalmers Adams. Included: Mirrors of Madeira, Rock Garden of the Atlantic. Photos by Wilhelm Tobien. 81-106, *July 1934*

Madeira, on the Way to Italy. By David Fairchild. 751-771, *Dec. 1907*

MADHYA PRADESH (State), India:

Purdah in India: Life Behind the Veil. By Doranne Wilson Jacobson. 270-286, *Aug. 1977*

MADISON, DOLLEY:

The Living White House. By Lonnelle Aikman. 593-643, *Nov. 1966*

Inside the White House. By Lonnelle Aikman. Photos by B. Anthony Stewart and Thomas Nebbia. 3-43, *Jan. 1961*

MADISON, JAMES:

James Madison, Architect of the Constitution. By Alice J. Hall. Photos by Sam Abell. 340-369, *Sept. 1987*

Profiles of the Presidents: I. The Presidency and How It Grew. By Frank Freidel. 642-687, *Nov. 1964*

MADOERA (Island), Java. *See* Madura

MADRID, Spain:

Madrid: The Change in Spain. By John J. Putman. Photos by O. Louis Mazzatenta. 142-181, *Feb. 1986*

Spain: It's a Changed Country. By Peter T. White. Photos by David Alan Harvey. 297-331, *Mar. 1978*

The Changing Face of Old Spain. By Bart McDowell. Photos by Albert Moldvay. 291-339, *Mar. 1965*

"Around the World in Eighty Days." By Newman Bumstead. 705-750, *Dec. 1951*

Speaking of Spain. By Luis Marden. 415-456, *Apr. 1950*

We Escape from Madrid. By Gretchen Schwinn. 251-268, *Feb. 1937*

Madrid Out-of-Doors. By Harriet Chalmers Adams. 225-256, *Aug. 1931*

International Literary Contest to be held in Madrid. 273-276, *July 1889*

MADRID CODEX:

The Maya. 729-811, *Dec. 1975*

MADSON, JOHN: *Author*

North American Waterfowl: Troubles and Triumphs. 562-599, *Nov. 1984*

South Dakota's Badlands: Castles in Clay. Photos by Jim Brandenburg. 524-539, *Apr. 1981*

Land of Long Sunsets: Nebraska's Sand Hills. Photos by Jodi Cobb. 493-517, *Oct. 1978*

MADURA (Madurai), India:

The Marriage of the Gods (Religious Festival). By John J. Banninga. 1314-1330, *Dec. 1913*

The Temples of India. By W. H. Zumbro. 922-971, *Nov. 1909*

The Madura Temples. By J. S. Chandler. 218-222, *Mar. 1908*

MADURA (Island), Indonesia:

Postwar Journey Through Java. By Ronald Stuart Kain. 675-700, *May 1948*

MAGADI, Lake, Kenya:

Freeing Flamingos From Anklets of Death. By John G. Williams. Photos by Alan Root. 934-944, *Dec. 1963*

MAGDALENA (River), Colombia:

Cruising Colombia's "Ol' Man River." By Amos Burg. 615-660, *May 1947*

Over the Andes to Bogotá. By Frank M. Chapman. 353-373, *Oct. 1921*

MAGDALENA BAY, Mexico:

A Land of Drought and Desert–Lower California. By E. W. Nelson. 443-474, *May 1911*

MAGEE, FRANK J.: *Author*

Transporting a Navy Through the Jungles of Africa in War Time. 331-362, *Oct. 1922*

MAGEE, GUY, Jr.: *Author*

"The Man in the Street" in China. 406-421, *Nov. 1920*

On the island of Madeira, a dapper gentleman in 1907 takes a cushioned downhill ride in a vehicle that is half carriage, half sled. DAVID FAIRCHILD

MAGEIK, Mount, Alaska:

The Valley of Ten Thousand Smokes: An Account of the Discovery and Exploration of the Most Wonderful Volcanic Region in the World. By Robert F. Griggs. 115-169, *Feb. 1918*
The Valley of Ten Thousand Smokes: National Geographic Society Explorations in the Katmai District of Alaska. By Robert F. Griggs. 13-68, *Jan. 1917*

MAGELLAN, FERDINAND:

Magellan: First Voyage Around the World. By Alan Villiers. Photos by Bruce Dale. Included: Strait of Magellan, discovered October 21, 1520. 721-753, *June 1976*
Nomination Page. *May 1976*
Triton Follows Magellan's Wake. By Edward L. Beach. Photos by J. Baylor Roberts. 585-615, *Nov. 1960*
The Greatest Voyage in the Annals of the Sea. By J. R. Hildebrand. 699-739, *Dec. 1932*
Discoverers of America. Annual Address by the President, Gardiner G. Hubbard. 1-20, *Apr. 7, 1893*

MAGELLAN, Strait of:

A Winter Voyage Through the Straits of Magellan. By R. W. Meade. 129-141, *May 1897*

MAGELLANIC CLOUDS:

Supernova–Death of a Star. By Robert P. Kirshner. Photos by Roger H. Ressmeyer. 619-647, *May 1988*

MAGGIORE, Lake, Italy-Switzerland:

Frontier Cities of Italy. By Florence Craig Albrecht. 533-586, *June 1915*
Gems of the Italian Lakes. By Arthur Ellis Mayer. 943-956, *Aug. 1913*

The **MAGIC** Beauty of Snow and Dew. By Wilson A. Bentley. 103-112, *Jan. 1923*

The **MAGIC** Lure of Sea Shells. By Paul A. Zahl. Photos by Victor R. Boswell, Jr. and author. 386-429, *Mar. 1969*

The **MAGIC** Mountain. By J. N. Patterson. 457-468, *July 1908*

The **MAGIC** of Aluminum. By Thomas Y. Canby. Photos by James L. Amos. 186-211, *Aug. 1978*

The **MAGIC** Road Round Ireland. By H. V. Morton. Photos by Robert F. Sisson. 293-333, *Mar. 1961*

The **MAGIC** World of Hans Christian Andersen. By Harvey Arden. Photos by Sisse Brimberg. 825-849, *Dec. 1979*

The **MAGIC** Worlds of Walt Disney. By Robert de Roos. Photos by Thomas Nebbia. 159-207, *Aug. 1963*

MAGIS, ROBERT C.: *Artist*

The Celts. By Merle Severy. Photos by James P. Blair. 582-633, *May 1977*
The Phoenicians, Sea Lords of Antiquity. By Samuel W. Matthews. Photos by Winfield Parks. 149-189, *Aug. 1974*

The small Transylvanian village of Banffy-hunyad in eastern Hungary was home to this Magyar farmer in 1918. ERDELYI

The Tower of the Winds. By Derek J. de Solla Price. 587-596, *Apr. 1967*

MAGNA CARTA:

The British Way. By Sir Evelyn Wrench. 421-541, *Apr. 1949*

MAGNESIA (Ancient City):

The Buried Cities of Asia Minor. By Ernest L. Harris. 1-18, *Jan. 1909*
Some Ruined Cities of Asia Minor. By Ernest L. Harris. 833-858, *Dec. 1908*

MAGNESS, J. R.: *Author*

How Fruit Came to America. Paintings by Else Bostelmann. 325-377, *Sept. 1951*

"MAGNETIC CITY," Core of Valiant Russia's Industrial Might. By John Scott. 525-556, *May 1943*

MAGNETIC Clues Help Date the Past. By Kenneth F. Weaver. 696-701, *May 1967*

MAGNETIC DATING METHOD:

Magnetic Clues Help Date the Past. By Kenneth F. Weaver. 696-701, *May 1967*

MAGNETIC Disturbance Caused by the Explosion of Mont Pelée. 208-209, *June 1902*

MAGNETIC Observations. By Harry Fielding Reid. 82, *Mar. 21, 1892*

MAGNETIC Observations in Alaska. By Daniel L. Hazard. 675-676, *July 1909*

MAGNETIC Observations in Iceland, Jan Mayen and Spitzbergen in 1892. By Cyrus C. Babb. 223-224, *Dec. 29, 1894*

MAGNETIC RESONANCE IMAGING (MRI):

Medicine's New Vision. By Howard Sochurek. Paintings by Davis Meltzer.

Illustrations text by Peter Miller. 2-41, *Jan. 1987*

MAGNETIC STORMS:

The Sun. By Herbert Friedman. 713-743, *Nov. 1965*
Unlocking Secrets of the Northern Lights. By Carl W. Gartlein. Paintings by William Crowder. NGS research grant. 673-704, *Nov. 1947*

The **MAGNETIC** Survey of Africa. By L. A. Bauer. 291-297, *Mar. 1909*

MAGNETIC Survey of the Pacific. 447-448, *June 1908*

MAGNETIC Survey of the Pacific Ocean. By L. A. Bauer. 237, *Apr. 1906*

MAGNETIC Survey of the United States. By L. A. Bauer. 92-95, *Mar. 1902*

MAGNETIC Work of the Coast and Geodetic Survey. By L. A. Bauer. 288-289, *Aug. 1899*

MAGNETISM:

The Compass in Modern Navigation. By G. W. Littlehales. 266-272, *Sept. 1897*

MAGNETISM, Terrestrial. *See* Geomagnetism

MAGNITOGORSK, Russian S.F.S.R., U.S.S.R.:

"Magnetic City," Core of Valiant Russia's Industrial Might. By John Scott. 525-556, *May 1943*

The **MAGNITUDE** of the New World Metropolis. 523-530, *Nov. 1930*

MAGNOLIA GARDENS, South Carolina:

The Ashley River and Its Gardens. By E.T.H. Shaffer. 525-550, *May 1926*

MAGNOLIA State Mosaic. By J. Baylor Roberts. 279-310, *Sept. 1937*

MAGPIES:

Crows, Magpies, and Jays: Unusual Intelligence Has Earned a Unique Position for These Birds. By T. Gilbert Pearson. Paintings by Allan Brooks. 51-79, *Jan. 1933*

MAGUBANE, PETER:

On Assignment in South Africa. *Feb. 1986*

Photographer
South Africa's Ndebele People. 260-282. Included: Dilemma of Independence. Introduction by The Editor. 260-261; Pioneers in Their Own Land. By David Jeffery. 262-282, *Feb. 1986*

MAGYARS:

Magyar Mirth and Melancholy. By John Patric. 1-55, *Jan. 1938*
The Races of Europe. By Edwin A. Grosvenor. 441-534, *Dec. 1918*
Hungary: A Land of Shepherd Kings. By C. Townley-Fullam. 311-393, *Oct. 1914*
The Land of Contrast: Austria-Hungary. By D. W. and A. S. Iddings. 1188-1217, 1284, *Dec. 1912*

MAH JONG (Yawl):

The Aegean Isles: Poseidon's Playground. By Gilbert M. Grosvenor. 733-781, *Dec. 1958*

MAHARASHTRA (State), India. *See* Shirala

MAHA-VAJIRAVUDH, King (Siam):

The Coronation of His Majesty King Maha-Vajiravudh of Siam. By Lea Febiger. 389-416, *Apr. 1912*

MAHDIA, Tunisia:

The Greek Bronzes of Tunisia. By Frank Edward Johnson. 89-103, *Jan. 1912*

MAHENDRA, King (Nepal):

Coronation in Katmandu. By E. Thomas Gilliard. Photos by Marc Riboud. 139-152, *July 1957*

MAHIEU, TED:

Nomination Page. *June 1968*

MAHOGANIES (Trees):

Among the Mahogany Forests of Cuba. By Walter D. Wilcox. 485-498, *July 1908*

The **MAID** of France Rides By: Compiègne, Where Joan of Arc Fought Her Last Battle, Celebrates Her Fifth Centenary. By Inez Buffington Ryan. 607-616, *Nov. 1932*

A **MAIDEN** Comes of Age. By Nita Quintero. 262-271, *Feb. 1980*

MAIL. *See* Mail Boat; Pony Express; Postage Stamps; U. S. Postal Service; *and* Boston Post Roads; Natchez Trace

MAIL BOAT:

J. W. Westcott, Postman for the Great Lakes. By Cy La Tour. 813-824, *Dec. 1950*

MAINE:

Maine's Working Coast. By David Jeffery. Photos by Kevin Fleming. 208-241, *Feb. 1985*

✦ *Northern Approaches: Maine and the Maritimes.* The Making of America series. On reverse: European Outreach, Northeast Contested, Shifting Population, A Changing Economy, The Cultural Imprint. *Feb. 1985*

The Incredible Potato. By Robert E. Rhoades. Photos by Martin Rogers. 668-694, *May 1982*

Thoreau, a Different Man. By William Howarth. Photos by Farrell Grehan. 349-387, *Mar. 1981*

Madawaska: Down East With a French Accent. By Perry Garfinkel. Photos by Cary Wolinsky. 380-409, *Sept. 1980*

A Way of Life Called Maine. By Ethel A. Starbird. Photos by David Hiser. 727-757, *June 1977*

✦ *Close-up: U.S.A., Maine, with the Maritime Provinces of Canada.* Text on reverse. *Mar. 1975*

The American Lobster, Delectable Cannibal. By Luis Marden. Photos by David Doubilet. 462-487, *Apr. 1973*

Stalking Wild Foods on a Desert Isle. By Euell Gibbons. Photos by David Hiser. 47-63, *July 1972*

Can We Save Our Salt Marshes? By Stephen W. Hitchcock. Photos by William R. Curtsinger. 729-765, *June 1972*

Character Marks the Coast of Maine. By John Scofield. Photos by B. Anthony Stewart. 798-843, *June 1968*

Seashore Summer: One Mother's Recipe for Smallboy Bliss. By Arline Strong. 436-444, *Sept. 1960*

Maine's Lobster Island, Monhegan. By William P. E. Graves. Photos by Kosti Ruohomaa. 285-298, *Feb. 1959*

Boatbuilder Bill Crampton, driven out of his native Ireland by high taxes, now makes his home in Maine. KEVIN FLEMING

Down East Cruise *(Nomad).* By Tom Horgan. Photos by Luis Marden. 329-369, *Sept. 1952*

Mountains Top Off New England. By F. Barrows Colton. Photos by Robert F. Sisson. 563-602, *May 1951*

Skyline Trail from Maine to Georgia. By Andrew H. Brown. Photos by Robert F. Sisson. 219-251, *Aug. 1949*

Aroostook County, Maine, Source of Potatoes. By Howell Walker. 459-478, *Oct. 1948*

The Worm Turns. By Samuel Sandrof. Included: Worm-digging industry. 775-786, *June 1946*

The Maine American and the American Lobster. By John D. Lucas. 523-543, *Apr. 1946*

Northeast of Boston. By Albert W. Atwood. 257-292, *Sept. 1945*

Maine, the Outpost State: Some Forgotten Incidents in the Life of an Old and Stout-Hearted Commonwealth. By George Otis Smith. 533-592, *May 1935*

In the Allagash Country. By Kenneth Fuller Lee. 505-520, *Apr. 1929*

First National Park East of Mississippi River. Contents: Sieur de Monts National Monument, Mount Desert Island. 623-626, *June 1916*

The Unique Island of Mount Desert. By George B. Dorr, Ernest Howe Forbush, and M. L. Fernald. 75-89, *July 1914*

The Leach's Petrel: His Nursery on Little Duck Island. By Arnold Wood. 360-365, *Apr. 1909*

All Around the Bay of Passamaquoddy. By Albert S. Gatschet. Included: A List of Indian Geographic Names Occurring Around Passamaquoddy

Duel to the death—attended by sea urchins and anemones—engages two lobsters, big-clawed crustaceans for which Maine's frigid coastal waters are famous. DAVID DOUBILET

Bay, Maine, with Their Derivations. 16-24, *Jan. 1897*

MAINE (Battleship):
Reception to Captain C. D. Sigsbee, U.S.N. By John Hyde. 251-252, *May 1898*

MAISEL, JAY: *Photographer*
Manhattan–Images of the City. By John J. Putman. 317-343, *Sept. 1981*

MAIURI, AMEDEO: *Author*
Last Moments of the Pompeians. Photos by Lee E. Battaglia. Paintings by Peter V. Bianchi. 651-669, *Nov. 1961*

MAJESTIC Island Worlds. Contents: Bali, Galapagos, Ireland, Japan, New Zealand, and Seychelles. 199 pages. *1987*

The MAJESTIC Rocky Mountains. By William S. Ellis. Photos by Dick Durrance II. 199 pages. *1976*

The **MAJESTY** of the Matterhorn. Pictorial supplement. *May 1912*

MAJOR, HARLAN: *Author*
The Delectable Shrimp: Once a Culinary Stepchild, Today a Gulf Coast Industry. 501-512, *Oct. 1944*

MAJORCA (Island), Balearic Islands, Spain:
Spain's Sun-blest Pleasure Isles. By Ethel A. Starbird. Photos by James A. Sugar. 679-701, *May 1976*
The Balearics Are Booming. By Jean and Franc Shor. 621-660, *May 1957*
Keeping House in Majorca. By Phoebe Binney Harnden. 425-440, *Apr. 1924*

MAJURO (Atoll), Marshall Islands:
Our New Military Wards, the Marshalls. By W. Robert Moore. 325-360, *Sept. 1945*

MAKALU NATURE PRESERVE, Nepal:
Editorial. By Wilbur E. Garrett. 283, *Mar. 1986*

MAKAT, Lake, Tanzania:
The Flamingo Eaters of Ngorongoro (Hyenas). By Richard D. Estes. 535-539, *Oct. 1973*

The **MAKERS** of the Flag. By Franklin K. Lane. 304, *Oct. 1917*

MAKIN (Atoll), Gilbert Islands:
Gilbert Islands in the Wake of Battle. By W. Robert Moore. 129-162, *Feb. 1945*

MAKING Friends With a Killer Whale. By Edward I. Griffin. 418-446, *Mar. 1966*

MAKING Friends With Mountain Gorillas. By Dian Fossey. Photos by Robert M. Campbell. NGS research grant. 48-67, *Jan. 1970*

The **MAKING** of a Japanese Newspaper. By Thomas E. Green. 327-334, *Oct. 1920*

The **MAKING** of a New Australia. By Howell Walker. 233-259, *Feb. 1956*

The **MAKING** of a West Pointer. By Howell Walker. 597-626, *May 1952*

THE MAKING OF AMERICA MAP SERIES:
Tidewater and Environs. Included: Maryland, Delaware, Virginia, North Carolina, South Carolina. On reverse: First Encounters, Farming and Frontiering, Rivalries and Rupture, Diversified Growth, Uneven Growth. *June 1988*
West Indies. On reverse: Spanish Caribbean, Imperial Rivalries, European Sea, American Sea, Forces of Change. *Nov. 1987*
Great Lakes. Included: Michigan, Wisconsin. On reverse: Indians, French, British; Creation of a Borderland; Influx of Settlers; Lake-country Lumber; Industrial Powerhouse; Region in Readjustment. *July 1987*
New England. Included: Maine, New Hampshire, Vermont, Massachusetts, Rhode Island, Connecticut, and eastern New York. On reverse: Indians and Outposts, Puritan Commonwealth, Greater New England, Industrial Hive, Immigrants and Industries, A New Vitality. *Feb. 1987*
Northern Plains. Included: Montana, Wyoming, North Dakota, South Dakota, Nebraska, Minnesota, Iowa, and in Canada: Saskatchewan, Manitoba, Ontario. On reverse: New Frontiers, Indians in Transition, Furs and Footholds, Steel Rails and Settlers, King Wheat, Patterns of Change. *Dec. 1986*
Pacific Northwest. Included: Idaho, Montana, Oregon, Washington. On reverse: Fur Trade Rivalries, Conquest-Colonization, Abrupt Change, Pacific Lumber Empire, Coming of Age. *Aug. 1986*
Texas. On reverse: Weak Spanish Frontier, Eras of Independence, Vigorous Expansion, A Broadening Base, New Frontiers, Mexican Borderland. *Mar. 1986*
Ohio Valley. Included: Tennessee-Tombigbee Waterway, West Virginia, Illinois, Tennessee, Kentucky, Ohio, Indiana. On reverse: Indians and Europeans, Speculation and Colonization, Transport Revolutions, Region Rent Asunder, Further Divergence, A New Era. *Dec. 1985*
Central Plains. Included: Iowa, Illinois, Missouri, Arkansas, Nebraska, Kansas, Oklahoma. On reverse: Indians and Entryways, Indian Land-White Land, The Great Assault, Indian Relocation, Indian Territory-The Last Stop, Last Frontiers, Dust Bowl of the Continent, Agricultural Heartland. *Sept. 1985*
Editorial. By Wilbur E. Garrett. 279, *Sept. 1985*
Northern Approaches: Maine and the Maritimes. On reverse: European Outreach, Northeast Contested, Shifting Population, A Changing Economy, The Cultural Imprint. *Feb. 1985*
Central Rockies. Included: Colorado,

Utah, Wyoming. On reverse: Fur and Frontier, Mission to Succeed, Mineral Riches, Lure of the Mountains. *Aug. 1984*
Far West. Included: California, Nevada. On reverse: Northern and Southern California–a Shifting Rivalry, Spanish Imprint, Sudden Transition, The New Eden, Water–the Key to Growth, Explosive Growth. *Apr. 1984*
Alaska. On reverse: Native Alaska, Russian America, Seward's Folly or New Eldorado?, Military Alaska, The 49th State. *Jan. 1984*
Hawaii. Included: Polynesian Arrival, Hawaii in Transition, Labor for Sugar, Hawaii as Territory, Hawaii as State. *Nov. 1983*
Deep South. Included: Alabama, Florida, Georgia, Louisiana, Mississippi, South Carolina, and parts of Arkansas, North Carolina, and Tennessee. On reverse: Indian Legacy, Imperial Footholds, Three Empires and Three Races, Cotton Kingdom, Postbellum, New Deep South, Subtropical Playground. *Aug. 1983*
Editorial. By Wilbur E. Garrett. 145, *Aug. 1983*
Atlantic Gateways. Included: Delaware, Maryland, New Jersey, New York, Pennsylvania, northern Virginia, West Virginia, and in Canada, southern Ontario and southern Quebec. On reverse: Indians and Trade, Nation in the Making, Peopling of the Gateways, Race for the Hinterlands, Growth of Industry, Spreading Urban Corridors. *Mar. 1983*
The Making of America: 17 New Maps Tie the Nation to Its Past. By Wilbur E. Garrett. 630-633, *Nov. 1982*
The Southwest. Included: Arizona, New Mexico, and parts of California, Colorado, Texas, Utah; and in Mexico: Baja California Norte, Chihuahua, Sonora. On reverse: 12,000 Years of History; Spanish Conquest; Anglo-American Entry and Occupancy. *Nov. 1982*

The **MAKING** of an Anzac. By Howell Walker. 409-456, *Apr. 1942*

The **MAKING** of an Astronaut. By Robert R. Gilruth. 122-144, *Jan. 1965*

The **MAKING** of Military Maps. By William H. Nicholas. 765-778, *June 1943*

MAKING the Fur Seal Abundant. By Hugh M. Smith. 1139-1165, *Dec. 1911*

MAKKAH, Saudi Arabia. *See* Mecca

MALABAR COAST, India:
Kerala, Jewel of India's Malabar Coast. By Peter Miller. Photos by Raghubir Singh. 592-617, *May 1988*
In the Wake of Sindbad. By Tim Severin. Photos by Richard Greenhill. 2-41, *July 1982*

MALAGASY REPUBLIC. *See* Madagascar

An Indian woman of Malaysia, tending a herd of water buffalo, takes shelter in a length of conduit from driving monsoon rains. DAVID ALAN HARVEY

MALARIA:

Mosquitoes, the Mighty Killers. By Lewis T. Nielsen. 427-440, *Sept. 1979*

Life Story of the Mosquito. By Graham Fairchild. 180-195, *Feb. 1944*

Saboteur Mosquitoes. By Harry H. Stage. 165-179, *Feb. 1944*

Map-Changing Medicine. By William Joseph Showalter. 303-330, *Sept. 1922*

Redeeming the Tropics. By William Joseph Showalter. 344-364, *Mar. 1914*

Economic Loss to the People of the United States Through Insects That Carry Disease. By L. O. Howard. 735-749, *Aug. 1909*

MALASPINA GLACIER, Alaska:

The National Geographic Society's Alaskan Expedition of 1909. By Ralph S. Tarr and Lawrence Martin. 1-54, *Jan. 1910*

MALAWI:

Tsetse–Fly of the Deadly Sleep. By Georg Gerster. 814-833, *Dec. 1986*

MALAY ARCHIPELAGO:

✤ *Indian Ocean, including Australia, New Zealand and Malaysia. Mar. 1941*

See also Bali; Borneo; Celebes; Java; Moluccas; New Guinea; Philippines; Sumatra; Timor

MALAYA, Federation of:

Malaya Meets Its Emergency. By George W. Long. Photos by J. Baylor Roberts. 185-228, *Feb. 1953*

See also British Malaya; *and* present name, Malaysia

MALAYS:

Brunei, Borneo's Abode of Peace. By Joseph Judge. Photos by Dean Conger. 207-225, *Feb. 1974*

Help for Philippine Tribes in Trouble. By Kenneth MacLeish. Photos by Dean Conger. Contents: The Higaonon, Mansaka, T'boli, and Ubo tribes of Malay stock (Southern Mongoloids) on Mindanao. 220-255, *Aug. 1971*

Singapore, Reluctant Nation. By Kenneth MacLeish. Photos by Winfield Parks. 269-300, *Aug. 1966*

MALAYSIA:

Saving the World's Largest Flower. By Willem Meijer. Photos by Edward S. Ross. NGS research grant. 136-140, *July 1985*

Tropical Rain Forests: Nature's Dwindling Treasures. By Peter T. White. Photos by James P. Blair. Paintings by Barron Storey. 2-47, *Jan. 1983*

Malaysia: Youthful Nation With Growing Pains. By William S. Ellis. Photos by David Alan Harvey. 635-667, *May 1977*

Asian Insects in Disguise. By Edward S. Ross. NGS research grant. 433-439, *Sept. 1965*

Malaysia's Giant Flowers and Insect-trapping Plants. By Paul A. Zahl. 680-701, *May 1964*

In Storied Lands of Malaysia. By Maurice Shadbolt. Photos by Winfield Parks. 734-783, *Nov. 1963*

See also former name, Malaya, Federation of

MALCOLM, IAN: *Author*

The Needs Abroad. 427-433, *May 1917*

MALDIVE ISLANDS, Indian Ocean:

The Marvelous Maldive Islands. By Alan Villiers. 829-849, *June 1957*

See also Maldives Republic

MALDIVES REPUBLIC, Indian Ocean:

Crosscurrents Sweep the Indian Ocean. By Bart McDowell. Photos by Steve Raymer. 422-457, *Oct. 1981*

See also Maldive Islands

MALEKULA (Island), New Hebrides:

Taboos and Magic Rule Namba Lives. By Kal Muller. 57-83, *Jan. 1972*

MALI:

Africa's Sahel: The Stricken Land. By William S. Ellis. Photos by Steve McCurry. 140-179, *Aug. 1987*

Finding West Africa's Oldest City. By Susan and Roderick McIntosh. Photos by Michael and Aubine Kirtley. Contents: Jenne-jeno (archaeological site), Mali. 396-418, *Sept. 1982*

The Niger: River of Sorrow, River of Hope. By Georg Gerster. 152-189, *Aug. 1975*

Foxes Foretell the Future in Mali's Dogon Country. By Pamela Johnson Meyer. 431-448, *Mar. 1969*

Freedom Speaks French in Ouagadougou. By John Scofield. 153-203, *Aug. 1966*

The **MALIGNED** Coyote. By Hope Ryden. Photos by author and David Hiser. 278-294, *Aug. 1974*

The **MALL**, Washington, D. C. Note: Plan showing building development to 1915 in accordance with the recommendations of the Park Commission of 1901. Supplement. *Mar. 1915*

MALLE, LOUIS: *Photographer*

Calypso Explores for Underwater Oil. By Jacques-Yves Cousteau. 155-184, *Aug. 1955*

MALLORCA (Island), Balearic Islands, Spain. *See* Majorca

MALLOWAN, MAX EDGAR LUCIEN: *Author*

New Light on Ancient Ur: Excavations at the Site of the City of Abraham Reveal Geographical Evidence of the Biblical Story of the Flood. 95-130, *Jan. 1930*

MALONEY, JOHN: *Author*

Chesapeake Odyssey: An 18-foot Sailboat Follows the Course of Captain John Smith around This Spacious Bay of History, Commerce, Sea Food, and Nautical Lore. 357-392, *Sept. 1939*

MALTA:

Democracy's Fortress: Unsinkable Malta. By Ernle Bradford. Photos by Ted H. Funk. 852-879, *June 1969*

Malta Invicta. By Bartimeus (A Captain in the Royal Navy). 375-400, *Mar. 1943*

Wanderers Awheel in Malta: British Stronghold Has Been a Stepping-stone of Conquest Since Phoenicians Cruised the Mediterranean and St. Paul Was Shipwrecked There. By Richard Walter. 253-272, *Aug. 1940*

The Maltese Islands: Cicero's Land of "Honey and Roses," and Stronghold of the Knights, Again Is Focus of

Rodents; Seals; Skunks; Ungulates (Hoofed Mammals); Walruses; Whales; Wolves; *and* Mammals, Prehistoric; Paleontology

MAMMALS, Prehistoric:

■■ *Giants from the Past: The Age of Mammals.* By Joseph H. Bailey. Juvenile. 104 pages. *1983*

Ancient Ashfall Creates a Pompeii of Prehistoric Animals. By Michael R. Voorhies. Photos by Annie Griffiths. Paintings by Jay Matternes. 66-75, *Jan. 1981*

Bison Kill By Ice Age Hunters. By Dennis Stanford. NGS research grant. 114-121, *Jan. 1979*

Exploring the Mind of Ice Age Man. By Alexander Marshack. Included: Mammals of the Ice Age as depicted in the art of Cro-Magnon man. NGS research grant. 64-89, *Jan. 1975*

✥ "Ice Age Mammals of the Alaskan Tundra," painting supplement. Map of Canada. *Mar. 1972*

Wyoming Muck Tells of Battle: Ice Age Man vs. Mammoth. By Cynthia Irwin, Henry Irwin, and George Agogino. NGS research grant. 828-837, *June 1962*

Big Game Hunting in the Land of Long Ago. By Joseph P. Connolly and James D. Bump. NGS research grant. 589-605, *May 1947*

MAMMOTH:

Uncovering the Bones in a Mammoth Graveyard. Geographica. *Dec. 1988*

Wyoming Muck Tells of Battle: Ice Age Man vs. Mammoth. By Cynthia

Irwin, Henry Irwin, and George Agogino. NGS research grant. 828-837, *June 1962*

A Strange and Remarkable Beast. 620, *Sept. 1907*

MAN, ERNEST A.: *Author*

The Nansen Polar Expedition. 339-344, *Oct. 1896*

MAN, Isle of:

The Manx and Their Isle of Man. By Veronica Thomas. Photos by Ted H. Funk. 426-444, *Sept. 1972*

The Isle of Man. By F. H. Mellor. 587-608, *May 1937*

MAN, Prehistoric:

"Where Did We Come From?" Editorial by Wilbur E. Garrett. Included: Map, The Peopling of the Earth. 434-437, *Oct. 1988*

The Search for Modern Humans. By John J. Putman. Photos by Sisse Brimberg and Ira Block. Paintings by Jack Unruh. 439-477, *Oct. 1988*

An Ice Age Ancestor? By Alexander Marshack. Photos by the author and Ira Block. 478-481, *Oct. 1988*

Mysteries of the Bog. By Louise E. Levathes. Photos by Fred Bavendam. Included: Peat holds clues to early American life. 397-420, *Mar. 1987*

Editorial. By Wilbur E. Garrett. 419, *Oct. 1986*

The Search for Our Ancestors. By Kenneth F. Weaver. Photos by David L. Brill. Paintings by Jay H. Matternes. 560-623, *Nov. 1985*

Tanzania's Stone Age Art. By Mary D.

Leakey. Photos by John Reader. 84-99, *July 1983*

A Bold New Look at Our Past. The Editor. NGS research grant. 62-63, *Jan. 1975*

Exploring the Mind of Ice Age Man. By Alexander Marshack. NGS research grant. 64-89, *Jan. 1975*

Adventures in the Search for Man *(Kenyapithecus wickeri).* By Louis S. B. Leakey. Photos by Hugo van Lawick. NGS research grant. 132-152, *Jan. 1963*

Vanished Mystery Men of Hudson Bay. By Henry B. Collins. Included: Dorset Eskimos, Sadlermiuts. NGS research grant. 669-687, *Nov. 1956*

See also Australopithecines; Hominids; Paleo-Indians

MAN Against the Sea, the Oosterschelde Barrier. By Larry Kohl. 526-537, *Oct. 1986*

MAN and Manatee: Can We Live Together? By Alice J. Hall. Photos by Fred Bavendam. Included: Man Can Save the Manatee. By Jesse R. White. 400-418, *Sept. 1984*

MAN and Nature Paint Italian Scenes in Prodigal Colors. Photos by Hans Hildenbrand. 443-466, *Apr. 1928*

The **MAN** Behind the Myths: George Washington. By Howard La Fay. Photos by Ted Spiegel. 90-111, *July 1976*

MAN-IN-SEA PROJECT:

A Taxi for the Deep Frontier. By

Members of a Neandertal group, after an ibex hunt, prepare a kill at their summer camp in southern France. PAINTING BY © JAY H. MATTERNES

In Florida's Crystal River a motherly manatee—or sea cow—nurses her yearling calf from a thumb-size teat under her flipper. FRED BAVENDAM, PETER ARNOLD, INC.

Kenneth MacLeish. Photos by Bates Littlehales. 139-150, *Jan. 1968*

The Deepest Days. By Robert Sténuit. NGS research grant. 534-547, *Apr. 1965*

Outpost Under the Ocean. By Edwin A. Link. Photos by Bates Littlehales. NGS research grant. 530-533, *Apr. 1965*

The Long, Deep Dive. By Lord Kilbracken. Photos by Bates Littlehales. NGS research grant. 718-731, *May 1963*

Our Man-in-Sea Project. By Edwin A. Link. NGS research grant. 713-717, *May 1963*

MAN in the Amazon: Stone Age Present Meets Stone Age Past. By W. Jesco von Puttkamer. NGS research grant. 60-83, *Jan. 1979*

"The MAN in the Street" in China. By Guy Magee, Jr. 406-421, *Nov. 1920*

MAN-OF-WAR:

The Deadly Fisher. By Charles E. Lane. 388-397, *Mar. 1963*

Man-of-war Fleet Attacks Bimini. By Paul A. Zahl. 185-212, *Feb. 1952*

MAN on the Moon in Idaho. By William Belknap, Jr. 505-525, *Oct. 1960*

MAN-POWERED FLIGHT. *See Daedalus; Gossamer Albatross; Gossamer Condor*

MAN Versus Nature. The Editor. 555, *Oct. 1969*

MAN Walks on Another World. By Neil A. Armstrong, Edwin E. Aldrin, Jr., and Michael Collins. 738-749, *Dec. 1969*

The MAN Who Made Time Stand Still–"Doc" Edgerton. By Erla Zwingle. Photos by Harold E. Edgerton and Bruce Dale. 464-483, *Oct. 1987*

The MAN Who Talks to Hummingbirds. By Luis Marden. Photos by James Blair. 80-99, *Jan. 1963*

The MAN Without the Hoe. 967-969, *Nov. 1910*

MANAGING Another Galápagos Species–Man. By Jerry Emory. Photos by Dieter and Mary Plage. 146-154, *Jan. 1988*

MANAGUA, Nicaragua:

A Land of Lakes and Volcanoes. By Luis Marden. 161-192, *Aug. 1944*

MANAMA, Bahrain:

Bahrain: Hub of the Persian Gulf. By Thomas J. Abercrombie. Photos by Steve Raymer. 300-329, *Sept. 1979*

Bahrein: Port of Pearls and Petroleum. By Maynard Owen Williams. 195-210, *Feb. 1946*

MANÁOS, Brazil. *See* Manaus

MANATEES:

Man and Manatee: Can We Live Together? By Alice J. Hall. Photos by Fred Bavendam. Included: Man Can Save the Manatee. By Jesse R. White. 400-418, *Sept. 1984*

Florida's Manatees, Mermaids in Peril. By Daniel S. Hartman. Photos by James A. Sugar. NGS research grant. 342-353, *Sept. 1969*

Guatemala Revisited. By Luis Marden. 525-564, *Oct. 1947*

MANAUS, Brazil:

Sea Fever. By John E. Schultz. 237-268, *Feb. 1949*

Air Cruising Through New Brazil: A National Geographic Reporter Spots Vast Resources Which the Republic's War Declaration Adds to Strength of United Nations. By Henry Albert Phillips. 503-536, *Oct. 1942*

MANCHESTER SHIP CANAL, England:

The Great Canals of the World. 475-479, *Oct. 1905*

MANCHUKUO. *See* Manchuria

MANCHURIA (Region), China:

In Manchuria Now. By W. Robert Moore. 389-414, *Mar. 1947*

Japan Faces Russia in Manchuria. By Willard Price. 603-634, *Nov. 1942*

Here in Manchuria: Many Thousand Lives Were Lost and More than Half the Crops Destroyed by the Floods of 1932. By Lilian Grosvenor Coville. 233-256, *Feb. 1933*

Byroads and Backwoods of Manchuria: Where Violent Contrasts of Modernism and Unaltered Ancient Tradition Clash. By Owen Lattimore. 101-130, *Jan. 1932*

Manchuria, Promised Land of Asia: Invaded by Railways and Millions of Settlers, This Vast Region Now Recalls Early Boom Days in the American West. By Frederick Simpich. 379-428, *Oct. 1929*

The Land of Promise. By A. W. Greely. 1078-1090, *Nov. 1912*

⊕ *Map of China and Its Territories.* Included: Mongolia, Manchuria, Chosen, East Turkestan, Tibet, Northern India. *Oct. 1912*

Mukden, the Manchu Home, and Its Great Art Museum. By Eliza R. Scidmore. 289-320, *Apr. 1910*

⊕ *Kirin, Harbin, Vladivostok.* Note: Map shows seat of war in Manchuria; map shows all roads, trails, and mountains over which the armies must pass. *June 1905*

Observations on the Russo-Japanese War, in Japan and Manchuria. By Louis Livingston Seaman. 80-82, *Feb. 1905*

Notes on Manchuria. By Henry B. Miller. 261-262, *June 1904*

Lumbering in Manchuria. By Henry B. Miller. 131-132, *Mar. 1904*

Russian Development of Manchuria. By Henry B. Miller. 113-127, *Mar. 1904*

⊕ *Map of Korea and Manchuria.* *Mar. 1904*

Building of Dalny (Dairen). 360, *Sept. 1903*

Railways, Rivers, and Strategic Towns in Manchuria. 326-327, *Aug. 1900*

MANDALAY, Burma:

Time and Again in Burma. By Bryan Hodgson. Photos by James L. Stanfield. 90-121, *July 1984*

Notes on Burma. By Thomas Barbour. 841-866, *Oct. 1909*

MANDARIN ROAD, Southeast Asia:

Along the Old Mandarin Road of Indo-China. By W. Robert Moore. 157-199, *Aug. 1931*

The **MANDATE** of Cameroun: A Vast African Territory Ruled by Petty Sultans Under French Sway. By John W. Vandercook. 225-260, *Feb. 1931*

MANDINGO TRIBESPEOPLE:

Rubber-cushioned Liberia. By Henry S.

Villard. Photos by Charles W. Allmon. 201-228, *Feb. 1948*

MANEUVERS of Military Planes Disclose Majestic Aërial Views. U. S. Army and Navy official photos. 599-614, *May 1933*

MANGANESE:

India's Treasures Helped the Allies. By John Fischer. 501-522, *Apr. 1946*

MANGBETTU TRIBESPEOPLE:

Trans-Africa Safari: A Motor Caravan Rolls Across Sahara and Jungle Through Realms of Dusky Potentates and the Land of Big-Lipped Women. By Lawrence Copley Thaw and Margaret Stout Thaw. 327-364, *Sept. 1938*

MANGOES:

New Plant Immigrants. By David Fairchild. 879-907, *Oct. 1911*
The Introduction of the Mango. 320-327, *Aug. 1903*

MANGROVES:

◗ Creatures of the Mangrove. President's Page. By Gilbert M. Grosvenor. Jan. 1986; cover, *Feb. 1986*
The Tree That Nobody Liked. By Rick Gore. Photos by Bianca Lavies. 669-689, *May 1977*

MANGYAN TRIBESPEOPLE:

Notes on Some Primitive Philippine Tribes. By Dean C. Worcester. 284-301, *June 1898*

MANHATTAN (Borough), New York, New York:

Manhattan–Images of the City. By John J. Putman. Photos by Jay Maisel. 317-343, *Sept. 1981*
Editorial. By Gilbert M. Grosvenor. 147, *Feb. 1977*
To Live in Harlem.... By Frank Hercules. Photos by LeRoy Woodson, Jr. 178-207, *Feb. 1977*
The World in New York City. By Peter T. White. 52-107, *July 1964*
✛ Tourist Manhattan; Greater New York. U. S. Atlas series. *July 1964*
Central Park: Manhattan's Big Outdoors. By Stuart E. Jones. Photos by Bates Littlehales. 781-811, *Dec. 1960*

MANHATTAN, S. S. (Tanker):

North for Oil: *Manhattan* Makes the Historic Northwest Passage. By Bern Keating. Photos by Tomas Sennett. 374-391, *Mar. 1970*

MANIHIKI (Atoll), Pacific Ocean:

Sailing the Seven Seas in the Interest of Science: Adventures Through 157,000 Miles of Storm and Calm, from Arctic to Antarctic and Around the World, in the Non-magnetic Yacht "Carnegie." By J. P. Ault. 631-690, *Dec. 1922*

MANILA, Philippines:

Hope and Danger in the Philippines. By Arthur Zich. Photos by Steve McCurry. 76-117, *July 1986*
The Philippines: Better Days Still Elude an Old Friend. By Don Moser.

Photos by Bruce Dale. 360-391, *Mar. 1977*
The Philippines, Freedom's Pacific Frontier. By Robert de Roos. Photos by Ted Spiegel. 301-351, *Sept. 1966*
What Luzon Means to Uncle Sam. By Frederick Simpich. 305-332, *Mar. 1945*
Facts about the Philippines. By Frederick Simpich. 185-202, *Feb. 1942*
Return to Manila. By Frederick Simpich. 409-451, *Oct. 1940*
Improvements in the City of Manila. 195-197, *May 1903*
The Manila Observatory. By José Algué. 427-438, *Nov. 1900*
The Economic Condition of the Philippines. By Max L. Tornow. 33-64, *Feb. 1899*
Manila and the Philippines. By A. Falkner von Sonnenburg. 65-72, *Feb. 1899*

MANION, ESTHER ANN:

Nomination Page. *Oct. 1965*

MANIPUR (State), India:

Manipur–Where Japan Struck at India. 743-750, *June 1944*

MANITOBA (Province), Canada:

The Hudson's Bay Company: Canada's Fur-Trading Empire. By Peter C. Newman. Photos by Kevin Fleming. 192-229, *Aug. 1987*
Western Grebes: The Birds That Walk on Water. By Gary L. Nuechterlein. 624-637, *May 1982*
Henry Hudson's Changing Bay. By Bill Richards. Photos by David Hiser. 380-405, *Mar. 1982*
◗ Polar Bear Alert. 395, cover, *Mar. 1982*
✛ Close-up, Canada: Saskatchewan, Manitoba, Northwest Territories. Text on reverse. *May 1979*

A Filipino father and son share a gentle moment in their home in one of the poorest sections of Manila. STEVE McCURRY

Manitoba's Fantastic Snake Pits. By Michael Aleksiuk. Photos by Bianca Lavies. 715-723, *Nov. 1975*
Canada's Heartland, the Prairie Provinces. By W. E. Garrett. 443-489, *Oct. 1970*
Across Canada by Mackenzie's Track. By Ralph Gray. 191-239, *Aug. 1955*
Trailing Cosmic Rays in Canada's North. By Martin A. Pomerantz. NGS research grant. 99-115, *Jan. 1953*

MANKATO, Minnesota:

Satellites Gave Warning of Midwest Floods. By Peter T. White. Photos by Thomas A. DeFeo. 574-592, *Oct. 1969*

MANKIND'S Best Friend: Companion of His Solitude, Advance Guard in the Hunt, and Ally of the Trenches. By Ernest Harold Baynes. 185-201, *Mar. 1919*

MANLESS Alpine Climbing: The First Woman to Scale the Grépon, the Matterhorn, and Other Famous Peaks Without Masculine Support Relates Her Adventures. By Miriam O'Brien Underhill. 131-170, *Aug. 1934*

The **MANLIKE** Apes of Jungle and Mountain. Paintings by Elie Cheverlange. 221-228, *Aug. 1940*

MANN, JAMES R.:

Honors to Colonel Goethals: The Presentation, by President Woodrow Wilson, of the National Geographic Society Special Gold Medal, and Addresses by Secretary of State Bryan, the French Ambassador, the German Ambassador, and Congressman James R. Mann. 677-690, *June 1914*

MANN, LUCILE Q.: *Author*

Around the World for Animals. By William M. and Lucile Q. Mann. 665-714, *June 1938*

MANN, WILLIAM M.: *Author*

The Wild Animals in My Life. 497-524, *Apr. 1957*
Man's Closest Counterparts: Heavyweight of Monkeydom Is the "Old Man" Gorilla, by Far the Largest of the Four Great Apes. Paintings by Elie Cheverlange. 213-236, *Aug. 1940*
Around the World for Animals. By William M. and Lucile Q. Mann. 665-714, *June 1938*
Monkey Folk. Paintings by Elie Cheverlange. 615-655, *May 1938*
Stalking Ants, Savage and Civilized: A Naturalist Braves Bites and Stings in Many Lands to Learn the Story of an Insect Whose Ways Often Parallel Those of Man. Paintings by Hashime Murayama. 171-192, *Aug. 1934*

MANNED SPACECRAFT CENTER, Houston, Texas:

First Explorers on the Moon: The Incredible Story of Apollo 11. 735-797, I. Man Walks on Another World. By Neil A. Armstrong, Edwin E. Aldrin, Jr., and Michael Collins. 738-

749; III. The Flight of Apollo 11: "One giant leap for mankind." By Kenneth F. Weaver. 752-787; IV. What the Moon Rocks Tell Us. By Kenneth F. Weaver. 788-791, *Dec. 1969*

"A Most Fantastic Voyage": The Story of Apollo 8's Rendezvous With the Moon. By Sam C. Phillips. 593-631, *May 1969*

Houston, Prairie Dynamo. By Stuart E. Jones. Photos by William Albert Allard. 338-377, *Sept. 1967*

MAN-O'-WAR BIRDS:

Birds of the High Seas: Albatrosses and Petrels; Gannets, Man-o'-war birds, and Tropic-birds. By Robert Cushman Murphy. Paintings by Allan Brooks. 226-251, *Aug. 1938*

MAN'S Amazing Progress in Conquering the Air. By J. R. Hildebrand. 93-122, *July 1924*

MAN'S *Best Friend.* Note: Originally ■■published as *The Book of Dogs.* 430 pages. 1958; rev. ed. *1966*

MAN'S Closest Counterparts: Heavyweight of Monkeydom Is the "Old Man" Gorilla, by Far the Largest of the Four Great Apes. By William M. Mann. Paintings by Elie Cheverlange. 213-236, *Aug. 1940*

MAN'S *Conquest of Space.* By William ■■R. Shelton. 199 pages. 1968; rev. ed. *1975*

MAN'S Deepest Dive. By Jacques Piccard. Photos by Thomas J. Abercrombie. 224-239, *Aug. 1960*

MAN'S Eighty Centuries in Veracruz. By S. Jeffrey K. Wilkerson. Photos by David Hiser. Paintings by Richard Schlecht. NGS research grant. 203-231, *Aug. 1980*

MAN'S Farthest Aloft: Rising to 13.71 Miles, the National Geographic Society-U. S. Army Stratosphere Expedition Gathers Scientific Data at Record Altitude. By Albert W. Stevens. Included: Action Photographs of the Balloon's Perfect Landing. 59-94, *Jan. 1936*

MAN'S Feathered Friends of Longest Standing: Peoples of Every Clime and Age Have Lavished Care and Affection Upon Lovely Pigeons. By Elisha Hanson. Paintings by Hashime Murayama. 63-110, *Jan. 1926*

MAN'S First Winter at the South Pole. By Paul A. Siple. 439-478, *Apr. 1958*

MAN'S Hunting Partner, the Field Dog. Paintings by Edward Herbert Miner. 89-104, *Jan. 1937*

MAN'S Mightiest Ally. Photos by Willard R. Culver. 423-450, *Apr. 1947*

MAN'S New Frontier: The Continental Shelf. By Luis Marden. Photos by Ira Block. 495-531, *Apr. 1978*

MAN'S New Servant, the Friendly Atom. By F. Barrows Colton. Photos by Volkmar Wentzel. 71-90, *Jan. 1954*

MAN'S Oldest Ally, the Dog: Since Cave-Dweller Days This Faithful Friend Has Shared the Work, Exploration, and Sport of Humankind. By Freeman Lloyd. Paintings by Edward Herbert Miner. 247-274, *Feb. 1936*

MAN'S Own Mountains, the Alps. By Ralph Gray. Photos by Walter Meayers Edwards and William Eppridge. 350-395, *Sept. 1965*

MAN'S Wildlife Heritage Faces Extinction. By H.R.H. The Prince Philip, Duke of Edinburgh. 700-703, *Nov. 1962*

MAN'S Winged Ally, the Busy Honeybee: Modern Research Adds a New Chapter to Usefulness of the Insect Which Has Symbolized Industry Since Early Bible Times. By James I. Hambleton. Paintings by Hashime Murayama. 401-428, *Apr. 1935*

MANSAKA TRIBESPEOPLE:

Help for Philippine Tribes in Trouble. By Kenneth MacLeish. Photos by Dean Conger. 220-255, *Aug. 1971*

MANSFIELD, Mount, Vermont:

Mountains Top Off New England. By F. Barrows Colton. Photos by Robert F. Sisson. 563-602, *May 1951*

MANTA RAYS:

A Strange Ride in the Deep (on Manta Rays). By Peter Benchley. 200-203, *Feb. 1981*

MANTFOMBI, Princess (Swaziland):

Zulu King Weds a Swazi Princess. By Volkmar Wentzel. 47-61, *Jan. 1978*

MANTIDS:

Mantids, the Praying Predators. By Edward S. Ross. Photos by Dwight Kuhn and the author. 268-280, *Feb. 1984*

Praying Mantis. Photos by John G. Pitkin. 685-692, *May 1950*

MANUFACTURING TECHNIQUES:

■■*How Things Are Made.* Juvenile. 104 pages. *1981*

MANUSCRIPTS, Medieval:

15th-Century Manuscript Yields First Look at *Niña.* By Eugene Lyon. 601-605, *Nov. 1986*

See also Henry E. Huntington Library and Art Gallery; Medieval Europe; St. Catherine's Monastery

The MANX and Their Isle of Man. By Veronica Thomas. Photos by Ted H. Funk. 426-444, *Sept. 1972*

The MANY-SIDED Diamond. By George S. Switzer. 568-586, *Apr. 1958*

MANY-SPLENDORED Glacierland. By George W. Long. Photos by Kathleen Revis. 589-636, *May 1956*

MAO TSE-TUNG:

Return to Changing China. By Audrey Topping. 801-833, *Dec. 1971*

MAORIS:

New Zealand: the Last Utopia? By Robert Paul Jordan. Photos by Kevin Fleming. 654-681, *May 1987*

Editorial. By Wilbur E. Garrett. 419, *Oct. 1984*

Maoris: At Home in Two Worlds. By Yva Momatiuk and John Eastcott. 522-541, *Oct. 1984*

Maoris: Treasures of the Tradition. By Douglas Newton. Photos by Brian Brake. 542-553, *Oct. 1984*

New Zealand's North Island: The Contented Land. By Charles McCarry. Photos by Bates Littlehales. 190-213, *Aug. 1974*

New Zealand's Cook Islands: Paradise in Search of a Future. By Maurice

Hanging on to hitchhiking remoras, a diver takes a ride on a manta ray, often called devilfish after the hornlike projections on its head.   HOWARD HALL

Shadbolt. Photos by William Albert Allard. 203-231, *Aug. 1967*

New Zealand: Gift of the Sea. By Maurice Shadbolt. Photos by Brian Brake. 465-511, *Apr. 1962*

New Zealand, Pocket Wonder World. By Howell Walker. 419-460, *Apr. 1952*

Hurdle Racing in Canoes: A Thrilling and Spectacular Sport Among the Maoris of New Zealand. By Walter Burke. 440-444, *May 1920*

The Maoris of New Zealand. 198-199, *Mar. 1907*

MAP (Island), Caroline Islands:

Mysterious Micronesia: Yap, Map, and Other Islands Under Japanese Mandate are Museums of Primitive Man. By Willard Price. 481-510, *Apr. 1936*

MAP-CHANGING Medicine. By William Joseph Showalter. 303-330, *Sept. 1922*

A **MAP** Maker Looks at the United States. By Newman Bumstead. 705-748, *June 1951*

MAP SERIES: Announcements:

The Making of America: 17 New Maps Tie the Nation to Its Past. By Wilbur E. Garrett. 630-633, *Nov. 1982*

Close-up: U.S.A.–a Fresh Look at Our Land and Its Heritage. By Gilbert M. Grosvenor. 287-289, *Mar. 1973*

New York City Map Launches United States Atlas Map Series. By Ralph E. McAleer. 108-110, *July 1964*

New Atlas Maps Announced by the Society: Expanded Map Program, Marking National Geographic's 70th Year. By James M. Darley. 66-68, *Jan. 1958*

MAP SUPPLEMENTS:

Africa

The Historic Mediterranean; The Mediterranean Seafloor. Dec. 1982
Africa; Africa, Its Political Development. Feb. 1980
The Heritage of Africa; The Peoples of Africa. Feb. 1971
Northwestern Africa. Atlas series. Aug. 1966
Nile Valley, Land of the Pharaohs. Atlas series. Text on reverse. May 1965
Africa: Countries of the Nile. Atlas series. Oct. 1963
Southern Africa. Atlas series. Nov. 1962
Africa. Atlas series. Sept. 1960
Northern Africa. Dec. 1954
Africa and the Arabian Peninsula. Mar. 1950
Africa. Feb. 1943
Theater of War in Europe, Africa, and Western Asia. July 1942
Africa. June 1935
Map of Africa and Adjoining Portions of Europe and Asia. Oct. 1922
Map of the Countries Bordering the Mediterranean Sea. Jan. 1912
Africa. Mar. 1909
Map of the Seat of War in Africa. Dec. 1899

Antarctica

Antarctica; Pinnipeds Around the World. Apr. 1987

A 1984 aerial survey covering 380 square miles of the Himalaya was used to produce the most detailed map ever drawn of the Mount Everest area.

Antarctica. Atlas series. Feb. 1963
Antarctica. Sept. 1957
Northern and Southern Hemispheres. Apr. 1943
The Antarctic Regions. Oct. 1932
South Polar Regions–Showing Routes of the Proposed Antarctic Expeditions. Aug. 1899

Arctic

Peoples of the Arctic; Arctic Ocean. Feb. 1983
Arctic Ocean; Arctic Ocean Floor. Oct. 1971
Top of the World. Atlas series. Nov. 1965
The Top of the World. Oct. 1949
Canada, Alaska, and Greenland. June 1947
Northern Hemisphere. Feb. 1946
Northern and Southern Hemispheres. Apr. 1943
The Arctic Regions. Nov. 1925

North Pole Regions. July 1907
The Arctic Regions. Included: Routes traversed by the Nansen Expedition of 1893-96. Oct. 1896
Carte Générale des Découvertes de l'Amiral de Fonte, et autres Navigateurs Espagnols, Anglois et Russes pour la recherche du Passage à la Mer du Sud. Par M. De l'Isle de l'Académie royale des Sciences &c. Jan. 28, 1892; Feb. 19, 1892

Asia

Mount Everest; High Himalaya. Nov. 1988
The Philippines; The History of the Philippines. Included: Archipelago; Cross, Crown, and Crescent; Manila Entrepôt; American Era; An Evolving Republic. July 1986
South Asia, with Afghanistan and Burma; Peoples of South Asia. Dec. 1984
Japan; Historical Japan. Included:

M N

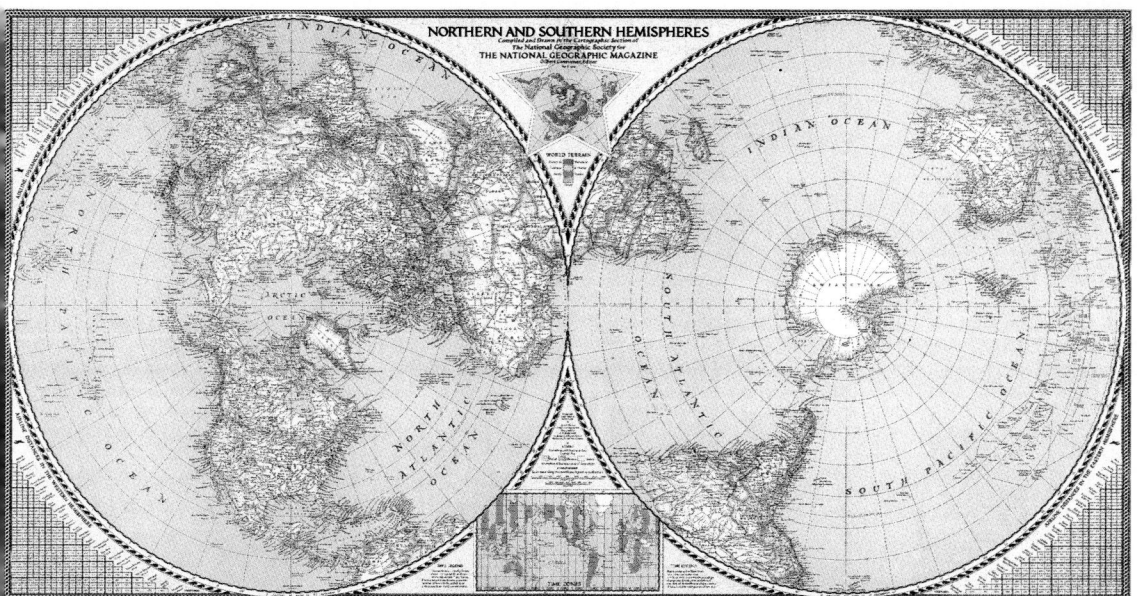

Society members received a polar-projection map of the Northern and Southern Hemispheres with their April 1943 magazine.

M
N

Land of the Feathered Serpent. Text on reverse. *Oct. 1968*

The United States and adjoining portions of Canada and Mexico. Dec. 1940

Mexico, Central America, and the West Indies. Dec. 1939

Mexico, Central America, and the West Indies. Dec. 1934

United States and adjoining portions of Canada and Mexico. May 1933

The Countries of the Caribbean, Including Mexico, Central America, the West Indies and the Panama Canal. Feb. 1922

Map of Mexico. July 1916

Mexico. May 1914

Mexico. May 1911

See also Central America; Mexico

Middle East

The Historic Mediterranean; The Mediterranean Seafloor. Dec. 1982

Two Centuries of Conflict in the Middle East; Mideast in Turmoil. Sept. 1980

Middle East, Eastern Mediterranean; Early Civilizations of the Middle East. Sept. 1978

The Peoples of the Middle East. Text on reverse. *July 1972*

Lands of the Bible Today. Dec. 1967

Holy Land Today. Atlas series. *Dec. 1963*

Lands of the Eastern Mediterranean. Atlas series. *Jan. 1959*

Lands of the Bible Today. Dec. 1956

Europe and the Near East. June 1949

Bible Lands and the Cradle of Western Civilization. Insets: Holy Land Today, Holy Land in Biblical Times, Jerusalem, Traditional Route of the Exodus, St. Paul's Travels and the Seven Churches, The Crusaders. *Dec. 1946*

Europe and the Near East. Inset: The Middle East. *June 1943*

Europe and the Near East. Inset: The Middle East. *May 1940*

Bible Lands and the Cradle of Western Civilization. Insets: Jerusalem, The Holy Land, Economic Development, Route of the Exodus, St. Paul's Travels and the Seven Churches, The Crusades, Empire of Alexander the Great. *Dec. 1938*

Europe and the Near East. Dec. 1929

North America

The Shaping of a Continent; Earth's Dynamic Crust. Included: Spreading, Subduction, Collision, Faulting, Accretion, Hot Spots, 90 Million Years of Drift. *Aug. 1985*

The Americas; Bird Migration in the Americas. Aug. 1979

Colonization and Trade in the New World. Text on reverse. *Dec. 1977*

North America Before Columbus; Indians of North America. Dec. 1972

North America. Atlas series. *Apr. 1964*

North America. Mar. 1952

North America. May 1942

North America. May 1924

A Chart Shewing part of the Coast of N. W. America (Vancouver's chart, No. I). *Nov. 1899*

A Chart Shewing part of the Coast of N. W. America (Vancouver's chart, No. II). *Nov. 1899*

Carte Générale des Découvertes de l'Amiral de Fonte, et autres Navigateurs Espagnols, Anglois et Russes pour la recherche du Passage à la Mer du Sud. Par M. de l'Isle de l'Académie royale des Sciences &c. Jan. 28, 1892; Feb. 19, 1892

See also Canada; Mexico; United States

Pacific Ocean

Islands of the Pacific; Discoverers of the Pacific. Dec. 1974

Pacific Ocean; Pacific Ocean Floor. Oct. 1969

Pacific Ocean; Pacific Islands. Atlas series. *Apr. 1962*

Pacific Ocean. Dec. 1952

Southeast Asia and Pacific Islands from the Indies and the Philippines to the Solomons. Oct. 1944

Japan and Adjacent Regions of Asia and the Pacific Ocean. Apr. 1944

Pacific Ocean and the Bay of Bengal. Sept. 1943

Theater of War in the Pacific Ocean. Feb. 1942

Pacific Ocean. Dec. 1936

Sovereignty and Mandate Boundary Lines in 1921 of the Islands of the Pacific. Dec. 1921

South America

Indians of South America; Archaeology of South America. Mar. 1982

The Americas; Bird Migration in the Americas. Aug. 1979

South America. Text on reverse. *Oct. 1972*

Northwestern South America. Atlas series. *Feb. 1964*

Eastern South America. Atlas series. *Sept. 1962*

South America. Atlas series. *Feb. 1960*

Southern South America. Atlas series. *Mar. 1958*

Eastern South America. Mar. 1955

South America. Oct. 1950

South America. Oct. 1942

South America. Dec. 1937

Map of South America. Oct. 1921

South America. Aug. 1906

Map of the Valley of the Orinoco River. Compiled by T. Heyward Gignilliat. *Feb. 1896*

Union of Soviet Socialist Republics

Soviet Union; Peoples of the Soviet Union. Feb. 1976

Eastern Soviet Union. Atlas series. *Mar. 1967*

Union of Soviet Socialist Republics. Wall map announced. *Dec. 1960*

Western Soviet Union. Atlas series. *Sept. 1959*

Union of Soviet Socialist Republics. Note: International boundaries shown as of October 1, 1944. Boundaries of January 1, 1938, are shown in red. *Dec. 1944*

Kirin, Harbin, Vladivostok. June 1905

Russia in Europe. Jan. 1896

Carte Générale des Découvertes de l'Amiral de Fonte, et autres Navigateurs Espagnols, Anglois et Russes pour la recherche du Passage à la Mer du Sud. Par M. De l'Isle de l'Académie royale des Sciences &c. Jan. 28, 1892; Feb. 19, 1892

United States

Tidewater and Environs. The Making of America series. Included: Maryland, Delaware, Virginia, North Carolina, South Carolina. On reverse: First Encounters, Farming and Frontiering, Rivalries and Rupture, Diversified Growth, Uneven Growth. *June 1988*

The United States; The Territorial Growth of the United States. Included: Europe Claims North America, A New Nation on Stage, Expanding West of the Mississippi, Coming of Age, Coast To Coast, The Union Holds, The Fifty States Today, A Broader View. *Sept. 1987*

Great Lakes. The Making of America series. Included: Michigan, Wisconsin. On reverse: Indians, French, British; Creation of a Borderland; Influx of Settlers; Lake-country Lumber; Industrial Powerhouse; Region in Readjustment. *July 1987*

New England. The Making of America series. Included: Maine, New Hampshire, Vermont, Massachusetts, Rhode Island, Connecticut, and eastern New York. On reverse: Indians and Outposts, Puritan Commonwealth, Greater New England, Industrial Hive, Immigrants and Industries, A New Vitality. *Feb. 1987*

Northern Plains. The Making of America series. Included: Montana, Wyoming, North Dakota, South Dakota, Nebraska, Minnesota, Iowa, and in Canada: Saskatchewan, Manitoba, Ontario. On reverse: New Frontiers, Indians in Transition, Furs and Footholds, Steel Rails and Settlers, King Wheat, Patterns of Change. *Dec. 1986*

Pacific Northwest. The Making of America series. Included: Idaho, Montana, Oregon, Washington.

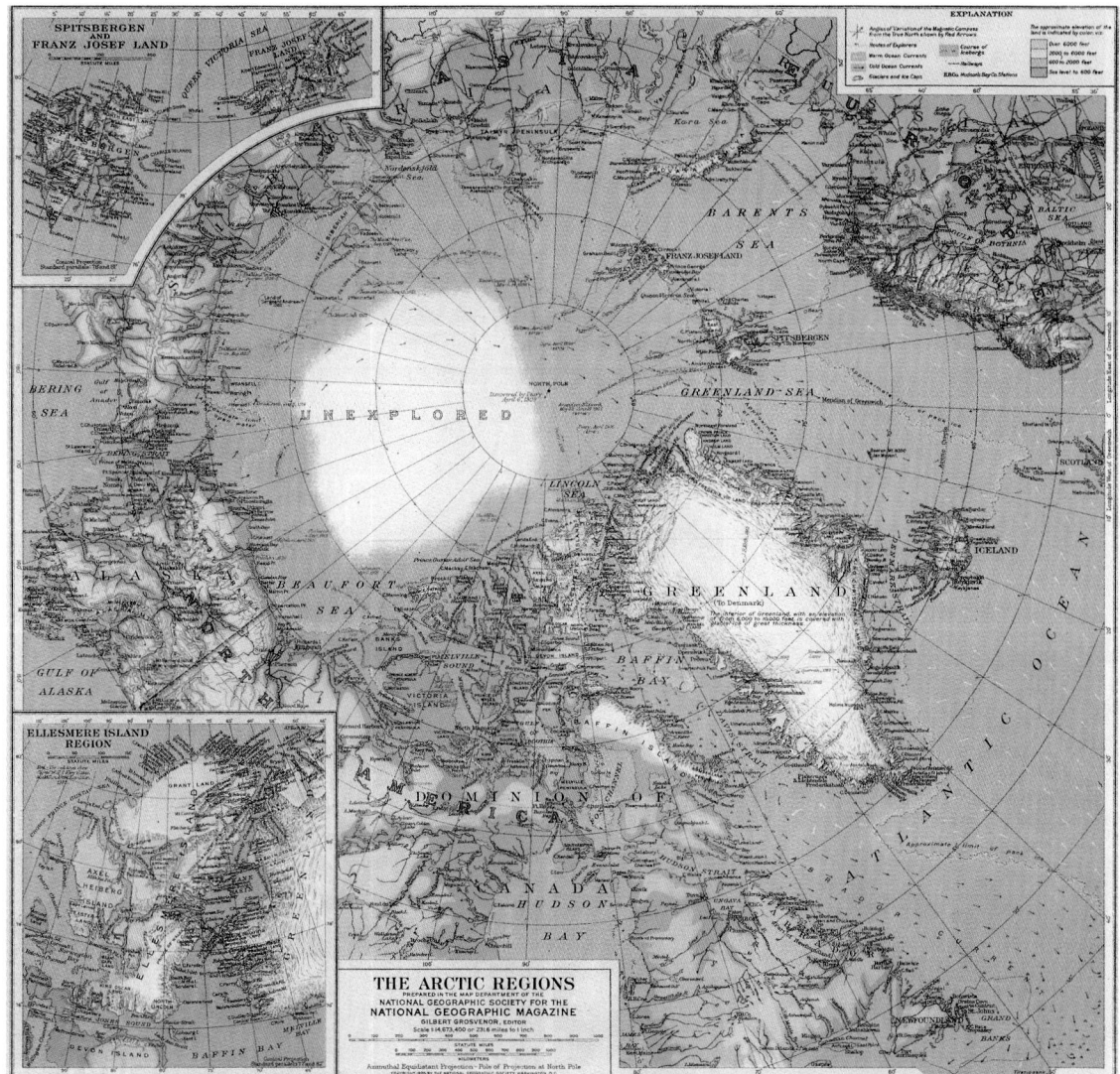

Map published in November 1925 with an account of the MacMillan Arctic Expedition shows some million square miles unexplored.

On reverse: Fur Trade Rivalries, Conquest-Colonization, Abrupt Change, Pacific Lumber Empire, Coming of Age. *Aug. 1986*

Texas. The Making of America series. On reverse: Weak Spanish Frontier, Eras of Independence, Vigorous Expansion, A Broadening Base, New Frontiers, Mexican Borderland. *Mar. 1986*

Ohio Valley. The Making of America series. Included: Tennessee-Tombigbee Waterway, West Virginia, Illinois, Tennessee, Kentucky, Ohio, Indiana. On reverse: Indians and Europeans, Speculation and Colonization, Transport Revolutions, Region Rent Asunder, Further Divergence, A New Era. *Dec. 1985*

Central Plains. The Making of America series. Included: Iowa, Illinois, Missouri, Arkansas, Nebraska, Kansas,

Oklahoma. On reverse: Indians and Entryways, Indian Land-White Land, The Great Assault, Indian Relocation, Indian Territory-The Last Stop, Last Frontiers, Dust Bowl of the Continent, Agricultural Heartland. *Sept. 1985*

Northern Approaches: Maine and the Maritimes. The Making of America series. Included: European Outreach, Northeast Contested, Shifting Population, A Changing Economy, The Cultural Imprint. *Feb. 1985*

Central Rockies. The Making of America series. Included: Colorado, Utah, Wyoming. On reverse: Fur and Frontier, Mission to Succeed, Mineral Riches, Lure of the Mountains. *Aug. 1984*

Far West. The Making of America series. Included: California, Nevada. On reverse: Northern and Southern

California—a Shifting Rivalry, Spanish Imprint, Sudden Transition, The New Eden, Water—the Key to Growth, Explosive Growth. *Apr. 1984*

Alaska. The Making of America series. On reverse: Native Alaska, Russian America, Seward's Folly or New Eldorado?, Military Alaska, The 49th State. *Jan. 1984*

Hawaii. The Making of America series. Included: Polynesian Arrival, Hawaii in Transition, Labor for Sugar, Hawaii as Territory, Hawaii as State. *Nov. 1983*

Deep South. The Making of America series. Included: Alabama, Florida, Georgia, Louisiana, Mississippi, South Carolina, and parts of Arkansas, North Carolina, and Tennessee. On reverse: Indian Legacy, Imperial Footholds, Three Empires and Three

Races, Cotton Kingdom, Post-bellum, New Deep South, Subtropical Playground. *Aug. 1983*

Atlantic Gateways. The Making of America series. Included: Delaware, Maryland, New Jersey, New York, Pennsylvania, northern Virginia, West Virginia, and in Canada, southern Ontario and southern Quebec. On reverse: Indians and Trade, Nation in the Making, Peopling of the Gateways, Race for the Hinterlands, Growth of Industry, Spreading Urban Corridors. *Mar. 1983*

Washington, D. C.: *Heart of Our Nation's Capital; Washington Inside the Beltway.* Detachable. 93-98, *Jan. 1983*

The Southwest. The Making of America series. Included: Arizona, New Mexico, and parts of California, Colorado, Texas, Utah; and in Mexico: Baja California Norte, Chihuahua, Sonora. On reverse: 12,000 Years of History; Spanish Conquest; Anglo-American Entry and Occupancy. *Nov. 1982*

America's Federal Lands; The United States. Sept. 1982

The Grand Canyon. Photomosaic and text on reverse. NGS research grant. *July 1978*

The Northeast. Close-up series. Text on reverse. Included: New Jersey, New York, Pennsylvania. *Jan. 1978*

The Southwest. Close-up series. Text on reverse. Included: Arizona, Colorado, New Mexico, Utah. *Oct. 1977*

Wild and Scenic Rivers of the United States. July 1977

Illinois, Indiana, Ohio, and Kentucky. Close-up series. Text on reverse. *Feb. 1977*

The Mid-Atlantic States. Close-up series. Text on reverse. Included: Delaware, Maryland, Virginia, West Virginia. *Oct. 1976*

The United States; Portrait U.S.A. (photomosaic). *July 1976*

Hawaii. Close-up series. Text on reverse. *Apr. 1976*

The Southeast. Close-up series. Text on reverse. Included: Alabama, Georgia, Mississippi, North Carolina, South Carolina, Tennessee. *Oct. 1975*

New England: *Western New England.* Close-up series. Text on reverse. Included: Connecticut, Massachusetts, New Hampshire, Rhode Island, Vermont. *July 1975*

Alaska. Close-up series. Text on reverse. *June 1975*

Maine, with the Maritime Provinces of Canada. Close-up series. Text on reverse. *Mar. 1975*

The South Central States. Close-up series. Text on reverse. Included: Arkansas, Louisiana, Oklahoma, Texas. *Oct. 1974*

California and Nevada. Close-up series. Text on reverse. *June 1974*

The North Central States. Close-up series. Text on reverse. Included: Iowa, Kansas, Minnesota, Missouri, Nebraska, North Dakota, South Dakota. *Mar. 1974*

Florida, with Puerto Rico and U. S. Virgin Islands. Close-up series. Text on reverse. *Nov. 1973*

Wisconsin, Michigan, and the Great Lakes. Close-up series. Text on reverse. *Aug. 1973*

Wisconsin, Michigan, and the Great Lakes. Close-up series. Text on reverse. *Aug. 1973*

The Northwest. Close-up series. Text on reverse. Included: Idaho, Montana, Oregon, Washington, Wyoming. *Mar. 1973*

The United States. Feb. 1968

Vacationlands of the United States and Southern Canada. Text on reverse. *July 1966*

Northern California; Southern California. U. S. Atlas series. *May 1966*

Tourist Washington; Suburban Washington. U. S. Atlas series. *Dec. 1964*

Greater New York; Tourist Manhattan. U. S. Atlas series. *July 1964*

United States: Washington to Boston. Atlas series. *Aug. 1962*

The United States. Atlas series. *July 1961*

Battlefields of the Civil War; Cockpit of the Civil War. Atlas series. *Apr. 1961*

South Central United States. Atlas series. Included: Arkansas, Louisiana, Mississippi, New Mexico, Oklahoma, Texas. *Feb. 1961*

Hawaii. Atlas series. *July 1960*

Northwestern United States. Atlas series. *Apr. 1960*

Southwestern United States. Atlas series. Included: Arizona, California, Colorado, Nevada, New Mexico, Utah. *Nov. 1959*

State of Alaska. Atlas series. *July 1959*

Northeastern United States, including the Great Lakes Region. Atlas series. Included: Connecticut, Delaware, Illinois, Indiana, Maine, Maryland, Massachusetts, Michigan, New Hampshire, New Jersey, New York, Ohio, Pennsylvania, Rhode Island, Vermont, Virginia, West Virginia, Wisconsin. *Apr. 1959*

North Central United States. Atlas series. Included: Illinois, Iowa, Kansas, Minnesota, Missouri, Nebraska, North Dakota, South Dakota, Wisconsin. *Nov. 1958*

National Parks, Monuments and Shrines of the United States and Canada. Atlas series. Text on reverse. *May 1958*

Southeastern United States. Atlas series. Included: Alabama, Florida, Georgia, Kentucky, Maryland, Mississippi, North Carolina, South Carolina, Tennessee, Virginia, West Virginia. *Jan. 1958*

The United States. Sept. 1956

Alaska. June 1956

Round About the Nation's Capital. Apr. 1956

New England. Included: Connecticut, Maine, Massachusetts, New Hampshire, New Jersey, New York, Pennsylvania, Rhode Island, Vermont. *June 1955*

A Map of California. June 1954

The Great Lakes Region of the United States and Canada. Dec. 1953

Historical Map of the United States. June 1953

The United States of America. June 1951

Northwestern United States and Neighboring Canadian Provinces. June 1950

Southwestern United States. Included: Arizona, California, Colorado, Nevada, New Mexico, Utah. *Dec. 1948*

A Pocket Map of Central Washington; A Pocket Map of Suburban Washington. Sept. 1948

North Central United States. Included: Illinois, Iowa, Kansas, Minnesota, Missouri, Nebraska, North Dakota, South Dakota, Wisconsin. *June 1948*

South Central United States. Included: Arkansas, Louisiana, Mississippi, New Mexico, Oklahoma, Texas. *Dec. 1947*

Southeastern United States. Included: Alabama, Florida, Georgia, Kentucky, Maryland, Mississippi, North Carolina, South Carolina, Tennessee, Virginia, West Virginia. *Feb. 1947*

The United States of America. Insets: United Nations area and East of Maine. *July 1946*

Northeastern United States. Sept. 1945

Map of Northwestern United States and Neighboring Canadian Provinces. June 1941

The United States and adjoining portions of Canada and Mexico. Dec. 1940

The Southwestern United States. June 1940

The Reaches of New York City. Included: Adjacent areas of Connecticut, New Jersey, and New York. *Apr. 1939*

Historic and Scenic Reaches of the Nation's Capital. July 1938

The White Mountains of New Hampshire. July 1937

United States and adjoining portions of Canada and Mexico. May 1933

Map of the Travels of George Washington. Insets: New York and the lower Hudson, Tidewater Virginia, Philadelphia, Boston, Mount Vernon. *Jan. 1932*

Illinois. May 1931

Louisiana. Apr. 1930

Florida. Insets: Miami-Palm Beach, Pensacola, Jacksonville-St. Augustine, Tampa-St. Petersburg-Sarasota. *Jan. 1930*

Maryland, Delaware, and District of Columbia. Feb. 1927

North Carolina, South Carolina, Georgia, and Eastern Tennessee. Sept. 1926

United States of America. Apr. 1923

The Mall, Washington, D. C. Mar. 1915

The Ultimate Washington (Plan laid out by the Commission of 1901). *Mar. 1915*

Alaska. Feb. 1914

Alaska. May 1904

Alaska Boundary Tribunal. Jan. 1904

The Gold And Coal Fields of Alaska, Together With the Principal Steamer Routes and Trails. Insets: Trails from Tide Water to the Headwaters of the Yukon River; The Klondike Gold Region, Canada. *Apr. 1898*

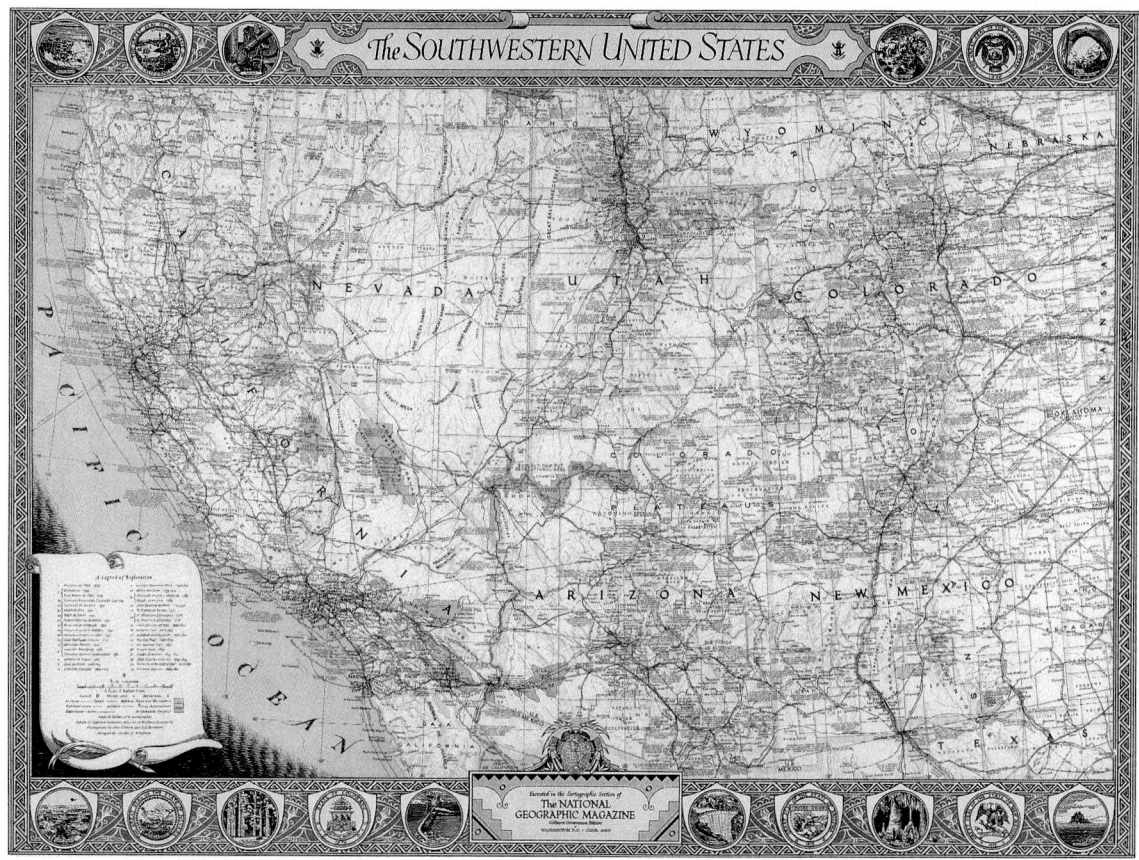

The SOUTHWESTERN UNITED STATES

Map of the southwestern United States in June 1940 traced routes of early explorers, pioneers, and the Pony Express in 1860-1861.

United States showing Estimates of the Map Value of Existing Mother Maps. By Henry Gannett. *Mar. 31, 1892*

Muir Glacier, Alaska. Mar. 21, 1892

North Carolina-Tennessee: Asheville Sheet. Section from the Cumberland Plateau to the Blue Ridge. Surveyed in 1882-3-7. Note: Reprinted 1965 as *Asheville Quadrangle.* Surveyed in 1898-99. *Oct. 1889*

Universe

Journey Into the Universe Through Time and Space; National Geographic-Palomar Sky Survey Charting the Heavens. June 1983

The Solar System; Saturn. July 1981

The Red Planet Mars. Text on reverse. *Feb. 1973*

A Map of the Heavens. Star charts on reverse. Dec. 1957; *Aug. 1970*

The Earth's Moon. Feb. 1969

World

World; Endangered Earth. Robinson projection. Included: Pastures of the Sea; The Continental Garden; Global Carbon Dioxide; Ice Age Vegetation 18,000 Years BP; Greenhouse-Effect Vegetation Zones; Population Explosion; Peru-Ecuador Upwelling; Minnesota's Boreal Forest; Population Projections; Growing Threats: Population Pressure, Air Pollution, Ozone Concerns, Acid Rain, Water Pollution, Species Extinctions, Fisheries Depletion, Deforestation, Desertification. *Dec. 1988*

Antarctica; Pinnipeds Around the World. Apr. 1987

Earth's Dynamic Crust; The Shaping of a Continent: North America's Active West. Aug. 1985

The World; The World Ocean Floor. Dec. 1981

The Great Whales: Migration and Range. Text on reverse. *Dec. 1976*

The Political World; The Physical World. Nov. 1975

The World. Text on reverse. *Dec. 1970*

The World. Feb. 1965

The World. Atlas series. *Nov. 1960*

The World. Mar. 1957

The World Map. Dec. 1951

Northern Hemisphere. Feb. 1946

The World Map. Dec. 1943

Northern and Southern Hemispheres. Apr. 1943

A Map of the World (in Eastern and Western Hemispheres). *Dec. 1941*

The World (in Eastern and Western Hemispheres). *Dec. 1935*

The World. Dec. 1932

The World. Dec. 1922

Cotidal Lines for the World; or, Lines of Simultaneous High Water at Each Hour and Half Hour of Greenwich Lunar Time. *June 1906*

Chart of the World on Mercator's Projection, showing Submarine Cables and Connections, and also Tracks for full-powered Steam Vessels. Feb. 1905

Submarine Cables of the World, with the Principal Connecting Land Lines, also Coaling, Docking, and Repairing Stations. Mar. 1896

Chronicon Nurembergense Map, 1493. Apr. 7, 1893

Juan de la Cosa Map, 1500. Apr. 7, 1893

Ruysch Map, 1508. Apr. 7, 1893

MAPLE SUGAR AND SYRUP:

Sugar Weather in the Green Mountains. By Stephen Greene. Photos by Robert F. Sisson. 471-482, *Apr. 1954*

MAPMAKING:

New Perspective on the World. By John B. Garver, Jr. 911-913, *Dec. 1988*

President's Page. By Gilbert M. Grosvenor. *May 1984*

Editorial. By Wilbur E. Garrett. 145, *Aug. 1983*

Editorial. By Wilbur E. Garrett. 685, *Dec. 1982*

Editorial. By Gilbert M. Grosvenor. 1, *July 1980*

MARBLEHEAD, Massachusetts:
Windjamming Around New England. By Tom Horgan. Photos by Robert F. Sisson. 141-169, *Aug. 1950*
Northeast of Boston. By Albert W. Atwood. 257-292, *Sept. 1945*

MARBLEHEAD-HALIFAX RACE:
Down East to Nova Scotia. By Winfield Parks. 853-879, *June 1964*

MARBORÉ (Massif), France-Spain:
Probing Ice Caves of the Pyrenees. By Norbert Casteret. 391-404, *Mar. 1953*

MARCHING Through Georgia Sixty Years After: Multifold Industries and Diversified Agriculture Are Restoring the Prosperity of America's Largest State East of the Mississippi. By Ralph A. Graves. 259-311, *Sept. 1926*

MARCHIONINI, ALFRED:
Author-Photographer
Peasants of Anatolia. 57-72, *July 1948*

MARCO POLO. *See* Polo, Marco

MARCOS, FERDINAND:
Hope and Danger in the Philippines. By Arthur Zich. Photos by Steve McCurry. 76-117, *July 1986*

MARCUS, OSCAR: *Photographer*
Pilgrims' Progress to Mecca. 627-642, *Nov. 1937*

MARDEN, LUIS:
On Assignment. *Nov. 1986*
Editorial. By Gilbert M. Grosvenor. 439, *Apr. 1978*
In Brazil. Nomination Page. *Mar. 1971*
Nomination Page. *Sept. 1961*
On Pitcairn Island. Nomination Page. *Dec. 1957*

Author
The First Landfall of Columbus. 572-577, *Nov. 1986*
Wreck of H.M.S. *Pandora*. 423-451, *Oct. 1985*
The Bird Men (Ultralight Fliers). Photos by Charles O'Rear. 198-217, *Aug. 1983*
Bamboo, the Giant Grass. Photos by Jim Brandenburg. 502-529, *Oct. 1980*
The Continental Shelf: Man's New Frontier. Photos by Ira Block. 495-531, *Apr. 1978*
The Renaissance Lives On In Tuscany. Photos by Albert Moldvay. 626-659, *Nov. 1974*
The American Lobster, Delectable Cannibal. Photos by David Doubilet. 462-487, *Apr. 1973*
The Exquisite Orchids. Included: The newly discovered *Epistephium mardeni*. 485-513, *Apr. 1971*
Titicaca, Abode of the Sun. Photos by Flip Schulke. 272-294, *Feb. 1971*
The Sailing Oystermen of Chesapeake Bay. 798-819, *Dec. 1967*
Madagascar: Island at the End of the Earth. Photos by Albert Moldvay. 443-487, *Oct. 1967*
Saga of a Ship, the *Yankee* (Brigantine). 263-269, *Feb. 1966*
The Man Who Talks to Hummingbirds.

Photos by James Blair. 80-99, *Jan. 1963*
Guatemala Revisited. 525-564, *Oct. 1947*
To Market in Guatemala. Photos by Giles Greville Healey and Charles S. Pineo. 87-104, *July 1945*

Author-Photographer
Ama, Sea Nymphs of Japan. 122-135, *July 1971*
The Friendly Isles of Tonga. 345-367, *Mar. 1968*

The remains of the **Bounty** *were discovered off Pitcairn Island by* GEOGRAPHIC *staffer Luis Marden.*   THOMAS CHRISTIAN

The Other Side of Jordan. 790-825, *Dec. 1964*
Tahiti, "Finest Island in the World." 1-47, *July 1962*
Huzza for Otaheite! (*Bounty* Voyage). 435-459, *Apr. 1962*
Amalfi, Italy's Divine Coast. 472-509, *Oct. 1959*
Dzibilchaltun: Up from the Well of Time. 110-129, *Jan. 1959*
The Islands Called Fiji. 526-561, *Oct. 1958*
I Found the Bones of the *Bounty*. 725-789, *Dec. 1957*
Camera Under the Sea. 162-200, *Feb. 1956*
Bruges, the City the Sea Forgot. 631-665, *May 1955*
Sicily the Three-cornered. 1-48, *Jan. 1955*
Gloucester Blesses Its Portuguese Fleet. 75-84, *July 1953*
Tropical Gardens of Key West. 116-124, *Jan. 1953*
Spain's Silkworm Gut. 100-108, *July 1951*
Holy Week and the Fair in Sevilla. 499-530, *Apr. 1951*
Speaking of Spain. 415-456, *Apr. 1950*
The Purple Land of Uruguay. 623-654, *Nov. 1948*
Land of the Painted Oxcarts (Costa Rica). 409-456, *Oct. 1946*
Coffee Is King in El Salvador. Photos by author and David D. Duncan. 575-616, *Nov. 1944*
A Land of Lakes and Volcanoes (Nicaragua). 161-192, *Aug. 1944*
Americans in the Caribbean. Included: War Echoes in the West Indies. 723-758, *June 1942*
Panama, Bridge of the World. Included: The Land That Links the Americas. 591-630, *Nov. 1941*
Hail Colombia! Included: Beneath Colombia's Azure Skies. 505-536, *Oct. 1940*
On the Cortés Trail. Included: In Montezuma's Painted Land. 335-375, *Sept. 1940*
Caracas, Cradle of the Liberator: The Spirit of Simón Bolívar, South American George Washington, Lives On in the City of His Birth. Included: Venezuela's Capital–City of Contrasts. 477-513, *Apr. 1940*

Photographer
Exploring the Drowned City of Port Royal. By Marion Clayton Link. 151-183, *Feb. 1960*
Cape Canaveral's 6,000-mile Shooting Gallery. By Allan C. Fisher, Jr. Photos by Luis Marden and Thomas Nebbia. 421-471, *Oct. 1959*
Reaching for the Moon (Rockets). By Allan C. Fisher, Jr. 157-171, *Feb. 1959*
Hydrofoil Ferry "Flies" the Strait of Messina. By Gilbert Grosvenor. 493-496, *Apr. 1957*
Exploring Davy Jones's Locker with *Calypso*. By Jacques-Yves Cousteau. 149-161, *Feb. 1956*
Aviation Medicine on the Threshold of Space. By Allan C. Fisher, Jr. 241-278, *Aug. 1955*

In the tiny submersible **Alvin,** *scientists explore the Mid-Ocean Ridge, finding startling marine life and mineral sources.*   EMORY KRISTOF AND ALVIN M. CHANDLER, BOTH NGS

The Strangest Sea. By Eugenie Clark. Photos by David Doubilet. 338-365. Included: Rainbow World Beneath the Red Sea. 344-365, *Sept. 1975*

Diving Beneath Arctic Ice. By Joseph B. MacInnis. Photos by William R. Curtsinger. 248-267, *Aug. 1973*

Antarctica's Nearer Side. By Samuel W. Matthews. Photos by William R. Curtsinger. 622-655, *Nov. 1971*

Tektite II. 256-296. I. Science's Window on the Sea. By John G. VanDerwalker. Photos by Bates Littlehales. 256-289; II. All-girl Team Tests the Habitat. By Sylvia A. Earle. Paintings by Pierre Mion. 291-296, *Aug. 1971*

Nature's Night Lights: Probing the Secrets of Bioluminescence. By Paul A. Zahl. 45-69, *July 1971*

Deepstar Explores the Ocean Floor. Photos by Ron Church. 110-129, *Jan. 1971*

At Home in the Sea. By Jacques-Yves Cousteau. 465-507, *Apr. 1964*

Oregon's Sidewalk on the Sea. By Paul A. Zahl. 708-734, *Nov. 1961*

How the Sun Gives Life to the Sea. By Paul A. Zahl. 199-225, *Feb. 1961*

Sailing a Sea of Fire (Phosphorescent Bay, Puerto Rico). By Paul A. Zahl. 120-129, *July 1960*

Diving Saucer Takes to the Deep. By Jacques-Yves Cousteau. NGS research grant. 571-586, *Apr. 1960*

Deep Diving off Japan. By Georges S. Houot. NGS research grant. 138-150, *Jan. 1960*

Four Years of Diving to the Bottom of the Sea. By Georges S. Houot. NGS research grant. 715-731, *May 1958*

Calypso Explores an Undersea Canyon (Romanche Trench). By Jacques-Yves Cousteau. Photos by Bates Littlehales. NGS research grant. 373-396, *Mar. 1958*

Camera Under the Sea. By Luis Marden. NGS research grant. 162-200, *Feb. 1956*

Exploring Davy Jones's Locker with *Calypso*. By Jacques-Yves Cousteau. Photos by Luis Marden. NGS research grant. 149-161, *Feb. 1956*

Glass Menageries of the Sea. By Paul A. Zahl. 797-822, *June 1955*

One Hundred Hours Beneath the Chesapeake. By Gilbert C. Klingel. Photos by Willard R. Culver. NGS research grant. 681-696, *May 1955*

Photographing the Sea's Dark Underworld. By Harold E. Edgerton. NGS research grant. 523-537, *Apr. 1955*

To the Depths of the Sea by Bathyscaphe. By Jacques-Yves Cousteau. NGS research grant. 67-79, *July 1954*

Two and a Half Miles Down. By Georges S. Houot. NGS research grant. 80-86, *July 1954*

Night Life in the Gulf Stream. By Paul A. Zahl. 391-418, *Mar. 1954*

Fishing in the Whirlpool of Charybdis. By Paul A. Zahl. 579-618, *Nov. 1953*

Miami's Expanding Horizons. By William H. Nicholas. Included: University of Miami marine biology study and National Geographic Society–University of Miami long-range

program to study plankton. 561-594, *Nov. 1950*

On the Bottom of a South Sea Pearl Lagoon. By Roy Waldo Miner. Paintings by Else Bostelmann. 365-390, *Sept. 1938*

Denizens of Our Warm Atlantic Waters. By Roy Waldo Miner. Paintings by Else Bostelmann. 199-219, *Feb. 1937*

Sea Creatures of Our Atlantic Shores. By Roy Waldo Miner. Paintings by Else Bostelmann. 209-231, *Aug. 1936*

A Half Mile Down: Strange Creatures, Beautiful and Grotesque as Figments of Fancy, Reveal Themselves at Windows of the Bathysphere. By William Beebe. Paintings by Else Bostelmann, Helen D. Tee-Van, and E. J. Geske. 661-704, *Dec. 1934*

A Wonderer Under Sea. By William Beebe. Paintings by E. Bostelmann. 741-758, *Dec. 1932*

The Depths of the Sea: Strange Life Forms a Mile Below the Surface. By William Beebe. Paintings by E. Bostelmann. 65-88, *Jan. 1932*

A Round Trip to Davy Jones's Locker: Peering into Mysteries a Quarter Mile Down in the Open Sea, by Means of the Bathysphere. By William Beebe. Paintings by E. Bostelmann. 653-678, *June 1931*

The First Autochromes from the Ocean Bottom: Marine Life in Its Natural Habitat Along the Florida Keys Is Successfully Photographed in Colors. Photos by W. H. Longley and Charles Martin. 56-60, *Jan. 1927*

Certain Citizens of the Warm Sea. By Louis L. Mowbray. Paintings by Hashime Murayama. 27-62, *Jan. 1922*

Treasure-House of the Gulf Stream: The Completion and Opening of the New Aquarium and Biological Laboratory at Miami, Florida. By John Oliver La Gorce. Paintings by Hashime Murayama. 53-68, *Jan. 1921*

Interesting Citizens of the Gulf Stream. By John T. Nichols. 69-84, *Jan. 1921*

Notes from a Naturalist's Experiences in British Guiana. By C. H. Eigenmann. 859-870, *Sept. 1911*

The Glass-Bottom Boat. By Charles Frederick Holder. 761-778, *Sept. 1909*

The Purple Veil: A Romance of the Sea. By H. A. Largelamb (Alexander Graham Bell). 337-341, *July 1905*

Deep-Sea Exploring Expedition of the Steamer "Albatross." By Hugh M. Smith. 291-296, *Aug. 1899*

See also Algae; Corals and Coral Reefs; Crustaceans; Dolphins; Fish Farming; Fisheries; Fishes; Manatees; Marine Worms; Mollusks; Octopuses; Plankton; Porpoises; Rotifers; Seals; Sharks; Sponges; Walruses; Whales

MARINE Hydrographic Surveys of the Coasts of the World. By George W. Littlehales. 63-67, *Feb. 1905*

MARINE MAMMALS. See Dolphins; Manatees; Porpoises; Sea Lions; Sea Otters; Seals; Walruses; Whales

A **MARINE** Park Is Born. By Soames Summerhays. Photos by Ron and Valerie Taylor. 630-635, *May 1981*

MARINE PARKS. See Buck Island Reef National Monument, St. Croix, Virgin Islands; Great Barrier Reef, Australia; John Pennekamp Coral Reef State Park, Florida; Ras Muhammad, Sinai Peninsula

MARINE RESEARCH. See Airborne Undersea Expeditions; Marine Biology; Oceanography; Underwater Exploration

MARINE WORMS:

The Worm Turns. By Samuel Sandrof. 775-786, *June 1946*

MARINELAND, Florida's Giant Fish Bowl. By Gilbert Grosvenor La Gorce. Photos by Luis Marden. 679-694, *Nov. 1952*

MARINER MISSIONS:

Mariner Unveils Venus and Mercury (Mariner 10). By Kenneth F. Weaver. 858-869, *June 1975*

Journey to Mars (Mariner 9). By Kenneth F. Weaver. Paintings by Ludek Pesek. 231-263, *Feb. 1973*

Voyage to the Planets. By Kenneth F. Weaver. Paintings by Ludek Pesek. Included: Mariner 2, Mariner 4, Mariner 5, Mariner 6, Mariner 7. 147-193, *Aug. 1970*

Mariner Scans a Lifeless Venus (Mariner 2). By Frank Sartwell. Paintings by Davis Meltzer. 733-742, *May 1963*

MARINES, U. S. See U. S. Marine Corps

MARISMAS (Marshes), Spain:

Rare Birds Flock to Spain's Marismas. By Roger Tory Peterson. 397-425, *Mar. 1958*

MARITIME ALPS, Europe:

Sheep Trek in the French Alps. By Maurice Moyal. Photos by Marcel Coen. 545-564, *Apr. 1952*

MARITIME PROVINCES, Canada:

✣ *Northern Approaches: Maine and the Maritimes.* The Making of America series. *Feb. 1985*

✣ *Close-up: U.S.A., Maine, with the Maritime Provinces of Canada.* Text on reverse. *Mar. 1975*

See also New Brunswick; Nova Scotia

MARK, MARY ELLEN:

On Assignment in Australia. *Feb. 1988*

Photographer

Brazil: Flight to the Cities. By Paul R. and Anne H. Ehrlich. 934-937, *Dec. 1988*

Sydney's Changing Face. By Elizabeth A. Moize. 246-265, *Feb. 1988*

MARK TWAIN: Mirror of America. By Noel Grove. Photos by James L. Stanfield. 300-337, *Sept. 1975*

MARKEN (Island), The Netherlands:

Glimpses of Holland. By William Wisner Chapin. 1-29, *Jan. 1915*

MARKING the Alaskan Boundary. 176-189, *Mar. 1908*

MARKING the Alaskan Boundary. By Thomas Riggs, Jr. 593-607, *July 1909*

MARKING Time in Grenada. By Charles E. Cobb, Jr. Photos by David Alan Harvey. 688-710, *Nov. 1984*

MARKWITH, CARL R.: *Author*

Skyway Below the Clouds. Photos by Ernest J. Cottrell. 85-108, *July 1949*

Farewell to Bikini. 97-116, *July 1946*

MARLATT, CHARLES LESTER: *Author*

Protecting the United States from Plant Pests. 205-218, *Aug. 1921*

Pests and Parasites: Why We Need a National Law to Prevent the Importation of Insect-Infested and Diseased Plants. 321-346, *Apr. 1911*

MARLINS:

Fighting Giants of the Humboldt. By David D. Duncan. 373-400, *Mar. 1941*

MARLOWE, CHRISTOPHER: *Author*

A Tour in the English Fenland. 605-634, *May 1929*

MARMORA, Sea of:

The Gates to the Black Sea: The Dardanelles, the Bosphorus, and the Sea of Marmora. By Harry Griswold Dwight. 435-459, *May 1915*

MAROON, FRED J.: *Photographer*

The Great Good Places: English Country Houses. By Mark Girouard. 658-694, *Nov. 1985*

MAROSTICA, Italy:

Chessmen Come to Life in Marostica. By Alexander Taylor. 658-668, *Nov. 1956*

MARQUEEN ISLANDS. *See* Tauu Islands

MARQUESAS ISLANDS, Pacific Ocean:

Shores and Sails in the South Seas. By Charles Allmon. Included: Fatu Hiva; Fatu Huku; Hiva Oa; Nuku Hiva; Tahuata; Ua Huka; Ua Pu. 73-104, *Jan. 1950*

Turning Back Time in the South Seas. By Thor Heyerdahl. 109-136, *Jan. 1941*

At Home on the Oceans: Whales and Sharks Make Exciting Neighbors for a Professor's Wife, Turned Able Seaman, On a Three-year Voyage Around the World. By Edith Bauer Strout. 33-86, *July 1939*

The Romance of Science in Polynesia: An Account of Five Years of Cruising Among the South Sea Islands. By Robert Cushman Murphy. Paintings by Hashime Murayama. 355-426, *Oct. 1925*

The Dream Ship: The Story of a Voyage of Adventure More Than Half Around the World in a 47-foot

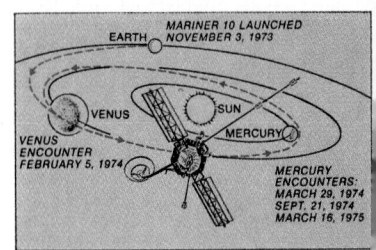

A 1974 mosaic of images made by Mariner 10 shows the meteorite-pocked surface of the planet Mercury. Diagram traces the spacecraft's path to encounter. NASA

A Mars colony, possible by the year 2050, would use an array of equipment to cope with the hostile environment. PAINTING BY ROY ANDERSEN

Lifeboat. By Ralph Stock. 1-52, *Jan. 1921*

A Vanishing People of the South Seas: The Tragic Fate of the Marquesan Cannibals, Noted for Their Warlike Courage and Physical Beauty. By John W. Church. 275-306, *Oct. 1919*

Diary of a Voyage from San Francisco to Tahiti and Return, 1901. By S. P. Langley. 413-429, *Dec. 1901*

MARQUESAS KEYS, Florida:

Treasure From the Ghost Galleon: *Santa Margarita*. By Eugene Lyon. Photos by Don Kincaid. 228-243, *Feb. 1982*

Atocha, Tragic Treasure Galleon of the Florida Keys. By Eugene Lyon. 787-809, *June 1976*

MARQUEZ, LUIS: *Photographer*

A Mexican Land of Lakes and Lacquers (Pátzcuaro Region). Photos by Helene Fischer and Luis Marquez. 633-648, *May 1937*

MARRAK POINT, Greenland:

Uncle Sam's Icebox Outposts. Photos by John E. Schneider and Robert B. Sykes, Jr. 473-496, *Oct. 1946*

MARRAKECH, Morocco:

Americans on the Barbary Coast. By Willard Price. 1-31, *July 1943*

The **MARRIAGE** of the Gods. By John J. Banninga. 1314-1330, *Dec. 1913*

MARRIAGES. *See* Weddings

MARRINER, J. THEODORE: *Author*

Transylvania and Its Seven Castles: A Motor Circuit Through Rumania's New Province of Racial Complexity and Architectural Charm. 319-352, *Mar. 1926*

MARS:

Mission to Mars. By Michael Collins. Photos by Roger H. Ressmeyer.

Paintings by Pierre Mion and Roy Andersen. 733-764, *Nov. 1988*

The Planets: Between Fire and Ice. By Rick Gore. 4-51, *Jan. 1985*

Editorial. By Gilbert M. Grosvenor. 1, *Jan. 1977*

Mars: Our First Close Look. 3-31. I. As Viking Sees It. 3-7; II. The Search For Life. By Rick Gore. 9-31, *Jan. 1977*

Journey to Mars. By Kenneth F. Weaver. Paintings by Ludek Pesek. 231-263, *Feb. 1973*

The Search for Life on Mars. By Kenneth F. Weaver. 264-265, *Feb. 1973*

⊕ *The Red Planet Mars;* "The Dusty Face of Mars," map-and-painting supplement. *Feb. 1973*

Voyage to the Planets. By Kenneth F. Weaver. Paintings by Ludek Pesek. 147-193, *Aug. 1970*

Mars: A New World to Explore. By Carl Sagan. 821-841, *Dec. 1967*

New Light on the Changing Face of Mars. By E. C. Slipher. NGS research grant. 427-436, *Sept. 1955*

MARS RESEARCH EXPEDITION: South Africa:

New Light on the Changing Face of Mars. By E. C. Slipher. NGS research grant. 427-436, *Sept. 1955*

MARSEILLE, France:

Provence, Empire of the Sun. By William Davenport. Photos by James A. Sugar. 692-715, *May 1975*

French Riviera: Storied Playground on the Azure Coast. By Carleton Mitchell. Photos by Thomas Nebbia. 798-835, *June 1967*

Marseille, Battle Port of Centuries. By a Staff Correspondent. Photos by W. Robert Moore. 425-448, *Oct. 1944*

MARSH, CODY: *Author*

Glimpses of Siberia, the Russian "Wild East." 513-536, *Dec. 1920*

MARSH, DONALD B.: *Author-Photographer*

Canada's Caribou Eskimos. 87-104, *Jan. 1947*

MARSH, O. C.:

Professor O. C. Marsh (Biography). By W J McGee. 181-182, *May 1899*

MARSH ARABS. *See* Ma'dan Tribespeople

MARSH DWELLERS of Southern Iraq. By Wilfred Thesiger. Photos by Gavin Maxwell. 205-239, *Feb. 1958*

MARSHACK, ALEXANDER:

A Bold New Look at Our Past. The Editor. 62-63, *Jan. 1975*

Author

Exploring the Mind of Ice Age Man. 64-89, *Jan. 1975*

Author-Photographer

An Ice Age Ancestor? Photos by the author and Ira Block. 478-481, *Oct. 1988*

MARSHALL, BOB:

A Short Hike With Bob Marshall. By Mike Edwards. Photos by Dewitt Jones. 664-689, *May 1985*

Battle For a Bigger Bob (Bob Marshall Wilderness). By Mike Edwards. Photos by Dewitt Jones. 690-692, *May 1985*

MARSHALL, GEORGE C.:

Tribute to General George C. Marshall. 113, *Jan. 1960*

Author

Our War Memorials Abroad: A Faith Kept. 731-737, *June 1957*

Giant Effigies of the Southwest. 389, *Sept. 1952*

MARSHALL, LAURENCE K.: *Photographer*

Bushmen of the Kalahari. By Elizabeth Marshall Thomas. 866-888, *June 1963*

MARSHALL ISLANDS, Pacific Ocean:

In the Far Pacific: At the Birth of Nations. By Carolyn Bennett Patterson. Photos by David Hiser and Melinda Berge. Included: Mariana Islands, Marshall Islands, Kosrae, Pohnpei, Truk, Yap, Palau. 460-499, *Oct. 1986*

Bikini—A Way of Life Lost. By William S. Ellis. Photos by James P. Blair. 813-834, *June 1986*

Pacific Wards of Uncle Sam. By W. Robert Moore. 73-104, *July 1948*

Farewell to Bikini. By Carl Markwith. 97-116, *July 1946*

American Pathfinders in the Pacific. By William H. Nicholas. 617-640, *May 1946*

Our New Military Wards, the Marshalls. By W. Robert Moore. Included: Marshallese Are Happy Again. 325-360, *Sept. 1945*

Hidden Key to the Pacific: Piercing the Web of Secrecy Which Long Has Veiled Japanese Bases in the Mandated Islands. By Willard Price. 759-785, *June 1942*

Yap and Other Pacific Islands Under Japanese Mandate. By Junius B. Wood. 591-627, *Dec. 1921*

See also Bikini; Kwajalein

MARSHALL KALAHARI EXPEDITIONS:

Bushmen of the Kalahari. By Elizabeth Marshall Thomas. Photos by Laurence K. Marshall. 866-888, *June 1963*

MARSHES. *See* Wetlands

MARSHFIELD, Massachusetts:

Land of the Pilgrims' Pride. By George W. Long. Photos by Robert F. Sisson. 193-219, *Aug. 1947*

MARSTON, JAY: *Author*

Uganda, "Land of Something New": Equatorial African Area Reveals Snow-crowned Peaks, Crater Lakes, Jungle-story Beasts, Human Giants, and Forest Pygmies. 109-130, *Jan. 1937*

MARSUPIALS:

■ Australia's Animal Mysteries. 824, *Dec. 1982*

Eden in the Outback. By Kay and Stanley Breeden. 189-203, *Feb. 1973*

Strange Animals of Australia. By David Fleay. Photos by Stanley Breeden. 388-411, *Sept. 1963*

What the Fighting Yanks See. By Wanda Burnett. 451-476, *Oct. 1944*

See also Kangaroos; Koalas; Opossums

MARTHA'S VINEYARD, Massachusetts:

Martha's Vineyard. By William P. E. Graves. Photos by James P. Blair. 778-809, *June 1961*

Windjamming Around New England. By Tom Horgan. Photos by Robert F. Sisson. 141-169, *Aug. 1950*

MARTIN, CHARLES: *Photographer*

Demon-Possessed Tibetans and Their Incredible Feats. 479-486, *Oct. 1935*

Winter Lights and Shadows in the Nation's Capital. 201-216, *Feb. 1935*

Our Colorful City of Magnificent Distances (Washington, D. C.). 531-610, *Nov. 1931*

Secrets of Washington's Lure. 377-384, *Mar. 1930*

Ever Changing California, Land of Startling Contrasts. 705-744, *June 1929*

Scenes and Shrines of the Cavalier Country. 425-432, *Apr. 1929*

Monticello, One of America's Most Historic Shrines. 489-496, *Apr. 1929*

Unique Gifts of Washington (D. C.) to the Nation. 473-480, *Apr. 1929*

The First Autochromes from the Ocean Bottom: Marine Life in Its Natural Habitat Along the Florida Keys Is Successfully Photographed in Colors. Photos by W. H. Longley and Charles Martin. 56-60, *Jan. 1927*

Exploring the Atlantic Seaboard with a Color Camera. 533-548, *May 1926*

Colorful Porto Rico. 631-642, *Dec. 1924*

Washington (D. C.), the Pride of the Nation. 617-632, *June 1923*

Philippines. Photos by Dean C. Worcester and Charles Martin. 1161-1192, *Nov. 1913*

MARTIN, DUDLEY B.: *Author*

Shad in the Shadow of Skyscrapers. Photos by Luis Marden. 359-376, *Mar. 1947*

MARTIN, ELINOR R.:

Nomination Page. *Sept. 1963*

MARTIN, ESMOND BRADLEY: *Author*

They're Killing Off the Rhino. Photos by Jim Brandenburg. 404-422, *Mar. 1984*

MARTIN, GEORGE C.: *Author*

The Recent Eruption of Katmai Volcano in Alaska. 131-181, *Feb. 1913*

MARTIN, LAWRENCE:

President's Page. By Gilbert M. Grosvenor. *Sept. 1988*

Author

■■ *Alaskan Glacier Studies of the National Geographic Society in the Yakutat Bay, Prince William Sound and Lower Copper River Regions.* By Ralph Stockman Tarr and Lawrence Martin. 498 pages. *1914*

The National Geographic Society Researches in Alaska. 537-561, *June 1911*

The National Geographic Society's Alaskan Expedition of 1909. By Ralph S. Tarr and Lawrence Martin. 1-54, *Jan. 1910*

MARTIN, PAUL D.: *Author*

■■ *Messengers to the Brain: Our Fantastic Five Senses.* Juvenile. 104 pages. *1984*

MARTIN, WILLIAM ALEXANDER PARSONS: *Author*

The Causes That Led Up to the Siege of Pekin. 53-63, *Feb. 1901*

MARTIN, Mount, Alaska:

Our Greatest National Monument: The National Geographic Society Completes Its Explorations in the Valley of Ten Thousand Smokes. By Robert F. Griggs. 219-292, *Sept. 1921*

The Valley of Ten Thousand Smokes: National Geographic Society Explorations in the Katmai District of Alaska. By Robert F. Griggs. 13-68, *Jan. 1917*

MARTINIQUE (Island), West Indies:

Martinique: Liberté, Egalité, and Uncertainty in the Caribbean. By Kenneth MacLeish. Photos by John Launois. 124-148, *Jan. 1975*

Finisterre Sails the Windward Islands. By Carleton Mitchell. Photos by Winfield Parks. 755-801, *Dec. 1965*

Martinique: A Tropical Bit of France. By Gwen Drayton Allmon. Photos by Charles Allmon. 255-283, *Feb. 1959*

Carib Cruises the West Indies. By Carleton Mitchell. 1-56, *Jan. 1948*

Martinique, Caribbean Question Mark. By Edward T. Folliard. 47-55, *Jan. 1941*

Southward Ho! In the "Alice." By Henry Howard. 265-312, *Mar. 1938*

The Shattered Obelisk of Mont Pelée. By Angelo Heilprin. 465-474, *Aug. 1906*

Destruction of Pompeii as Interpreted by the Volcanic Eruptions of Martinique. By Angelo Heilprin. 431, *Oct. 1904*

The New Cone of Mont Pelée. 422-423, *Nov. 1903*

Volcanic Eruptions on Martinique and St. Vincent. By Israel C. Russell. 415-436, *Dec. 1902*

Report by Robert T. Hill on the Volcanic Disturbances in the West Indies. 223-267, *July 1902*

The Recent Volcanic Eruptions in the West Indies. By Israel C. Russell. 267-285, *July 1902*

Volcanic Rocks of Martinique and St. Vincent: Collected by Robert T. Hill and Israel C. Russell. By J. S. Diller. 285-296, *July 1902*

Chemical Discussion of Analyses of Volcanic Ejecta from Martinique and St. Vincent. By W. F. Hillebrand. 296-299, *July 1902*

Reports of Vessels as to the Range of Volcanic Dust. By James Page. 299-301, *July 1902*

The National Geographic Society Expedition to Martinique and St. Vincent. 183-184, *June 1902*

Magnetic Disturbance Caused by the Explosion of Mont Pelée. 208-209, *June 1902*

The National Geographic Society Expedition in the West Indies. 209-213, *June 1902*

Lafcadio Hearn on the Island and People of Martinique. 214-216, *June 1902*

MARTIN'S HUNDRED (Settlement Tract), Virginia:

New Clues to an Old Mystery (Virginia's Wolstenholme Towne). By Ivor Noël Hume. Photos by Ira Block. Paintings by Richard Schlecht. 53-77, *Jan. 1982*

First Look at a Lost Virginia Settlement. By Ivor Noël Hume. Photos by

Ira Block. Paintings by Richard Schlecht. 735-767, *June 1979*

MARTINSBURG, West Virginia:

Potomac, River of Destiny. By Albert W. Atwood. 33-70, *July 1945*

The **MARVELOUS** Hummingbird Rediscovered. By Crawford H. Greenewalt. 98-101, *July 1966*

The **MARVELOUS** Maldive Islands. By Alan Villiers. 829-849, *June 1957*

The **MARVELOUS** Prosperity of the South. 685, *Oct. 1907*

MARVELS of a Coral Realm. By Walter A. Starck II. NGS research grant. 710-738, *Nov. 1966*

The **MARVELS** of Animal Behavior. ▪▪ 422 pages. *1972*

MARVELS of Fern Life. Paintings by E. J. Geske. 547-562, *May 1925*

MARVELS of Metamorphosis: A Scientific "G-man" Pursues Rare Trapdoor Spider Parasites for Three Years With a Spade and a Candid Camera. By George Elwood Jenks. 807-828, *Dec. 1938*

MARVELS of Mycetozoa: Exploration of a Long Island Swamp Reveals Some of the Secrets of the Slime Molds, Dwelling on the Borderland Between the Plant and Animal Kingdoms. By William Crowder. Paintings by author. 421-443, *Apr. 1926*

MARVIN, C. F.: *Author*

The Record of the Great Earthquake Written in Washington by the Seismograph of the U. S. Weather Bureau. 296-298, *May 1906*

MARY ROSE, H.M.S.:

Henry VIII's Lost Warship: *Mary Rose.* By Margaret Rule. Introduction and picture text by Peter Miller. Paintings by Richard Schlecht. 646-675, *May 1983*

MARY-ROUSSELIERE, GUY:
Author-Photographer

I Live With the Eskimos. 188-217, *Feb. 1971*

MARYLAND:

Citizens Band Together to Save Their Environment. Geographica. *Nov. 1988*

School Field Trip Yields Prehistoric Bone. Geographica. *Nov. 1988*

Annapolis: Camelot on the Bay. By Larry Kohl. Photos by Kevin Fleming. 162-189, *Aug. 1988*

George Washington's Patowmack Canal. By Wilbur E. Garrett. Photos by Kenneth Garrett. 716-753, *June 1987*

My Chesapeake–Queen of Bays. By Allan C. Fisher, Jr. Photos by Lowell Georgia. 428-467, *Oct. 1980*

The Nation's River. By Allan C. Fisher, Jr. Photos by James L. Stanfield. 432-469, *Oct. 1976*

Maryland on the Half Shell. By Stuart E. Jones. Photos by Robert W. Madden. 188-229, *Feb. 1972*

Elaborate jewelry adorns a married Masai woman in Kenya. Her earrings weigh more than a pound. © VERA WATKINS

Nature's Year in Pleasant Valley. By Paul A. Zahl. 488-525, *Apr. 1968*

The Sailing Oystermen of Chesapeake Bay. By Luis Marden. 798-819, *Dec. 1967*

Chesapeake Country. By Nathaniel T. Kenney. Photos by Bates Littlehales. 370-411, *Sept. 1964*

Waterway to Washington, the C & O Canal. By Jay Johnston. 419-439, *Mar. 1960*

Roving Maryland's Cavalier Country. By William A. Kinney. 431-470, *Apr. 1954*

"Delmarva," Gift of the Sea. By Catherine Bell Palmer. 367-399, *Sept. 1950*

Down the Susquehanna by Canoe. By Ralph Gray. Photos by Walter Meayers Edwards. 73-120, *July 1950*

Appalachian Valley Pilgrimage. By Catherine Bell Palmer. Photos by Justin Locke. 1-32, *July 1949*

Skyway Below the Clouds. By Carl R. Markwith. Photos by Ernest J. Cottrell. Included: Hyde Field, near Clinton. 85-108, *July 1949*

Down the Potomac by Canoe. By Ralph Gray. Photos by Walter Meayers Edwards. 213-242, *Aug. 1948*

Potomac, River of Destiny. By Albert W. Atwood. 33-70, *July 1945*

Wartime Washington. By William H. Nicholas. 257-290, *Sept. 1943*

Maryland Presents–. By W. Robert Moore. 401-448, *Apr. 1941*

Chesapeake Odyssey: An 18-foot Sailboat Follows the Course of Captain John Smith around This Spacious Bay of History, Commerce, Sea Food, and Nautical Lore. By John Maloney. 357-392, *Sept. 1939*

Roads from Washington. By John Patric. 1-56, *July 1938*

⊕ *Historic and Scenic Reaches of the Nation's Capital. July 1938*

Annapolis, Cradle of the Navy. By Arthur A. Ageton. 789-800, *June 1936*

The Travels of George Washington: Dramatic Episodes in His Career as the First Geographer of the United States. By William Joseph Showalter. 1-63, *Jan. 1932*

Approaching Washington by Tidewater Potomac. By Paul Wilstach. 372-392, *Mar. 1930*

A Maryland Pilgrimage: Visits to Hallowed Shrines Recall the Major Rôle Played by This Prosperous State in the Development of Popular Government in America. By Gilbert Grosvenor. 133-212, *Feb. 1927*

⊕ *Maryland, Delaware, and District of Columbia.* Inset: Baltimore. *Feb. 1927*

Colossal Work in Baltimore. By Calvin W. Hendrick. 365-373, *Apr. 1909*

The Geologist at Blue Mountain, Maryland. By Charles D. Walcott. 84-88, *July 10, 1893*

See also Assateague Island; Baltimore; Beltsville; Black Swamp Creek; Cabin John; Solomons Island; *and* Eastern Shore

MASAI TRIBESPEOPLE:

▪ Man of the Serengeti. 179A-179B, *Feb. 1972*

Preserving the Treasures of Olduvai Gorge. By Melvin M. Payne. Photos by Joseph J. Scherschel. 701-709, *Nov. 1966*

Spearing Lions with Africa's Masai. By Edgar Monsanto Queeny. 487-517, *Oct. 1954*

Wild Man and Wild Beast in Africa. By Theodore Roosevelt. 1-33, *Jan. 1911*

Where Roosevelt Will Hunt. By Sir Harry Johnston. 207-256, *Mar. 1909*

MASCARENE ISLANDS, Indian Ocean. *See* Mauritius

MASHHAD, Iran. *See* Meshed

MASKS:

Merry Maskers of Imst (Austria). Photos by Francis C. Fuerst. 201-208, *Aug. 1936*

MASON, BRIAN H.:

Nomination Page. *Oct. 1964*

MASON, J. ALDEN: *Author*

Preserving Ancient America's Finest Sculptures (Guatemala). Paintings by H. M. Herget. 537-570, *Nov. 1935*

MASQAT. *See* Muscat and Oman

MASSACHUSETTS:

Massachusetts' North Shore: Harboring Old Ways. By Randall S. Peffer. Photos by Nathan Benn. 568-590, *Apr. 1979*

Patriots in Petticoats. By Lonnelle Aikman. Paintings by Louis S. Glanzman. 475-493, *Oct. 1975*

New England's "Little Portugal." By O. Louis Mazzatenta. 90-109, *Jan. 1975*

The American Lobster, Delectable Cannibal. By Luis Marden. Photos by David Doubilet. 462-487, *Apr. 1973*

Yesterday Lingers Along the Connecticut. By Charles McCarry. Photos by David L. Arnold. 334-369, *Sept. 1972*

M N

Shadows stretching across the empty, open sands of the off-season meet the surf at Salisbury Beach, Massachusetts. NATHAN BENN

MASSANUTTEN MOUNTAIN, Virginia:

A **MASTER** Plan for Yellowstone: The Next 100 Years. By George B. Hartzog, Jr. 632-637, *May 1972*

MASTERPIECES on Tour. By Harry A. McBride. 717-750, *Dec. 1948*

MASTERS of Flight. 49-56, *July 1919*

MASTERWORK on the Mall. By J. Carter Brown. Photos by James A. Sugar. 680-701, *Nov. 1978*

MASTERWORKS of the Wild–a Portfolio From Our National Parks. Photos by David Alan Harvey. 3-17, *July 1979*

MASTIGIAS (Jellyfish):

Strange World of Palau's Salt Lakes. By William M. Hamner. Photos by David Doubilet. 264-282, *Feb. 1982*

MATHENY, RAY T.: *Author*

El Mirador: An Early Maya Metropolis Uncovered. Paintings by T. W. Rutledge. NGS research grant. 317-339, *Sept. 1987*

MATHER, STEPHEN T.:

Board of Trustees. 343, *Mar. 1936*
Awarded Jane M. Smith Life Membership. 342, *Apr. 1920*

MATILDAVILLE, Virginia:

George Washington's Patowmack Canal. By Wilbur E. Garrett. Photos by Kenneth Garrett. 716-753, *June 1987*

MATMATA, Tunisia:

The Mole Men: An Account of the Troglodytes of Southern Tunisia. By Frank Edward Johnson. 787-846, *Sept. 1911*

MATO GROSSO (State), Brazil:

Man in the Amazon: Stone Age Present Meets Stone Age Past. By W. Jesco von Puttkamer. NGS research grant. 60-83, *Jan. 1979*
Indians of the Amazon Darkness. By Harald Schultz. NGS research grant. 737-758, *May 1964*
The Jungle Was My Home. By Sasha Siemel. 695-712, *Nov. 1952*
Through Paraguay and Southern Matto Grosso. By Sir Christopher H. Gibson. 459-488, *Oct. 1943*
See also Cinta Larga Indians; Kreen-Akarores; Txukahameis

MATOS MOCTEZUMA, EDUARDO:
Author

New Finds in the Great Temple. Photos by David Hiser. 767-775, *Dec. 1980*

MATS: America's Long Arm of the Air. By Beverley M. Bowie. Photos by Robert F. Sisson. 283-317, *Mar. 1957*

MATSANG TSANGPO (now Yarlung Zangbo) River, Tibet:

The Tsangpo. By James Mascarene Hubbard. 32-35, *Jan. 1901*

MATSON, G. E.: *Photographer*

Multicolored Cones of Cappadocia. 769-800, *Dec. 1939*
The Rose-Red City of Rock (Petra). 145-160, *Feb. 1935*

MATTERHORN (Peak), Alps:

Manless Alpine Climbing: The First Woman to Scale the Grépon, the Matterhorn, and Other Famous Peaks Without Masculine Support Relates Her Adventures. By Miriam O'Brien Underhill. 131-170, *Aug. 1934*
The Majesty of the Matterhorn. Pictorial supplement. *May 1912*
A Woman's Climbs in the High Alps. By Dora Keen. 643-675, *July 1911*

MATTERNES, JAY H.:

Nomination Page. *Mar. 1972*
Artist
The Search for Our Ancestors. By Kenneth F. Weaver. Photos by David L. Brill. 560-623, *Nov. 1985*
Ancient Ashfall Creates a Pompeii of Prehistoric Animals. By Michael R.

Voorhies. Photos by Annie Griffiths. 66-75, *Jan. 1981*
Skull 1470. By Richard E. Leakey. Photos by Bob Campbell. 819-829, *June 1973*
⊕ "Ice Age Mammals of the Alaskan Tundra," painting supplement. Map of Canada. *Mar. 1972*

MATTHES, GERARD H.: *Author*

The Dikes of Holland. 219-234, *June 1901*

MATTHEWS, SAMUEL W.:

On Assignment in Alaska. *Jan. 1987*
Author
Ice on the World. 79-103, *Jan. 1987*
New World of the Ocean. 792-832, *Dec. 1981*
What's Happening to Our Climate? 576-615, *Nov. 1976*
The Phoenicians, Sea Lords of Antiquity. Photos by Winfield Parks. Paintings by Robert C. Magis. 149-189, *Aug. 1974*
This Changing Earth. 1-37, *Jan. 1973*
Antarctica's Nearer Side. Photos by William R. Curtsinger. 622-655, *Nov. 1971*
Antarctica: Icy Testing Ground for Space. Photos by Robert W. Madden. 569-592, *Oct. 1968*
Nevada's Mountain of Invisible Gold. Photos by David F. Cupp. 668-679, *May 1968*
Science Explores the Monsoon Sea. Photos by Robert F. Sisson. 554-575, *Oct. 1967*
Bali's Sacred Mountain Blows Its Top. Photos by Robert F. Sisson. 436-458. I. Disaster in Paradise. By Windsor P. Booth. 436-447; II. Devastated Land and Homeless People. By Samuel W. Matthews. 447-458, *Sept. 1963*
Scientists Drill at Sea to Pierce Earth's Crust (Project Mohole). Photos by J. Baylor Roberts. 686-697, *Nov. 1961*
The Night the Mountains Moved (Montana's 1959 Earthquake). Photos by J. Baylor Roberts. 329-359, *Mar. 1960*
Hunting the Heartbeat of a Whale. By Paul Dudley White and Samuel W. Matthews. 49-64, *July 1956*
America Goes to the Fair. 293-333, *Sept. 1954*
Beltsville Brings Science to the Farm. 199-218, *Aug. 1953*
Nevada Learns to Live With the Atom. 839-850, *June 1953*

MATTISON, JAMES A., Jr.:
Photographer

Return of the Sea Otter. By Karl W. Kenyon. 520-539, *Oct. 1971*

MATTO GROSSO (State), Brazil. *See* Mato Grosso

MAUGHAM, REGINALD CHARLES FULKE: *Author*

Hunting Big Game in Portuguese East Africa. 723-730, *Nov. 1907*

MAUI (Island), Hawaii:

New Light on the Singing Whales. Introduction by Roger Payne. Photos

by Flip Nicklin. NGS research grant. 463-477, *Apr. 1982*
Precious Corals, Hawaii's Deep-sea Jewels. By Richard W. Grigg. Photos by David Doubilet. 719-732, *May 1979*
Maui, Where Old Hawaii Still Lives. By Kenneth F. Weaver. Photos by Gordon W. Gahan. 514-543, *Apr. 1971*

MAUI WHALE WATCHERS:

Study Grant:
Humpback Whales. 466, *Apr. 1982*

MAUNEY, MICHAEL: *Photographer*

Milwaukee: More Than Beer. By Louise Levathes. 180-201, *Aug. 1980*

MAUNSELL, F. R.: *Author*

One Thousand Miles of Railway Built for Pilgrims and Not for Dividends (Damascus to Mecca). 156-172, *Feb. 1909*

MAURI, CARLO: *Photographer*

Tigris Sails Into the Past. By Thor Heyerdahl. Photos by Carlo Mauri and the crew of the *Tigris*. 806-827, *Dec. 1978*
The Voyage of *Ra II*. By Thor Heyerdahl. Photos by Carlo Mauri and Georges Sourial. 44-71, *Jan. 1971*

MAURITANIA:

Africa's Sahel: The Stricken Land. By William S. Ellis. Photos by Steve McCurry. 140-179, *Aug. 1987*
The Desert: An Age-old Challenge Grows. By Rick Gore. Photos by Georg Gerster and Bruce Dale. 586-639, *Nov. 1979*
Dry-land Fleet Sails the Sahara. By Jean du Boucher. Photos by Jonathan S. Blair. 696-725, *Nov. 1967*
Freedom Speaks French in Ouagadougou. By John Scofield. 153-203, *Aug. 1966*

MAURITIUS (Island), Indian Ocean:

Crosscurrents Sweep the Indian Ocean. By Bart McDowell. Photos by Steve Raymer. 422-457, *Oct. 1981*
Mauritius, Island of the Dodo. By Quentin Keynes. 77-104, *Jan. 1956*

MAURY, MATTHEW FONTAINE:

The Gem of the Ocean: Our American Navy. By Josephus Daniels. 313-335, *Apr. 1918*

MAXEY, ROBERT F.: *Photographer*

Pine-Scented, Harbor-Dented Maine. Photos by B. Anthony Stewart and Robert F. Maxey. 549-588, *May 1935*

MAXON, WILLIAM R.: *Author*

Ferns as a Hobby. Paintings by E. J. Geske. 541-586, *May 1925*

MAXWELL, GAVIN: *Photographer*

Marsh Dwellers of Southern Iraq. By Wilfred Thesiger. 205-239, *Feb. 1958*

MAYA:

Isla Cerritos, Maya Port Discovered. Geographica. *Oct. 1988*
El Mirador: An Early Maya Metropolis Uncovered. By Ray T. Matheny. Paintings by T. W. Rutledge. NGS research grant. 317-339, *Sept. 1987*

M
N

MAYER, ALFRED GOLDSBOROUGH: *Author*

MAYER, ARTHUR ELLIS: *Author*

MAYER, FRED: *Photographer*

Remnants of an ancient culture, a carved disk and an animal head were found in the early 1900s among Maya ruins at Quiriguá, Guatemala.   VALDEAVELLANO & CO.

MAYFLOWER. *See* Arbutus

MAYFLOWER (Ship):

Founders of New England. By Sir Evelyn Wrench. Photos by B. Anthony Stewart. 803-838, *June 1953*

MAYFLOWER II (Ship):

How We Sailed the New *Mayflower* to America. By Alan Villiers. 627-672, *Nov. 1957*
"Mayflower II," painting supplement. *Nov. 1957*
We're Coming Over on the *Mayflower*. By Alan Villiers. 708-728, *May 1957*

MAYNARD, CLARENCE F.:

The Valley of Ten Thousand Smokes: An Account of the Discovery and Exploration of the Most Wonderful Volcanic Region in the World. By Robert F. Griggs. 115-169, *Feb. 1918*

MAYOR DES PLANCHES, EDMOND, BARON:

The Discovery of the North Pole. Address by Baron Mayor des Planches. 63-82, *Jan. 1910*
Honors to Peary. Address by Baron Mayor des Planches. 49-60, *Jan 1907*

MAYTIME in the Heart of Maryland. Photos by B. Anthony Stewart and Charles Martin. 441-448, *Apr. 1941*

MAYTIME Miracle in Sherwood Gardens. By Nathaniel T. Kenney. 700-709, *May 1956*

MAZAMA, Mount, Oregon:

When Mt. Mazama Lost Its Top: The Birth of Crater Lake. By Lyman J. Briggs. 128-133, *July 1962*
Crater Lake Summer. By Walter Meayers Edwards. 134-148, *July 1962*

MAZAMAS (Association of Mountain Climbers):

The Mazamas. By J. S. Diller. 58-59, *Feb. 1897*
The Altitude of Mount Adams, Washington. By Edgar McClure. 151-153, *Apr. 1896*

MAZATLAN, Mexico:

Adventuring Down the West Coast of Mexico. By Herbert Corey. 449-503, *Nov. 1922*

MAZATZAL WILDERNESS, Arizona:

The Mazatzal's Harsh but Lovely Land Between. By François Leydet. Photos by Farrell Grehan. 161-167, *Feb. 1974*

MAZE, STEPHANIE:

On Assignment in Brazil. *Mar. 1987*
Photographer
Brazil: Moment of Promise and Pain. By Priit J. Vesilind. 348-385, *Mar. 1987*
Iberia's Vintage River (Douro-Duero). By Marion Kaplan. 460-489, *Oct. 1984*
Mexico City: An Alarming Giant. By Bart McDowell. 138-175, *Aug. 1984*
Catalonia: Spain's Country Within a Country. By Randall Peffer. 95-127, *Jan. 1984*

The Uncertain State of Puerto Rico. By Bill Richards. 516-543, *Apr. 1983*
The Mexican Americans: A People on the Move. By Griffin Smith, Jr. 780-809, *June 1980*

MAZZATENTA, O. LOUIS:

On Assignment in Italy. *May 1984*
Nomination Page. *Sept. 1974*
Author-Photographer
New England's "Little Portugal." 90-109, *Jan. 1975*
Photographer
The Eternal Etruscans. By Rick Gore. Paintings by James M. Gurney. 696-743, *June 1988*
Palio, Siena's Centuries-old 90-second Horse Race. 745-749, *June 1988*
Madrid: The Change in Spain. By John J. Putman. 142-181, *Feb. 1986*
The Dead Do Tell Tales at Vesuvius. By Rick Gore. NGS research grant. 557-613, *May 1984*
A Prayer for Pozzuoli. By Rick Gore. 615-625, *May 1984*
The Thames: That Noble River. By Ethel A. Starbird. 750-791, *June 1983*
Paraguay, Paradox of South America. By Gordon Young. 240-269, *Aug. 1982*
Down the Ancient Appian Way. By James Cerruti. 714-747, *June 1981*
The Gauchos, Last of a Breed. By Robert Laxalt. 478-501, *Oct. 1980*
The Azores, Nine Islands in Search of a Future. By Don Moser. 261-288, *Feb. 1976*

M'CHOPI TRIBESPEOPLE:

Impressions and Scenes of Mozambique. By O. W. Barrett. 807-830, *Oct. 1910*

MEAD, EDWIN D.: *Author*

The Expansion of England. 249-263, *July 1900*

MEADE, R. W.:

Admiral R. W. Meade, U.S.N. (Obituary). By John Hyde. 142, *May 1897*
Portrait. Plate 27, *May 1897*
Author
A Winter Voyage Through the Straits of Magellan. 129-141, *May 1897*

MEALY BUGS:

An Insect Community Lives in Flower Heads. By James G. Needham. 340-356, *Sept. 1946*

MEANCO (Raft):

Down Mark Twain's River on a Raft. By Rex E. Hieronymus. 551-574, *Apr. 1948*

MEANS, PHILIP AINSWORTH:
Author
The Incas: Empire Builders of the Andes. Paintings by H. M. Herget. 225-264, *Feb. 1938*

MEASURES. *See* Metric System; National Bureau of Standards

MEASURING the Sun's Heat and Forecasting the Weather: The National Geographic Society to Maintain a Solar Station in a Remote Part of the

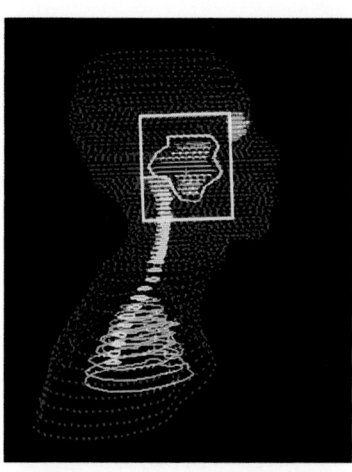

An advanced computer-imaging technique produces a three-dimensional view of a tumor of the nasopharynx. HOWARD SOCHUREK

World to Coöperate with Smithsonian Institution Stations in California and Chile. By C. G. Abbot. 111-126, *Jan. 1926*

MEAT INDUSTRY:

America's "Meat on the Hoof." By William H. Nicholas. 33-72, *Jan. 1952*
Farmers Keep Them Eating. By Frederick Simpich. 435-458, *Apr. 1943*
Revolution in Eating: Machine Food Age–Born of Roads, Research, and Refrigeration–Makes the United States the Best-fed Nation in History. By J. R. Hildebrand. 273-324, *Mar. 1942*
See Cattle Raising; Hog Raising; Poultry; Sheep Raising

MECCA, Saudi Arabia:

Saudi Arabia: The Kingdom and Its Power. By Robert Azzi. 286-333, *Sept. 1980*
Pilgrimage to Mecca. By Muhammad Abdul-Rauf. Photos by Mehmet Biber. 581-607, *Nov. 1978*
The Sword and the Sermon. By Thomas J. Abercrombie. 3-45, *July 1972*
Saudi Arabia: Beyond the Sands of Mecca. By Thomas J. Abercrombie. 1-53, *Jan. 1966*
From America to Mecca on Airborne Pilgrimage. By Abdul Ghafur. 1-60, *July 1953*
Pilgrims' Progress to Mecca. Photos by Oscar Marcus. 627-642, *Nov. 1937*
Mecca the Mystic: A New Kingdom Within Arabia. By S. M. Zwemer. 157-172, *Aug. 1917*
One Thousand Miles of Railway Built for Pilgrims and Not for Dividends. By F. R. Maunsell. 156-172, *Feb. 1909*
Damascus and Mecca Railway. 408, *Nov. 1901*

MECH, L. DAVID:

On Assignment in the Arctic. *May 1987*
Author
Ellesmere Island–Life in the High Arctic. Photos by Jim Brandenburg. 750-767, *June 1988*

Children caught in political conflict are fed at an International Committee of the Red Cross center on Atauro, a Pacific island near Timor.   STEVE RAYMER, NGS

Medieval teaching tool, frescoes on Voronet's 15th-century church depict Romanian folklore and Bible stories. JAMES L. STANFIELD, NGS

Crops. 145-217, *Aug. 1949*

The World in Your Garden. By W. H. Camp. Paintings by Else Bostelmann. 1-65, *July 1947*

From Africa to the Alps. U. S. Army Air Forces official photos. 161-168, *Feb. 1946*

Mediterranean Checkerboard. By Frederick Simpich. 527-550, *Apr. 1942*

⊕ *Central Europe and the Mediterranean as of September 1, 1939. Oct. 1939*

⊕ *Europe and the Mediterranean. Apr. 1938*

⊕ *Map of the Countries Bordering the Mediterranean Sea. Jan. 1912*

See also Balearic Islands; Capri; Corsica; Crete; Cyprus; Gibraltar; Ischia; Malta; Riviera; Sardinia; Sicily; *and* names of countries bordering the Mediterranean Sea: Albania; Algeria; Egypt; France; Greece; Israel; Italy; Lebanon; Monaco; Morocco; Spain; Syria; Tunisia; Turkey

MEDITERRANEAN SEA:

Oldest Known Shipwreck Reveals Splendors of the Bronze Age. By George F. Bass. Photos by William R. Curtsinger. NGS research grant. 693-733, *Dec. 1987*

Caesarea Maritima. By Robert L. Hohlfelder. Photos by Bill Curtsinger. Paintings by J. Robert Teringo. NGS research grant. 261-279, *Feb. 1987*

The Quest for Ulysses. By Tim Severin. Photos by Kevin Fleming. 197-225, *Aug. 1986*

Bronze Age Shipwreck. By Wilbur E. Garrett and George F. Bass. NGS research grant. 1-3, *Jan. 1985*

The Mediterranean–Sea of Man's Fate. By Rick Gore. Photos by Jonathan Blair. 694-737, *Dec. 1982*

⊕ *The Historic Mediterranean; The Mediterranean Seafloor. Dec. 1982*

Resurrecting the Oldest Known Greek Ship. By Michael L. Katsev. Photos by Bates Littlehales. NGS research grant. 841-857, *June 1970*

Yankee Cruises Turkey's History-haunted Coast. By Irving and Electa Johnson. Photos by Joseph J. Scherschel. 798-845, *Dec. 1969*

Ancient Shipwreck Yields New Facts– and a Strange Cargo. By Peter Throckmorton. Photos by Kim Hart and Joseph J. Scherschel. 282-300, *Feb. 1969*

New Tools for Undersea Archeology. By George F. Bass. Photos by Charles R. Nicklin, Jr. NGS research grant. 403-423, *Sept. 1968*

Working for Weeks on the Sea Floor. By Jacques-Yves Cousteau. Photos by Philippe Cousteau and Bates Littlehales. NGS research grant. 498-537, *Apr. 1966*

Underwater Archeology: Key to History's Warehouse. By George F. Bass. Photos by Thomas J. Abercrombie and Robert B. Goodman. NGS research grant. 138-156, *July 1963*

Oldest Known Shipwreck Yields Bronze Age Cargo. By Peter Throckmorton. NGS research grant. 697-711, *May 1962*

Thirty-three Centuries Under the Sea (Shipwreck). By Peter Throckmorton. 682-703, *May 1960*

Four Years of Diving to the Bottom of the Sea. By Georges S. Houot. NGS research grant. 715-731, *May 1958*

Diving Through an Undersea Avalanche. By Jacques-Yves Cousteau. NGS research grant. 538-542, *Apr. 1955*

Photographing the Sea's Dark Underworld. By Harold E. Edgerton. NGS research grant. 523-537, *Apr. 1955*

To the Depths of the Sea by Bathyscaphe. By Jacques-Yves Cousteau. NGS research grant. 67-79, *July 1954*

Two and a Half Miles Down. By Georges S. Houot. NGS research grant. 80-86, *July 1954*

Fish Men Discover a 2,200-year-old Greek Ship. By Jacques-Yves Cousteau. NGS research grant. 1-36, *Jan. 1954*

Fish Men Explore a New World Undersea. By Jacques-Yves Cousteau. 431-472, *Oct. 1952*

MEEN, V. BEN: *Author*

Solving the Riddle of Chubb Crater (Quebec). Photos by Richard H. Stewart. 1-32, *Jan. 1952*

MEGALOPOLIS, U.S.A.:

⊕ *Washington to Boston.* Atlas series. *Aug. 1962*

MEGARGEE, EDWIN: *Artist*

Dogs Work for Man. By Edward J. Linehan. Paintings by Edwin Megargee and R. E. Lougheed. 190-233, *Aug. 1958*

MEGASPELÆON, the Oldest Monastery in Greece. By Carroll Storrs Alden. 310-323, *Mar. 1913*

MEGGERS, BETTY J.: *Author-Photographer*

Life Among the Wai Wai Indians. By

An anguished mother from a Mekong River village in Laos comforts her son during a doctor's exam. WILBUR E. GARRETT, NGS

Clifford Evans and Betty J. Meggers. 329-346, *Mar. 1955*

MEGIDDO (Armageddon), Israel:

Bringing Old Testament Times to Life. By G. Ernest Wright. Paintings by Henry J. Soulen. 833-864, *Dec. 1957*

An Archeologist Looks at Palestine. By Nelson Glueck. 739-752, *Dec. 1947*

MEHRINGER, PETER J., Jr.: *Author*

Clovis Cache Found: Weapons of Ancient Americans. Photos by Warren Morgan. 500-503, *Oct. 1988*

MEIGS, MONTGOMERY C.:

The Washington Aqueduct and Cabin John Bridge. By D. D. Gaillard. 337-344, *Dec. 1897*

MEIJER, WILLEM: *Author*

Saving the World's Largest Flower. Photos by Edward S. Ross. NGS research grant. 136-140, *July 1985*

MEKONG (River), Southeast Asia:

The Mekong, River of Terror and Hope. By Peter T. White. Photos by W. E. Garrett. 737-787, *Dec. 1968*

Water War in Viet Nam. By Dickey Chapelle. 272-296, *Feb. 1966*

Through the Great River Trenches of Asia: National Geographic Society Explorer Follows the Yangtze, Mekong, and Salwin Through Mighty Gorges, Some of Whose Canyon Walls Tower to a Height of More Than Two Miles. By Joseph F. Rock. 133-186, *Aug. 1926*

MELANCON, JOHN M.:

Nomination Page. *June 1959*

MELANESIA:

Yankee Roams the Orient. By Irving and Electa Johnson. 327-370, *Mar. 1951*

Treasure Islands of Australasia: New Guinea, New Caledonia, and Fiji Trace across the South Pacific a Fertile Crescent Incredibly Rich in Minerals and Foods. By Douglas L. Oliver. 691-722, *June 1942*

North About. By Alan J. Villiers. 221-250, *Feb. 1937*

The Islands of the Pacific. By J. P. Thomson. 543-558, *Dec. 1921*

In the Savage South Seas. By Beatrice Grimshaw. 1-19, *Jan. 1908*

See also Bougainville; Fiji Islands; Louisiade Archipelago; Malekula; Munda; New Britain; New Caledonia; New Guinea; New Hebrides; Pentecost Island; Solomon Islands; Tanna

MELBOURNE, Australia:

Australia's Pacesetter State, Victoria. By Allan C. Fisher, Jr. Photos by Thomas Nebbia. 218-253, *Feb. 1971*

Sports-minded Melbourne, Host to the Olympics. 688-693, *Nov. 1956*

Capital Cities of Australia. By W. Robert Moore. 667-722, *Dec. 1935*

Lonely Australia: The Unique Continent. By Herbert E. Gregory. 473-568, *Dec. 1916*

MELDGAARD, JØRGEN: *Author*

The Mummies of Qilakitsoq. By Jens P.

Hart Hansen, Jørgen Meldgaard, and Jørgen Nordqvist. 191-207, *Feb. 1985*

MELGAREIO, A.: *Author*
The Greatest Volcanoes of Mexico. 741-760, *Sept. 1910*

MELHAM, TOM: *Author*
■■*John Muir's Wild America.* Photos by Farrell Grehan. Art by H. Tom Hall. 199 pages. *1976*
Cape Cod's Circle of Seasons. Photos by James P. Blair. 40-65, *July 1975*

MELLEN, IDA: *Author*
Tropical Toy Fishes: More Than 600 Varieties of Aquarium Pygmies Afford a Fascinating Field of Zoölogical Study in the Home. Paintings by Hashime Murayama. 287-317, *Mar. 1931*

MELLON, ANDREW:
The National Gallery After a Quarter Century. By John Walker. 348-371, *Mar. 1967*

MELLON, MR. and MRS. PAUL: Art Collection:
In Quest of Beauty. Text by Paul Mellon. 372-385, *Mar. 1967*

MELLON FAMILY:
Pittsburgh, Pattern for Progress. By William J. Gill. Photos by Clyde Hare. 342-371, *Mar. 1965*
Pittsburgh: Workshop of the Titans. By Albert W. Atwood. 117-144, *July 1949*

MELLOR, F. H.: *Author*
The Isle of Man. 587-608, *May 1937*

MELOY, THOMAS: *Author*
The Laser's Bright Magic. Photos by Howard Sochurek. 858-881, *Dec. 1966*

MELTZER, DAVIS: *Artist*
Medicine's New Vision. By Howard Sochurek. Illustrations text by Peter Miller. 2-41, *Jan. 1987*
The Awesome Worlds Within a Cell. By Rick Gore. Photos by Bruce Dale. 355-395, *Sept. 1976*
Project FAMOUS. 586-615, *May 1975*
The Incredible Universe. By Kenneth F. Weaver. Photos by James P. Blair. 589-625, *May 1974*
Sailors of the Sky. By Gordon Young. Photos by Emory Kristof and Jack Fields. 49-73, *Jan. 1967*
Footprints on the Moon. By Hugh L. Dryden. Paintings by Davis Meltzer and Pierre Mion. 357-401, *Mar. 1964*
Mariner Scans a Lifeless Venus. By Frank Sartwell. 733-742, *May 1963*

MELTZOFF, STANLEY: *Artist*
Plight of the Bluefin Tuna. By Michael J. A. Butler. Photos by David Doublet. 220-239, *Aug. 1982*

MELVILLE, GEORGE W.:
George W. Melville, Engineer-in-chief, U.S.N. By A. W. Greely. 187-190, *June 1897*
Portrait. Plate 28, *June 1897*
Vice-President. xix, *May 5, 1894*

Author
Geographic Literature. 212, *June 1896*

MELVILLE, HERMAN:
Literary Landmarks of Massachusetts. By William H. Nicholas. Photos by B. Anthony Stewart and John E. Fletcher. 279-310, *Mar. 1950*

MELVILLE BELL GROSVENOR, a Lifetime of Service. By Bart McDowell. 270-278, *Aug. 1982*

MELVILLE ISLAND, Australia:
Expedition to the Land of the Tiwi. By Charles P. Mountford. NGS research grant. 417-440, *Mar. 1956*

MEMORIAL DAY CEREMONIES:
'Known but to God' (Unknown Heroes). By Beverley M. Bowie. 593-605, *Nov. 1958*

MEMORIAL TRIBUTES:
Grosvenor, Melville Bell: Melville Bell Grosvenor, A Decade of Innovation, a Lifetime of Service. By Bart McDowell. 270-278, *Aug. 1982*
Carmichael, Leonard: An Appreciation. By Melvin M. Payne. 871-874, *Dec. 1973*
Leakey, Louis S. B.: The Leakey Tradition Lives On. By Melvin M. Payne. 143-144, *Jan. 1973*
Eisenhower, Dwight D.: World's Last Salute to a Great American. By William Graves and other members of the National Geographic staff. 40-51, *July 1969*
Fleming, Robert V.: 1890-1967. By Melville Bell Grosvenor. 526-529, *Apr. 1968*
Grosvenor, Gilbert Hovey: To Gilbert Grosvenor: a Monthly Monument 25 Miles High. By Frederick G. Vosburgh and the staff of the National Geographic Society. 445-487, *Oct. 1966*
Chapelle, Dickey: What Was a Woman Doing There? By W. E. Garrett. 270-271, *Feb. 1966*
Churchill, Winston. 153-225. Included: The Churchill I Knew. By Dwight D. Eisenhower. 153-157; "Be Ye Men of Valour." By Howard La Fay. 159-197; The Final Tribute. Text by Carolyn Bennett Patterson. 199-225, *Aug. 1965*
Grosvenor, Elsie May Bell: First Lady of the National Geographic. By Gilbert Hovey Grosvenor. 101-121, *July 1965*
Kennedy, John F.: The Last Full Measure. By Melville Bell Grosvenor. 307-355, *Mar. 1964*
Kennedy, John F.: To the Memory of Our Beloved President, Friend to All Mankind. 1A-1B, *Jan. 1964*
La Gorce, John Oliver: Colleague of the Golden Years. By Gilbert Grosvenor. 440-444, *Mar. 1960*
Marshall, George C.: 1880-1959. 113, *Jan. 1960*
Bowie, Beverley M.: 1914-1958. 214, *Feb. 1959*
Long, George W.: 1913-1958. 215, *Feb. 1959*
Hildebrand, Jesse Richardson: 1888-1951. 104, *Jan. 1952*

Arnold, H. H.: 1886-1950. 400, *Mar. 1950*
Wilkes, Charles: Monument to Rear Adm. Charles Wilkes. 633, *Nov. 1928*
Peary, Robert E.: A Memorial to Peary: The National Geographic Society Dedicates Monument in Arlington National Cemetery to Discoverer of the North Pole. 639-646, *June 1922*
See also Monuments and Memorials

MEN, Moose, and Mink of Northwest Angle. By William H. Nicholas. Photos by J. Baylor Roberts. 265-284, *Aug. 1947*

MEN, *Ships, and the Sea.* By Alan Vil-
■■liers and other adventurers on the sea. Maritime history. 436 pages. 1962; rev. ed. *1973*

MEN Against the Hurricane. By Andrew H. Brown. 537-560, *Oct. 1950*

MEN Against the Rivers. By Frederick Simpich. 767-794, *June 1937*

MEN and Gold. By Frederick Simpich. 481-518, *Apr. 1933*

MEN-BIRDS Soar on Boiling Air. By Frederick G. Vosburgh. 123-140, *July 1938*

MEN of the Eagle in Their Mountain Eyrie. Photos by Luigi Pellerano. 143-190, *Feb. 1970*

The **MEN** Who Hid the Dead Sea Scrolls. By A. Douglas Tushingham. Paintings by Peter V. Bianchi. 785-808, *Dec. 1958*

MEN Who Measure the Earth. By Robert Leslie Conly. Photos by John E. Fletcher. 335-362, *Mar. 1956*

MENDAÑA, ALVARO DE:
Revealing Earth's Mightiest Ocean (Pacific). By Albert W. Atwood. 291-306, *Sept. 1943*

MENDENHALL, T. C.:
Board of Managers. 294, Apr. 1891; xii, Feb. 19, 1892; xix, Feb. 20, 1893; 640, *Nov. 1944*
Vice-President. xix, May 5, 1894; ii, *Oct. 31, 1895*

Author
A Brief Account of the Geographic Work of the U. S. Coast and Geodetic Survey. By T. C. Mendenhall and Otto H. Tittmann. 294-299, *Oct. 1897*
The Geographical Position and Height of Mount Saint Elias. 63-67, *July 10, 1893*
The Alaskan Boundary Survey (Part I). 177-180, *Feb. 8, 1893*

MENDENHALL, WALTER C.: *Author*
The Colorado Desert. 681-701, *Aug. 1909*

Author-Photographer
The Wrangell Mountains, Alaska. Included: Panorama taken by author from ridge east of the Dadina River. 395-407, *Nov. 1903*

MENDING Dikes in the Netherlands. Photos by Lawrence Earl. 791-806, *Dec. 1946*

Through the mist of a chill November day an Amish buggy in Lancaster County, Pennsylvania, heads for home.   WILLIAM ALBERT ALLARD

MENEN, AUBREY: *Author*

St. Peter's, Rome's Church of Popes. Photos by Albert Moldvay. 865-879, *Dec. 1971*

MENÉNDEZ DE AVILÉS, DON PEDRO:

Exploring Our Forgotten Century: Between Columbus and Jamestown. By Joseph Judge. Photos by Bill Ballenberg. Paintings by John Berkey. Note: Menéndez was an explorer and colonizer of La Florida. 330-363, *Mar. 1988*

St. Augustine, Nation's Oldest City, Turns 400. By Robert L. Conly. 196-229, *Feb. 1966*

MENGO, Uganda:

Where Roosevelt Will Hunt. By Sir Harry Johnston. 207-256, *Mar. 1909*

MENHADEN–Uncle Sam's Top Commercial Fish. By Leonard C. Roy. Photos by Robert F. Sisson. 813-823, *June 1949*

MENNONITES:

The Plain People of Pennsylvania. Photo essay by Jerry Irwin. Text by Douglas Lee. Included: Amish Mennonites; Reidenbach Mennonites; Team Mennonites (Old Order Mennonites); Wenger Mennonites. 492-519, *Apr. 1984*

Pennsylvania: Faire Land of William Penn. By Gordon Young. Photos by Cary Wolinsky. 731-767, *June 1978*

Amish Folk: Plainest of Pennsylvania's Plain People. By Richard Gehman. Photos by William Albert Allard. Contents: The Plain sects in Pennsylvania, including the Brethren (Dunkards), Mennonites, and Old Order Amish. 227-253, *Aug. 1965*

Artists Look at Pennsylvania. By John Oliver La Gorce. 37-56, *July 1948*

MENOMINEE INDIANS:

Wisconsin's Menominees: Indians on a Seesaw. By Patricia Raymer. Photos by Steve Raymer. 228-251, *Aug. 1974*

America's First Settlers, the Indians. By Matthew W. Stirling. Paintings by W. Langdon Kihn. 535-596, *Nov. 1937*

MENZEL, DONALD H.: *Author*

Solar Eclipse, Nature's Super Spectacular. By Donald H. Menzel and Jay M. Pasachoff. 222-233, *Aug. 1970*

Exploring Our Neighbor World, the Moon. 277-296, *Feb. 1958*

Author-Designer

The Heavens Above: On Land, Sea, and in the Air the Stars Serve Modern Man as Map, Compass, and Clock. Included: Star charts designed by author. Drawings of the constellations by Carlotta Gonzales Lahey. 97-128, *July 1943*

Designer

✺ A Map of the Heavens. Star charts on reverse. *Dec. 1957*

MEO TRIBESPEOPLE. *See* Hmong

MERCHANT MARINE ACADEMY. *See* U. S. Merchant Marine Academy

MERCHANT MARINE TRAINING SHIPS. *See Dar Pomorza; Georg Stage; Joseph Conrad; and* U. S. Merchant Marine Academy

MERCURY (Metallic Element):

Graveyard of the Quicksilver Galleons. By Mendel Peterson. Photos by Jonathan Blair. Note: The *Nuestra Señora de Guadalupe* and the *Conde de Tolosa* sank off the coast of the Dominican Republic in 1724 while carrying a cargo of mercury to the New World. 850-876, *Dec. 1979*

Quicksilver and Slow Death. By John J. Putman. Photos by Robert W. Madden. 507-527, *Oct. 1972*

MERCURY (Planet):

The Planets: Between Fire and Ice. By Rick Gore. 4-51, *Jan. 1985*

Mariner Unveils Venus and Mercury. By Kenneth F. Weaver. Included: First geological maps of Mercury. 858-869, *June 1975*

Voyage to the Planets. By Kenneth F. Weaver. Paintings by Ludek Pesek. 147-193, *Aug. 1970*

MERCURY MISSIONS:

The Earth From Orbit. By Paul D. Lowman, Jr. 645-671, *Nov. 1966*

John Glenn Receives the Society's Hubbard Medal. 827, *June 1962*

John Glenn's Three Orbits in *Friendship 7*: A Minute-by-Minute Account of America's First Orbital Space Flight. By Robert B. Voas. 792-827, *June 1962*

Tracking America's Man in Orbit. By Kenneth F. Weaver. Photos by Robert F. Sisson. 184-217, *Feb. 1962*

The Flight of *Freedom 7*. By Carmault B. Jackson, Jr. 416-431, *Sept. 1961*

The Pilot's Story. By Alan B. Shepard,

Jr. Photos by Dean Conger. 432-444, *Sept. 1961*

Countdown for Space. By Kenneth F. Weaver. 702-734, *May 1961*

Exploring Tomorrow With the Space Agency. By Allan C. Fisher, Jr. Photos by Dean Conger. 48-89, *July 1960*

MERDSOY, BORA:

Nomination Page. *Jan. 1976*

MERMAID'S PURSE:

Miracle of the Mermaid's Purse. By Ernest L. Libby. 413-420, *Sept. 1959*

MERRIAM, C. HART:

Board of Managers. 191, June 1897; 792-793, June 1934; 694, *June 1944*

Vice-President. 165, Apr. 1889; 270, July 1889; 68, Apr. 1890; 294, Apr. 1891; xii, Feb. 19, 1892; xix, Feb. 20, 1893; xix, May 5, 1894; 216, June 1896; 134, *Jan. 1936*

Director of newly-formed U. S. Division of Biological Survey. 405, *Dec. 1896*

Laws of Temperature Control of the Geographic Distribution of Terrestrial Animals and Plants. Address by C. Hart Merriam. 229-238, *Dec. 29, 1894*

Author

The Acorn, a Possibly Neglected Source of Food. 129-137, *Aug. 1918*

Report–Geography of Life. 160-162, *Apr. 1889*

MERRILL, FULLERTON: *Author*

A Hunting Trip to Northern Greenland. 118-122, *Mar. 1900*

The **MERRIMACK:** River of Industry and Romance. By Albert W.

Atwood. Photos by B. Anthony Stewart. 106-140, *Jan. 1951*

MERRITT, Lake, Oakland, California:

Wild Ducks as Winter Guests in a City Park. By Joseph Dixon. 331-342, *Oct. 1919*

MERRITT ISLAND NATIONAL WILDLIFE REFUGE, Florida:

Island, Prairie, Marsh, and Shore. By Charlton Ogburn. Photos by Bates Littlehales. 350-381, *Mar. 1979*

MERRY Maskers of Imst. Photos by Francis C. Fuerst. 201-208, *Aug. 1936*

MESA DEL NAYAR, Mexico:

Mesa del Nayar's Strange Holy Week. By Guillermo Aldana E. 780-795, *June 1971*

MESA VERDE NATIONAL PARK, Colorado:

The Anasazi–Riddles in the Ruins. By Thomas Y. Canby. Photos by Dewitt Jones and David Brill. Paintings by Roy Andersen. 554-592, *Nov. 1982*

The Southwest. The Making of America series. Included: Arizona, New Mexico, and parts of California, Colorado, Texas, Utah; and in Mexico: Baja California Norte, Chihuahua, Sonora. On reverse: 12,000 Years of History; Spanish Conquest; Anglo-American Entry and Occupancy. *Nov. 1982*

I See America First. By Lynda Bird Johnson. Photos by William Albert Allard. 874-904, *Dec. 1965*

Solving the Riddles of Wetherill Mesa. By Douglas Osborne. Paintings by

Peter V. Bianchi. NGS research grant. 155-195, *Feb. 1964*

20th-century Indians Preserve Customs of the Cliff Dwellers. Photos by William Belknap, Jr. NGS research grant. 196-211, *Feb. 1964*

Searching for Cliff Dwellers' Secrets. By Carroll A. Burroughs. NGS research grant. 619-625, *Nov. 1959*

Your Society to Seek New Light on the Cliff Dwellers. NGS research grant. 154-156, *Jan. 1959*

Ancient Cliff Dwellers of Mesa Verde. By Don Watson. Photos by Willard R. Culver. 349-376, *Sept. 1948*

Our National Parks. By L. F. Schmeckebier. 531-579, *June 1912*

Mesa Verde. By F. A. Newell. 431-434, *Oct. 1898*

MESHED (Mashhad), Iran:

Gilded Domes Against an Azure Sky. Photos by Stephen H. Nyman. 339-346, *Sept. 1939*

MESOAMERICAN CIVILIZATIONS:

Lost Empires, Living Tribes. 402 pages. *1982*

Visitor's Guide to the Aztec World; Mexico and Central America. *Dec. 1980*

Man's Eighty Centuries in Veracruz. By S. Jeffrey K. Wilkerson. Photos by David Hiser. Paintings by Richard Schlecht. NGS research grant. 203-231, *Aug. 1980*

See also Aztecs; Maya

MESOPOTAMIA:

Ebla: Splendor of an Unknown Empire. By Howard La Fay. Photos by James L. Stanfield. Paintings by Louis S.

A catastrophic earthquake in 1909 left hundreds in temporary quarters in towns on both sides of the Strait of Messina in Italy.

Sparkling olivine shows in a backlighted section of rare stony iron held by meteorite collector Robert Haag. JONATHAN BLAIR

Nervously waiting for dark before crossing the Mexican border into the U.S., two teenagers rest by cardboard suitcases and a plastic jug of water. WILLIAM ALBERT ALLARD

Smith, Jr. Photos by Dan Dry. 210-234, *Feb. 1984*

The Mexican Americans: A People on the Move. By Griffin Smith, Jr. Photos by Stephanie Maze. 780-809, *June 1980*

MEXICO:

■ *America's Hidden Wilderness: Lands of Seclusion.* Included: Arctic Regions; Baxter State Park, Maine; l'Eau Claire Wilderness, Quebec; Grand Gulch Primitive Area, Utah; Great Burn Wilderness Area, Idaho-Montana; Lacandon Forest, Mexico; Mojave Desert, California. 200 pages. *1988*

Gray Whales of San Ignacio. By Steven L. Swartz and Mary Lou Jones. Photos by François Gohier. NGS research grant. 754-771, *June 1987*

Earthquake in Mexico. By Allen A. Boraiko. Photos by James L. Stanfield and Guillermo Aldana E. Included: The rise and fall of buildings–a portrait for survival in quake city. 654-675, *May 1986*

When the Earth Moves. The Editor. 638-639, *May 1986*

The Usumacinta River: Troubles on a Wild Frontier. By S. Jeffrey K. Wilkerson. Photos by David Hiser. 514-543, *Oct. 1985*

Life on the Line: U. S.-Mexican Border. By Mark Kramer. Photos by Danny Lehman. 720-749, *June 1985*

The Poppy. By Peter T. White. Photos by Steve Raymer. 143-189, *Feb. 1985*

Following Cortés: Path to Conquest. By S. Jeffrey K. Wilkerson. Photos by Guillermo Aldana E. Paintings by Ned Seidler and Rosalie Seidler. 420-459, *Oct. 1984*

Mexico City: An Alarming Giant. By Bart McDowell. Photos by Stephanie Maze. 138-175. Included: A Scholarly President Looks at Mexico's Future. The Editor. 175, *Aug. 1984*

The Disaster of El Chichón. By Boris Weintraub. Photos by Guillermo Aldana E. and Kenneth Garrett. 654-684. Included: Volcanic Cloud May Alter Earth's Climate. By Robert I. Tilling. 672-675, *Nov. 1982*

🌐 *The Southwest.* The Making of America series. Included: Arizona, New Mexico, and parts of California, Colorado, Texas, Utah; and in Mexico: Baja California Norte, Chihuahua, Sonora. On reverse: 12,000 Years of History; Spanish Conquest; Anglo-American Entry and Occupancy. *Nov. 1982*

Silver: A Mineral of Excellent Nature. By Allen A. Boraiko. Photos by Fred Ward. 280-313, *Sept. 1981*

Rediscovering America's Forgotten Crops. By Noel D. Vietmeyer. Photos by Burgess Blevins. Paintings by Paul M. Breeden. 702-712, *May 1981*

■ *The Mighty Aztecs.* By Gene S. Stuart. Photos by Mark Godfrey. Art by Louis S. Glanzman. 199 pages. *1981*

The Aztecs. 704-775. I. The Aztecs. By Bart McDowell. Photos by David Hiser. Paintings by Felipe Dávalos. 714-751; II. The Building of Tenoch-

titlan. By Augusto F. Molina Montes. Paintings by Felipe Dávalos. 753-765; III. New Finds in the Great Temple. By Eduardo Matos Moctezuma. Photos by David Hiser. 767-775, *Dec. 1980*

🌐 *Visitor's Guide to the Aztec World; Mexico and Central America. Dec. 1980*

Baja's Murals of Mystery. By Harry Crosby. Photos by Charles O'Rear. 692-702, *Nov. 1980*

Editorial. By Gilbert M. Grosvenor. 585, *May 1980*

Editorial. By Gilbert M. Grosvenor. 579, *May 1978*

Mexican Folk Art. By Fernando Horcasitas. Photos by David Hiser. 648-669, *May 1978*

Mexico: "A Very Beautiful Challenge." By Mike Edwards. Photos by Thomas Nebbia. 612-647, *May 1978*

The Huichols, Mexico's People of Myth and Magic. By James Norman. Photos by Guillermo Aldana E. 832-853, *June 1977*

■■ *The Mysterious Maya.* By George E. and Gene S. Stuart. Photos by David Alan Harvey and Otis Imboden. 199 pages. *1977*

Found at Last: the Monarch's Winter Home. By Fred A. Urquhart. Photos by Bianca Lavies. NGS research grant. 161-173, *Aug. 1976*

The Tarahumaras: Mexico's Long Distance Runners. By James Norman. Photos by David Hiser. 702-718, *May 1976*

The Maya. 729-811. I. Children of Time. By Howard La Fay. Photos by David Alan Harvey. Included: Archaeological sites: Becan; Bonampak; Chichén Itzá; Dzibilchaltún; Jaina Island; Palenque; Tancah; Tulum; Uxmal; and present-day Maya. 729-767; II. Riddle of the Glyphs. By George E. Stuart. With Otis Imboden. Included: Cobá; Kohunlich; Palenque; Tancah; Yaxchilán. 768-791, *Dec. 1975*

Into the Lairs of "Sleeping" Sharks. By Eugenie Clark. Photos by David Doubilet. NGS research grant. 570-584, *Apr. 1975*

A New Riviera: Mexico's West Coast. By Nathaniel T. Kenney. Photos by Charles O'Rear. 670-699, *Nov. 1973*

Mexico, the City That Founded a Nation. By Louis de la Haba. Photos by Albert Moldvay. 638-669, *May 1973*

🌐 *Mexico; Central America. May 1973*

Probing the Deep Reefs' Hidden Realm. By Walter A. Starck II and Jo D. Starck. NGS research grant. 867-886, *Dec. 1972*

Baja California's Rugged Outback. By Michael E. Long. 543-567, *Oct. 1972*

Rocks, Ruts, and Sand: Driving the Mexican 1000. By Michael E. Long. 569-575, *Oct. 1972*

Mesa del Nayar's Strange Holy Week. By Guillermo Aldana E. 780-795, *June 1971*

Two Wheels Along the Mexican Border. By William Albert Allard. 591-635, *May 1971*

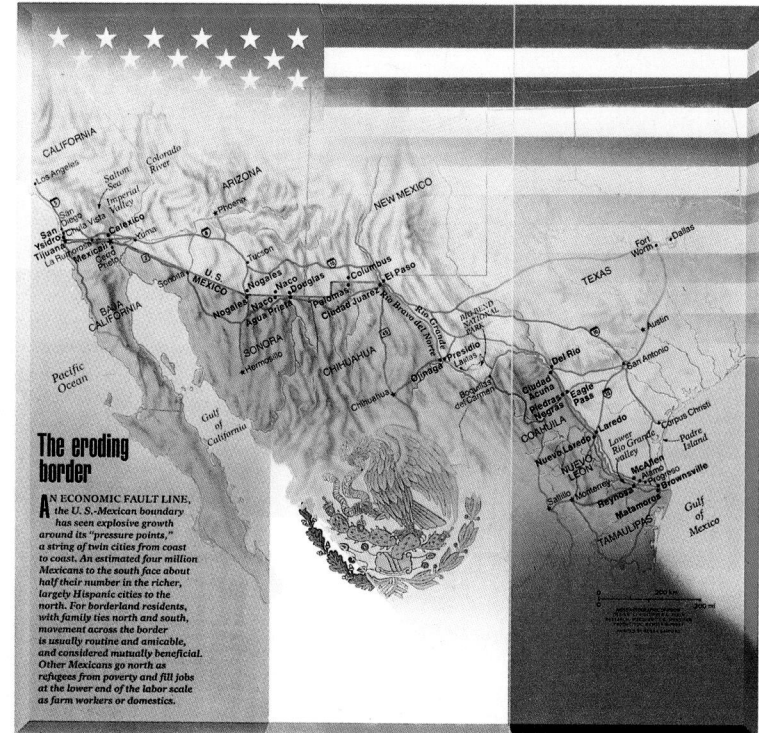

The eroding border

AN ECONOMIC FAULT LINE, the U. S.-Mexican boundary has seen explosive growth around its "pressure points," a string of twin cities from coast to coast. An estimated four million Mexicans to the south face about half their number in the richer, largely Hispanic cities to the north. For borderland residents, with family ties north and south, movement across the border is usually routine and amicable, and considered mutually beneficial. Other Mexicans go north as refugees from poverty and fill jobs at the lower end of the labor scale as farm workers or domestics.

Twin cities along the U.S.-Mexico border bond Hispanic families north and south—yet suffer from the crush of Mexicans fleeing poverty. NGS CARTOGRAPHIC DIVISION

During Mexico's bloody revolution seven decades ago, these veteran followers of Emiliano Zapata plundered the rich and gave land to the poor. THOMAS NEBBIA

The U.S. Sixth Infantry in pursuit of Pancho Villa in 1916 arrives near Namiquipa, Mexico. UNDERWOOD & UNDERWOOD/THE BETTMANN ARCHIVE

Refuge for swans and other birds, Wisconsin's Sturgeon Bay offers inspiration to conservationists battling pollution in Lake Michigan. RICHARD OLSENIUS

ATLANTIC OCEAN FLOOR

A map of the Atlantic Ocean floor showing the Mid-Atlantic Ridge was issued as a supplement to the June 1968 issue of NATIONAL GEOGRAPHIC magazine.

By James MacGillivray. 741-756, *Dec. 1928*

MICMAC INDIANS:

Nomads of the Far North. By Matthew W. Stirling. Paintings by W. Langdon Kihn. 471-504, *Oct. 1949*

MICROBIOLOGY:

The Awesome Worlds Within a Cell. By Rick Gore. Photos by Bruce Dale. Paintings by Davis Meltzer. 355-395, *Sept. 1976*

MICROELECTRONICS:

The Chip: Electronic Mini-marvel. By Allen A. Boraiko. Photos by Charles O'Rear. 421-457, *Oct. 1982*

Crystals, Magical Servants of the Space Age. By Kenneth F. Weaver. Photos by James P. Blair. 278-296, *Aug. 1968*

MICRONESIA:

In the Far Pacific: At the Birth of Nations. By Carolyn Bennett Patterson.

Photos by David Hiser and Melinda Berge. Note: Micronesia includes Guam, a U. S. territory; Kiribati; The Federated States of Micronesia, which include Kosrae, Pohnpei, Truk, Yap; The Commonwealth of Northern Marianas, which includes Rota, Saipan, Tinian; The Republic of the Marshall Islands, which includes Bikini Atoll, Enewetak, Kwajalein, Majuro Atoll; The Republic of Palau, which includes Babelthuap, Koror. 460-499, *Oct. 1986*

Micronesia: The Americanization of Eden. By David S. Boyer. 702-744, *May 1967*

Feast Day in Kapingamarangi. By W. Robert Moore. Note: The natives of Kapingamarangi and Nukuoro are Polynesian and differ in language and customs from the people of other island groups in Micronesia. 523-537, *Apr. 1950*

Pacific Wards of Uncle Sam. By W. Robert Moore. Contents: Trust

Territory of Pacific Islands. 73-104, *July 1948*

Hidden Key to the Pacific: Piercing the Web of Secrecy Which Long Has Veiled Japanese Bases in the Mandated Islands. By Willard Price. 759-785, *June 1942*

Mysterious Micronesia: Yap, Map, and Other Islands Under Japanese Mandate are Museums of Primitive Man. By Willard Price. 481-510, *Apr. 1936*

Nauru, the Richest Island in the South Seas. By Rosamond Dodson Rhone. 559-589, *Dec. 1921*

Yap and Other Pacific Islands Under Japanese Mandate. By Junius B. Wood. 591-627, *Dec. 1921*

See also Caroline Islands; Gilbert Islands; Mariana Islands; Marshall Islands; Nauru; Palau

MICROORGANISMS:

The Wild World of Compost. By Cecil E. Johnson. Photos by Bianca Lavies. 273-284, *Aug. 1980*

Those Marvelous, Myriad Diatoms. By Richard B. Hoover. 871-878, *June 1979*

Rotifers: Nature's Water Purifiers. By John Walsh. 287-292, *Feb. 1979*

Electronic Voyage Through an Invisible World. By Kenneth F. Weaver. 274-290, *Feb. 1977*

MICROPROCESSORS:

California's Silicon Valley. By Moira Johnston. Photos by Charles O'Rear. 459-477, *Oct. 1982*

The Chip: Electronic Mini-marvel. By Allen A. Boraiko. Photos by Charles O'Rear. 421-457, *Oct. 1982*

MICROSCOPICAL Examination of Wood from the Buried Forest, Muir Inlet, Alaska. By Francis H. Herrick. 75-78, *Mar. 21, 1892*

MICROSCOPY:

■■ *Hidden Worlds.* Vision, light, and magnification. Juvenile. 104 pages. *1981*

■ The Invisible World. 1, *Jan. 1980*; cover, *Mar. 1980*

Electronic Voyage Through an Invisible World. By Kenneth F. Weaver. 274-290, *Feb. 1977*

A Bold New Look at Our Past. The Editor. NGS research grant. 62-63, *Jan. 1975*

Exploring the Mind of Ice Age Man. By Alexander Marshack. NGS research grant. 64-89, *Jan. 1975*

Life in a "Dead" Sea–Great Salt Lake. By Paul A. Zahl. 252-263, *Aug. 1967*

Finding Rare Beauty in Common Rocks. By Lorence G. Collins. 121-129, *Jan. 1966*

Microscopical Examination of Wood from the Buried Forest, Muir Inlet, Alaska. By Francis H. Herrick. 75-78, *Mar. 21, 1892*

See also Microbiology; Photography, Microscope

MID-ATLANTIC RIDGE:

New Discoveries on the Mid-Atlantic Ridge. By Maurice Ewing. Photos by Robert F. Sisson. NGS research grant. 611-640, *Nov. 1949*

Exploring the Mid-Atlantic Ridge. By Maurice Ewing. NGS research grant. 275-294, *Sept. 1948*

MID-ATLANTIC RIFT:

Project FAMOUS. Photos by Emory Kristof. 586-615. I. Where the Earth Turns Inside Out. By J. R. Heirtzler. 586-603; II. Dive Into the Great Rift. By Robert D. Ballard. 604-615, *May 1975*

MID-ATLANTIC STATES:

🌐 *Close-up: U.S.A., The Mid-Atlantic States.* Text on reverse. Included: Delaware; Maryland; Virginia; West Virginia. *Oct. 1976*

See also Delaware; Maryland; Virginia; West Virginia

MID-CENTURY Holland Builds Her Future. By Sydney Clark. 747-778, *Dec. 1950*

MIDDLE AGES. *See* Byzantine Empire; Medieval Europe; *and* Crusades

MIDDLE AMERICA:

🌐 *Archeological Map of Middle America, Land of the Feathered Serpent.* Text on reverse. *Oct. 1968*

See also Central America; Mexico; *and* Aztecs; Maya

MIDDLE EAST:

The Persian Gulf–Living in Harm's Way. By Thomas J. Abercrombie. Photos by Steve Raymer. Included: Iraq, Iran, Saudi Arabia, Kuwait, Bahrain, Qatar, United Arab Emirates, Oman. 648-671, *May 1988*

Arabia's Frankincense Trail. By Thomas J. Abercrombie. Photos by Lynn Abercrombie. 474-513, *Oct. 1985*

Editorial. By Wilbur E. Garrett. 1, *July 1985*

Editorial. By Gilbert M. Grosvenor. 285, *Sept. 1980*

Islam's Heartland, Up in Arms. By Thomas J. Abercrombie. 335-345, *Sept. 1980*

🌐 *Two Centuries of Conflict in the Middle East; Mideast in Turmoil. Sept. 1980*

Ebla: Splendor of an Unknown Empire. By Howard La Fay. Photos by James L. Stanfield. Paintings by Louis S. Glanzman. Included: Akkad, Babylon, Ebla, Mari, Mesopotamia, Nippur, Sumer, Ugarit. 730-759, *Dec. 1978*

Editorial. By Gilbert M. Grosvenor. 729, *Dec. 1978*

Tigris Sails Into the Past. By Thor Heyerdahl. Photos by Carlo Mauri and the crew of the *Tigris.* Included: Probable trade routes of ancient Sumerians from Mesopotamia through the Persian Gulf east to the Indus Valley, and southwest in the Indian Ocean to the Horn of Africa. 806-827, *Dec. 1978*

🌐 *Middle East, Eastern Mediterranean; Early Civilizations of the Middle East. Sept. 1978*

Editorial. By Gilbert M. Grosvenor. 291, *Mar. 1977*

Editorial. By Gilbert M. Grosvenor. 295, *Mar. 1975*

Editorial. By Gilbert M. Grosvenor. 1, *Jan. 1975*

Editorial. By Gilbert M. Grosvenor. 587, *Nov. 1974*

Twilight of the Arab Dhow. By Marion Kaplan. 330-351, *Sept. 1974*

🌐 *The Peoples of the Middle East.* Text on reverse. *July 1972*

Eyewitness to War in the Holy Land. By Charles Harbutt. 782-795, *Dec. 1967*

Journey Into the Great Rift: the Northern Half. By Helen and Frank Schreider. 254-290, *Aug. 1965*

🌐 *Lands of the Eastern Mediterranean.* Atlas series. *Jan. 1959*

Troubled Waters East of Suez. By Ernest M. Eller. 483-522, *Apr. 1954*

Our Vegetable Travelers. By Victor R. Boswell. Paintings by Else Bostelmann. Included: Near Eastern Plant in American Pies (Rhubarb); Garden Peas and Spinach from the Middle East. 145-217, *Aug. 1949*

🌐 *Europe and the Near East. June 1949*

Sailing with Sindbad's Sons. By Alan Villiers. 675-688, *Nov. 1948*

🌐 *Europe and the Near East.* Inset: The Middle East. *June 1943*

🌐 *Europe and the Near East.* Inset: The Middle East. *May 1940*

🌐 *Europe and the Near East. Dec. 1929*

See also Bahrain; Cyprus; Egypt; Holy Land; Iran; Iraq; Israel; Jordan; Kurdistan; Lebanon; Oman; Red Sea; Saudi Arabia; Sinai Peninsula; Syria; Turkey; United Arab Emirates; Yemen Arab Republic; *and* Crusades

MIDDLE FORK SALMON (River), Idaho:

White-water Adventure on Wild Rivers of Idaho. By Frank Craighead, Jr., and John Craighead. 213-239, *Feb. 1970*

◼ *Wild River.* 239A-239B, *Feb. 1970*

MIDDLE ISLAND, Quebec, Canada:

Sea Bird Cities Off Audubon's Labrador. By Arthur A. Allen. Contents: Birds on Cliff, Harbour, and Middle Islands. NGS research grant. 755-774, *June 1948*

MIDDLETON GARDENS, South Carolina:

The Ashley River and Its Gardens. By E.T.H. Shaffer. 525-550, *May 1926*

MIDDLETON ISLAND, Alaska:

A Northern Crusoe's Island: Life on a Fox Farm Off the Coast of Alaska, Far from Contact with the World Eleven Months a Year. By Margery Pritchard Parker. 313-326, *Sept. 1923*

MIDDLETON PLACE, South Carolina:

The Ashley River and Its Gardens. By E.T.H. Shaffer. 525-550, *May 1926*

MIDGES:

An Insect Community Lives in Flower Heads. By James G. Needham. 340-356, *Sept. 1946*

MIDI (Region), France:

Across the Midi in a Canoe: Two Americans Paddle Along the Canals of Southern France from the Atlantic to the Mediterranean. By Melville Chater. 127-167, *Aug. 1927*

The **MIDLANDS,** England:

Exploring England's Canals. By Bryan Hodgson. Photos by Linda Bartlett. 76-111, *July 1974*

MIDNIGHT CAVE, Del Rio, Texas:

Six Months Alone in a Cave (Biorhythm Research). By Michel Siffre. 426-435, *Mar. 1975*

The **MIDNIGHT** Sun in the Klondike. By Alice Rollins Crane. 66-67, *Feb. 1901*

MID-OCEAN Color Log. Photos by E. John Long. 221-228, *Feb. 1939*

MID-OCEAN RIDGE SYSTEM:

Project FAMOUS. Photos by Emory Kristof. 586-615. I. Where the Earth Turns Inside Out. By J. R. Heirtzler. 586-603; II. Dive Into the Great Rift.

Limestone pillars provide a climbing challenge at ruins of a temple dedicated to the moon god Ilumquh in the Middle East's Democratic Yemen. LYNN ABERCROMBIE

Named for their resonant, brassy call, trumpeter swans migrate across the sky above Washington State's Skagit Valley. ART WOLFE

A young Greek island girl helps her grandmother, who spins yarn from wool of family sheep. ROBERT L'HOMMEDIEU

Mauney. Included: Maps tracing Milwaukee's history: Three settlements (1835); ethnic divisions (1900); present-day Milwaukee. 180-201, *Aug. 1980*

MIMICRY:
Deception: Formula for Survival. By Robert F. Sisson. Included: Insect mimicry. 394-415, *Mar. 1980*

MIN YUEN:
Malaya Meets Its Emergency. By George W. Long. Photos by J. Baylor Roberts and author. 185-228, *Feb. 1953*

MINAS GERAIS (State), Brazil:
Brazil's Land of Minerals. By W. Robert Moore. 479-508, *Oct. 1948*
Eclipse Hunting in Brazil's Ranchland. By F. Barrows Colton. NGS research grant. 285-324, *Sept. 1947*
Brazil's Potent Weapons. By W. Robert Moore. 41-78, *Jan. 1944*

MINDANAO (Island), Philippines:
Saving the Philippine Eagle. By Robert S. Kennedy. Photos by Alan R. Degen, Neil L. Rettig, and Wolfgang A. Salb. NGS research grant. 847-856, *June 1981*
The Tasadays, Stone Age Cavemen of Mindanao. By Kenneth MacLeish. Photos by John Launois. 219-249, *Aug. 1972*
◗ The Last Tribes of Mindanao. 882A-882B, *Dec. 1971*; 227, *Aug. 1972*
First Glimpse of a Stone Age Tribe. 881-882, *Dec. 1971*
Help for Philippine Tribes in Trouble. By Kenneth MacLeish. Photos by Dean Conger. 220-255, *Aug. 1971*
Seeking Mindanao's Strangest Creatures. By Charles Heizer Wharton. 389-408, *Sept. 1948*
Mindanao, on the Road to Tokyo. By Frederick Simpich. 539-574, *Nov. 1944*

MINDELEFF, COSMOS: *Author*
Topographic Models. 254-268, *July 1889*

A **MIND'S-EYE** Map of America. By Franklin K. Lane. 479-518, *June 1920*

MINER, EDWARD HERBERT:
Announcement of death. 769, *Dec. 1941*

Artist
Working Dogs of the World. 775-806, *Dec. 1941*
Hunters All: A Roll Call of the Hounds. 467-482, *Oct. 1937*
Man's Hunting Partner, the Field Dog. 89-104, *Jan. 1937*
Gallant Little Sportsmen of the Terrier Tribe. Note of acknowledgement: Painting the Terrier Series. 253-268, *Feb. 1936*
◗◗ *The Cattle of the World: Their Place in the Human Scheme–Wild Types and Modern Breeds in Many Lands.* By Alvin Howard Sanders. 142 pages. 1925; rev. ed. *1926*
The Cattle of the World. 639-678, *Dec. 1925*

Horses of the World. 479-526, *Nov. 1923*

MINER, ROY WALDO: *Author*
On the Bottom of a South Sea Pearl Lagoon. Paintings by Else Bostelmann. 365-390, *Sept. 1938*
Denizens of Our Warm Atlantic Waters. Paintings by Else Bostelmann. 199-219, *Feb. 1937*
Sea Creatures of Our Atlantic Shores. Paintings by Else Bostelmann. 209-231, *Aug. 1936*
Marauders of the Sea. Paintings by Else Bostelmann. 185-207, *Aug. 1935*
Coral Castle Builders of Tropic Seas. Paintings by Else Bostelmann. 703-728, *June 1934*

MINERALS:
Nauru, the World's Richest Nation. By Mike Holmes. 344-353, *Sept. 1976*
The Glittering World of Rockhounds. By David S. Boyer. 276-294, *Feb. 1974*
Questing for Gems. By George S. Switzer. 835-863, *Dec. 1971*
Colorado, the Rockies' Pot of Gold. By Edward J. Linehan. Photos by James L. Amos. Included: Gold, Lead, Molybdenum, Silver. 157-201, *Aug. 1969*
The Canadian North: Emerging Giant. By David S. Boyer. Included: Asbestos, Copper, Gold, Iron, Lead, Nickel, Silver, Uranium, Zinc. 1-43, *July 1968*
Finding Rare Beauty in Common Rocks. By Lorence G. Collins. 121-129, *Jan. 1966*
Sonora Is Jumping. By Mason Sutherland. Included: Cobalt, Copper, Gold, Graphite, Lead, Silver, Tungsten. 215-246, *Feb. 1955*
"Rockhounds" Uncover Earth's Mineral Beauty. By George S. Switzer. 631-660, *Nov. 1951*

Extracted from U.S. mines, coal in a plastic gas can symbolizes a problematical substitute for foreign oil. JONATHAN BLAIR

Exploring the World of Gems. By W. F. Foshag. 779-810, *Dec. 1950*
Brazil's Land of Minerals. By W. Robert Moore. Contents: Bauxite, Beryls, Diamonds, Gold, Iron Ore, Iron Pyrites, Manganese, Mica, Quartz. 479-508, *Oct. 1948*
India's Treasures Helped the Allies. By John Fischer. 501-522, *Apr. 1946*
Brazil's Potent Weapons. By W. Robert Moore. 41-78, *Jan. 1944*
Nauru, the Richest Island in the South Seas. By Rosamond Dodson Rhone. 559-589, *Dec. 1921*
Our Greatest Plant Food. By Guy Elliott Mitchell. 783-791, *Sept. 1910*
Modern Transmutation of the Elements. By Sir William Ramsay. 201-203, *Apr. 1906*
Alaska and Its Mineral Resources. By Samuel Franklin Emmons. 139-172, *Apr. 1898*
Mineral Production in the United States. 250, July 1896; 310, Sept. 1896; 201-202, *July-Aug. 1897*
An Expedition Through the Yukon District. By Charles Willard Hayes. 117-159, *May 15, 1892*
Report on Auriferous Sands from Yakutat Bay. By J. Stanley-Brown. 196-198, *May 29, 1891*
See also Crystals; Gems; Metals; *and* Coal; Salt

MINES, Submarine:
The Removal of the North Sea Mine Barrage. By Noel Davis. 103-133, *Feb. 1920*
The North Sea Mine Barrage. By Reginald R. Belknap. 85-110, *Feb. 1919*

MINES AND MINING:
Our National Forests: Problems in Paradise. By Rowe Findley. Photos by David Cupp. 306-339, *Sept. 1982*
Carrara Marble: Touchstone of Eternity. By Cathy Newman. Photos by Pierre Boulat. 42-59, *July 1982*
Synfuels: Fill 'er Up! With What? By Thomas Y. Canby. Photos by Jonathan Blair. Included: Oil-shale mines. 74-95, *Special Report on Energy. (Feb. 1981)*
Yukon Fever: Call of the North. By Robert Booth. Photos by George F. Mobley. Included: Gold, lead, silver, copper, and asbestos mines. 548-578, *Apr. 1978*
Should They Build a Fence Around Montana? By Mike W. Edwards. Photos by Nicholas deVore III. Included: Coal and copper mines. 614-649, *May 1976*
Questing for Gems. By George S. Switzer. Included: Mines in Africa; Asia; Australia. 835-863, *Dec. 1971*
The Canadian North: Emerging Giant. By David S. Boyer. Included: Asbestos, copper, gold, iron, lead, nickel, silver, uranium, and zinc mines. 1-43, *July 1968*
Colorado by Car and Campfire. By Kathleen Revis. Included: Blackhawk mines; Camp Bird Mine; Climax Mine; Leadville mines; Placer mines near Ute Pass; Smuggler Mine. 207-248, *Aug. 1954*
From Tucson to Tombstone. By Mason

MINIATURE HORSES:

MINIATURE Monaco. By Gilbert M. and Donna Kerkam Grosvenor. 546-573, *Apr. 1963*

MINIATURES of Macao. Photos by W. Robert Moore. 341-348, *Sept. 1932*

MINK:

MINNEAPOLIS, Minnesota:

MINNESOTA:

Fangs of steel scoop up oil-rich sand at Syncrude Canada Ltd., one of two immense mining facilities that process Canada's famous Athabasca tar sands. KENNETH GARRETT

Minnesota, Where Water Is the Magic Word. By David S. Boyer. Photos by author and David Brill. 200-229, *Feb. 1976*

Easter Greetings From the Ukrainians. By Robert Paul Jordan. Photos by James A. Sugar. 556-563, *Apr. 1972*

Satellites Gave Warning of Midwest Floods. By Peter T. White. Photos by Thomas A. DeFeo. 574-592, *Oct. 1969*

I See America First. By Lynda Bird Johnson. Photos by William Albert Allard. 874-904, *Dec. 1965*

Relics From the Rapids (Voyageurs). By Sigurd F. Olson. Photos by David S. Boyer. 413-435, *Sept. 1963*

Ice Fishing's Frigid Charms. By Thomas J. Abercrombie. 861-872, *Dec. 1958*

The Upper Mississippi. By Willard Price. 651-699, *Nov. 1958*

Minnesota Makes Ideas Pay. By Frederick G. Vosburgh. Photos by John E. Fletcher and B. Anthony Stewart. 291-336, *Sept. 1949*

Mapping the Nation's Breadbasket. By Frederick Simpich. 831-849, *June 1948*

Men, Moose, and Mink of Northwest Angle. By William H. Nicholas. Photos by J. Baylor Roberts. 265-284, *Aug. 1947*

Minnesota, Mother of Lakes and Rivers. By Glanville Smith. 273-318, *Mar. 1935*

The Wild Life of Lake Superior, Past and Present: The Habits of Deer, Moose, Wolves, Beavers. Muskrats, Trout, and Feathered Wood-Folk Studied with Camera and Flashlight. By George Shiras, 3d. 113-204, *Aug. 1921*

MINNESOTA (River), Minnesota:

Satellites Gave Warning of Midwest Floods. By Peter T. White. Photos by Thomas A. DeFeo. 574-592, *Oct. 1969*

MINNIGERODE, FITZHUGH LEE: *Author*

The Beauty of the Bavarian Alps. 632-649, *June 1926*

MINNIGERODE, H. GORDON: *Author*

Life Grows Grim in Singapore. 661-686, *Nov. 1941*

MINOAN CIVILIZATION:

Drama of Death in a Minoan Temple. By Yannis Sakellarakis and Efi Sapouna-Sakellaraki. Photos by Otis Imboden and Spyros Tsavdaroglou. 205-222, *Feb. 1981*

Joseph Alsop: A Historical Perspective (on Minoan Human Sacrifice). 223, *Feb. 1981*

Minoans and Mycenaeans: Greece's Brilliant Bronze Age. By Joseph Judge. Photos by Gordon W. Gahan. Paintings by Lloyd K. Townsend. 142-185, *Feb. 1978*

Thera, Key to the Riddle of Minos. By Spyridon Marinatos. Photos by Otis Imboden. 702-726, *May 1972*

VOL. 153, NO. 2   FEBRUARY 1978

NATIONAL GEOGRAPHIC

MINOANS AND MYCENAEANS: SEA KINGS OF THE AEGEAN 142
WHERE BALD EAGLES STILL SOAR 186
THE GULF'S WORKADAY WATERWAY 200
THE LIVING DEAD SEA 225
BRAZIL'S GOLDEN BEACHHEAD 246
THE PANAMA CANAL TODAY 279

SEE "THE GREAT WHALES" THURSDAY, FEBRUARY 16, ON PBS TV

MINOT, North Dakota:

Satellites Gave Warning of Midwest Floods. By Peter T. White. Photos by Thomas A. DeFeo. 574-592, *Oct. 1969*

North Dakota Comes into Its Own. By Leo A. Borah. Photos by J. Baylor Roberts. 283-322, *Sept. 1951*

MINSHALL, MERLIN: *Author*

By Sail Across Europe. 533-567, *May 1937*

MINTZ, BETTY:

Nomination Page. *June 1970*

MINUTEMEN of the Civil Air Patrol. By Allan C. Fisher, Jr. Photos by John E. Fletcher. 637-665, *May 1956*

MINYA KONKA (Mountain), China:

Climbing Mighty Minya Konka: Americans First Scaled Mountain That Now Is Landmark of China's New Skyway. By Richard L. Burdsall and Terris Moore. 625-650, *May 1943*

The Glories of the Minya Konka: Magnificent Snow Peaks of the China-Tibetan Border Are Photographed at Close Range by a National Geographic Society Expedition. By Joseph F. Rock. 385-437, *Oct. 1930*

MION, PIERRE: *Artist*

Mission to Mars. By Michael Collins. Photos by Roger H. Ressmeyer. Paintings by Pierre Mion and Roy Andersen. 733-764, *Nov. 1988*

Chernobyl—One Year After. By Mike Edwards. Photos by Steve Raymer. 632-653, *May 1987*

The Next Frontier? By Isaac Asimov. 76-89, *July 1976*

"Teammates in Mankind's Greatest Adventure" (Apollo Astronauts), painting supplement. *Sept. 1973*

Tektite II. 256-296. I. Science's Window on the Sea. By John G. VanDerwalker. Photos by Bates Littlehales. 256-289; II. All-girl Team Tests the

Habitat. By Sylvia A. Earle. 291-296, *Aug. 1971*

Footprints on the Moon. By Hugh L. Dryden. Paintings by Davis Meltzer and Pierre Mion. 357-401, *Mar. 1964*

Robots to the Moon. By Frank Sartwell. 557-571, *Oct. 1962*

MIQUELON (Island), St. Pierre and Miquelon:

White Mist Cruises to Wreck-haunted St. Pierre and Miquelon. By Melville Bell Grosvenor. 378-419, *Sept. 1967*

Islands Adrift: St. Pierre and Miquelon: In a Key Position on the North Atlantic Air Route, France's Oldest Colony Rides Out Another Storm. By Frederic K. Arnold. 743-768, *Dec. 1941*

MIRACLE Men of the Telephone. By F. Barrows Colton. 273-316, *Mar. 1947*

The **MIRACLE** Metal–Platinum. By Gordon Young. Photos by James L. Amos. 686-706, *Nov. 1983*

The **MIRACLE** of Talking by Telephone. By F. Barrows Colton. 395-433, *Oct. 1937*

MIRACLE of the Mermaid's Purse. By Ernest L. Libby. 413-420, *Sept. 1959*

MIRACLE of the Potholes. By Rowe Findley. Photos by Robert F. Sisson. 570-579, *Oct. 1975*

The **MIRACLE** of War Production: For Victory the United States Transforms Its Complex Industry into the Biggest Factory and Mightiest Arsenal the World Has Ever Known. By Albert W. Atwood. Paintings by Thornton Oakley. 693-715, *Dec. 1942*

MIRACLES of Fiber Optics. By Allen A. Boraiko. Photos by Fred Ward. 516-535, *Oct. 1979*

MIRAM SHAH, Pakistan:

South of Khyber Pass. By Maynard Owen Williams. 471-500, *Apr. 1946*

MIRROR of India: New Delhi. By Bryan Hodgson. Photos by Steve Raymer. 506-533, *Apr. 1985*

MIRRORS of Madeira, Rock Garden of the Atlantic. Photos by Wilhelm Tobien. 89-96, *July 1934*

MISHMI HILLS, Assam (State), India:

Caught in the Assam-Tibet Earthquake. By F. Kingdon-Ward. 403-416, *Mar. 1952*

MISSILE RANGE. *See* Atlantic Missile Range

MISSILES. *See* Guided Missiles; Rockets

MISSING in Action, 1972–U. S. Plane Found in Laos. By Peter T. White. Photos by Seny Norasingh. 692-696, *Nov. 1986*

The **MISSION** Called 66: Today in Our National Parks. By Conrad L. Wirth. 7-47, *July 1966*

The **MISSION** of the "Diana." 273, *July 1899*

M
N

MISSION to Mars. By Michael Collins. Photos by Roger H. Ressmeyer. Paintings by Pierre Mion and Roy Andersen. 733-764, *Nov. 1988*

MISSIONS:

I Live With the Eskimos (Canadian). By Guy Mary-Rousseliere. 188-217, *Feb. 1971*

San Diego, California's Plymouth Rock. By Allan C. Fisher, Jr. Photos by James L. Amos. 114-147, *July 1969*

California, the Golden Magnet. By William Graves. 595-679. I. The South. Photos by Thomas Nebbia. 595-639; II. Nature's North. Photos by James P. Blair and Jonathan S. Blair. Included: Spanish missions. 641-679, *May 1966*

From Tucson to Tombstone. By Mason Sutherland. 343-384, *Sept. 1953*

Far North with "Captain Mac." By Miriam MacMillan. Included: Catholic, Church of England, and Moravian missions. 465-513, *Oct. 1951*

Cruise to Stone Age Arnhem Land. By Howell Walker. Included: Mission stations: Croker Island, Elcho Island, Milingimbi Island, South Goulburn Island, and Yirrkala. NGS research grant. 417-430, *Sept. 1949*

Carnival in San Antonio. By Mason Sutherland. Photos by J. Baylor Roberts. Included: Espada, Mission Concepción, San José, San Juan Capistrano, and the Alamo. 813-844, *Dec. 1947*

Agriculture in the Yukon Valley. 189-190, *Apr. 1898*

The Metlakatla Mission in Danger. By William H. Dall. 187-189, *Apr. 1898*

See also Mesa del Nayar, Mexico; Sonora (State), Mexico

MISSISSIPPI:

The Tennessee-Tombigbee Waterway: Bounty or Boondoggle? By Carolyn Bennett Patterson. Photos by Sandy Felsenthal. Included: The Hidden Tenn-Tom: Bypassed But Still Striving. By Alice J. Hall. 364-387, *Mar. 1986*

Troubled Odyssey of Vietnamese Fishermen. By Harvey Arden. Photos by Steve Wall. 378-395, *Sept. 1981*

Mississippi's Grand Reunion at the Neshoba County Fair. By Carolyn Bennett Patterson. Photos by C. C. Lockwood. 854-866, *June 1980*

Today Along the Natchez Trace, Pathway Through History. By Bern Keating. Photos by Charles Harbutt. 641-667, *Nov. 1968*

Gettysburg and Vicksburg: the Battle Towns Today. By Robert Paul Jordan. Map notes by Carolyn Bennett Patterson. 4-57, *July 1963*

The Lower Mississippi. By Willard Price. Photos by W. D. Vaughn. 681-725, *Nov. 1960*

Skyway Below the Clouds. By Carl R. Markwith. Photos by Ernest J. Cottrell. Included: East Jackson Airport; Hawkins Field, Jackson; Vicksburg. 85-108, *July 1949*

Dixie Spins the Wheel of Industry. By

As the flooded Mississippi River breaks through a levee in 1919, refugees huddle on a tiny mound at Modoc, Arkansas. H. C. FRANKENFIELD

William H. Nicholas. Photos by J. Baylor Roberts. 281-324, *Mar. 1949*

History Repeats in Old Natchez. By William H. Nicholas. Photos by Willard R. Culver. 181-208, *Feb. 1949*

Machines Come to Mississippi. By J. R. Hildebrand. 263-318, *Sept. 1937*

Burning the Roads. 583-586, *Oct. 1906*

MISSISSIPPI (River), U. S.:

Drought Helps Uncover Life on the Mississippi. Geographica. *Nov. 1988*

Troubled Odyssey of Vietnamese Fishermen. By Harvey Arden. Photos by Steve Wall. 378-395, *Sept. 1981*

Minneapolis and St. Paul. By Thomas J. Abercrombie. Photos by Annie Griffiths. 665-691, *Nov. 1980*

Trouble in Bayou Country: Louisiana's Atchafalaya. By Jack and Anne Rudloe. Photos by C. C. Lockwood. Note: The Atchafalaya Basin is a major element in controlling floods on the Mississippi. 377-397, *Sept. 1979*

Mark Twain: Mirror of America. By Noel Grove. Photos by James L. Stanfield. 300-337, *Sept. 1975*

New Orleans and Her River. By Joseph Judge. Photos by James L. Stanfield. 151-187, *Feb. 1971*

▮▮ *The Mighty Mississippi.* By Bern Keating. Photos by James L. Stanfield. 199 pages. *1971*

St. Louis: New Spirit Soars in Mid-America's Proud Old City. By Robert Paul Jordan. Photos by Bruce Dale. 605-641, *Nov. 1965*

Gettysburg and Vicksburg: the Battle Towns Today. By Robert Paul Jor-

dan. Map notes by Carolyn Bennett Patterson. 4-57, *July 1963*

The Lower Mississippi. By Willard Price. Photos by W. D. Vaughn. 681-725, *Nov. 1960*

The Upper Mississippi. By Willard Price. 651-699, *Nov. 1958*

Land of Louisiana Sugar Kings. By Harnett T. Kane. Photos by Willard R. Culver. 531-567, *Apr. 1958*

Tom Sawyer's Town. By Jerry Allen. 121-140, *July 1956*

New Orleans: Jambalaya on the Levee. By Harnett T. Kane. Photos by Justin Locke. 143-184, *Feb. 1953*

Down Mark Twain's River on a Raft. By Rex E. Hieronymus. 551-574, *Apr. 1948*

Men Against the Rivers. By Frederick Simpich. 767-794, *June 1937*

Louisiana, Land of Perpetual Romance. By Ralph A. Graves. 393-482, *Apr. 1930*

The Great Mississippi Flood of 1927: Since White Man's Discovery This Mighty River Has Served Him Well, Yet It Has Brought Widespread Devastation Along Its Lower Reaches. By Frederick Simpich. 243-289, *Sept. 1927*

When the Father of Waters Goes on a Rampage: An Account of the Salvaging of Food-fishes from the Overflowed Lands of the Mississippi River. By Hugh M. Smith. 369-386, *Apr. 1920*

Honors for Amundsen. National Geographic Society Address by Theodore

Burton, on the Mississippi. 55-76, *Jan. 1908*

The Deep-Water Route from Chicago to the Gulf. 679-685, *Oct. 1907*

The Modern Mississippi Problem. By W J McGee. 24-27, *Jan. 1898*

Report–Geography of the Land. By Herbert G. Ogden. 31-48, *Apr. 1890*

MISSISSIPPI DELTA, Louisiana:

Mississippi Delta: The Land of the River. By Douglas Lee. Photos by C. C. Lockwood. 226-253, *Aug. 1983*

The Delta of the Mississippi River. By E. L. Corthell. 351-354, *Dec. 1897*

MISSISSIPPI VALLEY, U. S.:

Who Were the "Mound Builders"? By George E. Stuart. Included: Cahokia, Illinois; Koster farm site, Illinois; Monks Mound, East St. Louis, Illinois; Serpent Mound, Ohio. 783-801, *Dec. 1972*

"Pyramids" of the New World. By Neil Merton Judd. Note: Hundreds of mounds were built including Cahokia, Illinois; Grave Creek Mound, Moundsville, West Virginia; "Great Serpent," Ohio; St. Louis ("Mound City"), Missouri; Spiro, Oklahoma. 105-128, *Jan. 1948*

MISSISSIPPIAN CULTURE:

Who Were the "Mound Builders"? By George E. Stuart. 783-801, *Dec. 1972*

See also Russell Cave, Alabama

MISSOURI:

Kansas City, Heartland U.S.A. By Rowe Findley. Photos by Ted Spiegel. 112-139, *July 1976*

Mark Twain: Mirror of America. By Noel Grove. Photos by James L. Stanfield. 300-337, *Sept. 1975*

Through Ozark Hills and Hollows. By Mike W. Edwards. Photos by Bruce Dale. 656-689, *Nov. 1970*

St. Louis: New Spirit Soars in Mid-America's Proud Old City. By Robert Paul Jordan. Photos by Bruce Dale. 605-641, *Nov. 1965*

So Long, St. Louis, We're Heading West. By William C. Everhart. 643-669, *Nov. 1965*

The Upper Mississippi. By Willard Price. 651-699, *Nov. 1958*

Tom Sawyer's Town. By Jerry Allen. 121-140, *July 1956*

Following the Trail of Lewis and Clark. By Ralph Gray. 707-750, *June 1953*

Skyway Below the Clouds. By Carl R. Markwith. Photos by Ernest J. Cottrell. Included: The Ozarks; St. Louis; Springfield. 85-108, *July 1949*

The West Through Boston Eyes. By Stewart Anderson. 733-776, *June 1949*

Mapping the Nation's Breadbasket. By Frederick Simpich. 831-849, *June 1948*

"Pyramids" of the New World. By Neil Merton Judd. Included: "The Mound City." 105-128, *Jan. 1948*

These Missourians. By Frederick Simpich. Included: Missouri Mirrors of 1946. Photos by Richard H. Stewart. 277-310, *Mar. 1946*

Taming the Outlaw Missouri River. By Frederick Simpich. 569-598, *Nov. 1945*

Land of a Million Smiles (Ozarks). By Frederick Simpich. 589-623, *May 1943*

Missouri, Mother of the West. By Frederick Simpich. 421-460, *Apr. 1923*

MISSOURI (River), U. S.:

That Dammed Missouri River. By Gordon Young. Photos by David Hiser. 374-413, *Sept. 1971*

So Long, St. Louis, We're Heading West. By William C. Everhart. 643-669, *Nov. 1965*

Following the Trail of Lewis and Clark. By Ralph Gray. 707-750, *June 1953*

Taming the Outlaw Missouri River. By Frederick Simpich. 569-598, *Nov. 1945*

Trailing History Down the Big Muddy: In the Homeward Wake of Lewis and Clark, a Folding Steel Skiff Bears Its Lone Pilot on a 2,000-Mile Cruise on the Yellowstone-Missouri. By Lewis R. Freeman. 73-120, *July 1928*

MISSOURI (Battleship):

Battleship *Missouri* Comes of Age. 353-360, *Mar. 1945*

MISSOURI RIVER BASIN:

Taming the Outlaw Missouri River. By Frederick Simpich. 569-598, *Nov. 1945*

The **MIST** and Sunshine of Ulster. By Bernard F. Rogers, Jr. 571-610, *Nov. 1935*

MR. COOLIDGE Becomes a Member of The Society's Board of Trustees. 750, *June 1929*

MR. JEFFERSON'S Charlottesville. By Anne Revis. 553-592, *May 1950*

MR. JEFFERSON'S Monticello. By Joseph Judge. Photos by Dean Conger and Richard S. Durrance. 426-444, *Sept. 1966*

MR. ROOSEVELT'S "African Game Trails." 953-962, *Nov. 1910*

MR. ZIEGLER and the National Geographic Society. 251-254, *June 1903*

The **MISTLETOE.** 965, *Nov. 1910*

MISTRAL, FRÉDÉRIC:

Camargue, the Cowboy Country of Southern France. By André Vialles. 1-34, *July 1922*

MRS. BISHOP'S "The Yangtze Valley and Beyond." By Eliza Ruhamah Scidmore. 366-368, *Sept. 1900*

MRS. ROBINSON CRUSOE in Ecuador. By Mrs. Richard C. Gill. 133-172, *Feb. 1934*

MITCHELL, CARLETON: *Author*

Capri, Italy's Enchanted Rock. Photos by David F. Cupp. 795-809, *June 1970*

Our Virgin Islands, 50 Years Under the Flag. Photos by James L. Stanfield. 67-103, *Jan. 1968*

French Riviera: Storied Playground on the Azure Coast. Photos by Thomas Nebbia. 798-835, *June 1967*

More of Sea Than of Land: The Bahamas. Photos by James L. Stanfield. 218-267, *Feb. 1967*

A Fresh Breeze Stirs the Leewards. Photos by Winfield Parks. 488-537, *Oct. 1966*

■ *Isles of the Caribbees.* 208 pages. *1966*

Finisterre Sails the Windward Islands. Photos by Winfield Parks. 755-801, *Dec. 1965*

Time Turns Back in Picture-book Portofino. Photos by Winfield Parks. 232-253, *Feb. 1965*

To Europe with a Racing Start (*Finisterre*). 758-791, *June 1958*

The Bahamas, Isles of the Blue-green Sea. Photos by B. Anthony Stewart. 147-203, *Feb. 1958*

Ballerinas in Pink. Photos by B. Anthony Stewart. 553-571, *Oct. 1957*

Author-Photographer

Baltic Cruise of the *Caribbee.* 605-646, *Nov. 1950*

Carib Cruises the West Indies. 1-56, *Jan. 1948*

MITCHELL, EDGAR D.:

Photographer

The Climb Up Cone Crater. By Alice J. Hall. Photos by Edgar D. Mitchell and Alan B. Shepard, Jr. 136-148, *July 1971*

MITCHELL, GUY ELLIOTT: *Author*

Billions of Barrels of Oil Locked Up in Rocks. 195-205, *Feb. 1918*

American Potash for America. 399-405, *Apr. 1911*

An Ideal Fuel Manufactured Out of Waste Products: The American Coal Briquetting Industry. 1067-1074, *Dec. 1910*

A New Source of Power (Lignite). 935-944, *Nov. 1910*

Our Greatest Plant Food (Phosphorus). 783-791, *Sept. 1910*

Our Coal Lands. 446-451, *May 1910*

Landslides and Rock Avalanches. 277-287, *Apr. 1910*

A New National Park (Glacier National Park). 215-223, *Mar. 1910*

MITCHELL, HENRY:

Board of Managers. 165, *Apr. 1889*; 270, *July 1889*

MITCHELL, HENRY: *Author*

Washington, D. C.: Hometown Behind the Monuments. Photos by Adam Woolfitt. 84-125, *Jan. 1983*

MITCHELL, JOHN H.: *Author*

Oregon: Its History, Geography, and Resources. 239-284, *Apr. 20, 1895*

MITCHELL, SAMUEL ALFRED: *Author*

Nature's Most Dramatic Spectacle (Eclipse). 361-376, *Sept. 1937*

MITCHELL, WILLIAM: *Author*

Tiger-Hunting in India. 545-598, *Nov. 1924*

America in the Air: The Future of Airplane and Airship, Economically and as Factors in National Defense. 339-352, *Mar. 1921*

M
N

Building the Alaskan Telegraph System. 357-361, *Sept. 1904*

MITES:

The Wild World of Compost. By Cecil E. Johnson. Photos by Bianca Lavies. 273-284, *Aug. 1980*

MITLA, Mexico:

Hewers of Stone. By Jeremiah Zimmerman. 1002-1020, *Dec. 1910*

MITSUKURI, K.: *Author*

Cultivation of Marine and Fresh-Water Animals in Japan. 524-531, *Sept. 1906*

MITTELHOLZER, WALTER: *Author*

Flights from Arctic to Equator: Conquering the Alps, the Ice Peaks of Spitsbergen, of Persia, and Africa's Mountains of the Moon. 445-498, *Apr. 1932*

MITTERMEIER, RUSSELL A.: *Author*

Monkey in Peril: Rescuing Brazil's Muriqui. Photos by Andrew L. Young. 387-395, *Mar. 1987*

MIURA RANCH, Spain:

Holy Week and the Fair in Sevilla. By Luis Marden. 499-530, *Apr. 1951*

MIXTEC INDIANS:

Monte Albán, Richest Archeological Find in America: A Tomb in Oaxaca, Mexico, Yields Treasures Which Reveal the Splendid Culture of the Mixtecs. By Alfonso Caso. 487-512, *Oct. 1932*

MIXTER, GEORGE, 2D: *Author*

Hunting the Great Brown Bear of Alaska. 313-333, *Apr. 1909*

MIYAZAWA, EIJI: *Photographer*

Scientist Studies Japan's Fantastic Long-tailed Fowl. By Frank X. Ogasawara. 845-855, *Dec. 1970*
Snow Festival in Japan's Far North. 824-833, *Dec. 1968*
Japan's "Sky People," the Vanishing Ainu. By Mary Inez Hilger. 268-296, *Feb. 1967*

MNONG TRIBESPEOPLE:

Viet Nam's Montagnards. By Howard Sochurek. 443-487, *Apr. 1968*

MOBILE, Alabama:

Mobile, Alabama's City in Motion. By William Graves. Photos by Joseph J. Scherschel and Robert W. Madden. 368-397, *Mar. 1968*

MOBLEY, GEORGE F.:

On Assignment in Japan. *Aug. 1984*
Nomination Page. *Jan. 1964*

Photographer
■■ *Traveling the Trans-Canada: From Newfoundland to British Columbia.* By William Howarth. 199 pages. *1987*
Río Azul. 420-465. I. Lost City of the Maya. By Richard E. W. Adams. Included: Realm of the Maya (map). NGS research grant. 420-451; II. Looters Rob Graves and History. By Ian Graham. 452-461, *Apr. 1986*

Kluane: Canada's Icy Wilderness Park. By Douglas Lee. 630-653, *Nov. 1985*
■■ *We, The People: The Story of the United States Capitol, Its Past and Its Promise.* By Lonnelle Aikman. Photos by George F. Mobley and Joseph H. Bailey. Published in cooperation with the United States Capitol Historical Society. 143 pages. 1963; rev. ed. *1985*
The Japan Alps. By Charles McCarry. 238-259, *Aug. 1984*
■■ *Safari!* By Gene S. Stuart. Juvenile. 104 pages. *1982*
■■ *The Great Southwest.* By Charles McCarry. 199 pages. *1980*
The Society Islands, Sisters of the Wind. By Priit J. Vesilind. 844-869, *June 1979*
The Joy of Pigs. By Kent Britt. 398-415, *Sept. 1978*
Yukon Fever: Call of the North. By Robert Booth. 548-578, *Apr. 1978*
The Panama Canal Today. By Bart McDowell. 279-294, *Feb. 1978*
Kyoto and Nara: Keepers of Japan's Past. By Charles McCarry. 836-859. Included: Kyoto Says Happy New Year. 852-859, *June 1976*
■■ *Alaska: High Roads to Adventure.* 199 pages. *1976*
Greenland Feels the Winds of Change. By John J. Putman. 366-393, *Sept. 1975*
Firebrands of the Revolution. By Eric F. Goldman. 2-27, *July 1974*
Bavaria: Mod, Medieval–and Bewitching. By Gary Jennings. 409-431, *Mar. 1974*
Chile, Republic on a Shoestring. By Gordon Young. 437-477, *Oct. 1973*

A competitor at the 1985 national model airplane championships launches his plane on a practice flight. PETER ESSICK

Uganda, Africa's Uneasy Heartland. By Howard La Fay. 708-735, *Nov. 1971*
Norway, Land of the Generous Sea. By Edward J. Linehan. 1-43, *July 1971*
■■ *Alaska.* By Bern Keating. 207 pages. 1969; rev. ed. *1971*
Lebanon, Little Bible Land in the Crossfire of History. By William S. Ellis. 240-275, *Feb. 1970*
Finland: Plucky Neighbor of Soviet Russia. By William Graves. 587-629, *May 1968*
Parks, Plans, and People: How South America Guards Her Green Legacy. By Mary and Laurance Rockefeller. 74-119, *Jan. 1967*
900 Years Ago: the Norman Conquest. By Kenneth M. Setton. 206-251, *Aug. 1966*
World's Tallest Tree Discovered. By Melville Bell Grosvenor. 1-9, *July 1964*
Under the Dome of Freedom: The United States Capitol. By Lonnelle Aikman. 4-59, *Jan. 1964*

MOCHE CULTURE:

Discovering the New World's Richest Unlooted Tomb. By Walter Alva. Photos by Bill Ballenberg. Included: Into the Tomb of a Moche Lord. Paintings by Ned Seidler; Iconography of the Moche: Unraveling the Mystery of the Warrior-Priest. By Christopher B. Donnan. NGS research grant. 510-555, *Oct. 1988*
Finding the Tomb of a Warrior-God. By William Duncan Strong. Photos by Clifford Evans, Jr. 453-482, *Apr. 1947*

MOCHICA CULTURE. *See* Moche Culture

MOCTEZUMA II (Aztec Ruler):

Following Cortés: Path to Conquest. By S. Jeffrey K. Wilkerson. Photos by Guillermo Aldana E. Paintings by Ned Seidler and Rosalie Seidler. 420-459, *Oct. 1984*

MODEL AIRCRAFT:

Model Airplanes: To Dream, to Build ... And Then to Fly. By Michael E. Long. Photos by Peter Essick. Included: New wings for an old reptile. 132-144, *July 1986*

The **MODERN** Alchemist. By James Wilson. 781-795, *Dec. 1907*

A **MODERN** Dragon Hunt on Komodo: An English Yachting Party Traps and Photographs the Huge and Carnivorous Dragon Lizard of the Lesser Sundas. By Lady Broughton. 321-331, *Sept. 1936*

MODERN Ethiopia: Haile Selassie the First, Formerly Ras Tafari, Succeeds to the World's Oldest Continuously Sovereign Throne. By Addison E. Southard. 679-738, *June 1931*

MODERN House, Ancient Architecture. 42-43, *Special Report on Energy.* (*Feb. 1981*)

MODERN Life in Morocco, Western Outpost of Islam. Photos by M. Flandrin. 679-694, *June 1935*

Long ago, India's Mogul emperors ruled the Rajput ancestors of this Muslim bride from Pakistan. SABRINA MICHAUD

A cross section of a chambered nautilus reveals the mollusk's intricate shell structure. VICTOR R. BOSWELL, JR., NGS

Katarína Mišurová raises chickens and vegetables in Slovakia to add to erratically available store foods. YVA MOMATIUK AND JOHN EASTCOTT

Rejoicing at the arrival of the life-giving monsoon, women gather for a ceremonial bath in the Baghmati River in Kathmandu, Nepal. STEVE McCURRY

M
N

Frederick Simpich. 569-598, *Nov. 1945*

The Friendly Crows (Indians) in Festive Panoply. By Edwin L. Wisherd. 315-322, *Sept. 1927*

Our National Parks. By L. F. Schmeckebier. 531-579, *June 1912*

A New National Park (Glacier National Park). By Guy Elliott Mitchell. 215-223, *Mar. 1910*

The Call of the West. By C. J. Blanchard. 403-437, *May 1909*

A Bear Hunt in Montana. By Arthur Alvord Stiles. 149-154, *Feb. 1908*

Our Northern Rockies. By R. H. Chapman. 361-372, *Oct. 1902*

The Idaho and Montana Boundary Line. By Richard U. Goode. 23-29, *Jan. 1900*

Bitter Root Forest Reserve. By Richard U. Goode. 387-400, *Sept. 1898*

The Irrigation Problem in Montana. By H. Wilson. 212-229, *July 1890*

See also Glacier National Park; Padlock Ranch; Pryor Mountain Wild Horse Range; Red Rock Lakes National Wildlife Refuge; Scapegoat Wilderness; Surprise Creek Hutterite Colony

MONTANA TERRITORY, U. S.:

Ghosts on the Little Bighorn. By Robert Paul Jordan. Photos by Scott Rutherford. 787-813, *Dec. 1986*

✦ *Northern Plains.* The Making of America series. Included: Montana, Wyoming, North Dakota, South Dakota, Nebraska, Minnesota, Iowa,

and in Canada: Saskatchewan, Manitoba, Ontario. On reverse: New Frontiers, Indians in Transition, Furs and Footholds, Steel Rails and Settlers, King Wheat, Patterns of Change. *Dec. 1986*

C. M. Russell, Cowboy Artist. By Bart McDowell. Photos by Sam Abell. 60-95, *Jan. 1986*

MONTE Albán, Richest Archeological Find in America: A Tomb in Oaxaca, Mexico, Yields Treasures Which Reveal the Splendid Culture of the Mixtecs. By Alfonso Caso. 487-512, *Oct. 1932*

MONTENEGRO (Republic), Yugoslavia:

Montenegro: Yugoslavia's "Black Mountain." By Bryan Hodgson. Photos by Linda Bartlett. 663-683, *Nov. 1977*

Yugoslavia: Six Republics in One. By Robert Paul Jordan. Photos by James P. Blair. 589-633, *May 1970*

The New Map of Europe: Showing the Boundaries Established by the Peace Conference at Paris and by Subsequent Decisions of the Supreme Council of the Allied and Associate Powers. By Ralph A. Graves. 157-177, *Feb. 1921*

The Whirlpool of the Balkans. By George Higgins Moses. 179-197, *Feb. 1921*

The Races of Europe. By Edwin A. Grosvenor. 441-534, *Dec. 1918*

Greece and Montenegro. By George Higgins Moses. 281-310, *Mar. 1913*

East of the Adriatic: Notes on Dalmatia, Montenegro, Bosnia, and Herzegovina. By Kenneth McKenzie. 1159-1187, 1284, *Dec. 1912*

Servia and Montenegro. 774-789, *Nov. 1908*

Where East Meets West: Visit to Picturesque Dalmatia, Montenegro and Bosnia. By Marian Cruger Coffin. 309-344, *May 1908*

MONTEREY PENINSULA, California:

California's Land Apart–the Monterey Peninsula. By Mike W. Edwards. 682-703, *Nov. 1972*

California's Wonderful One (State Highway No. 1). By Frank Cameron. Photos by B. Anthony Stewart. 571-617, *Nov. 1959*

MONTESPAN GROTTO, France:

Discovering the Oldest Statues in the World: A Daring Explorer Swims Through a Subterranean River of the Pyrenees and Finds Rock Carvings Made 20,000 Years Ago. By Norbert Casteret. 123-152, *Aug. 1924*

MONTEVIDEO, Uruguay:

The Purple Land of Uruguay. By Luis Marden. 623-654, *Nov. 1948*

'Round the Horn by Submarine. By Paul C. Stimson. 129-144, *Jan. 1948*

MONTGOMERY, STEVEN L.: *Author*

The Case of the Killer Caterpillars.

A lone rider crosses meadows of Andrew Molera State Park in California's Big Sur, south of the Monterey Peninsula.   TOMAS W. SENNETT

First Explorers on the Moon: The Incredible Story of Apollo 11. 735-797. I. Man Walks on Another World. By Neil A. Armstrong, Edwin E. Aldrin, Jr., and Michael Collins. 738-749; II. Sounds of the Space Age, From Sputnik to Lunar Landing. A record narrated by Frank Borman. 750-751; III. The Flight of Apollo 11: "One giant leap for mankind." By Kenneth F. Weaver. 752-787, *Dec. 1969*

What the Moon Rocks Tell Us. By Kenneth F. Weaver. Included: Lunar Receiving Laboratory at the Manned Spacecraft Center in Houston, Texas. 788-791, *Dec. 1969*

And Now to Touch the Moon's Forbidding Face. By Kenneth F. Weaver. 633-635, *May 1969*

"A Most Fantastic Voyage": The Story of Apollo 8's Rendezvous With the Moon. By Sam C. Phillips. 593-631, *May 1969*

Awesome Views of the Forbidding Moonscape. Contents: Photos by Lunar Orbiter 2, 4, 5. 233-239, *Feb. 1969*

How We Mapped the Moon. By David W. Cook. 240-245, *Feb. 1969*

That Orbèd Maiden...the Moon. By Kenneth F. Weaver. 207-230, *Feb. 1969*

The Earth's Moon. Feb. 1969

Surveyor: Candid Camera on the Moon. By Homer E. Newell. Included: First color photographs from the surface of the moon. 578-592, *Oct. 1966*

The Moon Close Up. By Eugene M. Shoemaker. Photos by Ranger 7. 690-707, *Nov. 1964*

Footprints on the Moon. By Hugh L. Dryden. Paintings by Davis Meltzer and Pierre Mion. 357-401, *Mar. 1964*

Robots to the Moon. By Frank Sartwell. Paintings by Pierre Mion. 557-571, *Oct. 1962*

Reaching for the Moon. By Allan C. Fisher, Jr. Photos by Luis Marden. 157-171, *Feb. 1959*

Exploring Our Neighbor World, the Moon. By Donald H. Menzel. 277-296, *Feb. 1958*

First Photographs of Planets and Moon Taken with Palomar's 200-inch Telescope. By Milton L. Humason. 125-130, *Jan. 1953*

The Cartography and Observations of Bering's First Voyage. By A. W. Greely. Included: Lunar eclipse. 205-230, *Jan. 28, 1892; Feb. 19, 1892*

On the Alleged Observation of a Lunar Eclipse by Bering in 1728-9. By Marcus Baker. 167-169, *May 1890*

MOON JELLYFISH:

The Life of the Moon-Jelly. By William Crowder. Paintings by author. 187-202, *Aug. 1926*

MOORE, CHARLES: *Author*

The Transformation of Washington: A Glance at the History and Along the Vista of the Future of the Nation's Capital. 569-595, *June 1923*

MOORE, DAVID: *Photographer*

Okinawa, the Island Without a Country. By Jules B. Billard. Photos by Winfield Parks and David Moore. 422-448, *Sept. 1969*

New South Wales, the State That Cradled Australia. By Howell Walker. 591-635, *Nov. 1967*

"The Alice" in Australia's Wonderland. By Alan Villiers. Photos by Jeff Carter and David Moore. 230-257, *Feb. 1966*

MOORE, FREDERICK: *Author*

Rumania and Her Ambitions. 1057-1085, *Oct. 1913*

The Changing Map in the Balkans. 199-226, *Feb. 1913*

MOORE, HILARY B.: *Author*

X-Rays Reveal the Inner Beauty of Shells. 427-434, *Mar. 1955*

Strange Babies of the Sea (Plankton). Paintings by Craig Phillips and Jacqueline Hutton. 41-56, *July 1952*

MOORE, J. HAMPTON:

Pamphlet by J. Hampton Moore on Discovery of North Pole to be sent to Society members. 276, *Mar. 1910*

Honors for Amundsen. Address by J. Hampton Moore. 55-76, *Jan. 1908*

MOORE, J. Z.: *Photographer*

Scenes from the Land Where Everybody Dresses in White (Korea). 871-877, *Dec. 1908*

MOORE, KENNY: *Author*

Coober Pedy: Opal Capital of Australia's Outback. Photos by Penny Tweedie. 560-571, *Oct. 1976*

MOORE, TERRIS: *Author*

Climbing Mighty Minya Konka: Americans First Scaled Mountain That Now Is Landmark of China's New Skyway. By Richard L. Burdsall and Terris Moore. 625-650, *May 1943*

MOORE, W. ROBERT:

Nomination Page. At Angkor, Cambodia. *Apr. 1961*

Author

The Spotlight Swings to Suez. 105-115, *Jan. 1952*

Portrait of Indochina. By W. Robert Moore and Maynard Owen Williams. Paintings by Jean Despujols. 461-490, *Apr. 1951*

Power Comes Back to Peiping. By Nelson T. Johnson and W. Robert Moore. 337-368, *Sept. 1949*

Face of Japan. 753-768, *Dec. 1945*

Greens Grow for GI's on Soilless Ascension. 219-230, *Aug. 1945*

Capital and Chief Seaport of Chile. 477-500, *Oct. 1944*

Curaçao and Aruba on Guard. 169-192, *Feb. 1943*

Rehearsal at Dieppe (France). 495-502, *Oct. 1942*

Bombs over Bible Lands. By Frederick Simpich and W. Robert Moore. 141-180, *Aug. 1941*

Old-New Battle Grounds of Egypt and Libia. 809-820, *Dec. 1940*

As São Paulo Grows: Half the World's

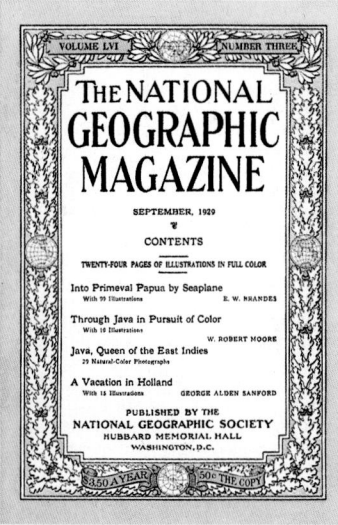

Coffee Beans Flavor the Life and Speed the Growth of an Inland Brazil City. 657-688, *May 1939*

The Garden Isles of Scilly: Geologists May Throw Stones at Legend of Lost Lyonnesse, But Natives Grow Flowers in Glass Houses for London. 755-774, *Dec. 1938*

When the Herring Fleet Comes to Great Yarmouth. 233-250, *Aug. 1934*

The Golden Isles of Guale (Sea Islands, Georgia). 235-264, *Feb. 1934*

Motor Trails in Japan. 303-318, *Mar. 1933*

Cosmopolitan Shanghai, Key Seaport of China. 311-335, *Sept. 1932*

Raft Life on the Hwang Ho. 743-752, *June 1932*

Coronation Days in Addis Ababa. 738-746, *June 1931*

Author-Photographer

Burma, Gentle Neighbor of India and Red China. 153-199, *Feb. 1963*

Cities of Stone in Utah's Canyonland. 653-677, *May 1962*

Thailand Bolsters Its Freedom. 811-849, *June 1961*

Angkor, Jewel of the Jungle. Paintings by Maurice Fiévet. 517-569, *Apr. 1960*

Progress and Pageantry in Changing Nigeria. 325-365, *Sept. 1956*

Alaska, the Big Land. 776-807, *June 1956*

Escalante: Utah's River of Arches. 399-425, *Sept. 1955*

War and Quiet on the Laos Frontier. 665-680, *May 1954*

Jamaica–Hub of the Caribbean. 333-362, *Mar. 1954*

Grass-skirted Yap. 805-830, *Dec. 1952*

White Magic in the Belgian Congo. 321-362, *Mar. 1952*

Clove-scented Zanzibar. 261-278, *Feb. 1952*

Republican Indonesia Tries Its Wings. 1-40, *Jan. 1951*

Strife-torn Indochina. 499-510, *Oct. 1950*

M
N

Odd fruits — such as red rambutan and spiny green durian — are displayed in a Bangkok, Thailand, stall in the 1930s. W. ROBERT MOORE, NGS

Through Java in Pursuit of Color. Included: Java, Queen of the East Indies. 333-362, *Sept. 1929*

Photographer

Three Whales That Flew. By Carleton Ray. 346-359, *Mar. 1962*

Bristlecone Pine, Oldest Known Living Thing. By Edmund Schulman. 355-372, *Mar. 1958*

Alaska's Warmer Side. By Elsie May Bell Grosvenor. 737-775, *June 1956*

South in the Sudan. By Harry Hoogstraal. 249-272, *Feb. 1953*

Because It Rains on Hawaii. By Frederick Simpich, Jr. 571-610, *Nov. 1949*

Operation Eclipse: 1948. By William A. Kinney. 325-372, *Mar. 1949*

Pageantry of the Siamese Stage. By D. Sonakul. 201-212, *Feb. 1947*

In the Land of Moses and Abraham. 711-742, *Dec. 1938*

Czechoslovakian Cyclorama. 181-220, *Aug. 1938*

Buddhist Calm Survives Along China's Great Wall. 321-328, *Mar. 1938*

Tradition Lingers in Modern Japan. 117-124, *Jan. 1938*

Castles, Shrines, and Parks of Japanese Pilgrimage. 457-464, *Apr. 1936*

England's Island Garden of Rocks and Flowers (Isle of Wight). 17-24, *Jan. 1935*

"Time Will Not Dim the Glory of Their Deeds" (World War Memorials). 17-24, *Jan. 1934*

Chromatic Highlights of Korea. 429-436, *Oct. 1933*

Life and Color Under the Rising Sun. Photos by W. Robert Moore and Kiyoshi Sakamoto. 289-296, *Mar. 1933*

Life Along the Central China Coast. 317-324, *Sept. 1932*

Miniatures of Macao (China). 341-348, *Sept. 1932*

The Color Camera Explores the Country That Moves by Night. 479-510, *Oct. 1931*

Shan Tribes Make Burma's Hills Flash With Color. 455-462, *Oct. 1931*

Present Day Scenes in the World's Oldest Empire (Ethiopia). 691-722, *June 1931*

Strange Tribes in the Shan States of Burma. 247-254, *Aug. 1930*

High Lights in the Peruvian and Bolivian Andes. 219-234, *Feb. 1927*

MOORE, WILLIS L.:

Board of Managers. 520, Dec. 1898; 88, *Jan. 1910*

The Discovery of the North Pole. Speeches by Willis L. Moore. 63-82, *Jan. 1910*

Honors to the American Navy. Speeches by Willis L. Moore. 77-95, *Jan. 1909*

Honors for Amundsen. Speeches by Willis L. Moore. 55-76, *Jan. 1908*

Portrait. 587, *Sept. 1907*

Honors to Peary. Speeches by Willis L. Moore. 49-60, *Jan. 1907*

The Annual Dinner of the National Geographic Society. Speeches by Willis L. Moore. 22-37, *Jan. 1906*

President. 87, *Feb. 1905*

Author

Forecasting the Weather and Storms. 255-305, *June 1905*

The Weather Bureau. 362-369, *Oct. 1901*

United States Daily Atmospheric Survey. 299-303, *Oct. 1897*

Storms and Weather Forecasts. 65-82, *Mar. 1897*

The Weather Bureau River and Flood System. 302-307, *Sept. 1896*

MOOREA (Island), Society Islands:

Tahiti, "Finest Island in the World." By Luis Marden. 1-47, *July 1962*

MOORISH Spain. Photos by Gervais Courtellemont. 163-178, *Aug. 1924*

MOORLANDS:

To Scotland Afoot Along the Pennine Way. By David Yeadon. Photos by Annie Griffiths. 388-418, *Mar. 1986*

MOORS (People):

Spain When the Moors Ruled Spain. By Thomas J. Abercrombie. Photos by Bruno Barbey. 86-119, *July 1988*

Toledo–El Greco's Spain Lives On. By Louise E. Levathes. Photos by James P. Blair. 726-753, *June 1982*

Andalusia, the Spirit of Spain. By Howard La Fay. Photos by Joseph J. Scherschel. 833-857, *June 1975*

Portugal at the Crossroads. By Howard La Fay. Photos by Volkmar Wentzel. 453-501, *Oct. 1965*

The Changing Face of Old Spain. By Bart McDowell. Photos by Albert Moldvay. 291-339, *Mar. 1965*

Speaking of Spain. By Luis Marden. 415-456, *Apr. 1950*

Portugal Is Different. By Clement E. Conger. 583-622, *Nov. 1948*

The Two Great Moorish Religious Dances. By George Edmund Holt. 777-785, *Aug. 1911*

An offering of cloth strips hangs from the doorway of a local saint's tomb in Tikirt, Morocco. THOMAS J. ABERCROMBIE, NGS

MOOSE:

Giants of the Wilderness: Alaskan Moose. By Victor Van Ballenberghe. Photos by Michio Hoshino. 260-280, *Aug. 1987*

Isle Royale, A North Woods Park Primeval. By John L. Eliot. Photos by Mitch Kezar. Included: Moose-wolf symbiosis. 534-550, *Apr. 1985*

Wolves Versus Moose on Isle Royale. By Durward L. Allen and L. David Mech. 200-219, *Feb. 1963*

Men, Moose, and Mink of Northwest Angle (Minnesota). By William H. Nicholas. Photos by J. Baylor Roberts. 265-284, *Aug. 1947*

Deer of the World: As Workers, Pets, and Graceful "Living Statuary" in Parks and Estates, These Versatile Creatures Have Endeared Themselves to Mankind. By Victor H. Cahalane. Paintings by Walter A. Weber. 463-510, *Oct. 1939*

Lords of the Rockies: Photographing Big Game Animals in Their Primeval Surroundings, from Arizona to Canada, Brings Adventure to Two Wilderness Wanderers. By Wendell and Lucie Chapman. 87-128, *July 1939*

The Wild Life of Lake Superior, Past and Present: The Habits of Deer, Moose, Wolves, Beavers, Muskrats, Trout, and Feathered Wood-Folk Studied with Camera and Flashlight. By George Shiras, 3d. 113-204, *Aug. 1921*

Wild Animals That Took Their Own Pictures by Day and by Night. By George Shiras, 3d. 763-834, *July 1913*

The White Sheep, Giant Moose, and Smaller Game of the Kenai Peninsula, Alaska. By George Shiras, 3d. 423-494, *May 1912*

The Big Game of Alaska. By Wilfred H. Osgood. 624-636, *July 1909*

One Season's Game-Bag with the Camera. By George Shiras, 3d. 387-446, *June 1908*

MORAN, EDMOND J.: *Author*

Stop-and-Go Sail Around South Norway. Photos by Randi Kjekstad Bull and Andrew H. Brown. 153-192, *Aug. 1954*

MORAN, KATHY:

On Assignment. *Sept. 1988*

MORAVIAN MISSIONARIES:

Two Hundred Miles up the Kuskokwim. By Charles Hallock. Included: Messrs. Hartmann and Weinland, Moravian missionaries. 85-92, *Mar. 1898*

MORAVJANS:

Old Salem, Morning Star of Moravian Faith. By Rowe Findley. Photos by Robert W. Madden. 818-837, *Dec. 1970*

Far North with "Captain Mac." By Miriam MacMillan. 465-513, *Oct. 1951*

MORDEN, FLORENCE H.: *Author*

House-Boat Days in the Vale of Kashmir. 437-463, *Oct. 1929*

A four-foot-drive vehicle idles with its high-tech cargo on a narrow cobbled street in the ancient city of Fez, in Morocco. BRUNO BARBEY, MAGNUM

MOSES:

Lost Outpost of the Egyptian Empire. By Trude Dothan. Photos by Sisse Brimberg. Paintings by Lloyd K. Townsend. NGS research grant. 739-769, *Dec. 1982*

Eternal Sinai. By Harvey Arden. Photos by David Doubilet and Kevin Fleming. 420-461, *Apr. 1982*

In Search of Moses. By Harvey Arden. Photos by Nathan Benn. 2-37, *Jan. 1976*

MOSES, GEORGE HIGGINS: *Author*

New Hampshire, the Granite State. 257-310, *Sept. 1931*

The Whirlpool of the Balkans. 179-197, *Feb. 1921*

Greece of Today. 295-329, *Oct. 1915*

Greece and Montenegro. 281-310, *Mar. 1913*

MOSES, Lake, Washington:

From Sagebrush to Roses on the Columbia. By Leo A. Borah. 571-611, *Nov. 1952*

MOSES SOLE (Fish):

The Red Sea's Sharkproof Fish. By Eugenie Clark. Photos by David Doubilet. 718-727, *Nov. 1974*

MOSIER, ROBERT H.:

Author-Photographer

The GI and the Kids of Korea. 635-664, *May 1953*

MOSLEMS. *See* Muslims

MOSQUES:

Saudi Arabia: The Kingdom and Its Power. By Robert Azzi. Included: The siege at Mecca. 286-333, *Sept. 1980*

Pilgrimage to Mecca. By Muhammad Abdul-Rauf. Photos by Mehmet Biber. Included: Mosque of Hudaybiyah, and al-Masjid al-Haram, the Sacred Mosque at Mecca. 581-607, *Nov. 1978*

From America to Mecca on Airborne Pilgrimage. By Abdul Ghafur. Included: The Kaaba, in the courtyard of the Great Mosque, Mecca; Masjid-al-Nabi (Mosque of the Prophet), in Medina; a mosque in Kuba; and Husain's tomb in Karbala. 1-60, *July 1953*

Journey Into Troubled Iran. By George W. Long. Photos by J. Baylor Roberts. Included: Masjid-i-Shah, Masjid Sheik Lutf Ullah, and the mosque at Qum. 425-464, *Oct. 1951*

Turkey Paves the Path of Progress. By Maynard Owen Williams. Included: Beyazit, Blue Mosque, Eyüp Ansari, Suleiman the Magnificent, Yeni Cami (New Mosque), Yeşil Cami (Green Mosque). 141-186, *Aug. 1951*

Gilded Domes Against an Azure Sky. 339-346, *Sept. 1939*

Constantinople Today. By Solita Solano. 647-680, *June 1922*

Constantinople and Sancta Sophia. By Edwin A. Grosvenor. 459-482, *May 1915*

MOSQUITO CAYS, Caribbean Sea:

Capturing Giant Turtles in the Caribbean. By David D. Duncan. 177-190, *Aug. 1943*

MOSQUITOES:

Mosquitoes, the Mighty Killers. By Lewis T. Nielsen. 427-440, *Sept. 1979*

Exploring Ancient Panama by Helicopter. By Matthew W. Stirling. Photos by Richard H. Stewart. Included: *Aedes aegypti* and *Haemagogus* mosquitoes. NGS research grant. 227-246, *Feb. 1950*

Keeping House for a Biologist in Colombia. By Nancy Bell Fairchild Bates. Photos by Marston Bates. Included: *Anopheles* and *Haemagogus* mosquitoes. 251-274, *Aug. 1948*

Life Story of the Mosquito. By Graham Fairchild. 180-195, *Feb. 1944*

Saboteur Mosquitoes. By Harry H. Stage. 165-179, *Feb. 1944*

MOST Curious Craft Afloat: The Compass in Navigation and the Work of the Non-Magnetic Yacht "Carnegie." By L. A. Bauer. 223-245, *Mar. 1910*

The **MOST** Extraordinary City in the World: Notes on Lhasa–The Mecca of the Buddhist Faith. By Shaoching H. Chuan. 959-995, *Oct. 1912*

The **MOST** Famous Battle Field in America. 66-75, *July 1931*

"A **MOST** Fantastic Voyage": The Story of Apollo 8's Rendezvous With the Moon. By Sam C. Phillips. 593-631, *May 1969*

The **MOST** Historic Lands on Earth. 615, *Dec. 1914*

The **MOST** Mexican City, Guadalajara. By Bart McDowell. Photos by Volkmar Wentzel. 412-441, *Mar. 1967*

A **MOST** Uncommon Town: Columbus, Indiana. By David Jeffery. Photos by J. Bruce Baumann. 383-397, *Sept. 1978*

The **MOST** Valuable Bird in the World. By Robert Cushman Murphy. 279-302, *Sept. 1924*

MOTAGUA FAULT, Guatemala:

Earthquake in Guatemala. By Bart McDowell. Photos by W. E. Garrett and Robert W. Madden. 810-829, *June 1976*

The **MOTHER MAPS** of the United States. By Henry Gannett. 101-116, *Mar. 31, 1892*

MOTHER-OF-PEARL:

Twenty Fathoms Down for Mother-of-Pearl. By Winston Williams. Photos by Bates Littlehales. 512-529, *Apr. 1962*

Goggle Fishing in California Waters. By David Hellyer. Photos by Lamar Boren. 615-632, *May 1949*

The **MOTHER** of Rivers: An Account of a Photographic Expedition to the Great Columbia Ice Field of the Canadian Rockies. By Lewis R. Freeman. 377-446, *Apr. 1925*

MOTHER Volga Defends Her Own. By Maynard Owen Williams. 793-811, *Dec. 1942*

MOTHERS of Many Lands. 549-564, *June 1917*

MOTHS:

New Tricks Outwit Our Insect Enemies. By Hal Higdon. Photos by Robert F. Sisson and Emory Kristof. Included: Gypsy moths. 380-399, *Sept. 1972*

Moths That Behave Like Hummingbirds. Photos by Treat Davidson. 770-775, *June 1965*

An Insect Community Lives in Flower Heads. By James G. Needham. 340-356, *Sept. 1946*

Exploring the Wonders of the Insect World. By William Joseph Showalter. Paintings by Hashime Murayama. 1-90, *July 1929*

Strange Habits of Familiar Moths and Butterflies. By William Joseph Showalter. 77-105, *July 1927*

Where Our Moths and Butterflies Roam. Contents: Arctiidae, Ceratocampidae, Lithosiidae Noctuidae, Saturniidae, Sphingidae. 105-126, *July 1927*

Explorers of a New Kind: Successful Introduction of Beetles and Parasites to Check Ravages of the Gipsy-moth and Brown-tail Moth. By L. O. Howard. 38-67, *July 1914*

Pests and Parasites: Why We Need a National Law to Prevent the Importation of Insect-Infested and Diseased Plants. By Charles Lester Marlatt. 321-346, *Apr. 1911*

The Gypsy Moth. 461-464, *Aug. 1906*

See also Inchworms; Silkworms

MOTILONE INDIANS:

Venezuela Builds on Oil. By Thomas J. Abercrombie. 344-387, *Mar. 1963*

MOTION PICTURE INDUSTRY:

Southern California at Work. By Frederick Simpich. 529-600, *Nov. 1934*

MOTOR-COACHING Through North Carolina. By Melville Chater. 475-523, *May 1926*

MOTOR Trails in Japan. By W. Robert Moore. 303-318, *Mar. 1933*

MOTORCYCLE RACES:

The Manx and Their Isle of Man. By Veronica Thomas. Photos by Ted H. Funk. Included: International Tourist Trophy Races ("T. T."); Manx Grand Prix. 426-444, *Sept. 1972*

MOTORCYCLE TRIPS:

Two Wheels Along the Mexican Border. By William Albert Allard. 591-635, *May 1971*

MOTZFELDT, JONATHAN:

Hunters of the Lost Spirit: Greenlanders. By Priit J. Vesilind. Photos by Ivars Šilis. 191-193, *Feb. 1983*

MOULIN, RAYMOND: *Photographer*

Saving Earth's Oldest Living Things. By Andrew H. Brown. Photos by Raymond Moulin and author. 679-695, *May 1951*

MOUND BUILDERS (Ancient Indians):

Piecing Together an Indian Heritage. Geographica. *Nov. 1988*

Who Were the "Mound Builders"? By George E. Stuart. 783-801, *Dec. 1972*

"Pyramids" of the New World. By Neil Merton Judd. 105-128, *Jan. 1948*

Indians of the Southeastern United States. By Matthew W. Stirling. Paintings by W. Langdon Kihn. 53-74, *Jan. 1946*

Ohio, the Gateway State. By Melville Chater. 525-591, *May 1932*

The Indian Village of Baum (Ohio). By H. C. Brown. 272-274, *July 1901*

MOUNDS:

Jericho Gives Up Its Secrets. By Kathleen M. Kenyon and A. Douglas

Tushingham. Photos by Nancy Lord. 853-870, *Dec. 1953*

The Ghosts of Jericho. By James L. Kelso. 825-844, *Dec. 1951*

Exploring Ancient Panama by Helicopter. By Matthew W. Stirling. Photos by Richard H. Stewart. Included: Archaeological sites in provinces of Chiriquí and Veraguas. NGS research grant. 227-246, *Feb. 1950*

Exploring the Past in Panama. By Matthew W. Stirling. Photos by Richard H. Stewart. Included: Azuero Peninsula, Tambor region. NGS research grant. 373-399, *Mar. 1949*

See also La Venta, Mexico; Tell Mardikh Excavation; Tepe Gawra; *and* Mound Builders

MOUNIER, BRUCE: *Photographer*

Strange March of the Spiny Lobster. By William F. Herrnkind. Photos by Rick Frehsee and Bruce Mounier. 819-831, *June 1975*

MOUNT ATHOS (Monastic Republic), Greece:

The Byzantine Empire. 709-777. I. Rome of the East. By Merle Severy. Photos by James L. Stanfield. 709-767; II. Mount Athos. 739-745, *Dec. 1983*

MOUNT DESERT ISLAND, Maine:

Northeast of Boston. By Albert W. Atwood. 257-292, *Sept. 1945*

First National Park East of Mississippi River. 623-626, *June 1916*

The Need of Conserving the Beauty and Freedom of Nature in Modern Life. By Charles W. Eliot. 67-74, *July 1914*

The Unique Island of Mount Desert. By George B. Dorr, Ernest Howe Forbush, and M. L. Fernald. 75-89, *July 1914*

MOUNT EVEREST: Surveying the Third Pole. By Bradford Washburn. NGS research grant. 653-659, *Nov. 1988*

MOUNT EVEREST NATIONAL PARK, Nepal:

A Fragile Heritage: The Mighty Himalaya. By Barry C. Bishop. Photos by William Thompson. 624-631, *Nov. 1988*

Preserving a Mountain Heritage. By Sir Edmund Hillary. 696-703, *June 1982*

Park at the Top of the World: Mount Everest National Park. By Rick Ridgeway. Photos by Nicholas deVore III. 704-725, *June 1982*

MOUNT KENNEDY YUKON EXPEDITION:

Canada's Mount Kennedy. 1-33. I. The Discovery. By Bradford Washburn. 1-3; II. A Peak Worthy of the President. By Robert F. Kennedy. 5-9; III. The First Ascent. By James W. Whittaker. Photos by William Albert Allard. NGS research grant. 11-33, *July 1965*

MOUNT McKINLEY NATIONAL PARK, Alaska:

New Mount McKinley Challenge–Trekking Around the Continent's

Highest Peak. By Ned Gillette. 66-79, *July 1979*

Mount McKinley Conquered by New Route. By Bradford Washburn. 219-248, *Aug. 1953*

Wildlife of Mount McKinley National Park. By Adolph Murie. Paintings by Walter A. Weber. 249-270, *Aug. 1953*

A Game Country Without Rival in America: The Proposed Mount McKinley National Park. By Stephen R. Capps. 69-84, *Jan. 1917*

Mount McKinley. By Robert Muldrow. 312-313, *Aug. 1901*

MOUNT RAINIER NATIONAL PARK, Washington:

Mount Rainier: Testing Ground for Everest. By Barry C. Bishop. NGS research grant. 688-711, *May 1963*

Climbing Our Northwest Glaciers. Photos by Bob and Ira Spring. 103-114, *July 1953*

The Great White Monarch of the Pacific Northwest. By A. H. Barnes. 593-626, *June 1912*

Our National Parks. By L. F. Schmeckebier. 531-579, *June 1912*

A Wonderland of Glaciers and Snow. By Milnor Roberts. 530-537, *June 1909*

The Height of Mt. Rainier. By Richard U. Goode. 97-98, *Mar. 1898*

See also Pacific Crest Trail

MOUNT RUSHMORE NATIONAL MEMORIAL, South Dakota:

Back to the Historic Black Hills. By Leland D. Case. Photos by Bates Littlehales. 479-509, *Oct. 1956*

South Dakota Keeps Its West Wild. By Frederick Simpich. 555-588, *May 1947*

Monks at the Thami Monastery in Nepal's Mount Everest National Park dance at a Buddhist festival . JONATHAN T. WRIGHT

A blizzard of ice hampers climbers attempting the peak of Tibet's 20,610-foot Anyemaqen mountain. GALEN ROWELL

The **MT. ST. ELIAS** Expedition of Prince Luigi Amadeo of Savoy, 1897. By Eliza Ruhamah Scidmore. 93-96, *Mar. 1898*

MOUNT ST. HELENS NATIONAL VOLCANIC MONUMENT, Washington:

Mount St. Helens Aftermath. By Rowe Findley. Photos by Steve Raymer. 713-733, *Dec. 1981*

Mount St. Helens. By Rowe Findley. 3-65, *Jan. 1981*

Mount St. Helens. By Charles P. Elliott. 226-230, *July-Aug. 1897*

MOUNT SINAI EXPEDITIONS:

Island of Faith in the Sinai Wilderness (St. Catherine's Monastery). By George H. Forsyth. Photos by Robert F. Sisson. Sponsors: University of Michigan, Princeton University, University of Alexandria. 82-106, *Jan. 1964*

Mount Sinai's Holy Treasures (St. Catherine's Monastery). By Kurt Weitzmann. Photos by Fred Anderegg. 109-127, *Jan. 1964*

Sinai Sheds New Light on the Bible. By Henry Field. Photos by William B. and Gladys Terry. Sponsor: University of California African Expedition. 795-815, *Dec. 1948*

MOUNT VERNON (Estate), Virginia:

Mount Vernon Lives On. By Lonnelle Aikman. 651-682, *Nov. 1953*

✣ *A Map of the Travels of George Washington.* Included: Inset of Mount Vernon. *Jan. 1932*

The Home of the First Farmer of America. By Worth E. Shoults. 603-628, *May 1928*

MOUNT VESUVIUS. 272-279, *May 1906*

MOUNT WEATHER METEOROLOGICAL OBSERVATORY, Virginia:

Scientific Work of Mount Weather Meteorological Observatory. By Frank H. Bigelow. 442-445, *Nov. 1904*

***MOUNTAIN** Adventure: Exploring the* ◾◾*Appalachian Trail.* By Ron Fisher. Photos by Sam Abell. 200 pages. *1988*

MOUNTAIN CLIMBING:

High Road to "Victory": Soviet and U. S. Climbers Conquer Pik Pobedy. By William Garner. Photos by Medford Taylor. 256-271, *Aug. 1986*

Kluane: A Century of Exploration. By Barry C. Bishop. 654-657, *Nov. 1985*

The Japan Alps. By Charles McCarry. Photos by George F. Mobley. 238-259, *Aug. 1984*

The Forgotten Face of Everest. By Andrew Harvard. Photos by Expedition Members. 71-89. Included: Conquest of the Summit. By James D. Morrissey. 79-89, *July 1984*

Park at the Top of the World: Mount Everest National Park. By Rick Ridgeway. Photos by Nicholas deVore III. 696-725. Included: Preserving a Mountain Heritage. By Sir Edmund Hillary. 696-703, *June 1982*

Nomads of China's West. By Galen Rowell. Photos by the author and Harold A. Knutson. Included: An American expedition to Anyemaqen peak. 244-263, *Feb. 1982*

At My Limit–I Climbed Everest Alone. By Reinhold Messner. Photos by the author and Nena Holguín. 552-566, *Oct. 1981*

American Skiers Find Adventure in Western China. By Ned Gillette. Photos by the author and Galen Rowell. 174-199. Included: Skiing From the Summit of China's Ice Mountain. 192-199, *Feb. 1981*

New Mount McKinley Challenge– Trekking Around the Continent's Highest Peak. By Ned Gillette. 66-79, *July 1979*

Americans Climb K2. Photos by members of the expedition. 623-649. I. The Ultimate Challenge. By James W. Whittaker. 624-639; II. On to the Summit. By James Wickwire. 641-649, *May 1979*

Triumph and Tragedy on Annapurna. By Arlene Blum. 295-313. Included: On the Summit. By Irene Miller, with Vera Komarkova. 312-313, *Mar. 1979*

To Torre Egger's Icy Summit. By Jim Donini. 813-823, *Dec. 1976*

First Conquest of Antarctica's Highest

A mountain goat in Montana's Glacier National Park checks out wildlife biologist Douglas Chadwick, busy noting the creature's lame leg. NICHOLAS DEVORE III

The violence of a Montana earthquake in 1959 caused shifting in this mountainous section of U.S. 191.   ALBERT MOLDVAY

M N

MOUNTAINS OF THE MOON
(Ruwenzori), Uganda-Zaire:

Mountains of the Moon. By Paul A. Zahl. 412-434, *Mar. 1962*

Flights from Arctic to Equator: Conquering the Alps, the Ice Peaks of Spitsbergen, of Persia, and Africa's Mountains of the Moon. By Walter Mittelholzer. 445-498, *Apr. 1932*

The World's Highest Altitudes and First Ascents. By Charles E. Fay. 493-530, *June 1909*

Amid the Snow Peaks of the Equator: A Naturalist's Explorations Around Ruwenzori, with an Excursion to the Congo State, and an Account of the Terrible Scourge of Sleeping Sickness. By A.F.R. Wollaston. 256-277, *Mar. 1909*

MOUNTAINS on Unimak Island, Alaska. By Ferdinand Westdahl. 91-99, *Mar. 1903*

MOUNTAINTOP War in Remote Ladakh. By W. E. Garrett. 664-687, *May 1963*

MOUNTFORD, CHARLES P.: *Author*

Expedition to the Land of the Tiwi. 417-440, *Mar. 1956*

Exploring Stone Age Arnhem Land. Photos by Howell Walker. 745-782, *Dec. 1949*

Author-Photographer

Earth's Most Primitive People: A Journey with the Aborigines of Central Australia. Included: Australia's Stone Age Men. 89-112, *Jan. 1946*

MOUSE (River), Canada-U. S.:

Satellites Gave Warning of Midwest Floods. By Peter T. White. Photos by Thomas A. DeFeo. 574-592, *Oct. 1969*

The **MOVEMENTS** of Our Population. By Henry Gannett. 21-44, *Mar. 20, 1893*

MOWBRAY, LOUIS L.: *Author*

Certain Citizens of the Warm Sea. Paintings by Hashime Murayama. 27-62, *Jan. 1922*

MOYAL, MAURICE: *Author*

Sheep Trek in the French Alps. Photos by Marcel Coen. 545-564, *Apr. 1952*

MOYNIHAN, MICHAEL: *Author*

The Swans of Abbotsbury. Photos by Barnet Saidman. 563-570, *Oct. 1959*

MOZABITES:

Oasis-hopping in the Sahara. By Maynard Owen Williams. 209-236, *Feb. 1949*

MOZAI, TORAO: *Author*

The Lost Fleet of Kublai Khan. Photos by Koji Nakamura. Paintings by Issho Yada. 634-649, *Nov. 1982*

MOZAMBIQUE:

Tsetse–Fly of the Deadly Sleep. By Georg Gerster. 814-833, *Dec. 1986*

Mozambique: Land of the Good People. By Volkmar Wentzel. 197-231, *Aug. 1964*

A gnarled, wind-flattened Jeffrey pine survives on Sentinel Dome in California's Sierra Nevada, a wilderness heralded by 19th-century naturalist John Muir. DEWITT JONES

Safari Through Changing Africa. By Elsie May Bell Grosvenor. Photos by Gilbert Grosvenor. 145-198, *Aug. 1953*

Wings Over Nature's Zoo in Africa. 527-542, *Oct. 1939*

Impressions and Scenes of Mozambique. By O. W. Barrett. 807-830, *Oct. 1910*

Hunting Big Game in Portugese East Africa. By R.C.F. Maugham. 723-730, *Nov. 1907*

MRU TRIBESPEOPLE:

The Peaceful Mrus of Bangladesh. By Claus-Dieter Brauns. 267-286, *Feb. 1973*

MUCH More Than Met the Eye: Halley's Comet 1986. By Rick Gore. 758-785, *Dec. 1986*

MUD-PUDDLE FROGS:

The Amazing Frog-Eating Bat. By Merlin D. Tuttle. NGS research grant. 78-91, *Jan. 1982*

MUDFLOWS:

Eruption in Colombia. By Bart McDowell. Photos by Steve Raymer. 640-653, *May 1986*

MUDIE, COLIN:

Braving the Atlantic by Balloon *(Small World)*. By Arnold Eiloart. 123-146, *July 1959*

MUDSKIPPERS:

Who Says Fish Can't Climb Trees? By Ivan Polunin. 85-91, *Jan. 1972*

MUDSLIDES:

Southern California's Trial by Mud and Water. By Nathaniel T. Kenney. Photos by Bruce Dale. 552-573, *Oct. 1969*

MUGH TRIBESPEOPLE:

India's Treasures Helped the Allies. By John Fischer. 501-522, *Apr. 1946*

MUHAMMAD (Prophet):

Pilgrimage to Mecca. By Muhammad Abdul-Rauf. Photos by Mehmet Biber. 581-607, *Nov. 1978*

The Sword and the Sermon. By Thomas J. Abercrombie. 3-45, *July 1972*

From America to Mecca on Airborne Pilgrimage. By Abdul Ghafur. 1-60, *July 1953*

MUHARRAQ (Town and Island), Bahrein Islands:

Bahrein: Port of Pearls and Petroleum. By Maynard Owen Williams. 195-210, *Feb. 1946*

MUIR, FRANCES:

Author-Photographer

India Mosaic. By Peter Muir and Frances Muir. Included: India at Work and Play. Photos by authors and Maynard Owen Williams. 443-470, *Apr. 1946*

MUIR, JOHN:

Yosemite–Forever? By David S. Boyer. Photos by Jonathan Blair. 52-79, *Jan. 1985*

■■*John Muir's Wild America.* By Tom Melham. Photos by Farrell Grehan. Art by H. Tom Hall. 199 pages. *1976*

John Muir's Wild America. By Harvey Arden. Photos by Dewitt Jones. 433-461, *Apr. 1973*

Portrait. 188, *May 1901*

The Discovery of Glacier Bay, Alaska. By Eliza Ruhamah Scidmore. Included: John Muir's discovery of Glacier Bay. 140-146, *Apr. 1896*

MUIR, PETER UPTON:

Author-Photographer

India Mosaic. By Peter Muir and Frances Muir. Included: India at Work and Play. Photos by authors and Maynard Owen Williams. 443-470, *Apr. 1946*

Photographer
Normandy and Brittany in Brighter Days. Photos by W. Robert Moore, Peter Upton Muir, and others. 209-232, *Aug. 1943*

MUIR GLACIER, Alaska:
Muir Glacier. By C. L. Andrews. 441-444, *Dec. 1903*
The Discovery of Glacier Bay, Alaska. By Eliza Ruhamah Scidmore. 140-146, *Apr. 1896*
Studies of Muir Glacier, Alaska. By Harry Fielding Reid. Appendices: List of Plants Collected near Muir Glacier, determined by W. W. Rowlee; Meteorological Observations; Magnetic Observations; Suggestions to Future Observers. Supplements: Notes on the Geology of the Vicinity of Muir Glacier, by H. P. Cushing; Notes on Some Eruptive Rocks from Alaska, by George H. Williams; Microscopical Examination of Wood from the Buried Forest, Muir Inlet, Alaska, by Francis H. Herrick. 19-84, *Mar. 21, 1892*
✣ *Muir Glacier, Alaska.* Surveyed with Plane Table in 1890, by Harry Fielding Reid. *Mar. 21, 1892*

MUIR INLET, Alaska:
Studies of Muir Glacier, Alaska. By Harry Fielding Reid. Supplement: Microscopical Examination of Wood from the Buried Forest, Muir Inlet, Alaska, by Francis H. Herrick. 19-84, *Mar. 21, 1892*

MUJERES, Isla, Mexico:
Into the Lairs of "Sleeping" Sharks. By Eugenie Clark. Photos by David Doubilet. NGS research grant. 570-584, *Apr. 1975*

MUKDEN, Manchuria, China. *See* Shenyang

MULA MULAI (Ship):
Seafarers of South Celebes. By G.E.P. Collins. 53-78, *Jan. 1945*

MULATAS ARCHIPELAGO, Panama:
Arch-Isolationists, the San Blas Indians: Coconuts Serve as Cash on Islands Off the Panama Coast Where Tribesmen Cling to Their Ancient Ways and Discourage Visitors. By Corine B. Feeney. 193-220, *Feb. 1941*

MULBERRY (Artificial Harbor), Normandy Coast, France:
Normandy's Made-in-England Harbors. 565-580, *May 1945*

MULDROW, ROBERT: *Author*
Mount McKinley. 312-313, *Aug. 1901*

MULE DEER:
High Country of Colorado. By Alfred M. Bailey. Photos by author, Robert J. Niedrach, and F. G. Brandenburg. 43-72, *July 1946*

MULES:
Trek by Mule Among Morocco's Berbers. By Victor Englebert. 850-875, *June 1968*

MULGREW, PETER:
Nomination Page. In the Himalaya. *June 1961*

MULI, Sichuan Province, China:
The Land of the Yellow Lama: National Geographic Society Explorer Visits the Strange Kingdom of Muli, Beyond the Likiang Snow Range of Yünnan Province, China. By Joseph F. Rock. 447-491, *Apr. 1925*

MULLER, JAMES ARTHUR: *Author*
Peking, the City of the Unexpected. 335-355, *Nov. 1920*

MULLER, KAL: *Author-Photographer*
Tanna Awaits the Coming of John Frum. 706-715, *May 1974*
Taboos and Magic Rule Namba Lives. 57-83, *Jan. 1972*
Land Diving With the Pentecost Islanders. 799-817, *Dec. 1970*

MULLIKIN, MARY AUGUSTA:
Author
Tai Shan, Sacred Mountain of the East. 699-719, *June 1945*

Author-Artist
China's Great Wall of Sculpture: Manhewn Caves and Countless Images Form a Colossal Art Wonder of Early Buddhism. Included: Buddhist Calm Survives Along China's Great Wall. Paintings by author and Anna M. Hotchkis. 313-348, *Mar. 1938*

MULTICOLORED Cones of Cappadocia. Photos by Eric Matson. 769-800, *Dec. 1939*

This 500-year-old mummy of an Inuit woman was discovered in Greenland in 1972. JOHN LEE, NATIONAL MUSEUM, COPENHAGEN

MULTI-HUED Marvels of a Coral Reef. Paintings by Else Bostelmann. 719-726, *June 1934*

MULU, Mount, Borneo (now Kalimantan), Indonesia:
Sarawak: The Land of the White Rajahs. By Harrison W. Smith. 110-167, *Feb. 1919*

MUMMIES:
Sealed in Time–Ice Entombs an Eskimo Family for Five Centuries. By Albert A. Dekin, Jr. Photos by Victor R. Boswell, Jr., and Scott Rutherford. Paintings by James M. Gurney. 824-836, *June 1987*
Mysteries of the Bog. By Louise E. Levathes. Photos by Fred Bavendam. Included: Peat holds clues to early American life. 397-420, *Mar. 1987*
The Mummies of Qilakitsoq. By Jens P. Hart Hansen, Jørgen Meldgaard, and Jørgen Nordqvist. 191-207, *Feb. 1985*
A Lady From China's Past. Photos from *China Pictorial.* Text by Alice J. Hall. 660-681, *May 1974*
The Lost Empire of the Incas. By Loren McIntyre. Art by Ned and Rosalie Seidler. 729-787. Included: A pictorial chronicle of the Incas. Contents: Mummified body of an Inca boy who froze to death 500 years ago. 747-753, *Dec. 1973*
Tutankhamun's Golden Trove. By Christiane Desroches Noblecourt. Photos by F. L. Kenett. 625-646, *Oct. 1963*
Lifelike Man Preserved 2,000 Years in Peat. By P. V. Glob. 419-430, *Mar. 1954*
Ancient Cliff Dwellers of Mesa Verde. By Don Watson. Photos by Willard R. Culver. Contents: Mummification by natural dehydration; the famous mummy "Esther." 349-376, *Sept. 1948*
At the Tomb of Tutankhamen: An Account of the Opening of the Royal Egyptian Sepulcher Which Contained the Most Remarkable Funeral Treasures Unearthed in Historic Times. By Maynard Owen Williams. Included: Egypt, Past and Present. 493-508, *May 1923*
The Sacred Ibis Cemetery and Jackal Catacombs at Abydos. By Camden M. Cobern. Contents: The preserved remains of ibises and jackals. 1042-1056, *Sept. 1913*

MUNDA, New Georgia (Island), Solomon Islands:
Painting History in the Pacific. Paintings by William F. Draper. 408-424, *Oct. 1944*

MUNGER, F. M.: *Author*
A Jack in the Box: An Account of the Strange Performances of the Most Wonderful Island in the World (Bogoslof Volcano, Alaska). 194-199, *Feb. 1909*

MUNICH, Germany:
Bavaria: Mod, Medieval–and Bewitching. By Gary Jennings. Photos by George F. Mobley. 409-431, *Mar. 1974*

MUÑOZ, JUAN: *Author-Photographer*
Cliff Dwellers of the Bering Sea. 129-146, *Jan. 1954*

MUNROE, JOE: *Photographer*
The Bonins and Iwo Jima Go Back to Japan. By Paul Sampson. 128-144, *July 1968*

MÜNSTER, Germany:
The Town of Many Gables. By Florence Craig Albrecht. 107-140, *Feb. 1915*

MURAYAMA, HASHIME: *Artist*
Rogues' Gallery of Imported Pests (Insects). 237-244, *Aug. 1941*
Fresh-Water Denizens of the Far West. 193-204, *Feb. 1939*
Gleaming Fishes of Pacific Coastal Waters. 467-498, *Oct. 1938*
Farmers' Friends Among the Wasps and Hornets. 57-64, *July 1937*
Nomads Among the Butterflies. Photos by Willard R. Culver. 569-584, *May 1937*
Winged Jewels from Many Lands. Photos by Willard R. Culver. 673-688, *May 1936*
In Field and Hive with the Busy Honeybee. 417-424, *Apr. 1935*
Work and War in the World of Ants. 179-186, *Aug. 1934*
Nature's Ingenious Spinners (Spiders). 167-174, *Aug. 1933*
The Iridescent Beauty of Frogs and Toads. 635-642, *May 1932*
Iridescent Denizens of the Miniature Aquarium. 293-300, *Mar. 1931*
Domestic Fowls of Field, Park, and Farmyard. 329-360, *Mar. 1930*
Insect Rivals of the Rainbow. 29, 53, 77, *July 1929*
Fowl of the Old and New World. 421-436, *Apr. 1927*
Pigeons of Resplendent Plumage. 65-76, *Jan. 1926*
Iridescent Isles of the South Seas (Birds). 403-418, *Oct. 1925*
Goldfish and Their Cultivation. 385-392, *Oct. 1924*
North Atlantic Fishes. 613-628, *Dec. 1923*
Fresh-Water Fishes of the United States. 133-148, *Aug. 1923*
Fish. 37-52, *Jan. 1922*
Fish. 61-68, *Jan. 1921*

MURCHISON MOUNTAINS, New Zealand:
Finding an "Extinct" New Zealand Bird. By R. V. Francis Smith. 393-401, *Mar. 1952*

MURCIA, Spain:
Spain's Silkworm Gut. By Luis Marden. 100-108, *July 1951*

MURDOCH, HELEN MESSINGER: *Photographer*
India and Ceylon. 281-288, *Mar. 1921*

MURDOCH, JOHN: *Author*
On Eskimo Geographic Names Ending in Miut. 190, *Apr. 1898*

MURDOCH, L. H.: *Author*
Why Great Salt Lake Has Fallen. 75-77, *Feb. 1903*

Lord of the trees, a male muriqui, or woolly spider monkey, feeds on a monstera plant in Brazil. ANDREW L. YOUNG

MURIA GONDS:
New Life for India's Villagers. By Anthony and Georgette Dickey Chapelle. 572-588, *Apr. 1956*

MURIE, ADOLPH: *Author*
Wildlife of Mount McKinley National Park. Paintings by Walter A. Weber. 249-270, *Aug. 1953*

MURIQUIS:
Monkey in Peril: Rescuing Brazil's Muriqui. By Russell A. Mittermeier. Photos by Andrew L. Young. 387-395, *Mar. 1987*

The **MURMAN COAST:** Arctic Gateway for American and Allied Expeditionary Forces in Northern European Russia. 331-348, *Apr. 1919*

MUROC DRY LAKE, California:
Flying in the "Blowtorch" Era. By Frederick G. Vosburgh. 281-322, *Sept. 1950*

MURPHY, GRACE E. BARSTOW: *Photographer*
Peru Profits from Sea Fowl. By Robert Cushman Murphy. Photos by author and Grace E. Barstow Murphy. 395-413, *Mar. 1959*

MURPHY, JOHN F., Jr.: *Author*
Ambassadors of Good Will: The Peace Corps. By Sargent Shriver and Peace Corps Volunteers. 297-345. Included: Gabon. 325-329, *Sept. 1964*

MURPHY, ROBERT CUSHMAN: *Author*
Birds of the High Seas: Albatrosses and Petrels; Gannets, Man-o'-war-birds, and Tropic-birds. Paintings by Allan Brooks. 226-251, *Aug. 1938*

The Timeless Arans: The Workaday World Lies Beyond the Horizon of Three Rocky Islets Off the Irish Coast. 747-775, *June 1931*
The Romance of Science in Polynesia: An Account of Five Years of Cruising Among the South Sea Islands. Paintings by Hashime Murayama. 355-426, *Oct. 1925*
The Most Valuable Bird in the World (Guanay). 279-302, *Sept. 1924*
South Georgia, an Outpost of the Antarctic. 409-444, *Apr. 1922*

Author-Photographer
Peru Profits from Sea Fowl. Photos by author and Grace E. Barstow Murphy. 395-413, *Mar. 1959*

MURRAY, EDWARD STEVENSON: *Author*
On the Turks' Russian Frontier: Everyday Life in the Fastnesses between the Black Sea and Ararat, Borderland of Oil and Minerals that Hitler Covets. 367-392, *Sept. 1941*
With the Nomads of Central Asia: A Summer's Sojourn in the Tekes Valley, Plateau Paradise of Mongol and Turkic Tribes. Paintings and drawings by Alexandre Iacovleff. 1-57, *Jan. 1936*

MURRAY, SIR JOHN:
Sir John Murray (Biography). 238-240, *June 1901*

MURRAY, LOUISE: *Author*
In Valais (Switzerland). 249-256, *Mar. 1910*

MURRAY (River), Australia:
The Land Where the Murray Flows. By Louise E. Levathes. Photos by David Robert Austen. 252-278, *Aug. 1985*

MURRELETS (Birds):
Birds of the Northern Seas. By Alexander Wetmore. Paintings by Allan Brooks. 95-122, *Jan. 1936*

MURRES:
Sea Bird Cities Off Audubon's Labrador. By Arthur A. Allen. NGS research grant. 755-774, *June 1948*
Birds of the Northern Seas. By Alexander Wetmore. Paintings by Allan Brooks. 95-122, *Jan. 1936*

MURUNGS:
Bangladesh: Hope Nourishes a New Nation. By William S. Ellis. Photos by Dick Durrance II. 295-333, *Sept. 1972*

MURZUCH, Libya:
The Mysteries of the Desert. By Hanns Vischer. 1056-1059, *Nov. 1911*

MÜSA, Gebel (Mountain), Egypt. See Sinai, Mount

MUSAN, North Korea:
Exploring Unknown Corners of the "Hermit Kingdom." By Roy Chapman Andrews. 25-48, *July 1919*

MUSANDAM PENINSULA, Oman:
Oman: Guardian of the Gulf. By Thomas J. Abercrombie. Photos by the author and Lynn Abercrombie. 344-377, *Sept. 1981*

Backstage at Nashville's Grand Ole Opry, in Tennessee, country singer Hank Snow awaits his cue. JODI COBB, NGS

In a last, vain attempt to protect their calves from a hungry pack of wolves, musk-oxen try to close ranks.   JIM BRANDENBURG

Johnson. Photos by Joseph J. Scherschel. 798-845, *Dec. 1969*
Turkey Paves the Path of Progress. By Maynard Owen Williams. 141-186, *Aug. 1951*
The Turkish Republic Comes of Age. By Maynard Owen Williams. 581-616, *May 1945*

MUTCH, THOMAS:
Nomination Page. *Jan. 1977*

MY Backyard, the Adirondacks. By Anne LaBastille. Photos by David Alan Harvey. 616-639, *May 1975*

MY Chesapeake–Queen of Bays. By Allan C. Fisher, Jr. Photos by Lowell Georgia. 428-467, *Oct. 1980*

MY Domestic Life in French Guinea: An American Woman Accompanies Her Husband, a Swiss Geologist, on His Explorations in a Little-Known Region. By Eleanor de Chételat. 695-730, *June 1935*

MY Flight Across Antarctica. By Lincoln Ellsworth. 1-35, *July 1936*

MY Flight from Hawaii. By Amelia Earhart. 593-609, *May 1935*

MY Four Antarctic Expeditions: Explorations of 1933-39 Have Stricken Vast Areas from the Realm of the Unknown. By Lincoln Ellsworth. 129-138, *July 1939*

MY Friends the Wild Chimpanzees. By ■■ Jane Goodall. Photos by Baron Hugo van Lawick. 204 pages. *1967*

MY Life Among Wild Chimpanzees. By Jane Goodall. Photos by Baron Hugo van Lawick and author. NGS research grant. 272-308, *Aug. 1963*

MY Life in Forbidden Lhasa. By Heinrich Harrer. 1-48, *July 1955*

MY Life in the Valley of the Moon. By H. H. Arnold. Photos by Willard R. Culver. 689-716, *Dec. 1948*

MY Life With Africa's Little People. By Anne Eisner Putnam. 278-302, *Feb. 1960*

MY Neighbors Hold to Mountain Ways. By Malcolm Ross. Photos by Flip Schulke. 856-880, *June 1958*

MYCENAEAN CIVILIZATION:
Minoans and Mycenaeans: Greece's Brilliant Bronze Age. By Joseph Judge. Photos by Gordon W. Gahan. Paintings by Lloyd K. Townsend. 142-185, *Feb. 1978*

MYCETOZOA:
Slime Mold: The Fungus That Walks. By Douglas Lee. Photos by Paul A. Zahl. 131-136, *July 1981*
Marvels of Mycetozoa: Exploration of a Long Island Swamp Reveals Some of the Secrets of the Slime Molds, Dwelling on the Borderland Between the Plant and Animal Kingdoms. By William Crowder. Paintings by author. Contents: Arcyria denudata, Arcyria ferruginea, Badhamia papaveracea, Comatricha pulchella, Diachea leucopoda, Dictydium

In the Holy Land of 1927, dignity graces the Muslim sheikh of Bethany, home of Lazarus. MAYNARD OWEN WILLIAMS, NGS

cancellatum, Diderma testaceum, Fuligo septica, Globuliferum, Lamproderma arcyrionema, Lamproderma violaceum, Leocarpus fragilis, Physarum lateritium, Physarum viride, Stemonitis splendens, Trichia persimilis. 421-443, *Apr. 1926*

MYCOLOGY:
Bizarre World of the Fungi. By Paul A. Zahl. 502-527, *Oct. 1965*
Common Mushrooms of the United States. By Louis C. C. Krieger. Paintings by author. 387-439, *May 1920*
See also Mycetozoa

MYKONOS (Island), Greece. *See* Mikonos

MYOJIN ISLAND (Volcano), Pacific Ocean:
The Explosive Birth of Myojin Island. By Robert S. Dietz. 117-128, *Jan. 1954*

MYSORE (State), India:
Wild Elephant Roundup in India. By Harry Miller. Photos by author and James P. Blair. 372-385, *Mar. 1969*
Mysore Celebrates the Death of a Demon. By Luc Bouchage. Photos by Ylla. 706-711, *May 1958*
India Mosaic. By Peter Muir and Frances Muir. 443-470, *Apr. 1946*

MYSTERIES of Bird Migration. By Allan C. Fisher, Jr. Photos by Jonathan Blair. 154-193, *Aug. 1979*

MYSTERIES of the Ancient World. ■■ Contents: ancient Indian cities, Easter Island, Egyptian pyramids, Etruscans, European megaliths, Ice Age cave art, Jericho, Minoans, and Mycenaeans. 223 pages. *1979*

MYSTERIES of the Bog. By Louise E. Levathes. Photos by Fred Bavendam.

Included: Peat holds clues to early American life. 397-420, *Mar. 1987*

The **MYSTERIES** of the Desert. By Hanns Vischer. 1056-1059, *Nov. 1911*

The **MYSTERIOUS** Life of the Common Eel. By Hugh M. Smith. 1140-1146, *Oct. 1913*

The MYSTERIOUS Maya. By George ■■ E. and Gene S. Stuart. Photos by David Alan Harvey and Otis Imboden. 199 pages. *1977*

MYSTERIOUS Micronesia: Yap, Map, and Other Islands Under Japanese Mandate are Museums of Primitive Man. By Willard Price. 481-510, *Apr. 1936*

The **MYSTERIOUS** Prehistoric Monuments of Brittany. By Charles Buxton Going. 53-69, *July 1923*

MYSTERIOUS Temples of the Jungle: The Prehistoric Ruins of Guatemala. By W. F. Sands. 325-338, *Mar. 1913*

The **MYSTERIOUS** Tomb of a Giant Meteorite. By William D. Boutwell. 721-730, *June 1928*

The MYSTERIOUS Undersea World. By ■■ Jan Leslie Cooke. Juvenile. 104 pages. *1980*

MYSTERY Mammals of the Twilight. By Donald R. Griffin. 117-134, *July 1946*

The **MYSTERY** of Auroras: National Geographic Society and Cornell University Study Spectacular Displays in the Heavens. 689-690, *May 1939*

The **MYSTERY** of Easter Island. By Mrs. Scoresby Routledge. 629-646, *Dec. 1921*

MYSTERY of the Ancient Nazca Lines. Photos by Loren McIntyre. NGS research grant. 716-728, *May 1975*

MYSTERY of the Medicine Wheels. By John A. Eddy. Photos by Thomas E. Hooper. 140-146, *Jan. 1977*

MYSTERY of the Monarch Butterfly. By Paul A. Zahl. 588-598, *Apr. 1963*

The **MYSTERY** of the Shroud. By Kenneth F. Weaver. 730-753, *June 1980*

MYSTERY Shrouds the Biggest Planet. By Kenneth F. Weaver. 285-294, *Feb. 1975*

MYSTIC Nedjef, the Shia Mecca. By Frederick Simpich. 589-598, *Dec. 1914*

MYSTIC SEAPORT, Connecticut:
The Age of Sail Lives On at Mystic. By Alan Villiers. Photos by Weston Kemp. 220-239, *Aug. 1968*

MYTILENE (Island), Greece. *See* Lesbos

MYXOMYCETES. *See* Slime Mold

MZABIS. *See* Mozabites

MZIMA SPRINGS, Tsavo National Park, Kenya:
Mzima, Kenya's Spring of Life. By Joan and Alan Root. 350-373, *Sept. 1971*

M
N

NR-1 (Submarine):
NR-1, the Navy's Inner-Space Shuttle. By Robert D. Ballard. Photos by Emory Kristof. 450-459, *Apr. 1985*

NABLUS (Shechem), Palestine:
The Last Israelitish Blood Sacrifice: How the Vanishing Samaritans Celebrate the Passover on Sacred Mount Gerizim. By John D. Whiting. 1-46, *Jan. 1920*

NABOURS, ROBERT K.: *Author*
The Land of Lambskins: An Expedition to Bokhara, Russian Central Asia, to Study the Karakul Sheep Industry. 77-88, *July 1919*

NABUCO, JOAQUIM:
What the Latin American Republics Think of the Pan-American Conferences. Address by the Brazilian Ambassador. 474-479, *Aug. 1906*

NACHTWEY, JAMES:
On Assignment in Guatemala. *June 1988*
Photographer
Guatemala: A Fragile Democracy. By Griffin Smith, Jr. 768-803, *June 1988*
Nicaragua: Nation in Conflict. By Mike Edwards. 776-811, *Dec. 1985*

NAGA HILLS, India-Burma:
Roaming India's Naga Hills. By S. Dillon Ripley. 247-264, *Feb. 1955*

NAGA TRIBESPEOPLE:
Women of All Nations. 49-61, *Jan. 1911*

NAGANA:
Tsetse–Fly of the Deadly Sleep. By Georg Gerster. Included: Nagana, a tsetse-borne livestock disease. 814-833, *Dec. 1986*

NAGEOMA (Canoe):
Across the Midi in a Canoe: Two Americans Paddle Along the Canals of Southern France from the Atlantic to the Mediterranean. By Melville Chater. Note: *Nageoma*, used by the author in his travels through Europe, was named after the *National Geographic Magazine*. 127-167, *Aug. 1927*
Through the Back Doors of Belgium: Artist and Author Paddle for Three Weeks Along 200 Miles of Low-Countries Canals in a Canadian Canoe. By Melville Chater. 499-540, *May 1925*
Through the Back Doors of France: A Seven Weeks' Voyage in a Canadian Canoe from St. Malo, Through Brittany and the Chateau Country, to Paris. By Melville Chater. 1-51, *July 1923*

NAGEOMA, giraffe named after the *National Geographic Magazine*. 714, *June 1938*

NAHA, Okinawa (Island), Ryukyu Islands:
Okinawa, the Island Without a Country. By Jules B. Billard. Photos by Winfield Parks and David Moore. 422-448, *Sept. 1969*

Peacetime Rambles in the Ryukyus. By William Leonard Schwartz. 543-561, *May 1945*

NAHANNI NATIONAL PARK, Northwest Territories, Canada:
Nahanni: Canada's Wilderness Park. By Douglas H. Chadwick. Photos by Matt Bradley. 396-420, *Sept. 1981*

NAIROBI, Kenya:
Kenya Says *Harambee!* By Allan C. Fisher, Jr. Photos by Bruce Dale. 151-205, *Feb. 1969*

NAIROBI NATIONAL PARK, Kenya:
Africa's Gentle Giants (Giraffes). By Bristol Foster. Photos by Bob Campbell and Thomas Nebbia. 402-417, *Sept. 1977*

NAIVASHA (Lake), Kenya:
Where Roosevelt Will Hunt. By Sir Harry Johnston. 207-256, *Mar. 1909*

NAJ TUNICH (Cave), Guatemala:
Maya Art Treasures Discovered in Cave. By George E. Stuart. Photos by Wilbur E. Garrett. 220-235, *Aug. 1981*

NAJAF, An, Iraq:
Mystic Nedjef, the Shia Mecca. By Frederick Simpich. 589-598, *Dec. 1914*

NAKAMURA, KOJI: *Photographer*
The Lost Fleet of Kublai Khan. By Torao Mozai. Paintings by Issho Yada. 634-649, *Nov. 1982*

"NAKWASINA" Goes North: A Man, a Woman, and a Pup Cruise from Tacoma to Juneau in a 17-Foot Canoe. By Jack Calvin. 1-42, *July 1933*

Poised with a seven-foot bow, Yoshishiro Shishime practices the age-old art of archery in Kyoto, Japan. GEORGE F. MOBLEY, NGS

NALTCHAYAN, HARRY N.:
Photographer
The Proud Armenians. By Robert Paul Jordan. 846-873, *June 1978*

NAMBA TRIBESPEOPLE:
Taboos and Magic Rule Namba Lives. By Kal Muller. 57-83, *Jan. 1972*

NAMBICUARA INDIANS. *See* Wasúsu Indians

NAMGYAL, PALDEN THONDUP, Maharaja (Sikkim):
Wedding of Two Worlds. By Lee E. Battaglia. 708-727, *Nov. 1963*
Nomination Page. *Oct. 1963*

NAMGYAL, SIR TASHI:
Nomination Page. *Oct. 1963*

NAMIB DESERT, Angola-Namibia-South Africa:
The Living Sands of the Namib. By William J. Hamilton III. Photos by Carol and David Hughes. 364-377, *Sept. 1983*
▪ The Living Sands of Namib. 439, Oct. 1977; cover, Mar. 1978; 1, *Jan. 1979*

NAMIBIA:
The Living Sands of the Namib. By William J. Hamilton III. Photos by Carol and David Hughes. 364-377, *Sept. 1983*
Etosha: Namibia's Kingdom of Animals. By Douglas H. Chadwick. Photos by Des and Jen Bartlett. 344-385, *Mar. 1983*
Family Life of Lions. By Des and Jen Bartlett. 800-819, *Dec. 1982*
Namibia: Nearly a Nation? By Bryan Hodgson. Photos by Jim Brandenburg. 755-797, *June 1982*
▪ Etosha: Place of Dry Water. 703, Dec. 1980; cover, *Jan. 1981*
▪ The Living Sands of Namib. 439, Oct. 1977; cover, Mar. 1978; 1, *Jan. 1979*
See also former name, South-West Africa

NAMU (Killer Whale):
Making Friends With a Killer Whale. By Edward I. Griffin. 418-446, *Mar. 1966*

NANCY, France:
A City Learns to Smile Again. By Frederick G. Vosburgh. 361-384, *Mar. 1945*
In French Lorraine: That Part of France Where the First American Soldiers Have Fallen. By Harriet Chalmers Adams. 499-518, *Nov.-Dec. 1917*

NANCY HANKS CENTER, Washington, D. C.:
A Preservation Victory Saves Washington's Old Post Office. By Wolf Von Eckardt. Photos by Volkmar Wentzel. 407-416, *Sept. 1983*

NANJING (Nanking), Jiangsu Province, China:
Along the Yangtze, Main Street of China. By W. Robert Moore. 325-356, *Mar. 1948*
The Rise and Fall of Nanking. By Julius Eigner. 189-224, *Feb. 1938*

Steam billowing in Moscow's Red Square recalls the events of 1812 when Napoleon I, marching in to conquer the city, found it deserted and ablaze. GORDON W. GAHAN

The Navy's aerobatic Blue Angels soar—on film—across a five-story-high screen at the National Air and Space Museum in Washington, D.C. CONTINENTAL OIL COMPANY

NATIONAL BUREAU OF STANDARDS:

NATIONAL CATHEDRAL, Washington, D. C. *See* Washington Cathedral

NATIONAL CIVIL WAR CENTENNIAL COMMISSION: United States:

NATIONAL EDUCATIONAL ASSOCIATION:

NATIONAL ELK REFUGE, Wyoming:

NATIONAL FOREST ASSOCIATION OF GERMANY:

NATIONAL FORESTS: United States:

Under South Africa's policy of apartheid, this Zulu child in the Natal region lives in a segregated township. DICK DURRANCE II

NATIONAL FOUNDATION FOR THE INDIAN (FUNAI): Brazil. *See* Cinta Larga Indians; Kreen-Akarores; Txukahameis; Wasúsu Indians

NATIONAL 4-H COUNCIL:

NATIONAL GALLERY OF ART, Washington, D. C.:

Great Masters of a Brave Era in Art (Impressionist). By Hereward Lester Cooke, Jr. Included: The Chester Dale Collection. 661-697, *May 1961*

The Nation's Newest Old Masters. By John Walker. Paintings from Kress Collection. 619-657, *Nov. 1956*

Your National Gallery of Art After 10 Years. By John Walker. Paintings from Kress Collection. 73-103, *Jan. 1952*

The Vienna Treasures and Their Collectors. By John Walker. 737-776, *June 1950*

Masterpieces on Tour. By Harry A. McBride. 717-750, *Dec. 1948*

American Masters in the National Gallery. By John Walker. 295-324, *Sept. 1948*

Washington: Home of the Nation's Great. By Albert W. Atwood. 699-738, *June 1947*

Old Masters in a New National Gallery. By Ruth Q. McBride. Included: Reproductions of masterpieces. 1-50, *July 1940*

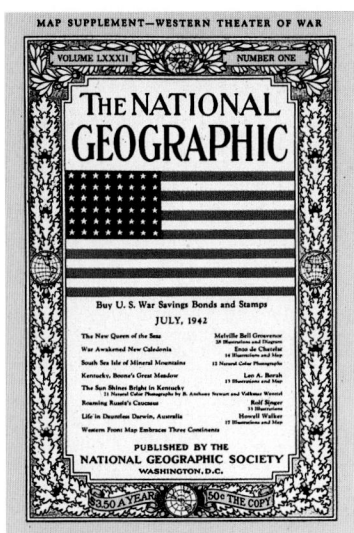

MAP SUPPLEMENT—WESTERN THEATER OF WAR

VOLUME LXXXII   NUMBER ONE

The NATIONAL GEOGRAPHIC

Buy U. S. War Savings Bonds and Stamps

JULY, 1942

PUBLISHED BY THE
NATIONAL GEOGRAPHIC SOCIETY
WASHINGTON, D.C.

They cover the world.... Awards to staff writers. Nomination Page. *July 1977*

Thomas J. Abercrombie, recipient of National Press Photographers Association awards. Editorial by Gilbert M. Grosvenor. 291, *Mar. 1977*

U. S. Camera Achievement Award medal (1951). 481, *Oct. 1966*

University of Missouri's Honor Award for Distinguished Service in Journalism (1954). 539, *Oct. 1963*

Photographers amass national awards. 898, 901, *Dec. 1962*

Photographers amass national awards. 878, 880-881, *Dec. 1961*

National Geographic Photographers Win Top Magazine Awards. 830-831, *June 1959*

Freedoms Foundation awards received by editor and two staff writers. 190, *Feb. 1954*

La Belle Award received by Franklin L. Fisher on behalf of the Society for outstanding contributions to the development of color photography in magazine illustration. 692, *Nov. 1953*

Braille Edition and Sound Recordings
Editorial. By Wilbur E. Garrett. 145, *Aug. 1986*

Centennial
Editorial. By Wilbur E. Garrett. 1-2, *Jan. 1988*

Cover Photographs: *Commentary in NGM*
Hologram of crystal globe. Geographica; On Assignment. *Dec. 1988*

Within the Yellow Border. Editorial by Wilbur E. Garrett. Included: Foldout displaying early covers and all cover illustrations since the first in July 1942. 270-286, *Sept. 1988*

Editorial. By Wilbur E. Garrett. Oregon Trail pioneers. 147, Feb. 1987; cover, *Aug. 1986*

Hologram of skull. 559, *Nov. 1985*

Hologram of eagle. 281, 372, *Mar. 1984*

Photographs appeared as a regular feature on the yellow-bordered cover during Melville Bell Grosvenor's tenure as Editor. 270, *Aug. 1982*

First color cover (American flag). *July 1942*

See also Covers, NGM, for brief descriptions

Editor
Gilbert Hovey Grosvenor (1899-1954); John Oliver La Gorce (1954-1957); Melville Bell Grosvenor (1957-1967); Frederick G. Vosburgh (1967-1970); Gilbert M. Grosvenor (1970-1980); Wilbur E. Garrett (1980-   )

NATIONAL GEOGRAPHIC ATLAS OF THE WORLD. *See* Atlases, NGS: World Atlas

NATIONAL GEOGRAPHIC ATLAS SERIES MAPS:
New Atlas Maps Announced by the Society: Expanded Map Program, Marking National Geographic's 70th Year. By James M. Darley. 66-68, *Jan. 1958*

NATIONAL GEOGRAPHIC EXPLORER (Cable Television Series):
Foreign-language broadcasts. President's Page. By Gilbert M. Grosvenor. *July 1988*

National Geographic Explorer–A New Series on Cable TV. President's Page. By Gilbert M. Grosvenor. *Apr. 1985*

NATIONAL GEOGRAPHIC MAGAZINE (NGM):
Spoofing the Geographic. By Roy Blount, Jr. 353-357, *Sept. 1988*

New missions for old magazines. President's Page. By Gilbert M. Grosvenor. *May 1987*

Atlases. *See* Atlases, NGS

Awards Received and Noted in NGM
Editorial. By Wilbur E. Garrett. 139, *Aug. 1987*

NGM award winners. On Assignment. *Aug. 1987*

NGM award winners. On Assignment. *Aug. 1985*

Editorial. By Wilbur E. Garrett. 553, *Nov. 1982*

Sigma Delta Chi award. 553, *Nov. 1982*

In the tradition of excellence (Awards for 1980 and 1981). 850, *Dec. 1981*

Photographers amass national awards. 850, *Dec. 1981*

Donated by the Imperial Russian Geographical Society of St. Petersburg, views of Lhasa, Tibet, were published in the GEOGRAPHIC's January 1905 issue (above).

NATIONAL GEOGRAPHIC's longest foldout was published in June 1911. Measuring eight feet in length, it showed a panorama of the Canadian Rockies.

CHARLES D. WALCOTT

Finisher Arthur Graf uses a natural gas flame to create a smooth electrotype plate for printing a NATIONAL GEOGRAPHIC cover in 1951. J. BAYLOR ROBERTS, NGS

Editor, Senior Associate
Joseph Judge (1985-)

Editor-at-Large
Charles McCarry (1988-)

Editorial Policy. 486, May 1909; 273-274, Mar. 1912; 253, Feb. 1913; 319, Mar. 1915; 123, 135, 145, 148, 149, Jan. 1936; 587, Nov. 1974; 1, Jan. 1978; 293, Mar. 1979; 427, Oct. 1980; 567, Nov. 1980; 279, Sept. 1981; 1, Jan. 1982; 553, Nov. 1982; 1, Jan. 1984; 561, Nov. 1984; 1, *Jan. 1986*

Editorials
Introduction as a regular feature. 587, *Nov. 1974*

Editors, Associate
John Oliver La Gorce (1914-1954); Melville Bell Grosvenor (1954-1957); Frederick G. Vosburgh (1957-1967); Gilbert M. Grosvenor (1967-1970); Franc Shor (1967-1974); John Scofield (1970-1978); Joseph Judge (1978-1985); Thomas R. Smith (1985-)

Geographica
Introduction of feature. *Oct. 1988*

History
Three Men Who Made the Magazine. By Charles McCarry. 287-316, *Sept. 1988*
"The Greatest Job in the World?" By Joseph Judge. Contents: Recollections of writers and photographers by the Senior Associate Editor. 317-321, *Sept. 1988*
Melville Bell Grosvenor, A Decade of Innovation, a Lifetime of Service. By Bart McDowell. 270-278, *Aug. 1982*
National Geographic Society Trustees Elect Key Executives. 576-590, *Oct. 1967*
To Gilbert Grosvenor: A Monthly Monument 25 Miles High. By Frederick G. Vosburgh and the staff of the National Geographic Society. 445-487, *Oct. 1966*
First Lady of the National Geographic (Elsie May Bell Grosvenor). By Gilbert Hovey Grosvenor. 101-121, *July 1965*

The Romance of the Geographic: National Geographic Magazine Observes Its Diamond Anniversary. By Gilbert Hovey Grosvenor. 516-585, *Oct. 1963*
75 Years Exploring Earth, Sea, and Sky: National Geographic Society Observes Its Diamond Anniversary. By Melvin M. Payne. 1-43, *Jan. 1963*
■■ *The National Geographic Society and Its Magazine.* By Gilbert Grosvenor. Reprint of the Foreword to the Cumulative Index to the National Geographic Magazine, 1899 to 1946. 116 pages. 1936; rev. ed. *1948*
The National Geographic Society and Its Magazine. By Gilbert Grosvenor. 123-164, *Jan. 1936*
History of the Magazine (Speech by Alexander Graham Bell). 273-274, *Mar. 1912*
Early years of the Magazine. 221-222, *June 1899*

Indexes: *Statements about*
Key to '83. 840, Dec. 1983; Key to '84. 848, Dec. 1984; Key to '85. 842, Dec. 1985; Key to '86. 834, Dec. 1986; Key to '87. 832, Dec. 1987; Key to '88. 946, *Dec. 1988*
Editorial, on cumulative and six-month indexes. By Wilbur E. Garrett. 423, *Apr. 1984*

Issues, Early
First issue, October 1888
Reprinting Brings Earliest Geographics to Life. By Melvin M. Payne. 688-689, *Nov. 1964*

Maps. *See* Map Supplements

Members Forum
Introduction of feature. 279, *Sept. 1981*

On Assignment
Introduction of feature. 709, *Dec. 1981*

Paintings. *See* Painting Supplements

Photographers: *Comments about*
Number of color photographs made by NGM photographers (7,500,000). 149, *July 1975*
Editorials. 295, Mar. 1975; 439, Apr. 1975; 1, July 1981; 553, *Nov. 1982*
See also NGM: Awards Received; Nomination Page; On Assignment; *and* names of individual photographers

Photographic Exhibit
Editorial. By Wilbur E. Garrett. Contents: Odyssey: The Art of Photography at National Geographic, a touring centennial exhibit. 1, *July 1988*

Photographs: *Commentary on*
Odyssey: The Art of Photography at National Geographic. By Jane Livingston. 322-351, *Sept. 1988*

Photographs appeared as a regular feature on the yellow-bordered cover during Melville Bell Grosvenor's tenure as Editor. 270, *Aug. 1982*

A never-before-published Autochrome of Mark Twain made in 1908. 299, 301, *Sept. 1975*

First extensive use of photographs: Gilbert H. Grosvenor's policy. 421, Mar. 1957; 574, *Oct. 1963*

Award-winning photos. 830-831, June 1959; 898, 901, *Dec. 1962*

First use of High Speed Ektachrome film. 864, *Dec. 1959*

Two NGM photographs were used in designing the Gadsden Purchase postage stamp. 135, *July 1954*

First aerial photographs of the North Pole. 478-479, *Oct. 1953*

First color cover of the magazine (the American flag). *July 1942*

First natural-color photograph taken in the stratosphere *(Explorer II)*. By Albert W. Stevens. 340, *Mar. 1937*

First natural-color photograph of an eclipse, showing the corona. By Irvine C. Gardiner. 178, *Feb. 1937*

First photograph ever made showing the division between the troposphere and stratosphere and also the actual curvature of the earth. By Albert W. Stevens (from *Explorer II*, November 11, 1935). Supplement. *May 1936*

List of pioneering achievements in photography. 128, *Jan. 1936*

First photograph ever made showing laterally the curvature of the earth. By Albert W. Stevens. 634, *May 1931*

First aerial color photographs published. 345-352, *Sept. 1930*

First successful natural-color photographs of life beneath the sea. 57-60, *Jan. 1927*

First series of natural-color photographs of the Arctic. 301-316, *Mar. 1926*

Autochromes: First natural-color series, "The Land of the Best." 379-405, *Apr. 1916*

First published Autochrome. 49, *July 1914*

Doe and twin fawns. Photo by George Shiras, 3d. Supplement. *July 1913*

First color series, hand-colored, "Scenes in Korea and China." 903-926, *Nov. 1910*

First photographic series: Eleven pages of pictures of the Forbidden City, Lhasa, Tibet. 28-38, *Jan. 1905*

First published photograph. *July 1890*

First appearance of hand-tinted illustrations. 315-335, *Oct. 1889*

See also NGM: Awards Received; *and* Photography

President's Page
Introduction of feature. *Jan. 1984*

Printing and Printers
Krueger Ringier (formerly W. F. Hall), Corinth, Mississippi, printers of the Magazine (1977-) 224, 226, *Aug. 1976*; 583, *Nov. 1977*; On Assignment, *Mar. 1988*

New presses printed an all-color magazine during Melville Bell Grosvenor's tenure. 270, *Aug. 1982*

R. R. Donnelley & Sons, Chicago, printers of the Magazine (1960-1977). 874-886, Dec. 1960; 878, 879, Dec.

1888 · CENTENNIAL · 1988
VOL. 173, NO. 1   JANUARY 1988

NATIONAL GEOGRAPHIC

One Hundred Years of increasing and diffusing geographic knowledge

SEE "AFRICAN ODYSSEY" WEDNESDAY, JANUARY 20, ON PBS TV

Historic photographs of exploration on the January 1988 cover kicked off the Society's centennial celebration.

1961; 582, Apr. 1962; 897, Dec. 1962; 772, June 1967; 529, *Apr. 1968*

Linofilm typesetting technique and high-speed web presses introduced. 836, Dec. 1959; 584, 588, *Oct. 1967*

Judd & Detweiler, Washington, D. C., printers of the Magazine (1891-1960). 465, Apr. 1914; 559, Oct. 1951; 561, *Oct. 1963*

McClure, Phillips & Company, New York. 559, 561, *Oct. 1963*

Beck Engraving Company, Philadelphia. 31, *July 1952*

Printing the Magazine. 474, 484, *Apr. 1942*

Recordings
Recorded edition of NGM loaned by Library of Congress to the visually impaired. 681, *Nov. 1975*
See also Records and Sound Sheets

Reprints: *Statements about*
Special Report on Energy. 849, *Dec. 1981*

■■ *The National Geographic Society and Its Magazine.* By Gilbert H. Grosvenor. 582A, Oct. 1957; 880, *Dec. 1964*

Reprinting Brings Earliest Geographics to Life. By Melvin M. Payne. 688-689, *Nov. 1964*

The Last Full Measure (Tribute to President Kennedy). By Melville Bell Grosvenor. 355, *Mar. 1964*

■■ *The National Geographic Society and Its Magazine.* By Gilbert Grosvenor. Reprint of the Foreword to the Cumulative Index to the National Geographic Magazine, 1899 to 1946. 116 pages. 1936; rev. ed. *1948*

Supplements. *See* Map Supplements; Painting Supplements; Photo Supplements; Records and Sound Sheets

Writers: *Comments about*
Editorials. By Gilbert M. Grosvenor. 295, Mar. 1975; 439, Apr. 1975; By Wilbur E. Garrett. 1, July 1981; 709, Dec. 1981; 553, *Nov. 1982*

NATIONAL Geographic Photographer's ■■ *Field Guide.* By Albert Moldvay. 120 pages. *1981*

NATIONAL Geographic Picture Atlas of ■■ *Our Fifty States.* Included: Pertinent information about the geography, climate, and population of each state. Juvenile. 304 pages. *1978*

NATIONAL Geographic Picture Atlas of ■■ *Our Universe.* By Roy A. Gallant. Juvenile. 284 pages. 1980; rev. ed. *1986*

NATIONAL Geographic Picture Atlas of ■■ *Our World.* Juvenile. 312 pages. *1979*

NATIONAL GEOGRAPHIC RESEARCH:
New journal announced. President's Page. By Gilbert M. Grosvenor. Aug. 1984; Nov. 1984; *May 1985*

NATIONAL GEOGRAPHIC SOCIETY (NGS):
Atlases. *See* Atlases, NGS

Awards Presented and Noted in NGM
The National Geographic Society Centennial Award. President's Page. By Gilbert M. Grosvenor. Recipients: Robert D. Ballard, George F. Bass, Jacques-Yves Cousteau, Frank C. Craighead, John J. Craighead, Harold E. Edgerton, Kenan T. Erim, John H. Glenn, Jr., Jane Goodall, Sir Edmund P. Hillary, Mary Leakey, Richard Leakey, Thayer Soule, and Bradford and Barbara Washburn. *Dec. 1988*

General Thomas D. White Space Trophy (USAF award) for 1973 presented to astronaut Henry W. Hartsfield, Jr., capsule communicator for Skylab I, at NGS headquarters. 452, *Oct. 1974*

Jane M. Smith Award recipients: Sir Bruce Ingram. 474, Apr. 1961; Lyndon B. Johnson. 906, Dec. 1962; 113, Jan. 1966; 468, *Oct. 1966*

Tenzing Norkey presented with cash award and replica of the Hubbard Medal given to the British Mount Everest Expedition. 846, *June 1955*
See also Grosvenor Medal; Hubbard Medal; La Gorce Medal; Special Gold Medal

Awards Received and Noted in NGM
Citation of Honor: Air Force Association's bronze plaque presented to the Society for providing cartographic aid to airmen during World War II. 846, *Dec. 1949*
See also NGM: Awards Received; NGS: Book Service; NGS: Television and Educational Films

Bequests
Pickering Bequest. President's Page. By Gilbert M. Grosvenor. *Oct. 1985*

Fund bequeathed by Mary C. Burr. 626, *May 1934*

Bequests by members of the National Geographic Society. 474, *Apr. 1926*

A. W. Cutler, photographic artist, leaves his entire collection of negatives to the Society. 34, *July 1922*

James C. Horgan bequest. 338, *Apr. 1920*

At the Cosmos Club on January 13, 1888, 33 uncommon men founded the National Geographic Society. PAINTING BY STANLEY MELTZOFF

M
N

Jane M. Smith bequest for life member-
ships. 104, *Jan. 1912;* 342-343,
Apr. 1920

Board of Managers
Resolution authorizing purchase of Big
Trees. 5, *Jan. 1917*
Resolution withdrawing subscription to
South Polar Expedition of Peary Arc-
tic Club. 365, *Apr. 1910*
Claims of Peary and Cook referred to
Committee on Research. 921-922,
Nov. 1909
Research fund established. 486,
May 1909
Resolution subscribing to Peary Expedi-
tion of 1907-1908. 281, *Apr. 1907*
Resolution concerning Wellman Polar
Expedition. 205, *Apr. 1906*
Standing rules of the Board of Manag-
ers. 308-310, *Apr. 1891*
See also Board of Trustees

Board of Trustees
1988: The Trustees Who Have Carried
On the Tradition. By Melvin M.
Payne. 38-43, *Jan. 1988*
Portraits. 65A-65B, July 1954; 834-835,
Dec. 1959; 113, Jan. 1960; 883, Dec.
1960; 553, Oct. 1965; 484-485, Oct.
1966; 588-589, Oct. 1967; 226-227,
Aug. 1976; 41-42, 1913 portrait 43,
Jan. 1988
Chairman of the Board. Gilbert Hovey
Grosvenor (1954-1966); Thomas W.
McKnew (1966-1967); Melville Bell
Grosvenor (1967-1976); Melvin M.
Payne (1976-1987); Gilbert M.
Grosvenor (1987-   )

Book Service
Established by Melville Bell Grosvenor
in 1954. 897, Dec. 1962; 585-586,
Oct. 1967; 275, *Aug. 1982*
Awards won. 848, 850, *Dec. 1981*
Book Service Division. 851-852,
Dec. 1981
See also Books, NGS, for titles

Cartographic Division
New Perspective on the World. By John
B. Garver, Jr. 911-913, *Dec. 1988*
President's Page. By Gilbert M.
Grosvenor. *May 1984*
First color photomosaic of the United
States produced by combining Land-
sat imagery and the General Electric
Company's color-mosaic expertise
with the Society's map program. 140-
147, *July 1976*
Mapping the moon. 240-245, *Feb. 1969*
Established in 1915. 576, Oct. 1963;
463, Oct. 1966; 585, *Oct. 1967*
Chamberlin Trimetric Projection. 841,
June 1947; 826, June 1949; 399, Mar.
1950; 417, Mar. 1952; 591, *Apr. 1964*
First known use of Two Point Equidis-
tant Projection in mapping Asia. 418,
Mar. 1951; 751, *Dec. 1959*
Awarded U. S. Air Force Association's
citation of honor for cartographic
aid during World War II. 846,
Dec. 1949
First use of Transverse Mercator Pro-
jection for mapping a long airplane
flight (1921). 524, *Oct. 1947*
See also Atlases, NGS; Globes, NGS;
Map Supplements; Satellite Finder

Centennial
The National Geographic Society Cen-
tennial Award. President's Page. By
Gilbert M. Grosvenor. *Dec. 1988*
President's Page. By Gilbert M.
Grosvenor. *Sept. 1988*
Editorial. By Wilbur E. Garrett. 1-2,
Jan. 1988
President's Page. By Gilbert M.
Grosvenor. *Sept. 1987*
Editorial. By Wilbur E. Garrett. 1,
Jan. 1987
Editorial. By Wilbur E. Garrett. 1,
Jan. 1986

**Committee for Research and
Exploration**
Sponsorship of symposium, "Earth '88:
Changing Geographic Perspectives."
President's Page. By Gilbert M.
Grosvenor. Jan. 1988; 766-771,
Dec. 1988
President's Page. By Gilbert M.
Grosvenor. *Dec. 1986*
Editorial. By Gilbert M. Grosvenor.
729, *June 1978*
Editorial. By Gilbert M. Grosvenor.
159, *Aug. 1976*
Chairman. Frederick V. Coville (1920-
1936); Lyman J. Briggs (1937-1959);
Leonard C. Carmichael (1960-1973);
Alexander Wetmore (1974-1975);
Melvin M. Payne (1975-   )
Chairman Emeritus. Alexander Wet-
more (1975-1978)
Vice Chairmen. Alexander Wetmore
(1937-1973); Melvin M. Payne (1964-
1975); T. Dale Stewart (1979-   );
Barry C. Bishop (1984-   )

Dues
Use of funds. 566, Oct. 1963; 679, May 1964; 880, Dec. 1964; 102, 105, July 1965; 587, *Oct. 1967*

Education Foundation
President's Page. By Gilbert M. Grosvenor. *Sept. 1988*
President Grosvenor Announces the National Geographic Society Education Foundation. By Lloyd H. Elliott. 329A-329D, *Mar. 1988*

Educational Products
President's Page. By Gilbert M. Grosvenor. Sept. 1984; Jan. 1987; *Sept. 1988*
Schoolroom aids provided by the National Geographic Society. 468, Apr. 1914; 343, Apr. 1920; 161-162, Jan. 1936; 366, Sept. 1941; 824, *Dec. 1941*
Sight-seeing in School: Taking Twenty Million Children on a Picture Tour of the World. By Jessie L. Burrall. 489-503, *June 1919*
Monographs on the physical features of the United States, to be prepared for use in the public schools. 225-227, *Dec. 29, 1894*
See also Atlases; Books; Films and Filmstrips; Globes; Map Supplements; NGM: Indexes; Records and Sound Sheets; Television Films; WORLD

Employees
Staff Awards for Distinguished Service. President's Page. By Gilbert M. Grosvenor. *June 1988*
President's Page. By Gilbert M. Grosvenor. *Aug. 1987*
Number of. 253, 261, Aug. 1949; 443, Mar. 1960; 585, Oct. 1963; 678, 679, May 1964; 102, 108, 112-113, 118, July 1965; 459, Oct. 1966; 208, *Feb. 1972*

Essay Contests
Prizes for Essays on Norse Discoveries in America. 31-32, Jan. 1899; 246, *June 1900*
Important Announcement Concerning Essays (Subject: River Systems of the United States). 227-228, *Dec. 29, 1894*
Geographic Prizes (Certificates and medals awarded annually to public high school students writing the best essay on geography). 206-208, *Feb. 8, 1893*

Excursions and Field Meetings
Luray Caverns, Virginia, May 26, 1906. 358-362, *June 1906*
Luray Caverns, Virginia, May 19, 1906. 302, May 1906; 358-362, *June 1906*
Annapolis, Maryland, May 9, 1903. 217, *May 1903*
Gettysburg, Pennsylvania, May 17, 1902. 150, *Apr. 1902*
Brandywine, Delaware, May 18, 1901. 208, *May 1901*
Eclipse expedition to Norfolk, Virginia, May 27-28, 1900. 320, *Aug. 1900*
Eclipse: The Scientific Work of the National Geographic Society's Eclipse Expedition to Norfolk, Virginia, May 27-28, 1900. By Simon Newcomb. 321-324, *Aug. 1900*
Harpers Ferry, West Virginia, May 14, 1898. 414, *Sept. 1898*

The National Geographic Society flag represents the blue sky, brown earth, and green ocean. ROBERT F. OAKES, NGS

Naval Observatory, Washington, D. C., November 13, 1897. 31, *Jan. 1898*
High Island, Potomac River, Maryland, November 6, 1897. 366, *Dec. 1897*
Cabin John Bridge, Maryland, October 2, 1897. 365-366, *Dec. 1897*
Manassas Gap, Virginia, May 22, 1897. 192, *June 1897*
Charlottesville, Virginia: Eighth Annual Field Meeting of the National Geographic Society: Monticello and University of Virginia, visited, May 16, 1896. 216, June 1896; 259-260, *Aug. 1896*
Virginia Beach and the Dismal Swamp, April 20, 1894. xvi, *Oct. 31, 1895*
Fredericksburg, Virginia: Announcement of the Seventh Annual Excursion and Field Meeting, Saturday, May 4, 1895. foldout, *Apr. 20, 1895*
Potomac River cruise to Indian Head and Marshall Hall, May 1, 1893. xiii, *May 5, 1894*
Annapolis, Maryland: State House, Naval Academy, Chase Mansion, visited, May 27, 1892. xvii, *Feb. 20, 1893*

Expeditions and Research
First expedition: Mount St. Elias Expedition. 288, Apr. 1891; 39-40, Apr. 30, 1891; vii-ix, Feb. 20, 1893; 177, *Jan. 31, 1894*
See also by subject; *and* NGS: Research and Exploration

Explorers Hall
Great Globe. 673-675, 677, 679, May 1964; 880, Dec. 1964; 578-579, Oct. 1967; President's Page. By Gilbert M. Grosvenor. *Oct. 1987*
History. 791, 794, June 1934.; 338, Mar. 1942; 657, May 1942; 91, Jan. 1957; 578-579, *Oct. 1967*
President Johnson Dedicates the Society's New Headquarters. 669-679, *May 1964*

Films and Filmstrips
President's Page. By Gilbert M. Grosvenor. *Sept. 1988*

Number of filmstrips. 851, *Dec. 1981*
The World in Geographic Filmstrips. By Melvin M. Payne. 134-137, *Jan. 1968*
See also Television Films

First Meetings
Editorial. By Wilbur E. Garrett. 1, *Jan. 1988*
Regular meeting, February 17, 1888, Law Lecture Room, Columbian University: Inaugural address, by the President of the Society. 87, Oct. 1888; 2-7, *Jan. 1988*
For organizing a geographic society, Cosmos Club, January 13, 1888. 164, Apr. 1889; 131, *Jan. 1936*
For the purpose of incorporating, January 20, 1888; 165, Apr., 1889; 131, *Jan. 1936*
Of the Society, after incorporation, January 27, 1888: Election of officers and adoption of by-laws. 165, Apr. 1889; 131, 134, *Jan. 1936*

Flag
NGS flag designed by Elsie May Bell Grosvenor. 637, May 1949; 145, Aug. 1953; 459, 516, 557, 564, Oct. 1963; 100, 101, 116, 118, *July 1965*

Founders and Founding
Editorial. By Wilbur E. Garrett. 1-2, *Jan. 1988*
1888: Introductory Address by the President, Mr. Gardiner Greene Hubbard. 2-7, *Jan. 1988*
"Tell me if your civilization is interesting": Those Electrifying Eighteen Eighties When the National Geographic Society Was Born. By William H. Goetzmann. Illustrated by Fred Otnes. Included: "Founding of the National Geographic Society, January 13, 1888" (painting by Stanley Meltzoff). 8-37, *Jan. 1988*
President's Page. By Gilbert M. Grosvenor. *Jan. 1984*
Thirty-three eminent men met at the Cosmos Club, January 13, 1888. 387, Mar. 1955; 807, 830, June 1960; 1-3, Jan. 1963; 518, 573-574, Oct. 1963; 880, *Dec. 1964*

Geography Education Programs
President's Page. By Gilbert M. Grosvenor. Feb. 1986; July 1986; Sept. 1986; Nov. 1987; Sept. 1988; *Nov. 1988*

Globes. *See* Globe, Great; Globes, NGS

Grants
President's Page. By Gilbert M. Grosvenor. Dec. 1986; Jan. 1987; *June 1987*
Titanic search. President's Page. By Gilbert M. Grosvenor. *Dec. 1985*
Amount of annual funding. 889, 893, 899, Dec. 1962; 571, Oct. 1963; 163, Feb. 1964; 582, 586, Oct. 1967; 148, July 1971; 873, Dec. 1973; 226, Aug. 1976; 274, Aug. 1982; 824, *Dec. 1982*
See also NGS: Research and Exploration; NGS: Land Grants

Headquarters
Hubbard Memorial Hall:
Mural and paintings by N. C. Wyeth. 568, Nov. 1928; 93, Jan. 1929; 77, July 1938; 38, July 1948; 105, *July 1965*

First headquarters of the Society. 273, Mar. 1947; 65, July 1954; 564, *Oct. 1963*

Laying of cornerstone (April 26, 1902). 420, *Mar. 1957*

A gift to the Society by the family of the first President, Gardiner Greene Hubbard. 24, Jan. 1906; 1008, Nov. 1909; 251, Feb. 1913; 124, 152, *Jan. 1936*

The Home of the National Geographic Society. 342, *July 1905*

The New Home of the National Geographic Society. 176-181, *Apr. 1904*

The Hubbard Memorial Building. 174-176, *May 1902*

M Street Building:

Our Society Opens New Doors. By Gilbert M. Grosvenor. 554-560, *Oct. 1984*

President's Page. By Gilbert M. Grosvenor. *Oct. 1984*

Groundbreaking for third headquarters building. 848, *Dec. 1981*

16th Street Building:

History. 410, Sept. 1948; 91, Jan. 1957; 669, May 1964; 588, *Oct. 1967*

The National Geographic Society and Its New Building. 455-470, *Apr. 1914*

Board of Managers, in December, 1912, authorized the construction of a building, on the property adjacent to Hubbard Memorial Hall. 251, *Feb. 1913*

17th Street Building:

Dedication: President Johnson Dedicates the Society's New Headquarters. 669-679, *May 1964*

See also NGS: Explorers Hall

History

■ The Explorers: A Century of Discovery. 316, Sept. 1988; cover, *Oct. 1988*

President's Page. By Gilbert M. Grosvenor. *Sept. 1988*

Three Men Who Made the Magazine. By Charles McCarry. 287-316, *Sept. 1988*

1888: Introductory Address by the President, Mr. Gardiner Greene Hubbard. 2-7, *Jan. 1988*

"Tell me if your civilization is interesting": Those Electrifying Eighteen Eighties When the National Geographic Society Was Born. By William H. Goetzmann. Illustrated by Fred Otnes. Included: "Founding of the National Geographic Society, January 13, 1888" (painting by Stanley Meltzoff). 8-37, *Jan. 1988*

■■ *The National Geographic Society: 100 Years of Adventure and Discovery* (Bryan). President's Page. By Gilbert M. Grosvenor. *Sept. 1987*

President's Page. By Gilbert M. Grosvenor. *Jan. 1984*

Melville Bell Grosvenor: A Decade of Innovation, a Lifetime of Service. By Bart McDowell. 270-278, *Aug. 1982*

Election of officers. 427, *Oct. 1980*

90th Anniversary. 1, *Jan. 1978*

Trustees Elect New Society Officers. 224-227, *Aug. 1976*

Frederick G. Vosburgh Retires as Editor; Gilbert M. Grosvenor Succeeds Him. By Melvin M. Payne. 838-843, *Dec. 1970*

Robert V. Fleming, 1890-1967. By Melville Bell Grosvenor. 526-529, *Apr. 1968*

National Geographic Society Trustees Elect Key Executives. 576-590, *Oct. 1967*

To Gilbert Grosvenor: A Monthly Monument 25 Miles High. By Frederick G. Vosburgh and the staff of the National Geographic Society. 445-487, *Oct. 1966*

First Lady of the National Geographic (Elsie May Bell Grosvenor). By Gilbert Hovey Grosvenor. 101-121, *July 1965*

The National Geographic Society and Its Magazine: A History. By Gilbert H. Grosvenor. 582A, Oct. 1957; 880, *Dec. 1964*

On the Geographic's 75th Birthday–Our Best to You. Introduction to anniversary issue. By Melville Bell Grosvenor. 459, *Oct. 1963*

The Romance of the Geographic: National Geographic Magazine Observes Its Diamond Anniversary. By Gilbert Hovey Grosvenor. 516-585, *Oct. 1963*

75 Years Exploring Earth, Sea, and Sky: National Geographic Society Observes Its Diamond Anniversary. By Melvin M. Payne. 1-43, *Jan. 1963*

First transcontinental telephone conversation (January 25, 1915). 58, *Jan. 1958*

John Oliver La Gorce Is Elected Vice-Chairman of the Board, Melville Bell Grosvenor President and Editor of the National Geographic Society. 419-423, *Mar. 1957*

Gilbert Grosvenor Is Elected Chairman of the Board, John Oliver La Gorce Chosen President and Editor of the National Geographic Society. 65, 65A-65H, 66, *July 1954*

Gilbert Grosvenor's Golden Jubilee. By Albert W. Atwood. 253-261, *Aug. 1949*

■■ *The National Geographic Society and Its Magazine.* By Gilbert Grosvenor. Reprint of the Foreword to the Cumulative Index to the National Geographic Magazine, 1899 to 1946. 116 pages. 1936; rev. ed. *1948*

First voice voyages via telephone taken to the four corners of the United States by 800 NGS members (January 7, 1916). 278, *Mar. 1947*

■■ *Henry Gannett, President of the National Geographic Society 1910-1914.* By S.N.D. North. 34 pages. *1915*

The National Geographic Society. By John Hyde. Note: Early history of the Society. 220-223, *June 1899*

Illustrations Library

World's largest library of color transparencies. 136, Jan. 1968; 149, *July 1975*

Franklin L. Fisher's contribution. 692, *Nov. 1953*

Intern Program

President's Page. By Gilbert M. Grosvenor. *Feb. 1985*

Inventions

Shutterless camera designed by Emory Kristof. 492, *Apr. 1975*

OceanEye camera housing, designed by Bates Littlehales. 271, 277, *Aug. 1971*

Chamberlin Trimetric Projection. 841, June 1947; 826, June 1949; 399, Mar. 1950; 417, Mar. 1952; 591, *Apr. 1964*

Compass invented by Albert H. Bumstead. 442, Oct. 1947; 469, Oct. 1953; 754, Dec. 1953; 160, Aug. 1956; 38, July 1957; 22, *Jan. 1963*

Explorers of the North and South polar areas pose in front of Society headquarters in 1913; Robert E. Peary, with cane, stands next to Roald Amundsen, third from left.

"Geometer," used with NGS globes. 698-701, May 1961; 875, Dec. 1961; 897, *Dec. 1962*

Photo-composing machine, invented by Albert H. Bumstead and further developed by his son, Newman Bumstead. 419, *Mar. 1953*

Land Grants
Russell Cave, Alabama, presented to the people of the United States. 438, Mar. 1958; 614, May 1958; 36, Jan. 1963; 808, June 1964; 440, Sept. 1967; 851, *June 1973*

Sequoia National Park, California: The NGS and its members contributed to the purchase of 2,239 acres. 679, 680, May 1951; 792, 794, June 1954; 552, Oct. 1957; 597, 614, May 1958; 162, 176, Aug. 1959; 38, Jan. 1963; 545, Oct. 1963; 107, July 1965; 627, 630, May 1966; 1, 2, *July 1966*

Shenandoah National Park, Virginia, increased by gift of 1,000 acres in 1926. 18, July 1949; 40, *Jan. 1963*

Lecturers
John Wesley Powell, first lecturer. President's Page. By Gilbert M. Grosvenor. *Sept. 1988*

Theodore Roosevelt. 587, Oct. 1958; 542, 585, Oct. 1963; 732, Nov. 1963; 468, *Oct. 1966*

William Howard Taft. 585, Oct. 1963; 549, *Oct. 1965*

Louis S. B. Leakey. 194-195, *Feb. 1965*

John W. Foster. 549, *Oct. 1963*

Richard E. Byrd. 42, 44, *July 1957*

Mrs. Robert E. Peary. 531, *Oct. 1954*

British Mount Everest Expedition members. 64, *July 1954*

Donald B. MacMillan. 563, *Apr. 1953*

William H. Fechtler. 614-615, *Nov. 1952*

H. H. Arnold. 400, *Mar. 1950*

Lectures
First lecture, Feb. 17, 1888. 113, July 1965; President's Page. By Gilbert M. Grosvenor. *Sept. 1988*

Chairman of Lecture Committee. 843, *Dec. 1970*

Annual series of lectures has been given in Constitution Hall since 1933. 565, 573, *Nov. 1951*

Lecture courses, self-supporting. 320, *Mar. 1915*

The National Geographic Society: The Forthcoming Course of Lectures on the Effects of Geographic Environment in Developing the Civilization of the World. 1-6, *Feb. 1897*

The National Geographic Society: Synopsis of a Course of Lectures on the Effects of Geographic Environment in Developing the Civilization of the World. By Gardiner G. Hubbard. 29-32, *Jan. 1897*

Lecture courses, defined. 257-258, *Aug. 1896*

Public lectures. 289, *Apr. 1891*

Maps. *See* Map Supplements

Medals
Resolutions concerning medals. 486-487, *May 1909*

Writer of best essay on geography to receive Gold Medal. 207, *Feb. 8, 1893*

See also Grosvenor Medal; Hubbard

Medal; La Gorce Medal; Special Gold Medal

Media Diversification
President's Page. By Gilbert M. Grosvenor. *Sept. 1988*

Melvin M. Payne encouraged diversification. 227, *Aug. 1976*

Members and Membership
President's Page. By Gilbert M. Grosvenor. Dec. 1984; Aug. 1987; May 1988; *Oct. 1988*

Editorial. By Wilbur E. Garrett. 139, *Aug. 1987*

One million new members joined for 1983. 1, *Jan. 1983*

Number of members. 848, *Dec. 1981*

Number of charter members (205). 689, *Nov. 1964*

Our Society Welcomes Its 3,000,000th Member. By Melville Bell Grosvenor. 579-582, *Apr. 1962*

Membership Center Building
President's Page. By Gilbert M. Grosvenor. *Aug. 1987*

Construction. 590, Oct. 1967; 225, *Aug. 1976*

Membership in the International Union for Conservation of Nature and Natural Resources
President's Page. By Gilbert M. Grosvenor. *Feb. 1988*

Museum
Exhibits. 579, Nov. 1931; 259, Sept. 1933; 481, 485, Oct. 1935; 670, *June 1937*

See also NGS: Explorers Hall

Musical Composition
The "National Geographic Society March," composed and dedicated by Captain Thomas F. Darcy, leader of the United States Army Band, Washington. 122, *Jan. 1936*

News Service
President's Page. By Gilbert M. Grosvenor. June 1984; *Aug. 1985*

News features sent to 2,500 editors of press, radio, and television. 836, *Dec. 1959*

Officers
Election of officers. 427, *Oct. 1980*

Trustees Elect New Society Officers. 224-227, *Aug. 1976*

National Geographic Society Trustees Elect Key Executives. 576-590, *Oct. 1967*

John Oliver La Gorce Is Elected Vice-Chairman of the Board, Melville Bell Grosvenor President and Editor of the National Geographic Society. 419-423, *Mar. 1957*

Gilbert Grosvenor Is Elected Chairman of the Board, John Oliver La Gorce Chosen President and Editor of the National Geographic Society. 65, 65A-65H, 66, *July 1954*

Photographic Laboratories. 308, Mar. 1948; 436, Apr. 1953; 567, Apr. 1959; 864, Dec. 1959; 540, 575, 581, Oct. 1963; 193, Feb. 1967; 729, Nov. 1967; 644, 675, May 1970; 785, Dec. 1970; 244, Feb. 1973; 237, 247, *Aug. 1976*

Photographic Library. *See* NGS: Illustrations Library

Photography. *See* NGM: Awards

Received; NGM: Photographs, *and* Photography

President
Gardiner Greene Hubbard (1888-1897); Alexander Graham Bell (1898-1903); W J McGee (1904); Grove Karl Gilbert (1904); Willis L. Moore (1905-1909); Henry Gannett (1910-1914); O. H. Tittmann (1915-1919); John Elliott Pillsbury (1919); Gilbert Hovey Grosvenor (1920-1954); John Oliver La Gorce (1954-1957); Melville Bell Grosvenor (1957-1967); Melvin M. Payne (1967-1976); Robert E. Doyle (1976-1980); Gilbert M. Grosvenor (1980-)

President's Report
President's Page. By Gilbert M. Grosvenor. *Dec. 1986*

President's Report to Members. By Gilbert M. Grosvenor. 848-852, Dec. 1981; 820-824, *Dec. 1982*

Your Society's President Reports: A Year of Widening Horizons. By Melville Bell Grosvenor. 888-906, *Dec. 1962*

Your Society Takes Giant New Steps: The President's Annual Message to Members. By Melville Bell Grosvenor. 874-886, *Dec. 1961*

Exploring an Epic Year. By Melville Bell Grosvenor. 874-886, *Dec. 1960*

Around the World and the Calendar with the Geographic. By Melville Bell Grosvenor. 832-866, *Dec. 1959*

Public Service Grants
President's Page. By Gilbert M. Grosvenor. *Apr. 1988*

Public Service Publications
▌▌ *Equal Justice Under the Law: The Supreme Court in American Life.* By Mary Ann Harrell. Published in cooperation with The Foundation of the Federal Bar Association. 151 pages. 1965; rev. ed. *1988*

▌▌ *The Living White House.* By Lonnelle Aikman. Published in cooperation with the White House Historical Association. 151 pages. 1966; rev. ed. *1987*

▌▌ *The President's House: A History.* By William Seale. Published in cooperation with the White House Historical Association. 2 volumes, 1224 pages. *1986*

▌▌ *Liberty: The Statue and the American Dream.* By Leslie Allen. The official book for the Centennial of the Statue of Liberty published by the Statue of Liberty–Ellis Island Foundation, Inc. Prepared and produced as a public service by NGS. 304 pages. *1985*

▌▌ *We, The People: The Story of the United States Capitol, Its Past and Its Promise.* By Lonnelle Aikman. Photos by George F. Mobley and Joseph H. Bailey. Published in cooperation with the United States Capitol Historical Society. 143 pages. 1963; rev. ed. *1985*

▌▌ *The First Ladies.* By Margaret Brown Klapthor. Published in cooperation with the White House Historical Association. 87 pages. 1975; rev. ed. *1983*

Gilbert Hovey Grosvenor, Editor of NATIONAL GEOGRAPHIC, examines a globe in 1922 with his father and his son Melville, later to be Editor himself. CHARLES MARTIN, NGS

■■ *The White House: An Historic Guide.* Published in cooperation with the White House Historical Association. 159 pages. 1962; rev. ed. *1982*

■ *George Washington–Man and Monument.* By Frank Freidel and Lonnelle Aikman. Published in cooperation with the Washington National Monument Association. 69 pages. 1965; rev. ed. *1973*

Publications. *See* Atlases; Books; National Geographic Magazine; NGM; Indexes; NGS: News Service; *National Geographic Research; National Geographic Traveler;* WORLD

Purpose of the Society
Editorial. By Wilbur E. Garrett. 1, Jan. 1986; 1, Jan. 1987; 1, *Jan. 1988*
President's Page. By Gilbert M. Grosvenor. *Jan. 1984*

Recordings. *See* Records and Sound Sheets

Research and Exploration
President's Page. By Gilbert M. Grosvenor. Jan. 1984; June 1984; Aug. 1984; Nov. 1984; July 1987; *Dec. 1987*
Amount spent annually. 824, *Dec. 1982*
Research fund established. 486, *May 1909*
See also NGS: Committee for Research and Exploration; Research Reports

Seal
The Seal of the National Geographic Society appears on one side of the Hubbard Medal. 564, *Apr. 1953*
Authorization and design of the Society's new seal. 215, June 1896; 28, 34, *July 1946*

Secretary
O. P. Austin (1904-1932); Thomas W. McKnew (1932-1962); Melvin M. Payne (1962-1967); Robert E. Doyle (1967-1976); Owen R. Anderson (1976-1980); Edwin W. Snider (1980-   )

Special Publications
Number of copies distributed (nearly eight million). 865, *June 1973*
Editorial Director: Gilbert M. Grosvenor. 843, *Dec. 1970*
Chief: Robert L. Breeden. 411, Mar. 1966; 884, *June 1970*
Adventure, science, history, exploration spring to life in your Society's new program of Special Publications. By Melville Bell Grosvenor. 408-417, *Mar. 1966*
See also Books, NGS, for titles

Symposium
Will We Mend Our Earth? By Gilbert M. Grosvenor. 766-771, *Dec. 1988*
"Earth '88: Changing Geographic Perspectives." President's Page. By Gilbert M. Grosvenor. *Jan. 1988*

Television and Educational Films
President's Page. By Gilbert M. Grosvenor. *Sept. 1988*
Foreign-language versions. President's Page. By Gilbert M. Grosvenor. *July 1988*
Cable TV programming (Explorer). President's Page. By Gilbert M. Grosvenor. Mar. 1985; Apr. 1985; *Jan. 1987*
Resource Guide. President's Page. By Gilbert M. Grosvenor. *Jan. 1986*
Great Moments With National Geographic. President's Page; cover, *Mar. 1985*
Awards received. President's Page. *Jan. 1985*
Director: Dennis Kane. President's Page. *Jan. 1985*
Awards Received. 848, 850, Dec. 1981; 824, *Dec. 1982*
Emmy Awards. 731, Dec. 1974; 1, Jan. 1979; 848, 850, Dec. 1981; 275, *Aug. 1982*
George Foster Peabody Award. 587, Oct. 1967; 850, *Dec. 1981*
Number of subjects available. 583, *Nov. 1975*

Director: Robert C. Doyle. 449-451, Sept. 1965; 586, 587, *Oct. 1967*
See also Television Films, for titles

Treasurer
John Joy Edson (1904-1935); Robert V. Fleming (1935-1967); Hilleary F. Hoskinson (1967-1982); Alfred J. Hayre (1982-   )

Vice President
John Oliver La Gorce (1922-1954); Melville Bell Grosvenor (1954-1957); Thomas W. McKnew (1954-1962); Melvin M. Payne (1958-1962); Robert V. Fleming (1958-1967); Frederick G. Vosburgh (1958-1970); Robert E. Doyle (1961-1976); Gilbert M. Grosvenor (1967-1980)

Vice President, Executive
Melvin M. Payne (1962-1967) 582, Apr. 1962; 865, June 1967; 583, Oct. 1967; 274, *Aug. 1982*
Thomas W. McKnew (1958-1961) 882, 883, Dec. 1960; 579, Apr. 1962; 148, Feb. 1965; 588, *Oct. 1967*

Vice President for Research and Exploration
Leonard C. Carmichael (1964-1973) 525, Apr. 1965; 864, June 1967; 441, 442, Sept. 1967; 582, 586, *Oct. 1967*

The NATIONAL Geographic Society:
■■ *100 Years of Adventure and Discovery.* By C.D.B. Bryan. Published by Harry N. Abrams, Inc. 484 pages. *1987*
The NATIONAL Geographic Society and
■■ *Its Magazine.* By Gilbert Grosvenor. 116 pages. 1936; rev. ed. *1948*

NATIONAL GEOGRAPHIC SOCIETY EDUCATION FOUNDATION:
President's Page. By Gilbert M. Grosvenor. *Sept. 1988*
President Grosvenor Announces the National Geographic Society Education Foundation. By Lloyd H. Elliott. 329A-329D, *Mar. 1988*

NATIONAL GEOGRAPHIC SOCIETY KIDS NETWORK:
President's Page. By Gilbert M. Grosvenor. *Apr. 1987*

NATIONAL GEOGRAPHIC SOCIETY–LIBRARY OF CONGRESS MAP PRESERVATION PROJECT:
President's Page. By Gilbert M. Grosvenor. *Apr. 1988*

NATIONAL GEOGRAPHIC SOCIETY–PALOMAR OBSERVATORY SKY SURVEYS:
✦ *Journey Into the Universe Through Time and Space; National Geographic-Palomar Sky Survey Charting the Heavens.* June 1983
Exploring the Farthest Reaches of Space. By George O. Abell. NGS research grant. 782-790, *Dec. 1956*
Sky Survey Charts the Universe. By Ira Sprague Bowen. NGS research grant. 780-781, *Dec. 1956*
Completing the Atlas of the Universe. By Ira Sprague Bowen. NGS research grant. 185-190, *Aug. 1955*
Our Universe Unfolds New Wonders. By Albert G. Wilson. NGS research grant. 245-260, *Feb. 1952*

MN

Mapping the Unknown Universe. By F. Barrows Colton. NGS research grant. 401-420, *Sept. 1950*

The NATIONAL Geographic Society- ▌▌*U. S. Army Air Corps Stratosphere Flight of 1934 in the Balloon* Explorer. 122 pages. *1935*

NATIONAL GEOGRAPHIC TRAVELER:
Foreign-language editions. President's Page. By Gilbert M. Grosvenor. *July 1988*
New journal announced. President's Page. By Gilbert M. Grosvenor. *Feb. 1984*

NATIONAL GEOGRAPHIC WORLD (Magazine for Young Readers):
Foreign-language editions. President's Page. By Gilbert M. Grosvenor. *July 1988*
Circulation. 851, *Dec. 1981*
Editorial. By Gilbert M. Grosvenor. The *School Bulletin* is retired after 56 years; replaced by WORLD. 299, *Sept. 1975*
Start the World, I Want to Get On! 148-150, *July 1975*

NATIONAL GEOGRAPHY BEE:
President's Page. By Gilbert M. Grosvenor. *Nov. 1988*

NATIONAL Growth and National Character. By W J McGee. 185-206, *June 1899*

NATIONAL HISTORICAL PARKS:
United States. *See* Chesapeake and Ohio Canal; Harpers Ferry

NATIONAL INSTITUTES OF HEALTH, Bethesda, Maryland:
Capturing Strange Creatures in Colombia. By Marte Latham. Photos by Tor Eigeland. 682-693, *May 1966*

NATIONAL MILITARY PARKS:
United States:
Echoes of Shiloh (Shiloh National Military Park, Tennessee). By Shelby Foote. 106-111, *July 1979*
Gettysburg and Vicksburg: the Battle Towns Today. By Robert Paul Jordan. Map notes by Carolyn Bennett Patterson. 4-57, *July 1963*
Heritage of Beauty and History. By Conrad L. Wirth. Included: Antietam, Chickamauga, Gettysburg, Kings Mountain, Shiloh, Vicksburg, Yorktown. 587-661, *May 1958*

NATIONAL MONUMENTS: United States:
Roosevelt Country: T. R.'s Wilderness Legacy. By John L. Eliot. Photos by Farrell Grehan. 340-363, *Sept. 1982*
✤ *America's Federal Lands; The United States. Sept. 1982*
▌▌*America's Wonderlands: The Scenic National Parks and Monuments of the United States.* 552 pages. 1959; rev. ed. *1980*
▌▌*Visiting Our Past: America's Historylands.* Included: Companion directory,

Granitic conservationist, President Theodore Roosevelt gazes from South Dakota's Mount Rushmore. FARRELL GREHAN

Visiting Our Past: A Supplemental Guide to Selected Sites. 400 pages. *1977*
Alaska: Rising Northern Star. By Joseph Judge. Photos by Bruce Dale. Included: Proposed monuments: Aniakchak Caldera, Cape Krusenstern, Harding Icefield-Kenai Fjords, Kobuk. 730-767, *June 1975*
Preserving America's Last Great Wilderness (Alaska). By David Jeffery. Included: Proposed monuments: Aniakchak Caldera, Cape Krusenstern, Harding Icefield-Kenai Fjords, Kobuk. 769-791, *June 1975*
▌▌*America's Historylands, Touring Our Landmarks of Liberty.* Companion volume to *America's Wonderlands.* 575 pages. 1962; rev. ed. *1967*
Today and Tomorrow in Our National Parks. By Melville Bell Grosvenor. Included: Glacier Bay National Monument. 1-5, *July 1966*
The Mission Called 66: Today in Our National Parks. By Conrad L. Wirth. Included: Death Valley, Dinosaur, Rainbow Bridge National Monuments. 7-47, *July 1966*
Parkscape, U.S.A.: Tomorrow in Our National Parks. By George B. Hartzog, Jr. Included: Buck Island Reef, Chesapeake and Ohio Canal, Glacier Bay, Muir Woods, Organ Pipe Cactus, Statue of Liberty. 48-93, *July 1966*
Heritage of Beauty and History. By Conrad L. Wirth. Included: Aztec Ruins, Bandelier, Castillo de San Marcos, Cedar Breaks, Custer Battlefield, Death Valley, Devils Tower, Dinosaur, Edison Laboratory, El Morro, Fort Frederica, Fort Laramie, Fort McHenry, Fort Sumter, Great Sand Dunes, Harpers Ferry, Lava Beds, Organ Pipe Cactus, Petrified Forest, Rainbow Bridge, Russell

Cave, Saguaro, Scotts Bluff, Tuzigoot, Walnut Canyon National Monuments. 587-661, *May 1958*
✤ *National Parks, Monuments and Shrines of the United States and Canada.* Atlas series. Text on reverse. *May 1958*
Shrines of Each Patriot's Devotion. By Frederick G. Vosburgh. Contents: Ackia Battleground, Andrew Johnson, Big Hole, Cabrillo, Custer Battlefield, El Morro, Father Millet Cross, Fort Matanzas, Fort Pulaski, Fort Vancouver, George Washington Birthplace, Homestead, Lava Beds, Perry's Victory and International Peace Memorial, Pipe Spring, Scotts Bluff, Statue of Liberty, Verendrye. 51-82, *Jan. 1949*
Utah's Arches of Stone. By Jack Breed. Contents: Arches National Monument. 173-192, *Aug. 1947*
Blizzard of Birds: The Tortugas Terns. By Alexander Sprunt, Jr. Included: Fort Jefferson National Monument. 213-230, *Feb. 1947*
New Mexico Melodrama. By Frederick Simpich. Included: Aztec Ruins; Bandelier; El Morro; Pueblo Bonito; White Sands. 529-569, *May 1938*
Arizona Sands, Home of the Cactus King. 521-528, *Apr. 1937*
The Saguaro Forest (Arizona). By H. L. Shantz. 515-532, *Apr. 1937*
Bursts of Color in Sculptured Utah. 593-616, *May 1936*
The White Sands of Alamogordo (New Mexico): A Dry Ocean of Granular Gypsum Billows Under Desert Winds in a New National Playground. By Carl P. Russell. 250-264, *Aug. 1935*
Photographing the Marvels of the West in Colors. By Fred Payne Clatworthy. 694-719, *June 1928*
Bats of the Carlsbad Cavern. By Vernon Bailey. 321-330, *Sept. 1925*
Everyday Life in Pueblo Bonito: As Disclosed by the National Geographic Society's Archeologic Explorations in the Chaco Canyon National Monument, New Mexico. By Neil M. Judd. 227-262, *Sept. 1925*
New Discoveries in Carlsbad Cavern (New Mexico): Vast Subterranean Chambers with Spectacular Decorations Are Explored, Surveyed, and Photographed. By Willis T. Lee. Note: Carlsbad Caverns was a national monument from 1923 until 1930, when it became a national park. 301-319, *Sept. 1925*
Among the "Craters of the Moon": An Account of the First Expeditions Through the Remarkable Volcanic Lava Beds of Southern Idaho. By R. W. Limbert. Note: Craters of the Moon became a national monument on May 2, 1924. 303-328, *Mar. 1924*
A Visit to Carlsbad Cavern: Recent Explorations of a Limestone Cave in the Guadalupe Mountains of New Mexico Reveal a Natural Wonder of the First Magnitude. By Willis T. Lee. 1-40, *Jan. 1924*
The Scenery of North America. By James Bryce. 339-389, *Apr. 1922*

Arizona Navajos unwind during a ceremony to cure a Vietnam veteran, wearing his finest jewelry, of illnesses ascribed to the spirits of his enemies. DAVID ALAN HARVEY

NATIONAL PARKS:

Africa

The Serengeti. 560-601. I. A Photographic Portfolio. Photos by Mitsuaki Iwago. Text by John Eliot. 563-585; II. The Glory of Life. By Shana Alexander. 585-601, *May 1986*

Africa's Elephants: Can They Survive? By Oria Douglas-Hamilton. Photos by Oria and Iain Douglas-Hamilton. Included: Addo Elephant National Park, South Africa; Kabalega Falls National Park, Uganda; Kruger National Park, South Africa; Lake Manyara National Park, Tanzania; Niokolo Koba National Park, Senegal; Ruwenzori National Park, Uganda; Selous Game Reserve, Tanzania; Tsavo National Park, Kenya; Wankie National Park, Zimbabwe; Wonga Wongué Reserve, Gabon; Zambesi National Park, Zimbabwe. 568-603, *Nov. 1980*

African Wildlife: Man's Threatened Legacy. By Allan C. Fisher, Jr. Photos by Thomas Nebbia. Paintings by Ned Seidler. Included: Albert National Park, Zaire; Amboseli Game Reserve, Kenya; Etosha National Park, South-West Africa; Gorongosa National Park, Mozambique; Kidepo Valley National Park, Uganda; Kruger National Park, South Africa; Lake Manyara National Park, Tanzania; Marsabit National Reserve, Kenya; Mkuzi Game Reserve, South Africa; Mountain Zebra National Park, South Africa; Murchison Falls National Park, Uganda; Nairobi National Park, Kenya; Ngorongoro Conservation Area, Tanzania; Serengeti National Park, Tanzania; Tsavo National Park, Kenya; Volcanoes National Park, Rwanda; Wankie National Park, Rhodesia. 147-187, *Feb. 1972*

Uganda, Africa's Uneasy Heartland. By Howard La Fay. Photos by George F. Mobley. Included: Kidepo Valley National Park, Murchison Falls National Park, Queen Elizabeth National Park. 708-735, *Nov. 1971*

The Last Great Animal Kingdom. Included: Albert National Park, Congo; Amboseli National Reserve, Kenya; Kruger National Park, South Africa; Serengeti National Park, Tanganyika. 390-409, *Sept. 1960*

Where Elephants Have Right of Way. By George and Jinx Rodger. Included: Amboseli National Reserve, Kenya; Garamba National Park, Congo; Murchison Falls National Park, Uganda; Nairobi Royal National Park, Kenya; Ngong National Reserve, Kenya; Queen Elizabeth National Park, Uganda; Tsavo Royal National Park, Kenya. 363-389, *Sept. 1960*

White Magic in the Belgian Congo. By W. Robert Moore. 321-362, *Mar. 1952*

Roaming Africa's Unfenced Zoos. By W. Robert Moore. Included: Hluhluwe Game Reserve, South Africa; Kruger National Park, South Africa;

VOL. 156, NO. 1   JULY 1979

NATIONAL GEOGRAPHIC

A SPECIAL ISSUE DEVOTED TO THE BEST OF THE LAND

Our National Parks

INCLUDING A VISITORS' GUIDE TO ALL 320 PARK SITES

Nairobi National Park, Kenya; Parc National Albert, Congo; Umfolozi Reserve, South Africa. 353-380, *Mar. 1950*

See also Etosha National Park, Namibia; Gombe Stream National Park, Tanzania; Kruger National Park, South Africa; Lake Manyara National Park, Tanzania; Nairobi National Park, Kenya; Serengeti National Park, Tanzania; Tassili-n-Ajjer, Algeria; Tsavo National Park, Kenya

Asia

The Mighty Himalaya: A Fragile Heritage. By Barry C. Bishop. Photos by William Thompson. Included: Sagarmatha National Park, Nepal. 624-631, *Nov. 1988*

Editorial. By Wilbur E. Garrett. 551, *Nov. 1987*

Return of Java's Wildlife. By Dieter and Mary Plage. 750-771, *June 1985*

Tiger! Lord of the Indian Jungle. By Stanley Breeden. Photos by Belinda Wright. 748-773, *Dec. 1984*

Japan's Izu Oceanic Park. By Eugenie Clark. Photos by David Doubilet. 465-491, *Apr. 1984*

Sri Lanka's Wildlife. 254-278. I. Sri Lanka's Wildlife Heritage: A Personal Perspective. By Arthur C. Clarke. 254-255; II. Legacy of Lively Treasures. By Dieter and Mary Plage. 256-273; III. A Nation Rises to the Challenge. By Lyn de Alwis. Photos by Dieter and Mary Plage. 274-278, *Aug. 1983*

Park at the Top of the World: Mount Everest National Park. By Rick Ridgeway. Photos by Nicholas deVore III. 696-725. Included: Preserving a Mountain Heritage. By Sir Edmund Hillary. 696-703, *June 1982*

India Struggles to Save Her Wildlife. By John J. Putman. Included: Borivli National Park, Corbett National Park, Kanha National Park, Kaziranga National Park. 299-343, *Sept. 1976*

Australia

A Walk and Ride on the Wild Side: Tasmania. By Carolyn Bennett Patterson. Photos by David Hiser and Melinda Berge. Included: Franklin-Lower Gordon Wild Rivers National Park; Southwest National Park. 676-693, *May 1983*

Australia's Great Barrier Reef. 630-663. I. A Marine Park Is Born. By Soames Summerhays. Photos by Ron and Valerie Taylor. 630-635; II. Paradise Beneath the Sea. By Ron and Valerie Taylor. 636-663, *May 1981*

Canada

Editorial. By Wilbur E. Garrett. 421, *Oct. 1987*

Heart of the Canadian Rockies. By Elizabeth A. Moize. Photos by Jim Brandenburg. Included: Banff, Jasper. 757-779, *June 1980*

Hiking the Backbone of the Rockies; Canada's Great Divide Trail. By Mike W. Edwards. Photos by Lowell Georgia. Included: Banff, Jasper, Kootenay, Yoho. 795-817, *June 1973*

Bikepacking Across Alaska and Canada. By Dan Burden. Included: Jasper. 682-695, *May 1973*

Canada's Heartland, the Prairie Provinces. By W. E. Garrett. Included: Banff, Elk Island, Jasper, Wood Buffalo. 443-489, *Oct. 1970*

Canadian Rockies, Lords of a Beckoning Land. By Alan Phillips. Photos by James L. Stanfield. Included: Banff, Jasper, Kootenay, Mount Robson, Waterton Lakes, Yoho. 353-393, *Sept. 1966*

On the Ridgepole of the Rockies. By Walter Meayers Edwards. Contents: Banff, Jasper. Included: Canada's Rocky Mountain Playground. 745-780, *June 1947*

Peaks and Parks of Western Canada. Photos by W. J. Oliver. 516-526, *Oct. 1941*

See also Kluane National Park Reserve; Nahanni National Park; Waterton Lakes National Park; Wood Buffalo National Park

Central America

Teeming Life of a Rain Forest. By Carol and David Hughes. 49-65, *Jan. 1983*

Resurrecting the Grandeur of Tikal (Maya Ruin). By William R. Coe. 792-798, *Dec. 1975*

New Zealand. *See* Milford Track, for Fiordland National Park

South America

Parks, Plans, and People: How South America Guards Her Green Legacy. By Mary and Laurance Rockefeller. Photos by George F. Mobley. Included: Cabo Polonio, Iguaçu, Los Glaciares, Nahuel Huapí, Robinson Crusoe Island, Tierra del Fuego, Torres del Paine. 74-119, *Jan. 1967*

See also Xingu National Park, Brazil

United States

Investing in Park Futures, a report on a three-year study by the National Parks and Conservation Association. Editorial by Wilbur E. Garrett. 551, *May 1988*

■■ *Exploring America's Scenic Highways.* 199 pages. *1985*

■■ *Alaska's Magnificent Parklands.* 199 pages. *1984*

■■ *A Guide to Our Federal Lands.* 227 pages. *1984*

■■ *Our Threatened Inheritance: Natural Treasures of the United States.* By Ron Fisher. Photos by James P. Blair. 400 pages. *1984*

Roosevelt Country: T. R.'s Wilderness Legacy. By John L. Eliot. Photos by Farrell Grehan. 340-363, *Sept. 1982*

✦ *America's Federal Lands; The United States.* Included: Arches, Bryce Canyon, Canyonlands, Capitol Reef, Zion. *Sept. 1982*

Coal vs. Parklands. By François Leydet. Photos by Dewitt Jones. 776-803, *Dec. 1980*

● National Parks: Playground or Paradise. 703, *Dec. 1980*

■■ *America's Wonderlands: The Scenic National Parks and Monuments of the United States.* 552 pages. 1959; rev. ed. *1980*

Editorial. By Gilbert M. Grosvenor. 1-2, *July 1979*

Our National Parks. Photos by David Alan Harvey. 1-152. I. The Best of Our Land. By Gilbert M. Grosvenor. 1-2; II. Parks Grandeur in Pictures. 3-17; III. A Long History of New Beginnings. By Melville Bell Grosvenor. 18-30; IV. Will Success Spoil Our Parks? By Robert Paul Jordan. 31-59; V. Sharing Alaska: How Much for Parks? Opposing views by Jay S. Hammond and Cecil D.

Andrus. 60-65; VI. Trekking Around the Continent's Highest Peak. By Ned Gillette. 66-79; VII. Our People, Our Past (Navajos). By Albert Laughter. 81-85; VIII. Gateway–Elbowroom for the Millions. By Louise Levathes. 86-97; IX. Golden Gate–Of City, Ships, and Surf. By David S. Boyer. 98-105; X. Echoes of Shiloh. By Shelby Foote. 106-111; XI. A Guide to Parklands. 111-123; XII. Spring Comes Late to Glacier. By Douglas Chadwick. 124-133; XIII. Guadalupe's Trails in Summer. By Edward Abbey. 135-141; XIV. Autumn–Season of the Smokies. By Gordon Young. 142-147; XV. Grand Teton–A Winter's Tale. By François Leydet. 148-152, *July 1979*

Alaska: Rising Northern Star. By Joseph Judge. Photos by Bruce Dale. Included: Mount McKinley, Sitka; *and* proposed parks: Gates of the Arctic, Lake Clark, Wrangell-St. Elias. 730-767, *June 1975*

Preserving America's Last Great Wilderness (Alaska). By David Jeffery. Included: Proposed parks: Gates of the Arctic, Katmai additional acreage, Lake Clark, Mount McKinley. 769-791, *June 1975*

■■ *The New America's Wonderlands: Our National Parks.* 464 pages. 1959; rev. ed. *1975*

John Muir's Wild America. By Harvey Arden. Photos by Dewitt Jones. Included: Petrified Forest, Sequoia, Yosemite. 433-461, *Apr. 1973*

■■ *Wilderness U.S.A.* 344 pages. *1973*

Mexico to Canada on the Pacific Crest Trail. By Mike W. Edwards. Photos by David Hiser. Included: Crater Lake, Lassen Volcanic, Mount Rainier, Sequoia, Yosemite. 741-779, *June 1971*

■■ *Vacationland U.S.A.* 424 pages. *1970*

● America's Wonderlands: The National Parks. 549A-549B, *Oct. 1968*

Today and Tomorrow in Our National Parks. By Melville Bell Grosvenor. Included: Kings Canyon, Mount McKinley, Sequoia. 1-5, *July 1966*

The Mission Called 66: Today in Our National Parks. By Conrad L. Wirth. Included: Acadia, Bryce Canyon, Crater Lake, Everglades, Grand Canyon, Grand Teton, Mesa Verde, Mount Rainier, Sequoia, Shenandoah, Yellowstone, Yosemite. 7-47, *July 1966*

Parkscape, U.S.A.: Tomorrow in Our National Parks. By George B. Hartzog, Jr. Included: Canyonlands, Everglades, Great Smoky Mountains, Haleakala, Mount McKinley, North Cascades (Proposed), Redwood (Proposed), Shenandoah, Virgin Islands; *and* National Capital Parks. 48-93, *July 1966*

✦ *Vacationlands of the United States and Southern Canada.* Text on reverse. *July 1966*

Wyoming: High, Wide, and Windy. By David S. Boyer. Included: Grand Teton, Yellowstone. 554-594, *Apr. 1966*

I See America First. By Lynda Bird Johnson. Photos by William Albert

Running red with silt-laden floodwaters, the Colorado River flushes a raft through Grand Canyon National Park. WILBUR E. GARRETT, NGS

■■ BOOKS ✦ MAPS ● TELEVISION

NATIONAL PARKS: Proposed. *See* North Cascades National Park; Tallgrass Prairie National Park

NATIONAL PRESERVES: Proposed. *See* Big Cypress Swamp, Florida; Big Thicket, Texas

NATIONAL RECREATION AREAS. *See* Gateway National Recreation Area; Glen Canyon National Recreation Area; Golden Gate National Recreation Area

NATIONAL RIVER. *See* Buffalo National River

NATIONAL SCENIC TRAILS: United States. *See* Appalachian Trail; Continental Divide National Scenic Trail; Pacific Crest Trail

NATIONAL SCIENCE FOUNDATION: Projects Funded:

Animal Studies
Alaskan Brown Bears 433, Sept. 1975; Andean Condors 686, May 1971; Baboons 674, May 1975; Coral Reefs

Threatened by loggers in 1915, a famous California sequoia is surrounded by a 20-man embrace. GILBERT H. GROSVENOR, NGS

710, 712, Nov. 1966; Fiddler Crabs 16, Jan. 1963; Galápagos Tortoises 639, Nov. 1972; Garden Eels 727, Nov. 1974; Green Turtles 879, 880, June 1967; Grizzly Bears 255, Aug. 1966; Krill 630, May 1984; Lions 496, Apr. 1969; Moose and Wolves of Isle Royale 202, Feb. 1963; Porpoises 403, Sept. 1966; Salmon 205, Aug. 1968; Wild Burros 506, *Apr. 1972*

Antarctica. *See* International Geophysical Year; U. S. Antarctic Research Program

Anthropology
Ethiopia 805, Dec. 1976; Karnali Zone, Nepal 662, Nov. 1971; New Britain Tribes 795, June 1966; Papua New Guinea 128, July 1977; Polynesians 736, Dec. 1974; Skull 1470 829, *June 1973*

Archaeology
Chan Chan 320, Mar. 1973; Dzibilchaltun 99, Jan. 1959; Jenne-jeno (site), Mali 408, Sept. 1982; *Monitor* search 49, Jan. 1975; Snaketown 675, 682, May 1967; Yassi Ada wrecks 404, *Sept. 1968*

Education
NGS Kids Network. President's Page. By Gilbert M. Grosvenor. Apr. 1987; Science projects in Pittsburgh high schools. 365, 368, *Mar. 1965*

Expeditions and Research
Bristlecone Pine Field Survey 361, Mar. 1958; Cayman Expedition 230, Aug. 1976; Deep Sea Drilling Project 650, Nov. 1978; Eclipse Expedition 224, Aug. 1970; Galapagos Rift Hydrothermal Expedition 443, Oct. 1977; 682, 685, Nov. 1979; International Biological Program (Tundra ecosystems) 305, Mar. 1972; Palau Lakes Survey 269, 271, Feb. 1982; Summer Institute of Glaciological and Arctic Sciences 796, June 1965; 201, Feb. 1967; University Corporation for Atmospheric Research 523, *Apr. 1972*
See also American Mount Everest Expedition; Deep Sea Drilling Project; FAMOUS; Mohole, Project

NATIONAL SEASHORES: United States. *See* Assateague Island; Cape Cod; Cape Hatteras National Seashore; Cumberland Island; Padre Island National Seashore

NATIONAL TRAIL SYSTEM. *See* listing under National Scenic Trails

NATIONAL TRUST FOR HISTORIC PRESERVATION:
Study Grant. 1, *July 1982*
Buildings Preserved. 93, Jan. 1957; 383, Mar. 1966; 834, Dec. 1970; 78, 83, *Jan. 1978*

NATIONAL TRUST FOR PLACES OF HISTORIC INTEREST OR NATURAL BEAUTY:
The Preservation of England's Historic and Scenic Treasures. By Eric Underwood. 413-440, *Apr. 1945*

NATIONAL WEATHER SERVICE:
The Year the Weather Went Wild. By Thomas Y. Canby. 799-829, *Dec. 1977*

Alaskan Amelia Sherman welcomes visitors to Noatak, the only village on the Arctic river that shares its name. SAM ABELL

We're Doing Something About the Weather! By Walter Orr Roberts. 518-555, *Apr. 1972*
See also former name, U. S. Weather Bureau

NATIONAL WILD AND SCENIC RIVERS SYSTEM:
■■ *America's Wild and Scenic Rivers.* 199 pages. *1983*
Our Wild and Scenic Rivers. 2-59. I. Rivers Wild and Pure: A Priceless Legacy. By Robert E. Doyle. 2-11; II. The Flathead. By Douglas H. Chadwick. Photos by Lowell Georgia. 13-19; III. The Suwannee. By Jack and Anne Rudloe. Photos by Jodi Cobb. 20-29; IV. The St. Croix. By David S. Boyer. 30-37; V. The Skagit. By David S. Boyer. 38-45; VI. The Rio Grande. By Nathaniel T. Kenney. Photos by Bank Langmore. 46-51; VII. The Noatak. By John M. Kauffmann. Photos by Sam Abell. 52-59, *July 1977*
⊕ *Wild and Scenic Rivers of the United States. July 1977*
America's Little Mainstream. By Harvey Arden. Photos by Matt Bradley. Note: In 1972, Congress created the Buffalo National River, a unique administrative unit. 344-359, *Mar. 1977*
White-water Adventure on Wild Rivers of Idaho. By Frank Craighead, Jr., and John Craighead. Included: Middle Fork Salmon; Salmon; and rivers protected or proposed for protection under the Wild and Scenic Rivers Act of 1968. 213-239, *Feb. 1970*
■ Wild River. Included: Middle Fork Salmon; Salmon. 239A-239B, *Feb. 1970*
See also protected rivers, by name

NATIONAL WILDFLOWER RESEARCH CENTER, Austin, Texas:
President's Page. By Gilbert M. Grosvenor. *Aug. 1988*

NATIONAL WILDLIFE REFUGES: United States:
North American Waterfowl: Troubles and Triumphs. By John Madson. 562-599, *Nov. 1984*
■■ *Wild Lands for Wildlife: America's National Refuges.* By Noel Grove. Photos by Bates Littlehales. 207 pages. *1984*
Delaware–Who Needs to Be Big? By Jane Vessels. Photos by Kevin Fleming. Included: Bombay Hook National Wildlife Refuge. 171-197, *Aug. 1983*
Roosevelt Country: T. R.'s Wilderness Legacy. By John L. Eliot. Photos by Farrell Grehan. 340-363, *Sept. 1982*
⊕ *America's Federal Lands; The United States. Sept. 1982*
Teamwork Helps the Whooping Crane. By Roderick C. Drewien, with Ernie Kuyt. Included: Bosque del Apache National Wildlife Refuge, New Mexico; Grays Lake National Wildlife Refuge, Idaho; Monte Vista National Wildlife Refuge, Colorado. 680-693, *May 1979*
Our National Wildlife Refuges. 342-381. I. A Chance to Grow. By Robert E. Doyle. 342-349; II. Island, Prairie, Marsh, and Shore. By Charlton Ogburn. Photos by Bates Littlehales. 350-381; III. Wildlife Refuges of the United States. Tear-out guide with maps. 363-370, *Mar. 1979*
Hawaii's Far-flung Wildlife Paradise. By John L. Eliot. Photos by Jonathan Blair. Contents: Hawaiian Islands National Wildlife Refuge. 670-691, *May 1978*
Tireless Voyager, the Whistling Swan. By William J. L. Sladen. Photos by Bianca Lavies. Included: Back Bay, Virginia; Blackwater, Maryland; Eastern Neck, Maryland; Mattamuskeet, North Carolina; Pungo, North Carolina; Upper Mississippi River Wild Life and Fish Refuge. NGS research grant. 134-147, *July 1975*
Alaska: Rising Northern Star. By Joseph Judge. Photos by Bruce Dale. Included: Map showing existing and proposed refuges. 730-767, *June 1975*
Preserving America's Last Great Wilderness (Alaska). By David Jeffery. 769-791, *June 1975*
Beyond the North Wind With the Snow Goose. By Des and Jen Bartlett. Included: De Soto, Missouri River; Sand Lake, South Dakota; Squaw Creek, Missouri. 822-843, *Dec. 1973*
See also Aransas National Wildlife Refuge; Arctic National Wildlife Range; National Elk Refuge; Okefenokee Swamp; Red Rocks Lake National Wildlife Refuge; Wichita Mountains Wildlife Refuge

NATIONAL ZOOLOGICAL PARK, Washington, D. C.:
Director: Theodore H. Reed. 630, May 1961; 875, Dec. 1968; 482, 484, 485,

Welders work on a section of the multibillion-dollar Alaska pipeline, which now carries crude oil 800 miles from Prudhoe Bay to the southern port of Valdez. STEVE RAYMER, NGS

A. Zahl. Photos by Victor R. Boswell, Jr., and author. 386-429, *Mar. 1969*

Nature's Year in Pleasant Valley. By Paul A. Zahl. 488-525, *Apr. 1968*

The Living Sand. By William H. Amos. 820-833, *June 1965*

Photographing Northern Wild Flowers. By Virginia L. Wells. 809-823, *June 1956*

In the Gardens of Olympus. By Paul A. Zahl. 85-123, *July 1955*

In the Wilds of a City Parlor. By Paul A. Zahl. 645-672, *Nov. 1954*

Shells Take You Over World Horizons. By Rutherford Platt. 33-84, *July 1949*

What the Fighting Yanks See. By Wanda Burnett. 451-476, *Oct. 1944*

The Magic Beauty of Snow and Dew. By Wilson A. Bentley. 103-112, *Jan. 1923*

See also the natural sciences; *and* listings under Animals

NATURAL RESOURCES:

✤ *America's Federal Lands; The United States.* Included: Managing Our Natural Heritage; Natural Resources Public and Private. *Sept. 1982*

This Land of Ours–How Are We Using It? By Peter T. White. Photos by Emory Kristof. 20-67, *July 1976*

See also Energy Sources; Forest Products; Metals; Minerals; Rain Forests; Water Resources

NATURAL Wonders of North America. ■ By Catherine O'Neill. Juvenile. 104 pages. *1984*

A **NATURALIST** in Penguin Land. By Niall Rankin. 93-116, *Jan. 1955*

A **NATURALIST** with MacMillan in the Arctic. By Walter N. Koelz. 299-318, *Mar. 1926*

A **NATURALIST'S** Journey Around Vera Cruz and Tampico. By Frank M. Chapman. 533-562, *May 1914*

NATURE and Man in Ethiopia. By Wilfred H. Osgood. 121-176, *Aug. 1928*

NATURE Carves Fantasies in Bryce Canyon. By William Belknap, Jr. 490-511, *Oct. 1958*

NATURE CONSERVANCY:

Prairie Preservation: Good News, Bad News. Geographica. *Dec. 1988*

Quietly Conserving Nature. By Noel Grove. Photos by Stephen J. Krasemann. 818-845, *Dec. 1988*

NATURE on the Rampage: Our Violent ■ *Earth.* 199 pages. *1986*

NATURE Paints New Mexico. Photos by Richard H. Stewart. 537-568, *May 1938*

NATURE PROTECTION AND WILD-LIFE MANAGEMENT SERVICE: Study Grant:

Orangutans. 449, Oct. 1975; 835, *June 1980*

NATURE RESERVES:

Editorial. By Wilbur E. Garrett. China-Nepal. 551, *Nov. 1987*

Madagascar: A World Apart. By Alison Jolly. Photos by Frans Lanting. 148-183, *Feb. 1987*

See also Bird Sanctuaries and Rookeries; Wildlife Refuges

NATURE STUDIES. *See* Biology; Birds; Crustaceans; Fishes; Flowers; Geology; Insects; Mammals; Marine Biology; Mollusks; Paleontology; Plants; Reptiles; Trees; Wildlife; *and* Natural History, for amateur studies

NATURE'S Alert Eyes. By Constance P. Warner. 558-569, *Apr. 1959*

NATURE'S Aquatic Engineers, Beavers. By Des and Jen Bartlett. 716-732, *May 1974*

NATURE'S Clown, the Penguin. By David Hellyer and Malcolm Davis. 405-428, *Sept. 1952*

NATURE'S Dwindling Treasures: Tropical Rain Forests. By Peter T. White. Photos by James P. Blair. Paintings by Barron Storey. 2-47, *Jan. 1983*

NATURE'S Gifts to Medicine. By Lonnelle Aikman. Paintings by Lloyd K. Townsend and Don Crowley. 420-440, *Sept. 1974*

NATURE'S Healing Arts: From Folk ■ *Medicine to Modern Drugs.* By Lonnelle Aikman. Photos by Nathan Benn and Ira Block. 199 pages. *1977*

NATURE'S Ingenious Spinners. Paintings by Hashime Murayama. 167-174, *Aug. 1933*

NATURE'S Kingdom on a High Rock Ledge. By William H. Amos. 558-566, *Oct. 1980*

NATURE'S Living, Jumping Jewels. By Paul A. Zahl. 130-146, *July 1973*

NATURE'S Most Amazing Mammal: Elephants, Unique Among Animals, Have Many Human Qualities When Wild That Make Them Foremost Citizens of Zoo and Circus. By Edmund Heller. 729-759, *June 1934*

NATURE'S Most Dramatic Spectacle. By S. A. Mitchell. 361-376, *Sept. 1937*

NATURE'S Night Lights: Probing the Secrets of Bioluminescence. By Paul A. Zahl. 45-69, *July 1971*

NATURE'S Scenic Marvels of the West. 17-32, *July 1933*

NATURE'S Tank, the Turtle. By Doris M. Cochran. Paintings by Walter A. Weber. 665-684, *May 1952*

NATURE'S Toy Train, the Railroad Worm. By Darwin L. Tiemann. Photos by Robert F. Sisson. NGS research grant. 56-67, *July 1970*

NATURE'S Transformation at Panama: Remarkable Changes in Faunal and Physical Conditions in the Gatun Lake Region. By George Shiras, 3d. 159-194, *Aug. 1915*

NATURE'S "Whirling" Water Purifiers. By John Walsh. 287-292, *Feb. 1979*

NATURE'S World of Wonders. 199 ■ pages. *1983*

NATURE'S Year in Pleasant Valley. By Paul A. Zahl. 488-525, *Apr. 1968*

NAURU:

Nauru, the World's Richest Nation. By Mike Holmes. 344-353, *Sept. 1976*

Nauru, the Richest Island in the South Seas. By Rosamond Dodson Rhone. 559-589, *Dec. 1921*

NAUTICAL Norfolk Turns to Azaleas. By William H. Nicholas. Photos by B. Anthony Stewart. 606-614, *May 1947*

NAUTILUS (Nuclear-powered Submarine):

The Arctic as a Sea Route of the Future. By William R. Anderson. 21-24, *Jan. 1959*

Submarine Through the North Pole. By William G. Lalor, Jr. Photos by John J. Krawczyk. 1-20, *Jan. 1959*

NAUTILUS, Chambered:

The Chambered Nautilus, Exquisite Living Fossil. Photos by Douglas Faulkner. 38-41, *Jan. 1976*

Shells Take You Over World Horizons. By Rutherford Platt. 33-84, *July 1949*

NAVAJO INDIAN RESERVATION, Utah-Arizona:

Flaming Cliffs of Monument Valley. By Jack Breed. Photos by author and Warren T. Mithoff. 452-461, *Oct. 1945*

NAVAJO INDIANS:

Inside the Sacred Hopi Homeland. By Jake Page. Photos by Susanne Page. Included: Hopi-Navajo land dispute. 607-629, *Nov. 1982*

✤ *The Southwest.* The Making of America series. Included: Arizona, New Mexico, and parts of California, Colorado, Texas, Utah; and in Mexico: Baja California Norte, Chihuahua, Sonora. On reverse: 12,000 Years of History; Spanish Conquest; Anglo-American Entry and Occupancy. *Nov. 1982*

Navajo Ranger Interprets–Our People, Our Past. By Albert Laughter. 81-85, *July 1979*

The Navajos. By Ralph Looney. Photos by Bruce Dale. 740-781, *Dec. 1972*

Better Days for the Navajos. By Jack Breed. Photos by Charles W. Herbert. 809-847, *Dec. 1958*

Desert River (San Juan) Through Navajo Land. By Alfred M. Bailey. Photos by author and Fred G. Brandenburg. 149-172, *Aug. 1947*

Flaming Cliffs of Monument Valley. By Jack Breed. Photos by author and Warren T. Mithoff. 452-461, *Oct. 1945*

Indian Tribes of Pueblo Land. By Matthew W. Stirling. Paintings by W. Langdon Kihn. 549-596, *Nov. 1940*

New Mexico Melodrama. By Frederick Simpich. 529-569, *May 1938*

NAVAJO MOUNTAIN, Utah:

Encircling Navajo Mountain with a

Pack-Train: An Expedition to a Hitherto Untraversed Region of Our Southwest Discovers a New Route to Rainbow Natural Bridge. By Charles L. Bernheimer. 197-224, *Feb. 1923*

NAVAJO NATIONAL MONUMENT, Arizona:

Navajo Ranger Interprets–Our People, Our Past. By Albert Laughter. 81-85, *July 1979*

NAVAL AFRICA EXPEDITION:

Transporting a Navy Through the Jungles of Africa in War Time. By Frank J. Magee. 331-362, *Oct. 1922*

NAVAL AIR TECHNICAL TRAINING UNIT:

Graduation by Parachute. By John E. Fletcher. 833-846, *June 1952*

NAVAL AIR TRANSPORT SERVICE:

Flying Our Wounded Veterans Home. By Catherine Bell Palmer. 363-384, *Sept. 1945*

NAVAL BASES, U. S.:

Crosscurrents Sweep the Indian Ocean. By Bart McDowell. Photos by Steve Raymer. 422-457, *Oct. 1981*

Four-ocean Navy in the Nuclear Age. By Thomas W. McKnew. 145-187, *Feb. 1965*

Our Navy in the Far East. By Arthur W. Radford. Photos by J. Baylor Roberts. 537-577, *Oct. 1953*

See also Guantánamo Bay; Hampton Roads; Honolulu, for Pearl Harbor; Key West; San Diego

The **NAVAL** Flags of the World. By Byron McCandless and Gilbert Grosvenor. 369, *Oct. 1917*

NAVARRO, DON JUAN N.: *Author*

Mexico of Today. 152-157, *Apr. 1901*; 176-179, *May 1901*; 235-238, *June 1901*

NAVASSA ISLAND, West Indies:

An Important New Guide for Shipping: Navassa Light, on a Barren Island in the West Indies, is the First Signal for the Panama Canal. By George R. Putnam. 401-406, *Nov. 1918*

NAVIDAD (Columbus's Colony). *See* La Navidad

NAVIGATING the "Norge" from Rome to the North Pole and Beyond: The Designer and Pilot of the First Dirigible to Fly Over the Top of the World Describes a Thrilling Voyage of More Than 8,000 Miles. By Umberto Nobile. 177-215, *Aug. 1927*

NAVIGATION:

Editorial. By Gilbert M. Grosvenor. 431, *Oct. 1976*

Editorial. By Gilbert M. Grosvenor. 731, *Dec. 1974*

Charting Our Sea and Air Lanes. By Stuart E. Jones. Photos by J. Baylor Roberts. 189-209, *Feb. 1957*

Revealing Earth's Mightiest Ocean. By Albert W. Atwood. 291-306, *Sept. 1943*

The Heavens Above: On Land, Sea, and in the Air the Stars Serve

Modern Man as Map, Compass, and Clock. Included: Star charts designed by the author. Drawings of the constellations by Carlotta Gonzales Lahey. 97-128, *July 1943*

The Compass in Modern Navigation. By G. W. Littlehales. 266-272, *Sept. 1897*

On the Telegraphic Determinations of Longitude by the Bureau of Navigation. By J. A. Norris. 1-30, *Apr. 1890*

See also Hokule'a; Mayflower II; Radar; Sonar; Submarines, Nuclear-powered; *and* Columbus, Christopher; Cook, James; Graham, Robin Lee; Henry, Prince, the Navigator; Heyerdahl, Thor; Lewis, David; Magellan, Ferdinand; Schultz, John E.; Severin, Timothy; Vikings

NAVIGATION, Flight:

Skyway Below the Clouds. By Carl R. Markwith. Photos by Ernest J. Cottrell. 85-108, *July 1949*

Our Air Age Speeds Ahead. By F. Barrows Colton. 249-272, *Feb. 1948*

See also Balloons

NAVIGATION SATELLITES:

Satellites That Serve Us. By Thomas Y. Canby. 281-335. Included: A portfolio: Images of Earth; Spacelab 1: *Columbia*. By Michael E. Long. 301-307, *Sept. 1983*

NAVIGATORS. *See* Explorers, Discoverers, and Navigators

NAVSTAR. *See* Global Positioning System

NAVY. *See* U. S. Navy

A **NAVY** Artist Paints the Aleutians. By Mason Sutherland. Paintings by William F. Draper. 157-176, *Aug. 1943*

Ndebele woman of South Africa wears a modern hat and a wife's traditional neck rings. PETER MAGUBANE, GAMMA-LIAISON

NAVY HURRICANE WEATHER CENTRAL, Miami, Florida:

Men Against the Hurricane. By Andrew H. Brown. 537-560, *Oct. 1950*

NAVY Wings over the Pacific. U. S. Navy official photos. 241-248, *Aug. 1944*

NAWANG GOMBU (Sherpa):

American and Geographic Flags Top Everest. By Melvin M. Payne. Photos by Barry C. Bishop. 157-157C, *Aug. 1963*

See also American Mount Everest Expedition

NAXOS (Island), Greece:

The Isles of Greece: Aegean Birthplace of Western Culture. By Melville Bell Grosvenor. Photos by Edwin Stuart Grosvenor and Winfield Parks. 147-193, *Aug. 1972*

NAYARIT (State), Mexico:

Mesa del Nayar's Strange Holy Week. By Guillermo Aldana E. 780-795, *June 1971*

Along the Old Spanish Road in Mexico: Life Among the People of Nayarit and Jalisco, Two of the Richest States of the Southern Republic. By Herbert Corey. 225-281, *Mar. 1923*

NAZARÉ, Portugal:

Portugal Is Different. By Clement E. Conger. 583-622, *Nov. 1948*

NAZARENOS (Penitents):

Holy Week and the Fair in Sevilla. By Luis Marden. 499-530, *Apr. 1951*

NAZARETH, Israel:

Where Jesus Walked. By Howard La Fay. Photos by Charles Harbutt. 739-781, *Dec. 1967*

The Land of Galilee. By Kenneth MacLeish. Photos by B. Anthony Stewart. 832-865, *Dec. 1965*

NAZCA LINES:

Mystery of the Ancient Nazca Lines. By Loren McIntyre. NGS research grant. 716-728, *May 1975*

NDEBELE TRIBESPEOPLE:

South Africa's Ndebele People. 260-282. Included: Dilemma of Independence. Introduction by The Editor. 260-261; Pioneers in Their Own Land. By David Jeffery. Photos by Peter Magubane. 262-282, *Feb. 1986*

NEALE, GUY: *Artist*

The High World of the Rain Forest. By William Beebe. 838-855, *June 1958*

NEALLEY, GEORGE TRUE:

Recent Bequests by Members of the National Geographic Society. 474, *Apr. 1926*

NEANDERTALS:

The Search for Our Ancestors. By Kenneth F. Weaver. Photos by David L. Brill. Paintings by Jay H. Matternes. 560-623, *Nov. 1985*

NEAPOLITAN Blues and Imperial Purple of Roman Italy. Photos by Hans

The old Dane Church in Webster County, Nebraska, rises from the prairie celebrated by novelist Willa Cather.   FARRELL GREHAN

Gazing in adoration, a figure of the god Garuda sits atop a pillar facing a temple devoted to Krishna, at right, in Nepal's capital city, Kathmandu. WILLIAM THOMPSON

W. E. Garrett and Thomas Nebbia. 420-436, *Mar. 1961*

The Fabulous State of Texas. By Stanley Walker. Photos by B. Anthony Stewart and Thomas Nebbia. 149-195, *Feb. 1961*

Inside the White House. By Lonnelle Aikman. Photos by B. Anthony Stewart and Thomas Nebbia. 3-43, *Jan. 1961*

Prince Henry, the Explorer Who Stayed Home. By Alan Villiers. 616-656, *Nov. 1960*

Philadelphia Houses a Proud Past. By Harold Donaldson Eberlein. 151-191, *Aug. 1960*

Hawaii, U.S.A. By Frederick Simpich, Jr. 1-45, *July 1960*

Cape Canaveral's 6,000-mile Shooting Gallery. By Allan C. Fisher, Jr. Photos by Luis Marden and Thomas Nebbia. 421-471, *Oct. 1959*

NEBI MUSA PROCESSION:

The Pageant of Jerusalem: The Capital of the Land of Three Great Faiths. By Edward Keith-Roach. 635-681, *Dec. 1927*

NEBRASKA:

The Country of Willa Cather. By William Howarth. Photos by Farrell Grehan. 71-93, *July 1982*

Ancient Ashfall Creates a Pompeii of Prehistoric Animals. By Michael R. Voorhies. Photos by Annie Griffiths. Paintings by Jay Matternes. Contents: Site of a ten-million-year-old ashfall near Orchard, Nebraska. NGS research grant. 66-75, *Jan. 1981*

Land of Long Sunsets: Nebraska's Sand Hills. By John Madson. Photos by Jodi Cobb. 493-517, *Oct. 1978*

Nebraska...the Good Life. By Robert Paul Jordan. Photos by Lowell Georgia. 378-407, *Mar. 1974*

Following the Trail of Lewis and Clark. By Ralph Gray. 707-750, *June 1953*

Taming the Outlaw Missouri River. By Frederick Simpich. 569-598, *Nov. 1945*

Nebraska, the Cornhusker State. By Leo A. Borah. 513-542, *May 1945*

NECK RINGS:

South Africa's Ndebele People. 260-282. Included: Dilemma of Independence. Introduction by The Editor. 260-261; Pioneers in Their Own Land. By David Jeffery. Photos by Peter Magubane. 262-282, *Feb. 1986*

Anatomy of a Burmese Beauty Secret. By John M. Keshishian. 798-801, *June 1979*

The **NECTAR** Connection. By Paul W. Ewald. Photos by Robert A. Tyrrell. 223-227, *Feb. 1982*

NEDJEF (An Najaf), Iraq:

Mystic Nedjef, the Shia Mecca. By Frederick Simpich. 589-598, *Dec. 1914*

The **NEED** of Conserving the Beauty and Freedom of Nature in Modern Life. By Charles W. Eliot. 67-74, *July 1914*

NEEDHAM, JAMES G.: *Author*

Dragonflies–Rainbows on the Wing. 215-229, *Aug. 1951*

An Insect Community Lives in Flower Heads. 340-356, *Sept. 1946*

NEEDLEWORK. *See* Bayeux Tapestry; Embroidery

The **NEEDS** Abroad. By Ian Malcolm. 427-433, *May 1917*

NEFERTITI, Queen (Egypt):

Computer Helps Scholars Re-create an Egyptian Temple. By Ray Winfield Smith. Photos by Emory Kristof. NGS research grant. 634-655, *Nov. 1970*

NEGRITOS:

The Last Andaman Islanders. By Raghubir Singh. 66-91, *July 1975*

NEILLIE, C. R.: *Author*

Fighting Insects With Airplanes: An Account of the Successful Use of the Flying-Machine in Dusting Tall Trees Infested With Leaf-Eating Caterpillars. By C. R. Neillie and J. S. Houser. 333-338, *Mar. 1922*

NEJD (Region), Saudi Arabia:

Guest in Saudi Arabia. By Maynard Owen Williams. 463-487, *Oct. 1945*

A Visit to Three Arab Kingdoms: Transjordania, Iraq, and the Hedjaz Present Many Problems to European Powers. By Junius B. Wood. 535-568, *May 1923*

NELLIS AIR FORCE BASE, Nevada. *See* Nevada Wild Horse Range

NELSON, DANIEL A.: *Author*

Ghost Ships of the War of 1812: *Hamilton* and *Scourge.* Photos by Emory Kristof. Paintings by Richard Schlecht. 289-313, *Mar. 1983*

NELSON, EDWARD WILLIAM:

Where Magic Ruled: Art of the Bering Sea. By William W. Fitzhugh and Susan A. Kaplan. Photos by Sisse Brimberg. Contents: The Nelson Collection of Eskimo artifacts. 198-205, *Feb. 1983*

Awarded Jane M. Smith Life Membership. 342, *Apr. 1920*

Author

Bird Banding, the Telltale of Migratory Flight: A Modern Method of Learning the Flight-Ways and Habits of Birds. 91-131, *Jan. 1928*

Smaller Mammals of North America. Paintings by Louis Agassiz Fuertes. 371*-493, *May 1918*

▪▪ *Wild Animals of North America: Intimate Studies of Big and Little Creatures of the Mammal Kingdom.* Natural Color Portraits from Paintings by Louis Agassiz Fuertes. Track Sketches by Ernest Thompson Seton. 612 pages. *1918*

The Rat Pest: The Labor of 200,000 Men in the United States Required to Support Rats, Man's Most Destructive and Dangerous Enemy. 1-23, *July 1917*

The Larger North American Mammals. Paintings by Louis Agassiz Fuertes. 385-472, *Nov. 1916*

A Land of Drought and Desert–Lower California: Two Thousand Miles on Horseback Through the Most Extraordinary Cacti Forests in the World. 443-474, *May 1911*

A Winter Expedition in Southwestern Mexico. 341-356, *Sept. 1904*

Notes on the Wild Fowl and Game Animals of Alaska. 121-132, *Apr. 1898*

A Winter Weather Record from the Klondike Region. 327-335, *Nov. 1897*

NELSON, HORATIO, Viscount:

Portsmouth, Britannia's Sally Port. By Thomas Garner James. Photos by B. Anthony Stewart. 513-544, *Apr. 1952*

The British Way. By Sir Evelyn Wrench. 421-541, *Apr. 1949*

NELSON, WILBUR A.: *Author*

Reelfoot–An Earthquake Lake (Tennessee). 95-114, *Jan. 1924*

NELSON ISLAND, Alaska:

Eskimo Hunters of the Bering Sea. By Brad Reynolds. Photos by Don Doll. 814-834, *June 1984*

NEMRUD DAGH (Mountain), Turkey:

Throne Above the Euphrates. By Theresa Goell. 390-405, *Mar. 1961*

NENE:

Saving the Nene, World's Rarest Goose. By S. Dillon Ripley. Photos by Jerry Chong. 745-754, *Nov. 1965*

NENETS:

People of the Long Spring. By Yuri Rytkheu. Photos by Dean Conger. 206-223, *Feb. 1983*

NEPAL:

The Mighty Himalaya: A Fragile Heritage. By Barry C. Bishop. Photos by William Thompson. 624-631, *Nov. 1988*

Heavy Hands on the Land. By Larry Kohl. Photos by William Thompson and Galen Rowell. 633-651, *Nov. 1988*

Mount Everest: Surveying the Third Pole. By Bradford Washburn. NGS research grant. 653-659, *Nov. 1988*

Honey Hunters of Nepal. By Eric Valli and Diane Summers. 660-671, *Nov. 1988*

Editorial. By Wilbur E. Garrett. 551, *Nov. 1988*

At the Crossroads of Kathmandu. By Douglas H. Chadwick. Photos by William Thompson. 32-65, *July 1987*

Tracking the Elusive Snow Leopard. By Rodney Jackson and Darla Hillard. NGS research grant. 793-809, *June 1986*

Editorial. By Wilbur E. Garrett. 283, *Mar. 1986*

Temple Monkeys of Nepal. By Jane Teas. NGS research grant. 575-584, *Apr. 1980*

Kathmandu's Remarkable Newars. By John Scofield. 269-285, *Feb. 1979*

Trek to Nepal's Sacred Crystal Mountain. By Joel F. Ziskin. 500-517, *Apr. 1977*

Karnali, Roadless World of Western Nepal. By Lila M. and Barry C. Bishop. NGS research grant. 656-689, *Nov. 1971*

Sherpaland, My Shangri-La. By Desmond Doig. 545-577, *Oct. 1966*

Mustang, Remote Realm in Nepal. By Michel Peissel. 579-604, *Oct. 1965*

We Build a School for Sherpa Children. By Sir Edmund Hillary. 548-551, *Oct. 1962*

Wintering on the Roof of the World. By Barry C. Bishop. NGS research grant. 503-547, *Oct. 1962*

Afoot in Roadless Nepal (Geological Survey). By Toni Hagen. 361-405, *Mar. 1960*

Coronation in Katmandu. By E. Thomas Gilliard. Photos by Marc Riboud. 139-152, *July 1957*

Peerless Nepal–A Naturalist's Paradise.

By S. Dillon Ripley. Photos by Volkmar Wentzel. NGS research grant. 1-40, *Jan. 1950*

Nepal, the Sequestered Kingdom. By Penelope Chetwode. 319-352, *Mar. 1935*

Nepal: A Little-Known Kingdom. By John Claude White. 245-283, *Oct. 1920*

See also Annapurna; Everest, Mount

NEPALESE:

Gangtok, Cloud-wreathed Himalayan Capital. By John Scofield. 698-713, *Nov. 1970*

NEPENTHES (Pitcher Plants):

Malaysia's Giant Flowers and Insect-trapping Plants. By Paul A. Zahl. 680-701, *May 1964*

NEPTUNE:

The Planets: Between Fire and Ice. By Rick Gore. 4-51, *Jan. 1985*

Voyage to the Planets. By Kenneth F. Weaver. Paintings by Ludek Pesek. 147-193, *Aug. 1970*

NERVION (River), Spain:

The Land of the Basques: Home of a Thrifty, Picturesque People, Who Take Pride in the Sobriquet, "The Yankees of Spain." By Harry A. McBride. 63-87, *Jan. 1922*

NESHOBA COUNTY FAIR, Mississippi:

Mississippi's Grand Reunion at the Neshoba County Fair. By Carolyn Bennett Patterson. Photos by C. C. Lockwood. 854-866, *June 1980*

NESS, Loch, Scotland:

Loch Ness: The Lake and the Legend. By William S. Ellis. Photos by Emory Kristof and David Doubilet. 759-779, *June 1977*

NET Results from Oceania: Collecting Aquarium Specimens in Tropical Pacific Waters. By Walter H. Chute. 347-372, *Mar. 1941*

The NETHERLANDS:

The Dutch Touch. By Bart McDowell. Photos by Nathan Benn and Farrell Grehan. 501-525, *Oct. 1986*

Man Against the Sea, the Oosterschelde Barrier. By Larry Kohl. 526-537, *Oct. 1986*

Tulips: Holland's Beautiful Business. By Elizabeth A. Moize. Photos by Farrell Grehan. 712-728, *May 1978*

Amiable Amsterdam. By William Davenport. Photos by Adam Woolfitt. 683-705, *May 1974*

◼ Holland Against the Sea. 588A-588B, *Apr. 1970*

The Netherlands: Nation at War With the Sea. By Alan Villiers. Photos by Adam Woolfitt. 530-571, *Apr. 1968*

Inside Europe Aboard *Yankee.* By Irving and Electa Johnson. Photos by Joseph J. Scherschel. 157-195, *Aug. 1964*

Rotterdam–Reborn From Ruins. By Helen Hill Miller. Photos by James Blair. 526-553, *Oct. 1960*

⬩ *France, Belgium, and the Netherlands.* Atlas series. *June 1960*

Under Canvas in the Atomic Age. By Alan Villiers. Included: Amsterdam, Hilversum, Marken Island, Spakenburg, Volendam. 49-84, *July 1955*

Helping Holland Rebuild Her Land. By Gilbert M. Grosvenor and Charles Neave. 365-413, *Sept. 1954*

"Around the World in Eighty Days." By Newman Bumstead. Included: Amsterdam, Edam, The Hague, Hook of Holland, Leiden, Noordwijk aan Zee, Rotterdam, Zuider Zee. 705-750, *Dec. 1951*

Mid-century Holland Builds Her

Skaters pass a window in Hindeloopen, the Netherlands, as competitors on television take part in the Elfstedentocht, a 200-kilometer race. MARTIN KERS

Survivor of a volcanic mudflow in 1985, a little girl in Lérida, Colombia, gets a dousing. ANTHONY SUAU, BLACK STAR

Injured woman is carried out of ruins in Armero, destroyed by a mudslide following the 1985 eruption of Colombia's volcano Nevado del Ruiz. CAROL GUZY, *MIAMI HERALD*/BLACK STAR

Portrait of a New England poet: Robert Frost sits quietly working in 1954 in the log cabin on his Vermont farm. TOM HOLLYMAN

Mud-smeared man with a clay helmet prepares to portray an evil spirit in a New Guinea tribal dance.   MALCOLM S. KIRK

Officers Koralja—Andrew, Joseph, and Robert, from left—back each other up on the streets of Jersey City, New Jersey, as only triplets can. MICHAEL S. YAMASHITA

A volcanic pinnacle on the Navajo reservation in northwestern New Mexico, Ship Rock is a sacred tribal site. DANNY LEHMAN

Everyday Life in Pueblo Bonito: As Disclosed by the National Geographic Society's Archeologic Explorations in the Chaco Canyon National Monument, New Mexico. By Neil M. Judd. 227-262, *Sept. 1925*

New Discoveries in Carlsbad Cavern: Vast Subterranean Chambers with Spectacular Decorations Are Explored, Surveyed, and Photographed. By Willis T. Lee. 301-319, *Sept. 1925*

A Visit to Carlsbad Cavern: Recent Explorations of a Limestone Cave in the Guadalupe Mountains of New Mexico Reveal a Natural Wonder of the First Magnitude. By Willis T. Lee. 1-40, *Jan. 1924*

Pueblo Bonito, the Ancient: The National Geographic Society's Third Expedition to the Southwest Seeks to Read in the Rings of Trees the Secret of the Age of Ruins. By Neil M. Judd. 99-108, *July 1923*

The Pueblo Bonito Expedition of the National Geographic Society. By Neil M. Judd. 323-331, *Mar. 1922*

A New National Geographic Society Expedition: Ruins of Chaco Canyon, New Mexico, Nature-Made Treasure-Chest of Aboriginal American History, To Be Excavated and Studied; Work Begins This Month. 637-643, *June 1921*

Scenes from America's Southwest. 651-664, *June 1921*

Notes on the Deserts of the United States and Mexico (from a publication of Daniel T. MacDougal). 691-714, *Aug. 1910*

The Southwest: Its Splendid Natural Resources, Agricultural Wealth, and Scenic Beauty. By N. H. Darton. 631-665, *Aug. 1910*

The Prehistoric Ruin of Tsankawi. By George L. Beam. 807-822, *Sept. 1909*

The Call of the West. By C. J. Blanchard. 403-437, *May 1909*

Arizona and New Mexico. By B. S. Rodey. 100-102, *Feb. 1906*

The Enchanted Mesa. By F. W. Hodge. 273-284, *Oct. 1897*

Descriptive Topographic Terms of Spanish America. By Robert T. Hill. 291-302, *Sept. 1896*

See also Four Corners Country; Los Alamos Scientific Laboratory; Philmont Scout Ranch; White Sands Proving Ground; *and* Navajo Indians

The **NEW** Mexico. By John W. Foster. 1-24, *Jan. 1902*

NEW Microscopes Reveal an Invisible World. By Kenneth F. Weaver. 274-290, *Feb. 1977*

NEW MILLS, Braintree, England:

Silkworms in England Spin for the Queen. By John E. H. Nolan. 689-704, *May 1953*

NEW Miracles of the Telephone Age. By Robert Leslie Conly. 87-120, *July 1954*

NEW Mount McKinley Challenge–Trekking Around the Continent's Highest Peak. By Ned Gillette. 66-79, *July 1979*

Reflected in an antique-shop window, a New Orleans carriage driver awaits hire in the French Quarter.   JAMES L. STANFIELD, NGS

NEW National Geographic Society Expedition: Ruins of Chaco Canyon, New Mexico, Nature-Made Treasure-Chest of Aboriginal American History, To Be Excavated and Studied. 637-643, *June 1921*

A **NEW** National Park: Glacier National Park. By Guy Elliott Mitchell. 215-223, *Mar. 1910*

NEW National Park Proposed: The Spectacular North Cascades. By Nathaniel T. Kenney. Photos by James P. Blair. 642-667, *May 1968*

NEW Nations in the Pacific. By Carolyn Bennett Patterson. Photos by David Hiser and Melinda Berge. Included: Mariana Islands, Marshall Islands, Kosrae, Pohnpei, Truk, Yap, Palau. 460-499, *Oct. 1986*

NEW ORLEANS, Louisiana:

New Orleans and Her River. By Joseph Judge. Photos by James L. Stanfield. 151-187, *Feb. 1971*

Mardi Gras in New Orleans. By Carolyn Bennett Patterson. Photos by Robert F. Sisson and John E. Fletcher. 726-732, *Nov. 1960*

New Orleans: Jambalaya on the Levee. By Harnett T. Kane. Photos by Justin Locke. 143-184, *Feb. 1953*

Louisiana Trades with the World. By Frederick Simpich. Photos by J. Baylor Roberts. 705-738, *Dec. 1947*

Louisiana, Land of Perpetual Romance. By Ralph A. Graves. 393-482, *Apr. 1930*

NEW Perspective on the World. By John B. Garver, Jr. 911-913, *Dec. 1988*

A **NEW** Peruvian Route to the Plain of the Amazon. By Solon I. Bailey. 432-448, *Aug. 1906*

NEW Plant Immigrants. By David Fairchild. 879-907, *Oct. 1911*

NEW PROVIDENCE (Island), Bahamas. *See* Nassau

The **NEW** Queen of the Seas. By Melville Bell Grosvenor. 1-30, *July 1942*

A **NEW** Riviera: Mexico's West Coast. By Nathaniel T. Kenney. Photos by Charles O'Rear. 670-699, *Nov. 1973*

NEW Road to Asia. By Owen Lattimore. 641-676, *Dec. 1944*

NEW Rush to Golden California. By George W. Long. 723-802, *June 1954*

NEW Safeguards for Ships in Fog and Storm. By George R. Putnam. 169-200, *Aug. 1936*

NEW St. Lawrence Seaway Opens the Great Lakes to the World. By Andrew H. Brown. 299-339, *Mar. 1959*

NEW SALEM, Illinois:

Vacation Tour Through Lincoln Land. By Ralph Gray. 141-184, *Feb. 1952*

NEW Scarlet Bird in Florida Skies. By Paul A. Zahl. 874-882, *Dec. 1967*

A **NEW** Source of Power: Billions of Tons of Lignite, Previously Thought Too Poor Coal for Commercial Use, Are Made Easily Available. By Guy Elliott Mitchell. 935-944, *Nov. 1910*

NEW SOUTH WALES (State), Australia:

The Land Where the Murray Flows. By Louise E. Levathes. Photos by David Robert Austen. 252-278, *Aug. 1985*

New South Wales, the State That Cradled Australia. By Howell Walker. Photos by David Moore. 591-635, *Nov. 1967*

The Paradise of the Tasman: A Pacific Island Provides the Palms Which Decorate Hotels, Churches, Steamships, and Homes. By Hubert Lyman Clark. Contents: Lord Howe Island. 115-136, *July 1935*

Shark Fishing–An Australian Industry. By Norman Ellison. 369-386, *Sept. 1932*

See also Sydney

NEW Stars for Old Glory. By Lonnelle Aikman. 86-121, *July 1959*

NEW Tools for Undersea Archeology. By George F. Bass. Photos by Charles R. Nicklin, Jr. NGS research grant. 403-423, *Sept. 1968*

The **NEW** Toronto. By Ethel A. Starbird. Photos by Robert W. Madden. 190-215, *Aug. 1975*

The **NEW** Trans-Canada Railway. 214-215, *May 1903*

NEW Tricks Outwit Our Insect Enemies. By Hal Higdon. Photos by Robert F. Sisson and Emory Kristof. 380-399, *Sept. 1972*

A **NEW** Volcano Bursts from the Atlantic. By John Scofield. Photos by Robert F. Sisson. 735-757, *June 1958*

NEW WORLD. *See* The Americas; Explorers, Discoverers, and Navigators; Pre-Columbian Civilization; Vinland

The Flatiron Building dominates New York City's Madison Square in 1917.
FROM NORMAN THOMAS AND W. W. ROCK

Joseph Showalter. 413-422, *May 1917*

The New Erie Canal. 568-570, *Dec. 1905*

Commercial Importance of the State of New York. 429, *Oct. 1904*

Shawangunk Mountain. By N. H. Darton. 23-34, *Mar. 17, 1894*

See also New York, New York; Rochester; *and* Old Rhinebeck Aerodrome; Thunder Hill Goat Farm; U. S. Merchant Marine Academy; U. S. Military Academy

NEW YORK, New York:

Liberty Lifts Her Lamp Once More. By Alice J. Hall. 2-19, *July 1986*

New York Harbor–The Golden Door. By Erla Zwingle. Photos by Bruce Davidson. 21-43, *July 1986*

■■ *Liberty: The Statue and the American Dream.* By Leslie Allen. The official book for the Centennial of the Statue of Liberty published by the Statue of Liberty-Ellis Island Foundation, Inc. Prepared and produced as a public service by NGS. 304 pages. *1985*

A Century Old, the Wonderful Brooklyn Bridge. By John G. Morris. Photos by Donal F. Holway. 565-579, *May 1983*

Brooklyn: The Other Side of the Bridge. By Alice J. Hall. Photos by Robert W. Madden. 580-613, *May 1983*

Manhattan–Images of the City. By John J. Putman. Photos by Jay Maisel. 317-343, *Sept. 1981*

To Live in Harlem…. By Frank Hercules. Photos by LeRoy Woodson, Jr. 178-207, *Feb. 1977*

The Pious Ones. By Harvey Arden. Photos by Nathan Benn. Contents: The Hasidic Jews of Brooklyn. 276-298, *Aug. 1975*

The Fair Reopens (World's Fair, 1964-1965). Photos by James P. Blair. Text by Carolyn Bennett Patterson. 505-529, *Apr. 1965*

The World in New York City. By Peter T. White. 52-107, *July 1964*

✥ *Greater New York; Tourist Manhattan.* U. S. Atlas series. *July 1964*

Central Park: Manhattan's Big Outdoors. By Stuart E. Jones. Photos by Bates Littlehales. 781-811, *Dec. 1960*

Staten Island Ferry, New York's Seagoing Bus. By John T. Cunningham and Jay Johnston. Photos by W. D. Vaughn. 833-843, *June 1959*

Immigrants Still Flock to Liberty's Land. By Albert W. Atwood. 708-724, *Nov. 1955*

Here's New York Harbor. By Stuart E. Jones. Photos by Robert F. Sisson and David S. Boyer. 773-813, *Dec. 1954*

In the Wilds of a City Parlor. By Paul A. Zahl. 645-672, *Nov. 1954*

New York Again Hails the Horse (National Horse Show). By Walter B. Devereux. 697-720, *Nov. 1954*

The Mohawks Scrape the Sky. By Robert L. Conly. Photos by B. Anthony Stewart. Contents: Brooklyn's steel-working Mohawk Indians. 133-142, *July 1952*

Long Island Outgrows the Country. By Howell Walker. Photos by B. Anthony Stewart. 279-326, *Mar. 1951*

The Romance of American Furs. By Wanda Burnett. 379-402, *Mar. 1948*

Shad in the Shadow of Skyscrapers. By Dudley B. Martin. Photos by Luis Marden. 359-376, *Mar. 1947*

Spin Your Globe to Long Island: Only Six States Have More People than the Insular Empire that Ranges from a World's Fair Through Potato Patches, Princely Estates, and Historic Shrines. By Frederick Simpich. 413-460, *Apr. 1939*

✥ *The Reaches of New York City.* Included: Adjacent areas of Connecticut, New Jersey, and New York. *Apr. 1939*

Greater New York…Metropolis of Mankind. Aërial photo by Albert W. Stevens. Pictorial supplement. *Nov. 1933*

✥ *A Map of the Travels of George Washington.* Included: Inset of New York and the lower Hudson. *Jan. 1932*

This Giant That Is New York. By Frederick Simpich. Included: Tempo and Color of a Great City. Photos by Clifton Adams and Edwin L. Wisherd. 517-583, *Nov. 1930*

New York–The Metropolis of Mankind. By William Joseph Showalter. 1-49, *July 1918*

See also American Museum of Natural History; Gateway National Recreation Area; New York Aquarium; New York Zoological Park; United Nations; Westminster Kennel Club Dog Show

Scaffolding swathes the Statue of Liberty during renovation of the lady who greets visitors to New York City. JOHN P. FILO

NEW YORK AQUARIUM, Coney Island, New York:

Three Whales That Flew. By Carleton Ray. Photos by W. Robert Moore. 346-359, *Mar. 1962*

NEW YORK GULF:

Gomez and the New York Gulf. By L. D. Scisco. 371-373, *Aug. 1898*

NEW YORK HARBOR–The Golden Door. By Erla Zwingle. Photos by Bruce Davidson. 21-43, *July 1986*

NEW YORK STATE BARGE CANAL:

Drums to Dynamos on the Mohawk. By Frederick G. Vosburgh. Photos by B. Anthony Stewart. 67-110, *July 1947*

See also Erie Canal

NEW YORK STATE THRUWAY:

New York State's New Main Street. By Matt C. McDade. 567-618, *Nov. 1956*

NEW YORK ZOOLOGICAL PARK, New York:

Flight of the Platypuses. By David Fleay. 512-525, *Oct. 1958*

Zoo Animals Go to School. By Marion P. McCrane. Photos by W. E. Garrett. 694-706, *Nov. 1956*

Biggest Worm Farm Caters to Platypuses. By W. H. Nicholas. 269-280, *Feb. 1949*

NEW YORK ZOOLOGICAL SOCIETY:

President's Page. By Gilbert M. Grosvenor. *June 1986*

Animal Studies

Humpback Whale. 2, Jan. 1979; 466, *Apr. 1982*

Elephant Survey. 578, 584, *Nov. 1980*

Giant Brazilian Otter. 132, *July 1980*

Orangutan. 449, Oct. 1975; 835, *June 1980*

Patagonian Wildlife. 297, *Mar. 1976*

Right Whale. 578, 581, 584, Oct. 1972; 328, 329, *Mar. 1976*

Snow Leopard. 706, *Nov. 1971*

Mountain Lion. 647, *Nov. 1969*

Lion. 496, *Apr. 1969*

Weddell Seal. 56, *Jan. 1966*

James's Flamingo. 91, 93, *July 1961*

Field Station, Trinidad

Keeping House for Tropical Butterflies. By Jocelyn Crane. Photos by M. Woodbridge Williams. 193-217, *Aug. 1957*

Vilcabamba Expedition

By Parachute Into Peru's Lost World. By G. Brooks Baekeland. Photos by author and Peter R. Gimbel. 268-296, *Aug. 1964*

NEW ZEALAND:

The Captivating Kiwifruit. By Noel D. Vietmeyer. Photos by Jim Brandenburg. 683-688, *May 1987*

New Zealand: the Last Utopia? By Robert Paul Jordan. Photos by Kevin Fleming. 654-681, *May 1987*

Red Deer and Man. By T. H. Clutton-Brock. Photos by Jim Brandenburg. 538-555, *Oct. 1986*

Monstrous eye of the Coney Island Light Station scans New York Harbor, aided by Frank Schubert, in 1985 the nation's last civilian lighthouse keeper. BRUCE DAVIDSON, MAGNUM

Maoris: At Home in Two Worlds. By Yva Momatiuk and John Eastcott. 522-541, *Oct. 1984*

Maoris: Treasures of the Tradition. By Douglas Newton. Photos by Brian Brake. 542-553, *Oct. 1984*

Park at the Top of the World: Mount Everest National Park. By Rick Ridgeway. Photos by Nicholas de-Vore III. 696-725. Contents: New Zealand's contribution to the establishment of Sagarmatha National Park, Nepal–funding for five years; construction of buildings; providing advisers; assisting the Nepalese in devising a plan of management. Included: Preserving a Mountain Heritage. By Sir Edmund Hillary. 696-703, *June 1982*

New Zealand's High Country. By Yva Momatiuk and John Eastcott. 246-265, *Aug. 1978*

New Zealand's Milford Track: "Walk of a Lifetime." By Carolyn Bennett Patterson. Photos by Robert E. Gilka. 117-129, *Jan. 1978*

New Zealand's North Island: The Contented Land. By Charles McCarry. Photos by Bates Littlehales. 190-213, *Aug. 1974*

New Zealand's Bountiful South Island. By Peter Benchley. Photos by James L. Amos. 93-123, *Jan. 1972*

Captain Cook: The Man Who Mapped the Pacific. By Alan Villiers. Photos by Gordon W. Gahan. 297-349, *Sept. 1971*

In the Wake of Darwin's *Beagle*. By Alan Villiers. Photos by James L. Stanfield. 449-495, *Oct. 1969*

New Zealand's Cook Islands: Paradise in Search of a Future. By Maurice Shadbolt. Photos by William Albert Allard. 203-231, *Aug. 1967*

First Flight Across the Bottom of the World (Cape Town to Christchurch). By James R. Reedy. Photos by Otis Imboden. 454-464, *Mar. 1964*

New Zealand: Gift of the Sea. By Maurice Shadbolt. Photos by Brian Brake. 465-511, *Apr. 1962*

The Kiwi, New Zealand's Wonder Bird. By Ron J. Anderson. 395-398, *Sept. 1955*

New Zealand, Pocket Wonder World. By Howell Walker. 419-460, *Apr. 1952*

Finding an "Extinct" New Zealand Bird. By R. V. Francis Smith. 393-401, *Mar. 1952*

The British Commonwealth of Nations: "Organized Freedom" Around the World. By Eric Underwood. 485-524, *Apr. 1943*

The Making of an Anzac. By Howell Walker. 409-456, *Apr. 1942*

🌐 *Indian Ocean, including Australia, New Zealand and Malaysia. Mar. 1941*

At Home on the Oceans: Whales and Sharks Make Exciting Neighbors for a Professor's Wife, Turned Able Seaman, On a Three-year Voyage Around the World. By Edith Bauer Strout. 33-86, *July 1939*

New Zealand "Down Under." By W. Robert Moore. 165-218, *Feb. 1936*

Tuatara: "Living Fossils" Walk on Well-Nigh Inaccessible Rocky Islands off the Coast of New Zealand. By Frieda Cobb Blanchard. 649-662, *May 1935*

Waimangu and the Hot-Spring Country of New Zealand: The World's Greatest Geyser Is One of Many Natural Wonders in a Land of Inferno and Vernal Paradise. By Joseph C. Grew. 109-130, *Aug. 1925*

Hurdle Racing in Canoes: A Thrilling and Spectacular Sport Among the Maoris of New Zealand. By Walter Burke. 440-444, *May 1920*

Great Britain's Bread Upon the Waters: Canada and Her Other Daughters. By William Howard Taft. 217-272, *Mar. 1916*

The World's Highest Altitudes and First Ascents. By Charles E. Fay. 493-530, *June 1909*

The Maoris of New Zealand. 198-199, *Mar. 1907*

Problems of the Pacific–New Zealand. By Henry Demarest Lloyd. 342-352, *Sept. 1902*

See also Waitomo Caves

NEWARS:

At the Crossroads of Kathmandu. By Douglas H. Chadwick. Photos by William Thompson. 32-65, *July 1987*

Kathmandu's Remarkable Newars. By John Scofield. 269-285, *Feb. 1979*

NEWBERRY, TRUMAN H.:

Honors to the American Navy. Address by Truman H. Newberry. 77-95, *Jan. 1909*

NEWBERT, CHRIS: *Photographer*

In Hawaii's Crystal Sea, A Galaxy of Life Fills the Night. By Kenneth Brower. Photos by William R. Curtsinger and Chris Newbert. 834-847, *Dec. 1981*

NEWBURYPORT, Massachusetts:

Northeast of Boston. By Albert W. Atwood. 257-292, *Sept. 1945*

NEWCOMB, H. T.: *Author*

Geographic Literature. 29-31, Jan. 1898; 253-256, *May 1898*

NEWCOMB, SIMON: *Author*

The Scientific Work of the National Geographic Society's Eclipse Expedition to Norfolk, Va. 321-324, *Aug. 1900*

NEWELL, FREDERICK H.:

Four Prominent Geographers. 425-428, *June 1907*

Portrait. 427, *June 1907*

Secretary. xii, Feb. 19, 1892; xix-xxi, Feb. 20, 1893; ii, May 5, 1894; 70, Feb. 1898; 416, Sept. 1898; 474, *Nov. 1899*

Board of Managers. ii, xix, May 5, 1894; 414, *Sept. 1898*

International Geographic Conference in Chicago, July 27-28, 1893: Minutes of the Conference. F. H. Newell and Eliza R. Scidmore, Secretaries. 101-111, *Jan. 31, 1894*

Author

The Reclamation of the West. 15-30, *Jan. 1904*

The Limited Water Supply of the Arid Region. 438-442, *Nov. 1900*

Mesa Verde. 431-434, *Oct. 1898*

Pollution of the Potomac River. 346-351, *Dec. 1897*

The National Forest Reserves. 177-187, *June 1897*

Recent Hydrographic Work. 347-348, *Oct. 1896*

Hydrography in the United States. 146-150, *Apr. 1896*

The Arid Regions of the United States. 167-172, *Jan. 31, 1894*

Fishermen haul a net stretched between two dories pitching in the North Atlantic off the coast of Newfoundland, Canada's easternmost province. SAM ABELL

NEWELL, HOMER E.: *Author*

Surveyor: Candid Camera on the Moon. 578-592, *Oct. 1966*

NEWEST Leakey Discovery: Footprints 3.6 Million Years Old. By Mary D. Leakey. 446-457, *Apr. 1979*

NEWFOUNDLAND (Province), Canada:

Newfoundland: The Enduring Rock. By Harry Thurston. Photos by Yva Momatiuk and John Eastcott. 676-700, *May 1986*
16th-Century Basque Whalers in America. Photos by Bill Curtsinger. Paintings by Richard Schlecht. 40-71. I. Discovery in Labrador: A 16th-Century Basque Whaling Port and Its Sunken Fleet. 40-49; II. Unearthing Red Bay's Whaling History. By James A. Tuck. 50-57; III. Excavating a 400-year-old Basque Galleon. By Robert Grenier. 58-67; IV. The Indomitable Basques. By Robert Laxalt. 69-71, *July 1985*
⊕ Close-up, Canada: Quebec, Newfoundland. Text on reverse. Inset: Southern Quebec. *May 1980*
Newfoundland Trusts in the Sea. By Gary Jennings. Photos by Sam Abell. 112-141, *Jan. 1974*
Vinland Ruins Prove Vikings Found the New World. By Helge Ingstad. 708-734, *Nov. 1964*
Atlantic Odyssey: Iceland to Antarctica. By Newman Bumstead. Photos by Volkmar Wentzel. 725-780, *Dec. 1955*
School for Survival. By Curtis E. Le-May. 565-602, *May 1953*
I Sailed with Portugal's Captains Courageous. By Alan Villiers. 565-596, *May 1952*
Far North with "Captain Mac." By Miriam MacMillan. 465-513, *Oct. 1951*
Labrador Canoe Adventure. By Andrew Brown and Ralph Gray. 65-99, *July 1951*

Milestones in My Arctic Journeys. By Willie Knutsen. Included: Activities of the Search and Rescue section of the Air Force at Goose Bay. 543-570, *Oct. 1949*
Newfoundland, Canada's New Province. By Andrew H. Brown. Photos by author and Robert F. Sisson. 777-812, *June 1949*
Sea Bird Cities Off Audubon's Labrador. By Arthur A. Allen. NGS research grant. 755-774, *June 1948*
Newfoundland, North Atlantic Rampart: From the "First Base of American Defense" Planes Fly to Britain's Aid over Stout Fishing Schooners of the Grand Banks. By George Whiteley, Jr. 111-140, *July 1941*
The Sealing Saga of Newfoundland. By Robert A. Bartlett. 91-130, *July 1929*
The MacMillan Arctic Expedition Returns: U. S. Navy Planes Make First Series of Overland Flights in the Arctic and National Geographic Society Staff Obtains Valuable Data and Specimens for Scientific Study. By Donald B. MacMillan. 477-518, *Nov. 1925*
Life on the Grand Banks: An Account of the Sailor-Fishermen Who Harvest the Shoal Waters of North America's Eastern Coasts. By Frederick William Wallace. 1-28, *July 1921*
A Land of Eternal Warring. By Sir Wilfrid T. Grenfell. 665-690, *Aug. 1910*
King Herring: An Account of the World's Most Valuable Fish, the Industries It Supports, and the Part It Has Played in History. By Hugh M. Smith. 701-735, *Aug. 1909*
Introducing Reindeer into Labrador. 686, *Oct. 1907*
Origin of "Labrador." 587-588, *Oct. 1906*
Labrador Expedition. 185, *Apr. 1904*

NEWMAN, CATHY:

On Assignment in Kyongju, South Korea. *Aug. 1988*

On Assignment. *Oct. 1984*
Author
Kyongju, Where Korea Began. Photos by H. Edward Kim. 258-268, *Aug. 1988*
Pollen: Breath of Life and Sneezes. Photos by Martha Cooper. 490-521, *Oct. 1984*
Carrara Marble: Touchstone of Eternity. Photos by Pierre Boulat. 42-59, *July 1982*
Pompidou Center, Rage of Paris. Photos by Marc Riboud. 469-477, *Oct. 1980*

NEWMAN, LARRY: *Author*

Double Eagle II Has Landed! Crossing the Atlantic by Balloon. By Ben L. Abruzzo, with Maxie L. Anderson and Larry Newman. 858-882, *Dec. 1978*

NEWMAN, OLIVER P.: *Author*

Bare Feet and Burros of Haiti. 307-328, *Sept. 1944*
The Land Columbus Loved (Dominican Republic). 197-224, *Feb. 1944*

NEWMAN, PETER C.: *Author*

The Hudson's Bay Company: Canada's Fur-Trading Empire. Photos by Kevin Fleming. 192-229, *Aug. 1987*

NEWPORT, Rhode Island:

By Square-rigger from Baltic to Bicentennial. By Kenneth Garrett. Note: Newport served as host to tall and small ships from 27 nations July 1-4, 1976. 824-857, *Dec. 1976*
New England's "Lively Experiment," Rhode Island. By Robert de Roos. Photos by Fred Ward. 370-401, *Sept. 1968*
Windjamming Around New England. By Tom Horgan. Photos by Robert F. Sisson. 141-169, *Aug. 1950*
Rhode Island, Modern City-State. By George W. Long. Photos by Willard R. Culver. 137-170, *Aug. 1948*

Since colonial times peanuts have been a staple of the economy of Virginia's Newport News area. KAREN KASMAUSKI

A Soviet-built reconnaissance vehicle, disabled by rebel forces in the early 1980s, turns to rust near Christina Blandon's home in northern Nicaragua. JAMES NACHTWEY, MAGNUM

NICE, France:

NICHOLAS, WILLIAM H.: *Author*

A boy shows the despair of those living on the edge of the desert in Africa's Sahel.
STEVE McCURRY

NICHOLDS, ELIZABETH: *Author*

NICHOLS, HERBERT B.: *Author*

NICHOLS, JOHN T.: *Author*

NICHOLS, RUTH ALEXANDER: *Author*

NICHOLSON, ROBERT W.:

Artist

NICKLIN, CHARLES R., Jr.:
Photographer

NICKLIN, FLIP:

Photographer

NICOLAIDIS-KARANIKOLAS, MARIA: *Author*

NICOSIA, Cyprus:

NIEDERMEYER, OSCAR VON ("Haji Mirza Hussein"): *Author*

NIEDRACH, ROBERT J.:
Author-Photographer

Photographer

NIELSEN, LEWIS T.: *Author*

NIETSCHMANN, BERNARD and JUDITH:

At the Torres Strait. Nomination Page. *Feb. 1978*

NIEZABITOWSKA, MAŁGORZATA:

On Assignment across America. *Jan. 1988*
On Assignment in Poland. *Sept. 1986*
Author
Discovering America. Photos by Tomasz Tomaszewski. 44-79, *Jan. 1988*
Remnants: The Last Jews of Poland. Photos by Tomasz Tomaszewski. 362-389, *Sept. 1986*

NIGER:

Africa's Sahel: The Stricken Land. By William S. Ellis. Photos by Steve McCurry. 140-179, *Aug. 1987*
Niger's Wodaabe: "People of the Taboo." By Carol Beckwith. 483-509, *Oct. 1983*
The Inadan: Artisans of the Sahara. By Michael and Aubine Kirtley. 282-298, *Aug. 1979*
Drought Threatens the Tuareg World. By Victor Englebert. 544-571, *Apr. 1974*
Freedom Speaks French in Ouagadougou. By John Scofield. 153-203, *Aug. 1966*
I Joined a Sahara Salt Caravan. By Victor Englebert. 694-711, *Nov. 1965*

NIGER (River), West Africa:

The Niger: River of Sorrow, River of Hope. By Georg Gerster. 152-189, *Aug. 1975*
In the Valley of the Niger. 164, *Mar. 1908*
Return of the Hourst Niger Expedition. By Ernest de Sasseville. 24-25, *Jan. 1897*

NIGER COLONY:

Three-Wheeling Through Africa: Two Adventurers Cross the So-called Dark Continent North of Lake Chad on Motorcycles with Side Cars. By James C. Wilson. 37-92, *Jan. 1934*

NIGERIA:

Nigeria Struggles With Boom Times. By Noel Grove. Photos by Bruno Barbey. 413-444, *Mar. 1979*
The Niger: River of Sorrow, River of Hope. By Georg Gerster. 152-189, *Aug. 1975*
Beyond the Bight of Benin. By Jeannette and Maurice Fiévet. 221-253, *Aug. 1959*
Progress and Pageantry in Changing Nigeria. By W. Robert Moore. 325-365, *Sept. 1956*
Safari Through Changing Africa. By Elsie May Bell Grosvenor. Photos by Gilbert Grosvenor. 145-198, *Aug. 1953*
Nigeria: From the Bight of Benin to Africa's Desert Sands. By Helen Trybulowski Gilles. 537-568, *May 1944*
The British Commonwealth of Nations: "Organized Freedom" Around the World. By Eric Underwood. 485-524, *Apr. 1943*
Timbuktu and Beyond: Desert City of Romantic Savor and Salt Emerges

into World Life Again as Trading Post of France's Vast African Empire. By Laura C. Boulton. 631-670, *May 1941*
Trans-Africa Safari: A Motor Caravan Rolls Across Sahara and Jungle Through Realms of Dusky Potentates and the Land of Big-Lipped Women. By Lawrence Copley Thaw and Margaret Stout Thaw. 327-364, *Sept. 1938*
Three-Wheeling Through Africa: Two Adventurers Cross the So-called Dark Continent North of Lake Chad on Motorcycles with Side Cars. By James C. Wilson. 37-92, *Jan. 1934*
The Tailed People of Nigeria. 1239-1242, *Dec. 1912*
Notes on the Ekoi. By P. A. Talbot. 33-38, *Jan. 1912*
The New English Province of Northern Nigeria. 433-442, *Nov. 1904*

NIGHT Life in the Gulf Stream. By Paul A. Zahl. 391-418, *Mar. 1954*

NIGHT of Terror: Alaska Earthquake. By Tay Pryor Thomas. 142-156, *July 1964*

The **NIGHT** the Mountains Moved. By Samuel W. Matthews. Photos by J. Baylor Roberts. 329-359, *Mar. 1960*

NIGHTINGALE, FLORENCE:

The British Way. By Sir Evelyn Wrench. 421-541, *Apr. 1949*
The Symbol of Service to Mankind. By Stockton Axson. 375-390, *Apr. 1918*

The **NIGHTMARE** of Famine. Photos by Steve Raymer. 33-39, *July 1975*

NIKE (Guided Missile):

New Miracles of the Telephone Age. By Robert Leslie Conly. 87-120, *July 1954*

NIKKO, Japan:

Glimpses of Japan. By William W. Chapin. 965-1002, *Nov. 1911*

Why Nik-ko Is Beautiful. By J. H. De Forest. 300-308, *Apr. 1908*

NIKOLAEVSK: A Bit of Old Russia Takes Root in Alaska. By Jim Rearden. Photos by Charles O'Rear. 401-425, *Sept. 1972*

NILE (River and Valley), Africa:

A Change of Fortunes on the River Nile. Geographica. *Dec. 1988*
Journey Up the Nile. By Robert Caputo. Included: Africa's River of Legend, a foldout map of the Nile; A Dam Against Famine. By Farouk El-Baz. 577-633, *May 1985*
Abu Simbel's Ancient Temples Reborn. By Georg Gerster. 724-744, *May 1969*
Saving the Ancient Temples at Abu Simbel. By Georg Gerster. Paintings by Robert W. Nicholson. 694-742, *May 1966*
The River Nile. By Bruce Brander. 207 pages. *1966*
Yankee Cruises the Storied Nile. By Irving and Electa Johnson. Photos by Winfield Parks. 583-633, *May 1965*
Nile Valley, Land of the Pharaohs. Atlas series. Text on reverse. *May 1965*
Threatened Treasures of the Nile. By Georg Gerster. 587-621, *Oct. 1963*
Africa: Countries of the Nile. Atlas series. *Oct. 1963*
Kayaks Down the Nile. By John M. Goddard. 697-732, *May 1955*
Safari from Congo to Cairo. By Elsie May Bell Grosvenor. Photos by Gilbert Grosvenor. 721-771, *Dec. 1954*
South in the Sudan. By Harry Hoogstraal. 249-272, *Feb. 1953*
By Felucca Down the Nile: Giant Dams Rule Egypt's Lifeline River, Yet Village Life Goes On As It Did in the Time of the Pharaohs. By Willard Price. 435-476, *Apr. 1940*
The Land of Egypt: A Narrow Green Strip of Fertility Stretching for a

Roving band of musicians and dancers pause before entertaining crowds admiring cherry trees along a Japanese road in 1911. WILLIAM W. CHAPIN

Thousand Miles Through Walls of Desert. By Alfred Pearce Dennis. 271-298, *Mar. 1926*

Along the Nile, Through Egypt and the Sudan. By Frederick Simpich. 379-410, *Oct. 1922*

The Barrage of the Nile. By Day Allen Willey. 175-184, *Feb. 1910*

NILE CROCODILE:

A Bad Time to Be a Crocodile. By Rick Gore. Photos by Jonathan Blair. 90-115, *Jan. 1978*

NILSON, ELIZABETH W.: *Author*

Rural Sweden Through American Eyes: A Visitor in Peacetime Finds Warmth, Welcome, and Strange Folkways On a Century-old Farm. 795-822, *June 1940*

NILSSON, LENNART:

On Assignment. *June 1986*

Photographer

Our Immune System: The Wars Within. By Peter Jaret. Illustrations text by Larry Kohl. 702-735, *June 1986*

Fishing in the Lofotens. 377-388, *Mar. 1947*

NIMBUS (Weather Satellite Series):

Studying Wildlife by Satellite. By Frank Craighead, Jr., and John Craighead. 120-123, *Jan. 1973*

Extraordinary Photograph Shows Earth Pole to Pole. Photos by Nimbus I. 190-193, *Feb. 1965*

NIMITZ, CHESTER W.:

How One of The Society's Maps (Pacific Ocean) Saved a Precious Cargo. 844, *June 1947*

Author

Your Navy as Peace Insurance. 681-736, *June 1946*

NIMKHERA (Village), Madhya Pradesh, India:

Purdah in India: Life Behind the Veil. By Doranne Wilson Jacobson. 270-286, *Aug. 1977*

NIMMO, JOSEPH, Jr.: *Author*

The Proposed American Interoceanic Canal in its Commercial Aspects. 297-310, *Aug. 1899*

NIÑA (Caravel):

15th-Century Manuscript Yields First Look at *Niña*. By Eugene Lyon. 601-605, *Nov. 1986*

⊕ *Where Did Columbus Discover America? New Evidence Marks Landfall at Samana Cay.* Included: Threading the Islands: Which Track Fits?; Samana Cay and the Columbus Log. *Nov. 1986*

NIÑA (Schooner):

Down East to Nova Scotia. By Winfield Parks. 853-879, *June 1964*

NINE-BANDED ARMADILLOS:

The Astonishing Armadillo. By Eleanor E. Storrs. Photos by Bianca Lavies. 820-830, *June 1982*

900 Years Ago: the Norman Conquest. By Kenneth M. Setton. Photos by

George F. Mobley. 206-251, *Aug. 1966*

1940 Paradox in Hong Kong. By Frederick Simpich. 531-558, *Apr. 1940*

1988: The Trustees Who Have Carried On the Tradition. By Melvin M. Payne. 38-43, *Jan. 1988*

NINEVEH (Ancient City):

Ancient Mesopotamia: A Light That Did Not Fail. By E. A. Speiser. Paintings by H. M. Herget. 41-105, *Jan. 1951*

NININGER, ROBERT D.: *Author*

Hunting Uranium Around the World. Photos by Volkmar Wentzel. 533-558, *Oct. 1954*

NIPPUR (Ancient City):

Excavations at Nippur. 392, *Oct. 1900*

NISBET, IAN: *Author*

Friend of the Wind: The Common Tern. Photos by Hope Alexander. 234-247, *Aug. 1973*

NITOBE, INAZU:

The National Geographic Society (Speech by Inazu Nitobe). 272-298, *Mar. 1912*

NITRATE INDUSTRY:

A Longitudinal Journey Through Chile. By Harriet Chalmers Adams. 219-273, *Sept. 1922*

NIUAFOŌ (Island), Tonga Islands:

Living on a Volcano: An Unspoiled Patch of Polynesia Is Niuafoō, Nicknamed "Tin Can Island" by Stamp Collectors. By Thomas A. Jaggar. 91-106, *July 1935*

Throngs of Poles press forth to greet Vice President Richard M. Nixon during a 1959 Warsaw visit. ELLIOTT ERWITT, MAGNUM

NIXON, RICHARD M.: *Author*

Russia as I Saw It. Photos by B. Anthony Stewart. 715-750, *Dec. 1959*

NIZHNI NOVGOROD. *See* Gorki

NO Man's Land–Spitzbergen. 455-458, *July 1907*

NO Place to Run: The Hmong of Laos. By W. E. Garrett. 78-111, *Jan. 1974*

NO Way to Run a Desert: The Rising Great Salt Lake. By Rick Gore. Photos by Jim Richardson. 694-719, *June 1985*

NOAA. *See* National Oceanic and Atmospheric Administration

NOATAK (River), Alaska:

Our Wild and Scenic Rivers: The Noatak. By John M. Kauffmann. Photos by Sam Abell. 52-59, *July 1977*

NOBILE, UMBERTO: *Author*

Navigating the "Norge" from Rome to the North Pole and Beyond: The Designer and Pilot of the First Dirigible to Fly Over the Top of the World Describes a Thrilling Voyage of More Than 8,000 Miles. 177-215, *Aug. 1927*

NOBLECOURT, CHRISTIANE DESROCHES: *Author*

Tutankhamun's Golden Trove. Photos by F. L. Kenett. 625-646, *Oct. 1963*

NOËL HUME, IVOR:

On Assignment. *Jan. 1982*

Nomination Page. *May 1979*

Author

New Clues to an Old Mystery (Virginia's Wolstenholme Towne). Photos by Ira Block. Paintings by Richard Schlecht. 53-77, *Jan. 1982*

First Look at a Lost Virginia Settlement (Martin's Hundred). Photos by Ira Block. Paintings by Richard Schlecht. 735-767, *June 1979*

"NOICEST Parrt o'England"–the Cotswolds. By James Cerruti. Photos by Adam Woolfitt. 846-869, *June 1974*

NOLAN, JOHN E. H.: *Author*

Life in the Land of the Basques. Photos by Justin Locke. 147-186, *Feb. 1954*

Silkworms in England Spin for the Queen. 689-704, *May 1953*

Pilgrimage to Holy Island and the Farnes. 547-570, *Oct. 1952*

Author-Photographer

Caldy, the Monks' Island. 564-578, *Oct. 1955*

NOMACHI, KAZUYOSHI:

Photographer

Oasis of Art in the Sahara. By Henri Lhote. Contents: Rock paintings of Tassili-n-Ajjer, Algeria. 180-191, *Aug. 1987*

NOMAD (Ketch):

Nomad Sails Long Island Sound. By Thomas Horgan. 295-338, *Sept. 1957*

Down East Cruise. By Tom Horgan. Photos by Luis Marden. 329-369, *Sept. 1952*

Windjamming Around New England.

By Tom Horgan. Photos by Robert F. Sisson. 141-169, *Aug. 1950*

NOMAD in Alaska's Outback. By Thomas J. Abercrombie. 540-567, *Apr. 1969*

NOMADS:

Niger's Wodaabe: "People of the Taboo." By Carol Beckwith. 483-509, *Oct. 1983*

Nomads of China's West. By Galen Rowell. Photos by the author and Harold A. Knutson. Contents: Gologs. 244-263, *Feb. 1982*

I Live With the Eskimos. By Guy Mary-Rousseliere. 188-217, *Feb. 1971*

■■*Nomads of the World.* 199 pages. *1971*

The Danakil: Nomads of Ethiopia's Wasteland. By Victor Englebert. 186-211, *Feb. 1970*

Afghanistan: Crossroad of Conquerors. By Thomas J. Abercrombie. 297-345, *Sept. 1968*

Abraham, the Friend of God. By Kenneth MacLeish. Photos by Dean Conger. 739-789, *Dec. 1966*

Saudi Arabia: Beyond the Sands of Mecca. By Thomas J. Abercrombie. 1-53, *Jan. 1966*

We Dwelt in Kashgai Tents. By Jean and Franc Shor. 805-832, *June 1952*

Journey Into Troubled Iran. By George W. Long. Photos by J. Baylor Roberts. Included: Bakhtiari, Kashgais, Kurds, Lurs. 425-464, *Oct. 1951*

Nomads of the Far North (Indians and Eskimos). By Matthew W. Stirling. Paintings by W. Langdon Kihn. 471-504, *Oct. 1949*

Mountain Tribes of Iran and Iraq. By Harold Lamb. 385-408, *Mar. 1946*

New Road to Asia. By Owen Lattimore. 641-676, *Dec. 1944*

The Nomads of Arctic Lapland: Mysterious Little People of a Land of the Midnight Sun Live Off the Country Above the Arctic Circle. By Clyde Fisher. 641-676, *Nov. 1939*

With the Nomads of Central Asia: A Summer's Sojourn in the Tekes Valley, Plateau Paradise of Mongol and Turkic Tribes. By Edward Murray. Paintings and drawings by Alexandre Iacovleff. 1-57, *Jan. 1936*

Nomad Life and Fossil Treasures of Mongolia. Photos by J. B. Shackelford. 669-700, *June 1933*

The People of the Wilderness: The Mongols, Once the Terror of All Christendom, Now a Primitive, Harmless, Nomad Race. By Adam Warwick. 507-551, *May 1921*

See also Aboriginal People of Australia; Bakhtiari Tribespeople; Bedouin; Brahui Tribespeople; Bushmen; Gypsies; Ice Age Man; Kazaks; Kirghiz; Lapps; Masai Tribespeople; Tuareg Tribespeople; Turkomans

NOMADS Among the Butterflies. Paintings by Hashime Murayama. Photos by Willard R. Culver. 569-584, *May 1937*

NOMADS' Land: A Journey Through Tibet. By Sorrel Wilby. 764-785, *Dec. 1987*

A child of the nomadic Golog people of China sports a Communist military-style hat, a reminder of past fighting between Golog and Chinese forces. GALEN ROWELL

The **NOMADS** of Arctic Lapland: Mysterious Little People of a Land of the Midnight Sun Live Off the Country Above the Arctic Circle. By Clyde Fisher. 641-676, *Nov. 1939*

NOME, Alaska:

The Nome Gold Fields. 384-385, *May 1908*

The Cape Nome Gold District. By F. C. Schrader. 15-23, *Jan. 1900*

NOME, Cape, Alaska:

Origin of the Name "Cape Nome." By George Davidson. 398, *Nov. 1901*

The Cape Nome Gold District. By F. C. Schrader. 15-23, *Jan. 1900*

NOMINATION PAGE:

National forests. *Aug. 1982*

Susman, Randall L., at Lomako River, Zaire. *July 1982*

Boraiko, Allen A. *June 1982*

Nuechterlein, Gary L. *May 1982*

Dale, Bruce, in Death Valley, California. *Apr. 1982*

Allard, William Albert, in Machu Picchu, Peru. *Mar. 1982*

Arden, Harvey, in Machu Picchu, Peru. *Mar. 1982*

Bingham, Hiram, in Peru. *Mar. 1982*

South, Stanley, in South Carolina. *Feb. 1982*

Jenkins, Farish A., Jr. *Jan. 1982*

McDowell, Bart, on the Indian Ocean. *Sept. 1981*

Erim, Kenan T., in Aphrodisias, Turkey. *Aug. 1981*

Payne, Melvin M., in Aphrodisias, Turkey. *Aug. 1981*

Abercrombie, Lynn and Thomas J., in Oman. *July 1981*

Clark, Eugenie. *June 1981*

Doubilet, David, in Australia. *June 1981*

Nicklin, Flip. *June 1981*

Schledermann, Peter, in Ellesmere Island. *May 1981*

Emerson, Ross. *Apr. 1981*

Gore, Rick. *Apr. 1981*

Jeffery, David. *Apr. 1981*

Rogers, Elie and Lesley. *Apr. 1981*

Sugar, James. *Apr. 1981*

Kennedy, Robert S. *Mar. 1981*

Rettig, Neil L. *Mar. 1981*

Salb, Wolfgang A. *Mar. 1981*

Grove, Noel, in Bangkok. *Feb. 1981*

Raymer, Steve, in San Diego. *Feb. 1981*

Cupp, David F., at Mount St. Helens, Washington. *Jan. 1981*

Findley, Rowe, at Mount St. Helens, Washington. *Jan. 1981*

Truman, Harry R., at Mount St. Helens, Washington. *Jan. 1981*

NGS membership. *Oct. 1980*

Douglas-Hamilton, Iain and Oria, in Africa. *Sept. 1980*

Bond, William H. *Aug. 1980*

Kristof, Emory. *Aug. 1980*

Royce, W. Allan. *Aug. 1980*

Weaver, Kenneth F. *Aug. 1980*

Dominguez Sanchez, Genaro. *July 1980*

Wilkerson, S. Jeffrey K. *July 1980*

Dale, Bruce. *June 1980*

Edwards, Mike. *June 1980*

Everingham, John. *May 1980*

Garrett, W. E. *May 1980*

Galdikas, Biruté, in Borneo. *Apr. 1980*

Voorhies, Michael R., in Nebraska. *Mar. 1980*

Gore, Rick, in Lanzhou, China. *Feb. 1980*

Park Chung Hee. *Jan. 1980*

Lockwood, C. C. *Sept. 1979*

Grove, Noel. *Aug. 1979*

Raymer, Steve. *Aug. 1979*

Morrison, R.I.G. *July 1979*

Harvey, David Alan. *June 1979*

Muir, John. *June 1979*

Noël Hume, Ivor. *May 1979*

Richie, Thomas. *Apr. 1979*

Southwick, Charles. *Apr. 1979*

Taylor, Henry. *Apr. 1979*

Teas, Jane. *Apr. 1979*

Bankoff, H. Arthur. *Mar. 1979*
Winter, Frederick A. *Mar. 1979*
Dillon, Luther E. *Feb. 1979*
McCausland, Bill. *Feb. 1979*
Bartlett, Des and Jen. *Jan. 1979*
Earle, Sylvia. *Oct. 1978*
Payne, Roger. *Oct. 1978*
Blair, James P. *Sept. 1978*
Conger, Dean. *Sept. 1978*
Gregg, Taylor. *Sept. 1978*
Harvey, David Alan. *Sept. 1978*
Jensen, James. *Aug. 1978*
Ostrom, John H. *Aug. 1978*
Garrett, Wilbur E., at the Grand
   Canyon. *July 1978*
Grosvenor, Gilbert H. *July 1978*
Duplaix, Nicole. *June 1978*
Toth, Tibor G. *May 1978*
Washburn, Barbara and Bradford, at
   the Grand Canyon. *May 1978*
Prestwich, Glenn D. *Apr. 1978*
Dyson, Robert, Jr., in Iran. *Mar. 1978*
Sumner, William, in Iran. *Mar. 1978*
Nietschmann, Bernard and Judith, at
   the Torres Strait. *Feb. 1978*
Blair, Jonathan, in Florida. *Jan. 1978*
Gore, Rick, in Florida. *Jan. 1978*
Werner, Dagmar I. *Oct. 1977*
Clark, Timothy W. *Sept. 1977*
Dale, Bruce. *Aug. 1977*
Royce, W. Allan. *Aug. 1977*
Canby, Thomas Y., in Explorers Hall.
   July 1977
Graves, William, in Japan. *July 1977*
Putman, John J., in Moscow. *July 1977*
Weaver, Kenneth F. *July 1977*
White, Peter T. *July 1977*
Gillison, David and Gillian. *June 1977*
Dorr, John F. *May 1977*
Pinny, Michael, in Pilsdon Pen,
   England. *May 1977*
Ross, Anne. *May 1977*
Ziskin, Joel, in Nepal. *Apr. 1977*
Cooney, John. *Mar. 1977*
Habachi, Labib. *Mar. 1977*
Silverman, David. *Mar. 1977*
Bass, George F. *Feb. 1977*
Cassils, John. *Feb. 1977*
Mutch, Thomas. *Jan. 1977*
Patterson, William. *Jan. 1977*
Smith, William W. *Jan. 1977*
Stucky, Rex. *Jan. 1977*
Hodgson, Bryan. *Oct. 1976*
Raymer, Steve. *Oct. 1976*
Breeden, Stanley. *Sept. 1976*
Putman, John J., in India. *Sept. 1976*
Chandler, Alvin M. *Aug. 1976*
Kristof, Emory. *Aug. 1976*
Chagnon, Napoleon A. *July 1976*
Garrett, Wilbur E., in Guatemala City.
   June 1976
McDowell, Bart, in Guatemala.
   June 1976
Madden, Robert W., in Guatemala.
   June 1976
Dale, Bruce. *May 1976*
Garcia, Mario Enrique. *May 1976*
Magellan, Ferdinand. *May 1976*
Earle, Sylvia. *Apr. 1976*
Hugho, Kimo. *Mar. 1976*
Kane, Herb. *Mar. 1976*
Bartlett, Des and Jen. *Feb. 1976*
Curtsinger, Bill. *Jan. 1976*
Lavigne, David. *Jan. 1976*
Merdsoy, Bora. *Jan. 1976*
Clark, Bob. *Oct. 1975*
Parks, Winfield. *Sept. 1975*

Putman, John J. *Sept. 1975*
Baumann, J. Bruce. *Aug. 1975*
Blair, James P. *Aug. 1975*
Canby, Thomas Y. *Aug. 1975*
deVore, Nicholas III. *Aug. 1975*
Kim, H. Edward. *Aug. 1975*
Laxalt, Robert. *Aug. 1975*
Weaver, Kenneth F. *Aug. 1975*
Lewis, David. *July 1975*
Sisson, Robert F. *June 1975*
Ellis, David H. *May 1975*
Eighteen months of NGM. *Apr. 1975*
Diamond, Billy, in Canada. *Mar. 1975*
Ward, Fred. *Mar. 1975*
Woodson, LeRoy, Jr. *Feb. 1975*
Gehrels, Tom. *Jan. 1975*
Pesek, Ludek. *Jan. 1975*
Weaver, Kenneth F. *Jan. 1975*
Royal Family of Bhutan. *Oct. 1974*
Todd, Burt Kerr, in Bhutan. *Oct. 1974*
White, John Claude, in Bhutan.
   Oct. 1974
Canby, Thomas Y. *Sept. 1974*
Mazzatenta, O. Louis. *Sept. 1974*
Schneeberger, Jon. *Sept. 1974*
Clark, Eugenie. *Aug. 1974*
Kim, H. Edward. *July 1974*
Ellis, William S. *June 1974*
Skylab. *May 1974*
Weaver, Kenneth F. *Apr. 1974*
Englebert, Victor, in Sahara. *Mar. 1974*
Irwin, Colin. *Feb. 1974*
Everingham, John, in Laos. *Jan. 1974*
Garrett, Wilbur E. *Jan. 1974*
Vang Pao. *Jan. 1974*
Michaud, Roland and Sabrina, in
   Afghanistan. *Oct. 1973*
McIntyre, Loren. *Sept. 1973*
Bartlett, Des and Jen. *Aug. 1973*
Judge, Joseph, and family. *Aug. 1973*
MacInnis, Joseph B., in the Arctic.
   Aug. 1973
Anderson, Carolyn H., in Heimaey,
   Iceland. *July 1973*
Grove, Noel, in Heimaey, Iceland.
   July 1973
Kristof, Emory, in Heimaey, Iceland.
   July 1973
Patton, Robert S., in Heimaey, Iceland.
   July 1973
Cano, José. *June 1973*
White, Peter T. *June 1973*
Rathbun, Galen B. *May 1973*
Galdikas-Brindamour, Biruté, in
   Borneo. *Apr. 1973*
Yen, Harry S. C. *Mar. 1973*
Brauns, Claus-Dieter, in Bangladesh.
   Feb. 1973
Beg, Tulah. *Jan. 1973*
Leaf, Alexander. *Jan. 1973*
Tarba, Temur. *Jan. 1973*
Tarkil, Markhti. *Jan. 1973*
Key deer, in Florida. *Oct. 1972*
Klimstra, W. D. *Oct. 1972*
Wheatcroft, Wilson, in New Guinea.
   Sept. 1972
Gardner, Beatrice T. and R. Allen.
   Aug. 1972
Washoe (chimpanzee). *Aug. 1972*
Abercrombie, Thomas J., in Saudi
   Arabia. *July 1972*
Schwartz, Douglas W., at the Grand
   Canyon. *June 1972*
Doyle, Gerald A. *May 1972*
Pinto, Dee, in South Africa. *May 1972*
Voss, Gilbert L. *Apr. 1972*
Matternes, Jay H. *Mar. 1972*

Estes, Richard D. and Runhild, in
   Africa. *Feb. 1972*
Polunin, Ivan. *Jan. 1972*
Fossey, Dian. *Oct. 1971*
Cook, James. *Sept. 1971*
Villiers, Alan. *Sept. 1971*
Conger, Dean, in the Philippines.
   Aug. 1971
Elizalde, Manuel. *Aug. 1971*
MacLeish, Kenneth, in the Philippines.
   Aug. 1971
Shepard, Alan B., Jr. *July 1971*
Andrews, E. Wyllys. *June 1971*
Alcock, Leslie, in Wales. *May 1971*
Zahl, Paul A. *Apr. 1971*
Marden, Luis, in Brazil. *Mar. 1971*
Ruschi, Augusto, in Brazil. *Mar. 1971*
MacFarland, Craig and Jan, in the Galá-
   pagos Islands. *Feb. 1971*
Reeder, William G., in the Galápagos
   Islands. *Feb. 1971*
Southeast Asia map. *Jan. 1971*
Moseley, Michael E. *Oct. 1970*
Walcott, Charles. *Sept. 1970*
Amos, William H. *Aug. 1970*
Pesek, Ludek. *Aug. 1970*
Weaver, Kenneth F. *Aug. 1970*
Carmichael, Leonard. *July 1970*
Griswold, Mary S. *July 1970*
Sisson, Robert F. *July 1970*
Tiemann, Darwin L. *July 1970*
Geographos (Asteroid). *June 1970*
Mintz, Betty. *June 1970*
Allen, Gerald R. *May 1970*
Baker, Bruce A. *May 1970*
Randall, John E. *May 1970*
Parsons, Lee A., in Guatemala.
   Apr. 1970
Shook, Edwin M. *Apr. 1970*
Diamond, Jared, at Mount Yule, New
   Guinea. *Mar. 1970*
Kunstadter, Peter, in Thailand.
   Feb. 1970
Craighead, John. *Jan. 1970*
Leakey, Richard E. *Jan. 1970*
Alvarez, Luis W. *Oct. 1969*
Chephren, Pharaoh. *Oct. 1969*
Gray, Ralph. *Sept. 1969*
Grosvenor, Melville Bell. *Sept. 1969*
Payne, Melvin M. *Sept. 1969*
Starck, Walter A. *Aug. 1969*
Carmichael, Leonard. *July 1969*
McGahan, Jerome. *June 1969*
Ross, Edward S. *May 1969*
Erim, Kenan T., in Aphrodisias,
   Turkey. *Apr. 1969*
Riopelle, Arthur J. *Mar. 1969*
Snowflake (gorilla). *Mar. 1969*
Webb, S. David. *Feb. 1969*
Cook, David W. *Jan. 1969*
Wilson, Barry. *Oct. 1968*
King, Mariel. *Oct. 1968*
Rehder, Harald, in the South Pacific.
   Oct. 1968
Richert, Thomas. *Oct. 1968*
Abell, Paul, in Ethiopia. *Sept. 1968*
Leakey, Richard E., in Ethiopia.
   Sept. 1968
Hartman, D. S., at Crystal River, Flori-
   da. *Aug. 1968*
Bass, George F., in Turkey. *July 1968*
Arnold, David, at Willamette National
   Forest. *June 1968*
Johnston, Jay, at Willamette National
   Forest. *June 1968*
Jones, Stuart E., at the Willamette
   National Forest. *June 1968*

Mahieu, Ted. *June 1968*
Schaller, George B., in Serengeti, Tanzania. *May 1968*
Haynes, C. Vance. *Apr. 1968*
Heard, William R. *Mar. 1968*
Idyll, Clarence P. *Mar. 1968*
Sisson, Robert F. *Mar. 1968*
Morris, William J. *Feb. 1968*
Fox, Evelyn. *Jan. 1968*
Ripley, S. Dillon, in Bhutan. *Oct. 1967*
Fox, Robert B., in Philippines. *Sept. 1967*
Townsend, Charles and Jean, in the Philippines. *Sept. 1967*
Craighead, Charles, Derek, Frank, and John. *Aug. 1967*
Judge, Joseph, in Florence. *July 1967*
Nicholson, Robert W. *July 1967*
Smith, Thomas R. *July 1967*
King Bhumibol and Queen Sirikit of Thailand. *June 1967*
Conger, Dean, in Thailand. *June 1967*
White, Peter T., in Thailand. *June 1967*
Clinch, Nicholas, at Vinson Massif. *May 1967*
Silverstein, Samuel, at Vinson Massif. *May 1967*
Wahlstrom, Richard, at Vinson Massif. *May 1967*
Peterson, Roger Tory. *Apr. 1967*
Jonch Cuspinera, Antonio. *Mar. 1967*
Riopelle, Arthur J. *Mar. 1967*
Snowflake (gorilla). *Mar. 1967*
Miller, Maynard M., in Alaska. *Feb. 1967*
Payne, Executive Vice-President and Mrs. Melvin M., at Taku Glacier, Alaska. *Feb. 1967*
Grazzini, Athos D. *Jan. 1967*
Peele, William T. *Jan. 1967*
Doig, Desmond, in Nepal. *Oct. 1966*
Hilger, Sister Mary Inez. *Sept. 1966*
Boswell, Victor R., Jr. *Aug. 1966*
Ford, Milton A. *Aug. 1966*
Griswold, Mary S. *Aug. 1966*
Allard, William Albert. *July 1966*
Blair, James P. *July 1966*
Boyer, David S. *July 1966*
Churchill, Winston. *July 1966*
Dale, Bruce. *July 1966*
Garrett, Wilbur E. *July 1966*
Moldvay, Albert. *July 1966*
Parks, Winfield. *July 1966*
Smith, Thomas R. *July 1966*
Edwards, Walter M. *June 1966*
Knight, Royce. *June 1966*
Wrather, William E., in Arizona. *June 1966*
Gerster, Georg, at Abu Simbel. *May 1966*
Cousteau, Philippe. *Apr. 1966*
Grosvenor, Gilbert M. *Mar. 1966*
Senanayake, Dudley (Prime Minister of Ceylon). *Mar. 1966*
Conger, Dean, in Mongolia. *Feb. 1966*
Conger, Lee, in Ulan Bator, Mongolia. *Feb. 1966*
Manion, Esther Ann. *Oct. 1965*
Booth, Cynthia, in Kenya. *Sept. 1965*
Carmichael, Leonard. *Sept. 1965*
Cousteau, Jacques-Yves. *Sept. 1965*
Goodall, Jane, at Gombe Stream Game Reserve, Tanzania. *Sept. 1965*
Leakey, Louis S. B., at Olduvai Gorge, Tanzania. *Sept. 1965*
Payne, Melvin M., in Tanzania. *Sept. 1965*

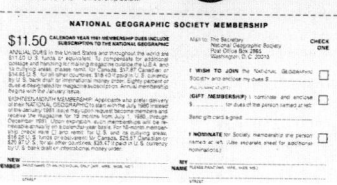

Nuclear energy coverage wins journalism award

Journalism award citation in the August 1980 issue gave readers reason to nominate a friend for Society membership.

Stewart, T. Dale. *Sept. 1965*
Brinkley, David. *Aug. 1965*
Schreider, Frank and Helen, in the Great Rift Valley. *July 1965*
Shor, Franc, in Budapest. *June 1965*
Goell, Theresa, at the tomb of Antiochus I. *May 1965*
Grant, Ulysses S., 3rd. *Apr. 1965*
Poggenpohl, Andrew. *Apr. 1965*
Estes, Richard D. *Mar. 1965*
Ross, Edward S. *Feb. 1965*
Chamberlin, Wellman. *Jan. 1965*
Hart, Catherine. *Jan. 1965*
Peele, William. *Jan. 1965*
Henderson, E. P. *Oct. 1964*
Mason, Brian H. *Oct. 1964*
Zahl, Paul A. *Sept. 1964*
Baekeland, G. Brooks. *Aug. 1964*
Gimbel, Peter R., in Peru. *Aug. 1964*
NGM reprints. *July 1964*
White, Peter T. *June 1964*
Carmichael, Leonard. *May 1964*
Shakespeare, William. *Apr. 1964*
Wright, Louis B. *Apr. 1964*
Gray, Ralph. *Mar. 1964*
Abercrombie, Thomas J., in Yemen. *Feb. 1964*
Mobley, George F. *Jan. 1964*
Nicholson, Robert W. *Nov. 1963*
Battaglia, Lee. *Oct. 1963*
Cooke, Hope (Crown Princess of Sikkim). *Oct. 1963*
Namgyal, Palden Thondup (Crown Prince of Sikkim). *Oct. 1963*
Namgyal, Sir Tashi (Denjong Chogyal, Maharaja of Sikkim). *Oct. 1963*
Martin, Elinor R. *Sept. 1963*
Montoya, Porfirio, and family. *Aug. 1963*
Kenyon, Kathleen. *July 1963*
Bass, George F. *June 1963*
Garrett, Wilbur E. *May 1963*
Kilbracken, Lord (John Godley, Third Baron Kilbracken). *Apr. 1963*
Stenuit, Robert and Mrs. *Apr. 1963*
Macbeth, James B. *Mar. 1963*

Zahl, Paul A. *Mar. 1963*
Abercrombie, Thomas J., at Angel Falls. *Feb. 1963*
Oliver, James A. *Jan. 1963*
Sisson, Robert F. *Jan. 1963*
Grosvenor, Melville Bell. *Nov. 1962*
Severy, Merle. *Nov. 1962*
Chapelle, Dickey, in Vietnam. *Oct. 1962*
Garrett, Wilbur E. *Oct. 1962*
Booth, Cynthia, in Nairobi, Kenya. *Sept. 1962*
Bass, George F. *Aug. 1962*
Womer, Susan. *Aug. 1962*
Schreider, Frank and Helen. *July 1962*
Fletcher, John E., in Peru. *June 1962*
McDowell, Bart, in Peru. *June 1962*
Moldvay, Albert. *May 1962*
Scott, Robert Falcon, at the South Pole. *May 1962*
Tyree, David M., in the Antarctic. *May 1962*
Scofield, John. *Apr. 1962*
Calleros, Cleofas. *Mar. 1962*
Conger, Dean, in Mongolia. *Feb. 1962*
Douglas, Mercedes and William O. *Feb. 1962*
Mercury missions. *Jan. 1962*
McDonald, Edwin A., in the Antarctic. *Nov. 1961*
Abercrombie, Thomas J., on Easter Island. *Oct. 1961*
La Fay, Howard, on Easter Island. *Oct. 1961*
Conger, Dean. *Sept. 1961*
Marden, Luis. *Sept. 1961*
Shepard, Alan B., Jr. *Sept. 1961*
Gilliard, E. Thomas, in British Guiana (Guyana). *Aug. 1961*
Schultz, Harald, in Brazil. *July 1961*
Bishop, Barry C., in the Himalaya. *June 1961*
Mulgrew, Peter, in the Himalaya. *June 1961*
Chamberlin, Wellman. *May 1961*
Lothers, John. *May 1961*
Moore, W. Robert, at Angkor. *Apr. 1961*
Booth, Windsor Peyton. *Mar. 1961*
Grimmer, J. Lear, in British Guiana (Guyana). *Feb. 1961*
Williams, M. Woodbridge, in British Guiana (Guyana). *Feb. 1961*
Bumstead, Newman. *Jan. 1961*
Nicholson, Robert W. *Jan. 1961*
Beach, Edward L. *Nov. 1960*
Roberts, Joseph Baylor. *Nov. 1960*
Conway, William G. *Oct. 1960*
Littlehales, Bates, in the Bolivian Andes. *Oct. 1960*
Gray, Ralph. *Sept. 1960*
NGS membership. *Aug. 1960*
Hayes, Alden. *July 1960*
Truslow, Frederick Kent, in the Everglades. *June 1960*
Carmichael, Leonard. *May 1960*
La Gorce, John Oliver. *May 1960*
Fisher, Allan C., Jr. *Apr. 1960*
Schreider, Frank. *Mar. 1960*
Schreider, Helen, and the Maharaja of Patiala. *Mar. 1960*
Singh, Sir Yadavindra, Maharaja of Patiala, in Punjab, India. *Mar. 1960*
Hagen, Toni, and family, in Nepal. *Feb. 1960*
Cousteau, Jacques-Yves. *Jan. 1960*
Craighead, Frank and John. *Nov. 1959*

M
N

The saga of the Norman Conquest of England unfolds on the 231-foot Bayeux Tapestry. MILTON A. FORD AND VICTOR R. BOSWELL, JR., BOTH NGS

Evidence of restless North America, the Rio Grande rift in New Mexico continues to widen from volcanic activity and movement of the earth's crust. JAMES A. SUGAR, BLACK STAR

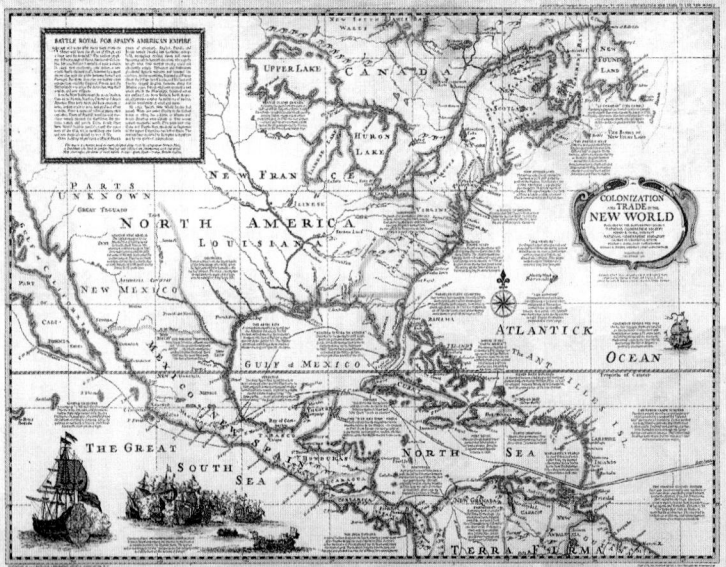

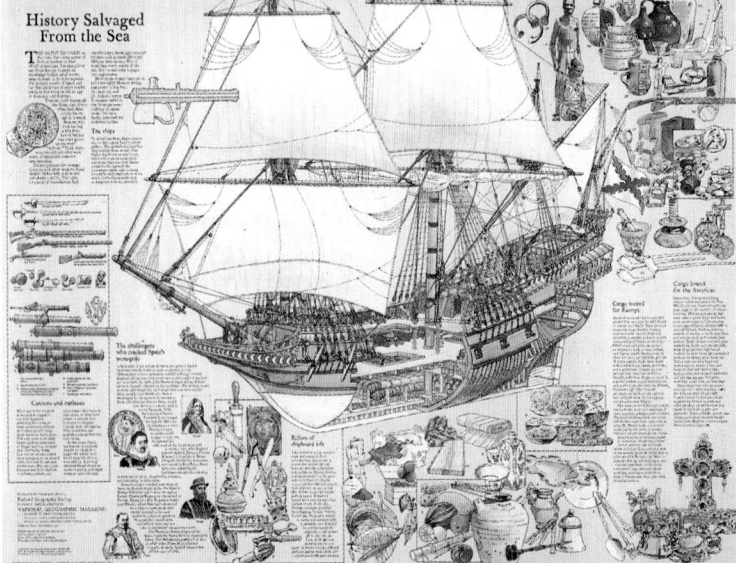

Based on charts designed about 1720 by Dutch cartographer Herman Moll, this December 1977 supplement map outlined the growth of colonies and trade in the New World.

Raymond Davis sells produce from his pickup truck at the State Farmer's Market in Raleigh, North Carolina. BILL WEEMS

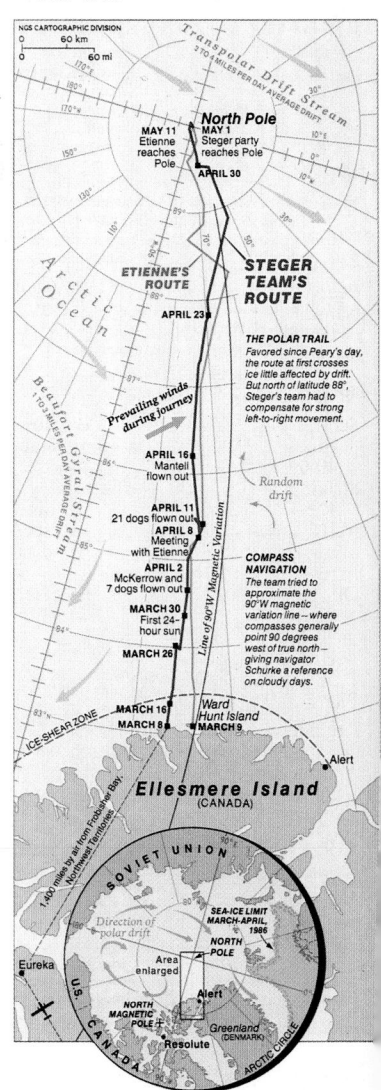

Similar paths led two expeditions to the North Pole in 1986: a six-person dogsled team and a solo skier.

For the first time since Peary's 1909 attempt, a 1986 expedition reached the North Pole by dogsled without resupplying. WILL STEGER

Peary on the North Pole. 29, *Jan. 1903*
Nansen's Polar Expedition. By A. W. Greely. 98-101, *Mar. 1896*
See also Arctic Regions

NORTH SEA:

Scotland, Ghosts, and Glory. By Rowe Findley. Photos by Peter Carmichael. 40-69, *July 1984*
Striking It Rich in the North Sea. By Rick Gore. Photos by Dick Durrance II. Included: Map showing five sectors of national rights over oil and gas reserves. 519-549, *Apr. 1977*
Oil, the Dwindling Treasure. By Noel Grove. Photos by Emory Kristof. 792-825, *June 1974*
◼ Holland Against the Sea. 588A-588B, *Apr. 1970*
Pilgrimage to Holy Island and the Farnes. By John E. H. Nolan. 547-570, *Oct. 1952*
Thumbs Up Round the North Sea's Rim. By Frances James. Photos by Erica Koch. 685-704, *May 1952*
Demolishing Germany's North Sea Ramparts (Helgoland). By Stuart E. Jones. 635-644, *Nov. 1946*
The Removal of the North Sea Mine Barrage. By Noel Davis. 103-133, *Feb. 1920*
The North Sea Mine Barrage. By Reginald R. Belknap. 85-110, *Feb. 1919*
Europe's Endangered Fish Supply: The War and the North Sea Fisheries. 141-152, *Feb. 1915*

NORTH SHORE, Massachusetts:

Massachusetts' North Shore: Harboring Old Ways. By Randall S. Peffer. Photos by Nathan Benn. 568-590, *Apr. 1979*

NORTH SLOPE, Alaska:

The Pipeline: Alaska's Troubled Colossus. By Bryan Hodgson. Photos by Steve Raymer. Included: Diagram, Anatomy of the pipeline; map showing potential and producing oil and gas areas. 684-717, *Nov. 1976*
Alaska: Rising Northern Star. By Joseph Judge. Photos by Bruce Dale. 730-767, *June 1975*
Oil, the Dwindling Treasure. By Noel Grove. Photos by Emory Kristof. 792-825, *June 1974*
Will Oil and Tundra Mix? Alaska's North Slope Hangs in the Balance. By William S. Ellis. Photos by Emory Kristof. 485-517, *Oct. 1971*

NORTH STAR Cruises Alaska's Wild West. By Amos Burg. 57-86, *July 1952*

NORTH Through History Aboard *White Mist.* By Melville Bell Grosvenor. Photos by Edwin Stuart Grosvenor. NGS research grant. 1-55, *July 1970*

NORTH to the Pole. By Will Steger. Photos by the author and Jim Brandenburg. 289-317, *Sept. 1986*

NORTH to the Tundra. 293-337. I. Recreating a Vanished World. By Russell D. Guthrie. Included: "Ice Age Mammals of the Alaskan Tundra." Painting supplement by Jay H. Matternes. 294-301; II. Portrait of a Fierce and Fragile Land. By Paul A. Zahl. 303-314; III. Plants of the Alaskan Tundra. 315-321; IV. Birds of the Alaskan Tundra. 322-327; V. Mammals of the Alaskan Tundra. 329-337, *Mar. 1972*

NORTH Toward the Pole on Skis. By Bjørn O. Staib. NGS research grant. 254-281, *Feb. 1965*

NORTH UIST (Island), Scotland:

Isles on the Edge of the Sea: Scotland's Outer Hebrides. By Kenneth Mac-Leish. Photos by Thomas Nebbia. 676-711, *May 1970*

NORTH VIETNAM:

Air Rescue Behind Enemy Lines. By Howard Sochurek. 346-369, *Sept. 1968*

NORTH With Finland's Lapps. By Jean and Franc Shor. 249-280, *Aug. 1954*

NORTH With the Snow Goose. By Des and Jen Bartlett. 822-843, *Dec. 1973*

NORTH With the Wheat Cutters. By Noel Grove. Photos by James A. Sugar. 194-217, *Aug. 1972*

A **NORTH** Woods Park Primeval: Isle Royale. By John L. Eliot. Photos by Mitch Kezar. 534-550, *Apr. 1985*

NORTH YEMEN. By Noel Grove. Photos by Steve Raymer. 244-269, *Aug. 1979*

NORTHAMPTON, Massachusetts:

Deaf Children Learn to Talk at Clarke School. By Lilian Grosvenor. Photos by Willard R. Culver. 379-397, *Mar. 1955*

NORTHEAST (Region), U. S.:

The Incredible Potato. By Robert E. Rhoades. Photos by Martin Rogers. Note: Potatoes were first introduced in New England in 1719 by Scotch-Irish immigrants. 668-694, *May 1982*

M N

NORTHWESTERN AERONAUTICAL CORPORATION, Minneapolis, Minnesota:

NORTHWIND (Coast Guard Icebreaker):

NORTON, WILSON K.: *Author*

NORWAY:

Dressed for her wedding in 1934, a young Norwegian bride wears a festive gown and a crown made of silver.   PER BRAATEN

NORWEGIAN Expedition to the Magnetic North Pole by Roald Amundsen. 293-294, *July 1903*

NORWEGIAN Fjords and Folkways. Photos by Jack Kuhne. 501-524, *Apr. 1939*

NORWEGIAN SEA:

NORWEGIANS:

NOTE on the Height of Mount Saint Elias. By Israel C. Russell. 215-216, *Dec. 29, 1894*

NOTES About Ants and Their Resemblance to Man. By William Morton Wheeler. 731-766, *Aug. 1912*

NOTES and Scenes from Korea. 498-508, *July 1908*

NOTES from a Naturalist's Experiences in British Guiana. By C. H. Eigenmann. 859-870, *Sept. 1911*

NOTES on a Zoological Collecting Trip to Dutch New Guinea. By Thomas Barbour. 469-484, *July 1908*

NOTES on Burma. By Thomas Barbour. 841-866, *Oct. 1909*

NOTES on Central America. 272-279, *Apr. 1907*

NOTES on Finland. By Baroness Alletta Korff. 493-494, *June 1910*

NOTES on Macedonia. 790-802, *Nov. 1908*

NOTES on Manchuria. By Henry B. Miller. 261-262, *June 1904*

NOTES on Morocco. 157, *Mar. 1906*

NOTES on Normandy. By Mrs. Geo. C. Bosson, Jr. 775-782, *Sept. 1910*

NOTES on Oman. By S. M. Zwemer. 89-98, *Jan. 1911*

NOTES on Panama and Colombia. 458-466, *Dec. 1903*

NOTES on Rumania. 1219-1225, 1239, *Dec. 1912*

NOTES on Some Eruptive Rocks from

Alaska. By George H. Williams. 63-74, *Mar. 21, 1892*

NOTES on Some Primitive Philippine Tribes. By Dean C. Worcester. 284-301, *June 1898*

NOTES on Southern Mexico. By G. N. Collins and C. B. Doyle. 301-320, *Mar. 1911*

NOTES on Tahiti. By H. W. Smith. 947-963, *Oct. 1911*

NOTES on the Deserts of the United States and Mexico (from a publication of Daniel T. MacDougal). 691-714, *Aug. 1910*

NOTES on the Distances Flies Can Travel. By N. A. Cobb. 380-383, *May 1910*

NOTES on the Ekoi. By P. A. Talbot. 33-38, *Jan. 1912*

NOTES on the Eucalyptus Tree from the United States Forest Service. 668-673, *July 1909*

NOTES on the Forest Service. 142-145, *Feb. 1907*

NOTES on the Geology of the Vicinity of Muir Glacier. By H. P. Cushing. 56-62, *Mar. 21, 1892*

NOTES on the Only American Colony in the World–Liberia. By Edgar Allen Forbes. 719-729, *Sept. 1910*

NOTES on the Panama Canal. By Theodore P. Shonts. 362-363, *June 1906*

NOTES on the Remarkable Habits of Certain Turtles and Lizards. By H. A. Largelamb (Alexander Graham Bell). 413-419, *June 1907*

NOTES on the Sea Dyaks of Borneo. By Edwin H. Gomes. 695-723, *Aug. 1911*

NOTES on the Wild Fowl and Game Animals of Alaska. By E. W. Nelson. 121-132, *Apr. 1898*

NOTES on Tibet. 292-294, *July 1904*

NOTES on Troy. By Ernest L. Harris. 531-532, *May 1915*

NOTES on Turbulent Nicaragua. 1102-1116, *Dec. 1909*

NOTRE DAME DE CHARTRES (Cathedral):

■ *Our World's Heritage.* Contents: UNESCO-designated World Heritage Sites. 312 pages. *1987*

Chartres: Legacy From the Age of Faith. By Kenneth MacLeish. Photos by Dean Conger. 857-882, *Dec. 1969*

NOTRE DAME DE PARIS (Cathedral):

Île de la Cité, Birthplace of Paris. By Kenneth MacLeish. Photos by Bruce Dale. 680-719, *May 1968*

NOURSE, MARY A.: *Author*

Women's Work in Japan. 99-132, *Jan. 1938*

How Half the World Works. By Alice Tisdale Hobart and Mary A. Nourse. 509-524, *Apr. 1932*

NOVA SCOTIA (Province), Canada:

Plight of the Bluefin Tuna. By Michael J. A. Butler. Photos by David Doubilet. Paintings by Stanley Meltzoff. 220-239, *Aug. 1982*

The Loyalists. By Kent Britt. Photos by Ted Spiegel. Included: Tories, American colonists who remained loyal to the British Empire and moved to Canada during and after the Revolution; their descendants today. 510-539, *Apr. 1975*

Nova Scotia, the Magnificent Anchorage. By Charles McCarry. Photos by Gordon W. Gahan. 334-363, *Mar. 1975*

Safe Landing on Sable, Isle of 500 Shipwrecks. By Melville Bell Grosvenor. Included: 1898: The Bells on Sable. Photos by Arthur W. McCurdy. 398-431, *Sept. 1965*

Down East to Nova Scotia. By Winfield Parks. Included: Baddeck, Boulaceet (Maskell's Harbour), Bras d'Or Lakes, Cape George Harbour, Halifax, Liscomb, Lunenburg, Peggy's Cove, St. Peters Canal. 853-879, *June 1964*

Canada, My Country. By Alan Phillips. Photos by David S. Boyer and Walter Meayers Edwards. 769-819, *Dec. 1961*

Canada's Winged Victory: the *Silver Dart*. By Gilbert M. Grosvenor. 254-267, *Aug. 1959*

The Giant Tides of Fundy. By Paul A. Zahl. 153-192, *Aug. 1957*

Far North with "Captain Mac." By Miriam MacMillan. Included: Big Harbour (Port Bevis), Cape Breton Island, Cape Canso, Cape Sable, Halifax, Sydney. 465-513, *Oct. 1951*

Salty Nova Scotia: In Friendly New Scotland Gaelic Songs Still Answer the Skirling Bagpipes. By Andrew H. Brown. 575-624, *May 1940*

The Charm of Cape Breton Island: The Most Picturesque Portion of Canada's Maritime Provinces–A Land Rich in Historic Associations, Natural Resources, and Geographic Appeal. By Catherine Dunlop Mackenzie. 34-60, *July 1920*

Tides in the Bay of Fundy. 71-76, *Feb. 1905*

See also Bell Museum

NOVAE:

The Once and Future Universe. By Rick Gore. Photos by James A. Sugar. Paintings by Barron Storey. Picture text by David Jeffery. 704-749, *June 1983*

NOVARUPTA (Volcano), Alaska:

The Valley of Ten Thousand Smokes: An Account of the Discovery and Exploration of the Most Wonderful Volcanic Region in the World. By Robert F. Griggs. 115-169, *Feb. 1918*

NOVICK, ALVIN: *Author*

Bats Aren't All Bad. Photos by Bruce Dale. 615-637, *May 1973*

NOVOSIBIRSK, U.S.S.R.:

Siberia's Empire Road, the River Ob. By Robert Paul Jordan. Photos by Dean Conger. 145-181, *Feb. 1976*

"NOWHERE To Lay Down Weary Head"–Sea Change in the Sea Islands. By Charles L. Blockson. Photos by Karen Kasmauski. 735-763, *Dec. 1987*

NOXONTOWN POND, Delaware:

Teeming Life of a Pond. By William H. Amos. 274-298, *Aug. 1970*

NOYES, PERLEY H.: *Author*

A Visit to Lonely Iceland. 731-741, *Nov. 1907*

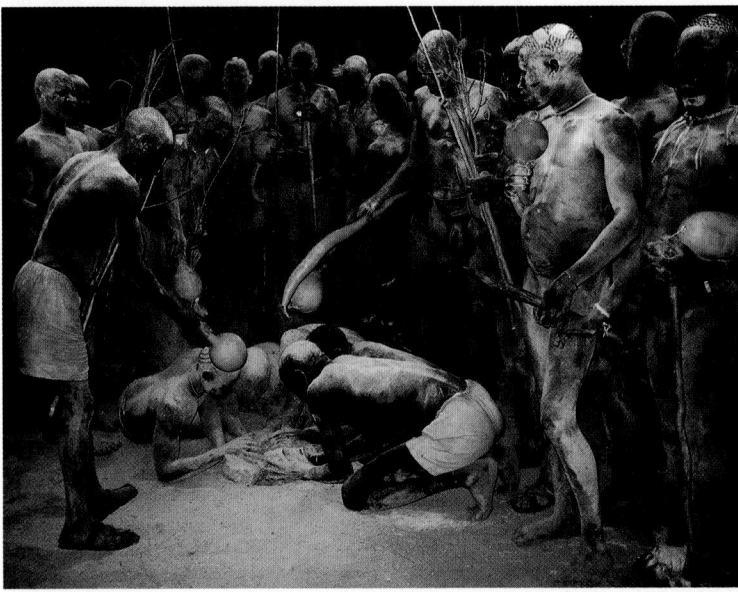

To ward off evil spirits, the Nuba people of Sudan bathe in ashes before a **sanda** *ceremony, a combination harvest feast, sports contest, and dance party.* HORST LUZ

NOYES, THEODORE W.: *Author*

The World's Great Waterfalls: Visits to Mighty Niagara, Wonderful Victoria, and Picturesque Iguazu. 29-59, *July 1926*

NUBA TRIBESPEOPLE:

Proud Primitives, the Nuba People. By Oskar Luz. Photos by Horst Luz. Contents: Masakin Qisar, Masakin Tiwal. 673-699, *Nov. 1966*

With the Nuba Hillmen of Kordofan. By Robin Strachan. Contents: Fungor, Kau, Koalib, and Korongo. 249-278, *Feb. 1951*

Two Fighting Tribes of the Sudan. By Merian C. Cooper. Photos by Ernest B. Schoedsack. 465-486, *Oct. 1929*

NUBIA (Region), Africa:

Abu Simbel's Ancient Temples Reborn. By Georg Gerster. 724-744, *May 1969*

Saving the Ancient Temples at Abu Simbel. By Georg Gerster. Paintings by Robert W. Nicholson. 694-742, *May 1966*

Threatened Treasures of the Nile. By Georg Gerster. 587-621, *Oct. 1963*

NUCLEAR ENERGY:

Chernobyl–One Year After. By Mike Edwards. Photos by Steve Raymer. Paintings by Pierre Mion. 632-653, *May 1987*

NR-1, the Navy's Inner-Space Shuttle. By Robert D. Ballard. Photos by Emory Kristof. 450-459, *Apr. 1985*

Contrary New Hampshire. By Robert Booth. Photos by Sandy Felsenthal. Included: Seabrook nuclear power plant. 770-799, *Dec. 1982*

An Atlas of Energy Resources. 58-69, *Special Report on Energy. (Feb. 1981)*

Editorial. By Gilbert M. Grosvenor. 445, *Apr. 1979*

The Promise and Peril of Nuclear Energy. By Kenneth F. Weaver. Photos by Emory Kristof. 459-493, *Apr. 1979*

Powerhouse of the Northwest (Columbia River). By David S. Boyer. 821-847, *Dec. 1974*

Whatever Happened to TVA? By Gordon Young. Photos by Emory Kristof. 830-863, *June 1973*

The Search for Tomorrow's Power. By Kenneth F. Weaver. Photos by Emory Kristof. 650-681, *Nov. 1972*

Four-ocean Navy in the Nuclear Age. By Thomas W. McKnew. 145-187, *Feb. 1965*

Our Nuclear Navy. By George W. Anderson, Jr. 449-450, *Mar. 1963*

New Era in the Loneliest Continent (Antarctica). By David M. Tyree. Photos by Albert Moldvay. 260-296, *Feb. 1963*

Nuclear Power for the Polar Regions (Camp Century). By George J. Dufek. 712-730, *May 1962*

You and the Obedient Atom. By Allan C. Fisher, Jr. 303-353, *Sept. 1958*

Man's New Servant, the Friendly Atom. By F. Barrows Colton. Photos by Volkmar Wentzel. 71-90, *Jan. 1954*

Uncle Sam's House of 1,000 Wonders. By Lyman J. Briggs and F. Barrows Colton. 755-784, *Dec. 1951*

Your New World of Tomorrow. By F. Barrows Colton. 385-410, *Oct. 1945*

See also Enterprise; Nautilus; Savannah, N. S.; Skate; Thresher; Triton

NUCLEAR POWER PLANT ACCIDENT:

Chernobyl–One Year After. By Mike Edwards. Photos by Steve Raymer. Paintings by Pierre Mion. 632-653, *May 1987*

NUCLEAR WEAPONS:

Profiles of the Presidents: V. The Atomic Age: Its Problems and Promises. By Frank Freidel. 66-119, *Jan. 1966*

Of Planes and Men. By Kenneth F. Weaver. Photos by Emory Kristof and Albert Moldvay. Included: Air Defense Command, Military Air Transport Service, Pacific Air Forces, Strategic Air Command, Tactical Air Command, U. S. Air Forces in Europe. 298-349, *Sept. 1965*

Four-ocean Navy in the Nuclear Age. By Thomas W. McKnew. 145-187, *Feb. 1965*

South Carolina Rediscovered. By Herbert Ravenel Sass. Photos by Robert F. Sisson. Included: Savannah River Plant of the Atomic Energy Commission which produces H-bombs. 281-321, *Mar. 1953*

See also Nuclear Weapons Testing

NUCLEAR WEAPONS TESTING:

Bikini–A Way of Life Lost. By William S. Ellis. Photos by James P. Blair. 813-834, *June 1986*

Nevada Learns to Live with the Atom. By Samuel W. Matthews. 839-850, *June 1953*

Operation Crossroads. Photos by Joint Task Force I. Paintings by Charles Bittinger. 519-530, *Apr. 1947*

Farewell to Bikini. By Carl Markwith. 97-116, *July 1946*

Air Power for Peace. By H. H. Arnold. 137-193, *Feb. 1946*

NUCLEIC ACIDS:

The Awesome Worlds Within a Cell. By Rick Gore. Photos by Bruce Dale. Paintings by Davis Meltzer. 355-395, *Sept. 1976*

NUDIBRANCHS:

Unsung Beauties of Hawaii's Coral Reefs. By Paul A. Zahl. 510-525, *Oct. 1959*

NUECHTERLEIN, GARY L.:

Nomination Page. *May 1982*

Author-Photographer

Western Grebes: The Birds That Walk on Water. 624-637, *May 1982*

NUER TRIBESPEOPLE:

Across Widest Africa. By A. Henry Savage Landor. 694-737, *Oct. 1908*

NUESTRA SEÑORA DE ATOCHA (Galleon):

Treasure From the Ghost Galleon:

Santa Margarita. By Eugene Lyon. Photos by Don Kincaid. Included: Sister galleon, *Atocha.* 228-243, *Feb. 1982*

■ Treasure! 575, Nov. 1976; cover, *Dec. 1976*

Atocha, Tragic Treasure Galleon of the Florida Keys. By Eugene Lyon. 787-809, *June 1976*

NULLARBOR PLAIN, Australia:

The Tea and Sugar Lifeline in Australia's Outback. By Erla Zwingle. Photos by William Albert Allard. 737-757, *June 1986*

NUNG TRIBESPEOPLE:

Cane Bridges of Asia. Photos by Paul Popper. 243-250, *Aug. 1948*

NUNIVAK (Island), Bering Sea:

Alaska–Our Northwestern Outpost. Photos by Ernest H. Gruening, Amos Burg, and Froelich Rainey. 297-308, *Sept. 1942*

NURSING:

The American Red Cross: A Century of Service. By Louise Levathes. Photos by Annie Griffiths. Included: A new role for home nursing. 777-791, *June 1981*

Flying Our Wounded Veterans Home. By Catherine Bell Palmer. 363-384, *Sept. 1945*

Heroes' Return. By William H. Nicholas. 333-352, *Mar. 1945*

The Symbol of Service to Mankind. By Stockton Axson. 375-390, *Apr. 1918*

See also Red Cross

NUTHATCHES:

Winged Denizens of Woodland, Stream, and Marsh. By Alexander Wetmore. Paintings by Allan Brooks. 577-596, *May 1934*

NUTRITION RESEARCH:

The Prodigious Soybean. By Fred Hapgood. Photos by Chris Johns. 67-91, *July 1987*

The Incredible Potato. By Robert E. Rhoades. Photos by Martin Rogers. 668-694, *May 1982*

NUTS and Their Uses as Foods. 800, *Dec. 1907*

NYAMLAGIRA (Volcano), Zaire:

We Keep House on an Active Volcano: After Flying to Study a Spectacular Eruption in Belgian Congo, a Geologist Settles Down on a Newborn Craterless Vent for Eight Months' Study. By Jean Verhoogen. 511-550, *Oct. 1939*

NYGAARD, ARNVID: *Author*

Native's Return to Norway. Photos by Andrew H. Brown. 683-691, *Nov. 1953*

NYMAN, STEPHEN H.: *Photographer*

Gilded Domes Against an Azure Sky (Iran). 339-346, *Sept. 1939*

NYOS, Lake, Cameroon:

Silent Death from Cameroon's Killer Lake. By Curt Stager. Photos by Anthony Suau. 404-420, *Sept. 1987*

O
P

*Risking encounters with leopard
seals, Adélie penguins take the plunge
to feed in Antarctic waters.*
JANNIK SCHOU

777

Jacques-Yves Cousteau prepares to test oceanauts' breathing apparatus for depths below 300 feet. BATES LITTLEHALES, NGS

OCEANOGRAPHY

A space-age diving suit will allow marine biologist Sylvia Earle to explore the seafloor at 1,250 feet off Oahu, Hawaii. PETE ROMANO

OCEANS:

A giant octopus in British Columbia's Strait of Georgia propels itself by jetting water past its eight arms.   DAVID DOUBILET

Steel mills, many built during the 19th century, line the Ohio River in Mingo Junction, Ohio. MARTIN ROGERS

William H. Nicholas. Photos by J. Baylor Roberts. 273-288, *Feb. 1948*

Men Against the Rivers. By Frederick Simpich. 767-794, *June 1937*

Ohio, the Gateway State. By Melville Chater. 525-591, *May 1932*

The Travels of George Washington: Dramatic Episodes in His Career as the First Geographer of the United States. By William Joseph Showalter. 1-63, *Jan. 1932*

OHIO VALLEY, U. S.:

Daniel Boone, First Hero of the Frontier. By Elizabeth A. Moize. Photos by William Strode. 812-841, *Dec. 1985*

🌐 Ohio Valley, The Making of America series. Included: Tennessee-Tombigbee Waterway, West Virginia, Illinois, Tennessee, Kentucky, Ohio, Indiana. On reverse: Indians and Europeans, Speculation and Colonization, Transport Revolutions, Region Rent Asunder, Further Divergence, A New Era. *Dec. 1985*

Who Were the "Mound Builders"? By George E. Stuart. 783-801, *Dec. 1972*

OIL:

Oil in the Wilderness: An Arctic Dilemma. By Douglas Lee. Photos by James P. Blair. 858-871, *Dec. 1988*

Scotland, Ghosts, and Glory. By Rowe Findley. Photos by Peter Carmichael. 40-69, *July 1984*

Calgary: Canada's Not-So-Wild West. By David S. Boyer. Photos by Ottmar Bierwagen. Included: Map showing Alberta's oil fields, natural gas fields, and tar sands. 378-403, *Mar. 1984*

High-Flying Tulsa. By Robert Paul Jordan. Photos by Annie Griffiths. 378-403, *Sept. 1983*

🌐 America's Federal Lands; The United States. Included: Inset map showing drilling sites. *Sept. 1982*

Oman: Guardian of the Gulf. By Thomas J. Abercrombie. Photos by the author and Lynn Abercrombie. 344-377, *Sept. 1981*

A Sumatran Journey. By Harvey Arden. Photos by David Alan Harvey. 406-430, *Mar. 1981*

An Atlas of Energy Resources. 58-69. Included: Oil: Lifeblood and Liability. 58-59. *Special Report on Energy. (Feb. 1981)*

Where Oil and Wildlife Mix. By Steven C. Wilson and Karen C. Hayden. 145-173, *Feb. 1981*

Saudi Arabia: The Kingdom and Its Power. By Robert Azzi. 286-333, *Sept. 1980*

Bahrain: Hub of the Persian Gulf. By Thomas J. Abercrombie. Photos by Steve Raymer. 300-329, *Sept. 1979*

Giants That Move the World's Oil: Superships. By Noel Grove. Photos by Martin Rogers. 102-124, *July 1978*

Pennsylvania: Faire Land of William Penn. By Gordon Young. Photos by Cary Wolinsky. 731-767, *June 1978*

Mexico: "A Very Beautiful Challenge." By Mike Edwards. Photos by Thomas Nebbia. 612-647, *May 1978*

The Continental Shelf: Man's New Frontier. By Luis Marden. Photos by Ira Block. 495-531, *Apr. 1978*

Striking It Rich in the North Sea. By Rick Gore. Photos by Dick Durrance II. 519-549, *Apr. 1977*

Canada's "Now" Frontier. By Robert Paul Jordan. Photos by Lowell Georgia. Included: Map showing oil pipeline, proposed gas pipeline, and tar sands. 480-511, *Oct. 1976*

Venezuela's Crisis of Wealth. By Noel Grove. Photos by Robert W. Madden. 175-209, *Aug. 1976*

Siberia's Empire Road, the River Ob. By Robert Paul Jordan. Photos by Dean Conger. 145-181, *Feb. 1976*

Editorial. By Gilbert M. Grosvenor. 443, *Oct. 1975*

The Arab World, Inc. By John J. Putman. Photos by Winfield Parks. 494-533, *Oct. 1975*

Iran: Desert Miracle. By William Graves. Photos by James P. Blair. 2-47, *Jan. 1975*

Oil, the Dwindling Treasure. By Noel Grove. Photos by Emory Kristof. 792-825, *June 1974*

Oman, Land of Frankincense and Oil. By Robert Azzi. 205-229, *Feb. 1973*

Oklahoma, the Adventurous One. By Robert Paul Jordan. Photos by Robert W. Madden. 149-189, *Aug. 1971*

Kuwait, Aladdin's Lamp of the Middle East. By John E. Frazer. Photos by David F. Cupp. 636-667, *May 1969*

The Canadian North: Emerging Giant. By David S. Boyer. 1-43, *July 1968*

Houston, Prairie Dynamo. By Stuart E. Jones. Photos by William Albert Allard. 338-377, *Sept. 1967*

Saudi Arabia: Beyond the Sands of Mecca. By Thomas J. Abercrombie. 1-53, *Jan. 1966*

Venezuela Builds on Oil. By Thomas J. Abercrombie. 344-387, *Mar. 1963*

The Fabulous State of Texas. By Stanley Walker. Photos by B. Anthony Stewart and Thomas Nebbia. 149-195, *Feb. 1961*

Alberta Unearths Her Buried Treasures. By David S. Boyer. 90-119, *July 1960*

Iraq–Where Oil and Water Mix. By Jean and Franc Shor. 443-489, *Oct. 1958*

Sand in My Eyes (Algerian Sahara). By Jinx Rodger. 664-705, *May 1958*

This Young Giant, Indonesia. By Beverley M. Bowie. Photos by J. Baylor Roberts. 351-392, *Sept. 1955*

Calypso Explores for Underwater Oil. By Jacques-Yves Cousteau. NGS research grant. 155-184, *Aug. 1955*

Troubled Waters East of Suez. By Ernest M. Eller. 483-522, *Apr. 1954*

Happy-go-lucky Trinidad and Tobago. By Charles Allmon. 35-75, *Jan. 1953*

Boom Time in Kuwait. By Paul Edward Case. 783-802, *Dec. 1952*

Journey into Troubled Iran. By George W. Long. Photos by J. Baylor Roberts. 425-464, *Oct. 1951*

Saudi Arabia, Oil Kingdom. Photos by Maynard Owen Williams. 497-512, *Apr. 1948*

Louisiana Trades with the World. By Frederick Simpich. Photos by J. Baylor Roberts. 705-738, *Dec. 1947*

Bahrein: Port of Pearls and Petroleum. By Maynard Owen Williams. 195-210, *Feb. 1946*

Oil for Victory Piped under the Sea. 721-726, *Dec. 1945*

Guest in Saudi Arabia. By Maynard Owen Williams. 463-487, *Oct. 1945*

Curaçao and Aruba on Guard. By W. Robert Moore. 169-192, *Feb. 1943*

Bombs over Bible Lands. By Frederick Simpich and W. Robert Moore. 141-180, *Aug. 1941*

Today's World Turns on Oil. By Frederick Simpich. Included: Petroleum Serves–From Lamps to Wheels. 703-748, *June 1941*

So Oklahoma Grew Up. By Frederick Simpich. 269-314, *Mar. 1941*

Where the World Gets Its Oil: But Where Will Our Children Get It When American Wells Cease to Flow? By George Otis Smith. 181-202, *Feb. 1920*

Billions of Barrels of Oil Locked up in Rocks. By Guy Elliott Mitchell. 195-205, *Feb. 1918*

The Nation's Undeveloped Resources. By Franklin K. Lane. 183-225, *Feb. 1914*

The Oil Treasure of Mexico. By Russell Hastings Millward. 803-805, *Nov. 1908*

A Vigorous Oil Well. By S. A. Cornelius. 348-349, *May 1907*

Natural-Gas, Oil, and Coal Supply of the United States. 186, *Apr. 1904*

Oil Fields of Texas and California. 276-278, *July 1901*

See also Alaskan Pipeline; North Slope, Alaska; *and* Conshelf Bases; Oil Shale; Tankers, Oil

OIL, Vegetable:

Rediscovering America's Forgotten Crops. By Noel D. Vietmeyer. Photos by Burgess Blevins. Paintings by Paul M. Breeden. Included: Jojoba oil. 702-712, *May 1981*

O
P

Piping crude oil to Britain and natural gas to West Germany, Phillips Petroleum's Ekofisk complex exploits the riches of the North Sea.   DICK DURRANCE II

■■ BOOKS   ✧ MAPS   ■ TELEVISION

At Olduvai Gorge in Tanzania, famed anthropologist Louis S. B. Leakey and his family probe one of earth's richest hoards of hominid fossils. ROBERT F. SISSON, NGS

Photos by John Launois. 93-119, *Jan. 1973*

OLDUVAI GORGE, Tanzania:

The Leakey Tradition Lives On. By Melvin M. Payne. NGS research grant. 143-144, *Jan. 1973*

Dr. Leakey and the Dawn of Man. 703A-703B, *Nov. 1966*

Preserving the Treasures of Olduvai Gorge. By Melvin M. Payne. Photos by Joseph J. Scherschel. NGS research grant. 701-709, *Nov. 1966*

The Leakeys of Africa: Family in Search of Prehistoric Man. By Melvin M. Payne. NGS research grant. 194-231, *Feb. 1965*

Adventures in the Search for Man. By Louis S. B. Leakey. Photos by Hugo van Lawick. NGS research grant. 132-152, *Jan. 1963*

Exploring 1,750,000 Years Into Man's Past. By L.S.B. Leakey. Photos by Robert F. Sisson. NGS research grant. 564-589, *Oct. 1961*

Finding the World's Earliest Man (*Zinjanthropus boisei*). By L.S.B. Leakey. Photos by Des Bartlett. NGS research grant. 420-435, *Sept. 1960*

O'LEARY, JOHN F.:

What Six Experts Say. 70-73, *Special Report on Energy. (Feb. 1981)*

OLFACTION. *See* Smell, Sense of

ÓLIMBOS, Kárpathos (Island), Greece:

Eternal Easter in a Greek Village. By Maria Nicolaidis-Karanikolas. Photos by James L. Stanfield. 768-777, *Dec. 1983*

OLIVER, DOUGLAS L.: *Author*

Treasure Islands of Australasia: New Guinea, New Caledonia, and Fiji Trace across the South Pacific a Fertile Crescent Incredibly Rich in Minerals and Foods. 691-722, *June 1942*

OLIVER, ELEANOR SCHIRMER: *Author*

A Woman's Experiences among Stone Age Solomon Islanders: Primitive Life Remains Unchanged in Tropical Jungleland Where United States Forces Now Are Fighting. 813-836, *Dec. 1942*

OLIVER, JAMES A.:

Nomination Page. *Jan. 1963*

Author

Behind New York's Window on Nature: The American Museum of Natural History. Photos by Robert F. Sisson. 220-259, *Feb. 1963*

OLIVER, MARION L.: *Author*

The Snake Dance (Hopi Indians). 107-137, *Feb. 1911*

OLIVER, R. L.: *Author*

Yucatan in 1895. 83-85, *Feb. 1896*

OLIVER, W. J.: *Photographer*

Peaks and Parks of Western Canada. 516-526, *Oct. 1941*

OLIVERIO, FRANK S.:

On Assignment. *Mar. 1988*

OLIVES:

How Fruit Came to America. By J. R. Magness. Paintings by Else Bostelmann. 325-377, *Sept. 1951*

Speaking of Spain. By Luis Marden. 415-456, *Apr. 1950*

OLMEC CULTURE:

Gifts for the Jaguar God. By Philip Drucker and Robert F. Heizer. 367-375, *Sept. 1956*

On the Trail of La Venta Man. By Matthew W. Stirling. Photos by Richard H. Stewart. 137-172, *Feb. 1947*

La Venta's Green Stone Tigers. By Matthew W. Stirling. 321-332, *Sept. 1943*

Finding Jewels of Jade in a Mexican Swamp. By Matthew W. and Marion Stirling. Included: Zoques, Zotzils, and Maya ruins at Palenque. 635-661, *Nov. 1942*

Expedition Unearths Buried Masterpieces of Carved Jade (Cerro de las Mesas). By Matthew W. Stirling. 277-302, *Sept. 1941*

Great Stone Faces of the Mexican Jungle: Five Colossal Heads and Numerous Other Monuments of Vanished Americans Are Excavated by the Latest National Geographic-Smithsonian Expedition. By Matthew W. Stirling. 309-334, *Sept. 1940*

Discovering the New World's Oldest Dated Work of Man: A Maya Monument Inscribed 291 B. C. is Unearthed Near a Huge Stone Head by a Geographic-Smithsonian Expedition in Mexico. By Matthew W. Stirling. Note: Later identified as Olmec. 183-218, *Aug. 1939*

OLMSTEAD, JUDITH: *Author*

Ethiopia's Artful Weavers. Photos by James A. Sugar. 125-141, *Jan. 1973*

OLSENIUS, RICHARD: *Photographer*

The Great Lakes' Troubled Waters. By Charles E. Cobb, Jr. Photos by Bob Sacha and Richard Olsenius. Included: A great meeting of waters; North America's fifth coast. 2-31, *July 1987*

OLSON, ALMA LUISE: *Author*

The Farthest-North Republic: Olympic Games and Arctic Flying Bring Sequestered Finland into New Focus of World Attention. 499-533, *Oct. 1938*

Sweden, Land of White Birch and White Coal. 441-484, *Oct. 1928*

OLSON, SIGURD F.: *Author*

Relics from the Rapids (Voyageurs). Photos by David S. Boyer. 413-435, *Sept. 1963*

OLSSON-SEFFER, HELEN: *Author*

The Isthmus of Tehuantepec (Mexico): "The Bridge of the World's Commerce." 991-1002, *Dec. 1910*

OLSSON-SEFFER, PEHR: *Author*

Agricultural Possibilities in Tropical Mexico. 1021-1040, *Dec. 1910*

The **OLYMPIC** Country: Washington. By S. C. Gilman. 133-140, *Apr. 1896*

Sixty-six feet in girth, the world's largest western red cedar stands in Washington's Olympic National Park.   PAUL A. ZAHL, NGS

OLYMPIC GAMES:

Tokyo, the Peaceful Explosion. By William Graves. Photos by Winfield Parks. 445-487, *Oct. 1964*

Again–the Olympic Challenge. By Alan J. Gould. 488-513, *Oct. 1964*

Sports-minded Melbourne, Host to the Olympics. 688-693, *Nov. 1956*

OLYMPIC MOUNTAINS, Washington:

The Olympics: Northwest Majesty. By François Leydet. Photos by Farrell Grehan. 188-197, *Feb. 1974*

A Map Maker Looks at the United States. By Newman Bumstead. 705-748, *June 1951*

The Olympic Country. By S. C. Gilman. 133-140, *Apr. 1896*

OLYMPIC NATIONAL PARK, Washington:

The Olympic Peninsula. By Bill Richards. Photos by Sam Abell. Included: Maps showing wildlife refuges, Indian reservations, and annual precipitation. 644-673, *May 1984*

The Olympics: Northwest Majesty. By François Leydet. Photos by Farrell Grehan. 188-197, *Feb. 1974*

In the Gardens of Olympus. By Paul A. Zahl. 85-123, *July 1955*

OLYMPIC PENINSULA, Washington. *See* Olympic National Park

OMAHA, Nebraska:

Nebraska...the Good Life. By Robert Paul Jordan. Photos by Lowell Georgia. 378-407, *Mar. 1974*

Nebraska, the Cornhusker State. By Leo A. Borah. 513-542, *May 1945*

OMAHA BEACH, Normandy Coast, France:

Normandy's Made-in-England Harbors. 565-580, *May 1945*

OMAN (Sultanate), Arabian Peninsula:

The Persian Gulf–Living in Harm's Way. By Thomas J. Abercrombie. Photos by Steve Raymer. 648-671, *May 1988*

Arabia's Frankincense Trail. By Thomas J. Abercrombie. Photos by Lynn Abercrombie. 474-513, *Oct. 1985*

In the Wake of Sindbad. By Tim Severin. Photos by Richard Greenhill. Note: The Sindbad project was sponsored by Oman's Ministry of National Heritage and Culture. The project was financed by the sultan on behalf of Oman and the Arab world. 2-41, *July 1982*

Editorial. By Wilbur E. Garrett. 279, *Sept. 1981*

Oman: Guardian of the Gulf. By Thomas J. Abercrombie. Photos by the author and Lynn Abercrombie. 344-377, *Sept. 1981*

The Arab World, Inc. By John J. Putman. Photos by Winfield Parks. 494-533, *Oct. 1975*

Oman, Land of Frankincense and Oil. By Robert Azzi. 205-229, *Feb. 1973*

Troubled Waters East of Suez. By Ernest M. Eller. 483-522, *Apr. 1954*

Notes on Oman. By S. M. Zwemer. 89-98, *Jan. 1911*

OMENS for a Better Tomorrow. By Thomas J. Abercrombie. 312-343, *Mar. 1977*

OMSK, R.S.F.S.R., U.S.S.R.:

The Land of Promise (Siberia). By A. W. Greely. 1078-1090, *Nov. 1912*

ON a Chilean Hacienda. Photos by E. P. Haddon. 489-496, *Oct. 1944*

ON a Peaceful Good Friday, Alaskans Feel the Dread Earthquake! By William P. E. Graves. 112-139, *July 1964*

ON ASSIGNMENT:

Dale, Bruce, making hologram of crystal globe. *Dec. 1988*

Summers, Diane, in Nepal. *Nov. 1988*

Thompson, William, in the Himalaya. *Nov. 1988*

Valli, Eric, in Nepal. *Nov. 1988*

Putman, John J., in France. *Oct. 1988*

Smith, Mary G., in France. *Oct. 1988*

Turnley, David, in South Africa. *Oct. 1988*

Andre, Dena. *Sept. 1988*

Fralin, Frances. *Sept. 1988*

Haun, Declan. *Sept. 1988*

Livingston, Jane. *Sept. 1988*

Moran, Kathy. *Sept. 1988*

Fleming, Kevin, in Annapolis, Maryland. *Aug. 1988*

Newman, Cathy, in Kyongju, South Korea. *Aug. 1988*

Boraiko, Allen A., in Chile. *July 1988*

Harvey, David Alan, in Chile. *July 1988*

Soren, David, in Kourion, Cyprus. *July 1988*

Archaeology, underwater. *June 1988*

Littlehales, Bates. *June 1988*

More than half a million miles were logged by the team that produced the February 1988 all-Australia issue.

Nachtwey, James, in Guatemala. *June 1988*

Watts, Gordon P. *June 1988*

Abercrombie, Thomas J., in Sharjah, United Arab Emirates. *May 1988*

Hyde, Nina, in China. *May 1988*

Ressmeyer, Roger H. *May 1988*

Telescopes. *May 1988*

Wolinsky, Cary, in China. *May 1988*

Benchley, Peter, in Papua New Guinea. *Apr. 1988*

El-Baz, Farouk, in Egypt. *Apr. 1988*

Garrett, Wilbur E., in Egypt. *Apr. 1988*

Petrone, Claude E., in Egypt. *Apr. 1988*

Barlett, Joe M. *Mar. 1988*

Judge, Joseph, in St. Augustine, Florida. *Mar. 1988*

King, Larry L., in Alaska and Texas. *Mar. 1988*

NGM printing (quality control). *Mar. 1988*

Oliverio, Frank S. *Mar. 1988*

Roberts, Jack. *Mar. 1988*

Austen, David Robert, in Australia. *Feb. 1988*

Breeden, Stanley, in Australia. *Feb. 1988*

Everingham, John, in Australia. *Feb. 1988*

Jamison, Anne, in Australia. *Feb. 1988*

Mark, Mary Ellen, in Australia. *Feb. 1988*

Moize, Elizabeth A., in Australia. *Feb. 1988*

O'Brien, Michael, in Australia. *Feb. 1988*

Phelps, Constance H., in Australia. *Feb. 1988*

Smith, Susan A., in Australia. *Feb. 1988*

Terrill, Ross, in Australia. *Feb. 1988*

Tipton, Abigail, in Australia. *Feb. 1988*

Welchman, Susan, in Australia. *Feb. 1988*

Wright, Belinda, in Australia. *Feb. 1988*

Goetzmann, William H. *Jan. 1988*

Niezabitowska, Małgorzata, across America. *Jan. 1988*

Otnes, Fred. *Jan. 1988*

Plage, Dieter and Mary, in the Galápagos Islands. *Jan. 1988*

Tomaszewski, Tomasz, across America. *Jan. 1988*

Bass, George, in Ulu Burun, Turkey. *Dec. 1987*

Hentschel, Faith, in Ulu Burun, Turkey. *Dec. 1987*

Blair, James P., in Haiti. *Nov. 1987*

Devillers, Carole, in Haiti. *Nov. 1987*

Alireza, Marianne, in Saudi Arabia. *Oct. 1987*

Cobb, Jodi, in Saudi Arabia. *Oct. 1987*

Gilbert, Avery N. *Oct. 1987*

Sense of smell. *Oct. 1987*

Wysocki, Charles J. *Oct. 1987*

Rutledge, T. W., in Guatemala. *Sept. 1987*

Stager, Curt, in Cameroon. *Sept. 1987*

Ward, Fred, in Guatemala. *Sept. 1987*

Canby, Thomas Y. *Aug. 1987*

McCurry, Steve. *Aug. 1987*

NGM award winners. *Aug. 1987*

Brown, William S., in New York. *July 1987*

Cobb, Charles E., Jr., in Ohio. *July 1987*

Norasingh, Seny, in Laos. *June 1987*

White, Peter T., in Laos. *June 1987*

Edwards, Mike, in the Ukraine. *May 1987*

Mech, L. David, in the Arctic. *May 1987*

Chmielinski, Piotr, in Peru. *Apr. 1987*

McIntyre, Loren, in Peru. *Apr. 1987*

Maze, Stephanie, in Brazil. *Mar. 1987*

Grove, Noel, on the Appalachian Trail. *Feb. 1987*

Lanting, Frans, in Madagascar. *Feb. 1987*

Matthews, Samuel W., in Alaska. *Jan. 1987*

Cormack, Patrick, in Great Britain. *Dec. 1986*

Moseley, Jennifer, in Great Britain. *Dec. 1986*

Woolfitt, Adam, in Great Britain. *Dec. 1986*

Auslander, Marc, on the track of Christopher Columbus. *Nov. 1986*

Devitt, Scott, on the track of Christopher Columbus. *Nov. 1986*

Marden, Luis, on the track of Christopher Columbus. *Nov. 1986*

Rogers, Richard K. *Nov. 1986*

Ryti, Carla, on the track of Christopher Columbus. *Nov. 1986*

Canby, Thomas Y., in Moscow. *Oct. 1986*

Niezabitowska, Małgorzata, in Poland. *Sept. 1986*

Tomaszewski, Tomasz, in Poland. *Sept. 1986*

Amos, Jim, on the Oregon Trail. *Aug. 1986*

Gibbons, Boyd, on the Oregon Trail. *Aug. 1986*

Graves, William, in the Philippines. *July 1986*

McCurry, Steve, in the Philippines. *July 1986*

Moments of drama, risk, and humor face writers, photographers, and editors on assignment for the magazine.

O
P

BOOKS ✦ MAPS ◼ TELEVISION

Massive 500-ton doors give access to eight locks that lower vessels 327 feet between Lake Erie and Lake Ontario. BOB SACHA

ONAGADORI (Long-tailed Fowl):
Scientist Studies Japan's Fantastic Long-tailed Fowl. By Frank X. Ogasawara. Photos by Eiji Miyazawa. 845-855, *Dec. 1970*

ONASSIS, JACQUELINE KENNEDY. *See* Kennedy, Jacqueline Bouvier

The **ONCE** and Future Universe. By Rick Gore. Photos by James A. Sugar. Paintings by Barron Storey. Picture text by David Jeffery. 704-749, *June 1983*

ONCE in a Lifetime: Black Bears Rarely Have Quadruplets, But Goofy Did–and the Camera Caught Her Nursing Her Remarkable Family. By Paul B. Kinney. 249-258, *Aug. 1941*

ONE Canada–or Two? By Peter T. White. Photos by Winfield Parks. 436-465, *Apr. 1977*

ONE Family's Odyssey to America. By John Everingham. 642-661, *May 1980*

ONE Hundred British Seaports. 84-94, *Jan. 1917*

ONE Hundred Hours Beneath the Chesapeake. By Gilbert C. Klingel. Photos by Willard R. Culver. NGS research grant. 681-696, *May 1955*

ONE Hundred Years of Increasing and Diffusing Geographic Knowledge: 1888: Introductory Address by the President, Mr. Gardiner Greene Hubbard. 2-7, *Jan. 1988*

ONE Hundred Years of Increasing and Diffusing Geographic Knowledge: "Tell me if your civilization is interesting": Those Electrifying Eighteen Eighties When the National Geographic Society Was Born. By William H. Goetzmann. Illustrated by Fred Otnes. 8-37, *Jan. 1988*

ONE Hundred Years of Increasing and Diffusing Geographic Knowledge: 1988: The Trustees Who Have Carried On the Tradition. By Melvin M. Payne. 38-43, *Jan. 1988*

"The **ONE** Less Traveled by...": A Journey Down Old U. S. 1. By Bruce Dale. 790-817, *Dec. 1984*

ONE Man's London. By Allan C. Fisher, Jr. Photos by James P. Blair. 743-791, *June 1966*

ONE on Skis. By Jean-Louis Etienne. 318-323, *Sept. 1986*

ONE Season's Game-Bag with the Camera. By George Shiras, 3d. 387-446, *June 1908*

ONE Strange Night on Turtle Beach. By Paul A. Zahl. 570-581, *Oct. 1973*

ONE Thousand Miles of Railway Built for Pilgrims and Not for Dividends. By F. R. Maunsell. 156-172, *Feb. 1909*

ONEIDA INDIANS:
"The Fire That Never Dies." By Harvey Arden. Photos by Steve Wall. 375-403, *Sept. 1987*

O'NEILL, CATHERINE: *Author*
◼️ *Dogs on Duty.* Juvenile. 104 pages. *1988*
◼️ *Natural Wonders of North America.* Juvenile. 104 pages. *1984*
◼️ *Amazing Mysteries of the World.* Contents: Mystifying phenomena such as auroras, black holes, Bigfoot, the Bermuda Triangle, and UFOs. 104 pages. *1983*

O'NEILL, THOMAS J.: *Author*
◼️ *Lakes, Peaks, and Prairies: Discovering the United States-Canadian Border.* Photos by Michael S. Yamashita. 199 pages. *1984*
◼️ *Back Roads America: A Portfolio of Her People.* Photos by Ira Block. 199 pages. *1980*
Dazzling Corals of Palau. Photos by Douglas Faulkner. 136-150, *July 1978*
The Four-eyed Fish Sees All. Photos by Paul A. Zahl. 390-395, *Mar. 1978*
Amber: Golden Window on the Past. Photos by Paul A. Zahl. 423-435, *Sept. 1977*

ONELLI, LUIGI: *Photographer*
Italy Smiles Again. By Edgar Erskine Hume. 693-732, *June 1949*

ONGES (Negrito Tribespeople):
The Last Andaman Islanders. By Raghubir Singh. 66-91, *July 1975*

ONIONS:
Black Acres: A Thrilling Sketch in the Vast Volume of Who's Who Among the Peoples That Make America. By Dorothea D. and Fred Everett. Contents: Mucklands of New York. 631-652, *Nov. 1941*

ONONDAGA INDIANS:
"The Fire That Never Dies." By Harvey Arden. Photos by Steve Wall. 375-403, *Sept. 1987*

ONTARIO (Province), Canada:
The Great Lakes' Troubled Waters. By Charles E. Cobb, Jr. Photos by Bob Sacha and Richard Olsenius. Included: A great meeting of waters; North America's fifth coast. 2-31, *July 1987*
Ontario, Canada's Keystone. By David S. Boyer. Photos by Sam Abell and the author. 760-795, *Dec. 1978*
✦ *Close-up, Canada: Ontario,* text on reverse. *Dec. 1978*
The Great Lakes: Is It Too Late? By Gordon Young. Photos by James L. Amos and Martin Rogers. 147-185, *Aug. 1973*
Relics from the Rapids (Voyageurs). By Sigurd F. Olson. Photos by David S. Boyer. 413-435, *Sept. 1963*
Canada's Dynamic Heartland, Ontario. By Marjorie Wilkins Campbell. Photos by Winfield Parks. 58-97, *July 1963*
Canada, My Country. By Alan Phillips. Photos by David S. Boyer and Walter Meayers Edwards. 769-819, *Dec. 1961*
Across Canada by Mackenzie's Track. By Ralph Gray. 191-239, *Aug. 1955*
Ontario, Pivot of Canada's Power. By Andrew H. Brown. Photos by B. Anthony Stewart and Bates Littlehales. 823-852, *Dec. 1953*
Ontario, Next Door: Alert, Energetic, and Resourceful, Its British Pluck and Skill in Arts and Trades Gain for This Province a High Place Under the Union Jack. By Frederick Simpich. 131-183, *Aug. 1932*
See also Kingston; Niagara Falls; Ottawa; St. Lawrence Seaway; Toronto

ONTARIO, Lake, Canada-U. S.:
The Great Lakes' Troubled Waters. By Charles E. Cobb, Jr. Photos by Bob Sacha and Richard Olsenius. Included: A great meeting of waters; North America's fifth coast. 2-31, *July 1987*

A Mohawk youth performs chores on the family farmstead at the St. Regis Indian Reservation in New York. STEVE WALL

Ghost Ships of the War of 1812: *Hamilton* and *Scourge*. By Daniel A. Nelson. Photos by Emory Kristof. Paintings by Richard Schlecht. 289-313, *Mar. 1983*

The Great Lakes: Is It Too Late? By Gordon Young. Photos by James L. Amos and Martin Rogers. 147-185, *Aug. 1973*

ONTONG JAVA (Islands), Solomon Islands:

Coconuts and Coral Islands. By H. Ian Hogbin. 265-298, *Mar. 1934*

OOSTERSCHELDE BARRIER, The Netherlands:

Man Against the Sea, the Oosterschelde Barrier. By Larry Kohl. 526-537, *Oct. 1986*

OPAL MINING:

Coober Pedy: Opal Capital of Australia's Outback. By Kenny Moore. Photos by Penny Tweedie. 560-571, *Oct. 1976*

South Australia, Gateway to the Great Outback. By Howell Walker. Photos by Joseph J. Scherschel. 441-481, *Apr. 1970*

OPEC. *See* Organization of Petroleum Exporting Countries

OPEN-AIR Law Courts of Ethiopia. Photos by Harald P. Lechenperg. 633-646, *Nov. 1935*

OPENING New Doors. By Gilbert M. Grosvenor. 554-560, *Oct. 1984*

OPENING of the Alaskan Territory. By Harrington Emerson. 99-106, *Mar. 1903*

The **OPENING** of the American West: Burr's 1840 Map. 762-763, *June 1953*

OPERATION CROSSROADS (Atomic Bomb Tests):

Operation Crossroads. Photos by Joint Task Force I. Paintings by Charles Bittinger. 519-530, *Apr. 1947*

Farewell to Bikini. By Carl Markwith. 97-116, *July 1946*

OPERATION DEEP FREEZE:

Antarctica: Icy Testing Ground for Space. By Samuel W. Matthews. Photos by Robert W. Madden. 569-592, *Oct. 1968*

Flight Into Antarctic Darkness. By J. Lloyd Abbot, Jr. Photos by David S. Boyer. 732-738, *Nov. 1967*

New Era in the Loneliest Continent. By David M. Tyree. Photos by Albert Moldvay. 260-296, *Feb. 1963*

What We've Accomplished in Antarctica. By George J. Dufek. 527-557, *Oct. 1959*

Man's First Winter at the South Pole. By Paul A. Siple. 439-478, *Apr. 1958*

Year of Discovery Opens in Antarctica. By David S. Boyer. 339-381, *Sept. 1957*

Across the Frozen Desert to Byrd Station. By Paul W. Frazier. Photos by Calvin L. Larsen. 383-398, *Sept. 1957*

We Are Living at the South Pole. By Paul A. Siple. Photos by David S. Boyer. 5-35, *July 1957*

All-out Assault on Antarctica. By Richard E. Byrd. 141-180, *Aug. 1956*

OPERATION ECLIPSE: 1948. By William A. Kinney. NGS research grant. 325-372, *Mar. 1949*

OPERATION HIGHJUMP:

Our Navy Explores Antarctica. By Richard E. Byrd. U. S. Navy official photos. 429-522, *Oct. 1947*

OPERATION PLUTO: World War II: Oil for Victory Piped under the Sea. 721-726, *Dec. 1945*

OPERATION SAIL:

By Square-rigger from Baltic to Bicentennial. By Kenneth Garrett. 824-857, *Dec. 1976*

OPIUM:

The Poppy. By Peter T. White. Photos by Steve Raymer. 143-189, *Feb. 1985*

Nature's Gifts to Medicine. By Lonnelle Aikman. Paintings by Lloyd K. Townsend and Don Crowley. 420-440, *Sept. 1974*

The Hmong of Laos: No Place to Run. By W. E. Garrett. 78-111, *Jan. 1974*

Spirits of Change Capture the Karens. By Peter Kunstadter. 267-285, *Feb. 1972*

OPORTO, Portugal:

Iberia's Vintage River (Douro-Duero). By Marion Kaplan. Photos by Stephanie Maze. 460-489, *Oct. 1984*

OPOSSUMS (American):

Br'er Possum, Hermit of the Lowlands. By Agnes Akin Atkinson. Photos by Charles Philip Fox. 405-418, *Mar. 1953*

OPOSSUMS (Phalangers):

Strange Animals of Australia. By David Fleay. Photos by Stanley Breeden. 388-411, *Sept. 1963*

Lisu mountain man of Thailand puffs on an opium pipe to celebrate the Chinese Lunar New Year. STEVE RAYMER, NGS

OPTICAL FIBERS:

Fiber Optics: Harnessing Light by a Thread. By Allen A. Boraiko. Photos by Fred Ward. 516-535, *Oct. 1979*

OPTICAL ILLUSIONS:

▌▌*You Won't Believe Your Eyes.* Contents: Optical illusions. 104 pages. *1987*

OPTICS. *See* Fiber Optics; Lasers; Photography, Microscope; Telescopes; *and* Newton, Isaac, for his spectrum experiments

ORAIBI, Arizona:

The Snake Dance (Hopi Indians). By Marion L. Oliver. 107-137, *Feb. 1911*

ORAN, Algeria:

Eastward from Gibraltar: Overland Route Across North Africa to Tunisia and Libia. By Cyrus French Wicker. 115-142, *Jan. 1943*

ORANGE COUNTY, California:

Orange, a Most California County. By Judith and Neil Morgan. Photos by Vince Streano. 750-779, *Dec. 1981*

ORANGE COUNTY, New York:

Black Acres: A Thrilling Sketch in the Vast Volume of Who's Who Among the Peoples That Make America. By Dorothea D. and Fred Everett. 631-652, *Nov. 1941*

ORANGE FREE STATE, South Africa:

The Afrikaners. By André Brink. Photos by David Turnley. 556-585, *Oct. 1988*

Orange Free State: The Prairie Province. By Melville Chater. 431-444, *Apr. 1931*

ORANGES:

Orange, a Most California County. By Judith and Neil Morgan. Photos by Vince Streano. Included: Encroachment of commercial and residential development into former orange-grove land. 750-779, *Dec. 1981*

Florida Rides a Space-age Boom. By Benedict Thielen. Photos by Winfield Parks and James P. Blair. 858-903, *Dec. 1963*

How Fruit Came to America. By J. R. Magness. Paintings by Else Bostelmann. 325-377, *Sept. 1951*

ORANGUTANS:

Living with the Great Orange Apes: Indonesia's Orangutans. By Biruté M. F. Galdikas. Photos by Rod Brindamour. NGS research grant. 830-853, *June 1980*

▌Search for the Great Apes. cover, *Jan. 1976*

Orangutans, Indonesia's "People of the Forest." By Biruté Galdikas-Brindamour. Photos by Rod Brindamour. NGS research grant. 444-473, *Oct. 1975*

Man's Closest Counterparts: Heavyweight of Monkeydom Is the "Old Man" Gorilla, by Far the Largest of the Four Great Apes. By William M. Mann. Paintings by Elie Cheverlange. 213-236, *Aug. 1940*

Primatologist Biruté Galdikas enlists an orphaned helper as she searches Borneo's jungle for wild orangutans, rarest of the apes. ROD BRINDAMOUR

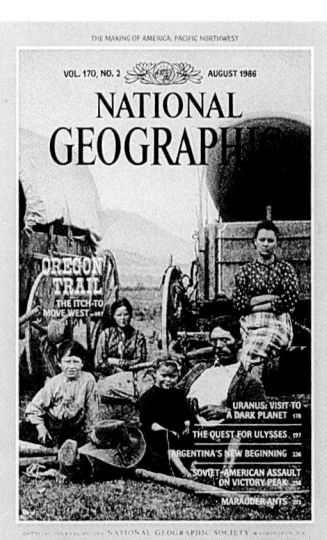

Expert pilots attract thousands to America's premier air show in Oshkosh, Wisconsin. JAMES A. SUGAR, BLACK STAR

OSGOOD, WILFRED H.: *Author*

The Big Game of Alaska. 624-636, *July 1909*

The Alaskan Brown Bear. 332-333, *Apr. 1909*

Lake Clark, a Little Known Alaskan Lake. 326-331, *Aug. 1904*

Author-Photographer

Nature and Man in Ethiopia. Photos by author and Alfred M. Bailey. 121-176, *Aug. 1928*

OSHKOSH, Wisconsin:

Oshkosh: America's Biggest Air Show. By Michael E. Long. Photos by James A. Sugar and the author. 365-375, *Sept. 1979*

OSLO, Norway:

Norway, Land of the Generous Sea. By Edward J. Linehan. Photos by George F. Mobley. 1-43, *July 1971*

The Vikings. By Howard La Fay. Photos by Ted Spiegel. 492-541, *Apr. 1970*

Stop-and-Go Sail Around South Norway. By Edmond J. Moran. Photos by Randi Kjekstad Bull and Andrew H. Brown. 153-192, *Aug. 1954*

"Around the World in Eighty Days." By Newman Bumstead. 705-750, *Dec. 1951*

Baltic Cruise of the *Caribbee.* By Carleton Mitchell. 605-646, *Nov. 1950*

Norway Cracks Her Mountain Shell. By Sydney Clark. Photos by Gilbert Grosvenor and Ole Friele Backer. 171-211, *Aug. 1948*

The White War in Norway. By Thomas R. Henry. 617-640, *Nov. 1945*

OSPREYS:

The Osprey, Endangered World Citizen. By Roger Tory Peterson. Photos by Frederick Kent Truslow. NGS research grant. 53-67, *July 1969*

Cruise of the *Kinkajou:* Among Desert Islands of Mexico Voyagers Find Outdoor Laboratories for the Naturalist and Ideal Fishing Grounds for the Sportsman. By Alfred M. Bailey. 339-366, *Sept. 1941*

The Eagle, King of Birds, and His Kin. By Alexander Wetmore. Paintings by Allan Brooks. 43-95, *July 1933*

Photographing the Nest Life of the Osprey. By C.W.R. Knight. 247-260, *Aug. 1932*

OSSABAW (Island), Georgia:

Sea Islands: Adventuring Along the South's Surprising Coast. By James Cerruti. Photos by Thomas Nebbia and James L. Amos. 366-393, *Mar. 1971*

OSTEND, Belgium:

Belgium Comes Back. By Harvey Klemmer. Photos by Maynard Owen Williams. 575-614, *May 1948*

OSTERHOUT, G. H., Jr.:
Author-Photographer

A Little-Known Marvel of the Western Hemisphere: Christophe's Citadel, a Monument to the Tyranny and Genius of Haiti's King of Slaves. 469-482, *Dec. 1920*

OSTIONAL BEACH, Costa Rica:

One Strange Night on Turtle Beach. By Paul A. Zahl. 570-581, *Oct. 1973*

OSTRICHES:

Ostrich Farming in the United States. 569-574, *Oct. 1906*

OSTROFF, EUGENE: *Photographer*

Vanished Mystery Men of Hudson Bay. By Henry B. Collins. 669-687, *Nov. 1956*

OSTROM, JOHN H.:

Nomination Page. *Aug. 1978*

Author

A New Look at Dinosaurs. Paintings by Roy Andersen. 152-185, *Aug. 1978*

OTAHEITE. *See* Tahiti

The **OTHER** Nevada. By Robert

A mother sea otter reclines casually while her pup nuzzles toward the two nipples on her lower abdomen. JAMES A. MATTISON, JR.

Laxalt. Photos by J. Bruce Baumann. 733-761, *June 1974*

The **OTHER** Side of Jordan. By Luis Marden. 790-825, *Dec. 1964*

OTHER Working Dogs and the Wild Species. By Stanley P. Young. Paintings by Walter A. Weber. 363-384, *Sept. 1944*

The **OTHER** Yosemite. By Nathaniel T. Kenney. Photos by Dean Conger. 762-781, *June 1974*

OTNES, FRED:

On Assignment. *Jan. 1988*

Illustrator

"Tell me if your civilization is interesting": Those Electrifying Eighteen Eighties When the National Geographic Society Was Born. By William H. Goetzmann. 8-37, *Jan. 1988*

OTOMI INDIANS:

The Mexican Indian Flying Pole Dance. By Helga Larsen. 387-400, *Mar. 1937*

OTSEGO COUNTY, New York:

The Goats of Thunder Hill. By Elizabeth Nicholds. Photos by Robert F. Sisson. Contents: Thunder Hill Goat Farm. 625-640, *May 1954*

OTTAWA, Ontario, Canada:

Ontario, Canada's Keystone. By David S. Boyer. Photos by Sam Abell and the author. 760-795, *Dec. 1978*

Queen of Canada (Elizabeth II). By Phyllis Wilson. Photos by Kathleen Revis. 825-829, *June 1959*

Exploring Ottawa. By Bruce Hutchison. 565-596, *Nov. 1947*

Ontario, Next Door: Alert, Energetic, and Resourceful, Its British Pluck and Skill in Arts and Trades Gain for This Province a High Place Under the Union Jack. By Frederick Simpich. 131-183, *Aug. 1932*

OTTERS:

Giant Otters: "Big Water Dogs" in Peril. By Nicole Duplaix. Photos by the

With patriotic pride Sister Mary Ann flies the Canadian flag during a visit by Prime Minister Pierre Trudeau to the Ontario village of Vankleek Hill. SAM ABELL

author and Bates Littlehales.
Contents: River otters. 130-142,
July 1980

Return of the Sea Otter. By Karl W.
Kenyon. Photos by James A. Mattison, Jr. 520-539, *Oct. 1971*

OTTOMAN EMPIRE:

The World of Süleyman the Magnificent. By Merle Severy. Photos by
James L. Stanfield. 552-601,
Nov. 1987

OUAGADOUGOU, Upper Volta:

Freedom Speaks French in Ouagadougou. By John Scofield. 153-203,
Aug. 1966

OUED SOUF (Region), Algeria:

The Country of the Ant Men. By Thomas R. Kearney. Included: panorama.
367-382, *Apr. 1911*

OUESSANT, Ile d', France:

Atlantic Odyssey: Iceland to Antarctica. By Newman Bumstead. Photos by
Volkmar Wentzel. 725-780,
Dec. 1955

OULIÉ, MARTHE: *Author*

Cruising to Crete: Four French Girls Set
Sail in a Breton Yawl for the Island of
the Legendary Minotaur. By Marthe
Oulié and Mariel Jean-Brunhes. 249-272, *Feb. 1929*

OUR Air Age Speeds Ahead. By F.
Barrows Colton. 249-272, *Feb. 1948*

OUR Air Frontier in Alaska. By H. H.
Arnold. 487-504, *Oct. 1940*

OUR Armies of Mercy. By Henry P.
Davison. 423-427, *May 1917*

OUR Army Versus a Bacillus. By Alton
G. Grinnell. 1146-1152, *Oct. 1913*

*OUR Awesome Earth: Its Mysteries and
Its Splendors.* 199 pages. *1986*

OUR Bald Eagle: Freedom's Symbol
Survives. By Thomas C. Dunstan.
Photos by Jeff Foott. NGS research
grant. 186-199, *Feb. 1978*

OUR Best to You–On the Geographic's
75th Birthday. By Melville Bell
Grosvenor. 459, *Oct. 1963*

OUR Big Trees Saved. 1-11, *Jan. 1917*

OUR Changing Atlantic Coastline. By
Nathaniel T. Kenney. Photos by B.
Anthony Stewart. 860-887,
Dec. 1962

OUR Coal Lands. By Guy Elliott Mitchell. 446-451, *May 1910*

OUR Colored Pictures. Contents:
Hand-tinted scenes of Korea and
China. 965, 967, *Nov. 1910*

OUR Colorful City of Magnificent Distances: Washington, D. C. Photos by
Albert W. Stevens and staff photographers. 531-610, *Nov. 1931*

OUR Common Dogs. By Louis Agassiz
Fuertes and Ernest Harold Baynes.
Paintings by Louis Agassiz Fuertes.
201-253, *Mar. 1919*

OUR Conquest of the Pacific: The

*A pilgrim rests after walking miles
through the Portuguese countryside to the
shrine of Fátima.* BRUNO BARBEY, MAGNUM

Narrative of the 7,400-Mile Flight
from San Francisco to Brisbane in
Three Ocean Hops. By Charles E.
Kingsford-Smith and Charles T. P.
Ulm. 371-402, *Oct. 1928*

OUR Country's Presidents. By Frank
Freidel. 279 pages. 1966; rev. ed.
1981

OUR Earth as a Satellite Sees It. By
W. G. Stroud. 293-302, *Aug. 1960*

OUR Ecological Crisis. By Gordon
Young. Photos by James P. Blair and
Harry S. C. Yen. 737-795, *Dec. 1970*

OUR Energy Predicament. By Kenneth
F. Weaver. 2-23, *Special Report on
Energy. (Feb. 1981)*

OUR First Alliance. By J. J. Jusserand.
518-548, *June 1917*

OUR Fish Immigrants. By Hugh M.
Smith. 383-400, *June 1907*

OUR Flag Number. By Gilbert Grosvenor. 281-284, *Oct. 1917*

OUR Foreign-Born Citizens. 95-130,
Feb. 1917

OUR Foreign Trade. By Henry Gannett. 27-28, *Jan. 1898*

OUR Friend From the Sea. By Robert
and Nina Horstman. Photos by Robert F. Sisson. 728-736, *Nov. 1968*

OUR Friend the Frog. By Doris M.
Cochran. Paintings by Hashime
Murayama. 629-654, *May 1932*

OUR Friends, the Bees. By A. I. and
E. R. Root. 675-694, *July 1911*

OUR Friends, the French: An Appraisal
of the Traits and Temperament of the
Citizens of Our Sister Republic. By
Carl Holliday. 345-377, *Nov. 1918*

OUR Global Ocean–Last and Vast
Frontier. By F. Barrows Colton. 105-128, *Jan. 1945*

OUR Global Strong Arm. Photos from
U. S. Army Air Forces. 145-152,
Feb. 1946

OUR Greatest National Monument:
The National Geographic Society
Completes Its Explorations in the
Valley of Ten Thousand Smokes. By
Robert F. Griggs. 219-292,
Sept. 1921

OUR Greatest Plant Food. By Guy Elliott Mitchell. 783-791, *Sept. 1910*

OUR Greatest Travelers: Birds that Fly
from Pole to Pole and Shun the Darkness: Birds that Make 2,500 Miles in a
Single Flight. By Wells W. Cooke.
346-365, *Apr. 1911*

OUR Green Treasury, the National Forests. By Nathaniel T. Kenney. Photos
by J. Baylor Roberts. 287-324,
Sept. 1956

OUR Growing Interstate Highway System. By Robert Paul Jordan. 195-219, *Feb. 1968*

OUR Guardians on the Deep. By William Joseph Showalter. 655-677,
June 1914

OUR Heralds of Storm and Flood. By
Gilbert H. Grosvenor. 586-601,
Sept. 1907

OUR Heritage of Liberty: An Address
Before the United States Senate by
M. Viviani, President of the French
Commission to the United States,
May 1, 1917. 365-367, *Apr. 1917*

OUR Heritage of the Fresh Waters: Biographies of the Most Widely Distributed of the Important Food and
Game Fishes of the United States. By
Charles Haskins Townsend. Paintings by Hashime Murayama. 109-159, *Aug. 1923*

OUR Heterogeneous System of Weights
and Measures. By Alexander Graham Bell. 158-169, *Mar. 1906*

OUR Home-town Planet, Earth. By F.
Barrows Colton. 117-139, *Jan. 1952*

OUR Immigration During 1904. 15-27,
Jan. 1905

OUR Immigration in 1905. 434-435,
Sept. 1905

OUR Immigration Laws from the Viewpoint of National Eugenics. By Robert De C. Ward. 38-41, *Jan. 1912*

OUR Immune System: The Wars Within. By Peter Jaret. Photos by Lennart
Nilsson. Illustrations text by Larry
Kohl. 702-735, *June 1986*

OUR Industrial Victory. By Charles M.
Schwab. 212-229, *Sept. 1918*

OUR Insect Fifth Column: Alien Enemies Take Steady Toll of Food,
Trees, and Treasure by Boring from
Within. By Frederick G. Vosburgh.
Paintings by Hashime Murayama.
225-248, *Aug. 1941*

O
P

North American constrictor, the bull snake feeds on small mammals such as Richardson's ground squirrel. PAINTING BY WALTER A. WEBER, NGS

Afternoon angler casts from a pier on North Carolina's Outer Banks, a sandy world stressed by man and the elements. DAVID ALAN HARVEY

OUTRAM, FRANK:
Author-Photographer

Burma Road, Back Door to China: Like the Great Wall of Ancient Times, This Mighty Mountain Highway Has Been Built by Myriad Chinese to Help Defend Their Homeland. By Frank Outram and G. E. Fane. 629-658, *Nov. 1940*

The **OUTSPEAKING** of a Great Democracy: The Proceedings of the Chamber of Deputies of France on Friday, April 6, 1917, as Reported in the "Journal Officiel de La République Française." 362-365, *Apr. 1917*

OUTWARD BOUND SCHOOL:

Journey to the Outer Limits. 150A-150B, *Jan. 1974*

OUTWITTING the Water Demons of Kashmir. By Maurice Pratt Dunlap. 499-511, *Nov. 1921*

OVAMBO TRIBESPEOPLE:

Namibia: Nearly a Nation? By Bryan Hodgson. Photos by Jim Brandenburg. 755-797, *June 1982*

OVER and Under Chesapeake Bay. By David S. Boyer. 593-612, *Apr. 1964*

OVER Plains and Hills of South Dakota. Photos by J. Baylor Roberts. 563-586, *May 1947*

OVER the Alps to Brenner Pass. 701-714, *Dec. 1943*

OVER the Andes to Bogotá. By Frank M. Chapman. 553-373, *Oct. 1921*

OVER the Roof of Our Continent. By Bradford Washburn. 78-98, *July 1938*

OVER the Sea to Scotland's Skye. By Robert J. Reynolds. 87-112, *July 1952*

OVER Trail and Through Jungle in Ecuador: Indian Headhunters of the Interior, an Interesting Study in the South American Republic. By H. E. Anthony. 327-352, *Oct. 1921*

OVERBECK, ALICIA O'REARDON:
Author

Tin, the Cinderella Metal. 659-684, *Nov. 1940*

Bolivia, Land of Fiestas. 645-660, *Nov. 1934*

Freiburg (Germany)–Gateway to the Black Forest. 213-252, *Aug. 1933*

OVERLAND Routes to the Klondike. By Hamlin Garland. 113-116, *Apr. 1898*

OWENS VALLEY, California:

California's Parched Oasis, the Owens Valley. By Judith and Neil Morgan. Photos by Jodi Cobb and Galen Rowell. 98-127, *Jan. 1976*

OWLS:

The Great Gray Owl. By Michael S. Quinton. 123-136, *July 1984*

Long-eared Owls–Masters of the Night. By Art Wolfe. 31-35, *Jan. 1980*

Photoflashing Western Owls. By Lewis W. Walker. Contents: Elf Owl, Great Horned Owl, Long-eared Owl, Screech Owl. 475-486, *Apr. 1945*

In Quest of the Golden Eagle: Over Lonely Mountain and Prairie Soars This Rare and Lordly Bird, But Three Youths from the East Catch Up With Him at Last. By John and Frank Craighead. Included: Barn Owl, Burrowing Owl, Great Horned Owl. 693-710, *May 1940*

Shadowy Birds of the Night. By Alexander Wetmore. Paintings by Allan Brooks. 217-240, *Feb. 1935*

American Birds of Prey–A Review of Their Value. 460-467, *Dec. 1920*

OXCARTS:

Land of the Painted Oxcarts (Costa Rica). By Luis Marden. 409-456, *Oct. 1946*

OXFORD, England:

The Thames: That Noble River. By Ethel A. Starbird. Photos by O. Louis Mazzatenta. 750-791, *June 1983*

Oxford, Mother of Anglo-Saxon Learning. By E. John Long. 563-596, *Nov. 1929*

Through the Heart of England in a Canadian Canoe. By R. J. Evans. 473-497, *May 1922*

OXHOLM, AXEL H.: *Author*

Country Life in Norway: The Beneficent Gulf Stream Enables One-third of the People in a Far-north, Mountainous Land to Prosper on Farms. 493-528, *Apr. 1939*

OXUS (River), Central Asia:

Surveying Through Khoresm: A Journey into Parts of Asiatic Russia Which Have Been Closed to Western Travelers Since the World War. By Lyman D. Wilbur. 753-780, *June 1932*

OYSTER FLEET:

Chincoteague: Watermen's Island Home. By Nathaniel T. Kenney.

Young long-eared owlets demonstrate their budding agility by lining up on a branch outside their nest. ART WOLFE

Photos by James L. Amos. 810-829, *June 1980*

The Sailing Oystermen of Chesapeake Bay. By Luis Marden. 798-819, *Dec. 1967*

OYSTERS:

The Pearl. By Fred Ward. 193-223, *Aug. 1985*

My Chesapeake–Queen of Bays. By Allan C. Fisher, Jr. Photos by Lowell Georgia. 428-467, *Oct. 1980*

Chesapeake Country. By Nathaniel T. Kenney. Photos by Bates Littlehales. 370-411, *Sept. 1964*

"Delmarva," Gift of the Sea. By Catherine Bell Palmer. 367-399, *Sept. 1950*

A Maryland Pilgrimage: Visits to Hallowed Shrines Recall the Major Rôle Played by This Prosperous State in the Development of Popular Government in America. By Gilbert Grosvenor. 133-212, *Feb. 1927*

The Dream Ship: The Story of a Voyage of Adventure More Than Half Around the World in a 47-foot Lifeboat. By Ralph Stock. 1-52, *Jan. 1921*

The Rise of the New Arab Nation. By Frederick Simpich. 369-393, *Nov. 1919*

America's Surpassing Fisheries: Their Present Condition and Future Prospects, and How the Federal Government Fosters Them. By Hugh M. Smith. 546-583, *June 1916*

Oysters: The World's Most Valuable Water Crop. By Hugh M. Smith. 257-281, *Mar. 1913*

The Pearl Fisheries of Ceylon. By Hugh M. Smith. 173-194, *Feb. 1912*

The Native Oysters of the West Coast. By Robert E. C. Stearns. 224-226, *Mar. 1908*

Cultivation of Marine and Fresh-Water Animals in Japan. By K. Mitsukuri. 524-531, *Sept. 1906*

OZARK PLATEAU, Arkansas-Missouri:

America's Little Mainstream. By Harvey Arden. Photos by Matt Bradley. Note: In 1972, Congress created the Buffalo National River, a unique administrative unit. 344-359, *Mar. 1977*

An Ozark Family Carves a Living and a Way of Life. Picture story by Bruce Dale. 124-133, *July 1975*

Through Ozark Hills and Hollows. By Mike W. Edwards. Photos by Bruce Dale. 656-689, *Nov. 1970*

Arkansas Rolls Up Its Sleeves. By Frederick Simpich. 273-312, *Sept. 1946*

Land of a Million Smiles. By Frederick Simpich. 589-623, *May 1943*

OZONE LAYER:

Air: An Atmosphere of Uncertainty. By Noel Grove. Photos by Ted Spiegel. Paintings by William H. Bond. Included: A deadly soup (a list of harmful chemicals), Careless neighbors, A global greenhouse, The ozone enigma, Getting the lead out, The enemy within. 502-537, *Apr. 1987*

O
P

Caledonia. Paintings by William F. Draper. 417-432, *Apr. 1944*

At Ease in the South Seas. By Frederick Simpich, Jr. 79-104, *Jan. 1944*

Revealing Earth's Mightiest Ocean. By Albert W. Atwood. 291-306, *Sept. 1943*

⊕ *Pacific Ocean and the Bay of Bengal. Sept. 1943*

Treasure Islands of Australasia: New Guinea, New Caledonia, and Fiji Trace across the South Pacific a Fertile Crescent Incredibly Rich in Minerals and Foods. By Douglas L. Oliver. 691-722, *June 1942*

Hidden Key to the Pacific: Piercing the Web of Secrecy Which Long Has Veiled Japanese Bases in the Mandated Islands. By Willard Price. 759-785, *June 1942*

⊕ *Theater of War in the Pacific Ocean. Feb. 1942*

Westward Bound in the *Yankee*. By Irving and Electa Johnson. Included: Easter Island; Galápagos Islands; Pitcairn; Samoa; Santa Cruz; Solomon Islands. 1-44, *Jan. 1942*

At Home on the Oceans: Whales and Sharks Make Exciting Neighbors for a Professor's Wife, Turned Able Seaman, On a Three-year Voyage Around the World. By Edith Bauer Strout. 33-86, *July 1939*

The "Pilgrim" Sails the Seven Seas: A Schooner Yacht Out of Boston Drops in at Desert Isles and South Sea Edens in a Leisurely Two-Year Voyage. By Harold Peters. 223-262, *Aug. 1937*

North About. By Alan J. Villiers. Included: Balabac, Philippines; Balimbing, Philippines; Barahun, Solomons; Bongao, Philippines;

Florida, Solomons; Guadalcanal, Solomons; Kawio, Pacific Ocean; Kiriwina, Trobriand Islands; Lusancay Islands, Pacific Ocean; Mambahenauhan, Sulu Sea; Nissan, Solomons; Santa Ana, Solomons; Santa Catalina, Solomons; Tawitawi, Philippines. 221-250, *Feb. 1937*

⊕ *Pacific Ocean. Dec. 1936*

Mysterious Micronesia: Yap, Map, and Other Islands Under Japanese Mandate are Museums of Primitive Man. By Willard Price. 481-510, *Apr. 1936*

Living on a Volcano: An Unspoiled Patch of Polynesia Is Niuafoō, Nicknamed "Tin Can Island" by Stamp Collectors. By Thomas A. Jaggar. 91-106, *July 1935*

Color Glimpses of the Changing South Seas. Photos by Amos Burg. 281-288, *Mar. 1934*

The Greatest Voyage in the Annals of the Sea. By J. R. Hildebrand. 699-739, *Dec. 1932*

A Modern Saga of the Seas: The Narrative of a 17,000-Mile Cruise on a 40-Foot Sloop by the Author, His Wife, and a Baby, Born on the Voyage. By Erling Tambs. 645-688, *Dec. 1931*

Around the World in the "Islander" (Yawl): A Narrative of the Adventures of a Solitary Voyager on His Four-Year Cruise in a Thirty-Four-Foot Sailing Craft. By Harry Pidgeon. 141-205, *Feb. 1928*

The Romance of Science in Polynesia: An Account of Five Years of Cruising Among the South Sea Islands. By Robert Cushman Murphy. Paintings by Hashime Murayama. 355-426, *Oct. 1925*

The Islands of the Pacific. By J. P. Thomson. 543-558, *Dec. 1921*

Yap and Other Pacific Islands Under Japanese Mandate. By Junius B. Wood. 591-627, *Dec. 1921*

⊕ *Sovereignty and Mandate Boundary Lines in 1921 of the Islands of the Pacific. Dec. 1921*

The Dream Ship: The Story of a Voyage of Adventure More Than Half Around the World in a 47-foot Lifeboat. By Ralph Stock. 1-52, *Jan. 1921*

In the Savage South Seas. By Beatrice Grimshaw. 1-19, *Jan. 1908*

Diary of a Voyage from San Francisco to Tahiti and Return, 1901. By S. P. Langley. 413-429, *Dec. 1901*

Our New Possessions and the Interest They Are Exciting. By O. P. Austin. 32-33, *Jan. 1900*

See also Melanesia; Micronesia; Polynesia; *and* islands of Pacific-bordering nations

PACIFIC MAP Played Providential Role: How One of the Society's Maps Saved a Precious Cargo. 844, *June 1947*

PACIFIC NORTHWEST (Region), U. S.:

⊕ *Pacific Northwest,* The Making of America series. Included: Idaho, Montana, Oregon, Washington. On reverse: Fur Trade Rivalries, Conquest-Colonization, Abrupt Change, Pacific Lumber Empire, Coming of Age. *Aug. 1986*

Wartime in the Pacific Northwest. By Frederick Simpich. 421-464, *Oct. 1942*

The Columbia Turns on the Power. By Maynard Owen Williams. 749-792, *June 1941*

The doomed brigantine Yankee *heels in the surf after breaking from her anchors off Rarotonga in the South Pacific.* FRANK J. DUNN

A young girl poses warily on the beach of Hereheretue Atoll in the Tuamotu Archipelago of the South Pacific Ocean.

Remnants of thousand-year-old Pagan, Burma's first imperial capital, include some 2,000 temples. JAMES L. STANFIELD, NGS

Painting of a woman holding an ermine reflects Leonardo da Vinci's mastery.

CZARTÓRYSKI MUSEUM, KRAKÓW, POLAND

A section of da Vinci's "Last Supper" shows the patch-by-patch restoration of the masterpiece after centuries of deterioration and abuse. VICTOR R. BOSWELL, JR., NGS

Training in bordering Pakistan in 1985, an Afghan boy wields a wooden version of the Soviet-made AK-47.   STEVE McCURRY

O
P

In the far Pacific a young student on Mogmog, an island of Yap state, heads for class in a grass skirt. DAVID HISER

Paleo-Indian hunters fashioned these Clovis spearpoints found in Washington State. WARREN MORGAN

Fossils in Alberta, Canada. By Barnum Brown. 407-429, *May 1919*

The Larger North American Mammals. By E. W. Nelson. Paintings by Louis Agassiz Fuertes. Included: Pictorial supplement. 385-472, *Nov. 1916*

Reptiles of All Lands. By Raymond L. Ditmars. Contents: Brontosaurus, Diplodocus, Stegosaurus. 601-633, *July 1911*

Our Coal Lands. By Guy Elliott Mitchell. 446-451, *May 1910*

A Strange and Remarkable Beast (Mammoth). 620, *Sept. 1907*

Extinct Reptiles Found in Nodules. By H. A. Largelamb. (Alexander Graham Bell). 170-173, *Mar. 1906*

The Wyoming Fossil Fields Expedition of July, 1899. By Wilbur C. Knight. 449-465, *Dec. 1900*

Report on Fossil Plants (Mount St. Elias Expedition). By Lester F. Ward. 199-200, *May 29, 1891*

See also Aepyornis; Brontosaurs; *and* American Museum of Natural History; Dinosaur National Monument; *and* Australopithecines; Hominids; Man, Prehistoric; Paleo-Indians

PALERMO, Sicily:

Sicily, Where All the Songs Are Sad. By Howard La Fay. Photos by Jonathan Blair. 407-436, *Mar. 1976*

Sicily Again in the Path of War. By Maynard Owen Williams. 307-320, *Sept. 1943*

Sicily, the Battle-Field of Nations and of Nature. By Mrs. George C. Bosson, Jr. 97-118, *Jan. 1909*

PALESTINE:

Palestine Today. By Francis Chase, Jr. 501-516, *Oct. 1946*

American Fighters Visit Bible Lands. By Maynard Owen Williams. 311-340, *Mar. 1946*

The Geography of the Jordan. By Nelson Glueck. 719-744, *Dec. 1944*

On the Trail of King Solomon's Mines: The Bible, in Addition to Its Spiritual Values, Continues to Prove a Rich Geography and Guide to Exploration of the Holy Land. By Nelson Glueck. 233-256, *Feb. 1944*

Bombs over Bible Lands. By Frederick Simpich and W. Robert Moore. 141-180, *Aug. 1941*

Canoeing Down the River Jordan: Voyagers in Rubber Boats Find the Bible Stream Little Tamed Today as It Plunges to the Dead Sea Over the Earth's Lowest River Bed. By John D. Whiting. 781-808, *Dec. 1940*

Change Comes to Bible Lands. By Frederick Simpich. 695-750, *Dec. 1938*

Changing Palestine. By Edward Keith-Roach. 493-527, *Apr. 1934*

The Road of the Crusaders: A Historian Follows the Steps of Richard the Lion Heart and Other Knights of the Cross Over the "Via Dei." By Harold Lamb. 645-693, *Dec. 1933*

Crusader Castles of the Near East. By William H. Hall. 369-390, *Mar. 1931*

Bethlehem and the Christmas Story. By John D. Whiting. 699-735, *Dec. 1929*

Skirting the Shores of Sunrise: Seeking and Finding "The Levant" in a Journey by Steamer, Motor-Car, and Train from Constantinople to Port Said. By Melville Chater. 649-728, *Dec. 1926*

Among the Bethlehem Shepherds: A Visit to the Valley Which David Probably Recalled When He Wrote the Twenty-third Psalm. By John D. Whiting. 729-753, *Dec. 1926*

Flying Over Egypt, Sinai, and Palestine: Looking Down Upon the Holy Land During an Air Journey of Two and a Half Hours from Cairo to Jerusalem. By P.R.C. Groves and J. R. McCrindle. 313-355, *Sept. 1926*

The Last Israelitish Blood Sacrifice: How the Vanishing Samaritans Celebrate the Passover on Sacred Mount Gerizim. By John D. Whiting. 1-46, *Jan. 1920*

An Old Jewel in the Proper Setting: An Eyewitness's Account of the Conquest of the Holy Land by Twentieth Century Crusaders. By Charles W. Whitehair. 325-344, *Oct. 1918*

Jerusalem's Locust Plague: Being a Description of the Recent Locust Influx into Palestine, and Comparing Same with Ancient Locust Invasions as Narrated in the Old World's History Book, the Bible. By John D. Whiting. 511-550, *Dec. 1915*

Impressions of Palestine. By James Bryce. 293-317, *Mar. 1915*

Village Life in the Holy Land. By John D. Whiting. 249-314, *Mar. 1914*

Palestine. Photos by the American Colony, Jerusalem. 265-313, *Mar. 1914*

See also Holy Land; Israel; Jerusalem; Jordan

PALESTINE LIBERATION ORGANIZATION (PLO):

Beirut–Up From the Rubble. By William S. Ellis. Photos by Steve McCurry. 262-286, *Feb. 1983*

Clutching prayer beads, a patriarch of Bethlehem dispenses wisdom to passersby from his window in a land called Palestine in 1929. AMERICAN COLONY PHOTOGRAPHERS

Tragedy strikes during the Palio—an annual race in Siena, Italy—as horses go down rounding a sharp turn. One prize gelding had to be destroyed. O. LOUIS MAZZATENTA, NGS

PALESTINIAN REFUGEES:

Jordan: Kingdom in the Middle. By Thomas J. Abercrombie. Photos by Jodi Cobb. 236-268, *Feb. 1984*

Beirut–Up From the Rubble. By William S. Ellis. Photos by Steve McCurry. 262-286, *Feb. 1983*

A **PALETTE** from Spain. By W. Langdon Kihn. 407-440, *Mar. 1936*

PALIO (Horse Race), Siena, Italy:

Palio, Siena's Centuries-Old 90-second Horse Race. Photos by O. Louis Mazzatenta. 745-749, *June 1988*

The Renaissance Lives On in Tuscany. By Luis Marden. Photos by Albert Moldvay. 626-659, *Nov. 1974*

The Palio of Siena. By Edgar Erskine Hume. 231-244, *Aug. 1951*

Siena's Palio, an Italian Inheritance from the Middle Ages. By Marie Louise Handley. 245-258, *Aug. 1926*

PALISADES, New York-New Jersey:

The Mighty Hudson. By Albert W. Atwood. Photos by B. Anthony Stewart. 1-36, *July 1948*

PALISADES INTERSTATE PARK, New York-New Jersey:

Skyline Trail from Maine to Georgia. By Andrew H. Brown. Photos by Robert F. Sisson. 219-251, *Aug. 1949*

PALM SPRINGS, California:

Californians Escape to the Desert. By Mason Sutherland. Photos by Charles W. Herbert. 675-724, *Nov. 1957*

PALM TREES:

What's Killing the Palm Trees? By Randolph E. McCoy. Photos by Guillermo Aldana E. 120-130, *July 1988*

The Paradise of the Tasman (Lord Howe Island): A Pacific Island Provides the Palms Which Decorate Hotels, Churches, Steamships, and Homes. By Hubert Lyman Clark. 115-136, *July 1935*

The Palms. Pictorial supplement. *Dec. 1911*

See also Coconut Palms; Date Palms

PALMAR, C. ERIC:
Author-Photographer

Scotland's Golden Eagles at Home. 273-286, *Feb. 1954*

PALMER, ALFRED MONROE:

Yemen–Southern Arabia's Mountain Wonderland. By Harlan B. Clark. 631-672, *Nov. 1947*

PALMER, ALFRED T.: *Photographer*

Great Lakes and Great Industries. Photos by B. Anthony Stewart, Alfred T. Palmer, and Willard R. Culver. 689-712, *Dec. 1944*

Changing Canton. Photos by Siukee Mack, Alfred T. Palmer, and Kinchue Wong. 711-726, *Dec. 1937*

PALMER, CATHERINE BELL:
Author

Crickets, Nature's Expert Fiddlers. 385-394, *Sept. 1953*

"Delmarva," Gift of the Sea. 367-399, *Sept. 1950*

Appalachian Valley Pilgrimage. 1-32, *July 1949*

Split-second Time Runs Today's World. By F. Barrows Colton and Catherine Bell Palmer. 399-428, *Sept. 1947*

Flying Our Wounded Veterans Home. 363-384, *Sept. 1945*

PALMER, HOWARD:
Author-Photographer

Some Tramps Across the Glaciers and Snowfields of British Columbia. 457-487, *June 1910*

PALMER, NATHANIEL:

New Stamps for Antarctic Explorers. Geographica. *Oct. 1988*

PALMER STATION, Antarctica:

Krill–Untapped Bounty From the Sea? By William M. Hamner. Photos by Flip Nicklin. 626-643, *May 1984*

PALMERSTON ISLAND, South Pacific Ocean:

The Dream Ship: The Story of a Voyage of Adventure More Than Half Around the World in a 47-foot Lifeboat. By Ralph Stock. 1-52, *Jan. 1921*

PALMS and Planes in the New Hebrides. By Robert D. Heinl, Jr. 229-256, *Aug. 1944*

PALMSTROM, WILLIAM N.: *Artist*

Space Satellites, Tools of Earth Research. By Heinz Haber. 487-509, *Apr. 1956*

PALOMAR OBSERVATORY, Mount Palomar, San Diego County, California:

✦ *Journey Into the Universe Through Time and Space; National Geographic-Palomar Sky Survey Charting the Heavens, June 1983*

Sky Survey Charts the Universe. By Ira Sprague Bowen. 780-781, *Dec. 1956*

Exploring the Farthest Reaches of Space. By George O. Abell. NGS research grant. 782-790, *Dec. 1956*

Completing the Atlas of the Universe (National Geographic Society-Palomar Observatory Sky Survey). By Ira Sprague Bowen. Included: Sky Survey Plates Unlock Secrets of the Stars. NGS research grant. 185-190, *Aug. 1955*

Our Universe Unfolds New Wonders

Cuna Indian women of Panama's San Blas Islands wear reverse appliqué blouses called **molas.** HILDA HARRISON

NATIONAL GEOGRAPHIC INDEX 1888-1988

BIRD'S-EYE VIEW OF THE PANAMA CANAL
Supplement to the National Geographic Magazine (Washington, D. C.) February, 1912, Gilbert H. Grosvenor, Editor

This bird's-eye view of the Panama Canal appeared with the February 1912 issue, two years before the waterway opened to traffic.

(National Geographic-Palomar Sky Survey). By Albert G. Wilson. 245-260, *Feb. 1952*

Mapping the Unknown Universe. By F. Barrows Colton. 401-420, *Sept. 1950*

PALOUSE HILLS, Idaho-Washington:

A Paradise Called the Palouse. By Barbara Austin. Photos by Phil Schofield. 798-819, *June 1982*

PAMIR (Ship):

Last of the Cape Horners. By Alan Villiers. Included: Square-rigger in a Tempest. 701-710, *May 1948*

PAMIRS (Mountains), Central Asia:

American Skiers Find Adventure in Western China. By Ned Gillette. Photos by the author and Galen Rowell. Included: Skiing From the Summit of China's Ice Mountain. 174-199, *Feb. 1981*

Winter Caravan to the Roof of the World. By Sabrina and Roland Michaud. 435-465, *Apr. 1972*

We Took the Highroad in Afghanistan. By Jean and Franc Shor. 673-706, *Nov. 1950*

PAMPA GALERAS NATIONAL VICUÑA RESERVE, Peru:

High, Wild World of the Vicuña. By William L. Franklin. 77-91, *Jan. 1973*

PAMPAS (Grasslands):

High, Wild World of the Vicuña. By William L. Franklin. 77-91, *Jan. 1973*

PANAMA:

Panama: Ever at the Crossroads. By Charles E. Cobb, Jr. Photos by Danny Lehman. 466-493, *Apr. 1986*

The Amazing Frog-Eating Bat. By Merlin D. Tuttle. 78-91, *Jan. 1982*

Troubled Times for Central America.

By Wilbur E. Garrett, Editor. 58-61, *July 1981*

The Panama Canal Today. By Bart McDowell. Photos by George F. Mobley. 279-294, *Feb. 1978*

Robin Sails Home. By Robin Lee Graham. 504-545, *Oct. 1970*

Panama, Link Between Oceans and Continents. By Jules B. Billard. Photos by Bruce Dale. 402-440, *Mar. 1970*

We Drove Panama's Darién Gap. By Kip Ross. 368-389, *Mar. 1961*

Hunting Prehistory in Panama Jungles. By Matthew W. Stirling. Photos by Richard H. Stewart. NGS research grant. 271-290, *Aug. 1953*

Exploring Ancient Panama by Helicopter. By Matthew W. Stirling. Photos by Richard H. Stewart. Included: Archaeological sites in provinces of Chiriquí and Veraguas. NGS research grant. 227-246, *Feb. 1950*

Exploring the Past in Panama. By Matthew W. Stirling. Photos by Richard H. Stewart. Included: Azuero Peninsula, Tambor region. NGS research grant. 373-399, *Mar. 1949*

Panama, Bridge of the World. By Luis Marden. 591-630, *Nov. 1941*

Arch-Isolationists, the San Blas Indians: Coconuts Serve as Cash on Islands Off the Panama Coast Where Tribesmen Cling to Their Ancient Ways and Discourage Visitors. By Corine B. Feeney. 193-220, *Feb. 1941*

Who Treads Our Trails? A Camera Trapper Describes His Experiences on an Island in the Canal Zone, a Natural-History Laboratory in the American Tropics. By Frank M. Chapman. 331-345, *Sept. 1927*

The Jungles of Panama. By David Fairchild. 131-145, *Feb. 1922*

Nature's Transformation at Panama:

Remarkable Changes in Faunal and Physical Conditions in the Gatun Lake Region. By George Shiras, 3d. 159-194, *Aug. 1915*

Redeeming the Tropics. By William Joseph Showalter. 344-364, *Mar. 1914*

Little-Known Parts of Panama. By Henry Pittier. 627-662, *July 1912*

Farming on the Isthmus of Panama. By Dillwyn M. Hazlett. 229-234, *Apr. 1906*

Improvements in the Republic of Panama. 441-442, *Sept. 1905*

The Republic of Panama. By William H. Burr. 57-73, *Feb. 1904*

Notes on Panama and Colombia. 458-466, *Dec. 1903*

The Latest Route Proposed for the Isthmian Canal–Mandingo Route. 64-70, *Feb. 1902*

The Panama Canal Route. By Robert T. Hill. 59-64, *Feb. 1896*

A Trip to Panama and Darien. By Richard U. Goode. 301-314, *Oct. 1889*

PANAMA CANAL:

Editorial. By Gilbert M. Grosvenor. 141, *Feb. 1978*

The Panama Canal Today. By Bart McDowell. Photos by George F. Mobley. 279-294, *Feb. 1978*

Panama, Link Between Oceans and Continents. By Jules B. Billard. Photos by Bruce Dale. 402-440, *Mar. 1970*

Panama, Bridge of the World. By Luis Marden. 591-630, *Nov. 1941*

⊕ *The Countries of the Caribbean, Including Mexico, Central America, the West Indies, and the Panama Canal. Feb. 1922*

The Dream Ship: The Story of a Voyage of Adventure More Than Half Around the World in a 47-foot Lifeboat. By Ralph Stock. 1-52, *Jan. 1921*

Honors to Colonel Goethals: The Presentation, by President Woodrow Wilson, of the National Geographic Society Special Gold Medal. 677-690, *June 1914*

Battling with the Panama Slides. By William Joseph Showalter. 133-153, *Feb. 1914*

The Panama Canal. By William L. Sibert. 153-183, *Feb. 1914*

The Probable Effect of the Panama Canal on the Commercial Geography of the World. By O. P. Austin. 245-248, *Feb. 1914*

The Panama Canal. By William Joseph Showalter. 195-205, 208, *Feb. 1912*

⊕ *Bird's-Eye View of the Panama Canal.* Relief map painting by H. H. Green. *Feb. 1912*

The Panama Canal. By George W. Goethals. 148-211, *Feb. 1911*

The Panama Canal. By George W. Goethals. 334-355, *Apr. 1909*

The Work on the Isthmus. 586-587, *Oct. 1906*

Notes on the Panama Canal. By Theodore P. Shonts. 362-363, *June 1906*

The Panama Canal. By Theodore P. Shonts. 55-68, *Feb. 1906*

What Has Been Accomplished by the United States Toward Building the Panama Canal. By Theodore P. Shonts. 558-564, *Dec. 1905*

The Panama Canal. By Colby M. Chester. 445-467, *Oct. 1905*

Progress on the Panama Canal. By Gilbert H. Grosvenor. 467-475, *Oct. 1905*

⊕ *Map Showing Location of Panama Canal,* as recommended by the Isthmian Canal Commission of 1899-1902. *Oct. 1905*

The Republic of Panama. By William H. Burr. 57-73, *Feb. 1904*

The completed report of the Isthmian Canal Commission. 441, *Dec. 1901*

The Proposed American Interoceanic Canal in Its Commercial Aspects. By Joseph Nimmo, Jr. 297-310, *Aug. 1899*

The Interoceanic Canal. By Emory R. Johnson. 311-316, *Aug. 1899*

Nicaragua and the Isthmian Routes. By Arthur P. Davis. 247-266, *July 1899*

Completion of the La Boca Dock. 84, *Mar. 1898*

The Panama Canal Route. By Robert T. Hill. 59-64, *Feb. 1896*

Geography of the Land. Annual Report by Vice-President Herbert G. Ogden. 31-40, *Apr. 30, 1891*

A Trip to Panama and Darien. By Richard U. Goode. 301-314, *Oct. 1889*

PANAMA-PACIFIC INTERNATIONAL EXPOSITION:

A City of Realized Dreams (San Francisco). By Franklin K. Lane. 169-171, *Feb. 1915*

PANAMA RAILROAD:

A Trip to Panama and Darien. By Richard U. Goode. 301-314, *Oct. 1889*

PAN AMERICAN AIRWAYS:

Over the Roof of Our Continent (Mount McKinley). By Bradford Washburn. 78-98, *July 1938*

Flying the Pacific. By William Burke Miller. 665-707, *Dec. 1936*

PAN-AMERICAN CONFERENCES:

What the Latin American Republics Think of the Pan-American Conferences. 474-479, *Aug. 1906*

Reasons Why the United States in Particular Should Encourage the Pan-American Conferences. By Elihu Root. 479-480, *Aug. 1906*

PAN-AMERICAN EXPOSITION:

The Philippine Exhibit at the Pan-American Exposition. By D. O. Noble Hoffmann. 119-122, *Mar. 1901*

PAN AMERICAN GOOD WILL FLYERS:

How Latin America Looks from the Air: U. S. Army Airplanes Hurdle the High Andes, Brave Brazil Jungles, and Follow Smoking Volcanoes to Map New Sky Paths Around South America. By Herbert A. Dargue. 451-502, *Oct. 1927*

PAN AMERICAN HIGHWAY:

We Drove Panama's Darién Gap. By Kip Ross. 368-389, *Mar. 1961*

PAN-AMERICAN RAILWAY:

Pan-American Railway. 232-233, *May 1904*

South America. Annual Address by the President, Gardiner G. Hubbard. 1-29, *Mar. 28, 1891*

PANAMIN. *See* Presidential Arm for National Minorities (Philippines)

PANAMINT RANGE, California:

Getting to Know the Wild Burros of Death Valley. By Patricia des Roses Moehlman. Photos by Ira S. Lerner and author. 502-517, *Apr. 1972*

PANDAS, Giant:

Secrets of the Wild Panda. By George B. Schaller. Included: Saving the panda. 284-309, *Mar. 1986*

■ Save the Panda. 824, *Dec. 1982*

Pandas in the Wild. By George B. Schaller. 735-749, *Dec. 1981*

What's Black and White and Loved All Over? By Theodore H. Reed. Photos by Donna K. Grosvenor. 803-815, *Dec. 1972*

PANDORA, H.M.S.:

Editorial. By Wilbur E. Garrett. 421, *Oct. 1985*

Wreck of H.M.S. *Pandora.* By Luis Marden. 423-451, *Oct. 1985*

PANORAMAS. *See* Painting Supplements *and* Photo Supplements

PANORAMIC View from the west side of Burgess Pass, 3280 feet above Field, British Columbia, in the Canadian Rockies. 521, *June 1911*

The **PANTHER** of the Hearth: Lithe Grace and Independence of Spirit Contribute to the Appeal of Cats, "The Only Domestic Animal Man Has Never Conquered." By Frederick B. Eddy. Included: Catdom's Royalty Photographed in Color. Photos by Willard R. Culver. 589-634, *Nov. 1938*

PANTHERS. *See* Mountain Lions

PAPAGO INDIANS:

The Old Yuma Trail. By W J McGee. 103-107, *Mar. 1901*; 129-143, *Apr. 1901*

Papagueria. By W J McGee. 345-371, *Aug. 1898*

PAPAGUERIA (U. S.-Mexico). By W J McGee. 345-371, *Aug. 1898*

PAPEETE, Tahiti, Society Islands:

The Society Islands, Sisters of the Wind. By Priit J. Vesilind. Photos by George F. Mobley. 844-869, *June 1979*

Tahiti: A Playground of Nature. By Paul Gooding. 301-326, *Oct. 1920*

Notes on Tahiti. By H. W. Smith. 947-963, *Oct. 1911*

PAPER PULP INDUSTRY:

Madawaska: Down East With a French Accent. By Perry Garfinkel. Photos by Cary Wolinsky. 380-409, *Sept. 1980*

Jari: A Billion-dollar Gamble. By Loren McIntyre. Contents: Daniel K. Ludwig's paper-pulp and food-production enterprise in Brazil's Amazon basin. 686-711, *May 1980*

Brazil's Wild Frontier. By Loren McIntyre. Included: Daniel K. Ludwig's three-million-acre agricultural and forestry experiment. 684-719, *Nov. 1977*

Timber: How Much Is Enough? By John J. Putman. Photos by Bruce Dale. 485-511, *Apr. 1974*

Amazon–The River Sea. By Loren McIntyre. Included: Daniel K. Ludwig's planned paper-pulp and food-production enterprise in Brazil's Amazon basin. 456-495, *Oct. 1972*

A River Restored: Oregon's Willamette. By Ethel A. Starbird. Photos by Lowell Georgia. 816-835, *June 1972*

From Sagebrush to Roses on the Columbia. By Leo A. Borah. 571-611, *Nov. 1952*

Versatile Wood Waits on Man. By Andrew H. Brown. 109-140, *July 1951*

Dixie Spins the Wheel of Industry. By William H. Nicholas. Photos by J. Baylor Roberts. 281-324, *Mar. 1949*

Massachusetts–Beehive of Business. By William Joseph Showalter. 203-245, *Mar. 1920*

Paper From Cotton Stalks. 425, *July 1906*

Lessons from Japan. 221-225, *May 1904*

PAPUA NEW GUINEA (Australian New Guinea and North-East New Guinea):

Ghosts of War in the South Pacific. By Peter Benchley. Photos by David Doubilet. 424-457, *Apr. 1988*

Living Theater in New Guinea's Highlands. By Gillian Gillison. Photos by David Gillison. 147-169, *Aug. 1983*

Tropical Rain Forests: Nature's Dwindling Treasures. By Peter T. White. Photos by James P. Blair. Paintings by Barron Storey. 2-47, *Jan. 1983*

Papua New Guinea. 143-171. I. Nation in the Making. By Robert J. Gordon. Photos by David Austen. 143-149; II

Female giant panda in China's Wolong Natural Reserve eats as much as 40 pounds of bamboo leaves and stems a day, her only easy wintertime food source. GEORGE B. SCHALLER

Unmapped Nooks of Sorcery and Cannibalism. By E. W. Brandes. 253-332, *Sept. 1929*
Pictorial Jaunt Through Papua. Photos by Frank Hurley. 109-124, *Jan. 1927*
Strange Sights in Far-Away Papua. By A. E. Pratt. 559-572, *Sept. 1907*
See also Australian New Guinea *and* New Britain

PAPYRUS SHIP:

The Voyage of *Ra II*. By Thor Heyerdahl. Photos by Carlo Mauri and Georges Sourial. 44-71, *Jan. 1971*

PARACHUTE JUMPS:

By Parachute Into Peru's Lost World. By G. Brooks Baekeland. Photos by author and Peter R. Gimbel. NGS research grant. 268-296, *Aug. 1964*
The Long, Lonely Leap. By Joseph W. Kittinger, Jr. Photos by Volkmar Wentzel. 854-873, *Dec. 1960*
Graduation by Parachute. By John E. Fletcher. 833-846, *June 1952*

PARACHUTE RIGGER SCHOOL, Lakehurst, New Jersey:

Graduation by Parachute. By John E. Fletcher. 833-846, *June 1952*

PARADE of Life Through the Ages: Records in Rocks Reveal a Strange Procession of Prehistoric Creatures, from Jellyfish to Dinosaurs, Giant Sloths, Saber-toothed Tigers, and Primitive Man. By Charles R. Knight. Paintings by author. 141-184, *Feb. 1942*

PARADISE Beneath the Sea. By Ron and Valerie Taylor. 636-663, *May 1981*

A **PARADISE** Called the Palouse. By Barbara Austin. Photos by Phil Schofield. 798-819, *June 1982*

PARADISE Comes of Age: the U. S. Virgin Islands. By Thomas J. Colin. Photos by William Albert Allard and Cary Wolinsky. 225-243, *Feb. 1981*

The **PARADISE** of the Tasman: A Pacific Island Provides the Palms Which Decorate Hotels, Churches, Steamships, and Homes. By Hubert Lyman Clark. 115-136, *July 1935*

"**PARADISE** on Earth": When the Moguls Ruled India. By Mike Edwards. Photos by Roland Michaud. 463-493, *Apr. 1985*

PARA-EXPLORERS Challenge Peru's Unknown Vilcabamba. By G. Brooks Baekeland. Photos by author and Peter R. Gimbel. NGS research grant. 268-296, *Aug. 1964*

PARAGUAY:

Paraguay, Paradox of South America. By Gordon Young. Photos by O. Louis Mazzatenta. 240-269, *Aug. 1982*
Through Paraguay and Southern Matto Grosso. By Sir Christopher H. Gibson. 459-488, *Oct. 1943*
River-Encircled Paraguay. By Harriet Chalmers Adams. 385-416, *Apr. 1933*
Buenos Aires and Its River of Silver: A

Journey Through Time. By François Leydet. Photos by David Austen. 150-171. *Aug. 1982*
Fertility Rites and Sorcery in a New Guinea Village (Gimi People). By Gillian Gillison. Photos by David Gillison. 124-146, *July 1977*
Change Ripples New Guinea's Sepik River. By Malcolm S. Kirk. 354-381, *Sept. 1973*
Journey Into Stone Age New Guinea. By Malcolm S. Kirk. 568-592, *Apr. 1969*
New Guinea. The Editor. 583, *May 1962*
Australian New Guinea. By John Scofield. 604-637, *May 1962*
New Guinea to Bali in *Yankee*. By Irving and Electa Johnson. 767-815, *Dec. 1959*
Off the Beaten Track of Empire (Prince Philip's Tour). By Beverley M.

Bowie. Photos by Michael Parker. 584-626, *Nov. 1957*
To the Land of the Head-hunters. By E. Thomas Gilliard. NGS research grant. 437-486, *Oct. 1955*
New Guinea's Rare Birds and Stone Age Mén. By E. Thomas Gilliard. NGS research grant. 421-488, *Apr. 1953*
Yankee Roams the Orient. By Irving and Electa Johnson. 327-370, *Mar. 1951*
Sheep Airlift in New Guinea. Photos by Ned Blood. Contents: The Hallstrom Trust's Nondugl Sheep Station in Australian New Guinea. 831-844, *Dec. 1949*
Adventures with the Survey Navy. By Irving Johnson. 131-148, *July 1947*
Into Primeval Papua by Seaplane: Seeking Disease-resisting Sugar Cane, Scientists Find Neolithic Man in

A ranch foreman in Paraguay's Chaco region greets his son while braiding a leather lasso. O. LOUIS MAZZATENTA, NGS

Riding down the Champs Elysées in September 1944, a U.S. soldier reads the first Paris edition of the **Stars and Stripes** *newspaper of World War II.* U.S. ARMY SIGNAL CORPS, OFFICIAL

His Gallic expression captured by the photographer, Quebec tobacco farmer Gérard Ricard speaks French, as do a quarter of his fellow Canadians. WINFIELD PARKS, NGS

Germany and Austria. 365-394, *Mar. 1932*

PARKER, FRANCIS W.: *Author*

The Relation of Geography to History. 125-131, *Jan. 31, 1894*

PARKER, MARGERY PRITCHARD: *Author*

A Northern Crusoe's Island: Life on a Fox Farm Off the Coast of Alaska, Far from Contact with the World Eleven Months a Year. 313-326, *Sept. 1923*

PARKER, MICHAEL: *Photographer*

Off the Beaten Track of Empire (Prince Philip's Tour). By Beverley M. Bowie. 584-626, *Nov. 1957*

PARKS, WINFIELD:

Nomination Page. *Sept. 1975*
Nomination Page. *July 1966*

Author

Down East to Nova Scotia. 853-879, *June 1964*

Photographer

The Danube: River of Many Nations, Many Names. By Mike Edwards. 455-485, *Oct. 1977*
One Canada–or Two? By Peter T. White. 436-465, *Apr. 1977*
Romania: Maverick on a Tightrope. By William S. Ellis. 688-713, *Nov. 1975*
The Arab World, Inc. By John J. Putman. 494-533, *Oct. 1975*
The Phoenicians, Sea Lords of Antiquity. By Samuel W. Matthews. Paintings by Robert C. Magis. 149-189, *Aug. 1974*
Istanbul, the City That Links Europe and Asia. By William S. Ellis. 501-533, *Oct. 1973*
The Isles of Greece: Aegean Birthplace of Western Culture. By Melville Bell Grosvenor. Photos by Edwin Stuart Grosvenor and Winfield Parks. 147-193, *Aug. 1972*

Cairo, Troubled Capital of the Arab World. By William S. Ellis. 639-667, *May 1972*
Carnival in Trinidad. By Howard La Fay. 693-701, *Nov. 1971*
The Arans, Ireland's Invincible Isles. By Veronica Thomas. 545-573, *Apr. 1971*
When in Rome.... By Stuart E. Jones. 741-789, *June 1970*
Okinawa, the Island Without a Country. By Jules B. Billard. Photos by Winfield Parks and David Moore. 422-448, *Sept. 1969*
Queensland: Young Titan of Australia's Tropic North. By Kenneth MacLeish. 593-639, *Nov. 1968*
Iran's Shah Crowns Himself and His Empress. By Franc Shor. Photos by James L. Stanfield and Winfield Parks. 301-321, *Mar. 1968*
The Highlands, Stronghold of Scottish Gaeldom. By Kenneth MacLeish. 398-435, *Mar. 1968*
Buenos Aires, Argentina's Melting-pot Metropolis. By Jules B. Billard. 662-695, *Nov. 1967*
Behind the Headlines in Viet Nam. By Peter T. White. 149-189, *Feb. 1967*
A Fresh Breeze Stirs the Leewards. By Carleton Mitchell. 488-537, *Oct. 1966*
Singapore, Reluctant Nation. By Kenneth MacLeish. 269-300, *Aug. 1966*
Finisterre Sails the Windward Islands. By Carleton Mitchell. 755-801, *Dec. 1965*
Yankee Cruises the Storied Nile. By Irving and Electa Johnson. 583-633, *May 1965*
Time Turns Back in Picture-book Portofino. By Carleton Mitchell. 232-253, *Feb. 1965*
Tokyo, the Peaceful Explosion. By William Graves. 445-487, *Oct. 1964*
Florida Rides a Space-age Boom. By Benedict Thielen. Photos by

Winfield Parks and James P. Blair. 858-903, *Dec. 1963*
In Storied Lands of Malaysia. By Maurice Shadbolt. 734-783, *Nov. 1963*
Canada's Dynamic Heartland, Ontario. By Marjorie Wilkins Campbell. 58-97, *July 1963*
Lonely Wonders of Katmai. By Ernest Gruening. 800-831, *June 1963*
Brazil, Ôba! By Peter T. White. 299-353, *Sept. 1962*

PARKS:

Parks, Plans, and People: How South America Guards Her Green Legacy. By Mary and Laurance Rockefeller. Photos by George F. Mobley. 74-119, *Jan. 1967*
The Parks in Your Backyard (U. S.). By Conrad L. Wirth. 647-707, *Nov. 1963*
See also Gardens; National Parks; National Recreation Areas; State Parks; Waterton-Glacier International Peace Park; World Heritage Sites

PARKSCAPE, U.S.A.: Tomorrow in Our National Parks. By George B. Hartzog, 48-93, *July 1966*

PARLIAMENT, British, London, England:

Westminster, the Palace That Became Parliament. 728-757. By Patrick Cormack. Photos by Adam Woolfitt. Included: Royal Pomp Before Debate: In Centuries-old Ceremonial, the Queen Opens Parliament. 730-732, *Dec. 1986*
Queen Elizabeth Opens Parliament. By W. E. Roscher. Photos by Robert B. Goodman. 699-707, *Nov. 1961*
Yanks at Westminster. By Leonard David Gammans. 223-252, *Aug. 1946*
The Oldest Free Assemblies: Address of Right Hon. Arthur J. Balfour, in the United States House of Representatives, May 5, 1917. 368-371, *Apr. 1917*

PARMA (Ship):

The Cape Horn Grain-Ship Race: The Gallant "Parma" Leads the Vanishing Fleet of Square-Riggers Through Raging Gales and Irksome Calms 16,000 Miles, from Australia to England. By A. J. Villiers. 1-39, *Jan. 1933*

PARNASSUS, Mount, Greece:

Festival Days on the Slopes of Mount Parnassus. Photos by Maynard Owen Williams. 713-720, *Dec. 1930*

PARO JONG (Fort), Bhutan:

Castles in the Air: Experiences and Journeys in Unknown Bhutan. By John Claude White. 365-455, *Apr. 1914*

PARO-TA-TSHANG (Monastery), Bhutan:

Castles in the Air: Experiences and Journeys in Unknown Bhutan. By John Claude White. 365-455, *Apr. 1914*

PARR, GRANT: *Author*

War Meets Peace in Egypt. By Grant Parr and G. E. Janssen. 503-526, *Apr. 1942*

O
P

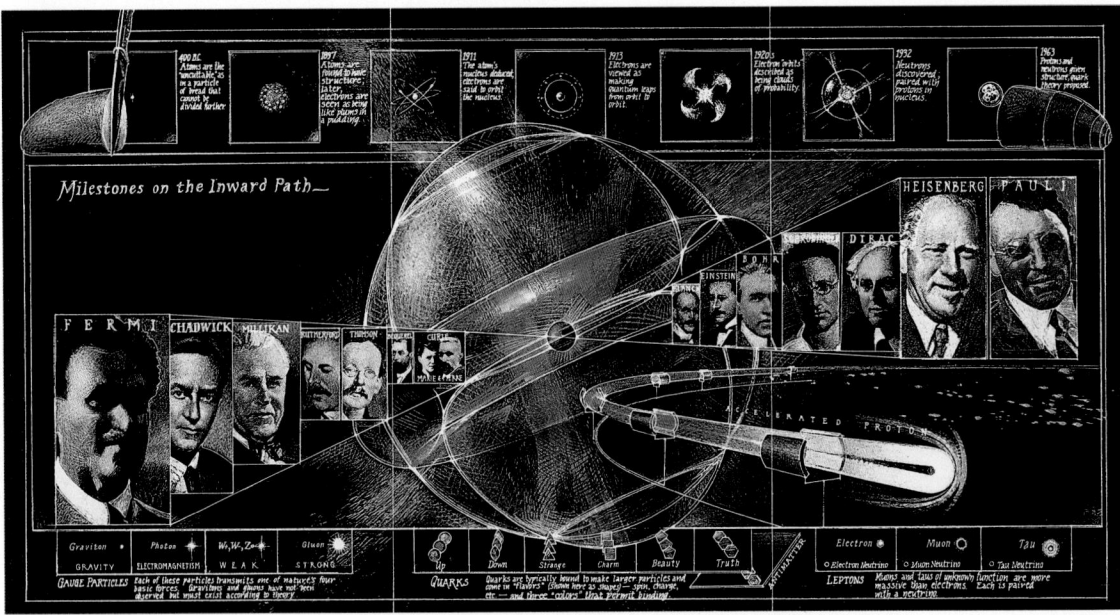

Milestones on the Inward Path—

Continuing a historical quest, modern researchers use particle accelerators to study the atom's structure. PAINTING BY BARRON STOREY

naming of Patagonia in 1520. 721-753, *June 1976*

Patagonia. 290-339. Photos by Des and Jen Bartlett. I. Argentina Protects Its Wildlife Treasures. By William G. Conway. 290-297; II. Where Two Worlds Meet. 298-321; III. At Home With Right Whales. By Roger Payne. NGS research grant. 322-339, *Mar. 1976*

Swimming With Patagonia's Right Whales. By Roger Payne. Photos by William R. Curtsinger and Charles R. Nicklin, Jr. NGS research grant. 576-587, *Oct. 1972*

Indian Tribes of Southern Patagonia, Tierra del Fuego, and the Adjoining Islands. By J. B. Hatcher. 12-22, *Jan. 1901*

Some Geographic Features of Southern Patagonia, with a Discussion of Their Origin. By J. B. Hatcher. 41-55, *Feb. 1900*

Patagonia. By J. B. Hatcher. 305-319, *Nov. 1897*

Hatcher's Work in Patagonia. By W J McGee. 319-322, *Nov. 1897*

See also Tierra del Fuego

PATAN, Nepal:

At the Crossroads of Kathmandu. By Douglas H. Chadwick. Photos by William Thompson. 32-65, *July 1987*

Nepal: A Little-Known Kingdom. By John Claude White. 245-283, *Oct. 1920*

PATENT PLANTS:

Patent Plants Enrich Our World. By Orville H. Kneen. Photos from U. S. Plant Patents. 357-378, *Mar. 1948*

PATHAN TRIBESPEOPLE:

Pakistan Under Pressure. By William S. Ellis. Photos by James L. Stanfield. 668-701, *May 1981*

An Eye for an Eye: Pakistan's Wild Frontier. By Mike W. Edwards. Photos by J. Bruce Baumann. 111-139, *Jan. 1977*

South of Khyber Pass (India). By Maynard Owen Williams. 471-500, *Apr. 1946*

The **PATHFINDER** of the East: Setting Sail to Find "Christians and Spices," Vasco da Gama Met Amazing Adventures, Founded an Empire, and Changed the History of Western Europe. By J. R. Hildebrand. Included: Pictorial supplement. 503-550, *Nov. 1927*

The **PATHFINDERS.** Paintings by Herb Kawainui Kane. 756-769, *Dec. 1974*

PATHS of Fury–This Century's Worst American Storms. 360-361, *Sept. 1980*

PATHWAY Through History: Today Along the Natchez Trace. By Bern Keating. Photos by Charles Harbutt. 641-667, *Nov. 1968*

PATMOS (Island), Greece:

The Isles of Greece: Aegean Birthplace of Western Culture. By Melville Bell Grosvenor. Photos by Edwin Stuart Grosvenor and Winfield Parks. 147-193, *Aug. 1972*

Rhodes, and Italy's Aegean Islands. By Dorothy Hosmer. 449-480, *Apr. 1941*

PATOWMACK CANAL, Maryland-Virginia:

Editorial. By Wilbur E. Garrett. 689, *June 1987*

George Washington's Patowmack Canal. By Wilbur E. Garrett. Photos by Kenneth Garrett. 716-753, *June 1987*

PATRIC, JOHN: *Author*

Italy, From Roman Ruins to Radio: History of Ancient Bridge Building and Road Making Repeats Itself in Modern Public Works and Engineering Projects. 347-394, *Mar. 1940*

Czechoslovaks, Yankees of Europe. 173-225, *Aug. 1938*

Roads from Washington (D. C.). 1-56, *July 1938*

Magyar Mirth and Melancholy. 1-55, *Jan. 1938*

Imperial Rome Reborn. 269-325, *Mar. 1937*

Friendly Journeys in Japan: A Young American Finds a Ready Welcome in the Homes of the Japanese During Leisurely Travels Through the Islands. 441-480, *Apr. 1936*

PATRICK, MARY MILLS: *Author*

Asia Minor in the Time of the Seven Wise Men. 47-67, *Jan. 1920*

The Emancipation of Mohammedan Women. 42-66, *Jan. 1909*

A **PATRIOTIC** Pilgrimage to Eastern National Parks: History and Beauty Live Along Paved Roads, Once Indian Trails, Through Virginia, North Carolina, Tennessee, Kentucky, and West Virginia. By Leo A. Borah. 663-702, *June 1934*

PATRIOTS in Petticoats. By Lonnelle Aikman. Paintings by Louis S. Glanzman. 475-493, *Oct. 1975*

A surveyor in his youth, George Washington championed the Patowmack Canal.

PAINTING BY FRANK SCHOONOVER, COURTESY VIRGINIA POLYTECHNIC INSTITUTE AND STATE UNIVERSITY

PATROLLING Troubled Formosa Strait. 573-588, *Apr. 1955*

PATTERNS of Plenty: The Art in Farming. Photo essay by Georg Gerster. 391-399, *Sept. 1984*

PATTERSON, CAROLYN BENNETT:

On Assignment on the Tennessee-Tombigbee Waterway. *Mar. 1986*

Author

In the Far Pacific: At the Birth of Nations. Photos by David Hiser and Melinda Berge. Included: Mariana Islands, Marshall Islands, Kosrae, Pohnpei, Truk, Yap, Palau. 460-499, *Oct. 1986*

The Tennessee-Tombigbee Waterway: Bounty or Boondoggle? Photos by Sandy Felsenthal. Included: The Hidden Tenn-Tom: Bypassed But Still Striving. By Alice J. Hall. 364-387, *Mar. 1986*

A Walk and Ride on the Wild Side: Tasmania. Photos by David Hiser and Melinda Berge. 676-693, *May 1983*

Mississippi's Grand Reunion at the Neshoba County Fair. Photos by C. C. Lockwood. 854-866, *June 1980*

Travels With a Donkey–100 Years Later. Photos by Cotton Coulson. 535-561, *Oct. 1978*

New Zealand's Milford Track: "Walk of a Lifetime." Photos by Robert E. Gilka. 117-129, *Jan. 1978*

Rescuing the Rothschild (Giraffe). 419-421, *Sept. 1977*

Haiti: Beyond Mountains, More Mountains. Photos by Thomas Nebbia. 70-97, *Jan. 1976*

The Final Tribute (Churchill Funeral). 199-225, *Aug. 1965*

The Fair Reopens (New York World's Fair, 1964-1965). Photos by James P. Blair. 505-529, *Apr. 1965*

Gettysburg and Vicksburg: the Battle Towns Today. By Robert Paul Jordan. Map notes by Carolyn Bennett Patterson. 4-57, *July 1963*

Seattle Fair Looks to the 21st Century. Photos by Thomas Nebbia. 402-427, *Sept. 1962*

Date Line: United Nations, New York. Photos by B. Anthony Stewart and John E. Fletcher. 305-331, *Sept. 1961*

Soaring on Skis in the Swiss Alps. Photos by Kathleen Revis. 94-121, *Jan. 1961*

Mardi Gras in New Orleans. Photos by Robert F. Sisson and John E. Fletcher. 726-732, *Nov. 1960*

Our Land Through Lincoln's Eyes. Photos by W. D. Vaughn. 243-277, *Feb. 1960*

PATTERSON, FRANCINE "PENNY":

On Assignment. *June 1985*

Editorial. By Wilbur E. Garrett. 409, *Apr. 1985*

On Assignment. *Jan. 1985*

Koko's Kitten. Text by Jane Vessels. Photos by Ronald H. Cohn. 110-113, *Jan. 1985*

Author

Conversations With a Gorilla. Photos by Ronald H. Cohn. 438-465, *Oct. 1978*

PATTERSON, J. N.: *Author*
The Magic Mountain (Mount Wilson, California). 457-468, *July 1908*

PATTERSON, WILLIAM:
Nomination Page. *Jan. 1977*

PATTON, GEORGE S., Jr.:
Luxembourg, Survivor of Invasions. By Sydney Clark. Photos by Maynard Owen Williams. 791-810, *June 1948*

PATTON, RAYMOND S.:
Board of Trustees. 640, *Nov. 1944*

PATTON, ROBERT S.:
Nomination Page. In Iceland. *July 1973*
Photographer
Vestmannaeyjar: Up From the Ashes. By Noel Grove. 690-701, *May 1977*

PÁTZCUARO (City and Lake), Mexico:
Lost Kingdom in Indian Mexico. By Justin Locke. 517-546, *Oct. 1952*
A Mexican Land of Lakes and Lacquers. Photos by Helene Fischer and Luis Marquez. 633-648, *May 1937*

PAUL, Saint:
Jerusalem to Rome in the Path of St. Paul. By David S. Boyer. 707-759, *Dec. 1956*

PAUL du Chaillu (Biography). 282-285, *July 1903*

PAVIA, Italy:
Frontier Cities of Italy. By Florence Craig Albrecht. 533-586, *June 1915*

PAVLOF VOLCANO, Alaska:
Mapping the Home of the Great Brown Bear: Adventures of the National Geographic Society's Pavlof Volcano Expedition to Alaska. By Thomas A. Jaggar. 109-134, *Jan. 1929*

Owned by European royalty for centuries, the pearl called La Peregrina now graces Elizabeth Taylor. FRED WARD, BLACK STAR

PAXOS (Island), Greece:
Homeward With Ulysses. By Melville Bell Grosvenor. Photos by Edwin Stuart Grosvenor. 1-39, *July 1973*

PAYNE, JOHN BARTON:
Board of Trustees. 793, *June 1934*

PAYNE, MELVIN M.:
NGS Offices. 852, Dec. 1981; 274, *Aug. 1982*
Nomination Page. In Turkey. *Aug. 1981*
Editorial. By Gilbert M. Grosvenor. 159, *Aug. 1976*
Board of Trustees, Chairman. 159, 225, 226, 227, *Aug. 1976*
President of NGS (1967-1976). 577, 583, 586, 589, 590, Oct. 1967; 843, Dec. 1970; 159, 225-227, *Aug. 1976*
Nomination Page. *Sept. 1969*
Vice President, Executive, of NGS. 579, 582, Apr. 1962; 4, Jan. 1963; 1, Jan. 1964; 689, Nov. 1964; 865, 867, June 1967; 583, 590, *Oct. 1967*
Nomination Page. *Feb. 1967*
Secretary. 4, Jan. 1963; 1, Jan. 1964; 485, *Oct. 1966*
Vice President of NGS. 108, 155, Jan. 1959; 834, Dec. 1959; 175, Feb. 1960; 883, Dec. 1960; 485, 486, *Oct. 1966*
Nomination Page. In Tanzania. *Sept. 1965*
Committee for Research and Exploration. 433, Mar. 1958; 827, Dec. 1965; 872-873, Dec. 1973; Chairman. 159, 225, Aug. 1976; Secretary. 155, Jan. 1959; 4, Jan. 1963; Vice Chairman. 198, *Feb. 1965*
Peak named for. 285, *Aug. 1964*
Secretary, Associate. 834, Dec. 1959; 883, *Dec. 1960*
Secretary, Senior Assistant. 420, 423, Mar. 1957; 867, *Dec. 1957*
Secretary, Assistant. 297, *Sept. 1947*
Author
1988: The Trustees Who Have Carried On the Tradition. 38-43, *Jan. 1988*
Leonard Carmichael: An Appreciation. 871-874, *Dec. 1973*
The Leakey Tradition Lives On. 143-144, *Jan. 1973*
Frederick G. Vosburgh Retires as Editor; Gilbert M. Grosvenor Succeeds Him. 838-843, *Dec. 1970*
The World in Geographic Filmstrips. 134-137, *Jan. 1968*
Preserving the Treasures of Olduvai Gorge. Photos by Joseph J. Scherschel. 701-709, *Nov. 1966*
The Leakeys of Africa: Family in Search of Prehistoric Man. 194-231, *Feb. 1965*
Reprinting Brings Earliest Geographics to Life. 688-689, *Nov. 1964*
American and Geographic Flags Top Everest. Photos by Barry C. Bishop. 157-157C, *Aug. 1963*
75 Years Exploring Earth, Sea, and Sky: National Geographic Society Observes Its Diamond Anniversary. 1-43, *Jan. 1963*

PAYNE, ROGER:
Nomination Page. *Oct. 1978*
Author
New Light on the Singing Whales.

Photos by Flip Nicklin. 463-477, *Apr. 1982*
Humpbacks: Their Mysterious Songs. Photos by Al Giddings. Included: Symphony of the Deep: "Songs of the Humpback Whale" (Sound sheet). 18-25, *Jan. 1979*
At Home With Right Whales. Photos by Des and Jen Bartlett. 322-339, *Mar. 1976*
Swimming With Patagonia's Right Whales. Photos by William R. Curtsinger and Charles R. Nicklin, Jr. 576-587, *Oct. 1972*

PEACE CONFERENCE: Paris, France:
Paris Lives Again. By M. O. Williams. 767-790, *Dec. 1946*

PEACE CORPS:
Ambassadors of Good Will. By Sargent Shriver and Peace Corps Volunteers. Contents: Bolivia, Ecuador, Gabon, Sarawak, Tanganyika, Turkey. 297-345, *Sept. 1964*

The **PEACE** of Latin America. 479-480, *Oct. 1905*

PEACE PARK. *See* Waterton-Glacier International Peace Park

The **PEACEFUL** Mrus of Bangladesh. By Claus-Dieter Brauns. 267-286, *Feb. 1973*

PEACETIME Plant Hunting About Peiping. By P. H. and J. H. Dorsett. 509-534, *Oct. 1937*

PEACETIME Rambles in the Ryukyus. By William Leonard Schwartz. 543-561, *May 1945*

PEAFOWL:
Fowls of Forest and Stream Tamed by Man. By Morley A. Jull. Paintings by Hashime Murayama. 327-371, *Mar. 1930*

The **PEAK** of Itambé. 476, *Nov. 1898*

PEAKS and Parks of Western Canada. Photos by W. J. Oliver. 516-526, *Oct. 1941*

PEAKS and Trails in the Canadian Alps. Photos by Byron Harmon and Clifford White. 627-642, *May 1934*

PEANUTS:
Britain Tackles the East African Bush. By W. Robert Moore. 311-352, *Mar. 1950*

PEARL HARBOR, Oahu, Hawaii:
Life on the Hawaii "Front": All-out Defense and Belt Tightening of Pacific Outpost Foreshadow the Things to Come on Mainland. By Frederick Simpich, Jr. 541-560, *Oct. 1942*
Hawaii, Then and Now: Boyhood Recollections by an American Whose Grandfather Came to the Islands 102 Years Ago. By William R. Castle. 419-462, *Oct. 1938*

PEARL INDUSTRY:
The Pearl. By Fred Ward. 193-223, *Aug. 1985*
The Philippines, Freedom's Pacific Frontier. By Robert de Roos. Photos by Ted Spiegel. 301-351, *Sept. 1966*

Aboard the **Roosevelt** *in 1908, Robert E. Peary steamed to wintering grounds on Elles-mere Island, Canada, on his final attempt to reach the North Pole.* THE BETTMANN ARCHIVE

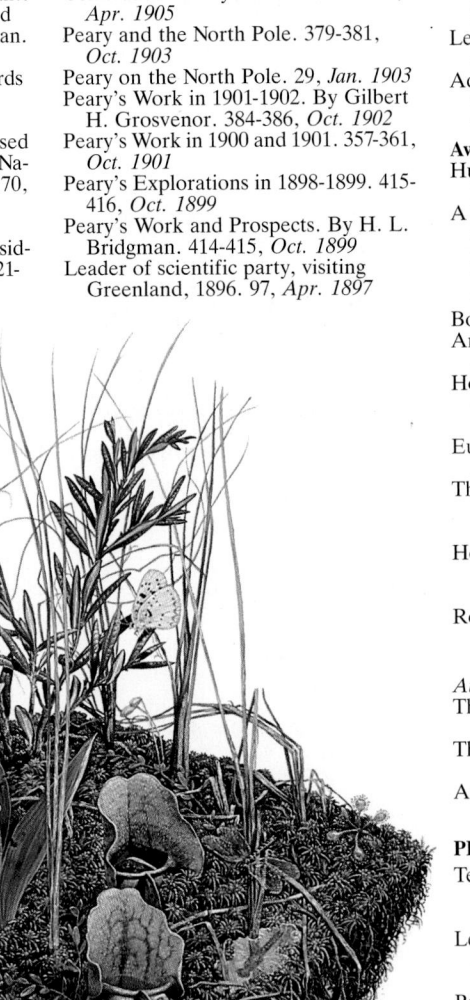

A bog's waterlogged sphagnum moss supports plants that, dying, will settle and become peat.

PAINTING BY JOHN DAWSON

American life. 397-420, *Mar. 1987*
California's Surprising Inland Delta. By Judith and Neil Morgan. Photos by Charles O'Rear. 409-430, *Sept. 1976*

PEAT-BOG BURIALS:

Mysteries of the Bog. By Louise E. Levathes. Photos by Fred Bavendam. Included: Peat holds clues to early American life. 397-420, *Mar. 1987*
Lifelike Man Preserved 2,000 Years in Peat. By P. V. Glob. 419-430, *Mar. 1954*

PECHKOFF, ZINOVI: *Author*

A Few Glimpses into Russia. 238-253, *Sept. 1917*

PECULIAR Caves of Asia Minor. By Elizabeth H. Brewer. 870-875, *Sept. 1911*

PEDALING Through Poland: An American Girl Free-wheels Alone from Kraków, and Its Medieval Byways, Toward Ukraine's Restive Borderland. By Dorothy Hosmer. 739-775, *June 1939*

PEEL ISLAND, Bonin Islands:

Springboards to Tokyo. By Willard Price. 385-407, *Oct. 1944*

PEELE, WILLIAM T.:

Nomination Page. *Jan. 1967*
Nomination Page. *Jan. 1965*

PEERLESS Nepal–A Naturalist's Paradise. By S. Dillon Ripley. Photos by Volkmar Wentzel. 1-40, *Jan. 1950*

PEFFER, RANDALL S.: *Author*

Catalonia: Spain's Country Within a Country. Photos by Stephanie Maze. 95-127, *Jan. 1984*
Massachusetts' North Shore: Harboring Old Ways. Photos by Nathan Benn. 568-590, *Apr. 1979*

PEIPING, China. *See* Beijing

A **PEIPING** Panorama in Vivid Pigments. Camera paintings by H. C. and J. H. White, Deng Bao-ling, Hwang Yao-tso. 753-784, *Dec. 1936*

PEISSEL, MICHEL:

Author-Photographer

Mustang, Remote Realm in Nepal. 579-604, *Oct. 1965*

PEKING, China. *See* Beijing

PEKING, the City of the Unexpected. By James Arthur Muller. 335-355, *Nov. 1920*

PELÉE, Mont (Volcano), Martinique:

The Shattered Obelisk of Mont Pelée. By Angelo Heilprin. 465-474, *Aug. 1906*
The New Cone of Mont Pelée. 422-423, *Nov. 1903*
Volcanic Eruptions on Martinique and St. Vincent. By Israel C. Russell. 415-436, *Dec. 1902*
The Recent Volcanic Eruptions in the West Indies. By Israel C. Russell. 267-285, *July 1902*
Report by Robert T. Hill on the Volcanic Disturbances in the West Indies. 223-267, *July 1902*

Western Hemisphere fisher that plunges into the sea after prey, a brown pelican makes a web-footed landing on its nest, which carries a typical clutch of three. LEWIS W. WALKER

Magnetic Disturbance Caused by the Explosion of Mont Pelée. 208-209, *June 1902*
The National Geographic Society Expedition in the West Indies. 209-213, *June 1902*

PELELIU (Island), Republic of Palau:

South from Saipan. By W. Robert Moore. 441-474, *Apr. 1945*

PELICANS:

Bad Days for the Brown Pelican. By Ralph W. Schreiber. Photos by William R. Curtsinger and author. 111-123, *Jan. 1975*
Pelican Profiles. By Lewis Wayne Walker. 589-598, *Nov. 1943*
Birds That Cruise the Coast and Inland Waters. By T. Gilbert Pearson. Paintings by Allan Brooks. 299-328, *Mar. 1934*
Peru's Wealth-Producing Birds: Vast Riches in the Guano Deposits of Cormorants, Pelicans, and Petrels which Nest on Her Barren, Rainless Coast. By R. E. Coker. 537-566, *June 1920*

PELLERANO, LUIGI: *Photographer*

Caesar's City Today (Rome). Photos by Bernard F. Rogers, Jr. and Luigi Pellerano. 285-316, *Mar. 1937*
Souvenirs of Knighthood in Rhodes. 665-672, *Dec. 1933*
Men of the Eagle in Their Mountain Eyrie (Albania). 143-190, *Feb. 1931*
Cirenaica, On the Edge of the Saharan Sands. 693-700, *June 1930*
Stone Beehive Homes of Italian Peasants. 235-242, *Feb. 1930*

Sicily: Island of Vivid Beauty and Crumbling Glory. 432-449, *Oct. 1927*
Where the Sard Holds Sway (Sardinia). 464-474, *Apr. 1926*
Under Italian Libya's Burning Sun. 141-148, *Aug. 1925*

PELLY BAY, Northwest Territories, Canada:

I Live With the Eskimos. By Guy Mary-Rousseliere. 188-217, *Feb. 1971*

PENCK, ALBRECHT: *Author*

Plan of a Map of the World. 405-408, *Oct. 1904*

PENDLETON, Oregon:

"Where Rolls the Oregon." Photos by Ray Atkeson. 689-728, *Dec. 1946*

PENEPLAINS:

Geomorphology of the Southern Appalachians. By Charles Willard Hayes and Marius R. Campbell. 63-126, *May 23, 1894*
The Rivers of Northern New Jersey, with Notes on the Classification of Rivers in General. By William Morris Davis. 81-110, *May 1890*

PENFIELD, JAMES K.: *Author*

Greenland Turns to America. Included: Greenland–U. S. Base in the Arctic. 369-383, *Sept. 1942*

PENGUINS:

Under Antarctic Ice. By Bill Curtsinger. 497-511, *Apr. 1986*
Icebound in Antarctica. By David Lewis. Photos by Mimi George. 634-663, *Nov. 1984*

Penguins and Their Neighbors. By Roger Tory Peterson. Photos by Des and Jen Bartlett. Included: Adélie, gentoo, and king penguins. 237-255, *Aug. 1977*

Oil and Penguins Don't Mix. Photos by Mike Holmes. Included: Jackass penguins. 384-397, *Mar. 1973*

Antarctica's Nearer Side. By Samuel W. Matthews. Photos by William R. Curtsinger. 622-655, *Nov. 1971*

People and Penguins of the Faraway Falklands. By Olin Sewall Pettingill, Jr. 387-416, *Mar. 1956*

A Naturalist in Penguin Land. By Niall Rankin. 93-116, *Jan. 1955*

Nature's Clown, the Penguin. By David Hellyer and Malcolm Davis. 405-428, *Sept. 1952*

Antarctica's Most Interesting Citizen: The Comical Penguin Is Both Romantic and Bellicose. By Worth E. Shoults. 251-260, *Feb. 1932*

South Georgia, an Outpost of the Antarctic. By Robert Cushman Murphy. 409-444, *Apr. 1922*

PENITENTS:

New Mexico: The Golden Land. By Robert Laxalt. Photos by Adam Woolfitt. 299-345, *Sept. 1970*

Easter Week in Indian Guatemala. By John Scofield. 406-417, *Mar. 1960*

Holy Week and the Fair in Sevilla. By Luis Marden. 499-530, *Apr. 1951*

Adobe New Mexico. By Mason Sutherland. Photos by Justin Locke. 783-830, *Dec. 1949*

PENN, WILLIAM:

The Historic City of Brotherly Love: Philadelphia, Born of Penn and Strengthened by Franklin, a Metropolis of Industries, Homes, and Parks. By John Oliver La Gorce. 643-697, *Dec. 1932*

The **PENN** Country in Sussex: Home of Pennsylvania's Founder Abounds in

Largest of the penguin species, Antarctic emperors may grow to four feet and weigh a hundred pounds. NATIONAL ARCHIVES

Quaker History and Memories of Adventurous Smugglers. By P. T. Etherton. 59-90, *July 1935*

PENNANTS of Patriotism 200 Years Ago. By Byron McCandless and Gilbert Grosvenor. 399-403, *Oct. 1917*

PENNINE CHAIN (Mountains), England:

To Scotland Afoot Along the Pennine Way. By David Yeadon. Photos by Annie Griffiths. 388-418, *Mar. 1986*

A Stroll to London. By Isobel Wylie Hutchison. Photos by B. Anthony Stewart. 171-204, *Aug. 1950*

PENNINGTON, JOHN: *Author*

Cumberland, My Island for a While. Photos by Jodi Cobb. 649-661, *Nov. 1977*

PENN'S Land of Modern Miracles. By John Oliver La Gorce. 1-58, *July 1935*

PENNSYLVANIA:

Susquehanna: America's Small-Town River. By Peter Miller. Photos by William T. Douthitt. 352-383, *Mar. 1985*

The Plain People of Pennsylvania. Photo essay by Jerry Irwin. Text by Douglas Lee. 492-519, *Apr. 1984*

Pennsylvania: Faire Land of William Penn. By Gordon Young. Photos by Cary Wolinsky. 731-767, *June 1978*

The Thousand-mile Glide. By Karl Striedieck. Photos by Otis Imboden. 431-438, *Mar. 1978*

⊕ *Close-up: U.S.A., New York, New Jersey, and Pennsylvania,* Text on reverse. *Jan. 1978*

Amish Folk: Plainest of Pennsylvania's Plain People. By Richard Gehman. Photos by William Albert Allard. 227-253, *Aug. 1965*

Gettysburg and Vicksburg: the Battle Towns Today. By Robert Paul Jordan. Map notes by Carolyn Bennett Patterson. 4-57, *July 1963*

Today on the Delaware, Penn's Glorious River. By Albert W. Atwood. Photos by Robert F. Sisson. 1-40, *July 1952*

Wonderland in Longwood Gardens. By Edward C. Ferriday, Jr. 45-64, *July 1951*

Down the Susquehanna by Canoe. By Ralph Gray. Photos by Walter Meayers Edwards. 73-120, *July 1950*

Appalachian Valley Pilgrimage. By Catherine Bell Palmer. Photos by Justin Locke. 1-32, *July 1949*

Shrines of Each Patriot's Devotion. By Frederick G. Vosburgh. 51-82, *Jan. 1949*

Artists Look at Pennsylvania. By John Oliver La Gorce. 37-56, *July 1948*

In the Pennsylvania Dutch Country. By Elmer C. Stauffer. Included: Pennsylvania's Land of Plenty. Photos by Harrison Howell Walker. 37-74, *July 1941*

Roads from Washington. By John Patric. 1-56, *July 1938*

⊕ *Historic and Scenic Reaches of the Nation's Capital. July 1938*

Penn's Land of Modern Miracles. By

John Oliver La Gorce. 1-58, *July 1935*

The Travels of George Washington: Dramatic Episodes in His Career as the First Geographer of the United States. By William Joseph Showalter. 1-63, *Jan. 1932*

⊕ *A Map of the Travels of George Washington.* Included: Inset of Philadelphia and vicinity. *Jan. 1932*

The Industrial Titan of America: Pennsylvania, Once the Keystone of the Original Thirteen, Now the Keystone of Forty-eight Sovereign States. By John Oliver La Gorce. 367-406, *May 1919*

The Rivers and Valleys of Pennsylvania. By William Morris Davis. 183-253, *July 1889*

See also Gettysburg; Kutztown; Philadelphia; Pittsburgh; Valley Forge

PENNSYLVANIA AVENUE, Washington, D. C.:

A Preservation Victory Saves Washington's Old Post Office. By Wolf Von Eckardt. Photos by Volkmar Wentzel. 407-416, *Sept. 1983*

New Grandeur for Flowering Washington. By Joseph Judge. Photos by James P. Blair. 500-539, *Apr. 1967*

Pennsylvania Avenue, Route of Presidents. By Dorothea and Stuart E. Jones. Photos by Volkmar Wentzel. 63-95, *Jan. 1957*

PENNSYLVANIA DUTCH:

The Plain People of Pennsylvania. Photo essay by Jerry Irwin. Text by Douglas Lee. 492-519, *Apr. 1984*

Pennsylvania's Old-time Dutch Treat. By Kent Britt. Photos by H. Edward Kim. 564-578, *Apr. 1973*

Pennsylvania's Amish Folk. By Richard Gehman. Photos by William Albert Allard. 227-253, *Aug. 1965*

Pennsylvania Dutch Folk Festival. By Maynard Owen Williams. 503-516, *Oct. 1952*

In the Pennsylvania Dutch Country. By Elmer C. Stauffer. Included: Pennsylvania's Land of Plenty. Photos by Harrison Howell Walker. 37-74, *July 1941*

Pennsylvania Dutch–In a Land of Milk and Honey. Photos by J. Baylor Roberts. 49-56, *July 1938*

PENOBSCOT BAY, Maine:

Atlantic Estuarine Tides. By Mark S. W. Jefferson. 400-409, *Sept. 1898*

PENOBSCOT INDIANS:

America's First Settlers, the Indians. By Matthew W. Stirling. Paintings by W. Langdon Kihn. 535-596, *Nov. 1937*

PENRHYN (Atoll) South Pacific Ocean. *See* Tongareva

PENROSE, C. B.:

The Bear Hunt. 222, *Mar. 1908*

A Bear Hunt in Montana. By Arthur Alvord Stiles. 149-154, *Feb. 1908*

PENSAR (Island), Finland:

Scenes of Postwar Finland. By La Verne Bradley. Photos by Jerry Waller. 233-264, *Aug. 1947*

As unhurried as the Susquehanna River across from the main street, a patron reads a newspaper in Steelton, a mill town near Harrisburg, Pennsylvania. WILLIAM T. DOUTHITT, NGS

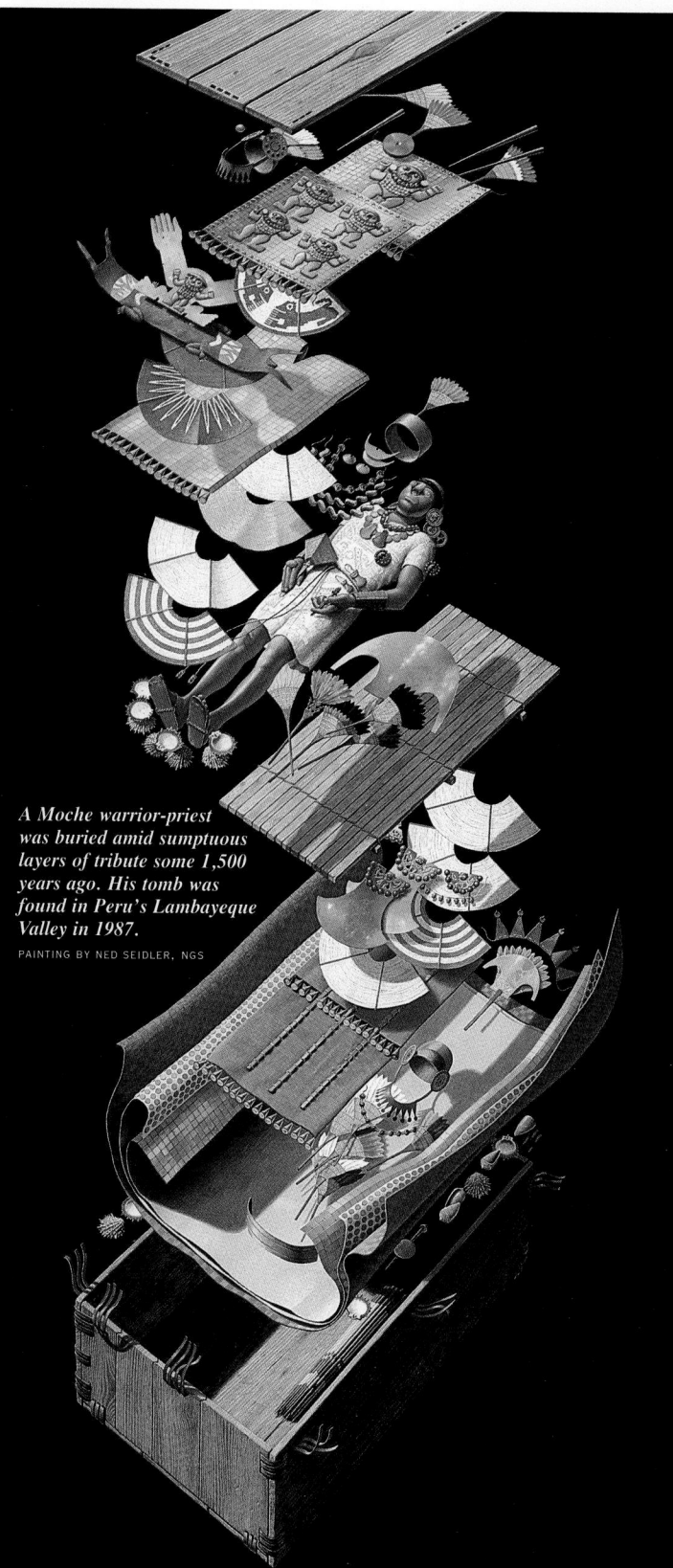

A Moche warrior-priest was buried amid sumptuous layers of tribute some 1,500 years ago. His tomb was found in Peru's Lambayeque Valley in 1987.

PAINTING BY NED SEIDLER, NGS

Republics, Covers 9,600 Miles of Mountain and Plain, Desert and Jungle. By A. F. Tschiffely. 135-196, *Feb. 1929*

How Latin America Looks from the Air: U. S. Army Airplanes Hurdle the High Andes, Brave Brazil Jungles, and Follow Smoking Volcanoes to Map New Sky Paths Around South America. By Herbert A. Dargue. 451-502, *Oct. 1927*

High Lights in the Peruvian and Bolivian Andes. Photos by W. Robert Moore. 219-234, *Feb. 1927*

The Most Valuable Bird in the World (Guanay). By Robert Cushman Murphy. 279-302, *Sept. 1924*

Peru's Wealth-Producing Birds: Vast Riches in the Guano Deposits of Cormorants, Pelicans, and Petrels which Nest on Her Barren, Rainless Coast. By R. E. Coker. 537-566, *June 1920*

Further Exploration in the Land of the Incas: The Peruvian Expedition of 1915 of the National Geographic Society and Yale University. By Hiram Bingham. Included: The Greatest Achievement of Ancient Man in America (Fortress of Sacsahuaman). Panorama from photo by author. 431-473, *May 1916*

Staircase Farms of the Ancients: Astounding Farming Skill of Ancient Peruvians, Who Were Among the Most Industrious and Highly Organized People in History. By O. F. Cook. 474-534, *May 1916*

The Story of Machu Picchu: The Peruvian Expeditions of the National Geographic Society and Yale University. By Hiram Bingham. 172-217, *Feb. 1915*

Some Personal Experiences with Earthquakes (Arica). By L. G. Billings. 57-71, *Jan. 1915*

In the Wonderland of Peru. By Hiram Bingham. Included: The Ruins of an Ancient Inca Capital, Machu Picchu. Panorama from photo by author. 387-573, *Apr. 1913*

Honors to Amundsen and Peary (Banquet: Address by Hiram Bingham, "The Expedition to Peru"). 113-130, *Jan. 1913*

Explorations in Peru. 417-422, *Apr. 1912*

Cuzco, America's Ancient Mecca. By Harriet Chalmers Adams. 669-689, *Oct. 1908*

Some Wonderful Sights in the Andean Highlands: The Oldest City in America. Sailing on the Lake of the Clouds: The Yosemite of Peru. By Harriet Chalmers Adams. 597-618, *Sept. 1908*

Along the Old Inca Highway. By Harriet Chalmers Adams. 231-250, *Apr. 1908*

A New Peruvian Route to the Plain of the Amazon. By Solon I. Bailey. 432-448, *Aug. 1906*

From Panama to Patagonia. By Charles M. Pepper. 449-452, *Aug. 1906*

Brazil and Peru. 203-204, *Apr. 1906*

Peru–Its Resources, Development, and Future. By Alfredo Alvarez Calderon. 311-323, *Aug. 1904*

Chile's Disputes with Peru and Bolivia. 401-402, *Nov. 1901*

The Road to Bolivia. By William E. Curtis. 209-224, June 1900; 264-280, *July 1900*

Geographic Work in Peru. 407, *Dec. 1896*

South America. Annual Address by the President, Gardiner G. Hubbard. 1-29, *Mar. 28, 1891*

See also Condor; Vicuñas

PERU CURRENT (Humboldt Current):

Fighting Giants of the Humboldt (Fish and Squid). By David D. Duncan. 373-400, *Mar. 1941*

PERUGIA, Italy:

Inexhaustible Italy. By Arthur Stanley Riggs. 273-368, *Oct. 1916*

PERUVIAN INDIANS:

Peru's Pilgrimage to the Sky. By Robert Randall. Photos by Loren McIntyre and Ira Block. 60-69, *July 1982*

The Incredible Potato. By Robert E. Rhoades. Photos by Martin Rogers. Included: *chuño*, a dehydrated potato product. 668-694, *May 1982*

The Two Souls of Peru. By Harvey Arden. Photos by William Albert Allard. 284-321, *Mar. 1982*

Mystery of the Ancient Nazca Lines. By Loren McIntyre. NGS research grant. 716-728, *May 1975*

Chan Chan, Peru's Ancient City of Kings. By Michael E. Moseley and Carol J. Mackey. Photos by David Brill. NGS research grant. 318-345, *Mar. 1973*

Amazon–The River Sea. By Loren McIntyre. 456-495, *Oct. 1972*

Titicaca, Abode of the Sun. By Luis Marden. Photos by Flip Schulke. 272-294, *Feb. 1971*

By Parachute Into Peru's Lost World. By G. Brooks Baekeland. Photos by author and Peter R. Gimbel. Included: Apurímac River, Cordillera Vilcabamba, Lake Parodi, Urubamba River. NGS research grant. 268-296, *Aug. 1964*

The Five Worlds of Peru. By Kenneth F. Weaver. Photos by Bates Littlehales. 213-265, *Feb. 1964*

At Home in the High Andes. By Harry Tschopik, Jr. 133-146, *Jan. 1955*

See also Incas; Moche Culture

PESCADORES (Islands), Taiwan:

Pescadores, Wind-swept Outposts of Formosa. By Horace Bristol, Sr. 265-284, *Feb. 1956*

Patrolling Troubled Formosa Strait. 573-588, *Apr. 1955*

PESEK, LUDEK:

Nomination Page. *Jan. 1975*

Nomination Page. *Aug. 1970*

Artist

Journey to Mars. By Kenneth F. Weaver. 231-263, *Feb. 1973*

⊕ *The Red Planet Mars;* "The Dusty Face of Mars," *Feb. 1973*

Voyage to the Planets. By Kenneth F. Weaver. 147-193, *Aug. 1970*

PESH MERGAS. *See* Kurds

PESHAWAR, India:

South of Khyber Pass. By Maynard Owen Williams. 471-500, *Apr. 1946*

Through the Heart of Hindustan: A Teeming Highway Extending for Fifteen Hundred Miles, from the Khyber Pass to Calcutta. By Maynard Owen Williams. 433-467, *Nov. 1921*

PEST CONTROL:

The Pesticide Dilemma. By Allen A. Boraiko. Photos by Fred Ward. 145-183, *Feb. 1980*

The Rat, Lapdog of the Devil. By Thomas Y. Canby. Photos by James L. Stanfield. 60-87, *July 1977*

See also Insect Control

The **PEST** of English Sparrows. By N. Dearborn. 948-952, *Nov. 1910*

PESTALOZZI, Switzerland:

Children's Village in Switzerland, Pestalozzi. Photos by Alfred Lammer. 268-282, *Aug. 1959*

PESTICIDE POLLUTION:

The Pesticide Dilemma. By Allen A. Boraiko. Photos by Fred Ward. 145-183, *Feb. 1980*

Can the Cooper's Hawk Survive? By Noel Snyder. Photos by author and Helen Snyder. NGS research grant. 433-442, *Mar. 1974*

Quicksilver and Slow Death (Mercury). By John J. Putman. Photos by Robert W. Madden. 507-527, *Oct. 1972*

Pollution, Threat to Man's Only Home. By Gordon Young. Photos by James P. Blair. 738-781, *Dec. 1970*

The Osprey, Endangered World Citizen. By Roger Tory Peterson. Photos by Frederick Kent Truslow. NGS research grant. 53-67, *July 1969*

PESTS and Parasites: Why We Need a National Law to Prevent the Importation of Insect-Infested and Diseased Plants. By Charles Lester Marlatt. 321-346, *Apr. 1911*

PET (Positron Emission Tomography):

Medicine's New Vision. By Howard Sochurek. Paintings by Davis Meltzer. Illustrations text by Peter Miller. 2-41, *Jan. 1987*

PETÉN, Department of the, Guatemala:

Maya Art Treasures Discovered in Cave. By George E. Stuart. Photos by Wilbur E. Garrett. 220-235, *Aug. 1981*

See also Tikal

PETER, Saint:

Vatican City. By James Fallows. Photos by James L. Stanfield. Included: The burial place of St. Peter. 723-761, *Dec. 1985*

St. Peter's, Rome's Church of Popes. By Aubrey Menen. Photos by Albert Moldvay. 865-879, *Dec. 1971*

PETER I, The Great:

Young Russia: The Land of Unlimited Possibilities. By Gilbert H. Grosvenor. 421-520, *Nov. 1914*

A car killed six of this young shepherd's flock near Puno, Peru. GEOGRAPHIC readers donated funds to replace them.   WILLIAM ALBERT ALLARD

Camera expert Claude Petrone readies a probe to penetrate an ancient Egyptian chamber. JAMES P. BLAIR, NGS

Man in the Amazon: Stone Age Present Meets Stone Age Past. By W. Jesco von Puttkamer. NGS research grant. 60-83, *Jan. 1979*
See also Rock Art

PETROGRAD (now Leningrad), Russian S.F.S.R., U.S.S.R.:
Young Russia: The Land of Unlimited Possibilities. By Gilbert H. Grosvenor. 421-520, *Nov. 1914*
Glimpses of the Russian Empire. By William Wisner Chapin. 1043-1078, *Nov. 1912*
See also Leningrad

PETROGRAPHY:
Finding Rare Beauty in Common Rocks. By Lorence G. Collins. 121-129, *Jan. 1966*

PETROLEUM. *See* Oil

PETRONE, CLAUDE E.:
On Assignment in Egypt. *Apr. 1988*
Photographer
Finding a Pharaoh's Funeral Bark. By Farouk El-Baz. Photos by James P. Blair and Claude E. Petrone. 513-533, *Apr. 1988*

PETS:
▓ *Your World of Pets.* By Susan McGrath. Art by Barbara L. Gibson. Juvenile. 104 pages. *1985*

PETSAMO REGION:
Scenes of Postwar Finland. By La Verne Bradley. Photos by Jerry Waller. 233-264, *Aug. 1947*

PETTINGILL, OLIN SEWALL, Jr.:
Author-Photographer
People and Penguins of the Faraway Falklands. 387-416, *Mar. 1956*

PEYOTE CULT:
The Huichols, Mexico's People of Myth and Magic. By James Norman.

Photos by Guillermo Aldana E. 832-853, *June 1977*

PEYTON, CAROLINAS:
A Long Life, a Good Life on the Potomac. By James L. Stanfield. 470-479, *Oct. 1976*

PFINGSTL, W.: *Photographer*
Behind the Scenes in the Home of the Passion Play (Oberammergau, Germany). 753-760, *Dec. 1935*

PFLEGER, MICHAEL: *Photographer*
Bicycles Are Back–and Booming! By Noel Grove. 671-681, *May 1973*

PHALANGERS:
Strange Animals of Australia. By David Fleay. Photos by Stanley Breeden. 388-411, *Sept. 1963*

PHALAROPES:
Mono Lake: A Vital Way Station for the Wilson's Phalarope. By Joseph R. Jehl, Jr. NGS research grant. 520-525, *Oct. 1981*

"PHANTOM COAST," Antarctica:
Exploring Antarctica's Phantom Coast. By Edwin A. McDonald. Photos by W. D. Vaughn. 251-273, *Feb. 1962*

PHARAOHS:
Finding a Pharaoh's Funeral Bark. By Farouk El-Baz. Photos by James P. Blair and Claude E. Petrone. Included: Craft for eternity; The world's oldest ship. 513-533, *Apr. 1988*
Riddle of the Pyramid Boats. By Peter Miller. Photos by Victor R. Boswell, Jr. 534-550, *Apr. 1988*
Tutankhamun's Golden Trove. By Christiane Desroches Noblecourt. Photos by F. L. Kenett. 625-646, *Oct. 1963*
Daily Life in Ancient Egypt. By William C. Hayes. Paintings by H. M. Herget. 419-515, *Oct. 1941*
At the Tomb of Tutankhamen: An Account of the Opening of the Royal Egyptian Sepulcher Which Contained the Most Remarkable Funeral Treasures Unearthed in Historic Times. By Maynard Owen Williams. Included: Egypt, Past and Present. 461-508, *May 1923*

PHELPS, CONSTANCE H.:
On Assignment in Australia. *Feb. 1988*

PHILADELPHIA (Ancient City):
The Buried Cities of Asia Minor. By Ernest L. Harris. 1-18, *Jan. 1909*

PHILADELPHIA, Pennsylvania:
They'd Rather Be in Philadelphia. By Ethel A. Starbird. Photos by Ted Spiegel. 314-343, *Mar. 1983*
Pennsylvania: Faire Land of William Penn. By Gordon Young. Photos by Cary Wolinsky. 731-767, *June 1978*
Benjamin Franklin, Philosopher of Dissent. By Alice J. Hall. Photos by Linda Bartlett. 93-123, *July 1975*
Philadelphia Houses a Proud Past. By Harold Donaldson Eberlein. Photos by Thomas Nebbia. 151-191, *Aug. 1960*

Artists Look at Pennsylvania. By John Oliver La Gorce. 37-56, *July 1948*
The Historic City of Brotherly Love: Philadelphia, Born of Penn and Strengthened by Franklin, a Metropolis of Industries, Homes, and Parks. By John Oliver La Gorce. 643-697, *Dec. 1932*
⊛ A Map of the Travels of George Washington. Included: Inset of Philadelphia and vicinity. *Jan. 1932*

PHILAE (Island), Egypt:
The Resurrection of Ancient Egypt. By James Baikie. 957-1020, *Sept. 1913*

PHILIP II, King (Macedon):
Regal Treasures From a Macedonian Tomb. By Manolis Andronicos. Photos by Spyros Tsavdaroglou. 55-77, *July 1978*

PHILIP, Prince, Duke of Edinburgh:
Windsor Castle. By Anthony Holden. Photos by James L. Stanfield. 604-631, *Nov. 1980*
President Eisenhower Presents to Prince Philip the National Geographic Society's Medal. 865-868, *Dec. 1957*
Off the Beaten Track of Empire. By Beverley M. Bowie. Photos by Michael Parker. 584-626, *Nov. 1957*
Author
Man's Wildlife Heritage Faces Extinction. 700-703, *Nov. 1962*
H.R.H. The Prince Philip, Duke of Edinburgh, Introduces to Members the Narrative of His Round-the-world Tour. 583-584, *Nov. 1957*

Workers remove objects in 1923 from the tomb of 14th-century B.C. Egyptian Pharaoh Tutankhamun. EDGAR ALDRICH

Alongside Egyptian Pharaoh Khufu's Great Pyramid in Giza, scientists unveil a 4,600-year-old funeral bark. JAMES P. BLAIR, NGS

Philippine tribesman of northern Luzon in the early 1900s belonged to the Tinguian ethnic community. DEAN C. WORCESTER

When Ferdinand Marcos claimed victory in the 1985 Philippine presidential race, supporters of opposition candidate Corazon Aquino took to the streets. STEVE McCURRY, MAGNUM

In the Philippines, where millions cannot find a full-time job, some Manilans stay alive by picking through a trash dump called "smoky mountain." STEVE McCURRY, MAGNUM

In a collage symbolizing the selection process, representatives from National Geographic and the Corcoran Gallery of Art sort images for "Odyssey," a photography exhibit celebrating the Society's centennial. DECLAN HAUN WITH DAVID ALAN HARVEY

Images made from space were used in this first coast-to-coast photomosaic of the 48 contiguous states.

PRODUCED FROM NASA LANDSAT IMAGERY BY THE NATIONAL GEOGRAPHIC SOCIETY WITH THE GENERAL ELECTRIC COMPANY BELTSVILLE PHOTOGRAPHIC ENGINEERING LABORATORY

Polaroid Corporation founder Edwin Land peers through filters at Harold Edgerton, father of high-speed photography. BRUCE DALE, NGS

PHOTOMAPPING:

Periscope on the Etruscan Past. By Carlo M. Lerici. 347-350, *Sept. 1959*

See also Inter-American Geodetic Survey; Landsat; U. S. Coast and Geodetic Survey

PHOTOMICROGRAPHY:

The Mystery of the Shroud. By Kenneth F. Weaver. 730-753, *June 1980*

■ The Invisible World. 1, Jan. 1980; cover, *Mar. 1980*

Those Marvelous, Myriad Diatoms. By Richard B. Hoover. Included: Light and electron micrographs. 871-878, *June 1979*

Rotifers: Nature's Water Purifiers. By John Walsh. 287-292, *Feb. 1979*

Electronic Voyage Through an Invisible World. By Kenneth F. Weaver. 274-290, *Feb. 1977*

PHOTOSYNTHESIS:

How the Sun Gives Life to the Sea. By Paul A. Zahl. 199-225, *Feb. 1961*

PHRYGIA (Ancient Kingdom):

The Lost Wealth of the Kings of Midas. By Ellsworth Huntington. 831-846, *Oct. 1910*

PHYLE (Fortress), Greece:

"The Glory That Was Greece." By Alexander Wilbourne Weddell. 571-630, *Dec. 1922*

PHYSALIA (Yacht):

Our Neglected Southern Coast. By Alfred Goldsborough Mayer. 859-871, *Dec. 1908*

PHYSICAL Features of the United States. By G. K. Gilbert. 308-317, *July 1898*

PHYSICS:

■■*Fun With Physics.* By Susan McGrath. Juvenile. 104 pages. *1986*

Worlds Within the Atom. By John Boslough. Photos by Kevin Fleming. Illustrations text by David Jeffery. Included: A Particle Factory: Tevatron; Search for the Atom. Paintings by Barron Storey; Inside the Atom; An Outbreak of Quarks; A Unification of Forces; Applications for the Future. 634-663, *May 1985*

Lasers–"A Splendid Light." By Allen A. Boraiko. Photos by Charles O'Rear. 335-363, *Mar. 1984*

The Once and Future Universe. By Rick Gore. Photos by James A. Sugar. Paintings by Barron Storey. Picture text by David Jeffery. 704-749, *June 1983*

■■*How Things Work.* Juvenile. 104 pages. *1983*

The Search for Tomorrow's Power. By Kenneth F. Weaver. Photos by Emory Kristof. Included: Electromagnets, Fission, Fusion, Magnetohydrodynamics, Nuclear reactors. 650-681, *Nov. 1972*

The British Way. By Sir Evelyn Wrench. 421-541, *Apr. 1949*

See also Electricity; Nuclear Energy; listing under Optics; *and* National Bureau of Standards

PHYSIOGRAPHY:

Physiography of the Nicaragua Canal Route. By C. Willard Hayes. 233-246, *July 1899*

Applied Physiography in South Carolina. By L. C. Glenn. 152-154, *May 1897*

The Relations of Geology to Physiography in Our Educational System. By T. C. Chamberlin. 154-160, *Jan. 31, 1894*

See also Geology

PHYTOPLANKTON:

Those Marvelous, Myriad Diatoms. By Richard B. Hoover. 871-878, *June 1979*

PIAZZA ARMERINA, Sicily:

Roman Life in 1,600-year-old Color Pictures. By Gino Vinicio Gentili. Photos by Duncan Edwards. 211-229, *Feb. 1957*

PICCANINNIE PONDS, South Australia:

Exploring a Sunken Realm in Australia. By Hillary Hauser. Photos by David Doubilet. 129-142, *Jan. 1984*

PICCARD, AUGUSTE:
Author-Photographer

Ballooning in the Stratosphere: Two Balloon Ascents to Ten-Mile Altitudes Presage New Mode of Aërial Travel. 353-384, *Mar. 1933*

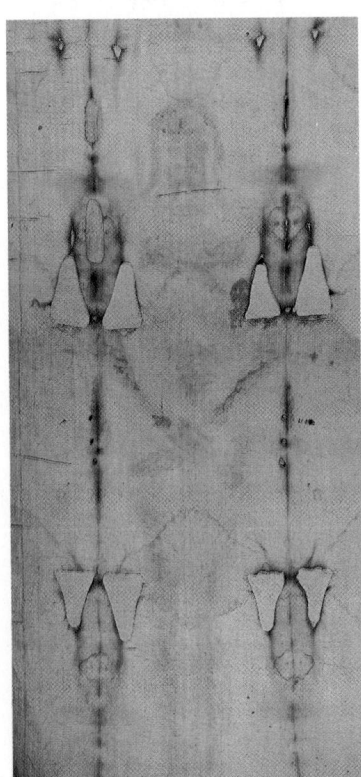

Photomicrographs taken in 1978 and compiled into a life-size image allow close study of the Shroud of Turin. VERNON MILLER

PICCARD, JACQUES: *Author*

Man's Deepest Dive. Photos by Thomas J. Abercrombie. 224-239, *Aug. 1960*

PICKERELL, JAMES H.:
Author-Photographer

Dory on the Banks: A Day in the Life of a Portuguese Fisherman. 573-583, *Apr. 1968*

PICKOW, GEORGE:
Author-Photographer

The Great St. Bernard Hospice Today. 49-62, *Jan. 1957*

PICTOGRAPHS:

Mystery of the Ancient Nazca Lines. By Loren McIntyre. NGS research grant. 716-728, *May 1975*

See also Gravel Pictographs

A PICTORIAL Chronicle of the Incas. Paintings by Ned Seidler and drawings by Rosalie Seidler. 747-753, *Dec. 1973*

PICTORIAL Jaunt Through Papua. Photos by Frank Hurley. 109-124, *Jan. 1927*

PICTORIAL SUPPLEMENTS. *See* Painting Supplements; Photo Supplements

PICTURE-BOOK Portofino. By Carleton Mitchell. Photos by Winfield Parks. 232-253, *Feb. 1965*

PICTURESQUE Paramaribo. By Harriet Chalmers Adams. 365-373, *June 1907*

The PICTURESQUE Side of Japanese Life. Photos by Kiyoshi Sakamoto. 283-298, *Sept. 1922*

PIDGEON, HARRY:
Author-Photographer

Around the World in the "Islander" (Yawl): A Narrative of the Adventures of a Solitary Voyager on His Four-Year Cruise in a Thirty-Four-Foot Sailing Craft. 141-205, *Feb. 1928*

PIECES of Silver. By Frederick Simpich. 253-292, *Sept. 1933*

PIED-À-TERRE (Motorboat):

French Riviera: Storied Playground on the Azure Coast. By Carleton Mitchell. Photos by Thomas Nebbia. 798-835, *June 1967*

PIEDMONT PLATEAU, U. S.:

Geographic History of the Piedmont Plateau. By W J McGee. 261-265, *Aug. 1896*

PIEDRA PARADA, Chiapas, Mexico:

On the Trail of La Venta Man. By Matthew W. Stirling. Photos by Richard H. Stewart. Included: Hunting Mexico's Buried Temples. 145-168. NGS research grant. 137-172, *Feb. 1947*

PIEL, GERARD: *Author*

Five Noted Thinkers Explore the Future. 70-71, *July 1976*

PIERCE, FRANKLIN:

Profiles of the Presidents: II. A Restless

A celebrant of the "Joy of Pigs," NATIONAL GEOGRAPHIC writer Kent Britt walks his 225-pound pet pig, Fido, near their suburban Washington, D.C., home. DAVID BRILL

The 800-mile trans-Alaska pipeline opened in 1977 to carry oil from north coast Prudhoe Bay, here lit by a gas flare, south to the ice-free port of Valdez. STEVE RAYMER, NGS

Pilgrims Still Stop at Plymouth (England). By Maynard Owen Williams. 59-77, *July 1938*

PILLSBURY, JOHN ELLIOTT:
President. 341, 345, *Apr. 1920*
Announcement of death. 345, *Apr. 1920*
Vice-President. 218, *Feb. 1915*
Board of Managers. 88, *Jan. 1910*
Author
The Grandest and Most Mighty Terrestrial Phenomenon: The Gulf Stream. 767-778, *Aug. 1912*
Wilkes' and D'Urville's Discoveries in Wilkes Land. 171-173, *Feb. 1910*

The **PILOT'S** Story. By Alan B. Shepard, Jr. Photos by Dean Conger. 432-444, *Sept. 1961*

PINCHOT, GIFFORD: *Author*
An American Fable (Conservation of Resources). 345-350, *May 1908*

Forestry Abroad and at Home. 375-388, *Aug. 1905*
Forest Reserves of the United States. 369-372, *Sept. 1900*
The Relation of Forests and Forest Fires. 393-403, *Oct. 1899*

PINE BARRENS (Region), New Jersey:
The People of New Jersey's Pine Barrens. By John McPhee. Photos by William R. Curtsinger. 52-77, *Jan. 1974*
The Wild Blueberry Tamed: The New Industry of the Pine Barrens of New Jersey. By Frederick V. Coville. 535-546, *June 1916*

PINE RIDGE RESERVATION, South Dakota:
South Dakota's Badlands: Castles in Clay. By John Madson. Photos by Jim Brandenburg. 524-539, *Apr. 1981*

PINE-SCENTED, Harbor-Dented Maine. Photos by B. Anthony Stewart and Robert F. Maxcy. 549-588, *May 1935*

PINEAPPLES:
Hawaii, U.S.A. By Frederick Simpich, Jr. Photos by Thomas Nebbia. 1-45, *July 1960*
How Fruit Came to America. By J. R. Magness. Paintings by Else Bostelmann. 325-377, *Sept. 1951*
Puya, the Pineapple's Andean Ancestor. By Mulford B. Foster. 463-480, *Oct. 1950*
Because It Rains on Hawaii. By Frederick Simpich, Jr. 571-610, *Nov. 1949*

PINEDO, FRANCESCO DE: *Author*
By Seaplane to Six Continents: Cruising 60,000 Miles, Italian Argonauts of the Air See World Geography Unroll and Break New Sky Trails Over Vast Brazilian Jungles. 247-301, *Sept. 1928*

PINEO, CHARLES S.: *Photographer*
To Market in Guatemala. Photos by Giles Greville Healey and Charles S. Pineo. 89-104, *July 1945*

PINES, Isle of, Cuba:
The Isle of Pines. 105-108, *Feb. 1906*
Cuba. By Robert T. Hill. 193-242, *May 1898*

The **PINK** Birds of Texas. By Paul A. Zahl. 641-654, *Nov. 1949*

PINKIANG, China. *See* Harbin

PINNIPEDS:
⊕ *Antarctica; Pinnipeds Around the World, Apr. 1987*
See also Sea Lions; Seals; Walruses

PINNY, MICHAEL:
Nomination Page. In England. *May 1977*

PINTO, DEE:
Nomination Page. In South Africa. *May 1972*

PIONEER Gaucho Days. Paintings by Cesáreo Bernaldo de Quirós. 453-460, *Oct. 1933*

PIONEER of Modern Geography: Humboldt's Way. By Loren McIntyre. 318-351, *Sept. 1985*

PIONEER PROBES:
Mystery Shrouds the Biggest Planet (Jupiter). By Kenneth F. Weaver. Included: Pioneer 10, Pioneer 11. 285-294, *Feb. 1975*
Voyage to the Planets. By Kenneth F. Weaver. Paintings by Ludek Pesek. Included: A Pioneer model; and plans for a future Pioneer F and Pioneer G. 147-193, *Aug. 1970*
Reaching for the Moon. By Allan C. Fisher, Jr. Photos by Luis Marden. Included: Pioneer I, Pioneer II, Pioneer III. 157-171, *Feb. 1959*

PIONEERS:
Editorial. By Wilbur E. Garrett. 147, *Feb. 1987*
Life and Death on the Oregon Trail:

The Itch to Move West. By Boyd Gibbons. Photos by James L. Amos. 147-177, *Aug. 1986*

Daniel Boone, First Hero of the Frontier. By Elizabeth A. Moize. Photos by William Strode. 812-841, *Dec. 1985*

PIONEERS Head North to Canada's "Now" Frontier. By Robert Paul Jordan. Photos by Lowell Georgia. 480-511, *Oct. 1976*

PIONEERS in Man's Search for the Universe. Paintings by Jean-Leon Huens. Text by Thomas Y. Canby. 627-633, *May 1974*

PIONEERS in Their Own Land: South Africa's Ndebele People. By David Jeffery. Photos by Peter Magubane. 262-282, *Feb. 1986*

The **PIOUS** Ones. By Harvey Arden. Photos by Nathan Benn. 276-298, *Aug. 1975*

PIPELINES, Natural Gas:

Natural Gas: The Search Goes On. By Bryan Hodgson. Photos by Lowell Georgia. Included: Map of United States locating existing, future, and proposed gas pipelines. 632-651, *Nov. 1978*

Striking It Rich in the North Sea. By Rick Gore. Photos by Dick Durrance II. Included: Map showing five sectors of national rights over oil and gas reserves; present and proposed oil and gas pipelines. 519-549, *Apr. 1977*

Canada's "Now" Frontier. By Robert Paul Jordan. Photos by Lowell Georgia. Included: Map showing oil pipeline, proposed gas pipeline, and tar sands. 480-511, *Oct. 1976*

The Eternal Flame: Millions of Years Old, Natural Gas Now Is a New Servant of Man. By Albert W. Atwood. Included: Construction and cost of pipeline-network in the United States ("Big Inch," "Little Big Inch," "Super Inch," and "Toughest Inch"); the Trans-Arabian pipeline. 540-564, *Oct. 1951*

PIPELINES, Oil:

Oil: Lifeblood and Liability. Included: Map of United States locating existing and proposed oil pipelines. 58-59, *Special Report on Energy. (Feb. 1981)*

Striking It Rich in the North Sea. By Rick Gore. Photos by Dick Durrance II. Included: Map showing five sectors of national rights over oil and gas reserves; present and proposed oil and gas pipelines. 519-549, *Apr. 1977*

The Pipeline: Alaska's Troubled Colossus. By Bryan Hodgson. Photos by Steve Raymer. Included: Diagram, Anatomy of the pipeline; map showing potential and producing oil and gas areas. 684-717, *Nov. 1976*

Canada's "Now" Frontier. By Robert Paul Jordan. Photos by Lowell Georgia. Included: Map showing oil pipeline, proposed gas pipeline, and tar sands. 480-511, *Oct. 1976*

Alaska: Rising Northern Star. By Joseph Judge. Photos by Bruce Dale.

Included: Map of Trans-Alaska pipeline (under construction). 730-767, *June 1975*

Oil, the Dwindling Treasure. By Noel Grove. Photos by Emory Kristof. Included: Oil pipelines in the North Sea, on the North Slope, Alaska, and Saudi Arabia. 792-825, *June 1974*

Will Oil and Tundra Mix? Alaska's North Slope Hangs in the Balance. By William S. Ellis. Photos by Emory Kristof. Included: Map of Alaska and northern Canada showing existing pipeline which carries crude oil to refineries in Canada and the United States from Alberta, and proposed Trans-Alaska and Trans-Canada pipelines; map of United States showing existing major crude-oil pipelines, and proposed pipelines; diagram of pipeline. 485-517, *Oct. 1971*

Colombia, from Amazon to Spanish Main. By Loren McIntyre. Included: The 194-mile Trans-Andean oil pipeline. 235-273, *Aug. 1970*

Oil for Victory Piped under the Sea. 721-726, *Dec. 1945*

PIRACY. *See* Pirates

PIRANHAS:

Seeking the Truth About the Feared Piranha. By Paul A. Zahl. 715-733, *Nov. 1970*

PIRATE Rivers and Their Prizes: The Warfare of Waterways Has Sometimes Changed the Geography of Our

Continents. By John Oliver La Gorce. 87-132, *July 1926*

PIRATES:

The Vikings. By Howard La Fay. Photos by Ted Spiegel. 492-541, *Apr. 1970*

Pirate-Fighters of the South China Sea. By Robert Cardwell. 787-796, *June 1946*

Tristan da Cunha, Isles of Contentment: On Lonely Sea Spots of Pirate Lore and Shipwrecks Seven Families Live Happily Far from War Rumors and World Changes. By W. Robert Foran. 671-694, *Nov. 1938*

The Haunts of the Caribbean Corsairs: The West Indies a Geographic Background for the Most Adventurous Episodes in the History of the Western Hemisphere. By Nell Ray Clarke. 147-187, *Feb. 1922*

PISA, Italy:

The Renaissance Lives On in Tuscany. By Luis Marden. Photos by Albert Moldvay. 626-659, *Nov. 1974*

From London to Australia by Aëroplane: A Personal Narrative of the First Aërial Voyage Half Around the World. By Sir Ross Smith. 229-339, *Mar. 1921*

Inexhaustible Italy. By Arthur Stanley Riggs. 273-368, *Oct. 1916*

PISAC (Fortress), Pisac, Peru:

Some Wonderful Sights in the Andean Highlands: The Oldest City in

Colonizers, merchants, and ruthless raiders, the Vikings swept out of Scandinavia to terrorize Europe in swift vessels like this Danish reproduction. TED SPIEGEL, BLACK STAR

America. Sailing on the Lake of the Clouds: The Yosemite of Peru. By Harriet Chalmers Adams. 597-618, *Sept. 1908*

PISCES VI (Submersible):

Sharks at 2,000 Feet. By Eugenie Clark and Emory Kristof as reported to Douglas Lee. NGS research grant. 681-691, *Nov. 1986*

PITCAIRN ISLAND, South Pacific Ocean:

Pitcairn and Norfolk–The Saga of *Bounty*'s Children. By Ed Howard. 510-541. Photos by David Hiser and Melinda Berge. Included: Pitcairn Island. 512-529; Norfolk Island. 530-541, *Oct. 1983*

I Found the Bones of the *Bounty.* By Luis Marden. 725-789, *Dec. 1957*

The *Yankee*'s Wander-world. By Irving and Electa Johnson. 1-50, *Jan. 1949*

Westward Bound in the *Yankee.* By Irving and Electa Johnson. 1-44, *Jan. 1942*

The **PITFALLS** of Success: Yellowstone at 100. By William S. Ellis. Photos by Jonathan Blair. 616-631, *May 1972*

The **PITH** of Peru: A Journey from Talara to Machu Picchu, with Memorable Stopovers. By Henry Albert Phillips. 167-196, *Aug. 1942*

PITKIN, JOHN G.: *Photographer*
Praying Mantis. 685-692, *May 1950*

PITTIER, HENRY:

Awarded Jane M. Smith Life Membership. 342, *Apr. 1920*

Author
Little-Known Parts of Panama. 627-662, *July 1912*
Costa Rica–Vulcan's Smithy. 494-525, *June 1910*

Sails of a model H.M.A.V. **Bounty** *catch the sun on Pitcairn Island, refuge of the ship's 18th-century mutineers.*   DAVID HISER

PITTMAN, BLAIR: *Photographer*
Big Thicket of Texas. By Don Moser. 504-529, *Oct. 1974*

PITTSBURGH, Pennsylvania:

Pennsylvania: Faire Land of William Penn. By Gordon Young. Photos by Cary Wolinsky. 731-767, *June 1978*
Pittsburgh, Pattern for Progress. By William J. Gill. Photos by Clyde Hare. 342-371, *Mar. 1965*
So Much Happens Along the Ohio River. By Frederick Simpich. Photos by Justin Locke. 177-212, *Feb. 1950*
Pittsburgh: Workshop of the Titans. By Albert W. Atwood. 117-144, *July 1949*
Artists Look at Pennsylvania. By John Oliver La Gorce. 37-56, *July 1948*

A **PLACE** Apart: Alaska's Southeast. By Bill Richards. 50-87, *Jan. 1984*

PLACE NAMES. *See* Geographic Names

PLACE Names in Canada. By Henry Gannett. 519-520, *Dec. 1899*

PLACE Names in Eastern Asia. 136, *Mar. 1904*

PLACE Names of the United States. 403-405, *Nov. 1902*

PLAGE, DIETER and MARY:

On Assignment in the Galápagos Islands. *Jan. 1988*

Author-Photographers
Galápagos Wildlife Under Pressure. 122-145, *Jan. 1988*
Return of Java's Wildlife. 750-771, *June 1985*

Photographers
Managing Another Galápagos Species–Man. By Jerry Emory. 146-154, *Jan. 1988*
Sri Lanka's Wildlife. 254-278. I. Sri Lanka's Wildlife Heritage: A Personal Perspective. By Arthur C. Clarke. 254-255; II. Legacy of Lively Treasures. 256-273; III. A Nation Rises to the Challenge. By Lyn de Alwis. 274-278. *Aug. 1983*

PLAGUE:

Fleas: The Lethal Leapers. By Nicole Duplaix. 672-694, *May 1988*
The Rat, Lapdog of the Devil. By Thomas Y. Canby. Photos by James L. Stanfield. Included: Map showing known and suspected plague areas of the Americas, Africa, and Asia; cases reported in 1975. 60-87, *July 1977*
See also Bubonic Plague

A **PLAGUE** of Mice. 479-485, *May 1909*

"PLAIN PEOPLE." *See* Amish; Hutterites; Mennonites

The **PLAIN** People of Pennsylvania. Photo essay by Jerry Irwin. Text by Douglas Lee. Included: Amish Mennonites; Old Order Amish; Old Order Mennonites (Team Mennonites); Reidenbach Mennonites; Wenger Mennonites. 492-519, *Apr. 1984*

PLAIN Tales from the Trenches: As Told Over the Tea Table in Blighty–

A Soldier's "Home" in Paris. By Carol Corey. 300-312, *Mar. 1918*

PLAINEST of Pennsylvania's Plain People: Amish Folk. By Richard Gehman. Photos by William Albert Allard. 227-253, *Aug. 1965*

PLAINS:

⊕ *Northern Plains,* The Making of America series. Included: Montana, Wyoming, North Dakota, South Dakota, Nebraska, Minnesota, Iowa, and in Canada: Saskatchewan, Manitoba, Ontario. On reverse: New Frontiers, Indians in Transition, Furs and Footholds, Steel Rails and Settlers, King Wheat, Patterns of Change. *Dec. 1986*
⊕ *Central Plains,* The Making of America series. Included: Iowa, Illinois, Missouri, Arkansas, Nebraska, Kansas, Oklahoma. On reverse: Indians and Entryways, Indian Land–White Land, The Great Assault, Indian Relocation, Indian Territory–The Last Stop, Last Frontiers, Dust Bowl of the Continent, Agricultural Heartland. *Sept. 1985*
Cloud Scenery of the High Plains (Kansas). By Willard D. Johnson. 493-496, *Dec. 1898*
The Sage Plains of Oregon. By Frederick V. Coville. 395-404, *Dec. 1896*
Geomorphology of the Southern Appalachians. By Charles Willard Hayes and Marius R. Campbell. 63-126, *May 23, 1894*
The Rivers of Northern New Jersey, with Notes on the Classification of Rivers in General. By William Morris Davis. 81-110, *May 1890*

PLAINS INDIANS:

Indians of Our Western Plains. By Matthew W. Stirling. Paintings by W. Langdon Kihn. 73-108, *July 1944*
See also Cheyenne Indians; Sioux Indians

PLAN for Climbing Mt. McKinley. By Alfred H. Brooks and D. L. Reaburn. 30-35, *Jan. 1903*

PLAN of a Map of the World. By Albrecht Penck. 405-408, *Oct. 1904*

PLANCHES, EDMOND MAYOR, BARON DES. *See* Mayor des Planches, Edmond, Baron

PLANETS:

▌▌*National Geographic Picture Atlas of Our Universe.* By Roy A. Gallant. 284 pages. 1980; rev. ed. *1986*
The Planets: Between Fire and Ice. By Rick Gore. 4-51, *Jan. 1985*
⊕ *The Solar System; Saturn, July 1981*
Voyager's Historic View of Earth and Moon. Note: NASA's Voyager 1 spacecraft begins its flight toward Jupiter, Saturn, Uranus, and the interstellar space beyond. 53, *July 1978*
Voyage to the Planets. By Kenneth F. Weaver. Paintings by Ludek Pesek. 147-193, *Aug. 1970*
First Photographs of Planets and Moon Taken with Palomar's 200-inch

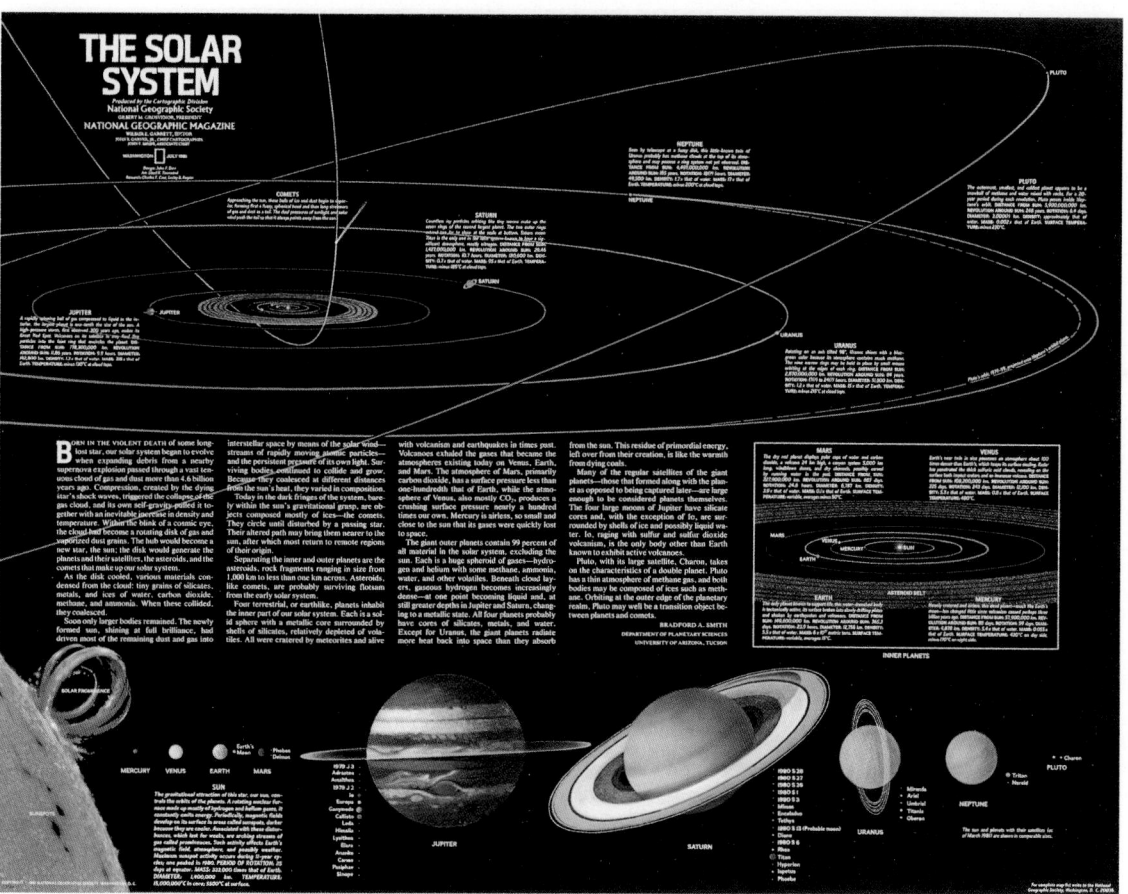

The planets in their courses, from Mercury to Pluto, were depicted on the July 1981 magazine supplement. NGS CARTOGRAPHIC DIVISION

■■ *Nature's Healing Arts: From Folk Medicine to Modern Drugs.* By Lonnelle Aikman. Photos by Nathan Benn and Ira Block. 199 pages. *1977*

Florida, Noah's Ark for Exotic Newcomers. By Rick Gore. Photos by David Doubilet. 538-559, *Oct. 1976*

Nature's Gifts to Medicine. By Lonnelle Aikman. Paintings by Lloyd K. Townsend and Don Crowley. 420-440, *Sept. 1974*

Abundant Life in a Desert Land. By Walter Meayers Edwards. 424-436, *Sept. 1973*

Stalking the West's Wild Foods. By Euell Gibbons. Photos by David Hiser. 186-199, *Aug. 1973*

Stalking Wild Foods on a Desert Isle. By Euell Gibbons. Photos by David Hiser. 47-63, *July 1972*

Plants of the Alaskan Tundra. 315-321, *Mar. 1972*

Nature's Year in Pleasant Valley. By Paul A. Zahl. 488-525, *Apr. 1968*

Malaysia's Giant Flowers and Insect-trapping Plants. By Paul A. Zahl. Included: Groundsels, Lichens, Lobelias. 680-701, *May 1964*

Mountains of the Moon (Ruwenzori). By Paul A. Zahl. 412-434, *Mar. 1962*

Plants That Eat Insects. By Paul A. Zahl. 643-659, *May 1961*

A Visit to the Living Ice Age (Far North). By Rutherford Platt. 525-545, *Apr. 1957*

In the Wilds of a City Parlor. By Paul A. Zahl. 645-672, *Nov. 1954*

Kew: The Commoners' Royal Garden. By Thomas Garner James. Photos by B. Anthony Stewart. 479-506, *Apr. 1950*

Patent Plants Enrich Our World. By Orville H. Kneen. Photos from U. S. Plant Patents. 357-378, *Mar. 1948*

An Insect Community Lives in Flower Heads (Shepherd's Needles). By James G. Needham. 340-356, *Sept. 1946*

Exploring a Grass Wonderland of Wild West China. By Ray G. Johnson. 713-742, *June 1944*

Riddle of the Aleutians: A Botanist Explores the Origin of Plants on Evermisty Islands Now Enshrouded in the Fog of War. By Isobel Wylie Hutchison. 769-792, *Dec. 1942*

Peacetime Plant Hunting About Peiping. By P. H. and J. H. Dorsett. 509-534, *Oct. 1937*

Hunting Useful Plants in the Caribbean. By David Fairchild. 705-737, *Dec. 1934*

Hunting for Plants in the Canary Islands. By David Fairchild. 607-652, *May 1930*

Round About Bogotá: A Hunt for New Fruits and Plants Among the Mountain Forests of Colombia's Unique Capital. By Wilson Popenoe. 127-160, *Feb. 1926*

Canyons and Cacti of the American Southwest. Photos by Edwin L. Wisherd, Jacob Gayer, Charles Martin. 275-290, *Sept. 1925*

Ferns as a Hobby. By William R. Maxon. Paintings by E. J. Geske. 541-586, *May 1925*

Goldfish and Their Cultivation in America. By Hugh M. Smith. Paintings by Hashime Murayama. Included: The following ornamental plants grown in aquaria: Fanwort, Spatterdock, Water Seedbox, Waterweed. 375-400, *Oct. 1924*

Exploring the Mysteries of Plant Life. By William Joseph Showalter. Paintings by Mary E. Eaton. 581-646, *June 1924*

Fantastic Plants of Our Western Deserts. Photos by Frank M. Campbell. 33-40, *Jan. 1924*

Protecting the United States from Plant Pests. By Charles Lester Marlatt. 205-218, *Aug. 1921*

Familiar Grasses and Their Flowers. By E. J. Geske and W. J. Showalter. Paintings by E. J. Geske. 625-636, *June 1921*

Common Mushrooms of the United States. By Louis C. C. Krieger. Paintings by author. 387-439, *May 1920*

A Hunter of Plants. By David Fairchild. 57-77, *July 1919*

The Discovery of Cancer in Plants. 53-70, *Jan. 1913*

The Kingdom of Flowers: An Account of the Wealth of Trees and Shrubs of China and of What the Arnold Arboretum, with China's Help, Is Doing to Enrich America. By Ernest H. Wilson. 1003-1035, *Nov. 1911*

New Plant Immigrants. By David Fairchild. 879-907, *Oct. 1911*

Pests and Parasites: Why We Need a National Law to Prevent the Importation of Insect-Infested and Diseased Plants. By Charles Lester Marlatt. 321-346, *Apr. 1911*

The Mistletoe. 965, *Nov. 1910*

Our Plant Immigrants. By David Fairchild. 179-201, *Apr. 1906*

The American Deserts. 153-163, *Apr. 1904*

Big Things of the West. By Charles F. Holder. 279-282, *July 1903*

Henequen–The Yucatan Fiber. By E. H. Thompson. 150-158, *Apr. 1903*

The Sage Plains of Oregon. By Frederick V. Coville. 395-404, *Dec. 1896*

Laws of Temperature Control of the Geographic Distribution of Terrestrial Animals and Plants. Annual Address by C. Hart Merriam. 229-238, *Dec. 29, 1894*

Cryptogams Collected by C. Willard Hayes in Alaska, 1891. By Clara E. Cummings. 160-162, *May 15, 1892*

List of Plants Collected near Muir Glacier, determined by W. W. Rowlee. *Mar. 21, 1892*

Report on Fossil Plants (Mount St. Elias Expedition). By Lester F. Ward. 199-200, *May 29, 1891*

See also Agriculture; Algae; Cactuses; Coffee; Flowers; Fruit Growing; Fruits; Fungi; Gardens; Grasses; Rain Forests; Seaweed; Shrubs; Trees; Vegetables

PLAQUEMINES PARISH, Louisiana:

New Orleans and Her River. By Joseph Judge. Photos by James L. Stanfield. 151-187, *Feb. 1971*

PLASTICS:

Chemists Make a New World: Creating Hitherto Unknown Raw Materials, Science Now Disrupts Old Trade Routes and Revamps the World Map of Industry. By Frederick Simpich. 601-640, *Nov. 1939*

PLATE TECTONICS:

Earthquake in Mexico. By Allen A. Boraiko. Photos by James L. Stanfield and Guillermo Aldana E. Included: The rise and fall of buildings–a primer for survival in quake city. 654-675, *May 1986*

Eruption in Colombia. By Bart McDowell. Photos by Steve Raymer. 640-653, *May 1986*

When the Earth Moves. The Editor. 638-639, *May 1986*

Tectonics to *Titanic.* President's Page. By Gilbert M. Grosvenor. *Dec. 1985*

Our Restless Planet Earth. 142-181. By Rick Gore. Photos by James A. Sugar. Included: Continents Adrift; Life's Triumph *and* Origin of Earth and Life. Painting by Ned M. Seidler. Text by Larry Kohl. 146-151. *Aug. 1985*

❖ *The Shaping of a Continent: North America's Active West; Earth's Dynamic Crust.* Included: Spreading, Subduction, Collision, Faulting, Accretion, Hot Spots, 90 Million Years of Drift. *Aug. 1985*

■■ *Exploring Our Living Planet.* By Robert D. Ballard. 366 pages. *1983*

The Mediterranean–Sea of Man's Fate. By Rick Gore. Photos by Jonathan Blair. Included: The unstable geologic history of its basin evidenced by volcanic eruptions, rising sea levels, and earthquakes; cross-section painting of African, Iberian, Apulian, and Eurasian Plates. 694-737, *Dec. 1982*

❖ *The Historic Mediterranean; The Mediterranean Seafloor. Dec. 1982*

● Born of Fire. 824, *Dec. 1982*

■■ *Our Violent Earth.* Juvenile. 104 pages. *1982*

New World of the Ocean. By Samuel W. Matthews. Included: Recent discoveries of forces at work in the ocean; rifting, crustal formation, drifting, and reabsorption; cross-section paintings of the anatomy of the seas, circulation of waters. 792-832, *Dec. 1981*

❖ *The World; The World Ocean Floor.* Included: Trenches, rifts, faults, and fracture zones; Undersea ridges, continental shelves, abyssal plains, and basins. *Dec. 1981*

Eruption of Mount St. Helens. By Rowe Findley. Included: Map, Shifting Plates Give Birth to Eruptions. 3-65, *Jan. 1981*

● Dive to the Edge of Creation: Galapagos II expedition. 682, Nov. 1979; 1, cover, *Jan. 1980*

Incredible World of the Deep-sea Rifts. 680-705 I. Strange World Without Sun. The Editor. 680-688; II. Return to Oases of the Deep. By Robert D. Ballard and J. Frederick Grassle. 689-705, *Nov. 1979*

■■ *Powers of Nature.* 199 pages. *1978*

Polish flag and religious portraits in a Lublin window welcome Pope John Paul II on a 1987 visit to his homeland.   JAMES L. STANFIELD, NGS

Frost encrusts the face of Paul Schurke, co-leader of a 1986 expedition to the North Pole by dogsled. WILL STEGER

POLO, MARCO:

POLONOROESTE (Development Program), Brazil:

POLPERRO, England:

POLUNIN, IVAN:

POLYNESIA:

Re-creating possible voyages of early Polynesians between Hawaii and Tahiti, the traditional sailing canoe **Hokule'a** *navigates the 3,000-nautical-mile route.* NICHOLAS DEVORE III

Starting in St. Joseph, Missouri, Pony Express riders moved mail day and night over their 1,840-mile route. PAINTING BY GEORGE S. GAADT

Diary of a Voyage from San Francisco to Tahiti and Return, 1901. By S. P. Langley. 413-429, *Dec. 1901*
See also Canton Island; Cook Islands; Easter Island; Ellice Islands; Falcon Island; Fatu-Hiva; Hawaii; Marquesas Islands; New Zealand; Norfolk Island; Pitcairn Island; Samoa; Society Islands; Tahiti; Tonga; Tongareva; Tuamotu Archipelago

POLYNESIAN CANOE. *See Hokule'a*

POLYNESIANS:

Isles of the Pacific. 732-793. I. The Coming of the Polynesians. By Kenneth P. Emory. 732-745; II. Wind, Wave, Star, and Bird. By David Lewis. Photos by Nicholas deVore III. 747-781; III. The Pathfinders. Paintings by Herb Kawainui Kane. 756-769; IV. Problems in Paradise. By Mary and Laurance S. Rockefeller. Photos by Thomas Nebbia. 782-793, *Dec. 1974*
Feast Day in Kapingamarangi. By W. Robert Moore. 523-537, *Apr. 1950*
See also Maoris

POLYPS (Marine Animals):

Coral Castle Builders of Tropic Seas. By Roy Waldo Miner. Paintings by Else Bostelmann. 703-728, *June 1934*

POMERANTZ, MARTIN A.: *Author*

Trailing Cosmic Rays in Canada's North. 99-115, *Jan. 1953*

The **POMP** and Pulse of Modern London. Photos by B. Anthony Stewart. 17-48, *Jan. 1937*

POMPEII (Ancient City), Italy:

The Dead Do Tell Tales at Vesuvius. By Rick Gore. Photos by O. Louis Mazzatenta. NGS research grant. 557-613, *May 1984*
Last Moments of the Pompeians. By Amedeo Maiuri. Photos by Lee E. Battaglia. Paintings by Peter V. Bianchi. 651-669, *Nov. 1961*

Destruction of Pompeii as Interpreted by the Volcanic Eruptions of Martinique. By Angelo Heilprin. 431, *Oct. 1904*

POMPEII of Prehistoric Animals in Nebraska. By Michael R. Voorhies. Photos by Annie Griffiths. Paintings by Jay Matternes. 66-75, *Jan. 1981*

POMPIDOU Center, Rage of Paris. Photos by Marc Riboud. Text by Cathy Newman. 469-477, *Oct. 1980*

PONAPE (Island), Caroline Islands:

Hidden Key to the Pacific: Piercing the Web of Secrecy Which Long Has Veiled Japanese Bases in the Mandated Islands. By Willard Price. 759-785, *June 1942*
Yap and Other Pacific Islands Under Japanese Mandate. By Junius B. Wood. 591-627, *Dec. 1921*
See also present name, Pohnpei

PONCE, ROJAS: *Artist*

Finding the Tomb of a Warrior-God. By William Duncan Strong. Photos by Clifford Evans, Jr. 453-482, *Apr. 1947*

POND INLET, Baffin Island, Canada:

I Live With the Eskimos. By Guy Mary-Rousseliere. 188-217, *Feb. 1971*

POND LIFE:

Life Around a Lily Pad. Photos by Bianca Lavies. Text by Charles R. Miller. 131-142, *Jan. 1980*
Rotifers: Nature's Water Purifiers. By John Walsh. 287-292, *Feb. 1979*
Teeming Life of a Pond. By William H. Amos. 274-298, *Aug. 1970*

PONIES:

England's Wild Moorland Ponies. 129-136, *Jan. 1946*
See also Assateague Island, for wild ponies; Devon, for Dartmoor ponies; Sable Island, for wild ponies; Shetland Islands, for Shetland ponies

PONTA DELGADA, Azores:

The Azores: Picturesque and Historic Half-way House of American Transatlantic Aviators. By Arminius T. Haeberle. 514-545, *June 1919*

PONTINE MARSHES, Italy:

Redemption of the Pontine Marshes: By Draining the Malarial Wastes Around Rome, Italy Has Created a Promised Land. By Gelasio Caetani. 201-217, *Aug. 1934*
The Story and the Legends of the Pontine Marshes: After Many Centuries of Fruitless Effort, Italy Is to Inaugurate a Gigantic Enterprise to Drain the Fertile Region Southeast of Rome. By Don Gelasio Caetani. 357-374, *Apr. 1924*

PONTING, HERBERT G.: *Photographer*

Nature's Clown, the Penguin. By David Hellyer and Malcolm Davis. Included: Photos taken on the second Scott Antarctic expedition (1911). 405-428, *Sept. 1952*
The Lure of the Land of Ice. Included: Photos taken on the Scott Antarctic expedition. 255-270, *Mar. 1924*
Life in the Antarctic. Included: Photos taken on the Scott Antarctic expedition. 655-662, *Dec. 1922*

PONY EXPRESS:

The Pony Express. By Rowe Findley. Photos by Craig Aurness. 45-71, *July 1980*

POOR Little Rich Land–Formosa. By Frederick G. Vosburgh. Photos by J. Baylor Roberts. 139-176, *Feb. 1950*

POORWILL Sleeps Away the Winter. By Edmund C. Jaeger. 273-280, *Feb. 1953*

POPENOE, PAUL B.: *Author*

Costa Rica, Land of the Banana. 201-220, *Feb. 1922*

POPENOE, WILSON: *Author*

Round About Bogotá: A Hunt for New Fruits and Plants Among the Mountain Forests of Colombia's Unique Capital. 127-160, *Feb. 1926*

POPES:

Vatican City. By James Fallows. Photos by James L. Stanfield. 723-775. Included: The Photographer's Perspective. By James L. Stanfield. 762-763; Treasures of the Vatican. Photos by James L. Stanfield and Victor R. Boswell, Jr. 764-775, *Dec. 1985*

St. Peter's, Rome's Church of Popes.

By Aubrey Menen. Photos by Albert Moldvay. Included: John XXIII, Julius II, Paul VI, Pius XII, and Saint Peter. 865-879, *Dec. 1971*

POPOCATEPETL (Volcano), Mexico:

The Greatest Volcanoes of Mexico. By A. Melgareio. 741-760, *Sept. 1910*

POPPER, PAUL: *Photographer*

Cane Bridges of Asia. 243-250, *Aug. 1948*

POPPIES, Opium:

The Poppy. By Peter T. White. Photos by Steve Raymer. 143-189, *Feb. 1985*

POPULATION:

Population, Plenty, and Poverty. By Paul R. and Anne H. Ehrlich. Included: Kenya: A Population Exploding. Photos by Robert Caputo; China: Back from the Brink. Photos by Patrick Zachmann; Hungary: A Static Society. Photos by Steve McCurry; India: Life on the Edge. Photos by Raghu Rai; Brazil: Flight to the Cities. Photos by Mary Ellen Mark; United States: Geared to Consumption. Photos by Pam Spaulding; Two Ways to Cope. 914-945, *Dec. 1988*

⊕ *World; Endangered Earth.* Included: Pastures of the Sea; The Continental Garden; Global Carbon Dioxide; Ice Age Vegetation 18,000 Years BP; Greenhouse-Effect Vegetation Zones; Population Explosion; Peru-Ecuador Upwelling; Minnesota's Boreal Forest; Population Projections; Population Time-line; Growing Threats: Population Pressure, Air Pollution, Ozone Concerns, Acid Rain, Water Pollution, Species Extinctions, Fisheries Depletion, Deforestation, Desertification. *Dec. 1988*

Mexico City: An Alarming Giant. By Bart McDowell. Photos by Stephanie Maze. Included: A Scholarly President Looks at Mexico's Future. The Editor. 138-175, *Aug. 1984*

The World's Urban Explosion. By Robert W. Fox. Graphics by Allen Carroll. 179-185, *Aug. 1984*

Editorial. By Gilbert M. Grosvenor. 1, *July 1975*

Census 1960: Profile of the Nation. By Albert W. Atwood and Lonnelle Aikman. 697-714, *Nov. 1959*

⊕ *A Map of the World* (in Eastern and Western Hemispheres). Included: Inset showing density of population. *Dec. 1941*

⊕ *The World.* Included: Inset showing density of population. *Dec. 1932*

The Remarkable Growth of Europe During 40 Years of Peace. By O. P. Austin. 272-274, *Sept. 1914*

Recent Population Figures. By Henry Gannett. 785-786, *Aug. 1911*

The Indian Census of 1911. By John J. Banninga. 633-638, *July 1911*

The Population of the United States. By Henry Gannett. 34-48, *Jan. 1911*

Proportion of Children in the United States. 504-508, *Nov. 1905*

The Population of Japan. By Walter J. Ballard. 482, *Oct. 1905*

European Populations. By Walter J. Ballard. 432, *Sept. 1905*

The Geographical Distribution of Insanity in the United States. By William A. White. 361-378, *Oct. 1903*

White Population of the Chief British Colonies. 360, *Sept. 1903*

Urban Population of United States. 345-346, *Sept. 1901*

Calculations of Population in June, 1900. By Henry Farquhar. 406-413, *Oct. 1899*

The Growth of the United States. By W J McGee. 377-386, *Sept. 1898*

The Russian Census of 1897. By A. W. Greely. 335-336, *Nov. 1897*

Suburb of Mexico City, world's largest megalopolis, Netzahualcóyotl rolls on, fueled by relentless population growth and rural emigration. STEPHANIE MAZE

The Mexican Census. 211, *June 1896*
The Great Populous Centers of the World. By A. W. Greely. 89-92, *July 10, 1893*
The Movements of Our Population (U. S.). By Henry Gannett. 21-44, *Mar. 20, 1893*
See also Census; Immigration

POPULOUS and Beautiful Szechuan: A Visit to the Restless Province of China, in which the Present Revolution Began. By Rollin T. Chamberlin. 1094-1119, *Dec. 1911*

PORCELAIN:
Yellow Sea Yields Shipwreck Trove. Photos by H. Edward Kim. Introduction by Donald H. Keith. 231-243, *Aug. 1979*
Treasures of Dresden. By John L. Eliot. Photos by Victor R. Boswell, Jr. Included: Europe's first porcelain; Meissen porcelain. 702-717, *Nov. 1978*
The Sunken Treasure of St. Helena. By Robert Sténuit. Photos by Bates Littlehales. Included: Porcelain of the Ming Dynasty. 562-576, *Oct. 1978*
The World's Ancient Porcelain Center (Kingtehchen, China). By Frank B. Lenz. 391-406, *Nov. 1920*

PORCUPINES:
Porcupines, Rambling Pincushions. By Donald A. Spencer. 247-264, *Aug. 1950*
Smaller Mammals of North America. By E. W. Nelson. Paintings by Louis Agassiz Fuertes. 371-493, *May 1918*
Wild Animals That Took Their Own Pictures by Day and by Night. By George Shiras, 3d. Included: Pictorial supplement. 763-834, *July 1913*
The Quills of a Porcupine. By Frederick V. Coville. 25-31, *Jan. 1912*
A Flashlight Story of an Albino Porcupine and of a Cunning but Unfortunate Coon. By George Shiras, 3d. 572-596, *June 1911*

PORPOISES:
The Trouble With Dolphins. By Edward J. Linehan. Photos by Bill Curtsinger. 506-541, *Apr. 1979*
Porpoises: Our Friends in the Sea. By Robert Leslie Conly. Photos by Thomas Nebbia. 396-425, *Sept. 1966*
Marineland, Florida's Giant Fish Bowl. By Gilbert Grosvenor La Gorce. Photos by Luis Marden. 679-694, *Nov. 1952*
Whales, Giants of the Sea: Wonder Mammals, Biggest Creatures of All Time, Show Tender Affection for Young, But Can Maim or Swallow Human Hunters. By Remington Kellogg. Paintings by Else Bostelmann. Included: Porpoises and dolphins. 35-90, *Jan. 1940*

PORT AU PRINCE, Haiti:
Haiti: Beyond Mountains, More Mountains. By Carolyn Bennett Patterson. Photos by Thomas Nebbia. 70-97, *Jan. 1976*
Bare Feet and Burros of Haiti. By Oliver P. Newman. 307-328, *Sept. 1944*

Haitian Vignettes. By John Houston Craige. 435-485, *Oct. 1934*
Haiti, the Home of Twin Republics. By Sir Harry Johnston. 483-496, *Dec. 1920*

PORT-OF-SPAIN, Trinidad:
Crossroads of the Caribbean. By Laurence Sanford Critchell. 319-344, *Sept. 1937*

PORT ROYAL, Jamaica:
Reach for the New World. By Mendel Peterson. Photos by David L. Arnold. Paintings by Richard Schlecht. 724-767, *Dec. 1977*
Exploring the Drowned City of Port Royal. By Marion Clayton Link. Photos by Luis Marden. NGS research grant. 151-183, *Feb. 1960*

PORT ROYAL SOUND, South Carolina:
Sea Islands: Adventuring Along the South's Surprising Coast. By James Cerruti. Photos by Thomas Nebbia and James L. Amos. 366-393, *Mar. 1971*

PORTER, ETHEL CHAMBERLAIN:
Author
The Clock Turns Back in Yugoslavia: Fortified Monastery of Mountain-girt Dečani Survives Its Six Hundredth Birthday. 493-512, *Apr. 1944*

PORTER, RUSSELL W.:
Member of Ziegler Polar Expedition. 35, *Jan. 1906*

PORTLAND, Oregon:
Powerhouse of the Northwest (Columbia River). By David S. Boyer. 821-847, *Dec. 1974*
A River Restored: Oregon's Willamette. By Ethel A. Starbird. Photos by Lowell J. Georgia. 816-835, *June 1972*
Oregon Finds New Riches. By Leo A. Borah. 681-728, *Dec. 1946*

PORTO ALEGRE, Rio Grande do Sul, Brazil:
Air Cruising Through New Brazil: A National Geographic Reporter Spots Vast Resources Which the Republic's War Declaration Adds to Strength of United Nations. By Henry Albert Phillips. 503-536, *Oct. 1942*

PORTO Rico. By Robert T. Hill. 93-112, *Mar. 1899*

PORTO Rico, the Gate of Riches: Amazing Prosperity Has Been the Lot of Ponce de León's Isle Under American Administration. By John Oliver La Gorce. 599-651, *Dec. 1924*

PORTO Rico or Puerto Rico? By R. T. Hill. 516-517, *Dec. 1899*

PORTO SANTO (Island), Atlantic Ocean:
The Treasure of Porto Santo. By Robert Sténuit. Photos by author and William R. Curtsinger. 260-275, *Aug. 1975*
Madeira, Like Its Wine, Improves With Age. By Veronica Thomas. Photos by Jonathan Blair. 488-513, *Apr. 1973*

PORTOFINO, Italy:
Time Turns Back in Picture-book Portofino. By Carleton Mitchell. Photos by Winfield Parks. 232-253, *Feb. 1965*

PORTRAIT of a Fierce and Fragile Land: Alaskan Tundra. By Paul A. Zahl. 303-314, *Mar. 1972*

PORTRAIT of Indochina. By W. Robert Moore and Maynard Owen Williams. Paintings by Jean Despujols. 461-490, *Apr. 1951*

PORTRAIT of Planet Earth. 53, *July 1978*

PORTRAIT ROSE (All-America Rose Selection):
Amateur Gardener Creates a New Rose. By Elizabeth A. Moize. Photos by Farrell Grehan. 286-294, *Aug. 1972*

PORTRAIT U.S.A., Landsat photomosaic. *July 1976*

PORTRAITS of Ancient Mayas, a Peace-Loving People. Paintings by H. M. Herget. 553-560, *Nov. 1935*

PORTRAITS of My Monkey Friends. By Ernest P. Walker. 105-119, *Jan. 1956*

PORTRAITS of the Land. 157-169, *Feb. 1988*

PORTS. *See* Harbors and Ports

PORTSMOUTH, England:
Portsmouth, Britannia's Sally Port. By Thomas Garner James. Photos by B. Anthony Stewart. 513-544, *Apr. 1952*

PORTSMOUTH, New Hampshire:
Northeast of Boston. By Albert W. Atwood. 257-292, *Sept. 1945*

O
P

PORTSMOUTH, Virginia:

PORTUGAL:

PORTUGUESE:

PORTUGUESE EAST AFRICA. See

Postage stamps issued in the United States in September 1988 commemorate four men who explored the continent of Antarctica by land, sea, and air. COURTESY U.S. POSTAL SERVICE

PORTUGUESE FISHING FLEET:

PORTUGUESE MAN-OF-WAR:

PORTUGUESE TIMOR:

PORTUGUESE WEST AFRICA. See

POSITRON EMISSION TOMOGRAPHY (PET):

POSSE-BRÁZDOVÁ, AMELIE:

Author

'POSSUMS (American):

POSSUMS (Phalangers):

POST OFFICE BUILDING, Washington, D. C.:

POST ROADS, U. S.:

POSTAGE STAMPS:

POSTAL SERVICE, U. S.:

POSTERS. See Painting Supplements; Photo Supplements

POSTWAR Journey Through Java. By

POSTWAR RECOVERY:

Maynard Owen Williams. 141-186, *Aug. 1951*

Occupied Austria, Outpost of Democracy. By George W. Long. Photos by Volkmar Wentzel. 749-790, *June 1951*

Mid-century Holland Builds Her Future. By Sydney Clark. 747-778, *Dec. 1950*

Japan Tries Freedom's Road. By Frederick G. Vosburgh. Photos by J. Baylor Roberts. 593-632, *May 1950*

Okinawa, Pacific Outpost. 538-552, *Apr. 1950*

War-torn Greece Looks Ahead. By Maynard Owen Williams. 711-744, *Dec. 1949*

Italy Smiles Again. By Edgar Erskine Hume. 693-732, *June 1949*

Airlift to Berlin. 595-614, *May 1949*

With Uncle Sam and John Bull in Germany. By Frederick Simpich. 117-140, *Jan. 1949*

Uncle Sam Bends a Twig in Germany. By Frederick Simpich. Photos by J. Baylor Roberts. 529-550, *Oct. 1948*

Pacific Wards of Uncle Sam. By W. Robert Moore. 73-104, *July 1948*

Luxembourg, Survivor of Invasions. By Sydney Clark. Photos by Maynard Owen Williams. 791-810, *June 1948*

Belgium Comes Back. By Harvey Klemmer. Photos by Maynard Owen Williams. 575-614, *May 1948*

Keeping House in London. By Frances James. 769-792, *Dec. 1947*

Scenes of Postwar Finland. By La Verne Bradley. Photos by Jerry Waller. 233-264, *Aug. 1947*

With the U. S. Army in Korea. By John R. Hodge. 829-840, *June 1947*

Backwoods Japan During American Occupation. By M. A. Huberman. 491-518, *Apr. 1947*

What I Saw Across the Rhine. By J. Frank Dobie. 57-86, *Jan. 1947*

POTALA (Palace), Lhasa, Tibet:

In Long-Forbidden Tibet. By Fred Ward. 218-259, *Feb. 1980*

My Life in Forbidden Lhasa. By Heinrich Harrer. 1-48, *July 1955*

Sky-high in Lama Land. Photos by C. Suydam Cutting. 185-196, *Aug. 1946*

The World's Strangest Capital (Lhasa, Tibet). By John Claude White. 273-295, *Mar. 1916*

POTASH:

American Potash for America. By Guy Elliott Mitchell. 399-405, *Apr. 1911*

POTASSIUM-ARGON DATING:

A Clock for the Ages: Potassium-Argon. By Garniss H. Curtis. 590-592, *Oct. 1961*

POTATOES:

The Incredible Potato. By Robert E. Rhoades. Photos by Martin Rogers. 668-694, *May 1982*

Madawaska: Down East With a French Accent. By Perry Garfinkel. Photos by Cary Wolinsky. 380-409, *Sept. 1980*

Our Vegetable Travelers. By Victor R. Boswell, Jr. Paintings by Else Bostelmann. 145-217, *Aug. 1949*

Aroostook County, Maine, Source of Potatoes. By Howell Walker. 459-478, *Oct. 1948*

POTENT Personalities–Wasps and Hornets: Though Often Painfully Stung, Mankind Profits Immeasurably from the Pest-killing Activities of These Fiery Little Flyers. By Austin H. Clark. Paintings by Hashime Murayama. 47-72, *July 1937*

POTHOLES, Desert:

Miracle of the Potholes. By Rowe Findley. Photos by Robert F. Sisson. 570-579, *Oct. 1975*

POTOMAC (River), Maryland-Virginia-West Virginia-D. C.:

George Washington's Patowmack Canal. By Wilbur E. Garrett. Photos by Kenneth Garrett. 716-753, *June 1987*

The Nation's River. 432-479. By Allan C. Fisher, Jr. Photos by James L. Stanfield. Included: A Good Life on the Potomac. 470-479, *Oct. 1976*

New Grandeur for Flowering Washington. By Joseph Judge. Photos by James P. Blair. 500-539, *Apr. 1967*

Waterway to Washington, the C & O Canal. By Jay Johnston. 419-439, *Mar. 1960*

Across the Potomac from Washington. By Albert W. Atwood. 1-33, *Jan. 1953*

Down the Potomac by Canoe. By Ralph Gray. Photos by Walter Meayers Edwards. 213-242, *Aug. 1948*

Potomac, River of Destiny. By Albert W. Atwood. 33-70, *July 1945*

Approaching Washington by Tidewater Potomac. By Paul Wilstach. 372-392, *Mar. 1930*

The Great Falls of the Potomac. By Gilbert Grosvenor. 385-400, *Mar. 1928*

Atlantic Estuarine Tides. By Mark S. W. Jefferson. 400-409, *Sept. 1898*

A church deacon, octogenarian Carolinas Peyton farms 50 acres on the Potomac River in Virginia. JAMES L. STANFIELD, NGS

The Washington Aqueduct and Cabin John Bridge. By D. D. Gaillard. 337-344, *Dec. 1897*

Pollution of the Potomac River. By F. H. Newell. 346-351, *Dec. 1897*

See also Harpers Ferry

POTOSI, Bolivia:

Bolivia–Tin Roof of the Andes. By Henry Albert Phillips. 309-332, *Mar. 1943*

POTTERY:

Pueblo Pottery–2,000 Years of Artistry. By David L. Arnold. 593-605, *Nov. 1982*

Finding West Africa's Oldest City. By Susan and Roderick McIntosh. Photos by Michael and Aubine Kirtley. Included: Pottery of ancient and modern Jenne. 396-418, *Sept. 1982*

Mexican Folk Art. By Fernando Horcasitas. Photos by David Hiser. 648-669, *May 1978*

20th-century Indians Preserve Customs of the Cliff Dwellers. Photos by William Belknap, Jr. NGS research grant. 196-211, *Feb. 1964*

The World's Ancient Porcelain Center (Kingtehchen, China). By Frank B. Lenz. 391-406, *Nov. 1920*

POTTERY FIGURES, Chinese:

China's Incredible Find. By Audrey Topping. Paintings by Yang Hsienmin. Included: The first emperor's burial mound, with guardian army of terra-cotta men and horses. 440-459, *Apr. 1978*

POUCH COVE, Newfoundland, Canada:

Newfoundland, Canada's New Province. By Andrew H. Brown. Photos by author and Robert F. Sisson. 777-812, *June 1949*

POULSEN, MOGENS BLOCH: *Author*

Greenland's "Place by the Icebergs." Photos by Thomas Nebbia. 849-869, *Dec. 1973*

POULTER, THOMAS C.:

The Society's Special Medal Is Awarded to Dr. Thomas C. Poulter: Admiral Byrd's Second-in-Command and Senior Scientist Is Accorded High Geographic Honor. 105-108, *July 1937*

POULTRY:

Delaware–Who Needs to Be Big? By Jane Vessels. Photos by Kevin Fleming. 171-197, *Aug. 1983*

Long Island Outgrows the Country. By Howell Walker. Photos by B. Anthony Stewart. Included: Duck raising. 279-326, *Mar. 1951*

"Delmarva," Gift of the Sea. By Catherine Bell Palmer. 367-399, *Sept. 1950*

Easter Egg Chickens. By Frederick G. Vosburgh. Photos by B. Anthony Stewart. 377-387, *Sept. 1948*

Fowls of Forest and Stream Tamed by Man. By Morley A. Jull. Paintings by Hashime Murayama. Contents: Ducks, Geese, Guinea Fowl, Peafowl, Swans, Turkeys. 327-371, *Mar. 1930*

The Races of Domestic Fowl. By M. A. Jull. Paintings by Hashime Murayama. Included: Ancona, Andalusian, Araucana, Bantam, Brahma, Campine, Cochin, Cornish, Dominique, Frizzle, Hamburg, Houdan, Jersey Black Giant, Langshan, Leghorn, Minorca, Plymouth Rock, Polish, Red Jungle Fowl, Rhode Island Red, Silkie, Sussex, Wyandotte, Yokohama. 379-452, *Apr. 1927*

America's Debt to the Hen. By Harry R. Lewis. 453-467, *Apr. 1927*

POWARS, NANCY LINK: Editor

■ *Research Reports.* 1976 Projects. 968 pages. *1984*
■ *Research Reports.* 1975 Projects. 844 pages. *1984*
■ *Research Reports.* 1971, 1973, or 1974 Projects. 787 pages. *1983*
■ *Research Reports.* 1973 Projects. 736 pages. *1982*
■ *Research Reports.* 1971 or 1972 Projects. 749 pages. *1981*
■ *Research Reports.* 1971 Projects. 771 pages. *1980*

POWDER EXPLOSION:

The Aberration of Sound as Illustrated by the Berkeley Powder Explosion. By Robert H. Chapman. 246-249, *July 1896*

POWDER RIVER BASIN, Wyoming:

Powder River Basin: New Energy Frontier. By Bill Richards. Photos by Louie Psihoyos. 96-113, *Special Report on Energy. (Feb. 1981)*

POWELL, IMOGENE:
Author-Photographer
"Compleat Angler" Fishes for Fossils. 251-258, *Aug. 1934*

POWELL, JOHN B.: *Author*
Today on the China Coast. 217-238, *Feb. 1945*

POWELL, JOHN WESLEY:
President's Page. By Gilbert M. Grosvenor. *Sept. 1988*
Retracing John Wesley Powell's Historic Voyage Down the Grand Canyon. By Joseph Judge. Photos by Walter Meayers Edwards. 668-713, *May 1969*
Surveying the Grand Canyon of the Colorado: An Account of the 1923 Boating Expedition of the United States Geological Survey. By Lewis R. Freeman. Included: Expeditions of John Wesley Powell in the Grand Canyon area. 471-548, *May 1924*
John Wesley Powell (Biography). By Gilbert H. Grosvenor. 393-394, *Nov. 1902*
Gardiner Greene Hubbard: Memorial Meeting. Address by John W. Powell. 59-63, *Feb. 1898*

POWELL, W. B.:
Chairman of National Geographic Society Prize Committee. 32, *Jan. 1899*
Board of Managers. 165, Apr. 1889; 270, July 1889; 68, Apr. 1890; 294, Apr. 1891; xii, Feb. 19, 1892; xix, Feb. 20, 1893; 191, *June 1897*
Vice-President. xix, *May 5, 1894*

Author
Geographic Instruction in the Public Schools. 137-153, *Jan. 31, 1894*

POWELL, Lake, Arizona-Utah:
Lake Powell: Waterway to Desert Wonders. By Walter Meayers Edwards. 44-75, *July 1967*

POWELL-COTTON, P.H.G.: *Author*
A Journey Through the Eastern Portion of the Congo State. 155-163, *Mar. 1908*

POWER. *See* Energy Sources

POWER Comes Back to Peiping. By Nelson T. Johnson and W. Robert Moore. 337-368, *Sept. 1949*

The **POWER** of Letting Off Steam. By Kenneth F. Weaver. 566-579, *Oct. 1977*

POWER PLANTS:
Coal vs. Parklands. By François Leydet. Photos by Dewitt Jones. 776-803, *Dec. 1980*
Jari: A Billion-dollar Gamble. By Loren McIntyre. Included: Daniel K. Ludwig's paper-pulp factory and the wood-burning plant that powers it. 686-711, *May 1980*
Geothermal Energy: The Power of Letting Off Steam. By Kenneth F. Weaver. 566-579, *Oct. 1977*
The Search for Tomorrow's Power. By Kenneth F. Weaver. Photos by Emory Kristof. 650-681, *Nov. 1972*
See also Hydroelectric Power; Nuclear Energy

POWERHOUSE of the Northwest: Columbia River. By David S. Boyer. 821-847, *Dec. 1974*

POWERS *of Nature.* 199 pages.
■■*1978*

POWHATAN CHIEFDOM:
New Clues to an Old Mystery (Virginia's Wolstenholme Towne). By Ivor Noël Hume. Photos by Ira Block. Paintings by Richard Schlecht. 53-77, *Jan. 1982*
Indians of the Southeastern United States. By Matthew W. Stirling. Paintings by W. Langdon Kihn. 53-74, *Jan. 1946*

POZZUOLI, Italy:
A Prayer for Pozzuoli. By Rick Gore. Photos by O. Louis Mazzatenta. 615-625, *May 1984*

PRACTICAL Exercises in Geography. By W. M. Davis. 62-78, *Feb. 1900*

PRACTICAL Patriotism. 279-280, Sept. 1917; 476, *Nov.-Dec. 1917*

PRAGUE (Praha), Czechoslovakia:
Old Prague in Winter. By Peter T. White. Photos by Nathan Benn. 546-567, *Apr. 1979*
Czechoslovakia: The Dream and the Reality. By Edward J. Linehan. Photos by James P. Blair. 151-193, *Feb. 1968*
A Tale of Three Cities. By Thomas R. Henry. 641-669, *Dec. 1945*

John Wesley Powell talks with a Paiute four years after leading a voyage down the Colorado River and through the Grand Canyon. JOHN K. HILLERS, COURTESY SMITHSONIAN INSTITUTION

Czechoslovaks, Yankees of Europe. By John Patric. 173-225, *Aug. 1938*

When Czechoslovakia Puts a Falcon Feather in Its Cap. By Maynard Owen Williams. 40-49, *Jan. 1933*

Czechoslovakia, Key-Land to Central Europe. By Maynard Owen Williams. 111-156, *Feb. 1921*

PRAIRIE DOGS:

The Hard Life of the Prairie Dog. By Tim W. Clark. Photos by Patricia Caulfield. NGS research grant. 270-281, *Aug. 1979*

PRAIRIE FALCONS:

In Quest of the Golden Eagle: Over Lonely Mountain and Prairie Soars This Rare and Lordly Bird, But Three Youths from the East Catch Up With Him at Last. By John and Frank Craighead. 693-710, *May 1940*

Week-Ends With the Prairie Falcon: A Commuter Finds Recreation in Scaling Cliffs to Observe the Nest Life and Flying Habits of These Elusive Birds. By Frederick Hall Fowler. 611-626, *May 1935*

PRAIRIE PROVINCES, Canada:

Canada's Heartland, the Prairie Provinces. By W. E. Garrett. Contents: Alberta, Manitoba, Saskatchewan. 443-489, *Oct. 1970*

PRAIRIES:

Prairie Preservation: Good News, Bad News. Geographica. *Dec. 1988*

▮▮ *Living on the Earth.* Contents: How various peoples have adapted to the world's environments. 320 pages. *1988*

✦ *Northern Plains,* The Making of America series. Included: Montana, Wyoming, North Dakota, South Dakota, Nebraska, Minnesota, Iowa, and in Canada: Saskatchewan, Manitoba, Ontario. On reverse: New Frontiers, Indians in Transition, Furs and Footholds, Steel Rails and Settlers, King Wheat, Patterns of Change. *Dec. 1986*

✦ *Central Plains,* The Making of America series. Included: Iowa, Illinois, Missouri, Arkansas, Nebraska, Kansas, Oklahoma. On reverse: Indians and Entryways, Indian Land-White Land, The Great Assault, Indian Relocation, Indian Territory-The Last Stop, Last Frontiers, Dust Bowl of the Continent, Agricultural Heartland. *Sept. 1985*

▮▮ *Lakes, Peaks, and Prairies: Discovering the United States-Canadian Border.* By Thomas O'Neill. Photos by Michael S. Yamashita. 199 pages. *1984*

The Tallgrass Prairie: Can It Be Saved? By Dennis Farney. Photos by Jim Brandenburg. 37-61, *Jan. 1980*

See also Kansas; North Dakota

PRATHER, VICTOR A., Jr.:

We Saw the World From the Edge of Space. By Malcolm D. Ross. Ground photos by Walter Meayers Edwards. 671-685, *Nov. 1961*

Swainson's hawk stretches on a prairie fence post while hunting for small rodents and grasshoppers. JIM BRANDENBURG

PRATT, A. E.: *Author*

Strange Sights in Far-Away Papua. 559-572, *Sept. 1907*

PRATT, WILLIAM V.:

Board of Trustees. 793, June 1934; 591, *May 1935*

PRAUS (Ships):

Seafarers of South Celebes. By G.E.P. Collins. 53-78, *Jan. 1945*

A **PRAYER** for Pozzuoli. By Rick Gore. Photos by O. Louis Mazzatenta. 615-625, *May 1984*

PRAYING MANTIS:

The Praying Predators. By Edward S. Ross. Photos by Dwight Kuhn and the author. 268-280, *Feb. 1984*

Praying Mantis. Photos by John G. Pitkin. 685-692, *May 1950*

PRECIOUS Corals, Hawaii's Deep-sea Jewels. By Richard W. Grigg. Photos by David Doubilet. 719-732, *May 1979*

PRECIOUS Stones. 451-458, *Dec. 1903*

PRE-COLUMBIAN CIVILIZATION:

Editorial. By Wilbur E. Garrett. 141, *Feb. 1986*

The Hohokam: First Masters of the American Desert. By Emil W. Haury. Photos by Helga Teiwes. 670-695, *May 1967*

Magnetic Clues Help Date the Past. By Kenneth F. Weaver. 696-701, *May 1967*

See also Anasazi; Mound Builders

Mexico

Mexico's Window on the Past. By Bart McDowell. Photos by B. Anthony Stewart. 492-519, *Oct. 1968*

"Pyramids" of the New World. By Neil Merton Judd. 105-128, *Jan. 1948*

See also Aztecs; Maya; Olmec Culture; Veracruz

South America

Gold, the Eternal Treasure. By Peter T. White. Photos by James L. Stanfield. Included: Golden Masterpieces. 1-51, *Jan. 1974*

Chan Chan, Peru's Ancient City of Kings. By Michael E. Moseley and Carol J. Mackey. Photos by David Brill. NGS research grant. 318-345, *Mar. 1973*

See also Incas; Moche Culture; *and* Nazca Lines

PRE-HISPANIC CIVILIZATION. *See* Pre-Columbian Civilization

PREHISTORIC ANIMALS. *See* Paleontology

PREHISTORIC CULTURES:

"Where Did We Come From?" Editorial by Wilbur E. Garrett. Included: Map, The Peopling of the Earth. 434-437, *Oct. 1988*

The Search for Modern Humans. By John J. Putman. Photos by Sisse Brimberg and Ira Block. Paintings by Jack Unruh. 439-477, *Oct. 1988*

Oasis of Art in the Sahara. By Henri Lhote. Photos by Kazuyoshi Nomachi. Contents: Rock paintings of Tassili-n-Ajjer, Algeria. 180-191, *Aug. 1987*

Ancient Bulgaria's Golden Treasures. By Colin Renfrew. Photos by James L. Stanfield. Paintings by Jean-Leon Huens. 112-129, *July 1980*

Ancient Europe Is Older Than We Thought. By Colin Renfrew. Photos by Adam Woolfitt. 615-623, *Nov. 1977*

New Light on a Forgotten Past (Southeast Asia). By Wilhelm G. Solheim II. 330-339, *Mar. 1971*

See also Arctic Small Tool Culture; Ice Age Man; Paleo-Indians

The **PREHISTORIC** Ruin of Tsankawi. By George L. Beam. 807-822, *Sept. 1909*

PREHISTORIC Telephone Days. By Alexander Graham Bell. 223-241, *Mar. 1922*

PREHISTORY. *See* Anthropology, Physical; Archaeology; Paleontology; Prehistoric Cultures

PRELUDE to Gettysburg. Map notes by Carolyn Bennett Patterson. 14-21, *July 1963*

PRELUDE to Vicksburg. Map notes by Carolyn Bennett Patterson. 42-45, *July 1963*

PREMANA, Italy:

Lombardy's Lakes, Blue Jewels in Italy's Crown. By Franc Shor. Photos by Joseph J. Scherschel. 58-99, *July 1968*

Sherpa Nawang Gombu presents President John F. Kennedy with a friendship scarf at a 1963 ceremony honoring the American Mount Everest Expedition. GEORGE F. MOBLEY, NGS

Stewart and Thomas Nebbia. 3-43, *Jan. 1961*

Profiles of the Presidents.
  By Frank Freidel:
  Part V. The Atomic Age: Its Problems and Promises. Contents: Franklin D. Roosevelt, Harry S. Truman, Dwight D. Eisenhower, John F. Kennedy, Lyndon B. Johnson. 66-119, *Jan. 1966*
  Part IV. America Enters the Modern Era. Contents: Theodore Roosevelt, William Howard Taft, Woodrow Wilson, Warren G. Harding, Calvin Coolidge, Herbert Hoover. 537-577, *Oct. 1965*
  Part III. The American Giant Comes of Age. Contents: Abraham Lincoln, Andrew Johnson, Ulysses S. Grant, Rutherford B. Hayes, James A. Garfield, Chester A. Arthur, Grover Cleveland, Benjamin Harrison, William McKinley. 660-711, *May 1965*
  Part II. A Restless Nation Moves West. Contents: Andrew Jackson, Martin Van Buren, William Henry Harrison, John Tyler, James K. Polk, Zachary Taylor, Millard Fillmore, Franklin Pierce, James Buchanan. 80-121, *Jan. 1965*
  Part I. The Presidency and How It Grew. Contents: George Washington, John Adams, Thomas Jefferson, James Madison, James Monroe, John Quincy Adams. 642-687, *Nov. 1964*
  See also Adams, John; Eisenhower, Dwight D.; Jackson, Andrew; Jefferson, Thomas; Johnson, Lyndon B.; Kennedy, John F.; Lincoln, Abraham; Roosevelt, Theodore; Washington, George

PRESTON, E. D.: *Author*
The Copper River Delta (Alaska). 29-31, *Jan. 1900*
Tides of Chesapeake Bay. 391-392, *Oct. 1899*
The Coast and Geodetic Survey: Its Present Work. 268-269, *July 1899*

PRESTWICH, GLENN D.:
Nomination Page. In East Africa. *Apr. 1978*
Author-Photographer
Termites: Dwellers in the Dark. 532-547, *Apr. 1978*

PRETORIA, South Africa:
South Africa Close-up. By Kip Ross. 641-681, *Nov. 1962*
The Cities That Gold and Diamonds Built: Transvaal Treasures Have Created Bustling Johannesburg and Fostered Pretoria, Administrative Capital of the South African Union. By W. Robert Moore. 735-766, *Dec. 1942*
The Transvaal: The Treasure-House Province. By Melville Chater. 479-512, *Apr. 1931*

The **PREVENTION** of Hailstorms by the Use of Cannon. 239-241, *June 1900*

PREVIOUS Explorations in the St. Elias Region. 58-74, *May 29, 1891*

PREWETT, GOLDA:
Our Society Welcomes Its 3,000,000th Member. By Melville Bell Grosvenor. 579-582, *Apr. 1962*

PRIBILOF ISLANDS, Bering Sea:
New Day for Alaska's Pribilof Islanders. By Susan Hackley Johnson. Photos by Tim Thompson. 536-552, *Oct. 1982*
The Fur Seal Herd Comes of Age. By Victor B. Scheffer and Karl W. Kenyon. 491-512, *Apr. 1952*
Making the Fur Seal Abundant. By Hugh M. Smith. 1139-1165, *Dec. 1911*

PRICE, DEREK J. DE SOLLA: *Author*
The Tower of the Winds. Paintings by Robert C. Magis. 587-596, *Apr. 1967*

PRICE, EDWIN C., Jr.: *Author*
Ambassadors of Good Will: The Peace Corps. By Sargent Shriver and Peace Corps Volunteers. Included: Sarawak. 297-345, *Sept. 1964*

PRICE, OVERTON W.: *Author*
The Influence of Forestry upon the Lumber Industry of the United States. 381-386, *Oct. 1903*

PRICE, THEODORA: *Artist*
Seals of Our Nation, States, and Territories. Paintings by Carlotta Gonzales Lahey, Irvin E. Alleman, Theodora Price. 17-32, *July 1946*

PRICE, WILLARD:
Author-Photographer
Japan Faces Russia in Manchuria. 603-634, *Nov. 1942*
Unknown Japan: A Portrait of the People Who Make Up One of the Two Most Fanatical Nations in the World. 225-252, *Aug. 1942*
Hidden Key to the Pacific: Piercing the Web of Secrecy Which Long Has Veiled Japanese Bases in the Mandated Islands. 759-785, *June 1942*
Grand Canal Panorama (China). 487-514, *Apr. 1937*
Mysterious Micronesia: Yap, Map, and Other Islands Under Japanese Mandate are Museums of Primitive Man. 481-510, *Apr. 1936*
Author
Henry Hudson's River. Photos by Wayne Miller. 364-403, *Mar. 1962*
The Lower Mississippi. Photos by W. D. Vaughn. 681-725, *Nov. 1960*
The Upper Mississippi. 651-699, *Nov. 1958*
The Thames Mirrors England's Varied Life. Photos by Robert F. Sisson. 45-93, *July 1958*
Cruising Japan's Inland Sea. 619-650, *Nov. 1953*
Behind the Mask of Modern Japan. 513-535, *Nov. 1945*
Jap Rule in the Hermit Nation (Korea). 429-451, *Aug. 1945*
Springboards to Tokyo. 385-407, *Oct. 1944*
Americans on the Barbary Coast (Africa). 1-31, *July 1943*
By Felucca Down the Nile: Giant Dams Rule Egypt's Lifeline River, Yet

Village Life Goes On As It Did in the Time of the Pharaohs. 435-476, *Apr. 1940*

PRICE of Free World Victory (Title of Address Delivered by the Honorable Henry A. Wallace at a Dinner of the Free World Association, May 8, 1942). 276-280, *Aug. 1942*

The **PRICE** of Liberty, Equality, Fraternity. 377, *Nov. 1918*

PRICELESS Relics of the Spanish Armada. By Robert Sténuit. Photos by Bates Littlehales. 745-777, *June 1969*

PRIDE of Two Nations: Waterton-Glacier International Peace Park. By David S. Boyer. Photos by Lowell Georgia. 796-823, *June 1987*

PRIENE, Turkey:
Some Ruined Cities of Asia Minor. By Ernest L. Harris. 833-858, *Dec. 1908*

PRIEST, CECIL D.: *Author*
Timbuktu, in the Sands of the Sahara. 73-85, *Jan. 1924*

PRIMATES:
◗ Search for the Great Apes. cover, *Jan. 1976*
◗ Monkeys, Apes, and Man. 585A-585B, *Oct. 1971*
See also Baboons; Chimpanzees; Gibbons; Gorillas; Hominids; Lemurs; Man, Prehistoric; Monkeys; Orangutans; Tarsiers

A **PRIMITIVE** Gyroscope in Liberia. By G. N. Collins. 531-535, *June 1910*

PRIMITIVE SOCIETIES:
Man in the Amazon: Stone Age Present Meets Stone Age Past. By W. Jesco von Puttkamer. NGS research grant. Contents: Wasúsu Indians. 60-83, *Jan. 1979*
Yanomamo, the True People. By Napoleon A. Chagnon. 211-223, *Aug. 1976*
The Last Andaman Islanders. By Raghubir Singh. Contents: Negritos. 66-91, *July 1975*
Brazil's Kreen-Akarores: Requiem for a Tribe? By W. Jesco von Puttkamer. 254-269, *Feb. 1975*
◗ Bushmen of the Kalahari. 578A-578B, Apr. 1973; 732A-732B, *May 1974*
■■ *Primitive Worlds: People Lost in Time.* Contents: Mbotgates, Sombas, Tarahumara Indians, Tifalmins, Turkanas, and Yanomamo. 211 pages. *1973*
Amazon–The River Sea. By Loren McIntyre. 456-495, *Oct. 1972*
◗ The Last Tribes of Mindanao. 882A-882B, Dec. 1971; 227, *Aug. 1972*
Taboos and Magic Rule Namba Lives. By Kal Muller. 57-83, *Jan. 1972*
Brazil Protects Her Cinta Larga Indians. By W. Jesco von Puttkamer. 420-444, *Sept. 1971*
Journey Into Stone Age New Guinea. By Malcolm S. Kirk. 568-592, *Apr. 1969*
Foxes Foretell the Future in Mali's Dogon Country. By Pamela Johnson Meyer. 431-448, *Mar. 1969*

Reformation leaders modified the teachings of Martin Luther, who challenged the Roman Catholic Church with tenets of Protestantism.   PAINTING BY ALLEN CARROLL, NGS

Robert Laxalt. Photos by David Hiser. 332-353, *Sept. 1973*
See also Gold; Gold Mining; *and* Death Valley National Monument

PROSPEROUS Idaho (An Interview with Governor Gooding, of Idaho, Published in the New York *Sun,* December, 1905). 16-22, *Jan. 1906*

PROSPEROUS Porto Rico. 712, *Dec. 1906*

PROTECTING Our Forests from Fire. By James Wilson. 98-106, *Jan. 1911*

PROTECTING the United States from Plant Pests. By Charles Lester Marlatt. 205-218, *Aug. 1921*

PROTESTANTISM:
The World of Martin Luther. By Merle Severy. Photos by James L. Amos. 418-463, *Oct. 1983*
The British Way. By Sir Evelyn Wrench. Included: James I and the Translation of the Bible; The Pilgrim Fathers; Oliver Cromwell; John Wesley. 421-541, *Apr. 1949*
See also Amish; Hutterites; Mennonites; Moravians; Mormons; Puritans; Shakers

The **PROUD** Armenians. By Robert Paul Jordan. Photos by Harry N. Naltchayan. 846-873, *June 1978*

PROUD Primitives, the Nuba People. By Oskar Luz. Photos by Horst Luz. 673-699, *Nov. 1966*

PROVENCE (Region), France:
Provence, Empire of the Sun. By William Davenport. Photos by James A. Sugar. 692-715, *May 1975*
Sheep Trek in the French Alps. By Maurice Moyal. Photos by Marcel Coen. 545-564, *Apr. 1952*
Camargue, the Cowboy Country of Southern France. By André Vialles. 1-34, *July 1922*

PROVIDENCE, Rhode Island:
New England's "Lively Experiment," Rhode Island. By Robert de Roos. Photos by Fred Ward. 370-401, *Sept. 1968*
Rhode Island, Modern City-State. By George W. Long. Photos by Willard R. Culver. 137-170, *Aug. 1948*

PROVINCETOWN, Massachusetts:
Cape Cod's Circle of Seasons. By Tom Melham. Photos by James P. Blair. 40-65, *July 1975*
Cape Cod, Where Sea Holds Sway Over Man and Land. By Nathaniel T. Kenney. Photos by Dean Conger. 149-187, *Aug. 1962*
Cape Cod People and Places. By Wanda Burnett. 737-774, *June 1946*

PRUDHOE BAY AREA, Alaska:
Oil in the Wilderness: An Arctic Dilemma. By Douglas Lee. Photos by James P. Blair. 858-871, *Dec. 1988*
Will Oil and Tundra Mix? Alaska's North Slope Hangs in the Balance.

By William S. Ellis. Photos by Emory Kristof. 485-517, *Oct. 1971*

PRUSSIA:
Flying Around the Baltic. By Douglas Chandler. 767-806, *June 1938*

PRUSSIANISM. By Robert Lansing. 546-557, *June 1918*

PRYOR, PAUL: *Photographer*
Exploring the World of Gems. By W. F. Foshag. 779-810, *Dec. 1950*

PRYOR, SAMUEL F.: *Author*
The World in Dolls. Photos by Kathleen Revis. 817-831, *Dec. 1959*

PRYOR MOUNTAIN WILD HORSE RANGE, Montana-Wyoming:
On the Track of the West's Wild Horses. By Hope Ryden. Photos by author and Dick Durrance II. 94-109, *Jan. 1971*

PSIHOYOS, LOUIE:
On Assignment in Pennsylvania. *July 1984*
On Assignment in Manila, Philippines. *Apr. 1983*
Photographer
What Is This Thing Called Sleep? By Michael E. Long. 787-821, *Dec. 1987*
The Intimate Sense of Smell. By Boyd Gibbons. Included: Smell Survey. 324-361, *Sept. 1986*
The Underground Railroad. By Charles L. Blockson. 3-39, *July 1984*
The Fascinating World of Trash. By Peter T. White. 424-457, *Apr. 1983*
Powder River Basin: New Energy Frontier. By Bill Richards. 96-113, *Special Report on Energy. (Feb. 1981)*

PTARMIGANS:
Birds of Timberline and Tundra. By Arthur A. Allen. Photos by author. 313-339, *Sept. 1946*
Game Birds of Prairie, Forest, and Tundra. By Alexander Wetmore. Paintings by Allan Brooks. 461-500, *Oct. 1936*
The White Sheep, Giant Moose, and Smaller Game of the Kenai Peninsula, Alaska. By George Shiras, 3d. 423-494, *May 1912*

PTERODACTYL FLIGHT:
Model Airplanes: To Dream, to Build ...And Then to Fly. By Michael E. Long. Photos by Peter Essick. Included: New wings for an old reptile. 132-144, *July 1986*

PUBERTY RITES:
The Threatened Ways of Kenya's Pokot People. By Elizabeth L. Meyerhoff. Photos by Murray Roberts. 120-140, *Jan. 1982*
Arnhem Land Aboriginals Cling to Dreamtime. By Clive Scollay. Photos by Penny Tweedie. 644-663, *Nov. 1980*
Coming of Age the Apache Way. By Nita Quintero. Photos by Bill Hess. 262-271, *Feb. 1980*
Tukuna Maidens Come of Age. By Harald Schultz. 629-649, *Nov. 1959*

PUBLIC HEALTH SERVICE, U. S.
See U. S. Public Health Service

Puget Sound area fishermen wait off Lummi Island for migrating salmon to swim into their nets. DAVID ALAN HARVEY

Its catch a beakful, a puffin fishes successfully off the Shetland Islands in the North Sea. DICK DURRANCE II

O
P

In the Belgian Congo, now Zaire, a Pygmy woman of the 1950s bears bunches of plantains with a tumpline. MICHEL HUET

Urueu-Wau-Wau have been studied for years by Jesco von Puttkamer, legendary chronicler of Brazilian Indians. LOREN MCINTYRE

Q
R

QIVIUT
QUARKS
QUASARS
QUECHUAS
QUEEN CHARLOTTE ISLANDS
QUEEN'S DOLLS' HOUSE
QUETZALS
QUIRIGUÁ
RA II
RADIATION
RADIOCARBON DATING
RAILROADS
RAIN FORESTS
RAJASTHAN
RAMAYANA
RAMSES II
RANCHES
RATS
RECLAMATION
RED SEA
REDWOODS
REFUGEES
REINDEER
RENAISSANCE
REPTILES
RESEARCH VESSELS
RHINOCEROSES
RIFTS
RING OF FIRE
RÍO AZUL
RIVER TRIPS
RIVIERA
ROBOTS
ROCK ART
ROCKY MOUNTAINS
ROMAN EMPIRE
RONDÔNIA
RUWENZORI

Scenes from the life of the
Hindu deity Krishna flank a window in
the Indian state of Rajasthan.
RAGHUBIR SINGH

859

QM, the Fighting Storekeeper. By Frederick Simpich. Paintings by Arthur Beaumont. 561-600, *Nov. 1942*

QATAR:
The Persian Gulf–Living in Harm's Way. By Thomas J. Abercrombie. Photos by Steve Raymer. 648-671, *May 1988*

QATIF, Saudi Arabia:
In Search of Arabia's Past. By Peter Bruce Cornwall. 493-522, *Apr. 1948*

QEQERTAT, Greenland:
Narwhal Hunters of Greenland. By Ivars Silis. 520-539, *Apr. 1984*

QILAKITSOQ (Abandoned Settlement), Greenland:
The Mummies of Qilakitsoq. By Jens P. Hart Hansen, Jørgen Meldgaard, and Jørgen Nordqvist. 191-207, *Feb. 1985*

QIN SHI HUANGDI, Emperor (China). *See* former spelling, Ch'in Shih Huang Ti

QINGHAI PROVINCE, China:
Nomads of China's West. By Galen Rowell. Photos by the author and Harold A. Knutson. 244-263, *Feb. 1982*
Seeking the Mountains of Mystery: An Expedition on the China-Tibet Frontier to the Unexplored Amnyi Machen Range, One of Whose Peaks Rivals Everest. By Joseph F. Rock. 131-185, *Feb. 1930*

See also former designation, Tsinghai Province

QIVIUT (Wool):
Domesticating the Wild and Woolly Musk Ox. By John J. Teal, Jr. Photos by Robert W. Madden. 862-879, *June 1970*

QOMOLANGMA NATURE PRESERVE, Tibet, China:
Editorial. By Wilbur E. Garrett. 551, *Nov. 1987*

QOMUL:
The Caves of the Thousand Buddhas. By Franc and Jean Shor. 383-415, *Mar. 1951*

QOYLLUR RITI (Star of the Snow), Peru:
Peru's Pilgrimage to the Sky. By Robert Randall. Photos by Loren McIntyre and Ira Block. 60-69, *July 1982*

QUAILS:
Game Birds of Prairie, Forest, and Tundra. By Alexander Wetmore. Paintings by Allan Brooks. 461-500, *Oct. 1936*

QUARKS:
Worlds Within the Atom. By John Boslough. Photos by Kevin Fleming. Illustrations text by David Jeffery. Paintings by Barron Storey. 634-663, *May 1985*

QUARRYING:
Carrara Marble: Touchstone of Eternity. By Cathy Newman. Photos by Pierre Boulat. 42-59, *July 1982*

QUASARS:
The Once and Future Universe. By Rick Gore. Photos by James A. Sugar. Paintings by Barron Storey. Picture text by David Jeffery. 704-749, *June 1983*

QUEBEC (City), Quebec, Canada:
The St. Lawrence River: Canada's Highway to the Sea. By William S. Ellis. Photos by Bruce Dale. 586-623, *May 1980*
Quebec: French City in an Anglo-Saxon World. By Kenneth MacLeish. Photos by James L. Stanfield and Declan Haun. 416-442, *Mar. 1971*
The St. Lawrence, River Key to Canada. By Howard La Fay. Photos by John Launois. 622-667, *May 1967*
Winter Brings Carnival Time to Quebec. By Kathleen Revis. 69-97, *Jan. 1958*
Old France in Modern Canada. By V. C. Scott O'Connor. 167-200, *Feb. 1935*
Quebec, Capital of French Canada. By William Dow Boutwell. 515-522, *Apr. 1930*

QUEBEC (Province), Canada:
Henry Hudson's Changing Bay. By Bill Richards. Photos by David Hiser. 380-405, *Mar. 1982*

On Quebec's Rue St. Louis a 1675 building restored by its owner reflects the pride of Canada's oldest city.   DECLAN HAUN

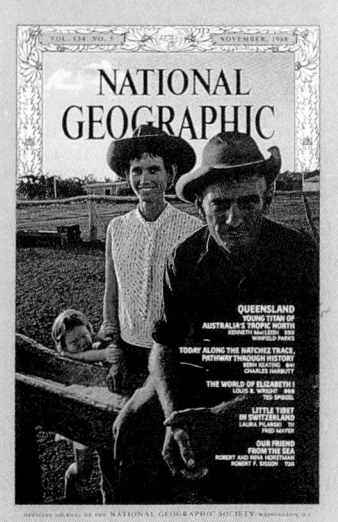

Quebec's Northern Dynamo. By Larry Kohl. Photos by Ottmar Bierwagen. Contents: La Grande Complex, a hydroelectric project. 406-418, *Mar. 1982*

The St. Lawrence River: Canada's Highway to the Sea. By William S. Ellis. Photos by Bruce Dale. 586-623, *May 1980*

⊕ *Close-up, Canada: Quebec, Newfoundland.* Text on reverse, inset Southern Quebec. *May 1980*

Editorial. By Gilbert M. Grosvenor. 435, *Apr. 1977*

One Canada–or Two? By Peter T. White. Photos by Winfield Parks. 436-465, *Apr. 1977*

North Through History Aboard *White Mist.* By Melville Bell Grosvenor. Photos by Edwin Stuart Grosvenor. 1-55, *July 1970*

The St. Lawrence, River Key to Canada. By Howard La Fay. Photos by John Launois. 622-667, *May 1967*

Canada, My Country. By Alan Phillips. Photos by David S. Boyer and Walter Meayers Edwards. 769-819, *Dec. 1961*

Solving the Riddle of Chubb Crater. By V. Ben Meen. Photos by Richard H. Stewart. NGS research grant. 1-32, *Jan. 1952*

Sea to Lakes on the St. Lawrence. By George W. Long. Photos by B. Anthony Stewart and John E. Fletcher. 323-366, *Sept. 1950*

Quebec's Forests, Farms, and Frontiers. By Andrew H. Brown. 431-470, *Oct. 1949*

Sea Bird Cities Off Audubon's Labrador. By Arthur A. Allen. NGS research grant. 755-774, *June 1948*

Servicing Arctic Airbases. By Robert A. Bartlett. 602-616, *May 1946*

Anticosti Island, Nugget of the North. By Eugene E. Wilson. 121-140, *Jan. 1942*

Gentle Folk Settle Stern Saguenay: On French Canada's Frontier Homespun

Colonists Keep the Customs of Old Norman Settlers. By Harrison Howell Walker. 595-632, *May 1939*

Gaspé Peninsula Wonderland. By Wilfrid Bovey. 209-230, *Aug. 1935*

Old France in Modern Canada. By V. C. Scott O'Connor. Contents: St. Lawrence and Saguenay Regions. 167-200, *Feb. 1935*

Quebec, Capital of French Canada. By William Dow Boutwell. 515-522, *Apr. 1930*

See also James Bay; Montreal; Quebec (City); St. Lawrence Seaway

QUECHUAS:

Ambassadors of Good Will: The Peace Corps. 297-345. By Sargent Shriver and Peace Corps Volunteers. Included: Bolivia. By Edward S. Dennison. 315-319, *Sept. 1964*

Peru, Homeland of the Warlike Inca. By Kip Ross. 421-462, *Oct. 1950*

Over Trail and Through Jungle in Ecuador: Indian Head-Hunters of the Interior, an Interesting Study in the South American Republic. By H. E. Anthony. 327-352, *Oct. 1921*

Cuzco, America's Ancient Mecca. By Harriet Chalmers Adams. 669-689, *Oct. 1908*

Along the Old Inca Highway. By Harriet Chalmers Adams. 231-250, *Apr. 1908*

QUEEN CHARLOTTE ISLANDS, British Columbia, Canada:

Editorial. By Wilbur E. Garrett. 421, *Oct. 1987*

Canada's Queen Charlotte Islands, Homeland of the Haida. By Moira Johnston. Photos by Dewitt Jones. 102-127, *July 1987*

Canada's Window on the Pacific: The British Columbia Coast. By Jules B. Billard. Photos by Ted Spiegel. 338-375, *Mar. 1972*

QUEEN ELIZABETH ISLANDS, Northwest Territories, Canada:

Weather from the White North. By Andrew H. Brown. Photos by John E. Fletcher. 543-572, *Apr. 1955*

QUEEN ELIZABETH Opens Parliament. By W. E. Roscher. Photos by Robert B. Goodman. 699-707, *Nov. 1961*

QUEEN ELIZABETH'S Favorite Sea Dog: Sir Francis Drake. By Alan Villiers. Photos by Gordon W. Gahan. 216-253, *Feb. 1975*

QUEEN of Canada. By Phyllis Wilson. Photos by Kathleen Revis. 825-829, *June 1959*

The **QUEEN** of Textiles: Silk. By Nina Hyde. Photos by Cary Wolinsky. 2-49, *Jan. 1984*

QUEEN'S DOLLS' HOUSE, Windsor Castle, England:

Royal House for Dolls. By David Jeffery. Photos by James L. Stanfield. 632-643, *Nov. 1980*

QUEENSLAND (State), Australia:

Queensland, Broad Shoulder of Australia. By William S. Ellis. Photos by David Robert Austen. Included: Queensland Fossils Expand Australia's Prehistoric Menagerie. 2-39, *Jan. 1986*

Queensland: Young Titan of Australia's Tropic North. By Kenneth MacLeish. Photos by Winfield Parks. 593-639, *Nov. 1968*

See also Great Barrier Reef

QUEENY, EDGAR MONSANTO:
Author

Spearing Lions with Africa's Masai. 487-517, *Oct. 1954*

The only children their age at Lawn Hill, an isolated cattle station in Queensland, Australia, Richard Kim, left, and Kristian Arthur enjoy a frolic. DAVID ROBERT AUSTEN

A world away from the capital of Quito, a Cayapa Indian baby gently bound with fiber sleeps on a hammock in the rain forest of northwestern Ecuador.   LOREN MCINTYRE

RNA. *See* Ribonucleic Acid

RPVS. *See* Remotely Piloted Vehicles

RA II (Papyrus Ship):

The Voyage of *Ra II*. By Thor Heyerdahl. Photos by Carlo Mauri and Georges Sourial. 44-71, *Jan. 1971*

RABAT, Morocco:

Eastward from Gibraltar: Overland Route Across North Africa to Tunisia and Libia. By Cyrus French Wicker. 115-142, *Jan. 1943*

RABBITS:

Smaller Mammals of North America. By E. W. Nelson. Paintings by Louis Agassiz Fuertes. 371-493, *May 1918*

Lonely Australia: The Unique Continent. By Herbert E. Gregory. 473-568, *Dec. 1916*

Wild Animals That Took Their Own Pictures by Day and by Night. By George Shiras, 3d. 763-834, *July 1913*

RABOT, CHARLES: *Author*

French Conquest of the Sahara. 76-80, *Feb. 1905*

A Notable Norwegian Publication. 370-371, *Sept. 1904*

Recent French Explorations in Africa. 119-132, *Apr. 1902*

RACCOONS:

Raccoon: Amiable Rogue in a Black Mask. By Melvin R. Ellis. 841-854, *Dec. 1956*

A Flashlight Story of an Albino Porcupine and of a Cunning but Unfortunate Coon. By George Shiras, 3d. 572-596, *June 1911*

The **RACE** for the South Pole (Presentation of Hubbard Medal to Shackleton). 185-186, *Mar. 1910*

RACE Prejudice in the Far East. By Melville E. Stone. 973-985, *Dec. 1910*

RACEHORSES:

Heart of the Bluegrass. By Charles McCarry. Photos by J. Bruce Baumann. 634-659, *May 1974*

RACES. *See* Automobile Race; Balloon Races; Boat Races; Bull Derby; Horse Races; Iditarod Trail Sled Dog Race; Land Yachts; Motorcycle Races; Olympic Games; Tall-Ships Race

RACES, Human. *See* Ethnology

The **RACES** and Religions of Macedonia. By Luigi Villari. 1118-1132, *Nov. 1912*

The **RACES** of Domestic Fowl. By M. A. Jull. Paintings by Hashime Murayama. 379-452, *Apr. 1927*

The **RACES** of Europe: The Graphic Epitome of a Never-ceasing Human Drama. The Aspirations, Failures, Achievements, and Conflicts of the Polyglot People of the Most Densely Populated Continent. By Edwin A. Grosvenor. 441-534, *Dec. 1918*

RADAR:

Our Air Age Speeds Ahead. By F. Barrows Colton. 249-272, *Feb. 1948*

Miracle Men of the Telephone. By F. Barrows Colton. 273-316. Included: Birthplace of Telephone Magic. Photos by Willard R. Culver. 289-312, *Mar. 1947*

New Frontier in the Sky. By F. Barrows Colton. 379-408, *Sept. 1946*

Air Power for Peace. By H. H. Arnold. 137-193, *Feb. 1946*

Your New World of Tomorrow. By F. Barrows Colton. 385-410, *Oct. 1945*

See also DEW Line; Remote Sensing

RADFORD, ARTHUR W.: *Author*

Our Navy in the Far East. Photos by J. Baylor Roberts. 537-577, *Oct. 1953*

RADIATION, Electromagnetic:

Eyes of Science. By Rick Gore. Photos by James P. Blair. 360-389, *Mar. 1978*

The Incredible Universe. By Kenneth F. Weaver. Photos by James P. Blair. 584-625, *May 1974*

Remote Sensing: New Eyes to See the World. By Kenneth F. Weaver. Included: Cosmic Rays, Gamma Rays, Infrared Radiation, Microwaves, Radar and Sonar, Ultraviolet Rays. 46-73, *Jan. 1969*

See also Cosmic Rays; Lasers; Radar; Radio; Solar Energy

RADIATION CONTAMINATION:

Chernobyl–One Year After. By Mike Edwards. Photos by Steve Raymer. Paintings by Pierre Mion. 632-653, *May 1987*

Air: An Atmosphere of Uncertainty. By Noel Grove. Photos by Ted Spiegel. Paintings by William H. Bond. 502-537, *Apr. 1987*

Bikini–A Way of Life Lost. By William S. Ellis. Photos by James P. Blair. 813-834, *June 1986*

The Promise and Peril of Nuclear Energy. By Kenneth F. Weaver. Photos by Emory Kristof. 459-493, *Apr. 1979*

See also Nuclear Weapons Testing

RADIO:

New Miracles of the Telephone Age. By Robert Leslie Conly. 87-120, *July 1954*

Uncle Sam's House of 1,000 Wonders. By Lyman J. Briggs and F. Barrows Colton. Contents: National Bureau of Standards. 755-784, *Dec. 1951*

Our Air Age Speeds Ahead. By F. Barrows Colton. 249-272, *Feb. 1948*

Unlocking Secrets of the Northern Lights. By Carl W. Gartlein. Paintings by William Crowder. Included: The effect of magnetic storms on radio transmission. NGS research grant. 673-704, *Nov. 1947*

Miracle Men of the Telephone. By F. Barrows Colton. Included: Birthplace of Telephone Magic. Photos by Willard R. Culver. 273-316, *Mar. 1947*

New Frontier in the Sky. By F. Barrows Colton. 379-408, *Sept. 1946*

Air Power for Peace. By H. H. Arnold. 137-193, *Feb. 1946*

Your New World of Tomorrow. By F. Barrows Colton. 385-410, *Oct. 1945*

Winged Words–New Weapon of War. By F. Barrows Colton. 663-692, *Nov. 1942*

The Miracle of Talking by Telephone. By F. Barrows Colton. 395-433, *Oct. 1937*

New Safeguards for Ships in Fog and Storm. By George R. Putnam. 169-200, *Aug. 1936*

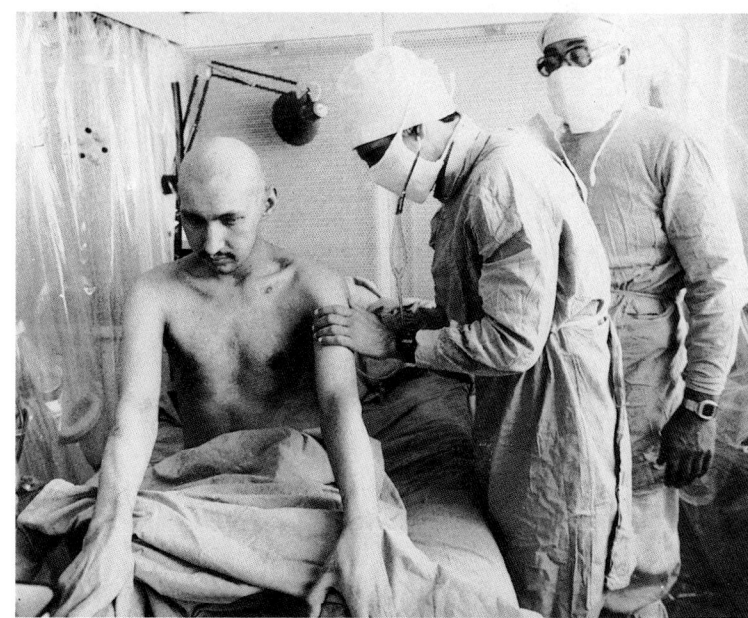

Doctors examine a patient contaminated by radiation while fighting the fire following the Soviet nuclear power plant explosion in Chernobyl. VLADIMIR VYATKIN, NOVOSTI PRESS AGENCY

Streaking through Kowloon in Hong Kong, a diesel train featuring duty-free shopping makes four round-trips daily to Guangzhou (Canton), China. BRUCE DALE, NGS

RAFFLESIA (Flower):

Saving the World's Largest Flower. By Willem Meijer. Photos by Edward S. Ross. NGS research grant. 136-140, *July 1985*

Malaysia's Giant Flowers and Insect-trapping Plants. By Paul A. Zahl. 680-701, *May 1964*

RAFT Life on the Hwang Ho. By W. Robert Moore. 743-752, *June 1932*

RAFT TRIPS:

A Walk and Ride on the Wild Side: Tasmania. By Carolyn Bennett Patterson. Photos by David Hiser and Melinda Berge. 676-693, *May 1983*

Chattooga River Country: Wild Water, Proud People. By Don Belt. Photos by Steve Wall. 458-477, *Apr. 1983*

Rafting Down the Yukon. By Keith Tryck. Photos by Robert Clark. 830-861, *Dec. 1975*

White-water Adventure on Wild Rivers of Idaho. By Frank Craighead, Jr., and John Craighead. 213-239, *Feb. 1970*

Retracing John Wesley Powell's Historic Voyage Down the Grand Canyon. By Joseph Judge. Photos by Walter Meayers Edwards. 668-713, *May 1969*

Down Mark Twain's River on a Raft. By Rex E. Hieronymus. 551-574, *Apr. 1948*

RAI, RAGHU: *Photographer*

India: Life on the Edge. By Paul R. and Anne H. Ehrlich. 930-933, *Dec. 1988*

RAILROAD WORM:

Nature's Toy Train, the Railroad Worm. By Darwin L. Tiemann. Photos by Robert F. Sisson. NGS research grant. 56-67, *July 1970*

RAILROADS:

China Passage by Rail. By Paul Theroux. Photos by Bruce Dale. 296-329, *Mar. 1988*

The Tea and Sugar Lifeline in Australia's Outback. By Erla Zwingle. Photos by William Albert Allard. 737-757, *June 1986*

By Rail Across the Indian Subcontinent. By Paul Theroux. Photos by Steve McCurry. 696-743, *June 1984*

India's Railway Lifeline. By Michael G. Satow. 744-749, *June 1984*

■ Love Those Trains. cover, *Feb. 1984*

■■ *Railroads: The Great American Adventure.* By Charlton Ogburn. Photos by James A. Sugar. 203 pages. *1977*

Slow Train Through Viet Nam's War. By Howard Sochurek. 412-444, *Sept. 1964*

Winning the War of Supply. By F. Barrows Colton. 705-736, *Dec. 1945*

Trains of Today–and Tomorrow. By J. R. Hildebrand. 535-589, *Nov. 1936*

Manchuria, Promised Land of Asia: Invaded by Railways and Millions of Settlers, This Vast Region Now Recalls Early Boom Days in the American West. By Frederick Simpich. 379-428, *Oct. 1929*

A Maryland Pilgrimage: Visits to Hallowed Shrines Recall the Major Rôle Played by This Prosperous State in the Development of Popular Government in America. By Gilbert Grosvenor. 133-212, *Feb. 1927*

America's Amazing Railway Traffic. By William Joseph Showalter. 353-404, *Apr. 1923*

Alaska's New Railway. 567-589, *Dec. 1915*

The First Transandine Railroad from Buenos Aires to Valparaiso. By Harriet Chalmers Adams. 397-417, *May 1910*

Railway Routes in Alaska. By Alfred H. Brooks. 165-190, *Mar. 1907*

The Commercial Valuation of Railway Operating Property in the United States. 438-439, *Sept. 1905*

A chef caters to tastes on a luxury train in India's railroad system, which carries ten million passengers a day. STEVE McCURRY

Pan-American Railway. 232-233, *May 1904*

Shortening Time Across the Continent. By Henry Herbert McClure. 319-321, *Aug. 1902*

Cuban Railways. By Albert G. Robinson. 108-110, *Mar. 1902*

Railways, Rivers, and Strategic Towns in Manchuria. By G. H. Grosvenor. 326-327, *Aug. 1900*

Russian Railways. 243, *June 1900*

Railway Construction and Improvements. 163, *Apr. 1900*

Railroads and Canals. 420, *Oct. 1899*

Statistics of Railways in the United States. By Henry Gannett. 406-407, *Dec. 1896*

Across the Gulf by Rail to Key West. By Jefferson B. Browne. 203-207, *June 1896*

The Tehuantepec Ship Railway. By Elmer L. Corthell. Included: National Railroad of Tehuantepec. 64-72, *Feb. 1896*

South America. Annual Address by the President, Gardiner G. Hubbard. 1-29, *Mar. 28, 1891*

See also California Western Railroad; Damascus and Mecca Railway; Trans-Siberian Railway; *and* Trains

RAILS (Birds):

Finding an "Extinct" New Zealand Bird. By R. V. Francis Smith. Contents: Takahe. 393-401, *Mar. 1952*

The Shore Birds, Cranes, and Rails: Willets, Plovers, Stilts, Phalaropes, Sandpipers, and Their Relatives Deserve Protection. By Arthur A. Allen. Paintings by Allan Brooks. 183-222, *Aug. 1937*

RAILS-TO-TRAILS CONSERVANCY:

President's Page. By Gilbert M. Grosvenor. *May 1988*

RAILWAY Construction and Improvements. 163, *Apr. 1900*

RAILWAY Routes in Alaska. By Alfred H. Brooks. 165-190, *Mar. 1907*

RAILWAYS. *See* Electric Street Railways; Railroads; Ship Railways

RAILWAYS, Rivers, and Strategic Towns in Manchuria. By G. H. Grosvenor. 326-327, *Aug. 1900*

RAIN FORESTS:

Rondônia: Brazil's Imperiled Rain Forest. By William S. Ellis. Photos by William Albert Allard and Loren McIntyre. 772-779, *Dec. 1988*

Canada's Queen Charlotte Islands, Homeland of the Haida. By Moira Johnston. Photos by Dewitt Jones. 102-127, *July 1987*

Monkey in Peril: Rescuing Brazil's Muriqui. By Russell A. Mittermeier. Photos by Andrew L. Young. 387-395, *Mar. 1987*

Madagascar: A World Apart. By Alison Jolly. Photos by Frans Lanting. 148-183, *Feb. 1987*

The Usumacinta River: Troubles on a Wild Frontier. By S. Jeffrey K. Wilkerson. Photos by David Hiser. 514-543, *Oct. 1985*

A small tsunami in 1981 echoes the 1883 Krakatau waves that devastated Java's Ujung Kulon Peninsula rain forest. DIETER AND MARY PLAGE

Discovering Alaska's Oldest Arctic Town: A Scientist Finds Ivory-eyed Skeletons of a Mysterious People and Joins Modern Eskimos in the Dangerous Spring Whale Hunt. 319-336, *Sept. 1942*

RAINFALL:

Salton Sea and the Rainfall of the Southwest. By Alfred J. Henry. 244-248, *Apr. 1907*

Rainfall and the Level of Lake Erie. By E. L. Moseley. 327-328, *Aug. 1903*

The Economic Aspects of Soil Erosion (Part II). By N. S. Shaler. 368-377, *Nov. 1896*

The Economic Aspects of Soil Erosion (Part I). By N. S. Shaler. 328-338, *Oct. 1896*

Relations of Air and Water to Temperature and Life. By Gardiner G. Hubbard. 112-124, *Jan. 31, 1894*

Rainfall Types of the United States. Annual Report by A. W. Greely. 45-58, *Apr. 29, 1893*

Report–Geography of the Air. By A. W. Greely. 49-63, *Apr. 1890*

See also Acid Rain; Floods; Meteorology; Rainmaking; Storms

RAINIER, Mount, Washington:

Mount Rainier: Testing Ground for Everest. By Barry C. Bishop. NGS research grant. 688-711, *May 1963*

Climbing Our Northwest Glaciers. Photos by Bob and Ira Spring. 103-114, *July 1953*

The Great White Monarch of the Pacific Northwest. By A. H. Barnes. 593-626, *June 1912*

Our National Parks. By L. F. Schmeckebier. 531-579, *June 1912*

A Wonderland of Glaciers and Snow. By Milnor Roberts. 530-537, *June 1909*

The Height of Mt. Rainier. By Richard U. Goode. 97-98, *Mar. 1898*

RAINMAKING:

Weather Making, Ancient and Modern. By Mark W. Harrington. Included: Bibliography on artificial production of rain. 35-62, *Apr. 25, 1894*

RAJASTHAN (State), India:

The Pageant of Rajasthan. By Raghubir Singh. 219-243, *Feb. 1977*

See also Jaipur; Jaisalmer; Jodhpur; *and* former name, Rajputana

RAJPUTANA (Region), India:

Feudal Splendor Lingers in Rajputana. By Volkmar Wentzel. 411-458, *Oct. 1948*

The Marble Dams of Rajputana. By Eleanor Maddock. 469-499, *Nov. 1921*

See also present name, Rajasthan

RAJ SAMAND (Lake), India:

The Marble Dams of Rajputana. By Eleanor Maddock. 469-499, *Nov. 1921*

RALEIGH, SIR WALTER:

Founders of Virginia. By Sir Evelyn Wrench. Photos by B. Anthony Stewart. 433-462, *Apr. 1948*

Boyhood of Sir Walter Raleigh. Painting by Sir John Millais, Tate Gallery, London. Supplement, *May 1926*

RALEIGH Rock. 148, *Apr. 1903*

RALIK CHAIN, Marshall Islands. *See* Bikini

RAMA IX, King (Thailand). *See* Bhumibol Adulyadej

RAMAYANA (Epic):

Pageantry of the Siamese Stage. By D. Sonakul. Photos by W. Robert Moore. 201-212, *Feb. 1947*

RAMBLES Through the Prairie State. Photos by Clifton Adams. 545-552, *May 1931*

RAMBLES Through Ulster, Northern Tip of the Shamrock Isle. Photos by Bernard F. Rogers, Jr. 577-600, *Nov. 1935*

RAMBLING Around the Roof of Eastern America. By Leonard C. Roy. Contents: Great Smoky Mountains. 243-266, *Aug. 1936*

RAMESSES II (Pharaoh). *See* Ramses II

RAMSAY, SIR WILLIAM:

The British Way. By Sir Evelyn Wrench. 421-541, *Apr. 1949*

Author

A Sketch of the Geographical History of Asia Minor. 553-570, *Nov. 1922*

Modern Transmutation of the Elements. 201-203, *Apr. 1906*

RAMSES II (Pharaoh):

Lost Outpost of the Egyptian Empire. By Trude Dothan. Photos by Sisse

---

Brimberg. Paintings by Lloyd K. Townsend. NGS research grant. 739-769, *Dec. 1982*

In Search of Moses. By Harvey Arden. Photos by Nathan Benn. 2-37, *Jan. 1976*

Abu Simbel's Ancient Temples Reborn. By Georg Gerster. 724-744, *May 1969*

Saving the Ancient Temples at Abu Simbel. By Georg Gerster. Paintings by Robert W. Nicholson. 694-742, *May 1966*

Yankee Cruises the Storied Nile. By Irving and Electa Johnson. Photos by Winfield Parks. 583-633, *May 1965*

Threatened Treasures of the Nile. By Georg Gerster. 587-621, *Oct. 1963*

RANCHES:

C. M. Russell, Cowboy Artist. By Bart McDowell. Photos by Sam Abell. 60-95, *Jan. 1986*

Orange, a Most California County. By Judith and Neil Morgan. Photos by Vince Streano. Included: The urbanization of Irvine Ranch. 750-779, *Dec. 1981*

Buffalo Bill and the Enduring West. By Alice J. Hall. Photos by James L. Amos. Included: M Bar Ranch, Wyoming; Scout's Rest Ranch, Nebraska; TE Ranch, Wyoming. 76-103, *July 1981*

Texas! By Howard La Fay. Photos by Gordon W. Gahan. Included: O-6 Ranch. 440-483, *Apr. 1980*

The Tallgrass Prairie: Can It Be Saved? By Dennis Farney. Photos by Jim

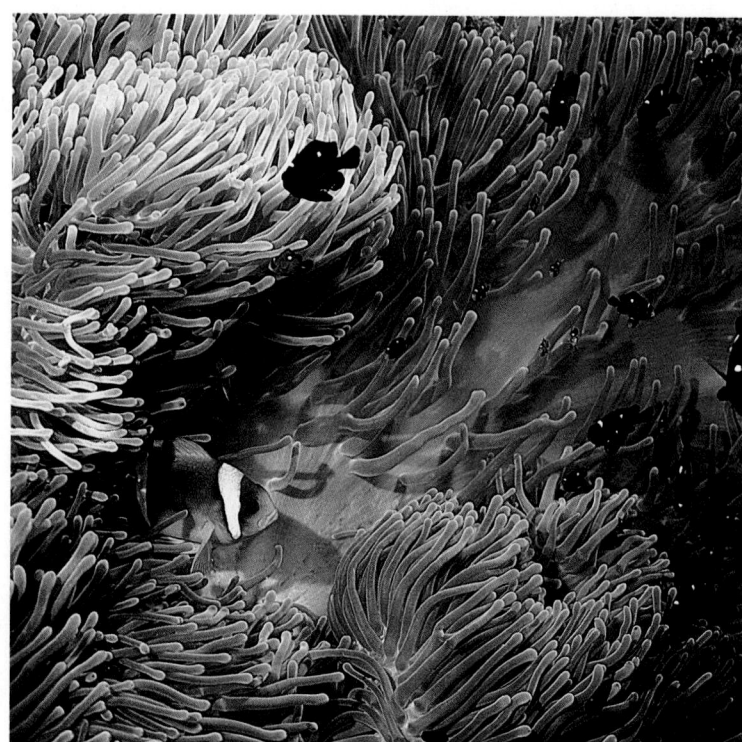

The usually lethal tentacles of sea anemones shelter spotted damselfish and striped clown fish in the rainbow-hued world of the Red Sea. DAVID DOUBILET

Gerald Mack wrangles horses on a Montana ranch, as cowboy artist C. M. Russell did in 1882. SAM ABELL

A century of hunting and habitat destruction has shrunk the tiger population. India protects 3,000 on reserves such as Ranthambhor National Park. BELINDA WRIGHT

Palace of Darius the Great. 325-355, *Sept. 1939*

RAY, G. CARLETON: *Author*

Learning the Ways of the Walrus. Photos by Bill Curtsinger. 565-580, *Oct. 1979*
Three Whales That Flew. Photos by W. Robert Moore. 346-359, *Mar. 1962*
Author-Photographer
Stalking Seals Under Antarctic Ice. 54-65, *Jan. 1966*

RAYLEIGH, LORD (John William Strutt):

The British Way. By Sir Evelyn Wrench. 421-541, *Apr. 1949*

RAYMER, PATRICIA: *Author*

Wisconsin's Menominees: Indians on a Seesaw. Photos by Steve Raymer. 228-251, *Aug. 1974*

RAYMER, STEVE:

On Assignment in Mexico; Awards. *Feb. 1985*
Nomination Page. In San Diego, California. *Feb. 1981*
Nomination Page. In Yemen Arab Republic (North Yemen). *Aug. 1979*
Nomination Page. In Alaska. *Oct. 1976*
Photographer
Air Bridge to Siberia. By Wilbur E. Garrett. 504-509, *Oct. 1988*
The Persian Gulf–Living in Harm's Way. By Thomas J. Abercrombie. 648-671, *May 1988*
The Falkland Islands–Life After the War. By Bryan Hodgson. 390-411, *Mar. 1988*
Chernobyl–One Year After. By Mike Edwards. Paintings by Pierre Mion. 632-653, *May 1987*
Ukraine. By Mike Edwards. 595-631, *May 1987*
A Little Humanity Amid the Horrors of War. By Peter T. White. 647-679, *Nov. 1986*
Eruption in Colombia. By Bart McDowell. 640-653, *May 1986*
Afghanistan's Troubled Capital–Kabul. By Mike Edwards. 494-505, *Apr. 1985*
New Delhi: Mirror of India. By Bryan Hodgson. 506-533, *Apr. 1985*
The Poppy. By Peter T. White. 143-189, *Feb. 1985*
Kamehameha–Hawaii's Warrior King. By Louise E. Levathes. Paintings by Herb Kawainui Kane. 558-599, *Nov. 1983*
Thailand: Luck of a Land in the Middle. By Bart McDowell. 500-535, *Oct. 1982*
Mount St. Helens Aftermath: The Mountain That Was–and Will Be. By Rowe Findley. 713-733, *Dec. 1981*
Crosscurrents Sweep the Indian Ocean. By Bart McDowell. 422-457, *Oct. 1981*
Wild Cargo: the Business of Smuggling Animals. By Noel Grove. 287-315, *Mar. 1981*
The Caribbean: Sun, Sea, and Seething. By Noel Grove. 244-271, *Feb. 1981*
Bahrain: Hub of the Persian Gulf. By Thomas J. Abercrombie. 300-329, *Sept. 1979*

A 1982 monumental salute to Kiev's 1,500th birthday commemorates the 1654 reunification of Russia and Ukraine. STEVE RAYMER, NGS

North Yemen. By Noel Grove. 244-269, *Aug. 1979*
Risk and Reward on Alaska's Violent Gulf. By Boyd Gibbons. 237-267, *Feb. 1979*
Chicago! By Harvey Arden. 463-493, *Apr. 1978*
The Pipeline: Alaska's Troubled Colossus. By Bryan Hodgson. 684-717, *Nov. 1976*
Iowa's Enduring Amana Colonies. By Laura Longley Babb. 863-878, *Dec. 1975*
Can the World Feed Its People? By Thomas Y. Canby. 2-31, *July 1975*
Bangladesh: The Nightmare of Famine. 33-39, *July 1975*
Wisconsin's Menominees: Indians on a Seesaw. By Patricia Raymer. 228-251, *Aug. 1974*
In Touch With Nature. Text by Elizabeth A. Moize. 537-543, *Apr. 1974*

RAZA, Isla, Mexico:
Sea Birds of Isla Raza. By Lewis Wayne Walker. 239-248, *Feb. 1951*

REABURN, D. L.: *Author*
Plan for Climbing Mt. McKinley. By Alfred H. Brooks and D. L. Reaburn. 30-35, *Jan. 1903*

REACH for the New World. By Mendel Peterson. Photos by David L. Arnold. Paintings by Richard Schlecht. 724-767, *Dec. 1977*

REACHING for the Moon. By Allan C. Fisher, Jr. Photos by Luis Marden. 157-171, *Feb. 1959*

READER, JOHN: *Photographer*
Tanzania's Stone Age Art. By Mary D. Leakey. 84-99, *July 1983*

REAGAN, RONALD:
Dedication of new NGS building.

President's Page. By Gilbert M. Grosvenor. *Oct. 1984*

REARDEN, JIM: *Author*

Nikolaevsk: A Bit of Old Russia Takes Root in Alaska. Photos by Charles O'Rear. 401-425, *Sept. 1972*

Author-Photographer

Caribou: Hardy Nomads of the North. 858-878, *Dec. 1974*

The **REBIRTH** of Religion in Russia: The Church Reorganized While Bolshevik Cannon Spread Destruction in the Nation's Holy of Holies. By Thomas Whittemore. 379-401, *Nov. 1918*

The **RECENT** Ascent of Itambé. By J. C. Branner. 183, *May 1899*

RECENT Bequests by Members of the National Geographic Society. 474, *Apr. 1926*

RECENT Contributions to Our Knowledge of the Earth's Shape and Size, by the United States Coast and Geodetic Survey. By C. A. Schott. 36-41, *Jan. 1901*

RECENT Disclosures Concerning Pre-Columbian Voyages to America in the Archives of the Vatican. By William Eleroy Curtis. 197-234, *Jan. 31, 1894*

RECENT Discoveries in Egypt. 396-397, *Nov. 1901*

The **RECENT** Earthquake Wave on the Coast of Japan. By Eliza Ruhamah Scidmore. 285-289, *Sept. 1896*

The **RECENT** Eruption of Katmai Volcano in Alaska. By George C. Martin. 131-181, *Feb. 1913*

RECENT Exploration in the Canadian Rockies. By Walter D. Wilcox. 151-168, May 1902; Part II, 185-200, *June 1902*

RECENT Explorations in Alaska. By Eliza Ruhamah Scidmore. 173-179, *Jan. 31, 1894*

RECENT Explorations in Equatorial Africa. By Ernest de Sasseville. 88-91, *Mar. 1897*

RECENT French Explorations in Africa. By Charles Rabot. 119-132, *Apr. 1902*

RECENT Geographic Advances, Especially in Africa. By A. W. Greely. 383-398, *Apr. 1911*

RECENT Hydrographic Work. By F. H. Newell. 347-348, *Oct. 1896*

RECENT Magnetic Work by the Carnegie Institution of Washington. 648, *Nov. 1906*

RECENT Observations in Albania. By George P. Scriven. 90-114, *Aug. 1918*

RECENT Population Figures. By Henry Gannett. 785-786, *Aug. 1911*

A **RECENT** Report from the "Doubtful Island Region." By James D. Hague. 205-208, *Mar. 1907*

RECENT Triangulation in the Cascades. By S. S. Gannett. 150, *Apr. 1896*

The **RECENT** Volcanic Eruptions in the West Indies. By Israel C. Russell. 267-285, *July 1902*

RECEPTION to Captain C. D. Sigsbee, USN. By John Hyde. 251-252, *May 1898*

The **RECESSION** of the Glaciers of Glacier Bay, Alaska. By Fremont Morse. 76-78, *Jan. 1908*

RECIFE (Pernambuco), Brazil:

Air Cruising Through New Brazil: A National Geographic Reporter Spots Vast Resources Which the Republic's War Declaration Adds to Strength of United Nations. By Henry Albert Phillips. 503-536, *Oct. 1942*

RECK, DAISY: *Author*

The American Virgins: After Dark Days, These Adopted Daughters of the United States Are Finding a New Place in the Caribbean Sun. By Du-Bose Heyward and Daisy Reck. 273-308, *Sept. 1940*

RECLAIMING the Swamp Lands of the United States. By Herbert M. Wilson. 292-301, *May 1907*

RECLAMATION:

The Dutch Touch. By Bart McDowell. Photos by Nathan Benn and Farrell Grehan. 501-525, *Oct. 1986*
Man Against the Sea, the Oosterschelde Barrier. By Larry Kohl. 526-537, *Oct. 1986*
Roosevelt Country: T. R.'s Wilderness Legacy. By John L. Eliot. Photos by Farrell Grehan. 340-363, *Sept. 1982*
Egypt's Desert of Promise. By Farouk El-Baz. Photos by Georg Gerster. 190-221, *Feb. 1982*
The Desert: An Age-old Challenge Grows. By Rick Gore. Photos by Georg Gerster and Bruce Dale. 586-639, *Nov. 1979*
Pennsylvania: Faire Land of William Penn. By Gordon Young. Photos by Cary Wolinsky. 731-767, *June 1978*
California's Surprising Inland Delta. By Judith and Neil Morgan. Photos by Charles O'Rear. 409-430, *Sept. 1976*
A River Restored: Oregon's Willamette. By Ethel A. Starbird. Photos by Lowell J. Georgia. 816-835, *June 1972*
⬛ Holland Against the Sea. 588A-588B, *Apr. 1970*
The Netherlands: Nation at War With the Sea. By Alan Villiers. Photos by Adam Woolfitt. 530-571, *Apr. 1968*
Californians Escape to the Desert. By Mason Sutherland. Photos by Charles W. Herbert. 675-724, *Nov. 1957*
Helping Holland Rebuild Her Land. By Gilbert M. Grosvenor and Charles Neave. 365-413, *Sept. 1954*
Mid-century Holland Builds Her Future. By Sydney Clark. 747-778, *Dec. 1950*
Mending Dikes in the Netherlands.

Photos by Lawrence Earl. 791-806, *Dec. 1946*
More Water for California's Great Central Valley. By Frederick Simpich. 645-664, *Nov. 1946*
Taming the Outlaw Missouri River. By Frederick Simpich. 569-598, *Nov. 1945*
China Fights Erosion with U. S. Aid. By Walter C. Lowdermilk. 641-680, *June 1945*
Redemption of the Pontine Marshes: By Draining the Malarial Wastes Around Rome, Italy Has Created a Promised Land. By Gelasio Caetani. 201-217, *Aug. 1934*
A New Country Awaits Discovery: The Draining of the Zuider Zee Makes Room for the Excess Population of the Netherlands. By J.C.M. Kruisinga. 293-320, *Sept. 1933*
Surveying Through Khoresm: A Journey into Parts of Asiatic Russia Which Have Been Closed to Western Travelers Since the World War. By Lyman D. Wilbur. 753-780, *June 1932*
Farmers Since the Days of Noah: China's Remarkable System of Agriculture Has Kept Alive the Densest Population in the World. By Adam Warwick. 469-500, *Apr. 1927*
The Land of Egypt: A Narrow Green Strip of Fertility Stretching for a Thousand Miles Through Walls of Desert. By Alfred Pearce Dennis. 271-298, *Mar. 1926*
The Story and the Legends of the Pontine Marshes: After Many Centuries of Fruitless Efforts, Italy Is to Inaugurate a Gigantic Enterprise to Drain the Fertile Region Southeast of Rome. By Don Gelasio Caetani. 357-374, *Apr. 1924*
Holland's War With the Sea. By James Howard Gore. 283-325, *Mar. 1923*
Staircase Farms of the Ancients: Astounding Farming Skill of Ancient Peruvians, Who Were Among the Most Industrious and Highly Organized People in History. By O. F. Cook. 474-534, *May 1916*
The Nation's Undeveloped Resources. By Franklin K. Lane. 183-225, *Feb. 1914*
The Spirit of the West: The Wonderful Agricultural Development Since the Dawn of Irrigation. By C. J. Blanchard. 333-360, *Apr. 1910*
The Call of the West. By C. J. Blanchard. 403-437, *May 1909*
Home-Making by the Government: An Account of the Eleven Immense Irrigating Projects. By C. J. Blanchard. 250-287, *Apr. 1908*
A Drowned Empire. By Robert H. Chapman. 190-199, *Mar. 1908*
Reclamation: Drainage; Planting Denuded State Land; Control of the Boll Weevil. 778-780, *Dec. 1907*
Reclaiming the Swamp Lands of the United States. By Herbert M. Wilson. 292-301, *May 1907*
Millions for Moisture: An Account of the Work of the U. S. Reclamation Service. By C. J. Blanchard. 217-243, *Apr. 1907*

Q R

Introduced from Great Britain last century, red deer are farm raised in New Zealand for venison and trophy antlers. JIM BRANDENBURG

Century Basque Whaling Port and Its Sunken Fleet. 40-49; II. Unearthing Red Bay's Whaling History. By James A. Tuck. 50-57; III. Excavating a 400-year-old Basque Galleon. By Robert Grenier. 58-67; IV. The Indomitable Basques. By Robert Laxalt. 69-71, *July 1985*

RED CRABS:

Red Crabs on the March on Christmas Island. By John W. Hicks. 822-831, *Dec. 1987*

RED CROSS:

A Little Humanity Amid the Horrors of War. By Peter T. White. Photos by Steve Raymer. Contents: The International Committee of the Red Cross (ICRC). 647-679, *Nov. 1986*

Scenes of Postwar Finland. By La Verne Bradley. Photos by Jerry Waller. Included: Finnish Red Cross. 233-264, *Aug. 1947*

The Symbol of Service to Mankind. By Stockton Axson. 375-390, *Apr. 1918*

The Needs Abroad. By Ian Malcolm. 427-433, *May 1917*

Bind the Wounds of France. By Herbert C. Hoover. 439-444, *May 1917*

American Red Cross

The American Red Cross: A Century of Service. By Louise Levathes. Photos by Annie Griffiths. 777-791, *June 1981*

Scenes of Postwar Finland. By La Verne Bradley. Photos by Jerry Waller. 233-264, *Aug. 1947*

Red Cross Girl Overseas. By Margaret Cotter. 745-768, *Dec. 1944*

Heroes of Wartime Science and Mercy. By Elizabeth W. King. 715-740, *Dec. 1943*

The Great Mississippi Flood of 1927: Since White Man's Discovery This Mighty River Has Served Him Well, Yet It Has Brought Widespread Devastation Along Its Lower Reaches. By Frederick Simpich. 243-289, *Sept. 1927*

The Healer of Humanity's Wounds. 308-324, *Oct. 1918*

The Symbol of Service to Mankind. By Stockton Axson. 375-390, *Apr. 1918*

Help Our Red Cross. By Woodrow Wilson. 422, *May 1917*

Our Armies of Mercy. By Henry P. Davison. 423-427, *May 1917*

Bind the Wounds of France. By Herbert C. Hoover. 439-444, *May 1917*

America's Duty. By Newton D. Baker. 453-457, *May 1917*

Stand by the Soldier. By John J. Pershing. 457-459, *May 1917*

A Poisoned World. By William Howard Taft. 459-467, *May 1917*

The Red Cross Spirit. By Eliot Wadsworth. Included: The Red Cross Spirit Speaks, a poem by John H. Finley. 467-474, *May 1917*

The National Geographic Society. Speech by Mabel Boardman. 272-298, *Mar. 1912*

The American Red Cross in Italy. By Mabel Boardman. 396-397, *Apr. 1909*

Honors to the American Navy. National Geographic Society Banquet Speech by Mabel Boardman. 77-95, *Jan. 1909*

RED DEER:

Red Deer and Man. By T. H. Clutton-Brock. Included: Red Deer: A Scottish Dynasty. 538-555, *Oct. 1986*

RED MANGROVES:

The Tree Nobody Liked. By Rick Gore. Photos by Bianca Lavies. 669-689, *May 1977*

RED Men of the Southwest. Paintings by W. Langdon Kihn. Contents: Pueblo Indians. 557-596, *Nov. 1940*

RED ROCK LAKES NATIONAL WILDLIFE REFUGE, Montana:

The Triumphant Trumpeter. By Charles A. Bergman. Photos by Art Wolfe. 554-558, *Oct. 1985*

Return of the Trumpeter. By Frederick Kent Truslow. 134-150, *July 1960*

RED SEA:

Scorpionfish: Danger in Disguise. By David Doubilet. 634-643, *Nov. 1987*

Hidden Life of an Undersea Desert. By Eugenie Clark. Photos by David Doubilet. 129-144, *July 1983*

Flashlight Fish of the Red Sea. By Eugenie Clark. Photos by David Doubilet. 719-728, *Nov. 1978*

The Strangest Sea. By Eugenie Clark. Photos by David Doubilet. 338-365, *Sept. 1975*

The Red Sea's Sharkproof Fish. By Eugenie Clark. Photos by David Doubilet. NGS research grant. 718-727, *Nov. 1974*

The Red Sea's Gardens of Eels. By Eugenie Clark. Photos by James L. Stanfield and David Doubilet. NGS research grant. 724-735, *Nov. 1972*

At Home in the Sea. By Jacques-Yves Cousteau. Contents: Conshelf Two underwater lodge. 465-507, *Apr. 1964*

Exploring Davy Jones's Locker with *Calypso.* By Jacques-Yves Cousteau. Photos by Luis Marden. NGS research grant. 149-161, *Feb. 1956*

Camera Under the Sea. By Luis Marden. NGS research grant. 162-200, *Feb. 1956*

Calypso Explores for Underwater Oil. By Jacques-Yves Cousteau. NGS research grant. 155-184, *Aug. 1955*

Fish Men Explore a New World Undersea. By Jacques-Yves Cousteau. 431-472, *Oct. 1952*

Pearl Fishing in the Red Sea. By Henri de Monfreid. 597-626, *Nov. 1937*

REDEEMING the Tropics. By William Joseph Showalter. 344-364, *Mar. 1914*

REDEMPTION of the Pontine Marshes: By Draining the Malarial Wastes Around Rome, Italy Has Created a Promised Land. By Gelasio Caetani. 201-217, *Aug. 1934*

REDFIELD, WILLIAM C.:

Honors to Amundsen and Peary. Speech by William C. Redfield. 113-130, *Jan. 1913*

REDFORD, ROBERT: *Author*

Riding the Outlaw Trail. Photos by Jonathan Blair. 622-657, *Nov. 1976*

REDISCOVERING America's Forgotten Crops. By Noel D. Vietmeyer. Photos by Burgess Blevins. Paintings by Paul M. Breeden. 702-712, *May 1981*

REDISCOVERING the Rhine: A Trip by Barge from the Sea to the Headwaters of Europe's Storied Stream. By Melville Chater. 1-43, *July 1925*

The **REDISCOVERY** of Puerto Rico. 359-360, *Sept. 1899*

Retracing the Outlaw Trail, actor Robert Redford rides with Arthur Ekker, whose Utah ranch lies near the escape route of Old West desperadoes. JONATHAN BLAIR

Q R

REDWAY, JACQUES W.: *Author*

The First Landfall of Columbus. 179-192, *Dec. 29, 1894*

The **REDWOOD** Forest of the Pacific Coast. By Henry Gannett. 145-159, *May 1899*

REDWOOD NATIONAL PARK, California:

Editorial. By Gilbert M. Grosvenor. 295, *Sept. 1977*

A Park to Save the Tallest Trees. By Melville Bell Grosvenor. 62-64, *July 1966*

REDWOODS:

Editorial. By Gilbert M. Grosvenor. 295, *Sept. 1977*

Redwoods, Rain, and Lots of Room: California's North Coast. By Judith and Neil Morgan. Photos by Dewitt Jones. 330-363, *Sept. 1977*

A Park to Save the Tallest Trees. By Melville Bell Grosvenor. 62-64, *July 1966*

World's Tallest Tree Discovered. By Melville Bell Grosvenor. Photos by George F. Mobley. 1-9, *July 1964*

Finding the Mt. Everest of All Living Things. By Paul A. Zahl. 10-51, *July 1964*

California's Coastal Redwood Realm. By J. R. Hildebrand. 133-184, *Feb. 1939*

Among the Big Trees of California. By John R. White. 219-232, *Aug. 1934*

Saving the Redwoods. By Madison Grant. 519-536, *June 1920*

The Redwood Forest of the Pacific Coast. By Henry Gannett. 145-159, *May 1899*

See also Sequoia gigantea

REED, ELIZABETH C.: *Author*

White Tiger in My House. Photos by Donna K. Grosvenor. 482-491, *Apr. 1970*

REED, JOHN C.: *Author*

Down Idaho's River of No Return. By Philip J. Shenon and John C. Reed. Contents: Salmon River. 95-136, *July 1936*

REED, MACON, Jr.: *Author*

Behind the Lines in Italy. 109-128, *July 1944*

REED, NATHANIEL P.:

Board of Trustees. President's Page. By Gilbert M. Grosvenor. *Aug. 1988*

REED, NORMAN D.: *Photographer*

The Swallow-tailed Kite: Graceful Aerialist of the Everglades. 496-505, *Oct. 1972*

REED, THEODORE H.: *Author*

What's Black and White and Loved All Over? Photos by Donna K. Grosvenor. 803-815, *Dec. 1972*

Enchantress! (White Tigress). Photos by Thomas J. Abercrombie. 628-641, *May 1961*

REED SHIPS. *See* Ra II; Tigris

REEDER, WILLIAM G.:

Nomination Page. In the Galápagos Islands. *Feb. 1971*

REEDY, JAMES R.: *Author*

First Flight Across the Bottom of the World. Photos by Otis Imboden. 454-464, *Mar. 1964*

REEF SHARKS:

Into the Lairs of "Sleeping" Sharks. By Eugenie Clark. Photos by David Doubilet. NGS research grant. 570-584, *Apr. 1975*

REEFS. *See* Corals and Coral Reefs; Great Bahama Bank; Great Sand Barrier Reef

REELFOOT–An Earthquake Lake. By Wilbur A. Nelson. 95-114, *Jan. 1924*

REFORESTATION:

Park at the Top of the World: Mount Everest National Park. By Rick Ridgeway. Photos by Nicholas de-Vore III. 704-725, *June 1982*

Timber: How Much Is Enough? By John J. Putman. Photos by Bruce Dale. 485-511, *Apr. 1974*

The **REFORMATION:**

The World of Martin Luther. By Merle Severy. Photos by James L. Amos. 418-463, *Oct. 1983*

REFUGEES:

The Hmong in America: Laotian Refugees in the "Land of the Giants." By Spencer Sherman. Photos by Dick Swanson. 586-610, *Oct. 1988*

Africa's Sahel: The Stricken Land. By William S. Ellis. Photos by Steve McCurry. 140-179, *Aug. 1987*

The Usumacinta River: Troubles on a Wild Frontier. By S. Jeffrey K. Wilkerson. Photos by David Hiser.

Refugees of the drought-stricken African Sahel, a family receives food aid in Mauritania. STEVE McCURRY, MAGNUM

Included: Guatemalan refugees in Mexican camps. 514-543, *Oct. 1985*

Along Afghanistan's War-torn Frontier. By Debra Denker. Photos by Steve McCurry. 772-797, *June 1985*

Honduras: Eye of the Storm. By Mike Edwards. Photos by David Alan Harvey. Included: Nicaraguan and Salvadoran refugees. 608-637, *Nov. 1983*

Ethiopia: Revolution in an Ancient Empire. By Robert Caputo. 614-645, *May 1983*

Beirut–Up From the Rubble. By William S. Ellis. Photos by Steve McCurry. Included: Palestinian refugees. 262-286, *Feb. 1983*

Florida–A Time for Reckoning. By William S. Ellis. Photos by Nathan Benn and Kevin Fleming. Included: Cuban and Haitian refugees. 172-219, *Aug. 1982*

Troubled Odyssey of Vietnamese Fishermen. By Harvey Arden. Photos by Steve Wall. 378-395, *Sept. 1981*

Editorial. By Wilbur E. Garrett. 713, *June 1981*

Somalia's Hour of Need. By Robert Paul Jordan. Photos by Michael S. Yamashita and Kevin Fleming. 748-775. Included: Encampments of the Dispossessed (Ethiopians from Ogaden region). By Larry Kohl. 756-763, *June 1981*

Pakistan Under Pressure. By William S. Ellis. Photos by James L. Stanfield. Included: Afghan refugees. 668-701, *May 1981*

Thailand: Refuge From Terror. By W. E. Garrett. Included: Cambodian, Laotian, Vietnamese refugees. 633-642, *May 1980*

One Family's Odyssey to America. By John Everingham. Contents: Laotian refugees. 642-661, *May 1980*

Hong Kong's Refugee Dilemma. By William S. Ellis. Photos by William Albert Allard. Included: Ethnic Chinese from Vietnam. 709-732, *Nov. 1979*

The Niger: River of Sorrow, River of Hope. By Georg Gerster. 152-189, *Aug. 1975*

Bangladesh: The Nightmare of Famine. By Steve Raymer. 33-39, *July 1975*

The Hmong of Laos: No Place to Run. By W. E. Garrett. 78-111, *Jan. 1974*

The Mekong, River of Terror and Hope. By Peter T. White. Photos by W. E. Garrett. 737-787, *Dec. 1968*

Little Tibet in Switzerland. By Laura Pilarski. Photos by Fred Mayer. 711-727, *Nov. 1968*

Hong Kong Has Many Faces. By John Scofield. 1-41, *Jan. 1962*

Jerusalem, the Divided City. By John Scofield. Photos by Brian Brake. 492-531, *Apr. 1959*

Freedom Flight from Hungary. By Robert F. Sisson. 424-436, *Mar. 1957*

Passage to Freedom in Viet Nam. By Gertrude Samuels. 858-874, *June 1955*

How the Kazakhs Fled to Freedom. By Milton J. Clark. 621-644, *Nov. 1954*

Hong Kong Hangs On. By George W. Long. Photos by J. Baylor Roberts. 239-272, *Feb. 1954*

British Army Gurkhas round up Chinese refugees who have illegally entered Hong Kong seeking better lives.   WILLIAM ALBERT ALLARD

First Polish boy in decades to celebrate his bar mitzvah, Mateusz Kos in 1985 prepares for the ceremony that will make him a man under Jewish law. TOMASZ TOMASZEWSKI

Calligrapher to the government of Palestine in 1927, Abdel Kader Shihabi of Jerusalem practices a treasured Islamic art.   MAYNARD OWEN WILLIAMS, NGS

Muddy residue covers the square of the Church of Santa Croce in 1966 after the Arno River flooded the Renaissance city of Florence. DANIELE PETTINARI

Edwin A. Link. NGS research grant. 778-801, *June 1964*
See also Helicopters

RESCUE WORK:

A Little Humanity Amid the Horrors of War. By Peter T. White. Photos by Steve Raymer. 647-679, *Nov. 1986*
The American Red Cross: A Century of Service. By Louise Levathes. Photos by Annie Griffiths. 777-791, *June 1981*
Earthquake in Guatemala. By Bart McDowell. Photos by W. E. Garrett and Robert W. Madden. 810-829, *June 1976*
The Great St. Bernard Hospice Today. By George Pickow. 49-62, *Jan. 1957*
School for Survival. By Curtis E. LeMay. 565-602, *May 1953*
New Guinea's Mountain and Swampland Dwellers. By Ray T. Elsmore. Included: U. S. Army plane crash (May, 1945). 671-694, *Dec. 1945*
They Survived at Sea. By Samuel F. Harby. 617-640, *May 1945*
See also Air Rescue Squadrons; Civil Air Patrol; Diving Bell; Military Air Transport Service; U. S. Coast Guard; U. S. Revenue Cutter Service

RESCUING Brazil's Muriqui. By Russell A. Mittermeier. Photos by Andrew L. Young. 387-395, *Mar. 1987*

RESCUING the Rothschild. By Carolyn Bennett Patterson. 419-421, *Sept. 1977*

RESEARCH, National Geographic:
President's Page. By Gilbert M. Grosvenor. Aug. 1984; Nov. 1984; *May 1985*

RESEARCH REPORTS, NGS:

■■ *Research Reports.* 1980-1983 Projects. 531 pages. *1985*
■■ *Research Reports.* 1979 Projects. 900 pages. *1985*
■■ *Research Reports.* 1978 Projects. 764 pages. *1985*
■■ *Research Reports.* 1977 Projects. 803 pages. *1985*
■■ *Research Reports.* 1976 Projects. 968 pages. *1984*
■■ *Research Reports.* 1975 Projects. 844 pages. *1984*
■■ *Research Reports.* 1971, 1973, or 1974 Projects. 787 pages. *1983*
■■ *Research Reports.* 1973 Projects. 736 pages. *1982*
■■ *Research Reports.* 1971 or 1972 Projects. 749 pages. *1981*
■■ *Research Reports.* 1971 Projects. 771 pages. *1980*
■■ *Research Reports.* 1970 Projects. 628 pages. *1979*
■■ *Research Reports.* 1969 Projects. 658 pages. *1978*
■■ *Research Reports.* 1968 Projects. 527 pages. *1976*
■■ *Research Reports.* 1890-1954 Projects. 399 pages. *1975*
■■ *Research Reports.* 1967 Projects. 323 pages. *1974*
■■ *Research Reports.* 1966 Projects. 325 pages. *1973*
■■ *Research Reports.* 1955-1960 Projects. 205 pages. *1972*

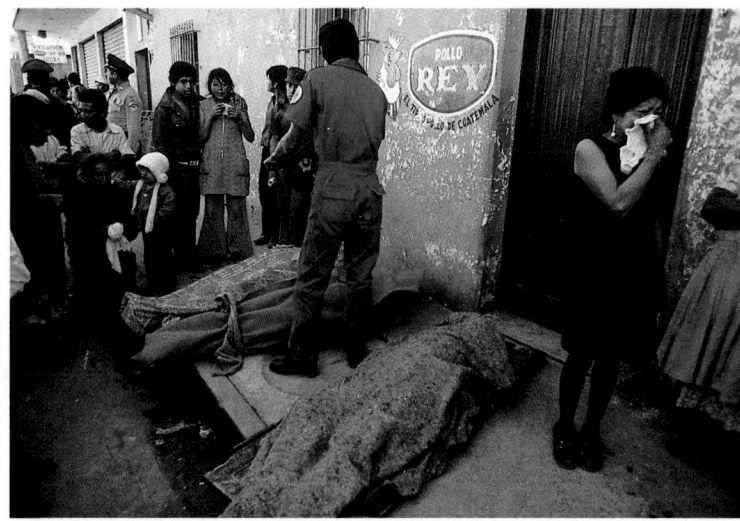

Despite valiant rescue efforts following Guatemala's devastating 1976 earthquake some 23,000 people were lost. LEE ROMERO, EL SOL DE MEXICO

■■ *Research Reports.* 1965 Projects. 305 pages. *1971*
■■ *Research Reports.* 1961-1962 Projects. 235 pages. *1970*
■■ *Research Reports.* 1964 Projects. 275 pages. *1969*
■■ *Research Reports.* 1963 Projects. 251 pages. *1968*

RESEARCH VESSELS:

Project FAMOUS. Photos by Emory Kristof. 586-615. I. Where the Earth Turns Inside Out. By J. R. Heirtzler. Included: *Glomar Challenger; Knorr, R. V.; Lulu; Mizar,* U.S.N.S.; and submersibles *Alvin; Archimède; Cyana.* 586-603; II. Dive Into the Great Rift. By Robert D. Ballard. Included: *Alvin; Lulu.* 604-615, *May 1975*
How We Found the *Monitor.* By John G. Newton. Included: *Alcoa Seaprobe, Eastward.* NGS research grant. 48-61, *Jan. 1975*
Antarctica's Nearer Side. By Samuel W. Matthews. Photos by William R. Curtsinger. Included: *Alpha Helix, Bransfield, Endurance, Hero, Professor Viese.* 622-655, *Nov. 1971*
Science Explores the Monsoon Sea. By Samuel W. Matthews. Photos by Robert F. Sisson. 554-575, *Oct. 1967*
Thresher: Lesson and Challenge. By James H. Wakelin, Jr. Included: *Atlantis II, Conrad, Gilliss.* 759-763, *June 1964*
Scientists Drill at Sea to Pierce Earth's Crust. By Samuel W. Matthews. Photos by J. Baylor Roberts. Included: *CUSS I* drilling barge. 686-697, *Nov. 1961*
See also Amphitrite; Benjamin Bowring; Calypso; Glomar Challenger; John Elliott Pillsbury; Sea Diver; and Submersibles

RESOLUTE BAY, Canada:

Diving Beneath Arctic Ice. By Joseph B. MacInnis. Photos by William R. Curtsinger. 248-267, *Aug. 1973*

RESOLUTION (Sloop):
Captain Cook: The Man Who Mapped the Pacific. By Alan Villiers. Photos by Gordon W. Gahan. 297-349, *Sept. 1971*
The Columbus of the Pacific: Captain James Cook, Foremost British Navigator, Expanded the Great Sea to Correct Proportions and Won for Albion an Insular Empire by Peaceful Exploration and Scientific Study. By J. R. Hildebrand. 85-132, *Jan. 1927*

RESOURCE MANAGEMENT. *See* Deforestation; Energy Sources; Erosion; Land Use; Recycling; Waste Disposal; Water Resources

RESSMEYER, ROGER H.:

On Assignment. *May 1988*
Photographer
Mission to Mars. By Michael Collins. Paintings by Pierre Mion and Roy Andersen. 733-764, *Nov. 1988*
Supernova–Death of a Star. By Robert P. Kirshner. 619-647, *May 1988*

A **RESTLESS** Nation Moves West. By Frank Freidel. 80-121, *Jan. 1965*

The **RESTORATION** of Colonial Williamsburg. By W.A.R. Goodwin. 402-443, *Apr. 1937*

RESTORATION Reveals the "Last Supper." By Carlo Bertelli. Photos by Victor R. Boswell, Jr. 664-685, *Nov. 1983*

RESURRECTING the Grandeur of Tikal. By William R. Coe. 792-798, *Dec. 1975*

RESURRECTING the Oldest Known Greek Ship. By Michael L. Katzev. Photos by Bates Littlehales. NGS research grant. 841-857, *June 1970*

The **RESURRECTION** of Ancient Egypt. By James Baikie. 957-1020, *Sept. 1913*

Amid Uganda's turmoil after the fall of Idi Amin in 1979, Bishop Theodoros Nankyama leads a service in a village church. SARAH LEEN

The **REVOLT** of the Ashantis. 244, *June 1900*

REVOLUTION, American. *See* American Revolution

The **REVOLUTION** in American Agriculture. By Jules B. Billard. Photos by James P. Blair. 147-185, *Feb. 1970*

REVOLUTION in Eating: Machine Food Age–Born of Roads, Research, and Refrigeration–Makes the United States the Best-fed Nation in History. By J. R. Hildebrand. 273-324, *Mar. 1942*

The **REVOLUTION** in Russia. By William Eleroy Curtis. 302-316, *May 1907*

REVOLUTIONARY View of the 48 States. By Barry C. Bishop. 140-147, *July 1976*

REVOLUTIONARY WAR. *See* American Revolution

The REVOLUTIONARY War: America's Fight for Freedom. By Bart McDowell. 199 pages. *1967*

The **REWARDS** of Walrus-watching. By G. Carleton Ray. Photos by Bill Curtsinger. NGS research grant. 565-580, *Oct. 1979*

REWATI (White Tiger):

White Tiger in My House. By Elizabeth C. Reed. Photos by Donna K. Grosvenor. 482-491, *Apr. 1970*

REYKJAVÍK, Iceland:

Iceland: Life Under the Glaciers. By Louise E. Levathes. Photos by Bob Krist. 184-215, *Feb. 1987*
Sailing Iceland's Rugged Coasts. By Wright Britton. Photos by James A. Sugar. 228-265, *Aug. 1969*
Iceland Tapestry. By Deena Clark. 599-630, *Nov. 1951*
American Soldier in Reykjavík. By Luther M. Chovan. 536-568, *Nov. 1945*

REYNOLDS, BRAD: *Author*

Eskimo Hunters of the Bering Sea. Photos by Don Doll. 814-834, *June 1984*

REYNOLDS, ROBERT J.:
Author-Photographer

Over the Sea to Scotland's Skye. 87-112, *July 1952*

RHESUS MONKEYS:

Temple Monkeys of Nepal. By Jane Teas. 575-584, *Apr. 1980*

RHINE (River), Europe:

The Rhine: Europe's River of Legend. By William Graves. Photos by Bruce Dale. 449-499, *Apr. 1967*
Rediscovering the Rhine: A Trip by Barge from the Sea to the Headwaters of Europe's Storied Stream. By Melville Chater. 1-43, *July 1925*
The Story of the Ruhr. By Frederick Simpich. 553-564, *May 1922*

RHINEBECK, New York:

World War I Aircraft Fly Again in Rhinebeck's Rickety Rendezvous. By Harvey Arden. Photos by Howard Sochurek. 578-587, *Oct. 1970*

RHINELAND (Region), Germany:

War's Wake in the Rhineland. By Thomas R. Henry. 1-32, *July 1945*
Cologne, Key City of the Rhineland. By Francis Woodworth. 829-848, *June 1936*

RHINOCEROSES:

They're Killing Off the Rhino. By Esmond Bradley Martin. Photos by Jim Brandenburg. 404-422, *Mar. 1984*
Wild Cargo: the Business of Smuggling Animals. By Noel Grove. Photos by Steve Raymer. Included: Black Rhinoceros, White Rhinoceros; and Rhino horn trade. 287-315, *Mar. 1981*
Ancient Ashfall Creates a Pompeii of Prehistoric Animals. By Michael R. Voorhies. Photos by Annie Griffiths. Paintings by Jay Matternes. 66-75, *Jan. 1981*
Where Elephants Have Right of Way. By George and Jinx Rodger. Included: Black Rhinoceros, White Rhinoceros. 363-389, *Sept. 1960*
Stalking the Great Indian Rhino. By Lee Merriam Talbot. 389-398, *Mar. 1957*

RHOADES, ROBERT E.: *Author*

The Incredible Potato. Photos by Martin Rogers. 668-694, *May 1982*

RHODE, CECIL E.:
Author-Photographer

When Giant Bears Go Fishing. 195-205, *Aug. 1954*

RHODE ISLAND:

New England's "Little Portugal." By O. Louis Mazzatenta. 90-109, *Jan. 1975*
New England's "Lively Experiment," Rhode Island. By Robert de Roos. Photos by Fred Ward. 370-401, *Sept. 1968*
Rhode Island, Modern City-State. By George W. Long. Photos by Willard R. Culver. 137-170, *Aug. 1948*

Sauntering Through the Land of Roger Williams. Photos by Clifton Adams. 311-318, *Sept. 1931*
See also Newport

RHODE ISLAND (Sidewheeler):

How We Found the *Monitor.* By John G. Newton. Note: A search area was established for the *Monitor* based on the log of *Rhode Island,* which had the *Monitor* in tow. 48-61, *Jan. 1975*

RHODES, CECIL:

The British Way. By Sir Evelyn Wrench. 421-541, *Apr. 1949*
Rhodesia, Hobby and Hope of Cecil Rhodes. By W. Robert Moore. 281-306, *Sept. 1944*

RHODES (Island), Aegean Sea:

The Isles of Greece: Aegean Birthplace of Western Culture. By Melville Bell Grosvenor. Photos by Edwin Stuart Grosvenor and Winfield Parks. 147-193, *Aug. 1972*
On the Winds of the Dodecanese. By Jean and Franc Shor. 351-390, *Mar. 1953*
Rhodes, and Italy's Aegean Islands. By Dorothy Hosmer. 449-480, *Apr. 1941*
Ageless Luster of Greece and Rhodes. Photos by Arnold Genthe. 477-492, *Apr. 1938*
Souvenirs of Knighthood in Rhodes. Photos by Luigi Pellerano. 665-672, *Dec. 1933*
Historic Islands and Shores of the Ægean Sea. By Ernest Lloyd Harris. 231-261, *Sept. 1915*

RHODESIA:

Rhodesia, a House Divided. By Allan C. Fisher, Jr. Photos by Thomas Nebbia. 641-671, *May 1975*
Freedom's Progress South of the Sahara. By Howard La Fay. Photos by

Prehensile lip of a black rhinoceros bull folds and flattens an acacia thorn, a favorite browse. Riding above, a red-billed oxpecker searches for ticks and flies. JIM BRANDENBURG

Joseph J. Scherschel. 603-637, *Nov. 1962*

Africa: The Winds of Freedom Stir a Continent. By Nathaniel T. Kenney. Photos by W. D. Vaughn. 303-359, *Sept. 1960*

Safari Through Changing Africa. By Elsie May Bell Grosvenor. Photos by Gilbert Grosvenor. 145-198, *Aug. 1953*

Rhodesia, Hobby and Hope of Cecil Rhodes. By W. Robert Moore. 281-306, *Sept. 1944*

Rhodesia, the Pioneer Colony: In the Land of Sheba's Gold and Rhodes' Diamonds Emerge Model Towns and Modern Mines. By Melville Chater. 753-782, *June 1935*

The World's Great Waterfalls: Visits to Mighty Niagara, Wonderful Victoria, and Picturesque Iguazu. By Theodore W. Noyes. 29-59, *July 1926*

The Wonders of the Mosi-oa-Tunga: The Falls of the Zambesi. By Louis Livingston Seaman. 561-571, *June 1911*

See also present name, Zimbabwe

RHODESIA, Northern. *See* present name, Zambia

RHODODENDRONS:

Rhododendron Time on Roan Mountain. By Ralph Gray. 819-828, *June 1957*

Rhododendron Glories of Southwest Scotland. By David S. Boyer. Photos by B. Anthony Stewart and author. 641-664, *May 1954*

Pack Trip Through the Smokies. By Val Hart. Photos by Robert F. Sisson. 473-502, *Oct. 1952*

See also Azaleas

RHONE, ROSAMOND DODSON: *Author*

Nauru, the Richest Island in the South Seas. 559-589, *Dec. 1921*

RHÔNE, France:

Here Rest in Honored Glory; The United States Dedicates Six New Battle Monuments in Europe to Americans Who Gave Their Lives During World War II. By Howell Walker. Included: Rhône American Cemetery and Memorial. 739-768, *June 1957*

RHÔNE RIVER DELTA, France. *See* Camargue

RHUM (Island), Scotland:

Red Deer: A Scottish Dynasty. By T. H. Clutton-Brock. 556-562, *Oct. 1986*

Red Deer and Man. By T. H. Clutton-Brock. Photos by Jim Brandenburg. 538-555, *Oct. 1986*

RIACE BRONZES:

Warriors From a Watery Grave. By Joseph Alsop. 821-827, *June 1983*

RIATAS and Romance on the Rio Grande. Photos by Luis Marden. 431-462, *Oct. 1939*

RIBONUCLEIC ACID (RNA):

The Awesome Worlds Within a Cell. By Rick Gore. Photos by Bruce Dale.

Paintings by Davis Meltzer. Included: The Language of Life, foldout showing replication of DNA and manufacture of RNA and proteins. 355-395, *Sept. 1976*

RIBOUD, MARC: *Photographer*

Pompidou Center, Rage of Paris. By Cathy Newman. 469-477, *Oct. 1980*

Cappadocia: Turkey's Country of Cones. 122-146, *Jan. 1958*

Coronation in Katmandu. By E. Thomas Gilliard. 139-152, *July 1957*

RICE, WILLIAM GORHAM: *Author*

The Singing Towers of Holland and Belgium. 357-376, *Mar. 1925*

RICE GROWING:

Day of the Rice God. Photos by H. Edward Kim. Text by Douglas Lee. 78-85, *July 1978*

Bangladesh: Hope Nourishes a New Nation. By William S. Ellis. Photos by Dick Durrance II. 295-333, *Sept. 1972*

Spirits of Change Capture the Karens. By Peter Kunstadter. 267-285, *Feb. 1972*

Backwoods Japan During American Occupation. By M. A. Huberman. 491-518, *Apr. 1947*

How Half the World Works. By Alice Tisdale Hobart and Mary A. Nourse. 509-524, *Apr. 1932*

Some Aspects of Rural Japan. By Walter Weston. 275-301, *Sept. 1922*

RICHARD THE LION-HEARTED:

The British Way. By Sir Evelyn Wrench. 421-541, *Apr. 1949*

The Road of the Crusaders. By Harold Lamb. 645-693, *Dec. 1933*

RICHARDS, BILL: *Author*

The Olympic Peninsula. Photos by Sam Abell. Included: Maps showing wildlife refuges, Indian reservations, and

Government troops fought black guerrillas in Rhodesia until 1980 when the nation of Zimbabwe was declared. THOMAS NEBBIA

---

annual precipitation. 644-673, *May 1984*

Alaska's Southeast: A Place Apart. 50-87, *Jan. 1984*

The Uncertain State of Puerto Rico. Photos by Stephanie Maze. 516-543, *Apr. 1983*

Henry Hudson's Changing Bay. Photos by David Hiser. 380-405, *Mar. 1982*

The Untamed Yellowstone. Photos by Dean Krakel II. 257-278, *Aug. 1981*

Powder River Basin: New Energy Frontier. Photos by Louie Psihoyos. 96-113, *Special Report on Energy. (Feb. 1981)*

RICHARDSON, JIM: *Photographer*

Atlanta: Energy and Optimism in the New South. By Erla Zwingle. 3-29, *July 1988*

The Rising Great Salt Lake: No Way to Run a Desert. By Rick Gore. 694-719, *June 1985*

RICHELIEU (River), Canada:

North Through History Aboard *White Mist.* By Melville Bell Grosvenor. Photos by Edwin Stuart Grosvenor. 1-55, *July 1970*

RICHERT, THOMAS:

Nomination Page. *Oct. 1968*

RICHEST Unlooted Tomb of a Moche Lord. By Walter Alva. Photos by Bill Ballenberg. Included: Into the Tomb of a Moche Lord. Paintings by Ned Seidler; Iconography of the Moche: Unraveling the Mystery of the Warrior-Priest. By Christopher B. Donnan. NGS research grant. 510-555, *Oct. 1988*

RICHIE, THOMAS:

Nomination Page. *Apr. 1979*

RICHMOND, Virginia:

Virginia–A Commonwealth That Has Come Back. By William Joseph Showalter. 403-472, *Apr. 1929*

RICHTHOFEN, MANFRED VON:

Aces Among Aces. By Laurence La Tourette Driggs. 568-580, *June 1918*

RICKER, P. L.: *Author-Photographer*

American Wild Flower Odyssey. 603-634, *May 1953*

RIDDIFORD, CHARLES E.: *Artist*

■■ *The Round Earth on Flat Paper: Map Projections Used By Cartographers.* By Wellman Chamberlin. 126 pages. *1947*

RIDDLE of the Aleutians: A Botanist Explores the Origin of Plants on Ever-misty Islands Now Enshrouded in the Fog of War. By Isobel Wylie Hutchison. 769-792, *Dec. 1942*

RIDDLE of the Glyphs. By George E. Stuart. Photos by Otis Imboden. 768-791, *Dec. 1975*

RIDDLE of the Pyramid Boats. By Peter Miller. Photos by Victor R. Boswell, Jr. 534-550, *Apr. 1988*

RIDGEWAY, RICK: *Author*

Park at the Top of the World: Mount Everest National Park. Photos by

Tracks in tiers allowed three trains in 1929 to pass each other without stopping in Richmond, Virginia. VIRGINIA DEPARTMENT OF AGRICULTURE

Nicholas deVore III. 704-725, *June 1982*

RIDING SCHOOL:

The White Horses of Vienna. By Beverley M. Bowie. Photos by Volkmar Wentzel. Included: Spanish Riding School. 401-419, *Sept. 1958*

RIDING the Outlaw Trail. By Robert Redford. Photos by Jonathan Blair. 622-657, *Nov. 1976*

RIDLEY TURTLES. *See* Pacific Ridley Turtles

RIFT VALLEY, Africa-Asia. *See* Great Rift Valley

RIFTS, Ocean-floor:

New World of the Ocean. By Samuel W. Matthews. 792-832, *Dec. 1981*
Incredible World of the Deep-sea Rifts. NGS research grant. 680-705, *Nov. 1979*
Window on Earth's Interior. By Robert D. Ballard. Photos by Emory Kristof. Contents: Cayman Trough. 228-249, *Aug. 1976*
Project FAMOUS. Photos by Emory Kristof. 586-615. Contents: Mid-Atlantic Rift. I. Where the Earth Turns Inside Out. By J. R. Heirtzler. 586-603; II. Dive Into the Great Rift. By Robert D. Ballard. 604-615, *May 1975*
This Changing Earth. By Samuel W. Matthews. 1-37, *Jan. 1973*
Man's Deepest Dive. By Jacques Piccard. Photos by Thomas J.

Abercrombie. Contents: Challenger Deep of the Mariana Trench. 224-239, *Aug. 1960*
Deep Diving off Japan. By Georges S. Houot. NGS research grant. Contents: Japan Trench. 138-150, *Jan. 1960*
Calypso Explores an Undersea Canyon. By Jacques-Yves Cousteau. Photos by Bates Littlehales. Contents: Romanche Trench. NGS research grant. 373-396, *Mar. 1958*
See also Galapagos Rift; Oases, Oceanfloor

RĪGA, Latvia:

Flying Around the Baltic. By Douglas Chandler. 767-806, *June 1938*

RIGAUD, JEAN-PHILIPPE: *Author*

Art Treasures from the Ice Age: Lascaux Cave. Photos by Sisse Brimberg and Norbert Aujoulat. 482-489, *Oct. 1988*

RIGGERT, TOM: *Author*

Skylab's Fiery Finish. 581-584, *Oct. 1979*

RIGGS, ARTHUR STANLEY: *Author*

Inexhaustible Italy. 273-368, *Oct. 1916*
The Beauties of France. 391-491, *Nov. 1915*

RIGGS, THOMAS, Jr.: *Author*

Surveying the 141st Meridian. 685-713, *July 1912*
Marking the Alaskan Boundary. 593-607, *July 1909*

RIGHT WHALES:

At Home With Right Whales. By Roger Payne. Photos by Des and Jen Bartlett. NGS research grant. 322-339, *Mar. 1976*
Swimming With Patagonia's Right Whales. By Roger Payne. Photos by William R. Curtsinger and Charles R. Nicklin, Jr. NGS research grant. 576-587, *Oct. 1972*

RINARD, JUDITH E.: *Author*

■■*Wildlife: Making a Comeback.* Juvenile. 104 pages. *1987*
■□*Dolphins: Our Friends in the Sea.* Juvenile. 104 pages. *1986*
■■*Zoos Without Cages.* Juvenile. 104 pages. *1981*

RING OF FIRE (Volcanic Zone):

When the Earth Moves. The Editor. 638-639, *May 1986*
Eruption in Colombia. By Bart McDowell. Photos by Steve Raymer. 640-653, *May 1986*
Earthquake in Mexico. By Allen A. Boraiko. Photos by James L. Stanfield and Guillermo Aldana E. Included: The rise and fall of buildings– a primer for survival in quake city. 654-675, *May 1986*
See also Plate Tectonics

RINGLING BROS. AND BARNUM & BAILEY CIRCUS:

The Wonder City That Moves by Night. By Francis Beverly Kelley. 289-324, *Mar. 1948*

RÍO AZUL (Site), Guatemala:

Editorial. By Wilbur E. Garrett. 561, *May 1987*

Editorial. By Wilbur E. Garrett. 419, *Apr. 1986*

Río Azul. Photos by George F. Mobley. 420-465. I. Lost City of the Maya. By Richard E. W. Adams. Included: Realm of the Maya (map). NGS research grant. 420-451; II. Looters Rob Graves and History. By Ian Graham. 452-461; III. In Defense of the Collector. By Gillett G. Griffin. 462-465, *Apr. 1986*

Editorial. By Wilbur E. Garrett. 137-137B, *Aug. 1984*

RIO BRANCO, MIGUEL:
Photographer

Brazil's Kayapo Indians, Beset by a Golden Curse. By Vanessa Lea. 675-694, *May 1984*

RIO DE JANEIRO, Brazil:

Brazil: Moment of Promise and Pain. By Priit J. Vesilind. Photos by Stephanie Maze. 348-385, *Mar. 1987*

Brazil's Golden Beachhead. By Bart McDowell. Photos by Nicholas deVore III. 246-277, *Feb. 1978*

Brazil, Ôba! By Peter T. White. Photos by Winfield Parks. 299-353, *Sept. 1962*

Spectacular Rio de Janeiro. By Hernane Tavares de Sá. Photos by Charles Allmon. 289-328, *Mar. 1955*

Brazil's Potent Weapons. By W. Robert Moore. 41-78, *Jan. 1944*

Air Cruising Through New Brazil: A National Geographic Reporter Spots Vast Resources Which the Republic's War Declaration Adds to Strength of United Nations. By Henry Albert Phillips. 503-536, *Oct. 1942*

Rio Panorama: Breath-taking Is This Fantastic City amid Peaks, Palms, and Sea, and in Carnival Time It Moves to the Rhythm of Music. By W. Robert Moore. 283-324, *Sept. 1939*

Gigantic Brazil and Its Glittering Capital. By Frederick Simpich. 733-778, *Dec. 1930*

Rio de Janeiro, in the Land of Lure. By Harriet Chalmers Adams. 165-210, *Sept. 1920*

RIO GRANDE (River), U. S.-Mexico:

Our Wild and Scenic Rivers: The Rio Grande. By Nathaniel T. Kenney. Photos by Bank Langmore. 46-51, *July 1977*

Two Wheels Along the Mexican Border. By William Albert Allard. 591-635, *May 1971*

Big Bend: Jewel in the Texas Desert. By Nathaniel T. Kenney. Photos by James L. Stanfield. 104-133, *Jan. 1968*

Down the Rio Grande: Tracing this Strange, Turbulent Stream on Its Long Course from Colorado to the Gulf of Mexico. By Frederick Simpich. 415-462, *Oct. 1939*

Rio Grande Cornucopia Under a Winter Sun. Photos by B. Anthony Stewart. 65-96, *Jan. 1939*

Wandering Islands in the Rio Grande. By Mrs. Albert S. Burleson. 381-386, *Mar. 1913*

RIO GRANDE NATIONAL FOREST, Colorado:

The Wheeler National Monument. 837-840, *Sept. 1909*

RÍO INDIO, Panama:

Hunting Prehistory in Panama Jungles. By Matthew W. Stirling. Photos by Richard H. Stewart. 271-290, *Aug. 1953*

RÍO MUNI, Equatorial Guinea:

In Quest of the World's Largest Frog. By Paul A. Zahl. 146-152, *July 1967*

"Snowflake," the World's First White Gorilla. By Arthur J. Riopelle. Photos by Paul A. Zahl. NGS research grant. 443-448, *Mar. 1967*

RIOPELLE, ARTHUR J.:
Nomination Page. *Mar. 1969*
Nomination Page. *Mar. 1967*

Author
Growing Up With Snowflake. Photos by Michael Kuh. 491-503, *Oct. 1970*

"Snowflake," the World's First White Gorilla. Photos by Paul A. Zahl. 443-448, *Mar. 1967*

RIP VAN WINKLE of the Underground. By Kenneth F. Weaver. 133-142, *July 1953*

RIPLEY, S. DILLON:
Nomination Page. In Bhutan. *Oct. 1967*

Author
Saving the Nene, World's Rarest Goose. Photos by Jerry Chong. 745-754, *Nov. 1965*

Strange Courtship of Birds of Paradise. Paintings by Walter A. Weber. 247-278, *Feb. 1950*

Peerless Nepal–A Naturalist's Paradise.

In the Rio de Janeiro slum of Rocinha, cinder block and brick replace sheet metal and cardboard in homes as Brazilians gain title to land and city services. STEPHANIE MAZE

Elegant cars of the 1920s parade up and down the broad and breezy Avenida Rio Branco, called Rio de Janeiro's "finest thoroughfare." FROM HARRIET CHALMERS ADAMS

Spawning ground for cutthroat trout and Dolly Varden char, Montana's Flathead is part of the National Wild and Scenic Rivers System, mapped for the July 1977 GEOGRAPHIC.

Pirate Rivers and Their Prizes: The Warfare of Waterways Has Sometimes Changed the Geography of Our Continents. By John Oliver La Gorce. 87-132, *July 1926*

The Mother of Rivers: An Account of a Photographic Expedition to the Great Columbia Ice Field of the Canadian Rockies. By Lewis R. Freeman. Included: Alexandra; Athabaska; Bow; Bush; Castleguard; Chaba; Cline; Columbia; Howse; Mackenzie; Mistaya; North Fork; Saskatchewan; Sunwapta; Wood. 377-446, *Apr. 1925*

The Deep-Water Route from Chicago to the Gulf. 679-685, *Oct. 1907*

Limiting Width of Meander Belts. By Mark S. W. Jefferson. 373-384, *Oct. 1902*

Atlantic Estuarine Tides. By Mark S. W. Jefferson. 400-409, *Sept. 1898*

Alaska and Its Mineral Resources. By Samuel Franklin Emmons. 139-172, *Apr. 1898*

Important Announcement Concerning Essays (Subject: River Systems of the United States). 227-228, *Dec. 29, 1894*

Geomorphology of the Southern Appalachians. By Charles Willard Hayes and Marius R. Campbell. 63-126, *May 23, 1894*

South America. Annual Address by the President, Gardiner G. Hubbard. Included: Amazon; Orinoco; Rio de la Plata; San Francisco. 1-29, *Mar. 28, 1891*

The Rivers of Northern New Jersey, with Notes on the Classification of Rivers in General. By William Morris Davis. 81-110, *May 1890*

Report–Geography of the Air. By A. W. Greely. Included: Interrelation of rainfall and river outflows. 49-63, *Apr. 1890*

The Rivers and Valleys of Pennsylvania. By William Morris Davis. 183-253, *July 1889*

See also Amazon Basin; Amu Darya; Arno; Avon (River); Balim; Bow; Brahmaputra; Cauca; Chattooga (River); Clearwater; Colorado River and Basin; Columbia River and Basin; Congo (River); Connecticut River and Valley; Copper River Delta; Crystal (River); Danube; Delaware (River); Detroit (River); Douro (River); East River; Escalante Canyon, for Escalante; Euphrates; Feni (River); Franklin (River); Fraser (River); Ganges; Green (River); Hudson (River); Hwang Ho; Irrawaddy; James (River); Jhelum; Jordan (River); Juruena; Kansas (River); Knik Glacier and River; Koksoak; Kowak (River); Li; Loire River and Valley; Luhit; Mackenzie (River); Magdalena; Mekong; Merrimack; Meuse; Mississippi (River); Missouri (River); Mohawk; Moselle; Murray (River); Nervion (River); Niger; Nile; Ob; Ohio (River); Orinoco; Paraguay (River); Paraná; Parima; Potomac; Rhine; Rio Grande; Ruhr; Sacramento (River); Saint

John River and Valley; St. Lawrence (River); Salmon (River); Salween; San Joaquin; San Juan (River); Saskatchewan (River); Seine; Sepik (River); Shannon; Snake; Stikine (River); Sungari; Sushitna; Susquehanna; Suwannee (River); Tejo; Tennessee Valley Authority; Thames; Tigris (River); Tonlé Sap; Tumen; Ucayali; Usumacinta (River); Virgin (River); Volga; White (River); Willamette River and Valley; Yalu; Yangtze; Yellowstone (River); Yukon (River); Zambezi; *and* Floods; River Trips

RIVERSLEIGH STATION FOSSILS:

Queensland, Broad Shoulder of Australia. By William S. Ellis. Photos by David Robert Austen. Included: Queensland Fossils Expand Australia's Prehistoric Menagerie. 2-39, *Jan. 1986*

RIVIERA (Region), France-Italy:

French Riviera: Storied Playground on the Azure Coast. By Carleton Mitchell. Photos by Thomas Nebbia. 798-835, *June 1967*

Time Turns Back in Picture-book Portofino. By Carleton Mitchell. Photos by Winfield Parks. 232-253, *Feb. 1965*

Italian Riviera, Land That Winter Forgot. By Howell Walker. 743-789, *June 1963*

Miniature Monaco. By Gilbert M. and Donna Kerkam Grosvenor. 546-573, *Apr. 1963*

Wet-suited against water near 40°F, canoeists shoot Big Kahuna, a major rapids on the Snake River in Wyoming. SAM ABELL

Life's Pattern on the Italian Riviera. By Helen Churchill Candee. 67-100, *Jan. 1935*

Carnival Days on the Riviera. By Maynard Owen Williams. 467-501, *Oct. 1926*

RIYADH, Saudi Arabia:

Saudi Arabia: The Kingdom and Its Power. By Robert Azzi. 286-333, *Sept. 1980*

Guest in Saudi Arabia. By Maynard Owen Williams. 463-487, *Oct. 1945*

ROACHES. *See* Cockroaches

The **ROAD** of the Crusaders: A Historian Follows the Steps of Richard the Lion Heart and Other Knights of the Cross Over the "Via Dei." By Harold Lamb. 645-693, *Dec. 1933*

The **ROAD** to Bolivia. By William E. Curtis. 209-224, June 1900; 264-280, *July 1900*

The **ROAD** to Wang Ye Fu: An Account of the Work of the National Geographic Society's Central-China Expedition in the Mongol Kingdom of Ala Shan. By Frederick R. Wulsin. 197-234, *Feb. 1926*

ROADRUNNERS:

The Roadrunner–Clown of the Desert. By Martha A. Whitson. Photos by Bruce Dale. 694-702, *May 1983*

ROADS. *See* Highways and Roads

ROADS from Washington. By John Patric. 1-56, *July 1938*

ROAMING Africa's Unfenced Zoos. By W. Robert Moore. 353-380, *Mar. 1950*

ROAMING India's Naga Hills. By S. Dillon Ripley. 247-264, *Feb. 1955*

ROAMING Korea South of the Iron Curtain. By Enzo de Chetelat. 777-808, *June 1950*

ROAMING Russia's Caucasus: Rugged Mountains and Hardy Fighters Guard the Soviet Union's Caucasian Treasury of Manganese and Oil. By Rolf Singer. 91-121, *July 1942*

ROAMING the West's Fantastic Four Corners. By Jack Breed. 705-742, *June 1952*

ROAN MOUNTAIN, North Carolina-Tennessee:

Rhododendron Time on Roan Mountain. By Ralph Gray. 819-828, *June 1957*

ROANOKE ISLAND, North Carolina:

Lonely Cape Hatteras, Besieged by the Sea. By William S. Ellis. Photos by Emory Kristof. 393-421, *Sept. 1969*

October Holiday on the Outer Banks. By Nike Anderson. Photos by J. Baylor Roberts. 501-529, *Oct. 1955*

Exploring America's Great Sand Barrier Reef. By Eugene R. Guild. Photos by John E. Fletcher and author. 325-350, *Sept. 1947*

Indian Life Before the Colonists Came. By Stuart E. Jones. Engravings by Theodore de Bry (1590). 351-368, *Sept. 1947*

A Bit of Elizabethan England in America: Fisher Folk of the Islands Off North Carolina Conserved the Speech and Customs of Sir Walter Raleigh's Colonists. By Blanch Nettleton Epler. 695-730, *Dec. 1933*

ROBBINS, MICHAEL: *Author*

■ *High Country Trail: Along the Continental Divide.* Photos by Paul Chesley. 199 pages. *1981*

ROBERT COLLEGE, Turkey:

Robert College, Turkish Gateway to the Future. By Franc Shor. 399-418, *Sept. 1957*

American Alma Maters in the Near East. By Maynard Owen Williams. 237-256, *Aug. 1945*

ROBERT FROST and New England. By Archibald MacLeish. 438-444, *Apr. 1976*

ROBERT REDFORD Rides the Outlaw Trail. By Robert Redford. Photos by Jonathan Blair. 622-657, *Nov. 1976*

ROBERT V. FLEMING, 1890-1967. By Melville Bell Grosvenor. 526-529, *Apr. 1968*

ROBERTS, FRANK H. H., Jr.: *Author*

In the Empire of the Aztecs: Mexico City Is Rich in Relics of a People Who Practiced Human Sacrifice, Yet Loved Flowers, Education, and Art. Paintings by H. M. Herget. 725-750, *June 1937*

ROBERTS, J. BAYLOR:

Nomination Page. *Nov. 1960*

Author-Photographer

Focusing on the Tournament of Roses. By B. Anthony Stewart and J. Baylor Roberts. 805-816, *June 1954*

Photographer

Scientists Drill at Sea to Pierce Earth's Crust. By Samuel W. Matthews. Contents: Project Mohole. 686-697, *Nov. 1961*

Triton Follows Magellan's Wake. By Edward L. Beach. 585-615, *Nov. 1960*

Bounty Descendants Live on Remote Norfolk Island. By T. C. Roughley. 559-584, *Oct. 1960*

The Night the Mountains Moved. By Samuel W. Matthews. 329-359, *Mar. 1960*

Iraq–Where Oil and Water Mix. By Jean and Franc Shor. 443-489, *Oct. 1958*

Heritage of Beauty and History. By Conrad L. Wirth. 587-661, *May 1958*

Slow Boat to Florida. By Dorothea and Stuart E. Jones. 1-65, *Jan. 1958*

Charting Our Sea and Air Lanes. By Stuart E. Jones. 189-209, *Feb. 1957*

Our Green Treasury, the National Forests. By Nathaniel T. Kenney. 287-324, *Sept. 1956*

Hunting the Heartbeat of a Whale. By Paul Dudley White and Samuel W. Matthews. 49-64, *July 1956*

October Holiday on the Outer Banks. By Nike Anderson. 501-529, *Oct. 1955*

This Young Giant, Indonesia. By Beverley M. Bowie. 351-392, *Sept. 1955*

Across Canada by Mackenzie's Track. By Ralph Gray. 191-239, *Aug. 1955*

Saving Man's Wildlife Heritage. By John H. Baker. 581-620, *Nov. 1954*

America Goes to the Fair. By Samuel W. Matthews. 293-333, *Sept. 1954*

New Rush to Golden California. By George W. Long. 723-802, *June 1954*

Hong Kong Hangs On. By George W. Long. 239-272, *Feb. 1954*

Cruising Japan's Inland Sea. By Willard Price. 619-650, *Nov. 1953*

Our Navy in the Far East. By Arthur W. Radford. 537-577, *Oct. 1953*

Macau, a Hole in the Bamboo Curtain. By George W. Long. 679-688, *May 1953*

Malaya Meets Its Emergency. By George W. Long. 185-228, *Feb. 1953*

La Jolla, a Gem of the California Coast. By Deena Clark. 755-782, *Dec. 1952*

Indochina Faces the Dragon. By George W. Long. 287-328, *Sept. 1952*

"Around the World in Eighty Days." By Newman Bumstead. 705-750, *Dec. 1951*

Journey Into Troubled Iran. By George W. Long. 425-464, *Oct. 1951*

North Dakota Comes into Its Own. By Leo A. Borah. 283-322, *Sept. 1951*

Dog Mart Day in Fredericksburg. By Frederick G. Vosburgh. 817-832, *June 1951*

Seeing the Earth from 80 Miles Up. By Clyde T. Holliday. 511-528, *Oct. 1950*

Japan Tries Freedom's Road. By Frederick G. Vosburgh. 593-632, *May 1950*

Formosa–Hot Spot of the East. By Frederick G. Vosburgh. 139-176, *Feb. 1950*

From Indian Canoes to Submarines at Key West. By Frederick Simpich. 41-72, *Jan. 1950*

Pittsburgh: Workshop of the Titans. By Albert W. Atwood. 117-144, *July 1949*

Dixie Spins the Wheel of Industry. By William H. Nicholas. 281-324, *Mar. 1949*

Uncle Sam Bends a Twig in Germany. By Frederick Simpich. 529-550, *Oct. 1948*

Around the "Great Lakes of the South." By Frederick Simpich. 463-491, *Apr. 1948*

The Wonder City That Moves by Night. By Francis Beverly Kelley. 289-324, *Mar. 1948*

Shawneetown Forsakes the Ohio. By William H. Nicholas. 273-288, *Feb. 1948*

Carnival in San Antonio. By Mason Sutherland. 813-844, *Dec. 1947*

Louisiana Trades with the World. By Frederick Simpich. 705-738, *Dec. 1947*

Men, Moose, and Mink of Northwest Angle. By William H. Nicholas. 265-284, *Aug. 1947*

Deep in the Heart of "Swissconsin." By William H. Nicholas. 781-800, *June 1947*

Performing swimmers put on lipstick in Wakulla Springs, a northern Florida site near the Gulf of Mexico used as a set for underwater films in the 1940s. J. BAYLOR ROBERTS, NGS

Over Plains and Hills of South Dakota. 563-586, *May 1947*
America on the Move. Photos by J. Baylor Roberts, B. Anthony Stewart, and others. 357-378, *Sept. 1946*
Camera Cruising in the Philippines. Photos by J. Baylor Roberts, Fenno Jacobs, and others. 545-552, *Nov. 1944*
Gulf Coast Towns Get into the Fight. 17-40, *Jan. 1944*
Work and Play in the Ozarks. Photos by B. Anthony Stewart and J. Baylor Roberts. 597-620, *May 1943*
Pacific Northwest: Where Fog and Sun Paint the Pacific. 437-460, *Oct. 1942*
Flavor and Savor of American Foods. Photos by J. Baylor Roberts, Willard R. Culver, and others. 289-320, *Mar. 1942*
Empire State Onions and Pageantry. Photos by J. Baylor Roberts and Volkmar Wentzel. 641-648, *Nov. 1941*
Singapore–Britain's Outpost of Empire. 665-672, *Nov. 1941*
North Carolina Colorcade. 189-220, *Aug. 1941*
Smiling, Happy Philippines. 425-448, *Oct. 1940*
Rubber: From Trees to Tires and Toys. Photos by Willard R. Culver and J. Baylor Roberts. 159-190, *Feb. 1940*
Corn and Color in the Hawkeye State. 151-174, *Aug. 1939*
Tennessee Tableaux. 569-592, *May 1939*
Pennsylvania Dutch–In a Land of Milk and Honey. 49-56, *July 1938*
Magnolia State Mosaic. 279-310, *Sept. 1937*
The Washington of Tradition Builds for the Future. Photos by J. Baylor Roberts and others. 671-694, *June 1937*

ROBERTS, JACK:
On Assignment. *Mar. 1988*

ROBERTS, MRS. KENNETH: *Author*
Sojourning in the Italy of Today. 351-396, *Sept. 1936*

ROBERTS, LEO B.: *Author*
Traveling in the Highlands of Ethiopia. 297-328, *Sept. 1935*

ROBERTS, MILNOR: *Author*
A Wonderland of Glaciers and Snow. 530-537, *June 1909*

ROBERTS, MURRAY: *Photographer*
The Threatened Ways of Kenya's Pokot People. By Elizabeth L. Meyerhoff. 120-140, *Jan. 1982*

ROBERTS, WALTER ORR: *Author*
We're Doing Something About the Weather! 518-555, *Apr. 1972*

ROBERTS, WILLIAM H.: *Author*
The Five Thousand Temples of Pagān: Burma's Sacred City Is a Place of Enchantment in the Midst of Ruins. 445-454, *Oct. 1931*

ROBERTSON, RUTH:
Author-Photographer
Jungle Journey to the World's Highest Waterfall. 655-690, *Nov. 1949*

ROBIN HOOD'S BAY, England:
Between the Heather and the North Sea: Bold English Headlands Once Sheltered Sea Robbers, Later Were Ports of Wooden Ships, Centers of the Jet and Alum Trades, To-day Are Havens of Adventurous Fishing Fleets. By Leo Walmsley. 197-232, *Feb. 1933*

ROBIN Sails Home. By Robin Lee Graham. 504-545, *Oct. 1970*

ROBINSON, ALBERT G.: *Author*
Cuban Railways. 108-110, *Mar. 1902*

ROBINSON, ANNE GROSVENOR: *Author*
Seattle, City of Two Voices. Photos by B. Anthony Stewart. 494-513, *Apr. 1960*

ROBINSON, G. D.: *Author*
Exploring Aleutian Volcanoes. 509-528, *Oct. 1948*

ROBINSON, H. W.: *Author*
The Hairnet Industry in North China. 327-336, *Sept. 1923*

ROBINSON, NANCY: *Author*
Alaskan Family Robinson. Photos by John Metzger and Peter Robinson. 55-75, *Jan. 1973*

ROBINSON, PETER: *Photographer*
Alaskan Family Robinson. By Nancy Robinson. Photos by John Metzger and Peter Robinson. 55-75, *Jan. 1973*

ROBOT AIRPLANES:
Air Power for Peace. By H. H. Arnold. 137-193, *Feb. 1946*

ROBOT BOMBS:
Air Power for Peace. By H. H. Arnold. 137-193, *Feb. 1946*
London Wins the Battle. By Marquis W. Childs. 129-152, *Aug. 1945*

ROBOTS:
The Chip: Electronic Mini-marvel. By Allen A. Boraiko. Photos by Charles O'Rear. 421-457, *Oct. 1982*
See also Jason Jr.

ROBOTS to the Moon. By Frank Sartwell. Paintings by Pierre Mion. 557-571, *Oct. 1962*

ROBSON, Mount, British Columbia, Canada:
The Monarch of the Canadian Rockies. By Charles D. Walcott. Included: The Monarch of the Canadian Rockies–Robson Peak (panorama). 626-639, *May 1913*

ROCHAMBEAU, JEAN-BAPTISTE DONATIEN DE VIMEUR, COMTE DE:
Our First Alliance. By J. J. Jusserand. 518-548, *June 1917*

ROCHESTER, New York:
Eastman of Rochester: Photographic Pioneer. By Allan C. Fisher, Jr. 423-438, *Sept. 1954*

ROCHFORD, DANIEL: *Author*
New England Ski Trails: Snow and Ice Sports Transform Whittier's Winters of Snowbound Seclusion Into Seasons of Outdoor Recreation. 645-664, *Nov. 1936*

ROCK, JOSEPH F.:
Author-Photographer
Sungmas, the Living Oracles of the Tibetan Church. Included: Demon-

Possessed Tibetans and Their Incredible Feats. 475-486, *Oct. 1935*

Konka Risumgongba, Holy Mountain of the Outlaws. Included: With the Devil Dancers of China and Tibet. 1-65, *July 1931*

The Glories of the Minya Konka: Magnificent Snow Peaks of the China-Tibetan Border Are Photographed at Close Range by a National Geographic Society Expedition. Included: Carrying the Color Camera Through Unmapped China. 385-437, *Oct. 1930*

Seeking the Mountains of Mystery: An Expedition on the China-Tibet Frontier to the Unexplored Amnyi Machen Range, One of Whose Peaks Rivals Everest. 131-185, *Feb. 1930*

Life Among the Lamas of Choni: Describing the Mystery Plays and Butter Festival in the Monastery of an Almost Unknown Tibetan Principality in Kansu Province, China. Included: Demon Dancers and Butter Gods of Choni. 569-619, *Nov. 1928*

Through the Great River Trenches of Asia: National Geographic Society Explorer Follows the Yangtze, Mekong, and Salwin Through Mighty Gorges, Some of Whose Canyon Walls Tower to a Height of More Than Two Miles. 133-186, *Aug. 1926*

Experiences of a Lone Geographer: An American Agricultural Explorer Makes His Way Through Brigand-infested Central China en Route to the Amne Machin Range, Tibet. 331-347, *Sept. 1925*

The Land of the Yellow Lama: National Geographic Society Explorer Visits the Strange Kingdom of Muli, Beyond the Likiang Snow Range of Yünnan Province, China. 447-491, *Apr. 1925*

Banishing the Devil of Disease Among the Nashi: Weird Ceremonies Performed by an Aboriginal Tribe in the Heart of Yünnan Province, China. 473-499, *Nov. 1924*

Hunting the Chaulmoogra Tree. 243-276, *Mar. 1922*

ROCK ART:

Oasis of Art in the Sahara. By Henri Lhote. Photos by Kazuyoshi Nomachi. Contents: Rock paintings of Tassili-n-Ajjer, Algeria. 180-191, *Aug. 1987*

Tanzania's Stone Age Art. By Mary D. Leakey. Photos by John Reader. 84-99, *July 1983*

Maya Art Treasures Discovered in Cave. By George E. Stuart. Photos by Wilbur E. Garrett. 220-235, *Aug. 1981*

Baja's Murals of Mystery. By Harry Crosby. Photos by Charles O'Rear. 692-702, *Nov. 1980*

Utah's Rock Art: Wilderness Louvre. A picture essay by Gary Smith, with Michael E. Long. 97-117, *Jan. 1980*

Man in the Amazon: Stone Age Present Meets Stone Age Past. By W. Jesco von Puttkamer. NGS research grant. 60-83, *Jan. 1979*

A Bold New Look at Our Past. The Editor. NGS research grant. 62-63, *Jan. 1975*

Exploring the Mind of Ice Age Man. By Alexander Marshack. NGS research grant. 64-89, *Jan. 1975*

Rock Paintings of the Aborigines. By Kay and Stanley Breeden. 174-187, *Feb. 1973*

Africa's Bushman Art Treasures. By Alfred Friendly. Photos by Alex R. Willcox. 848-865, *June 1963*

Exploring Stone Age Arnhem Land. By Charles P. Mountford. Photos by Howell Walker. Included: Cave

paintings of Oenpelli and Groote Eylandt, Australia. NGS research grant. 745-782, *Dec. 1949*

Lascaux Cave, Cradle of World Art. By Norbert Casteret. Photos by Maynard Owen Williams. Contents: La Baume Ladrone, La Henne Morte, La Mouthe, Lascaux, Montespan, Niaux, Trois Frères, Tuc D'Audoubert, in France; and Altamira in Spain. NGS research grant. 771-794, *Dec. 1948*

Discovering the Oldest Statues in the World: A Daring Explorer Swims Through a Subterranean River of the Pyrenees and Finds Rock Carvings Made 20,000 Years Ago. By Norbert Casteret. 123-152, *Aug. 1924*

See also Cave Art; Petroglyphs

ROCK CARVINGS:

Searching Out Medieval Churches in Ethiopia's Wilds. By Georg Gerster. 856-884, *Dec. 1970*

India's Sculptured Temple Caves. By Volkmar Wentzel. 665-678, *May 1953*

The Caves of the Thousand Buddhas. By Franc and Jean Shor. 383-415, *Mar. 1951*

Darius Carved History on Ageless Rock. By George G. Cameron. 825-844, *Dec. 1950*

China's Great Wall of Sculpture: Manhewn Caves and Countless Images Form a Colossal Art Wonder of Early Buddhism. By Mary Augusta Mullikin. Paintings by author and Anna M. Hotchkis. 313-348, *Mar. 1938*

See also Abu Simbel; Cappadocia; Petra

The **ROCK** City of Petra. By Franklin E. Hoskins. 283-291, *May 1907*

ROCK CLIMBING:

Climbing Half Dome the Hard Way. By Galen Rowell. 782-791, *June 1974*

We Climbed Utah's Skyscraper Rock. By Huntley Ingalls. Photos by author and Barry C. Bishop. 705-721, *Nov. 1962*

ROCK-LEDGE LIFE:

Life on a Rock Ledge. By William H. Amos. 558-566, *Oct. 1980*

The **ROCK** of Aden: The Volcanic Mountain Fortress, on the Sea Route from Suez to India, Assumes New Importance. By H.G.C. Swayne. 723-742, *Dec. 1935*

The **ROCK** of Gibraltar: Key to the Mediterranean. 376-391, *Sept. 1940*

ROCK PAINTINGS. *See* Rock Art

ROCKEFELLER, JOHN D., Jr.:
Author

The Genesis of the Williamsburg Restoration. 401, *Apr. 1937*

ROCKEFELLER, LAURANCE S.:

Board of Trustees, member. 647, 655, May 1958; 5, 46, 55, July 1966; 531, 533, Oct. 1966; 80, Jan. 1967; 588, Oct. 1967; 542, Apr. 1971; 227, *Aug. 1976*

Nomination Page. In the Virgin Islands. *Feb. 1958*

The father of popular photography, Eastman Kodak Company founder George Eastman, left, confers with the wizard of light, Thomas Edison, in 1928. EASTMAN HOUSE

Pilloried murderers from a Chinese dungeon were photographed in 1928 by legendary explorer Joseph Rock. JOSEPH F. ROCK

RODENTS:

RODEOS:

RODEY, B. S.: *Author*

RODGER, GEORGE:
Author-Photographer

RODGER, JINX: *Author*

RODNEY THE JAZZ BIRD (Balloon):

ROEBLING, JOHN A.:

ROEBLING, WASHINGTON A.:

A bighorn ram seeks an illegal handout on the Trans-Canada Highway in Banff National Park in the heart of the Canadian Rockies.   JIM BRANDENBURG

ROGERS, BERNARD F., Jr.:
Author-Photographer

The Mist and Sunshine of Ulster. 571-610, *Nov. 1935*

Photographer

Old Pattern and New in Turkey. 17-48, *Jan. 1939*

Caesar's City Today. Photos by Bernard F. Rogers, Jr. and Luigi Pellerano. 285-316, *Mar. 1937*

Green Gruyère, Home of a Swiss Cheese. 145-168, *Aug. 1936*

ROGERS, ELIE:
Nomination Page. *Apr. 1981*

ROGERS, G. SHERBURNE: *Author*
Helium, the New Balloon Gas. 441-456, *May 1919*

ROGERS, LESLEY:
Nomination Page. *Apr. 1981*

ROGERS, MARTIN: *Photographer*

The Incredible Potato. By Robert E. Rhoades. 668-694, *May 1982*

Belgium: One Nation Divisible. By James Cerruti. 314-341, *Mar. 1979*

Norway's Strategic Arctic Islands. By Gordon Young. 267-283, *Aug. 1978*

Giants That Move the World's Oil: Superships. By Noel Grove. 102-124, *July 1978*

Superspill: Black Day for Brittany. Text by Noel Grove. 124-135, *July 1978*

The Dominican Republic: Caribbean Comeback. By James Cerruti. 538-565, *Oct. 1977*

The Ohio—River With a Job to Do. By Priit J. Vesilind. 245-273, *Feb. 1977*

Baltimore: The Hidden City. By Fred Kline. 188-215, *Feb. 1975*

The Great Lakes: Is It Too Late? By Gordon Young. Photos by James L. Amos and Martin Rogers. 147-185, *Aug. 1973*

ROGERS, RICHARD K.:
On Assignment. *Nov. 1986*

ROGUES' Gallery of Imported Pests.
Paintings by Hashime Murayama. 237-244, *Aug. 1941*

ROHE, ALICE: *Author*
Our Littlest Ally. 139-163, *Aug. 1918*

ROLAND, ARTHUR (Pseudonym). *See*
Kilbon, Roland

ROMAN CATHOLICISM:

Vatican City. By James Fallows. Photos by James L. Stanfield. 723-775. Included: The Photographer's Perspective. By James L. Stanfield. 762-763; Treasures of the Vatican. Photos by James L. Stanfield and Victor R. Boswell, Jr. 764-775, *Dec. 1985*

The World of Martin Luther. By Merle Severy. Photos by James L. Amos. 418-463, *Oct. 1983*

Peru's Pilgrimage to the Sky. By Robert Randall. Photos by Loren McIntyre and Ira Block. Included: Syncretism of Indian beliefs and Roman Catholicism. 60-69, *July 1982*

Toledo—El Greco's Spain Lives On. By Louise E. Levathes. Photos by James P. Blair. 726-753, *June 1982*

⊕ The Face and Faith of Poland. Map,

Pope John Paul II delivers Easter tidings in 56 languages from the balcony of St. Peter's. JAMES L. STANFIELD, NGS

photo, and essay supplement. By Peter Miller. Essay by Czesław Miłosz. Photos by Bruno Barbey. *Apr. 1982*

Fátima: Beacon for Portugal's Faithful. By Jane Vessels. Photos by Bruno Barbey. 832-839, *Dec. 1980*

New Mexico's Mountains of Mystery. By Robert Laxalt. Photos by Craig Aurness. Included: Penitente sect of Sangre de Cristo. 416-436, *Sept. 1978*

St. Peter's, Rome's Church of Popes. By Aubrey Menen. Photos by Albert Moldvay. 865-879, *Dec. 1971*

Mesa del Nayar's Strange Holy Week. By Guillermo Aldana E. Included: Syncretism with Cora Indians' ancient religion. 780-795, *June 1971*

Rome: Eternal City with a Modern Air. By Harnett T. Kane. Photos by B. Anthony Stewart. 437-491, *Apr. 1957*

Caldy, the Monks' Island. By John E. H. Nolan. 564-578, *Oct. 1955*

The Smallest State in the World: Vatican City on Its 108 Acres Is a Complete Sovereignty Internationally

Recognized. By W. Coleman Nevils. Included: Vatican City: Treasure House of the Ages. 377-412, *Mar. 1939*

ROMAN EMPIRE:

The Day the World Ended at Kourion. By David Soren. Photos by Martha Cooper. NGS research grant. 30-53, *July 1988*

The Eternal Etruscans. By Rick Gore. Photos by O. Louis Mazzatenta. Paintings by James M. Gurney. 696-743, *June 1988*

A Buried Roman Town Gives Up Its Dead. By Joseph Judge. Photos by Jonathan Blair. Contents: Herculaneum. NGS research grant. 687-693, *Dec. 1982*

Ancient Aphrodisias Lives Through Its Art. By Kenan T. Erim. Photos by David Brill. NGS research grant. 527-551, *Oct. 1981*

Down the Ancient Appian Way. By James Cerruti. Photos by O. Louis Mazzatenta. 714-747, *June 1981*

▌▌ *Greece and Rome: Builders of Our World.* 448 pages. *1968*

A New Look at Medieval Europe. By Kenneth M. Setton. Paintings by Andre Durenceau and Birney Lettick. 799-859, *Dec. 1962*

Roman Life in 1,600-year-old Color Pictures. By Gino Vinicio Gentili. Photos by Duncan Edwards. 211-229, *Feb. 1957*

⊕ Classical Lands of the Mediterranean. *Dec. 1949*

The Roman Way. By Edith Hamilton. 545-565, *Nov. 1946*

Ancient Rome Brought to Life. By Rhys Carpenter. Paintings by H. M. Herget. Contents: Before Rome Was Founded.—Etruscan Funeral.—Etruscan Festival.—Bridge over the Tiber.—Market and Wharf at a Roman Port.—At the Slave Market.—The Roman Army Crosses Alcántara in Spain.—Siege of a Walled City.—Triumphal Procession.—Unconditional Surrender.—An Embassy to Caligula.—An Empress Makes Ready.—In the Gardens of Lucullus.—A Distinguished Dinner Party.—Horace's Villa in the Sabine Hills.—Interior of a Rich Man's House.—Vegetable Market.—Tunisian Farm.—Street Scene in Pompeii.—In a Pompeian Tavern.—Seaside Villas.—Roman Baths: Tepidarium.—Furnaces Beneath the Baths.—Worship of Isis.—Rehearsal for the Mysteries.—Sacrifice of the "Suovetaurilia."—In a Court of Law.—The Library in Timgad.—At the Theater.—Sea Battle in the Arena.—Diocletian's Palace at Spalato.—Dusk on the Street of Tombs. 567-633, *Nov. 1946*

⊕ Classical Lands of the Mediterranean. Included: Inset of the Roman Empire at the time of Trajan. *Mar. 1940*

Augustus—Emperor and Architect: Two Thousand Years Ago Was Born the Physically Frail But Spiritually Great Roman Who Became the Master of His World. By W. Coleman Nevils. 535-556, *Oct. 1938*

The Perennial Geographer: After 2,000 Years Vergil Is Still the Most Widely Read of Latin Poets–First to Popularize the Geography of the Roman Empire. By W. Coleman Nevils. 439-465, *Oct. 1930*

The Isle of Capri: An Imperial Residence and Probable Wireless Station of Ancient Rome. By John A. Kingman. 213-231, *Sept. 1919*

Geographic Progress of Civilization. Annual Address by the President, Gardiner G. Hubbard. 1-22, *Feb. 14, 1894*

See also Byzantine Empire

ROMAN RUINS:

Caesarea Maritima. By Robert L. Hohlfelder. Photos by Bill Curtsinger. Paintings by J. Robert Teringo. NGS research grant. 261-279, *Feb. 1987*

◼ In the Shadow of Vesuvius. President's Page. By Gilbert M. Grosvenor. Jan. 1987; cover, *Feb. 1987*

The Dead Do Tell Tales at Vesuvius. By Rick Gore. Photos by O. Louis Mazzatenta. NGS research grant. 557-613, *May 1984*

Down the Ancient Appian Way. By James Cerruti. Photos by O. Louis Mazzatenta. 714-747, *June 1981*

Yankee Cruises the Storied Nile. By Irving and Electa Johnson. Photos by Winfield Parks. 583-633, *May 1965*

A Stroll to London. By Isobel Wylie Hutchison. Photos by B. Anthony Stewart. 171-204, *Aug. 1950*

The British Way: Great Britain's Major Gifts to Freedom, Democratic Government, Science, and Society. By Sir Evelyn Wrench. 421-541, *Apr. 1949*

Italy's Monuments Tell Rome's Magnificence. Photos by B. Anthony Stewart. 371-378, *Mar. 1940*

Augustus–Emperor and Architect: Two Thousand Years Ago Was Born the Physically Frail But Spiritually Great Roman Who Became the Master of His World. By W. Coleman Nevils. 535-556, *Oct. 1938*

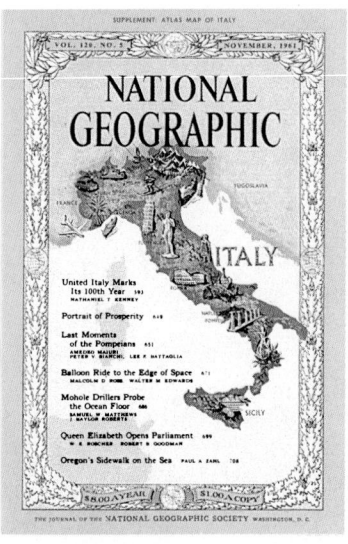

The Splendor of Rome. By Florence Craig Albrecht. 593-626, *June 1922*

The Isle of Capri: An Imperial Residence and Probable Wireless Station of Ancient Rome. By John A. Kingman. 213-231, *Sept. 1919*

See also Aphrodisias; Pompeii

The **ROMANCE** of American Furs. By Wanda Burnett. 379-402, *Mar. 1948*

ROMANCE OF DISCOVERY SERIES:

The "Map of Discovery" (Western Hemisphere). Painting by N. C. Wyeth, National Geographic Society, Washington, D. C. Supplement, *Jan. 1929*

The "Map of Discovery" (Eastern Hemisphere). Painting by N. C. Wyeth, National Geographic Society, Washington, D. C. Supplement, *Nov. 1928*

The Caravels of Columbus. Painting by N. C. Wyeth, National Geographic Society, Washington, D. C. Supplement, *July 1928*

Commander Byrd at the North Pole (Through Pathless Skies to the North Pole). Painting by N. C. Wyeth, National Geographic Society, Washington, D. C. Supplement, *May 1928*

The Discoverer. Painting by N. C. Wyeth, National Geographic Society, Washington, D. C. Supplement, *Mar. 1928*

The **ROMANCE** of Military Insignia: How the United States Government Recognizes Deeds of Heroism and Devotion to Duty. By Robert E. Wyllie. 463-501, *Dec. 1919*

The **ROMANCE** of Science in Polynesia: An Account of Five Years of Cruising Among the South Sea Islands. By Robert Cushman Murphy. Paintings by Hashime Murayama. 355-426, *Oct. 1925*

The **ROMANCE** of the Geographic: National Geographic Magazine Observes Its Diamond Anniversary. By Gilbert Hovey Grosvenor. 516-585, *Oct. 1963*

ROMANCE of the Sea. Contents: Maritime history. 312 pages. *1981*

ROMANCHE TRENCH, Atlantic Ocean:

Calypso Explores an Undersea Canyon. By Jacques-Yves Cousteau. Photos by Bates Littlehales. NGS research grant. 373-396, *Mar. 1958*

ROMANIA:

The Danube: River of Many Nations, Many Names. By Mike Edwards. Photos by Winfield Parks. 455-485, *Oct. 1977*

Romania: Maverick on a Tightrope. By William S. Ellis. Photos by Winfield Parks. 688-713, *Nov. 1975*

Americans Afoot in Rumania. By Dan Dimancescu. Photos by Dick Durrance II and Christopher G. Knight. 810-845, *June 1969*

Down the Danube by Canoe. By William Slade Backer. Photos by Richard S. Durrance and Christopher G. Knight. 34-79, *July 1965*

🌐 *The Balkans*. Atlas series. *Feb. 1962*

Caviar Fishermen of Romania: From Vâlcov, "Little Venice" of the Danube Delta, Bearded Russian Exiles Go Down to the Sea. By Dorothy Hosmer. 407-434, *Mar. 1940*

An American Girl Cycles Across Romania: Two-wheel Pilgrim Pedals the Land of Castles and Gypsies, Where Roman Empire Traces Mingle With Remnants of Oriental Migration. By Dorothy Hosmer. 557-588, *Nov. 1938*

The Spell of Romania: An American Woman's Narrative of Her Wanderings Among Colorful People and Long-Hidden Shrines. By Henrietta Allen Holmes. Included: Romania, Land of Color and Contrast. Photos by Wilhelm Tobien. 399-450, *Apr. 1934*

Columbus sails to the New World in one of five murals at Society headquarters painted by N. C. Wyeth and published as "The Romance of Discovery." PAINTING BY N. C. WYETH

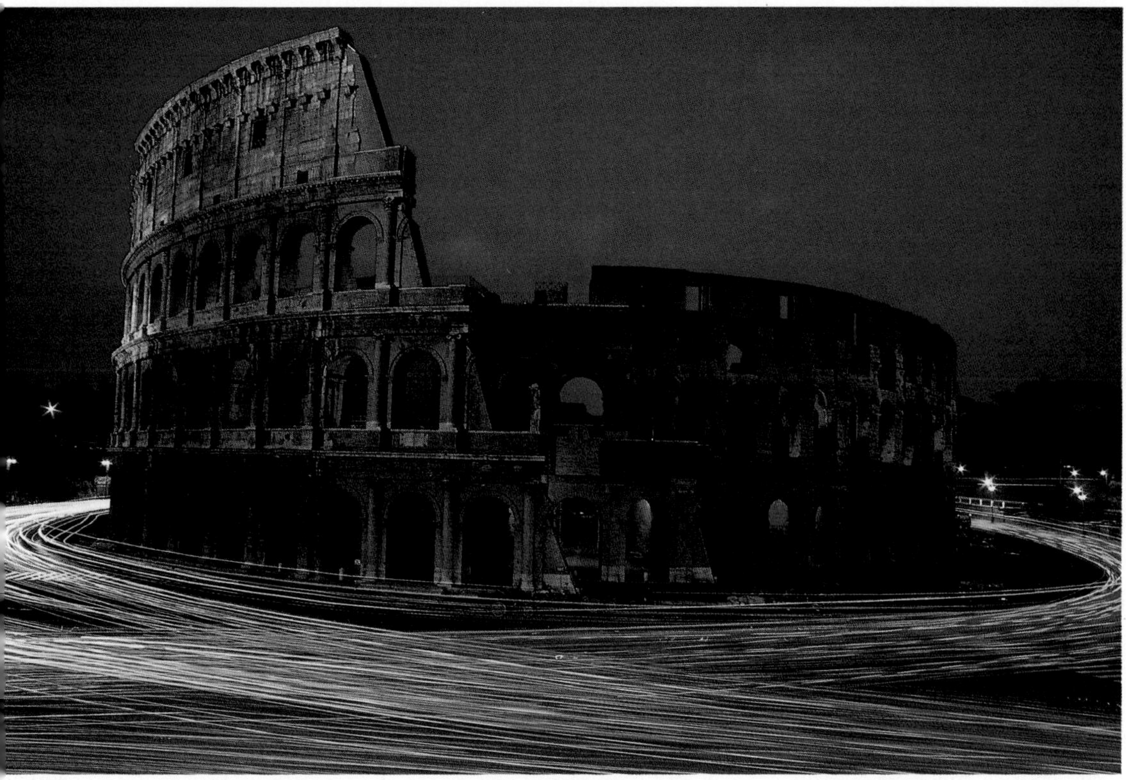

Ringed at rush hour in a time exposure, Rome's Colosseum today witnesses contests by cars instead of gladiators. WINFIELD PARKS, NGS

Theodore Roosevelt preached conservation of forests and wildlife. THEODORE
ROOSEVELT COLLECTION, HARVARD COLLEGE LIBRARY

The Living White House. By Lonnelle Aikman. 593-643, *Nov. 1966*

Profiles of the Presidents: IV. America Enters the Modern Era. By Frank Freidel. 537-577, *Oct. 1965*

Inside the White House. By Lonnelle Aikman. Photos by B. Anthony Stewart and Thomas Nebbia. 3-43, *Jan. 1961*

Theodore Roosevelt: a Centennial Tribute. By Bart McDowell. 572-590, *Oct. 1958*

North Dakota Comes into Its Own. By Leo A. Borah. Photos by J. Baylor Roberts. Included: Roosevelt's log cabin, now a museum on the State Capitol grounds. 283-322, *Sept. 1951*

The Roosevelt African Trophies. 103-106, *Jan. 1911*

Mr. Roosevelt's "African Game Trails." 953-962, *Nov. 1910*

National Geographic Society (Cables and Report by Theodore Roosevelt on the African Expedition). 365-370, *Apr. 1910*

Lessons from China (From President Roosevelt's Message to Congress, December 8, 1908). 18-29, *Jan. 1909*

Honors to Peary (Address by President Roosevelt). 49-60, *Jan. 1907*

Forests Vital to Our Welfare (From an Address by President Roosevelt). 515-516, *Nov. 1905*

Cotton and the Chinese Boycott (From an Address by President Roosevelt). 516-517, *Nov. 1905*

Author
How Old Is Man? 111-127, *Feb. 1916*
Wild Man and Wild Beast in Africa. 1-33, *Jan. 1911*

ROOSEVELT (Ship):
Commander Peary's New Vessel. 192, *Apr. 1905*

ROOSEVELT DAM, Arizona:
The Spirit of the West: The Wonderful

Agricultural Development Since the Dawn of Irrigation. By C. J. Blanchard. 333-360, *Apr. 1910*

Home-Making by the Government: An Account of the Eleven Immense Irrigating Projects to be Opened in 1908. By C. J. Blanchard. 250-287, *Apr. 1908*

The Highest Dam in the World. 440-441, *Sept. 1905*

ROOT, A. I.: *Author*
Our Friends, the Bees. By A. I. and E. R. Root. 675-694, *July 1911*

ROOT, ALAN: *Photographer*
Mzima, Kenya's Spring of Life. Photos by Joan and Alan Root. 350-373, *Sept. 1971*

Inside a Hornbill's Walled-up Nest. Photos by Joan and Alan Root. 846-855, *Dec. 1969*

The Galapagos, Eerie Cradle of New Species. By Roger Tory Peterson. Photos by Alan and Joan Root. 541-585, *Apr. 1967*

Freeing Flamingos From Anklets of Death. By John G. Williams. 934-944, *Dec. 1963*

ROOT, E. R.: *Author*
Our Friends, the Bees. By A. I. and E. R. Root. 675-694, *July 1911*

ROOT, ELIHU: *Author*
An Awakened Continent to the South of Us. 61-72, *Jan. 1907*

Reasons Why the United States in Particular Should Encourage the Pan-American Conferences. 479-480, *Aug. 1906*

ROOT, JOAN: *Photographer*
Mzima, Kenya's Spring of Life. Photos by Joan and Alan Root. 350-373, *Sept. 1971*

Inside a Hornbill's Walled-up Nest. Photos by Joan and Alan Root. 846-855, *Dec. 1969*

The Galapagos, Eerie Cradle of New Species. By Roger Tory Peterson. Photos by Alan and Joan Root. 541-585, *Apr. 1967*

RORAIMA, Mount, Brazil-Colombia-Guyana:
Through Brazil to the Summit of Mount Roraima. By G.H.H. Tate. 585-605, *Nov. 1930*

Kaieteur and Roraima: The Great Falls and the Great Mountain of the Guianas. By Henry Edward Crampton. 227-244, *Sept. 1920*

ROSA, Monte, Alps:
A Woman's Climbs in the High Alps. By Dora Keen. 643-675, *July 1911*

ROSALES, LOUISE, MARCHESA DE:
Author
Letters from the Italian Front. By Marchesa Louise de Rosales to Ethel Mather Bagg. 47-67, *July 1917*

ROSCHER, W. E.: *Author*
Queen Elizabeth Opens Parliament. Photos by Robert B. Goodman. 699-707, *Nov. 1961*

ROSE APHIDS. By Treat Davidson. 851-859, *June 1961*

The **ROSE-RED** City of Rock. Photos by G. E. Matson. Contents: Petra, Jordan. 145-160, *Feb. 1935*

ROSEATE SPOONBILLS:
Roseate Spoonbills, Radiant Birds of the Gulf Coast. By Robert Porter Allen. Photos by Frederick Kent Truslow. 274-288, *Feb. 1962*

Saving Man's Wildlife Heritage. By John H. Baker. Photos by Robert F. Sisson. 581-620, *Nov. 1954*

The Pink Birds of Texas. By Paul A. Zahl. 641-654, *Nov. 1949*

The Large Wading Birds: Long Legs and Immense Beaks, as Well as Size, Form, and Color, Distinguish the Herons, Ibises, and Flamingos. By T. Gilbert Pearson. Painting by Allan Brooks. 441-469, *Oct. 1932*

ROSENQUIST, GARY:
Mountain With a Death Wish. By Rowe Findley. Included: Gary Rosenquist's photos of Mount St. Helens' eruption taken just before he fled the area. 3-33, *Jan. 1981*

ROSES:
Amateur Gardener Creates a New Rose. By Elizabeth A. Moize. Photos by Farrell Grehan. Contents: Portrait rose. 286-294, *Aug. 1972*

Focusing on the Tournament of Roses. By B. Anthony Stewart and J. Baylor Roberts. 805-816, *June 1954*

Patent Plants Enrich Our World. By Orville H. Kneen. Photos from U. S. Plant Patents. 357-378, *Mar. 1948*

Bulgaria's Valley of Roses. Photos by Wilhelm Tobien and Georg Paskoff. Included: Rose oil industry. 187-194, *Aug. 1932*

ROSIE O'GRADY (Helium Balloon):
The Long, Lonely Flight. By Joe W. Kittinger, Jr. Contents: Transatlantic solo. 270-276, *Feb. 1985*

ROSIER CREEK, Virginia:
A Good Life on the Potomac. By James L. Stanfield. 470-479, *Oct. 1976*

ROSS, ANNE:
Nomination Page. *May 1977*

ROSS, EDWARD S.:
Nomination Page. *May 1969*
Nomination Page. *Feb. 1965*

Author
Hunting Africa's Smallest Game. 406-419, *Mar. 1961*

Author-Photographer
Mantids, the Praying Predators. Photos by Dwight Kuhn and the author. 268-280, *Feb. 1984*

Asian Insects in Disguise. 433-439, *Sept. 1965*

Birds That "See" in the Dark With Their Ears. 282-290, *Feb. 1965*

Photographer
Saving the World's Largest Flower. By Willem Meijer. Contents: *Rafflesia*

---

arnoldii. NGS research grant. 136-140, *July 1985*

Crossroads of the Insect World. By J. W. MacSwain. 844-857, *Dec. 1966*

ROSS, JOHN W.:

Gardiner Greene Hubbard: Memorial Meeting. Address by John W. Ross. 66-67, *Feb. 1898*

ROSS, KIP: *Author-Photographer*

South Africa Close-up. 641-681, *Nov. 1962*

We Drove Panama's Darién Gap. 368-389, *Mar. 1961*

Chile, the Long and Narrow Land. 185-235, *Feb. 1960*

Peru, Homeland of the Warlike Inca. 421-462, *Oct. 1950*

Photographer

Mexico in Motion. By Bart McDowell. 490-537, *Oct. 1961*

ROSS, MALCOLM D.: *Author*

North Carolina, Dixie Dynamo. Photos by B. Anthony Stewart. 141-183, *Feb. 1962*

We Saw the World From the Edge of Space. Ground photos by Walter Meayers Edwards. 671-685, *Nov. 1961*

My Neighbors Hold to Mountain Ways. Photos by Flip Schulke. 856-880, *June 1958*

To 76,000 Feet by *Strato-Lab* Balloon. By Malcolm D. Ross and M. Lee Lewis. 269-282, *Feb. 1957*

ROTARY CLUBS:

New missions for old magazines.

President's Page. By Gilbert M. Grosvenor. *May 1987*

ROTCH, A. LAWRENCE: *Author*

Project for the Exploration of the Atmosphere Over the Tropical Oceans. 430, *Oct. 1904*

ROTH, TOM and TOMMY:

Down Mark Twain's River on a Raft. By Rex E. Hieronymus. 551-574, *Apr. 1948*

ROTHENBURG, West Germany:

"Around the World in Eighty Days." By Newman Bumstead. Included: Darmstadt; Frankfurt; Rothenburg. 705-750, *Dec. 1951*

Rothenburg, the City Time Forgot. By Charles W. Beck, Jr. 184-194, *Feb. 1926*

ROTHSCHILD'S GIRAFFE:

Rescuing the Rothschild. By Carolyn Bennett Patterson. 419-421, *Sept. 1977*

ROTIFERS: Nature's Water Purifiers. By John Walsh. 287-292, *Feb. 1979*

ROTTERDAM, The Netherlands:

Rotterdam–Reborn From Ruins. By Helen Hill Miller. Photos by James Blair. 526-553, *Oct. 1960*

Holland Rises from War and Water. By Thomas R. Henry. 237-260, *Feb. 1946*

ROUEN, France:

The Coasts of Normandy and Brittany.

Ghostly and graceful underwater, a hippopotamus investigates a tunnel of vegetation in Mzima Springs, part of Kenya's Tsavo National Park.   ALAN ROOT

By W. Robert Moore. 205-232, *Aug. 1943*

The Beauties of France. By Arthur Stanley Riggs. 391-491, *Nov. 1915*

ROUGHEST Road Race: the Mexican 1000. By Michael E. Long. 569-575, *Oct. 1972*

ROUGHLEY, T. C.: *Author*

Bounty Descendants Live on Remote Norfolk Island. Photos by J. Baylor Roberts. 559-584, *Oct. 1960*

Author-Photographer

Where Nature Runs Riot: On Australia's Great Barrier Reef Marine Animals Grow to Unusual Size, Develop Strange Weapons of Attack and Defense, and Acquire Brilliant Colors. Included: Fantastic Dwellers in a Coral Fairyland. 823-850, *June 1940*

ROUMANIA. *See* Romania

ROUMANIA, the Pivotal State. By James Howard Gore. 360-390, *Oct. 1915*

ROUMANIA and Its Rubicon. By John Oliver La Gorce. 185-202, *Sept. 1916*

ROUND About Asheville. By Bailey Willis. 291-300, *Oct. 1889*

ROUND About Bogotá: A Hunt for New Fruits and Plants Among the Mountain Forests of Colombia's Unique Capital. By Wilson Popenoe. 127-160, *Feb. 1926*

ROUND About Grim Tarawa. Photos by W. Robert Moore. 137-160, *Feb. 1945*

ROUND About Liechtenstein: A Tiny Principality Which the Visitor May Encompass in a Single View Affords Adventurous Climbs Among Steep Pastures and Quaint Villages. By Maynard Owen Williams. 611-634, *Nov. 1927*

The **ROUND** Earth on Flat Paper: Map ■■ Projections Used By Cartographers. By Wellman Chamberlin. Art by Charles E. Riddiford. 126 pages. *1947*

'**ROUND** the Horn by Submarine. By Paul C. Stimson. 129-144, *Jan. 1948*

ROUND THE WORLD SCHOOL. By Paul Antze. Photos by William Eppridge. 96-127, *July 1962*

A **ROUND** Trip to Davy Jones's Locker: Peering into Mysteries a Quarter Mile Down in the Open Sea, by Means of the Bathysphere. By William Beebe. Paintings by E. Bostelmann. 653-678, *June 1931*

ROUNDING the Horn in a Windjammer. By A. J. Villiers. 191-224, *Feb. 1931*

ROUNDUPS:

Wild Elephant Roundup in India. By Harry Miller. Photos by author and James P. Blair. 372-385, *Mar. 1969*

See also Cattle Raising; Reindeer

The **ROUTE** Over Which Moses Led the Children of Israel Out of Egypt.

Q
R

By Franklin E. Hoskins. 1011-1038, *Dec. 1909*

ROUTLEDGE, MRS. SCORESBY:
Author

The Mystery of Easter Island. 629-646, *Dec. 1921*

ROVER (Lunar Vehicle):

Exploring Taurus-Littrow. By Harrison H. Schmitt. Photos by the crew of Apollo 17. 290-307, *Sept. 1973*

What Is It Like to Walk on the Moon? By David R. Scott. 326-331, *Sept. 1973*

Apollo 15 Explores the Mountains of the Moon. By Kenneth F. Weaver. Photos from NASA. 233-265, *Feb. 1972*

Detailed diagram of Rover. 148, *July 1971*

ROVING Maryland's Cavalier Country. By William A. Kinney. 431-470, *Apr. 1954*

ROWELL, BARBARA CUSHMAN:
Photographer

Baltistan–The 20th Century Comes to Shangri-la. By Galen Rowell. Photos by the author and Barbara Cushman Rowell. Included: War among the peaks. 526-550, *Oct. 1987*

ROWELL, GALEN:
Author-Photographer

Baltistan–The 20th Century Comes to Shangri-la. Photos by the author and Barbara Cushman Rowell. Included: War among the peaks. 526-550, *Oct. 1987*

Nomads of China's West. Photos by the author and Harold A. Knutson. Included: The climb of Anyemaqen. 244-263, *Feb. 1982*

Climbing Half Dome the Hard Way. 782-791, *June 1974*

Photographer

Heavy Hands on the Land. By Larry Kohl. Photos by William Thompson and Galen Rowell. 633-651, *Nov. 1988*

Long Journey of the Brahmaputra. By Jere Van Dyk. Photos by Raghubir Singh and Galen Rowell. Included: A Rare Visit to a World Unto Itself. 672-711, *Nov. 1988*

American Skiers Find Adventure in Western China. By Ned Gillette. Photos by the author and Galen Rowell. Included: Skiing From the Summit of China's Ice Mountain. 174-199, *Feb. 1981*

California's Parched Oasis, the Owens Valley. By Judith and Neil Morgan. Photos by Jodi Cobb and Galen Rowell. 98-127, *Jan. 1976*

ROWLEE, W. W.:

List of Plants Collected near Muir Glacier, determined by W. W. Rowlee. 79, *Mar. 21, 1892*

ROY, LEONARD C.: *Author*

Menhaden–Uncle Sam's Top Commercial Fish. Photos by Robert F. Sisson. 813-823, *June 1949*

Tarheelia on Parade: Versatile and Vibrant, North Carolina in a Genera-

Soil sampler in hand, an astronaut leaps into the battery-powered rover to explore the moon during Apollo 17, last of that mission series.   NASA/APOLLO 17 CREW

tion Has Climbed New Economic Heights. 181-224, *Aug. 1941*

Highlights of the Volunteer State: Men and Industry in Tennessee Range from Pioneer Stages to Modern Machine Age. 553-594, *May 1939*

From Notch to Notch in the White Mountains: Soaring Heights of New Hampshire Attract Multitudes to America's Oldest Mountain Recreation Area. 73-104, *July 1937*

Rambling Around the Roof of Eastern America. 243-266, *Aug. 1936*

ROYAL ACADEMY OF ARTS,
London:

Our Search for British Paintings. By Franklin L. Fisher. 543-550, *Apr. 1949*

ROYAL AIR FORCE (RAF):
Airlift to Berlin. 595-614, *May 1949*

ROYAL BOTANIC GARDENS,
England:

Kew: The Commoners' Royal Garden. By Thomas Garner James. Photos by B. Anthony Stewart. 479-506, *Apr. 1950*

ROYAL Copenhagen, Capital of a Farming Kingdom: A Fifth of Denmark's Thrifty Population Resides in a Metropolis Famous for Its Porcelains, Its Silver, and Its Lace. By J. R. Hildebrand. 217-250, *Feb. 1932*

ROYAL GEOGRAPHICAL SOCIETY,
London:

Medal presented to A. W. Greely. Frontispiece, June 1896; 355, *Oct. 1901*

The British Antarctic Expedition (Instructions given by the Presidents of the Royal Society and the Royal Geographical Society to Capt. Scott and Dr. George Murray). 339-345, *Sept. 1901*

Medals presented to Sven Hedin and Robert E. Peary. 342, *July 1898*

A Geographical Description of the British Islands. By W. M. Davis. 208-211, *June 1896*

Expeditions. *See* British Mount Everest Expedition

ROYAL House for Dolls. By David Jeffery. Photos by James L. Stanfield. 632-643, *Nov. 1980*

ROYAL Pomp Before Debate: In Centuries-old Ceremonial, the Queen Opens Parliament. 730-732, *Dec. 1986*

The **ROYAL** Spoonbill. By M. Philip Kahl. NGS research grant. 281-284, *Feb. 1987*

ROYAL Wedding at Jaisalmer. By Marilyn Silverstone. 66-79, *Jan. 1965*

ROYALE, Isle, Michigan. *See* Isle Royale National Park

ROYALTY at Work. Photos by John Everingham. 486-499, *Oct. 1982*

ROYCE, W. ALLAN:
On Assignment. *June 1983*
Nomination Page. *Aug. 1980*
Nomination Page. *Aug. 1977*

ROZUMALSKI, TED: *Photographer*
Wisconsin's Door Peninsula. By William S. Ellis. 347-371, *Mar. 1969*

RUANDA (Region), Belgian Congo:
A Land of Giants and Pygmies. By the Duke Adolphus Frederick of Mecklenburg. 369-388, *Apr. 1912*
See also Virunga Mountains

RUBBER:
Rediscovering America's Forgotten Crops. By Noel D. Vietmeyer. Photos by Burgess Blevins. Paintings by Paul M. Breeden. Included: Guayule rubber. 702-712, *May 1981*
Our Most Versatile Vegetable Product: Rubber Drops from Millions of Tropical Trees Are Transformed by Genii Chemists into Myriad Articles, from Tires to Teething Rings. By J. R. Hildebrand. Included: From Trees to Tires and Toys. Photos by Willard R. Culver and J. Baylor Roberts. 143-200, *Feb. 1940*
The Amazon, Father of Waters: The Earth's Mightiest River Drains a Basin of More Than 2,700,000 Square Miles, from Which Came Originally the World's Finest Rubber. By W. L. Schurz. 445-463, *Apr. 1926*
Singapore, Crossroads of the East: The World's Greatest Mart for Rubber and Tin Was in Recent Times a Pirate-haunted, Tiger-infested Jungle Isle. By Frederick Simpich. 235-269, *Mar. 1926*
Rubber Plantations in Mexico and Central America. 409-414, *Nov. 1903*
Rubber Forests of Nicaragua and Sierra Leone. By A. W. Greely. 83-88, *Mar. 1897*

RUBBER-CUSHIONED Liberia. By Henry S. Villard. Photos by Charles W. Allmon. 201-228, *Feb. 1948*

RUBIES:
Questing for Gems. By George S. Switzer. 835-863, *Dec. 1971*

RUDLOE, ANNE and JACK: *Authors*
The Changeless Horseshoe Crab. Photos by Robert F. Sisson. 562-572, *Apr. 1981*
Trouble in Bayou Country: Louisiana's Atchafalaya. Photos by C. C. Lockwood. 377-397, *Sept. 1979*
Our Wild and Scenic Rivers: The Suwannee. Photos by Jodi Cobb. 20-29, *July 1977*

RUDOLF, Lake, Kenya:
Skull 1470. By Richard E. Leakey. Photos by Bob Campbell. 819-829, *June 1973*
In Search of Man's Past at Lake Rudolf. By Richard E. Leakey. Photos by Gordon W. Gahan. NGS research grant. 712-734, *May 1970*
See also present name, Turkana, Lake

RUGGED Is the Word for Bravo. By Phillip M. Swatek. 829-843, *Dec. 1955*

RUGS:
Afghanistan: Crossroad of Conquerors. By Thomas J. Abercrombie. 297-345, *Sept. 1968*
Journey into Troubled Iran. By George W. Long. Photos by J. Baylor Roberts. 425-464, *Oct. 1951*
The Idyllic Vale of Kashmir. By Volkmar Wentzel. 523-550, *Apr. 1948*
See also Kashgai Tribespeople; Navajo Indians; Turkomans

RUHEN, OLAF: *Author*
■■ *Isles of the South Pacific.* By Maurice Shadbolt and Olaf Ruhen. 211 pages. *1968*

RUHR RIVER AND VALLEY, West Germany:
With Uncle Sam and John Bull in Germany. By Frederick Simpich. 117-140, *Jan. 1949*
The Story of the Ruhr. By Frederick Simpich. 553-564, *May 1922*

The **RUINED** Cities of Asia Minor. By Ernest L. Harris. 741-760, *Nov. 1908*

RUINS. See Angkor; Athens; Machu Picchu; Pagan; Persepolis; Roman Ruins; Stonehenge; Zimbabwe (Ruins); *and* Archaeology

The **RUINS** at Selinus. By Marion Crawford. 117, *Jan. 1909*

The **RUINS** of an Ancient Inca Capital, Machu Picchu. Panorama. *Apr. 1913*

RUINS of Cuicuilco May Revolutionize Our History of Ancient America: Lofty Mound Sealed and Preserved by Great Lava Flow for Perhaps Seventy Centuries Is Now Being Excavated in Mexico. By Byron Cummings. 203-220, *Aug. 1923*

RULE, MARGARET: *Author*
Henry VIII's Lost Warship: *Mary Rose.* Introduction and picture text by Peter Miller. Paintings by Richard Schlecht. 646-675, *May 1983*

RULES for the Orthography of Geographic Names. By Gustave Herrle. 279-285, *Aug. 1890*

RUMANIA. See Romania

RUMANIA and Her Ambitions. By Frederick Moore. 1057-1085, *Oct. 1913*

RUMANIAN Peasant Girl. Enlargement for framing. 1084, Oct. 1913; 467, *Dec. 1918*

RUMBUR VALLEY, Pakistan:
Pakistan's Kalash: People of Fire and Fervor. By Debra Denker. Photos by Steve McCurry. 458-473, *Oct. 1981*

RUMELI HISSAR (Castle), Turkey:
American Alma Maters in the Near East. By Maynard Owen Williams. 237-256, *Aug. 1945*

RUMTEK MONASTERY, Gangtok, Sikkim:
Gangtok, Cloud-wreathed Himalayan

Capital. By John Scofield. 698-713, *Nov. 1970*

RUNNING the Jökulsá á Fjöllum, Iceland's Wild Glacier-born River. By Paul Vander-Molen. Photos by Robert Grégoire and Jean-Luc Chéron. 306-321, *Sept. 1984*

RUOHOMAA, KOSTI: *Photographer*
Maine's Lobster Island, Monhegan. By William P. E. Graves. 285-298, *Feb. 1959*

RUPERT HOUSE, Quebec, Canada:
The Changing World of Canada's Crees. By Fred Ward. 541-569, *Apr. 1975*

RURAL Britain Carries On. By Harvey Klemmer. 527-552, *Oct. 1941*

RURAL Hungarian Rhapsody. Photos by Rudolf Balogh and Hans Hildenbrand. 17-48, *Jan. 1938*

RURAL Scenes in Brittany. 11-26, *July 1923*

RURAL Sweden Through American Eyes: A Visitor in Peacetime Finds Warmth, Welcome, and Strange Folkways On a Century-old Farm. By Elizabeth W. Nilson. 795-822, *June 1940*

RUS:
Viking Trail East. By Robert Paul Jordan. Photos by Jim Brandenburg. Paintings by Michael A. Hampshire. 278-317, *Mar. 1985*

RUSCHI, AUGUSTO:
Nomination Page. In Brazil. *Mar. 1971*
The Man Who Talks to Hummingbirds. By Luis Marden. Photos by James Blair. 80-99, *Jan. 1963*

RUSHMORE, Mount, South Dakota:
Back to the Historic Black Hills. By Leland D. Case. Photos by Bates Littlehales. 479-509, *Oct. 1956*
South Dakota Keeps Its West Wild. By Frederick Simpich. 555-588, *May 1947*

RUSSELL, CARL P.: *Author*
The White Sands of Alamogordo: A Dry Ocean of Granular Gypsum Billows Under Desert Winds in a New National Playground. 250-264, *Aug. 1935*

RUSSELL, CHARLES MARION:
C. M. Russell, Cowboy Artist. By Bart McDowell. Photos by Sam Abell. 60-95, *Jan. 1986*

RUSSELL, ISRAEL C.:
Volcanic Rocks of Martinique and St. Vincent: Collected by Robert T. Hill and Israel C. Russell. By J. S. Diller. 285-296, *July 1902*
The National Geographic Society Expedition to Martinique and St. Vincent. 183-184, *June 1902*
The National Geographic Society Expedition in the West Indies. 209-213, *June 1902*
Board of Managers. 218-219, *June 1902*
Mount St. Elias Expedition, the Society's first scientific exploration,

A cascade of weathered ice spills from a 14-square-mile glacier in Russia's Greater Caucasus Mountains. VITTORIO SELLA

RUSSIA of the Hour: Giant Battle Ground for Theories of Economy, Society, and Politics, as Observed by an Unbiased Correspondent. By Junius B. Wood. 519-598, *Nov. 1926*

RUSSIAN ORTHODOX CHURCH:

The Byzantine Empire: Rome of the East. By Merle Severy. Photos by James L. Stanfield. 709-767, *Dec. 1983*

Nikolaevsk: A Bit of Old Russia Takes Root in Alaska. By Jim Rearden. Photos by Charles O'Rear. Contents: Old Believers. 401-425, *Sept. 1972*

The Rebirth of Religion in Russia: The Church Reorganized While Bolshevik Cannon Spread Destruction in the Nation's Holy of Holies. By Thomas Whittemore. 379-401, *Nov. 1918*

The **RUSSIAN** Situation and Its Significance to America. By Stanley Washburn. 371-382, *Apr. 1917*

RUSSIAN SOVIET FEDERATED SOCIALIST REPUBLIC, U.S.S.R.:

New Road to Asia. By Owen Lattimore. 641-676, *Dec. 1944*

I Learn About the Russians. By Eddy Gilmore. 619-640, *Nov. 1943*

One of the magazine's first color pictures, St. Basil's Cathedral was hand tinted and published in 1914. GILBERT H. GROSVENOR, NGS

Roaming Russia's Caucasus: Rugged Mountains and Hardy Fighters Guard the Soviet Union's Caucasian Treasury of Manganese and Oil. By Rolf Singer. 91-121, *July 1942*

The Murman Coast: Arctic Gateway for American and Allied Expeditionary Forces in Northern European Russia. 331-348, *Apr. 1919*

See also Crimea; Daghestan Autonomous Soviet Socialist Republic; Leningrad; Moscow; Siberia; Volga

RUSSIAN TURKISTAN. *See* Soviet Central Asia

RUSSIA'S Democrats. By Montgomery Schuyler. 210-240, *Mar. 1917*

RUSSIA'S Man of the Hour: Alexander Kerensky's First Speeches and Proclamations. 24-45, *July 1917*

RUSSIA'S Mighty River Road, the Volga. By Howard Sochurek. 579-613, *May 1973*

RUSSIA'S Orphan Races: Picturesque Peoples Who Cluster on the Southeastern Borderland of the Vast Slav Dominions. By Maynard Owen Williams. 245-278, *Oct. 1918*

RUSSIA'S Window on the West: Leningrad. By Howard La Fay. Photos by Dick Durrance II. 636-673, *May 1971*

The **RUSSO-AMERICAN** Telegraph Project of 1864-'67. By William H. Dall. 110-111, *Mar. 1896*

RUTHERFORD, ERNEST, LORD:

The British Way. By Sir Evelyn Wrench. 421-541, *Apr. 1949*

RUTHERFORD, SCOTT:

Photographer

Sealed in Time–Ice Entombs an Eskimo Family for Five Centuries. By Albert A. Dekin, Jr. Photos by Victor R. Boswell, Jr., and Scott Rutherford. Paintings by James M. Gurney. 824-836, *June 1987*

Ghosts on the Little Bighorn. By Robert Paul Jordan. 787-813, *Dec. 1986*

RUTLEDGE, T. W.:

On Assignment in Guatemala. *Sept. 1987*

Artist

El Mirador: An Early Maya Metropolis Uncovered. By Ray T. Matheny. NGS research grant. 317-339, *Sept. 1987*

RUWENZORI (Mountains of the Moon), Uganda-Zaire:

Mountains of the Moon. By Paul A. Zahl. 412-434, *Mar. 1962*

Flights from Arctic to Equator: Conquering the Alps, the Ice Peaks of Spitsbergen, of Persia, and Africa's Mountains of the Moon. By Walter Mittelholzer. 445-498, *Apr. 1932*

The World's Highest Altitudes and First Ascents. By Charles E. Fay. 493-530, *June 1909*

Amid the Snow Peaks of the Equator: A Naturalist's Explorations Around Ruwenzori, with an Excursion to the Congo State, and an Account of the Terrible Scourge of Sleeping Sickness. By A.F.R. Wollaston. 256-277, *Mar. 1909*

RWANDA. *See* Virunga Mountains; *and* former name, Ruanda

RYAN, INEZ BUFFINGTON: *Author*

The Maid of France Rides By: Compiègne, Where Joan of Arc Fought Her Last Battle, Celebrates Her Fifth Centenary. 607-616, *Nov. 1932*

The Land of William the Conqueror: Where Northmen Came to Build Castles and Cathedrals. 89-99, *Jan. 1932*

RYDEN, HOPE:

Author-Photographer

The "Lone" Coyote Likes Family Life. Photos by author and David Hiser. 278-294, *Aug. 1974*

On the Track of the West's Wild Horses. Photos by author and Dick Durrance II. 94-109, *Jan. 1971*

RYDER, C. H.:

Three Weeks in Hubbard Bay, West Greenland. By Robert Stein. 1-11, *Jan. 1898*

RYTI, CARLA:

On Assignment. *Nov. 1986*

RYTKHEU, YURI:

On Assignment in the Soviet Arctic. *Feb. 1983*

Author

People of the Long Spring. Photos by Dean Conger. 206-223, *Feb. 1983*

RYUKYU ISLANDS, Japan:

Peacetime Rambles in the Ryukyus. By William Leonard Schwartz. 543-561, *May 1945*

See also Okinawa

Q R

S
T

*A farmer and his donkey
haul flowering* nabiza, *turnip plants,
in Zamora Province, Spain.*

DAVID ALAN HARVEY

Egypt's President Anwar Sadat reviews troops commemorating the 1973 Suez Canal battle. THOMAS J. ABERCROMBIE, NGS

SÁ, HERNANE TAVARES DE: *Author*

Brasília, Metropolis Made to Order. Photos by Thomas J. Abercrombie. 704-724, *May 1960*

Spectacular Rio de Janeiro. Photos by Charles Allmon. 289-328, *Mar. 1955*

SAAMI. *See* Lapps

SAAR (Region), West Germany:

Coal Makes the Saar a Prize. By Franc Shor. 561-576, *Apr. 1954*

What Is the Saar? By Frederick Simpich. 241-264, *Feb. 1935*

SAARINEN, EERO:

St. Louis: New Spirit Soars in Mid-America's Proud Old City. By Robert Paul Jordan. Photos by Bruce Dale. Included: Saarinen's Gateway Arch. 605-641, *Nov. 1965*

SABA (Island), Netherlands Antilles:

The Netherlands Antilles: Holland in the Caribbean. By James Cerruti. Photos by Emory Kristof. 115-146, *Jan. 1970*

A Fresh Breeze Stirs the Leewards. By Carleton Mitchell. Photos by Winfield Parks. 488-537, *Oct. 1966*

Saba, Crater Treasure of the Indies. By Charles W. Herbert. 597-620, *Nov. 1940*

SABAH (North Borneo), Malaysia:

Malaysia's Giant Flowers and Insect-trapping Plants. By Paul A. Zahl. 680-701, *May 1964*

In Storied Lands of Malaysia. By Maurice Shadbolt. Photos by Winfield Parks. 734-783, *Nov. 1963*

SABLE ISLAND, Nova Scotia, Canada:

Safe Landing on Sable, Isle of 500 Shipwrecks. By Melville Bell Grosvenor. Included: 1898: The Bells on Sable. Photos by Arthur W. McCurdy, with maps, 1766 to 1964, indicating

eastward shift of the island; and map of known shipwreck sites. 398-431, *Sept. 1965*

SABOTEUR Mosquitoes. By Harry H. Stage. 165-179, *Feb. 1944*

SACHA, BOB: *Photographer*

Descendants of the Expeditions. 414-429. I. The Peary Family. By Edward Peary Stafford. 417-421; II. The Henson Family. By S. Allen Counter. 422-429, *Sept. 1988*

The Great Lakes' Troubled Waters. By Charles E. Cobb, Jr. Photos by Bob Sacha and Richard Olsenius. Included: A great meeting of waters; North America's fifth coast. 2-31, *July 1987*

SACRAMENTO, California:

California, the Golden Magnet. By William Graves. 595-679. Included: Nature's North. Photos by James P. Blair and Jonathan S. Blair. 641-679, *May 1966*

New Rush to Golden California. By George W. Long. 723-802, *June 1954*

California, Horn of Plenty. By Frederick Simpich. Photos by Willard R. Culver. 553-594, *May 1949*

SACRAMENTO (River), California:

California's Surprising Inland Delta. By Judith and Neil Morgan. Photos by Charles O'Rear. 409-430, *Sept. 1976*

More Water for California's Great Central Valley. By Frederick Simpich. 645-664, *Nov. 1946*

SACRAMENTO-SAN JOAQUIN RIVER DELTA, California:

San Francisco Bay: The Beauty and the Battles. By Cliff Tarpy. Photos by James A. Sugar. 814-845, *June 1981*

California's Surprising Inland Delta. By Judith and Neil Morgan. Photos by Charles O'Rear. 409-430, *Sept. 1976*

The **SACRED** City of the Sands. By Frank Edward Johnson. Contents: Kairouan, Tunisia. 1061-1093, *Dec. 1911*

The **SACRED** Ibis Cemetery and Jackal Catacombs at Abydos. By Camden M. Cobern. 1042-1056, *Sept. 1913*

A **SACRED** Symbol Comes Home: Afo-A-Kom. By William S. Ellis. Photos by James P. Blair. 141-148, *July 1974*

The **SACRED** Tooth (of Buddha). 745, *Nov. 1907*

SACRIFICE. *See* Animal Sacrifice; Human Sacrifice

SACSAHUAMAN (Fortress), Peru:

The Greatest Achievement of Ancient Man in America. Panorama. *May 1916*

SADAT, ANWAR:

Eternal Sinai. By Harvey Arden. Photos by David Doubilet and Kevin Fleming. Included: First-hand account of Anwar Sadat's assassination. 420-461, *Apr. 1982*

On Assignment. *Apr. 1982*

Egypt's Desert of Promise. By Farouk El-Baz. Photos by Georg Gerster.

190-221, *Feb. 1982*

On Assignment. In Egypt. *Feb. 1982*

Egypt: Two Perspectives. Included: Omens for a Better Tomorrow. By Thomas J. Abercrombie. 293-343, *Mar. 1977*

SADLERMIUTS (Inuit):

Vanished Mystery Men of Hudson Bay. By Henry B. Collins. NGS research grant. 669-687, *Nov. 1956*

SAFARI! By Gene S. Stuart. Photos by George F. Mobley. Juvenile. 104 pages. *1982*

SAFARI from Congo to Cairo. By Elsie May Bell Grosvenor. Photos by Gilbert Grosvenor. 721-771, *Dec. 1954*

SAFARI Through Changing Africa. By Elsie May Bell Grosvenor. Photos by Gilbert Grosvenor. 145-198, *Aug. 1953*

SAFE Landing on Sable, Isle of 500 Shipwrecks. By Melville Bell Grosvenor. 398-431, *Sept. 1965*

SAFFORD, WILLIAM E.: *Author*

Our Smallest Possession–Guam. 229-237, *May 1905*

SAGA of a Ship, the *Yankee.* By Luis Marden. 263-269, *Feb. 1966*

SAGA of the Carrier *Princeton.* By William H. Buracker. 189-218, *Aug. 1945*

The **SAGACITY** and Courage of Dogs. 253-275, *Mar. 1919*

SAGAMORE HILL, Long Island, New York:

Roosevelt Country: T. R.'s Wilderness Legacy. By John L. Eliot. Photos by Farrell Grehan. 340-363, *Sept. 1982*

SAGAN, CARL: *Author*

Mars: a New World to Explore. 821-841, *Dec. 1967*

SAGARMATHA NATIONAL PARK, Nepal:

The Mighty Himalaya: A Fragile Heritage. By Barry C. Bishop. Photos by William Thompson. 624-631, *Nov. 1988*

Heavy Hands on the Land. By Larry Kohl. Photos by William Thompson and Galen Rowell. 633-651, *Nov. 1988*

Editorial. By Wilbur E. Garrett. 551, *Nov. 1987*

Park at the Top of the World: Mount Everest National Park. By Rick Ridgeway. Photos by Nicholas de-Vore II. 696-725. Included: Preserving a Mountain Heritage. By Sir Edmund Hillary. 696-703, *June 1982*

SAGAS:

Iceland: Life Under the Glaciers. By Louise E. Levathes. Photos by Bob Krist. 184-215, *Feb. 1987*

The Vikings. By Howard La Fay. Photos by Ted Spiegel. 492-541, *Apr. 1970*

Dwellings of the Saga-Time in Iceland, Greenland, and Vineland. By Cornelia Horsford. 73-84, *Mar. 1898*

Veiled against wind, sand, and sun, a Tuareg tribesman rides his camel in the Algerian Sahara. GEORGE RODGER, MAGNUM

North Africans cross the Sahara on camels, whose two-toed feet keep them from sinking into the sand and whose pacing gait can carry them 100 miles a day. LEHNERT AND LANDROCK

Michael and Aubine Kirtley. 282-298, *Aug. 1979*

The Niger: River of Sorrow, River of Hope. By Georg Gerster. 152-189, *Aug. 1975*

Drought Threatens the Tuareg World. By Victor Englebert. 544-571, *Apr. 1974*

SAIDMAN, BARNET: *Photographer*

The Swans of Abbotsbury. By Michael Moynihan. 563-570, *Oct. 1959*

SAIGON, Vietnam:

Saigon: Eye of the Storm. By Peter T. White. Photos by W. E. Garrett. 834-872, *June 1965*

Slow Train Through Viet Nam's War. By Howard Sochurek. 412-444, *Sept. 1964*

South Viet Nam Fights the Red Tide. By Peter T. White. Photos by W. E. Garrett. 445-489, *Oct. 1961*

Indochina Faces the Dragon. By George W. Long. Photos by J. Baylor Roberts. 287-328, *Sept. 1952*

Portrait of Indochina. By W. Robert Moore and Maynard Owen Williams. Paintings by Jean Despujols. 461-490, *Apr. 1951*

SAILFISH:

Solving Life Secrets of the Sailfish. By Gilbert Voss. Photos by B. Anthony Stewart. Paintings by Craig Phillips. NGS research grant. 859-872, *June 1956*

SAILING. *See* Cruises and Voyages; Sailing Vessels; Yachting

SAILING a Sea of Fire. By Paul A. Zahl. 120-129, *July 1960*

SAILING CARS:

◼ Wind Raiders of the Sahara. 436A-436B, *Sept. 1973*

Dry-land Fleet Sails the Sahara. By Jean du Boucher. Photos by Jonathan S. Blair. 696-725, *Nov. 1967*

SAILING Forbidden Coasts. By Ida Treat. 357-386, *Sept. 1931*

SAILING Iceland's Rugged Coasts. By Wright Britton. Photos by James A. Sugar. 228-265, *Aug. 1969*

The **SAILING** Oystermen of Chesapeake Bay. By Luis Marden. 798-819, *Dec. 1967*

SAILING Ship and the Panama Canal. By James Page. 167-176, *Apr. 1904*

SAILING the Seven Seas in the Interest of Science: Adventures Through 157,000 Miles of Storm and Calm, from Arctic to Antarctic and Around the World, in the Non-magnetic Yacht "Carnegie." By J. P. Ault. 631-690, *Dec. 1922*

SAILING VESSELS:

By Square-rigger from Baltic to Bicentennial. By Kenneth Garrett. Included: The tall-ships race. 824-857, *Dec. 1976*

Life's Tempo on Nantucket. By Peter Benchley. Photos by James L. Stanfield. 810-839, *June 1970*

The Age of Sail Lives On at Mystic. By

Alan Villiers. Photos by Weston Kemp. Included: *Alice, Charles W. Morgan, Joseph Conrad, L. A. Dunton.* 220-239, *Aug. 1968*

The Sailing Oystermen of Chesapeake Bay. By Luis Marden. 798-819, *Dec. 1967*

Windjamming Around New England. By Tom Horgan. Photos by Robert F. Sisson. Included: *Abigail Chandler, Bluenose, Bolero, Bowdoin, Charles W. Morgan, Daniel I. Tenny, Fiddlers' Green, Gertrude L. Thebaud, Great Republic, Hannah, Hero, Joseph Conrad, Lagoda, Malabar XIII, Manxman, Nomad, Regina M., Telegraph, Wanderer, Yankee.* 141-169, *Aug. 1950*

Last of the Cape Horners. By Alan Villiers. Included: Square-rigger in a Tempest *(Pamir).* Contents: *Abraham Rydberg, Archibald Russell, Grace Harwar, Kjøbenhavn, Kommodore Johnsen, Lawhill, Moshulu, Padua, Pamir, Parma, Passat, Pommern, Viking.* 701-710, *May 1948*

See also Caravels; Dhows; Galleasses; Galleons; Galleys; Junks; *Lipas*; Longships; Schooners; Square-riggers; Training Ships; listing under Yachts; *and Beagle; Bounty; Brendan; Dick Smith Explorer; Dove; Endeavour* (Bark); *Hamilton; Hokule'a; Ice Bird; Isbjorn; Kublai Khan* (Fleet); *Mary Rose; Mayflower II; Ra II; Scourge; Sohar; Tigris; Witte Leeuw; Yorktown Shipwreck*

SAILING with Sindbad's Sons. By Alan Villiers. 675-688, *Nov. 1948*

SAILING With the Supertankers. By Noel Grove. Photos by Martin Rogers. 102-124, *July 1978*

The **SAILOR** Who Gave Us the New World: Christopher Columbus. By John Scofield. Photos by Adam Woolfitt. 584-625, *Nov. 1975*

SAILORS, U. S. *See* U. S. Navy

SAILORS in the Sky: Fifty Years of

Naval Aviation. By Patrick N. L. Bellinger. 276-296, *Aug. 1961*

SAILPLANES:

The Thousand-mile Glide. By Karl Striedieck. Photos by Otis Imboden. 431-438, *Mar. 1978*

Happy Birthday, Otto Lilienthal! By Russell Hawkes. Photos by James Collison. 286-292, *Feb. 1972*

Sailors of the Sky. By Gordon Young. Photos by Emory Kristof and Jack Fields. Paintings by Davis Meltzer. 49-73, *Jan. 1967*

Men-Birds Soar on Boiling Air. By Frederick G. Vosburgh. 123-140, *July 1938*

On the Wings of the Wind: In Motorless Planes, Pilots Ride in Flying-Fox Fashion Cruising on Upward Air Streams and Lifted by the Suction of Moving Clouds. By Howard Siepen. 751-780, *June 1929*

ST. ANDREWS, Scotland:

Bonnie Scotland, Postwar Style. By Isobel Wylie Hutchison. 545-601, *May 1946*

ST. AUBYN, SIR FRANCIS CECIL. *See* St. Levan, Baron

ST. AUGUSTINE, Florida:

Exploring Our Forgotten Century: Between Columbus and Jamestown. By Joseph Judge. Photos by Bill Ballenberg. Paintings by John Berkey. 330-363, *Mar. 1988*

St. Augustine, Nation's Oldest City, Turns 400. By Robert L. Conly. 196-229, *Feb. 1966*

ST. BERNARD DOGS:

The Great St. Bernard Hospice Today. By George Pickow. 49-62, *Jan. 1957*

ST. BERNARD HOSPICE, Switzerland:

The Great St. Bernard Hospice Today. By George Pickow. 49-62, *Jan. 1957*

ST. BOTOLPH'S Town: the Original Boston. By Veronica Thomas. Photos by James L. Amos. 382-389, *Sept. 1974*

ST. CATHERINES (Island), Georgia:

Sea Islands: Adventuring Along the South's Surprising Coast. By James Cerruti. Photos by Thomas Nebbia and James L. Amos. 366-393, *Mar. 1971*

ST. CATHERINE'S MONASTERY, Sinai Peninsula, Egypt:

Island of Faith in the Sinai Wilderness. By George H. Forsyth. Photos by Robert F. Sisson. 82-106, *Jan. 1964*

Mount Sinai's Holy Treasures. By Kurt Weitzmann. Photos by Fred Anderegg. 109-127, *Jan. 1964*

Sinai Sheds New Light on the Bible. By Henry Field. Photos by William B. and Gladys Terry. 795-815, *Dec. 1948*

The Route Over Which Moses Led the Children of Israel Out of Egypt. By Franklin E. Hoskins. 1011-1038, *Dec. 1909*

Avian casualty lies in ash erupted from Mount St. Helens, in Washington State, on May 18, 1980. KEN WHITMIRE, IMAGES WEST

ST. JOHN'S, Newfoundland, Canada:

Newfoundland Trusts in the Sea. By Gary Jennings. Photos by Sam Abell. 112-141, *Jan. 1974*

Newfoundland, Canada's New Province. By Andrew H. Brown. Photos by author and Robert F. Sisson. 777-812, *June 1949*

Newfoundland, North Atlantic Rampart: From the "First Base of American Defense" Planes Fly to Britain's Aid over Stout Fishing Schooners of the Grand Banks. By George Whiteley, Jr. 111-140, *July 1941*

ST. KITTS AND NEVIS, Federation of. *See* St. Christopher

ST. LAWRENCE, Gulf of:

Sea Bird Cities Off Audubon's Labrador. By Arthur A. Allen. NGS research grant. 755-774, *June 1948*

Atlantic Coast Tides. By Mark S. W. Jefferson. 497-509, *Dec. 1898*

ST. LAWRENCE (River), Canada-U. S.:

The St. Lawrence River: Canada's Highway to the Sea. By William S. Ellis. Photos by Bruce Dale. 586-623, *May 1980*

North Through History Aboard *White Mist.* By Melville Bell Grosvenor. Photos by Edwin Stuart Grosvenor. 1-55, *July 1970*

The St. Lawrence, River Key to Canada. By Howard La Fay. Photos by John Launois. 622-667, *May 1967*

Sea to Lakes on the St. Lawrence. By George W. Long. Photos by B. Anthony Stewart and John E. Fletcher. 323-366, *Sept. 1950*

Quebec's Forests, Farms, and Frontiers. By Andrew H. Brown. 431-470, *Oct. 1949*

Atlantic Estuarine Tides. By Mark S. W. Jefferson. 400-409, *Sept. 1898*

See also Montreal; Quebec (City)

ST. LAWRENCE SEAWAY, Canada-U. S.:

The St. Lawrence River: Canada's Highway to the Sea. By William S. Ellis. Photos by Bruce Dale. 586-623, *May 1980*

New St. Lawrence Seaway Opens the Great Lakes to the World. By Andrew H. Brown. 299-339, *Mar. 1959*

ST. LEVAN, BARON and BARONESS:

Fabled Mount of St. Michael. By Alan Villiers. Photos by Bates Littlehales. Note: Baron St. Levan is the owner of Mount St. Michael. 880-898, *June 1964*

ST. LOUIS, Île, Paris, France:

The More Paris Changes…. By Howell Walker. Photos by Gordon W. Gahan. 64-103, *July 1972*

Île de la Cité, Birthplace of Paris. By Kenneth MacLeish. Photos by Bruce Dale. 680-719, *May 1968*

ST. LOUIS, Missouri:

St. Louis: New Spirit Soars in Mid-America's Proud Old City. By Robert Paul Jordan. Photos by Bruce Dale. 605-641, *Nov. 1965*

So Long, St. Louis, We're Heading West. By William C. Everhart. 643-669, *Nov. 1965*

"Pyramids" of the New World. By Neil Merton Judd. Included: "The Mound City." 105-128, *Jan. 1948*

These Missourians. By Frederick Simpich. 277-310, *Mar. 1946*

ST. LUCIA (Island), West Indies:

Finisterre Sails the Windward Islands. By Carleton Mitchell. Photos by Winfield Parks. 755-801, *Dec. 1965*

Americans in the Caribbean. By Luis Marden. 723-758, *June 1942*

British West Indian Interlude. By Anne Rainey Langley. 1-46, *Jan. 1941*

ST. MAGNUS CATHEDRAL, Orkney Islands, Scotland:

The Orkneys and Shetlands–A Mysterious Group of Islands. By Charles S. Olcott. 197-228, *Feb. 1921*

ST. MALO, France:

St. Malo, Ancient City of Corsairs: An Old Brittany Seaport Whose Past Bristles with Cannons and Cutlasses. By Junius B. Wood. 131-177, *Aug. 1929*

ST. MARGARETS BAY, Nova Scotia, Canada:

Plight of the Bluefin Tuna. By Michael J. A. Butler. Photos by David Doubilet. Paintings by Stanley Meltzoff. 220-239, *Aug. 1982*

ST. MARK'S CATHEDRAL, Venice, Italy:

Venice. By Karl Stieler. 587-630, *June 1915*

Leg of the stainless steel Gateway Arch in St. Louis glows in the afternoon sun during construction in 1964. BRUCE DALE, NGS

ST. MARTIN (Island), Netherlands Antilles. *See* Sint Maarten

ST. MARY ISLANDS SANCTUARY, Quebec, Canada:

Sea Bird Cities Off Audubon's Labrador. By Arthur A. Allen. Contents: Birds on Cliff, Harbour, and Middle Islands. NGS research grant. 755-774, *June 1948*

ST. MARYS, West Virginia:

So Much Happens Along the Ohio River. By Frederick Simpich. Photos by Justin Locke. 177-212, *Feb. 1950*

ST. MICHAEL'S (Island), Azores:

The Azores: Picturesque and Historic Half-way House of American Transatlantic Aviators. By Arminius T. Haeberle. 514-545, *June 1919*

ST. MICHAEL'S MOUNT, England:

Fabled Mount of St. Michael. By Alan Villiers. Photos by Bates Littlehales. 880-898, *June 1964*

ST. PAUL (Apostle). *See* Paul, Saint

ST. PAUL, Minnesota:

Minneapolis and St. Paul. By Thomas J. Abercrombie. Photos by Annie Griffiths. 665-691, *Nov. 1980*

Minnesota, Where Water Is the Magic Word. By David S. Boyer. Photos by author and David Brill. 200-229, *Feb. 1976*

The Upper Mississippi. By Willard Price. 651-699, *Nov. 1958*

Minnesota Makes Ideas Pay. By Frederick G. Vosburgh. Photos by John E. Fletcher and B. Anthony Stewart. 291-336, *Sept. 1949*

ST. PETER'S (Basilica), Vatican City:

Vatican City. By James Fallows. Photos by James L. Stanfield. 723-775, *Dec. 1985*

St. Peter's, Rome's Church of Popes. By Aubrey Menen. Photos by Albert Moldvay. 865-879, *Dec. 1971*

When in Rome…. By Stuart E. Jones. Photos by Winfield Parks. 741-789, *June 1970*

Rome: Eternal City with a Modern Air. By Harnett T. Kane. Photos by B. Anthony Stewart. 437-491, *Apr. 1957*

The Splendor of Rome. By Florence Craig Albrecht. 593-626, *June 1922*

Inexhaustible Italy. By Arthur Stanley Riggs. 273-368, *Oct. 1916*

ST. PIERRE, Martinique:

Martinique: A Tropical Bit of France. By Gwen Drayton Allmon. Photos by Charles Allmon. 255-283, *Feb. 1959*

The Recent Volcanic Eruptions in the West Indies. By Israel C. Russell. 267-285, *July 1902*

Lafcadio Hearn on the Island and People of Martinique. 214-216, *June 1902*

ST. PIERRE AND MIQUELON (Islands), North Atlantic Ocean:

White Mist Cruises to Wreck-haunted St. Pierre and Miquelon. By Melville Bell Grosvenor. 378-419, *Sept. 1967*

Islands Adrift: St. Pierre and Miquelon: In a Key Position on the North Atlantic Air Route, France's Oldest Colony Rides Out Another Storm. By Frederic K. Arnold. 743-768, *Dec. 1941*

ST. SIMONS ISLAND, Sea Islands, Georgia:

Sea Islands: Adventuring Along the South's Surprising Coast. By James Cerruti. Photos by Thomas Nebbia and James L. Amos. 366-393, *Mar. 1971*

The Golden Isles of Guale. By W. Robert Moore. 235-264, *Feb. 1934*

SAINT STEPHEN'S Fete in Budapest. By De Witt Clinton Falls. 548-558, *Aug. 1907*

ST. THOMAS (Island), U. S. Virgin Islands:

The U. S. Virgin Islands. By Thomas J. Colin. Photos by William Albert Allard and Cary Wolinsky. 225-243, *Feb. 1981*

A Fresh Breeze Stirs the Leewards. By Carleton Mitchell. Photos by Winfield Parks. 488-537, *Oct. 1966*

Virgin Islands: Tropical Playland, U.S.A. By John Scofield. Photos by Charles Allmon. 201-232, *Feb. 1956*

The American Virgins: After Dark Days, These Adopted Daughters of the United States Are Finding a New Place in the Caribbean Sun. By DuBose Heyward and Daisy Reck. 273-308, *Sept. 1940*

The Haunts of the Caribbean Corsairs: The West Indies a Geographic Background for the Most Adventurous Episodes in the History of the Western Hemisphere. By Nell Ray Clarke. 147-187, *Feb. 1922*

An American Gibraltar: Notes on the Danish West Indies. 89-96, *July 1916*

SAINT VÉRAN, France's Highest Village. By Robert K. Burns, Jr. 571-588, *Apr. 1959*

ST. VINCENT (Island), West Indies:

St. Vincent, the Grenadines, and Grenada: Taking It as It Comes. By Ethel A. Starbird. Photos by Cotton Coulson. 399-425, *Sept. 1979*

Finisterre Sails the Windward Islands. By Carleton Mitchell. Photos by Winfield Parks. 755-801, *Dec. 1965*

British West Indian Interlude. By Anne Rainey Langley. 1-46, *Jan. 1941*

A Report of the Eruption of the Soufrière of St. Vincent, 1812 (From the *Evening News* of June 30, 1812). 158-161, *Apr. 1903*

Volcanic Eruptions on Martinique and St. Vincent. By Israel C. Russell. 415-436, *Dec. 1902*

The Eruptions of La Soufrière, St. Vincent, in May 1902. By Edmund Otis Hovey. 444-459, *Dec. 1902*

Report by Robert T. Hill on the Volcanic Disturbances in the West Indies. 223-267, *July 1902*

The Recent Volcanic Eruptions in the West Indies. By Israel C. Russell. 267-285, *July 1902*

Volcanic Rocks of Martinique and St.

Girl gazes seaward from Sailors' Island off the coast of St. Pierre, one of a cluster of French isles near Newfoundland's south coast. WILBUR E. GARRETT, NGS

Vincent: Collected by Robert T. Hill and Israel C. Russell. By J. S. Diller. 285-296, *July 1902*

Chemical Discussion of Analyses of Volcanic Ejecta from Martinique and St. Vincent. By W. F. Hillebrand. 296-299, *July 1902*

Reports of Vessels as to the Range of Volcanic Dust. By James Page. 299-301, *July 1902*

The National Geographic Society Expedition to Martinique and St. Vincent. 183-184, *June 1902*

STE. CÉCILE, Cathedral of, Albi, France:

France's Past Lives in Languedoc. By Walter Meayers Edwards. 1-43, *July 1951*

SAIPAN (Island), Mariana Islands:

Victory's Portrait in the Marianas. By William Franklin Draper. Paintings by author. 599-616, *Nov. 1945*

South from Saipan. By W. Robert Moore. Included: Saipan and Tinian, Take-offs to Tokyo. 441-474, *Apr. 1945*

Springboards to Tokyo. By Willard Price. 385-407, *Oct. 1944*

Hidden Key to the Pacific: Piercing the Web of Secrecy Which Long Has Veiled Japanese Bases in the Mandated Islands. By Willard Price. 759-785, *June 1942*

SAKAMOTO, KIYOSHI:
Photographer

The Picturesque Side of Japanese Life. 283-298, *Sept. 1922*

Japan. 61-76, *July 1921*

SAKELLARAKIS, YANNIS: *Author*

Drama of Death in a Minoan Temple. By Yannis Sakellarakis and Efi Sapouna-Sakellaraki. Photos by Otis Imboden and Spyros Tsavdaroglou. 205-222, *Feb. 1981*

SAKURAJIMA, Japan's Greatest Volcanic Eruption: A Convulsion of Nature Whose Ravages Were Minimized by Scientific Knowledge, Compared with the Terrors and Destruction of the Recent Tokyo Earthquake. By Thomas Augustus Jaggar. 441-470, *Apr. 1924*

SALAMANDERS:

The Shadowy World of Salamanders. By Paul A. Zahl. 104-117, *July 1972*

In the Wilds of a City Parlor. By Paul A. Zahl. 645-672, *Nov. 1954*

SALB, WOLFGANG A.:

Nomination Page. *Mar. 1981*

Photographer

Saving the Philippine Eagle. By Robert S. Kennedy. Photos by Alan R. Degen, Neil L. Rettig, and Wolfgang A. Salb. 847-856, *June 1981*

SALE, GEORGE: *Author*

Conditions in Liberia. By Roland P. Folkner, George Sale, and Emmett J. Scott. 729-741, *Sept. 1910*

SALÉ, Morocco:

Eastward from Gibraltar: Overland Route Across North Africa to Tunisia and Libya. By Cyrus French Wicker. 115-142, *Jan. 1943*

SALEM, Massachusetts:

Literary Landmarks of Massachusetts. By William H. Nicholas. Photos by B. Anthony Stewart and John E. Fletcher. 279-310, *Mar. 1950*

Northeast of Boston. By Albert W. Atwood. 257-292, *Sept. 1945*

SALEM, Oregon:

Oregon Finds New Riches. By Leo A. Borah. 681-728, *Dec. 1946*

SALERNO, Gulf of:

Amalfi, Italy's Divine Coast. By Luis Marden. 472-509, *Oct. 1959*

S
T

SALERNO, Italy:

Italy Smiles Again. By Edgar Erskine Hume. 693-732, *June 1949*

SALGADO, JOSÉ VELLOSO: *Artist*

Vasco da Gama at the Court of the Zamorin of Calicut. Supplement, *Nov. 1927*

SALISBURY, Rhodesia (now Harare, Zimbabwe):

Rhodesia, a House Divided. By Allan C. Fisher, Jr. Photos by Thomas Nebbia. 641-671, *May 1975*

Rhodesia, Hobby and Hope of Cecil Rhodes. By W. Robert Moore. 281-306, *Sept. 1944*

SALMON, H. MORREY: *Photographer*

We Live Alone, and Like It–On an Island. By R. M. Lockley. Photos by author and H. Morrey Salmon. 252-278, *Aug. 1938*

SALMON (River), Idaho:

White-water Adventure on Wild Rivers of Idaho. By Frank Craighead, Jr., and John Craighead. 213-239, *Feb. 1970*

◼ Wild River. 239A-239B, *Feb. 1970*

Down Idaho's River of No Return. By Philip J. Shenon and John C. Reed. 95-136, *July 1936*

SALMON:

Atlantic Salmon: The "Leaper" Struggles to Survive. By Art Lee. Photos by Bianca Lavies. 600-615, *Nov. 1981*

The Columbia River, Powerhouse of the Northwest. By David S. Boyer. 821-847, *Dec. 1974*

A River Restored: Oregon's Willamette. By Ethel A. Starbird. Photos by Lowell J. Georgia. 816-835, *June 1972*

The Incredible Salmon. By Clarence P. Idyll. Photos by Robert F. Sisson. Paintings by Walter A. Weber.

195-219. Included: Life portraits of a famous family: Pacific salmon. 214-216, *Aug. 1968*

When Giant Bears Go Fishing. By Cecil E. Rhode. 195-205, *Aug. 1954*

Endeavour Sails the Inside Passage. By Amos Burg. 801-828, *June 1947*

Fishing in Pacific Coast Streams. By Leonard P. Schultz. Paintings by Hashime Murayama. 185-212, *Feb. 1939*

The White Sheep, Giant Moose, and Smaller Game of the Kenai Peninsula, Alaska. By George Shiras, 3d. 423-494, *May 1912*

America's Most Valuable Fishes. By Hugh M. Smith. 494-514, *May 1912*

Federal Fish Farming; or, Planting Fish by the Billion. By Hugh M. Smith. 418-446, *May 1910*

A Jumping Salmon. 124-125, *Feb. 1908*

SALONIKI (Greece). By H. G. Dwight. 203-232, *Sept. 1916*

SALT:

Salt–The Essence of Life. By Gordon Young. Photos by Volkmar Wentzel and Georg Gerster. 381-401, *Sept. 1977*

I Joined a Sahara Salt Caravan. By Victor Englebert. 694-711, *Nov. 1965*

Salt for China's Daily Rice. 329-336, *Sept. 1944*

The Eden of the Flowery Republic. By Joseph Beech. 355-390, *Nov. 1920*

Methods of Obtaining Salt in Costa Rica. 28-34, *Jan. 1908*

An Interesting Photograph (Salt Deposit, Athabasca District, Alberta). 236-237, *Apr. 1906*

A Remarkable Salt Deposit. By Charles F. Holder. 391-392, *Nov. 1901*

See also Salt Lakes; Salzkammergut

SALT LAKE CITY, Utah:

The Rising Great Salt Lake: No Way to Run a Desert. By Rick Gore. Photos by Jim Richardson. 694-719, *June 1985*

Utah's Shining Oasis. By Charles McCarry. Photos by James L. Amos. 440-473, *Apr. 1975*

SALT LAKES:

Strange World of Palau's Salt Lakes. By William M. Hamner. Photos by David Doubilet. 264-282, *Feb. 1982*

See also Dead Sea; Great Salt Lake; Mono Lake

SALT MARSHES:

Can We Save Our Salt Marshes? By Stephen W. Hitchcock. Photos by William R. Curtsinger. 729-765, *June 1972*

Sea Islands: Adventuring Along the South's Surprising Coast. By James Cerruti. Photos by Thomas Nebbia and James L. Amos. 366-393, *Mar. 1971*

SALT MINES:

Salt–The Essence of Life. By Gordon Young. Photos by Volkmar Wentzel and Georg Gerster. 381-401, *Sept. 1977*

Salzkammergut, Austria's Alpine Playground. By Beverley M. Bowie. Photos by Volkmar Wentzel. 246-275, *Aug. 1960*

SALTON SEA, California:

The Colorado Desert. By W. C. Mendenhall. 681-701, *Aug. 1909*

Studies on the Rate of Evaporation at Reno, Nevada, and in the Salton Sink. By Frank H. Bigelow. 20-28, *Jan. 1908*

Salton Sea and the Rainfall of the Southwest. By Alfred J. Henry. 244-248, *Apr. 1907*

The New Inland Sea. By Arthur P. Davis. 37-49, *Jan. 1907*

A Remarkable Salt Deposit. By Charles F. Holder. 391-392, *Nov. 1901*

SALTON SEA BIRD REFUGE, California:

Pelican Profiles. By Lewis Wayne Walker. 589-598, *Nov. 1943*

SALTY Nova Scotia: In Friendly New Scotland Gaelic Songs Still Answer the Skirling Bagpipes. By Andrew H. Brown. 575-624, *May 1940*

SALUT, Îles du, French Guiana. *See* Devil's Island

SALVADOR (Bahia), Brazil:

Air Cruising Through New Brazil: A National Geographic Reporter Spots Vast Resources Which the Republic's War Declaration Adds to Strength of United Nations. By Henry Albert Phillips. 503-536, *Oct. 1942*

SALVAGE:

Yorktown Shipwreck. By John D. Broadwater. Photos by Bates Littlehales. 804-823, *June 1988*

Oldest Known Shipwreck Reveals Splendors of the Bronze Age. By George F. Bass. Photos by William R. Curtsinger. Included: Bronze Age Trade, The Cosmopolitan World of the Late Bronze Age, The Painstaking Art of Marine Archaeology. NGS research grant. 693-733, *Dec. 1987*

During spawning-season migration back to its birthplace, a salmon struggles up the Brooks River in Alaska's Katmai National Park and Preserve. WINFIELD PARKS, NGS

SALVATION ARMY:

SALWEEN (River), Tibet-Burma-China:

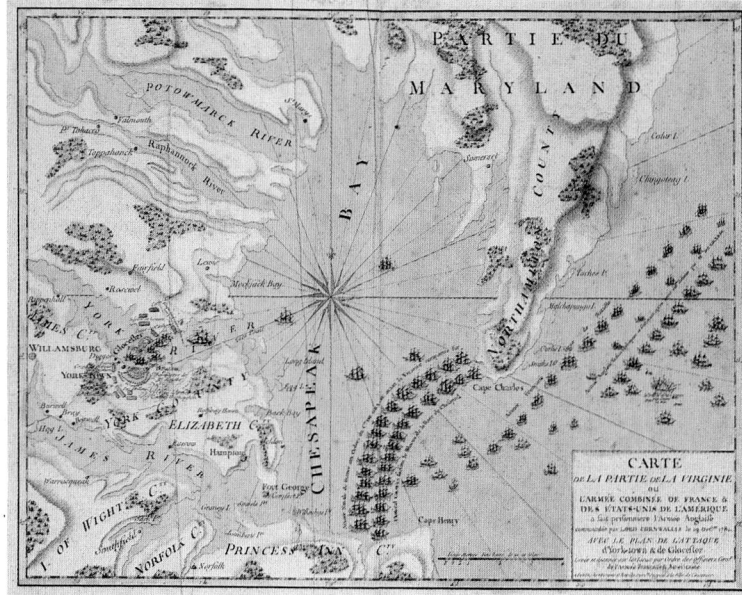

French map shows the Yorktown blockade during the American Revolution; artifacts have been salvaged from a sunken British ship. FREDERICK S. HICKS COLLECTION, 1967

SALYUT 7 (Soviet Space Station):

SALZBURG, Austria:

SALZKAMMERGUT (Region), Austria:

SAM HOUSTON: A Man Too Big for

SAMANA CAY, Bahama Islands:

SAMARITANS (Sect):

SAMARKAND, Uzbek S.S.R., U.S.S.R.:

SAMOA (Islands), South Pacific Ocean:

Nation. By Maurice Shadbolt.
Photos by Robert B. Goodman.
573-602, *Oct. 1962*

Samoa–South Sea Outpost of the U. S.
Navy. Photos by Truman Bailey. 615-
630, *May 1941*

Sailing the Seven Seas in the Interest of
Science: Adventures Through
157,000 Miles of Storm and Calm,
from Arctic to Antarctic and Around
the World, in the Non-magnetic
Yacht "Carnegie." By J. P. Ault.
631-690, *Dec. 1922*

America's South Sea Soldiers. By Lorena MacIntyre Quinn. 267-274,
Sept. 1919

The Samoan Islands. By Edwin V. Morgan. 417-426, *Nov. 1900*

The Commercial Importance of Samoa.
By O. P. Austin. 218-220, *June 1899*

Samoa: Navigators Islands. By H. Webster. 207-217, *June 1899*

The Samoan Cocoanut. Article compiled by A. W. Greely. 12-24,
Jan. 1898

SAMOS (Island), Aegean Sea:

Historic Islands and Shores of the
Ægean Sea. By Ernest Lloyd Harris.
231-261, *Sept. 1915*

SAMPSON, PAUL: *Author*

The Bonins and Iwo Jima Go Back to
Japan. Photos by Joe Munroe. 128-
144, *July 1968*

SAMUELS, GERTRUDE: *Author*

Passage to Freedom in Viet Nam. 858-
874, *June 1955*

SAMURAI:

Hagi: Where Japan's Revolution Be-
gan. By N. Taylor Gregg. Photos by
Sam Abell. Paintings by Kinuko Y.
Craft. 751-773, *June 1984*

SAN. *See Bushmen*

SAN AGUSTÍN REGION, Colombia:

Stone Idols of the Andes Reveal a Vanished People: Remarkable Relics of
One of the Oldest Aboriginal Cultures of America are Unearthed in
Colombia's San Agustín Region. By
Hermann von Walde-Waldegg. 627-
647, *May 1940*

SAN ANDREAS FAULT, California:

California's San Andreas Fault. By
Thomas Y. Canby. Photos by James
P. Blair. 38-53, *Jan. 1973*

SAN ANTONIO, Texas:

The Mexican Americans: A People on
the Move. By Griffin Smith, Jr. Photos by Stephanie Maze. 780-809,
June 1980

San Antonio: "Texas, Actin' Kind of
Natural." By Fred Kline. Photos by
David Hiser. 524-549, *Apr. 1976*

The Fabulous State of Texas. By Stanley Walker. Photos by B. Anthony
Stewart and Thomas Nebbia. 149-
195, *Feb. 1961*

Carnival in San Antonio. By Mason
Sutherland. Photos by J. Baylor Roberts. 813-844, *Dec. 1947*

SAN BENITO ISLANDS, Mexico:

Cruise of the *Kinkajou:* Among Desert

*San Francisco's high-flying Bay Bridge
spans eight miles of water and an island to
reach Oakland.* LUIS MARDEN, NGS

Islands of Mexico Voyagers Find
Outdoor Laboratories for the Naturalist and Ideal Fishing Grounds for
the Sportsman. By Alfred M. Bailey.
339-366, *Sept. 1941*

SAN BLAS INDIANS:

The Land That Links the Americas.
Photos by Luis Marden. 601-624,
Nov. 1941

Arch-Isolationists, the San Blas Indi-
ans: Coconuts Serve as Cash on Is-
lands Off the Panama Coast Where
Tribesmen Cling to Their Ancient
Ways and Discourage Visitors. By
Corinne B. Feeney. 193-220,
Feb. 1941

Little-Known Parts of Panama. By Henry Pittier. 627-662, *July 1912*

SAN CRISTÓBAL (Island), Galápagos
Islands:

The Dream Ship: The Story of a Voyage
of Adventure More Than Half
Around the World in a 47-foot Lifeboat. By Ralph Stock. 1-52,
Jan. 1921

SAN DIEGO, California:

San Diego, California's Plymouth
Rock. By Allan C. Fisher, Jr. Photos
by James L. Amos. 114-147,
July 1969

California, the Golden Magnet. By Wil-
liam Graves. 595-679. I. The South.
Photos by Thomas Nebbia. 595-639,
May 1966

New Rush to Golden California. By
George W. Long. 723-802, *June 1954*

California, Horn of Plenty. By Frederick Simpich. Photos by Willard R.
Culver. 553-594, *May 1949*

San Diego Can't Believe It. By Frederick Simpich. 45-80, *Jan. 1942*

SAN FRANCISCO, California:

San Francisco Bay: The Beauty and the
Battles. By Cliff Tarpy. Photos by

James A. Sugar. 814-845, *June 1981*

Chinatown, the Gilded Ghetto. By William Albert Allard. 627-643,
Nov. 1975

This Changing Earth. By Samuel W.
Matthews. Included: 1906 earthquake. 1-37, *Jan. 1973*

Barehanded Battle to Cleanse the Bay.
By Peter T. White. Photos by Jonathan S. Blair. 866-881, *June 1971*

San Francisco Bay, the Westward Gate.
By William Graves. Photos by James
L. Stanfield. 593-637, *Nov. 1969*

California, the Golden Magnet. By Wil-
liam Graves. 595-679. II. Nature's
North. Photos by James P. Blair and
Jonathan S. Blair. 641-679, *May 1966*

⊕ *Northern California; Southern California.* Atlas series. *May 1966*

Boom on San Francisco Bay. By Franc
Shor. Photos by David S. Boyer. 181-
226, *Aug. 1956*

New Rush to Golden California. By
George W. Long. 723-802, *June 1954*

California, Horn of Plenty. By Frederick Simpich. Photos by Willard R.
Culver. 553-594, *May 1949*

San Francisco: Gibraltar of the West
Coast. By La Verne Bradley. 279-
308, *Mar. 1943*

Out in San Francisco: Fed on Gold Dust
and Fattened by Sea Trade, a Pioneer
Village Becomes a Busy World Port.
By Frederick Simpich. 395-434,
Apr. 1932

The Wonderland of California. By Herman Whitaker. 57-104, *July 1915*

A City of Realized Dreams. By Franklin
K. Lane. 169-171, *Feb. 1915*

Echoes of the San Francisco Earthquake. By Robert E. C. Stearns. 351-
353, *May 1907*

The California Earthquake. 325-343,
June 1906

The Probable Cause of the San Francisco Earthquake. By Frederick Leslie
Ransome. 280-296, *May 1906*

The Record of the Great Earthquake
Written in Washington by the Seismograph of the U. S. Weather Bureau. By C. F. Marvin. 296-298,
May 1906

The San Francisco Earthquake of April
18, 1906, as Recorded by the Coast
and Geodetic Survey Magnetic Observatories. By L. A. Bauer and J. E.
Burbank. 298-300, *May 1906*

The Sea Fogs of San Francisco. 108-114,
Mar. 1901

SAN FRANCISCO BAY, California:

San Francisco Bay: The Beauty and the
Battles. By Cliff Tarpy. Photos by
James A. Sugar. 814-845, *June 1981*

Golden Gate–Of City, Ships, and Surf.
By David S. Boyer. 98-105, *July 1979*

Barehanded Battle to Cleanse the Bay.
By Peter T. White. Photos by Jonathan S. Blair. 866-881, *June 1971*

San Francisco Bay, the Westward Gate.
By William Graves. Photos by James
L. Stanfield. 593-637, *Nov. 1969*

Boom on San Francisco Bay. By Franc
Shor. Photos by David S. Boyer. 181-
226, *Aug. 1956*

SAN IGNACIO LAGOON, Baja California Sur, Mexico:

Gray Whales of San Ignacio. By Steven L. Swartz and Mary Lou Jones. Photos by François Gohier. NGS research grant. 754-771, *June 1987*

SAN JACINTO WEEK (Fiesta):

Carnival in San Antonio. By Mason Sutherland. Photos by J. Baylor Roberts. 813-844, *Dec. 1947*

SAN JOAQUIN (River), California:

California's Surprising Inland Delta. By Judith and Neil Morgan. Photos by Charles O'Rear. 409-430, *Sept. 1976*
More Water for California's Great Central Valley. By Frederick Simpich. 645-664, *Nov. 1946*

SAN JOSÉ, Costa Rica:

Land of the Painted Oxcarts. By Luis Marden. 409-456, *Oct. 1946*
Costa Rica, Land of the Banana. By Paul B. Popenoe. 201-220, *Feb. 1922*
Costa Rica–Vulcan's Smithy. By H. Pittier. 494-525, *June 1910*

SAN JUAN, Puerto Rico:

The Uncertain State of Puerto Rico. By Bill Richards. Photos by Stephanie Maze. 516-543, *Apr. 1983*
Puerto Rico's Seven-league Bootstraps. By Bart McDowell. Photos by B. Anthony Stewart. 755-793, *Dec. 1962*
Growing Pains Beset Puerto Rico. By William H. Nicholas. Photos by Justin Locke. 419-460, *Apr. 1951*
Puerto Rico: Watchdog of the Caribbean: Venerable Domain Under American Flag Has New Role as West Indian Stronghold and Sentinel of the

Panama Canal. By E. John Long. 697-738, *Dec. 1939*

SAN JUAN (River), Colorado-New Mexico-Utah:

Lake Powell: Waterway to Desert Wonders. By Walter Meayers Edwards. 44-75, *July 1967*
Desert River Through Navajo Land. By Alfred M. Bailey. Photos by author and Fred G. Brandenburg. 149-172, *Aug. 1947*
Beyond the Clay Hills: An Account of the National Geographic Society's Reconnaissance of a Previously Unexplored Section in Utah. By Neil M. Judd. 275-302, *Mar. 1924*

SAN JUAN ISLANDS, Washington:

Puget Sound, Sea Gate of the Pacific Northwest. By William Graves. Photos by David Alan Harvey. 71-97, *Jan. 1977*

SAN JUAN MOUNTAINS, Colorado-New Mexico:

Colorado's Friendly Topland. By Robert M. Ormes. 187-214, *Aug. 1951*
Landslides and Rock Avalanches. By Guy Elliott Mitchell. 277-287, *Apr. 1910*

SAN JUAN TEOTIHUACAN, Mexico:

An Interesting Visit to the Ancient Pyramids of San Juan Teotihuacan. By A. C. Galloway. 1041-1050, *Dec. 1910*
See also Teotihuacán

SAN LORENZO, Veracruz, Mexico:

On the Trail of La Venta Man. By

Matthew W. Stirling. Photos by Richard H. Stewart. Included: Hunting Mexico's Buried Temples. NGS research grant. 137-172, *Feb. 1947*

SAN MARCOS, Castillo de, St. Augustine, Florida. *See* Castillo de San Marcos

SAN MARINO:

San Marino, Little Land of Liberty. By Donna Hamilton Shor. Photos by Ted H. Funk. 233-251, *Aug. 1967*
United Italy Marks Its 100th Year. By Nathaniel T. Kenney. 593-647, *Nov. 1961*
Our Littlest Ally. By Alice Rohe. 139-163, *Aug. 1918*

SAN MARINO, California. *See* Henry E. Huntington Library and Art Gallery

SAN MIGUEL MOUNTAINS, Colorado:

Colorado's Friendly Topland. By Robert M. Ormes. 187-214, *Aug. 1951*

SAN SALVADOR, El Salvador:

Coffee Is King in El Salvador. By Luis Marden. 575-616, *Nov. 1944*
Volcano-Girded Salvador: A Prosperous Central American State with the Densest Rural Population in the Western World. By Harriet Chalmers Adams. 189-200, *Feb. 1922*

SAN SALVADOR (First Landfall of Columbus):

Where Columbus Found the New World. By Joseph Judge. Photos by James L. Stanfield. Note: The

Wine maker in San Marino, the world's oldest independent republic, stomps juice from grapes in the early 1900s. ALICE ROHE

Lincoln's life mask breathes the dignity evoked by biographer-poet Carl Sandburg. EDWARD STEICHEN

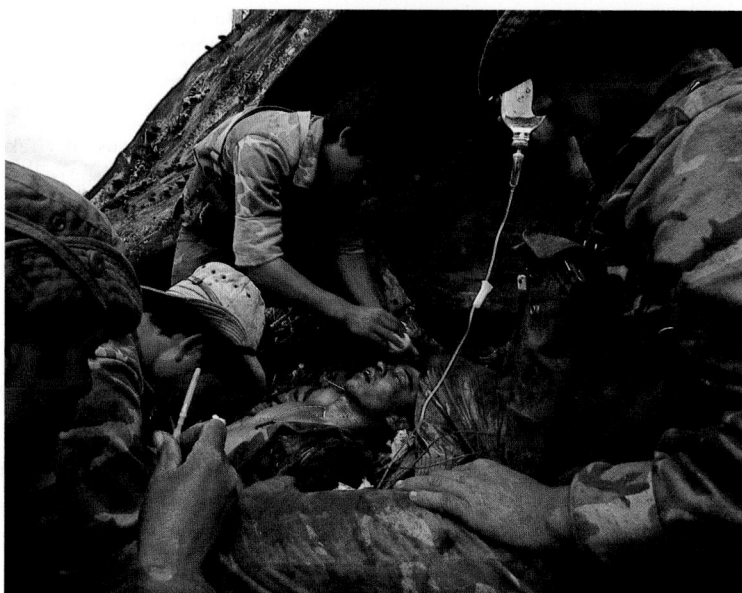

Sandinista soldier lies dying after his battalion, on patrol near San José de Bocay, Nicaragua, engaged some 300 rebels in a firefight in July 1985. JAMES NACHTWEY, MAGNUM

Carry Disease. By L. O. Howard. 735-749, *Aug. 1909*

See also Cockroaches; Rats; Waste Disposal

SANTA BARBARA (Island), Channel Islands, California:

Off Santa Barbara: California's Ranches in the Sea. By Earl Warren, Jr. Photos by Bates Littlehales. 257-283, *Aug. 1958*

Early Voyages on the Northwestern Coast of America. By George Davidson. 235-256, *Jan. 31, 1894*

SANTA CATALINA (Island), California:

Undersea World of a Kelp Forest. By Sylvia A. Earle. Photos by Al Giddings. 411-426, *Sept. 1980*

Santa Catalina—400 Years a Lure to Californian Travelers. Photos by B. Anthony Stewart. 81-88, *Jan. 1942*

SANTA CLARA COUNTY, California:

California's Silicon Valley. By Moira Johnston. Photos by Charles O'Rear. 459-477, *Oct. 1982*

SANTA CRUZ (Island), California:

Off Santa Barbara: California's Ranches in the Sea. By Earl Warren, Jr. Photos by Bates Littlehales. 257-283, *Aug. 1958*

SANTA CRUZ (Island), Galápagos Islands:

Managing Another Galápagos Species— Man. By Jerry Emory. Photos by Dieter and Mary Plage. 146-154, *Jan. 1988*

SANTA ELENA (Colonial Settlement), Parris Island, South Carolina:

Exploring Our Forgotten Century:

Between Columbus and Jamestown. By Joseph Judge. Photos by Bill Ballenberg. Paintings by John Berkey. 330-363, *Mar. 1988*

SANTA FE, New Mexico:

Goal at the End of the Trail: Santa Fe. By William S. Ellis. Photos by Gordon W. Gahan and Otis Imboden. 323-345, *Mar. 1982*

New Mexico: The Golden Land. By Robert Laxalt. Photos by Adam Woolfitt. 299-345, *Sept. 1970*

Adobe New Mexico. By Mason Sutherland. Photos by Justin Locke. 783-830, *Dec. 1949*

New Mexico Melodrama. By Frederick Simpich. 529-569, *May 1938*

The **SANTA FE TRAIL,** Path to Empire. By Frederick Simpich. 213-252, *Aug. 1929*

SANTA LUISA (Site), Mexico:

Man's Eighty Centuries in Veracruz. By S. Jeffrey K. Wilkerson. Photos by David Hiser. Paintings by Richard Schlecht. NGS research grant. 203-231, *Aug. 1980*

SANTA MARGARITA (Galleon):

Treasure From the Ghost Galleon: *Santa Margarita.* By Eugene Lyon. Photos by Don Kincaid. 228-243, *Feb. 1982*

SANTA MARÍA (Seaplane):

By Seaplane to Six Continents: Cruising 60,000 Miles, Italian Argonauts of the Air See World Geography Unroll, and Break New Sky Trails Over Vast Brazilian Jungles. By Francesco de Pinedo. 247-301, *Sept. 1928*

SANTA ROSA ISLAND, California:

Off Santa Barbara: California's Ranches in the Sea. By Earl Warren, Jr. Photos by Bates Littlehales. 257-283, *Aug. 1958*

SANTA TECLA, El Salvador:

Coffee Is King in El Salvador. By Luis Marden. 575-616, *Nov. 1944*

SANTANDER, Spain:

Under Canvas in the Atomic Age. By Alan Villiers. Contents: United States Coast Guard Cadets. 49-84, *July 1955*

SANTAREM, Brazil:

Air Cruising Through New Brazil: A National Geographic Reporter Spots Vast Resources Which the Republic's War Declaration Adds to Strength of United Nations. By Henry Albert Phillips. 503-536, *Oct. 1942*

SANTIAGO, Chile:

Chile, Republic on a Shoestring. By Gordon Young. Photos by George F. Mobley. 437-477, *Oct. 1973*

Chile, the Long and Narrow Land. By Kip Ross. 185-235, *Feb. 1960*

Capital and Chief Seaport of Chile. By W. Robert Moore. 477-500, *Oct. 1944*

Twin Stars of Chile: Valparaiso, the Gateway, and Santiago, the Capital— Key Cities with a Progressive Present and a Romantic Past. By William Joseph Showalter. 197-247, *Feb. 1929*

SANTIAGO ATITLÁN, Guatemala:

Guatemala, Maya and Modern. By Louis de la Haba. Photos by Joseph J. Scherschel. 661-689, *Nov. 1974*

Guatemala Revisited. By Luis Marden. 525-564, *Oct. 1947*

To Market in Guatemala. By Luis Marden. Photos by Giles Greville Healey and Charles S. Pineo. 87-104, *July 1945*

SANTO DOMINGO, Dominican Republic:

The Land Columbus Loved. By Oliver P. Newman. 197-224, *Feb. 1944*

SANTORIN (Island), Aegean Sea:

The Isles of Greece. By Richard Stillwell. 593-622, *May 1944*

Santorin and Mýkonos, Aegean Gems. Photos by B. Anthony Stewart. 339-346, *Mar. 1940*

See also Thera

SANTOS, Brazil:

As São Paulo Grows: Half the World's Coffee Beans Flavor the Life and Speed the Growth of an Inland Brazil City. By W. Robert Moore. 657-688, *May 1939*

SÃO MIGUEL (Island), Azores. *See* St. Michael's

SÃO PAULO (City), Brazil:

Brazil: Moment of Promise and Pain. By Priit J. Vesilind. Photos by Stephanie Maze. 348-385, *Mar. 1987*

Brazil's Golden Beachhead. By Bart McDowell. Photos by Nicholas deVore III. 246-277, *Feb. 1978*

A collector and seller of junk in São Paulo, Brazil, Augusto Procopio Pinto takes time out for music. DICK DURRANCE II

As São Paulo Grows: Half the World's Coffee Beans Flavor the Life and Speed the Growth of an Inland Brazil City. By W. Robert Moore. 657-688, *May 1939*
See also São Paulo (State)

SÃO PAULO (State), Brazil:
Brazil's Potent Weapons. By W. Robert Moore. 41-78, *Jan. 1944*
Air Cruising Through New Brazil: A National Geographic Reporter Spots Vast Resources Which the Republic's War Declaration Adds to Strength of United Nations. By Henry Albert Phillips. 503-536, *Oct. 1942*
A Visit to the Brazilian Coffee Country. By Robert De C. Ward. 908-931, *Oct. 1911*
See also São Paulo (City)

SÃO TOMÉ (Island), Gulf of Guinea:
São Tomé, the Chocolate Island. By William Leon Smyser. 657-680, *May 1946*

SAPELO ISLAND, Sea Islands, Georgia:
Sea Islands: Adventuring Along the South's Surprising Coast. By James Cerruti. Photos by Thomas Nebbia and James L. Amos. 366-393, *Mar. 1971*
The Golden Isles of Guale. By W. Robert Moore. 235-264, *Feb. 1934*

SAPOUNA-SAKELLARAKI, EFI:
Author
Drama of Death in a Minoan Temple. By Yannis Sakellarakis and Efi Sapouna-Sakellaraki. Photos by Otis Imboden and Spyros Tsavdaroglou. 205-222, *Feb. 1981*

SAPPORO, Japan:
Snow Festival in Japan's Far North. By Eiji Miyazawa. 824-833, *Dec. 1968*

SAPSUCKER WOODS, Cornell University's Exciting New Bird Sanctuary. By Arthur A. Allen. 530-551, *Apr. 1962*

SARA TRIBESPEOPLE:
Into the Heart of Africa. By Gertrude S. Weeks. NGS research grant. 257-263, *Aug. 1956*

SARAWAK (State), Borneo, Malaysia:
Ambassadors of Good Will: The Peace Corps. By Sargent Shriver and Peace Corps Volunteers. Included: Sarawak. By Edwin C. Price, Jr. 297-345, *Sept. 1964*
In Storied Lands of Malaysia. By Maurice Shadbolt. Photos by Winfield Parks. 734-783, *Nov. 1963*
Jungle Journeys in Sarawak. By Hedda Morrison. 710-736, *May 1956*
Keeping House in Borneo. By Virginia Hamilton. 293-324, *Sept. 1945*
Sarawak: The Land of the White Rajahs. By Harrison W. Smith. 110-167, *Feb. 1919*
Notes on the Sea Dyaks of Borneo. By Edwin H. Gomes. 695-723, *Aug. 1911*
Colonial Government in Borneo. By James M. Hubbard. 359-363, *Sept. 1900*

SARCOPHAGI:
Ancient Shipwreck Yields New Facts–and a Strange Cargo. By Peter Throckmorton. Photos by Kim Hart and Joseph J. Scherschel. 282-300, *Feb. 1969*
Fresh Treasures from Egypt's Ancient Sands. By Jefferson Caffery. Photos by David S. Boyer. 611-650, *Nov. 1955*

SARDINES:
Brittany: The Land of the Sardine. By Hugh M. Smith. 541-573, *June 1909*

SARDINIA (Island), Italy:
Where the Sard Holds Sway. By Luigi Pellerano. 464-474, *Apr. 1926*
The Island of Sardinia and Its People: Traces of Many Civilizations to Be Found in the Speech, Customs, and Costumes of This Picturesque Land. By Guido Costa. Included: Sardinian Smiles. Photos by Clifton Adams. 1-75, *Jan. 1923*
Little-Known Sardinia. By Helen Dunstan Wright. 97-120, *Aug. 1916*

SARDIS (Ancient City):
The Buried Cities of Asia Minor. By Ernest L. Harris. 1-18, *Jan. 1909*

SARGASSO SEA:
Adrift on a Raft of Sargassum. Photos by Robert F. Sisson. 188-199, *Feb. 1976*
Night Life in the Gulf Stream. By Paul A. Zahl. 391-418, *Mar. 1954*
Sindbads of Science: Narrative of a Windjammer's Specimen-Collecting Voyage to the Sargasso Sea, to Senegambian Africa and Among Islands of High Adventure in the South Atlantic. By George Finlay Simmons. 1-75, *July 1927*

SARGASSUM:
Adrift on a Raft of Sargassum. Photos by Robert F. Sisson. 188-199, *Feb. 1976*

SARGASSUM FISH:
Adrift on a Raft of Sargassum. Photos by Robert F. Sisson. 188-199, *Feb. 1976*

SARGENT, R. H.: *Author*
The Monarchs of Alaska. 610-623, *July 1909*

SARGON II, King (Assyria):
Ancient Mesopotamia: A Light That Did Not Fail. By E. A. Speiser. Paintings by H. M. Herget. 41-105, *Jan. 1951*

SARICHEF'S Atlas, 1826. By Marcus Baker. 86-92, *Mar. 1902*

Erected along the railroad tracks that linked Canada's wheat belt with world markets in the 1880s, grain elevators punctuate the plains of Saskatchewan. CRAIG AURNESS, WEST LIGHT

S
T

An Unbeliever Joins the Hadj: On the Age-Old Pilgrimage to Mecca, Babies Are Born, Elders Die, and Families May Halt a Year to Earn Funds in Distant Lands. By Owen Tweedy. 761-789, *June 1934*

A Visit to Three Arab Kingdoms: Transjordania, Iraq, and the Hedjaz Present Many Problems to European Powers. By Junius B. Wood. 535-568, *May 1923*

The Rise of the New Arab Nation. By Frederick Simpich. 369-393, *Nov. 1919*

Mecca the Mystic: A New Kingdom Within Arabia. By S. M. Zwemer. 157-172, *Aug. 1917*

Arabia, the Desert of the Sea. By Archibald Forder. 1039-1062, 1117, *Dec. 1909*

One Thousand Miles of Railway Built for Pilgrims and Not for Dividends. By F. R. Maunsell. Contents: Damascus to Mecca railway. 156-172, *Feb. 1909*

Damascus and Mecca Railway. 408, *Nov. 1901*

SAUK AND FOX INDIANS:

America's First Settlers, the Indians. By Matthew W. Stirling. Paintings by W. Langdon Kihn. 535-596, *Nov. 1937*

SAUNTERING Through the Land of Roger Williams. Photos by Clifton Adams. 311-318, *Sept. 1931*

SAUSSURE, H. B. DE:

The Ascent of Mont Blanc. By Walter Woodburn Hyde. 861-942, *Aug. 1913*

SAVANNAH, N. S.:

Aboard the N. S. *Savannah:* World's First Nuclear Merchantman. By Alan Villiers. Photos by John E. Fletcher. 280-298, *Aug. 1962*

SAVANNAH to Charleston–A Good Life in the Low Country. By John J. Putman. Photos by Annie Griffiths. Included: Savannah, Georgia. 798-829, *Dec. 1983*

SAVE-THE-REDWOODS League. 682, May 1951; 510, Oct. 1957; 658, Nov. 1963; 15, 28, 44, July 1964; 60, 63, 67, *July 1966*

SAVING Brazil's Stone Age Tribes From Extinction. By Orlando and Claudio Villas Boas. Photos by W. Jesco von Puttkamer. 424-444, *Sept. 1968*

SAVING Earth's Oldest Living Things. By Andrew H. Brown. Photos by Raymond Moulin and author. 679-695, *May 1951*

SAVING Man's Wildlife Heritage. By John H. Baker. Photos by Robert F. Sisson. 581-620, *Nov. 1954*

SAVING Père David's Deer. By Larry Kohl. Photos by Bates Littlehales. 478-485, *Oct. 1982*

SAVING the Ancient Temples at Abu Simbel. By Georg Gerster. Paintings by Robert W. Nicholson. 694-742, *May 1966*

SAVING the Ducks and Geese. By Wells W. Cooke. 361-380, *Mar. 1913*

SAVING the Forests. By Herbert A. Smith. 519-534, *Aug. 1907*

SAVING the Nene, World's Rarest Goose. By S. Dillon Ripley. Photos by Jerry Chong. 745-754, *Nov. 1965*

SAVING the Philippine Eagle. By Robert S. Kennedy. Photos by Alan R. Degen, Neil L. Rettig, and Wolfgang A. Salb. NGS research grant. 847-856, *June 1981*

SAVING the Redwoods. By Madison Grant. 519-536, *June 1920*

SAVING the Rothschild's Giraffe. By Carolyn Bennett Patterson. 419-421, *Sept. 1977*

SAVING the World's Largest Flower. By Willem Meijer. Photos by Edward S. Ross. 136-140, *July 1985*

SAVOY, PRINCE OF. *See* Abruzzi, Duke of the

SAXONY (Region), East Germany:

Treasures of Dresden. By John L. Eliot. Photos by Victor R. Boswell, Jr. 702-717, *Nov. 1978*

SAYRE, J. D.:

The Valley of Ten Thousand Smokes: An Account of the Discovery and Exploration of the Most Wonderful Volcanic Region in the World. By Robert F. Griggs. 115-169, *Feb. 1918*

SCALLOPS:

The Magic Lure of Sea Shells. By Paul A. Zahl. Photos by Victor R. Boswell, Jr. and author. 386-429, *Mar. 1969*

Shells Take You Over World Horizons. By Rutherford Platt. 33-84, *July 1949*

SCAMMON LAGOON, Baja California, Mexico:

The California Gray Whale Comes Back. By Theodore J. Walker. 394-415, *Mar. 1971*

Hunting the Heartbeat of a Whale. By Paul Dudley White and Samuel W. Matthews. NGS research grant. 49-64, *July 1956*

SCANDINAVIA:

Hunters of the Lost Spirit: Lapps. By Priit J. Vesilind. Photos by Sisse Brimberg. 194-197, *Feb. 1983*

⊕ *Peoples of the Arctic; Arctic Ocean.* *Feb. 1983*

■ The Last Vikings. 434A-434B, *Mar. 1972*

Friendly Flight to Northern Europe. By Lyndon B. Johnson. Photos by Volkmar Wentzel. 268-293, *Feb. 1964*

⊕ *Scandinavia.* Atlas series. *Apr. 1963*

⊕ *Northern Europe. Aug. 1954*

See also Denmark; Finland; Iceland; Norway; Sweden

SCAPEGOAT WILDERNESS, Montana:

Studying Grizzly Habitat by Satellite. By John Craighead. NGS research grant. 148-158, *July 1976*

SCARLET IBIS:

New Scarlet Bird in Florida Skies. By Paul A. Zahl. 874-882, *Dec. 1967*

Search for the Scarlet Ibis in Venezuela. By Paul A. Zahl. NGS research grant. 633-661, *May 1950*

SCAT. *See* South Pacific Combat Air Transport

SCAVENGERS:

The Fascinating World of Trash. By Peter T. White. Photos by Louie Psihoyos. 424-457, *Apr. 1983*

SCENE in Liberia. 298-301, *Mar. 1909*

The **SCENERY** of North America. By James Bryce. 339-389, *Apr. 1922*

SCENES Along the Byways of Hellas. Photos by Maynard Owen Williams. 689-696, *Dec. 1930*

SCENES Among the High Cascades in Central Oregon. By Ira A. Williams. 579-592, *June 1912*

SCENES and Round-Ups of the Beaver State. Photos by Amos Burg. 181-212, *Feb. 1934*

SCENES and Shrines of the Cavalier Country. Photos by Charles Martin, Edwin L. Wisherd, Jacob Gayer, Clifton Adams. 425-432, *Apr. 1929*

SCENES from America's Southwest. 651-664, *June 1921*

SCENES From Every Land: A Collection of Illustrations From NGM Picturing the People, Natural Phenomena, and Animal Life in All Parts of the World. 224 pages. *1907*

SCENES From Every Land: Illustrations Picturing the People, Natural Phenomena, and Animal Life in All Parts of the World (Second Series). 223 pages. *1909*

SCENES From Every Land: Picturing the People, Natural Phenomena, and Animal Life in All Parts of the World (Third Series). 216 pages. *1912*

SCENES From Every Land: Picturing ▪▪ the People, Natural Phenomena, and Animal Life in All Parts of the World (Fourth Series). 216 pages. *1918*

SCENES from France. 29-44, *July 1921*

SCENES from Greenland. 877-891, *Oct. 1909*

SCENES from North Africa. Photos from David Fairchild. 615-619, *Sept. 1907*

SCENES from the Land Where Everybody Dresses in White. Photos by Rev. J. Z. Moore. 871-877, *Dec. 1908*

SCENES in Asia Minor. 173-193, *Feb. 1909*

SCENES in Italy. 321-332, *Apr. 1910*

SCENES in Korea and China. Photos by William W. Chapin. 903-926, *Nov. 1910*

SCENES in Many Lands. Photos by Franklin Price Knott. 233-248, *Sept. 1916*

SCENES in Out-of-the-Way Places. 854-860, *July 1913*

SCENES in Scotland. 519-534, *Nov.-Dec. 1917*

SCENES in South America. 375-390, *Oct. 1921*

SCENES in Switzerland. 257-268, *Mar. 1910*

SCENES in the British Isles. Photos by A. W. Cutler. 551-566, *Dec. 1915*

SCENES in the Celestial Republic. 217-232, *Feb. 1926*

SCENES in the Fortunate Isles. Photos by Wilhelm Tobien. 599-606, *May 1930*

SCENES of Beauty in Copper Land. Photos by Jacob Gayer. 199-214, *Feb. 1929*

SCENES of Postwar Finland. By La Verne Bradley. Photos by Jerry Waller. 233-264, *Aug. 1947*

SCENES of Sunny Africa. 735-750, *June 1935*

SCENES on High Veld and Low. Photos by Melville Chater. 493-500, *Apr. 1931*

SCENIC Glories of Western United States. Photos by Fred Payne Clatworthy. 223-230, *Aug. 1929*

SCENIC Guilin Links China's Past and Present. By W. E. Garrett. 536-563, *Oct. 1979*

SCENIC Resources of the Dominican Republic. Photos by Jacob Gayer. 81-104, *Jan. 1931*

SCHAEFFER, CLAUDE F. A.: *Author*

Secrets from Syrian Hills: Explorations Reveal World's Earliest Known Alphabet, Deciphered from Schoolboy Slates and Dictionaries of 3,000 Years Ago. 97-126, *July 1933*

A New Alphabet of the Ancients Is Unearthed: An Inconspicuous Mound in Northern Syria Yields Archeological Treasures of Far-reaching Significance. 477-516, *Oct. 1930*

SCHALLER, GEORGE B.:

On Assignment in China. *Dec. 1981*

Nomination Page. In Tanzania. *May 1968*

Author-Photographer

Secrets of the Wild Panda. Included: Saving the panda. 284-309, *Mar. 1986*

Pandas in the Wild. 735-749, *Dec. 1981*

Imperiled Phantom of Asian Peaks: First Photographs of Snow Leopards in the Wild. 702-707, *Nov. 1971*

Life with the King of Beasts. 494-519, *Apr. 1969*

SCHANTZ, ORPHEUS MOYER:

Author

Indiana's Unrivaled Sand-Dunes–A National Park Opportunity. 430-441, *May 1919*

SCHEFFER, VICTOR B.: *Author*

Exploring the Lives of Whales. 752-767, *Dec. 1976*

Author-Photographer

The Fur Seal Herd Comes of Age. By Victor B. Scheffer and Karl W. Kenyon. 491-512, *Apr. 1952*

SCHELLBACH, LOUIS: *Author*

Grand Canyon: Nature's Story of Creation. Photos by Justin Locke. 589-629, *May 1955*

SCHERSCHEL, JOSEPH J.:

Photographer

The Preposterous Puffer. By Noel D. Vietmeyer. 260-270, *Aug. 1984*

The Journey of Burke and Wills: First Across Australia. By Joseph Judge. 152-191, *Feb. 1979*

Andalusia, the Spirit of Spain. By Howard La Fay. 833-857, *June 1975*

Guatemala, Maya and Modern. By Louis de la Haba. 661-689, *Nov. 1974*

Sunny Corsica: French Morsel in the Mediterranean. By Robert Cairns. 401-423, *Sept. 1973*

Hungary: Changing Homeland of a Tough, Romantic People. By Bart McDowell. Photos by Albert Moldvay and Joseph J. Scherschel. 443-483, *Apr. 1971*

South Australia, Gateway to the Great Outback. By Howell Walker. 441-481, *Apr. 1970*

Yankee Cruises Turkey's History-haunted Coast. By Irving and Electa Johnson. 798-845, *Dec. 1969*

Macao Clings to the Bamboo Curtain. By Jules B. Billard. 521-539, *Apr. 1969*

Ancient Shipwreck Yields New Facts–and a Strange Cargo. By Peter Throckmorton. Photos by Kim Hart and Joseph J. Scherschel. 282-300, *Feb. 1969*

Lombardy's Lakes, Blue Jewels in Italy's Crown. By Franc Shor. 58-99, *July 1968*

Mobile, Alabama's City in Motion. By William Graves. Photos by Joseph J. Scherschel and Robert W. Madden. 368-397, *Mar. 1968*

Illinois: The City and the Plain. By Robert Paul Jordan. Photos by James L. Stanfield and Joseph J. Scherschel. 745-797, *June 1967*

Shielding themselves from view, women of Saudi Arabia don veils when appearing in public and retire in private behind latticed windows. JODI COBB, NGS

*An artist portrays the fateful moment when Henry VIII's warship **Mary Rose** sank off Portsmouth harbor.*   PAINTING BY RICHARD SCHLECHT

SCHOEDSACK, ERNEST B.:
Photographer

Two Fighting Tribes of the Sudan. By Merian C. Cooper. 465-486, *Oct. 1929*

The Warfare of the Jungle Folk: Campaigning Against Tigers, Elephants, and Other Wild Animals in Northern Siam. By Merian C. Cooper. 233-268, *Feb. 1928*

SCHOFIELD, PHIL: *Photographer*

A Paradise Called the Palouse. By Barbara Austin. 798-819, *June 1982*

A **SCHOLARLY** President Looks at Mexico's Future. The Editor. 175, *Aug. 1984*

SCHOOL BULLETIN, NGS:

President's Page. By Gilbert M. Grosvenor. *Sept. 1988*
The *School Bulletin* is retired after 56 years; replaced by *WORLD.* 299, *Sept. 1975*

SCHOOL for Space Monkeys. 725-729, *May 1961*

SCHOOL for Survival. By Curtis E. LeMay. 565-602, *May 1953*

SCHOOLS:

Gallup Survey of Geographic Knowledge. President's Page. By Gilbert M. Grosvenor. *Nov. 1988*
We Build a School for Sherpa Children. By Sir Edmund Hillary. 548-551, *Oct. 1962*
Round the World School. By Paul Antze. Photos by William Eppridge. Contents: International School of America. 96-127, *July 1962*
Zoo Animals Go to School. By Marion P. McCrane. Photos by W. E. Garrett. 694-706, *Nov. 1956*
The DAR Story. By Lonnelle Aikman. Photos by B. Anthony Stewart and John E. Fletcher. Note: DAR partially supports a dozen schools and colleges in this country, maintains a large student-loan fund, presents annual awards for high standing in certain subjects, and operates two schools of its own, the Kate Duncan Smith School, Grant, Alabama, and Tamassee School, South Carolina. 565-598, *Nov. 1951*
Turkey Goes to School. By Maynard Owen Williams. 95-108, *Jan. 1929*
See also The Deaf, Schools for; National Outdoor Leadership School; Outward Bound School; Public Schools; Training Schools; U. S. Air Force Academy; U. S. Merchant Marine Academy; U. S. Military Academy; U. S. Naval Academy; Universities and Colleges; *and* Education

SCHOONERS:

Down East Cruise. By Tom Horgan. Photos by Luis Marden. 329-369, *Sept. 1952*
Newfoundland, North Atlantic Rampart: From the "First Base of American Defense" Planes Fly to Britain's Aid over Stout Fishing Schooners of the Grand Banks. By George Whiteley, Jr. 111-140, *July 1941*

The Sealing Saga of Newfoundland. By Robert A. Bartlett. 91-130, *July 1929*
Life on the Grand Banks: An Account of the Sailor-Fishermen Who Harvest the Shoal Waters of North America's Eastern Coasts. By Frederick William Wallace. 1-28, *July 1921*
Reports of Sealing Schooners Cruising in the Neighborhood of Tuscarora Deep in May and June 1896. By Eliza Ruhamah Scidmore. 310-312, *Sept. 1896*
See also Portuguese Fishing Fleet; *and* Adams; Bowdoin; Effie M. Morrissey; Georg Stage; Kinkajou; Vaitere; Yankee

SCHOTT, C. A.: *Author*

Recent Contributions to Our Knowledge of the Earth's Shape and Size, by the United States Coast and Geodetic Survey. 36-41, *Jan. 1901*

SCHRADER, F. C.: *Author*

The Cape Nome Gold District. 15-23, *Jan. 1900*

SCHREIBER, RALPH W.:
Author-Photographer

Bad Days for the Brown Pelican. Photos by William R. Curtsinger and author. 111-123, *Jan. 1975*

SCHREIDER, HELEN and FRANK:

Nomination Page. In the Great Rift Valley. *July 1965*
Nomination Page. On Timor, Indonesia. *July 1962*
Nomination Page. *Mar. 1960*
Author-Photographers
■■ *Exploring the Amazon.* 207 pages. *1970*
Taiwan: The Watchful Dragon. 1-45, *Jan. 1969*
In the Footsteps of Alexander the Great. Paintings by Tom Lovell. 1-65, *Jan. 1968*
Journey Into the Great Rift: the Northern Half. 254-290, *Aug. 1965*
East From Bali by Seagoing Jeep to Timor. 236-279, *Aug. 1962*
Indonesia, the Young and Troubled Island Nation. 579-625, *May 1961*
From the Hair of Siva. 445-503, *Oct. 1960*

SCHROEDER, ROBERT E.:
Author-Photographer

Photographing the Night Creatures of Alligator Reef. Photos by author and Walter A. Starck. 124-154, *Jan. 1964*
Photographer
Imperiled Gift of the Sea: Caribbean Green Turtle. By Archie Carr. 876-890, *June 1967*

SCHULKE, FLIP: *Photographer*

Titicaca, Abode of the Sun. By Luis Marden. 272-294, *Feb. 1971*
My Neighbors Hold to Mountain Ways. By Malcolm Ross. Contents: Blue Ridge, North Carolina. 856-880, *June 1958*

SCHULMAN, EDMUND: *Author*

Bristlecone Pine, Oldest Known Living Thing. Photos by W. Robert Moore. 355-372, *Mar. 1958*

SCHULTZ, HARALD:

Nomination Page. In Brazil. *July 1961*
Author-Photographer
The Waurá: Brazilian Indians of the Hidden Xingu. 130-152, *Jan. 1966*
Indians of the Amazon Darkness. 737-758, *May 1964*
Brazil's Big-lipped Indians. 118-133, *Jan. 1962*
Blue-eyed Indian. 65-89, *July 1961*
Tukuna Maidens Come of Age. 629-649, *Nov. 1959*
Children of the Sun and Moon. Translated from German by Curtis T. Everett. Contents: Kraho Indians. 340-363, *Mar. 1959*

SCHULTZ, JOHN E.: *Author*

Sea Fever. 237-268, *Feb. 1949*

SCHULTZ, LEONARD P.: *Author*

Fishing in Pacific Coast Streams. Paintings by Hashime Murayama. 185-212, *Feb. 1939*
Treasures of the Pacific: Marine Fishes and Fisheries Yield Vast Wealth from Alaska to Baja California. Paintings by Hashime Murayama. 463-498, *Oct. 1938*

SCHURZ, W. L.: *Author*

The Amazon, Father of Waters: The Earth's Mightiest River Drains a Basin of More Than 2,700,000 Square Miles, from Which Came Originally the World's Finest Rubber. 445-463, *Apr. 1926*

SCHUYLER, MONTGOMERY:
Author

Russia's Democrats. 210-240, *Mar. 1917*

SCHWAB, CHARLES M.: *Author*

Our Industrial Victory. 212-229, *Sept. 1918*

SCHWARTZ, DOUGLAS W.:

Nomination Page. At the Grand Canyon. *June 1972*

SCHWARTZ, WILLIAM LEONARD:
Author

Peacetime Rambles in the Ryukyus. 543-561, *May 1945*

SCHWINN, GRETCHEN: *Author*

We Escape from Madrid. 251-268, *Feb. 1937*

SCIDMORE, ELIZA RUHAMAH:

Corresponding Secretary. xii, Feb. 19, 1892; xix, xx-xxi, Feb. 20, 1893; xix, xx-xxi, May 5, 1894; 416, *Sept. 1898*
International Geographic Conference in Chicago, July 27-28, 1893: Minutes of the Conference. F. H. Newell and Eliza R. Scidmore, Secretaries. 101-111, *Jan. 31, 1894*
Author
Adam's Second Eden. 105-173, 206, *Feb. 1912*
Mukden, the Manchu Home, and Its Great Art Museum. 289-320, *Apr. 1910*
Koyasan, the Japanese Valhalla. 650-670, *Oct. 1907*
Archaeology in the Air. 151-163, *Mar. 1907*

SCIENCE:

This hand-tinted portrait was the work of the first woman on the Society's Board of Managers. ELIZA R. SCIDMORE

SCIENTIST CLIFFS, Maryland:

SCILLY, Isles of, England:

SCISCO, L. D.: *Author*

SCOFIELD, JOHN:

Hong Kong Has Many Faces. 1-41, *Jan. 1962*

Haiti–West Africa in the West Indies. 226-259, *Feb. 1961*

Easter Week in Indian Guatemala. 406-417, *Mar. 1960*

Hashemite Jordan, Arab Heartland. 841-856, *Dec. 1952*

Photographer

Venice, City of Twilight Splendor. By Joe Alex Morris. 543-569, *Apr. 1961*

SCOLLAY, CLIVE: *Author*

Arnhem Land Aboriginals Cling to Dreamtime. Photos by Penny Tweedie. 644-663, *Nov. 1980*

The **SCOPE** and Value of Arctic Explorations. By A. W. Greely. 32-39, *Jan. 1896*

SCORPIONFISH:

Scorpionfish: Danger in Disguise. By David Doubilet. 634-643, *Nov. 1987*

Something's Fishy About That Fin! Photos by Robert J. Shallenberger and William D. Madden. 224-227, *Aug. 1974*

SCORPIONS: Living Fossils of the Sands. By Paul A. Zahl. 436-442, *Mar. 1968*

SCOTLAND:

Red Deer and Man. By T. H. Clutton-Brock. Photos by Jim Brandenburg. 538-555, *Oct. 1986*

Red Deer: A Scottish Dynasty. By T. H. Clutton-Brock. 556-562, *Oct. 1986*

To Scotland Afoot Along the Pennine Way. By David Yeadon. Photos by Annie Griffiths. 388-418, *Mar. 1986*

■ *Discovering Britain & Ireland.* 448 pages. *1985*

Scotland, Ghosts, and Glory. By Rowe Findley. Photos by Peter Carmichael. 40-69, *July 1984*

The Celts. By Merle Severy. Photos by James P. Blair. Paintings by Robert C. Magis. 582-633, *May 1977*

Striking It Rich in the North Sea. By Rick Gore. Photos by Dick Durrance II. 519-549, *Apr. 1977*

✣ *A Traveler's Map of the British Isles.* Text on reverse. *Apr. 1974*

The Highlands, Stronghold of Scottish Gaeldom. By Kenneth MacLeish. Photos by Winfield Parks. 398-435, *Mar. 1968*

Home to Arran, Scotland's Magic Isle. By J. Harvey Howells. 80-99, *July 1965*

The Britain That Shakespeare Knew. By Louis B. Wright. Photos by Dean Conger. 613-665, *May 1964*

Scotland From Her Lovely Lochs and Seas. By Alan Villiers. Photos by Robert F. Sisson. 492-541, *Apr. 1961*

✣ *British Isles.* Atlas series. *July 1958*

Poets' Voices Linger in Scottish Shrines. By Isobel Wylie Hutchison. Photos by Kathleen Revis. 437-488, *Oct. 1957*

A Stroll to John o'Groat's. By Isobel Wylie Hutchison. 1-48, *July 1956*

Rhododendron Glories of Southwest Scotland. By David S. Boyer. Photos

by B. Anthony Stewart and author. 641-664, *May 1954*

Scotland's Golden Eagles at Home. By C. Eric Palmar. 273-286, *Feb. 1954*

Playing 3,000 Golf Courses in Fourteen Lands. By Ralph A. Kennedy. 113-132, *July 1952*

A Stroll to London. By Isobel Wylie Hutchison. Photos by B. Anthony Stewart. 171-204, *Aug. 1950*

The British Way. By Sir Evelyn Wrench. Included: James I, James Watt. 421-541, *Apr. 1949*

✣ *The British Isles. Apr. 1949*

Midshipmen's Cruise. By William J. Aston and Alexander G. B. Grosvenor. 711-754, *June 1948*

British Castles, History in Stone. By Norman Wilkinson. 111-129, *July 1947*

Bonnie Scotland, Postwar Style. By Isobel Wylie Hutchison. 545-601, *May 1946*

Scotland in Wartime. By Isobel Wylie Hutchison. 723-743, *June 1943*

✣ *A Modern Pilgrim's Map of the British Isles or More Precisely the Kingdom of Great Britain and Northern Ireland and the Irish Free State. June 1937*

Low Road, High Road, Around Dundee. By Maurice P. Dunlap. 547-576, *Apr. 1936*

Great Britain on Parade. By Maynard Owen Williams. 137-184, *Aug. 1935*

The Orkneys and Shetlands–A Mysterious Group of Islands. By Charles S. Olcott. 197-228, *Feb. 1921*

The Races of Europe. By Edwin A. Grosvenor. 441-534, *Dec. 1918*

Gems from Scotland. 519-534, *Nov.-Dec. 1917*

The Ordnance Survey of Great Britain–Its History and Object. By Josiah Pierce, Jr. 243-260, *Aug. 1890*

See also Edinburgh; Inner Hebrides; Ness, Loch; Orkney Islands; Outer Hebrides; Shetland Islands

SCOTT, CHARLES F.:

The Annual Dinner of the National Geographic Society (Speech by Charles F. Scott). 22-37, *Jan. 1906*

SCOTT, DAVID R.:

Apollo 15 Explores the Mountains of the Moon. By Kenneth F. Weaver. Photos from NASA. 233-265, *Feb. 1972*

Author

What Is It Like to Walk on the Moon? 326-331, *Sept. 1973*

SCOTT, DOUGLAS: *Photographer*

High Adventure in the Himalayas. By Thomas Weir. 193-234, *Aug. 1952*

SCOTT, EMMETT J.: *Author*

Conditions in Liberia. By Roland P. Folkner, George Sale, Emmett J. Scott. 729-741, *Sept. 1910*

SCOTT, SIR GEORGE: *Author*

Among the Hill Tribes of Burma–An Ethnological Thicket. 293-321, *Mar. 1922*

SCOTT, GEORGE W.: *Photographer*

Kano, Mud-made City. Photos by George W. Scott and K. S. Twitchell. 545-552, *May 1944*

SCOTT, JOHN: *Author*

"Magnetic City," Core of Valiant Russia's Industrial Might. 525-556, *May 1943*

SCOTT, JOHN ANTHONY: *Author*

■ *The Story of America: A National Geographic Picture Atlas.* Juvenile. 324 pages. *1984*

SCOTT, SIR PETER: *Author*

The Antarctic Challenge. 538-543, *Apr. 1987*

SCOTT, ROBERT FALCON:

The Antarctic Challenge. By Sir Peter Scott. 538-543, *Apr. 1987*

Frilled, flamboyant, and dangerous, this turkeyfish is one of some dozen species of poisonous scorpionfish that range the Gulf of Aqaba, an arm of the Red Sea. DAVID DOUBILET

In the Footsteps of Scott. By Robert Swan. 544-555, *Apr. 1987*

Nomination Page. At the South Pole. *May 1962*

All-out Assault on Antarctica. By Richard E. Byrd. 141-180, *Aug. 1956*

The British Way. By Sir Evelyn Wrench. 421-541, *Apr. 1949*

Our Navy Explores Antarctica. By Richard E. Byrd. U. S. Navy official photos. 429-522, *Oct. 1947*

The Lure of the Land of Ice. Photos by Herbert G. Ponting, official photographer of the British Antarctic Expedition under Capt. Robert F. Scott. 255-270, *Mar. 1924*

An Ice Wrapped Continent. By G. H. Grosvenor. 95-117, *Feb. 1907*

Some Recent English Statements About the Antarctic. By Edwin Swift Balch. 266, *June 1904*

The British South Polar Expedition. 210-212, *May 1903*

The British Antarctic Expedition. 339-345, *Sept. 1901*

SCOTT, SIR WALTER:

Poets' Voices Linger in Scottish Shrines. By Isobel Wylie Hutchison. Photos by Kathleen Revis. 437-488, *Oct. 1957*

A Stroll to London. By Isobel Wylie Hutchison. Photos by B. Anthony Stewart. 171-204, *Aug. 1950*

The British Way. By Sir Evelyn Wrench. 421-541, *Apr. 1949*

SCOTT EXPEDITION:

The Antarctic Challenge. By Sir Peter Scott. 538-543, *Apr. 1987*

In the Footsteps of Scott. By Robert Swan. 544-555, *Apr. 1987*

The British Way. By Sir Evelyn Wrench. Included: A Very Gallant Gentleman–Lawrence Edward Grace Oates (1880-1912). 421-541, *Apr. 1949*

See also Scott, Robert Falcon

SCOTTISH TRANS-GREENLAND EXPEDITION:

First Woman Across Greenland's Ice. By Myrtle Simpson. Photos by Hugh Simpson. 264-279, *Aug. 1967*

SCOUGALL, IRENE. *See* Burdett-Scougall, Irene

SCOURGE (Warship):

Ghost Ships of the War of 1812: *Hamilton* and *Scourge.* By Daniel A. Nelson. Photos by Emory Kristof. Paintings by Richard Schlecht. 289-313, *Mar. 1983*

SCOUTS AND SCOUTING. *See* Boy Scouts; Girl Scouts

SCRIPPS INSTITUTION OF OCEANOGRAPHY:

This Changing Earth. By Samuel W. Matthews. Included: Deep Sea Drilling Project which was directed by the Scripps Institution. 1-37, *Jan. 1973*

La Jolla, a Gem of the California Coast. By Deena Clark. Photos by J. Baylor Roberts. 755-782, *Dec. 1952*

SCRIVEN, GEORGE P.: *Author*

Recent Observations in Albania. 90-114, *Aug. 1918*

SCRUGGS, JAN C.:

Vietnam Veterans Memorial: America Remembers. Included: Echoes of a War. By Timothy S. Kolly; To Heal a Nation. By Joel L. Swerdlow; An Interview with Maya Lin, designer; Editor's Postscript: Southeast Asia Ten Years Later. 552-575, *May 1985*

SCULPTURE:

An Ice Age Ancestor? By Alexander Marshack. Photos by the author and Ira Block. 478-481, *Oct. 1988*

Warriors From a Watery Grave. By Joseph Alsop. Contents: Riace Bronzes. 821-827, *June 1983*

Indonesia Rescues Ancient Borobudur. By W. Brown Morton III. Photos by Dean Conger. 126-142, *Jan. 1983*

Carrara Marble: Touchstone of Eternity. By Cathy Newman. Photos by Pierre Boulat. 42-59, *July 1982*

Ancient Aphrodisias Lives Through Its Art. By Kenan T. Erim. Photos by David Brill. 527-551, *Oct. 1981*

The National Gallery's New Masterwork on the Mall. By J. Carter Brown. Photos by James A. Sugar. 680-701, *Nov. 1978*

China's Incredible Find. By Audrey Topping. Paintings by Yang Hsien-min. Included: The first emperor's burial mound, with guardian army of terra-cotta men and horses. 440-459, *Apr. 1978*

The Maya. 729-811. I. Children of Time. By Howard La Fay. Photos by David Alan Harvey. 729-767; II. Riddle of the Glyphs. By George E. Stuart. Photos by Otis Imboden. 768-791; III. Resurrecting the Grandeur of Tikal. By William R. Coe. 792-798, *Dec. 1975*

China Unveils Her Newest Treasures. Photos by Robert W. Madden. 848-857, *Dec. 1974*

Aphrodisias, Awakened City of Ancient Art. By Kenan T. Erim. Photos by Jonathan S. Blair. NGS research grant. 766-791, *June 1972*

The Louvre, France's Palace of the Arts. By Hereward Lester Cooke, Jr. 796-831, *June 1971*

Searching Out Medieval Churches in Ethiopia's Wilds. By Georg Gerster. 856-884, *Dec. 1970*

Ancient Aphrodisias and Its Marble Treasures. By Kenan T. Erim. Photos by Jonathan S. Blair. NGS research grant. 280-294, *Aug. 1967*

Petra, Rose-red Citadel of Biblical Edom. By David S. Boyer. 853-870, *Dec. 1955*

India's Sculptured Temple Caves. By Volkmar Wentzel. 665-678, *May 1953*

The Caves of the Thousand Buddhas. By Franc and Jean Shor. 383-415, *Mar. 1951*

Darius Carved History on Ageless Rock. By George G. Cameron. 825-844, *Dec. 1950*

The British Way. By Sir Evelyn

Wrench. Included: Landseer Lions. 421-541, *Apr. 1949*

Lascaux Cave, Cradle of World Art. By Norbert Casteret. Photos by Maynard Owen Williams. Included: Clay statues of the Old Stone Age. 771-794, *Dec. 1948*

Great Stone Faces of Easter Island. 225-232, *Feb. 1944*

Storied Islands of the South Sea. Photos by Irving Johnson, Malcolm Evans, and others. 9-40, *Jan. 1942*

Great Stone Faces of the Mexican Jungle: Five Colossal Heads and Numerous Other Monuments of Vanished Americans Are Excavated by the Latest National Geographic-Smithsonian Expedition. By Matthew W. Stirling. 309-334, *Sept. 1940*

Stone Idols of the Andes Reveal a Vanished People: Remarkable Relics of One of the Oldest Aboriginal Cultures of America Are Unearthed in Colombia's San Agustín Region. By Hermann von Walde-Waldegg. 627-647, *May 1940*

The Nation's Capital by Night. By Volkmar Wentzel. 514-530, *Apr. 1940*

Modern Odyssey in Classic Lands: Troy's Treasures, Athens' Parthenon, and Rome's First "Broad Way" Influence Today's Banks, Costumes, Jewelry, and Railroad Timetables. By Maynard Owen Williams. 291-337, *Mar. 1940*

Italy's Monuments Tell Rome's Magnificence. Photos by B. Anthony Stewart. 371-378, *Mar. 1940*

Discovering the New World's Oldest Dated Work of Man: A Maya Monument Inscribed 291 B.C. is Unearthed Near a Huge Stone Head by a Geographic-Smithsonian Expedition in Mexico. By Matthew W. Stirling. 183-218, *Aug. 1939*

The Smallest State in the World: Vatican City on Its 108 Acres Is a Complete Sovereignty Internationally Recognized. By W. Coleman Nevils. 377-412, *Mar. 1939*

China's Great Wall of Sculpture: Man-hewn Caves and Countless Images Form a Colossal Art Wonder of Early Buddhism. By Mary Augusta Mullikin. Paintings by author and Anna M. Hotchkis. 313-348, *Mar. 1938*

Exploring the Secrets of Persepolis. By Charles Breasted. 381-420, *Oct. 1933*

Discovering the Oldest Statues in the World: A Daring Explorer Swims Through a Subterranean River of the Pyrenees and Finds Rock Carvings Made 20,000 Years Ago. By Norbert Casteret. 123-152, *Aug. 1924*

The Mystery of Easter Island. By Mrs. Scoresby Routledge. 629-646, *Dec. 1921*

The Greek Bronzes of Tunisia. By Frank Edward Johnson. 89-103, *Jan. 1912*

See also Afo-A-Kom; Akhenaten Temple Project; Dreyfus Collection; Statue of Liberty; War Memorials; *and* Abu Simbel; Athens; Florence; Rome; Tuscany; Washington, D. C.; *and* Ceramics; Goldsmithing; Wood Carving

SCULPTURE, Gravel. *See* Gravel Pictographs

SCULPTURE, Ice:

Snow Festival in Japan's Far North. By Eiji Miyazawa. 824-833, *Dec. 1968*

SCULPTURED Gates to English Learning. Photos by B. Anthony Stewart. 417-440, *Apr. 1946*

SEA AND SPACE RESEARCH PROJECT. *See* Tektite II

SEA ANEMONES:

Oregon's Sidewalk on the Sea. By Paul A. Zahl. 708-734, *Nov. 1961*

Camera Under the Sea. By Luis Marden. NGS research grant. 162-200, *Feb. 1956*

SEA Change in the Sea Islands. By Charles L. Blockson. Photos by Karen Kasmauski. 735-763, *Dec. 1987*

SEA-CORE DATING:

What's Happening to Our Climate? By Samuel W. Matthews. 576-615, *Nov. 1976*

SEA COWS. *See* Manatees

SEA Creatures of Our Atlantic Shores. By Roy Waldo Miner. Paintings by Else Bostelmann. 209-231, *Aug. 1936*

SEA DIVER (Research Vessel):

A Taxi for the Deep Frontier. By Kenneth MacLeish. Photos by Bates Littlehales. 139-150, *Jan. 1968*

Outpost Under the Ocean. By Edwin A. Link. Photos by Bates Littlehales. NGS research grant. 530-533, *Apr. 1965*

The Deepest Days. By Robert Sténuit. NGS research grant. 534-547, *Apr. 1965*

Tomorrow on the Deep Frontier. By Edwin A. Link. NGS research grant. 778-801, *June 1964*

Our Man-in-Sea Project. By Edwin A.

Link. NGS research grant. 713-717, *May 1963*

The Long, Deep Dive. By Lord Kilbracken. Photos by Bates Littlehales. NGS research grant. 718-731, *May 1963*

SEA DRAGONS:

Dragons of the Deep. Photos by Paul A. Zahl. 838-845, *June 1978*

SEA DYAKS. *See* Iban

SEA ELEPHANTS:

Off Santa Barbara: California's Ranches in the Sea. By Earl Warren, Jr. Photos by Bates Littlehales. 257-283, *Aug. 1958*

Cruise of the *Kinkajou:* Among Desert Islands of Mexico Voyagers Find Outdoor Laboratories for the Naturalist and Ideal Fishing Grounds for the Sportsman. By Alfred M. Bailey. 339-366, *Sept. 1941*

South Georgia, an Outpost of the Antarctic. By Robert Cushman Murphy. 409-444, *Apr. 1922*

SEA Fever. By John E. Schultz. 237-268, *Feb. 1949*

SEA Floor Aquarelles from Tongareva. Paintings by Else Bostelmann under direction of Roy W. Miner. 383-390, *Sept. 1938*

The **SEA** Fogs of San Francisco. 108-114, *Mar. 1901*

SEA Gate of the Pacific Northwest, Puget Sound. By William Graves. Photos by David Alan Harvey. 71-97, *Jan. 1977*

SEA Gypsies of the Philippines. By Anne de Henning Singh. Photos by Raghubir Singh. 659-677, *May 1976*

SEA HORSES:

Little Horses of the Sea. By Paul A. Zahl. 131-153, *Jan. 1959*
See also Sea Dragons

SEA ISLANDS, South Carolina-Georgia-Florida:

Sea Change in the Sea Islands. By Charles L. Blockson. Photos by Karen Kasmauski. 735-763, *Dec. 1987*

Sea Islands: Adventuring Along the South's Surprising Coast. By James Cerruti. Photos by Thomas Nebbia and James L. Amos. Included: Blackbeard, Cumberland, Jekyll, Ossabaw, St. Catherines, St. Simons, Sapelo, Sea Island, Wassaw, in Georgia; Daufuskie, Hilton Head, Johns, Port Royal Sound, in South Carolina. 366-393, *Mar. 1971*

The Golden Isles of Guale. By W. Robert Moore. 235-264, *Feb. 1934*
See also Cumberland Island

The **SEA-KINGS** of Crete. By James Baikie. 1-25, *Jan. 1912*

SEA LAMPREYS:

New Era on the Great Lakes. By Nathaniel T. Kenney. 439-490, *Apr. 1959*

SEA LIONS:

Seals and Their Kin. By Roger L. Gentry. 475-501, *Apr. 1987*
⊕ *Antarctica; Pinnipeds Around the World. Apr. 1987*

Undersea Wonders of the Galapagos. By Gerard Wellington. Photos by David Doubilet. 363-381, *Sept. 1978*

Where Two Worlds Meet. Photos by Des and Jen Bartlett. Contents: Patagonia region, Argentina-Chile. 298-321, *Mar. 1976*

The Galapagos, Eerie Cradle of New Species. By Roger Tory Peterson. Photos by Alan and Joan Root. 541-585, *Apr. 1967*

Lost World of the Galapagos. By Irving and Electa Johnson. 681-703, *May 1959*

SEA Nymphs of Japan. By Luis Marden. 122-135, *July 1971*

SEA OTTERS:

Return of the Sea Otter. By Karl W. Kenyon. Photos by James A. Mattison, Jr. 520-539, *Oct. 1971*

SEA RESCUES:

They Survived at Sea. By Samuel F. Harby. 617-640, *May 1945*

SEA ROBIN (Submarine):

'Round the Horn by Submarine. By Paul C. Stimson. 129-144, *Jan. 1948*

SEA SLUGS. *See* Nudibranchs

SEA SNAKES:

Diving With Sea Snakes. By Kenneth MacLeish. Photos by Ben Cropp. 565-578, *Apr. 1972*

SEA to Lakes on the St. Lawrence. By George W. Long. Photos by B. Anthony Stewart and John E. Fletcher. 323-366, *Sept. 1950*

SEA TURTLES:

Wild Cargo: the Business of Smuggling Animals. By Noel Grove. Photos by Steve Raymer. Included: Green Sea Turtle, Hawksbill Turtle, Pacific Ridley Turtle; and Turtle farming, Turtle shell trade. 287-315, *Mar. 1981*
See also Green Turtles

SEA URCHINS:

Giant Kelp, Sequoias of the Sea. By Wheeler J. North. Photos by Bates Littlehales. Included: Destruction of kelp by sea urchins. 251-269, *Aug. 1972*

SEABEES:

Your Navy as Peace Insurance. By Chester W. Nimitz. 681-736, *June 1946*

SEABIRDS:

New Day for Alaska's Pribilof Islanders. By Susan Hackley Johnson. Photos by Tim Thompson. 536-552, *Oct. 1982*

Hawaii's Far-flung Wildlife Paradise. By John L. Eliot. Photos by Jonathan Blair. 760-791, *May 1978*

Penguins and Their Neighbors. By Roger Tory Peterson. Photos by Des and Jen Bartlett. Included: Albatrosses,

S
T

Seals and their kin were featured on the obverse side of the April 1987 map supplement of Antarctica. NGS CARTOGRAPHIC DIVISION

SEAWEED:

Undersea World of a Kelp Forest. By Sylvia A. Earle. Photos by Al Giddings. 411-426, *Sept. 1980*

Adrift on a Raft of Sargassum. Photos by Robert F. Sisson. 188-199, *Feb. 1976*

Algae: the Life-givers. By Paul A. Zahl. 361-377, *Mar. 1974*

Giant Kelp, Sequoias of the Sea. By Wheeler J. North. Photos by Bates Littlehales. 251-269, *Aug. 1972*

Undersea Gardens of the North Atlantic Coast. Paintings by Else Bostelmann under direction of Roy W. Miner. 217-224, *Aug. 1936*

The Fisheries of Japan. By Hugh M. Smith. 201-220, *May 1905*

Seaweeds of the United States. 244, *May 1905*

SECOND MARINE DIVISION, U. S.:

Gilbert Islands in the Wake of Battle. By W. Robert Moore. 129-162, *Feb. 1945*

SECRET Corners of the World. Contents: Northern Afghanistan, the Alpujarras, the Santa Martas, the Marquesas, Tierra Del Fuego, and the Ruwenzori. 199 pages. *1982*

SECRET of the Discus Fish. By Gene Wolfsheimer. 675-681, *May 1960*

The SECRET of the Southwest Solved by Talkative Tree Rings: Horizons of American History Are Carried Back to A.D. 700 and a Calendar for 1,200 Years Established by National Geographic Society Expeditions. By Andrew Ellicott Douglass. 737-770, *Dec. 1929*

SECRETS from Syrian Hills: Explorations Reveal World's Earliest Known Alphabet, Deciphered from Schoolboy Slates and Dictionaries of 3,000 Years Ago. By Claude F. A. Schaeffer. 97-126, *July 1933*

SECRETS From the Past. By Gene S. Stuart. Juvenile. 104 pages. *1979*

SECRETS of Animal Survival. Juvenile. 104 pages. *1983*

The SECRETS of Nature's Night Lights. By Paul A. Zahl. 45-69, *July 1971*

SECRETS of the Wild Panda. By George B. Schaller. Included: Saving the panda. 284-309, *Mar. 1986*

SECRETS of Washington's Lure. Photos by staff photographers. 377-384, *Mar. 1930*

SEED Farms in California. By A. J. Wells. 515-530, *May 1912*

SEED INDUSTRY:

The Flower Seed Growers: Gardening's Color Merchants. By Robert de Roos. Photos by Jack Fields. 720-738, *May 1968*

Seed Farms in California. By A. J. Wells. 515-530, *May 1912*

SEEING America from the "Shenandoah": An Account of the Record-making 9,000-mile Flight from the Atlantic to the Pacific Coast and Return in the Navy's American-built American-manned Airship. By Junius B. Wood. 1-47, *Jan. 1925*

SEEING America with Lindbergh: The Record of a Tour of More than 20,000 Miles by Airplane Through Forty-eight States on Schedule Time. By Donald E. Keyhoe. 1-46, *Jan. 1928*

SEEING Birds as Real Personalities. By Hance Roy Ivor. 523-530, *Apr. 1954*

SEEING EYE (School), Morristown, New Jersey:

Dogs of Duty and Devotion. By Frederick G. Vosburgh. 769-774, *Dec. 1941*

SEEING-EYE DOGS:

Dogs Work for Man. By Edward J. Linehan. Paintings by Edward Megargee and R. E. Lougheed. 190-233, *Aug. 1958*

Dogs of Duty and Devotion. By Frederick G. Vosburgh. 769-774, *Dec. 1941*

SEEING Our Spanish Southwest. By Frederick Simpich. 711-756, *June 1940*

SEEING Paris on a 48-Hour Pass. U. S. Army official photos. 401-412, *Apr. 1945*

SEEING the Earth from 80 Miles Up. By Clyde T. Holliday. 511-528, *Oct. 1950*

SEEING the World from the Air. By Sir Alan J. Cobham. 349-384, *Mar. 1928*

SEEING 3,000 Years of History in Four Hours: A Panorama of Ancient, Medieval, and Modern Events Against a Background of Mythology Unfolds During an Airplane Journey from Constantinople to Athens. By Maynard Owen Williams. 719-739, *Dec. 1928*

SEEKING Mindanao's Strangest Creatures. By Charles Heizer Wharton. 389-408, *Sept. 1948*

SEEKING the Best of Two Worlds. By Bill Hess. 272-290, *Feb. 1980*

SEEKING the Mountains of Mystery: An Expedition on the China-Tibet Frontier to the Unexplored Amnyi Machen Range, One of Whose Peaks Rivals Everest. By Joseph F. Rock. 131-185, *Feb. 1930*

SEEKING the Oldest Known Maya. By Norman Hammond. Photos by Lowell Georgia and Martha Cooper. NGS research grant. 126-140, *July 1982*

SEEKING the Secret of the Giants. By Frank M. Setzler. Photos by Richard H. Stewart. 390-404, *Sept. 1952*

SEEKING the Smallest Feathered Creatures: Humming Birds, Peculiar to the New World, Are Found from Canada and Alaska to the Straits of Magellan. Swifts and Goatsuckers, Their Nearest Relatives. By Alexander Wetmore. Paintings by Allan Brooks. 65-89, *July 1932*

SEEKING the Tomb of Philip of Macedon. By Manolis Andronicos. Photos by Spyros Tsavdaroglou. 55-77, *July 1978*

SEEKING the Truth About the Feared Piranha. By Paul A. Zahl. 715-733, *Nov. 1970*

The SEETHING Caribbean. By Noel Grove. Photos by Steve Raymer. 244-271, *Feb. 1981*

SEGERSTROM, KENNETH:
Photographer

Down Mexico's Río Balsas. Photos by John W. Webber, Kenneth Segerstrom, and Jack Breed. 257-264, *Aug. 1946*

Stunt at an Indiana kennel in the 1930s shows athletic power of a Doberman pinscher, one of the breeds used as guide dogs and canine police partners. WILLARD R. CULVER, NGS

Francisco Pizarro conquered the Inca in the 16th century, captured Emperor Atahuallpa, held him for ransom, then had him killed. PAINTING BY NED SEIDLER, NGS, AND ROSALIE SEIDLER

S
T

Indians of the Southeastern United States. By Matthew W. Stirling. Paintings by W. Langdon Kihn. 53-74, *Jan. 1946*

South Florida's Amazing Everglades: Encircled by Populous Places Is a Seldom-visited Area of Rare Birds, Prairies, Cowboys, and Teeming Wild Life of Big Cypress Swamp. By John O'Reilly. 115-142, *Jan. 1940*

The Five Civilized Tribes and the Survey of Indian Territory. By C. H. Fitch. 481-491, *Dec. 1898*

SENANAYAKE, DUDLEY:

Nomination Page. *Mar. 1966*

SENECA INDIANS:

"The Fire That Never Dies." By Harvey Arden. Photos by Steve Wall. 375-403, *Sept. 1987*

America's First Settlers, the Indians. By Matthew W. Stirling. Paintings by W. Langdon Kihn. 535-596, *Nov. 1937*

SENEGAL:

Africa's Sahel: The Stricken Land. By William S. Ellis. Photos by Steve McCurry. 140-179, *Aug. 1987*

Senegambia: A Now and Future Nation. By Michael and Aubine Kirtley. 224-251, *Aug. 1985*

Freedom Speaks French in Ouagadougou. By John Scofield. 153-203, *Aug. 1966*

French West Africa in Wartime. By Paul M. Atkins. 371-408, *Mar. 1942*

Timbuktu and Beyond: Desert City of Romantic Savor and Salt Emerges into World Life Again as Trading Post of France's Vast African Empire. By Laura C. Boulton. 631-670, *May 1941*

SENEGAMBIA:

Senegambia: A Now and Future Nation. By Michael and Aubine Kirtley. Note: Senegambia is a confederation

Drought dried the carcasses of a Fulani herdsman's cattle in Senegal, which is allied with Gambia in the Confederation of Senegambia. MICHAEL AND AUBINE KIRTLEY

of the Gambia and Senegal. 224-251, *Aug. 1985*

SENGSENG TRIBESPEOPLE:

Blowgun Hunters of the South Pacific. By Jane C. Goodale. Photos by Ann Chowning. 793-817, *June 1966*

SENNETT, TOMAS: *Photographer*

North for Oil: *Manhattan* Makes the Historic Northwest Passage. By Bern Keating. 374-391, *Mar. 1970*

SENSES:

The Smell Survey Results. By Avery N. Gilbert and Charles J. Wysocki. Graphics designed by Allen Carroll and painted by Mark Seidler. 514-525, *Oct. 1987*

Editorial. By Wilbur E. Garrett. 285, *Mar. 1987*

The Intimate Sense of Smell. By Boyd Gibbons. Photos by Louie Psihoyos. Included: Smell Survey. 324-361, *Sept. 1986*

Messengers to the Brain: Our Fantastic Five Senses. By Paul D. Martin. Juvenile. 104 pages. *1984*

SENTINEL RANGE, Antarctica:

First Conquest of Antarctica's Highest Peaks. By Nicholas B. Clinch. NGS research grant. 836-863, *June 1967*

SENTINELESE (Negrito Tribespeople):

The Last Andaman Islanders. By Raghubir Singh. 66-91, *July 1975*

SEOUL, South Korea:

The South Koreans. By Boyd Gibbons. Photos by Nathan Benn. 232-257, *Aug. 1988*

Seoul: Korean Showcase. By H. Edward Kim. 770-797, *Dec. 1979*

South Korea: What Next? By Peter T. White. Photos by H. Edward Kim. 394-427, *Sept. 1975*

South Korea: Success Story in Asia. By

Howard Sochurek. 301-345, *Mar. 1969*

Roaming Korea South of the Iron Curtain. By Enzo de Chetelat. 777-808, *June 1950*

With the U. S. Army in Korea. By John R. Hodge. 829-840, *June 1947*

Jap Rule in the Hermit Nation. By Willard Price. 429-451, *Oct. 1945*

Chosen–Land of Morning Calm. By Mabel Craft Deering. 421-448, *Oct. 1933*

Glimpses of Korea and China. By William W. Chapin. 895-934, *Nov. 1910*

SEPIK RIVER AND REGION, Papua New Guinea:

Change Ripples New Guinea's Sepik River. By Malcolm S. Kirk. 354-381, *Sept. 1973*

To the Land of the Head-hunters. By E. Thomas Gilliard. NGS research grant. 437-486, *Oct. 1955*

SEPTEMBER, Remember...Atlantic Waters Spawn the Deadly, Unpredictable Hurricane! By Ben Funk. Photos by Robert W. Madden. 346-379, *Sept. 1980*

SEQUOIA GIGANTEA (now *Sequoiadendron giganteum*):

The General Sherman: Earth's Biggest Living Thing. 605-608, *May 1958*

Among the Big Trees of California. By John R. White. 219-232, *Aug. 1934*

The Oldest Living Thing. Contents: "General Sherman Tree." Pictorial supplement, *Apr. 1916*

See also Big Trees

SEQUOIA NATIONAL PARK, California:

Giant Sequoias Draw Millions to California Parks. By John Michael Kauffmann. Photos by B. Anthony Stewart. 147-187, *Aug. 1959*

Saving Earth's Oldest Living Things. By Andrew H. Brown. Photos by Raymond Moulin and author. 679-695, *May 1951*

Among the Big Trees of California. By John R. White. 219-232, *Aug. 1934*

The National Geographic Society Completes Its Gifts of Big Trees. 85-86, *July 1921*

Our Big Trees Saved. 1-11, *Jan. 1917*

The Land of the Best. By Gilbert H. Grosvenor. Included: The Oldest Living Thing ("General Sherman Tree"). 327-430, *Apr. 1916*

Our National Parks. By L. F. Schmeckebier. 531-579, *June 1912*

SEQUOIA SEMPERVIRENS. See Redwoods

SEQUOIAS (Trees):

The National Geographic Society Completes Its Gifts of Big Trees. 85-86, *July 1921*

Our Big Trees Saved. 1-11, *Jan. 1917*

Our National Parks. By L. F. Schmeckebier. 531-579, *June 1912*

See also Redwoods; *Sequoia gigantea*

SEQUOIAS of the Sea: Giant Kelp. By Wheeler J. North. Photos by Bates Littlehales. 251-269, *Aug. 1972*

Powerful grip of a lion's paws brings a wildebeest to its knees on the savanna of the Serengeti National Park, Tanzania's 5,700-square-mile wildlife refuge. MITSUAKI IWAGO

Cosmos. Paintings by Jean-Leon Huens. Text by Thomas Y. Canby. 627-633, *May 1974*

SEVENTH ANNUAL NEWSPAPER NATIONAL SNAPSHOT AWARDS:

Americana. Contents: Winning photos in the Seventh Annual Newspaper National Snapshot Awards. 657-666, *May 1942*

SEVENTH FLEET, U. S.:

Crosscurrents Sweep the Indian Ocean. By Bart McDowell. Photos by Steve Raymer. 422-457, *Oct. 1981*

Pacific Fleet: Force for Peace. By Franc Shor. Photos by W. E. Garrett. 283-335, *Sept. 1959*

Patrolling Troubled Formosa Strait. 573-588, *Apr. 1955*

Our Navy in the Far East. By Arthur W. Radford. Photos by J. Baylor Roberts. 537-577, *Oct. 1953*

SEVENTH U. S. CAVALRY:

Ghosts on the Little Bighorn. By Robert Paul Jordan. Photos by Scott Rutherford. 787-813, *Dec. 1986*

SEVENTY-FIVE Days in the Arctics. By Max Fleischman. 439-446, *July 1907*

75 YEARS Exploring Earth, Sea, and Sky: National Geographic Society Observes Its Diamond Anniversary. By Melvin M. Payne. 1-43, *Jan. 1963*

SEVERIN, TIMOTHY:

On Assignment in Asia Minor. *Sept. 1985*

On Assignment. *July 1982*

Author

The Quest for Ulysses. Photos by Kevin Fleming. 197-225, *Aug. 1986*

Jason's Voyage: In Search of the Golden Fleece. Photos by John Egan and Seth Mortimer. 406-420, *Sept. 1985*

In the Wake of Sindbad. Photos by Richard Greenhill. 2-41, *July 1982*

The Voyage of *Brendan.* Photos by Cotton Coulson. 770-797, *Dec. 1977*

SEVERN VALLEY, England:

The Beauties of the Severn Valley. By Frank Wakeman. 417-452, *Apr. 1933*

SEVERY, MERLE:

On Assignment in Vatican City. *Oct. 1983*

Nomination Page. *Nov. 1962*

Nomination Page. *Aug. 1958*

Author

The World of Süleyman the Magnificent. Photos by James L. Stanfield. 552-601, *Nov. 1987*

Shakespeare Lives at the Folger. Photos by Nathan Benn. 244-259, *Feb. 1987*

The Byzantine Empire: Rome of the East. Photos by James L. Stanfield. 709-767, *Dec. 1983*

The World of Martin Luther. Photos by James L. Amos. 418-463, *Oct. 1983*

The Celts. Photos by James P. Blair. Paintings by Robert C. Magis. 582-633, *May 1977*

Northwest Wonderland: Washington State. Photos by B. Anthony Stewart. 445-493, *Apr. 1960*

In 1951 actor Charles Laughton, right, and associate William Cottrell view a model of the Globe Theatre, hall where Shakespeare's plays were performed.   J. BAYLOR ROBERTS, NGS

SEVILLA (Seville), Spain:

Andalusia, the Spirit of Spain. By Howard La Fay. Photos by Joseph J. Scherschel. 833-857, *June 1975*

Holy Week and the Fair in Sevilla. By Luis Marden. 499-530, *Apr. 1951*

Seville, More Spanish Than Spain: The City of the Ibero-American Exposition, Which Opens This Spring, Presents a Tapestry of Many Ages and of Nations Old and New. By Richard Ford. 273-310, *Mar. 1929*

The **SEX,** Nativity, and Color of the People of the United States. By G. H. Grosvenor. 381-389, *Nov. 1901*

SEYCHELLES, Indian Ocean:

Crosscurrents Sweep the Indian Ocean. By Bart McDowell. Photos by Steve Raymer. 422-457, *Oct. 1981*

Seychelles, Tropic Isles of Eden. By Quentin Keynes. 670-695, *Nov. 1959*

See also Assumption Island

'S GRAVENHAGE (The Hague), The Netherlands:

The Netherlands: Nation at War With the Sea. By Alan Villiers. Photos by Adam Woolfitt. 530-571, *Apr. 1968*

Mid-century Holland Builds Her Future. By Sydney Clark. 747-778, *Dec. 1950*

Holland Rises from War and Water. By Thomas R. Henry. 237-260, *Feb. 1946*

Glimpses of Holland. By William Wisner Chapin. 1-29, *Jan. 1915*

SHA'AB RÜMI (Reef), Red Sea:

At Home in the Sea. By Jacques-Yves Cousteau. 465-507, *Apr. 1964*

SHAANXI PROVINCE, China:

China's Incredible Find. By Audrey Topping. Paintings by Yang Hsien-min. Included: The first emperor's guardian army of terra-cotta men and horses. 440-459, *Apr. 1978*

See also former spelling, Shensi

SHACKELFORD, J. B.: *Photographer*

Nomad Life and Fossil Treasures of Mongolia. 669-700, *June 1933*

SHACKLETON, SIR ERNEST H.:

In the Footsteps of Scott. By Robert Swan. 544-555, *Apr. 1987*

Our Navy Explores Antarctica. By Richard E. Byrd. U. S. Navy official photos. 429-522, *Oct. 1947*

South Georgia, an Outpost of the Antarctic. By Robert Cushman Murphy. 409-444, *Apr. 1922*

The Race for the South Pole (Presentation of Hubbard Medal by President Taft). 185-186, *Mar. 1910*

Shackleton's Farthest South. 398-402, *Apr. 1909*

Author

The Heart of the Antarctic. 972-1007, *Nov. 1909*

SHAD:

Shad in the Shadow of Skyscrapers. By Dudley B. Martin. Photos by Luis Marden. 359-376, *Mar. 1947*

Federal Fish Farming; or, Planting Fish by the Billion. By Hugh M. Smith. 418-446, *May 1910*

SHADBOLT, MAURICE: *Author*

■■ *Isles of the South Pacific.* By Maurice Shadbolt and Olaf Ruhen. 211 pages. *1968*

New Zealand's Cook Islands: Paradise in Search of a Future. Photos by William Albert Allard. 203-231, *Aug. 1967*

In Storied Lands of Malaysia. Photos by Winfield Parks. 734-783, *Nov. 1963*

Western Samoa, the Pacific's Newest Nation. Photos by Robert B. Goodman. 573-602, *Oct. 1962*

New Zealand: Gift of the Sea. Photos by Brian Brake. 465-511, *Apr. 1962*

SHADOWY Birds of the Night. By Alexander Wetmore. Paintings by Allan Brooks. 217-240, *Feb. 1935*

SHADOWY London by Night. Photos by H. B. Burdekin. 177-184, *Aug. 1935*

The **SHADOWY** World of Salamanders. By Paul A. Zahl. 104-117, *July 1972*

SHAFFER, E.T.H.: *Author*

The Ashley River and Its Gardens. 525-550, *May 1926*

SHAH JAHAN:

When the Moguls Ruled India. By Mike Edwards. Photos by Roland Michaud. 463-493, *Apr. 1985*

SHAHR KURD, Iran:

Mountain Tribes of Iran and Iraq. By Harold Lamb. 385-408, *Mar. 1946*

SHAKERS (Religious Sect):

Home to the Enduring Berkshires. By Charles McCarry. Photos by Jonathan S. Blair. 196-221, *Aug. 1970*

SHAKESPEARE, WILLIAM:

Shakespeare Lives at the Folger. By Merle Severy. Photos by Nathan Benn. 244-259, *Feb. 1987*
The World of Elizabeth I. By Louis B. Wright. 668-709, *Nov. 1968*
The Britain That Shakespeare Knew. By Louis B. Wright. Photos by Dean Conger. 613-665, *May 1964*
◉ Shakespeare's Britain. May 1964
Nomination Page. *Apr. 1964*
Folger: Biggest Little Library in the World. By Joseph T. Foster. Photos by B. Anthony Stewart and John E. Fletcher. 411-424, *Sept. 1951*
A Stroll to London. By Isobel Wylie Hutchison. Photos by B. Anthony Stewart. 171-204, *Aug. 1950*
The British Way. By Sir Evelyn Wrench. 421-541, *Apr. 1949*
Founders of Virginia. By Sir Evelyn Wrench. Photos by B. Anthony Stewart. Included: Stratford on Avon and *The Tempest*. 433-462, *Apr. 1948*

SHALE OIL:

Synfuels: Fill 'er Up! With What? By Thomas Y. Canby. Photos by Jonathan Blair. 74-95. Included: Wresting Oil From Reluctant Rock. 78-79, *Special Report on Energy. (Feb. 1981)*
Billions of Barrels of Oil Locked up in Rocks. By Guy Elliott Mitchell. 195-205, *Feb. 1918*

SHALER, N. S.: *Author*

The Economic Aspects of Soil Erosion. Part II. 368-377, *Nov. 1896*
The Economic Aspects of Soil Erosion. Part I. 328-338, *Oct. 1896*

SHALLENBERGER, ROBERT J.: *Photographer*

Something's Fishy About That Fin! Photos by Robert J. Shallenberger and William D. Madden. 224-227, *Aug. 1974*

SHAMANISM:

The White Mountain Apache. 260-290. I. At Peace With the Past, In Step With the Future. By Ronnie Lupe. 260-261; II. Coming of Age the Apache Way. By Nita Quintero. Photos by Bill Hess. 262-271; III. Seeking the Best of Two Worlds. By Bill Hess. 272-290, *Feb. 1980*
The Huichols, Mexico's People of Myth and Magic. By James Norman. Photos by Guillermo Aldana E. 832-853, *June 1977*
◼ Bushmen of the Kalahari. 578A-578B, Apr. 1973; 732A-732B, May 1973
Bushmen of the Kalahari. By Elizabeth Marshall Thomas. Photos by Laurence K. Marshall. 866-888, *June 1963*
Better Days for the Navajos. By Jack Breed. Photos by Charles W. Herbert. 809-847, *Dec. 1958*
Nomads of the Far North. By Matthew W. Stirling. 471-504, *Oct. 1949*
Banishing the Devil of Disease Among the Nashi: Weird Ceremonies Performed by an Aboriginal Tribe in the Heart of Yünnan Province, China. By Joseph F. Rock. 473-499, *Nov. 1924*
See also Kachinas

SHAN TRIBESPEOPLE:

Burma: Where India and China Meet: In the Massive Mountains of Southeast Asia, Swarming Road Builders Wage the "War of the Highways" for Free China and Her Allies. By John LeRoy Christian. 489-512, *Oct. 1943*
Shan Tribes Make Burma's Hills Flash With Color. Photos by W. Robert Moore. 455-462, *Oct. 1931*
Strange Tribes in the Shan States of Burma. Photos by W. Robert Moore. 247-254, *Aug. 1930*

Birdcage brightens Shanghai's Happiness Concentrated, once an alley of brothels and opium dens. BRUCE DALE, NGS

SHAN STATE, Burma:

Burma's Leg Rowers and Floating Farms. Photos by W. E. Garrett. Text by David Jeffery. 826-845, *June 1974*
Burma: Where India and China Meet: In the Massive Mountains of Southeast Asia, Swarming Road Builders Wage the "War of the Highways" for Free China and Her Allies. By John LeRoy Christian. 489-512, *Oct. 1943*
Shan Tribes Make Burma's Hills Flash With Color. Photos by W. Robert Moore. 455-462, *Oct. 1931*
Strange Tribes in the Shan States of Burma. Photos by W. Robert Moore. 247-254, *Aug. 1930*

SHANDONG PROVINCE, China. *See* former spelling, Shantung

SHANGHAI, China:

Shanghai: Born-again Giant. By Mike Edwards. Photos by Bruce Dale. Included: "Muscle and smoke, commerce and crowds." A Shanghai portfolio by Bruce Dale. 2-43, *July 1980*
This Is the China I Saw. By Jørgen Bisch. 591-639, *Nov. 1964*
Eyes on the China Coast. By George W. Long. 505-512, *Apr. 1953*
Along the Yangtze, Main Street of China. By W. Robert Moore. 325-356, *Mar. 1948*
Today on the China Coast. By John B. Powell. 217-238, *Feb. 1945*
Changing Shanghai. By Amanda Boyden. 485-508, *Oct. 1937*
Cosmopolitan Shanghai, Key Seaport of China. By W. Robert Moore. 311-335, *Sept. 1932*

"SHANGRI-LA" in Panorama. Photos by Ray T. Elsmore. Contents: Grand Valley, New Guinea. 681-688, *Dec. 1945*

SHANNON (River), Ireland:

Where the River Shannon Flows. By Allan C. Fisher, Jr. Photos by Adam Woolfitt. 652-679, *Nov. 1978*

SHANSI PROVINCE, China:

China's Great Wall of Sculpture: Man-hewn Caves and Countless Images Form a Colossal Art Wonder of Early Buddhism. By Mary Augusta Mullikin. Paintings by author and Anna M. Hotchkis. 313-348, *Mar. 1938*

SHANTOU SPECIAL ECONOMIC ZONE, Guangdong, China:

China's Opening Door. By John J. Putman. Photos by H. Edward Kim. 64-83, *July 1983*

SHANTUNG PROVINCE, China:

Tai Shan, Sacred Mountain of the East. By Mary Augusta Mullikin. 699-719, *June 1945*
Shantung–China's Holy Land. By Charles K. Edmunds. 231-252, *Sept. 1919*
The Descendants of Confucius. By Maynard Owen Williams. 253-265, *Sept. 1919*

SHANTZ, H. L.: *Author*

The Saguaro Forest (Arizona). 515-532, *Apr. 1937*

SHANXI PROVINCE, China. *See* former spelling, Shansi

SHARECROPPERS:

The Okies–Beyond the Dust Bowl. By William Howarth. Photos by Chris Johns. 322-349, *Sept. 1984*

SHARING Alaska: How Much for Parks? Opposing views by Jay S. Hammond and Cecil D. Andrus. 60-65, *July 1979*

SHARING the Lives of Wild Golden Eagles. By John Craighead. Photos by Charles and Derek Craighead. 420-439, *Sept. 1967*

SHARJAH, United Arab Emirates:

The Persian Gulf–Living in Harm's Way. By Thomas J. Abercrombie. Photos by Steve Raymer. 648-671, *May 1988*

SHARK FISHING–An Australian Industry. By Norman Ellison. 369-386, *Sept. 1932*

SHARKS:

Australia's Southern Seas. By Richard Ellis. Photos by David Doubilet. 286-319, *Mar. 1987*

Sharks at 2,000 Feet. By Eugenie Clark and Emory Kristof as reported to Douglas Lee. NGS research grant. 681-691, *Nov. 1986*

■ The Sharks. Cover, Jan. 1982; President's Page. *Jan. 1985*

Sharks: Magnificent and Misunderstood. By Eugenie Clark. Photos by David Doubilet. 138-187, *Aug. 1981*

A Jawbreaker for Sharks. By Valerie Taylor. Contents: A chain-mail diving suit. 664-667, *May 1981*

Into the Lairs of "Sleeping" Sharks. By Eugenie Clark. Photos by David Doubilet. NGS research grant. 570-584, *Apr. 1975*

The Red Sea's Sharkproof Fish. By Eugenie Clark. Photos by David Doubilet. 718-727, *Nov. 1974*

Sharks: Wolves of the Sea. By Nathaniel T. Kenney. 222-257, *Feb. 1968*

Calypso Explores for Underwater Oil. By Jacques-Yves Cousteau. Included: Aqualung divers' war on sharks in the Indian Ocean. NGS research grant. 155-184, *Aug. 1955*

Marineland, Florida's Giant Fish Bowl. By Gilbert Grosvenor La Gorce. Photos by Luis Marden. 679-694, *Nov. 1952*

Fish Men Explore a New World Undersea. By Jacques-Yves Cousteau. 431-472, *Oct. 1952*

Shark Fishing–An Australian Industry. By Norman Ellison. 369-386, *Sept. 1932*

SHARMAN, GEOFFREY B.: *Author*

Those Kangaroos! They're a Marvelous Mob. Photos by Des and Jen Bartlett. 192-209, *Feb. 1979*

SHARPS (Sonic High-accuracy Ranging and Positioning System):

President's Page. By Gilbert M. Grosvenor. *July 1987*

SHASTA DAM, California:

More Water for California's Great Central Valley. By Frederick Simpich. 645-664, *Nov. 1946*

SHATTERED Capitals of Central America. By Herbert J. Spinden. 185-212, *Sept. 1919*

SHATTERED Obelisk of Mont Pelée. By Angelo Heilprin. 465-474, *Aug. 1906*

SHAW, WILLIAM T.: *Author-Photographer*

Tracking the Columbian Ground-Squirrel to Its Burrow: Loss of Millions to Crops and Danger of the Spread of Spotted Fever Necessitated Study of

Peculiar Rodent of Western North America. 587-596, *May 1925*

SHAWANGUNK Mountain. By N. H. Darton. 23-34, *Mar. 17, 1894*

SHAWNEE INDIANS:

America's First Settlers, the Indians. By Matthew W. Stirling. Paintings by W. Langdon Kihn. 535-596, *Nov. 1937*

SHAWNEETOWN Forsakes the Ohio. By William H. Nicholas. Photos by J. Baylor Roberts. 273-288, *Feb. 1948*

SHAY, FELIX: *Author*

Cairo to Cape Town, Overland: An Adventurous Journey of 135 Days, Made by an American Man and His Wife, Through the Length of the African Continent. 123-260, *Feb. 1925*

SHEARWATERS:

Birds of the High Seas: Albatrosses and Petrels; Gannets, Man-o'-war-birds, and Tropic-birds. By Robert Cushman Murphy. Paintings by Allan Brooks. 226-251, *Aug. 1938*

SHEATS, DOROTHEA:
Author-Photographer

I Walked Some Irish Miles. 653-678, *May 1951*

See also Jones, Dorothea Sheats

SHECHEM, Palestine. *See* Nablus

SHEDD AQUARIUM, Chicago, Illinois: Expedition:

Net Results from Oceania: Collecting Aquarium Specimens in Tropical Pacific Waters. By Walter H. Chute. 347-372, *Mar. 1941*

SHEEP. *See* Bighorn Sheep; Sheep Raising; Sheep Trek

SHEEP DOGS:

Working Dogs of the World. By Freeman Lloyd. Paintings by Edward Herbert Miner. 776-806, *Dec. 1941*

Sheep Dog Trials in Llangollen: Trained Collies Perform Marvels of Herding in the Cambrian Stakes, Open to the World. By Sara Bloch. 559-574, *Apr. 1940*

SHEEP-KILLERS–The Pariahs of Dogkind. 275-280, *Mar. 1919*

SHEEP RAISING:

Wool–Fabric of History. By Nina Hyde. Photos by Cary Wolinsky. Included: Living in Wool. 552-591, *May 1988*

Perth–Fair Winds and Full Sails. By Thomas J. Abercrombie. Photos by Cary Wolinsky. 638-667, *May 1982*

New Zealand's High Country. By Yva Momatiuk and John Eastcott. 246-265, *Aug. 1978*

Scotland's Inner Hebrides: Isles of the Western Sea. By Kenneth MacLeish. Photos by R. Stephen Uzzell III. 690-717, *Nov. 1974*

New Zealand's North Island: The Contented Land. By Charles McCarry. Photos by Bates Littlehales. 190-213, *Aug. 1974*

The Navajos. By Ralph Looney. Photos by Bruce Dale. 740-781, *Dec. 1972*

Winter Caravan to the Roof of the

Fifty feet underwater off the Cape Verde Islands a diver overtakes an eight-foot shark and its attendant pilot fish. JACQUES-YVES COUSTEAU, PHILIPPE TAILLIEZ, FRÉDÉRIC DUMAS

SHEEP TREKS:

SHEIK SAID. By Ernest de Sasseville. 155-156, *May 1897*

Merino sheep brought wealth to the Iberian Peninsula, where the breed was developed for its fine white wool. CARY WOLINSKY, STOCK, BOSTON

SHELLFISH. *See* Crabs; Lobsters; Mollusks; Oysters; Scallops; Shrimp

SHELLFISH INDUSTRY:

See also Crabs; Crayfish; Lobsters; Shrimp Fishing

SHELLS:

See also Mother-of-Pearl; Nautilus, Chambered

SHELTER OF THE SUN (Archaeological Site), Brazil:

SHELTON, A. L.: *Author*

SHELTON, WILLIAM R.: *Author*

SHENANDOAH (Airship):

SHENANDOAH NATIONAL PARK, Virginia:

SHENANDOAH VALLEY, Virginia-West Virginia:

Mike W. Edwards. Photos by Thomas Anthony DeFeo. 554-588, *Apr. 1970*

Appalachian Valley Pilgrimage. By Catherine Bell Palmer. Photos by Justin Locke. 1-32, *July 1949*

SHENON, PHILIP J.: *Author*

Down Idaho's River of No Return. By Philip J. Shenon and John C. Reed. 95-136, *July 1936*

SHENSI PROVINCE, China:

China's Incredible Find. By Audrey Topping. Paintings by Yang Hsien-min. Included: The first emperor's burial mound, with guardian army of terra-cotta men and horses. 440-459, *Apr. 1978*

China Fights Erosion with U. S. Aid. By Walter C. Lowdermilk. 641-680, *June 1945*

See also Sian

SHENYANG (Mukden), Liaoning Province, China:

In Manchuria Now. By W. Robert Moore. 389-414, *Mar. 1947*

Japan Faces Russia in Manchuria. By Willard Price. 603-634, *Nov. 1942*

Mukden, the Manchu Home, and Its Great Art Museum. By Eliza R. Scidmore. 289-320, *Apr. 1910*

SHENZEN SPECIAL ECONOMIC ZONE, Guangdong Province, China:

China's Opening Door. By John J. Putman. Photos by H. Edward Kim. 64-83, *July 1983*

SHEPARD, ALAN B., Jr.:

Nomination Page. *July 1971*

The Flight of *Freedom 7.* By Carmault B. Jackson, Jr. 416-431, *Sept. 1961*

Nomination Page. *Sept. 1961*

Author

The Pilot's Story. Photos by Dean Conger. 432-444, *Sept. 1961*

Photographer

The Climb Up Cone Crater. By Alice J. Hall. Photos by Edgar D. Mitchell and Alan B. Shepard, Jr. 136-148, *July 1971*

SHEPARD, OLIVER:

Circling Earth From Pole to Pole. By Sir Ranulph Fiennes. 464-481, *Oct. 1983*

SHEPHERD'S NEEDLES (Plants):

An Insect Community Lives in Flower Heads. By James G. Needham. 340-356, *Sept. 1946*

SHERMAN, SPENCER: *Author*

The Hmong in America: Laotian Refugees in the "Land of the Giants." Photos by Dick Swanson. 586-610, *Oct. 1988*

SHERPAS:

Park at the Top of the World: Mount Everest National Park. By Rick Ridgeway. Photos by Nicholas de-Vore III. Included: Preserving a Mountain Heritage. By Sir Edmund Hillary. 696-725, *June 1982*

Sherpaland, My Shangri-La. By Desmond Doig. 545-577, *Oct. 1966*

We Build a School for Sherpa Children.

As part of funeral rites for his father, Khufu, Egyptian Pharaoh Djedefre buried a ship near the Great Pyramid at Giza, Khufu's tomb. Uncovered in 1954, the cedar bark has been reconstructed.

VICTOR R. BOSWELL, JR., NGS

By Sir Edmund Hillary. 548-551, *Oct. 1962*

See also American Mount Everest Expedition; British Mount Everest Expedition

SHERWOOD GARDENS, Baltimore, Maryland:

Maytime Miracle in Sherwood Gardens. By Nathaniel T. Kenney. 700-709, *May 1956*

Maytime in the Heart of Maryland. Photos by B. Anthony Stewart and Charles Martin. 441-448, *Apr. 1941*

SHETLAND ISLANDS, Scotland:

Striking It Rich in the North Sea. By Rick Gore. Photos by Dick Durrance II. 519-549, *Apr. 1977*

Viking Festival in the Shetlands. Photos by Karl Gullers. 853-862, *Dec. 1954*

Shetland and Orkney, Britain's Far North. By Isobel Wylie Hutchison. 519-536, *Oct. 1953*

The Orkneys and Shetlands–A Mysterious Group of Islands. By Charles S. Olcott. 197-228, *Feb. 1921*

SHIELDS, CYNTHIA: *Author*

The Fantastic Flight of *Cote d'Or.* 789-793, *Dec. 1983*

SHIFTING Scenes on the Stage of New China. 423-428, *Nov. 1920*

SHIGATSE, Tibet:

Sky-high in Lama Land. Photos by C. Suydam Cutting. 185-196, *Aug. 1946*

SHIISM:

Iran Under the Ayatollah. By Michael Coyne. 108-135, *July 1985*

Mystic Nedjef, the Shia Mecca. By Frederick Simpich. 589-598, *Dec. 1914*

SHILOH NATIONAL MILITARY PARK, Tennessee:

Echoes of Shiloh. By Shelby Foote. 106-111, *July 1979*

SHINTOISM:

Day of the Rice God. Photos by H. Edward Kim. Text by Douglas Lee. 78-85, *July 1978*

Kyoto and Nara: Keepers of Japan's Past. By Charles McCarry. Photos by George F. Mobley. 836-851, *June 1976*

Kansai, Japan's Historic Heartland. By Thomas J. Abercrombie. Included: Expo '70. 295-339, *Mar. 1970*

Kayak Odyssey: From the Inland Sea to Tokyo. By Dan Dimancescu. Photos by Christopher G. Knight. 295-337, *Sept. 1967*

Cruising Japan's Inland Sea. By Willard Price. 619-650, *Nov. 1953*

Behind the Mask of Modern Japan. By Willard Price. 513-535, *Nov. 1945*

SHIP BURIAL:

Ancestor of the British Navy: England's Oldest Known War Vessel Is Unearthed, Laden with Remarkable Treasures of an Anglo-Saxon Ruler. By C. W. Phillips. 247-268, *Feb. 1941*

See also Funerary Boats

SHIP CRAFTING:

In the Wake of Sindbad. By Tim Severin. Photos by Richard Greenhill. 2-41, *July 1982*

See also Brendan; Tigris

SHIP RAILWAYS:

The Tehuantepec Ship Railway. By Elmer L. Corthell. 64-72, *Feb. 1896*

SHIPBUILDING:

Helsinki: City With Its Heart in the Country. By Priit J. Vesilind. Photos by Jodi Cobb. Included: Icebreakers; Ice-breaking freighters; Drydock operations. 237-255, *Aug. 1981*

Ships Through the Ages: A Saga of the Sea. By Alan Villiers. 494-545, *Apr. 1963*

American Industries Geared for War. By Thornton Oakley. Paintings by author. 716-734, *Dec. 1942*

As 2,000 Ships Are Born. By Frederick Simpich. 551-588, *May 1942*

The American People Must Become Ship-Minded. By Edward N. Hurley. 201-211, *Sept. 1918*

Our Industrial Victory. By Charles M. Schwab. 212-229, *Sept. 1918*

Ships for the Seven Seas: The Story of America's Maritime Needs, Her Capabilities and Her Achievements. By Ralph A. Graves. 165-200, *Sept. 1918*

Shipbuilding in the United Kingdom in 1898. 138-139, *Apr. 1899*

See also Kyrenia Ship; *Mayflower II;* Vikings; *and* Ship Crafting

During World War I the United States made building supply ships a priority.

S T

Victory's Portrait in the Marianas. By William Franklin Draper. Paintings by author. 599-616, *Nov. 1945*

Battleship *Missouri* Comes of Age. 353-369, *Mar. 1945*

Seafarers of South Celebes. By G.E.P. Collins. 53-78, *Jan. 1945*

Landing Craft for Invasion. By Melville Bell Grosvenor. 1-30, *July 1944*

Heroes of Wartime Science and Mercy. By Elizabeth W. King. 715-740, *Dec. 1943*

Ships That Guard Our Ocean Ramparts. By F. Barrows Colton. Paintings by Arthur Beaumont. 328-337, *Sept. 1941*

Life in Our Fighting Fleet. By F. Barrows Colton. 671-702, *June 1941*

Ancestor of the British Navy: England's Oldest Known War Vessel Is Unearthed, Laden with Remarkable Treasures of an Anglo-Saxon Ruler. By C. W. Phillips. 247-268, *Feb. 1941*

Time and Tide on the Thames. By Frederick Simpich. 239-272, *Feb. 1939*

Ships, from Dugouts to Dreadnoughts. By Dudley W. Knox. Included: Ships of the Centuries. Gravure etchings by Norman Wilkinson. 57-98, *Jan. 1938*

New Safeguards for Ships in Fog and Storm. By George R. Putnam. 169-200, *Aug. 1936*

Where the Sailing Ship Survives. By A. J. Villiers. Contents: Åland Islands. 101-128, *Jan. 1935*

The Caravels of Columbus. Painting by N. C. Wyeth, National Geographic Society, Washington, D. C. Supplement, *July 1928*

The Argosy of Geography. Pictorial supplement, *Jan. 1921*

Most Curious Craft Afloat: The Compass in Navigation and the Work of the Non-Magnetic Yacht "Carnegie." By L. A. Bauer. 223-245, *Mar. 1910*

The Sailing Ship and the Panama Canal. By James Page. 167-176, *Apr. 1904*

The Caravels of Columbus. By Victor Maria Concas. 180-186, *Jan. 31, 1894*

Norway and the Vikings. By Magnus Andersen. Note: Voyage of the *Viking*, Bergen to New London. 132-136, *Jan. 31, 1894*

See also Cruises and Voyages; Galleasses; Galleons; Galleys, Bronze Age; Junks; Research Vessels; Sailing Vessels; Shipbuilding; Shipwrecks; Submarines; Tankers; U. S. Coast Guard; U. S. Navy; Windjammers; listing under Yachts; *and Af Chapman; Hickory; J. W. Westcott; Savannah, N. S.*

SHIPTON, JAMES A.:

The Peak of Itambé (Brazil). 476, *Nov. 1898*

SHIPWORMS, Saboteurs of the Sea. By F. G. Walton Smith. 559-566, *Oct. 1956*

Combination of 108 photographs creates a portrait of a shipwreck: the battered forward section of the **Titanic,** *which has lain on the floor of the North Atlantic since 1912.* © 1987 BALLARD & FAMILY

SHIPWRECKS:

Drought Helps Uncover Life on the Mississippi. Geographica. *Nov. 1988*

Yorktown Shipwreck. By John D. Broadwater. Photos by Bates Littlehales. Contents: Wreck of British ship sunk in 1781. 804-823, *June 1988*

Ghosts of War in the South Pacific. By Peter Benchley. Photos by David Doubilet. Contents: World War II shipwrecks. 424-457, *Apr. 1988*

Wreck of the *Coolidge*. Text and photos by David Doubilet. Note: The U.S.S. *Coolidge* was sunk off the coast of Espiritu Santo in the New Hebrides on Oct. 26, 1942. 458-467, *Apr. 1988*

▓▓ *Hidden Treasures of the Sea.* Juvenile. 104 pages. *1988*

Oldest Known Shipwreck Reveals Splendors of the Bronze Age. By George F. Bass. Photos by Bill Curtsinger. Included: Bronze Age Trade, The Cosmopolitan World of the Late Bronze Age, The Painstaking Art of Marine Archaeology. Note: Found near Kaş, Turkey. NGS research grant. 693-733, *Dec. 1987*

Epilogue for *Titanic*. By Robert D. Ballard. 454-463, *Oct. 1987*

A Long Last Look at *Titanic*. By Robert D. Ballard. Included: High-tech partners plumb new depths; Poignant relics of a disaster. Illustrations text by Cliff Tarpy. 698-727, *Dec. 1986*

How We Found *Titanic*. By Robert D. Ballard, with Jean-Louis Michel. 696-719, *Dec. 1985*

Tectonics to *Titanic*. President's Page. By Gilbert M. Grosvenor. *Dec. 1985*

Editorial. By Wilbur E. Garrett. Contents: *Atocha;* H.M.S. *Pandora; San José; Santa Margarita.* 421, *Oct. 1985*

Wreck of H.M.S. *Pandora*. By Luis Marden. Note: The wreck was found on Australia's Great Barrier Reef. 423-451, *Oct. 1985*

16th-Century Basque Whalers in America. Photos by Bill Curtsinger. Paintings by Richard Schlecht. Included:

Basque shipwrecks in Red Bay, Labrador, Canada. 40-71, *July 1985*

Bronze Age Shipwreck. By Wilbur E. Garrett and George F. Bass. Note: Found near Kaş, Turkey. NGS research grant. 1-3, *Jan. 1985*

Exploring a 140-year-old Ship Under Arctic Ice. By Joseph B. MacInnis. Photos by Emory Kristof. Contents: *Breadalbane.* 104A-104D, *July 1983*

Henry VIII's Lost Warship: *Mary Rose.* By Margaret Rule. Introduction and picture text by Peter Miller. Paintings by Richard Schlecht. Note: *Mary Rose* sank off Portsmouth, England on July 19, 1545. 646-675, *May 1983*

Ghost Ships of the War of 1812: *Hamilton* and *Scourge*. By Daniel A. Nelson. Photos by Emory Kristof. Paintings by Richard Schlecht. Note: The ships sank in Lake Ontario on Aug. 8, 1813. 289-313, *Mar. 1983*

The Lost Fleet of Kublai Khan. By Torao Mozai. Photos by Koji Nakamura. Paintings by Issho Yada. Contents: Mongol invasion fleet sunk off Japan in 1281. 634-649, *Nov. 1982*

Treasure From the Ghost Galleon: *Santa Margarita*. By Eugene Lyon. Photos by Don Kincaid. Included: *Atocha; Santa Margarita*. Note: The ships sank off the Florida Keys in 1622. 228-243, *Feb. 1982*

Graveyard of the Quicksilver Galleons. By Mendel Peterson. Photos by Jonathan Blair. Included: The *Nuestra Señora de Guadalupe* and the *Conde de Tolosa*. Note: The ships sank off Santo Domingo on Aug. 24, 1724. 850-876, *Dec. 1979*

Yellow Sea Yields Shipwreck Trove. Photos by H. Edward Kim. Introduction by Donald H. Keith. Contents: 14th-century shipwreck off the coast of Korea. 231-243, *Aug. 1979*

The Sunken Treasure of St. Helena. By Robert Sténuit. Photos by Bates Littlehales. Contents: *Witte Leeuw* wreck. 562-576, *Oct. 1978*

In 1898 pioneer wildlife photographer George Shiras 3d rigged a trip wire to a camera and flashgun to get nighttime shots. GEORGE SHIRAS 3D

At California's Mono Lake a Wilson's phalarope picks through shallow water for food with its long beak. JOSEPH R. JEHL, JR.

A New York City street is seen in a 1918 article by NATIONAL GEOGRAPHIC Assistant Editor William Joseph Showalter. EDWIN LEVICK

Mexico and Mexicans. 471-493, *May 1914*
Redeeming the Tropics. 344-364, *Mar. 1914*
Battling with the Panama Slides. 133-153, *Feb. 1914*
The Countries of the Caribbean. 227-250, *Feb. 1913*
The Panama Canal. 195-205, *Feb. 1912*

SHOWCASE of Red China. By Franc Shor. Photos by Brian Brake. 193-223, *Aug. 1960*

SHREVE, FORREST: *Author*
The Saguaro, Cactus Camel of Arizona. 695-704, *Dec. 1945*

SHREWS. *See* Tree Shrews

SHRIMP:
Miracle of the Potholes. By Rowe Findley. Photos by Robert F. Sisson. 570-579, *Oct. 1975*
Life in a "Dead" Sea–Great Salt Lake. By Paul A. Zahl. Included: Brine shrimp. 252-263, *Aug. 1967*
Shrimp Nursery: Science Explores New Ways to Farm the Sea. By Clarence P. Idyll. Photos by Robert F. Sisson. NGS research grant. 636-659, *May 1965*
Night Life in the Gulf Stream. By Paul A. Zahl. 391-418, *Mar. 1954*
The Delectable Shrimp: Once a Culinary Stepchild, Today a Gulf Coast Industry. By Harlan Major. 501-512, *Oct. 1944*

SHRIMP, Krill:
Krill–Untapped Bounty From the Sea? By William M. Hamner. Photos by Flip Nicklin. 626-643, *May 1984*

SHRIMP FISHING:
Troubled Odyssey of Vietnamese Fishermen. By Harvey Arden. Photos by Steve Wall. 378-395, *Sept. 1981*
Greenland's "Place by the Icebergs." By Mogens Bloch Poulsen. Photos by Thomas Nebbia. 849-869, *Dec. 1973*
Shrimp Nursery: Science Explores New Ways to Farm the Sea. By Clarence P. Idyll. Photos by Robert F. Sisson. NGS research grant. 636-659, *May 1965*
Shrimpers Strike Gold in the Gulf. By Clarence P. Idyll. Photos by Robert F. Sisson. 699-707, *May 1957*

SHRINES, Historic:
■■ *Visiting Our Past: America's Historylands.* Included: Companion directory, *Visiting Our Past: A Supplemental Guide to Selected Sites.* 400 pages. *1977*
■■ *America's Historylands, Touring Our Landmarks of Liberty.* Companion volume to *America's Wonderlands.* 575 pages. 1962; rev. ed. *1967*
Vacation Tour Through Lincoln Land. By Ralph Gray. 141-184, *Feb. 1952*
Dog Mart Day in Fredericksburg. By Frederick G. Vosburgh. Included: Kenmore, Mary Washington House, Ferry Farm, James Monroe Law Office, the John Paul Jones house, and Civil War battlesites. 817-832, *June 1951*

Shrines of Each Patriot's Devotion. By Frederick G. Vosburgh. Contents: Ackia Battleground, Andrew Johnson, Big Hole, Cabrillo, Custer Battlefield, Fort Matanzas, Fort Pulaski, Fort Vancouver, George Washington Birthplace, Homestead, Lava Beds, Perry's Victory and International Peace Memorial, Pipe Spring, Scotts Bluff, Statue of Liberty, Verendrye. 51-82, *Jan. 1949*
Founders of Virginia. By Sir Evelyn Wrench. Photos by B. Anthony Stewart. Included: Historic and hallowed places in England. 433-462, *Apr. 1948*
See also Monticello, Virginia; Monuments and Memorials

SHRIVER, SARGENT: *Author*
Ambassadors of Good Will: The Peace Corps. By Sargent Shriver and Peace Corps Volunteers. 297-345, *Sept. 1964*

SHROUD OF TURIN:
Editorial. By Gilbert M. Grosvenor. 729, *June 1980*
The Mystery of the Shroud. By Kenneth F. Weaver. Note: The Shroud of Turin is believed by some to be the burial shroud of Jesus. 730-753, *June 1980*

SHRUBS:
American Berries of Hill, Dale, and Wayside. Paintings by Mary E. Eaton. 168-184, *Feb. 1919*
The Kingdom of Flowers: An Account of the Wealth of Trees and Shrubs of China and of What the Arnold Arboretum, with China's Help, Is Doing to Enrich America. By Ernest H. Wilson. 1003-1035, *Nov. 1911*
See also Rhododendrons

Siberian resident Maria Malikov is one of about 800 Yukaghir, among the smallest of Soviet ethnic groups. DEAN CONGER, NGS

SHURI, Okinawa (Island), Ryukyu Islands:
Peacetime Rambles in the Ryukyus. By William Leonard Schwartz. 543-561, *May 1945*

SHUSH, Iran. *See* Susa

SHUSTER, ERNEST A., Jr.: *Author*
The Original Boundary Stones of the District of Columbia. 356-359, *Apr. 1909*

The **SHY** and Spectacular Kingfisher. Photos by Carl-Johan Junge and Emil Lütken. 413-419, *Sept. 1974*

SHY Monster, the Octopus. By Gilbert L. Voss. Photos by Robert F. Sisson. 776-799, *Dec. 1971*

SIAM. *See* Thailand

SIAMESE CATS:
The Panther of the Hearth: Lithe Grace and Independence of Spirit Contribute to the Appeal of Cats, "The Only Domestic Animal Man Has Never Conquered." By Frederick B. Eddy. 589-634, *Nov. 1938*

SIAN (Siking, now Xian), Shaanxi Province, China:
China's Incredible Find. By Audrey Topping. Paintings by Yang Hsienmin. Included: The first emperor's burial mound, with guardian army of terra-cotta men and horses. 440-459, *Apr. 1978*
Singan–The Present Capital of the Chinese Empire. By James Mascarene Hubbard. 63-66, *Feb. 1901*

SIASCONSET, Nantucket (Island), Massachusetts:
Nantucket–Little Gray Lady. By William H. Nicholas. 433-458, *Apr. 1944*

SIBERIA (Region), Russian S.F.S.R., U.S.S.R.:
Celebrating Peoples of the Bering Strait. Geographica. *Nov. 1988*
Air Bridge to Siberia. By Wilbur E. Garrett. Photos by Steve Raymer. 504-509, *Oct. 1988*
People of the Long Spring. By Yuri Rytkheu. Photos by Dean Conger. 206-223, *Feb. 1983*
⊕ *Peoples of the Arctic; Arctic Ocean. Feb. 1983*
Five Times to Yakutsk. By Dean Conger. 256-269, *Aug. 1977*
Siberia's Empire Road, the River Ob. By Robert Paul Jordan. Photos by Dean Conger. 145-181, *Feb. 1976*
■ Siberia: The Endless Horizon. 734A-734B, *Nov. 1969*
Siberia: Russia's Frozen Frontier. By Dean Conger. 297-345, *Mar. 1967*
⊕ *Eastern Soviet Union.* Atlas series. *Mar. 1967*
New Road to Asia. By Owen Lattimore. 641-676, *Dec. 1944*
"Magnetic City," Core of Valiant Russia's Industrial Might. By John Scott. Contents: Magnitogorsk. 525-556, *May 1943*
With an Exile in Arctic Siberia: The Narrative of a Russian Who Was Compelled to Turn Polar Explorer

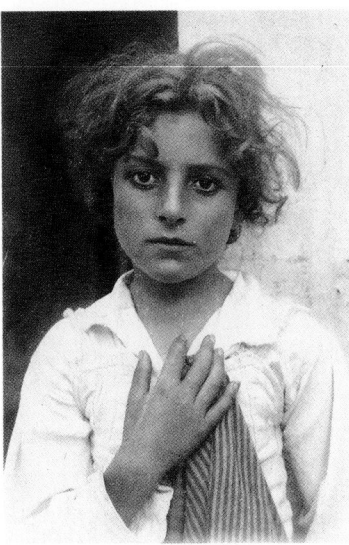

Vast numbers of emigrants left Sicily, home of this youngster, for the U.S. at the turn of the century. W. VON GLÖDEN

for Two Years. By Vladimir M. Zenzinov. 695-718, *Dec. 1924*

The Far Eastern Republic. By Junius B. Wood. 565-592, *June 1922*

Western Siberia and the Altai Mountains: With Some Speculations on the Future of Siberia. By James Bryce. 469-507, *May 1921*

Glimpses of Siberia, the Russian "Wild East." By Cody Marsh. 513-536, *Dec. 1920*

The Land of Promise. By A. W. Greely. 1078-1090, *Nov. 1912*

A Strange and Marvelous Beast (Mammoth). 620, *Sept. 1907*

✿ Kirin, Harbin, Vladivostok. *June 1905*

A Trip Through Siberia. By Ebenezer J. Hill. 37-54, *Feb. 1902*

Butter Exports from Siberia. 34, *Jan. 1902*

Siberia. By Edwin A. Grosvenor. 317-324, *Sept. 1901*

The Siberian Transcontinental Railroad. By A. W. Greely. 121-124, *Apr. 1897*

✿ Carte Générale des Découvertes de l'Amiral de Fonte, et autres Navigateurs Espagnols, Anglois et Russes pour la recherche du Passage à la Mer du Sud. Par M. De l'Isle de l'Académie royale des Sciences &c. Jan. 28, 1892; *Feb. 19, 1892*

A Critical Review of Bering's First Expedition, 1725-30, Together with a Translation of His Original Report Upon It. By Wm. H. Dall. 111-169, *May 1890*

See also Trans-Siberian Railway

The **SIBERIAN** Transcontinental Railroad. By A. W. Greely. 121-124, *Apr. 1897*

SIBERT, WILLIAM L.: *Author*

The Panama Canal. 153-183, *Feb. 1914*

SICHUAN PROVINCE, China:

Secrets of the Wild Panda. By George B. Schaller. Included: Saving the panda. 284-309, *Mar. 1986*

Sichuan: Where China Changes Course. By Ross Terrill. Photos by Cary Wolinsky. 280-317, *Sept. 1985*

Peoples of China's Far Provinces. By Wong How-Man. 283-333, *Mar. 1984*

Pandas in the Wild. By George B. Schaller. 735-749, *Dec. 1981*

See also former spelling, Szechwan; *and* Sikang

SICILY (Island), Italy:

Sicily, Where All the Songs Are Sad. By Howard La Fay. Photos by Jonathan Blair. 407-436, *Mar. 1976*

Roman Life in 1,600-year-old Color Pictures. By Gino Vinicio Gentili. Photos by Duncan Edwards. Contents: Mosaics from the imperial villa near Piazza Armerina. 211-229, *Feb. 1957*

Sicily the Three-cornered. By Luis Marden. 1-48, *Jan. 1955*

Fishing in the Whirlpool of Charybdis. By Paul A. Zahl. 579-618, *Nov. 1953*

Sicily Again in the Path of War. By Maynard Owen Williams. 307-320, *Sept. 1943*

Africa First of 1943 Global Warfare Maps. By William H. Nicholas. Included: Portfolio of pictures of Sicily. 261-276, *Feb. 1943*

Sicily: Island of Vivid Beauty and Crumbling Glory. 432-449, *Oct. 1927*

Zigzagging Across Sicily. By Melville Chater. 303-352, *Sept. 1924*

Inexhaustible Italy. By Arthur Stanley Riggs. 273-368, *Oct. 1916*

A Country Where Going to America Is an Industry. By Arthur H. Warner. 1063-1102, *Dec. 1909*

The World's Most Cruel Earthquake. By Charles W. Wright. Contents: The Messina earthquake of Dec. 28, 1908. 373-396, *Apr. 1909*

The Ruins at Selinus. By Marion Crawford. 117, *Jan. 1909*

Sicily, the Battle-Field of Nations and of Nature. By Mrs. George C. Bosson, Jr. 97-118, *Jan. 1909*

SICKLES, NOEL: *Artist*

Alone to Antarctica. By David Lewis. 808-821, *Dec. 1973*

SIDEWHEELER. See Rhode Island

SIEMEL, SASHA: *Author-Photographer*

The Jungle Was My Home. 695-712, *Nov. 1952*

SIENA, Italy:

Palio, Siena's Centuries-Old 90-second Horse Race. Photos by O. Louis Mazzatenta. 745-749, *June 1988*

The Renaissance Lives On in Tuscany. By Luis Marden. Photos by Albert Moldvay. Included: The Palio. 626-659, *Nov. 1974*

The Palio of Siena. By Edgar Erskine Hume. 231-244, *Aug. 1951*

Siena's Palio, an Italian Inheritance from the Middle Ages. By Marie Louise Handley. 245-258, *Aug. 1926*

Inexhaustible Italy. By Arthur Stanley Riggs. 273-368, *Oct. 1916*

SIEPEN, HOWARD: *Author*

On the Wings of the Wind: In Motorless Planes, Pilots Ride in Flying-Fox Fashion, Cruising on Upward Air Streams and Lifted by the Suction of Moving Clouds. 751-780, *June 1929*

SIERRA LEONE:

The Loyalists. By Kent Britt. Photos by Ted Spiegel. Note: Slaves of Patriot colonists, liberated by the British during the American Revolution, founded Freetown after the war. 510-539, *Apr. 1975*

Rubber Forests of Nicaragua and Sierra Leone. By A. W. Greely. 83-88, *Mar. 1897*

SIERRA MADRE OCCIDENTAL (Mountain Range), Mexico:

Following Cortés: Path to Conquest. By S. Jeffrey K. Wilkerson. Photos by Guillermo Aldana E. Paintings by Ned Seidler and Rosalie Seidler. 420-459, *Oct. 1984*

Found at Last: the Monarch's Winter Home. By Fred A. Urquhart. Photos by Bianca Lavies. NGS research grant. 161-173, *Aug. 1976*

The Tarahumaras: Mexico's Long-Distance Runners. By James Norman. Photos by David Hiser. 702-718, *May 1976*

SIERRA NEVADA (Mountains), California:

Avalanche! "I'm OK, I'm Alive!" By David Cupp. Photos by Lanny Johnson and Andre Benier. 282-289, *Sept. 1982*

The Troubled Waters of Mono Lake. By Gordon Young. Photos by Craig Aurness. 504-519, *Oct. 1981*

Golden Ghosts of the Lost Sierra. By Robert Laxalt. Photos by David Hiser. 332-353, *Sept. 1973*

John Muir's Wild America. By Harvey Arden. Photos by Dewitt Jones. 433-461, *Apr. 1973*

Mexico to Canada on the Pacific Crest

Trail. By Mike W. Edwards. Photos by David Hiser. 741-779, *June 1971*

Giant Sequoias Draw Millions to California Parks. By John Michael Kauffmann. Photos by B. Anthony Stewart. 147-187, *Aug. 1959*

The Fabulous Sierra Nevada. By J. R. Challacombe. 825-843, *June 1954*

Sierra High Trip. By David R. Brower. 844-868, *June 1954*

School for Survival. By Curtis E. LeMay. 565-602, *May 1953*

See also Yosemite National Park

SIEUR DE MONTS NATIONAL MONUMENT, Mount Desert Island, Maine:

First National Park East of Mississippi River. Note: Now called Acadia National Park. 623-626, *June 1916*

SIFFRE, MICHEL:
Author-Photographer

Six Months Alone in a Cave. 426-435, *Mar. 1975*

SIFTING for Life in the Sands of Mars. By Rick Gore. 9-31, *Jan. 1977*

SIGHT-SEEING in School: Taking Twenty Million Children on a Picture Tour of the World. By Jessie L. Burrall. 489-503, *June 1919*

SIGHTS and Sounds of the Winged World: Study of Birds to Make National Geographic Color Photographs Yields Rich Scientific Knowledge of Their Habits and Behavior. By Arthur A. Allen. 721-744, *June 1945*

SIGIRIYA (Sigiri), Sri Lanka:

Sigiriya, "A Fortress in the Sky." By Wilson K. Norton. 665-680, *Nov. 1946*

Archaeology in the Air. By Eliza R. Scidmore. 151-163, *Mar. 1907*

SIGNAL CORPS, U. S. Army. *See* U. S. Army Signal Corps

SIGSBEE, CHARLES D.:

Portrait. Frontispiece. *May 1898*

Captain Charles D. Sigsbee, U.S.N. By Henry Gannett. 250, *May 1898*

Reception to Captain C. D. Sigsbee, U.S.N. By John Hyde. 251-252, *May 1898*

SIGURDSSON, HARALDUR:

The Dead Do Tell Tales at Vesuvius. By Rick Gore. Photos by O. Louis Mazzatenta. NGS research grant. 557-613, *May 1984*

SIKANG (Former Province), China:

Adventures in Lololand. By Rennold L. Lowy. 105-118, *Jan. 1947*

Exploring a Grass Wonderland of Wild West China. By Ray G. Johnson. 713-742, *June 1944*

Climbing Mighty Minya Konka: Americans First Scaled Mountain That Now Is Landmark of China's New Skyway. By Richard L. Burdsall and Terris Moore. 625-650, *May 1943*

Konka Risumgongba, Holy Mountain of the Outlaws. By Joseph F. Rock. 1-65, *July 1931*

Fisherman mends his nets while his wife starts down the steps of their home, flanked by a fish trap and the day's wash, in Taormina, Sicily, in the early 1900s.   A. W. CUTLER

The Glories of the Minya Konka: Magnificent Snow Peaks of the China-Tibetan Border Are Photographed at Close Range by a National Geographic Society Expedition. By Joseph F. Rock. 385-437, *Oct. 1930*

See also Sichuan; Szechwan

SIKANG EXPEDITION:

Climbing Mighty Minya Konka: Americans First Scaled Mountain That Now Is Landmark of China's New Skyway. By Richard L. Burdsall and Terris Moore. 625-650, *May 1943*

A **SIKH** Discovers America. By Joginder Singh Rekhi. 558-590, *Oct. 1964*

SIKHS:

India's Energetic Sikhs. By John E. Frazer. Photos by James P. Blair. 528-541, *Oct. 1972*

In the Realms of the Maharajas. By Lawrence Copley Thaw and Margaret S. Thaw. 727-780, *Dec. 1940*

SIKING, Shaanxi Province, China. *See* Sian

SIKKIM:

Gangtok, Cloud-wreathed Himalayan Capital. By John Scofield. 698-713, *Nov. 1970*

Wedding of Two Worlds. By Lee E. Battaglia. 708-727, *Nov. 1963*

Sikkim. By Desmond Doig. 398-429, *Mar. 1963*

SILENT-WINGED Owls of North America. Paintings by Allan Brooks. 225-240, *Feb. 1935*

SILICON VALLEY (Industrial District), California:

The Chip: Electronic Mini-marvel. By Allen A. Boraiko. Photos by Charles O'Rear. 421-457, *Oct. 1982*

California's Silicon Valley. By Moira

Johnston. Photos by Charles O'Rear. 459-477, *Oct. 1982*

SILIS, IVARS:
On Assignment in Greenland. *Feb. 1983*

Author-Photographer
Narwhal Hunters of Greenland. 520-539, *Apr. 1984*

Photographer
Hunters of the Lost Spirit: Greenlanders. By Priit J. Vesilind. 191-193, *Feb. 1983*

SILK:
Silk–The Queen of Textiles. By Nina Hyde. Photos by Cary Wolinsky. 2-49, *Jan. 1984*

A Lady From China's Past. Photos from *China Pictorial*. Text by Alice J. Hall. 660-681, *May 1974*

Thailand Bolsters Its Freedom. By W. Robert Moore. 811-849, *June 1961*

How Half the World Works. By Alice Tisdale Hobart and Mary A. Nourse. 509-524, *Apr. 1932*

Strange Habits of Familiar Moths and Butterflies. By William Joseph Showalter. 77-105, *July 1927*

Massachusetts–Beehive of Business. By William Joseph Showalter. 203-245, *Mar. 1920*

The Industrial Titan of America: Pennsylvania, Once the Keystone of the Original Thirteen, Now the Keystone of Forty-eight Sovereign States. By John Oliver La Gorce. 367-406, *May 1919*

SILK ROAD:
Silk–The Queen of Textiles. By Nina Hyde. Photos by Cary Wolinsky. Included: Map of the caravan network across Asia. 2-49, *Jan. 1984*

SILKWORMS:
Silk–The Queen of Textiles. By Nina Hyde. Photos by Cary Wolinsky. 2-49, *Jan. 1984*

This Is the China I Saw. By Jørgen Bisch. 591-639, *Nov. 1964*

Silkworms in England Spin for the Queen. By John E. H. Nolan. 689-704, *May 1953*

Spain's Silkworm Gut. By Luis Marden. 100-108, *July 1951*

SILVER:
Viking Trail East. By Robert Paul Jordan. Photos by Jim Brandenburg. Paintings by Michael A. Hampshire. 278-317, *Mar. 1985*

Silver: A Mineral of Excellent Nature. By Allen A. Boraiko. Photos by Fred Ward. 280-313, *Sept. 1981*

The Treasure of Porto Santo. By Robert Sténuit. Photos by author and William R. Curtsinger. Included: Silver ingots and coins from the wreck of the *Slot ter Hooge*. 260-275, *Aug. 1975*

Pieces of Silver. By Frederick Simpich. 253-292, *Sept. 1933*

The Treasure Chest of Mercurial Mexico. By Frank H. Probert. Contents: Silver mines in Guanajuato. 33-68, *July 1916*

See also Spanish Treasure

Worker from the Dongshan People's Commune in eastern China hefts a harvest of silk cocoons destined for a government purchasing station. CARY WOLINSKY, STOCK, BOSTON

SILVER-BACKED JACKALS:
Jackals of the Serengeti. By Patricia D. Moehlman. NGS research grant. 840-850, *Dec. 1980*

SILVER DART I and II (Airplanes):
Canada's Winged Victory: the *Silver Dart*. By Gilbert M. Grosvenor. 254-267, *Aug. 1959*

SILVER FOX (Balloon):
The Longest Manned Balloon Flight. By Ed Yost. 208-217, *Feb. 1977*

SILVERMAN, DAVID:
Nomination Page. *Mar. 1977*

SILVERSMITHS:
Better Days for the Navajos. By Jack Breed. Photos by Charles W. Herbert. 809-847, *Dec. 1958*

SILVERSTEIN, SAMUEL:
Nomination Page. In Antarctica. *May 1967*

SILVERSTONE, MARILYN:
Photographer
Royal Wedding at Jaisalmer. 66-79, *Jan. 1965*

SILVERWARE:
Pieces of Silver. By Frederick Simpich. 253-292, *Sept. 1933*

SIMI (Island), Aegean Sea:
Rhodes, and Italy's Aegean Islands. By Dorothy Hosmer. 449-480, *Apr. 1941*

SIMLA, Trinidad:
Keeping House for Tropical Butterflies. By Jocelyn Crane. Photos by M. Woodbridge Williams. NGS research grant. 193-217, *Aug. 1957*

SIMMONS, GEORGE FINLAY:
Author
Sindbads of Science: Narrative of a Windjammer's Specimen-Collecting

Voyage to the Sargasso Sea, to Senegambian Africa and Among Islands of High Adventure in the South Atlantic. 1-75, *July 1927*

SIMONS, VERA: *Author*
Laboratory in a Dirty Sky. By Rudolf J. Engelmann and Vera Simons. 616-621, *Nov. 1976*

SIMPICH, FREDERICK: *Author*
Here Come the Marines. 647-672, *Nov. 1950*

So Much Happens Along the Ohio River. Photos by Justin Locke. 177-212, *Feb. 1950*

From Indian Canoes to Submarines at Key West. Photos by J. Baylor Roberts. 41-72, *Jan. 1950*

California, Horn of Plenty. Photos by Willard R. Culver. 553-594, *May 1949*

With Uncle Sam and John Bull in Germany. 117-140, *Jan. 1949*

4-H Boys and Girls Grow More Food. 551-582, *Nov. 1948*

Uncle Sam Bends a Twig in Germany. Photos by J. Baylor Roberts. 529-550, *Oct. 1948*

Mapping the Nation's Breadbasket. 831-849, *June 1948*

Around the "Great Lakes of the South." Photos by J. Baylor Roberts. 463-491, *Apr. 1948*

Louisiana Trades with the World. Photos by J. Baylor Roberts. 705-738, *Dec. 1947*

South Dakota Keeps Its West Wild. 555-588, *May 1947*

More Water for California's Great Central Valley. 645-664, *Nov. 1946*

Arkansas Rolls Up Its Sleeves. 273-312, *Sept. 1946*

These Missourians. 277-310, *Mar. 1946*

Taming the Outlaw Missouri River. 569-598, *Nov. 1945*

Grass Makes Wyoming Fat. 153-188, *Aug. 1945*

Elegant 18th-century shoe is made of silk brocade woven in London.

SIMPSON, HUGH: *Photographer*

First Woman Across Greenland's Ice.
By Myrtle Simpson. 264-279,
Aug. 1967

SIMPSON, MYRTLE: *Author*

First Woman Across Greenland's Ice.
Photos by Hugh Simpson. 264-279,
Aug. 1967

SIMPSON, W. A.: *Author*

Influence of Geographical Conditions
on Military Operations in South Africa. 186-192, *May 1900*

SIMSON, SPICER:

Transporting a Navy Through the Jun-
gles of Africa in War Time. By Frank
J. Magee. Note: Commander Spicer
Simson, R. N., was the organizer and
leader of the expedition. 331-362,
Oct. 1922

SINAI, Mount, Egypt:

In Search of Moses. By Harvey Arden.
Photos by Nathan Benn. 2-37,
Jan. 1976

Island of Faith in the Sinai Wilderness.
By George H. Forsyth. Photos by
Robert F. Sisson. Contents: St. Cath-
erine's Monastery. 82-106, *Jan. 1964*

Mount Sinai's Holy Treasures. By Kurt
Weitzmann. Photos by Fred Anderegg. Contents: St. Catherine's Monastery. 109-127, *Jan. 1964*

Sinai Sheds New Light on the Bible. By
Henry Field. Photos by William B.
and Gladys Terry. 795-815,
Dec. 1948

Sunrise and Sunset from Mount Sinai.
By Sartell Prentice, Jr. 1242-1282,
Dec. 1912

SINAI PENINSULA, Egypt:

Eternal Sinai. By Harvey Arden. 420-
461. Included: Egyptian Sector. Photos by Kevin Fleming. 430-443;
Israeli Sector. Photos by David Doubilet. Contents: Israeli withdrawal
from the Sinai Peninsula by April 25,

1982, as part of the Camp David
accords. 444-461, *Apr. 1982*

In Search of Moses. By Harvey Arden.
Photos by Nathan Benn. 2-37,
Jan. 1976

New Life for the Troubled Suez Canal.
By William Graves. Photos by Jonathan Blair. 792-817, *June 1975*

Island of Faith in the Sinai Wilderness.
By George H. Forsyth. Photos by
Robert F. Sisson. Contents: St. Cath-
erine's Monastery. 82-106, *Jan. 1964*

Mount Sinai's Holy Treasures. By Kurt
Weitzmann. Photos by Fred Anderegg. Contents: St. Catherine's Monastery. 109-127, *Jan. 1964*

Sinai Sheds New Light on the Bible. By
Henry Field. Photos by William B.
and Gladys Terry. 795-815,
Dec. 1948

East of Suez to the Mount of the Deca-
logue: Following the Trail Over
Which Moses Led the Israelites from
the Slave-Pens of Egypt to Sinai. By
Maynard Owen Williams. 709-743,
Dec. 1927

Flying Over Egypt, Sinai, and Palestine:
Looking Down Upon the Holy Land
During an Air Journey of Two and a
Half Hours from Cairo to Jerusalem.
By P.R.C. Groves and J. R. McCrin-
dle. 313-355, *Sept. 1926*

Sunrise and Sunset from Mount Sinai.
By Sartell Prentice, Jr. 1242-1282,
Dec. 1912

The Route Over Which Moses Led the
Children of Israel Out of Egypt. By
Franklin E. Hoskins. 1011-1038,
Dec. 1909

See also Ras Muhammad; Suez Canal

SINAN (District), South Korea:

Yellow Sea Yields Shipwreck Trove.
Photos by H. Edward Kim. Introduc-
tion by Donald H. Keith. 231-243,
Aug. 1979

SINCLAIR, C. H.: *Author*

The California and Nevada Boundary.
416-417, *Oct. 1899*

SINDBAD THE SAILOR:

In the Wake of Sindbad. By Tim
Severin. Photos by Richard Greenhill. 2-41, *July 1982*

Sailing with Sindbad's Sons. By Alan
Villiers. 675-688, *Nov. 1948*

SINDBADS of Science: Narrative of a
Windjammer's Specimen-Collecting
Voyage to the Sargasso Sea, to Senegambian Africa and Among Islands
of High Adventure in the South Atlantic. By George Finlay Simmons. 1-
75, *July 1927*

SINDONOLOGY. *See* Shroud of Turin

SING-SING (Fair):

New Guinea Festival of Faces. By Malcolm S. Kirk. 148-156, *July 1969*

Blowgun Hunters of the South Pacific.
By Jane C. Goodale. Photos by Ann
Chowning. 793-817, *June 1966*

Australian New Guinea. By John Scofield. 604-637, *May 1962*

To the Land of the Head-hunters. By E.
Thomas Gilliard. NGS research
grant. 437-486, *Oct. 1955*

New Guinea's Rare Birds and Stone
Age Men. By E. Thomas Gilliard.
NGS research grant. 421-488,
Apr. 1953

SINGAN–The Present Capital of the
Chinese Empire. By James Mascarene Hubbard. 63-66, *Feb. 1901*

SINGAPORE:

Singapore: Mini-size Superstate. By
Bryan Hodgson. Photos by Dean
Conger. 540-561, *Apr. 1981*

Singapore, Reluctant Nation. By Kenneth MacLeish. Photos by Winfield
Parks. 269-300, *Aug. 1966*

In Storied Lands of Malaysia. By Maurice Shadbolt. Photos by Winfield
Parks. 734-783, *Nov. 1963*

Malaya Meets Its Emergency. By
George W. Long. Photos by J. Baylor
Roberts and author. 185-228,
Feb. 1953

Life Grows Grim in Singapore. By H.
Gordon Minnigerode. Included: Singapore–Britain's Outpost of Empire.
Photos by J. Baylor Roberts. 661-
686, *Nov. 1941*

Behind the News in Singapore. By Frederick Simpich. 83-110, *July 1940*

Singapore: Far East Gibraltar in the
Malay Jungle. 599-614, *May 1938*

The Fire-Walking Hindus of Singapore.
By L. Elizabeth Lewis. 513-522,
Apr. 1931

Singapore, Crossroads of the East: The
World's Greatest Mart for Rubber
and Tin Was in Recent Times a Pi-
rate-haunted, Tiger-infested Jungle
Isle. By Frederick Simpich. 235-269,
Mar. 1926

SINGER, ARTHUR: *Artist*

✤ "Bird Migration in the Americas,"
painting supplement. Map on reverse. *Aug. 1979*

SINGER, ROLF: *Author*

Roaming Russia's Caucasus: Rugged
Mountains and Hardy Fighters
Guard the Soviet Union's Caucasian

*Bedouin prays on Gebel Musa, believed to be biblical Mount Sinai, where Moses
received the Ten Commandments after the Israelites' exodus from Egypt.* KEVIN FLEMING

Treasury of Manganese and Oil. 91-121, *July 1942*

SINGH, ANNE DE HENNING: *Author*

Sea Gypsies of the Philippines. Photos by Raghubir Singh. 659-677, *May 1976*

SINGH, RAGHUBIR:

Author-Photographer

The Pageant of Rajasthan. 219-243, *Feb. 1977*

The Last Andaman Islanders. 66-91, *July 1975*

Photographer

Long Journey of the Brahmaputra. By Jere Van Dyk. Photos by Raghubir Singh and Galen Rowell. Included: A Rare Visit to a World Unto Itself. 672-711, *Nov. 1988*

Kerala, Jewel of India's Malabar Coast. By Peter Miller. 592-617, *May 1988*

Bombay, the Other India. By John Scofield. 104-129, *July 1981*

Sri Lanka: Time of Testing for an Ancient Land. By Robert Paul Jordan. 123-150, *Jan. 1979*

Sea Gypsies of the Philippines. By Anne de Henning Singh. 659-677, *May 1976*

Calcutta, India's Maligned Metropolis. By Peter T. White. 534-563, *Apr. 1973*

The Ganges, River of Faith. By John J. Putman. 445-483, *Oct. 1971*

SINGH, SIR YADAVINDRA, Maharaja of Patiala:

Nomination Page. In India. *Mar. 1960*

The **SINGING** Towers of Holland and Belgium. By William Gorham Rice. 357-376, *Mar. 1925*

SINGLE PHOTON EMISSION COMPUTED TOMOGRAPHY (SPECT):

Medicine's New Vision. By Howard Sochurek. Paintings by Davis Meltzer. Illustrations text by Peter Miller. 2-41, *Jan. 1987*

SINHALESE:

Sri Lanka: Time of Testing for an Ancient Land. By Robert Paul Jordan. Photos by Raghubir Singh. 123-150, *Jan. 1979*

SINKHOLES:

Exploring a Sunken Realm in Australia. By Hillary Hauser. Photos by David Doubilet. 129-142, *Jan. 1984*

SINKIANG (Autonomous Region), China:

How the Kazakhs Fled to Freedom. By Milton J. Clark. 621-644, *Nov. 1954*

The Caves of the Thousand Buddhas. By Franc and Jean Shor. Included: Urumchi, Turfan, and Qomul (Hami), visited on way to the caves in Kansu Province. 383-415, *Mar. 1951*

With the Nomads of Central Asia: A Summer's Sojourn in the Tekes Valley, Plateau Paradise of Mongol and Turkic Tribes. By Edward Murray. Paintings and drawings by Alexandre Iacovleff. 1-57, *Jan. 1936*

From the Mediterranean to the Yellow Sea by Motor: The Citroën-Haardt Expedition Successfully Completes Its Dramatic Journey. By Maynard Owen Williams. 513-580, *Nov. 1932*

First Over the Roof of the World by Motor: The Trans-Asiatic Expedition Sets New Records for Wheeled Transport in Scaling Passes of the Himalaya. By Maynard Owen Williams. 321-363, *Mar. 1932*

On the World's Highest Plateaus: Through an Asiatic No Man's Land to the Desert of Ancient Cathay. By Hellmut de Terra. 319-367, *Mar. 1931*

The Desert Road to Turkestan: Twentieth Century Travel Through Innermost Asia, Along Caravan Trails Over Which Oriental Commerce Was Once Borne from China to the Medieval Western World. By Owen Lattimore. 661-702, *June 1929*

By Coolie and Caravan Across Central Asia: Narrative of a 7,900-Mile Journey of Exploration and Research Over "the Roof of the World," from the Indian Ocean to the Yellow Sea. By William J. Morden. 369-431, *Oct. 1927*

Tales of the Lop Basin in Central Asia. By Ellsworth Huntington. 289-295, *Apr. 1908*

Sven Hedin's Explorations in Central Asia. 393-395, *Nov. 1901*

See also present name, Xinjiang Uygur Autonomous Region

SINT EUSTATIUS (Island), Netherlands Antilles:

The Netherlands Antilles: Holland in the Caribbean. By James Cerruti. Photos by Emory Kristof. 115-146, *Jan. 1970*

A Fresh Breeze Stirs the Leewards. By Carleton Mitchell. Photos by Winfield Parks. 488-537, *Oct. 1966*

SINT MAARTEN (Island), Netherlands Antilles:

The Netherlands Antilles: Holland in the Caribbean. By James Cerruti. Photos by Emory Kristof. 115-146, *Jan. 1970*

SIOUX FALLS, South Dakota:

Satellites Gave Warning of Midwest Floods. By Peter T. White. Photos by Thomas A. DeFeo. 574-592, *Oct. 1969*

SIOUX INDIANS:

Ghosts on the Little Bighorn. By Robert Paul Jordan. Photos by Scott Rutherford. 787-813, *Dec. 1986*

✦ *Northern Plains,* The Making of America series. Included: Montana, Wyoming, North Dakota, South Dakota, Nebraska, Minnesota, Iowa, and in Canada: Saskatchewan, Manitoba, Ontario. On reverse: New Frontiers, Indians in Transition, Furs and Footholds, Steel Rails and

Billowing dye allows scientists to time the rate of water exchange in the largest of Ewens Ponds, a trio of interconnected sinkholes in southeastern Australia. DAVID DOUBILET

■■ BOOKS ✦ MAPS ■ TELEVISION

Red Horse's drawing of the 1876 Battle of Little Bighorn probably combines personal and Sioux tribal memories. NATIONAL ANTHROPOLOGICAL ARCHIVES, SMITHSONIAN INSTITUTION

In 1881 Sioux Chief Red Horse depicted Custer's last stand in colored-pencil pictures. BY D. F. BARRY, THOMAS HESKI COLLECTION

Only three-eighths of an inch long, the wentletrap snail can extend its snout three times the length of its shell to feed off the tip of a sea anemone.   ROBERT F. SISSON, NGS

The nuclear submarine U.S.S. Skate breaks through ice 300 miles from the North Pole on a 1959 voyage. COMDR. JAMES F. CALVERT, USN

Skiing Over the New Hampshire Hills. By Fred H. Harris. 151-164, *Feb. 1920*

SKINGLE, DEREK:

Journey Into Stone Age New Guinea. By Malcolm S. Kirk. 568-592, *Apr. 1969*

SKINNER, ROBERT P.:

Consul Skinner's Mission to Abyssinia. 165-166, *Apr. 1904*

SKIRTING the Shores of Sunrise: Seeking and Finding "The Levant" in a Journey by Steamer, Motor-Car, and Train from Constantinople to Port Said. By Melville Chater. 649-728, *Dec. 1926*

SKOKHOLM ISLAND, Wales:

We Live Alone, and Like It–On an Island. By R. M. Lockley. 252-278, *Aug. 1938*

SKOMER ISLAND, Wales:

The Solemn, Sociable Puffins. By R. M. Lockley. 414-422, *Sept. 1954*

SKOPJE, Yugoslavia:

Yugoslavia: Six Republics in One. By Robert Paul Jordan. Photos by James P. Blair. Included: 1963 earthquake. 589-633, *May 1970*

SKRAELING ISLAND, Northwest Territories, Canada:

Eskimo and Viking Finds in the High Arctic: Ellesmere Island. By Peter Schledermann. Photos by Sisse Brimberg. Included: Artifacts from Thule sites. 575-601, *May 1981*

SKUAS:

South Georgia, an Outpost of the Antarctic. By Robert Cushman Murphy. 409-444, *Apr. 1922*

SKULL, 1.6-Million-Year-Old Hominid:

Editorial. By Wilbur E. Garrett. Note: The skull was found near Lake Turkana, Kenya. 419, *Oct. 1986*

SKULL 1470. By Richard E. Leakey. Photos by Bob Campbell. NGS research grant. 819-829, *June 1973*

"SKUNK" (Train):

The Friendly Train Called Skunk. By Dean Jennings. Photos by B. Anthony Stewart. 720-734, *May 1959*

SKUNKS:

Skunks Want Peace–or Else! By Melvin R. Ellis. Photos by Charles Philip Fox. 279-294, *Aug. 1955*

Wild Animals That Took Their Own Pictures by Day and by Night. By George Shiras, 3d. 763-834, *July 1913*

SKY CHARTS. See Star Charts

SKY-HIGH Bolivia. 481-496, *Oct. 1950*

SKY-HIGH in Lama Land. Photos by C. Suydam Cutting. 185-196, *Aug. 1946*

"SKY PEOPLE." *See* Ainu

SKY Road East. By Tay and Lowell Thomas, Jr. 71-112, *Jan. 1960*

SKY SURVEY:

⊕ *Journey Into the Universe Through Time and Space; National Geographic-Palomar Sky Survey Charting the Heavens. June 1983*

Sky Survey Charts the Universe. By Ira Sprague Bowen. NGS research grant. 780-781, *Dec. 1956*

Exploring the Farthest Reaches of Space. By George O. Abell. NGS research grant. 782-790, *Dec. 1956*

Completing the Atlas of the Universe. By Ira Sprague Bowen. Contents: National Geographic Society-Palomar Observatory Sky Survey; Sky Survey Plates Unlock Secrets of the Stars. NGS research grant. 185-190, *Aug. 1955*

Twelve National Geographic Society Scientific Projects Under Way. 869-870, *June 1954*

Current Scientific Projects of the National Geographic Society. NGS research grant. 143-144, *July 1953*

Our Universe Unfolds New Wonders. By Albert G. Wilson. Contents: National Geographic-Palomar Sky Survey. NGS research grant. 245-260, *Feb. 1952*

Mapping the Unknown Universe. By F. Barrows Colton. NGS research grant. 401-420, *Sept. 1950*

SKYE, Isle of, Inner Hebrides, Scotland:

Over the Sea to Scotland's Skye. By Robert J. Reynolds. 87-112, *July 1952*

SKYLAB MISSIONS:

Skylab's Fiery Finish. By Tom Riggert. 581-584, *Oct. 1979*

Skylab. Photos by the nine mission astronauts. 441-503. I. Outpost in Space. By Thomas Y. Canby. 441-469; II. Its View of Earth. 471-493; III. The Sun Unveiled. By Edwin G. Gibson. 494-503, *Oct. 1974*

A **SKYLINE** Drive in the Pyrenees. By W. Robert Moore. 434-452, *Oct. 1937*

SKYLINE Trail from Maine to Georgia. By Andrew H. Brown. Photos by Robert F. Sisson. 219-251, *Aug. 1949*

SKYPATHS Through Latin America: Flying From Our Nation's Capital Southward Over Jungles, Remote Islands, and Great Cities on an Aërial Survey of the East Coast of South America. By Frederick Simpich. 1-79, *Jan. 1931*

SKÝROS (Island), Aegean Sea:

The Isles of Greece. By Richard Stillwell. 593-622, *May 1944*

SKYSCRAPERS:

The Mohawks Scrape the Sky. By Robert L. Conly. Photos by B. Anthony Stewart. 133-142, *July 1952*

SKYWAY Below the Clouds. By Carl R. Markwith. Photos by Ernest J. Cottrell. Contents: Skyway 1 (Wright Way), a route planned and marked especially for the use of private flyers. 85-108, *July 1949*

SLADEN, WILLIAM J. L.: *Author*

Tireless Voyager, the Whistling Swan. Photos by Bianca Lavies. 134-147, *July 1975*

SLAVERY:

The Underground Railroad. By Charles L. Blockson. Photos by Louie Psihoyos. 3-39, *July 1984*

Africa, Its Past and Future. By Gardiner G. Hubbard. 99-124, *Apr. 1889*

SLAVS:

Ukraine. By Mike Edwards. Photos by Steve Raymer. 595-631, *May 1987*

Slovakia's Spirit of Survival. By Yva Momatiuk and John Eastcott. 120-146, *Jan. 1987*

Viking Trail East. By Robert Paul Jordan. Photos by Jim Brandenburg. Paintings by Michael A. Hampshire. 278-317, *Mar. 1985*

SLAYTON, DONALD K.:

Apollo-Soyuz: Handclasp in Space. By Thomas Y. Canby. 183-187, *Feb. 1976*

SLED-DOG RACE:

Thousand-mile Race to Nome: A Woman's Icy Struggle. By Susan Butcher. Photos by Kerby Smith. 411-422, *Mar. 1983*

SLED DOGS:

North to the Pole. By Will Steger. Photos by the author and Jim Brandenburg. 289-317, *Sept. 1986*

Thousand-mile Race to Nome: A Woman's Icy Struggle. By Susan Butcher. Photos by Kerby Smith. 411-422, *Mar. 1983*

Solo to the Pole. By Naomi Uemura. Photos by the author and Ira Block. 298-325, *Sept. 1978*

Trek Across Arctic America. By Colin Irwin. 295-321, *Mar. 1974*

Dogs of Duty and Devotion. By Frederick G. Vosburgh. 769-774, *Dec. 1941*

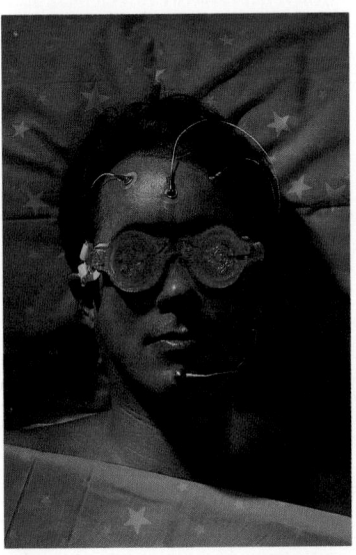

Stanford University psychologist Stephen LaBerge wears goggles he designed for a dreaming experiment. LOUIE PSIHOYOS

Smell Survey, containing scratch-and-sniff panels, was issued with the September 1986 magazine. LOUIE PSIHOYOS

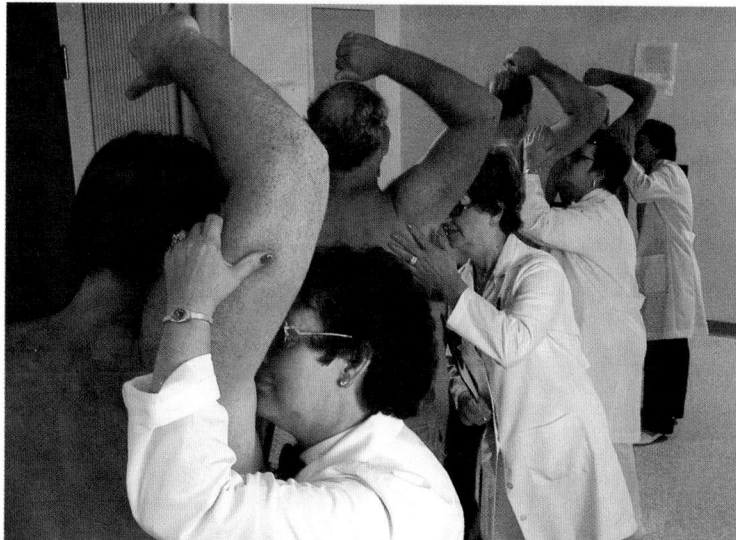

Judges at a research firm sniff the natural odors of volunteers testing a deodorant. Smell can be memorable but is our least understood sense. LOUIE PSIHOYOS

Young museum visitor mimics a bronze witch doctor at an exhibit in the Smithsonian Institution, Washington, D.C.   WILLIS D. VAUGHN

Jungle Housekeeping for a Geographic Expedition. By Marion Stirling. 303-327, *Sept. 1941*

Great Stone Faces of the Mexican Jungle: Five Colossal Heads and Numerous Other Monuments of Vanished Americans Are Excavated by the Latest National Geographic-Smithsonian Expedition. By Matthew W. Stirling. 309-334, *Sept. 1940*

Discovering the New World's Oldest Dated Work of Man: A Maya Monument Inscribed 291 B. C. is Unearthed Near a Huge Stone Head by a Geographic-Smithsonian Expedition in Mexico. By Matthew W. Stirling. 183-218, *Aug. 1939*

Exploring Frozen Fragments of American History: On the Trail of Early Eskimo Colonists Who Made a 55-Mile Crossing from the Old World to the New. By Henry B. Collins, Jr. 633-656, *May 1939*

Around the World for Animals. By William M. and Lucile Q. Mann. 665-714, *June 1938*

Measuring the Sun's Heat and Forecasting the Weather: The National Geographic Society to Maintain a Solar Station in a Remote Part of the World to Coöperate with Smithsonian Institution Stations in California and Chile. By C. G. Abbot. 111-126, *Jan. 1926*

Wild Man and Wild Beast in Africa. By Theodore Roosevelt. 1-33, *Jan. 1911*

National Geographic Society (Cables and Report by Theodore Roosevelt on the African Expedition Sponsored by the Smithsonian Institution). 365-370, *Apr. 1910*

Museums

U. S. National Museum. 792, 798, 800, 803, 805, 806, Dec. 1950, 367, Mar. 1954, 90, Jan. 1956, 264, Feb. 1956, 276, Aug. 1956, 829, 832, Dec. 1956; First Lady exhibit. 328, 347, Sept. 1948, 90, Jan. 1957; Fossil collection. 363, 365, 376, 379, 381, Mar. 1956; Mineral collection. 631, 638-641, Nov. 1951; Shell collection. 39, 68, 71, July 1949; Eskimo artifacts. 198, Feb. 1983

National Air and Space Museum: Of Air and Space. By Michael Collins. 819-837. Included: Picture portfolio by Nathan Benn, Robert S. Oakes, and Joseph D. Lavenburg, with text by Michael E. Long. 825-837, *June 1978*

Museum of History and Technology. 741, 743, Dec. 1964, 873, 874, Dec. 1973, 95-97, 99, *July 1975*

Natural History Museum. 874, Dec. 1973; Hall of Gems and Minerals. 568, 575, 579, 584, Apr. 1958, 835-839, 852-853, 858-863, Dec. 1971; Ice Age "Mummy." 297, Mar. 1972; Mural. 294-295, *Mar. 1972*

National Collection of Fine Arts. 798, 831, 838, June 1960, 508, 511, *Apr. 1967*

Freer Gallery of Art. 348, Sept. 1948, 798, 805, 832-833, 838, June 1960, 363, *Sept. 1964*

The Smithsonian, Magnet on the Mall. By Leonard Carmichael. Photos by

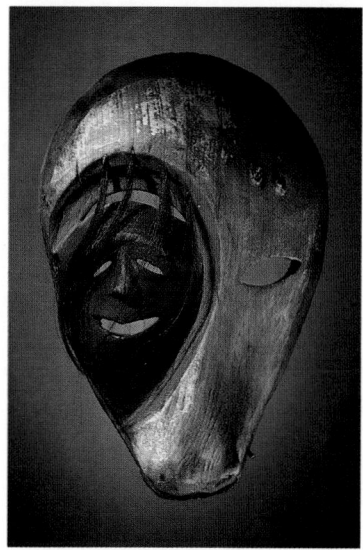

Eskimo ceremonial mask is preserved in the Smithsonian's National Museum of Natural History. SISSE BRIMBERG

Volkmar Wentzel. 796-845, *June 1960*

National Herbarium. 477, *Oct. 1950*

The Smithsonian Institution. By Thomas R. Henry. 325-348, *Sept. 1948*

Research Facilities

Smithsonian Astrophysical Observatory, Cambridge, Massachusetts. 190, Feb. 1962, 808, 812, Dec. 1966; Comet Kohoutek. 148, Jan. 1974; Ikeya-Seki comet. 260, 261, Feb. 1966; Solar Eclipse, Nature's Super Spectacular. By Donald H. Menzel and Jay M. Pasachoff. 222-233, Aug. 1970; Solar studies. 334, 343, 344, 346, Sept. 1948; Supernova SN 1987A. 622, *May 1988*

Canal Zone Biological Area: Sea level canal study. 772, Dec. 1970; Tropical Research Institute. 417, 440, Mar. 1970, 575, Apr. 1972, 282, 288, 292, Feb. 1978, 78, 80, *Jan. 1982*

Chesapeake Bay Center for Environmental Studies: Whistling swan. 140, 141, 144, *July 1975*

Center for Short-Lived Phenomena, Cambridge, Massachusetts. 286B, *Feb. 1973*

"Science City," Maui. 515, 527, *Apr. 1971*

Science Information Exchange. 614, *Nov. 1970*

International Exchange Service. 798, 816, *June 1960*

See also National Gallery of Art; National Zoological Park

SMOG. *See* Air Pollution

SMOKE Over Alabama. By Frederick Simpich. 703-758, *Dec. 1931*

SMOKEJUMPING:

Forest Fire: The Devil's Picnic. By Stuart E. Jones and Jay Johnston. 100-127, *July 1968*

SMOKY JUNGLE FROG:

A Frog That Eats Bats and Snakes: In Captivity, This Big Jungle Amphibian Exhibits an Extraordinary Appetite. By Kenneth W. Vinton. 657-664, *May 1938*

SMOKY MOUNTAINS, North Carolina-Tennessee. *See* Great Smoky Mountains

SMOLAN, RICK: *Photographer*

Alone Across the Outback. By Robyn Davidson. 581-611, *May 1978*

SMUGGLING:

Jade: Stone of Heaven. By Fred Ward. 282-315, *Sept. 1987*

Editorial. By Wilbur E. Garrett. 141, *Feb. 1985*

The Poppy. By Peter T. White. Photos by Steve Raymer. 143-189, *Feb. 1985*

Wild Cargo: the Business of Smuggling Animals. By Noel Grove. Photos by Steve Raymer. 287-315, *Mar. 1981*

SMYRNA, Turkey. *See* İzmir

SMYSER, WILLIAM LEON: *Author*

São Tomé, the Chocolate Island. 657-680, *May 1946*

SNAILS:

Blue-water Plankton: Ghosts of the Gulf Stream. By William M. Hamner. Included: Planktonic snails. NGS research grant. 530-545, *Oct. 1974*

Tree Snails, Gems of the Everglades. By Treat Davidson. 372-387, *Mar. 1965*

Formosa–Hot Spot of the East. By Frederick G. Vosburgh. Photos by J. Baylor Roberts. Included: Giant African land snails. 139-176, *Feb. 1950*

Shells Take You Over World Horizons. By Rutherford Platt. Included: Land, marine, and tree snails. 33-84, *July 1949*

SNAKE (River), Wyoming-Idaho-Washington:

Wildlife Adventuring in Jackson Hole. By Frank and John Craighead. 1-36, *Jan. 1956*

A Map Maker Looks at the United States. By Newman Bumstead. 705-748, *June 1951*

SNAKE DANCE:

The Snake Dance. By Marion L. Oliver. Contents: Snake dance ritual of the Hopi Indians. 107-137, *Feb. 1911*

The Forests and Deserts of Arizona. By Bernhard E. Fernow. 203-226, *July-Aug. 1897*

SNAKES:

Hidden Life of the Timber Rattler. By William S. Brown. Photos by Bianca Lavies. NGS research grant. 128-138, *July 1987*

Manitoba's Fantastic Snake Pits. By Michael Aleksiuk. Photos by Bianca Lavies. Contents: Garter snake hibernation pits. 715-723, *Nov. 1975*

Diving With Sea Snakes. By Kenneth MacLeish. Photos by Ben Cropp. 565-578, *Apr. 1972*

Finger-thin green tree snake hunts birds, lizards, and frogs in the Venezuelan jungle.

LOREN McINTYRE

Volkmar Wentzel. 266-293, *Aug. 1969*

SOC (Sub-ice Observation Chamber): Stalking Seals Under Antarctic Ice. By Carleton Ray. 54-65, *Jan. 1966*

SOCHUREK, HOWARD:

Author-Photographer

Medicine's New Vision. Paintings by Davis Meltzer. Illustrations text by Peter Miller. 2-41, *Jan. 1987*

The Volga, Russia's Mighty River Road. 579-613, *May 1973*

Berlin, on Both Sides of the Wall. 1-47, *Jan. 1970*

South Korea: Success Story in Asia. 301-345, *Mar. 1969*

Air Rescue Behind Enemy Lines. 346-369, *Sept. 1968*

Viet Nam's Montagnards. 443-487, *Apr. 1968*

American Special Forces in Action in Viet Nam. 38-65, *Jan. 1965*

Slow Train Through Viet Nam's War. 412-444, *Sept. 1964*

Photographer

World War I Aircraft Fly Again in Rhinebeck's Rickety Rendezvous. By Harvey Arden. 578-587, *Oct. 1970*

The Laser's Bright Magic. By Thomas Meloy. 858-881, *Dec. 1966*

SOCIAL INSECTS. *See* Ants; Bees; Termites

SOCIÉTÉ D'ÉNERGIE DE LA BAIE JAMES: Quebec Province, Canada:

Quebec's Northern Dynamo. By Larry Kohl. Photos by Ottmar Bierwagen. 406-418, *Mar. 1982*

The **SOCIETY** Announces New Flight into the Stratosphere. By Gilbert Grosvenor. 265-272, *Feb. 1935*

The **SOCIETY** Awards Hubbard Medal to Anne Morrow Lindbergh. 791-794, *June 1934*

SOCIETY Honors the Conquerors of Antarctica. 589-590, *Apr. 1959*

SOCIETY ISLANDS, South Pacific Ocean:

The Society Islands, Sisters of the Wind. By Priit J. Vesilind. Photos by George F. Mobley. 844-869, *June 1979*

The *Yankee's* Wander-world. By Irving and Electa Johnson. 1-50, *Jan. 1949*

The Dream Ship: The Story of a Voyage of Adventure More Than Half Around the World in a 47-foot Lifeboat. By Ralph Stock. 1-52, *Jan. 1921*

Tahiti: A Playground of Nature. By Paul Gooding. 301-326, *Oct. 1920*

Notes on Tahiti. By H. W. Smith. 947-963, *Oct. 1911*

Diary of a Voyage from San Francisco to Tahiti and Return, 1901. By S. P. Langley. 413-429, *Dec. 1901*

See also Tahiti

The **SOCIETY** Reports to Its Members on Russia Today. The Editor. 351, *Sept. 1959*

The **SOCIETY** Takes Part in Three

Geographic Expeditions. 625-626, *May 1934*

The **SOCIETY'S** Great 75th Anniversary Issue. Introduction by Melville Bell Grosvenor. 459, *Oct. 1963*

The **SOCIETY'S** Hubbard Medal Awarded to Commander MacMillan. 563-564, *Apr. 1953*

The **SOCIETY'S** Map of South America. By Gilbert Grosvenor. 809-810, *Dec. 1937*

The **SOCIETY'S** New Map of Canada. 769-776, *June 1936*

The **SOCIETY'S** New Map of China. By James M. Darley. 745-746, *June 1945*

The **SOCIETY'S** New Map of Europe. By Gilbert Grosvenor. 771-774, *Dec. 1929*

The **SOCIETY'S** New Map of South America. Included: Scenes in South America. 374-392, *Oct. 1921*

The **SOCIETY'S** New Map of the Pacific. By Gilbert Grosvenor. 793-796, *Dec. 1936*

The **SOCIETY'S** Special Medal Awarded to Amelia Earhart: First Woman to Receive Geographic Distinction at

Brilliant Ceremony in the National Capital. 358-367, *Sept. 1932*

The **SOCIETY'S** Special Medal Is Awarded to Dr. Thomas C. Poulter: Admiral Byrd's Second-in-Command and Senior Scientist Is Accorded High Geographic Honor. 105-108, *July 1937*

The **SOCIETY'S** Trustees: 1988: The Trustees Who Have Carried On the Tradition. By Melvin M. Payne. 38-43, *Jan. 1988*

SOCKEYE SALMON:

The Incredible Salmon. By Clarence P. Idyll. Photos by Robert F. Sisson. Paintings by Walter A. Weber. 195-219, *Aug. 1968*

SOCOTRA (Island), South Yemen:

The Isle of Frankincense. By Charles K. Moser. 267-278, *Mar. 1918*

SOFIA, Bulgaria:

Bulgaria, Farm Land Without a Farmhouse: A Nation of Villagers Faces the Challenge of Modern Machinery and Urban Life. By Maynard Owen Williams. 185-218, *Aug. 1932*

SOHAR (Dhow):

In the Wake of Sindbad. By Tim

Canadian sockeye salmon fill the Adams River in British Columbia during their summer spawning run. ROBERT F. SISSON, NGS

Firewood vendor travels the drought-stricken Sahel. Overcut since 1950, the area has lost more than half its forest.   STEVE McCURRY, MAGNUM

An Atlas of Energy Resources. Included: Maps of the United States showing the average daily radiation. 58-69, *Special Report on Energy.* (Feb. 1981)

Conservation: Can We Live Better on Less? By Rick Gore. 34-57, *Special Report on Energy. (Feb. 1981)*

Electricity From the Sun. Contents: The solar-powered aircraft, *Gossamer Penguin.* 40-41, *Special Report on Energy. (Feb. 1981)*

What's Happening to Our Climate? By Samuel W. Matthews. 576-615, *Nov. 1976*

The Next Frontier? By Isaac Asimov. Paintings by Pierre Mion. 76-89, *July 1976*

Editorial. By Gilbert M. Grosvenor. 289, *Mar. 1976*

Solar Energy, the Ultimate Powerhouse. By John L. Wilhelm. Photos by Emory Kristof. 381-397, *Mar. 1976*

The Search for Tomorrow's Power. By Kenneth F. Weaver. Photos by Emory Kristof. 650-681, *Nov. 1972*

The Sun. By Herbert Friedman. 713-743, *Nov. 1965*

Keeping House for the "Shepherds of the Sun." By Mrs. William H. Hoover. Contents: The Solar Radiation Observatory at Mount Burkkaros, South-West Africa. 483-506, *Apr. 1930*

Hunting an Observatory: A Successful Search for a Dry Mountain on Which to Establish the National Geographic Society's Solar Radiation Station. By C. G. Abbot. Contents: The Solar Radiation Observatory at Mount Burkkaros, South-West Africa. 503-518, *Oct. 1926*

Measuring the Sun's Heat and Forecasting the Weather: The National Geographic Society to Maintain a Solar Station in a Remote Part of the World to Coöperate with Smithsonian Institution Stations in California and Chile. By C. G. Abbot. Contents: Proposal for NGS-sponsored solar radiation observatory. 111-126, *Jan. 1926*

SOLAR-POWERED CAR:

Across Australia by Sunpower. By Hans Tholstrup and Larry Perkins. Photos by David Austen. 600-607, *Nov. 1983*

SOLAR SYSTEM:

Meteorites–Invaders From Space. By Kenneth F. Weaver. Photos by Jonathan Blair. 390-418, *Sept. 1986*

■■ *National Geographic Picture Atlas of Our Universe.* By Roy A. Gallant. 284 pages. 1980; rev. ed. *1986*

The Planets: Between Fire and Ice. By Rick Gore. 4-51, *Jan. 1985*

✧ *The Solar System; Saturn. July 1981*

Voyage to the Planets. By Kenneth F. Weaver. Paintings by Ludek Pesek. 147-193, *Aug. 1970*

News of the Universe: Mars Swings Nearer the Earth, Sunspots Wane, and a Giant New Telescopic Eye Soon Will Peer Into Unexplored Depths of Space. By F. Barrows

Colton. Included: Solar System's Eternal Show. Paintings by Charles Bittinger. 1-32, *July 1939*

See also Comets; Moon; Planets; Sun

SOLDIER CRABS:

Strange Sights in Far-Away Papua. By A. E. Pratt. 559-572, *Sept. 1907*

SOLDIERS:

Americans Stand Guard in Greenland. By Andrew H. Brown. 457-500, *Oct. 1946*

American Fighters Visit Bible Lands. By Maynard Owen Williams. 311-340, *Mar. 1946*

This Is My Own: How the United States Seems to a Citizen Soldier Back from Three Years Overseas. By Frederick G. Vosburgh. 113-128, *Jan. 1946*

American Soldier in Reykjavík. By Luther M. Chovan. 536-568, *Nov. 1945*

The White War in Norway. By Thomas R. Henry. 617-640, *Nov. 1945*

Flying Our Wounded Veterans Home. By Catherine Bell Palmer. 363-384, *Sept. 1945*

Yank Meets Native. By Wanda Burnett. 105-128, *July 1945*

Paris Freed. By Frederick Simpich, Jr. 385-412, *Apr. 1945*

Heroes' Return. By William H. Nicholas. 333-352, *Mar. 1945*

Fiji Patrol on Bougainville. By David D. Duncan. 87-104, *Jan. 1945*

Paris Delivered. 79-86, *Jan. 1945*

Infantrymen–The Fighters of War. By W. H. Wilbur. 513-538, *Nov. 1944*

When GI Joes Took London. By Frederick Simpich, Jr. 337-354, *Sept. 1944*

The Aerial Invasion of Burma. By H. H. Arnold. Included: Allied troops who served with Major General Wingate. 129-148, *Aug. 1944*

Yanks in Northern Ireland. 191-204, *Aug. 1943*

Painting the Army on Maneuvers. By Arthur Beaumont. Paintings by author. 601-602, *Nov. 1942*

Proud soldier wears the Medal of Honor, French Croix de Guerre, and a Montenegrin medal. PAUL THOMPSON

The Making of an Anzac. By Howell Walker. 409-456, *Apr. 1942*

Around the Clock with Your Soldier Boy. By Frederick Simpich. 1-36, *July 1941*

America's South Sea Soldiers. By Lorena MacIntyre Quinn. 267-274, *Sept. 1919*

See also Korean War; U. S. Army; U. S. Army Air Forces; U. S. Army Corps of Engineers; U. S. Army Quartermaster Corps; U. S. Army Signal Corps; Vietnam War; War Memorials; World War I; World War II

SOLDIERS of the Soil: Our Food Crops Must Be Greatly Increased. By David F. Houston. 273-280, *Mar. 1917*

SOLE:

The Red Sea's Sharkproof Fish. By Eugenie Clark. Photos by David Doubilet. Contents: Moses sole. NGS research grant. 718-727, *Nov. 1974*

The **SOLEMN,** Sociable Puffins. By R. M. Lockley. 414-422, *Sept. 1954*

SOLHEIM, WILHELM G., II: *Author*

New Light on a Forgotten Past. 330-339, *Mar. 1971*

SOLIDARITY (Trade Union):

Poland: The Hope That Never Dies. By Tad Szulc. Photos by James L. Stanfield. 80-121, *Jan. 1988*

✧ *The Face and Faith of Poland.* Map, photo, and essay supplement. By Peter Miller. Essay by Czesław Miłosz. Photos by Bruno Barbey. *Apr. 1982*

SOLO to the Pole. By Naomi Uemura. Photos by the author and Ira Block. 298-325, *Sept. 1978*

SOLOMON, King (Israel):

On the Trail of King Solomon's Mines: The Bible, in Addition to Its Spiritual Values, Continues to Prove a Rich Geography. By Nelson Glueck. 233-256, *Feb. 1944*

SOLOMON ISLANDS, South Pacific Ocean:

A Teen-ager Sails the World Alone. By Robin Lee Graham. 445-491, *Oct. 1968*

Yankee Roams the Orient. By Irving and Electa Johnson. 327-370, *Mar. 1951*

Adventures with the Survey Navy. By Irving Johnson. 131-148, *July 1947*

American Pathfinders in the Pacific. By William H. Nicholas. 617-640, *May 1946*

Fiji Patrol on Bougainville. By David D. Duncan. 87-104, *Jan. 1945*

Painting History in the Pacific. Paintings by William F. Draper. 408-424, *Oct. 1944*

What the Fighting Yanks See. By Wanda Burnett. 451-476, *Oct. 1944*

✧ *Southeast Asia and Pacific Islands from the Indies and the Philippines to the Solomons. Oct. 1944*

Jungle War: Bougainville and New Caledonia. Paintings by William F. Draper. 417-432, *Apr. 1944*

At Ease in the South Seas. By Frederick Simpich. Jr. 79-104, *Jan. 1944*

S T

A Woman's Experiences among Stone Age Solomon Islanders: Primitive Life Remains Unchanged in Tropical Jungleland Where United States Forces Now Are Fighting. By Eleanor Schirmer Oliver. 813-836, *Dec. 1942*

Coconuts and Coral Islands. By H. Ian Hogbin. 265-298, *Mar. 1934*

The Islands of the Pacific. By J. P. Thomson. 543-558, *Dec. 1921*

SOLOMONS ISLAND, Maryland:

Landing Craft for Invasion. By Melville Bell Grosvenor. Included: Amphibious Training Base. 1-30, *July 1944*

SOLUKA CREEK, Alaska:

The Valley of Ten Thousand Smokes: National Geographic Society Explorations in the Katmai District of Alaska. By Robert F. Griggs. 13-68, *Jan. 1917*

SOLVING Life Secrets of the Sailfish. By Gilbert Voss. Photos by B. Anthony Stewart. Paintings by Craig Phillips. 859-872, *June 1956*

SOLVING the Mystery of Mexico's Great Stone Spheres. By Matthew W. Stirling. Photos by David F. Cupp. 295-300, *Aug. 1969*

SOLVING the Riddle of Chubb Crater. By V. Ben Meen. Photos by Richard H. Stewart. 1-32, *Jan. 1952*

SOLVING the Riddles of Wetherill Mesa. By Douglas Osborne. Paintings by Peter V. Bianchi. 155-195, *Feb. 1964*

SOMALIA:

Somalia's Hour of Need. By Robert Paul Jordan. Photos by Michael S. Yamashita and Kevin Fleming. Included: Encampments of the Dispossessed. By Larry Kohl. 748-775, *June 1981*

SOMALILAND. *See* French Somaliland

SOME Aspects of Rural Japan. By Walter Weston. 275-301, *Sept. 1922*

SOME Early Geographers of the United States. By Colby M. Chester. 392-404, *Oct. 1904*

SOME Facts About Japan. 446-448, *Nov. 1904*

SOME Forgotten Corners of London: Many Places of Beauty and Historic Interest Repay the Search of the Inquiring Visitor. By Harold Donaldson Eberlein. 163-198, *Feb. 1932*

SOME French Pastorals. Photos by Harrison Howell Walker. 207-230, *Feb. 1940*

SOME Geographic Features of Southern Patagonia, with a Discussion of Their Origin. By J. B. Hatcher. 41-55, *Feb. 1900*

SOME Giant Fishes of the Seas. By Hugh M. Smith. 637-644, *July 1909*

SOME Human Habitations. By Collier Cobb. 509-515, *July 1908*

SOME Impressions of 150,000 Miles of Travel. By William Howard Taft. 523-598, *May 1930*

SOME Indications of Land in the Vicinity of the North Pole. By R. A. Harris. 255-261, *June 1904*

SOME Lessons in Geography. By Edward Atkinson. 193-198, *Apr. 1905*

SOME Mexican Transportation Scenes. By Walter W. Bradley. 985-991, *Dec. 1910*

SOME Notes on the Fox Island Passes, Alaska. By J. J. Gilbert. 427-429, *Sept. 1905*

SOME Notes on Venezuela. 17-21, *Jan. 1903*

SOME Odd Pages from the Annals of the Tulip: A "Made" Flower of

Unknown Origin Took Medieval Europe by Storm and Caused a Financial Panic in the Netherlands. By Leo A. Borah. 321-343, *Sept. 1933*

SOME of Nature's Scenic Gifts to Hawaii. Photos by Henry W. Henshaw and others. 159-174, *Feb. 1924*

SOME of Our Immigrants. 317-334, *May 1907*

SOME of the Conditions and Possibilities of Agriculture in Alaska. By Walter H. Evans. 178-187, *Apr. 1898*

SOME Peculiar Features of Central African Geography. By Samuel P. Verner. 448, *Nov. 1904*

SOME Personal Experiences with Earthquakes. By L. G. Billings. 57-71, *Jan. 1915*

SOME Recent Geographic Events. By John Hyde. 359-362, *Dec. 1897*

SOME Recent Instances of National Altruism: The Efforts of the United States to Aid the Peoples of Cuba, Porto Rico and the Philippines. By William H. Taft. 429-438, *July 1907*

SOME Ruined Cities of Asia Minor. By Ernest L. Harris. 833-858, *Dec. 1908*

SOME Songsters and Flyers of Wide Repute. Paintings by Allan Brooks. 529-544, *Apr. 1936*

SOME Tramps Across the Glaciers and Snowfields of British Columbia. By Howard Palmer. 457-487, *June 1910*

SOME Wonderful Sights in the Andean Highlands: The Oldest City in America. Sailing on the Lake of the Clouds: The Yosemite of Peru. By Harriet Chalmers Adams. 597-618, *Sept. 1908*

SOMERS, SIR GEORGE:

The Islands of Bermuda: A British Colony with a Unique Record in Popular Government. By William Howard Taft. 1-26, *Jan. 1922*

SOMETHING'S Fishy About That Fin! Photos by Robert J. Shallenberger and William D. Madden. 224-227, *Aug. 1974*

SONAKUL, D.: *Author*

Pageantry of the Siamese Stage. Photos by W. Robert Moore. 201-212, *Feb. 1947*

SONAR (Sound Navigation and Ranging):

Down to *Thresher* by Bathyscaph. By Donald L. Keach. 764-777, *June 1964*

Our Navy's Long Submarine Arm. By Allan C. Fisher, Jr. 613-636, *Nov. 1952*

From Indian Canoes to Submarines at Key West. By Frederick Simpich. Photos by J. Baylor Roberts. 41-72, *Jan. 1950*

SONAR ABILITY. *See* Echolocation

SONG and Garden Birds of North America. 400 pages. *1964*

Though he walks unarmed in his village, a Solomon Islander from Ulawa carries spears as a precaution on a shoreside excursion in the early 1900s.   J. W. BEATTIE

SONG of Hope for the Bluebird. By Lawrence Zeleny. Photos by Michael L. Smith. 855-865, *June 1977*

SONGDO (Kaijo), Korea:

Chosen–Land of Morning Calm. By Mabel Craft Deering. 421-448, *Oct. 1933*

SONGHAI TRIBESPEOPLE:

The Niger: River of Sorrow, River of Hope. By Georg Gerster. 152-189, *Aug. 1975*

SONGHUA (River), China. *See* former name, Sungari

SONGS:

Hunting Musical Game in West Africa. By Arthur S. Alberts. 262-282, *Aug. 1951*

Hunting Folk Songs in the Hebrides. By Margaret Shaw Campbell. 249-272, *Feb. 1947*

SONNENBURG, A. FALKNER VON: *Author*

Manila and the Philippines. 65-72, *Feb. 1899*

SONOGRAPHY (SONO):

Medicine's New Vision. By Howard Sochurek. Paintings by Davis Meltzer. Illustrations text by Peter Miller. 2-41, *Jan. 1987*

SONOMA VALLEY, California. *See* Valley of the Moon

SONORA (State), Mexico:

From Sun-clad Sea to Shining Mountains. By Ralph Gray. Photos by James P. Blair. 542-589, *Apr. 1964*

Sonora Is Jumping. By Mason Sutherland. 215-246, *Feb. 1955*

Adventuring Down the West Coast of Mexico. By Herbert Corey. 449-503, *Nov. 1922*

A Mexican Land of Canaan: Marvelous Riches of the Wonderful West Coast of Our Neighbor Republic. By Frederick Simpich. 307-330, *Oct. 1919*

Papagueria. By W J McGee. 345-371, *Aug. 1898*

Seriland. By W J McGee and Willard D. Johnson. 125-133, *Apr. 1896*

SONORAN DESERT, Arizona-California-Mexico:

California Desert, A Worldly Wilderness. By Barry Lopez. Photos by Craig Aurness. 42-77, *Jan. 1987*

Arizona's Suburbs of the Sun. By David Jeffery. Photos by H. Edward Kim. 486-517, *Oct. 1977*

Abundant Life in a Desert Land. By Walter Meayers Edwards. 424-436, *Sept. 1973*

SOOCHOW CREEK, China:

Ho for the Soochow Ho. By Mabel Craft Deering. 623-649, *June 1927*

SORATA, Bolivia:

Bolivia–Tin Roof of the Andes. By Henry Albert Phillips. 309-332, *Mar. 1943*

SORCERY:

Fertility Rites and Sorcery in a New Guinea Village. By Gillian Gillison.

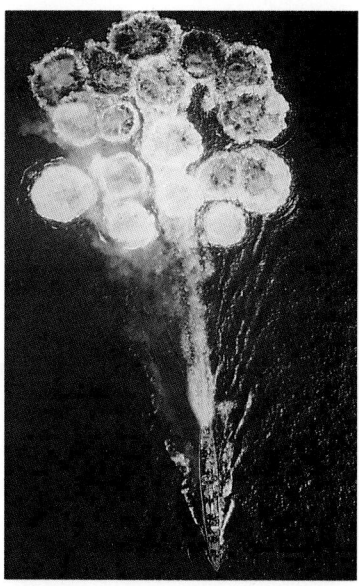

U.S. destroyer of the 1950s lays depth charges that could have sunk a submarine located by sonar. U.S. NAVY, OFFICIAL

Photos by David Gillison. Included: Sorcery trials, involving divination, to affix guilt in cases of illness and death among the Gimis. 124-146, *July 1977*

Journey Into Stone Age New Guinea. By Malcolm S. Kirk. Included: Sorcerers of Nomad River and Oksapmin. 568-592, *Apr. 1969*

Viet Nam's Montagnards. By Howard Sochurek. Included: Mnong tribe sorcerers. 443-487, *Apr. 1968*

American Special Forces in Action in Viet Nam. By Howard Sochurek. Included: Rhadé tribe sorcerers. 38-65, *Jan. 1965*

SOREN, DAVID:

On Assignment in Cyprus. *July 1988*

Author

The Day the World Ended at Kourion. Photos by Martha Cooper. NGS research grant. 30-53, *July 1988*

SOUF (Region), Algeria:

The Country of the Ant Men. By Thomas H. Kearney. 367-382, *Apr. 1911*

SOUFRIÈRE (Volcano), St. Vincent (Island), West Indies:

A Report of the Eruption of the Soufrière of St. Vincent, 1812. 158-161, *Apr. 1903*

The Eruptions of La Soufrière, St. Vincent, in May, 1902. By Edmund Otis Hovey. 444-459, *Dec. 1902*

The Recent Volcanic Eruptions in the West Indies. By Israel C. Russell. 267-285, *July 1902*

The National Geographic Society Expedition in the West Indies. 209-213, *June 1902*

The **SOUL** of a Tribe Returns to Africa.

By William S. Ellis. Photos by James P. Blair. 141-148, *July 1974*

SOULE, THAYER:

Recipient of the National Geographic Society Centennial Award. President's Page. By Gilbert M. Grosvenor. *Dec. 1988*

SOULEN, HENRY J.: *Artist*

The Last Thousand Years Before Christ. By G. Ernest Wright. Paintings by H. J. Soulen and Peter V. Bianchi. 812-853, *Dec. 1960*

Bringing Old Testament Times to Life. By G. Ernest Wright. 833-864, *Dec. 1957*

SOUND:

The Aberration of Sound as Illustrated by the Berkeley Powder Explosion. By Robert H. Chapman. 246-249, *July 1896*

SOUND SHEETS:

■■ *The Wonder of Birds.* Included: *Guide to Birds* sound sheets. 280 pages. *1983*

Symphony of the Deep: "Songs of the Humpback Whale." Sound sheet, *Jan. 1979*

"Sounds of the Space Age, from Sputnik to Lunar Landing." Narrated by Frank Borman. Sound sheet, *Dec. 1969*

"The Funeral of Sir Winston Churchill, with Excerpts From His Speeches." Sound sheet, Aug. 1965; 580, 581, *Oct. 1967*

■■ *Water, Prey, and Game Birds of North America.* Included: Bird song sound sheets. 464 pages. *1965*

■■ *Song and Garden Birds of North America.* Included: Bird song sound sheets. 400 pages. *1964*

SOURCES of the Saskatchewan. By Walter D. Wilcox. 113-134, *Apr. 1899*

The **SOURCES** of Washington's Charm. By J. R. Hildebrand. 639-680, *June 1923*

SOURIAL, GEORGES: *Photographer*

The Voyage of *Ra II.* By Thor Heyerdahl. Photos by Carlo Mauri and Georges Sourial. 44-71, *Jan. 1971*

SOUTH, STANLEY:

Nomination Page. In South Carolina. *Feb. 1982*

The **SOUTH** (Region), U. S.:

Atlanta: Energy and Optimism in the New South. By Erla Zwingle. Photos by Jim Richardson. 3-29, *July 1988*

Sea Change in the Sea Islands. By Charles L. Blockson. Photos by Karen Kasmauski. 735-763, *Dec. 1987*

Rising, Shining Tennessee. By Priit J. Vesilind. Photos by Karen Kasmauski. 602-637, *May 1986*

The Underground Railroad. By Charles L. Blockson. Photos by Louie Psihoyos. 3-39, *July 1984*

Savannah to Charleston–A Good Life in the Low Country. By John J. Putman. Photos by Annie Griffiths. 798-829, *Dec. 1983*

S
T

Midwife Etta Nichols of Del Rio, Tennessee, learned her trade by watching her father, a country doctor, and has delivered more than 2,000 babies. KAREN KASMAUSKI

Africa Since 1888, with Special Reference to South Africa and Abyssinia. By Gardiner G. Hubbard. 157-175, *May 1896*

SOUTH AMERICA:

The High Andes: South America's Islands in the Sky. By Loren McIntyre. 422-459, *Apr. 1987*

Humboldt's Way. By Loren McIntyre. 318-351, *Sept. 1985*

El Niño's Ill Wind. By Thomas Y. Canby. Included: Severe storms and flooding caused by the current. 144-183, *Feb. 1984*

Tropical Rain Forests: Nature's Dwindling Treasures. By Peter T. White. Photos by James P. Blair. Paintings by Barron Storey. 2-47, *Jan. 1983*

The Incredible Potato. By Robert E. Rhoades. Photos by Martin Rogers. 668-694, *May 1982*

⊕ *Indians of South America; Archaeology of South America. Mar. 1982*

The Gauchos, Last of a Breed. By Robert Laxalt. Photos by O. Louis Mazzatenta. 478-501, *Oct. 1980*

The Desert: An Age-old Challenge Grows. By Rick Gore. Photos by Georg Gerster and Bruce Dale. 586-639, *Nov. 1979*

The Search for the First Americans. By Thomas Y. Canby. Photos by Kerby Smith. Paintings by Roy Andersen. Included: Paleo-Indian sites in Argentina, Chile, Peru, and Venezuela. 330-363, *Sept. 1979*

Mysteries of Bird Migration. By Allan C. Fisher, Jr. Photos by Jonathan Blair. 154-193, *Aug. 1979*

⊕ *Bird Migration in the Americas; The Americas. Aug. 1979*

Magellan: First Voyage Around the World. By Alan Villiers. Photos by Bruce Dale. 721-753, *June 1976*

Editorial. By Gilbert M. Grosvenor. 295, *Mar. 1975*

Sir Francis Drake. By Alan Villiers. 216-253, *Feb. 1975*

Gold, the Eternal Treasure. By Peter T.

White. Photos by James L. Stanfield. 1-51, *Jan. 1974*

The Amazon. Photos by Loren McIntyre. 445-455, *Oct. 1972*

Amazon–The River Sea. By Loren McIntyre. 456-495, *Oct. 1972*

⊕ *South America. Text on reverse. Oct. 1972*

In the Wake of Darwin's *Beagle*. By Alan Villiers. Photos by James L. Stanfield. Included: Argentina; Brazil; Chile; Peru; Uruguay. 449-495, *Oct. 1969*

Parks, Plans, and People: How South America Guards Her Green Legacy. By Mary and Laurance Rockefeller. Photos by George F. Mobley. 74-119, *Jan. 1967*

Ambassadors of Good Will: The Peace Corps. By Sargent Shriver and Peace Corps Volunteers. Included: Bolivia; Ecuador. 297-345, *Sept. 1964*

⊕ *Northwestern South America. Atlas series. Feb. 1964*

⊕ *Eastern South America. Atlas series. Sept. 1962*

⊕ *South America. Atlas series. Feb. 1960*

Theodore Roosevelt: a Centennial Tribute. By Bart McDowell. Included: Travels in South America. 572-590, *Oct. 1958*

⊕ *Southern South America. Atlas series. Mar. 1958*

⊕ *Eastern South America. Mar. 1955*

Jungle Jaunt on Amazon Headwaters. By Bernice M. Goetz. 371-388, *Sept. 1952*

Playing 3,000 Golf Courses in Fourteen Lands. By Ralph A. Kennedy. 113-132, *July 1952*

How Fruit Came to America. By J. R. Magness. Paintings by Else Bostelmann. Included: Origin of the pineapple; Development of the strawberry. 325-377, *Sept. 1951*

⊕ *South America. Oct. 1950*

Flags of the Americas. By Elizabeth W. King. Included: Argentina; Bolivia;

Daniel Brits is an unemployed white South African of the 1980s.

DAVID TURNLEY, DETROIT *FREE PRESS*

Brazil; Chile; Colombia; Ecuador; Paraguay; Peru; Uruguay; Venezuela. 633-657, *May 1949*

Sea Fever. By John E. Schultz. Contents: The author's 6,000-mile trip from Quito, Ecuador, to Miami, Florida, by way of the Napo and Amazon Rivers and the West Indies. 237-268, *Feb. 1949*

The World in Your Garden. By W. H. Camp. Paintings by Else Bostelmann. Included: South America Rich in Plant Life (Fuchsia, Petunia, Cupflower, Garden verbena, Scarlet sage); From South American Jungles (Spider flower, Morning glory, Cypress vine, Nasturtium, Victoria waterlily, Canna). 1-65, *July 1947*

⊕ *South America. Oct. 1942*

Bonds Between the Americas. By Frederick Simpich. 785-808, *Dec. 1937*

⊕ *South America. Dec. 1937*

In Humboldt's Wake: Narrative of a National Geographic Society Expedition Up the Orinoco and Through the Strange Casiquiare Canal to Amazonian Waters. By Ernest G. Holt. 621-644, *Nov. 1931*

Flying the "Hump" of the Andes. By Albert W. Stevens. 595-636, *May 1931*

Skypaths Through Latin America: Flying From Our Nation's Capital Southward Over Jungles, Remote Islands, and Great Cities on an Aërial Survey of the East Coast of South America. By Frederick Simpich. 1-79, *Jan. 1931*

The World's Highest International Telephone Cable. 722-731, *Dec. 1930*

Flying the World's Longest Air-Mail Route: From Montevideo, Uruguay, Over the Andes, Up the Pacific Coast, Across Central America and

Around 1930 a young South African listens to an old timer in a museum as he leans against a wagon used by the Boers in their Great Trek of the mid-1800s. MELVILLE CHATER

A Machiguenga tribesman examines his corn crop in the Amazon region of Peru in South America. LOREN MCINTYRE

SOUTH American Immigration. 587, *Oct. 1906*

SOUTH ASIA:

SOUTH AUSTRALIA (State), Australia:

SOUTH CALAVERAS GROVE, California:

SOUTH CAROLINA:

SOUTH CENTRAL STATES:

SOUTH CHINA SEA VOYAGE:

SOUTH DAKOTA:

In the land of her ancestors a young Sioux girl, DeVonna Lone Hill, graces a field near South Dakota's Badlands National Park. JIM BRANDENBURG

A World War II Japanese Zero rests forever on the seafloor off Rabaul in the South Pacific. DAVID DOUBILET

The Singaporean antler-jawed ant of Southeast Asia wields mandibles that can open 280 degrees. MARK W. MOFFETT

Climbers—part of a joint Soviet-American team—train in Soviet Central Asia to scale 24,406-foot Pik Pobedy, which straddles the Soviet-Chinese border.   MEDFORD TAYLOR

Paintings by Pierre Mion and Roy Andersen. 733-764, *Nov. 1988*

Halley's Comet 1986. By Rick Gore. Included: European Space Agency's Giotto mission, Soviet VEGA 1 and 2 probes, Japanese Sakigake and Suisei missions. 758-785, *Dec. 1986*

Are the Soviets Ahead in Space? By Thomas Y. Canby. 420-459, *Oct. 1986*

■■*Man's Conquest of Space.* By William R. Shelton. 199 pages. 1968; rev. ed. *1975*

Behold the Computer Revolution. By Peter T. White. Photos by Bruce Dale and Emory Kristof. 593-633, *Nov. 1970*

Awesome Views of the Forbidding Moonscape. 233-239, *Feb. 1969*

The Sun. By Herbert Friedman. Included: U. S. Naval Research Laboratory studies. 713-743, *Nov. 1965*

I Fly the X-15. By Joseph A. Walker. Photos by Dean Conger. 428-450, *Sept. 1962*

We Saw the World From the Edge of Space. By Malcolm D. Ross. Ground photos by Walter Meayers Edwards. 671-685, *Nov. 1961*

The Long, Lonely Leap. By Joseph W. Kittinger, Jr. Photos by Volkmar Wentzel. 854-873, *Dec. 1960*

See also Apollo Missions; Gemini Missions; Mariner Missions; Mercury Missions; Pioneer Probes; Ranger Spacecraft; Rockets; Satellites; Skylab Missions; Space Medicine; Space Shuttles; Surveyor Spacecraft; Viking Spacecraft Missions; Voyager; Voyager 2

SPACE MEDICINE:

Spacelab 1: *Columbia.* By Michael E. Long. 301-307, *Sept. 1983*

Six Months Alone in a Cave. By Michel Siffre. Contents: Biorhythm research. 426-435, *Mar. 1975*

Skylab, Outpost on the Frontier of Space. By Thomas Y. Canby. Photos by the nine mission astronauts. 441-469, *Oct. 1974*

The Making of an Astronaut. By Robert R. Gilruth. 122-144, *Jan. 1965*

We Saw the World From the Edge of Space. By Malcolm D. Ross. Ground photos by Walter Meayers Edwards. 671-685, *Nov. 1961*

The Flight of *Freedom 7.* By Carmault B. Jackson, Jr. 416-431, *Sept. 1961*

School for Space Monkeys. 725-729, *May 1961*

Aviation Medicine on the Threshold of Space. By Allan C. Fisher, Jr. Photos by Luis Marden. 241-278, *Aug. 1955*
See also Tektite II

SPACE PIONEERS of NASA Journey Into Tomorrow. By Allan C. Fisher, Jr. Photos by Dean Conger. 48-89, *July 1960*

SPACE RENDEZVOUS, Milestone on the Way to the Moon. By Kenneth F. Weaver. 539-553, *Apr. 1966*

SPACE SATELLITES. *See* Satellites

SPACE SHUTTLES:

Satellites That Serve Us. By Thomas Y.

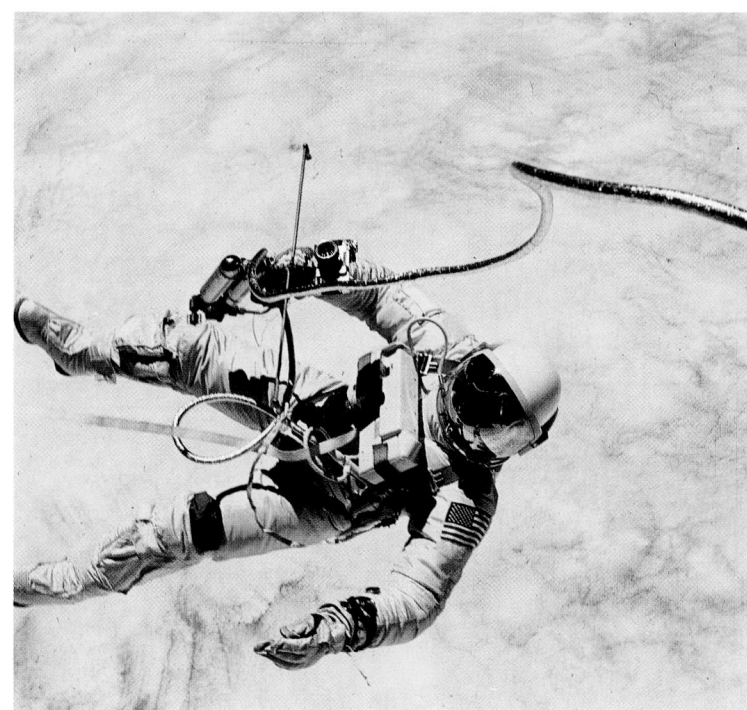

A golden umbilical cord tethers Maj. Edward H. White II, the first American to take a walk in space, on June 3, 1965. JAMES A. McDIVITT, NASA

Canby. 281-335. Included: Images of Earth; Spacelab 1: *Columbia.* By Michael E. Long. 301-307, *Sept. 1983*

Heat Paints *Columbia's* Portrait. By Cliff Tarpy. 650-653, *Nov. 1982*

Columbia's Landing Closes a Circle. By Tom Wolfe. 474-477, *Oct. 1981*

Columbia's Astronauts' Own Story: Our Phenomenal First Flight. By John W. Young and Robert L. Crippen. Paintings by Ken Dallison. 478-503, *Oct. 1981*

When the Space Shuttle Finally Flies. By Rick Gore. Photos by Jon Schneeberger. Paintings by Ken Dallison. Note: Names chosen for the space shuttles are *Columbia, Challenger, Discovery,* and *Atlantis.* 317-347, *Mar. 1981*

SPACE STATIONS:

Are the Soviets Ahead in Space? By Thomas Y. Canby. Included: Salyut 7. 420-459, *Oct. 1986*

The Next Frontier? By Isaac Asimov. Paintings by Pierre Mion. 76-89, *July 1976*

Solar Energy, the Ultimate Powerhouse. By John L. Wilhelm. Photos by Emory Kristof. 381-397, *Mar. 1976*
See also Skylab Missions

SPACE WALK:

America's 6,000-mile Walk in Space. 440-447, *Sept. 1965*

SPACECRAFT:

Of Air and Space. By Michael Collins. Contents: National Air and Space Museum. Included: Picture portfolio

by Nathan Benn, Robert S. Oakes, and Joseph D. Lavenburg, with text by Michael E. Long. 819-837, *June 1978*

See also Apollo Missions; Gemini Missions; Mariner Missions; Mercury Missions; Pioneer Probes; Ranger Spacecraft; Skylab Missions; Space Shuttles; Surveyor Spacecraft; Viking Spacecraft Missions; Voyager; Voyager 2; *and* Satellites

SPACELAB:

Spacelab 1: *Columbia.* By Michael E. Long. 301-307, *Sept. 1983*

When the Space Shuttle Finally Flies. By Rick Gore. Photos by Jon Schneeberger. Paintings by Ken Dallison. Note: Spacelab is a European-built laboratory for use aboard the space shuttle. 317-347, *Mar. 1981*

SPAFFORD MEMORIAL CHILDREN'S HOSPITAL, Jerusalem:

Jerusalem, My Home. By Bertha Spafford Vester. 826-847, *Dec. 1964*

SPAIN:

When the Moors Ruled Spain. By Thomas J. Abercrombie. Photos by Bruno Barbey. 86-119, *July 1988*

Exploring Our Forgotten Century: Between Columbus and Jamestown. By Joseph Judge. Photos by Bill Ballenberg. Paintings by John Berkey. Included: Exploration and colonization of La Florida. 330-363, *Mar. 1988*

Madrid: The Change in Spain. By John J. Putman. Photos by O. Louis Mazzatenta. 142-181, *Feb. 1986*

S
T

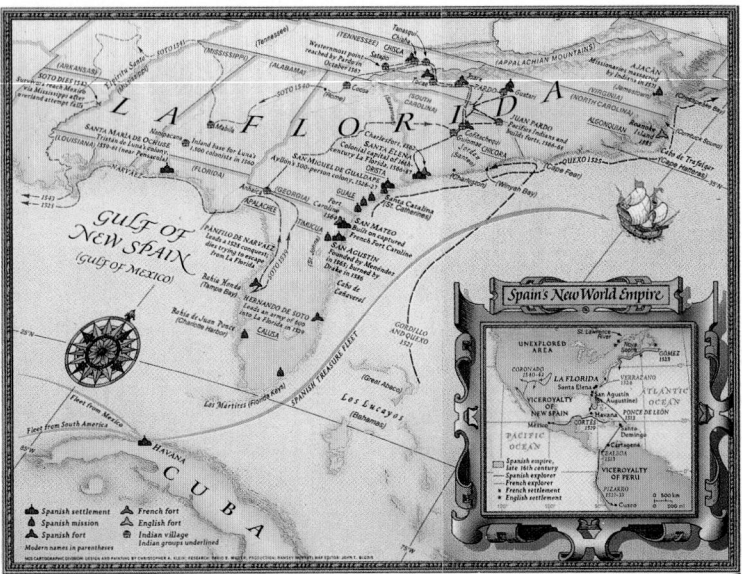

Spain's tenuous foothold in North America in the 1500s covered much of the south-eastern United States. NGS CARTOGRAPHIC DIVISION

Sparrows, Towhees, and Longspurs: These Happy Little Singers Make Merry in Field, Forest, and Desert Throughout North America. By T. Gilbert Pearson. Paintings by Allan Brooks and Walter A. Weber. 353-376, *Mar. 1939*

The Pest of English Sparrows. By N. Dearborn. 948-952, *Nov. 1910*

SPARROWS POINT, Maryland:

Man's Mightiest Ally. Photos by Willard R. Culver. Included: Bethlehem Steel Company plant. 432-450, *Apr. 1947*

SPARS (Women's Reserve of the U. S. Coast Guard Reserve):

Decorations, Medals, Service Ribbons, Badges, and Women's Insignia. 414-444, *Oct. 1943*

Women in Uniform. By La Verne Bradley. 445-458, *Oct. 1943*

SPAULDING, PAM: *Photographer*

United States: Geared to Consumption. By Paul R. and Anne H. Ehrlich. 938-941, *Dec. 1988*

SPAWNING:

Grunion, the Fish That Spawns on Land. By Clarence P. Idyll. Photos by Robert F. Sisson. 714-723, *May 1969*
See also Salmon

SPEAKING of Kansas. By Frederick Simpich. 135-182, *Aug. 1937*

SPEAKING of Spain. By Luis Marden. 415-456, *Apr. 1950*

SPEARING Lions with Africa's Masai. By Edgar Monsanto Queeny. 487-517, *Oct. 1954*

SPEARS, JOSEPH F.: *Author*

The Flying Telegraph. Official U. S. Army Signal Corps photos. 531-554, *Apr. 1947*

SPECIAL Economic Zones: China's Opening Door. By John J. Putman. Photos by H. Edward Kim. 64-83, *July 1983*

SPECIAL FORCES, U. S. Army. *See* U. S. Army Special Forces

SPECIAL GOLD MEDAL, NGS:

Design by Peter V. Bianchi. 146, *July 1961*
Design by Felix W. deWeldon. 868, *Dec. 1957*
Design by Laura Gardin Fraser. 45, *July 1957*

Recipients

Amundsen, Roald:
Honors to Amundsen and Peary (Special Gold Medal Presented to Amundsen by Peary). 113-130, Jan. 1913; 127, 149, Jan. 1936; 65F, *July 1954*

Bennett, Floyd:
Awarded Gold Medal; presentation by President Coolidge. 377-379, Sept. 1926; 238, Aug. 1927; 868, *Dec. 1957*

Byrd, Richard E.:
Admiral Byrd Receives New Honor From The Society (Presentation by President Hoover of Special Medal of Honor). 228-238, Aug. 1930; 38, 45, July 1957; 868, Dec. 1957; 574, 576, *Apr. 1962*

Cousteau, Jacques-Yves:
Jacques-Yves Cousteau Receives National Geographic Society Medal at White House; presentation by President Kennedy. 146-147, *July 1961*

Earhart, Amelia:
The Society's Special Medal Awarded to Amelia Earhart: First Woman to Receive Geographic Distinction at Brilliant Ceremony in the National Capital (Presentation of Special Gold Medal by President Hoover). 358-367, Sept. 1932; 134, Jan. 1936; 566, Nov. 1951; 868, Dec. 1957; 571, 582, Oct. 1963; 619, *Nov. 1966*

Eckener, Hugo:
The First Airship Flight Around the World: Dr. Hugo Eckener Tells of an Epochal Geographic Achievement upon the Occasion of the Bestowal of the National Geographic Society's Special Gold Medal (Presentation of Medal by Gilbert Grosvenor). 653-688, *June 1930*

Goethals, George W.:
Honors to Colonel Goethals: The Presentation, by President Woodrow Wilson, of the National Geographic Society Special Gold Medal. 677-690, June 1914; 868, Dec. 1957; 585, Oct. 1963; 141, *Feb. 1978*

Peary, Robert E.:
Resolution awarding a special medal to Commander Peary. 1008, Nov. 1909; The Discovery of the North Pole (Special Gold Medal presented to Peary). 63-82, Jan. 1910; 540, June, 1910; 149, 154, Jan., 1936; 18, Jan. 1963; Medal in the Smithsonian Institution. 347, *Sept. 1948*

Peary, Mrs. Robert E.:
Gold Medal Awarded to Mrs. Robert E. Peary. 148, *Jan. 1956*

Prince Philip, Duke of Edinburgh:
President Eisenhower Presents to Prince Philip the National Geographic Society's Medal. 865-868, *Dec. 1957*

Poulter, Thomas C.:
The Society's Special Medal Is Awarded to Dr. Thomas C. Poulter: Admiral Byrd's Second-in-Command and Senior Scientist Is Accorded High Geographic Honor. 105-108, July 1937; 205, *Feb. 1967*

SPECIAL *Report on Energy,* an extra issue of NGM. 115 pages. *Feb. 1981*

The **SPECIAL** Telegraphic Time Signal from the Naval Observatory. 411-415, *Oct. 1904*

SPECT (Single Photon Emission Computed Tomography):

Medicine's New Vision. By Howard Sochurek. Paintings by Davis Meltzer. Illustrations text by Peter Miller. 2-41, *Jan. 1987*

The **SPECTACULAR** North Cascades: New National Park Proposed. By Nathaniel T. Kenney. Photos by James P. Blair. 642-667, *May 1968*

SPECTACULAR Rio de Janeiro. By Hernane Tavares de Sá. Photos by Charles Allmon. 289-328, *Mar. 1955*

SPECTACULAR Treasures From a Chinese Tomb. Photos from *China*

Fury on the hoof, a bull maddened by banderillas in his back charges past a daring matador in a popular Spanish spectacle. DAVID ALAN HARVEY

Like a vision from **Moby Dick,** *a giant sperm whale—long hunted for its oil—travels the depths of the Indian Ocean.* FLIP NICKLIN

The Hudson: "That River's Alive." By Alice J. Hall. 62-89, *Jan. 1978*

George Washington: The Man Behind the Myths. By Howard La Fay. 90-111, *July 1976*

Kansas City, Heartland U.S.A. By Rowe Findley. 112-139, *July 1976*

The Loyalists. By Kent Britt. 510-539, *Apr. 1975*

Those Proper and Other Bostonians. By Joseph Judge. 352-381, *Sept. 1974*

Canada's Window on the Pacific: The British Columbia Coast. By Jules B. Billard. 338-375, *Mar. 1972*

■■ *The Vikings.* By Howard La Fay. Art by Louis S. Glanzman. 207 pages. *1972*

The Vikings. By Howard La Fay. 492-541, *Apr. 1970*

Reunited Jerusalem Faces Its Problems. By Kenneth MacLeish. 835-871, *Dec. 1968*

The World of Elizabeth I. By Louis B. Wright. 668-709, *Nov. 1968*

The Philippines, Freedom's Pacific Frontier. By Robert de Roos. 301-351, *Sept. 1966*

Scientists Ride Ice Islands on Arctic Odysseys. By Lowell Thomas, Jr. 670-691, *Nov. 1965*

SPIER, PETER: *Artist*

A Traveler's Tale of Ancient Tikal. Text by Alice J. Hall. 799-811, *Dec. 1975*

SPIN Your Globe to Long Island: Only Six States Have More People than the Insular Empire that Ranges from a World's Fair Through Potato Patches, Princely Estates, and Historic Shrines. By Frederick Simpich. Included: Bright Patterns of Long Island Life. Photos by Willard R. Culver. 413-459, *Apr. 1939*

SPINDEN, HERBERT J.: *Author*

Shattered Capitals of Central America. 185-212, *Sept. 1919*

SPINY BABBLER (Bird):

Peerless Nepal–A Naturalist's Paradise. By S. Dillon Ripley. Photos by Volkmar Wentzel. NGS research grant. 1-40, *Jan. 1950*

SPINY LOBSTERS:

Strange March of the Spiny Lobster. By William F. Herrnkind. Photos by Rick Frehsee and Bruce Mounier. NGS research grant. 819-831, *June 1975*

Tektite II: Science's Window on the Sea. By John G. VanDerwalker. Photos by Bates Littlehales. 256-289, *Aug. 1971*

New Life for the "Loneliest Isle." By Lewis Lewis. 105-116, *Jan. 1950*

SPIRIT OF ST. LOUIS (Airplane):

To Bogotá and Back by Air: The Narrative of a 9,500-Mile Flight from Washington, Over Thirteen Latin-American Countries and Return, in the Single-Seater Airplane "Spirit of St. Louis." By Charles A. Lindbergh. 529-601, *May 1928*

Seeing America with Lindbergh: The Record of a Tour of More Than

Royal spoonbill of Australia scratches its head through plumage usually flared during social displays. M. PHILIP KAHL

20,000 Miles by Airplane Through Forty-eight States on Schedule Time. By Donald E. Keyhoe. 1-46, *Jan. 1928*

The **SPIRIT** of the Geographic. 434-440, *Nov. 1918*

The **SPIRIT** of the West: The Wonderful Agricultural Development Since the Dawn of Irrigation. By C. J. Blanchard. 333-360, *Apr. 1910*

SPIRITS of Change Capture the Karens. By Peter Kunstadter. 267-285, *Feb. 1972*

SPIRO MOUNDS, Oklahoma:

Piecing Together an Indian Heritage. Geographica. *Nov. 1988*

SPITSBERGEN, Svalbard (Archipelago), Arctic Ocean:

Norway's Strategic Arctic Islands. By Gordon Young. Photos by Martin Rogers. 267-283, *Aug. 1978*

Spitsbergen Mines Coal Again. 113-120, *July 1948*

Flights from Arctic to Equator: Conquering the Alps, the Ice Peaks of Spitsbergen, of Persia, and Africa's Mountains of the Moon. By Walter Mittelholzer. 445-498, *Apr. 1932*

A Woman's Winter on Spitsbergen. By Martha Phillips Gilson. 227-246, *Aug. 1928*

No Man's Land–Spitzbergen. 455-458, *July 1907*

The Russian Expedition to Spitzbergen. 404, *Nov. 1901*

Magnetic Observations in Iceland, Jan Mayen and Spitzbergen in 1892. By Cyrus C. Babb. 223-224, *Dec. 29, 1894*

SPLENDOR of an Unknown Empire: Ebla. By Howard La Fay. Photos by James L. Stanfield. Paintings by Louis S. Glanzman. 730-759, *Dec. 1978*

The **SPLENDOR** of Rome. By Florence Craig Albrecht. 593-626, *June 1922*

SPLENDORS *of the Past: Lost Cities of* ■■ *the Ancient World.* 295 pages. *1981*

SPLIT, Yugoslavia:

Yugoslavia's Window on the Adriatic. By Gilbert M. Grosvenor. 219-247, *Feb. 1962*

Yugoslavia, Between East and West. By George W. Long. Photos by Volkmar Wentzel. 141-172, *Feb. 1951*

SPLIT-SECOND Time Runs Today's World. By F. Barrows Colton and Catherine Bell Palmer. 399-428, *Sept. 1947*

SPLIT Seconds in the Lives of Birds. By Arthur A. Allen. 681-706, *May 1954*

SPOFFORD, A. R.:

Gardiner Greene Hubbard: Memorial Meeting. Address by A. R. Spofford. 63-65, *Feb. 1898*

SPONGE-FISHING INDUSTRY:

On the Winds of the Dodecanese. By Jean and Franc Shor. 351-390, *Mar. 1953*

Sponge Fishermen of Tarpon Springs. By Jennie E. Harris. 119-136, *Jan. 1947*

Here and There in Northern Africa. By Frank Edward Johnson. Included: Greek sponge divers in Tripoli. 1-132, *Jan. 1914*

Federal Fish Farming; or, Planting Fish by the Billion. By Hugh M. Smith. 418-446, *May 1910*

The Bureau of Fisheries. By Barton Warren Evermann. Included: Experiments in Sponge Culture. 191-212, *May 1904*

SPONGES:

Consider the Sponge.... Photos by David Doubilet. Text by Michael E. Long. 392-407, *Mar. 1977*

See also Sponge-Fishing Industry

SPOOFING the Geographic. By Roy Blount, Jr. 353-357, *Sept. 1988*

SPOOKY LAKE, Eil Malk (Island), Palau Islands:

Strange World of Palau's Salt Lakes. By William M. Hamner. Photos by David Doubilet. 264-282, *Feb. 1982*

SPOONBILLS:

The Royal Spoonbill. By M. Philip Kahl. NGS research grant. 281-284, *Feb. 1987*

Roseate Spoonbills, Radiant Birds of the Gulf Coast. By Robert Porter Allen. Photos by Frederick Kent Truslow. 274-288, *Feb. 1962*

Saving Man's Wildlife Heritage. By John H. Baker. Photos by Robert F. Sisson. 581-620, *Nov. 1954*

The Pink Birds of Texas. By Paul A. Zahl. Contents: Roseate spoonbills. 641-654, *Nov. 1949*

The Large Wading Birds: Long Legs and Remarkable Beaks, as Well as Size, Form, and Color, Distinguish the Herons, Ibises, and Flamingos. By T. Gilbert Pearson. Painting by Allan Brooks. 441-469, *Oct. 1932*

SPORADES, Northern (Islands), Greece. *See* Skýros

SPORADES, Southern (Islands). *See* Dodecanese Islands; Rhodes (Island)

SPORANGIA:

Slime Mold: The Fungus That Walks. By Douglas Lee. Photos by Paul A. Zahl. 131-136, *July 1981*

SPORT and Color Amid New England Snows. Photos by B. Anthony Stewart. 647-654, *Nov. 1936*

SPORTS:

Mexico's Booming Capital. By Mason Sutherland. Photos by Justin Locke. Included: Baseball, Bowling, Bullfighting, Football, Swimming. 785-824, *Dec. 1951*

Long Island Outgrows the Country. By Howell Walker. Photos by B. Anthony Stewart. Included: Baseball, Fishing, Golf, Lawn bowling, Sailing, Swimming, Tennis. 279-326, *Mar. 1951*

Around the "Great Lakes of the South." By Frederick Simpich. Photos by J. Baylor Roberts. Included: Boating, Fishing, Horseback riding, Swimming. 463-491, *Apr. 1948*

Clans in Kilt and Plaidie Gather at Braemar (Scotland). Photos by Maynard Owen Williams. 153-160, *Aug. 1935*

When Czechoslovakia Puts a Falcon Feather in Its Cap. By Maynard Owen Williams. Included: Gymnastics. 40-49, *Jan. 1933*

Hurdle Racing in Canoes: A Thrilling and Spectacular Sport Among the Maoris of New Zealand. By Walter Burke. 440-444, *May 1920*

The Geography of Games: How the Sports of Nations Form a Gazetteer of the Habits and Histories of Their Peoples. By J. R. Hildebrand. 89-144, *Aug. 1919*

Devil-Fishing in the Gulf Stream. By John Oliver La Gorce. 476-488, *June 1919*

Field Sports Among the Wild Men of Northern Luzon. By Dean C. Worcester. 215-267, *Mar. 1911*

See also Cockfights; Falconry; Horse Races; Skiing; Surfboarding; *and* Games; Olympic Games

SPORTS-MINDED Melbourne, Host to the Olympics. 688-693, *Nov. 1956*

The **SPOTLIGHT** Swings to Suez. By W. Robert Moore. 105-115, *Jan. 1952*

SPOTTED FEVER:

Tracking the Columbian Ground-Squirrel to Its Burrow: Loss of Millions to Crops and Danger of the Spread of Spotted Fever Necessitated Study of Peculiar Rodent of Western North America. By William T. Shaw. 587-596, *May 1925*

SPOTTSWOOD, ALEXANDER:

Spottswood's Expedition of 1716. By William M. Thornton. 265-269, *Aug. 1896*

All sails set, the four-masted, square-rigged **Nereos** *illustrated a 1924 article by Joseph Conrad.*

SPREEWALD (Region), East Germany:

The Wends of the Spreewald. By Frederick Simpich. 327-336, *Mar. 1923*

SPRING, BOB and IRA: *Photographers*

Climbing Our Northwest Glaciers. 103-114, *July 1953*

SPRING:

Spring Comes Late to Glacier. By Douglas H. Chadwick. Contents: Glacier National Park, Montana. 125-133, *July 1979*

Springtime Comes to Yellowstone National Park. By Paul A. Zahl. 761-779, *Dec. 1956*

Maytime in the Heart of Maryland. Photos by B. Anthony Stewart and Charles Martin. 441-448, *Apr. 1941*

Spring's Gay Bouquets Deck the Nation's Capital. Photos by Harrison Howell Walker. 17-24, *July 1938*

Springtime Wreathes a Garland for the Nation's Capital. 473-480, *Apr. 1935*

SPRING CREEK HUTTERITE COLONY, Montana:

The Hutterites, Plain People of the West. By William Albert Allard. 98-125, *July 1970*

SPRINGBOARDS to Tokyo. By Willard Price. 385-407, *Oct. 1944*

SPRINGBOKS:

Etosha: Namibia's Kingdom of Animals. By Douglas H. Chadwick. Photos by Des and Jen Bartlett. 344-385, *Mar. 1983*

SPRINGFIELD, Illinois:

Illinois–Healthy Heart of the Nation. By Leo A. Borah. Photos by B. Anthony Stewart and Willard R. Culver. 781-820, *Dec. 1953*

Vacation Tour Through Lincoln Land. By Ralph Gray. 141-184, *Feb. 1952*

SPRING'S Gay Bouquets Deck the Nation's Capital. Photos by Harrison Howell Walker. 17-24, *July 1938*

SPRINGTAILS:

The Wild World of Compost. By Cecil E. Johnson. Photos by Bianca Lavies. 273-284, *Aug. 1980*

SPRINGTIME Comes to Yellowstone National Park. By Paul A. Zahl. 761-779, *Dec. 1956*

SPRINGTIME of Hope in Poland. By Peter T. White. Photos by James P. Blair. 467-501, *Apr. 1972*

SPRINGTIME Wreathes a Garland for the Nation's Capital. 473-480, *Apr. 1935*

SPRUNT, ALEXANDER, Jr.: *Author*

Blizzard of Birds: The Tortugas Terns. 213-230, *Feb. 1947*

SQUARE-RIGGERS:

By Square-rigger from Baltic to Bicentennial. By Kenneth Garrett. Included: *Amerigo Vespucci, Christian Radich, Danmark, Dar Pomorza, Eagle, Esmeralda, Gazela Primeiro, Gloria, Gorch Fock, Juan Sebastián de Elcano, Kruzenshtern, Libertad, Mircea, Nippon Maru, Sagres II, Tovarishch.* 824-857, *Dec. 1976*

Windjamming Around New England. By Tom Horgan. Photos by Robert F. Sisson. 141-169, *Aug. 1950*

See also Breadalbane; Charles W. Morgan; Eagle; Georg Stage; Joseph Conrad; Pamir; Vasa; Yankee (Brigantine)

SQUAWS Along the Yukon. By Ginny Hill Wood. 245-265, *Aug. 1957*

SQUIDS:

Nature's Night Lights: Probing the Secrets of Bioluminescence. By Paul A. Zahl. 45-69, *July 1971*

Squids: Jet-powered Torpedoes of the Deep. By Gilbert L. Voss. Photos by Robert F. Sisson. NGS research grant. 386-411, *Mar. 1967*

Fighting Giants of the Humboldt. By David D. Duncan. 373-400, *Mar. 1941*

Marauders of the Sea. By Roy Waldo

Miner. Paintings by Else Bostelmann. 185-207, *Aug. 1935*

SQUIER, GEORGE O.: *Author*

The Influence of Submarine Cables
Upon Military and Naval Supremacy.
1-12, *Jan. 1901*

SQUIRES, GRANT:

First award by the Society from the
Grant Squires fund, to F. H. King,
author of "Farmers of Forty Centuries." 115, *Jan. 1913*

SQUIRRELS:

Tracking the Columbian Ground-Squir-
rel to Its Burrow: Loss of Millions to
Crops and Danger of the Spread of
Spotted Fever Necessitated Study of
Peculiar Rodent of Western North
America. By William T. Shaw. 587-
596, *May 1925*

SQUIRRELS, Flying:

"Flying" Squirrels, Nature's Gliders.
By Ernest P. Walker. 663-674,
May 1947

SRI LANKA:

The Prodigious Soybean. By Fred Hapgood. Photos by Chris Johns. Note:
In the 1970s Sri Lanka began a program to improve the national diet
through the introduction of soya. 67-
91, *July 1987*
Rare Look At Sperm and Blue Whales,
The Unknown Giants. By Hal Whitehead. Photos by Flip Nicklin. 774-
789, *Dec. 1984*
Sri Lanka's Wildlife. 254-278. I. Sri
Lanka's Wildlife Heritage: A Personal Perspective. By Arthur C. Clarke.
254-255; II. Legacy of Lively Treasures. By Dieter and Mary Plage.
256-273; III. A Nation Rises to the
Challenge. By Lyn de Alwis. Photos
by Dieter and Mary Plage. 274-278,
Aug. 1983
Sri Lanka: Time of Testing For an An-
cient Land. By Robert Paul Jordan.
Photos by Raghubir Singh. 123-150,
Jan. 1979
See also former name, Ceylon

SRINAGAR, Jammu and Kashmir,
India:

The Idyllic Vale of Kashmir. By Volkmar Wentzel. 523-550, *Apr. 1948*
House-Boat Days in the Vale of Kashmir. By Florence H. Morden. 437-
463, *Oct. 1929*
The Oriental Pageantry of Northern India. Photos by Franklin Price Knott.
429-460, *Oct. 1929*
Outwitting the Water Demons of Kashmir. By Maurice Pratt Dunlap. 499-
511, *Nov. 1921*
A Pilgrimage to Amernath, Himalayan
Shrine of the Hindu Faith. By Louise
Ahl Jessop. 513-542, *Nov. 1921*

STAFFORD, EDWARD PEARY:
Author

Descendants of the Expeditions. Photos
by Bob Sacha. 414-429. I. The Peary
Family. 417-421, *Sept. 1988*

STAFFORD, MARIE PEARY:

Gold Medal Awarded to Mrs. Robert

E. Peary. Note: Mrs. Stafford accept-
ed the Special Gold Medal on behalf
of her mother. 148, *Jan. 1956*
Author
The Peary Flag Comes to Rest. 519-532,
Oct. 1954

STAFFORD, THOMAS P.:

Apollo-Soyuz: Handclasp in Space. By
Thomas Y. Canby. 183-187,
Feb. 1976
Space Rendezvous, Milestone on the
Way to the Moon. By Kenneth F.
Weaver. 539-553, *Apr. 1966*

STAGE, HARRY H.: *Author*

Saboteur Mosquitoes. 165-179,
Feb. 1944

STAGER, CURT:

On Assignment in Cameroon.
Sept. 1987
Author
Silent Death from Cameroon's Killer
Lake. Photos by Anthony Suau. 404-
420, *Sept. 1987*

STAIB, BJØRN O.: *Author*

North Toward the Pole on Skis. 254-
281, *Feb. 1965*

STAINED GLASS:

Washington Cathedral: "House of Prayer for All People." By Robert Paul
Jordan. Photos by Sisse Brimberg.
552-573, *Apr. 1980*
Chartres: Legacy From the Age of
Faith. By Kenneth MacLeish. Photos
by Dean Conger. 857-882, *Dec. 1969*

STAIRCASE Farms of the Ancients:
Astounding Farming Skill of Ancient
Peruvians, Who Were Among the
Most Industrious and Highly Orga-
nized People in History. By O. F.
Cook. 474-534, *May 1916*

STALINGRAD, Russian S.F.S.R.,
U.S.S.R. *See* Volgograd

STALKING Ants, Savage and Civi-
lized: A Naturalist Braves Bites and
Stings in Many Lands to Learn the
Story of an Insect Whose Ways Often
Parallel Those of Man. By W. M.

*Young novice accompanies Buddhist monk in the 1920s; both are members of the Sinha-
lese ethnic majority in Ceylon, known as Sri Lanka since 1972.* GERVAIS COURTELLEMONT

Mann. Paintings by Hashime Murayama. 171-192, *Aug. 1934*

STALKING Big Game with Color Camera. Photos by Wendell Chapman. 89-128, *July 1939*

STALKING Birds With a Color Camera: An Expert in Avian Habits Persuades His Subjects to Sit Where He Wants Them, Even in His Hat. By Arthur A. Allen. 777-789, *June 1939*

STALKING Birds with Color Camera. ■■By Arthur A. Allen. 328 pages. *1951*

STALKING Central Africa's Wildlife. By T. Donald Carter. Paintings by Walter A. Weber. 264-286, *Aug. 1956*

STALKING Seals Under Antarctic Ice. By Carleton Ray. 54-65, *Jan. 1966*

STALKING the Dragon Lizard on the Island of Komodo. By W. Douglas Burden. 216-232, *Aug. 1927*

STALKING the Great Indian Rhino. By Lee Merriam Talbot. 389-398, *Mar. 1957*

STALKING the Mountain Lion–to Save Him. By Maurice G. Hornocker. 638-655, *Nov. 1969*

STALKING the West's Wild Foods. By Euell Gibbons. Photos by David Hiser. 186-199, *Aug. 1973*

STALKING Wild Foods on a Desert Isle. By Euell Gibbons. Photos by David Hiser. 47-63, *July 1972*

STAMPS, Postage:

New Stamps for Antarctic Explorers. Geographica. *Oct. 1988*

Those Outlandish Goldfish! By Paul A. Zahl. Included: China's 1960 goldfish postage stamp series. 514-533, *Apr. 1973*

Everyone's Servant, the Post Office. By Allan C. Fisher, Jr. Photos by Volkmar Wentzel. 121-152, *July 1954*

Liechtenstein Thrives on Stamps. By Ronald W. Clark. 105-112, *July 1948*

STAND by the Soldier. By John J. Pershing. 457-459, *May 1917*

STANDARD OIL COMPANY OF CALIFORNIA:

Barehanded Battle to Cleanse the Bay. By Peter T. White. Photos by Jonathan S. Blair. 866-881, *June 1971*

STANDARD WEIGHTS AND MEASURES:

Uncle Sam's House of 1,000 Wonders. By Lyman J. Briggs and F. Barrows Colton. Contents: National Bureau of Standards. 755-784, *Dec. 1951*

STANDING Iceberg Guard in the North Atlantic: International Patrol Safeguards the Lives of Thousands of Travelers and Protects Trans-Atlantic Liners from a "Titanic" Fate. By F. A. Zeusler. 1-28, *July 1926*

STANFIELD, JAMES L.:

On Assignment in Rome. *Dec. 1985*
On Assignment in Israel. *July 1985*
On Assignment in Yugoslavia. *Dec. 1983*

Author-Photographer

Vatican City. By James Fallows. Included: The Photographer's Perspective. By James L. Stanfield; Treasures of the Vatican. Photos by James L. Stanfield and Victor R. Boswell, Jr. 723-775, *Dec. 1985*

Photographer

Poland: The Hope That Never Dies. By Tad Szulc. 80-121, *Jan. 1988*

The World of Süleyman the Magnificent. By Merle Severy. 552-601, *Nov. 1987*

Where Columbus Found the New World. By Joseph Judge. 566-599, *Nov. 1986*

Earthquake in Mexico. By Allen A. Boraiko. Photos by James L. Stanfield and Guillermo Aldana E. 654-675, *May 1986*

Israel: Searching for the Center. By Priit J. Vesilind. 2-39, *July 1985*

Chocolate: Food of the Gods. By Gordon Young. Photos by James L. Stanfield and Sisse Brimberg. 664-687, *Nov. 1984*

Time and Again in Burma. By Bryan Hodgson. 90-121, *July 1984*

The Byzantine Empire. 709-777. I. Rome of the East. By Merle Severy. 709-767; II. Mount Athos. 739-745; III. Eternal Easter in a Greek Village. By Maria Nicolaidis-Karanikolas. 768-777, *Dec. 1983*

After Rhodesia, a Nation Named Zimbabwe. By Charles E. Cobb, Jr. Photos by James L. Stanfield and LeRoy Woodson, Jr. 616-651, *Nov. 1981*

Pakistan Under Pressure. By William S. Ellis. 668-701, *May 1981*

Windsor Castle. By Anthony Holden. 604-631, *Nov. 1980*

Royal House for Dolls. By David Jeffery. 632-643, *Nov. 1980*

The Bulgarians. By Boyd Gibbons. 91-111, *July 1980*

Ancient Bulgaria's Golden Treasures. By Colin Renfrew. Paintings by Jean-Leon Huens. 112-129, *July 1980*

Ebla: Splendor of an Unknown Empire. By Howard La Fay. Paintings by Louis S. Glanzman. 730-759, *Dec. 1978*

Syria Tests a New Stability. By Howard La Fay. 326-361, *Sept. 1978*

Japan's Amazing Inland Sea. By William S. Ellis. 830-863, *Dec. 1977*

The Rat, Lapdog of the Devil. By Thomas Y. Canby. 60-87, *July 1977*

The Nation's River. By Allan C. Fisher, Jr. 432-469. Included: A Good Life on the Potomac. 470-479, *Oct. 1976*

Mark Twain: Mirror of America. By Noel Grove. 300-337, *Sept. 1975*

Western Australia, the Big Country. By Kenneth MacLeish. 150-187, *Feb. 1975*

Gold, the Eternal Treasure. By Peter T. White. Included: Golden Masterpieces. 1-51, *Jan. 1974*

The Red Sea's Gardens of Eels. By Eugenie Clark. Photos by James L. Stanfield and David Doubilet. 724-735, *Nov. 1972*

Human Treasures of Japan. By William Graves. 370-379, *Sept. 1972*

Living in a Japanese Village. By William Graves. 668-693, *May 1972*

Quebec: French City in an Anglo-Saxon World. By Kenneth MacLeish. Photos by James L. Stanfield and Declan Haun. 416-442, *Mar. 1971*

New Orleans and Her River. By Joseph Judge. 151-187, *Feb. 1971*

Housewife at the End of the World. By Rae Natalie P. Goodall. 130-150, *Jan. 1971*

■■*The Mighty Mississippi.* By Bern Keating. 199 pages. *1971*

In a museum at Auschwitz-Birkenau, Poland, New York Rabbi Pinchas Goldberg views footwear taken from prisoners at the Nazi concentration camp. JAMES L. STANFIELD, NGS

Father Spiridon feeds the cats at one of 20 monasteries in Greece's Mount Athos religious community. JAMES L. STANFIELD, NGS

S
T

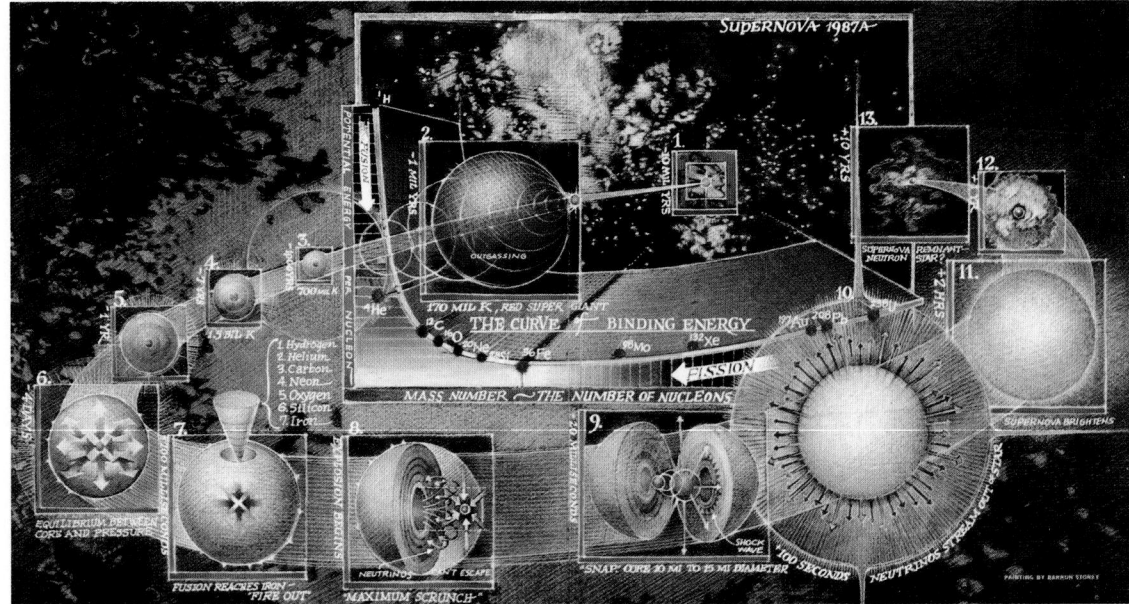

Life cycle of a star is traced from its beginning as a hot blue-white star to its suspected end as a neutron star. PAINTING BY BARRON STOREY

STATE SEALS:

Seals of Our Nation, States, and Territories. By Elizabeth W. King. Paintings by Carlotta Gonzales Lahey, Irvin E. Alleman, Theodora Price. Contents: Seals of the States and the District of Columbia; Seals of the Territories, Island Possessions, the Canal Zone, and the Philippine Commonwealth; Great Seal of the United States and Other Federal Seals; Seals of the President and of the Government Departments. 1-42, *July 1946*

STATELY HOMES:

The Great Good Places: English Country Houses. By Mark Girouard. Photos by Fred J. Maroon. 658-694, *Nov. 1985*
Stately Homes of Old Virginia. By Albert W. Atwood. 787-802, *June 1953*

STATEN ISLAND FERRY, New York's

Seagoing Bus. By John T. Cunningham and Jay Johnston. Photos by W. D. Vaughn. 833-843, *June 1959*

STATIA (Island), Netherlands Antilles.
See Sint Eustatius

STATION WAGON Odyssey: Baghdad to Istanbul. By William O. Douglas. 48-87, *Jan. 1959*

STATISTICAL Atlas of the United States. 50-52, *Jan. 1904*

STATISTICS:

Commercial and Financial Statistics of the Principal Countries of the World. 420-423, *June 1907*
Useful Facts About the Countries of the World. 424-425, *June 1907*
Statistics of Cities. 437, *Sept. 1905*
Some Significant Facts Concerning the Foreign Trade of Great Britain. 480, *Dec. 1900*
Shipbuilding in the United Kingdom in 1898. 138-139, *Apr. 1899*
Electric Street Railways. By John Hyde. 284, *Oct. 1897*
Statistics of Railways in the United States. By Henry Gannett. 406-407, *Dec. 1896*
See also Census; Population

STATUE OF LIBERTY:

Editorial. By Wilbur E. Garrett. 1, *July 1986*
Liberty Lifts Her Lamp Once More. By Alice J. Hall. 2-19, *July 1986*
■■ *Liberty: The Statue and the American Dream.* By Leslie Allen. The official book for the Centennial of the Statue of Liberty published by the Statue of Liberty–Ellis Island Foundation, Inc. Prepared and produced as a public service by NGS. 304 pages. *1985*

STATUES:

Warriors From a Watery Grave. By Joseph Alsop. Contents: Riace Bronzes. 821-827, *June 1983*
Carrara Marble: Touchstone of Eternity. By Cathy Newman. Photos by Pierre Boulat. 42-59, *July 1982*
The Nation Honors Admiral Richard E. Byrd. Included: Byrd Memorial statue. 567-578, *Apr. 1962*
See also Buddhism, for Buddhas;

Sculpture; Stone Faces; War Memorials; *and* Abu Simbel; Aegean Islands; Aphrodisias; Athens; Florence; Rome

STAUFFER, ELMER C.: *Author*

In the Pennsylvania Dutch Country. 37-74, *July 1941*

STAVANGER, Norway:

Striking It Rich in the North Sea. By Rick Gore. Photos by Dick Durrance II. 519-549, *Apr. 1977*
Norway, Land of the Generous Sea. By Edward J. Linehan. Photos by George F. Mobley. 1-43, *July 1971*

STEAD AIR FORCE BASE, Nevada:

School for Survival. By Curtis E. Le-May. 565-602, *May 1953*

STEAMBOATS:

Mark Twain: Mirror of America. By Noel Grove. Photos by James L. Stanfield. 300-337, *Sept. 1975*
How We Found the *Monitor.* By John G. Newton. Note: A search area was established for the *Monitor* based on the log of *Rhode Island,* which had the *Monitor* in tow. 48-61, *Jan. 1975*
That Dammed Missouri River. By Gordon Young. Photos by David Hiser. Included: The discovery of sunken steamer, *Bertrand.* 374-413, *Sept. 1971*
Ships Through the Ages: A Saga of the Sea. By Alan Villiers. 494-545, *Apr. 1963*
Henry Hudson's River. By Willard Price. Photos by Wayne Miller. 364-403, *Mar. 1962*
The Upper Mississippi. By Willard Price. 651-699, *Nov. 1958*
Squaws Along the Yukon. By Ginny Hill Wood. 245-265, *Aug. 1957*
Tom Sawyer's Town. By Jerry Allen. 121-140, *July 1956*
The Mighty Hudson. By Albert W. Atwood. Photos by B. Anthony Stewart. 1-36, *July 1948*

Cruising Colombia's "Ol' Man River." By Amos Burg. 615-660, *May 1947*

STEARNS, ROBERT E. C.: *Author*

The Native Oysters of the West Coast. 224-226, *Mar. 1908*
Echoes of the San Francisco Earthquake. 351-353, *May 1907*

STEARNS, WALLACE N.: *Author*

Reconstructing Egypt's History. 1021-1042, *Sept. 1913*

STEEL BANDS:

Carnival in Trinidad. By Howard La Fay. Photos by Winfield Parks. 693-701, *Nov. 1971*
"The Music of Trinidad." NGS recording announced. 701, *Nov. 1971*

STEEL INDUSTRY:

Pennsylvania: Faire Land of William Penn. By Gordon Young. Photos by Cary Wolinsky. 731-767, *June 1978*
Luxembourg, the Quiet Fortress. By Robert Leslie Conly. Photos by Ted H. Funk. 69-97, *July 1970*
Pittsburgh, Pattern for Progress. By William J. Gill. Photos by Clyde Hare. 342-371, *Mar. 1965*
Ohio Makes Its Own Prosperity. By Leo A. Borah. Photos by B. Anthony Stewart. 435-484, *Apr. 1955*
Coal Makes the Saar a Prize. By Franc Shor. 561-576, *Apr. 1954*
Today on the Delaware, Penn's Glorious River. By Albert W. Atwood. Photos by Robert F. Sisson. 1-40, *July 1952*
Pittsburgh: Workshop of the Titans. By Albert W. Atwood. 117-144, *July 1949*
Steel: Master of Them All. By Albert W. Atwood. 415-452. Included: Man's Mightiest Ally. Photos by Willard R. Culver. 423-450, *Apr. 1947*
India's Treasures Helped the Allies. By John Fischer. 501-522, *Apr. 1946*
"Magnetic City," Core of Valiant

The object of great affection, the Statue of Liberty gets a kiss from Tony Soraci, who helped erect scaffolding for her restoration. KONI NORDMANN, CONTACT PRESS IMAGES

■■ BOOKS ✦ MAPS ■ TELEVISION

Russia's Industrial Might. By John Scott. Included: Steel mills of Magnitogorsk. 525-556, *May 1943*

Industry's Greatest Asset–Steel. By William Joseph Showalter. 121-156, *Aug. 1917*

STEFANSSON, JON: *Author*

The Land of Fire. Contents: Iceland. 741-744, *Nov. 1907*

STEFANSSON, VILHJALMUR:

The National Geographic Society's Notable Year (Award of Hubbard Gold Medal). 338-345, *Apr. 1920*

The Origin of Stefansson's Blond Eskimo. By A. W. Greely. 1225-1238, *Dec. 1912*

Author

The Arctic as an Air Route of the Future. 205-218, *Aug. 1922*

STEGER, WILL: *Author-Photographer*

North to the Pole. Photos by the author and Jim Brandenburg. 289-317, *Sept. 1986*

STEGER INTERNATIONAL POLAR EXPEDITION:

Editorial. By Wilbur E. Garrett. 287, *Sept. 1986*

North to the Pole. By Will Steger. Photos by the author and Jim Brandenburg. 289-317, *Sept. 1986*

STEHEKIN, Washington:

Snow-mantled Stehekin: Where Solitude Is in Season. Photos by Bruce Dale. Text by Pat Hutson. 572-588, *Apr. 1974*

STEIN, ROBERT:

Geographic Names in West Greenland. By Ralph S. Tarr. 103-104, *Mar. 1898*

Author

Three Weeks in Hubbard Bay, West Greenland. 1-11, *Jan. 1898*

STEINEMANN, PAUL: *Photographer*

Jambo–First Gorilla Raised by Its Mother in Captivity. By Ernst M. Lang. 446-453, *Mar. 1964*

STEINER, ALBERT: *Photographer*

Amid the Snows of Switzerland. 277-292, *Mar. 1922*

STÉNUIT, ROBERT:

Outpost Under the Ocean. By Edwin A. Link. Photos by Bates Littlehales. 530-533, *Apr. 1965*

The Long, Deep Dive. By Lord Kilbracken. Photos by Bates Littlehales. 718-731, *May 1963*

Nomination Page. *Apr. 1963*

Author

The Sunken Treasure of St. Helena. Photos by Bates Littlehales. 562-576, *Oct. 1978*

Priceless Relics of the Spanish Armada. Photos by Bates Littlehales. 745-777, *June 1969*

The Deepest Days. 534-547, *Apr. 1965*

Author-Photographer

The Treasure of Porto Santo. Photos by author and William R. Curtsinger. 260-275, *Aug. 1975*

The **STEPPE.** *See* Ukrainian S.S.R.

STERNBERG, GEORGE M.:

Gardiner Greene Hubbard: Memorial Meeting. Address by George M. Sternberg, Surgeon-General, U.S.A. 41-43, *Feb. 1898*

Author

The History and Geographic Distribution of Bubonic Plague. 97-113, *Mar. 1900*

STERRETT, J. R. SITLINGTON:
Author

The Cone-Dwellers of Asia Minor: A Primitive People Who Live in Nature-Made Apartment Houses, Fashioned by Volcanic Violence and

Trickling Streams. 281-331, *Apr. 1919*

STEVENS, ALBERT W.:

National Geographic Society-U. S. Army Air Corps Stratosphere Flight of 1935 in Balloon *Explorer II* (Contributed Technical Papers, *Stratosphere Series No. 2*). 340, *Mar. 1937*; 802, *June 1937*

Hubbard Medals Awarded to Stratosphere Explorers: Presentation by General Pershing. 712-714, *May 1936*

Franklin L. Burr Prize awarded to Captain Stevens. 626, *May 1934*

The Society Takes Part in Three Geographic Expeditions. 625-626, *May 1934*

Your Society Sponsors an Expedition to Explore the Stratosphere. 528-530, *Apr. 1934*

Author

Exploring the Valley of the Amazon in a Hydroplane: Twelve Thousand Miles of Flying Over the World's Greatest River and Greatest Forest to Chart the Unknown Parima River from the Sky. 353-420, *Apr. 1926*

Author-Photographer

The Scientific Results of the World-Record Stratosphere Flight. 693-712, *May 1936*

Man's Farthest Aloft: Rising to 13.71 Miles, the National Geographic Society-U. S. Army Stratosphere Expedition Gathers Scientific Data at Record Altitude. Included: Action Photographs of the Balloon's Perfect Landing. 59-94, *Jan. 1936*

Exploring the Stratosphere. 397-434, *Oct. 1934*

Photographing the Eclipse of 1932 from the Air: From Five Miles Above the Earth's Surface, the National Geographic Society-Army Air Corps Survey Obtains Successful Photographs of the Moon's Shadow. 581-596, *Nov. 1932*

Flying the "Hump" of the Andes. Included: First photo showing the curvature of the earth. (Reprint: 142, Jan. 1936.) 595-636, *May 1931*

Photographer

First natural-color photograph taken in the stratosphere. 340, *Mar. 1937*

Curvature of the Earth: The First Photograph Ever Made Showing the Division Between the Troposphere and Stratosphere and also the Actual Curvature of the Earth. Pictorial supplement, *May 1936*

Greater New York...Metropolis of Mankind. Pictorial supplement, *Nov. 1933*

Our Colorful City of Magnificent Distances. Photos by A. W. Stevens and others. 531-610, *Nov. 1931*

The Non-Stop Flight Across America. By John A. Macready. 1-83, *July 1924*

America from the Air: No Such Series of Airplane Views Has Ever Before Been Printed. 85-92, *July 1924*

STEVENS, D. W.: *Author*

Japan. 193-199, *Dec. 29, 1894*

A monk worships at Our Lady of the Snows, rebuilt after fire ruined the Trappist monastery Robert Louis Stevenson saw on his 1878 trek in southern France.   COTTON COULSON

The National Trust for Scotland preserves the showplace 18th-century Culzean Castle, on a seaside cliff in Ayr. B. ANTHONY STEWART, NGS

Diesel train services a Ford Motor Company power plant in Dearborn, Michigan, in World War II. B. ANTHONY STEWART, NGS

Under Egypt's Golden Sun. 451-466, *Apr. 1940*

Today's Evidence of Grecian Glory. 307-322, *Mar. 1940*

Bright Facets of Italy's Grandeur. 355-362, *Mar. 1940*

Italy's Monuments Tell Rome's Magnificence. 371-378, *Mar. 1940*

Santorin and Mýkonos, Aegean Gems. 339-346, *Mar. 1940*

Charleston: A Colonial Rhapsody. 289-312, *Mar. 1939*

The Golden Gate, and Redwood Evergreens. 149-160, *Feb. 1939*

The Thames, England's Gateway to the World. 253-260, *Feb. 1939*

Rio Grande Cornucopia Under a Winter Sun. 65-96, *Jan. 1939*

The Scillies: Isles of Wrecks and Golden Daffodils. Photos by B. Anthony Stewart. 759-766, *Dec. 1938*

Old and New Blend in Yankeeland. Photos by B. Anthony Stewart and others. 295-326, *Sept. 1938*

Belgian Portraits. 413-444, *Apr. 1938*

Contented Guernsey. 377-384, *Mar. 1938*

Life's Color in Wisconsin. 17-40, *July 1937*

Sunny Corners in a Friendly Isle. Contents: Isle of Man. 601-608, *May 1937*

The Pomp and Pulse of Modern London. 17-48, *Jan. 1937*

Sport and Color Amid New England Snows. 647-654, *Nov. 1936*

The Hub City, Cradle of American Liberty. Photos by B. Anthony Stewart and others. Contents: Boston, Massachusetts. 49-72, *July 1936*

California—85 Years After the Gold Rush. 325-356, *Mar. 1936*

Where Spring Paints a State with Wild Flowers. Contents: California. 365-380, *Mar. 1936*

First in Statehood, Delaware Retains Its Graciousness. 377-384, *Sept. 1935*

Remnants of Royal France in Canada. 217-224, *Aug. 1935*

Pine-Scented, Harbor-Dented Maine. Photos by B. Anthony Stewart and Robert F. Maxey. 549-588, *May 1935*

Winter Lights and Shadows in the Nation's Capital. 201-216, *Feb. 1935*

STEWART, RICHARD H.:
Photographer

Hunting Prehistory in Panama Jungles. By Matthew W. Stirling. 271-290, *Aug. 1953*

Seeking the Secret of the Giants. By Frank M. Setzler. 390-404, *Sept. 1952*

Solving the Riddle of Chubb Crater. By V. Ben Meen. 1-32, *Jan. 1952*

Exploring Ancient Panama by Helicopter. By Matthew W. Stirling. 227-246, *Feb. 1950*

Exploring the Past in Panama. By Matthew W. Stirling. 373-399, *Mar. 1949*

Eclipse Hunting in Brazil's Ranchland. By F. Barrows Colton. Photos by Richard H. Stewart and Guy W. Starling. 285-324, *Sept. 1947*

On the Trail of La Venta Man. By Matthew W. Stirling. Included: Hunting Mexico's Buried Temples. 137-172, *Feb. 1947*

Missouri Mirrors of 1946. 285-308, *Mar. 1946*

From the Halls of Montezuma. Photos by Richard H. Stewart and others. 137-164, *Feb. 1944*

La Venta's Green Stone Tigers. 329-332, *Sept. 1943*

Mexico's Deep South Yields New Treasure. 649-656, *Nov. 1942*

Treasure-trove of Old Mexican Jade. 293-316, *Sept. 1941*

Leis from Aloha Land. 435-442, *Oct. 1938*

Unfurling Old Glory on Canton Island. Photos by Richard H. Stewart and others. 753-760, *June 1938*

Nature Paints New Mexico. 537-568, *May 1938*

Views and Hues of the Sunflower State. 151-158, *Aug. 1937*

Bursts of Color in Sculptured Utah. 593-616, *May 1936*

The Color Camera Explores the Country That Moves by Night. 479-510, *Oct. 1931*

STEWART, T. DALE:
Nomination Page. *Sept. 1965*

STEWART ISLAND, New Zealand:
New Zealand: the Last Utopia? By Robert Paul Jordan. Photos by Kevin Fleming. 654-681, *May 1987*

STIELER, KARL: *Author*
Venice. 587-630, *June 1915*

STIKINE (River), Alaska-Canada:
Life on a Yukon Trail. By Alfred Pearce Dennis. 377-391, Oct. 1899; 457-466, *Nov. 1899*

The Stikine River in 1898. By Eliza Ruhamah Scidmore. 1-15, *Jan. 1899*

STILES, ARTHUR ALVORD: *Author*
A Bear Hunt in Montana. 149-154, *Feb. 1908*

STILL Eskimo, Still Free: The Inuit of Umingmaktok. By Yva Momatiuk and John Eastcott. 624-647, *Nov. 1977*

STILL Waters, White Waters: Exploring ■■ *America's Rivers and Lakes.* By Ron Fisher. Photos by Sam Abell. Contents: Touring by canoe. 199 pages. *1977*

STILLWELL, AGNES N.: *Author*
Crete, Where Sea-Kings Reigned. 547-568, *Nov. 1943*

STILLWELL, RICHARD: *Author*
The Isles of Greece. 593-622, *May 1944*

Greece—the Birthplace of Science and Free Speech: Explorations on the Mainland and in Crete and the Aegean Isles Reveal Ancient Life Similar to That of the Present. Paintings by H. M. Herget. 273-353, *Mar. 1944*

STILTS (Birds):
The Dauntless Little Stilt. By Frederick Kent Truslow. 241-245, *Aug. 1960*

STILWELL Road—Land Route to China. By Nelson Grant Tayman. 681-698, *June 1945*

STIMSON, PAUL C.: *Author*
'Round the Horn by Submarine. 129-144, *Jan. 1948*

STIRLING, MARION: *Author*
Finding Jewels of Jade in a Mexican Swamp. By Matthew W. and Marion Stirling. 635-661, *Nov. 1942*

Jungle Housekeeping for a Geographic Expedition. 303-327, *Sept. 1941*

STIRLING, MATTHEW W.: *Author*
Solving the Mystery of Mexico's Great Stone Spheres. Photos by David F. Cupp. 295-300, *Aug. 1969*

Hunting Prehistory in Panama Jungles. Photos by Richard H. Stewart. 271-290, *Aug. 1953*

Exploring Ancient Panama by Helicopter. Photos by Richard H. Stewart. 227-246, *Feb. 1950*

Nomads of the Far North. Paintings by W. Langdon Kihn. 471-504, *Oct. 1949*

Exploring the Past in Panama. Photos by Richard H. Stewart. 373-399, *Mar. 1949*

Indians of the Far West. Paintings by W. Langdon Kihn. 175-200, *Feb. 1948*

On the Trail of La Venta Man. Photos by Richard H. Stewart. 137-172, *Feb. 1947*

Indians of the Southeastern United States. Paintings by W. Langdon Kihn. 53-74, *Jan. 1946*

Indians of Our North Pacific Coast. Paintings by W. Langdon Kihn. 25-52, *Jan. 1945*

Indians of Our Western Plains. Paintings by W. Langdon Kihn. 73-108, *July 1944*

La Venta's Green Stone Tigers. 321-332, *Sept. 1943*

Finding Jewels of Jade in a Mexican Swamp. By Matthew W. and Marion Stirling. 635-661, *Nov. 1942*

Expedition Unearths Buried Masterpieces of Carved Jade. 277-302, *Sept. 1941*

Indian Tribes of Pueblo Land. Paintings by W. Langdon Kihn. 549-596, *Nov. 1940*

Great Stone Faces of the Mexican Jungle: Five Colossal Heads and Numerous Other Monuments of Vanished Americans Are Excavated by the Latest National Geographic-Smithsonian Expedition. 309-334, *Sept. 1940*

Discovering the New World's Oldest Dated Work of Man: A Maya Monument Inscribed 291 B.C. Is Unearthed Near a Huge Stone Head by a Geographic-Smithsonian Expedition in Mexico. 183-218, *Aug. 1939*

America's First Settlers, the Indians. Paintings by W. Langdon Kihn. 535-596, *Nov. 1937*

STOBAUGH, ROBERT B.:
What Six Experts Say. 70-73, *Special Report on Energy. (Feb. 1981)*

STOCK, RALPH: *Author*
The Dream Ship: The Story of a Voyage of Adventure More Than Half Around the World in a 47-foot Lifeboat. 1-52, *Jan. 1921*

Illustration of the big bang theory portrays famous scientists and the explosion that created our universe.   PAINTING BY BARRON STOREY

Archaeologist Matthew W. Stirling measures Olmec stone head at Tres Zapotes, Mexico, in 1938. RICHARD H. STEWART, NGS

School of transparent tropical fish called sweepers passes the opening of a Red Sea cave. DAVID DOUBILET

S
T

STRASBOURG, France:

The Rhine: Europe's River of Legend. By William Graves. Photos by Bruce Dale. 449-499, *Apr. 1967*

STRATEGIC AIR COMMAND (SAC):

Of Planes and Men. By Kenneth F. Weaver. Photos by Emory Kristof and Albert Moldvay. 298-349, *Sept. 1965*

DEW Line, Sentry of the Far North. By Howard La Fay. Contents: Distant Early Warning Line. 128-146, *July 1958*

School for Survival. By Curtis E. Le-May. 565-602, *May 1953*

STRATEGIC Alaska Looks Ahead: Our Vast Territory, Now Being More Closely Linked to Us by Road and Rail, Embodies the American Epic of Freedom, Adventure, and the Pioneer Spirit. By Ernest H. Gruening. 281-315, *Sept. 1942*

STRATEGIC Spitsbergen. By Gordon Young. Photos by Martin Rogers. 267-283, *Aug. 1978*

STRATFORD-UPON-AVON, England:

The Britain That Shakespeare Knew. By Louis B. Wright. Photos by Dean Conger. 613-665, *May 1964*

Through the Heart of England in a Canadian Canoe. By R. J. Evans. 473-497, *May 1922*

STRATOBOWL, South Dakota:

To 76,000 Feet by *Strato-Lab* Balloon. By Malcolm D. Ross and M. Lee Lewis. 269-282, *Feb. 1957*

STRATO-LAB (Balloon):

We Saw the World From the Edge of Space. By Malcolm D. Ross. Ground photos by Walter Meayers Edwards. 671-685, *Nov. 1961*

To 76,000 Feet by *Strato-Lab* Balloon. By Malcolm D. Ross and M. Lee Lewis. 269-282, *Feb. 1957*

STRATOSPHERE RESEARCH:

Ballooning in the Stratosphere: Two Balloon Ascents to Ten-Mile Altitudes Presage New Mode of Aërial Travel. By Auguste Piccard. 353-384, *Mar. 1933*

Exploring the Earth's Stratosphere: The Holder of the American Altitude Record Describes His Experiences in Reaching the "Ceiling" of His Plane at an Elevation of Nearly Eight Miles. By John A. Macready. 755-776, *Dec. 1926*

See also Explorer I; Explorer II

STRAUSS, JOSEPH:

Awarded Jane M. Smith Life Membership. 342, *Apr. 1920*

STREANO, VINCE: *Photographer*

Orange, a Most California County. By Judith and Neil Morgan. 750-779, *Dec. 1981*

STREETCARS:

Electric Street Railways. By John Hyde. 284, *Oct. 1897*

STREETS and Palaces of Colorful

India. Photos by Gervais Courtellemont. 60-85, *July 1926*

STREETT, ST. CLAIR: *Author*

The First Alaskan Air Expedition. 499-552, *May 1922*

STRIEDIECK, KARL: *Author*

The Thousand-mile Glide. Photos by Otis Imboden. 431-438, *Mar. 1978*

STRIFE-TORN Indochina. By W. Robert Moore. 499-510, *Oct. 1950*

STRIKING It Rich in the North Sea. By Rick Gore. Photos by Dick Durrance II. 519-549, *Apr. 1977*

STRIP MINING:

Coal vs. Parklands. By François Leydet. Photos by Dewitt Jones. 776-803, *Dec. 1980*

This Land of Ours–How Are We Using It? By Peter T. White. Photos by Emory Kristof. 20-67, *July 1976*

Should They Build a Fence Around Montana? By Mike W. Edwards. Photos by Nicholas deVore III. 614-649, *May 1976*

Will Coal Be Tomorrow's "Black Gold"? By Gordon Young. Photos by James P. Blair. 234-259, *Aug. 1975*

The People of Cumberland Gap. By John Fetterman. Photos by Bruce Dale. 591-621, *Nov. 1971*

Illinois–Healthy Heart of the Nation. By Leo A. Borah. Photos by B. Anthony Stewart and Willard R. Culver. 781-820, *Dec. 1953*

Coal: Prodigious Worker for Man. By Albert W. Atwood. 569-592, *May 1944*

STRÖBECK, East Germany:

Ströbeck, Home of Chess: A Medieval Village in the Harz Mountains of Germany Teaches the Royal Game in Its Public School. By Harriet Geithmann. 637-652, *May 1931*

Stroboscopic lamp freezes the action of splashing milk in a red cookie tin.

HAROLD E. EDGERTON

STROBOSCOPIC LAMPS:

"Doc" Edgerton–The Man Who Made Time Stand Still. By Erla Zwingle. Photos by Harold E. Edgerton and Bruce Dale. 464-483, *Oct. 1987*

Mystery Mammals of the Twilight (Bats). By Donald R. Griffin. Included: Photographs taken by the high-speed camera developed by Harold E. Edgerton. 117-134, *July 1946*

STRODE, WILLIAM: *Photographer*

Daniel Boone, First Hero of the Frontier. By Elizabeth A. Moize. 804-839, *Dec. 1985*

Home to the Heart of Kentucky. By Nadine Brewer. 522-546, *Apr. 1982*

A **STROLL** to John o' Groat's. By Isobel Wylie Hutchison. 1-48, *July 1956*

A **STROLL** to London. By Isobel Wylie Hutchison. Photos by B. Anthony Stewart. 171-204, *Aug. 1950*

A **STROLL** to Venice. By Isobel Wylie Hutchison. Contents: Trek from Innsbruck, through the Alps to Venice. 378-410, *Sept. 1951*

STRONG, ARLINE:
Author-Photographer

Seashore Summer. 436-444, *Sept. 1960*

STRONG, WILLIAM DUNCAN:
Author

Finding the Tomb of a Warrior-God. Photos by Clifford Evans, Jr. 453-482, *Apr. 1947*

STROUD, W. G.: *Author*

Our Earth as a Satellite Sees It. 293-302, *Aug. 1960*

STROUT, EDITH BAUER: *Author*

At Home on the Oceans: Whales and Sharks Make Exciting Neighbors for a Professor's Wife, Turned Able Seaman, On a Three-year Voyage Around the World. 33-86, *July 1939*

STRUGGLING Poland: A Journey in Search of the Picturesque Through the Most Populous of the New States of Europe. By Maynard Owen Williams. 203-244, *Aug. 1926*

STRUM, SHIRLEY C.: *Author*

Life with the "Pumphouse Gang": New Insights Into Baboon Behavior. Photos by Timothy W. Ransom. 672-691, *May 1975*

Author-Photographer

The "Gang" Moves to a Strange New Land. Note: The baboons of the "Pumphouse Gang" are translocated in Kenya. NGS research grant. 676-690, *Nov. 1987*

STRUTT, JOHN WILLIAM (Third Baron Rayleigh):

The British Way. By Sir Evelyn Wrench. 421-541, *Apr. 1949*

STUART, DAVID:

Editorial. By Wilbur E. Garrett. 561, *May 1987*

STUART, ELEANOR (Mrs. Harris R. Childs): *Author*

Zanzibar. 810-824, *Aug. 1912*

STUART, GENE S.: *Author*

■■ *America's Ancient Cities.* Photos by Richard Alexander Cooke III. Art by H. Tom Hall. 199 pages. *1988*
■■ *Safari!* Photos by George F. Mobley. Juvenile. 104 pages. *1982*
■■ *The Mighty Aztecs.* Photos by Mark Godfrey. Art by Louis S. Glanzman. 199 pages. *1981*
■■ *Secrets From the Past.* Juvenile. 104 pages. *1979*
■■ *The Mysterious Maya.* By George E. and Gene S. Stuart. Photos by David Alan Harvey and Otis Imboden. 199 pages. *1977*
■■ *Discovering Man's Past in the Americas.* By George E. and Gene S. Stuart. 211 pages. *1969*

STUART, GEORGE E.: *Author*

Maya Art Treasures Discovered in Cave. Photos by Wilbur E. Garrett. 220-235, *Aug. 1981*
■■ *The Mysterious Maya.* By George E. and Gene S. Stuart. Photos by David Alan Harvey and Otis Imboden. 199 pages. *1977*
The Maya: Riddle of the Glyphs. Photos by Otis Imboden. 768-791, *Dec. 1975*
Who Were the "Mound Builders"? 783-801, *Dec. 1972*
■■ *Discovering Man's Past in the Americas.* By George E. and Gene S. Stuart. 211 pages. *1969*

STUBENRAUCH, ROBERT: *Photographer*

Okinawa, Pacific Outpost. 538-552, *Apr. 1950*

STUCKY, REX:

Nomination Page. *Jan. 1977*

STUDENTS:

Geographic education. President's Page. By Gilbert M. Grosvenor. Aug. 1984; Sept. 1984; Feb. 1985; June 1985; Sept. 1985; Oct. 1985; Feb. 1986; July 1986; Aug. 1986; Sept. 1986; Dec. 1986; Nov. 1987; Jan. 1988
YWCA: International Success Story. By Mary French Rockefeller. Photos by Otis Imboden. 904-933, *Dec. 1963*
Helping Holland Rebuild Her Land. By Gilbert M. Grosvenor and Charles Neave. 365-413, *Sept. 1954*
Experiment in International Living. By Hugh M. Hamill, Jr. Contents: American college students in Guanajuato, Mexico. 323-350, *Mar. 1953*
Norway Cracks Her Mountain Shell. By Sydney Clark. Photos by Gilbert H. Grosvenor and Ole Friele Backer. 171-211, *Aug. 1948*
See also Schools; Universities and Colleges

STUDIES of Muir Glacier, Alaska. By Harry Fielding Reid. 19-55, *Mar. 21, 1892*

STUDIES on the Rate of Evaporation at Reno, Nevada, and in the Salton Sink. By Frank H. Bigelow. 20-28, *Jan. 1908*

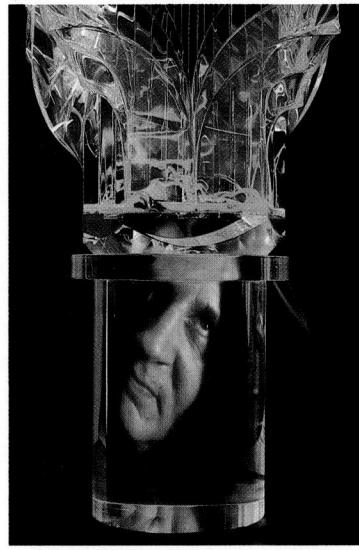

A light guide in a West German laboratory bends the paths of photons, subatomic particles without mass. KEVIN FLEMING

STUDIES Planned for New Stratosphere Flight with Helium. 795-800, *June 1935*

STUDYING Grizzly Habitat by Satellite. By John Craighead. 148-158, *July 1976*

STUDYING Scotland's Red Deer. By T. H. Clutton-Brock. 556-562, *Oct. 1986*

STUDYING Wildlife by Satellite. By Frank Craighead, Jr., and John Craighead. 120-123, *Jan. 1973*

STYRIA (State), Austria:

This Was Austria. 71-86, *July 1945*
Styria, a Favored Vacation Land of Central Europe. By Melville Bell Grosvenor. 430-439, *Oct. 1932*

SUAU, ANTHONY:
Author-Photographer
Eritrea: Region in Rebellion. 384-405, *Sept. 1985*

Photographer
Silent Death from Cameroon's Killer Lake. By Curt Stager. 404-420, *Sept. 1987*

SUBATOMIC PARTICLES:

Worlds Within the Atom. By John Boslough. Photos by Kevin Fleming. Illustrations text by David Jeffery. Paintings by Barron Storey. 634-663, *May 1985*

SUB-IGLOO (Underwater Workshop):

Diving Beneath Arctic Ice. By Joseph B. MacInnis. Photos by William R. Curtsinger. 248-267, *Aug. 1973*

The **SUBMARINE** Cables of the World. By Gustave Herrle. Included: Chart compiled by U. S. Hydrographic Office. 102-107, *Mar. 1896*

SUBMARINES:

Pacific Fleet: Force for Peace. By Franc

Shor. Photos by W. E. Garrett. Included: *Grayback, Gudgeon, Sterlet.* 283-335, *Sept. 1959*
Our Navy's Long Submarine Arm. By Allan C. Fisher, Jr. 613-636, *Nov. 1952*
From Indian Canoes to Submarines at Key West. By Frederick Simpich. Photos by J. Baylor Roberts. 41-72, *Jan. 1950*
'Round the Horn by Submarine. By Paul C. Stimson. Contents: *Sea Robin.* 129-144, *Jan. 1948*
Your Navy as Peace Insurance. By Chester W. Nimitz. 681-736, *June 1946*
See also Submersibles

Nuclear-powered
NR-1, the Navy's Inner-Space Shuttle. By Robert D. Ballard. Photos by Emory Kristof. 450-459, *Apr. 1985*
Four-ocean Navy in the Nuclear Age. By Thomas W. McKnew. Included: *Nautilus, Shark, Skate, Triton.* 145-187, *Feb. 1965*
Our Nuclear Navy. By George W. Anderson, Jr. 449-450, *Mar. 1963*
You and the Obedient Atom. By Allan C. Fisher, Jr. Included: *Nautilus, Seawolf.* 303-353, *Sept. 1958*
Man's New Servant, the Friendly Atom. By F. Barrows Colton. Photos by Volkmar Wentzel. Included: *Nautilus, Seawolf.* 71-90, *Jan. 1954*
See also Nautilus; Skate; Thresher; Triton

SUBMERGED Valleys in Sandusky Bay. By E. L. Moseley. 398-403, *Nov. 1902*

SUBMERSIBLES:

Down the Cayman Wall. By Eugenie Clark. Included: *Atlantis I* submersible, Perry research submersible, *Pisces II.* NGS research grant. 712-731, *Nov. 1988*
Coelacanths, the Fish That Time Forgot. Article and photos by Hans Fricke. Included: The submersible *Geo.* 824-838, *June 1988*
Epilogue for *Titanic.* By Robert D. Ballard. 454-463, *Oct. 1987*
A Long Last Look at *Titanic.* By Robert D. Ballard. Included: High-tech partners *(Alvin* and *Jason Jr.)* plumb new depths; Poignant relics of a disaster. Illustrations text by Cliff Tarpy. 698-727, *Dec. 1986*
Sharks at 2,000 Feet. By Eugenie Clark and Emory Kristof as reported to Douglas Lee. *Included: Pisces VI.* NGS research grant. 681-691, *Nov. 1986*
How We Found *Titanic.* By Robert D. Ballard in association with Jean-Louis Michel. Included: *Argo.* 696-719, *Dec. 1985*
Exploring a 140-year-old Ship Under Arctic Ice. By Joseph B. MacInnis. Photos by Emory Kristof. Included: WASP submersible. 104A-104D, *July 1983*
Project FAMOUS. 586-615. I. Where the Earth Turns Inside Out. By J. R. Heirtzler. Photos by Emory Kristof. 586-603; Included: *Alvin, Archimède, Cyana.* II. Dive Into the Great

SUCCESSFUL Shots With a Friendly Camera. Photos by H. T. Bohlman, Irene Finley, and William L. Finley. 165-180, *Aug. 1923*

SUDAN:

The **SUDD** (Swamp), Sudan:

SUEHSDORF, ADOLPH: *Author*

The Cats in Our Lives. Photos by Walter Chandoha. 508-541, *Apr. 1964*

SUEZ CANAL, Egypt:

New Life for the Troubled Suez Canal.

A south Sudanese woman displays the traditional scarification and haircut of the isolated Mondari tribe. ROBERT CAPUTO

SUGAR, JAMES A.:

SUGAR CANE:

SUGAR INDUSTRY:

A **SUGGESTED** Field for Exploration. 290-291, *July 1903*

SUGGESTIONS to Future Observers. By H. F. Reid. 83-84, *Mar. 21, 1892*

SULAIMANIYA, Iraq:

Mountain Tribes of Iran and Iraq. By Harold Lamb. 385-408, *Mar. 1946*

SULAWESI (Island), Indonesia:

Life and Death in Tana Toradja. By Pamela and Alfred Meyer. 793-815, *June 1972*

See also former name, Celebes

SÜLEYMAN THE MAGNIFICENT:

The World of Süleyman the Magnificent. By Merle Severy. Photos by James L. Stanfield. 552-601, *Nov. 1987*

SULFUR DIOXIDE:

Acid Rain–How Great a Menace? By Anne LaBastille. Photos by Ted Spiegel. 652-681, *Nov. 1981*

SULLIVAN, SIR ARTHUR:

The British Way. By Sir Evelyn Wrench. 421-541, *Apr. 1949*

SULPHUR Mine in Nevada. 498, *Dec. 1904*

SULTAN, DAN I.: *Author*

An Army Engineer Explores Nicaragua: Mapping a Route for a New Canal Through the Largest of Central American Republics. 593-627, *May 1932*

SULU ARCHIPELAGO, Philippines:

Sea Gypsies of the Philippines. By Anne de Henning Singh. Photos by Raghubir Singh. 659-677, *May 1976*

"As the Tuan Had Said." By George M. Hanson. 631-644, *Nov. 1933*

SUMATRA (Island), Indonesia:

A Sumatran Journey. By Harvey Arden. Photos by David Alan Harvey. 406-430, *Mar. 1981*

Indonesia, the Young and Troubled Island Nation. By Helen and Frank Schreider. 579-625, *May 1961*

This Young Giant, Indonesia. By Beverley M. Bowie. Photos by J. Baylor Roberts. 351-392, *Sept. 1955*

Republican Indonesia Tries Its Wings. By W. Robert Moore. 1-40, *Jan. 1951*

The Face of the Netherlands Indies. Photos by Maynard Owen Williams and others. 261-276, *Feb. 1946*

Around the World for Animals. By William M. and Lucile Q. Mann. 665-714, *June 1938*

Among the Hill Tribes of Sumatra. By W. Robert Moore. Included: Sumatra, a Ribbon of Color on the Equator. Photos by W. Robert Moore. 187-227, *Feb. 1930*

By Motor Through the East Coast and Batak Highlands of Sumatra. By Melvin A. Hall. 69-102, *Jan. 1920*

Sumatra's West Coast. By David G. Fairchild. 449-464, *Nov. 1898*

SUMERIAN CIVILIZATION:

■ The *Tigris* Expedition. 826, Dec. 1978; 1, Jan. 1979; cover, *Apr. 1979*

Tigris Sails Into the Past. By Thor Heyerdahl. Photos by Carlo Mauri and the crew of the *Tigris.* 806-827, *Dec. 1978*

Ancient Mesopotamia: A Light That Did Not Fail. By E. A. Speiser.

Paintings by H. M. Herget. 41-105, *Jan. 1951*

New Light on Ancient Ur: Excavations at the Site of the City of Abraham Reveal Geographical Evidence of the Biblical Story of the Flood. By M.E.L. Mallowan. 95-130, *Jan. 1930*

SUMMARY of Reports on the Mt. St. Elias Expedition. 302-304, *Apr. 1891*

SUMMER GEOGRAPHY INSTITUTE (NGS):

President's Page. By Gilbert M. Grosvenor. Feb. 1986; Aug. 1986; Dec. 1986; *Nov. 1987*

SUMMER Holidays on the Bosporus. By Maynard Owen Williams. 487-508, *Oct. 1929*

SUMMER INSTITUTE OF GLACIOLOGICAL AND ARCTIC SCIENCES, Alaska:

Alaska's Mighty Rivers of Ice. By Maynard M. Miller. Photos by Christopher G. Knight. NGS research grant. 194-217, *Feb. 1967*

SUMMER Meeting of the American Forestry Association. 352-358, *Sept. 1902*

A **SUMMER** Voyage to the Arctic. By G. R. Putnam. 97-110, *Apr. 1897*

SUMMERHAYS, SOAMES: *Author*

A Marine Park Is Born: Australia's Great Barrier Reef. Photos by Ron and Valerie Taylor. 630-635, *May 1981*

Amara tribesmen of Sudan's Red Sea hills earned a reputation for fierceness in colonial-era conflicts. ERNEST B. SCHOEDSACK

Supertanker **Amoco Cadiz** *breaks up off Brittany after foundering on March 16, 1978, and coating beaches with oil.* MARTIN ROGERS

Cartographer Bradford Washburn takes survey readings for the magazine's Grand Canyon map. CHARLES O'REAR, WEST LIGHT

Report of Ernest A. Man. 339-344, *Oct. 1896*

The Return of Dr. Nansen. 290, *Sept. 1896*

The SWALLOW-TAILED KITE:
Graceful Aerialist of the Everglades. Photos by Ray O. Green, Jr., Norman D. Reed, and Myron H. Wright, Jr. 496-505, *Oct. 1972*

SWALLOWS:
Thrushes, Thrashers, and Swallows: Robins and Bluebirds are Familiar Members of a Famous Musical Family Which Includes the Hermit Thrush and European Nightingale. By T. Gilbert Pearson. Paintings by Allan Brooks. 523-546, *Apr. 1936*

SWAMPS:
■ Realm of the Alligator. President's Page. By Gilbert M. Grosvenor. Jan. 1986; cover, *Apr. 1986*

■ Creatures of the Mangrove. President's Page. By Gilbert M. Grosvenor. Jan. 1986; cover, *Feb. 1986*

Journey Up the Nile. By Robert Caputo. Included: The Sudd. 577-633, *May 1985*

Sudan: Arab-African Giant. By Robert Caputo. Included: The Sudd. 346-379, *Mar. 1982*

Trouble in Bayou Country. By Jack and Anne Rudloe. Photos by C. C. Lockwood. 377-397, *Sept. 1979*

Twilight Hope for Big Cypress. By Rick Gore. Photos by Patricia Caulfield. 251-273, *Aug. 1976*

Okefenokee, the Magical Swamp. By François Leydet. Photos by Farrell Grehan. 169-175, *Feb. 1974*

The People of New Jersey's Pine Barrens. By John McPhee. Photos by William R. Curtsinger. 52-77, *Jan. 1974*

The Top End of Down Under. By Kenneth MacLeish. Photos by Thomas Nebbia. 145-174, *Feb. 1973*

The Okefenokee Wilderness: Exploring the Mystery Land of the Suwannee River. By Francis Harper. 597-624, *May 1934*

See also Everglades

SWAN, ROBERT: *Author*
In the Footsteps of Scott. 544-555, *Apr. 1987*

SWAN EXPEDITION:
In the Footsteps of Scott. By Robert Swan. 544-555, *Apr. 1987*

SWANS:
The Triumphant Trumpeter. By Charles A. Bergman. Photos by Art Wolfe. 544-558, *Oct. 1985*

Tireless Voyager, the Whistling Swan. By William J. L. Sladen. Photos by Bianca Lavies. NGS research grant. 134-147, *July 1975*

Return of the Trumpeter. By Frederick Kent Truslow. 134-150, *July 1960*

The Swans of Abbotsbury. By Michael Moynihan. Photos by Barnet Saidman. 563-570, *Oct. 1959*

Far-Flying Wild Fowl and Their Foes. By Allan Brooks. Paintings from life by author. 487-528, *Oct. 1934*

Fowls of Forest and Stream Tamed by Man. By Morley A. Jull. Paintings by Hashime Murayama. 327-371, *Mar. 1930*

SWANSON, DICK: *Photographer*
The Hmong in America: Laotian Refugees in the "Land of the Giants." By Spencer Sherman. 586-610, *Oct. 1988*

SWANSON, WINFIELD: *Editor*
■■*Research Reports.* 1980-1983 Projects. 531 pages. *1985*

■■*Research Reports.* 1979 Projects. 900 pages. *1985*

■■*Research Reports.* 1978 Projects. 764 pages. *1985*

■■*Research Reports.* 1977 Projects. 803 pages. *1985*

■■*Research Reports.* 1976 Projects. 968 pages. *1984*

SWAPO (South-West Africa People's Organization):
Namibia: Nearly a Nation? By Bryan Hodgson. Photos by Jim Brandenburg. Note: SWAPO members are recognized by the United Nations as representatives of Namibia. 755-797, *June 1982*

SWARTZ, STEVEN L.: *Author*
Gray Whales of San Ignacio. By Steven L. Swartz and Mary Lou Jones. Photos by François Gohier. NGS research grant. 754-771, *June 1987*

SWAT (State), Pakistan:
Pakistan, New Nation in an Old Land. By Jean and Franc Shor. 637-678, *Nov. 1952*

SWATEK, PHILLIP M.: *Author*
Rugged Is the Word for Bravo. 829-843, *Dec. 1955*

SWATOW, Guangdong, China. *See* Shantou Special Economic Zone

SWAYNE, H.G.C.: *Author*
The Rock of Aden: The Volcanic Mountain Fortress, on the Sea Route from Suez to India, Assumes New Importance. 723-742, *Dec. 1935*

SWAZILAND:
Zulu King Weds a Swazi Princess. By Volkmar Wentzel. 47-61, *Jan. 1978*

Swaziland Tries Independence. By Volkmar Wentzel. 266-293, *Aug. 1969*

SWEDEN:
Stockholm, Where "Kvalitet" Is a Way of Life. By James Cerruti. Photos by Albert Moldvay and Jonathan Blair. 43-69, *Jan. 1976*

Gotland: Sweden's Treasure Island. By James Cerruti. Photos by Albert Moldvay. 268-288, *Aug. 1973*

The Vikings. By Howard La Fay. Photos by Ted Spiegel. 492-541, *Apr. 1970*

Friendly Flight to Northern Europe. By Lyndon B. Johnson. Photos by Volkmar Wentzel. 268-293, *Feb. 1964*

Sweden, Quiet Workshop for the World. By Andrew H. Brown. 451-491, *Apr. 1963*

Ghost From the Depths: the Warship *Vasa*. By Anders Franzén. 42-57, *Jan. 1962*

Thumbs Up Round the North Sea's Rim. By Frances James. Photos by Erica Koch. 685-704, *May 1952*

Baltic Cruise of the *Caribbee*. By Carleton Mitchell. 605-646, *Nov. 1950*

Rural Sweden Through American Eyes: A Visitor in Peacetime Finds Warmth, Welcome, and Strange Folkways On a Century-old Farm. By Elizabeth W. Nilson. 795-822, *June 1940*

The Nomads of Arctic Lapland: Mysterious Little People of a Land of the Midnight Sun Live Off the Country Above the Arctic Circle. By Clyde Fisher. 641-676, *Nov. 1939*

Life's Flavor on a Swedish Farm: From the Rocky Hills of Småland Thousands of Sturdy Citizens Have Emigrated to the United States. By Willis Lindquist. 393-414, *Sept. 1939*

Flying Around the Baltic. By Douglas Chandler. 767-806, *June 1938*

Country-House Life in Sweden: In Castle and Cottage the Landed Gentry Gallantly Keep the Old Traditions. By Amelie Posse-Brázdová. 1-64, *July 1934*

The Granite City of the North: Austere Stockholm, Sweden's Prosperous Capital, Presents a Smiling Aspect in Summer. By Ralph A. Graves. 403-424, *Oct. 1928*

Types and Costumes of Old Sweden. Photos by Gustav Heurlin, G. W. Cronquist, Wilhelm Tobien, and Charles Martin. 425-440, *Oct. 1928*

Sweden, Land of White Birch and White Coal. By Alma Luise Olson. 441-484, *Oct. 1928*

King Herring: An Account of the World's Most Valuable Fish, the Industries It Supports, and the Part It Has Played in History. By Hugh M. Smith. 701-735, *Aug. 1909*

In Beautiful Delecarlia. By Lillian Gore. 464-477, *May 1909*

A Comparison of Norway and Sweden. 429-431, *Sept. 1905*

SWEDES:
Viking Trail East. By Robert Paul Jordan. Photos by Jim Brandenburg. Paintings by Michael A. Hampshire. 278-317, *Mar. 1985*

SWEET, O. C.: *Photographer*
Busy Fairbanks Sets Alaska's Pace. By Bruce A. Wilson. 505-523, *Oct. 1949*

SWELLFISH. *See* Puffer Fish

SWERDLOW, JOEL L.: *Author*
To Heal a Nation. 555-573, *May 1985*

SWIFTS:
Seeking the Smallest Feathered Creatures: Humming Birds, Peculiar to the New World, Are Found from Canada and Alaska to the Strait of Magellan. Swifts and Goatsuckers, Their Nearest Relatives. By Alexander Wetmore. Paintings by Allan Brooks. 65-89, *July 1932*

S T

Men from the Swiss canton Appenzell-Inner Rhoden assemble in a spring snow for their annual vote by show of hands.   COTTON COULSON

The Races of Europe. By Edwin A. Grosvenor. 441-534, *Dec. 1918*

Republics–The Ladder to Liberty. By David Jayne Hill. 240-254, *Mar. 1917*

The Citizen Army of Switzerland. 503-510, *Nov. 1915*

Italian, French, and Swiss Scenes. Photos by Donald McLeish and Arthur Stanley Riggs. 439-454, *Nov. 1915*

The Ascent of Mont Blanc. By Walter Woodburn Hyde. 861-942, *Aug. 1913*

The Majesty of the Matterhorn. Pictorial supplement, *May 1912*

A Woman's Climbs in the High Alps. By Dora Keen. 643-675, *July 1911*

Landslides and Rock Avalanches. By Guy Elliott Mitchell. 277-287, *Apr. 1910*

In Valais. By Louise Murray. 249-256, *Mar. 1910*

Scenes in Switzerland. 257-268, *Mar. 1910*

SWOPE, JOHN: *Photographer*

Sunshine Over the Chilean Lakes. Photos by W. Robert Moore and John Swope. 97-104, *July 1941*

The **SWORD** and the Sermon. By Thomas J. Abercrombie. 3-45, *July 1972*

SWORDFISH:

Fighting Giants of the Humboldt. By David D. Duncan. 373-400, *Mar. 1941*

SYDNEY, Australia:

Sydney's Changing Face. Photos by Mary Ellen Mark. Introduction by Elizabeth A. Moize. 246-265, *Feb. 1988*

Sydney: Big, Breezy, and a Bloomin' Good Show. By Ethel A. Starbird. Photos by Robert W. Madden. 211-235, *Feb. 1979*

New South Wales, the State That Cradled Australia. By Howell Walker. Photos by David Moore. 591-635, *Nov. 1967*

Australia. By Alan Villiers. 309-385, *Sept. 1963*

The Making of a New Australia. By Howell Walker. 233-259, *Feb. 1956*

Sydney Faces the War Front Down Under. By Howell Walker. 359-374, *Mar. 1943*

Capital Cities of Australia. By W. Robert Moore. 667-722, *Dec. 1935*

Lonely Australia: The Unique Continent. By Herbert E. Gregory. 473-568, *Dec. 1916*

SYKES, ELLA C.: *Author*

A Talk About Persia and Its Women. 847-866, *Oct. 1910*

SYKES, ROBERT B., Jr.: *Photographer*

Uncle Sam's Icebox Outposts. Photos by John E. Schneider and Robert B. Sykes, Jr. 473-496, *Oct. 1946*

SYLVESTER, A. H.: *Author*

Is Our Noblest Volcano Awakening to New Life: Glaciers and Evidences of Volcanic Activity of Mount Hood. 515-525, *July 1908*

The **SYMBOL** of Service to Mankind. By Stockton Axson. 375-390, *Apr. 1918*

SYMPHONY of the Deep: "Songs of the Humpback Whale"(Sound Sheet). 24-24B, *Jan. 1979*

SYNFUELS:

Synfuels: Fill 'er Up! With What? By Thomas Y. Canby. Photos by Jonathan Blair. 74-95, *Special Report on Energy. (Feb. 1981)*

SYNTHETIC PRODUCTS:

Chemists Make a New World: Creating Hitherto Unknown Raw Materials, Science Now Disrupts Old Trade Routes and Revamps the World Map of Industry. By Frederick Simpich. 601-640, *Nov. 1939*

SYRACUSE, Sicily. *See* Siracusa

SYRIA:

Ebla: Splendor of an Unknown Empire. By Howard La Fay. Photos by James L. Stanfield. Paintings by Louis S. Glanzman. 730-759, *Dec. 1978*

Syria Tests a New Stability. By Howard La Fay. Photos by James L. Stanfield. 326-361, *Sept. 1978*

Damascus, Syria's Uneasy Eden. By Robert Azzi. 512-535, *Apr. 1974*

Abraham, the Friend of God. By Kenneth MacLeish. Photos by Dean Conger. 739-789, *Dec. 1966*

Journey Into the Great Rift: the Northern Half. By Helen and Frank Schreider. 254-290, *Aug. 1965*

The Arab World. 712-732, *Nov. 1958*

Syria and Lebanon Taste Freedom. By Maynard Owen Williams. 729-763, *Dec. 1946*

Ali Goes to the Clinic. By Herndon and Mary Hudson. 764-766, *Dec. 1946*

Bombs over Bible Lands. By Frederick Simpich and W. Robert Moore. 141-180, *Aug. 1941*

Change Comes to Bible Lands. By Frederick Simpich. 695-750, *Dec. 1938*

Secrets from Syrian Hills: Explorations Reveal World's Earliest Known Alphabet, Deciphered from Schoolboy Slates and Dictionaries of 3,000 Years Ago. By Claude F. A. Schaeffer. 97-126, *July 1933*

A New Alphabet of the Ancients Is Unearthed: An Inconspicuous Mound in Northern Syria Yields Archeological Treasures. By F. A. Schaeffer. 477-516, *Oct. 1930*

Skirting the Shores of Sunrise: Seeking and Finding "The Levant" in a Journey by Steamer, Motor-Car, and Train from Constantinople to Port Said. By Melville Chater. 649-728, *Dec. 1926*

Antioch the Glorious. By William H. Hall. 81-103, *Aug. 1920*

Syria: The Land Link of History's Chain. By Maynard Owen Williams. 437-462, *Nov. 1919*

Impressions of Asiatic Turkey. By Stephen van Rensselaer Trowbridge. 598-609, *Dec. 1914*

From Jerusalem to Aleppo. By John D. Whiting. 71-113, *Jan. 1913*

Damascus, the Pearl of the Desert. By A. Forder. 62-82, *Jan. 1911*

One Thousand Miles of Railway Built for Pilgrims and Not for Dividends. By F. R. Maunsell. 156-172, *Feb. 1909*

Damascus and Mecca Railway. 408, *Nov. 1901*

Geographic Progress of Civilization. Annual Address by the President, Gardiner G. Hubbard. 1-22, *Feb. 14, 1894*

SZECHWAN PROVINCE, China:

Adventures in Lololand. By Rennold L. Lowy. 105-118, *Jan. 1947*

China Fights Erosion with U. S. Aid. By Walter C. Lowdermilk. 641-680, *June 1945*

Salt for China's Daily Rice. 329-336, *Sept. 1944*

Experiences of a Lone Geographer: An American Agricultural Explorer Makes His Way Through Brigand-infested Central China en Route to the Amne Machin Range, Tibet. By Joseph F. Rock. 331-347, *Sept. 1925*

The Land of the Yellow Lama: National Geographic Society Explorer Visits the Strange Kingdom of Muli, Beyond the Likiang Snow Range of Yünnan Province, China. By Joseph F. Rock. 447-491, *Apr. 1925*

The Eden of the Flowery Republic. By Joseph Beech. 355-390, *Nov. 1920*

Populous and Beautiful Szechuan: A Visit to the Restless Province of China, in which the Present Revolution Began. By Rollin T. Chamberlin. 1094-1119, *Dec. 1911*

See also present spelling, Sichuan; *and* Sikang; Yangtze River and Basin

SZULC, TAD: *Author*

Poland: The Hope That Never Dies. Photos by James L. Stanfield. 80-121, *Jan. 1988*

A highly lustrous, synthetic fiber made from cellulose, rayon was developed as a silk substitute. WILLARD R. CULVER, NGS

A child enjoys hot noodles on Quemoy (now Chinmen Tao), Taiwan. Gastronomy reigns in Taipei, where some restaurants serve 400 different dishes.   HELEN AND FRANK SCHREIDER

Above a pool's reflection of perfection stands the Taj Mahal, begun by Mogul Emperor Shah Jahan near Agra in 1632 and completed 22 years later. MAYNARD OWEN WILLIAMS, NGS

■■ BOOKS ✤ MAPS ■ TELEVISION

TAKING It as It Comes: St. Vincent, the Grenadines, and Grenada. By Ethel A. Starbird. Photos by Cotton Coulson. 399-425, *Sept. 1979*

TALBOT, LEE MERRIAM:
Author-Photographer
Stalking the Great Indian Rhino. 389-398, *Mar. 1957*

TALBOT, P. A.: *Author*
Notes on the Ekoi (Nigeria). 33-38, *Jan. 1912*

TALBOT, PHILLIPS: *Author*
Delhi, Capital of a New Dominion. 597-630, *Nov. 1947*

TALC (Block Talc):
India's Treasures Helped the Allies. By John Fischer. 501-522, *Apr. 1946*

A **TALE** of Three Cities. Contents: Prague, Vienna, Budapest. By Thomas R. Henry. 641-669, *Dec. 1945*

A **TALE** of Twin Cities: Minneapolis and St. Paul. By Thomas J. Abercrombie. Photos by Annie Griffiths. 665-691, *Nov. 1980*

TALES of the British Air Service. By William A. Bishop. 27-37, *Jan. 1918*

TALK About Persia and Its Women. By Ella C. Sykes. 847-866, *Oct. 1910*

TALL-SHIPS RACE:
By Square-rigger from Baltic to Bicentennial. By Kenneth Garrett. Included: Training ships from Argentina, Chile, Colombia, Denmark, England, Italy, Japan, Norway, Poland, Portugal, Romania, Spain, Union of Soviet Socialist Republics, United States, West Germany. 824-857, *Dec. 1976*

The **TALLEST** Tree That Grows. By Edgerton R. Young. 664-667, *July 1909*

TALLGRASS PRAIRIE:
The Tallgrass Prairie: Can It Be Saved? By Dennis Farney. Photos by Jim Brandenburg. 37-61, *Jan. 1980*

TALLINN, Estonia, U.S.S.R.:
Estonia: At Russia's Baltic Gate: War Often Has Ravaged This Little Nation Whose Identity Was Long Submerged in the Vast Sea of Russian Peoples. By Baroness Irina Ungern-Sternberg. 803-834, *Dec. 1939*
Flying Around the Baltic. By Douglas Chandler. 767-806, *June 1938*

TAMBS, ERLING: *Author*
A Modern Saga of the Seas: The Narrative of a 17,000-Mile Cruise on a 40-Foot Sloop by the Author, His Wife, and a Baby, Born on the Voyage. 645-688, *Dec. 1931*

TAMILS:
Sri Lanka: Time of Testing for an Ancient Land. By Robert Paul Jordan. Photos by Raghubir Singh. 123-150, *Jan. 1979*

TAMING "Flood Dragons" Along China's Hwang Ho. By Oliver J. Todd. 205-234, *Feb. 1942*

TAMING the Outlaw Missouri River. By Frederick Simpich. 569-598, *Nov. 1945*

TAMING the Wild Blueberry. By Frederick V. Coville. 137-147, *Feb. 1911*

TAMPA, Florida:
America Goes to the Fair. By Samuel W. Matthews. Included: Florida State Fair, Gasparilla Celebration. 293-333, *Sept. 1954*

TAMPA BAY, Gulf of Mexico:
Cruising Florida's Western Waterways. By Rube Allyn. Photos by Bates Littlehales. 49-76, *Jan. 1955*

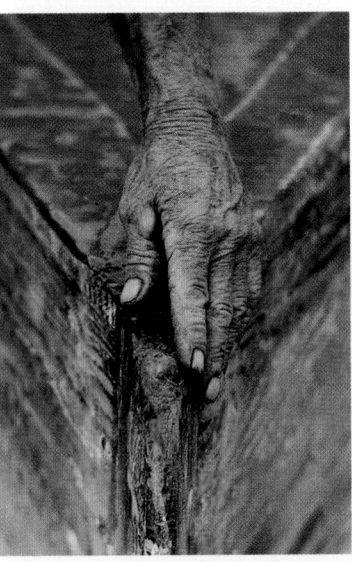

Waterman's weathered hand feels the hull of a crab boat on Tangier Island in Chesapeake Bay. DAVID ALAN HARVEY

TAMPICO, Mexico:
A Naturalist's Journey Around Vera Cruz and Tampico. By Frank M. Chapman. 533-562, *May 1914*

TANA TORADJA (Region), Sulawesi:
Life and Death in Tana Toradja. By Pamela and Alfred Meyer. 793-815, *June 1972*
Life and Death in Toradjaland (Celebes). Photos by Maynard Owen Williams and Helene Fischer. 65-80, *July 1940*

TANAGER (Ship):
Bird Life Among Lava Rock and Coral Sand: The Chronicle of a Scientific Expedition to Little-known Islands of Hawaii. By Alexander Wetmore. 77-108, *July 1925*

TANAGERS:
The Tanagers and Finches: Their Flashes of Color and Lilting Songs Gladden the Hearts of American Bird Lovers East and West. By Arthur A. Allen. Paintings by Allan Brooks. 505-532, *Apr. 1935*

TANAHMERAH, Irian Jaya, Indonesia:
New Guinea's Mountain and Swampland Dwellers. By Ray T. Elsmore. 671-694, *Dec. 1945*

TANGANYIKA:
Ambassadors of Goodwill: The Peace Corps. By Sargent Shriver and Peace Corps Volunteers. Included: Tanganyika. By Ruth E. Dygert. 297-345, *Sept. 1964*
The Last Great Animal Kingdom. 390-409, *Sept. 1960*
Spearing Lions with Africa's Masai. By Edgar Monsanto Queeny. 487-517, *Oct. 1954*
Britain Tackles the East African Bush. By W. Robert Moore. 311-352, *Mar. 1950*
Roaming Africa's Unfenced Zoos. By W. Robert Moore. 353-380, *Mar. 1950*
Weighing the Aga Khan in Diamonds. Photos by David J. Carnegie. 317-324, *Mar. 1947*
Wings Over Nature's Zoo in Africa. Photos by Reginald A. Bourlay. 527-542, *Oct. 1939*
Flashlights from the Jungle. 534-548, *Aug. 1907*
The Heart of Africa. By E. C. Hore. 238-247, *Feb. 19, 1892*
See also present name, Tanzania

TANGANYIKA, Lake, Tanzania-Zaire:
Where Exploration Is Needed (Africa). 163-164, *Apr. 1900*

TANGIER, Morocco:
Eastward from Gibraltar: Overland Route Across North Africa to Tunisia and Libia. By Cyrus French Wicker. 115-142, *Jan. 1943*
A Journey in Morocco: "The Land of the Moors." By Thomas Lindsey Blayney. 750-775, *Aug. 1911*
The Two Great Moorish Religious

Shutterless camera captures the grace of a bounding zebra, whose striped hide tempts Tanzanian poachers. EMORY KRISTOF, NGS

S
T

Searching for the ultimate defense against shark attack, Valerie Taylor, clad in a chain-mail suit, offers an armored arm to a blue shark off the California coast. RON TAYLOR

Volcano (Mexico). By James A. Green. 129-164, *Feb. 1944*
A Mexican Land of Lakes and Lacquers (Pátzcuaro Region). Photos by Helene Fischer and Luis Marquez. 633-648, *May 1937*

TARAWA (Atoll), Kiribati:
Adventures with the Survey Navy. By Irving Johnson. 131-148, *July 1947*
Gilbert Islands in the Wake of Battle. By W. Robert Moore. 129-162, *Feb. 1945*

TARBA, TEMUR:
Nomination Page. *Jan. 1973*

TARHEELIA on Parade: Versatile and Vibrant, North Carolina in a Generation Has Climbed New Economic Heights. By Leonard C. Roy. 181-224, *Aug. 1941*

TARKIL, MARKHTI:
Nomination Page. *Jan. 1973*

TARPON KEY, Florida:
Bad Days for the Brown Pelican. By Ralph W. Schreiber. Photos by William R. Curtsinger and author. 111-123, *Jan. 1975*

TARPON SPRINGS, Florida:
Sponge Fishermen of Tarpon Springs. By Jennie E. Harris. 119-136, *Jan. 1947*

TARPY, CLIFF: *Author*
High-tech Partners Plumb New Depths; Poignant Relics of a Disaster *(Titanic).* 706-727, *Dec. 1986*
Home to Kansas. Photos by Cotton Coulson. 352-383, *Sept. 1985*

Heat Paints *Columbia*'s Portrait. 650-653, *Nov. 1982*
San Francisco Bay: The Beauty and the Battles. Photos by James A. Sugar. 814-845, *June 1981*
Killer Whale Attack! 542-545, *Apr. 1979*

TARQUINIA, Italy:
The Eternal Etruscans. By Rick Gore. Photos by O. Louis Mazzatenta. Paintings by James M. Gurney. 696-743, *June 1988*

TARR, RALPH S.:
President's Page. By Gilbert M. Grosvenor. *Sept. 1988*
Author
█ *Alaskan Glacier Studies of the National Geographic Society in the Yakutat Bay, Prince William Sound and Lower Copper River Regions.* By Ralph Stockman Tarr and Lawrence Martin. 498 pages. *1914*
The National Geographic Society's Alaskan Expedition of 1909. By Ralph S. Tarr and Lawrence Martin. 1-54, *Jan. 1910*
The Teaching of Geography. 55-64, *Feb. 1902*
Geographic Names in West Greenland. 103-104, *Mar. 1898*

TARSIERS:
Seeking Mindanao's Strangest Creatures. By Charles Heizer Wharton. 389-408, *Sept. 1948*

TARTAN Tints New Scotland. Photos by John Mills, Jr. and W. R. MacAskill. 591-622, *May 1940*

TARXIEN TEMPLE, Malta:
Malta: The Halting Place of Nations: First Account of Remarkable Prehistoric Tombs and Temples Recently Unearthed on the Island. By William Arthur Griffiths. 445-478, *May 1920*

TASADAYS:
The Tasadays, Stone Age Cavemen of Mindanao. By Kenneth MacLeish. Photos by John Launois. 219-249, *Aug. 1972*
First Glimpse of a Stone Age Tribe. 881-882, *Dec. 1971*
■ The Last Tribes of Mindanao. 227, *Aug. 1972;* 882A-882B, *Dec. 1971*
Help for Philippine Tribes in Trouble. By Kenneth MacLeish. Photos by Dean Conger. 220-255, *Aug. 1971*

TASHI-CHO-JONG (Fort), Bhutan:
Castles in the Air: Experiences and Journeys in Unknown Bhutan. By John Claude White. 365-455, *Apr. 1914*

TASMANIA (Island), Australia:
A Walk and Ride on the Wild Side: Tasmania. By Carolyn Bennett Patterson. Photos by David Hiser and Melinda Berge. 676-693, *May 1983*
Tasmania, Australia's Island State. By Howell Walker. 791-818, *Dec. 1956*

TASSILI-N-AJJER, Algeria:
Oasis of Art in the Sahara. By Henri Lhote. Photos by Kazuyoshi Nomachi. 180-191, *Aug. 1987*

TATARS (People):
Young Russia: The Land of Unlimited Possibilities. By Gilbert H. Grosvenor. 421-520, *Nov. 1914*

TATE, G.H.H.: *Author*
Through Brazil to the Summit of Mount Roraima. 585-605, *Nov. 1930*

TATRA MOUNTAINS, Czechoslovakia-Poland:
Poland's Mountain People. By Yva Momatiuk and John Eastcott. 104-129, *Jan. 1981*

TAUFA'AHAU TUPOU IV, King (Tonga):
South Seas' Tonga Hails a King. By Melville Bell Grosvenor. Photos by Edwin Stuart Grosvenor. 322-343, *Mar. 1968*

The **TAURINE** World: Cattle and Their Place in the Human Scheme–Wild Types and Modern Breeds in Many Lands. By Alvin Howard Sanders. Paintings by Edward Herbert Miner. 591-710, *Dec. 1925*

TAURUS-LITTROW (Valley), Moon:
Exploring Taurus-Littrow. By Harrison H. Schmitt. 290-307, *Sept. 1973*

TAUTIRA, Tahiti:
Notes on Tahiti. By H. W. Smith. 947-963, *Oct. 1911*

TAUU ISLANDS, South Pacific Ocean:
American Pathfinders in the Pacific. By William H. Nicholas. 617-640, *May 1946*

TAVARES DE SÁ, HERNANE: *Author*

Brasília, Metropolis Made to Order. Photos by Thomas J. Abercrombie. 704-724, *May 1960*

Spectacular Rio de Janeiro. Photos by Charles Allmon. 289-328, *Mar. 1955*

A **TAXI** for the Deep Frontier. By Kenneth MacLeish. Photos by Bates Littlehales. 139-150, *Jan. 1968*

TAYLOR, ALEXANDER:
Author-Photographer

Chessmen Come to Life in Marostica. 658-668, *Nov. 1956*

Photographer

Paris Flea Market. By Franc Shor. 318-326, *Mar. 1957*

By Full-rigged Ship to Denmark's Fairyland. By Alan Villiers. Photos by Alexander Taylor and author. 809-828, *Dec. 1955*

TAYLOR, HENRY:

Nomination Page. *Apr. 1979*

TAYLOR, MEDFORD: *Photographer*

High Road to "Victory": Soviet and U. S. Climbers Conquer Pik Pobedy. By William Garner. 256-271, *Aug. 1986*

TAYLOR, RON: *Author-Photographer*

Paradise Beneath the Sea: Australia's Great Barrier Reef. By Ron and Valerie Taylor. 636-663, *May 1981*

Photographer

A Marine Park Is Born: Australia's Great Barrier Reef. By Soames Summerhays. Photos by Ron and Valerie Taylor. 630-635, *May 1981*

Australia's Great Barrier Reef. 728-741, *June 1973*

Exploring Australia's Coral Jungle. By Kenneth MacLeish. 743-779, *June 1973*

TAYLOR, VALERIE: *Author*

A Jawbreaker for Sharks (Chain-Mail Diving Suit). 664-667, *May 1981*

Author-Photographer

Paradise Beneath the Sea: Australia's Great Barrier Reef. By Ron and Valerie Taylor. 636-663, *May 1981*

Photographer

A Marine Park Is Born: Australia's Great Barrier Reef. By Soames Summerhays. Photos by Ron and Valerie Taylor. 630-635, *May 1981*

Australia's Great Barrier Reef. 728-741, *June 1973*

Exploring Australia's Coral Jungle. By Kenneth MacLeish. 743-779, *June 1973*

TAYLOR, ZACHARY:

Profiles of the Presidents: II. A Restless Nation Moves West. By Frank Freidel. 80-121, *Jan. 1965*

TAYLOR COUNTY, Kentucky:

Home to the Heart of Kentucky. By Nadine Brewer. Photos by William Strode. 522-546, *Apr. 1982*

TAYMAN, NELSON GRANT: *Author*

Stilwell Road–Land Route to China. 681-698, *June 1945*

T'BOLI TRIBESPEOPLE:

The Last Tribes of Mindanao. 882A-882B, *Dec. 1971*; 227, *Aug. 1972*

Help for Philippine Tribes in Trouble. By Kenneth MacLeish. Photos by Dean Conger. 220-255, *Aug. 1971*

TCHIKAO INDIANS:

Saving Brazil's Stone Age Tribes From Extinction. By Orlando and Claudio Villas Boas. Photos by W. Jesco von Puttkamer. 424-444, *Sept. 1968*

TE ANAU (Lake), New Zealand:

Finding an "Extinct" New Zealand Bird. By R. V. Francis Smith. 393-401, *Mar. 1952*

TEA AND SUGAR TRAIN:

The Tea and Sugar Lifeline in Australia's Outback. By Erla Zwingle. Photos by William Albert Allard. 737-757, *June 1986*

The **TEACHING** of Geography. By Ralph S. Tarr. 55-64, *Feb. 1902*

The **TEACHING** of Physical Geography in Elementary Schools. By Richard E. Dodge. 470-475, *Dec. 1900*

TEAK:

Working Teak in the Burma Forests: The Sagacious Elephant Is Man's Ablest Ally in the Logging Industry of the Far East. By A. W. Smith. 239-256, *Aug. 1930*

TEAL, JOHN J., Jr.: *Author*

Domesticating the Wild and Woolly Musk Ox. Photos by Robert W. Madden. 862-879, *June 1970*

TEAMWORK Helps the Whooping Crane. By Roderick C. Drewien, with Ernie Kuyt. 680-693, *May 1979*

TEAS, JANE:

Nomination Page. *Apr. 1979*

Author

Temple Monkeys of Nepal. 575-584, *Apr. 1980*

TECHNICAL EDUCATION RESEARCH CENTERS (TERC):

President's Page. By Gilbert M. Grosvenor. *Apr. 1987*

TECHNOLOGY:

Medicine's New Vision. By Howard Sochurek. Paintings by Davis Meltzer. Illustrations text by Peter Miller. Included: Computed Tomography, Magnetic Resonance Imaging, Sonography, Digital Subtraction Angiography, Radioisotope imaging. 2-41, *Jan. 1987*

Editorial. By Wilbur E. Garrett. 701, *June 1986*

Miraculous Machines. cover, *Apr. 1985*

Computers: Those Amazing Machines. By Catherine O'Neill. Juvenile. 104 pages. *1985*

Science: It's Changing Your World. Contents: Fuel and food, industry, medicine, transportation, and space. Juvenile. 104 pages. *1985*

Editorial. By Wilbur E. Garrett. 281, *Mar. 1984*

Lasers–"A Splendid Light." By Allen A. Boraiko. Photos by Charles O'Rear. 335-363, *Mar. 1984*

The Wonder of Holography. By H. John Caulfield. Photos by Charles O'Rear. 364-377, *Mar. 1984*

Across Australia by Sunpower. By Hans Tholstrup and Larry Perkins. Photos by David Austen. 600-607, *Nov. 1983*

The Miracle Metal–Platinum. By Gordon Young. Photos by James L. Amos. 686-706, *Nov. 1983*

Satellites That Serve Us. By Thomas Y. Canby. Included: Images of Earth; Spacelab 1: *Columbia.* By Michael E. Long. 301-307. 81-335, *Sept. 1983*

Swing Low, Sweet Chariot! By Noel Grove. Photos by Bruce Dale. 2-35, *July 1983*

How Things Work. Juvenile. 104 pages. *1983*

On the Brink of Tomorrow: Frontiers

In need of a cold beer beneath South Australia's beating sun, Henry Cox takes a break from his job as an examiner for the Tea and Sugar Train. WILLIAM ALBERT ALLARD

Burgeoning technology of the automobile helps spread education as a thousand-volume book wagon visits a Maryland country cabin in 1922. CLIFTON ADAMS, NGS

A portable television was demonstrated in 1954 when RCA produced a battery-powered transistorized model, weighing 27 pounds, with a five-inch screen. WILLARD R. CULVER, NGS

TEKES VALLEY, Xinjiang Uygur Autonomous Region, China:

With the Nomads of Central Asia: A Summer's Sojourn in the Tekes Valley, Plateau Paradise of Mongol and Turkic Tribes. By Edward Murray. Paintings and drawings by Alexandre Iacovleff. 1-57, *Jan. 1936*

TEKTITE II (Sea and Space Research Project):

Tektite II: I. Science's Window on the Sea. By John G. VanDerwalker. Photos by Bates Littlehales. II. All-girl Team Tests the Habitat. By Sylvia A. Earle. Paintings by Pierre Mion. 256-296, *Aug. 1971*

TEL AVIV-JAFFA, Israel:

Israel–The Seventh Day. By Joseph Judge. Photos by Gordon W. Gahan. 816-855, *Dec. 1972*

Eyewitness to War in the Holy Land. By Charles Harbutt. 782-795, *Dec. 1967*

Israel: Land of Promise. By John Scofield. Photos by B. Anthony Stewart. 395-434, *Mar. 1965*

Home to the Holy Land. By Maynard Owen Williams. 707-746, *Dec. 1950*

Palestine Today. By Francis Chase, Jr. 501-516, *Oct. 1946*

American Fighters Visit Bible Lands. By Maynard Owen Williams. 311-340, *Mar. 1946*

TELEGRAPHY:

The United States Government Telegraph and Cable Lines. 490-494, *Dec. 1904*

The Special Telegraphic Time Signal from the Naval Observatory. 411-415, *Oct. 1904*

Building the Alaskan Telegraph System. By William Mitchell. 357-361, *Sept. 1904*

The Cape to Cairo Telegraph. 76-77, *Feb. 1902*

Cape to Cairo Telegraph. 162-163, *Apr. 1901*

Peter Cooper and Submarine Telegraphy. 108-110, *Mar. 1896*

The Russo-American Telegraph Project of 1864-'67. By William H. Dall. 110-111, *Mar. 1896*

On the Telegraphic Determinations of Longitude by the Bureau of Navigation. By J. A. Norris. 1-30, *Apr. 1890*

See also Cables

TELEMETRY. *See* Radiotelemetry

TELEPHONE:

Fiber Optics: Harnessing Light by a Thread. By Allen A. Boraiko. Photos by Fred Ward. 516-535, *Oct. 1979*

New Miracles of the Telephone Age. By Robert Leslie Conly. 87-120, *July 1954*

Miracle Men of the Telephone. By F. Barrows Colton. Included: Birthplace of Telephone Magic. Photos by Willard R. Culver. 273-316, *Mar. 1947*

The Miracle of Talking by Telephone. By F. Barrows Colton. 395-433, *Oct. 1937*

The World's Highest International Telephone Cable. 722-731, *Dec. 1930*

Prehistoric Telephone Days. By Alexander Graham Bell. 223-241, *Mar. 1922*

Voice Voyages by the National Geographic Society: A Tribute to the Geographical Achievements of the Telephone. 296-326, *Mar. 1916*

TELEPHONE a Star: the Story of Communications Satellites. By Rowe Findley. 638-651, *May 1962*

TELESCOPES:

Halley's Comet 1986. By Rick Gore. 758-785, *Dec. 1986*

The Once and Future Universe. By Rick Gore. Photos by James A. Sugar. Paintings by Barron Storey. Picture text by David Jeffery. 704-749, *June 1983*

The Incredible Universe. By Kenneth F. Weaver. Photos by James P. Blair. 589-625, *May 1974*

Pioneers in Man's Search for the Universe. Paintings by Jean-Leon Huens. Text by Thomas Y. Canby. 627-633, *May 1974*

First Photographs of Planets and Moon Taken with Palomar's 200-inch Telescope. By Milton L. Humason. 125-130, *Jan. 1953*

Mapping the Unknown Universe. By F. Barrows Colton. Included: "Big Schmidt" and the 200-inch Hale telescope or "Big Eye." NGS research grant. 401-420, *Sept. 1950*

News of the Universe: Mars Swings Nearer the Earth, Sunspots Wane, and a Giant New Telescopic Eye Soon Will Peer Into Unexplored Depths of Space. By F. Barrows Colton. Paintings by Charles Bittinger. 1-32, *July 1939*

Exploring the Glories of the Firmament. By William Joseph Showalter. 153-181, *Aug. 1919*

See also Sky Survey; Skylab Missions

TELEVISION:

New Miracles of the Telephone Age. By Robert Leslie Conly. 87-120, *July 1954*

Fish Men Discover a 2,200-year-old Greek Ship. By Jacques-Yves Cousteau. NGS research grant. 1-36, *Jan. 1954*

Your Society Observes Eclipse in Brazil. NGS research grant. 661, *May 1947*

Your New World of Tomorrow. By F. Barrows Colton. 385-410, *Oct. 1945*

TELEVISION FILMS, NGS:

History. President's Page. By Gilbert M. Grosvenor. *Sept. 1988*

Foreign-language versions. President's

Telephone engineers developed picture-by-wire systems in the 1930s to transmit photographs. J. BAYLOR ROBERTS, NGS

Hugo the chimpanzee hoots a greeting to another Tanzanian ape, a scene recorded in a 1971 TV documentary.

Page. By Gilbert M. Grosvenor. *July 1988*

President's Page. By Gilbert M. Grosvenor. Mar. 1985; Jan. 1986; Dec. 1986; *Jan. 1987*

National Geographic's Newest Adventure: a Color Television Series. By Melville Bell Grosvenor. Note: The first program was "Americans on Everest." 448-452, *Sept. 1965*

Awards

Emmys. President's Page. *Jan. 1985*

Emmy. 731, Dec. 1974; 1, Jan. 1979; 848, 850, Dec. 1981; 275, *Aug. 1982*

George Foster Peabody Award. 587, Oct. 1967; 848, 850, *Dec. 1981*

Editorials

Editorial. By Wilbur E. Garrett. 703, *Dec. 1980*

Editorials. By Gilbert M. Grosvenor. 731, Dec. 1974; 299, Sept. 1975; 583, Nov. 1975; 575, Nov. 1976; 439, Oct. 1977; 1, Jan. 1979; 1, *Jan. 1980*

Explorer Cable Series

National Geographic Explorer–A New Series on Cable TV. President's Page. By Gilbert M. Grosvenor. *Apr. 1985*

Off-air Taping Policy

President's Page. By Gilbert M. Grosvenor. Jan. 1986; *Jan. 1987*

Resource Guide for Educators

President's Page. By Gilbert M. Grosvenor. Jan. 1986; *Jan. 1987*

Specials (S) and Videos (V)

African Odyssey (S). cover, *Jan. 1988*

Alaska! (S). 215A-215B, *Feb. 1967*

Amazon (S). 295A-295B, *Feb. 1968*

Americans on Everest (S). 448-452, Sept. 1965; 575, Nov. 1976; President's Page. *Jan. 1985*

America's Wonderlands: The National Parks (S). 549A-549B, *Oct. 1968*

Among the Wild Chimpanzees (S, V). cover, *Jan. 1984*

The Animals Nobody Loved (S). cover, *Feb. 1976*

Australia: The Timeless Land (S). 300A-300B, *Feb. 1969*

Australia's Animal Mysteries (S). 824, Dec. 1982; cover, *Feb. 1983*

Australia's Improbable Animals (V). *1988*

Australia's Twilight of the Dreamtime (S). 270, cover, *Feb. 1988*

Ballad of the Irish Horse (S, V). cover, *Mar. 1985*

The Big Cats (S). 442A, *Mar. 1974*

Born of Fire (S, V). 824, Dec. 1982; cover, *Apr. 1983*

Bushmen of the Kalahari (S). 578A-578B, Apr. 1973; 732A-732B, *May 1974*

Chesapeake Borne (S). President's Page; cover, *Jan. 1986*

Creatures of the Mangrove (S, V). President's Page. Jan. 1986; cover, *Feb. 1986*

Dive to the Edge of Creation (S). Contents: Galapagos Rift expedition. 682, Nov. 1979; 1, cover, *Jan. 1980*

Dr. Leakey and the Dawn of Man (S). 703A-703B, *Nov. 1966*

Egypt: Quest for Eternity (S, V). cover, *Feb. 1982*

Ethiopia: The Hidden Empire (S). 884A-884B, *Dec. 1970*

Etosha: Place of Dry Water (S, V). Note: Video retitled African Wildlife. 703, Dec. 1980; cover, *Jan. 1981*

The Explorers: A Century of Discovery (S, V). 316, Sept. 1988; cover, *Oct. 1988*

Flight of the Whooping Crane (S). President's Page; cover, *Apr. 1984*

Four Americans in China (S). cover, *Feb. 1985*

Gold! (S). 1, cover, *Jan. 1979*

Gorilla (S, V). 703, Dec. 1980; cover, *Apr. 1981*

The Great Mojave Desert (S). 294A-294B, *Feb. 1971*

Great Moments With National

Geographic (S). President's Page; cover, *Mar. 1985*

The Great Whales (S, V). 439, Oct. 1977; cover, Feb. 1978; Emmy Award. 1, *Jan. 1979*

The Grizzlies (S, V). President's Page. Jan. 1987; cover, *Mar. 1987*

Grizzly! (S). 639A-639B, *Nov. 1967*

The Haunted West (S). *Apr. 1973*

The Hidden World (S). 853A-853B, *Dec. 1966*

Himalayan River Run (V). *1988*

Holland Against the Sea (S). 588A-588B, *Apr. 1970*

Hong Kong: A Family Portrait (S). 1, Jan. 1979; cover, *Feb. 1979*

Iceland River Challenge (V). *1986*

In the Shadow of Vesuvius (S, V). President's Page. Jan. 1987; cover, *Feb. 1987*

The Incredible Machine (S, V). Note: Video retitled The Incredible Human Machine. 299, Sept. 1975; cover, Oct. 1975; 583, Nov. 1975; 575, Nov. 1976; President's Page. *Jan. 1985*

Inside the Soviet Circus (S). cover, *Mar. 1988*

The Invisible World (S, V). 1, Jan. 1980; cover, *Mar. 1980*

Jerusalem: Within These Walls (S, V). President's Page. Jan. 1986; cover, *Mar. 1986*

Journey to the High Arctic (S). 590A-590B, *Apr. 1971*

Journey to the Outer Limits (S). 150A-150B, *Jan. 1974*

Land of the Tiger (S, V). 754, Dec. 1984; President's Page; cover, *Jan. 1985*

Last Stand in Eden (S). 1, Jan. 1979; cover, *Mar. 1979*

The Last Tribes of Mindanao (S). 882A-882B, Dec. 1971; 227, *Aug. 1972*

The Last Vikings (S). 434A-434B, *Mar. 1972*

The Legacy of L.S.B. Leakey (S). 439, Oct. 1977; cover, *Jan. 1978*

Lions of the African Night (S, V). President's Page. Jan. 1987; cover, *Jan. 1987*

The Living Sands of Namib (S, V). Note: Video retitled Creatures of the Namib Desert. 439, Oct. 1977; cover, Mar. 1978; 1, *Jan. 1979*

Living Treasures of Japan (S, V). 703, Dec. 1980; cover, *Feb. 1981*

The Lonely Dorymen (S). 579A-579B, *Apr. 1968*

Love Those Trains (S). cover, *Feb. 1984*

Man-eaters of India (V). *1987*

Man of the Serengeti (S). 179A-179B, *Feb. 1972*

Miraculous Machines (S, V). Note: Video retitled Miniature Miracle: The Computer Chip. cover, *Apr. 1985*

Miss Goodall and the Wild Chimpanzees (S). 448, 451, Sept. 1965; 831A-831B, *Dec. 1965*

Monkeys, Apes, and Man (S). 585A-585B, *Oct. 1971*

Mysteries of Mankind (S). cover, *Apr. 1988*

Mysteries of the Mind (S). 1, Jan. 1980; cover, *Feb. 1980*

The Mystery of Animal Behavior (S). 592A-592B, *Oct. 1969*

TELL EL-KHELEIFEH (Ezion-geber), Jordan:

TELL EL MUTASALLIM, Israel. *See* Megiddo

TELL MARDIKH EXCAVATION, Syria:

TELSTAR (Satellite):

TEMPERATURE:

TEMPLE CAVES:

TEMPLE Monkeys of Nepal. By Jane Teas. NGS research grant. 575-584, *Apr. 1980*

TEMPLE MOUNDS:

TEMPLES:

Tokens of the late 1800s illustrated the Society's centennial-year story "Tell Me If Your Civilization Is Interesting." FRED OTNES

William Howard Taft. 141-148, *Feb. 1908*

TEN Years of the Peary Arctic Club. By Herbert L. Bridgman. 661-668, *Sept. 1908*

TENNESSEE:

Rising, Shining Tennessee. By Priit J. Vesilind. Photos by Karen Kasmauski. 602-637, *May 1986*

⊕ *Deep South,* The Making of America series. Included: Alabama, Florida, Georgia, Louisiana, Mississippi, South Carolina, and parts of Arkansas, North Carolina, and Tennessee. On reverse: Indian Legacy, Imperial Footholds, Three Empires and Three Races, Cotton Kingdom, Postbellum, New Deep South, Subtropical Playground. *Aug. 1983*

Echoes of Shiloh. By Shelby Foote. 106-111, *July 1979*

There's More to Nashville than Music. By Michael Kernan. Photos by Jodi Cobb. 692-711, *May 1978*

A Walk Across America. By Peter Gorton Jenkins. 466-499, *Apr. 1977*

Whatever Happened to TVA? By Gordon Young. Photos by Emory Kristof. 830-863, *June 1973*

Today Along the Natchez Trace, Pathway Through History. By Bern Keating. Photos by Charles Harbutt. 641-667, *Nov. 1968*

The People of Cades Cove. By William O. Douglas. Photos by Thomas Nebbia and Otis Imboden. 60-95, *July 1962*

The Lower Mississippi. By Willard Price. Photos by W. D. Vaughn. 681-725, *Nov. 1960*

Rhododendron Time on Roan Mountain. By Ralph Gray. 819-828, *June 1957*

Pack Trip Through the Smokies. By Val Hart. Photos by Robert F. Sisson. 473-502, *Oct. 1952*

Skyline Trail from Maine to Georgia. By Andrew H. Brown. Photos by Robert F. Sisson. 219-251, *Aug. 1949*

Dixie Spins the Wheel of Industry. By William H. Nicholas. Photos by J. Baylor Roberts. 281-324, *Mar. 1949*

Around the "Great Lakes of the South." By Frederick Simpich. Photos by J. Baylor Roberts. 463-491, *Apr. 1948*

Highlights of the Volunteer State: Men and Industry in Tennessee Range from Pioneer Stages to Modern Machine Age. By Leonard Cornell Roy. Included: Tennessee Tableaux. Photos by J. Baylor Roberts. 553-594, *May 1939*

Rambling Around the Roof of Eastern America. By Leonard C. Roy. Contents: Great Smoky Mountains. 243-266, *Aug. 1936*

⊕ *North Carolina, South Carolina, Georgia, and Eastern Tennessee. Sept. 1926*

Reelfoot–An Earthquake Lake. By Wilbur A. Nelson. 95-114, *Jan. 1924*

⊕ *North Carolina-Tennessee: Asheville Sheet.* Section from the Cumberland Plateau to the Blue Ridge. Surveyed in 1882-3-7. Note: Reprinted 1965 as

Asheville Quadrangle. Surveyed in 1898-99. *Oct. 1889*
See also Cumberland Gap; Great Smoky Mountains National Park; Oak Ridge

TENNESSEE (Battleship):

Victory's Portrait in the Marianas. By William Franklin Draper. Paintings by author. 599-616, *Nov. 1945*

TENNESSEE–TOMBIGBEE WATERWAY, Mississippi-Alabama:

The Tennessee-Tombigbee Waterway: Bounty or Boondoggle? By Carolyn Bennett Patterson. Photos by Sandy Felsenthal. Included: The Hidden Tenn-Tom: Bypassed But Still Striving. By Alice J. Hall. 364-387, *Mar. 1986*

TENNESSEE VALLEY AUTHORITY:

Whatever Happened to TVA? By Gordon Young. Photos by Emory Kristof. 830-863, *June 1973*

Around the "Great Lakes of the South." By Frederick Simpich. Photos by J. Baylor Roberts. 463-491, *Apr. 1948*

TENOC (Ten-year Oceanographic Program). *See* National Oceanographic Program

TENOCHTITLAN (Aztec Capital):

Following Cortés: Path to Conquest. By S. Jeffrey K. Wilkerson. Photos by Guillermo Aldana E. Paintings by Ned Seidler and Rosalie Seidler. 420-459, *Oct. 1984*

The Aztecs. 704-775. I. The Aztecs. By Bart McDowell. Photos by David Hiser. Paintings by Felipe Dávalos. 714-751; II. The Building of Tenochtitlan. By Augusto F. Molina Montes. Paintings by Felipe Dávalos. 753-765; III. New Finds in the Great Temple. By Eduardo Matos Moctezuma. Photos by David Hiser. 767-775, *Dec. 1980*

⊕ *Visitor's Guide to the Aztec World; Mexico and Central America. Dec. 1980*

TENOS (Island), Aegean Sea:

The Isles of Greece. By Richard Stillwell. 593-622, *May 1944*

TENZING NORGAY:

President Eisenhower Presents the Hubbard Medal to Everest's Conquerors. 64, *July 1954*

Triumph on Everest. 1-63. I. Siege and Assault. By Sir John Hunt. 1-43; II. The Conquest of the Summit. By Sir Edmund Hillary. 45-63, *July 1954*

TEOTIHUACÁN, Mexico:

South to Mexico City. By W. E. Garrett. 145-193, *Aug. 1968*

Mexico's Booming Capital. By Mason Sutherland. Photos by Justin Locke. 785-824, *Dec. 1951*

"Pyramids" of the New World. By Neil Merton Judd. 105-128, *Jan. 1948*

An Interesting Visit to the Ancient Pyramids of San Juan Teotihuacan. By A. C. Galloway. 1041-1050, *Dec. 1910*

TEPARY BEANS:

Rediscovering America's Forgotten Crops. By Noel D. Vietmeyer. Photos by Burgess Blevins. Paintings by Paul M. Breeden. 702-712, *May 1981*

TEPE GAWRA (Archaeological Site), Iraq:

Ancient Mesopotamia: A Light That Did Not Fail. By E. A. Speiser. Paintings by H. M. Herget. 41-105, *Jan. 1951*

TER GOES, The Netherlands. *See* Goes

TERCEIRA (Island), Azores:

American Airmen in the Azores. 177-184, *Feb. 1946*

TEREDOS:

Shipworms, Saboteurs of the Sea. By F. G. Walton Smith. 559-566, *Oct. 1956*

TERINGO, J. ROBERT: *Artist*

Caesarea Maritima. By Robert L. Hohlfelder. Photos by Bill Curtsinger. NGS research grant. 261-279, *Feb. 1987*

TERMINATION Land. By Edwin Swift Balch. 220-221, *May 1904*

TERMITES:

Termites: Dwellers in the Dark. By Glenn D. Prestwich. 532-547, *Apr. 1978*

TERNATE (Island), Moluccas, Indonesia:

Yankee Roams the Orient. By Irving and Electa Johnson. 327-370, *Mar. 1951*

TERNS:

Friend of the Wind: The Common Tern. By Ian Nisbet. Photos by Hope Alexander. 234-247, *Aug. 1973*

What A Place to Lay an Egg! By Thomas R. Howell. Contents: Fairy terns.

NGS research grant. 414-419, *Sept. 1971*

Sea Birds of Isla Raza. By Lewis Wayne Walker. Included: Elegant terns; Royal terns. 239-248, *Feb. 1951*

Blizzard of Birds: The Tortugas Terns. By Alexander Sprunt, Jr. Included: Noddy terns; Sooty terns. 213-230, *Feb. 1947*

Fairy Terns of the Atolls. By Lewis Wayne Walker. 807-814, *Dec. 1946*

Pelican Profiles. By Lewis Wayne Walker. Included: The gull-billed tern of the Salton Sea area, California. 589-598, *Nov. 1943*

TERRA, HELLMUT DE: *Author*

On the World's Highest Plateaus: Through an Asiatic No Man's Land to the Desert of Ancient Cathay. 319-367, *Mar. 1931*

TERRA-COTTA ARMY:

China's Incredible Find. By Audrey Topping. Paintings by Yang Hsien-min. Included: The first emperor's burial mound, with guardian army of terra-cotta men and horses. 440-459, *Apr. 1978*

TERRANES:

Our Restless Planet Earth. By Rick Gore. Photos by James A. Sugar. Painting by Ned M. Seidler. Text by Larry Kohl. 142-181, *Aug. 1985*

◈ The Shaping of a Continent: North America's Active West; Earth's Dynamic Crust. Included: Spreading, Subduction, Collision, Faulting, Accretion, Hot Spots, 90 Million Years of Drift. *Aug. 1985*

TERRANOVA:

16th-Century Basque Whalers in America. Photos by Bill Curtsinger. Paintings by Richard Schlecht. 40-71. I. Discovery in Labrador: A 16th-Century Basque Whaling Port and Its Sunken Fleet. 40-49; II. Unearthing Red Bay's Whaling History. By James A. Tuck. 50-57; III. Excavating a 400-year-old Basque Galleon. By Robert Grenier. 58-67; IV. The Indomitable Basques. By Robert Laxalt. 69-71, *July 1985*

TERRESTRIAL MAGNETISM. *See* Geomagnetism

TERRIERS:

Toy Dogs, Pets of Kings and Commoners. By Freeman Lloyd. 459-480, *Apr. 1944*

Man's Oldest Ally, the Dog: Since Cave-Dweller Days This Faithful Friend Has Shared the Work, Exploration, and Sport of Humankind. By Freeman Lloyd. Paintings by Edward Herbert Miner. Included: Airedale Terrier, Bedlington Terrier, Bull Terrier, Cairn Terrier, Dandie Dinmont Terrier, Irish Terrier, Kerry Blue Terrier, Lakeland Terrier, Manchester Terrier, Scottish Terrier, Sealyham Terrier, Skye Terrier, Smooth Fox Terrier, Welsh Terrier, West Highland White Terrier, Wire-haired Fox Terrier. 247-274, *Feb. 1936*

TERRILL, ROSS:

On Assignment in Australia. *Feb. 1988*

Author

Australia at 200. Photos by David Robert Austen. 181-211, *Feb. 1988*

Sichuan: Where China Changes Course. Photos by Cary Wolinsky. 280-317, *Sept. 1985*

TERRY, WILLIAM B. and GLADYS:
Photographers

Sinai Sheds New Light on the Bible. By Henry Field. 795-815, *Dec. 1948*

The **TESTING** of Arctic Currents. 404, *Nov. 1901*

TESTING the Currents of Lake Erie. By E. L. Moseley. 41-42, *Jan. 1903*

TETON RANGE, Wyoming:

Cloud Gardens in the Tetons. By Frank and John Craighead. 811-830, *June 1948*

See also Grand Teton National Park

TETRAHEDRAL KITES:

Aërial Locomotion: With a Few Notes of Progress in the Construction of an Aërodrome. By Alexander Graham Bell. 1-34, *Jan. 1907*

The Tetrahedral Kite. 294, *July 1903*

The Tetrahedral Principle in Kite Structure. By Alexander Graham Bell. 219-251, *June 1903*

TETRAHEDRAL TOWER:

Dr. Bell's Tetrahedral Tower. By Gilbert H. Grosvenor. 672-675, *Oct. 1907*

A **TEXAN** Teaches American History at Cambridge University. By J. Frank Dobie. 409-441, *Apr. 1946*

TEXAS:

Texas in Bloom. By Lady Bird Johnson. 493-499, *Apr. 1988*

Sam Houston: A Man Too Big for

Texans cool down under spray from a water hose at a Willie Nelson concert in the Cotton Bowl. GORDON W. GAHAN

Texas. By Bart McDowell. Photos by Charles O'Rear. Included: The Battle of San Jacinto. 311-329, *Mar. 1986*

◈ *Texas,* The Making of America series. On reverse: Weak Spanish Frontier, Eras of Independence, Vigorous Expansion, A Broadening Base, New Frontiers, Mexican Borderland. *Mar. 1986*

Life on the Line: U. S.-Mexican Border. By Mark Kramer. Photos by Danny Lehman. 720-749, *June 1985*

Dallas! By Griffin Smith, Jr. Photos by David Alan Harvey. 272-305, *Sept. 1984*

Texas West of the Pecos. By Griffin Smith, Jr. Photos by Dan Dry. 210-234, *Feb. 1984*

Where Oil and Wildlife Mix. By Steven C. Wilson and Karen C. Hayden. 145-173, *Feb. 1981*

The Mexican Americans: A People on the Move. By Griffin Smith, Jr. Photos by Stephanie Maze. 780-809, *June 1980*

Texas! By Howard La Fay. Photos by Gordon W. Gahan. 440-483, *Apr. 1980*

A Walk Across America: Part II. By Peter and Barbara Jenkins. 194-229, *Aug. 1979*

Guadalupe's Trails in Summer. By Edward Abbey. Contents: Guadalupe Mountains National Park. 135-141, *July 1979*

The Gulf's Workaday Waterway. By Gordon Young. Photos by Charles O'Rear. 200-223, *Feb. 1978*

Our Wild and Scenic Rivers: The Rio Grande. By Nathaniel T. Kenney. Photos by Bank Langmore. 46-51, *July 1977*

Big Thicket of Texas. By Don Moser. Photos by Blair Pittman. 504-529, *Oct. 1974*

North With the Wheat Cutters. By Noel Grove. Photos by James A. Sugar. 194-217, *Aug. 1972*

Two Wheels Along the Mexican Border. By William Albert Allard. 591-635, *May 1971*

Houston, Prairie Dynamo. By Stuart E. Jones. Photos by William Albert Allard. 338-377, *Sept. 1967*

Roseate Spoonbills, Radiant Birds of the Gulf Coast. By Robert Porter Allen. Photos by Frederick Kent Truslow. 274-288, *Feb. 1962*

The Fabulous State of Texas. By Stanley Walker. Photos by B. Anthony Stewart and Thomas Nebbia. 149-195, *Feb. 1961*

Whooping Cranes Fight for Survival. By Robert Porter Allen. Photos by Frederick Kent Truslow. Contents: Aransas National Wildlife Refuge. 650-669, *Nov. 1959*

Saving Man's Wildlife Heritage. By John H. Baker. Photos by Robert F. Sisson. Included: Audubon sanctuaries in Texas. 581-620, *Nov. 1954*

America Goes to the Fair. By Samuel W. Matthews. Included: Texas State Fair at Dallas. 293-333, *Sept. 1954*

We Captured a 'Live' Brontosaur. By Roland T. Bird. 707-722, *May 1954*

May storm drenches a farm on the Texas Gulf coast, where fertile land and abundant rain yield good crops. JOHN VACHON, O.W.I., OFFICIAL

Playing her part in Thailand's booming 1960s, a merchant in a boat named **Lucky Commerce** *sells vegetables to homes along the canals of Bangkok.* DEAN CONGER, NGS

Thermogram registers levels of infrared heat lost from buildings in Plymouth, Michigan. VANSCAN™ THERMOGRAM BY DAEDALUS ENTERPRISES, INC.

The Sumerian-style reed boat Tigris *burns in Djibouti after local wars and politics halted Thor Heyerdahl's voyage from southern Iraq into the Red Sea.* TIGRIS EXPEDITION

The Manx and Their Isle of Man. Photos by Ted H. Funk. 426-444, *Sept. 1972*

The Arans, Ireland's Invincible Isles. Photos by Winfield Parks. 545-573, *Apr. 1971*

THOMAS JEFFERSON: Architect of Freedom. By Mike W. Edwards. Photos by Linda Bartlett. 231-259, *Feb. 1976*

THOMASON, JOHN W., Jr.: *Author*

Approach to Peiping. 275-308, *Feb. 1936*

THOMPSON, A. H.:

Vice President. 165, *Apr. 1889*; 270, *July 1889*; 68, *Apr. 1890*; 134, *Jan. 1936*

Author

Geographic Nomenclature. Remarks by Herbert G. Ogden, Gustave Herrle, Marcus Baker, and A. H. Thompson. 261-278, *Aug. 1890*

THOMPSON, EDWARD H.: *Author*

The Home of a Forgotten Race: Mysterious Chichen Itza, in Yucatan, Mexico. 585-648, *June 1914*

Henequen–The Yucatan Fiber. 150-158, *Apr. 1903*

THOMPSON, J. CHARLES: *Photographer*

Trawling the China Seas. 381-395, *Mar. 1950*

THOMPSON, TIM: *Photographer*

New Day for Alaska's Pribilof Islanders. By Susan Hackley Johnson. 536-552, *Oct. 1982*

THOMPSON, WILLIAM:

On Assignment in Himalaya. *Nov. 1988*

Photographer

Roof of the World. 613-623, *Nov. 1988*

The Mighty Himalaya: A Fragile Heritage. By Barry C. Bishop. 624-631, *Nov. 1988*

Heavy Hands on the Land. By Larry Kohl. Photos by William Thompson and Galen Rowell. 633-651, *Nov. 1988*

At the Crossroads of Kathmandu. By Douglas H. Chadwick. 32-65, *July 1987*

THOMSON, DONALD F.: *Author-Photographer*

An Arnhem Land Adventure. 403-430, *Mar. 1948*

THOMSON, SIR J. J.:

The British Way. By Sir Evelyn Wrench. 421-541, *Apr. 1949*

THOMSON, J. P.: *Author*

The Islands of the Pacific. 543-558, *Dec. 1921*

THOR HEYERDAHL Sails in the Wake of Sumerian Voyagers. By Thor Heyerdahl. Photos by Carlo Mauri and the crew of the *Tigris*. 806-827, *Dec. 1978*

THOR HEYERDAHL'S Own Story of *Ra II*. Photos by Carlo Mauri and Georges Sourial. 44-71, *Jan. 1971*

THORARINSSON, SIGURDUR: *Author*

Surtsey: Island Born of Fire. 713-726, *May 1965*

THOREAU, HENRY DAVID:

Thoreau, a Different Man. By William Howarth. Photos by Farrell Grehan. 349-387, *Mar. 1981*

Literary Landmarks of Massachusetts. By William H. Nicholas. Photos by B. Anthony Stewart and John E. Fletcher. 279-310, *Mar. 1950*

Winter Rambles in Thoreau's Country. By Herbert W. Gleason. 165-180, *Feb. 1920*

THORNDIKE, TOWNSEND W.: *Author*

Game and Fur-Bearing Animals and Their Influence on the Indians of the Northwest. 431, *Oct. 1904*

THORNTON, WILLIAM M.: *Author*

Spottswood's Expedition of 1716. 265-269, *Aug. 1896*

THOROUGHBREDS:

Heart of the Bluegrass (Kentucky). By Charles McCarry. Photos by J. Bruce Baumann. 634-659, *May 1974*

THOSE Electrifying Eighteen Eighties When the National Geographic Society Was Born: "Tell me if your civilization is interesting." By William H. Goetzmann. Illustrated by Fred Otnes. 8-37, *Jan. 1988*

THOSE Eternal Austrians. By John J. Putman. Photos by Adam Woolfitt. 410-449, *Apr. 1985*

THOSE Fiery Brazilian Bees. By Rick Gore. Photos by Bianca Lavies. 491-501, *Apr. 1976*

THOSE *Inventive Americans*. 231 pages. ■■*1971*

THOSE Kangaroos! They're a Marvelous Mob. By Geoffrey B. Sharman.

Photos by Des and Jen Bartlett. 192-209, *Feb. 1979*

THOSE Marvelous, Myriad Diatoms. By Richard B. Hoover. 871-878, *June 1979*

THOSE Outlandish Goldfish! By Paul A. Zahl. 514-533, *Apr. 1973*

THOSE Popular Pandas. By Theodore H. Reed. Photos by Donna K. Grosvenor. 803-815, *Dec. 1972*

THOSE Proper and Other Bostonians. By Joseph Judge. Photos by Ted Spiegel. 352-381, *Sept. 1974*

THOSE Successful Japanese. By Bart McDowell. Photos by Fred Ward. 323-359, *Mar. 1974*

The **THOUSAND AND ONE NIGHTS** (The Arabian Nights Entertainments):

In the Wake of Sindbad. By Tim Severin. Photos by Richard Greenhill. 2-41, *July 1982*

The **THOUSAND-MILE** Glide. By Karl Striedieck. Photos by Otis Imboden. 431-438, *Mar. 1978*

THOUSAND-MILE Race to Nome: A Woman's Icy Struggle. By Susan Butcher. Photos by Kerby Smith. 411-422, *Mar. 1983*

A **THOUSAND** Miles Along the Great Wall of China: The Mightiest Barrier Ever Built by Man Has Stood Guard Over the Land of Chin for Twenty Centuries. By Adam Warwick. 113-143, *Feb. 1923*

THRACIANS:

Ancient Bulgaria's Golden Treasures. By Colin Renfrew. Photos by James L. Stanfield. Paintings by Jean-Leon Huens. 112-129, *July 1980*

THRASHERS:

Thrushes, Thrashers, and Swallows: Robins and Bluebirds are Familiar Members of a Famous Musical Family Which Includes the Hermit Thrush and European Nightingale. By T. Gilbert Pearson. Paintings by Allan Brooks. 523-546, *Apr. 1936*

THREATENED Glories of Everglades National Park. By Frederick Kent Truslow and Frederick G. Vosburgh. Photos by Frederick Kent Truslow and Otis Imboden. 508-553, *Oct. 1967*

THREATENED Treasures of the Nile. By Georg Gerster. 587-621, *Oct. 1963*

The **THREATENED** Ways of Kenya's Pokot People. By Elizabeth L. Meyerhoff. Photos by Murray Roberts. NGS research grant. 120-140, *Jan. 1982*

THREE Centuries of the Hudson's Bay Company–Canada's Fur-Trading Empire. By Peter C. Newman. Photos by Kevin Fleming. 192-229, *Aug. 1987*

Dressed in splendid robes, this shaman was believed by Tibetan lamas to embody a spirit with great physical strength. JOSEPH F. ROCK

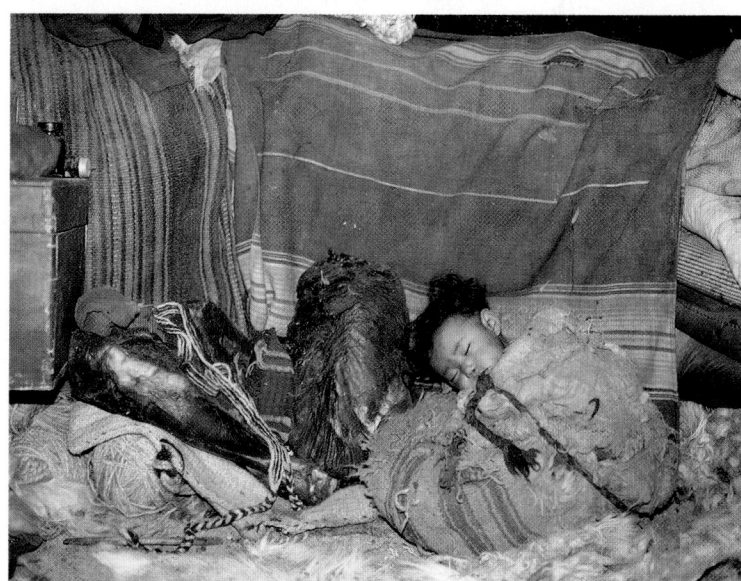

Secure in her loving and attentive extended family, a nomad girl of mountainous Tibet slumbers in a sheepskin cocoon beside dried yak meat. SORREL WILBY

TIBETAN BUDDHISM:

TIBETANS:

TIBURON (Island), Mexico:

TICONDEROGA, New York:

TIDAL BORES:

TIDAL WAVES. *See* Tsunamis

TIDES:

TIDEWATER AREA:

TIEMANN, DARWIN L.:

TIERRA DEL FUEGO (Archipelago), South America:

Guanacos: Wild Camels of South America. By William L. Franklin. NGS research grant. 63-75, *July 1981*

Housewife at the End of the World. By Rae Natalie P. Goodall. Photos by James L. Stanfield. 130-150, *Jan. 1971*

In the Wake of Darwin's *Beagle.* By Alan Villiers. Photos by James L. Stanfield. 449-495, *Oct. 1969*

Chile, the Long and Narrow Land. By Kip Ross. 185-235, *Feb. 1960*

Argentina: Young Giant of the Far South. By Jean and Franc Shor. 297-352, *Mar. 1958*

Inside Cape Horn. By Amos Burg. 743-783, *Dec. 1937*

A Longitudinal Journey Through Chile. By Harriet Chalmers Adams. 219-273, *Sept. 1922*

The Indian Tribes of Southern Patagonia, Tierra del Fuego, and the Adjoining Islands. By J. B. Hatcher. 12-22, *Jan. 1901*

The **TIES** That Bind: Our Natural Sympathy with English Traditions, the French Republic, and the Russian Outburst for Liberty. By John Sharp Williams. 281-286, *Mar. 1917*

TIFLIS, Georgian S.S.R., U.S.S.R.:

The Land of the Stalking Death: A Journey Through Starving Armenia on an American Relief Train. By Melville Chater. 393-420, *Nov. 1919*

TIGARA, Alaska:

Discovering Alaska's Oldest Arctic Town: A Scientist Finds Ivory-eyed Skeletons of a Mysterious People and Joins Modern Eskimos in the Dangerous Spring Whale Hunt. By Froelich G. Rainey. 319-336, *Sept. 1942*

TIGERS:

■ Land of the Tiger. 754, Dec. 1984; President's Page, cover, *Jan. 1985*

Tiger! Lord of the Indian Jungle. By Stanley Breeden. Photos by Belinda Wright. 748-773, *Dec. 1984*

India Struggles to Save Her Wildlife. By John J. Putman. 299-343, *Sept. 1976*

White Tiger in My House. By Elizabeth C. Reed. Photos by Donna K. Grosvenor. 482-491, *Apr. 1970*

Enchantress! (White Tigress). By Theodore H. Reed. Photos by Thomas J. Abercrombie. 628-641, *May 1961*

King of Cats and His Court. By Victor H. Cahalane. Paintings by Walter A. Weber. 217-259, *Feb. 1943*

The Warfare of the Jungle Folk: Campaigning Against Tigers, Elephants, and Other Wild Animals in Northern Siam. By Merian C. Cooper. Photos by Ernest B. Schoedsack. 233-268, *Feb. 1928*

Tiger-Hunting in India. By William Mitchell. 545-598, *Nov. 1924*

TIGRIS (River), Turkey-Iraq:

The Cradle of Civilization: The Historic Lands Along the Euphrates and Tigris Rivers Where Briton Is Fighting

Turk. By James Baikie. 127-162, *Feb. 1916*

Where Adam and Eve Lived. By Frederick and Margaret Simpich. 546-588, *Dec. 1914*

TIGRIS (Reed Ship):

■ The Voyage of the *Tigris.* 826, Dec. 1978; 1, Jan. 1979; cover, *Apr. 1979*

Tigris Sails Into the Past. By Thor Heyerdahl. Photos by Carlo Mauri and the crew of the *Tigris.* 806-827, *Dec. 1978*

TIHWA, Xinjiang Uygur Autonomous Region, China. *See* Ürümqi

TIJUANA, Mexico:

Two Wheels Along the Mexican Border. By William Albert Allard. 591-635, *May 1971*

TIKAL (Maya Ruin), Guatemala:

The Maya. 729-811. III. Resurrecting the Grandeur of Tikal. By William R. Coe. 792-798; IV. A Traveler's Tale of Ancient Tikal. Paintings by Peter

Spier. Text by Alice J. Hall. 799-811, *Dec. 1975*

Guatemala, Maya and Modern. By Louis de la Haba. Photos by Joseph J. Scherschel. 661-689, *Nov. 1974*

TIKOPIA (Island), Santa Cruz Islands:

Yankee Roams the Orient. By Irving and Electa Johnson. 327-370, *Mar. 1951*

TILEFISH:

The Relations of the Gulf Stream and the Labrador Current. By William Libbey, Junior. 161-166, *Jan. 31, 1894*

TILLING, ROBERT I.: *Author*

Volcanic Cloud May Alter Earth's Climate. 672-675, *Nov. 1982*

TIMBER:

Timber: How Much Is Enough? By John J. Putman. Photos by Bruce Dale. 485-511, *Apr. 1974*

Timberlines. By Israel C. Russell. 47-49, *Jan. 1904*

A tigress drinks from a forest pool in Kanha National Park, one of several sanctuaries created in India, where the tiger population has shrunk dramatically. BELINDA WRIGHT

Timber Lines. 80-81, *Feb. 1903*
See also Forests; Lumber Industry

TIMBER RATTLESNAKES:
Hidden Life of the Timber Rattler. By William S. Brown. Photos by Bianca Lavies. NGS research grant. 128-138, *July 1987*

TIMBER WOLVES. *See* Gray Wolves

TIMBUKTU (Tombouctou), Mali:
Timbuktu and Beyond: Desert City of Romantic Savor and Salt Emerges into World Life Again as Trading Post of France's Vast African Empire. By Laura C. Boulton. Included: Dusky Tribesmen of French West Africa. Photos by Enzo de Chetelat. 631-670, *May 1941*
Timbuktu, in the Sands of the Sahara. By Cecil D. Priest. 73-85, *Jan. 1924*

TIME and Again in Burma. By Bryan Hodgson. Photos by James L. Stanfield. 90-121, *July 1984*

TIME and Tide on the Thames. By Frederick Simpich. 239-272, *Feb. 1939*

TIME Catches Up With Mongolia. By Thomas B. Allen. Photos by Dean Conger. 242-269, *Feb. 1985*

TIME of Testing for Sri Lanka. By Robert Paul Jordan. Photos by Raghubir Singh. 123-150, *Jan. 1979*

TIME Turns Back in Picture-book Portofino. By Carleton Mitchell. Photos by Winfield Parks. 232-253, *Feb. 1965*

"TIME Will Not Dim the Glory of Their Deeds." Photos by W. Robert Moore. Contents: World War I memorials. 17-24, *Jan. 1934*

TIMEKEEPING:
The Tower of the Winds. By Derek J.

de Solla Price. Paintings by Robert C. Magis. NGS research grant. 587-596, *Apr. 1967*
Split-second Time Runs Today's World. By F. Barrows Colton and Catherine Bell Palmer. 399-428, *Sept. 1947*

The **TIMELESS** Arans: The Workaday World Lies Beyond the Horizon of Three Rocky Islets Off the Irish Coast. By Robert Cushman Murphy. 747-775, *June 1931*

TIMELY Articles and Maps Give Geographic Members Background of European Drama. 550, *Oct. 1939*

TIME'S Footprints in Tunisian Sands. By Maynard Owen Williams. 345-386, *Mar. 1937*

TIMOR (Island), Malay Archipelago:
East From Bali by Seagoing Jeep to Timor. By Helen and Frank Schreider. 236-279, *Aug. 1962*
Timor a Key to the Indies. By Stuart St. Clair. 355-384, *Sept. 1943*

TIN:
Malaya Meets Its Emergency. By George W. Long. Photos by J. Baylor Roberts. Included: Tin mining. 185-228, *Feb. 1953*
Bolivia–Tin Roof of the Andes. By Henry Albert Phillips. 309-332, *Mar. 1943*
Tin, the Cinderella Metal. By Alicia O'Reardon Overbeck. 659-684, *Nov. 1940*

TIN CAN ISLAND. *See* Niuafoō

TINAJAS ALTAS (Water Basins). *See* Yuma Trail

TINGMISSARTOQ (Seaplane):
Flying Around the North Atlantic. By Anne Morrow Lindbergh. Foreword by Charles A. Lindbergh. 259-337, *Sept. 1934*

TINIAN (Island), Mariana Islands, Pacific Ocean:
South from Saipan. By W. Robert Moore. 441-474, *Apr. 1945*
Springboards to Tokyo. By Willard Price. 385-407, *Oct. 1944*

TINKER, CLIFFORD ALBION:
Author
Lisbon, the City of the Friendly Bay. 505-552, *Nov. 1922*

TINKERS, Irish. *See* Appleby Fair

TINOS (Island), Greece:
The Isles of Greece: Aegean Birthplace of Western Culture. By Melville Bell Grosvenor. Photos by Edwin Stuart Grosvenor and Winfield Parks. 147-193, *Aug. 1972*

TINTAGEL, England:
Channel Ports–And Some Others. By Florence Craig Albrecht. 1-55, *July 1915*

TIPTON, ABIGAIL:
On Assignment in Australia. *Feb. 1988*

TIRELESS Voyager, the Whistling Swan. By William J. L. Sladen. Photos by Bianca Lavies. NGS research grant. 134-147, *July 1975*

TIRNOVA, Bulgaria:
Tirnova, the City of Hanging Gardens. By Felix J. Koch. 632-640, *Oct. 1907*

TIROL (Region), Austria-Italy:
Tirol, Austria's Province in the Clouds. By Peter T. White. Photos by Volkmar Wentzel. 107-141, *July 1961*
A Stroll to Venice. By Isobel Wylie Hutchison. 378-410, *Sept. 1951*
Occupied Austria, Outpost of Democracy. By George W. Long. Photos by Volkmar Wentzel. 749-790, *June 1951*
This Was Austria. 71-86, *July 1945*
Over the Alps to Brenner Pass. 701-714, *Dec. 1943*

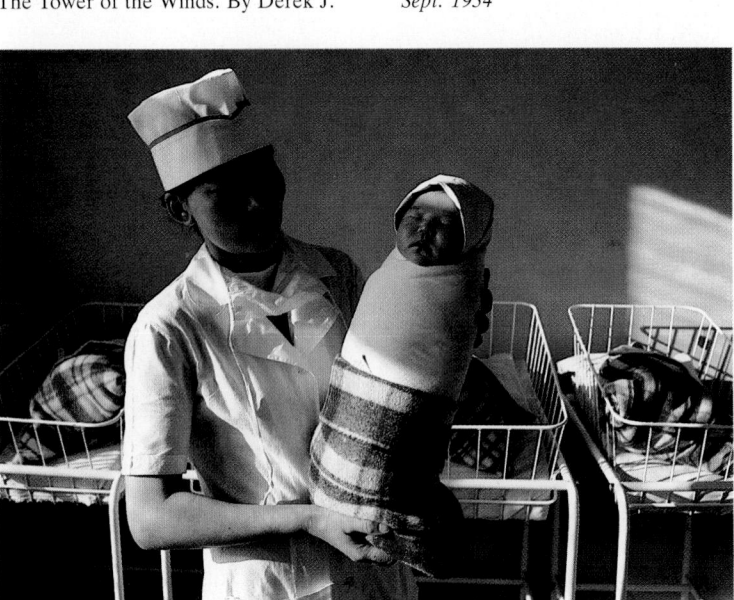

Time catches up with sparsely populated Mongolia: In the move toward modernization a healthy birthrate is seen as crucial to national development. DEAN CONGER, NGS

Merry Maskers of Imst. Photos by Francis C. Fuerst. 201-208, *Aug. 1936*

Entering the Front Doors of Medieval Towns: The Adventures of an American Woman and Her Daughter in a Folding Boat on Eight Rivers of Germany and Austria. By Cornelia Parker. Included: Tyrol, the Happy Mountain Land. Photos by Hans Hildenbrand. 365-394, *Mar. 1932*

Austro-Italian Mountain Frontiers. By Florence Craig Albrecht. 321-376, *Apr. 1915*

The Land of Contrast: Austria-Hungary. By D. W. and A. S. Iddings. 1188-1217, 1284, *Dec. 1912*

TIROS I (Weather Satellite):

Our Earth as a Satellite Sees It. By W. G. Stroud. 293-302, *Aug. 1960*

TISDEL, EDINE FRANCES: *Author*

Guatemala, the Country of the Future. 596-624, *July 1910*

TITAN (Rock Spire), Fisher Towers, Utah:

We Climbed Utah's Skyscraper Rock. By Huntley Ingalls. Photos by author and Barry C. Bishop. 705-721, *Nov. 1962*

TITAN II (Rocket). *See* Gemini Missions

TITANIC, R.M.S.:

Editorial. By Wilbur E. Garrett. 691, *Dec. 1987*

Epilogue for *Titanic.* By Robert D. Ballard. 454-463, *Oct. 1987*

◖ Secrets of the *Titanic.* President's Page. By Gilbert M. Grosvenor. *Jan. 1987*

Editorial. By Wilbur E. Garrett. 697, *Dec. 1986*

A Long Last Look at *Titanic.* By Robert D. Ballard. Included: High-tech partners plumb new depths; Poignant relics of a disaster. Illustrations text by Cliff Tarpy. 698-727, *Dec. 1986*

Tectonics to *Titanic.* President's Page. By Gilbert M. Grosvenor. *Dec. 1985*

Robot records the manned submersible **Alvin** *taking a last look at the sunken* **Titanic** *in 1986.* ROBERT D. BALLARD AND MARTIN BOWEN, © WOODS HOLE OCEANOGRAPHIC INSTITUTION

Editorial. By Wilbur E. Garrett. 695, *Dec. 1985*

How We Found *Titanic.* By Robert D. Ballard in association with Jean-Louis Michel. 696-719, *Dec. 1985*

TITICACA, Lake, Bolivia-Peru:

The High Andes: South America's Islands in the Sky. By Loren McIntyre. 422-459, *Apr. 1987*

The Lost Empire of the Incas. By Loren McIntyre. Art by Ned and Rosalie Seidler. 729-787, *Dec. 1973*

Titicaca, Abode of the Sun. By Luis Marden. Photos by Flip Schulke. 272-294, *Feb. 1971*

Flamboyant Is the Word for Bolivia. By Loren McIntyre. 153-195, *Feb. 1966*

Sky-high Bolivia. 481-496, *Oct. 1950*

The Heart of Aymará Land: A Visit to Tiahuanacu, Perhaps the Oldest City of the New World, Lost Beneath the Drifting Sand of Centuries in the Bolivian Highlands. By Stewart E. McMillin. 213-256, *Feb. 1927*

Some Wonderful Sights in the Andean Highlands: The Oldest City in America. Sailing on the Lake of the Clouds: The Yosemite of Peru. By Harriet Chalmers Adams. 597-618, *Sept. 1908*

TITMICE:

Winged Denizens of Woodland, Stream, and Marsh. By Alexander Wetmore. Paintings by Allan Brooks. 577-596, *May 1934*

TITO, JOSIP BROZ:

Yugoslavia: Six Republics in One. By Robert Paul Jordan. Photos by James P. Blair. 589-633, *May 1970*

Yugoslavia's Window on the Adriatic. By Gilbert M. Grosvenor. 219-247, *Feb. 1962*

TITTMANN, O. H.:

Board of Managers. 270, July 1889; 87, Feb. 1905; 211, Feb. 1911; 640, *Nov. 1944*

Charter member of NGS. 793, *June 1934*

President. 218, *Feb. 1915*

Speech. 272-298, *Mar. 1912*

Vice President. 88, *Jan. 1910*

Portrait. 37, *Jan. 1901*

Author

Progress in Surveying the United States. 110-112, *Feb. 1906*

Ketchikan. 508-509, *Nov. 1905*

The U. S. Coast and Geodetic Survey. 1-9, *Jan. 1903*

The Definite Location of Bouvet Island. 413-414, *Oct. 1899*

Jobos Harbor. 206, *June 1899*

A Brief Account of the Geographic Work of the U. S. Coast and Geodetic Survey. By T. C. Mendenhall and Otto H. Tittmann. 294-299, *Oct. 1897*

TIVOLI, Copenhagen, Denmark:

Denmark, Field of the Danes. By William Graves. Photos by Thomas Nebbia. 245-275, *Feb. 1974*

Private-school student waits for her train at Tokyo's Shinjuku station, Japan's largest, used by almost a quarter of the capital's 12 million residents every day. DAVID ALAN HARVEY

Copenhagen, Wedded to the Sea. By Stuart E. Jones. Photos by Gilbert M. Grosvenor. 45-79, *Jan. 1963*

TIWIS:

Expedition to the Land of the Tiwi. By Charles P. Mountford. NGS research grant. 417-440, *Mar. 1956*

TLAPEHUALA, Mexico:

Down Mexico's Río Balsas. By John W. Webber. Photos by author, Kenneth Segerstrom, and Jack Breed. 253-272, *Aug. 1946*

TLAXCALANS:

Following Cortés: Path to Conquest. By S. Jeffrey K. Wilkerson. Photos by Guillermo Aldana E. Paintings by Ned Seidler and Rosalie Seidler. 420-459, *Oct. 1984*

TLINGIT INDIANS:

Alaska's Southeast: A Place Apart. By Bill Richards. 50-87, *Jan. 1984*
New Day for Alaska's Pribilof Islanders. By Susan Hackley Johnson. Photos by Tim Thompson. 536-552, *Oct. 1982*
Alaska's Marine Highway: Ferry Route to the North. By W. E. Garrett. 776-819, *June 1965*
Indians of Our North Pacific Coast. By Matthew W. Stirling. Paintings by W. Langdon Kihn. 25-52, *Jan. 1945*

"**TO** Be Indomitable, To be Joyous": Greece. By Peter T. White. Photos by James P. Blair. 360-393, *Mar. 1980*

TO Bogotá and Back by Air: The Narrative of a 9,500-Mile Flight from Washington, Over Thirteen Latin-American Countries and Return, in the Single-Seater Airplane "Spirit of St. Louis." By Charles A. Lindbergh. 529-601, *May 1928*

TO Europe with a Racing Start. By Carleton Mitchell. 758-791, *June 1958*

TO Gilbert Grosvenor: a Monthly Monument 25 Miles High. By Frederick G. Vosburgh and the staff of the National Geographic Society. 445-487, *Oct. 1966*

TO Heal a Nation. By Joel L. Swerdlow. 555-573, *May 1985*

TO Live in Harlem.... By Frank Hercules. Photos by LeRoy Woodson, Jr. 178-207, *Feb. 1977*

TO Market in Guatemala. By Luis Marden. Photos by Giles Greville Healey and Charles S. Pineo. 87-104, *July 1945*

TO Scotland Afoot Along the Pennine Way. By David Yeadon. Photos by Annie Griffiths. 388-418, *Mar. 1986*

TO Seek the Unknown in the Arctic: United States Navy Fliers to Aid MacMillan Expedition Under the Auspices of the National Geographic Society in Exploring Vast Area. 673-675, *June 1925*

TO 76,000 Feet by *Strato-Lab* Balloon. By Malcolm D. Ross and M. Lee Lewis. 269-282, *Feb. 1957*

TO the Depths of the Sea by Bathyscaphe. By Jacques-Yves Cousteau. NGS research grant. 67-79, *July 1954*

TO the Land of the Head-hunters. By E. Thomas Gilliard. NGS research grant. 437-486, *Oct. 1955*

TO the Memory of Our Beloved President, Friend to All Mankind. 1A-1B, *Jan. 1964*

TO the Men at South Pole Station. By Richard E. Byrd. 1-4, *July 1957*

TO the Mountains of the Moon. By Kenneth F. Weaver. Photos from NASA. 233-265, *Feb. 1972*

TO Torre Egger's Icy Summit. By Jim Donini. 813-823, *Dec. 1976*

TOADS:

Voices of the Night. By Arthur A. Allen. Included: Canadian toad, Common toad, Common tree toad, Oak toad, Spadefoot toad, Western toad. NGS research grant. 507-522, *Apr. 1950*
Our Friend the Frog. By Doris M. Cochran. Paintings by Hashime Murayama. 629-654, *May 1932*

TOADSTOOLS:

Bizarre World of the Fungi. By Paul A. Zahl. 502-527, *Oct. 1965*

TOBA, Lake, Sumatra (Island), Indonesia:

By Motor Through the East Coast and Batak Highlands of Sumatra. By Melvin A. Hall. 69-102, *Jan. 1920*

TOBACCO:

The Bulgarians. By Boyd Gibbons. Photos by James L. Stanfield. 91-111, *July 1980*
Home to North Carolina. By Neil Morgan. Photos by Bill Weems. 333-359, *Mar. 1980*
Inside Cuba Today. By Fred Ward. 32-69, *Jan. 1977*
Heart of the Bluegrass. By Charles McCarry. Photos by J. Bruce Baumann. 634-659, *May 1974*
Yesterday Lingers Along the Connecticut. By Charles McCarry. Photos by David L. Arnold. 334-369, *Sept. 1972*
North Carolina, Dixie Dynamo. By Malcolm Ross. Photos by B. Anthony Stewart. 141-183, *Feb. 1962*
Cuba–American Sugar Bowl. By Melville Bell Grosvenor. 1-56, *Jan. 1947*
Cuba–The Sugar Mill of the Antilles. By William Joseph Showalter. Included: Tobacco lands of Pinar del Rio. 1-33, *July 1920*
Helping the Farmers. 82-85, *Feb. 1905*

TOBAGO (Island), West Indies. *See* Trinidad and Tobago

TOBIAS, PHILIP V.:

On Assignment in South Africa. *Nov. 1985*

TOBIEN, WILHELM: *Photographer*
Demolishing Germany's North Sea Ramparts. 637-644, *Nov. 1946*
Life and Luster of Berlin. Photos by Wilhelm Tobien and Hans Hildenbrand. 147-177, *Feb. 1937*
The Azores, Communications Hub of the Atlantic. 41-48, *Jan. 1935*
Mirrors of Madeira, Rock Garden of the Atlantic. 89-96, *July 1934*
Palaces and Peasants in Rome's Old Colony. 439-446, *Apr. 1934*
Romania, Land of Color and Contrast. 415-422, *Apr. 1934*
Nooks and Bays Around the Zuider Zee. 301-308, *Sept. 1933*
Tulip Time in the Netherlands. 325-332, *Sept. 1933*

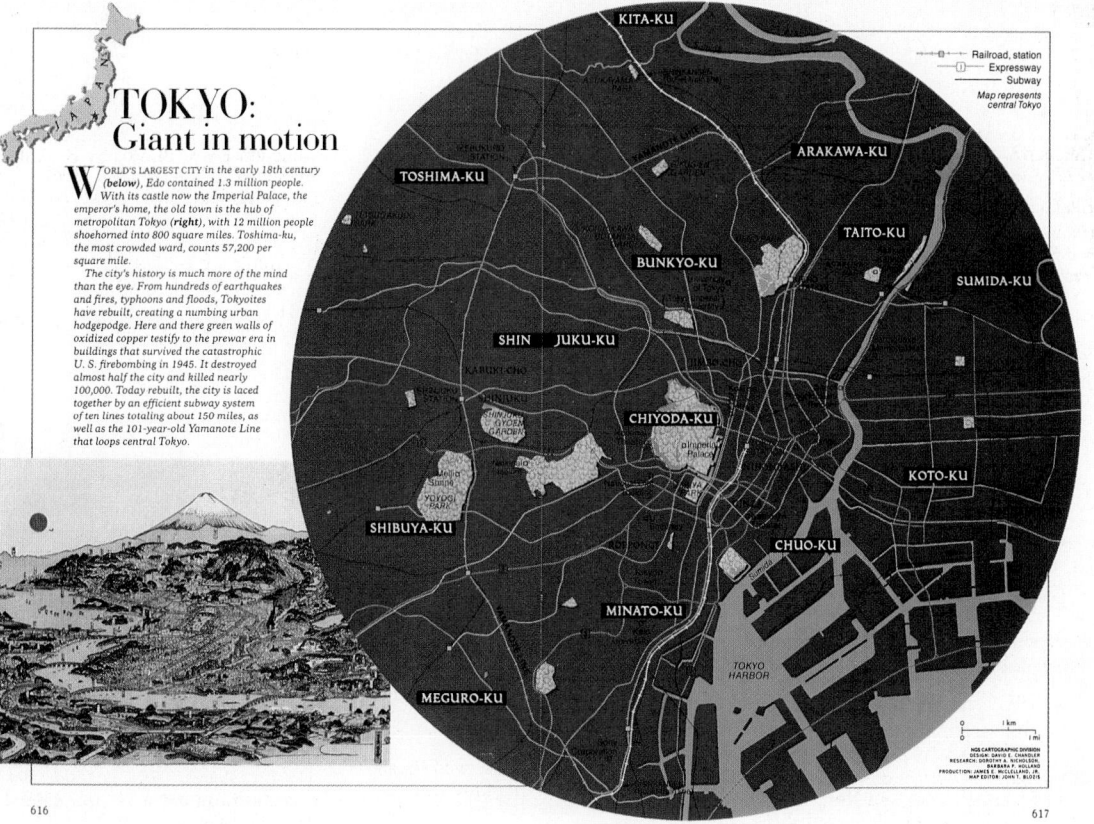

KITA-KU

Railroad, station
Expressway
Subway
Map represents central Tokyo

TOKYO:
Giant in motion

WORLD'S LARGEST CITY in the early 18th century (below), Edo contained 1.3 million people. With its castle now the Imperial Palace, the emperor's home, the old town is the hub of metropolitan Tokyo (right), with 12 million people shoehorned into 800 square miles. Toshima-ku, the most crowded ward, counts 57,200 per square mile.

The city's history is much more of the mind than the eye. From hundreds of earthquakes and fires, typhoons and floods, Tokyoites have rebuilt, creating a numbing urban hodgepodge. Here and there green walls of oxidized copper testify to the prewar era in buildings that survived the catastrophic U. S. firebombing in 1945. It destroyed almost half the city and killed nearly 100,000. Today rebuilt, the city is laced together by an efficient subway system of ten lines totaling about 150 miles, as well as the 101-year-old Yamanote Line that loops central Tokyo.

ARAKAWA-KU
TOSHIMA-KU
TAITO-KU
BUNKYO-KU
SUMIDA-KU
SHIN JUKU-KU
CHIYODA-KU
KOTO-KU
SHIBUYA-KU
CHUO-KU
MINATO-KU
TOKYO HARBOR
MEGURO-KU

616 617

Old town of Edo, at left, and its castle, now the emperor's Imperial Palace, sit at the center of modern metropolitan Tokyo.

Tokyo, the Peaceful Explosion. By William Graves. Photos by Winfield Parks. 445-487, *Oct. 1964*

Japan, the Exquisite Enigma. By Franc Shor. 733-777, *Dec. 1960*

The Yankee Sailor Who Opened Japan. By Ferdinand Kuhn. 85-102, *July 1953*

Japan Tries Freedom's Road. By Frederick G. Vosburgh. Photos by J. Baylor Roberts. 593-632, *May 1950*

Operation Eclipse: 1948. By William A. Kinney. Note: Tokyo's location error was discovered by expedition scientists. NGS research grant. 325-372, *Mar. 1949*

Sunset in the East. By Blair A. Walliser. 797-812, *June 1946*

Behind the Mask of Modern Japan. By Willard Price. 513-535, *Nov. 1945*

South from Saipan. By W. Robert Moore. Included: Aerial photo of Tokyo. 441-474, *Apr. 1945*

Japan, Child of the World's Old Age: An Empire of Mountainous Islands, Whose Alert People Constantly Conquer Harsh Forces of Land, Sea, and Sky. By William Elliott Griffis. 257-301, *Mar. 1933*

Tokyo To-day. By William R. Castle, Jr. 131-162, *Feb. 1932*

Sakurajima, Japan's Greatest Volcanic Eruption: A Convulsion of Nature Whose Ravages Were Minimized by Scientific Knowledge, Compared with the Terrors and Destruction of the Recent Tokyo Earthquake. By Thomas Augustus Jaggar. 441-470, *Apr. 1924*

TOKYO BAY, Japan:

The Yankee Sailor Who Opened Japan. By Ferdinand Kuhn. 85-102, *July 1953*

TOLEDO, Spain:

Toledo–El Greco's Spain Lives On. By Louise E. Levathes. Photos by James P. Blair. Included: The Genius of El Greco. Introduction by J. Carter Brown. 736-744. 726-753, *June 1982*

TOLLUND MAN:

Lifelike Man Preserved 2,000 Years in Peat. By P. V. Glob. 419-430, *Mar. 1954*

TOLOSA, CONDE DE (Spanish Galleon):

Graveyard of the Quicksilver Galleons. By Mendel Peterson. Photos by Jonathan Blair. 850-876, *Dec. 1979*

TOLSTOY, ILIA: *Author*

Across Tibet from India to China. 169-222, *Aug. 1946*

TOLSTOY, LEO NIKOLAYEVICH:

The World of Tolstoy. By Peter T. White. Photos by Sam Abell. 758-791, *June 1986*

TOLTECS:

The Luster of Ancient Mexico. By William H. Prescott. 1-32, *July 1916*

An Interesting Visit to the Ancient Pyramids of San Juan Teotihuacan. By A. C. Galloway. 1041-1050, *Dec. 1910*

See also Teotihuacán

TOM SAWYER'S Town. By Jerry Allen. 121-140, *July 1956*

TOMASZEWSKI, TOMASZ:

On Assignment in the United States. *Jan. 1988*

On Assignment in Poland. *Sept. 1986*

Photographer

Discovering America. By Małgorzata Niezabitowska. 44-79, *Jan. 1988*

Remnants: The Last Jews of Poland. By Małgorzata Niezabitowska. 362-389, *Sept. 1986*

TOMBOUCTOU, Mali. *See* former name, Timbuktu

TOMBS:

Discovering the New World's Richest Unlooted Tomb. By Walter Alva. Photos by Bill Ballenberg. Paintings by Ned Seidler. NGS research grant. Contents: Tomb of a Moche lord. 510-549, *Oct. 1988*

Iconography of the Moche: Unraveling the Mystery of the Warrior-Priest. By Christopher B. Donnan. 551-555, *Oct. 1988*

The Eternal Etruscans. By Rick Gore. Photos by O. Louis Mazzatenta. Paintings by James M. Gurney. 696-743, *June 1988*

Riddle of the Pyramid Boats. By Peter Miller. Photos by Victor R. Boswell, Jr. 534-550, *Apr. 1988*

The Mummies of Qilakitsoq. By Jens P. Hart Hansen, Jørgen Meldgaard, and Jørgen Nordqvist. 191-207, *Feb. 1985*

Río Azul. 420-465. Photos by George F. Mobley. I. Lost City of the Maya. By Richard E. W. Adams. NGS research grant. Included: Realm of the Maya (map). 420-451; II. Looters Rob Graves and History. By Ian Graham. 452-461; III. In Defense of the Collector. By Gillett G. Griffin. 462-465, *Apr. 1986*

Ancient Bulgaria's Golden Treasures. By Colin Renfrew. Photos by James L. Stanfield. Paintings by Jean-Leon Huens. 112-129, *July 1980*

Treasure From a Celtic Tomb. By Jörg Biel. Photos by Volkmar Wentzel. 428-438, *Mar. 1980*

Regal Treasures From a Macedonian Tomb. By Manolis Andronicos. Photos by Spyros Tsavdaroglou. 55-77, *July 1978*

China's Incredible Find. By Audrey Topping. Paintings by Yang Hsienmin. Included: The first emperor's burial mound, with terra-cotta soldiers and horses. 440-459, *Apr. 1978*

Egypt: Two Perspectives. 293-343. I. Legacy of a Dazzling Past. By Alice J. Hall. 293-311; II. Omens for a Better Tomorrow. By Thomas J. Abercrombie. 312-343, *Mar. 1977*

Fresh Treasures from Egypt's Ancient Sands. By Jefferson Caffery. Photos by David S. Boyer. 611-650, *Nov. 1955*

An Archeologist Looks at Palestine. By Nelson Glueck. 739-752, *Dec. 1947*

Finding the Tomb of a Warrior-God. By William Duncan Strong. Photos by Clifford Evans, Jr. 453-482, *Apr. 1947*

Exploration party returns from visiting Japan's Sakurajima (now Ontake) volcano in 1914; an earthquake nine years later devastated unprepared Tokyo. OSAKA MAINICHI SHIMBUN

Secrets from Syrian Hills: Explorations Reveal World's Earliest Known Alphabet, Deciphered from Schoolboy Slates and Dictionaries of 3,000 Years Ago. By Claude F. A. Schaeffer. 97-126, *July 1933*

Monte Albán, Richest Archeological Find in America: A Tomb in Oaxaca, Mexico, Yields Treasures Which Reveal the Splendid Culture of the Mixtecs. By Alfonso Caso. 487-512, *Oct. 1932*

Malta: The Halting Place of Nations: First Account of Remarkable Prehistoric Tombs and Temples Recently Unearthed on the Island. By William Arthur Griffiths. 445-478, *May 1920*

China's Treasures. By Frederick McCormick. 996-1040, *Oct. 1912*

Mukden, the Manchu Home, and Its Great Art Museum. By Eliza R. Scidmore. 289-320, *Apr. 1910*

See also Arlington National Cemetery; Egypt, ancient; Etruscans; Han Dynasty Tombs; La Venta; Maya; Petra; Pyramids; Taj Mahal; Ur

TOMBSTONE, Arizona:

From Tucson to Tombstone. By Mason Sutherland. 343-384, *Sept. 1953*

TOMORROW on the Deep Frontier. By Edwin A. Link. NGS research grant. 778-801, *June 1964*

TOMSK, Siberia (Region), U.S.S.R.:

Western Siberia and the Altai Mountains: With Some Speculations on the Future of Siberia. By James Bryce. 469-507, *May 1921*

TONDORF, FRANCIS A.: *Author*

How the Earth Telegraphed Its Tokyo Quake to Washington. 453-454, *Oct. 1923*

TONGA ISLANDS, Pacific Ocean:

Problems in Paradise. By Mary and Laurance S. Rockefeller. Photos by Thomas Nebbia. 782-793, *Dec. 1974*

Coronations a World Apart. By the Editor. 299, *Mar. 1968*

South Seas' Tonga Hails a King. By Melville Bell Grosvenor. Photos by Edwin Stuart Grosvenor. 322-343, *Mar. 1968*

The Friendly Isles of Tonga. By Luis Marden. 345-367, *Mar. 1968*

Living on a Volcano: An Unspoiled Patch of Polynesia Is Niuafoʻou, Nicknamed "Tin Can Island" by Stamp Collectors. By Thomas A. Jaggar. 91-106, *July 1935*

Falcon, the Pacific's Newest Island. By J. Edward Hoffmeister and Harry S. Ladd. 757-766, *Dec. 1928*

The Dream Ship: The Story of a Voyage of Adventure More Than Half Around the World in a 47-foot Lifeboat. By Ralph Stock. 1-52, *Jan. 1921*

TONGAREVA (Penrhyn), Pacific Ocean:

On the Bottom of a South Sea Pearl Lagoon. By Roy Waldo Miner. Paintings by Else Bostelmann. 365-390, *Sept. 1938*

Youngsters peek inside an Etruscan tomb in Tarquinia, Italy. A fresco depicting underworld demons frames the entrance. O. LOUIS MAZZATENTA, NGS

Sailing the Seven Seas in the Interest of Science: Adventures Through 157,000 Miles of Storm and Calm, from Arctic to Antarctic and Around the World, in the Non-magnetic Yacht "Carnegie." By J. P. Ault. 631-690, *Dec. 1922*

TONGSA JONG (Fort), Bhutan:

Castles in the Air: Experiences and Journeys in Unknown Bhutan. By John Claude White. 365-455, *Apr. 1914*

TONKIN, Vietnam:

Along the Old Mandarin Road of Indo-China. By W. Robert Moore. 157-199, *Aug. 1931*

TONLÉ SAP (Lake and River), Kampuchea:

The Temples of Angkor. 548-589. I. Will They Survive? Introduction by Wilbur E. Garrett. 548-551. II. Ancient Glory in Stone. By Peter T. White. Photos by Wilbur E. Garrett. 552-589, *May 1982*

Cambodia: Indochina's "Neutral" Corner. By Thomas J. Abercrombie. 514-551, *Oct. 1964*

Angkor, Jewel of the Jungle. By W. Robert Moore. Paintings by Maurice Fiévet. 517-569, *Apr. 1960*

TOOGOOD, STANLEY: *Author*

Southampton–Gateway to London: The Port of Double Tides Where the "Mayflower" Moored is Rich in Sea History and Lore of Early England. 91-114, *Jan. 1940*

TOOL-USING ANIMALS:

Aha! It Really Works! By Robert F. Sisson. Contents: A heron fishes with bait. 143-147, *Jan. 1974*

Return of the Sea Otter. By Karl W.

Kenyon. Photos by James A. Mattison, Jr. 520-539, *Oct. 1971*

Tool-using Bird: The Egyptian Vulture. By Baroness Jane van Lawick-Goodall. Photos by Baron Hugo van Lawick. 631-641, *May 1968*

The Galapagos, Eerie Cradle of New Species. By Roger Tory Peterson. Photos by Alan and Joan Root. Included: Tool-using finches. 541-585, *Apr. 1967*

See also Chimpanzees

TOOLS, Primitive:

The Search for the First Americans. By Thomas Y. Canby. Photos by Kerby Smith. Paintings by Roy Andersen. 330-363, *Sept. 1979*

The Tasadays, Stone Age Cavemen of Mindanao. By Kenneth MacLeish. Photos by John Launois. 219-249, *Aug. 1972*

First Glimpse of a Stone Age Tribe. 881-882, *Dec. 1971*

Brazil Protects Her Cinta Larga Indians. By W. Jesco von Puttkamer. 420-444, *Sept. 1971*

New Light on a Forgotten Past. By Wilhelm G. Solheim II. Contents: Hoabinhian Culture. 330-339, *Mar. 1971*

See also Asmat Tribespeople; Clovis Points; Ice Age Man

The **TOP** End of Down Under. By Kenneth MacLeish. Photos by Thomas Nebbia. 145-174, *Feb. 1973*

TOP of the World: Once Immutable, Now Threatened. By Barry C. Bishop. Photos by William Thompson. 612-631, *Nov. 1988*

TOPOGRAPHIC SURVEYS. See Surveying

TOPOGRAPHY:

Topographic Maps Issued by the

Geological Survey in 1907. 226-227, *Mar. 1908*

Topographic Work of the U. S. Geological Survey in 1902. 326-328, *Aug. 1902*

The Topographic Atlas of the United States. By W J McGee. 343-344, *July 1898*

Cuba. By Robert T. Hill. 193-242, *May 1898*

Descriptive Topographic Terms of Spanish America. By Robert T. Hill. 291-302, *Sept. 1896*

The Improvement of Geographical Teaching. By William Morris Davis. 68-75, *July 10, 1893*

An Expedition through the Yukon District. By Charles Willard Hayes. 117-159, *May 15, 1892*

Report on Topographic Work (Mount St. Elias Expedition). By Mark B. Kerr. 195, *May 29, 1891*

Round About Asheville (North Carolina). By Bailey Willis. 291-300, *Oct. 1889*

The Rivers and Valleys of Pennsylvania. By William Morris Davis. 183-253, *July 1889*

Topographic Models. By Cosmos Mindeleff. 254-268, *July 1889*

Geographic Methods in Geologic Investigation. By W. M. Davis. 11-26, *Oct. 1888*

The Classification of Geographic Forms by Genesis. By W J McGee. 27-36, *Oct. 1888*

TOPPING, AUDREY: *Author*

China's Incredible Find. Paintings by Yang Hsien-min. 440-459, *Apr. 1978*

Author-Photographer
Return to Changing China. 801-833, *Dec. 1971*

TOPS:

A Primitive Gyroscope in Liberia. By G. N. Collins. 531-535, *June 1910*

TOPSOIL:

Editorial. By Wilbur E. Garrett. 271, *Sept. 1984*

Do We Treat Our Soil Like Dirt? By Boyd Gibbons. Photos by Steven C. Wilson. 350-389, *Sept. 1984*

TORADJA TRIBESPEOPLE:

Life and Death in Tana Toradja. By Pamela and Alfred Meyer. 793-815, *June 1972*

Life and Death in Toradjaland (Celebes). Photos by Maynard Owen Williams and Helène Fischer. 65-80, *July 1940*

TORBERT, JOHN B.: *Author*

Africa the Largest Game Preserve in the World. 445-448, *Nov. 1900*

TORCHBEARERS of the Twilight. By Frederick G. Vosburgh. 697-704, *May 1951*

TORDAY, E.: *Author*

Curious and Characteristic Customs of Central African Tribes (Belgian Congo). 342-368, *Oct. 1919*

Among the Cannibals of Belgian Kongo. 969-971, *Nov. 1910*

TORIES:

The Loyalists. By Kent Britt. Photos by Ted Spiegel. 510-539, *Apr. 1975*

TORII GATE, Japan. Enlargement for framing. 982, *Nov. 1911*

TORLANINI, ENRICO:

The Speediest Boat. 875-878, *Sept. 1911*

TORNADOES:

Tornado! By Peter Miller. Photos by Chris Johns. Included: Map of tornado activity, 1950-1985; Diagram of tornado dynamics. 690-715, *June 1987*

We're Doing Something About the Weather! By Walter Orr Roberts. 518-555, *Apr. 1972*

Forecasting the Weather and Storms. By Willis L. Moore. 255-305, *June 1905*

TORNOW, MAX L.: *Author*

The Economic Condition of the Philippines. 33-64, *Feb. 1899*

TORONTO, Ontario, Canada:

Ontario, Canada's Keystone. By David S. Boyer. Photos by Sam Abell and the author. 760-795, *Dec. 1978*

Toronto: Canada's Dowager Learns to Swing. By Ethel A. Starbird. Photos by Robert W. Madden. 190-215, *Aug. 1975*

Canada's Dynamic Heartland, Ontario. By Marjorie Wilkins Campbell. Photos by Winfield Parks. 58-97, *July 1963*

Ontario, Pivot of Canada's Power. By Andrew H. Brown. Photos by B. Anthony Stewart and Bates Littlehales. 823-852, *Dec. 1953*

Ontario, Next Door: Alert, Energetic, and Resourceful, Its British Pluck and Skill in Arts and Trades Gain for This Province a High Place Under the Union Jack. By Frederick Simpich. 131-183, *Aug. 1932*

The Toronto Meeting of the British Association for the Advancement of Science. By John Hyde. 247-251, *Sept. 1897*

Royal Ontario Museum of Geology and Mineralogy: Expedition. *See* Chubb Crater

See also Little Norway (Training Center)

TORRE EGGER (Mountain), Argentina-Chile:

To Torre Egger's Icy Summit. By Jim Donini. 813-823, *Dec. 1976*

TORRE SGARRATA EXPEDITION: Italy:

Ancient Shipwreck Yields New Facts–and a Strange Cargo. By Peter Throckmorton. Photos by Kim Hart and Joseph J. Scherschel. 282-300, *Feb. 1969*

TÓRSHAVN, Faeroe Islands:

The Faeroes, Isles of Maybe. By Ernle Bradford. Photos by Adam Woolfitt. 410-442, *Sept. 1970*

TORTOISES:

Giant Tortoises: Goliaths of the Galapagos. By Craig MacFarland. Photos

by author and Jan MacFarland. 632-649, *Nov. 1972*

TORTOLI, GIANNI: *Photographer*

Locusts: "Teeth of the Wind." By Robert A. M. Conley. 202-227, *Aug. 1969*

TORTUGA II (Amphibious Jeep):

East From Bali by Seagoing Jeep to Timor. By Helen and Frank Schreider. 236-279, *Aug. 1962*

Indonesia, the Young and Troubled Island Nation. By Helen and Frank Schreider. 579-625, *May 1961*

From the Hair of Siva (Ganges River, India). By Helen and Frank Schreider. 445-503, *Oct. 1960*

TORTUGAS (Islands), Florida. *See* Dry Tortugas

TORTUGUERO BEACH, Costa Rica:

Imperiled Gift of the Sea: Caribbean Green Turtle. By Archie Carr. Photos by Robert E. Schroeder. 876-890, *June 1967*

The **TOTAL** Eclipse of the Sun, May 28, 1900. By F. H. Bigelow. 33-34, *Jan. 1900*

TOTAL Victory Over Smallpox? By Donald A. Henderson. Photos by Marion Kaplan. 796-805, *Dec. 1978*

TOTEM POLES:

Canada's Queen Charlotte Islands, Homeland of the Haida. By Moira Johnston. Photos by Dewitt Jones. 102-127, *July 1987*

Indians of Our North Pacific Coast. By Matthew W. Stirling. Included: Totem-Pole Builders. Paintings by W. Langdon Kihn. 25-52, *Jan. 1945*

TOTH, TIBOR G.:

Nomination Page. *May 1978*

TOTONAC INDIANS:

Following Cortés: Path to Conquest. By S. Jeffrey K. Wilkerson. Photos by Guillermo Aldana E. Paintings by Ned Seidler and Rosalie Seidler. 420-459, *Oct. 1984*

Man's Eighty Centuries in Veracruz. By S. Jeffrey K. Wilkerson. Photos by David Hiser. Paintings by Richard Schlecht. 203-231, *Aug. 1980*

TOUGH Times on the Prairie–North Dakota. By Bryan Hodgson. Photos by Annie Griffiths. 320-347, *Mar. 1987*

TOULON CANYON, Mediterranean Sea:

Diving Through an Undersea Avalanche. By Jacques-Yves Cousteau. NGS research grant. 538-542, *Apr. 1955*

To the Depths of the Sea by Bathyscaphe. By Jacques-Yves Cousteau. NGS research grant. 67-79, *July 1954*

TOULOUSE, France:

France's Past Lives in Languedoc. By Walter Meayers Edwards. Included: Academy of the Floral Games, Canal du Midi, Cathedral of St. Etienne, and St. Sernin. 1-43, *July 1951*

A **TOUR** in the English Fenland. By Christopher Marlowe. 605-634, *May 1929*

TOURING for Birds with Microphone and Color Cameras. By Arthur A. Allen. 689-712, *June 1944*

TOURNAMENT OF ROSES, Pasadena, California:

Focusing on the Tournament of Roses. By B. Anthony Stewart and J. Baylor Roberts. 805-816, *June 1954*

TOWBOATS:

The Gulf's Workaday Waterway. By Gordon Young. Photos by Charles O'Rear. 200-223, *Feb. 1978*

The Ohio–River With a Job to Do. By Priit J. Vesilind. Photos by Martin Rogers. Included: The *Northern,* working the 981-mile length of the Ohio River. 245-273, *Feb. 1977*

That Dammed Missouri River. By Gordon Young. Photos by David Hiser. 374-413, *Sept. 1971*

TOWERS:

The Tower of the Winds. By Derek J. de Solla Price. Paintings by Robert C. Magis. NGS research grant. 587-596, *Apr. 1967*

The Singing Towers of Holland and Belgium. By William Gorham Rice. 357-376, *Mar. 1925*

Dr. Bell's Tetrahedral Tower. By Gilbert H. Grosvenor. 672-675, *Oct. 1907*

The Parsees and the Towers of Silence at Bombay, India. By William Thomas Fee. 529-554, *Dec. 1905*

TOWERS, Rock. *See* Fisher Towers

TOWHEES:

Sparrows, Towhees, and Longspurs: These Happy Little Singers Make Merry in Field, Forest, and Desert Throughout North America. By T. Gilbert Pearson. Paintings by Allan Brooks and Walter A. Weber. 353-376, *Mar. 1939*

A **TOWN**...a Mountain...a Way of Life. By Jill Durrance and Dick Durrance II. 788-807, *Dec. 1973*

The **TOWN** of Many Gables. By Florence Craig Albrecht. 107-140, *Feb. 1915*

TOWNLEY-FULLAM, C.: *Author*

Hungary: A Land of Shepherd Kings. 311-393, *Oct. 1914*

TOWNSEND, CHARLES and JEAN:

Nomination Page. In the Philippines. *Sept. 1967*

TOWNSEND, CHARLES HASKINS: *Author*

Our Heritage of the Fresh Waters: Biographies of the Most Widely Distributed of the Important Food and Game Fishes of the United States. Paintings by Hashime Murayama. 109-159, *Aug. 1923*

TOWNSEND, LLOYD K.: *Artist*

"Journey Into the Universe Through Time and Space." Sky Survey photos on reverse. Supplement. *June 1983*

Lost Outpost of the Egyptian Empire. By Trude Dothan. Photos by Sisse Brimberg. 739-769, *Dec. 1982*

"The Solar System," painting supplement. NASA photo of Saturn on reverse. *July 1981*

✣ "Early Civilizations," painting supplement. Map on reverse. *Sept. 1978*

Minoans and Mycenaeans: Greece's Brilliant Bronze Age. By Joseph Judge. Photos by Gordon W. Gahan. 142-185, *Feb. 1978*

Nature's Gifts to Medicine. By Lonnelle Aikman. Paintings by Lloyd K. Townsend and Don Crowley. 420-440, *Sept. 1974*

TOXIC POLLUTION:

The Great Lakes' Troubled Waters. By Charles E. Cobb, Jr. Photos by Bob Sacha and Richard Olsenius. Included: A great meeting of waters; North America's fifth coast. 2-31, *July 1987*

Air: An Atmosphere of Uncertainty. By Noel Grove. Photos by Ted Spiegel. Paintings by William H. Bond. Included: A deadly soup (a list of harmful chemicals), Careless neighbors, A global greenhouse, The ozone enigma, Getting the lead out, The enemy within. 502-537, *Apr. 1987*

A crop duster begins its run over a North Dakota field during "Tough Times on the Prairie."   ANNIE GRIFFITHS BELT

Editorial. By Wilbur E. Garrett. 277, *Mar. 1985*

Hazardous Waste...Storing Up Trouble. By Allen A. Boraiko. Photos by Fred Ward. 318-351, *Mar. 1985*

TOY DOGS, Pets of Kings and Commoners. By Freeman Lloyd. 459-480, *Apr. 1944*

TOY FISHES:

Tropical Toy Fishes: More Than 600 Varieties of Aquarium Pygmies Afford a Fascinating Field of Zoölogical Study in the Home. By Ida Mellen. Paintings by Hashime Murayama. 287-317, *Mar. 1931*

TOZEUR, Tunisia:

The Date Gardens of the Jerid. By Thomas H. Kearney. 543-567, *July 1910*

TOZZI, PASQUALE: *Author*

Italy's Eagles of Combat and Defense: Heroic Achievements of Aviators Above the Adriatic, the Apennines, and the Alps. 38-47, *Jan. 1918*

TRACKING America's Man in Orbit. By Kenneth F. Weaver. Photos by Robert F. Sisson. 184-217, *Feb. 1962*

TRACKING AND DATA RELAY SATELLITES (TDRS):

Satellites That Serve Us. By Thomas Y. Canby. Included: Spacelab 1: *Columbia.* By Michael E. Long. 301-307. 281-335, *Sept. 1983*

TRACKING Columbus Across the Atlantic. By Luis Marden. 572-577, *Nov. 1986*

TRACKING Danger With the Ice Patrol. By William S. Ellis. Photos by James R. Holland. 780-793, *June 1968*

TRACKING the Columbian Ground-Squirrel to Its Burrow: Loss of Millions to Crops and Danger of the Spread of Spotted Fever Necessitated

Study of Peculiar Rodent of Western North America. By William T. Shaw. 587-596, *May 1925*

TRACKING the Elusive Snow Leopard. By Rodney Jackson and Darla Hillard. NGS research grant. 793-809, *June 1986*

TRACKING the Shore Dwellers From Canada to Suriname. 175-179, *Aug. 1979*

TRACKING Tornadoes. By Peter Miller. Photos by Chris Johns. Included: Map of tornadoes, 1950-1985; Diagram of tornado dynamics. 690-715, *June 1987*

TRADE:

Wild Cargo: the Business of Smuggling Animals. By Noel Grove. Photos by Steve Raymer. 287-315, *Mar. 1981*

The Bonanza Bean–Coffee. By Ethel A. Starbird. Photos by Sam Abell. 388-405, *Mar. 1981*

Reach for the New World. By Mendel Peterson. Photos by David L. Arnold. Paintings by Richard Schlecht. 724-767, *Dec. 1977*

⊕ Colonization and Trade in the New World. Text on reverse. *Dec. 1977*

Spices, the Essence of Geography. By Stuart E. Jones. 401-420, *Mar. 1949*

With Uncle Sam and John Bull in Germany. By Frederick Simpich. 117-140, *Jan. 1949*

Louisiana Trades with the World. By Frederick Simpich. Photos by J. Baylor Roberts. 705-738, *Dec. 1947*

Bonds Between the Americas. By Frederick Simpich. 785-808, *Dec. 1937*

Commercial and Financial Statistics of the Principal Countries of the World. 420-425, *June 1907*

Commercial Prize of the Orient. By O. P. Austin. 399-423, *Sept. 1905*

The Commercial Valuation of Railway Operating Property in the United States. 438-439, *Sept. 1905*

Commercial Importance of the State of New York. 429, *Oct. 1904*

Foreign Commerce of the United States in 1903. 359-360, *Sept. 1903*

Commerce of Mexico and the United States. By O. P. Austin. 25-26, *Jan. 1902*

The Commercial Development of Japan. By O. P. Austin. 329-337, *Sept. 1899*

The Commercial Importance of Samoa. By O. P. Austin. 218-220, *June 1899*

Commerce of the Philippine Islands. By John Hyde. 301-303, *June 1898*

Trade of the United States with Cuba. By John Hyde. 247-249, *May 1898*

Our Foreign Trade. By Henry Gannett. 27-28, *Jan. 1898*

The Evolution of Commerce. Annual Address by the President, Hon. Gardiner G. Hubbard. 1-18, *Mar. 26, 1892*

See also Hudson's Bay Company; *Witte Leeuw; and* Shipping

TRADE ROUTES:

Crosscurrents Sweep the Indian Ocean. By Bart McDowell. Photos by Steve Raymer. 422-457, *Oct. 1981*

See also Persian Gulf; St. Lawrence Seaway

Historic

Oldest Known Shipwreck Reveals Splendors of the Bronze Age. By George F. Bass. Photos by William R. Curtsinger. Included: Bronze Age Trade, The Cosmopolitan World of the Late Bronze Age, The Painstaking Art of Marine Archaeology. NGS research grant. 693-733, *Dec. 1987*

Arabia's Frankincense Trail. By Thomas J. Abercrombie. Photos by Lynn Abercrombie. 474-513, *Oct. 1985*

Silk–The Queen of Textiles. By Nina Hyde. Photos by Cary Wolinsky. Included: Map of the caravan network across Asia. 2-49, *Jan. 1984*

In the Wake of Sindbad. By Tim Severin. Photos by Richard Greenhill. 2-41, *July 1982*

Journey to China's Far West. By Rick Gore. Photos by Bruce Dale. Included: Silk Road. 292-331, *Mar. 1980*

The Phoenicians, Sea Lords of Antiquity. By Samuel W. Matthews. Photos by Winfield Parks. Paintings by Robert C. Magis. 149-189, *Aug. 1974*

See also Mesopotamia; *and* Vikings

TRADEWINDS (Ketch):

Slow Boat to Florida. By Dorothea and Stuart E. Jones. 1-65, *Jan. 1958*

TRADITION Lingers in Modern Japan. Photos by W. Robert Moore. 117-124, *Jan. 1938*

The **TRADITIONS** and Glamour of Insignia. By Arthur E. Du Bois. 652-655, *June 1943*

TRAFALGAR, Battle of (1805):

Portsmouth, Britannia's Sally Port. By Thomas Garner James. Photos by B. Anthony Stewart. 513-544, *Apr. 1952*

Girls in Nuapatna, India, spin silk, noble textile of the Orient sent west on ancient trade routes. CARY WOLINSKY, STOCK, BOSTON

NATIONAL GEOGRAPHICS bring the world to foreign soldiers studying English in a training school at Camp Kearny, California, during World War I. CHRISTINA KRYSTO

Billowing steam into the frosty morning air, a Chinese train starts its daily passage through towns near Langxiang. BRUCE DALE, NGS

TRANSCONTINENTAL BALLOON FLIGHT:

TRANS-DARIÉN EXPEDITION:

TRANS-JORDAN. *See* Jordan

TRANSPORT AIR GROUP (TAG):

TRANSPORTATION:

See also Automobiles; Aviation; Boats; Highways and Roads; Railroads; Shipping; Trade Routes; U. S. Army Transportation Corps

TRANS-SAHARA SAND AND LAND YACHT RALLY:

TRANS-SIBERIAN RAILWAY, U.S.S.R.:

Aboard **Double Eagle II** *in August 1978, Ben Abruzzo breathes bottled oxygen at 23,000 feet on the first successful transatlantic balloon flight.* DOUBLE EAGLE II

National Geographic **Traveler** Spring 1986

Colorful, Casual, Cultured San Diego

Casco Bay •
Ramsey Canyon •
Civil War Battlefields •
Kennedy Space Center •
Salzburg, Austria •
Colorado Rock Climbing •
Ontario's Shakespeare Festival •
New Harmony, Indiana •
Rajasthan, India •

Future of Siberia. By James Bryce. 469-507, *May 1921*

The Land of Promise. By A. W. Greely. 1078-1090, *Nov. 1912*

Siberia. By Edwin A. Grosvenor. 317-324, *Sept. 1901*

Railways, Rivers, and Strategic Towns in Manchuria. By Gilbert H. Grosvenor. 326-327, *Aug. 1900*

The Siberian Transcontinental Railroad. By A. W. Greely. 121-124, *Apr. 1897*

TRANSVAAL (Province), South Africa:

The Afrikaners. By André Brink. Photos by David Turnley. 556-585, *Oct. 1988*

South Africa's Lonely Ordeal. By William S. Ellis. Photos by James P. Blair. 780-819, *June 1977*

The Cities That Gold and Diamonds Built. By W. Robert Moore. 735-766, *Dec. 1942*

The Transvaal: The Treasure-House Province. By Melville Chater. 479-512, *Apr. 1931*

British South Africa and the Transvaal. By F. F. Hilder. 81-96, *Mar. 1900*

The Witwatersrand and the Revolt of the Uitlanders. By George F. Becker. 349-367, *Nov. 1896*

A Critical Period in South African History. By John Hyde. 377-379, *Nov. 1896*

Africa Since 1888, with Special Reference to South Africa and Abyssinia. By Gardiner G. Hubbard. 157-175, *May 1896*

See also Johannesburg; Pretoria

TRANSYLVANIA (Region), Romania:

An American Girl Cycles Across Romania: Two-wheel Pilgrim Pedals the Land of Castles and Gypsies, Where Roman Empire Traces Mingle With Remnants of Oriental Migration. By Dorothy Hosmer. 557-588, *Nov. 1938*

Transylvania and Its Seven Castles. By J. Theodore Marriner. 319-352, *Mar. 1926*

Roumania and Its Rubicon. By John Oliver La Gorce. 185-202, *Sept. 1916*

TRAPDOOR SPIDERS:

Marvels of Metamorphosis: A Scientific "G-man" Pursues Rare Trapdoor Spider Parasites for Three Years With a Spade and a Candid Camera. By George Elwood Jenks. 807-828, *Dec. 1938*

California Trapdoor Spider Performs Engineering Marvels. By Lee Passmore. 195-211, *Aug. 1933*

TRASH:

The Fascinating World of Trash. By Peter T. White. Photos by Louie Psihoyos. 424-457, *Apr. 1983*

The **TRAVAIL** of Ireland. By Joseph Judge. Photos by Cotton Coulson. 432-441, *Apr. 1981*

***TRAVELER**, National Geographic:*

President's Page. By Gilbert M. Grosvenor. *Feb. 1984*

A **TRAVELER'S** Notes on Java. By Henry G. Bryant. 91-111, *Feb. 1910*

A **TRAVELER'S** Tale of Ancient Tikal. Paintings by Peter Spier. Text by Alice J. Hall. 799-811, *Dec. 1975*

TRAVELING in the Highlands of Ethiopia. By Leo B. Roberts. 297-328, *Sept. 1935*

***TRAVELING** the Trans-Canada: From Newfoundland to British Columbia. By William Howarth. Photos by George F. Mobley. 199 pages. 1987*

TRAVELS in Arabia and Along the Persian Gulf. By David G. Fairchild. 139-151, *Apr. 1904*

The **TRAVELS** of George Washington: Dramatic Episodes in His Career as the First Geographer of the United States. By William Joseph Showalter. 1-63, *Jan. 1932*

TRAVELS With a Donkey–100 Years Later. By Carolyn Bennett Patterson. Photos by Cotton Coulson. 535-561, *Oct. 1978*

TRAVELS with a Donkey in Mexico: Three Adventurers Trudge from Oaxaca to Acapulco, 400 Miles, Through Back Country, Their Equipment Carried by Burros. By Bernard Bevan. 757-788, *Dec. 1934*

TRAWLERS:

Chincoteague: Watermen's Island Home. By Nathaniel T. Kenney. Photos by James L. Amos. 810-829, *June 1980*

The Sailing Oystermen of Chesapeake Bay. By Luis Marden. 798-819, *Dec. 1967*

Trawling the China Seas. Photos by J. Charles Thompson. 381-395, *Mar. 1950*

See also Shrimp Fishing

TREASURE, Sunken:

Hidden Treasures of the Sea. Juvenile. 104 pages. *1988*

Oldest Known Shipwreck Reveals Splendors of the Bronze Age. By

George F. Bass. Photos by William R. Curtsinger. Included: Bronze Age Trade, The Cosmopolitan World of the Late Bronze Age, The Painstaking Art of Marine Archaeology. NGS research grant. 693-733, *Dec. 1987*

Bronze Age Shipwreck. By Wilbur E. Garrett and George F. Bass. NGS research grant. 1-3, *Jan. 1985*

The Lost Fleet of Kublai Khan. By Torao Mozai. Photos by Koji Nakamura. Paintings by Issho Yada. 634-649, *Nov. 1982*

Treasure From the Ghost Galleon: *Santa Margarita.* By Eugene Lyon. Photos by Don Kincaid. 228-243, *Feb. 1982*

Graveyard of the Quicksilver Galleons. By Mendel Peterson. Photos by Jonathan Blair. 850-876, *Dec. 1979*

Yellow Sea Yields Shipwreck Trove. Photos by H. Edward Kim. Introduction by Donald H. Keith. Included: Earthenware, porcelain, and stoneware. 231-243, *Aug. 1979*

The Sunken Treasure of St. Helena. By Robert Sténuit. Photos by Bates Littlehales. Included: Porcelain of the Ming Dynasty. 562-576, *Oct. 1978*

Glass Treasure From the Aegean. By George F. Bass. Photos by Jonathan Blair. NGS research grant. 768-793, *June 1978*

Reach for the New World. By Mendel Peterson. Photos by David L. Arnold. Paintings by Richard Schlecht. 724-767, *Dec. 1977*

❖ "History Salvaged From the Sea," painting supplement. Map on reverse. *Dec. 1977*

▉ Treasure! 575, Nov. 1976; cover, *Dec. 1976*

Atocha, Tragic Treasure Galleon of the Florida Keys. By Eugene Lyon. 787-809, *June 1976*

The Treasure of Porto Santo. By Robert Sténuit. Photos by author and William R. Curtsinger. 260-275, *Aug. 1975*

Undersea Treasures. 199 pages. *1974*

Bermuda–Balmy, British, and Beautiful. By Peter Benchley. Photos by Emory Kristof. 93-121, *July 1971*

Priceless Relics of the Spanish Armada. By Robert Sténuit. Photos by Bates Littlehales. 745-777, *June 1969*

Drowned Galleons Yield Spanish Gold. By Kip Wagner. Photos by Otis Imboden. 1-37, *Jan. 1965*

The **TREASURE** Chest of Mercurial Mexico. By Frank H. Probert. 33-68, *July 1916*

TREASURE Chest or Pandora's Box? Brazil's Wild Frontier. By Loren McIntyre. 684-719, *Nov. 1977*

TREASURE From a Celtic Tomb. By Jörg Biel. Photos by Volkmar Wentzel. 428-438, *Mar. 1980*

TREASURE From the Ghost Galleon: *Santa Margarita.* By Eugene Lyon. Photos by Don Kincaid. 228-243, *Feb. 1982*

TREASURE-HOUSE of the Gulf Stream: The Completion and Opening of the New Aquarium and

Biological Laboratory at Miami, Florida. By John Oliver La Gorce. Paintings by Hashime Murayama. 53-68, *Jan. 1921*

TREASURE Islands of Australasia: New Guinea, New Caledonia, and Fiji Trace across the South Pacific a Fertile Crescent Incredibly Rich in Minerals and Foods. By Douglas L. Oliver. 691-722, *June 1942*

TREASURE-TROVE of Old Mexican Jade. Photos by Richard H. Stewart. 293-316, *Sept. 1941*

TREASURES of Dresden. By John L. Eliot. Photos by Victor R. Boswell, Jr. 702-717, *Nov. 1978*

TREASURES of Lascaux Cave. By Jean-Philippe Rigaud. Photos by Sisse Brimberg and Norbert Aujoulat. 482-499, *Oct. 1988*

TREASURES of the Pacific: Marine Fishes and Fisheries Yield Vast Wealth from Alaska to Baja California. By Leonard P. Schultz. Paintings by Hashime Murayama. 463-498, *Oct. 1938*

TREASURES of the Tsars. 24-33, *Jan. 1978*

TREASURES of the Vatican. Photos by James L. Stanfield and Victor R. Boswell, Jr. 764-775, *Dec. 1985*

TREAT, IDA: *Author-Photographer*
Sailing Forbidden Coasts. 357-386, *Sept. 1931*

TREE FROGS:
Teeming Life of a Rain Forest. By Carol and David Hughes. 49-65, *Jan. 1983*
Nature's Living, Jumping Jewels. By Paul A. Zahl. 130-146, *July 1973*
Voices of the Night. By Arthur A. Allen. 507-522, *Apr. 1950*

TREE PLANTATIONS:
Tropical Rain Forests: Nature's Dwindling Treasures. By Peter T. White. Photos by James P. Blair. Paintings by Barron Storey. 2-47, *Jan. 1983*
Jari: A Billion-dollar Gamble. By Loren McIntyre. 686-711, *May 1980*
Brazil's Wild Frontier. By Loren McIntyre. Included: Daniel K. Ludwig's three-million-acre forestry experiment. 684-719, *Nov. 1977*
Amazon–The River Sea. By Loren McIntyre. Included: Daniel K. Ludwig's planned paper-pulp and food-production enterprise in Brazil's Amazon basin. 456-495, *Oct. 1972*

TREE-RING DATING:
What's Happening to Our Climate? By Samuel W. Matthews. 576-615, *Nov. 1976*
Bristlecone Pine, Oldest Known Living Thing. By Edmund Schulman. Photos by W. Robert Moore. 355-372, *Mar. 1958*
The Secret of the Southwest Solved by Talkative Tree Rings: Horizons of American History Are Carried Back to A.D. 700 and a Calendar for 1,200 Years Established by National Geographic Society Expeditions. By

With spring busting out all over, a robin guards his nest of chicks in a blossoming apple tree. ROBERT F. SISSON, NGS

Andrew Ellicott Douglass. 737-770, *Dec. 1929*
Pueblo Bonito, the Ancient: The National Geographic Society's Third Expedition to the Southwest Seeks to Read in the Rings of Trees the Secret of the Age of Ruins. By Neil M. Judd. 99-108, *July 1923*

TREE SHREWS:
Seeking Mindanao's Strangest Creatures. By Charles Heizer Wharton. 389-408, *Sept. 1948*

TREE SNAILS:
Tree Snails, Gems of the Everglades. By Treat Davidson. 372-387, *Mar. 1965*

TREES:
Jari: A Billion-dollar Gamble. By Loren McIntyre. Contents: Daniel K. Ludwig's paper-pulp and food-production enterprise in Brazil's Amazon basin. 686-711, *May 1980*
Brazil's Wild Frontier. By Loren McIntyre. Included: Daniel K. Ludwig's three-million-acre agricultural and forestry experiment. 684-719, *Nov. 1977*
The Tree Nobody Liked. By Rick Gore. Photos by Bianca Lavies. Contents: Red mangroves. 669-689, *May 1977*
The World of My Apple Tree. By Robert F. Sisson. 836-847, *June 1972*
Bristlecone Pine, Oldest Known Living Thing. By Edmund Schulman. Photos by W. Robert Moore. 355-372, *Mar. 1958*
Beauty and Bounty of Southern State Trees. By William A. Dayton. Paintings by Walter A. Weber. Contents: Cottonwood, Eastern (Kansas); Dogwood (Missouri, Virginia); Live Oak (Georgia); Magnolia (Mississippi); Palmetto, Cabbage (Florida, South Carolina); Paloverde, Blue (Arizona); Pecan (Texas); Pine,

On a Virginia hillside painted in spring's pastels an Angus cow and her calves stand under an apple tree that awaits the greening of its branches. ROBERT F. SISSON, NGS

This immense tree of the fig family was photographed in China in 1911 during a botanical expedition.   E. H. WILSON, ARNOLD ARBORETUM

TREKKING:

Nomads' Land: A Journey Through Tibet. By Sorrel Wilby. 764-785, *Dec. 1987*

Preserving a Mountain Heritage. By Sir Edmund Hillary. 696-703, *June 1982*

Park at the Top of the World: Mount Everest National Park. By Rick Ridgeway. Photos by Nicholas deVore III. 704-725, *June 1982*

Trekking Around the Continent's Highest Peak (Mount McKinley). By Ned Gillette. 66-79, *July 1979*

Trek to Nepal's Sacred Crystal Mountain. By Joel F. Ziskin. 500-517, *Apr. 1977*

Trek to Lofty Hunza–and Beyond. By Sabrina and Roland Michaud. 644-669, *Nov. 1975*

Trek Across Arctic America. By Colin Irwin. 295-321, *Mar. 1974*

Trek by Mule Among Morocco's Berbers. By Victor Englebert. 850-875, *June 1968*

Trekking South Africa with a Color Camera. Photos by Melville Chater. 413-420, *Apr. 1931*

TRENCHES, Undersea:

Window on Earth's Interior. By Robert D. Ballard. Photos by Emory Kristof. Contents: Cayman Trough. 228-249, *Aug. 1976*

Man's Deepest Dive. By Jacques Piccard. Photos by Thomas J. Abercrombie. Contents: Challenger Deep of the Mariana Trench. 224-239, *Aug. 1960*

Deep Diving off Japan. By Georges S. Houot. Contents: Japan Trench. NGS research grant. 138-150, *Jan. 1960*

Calypso Explores an Undersea Canyon. By Jacques-Yves Cousteau. Photos by Bates Littlehales. Contents: Romanche Trench. NGS research grant. 373-396, *Mar. 1958*

TRES ZAPOTES, Mexico:

Great Stone Faces of the Mexican Jungle: Five Colossal Heads and Numerous Other Monuments of Vanished Americans Are Excavated by the Latest National Geographic-Smithsonian Expedition. By Matthew W. Stirling. 309-334, *Sept. 1940*

Discovering the New World's Oldest Dated Work of Man: A Maya Monument Inscribed 291 B.C. is Unearthed Near a Huge Stone Head by a Geographic-Smithsonian Expedition in Mexico. By Matthew W. Stirling. 183-218, *Aug. 1939*

TRIANGULATION:

Recent Triangulation in the Cascades (Washington). By S. S. Gannett. 150, *Apr. 1896*

TRIBAL FAIRS. See Sing-Sing

TRIBESPEOPLE. See Ethnology

A **TRIBUTE** to America. By Herbert Henry Asquith. 295-296, *Apr. 1917*

TRIBUTE to American Topographers. By Alfred H. Brooks. 358, *July 1905*

The **TRICOLOR** Rules the Rainbow in French Indo-China. Photos by Maynard Owen Williams. 495-518, *Oct. 1935*

TRIESTE, Italy:

Trieste–Side Door to Europe. By Harnett T. Kane. 824-857, *June 1956*

TRIESTE (Bathyscaph):

Down to *Thresher* by Bathyscaph. By Donald L. Keach. 764-777, *June 1964*

Man's Deepest Dive. By Jacques Piccard. Photos by Thomas J. Abercrombie. 224-239, *Aug. 1960*

TRINIDAD, Cuba:

Cuba–American Sugar Bowl. By Melville Bell Grosvenor. 1-56, *Jan. 1947*

TRINIDAD AND TOBAGO, West Indies:

Carnival in Trinidad. By Howard La Fay. Photos by Winfield Parks. 693-701, *Nov. 1971*

"The Music of Trinidad." NGS recording announced. 701, *Nov. 1971*

Feathered Dancers of Little Tobago. By E. Thomas Gilliard. Photos by Frederick Kent Truslow. NGS research grant. 428-440, *Sept. 1958*

The High World of the Rain Forest. By William Beebe. Paintings by Guy Neale. 838-855, *June 1958*

Keeping House for Tropical Butterflies. By Jocelyn Crane. Photos by M. Woodbridge Williams. NGS research grant. 193-217, *Aug. 1957*

Happy-go-lucky Trinidad and Tobago. By Charles Allmon. 35-75, *Jan. 1953*

Sea Fever. By John E. Schultz. 237-268, *Feb. 1949*

Carib Cruises the West Indies. By Carleton Mitchell. 1-56, *Jan. 1948*

Americans in the Caribbean. By Luis Marden. 723-758, *June 1942*

Crossroads of the Caribbean. By Laurence Sanford Critchell. 319-344, *Sept. 1937*

Calypso dancer steps to the lively form of a folk ballad born on the West Indian island of Trinidad. CHARLES ALLMON

The East Indians in the New World. By Harriet Chalmers Adams. 485-491, *July 1907*

See also Caroni Swamp Sanctuary

A **TRIP** Through Siberia. By Ebenezer J. Hill. 37-54, *Feb. 1902*

A **TRIP** to Panama and Darien. By Richard U. Goode. 301-314, *Oct. 1889*

TRIPOLI, Lebanon:

From Jerusalem to Aleppo. By John D. Whiting. 71-113, *Jan. 1913*

TRIPOLI, Libya:

Americans on the Barbary Coast. By Willard Price. 1-31, *July 1943*

Tripoli: A Land of Little Promise. By Adolf L. Vischer. 1035-1047, *Nov. 1911*

TRIPOLITANIA (Region), North Africa:

Americans on the Barbary Coast. By Willard Price. 1-31, *July 1943*

Tripolitania, Where Rome Resumes Sway: The Ancient Trans-Mediterranean Empire, on the Fringe of the Libyan Desert, Becomes a Promising Modern Italian Colony. By Gordon Casserly. 131-161, *Aug. 1925*

Here and There in Northern Africa. By Frank Edward Johnson. 1-132, *Jan. 1914*

Tripoli: A Land of Little Promise. By Adolf L. Vischer. 1035-1047, *Nov. 1911*

The Mysteries of the Desert. By Hanns Vischer. 1056-1059, *Nov. 1911*

TRIPPE, JUAN T.:

National Geographic Society Honors Air Pioneer Juan Trippe. 584-586, *Apr. 1968*

TRISTAN DA CUNHA ISLANDS, South Atlantic Ocean:

Home to Lonely Tristan da Cunha. By James P. Blair. 60-81, *Jan. 1964*

Death of an Island, Tristan da Cunha. By P.J.F. Wheeler. 678-695, *May 1962*

New Life for the "Loneliest Isle." By Lewis Lewis. 105-116, *Jan. 1950*

Tristan da Cunha, Isles of Contentment: On Lonely Sea Spots of Pirate Lore and Shipwrecks Seven Families Live Happily Far from War Rumors and World Changes. By W. Robert Foran. 671-694, *Nov. 1938*

TRI-STATE Medley. Photos by Willard R. Culver. 33-40, *July 1938*

TRITON Follows Magellan's Wake. By Edward L. Beach. Photos by J. Baylor Roberts. 585-615, *Nov. 1960*

TRIUMPH and Tragedy on Annapurna. By Arlene Blum. 295-313. Included: On the Summit. By Irene Miller, with Vera Komarkova. 312-313, *Mar. 1979*

TRIUMPH of *Daedalus*. By John S. Langford. Photos by Charles O'Rear. 191-199, *Aug. 1988*

TRIUMPH of the First Crusade to the Holy Land. By Franc Shor. Photos by Thomas Nebbia. 797-855, *Dec. 1963*

The trouble with this spotted dolphin near Hawaii is its hitchhiker—a remora, or scavenger fish—which it hopes to dislodge with a series of high leaps. BILL CURTSINGER

TROUBLED Waters East of Suez. By Ernest M. Eller. 483-522, *Apr. 1954*

The **TROUBLED** Waters of Mono Lake. By Gordon Young. Photos by Craig Aurness. 504-519, *Oct. 1981*

TROUT:

Freezing the Trout's Lightning Leap. By Treat Davidson. 525-530, *Apr. 1958*

Lake Sunapee's Golden Trout. Photos by Robert F. Sisson. 529-536, *Oct. 1950*

Fishing in Pacific Coast Streams. By Leonard P. Schultz. Paintings by Hashime Murayama. 185-212, *Feb. 1939*

The Wild Life of Lake Superior, Past and Present: The Habits of Deer, Moose, Wolves, Beavers, Muskrats, Trout, and Feathered Wood-Folk Studied with Camera and Flashlight. By George Shiras, 3d. Included: Pictorial supplement. 113-204, *Aug. 1921*

The Golden Trout. 424, *July 1906*

TROWBRIDGE, STEPHEN VAN RENSSELAER: *Author*

Impressions of Asiatic Turkey. 598-609, *Dec. 1914*

TROY (Ancient City), Turkey:

Homer's Troy Today. By Jacob E. Conner. Included: Notes on Troy. By Ernest L. Harris. 521-532, *May 1915*

TRUCIAL COAST:

Desert Sheikdoms of Arabia's Pirate Coast. By Ronald Codrai. 65-104, *July 1956*

Troubled Waters East of Suez. By Ernest M. Eller. 483-522, *Apr. 1954*

See also present designation, United Arab Emirates

TRUCKING:

Trucks Race the Clock From Coast to Coast. By James A. Sugar. 226-243, *Feb. 1974*

North With the Wheat Cutters. By Noel Grove. Photos by James A. Sugar. 194-217, *Aug. 1972*

"TRUE PEOPLE" of the Jungle. By Napoleon A. Chagnon. 211-223, *Aug. 1976*

TRUFFLES:

The Diffident Truffle, France's Gift to Gourmets. 419-426, *Sept. 1956*

TRUJILLO (City), Dominican Republic. *See* Santo Domingo

TRUK ISLANDS, Micronesia:

In the Far Pacific: At the Birth of Nations. By Carolyn Bennett Patterson. Photos by David Hiser and Melinda Berge. Included: Mariana Islands, Marshall Islands, Kosrae, Pohnpei, Truk, Yap, Palau. 460-499, *Oct. 1986*

Life Springs From Death in Truk Lagoon. By Sylvia A. Earle. Photos by Al Giddings. 578-613, *May 1976*

Micronesia: The Americanization of Eden. By David S. Boyer. 702-744, *May 1967*

Pacific Wards of Uncle Sam. By W. Robert Moore. 73-104, *July 1948*

Hidden Key to the Pacific: Piercing the Web of Secrecy Which Long Has

Veiled Japanese Bases in the Mandated Islands. By Willard Price. 759-785, *June 1942*

Yap and Other Pacific Islands Under Japanese Mandate. By Junius B. Wood. 591-627, *Dec. 1921*

TRUK LAGOON, Truk Islands, Micronesia:

Life Springs From Death in Truk Lagoon. By Sylvia A. Earle. Photos by Al Giddings. Included: From Graveyard to Garden. 578-613, *May 1976*

TRULLI (Dwellings):

The Stone Beehive Homes of the Italian Heel: In Trulli-Land the Native Builds His Dwelling and Makes His Field Arable in the Same Operation. By Paul Wilstach. 229-260, *Feb. 1930*

TRUMAN, HARRY R.:

Mount St. Helens Aftermath: The Mountain That Was–and Will Be. By Rowe Findley. Photos by Steve Raymer. 713-733, *Dec. 1981*

Mountain With a Death Wish (Mount St. Helens). By Rowe Findley. Note: Harry R. Truman was a casualty of the eruption of Mount St. Helens. 3-33, *Jan. 1981*

Nomination Page. At Mount St. Helens, Washington. *Jan. 1981*

TRUMAN, HARRY S.:

The Living White House. By Lonnelle Aikman. 593-643, *Nov. 1966*

Profiles of the Presidents: V. The Atomic Age: Its Problems and Promises. By Frank Freidel. 66-119, *Jan. 1966*

Locusts swarm across the sky of Dubayy, a desert sheikhdom on the Trucial Coast now part of the United Arab Emirates. RONALD CODRAI

After working in family tulip fields, a Dutch boy on his mother's bicycle takes blooms to school.　FARRELL GREHAN

TUAREG TRIBESPEOPLE:

Oursi, Magnet in the Desert. By Carole E. Devillers. 512-525, *Apr. 1980*

The Inadan: Artisans of the Sahara. By Michael and Aubine Kirtley. Contents: A study of the symbiotic relationship between Tuareg nobles and artisans. 282-298, *Aug. 1979*

The Niger: River of Sorrow, River of Hope. By Georg Gerster. 152-189, *Aug. 1975*

Drought Threatens the Tuareg World. By Victor Englebert. 544-571, *Apr. 1974*

I Joined a Sahara Salt Caravan. By Victor Englebert. 694-711, *Nov. 1965*

Sand in My Eyes. By Jinx Rodger. 664-705, *May 1958*

Trans-Africa Safari: A Motor Caravan Rolls Across Sahara and Jungle Through Realms of Dusky Potentates and the Land of Big-Lipped Women. By Lawrence Copley Thaw and Margaret Stout Thaw. 327-364, *Sept. 1938*

The Mysteries of the Desert. By Hanns Vischer. Contents: Sahara Desert. 1056-1059, *Nov. 1911*

TUATARA:

Tuatara: "Living Fossils" Walk on Well-Nigh Inaccessible Rocky Islands off the Coast of New Zealand. By Frieda Cobb Blanchard. 649-662, *May 1935*

TUCK, JAMES A.: *Author*

Unearthing Red Bay's Whaling History. Photos by Bill Curtsinger. 50-57, *July 1985*

TUCK, JOHN, Jr.:

Man's First Winter at the South Pole. By Paul A. Siple. 439-478, *Apr. 1958*

We Are Living at the South Pole. By Paul A. Siple. Photos by David S. Boyer. 5-35, *July 1957*

TUCSON, Arizona:

Arizona's Suburbs of the Sun. By David Jeffery. Photos by H. Edward Kim. 486-517, *Oct. 1977*

Arizona's Window on Wildlife. By Lewis Wayne Walker. 240-250, *Feb. 1958*

From Tucson to Tombstone. By Mason Sutherland. 343-384, *Sept. 1953*

TUGERI TRIBESPEOPLE:

Strange Sights in Far-Away Papua. By A. E. Pratt. 559-572, *Sept. 1907*

TUKUNA INDIANS:

Tukuna Maidens Come of Age. By Harald Schultz. 629-649, *Nov. 1959*

TULANE UNIVERSITY, New Orleans, Louisiana:

Delta Regional Primate Research Center. *See* Snowflake (Albino Gorilla)

Expedition. *See* Dzibilchaltun

TULASNE, JOSEPH: *Author*

America's Part in the Allies' Mastery of the Air. 1-5, *Jan. 1918*

TULES INDIANS. *See* San Blas Indians

TULIPS:

Tulips: Holland's Beautiful Business. By Elizabeth A. Moize. Photos by Farrell Grehan. 712-728, *May 1978*

Some Odd Pages from the Annals of the Tulip: A "Made" Flower of Unknown Origin Took Medieval Europe by Storm and Caused a Financial Panic in the Netherlands. By Leo A. Borah. Included: Tulip Time in the Netherlands. Photos by Wilhelm Tobien and A. Buyssens. 321-343, *Sept. 1933*

TULSA, Oklahoma:

High-Flying Tulsa. By Robert Paul Jordan. Photos by Annie Griffiths. 378-403, *Sept. 1983*

Oklahoma, the Adventurous One. By Robert Paul Jordan. Photos by Robert W. Madden. 149-189, *Aug. 1971*

So Oklahoma Grew Up. By Frederick Simpich. 269-314, *Mar. 1941*

TUMEN (River), China-North Korea:

Exploring Unknown Corners of the "Hermit Kingdom." By Roy Chapman Andrews. 25-48, *July 1919*

TUNA:

Plight of the Bluefin Tuna. By Michael J. A. Butler. Photos by David Doubilet. Paintings by Stanley Meltzoff. 220-239, *Aug. 1982*

Quicksilver and Slow Death. By John J. Putman. Photos by Robert W. Madden. Included: Mercury found in tuna. 507-527, *Oct. 1972*

Golden Beaches of Portugal. By Alan Villiers. 673-696, *Nov. 1954*

The *Yankee*'s Wander-world. By Irving and Electa Johnson. Included: Tuna fishing in Tagus Cove, Galapagos Islands. 1-50, *Jan. 1949*

The Tuna Harvest of the Sea: A Little-known Epic of the Ocean Is the Story of Southern California's Far-ranging Tuna Fleet. By John Degelman. 393-408, *Sept. 1940*

TUNDRA: North America:

Our Wildest Wilderness: Alaska's Arctic National Wildlife Range. By Douglas H. Chadwick. Photos by Lowell Georgia. 737-769, *Dec. 1979*

The Pipeline: Alaska's Troubled Colossus. By Bryan Hodgson. Photos by Steve Raymer. 684-717, *Nov. 1976*

Caribou: Hardy Nomads of the North. By Jim Rearden. 858-878, *Dec. 1974*

Beyond the North Wind With the Snow Goose. By Des and Jen Bartlett. 822-843, *Dec. 1973*

North to the Tundra. 293-337. I. Re-creating a Vanished World. By Russell D. Guthrie. Included: "Ice Age Mammals of the Alaskan Tundra." Painting supplement by Jay H. Matternes. 294-301; II. Portrait of a Fierce and Fragile Land. By Paul A. Zahl. 303-314; III. Plants of the Alaskan Tundra. 315-321; IV. Birds of the Alaskan Tundra. 322-327; V. Mammals of the Alaskan Tundra. 329-337, *Mar. 1972*

Will Oil and Tundra Mix? Alaska's North Slope Hangs in the Balance. By William S. Ellis. Photos by Emory Kristof. 485-517, *Oct. 1971*

Birds of Timberline and Tundra. By Arthur A. Allen. Photos by author. 313-339, *Sept. 1946*

TUNDRA SWAN. *See* Whistling Swan

TUNHWANG, Gansu Province, China:

The Caves of the Thousand Buddhas. By Franc and Jean Shor. 383-415, *Mar. 1951*

TUNIS, Tunisia:

Eastward from Gibraltar: Overland Route Across North Africa to Tunisia and Libia. By Cyrus French Wicker. 115-142, *Jan. 1943*

Tunis of Today. By Frank Edward Johnson. 723-749, *Aug. 1911*

TUNISIA:

Tunisia: Sea, Sand, Success. By Mike Edwards. Photos by David Alan Harvey. 184-217, *Feb. 1980*

The Phoenicians, Sea Lords of

Even children in remote Tunisian villages were able to receive an education during France's years of control in northern Africa. LEHNERT AND LANDROCK

A TUNNEL Through Time: The Appalachian Trail. By Noel Grove. Photos by Sam Abell. 216-243, *Feb. 1987*

TUNNELS:

TURBULENT Spain. By Ruth Q. McBride. 397-427, *Oct. 1936*

TURCIANSKY SVATY MARTIN (Turocz Szent Martin), Czechoslovakia:

TURIN, Italy. *See* Shroud of Turin

TURKANA, Lake, Kenya:

See also former name, Rudolf, Lake

TURKESTAN. *See* Sinkiang; Soviet Central Asia

TURKEY:

The Turkish Army retreats to Çatalca in 1912 during wars that ended the Ottoman Empire's rule in the Balkans. FREDERICK MOORE

TURKEYS:

TURKIC TRIBES:

Valley, Plateau Paradise of Mongol and Turkic Tribes. By Edward Murray. Paintings and drawings by Alexandre Iacovleff. 1-57, *Jan. 1936*
See also Tatars; Turkomans

TURKISTAN. *See* Sinkiang; Soviet Central Asia

TURKMEN SOVIET SOCIALIST REPUBLIC:
The Afghan Borderland. By Ellsworth Huntington. Part I: The Russian Frontier. 788-799, *Sept. 1909*
Life in the Great Desert of Central Asia. By Ellsworth Huntington. 749-760, *Aug. 1909*

TURKOMANS:
Bold Horsemen of the Steppes. By Sabrina and Roland Michaud. 634-669, *Nov. 1973*
Russia's Orphan Races: Picturesque Peoples Who Cluster on the Southeastern Borderland of the Vast Slav Dominions. By Maynard Owen Williams. 245-278, *Oct. 1918*
Life in the Great Desert of Central Asia. By Ellsworth Huntington. 749-760, *Aug. 1909*

TURKS:
Cyprus Under Four Flags: A Struggle for Unity. By Kenneth MacLeish. Photos by Jonathan Blair. 356-383, *Mar. 1973*
The Isles of Greece: Aegean Birthplace of Western Culture. By Melville Bell Grosvenor. Photos by Edwin Stuart Grosvenor and Winfield Parks. 147-193, *Aug. 1972*

TURKU ARCHIPELAGO, Finland:
Scenes of Postwar Finland. By La Verne Bradley. Photos by Jerry Waller. 233-264, *Aug. 1947*

TURNAROUND Time in West Virginia. By Elizabeth A. Moize. Photos by Jodi Cobb. 755-785, *June 1976*

TURNER, DANIEL S.: *Photographer*
Voyage of the *Morrissey*. Photos by Daniel S. Turner and Sherman A. Wengerd. 609-616, *May 1946*

TURNER, J. HENRY: *Author*
The Alaskan Boundary Survey. III–The Boundary North of Fort Yukon. 189-197, *Feb. 8, 1893*

TURNING Back Time in the South Seas. By Thor Heyerdahl. Contents: Fatu-Hiva Island. 109-136, *Jan. 1941*

TURNLEY, DAVID:
On Assignment in South Africa. *Oct. 1988*
Photographer
The Afrikaners. By André Brink. 556-585, *Oct. 1988*

TUROCZ SZENT MARTIN, Czechoslovakia. *See* Turciansky Svaty Martin

TURPAN DEPRESSION (Region), China:
Journey to China's Far West. By Rick

Gore. Photos by Bruce Dale. 292-331, *Mar. 1980*

TURTLE BOGUE. *See* Tortuguero Beach, Costa Rica

TURTLES:
Freshwater Turtles–Designed for Survival. By Christopher P. White. Photos by Bill Curtsinger. Contents: Alligator snapper, Black-knobbed sawback, Common snapping, Eastern painted, Gulf Coast spiny softshell, Map turtle, Painted, Peninsula cooter, Plymouth red-belly white, River cooter, Softshell, Spotted, Stinkpot, Stripe-necked musk, Suwannee cooter, Yellow-belly sliders, Yellow-blotched sawback. 40-59, *Jan. 1986*
One Strange Night on Turtle Beach. By Paul A. Zahl. 570-581, *Oct. 1973*
In the Wilds of a City Parlor. By Paul A. Zahl. 645-672, *Nov. 1954*
Nature's Tank, the Turtle. By Doris M. Cochran. Paintings by Walter A. Weber. 665-684, *May 1952*
Capturing Giant Turtles in the Caribbean. By David D. Duncan. 177-190, *Aug. 1943*
Certain Citizens of the Warm Sea. By Louis L. Mowbray. Paintings by Hashime Murayama. 27-62, *Jan. 1922*
Reptiles of All Lands. By Raymond L. Ditmars. 601-633, *July 1911*
Notes on the Remarkable Habits of Certain Turtles and Lizards. By H. A. Largelamb (Alexander Graham Bell). 413-419, *June 1907*
Cultivation of Marine and Fresh-Water Animals in Japan. By K. Mitsukuri. 524-531, *Sept. 1906*
See also Green Turtles; Tortoises

TUSCANY (Region), Italy:
The Eternal Etruscans. By Rick Gore. Photos by O. Louis Mazzatenta. Paintings by James M. Gurney. 696-743, *June 1988*
Carrara Marble: Touchstone of Eternity. By Cathy Newman. Photos by Pierre Boulat. 42-59, *July 1982*
Leonardo da Vinci: A Man for All Ages. By Kenneth MacLeish. Photos by James L. Amos. 296-329, *Sept. 1977*
The Renaissance Lives On in Tuscany. By Luis Marden. Photos by Albert Moldvay. 626-659, *Nov. 1974*
Italy, From Roman Ruins to Radio: History of Ancient Bridge Building and Road Making Repeats Itself in Modern Public Works and Engineering Projects. By John Patric. 347-394, *Mar. 1940*
Holidays Among the Hill Towns of Umbria and Tuscany. By Paul Wilstach. 401-442, *Apr. 1928*
Inexhaustible Italy. By Arthur Stanley Riggs. 273-368, *Oct. 1916*
See also Florence; Siena

TUSCARORA DEEP, Pacific Ocean:
The Recent Earthquake Wave on the Coast of Japan. By Eliza Ruhamah Scidmore. 285-289, *Sept. 1896*
Reports of Sealing Schooners Cruising in the Neighborhood of Tuscarora Deep in May and June, 1896. By

Eliza Ruhamah Scidmore. 310-312, *Sept. 1896*

TUSCARORA INDIANS:
"The Fire That Never Dies." By Harvey Arden. Photos by Steve Wall. 375-403, *Sept. 1987*

TUSHINGHAM, A. DOUGLAS:
Author
The Men Who Hid the Dead Sea Scrolls. Paintings by Peter V. Bianchi. 785-808, *Dec. 1958*
Jericho Gives Up Its Secrets. By Kathleen M. Kenyon and A. Douglas Tushingham. Photos by Nancy Lord. 853-870, *Dec. 1953*

TUTANKHAMUN:
■■*Ancient Egypt: Discovering its Splendors.* 256 pages. *1978*
Dazzling Legacy of an Ancient Quest. By Alice J. Hall. 293-311, *Mar. 1977*
Golden Masterpieces. 36-39, *Jan. 1974*
Tutankhamun's Golden Trove. By Christiane Desroches Noblecourt. Photos by F. L. Kenett. 625-646, *Oct. 1963*
At the Tomb of Tutankhamen: An Account of the Opening of the Royal Egyptian Sepulcher. By Maynard Owen Williams. 461-508, *May 1923*

TUTTLE, MERLIN D.:
President's Page. By Gilbert M. Grosvenor. *Feb. 1987*
On Assignment in Kenya. *Apr. 1986*
On Assignment in Thailand. *Jan. 1982*
Author-Photographer
Gentle Fliers of the African Night. Contents: Bats. NGS research grant. 540-558, *Apr. 1986*
The Amazing Frog-Eating Bat. 78-91, *Jan. 1982*

TUTUILA (Island), American Samoa, Pacific Ocean:
The Two Samoas, Still Coming of Age. By Robert Booth. Photos by Melinda Berge. 452-473, *Oct. 1985*
America's South Sea Soldiers. By Lorena MacIntyre Quinn. 267-274, *Sept. 1919*

TUVALU. *See* former name, Ellice Islands

TWAIN, MARK:
Editorial. By Gilbert M. Grosvenor. 577, *May 1976*
Editorial. By Gilbert M. Grosvenor. 299, *Sept. 1975*
Mark Twain: Mirror of America. By Noel Grove. Photos by James L. Stanfield. 300-337, *Sept. 1975*
Tom Sawyer's Town. By Jerry Allen. 121-140, *July 1956*
The West Through Boston Eyes. By Stewart Anderson. Included: Today in Mark Twain's Home Town; Exploring Tom Sawyer's Cave. 733-776, *June 1949*

TWEED:
From Barra to Butt in the Hebrides. By Isobel Wylie Hutchison. 559-580, *Oct. 1954*
Over the Sea to Scotland's Skye. By Robert J. Reynolds. 87-112, *July 1952*

TWEEDIE, PENNY: *Photographer*
Arnhem Land Aboriginals Cling to Dreamtime. By Clive Scollay. 644-663, *Nov. 1980*
Coober Pedy: Opal Capital of Australia's Outback. By Kenny Moore. 560-571, *Oct. 1976*

TWEEDSMUIR OF ELSFIELD, SUSAN CHARLOTTE BUCHAN, LADY: *Author*
The Diary of a Pilgrimage. 451-476, *Apr. 1938*

TWEEDSMUIR PARK, British Columbia, Canada:
The Diary of a Pilgrimage. By Lady Tweedsmuir of Elsfield. 451-476, *Apr. 1938*

TWEEDY, OWEN: *Author*
An Unbeliever Joins the Hadj: On the Age-Old Pilgrimage to Mecca, Babies Are Born, Elders Die, and Families May Halt a Year to Earn Funds in Distant Lands. 761-789, *June 1934*

TWELVE National Geographic Society Scientific Projects Under Way. 869-870, *June 1954*

TWENTIETH Anniversary of the Epoch-making Stratosphere Flight by *Explorer II.* NGS research grant. 707, *Nov. 1955*

The **TWENTIETH** Century Comes to Shangri-la–Baltistan. By Galen Rowell. Photos by the author and Barbara Cushman Rowell. Included: War among the peaks. 526-550, *Oct. 1987*

20TH-CENTURY Indians Preserve Customs of the Cliff Dwellers. Photos by William Belknap, Jr. NGS research grant. 196-211, *Feb. 1964*

TWENTY Fathoms Down for Mother-of-Pearl. By Winston Williams. Photos by Bates Littlehales. 512-529, *Apr. 1962*

TWILIGHT Hope for Big Cypress. By Rick Gore. Photos by Patricia Caulfield. 251-273, *Aug. 1976*

TWILIGHT of the Arab Dhow. By Marion Kaplan. 330-351, *Sept. 1974*

TWIN CITIES, Minnesota:
Minneapolis and St. Paul. By Thomas J. Abercrombie. Photos by Annie Griffiths. 665-691, *Nov. 1980*

TWIN Stars of Chile: Valparaiso, the Gateway, and Santiago, the Capital–Key Cities with a Progressive Present and a Romantic Past. By William Joseph Showalter. 197-247, *Feb. 1929*

TWITCHELL, K. S.: *Photographer*
Kano, Mud-made City. Photos by George W. Scott and K. S. Twitchell. 545-552, *May 1944*

2, 4, 5-T (Herbicide):
The Pesticide Dilemma. By Allen A. Boraiko. Photos by Fred Ward. 145-183, *Feb. 1980*

The **TWO** Acapulcos. By James Cerruti. Photos by Thomas Nebbia. 848-878, *Dec. 1964*

Turkoman hunter of Afghanistan sips tea in a guesthouse near Towz Bulaq.
SABRINA AND ROLAND MICHAUD

TWO American Teachers in China. By Elisabeth B. Booz. Photos by Thomas Nebbia. 793-813, *June 1981*

TWO and a Half Miles Down. By Georges S. Houot. NGS research grant. 80-86, *July 1954*

TWO Berlins–A Generation Apart. By Priit J. Vesilind. Photos by Cotton Coulson. 2-51, *Jan. 1982*

TWO Englands. By Allan C. Fisher, Jr. Photos by Cary Wolinsky. 442-481, *Oct. 1979*

TWO Fighting Tribes of the Sudan. By Merian C. Cooper. Photos by Ernest B. Schoedsack. 465-486, *Oct. 1929*

The **TWO** Great Moorish Religious Dances. By George Edmund Holt. 777-785, *Aug. 1911*

TWO Great Undertakings. Contents: Work of U. S. Bureau of Reclamation and U. S. Forest Service. 645-647, *Nov. 1906*

TWO Hundred Miles up the Kuskokwim. By Charles Hallock. 85-92, *Mar. 1898*

TWO Possible Solutions for the Eastern Problem. By James Bryce. 1149-1157, *Nov. 1912*

The **TWO** Samoas, Still Coming of Age. By Robert Booth. Photos by Melinda Berge. 452-473, *Oct. 1985*

The **TWO** Souls of Peru. By Harvey Arden. Photos by William Albert Allard. 284-321, *Mar. 1982*

2,000 Miles Through Europe's Oldest Kingdom. By Isobel Wylie Hutchison. Photos by Maynard Owen Williams. 141-180, *Feb. 1949*

2,300-YEAR-OLD Greek Ship Reaches Port at Last. By Susan W. and

Michael L. Katzev. NGS research grant. 618-625, *Nov. 1974*

TWO Wheels Along the Mexican Border. By William Albert Allard. 591-635, *May 1971*

The **TWO** Worlds of Michigan. By Noel Grove. Photos by James L. Amos. 802-843, *June 1979*

TXUKAHAMEI INDIANS:
Brazil's Txukahameis: Good-bye to the Stone Age. Photos by W. Jesco von Puttkamer. 270-283, *Feb. 1975*
Amazon–The River Sea. By Loren McIntyre. 456-495, *Oct. 1972*

TYLER, JOHN:
Profiles of the Presidents: II. A Restless Nation Moves West. By Frank Freidel. 80-121, *Jan. 1965*

TYOSEN. *See* Korea

TYPES and Costumes of Old Sweden. Photos by Gustav Heurlin, G. W. Cronquist, Wilhelm Tobien, Charles Martin. 425-440, *Oct. 1928*

TYPHOONS:
The Lost Fleet of Kublai Khan. By Torao Mozai. Photos by Koji Nakamura. Paintings by Issho Yada. 634-649, *Nov. 1982*

TYPHOID FEVER:
Redeeming the Tropics. By William Joseph Showalter. 344-364, *Mar. 1914*
Our Army Versus a Bacillus. By Alton G. Grinnell. 1146-1152, *Oct. 1913*
Economic Loss to the People of the United States Through Insects That Carry Disease. By L. O. Howard. 735-749, *Aug. 1909*

TYREE, DAVID M.:
Nomination Page. In Antarctica. *May 1962*
Author
New Era in the Loneliest Continent. Photos by Albert Moldvay. Contents: Antarctica. 260-296, *Feb. 1963*

TYROL (Region), Austria-Italy. *See* Tirol

TYRRELL, ROBERT A.:
Photographer
Hummingbirds: The Nectar Connection. By Paul W. Ewald. 223-227, *Feb. 1982*

TYRRHENIAN SEA:
Fishing in the Whirlpool of Charybdis. By Paul A. Zahl. 579-618, *Nov. 1953*

TYUMEN OBLAST (Region), U.S.S.R.:
Siberia's Empire Road, the River Ob. By Robert Paul Jordan. Photos by Dean Conger. 145-181, *Feb. 1976*

TZELIUTSING, Sichuan Province, China:
Salt for China's Daily Rice. 329-336, *Sept. 1944*

TZOTZIL INDIANS. *See* Zotzil Indians

TZU-KUNG, Sichuan Province, China. *See* Tzeliutsing

U
V

UAXACTÚN
UKRAINIANS
ULTRALIGHT AIRCRAFT
ULU BURUN
ULYSSES
UNDERGROUND RAILROAD
UNDERWATER EXPLORATION
UNITED NATIONS
UNITED STATES
UNIVERSE
UR
URANIUM
URANUS
URBAN LIFE
VALLEY FORGE
VALLEY OF THE MOON
VANCOUVER ISLAND
VASA
VEGETABLES
VENUS
VERACRUZ
VERSAILLES
VESTMANNAEYJAR
VESUVIUS
VICTORIA FALLS
VICUÑAS
VIETNAM VETERANS MEMORIAL
VIETNAMESE REFUGEES
VIKINGS
VILCABAMBA
VIRGIN ISLANDS
VIRUNGA MOUNTAINS
VIRUSES
VOLCANOES
VOLGA
VOODOO
VOYAGER
VULTURES

*In the South Pacific near New Hanover Island
barracuda enchant both diver and photographer
as they rotate in a slow ballet.*

DAVID DOUBILET

1045

USBR. *See* U. S. Bureau of Reclamation

U.S.S.R. *See* Union of Soviet Socialist Republics

UAUPÉS (River), South America. *See* Vaupés (River)

UAXACTÚN, Guatemala:

Unearthing America's Ancient History: Investigation Suggests That the Maya May Have Designed the First Astronomical Observatory in the New World in Order to Cultivate Corn. By Sylvanus Griswold Morley. 99-126, *July 1931*

UBAIGUBI, Papua New Guinea:

Fertility Rites and Sorcery in a New Guinea Village. By Gillian Gillison. Photos by David Gillison. 124-146, *July 1977*

"UBANGI" TRIBESPEOPLE. *See* Sara Tribespeople

UBO TRIBESPEOPLE:

■ The Last Tribes of Mindanao. 882A-882B, *Dec. 1971*
Help for Philippine Tribes in Trouble. By Kenneth MacLeish. Photos by Dean Conger. 220-255, *Aug. 1971*

UCAYALI (River), Peru:

Some Wonderful Sights in the Andean Highlands: The Oldest City in America. Sailing on the Lake of the Clouds: The Yosemite of Peru. By Harriet Chalmers Adams. 597-618, *Sept. 1908*

UDAIPUR, India:

The Marble Dams of Rajputana. By Eleanor Maddock. 469-499, *Nov. 1921*

UDORN ROYAL THAI AIR FORCE BASE, Thailand:

Air Rescue Behind Enemy Lines. By Howard Sochurek. 346-369, *Sept. 1968*

UEMURA, NAOMI:
Author-Photographer

Solo to the Pole. Photos by the author and Ira Block. 298-325, *Sept. 1978*

UGANDA:

Uganda–Land Beyond Sorrow. Article and photos by Robert Caputo. 468-491, *Apr. 1988*
Journey Up the Nile. By Robert Caputo. 577-633, *May 1985*
Return to Uganda. By Jerry and Sarah Kambites. Photos by Sarah Leen. 73-89, *July 1980*
Uganda, Africa's Uneasy Heartland. By Howard La Fay. Photos by George F. Mobley. 708-735, *Nov. 1971*
Orphans of the Wild. By Bruce G. Kinloch. 683-699, *Nov. 1962*
Where Elephants Have Right of Way. By George and Jinx Rodger. Photos by George Rodger. 363-389, *Sept. 1960*
Kayaks Down the Nile. By John M. Goddard. 697-732, *May 1955*
Safari from Congo to Cairo. By Elsie May Bell Grosvenor. Photos by Gilbert Grosvenor. 721-771, *Dec. 1954*
Britain Tackles the East African Bush. By W. Robert Moore. 311-352, *Mar. 1950*
Roaming Africa's Unfenced Zoos. By W. Robert Moore. 353-380, *Mar. 1950*
Uganda, "Land of Something New": Equatorial African Area Reveals Snow-crowned Peaks, Crater Lakes, Jungle-story Beasts, Human Giants, and Forest Pygmies. By Jay Marston. 109-130, *Jan. 1937*
Elephant Hunting in Equatorial Africa with Rifle and Camera. By Carl E. Akeley. 779-810, *Aug. 1912*
Wild Man and Wild Beast in Africa. By Theodore Roosevelt. 1-33, *Jan. 1911*
Where Roosevelt Will Hunt. By Sir Harry Johnston. 207-256, *Mar. 1909*
Amid the Snow Peaks of the Equator: A Naturalist's Explorations Around Ruwenzori, with an Excursion to the Congo State, and an Account of the Terrible Scourge of Sleeping Sickness. By A.F.R. Wollaston. 256-277, *Mar. 1909*
A Great African Lake. By Sir Henry M. Stanley. Contents: Lake Victoria. 169-172, *May 1902*
See also Ruwenzori; Virunga Mountains

UIGHURS. *See* Uygurs

UIST, North, and South Uist (Islands), Scotland:

Isles on the Edge of the Sea: Scotland's Outer Hebrides. By Kenneth MacLeish. Photos by Thomas Nebbia. 676-711, *May 1970*

UITLANDERS:

The Witwatersrand and the Revolt of the Uitlanders. By George F. Becker. 349-367, *Nov. 1896*
Africa Since 1888, with Special Reference to South Africa and Abyssinia. By Gardiner G. Hubbard. 157-175, *May 1896*

UJUNG KULON NATIONAL PARK, Java (Island), Indonesia: ·

Return of Java's Wildlife. By Dieter and Mary Plage. 750-771, *June 1985*

UKRAINIAN S.S.R., U.S.S.R.:

Ukraine. By Mike Edwards. Photos by Steve Raymer. 595-631, *May 1987*
Chernobyl–One Year After. By Mike Edwards. Photos by Steve Raymer. Paintings by Pierre Mion. 632-653, *May 1987*
The Society's New Map of Soviet Russia. 716-718, *Dec. 1944*
Liberated Ukraine. By Eddy Gilmore. 513-536, *May 1944*
The Races of Europe. By Edwin A. Grosvenor. 441-534, *Dec. 1918*
The Ukraine, Past and Present. By Nevin O. Winter. 114-128, *Aug. 1918*
See also The Crimea

UKRAINIANS:

Easter Greetings From the Ukrainians. By Robert Paul Jordan. Photos by James A. Sugar. 556-563, *Apr. 1972*

ULITHI (Atoll), Caroline Islands:

Adventures with the Survey Navy. By Irving Johnson. 131-148, *July 1947*
American Pathfinders in the Pacific. By William H. Nicholas. 617-640, *May 1946*

ULM, CHARLES T. P.: *Author*

Our Conquest of the Pacific: The Narrative of the 7,400-Mile Flight from San Francisco to Brisbane in Three Ocean Hops. By Charles E. Kingsford-Smith and Charles T. P. Ulm. 371-402, *Oct. 1928*

ULSTER. *See* Ireland, Northern

ULSTER COUNTY, New York:

Shawangunk Mountain. By N. H. Darton. 23-34, *Mar. 17, 1894*

The **ULTIMATE** Challenge. By James Whittaker. 624-639, *May 1979*

The **ULTIMATE** Washington. Panorama. *Mar. 1915*

In an exuberant dance, Tutsi men in Uganda recall their days of glory when they ruled neighboring Rwanda until deposed by a rival tribe in 1959. GEORGE F. MOBLEY, NGS

Struggling to walk even with support from her mother, Jane Namirimu, left, is one of thousands of Ugandans infected by the AIDS virus. ROBERT CAPUTO

U
V

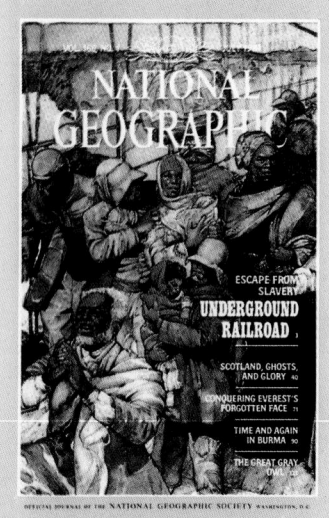

Tektite II. 256-296. I. Science's Window on the Sea. By John G. VanDerwalker. Photos by Bates Littlehales. 256-289; II. All-girl Team Tests the Habitat. By Sylvia A. Earle. Paintings by Pierre Mion. 291-296, *Aug. 1971*

Working for Weeks on the Sea Floor. By Jacques-Yves Cousteau. Photos by Philippe Cousteau and Bates Littlehales. NGS research grant. 498-537, *Apr. 1966*

Outpost Under the Ocean. By Edwin A. Link. Photos by Bates Littlehales. NGS research grant. 530-533, *Apr. 1965*

The Deepest Days. By Robert Sténuit. NGS research grant. 534-547, *Apr. 1965*

Tomorrow on the Deep Frontier. By Edwin A. Link. NGS research grant. 778-801, *June 1964*
See also Conshelf Bases

UNDERWATER PARKS. *See* Buck Island Reef National Monument; Great Barrier Reef, Australia; Izu Oceanic Park, Japan; John Pennekamp Coral Reef State Park; Ras Muhammad

UNDERWOOD, ERIC: *Author*
The Preservation of England's Historic and Scenic Treasures. 413-440, *Apr. 1945*
The British Commonwealth of Nations:

"Organized Freedom" Around the World. 485-524, *Apr. 1943*

An **UNDISCOVERED** Island Off the Northern Coast of Alaska. By Marcus Baker, Edward Perry Herendeen, and A. W. Greely. 76-83, *July 10, 1893*

UNEARTHING America's Ancient History: Investigation Suggests That the Maya May Have Designed the First Astronomical Observatory in the New World in Order to Cultivate Corn. By Sylvanus Griswold Morley. 99-126, *July 1931*

UNEARTHING Red Bay's Whaling History. By James A. Tuck. Photos by Bill Curtsinger. Paintings by Richard Schlecht. 50-57, *July 1985*

UNEARTHING the Oldest Known Maya. By Norman Hammond. Photos by Lowell Georgia and Martha Cooper. NGS research grant. 126-140, *July 1982*

UNESCO WORLD HERITAGE SITES. *See* World Heritage Sites

UNEXPECTED Glory in Canada's Cold Seas. Photos by David Doubilet. Text by Larry Kohl. 526-551, *Apr. 1980*

The **UNEXPLORED** Philippines from the Air: Map-making Over Jungle Lands Never Before Seen By White

Men. By George W. Goddard. 311-343, *Sept. 1930*

UNFAMILIAR Glories of the West. 733-791, *June 1974*

UNFURLING Old Glory on Canton Island. Photos by Richard H. Stewart and others. Painting by Charles Bittinger. 753-760, *June 1938*

UNGAVA (Region), Quebec, Canada. *See* Chubb Crater

UNGERN-STERNBERG, IRINA, BARONESS: *Author*
Estonia: At Russia's Baltic Gate: War Often Has Ravaged This Little Nation Whose Identity Was Long Submerged in the Vast Sea of Russian Peoples. 803-834, *Dec. 1939*

UNGULATES:
The Joy of Pigs. By Kent Britt. Photos by George F. Mobley. 398-415, *Sept. 1978*
Deer of the World: As Workers, Pets, and Graceful "Living Statuary" in Parks and Estates, These Versatile Creatures Have Endeared Themselves to Mankind. By Victor H. Cahalane. Paintings by Walter A. Weber. 463-510, *Oct. 1939*
The Indispensable Sheep. 512-528, *Apr. 1928*
The Taurine World: Cattle and Their Place in the Human Scheme–Wild Types and Modern Breeds in Many Lands. By Alvin Howard Sanders. Paintings by Edward Herbert Miner. Contents: Aberdeen-Angus, Ayrshire, Banteng, Brahman, Brown Swiss, Devon, Dutch Belted, Gaur, Guernsey, Hereford, Holstein-Friesian, Indian Buffalo, Jersey, Nivernais-Charolais, Red Africander, Red Polls, Shorthorn, Texas Longhorn, West Highlander, Wild White, Yak. Paintings by Edward Herbert Miner. 591-710, *Dec. 1925*
The Story of the Horse: The Development of Man's Companion in War Camp, on Farm, in the Marts of Trade, and in the Field of Sports. By William Harding Carter. Paintings by Edward Herbert Miner. Included: Horses of the World (paintings). 455-566, *Nov. 1923*
■■ *The Horses of the World: The Development of Man's Companion in War Camp, on Farm, in the Marts of Trade, and in the Field of Sports. By William Harding Carter. Art by Edward Herbert Miner. 118 pages. 1923*
See also Antelopes; Bighorn Sheep; Bison, American; Burros, Wild; Camels; Caribou; Cattle Raising; Deer; Giraffes; Goats; Hippopotamuses; Hog Raising; Horses; Horses, Wild; Lamoids; Moose; Mountain Goats; Mule Deer; Musk-Oxen; Reindeer; Rhinoceroses; Sheep Raising; Water Buffalo

U
V

UNIMAK (Island), Alaska:
Mountains on Unimak Island, Alaska. By Ferdinand Westdahl. 91-99, *Mar. 1903*

Nearly as revolutionary an invention as the Aqua-Lung, a small submersible takes scientists past the Cayman Wall, an undersea escarpment in the Caribbean. EMORY KRISTOF, NGS

Ukrainian poet Taras Shevchenko condemned the 1654 unification of Ukraine and Russia. STEVE RAYMER, NGS

In a scene of primeval beauty, reindeer course through a valley in Siberia. DEAN CONGER, NGS

U
V

of America series. Included: Maryland, Delaware, Virginia, North Carolina, South Carolina. On reverse: First Encounters, Farming and Frontiering, Rivalries and Rupture, Diversified Growth, Uneven Growth. *June 1988*

Discovering America. By Małgorzata Niezabitowska. Photos by Tomasz Tomaszewski. 44-79, *Jan. 1988*

■■ *America's Hidden Wilderness: Lands of Seclusion.* Contents: Arctic regions; Baxter State Park, Maine; l'Eau Claire wilderness, Quebec; Grand Gulch Primitive Area, Utah; Great Burn wilderness area, Idaho-Montana; Lacandon Forest, Mexico; Mojave Desert. 200 pages. *1988*

■■ *Historical Atlas of the United States.* 289 pages. *1988*

■■ *Mountain Adventure: Exploring the Appalachian Trail.* By Ron Fisher. Photos by Sam Abell. 200 pages. *1988*

✣ *The United States; The Territorial Growth of the United States.* Included: Europe Claims North America, A New Nation on Stage, Expanding West of the Mississippi, Coming of Age, Coast To Coast, The Union Holds, The Fifty States Today, A Broader View. *Sept. 1987*

✣ *Great Lakes,* The Making of America series. Included: Michigan, Wisconsin. On reverse: Indians, French, British; Creation of a Borderland; Influx of Settlers; Lake-country Lumber; Industrial Powerhouse; Region in Readjustment. *July 1987*

Tornado! By Peter Miller. Photos by Chris Johns. Included: Map of tornado activity, 1950-1985; diagram of tornado dynamics. 690-715, *June 1987*

✣ *New England,* The Making of America series. Included: Maine, New Hampshire, Vermont, Massachusetts, Rhode Island, Connecticut, and eastern New York. On reverse: Indians and Outposts, Puritan Commonwealth, Greater New England, Industrial Hive, Immigrants and Industries, A New Vitality. *Feb. 1987*

■■ *America's Outdoor Wonders: State Parks and Sanctuaries.* 199 pages. *1987*

■■ *Window on America.* Contents: America's scenic treasures. 199 pages. *1987*

✣ *Northern Plains,* The Making of America series. Included: Montana, Wyoming, North Dakota, South Dakota, Nebraska, Minnesota, Iowa, and in Canada: Saskatchewan, Manitoba, Ontario. On reverse: New Frontiers, Indians in Transition, Furs and Footholds, Steel Rails and Settlers, King Wheat, Patterns of Change. *Dec. 1986*

✣ *Pacific Northwest,* The Making of America series. Included: Idaho, Montana, Oregon, Washington. On reverse: Fur Trade Rivalries, Conquest-Colonization, Abrupt Change, Pacific Lumber Empire, Coming of Age. *Aug. 1986*

Japanese Americans: Home at Last. By

Arthur Zich. Photos by Michael S. Yamashita. 512-539, *Apr. 1986*

✣ *Texas,* The Making of America series. On reverse: Weak Spanish Frontier, Eras of Independence, Vigorous Expansion, A Broadening Base, New Frontiers, Mexican Borderland. *Mar. 1986*

■■ *America's Great Hideaways.* Contents: Arizona, Baja California, California, Canadian Rockies, Finger Lakes, Kauai, Martha's Vineyard and Nantucket, Minnesota, Montana, Oregon, Suwannee River, Virgin Islands, and West Virginia. 199 pages. *1986*

✣ *Ohio Valley,* The Making of America series. Included: Tennessee-Tombigbee Waterway, West Virginia, Illinois, Tennessee, Kentucky, Ohio, Indiana. On reverse: Indians and Europeans, Speculation and Colonization, Transport Revolutions, Region Rent Asunder, Further Divergence, A New Era. *Dec. 1985*

✣ *Central Plains,* The Making of America series. Included: Iowa, Illinois, Missouri, Arkansas, Nebraska, Kansas, Oklahoma. On reverse: Indians and Entryways, Indian Land-White Land, The Great Assault, Indian Relocation, Indian Territory-The Last Stop, Last Frontiers, Dust Bowl of the Continent, Agricultural Heartland. *Sept. 1985*

Life on the Line: U. S.-Mexican Border. By Mark Kramer. Photos by Danny Lehman. 720-749, *June 1985*

Designer of the Vietnam Veterans Memorial, Maya Lin incorporated 58,000 names of those who died in that war. JAMES P. BLAIR, NGS

VOL. 167, NO. 5   MAY 1985

NATIONAL
GEOGRAPHIC

VIETNAM
MEMORIAL
ECHOES OF A WAR 552
TO HEAL A NATION 555
TEN YEARS LATER 574

JOURNEY UP THE NILE 577

WORLDS WITHIN
THE ATOM 634

BOB MARSHALL 664
BATTLE FOR
HIS WILDERNESS 690

SEE NATIONAL GEOGRAPHIC EXPLORER EVERY SUNDAY ON NICKELODEON CABLE TV

Vietnam Veterans Memorial: America Remembers. Included: Echoes of a War. By Timothy S. Kolly; To Heal a Nation. By Joel L. Swerdlow; An Interview with Maya Lin, designer; Editor's Postscript: Southeast Asia Ten Years Later. 552-575, *May 1985*

Hazardous Waste...Storing Up Trouble. By Allen A. Boraiko. Photos by Fred Ward. 318-351, *Mar. 1985*

Susquehanna: America's Small-Town River. By Peter Miller. Photos by William T. Douthitt. 352-383, *Mar. 1985*

Northern Approaches: Maine and the Maritimes, The Making of America series. Included: European Outreach, Northeast Contested, Shifting Population, A Changing Economy, The Cultural Imprint. *Feb. 1985*

The Poppy. By Peter T. White. Photos by Steve Raymer. Included: Drug traffic control efforts; Drug addiction research and treatment; Funding poppy eradication programs abroad. 143-189, *Feb. 1985*

America's Seashore Wonderlands. 199 pages. *1985*

America's Wild Woodlands. 199 pages. *1985*

Exploring America's Scenic Highways. 199 pages. *1985*

Liberty: The Statue and the American Dream. By Leslie Allen. The official book for the Centennial of the Statue of Liberty published by the Statue of Liberty-Ellis Island Foundation, Inc. Prepared and produced as a public service by NGS. 304 pages. *1985*

Do We Treat Our Soil Like Dirt? By Boyd Gibbons. Photos by Steven C. Wilson. 350-389, *Sept. 1984*

Patterns of Plenty: The Art in Farming. Photo essay by Georg Gerster. 391-399, *Sept. 1984*

Central Rockies, The Making of America series. Included: Colorado, Utah, Wyoming. On reverse: Fur and Frontier, Mission to Succeed,

Mineral Riches, Lure of the Mountains. *Aug. 1984*

Far West, The Making of America series. Included: California and Nevada. On reverse: Northern and Southern California–a Shifting Rivalry, Spanish Imprint, Sudden Transition, The New Eden, Water–the Key to Growth, Explosive Growth. *Apr. 1984*

El Niño's Ill Wind. By Thomas Y. Canby. Included: Severe storms and flooding caused by the current. 144-183, *Feb. 1984*

Alaska, The Making of America series. Included: Native Alaska, Russian America, Seward's Folly or New Eldorado?, Military Alaska, The 49th State. *Jan. 1984*

Exploring America's Valleys: From the Shenandoah to the Rio Grande. 199 pages. *1984*

Lakes, Peaks, and Prairies: Discovering the United States-Canadian Border. By Thomas O'Neill. Photos by Michael S. Yamashita. 199 pages. *1984*

Natural Wonders of North America. By Catherine O'Neill. Juvenile. 104 pages. *1984*

Our Threatened Inheritance: Natural Treasures of the United States. By Ron Fisher. Photos by James P. Blair. 400 pages. *1984*

A Guide to Our Federal Lands. 227 pages. *1984*

The Story of America: A National Geographic Picture Atlas. By John Anthony Scott. Juvenile. 324 pages. *1984*

Wild Lands for Wildlife: America's National Refuges. By Noel Grove. Photos by Bates Littlehales. 207 pages. *1984*

Humble Masterpieces: Decoys. By George Reiger. Photos by Kenneth Garrett. Included: Waterfowl hunting in the United States. 639-663, *Nov. 1983*

Satellites That Serve Us. By Thomas Y. Canby. Included: Images of Earth. 281-335, *Sept. 1983*

Deep South, The Making of America series. Included: Alabama, Florida, Georgia, Louisiana, Mississippi, South Carolina, and parts of Arkansas, North Carolina, and Tennessee. On reverse: Indian Legacy, Imperial Footholds, Three Empires and Three Races, Cotton Kingdom, Postbellum, New Deep South, Subtropical Playground. *Aug. 1983*

Swing Low, Sweet Chariot! By Noel Grove. Photos by Bruce Dale. 2-35, *July 1983*

Wrestlin' for a Livin' With King Coal. By Michael E. Long. Photos by Michael O'Brien. 793-819, *June 1983*

The Fascinating World of Trash. By Peter T. White. Photos by Louie Psihoyos. 424-457, *Apr. 1983*

Atlantic Gateways, The Making of America series. Included: Delaware, Maryland, New Jersey, New York, Pennsylvania, northern Virginia, West Virginia, and in Canada, southern Ontario and southern Quebec.

On reverse: Indians and Trade, Nation in the Making, Peopling of the Gateways, Race for the Hinterlands, Growth of Industry, Spreading Urban Corridors. *Mar. 1983*

Herbs for All Seasons. By Lonnelle Aikman. Photos by Sam Abell. Picture portfolio text by Larry Kohl. 386-409, *Mar. 1983*

America's Hidden Corners: Places Off the Beaten Path. Contents: Badlands, Chesapeake Bay, Four Corners, Great Basin, Gulf Coast, Michigan's Upper Peninsula, and Ozarks. 199 pages. *1983*

America's Wild and Scenic Rivers. 199 pages. *1983*

Preserving America's Past. 199 pages. *1983*

The Making of America: 17 New Maps Tie the Nation to Its Past. By Wilbur E. Garrett, Editor. 630-633, *Nov. 1982*

The Southwest, The Making of America series. *Nov. 1982*

The Chip: Electronic Mini-marvel. By Allen A. Boraiko. Photos by Charles O'Rear. 421-457, *Oct. 1982*

America's Federal Lands; The United States. *Sept. 1982*

The Incredible Potato. By Robert E. Rhoades. Photos by Martin Rogers. 668-694, *May 1982*

Silver: A Mineral of Excellent Nature. By Allen A. Boraiko. Photos by Fred Ward. 280-313, *Sept. 1981*

The American Red Cross: A Century of Service. By Louise Levathes. Photos by Annie Griffiths. 777-791, *June 1981*

Wild Cargo: the Business of Smuggling Animals. By Noel Grove. Photos by Steve Raymer. 287-315, *Mar. 1981*

Special Report on Energy, an extra issue of NGM. Included: An atlas of America's energy resources. *(Feb. 1981)*

With love for the U.S., a Mardi Gras celebrator stated: "My name doesn't matter, I'm just an American." TOMASZ TOMASZEWSKI

BOOKS   MAPS   TELEVISION

Anchored by a reproduction of a 1784 United States map, a supplement to the September 1987 issue traces the country's territorial growth from colonial to modern times.

At the end of a 4,751-mile, five-year walk across America, Peter and Barbara Jenkins near an Oregon beach in 1979.   COTTON COULSON

U
V

AGRICULTURE

Bittersweet tunes on a horn of plenty

FROM BRITISH BOILERS TO CASEY JONES

Railroads roar into the picture

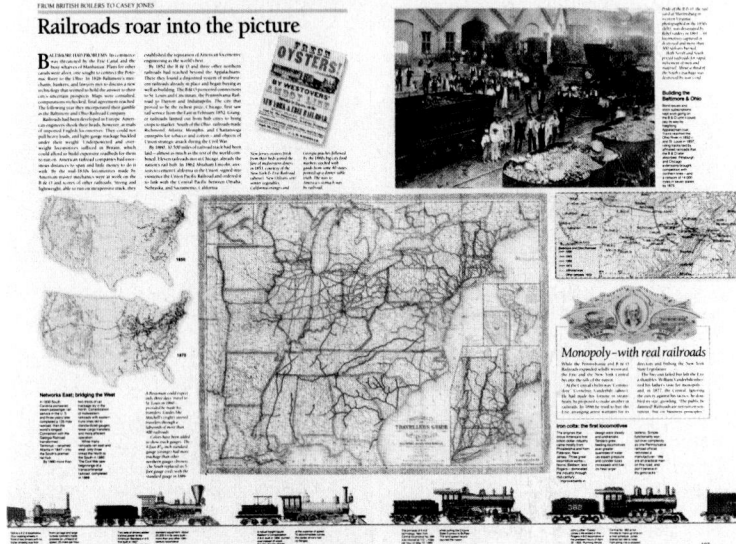

Monopoly—with real railroads

The Society's **Historical Atlas of the United States** *tracks the country's growth with illustrations, text, and some 600 maps—from railroads and bumper crops to languages.*

Turbulence and triumphs of recent decades fill this chronology section in the historical atlas.

To supply four million U.S. soldiers fighting in France during World War I, an industrial army of 400,000 riveters, machinists, and other workers manned the shipyards to build up the nation's merchant fleet.

© COMMITTEE ON PUBLIC INFORMATION

U. S. AGRICULTURAL RESEARCH CENTER, Beltsville, Maryland:

U. S. AIR FORCE:

U. S. AIR FORCE ACADEMY, Colorado:

U. S. ANTARCTIC RESEARCH PROGRAM (USARP):

U. S. ARMED FORCES:

Capable of carrying an eight-ton arsenal, F-4C Phantom II was the fastest tactical fighting plane that the U.S. Air Force used in the mid-1960s. EMORY KRISTOF, NGS

Army; U. S. Coast Guard; U. S. Marine Corps; U. S. Navy; *and* War Memorials

U. S. ARMY:

U. S. ARMY AIR FORCES:

A World War II GI leads a mule laden with cans of plasma and other medical supplies up a mountain trail toward troops at the Italian front. OLLIE ATKINS FROM AMERICAN RED CROSS

A section of an offshore-drilling rig is towed through Louisiana's Atchafalaya swamp, largely managed by the U.S. Army Corps of Engineers for flood control. C. C. LOCKWOOD

Vietnamese gunman and Capt. Vernon Gillespie, of the U.S. Army Special Forces, flank a montagnard wounded in his people's fight for autonomy. HOWARD SOCHUREK

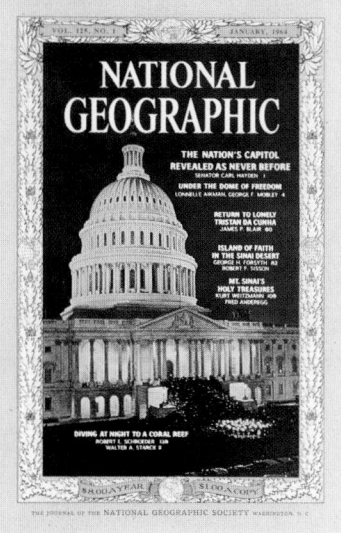

U. S. BUREAU OF STANDARDS. *See* National Bureau of Standards

U. S. BUREAU OF THE CENSUS:

U. S. CAPITOL, Washington, D. C.:

U. S. COAST AND GEODETIC SURVEY:

U. S. COAST GUARD:

Geographers get down to business preparing the 1960 census at the U.S. Census Bureau. THOMAS J. ABERCROMBIE, NGS

Capt. Lilbourn Pharris directs a U.S. Coast Guard icebreaker through Lake Superior's winter armor. JAMES L. AMOS, NGS

Electronic examinations of the U.S. Constitution at the National Archives record signs of deterioration. SAM ABELL

At the National Archives in Washington, D.C., visitors view the U.S. Constitution on September 17, anniversary of its signing.   SAM ABELL

U. S. GOVERNMENT AGENCIES:

U. S. HYDROGRAPHIC OFFICE:

U. S. IMMIGRATION AND NATURALIZATION SERVICE:

U. S. MARINE CORPS:

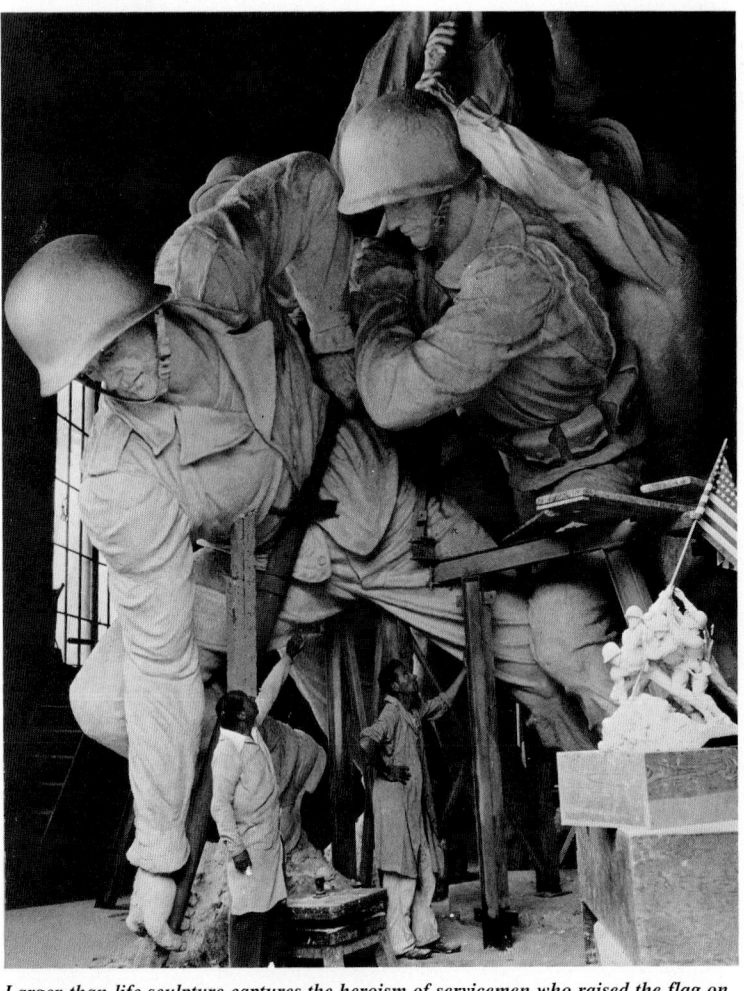

Larger-than-life sculpture captures the heroism of servicemen who raised the flag on Iwo Jima in 1945. U.S. MARINE CORPS, OFFICIAL

Catapult officer sends a fighter down the flight deck of a U.S. Navy aircraft carrier in the Pacific in the 1950s. WILBUR E. GARRETT, NGS

Balloons and bunting send the U.S. Navy submarine Chicago *into the James River near the Hampton Roads waterway to Chesapeake Bay.* KAREN KASMAUSKI

In the early 1900s the U.S. Navy's **New Hampshire** *fires a broadside of more than eight tons.*   UNDERWOOD & UNDERWOOD/THE BETTMANN ARCHIVE

■■ BOOKS ✧ MAPS ■ TELEVISION

Rainwater-filled pool on St. Thomas overlooks the harbor of Charlotte Amalie, capital of the U.S. Virgin Islands. JODI COBB, NGS

The U. S. Weather Bureau at the Paris Exposition. 81-82, *Feb. 1901*

Loss of Property from Lightning. 82, *Feb. 1901*

Kite Work of the Weather Bureau. By H. C. Frankenfield. 55-62, *Feb. 1900*

The International Cloud Work of the Weather Bureau. By Frank H. Bigelow. 351-354, *Sept. 1899*

Geographic Work of the General Government. By Henry Gannett. 329-338, *July 1898*

Geographical Research in the United States. By Gardiner G. Hubbard and Marcus Baker. 285-293, *Oct. 1897*

United States Daily Atmospheric Survey. By Willis L. Moore. 299-303, *Oct. 1897*

The Weather Bureau River and Flood System. By Willis L. Moore. 302-307, *Sept. 1896*

See also present designation, National Weather Service; *and* U. S. Signal Service

UNIVERSE:

Rethinking the Big Bang: Maybe It Didn't Happen. Geographica. *Dec. 1988*

■■ *National Geographic Picture Atlas of Our Universe.* By Roy A. Gallant. Juvenile. 284 pages. 1980; rev. ed. *1986*

The Once and Future Universe. By Rick Gore. Photos by James A. Sugar. Paintings by Barron Storey. Picture text by David Jeffery. 704-749, *June 1983*

Journey Into the Universe Through Time and Space; National Geographic-Palomar Sky Survey Charting the Heavens. Supplement. *June 1983*

■■ *The Amazing Universe.* By Herbert Friedman. Included: Theories of astronomy. 199 pages. *1975*

The Incredible Universe. By Kenneth F. Weaver. Photos by James P. Blair. 589-625, *May 1974*

Pioneers in Man's Search for the Universe. Paintings by Jean-Leon Huens. Text by Thomas Y. Canby. 627-633, *May 1974*

Sky Survey Charts the Universe. By Ira Sprague Bowen. NGS research grant. 780-781, *Dec. 1956*

Completing the Atlas of the Universe (National Geographic Society-Palomar Observatory Sky Survey). By Ira Sprague Bowen. Included: Sky Survey Plates Unlock Secrets of the Stars. NGS research grant. 185-190, *Aug. 1955*

Our Universe Unfolds New Wonders. By Albert G. Wilson. NGS research grant. 245-260, *Feb. 1952*

Mapping the Unknown Universe. By F. Barrows Colton. NGS research grant. 401-420, *Sept. 1950*

News of the Universe: Mars Swings Nearer the Earth, Sunspots Wane, and a Giant New Telescopic Eye Soon Will Peer Into Unexplored Depths of Space. By F. Barrows Colton. Included: Solar System's Eternal Show. Paintings by Charles Bittinger. 1-32, *July 1939*

See also Solar System; Stars

SPECIAL DOUBLE SUPPLEMENT: THE UNIVERSE

VOL. 163, NO. 6   JUNE 1983

NATIONAL GEOGRAPHIC

THE ONCE AND FUTURE UNIVERSE 704

THAT NOBLE RIVER, THE THAMES 750

GOOD TIMES AND BAD IN COAL COUNTRY 793

WARRIORS FROM A WATERY GRAVE 821

LAST OF THE BLACK-FOOTED FERRETS? 828

OFFICIAL JOURNAL OF THE NATIONAL GEOGRAPHIC SOCIETY WASHINGTON D.C.

UNIVERSITIES AND COLLEGES:

Atlanta, Pacesetter City of the South. By William S. Ellis. Photos by James L. Amos. Included: Atlanta University Center (Atlanta University, Clark, Interdenominational Theological Center, Morehouse, Morris Brown, Spelman); Emory University; Georgia Institute of Technology. 246-281, *Feb. 1969*

California, the Golden Magnet. By William Graves. Included: Stanford University, University of California, University of Southern California. 595-679, *May 1966*

Pittsburgh, Pattern for Progress. By William J. Gill. Photos by Clyde Hare. Included: Carnegie Institute of Technology, University of Pittsburgh. 342-371, *Mar. 1965*

Young-Old Lebanon Lives by Trade. By Thomas J. Abercrombie. Included: American University of Beirut. 479-523, *Apr. 1958*

Robert College, Turkish Gateway to the Future. By Franc Shor. Included: American College for Girls, Robert Academy. 399-418, *Sept. 1957*

Washington's Historic Georgetown. By William A. Kinney. 513-544, *Apr. 1953*

Literary Landmarks of Massachusetts. By William H. Nicholas. Photos by B. Anthony Stewart and John E. Fletcher. Included: Amherst College, Boston College, College of the Holy Cross, Harvard University, Smith College. 279-310, *Mar. 1950*

Pittsburgh: Workshop of the Titans. By Albert W. Atwood. Included: Carnegie Institute of Technology, University of Pittsburgh. 117-144, *July 1949*

A Texan Teaches American History at Cambridge University. By J. Frank Dobie. 409-441, *Apr. 1946*

American Alma Maters in the Near East. By Maynard Owen Williams. Contents: American University at Cairo; American University of

Beirut; İstanbul Woman's College; Robert College. 237-256, *Aug. 1945*

The Long River of New England: In War and Peace, from Mountain Wilderness to the Sea, Flows the Connecticut River, Through a Valley Abounding in History, Scenery, Inventive Genius, and Industry. By Albert W. Atwood. Included: Amherst College; Dartmouth College; Mount Holyoke College; Smith College; Wesleyan University; Yale University. 401-434, *Apr. 1943*

Within the Halls of Cambridge. By Philip Broad. 333-349, *Sept. 1936*

Oxford, Mother of Anglo-Saxon Learning. By E. John Long. 563-596, *Nov. 1929*

Geography in the University of Chicago. 163-164, *Apr. 1903*

See also universities by name

UNIVERSITY OF ALASKA: Arctic Research Laboratory:

Scientists Ride Ice Islands on Arctic Odysseys. By Lowell Thomas, Jr. Photos by Ted Spiegel. 670-691, *Nov. 1965*

UNIVERSITY OF ALEXANDRIA:
Expeditions and Research:

Island of Faith in the Sinai Wilderness. By George H. Forsyth. Photos by Robert F. Sisson. 82-106, *Jan. 1964*

UNIVERSITY OF ARIZONA-ARIZONA STATE MUSEUM EXPEDITION. *See* Snaketown

UNIVERSITY OF CALIFORNIA:
Expeditions and Research:

Giant Kelp, Sequoias of the Sea. By Wheeler J. North. Photos by Bates Littlehales. 251-269, *Aug. 1972*

Gifts for the Jaguar God. By Philip Drucker and Robert F. Heizer. Contents: Olmec archaeological expedition. NGS research grant. 367-375, *Sept. 1956*

La Jolla, a Gem of the California Coast. By Deena Clark. Photos by J. Baylor Roberts. Included: Scripps Institution of Oceanography. 755-782, *Dec. 1952*

Sinai Sheds New Light on the Bible. By Henry Field. Photos by William B. and Gladys Terry. 795-815, *Dec. 1948*

UNIVERSITY OF COSTA RICA:
Research:

One Strange Night on Turtle Beach. By Paul A. Zahl. 570-581, *Oct. 1973*

UNIVERSITY OF FLORIDA:
Research:

Imperiled Gift of the Sea: Caribbean Green Turtle. By Archie Carr. Photos by Robert E. Schroeder. 876-890, *June 1967*

UNIVERSITY OF HAWAII: Sea Grant Program:

Precious Corals, Hawaii's Deep-sea Jewels. By Richard W. Grigg. 719-732, May 1979

UNIVERSITY OF MIAMI:

Miami's Expanding Horizons. By

William H. Nicholas. Included: College of Arts and Sciences, Drama Department, Food Technology Department, Graduate School, Marine Biology Department, Medical Research Unit, School of Business Administration, School of Education, School of Engineering, School of Law, School of Music. 561-594, *Nov. 1950*

Marine Research

The Changeless Horseshoe Crab. By Anne and Jack Rudloe. Photos by Robert F. Sisson. Note: These arthropods are not true crabs. 562-572, *Apr. 1981*

Shy Monster, the Octopus. By Gilbert L. Voss. Photos by Robert F. Sisson. 776-799, *Dec. 1971*

New Florida Resident, the Walking Catfish. By Clarence P. Idyll. Photos by Robert F. Sisson. 847-851, *June 1969*

The Incredible Salmon. By Clarence P. Idyll. Photos by Robert F. Sisson. Paintings by Walter A. Weber. 195-219, *Aug. 1968*

Squids: Jet-powered Torpedoes of the Deep. By Gilbert L. Voss. Photos by Robert F. Sisson. NGS research grant. 386-411, *Mar. 1967*

Shrimp Nursery: Science Explores New Ways to Farm the Sea. By Clarence P. Idyll. Photos by Robert F. Sisson. NGS research grant. 636-659, *May 1965*

The Deadly Fisher. By Charles E. Lane. 388-397, *Mar. 1963*

Shrimpers Strike Gold in the Gulf. By Clarence P. Idyll. Photos by Robert F. Sisson. 699-707, *May 1957*

Shipworms, Saboteurs of the Sea. By F. G. Walton Smith. 559-566, *Oct. 1956*

X-Rays Reveal the Inner Beauty of Shells. By Hilary B. Moore. 427-434, *Mar. 1955*

Strange Babies of the Sea. By Hilary B. Moore. Paintings by Craig Phillips and Jacqueline Hutton. Contents: Plankton study and other marine life. NGS research grant. 41-56, *July 1952*

UNIVERSITY OF MICHIGAN: Expeditions and Research:

Island of Faith in the Sinai Wilderness. By George H. Forsyth. Photos by Robert F. Sisson. 82-106, *Jan. 1964*

UNIVERSITY OF MINNESOTA: Bell Museum of Natural History Study Grant:

Western Grebes: The Birds That Walk on Water. By Gary L. Nuechterlein. NGS research grant. 624-637, *May 1982*

UNIVERSITY OF MISSOURI SCHOOL OF JOURNALISM:

Photography awards. 830-831, June 1959; 898, 901, Dec. 1962; 539, *Oct. 1963*

UNIVERSITY OF OXFORD:

Oxford, Mother of Anglo-Saxon Learning. By E. John Long. 563-596, *Nov. 1929*

UNIVERSITY OF PENNSYLVANIA: University Museum Expeditions and Research:

The Maya: Resurrecting the Grandeur of Tikal. By William R. Coe. 792-798, *Dec. 1975*

Computer Helps Scholars Re-create an Egyptian Temple. By Ray Winfield Smith. Photos by Emory Kristof. NGS research grant. 634-655, *Nov. 1970*

New Tools for Undersea Archeology. By George F. Bass. Photos by Charles R. Nicklin, Jr. NGS research grant. 403-423, *Sept. 1968*

Medical Research: Undersea Living (Man-in-Sea Project). 530, 541, *Apr. 1965*

Underwater Archeology: Key to History's Warehouse. By George F. Bass. Photos by Thomas J. Abercrombie and Robert B. Goodman. NGS research grant. 138-156, *July 1963*

Oldest Known Shipwreck Yields Bronze Age Cargo. By Peter Throckmorton. NGS research grant. 697-711, *May 1962*

UNIVERSITY OF SOUTHERN CALIFORNIA: Study Grant:

Undersea World of a Kelp Forest. By Sylvia A. Earle. Photos by Al Giddings. 411-426, *Sept. 1980*

UNIVERSITY OF VIRGINIA:

Thomas Jefferson: Architect of Freedom. By Mike W. Edwards. Photos by Linda Bartlett. 231-259, *Feb. 1976*

Mr. Jefferson's Charlottesville. By Anne Revis. 553-592, *May 1950*

UNIVERSITY OF WISCONSIN: Study Grant:

Jackals of the Serengeti. By Patricia D. Moehlman. NGS research grant. 840-850, *Dec. 1980*

UNKNOWN FALLS, Upper and Lower, Labrador, Canada:

Labrador Canoe Adventure. By Andrew H. Brown and Ralph Gray. 65-99, *July 1951*

The **UNKNOWN** Giants: Rare Look At Sperm and Blue Whales. By Hal Whitehead. Photos by Flip Nicklin. 774-789, *Dec. 1984*

UNKNOWN Japan: A Portrait of the People Who Make Up One of the Two Most Fanatical Nations of the World. By Willard Price. 225-252, *Aug. 1942*

UNKNOWN New Guinea: Circumnavigating the World in a Flying Boat, American Scientists Discover a Valley of 60,000 People Never Before Seen by White Men. By Richard Archbold. 315-344, *Mar. 1941*

UNKNOWN SERVICEMEN:

'Known But to God.' By Beverley M. Bowie. 593-605, *Nov. 1958*

UNLOCKING Secrets of the Northern Lights. By Carl W. Gartlein. Paintings by William Crowder. NGS research grant. 673-704, *Nov. 1947*

UNOTO (Masai Ceremony):

Spearing Lions with Africa's Masai. By Edgar Monsanto Queeny. 487-517, *Oct. 1954*

UNRAVELING the Mystery of the Warrior-Priest. By Christopher B. Donnan. 551-555, *Oct. 1988*

UNRUH, JACK: *Artist*

The Search for Modern Humans. By John J. Putman. Photos by Sisse Brimberg and Ira Block. 439-477, *Oct. 1988*

Wildflowers Across America. Text by Michael E. Long. Included: Wildflowers of Texas, Southern Woodlands, Southwest Desert, Eastern Wetland, Tallgrass Prairie, Alpine Tundra. 500-511, *Apr. 1988*

Arctic Odyssey. By John Bockstoce.

In 1952 a dam on the Nechako, tributary of British Columbia's untamed Fraser River, flooded lands of the Cheslatta Indian tribe of Pat Edmund and his son. CHRIS JOHNS

Wildflowers of rolling central Texas, abloom in May, survive years of drought to flourish when the rains come. PAINTING BY JACK UNRUH

U
V

URBAN NATIONAL PARKS. *See* Gateway National Recreation Area, New Jersey-New York; Golden Gate National Recreation Area, California

"URBAN ORE":

The Fascinating World of Trash. By Peter T. White. Photos by Louie Psihoyos. 424-457, *Apr. 1983*

URBAN Population of United States. 345-346, *Sept. 1901*

URBAN RENEWAL. *See* Atlanta, Georgia; Baltimore, Maryland; Brooklyn, New York; Indianapolis, Indiana; Kansas City, Missouri; Philadelphia, Pennsylvania; Pittsburgh, Pennsylvania; St. Louis, Missouri; Stockholm, Sweden; Tulsa, Oklahoma; Venice, Italy; Washington, D. C.; Wilmington, Delaware

URGA, Mongolia:

The Lama's Motor-Car: A Trip Across the Gobi Desert by Motor-Car. By Ethan C. Le Munyon. 641-670, *May 1913*

URGUB, Turkey:

Peculiar Caves of Asia Minor. By Elizabeth H. Brewer. 870-875, *Sept. 1911*

URICK, FRANK, and Family:

Growing Up in Montana. Photos by Nicholas deVore III. 650-657, *May 1976*

URQUHART, FRED A.: *Author*

Found at Last: the Monarch's Winter Home. Photos by Bianca Lavies. 161-173, *Aug. 1976*

URU INDIANS:

Titicaca, Abode of the Sun. By Luis Marden. Photos by Flip Schulke. 272-294, *Feb. 1971*

URUEU-WAU-WAU INDIANS:

"Last Days of Eden," Rondônia's Urueu-Wau-Wau Indians. By Loren McIntyre. Photos by W. Jesco von Puttkamer. 800-817, *Dec. 1988*

URUGUAY:

Parks, Plans, and People: How South America Guards Her Green Legacy. By Mary and Laurance Rockefeller. Photos by George F. Mobley. 74-119, *Jan. 1967*

The Purple Land of Uruguay. By Luis Marden. 623-654, *Nov. 1948*

URUMCHI (Wulumuchi), Sinkiang, China. *See present designation,* Ürümqi, Xinjiang Uygur Zizhiqu

ÜRÜMQI, Xinjiang Uygur Zizhiqu:

The Caves of the Thousand Buddhas. By Franc and Jean Shor. 383-415, *Mar. 1951*

USE and Abuse of Our National Forests: Problems in Paradise. By Rowe Findley. Photos by David Cupp. 306-339, *Sept. 1982*

USEFUL Facts About the Countries of the World. 424-425, *June 1907*

USHER, ROLAND G.: *Author*

The Oldest Nation of Europe: Geographical Factors in the Strength of Modern England. 393-414, *Oct. 1914*

USUMACINTA (River), Guatemala-Mexico:

The Usumacinta River: Troubles on a Wild Frontier. By S. Jeffrey K. Wilkerson. Photos by David Hiser. 514-543, *Oct. 1985*

UTAH:

The Rising Great Salt Lake: No Way to Run a Desert. By Rick Gore. Photos by Jim Richardson. 694-719, *June 1985*

The Anasazi–Riddles in the Ruins. By Thomas Y. Canby. Photos by Dewitt Jones and David Brill. Paintings by Roy Andersen. 554-592, *Nov. 1982*

Coal vs. Parklands. By François Leydet. Photos by Dewitt Jones. 776-803, *Dec. 1980*

Utah's Rock Art: Wilderness Louvre. Picture essay by Gary Smith, with Michael E. Long. 97-117, *Jan. 1980*

⊕ *Close-up: U.S.A., The Southwest.* Text on reverse. *Oct. 1977*

Riding the Outlaw Trail. By Robert Redford. Photos by Jonathan Blair. 622-657, *Nov. 1976*

Miracle of the Potholes. By Rowe Findley. Photos by Robert F. Sisson. 570-579, *Oct. 1975*

Utah's Shining Oasis. By Charles McCarry. Photos by James L. Amos. 440-473, *Apr. 1975*

Life in a "Dead" Sea–Great Salt Lake. By Paul A. Zahl. Included: Ancient inland sea, Lake Bonneville. 252-263, *Aug. 1967*

From Sun-clad Sea to Shining Mountains. By Ralph Gray. Photos by James P. Blair. 542-589, *Apr. 1964*

Skiing in the United States. By Kathleen Revis. 216-254, *Feb. 1959*

Geographical Twins a World Apart. By David S. Boyer. Included: Great Salt Lake and the Dead Sea. 848-859, *Dec. 1958*

A Map Maker Looks at the United States. By Newman Bumstead. Included: Arches National Monument, Bryce Canyon, Price, Provo, Roan (Brown) Cliffs, Salt Lake City. 705-748, *June 1951*

Utah's Arches of Stone. By Jack Breed. 173-192, *Aug. 1947*

Flaming Cliffs of Monument Valley. By Jack Breed. Photos by author and Warren T. Mithoff. 452-461, *Oct. 1945*

Utah, Carved by Winds and Waters: The Beehive State, Settled Only 89 Years Ago, Stands a Monument to the Courage of Its Founders. By Leo A. Borah. 577-623, *May 1936*

Beyond the Clay Hills: An Account of the National Geographic Society's Reconnaissance of a Previously Unexplored Section in Utah. By Neil M. Judd. 275-302, *Mar. 1924*

Encircling Navajo Mountain with a Pack-Train: An Expedition to a Hitherto Untraversed Region of Our Southwest Discovers a New Route to Rainbow Natural Bridge. By Charles L. Bernheimer. 197-224, *Feb. 1923*

Experiences in the Grand Canyon. By Ellsworth and Emery Kolb. 99-184, *Aug. 1914*

The Great Rainbow Natural Bridge of Southern Utah. By Joseph E. Pogue. 1048-1056, *Nov. 1911*

The Great Natural Bridges of Utah. By Byron Cummings. 157-167, *Feb. 1910*

The Great Natural Bridges of Utah. 199-204, *Mar. 1907*

Colossal Natural Bridges of Utah. 367-369, *Sept. 1904*

Why Great Salt Lake Has Fallen. By L. H. Murdoch. 75-77, *Feb. 1903*

See also Bear River Migratory Bird Refuge; Bryce Canyon National Park; Canyonlands National Park; Dinosaur National Monument; Escalante Canyon; Fisher Towers; Four Corners Country; Powell, Lake; Rainbow Bridge National Monument; San Juan (River); Wasatch Range; Zion National Park

The **UTILIZATION** of the Vacant Public Lands. By Emory F. Best. 49-57, *Feb. 1897*

UTQIAGVIK (Site), Barrow, Alaska:

Sealed in Time–Ice Entombs an Eskimo Family for Five Centuries. By Albert A. Dekin, Jr. Photos by Victor R. Boswell, Jr., and Scott Rutherford. Paintings by James M. Gurney. 824-836, *June 1987*

UTRECHT, The Netherlands:

Holland Rises from War and Water. By Thomas R. Henry. 237-260, *Feb. 1946*

UVÉA (Island), Wallis Islands, Pacific Ocean:

Adventures with the Survey Navy. By Irving Johnson. 131-148, *July 1947*

UYGURS:

Journey to China's Far West. By Rick Gore. Photos by Bruce Dale. 292-331, *Mar. 1980*

UZBEK S.S.R., U.S.S.R.:

New Road to Asia. By Owen Lattimore. 641-676, *Dec. 1944*

Surveying Through Khoresm: A Journey Into Parts of Asiatic Russia Which Have Been Closed to Western Travelers Since the World War. By Lyman D. Wilbur. 753-780, *June 1932*

Where Slav and Mongol Meet. 421-436, *Nov. 1919*

The Land of Lambskins: An Expedition to Bokhara, Russian Central Asia, to Study the Karakul Sheep Industry. By Robert K. Nabours. 77-88, *July 1919*

Russia's Orphan Races: Picturesque Peoples Who Cluster on the Southeastern Borderland of the Vast Slav Dominions. By Maynard Owen Williams. 245-278, *Oct. 1918*

UZZELL, R. STEPHEN, III:
Photographer

Scotland's Inner Hebrides: Isles of the Western Sea. By Kenneth MacLeish. 690-717, *Nov. 1974*

V-1 (Buzz Bomb):

Air Power for Peace. By H. H. Arnold. 137-193, *Feb. 1946*

London Wins the Battle. By Marquis W. Childs. 129-152, *Aug. 1945*

V-2 (Rocket):

Seeing the Earth from 80 Miles Up. By Clyde T. Holliday. 511-528, *Oct. 1950*

New Frontier in the Sky. By F. Barrows Colton. 379-408, *Sept. 1946*

Air Power for Peace. By H. H. Arnold. 137-193, *Feb. 1946*

London Wins the Battle. By Marquis W. Childs. 129-152, *Aug. 1945*

A **VACATION** in a Fifteenth Century English Manor House. By George Alden Sanford. 629-636, *May 1928*

A **VACATION** in Holland. By George Alden Sanford. 363-378, *Sept. 1929*

VACATION Tour Through Lincoln Land. By Ralph Gray. 141-184, *Feb. 1952*

VACATIONLAND U.S.A. 424 pages. ▪▪*1970*

VACCINATIONS:

Smallpox–Epitaph for a Killer? By Donald A. Henderson. Photos by Marion Kaplan. 796-805, *Dec. 1978*

VADUZ, Liechtenstein:

Liechtenstein Thrives on Stamps. By Ronald W. Clark. 105-112, *July 1948*

VAGABONDING in England: A Young American Works His Way Around the British Isles and Sees Sights from an Unusual Point of View. By John McWilliams. 357-398, *Mar. 1934*

VAI TRIBESPEOPLE:

The Land of the Free in Africa. By Harry A. McBride. 411-430, *Oct. 1922*

VAIL, THEODORE N.:

Voice Voyages by the National Geographic Society: A Tribute to the Geographical Achievements of the Telephone. Address by Theodore N. Vail. 296-326, *Mar. 1916*

VAITERE (Schooner):

Shores and Sails in the South Seas. By Charles Allmon. 73-104, *Jan. 1950*

VAL D'HÉRENS, Switzerland:

Switzerland's Enchanted Val d'Hérens. By Georgia Engelhard Cromwell. 825-848, *June 1955*

VALAIS (Canton), Switzerland:

In Valais. By Louise Murray. 249-256, *Mar. 1910*

VÂLCOV, Romania:

Caviar Fishermen of Romania: From Vâlcov, "Little Venice" of the Danube Delta, Bearded Russian Exiles Go Down to the Sea. By Dorothy Hosmer. 407-434, *Mar. 1940*

VALDEZ, Alaska:

Earthquake! By William P. E. Graves. 112-139, *July 1964*

The National Geographic Society's Alaskan Expedition of 1909. By

Holding their grandfather's musket, Sri Lal joins brother Mani at the start of a three-week honey hunt in the Himalayan foothills of central Nepal. ERIC VALLI AND DIANE SUMMERS

Ralph S. Tarr and Lawrence Martin. 1-54, *Jan. 1910*

VALENCIA, Spain:

The Changing Face of Old Spain. By Bart McDowell. Photos by Albert Moldvay. 291-339, *Mar. 1965*

Speaking of Spain. By Luis Marden. 415-456, *Apr. 1950*

VALLADOLID, Spain:

Iberia's Vintage River (Douro-Duero). By Marion Kaplan. Photos by Stephanie Maze. 460-489, *Oct. 1984*

VALLEY FORGE, Pennsylvania:

Patriots in Petticoats. By Lonnelle Aikman. Paintings by Louis S. Glanzman. 475-493, *Oct. 1975*

Washington Lives Again at Valley Forge. By Howell Walker. 187-202, *Feb. 1954*

VALLEY OF TEN THOUSAND SMOKES (Volcanic Region), Alaska:

President's Page. By Gilbert M. Grosvenor. *Sept. 1988*

Lonely Wonders of Katmai. By Ernest Gruening. Photos by Winfield Parks. 800-831, *June 1963*

▪▪*The Valley of Ten Thousand Smokes.* By Robert F. Griggs. 341 pages. 1912; rev. ed. *1922*

Our Greatest National Monument: The National Geographic Society Completes Its Explorations in the Valley of Ten Thousand Smokes. By Robert F. Griggs. 219-292, *Sept. 1921*

The Ten Thousand Smokes Now a National Monument: The President of the United States Sets Aside for the American People the Extraordinary Valley Discovered and Explored by

St. Peter's Basilica, with adjacent piazza, is the masterpiece of Vatican City, the world's smallest nation.   PAINTING BY HARRY J. BLISS

the National Geographic Society. 359-366, *Apr. 1919*

The Valley of Ten Thousand Smokes: An Account of the Discovery and Exploration of the Most Wonderful Volcanic Region in the World. By Robert F. Griggs. Included: The Awe-Inspiring Spectacle of the Valley of Ten Thousand Smokes, Discovered and Explored by National Geographic Society Expeditions (panorama). 115-169, *Feb. 1918*

The Valley of Ten Thousand Smokes: National Geographic Society Explorations in the Katmai District of Alaska. By Robert F. Griggs. 13-68, *Jan. 1917*

VALLEY OF THE MOON (Sonoma Valley), California:

Wildlife In and Near the Valley of the Moon. By H. H. Arnold. Photos by Paul J. Fair. 401-414, *Mar. 1950*

My Life in the Valley of the Moon. By H. H. Arnold. Photos by Willard R. Culver. 689-716, *Dec. 1948*

The **VALLEY** of the Orinoco. By T. H. Gignilliat. 92, *Feb. 1896*

VALLI, ERIC:

On Assignment in Nepal. *Nov. 1988*

Author-Photographer

Honey Hunters of Nepal. By Eric Valli and Diane Summers. 660-671, *Nov. 1988*

VALPARAÍSO, Chile:

Chile, the Long and Narrow Land. By Kip Ross. 185-235, *Feb. 1960*

Capital and Chief Seaport of Chile. By W. Robert Moore. 477-500, *Oct. 1944*

Twin Stars of Chile: Valparaiso, the Gateway, and Santiago, the Capital–Key Cities with a Progressive Present and a Romantic Past. By William Joseph Showalter. 197-247, *Feb. 1929*

A Longitudinal Journey Through Chile. By Harriet Chalmers Adams. 219-273, *Sept. 1922*

From Panama to Patagonia. By Charles M. Pepper. 449-452, *Aug. 1906*

The **VALUE** of Arctic Exploration. By Robert E. Peary. 429-436, *Dec. 1903*

The **VALUE** of the United States Forest Service. 29-41, *Jan. 1909*

VAN, Turkey:

Between Massacres in Van. By Maynard Owen Williams. 181-184, *Aug. 1919*

VAN BALLENBERGHE, VICTOR: *Author*

Giants of the Wilderness: Alaskan Moose. Photos by Michio Hoshino. 260-280, *Aug. 1987*

VAN BIESBROECK, GEORGE:

Burr Prizes Awarded to Dr. Edgerton and Dr. Van Biesbroeck. 705-706, *May 1953*

South in the Sudan. By Harry Hoogstraal. 249-272, *Feb. 1953*

Operation Eclipse: 1948. By William A. Kinney. 325-372, *Mar. 1949*

Eclipse Hunting in Brazil's Ranchland. By F. Barrows Colton. Photos by Richard H. Stewart and Guy W. Starling. 285-324, *Sept. 1947*

VAN BUREN, MARTIN:

Profiles of the Presidents: II. A Restless Nation Moves West. By Frank Freidel. 80-121, *Jan. 1965*

VANCOUVER, British Columbia, Canada:

The Untamed Fraser River, British Columbia's Lifeline. By David S. Boyer. Photos by Chris Johns. 44-75, *July 1986*

Dream On, Vancouver. By Mike Edwards. Photos by Charles O'Rear. 467-491, *Oct. 1978*

VANCOUVER AQUARIUM: Study Grant:

Humpback Whales. 466, *Apr. 1982*

VANCOUVER ISLAND, British Columbia, Canada:

The Whales Called "Killer." By Erich Hoyt. 220-237, *Aug. 1984*

Canada's Window on the Pacific: The British Columbia Coast. By Jules B. Billard. Photos by Ted Spiegel. 338-375, *Mar. 1972*

British Columbia: Life Begins at 100. By David S. Boyer. 147-189, *Aug. 1958*

VANDERCOOK, JOHN W.: *Author*

The Mandate of Cameroun: A Vast African Territory Ruled by Petty Sultans Under French Sway. 225-260, *Feb. 1931*

VANDERLIP, F. A.:

The World's Production of Gold (From an Address to the American Bankers' Convention by F. A. Vanderlip, October 11, 1905). 571-572, *Dec. 1905*

VAN DER MEULEN, D.: *Author*

Into Burning Hadhramaut: The Arab Land of Frankincense and Myrrh. 387-429, *Oct. 1932*

VANDER-MOLEN, PAUL:

On Assignment in Iceland. *Sept. 1984*
Author
Iceland's Wild Glacier-born River. Photos by Robert Grégoire and Jean-Luc Chéron. 306-321, *Sept. 1984*

VANDERWALKER, JOHN G.: *Author*

Tektite II: Science's Window on the Sea. Photos by Bates Littlehales. 256-289, *Aug. 1971*

VAN DUIVENDIJK, HANS: *Author*

They Stopped the Sea. Photos by Pablo Bartholomew. 92-101, *July 1987*

VAN DYK, JERE: *Author*

Long Journey of the Brahmaputra. Photos by Raghubir Singh and Galen Rowell. Included: A Rare Visit to a World Unto Itself. 672-711, *Nov. 1988*

VAN ESS, JOHN: *Author*

Forty Years Among the Arabs. 385-420, *Sept. 1942*

VANG PAO:

Nomination Page. *Jan. 1974*

VANISHED Mystery Men of Hudson Bay. By Henry B. Collins. NGS research grant. 669-687, *Nov. 1956*

A **VANISHING** People of the South Seas: The Tragic Fate of the Marquesan Cannibals, Noted for their Warlike Courage and Physical Beauty. By John W. Church. 275-306, *Oct. 1919*

VANISHING *Peoples of the Earth.*
■■ Included: Ainu, Asmat, Australian Aborigines, Brazilian Indians, Bushmen, Eskimos, Hopis, Lapps, Nilgiri. 207 pages. *1968*

VANISHING *Wildlife of North America.* By Thomas B. Allen. Included: Some of the 109 species or subspecies on the federal list of endangered wildlife in the U. S. 207 pages. *1974*

VAN LAWICK, HUGO. *See* Lawick, Hugo van

VAN LAWICK-GOODALL, JANE. *See* Goodall, Jane

VAN LOON, HENRIK WILLEM: *Author*

The Citizen Army of Holland. 609-622, *June 1916*

VAN RIPER, WALKER: *Author-Photographer*

Freezing the Flight of Hummingbirds. By Harold E. Edgerton, R. J. Niedrach, and Walker Van Riper. 245-261, *Aug. 1951*

VAN TIENHOVEN FOUNDATION OF THE NETHERLANDS: Study Grant: Orangutans. 835, *June 1980*

VANUATU (formerly New Hebrides):

Yankee Roams the Orient. By Irving and Electa Johnson. 327-370, *Mar. 1951*

Meticulous stitches repair a Vatican tapestry designed by the Italian Renaissance artist Raphael. JAMES L. STANFIELD, NGS

Palms and Planes in the New Hebrides. By Robert D. Heinl, Jr. 229-256, *Aug. 1944*
In the Savage South Seas. By Beatrice Grimshaw. 1-19, *Jan. 1908*
See also Espíritu Santo; Malekula; Pentecost Island; Tanna

VAN ZANDT, J. PARKER: *Author*

Looking Down on Europe Again: Crisscrossing Air Tracks Reveal Nature's Scenic Masterpieces and Man's Swiftchanging Boundaries and Structures. 791-822, *June 1939*
On the Trail of the Air Mail. A Narrative of the Experiences of the Flying Couriers Who Relay the Mail Across

America at a Speed of More than 2,000 Miles a Day. 1-61, *Jan. 1926*
Looking Down on Europe: The Thrills and Advantages of Sight-seeing by Airplane, as Demonstrated on a 6,500-mile Tour Over Commercial Aviation Routes. 261-326, *Mar. 1925*

VARANASI, India. *See* Banaras

VARANGIANS:

Viking Trail East. By Robert Paul Jordan. Photos by Jim Brandenburg. Paintings by Michael A. Hampshire. 278-317, *Mar. 1985*

VARIATIONS in Lake Levels and Atmospheric Precipitation. By Alfred J. Henry. 403-406, *Oct. 1899*

VASA (Swedish Warship):

Ghost From the Depths: the Warship *Vasa*. By Anders Franzén. 42-57, *Jan. 1962*

VASCO DA GAMA. *See* Gama, Vasco da

VASCO da Gama at the Court of the Zamorin of Calicut. Contents: Reproduction of the painting by José Velloso Salgado, Sociedade de Geographia de Lisboa. Supplement, *Nov. 1927*

The **VAST** Timber Belts of Canada. 509-511, *Sept. 1906*

VATICAN CITY:

Vatican City. By James Fallows. Photos by James L. Stanfield. 723-775. Included: The Photographer's Perspective. By James L. Stanfield. 762-763; Treasures of the Vatican. Photos by James L. Stanfield and Victor R. Boswell, Jr. 764-775, *Dec. 1985*
St. Peter's, Rome's Church of Popes. By Aubrey Menen. Photos by Albert Moldvay. 865-879, *Dec. 1971*
When in Rome.... By Stuart E. Jones. Photos by Winfield Parks. 741-789, *June 1970*

In his role as peacemaker, Pope John Paul II signs the final papers of a Vatican-negotiated treaty between Argentina and Chile. JAMES L. STANFIELD, NGS

When the President Goes Abroad (Eisenhower Tour). By Gilbert M. Grosvenor. 588-649, *May 1960*
Rome: Eternal City with a Modern Air. By Harnett T. Kane. Photos by B. Anthony Stewart. 437-491, *Apr. 1957*
The Smallest State in the World: Vatican City on Its 108 Acres Is a Complete Sovereignty Internationally Recognized. By W. Coleman Nevils. Included: Treasure House of the Ages. 377-412, *Mar. 1939*
Recent Disclosures Concerning Pre-Columbian Voyages to America in the Archives of the Vatican. By William Eleroy Curtis. 197-234, *Jan. 31, 1894*

VATOPÉTHI (Monastery), Greece:
The Hoary Monasteries of Mt. Athos. By H. G. Dwight. 249-272, *Sept. 1916*

VAUGHN, W. D.:
Nomination Page. *Mar. 1959*
Photographer
Exploring Antarctica's Phantom Coast. By Edwin S. McDonald. 251-273, *Feb. 1962*
The Lower Mississippi. By Willard Price. 681-725, *Nov. 1960*
Africa: The Winds of Freedom Stir a Continent. By Nathaniel T. Kenney. 303-359, *Sept. 1960*
Our Land Through Lincoln's Eyes. By Carolyn Bennett Patterson. 243-277, *Feb. 1960*
Staten Island Ferry, New York's Seagoing Bus. By John T. Cunningham and Jay Johnston. 833-843, *June 1959*
New Era on the Great Lakes. By Nathaniel T. Kenney. 439-490, *Apr. 1959*

VAUPÉS (River), Colombia-Brazil:
Jungle Jaunt on Amazon Headwaters. By Bernice M. Goetz. 371-388, *Sept. 1952*

VEGETABLES:
■■ *The World in Your Garden.* Art by Else Bostelmann. 231 pages. *1957*
Our Vegetable Travelers. By Victor R. Boswell. Paintings by Else Bostelmann. Contents: Artichoke, Asparagus, Beans (Great Northern, Kidney, Lima, Marrow, Navy or Pea, Pinto, Stringless or Snap, Yellow), Broccoli, Brussels Sprouts, Cabbage, Cardoon, Carrots, Cauliflower, Celery, Chard, Chinese Cabbage, Collards, Corn, Cowpea, Cucumber, Eggplant, Endive, Kale, Kohlrabi, Lettuce, Muskmelons (Banana Melon, Cantaloupe, Casaba, Honey Dew, Montreal, Santa Claus), Mustard, Okra, Onions (Chive, Garlic, Leek), Parsnip, Peas, Peppers (Garden Pepper, Pimiento), Potato, Radish, Rhubarb, Romaine, Rutabaga, Salsify, Soybeans, Spinach, Squash (Acorn, Boston Marrow, Cocozelle, Crookneck, Cushaw, Cymling, Delicious, Hubbard, Marblehead, Pumpkin, Straightneck, Turks Turban, White Bush Scallop, Zucchini), Sweet Potato, Tomato, Turnip, Watermelon. 145-217, *Aug. 1949*

California, Horn of Plenty. By Frederick Simpich. Photos by Willard R. Culver. 553-594, *May 1949*
More Water for California's Great Central Valley. By Frederick Simpich. 645-664, *Nov. 1946*
Greens Grow for GI's on Soilless Ascension. By W. Robert Moore. 219-230, *Aug. 1945*
America Fights on the Farms. 33-48, *July 1944*
Farmers Keep Them Eating. By Frederick Simpich. 435-458, *Apr. 1943*
Black Acres (Mucklands of New York): A Thrilling Sketch in the Vast Volume of Who's Who Among the Peoples That Make America. By Dorothea D. and Fred Everett. 631-652, *Nov. 1941*
Fruitful Shores of the Finger Lakes (New York). By Harrison Howell Walker. 559-594, *May 1941*
The Texas Delta of an American Nile: Orchards and Gardens Replace Thorny Jungle in the Southmost Tip of the Lone Star State. By McFall Kerbey. 51-96, *Jan. 1939*
Forming New Fashions in Food: The Bearing of Taste on One of Our Great Food Economies, the Dried Vegetable, Which Is Developing Into a Big War Industry. By David Fairchild. 356-368, *Apr. 1918*
Reviving a Lost Art (Drying Fruits and Vegetables). 475-481, *June 1917*
See also Dasheen; Potatoes; Soybeans; *and* Wild Foods

VEIT, PETER G.: *Photographer*
Death of Marchessa (Mountain Gorilla). 508-511, *Apr. 1981*

VENEZUELA:
Venezuela's Crisis of Wealth. By Noel Grove. Photos by Robert W. Madden. 175-209, *Aug. 1976*

Male gorilla beats his chest after killing an ailing female in a gorilla family studied by Dian Fossey in Rwanda.   PETER G. VEIT

Yanomamo, the True People. By Napoleon A. Chagnon. 211-223, *Aug. 1976*
Venezuela Builds on Oil. By Thomas J. Abercrombie. 344-387, *Mar. 1963*
Search for the Scarlet Ibis in Venezuela. By Paul A. Zahl. NGS research grant. 633-661, *May 1950*
Jungle Journey to the World's Highest Waterfall. By Ruth Robertson. 655-690, *Nov. 1949*
Caracas, Cradle of the Liberator: The Spirit of Simón Bolívar, South American George Washington, Lives On in the City of His Birth. By Luis Marden. 477-513, *Apr. 1940*
I Kept House in a Jungle: The Spell of Primeval Tropics in Venezuela, Riotous With Strange Plants, Animals, and Snakes, Enthralls a Young American Woman. By Anne Rainey Langley. 97-132, *Jan. 1939*
A Journey by Jungle Rivers to the Home of the Cock-of-the-rock: Naturalists Enter the Amazon, Voyage Through the Heart of Tropical South America, and Emerge at the Mouth of the Orinoco. By Ernest G. Holt. 585-630, *Nov. 1933*
In Humboldt's Wake: Narrative of a National Geographic Society Expedition Up the Orinoco and Through the Strange Casiquiare Canal to Amazonian Waters. By Ernest G. Holt. 621-644, *Nov. 1931*
The Countries of the Caribbean. By William Joseph Showalter. 227-250, *Feb. 1913*
Three Old Ports on the Spanish Main. By G.M.L. Brown. 622-638, *Nov. 1906*
Some Notes on Venezuela. 17-21, *Jan. 1903*
The Anglo-Venezuelan Boundary Dispute. By Marcus Baker. 129-144, *Apr. 1900*
The Venezuelan Boundary Commission and Its Work. By Marcus Baker. 193-201, *July-Aug. 1897*
Venezuela: Her Government, People, and Boundary. By William E. Curtis. 49-58, *Feb. 1896*
⊕ *Map of the Valley of the Orinoco River.* Compiled by T. Heyward Gignilliat. *Feb. 1896*

VENICE, Italy:
Venice Fights for Life. By Joseph Judge. Photos by Albert Moldvay. Included: Venice's Golden Legacy. Photos by Victor R. Boswell, Jr. 591-631, *Nov. 1972*
Venice, City of Twilight Splendor. By Joe Alex Morris. Photos by John Scofield. 543-569, *Apr. 1961*
A Stroll to Venice. By Isobel Wylie Hutchison. 378-410, *Sept. 1951*
Italy Smiles Again. By Edgar Erskine Hume. 693-732, *June 1949*
Northern Italy: Scenic Battleground. Photos by B. Anthony Stewart and Benjamin C. McCartney. 265-288, *Mar. 1945*
Venice: Home City of Marco Polo. 559-566, *Nov. 1928*
The Geography of Medicines: War's Effect Upon the World's Sources of

Statue of Venice's patron, backlit by moonlight, crowns the Basilica of St. Mark, whose piazza has been the center of the city's public life for centuries.   ALBERT MOLDVAY

Supply. By John Foote. 213-238, *Sept. 1917*

Republics–The Ladder to Liberty. By David Jayne Hill. 240-254, *Mar. 1917*

Frontier Cities of Italy. By Florence Craig Albrecht. 533-586, *June 1915*

Venice. By Karl Stieler. 587-630, *June 1915*

The **VENICE** of Mexico. By Walter Hough. 69-88, *July 1916*

VENIZELOS, ELEUTHERIOS:

Greece and Montenegro. By George Higgins Moses. 281-310, *Mar. 1913*

VENUS (Planet):

The Planets: Between Fire and Ice. By Rick Gore. 4-51, *Jan. 1985*

Mariner Unveils Venus and Mercury. By Kenneth F. Weaver. 858-869, *June 1975*

Voyage to the Planets. By Kenneth F. Weaver. Paintings by Ludek Pesek. 147-193, *Aug. 1970*

Mariner Scans a Lifeless Venus. By Frank Sartwell. Paintings by Davis Meltzer. 733-742, *May 1963*

VENUS FLYTRAP:

Plants That Eat Insects. By Paul A. Zahl. 643-659, *May 1961*

VERACRUZ (State), Mexico:

Man's Eighty Centuries in Veracruz. By S. Jeffrey K. Wilkerson. Photos by David Hiser. Paintings by Richard Schlecht. NGS research grant. 203-231, *Aug. 1980*

On the Trail of La Venta Man. By Matthew W. Stirling. Photos by Richard H. Stewart. Included: Hunting Mexico's Buried Temples. NGS research grant. 137-172, *Feb. 1947*

Wildlife of Tabasco and Vera Cruz. By Walter A. Weber. Paintings by author. 187-216, *Feb. 1945*

Expedition Unearths Buried Masterpieces of Carved Jade. By Matthew W. Stirling. 277-302, *Sept. 1941*

Jungle Housekeeping for a Geographic Expedition. By Marion Stirling. 303-327, *Sept. 1941*

Great Stone Faces of the Mexican Jungle: Five Colossal Heads and Numerous Other Monuments of Vanished Americans Are Excavated by the Latest National Geographic-Smithsonian Expedition. By Matthew W. Stirling. 309-334, *Sept. 1940*

Discovering the New World's Oldest Dated Work of Man: A Mayan Monument Inscribed 291 B.C. is Unearthed Near a Huge Stone Head by a Geographic-Smithsonian

Expedition in Mexico. By Matthew W. Stirling. 183-218, *Aug. 1939*

A Naturalist's Journey Around Vera Cruz and Tampico. By Frank M. Chapman. 533-562, *May 1914*

VERAGUAS (Province), Panama:

Exploring Ancient Panama by Helicopter. By Matthew W. Stirling. Photos by Richard H. Stewart. NGS research grant. 227-246, *Feb. 1950*

VERGIL:

The Perennial Geographer: After 2,000 Years Vergil Is Still the Most Widely Read of Latin Poets–First to Popularize the Geography of the Roman Empire. By W. Coleman Nevils. 439-465, *Oct. 1930*

VERHOOGEN, JEAN: *Author*

We Keep House on an Active Volcano: After Flying to Study a Spectacular Eruption in Belgian Congo, a Geologist Settles Down on a Newborn Craterless Vent for Eight Months' Study. By Jean Verhoogen. 511-550, *Oct. 1939*

VERMONT:

Life on a Rock Ledge. By William H. Amos. 558-566, *Oct. 1980*

Robert Frost and New England. By Archibald MacLeish. 438-467. Included: Look of a Land Beloved. Photos by Dewitt Jones. 444-467, *Apr. 1976*

Vermont–a State of Mind and Mountains. By Ethel A. Starbird. Photos by Nathan Benn. 28-61, *July 1974*

Skiing in the United States. By Kathleen Revis. 216-254, *Feb. 1959*

New England, a Modern Pilgrim's Pride. By Beverley M. Bowie. 733-796, *June 1955*

The Long River of New England: In War and Peace, from Mountain Wilderness to the Sea, Flows the Connecticut River, Through a Valley Abounding in History, Scenery, Inventive Genius, and Industry. By Albert W. Atwood. 401-434, *Apr. 1943*

Francesco Morosini, a 17th-century doge of Venice, packed a pistol in his prayer book.   VICTOR R. BOSWELL, JR., NGS

Windblown ash from Eldfell, a volcano born in 1973, scoured this window in Vestman-naeyjar, a fishing port on the Icelandic island of Heimaey. ROBERT S. PATTON, NGS

New England's Wonderland of Mountain, Lake, and Seascape. Photos by Clifton Adams. 263-270, *Sept. 1931*
The Green Mountain State. By Herbert Corey. 333-369, *Mar. 1927*
See also Champlain, Lake; Connecticut River and Valley; Green Mountains; Stark Brook

VERNER, SAMUEL P.: *Author*
Some Peculiar Features of Central African Geography. 448, *Nov. 1904*

VERONA, Italy:
Italy Smiles Again. By Edgar Erskine Hume. 693-732, *June 1949*
Frontier Cities of Italy. By Florence Craig Albrecht. 533-586, *June 1915*

VERREAUX'S EAGLES. See Black Eagles

VERSAILLES (Palace), France:
The Palace of Versailles, Its Park and the Trianons. By Franklin L. Fisher. Included: Versailles the Magnificent. Photos by Gervais Courtellemont. 49-62, *Jan. 1925*
From the Trenches to Versailles. By Carol Corey. 535-550, *Nov.-Dec. 1917*

VERSATILE Wood Waits on Man. By Andrew H. Brown. 109-140, *July 1951*

VESILIND, PRIIT J.:
On Assignment in Israel. *July 1985*
On Assignment in Alaska. *Feb. 1983*
Author
Antarctica. 556-560, *Apr. 1987*
Brazil: Moment of Promise and Pain. Photos by Stephanie Maze. 348-385, *Mar. 1987*
Rising, Shining Tennessee. Photos by

Karen Kasmauski. 602-637, *May 1986*
Israel: Searching for the Center. Photos by James L. Stanfield. 2-39, *July 1985*
Monsoons: Life Breath of Half the World. Photos by Steve McCurry. 712-747, *Dec. 1984*
Hunters of the Lost Spirit: Alaskans, Canadians, Greenlanders, Lapps. Photos by David Alan Harvey, Ivars Silis, and Sisse Brimberg. 150-197, *Feb. 1983*
Two Berlins–A Generation Apart. Photos by Cotton Coulson. 2-51, *Jan. 1982*
Helsinki: City With Its Heart in the Country. Photos by Jodi Cobb. 237-255, *Aug. 1981*
Return to Estonia. Photos by Cotton Coulson. 485-511, *Apr. 1980*
The Society Islands, Sisters of the Wind. Photos by George F. Mobley. 844-869, *June 1979*
The Ohio–River With a Job to Do. Photos by Martin Rogers. 245-273, *Feb. 1977*

VESSELS, JANE: *Author*
Koko's Kitten. Photos by Ronald H. Cohn. 110-113, *Jan. 1985*
Delaware–Who Needs to Be Big? Photos by Kevin Fleming. 171-197, *Aug. 1983*
Fátima: Beacon for Portugal's Faithful. Photos by Bruno Barbey. 832-839, *Dec. 1980*

VEST SPITSBERGEN (Island). See Spitsbergen

VESTER, BERTHA SPAFFORD:
Author-Photographer-Artist
Jerusalem, My Home. 826-847, *Dec. 1964*

VESTFJORDEN, Norway:
Fishing in the Lofotens. Photos by Lennart Nilsson. 377-388, *Mar. 1947*

VESTMANNAEYJAR, Heimaey, Iceland:
Vestmannaeyjar: Up From the Ashes. By Noel Grove. Photos by Robert S. Patton. 690-701, *May 1977*
A Village Fights for Its Life. By Noel Grove. 40-67, *July 1973*

VESUVIUS (Volcano), Italy:
■ In the Shadow of Vesuvius. President's Page. By Gilbert M. Grosvenor. Jan. 1987; cover, *Feb. 1987*
The Dead Do Tell Tales at Vesuvius. By Rick Gore. Photos by O. Louis Mazzatenta. NGS research grant. 557-613, *May 1984*
A Buried Roman Town Gives Up Its Dead (Herculaneum). By Joseph Judge. Photos by Jonathan Blair. NGS research grant. 687-693, *Dec. 1982*
Behind the Lines in Italy. By Macon Reed, Jr. 109-128, *July 1944*
The Eruption of Mount Vesuvius, April 7-8, 1906. By Thomas Augustus Jaggar, Jr. 318-325, *June 1906*
Mount Vesuvius. 272-279, *May 1906*

VEVEY, Switzerland:
Switzerland's Once-in-a-generation Festival. By Jean and Franc Shor. 563-571, *Oct. 1958*

VÉZELAY, Hill of the Pilgrims. By Melvin Hall. 229-247, *Feb. 1953*

VIA APPIA, Italy. See Appian Way

VIALLES, ANDRÉ: *Author*
Camargue, the Cowboy Country of Southern France. 1-34, *July 1922*

VICKSBURG, Mississippi:
Gettysburg and Vicksburg: the Battle Towns Today. By Robert Paul Jordan. Map notes by Carolyn Bennett Patterson. 4-57, *July 1963*

VICTOR, PAUL-EMILE: *Author*
Wringing Secrets from Greenland's Icecap. 121-147, *Jan. 1956*

VICTORIA, Queen (Great Britain and Ireland):
The British Way. By Sir Evelyn Wrench. 421-541, *Apr. 1949*

VICTORIA (State), Australia:
Australia's Pacesetter State, Victoria. By Allan C. Fisher, Jr. Photos by Thomas Nebbia. 218-253, *Feb. 1971*
See also Melbourne

VICTORIA, British Columbia, Canada:
Canada's Window on the Pacific: The British Columbia Coast. By Jules B. Billard. Photos by Ted Spiegel. 338-375, *Mar. 1972*
British Columbia: Life Begins at 100. By David S. Boyer. 147-189, *Aug. 1958*
Factors Which Modify the Climate of Victoria. By Arthur W. McCardy. 345-348, *May 1907*

VICTORIA, Kansas:
Hays, Kansas, at the Nation's Heart. By

Margaret M. Detwiler. Photos by
John E. Fletcher. 461-490, *Apr. 1952*

VICTORIA, Lake, Kenya-Tanzania-
Uganda:

Uganda, Africa's Uneasy Heartland. By
Howard La Fay. Photos by George F.
Mobley. 708-735, *Nov. 1971*
Adventures in the Search for Man. By
Louis S. B. Leakey. Photos by Hugo
van Lawick. NGS research grant.
132-152, *Jan. 1963*
Britain Tackles the East African Bush.
By W. Robert Moore. 311-353,
Mar. 1950
Where Roosevelt Will Hunt. By Sir
Harry Johnston. 207-256, *Mar. 1909*
A Great African Lake. By Sir Henry M.
Stanley. 169-172, *May 1902*

VICTORIA FALLS, Zambia-
Zimbabwe:

Rhodesia, a House Divided. By Allan
C. Fisher, Jr. Photos by Thomas Neb-
bia. 641-671, *May 1975*
Africa: The Winds of Freedom Stir a
Continent. By Nathaniel T. Kenney.
Photos by W. D. Vaughn. 303-359,
Sept. 1960
Rhodesia, Hobby and Hope of Cecil
Rhodes. By W. Robert Moore. 281-
306, *Sept. 1944*
The World's Great Waterfalls: Visits to
Mighty Niagara, Wonderful Victoria,
and Picturesque Iguazu. By Theo-
dore W. Noyes. 29-59, *July 1926*
The Wonders of the Mosi-oa-Tunga:
The Falls of the Zambesi. By Louis
Livingston Seaman. 561-571,
June 1911

VICTORIA ISLAND, Northwest
Territories, Canada:

The Origin of Stefansson's Blond Eskimo. By A. W. Greely. 1225-1238,
Dec. 1912

VICTORIAN AGE:

The England of Charles Dickens. By
Richard L. Long. Photos by Adam
Woolfitt. 443-483, *Apr. 1974*

VICTORY PEAK, China-U.S.S.R. *See*
Pobedy, Pik

VICTORY'S Portrait in the Marianas.
By William Franklin Draper. Paintings by author. 599-616, *Nov. 1945*

VICUÑAS:

High, Wild World of the Vicuña. By
William L. Franklin. 77-91, *Jan. 1973*
Camels of the Clouds. By W. H. Hodge.
641-656, *May 1946*

VIDEOS, NGS. *See* Television Films,
NGS: Specials (S) and Videos (V)

VIENNA, Austria:

Those Eternal Austrians. By John J.
Putman. Photos by Adam Woolfitt.
410-449, *Apr. 1985*
Vienna, City of Song. By Peter T.
White. Photos by John Launois. 739-
779, *June 1968*
Building a New Austria. By Beverley
M. Bowie. Photos by Volkmar Went-
zel. 172-213, *Feb. 1959*
Occupied Austria, Outpost of Democ-
racy. By George W. Long. Photos by

Volkmar Wentzel. 749-790,
June 1951
The Vienna Treasures and Their Collec-
tors. By John Walker. Included:
Kunsthistorisches Museum. 737-776,
June 1950
What I Saw Across the Rhine. By J.
Frank Dobie. 57-86, *Jan. 1947*
A Tale of Three Cities. By Thomas R.
Henry. 641-669, *Dec. 1945*
Vienna–A Capital Without a Nation.
By Solita Solano. 77-102, *Jan. 1923*
See also Spanish Riding School

VIENTIANE, Laos:

Laos Today. By Peter T. White. Photos
by Seny Norasingh. Included: Map of
plane-crash sites. 772-795, *June 1987*

VIETMEYER, NOEL D.: *Author*

The Captivating Kiwifruit. Photos by
Jim Brandenburg. 683-688,
May 1987
The Preposterous Puffer. Photos by
Joseph J. Scherschel. 260-270,
Aug. 1984
Rediscovering America's Forgotten
Crops. Photos by Burgess Blevins.
Paintings by Paul M. Breeden. 702-
712, *May 1981*

VIETNAM:

Kampuchea Wakens From a Night-
mare. By Peter T. White. Photos by
David Alan Harvey. Included: Viet-
nam's occupation of Kampuchea.
590-623, *May 1982*
The Lands and Peoples of Southeast
Asia. 295-365. I. Mosaic of Cultures.
By Peter T. White. Photos by W. E.

Dancers of the 1950s take a bow in Vienna's Opera House, rebuilt after World War II bombs wrecked the original. VOLKMAR WENTZEL, NGS

Taps sounds at the Vietnam Veterans Memorial, inscribed with the names of those who died in the conflict.   MICHAEL S. WILSON

VIEWS of the Lincoln Memorial in Washington. 197-204, *Aug. 1922*

VIGNETTES of Guadalajara. By Frederick Simpich. 329-356, *Mar. 1934*

VIGOROUS Young Nation in the South Sea. By Alan Villiers. 309-385, *Sept. 1963*

VIKING FESTIVAL in the Shetlands. Photos by Karl W. Gullers. 853-862, *Dec. 1954*

VIKING LANDER (Spacecraft):
The Search for Life on Mars. By Kenneth F. Weaver. 264-265, *Feb. 1973*
See also Viking Spacecraft Missions

VIKING Life in the Storm-Cursed Faeroes. By Leo Hansen. 607-648, *Nov. 1930*

VIKING MARU (Balloon):
Last Ascent of a Heroic Team (Maxie Anderson and Don Ida). 794-797, *Dec. 1983*

VIKING SPACECRAFT MISSIONS:
Mars: Our First Close Look. 3-31. I. As Viking Sees It. 3-7; II. The Search for Life. By Rick Gore. 9-31, *Jan. 1977*
Mars: A New World to Explore. By Carl Sagan. Note: The proposed name Voyager was later changed to Viking. 821-841, *Dec. 1967*

VIKINGS:
Viking Trail East. By Robert Paul Jordan. Photos by Jim Brandenburg. Paintings by Michael A. Hampshire. 278-317, *Mar. 1985*
Eskimo and Viking Finds in the High Arctic: Ellesmere Island. By Peter Schledermann. Photos by Sisse Brimberg. 575-601, *May 1981*
■■ *The Vikings.* By Howard La Fay. Photos by Ted Spiegel. Art by Louis S. Glanzman. 207 pages. *1972*
The Vikings. By Howard La Fay. Photos by Ted Spiegel. 492-541, *Apr. 1970*
Vinland Ruins Prove Vikings Found the New World. By Helge Ingstad. NGS research grant. 708-734, *Nov. 1964*
A New Look at Medieval Europe. By Kenneth M. Setton. Paintings by Andre Durenceau and Birney Lettick. 799-859, *Dec. 1962*
Dwellings of the Saga-Time in Iceland, Greenland, and Vineland. By Cornelia Horsford. 73-84, *Mar. 1898*
Norway and the Vikings. By Magnus Andersen. 132-136, *Jan. 31, 1894*
Recent Disclosures Concerning Pre-Columbian Voyages to America in the Archives of the Vatican. By William Eleroy Curtis. 197-234, *Jan. 31, 1894*
Discoverers of America. Annual Address by Gardiner G. Hubbard. 1-20, *Apr. 7, 1893*

VILA, Efate (Island), New Hebrides:
Palms and Planes in the New Hebrides. By Robert D. Heinl, Jr. 229-256, *Aug. 1944*

VILCABAMBA, Cordillera, Andes (Mountains), Peru:
By Parachute Into Peru's Lost World. By G. Brooks Baekeland. Photos by

Vietnam Veterans Memorial reunites buddies and begins to heal the nation's wounds of war. MEDFORD TAYLOR, BLACK STAR

author and Peter R. Gimbel. NGS research grant. 268-296, *Aug. 1964*

VILCABAMBA, Ecuador:
"Every Day Is a Gift When You Are Over 100." By Alexander Leaf. Photos by John Launois. 93-119, *Jan. 1973*

VILLAFRANCA, RICARDO: *Author*
Costa Rica. 143-151, *May 1897*

A VILLAGE Fights for Its Life. By Noel Grove. 40-67, *July 1973*

VILLAGE From the Past. By Maria Nicolaidis-Karanikolas. Photos by James L. Stanfield. 768-777, *Dec. 1983*

VILLAGE Life in the Holy Land. By John D. Whiting. 249-314, *Mar. 1914*

A VILLAGE Rises From Ashes. By Noel Grove. Photos by Robert S. Patton. 690-701, *May 1977*

VILLARD, HENRY S.: *Author*
Rubber-cushioned Liberia. Photos by Charles W. Allmon. 201-228, *Feb. 1948*

VILLARI, LUIGI: *Author*
The Races and Religions of Macedonia. 1118-1132, *Nov. 1912*

VILLAS BOAS, CLAUDIO and ORLANDO: *Authors*
Saving Brazil's Stone Age Tribes From Extinction. Photos by W. Jesco von Puttkamer. 424-444, *Sept. 1968*

VILLAVICENCIO, Colombia:
Keeping House for a Biologist in Colombia. By Nancy Bell Fairchild Bates. Photos by Marston Bates. 251-274, *Aug. 1948*

VILLIERS, ALAN:
Editorial. By Gilbert M. Grosvenor. 149, *Feb. 1975*
Nomination Page. *Sept. 1971*
Nomination Page. *Nov. 1957*
Author
Magellan: First Voyage Around the World. Photos by Bruce Dale. 721-753, *June 1976*
Sir Francis Drake. Photos by Gordon W. Gahan. 216-253, *Feb. 1975*
■■ *Men, Ships, and the Sea.* By Alan Villiers and other adventurers on the sea. Contents: Maritime history. 436 pages. 1962; rev. ed. *1973*
Captain Cook: The Man Who Mapped the Pacific. Photos by Gordon W. Gahan. 297-349, *Sept. 1971*
In the Wake of Darwin's *Beagle.* Photos by James L. Stanfield. 449-495, *Oct. 1969*

Remembering loved ones, visitors to the Vietnam Veterans Memorial in Washington, D.C., touch the names chiseled into polished granite. MEDFORD TAYLOR, BLACK STAR

Captained by Alan Villiers, a replica of the **Mayflower** *braves a stormy sea in 1957 to retrace the Pilgrims' journey from England to America.* GORDON TENNEY, BLACK STAR

The Age of Sail Lives On at Mystic. Photos by Weston Kemp. 220-239, *Aug. 1968*

The Netherlands: Nation at War With the Sea. Photos by Adam Woolfitt. 530-571, *Apr. 1968*

England's Scillies, the Flowering Isles. Photos by Bates Littlehales. 126-145, *July 1967*

"The Alice" in Australia's Wonderland. Photos by Jeff Carter and David Moore. 230-257, *Feb. 1966*

Wales, Land of Bards. Photos by Thomas Nebbia. 727-769, *June 1965*

Fabled Mount of St. Michael. Photos by Bates Littlehales. 880-898, *June 1964*

Australia. 309-385, *Sept. 1963*

Channel Cruise to Glorious Devon. Photos by Bates Littlehales. 208-259, *Aug. 1963*

Ships Through the Ages: A Saga of the Sea. 494-545, *Apr. 1963*

Aboard the N. S. *Savannah:* World's First Nuclear Merchantman. Photos by John E. Fletcher. 280-298, *Aug. 1962*

Cowes to Cornwall. Photos by Robert B. Goodman. 149-201, *Aug. 1961*

Scotland From Her Lovely Lochs and Seas. Photos by Robert F. Sisson. 492-541, *Apr. 1961*

Prince Henry, the Explorer Who Stayed Home. Photos by Thomas Nebbia. 616-656, *Nov. 1960*

We're Coming Over on the *Mayflower.* 708-728, *May 1957*

Last of the Cape Horners. 701-710, *May 1948*

North About *(Joseph Conrad).* 221-250, *Feb. 1937*

Where the Sailing Ship Survives (Åland Islands). 101-128, *Jan. 1935*

The Cape Horn Grain-Ship Race: The Gallant "Parma" Leads the Vanishing Fleet of Square-Riggers Through Raging Gales and Irksome Calms 16,000 Miles, from Australia to England. 1-39, *Jan. 1933*

Rounding the Horn in a Windjammer *(Grace Harwar).* 191-224, *Feb. 1931*

Author-Photographer

How We Sailed the New *Mayflower* to America. 627-672, *Nov. 1957*

The Marvelous Maldive Islands. 829-849, *June 1957*

By Full-rigged Ship to Denmark's Fairyland. Photos by Alexander Taylor and author. 809-828, *Dec. 1955*

Under Canvas in the Atomic Age. 49-84, *July 1955*

Golden Beaches of Portugal. 673-696, *Nov. 1954*

I Sailed with Portugal's Captains Courageous. 565-596, *May 1952*

Sailing with Sindbad's Sons. 675-688, *Nov. 1948*

VILNIUS, Lithuania, U.S.S.R.:

Wilno, Stepchild of the Polish Frontier. 777-784, *June 1938*

VINCI, LEONARDO DA. *See* Leonardo da Vinci

VINELAND. *See* Vinland

VINEYARDS. *See* Grape Culture; Grapes

VINLAND (Coastal Region), North America:

Vinland Ruins Prove Vikings Found the New World. By Helge Ingstad. NGS research grant. 708-734, *Nov. 1964*

Dwellings of the Saga-Time in Iceland, Greenland, and Vineland. By Cornelia Horsford. 73-84, *Mar. 1898*

VINTON, KENNETH W.: *Author*

A Frog That Eats Bats and Snakes: In Captivity, This Big Jungle Amphibian Exhibits an Extraordinary Appetite. 657-664, *May 1938*

VINTON, S. R.: *Photographer*

China. 382-390, *Nov. 1920*

The **VIOLENT** Gulf of Alaska. By Boyd Gibbons. Photos by Steve Raymer. 237-267, *Feb. 1979*

VIREOS:

Blackbirds and Orioles. By Arthur A. Allen. Paintings by Allan Brooks. 111-130, *July 1934*

VIRGIL. *See* Vergil

VIRGIN (River), Arizona-Nevada-Utah:

Amid the Mighty Walls of Zion. By Lewis F. Clark. 37-70, *Jan. 1954*

VIRGIN ISLANDS, West Indies:

The U. S. Virgin Islands. By Thomas J. Colin. Photos by William Albert Allard and Cary Wolinsky. 225-243, *Feb. 1981*

Buck Island–Underwater Jewel. By Jerry and Idaz Greenberg. 677-683, *May 1971*

Our Virgin Islands, 50 Years Under the Flag. By Carleton Mitchell. Photos by James L. Stanfield. 67-103, *Jan. 1968*

A Fresh Breeze Stirs the Leewards. By Carleton Mitchell. Photos by Winfield Parks. 488-537, *Oct. 1966*

Virgin Islands: Tropical Playland, U.S.A. By John Scofield. Photos by Charles Allmon. 201-232, *Feb. 1956*

The American Virgins: After Dark Days, These Adopted Daughters of

Antonio Rodrigues steers the Portuguese ship **Argus** *as it travels to the Grand Banks to fish for cod in 1950.* ALAN VILLIERS

VIRGINIA:

Virginia was "founded upon smoak," an early settler wrote. Tobacco guaranteed economic survival of the colony and remains the state's major cash crop. DAVID ALAN HARVEY

Plateau. By W J McGee. 261-265, *Aug. 1896*

Spottswood's Expedition of 1716. By William M. Thornton. 265-269, *Aug. 1896*

"Free Burghs" in the United States. By James H. Blodgett. 116-122, *Mar. 1896*

The Natural Bridge of Virginia. By Charles D. Walcott. 59-62, *July 10, 1893*

See also Appomattox; Arlington County; Arlington National Cemetery; Chincoteague Island; Delmarva Peninsula; Fredericksburg; Harmony Hollow; Jamestown; Monticello; Mount Vernon; Norfolk; Shenandoah National Park; Tangier Island; Williamsburg

VIRGINIA BEACH, Virginia:

Hampton Roads, Where the Rivers End. By William S. Ellis. Photos by Karen Kasmauski. 72-107, *July 1985*

VIRÚ VALLEY, Peru:

Finding the Tomb of a Warrior-God. By William Duncan Strong. Photos by Clifford Evans, Jr. 453-482, *Apr. 1947*

VIRUNGA MOUNTAINS, Rwanda-Uganda-Zaire:

The Imperiled Mountain Gorilla. By Dian Fossey. Included: Death of Marchessa. Photos by Peter G. Veit. NGS research grant. 501-523, *Apr. 1981*

More Years With Mountain Gorillas. By Dian Fossey. Photos by Robert M. Campbell. NGS research grant. 574-585, *Oct. 1971*

Making Friends With Mountain Gorillas. By Dian Fossey. Photos by Robert M. Campbell. NGS research grant. 48-67, *Jan. 1970*

VIRUSES:

Our Immune System: The Wars Within. By Peter Jaret. Photos by Lennart Nilsson. Illustrations text by Larry Kohl. 702-735, *June 1986*

VISBY, Gotland, Sweden:

Gotland: Sweden's Treasure Island. By James Cerruti. Photos by Albert Moldvay. 268-288, *Aug. 1973*

VISCHER, ADOLF L.: *Author*

Tripoli: A Land of Little Promise. 1035-1047, *Nov. 1911*

VISCHER, HANNS: *Author*

The Mysteries of the Desert (Sahara). 1056-1059, *Nov. 1911*

A **VISIT** From House Doctors. 48-49, *Special Report on Energy. (Feb. 1981)*

A **VISIT** to Carlsbad Cavern: Recent Explorations of a Limestone Cave in the Guadalupe Mountains of New Mexico Reveal a Natural Wonder of the First Magnitude. By Willis T. Lee. 1-40, *Jan. 1924*

VISIT to Forbidden Tibet. By Fred Ward. 218-259, *Feb. 1980*

A **VISIT** to Lonely Iceland. By Perley H. Noyes. 731-741, *Nov. 1907*

A **VISIT** to the Brazilian Coffee Country. By Robert De C. Ward. 908-931, *Oct. 1911*

A **VISIT** to the Living Ice Age. By Rutherford Platt. 525-545, *Apr. 1957*

A **VISIT** to Three Arab Kingdoms: Transjordania, Iraq, and the Hedjaz Present Many Problems to European Powers. By Junius B. Wood. 535-568, *May 1923*

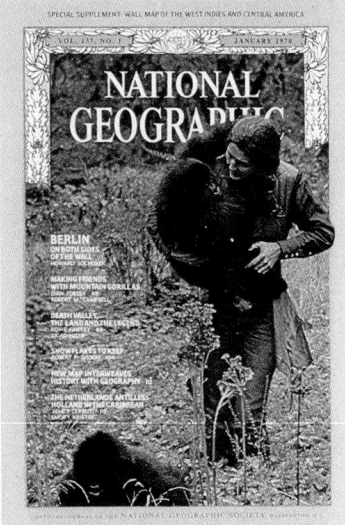

VISITING *Our Past: America's* **▣** *Historylands.* Included: Companion directory, *Visiting Our Past: A Supplemental Guide to Selected Sites.* 400 pages. *1977*

A **VISITORS'** Guide to All 320 Park Sites. 111-123, *July 1979*

VISITS to the Old Inns of England: Historic Homes of Hospitality for the Wayfarer Dot the Length and Breadth of the Kingdom. By Harold Donaldson Eberlein. 261-285, *Mar. 1931*

VISOKE, Mount, Rwanda-Zaire:

The Imperiled Mountain Gorilla. By Dian Fossey. Included: Death of Marchessa. Photos by Peter G. Veit. NGS research grant. 501-523, *Apr. 1981*

VISOKI DEČANI (Monastery), Yugoslavia:

The Clock Turns Back in Yugoslavia: The Fortified Monastery of Mountain-girt Dečani Survives Its Six Hundredth Birthday. By Ethel Chamberlain Porter. 493-512, *Apr. 1944*

VIVIANI, RENÉ RAPHAËL:

Our Heritage of Liberty: An Address Before the United States Senate by M. Viviani, President of the French Commission to the United States. 365-367, *Apr. 1917*

Their Monument Is in Our Hearts: Address by M. Viviani Before the Tomb of Washington, at Mount Vernon, April 29, 1917. 367, *Apr. 1917*

VIZCAYA: An Italian Palazzo in Miami. By William H. Nicholas. Photos by Justin Locke. 595-604, *Nov. 1950*

VIZETELLY, FRANK:

Witness to a War: British Correspondent Frank Vizetelly. By Robert T. Cochran, Jr. 453-491, *Apr. 1961*

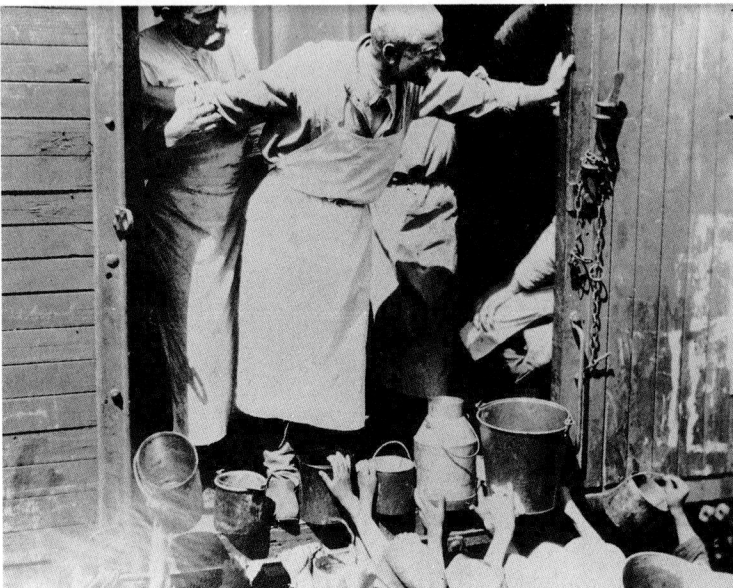

Freed during the Bolshevik Revolution, Czech soldiers on their way to join Allied forces at Vladivostok feed hungry Siberians—victims of the civil strife. CODY MARSH

Earthmovers help remove some of the 23,000 who died when Colombia's Nevado del Ruiz volcano erupted in 1985 and set off a 130-foot-high mudflow. SHELLY KATZ, BLACK STAR

Tumbling lava blocks startle an onlooker as planet earth lets off volcanic steam from Sakurajima on Japan's island of Kyushu. BOB BRYANT, INTERNATIONAL NEWS SERVICE

A blast with the force of ten megatons of TNT blew the top off Mount St. Helens on May 18, 1980, spewing a cloud of hot gases, rock, and ash. GARY ROSENQUIST, EARTH IMAGES

A Soviet carpenter in Gorodnya stands in front of a shed that protects his vegetables from the winter cold that freezes much of the nearby Volga River. HOWARD SOCHUREK

and Israel C. Russell. By J. S. Diller. 285-296, *July 1902*

Chemical Discussion of Analyses of Volcanic Ejecta from Martinique and St. Vincent. By W. F. Hillebrand. 296-299, *July 1902*

Reports of Vessels as to the Range of Volcanic Dust (Martinique and St. Vincent). By James Page. 299-301, *July 1902*

The Eruption of Krakatoa. By Sir Robert Ball. 200-204, *June 1902*

Volcanoes. By Gilbert H. Grosvenor. 204-208, *June 1902*

Magnetic Disturbance Caused by the Explosion of Mont Pelée (Martinique). 208-209, *June 1902*

The National Geographic Society Expedition in the West Indies. 209-213, *June 1902*

Shishaldin as a Field for Exploration. By Joseph Stanley-Brown. 281-288, *Aug. 1899*

Mount St. Helens. By Charles P. Elliott. 226-230, *July-Aug. 1897*

Crater Lake, Oregon. By J. S. Diller. 33-48, *Feb. 1897*

Reports of Sealing Schooners Cruising in the Neighborhood of Tuscarora Deep in May and June, 1896. By Eliza Ruhamah Scidmore. 310-312, *Sept. 1896*

Fundamental Geographic Relation of the Three Americas. By Robert T. Hill. 175-181, *May 1896*

Our Youngest Volcano. By J. S. Diller. 93-96, *July 10, 1893*

An Expedition through the Yukon District. By Charles Willard Hayes. 117-159, *May 15, 1892*

VOLENDAM, The Netherlands:

Glimpses of Holland. By William Wisner Chapin. 1-29, *Jan. 1915*

VOLGA (River), U.S.S.R.:

Viking Trail East. By Robert Paul Jordan. Photos by Jim Brandenburg.

Paintings by Michael A. Hampshire. 278-317, *Mar. 1985*

■ The Volga. 575, Nov. 1976; cover, *Mar. 1977*

The Volga, Russia's Mighty River Road. By Howard Sochurek. 579-613, *May 1973*

Mother Volga Defends Her Own. By Maynard Owen Williams. 793-811, *Dec. 1942*

Voyaging on the Volga Amid War and Revolution: War-time Sketches on Russia's Great Waterway. By William T. Ellis. 245-265, *Mar. 1918*

VOLGOGRAD (Stalingrad), Russian S.F.S.R., U.S.S.R.:

The Volga, Russia's Mighty River Road. By Howard Sochurek. 579-613, *May 1973*

VOLTA BUREAU, Georgetown, Washington, D. C.:

Washington's Historic Georgetown. By William A. Kinney. 513-544, *Apr. 1953*

VON BERNSTORFF, JOHANN HEINRICH:

Honors to Colonel Goethals: The Presentation, by President Woodrow Wilson, of the National Geographic Society Special Gold Medal, and Addresses by Secretary of State Bryan, the French Ambassador, the German Ambassador, and Congressman James R. Mann. 677-690, *June 1914*

In Honor of the Army and Aviation. Address by Count von Bernstorff. 267-284, *Mar. 1911*

VON ECKARDT, WOLF:

On Assignment in Washington, D. C. *Sept. 1983*

Author

A Preservation Victory Saves Washington's Old Post Office. Photos by Volkmar Wentzel. 407-416, *Sept. 1983*

VON PUTTKAMER, W. JESCO:

Author-Photographer

Man in the Amazon: Stone Age Present Meets Stone Age Past. 60-83, *Jan. 1979*

Brazil's Beleaguered Indians. 254-283. I. Requiem for a Tribe? (Kreen-Akarores). 254-269; II. Good-bye to the Stone Age (Txukahameis). 270-283, *Feb. 1975*

Brazil Protects Her Cinta Larga Indians. 420-444, *Sept. 1971*

Photographer

"Last Days of Eden," Rondônia's Urueu-Wau-Wau Indians. By Loren McIntyre. 800-817, *Dec. 1988*

Saving Brazil's Stone Age Tribes From Extinction. By Orlando and Claudio Villas Boas. 424-444, *Sept. 1968*

VOODOO:

Haiti–Against All Odds. By Charles E. Cobb, Jr. Photos by James P. Blair. 645-671, *Nov. 1987*

Haiti's Voodoo Pilgrimages: Of Spirits and Saints. By Carole Devillers. 395-408, *Mar. 1985*

Haiti: Beyond Mountains, More Mountains. By Carolyn Bennett Patterson. Photos by Thomas Nebbia. 70-97, *Jan. 1976*

Haiti–West Africa in the West Indies. By John Scofield. 226-259, *Feb. 1961*

VOORHIES, MICHAEL R.:

Nomination Page. In Nebraska. *Mar. 1980*

Author

Ancient Ashfall Creates a Pompeii of Prehistoric Animals. Photos by Annie Griffiths. Paintings by Jay Matternes. 66-75, *Jan. 1981*

VOSBURGH, FREDERICK G.:

Editor (1967-1970). 576, 577, 579, 586, 588, Oct. 1967; 861, June 1970; 841, Dec. 1970; 270, 276, *Aug. 1982*

Board of Trustees. 867, Dec. 1957; 485, Oct. 1966; 589, Oct. 1967; 838, Dec. 1970; 226, *Aug. 1976*

Vice President. 585, Oct. 1963; 485, Oct. 1966; 576, 577, 588, Oct. 1967; 861, June 1970; 838, *Dec. 1970*

Editor, Associate. 419, 420, 423, Mar. 1957; 867, Dec. 1957; 834, Dec. 1959; 585, Oct. 1963; 485, Oct. 1966; 579, Oct. 1967; 841, *Dec. 1970*

Editor, Assistant. 841, *Dec. 1970*

Author

Threatened Glories of Everglades National Park. By Frederick Kent Truslow and Frederick G. Vosburgh. Photos by Frederick Kent Truslow and Otis Imboden. 508-553, *Oct. 1967*

To Gilbert Grosvenor: a Monthly Monument 25 Miles High. By Frederick G. Vosburgh and the staff of the National Geographic Society. 445-487, *Oct. 1966*

Berlin, Island in a Soviet Sea. Photos by Volkmar Wentzel. 689-704, *Nov. 1951*

Dog Mart Day in Fredericksburg. 817-832, *June 1951*

Torchbearers of the Twilight. 697-704, *May 1951*

VOSS, GILBERT L.:

VOURAIKOS RIVER WATERSHED, Greece:

VOYAGER (Spacecraft):

VOYAGER 2 (Spacecraft):

VOYAGEURS:

VULTURES:

Andean condor, the largest of American vultures, glides on an updraft above Río Pasto canyon, one of the birds' few remaining retreats in Colombia. LIBBY McGAHAN

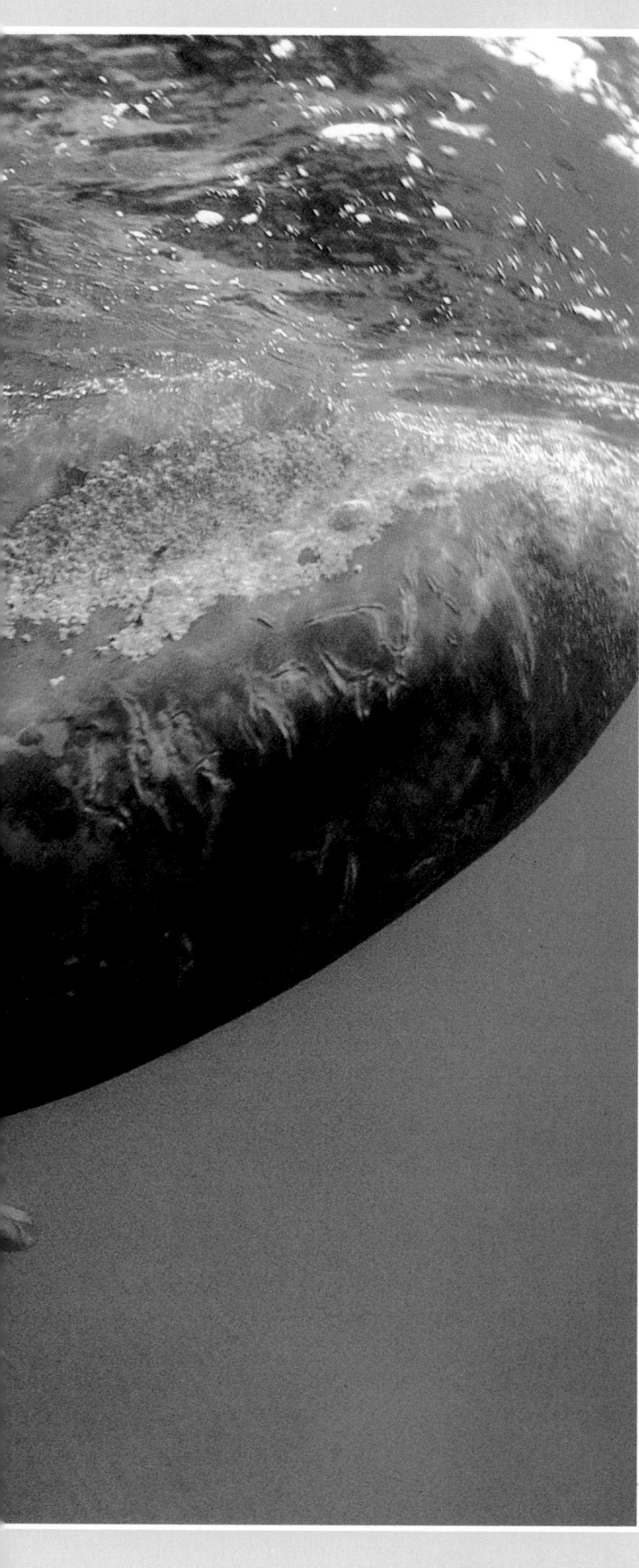

W

X

A young southern right whale,
a species hunted nearly to extinction,
cavorts off Argentina.
FLIP NICKLIN

Welsh faces, reflecting strength born of struggle with an infertile land, appear in **Discovering Britain & Ireland.**

Two Famous Maps of America. 72,
Feb. 1902

WALES:

◼ *Discovering Britain & Ireland.* 448
pages. *1985*
Wales, the Lyric Land. By Bryan Hodg-
son. Photos by Farrell Grehan. 36-63,
July 1983
The Celts. By Merle Severy. Photos by
James P. Blair. Paintings by Robert
C. Magis. 582-633, *May 1977*
⊕ *A Traveler's Map of the British Isles.*
Text on reverse. *Apr. 1974*
The Investiture of Great Britain's
Prince of Wales. By Allan C. Fisher,
Jr. Photos by James L. Stanfield and
Adam Woolfitt. Included: Caernar-
von Castle. 698-715, *Nov. 1969*
Wales, Land of Bards. By Alan Villiers.
Photos by Thomas Nebbia. 727-769,
June 1965
Caldy, the Monks' Island. By John E.
H. Nolan. 564-578, *Oct. 1955*
The Solemn, Sociable Puffins. By R. M.
Lockley. 414-422, *Sept. 1954*
British Castles, History in Stone. By
Norman Wilkinson. 111-129,
July 1947
Wales in Wartime. By Isobel Wylie
Hutchison. 751-768, *June 1944*
Sheep Dog Trials in Llangollen:
Trained Collies Perform Marvels of
Herding in the Cambrian Stakes,
Open to the World. By Sara Bloch.
559-574, *Apr. 1940*
We Live Alone, and Like It–On an Is-
land. By R. M. Lockley. 252-278,
Aug. 1938
⊕ *A Modern Pilgrim's Map of the Brit-
ish Isles or More Precisely the King-
dom of Great Britain and Northern
Ireland and the Irish Free State.*
June 1937
A Short Visit to Wales: Historic Associ-
ations and Scenic Beauties Contend
for Interest in the Little Land Behind
the Hills. By Ralph A. Graves. 635-
675, *Dec. 1923*
The Races of Europe. By Edwin A.
Grosvenor. 441-534, *Dec. 1918*

WALES, Alaska:

Exploring Frozen Fragments of American History: On the Trail of Early Eskimo Colonists Who Made a 55-Mile
Crossing from the Old World to the
New. By Henry B. Collins, Jr. 633-
656, *May 1939*

A **WALK** Across America. By Peter
Gorton Jenkins. 466-499, *Apr. 1977*

A **WALK** Across America: Part II. By
Peter and Barbara Jenkins. 194-229,
Aug. 1979

A **WALK** and Ride on the Wild Side:
Tasmania. By Carolyn Bennett Pat-
terson. Photos by David Hiser and
Melinda Berge. 676-693, *May 1983*

A **WALK** in the Deep. By Sylvia A.
Earle. Photos by Al Giddings and
Chuck Nicklin. 624-631, *May 1980*

A **WALK** Through the Wilderness: Yellowstone at 100. By Karen and Derek
Craighead. Photos by Sam Abell.
579-603, *May 1972*

WALKER, ALAN:

Editorial. By Wilbur E. Garrett. 419,
Oct. 1986
Author
Homo Erectus Unearthed: A Fossil
Skeleton 1,600,000 Years Old. By
Richard Leakey and Alan Walker.
Photos by David L. Brill. NGS re-
search grant. 624-629, *Nov. 1985*

WALKER, ERNEST P.: *Author*
"Flying" Squirrels, Nature's Gliders.
663-674, *May 1947*
Author-Photographer
Portraits of My Monkey Friends. 105-
119, *Jan. 1956*
Photographer
The Wild Animals in My Life. By Wil-
liam M. Mann. 497-524, *Apr. 1957*

WALKER, HOWELL: *Author*
The More Paris Changes.... Photos by
Gordon W. Gahan. 64-103, *July 1972*
South Australia, Gateway to the Great
Outback. Photos by Joseph J. Scher-
schel. 441-481, *Apr. 1970*
New South Wales, the State That Cra-
dled Australia. Photos by David
Moore. 591-635, *Nov. 1967*
Italian Riviera, Land That Winter For-
got. 743-789, *June 1963*
Washington Lives Again at Valley
Forge. 187-202, *Feb. 1954*
The Making of a West Pointer. 597-626,
May 1952
Long Island Outgrows the Country.
Photos by B. Anthony Stewart. 279-
326, *Mar. 1951*
Sydney Faces the War Front Down Un-
der. 359-374, *Mar. 1943*
American Bombers Attacking from
Australia. 49-70, *Jan. 1943*
Life in Dauntless Darwin: A National
Geographic Staff Writer Gives a Viv-
id Description of the Australian
Town That Guards the Continent's
Northern Door. 123-138, *July 1942*

*Dylan Thomas lies beneath a simple cross
in Laugharne, Wales, lyric land that
inspired his poetry.* FARRELL GREHAN

Fruitful Shores of the Finger Lakes.
559-594, *May 1941*
Author-Photographer
France Meets the Sea in Brittany. 470-
503, *Apr. 1965*
Normandy Blossoms Anew. 591-631,
May 1959
Belgium Welcomes the World (1958
World's Fair). 795-837, *June 1958*
Lafayette's Homeland, Auvergne. 419-
436, *Sept. 1957*
Here Rest in Honored Glory...The
United States Dedicates Six New
Battle Monuments in Europe to
Americans Who Gave Their Lives
During World War II. 739-768,
June 1957
Tasmania, Australia's Island State. 791-
818, *Dec. 1956*
History Keeps House in Virginia. 441-
484, *Apr. 1956*
The Making of a New Australia. 233-
259, *Feb. 1956*
Cities Like Worcester Make America.
189-214, *Feb. 1955*
Air Age Brings Life to Canton Island.
117-132, *Jan. 1955*
The Greener Fields of Georgia. Photos
by author and B. Anthony Stewart.
287-330, *Mar. 1954*
From Spear to Hoe on Groote Eylandt.
131-142, *Jan. 1953*
New Zealand, Pocket Wonder World.
419-460, *Apr. 1952*
You Can't Miss America by Bus. Paint-
ings by Walter A. Weber. 1-42,
July 1950
Cruise to Stone Age Arnhem Land.
417-430, *Sept. 1949*
Aroostook County, Maine, Source of
Potatoes. 459-478, *Oct. 1948*
The Making of an Anzac. Included:
Facing War's Challenge "Down Un-
der." 409-456, *Apr. 1942*
Old Ireland, Mother of New Eire: By
Whatever Name, 'Tis the Same Fair
Land With the Grass Growing Green
on the Hills of Her and the Peat
Smoke Hanging Low. Included:
When Irish Skies Are Smiling. 649-
691, *May 1940*
France Farms as War Wages: An Amer-
ican Explores the Rich Rural Region
of the Historic Paris Basin. Included:
Some French Pastorals. 201-238,
Feb. 1940
Gentle Folk Settle Stern Saguenay: On
French Canada's Frontier Homespun
Colonists Keep the Customs of Old
Norman Settlers. Included: Camera
Pastels in French Canada. 595-632,
May 1939
Photographer
King Ranch, Cattle Empire in Texas.
41-64, *Jan. 1952*
Exploring Stone Age Arnhem Land. By
Charles P. Mountford. 745-782,
Dec. 1949
Pennsylvania's Land of Plenty. 41-64,
July 1941
Spring's Gay Bouquets Deck the Na-
tion's Capital. 17-24, *July 1938*
Adirondack Idyls. 729-736, *June 1938*

WALKER, J. BERNARD: *Author*
Cathedrals of the Old and New World.
61-114, *July 1922*

WALKER, JOHN: *Author*

The National Gallery After a Quarter Century. 348-371, *Mar. 1967*

The Nation's Newest Old Masters. Paintings from Kress Collection. 619-657, *Nov. 1956*

Your National Gallery of Art After 10 Years. Paintings from Kress Collection. 73-103, *Jan. 1952*

The Vienna Treasures and Their Collectors. 737-776, *June 1950*

American Masters in the National Gallery. 295-324, *Sept. 1948*

Europe's Looted Art. 39-52, *Jan. 1946*

WALKER, JOSEPH A.: *Author*

I Fly the X-15. Photos by Dean Conger. 428-450, *Sept. 1962*

WALKER, LEWIS WAYNE: *Author*

Fairy Terns of the Atolls. 807-814, *Dec. 1946*

Photoflashing Western Owls. 475-486, *Apr. 1945*

Pelican Profiles. 589-598, *Nov. 1943*

Author-Photographer

Arizona's Window on Wildlife. 240-250, *Feb. 1958*

Sea Birds of Isla Raza. 239-248, *Feb. 1951*

WALKER, PHIL: *Author*

Across the Alps in a Wicker Basket *(Bernina).* 117-131, *Jan. 1963*

WALKER, STANLEY: *Author*

The Fabulous State of Texas. Photos by B. Anthony Stewart and Thomas Nebbia. 149-195, *Feb. 1961*

WALKER, THEODORE J.: *Author*

The California Gray Whale Comes Back. 394-415, *Mar. 1971*

WALKING Britain's Pennine Way. By David Yeadon. Photos by Annie Griffiths. 388-418, *Mar. 1986*

WALKING CATFISH:

New Florida Resident, the Walking Catfish. By Clarence P. Idyll. Photos by Robert F. Sisson. 847-851, *June 1969*

WALKING TOURS:

■■ *Mountain Adventure: Exploring the Appalachian Trail.* By Ron Fisher. Photos by Sam Abell. 200 pages. *1988*

A Tunnel Through Time: The Appalachian Trail. By Noel Grove. Photos by Sam Abell. 216-243, *Feb. 1987*

To Scotland Afoot Along the Pennine Way. By David Yeadon. Photos by Annie Griffiths. 388-418, *Mar. 1986*

A Short Hike With Bob Marshall. By Mike Edwards. Photos by Dewitt Jones. 664-689, *May 1985*

Battle For a Bigger Bob (Bob Marshall Wilderness). By Mike Edwards. Photos by Dewitt Jones. 690-692, *May 1985*

A Walk and Ride on the Wild Side: Tasmania. By Carolyn Bennett Patterson. Photos by David Hiser and Melinda Berge. 676-693, *May 1983*

Park at the Top of the World: Mount Everest National Park. By Rick Ridgeway. Photos by Nicholas deVore III. 704-725. Included: Preserv-

ing a Mountain Heritage. By Sir Edmund Hillary. 696-703, *June 1982*

Along the Great Divide. By Mike Edwards. Photos by Nicholas deVore III. 483-515, *Oct. 1979*

A Walk Across America: Part II. By Peter and Barbara Jenkins. 194-229, *Aug. 1979*

New Mount McKinley Challenge–Trekking Around the Continent's Highest Peak. By Ned Gillette. 66-79, *July 1979*

Travels With a Donkey–100 Years Later. By Carolyn Bennett Patterson. Photos by Cotton Coulson. 535-561, *Oct. 1978*

New Zealand's Milford Track: "Walk of a Lifetime." By Carolyn Bennett Patterson. Photos by Robert E. Gilka. 117-129, *Jan. 1978*

A Walk Across America. By Peter Gorton Jenkins. 466-499, *Apr. 1977*

■ *The Pacific Crest Trail.* By William R. Gray. Photos by Sam Abell. 199 pages. *1975*

Hiking the Backbone of the Rockies: Canada's Great Divide Trail. By Mike W. Edwards. Photos by Lowell Georgia. 795-817, *June 1973*

Yellowstone at 100: A Walk Through the Wilderness. By Karen and Derek Craighead. Photos by Sam Abell. 579-603, *May 1972*

■ *The Appalachian Trail.* By Ronald M. Fisher. Photos by Dick Durrance II. 199 pages. *1972*

Karnali, Roadless World of Western Nepal. By Lila M. and Barry C. Bishop. NGS research grant. 656-689, *Nov. 1971*

Mexico to Canada on the Pacific Crest Trail. By Mike W. Edwards. Photos by David Hiser. 741-779, *June 1971*

Americans Afoot in Rumania. By Dan Dimancescu. Photos by Dick Durrance II and Christopher G. Knight. 810-845, *June 1969*

An outing club's outhouse provides convenience for those walking the Appalachian Trail in central Vermont. SAM ABELL

The Friendly Huts of the White Mountains. By William O. Douglas. Photos by Kathleen Revis. 205-239, *Aug. 1961*

Afoot in Roadless Nepal. By Toni Hagen. 361-405, *Mar. 1960*

A Stroll to John o'Groat's. By Isobel Wylie Hutchison. 1-48, *July 1956*

From Barra to Butt in the Hebrides. By Isobel Wylie Hutchison. 559-580, *Oct. 1954*

Sierra High Trip. By David R. Brower. 844-868, *June 1954*

Pack Trip Through the Smokies. By Val Hart. Photos by Robert F. Sisson. 473-502, *Oct. 1952*

Thumbs Up Round the North Sea's Rim. By Frances James. Photos by Erica Koch. 685-704, *May 1952*

A Stroll to Venice. By Isobel Wylie Hutchison. 378-410, *Sept. 1951*

I Walked Some Irish Miles. By Dorothea Sheats. 653-678, *May 1951*

A Stroll to London. By Isobel Wylie Hutchison. Photos by B. Anthony Stewart. 171-204, *Aug. 1950*

Skyline Trail from Maine to Georgia. By Andrew H. Brown. Photos by Robert F. Sisson. 219-251, *Aug. 1949*

A Tour in the English Fenland. 605-634, *May 1929*

A Walking Tour Across Iceland. By Isobel Wylie Hutchison. 467-497, *Apr. 1928*

See also Hostels

WALL, STEVE: *Photographer*

"The Fire That Never Dies." By Harvey Arden. Contents: Iroquois Confederacy. 375-403, *Sept. 1987*

Chattooga River Country: Wild Water, Proud People. By Don Belt. 458-477, *Apr. 1983*

Troubled Odyssey of Vietnamese Fishermen. By Harvey Arden. 378-395, *Sept. 1981*

WALL Against the Sea, the Oosterschelde Barrier. By Larry Kohl. 526-537, *Oct. 1986*

WALL OF CHINA. *See* Great Wall of China

WALLACE, FREDERICK WILLIAM: *Author*

Life on the Grand Banks: An Account of the Sailor-Fishermen Who Harvest the Shoal Waters of North America's Eastern Coasts. 1-28, *July 1921*

WALLACE, HENRY A.:

The People's Fight Against Slavery. Reprint of address delivered at a dinner of the Free World Association by Henry A. Wallace, May 8, 1942. 276-280, *Aug. 1942*

WALLER, JERRY: *Photographer*

Scenes of Postwar Finland. By La Verne Bradley. 233-264, *Aug. 1947*

WALLIS ISLANDS, Pacific Ocean. *See* Uvéa

WALLISER, BLAIR A.: *Author*

Sunset in the East (Japan). 797-812, *June 1946*

WALLO (Province), Ethiopia. *See* Lalibala

Train shares this countryside view with the Pennine Way, a walking path to Scotland along the spine of England. ANNIE GRIFFITHS BELT

Painting of Pickett's Charge is on display at Gettysburg National Military Park. DETAIL OF GETTYSBURG CYCLORAMA, PAINTING BY PAUL PHILIPPOTEAUX

Jade carver in Hotan, China, creates a bangle with his traditional treadle-driven blade. FRED WARD, BLACK STAR

W
X

Riverboat reproduction navigates Virginia's Seneca Bypass, a remnant of George Washington's Patowmack Canal.   KENNETH GARRETT

Member of a 1934 climbing party films Mount Crillon during the first conquest of the Alaska peak. BRADFORD WASHBURN

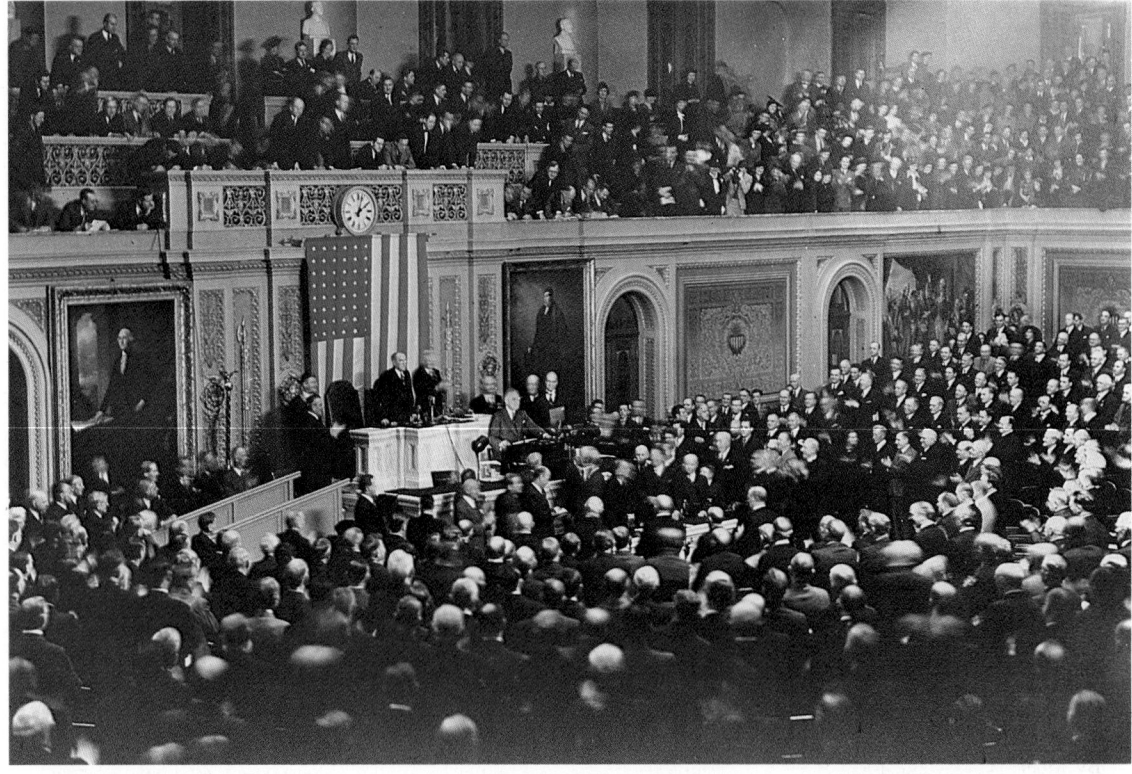

First color photograph of a joint session of Congress captured President Franklin D. Roosevelt's 1937 address.   J. BAYLOR ROBERTS, NGS

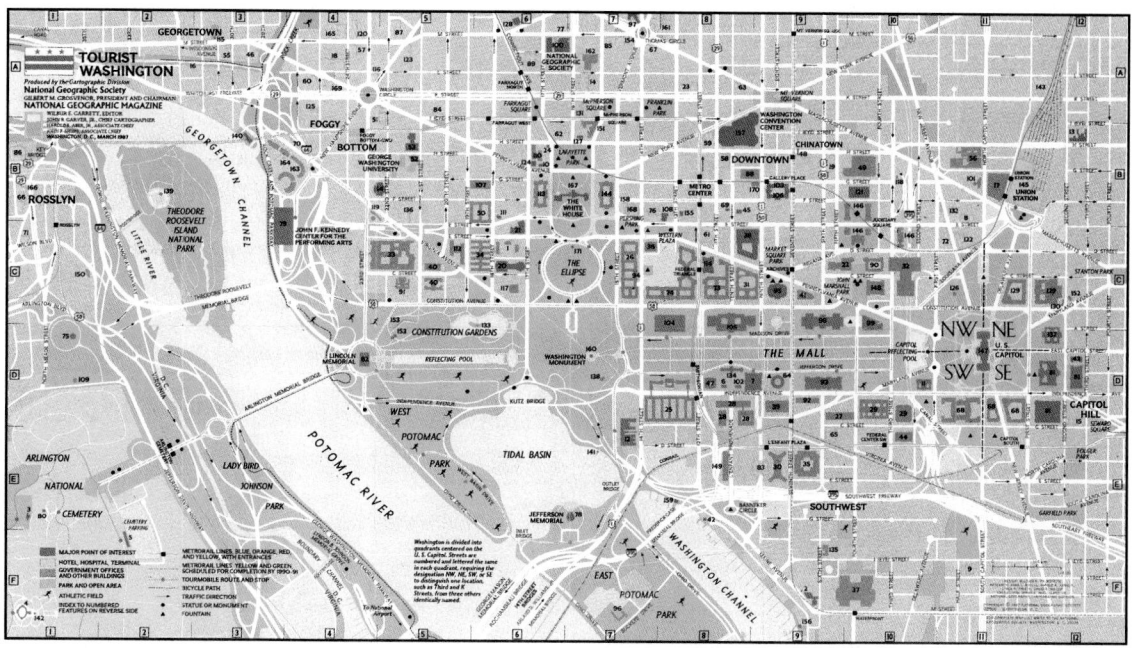

Tear-out map of Washington, D.C., in the January 1983 magazine charts the monuments and landmarks that line downtown streets.

Vista of the Future of the Nation's Capital. By Charles Moore. 569-595, *June 1923*

Washington, the Pride of the Nation. Photos by Charles Martin. 617-632, *June 1923*

■■ *The Capital of Our Country.* 154 pages. *1923*

Views of the Lincoln Memorial in Washington. 197-204, *Aug. 1922*

Washington: Its Beginning, Its Growth, and Its Future. By William Howard Taft. Included: The Mall (panorama); The Ultimate Washington: Plan Laid Out by the Commission of 1901 for the National Capital (panorama). 221-292, *Mar. 1915*

⊕ *The Mall, Washington, D. C. Mar. 1915*

⊕ *The Ultimate Washington* (Plan laid out by the Commission of 1901). *Mar. 1915*

■■ *Washington, The Nation's Capital.* By William Howard Taft and James Bryce. Reprint of two articles: "Washington: Its Beginning, Its Growth, and Its Future" by William Howard Taft; and "The Nation's Capital" by James Bryce. 101 pages. 1913; rev. ed. *1915*

The Nation's Capital. By James Bryce. 717-750, *June 1913*

The Original Boundary Stones of the District of Columbia. By Ernest A. Shuster, Jr. 356-359, *Apr. 1909*

Next International Geographical Congress To Be Held in Washington. By Gilbert H. Grosvenor. 351-357, *Oct. 1901*

American Geographic Education. By W J McGee. 305-307, *July 1898*

Geographic Development of the District of Columbia. By W J McGee. 317-323, *July 1898*

The Historical Development of the National Capital. By Marcus Baker. 323-329, *July 1898*

The Washington Aqueduct and Cabin John Bridge. By D. D. Gaillard. 337-344, *Dec. 1897*

Surveys and Maps of the District of Columbia. By Marcus Baker. Included: List of Maps of Washington and the District of Columbia. 149-178, *Nov. 1, 1894*

See also National Bureau of Standards; National Gallery of Art; National Geographic Society; National Zoological Park; Smithsonian Institution; *and* names of U. S. government agencies

WASHINGTON, Mount, New Hampshire:

The Friendly Huts of the White Mountains. By William O. Douglas. Photos by Kathleen Revis. 205-239, *Aug. 1961*

Mountains Top Off New England. By F. Barrows Colton. Photos by Robert F. Sisson. 563-602, *May 1951*

Skyline Trail (Appalachian Trail) from Maine to Georgia. By Andrew H. Brown. Photos by Robert F. Sisson. 219-251, *Aug. 1949*

WASHINGTON ACADEMY OF SCIENCES:

The Harriman Alaska Expedition in Cooperation with the Washington Academy of Sciences. By Gilbert H. Grosvenor. 225-227, *June 1899*

WASHINGTON AND OLD DOMINION RAILROAD REGIONAL PARK, Virginia:

President's Page. By Gilbert M. Grosvenor. *May 1988*

WASHINGTON CATHEDRAL, Washington, D. C.:

Washington Cathedral: "House of Prayer for All People." By Robert Paul Jordan. Photos by Sisse Brimberg. 552-573, *Apr. 1980*

Cathedrals of the Old and New World. By J. Bernard Walker. 61-114, *July 1922*

WASHINGTON MONUMENT, Washington, D. C.:

■■ *George Washington–Man and Monument.* By Frank Freidel and Lonnelle Aikman. Published in cooperation with the Washington National Monument Association. 69 pages. 1965; rev. ed. *1973*

The Washington National Monument Society. By Charles Warren. 739-744, *June 1947*

WASP (Submersible):

Exploring a 140-year-old Ship Under Arctic Ice *(Breadalbane).* By Joseph B. MacInnis. Photos by Emory Kristof. 104A-104D, *July 1983*

WASPS. *See* Women's AirForce Service Pilots

WASPS (Insects):

New Tricks Outwit Our Insect Enemies. By Hal Higdon. Photos by Robert F. Sisson and Emory Kristof. 380-399, *Sept. 1972*

The Wasp That Plays Cupid to a Fig. By Robert F. Sisson. 690-697, *Nov. 1970*

Marvels of Metamorphosis: A Scientific "G-man" Pursues Rare Trapdoor Spider Parasites for Three Years With a Spade and a Candid Camera. By George Elwood Jenks. 807-828, *Dec. 1938*

Potent Personalities–Wasps and Hornets: Though Often Painfully Stung, Mankind Profits Immeasurably from the Pest-killing Activities of These Fiery Little Flyers. By Austin H. Clark. Paintings by Hashime Murayama. 47-72, *July 1937*

WASSAW (Island), Georgia:

Sea Islands: Adventuring Along the South's Surprising Coast. By James Cerruti. Photos by Thomas Nebbia and James L. Amos. 366-393, *Mar. 1971*

WASTE DISPOSAL:

Editorial. By Wilbur E. Garrett. 277, *Mar. 1985*

Hazardous Waste...Storing Up Trouble. By Allen A. Boraiko. Photos by Fred Ward. 318-351, *Mar. 1985*

The Fascinating World of Trash. By Peter T. White. Photos by Louie Psihoyos. 424-457, *Apr. 1983*

The Wild World of Compost. By Cecil E. Johnson. Photos by Bianca Lavies. 273-284, *Aug. 1980*

A **WASTEFUL** Nation. 203-206, *Feb. 1909*

WASÚSU INDIANS:

Man in the Amazon: Stone Age Present Meets Stone Age Past. By W. Jesco von Puttkamer. NGS research grant. 60-83, *Jan. 1979*

Women in Washington, D.C., stroll around the Tidal Basin beneath blooming cherry trees, given to the nation by Japan and planted in 1912. © NATIONAL PHOTO COMPANY

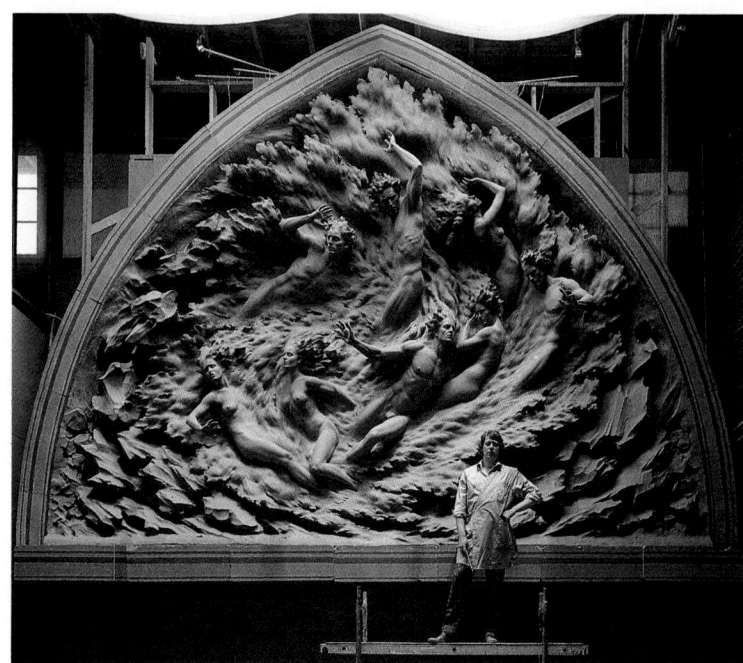

Stone carvers copied Frederick Hart's sculpture of the creation for the central west portal of Washington Cathedral, the capital's majestic house of prayer. SISSE BRIMBERG

W
X

Potomac, River of Destiny. By Albert W. Atwood. 33-70, *July 1945*

Rhodesia, Hobby and Hope of Cecil Rhodes. By W. Robert Moore. 281-306, *Sept. 1944*

The Great Falls of the Potomac. By Gilbert Grosvenor. 385-400, *Mar. 1928*

The World's Great Waterfalls: Visits to Mighty Niagara, Wonderful Victoria, and Picturesque Iguazu. By Theodore W. Noyes. 29-59, *July 1926*

The Geography of Japan: With Special Reference to Its Influence on the Character of the Japanese People. By Walter Weston. 45-84, *July 1921*

Kaieteur and Roraima: The Great Falls and the Great Mountain of the Guianas. By Henry Edward Crampton. 227-244, *Sept. 1920*

Niagaras of Five Continents. 211-226, *Sept. 1920*

Niagara at the Battle Front. By William Joseph Showalter. 413-422, *May 1917*

The World's Greatest Waterfall: The Kaieteur Fall, in British Guiana. By Leonard Kennedy. 846-859, *Sept. 1911*

The Wonders of the Mosi-oa-Tunga: The Falls of the Zambesi. By Louis Livingston Seaman. 561-571, *June 1911*

The Falls of Iguazu. By Marie Robinson Wright. 456-460, *Aug. 1906*

The American Association (for the Advancement of Science) at Buffalo. 315-316, *Sept. 1896*

WATERFOWL:

North Dakota–Tough Times on the Prairie. By Bryan Hodgson. Photos by Annie Griffiths. Included: Loss of pothole habitats for ducks, gulls, and pelicans. 320-347, *Mar. 1987*

North American Waterfowl: Troubles and Triumphs. By John Madson. 562-599, *Nov. 1984*

Humble Masterpieces: Decoys. By George Reiger. Photos by Kenneth Garrett. 639-663, *Nov. 1983*

Ice veils the Cave of the Winds on the Niagara River, whose surging waters generated hydroelectric power for industries that supplied the World War I battlefront. ERNEST FOX

Where Oil and Wildlife Mix. By Steven C. Wilson and Karen C. Hayden. 145-173, *Feb. 1981*

◼◼ *Wildlife Alert! The Struggle to Survive.* By Gene S. Stuart. Juvenile. 104 pages. *1980*

Mysteries of Bird Migration. By Allan C. Fisher, Jr. Photos by Jonathan Blair. 154-193. Included: Tracking the Shore Dwellers: From Canada to Suriname. 175-179, *Aug. 1979*

❁ *Bird Migration in the Americas.* *Aug. 1979*

Island, Prairie, Marsh, and Shore. By Charlton Ogburn. Photos by Bates Littlehales. 350-381, *Mar. 1979*

Can We Save Our Salt Marshes? By Stephen W. Hitchcock. Photos by William R. Curtsinger. 729-765, *June 1972*

Barehanded Battle to Cleanse the Bay. By Peter T. White. Photos by Jonathan S. Blair. Included: Oil-crippled birds. 866-881, *June 1971*

Businessman in the Bush (Everglades). By Frederick Kent Truslow. 634-675, *May 1970*

Threatened Glories of Everglades National Park. By Frederick Kent Truslow and Frederick G. Vosburgh. Photos by Frederick Kent Truslow and Otis Imboden. 508-553, *Oct. 1967*

◼◼ *Water, Prey, and Game Birds of North America.* 464 pages. *1965*

Corkscrew Swamp–Florida's Primeval Show Place. By Melville Bell Grosvenor. 98-113, *Jan. 1958*

Saving Man's Wildlife Heritage. By John H. Baker. Photos by Robert F. Sisson. 581-620, *Nov. 1954*

Wildlife of Everglades National Park. By Daniel B. Beard. Paintings by Walter A. Weber. 83-116, *Jan. 1949*

The Curlew's Secret. By Arthur A. Allen. Included: Alaska longspur, Alaska yellow wagtail, Baird's sandpiper, Black-bellied plover, Bristle-thighed curlew, Cackling goose, Emperor goose, Frigate bird, Golden plover, Hoary redpoll, Hudsonian curlew, Little brown crane, Northern phalarope, Old-squaw, Pacific godwit, Parasitic jaeger, Pectoral sandpiper, Ruddy turnstone, Sabine's gull, Savannah sparrow, Snow bunting, Spectacled eider, Tree sparrow, Varied thrush, Western sandpiper, Whistling swan, White-fronted goose, Wilson's snipe. 751-770, *Dec. 1948*

Born Hunters, the Bird Dogs. By Roland Kilbon. Paintings by Walter A. Weber. 369-398, *Sept. 1947*

Birds of Timberline and Tundra. By Arthur A. Allen. Contents: Arctic Loons, Arctic Terns, Black-poll Warblers, Bonaparte's Gulls, Dowitchers, Golden Plovers, Harris's Sparrows, Herring Gulls, Horned Grebes, Hoyt's Horned Larks, Hudsonian Curlews, Lapland Longspurs, Least Sandpipers, Lesser Yellowlegs, Northern Phalaropes, Northern Shrikes, Parasitic Jaeger, Pintail Ducks, Pipits, Red-backed Sandpipers, Semipalmated Plovers, Semipalmated Sandpipers, Snow Buntings,

Starlings, Stilt Sandpipers, Tree Sparrows, White-crowned Sparrows, Wild Geese, Willow Ptarmigans, Yellow Warblers. 313-339, *Sept. 1946*

Wildlife of Tabasco and Veracruz (Mexico). By Walter A. Weber. Paintings by author. Contents: Ant Tanager, Araçari Toucan, Black-bellied Tree Duck, Black-headed Trogon, Black Vulture, Blue Tanager, Crested Curassow, Crimson-collared Tanager, Finfoot, Forest Sparrow, Jacamar, King Vulture, Laughing Falcon, Least Kingfisher, Lesson's Oriole, Massena Trogon, Mexican Ant Thrush, Mexican Black Hawk, Mexican Jaçana, Mexican Motmot, Muscovy Duck, Oropendola, Plush Tanager, Quail Dove, Redstart, Ringed Kingfisher, Royal Flycatcher, Squirrel Cuckoo, Sulphur-breasted Toucan, Tiger Bittern, Veracruz Ivory-billed Woodpecker, White Snake Hawk, White-throated Bat Falcon, Yellow-headed Amazon, Yellow-tailed Oriole, Yellow-thighed Manakin. 187-216, *Feb. 1945*

Touring for Birds with Microphone and Color Cameras. By Arthur A. Allen. Contents: Burrowing Owl, California Blue Grosbeak, California Clapper Rail, California Woodpecker, Clark's Nutcracker, Coppery-tailed Trogon, Eastern Brown Pelican, Eastern Song Sparrow, Florida Ground Dove, Gambel's Quail, Hoyt's Horned Lark, Mourning Dove, Nighthawk, Purple Gallinule, Red-eyed Towhee, Reddish Egret, Sandhill Crane, Saw-whet Owl, Scissor-tailed Flycatcher, Sennett's Oriole, Snow Bunting, Snowy Egret, Western Gull, Western Horned Owl, Yellow Warbler. 689-712, *June 1944*

Birds on the Home Front. By Arthur A. Allen. Contents: Canada Geese, Catbirds, Chickadees, Chuck-will's-widow, Cowbirds, Flickers, Flycatchers, Gallinules, Grebes, Grouse,

Hummingbirds, Meadowlarks, Orioles, Owls, Peregrines, Plovers, Ptarmigans, Puffins, Rails, Redstarts, Shrikes, Skimmers, Swallows, Vireos, Warblers, Waxwings. 32-56, *July 1943*

Cruise of the *Kinkajou:* Among Desert Islands of Mexico Voyagers Find Outdoor Laboratories for the Naturalist and Ideal Fishing Grounds for the Sportsman. By Alfred M. Bailey. Contents: Auklets, Belding's Plovers, Black Oyster-catchers, Black Turnstones, Black-vented Shearwaters, Blue-footed Boobies, Brewster's Boobies, Brown Towhees, Cactus Wrens, Cape Gilded Flickers, Caracaras, Cardinals, Cardon Woodpeckers, Cormorants, Frazar's Oyster-catchers, Gnat-catchers, Heermann's Gulls, Horned Larks, Hudsonian Curlews, Lark Buntings, Man-o'-war-birds, Mockingbirds, Noddy Terns, Ospreys, Pelicans, Petrels, Ravens, Red-billed Tropicbirds, Redfooted Boobies, Red Phalaropes, Rock Wrens, San Lucas Quail, San Lucas Sparrows, San Lucas Woodpeckers, Sooty Terns, Thrashers, Townsend's Shearwaters, Verdins, Vultures, Wandering Tattlers, White-winged Doves, Willets, Wyman's Gulls, Yellow-legged Gulls. 339-366, *Sept. 1941*

South Florida's Amazing Everglades: Encircled by Populous Places Is a Seldom-visited Area of Rare Birds, Prairies, Cowboys, and Teeming Wild Life of Big Cypress Swamp. By John O'Reilly. Contents: Burrowing Owl, Everglade Kite, Florida Cormorant, Florida Crane, Great White Heron, Limpkin, Pelican, Roseate Spoonbill, Snakebird, Snowy Egret, White Ibis, Wood Ibis. 115-142, *Jan. 1940*

National Geographic Society's New "Book of Birds." 723, June 1937;

183, Aug. 1937; 226, Aug. 1938; 775, Dec. 1938; 121, *Jan. 1940*

The Shore Birds, Cranes, and Rails: Willets, Plovers, Stilts, Phalaropes, Sandpipers, and Their Relatives Deserve Protection. By Arthur A. Allen. Paintings by Allan Brooks. 183-222, *Aug. 1937*

Parrots, Kingfishers, and Flycatchers: Strange Trogons and Curious Cuckoos are Pictured with these Other Birds of Color, Dash, and Courage. By Alexander Wetmore. Paintings by Allan Brooks. Contents: Anis, Cuckoos, Flycatchers, Kingbirds, Kingfishers, Parakeets, Parrots, Pewees, Phoebes, Trogons. 801-828, *June 1936*

Winged Denizens of Woodland, Stream, and Marsh. By Alexander Wetmore. Paintings by Allan Brooks. Contents: Chickadees, Creepers, Dippers, Gnatcatchers, Kinglets, Nuthatches, Titmice, Wren-tits, Wrens. 577-596, *May 1934*

Birds That Cruise the Coast and Inland Waters. By T. Gilbert Pearson. Paintings by Allan Brooks. Contents: Cormorants, Grebes, Loons, Pelicans, Water Turkeys. Included: Birds of Lake and Lagoon, Marsh, and Seacoast. 299-328, *Mar. 1934*

The Large Wading Birds: Long Legs and Remarkable Beaks, as Well as Size, Form, and Color, Distinguish the Herons, Ibises, and Flamingos. By T. Gilbert Pearson. Paintings by Allan Brooks. 441-469, *Oct. 1932*

Wild Life of the Atlantic and Gulf Coasts: A Field Naturalist's Photographic Record of Nearly Half a Century of Fruitful Exploration. By George Shiras, 3d. 261-309, *Sept. 1932*

American Game Birds. By Henry Wetherbee Henshaw. Paintings by Louis Agassiz Fuertes. Contents:

Once imperiled, the trumpeter swan is on the rebound, but shrinking habitat threatens the future of other North American waterfowl species. STEVEN C. WILSON, ENTHEOS

Cranes, Ducks, Geese, Grouse, Pheasants, Pigeons, Plovers, Quails, Rails, Sandpipers, Snipes, Stilts, Swans. 105-158, *Aug. 1915*
Birds of Town and Country. By Henry Wetherbee Henshaw. Paintings by Louis Agassiz Fuertes. Contents: Blackbirds, Eagles, Finches, Flycatchers, Gulls, Hawks, Herons, Hummingbirds, Jays, Kingfishers, Orioles, Owls, Sparrows, Starlings, Swallows, Swifts, Tanagers, Terns, Thrushes, Titmice, Vireos, Vultures, Waxwings, Whip-poor-wills, Wood Warblers, Woodpeckers. 494-531, *May 1914*
Fifty Common Birds of Farm and Orchard. By Henry Wetherbee Henshaw. Paintings by Louis Agassiz Fuertes. Included: Blackbirds, Creepers, Crows, Cuckoos, Doves, Flycatchers, Grouse, Gulls, Hawks, Jays, Kinglets, Larks, Nighthawks, Nuthatches, Orioles, Owls, Plovers, Quail, Shrikes, Sparrows, Swallows, Terns, Thrashers, Thrushes, Titmice, Wood Warblers, Woodpeckers, Wrens. 669-697, *June 1913*
See also Cranes; Ducks; Egrets; Flamingos; Geese; Grebes; Herons; Ibises; Limpkin; Penguins; Spoonbills; Storks; Swans; Wilson's Phalarope; *and* Seabirds

WATERMEN:

My Chesapeake–Queen of Bays. By Allan C. Fisher, Jr. Photos by Lowell Georgia. 428-467, *Oct. 1980*
Chincoteague: Watermen's Island Home. By Nathaniel T. Kenney. Photos by James L. Amos. 810-829, *June 1980*
This Is My Island, Tangier. By Harold G. Wheatley. Photos by David Alan Harvey. 700-725, *Nov. 1973*
The Sailing Oystermen of Chesapeake Bay. By Luis Marden. 798-819, *Dec. 1967*

WATERPOWER. *See* Hydroelectric Power

WATERTON-GLACIER INTERNATIONAL PEACE PARK, Alberta-Montana:

Waterton-Glacier International Peace Park: Pride of Two Nations. By David S. Boyer. Photos by Lowell Georgia. 796-823, *June 1987*
Canadian Rockies, Lords of a Beckoning Land. By Alan Phillips. Photos by James L. Stanfield. 353-393, *Sept. 1966*
Many-splendored Glacierland. By George W. Long. Photos by Kathleen Revis. 589-636, *May 1956*

WATERTON LAKES NATIONAL PARK, Alberta, Canada:

Waterton-Glacier International Peace Park: Pride of Two Nations. By David S. Boyer. Photos by Lowell Georgia. 796-823, *June 1987*

WATERWAY That Led to the Constitution: George Washington's Patowmack Canal. By Wilbur E. Garrett. Photos by Kenneth Garrett. 716-753, *June 1987*

Waterman "Sonny" Parks enjoys the small-town life-style of Chesapeake Bay's Tangier Island. DAVID ALAN HARVEY

WATERWAY to Washington, the C & O Canal. By Jay Johnston. 419-439, *Mar. 1960*

WATERWAYS. *See* Chesapeake Bay; Great Lakes; Inland Sea, Japan; Inside Passage; Panama Canal; St. Lawrence Seaway; Tennessee-Tombigbee Waterway; *and* Canals; Intracoastal Waterways; River Trips; Rivers

WATLING ISLAND (now San Salvador), Bahama Islands:

Where Columbus Found the New World. By Joseph Judge. Photos by James L. Stanfield. Note: Samuel Morison believed Watling Island to be the first landfall of Columbus in the Americas. 566-599, *Nov. 1986*
The First Landfall of Columbus. By Jacques W. Redway. Included: Mariguana (Mayaguana); Samaná; Watling (San Salvador). 179-192, *Dec. 29, 1894*

WATSON, DON: *Author*

Ancient Cliff Dwellers of Mesa Verde. Photos by Willard R. Culver. 349-376, *Sept. 1948*

WATSON, THOMAS:

Voice Voyages by the National Geographic Society: A Tribute to the Geographical Achievements of the Telephone (Address by Thomas Watson). 296-326, *Mar. 1916*

WATT, JAMES:

The British Way. By Sir Evelyn Wrench. 421-541, *Apr. 1949*

WATTS, HARVEY MAITLAND: *Author*

The Chinese Paradox. 352-358, *Sept. 1900*

WATTS, W. A.: *Author*

Flame-Feathered Flamingos of Florida. Photos by W. F. Gerecke. 56-65, *Jan. 1941*

WATUSSI TRIBESPEOPLE:

Uganda, "Land of Something New": Equatorial African Area Reveals Snow-crowned Peaks, Crater Lakes, Jungle-story Beasts, Human Giants, and Forest Pygmies. By Jay Marston. 109-130, *Jan. 1937*
A Land of Giants and Pygmies (Ruanda). By Duke Adolphus Frederick of Mecklenburg. 369-388, *Apr. 1912*

WAURÁ INDIANS:

Amazon–The River Sea. By Loren McIntyre. 456-495, *Oct. 1972*
The Waurá: Brazilian Indians of the Hidden Xingu. By Harald Schultz. 130-152, *Jan. 1966*

WAVES. *See* Women's Reserve of the U. S. Naval Reserve

WAVES, Tidal. *See* Tsunamis

WAVES and Thrills at Waikiki. Photos by Thomas Edward Blake. 597-604, *May 1935*

WAXEL, SWEN:

The Cartography and Observations of Bering's First Voyage. By A. W. Greely. 205-230, Jan. 28, 1892; *Feb. 19, 1892*

A **WAY** of Life Called Maine. By Ethel A. Starbird. Photos by David Hiser. 727-757, *June 1977*

WAY of the Jackal. By Patricia D. Moehlman. 840-850, *Dec. 1980*

WAY Station for the Wilson's Phalarope. By Joseph R. Jehl, Jr. 520-525, *Oct. 1981*

WAYANA INDIANS:

What Future for the Wayana Indians? By Carole Devillers. 66-83, *Jan. 1983*

WAYFARING Down the Winding Severn. Photos by Frank and Bernard Wakeman. 433-440, *Apr. 1933*

WAYS and Byways of an Island Paradise. 345-352, *Mar. 1939*

WAYS of the Ant. By Bert Hölldobler. Paintings by John D. Dawson. Illustrations text by Alice J. Hall. NGS research grant. 779-813, *June 1984*

WAYSIDE Scenes in Europe. 229-244, *Feb. 1914*

WAYSIDE Scenes in Europe. 401-416, *Apr. 1915*

WAZIRISTAN (Region), Pakistan:

South of Khyber Pass. By Maynard Owen Williams. 471-500, *Apr. 1946*

WE, *The People: The Story of the* ▪▪ *United States Capitol, Its Past and Its Promise.* By Lonnelle Aikman. Photos by George F. Mobley and Joseph H. Bailey. Published in cooperation with the United States Capitol Historical Society. 143 pages. 1963; rev. ed. *1985*

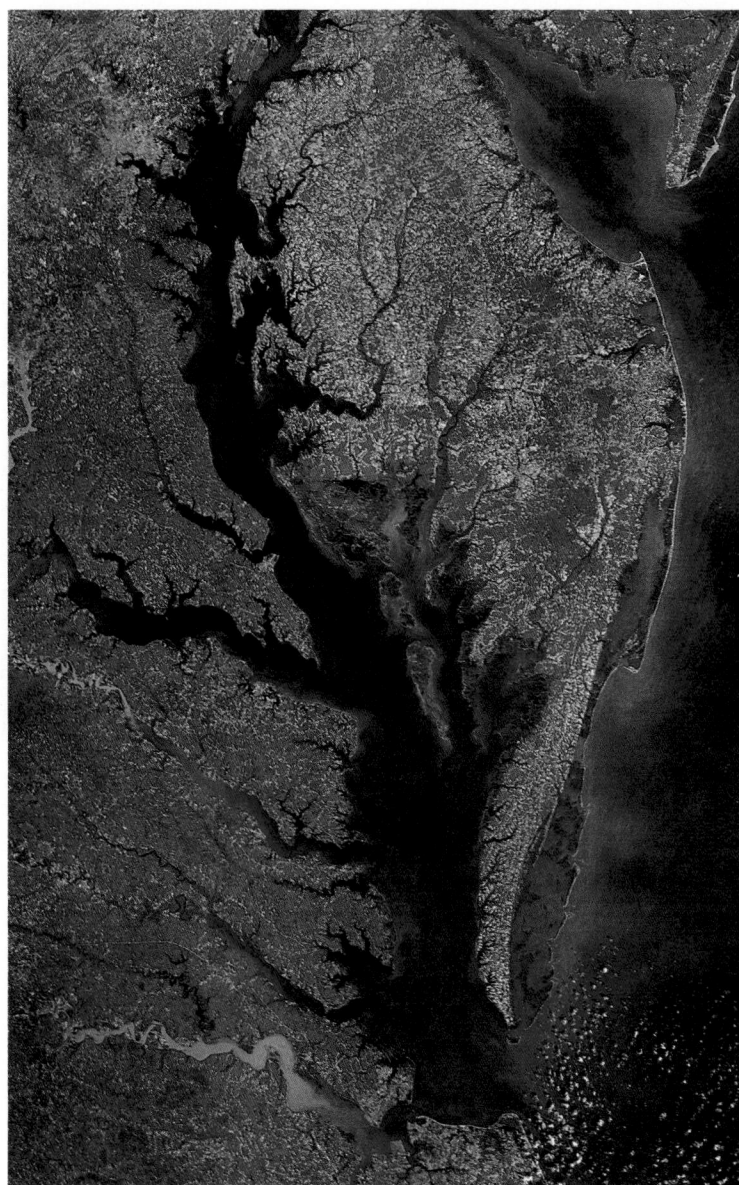

Ecological problems threaten the bounty watermen win from the Chesapeake Bay.

EARTH SATELLITE CORPORATION ENHANCEMENT AND MOSAIC FROM LANDSAT DATA

Keeping his eyes on a ghostly white tornado, young Kent Otto races back toward his North Dakota farmhouse.   EDI ANN OTTO

WEATHER BUREAU. *See* U. S. Weather Bureau

WEATHER SATELLITES:

WEATHER STATIONS AND RESEARCH:

WEATHERIZATION PROGRAMS:

Weather puts on a show above the Grand Canyon as an electrical storm lights up the night with natural fireworks. KOLB BROTHERS

WEAVER, KENNETH F.:

Nomination Page. *Aug. 1980*
Editorial. By Gilbert M. Grosvenor.
729, *June 1980*
Nomination Page. *July 1977*
Nomination Page. *Aug. 1975*
Nomination Page. *Jan. 1975*
Nomination Page. *Apr. 1974*
Nomination Page. *Aug. 1970*

Author

Meteorites–Invaders From Space. Photos by Jonathan Blair. 390-418, *Sept. 1986*
The Search for Our Ancestors. Photos by David L. Brill. Paintings by Jay H. Matternes. 560-623, *Nov. 1985*
Our Energy Predicament. 2-23, *Special Report on Energy. (Feb. 1981)*
The Mystery of the Shroud. 730-753, *June 1980*
The Promise and Peril of Nuclear Energy. Photos by Emory Kristof. 459-493, *Apr. 1979*
Geothermal Energy: The Power of Letting Off Steam. 566-579, *Oct. 1977*
How Soon Will We Measure In Metric? Drawings by Donald A. Mackay. 287-294, *Aug. 1977*
Electronic Voyage Through an Invisible World. 274-290, *Feb. 1977*
Mariner Unveils Venus and Mercury. 858-869, *June 1975*
Mystery Shrouds the Biggest Planet (Jupiter). 285-294, *Feb. 1975*
What You Didn't See in Kohoutek. 214-223, *Aug. 1974*
The Incredible Universe. Photos by James P. Blair. 589-625, *May 1974*
How to Catch a Passing Comet. 148-150, *Jan. 1974*
Have We Solved the Mysteries of the Moon? Paintings by William H. Bond. 309-325, *Sept. 1973*
Journey to Mars. Paintings by Ludek Pesek. 231-263, *Feb. 1973*
The Search for Life on Mars. 264-265, *Feb. 1973*
The Search for Tomorrow's Power. Photos by Emory Kristof. 650-681, *Nov. 1972*
Apollo 15 Explores the Mountains of the Moon. Photos from NASA. 233-265, *Feb. 1972*
Maui, Where Old Hawaii Still Lives. Photos by Gordon W. Gahan. 514-543, *Apr. 1971*
Voyage to the Planets. Paintings by Ludek Pesek. 147-193, *Aug. 1970*
The Flight of Apollo 11: "One giant leap for mankind." 752-787, *Dec. 1969*
What the Moon Rocks Tell Us. 788-791, *Dec. 1969*
And Now to Touch the Moon's Forbidding Face. 633-635, *May 1969*
That Örbèd Maiden...the Moon. 207-230, *Feb. 1969*
Remote Sensing: New Eyes to See the World. 46-73, *Jan. 1969*
Crystals, Magical Servants of the Space Age. Photos by James P. Blair. 278-296, *Aug. 1968*
Historic Color Portrait of Earth From Space. Photos by DODGE Satellite. 726-731, *Nov. 1967*
Magnetic Clues Help Date the Past. 696-701, *May 1967*

Space Rendezvous, Milestone on the Way to the Moon. 539-553, *Apr. 1966*
Giant Comet Grazes the Sun. 259-261, *Feb. 1966*
Of Planes and Men. Photos by Emory Kristof and Albert Moldvay. 298-349, *Sept. 1965*
The Five Worlds of Peru. Photos by Bates Littlehales. 213-265, *Feb. 1964*
Athens: Her Golden Past Still Lights the World. Photos by Phillip Harrington. 100-137, *July 1963*
Tracking America's Man in Orbit. Photos by Robert F. Sisson. 184-217, *Feb. 1962*
Countdown for Space. 702-734, *May 1961*
How Old Is It? By Lyman J. Briggs and Kenneth F. Weaver. 234-255, *Aug. 1958*
Rip Van Winkle of the Underground (Cicada). 133-142, *July 1953*

WEAVER, ROBERT F.: *Author*

Beyond Supermouse: Changing Life's Genetic Blueprint. Photos by Ted Spiegel. 818-847, *Dec. 1984*
The Cancer Puzzle. 396-399, *Sept. 1976*

WEAVER ANTS:

Ways of the Ant. By Bert Hölldobler. Paintings by John D. Dawson. Illustrations text by Alice J. Hall. NGS research grant. 779-813, *June 1984*

WEAVERBIRDS:

Canaries and Other Cage-Bird Friends. By Alexander Wetmore. Paintings by Allan Brooks. 775-806, *Dec. 1938*

WEAVING:

Ethiopia's Artful Weavers. By Judith Olmstead. Photos by James A. Sugar. 125-141, *Jan. 1973*
Weavers of the World. 145-152, *Aug. 1919*
See also Bayeux Tapestry; Rugs; Tweed; *and* Cotton; Silk; Wool

WEBB, S. DAVID:

Nomination Page. *Feb. 1969*

WEBBER, JOHN:

Captain Cook: The Man Who Mapped the Pacific. By Alan Villiers. Photos by Gordon W. Gahan. Included: Oil painting by *Resolution* artist John Webber. 297-349, *Sept. 1971*

WEBBER, JOHN W.:

Author-Photographer

Down Mexico's Río Balsas. Photos by author, Kenneth Segerstrom, and Jack Breed. 253-272, *Aug. 1946*

WEBER, WALTER A.: *Artist*

Life Portraits of a Famous Family: Pacific Salmon. 214-216, *Aug. 1968*
Beauty and Bounty of Southern State Trees. By William A. Dayton. 508-552, *Oct. 1957*
Stalking Central Africa's Wildlife. By T. Donald Carter. 264-286, *Aug. 1956*
Wealth and Wonder of Northern State Trees. By William A. Dayton. 651-691, *Nov. 1955*
Our Snake Friends and Foes. By Doris M. Cochran. 334-364, *Sept. 1954*
Honey-Guide: The Bird That Eats Wax. By Herbert Friedmann. 551-560, *Apr. 1954*
Wildlife of Mount McKinley National Park. By Adolph Murie. 249-270, *Aug. 1953*
Nature's Tank, the Turtle. By Doris M. Cochran. 665-684, *May 1952*
An Artist's Glimpses of Our Roadside Wildlife. 16-32, *July 1950*
Strange Courtship of Birds of Paradise. By S. Dillon Ripley. 247-278, *Feb. 1950*
Wildlife of Everglades National Park. By Daniel B. Beard. 83-116, *Jan. 1949*
Born Hunters, the Bird Dogs. By Roland Kilbon. 369-398, *Sept. 1947*

Author-Artist

Wildlife of Tabasco and Veracruz (Mexico). 187-216, *Feb. 1945*
Wild Dogs and Working Dogs. 369-376, *Sept. 1944*
Non-sporting Dogs. 577-584, *Nov. 1943*
King of Cats and His Court. 223-254, *Feb. 1943*
Antlered Majesties of Many Lands. 479-510, *Oct. 1939*
Sparrows, Towhees, and Longspurs. Paintings by Allan Brooks and Walter A. Weber. 361-375, *Mar. 1939*

WEBSTER, HARRIE: *Author*

Japan and China–Some Comparisons. 69-77, *Feb. 1901*
China and Her People–Some Reflections on Their Manners and Customs, Habits and Lives. 309-319, *Aug. 1900*
Korea–The Hermit Nation. 145-155, *Apr. 1900*
Samoa: Navigators Islands. 207-217, *June 1899*

WEBSTER, NOAH:

Literary Landmarks of Massachusetts. By William H. Nicholas. Photos by B. Anthony Stewart and John E. Fletcher. 279-310, *Mar. 1950*

WEDDELL, ALEXANDER WILBOURNE: *Author*

"The Glory That Was Greece." 571-630, *Dec. 1922*

WEDDELL SEALS:

Under Antarctic Ice. By Bill Curt-singer. 497-511, *Apr. 1986*
Stalking Seals Under Antarctic Ice. By Carleton Ray. 54-65, *Jan. 1966*

WEDDINGS:

Zulu King Weds a Swazi Princess. By Volkmar Wentzel. 47-61, *Jan. 1978*
Royal Wedding at Jaisalmer. By Marilyn Silverstone. 66-79, *Jan. 1965*
Wedding of Two Worlds. By Lee E. Battaglia. Contents: The wedding uniting Hope Cooke of New York and Palden Thondup Namgyal, Crown Prince of Sikkim. 708-727, *Nov. 1963*

WEEDS:

Pollen: Breath of Life and Sneezes. By Cathy Newman. Photos by Martha Cooper. Included: Anatomy of a Sneeze; Yellow Rain; A Misery Index. 490-521, *Oct. 1984*

WEEDS, Aquatic:

Undersea World of a Kelp Forest. By Sylvia A. Earle. Photos by Al Giddings. 411-426, *Sept. 1980*
Florida, Noah's Ark for Exotic Newcomers. By Rick Gore. Photos by David Doubilet. 538-559, *Oct. 1976*
Adrift on a Raft of Sargassum. Photos by Robert F. Sisson. 188-199, *Feb. 1976*
Algae: the Life-givers. By Paul A. Zahl. 361-377, *Mar. 1974*
Giant Kelp, Sequoias of the Sea. By Wheeler J. North. Photos by Bates Littlehales. 251-269, *Aug. 1972*
Undersea Gardens of the North

Hokkaido farmer hauls ashore a harvest of kelp, an aquatic weed belonging to the brown algae group that is used as a vegetable and condiment in Japan. EIJI MIYAZAWA, BLACK STAR

Atlantic Coast. Paintings by Else Bostelmann under direction of Roy W. Miner. 217-224, *Aug. 1936*
Seaweeds of the United States. 244, *May 1905*

WEEK-ENDS with the Prairie Falcon: A Commuter Finds Recreation in Scaling Cliffs to Observe the Nest Life and Flying Habits of These Elusive Birds. By Frederick Hall Fowler. 611-626, *May 1935*

WEEKS, GERTRUDE S.: *Author*

Into the Heart of Africa. 257-263, *Aug. 1956*

WEEKS, JOHN M.:

Honors to the American Navy (Address by John M. Weeks). 77-95, *Jan. 1909*

WEEKS EXPEDITION:

Into the Heart of Africa. By Gertrude S. Weeks. 257-263, *Aug. 1956*
Stalking Central Africa's Wildlife. By T. Donald Carter. Paintings by Walter A. Weber. 264-286, *Aug. 1956*

WEEMS, BILL: *Photographer*

Hungary's New Way: A Different Communism. By John J. Putman. 225-261, *Feb. 1983*
Home to North Carolina. By Neil Morgan. 333-359, *Mar. 1980*
Georgia, Unlimited. By Alice J. Hall. 212-245, *Aug. 1978*

WEEVILS. *See* Boll Weevils

WEIGHING the Aga Khan in Diamonds. Photos by David J. Carnegie. 317-324, *Mar. 1947*

WEIGHTS AND MEASURES:

Editorial. By Wilbur E. Garrett. 693, *June 1985*
How Soon Will We Measure In Metric? By Kenneth F. Weaver. Drawings by Donald A. Mackay. 287-294, *Aug. 1977*

Uncle Sam's House of 1,000 Wonders. By Lyman J. Briggs and F. Barrows Colton. 755-784, *Dec. 1951*
Split-second Time Runs Today's World. By F. Barrows Colton and Catherine Bell Palmer. 399-428, *Sept. 1947*
A Wonderland of Science. 153-169, *Feb. 1915*
Our Heterogeneous System of Weights and Measures. By Alexander Graham Bell. 158-169, *Mar. 1906*

WEINTRAUB, BORIS:

On Assignment in Mexico. *Nov. 1982*
Author
The Disaster of El Chichón. Photos by Guillermo Aldana E. and Kenneth Garrett. 654-684, *Nov. 1982*

WEIR, THOMAS: *Author*

High Adventure in the Himalayas. 193-234, *Aug. 1952*

WEISSHORN (Peak), Switzerland:

A Woman's Climbs in the High Alps. By Dora Keen. 643-675, *July 1911*

WEITZ, PAUL J.:

Skylab, Outpost on the Frontier of Space. By Thomas Y. Canby. Photos by the nine mission astronauts. 441-469, *Oct. 1974*

WEITZMANN, KURT: *Author*

Mount Sinai's Holy Treasures. Photos by Fred Anderegg. 109-127, *Jan. 1964*

WELCHMAN, SUSAN:

On Assignment in Australia. *Feb. 1988*

WELCOME to Wyoming. Photos by B. Anthony Stewart. 161-184, *Aug. 1945*

WELKER, P. A.: *Author*

Surveys in the Philippines. 82-83, *Jan. 1911*

Coho, or silver salmon, is prized by commercial and sports fishermen of the North Pacific. PAINTING BY WALTER A. WEBER, NGS

An 1867 New Zealand law gives the Maori four parliamentary seats in Wellington.
BRIAN BRAKE, MAGNUM

WELLFLEET, Massachusetts:
Cape Cod People and Places. By Wanda Burnett. 737-774, *June 1946*

WELLING, JAMES C.:
Board of Managers. 165, Apr. 1889; 270, July 1889; 68, Apr. 1890; 297, *Apr. 1891*

WELLINGTON, GERARD: *Author*
Undersea Wonders of the Galapagos. Photos by David Doubilet. 363-381, *Sept. 1978*

WELLINGTON, New Zealand:
New Zealand's North Island: The Contented Land. By Charles McCarry. Photos by Bates Littlehales. 190-213, *Aug. 1974*
New Zealand: Gift of the Sea. By Maurice Shadbolt. Photos by Brian Brake. 465-511, *Apr. 1962*
New Zealand, Pocket Wonder World. By Howell Walker. 419-460, *Apr. 1952*

WELLIVER, JUDSON C.: *Author*
What the War Has Done for Britain. 278-297, *Oct. 1918*

WELLMAN, WALTER:
Portraits. 349, Sept. 1899; 237, *Apr. 1906*
Author
The Polar Airship. 208-228, *Apr. 1906*

WELLMAN POLAR EXPEDITION:
No Man's Land–Spitzbergen. 455-458, *July 1907*
The Wellman Polar Expedition. 712, *Dec. 1906*
Walter Wellman's Expedition to the North Pole. 205-207, *Apr. 1906*
The Wellman Polar Expedition. By Walter Wellman. 481-505, *Dec. 1899*
The Meteorological Observations of the Second Wellman Expedition. By

Evelyn B. Baldwin. 512-516, *Dec. 1899*
The Return of Wellman. By J. Howard Gore. 348-351, *Sept. 1899*
The Wellman Polar Expedition. 361-362, *Sept. 1899*
The Wellman Polar Expedition. By J. Howard Gore. 267-268, *July 1899*
Wellman Polar Expedition. 373-375, *Aug. 1898*

WELLS, A. J.: *Author*
Seed Farms in California. 515-530, *May 1912*

WELLS, MARGARETTA BURR:
Author
The Ape with Friends in Washington. 61-74, *July 1953*

WELLS, VIRGINIA L.:
Author-Photographer
Photographing Northern Wild Flowers. 809-823, *June 1956*

WENDLE, JOSEPH: *Author*
Hunting the Grizzly in British Columbia. 612-615, *Sept. 1907*

The **WENDS** of the Spreewald. By Frederick Simpich. 327-336, *Mar. 1923*

WENKAM, ROBERT: *Photographer*
Fountain of Fire in Hawaii. By Frederick Simpich, Jr. Photos by Robert B. Goodman and Robert Wenkam. 303-327, *Mar. 1960*

WENTZEL, VOLKMAR:
On Assignment in Washington, D. C. *Sept. 1983*
Author-Photographer
Zulu King Weds a Swazi Princess. 47-61, *Jan. 1978*
Swaziland Tries Independence. 266-293, *Aug. 1969*
Mozambique: Land of the Good People. 197-231, *Aug. 1964*
Life in Walled-off West Berlin. By Nathaniel T. Kenney and Volkmar Wentzel. 735-767, *Dec. 1961*
Angola, Unknown Africa. 347-383, *Sept. 1961*
History Awakens at Harpers Ferry. 399-416, *Mar. 1957*
India's Sculptured Temple Caves. 665-678, *May 1953*
Feudal Splendor Lingers in Rajputana. 411-458, *Oct. 1948*
The Idyllic Vale of Kashmir. 523-550, *Apr. 1948*
Washington, D. C.: The Nation's Capital by Night. 514-530, *Apr. 1940*
Photographer
A Preservation Victory Saves Washington's Old Post Office. By Wolf Von Eckardt. 407-416, *Sept. 1983*
Treasure From a Celtic Tomb. By Jörg Biel. 428-438, *Mar. 1980*
Salt–The Essence of Life. By Gordon Young. Photos by Volkmar Wentzel and Georg Gerster. 381-401, *Sept. 1977*
The Most Mexican City, Guadalajara. By Bart McDowell. 412-441, *Mar. 1967*
Portugal at the Crossroads. By Howard La Fay. 453-501, *Oct. 1965*

Friendly Flight to Northern Europe. By Lyndon B. Johnson. 268-293, *Feb. 1964*
Tirol, Austria's Province in the Clouds. By Peter T. White. 107-141, *July 1961*
The Long, Lonely Leap (Parachute Jump). By Joseph W. Kittinger, Jr. 854-873, *Dec. 1960*
Salzkammergut, Austria's Alpine Playground. By Beverley M. Bowie. 246-275, *Aug. 1960*
The Smithsonian, Magnet on the Mall. By Leonard Carmichael. 796-845, *June 1960*
I'm From New Jersey. By John T. Cunningham. 1-45, *Jan. 1960*
Building a New Austria. By Beverley M. Bowie. 172-213, *Feb. 1959*
The White Horses of Vienna. By Beverley M. Bowie. 401-419, *Sept. 1958*
Wisconsin, Land of the Good Life. By Beverley M. Bowie. 141-187, *Feb. 1957*
Pennsylvania Avenue, Route of Presidents. By Dorothea and Stuart E. Jones. 63-95, *Jan. 1957*
Atlantic Odyssey: Iceland to Antarctica. By Newman Bumstead. 725-780, *Dec. 1955*
Kings Point: Maker of Mariners. By Nathaniel T. Kenney. 693-706, *Nov. 1955*
Hunting Uranium Around the World. By Robert D. Nininger. 533-558, *Oct. 1954*
Everyone's Servant, the Post Office. By Allan C. Fisher, Jr. 121-152, *July 1954*
Man's New Servant, the Friendly Atom.

Narrow street frames a Gothic church and St. Magdalena's Chapel in the Austrian town of Solbad Hall. VOLKMAR WENTZEL, NGS

Frederic Remington chronicled the American West's final frontier days in works such as "The Old Stage Coach of the Plains" (1901). AMON CARTER MUSEUM, FORT WORTH, TEXAS

W
X

A camp stove cooks vittles on a pack trip in the Big Horn region of Wyoming, a reminder of life in the Old West that attracted Frederic Remington. CHRIS JOHNS

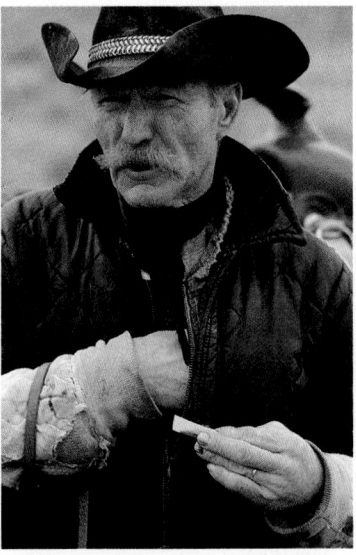

In the way of the Old West, cowhand Vern Torrance rolls a smoke on a Wyoming ranch. WILLIAM ALBERT ALLARD

Is Climatic Aridity Impending on the
Pacific Slope? The Testimony of the
Forest. By J. B. Leiberg. 160-181,
May 1899

The National Forest Reserves. By Frederick H. Newell. 177-187, *June 1897*

The Sage Plains of Oregon. By Frederick V. Coville. 395-404, *Dec. 1896*

The Arid Regions of the United States.
By F. H. Newell. 167-172,
Jan. 31, 1894

The North American Deserts. By Johannes Walther. 163-176,
Feb. 8, 1893

See also names of states

WEST AFRICA:

Africa's Sahel: The Stricken Land. By
William S. Ellis. Photos by Steve
McCurry. 140-179, *Aug. 1987*

Tsetse–Fly of the Deadly Sleep. By
Georg Gerster. 814-833, *Dec. 1986*

Senegambia: A Now and Future Nation. By Michael and Aubine Kirtley.
224-251, *Aug. 1985*

Finding West Africa's Oldest City
(Jenne-jeno). By Susan and Roder-
ick McIntosh. Photos by Michael and
Aubine Kirtley. 396-418, *Sept. 1982*

The Desert: An Age-old Challenge
Grows. By Rick Gore. Photos by
Georg Gerster and Bruce Dale. 586-
639, *Nov. 1979*

The Niger: River of Sorrow, River of
Hope. By Georg Gerster. 152-189,
Aug. 1975

Dry-land Fleet Sails the Sahara. By Jean
du Boucher. Photos by Jonathan S.
Blair. 696-725, *Nov. 1967*

Freedom Speaks French in Ouagadougou. By John Scofield. 153-203,
Aug. 1966

Africa: The Winds of Freedom Stir a
Continent. By Nathaniel T. Kenney.
Photos by W. D. Vaughn. 303-359,
Sept. 1960

Beyond the Bight of Benin. By Jeannette and Maurice Fiévet. 221-253,
Aug. 1959

Safari Through Changing Africa. By El-
sie May Bell Grosvenor. Photos by
Gilbert Grosvenor. 145-198,
Aug. 1953

Hunting Musical Game in West Africa.
By Arthur S. Alberts. 262-282,
Aug. 1951

The British Commonwealth of Nations:
"Organized Freedom" Around the
World. By Eric Underwood. 485-
524, *Apr. 1943*

Trans-Africa Safari: A Motor Caravan
Rolls Across Sahara and Jungle
Through Realms of Dusky Poten-
tates and the Land of Big-Lipped
Women. By Lawrence Copley Thaw
and Margaret Stout Thaw. 327-364,
Sept. 1938

Three-Wheeling Through Africa: Two
Adventurers Cross the So-called
Dark Continent North of Lake Chad
on Motorcycles with Side Cars. By
James C. Wilson. 37-92, *Jan. 1934*

In the Valley of the Niger. 164,
Mar. 1908

The Gold Coast, Ashanti, and Kumassi.
By George K. French. 1-15,
Jan. 1897

Return of the Hourst Niger Expedition.
By Ernest de Sasseville. 24-25,
Jan. 1897

See also Cameroon; Ivory Coast; Libe-
ria; Mali; Mauritania; Niger; Nigeria;
Sierra Leone; Upper Volta; *and*
French West Africa

WEST BANK:

Israel: Searching for the Center. By
Priit J. Vesilind. Photos by James L.
Stanfield. 2-39, *July 1985*

Jordan: Kingdom in the Middle. By
Thomas J. Abercrombie. Photos by
Jodi Cobb. 236-268, *Feb. 1984*

The Living Dead Sea. By Harvey Arden. Photos by Nathan Benn. 225-
245, *Feb. 1978*

See also Jerusalem

WEST from the Khyber Pass. By William O. Douglas. Photos by Mercedes H. Douglas and author. 1-44,
July 1958

WEST GERMANY: Continuing Mir-
acle. By John J. Putman. Photos by
Robert W. Madden. 149-181,
Aug. 1977

The **WEST** Indian Hurricane of August
7-14, 1899. By E. B. Garriott. 343-
348, *Sept. 1899*

The **WEST** Indian Hurricane of September 10-11, 1898. By E. B. Garriott. 17-20, *Jan. 1899*

The **WEST** Indian Hurricane of September 1-12, 1900. By E. B. Garriott.
384-392, *Oct. 1900*

*Not yet ready to mate, a female manatee in estrus, center, wards off a tumbling
entourage of pursuing males in Florida's Crystal River.* FRED BAVENDAM, PETER ARNOLD, INC.

WEST INDIAN MANATEE:

Man and Manatee: Can We Live To-
gether? By Alice J. Hall. Photos by
Fred Bavendam. Included: Man Can
Save the Manatee. By Jesse R.
White. 400-418, *Sept. 1984*

WEST INDIES:

⊕ *West Indies. The Making of America
series. On reverse: Spanish Caribbean, Imperial Rivalries, European
Sea, American Sea, Forces of
Change. Nov. 1987*

Fair Skies for the Cayman Islands. By
Peter Benchley. Photos by David
Doubilet. 798-824, *June 1985*

Marking Time in Grenada. By Charles
E. Cobb, Jr. Photos by David Alan
Harvey. 688-710, *Nov. 1984*

The Caribbean: Sun, Sea, and Seething.
By Noel Grove. Photos by Steve
Raymer. 244-271, *Feb. 1981*

⊕ *Tourist Islands of the West Indies;
West Indies and Central America.
Feb. 1981*

▪▪ *Isles of the Caribbean. 215 pages.
1980*

St. Vincent, the Grenadines, and Grenada: Taking It as It Comes. By Ethel
A. Starbird. Photos by Cotton Coulson. 399-425, *Sept. 1979*

Reach for the New World. By Mendel
Peterson. Photos by David L. Arnold. Paintings by Richard Schlecht.
724-767, *Dec. 1977*

Christopher Columbus and the New
World He Found. By John Scofield.
Photos by Adam Woolfitt. 584-625,
Nov. 1975

WEST IRIAN (Indonesian New Guinea). *See* Irian Jaya

WEST POINT, New York:

A hurricane brushes by Robin Lee Graham early in 1970 on the final West Indies-to-California leg of his five-year round-the-world solo sail. ROBIN LEE GRAHAM

West Virginia's first woman coal miner, Carol Bain, leaves her shift with David "Hoot" Frost. JODI COBB, NGS

W. Atwood. Photos by B. Anthony Stewart. 1-36, *July 1948*
West Point and the Gray-Clad Corps. By Herman Beukema. 777-788, *June 1936*

WEST VIRGINIA:

Wrestlin' for a Livin' With King Coal. By Michael E. Long. Photos by Michael O'Brien. 793-819, *June 1983*
The Nation's River. By Allan C. Fisher, Jr. Photos by James L. Stanfield. 432-469, *Oct. 1976*
Turnaround Time in West Virginia. By Elizabeth A. Moize. Photos by Jodi Cobb. 755-785, *June 1976*
Mountain Voices, Mountain Days. By Bryan Hodgson. Photos by Linda Bartlett. 118-146, *July 1972*
Shenandoah, I Long to Hear You. By Mike W. Edwards. Photos by Thomas Anthony DeFeo. 554-588, *Apr. 1970*
History Awakens at Harpers Ferry. By Volkmar Wentzel. 399-416, *Mar. 1957*
So Much Happens Along the Ohio River. By Frederick Simpich. Photos by Justin Locke. 177-212, *Feb. 1950*
Appalachian Valley Pilgrimage. By Catherine Bell Palmer. Photos by Justin Locke. 1-32, *July 1949*
Down the Potomac by Canoe. By Ralph Gray. Photos by Walter Meayers Edwards. 213-242, *Aug. 1948*
Potomac, River of Destiny. By Albert W. Atwood. 33-70, *July 1945*
West Virginia: Treasure Chest of Industry. By Enrique C. Canova. 141-184, *Aug. 1940*
Roads from Washington. By John Patric. 1-56, *July 1938*
❖ *Historic and Scenic Reaches of the Nation's Capital. July 1938*
The Travels of George Washington: Dramatic Episodes in His Career as the First Geographer of the United

States. By William Joseph Showalter. 1-63, *Jan. 1932*
WESTCOTT (Mail Boat). *See J. W. Westcott*

WESTDAHL, FERDINAND: *Author*
Mountains on Unimak Island, Alaska. 91-99, *Mar. 1903*

WESTERN AUSTRALIA (State), Australia:
The Tea and Sugar Lifeline in Australia's Outback. By Erla Zwingle. Photos by William Albert Allard. 737-757, *June 1986*
Perth–Fair Winds and Full Sails. By Thomas J. Abercrombie. Photos by Cary Wolinsky. 638-667, *May 1982*
Western Australia, the Big Country. By Kenneth MacLeish. Photos by James L. Stanfield. 150-187, *Feb. 1975*

WESTERN DESERT, Egypt:
Egypt's Desert of Promise. By Farouk El-Baz. Photos by Georg Gerster. 190-221, *Feb. 1982*
The Desert: An Age-old Challenge Grows. By Rick Gore. Photos by Georg Gerster and Bruce Dale. 586-639, *Nov. 1979*

WESTERN GREBES:
Western Grebes: The Birds That Walk on Water. By Gary L. Nuechterlein. NGS research grant. 624-637, *May 1982*

WESTERN HEMISPHERE:
❖ *A Map of the World* (in Eastern and Western Hemispheres). *Dec. 1941*
❖ *The World* (in Eastern and Western Hemispheres). *Dec. 1935*
The "Map of Discovery." Reproduction in color of the painting by N. C. Wyeth, National Geographic Society, Washington, D. C. 93, *Jan. 1929*

WESTERN Indian Ocean: Crosscurrents Sweep a Strategic Sea. By Bart McDowell. Photos by Steve Raymer. 422-457, *Oct. 1981*

WESTERN National Parks Invite America Out of Doors. Photos by G. A. Grant, W. M. Rush, Merl La Voy, and J. S. Dixon. 65-80, *July 1934*

WESTERN Progress in China. 434-436, *Dec. 1901*

WESTERN SAMOA, Pacific Ocean:
The Two Samoas, Still Coming of Age. By Robert Booth. Photos by Melinda Berge. 452-473, *Oct. 1985*
Western Samoa, the Pacific's Newest Nation. By Maurice Shadbolt. Photos by Robert B. Goodman. 573-602, *Oct. 1962*

WESTERN Siberia and the Altai Mountains: With Some Speculations on the Future of Siberia. By James Bryce. 469-507, *May 1921*

WESTERN Views in the Land of the Best. Photos by Fred Payne Clatworthy. 405-420, *Apr. 1923*

WESTMAN ISLANDS, Iceland. *See Vestmannaeyjar*

WESTMINSTER, Palace of, London, England:
Westminster, the Palace That Became Parliament. By Patrick Cormack. Photos by Adam Woolfitt. 728-757, *Dec. 1986*
Queen Elizabeth Opens Parliament. By W. E. Roscher. Photos by Robert B. Goodman. 699-707, *Nov. 1961*
Yanks at Westminster. By Leonard David Gammans. 223-252, *Aug. 1946*

A run of more than a thousand miles across Australia's desolate Nullarbor Plain leaves plenty of time for reflection by the Tea and Sugar Train's engineer. WILLIAM ALBERT ALLARD

Handful of sphagnum moss drips water into a bog, the wetland world where the spongy plant thrives. SANDY FELSENTHAL

WETMORE, ALEXANDER:

Board of Trustees, Trustee Emeritus. 672, *May 1978*

Board of Trustees, member. 161, Aug. 1944; 595, May 1947; 344, Sept. 1948; 65A-65B, July 1954; 364, Mar. 1956; 835, Dec. 1959; 883, Dec. 1960; 555, Oct. 1964; 485, Oct. 1966; 839, Dec. 1970; 151, Aug. 1975; 227, *Aug. 1976*

Editorial. By Gilbert M. Grosvenor. 151, *Aug. 1975*

Hubbard Medal recipient (1975). 151, *Aug. 1975*

Committee for Research and Exploration, Vice Chairman. 705, June 1947; 532, Oct. 1965; 489, Oct. 1967; 881-882, *Dec. 1967*

Nomination Page. In Panama. *July 1959*

The Book of Birds: The First Work Presenting in Full Color All the Major Species of the United States and Canada. Edited by Gilbert H. Grosvenor and Alexander Wetmore. Art by Allan Brooks. 2 volumes: I, 355 pages; II, 374 pages. 1932; rev. ed. *1937*

Author

Re-creating Madagascar's Giant Extinct Bird. 488-493, *Oct. 1967*

Canaries and Other Cage-Bird Friends. Paintings by Allan Brooks. 775-806, *Dec. 1938*

Game Birds of Prairie, Forest, and Tundra. Paintings by Allan Brooks. 461-500, *Oct. 1936*

Parrots, Kingfishers, and Flycatchers; Strange Trogons and Curious Cuckoos are Pictured with these Other Birds of Color, Dash, and Courage. Paintings by Allan Brooks. 801-828, *June 1936*

Birds of the Northern Seas. Paintings by Allan Brooks. 95-122, *Jan. 1936*

Shadowy Birds of the Night (Owls). Paintings by Allan Brooks. 217-240, *Feb. 1935*

Winged Denizens of Woodland, Stream, and Marsh. Paintings by Allan Brooks. 577-596, *May 1934*

The Eagle, King of Birds, and His Kin. Paintings by Allan Brooks. 43-95, *July 1933*

Seeking the Smallest Feathered Creatures: Humming Birds, Peculiar to the New World, Are Found from Canada and Alaska to the Strait of Magellan. Swifts and Goatsuckers, Their Nearest Relatives. Paintings by Allan Brooks. 65-89, *July 1932*

Bird Life Among Lava Rock and Coral Sand: The Chronicle of a Scientific Expedition to Little-known Islands of Hawaii. 77-108, *July 1925*

WHALERS (Ships):

American Pathfinders in the Pacific. By William H. Nicholas. 617-640, *May 1946*

WHALES:

Whales: An Era of Discovery. By James D. Darling. Photos by Flip Nicklin. 872-909, *Dec. 1988*

Gray Whales of San Ignacio. By Steven L. Swartz and Mary Lou Jones. Photos by François Gohier. NGS research grant. 754-771, *June 1987*

Narwhal: Unicorn of the Arctic Seas. By John and Deborah Ford. Photos by Flip Nicklin. 354-363, *Mar. 1986*

Rare Look At Sperm and Blue Whales, The Unknown Giants. By Hal Whitehead. Photos by Flip Nicklin. 774-789, *Dec. 1984*

The Whales Called "Killer." By Erich Hoyt. 220-237, *Aug. 1984*

Narwhal Hunters of Greenland. By Ivars Silis. 520-539, *Apr. 1984*

An Incredible Feasting of Whales. By Al Giddings. 88-93, *Jan. 1984*

New Light on the Singing Whales. Introduction by Roger Payne. Photos by Flip Nicklin. NGS research grant. 463-477, *Apr. 1982*

Killer Whale Attack! Text by Cliff Tarpy. Contents: Blue whale attacked by thirty killer whales. 542-545, *Apr. 1979*

Humpback Whales. 2-25. I. The Gentle Giants. By Sylvia A. Earle. Photos by Al Giddings. 2-17; II. Their Mysterious Songs. By Roger Payne. Photos by Al Giddings. 18-25; III. Symphony of the Deep: "Songs of the Humpback Whale" (Sound sheet). NGS research grant. 24-24B, *Jan. 1979*

The Great Whales. 439, Oct. 1977; cover, Feb. 1978; Emmy Award. 1, *Jan. 1979*

Editorial. By Gilbert M. Grosvenor. 721, *Dec. 1976*

Whales of the World. 722-767. I. The Imperiled Giants. By William Graves. 722-751; II. Exploring the Lives of Whales. By Victor B. Scheffer. 752-767, *Dec. 1976*

❖ "Whales of the World." Painting supplement. Map on reverse, *The Great Whales: Migration and Range. Dec. 1976*

At Home With Right Whales. By Roger Payne. Photos by Des and Jen Bartlett. NGS research grant. 322-339, *Mar. 1976*

Where Two Worlds Meet (Patagonia). Photos by Des and Jen Bartlett. Included: Dolphins; Killer Whales. 298-321, *Mar. 1976*

The Last U. S. Whale Hunters. By

Contemporaries of dinosaurs and the world's oldest surviving reptiles, turtles include a Suwannee cooter cruising Florida's Rainbow Run. BILL CURTSINGER

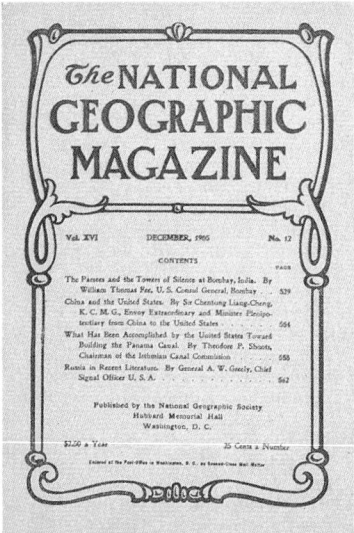

The NATIONAL GEOGRAPHIC MAGAZINE

A Wayana boy cools off in the cascading Itany River. Fewer than 1,000 Wayanas survive along the Suriname-French Guiana border in South America. CAROLE DEVILLERS

In a furious display, one male humpback whale lashes his tail as other suitors compete for a female in Hawaiian waters. FLIP NICKLIN

WHEELER, WILLIAM MORTON:
Author
Notes About Ants and Their Resemblance to Man. 731-766, *Aug. 1912*

WHEELER MOUNTAIN, Vermont:
Life on a Rock Ledge. By William H. Amos. 558-566, *Oct. 1980*

WHEELER NATIONAL MONUMENT, Colorado:
The Wheeler National Monument. 837-840, *Sept. 1909*

WHEELING, West Virginia:
So Much Happens Along the Ohio River. By Frederick Simpich. Photos by Justin Locke. 177-212, *Feb. 1950*

WHEN a Drought Blights Africa: Hippos and Elephants Are Driven Insane by Suffering, in the Lorian Swamp, Kenya Colony. By A. T. Curle. 521-528, *Apr. 1929*

WHEN Czechoslovakia Puts a Falcon Feather in Its Cap. By Maynard Owen Williams. 40-49, *Jan. 1933*

WHEN Disaster Struck a Woodpecker's Home. By Frederick Kent Truslow. 882-884, *Dec. 1966*

WHEN GI Joes Took London. By Frederick Simpich, Jr. 337-354, *Sept. 1944*

WHEN Giant Bears Go Fishing. By Cecil E. Rhode. 195-205, *Aug. 1954*

WHEN Golden Praha Entertains the Majestic Sokol Festival. Photos by Hans Hildenbrand. 41-48, *Jan. 1933*

WHEN Gypsies Gather at Appleby Fair. Photos by Bruce Dale. 848-869, *June 1972*

WHEN Ice Entombed an Eskimo Family. By Albert A. Dekin, Jr. Photos by Victor R. Boswell, Jr., and Scott Rutherford. Paintings by James M. Gurney. 824-836, *June 1987*

WHEN in Rome.... By Stuart E. Jones. Photos by Winfield Parks. 741-789, *June 1970*

WHEN Irish Skies Are Smiling. Photos by Harrison Howell Walker. 663-686, *May 1940*

WHEN Mt. Mazama Lost Its Top: The Birth of Crater Lake. By Lyman J. Briggs. 128-133, *July 1962*

WHEN Our Country Is Fifty Years Older. By Raphael Zon. 573-580, *June 1909*

WHEN Red Men Ruled Our Forests. Paintings by W. Langdon Kihn. 551-590, *Nov. 1937*

WHEN the Earth Moves. The Editor. 638-639, *May 1986*

WHEN the Father of Waters Goes on a Rampage: An Account of the Salvaging of Food-fishes from the Overflowed Lands of the Mississippi River. By Hugh M. Smith. 369-386, *Apr. 1920*

WHEN the Herring Fleet Comes to Great Yarmouth. By W. Robert Moore. 233-250, *Aug. 1934*

WHEN the Moguls Ruled India. By Mike Edwards. Photos by Roland Michaud. 463-493, *Apr. 1985*

WHEN the Moors Ruled Spain. By Thomas J. Abercrombie. Photos by Bruno Barbey. 86-119, *July 1988*

WHEN the President Goes Abroad. By Gilbert M. Grosvenor. 588-649, *May 1960*

WHEN the Rus Invaded Russia: Viking Trail East. By Robert Paul Jordan. Photos by Jim Brandenburg. Paintings by Michael A. Hampshire. 278-317, *Mar. 1985*

WHEN the Space Shuttle Finally Flies. By Rick Gore. Photos by Jon Schneeberger. Paintings by Ken Dallison. 317-347, *Mar. 1981*

WHEN Will We Measure In Metric? By Kenneth F. Weaver. Drawings by Donald A. Mackay. 287-294, *Aug. 1977*

WHERE Adam and Eve Lived. By Frederick and Margaret Simpich. 546-588, *Dec. 1914*

WHERE Ancient Sea Kings Held Sway. Photos by Maynard Owen Williams. 255-262, *Feb. 1929*

WHERE Bald Eagles Soar. By Thomas C. Dunstan. Photos by Jeff Foott. 186-199, *Feb. 1978*

WHERE Bible Characters Live Again: Everyday Life in Oberammergau, World Famous for Its Passion Play, Reaches a Climax at Christmas. By Anton Lang, Jr. 743-769, *Dec. 1935*

WHERE Birds and Little Animals Find Haven. By Agnes Akin Atkinson. 232-241, *Aug. 1936*

WHERE Bretons Wrest a Living from the Sea. Photos by F. W. Goro. 751-766, *June 1937*

WHERE Can the Wolf Survive? By L. David Mech. 518-537, *Oct. 1977*

WHERE Columbus Found the New World. By Joseph Judge. Photos by James L. Stanfield. 566-599, *Nov. 1986*

"WHERE Did We Come From?" Editorial by Wilbur E. Garrett. Included: Map, The Peopling of the Earth. 434-437, *Oct. 1988*

WHERE Do Society Members Stand? 52-53, *Special Report on Energy. (Feb. 1981)*

WHERE Early Christians Lived in Cones of Rock: A Journey to Cappadocia in Turkey Where Strange Volcanic Pinnacles Are Honeycombed With Hermit Cells and Monasteries. By John D. Whiting. 763-802, *Dec. 1939*

WHERE East Meets West: Visit to Picturesque Dalmatia, Montenegro and Bosnia. By Marian Cruger Coffin. 309-344, *May 1908*

WHERE Elephants Have Right of Way. By George and Jinx Rodger. 363-389, *Sept. 1960*

WHERE Everybody Dresses in White. Photos by J. Z. Moore. 872-877, *Dec. 1908*

WHERE Exploration Is Needed. 163-164, *Apr. 1900*

WHERE Falcons Wear Air Force Blue, United States Air Force Academy. By Nathaniel T. Kenney. Photos by William Belknap, Jr. 845-873, *June 1959*

WHERE Fog and Sun Paint the Pacific. Photos by J. Baylor Roberts. 437-460, *Oct. 1942*

WHERE Gods Dwelled–The Japan Alps. By Charles McCarry. Photos by George F. Mobley. 238-259, *Aug. 1984*

WHERE Hot Pools Seethe and Geysers Spout. Photos by Edwin L. Wisherd. 775-782, *June 1940*

WHERE Jesus Walked. By Howard La Fay. Photos by Charles Harbutt. 739-781, *Dec. 1967*

WHERE Magic Ruled: Art of the Bering Sea. By William W. Fitzhugh and Susan A. Kaplan. Photos by Sisse Brimberg. 198-205, *Feb. 1983*

WHERE Man's Garb Rivals the Quetzal. Photos by Luis Marden. 437-444, *Oct. 1936*

WHERE Nature Runs Riot: On Australia's Great Barrier Reef Marine Animals Grow to Unusual Size, Develop Strange Weapons of Attack and Defense, and Acquire Brilliant Colors. By T. C. Roughley. 823-850, *June 1940*

WHERE New England Meets the Sea. Photos by B. Anthony Stewart. 265-288, *Sept. 1945*

WHERE Oil and Wildlife Mix. By Steven C. Wilson and Karen C. Hayden. 145-173, *Feb. 1981*

WHERE Old Hawaii Still Lives: Maui. By Kenneth F. Weaver. Photos by Gordon W. Gahan. 514-543, *Apr. 1971*

WHERE Our Bananas Come From. By Edwin R. Fraser. 713-730, *July 1912*

WHERE Our Moths and Butterflies Roam. 105-126, *July 1927*

"WHERE Rolls the Oregon." Photos by Ray Atkeson. 689-728, *Dec. 1946*

WHERE Roosevelt Will Hunt. By Sir Harry Johnston. 207-256, *Mar. 1909*

WHERE Slav and Mongol Meet. 421-436, *Nov. 1919*

WHERE Snow Peaks Temper the Tropics. Photos by W. Robert Moore. 727-734, *Dec. 1941*

WHERE Solitude Is in Season: Snow-mantled Stehekin. Photos by Bruce Dale. Text by Pat Hutson. 572-588, *Apr. 1974*

WHERE Spring Paints a State with Wild Flowers. Photos by B. Anthony Stewart. 365-380, *Mar. 1936*

When Gypsies gather each June at Appleby Fair in northern England, children shoulder their share of work—here a trio fetches water while minding baby sister. BRUCE DALE, NGS

WHERE the Blue Begins on the Italian Coast. Photos by Hans Hildenbrand. 81-88, *Jan. 1935*

WHERE the Earth Turns Inside Out. By J. R. Heirtzler. Photos by Emory Kristof. 586-603, *May 1975*

WHERE the Last of the West Was Won. Photos by Clifton Adams and Asahel Curtis. 179-186, *Feb. 1933*

"**WHERE** the Mountains Walked": An Account of the Recent Earthquake in Kansu Province, China, Which Destroyed 100,000 Lives. By Upton Close and Elsie McCormick. 445-464, *May 1922*

WHERE the New South Challenges the Old. Photos by Edwin L. Wisherd. 717-748, *Dec. 1931*

WHERE the River Shannon Flows. By Allan C. Fisher, Jr. Photos by Adam Woolfitt. 652-679, *Nov. 1978*

WHERE the Sailing Ship Survives. By A. J. Villiers. 101-128, *Jan. 1935*

WHERE the Sard Holds Sway. By Luigi Pellerano. 464-474, *Apr. 1926*

WHERE the Wind Does the Work. By Collier Cobb. 310-317, *June 1906*

WHERE the Winding Cam Mirrors Cambridge Spires. Photos by Bernard Wakeman and Walter M. Edwards. 339-346, *Sept. 1936*

WHERE the Winning of the West Began. Photos by Jacob Gayer. 563-570, *May 1932*

WHERE the World Gets Its Oil: But Where Will Our Children Get It When American Wells Cease to Flow? By George Otis Smith. 181-202, *Feb. 1920*

WHERE Turk and Russian Meet. By Ferdinand Kuhn. 743-766, *June 1952*

WHERE Two Worlds Meet. Photos by Des and Jen Bartlett. 298-321, *Mar. 1976*

WHERE Women Vote. By Baroness Alletta Korff. 487-493, *June 1910*

WHERE Would We Be Without Algae? By Paul A. Zahl. 361-377, *Mar. 1974*

WHICH Way Now for Argentina? By Loren McIntyre. 296-333, *Mar. 1975*

WHICH Way Oahu? By Gordon Young. Photos by Robert W. Madden. 653-679, *Nov. 1979*

WHIPSNADE ZOOLOGICAL PARK, Dunstable Downs, England:

London's Zoo of Zoos. By Thomas Garner James. Included: Regent's Park; Whipsnade. 771-786, *June 1953*

The **WHIRLPOOL** of the Balkans. By George Higgins Moses. 179-197, *Feb. 1921*

WHISTLING SWANS:

Tireless Voyager, the Whistling Swan. By William J. L. Sladen. Photos by Bianca Lavies. NGS research grant. 134-147, *July 1975*

WHITAKER, HERMAN: *Author*

The Wonderland of California. 57-99, *July 1915*

WHITBECK, RAY HUGHES: *Author*

Geographic Names in the United States and the Stories They Tell. 100-104, *Mar. 1905*

WHITBY, England:

Between the Heather and the North Sea: Bold English Headlands Once Sheltered Sea Robbers, Later Were

Ports of Wooden Ships, Centers of the Jet and Alum Trades, To-day Are Havens of Adventurous Fishing Fleets. By Leo Walmsley. 197-232, *Feb. 1933*

WHITE, ABBIE M.:
Bequests by members. 474, *Apr. 1926*

WHITE, CHRISTOPHER P.: *Author*
Freshwater Turtles–Designed for Survival. Photos by Bill Curtsinger. 40-59, *Jan. 1986*

WHITE, CLIFFORD: *Photographer*
Peaks and Trails in the Canadian Alps. 627-642, *May 1934*

WHITE, EDWARD H.:
America's 6,000-mile Walk in Space. 440-447, *Sept. 1965*

WHITE, H. C.: *Photographer*
China's Wonderland–Yen Tang Shan. Photos by Herbert Clarence White, Clarence C. Crisler, Deng Bao-ling, and Hwang Yao-tso. 687-694, *Dec. 1937*
A Peiping Panorama in Vivid Pigments. Photos by H. C. and J. H. White, Deng Bao-ling, and Hwang Yao-tso. 753-784, *Dec. 1936*

WHITE, J. H.: *Photographer*
A Peiping Panorama in Vivid Pigments. Photos by H. C. and J. H. White, Deng Bao-ling, and Hwang Yao-tso. 753-784, *Dec. 1936*

WHITE, JAMES: *Author*
Location of the Sir John Franklin Monument. 596, *Aug. 1908*

WHITE, JESSE R.: *Author*
Man Can Save the Manatee. 414-418, *Sept. 1984*

WHITE, JOHN:
Indian Life Before the Colonists Came. By Stuart E. Jones. Engravings by Theodore de Bry, 1590. Included: John White, one of Sir Walter Raleigh's colonists on Roanoke Island, 1585, and reproductions of his paintings from De Bry's copper plate engravings. 351-368, *Sept. 1947*

WHITE, JOHN CLAUDE:
Nomination Page. In Bhutan. *Oct. 1974*
Author
Nepal: A Little-Known Kingdom. 245-283, *Oct. 1920*
The World's Strangest Capital (Lhasa, Tibet). 273-295, *Mar. 1916*
Castles in the Air: Experiences and Journeys in Unknown Bhutan. 365-455, *Apr. 1914*

WHITE, JOHN R.: *Author*
Among the Big Trees of California. 219-232, *Aug. 1934*

WHITE, PAUL DUDLEY: *Author*
Hunting the Heartbeat of a Whale. By Paul Dudley White and Samuel W. Matthews. 49-64, *July 1956*

WHITE, PETER T.:
On Assignment in Laos. *June 1987*
On Assignment in Pakistan. *Feb. 1985*

On Assignment in Tucson, Arizona. *Apr. 1983*

On Assignment in Southeast Asia. *May 1982*

Nomination Page. *July 1977*

Nomination Page. *June 1973*

Nomination Page. In Thailand. *June 1967*

Nomination Page. *June 1964*

Author

Laos Today. Photos by Seny Norasingh. 772-795, *June 1987*

A Little Humanity Amid the Horrors of War. Photos by Steve Raymer. 647-679, *Nov. 1986*

Missing in Action, 1972–U. S. Plane Found in Laos. Photos by Seny Norasingh. 692-696, *Nov. 1986*

The World of Tolstoy. Photos by Sam Abell. 758-791, *June 1986*

The Poppy. Photos by Steve Raymer. 143-189, *Feb. 1985*

The Fascinating World of Trash. Photos by Louie Psihoyos. 424-457, *Apr. 1983*

Tropical Rain Forests: Nature's Dwindling Treasures. Photos by James P. Blair. Paintings by Barron Storey. 2-47, *Jan. 1983*

The Temples of Angkor: Ancient Glory in Stone. Photos by Wilbur E. Garrett. 552-589, *May 1982*

Kampuchea Wakens From a Nightmare. Photos by David Alan Harvey. 590-623, *May 1982*

Greece: "To Be Indomitable, To Be Joyous." Photos by James P. Blair. 360-393, *Mar. 1980*

Old Prague in Winter. Photos by Nathan Benn. 546-567, *Apr. 1979*

Spain: It's a Changed Country. Photos by David Alan Harvey. 297-331, *Mar. 1978*

One Canada–or Two? Photos by Winfield Parks. 436-465, *Apr. 1977*

This Land of Ours–How Are We Using

It? Photos by Emory Kristof. 20-67, *July 1976*

South Korea: What Next? Photos by H. Edward Kim. 394-427, *Sept. 1975*

Tanzania Marches to Its Own Drum. Photos by Emory Kristof. 474-509, *Apr. 1975*

Gold, the Eternal Treasure. Photos by James L. Stanfield. 1-51, *Jan. 1974*

Calcutta, India's Maligned Metropolis. Photos by Raghubir Singh. 534-563, *Apr. 1973*

Springtime of Hope in Poland. Photos by James P. Blair. 467-501, *Apr. 1972*

Barehanded Battle to Cleanse the Bay. Photos by Jonathan S. Blair. 866-881, *June 1971*

Mosaic of Cultures (Southeast Asia). Photos by W. E. Garrett. 296-329, *Mar. 1971*

Behold the Computer Revolution. Photos by Bruce Dale and Emory Kristof. 593-633, *Nov. 1970*

Satellites Gave Warning of Midwest Floods. Photos by Thomas A. De-Feo. 574-592, *Oct. 1969*

The Mekong, River of Terror and Hope. Photos by W. E. Garrett. 737-787, *Dec. 1968*

Vienna, City of Song. Photos by John Launois. 739-779, *June 1968*

Hopes and Fears in Booming Thailand. Photos by Dean Conger. 76-125, *July 1967*

Behind the Headlines in Viet Nam. Photos by Winfield Parks. 149-189, *Feb. 1967*

Saigon: Eye of the Storm. Photos by W. E. Garrett. 834-872, *June 1965*

The World in New York City. 52-107, *July 1964*

Brazil, Ôba! Photos by Winfield Parks. 299-353, *Sept. 1962*

South Viet Nam Fights the Red Tide. Photos by W. E. Garrett. 445-489, *Oct. 1961*

Report on Laos. Photos by W. E. Garrett. 241-275, *Aug. 1961*

Tirol, Austria's Province in the Clouds. Photos by Volkmar Wentzel. 107-141, *July 1961*

The Incredible Helicopter. 533-557, *Apr. 1959*

WHITE, WILLIAM A.: *Author*

The Geographical Distribution of Insanity in the United States. 361-378, *Oct. 1903*

WHITE (River), Yukon Territory, Canada:

Ice Cliffs on White River, Yukon Territory. By C. Willard Hayes and Alfred H. Brooks. 199-201, *May 1900*

Ice-Cliffs on White River, Yukon Territory. By Martin W. Gorman. 113-117, *Mar. 1900*

The **WHITE** City of Algiers. By Gordon Casserly. Included: On the Fringe of the Great Desert. Photos by Gervais Courtellemont. 206-232, *Feb. 1928*

The **WHITE HORSES** of Vienna. By Beverley M. Bowie. Photos by Volkmar Wentzel. 401-419, *Sept. 1958*

WHITE HOUSE, Washington, D. C.:

▪▪ *The Living White House.* By Lonnelle Aikman. Published in cooperation with the White House Historical Association. 151 pages. 1966; rev. ed. *1987*

▪▪ *The President's House: A History.* By William Seale. Published in cooperation with the White House Historical Association. 2 volumes, 1224 pages. *1986*

▪▪ *The White House: An Historic Guide.* Published in cooperation with the White House Historical Association. 159 pages. 1962; rev. ed. *1982*

The Living White House. By Lonnelle Aikman. 593-643, *Nov. 1966*

The Last Full Measure (Tribute to President Kennedy). By Melville Bell Grosvenor. 307-355, *Mar. 1964*

Inside the White House. By Lonnelle Aikman. Photos by B. Anthony Stewart and Thomas Nebbia. 3-43, *Jan. 1961*

Washington: Home of the Nation's Great. By Albert W. Atwood. 699-738, *June 1947*

See also Presidents, U. S.

WHITE LION (Dutch East Indiaman). *See Witte Leeuw*

WHITE MAGIC in the Belgian Congo. By W. Robert Moore. 321-362, *Mar. 1952*

WHITE MIST (Yawl):

Homeward With Ulysses. By Melville Bell Grosvenor. Photos by Edwin Stuart Grosvenor. 1-39, *July 1973*

The Isles of Greece: Aegean Birthplace of Western Culture. By Melville Bell Grosvenor. Photos by Edwin Stuart Grosvenor and Winfield Parks. 147-193, *Aug. 1972*

North (U. S. and Canada) Through History Aboard *White Mist.* By Melville Bell Grosvenor. Photos by Edwin Stuart Grosvenor. 1-55, *July 1970*

On assignment for a story on gold, writer Peter White, front, and photographer Jim Stanfield soak in a Japanese hotel's 313.5-pound, 22-karat-gold tub. JAMES L. STANFIELD, NGS

Returning from a voyage among the isles of Greece, **White Mist** *passes Cape Sounion at dawn.* EDWIN STUART GROSVENOR

WHITMAN, MARCUS:

Oregon: Its History, Geography, and Resources. By John H. Mitchell. 239-284, *Apr. 20, 1895*

WHITMAN COUNTY, Washington:

A Paradise Called the Palouse. By Barbara Austin. Photos by Phil Schofield. 798-819, *June 1982*

WHITNEY, Mount, California:

Sierra High Trip. By David R. Brower. 844-868, *June 1954*

WHITSON, MARTHA A.: *Author*

The Roadrunner–Clown of the Desert. Photos by Bruce Dale. 694-702, *May 1983*

WHITTAKER, JAMES W.:

Six to the Summit. By Norman G. Dyhrenfurth. Photos by Barry C. Bishop. Note: Jim Whittaker was the first American to reach the summit of Everest. 460-473, *Oct. 1963*

Author

Americans Climb K2: The Ultimate Challenge. 624-639, *May 1979*

Canada's Mount Kennedy: III. The First Ascent. Photos by William Albert Allard. 11-33, *July 1965*

WHITTEMORE, THOMAS: *Author*

The Rebirth of Religion in Russia: The Church Reorganized While Bolshevik Cannon Spread Destruction in the Nation's Holy of Holies. 379-401, *Nov. 1918*

WHITTIER, JOHN GREENLEAF:

Literary Landmarks of Massachusetts. By William H. Nicholas. Photos by B. Anthony Stewart and John E. Fletcher. 279-310, *Mar. 1950*

WHO Are Earth's Richest People? By Mike Holmes. 344-353, *Sept. 1976*

WHO Discovered America? A New Look at an Old Question. The Editor. 769, *Dec. 1977*

WHO Says Fish Can't Climb Trees? By Ivan Polunin. 85-91, *Jan. 1972*

WHO Shall Inherit Long Life? On the Existence of a Natural Process at Work Among Human Beings Tending to Improve the Vigor and Vitality of Succeeding Generations. By Alexander Graham Bell. 505-514, *June 1919*

WHO Treads Our Trails? A Camera Trapper Describes His Experiences on an Island in the Canal Zone, a Natural-History Laboratory in the American Tropics. By Frank M. Chapman. 331-345, *Sept. 1927*

WHO Were the "Mound Builders"? By George E. Stuart. 783-801, *Dec. 1972*

WHOOPING CRANES:

■ Flight of the Whooping Crane. President's Page; cover, *Apr. 1984*

Where Oil and Wildlife Mix. By Steven C. Wilson and Karen C. Hayden. 145-173, *Feb. 1981*

Teamwork Helps the Whooping Crane.

By Roderick C. Drewien, with Ernie Kuyt. 680-693, *May 1979*

Whooping Cranes Fight for Survival. By Robert Porter Allen. Photos by Frederick Kent Truslow. 650-669, *Nov. 1959*

WHO'S Who Among the Butterflies. By Austin H. Clark. Paintings by Hashime Murayama. 679-692, *May 1936*

WHO'S Who in the Monkey World. Paintings by Elie Cheverlange. 625-648, *May 1938*

WHY Great Salt Lake Has Fallen. By L. H. Murdoch. 75-77, *Feb. 1903*

WHY in the World? Contents: Ques-
■ tions and answers on a variety of subjects. Juvenile. 104 pages. *1985*

WHY Is It That Calcutta–the World's Most Maligned Metropolis–Is Where So Many People Want To Be? By Peter T. White. Photos by Raghubir Singh. 534-563, *Apr. 1973*

WHY Nik-ko Is Beautiful. By J. H. De Forest. 300-308, *Apr. 1908*

WHY on Earth? Contents: Questions
■ and answers on a variety of subjects. Juvenile. 96 pages. *1988*

WICHITA MOUNTAINS WILDLIFE REFUGE, Oklahoma:

The Wichitas: Land of the Living Prairie. By M. Woodbridge Williams. 661-697, *May 1957*

WICKER, CYRUS FRENCH: *Author*

Eastward from Gibraltar: Overland Route Across North Africa to Tunisia and Libia. 115-142, *Jan. 1943*

WICKWIRE, JAMES: *Author*

Americans Climb K2: On to the Summit. 641-649, *May 1979*

WIDEAWAKE FIELD, Ascension Island:

Ascension Island, an Engineering Victory. By Frederick J. Clarke. 623-640, *May 1944*

WIGHT, Isle of, England:

Cowes to Cornwall. By Alan Villiers. Photos by Robert B. Goodman. 149-201, *Aug. 1961*

Portsmouth, Britannia's Sally Port. By Thomas Garner James. Photos by B. Anthony Stewart. 513-544, *Apr. 1952*

The British Way. By Sir Evelyn Wrench. 421-541, *Apr. 1949*

England's Sun Trap Isle of Wight. By J. R. Hildebrand. 1-33, *Jan. 1935*

WILBUR, CURTIS D.:

Commander Byrd Receives the Hubbard Gold Medal: The First Explorer to Reach the North Pole by Air Receives Coveted Honor at Brilliant National Geographic Society Reception. Address by Secretary Wilbur. 377-388, *Sept. 1926*

WILBUR, LYMAN D.: *Author*

Surveying Through Khoresm: A Journey Into Parts of Asiatic Russia Which Have Been Closed to Western Travelers Since the World War. 753-780, *June 1932*

WILBUR, W. H.: *Author*

Infantrymen–The Fighters of War. 513-538, *Nov. 1944*

WILBY, SORREL:

Author-Photographer

Nomads' Land: A Journey Through Tibet. 764-785, *Dec. 1987*

WILCOX, WALTER D.: *Author*

Among the Mahogany Forests of Cuba. 485-498, *July 1908*

Recent Exploration in the Canadian Rockies (Part II). 185-200, *June 1902*

Recent Exploration in the Canadian Rockies (Part I). 151-168, *May 1902*

Sources of the Saskatchewan. 113-134, *Apr. 1899*

A **WILD,** Ill-fated Balloon Race. 778-797. I. Wild Launch. 778-787; II. The Fantastic Flight of *Cote d'Or.* By Cynthia Shields. 789-793; III. Last Ascent of a Heroic Team. 794-797, *Dec. 1983*

WILD AND SCENIC RIVERS SYSTEM:

■ *America's Wild and Scenic Rivers.* 199 pages. *1983*

Our Wild and Scenic Rivers. 2-59. I. Rivers Wild and Pure: A Priceless Legacy. By Robert E. Doyle. 2-11; II. The Flathead. By Douglas H. Chadwick. Photos by Lowell Georgia. 13-19; III. The Suwannee. By Jack and Anne Rudloe. Photos by Jodi Cobb. 20-29; IV. The St. Croix. By David S. Boyer. 30-37; V. The Skagit. By David S. Boyer. 38-45; VI. The Rio Grande. By Nathaniel T. Kenney. Photos by Bank Langmore. 46-51; VII. The Noatak. By John M. Kauffmann. Photos by Sam Abell. 52-59, *July 1977*

⊕ *Wild and Scenic Rivers of the United States. July 1977*

America's Little Mainstream. By Harvey Arden. Photos by Matt Bradley. Note: In 1972, Congress created the

Buffalo National River, a unique administrative unit. 344-359, *Mar. 1977*
White-water Adventure on Wild Rivers of Idaho. By Frank Craighead, Jr., and John Craighead. Included: Middle Fork Salmon; Salmon; and rivers protected or proposed for protection under the Wild and Scenic Rivers Act of 1968. 213-239, *Feb. 1970*
● Wild River. Included: Middle Fork Salmon; Salmon. 239A-239B, *Feb. 1970*
See also protected rivers, by name

The **WILD** Animals in My Life. By William M. Mann. 497-524, *Apr. 1957*

WILD Animals of North America. 406
■■ pages. 1979; rev. ed. *1987*

WILD Animals of North America. 400
■■ pages. *1960*

WILD Animals of North America: Intimate Studies of Big and Little Creatures of the Mammal Kingdom. By Edward W. Nelson. Paintings by Louis Agassiz Fuertes. Sketches by Ernest Thompson Seton. 612 pages. *1918*

WILD Animals That Took Their Own Pictures by Day and by Night. By George Shiras, 3d. 763-834, *July 1913*

The **WILD** Blueberry Tamed: The New Industry of the Pine Barrens of New Jersey. By Frederick V. Coville. 535-546, *June 1916*

The **WILD BUNCH:**
Riding the Outlaw Trail. By Robert Redford. Photos by Jonathan Blair. 622-657, *Nov. 1976*

The **WILD** Burros of Death Valley. By Patricia des Roses Moehlman. Photos by Ira S. Lerner and author. NGS research grant. 502-517, *Apr. 1972*

WILD CARGO: the Business of Smuggling Animals. By Noel Grove. Photos by Steve Raymer. 287-315, *Mar. 1981*

WILD Dogs and Working Dogs. Paintings by Walter A. Weber. 369-376, *Sept. 1944*

WILD Ducks as Winter Guests in a City Park. By Joseph Dixon. 331-342, *Oct. 1919*

WILD Elephant Roundup in India. By Harry Miller. Photos by author and James P. Blair. 372-385, *Mar. 1969*

WILD FOODS:
Stalking the West's Wild Foods. By Euell Gibbons. Photos by David Hiser. 186-199, *Aug. 1973*
Stalking Wild Foods on a Desert Isle. By Euell Gibbons. Photos by David Hiser. 47-63, *July 1972*
The Making of an Astronaut. By Robert R. Gilruth. 122-144, *Jan. 1965*
Philmont Scout Ranch Helps Boys Grow Up. By Andrew H. Brown. 399-416, *Sept. 1956*
We Survive on a Pacific Atoll. By John and Frank Craighead. 73-94, *Jan. 1948*

Led by James W. Whittaker in 1978, the first American team to reach the top of K2 traces its route along a razor-sharp ridge on the Chinese-Pakistan border. JOHN ROSKELLEY

The Acorn, a Possibly Neglected Source of Food. By C. Hart Merriam. 129-137, *Aug. 1918*
Nuts and Their Uses as Foods. 800, *Dec. 1907*
Wokas, a Primitive Indian Food. 183-185, *Apr. 1904*

The **WILD** Fowl and Game Animals of Alaska. By E. W. Nelson. 121-132, *Apr. 1898*

WILD Gardens of the Southern Appalachians. Photos by Edwin L. Wisherd, Laurence V. Jolliffe, and Clifton Adams. 679-686, *June 1934*

WILD Geese, Ducks, and Swans. Paintings by Allan Brooks. 493-524, *Oct. 1934*

WILD Lands for Wildlife: America's
■■ *National Refuges.* By Noel Grove.

Photos by Bates Littlehales. 207 pages. *1984*

WILD Man and Wild Beast in Africa. By Theodore Roosevelt. 1-33, *Jan. 1911*

WILD Nursery of the Mangroves. By Rick Gore. Photos by Bianca Lavies. 669-689, *May 1977*

The WILD Realm: Animals of East
■■ *Africa.* By Louis S. B. Leakey. 199 pages. *1969*

A **WILD** Shore Where Two Worlds Meet. Photos by Des and Jen Bartlett. 298-321, *Mar. 1976*

The WILD Shores: America's Begin-
■■ *nings.* By Tee Loftin Snell. Photos by Walter Meayers Edwards. Art by Louis S. Glanzman. 203 pages. *1974*

Spirit of the Wild West endured in Buffalo Bill Cody's traveling troupe.

THE HUNTINGTON LIBRARY, SAN MARINO, CALIFORNIA

Bull caribou grazes the tundra in the wilderness south of Alaska's Brooks Range in early September. MICHIO HOSHINO

American Wild Flower Odyssey. By P. L. Ricker. 603-634, *May 1953*

Cloud Gardens in the Tetons. By Frank and John Craighead. 811-830, *June 1948*

The World in Your Garden. By W. H. Camp. Paintings by Else Bostelmann. Contents: Abelia, African Violet, Azalea, Bellflower, Bird-of-Paradise Flower, Blackberry-Lily, Blanket-Flower, Bleeding Heart, Blue Lace-Flower, Bottle-Brush, California Poppy, Calla, Camellia, Candytuft, Canna, Cape Marigold, Castor-Oil-Plant, Catawba Rhododendron, China Aster, Chrysanthemum, Clarkia, Clematis, Common Hyacinth, Cosmos, Crown Imperial, Crown-of-Thorns, Cup-Flower, Cypress Vine, Dahlia, Daisy, East Indian Lotus, Eucalyptus (Gum-Tree), Flamboyant (Royal) Poinciana, Flame Azalea, Forsythia, Foxglove, Frangipani, French and African Marigolds, Fringed Hibiscus, Fuchsia, Garden Verbena, Gerbera, Gladiolus, Grape-Hyacinth, Hibiscus, Hollyhock, Impatiens, Japanese Iris, Japanese Wisteria, Lobelia, Lupine, Michaelmas Daisies, Morning Glory, Nasturtium, Oleander, Oriental Poppy, Oswego Tea, Pansy (Heartsease), Pelargonium ("Geranium"), Peony, Petunia, Poinsettia, Poker-Plant, Pot Marigold, Primrose, Regal Lily, Rose, Scarlet Sage, Snakes-Head (Checkered-Lily), Snapdragon, Snowdrop, Spider Flower, Spring Crocus, Star-of-Bethlehem, Stock (Gilliflower), Strawflower, Summer Perennial Phlox, Swan River Daisy, Sweet Scabious, Tiger-Flower, Travelers-Tree, Tulip, Victoria Waterlily, Wallflower, Zinnia. 1-65, *July 1947*

An Insect Community Lives in Flower Heads. By James G. Needham. 340-356, *Sept. 1946*

High Country of Colorado. By Alfred M. Bailey. Photos by author, Robert J. Niedrach, and F. G. Brandenburg. Included: Arnica, Columbine, Marigolds, Shooting Stars, Snow Lily, Wild Onion, Wood Lilies. 43-72, *July 1946*

California Says It with Wild Flowers. By Francis Woodworth. Photos by B. Anthony Stewart. Contents: Baby-blue-eyes, Blazingstar, Blue-blossom, Collinsia, Coreopsis, Dandelion, Eveningprimrose, Farewell-to-spring, Flannel Bush, Ithuriel's Spear, Lupine, Monkeyflower, Mustard, Owlclover, Poppy, *Rosa californica*, Toyon, Yellowdaisy, Tidytip. 492-501, *Apr. 1942*

Flower Pageant of the Midwest: From March to November Nature Embroiders an Ever-changing Pattern of Living Color. By Edith S. and Frederic E. Clements. Paintings by Edith S. Clements. Contents: Acanthus, Amaryllis, Aster, Bluebell, Borage, Buckwheat, Buttercup, Cactus, Caper, Dogbane, Evening Primrose, Evening Star, Gentian, Geranium, Heath, Iris, Lily, Mallow, Meadow Beauty, Mint, Morning-Glory, Mustard, Orchid, Oxalis, Pea, Phlox, Pink, Poppy, Potato, Primrose, Purslane, Snapdragon, Spiderwort, Spurge, Touch-Me-Not, Verbena, Violet, Witch Hazel. 219-271, *Aug. 1939*

Where Spring Paints a State with Wild Flowers (California). Photos by B. Anthony Stewart. 365-380, *Mar. 1936*

■■ The Book of Wild Flowers: An Introduction to the Ways of Plant Life, Together with Biographies of 250 Representative Species and Chapters on Our State Flowers and Familiar Grasses. 243 pages. 1924; rev. ed. 1933

Wild Flowers of the West (U. S.). By Edith S. Clements. Paintings by author. Contents: Aster, Bellflower, Borage, Broom-Rape, Buckthorn, Buckwheat, Cactus, Caper, Chicory, Crowfoot, Dogbane, Evening-Primrose, Evening-Star, Figwort, Flax, Four-O'Clock, Fumitory, Gentian, Geranium, Gooseberry, Heath, Honeysuckle, Indianpipe, Iris, Leadwort, Lily, Lobelia, Mallow, Mesembryanthemum, Milkweed, Milkwort, Mint, Morning-Glory, Mustard, Orchid, Orpine, Parsley, Pea, Phlox, Pink, Poppy, Potato, Primrose, Purslane, Rockrose, Rose, St. Johnswort, Saxifrage, Violet, Waterleaf, Wintergreen, Woodsorrel. 566-622, *May 1927*

Pages from the Floral Life of America. Paintings by Mary E. Eaton. Contents: Acanthus, Amaranth, Amaryllis, Apple, Arum, Aster, Bicknell, Bladderwort, Borage, Broom-Rape, Buckthorn, Buckwheat, Bunchflower, Caper, Chicory, Diapensia, Dogwood, Evening-Primrose, Figwort, Four-O'Clock, Fumitory, Gentian, Ginseng, Gooseberry, Goosefoot, Gourd, Heath, Horsetail, Indianpipe, Lily-of-the-Valley, Logania, Madder, Magnolia, Meadowbeauty, Milkweed, Milkwort, Mimosa, Nettle, Olive, Parsley, Passion-flower, Pea, Plantain, Pondweed, Ragweed, Rush, Saxifrage, Senna, Sundew, Waterlily. 44-75, *July 1925*

Exploring the Mysteries of Plant Life. By William Joseph Showalter. Paintings by Mary E. Eaton. Included: Alfalfa, Amsonia, Arethusa, Bindweed, Blackberry-Lily, Checkerbloom, Cobaea Pentstemon, Coneflower, Creeping Polemonium, Daylily, Goldmoss, Grays Lily, Ground-Ivy, Honeysuckle, Meadow-Parsnip, Phlox, Pitcher-plant, Poppy-Mallow, Rhododendron, Rose Pogonia, St. Johnswort, Shooting-star, Snow-on-the-Mountain, Spatterdock, Springbeauty, Wild-bergamot, Woodbetony, Woodsorrel, Yellow Ladyslipper. 581-646, *June 1924*

Midsummer Wild Flowers. Paintings by Mary E. Eaton. Included: American Waterlily, Aster, Beach Pea, Blue Vervain, Bluebell, Broom Flax, Corn Cockle, Corydalis, Dodder,

Spectacular wildflowers of southwest Australia include ten-inch-long blossoms of a cut-leaf banksia. PAUL A. ZAHL, NGS

Early Goldenrod, English Plaintain, False-Foxglove, Field Mustard, Gayfeather, Gentian, Golden St. John's-Wort, Groundcherry, Hairy Pentstemon, Hyssop Skullcap, Milkweed, Milkwort, Mistflower, Pickerelweed, Pokeweed, Pricklepoppy, Purple Avens, Purple Wild-Bergamot, Rosemallow, Sheep Laurel, Sheep Sorrel, Spiderwort, Sweetshrub, Tansy, Teasel, Turtlehead, Venus Looking-Glass, Yellow Fringed Orchid. 35-59, *July 1922*

Familiar Grasses and Their Flowers. By E. J. Geske and W. J. Showalter. Paintings by E. J. Geske. 625-636, *June 1921*

American Berries of Hill, Dale, and Wayside. Paintings by Mary E. Eaton. 168-184, *Feb. 1919*

Our State Flowers: The Floral Emblems Chosen by the Commonwealths. By Gilbert Grosvenor. Paintings by Mary E. Eaton. Contents: Apple, Bitter Root, Cactus, Carnation, Colorado Columbine, Daisy, Golden Poppy, Goldenrod, Indian Paintbrush, Magnolia, Mistletoe, Moccasin Flower, Mountain Laurel, Orange, Oregon Grape, Pasque Flower, Peach, Pine, Red Clover, Rhododendron, Rose, Sagebrush, Sahuaro, Sego Lily, Sunflower, Syringa, Texas Bluebonnet, Trumpet Vine, Violet. 481-517, 567, *June 1917*

Common American Wild Flowers. Paintings by Mary E. Eaton. Contents: Butter-and-Eggs, Butterfly-Weed, Button Bush, Chicory, Common Mullen, Fireweed, Forget-Me-Not, Fringed Gentian, Jack-in-the-Pulpit, New England Aster, Poison Ivy, Spotted Boneset, Steeple Bush, Swamp Rose-Mallow, Virginia Creeper, Wild Yellow Plum, Yarrow. 584-609, *June 1916*

American Wild Flowers. Paintings by Mary E. Eaton. Included: American Holly, Bindweed, Bittersweet, Black Haw, Black-Eyed Susan, Blue Flag, Bluebell, Blue-Eyed Grass, Broad-Leaved Arrow-Head, Bulb-Bearing Loosestrife, Buttercup, Canada Lily, Cardinal Flower, Day Flower, Evening Primrose, Jewel Weed, Moth Mullen, Partridge Berry, Purple Flowering Raspberry, Purple Loosestrife, Showy Lady's-Slipper, Star Grass, Trailing Arbutus, Turk's Cap Lily, Virginia Strawberry, Wild Columbine, Wild Geranium, Wild Pink, Witch Hazel. 507-517, *May 1915*

The Cultivation of the Mayflower. By Frederick V. Coville. 518-519, *May 1915*

WILDLIFE:

■■ *Wildlife: Making a Comeback.* By Judith E. Rinard. Juvenile. 104 pages. *1987*

■■ *How Animals Behave: A New Look at Wildlife.* Juvenile. 104 pages. *1984*

Nature's Dwindling Treasures. By Peter T. White. Photos by James P. Blair. Paintings by Barron Storey. Included: Tropical rain forests: earth's green belt. 2-47, *Jan. 1983*

Wild Cargo: the Business of Smuggling Animals. By Noel Grove. Photos by Steve Raymer. 287-315, *Mar. 1981*

■■ *Wildlife Alert! The Struggle to Survive.* By Gene S. Stuart. Juvenile. 104 pages. *1980*

Studying Wildlife by Satellite. By Frank Craighead, Jr., and John Craighead. NGS research grant. 120-123, *Jan. 1973*

Man's Wildlife Heritage Faces Extinction. By H.R.H. The Prince Philip, Duke of Edinburgh. 700-703, *Nov. 1962*

Nature's Alert Eyes (Animal Eyes). By Constance P. Warner. 558-569, *Apr. 1959*

See also Amphibians; Birds; Fishes; Mammals; Reptiles; *and* Animal Introduction; Endangered and Threatened Species; Extinct Species; Game Preserves; National Parks; Wildlife Refuges

African

■ African Odyssey. cover, *Jan. 1988*

Madagascar: A World Apart. By Alison Jolly. Photos by Frans Lanting. Included: Rare species. 148-183, *Feb. 1987*

The Serengeti. 560-601. I. A Photographic Portfolio. Photos by Mitsuaki Iwago. Text by John Eliot. 563-585; II. The Glory of Life. By Shana Alexander. 585-601, *May 1986*

The Living Sands of the Namib. By William J. Hamilton III. Photos by Carol and David Hughes. Contents: Unique desert creatures. 364-377, *Sept. 1983*

Etosha: Namibia's Kingdom of Animals. By Douglas H. Chadwick. Photos by Des and Jen Bartlett. 344-385, *Mar. 1983*

■■ *Safari!* By Gene S. Stuart. Photos by George F. Mobley. Juvenile. 104 pages. *1982*

■ Etosha: Place of Dry Water. 703, *Dec. 1980*

■ Last Stand in Eden. 1, *Jan. 1979*

■ The Living Sands of Namib. 439, Oct. 1977; cover, Mar. 1978; 1, *Jan. 1979*

African Wildlife: Man's Threatened Legacy. By Allan C. Fisher, Jr. Photos by Thomas Nebbia. 147-187. Included: A Continent's Living Treasure. Paintings by Ned Seidler. 164-167, *Feb. 1972*

Mzima, Kenya's Spring of Life. By Joan and Alan Root. 350-373, *Sept. 1971*

■ *The Wild Realm: Animals of East Africa.* By Louis S. B. Leakey. 199 pages. *1969*

Orphans of the Wild (Animal Orphanage, Uganda). By Bruce G. Kinloch. 683-699, *Nov. 1962*

Where Elephants Have Right of Way. By George and Jinx Rodger. Included: Buffaloes, giraffes, hippopotamuses, lyrehorned ankoles, rhinoceroses. 363-389, *Sept. 1960*

The Last Great Animal Kingdom. 390-409, *Sept. 1960*

A New Look at Kenya's "Treetops." By Quentin Keynes. 536-541, *Oct. 1956*

Stalking Central Africa's Wildlife. By T. Donald Carter. Paintings by Walter A. Weber. NGS research grant. 264-286, *Aug. 1956*

Safari from Congo to Cairo. By Elsie May Bell Grosvenor. Photos by Gilbert Grosvenor. 721-771, *Dec. 1954*

Safari Through Changing Africa. By Elsie May Bell Grosvenor. Photos by Gilbert Grosvenor. 145-198, *Aug. 1953*

Roaming Africa's Unfenced Zoos. By W. Robert Moore. 353-380, *Mar. 1950*

Antarctic

Penguins and Their Neighbors. By Roger Tory Peterson. Photos by Des and Jen Bartlett. 237-255, *Aug. 1977*

Antarctica's Nearer Side. By Samuel W. Matthews. Photos by William R. Curtsinger. 622-655, *Nov. 1971*

Arctic

Ellesmere Island–Life in the High Arctic. By L. David Mech. Photos by Jim Brandenburg. 750-767, *June 1988*

Our Wildest Wilderness: Alaska's Arctic National Wildlife Range. By Douglas H. Chadwick. Photos by Lowell Georgia. 737-769, *Dec. 1979*

✣ "Ice Age Mammals of the Alaskan Tundra," painting supplement. Map of Canada. *Mar. 1972*

■ Journey to the High Arctic. 590A-590B, *Apr. 1971*

Nomad in Alaska's Outback. By Thomas J. Abercrombie. 540-567, *Apr. 1969*

Asian

Return of Java's Wildlife. By Dieter and Mary Plage. 750-771, *June 1985*

Sri Lanka's Wildlife. 254-278. I. Sri Lanka's Wildlife Heritage: A Personal Perspective. By Arthur C. Clarke. 254-255; II. Legacy of Lively Treasures. By Dieter and Mary Plage. 256-273; III. A Nation Rises to the Challenge. By Lyn de Alwis. Photos by Dieter and Mary Plage. 274-278, *Aug. 1983*

India Struggles to Save Her Wildlife. By John J. Putman. Paintings by Ned Seidler. 299-343, *Sept. 1976*

Seeking Mindanao's Strangest Creatures. By Charles Heizer Wharton. 389-408, *Sept. 1948*

Australian

■ Australia's Animal Mysteries. 824, *Dec. 1982*

✣ "Land of Living Fossils," painting supplement. Map on reverse. *Feb. 1979*

Pounding hooves and a hunter's snarl sound as a cheetah fells a Thomson's gazelle in the wildlife spectacle of Tanzania's Serengeti National Park. MITSUAKI IWAGO

On the Galápagos Islands pressure from people and predators threatens wildlife such as these giant tortoises. DIETER AND MARY PLAGE

Eden in the Outback. By Kay and Stanley Breeden. 189-203, *Feb. 1973*

Strange Animals of Australia. By David Fleay. Photos by Stanley Breeden. 388-411, *Sept. 1963*

Central American

Teeming Life of a Rain Forest. By Carol and David Hughes. 49-65, *Jan. 1983*

Falkland Islands

Falkland Islands Wildlife. A photographic portfolio by Frans Lanting. 413-422, *Mar. 1988*

Galápagos Islands

Galápagos Wildlife Under Pressure. Photo essay by Dieter and Mary Plage. 122-145, *Jan. 1988*

Undersea Wonders of the Galapagos. By Gerard Wellington. Photos by David Doubilet. 363-381, *Sept. 1978*

The Galapagos, Eerie Cradle of New Species. By Roger Tory Peterson. Photos by Alan and Joan Root. 541-585, *Apr. 1967*

Lost World of the Galapagos. By Irving and Electa Johnson. 681-703, *May 1959*

Hawaiian

Hawaii's Far-flung Wildlife Paradise. By John L. Eliot. Photos by Jonathan Blair. 670-691, *May 1978*

North American

▪▪ *Wild Animals of North America.* 406 pages. 1979; rev. ed. *1987*

Isle Royale, A North Woods Park Primeval. By John L. Eliot. Photos by Mitch Kezar. Included: Foxes, Moose, Wolves. 534-550, *Apr. 1985*

▪▪ *Wild Lands for Wildlife: America's National Refuges.* By Noel Grove. Photos by Bates Littlehales. 207 pages. *1984*

▪▪ *Field Guide to the Birds of North America.* 464 pages. *1983*

▪▪ *The Wonder of Birds.* Included: *Guide to Birds* recording and *Field Guide to the Birds of North America.* 280 pages. *1983*

Henry Hudson's Changing Bay. By Bill Richards. Photos by David Hiser. Included: Arctic fox, Beluga whales, Caribou, Murres, Polar bears. 380-405, *Mar. 1982*

Heart of the Canadian Rockies. By Elizabeth A. Moize. Photos by Jim Brandenburg. 757-779, *June 1980*

Our National Wildlife Refuges. 342-381, *Mar. 1979*

Florida, Noah's Ark for Exotic Newcomers. By Rick Gore. Photos by David Doubilet. Included: The introduction of tropical birds: budgerigar, bulbul, myna, parakeet, and parrot. 538-559, *Oct. 1976*

Twilight Hope for Big Cypress. By Rick Gore. Photos by Patricia Caulfield. 251-273, *Aug. 1976*

▪▪ *Our Continent: A Natural History of North America.* 398 pages. *1976*

Preserving America's Last Great Wilderness (Alaska). By David Jeffery. 769-791, *June 1975*

▪▪ *Vanishing Wildlife of North America.* By Thomas B. Allen. 207 pages. *1974*

Can We Save Our Salt Marshes? By Stephen W. Hitchcock. Photos by

William R. Curtsinger. 729-765, *June 1972*

Yellowstone at 100: A Walk Through the Wilderness. By Karen and Derek Craighead. Photos by Sam Abell. 579-603, *May 1972*

Businessman in the Bush. By Frederick Kent Truslow. Contents: Everglades. 634-675, *May 1970*

Nature's Year in Pleasant Valley. By Paul A. Zahl. 488-525, *Apr. 1968*

Yellowstone Wildlife in Winter. By William Albert Allard. 637-661, *Nov. 1967*

Threatened Glories of Everglades National Park. By Frederick Kent Truslow and Frederick G. Vosburgh. Photos by Frederick Kent Truslow and Otis Imboden. 508-553, *Oct. 1967*

▪▪ *Water, Prey, and Game Birds of North America.* 464 pages. *1965*

▪▪ *Song and Garden Birds of North America.* 400 pages. *1964*

▪▪ *Wild Animals of North America.* 400 pages. *1960*

Arizona's Window on Wildlife. By Lewis Wayne Walker. 240-250, *Feb. 1958*

Corkscrew Swamp–Florida's Primeval Show Place. By Melville Bell Grosvenor. 98-113, *Jan. 1958*

The Wichitas: Land of the Living Prairie. By M. Woodbridge Williams. 661-697, *May 1957*

Springtime Comes to Yellowstone National Park. By Paul A. Zahl. 761-779, *Dec. 1956*

Wildlife Adventuring in Jackson Hole.

A pack of wolves circles a tiring moose, part of the natural cycle among north woods wildlife in the 210-square-mile Isle Royale National Park in Lake Superior. ROLF PETERSON

WILDLIFE CONSERVATION:

WILDLIFE MANAGEMENT:

Photos by Des and Jen Bartlett. 344-385, *Mar. 1983*

WILDLIFE MANAGEMENT INSTITUTE: Expeditions and Research.
See Isle Royale, Michigan

WILDLIFE REFUGES:

Africa
They're Killing Off the Rhino. By Esmond Bradley Martin. Photos by Jim Brandenburg. 404-422, *Mar. 1984*
See also Entebbe Animal Refuge; Etosha National Park; Serengeti National Park; *and* National Parks

Asia
They're Killing Off the Rhino. By Esmond Bradley Martin. Photos by Jim Brandenburg. Included: Refuges in India, Nepal, and Indonesia. 404-422, *Mar. 1984*
Sri Lanka's Wildlife. 254-278. I. Sri Lanka's Wildlife Heritage: A Personal Perspective. By Arthur C. Clarke. 254-255; II. Legacy of Lively Treasures. By Dieter and Mary Plage. 256-273; III. A Nation Rises to the Challenge. By Lyn de Alwis. Photos by Dieter and Mary Plage. 274-278, *Aug. 1983*
See also Kanha National Park; Kaziranga Wild Life Sanctuary; Ranthambhor National Park; Tanjung Puting Reserve; Ujung Kulon National Park; Wolong Natural Reserve; *and* National Parks
Australia. *See* National Parks
Caribbean. *See* Little Tobago (Island)
Europe. *See* Abbotsbury Swannery; The Camargue; Marismas

Indian Ocean
Rare Look At Sperm and Blue Whales, The Unknown Giants. By Hal Whitehead. Photos by Flip Nicklin. Included: The International Marine Mammals Sanctuary in the Indian Ocean. 774-789, *Dec. 1984*
South America. *See* Pampa Galeras National Vicuña Reserve; *and* National Parks

United States
The Aleutians: Alaska's Far-out Islands. By Lael Morgan. Photos by Steven C. Wilson. Note: 95 percent of the islands are claimed by the federal government as wildlife refuges and military sites. 336-363, *Sept. 1983*
Delaware–Who Needs to Be Big? By Jane Vessels. Photos by Kevin Fleming. Included: Bombay Hook National Wildlife Refuge. 171-197, *Aug. 1983*
Our National Forests: Problems in Paradise. By Rowe Findley. Photos by David Cupp. 306-339, *Sept. 1982*
Roosevelt Country: T. R.'s Wilderness Legacy. By John L. Eliot. Photos by Farrell Grehan. 340-363, *Sept. 1982*
✦ America's Federal Lands; The United States. *Sept. 1982*
Teamwork Helps the Whooping Crane. By Roderick C. Drewien, with Ernie Kuyt. 680-693, *May 1979*
Our National Wildlife Refuges. 342-381. I. A Chance to Grow. By Robert

E. Doyle. 342-349; II. Island, Prairie, Marsh, and Shore. By Charlton Ogburn. Photos by Bates Littlehales. 350-381; III. Wildlife Refuges of the United States. Tear-out guide with maps. 363-370, *Mar. 1979*
Hawaii's Far-flung Wildlife Paradise. By John L. Eliot. Photos By Jonathan Blair. 670-691, *May 1978*
Tireless Voyager, the Whistling Swan. By William J. L. Sladen. Photos by Bianca Lavies. NGS research grant. 134-147, *July 1978*
Alaska: Rising Northern Star. By Joseph Judge. Photos by Bruce Dale. Included: Mount McKinley, Sitka; *and* proposed parks: Gates of the Arctic, Lake Clark, Wrangell-St. Elias. 730-767, *June 1975*
Preserving America's Last Great Wilderness (Alaska). By David Jeffery. Included: Proposed parks: Gates of the Arctic, Katmai additional acreage, Lake Clark, Mount McKinley. 769-791, *June 1975*
Beyond the North Wind With the Snow Goose. By Des and Jen Bartlett. 822-843, *Dec. 1973*
See also Aransas National Wildlife Refuge; Arctic National Wildlife Refuge; Bear River Migratory Bird Refuge; Chincoteague Island; Corkscrew Swamp; Denali National Park and Preserve; Desert Museum; Everglades; Glacier National Park; McNeil River State Game Sanctuary; National Elk Refuge; Okefenokee Swamp; Pribilof Islands; Red Rock Lakes National Wildlife Refuge; Santa Barbara Islands; Sapsucker Woods; Wichita Mountains Wildlife Refuge; *and* Bird Sanctuaries; Game Preserves; National Parks

WILDLIFE TRADE:
They're Killing Off the Rhino. By Esmond Bradley Martin. Photos by Jim Brandenburg. 404-422, *Mar. 1984*
Wild Cargo: the Business of Smuggling Animals. By Noel Grove. Photos by Steve Raymer. 287-315, *Mar. 1981*
Animal Wealth of the United States. By Francis E. Warren. 511-524, *Sept. 1906*

WILES, WILBUR:
Stalking the Mountain Lion–to Save Him. By Maurice G. Hornocker. 638-655, *Nov. 1969*

WILEY, HARVEY W.:
The National Geographic Society. Speech by Harvey W. Wiley. 272-298, *Mar. 1912*
Author
The United States; Its Soils and Their Products. 263-279, *July 1903*

WILHELM, JOHN L.: *Author*
Solar Energy, the Ultimate Powerhouse. Photos by Emory Kristof. 381-397, *Mar. 1976*

WILKERSON, S. JEFFREY K.:
On Assignment in Guatemala. *Oct. 1985*
On Assignment in Mexico City. *Oct. 1984*

Nomination Page. *July 1980*
Author
The Usumacinta River: Troubles on a Wild Frontier. Photos by David Hiser. 514-543, *Oct. 1985*
Following Cortés: Path to Conquest. Photos by Guillermo Aldana E. Paintings by Ned Seidler and Rosalie Seidler. 420-459, *Oct. 1984*
Man's Eighty Centuries in Veracruz. Photos by David Hiser. Paintings by Richard Schlecht. 203-231, *Aug. 1980*

WILKES, CHARLES:
New Stamps for Antarctic Explorers. Geographica. *Oct. 1988*
Revealing Earth's Mightiest Ocean (Pacific). By Albert W. Atwood. 291-306, *Sept. 1943*
Memorial monument. 633, *Nov. 1928*
The Gem of the Ocean: Our American Navy. By Josephus Daniels. 313-335, *Apr. 1918*
American Discoverers of the Antarctic Continent. By A. W. Greely. 298-312, *Mar. 1912*
Wilkes' and D'Urville's Discoveries in Wilkes Land. By John E. Pillsbury. 171-173, *Feb. 1910*
Some Early Geographers of the United States. By Colby M. Chester. 392-404, *Oct. 1904*
Termination Land (Antarctica). By Edwin Swift Balch. 220-221, *May 1904*

WILKINS, SIR HUBERT: *Author*
Our Search for the Lost Aviators: An Arctic Area Larger Than Montana First Explored in Hunt for Missing Russians. 141-172, *Aug. 1938*

WILKINSON, NORMAN: *Artist*
Ships of the Centuries. Etchings by Norman Wilkinson. 65-80, *Jan. 1938*

South African wildlife officials examine a potential fortune in rhinoceros horns confiscated from poachers. JIM BRANDENBURG

Author-Artist

British Castles, History in Stone. 111-129, *July 1947*

Cathedrals of England: An Artist's Pilgrimage to These Majestic Monuments of Man's Genius and Faith. 741-762, *Dec. 1939*

WILL Brazil's Fiery Bees Reach the U. S.? By Rick Gore. Photos by Bianca Lavies. 491-501, *Apr. 1976*

WILL Coal Be Tomorrow's "Black Gold"? By Gordon Young. Photos by James P. Blair. 234-259, *Aug. 1975*

WILL Oil and Tundra Mix? Alaska's North Slope Hangs in the Balance. By William S. Ellis. Photos by Emory Kristof. 485-517, *Oct. 1971*

WILL Success Spoil Our Parks? By Robert Paul Jordan. 31-59, *July 1979*

WILL We Mend Our Earth? Introduction by Gilbert M. Grosvenor. 766-771, *Dec. 1988*

WILLA CATHER: Voice of the Frontier. By William Howarth. Photos by Farrell Grehan. 71-93, *July 1982*

WILLAMETTE RIVER AND VALLEY, Oregon:

A River Restored: Oregon's Willamette. By Ethel A. Starbird. Photos by Lowell J. Georgia. 816-835, *June 1972*

WILLCOX, ALEX R.: *Photographer*

Africa's Bushman Art Treasures. By Alfred Friendly. 848-865, *June 1963*

WILLEMSTAD, Curaçao, Netherlands Antilles:

The Netherlands Antilles: Holland in the Caribbean. By James Cerruti. Photos by Emory Kristof. 115-146, *Jan. 1970*

Curaçao and Aruba on Guard. By W. Robert Moore. 169-192, *Feb. 1943*

WILLEY, DAY ALLEN: *Author*

The Barrage of the Nile. 175-184, *Feb. 1910*

WILLIAM THE CONQUEROR:

900 Years Ago: the Norman Conquest. By Kenneth M. Setton. Photos by George F. Mobley. 206-251, *Aug. 1966*

A New Look at Medieval Europe. By Kenneth M. Setton. Paintings by Andre Durenceau and Birney Lettick. 799-859, *Dec. 1962*

The British Way. By Sir Evelyn Wrench. 421-541, *Apr. 1949*

The Land of William the Conqueror (Normandy): Where Northmen Came to Build Castles and Cathedrals. By Inez Buffington Ryan. 89-99, *Jan. 1932*

WILLIAM AND MARY COLLEGE, Williamsburg, Virginia:

Williamsburg: Its College and Its Cinderella City. By Beverley M. Bowie. 439-486, *Oct. 1954*

WILLIAM PENN'S Faire Land. By Gordon Young. Photos by Cary Wolinsky. 731-767, *June 1978*

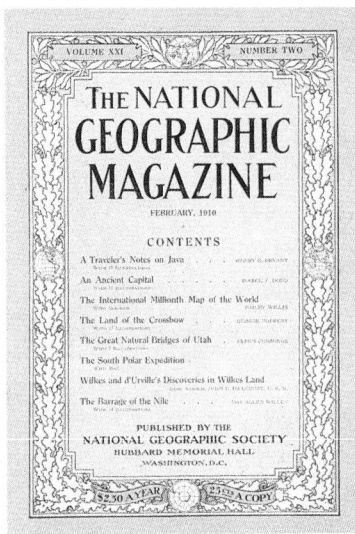

THE NATIONAL GEOGRAPHIC MAGAZINE

WILLIAM T. GRANT FOUNDATION: Study Grant:

Chimpanzees. 598, *May 1979*

WILLIAMS, C. B.: *Author*

Butterfly Travelers: Some Varieties Migrate Thousands of Miles. Paintings by Hashime Murayama. 568-585, *May 1937*

WILLIAMS, GARDINER F.: *Author*

The Diamond Mines of South Africa. 344-356, *June 1906*

WILLIAMS, GEORGE H.: *Author*

Notes on Some Eruptive Rocks from Alaska. 63-74, *Mar. 21, 1892*

WILLIAMS, IRA A.: *Author*

Scenes Among the High Cascades in Central Oregon. 579-592, *June 1912*

WILLIAMS, JOHN G.: *Author*

Freeing Flamingos From Anklets of Death. Photos by Alan Root. 934-944, *Dec. 1963*

WILLIAMS, JOHN SHARP: *Author*

The Ties That Bind: Our Natural Sympathy with English Traditions, the French Republic, and the Russian Outburst for Liberty. 281-286, *Mar. 1917*

WILLIAMS, M. WOODBRIDGE:

Nomination Page. In British Guiana (Guyana). *Feb. 1961*

Author-Photographer

The Wichitas: Land of the Living Prairie. 661-697, *May 1957*

Photographer

Strange Little World of the Hoatzin. By J. Lear Grimmer. 391-401, *Sept. 1962*

History and Beauty Blend in a Concord Iris Garden. By Robert T. Cochran, Jr. 705-719, *May 1959*

Keeping House for Tropical Butterflies. By Jocelyn Crane. 193-217, *Aug. 1957*

WILLIAMS, MAYNARD OWEN:

Chief of the NGS Foreign Staff for 20 years; total service, 34 years. 627, *Oct. 1963*

Author

Pilgrims Follow the Christmas Star. 831-840, *Dec. 1952*

Turkey Paves the Path of Progress. 141-186, *Aug. 1951*

Portrait of Indochina. By W. Robert Moore and Maynard Owen Williams. Paintings by Jean Despujols. 461-490, *Apr. 1951*

Home to the Holy Land. 707-746, *Dec. 1950*

Paris Lives Again. 767-790, *Dec. 1946*

The Turkish Republic Comes of Age. Included: Star and Crescent on Parade. 581-616, *May 1945*

Sicily Again in the Path of War. 307-320, *Sept. 1943*

The Columbia (River) Turns on the Power. 749-792, *June 1941*

The Celebes: New Man's Land of the Indies. Included: Life and Death in Toradjaland. 51-82, *July 1940*

Buenos Aires: Queen of the River of Silver. Included: Buenos Aires–Metropolis of the Pampas. 561-600, *Nov. 1939*

Bali and Points East: Crowded, Happy Isles of the Flores Sea Blend Rice Terraces, Dance Festivals, and Amazing Music in Their Pattern of Living. Included: Bali, Gem of the Netherlands Indies. 313-352, *Mar. 1939*

Pilgrims Still Stop at Plymouth (England). 59-77, *July 1938*

Along London's Coronation Route. 609-632, *May 1937*

Paris in Spring. 501-534, *Oct. 1936*

Informal Salute to the English Lakes. 511-521, *Apr. 1936*

Great Britain on Parade. Included: Clans in Kilt and Plaidie Gather at Braemar (Scotland). 137-184, *Aug. 1935*

The Poland of the Present. 319-344, *Mar. 1933*

When Czechoslovakia Puts a Falcon Feather in Its Cap. 40-49, *Jan. 1933*

From the Mediterranean to the Yellow Sea by Motor: The Citroën-Haardt Expedition Successfully Completes Its Dramatic Journey. Included: Bright Pages from an Asiatic Travel Log; The Land of Genghis Khan in Its True Colors. 513-580, *Nov. 1932*

Bulgaria, Farm Land Without a Farmhouse: A Nation of Villagers Faces the Challenge of Modern Machinery and Urban Life. 185-218, *Aug. 1932*

The Grand Duchy of Luxemburg: A Miniature Democratic State of Many Charms Against a Feudal Background. 501-528, *Nov. 1924*

Latvia, Home of the Letts: One of the Baltic Republics Which Is Successfully Working Its Way to Stability. 401-443, *Oct. 1924*

The Coasts of Corsica: Impressions of a Winter's Stay in the Island Birthplace of Napoleon. 221-312, *Sept. 1923*

At the Tomb of Tutankhamen: An

Awaiting the 1925 MacMillan Arctic Expedition's return, photographer Maynard Owen Williams joined young Inuit framed by whale bones at Holsteinsborg, Greenland.

W X

Boy Scouts charged up New York's Fifth Avenue after Woodrow Wilson's 1917 call to arms.   UNDERWOOD & UNDERWOOD/THE BETTMANN ARCHIVE

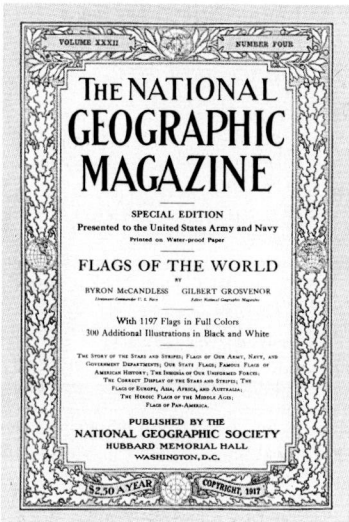

The December 1917 issue published a letter from President Woodrow Wilson, right, congratulating the Society on its October issue, devoted to historical and contemporary flags of the world. The 32 pages of color banners for 700,000 copies took three months to print.

Round About Asheville. 291-300, *Oct. 1889*

WILLITS, EDWIN:
Board of Managers. xii, Feb. 19, 1892; xix, Feb. 20, 1893; xix, *May 5, 1894*

WILLM, PIERRE HENRI:
Two and a Half Miles Down. By Georges S. Houot. NGS research grant. 80-86, *July 1954*

WILLOUGHBY, WILLIAM F.:
Proceedings of the National Geographic Society (Abstract of Address on Puerto Rico by William F. Willoughby). 466-470, *Dec. 1902*

WILLOW RUN, Michigan:
Michigan Fights (Bomber Plant). By Harvey Klemmer. 677-715, *Dec. 1944*

WILLS, WILLIAM JOHN:
The Journey of Burke and Wills: First Across Australia. By Joseph Judge. Photos by Joseph J. Scherschel. 152-191, *Feb. 1979*

WILMINGTON, Delaware:
Delaware—Who Needs to Be Big? By Jane Vessels. Photos by Kevin Fleming. 171-197, *Aug. 1983*

WILNO, Stepchild of the Polish Frontier. 777-784, *June 1938*

WILSON, ALAN D.: *Author*
Hunting Bears on Horseback. 350-356, *May 1908*

WILSON, ALBERT G.: *Author*
Our Universe Unfolds New Wonders. 245-260, *Feb. 1952*

WILSON, BARRY:
Nomination Page. *Oct. 1968*

WILSON, BRUCE A.: *Author*
Busy Fairbanks Sets Alaska's Pace. 505-523, *Oct. 1949*

WILSON, ERNEST H.: *Author*
The Kingdom of Flowers: An Account of the Wealth of Trees and Shrubs of China and of What the Arnold Arboretum, with China's Help, Is Doing to Enrich America. 1003-1035, *Nov. 1911*

WILSON, EUGENE E.: *Author*
Anticosti Island, Nugget of the North. 121-140, *Jan. 1942*

WILSON, HERBERT M.: *Author*
Reclaiming the Swamp Lands of the United States. 292-301, *May 1907*
The Irrigation Problem in Montana. 212-229, *July 1890*

WILSON, J. A.: *Author*
Gentlemen Adventurers of the Air: Many Regions of Canada's Vast Wilderness, Long Hidden Even from Fur Trappers, Are Now Revealed by Exploring Airmen. 597-642, *Nov. 1929*
Canada from the Air: Flights Aggregating 10,000 Miles Reveal the Marvelous Scenic Beauties and Amazing Natural Resources of the Dominion. 389-466, *Oct. 1926*

WILSON, JAMES: *Author*
Protecting Our Forests from Fire. 98-106, *Jan. 1911*
The Modern Alchemist (Work of the Department of Agriculture). 781-795, *Dec. 1907*
The U. S. Weather Bureau. 37-39, *Jan. 1904*

WILSON, JAMES C.: *Author*
Three-Wheeling Through Africa: Two Adventurers Cross the So-called Dark Continent North of Lake Chad on Motorcycles with Side Cars. 37-92, *Jan. 1934*

WILSON, JAMES H.: *Author*
The Great Wall of China. 372-374, *Sept. 1900*

WILSON, JAY: *Photographer*
To Torre Egger's Icy Summit. By Jim Donini. 813-823, *Dec. 1976*

WILSON, JOHN: *Author*
Drought Bedevils Brazil's Sertão. Photos by Gordon W. Gahan. 704-723, *Nov. 1972*

WILSON, JOHN M.:
Photograph. 129, *Jan. 1936*
Announcement of death. 345, *Apr. 1920*
In Honor of the Army and Aviation. Speeches by John M. Wilson. 267-284, *Mar. 1911*
Board of Managers. 87, Feb. 1905; 211, *Feb. 1911*

WILSON, PHYLLIS: *Author*
Queen of Canada (Elizabeth II). Photos by Kathleen Revis. 825-829, *June 1959*

WILSON, STEVEN C.:
On Assignment. *Sept. 1984*
What Six Experts Say. 70-73, *Special Report on Energy. (Feb. 1981)*
Author-Photographer
Where Oil and Wildlife Mix. By Steven C. Wilson and Karen C. Hayden. 145-173, *Feb. 1981*
Photographer
Do We Treat Our Soil Like Dirt? By Boyd Gibbons. 350-389, *Sept. 1984*
The Aleutians: Alaska's Far-out Islands. By Lael Morgan. 336-363, *Sept. 1983*

WILSON, WILLIAM L.:
Gardiner Greene Hubbard: Memorial Meeting. Address by William L. Wilson. 43-45, *Feb. 1898*

WILSON, WOODROW:
The Living White House. By Lonnelle Aikman. 593-643, *Nov. 1966*
Profiles of the Presidents: IV. America Enters the Modern Era. By Frank Freidel. 537-577, *Oct. 1965*

> THE WHITE HOUSE
> WASHINGTON
>
> 14 December, 1917
>
> My dear Mr. Grosvenor:
>   The Flag Number of the National Geographic Magazine is indeed most interesting and most valuable. I sincerely congratulate you on the thoroughness and intelligence with which the work has been done. It constitutes a very valuable document indeed.
>
> Cordially and sincerely yours,
>
> *Woodrow Wilson*
>
> Mr. Gilbert H. Grosvenor, Director,
> National Geographic Society.

Inside the White House. By Lonnelle Aikman. Photos by B. Anthony Stewart and Thomas Nebbia. 3-43, *Jan. 1961*
Election of Woodrow Wilson as Honorary Member. 369, *Apr. 1918*
Letter to Gilbert H. Grosvenor (Flag Number). 549, *Nov.-Dec. 1917*
Do Your Bit for America: A Proclamation by President Wilson to the American People. 287-293, *Apr. 1917*
Honors to Colonel Goethals: The Presentation, by President Woodrow Wilson, of the National Geographic Society Special Gold Medal, and Addresses by Secretary of State Bryan, the French Ambassador, the German Ambassador, and Congressman James R. Mann. 677-690, *June 1914*

W
X

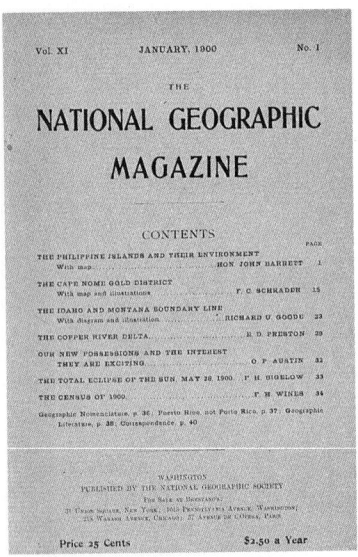

Vol. XI   JANUARY, 1900   No. 1

THE

NATIONAL GEOGRAPHIC MAGAZINE

CONTENTS

THE PHILIPPINE ISLANDS AND THEIR ENVIRONMENT
With map .... HON JOHN BARRETT   1

THE CAPE NOME GOLD DISTRICT
With map and illustrations .... F. C. SCHRADER   15

THE IDAHO AND MONTANA BOUNDARY LINE
With diagram and illustration .... RICHARD U. GOODE   23

THE COPPER RIVER DELTA .... H. D. PRESTON   29

OUR NEW POSSESSIONS AND THE INTEREST
THEY ARE EXCITING .... O. P. AUSTIN   32

THE TOTAL ECLIPSE OF THE SUN, MAY 28 1900. F. H. BIGELOW   33

THE CENSUS OF 1900 .... F. H. WINES   34

Geographic Nomenclature, p. 36. Puerto Rico, not Porto Rico, p. 37; Geographic
Literature, p. 38; Correspondence, p. 40

WASHINGTON
PUBLISHED BY THE NATIONAL GEOGRAPHIC SOCIETY

Price 25 Cents $2.50 a Year

Author
Help Our Red Cross. 422, *May 1917*

WILSON, Mount, California:
The Magic Mountain. By J. N. Patterson. 457-468, *July 1908*

WILSON'S PHALAROPE:
Mono Lake: A Vital Way Station for the Wilson's Phalarope. By Joseph R. Jehl, Jr. 520-525, *Oct. 1981*

WILSTACH, PAUL: *Author*
Approaching Washington by Tidewater Potomac. 372-392, *Mar. 1930*
The Stone Beehive Homes of the Italian Heel: In Trulli-Land the Native Builds His Dwelling and Makes His Field Arable in the Same Operation. 229-260, *Feb. 1930*
Jefferson's Little Mountain: Romance Enfolds Monticello, the Restored Home of the Author of the Declaration of Independence. 481-503, *Apr. 1929*
Holidays Among the Hill Towns of Umbria and Tuscany. 401-442, *Apr. 1928*

WINCHELL, N. H.: *Author*
Origin of the Word Canada. 215, *Mar. 1907*

WINCHESTER, England:
Winchester, England's Early Capital. By Frederick Simpich. 67-92, *Jan. 1941*

WINCHESTER (Ship):
Cannon on Florida Reefs Solve Mystery of Sunken Ship. By Charles M. Brookfield. 807-824, *Dec. 1941*

WIND, Wave, Star, and Bird. By David Lewis. Photos by Nicholas deVore III. 747-781, *Dec. 1974*

WIND POWER:
Harnessing the Wind. 34-57, *Special Report on Energy. (Feb. 1981)*
Can We Harness the Wind? By Roger Hamilton. Photos by Emory Kristof. 812-829, *Dec. 1975*

WIND RIVER RANGE, Wyoming:
Wind River Range: Many-treasured Splendor. By Joseph Judge. 198-205, *Feb. 1974*

WINDERMERE LAKE, British Columbia, Canada:
On the Trail of a Horse Thief. By Herbert W. Gleason. 349-358, *Apr. 1919*

WINDJAMMERS:
Windjamming Around New England. By Tom Horgan. Photos by Robert F. Sisson. 141-169, *Aug. 1950*
The Cape Horn Grain-Ship Race: The Gallant "Parma" Leads the Vanishing Fleet of Square-Riggers Through Raging Gales and Irksome Calms 16,000 Miles, from Australia to England. By A. J. Villiers. 1-39, *Jan. 1933*
Rounding the Horn in a Windjammer. By A. J. Villiers. 191-224, *Feb. 1931*
Sindbads of Science: Narrative of a Windjammer's Specimen-Collecting Voyage to the Sargasso Sea, to Senegambian Africa and Among Islands of High Adventure in the South Atlantic. By George Finlay Simmons. 1-75, *July 1927*

WINDMILLS:
Can We Harness the Wind? By Roger Hamilton. Photos by Emory Kristof. 812-829, *Dec. 1975*

WINDOVER ARCHAEOLOGICAL RESEARCH PROJECT, Titusville, Florida:
Mysteries of the Bog. By Louise E. Levathes. Photos by Fred Bavendam. Included: Peat holds clues to early American life. 397-420, *Mar. 1987*

WINDOW on America. Contents:
■ America's scenic treasures. 199 pages. *1987*

WINDOW on Earth's Interior. By Robert D. Ballard. Photos by Emory Kristof. 228-249, *Aug. 1976*

WINDOW on Nature: The American Museum of Natural History. By James A. Oliver. Photos by Robert F. Sisson. 220-259, *Feb. 1963*

WINDS:
Americans Stand Guard in Greenland. By Andrew H. Brown. 457-500, *Oct. 1946*
Weather Fights and Works for Man. By F. Barrows Colton. 641-670, *Dec. 1943*
Where the Wind Does the Work (Cape Hatteras). By Collier Cobb. 310-317, *June 1906*
The Polar Airship. By Walter Wellman. 208-228, *Apr. 1906*
Forecasting the Weather. By Alfred J. Henry. 285-292, *July 1904*
The Sailing Ship and the Panama Canal. By James Page. 167-176, *Apr. 1904*
Weather Making, Ancient and Modern. By Mark W. Harrington. 35-62, *Apr. 25, 1894*
Relations of Air and Water to Temperature and Life. By Gardiner G. Hubbard. 112-124, *Jan. 31, 1894*
Report–Geography of the Air. By A. W. Greely. 49-63, *Apr. 1890*
See also Hurricanes; Tornadoes; *and* Marine Erosion

The **WINDS** of Freedom Stir a Continent. By Nathaniel T. Kenney. Photos by W. D. Vaughn. 303-359, *Sept. 1960*

WINDSOR, MERRILL: *Author*
■ America's Sunset Coast. Photos by James A. Sugar. 211 pages. *1978*

WINDSOR CASTLE, England:
Windsor Castle. By Anthony Holden. Photos by James L. Stanfield. 604-631. Included: The Grandeur of Windsor. Text by David Jeffery. 616-625, *Nov. 1980*
Royal House for Dolls. By David Jeffery. Photos by James L. Stanfield. 632-643, *Nov. 1980*

Oklahoma State University's Super Speed Turbine harnesses the wind with wheels of aerodynamically shaped aluminum blades inspired by the bicycle. EMORY KRISTOF, NGS

Prince Philip drives a four-in-hand past snowy Windsor Castle, a residence of British monarchs since about 1070. JAMES L. STANFIELD, NGS

WINDWARD ISLANDS, West Indies:
St. Vincent, the Grenadines, and Grenada: Taking It as It Comes. By Ethel A. Starbird. Photos by Cotton Coulson. 399-425, *Sept. 1979*
Finisterre Sails the Windward Islands. By Carleton Mitchell. Photos by Winfield Parks. 755-801, *Dec. 1965*
Carib Cruises the West Indies. By Carleton Mitchell. 1-56, *Jan. 1948*
British West Indian Interlude. By Anne Rainey Langley. 1-46, *Jan. 1941*
See also Martinique; St. Lucia; St. Vincent

WINE MAKING:
The Captivating Kiwifruit. By Noel D. Vietmeyer. Photos by Jim Brandenburg. 683-688, *May 1987*
Iberia's Vintage River (Douro-Duero). By Marion Kaplan. Photos by Stephanie Maze. 460-489, *Oct. 1984*
Bordeaux: Fine Wines and Fiery Gascons. By William Davenport. Photos by Adam Woolfitt. 233-259, *Aug. 1980*
Napa, California's Valley of the Vine. By Moira Johnston. Photos by Charles O'Rear. 695-717, *May 1979*
Living the Good Life in Burgundy. By William Davenport. Photos by Robert Freson. 794-817, *June 1978*
Provence, Empire of the Sun. By William Davenport. Photos by James A. Sugar. 692-715, *May 1975*
The Renaissance Lives On in Tuscany. By Luis Marden. Photos by Albert Moldvay. 626-659, *Nov. 1974*
Madeira, Like Its Wine, Improves With

Age. By Veronica Thomas. Photos by Jonathan Blair. 488-513, *Apr. 1973*
Portugal at the Crossroads. By Howard La Fay. Photos by Volkmar Wentzel. 458-501, *Oct. 1965*
Italian Riviera, Land That Winter Forgot. By Howell Walker. 743-789, *June 1963*
My Life in the Valley of the Moon (California). By H. H. Arnold. Photos by Willard R. Culver. Included: Vineyards and wineries of the Sonoma, Napa, and Petaluma Valleys. 689-716, *Dec. 1948*

WINEGROWERS' FESTIVAL:
Switzerland's Once-in-a-generation Festival. By Jean and Franc Shor. 563-571, *Oct. 1958*

WINES, F. H.: *Author*
The Census of 1900 (U. S.). 34-36, *Jan. 1900*

WING-BORNE Lamps of the Summer Night. By Paul A. Zahl. 48-59, *July 1962*

WINGATE, ORDE C.:
The Aerial Invasion of Burma. By H. H. Arnold. 129-148, *Aug. 1944*

WINGED Denizens of Woodland, Stream, and Marsh. By Alexander Wetmore. Paintings by Allan Brooks. 577-596, *May 1934*

WINGED Jewels from Many Lands. Photos by Willard R. Culver.

Paintings by Hashime Murayama. 673-688, *May 1936*

WINGED Victory of *Gossamer Albatross.* By Bryan Allen. 640-651, *Nov. 1979*

WINGED Words–New Weapon of War. By F. Barrows Colton. 663-692, *Nov. 1942*

WINGS Over Nature's Zoo in Africa. Photos by Reginald A. Bourlay. 527-542, *Oct. 1939*

WINGS Over the Bounding Main (Ocean Birds). Paintings by Allan Brooks. 237-251, *Aug. 1938*

WINNING the War of Supply. By F. Barrows Colton. 705-736, *Dec. 1945*

WINNING the West. By C. J. Blanchard. 82-98, *Feb. 1906*

WINNIPESAUKEE, Lake, New Hampshire:
Contrary New Hampshire. By Robert Booth. Photos by Sandy Felsenthal. 770-799, *Dec. 1982*
The Merrimack: River of Industry and Romance. By Albert W. Atwood. Photos by B. Anthony Stewart. 106-140, *Jan. 1951*

WINSTON-SALEM, North Carolina:
Old Salem, Morning Star of Moravian Faith. By Rowe Findley. Photos by Robert W. Madden. 818-837, *Dec. 1970*

WINTER, FREDERICK A.:
Nomination Page. *Mar. 1979*

A great meeting of waters

These immense natural reservoirs share an increasingly troublesome set of problems.

Wisconsin and other Great Lakes states share concern over ecological problems afflicting these waters. PAINTING BY DAVIS MELTZER

Sturdy Nationalities. By Glanville Smith. 1-46, *July 1937*

WISCONSIN, U.S.S.:

Midshipmen's Cruise. By William J. Aston and Alexander G. B. Grosvenor. 711-754, *June 1948*

WISHERD, EDWIN L.: *Photographer*

The Wonder City That Moves by Night. By Francis Beverly Kelley. 289-324, *Mar. 1948*

West Indies Links in a Defense Chain. 9-32, *Jan. 1941*

Island Treasures of the Caribbean. Photos by Edwin L. Wisherd and C. W. Herbert. 281-304, *Sept. 1940*

Where Hot Pools Seethe and Geysers Spout (Yellowstone). 775-782, *June 1940*

Puerto Rico Polychromes. 713-736, *Dec. 1939*

Old and New Blend in Yankeeland. 295-326, *Sept. 1938*

Colorful Paths in Martinique and Guadeloupe. 281-288, *Mar. 1938*

Tropic Color in Trinidad. 327-334, *Sept. 1937*

Virginia's Colonial Heritage (Williamsburg). 417-440, *Apr. 1937*

West Point, Mother of Army Men. 779-786, *June 1936*

Today in the Land of Penn and Franklin. 13-52, *July 1935*

Springtime Wreathes a Garland for the Nation's Capital. 473-480, *Apr. 1935*

The State of Sky-Blue Water and Verdure (Minnesota). Photos by Clifton Adams and Edwin L. Wisherd. 289-296, *Mar. 1935*

Winter Lights and Shadows in the Nation's Capital. 201-216, *Feb. 1935*

Wild Gardens of the Southern Appalachians. 679-686, *June 1934*

Modern Scenes in the Land of Lincoln's Birth. 695-702, *June 1934*

Rainbow Denizens of the Aquarium. 97-104, *Jan. 1934*

Color Highlights of the Empire State. 569-576, *Nov. 1933*

Beaches and Bathers of the Jersey Shore. 535-542, *May 1933*

Farms and Workshops of "The Garden State." 559-566, *May 1933*

Colorful Corners of the City of Homes (Philadelphia). Photos by Clifton Adams and Edwin L. Wisherd. 675-682, *Dec. 1932*

Where the New South Challenges the Old. 717-748, *Dec. 1931*

Tempo and Color of a Great City. Photos by Clifton Adams and Edwin L. Wisherd. 539-578, *Nov. 1930*

Flecks of Color in the Fertile Fields of Louisiana. 419-426, *Apr. 1930*

Color Camera Records of New Orleans. 459-466, *Apr. 1930*

Insect Rivals of the Rainbow. 28-90, *July 1929*

Scenes and Shrines of the Cavalier Country. 425-432, *Apr. 1929*

Unique Gifts of Washington to the Nation. 473-480, *Apr. 1929*

Monticello, One of America's Most Historic Shrines. 489-496, *Apr. 1929*

The Friendly Crows (Indians) in Festive Panoply. 315-322, *Sept. 1927*

Canyons and Cacti of the American Southwest. 275-290, *Sept. 1925*

WITH an Exile in Arctic Siberia: The Narrative of a Russian Who Was Compelled to Turn Polar Explorer for Two Years. By Vladimir M. Zenzinov. 695-718, *Dec. 1924*

WITH the Devil Dancers of China and Tibet. Photos by Joseph F. Rock. 19-58, *July 1931*

WITH the Italians in Eritrea: Torrid Colony Between the Red Sea and Ethiopia, 2,600 Miles by Sea from Rome, Is Mobilization Place of Fascist Troops and Planes. By Harald P. Lechenperg. 265-295, *Sept. 1935*

WITH the Monks at Meteora: The Monasteries of Thessaly. By Elizabeth Perkins. 799-807, *Sept. 1909*

WITH the Nomads of Central Asia: A Summer's Sojourn in the Tekes Valley, Plateau Paradise of Mongol and Turkic Tribes. By Edward Murray. Paintings and drawings by Alexandre Iacovleff. 1-57, *Jan. 1936*

WITH the Nuba Hillmen of Kordofan. By Robin Strachan. 249-278, *Feb. 1951*

WITH the U. S. Army in Korea. By John R. Hodge. 829-840, *June 1947*

WITH Uncle Sam and John Bull in Germany. By Frederick Simpich. 117-140, *Jan. 1949*

WITH Wild Animals in the Rockies. By Lucie and Wendell Chapman. 231-249, *Aug. 1935*

WITHIN the Halls of Cambridge. By Philip Broad. 333-349, *Sept. 1936*

WITHIN the Yellow Border. Editorial by Wilbur E. Garrett. Included:

April snowmelt leaves its signature on the Wisconsin farm once owned by naturalist Aldo Leopold. JIM BRANDENBURG

Foldout displaying early covers and all cover illustrations since the first in July 1942. 270-286, *Sept. 1988*

WITNESS to a War: British Correspondent Frank Vizetelly. By Robert T. Cochran, Jr. 453-491, *Apr. 1961*

WITTE LEEUW (Dutch East Indiaman):

The Sunken Treasure of St. Helena. By Robert Sténuit. Photos by Bates Littlehales. 562-576, *Oct. 1978*

WITWATERSRAND (Region), South Africa:

The Transvaal: The Treasure-House Province. By Melville Chater. 479-512, *Apr. 1931*

The Witwatersrand and the Revolt of the Uitlanders. By George F. Becker. 349-367, *Nov. 1896*

A Critical Period in South African History. By John Hyde. 377-379, *Nov. 1896*

WIZARD ISLAND (Volcano), Oregon:

Crater Lake Summer. By Walter Meayers Edwards. 134-148, *July 1962*

WOBURN ABBEY (Estate), England:

Père David's Deer Saved From Extinction. By Larry Kohl. Photos by Bates Littlehales. 478-485, *Oct. 1982*

WODAABE TRIBESPEOPLE:

Niger's Wodaabe: "People of the Taboo." By Carol Beckwith. 483-509, *Oct. 1983*

WOKAS, a Primitive Indian Food. 183-185, *Apr. 1904*

WOLFE, ART: *Author-Photographer*

Long-eared Owls–Masters of the Night. 31-35, *Jan. 1980*

Photographer

The Triumphant Trumpeter. By Charles A. Bergman. 544-558, *Oct. 1985*

WOLFE, JAMES:

The British Way. By Sir Evelyn Wrench. 421-541, *Apr. 1949*

WOLFE, TOM: *Author*

Columbia's Landing Closes a Circle. 474-477, *Oct. 1981*

WOLFSHEIMER, GENE:

Author-Photographer

The Discus Fish Yields a Secret. 675-681, *May 1960*

WOLINSKY, CARY:

On Assignment in China. *May 1988*

Photographer

Wool–Fabric of History. By Nina Hyde. Included: Living in Wool. 552-591, *May 1988*

Sichuan: Where China Changes Course. By Ross Terrill. 280-317, *Sept. 1985*

Silk–The Queen of Textiles. By Nina Hyde. 2-49, *Jan. 1984*

Perth–Fair Winds and Full Sails. By Thomas J. Abercrombie. 638-667, *May 1982*

War and Peace in Northern Ireland. By Bryan Hodgson. 470-499, *Apr. 1981*

While adults hunt on the tundra of Canada's Ellesmere Island, a yearling arctic wolf supervises pups outside their den.   JIM BRANDENBURG

Pierre Mion. 291-296, *Aug. 1971*
Ama, Sea Nymphs of Japan. By Luis Marden. 122-135, *July 1971*

WOMEN in Uniform. By La Verne Bradley. 445-458, *Oct. 1943*

WOMEN of All Nations. 49-61, *Jan. 1911*

WOMEN of Saudi Arabia. By Marianne Alireza. Photos by Jodi Cobb. 423-453, *Oct. 1987*

WOMEN of the Revolution: Patriots in Petticoats. By Lonnelle Aikman. Paintings by Louis S. Glanzman. 475-493, *Oct. 1975*

WOMEN'S AIRFORCE SERVICE PILOTS (WASPS):
Women in Uniform. By La Verne Bradley. 445-458, *Oct. 1943*

WOMEN'S ARMY CORPS (WAC):
Paris Freed. By Frederick Simpich, Jr. 385-412, *Apr. 1945*
Decorations, Medals, Service Ribbons, Badges, and Women's Insignia. 414-444, *Oct. 1943*
Women in Uniform. By La Verne Bradley. 445-458, *Oct. 1943*

WOMEN'S INSIGNIA:
Decorations, Medals, Service Ribbons, Badges, and Women's Insignia. 414-444, *Oct. 1943*

WOMEN'S RESERVE OF THE U. S. COAST GUARD RESERVE (SPARS):
Decorations, Medals, Service Ribbons, Badges, and Women's Insignia. 414-444, *Oct. 1943*
Women in Uniform. By La Verne Bradley. 445-458, *Oct. 1943*

WOMEN'S RESERVE OF THE U. S. NAVAL RESERVE (WAVES):
Graduation by Parachute. By John E. Fletcher. 833-846, *June 1952*
Decorations, Medals, Service Ribbons, Badges, and Women's Insignia. 414-444, *Oct. 1943*
Women in Uniform. By La Verne Bradley. 445-458, *Oct. 1943*

WOMEN'S Work in Japan. By Mary A. Nourse. 99-132, *Jan. 1938*

WOMER, SUSAN:
Nomination Page. *Aug. 1962*

The **WONDER** City That Moves by Night. By Francis Beverly Kelley. 289-324, *Mar. 1948*

WONDER Island of the Amazon Delta: On Marajó Cowboys Ride Oxen, Tree-dwelling Animals Throng Dense Forests, While Strange Fishes and Birds Help Make a Zoologist's Paradise. By Hugh B. Cott. 635-670, *Nov. 1938*

The **WONDER** *of Birds.* Included:
■■ *Guide to Birds* recording and *Field Guide to the Birds of North America.* 280 pages. *1983*

The **WONDER** of Holography. By H. John Caulfield. Photos by Charles O'Rear. 364-377, *Mar. 1984*

A **WONDERER** Under Sea. By William Beebe. Paintings by E. Bostelmann. 741-758, *Dec. 1932*

The **WONDERFUL** Brooklyn Bridge. By John G. Morris. Photos by Donal F. Holway. 565-579, *May 1983*

The **WONDERFUL** Canals of China. By F. H. King. 931-958, *Oct. 1912*

The **WONDERFUL** Canals of China. By George E. Anderson. 68-69, *Feb. 1905*

WONDERFUL Strides of Africa. 176-177, *Mar. 1906*

The **WONDERFULLY** Diverse Ways of the Ant. By Bert Hölldobler. Paintings by John D. Dawson. Illustrations text by Alice J. Hall. NGS research grant. 779-813, *June 1984*

WONDERLAND in Longwood Gardens. By Edward C. Ferriday, Jr. 45-64, *July 1951*

The **WONDERLAND** of California. By Herman Whitaker. 57-99, *July 1915*

A **WONDERLAND** of Glaciers and Snow. By Milnor Roberts. 530-537, *June 1909*

A **WONDERLAND** of Science. 153-169, *Feb. 1915*

The **WONDERS** of the Mosi-oa-Tunga: The Falls of the Zambesi. By Louis Livingston Seaman. 561-571, *June 1911*

WONDERS of the New Washington: Efficient Modern Structures Rise in the Biggest Government Building Program Since the Capital City Was Founded in a Wilderness. By Frederick G. Vosburgh. 457-488, *Apr. 1935*

The **WONDROUS** Eyes of Science. By Rick Gore. Photos by James P. Blair. 360-389, *Mar. 1978*

WONDROUS *World of Fishes.* 373 ■■ pages. 1965; rev. ed. *1969*

WONG HOW-MAN:
On Assignment in China. *Mar. 1984*
Author-Photographer
Peoples of China's Far Provinces. 283-333, *Mar. 1984*

WONG, KINCHUE: *Photographer*
Changing Canton (China). Photos by Siukee Mack, Alfred T. Palmer, and Kinchue Wong. 711-726, *Dec. 1937*

WOOD, ARNOLD: *Author*
The Leach's Petrel: His Nursery on Little Duck Island. 360-365, *Apr. 1909*

WOOD, EDWARD FREDERICK LINDLEY. See Halifax, Lord

WOOD, GINNY HILL: *Author*
Squaws Along the Yukon. 245-265, *Aug. 1957*

WOOD, H. P.: *Author*
Hawaii for Homes. 298-299, *Apr. 1908*

WOOD, JUNIUS B.: *Author*
Illinois, Crossroads of the Continent. 523-594, *May 1931*
Flying the World's Longest Air-Mail Route: From Montevideo, Uruguay, Over the Andes, Up the Pacific Coast, Across Central America and the Caribbean to Miami, Florida, in 67 Thrilling Flying Hours. 261-325, *Mar. 1930*
St. Malo (France), Ancient City of Corsairs: An Old Brittany Seaport Whose Past Bristles with Cannons and Cutlasses. 131-177, *Aug. 1929*
Russia of the Hour: Giant Battleground for Theories of Economy, Society, and Politics, as Observed by an Unbiased Correspondent. 519-598, *Nov. 1926*
Seeing America from the "Shenandoah": An Account of the Record-making 9,000-mile Flight from the Atlantic to the Pacific Coast and Return in the Navy's American-built, American-manned Airship. 1-47, *Jan. 1925*
A Visit to Three Arab Kingdoms: Transjordania, Iraq, and the Hedjaz Present Many Problems to European Powers. 535-568, *May 1923*
The Far Eastern Republic (U.S.S.R.). 565-592, *June 1922*
Yap and Other Pacific Islands Under Japanese Mandate. 591-627, *Dec. 1921*

WOOD, LEONARD:
In Honor of the Army and Aviation. Speech by Leonard Wood. 267-284, *Mar. 1911*

WOOD, R. W.: *Photographer*
Remarkable Photograph of Lilienthal's Gliding Machine. 596, Aug. 1908; 271, Mar. 1911; 235, *Aug. 1927*

WOOD:
Versatile Wood Waits on Man. By Andrew H. Brown. 109-140, *July 1951*
Microscopical Examination of Wood from the Buried Forest, Muir Inlet, Alaska. By Francis H. Herrick. 75-78, *Mar. 21, 1892*
See also Lumber Industry; Paper Pulp Industry

Yellow cedar wood carving depicts the first men being discovered by the Raven, a belief of the Haida, islanders off the coast of British Columbia. DEWITT JONES

WOOD BUFFALO NATIONAL PARK, Canada:

Teamwork Helps the Whooping Crane. By Roderick C. Drewien, with Ernie Kuyt. 680-693, *May 1979*

WOOD CARVING:

Canada's Queen Charlotte Islands, Homeland of the Haida. By Moira Johnston. Photos by Dewitt Jones. Included: Totem poles. 102-127, *July 1987*

Humble Masterpieces: Decoys. By George Reiger. Photos by Kenneth Garrett. 639-663, *Nov. 1983*

Eskimo and Viking Finds in the High Arctic: Ellesmere Island. By Peter Schledermann. Photos by Sisse Brimberg. 575-601, *May 1981*

An Ozark Family Carves a Living and a Way of Life. By Bruce Dale. 124-133, *July 1975*

Afo-A-Kom: A Sacred Symbol Comes Home. By William S. Ellis. Photos by James P. Blair. 141-148, *July 1974*

Indians of Our North Pacific Coast. By Matthew W. Stirling. Paintings by W. Langdon Kihn. Included: Totem-Pole Builders. 25-52, *Jan. 1945*

WOOD IBIS. See Wood Storks

WOOD STORKS:

Our Only Native Stork, the Wood Ibis. By Robert Porter Allen. Photos by Frederick Kent Truslow. 294-306, *Feb. 1964*

WOODLAND PERIOD. See Russell Cave, Alabama

WOODPECKERS:

When Disaster Struck a Woodpecker's Home. By Frederick Kent Truslow. 882-884, *Dec. 1966*

The Bird's Year. By Arthur A. Allen. Included: Gila, Golden-fronted, Red-bellied woodpeckers. 791-816, *June 1951*

Woodpeckers, Friends of Our Forests. By T. Gilbert Pearson. Paintings by Allan Brooks. 453-479, *Apr. 1933*

WOODS, Lake of the, Canada-U. S.:

Men, Moose, and Mink of Northwest Angle. By William H. Nicholas. Photos by J. Baylor Roberts. 265-284, *Aug. 1947*

The **WOODS** and Gardens of Portugal. By Martin Hume. 883-894, *Oct. 1910*

WOODS HOLE, Massachusetts:

Cape Cod, Where Sea Holds Sway Over Man and Land. By Nathaniel T. Kenney. Photos by Dean Conger. 149-187, *Aug. 1962*

Windjamming Around New England. By Tom Horgan. Photos by Robert F. Sisson. 141-169, *Aug. 1950*

WOODS HOLE OCEANOGRAPHIC INSTITUTION:

Expeditions and Research. *See* Galapagos Rift; Mid-Atlantic Ridge; Mid-Atlantic Rift; *Titanic,* R.M.S.; *and* Weddell Seals

WOODSON, LeROY, Jr.:

Editorial. By Gilbert M. Grosvenor. 295, *Mar. 1975*

Nomination Page. *Feb. 1975*

Author-Photographer

The Kurds of Iraq: "We Who Face Death." 364-387, *Mar. 1975*

Photographer

After Rhodesia, a Nation Named Zimbabwe. By Charles E. Cobb, Jr. Photos by James L. Stanfield and LeRoy Woodson, Jr. 616-651, *Nov. 1981*

To Live in Harlem.... By Frank Hercules. 178-207, *Feb. 1977*

WOODWORTH, FRANCIS: *Author*

California Says It with Wild Flowers. Photos by B. Anthony Stewart. 492-501, *Apr. 1942*

Cologne, Key City of the Rhineland. 829-848, *June 1936*

WOOL:

Wool–Fabric of History. By Nina Hyde. Photos by Cary Wolinsky. Included: Living in Wool. 552-591, *May 1988*

The Cotswolds, "Noicest Parrt o'England." By James Cerruti. Photos by Adam Woolfitt. 846-869, *June 1974*

High, Wild World of the Vicuña. By William L. Franklin. 77-91, *Jan. 1973*

Beyond Australia's Cities. By W. Robert Moore. 709-747, *Dec. 1936*

The Indispensable Sheep. 512-528, *Apr. 1928*

See also Qiviut; Tweed

WOOLF, BELLA SIDNEY: *Author*

Fishing for Pearls in the Indian Ocean. 161-183, *Feb. 1926*

WOOLFITT, ADAM:

On Assignment in Great Britain. *Dec. 1986*

Photographer

Westminster, the Palace That Became Parliament. By Patrick Cormack. 728-757. Included: Royal Pomp Before Debate: In Centuries-old Ceremonial, the Queen Opens Parliament. 730-732, *Dec. 1986*

Those Eternal Austrians. By John J. Putman. 410-449, *Apr. 1985*

Washington, D. C.: Hometown Behind the Monuments. By Henry Mitchell. 84-125, *Jan. 1983*

Bordeaux: Fine Wines and Fiery Gascons. By William Davenport. 233-259, *Aug. 1980*

Where the River Shannon Flows. By Allan C. Fisher, Jr. 652-679, *Nov. 1978*

Ancient Europe Is Older Than We Thought. By Colin Renfrew. 615-623, *Nov. 1977*

Edinburgh: Capital in Search of a Country. By James Cerruti. 274-296, *Aug. 1976*

Christopher Columbus and the New World He Found. By John Scofield. 584-625, *Nov. 1975*

The Cotswolds, "Noicest Parrt o'England." By James Cerruti. 846-869, *June 1974*

Amiable Amsterdam. By William Davenport. 683-705, *May 1974*

The England of Charles Dickens. By Richard W. Long. 443-483, *Apr. 1974*

Chelsea, London's Haven of Individualists. By James Cerruti. 28-55, *Jan. 1972*

The Faeroes, Isles of Maybe. By Ernle Bradford. 410-442, *Sept. 1970*

New Mexico: The Golden Land. By Robert Laxalt. 299-345, *Sept. 1970*

The Investiture of Great Britain's Prince of Wales. By Allan C. Fisher, Jr. Photos by James L. Stanfield and Adam Woolfitt. 698-715, *Nov. 1969*

The Netherlands: Nation at War With the Sea. By Alan Villiers. 530-571, *Apr. 1968*

WOOLLEY, C. LEONARD: *Author*

Archeology, the Mirror of the Ages: Our Debt to the Humble Delvers in the Ruins at Carchemish and at Ur. 207-226, *Aug. 1928*

WOOLLY SPIDER MONKEYS:

Monkey in Peril: Rescuing Brazil's Muriqui. By Russell A. Mittermeier. Photos by Andrew L. Young. 387-395, *Mar. 1987*

WORCESTER, DEAN C.: *Author*

Head-Hunters of Northern Luzon. 833-930, *Sept. 1912*
Taal Volcano and Its Recent Destructive Eruption (Philippine Islands). 313-367, *Apr. 1912*
Field Sports Among the Wild Men of Northern Luzon. 215-267, *Mar. 1911*
Notes on Some Primitive Philippine Tribes. 284-301, *June 1898*
Author-Photographer
The Non-Christian Peoples of the Philippine Islands. Photos by author and Charles Martin. 1157-1256, *Nov. 1913*

WORCESTER, Massachusetts:

Cities Like Worcester Make America. By Howell Walker. 189-214, *Feb. 1955*

WORDEN, ALFRED M.:

Apollo 15 Explores the Mountains of the Moon. By Kenneth F. Weaver. Photos from NASA. 233-265, *Feb. 1972*

WORDSWORTH, WILLIAM:

Lake District, Poets' Corner of England. By H. V. Morton. Photos by David S. Boyer. 511-545, *Apr. 1956*
The British Way. By Sir Evelyn Wrench. 421-541, *Apr. 1949*

As her child sleeps, a Peruvian woman spins wool—sometimes turning the spindle counterclockwise to ward off evil spirits. CARY WOLINSKY, STOCK, BOSTON

WORK and Play in the Ozarks. Photos by B. Anthony Stewart and J. Baylor Roberts. 597-620, *May 1943*

WORK and War in the World of Ants. Paintings by Hashime Murayama. 179-186, *Aug. 1934*

WORK-HARD, Play-hard Michigan. By Andrew H. Brown. 279-320, *Mar. 1952*

WORK in the Arctic and Antarctic. 164-165, *Apr. 1900*

WORK in the Far South. 109, *Mar. 1903*

The **WORK** in the Pacific Ocean of the Magnetic Survey Yacht "Galilee." By L. A. Bauer. 601-611, *Sept. 1907*

WORK of the Bureau of American Ethnology. By W J McGee. 369-372, *Oct. 1901*

The **WORK** of the Bureau of Insular Affairs. By Clarence R. Edwards. 239-255, *June 1904*

The **WORK** of the National Geographic Society. By W J McGee. 253-259, *Aug. 1896*

The **WORK** of the United States Board on Geographic Names. By Henry Gannett. 221-227, *July 1896*

The **WORK** of the U. S. Hydrographic Office. By W.H.H. Southerland. 61-75, *Feb. 1903*

The **WORK** on the Isthmus (Panama). 586-587, *Oct. 1906*

WORKING Dogs of the World. By Freeman Lloyd. Paintings by Edward Herbert Miner. 776-806, *Dec. 1941*

WORKING for Weeks on the Sea Floor. By Jacques-Yves Cousteau. Photos by Philippe Cousteau and Bates Littlehales. NGS research grant. 498-537, *Apr. 1966*

WORKING Teak in the Burma Forests: The Sagacious Elephant Is Man's Ablest Ally in the Logging Industry of the Far East. By A. W. Smith. 239-256, *Aug. 1930*

WORLD:

New Perspective on the World. By John B. Garver, Jr. 911-913, *Dec. 1988*
Population, Plenty, and Poverty. By Paul R. and Anne H. Ehrlich. Included: Kenya: A Population Exploding. Photos by Robert Caputo; China: Back from the Brink. Photos by Patrick Zachmann; Hungary: A Static Society. Photos by Steve McCurry; India: Life on the Edge. Photos by Raghu Rai; Brazil: Flight to the Cities. Photos by Mary Ellen Mark;

Humble masterpieces in the world of wood carving, lifelike pintail, top, and blue-winged teal decoys fill collectors' shelves, not hunters' bags.

KENNETH GARRETT

W X

Ranchod Patel's family lives in one of more than half a million rural villages in India, a nation increasing the world's population by 16 million a year. RAGHU RAI, MAGNUM

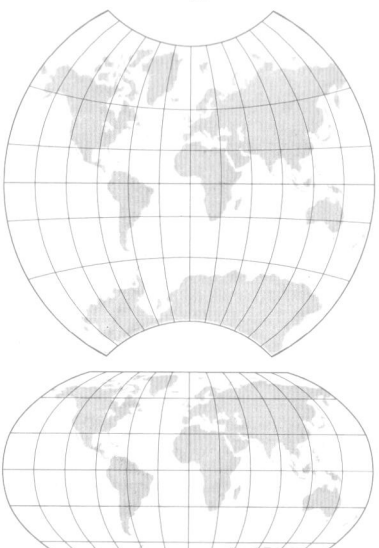

Arthur H. Robinson's new world map projection, bottom, improves upon Alphons van der Grinten's 1904 effort.

(Fourth Series). Edited by Gilbert H. Grosvenor. 216 pages. *1918*

■ *Scenes From Every Land: Picturing the People, Natural Phenomena, and Animal Life in All Parts of the World (Third Series).* Edited by Gilbert H. Grosvenor. 216 pages. *1912*

■ *Scenes From Every Land: Illustrations Picturing the People, Natural Phenomena, and Animal Life in All Parts of the World (Second Series).* Edited by Gilbert H. Grosvenor. 223 pages. *1909*

■ *Scenes From Every Land: A Collection of Illustrations From NGM Picturing the People, Natural Phenomena, and Animal Life in All Parts of the World.* Edited by Gilbert H. Grosvenor. 224 pages. *1907*

Cotidal Lines for the World. By R. A. Harris. 303-309, *June 1906*

✤ *Cotidal Lines for the World;* or, Lines of Simultaneous High Water at Each Hour and Half Hour of Greenwich Lunar Time. *June 1906*

Marine Hydrographic Surveys of the Coasts of the World. By George W. Littlehales. 63-67, *Feb. 1905*

✤ *Chart of the World on Mercator's Projection, showing Submarine Cables and Connections, and also Tracks for full-powered Steam Vessels. Feb. 1905*

Advances in Geographic Knowledge During the Nineteenth Century. By A. W. Greely. 143-152, *Apr. 1901*

Recent Contributions to Our Knowledge of the Earth's Shape and Size, by the United States Coast and Geodetic Survey. By C. A. Schott. 36-41, *Jan. 1901*

The Great Unmapped Areas on the Earth's Surface Awaiting the Explorer and Geographer. By J. Scott Keltie. 251-266, *Sept. 1897*

✤ *Submarine Cables of the World, with the Principal Connecting Land Lines, also Coaling, Docking, and Repairing Stations. Mar. 1896*

The Great Populous Centers of the World. By A. W. Greely. 89-92, *July 10, 1893*

✤ *Chronicon Nurembergense Map, 1493. Apr. 7, 1893*

✤ *Juan de la Cosa Map, 1500. Apr. 7, 1893*

✤ *Ruysch Map, 1508. Apr. 7, 1893*

See also Earth; *and* Atlases, NGS

WORLD (Magazine for Young Readers):

Circulation. 851, *Dec. 1981*

Editorial. The *School Bulletin* is retired after 56 years; replaced by WORLD. By Gilbert M. Grosvenor. 299, *Sept. 1975*

Start the World, I Want to Get On! Announcing National Geographic WORLD. 148-150, *July 1975*

WORLD ATLAS. *See* Atlases, NGS: World

WORLD CENTER FOR BIRDS OF PREY, Boise, Idaho:

Raptor Nursery Raises Birds for the Wild. Geographica. *Nov. 1988*

WORLD COMMUNICATIONS. *See* Cables; Radio; Satellites; Telegraphy; Telephone; Television

WORLD CONGRESSES. *See* International Congress of Orientalists; International Geographic Congress; World's Congress of Education

WORLD CRUISES AND VOYAGES:

Circling Earth From Pole to Pole. By Sir Ranulph Fiennes. 464-481, *Oct. 1983*

■ *Voyages to Paradise: Exploring in the Wake of Captain Cook.* By William R. Gray. Photos by Gordon W. Gahan. 215 pages. *1981*

Magellan: First Voyage Around the World. By Alan Villiers. Photos by Bruce Dale. 721-753, *June 1976*

Sir Francis Drake. By Alan Villiers. Photos by Gordon W. Gahan. 216-253, *Feb. 1975*

Captain Cook: The Man Who Mapped the Pacific. By Alan Villiers. Photos by Gordon W. Gahan. 297-349, *Sept. 1971*

Robin Sails Home. By Robin Lee Graham. 504-545, *Oct. 1970*

In the Wake of Darwin's *Beagle.* By Alan Villiers. Photos by James L. Stanfield. 449-495, *Oct. 1969*

World-roaming Teen-ager Sails On. By Robin Lee Graham. 449-493, *Apr. 1969*

A Teen-ager Sails the World Alone. By Robin Lee Graham. 445-491, *Oct. 1968*

Saga of a Ship, the *Yankee.* By Luis Marden. 263-269, *Feb. 1966*

■ The Voyage of the Brigantine *Yankee.* 265A-265B, *Feb. 1966*

Triton Follows Magellan's Wake. By Edward L. Beach. Photos by J. Baylor Roberts. 585-616, *Nov. 1960*

Off the Beaten Track of Empire (Prince Philip's Tour). By Beverley M. Bowie. Photos by Michael Parker. 584-626, *Nov. 1957*

"Around the World in Eighty Days." By Newman Bumstead. 705-750, *Dec. 1951*

National Geographic WORLD teaches 8-to-13-year olds through innovative articles, games, and puzzles.

WORLD FAIRS AND EXPOSITIONS. *See* World's Fairs

WORLD HEALTH ORGANIZATION (WHO). *See* United Nations: World Health Organization

WORLD HERITAGE FUND: Grant: Buddhist temple restoration: Nepal. 716, *June 1982*

WORLD HERITAGE SITES (UNESCO-Designated):

■ *Our World's Heritage.* Contents: UNESCO-designated World Heritage Sites. 312 pages. *1987*

See also by name

The **WORLD** in Dolls. By Samuel F. Pryor. Photos by Kathleen Revis. 817-831, *Dec. 1959*

The **WORLD** in New York City. By Peter T. White. 52-107, *July 1964*

The **WORLD** *in Your Garden.* Art by ■ Else Bostelmann. 231 pages. *1957*

The **WORLD** in Your Garden. By W. H. Camp. Paintings by Else Bostelmann. 1-65, *July 1947*

A **WORLD** Inside a Mountain: Aniakchak, the New Volcanic Wonderland of the Alaska Peninsula, Is Explored. By Bernard R. Hubbard. 319-345, *Sept. 1931*

The **WORLD** of Elizabeth I. By Louis B. Wright. Photos by Ted Spiegel. 668-709, *Nov. 1968*

The **WORLD** of Martin Luther. By Merle Severy. Photos by James L. Amos. 418-463, *Oct. 1983*

The **WORLD** of My Apple Tree. By Robert F. Sisson. 836-847, *June 1972*

The **WORLD** of Süleyman the Magnificent. By Merle Severy. Photos by James L. Stanfield. 552-601, *Nov. 1987*

The **WORLD** *of the American Indian.* ■ 399 pages. *1974*

A **WORLD** *of Things To Do.* Contents: Crafts, activities, games, puzzles, and recipes to be done alone or with others. Juvenile. 104 pages. *1986*

The **WORLD** of Tolstoy. By Peter T. White. Photos by Sam Abell. 758-791, *June 1986*

The **WORLD** Pays Final Tribute (Churchill Funeral). Text by Carolyn Bennett Patterson. 199-225, *Aug. 1965*

WORLD WAR I:

Our National War Memorials in Europe. By John J. Pershing. 1-36, *Jan. 1934*

Armistice Day and the American Battle Fields. By J. J. Jusserand. 509-554, *Nov. 1929*

The National Geographic Society's Memorial to American Troops: Fountain and Water Supply System Presented to Historic French Town of Cantigny, Where Our Overseas Soldiers Won Their First Victory in the World War. 675-678, *Dec. 1923*

Transporting a Navy Through the

Many troops could not have borne the terrors and rigors of World War I without the indomitable Salvation Army cook.

After four years of German occupation a French couple joyously greet World War I doughboys who helped liberate their town in 1918. COURTESY *AMERICAN LEGION MONTHLY*

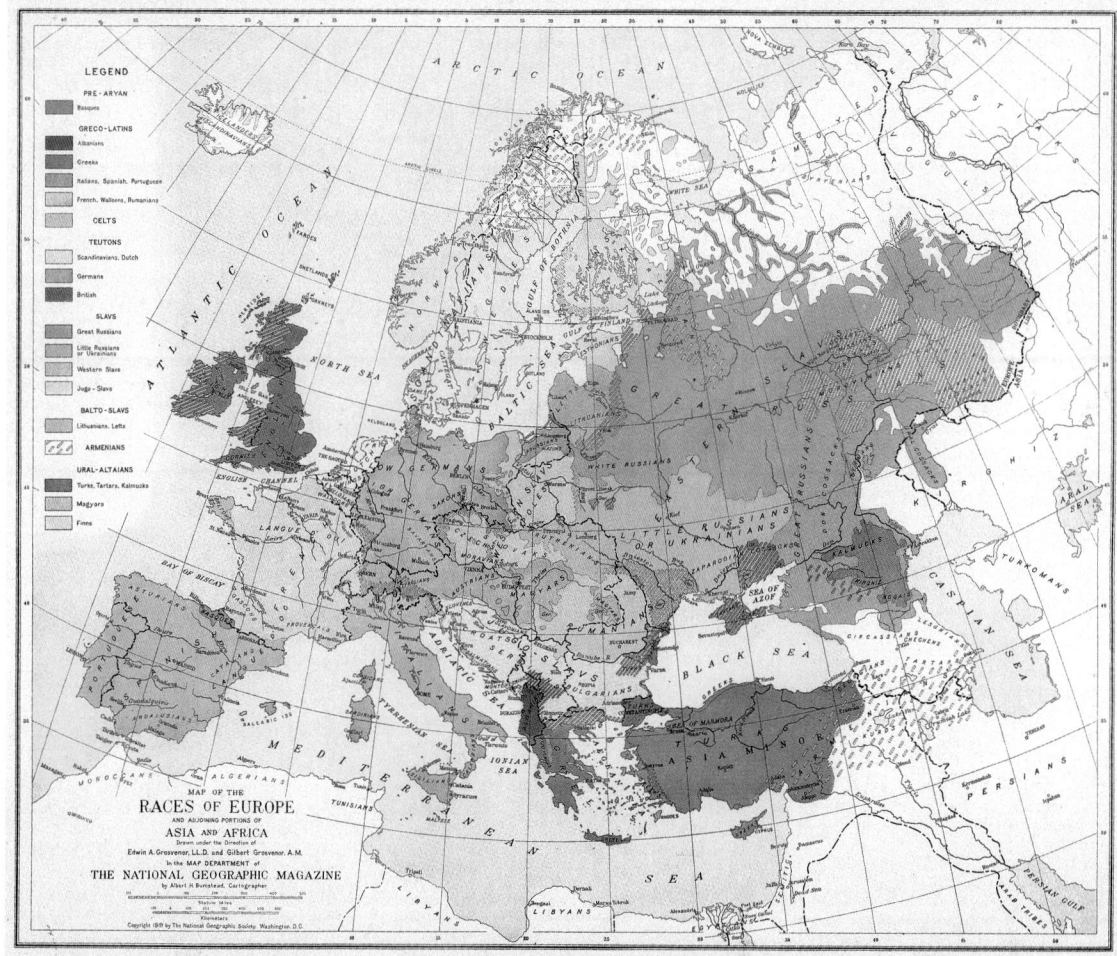

A 1918 NATIONAL GEOGRAPHIC map shows the distribution of ethnic groups in Europe at the conclusion of World War I.

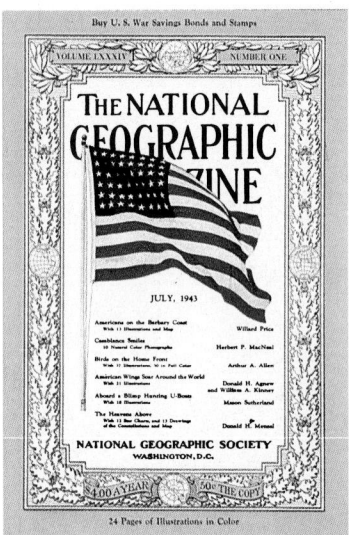

Patriotism during World War II inspired the magazine cover's first photograph, in July 1943.

Taking time out from the intense fighting that racked Italy during World War II, a pair of GIs pose for a photographer. U.S. ARMY SIGNAL CORPS, OFFICIAL

Prime Minister Winston Churchill is mobbed on V-E day, May 8, 1945, following Germany's World War II surrender. BRITISH COMBINE

Testing German strength, U.S. infantrymen fire machine guns from a house 400 yards from the front near Anzio, Italy, during World War II. U.S. ARMY SIGNAL CORPS, OFFICIAL

Pools Resources of United Nations, and Supplies American Forces. By Francis Flood. 745-761, *June 1943*

Scotland in Wartime. By Isobel Wylie Hutchison. 723-743, *June 1943*

San Francisco: Gibraltar of the West Coast. By La Verne Bradley. 279-308, *Mar. 1943*

Sydney Faces the War Front Down Under. By Howell Walker. 359-374, *Mar. 1943*

Malta Invicta. By Bartimeus (A Captain in the Royal Navy). 375-400, *Mar. 1943*

Norway, an Active Ally. By Wilhelm Morgenstierne. 333-357, *Mar. 1943*

Your Society Aids War Effort. 277-278, *Feb. 1943*

Convoys to Victory. By Harvey Klemmer. 193-216, *Feb. 1943*

American Bombers Attacking from Australia. By Howell Walker. 49-70, *Jan. 1943*

Your Dog Joins Up. By Frederick Simpich. 93-113, *Jan. 1943*

The Miracle of War Production: For Victory the United States Transforms Its Complex Industry into the Biggest Factory and Mightiest Arsenal the World Has Ever Known. By Albert W. Atwood. Paintings by Thornton Oakley. 693-715, *Dec. 1942*

American Industries Geared for War. By Thornton Oakley. Paintings by author. 716-734, *Dec. 1942*

Japan Faces Russia in Manchuria. By Willard Price. 603-634, *Nov. 1942*

QM the Fighting Storekeeper. By Frederick Simpich. Paintings by Arthur Beaumont. 561-600, *Nov. 1942*

Life on the Hawaii "Front": All-out Defense and Belt Tightening of Pacific Outpost Foreshadow the Things to Come on Mainland. By Frederick Simpich, Jr. 541-560, *Oct. 1942*

Rehearsal at Dieppe (France). By W. Robert Moore. 495-502, *Oct. 1942*

Wartime in the Pacific Northwest. By Frederick Simpich. 421-464, *Oct. 1942*

China Opens Her Wild West. By Owen Lattimore. 337-367, *Sept. 1942*

"Blood, Toil, Tears, and Sweat": An American Tells the Story of Britain's War Effort, Summed up in Prime Minister Churchill's Unflinching Words. By Harvey Klemmer. 141-166, *Aug. 1942*

The People's Fight Against Slavery. By Henry A. Wallace. Reprint of address delivered at a dinner of the Free World Association, May 8, 1942. 276-280, *Aug. 1942*

Life in Dauntless Darwin: A National Geographic Staff Writer Gives a Vivid Description of the Australian Town That Guards the Continent's Northern Door. By Howell Walker. 123-138, *July 1942*

The New Queen of the Seas (Aircraft Carrier). By Melville Bell Grosvenor. 1-30, *July 1942*

⊕ *Theater of War in Europe, Africa, and Western Asia. July 1942*

As 2,000 Ships Are Born. By Frederick Simpich. 551-588, *May 1942*

The Making of an Anzac. By Howell Walker. 409-456, *Apr. 1942*

Mediterranean Checkerboard. By Frederick Simpich. 527-550, *Apr. 1942*

Metal Sinews of Strength: This Is a War of Many Metals for We Live in an Age of Alloys. By Frederick G. Vosburgh. 457-491, *Apr. 1942*

War Meets Peace in Egypt. By Grant Parr and G. E. Janssen. 503-526, *Apr. 1942*

French West Africa in Wartime. By Paul M. Atkins. 371-408, *Mar. 1942*

⊕ *Theater of War in the Pacific Ocean. Feb. 1942*

San Diego Can't Believe It. By Frederick Simpich. 45-80, *Jan. 1942*

Canada's War Effort: A Canadian Pictures the Swift and Sweeping Transformation from a Peaceful Dominion to a Nation Geared for War. By Bruce Hutchison. 553-590, *Nov. 1941*

Life Grows Grim in Singapore. By H. Gordon Minnigerode. 661-686, *Nov. 1941*

Rural Britain Carries On. By Harvey Klemmer. 527-552, *Oct. 1941*

Bombs over Bible Lands. By Frederick Simpich and W. Robert Moore. 141-180, *Aug. 1941*

Lisbon–Gateway to Warring Europe. By Harvey Klemmer. 259-276, *Aug. 1941*

Ancient Iceland, New Pawn of War. 75-90, *July 1941*

Newfoundland, North Atlantic Rampart: From the "First Base of American Defense" Planes Fly to Britain's Aid over Stout Fishing Schooners of the Grand Banks. By George Whiteley, Jr. 111-140, *July 1941*

Everyday Life in Wartime England. By Harvey Klemmer. 497-534, *Apr. 1941*

See also U. S. Army; U. S. Army Air Forces; U. S. Army Corps of Engineers; U. S. Army Map Service; U. S. Army Quartermaster Corps; U. S. Army Signal Corps; U. S. Coast Guard; U. S. Defense Bases; U. S. Marine Corps; U. S. Navy; *and* Churchill, Sir Winston; Insignia; Maps; Unknown Servicemen; War Agencies; War Memorials

WORLD WILDLIFE FUND:

Secrets of the Wild Panda. By George B. Schaller. Included: Saving the panda. 284-309, *Mar. 1986*

Man's Wildlife Heritage Faces Extinction. By H.R.H. The Prince Philip. 700-703, *Nov. 1962*

Grants

Humpback whales. 466, *Apr. 1982*

Pandas. 735, *Dec. 1981*

TRAFFIC (monitoring of wildlife shipments). 296, *Mar. 1981*

African elephant survey. 578, 584, *Nov. 1980*

Giant Brazilian otters. 132, *July 1980*

Orangutans. 835, *June 1980*

Humpback whales. 1, *Jan. 1979*

The **WORLD'S** Ancient Porcelain Center. By Frank B. Lenz. 391-406, *Nov. 1920*

WORLD'S COLUMBIAN EXPOSITION:

Proceedings of the International Geographic Conference, held in conjunction with the World's Columbian Exposition, Chicago, May 1- October 30, 1893. 97-256, *Jan. 31, 1894*

WORLD'S CONGRESS OF EDUCATION:

The International Geographic Conference, Chicago, July 27-28, 1893, sponsored by the National Geographic Society, held in conjunction with the World's Congress of Education. 98-100, *Jan. 31, 1894*

The **WORLD'S** Debt to France. 491-501, *Nov. 1915*

WORLD'S FAIRS:

Kansai, Japan's Historic Heartland, Hosts Expo '70. By Thomas J. Abercrombie. 295-339, *Mar. 1970*

In a World War II vignette an aircraft carrier's crewmen relax in a lagoon after attacking Japanese troops on Kwajalein Atoll.   U.S. NAVY, OFFICIAL

Fish teem around a three-inch gun of the **President Coolidge,** *a U.S. liner converted to a troop transport that sank in the western Pacific during World War II.*   DAVID DOUBILET

W
X

WRECK of H.M.S. *Pandora.* By Luis Marden. 423-457, *Oct. 1985*

WRECK of the *Coolidge.* Text and photos by David Doubilet. 458-467, *Apr. 1988*

WREN, CHRISTOPHER:
The British Way. By Sir Evelyn Wrench. 421-541, *Apr. 1949*

WRENCH, SIR EVELYN: *Author*
Founders of New England. Photos by B. Anthony Stewart. 803-838, *June 1953*
The British Way. 421-541, *Apr. 1949*
Founders of Virginia. Photos by B. Anthony Stewart. 433-462, *Apr. 1948*

WRENS:
The Fairy Wrens of Australia: The Little Longtailed "Blue Birds of Happiness" Rank High Among the Island Continent's Remarkable Birds. By Neville W. Cayley. Paintings by author. 488-498, *Oct. 1945*
Winged Denizens of Woodland, Stream, and Marsh. By Alexander Wetmore. Paintings by Allan Brooks. 577-596, *May 1934*

WRESTING Oil From Reluctant Rock. 78-79, *Special Report on Energy. (Feb. 1981)*

WRESTLIN' for a Livin' With King Coal. By Michael E. Long. Photos by Michael O'Brien. 793-819, *June 1983*

WRIGHT, BELINDA:
On Assignment in Australia. *Feb. 1988*
Author-Photographer
The First Australians: Living in Two Worlds. By Belinda Wright and Stanley Breeden. 291-294, *Feb. 1988*
Photographer
The First Australians. By Stanley Breeden. 266-289, *Feb. 1988*
Tiger! Lord of the Indian Jungle. By Stanley Breeden. 748-773, *Dec. 1984*
India Struggles to Save Her Wildlife. By John J. Putman. 299-343, *Sept. 1976*

WRIGHT, CHARLES W.: *Author*
The World's Most Cruel Earthquake (Messina, Sicily). 373-396, *Apr. 1909*

WRIGHT, G. ERNEST: *Author*
The Last Thousand Years Before Christ. Paintings by H. J. Soulen and Peter V. Bianchi. 812-853, *Dec. 1960*
Bringing Old Testament Times to Life. Paintings by Henry J. Soulen. 833-864, *Dec. 1957*

WRIGHT, HELEN DUNSTAN: *Author*
Little-Known Sardinia. 97-120, *Aug. 1916*

WRIGHT, JONATHAN:
On Assignment in the Canadian Arctic. *July 1983*
Photographer
Arctic Odyssey. By John Bockstoce. Paintings by Jack Unruh. 100-127, *July 1983*
Jackson Hole: Good-bye to the Old Days? By François Leydet. 768-789, *Dec. 1976*

WRIGHT, LOUIS B.:
Nomination Page. *Apr. 1964*
Author
The World of Elizabeth I. Photos by Ted Spiegel. 668-709, *Nov. 1968*
The Britain That Shakespeare Knew. Photos by Dean Conger. 613-665, *May 1964*

WRIGHT, MARIE ROBINSON:
Author
The Falls of Iguazu. 456-460, *Aug. 1906*

WRIGHT, MYRON H., Jr.:
Photographer
The Swallow-tailed Kite: Graceful Aerialist of the Everglades. 496-505, *Oct. 1972*

WRIGHT, ORVILLE:
Lonely Cape Hatteras, Besieged by the Sea. By William S. Ellis. Photos by Emory Kristof. 393-421, *Sept. 1969*
Fledgling Wings of the Air Force. By Thomas W. McKnew. 266-271, *Aug. 1957*
Aviation Looks Ahead on Its 50th Birthday. By Emory S. Land. 721-739, *Dec. 1953*
Fifty Years of Flight. 740-756, *Dec. 1953*
Air Conquest: From the Early Days of Giant Kites and Birdlike Gliders, the National Geographic Society Has Aided and Encouraged the Growth of Aviation. 233-242, *Aug. 1927*

WRIGHT, WILBUR:
Lonely Cape Hatteras, Besieged by the Sea. By William S. Ellis. Photos by Emory Kristof. 393-421, *Sept. 1969*
Fledgling Wings of the Air Force. By Thomas W. McKnew. 266-271, *Aug. 1957*
Aviation Looks Ahead on Its 50th Birthday. By Emory S. Land. 721-739, *Dec. 1953*
Fifty Years of Flight. 740-756, *Dec. 1953*
Air Conquest: From the Early Days of Giant Kites and Birdlike Gliders, the National Geographic Society Has Aided and Encouraged the Growth of Aviation. 233-242, *Aug. 1927*
In Honor of the Army and Aviation. Speech by Wilbur Wright. 267-284, *Mar. 1911*

WRIGHT, WILLIAM:
The Journey of Burke and Wills: First Across Australia. By Joseph Judge. Photos by Joseph J. Scherschel. 152-191, *Feb. 1979*

WRIGHT FIELD, Ohio:
New Frontier in the Sky. By F. Barrows Colton. 379-408, *Sept. 1946*

WRIGHT WAY (Skyway 1):
Skyway Below the Clouds. By Carl R. Markwith. Photos by Ernest J. Cottrell. Contents: An airway route planned and marked especially for the use of private flyers. 85-108, *July 1949*

WRINGING Secrets from Greenland's Icecap. By Paul-Emile Victor. 121-147, *Jan. 1956*

WRIOTHESLEY, HENRY (Third Earl of Southampton):
Founders of Virginia. By Sir Evelyn Wrench. Photos by B. Anthony Stewart. 433-462, *Apr. 1948*

WRITING:
Ebla: Splendor of an Unknown Empire. By Howard La Fay. Photos by James L. Stanfield. Paintings by Louis S. Glanzman. 730-759, *Dec. 1978*
The Phoenicians, Sea Lords of Antiquity. By Samuel W. Matthews. Photos by Winfield Parks. Paintings by Robert C. Magis. 149-189, *Aug. 1974*
Ancient Mesopotamia: A Light That Did Not Fail. By E. A. Speiser. Paintings by H. M. Herget. Included: How Seal Engraving Led to the Invention of Writing. 41-105, *Jan. 1951*
See also Cuneiform Script; Glyphs

WULSIN, FREDERICK R.: *Author*
The Road to Wang Ye Fu: An Account of the Work of the National Geographic Society's Central-China Expedition in the Mongol Kingdom of Ala Shan. 197-234, *Feb. 1926*

WULUMUCH'I, Sinkiang Province, China. *See* Ürümqi

WÜRTTEMBERG (Former State), Germany:
A Corner of Old Württemberg. By B. H. Buxton. 931-947, *Oct. 1911*

WYATT EARP (Ship):
My Four Antarctic Expeditions: Explorations of 1933-1939 Have Stricken Vast Areas from the Realm of the Unknown. By Lincoln Ellsworth. 129-138, *July 1939*

WYETH, NEWELL CONVERS:
The "Map of Discovery" (Western Hemisphere). Reproduction of the painting by N. C. Wyeth, National Geographic Society, Washington, D. C. 93, *Jan. 1929*
The "Map of Discovery" (Eastern Hemisphere). Reproduction of the painting by N. C. Wyeth, National Geographic Society, Washington, D. C. 568, *Nov. 1928*
The Caravels of Columbus. Reproduction of the painting by N. C. Wyeth, National Geographic Society, Washington, D. C. 55, *July 1928*
Commander Byrd at the North Pole (Through Pathless Skies to the North Pole). Reproduction of the painting by N. C. Wyeth, National Geographic Society, Washington, D. C. *May 1928*
The Discoverer. Reproduction of the painting by N. C. Wyeth, National Geographic Society, Washington, D. C. 347, *Mar. 1928*

WYLLIE, ROBERT E.: *Author*
The Romance of Military Insignia: How the United States Government Recognizes Deeds of Heroism and Devotion to Duty. 463-501, *Dec. 1919*

"Map of Discovery of the Western Hemisphere," a supplement reproduced from a mural painted by N. C. Wyeth for Society headquarters, graced the January 1929 issue.

Y
Z

YACHTING
YAKIMA VALLEY
YAKUTAT BAY
YAKUTSK
YANGTZE RIVER AND BASIN
YANKEE
YANOMAMO
YAP ISLANDS
YASSI ADA
YELLOW FEVER
YELLOWSTONE NATIONAL PARK
YEREVAN
YORKSHIRE
YORKTOWN SHIPWRECK
YOSEMITE NATIONAL PARK
YUCATÁN PENINSULA
YUKAGHIRS
YUKON TERRITORY
YUMA TRAIL
YUNNAN PROVINCE
YUPIK ESKIMOS
ZAGREB
ZAMBEZI
ZANZIBAR
ZAPOTEC INDIANS
ZEN BUDDHISM
ZHEJIANG PROVINCE
ZHUHAI SPECIAL ECONOMIC ZONE
ZIMBABWE
ZINJANTHROPUS
ZION NATIONAL PARK
ZOOS
ZOQUE INDIANS
ZOROASTRIANISM
ZUIDER ZEE
ZULUS
ZUNI INDIANS
ZÜRICH

*Nevada and Vernal Falls
drop the frothing Merced River into
the Yosemite Valley.*

JONATHAN BLAIR

1161

Under full sail the brigantine Yankee *in 1949 glides past New York City after an 18-month, 45,000-mile voyage around the world.* TED KELL, NEW YORK HERALD TRIBUNE

YWCA. *See* Young Women's Christian Association

YWCA: International Success Story. By Mary French Rockefeller. Photos by Otis Imboden. 904-933, *Dec. 1963*

YACHTING:

More of Sea Than of Land: The Bahamas. By Carleton Mitchell. Photos by James L. Stanfield. Included: Out-Island Regatta. 218-267, *Feb. 1967*

Inside Europe Aboard *Yankee.* By Irving and Electa Johnson. Photos by Joseph J. Scherschel. Included: Fastnet race. 157-195, *Aug. 1964*

Down East to Nova Scotia. By Winfield Parks. Included: Marblehead-Halifax race, Bras d'Or McCurdy Cup race, Jones Trophy. 853-879, *June 1964*

To Europe with a Racing Start. By Carleton Mitchell. Included: Newport-to-Bermuda race. 758-791, *June 1958*

Down East Cruise. By Tom Horgan. Photos by Luis Marden. 329-369, *Sept. 1952*

Baltic Cruise of the *Caribbee.* By Carleton Mitchell. Included: Sandhamn Regatta Week. 605-646, *Nov. 1950*

"Delmarva," Gift of the Sea. By Catherine Bell Palmer. Included: Cambridge Yacht Club's championship races for Hampton-class sloops; and log canoe, *Jay Dee,* racing on the Choptank. 367-399, *Sept. 1950*

Windjamming Around New England. By Tom Horgan. Photos by Robert F. Sisson. Contents: Weekly regattas of Cape Cod in the summer, the annual Provincetown-Wellfleet competition, Squam Day Regatta on Ipswich Bay, and Race Week at Marblehead. 141-169, *Aug. 1950*

The British Way. By Sir Evelyn Wrench. Included: Cowes: Cradle of Yachting. 421-541, *Apr. 1949*

YACHTS. *See* Alice; Argyll; Betelgeuse; Bonita; Britannia; Carib; Caribbee; Carnegie; Delight; Elsie; Finisterre; Galilee; Great Britain II; Kinkajou; Mah Jong; Nomad; Physalia; Pilgrim; Tectona; Tradewinds; White Mist; Yankee

YACHTS, Land. *See* Land Yachts

YACHTS, Sand. *See* Sand Yachts

YADA, ISSHO: *Artist*

The Lost Fleet of Kublai Khan. By Torao Mozai. Photos by Koji Nakamura. 634-649, *Nov. 1982*

YAHGAN INDIANS:

Inside Cape Horn. By Amos Burg. 743-783, *Dec. 1937*

The Indian Tribes of Southern Patagonia, Tierra del Fuego, and the Adjoining Islands. By J. B. Hatcher. 12-22, *Jan. 1901*

YAKIMA VALLEY, Washington:

Mount St. Helens Aftermath: The Mountain That Was–and Will Be. By Rowe Findley. Photos by Steve Raymer. 713-733, *Dec. 1981*

The Day the Sky Fell. By Rowe Findley. Included: Ashfall and cleanup after the eruption of Mount St. Helens. 50-65, *Jan. 1981*

Washington's Yakima Valley. By Mark Miller. Photos by Sisse Brimberg. 609-631, *Nov. 1978*

YAKUTAT BAY, Alaska:

Glaciers on the Move. By John L. Eliot. Photos by Chris Johns. Included: Anatomy of a tidewater glacier. 107-119, *Jan. 1987*

The National Geographic Society's Alaskan Expedition of 1909. By Ralph S. Tarr and Lawrence Martin. 1-54, *Jan. 1910*

Report on Auriferous Sands from Yakutat Bay. By J. Stanley-Brown. 196-198, *May 29, 1891*

YAKUTS:

New Road to Asia. By Owen Lattimore. 641-676, *Dec. 1944*

YAKUTSK, U.S.S.R.:

Five Times to Yakutsk. By Dean Conger. 256-269, *Aug. 1977*

YALE, CAROLINE A.:

Gardiner Greene Hubbard: Memorial Meeting. Address by Caroline A. Yale. 46-50, *Feb. 1898*

YALU (River), Korea-Manchuria:

Exploring Unknown Corners of the "Hermit Kingdom." By Roy Chapman Andrews. 25-48, *July 1919*

YAMASHITA, MICHAEL S.: *Photographer*

Japanese Americans: Home at Last. By Arthur Zich. 512-539, *Apr. 1986*

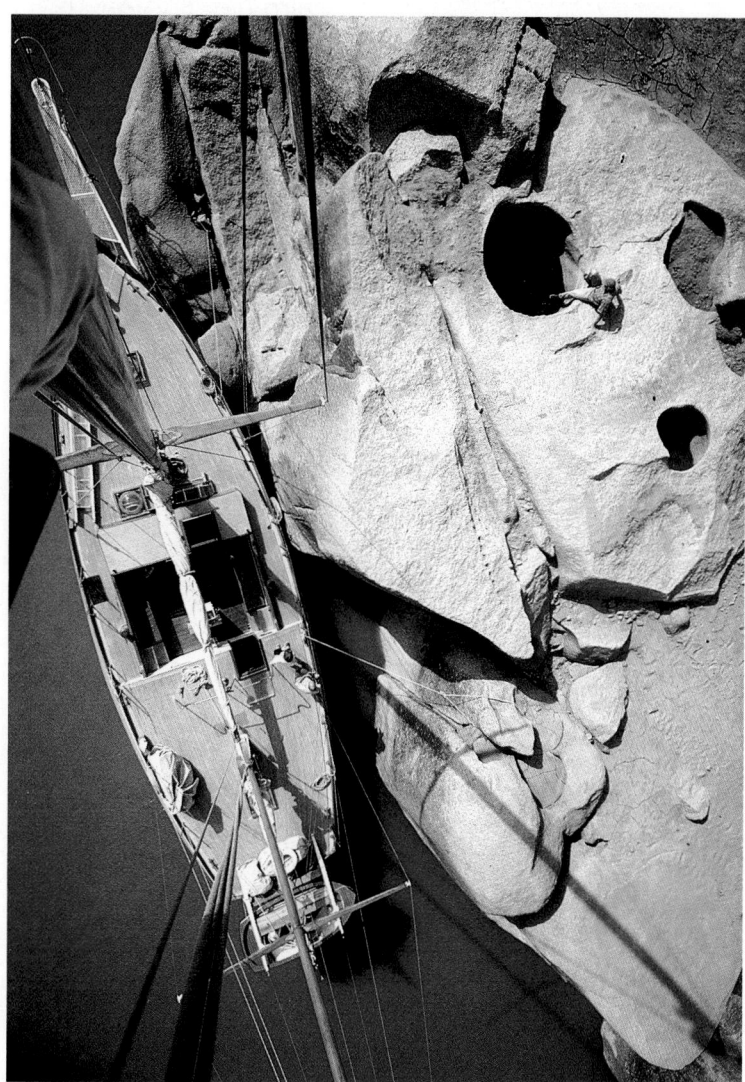

The new **Yankee,** *a ketch, pauses by an ancient Egyptian granite quarry on a mid-1960s cruise up the Nile River from the northern delta into the Sudan.* WINFIELD PARKS, NGS

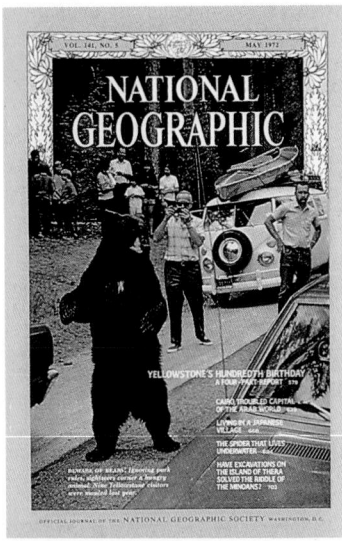

Pacific Wards of Uncle Sam. By W.
   Robert Moore. 73-104, *July 1948*
Yap Meets the Yanks. By David D.
   Duncan. 364-372, *Mar. 1946*
Hidden Key to the Pacific: Piercing the
   Web of Secrecy Which Long Has
   Veiled Japanese Bases in the Man-
   dated Islands. By Willard Price. 759-
   785, *June 1942*
Mysterious Micronesia: Yap, Map, and
   Other Islands Under Japanese Man-
   date are Museums of Primitive Man.
   By Willard Price. 481-510, *Apr. 1936*
Yap and Other Pacific Islands Under
   Japanese Mandate. By Junius B.
   Wood. 591-627, *Dec. 1921*

YAQUI INDIANS:

Adventuring Down the West Coast of
   Mexico. By Herbert Corey. 449-503,
   Nov. 1922
A Mexican Land of Canaan: Marvelous
   Riches of the Wonderful West Coast
   of Our Neighbor Republic. By Fred-
   erick Simpich. 307-330, *Oct. 1910*

YARLUNG ZANGBO (River), India-
   Tibet. *See* Brahmaputra

YARMOUTH (Great Yarmouth),
   England:

When the Herring Fleet Comes to Great
   Yarmouth. By W. Robert Moore.
   233-250, *Aug. 1934*
King Herring: An Account of the
   World's Most Valuable Fish, the In-
   dustries It Supports, and the Part It
   Has Played in History. By Hugh M.
   Smith. 701-735, *Aug. 1909*

YARMOUTH PORT, Massachusetts:

Cape Cod People and Places. By Wanda
   Burnett. 737-774, *June 1946*

YASSI ADA (Island), Turkey:

New Tools for Undersea Archeology.
   By George F. Bass. Photos by
   Charles R. Nicklin, Jr. NGS research
   grant. 403-423, *Sept. 1968*
Underwater Archeology: Key to Histo-
   ry's Warehouse. By George F. Bass.
   Photos by Thomas J. Abercrombie

and Robert B. Goodman. NGS
   research grant. 138-156, *July 1963*
Thirty-three Centuries Under the Sea.
   By Peter Throckmorton. 682-703,
   May 1960

YAWLS. *See* Argyll; Bonita; Caribbee;
   *Delight; Elsie; Finisterre; Islander;
   Mah Jong; White Mist*

YAZD-E KHVAST, Iran. *See*
   Yezdikhast

YEADON, DAVID: *Author*

To Scotland Afoot Along the Pennine
   Way. Photos by Annie Griffiths. 388-
   418, *Mar. 1986*

YEAGER, CHUCK:

Columbia's Landing Closes a Circle. By
   Tom Wolfe. 474-477, *Oct. 1981*
Flying in the "Blowtorch" Era. By
   Frederick G. Vosburgh. 281-322,
   Sept. 1950

YEAR of Discovery Opens in Antarctica. By David S. Boyer. 339-381,
   Sept. 1957

A **YEAR** of Widening Horizons: The
   President's Message to Members. By
   Melville Bell Grosvenor. 888-906,
   Dec. 1962

The **YEAR** the Weather Went Wild. By
   Thomas Y. Canby. 799-829,
   Dec. 1977

YELLOW (River), China:

Taming "Flood Dragons" Along
   China's Hwang Ho. By Oliver J.
   Todd. 205-234, *Feb. 1942*
Raft Life on the Hwang Ho. By W.
   Robert Moore. 743-752, *June 1932*
Shantung–China's Holy Land. By
   Charles K. Edmunds. 231-252,
   Sept. 1919

YELLOW FEVER:

Mosquitoes, the Mighty Killers. By
   Lewis T. Nielsen. 427-440, *Sept. 1979*
Exploring Ancient Panama by Helicop-
   ter. By Matthew W. Stirling. Photos
   by Richard H. Stewart. NGS re-
   search grant. 227-246, *Feb. 1950*
Keeping House for a Biologist in Co-
   lombia. By Nancy Bell Fairchild
   Bates. Photos by Marston Bates. 251-
   274, *Aug. 1948*
Map-Changing Medicine. By William
   Joseph Showalter. 303-330,
   Sept. 1922
Economic Loss to the People of the
   United States Through Insects That
   Carry Disease. By L. O. Howard.
   735-749, *Aug. 1909*

YELLOW SEA Yields Shipwreck
   Trove. Photos by H. Edward Kim.
   Introduction by Donald H. Keith.
   231-243, *Aug. 1979*

*Tired trekker, the photographer's son, Dean, nods off in a warm bath after a pack trip to
the headwaters of the Yellowstone River in Wyoming's Absaroka Range.* DEAN KRAKEL II

YELLOWSTONE (River), Wyoming-Montana-North Dakota:

The Untamed Yellowstone. By Bill Richards. Photos by Dean Krakel II. 257-278, *Aug. 1981*

Trailing History Down the Big Muddy: In the Homeward Wake of Lewis and Clark, a Folding Steel Skiff Bears Its Lone Pilot on a 2,000-Mile Cruise on the Yellowstone-Missouri. By Lewis R. Freeman. 73-120, *July 1928*

YELLOWSTONE NATIONAL PARK, Wyoming-Montana-Idaho:

Winterkeeping in Yellowstone. By R. Steven Fuller. 829-857, *Dec. 1978*

The "Lone" Coyote Likes Family Life. By Hope Ryden. Photos by author and David Hiser. 278-294, *Aug. 1974*

Studying Wildlife by Satellite. By Frank Craighead, Jr., and John Craighead. NGS research grant. 120-123, *Jan. 1973*

Yellowstone's Hundredth Birthday: A Four-part Report. 579-637. I. A Walk Through the Wilderness. By Karen and Derek Craighead. Photos by Sam Abell. 579-603; II. Ageless Splendors of Our Oldest Park. 604-615; III. The Pitfalls of Success. By William S. Ellis. 616-631; IV. The Next 100 Years: A Master Plan for Yellowstone. By George B. Hartzog, Jr. 632-637, *May 1972*

Yellowstone Wildlife in Winter. By William Albert Allard. 637-661, *Nov. 1967*

◼ Grizzly! 639A-639B, *Nov. 1967*

Trailing Yellowstone's Grizzlies by Radio. By Frank Craighead, Jr., and John Craighead. NGS research grant. 252-267, *Aug. 1966*

Wyoming: High, Wide, and Windy. By David S. Boyer. 554-594, *Apr. 1966*

Knocking Out Grizzly Bears for Their Own Good. By Frank and John Craighead. NGS research grant. 276-291, *Aug. 1960*

The Night the Mountains Moved. By Samuel W. Matthews. Photos by J. Baylor Roberts. 329-359, *Mar. 1960*

Springtime Comes to Yellowstone National Park. By Paul A. Zahl. 761-779, *Dec. 1956*

The West Through Boston Eyes. By Stewart Anderson. 733-776, *June 1949*

Fabulous Yellowstone: Even Stranger Than the Tales of Early Trappers is the Truth About This Steaming Wonderland. By Frederick G. Vosburgh. 769-794, *June 1940*

The Land of the Best. By Gilbert H. Grosvenor. 327-430, *Apr. 1916*

Wild Animals That Took Their Own Pictures by Day and by Night. By George Shiras, 3d. 763-834, *July 1913*

Our National Parks. By L. F. Schmeckebier. 531-579, *June 1912*

YEMEN:

Arabia's Frankincense Trail. By Thomas J. Abercrombie. Photos by Lynn Abercrombie. 474-513, *Oct. 1985*

Along the Storied Incense Roads of

Climbers ascend 2,000-foot Half Dome in Yosemite National Park, using aluminum wedges and nuts instead of hammering steel pitons that deface the rock. GALEN ROWELL

Aden. By Hermann F. Eilts. Photos by Brian Brake. 230-254, *Feb. 1957*

Sailing with Sindbad's Sons. By Alan Villiers. 675-688, *Nov. 1948*

The Rock of Aden: The Volcanic Mountain Fortress, on the Sea Route from Suez to India, Assumes New Importance. By H.G.C. Swayne. 723-742, *Dec. 1935*

Into Burning Hadhramaut: The Arab Land of Frankincense and Myrrh, Ever a Lodestone of Western Exploration. By D. van der Meulen. 387-429, *Oct. 1932*

"The Flower of Paradise": The Part Which Khat Plays in the Life of the Yemen Arab. By Charles Moser. 173-186, *Aug. 1917*

Arabia, the Desert of the Sea. By Archibald Forder. 1039-1062, 1117, *Dec. 1909*

See also Yemen Arab Republic

YEMEN, People's Democratic Republic of (Southern Yemen):

Arabia's Frankincense Trail. By Thomas J. Abercrombie. Photos by Lynn Abercrombie. 474-513, *Oct. 1985*

YEMEN ARAB REPUBLIC (North Yemen):

Arabia's Frankincense Trail. By Thomas J. Abercrombie. Photos by Lynn Abercrombie. 474-513, *Oct. 1985*

North Yemen. By Noel Grove. Photos by Steve Raymer. 244-269, *Aug. 1979*

Behind the Veil of Troubled Yemen. By Thomas J. Abercrombie. 403-445, *Mar. 1964*

Yemen Opens the Door to Progress. By Harry Hoogstraal. 213-244, *Feb. 1952*

Yemen–Southern Arabia's Mountain Wonderland. 631-672. By Harlan B. Clark. Included: Ancient "Skyscrapers" of the Yemen. Photos by Richard H. Sanger. 645-668, *Nov. 1947*

YEN, HARRY S. C.:

Nomination Page. *Mar. 1973*

Photographer

The Fragile Beauty All About Us. 785-795, *Dec. 1970*

YEN TANG SHAN (Yandang Shan), Chekiang Province, China:

China's Wonderland–Yen Tang Shan. Photos by Herbert Clarence White, Clarence C. Crisler, Deng Bao-ling, and Hwang Yao-tso. 687-694, *Dec. 1937*

YEREVAN, Armenian S.S.R., U.S.S.R.:

The Proud Armenians. By Robert Paul Jordan. Photos by Harry N. Naltchayan. 846-873, *June 1978*

YESTERDAY Lingers Along the Connecticut. By Charles McCarry. Photos by David L. Arnold. 334-369, *Sept. 1972*

YESTERDAY Lingers on Lake Erie's Bass Islands. By Terry and Lyntha Eiler. 86-101, *July 1978*

YESTERDAY'S Congo, Today's Zaire. By John J. Putman. Photos by Eliot Elisofon. 398-432, *Mar. 1973*

YEZDIKHAST (Yazd-e Khvast), Iran:

Persian Caravan Sketches: The Land of the Lion and the Sun as Seen on a Summer Caravan Trip. By Harold F. Weston. 417-468, *Apr. 1921*

YEZIDI:

Mountain Tribes of Iran and Iraq. By Harold Lamb. 385-408, *Mar. 1946*

The **YIELD** of Texas. By Frederick Simpich. 163-184, *Feb. 1945*

YLLA (Camilla Koffler): *Photographer*

Mysore Celebrates the Death of a Demon. By Luc Bouchage. 706-711, *May 1958*

Y
Z

Silhouetted on a wooden bridge, a worker returns from a strenuous day in the rice fields, a hand-tinted image from "Young Japan," July 1914. ELIZA R. SCIDMORE

Ranch hand Moses Sibanda is among the 7.2 million blacks who began to govern themselves in 1980 after Rhodesia was renamed Zimbabwe. JAMES L. STANFIELD, NGS

ZAANDAM, The Netherlands:
Glimpses of Holland. By William Wisner Chapin. 1-29, *Jan. 1915*

ZACATECAS (State), Mexico:
A Mexican Hacienda. By J. E. Kirkwood. 563-584, *May 1914*

ZACHMANN, PATRICK: *Photographer*
China: Back from the Brink. By Paul R. and Anne H. Ehrlich. 922-925, *Dec. 1988*

ZADAR, Yugoslavia. *See* Zara

ZAGREB, Yugoslavia:
Yugoslavia: Six Republics in One. By Robert Paul Jordan. Photos by James P. Blair. 589-633, *May 1970*
Yugoslavia, Between East and West. By George W. Long. Photos by Volkmar Wentzel. 141-172, *Feb. 1951*

ZAHL, PAUL A.:
Nomination Page. *Apr. 1971*
Nomination Page. *Sept. 1964*
Nomination Page. *Mar. 1963*
Nomination Page. In the Amazon. *Oct. 1957*
Author-Photographer
Australia's Bizarre Wild Flowers. 858-868, *Dec. 1976*
Hidden Worlds in the Heart of a Plant. 389-397, *Mar. 1975*
Algae: the Life-givers. 361-377, *Mar. 1974*
One Strange Night on Turtle Beach. 570-581, *Oct. 1973*
Nature's Living, Jumping Jewels. 130-146, *July 1973*
Those Outlandish Goldfish! 514-533, *Apr. 1973*
The Shadowy World of Salamanders. 104-117, *July 1972*
Portrait of a Fierce and Fragile Land. 303-314, *Mar. 1972*

What's So Special About Spiders? 190-219, *Aug. 1971*
Nature's Night Lights: Probing the Secrets of Bioluminescence. 45-69, *July 1971*
Seeking the Truth About the Feared Piranha. 715-733, *Nov. 1970*
The Magic Lure of Sea Shells. Photos by Victor R. Boswell, Jr. and author. 386-429, *Mar. 1969*
Nature's Year in Pleasant Valley. 488-525, *Apr. 1968*
Scorpions: Living Fossils of the Sands. 436-442, *Mar. 1968*
New Scarlet Bird in Florida Skies. 874-882, *Dec. 1967*
Life in a "Dead" Sea–Great Salt Lake. 252-263, *Aug. 1967*
In Quest of the World's Largest Frog. 146-152, *July 1967*
Bizarre World of the Fungi. 502-527, *Oct. 1965*
Finding the Mt. Everest of All Living Things. 10-51, *July 1964*
Malaysia's Giant Flowers and Insect-trapping Plants. 680-701, *May 1964*
Fluorescent Gems From Davy Jones's Locker. 260-271, *Aug. 1963*
Mystery of the Monarch Butterfly. 588-598, *Apr. 1963*
Wing-borne Lamps of the Summer Night. 48-59, *July 1962*
Mountains of the Moon. 412-434, *Mar. 1962*
Oregon's Sidewalk on the Sea. 708-734, *Nov. 1961*
Plants That Eat Insects. 643-659, *May 1961*
How the Sun Gives Life to the Sea. 199-225, *Feb. 1961*
Sailing a Sea of Fire. 120-129, *July 1960*
Face to Face With Gorillas in Central Africa. 114-137, *Jan. 1960*
Unsung Beauties of Hawaii's Coral Reefs. 510-525, *Oct. 1959*

Volcanic Fires of the 50th State: Hawaii National Park. 793-823, *June 1959*
Giant Insects of the Amazon. 632-669, *May 1959*
Little Horses of the Sea. 131-153, *Jan. 1959*
Hatchetfish, Torchbearers of the Deep. 713-714, *May 1958*
The Giant Tides of Fundy. 153-192, *Aug. 1957*
On Australia's Coral Ramparts. 1-48, *Jan. 1957*
Springtime Comes to Yellowstone National Park. 761-779, *Dec. 1956*
Honey Eaters of Currumbin. 510-519, *Oct. 1956*
In the Gardens of Olympus. 85-123, *July 1955*
Glass Menageries of the Sea. 797-822, *June 1955*
In the Wilds of a City Parlor. 645-672, *Nov. 1954*
Night Life in the Gulf Stream. 391-418, *Mar. 1954*
Fishing in the Whirlpool of Charybdis. 579-618, *Nov. 1953*
Exotic Birds in Manhattan's Bowery. 77-98, *Jan. 1953*
Back-yard Monsters in Color. 235-260, *Aug. 1952*
Man-of-war Fleet Attacks Bimini. 185-212, *Feb. 1952*
Flamingos' Last Stand on Andros Island. 635-652, *May 1951*
Search for the Scarlet Ibis in Venezuela. 633-661, *May 1950*
The Pink Birds of Texas. 641-654, *Nov. 1949*
Photographer
Slime Mold: The Fungus That Walks. By Douglas Lee. 131-136, *July 1981*
Dragons of the Deep. 838-845, *June 1978*
The Four-eyed Fish Sees All. Text by Thomas O'Neill. 390-395, *Mar. 1978*
Amber: Golden Window on the Past. Text by Thomas J. O'Neill. 423-435, *Sept. 1977*
"Snowflake," the World's First White Gorilla. By Arthur J. Riopelle. 443-448, *Mar. 1967*

ZAIRE, Republic of:
Tropical Rain Forests: Nature's Dwindling Treasures. By Peter T. White. Photos by James P. Blair. Paintings by Barron Storey. 2-47, *Jan. 1983*
The Imperiled Mountain Gorilla. By Dian Fossey. 501-523. Included: Death of Marchessa. Photos by Peter G. Veit. NGS research grant. 508-511, *Apr. 1981*
Yesterday's Congo, Today's Zaire. By John J. Putman. Photos by Eliot Elisofon. 398-432, *Mar. 1973*
See also Virunga Mountains; *and* former names, Belgian Congo; Congo, Democratic Republic of the

ZAIRE (River). *See* Congo (River)

ZAMBEZI (River), Africa:
The Wonders of the Mosi-oa-Tunga: The Falls of the Zambesi. By Louis Livingston Seaman. 561-571, *June 1911*
Impressions and Scenes of

Mozambique. By O. W. Barrett. 807-830, *Oct. 1910*

ZAMBIA:
Tsetse–Fly of the Deadly Sleep. By Georg Gerster. 814-833, *Dec. 1986*

ZANGBO-BRAHMAPUTRA (River). *See* Brahmaputra (River)

ZANTE (Island), Greece:
Homeward With Ulysses. By Melville Bell Grosvenor. Photos by Edwin Stuart Grosvenor. 1-39, *July 1973*

ZANZIBAR, Tanzania:
Tanzania Marches to Its Own Drum. By Peter T. White. Photos by Emory Kristof. 474-509, *Apr. 1975*
Safari from Congo to Cairo. By Elsie May Bell Grosvenor. Photos by Gilbert Grosvenor. 721-771, *Dec. 1954*
Clove-scented Zanzibar. By W. Robert Moore. 261-278, *Feb. 1952*
Yankee Roams the Orient. By Irving and Electa Johnson. 327-370, *Mar. 1951*
Zanzibar. By Mrs. Harris R. Childs. 810-824, *Aug. 1912*

ZAPOTEC INDIANS:
Monte Albán, Richest Archeological Find in America: A Tomb in Oaxaca, Mexico, Yields Treasures Which Reveal the Splendid Culture of the Mixtecs. By Alfonso Caso. 487-512, *Oct. 1932*
Among the Zapotecs of Mexico: A Visit to the Indians of Oaxaca, Home State of the Republic's Great Liberator, Juarez, and Its Most Famous Ruler, Diaz. By Herbert Corey. 501-553, *May 1927*
The Isthmus of Tehuantepec: "The Bridge of the World's Commerce." By Helen Olsson-Seffer. 991-1002, *Dec. 1910*
Hewers of Stone (Mitla, Mexico). By Jeremiah Zimmerman. 1002-1020, *Dec. 1910*

ZARA (Zadar), Yugoslavia:
East of the Adriatic: Notes on Dalmatia, Montenegro, Bosnia, and Herzegovina. By Kenneth McKenzie. 1159-1187, 1284, *Dec. 1912*

ZEELAND (Province), The Netherlands:
The City of Jacqueline (Goes, The Netherlands). By Florence Craig Albrecht. 29-56, *Jan. 1915*
See also Walcheren (Island)

ZELENY, LAWRENCE: *Author*
Song of Hope for the Bluebird. Photos by Michael L. Smith. 855-865, *June 1977*

ZEN BUDDHISM:
Kyoto and Nara: Keepers of Japan's Past. By Charles McCarry. Photos by George F. Mobley. Included: Kyoto Says Happy New Year. 836-859, *June 1976*

ZENZINOV, VLADIMIR M.: *Author*
With an Exile in Arctic Siberia: The Narrative of a Russian Who Was

Compelled to Turn Polar Explorer for Two Years. 695-718, *Dec. 1924*

ZEUSLER, F. A.: *Author*
Standing Iceberg Guard in the North Atlantic: International Patrol Safeguards the Lives of Thousands of Travelers and Protects TransAtlantic Liners from a "Titanic" Fate. 1-28, *July 1926*

ZHEJIANG PROVINCE (now Chekiang), China:
Operation Eclipse: 1948. By William A. Kinney. NGS research grant. 325-372, *Mar. 1949*
China's Wonderland–Yen Tang Shan. Photos by Herbert Clarence White, Clarence C. Crisler, Deng Bao-ling, and Hwang Yao-tso. 687-694, *Dec. 1937*

ZHUHAI SPECIAL ECONOMIC ZONE, China:
China's Opening Door. By John J. Putman. Photos by H. Edward Kim. 64-83, *July 1983*

ZICH, ARTHUR: *Author*
Hope and Danger in the Philippines. Photos by Steve McCurry. 76-117, *July 1986*
Japanese Americans: Home at Last. Photos by Michael S. Yamashita. 512-539, *Apr. 1986*

ZIEGLER, WILLIAM:
Polar Photography. By Anthony Fiala. 140-142, *Feb. 1907*
Fighting the Polar Ice. 72-77, *Jan. 1907*
The Annual Dinner of the National Geography Society. 32-36, *Jan. 1906*
The Ziegler Polar Expedition. 439-440, *Sept. 1905*
Biography of William Ziegler. 355-357, *July 1905*
The Ziegler Polar Expedition. 198, *Apr. 1905*
Ziegler Polar Expedition. 427-428, *Oct. 1904*
The Ziegler Polar Expedition. 414-417, *Nov. 1903*
Mr. Ziegler and the National Geographic Society. 251-254, *June 1903*
The Baldwin-Ziegler Arctic Expedition. 358-359, *Sept. 1902*

ZIGONG, Sichuan Province, China. *See* former designation, Tzeliutsing

ZIGZAGGING Across Sicily. By Melville Chater. 303-352, *Sept. 1924*

ZIMBABWE:
Tsetse–Fly of the Deadly Sleep. By Georg Gerster. 814-833, *Dec. 1986*
Editorial. By Wilbur E. Garrett. 567, *Nov. 1981*
After Rhodesia, a Nation Named Zimbabwe. By Charles E. Cobb, Jr. Photos by James L. Stanfield and LeRoy Woodson, Jr. 616-651, *Nov. 1981*
See also former name, Rhodesia

ZIMBABWE (Ruins), Zimbabwe:
Safari Through Changing Africa. By Elsie May Bell Grosvenor. Photos by Gilbert Grosvenor. 145-198, *Aug. 1953*

Rhodesia, Hobby and Hope of Cecil Rhodes. By W. Robert Moore. 281-306, *Sept. 1944*

ZIMMERMAN, JEREMIAH: *Author*
Hewers of Stone (Mitla, Mexico). 1002-1020, *Dec. 1910*

ZINJANTHROPUS:
Preserving the Treasures of Olduvai Gorge. By Melvin M. Payne. Photos by Joseph J. Scherschel. NGS research grant. 701-709, *Nov. 1966*
Finding the World's Earliest Man. By L.S.B. Leakey. Photos by Des Bartlett. NGS research grant. 420-435, *Sept. 1960*
See also Australopithecines

ZION NATIONAL PARK, Utah:
Amid the Mighty Walls of Zion. By Lewis F. Clark. 37-70, *Jan. 1954*
Bursts of Color in Sculptured Utah. 593-616, *May 1936*
Photographing the Marvels of the West in Colors. By Fred Payne Clatworthy. 694-719, *June 1928*

ZISKIN, JOEL F.:
Nomination Page. In Nepal. *Apr. 1977*
Author-Photographer
Trek to Nepal's Sacred Crystal Mountain. 500-517, *Apr. 1977*

ZON, RAPHAEL: *Author*
When Our Country Is Fifty Years Older. 573-580, *June 1909*

ZOOS:
President's Page. By Gilbert M. Grosvenor. *June 1986*
■■ *Zoos Without Cages.* By Judith E. Rinard. Juvenile. 104 pages. *1981*
What's Black and White and Loved All Over? By Theodore H. Reed. Photos by Donna K. Grosvenor. Contents: Giant pandas at the National Zoological Park, Washington, D. C. 803-815, *Dec. 1972*
Growing Up With Snowflake. By Arthur J. Riopelle. Photos by Michael Kuh. Contents: Albino gorilla at zoo in Barcelona, Spain. NGS research grant. 491-503, *Oct. 1970*
■ Zoos of the World. 503A-503B, *Oct. 1970*
Jambo–First Gorilla Raised by Its Mother in Captivity. By Ernst M. Lang. Photos by Paul Steinemann. Included: The Zoological Gardens of Basel, Switzerland. 446-453, *Mar. 1964*
Enchantress! By Theodore H. Reed. Photos by Thomas J. Abercrombie. Included: Albino tigress at the National Zoological Park, Washington, D. C. 628-641, *May 1961*
The Wild Animals in My Life. By William M. Mann. Included: Establishment and growth of the National Zoological Park, Washington, D. C. 497-524, *Apr. 1957*
Zoo Animals Go to School. By Marion P. McCrane. Photos by W. E. Garrett. Contents: Animals from New York Zoological Park (Bronx Zoo). 694-706, *Nov. 1956*
Portraits of My Monkey Friends. By Ernest P. Walker. Included: Primates at

the National Zoological Park, Washington, D. C. 105-119, *Jan. 1956*

The Ape with Friends in Washington. By Margaretta Burr Wells. Included: The National Zoological Park, Washington, D. C. 61-74, *July 1953*

London's Zoo of Zoos. By Thomas Garner James. Included: Regent's Park; Whipsnade. 771-786, *June 1953*

Biggest Worm Farm Caters to Platypuses. By W. H. Nicholas. Note: Bronx zookeepers (New York Zoological Park) learned to raise 25,000 worms needed as food each month. 269-280, *Feb. 1949*

See also Animal Orphanage; Animal Safari

ZOQUE INDIANS:

Finding Jewels of Jade in a Mexican Swamp. By Matthew W. and Marion Stirling. 635-661, *Nov. 1942*

The Isthmus of Tehuantepec: "The Bridge of the World's Commerce." By Helen Olsson-Seffer. 991-1002, *Dec. 1910*

ZOROASTRIANISM:

The Parsees and the Towers of Silence at Bombay, India. By William Thomas Fee. 529-554, *Dec. 1905*

ZOTZIL INDIANS:

Finding Jewels of Jade in a Mexican Swamp. By Matthew W. and Marion Stirling. 635-661, *Nov. 1942*

ZUIDER ZEE (now IJsselmeer), The Netherlands:

A New Country Awaits Discovery: The Draining of the Zuider Zee Makes Room for the Excess Population of the Netherlands. By J.C.M. Kruisinga. 293-320, *Sept. 1933*

Glimpses of Holland. By William Wisner Chapin. 1-29, *Jan. 1915*

ZULULAND (Region), Natal, Republic of South Africa:

The Zulus: Black Nation in a Land of Apartheid. By Joseph Judge. Photos by Dick Durrance II. 738-775, *Dec. 1971*

Safari Through Changing Africa. By Elsie May Bell Grosvenor. Photos by Gilbert Grosvenor. 145-198, *Aug. 1953*

Roaming Africa's Unfenced Zoos. By W. Robert Moore. 353-380, *Mar. 1950*

Natal: The Garden Province. By Melville Chater. 447-478, *Apr. 1931*

Natal: The Garden Colony. By Russell Hastings Millward. 278-291, *Mar. 1909*

ZULUS:

Zulu King Weds a Swazi Princess. By Volkmar Wentzel. 47-61, *Jan. 1978*

The Zulus: Black Nation in a Land of Apartheid. By Joseph Judge. Photos by Dick Durrance II. 738-775, *Dec. 1971*

The Diamond Mines of South Africa. By Gardiner F. Williams. 344-356, *June 1906*

See also Zululand

ZUMBACH, EARL:

The Family Farm Ain't What It Used to Be. By James A. Sugar. 391-411, *Sept. 1974*

ZUMBRO, W. M.: *Author*

Religious Penances and Punishments Self-Inflicted by the Holy Men of India. 1257-1314, *Dec. 1913*

Photographer

The Temples of India. 922-971, *Nov. 1909*

ZUNI INDIANS:

Indian Tribes of Pueblo Land. By Matthew W. Stirling. Paintings by W. Langdon Kihn. 549-596, *Nov. 1940*

Everyday Life in Pueblo Bonito: As Disclosed by the National Geographic Society's Archeologic Explorations in the Chaco Canyon National Monument, New Mexico. By Neil M. Judd. 227-262, *Sept. 1925*

ZÜRICH, Switzerland:

Switzerland, Europe's High-rise Republic. By Thomas J. Abercrombie. 68-113, *July 1969*

ZWELITHINI, GOODWILL, King of the Zulus:

Zulu King Weds a Swazi Princess. By Volkmar Wentzel. 47-61, *Jan. 1978*

ZWEMER, S. M.: *Author*

Mecca the Mystic: A New Kingdom Within Arabia. 157-172, *Aug. 1917*

Notes on Oman. 89-98, *Jan. 1911*

ZWINGLE, ERLA: *Author*

Atlanta: Energy and Optimism in the New South. Photos by Jim Richardson. 3-29, *July 1988*

"Doc" Edgerton–The Man Who Made Time Stand Still. Photos by Harold E. Edgerton and Bruce Dale. 464-483, *Oct. 1987*

New York Harbor–The Golden Door. Photos by Bruce Davidson. 21-43, *July 1986*

The Tea and Sugar Lifeline in Australia's Outback. Photos by William Albert Allard. 737-757, *June 1986*

Descendant of fierce warriors, a Zulu youth strumming his guitar strolls the grassy hills of Zululand, a region of the Republic of South Africa. DICK DURRANCE II

Scientific Research and Exploration

By MELVIN M. PAYNE   CHAIRMAN, COMMITTEE FOR RESEARCH AND EXPLORATION

I N ITS CENTENNIAL YEAR the National Geographic Society celebrated its substantial contribution to uncovering new knowledge through ever expanding investment in scientific research. When the Society's 10,500,000 members open their monthly NATIONAL GEOGRAPHIC magazines, they enjoy the principal benefit of membership. Many will note that certain articles—undersea discoveries, archaeological investigations, and natural history examinations, for example—carry a note saying "a research project supported in part by your Society." This is a reminder that members can take pride in the contribution that their dues make to supporting these as well as the many other Society research efforts not reported in the GEOGRAPHIC.

Since 1890 the Society has backed worldwide explorations and has supported basic research related to geography. Through its Committee for Research and Exploration, the Society has made close to 4,000 grants to assist the efforts of scholars and scientists around the world in increasing knowledge of our planet, its environment, and its inhabitants, from the tiniest mite to the most exalted achievements of humankind—and even of the cosmos beyond. In the past ten years funds allocated to research have exceeded the total amount spent in the prior 88 years. In 1988 alone 260 grants were made with a total budget of about six million dollars, a figure that exceeded the 1983 budget by nearly three million dollars.

Time and again this support has yielded important, even spectacular, finds. In Peru recent excavations at a site of the pre-Inca Moche people uncovered the richest cache of pre-Columbian artifacts ever scientifically excavated in the Americas. Principal investigator Walter Alva, with Christopher B. Donnan, brought to light some of the most finely crafted goldwork yet found in the New World—an archaeological discovery among the most astonishing in the modern era.

Across the world in Kenya, Alan Walker of Johns Hopkins University found jaws of an apelike creature that lived 17 million years ago—possibly a common ancestor of human beings and all the great apes. Team member Kamoya Kimeu came upon a remarkably complete 1.6-million-year-old skeleton of *Homo erectus*.

The results of many Society-backed research projects appear within the pages of NATIONAL GEOGRAPHIC RESEARCH, a scientific quarterly launched in 1985 that features Society-funded studies but

Forging a bond with an endangered species, Dian Fossey picks leaves that she chewed like a mountain gorilla to reassure an onlooker. For more than a decade this extraordinary woman was supported by the Society's Committee for Research and Exploration. Research grants also aid the search for the past. A thousand-year-old jar rises from a natural well at Dzibilchaltún, a Maya city explored by E. Wyllys Andrews IV of Tulane University.

ALAN ROOT (OPPOSITE); LUIS MARDEN, NGS

Bold steps leading to nearly 4,000 grants began in 1890 with the Society's first expedition. Its members, standing atop an uncharted moraine (above), made a landmark survey of North America's highest range, the St. Elias Mountains on the Alaska-Canada border.

Society-supported research now plumbs the depths of the sea, where marine zoologist Eugenie Clark has studied deepwater sharks. Here, at 150 feet, she attempts to cut free a tangle of sixgill sharks and a gummy shark hooked on the same longline.

ISRAEL C. RUSSELL, U.S. GEOLOGICAL SURVEY, (ABOVE); EMORY KRISTOF, NGS

welcomes contributions from independent scholars and scientists. RESEARCH immediately took its place as an authoritative peer in the world of scientific publications. The highest quality drawings, charts, maps, and color photographs enliven each issue.*

In 1988, as part of its centennial celebration, the Society convened a symposium sponsored by the Committee for Research and Exploration at which 22 international experts recounted advances in science, technology, and exploration over the past century. Their primary emphasis, however, struck at concerns for the future—concerns that demand solutions if humanity is to maintain and improve its quality of life. The symposium focused on major issues that affect the future of air and water quality, land availability, forest conservation, environmental stability, and the protection of biological diversity.†

Here follow, under 42 category headings, summaries of the research projects. Even a casual glance at this body of work must impress the reader with the breadth and variety of findings made possible by member support of their Society's research objectives.

*A subscription to NATIONAL GEOGRAPHIC RESEARCH is $40 for one year; Canada $58; all other countries $66 airmail, $46 surface. Remit to National Geographic Society, P.O. Box 1111, Washington, D. C. 20013-9990.

†The symposium proceedings, published as *Earth '88: Changing Geographic Perspectives,* are available for $20 from National Geographic Society, P.O. Box 1640, Washington, D. C. 20077-9952.

Aeronautics and Atmospheric Science

Capts. Albert W. Stevens and Orvil A. Anderson soared in Explorer II *to a record 72,395 feet in 1935.* RICHARD H. STEWART, NGS

Air-quality measurement device: development. John S. Hall. 1974
Atmospheric pollution. Beijing, China. Edward D. Goldberg. 1986
Da Vinci–Trans-America Manned Scientific Balloon Flight. Rudolf J. Engelmann. 1973
Explorer I (balloon). William E. Kepner, Albert W. Stevens, and Orvil A. Anderson. 1934
Explorer II (balloon): altitude record. Albert W. Stevens and Orvil A. Anderson. 1935
Pollution: basic standards of air quality from telephotometer measurements. John S. Hall. 1977
Stratosphere sampling. Bismarck, North Dakota. National Bureau of Standards. 1940-41

Anthropology

ARCHAEOLOGY

General

Dating archaeological ceramics: electron spin resonance spectroscopy. Thomas J. Riley. 1978
Fire: man's use to shape earths and metals. Theodore A. Wertime. 1968, 1970, 1972

North America

Adaptation under stress: archaeology of the altithermal period. Texas. David J. Meltzer. 1987-88
Agate Basin: ancient Indian camp. Wyoming. Frank H. H. Roberts and William M. Bass. 1959, 1961
Aleutian Islands: protohistoric settlement patterns. Unalaska Island. Jean Aigner and Lydia Black. 1988
American Southwest: bat cave and early agriculture. Richard I. Ford and John D. Speth. 1982
—— emergence of agricultural communities. New Mexico. Wirt H. Wills. 1988
Anasazi: rock-shelter survey. Tsegi Canyon, Arizona. Jonathan Haas. 1986
Arizona, central: prehistoric human adaptation in an environmental transition zone. George J. Gumerman. 1973
Avalon: 17th-century English colony. Newfoundland. James A. Tuck. 1986
Baffin Island. Northwest Territories, Canada. Lorna M. McKenzie-Pollock. 1968-69
Barker Creek Village: high-altitude desert ecology. Nevada. David H. Thomas. 1981
Basket Maker occupation. Upper Grand Gulch, Utah. William D.

Lipe. 1968-69
Basque whaling stations, 16th-century. Labrador. James A. Tuck. 1978
Baucom site: Paleo-Indian geoarchaeology. North Carolina. Albert C. Goodyear and C. Vance Haynes. 1987
Bering Strait. Alaska. Henry B. Collins. 1936
Bison-kill site: Jones-Miller Paleo-Indian. Colorado. Dennis J. Stanford. 1973-76
Blackwater Draw site. New Mexico. Dennis J. Stanford. 1983-84
Boland site. New York. Vincas P. Steponaitis. 1987
Bourbon Field site. Georgia. Morgan Ray Crook, Jr. 1980
Carter's Grove site. Virginia. Ivor Noël Hume. 1976-78
Chaco Canyon: Holocene paleoecology. New Mexico. Paul S. Martin. 1981
—— remote-sensing analysis of prehistoric human occupations. Thomas R. Lyons. 1973
Chinese gold-mining camp, 19th-century. Pierce, Idaho. Roderick Sprague. 1985
Donner Party camp: the Murphy's Cabin Project. California. Donald L. Hardesty. 1984
Dorset Eskimo sites. Southampton Island, Hudson Bay. Henry B. Collins. 1954
Dry Creek, central Alaska. William R. Powers. 1976
Engelbert site: Indian burials. Nichols, New York. William D. Lipe. 1968
Environmental archaeology and cultural systems. Hamilton Inlet, Labrador. William W. Fitzhugh. 1971-72
Exploration of Early Human Sites in Alaska Project. National Park Service. 1976
Finger Lakes region. New York. Marian E. White. 1975
Fletcher site. Michigan. William A. Lovis. 1987
Four Corners: pre-Columbian towers. Colorado and Utah. Ray A. Williamson and Florence H. Ellis. 1977
Fox Islands: faunal remains. Penobscot Bay, Maine. Bruce J. Bourque. 1978
Gatecliff Shelter. Nevada. David H. Thomas. 1975-76
Glyph caves: cultural associations of mud glyphs and petroglyphs. Tennessee, Virginia, and West Virginia. Charles H. Faulkner. 1984
Grand Canyon: North Rim. Arizona. Douglas W. Schwartz. 1968-71
Grasshopper Pueblo: habitat. Arizona. William A. Longacre. 1974
Hell Gap site. Wyoming. Cynthia and Henry T. Irwin and George A. Agogino. 1962-66
Hirundo site. Maine. David Sanger. 1972-73, 1975
Hontoon Island: identification of woods from a wet site. Florida. Barbara A. Purdy. 1982-83
Indian farming community, 13th-century. Ohio. C. Wesley Cowan. 1986
Jeffrey-Harris Rock-shelter. Virginia. Charles W. McNett, Jr. 1978
Kagati Lake: Southwestern Alaska. Robert E. Ackerman. 1979

In the New Mexico sun, thousand-year-old ruins of Pueblo Bonito, built by the Anasazi, lie in Chaco Canyon. DAVID L. BRILL

Katmai National Monument: ancient Aleut and Eskimo site. Alaska. Don E. Dumond. 1967-68

Kimmswick: Clovis adaptations in the Midwest. Missouri. Russell W. Graham. 1980

King site. Floyd County, Georgia. David J. Hally. 1973

Kuskokwim region. Alaska. Robert E. Ackerman. 1978, 1981-82

Lac Labelle site. Michigan. Patrick E. Martin. 1988

Lahonton Lake. Nevada. Phil C. Orr. 1957

Lange-Ferguson site: a Clovis locality. South Dakota. Lucien A. Hannus. 1984

Larsen site. South Dakota. William M. Bass. 1970

Lehner Paleo-Indian site. San Pedro Valley, Arizona. C. Vance Haynes and Emil W. Haury. 1973, 1975

Manis Mastodon Archaeological Project. Washington. Carl E. Gustafson. 1979

Meadowcroft Rock-shelter and Cross Creek drainage. Pennsylvania. James M. Adovasio. 1976-77, 1984

Mill Iron site: Goshen Paleo-Indian cultural complex. Montana. George C. Frison. 1986-87

Mimbres Mogollon. New Mexico. Harry J. Shafer. 1978

——— social stratification. New Mexico. Harry J. Shafer. 1987

Mississippi, southwestern. Stephen Williams. 1970, 1972

Mississippi Valley: protohistoric and early 18th-century period. Jeffrey P. Brain. 1974

Modoc Rock-shelter: Late archaic component. Illinois. Steven R. Ahler. 1987

Mohawk Valley Project. Oak Hill, New York. Dean R. Snow. 1983, 1985

Morgan site: mound complex. Louisiana. Stephen Williams. 1986

Mount Jasper mine. New Hampshire. Richard M. Gramly. 1979

Mummy Cave. Wyoming. Harold McCracken. 1965

Natchez Indians. Mississippi. Stephen Williams. 1981-82

Nenana complex: early human occupation. Alaska. William R. Powers. 1986

Occaneechi village: archaeological study of 1680-1710 Indian site. North Carolina. Roy S. Dickens, Jr. 1984-86

Olive Branch site: Paleo-Indian to Archaic transition. Illinois. Richard Gramly. 1988

Paleo-Indians: culture, fauna, and flora. Half-Mile Rise, Florida. S. David Webb. 1986, 1988

——— habitation area. Little Salt Spring, Florida. Carl J. Clausen. 1977

——— kill sites. Tennessee River Valley, Alabama. Gregory A. Waselkov. 1985

——— Little Salt Spring, Florida. Arthur D. Cohen. 1980

——— quarry and living sites. Shenandoah Valley, Virginia. William M. Gardner. 1970

Patuxent River: prehistoric settlement and subsistence. Maryland. Laurie C. Steponaitis. 1988

Pilcher Creek Project. Oregon. David R. Brauner. 1983

Porcupine River: Pleistocene cave deposits and alluvial sediments. Alaska. Edward J. Dixon, Jr. 1979-81

Post-Hopewell culture subsistence change: testing a model for. Stuart Struever. 1973

Potomac Valley: prehistoric shell middens. Gregory A. Waselkov. 1979

Potts Farm Clovis site. New York. Richard M. Gramly. 1982

Prehistoric cave art. Tennessee. Charles H. Faulkner. 1982

Pryor Mountain: environmental archaeological project. Montana. Robson Bonnichsen. 1979, 1982

Pueblo Bonito. New Mexico. Andrew Ellicott Douglass, 1923-29; Neil M. Judd, 1920-27, 1929

Puerco River Valley: resettlement of Pueblo populations. New Mexico. Cynthia Irwin-Williams. 1970-73

Richey-Roberts Clovis cache. Washington. Peter J. Mehringer. 1988

River of No Return Wilderness: prehistoric archaeology. Idaho. Frank C. Leonhardy. 1984

Rock art: prehistoric caves. Nevada. Robert F. Heizer. 1975

Rocky Dell Rock-shelter: archaeology and geomorphology. Allegheny County, Pennsylvania. James M. Adovasio. 1980

Russell Cave. Jackson County, Alabama. Carl F. Miller. 1956-58

Salts Cave. Mammoth Cave National Park, Kentucky. Patty Jo Watson. 1968-69

Sand Canyon Pueblo: archaeology of a 13th-century Anasazi town. Colorado. E. Charles Adams. 1984

Sandia Cave. New Mexico. George A. Agogino. 1961

San Juan County. Utah. Neil M. Judd. 1923

Santa Elena: 16th-century Spanish occupation. Parris Island, South Carolina. Stanley A. South. 1979

——— Robert L. Stephenson. 1981

——— Stanley A. South and Robert L. Stephenson. 1982

Santa Rosa Island. California. Phil C. Orr. 1957

Shumagin Island and Alaska Peninsula prehistory. Lucille L. Johnson and Margaret A. Winslow. 1986-88

Southeastern U. S.: early human sites. South Carolina. Albert C. Goodyear. 1985

"Spanish Diggings": aboriginal flint quarries. Southeastern Wyoming. John M. Saul. 1964

Tellico Reservoir. Tennessee. Jefferson Chapman. 1976

Towers of Hovenweep National Monument. Mesa Verde, Colorado. Ray A. Williamson. 1976

Town-planning archaeology. Annapolis, Maryland. Mark P. Leone. 1985

Tunica Treasure Project. Louisiana. Jeffrey P. Brain. 1977

Turner Farm site. North Haven, Maine. Bruce J. Bourque. 1974-75

Upper Delaware Valley Early Human
Project. Charles W. McNett, Jr. 1974-76

Vail Paleo-Indian site. Oxford County, Maine. Richard M. Gramly. 1980

Viking site. L'Anse aux Meadows, Newfoundland. Helge Ingstad. 1963-65

Voyageurs: Fort Charlotte Underwater Project. Grand Portage National Monument, Minnesota. Robert C. Wheeler. 1975

——— fur-trade materials. Minnesota-Ontario border. Robert C. Wheeler. 1963-66

Walker Road early human site: paleoenvironments and sedimentary history. Alaska. Christopher F. Waythomas. 1988

Wetherill Mesa. Colorado. Douglas Osborne. 1958-63

Whalen site: early Archaic settlement. Cumberland River, Kentucky. Jack D. Nance. 1984

Windover site: analysis and preservation of perishable artifacts. Florida. Glen H. Doran. 1987

Mesoamerica and South America

Abaj Takalik. Guatemala. John A. Graham. 1975-79

Abrigo do Sol Rock-shelter. Mato Grosso, Brazil. Eurico T. Miller. 1977

Agronomy potential. Bajo de Santa Fe, Petén, Guatemala. Bruce H. Dahlin. 1975

Andean walls, Pre-Columbian: techniques for precision fitting of stone. U. S. museums and Peru. J. Lee Hollowell. 1984

Andes: cultivation. Augusto R. Cardich. 1979, 1982

——— early civilization. Pativilca, Peru. Arturo Ruiz. 1985

——— ruins. Johan G. Reinhard. 1982

——— Sicán metallurgy. Batan Grande, Peru. Izumi Shimada. 1981-83, 1985

——— Titicaca Basin. South-Central Andes. Elias J. Mujica. 1981

Archaeological reconnaissance: via satellites. Yucatán, Mexico. Edward B. Kurjack. 1985

Architectural stones and sculpture. Peru and Bolivia. Robert F. Heizer. 1963

Arenal area: settlement and volcanism. Costa Rica. Payson D. Sheets. 1983

Arenal Lake and volcano region. Costa Rica. Carlos Aguilar P. 1977

Ariari River Basin: archaeological chronology. Colombia. John P. Marwitt. 1973-74

Balankanche Cave. Chichén Itzá, Mexico. E. Wyllys Andrews IV. 1959

Balberta Project. Guatemala. Frederick J. Bove. 1984-85

Beagle Channel: early human adaptation to a marine environment. Tierra del Fuego, Argentina. Luis Abel Orquera. 1984-85

Belize, southern. Richard M. Leaventhal. 1979

Beni. Bolivia. Bernardo Dougherty. 1982

Calakmul tomb excavation. Campeche, Mexico. William Folan. 1988

Callejon de Huaylas. Peru. Richard L. Burger. 1978-79, 1982

Campeche, southeastern: hieroglyphic inscriptions and figurative art. Mexico. Ian J. A. Graham. 1977

Cardal site: polychrome friezes. Peru. Richard Burger. 1987

Cave paintings: salvage and identification. El Medano, Chile. Hans F. Niemeyer. 1984

Caves and rock-shelters: art. Chile. Calogero M. Santoro. 1983-84
—— Dominican Republic. Marcio Veloz Maggiolo. 1976

Chalcatzingo. Morelos, Mexico. David C. Grove. 1971-72

Chan Chan-Moche Valley Project. Peru. Carol J. Mackey and Michael E. Moseley. 1969-74

Chiapas: Archaic and late Postclassic research. Mexico. Barbara Voorhies. 1978, 1980, 1982, 1987

Chicama-Moche Canal Project. Peru. James S. Kus. 1968-69

Chichén Itzá. Yucatán, Mexico. Charles E. Lincoln. 1983

Chincha and Pisco Valleys: Inca Empire trade and cultural development. Peru. Edward C. Morris and Heather N. Lechtman. 1984, 1986

Chotuna and Chornancap. Peru. Christopher B. Donnan. 1981-82

Cobá Mapping Project. Quintana Roo, Mexico. George E. Stuart. 1974-75, 1978

Cochabamba Valley: archaeology survey. Bolivia. Donald L. Brockington. 1984-86, 1988

Colha: main pyramidal mound. Belize. Thomas R. Hester. 1983

Colima. Mexico. Isabel T. Kelly. 1968, 1970

Copan: hieroglyphic stairway and temple sculptures. Honduras. William L. Fash, Jr. 1986-88
—— settlement patterns. Honduras. Wendy A. Ashmore. 1988

Coxcatlán. Mexico. Richard S. MacNeish. 1971-73

Cuello site. Belize. Norman Hammond. 1978-80, 1987

Cuicuilco ruins. Mexico. Byron Cummings. 1924-25

Culebra Bay. Costa Rica. Frederick W. Lange. 1976

Cultural ecology. Mexican Gulf Coast. S. Jeffrey K. Wilkerson. 1973-75, 1977, 1979

Cupisnique culture: Caballo Muerto complex. Peru. Thomas G. Pozorski. 1973

Dzibilchaltún. Yucatán, Mexico. E. Wyllys Andrews IV. 1957-66
—— E. Wyllys Andrews V. 1978

Easter Island Statue Project. Chile. JoAnne Van Tilburg. 1988

Economic exchange: Aztec communities. Ceramics collections. Mary G. Hodge. 1987

Ecuador Indians: pre-Columbian sites. Matthew W. Stirling. 1957

Ek Balam: a northern Maya center. Yucatán, Mexico. William M. Ringle III. 1987-88

El Mirador Project. Petén, Guatemala. Bruce H. Dahlin and Ray T. Matheny. 1979, 1981-82

El Perenal and Bajabonico: archaeological survey. Dominican Republic.

Marcio E. Velozmaggiolo. 1985

Etzna: prehistoric house mounds and canals. Campeche, Mexico. Ray T. Matheny. 1974

Gold artifacts, pre-Columbian: catalog. Panama. Reina Torres de Araúz. 1971

Honduras cultural change (pre-Columbian Mesoamerican frontier). Paul F. Healy. 1975-76

Inca city of Bombon (Pumpu-tampu). Peru. Matos M. Ramiro. 1986

Inca Project: the empire's outreach to the south. Argentina. Rodolfo A. Raffino. 1984

Inca roads. Chile. Ruben F. Stehberg. 1985

Incas. Machu Picchu, Peru. Hiram Bingham. 1912, 1914-15

Isla Cerritos Project. Yucatán, Mexico. Anthony P. Andrews. 1984-85

La Mixtequilla: ceramic periods. Mexico. Barbara L. Stark. 1984

Lenca Indians: archaeology and ethnohistory. Honduras. John M. Weeks. 1987

Lucayan Indian settlements: Columbus's route. Bahamas. Charles A. Hoffman. 1986

Lurin Valley: early civilization. Peru. Richard L. Burger. 1984-85

Macal-Tipu Project. Belize. Robert R. Kautz, Grant D. Jones, and Elizabeth A. Graham. 1982, 1984

Malhada I site. Brazil. Ondemar F. Dias, Jr. 1984, 1986

Maya: Classic settlement organization and internal function. Belize. Joseph W. Ball. 1980
—— Cozumel: animal utilization. William L. Rathje. 1977
—— highlands. Guatemala. Robert J. Sharer. 1972-73
—— housing. El Salvador. Payson D. Sheets. 1979
—— search for evidence of seaborne contact with highland cultures of Mesoamerica. Nancy M. Farriss. 1974-75

Maya sculpture: cataloging remaining color. Chiapas, Yucatán, Quintana Roo, and Campeche, Mexico. Merle Greene Robertson. 1985, 1987

Maya sites. Becan, Campeche, Mexico. Prentice M. Thomas, Jr. 1972-73
—— Yucatán Peninsula, Mexico. E. Wyllys Andrews IV. 1968, 1970

Maya writing. Mexico. George E. Stuart. 1983-84

Middle American Research Institute: archaeological publications. New Orleans, Louisiana. E. Wyllys Andrews V. 1975, 1977

Monte Alto. Guatemala. Lee A. Parsons. 1968-70
—— Edwin Martin Shook. 1972

Monte Verde. Chile. Tom D. Dillehay. 1978

Morelos: Postclassic settlement and land use. Mexico. Michael E. Smith. 1988

Naj Tunich cave site: photographic documentation. Guatemala. Andrea J. Stone. 1988

Navigational aids, pre-Columbian. Yucatán coast, Mexico. Pilar Luna. 1984

Nazca culture: settlement pattern. Peru. Helaine I. Silverman. 1987

Nazca lines. Peru. Gerald S. Hawkins. 1967
—— Maria Reiche. 1974
—— geometric and astronomical order. Anthony F. Aveni. 1981

Nohmul Project. Belize. Norman Hammond. 1981-86

Oaxaca: late Formative human ecology. Río Verde Valley, Mexico. Marcus C. Winter. 1988
—— Zapotec murals. Mexico. Arthur G. Miller. 1983, 1988

Olmec sites. La Venta, Tres Zapotes, and San Lorenzo, Mexico. Philip Drucker, 1955; Robert F. Heizer, 1955, 1965-69; Matthew W. Stirling, 1938-46

Otomi: maguey utilization. Mexico. Jeffrey R. Parsons. 1984, 1986

Pacatnamu: multidisciplinary study of an ancient city. Peru. Christopher B. Donnan. 1983-87

Pachamachay Cave. Peru. Ramiro Matos. 1981

Paleo-Indian technology. South America. Clifford Evans. 1978

Panama. Matthew W. Stirling. 1948-49, 1951, 1953

Pedernales Province. Dominican Republic. Marcio E. Veloz M. 1978

Peruvian highlands: early populations. Ruth M. Shady. 1982, 1988
—— Ruth M. Shady and Hermilio Rosas. 1978

Petén savanna. Guatemala. Don S. Rice. 1978

Petexbatún Project: Maya political geography. Guatemala. Arthur A. Demarest. 1988

Port Royal. Jamaica. Edwin A. Link. 1959

Preceramic sites. Eastern Venezuela. Mario J. Sanoja. 1977, 1984
—— Cajamarca caves. Peru. Augusto Ricardo Cardich. 1987

Preclassic survey: Olmec interaction. Honduras. Robert J. Sharer. 1985

Prehistoric maize dissemination: ceramic evidence. Peru. Mary Eubanks Dunn. 1975

Querero, Los Vilos: Paleo-Indian archaeology, paleoclimate, and paleontology. Chile. Lautaro Nuñez A. 1977-78

Quichean civilization. Central Guatemala. Kenneth L. Brown. 1976-77

Quintana Roo: murals and architecture. Mexico. Arthur G. Miller. 1972-75
—— San Angel Project. Mexico. Karl A. Taube. 1988

Quiriguá. Guatemala. William R. Coe, 1974-75; Robert J. Sharer, 1976-79

Río Azul: history as recorded in Maya skeletons. Guatemala. Frank P. Saul. 1988

Río Azul Project. Guatemala. Richard E. W. Adams. 1983-86

Río Bec region: ecological change and cultural history. Yucatán Peninsula, Mexico. Richard E. W. Adams. 1972

Río Verde Project. Oaxaca, Mexico. David C. Grove. 1985

Sakajut site. Guatemala. Robert J. Sharer. 1988

Salt making, pre-Columbian. Nexquipayac, Mexico. Jeffery R. Parsons. 1988

Sangay site. Morona-Santiago Province,

Ecuador. P. Pedro I. Porras G. 1980, 1983

Santa Barbara Project. Honduras. Edward M. Schortman. 1983, 1985
———— settlement and cultural sequence. Honduras. Wendy A. Ashmore. 1984

Sigchos culture: burial by eruption of Quilotoa volcano. Ecuador. Minard L. Hall. 1987

Sipán: Royal Moche tombs. Peru. Christopher B. Donnan. 1987

Stone spheres. Jalisco, Mexico. Matthew W. Stirling. 1967-68

Terrace abandonment. Colca Valley, Peru. William M. Denevan. 1985

Tetzcotzingo: mapping of a ritual hill. Mexico. Richard F. Townsend. 1979

Textiles, pre-Columbian. Los Ríos Province, Ecuador. Joan S. Gardner. 1977, 1979

Tiahuanacoid Temple. Huari, Peru. William H. Isbell. 1980

Túnel site. Argentina. Luis Abel Orquera. 1981-85

Water distribution systems, Pre-classical. Mexico. Melvin L. Fowler. 1983

Well of Sacrifice probe. Chichén Itzá, Mexico. William J. Folan. 1960-61

Williamsburg and Palmar Sur. Costa Rica. Matthew W. Stirling. 1964

Wineries, colonial: comparative study. Moquegua Valley, Peru and Spain. Prudence M. Rice. 1986-87

Xitle (volcano) and Cuicuilco (pyramid). Mexico. Robert F. Heizer. 1957

Xochicalco: pre-Columbian residential and public architecture. Mexico. Kenneth G. Hirth. 1985
———— mapping. Mexico. Kenneth G. Hirth. 1978
———— Richard F. Townsend. 1980

Yaxuna site: Yucatán, Mexico. David A. Freidel. 1986-87

Yucatán Peninsula: pre-Columbian settlement patterns, Mexico. Edward B. Kurjack. 1975

Pacific

Huahine. Society Islands. Yosihiko H. Sinoto. 1974-75, 1977

Lapita culture: Homeland Project. Bismarck Archipelago, Papua New Guinea. Frederick James Allen. 1984
———— Mussau Islands, Papua New Guinea. Patrick V. Kirch. 1986

Lau Island. Fiji. Roger C. Green. 1976

Lelu stone ruins. Kosrae, Micronesia. Ross H. Cordy. 1982

Micronesia: origins of human settlement. Guam. Hiro Kurashina. 1983

Nanmatol site: a Micronesian chiefdom center. Ponape Island, Caroline Islands, Micronesia. J. Stephen Athens. 1984
———— William S. Ayres. 1983

New Britain: prehistoric settlement and trade. Papua New Guinea. Ian A. Lilley. 1988

Papua New Guinea islands: human prehistory and zoogeography. John P. White. 1988

Tataga-Matau adze quarry. American Samoa. Roger C. Green. 1988

Torres Strait: recent paleoenviron-mental history. Northern Australia. Anthony J. Barham and David R. Harris. 1982, 1984-85

Asia

Abu Salabikh: Sumerian city. Iraq. John N. Postgate. 1976, 1978, 1980, 1982, 1984, 1987
———— Uruk Mound. Iraq. Susan M. Pollock. 1986

Afrin Valley Project: beginnings of agriculture. Syria. Andrew M.T. Moore. 1988

Ain Ghazal: a Neolithic village. Jordan. Gary O. Rollefson. 1983-85, 1988

Alisia, ancient: geochemical location search. Turkey. Allan S. Gilbert. 1984

Akrotiri-Aetokremnos. Cyprus. Alan H. Simmons. 1988

Animal domestication. China. Stanley J. Olsen. 1981

Antiochus I: tomb. Nemrud Dagh, Turkey. Theresa Goell. 1963-64

Aphrodisias. Turkey. Kenan T. Erim. 1966-84

Aqaba: medieval trade. Jordan. Donald S. Whitcomb. 1987-88

Archaeometallurgy: prehistoric copper mine. Thailand. Vincent C. Pigott. 1985-86
———— silver. Anatolia, Turkey. K. Aslihan Yener. 1984-85, 1987

Asia, southern: trade. Janice M. Stargardt. 1979

Azraq Basin. Jordan. Andrew N. Garrard. 1985

Bakhtiari Mountains: routes. Iran. Allen Zagarell. 1976

Baqcah Valley Project: test soundings of magnetometer and resistivity anomalies. Jordan. Patrick E. McGovern. 1979-81

Bronze Age: life patterns. Dead Sea, Jordan. Walter E. Rast. 1979, 1981
———— settlement. Cyprus. James R. Carpenter. 1974

Caesarea Maritima: ancient harbors. Israel. Robert L. Hohlfelder. 1983-84, 1986

Camel and horse: early domestication. China and U.S.S.R. Stanley J. Olsen. 1983, 1985

Chalcolithic culture of the Golan. Palestine. Claire Epstein. 1985

Crafts and labor in the ancient Middle East. Mohenjodaro, Pakistan. Maurizio Tosi. 1985

Cyprus: Mesolithic occupations. James M. Adovasio. 1972-73

Deir el Balah Regional Project. Gaza Strip. Trude Dothan. 1980-82

Dishon Basin, upper. Israel. Milla Y. Ohel. 1979

Early pastoralists. Sinai Peninsula. Israel Hershkovitz. 1985

El Qitar site. Syria. Thomas L. McClellan. 1984-85

En Nabratein. Israel. Eric M. Meyers. 1980

Erbaba: Neolithic site. South-central Turkey. Jacques Bordaz and Louise A. Bordaz. 1977-78

Farming communities. Jordan Valley. Ofer Bar-Yosef. 1982

Gezer: late Bronze and Iron Age

To loosen grime, wet fabric drapes a second-century A.D. Aphrodite from the ancient city of Aphrodisias. DAVID L. BRILL

Project director Walter Alva cleans jars dug from the spectacular tomb of a Moche nobleman at Sipán, Peru. BILL BALLENBERG

Physical anthropologist Sara Bisel preserves skeletons buried at Herculaneum by the eruption of Mount Vesuvius in A.D. 79. A gold coin was found in the purse of an armed man trapped on the beach.

CHERYL NUSS, SISSE BRIMBERG, JONATHAN BLAIR

defenses. Israel. William G. Dever. 1984

Gordion: cultural history. Turkey. Mary M. Voigt. 1988

Hartuv site: protohistory of Judaean urbanization. Israel. A. Mazar and Pierre de Miroschedji. 1986

Jericho: Hasmonean and Herodian winter palace complexes. Jordan. Ehud Netzer. 1979

Jerusalem. Israel. Kathleen M. Kenyon. 1962-67

Ko Kho Khao site. Thailand. Bennet Bronson. 1988

Kourion: excavations of a Roman city. Cyprus. Howard D. Soren. 1985-87

Lemba Project. Cyprus. Edgar J. Peltenburg. 1986, 1988

Mahurjhari: Iron Age megalithic culture. India. Shantaram B. Deo. 1985

Malay Peninsula and Indonesia. Janice M. Stargardt. 1978

Nahal Hemar Cave: early Neolithic organic craft remains. Israel. Ofer Bar-Yosef. 1985

Negev Desert: prehistoric farming societies. Israel. Thomas E. Levy. 1982-84

Nestorian archives. Anatolia. James Hamilton Charlesworth. 1982

Nippur site: archaeological-environmental investigations. Iraq. McGuire Gibson. 1988

Nomadism in the Jezireh. Syria. Frank Hole. 1988

North Jasira Rescue Project. Iraq. Tony J. Wilkinson. 1988

Oman: ancient subsistence and settlement systems. Christopher M. Edens. 1988

Palawan caves. Palawan Island, Philippines. Robert B. Fox. 1965-66

Pella. Jordan. Robert H. Smith. 1979-80, 1982, 1984

Radiometric dating of Paleolithic sites. Israel and Hungary. Henry P. Schwarcz. 1975

Salibiya I. Jordan Valley, Israel. Pam J. Crabtree. 1987

Samosata Mound. Turkey. Theresa Goell. 1967, 1969

Sarepta (Zarephath): Phoenician and biblical city. Lebanon. James B. Pritchard. 1968-72

Shahr-i Qumis: lost capital of Parthian Iran. John F. Hansman. 1970, 1975

Shanidar Cave. Northern Iraq. Ralph S. Solecki. 1978

Sri Lanka: 10th- to 12th-century trading site. John Carswell. 1978

Susa: early fourth millennium strata. Iran. Henry T. Wright. 1978

Syria. Trevor F. Watkins. 1975

Tal-i Malyan. Fars, Iran. Robert H. Dyson, Jr. 1976, 1978

Tell Abu Duwari: anatomy of a Mesopotamian city. Iraq. Elizabeth C. Stone. 1988

Tell Abu Hamid: study of a fifth to fourth millennium site. Jordan. Genevieve L. Dollfus. 1985, 1987

Tell Ain Dara. Syria. Elizabeth C. Stone and Paul E. Zimansky. 1983-84

Tell Brak. Northeastern Syria. David Oates. 1983, 1985-86

Tell el Hayyat Project. Jordan. William G. Dever. 1983

———— Jordan. Steven E. Falconer and

Bonnie S. Magness-Gardiner. 1984

Tell Gabi and Tell al Raqai: salvage excavations. Habur Valley, Syria. Maurits N. van Loon. 1986, 1988

Tell Hadidi. Syria. Rudolph H. Dornemann. 1977-78

Tell Jemmeh. Israel. Gus W. Van Beek. 1975-78, 1984

———— Paula Wapnish-Hesse. 1980

Tell Keisan. Israel. Roland DeVaux. 1971

Tell Miqne (Ekron): Iron Age occupation. Israel. Trude Dothan. 1984

Thailand, prehistoric. Douglas D. Anderson. 1983

Tigris and Euphrates River Basins: ancient settlement. Anatolia, Turkey. Guillermo Algaze. 1988

Tor Hamar Rock-shelter. Jordan. Donald O. Henry. 1988

Turkey, northwestern. Mehmet C. Ozdogan. 1979, 1981

———— southeastern: early village site. Robert J. Braidwood. 1980-81

Umm Qseir: prehistoric site. Syria. Frank Hole. 1986

Upper Paleolithic sites. Wadi Elhasa, Jordan. Geoffrey A. Clark. 1984

Urbanism in northern Mesopotamia: Nineveh. Iraq. David B. Stronach. 1987

Yabrud rock-shelters: Paleolithic culture. Syria. William R. Farrand. 1988

Yagi site: social dynamics and subsistence strategies. Japan. William M. Hurley and Peter Bleed. 1978-80

Yemen Arab Republic: archaeological-environmental survey. McGuire Gibson. 1978

Europe

Aegean Dendrochronology Project. Southeastern Europe and Turkey. Peter L. Kuniholm. 1979-80, 1982-83, 1986

Aisne Valley: Neolithic settlement processes. France. Anick Coudart. 1987

Amber: prehistoric trade. A. Colin Renfrew and Curt W. Beck. 1975

———— spectroscopic provenance analysis. Curt W. Beck. 1973

Anglo-Saxon royal burial ground. Sutton Hoo, Suffolk, England. Rupert L. S. Bruce-Mitford. 1968, 1970

Apollo sanctuary. Halieis, Greece. Michael H. Jameson. 1973-74

Architecture and village layout. Ancient Greece. William A. McDonald. 1971

Argolid Peninsula. Greece. Michael H. Jameson. 1979

———— postglacial environmental history. Donald R. Whitehead. 1972-73

Assiros tombs. Macedonia, Greece. Kenneth A. Wardle. 1986-88

Bally Lough: Mesolithic and Neolithic settlements. Ireland. Mark Zvelebil. 1984, 1986

Britain: search for earliest humans. Ronald Singer. 1978-79

Bronze Age: copper-mining settlement. St. Veit-Klingleberg, Austria. Stephen J. Shennan. 1986-88

———— marble sources in the Aegean. Greece. Norman Herz. 1988

———— political landscapes in the Mancha. Spain. Antonio Gilman. 1988

"Camelot." South Cadbury, Somerset, England. Leslie Alcock. 1970

Caves: Jumilla, Yecla, and Villena. Southeastern Spain. Michael J. Walker. 1979

—— Quaternary and Holocene origins. Spain. William H. Waldren. 1971, 1973

Central Russian Plain: Upper Paleolithic settlements and exchange networks. Olga Soffer. 1982

Chalosse district. Southwestern France. Lawrence G. Straus. 1980

Classical marble: stable isotopic signatures applied. Norman Herz. 1979, 1981-82

Cretan Exploration Project. Livingston V. Watrous. 1983-85, 1987

—— multidisciplinary collaboration. Despoina Vallianou. 1985, 1987

Dalmatia: ancient settlement patterns. Yugoslavia. John C. Chapman. 1984-86

Dog domestication, prehistoric. Soviet Union and Sweden. Stanley J. Olsen. 1987

Dolní Věstonice: Paleolithic cultural change from faunal remains. Czechoslovakia. Olga Soffer. 1987

Etruscan tomb painting: scientific record. Tarquinia, Italy. Richard C. Bronson. 1986

Federsee: Mesolithic survey beneath peat deposits. West Germany. Michael A. Jochim. 1987

Franchthi Cave. Greece. John A. Gifford. 1981, 1983

Gatas Bronze Age Project. Spain. Robert W. Chapman. 1986-88

Geissenklosterle: early human site. West Germany. Joachim Hahn. 1987

Great Hungarian Plain: prehistoric settlement history. Andrew G. Sherratt. 1980

Greece: society, culture, economy in the later Roman period. Timothy E. Gregory. 1974

Grubgraben site: excavations. Austria. Anta Montet-White. 1986-87

Gubbio Project. Umbria, Italy. Caroline Ann T. Malone and Simon Kenneth Stoddart. 1984, 1987

Guipúzcoa Province. Spain. Lawrence G. Straus. 1979

Hascherkeller site: prehistoric economy. West Germany. Peter S. Wells. 1980, 1983

Helice. Greece. Harold E. Edgerton and Peter Throckmorton. 1970-71

Herculaneum: ancient Roman population. Italy. Sara C. Bisel. 1982-83, 1988

—— boat. Italy. J. Richard Steffy. 1983

Ice Age Franco-Cantabrian caves: photography and analysis. Alexander Marshack. 1973

Ithaka: Mycenaean settlement. Greece. Sarantis Symeonoglou. 1984-85

Kamegg site: excavations. Austria. Anta Montet-White. 1984

Kavousi Project. Crete. William D. E. Coulson. 1984-85, 1987

Klithi Rock-shelter: Paleolithic excavations. Epirus, Greece. Geoff N. Bailey. 1984, 1986

Koukounaries: Mycenaean acropolis.

Demetrius U. Schilardi. 1977

Lucania. Italy. Sterling P. Vinson. 1978-79

Manika Bronze Age Project. Euboea, Greece. Adamantios Sampson. 1986

Mezhirichi. Ukrainian S.S.R. Olga Soffer. 1979

Mirobriga Project. Portugal. William R. Biers. 1982-84

Mochlos: field survey. Crete. Jeffrey S. Soles. 1983

Molise Project. Biferno Valley, Italy. Graeme W. Barker. 1977-78

Monastery, seventh-century. Jarrow, England. Rosemary J. Cramp. 1973

Morava Valley: ecology and cultural change. Yugoslavia. H. Arthur Bankoff. 1977, 1980-81

Mycenaean palace. Páros, Greece. Demetrius U. Schilardi. 1978

Nemea Valley Project. Peloponnesus, Greece. James C. Wright. 1984, 1986

Neolithic fortress site and rock paintings. Sierra de Taibilla, Spain. Michael J. Walker. 1968-70

Pantanello Necropolis: Greek colonial population dynamics: Metaponto, Italy. Joseph C. Carter. 1986

Pantelleria. David P. S. Peacock. 1977

Pompeii and other Vesuvian sites: natural history in Roman times. Italy. Wilhelmina Jashemski. 1988

Porto Longo harbor. Sapienza Island, Greece. Harold E. Edgerton and Peter Throckmorton. 1970

Prehistoric settlement: sites in peat. Cumbria, England. Joan J. Taylor. 1986-87

Remote sensing: applied to regional archaeology. Burgundy, France. Carole L. Crumley. 1986

Rome, ancient: environmental studies. Albert J. Ammerman. 1985, 1988

Solutre: Paleolithic kill site. France. Sandra L. Olsen. 1986

Son Ferrandell Oleza Project: cultural adaptations to environmental change. Mallorca. Robert W. Chapman. 1984

Stanwick Project. Yorkshire, England. R. Leon Fitts. 1988

Stonehenge, England, and Callanish, Scotland. Gerald S. Hawkins. 1965

Syme: sanctuary of Hermes and Aphrodite. Crete. Angeliki Lebessi. 1984-85, 1987-88

Thessaly: Paleolithic survey. Greece. Curtis N. Runnels. 1987

Thisbe Basin: Ohio Boeotia Expedition. Greece. Timothy E. Gregory. 1981

Tower of the Winds. Athens, Greece. Derek J. de Solla Price. 1964

Ukrina Valley: paleoliths. Yugoslavia. Anta Montet-White. 1980

Voidokoilia: pre-Mycenaean tumulus. Greece. George S. Korres. 1977-78, 1982

Africa

Abydos: royal funerary enclosures. Egypt. David B. O'Connor. 1988

Akhmim: excavations. Upper Egypt. Naguib Kanawati. 1979-85

Asante people: early sites. Ghana. Peter L. Shinnie. 1985, 1987

Aten temple: computerized study. Karnak, Egypt. Ray W. Smith. 1968-69

Bamenda-Koumbo area. West Cameroon. Donald D. Hartle. 1967

Bantu culture: Congo coast excavations. James R. Denbow. 1988

Berenice: ancient Red Sea port. Egypt. Steven E. Sidebotham. 1988

Botswana, western: Iron Age penetration. Edwin N. Wilmsen. 1987

Cambyses: Lost Army. Egypt. Gary S. Chafetz. 1983

Carthage: port and sacrificial precinct. Tunisia. Lawrence Stager. 1978

—— Punic harbor development. George Rapp, Jr. 1985

Chad and Libya: archaeological reconnaissance. Carleton S. Coon. 1966-67

Colossi of Memnon. Egypt. Robert F. Heizer. 1971

Comoro Islands: archaeology of early Islamic centers. Henry T. Wright, 1984

—— early settlements. Claude J. Allibert. 1987

Deir el Ballas: survey and excavation. Egypt. Peter Lacovara. 1984

Dia region. Mali. Susan K. and Roderick J. McIntosh. 1986

Eastern Desert: early pastoral nomadism. Egypt. Juris Zarins. 1988

El Amarna Project: boundary stelae. Egypt. William J. Murnane. 1985

Engaruka: cultural site of early humans. Tanzania. Hamo Sassoon. 1967

Gebel Adda. Egypt. Nicholas B. Millet. 1963-65

Houlouf Project: prehistoric settlement. Cameroon. Augustin F. C. Holl. 1987

Iron Age settlement survey. Upper Zambezi Valley, Zambia. Joseph O. Vogel. 1976

Karamoja District. Uganda. Hamo Sassoon. 1972

Kasserine Project: semiarid land-use history. Tunisia. Robert B. Hitchner. 1985, 1987

Kramo excavation. Begho, Ghana. Merrick Posnansky. 1978

Lake Ndutu Research Project. Tanzania. Amini A. Mturi. 1983

Libyan Desert: geological-anthropological survey. Egypt. C. Vance Haynes. 1974-76

Madagascar, southwest. Robert E. Dewar. 1979

Mali caves. Johan Huizinga. 1970

Medieval Luxor Project. Egypt. Donald S. Whitcomb. 1985

Megaliths. Central Africa. Nicholas C. David. 1974

Mosaics. Tunisia. Margaret A. Alexander. 1973, 1976

Ngamiland. Botswana. John E. Yellen. 1973

Northern Volta Basin. Ghana. Emmanuel K. Agorsah. 1983

Pyramids: cosmic-ray research. Egypt. Luis W. Alvarez. 1968

Queir Project. Egypt. Janet H. Johnson. 1977, 1979, 1981

Rock art, prehistoric. Tanzania. Amini A. Mturi. 1985

Roman quarries. Mons Claudianus, Egypt. David P. S. Peacock. 1987-88

Serengeti National Park: Middle Stone Age. Tanzania. John R. F. Bower. 1979

Sijilmasa: survey. Morocco. Ronald A. Messier. 1988

Timbuktu. Mali. Roderick J. McIntosh. 1983

Tsodilo Hills: Stone Age archaeology. Botswana. Lawrence H. Robbins. 1987

Tumuli. Senegal. Susan K. and Roderick J. McIntosh. 1988

Underwater

American Revolutionary gunboat. Lake Champlain. Philip K. Lundeberg. 1968

Atlit Yam: excavation of a submerged prehistoric site. Israel. Ehud Galili. 1988

Battle of Lepanto shipwrecks. Greece. Spyridon Marinatos. 1971

Bermuda waters. Mendel L. Peterson. 1965-67

Breadalbane: scientific and photographic survey. Barrow Strait, Canada. Joseph B. MacInnis. 1981

Bronze Age shipwreck. Kas, Turkey. George F. Bass. 1984-86.

Byzantine shipwrecks. Turkey. George F. Bass. 1961-69, 1976

Columbus's caravel *Gallega:* search. Río Belen, Panama. David H. Keith. 1987

Defence: Revolutionary War privateer. David C. Switzer. 1977

Greek cargo ship, seventh-century. Sicilian waters. Edwin A. Link. 1962

Iron Age shipwreck. Turkey. George F. Bass. 1974-75

JASON Project: expedition to the Mediterranean. Robert D. Ballard. 1988

Kyrenia Ship Project: film documentary. Susan W. Katzev. 1975

Kyrenia shipwreck. Cyprus. Michael L. Katzev. 1967-72

Medieval Islamic shipwreck. Turkey. George F. Bass. 1978-79

Mediterranean Sea: search. Peter Throckmorton. 1975

—— survey. George F. Bass. 1973

Molasses Reef shipwreck, 16th-century. Caribbean. Donald H. Keith. 1983, 1985

Mombasa wreck excavation. Kenya. Robin C. M. Piercy. 1979

Monitor search. Cape Hatteras area, North Carolina. John J. Newton and Harold E. Edgerton. 1973-74

Ottoman shipwreck, 16th-century. Turkey. George F. Bass. 1982

Porto Longo: sonar search. Greece. Peter Throckmorton. 1968-69

Portuguese frigate search. Mombasa Harbor, Kenya. Hamo Sassoon. 1975

Program of nautical archaeology. New World. George F. Bass. 1981

Punic ship, third-century B.C. Sicily. Honor E. Frost. 1973

Sackets Harbor Project: U.S. Navy brig *Jefferson.* New York. Kevin J. Crisman. 1986, 1988

Sonar gear. Eastern Mediterranean. Harold E. Edgerton. 1968

Spanish Plate Fleet. Florida. Kip L. Wagner. 1965

Strait of Otranto: submerged Paleolithic occupation and sea levels. Nicholas C. Flemming. 1987

Turkey: survey of ancient shipwrecks. George F. Bass. 1980

ETHNOLOGY

Chewing sticks. West Africa, Egypt, and Pakistan. Memory Elvin-Lewis and Walter H. Lewis. 1975

Facial expressions: cross-cultural comparison of patterns. Wolfgang M. Schleidt. 1980

North America

Aleutian survivors of the Bering land bridge. William S. Laughlin. 1972

Aleuts: Russian influence on ecology, culture, and physical anthropology. Alaska. Christy G. Turner II. 1972-73

Eskimos: linguistics and religion. Canada. Svend Frederiksen. 1965

—— prehistoric Thule culture. Northwest Hudson Bay, Canada. Charles F. Merbs. 1968-70

Hinds Cave. Val Verde County, Texas. Vaughn M. Bryant, Jr. 1975

Indian ethnobotany. California. Lowell J. Bean. 1975

Pima people: ethnobotany. Gila River, Arizona. Amadeo M. Rea. 1985

Washo Indians: art. Nevada. Norval C. Kern, Jr. 1970

Mesoamerica and South America

Afkodre **magic and religion:** Creoles. Suriname. Benjamin E. Pierce. 1971

Amazonia: aboriginal animal domestication. Daniel W. Gade. 1977

—— forest-living Indians: comparative dietary ecology. Katherine Milton. 1985

—— Mestizo floodplain subsistence. Peru. Mario Hiraoka. 1982-83

—— relationships between the Tukanoan fishing and Maduan hunting tribes. Katharine Milton. 1980

Andes: oral tradition and sacred monuments. Casma, Peru. Luis Millones. 1988

Ayoreo Indians. Southeastern Bolivia. Paul E. Bugos, Jr. 1980

Basketwork technology and barter system. Upper Negro River, Brazil. Berta Gleizer Ribeiro. 1984

Black Caribs. Central America. William V. Davidson. 1973-74

Brazilian Indian fabrics. Berta G. Ribeiro. 1980

Chickens, black-boned: distribution and use. Central and South America. Carl L. Johannessen. 1976-77

Chimu Empire. Peru. Carol J. Mackey. 1982

Copablanca Festival: ethnographic and ethnomusicological survey. Bolivia. Edwin E. Erickson. 1973

Hunter-gatherers, lowland. Peru. Kim Hill. 1986

Jivaro people: medical ethnobotany. Upper Amazon Basin. Memory Elvin-Lewis and Walter H. Lewis. 1985-86, 1988

Kayapo Indians: resource management. Brazil. Darrell A. Posey. 1985

Maya: salt trade. Guatemala and Mexico. Anthony P. Andrews. 1975

—— textile designs. Chiapas, Mexico. Walter F. Morris, Jr. 1977, 1979

—— village curer-priest. Coba, Quintana Roo, Mexico. Eileen R. Kintz. 1984

Mesoamerica: food and cosmology. Mexico. Nancy M. Farriss. 1983

—— pottery techniques. Lewis A. Krevolin. 1972

—— textile traditions. Mexico and Guatemala. Patricia R. Anawalt. 1982, 1984

—— and Southwestern cosmology. Evon Z. Vogt. 1982

Otomi Indians: resource cognition. Mexico. Kirsten J. Haring. 1973

Peasant livelihood behavior. Trinidad. Bonham C. Richardson. 1971

Peruvian highlands: prehistoric cultural development. Clifford Evans and Betty Meggers. 1968-69

Preceramic culture. Chiapas, Mexico. Philip Drucker. 1947

Pre-Columbian cultural change. Cozumel, Mexico. Jeremy A. Sabloff. 1971-73

Quechua communities: subsistence economy. North Peruvian Andes. Cesar A. Fonseca. 1980

Tarahumara people. Mexico. Robert A. Bye, Jr. 1972

Tlapanec Indians. Tlacoapa, Mexico. Marion Oettinger, Jr. 1971

Tooth extraction. Peru and Colombia. Memory Elvin-Lewis and Walter H. Lewis. 1982

Waurá Indians. Mato Grosso, Brazil. Harald Schultz. 1961-64

Welsh colony. Patagonia. Glyn Williams. 1968-69

Zinacantan. Mexico. John B. Haviland. 1983

Pacific

Caroline Islanders: ethnohistory. Saul H. Riesenberg. 1973

Child behavior. New Hebrides. E. Richard Sorenson. 1971

Dani people: material culture. Netherlands New Guinea. Robert G. Gardner. 1962

Diseases and cures. Torres Strait Islands. George J. Simeon. 1974

Fore and Bahinemo peoples: facial expression of emotions. New Guinea. E. Richard Sorenson. 1968-69

Hagahai people: cultural history and biological adaptation. Papua New Guinea. Carol L. Jenkins. 1983, 1985, 1987

Ifalik Island: food production and reproduction. Western Caroline Islands. Laura L. Betzig. 1986

Maisin society: tapa cloth. Melanesia. John H. Barker. 1986

Maoris. New Zealand. William N. Fenton. 1974

New Guinea: native religious symbolism. Wilson G. Wheatcroft. 1968-70

Polynesians: dances. Cook Island. E. Richard Sorenson. 1975

——— origins. Roger C. Green. 1977

Tanna Island. New Hebrides. Kalman A. Muller. 1974

Tattooing. Palau, Micronesia. Philip J. C. Dark. 1986

Taut Batu people: shelter in a small society. Palawan Island, Philippines. Barton M. Brown. 1987

Trade, migration, and marriage. New Guinea. Deborah Gewertz. 1974

Australia

Aborigines. Arnhem Land, northern Australia. Charles P. Mountford. 1948

——— Pintupi Christianity. Fred E. Myers. 1988

Art sanctuary. Koonalda Cave, South Australia. Christine Elvera Sharpe. 1975

Tiwi culture. Melville Island, Australia. Charles P. Mountford. 1954

——— Jane C. Goodale. 1980

Asia

Ainu. Hokkaido, Japan. M. Inez Hilger. 1965-66

Arab potters. Israel. Owen S. Rye. 1976

Bakhtiari tribe: role in history. Iran. Gene R. Garthwaite. 1971

Bedouin tribes: traditional medicine. Negev Desert, Israel. Aref I. Abu-Rabia. 1984-85

Buddhist monasticism. Melvyn C. Goldstein. 1980

Burial ritual. North Borneo. Peter A. Metcalf. 1975

Forest cultures and product technology. Malaysia and Sumatra. Rosemary Gianno. 1986

Himalayan village: environmental adaptation. Melemchi, Nepal. Naomi H. Bishop. 1986

Hindu pilgrimage: cultural symbolism. Muktinath, Nepal. Donald A. Messerschmidt. 1980

Hmong people: effect on forests and primate population. Huai Kha Khaeng Wildlife Sanctuary, Thailand. Ardith A. Eudey. 1985

Humans, protohistoric and early historic: interaction with the environment. Isthmian Thailand. Janice M. Stargardt. 1973

Karnali zone: cultural-ecological analysis. Western Nepal. Barry C. Bishop. 1968-69, 1971

——— livelihood strategies and seasonal rhythms. Nepal. Barry C. Bishop. 1980

Kenyah Dayaks: religion and social organization. Sarawak, Malaysia. Herbert L. Whittier. 1973

Kinship and marriage: hierarchy and amity. South Asia. Anthony T. Carter. 1973

Kurds. Khorasan, Iran. Robert E. Peck. 1967

Lejjun: nomadism and sedentarism on the Roman frontier. Jordan. S. Thomas Parker. 1985, 1987

Lua tribe. Northern Thailand. Peter Kunstadter. 1963-64

Nagas: cultural development. Southeast Asia. Vikuosa O. Nienu. 1977

Pashtoon: pastoral nomadism. Afghanistan. Asen Balikci. 1972

Pastoralism. Southern Sinai. Ofer Bar-Yosef. 1976

——— yak. Western Tibet. Melvyn C. Goldstein. 1986-87

Religious centers. Himalaya. Barbara N. Aziz. 1975

Shabakites. Northern Iraq. Sami Said Ahmed. 1973

Sherpa culture. Nepal and Sikkim. Luther G. Jerstad. 1965

Tugitils, highland: ethnobiology. Halmahera Island, Indonesia. Paul M. Taylor. 1980-81

Yazidi religious group. Middle East. Sami Said Ahmed. 1967

Europe

Depopulation and cultural change. Islands of western Ireland. Kevin C. Kearns. 1975

Grevena Project: regional study. Greece. Nancy C. Wilke. 1987

Symbol systems, Paleolithic. Eastern Europe and the Soviet Union. Alexander Marshack. 1975-76

Africa

Afar nomadism. Ethiopia. Robert G. Gardner. 1965

Anosy society: human ecology. Madagascar. Jean Aime Rakotoarisoa. 1987

Ariaal Rendille people: nomadic economic organization. Kenya. Elliot Fratkin. 1985

Bani-Niger people: African migrants. Johan Huizinga. 1974

Barabaig people: testing evolutionary predictions. Tanzania. Monique E. Borgerhoff Mulder. 1987

Bayei people: ethnography. Okavango Delta, Botswana. Thomas J. Larson. 1986

Fulani people: social system with their cattle. Northern Nigeria. Dale F. Lott. 1973

Kabiye society: social change. Togo. Thomas J. Larson. 1984

Kipsigis. Kenya. Monique Borgerhoff-Mulder. 1983

Kisii: migration and communication. Kenya. Ronald D. Garst. 1975

Kwanyama linguistic group: ethnobotany. Ovamboland, Namibia. Robert J. Rodin. 1972

Malagasy: origins and prehistory. Robert E. Dewar, Jr. 1978

Mandinko people: history, social structure, and ethnobotany. Pakao, southern Senegal. David M. Schaffer. 1973, 1975

Mayotte: religion, ethnomedicine, and social structure of Malagasy speakers. Comoro Islands. Michael J. Lambek. 1985

Mbuti Pygmies. Ituri Forest, Zaire. Robert C. Bailey. 1979

Ngamiland peoples: demography. Okavango River and Delta, Africa. Thomas J. Larson. 1971

Pokot tribe: women's role. Kenya.

A mother and daughter belonging to the Lua, Thai mountain people, prepare rice for transplanting. PETER KUNSTADTER

An archaeologist removes an amphora from the oldest known shipwreck, sunk off Turkey 34 centuries ago. DONALD FREY

Palomar Observatory-National Geographic Society Sky Survey photographed Andromeda. WILLIAM C. MILLER

Alan Walker, left, and Richard Leakey examine a 1.6-million-year-old human jawbone found in East Africa. DAVID L. BRILL

Elizabeth L. Meyerhoff. 1976

Rural migration: relationship to expansion of commercial agriculture. Tanzania. Marilyn Silberfein. 1973

Swahili ethno-archaeology: social uses of houses and artifacts. Lamu, Kenya. Linda W. Donley. 1985
—— medical beliefs and practices. Mombasa, Kenya. Marc J. Swartz. 1985, 1987

Turkana people: nomadic co-residence, conflict, and cooperation. Kenya. V. Rada Dyson-Hudson. 1984, 1987

West African settlement geography along a linguistic and environmental transect. Reed F. Stewart. 1976

Yoruba geophagy. Nigeria. Donald E. Vermeer. 1975

Yoruba people: festivals, rituals, and sacred kingship. Nigeria and Benin. John Pemberton III. 1984
—— Odun Aje Festival and the status of urban women. Ondo Town, Nigeria. Elizabeth Anne Eames. 1985

PHYSICAL ANTHROPOLOGY and PALEOANTHROPOLOGY

African sites: Fort Ternan, Kenya; Lake Turkana, Kenya; Olduvai Gorge, Tanzania; Omo Valley, Ethiopia. Louis S. B. Leakey, Mary D. Leakey, and Richard E. Leakey. 1960-69, 1971
—— Louis S. B. Leakey. 1971-72.

Aging, biological. Nepal. Cynthia M. Beall. 1983

Ambrona. Soria Province, Spain. F. Clark Howell. 1981

Americans, first: dental evidence. Christy G. Turner II. 1978-80, 1982

Arikara: burial sites. South Dakota. T. Dale Stewart. 1971
—— skeletons. North Dakota. William M. Bass. 1968-69

Buluk: Miocene hominid site. Kenya. Alan C. Walker. 1983

Calico Mountains. Mojave Desert, California. Louis S. B. Leakey, Thomas Clements, Gerald A. Smith, and Ruth D. Simpson. 1964-67

Centre for Prehistory and Palaeontology. Nairobi, Kenya. Louis S. B. Leakey. 1971

Cerebral function at extreme high altitude. Thomas F. Hornbein. 1981

Colonsay and Jura: historical demography. Scotland. John W. Sheets II. 1983

Disease, pre-Columbian American. Marvin J. Allison. 1971, 1973-74, 1976-77, 1979-81, 1983

Early humans: taphonomic perspectives. Gary A. Haynes. 1982

East Africa Early Humans Program. Kenya. Richard E. Leakey. 1985

Ecuador, coastal: demography. Douglas H. Ubelaker. 1974

Ethiopia: Upper Pliocene localities. Francis H. Brown and F. Clark Howell. 1974

Extinct fauna and early humans. Mojave Desert, California. Emma Lou Davis. 1970-71

Fossil bones: amino-acid dating. East Africa. Jeffrey L. Bada. 1978

Fossiliferous deposits, Cenozoic. Yemen. Ian Tattersall. 1988

Grotte XVI: Pleistocene biocultural evolution. Dordogne, France. Jean-Philippe Rigaud. 1987-88

Hadar. Central Afar, Ethiopia. Donald C. Johanson. 1975-76, 1980

High-altitude physiological adaptation: Himalayan and Andean natives. F. Duane Blume. 1986

Hominid corridor: Plio-Pleistocene deposits. Malawi. Timothy G. Bromage. 1983-84, 1987

Hominids, middle Pleistocene. Lainyamok, Kenya. Richard B. Potts and Pat L. Shipman. 1984

Homo erectus: killing-butchering site. Evron Quarry, Israel. Avraham Ronen. 1984
—— Olduvai Gorge, Africa. G. Philip Rightmire. 1978

Hubei Province. China. Frank E. Poirier. 1981

Human crania: paleoanthropology. Vietnam. Michael Pietrusewsky. 1985

Iceland Paleoeconomy Project. Thomas H. McGovern. 1988

Kathmandu Valley. Nepal. Elwyn L. Simons. 1974

Laetoli Beds and Olduvai Gorge. Tanzania. Raymonde Bonnefille. 1976
—— Mary D. Leakey. 1975-82

Lake Turkana (Rudolf). Kenya. Richard E. Leakey. 1965-81
—— hominid locality. Kenya. John M. Harris. 1982
—— report of discoveries. F. Clark Howell. 1974

Lamb Springs Early Human Project. Douglas County, Colorado. Dennis J. Stanford. 1980-81

La Quina: Paleolithic sequence. France. Arthur J. Jelinek. 1986-88

Makau and Olduvai, and continued preparation of Laetoli monograph. Tanzania. Mary D. Leakey. 1982

Men: physiological responses to hypoxia and cold at altitude. John B. West. 1980

Middle Awash Valley. Ethiopia. John D. Clark. 1982

Nomads, pastoral: desert physiology. Northern Kenya. Geoffrey M. O. Maloiy. 1977

Olduvai Gorge. Tanzania. Mary D. Leakey. 1970-75, 1983
—— publication. Philip V. Tobias. 1977, 1987
—— reevaluation of putative bone tools. Pat L. Shipman. 1982

Paleomagnetic dating: earliest human occupations. Italy. Alan L. McPherron. 1981

Peopling of the Americas: conference and workshop. University of Maine. Robson Bonnichsen. 1987

Pleistocene karst caves. Vietnam. Russell L. Ciochan. 1988

Portugal: Upper Paleolithic research. Lawrence G. Straus. 1987-88

Primates: adaptive strategies of and evolution of suspensory locomotion. John G. H. Cant. 1981
—— Outamba-Kilimi National Park, Sierra Leone. Robert S. O. Harding. 1981

Sahabi. Northern Libya. Noel T. Boaz. 1978
Semliki Valley. Zaire. Noel T. Boaz. 1983, 1986
Sherpas: high-altitude adaptation and genetics. Georgio P. Morpurgo. 1976
Skeletal biology. Bahrain. Bruno Frøhlich. 1980
—— Corinth, Greece. Henry S. Robinson. 1975
—— dental anthropology and biological affinities. Indus Valley, Pakistan, and Ganga Valley, India. John R. Lukacs. 1982, 1984-87
—— Maya. Cozumel, Mexico. Frank P. Saul. 1979
—— Neandertal. Egypt. T. Dale Stewart. 1982
—— prehistoric human. Easter Island. George W. Gill. 1980
—— Southwest Indians: prehistory through dentition. Christy G. Turner II. 1988
Toromoja: potential early human site. Alison S. Brooks. 1980
West Africa: paleobiology and paleoecology. Cameroon. David Pilbeam. 1984
West Turkana area: Paleontological exploration. Kenya. Alan C. Walker. 1984-88
Women: physiological responses to hypoxia and cold at altitude. Barbara L. Drinkwater. 1980
Yarimburgaz Cave: early Paleolithic artifacts. Turkey. F. Clark Howell. 1987-88

Astronomy and Astrophysics

Atlas of Local Group Galaxies. Five astronomical observatories. Paul W. Hodge. 1988
Asteroid geography: a study of asteroid topography. A.M.J. Gehrels. 1980
Asteroids: Ceres. Measurement, diameter, and bulk density of the largest asteroid. Robert L. Millis. 1984
—— Geographos (1620). Betty F. Mintz. 1968-69
—— Geographos orbit study. Samuel Herrick. 1968-69
—— Geographos and others. A.M.J. Gehrels. 1971
—— satellites. Steward Observatory, Kitt Peak, Arizona. Tom Gehrels. 1985
Astronomical alignment: Canadian Indian cairns and medicine wheels. John A. Eddy. 1975
Atlas of the Andromeda Galaxy. Paul W. Hodge. 1977, 1979
Auroras: observations on brightness, color, variety, and sequence. Carl W. Gartlein. 1938-56
Beta Scorpii and companion: occultation by Jupiter. David S. Evans. 1971
Chromospheric activity in sunlike stars: age dependence. Mount Wilson Observatory, California. Arthur H. Vaughan. 1984

Cosmic-ray monitoring. Martin A. Pomerantz. 1946-53, 1956-58, 1964
Cygnus XI: optical studies. Pine Mountain Observatory, Oregon. James C. Kemp. 1984
Disk characteristics of Sc I galaxies. Gregory O. Boeshaar. 1979
"Einstein Shift" verification: 1952 solar eclipse. Khartoum, Sudan. George A. Van Biesbroeck. 1952
Epsilon Aurigae: polarimetry of the eclipsing star system. James C. Kemp. 1983
Galaxy clusters: size. Hale Observatories. Thomas W. Noonan. 1974
Gravitational light-deflection effect: improved measurement. Bryce S. DeWitt. 1973
Halley's comet: near perihelion. Haleakala Observatory, Hawaii. Jay M. Pasachoff. 1985
Infrared images: star formation, bipolar nebulae, and galaxies. Observatories in Arizona, California, Chile, and Hawaii. Judith L. Pipher. 1984, 1987
Interstellar deuterium. Jay M. Pasachoff. 1974
Interstellar molecular clouds: exploration by submillimeter polarimetry. Roger H. Hildebrand. 1979
Kohoutek comet and the annular solar eclipse. Donald H. Menzel. 1973
Mars: greenish patches and mysterious "canals." Bloemfontein Observatory, South Africa. E. C. Slipher. 1954-56
—— telescopic monitoring of 1986 opposition. Philip B. James. 1986
Mars and Jupiter: spectroscopic studies. Mauna Loa, Hawaii. C. C. Kiess and C. H. Corliss. 1956-57
"Martian Pavilion." Georgetown College Observatory, presented by the National Geographic Society. 1956
Planetary systems search. A.M.J. Gehrels and Krzysztof M. Serkowski. 1974-76
—— Krzysztof M. Serkowski. 1978, 1980
Planets: brighter, photographic atlas. E. C. Slipher and John S. Hall. 1962-63
Sky survey: infrared photographs. Eric R. Craine. 1976
—— Palomar Observatory–National Geographic Society: photomapping. 1949-58
—— Palomar Observatory–National Geographic Society: transparent overlay map preparation. John D. Kraus. 1976
—— Palomar Observatory. Wallace L. W. Sargent. 1980
—— radio-telescope monitoring of infrared emissions. James N. Douglas. 1973-75
Solar corona: heating studies, 1980 eclipse. Jay M. Pasachoff. 1979
—— photography of the spectrum, polarization, and form. Donald H. Menzel. 1972
—— spectrographic study, 1970 eclipse. Donald H. Menzel. 1969
—— temperature and density studies, 1977 eclipse. Jay M. Pasachoff. 1977
Solar eclipse: aerial photographs. Bo-

caiúva, Brazil. Lyman J. Briggs. 1947
—— Africa. Donald H. Menzel. 1972
—— Australia. Donald H. Menzel. 1976
—— Burma to the Aleutian Islands. Lyman J. Briggs. 1948
—— Canton Island, Pacific. Samuel A. Mitchell. 1937
—— Maine-New Hampshire. Albert W. Stevens and Paul A. McNally. 1932
—— Norfolk, Virginia. Simon Newcomb and Alexander Graham Bell. 1900
—— Northern Canada. Wolfgang B. Klemperer. 1963
—— Patos, Brazil. Irvine C. Gardner. 1940
—— Trans-African baseline. Jay M. Pasachoff. 1973
—— U.S.S.R. Irvine C. Gardner. 1936
—— U.S.S.R. Paul A. McNally and W. Robert Moore. 1936
—— and occultation by Neptune. Indonesia. Jay M. Pasachoff. 1982
Solar radiation. Mount Brukkaros, Namibia. Charles G. Abbot. 1925-29
Spacewatch Camera: microwave data link. A.M.J. Gehrels. 1983
Stars: peculiar early type. Deane M. Peterson. 1974
Stellar remnants: measuring the age of the universe. Worldwide observatories. Donald E. Winget. 1987
Structure of the early universe. Richard A. Matzner. 1980
Sunlike stars: synoptic observation of magnetically induced chromospheric variations. Arthur H. Vaughan, George W. Preston, and Robert W. Noyes. 1982
Uranus occultation: 1977. William B. Hubbard, Jr. 1976
Venus and ritual warfare in Mesoamerica: Maya Grolier Codex. John B. Carlson. 1985
Zodiacal light. Colorado-Nebraska border. George A. Van Biesbroeck. 1954

Biology

Animal hard parts: biological destruction in a marine environment. Peter M. Kranz. 1973
Aquatic animals: behavior in relation to polarized light. Talbot H. Waterman. 1970-71
Aquatic biota: river survey. Eastern Panama. Wayne C. Starnes. 1984
Biogeography, vicariance: empirical test. Spain and Morocco. Stephen D. Busack. 1983
—— historical relationships of biota. Argentina, Bolivia, Chile, and Uruguay. Jorge V. Crisci. 1988
Biological and archaeological expedition. Southeast Oceania. John E. Randall. 1969
Biological colonization of a recently formed volcanic island. Motmot, Papua New Guinea. Eldon E. Ball. 1972, 1974, 1976, 1978, 1980, 1983

Biological investigation: disease study. Bolivia. Richard G. Van Gelder. 1964

Biological studies of the northern Cordillera Vilcabamba. Peru. John W. Terborgh. 1966-68

Bioluminescent and optical attenuation measurements. Maui Basin, Hawaii. Guy C. McLeod. 1977

Bird and plant communities: convergent evolution. Africa and North America. Martin L. Cody. 1977

Central Australia: biological exploration of remote mountain chains. G. Alan Solem. 1982

Cerro Tacarcuna: biological exploration. Panama-Colombia border. Alwyn H. Gentry. 1974

Cordella Bank Expedition. Pacific Ocean. Robert W. Schmieder. 1979

Deep reefs: ecology. Western Caribbean. Walter A. Starck II. 1970

Deep-sea fauna: biology and distribution. Tropical Atlantic Ocean. Gilbert L. Voss. 1963-73

—— hydrothermal-vent: photographic documentation. Pacific. Robert R. Hessler. 1983

—— pressure tolerance. Bermuda. Alister G. MacDonald. 1980

El Niño: biological impact. Costa Rica. Yan B. Linhart. 1984

Gombe National Park: establishment. Tanzania. 1968

—— support. D. N. Bryceson. 1973

Herbivory: transatlantic variation in plant and insect communities. Great Britain and Iowa. Valerie K. Brown and Stephen D. Hendrix. 1987

Hiscock site: Quaternary paleoecology. New York. David W. Steadman. 1986

Hudson Bay and Labrador: biological expedition. W. E. Clyde Todd. 1912, 1914, 1917

Lake Baikal: freshwater fauna. U.S.S.R. Ralph W. Brauer. 1977-79

Lizard malaria: ecology. Sierra Leone. Joseph J. Schall. 1982

Magnetic bacteria search. Southern Hemisphere. Richard P. Blakemore. 1979

Myxomycetes and their insect associates: Arctic and subarctic ecosystems. Alaska. Steven L. Stephenson. 1988

Natural history collection. Inner Mongolia, China. Frederick R. Wulsin. 1923-24

Netherlands Indies: collection of rare species for zoos. Sumatra. William M. Mann. 1937

Organisms from simple environments. Nicholas C. Collins. 1976

Photorefraction and penguin vision. Falkland Islands. Jacob G. Sivak. 1980

Prochloron and ascidian symbioses. Palau. Rosevelt L. Pardy. 1981

Rain forest, tropical: biological exploration. Costa Rica. Donald E. Stone. 1985

Río Camuy Cave. Northwestern Puerto Rico. Russell H. Gurnee, Brother G. Nicholas, and John V. Thrailkill. 1963

Tambopata Reserve: flora and fauna. Peru. David L. Pearson. 1979

Taphonomy: plant remains in thaw lakes. Seward Peninsula, Alaska. David M. Hopkins. 1988

Tierra del Fuego: natural history. Argentina-Chile. Rae Natalie P. Goodall. 1970-72, 1977-79, 1982-84, 1986

United States natural reserves: biogeographical assessment. David W. Crumpacker. 1985

Urubamba Valley: biological expedition. Peru. Frank M. Chapman. 1916

Uzungwa Mountains: international plant and animal survey. Tanzania. Jonathan C. Lovett. 1984

BOTANY

Agave sebastiana: pollination ecology. Cedros Island, Mexico. James H. Brown. 1981

Algae. Australia. Ralph A. Lewin. 1976

—— calcareous. North Atlantic Ocean. Walter H. Adey. 1964-65

Algal communities: structure: physical and biological factors. Qingdao, China. Susan H. Brawley. 1985

—— tide pools. New England coast. Philip Sze. 1981

Alpine cushion plants. George G. Spomer. 1974

Andean desert loma formations: botanical response to El Niño. Peru and Chile. Michael O. Dillon. 1983

Andean high-altitude plants: reproductive biology. Patagonia, Chile. Mary T. Kalin de Arroyo. 1984-85

Angiosperms, ancient: reproductive biology. New Caledonia. Leonard B. Thien. 1985

—— Degeneria vitiensis: phytogeography and pollination biology. Fiji. John M. Miller. 1986

—— pollination mechanisms. New Caledonia. Leonard B. Thien. 1983

Anthurium. Central America. Thomas B. Croat. 1977

Araceae: Caribbean coast. Vera Cruz to Panama, Central America. Thomas B. Croat. 1986

Araliaceae. Madagascar and Comoros. Porter P. Lowry II. 1987

Araucarian cones. Southern Argentina. Thomas N. Taylor. 1973

Asteraceae: biosystematic studies. South America. Robert Merrill King. 1973

—— genus Bidens: adaptive radiation. Hawaii. Barbara A. Schaal. 1984

Bahama, Turks, and Caicos Islands. William Thomas Gillis, Jr. 1973

Bali and Celebes Islands. Willem Meijer. 1976

Bambara groundnut: variation and evolution. Sub-Saharan Africa. W. Hardy Eshbaugh. 1987

Bamboos: new species reproduction. Costa Rica. Richard W. Pohl. 1982, 1984

—— and bambusoid grasses. Brazil. Thomas R. Soderstrom. 1971, 1975

Beach heather. Ralph P. Collins. 1980

Boraginaceae: phylogenetic study. Mexico. James S. Miller. 1986

Botanical explorations. Chiapas, Mexico. David A. Sutton. 1988

—— Guizhou Province, China. David E. Boufford. 1986-87

—— Río Peñas Blancas Valley. Costa Rica. William A. Haber. 1988

—— southern Andes. Argentina and Chile. Roberto Kiesling. 1988

Botanical survey: Cordillera de Talamanca. Costa Rica. Michael H. Grayum. 1986

—— hills of the northern Kalahari. Africa. David G. Long. 1986

Bracken-fern gametophytes: comparative normal and abnormal development. Carl R. Partanen. 1971

Bromeliaceae, genus Puya: evolution and migration. South America. Amy Jean Gilmartin. 1986

Bromeliads. Brazilian mountains. Margaret U. Mee. 1966

—— carnivorism. South America. Thomas J. Givnish. 1983

Bryophytes. Bolivia. John J. Engel. 1984

—— Chaillu Massif, Gabon. Robert E. Magill. 1986

—— rain forest: collection. Yunnan and Sichuan, China. Paul L. Redfearn, Jr. 1986, 1988

—— South America. John J. Engel. 1975, 1981

—— Southern Africa. Robert E. Magill. 1983

Buttercups, alpine: species formation. New Zealand. George B. Johnson. 1984

Capsicum pubescens complex: biosystematics and evolution. W. Hardy Eshbaugh. 1970-71

Cerro de la Neblina. Venezuela. Thomas B. Croat. 1983

Cerro del Torra: floristic study and collections. Colombia. Philip A. Silverstone-Sopkin. 1988

Cerro El Gigante: flora and vegetation. Nicaragua. Warren D. Stevens. 1984

Cerro Sumaco. Ecuador. Michael T. Madison. 1978

Cerro Tacarcuna: botanical survey. Panama. Barry E. Hammel. 1986

Chenopodium germplasm. South America. Hugh D. Wilson. 1978

Chondrus crispus alga. Esther L. McCandless. 1970

Cycads (Zamia). Knut Norstog. 1975

—— Australian: reproductive ecology. New South Wales and Queensland. Robert Ornduff. 1985

Cyclanthaceae (Monotyledoneae). Ecuadoran Andes. George J. Wilder. 1988

Death Valley. California. Frederick V. Coville. 1931

Desert Plants. Chile. Harold A. Mooney and Sherry L. Gulmon. 1978

—— community analysis of perennials. Mojave Desert, California. Henry F. Howe. 1984

—— population dynamics of annuals. Sonora Desert, Arizona. David L. Venable. 1988

—— (Welwitschia). Namibia. Chris H. Bornman. 1968

Dioecy: evolution in Schiedea. Hawaii. Ann K. Sakai and Stephen G. Weller. 1987

Epilobium (Onagraceae). Tian Shan, Xinjiang Province, China, and

Taiwan. Peter C. Hoch. 1986

Erythronium: field studies. Appalachians and Pacific Northwest, United States. Bruce L. Carr. 1987

Euphorbiaceae. New Caledonia. Gordon D. McPherson. 1983

Ferns, tropical. Eastern United States. Donald R. Farrar. 1981

Figs, strangler. Venezuela. Francis E. Putz. 1984

Flax *(Linum).* Mediterranean region. Claude M. Rogers. 1971

Floral odors in beetle-pollinated plants. Costa Rica. Helen J. Young. 1988

Floristic inventory: Amazonian flora. Upper Río Napo, Ecuador. David A. Neill. 1987

—— eastern cordilleras, Paraguay. Elsa N. Zardini. 1988

—— Huascarán National Park. Peru. David N. Smith. 1985

Forest reserves in the "Green Plan." Austria. Else A. Schmidt. 1968-69

Forest types. North Cascade Range, Washington. Richard N. Mack. 1973

Forests: conservation. Malawi. Françoise B. Dowsett-Lemaire. 1982

—— conservation sites. Cameroon. Duncan W. Thomas. 1987

—— establishment. Celebes. Willem Meijer. 1975

—— evergreen. Cameroon. Duncan W. Thomas. 1983

—— paleotropical. Africa and Asia. Alwyn H. Gentry. 1981, 1988

—— tropical: pathogen-plant interactions. Los Tuxtlas Biological Station, Mexico. Rodolfo Dirzo. 1987

—— tropical: regeneration. Panama. Nicholas V. L. Brokaw. 1982, 1984

—— tropical: sample observation plots. Kolombangara Island, Solomon Islands. Timothy C. Whitmore. 1985

—— tropical lowland: evolutionary relationships. Thailand, Malaysia, Indonesia, and Papua New Guinea. Steven H. Rogstad. 1987

—— wet tropical: biomass allocation and growth in saplings. Costa Rica. David A. King. 1987

Fuchsias: evolutionary mechanisms. Colombia, Ecuador, Peru, and Chile. Paul E. Berry. 1988

Fungi. Brazil. Gary J. Samuels. 1983

—— high arctic lowland. Alexandra Fjord, Ellesmere Island. Linda M. Kohn. 1984

—— Sulawesi. Gary J. Samuels. 1985

Galápagos Islands: post-eruption revegetation on Isla Fernandina. Lynn B. Hendrix. 1984

Gondwana conifers: reproductive biology. Chile. Philip B. Tomlinson. 1985

Grasses: biosystematic investigation. Oaxaca and Chiapas, Mexico. Frank W. Gould. 1973

Gustavia superba: population ecology. Panama. Victoria L. Sork. 1983

Hanging gardens. Colorado Plateau. Stanley L. Welsh. 1972

Hawaiian Islands. Ron Scogin. 1978

Heliconia. Melanesia. Walter J. E. Kress. 1982

—— pollinator behavior and genetic variation. Costa Rica. W. John Kress. 1988

Iridaceae: *Gladiolus* and *Geissorhiza.* Madagascar. Peter Goldblatt. 1988

—— *Lapeyrousia:* systematics. Namibia. Peter Goldblatt. 1988

Isoetacae, tropical alpine: sediment-based autotrophy. Peru. Jon E. Keeley. 1985

Kakabekia: microorganism with Precambrian affinities. Iceland. Sanford M. Siegel. 1971

Kanga Mountain expedition: altitudinal variation in forest trees. Tanzania. Jonathan C. Lovett. 1986

Kokechik Bay area. Alaska. Charles M. Kirkpatrick. 1972

Krakatoa: resurvey of flora. John R. Flenley. 1979

Kwangsi. China. G. Weidman Groff. 1937

Lauraceae (avocado). Costa Rica and museums. William C. Burger. 1986

—— Iquitos area, Peru. Henrik H. van der Werff. 1988

—— montane forest field study. Ecuador. Hendrik H. van der Werff. 1986

Leaf herbivory: variation in rain-forest shrub, *Piper arieianum.* Costa Rica. Robert J. Marquis. 1986, 1988

Lepidoptera: host plants. Aldabra Atoll, Indian Ocean. Jay C. Shaffer. 1967

Lichen growths on Maya ruins. Mason E. Hale. 1975, 1978-79

Lichens, rain-forest. Australia. Mason E. Hale, Jr. 1983

—— *(Stereocaulon paschale)* as caribou fodder. K. A. Kershaw. 1976

—— survey and inventory. Namibia and Namaqualand. Mason E. Hale. 1988

—— (Thelotremataceae): systematics and evolution. Lesser Antilles. Mason E. Hale. 1971

—— and bryophytes. Galápagos Islands. William A. Weber. 1975

Lobelioids. Hawaii. Thomas J. Givnish. 1988

Lodgepole pine forests: biotic succession following fire. Yellowstone National Park. Dale L. Taylor. 1971

Log-fern hybrids *(Dryopteris).* Great Dismal Swamp, Virginia. Lytton J. Musselman. 1976-77

Luangwa Valley National Park: vegetation changes. Zambia. Stephen D. Prince. 1987

Madagascar. Peter Goldblatt. 1973

—— biological evaluation. Anjozorobe Forest. Voara A. Randrianasolo. 1988

—— botanical inventory. Marojejy Massif. Marion F. Nicoll. 1987

—— floristic inventory. Beza-Mahafaly region. Linda K. Sussman. 1986

—— floristic inventory. Nosy Mangabe rain forest. George E. Schatz. 1987

—— Mimosaceae: phytogeographic study. Jean-Francois Villiers. 1987

—— primary vegetation: remote sensing. Southern Madagascar. Glen M. Green. 1987

—— xerophyte flora. South and southwest. Peter B. Phillipson. 1987

Marine biologist Walter Starck and his wife, Jo, explore reefs off Andros Island in the Bahamas. BATES LITTLEHALES, NGS

Snug in a self-made shell, a female paper nautilus jets about by ejecting water through a siphon. ROBERT F. SISSON, NGS

A camera's click alerts a timber wolf, subject of a field study of moose and wolves on Isle Royale in Lake Superior. L. DAVID MECH

This average-size rafflesia measures 27.5 inches; some specimens of the world's largest flower span a yard. YVES LAUMONIER

Maize, sweet stalk: high elevation. Himalaya. Carl L. Johannessen. 1985

Mangroves: evolutionary mechanisms. Philip B. Tomlinson. 1976.

—— Old World. Indo-Pacific. Philip B. Tomlinson. 1973

—— Oriental. A. Malcolm Gill. 1968-69

Marquesas Islands. Marie-Helene Sachet. 1974

Maya Mountains. British Honduras. John D. Dwyer. 1972

Microflora: composition, variation, and ecology. Arctic Sea. Spencer Apollonio. 1971

Mistletoes: biogeographical affinities and chromosomal relationships. Africa. Delbert Wiens. 1971

Mosses. Society Islands. Henry O. Whittier. 1979

—— entomophilous. Alberta, Canada. Dale H. Vitt. 1985

—— flora. Southern Patagonia, Argentina. Celina M. Matteri. 1986, 1988

Mount Mulanje Massif. Malawi. J. D. Chapman. 1983, 1986

Mycorrhizae in vascular epiphytes. Costa Rica. Robert K. Antibus. 1986

Myrtaceae. Mexico and Central America. Leslie R. Landrum. 1988

Natural diversity in an arborescent legume, *Acacia caven*. Chile and Argentina. James C. Aronson. 1988

Orchids, slipper: pollination biology. Borneo, Malaysia, and Philippines. John T. Atwood. 1984-86

—— *Telipogon*. Ecuador. Calaway H. Dodson. 1986

—— terrestrial: pollination. Australia. Warren P. Stoutamire. 1972-73

Palms: key to Neotropical mammal abundance. Peru. Louise H. Emmons. 1979

—— Madagascan: reproductive biology. James H. Beach. 1986

—— Madagascan. Andrew J. Henderson. 1988

—— taxonomic studies. Papua New Guinea. Frederick B. Essig. 1977

Pandanaceae: floral evolution. South Pacific. Paul A. Cox. 1982

Paniceae, Poaceae, Panicoideae: revision of Neotropical genera. Colombia and Venezuela. Fernando O. Zuloaga. 1988

Paraguayan Chaco: floristic and biogeographic study. Paraguay and Bolivia. R. E. Spichiger. 1986

Patagonia: flora and vegetation. Argentina. Maevia N. Correa. 1988

Perennial shrubs *(Galvezia)*. Ecuador. Wayne J. Elisens. 1984

Phenakosperum: pollination biology. French Guiana. Donald E. Stone. 1987

Phytogeographic studies. Burica Peninsula, Panama and Costa Rica. Thomas B. Croat. 1972

Pico das Almas Project: flora of the Campos Rupestres. Brazil. Raymond M. Harley. 1988

Plankton, blue-water. William M. Hamner. 1970

Plant collecting: areas with serpentine soils. Goias State, Brazil. Robert R. Brooks. 1987

—— Bhutan. Bruce M. Bartholomew. 1985

—— China. Robert Ornduff. 1980

—— Costa Rica. Gerrit Davidse. 1983

—— Japan. John L. Creech. 1978

—— New Britain, Papua New Guinea. Frederick B. Essiq. 1988

—— Sierra de San Lazaro, Baja California. Amy Jean Gilmartin. 1968-69

—— Venezuelan Guyana. Julian A. Steyermark. 1986

Plant communities: distribution and diversity. Amazonian Peru. Alwyn H. Gentry. 1979

—— effects of pollinating bats. Costa Rica and Arizona. Donna J. Howell. 1974

Plant invader (guava): Hawaii Volcanoes National Park, Hawaii. Peter M. Vitousek. 1987

Plant mating systems: measuring natural selection. Spain and North Africa. Denise E. Costich. 1986-87

Plant species: *Beagle* voyage. Duncan M. Porter. 1980, 1982

—— Cook and Flinders voyages. Society Islands and Australia. Francis R. Fosberg. 1981-82

Plant succession: Soufrière. St. Vincent, Leeward Islands. John Stanley Beard. 1971

Plant zonation: around geothermal vents. Japan, New Zealand, and Iceland. Janice M. Glime. 1986

Plants and landforms. Tristan da Cunha and St. Helena Islands. Nigel M. Wace. 1975

Psilotum: classical culture, mutants, and wild occurrences. Japan. Albert S. Rouffa. 1972

Pteridophytic plants: phytogeography. Chocó, Colombia. David B. Lellinger. 1968-69

Qinling Mountains: vegetation analysis. China. Tsen-shen Ying. 1987

Quercus (oak), wet-forest. Mexico. Dennis E. Breedlove. 1986

Rafflesiaceae. Southeast Asia. Willem Meijer. 1982

Rain forests: collecting *Chisocheton* (Meliaceae). Papua New Guinea, Java, and Borneo. Jack B. Fisher. 1985

—— plant inventory in threatened areas. Indonesia. Peter S. Ashton. 1988

—— tropical montane: fertilization effects on growth. Venezuela. Edmund V. J. Tanner. 1985

Rattan palm: collection. Asian rain forests. Jack B. Fisher. 1976

Redwoods: preservation. California. Chester C. Brown. 1963

Sage *(Salvia)*. James L. Reveal. 1974

Sichuan Province: China. Bruce M. Bartholomew. 1983

Solanaceae. Comoros and Madagascar. William G. D'Arcy. 1982, 1987

Spore research. West Indies and northern South and Central America. Fred C. Meier. 1935

Stromatolites and algal carbonate structures of the Recent Epoch: ecology. Shark Bay, Australia. Stjepko Golubic. 1973

Subarctic plant systems and water conservation. Wayne R. Rouse. 1971
Sunflower family (Compositae): source of fish poisons. Tod F. Stuessy. 1976
Tariquia Forest: botanical inventory. Bolivia. James C. Solomon. 1981
Tibet: botanical expedition. Ronald H. Petersen. 1979
Tian Shan: ecology. Xinjiang Province, China. David H. Chang. 1987
Tiliaceae. Cameroon, West Africa. Willem Meijer. 1981
Tree-limit ecotone: vegetational dynamics. Central Brooks Range, Alaska. Ann M. Odasz. 1981
Tree regeneration: tropical forest gaps. Western Malaysia. James W. Raich. 1985
Tree-species diversity. Upper Amazonia, Peru. Alwyn H. Gentry. 1983
Trigger plants: pollinating mechanisms. Australia. Sherwin J. Carlquist. 1977
Tristan da Cunha Islands: atmospheric pollen and spores. Nigel M. Wace. 1982
Tropical botany: exploration of Bocas del Toro. Panama. Gordon D. McPherson. 1985-86
——— exploration of the Sierra Nevada de Santa Marta. Colombia. Hermes Cuadros. 1985
Truffles and trees: post-glaciopluvial co-dispersal. Nevada and Utah. Robert D. Fogel. 1986
Viticulture. South Africa. Harm J. de Blij. 1983
Wheats, cultivated: origin and ancestry. B. Lennart Johnson. 1972
Wildflowers of the United States. New York Botanical Garden. 1965
Willow, Setchell: demography. Denali National Park, Alaska. Dorothy A. Douglas. 1987-88
Witchweeds: fertility patterns. Lytton J. Musselman. 1979
Wokomung, sandstone massif: botanical reconnaissance. Guyana. Brian M. Boom. 1988
Xyridaceae: survey. Brazil. Robert Kral. 1986

ECOLOGY

Amazon Basin: ecosystem rehabilitation. Brazil. Christopher Uhl. 1982, 1985, 1988
Amazonian Brazil: species area requirements. David C. Oren. 1979-80
Ants and giant anteaters: ecologic interaction. Venezuela. Yael D. Lubin. 1977
Arctic grayling: ecological growth limits. Alaska. Linda A. Deegan. 1987
Argentina: impact of introduced red deer on Andean forest vegetation. Thomas T. Veblen. 1987
Asses, feral: distribution and ecological impact. Galápagos Islands. Patricia D. Moehlman. 1980
Camera equipment for marine biology research. Harold E. Edgerton. 1974
Capelin crash: effects on seabirds. Norway. Robert W. Furness. 1988
Chelation: sea-ice algae and phytoplankton growth. Arctic waters.

Spencer Apollonio. 1986
Coastal lagoons: hydrology. Brazil. Bjorn Kjerfve. 1988
Coral reefs: siltation effects of deforestation. Panama. Ann B. Foster. 1987
Computer extrapolation of Landsat spectral signatures to classify vegetation. John J. Craighead. 1981
Dead Sea system: limnology and ecology. Joel R. Gat. 1976-77
Desert buttes: testing island biogeography theories. David M. Armstrong. 1981
Dugongs and sea turtles: exploitation. Torres Strait. Bernard Nietschmann. 1976
Earth mounds: hypotheses of origin. Kenya, Cameroon, Central African Republic, and Cape Province, South Africa. George W. Cox. 1985, 1987
Ecological effects of exotic grasses in semidesert Southwest. Arizona. Carl E. and Jane H. Bock. 1984, 1988
Ecological influences of the Tarahumara Indians on three plants. Mexico. Robert A. Bye, Jr. 1977
Ecological surveying. East Lake Turkana (Rudolf), Kenya. Michael Norton-Griffiths. 1976
Epiphyte ecology: rain-forest tree canopies. Costa Rica. Nalini M. Nadkarni. 1984, 1986
Everglades ecology. Everglades National Park, Florida. Frank C. Craighead, Sr. 1966, 1970
Falkland Islands: natural history and ecology. Olin S. Pettingill, Jr. 1970
Fish herbivory: effects on tropical-stream algae. Costa Rica. Catherine M. Pringle. 1988
Fish ecology. Orinoco floodplain, Venezuela. William M. Lewis, Jr. 1988
Forests, old growth: effects of early eruptions. Mount St. Helens, Washington. David K. Yamaguchi. 1985
——— semideciduous: ecology of the canopy. Panama. Pedro Galindo. 1973
——— tropical plantations and natural systems: avian community structure. Puerto Rico. Alexander Cruz. 1985
Fruiting phenology: Amazonian rain forest. Colombia. Sara B. Defler. 1986, 1988
Geckos: competitive displacement in an introduced assemblage. Fiji. Douglas T. Bolger. 1988
Goats, feral: ecological impact. Aldabra Atoll, Seychelles. Margaret G. Burke. 1985
Great Plains: comparative competition and diversity of herbivores. Gary E. Belovsky. 1979
Hawaii: introduced avifauna. Stuart L. Pimm. 1982
Island factors and density regulation on land-bird populations in Hawaii. John T. Emlen. 1977
Isthmus of Panama: environmental and climatic history. Paul A. Colinvaux. 1987
Kruger National Park: biomass production of selected woody species utilized by browsing game. South Africa. Bruce R. Dayton. 1977
Larval amphibians: growth and survival in the Asian frog (Bombina orienta-

lis). Korea. Robert H. Kaplan. 1988
Laysan Lagoon: ecology in relation to Laysan duck. Hawaii. Petra H. Lenz. 1984
Little Dunk's Bay: ecosystem. Great Lakes. Joseph B. MacInnis and Alan R. Emery. 1970
Mangrove trees and associated epifauna. Belize. Aaron M. Ellison. 1988
Marine communities. St. Matthew Island, Alaska. John S. Oliver. 1986
Masai land: ecology. Tanzania. Tepilit Ole-Saitoti. 1978
Monarch butterflies: microclimatic determinants. Mexico. William H. Calvert. 1988
Mono Lake. California. John M. Melack. 1979-80
Moose and wolf relationships. Isle Royale, Michigan. Rolf O. Peterson. 1980, 1983, 1985, 1987
——— Isle Royale, Michigan. Durward L. Allen and Peter A. Jordan. 1964-65.
Nautilus: ecology of sympatric species. Palau and Manus Island, Papua New Guinea. William B. Saunders. 1984-85
Neotropical plant communities: diversity and floristic composition. Andes, Colombia. Alwyn H. Gentry. 1985
New Guinea mountains. J. Linsley Gressitt. 1968-69
Northern Thailand: highland land use and environmental change. Peter Kunstadter. 1982
Northern Waterfowl Project: U. S.-U.S.S.R. Environmental Protection Agreement. William J. L. Sladen. 1977
Panama: recovery of vegetation from earthquake-caused landslides. Nancy C. Garwood. 1980
Papyrus swamps: effect on ecology. Lake Naivasha, Kenya. John J. Gaudet. 1971, 1973, 1975, 1977
Plant-insect interactions in a tropical herb. Mexico. Carol C. Horvitz. 1982
Plant-vertebrate interactions: fruit dispersal and evolutionary ecology. Borneo. Mark Leighton. 1984
Plant-water relationships in an extreme desert. Atacama Desert, Chile. Harold A. Mooney. 1988
Pollution: 70-year evaluation. Dry Tortugas, Florida. Richard H. Chesher. 1972
Protozoan communities: ecology. Lake Waiau, Hawaii. Raymond D. Dillon. 1970
Rain forests: destruction and ecology. Moorea Island, French Polynesia. John R. Flenley. 1984
——— fruit and vertebrate frugivore interaction. Gabon. Louise H. Emmons. 1980
——— fruit and vertebrate frugivore interaction. Panama. Thomas E. Martin. 1985
——— production and nutrient cycling. Sarawak. John Proctor. 1977-78
——— Valdivian: gap dynamics. Chile. Thomas T. Veblen. 1983
Red Sea mountains: plant and animal ecology. Egypt. Steven M. Goodman. 1984
Saltville Valley: paleoecology. Virginia.

Jerry N. McDonald. 1982

Sea otters: foraging effect on mussels. Alaska. James A. Estes. 1984

Seaweed: chemical defenses against marine herbivores. Atlantic and Caribbean. Mark E. Hay. 1986

Slime mold *(Myxomycete):* beetle associates and forest ecology. Northern India. Steven L. Stephenson. 1986

Soil erosion: natural and man-induced. Sagarmatha (Mount Everest) National Park, Nepal. Alton C. Byers. 1985

Sub-lacustrine fumarole communities. Yellowstone Lake, Yellowstone National Park, Wyoming. Jerry L. Kaster, J. V. Klump, and Charles C. Remsen. 1985

Submarine limnological study. Great Lakes. Joseph B. MacInnis. 1968-69

Subtidal fauna: ecological reconnaissance. Easter Island. Louis H. DiSalvo. 1984

Tidal marsh: ecosystem. Trenton, New Jersey. Dennis F. Whigham. 1974

Titicaca, Lake. Peru-Bolivia. Carl Widmer. 1972

United States-Mexico boundary: vegetation and landform study. Robert R. Humphrey. 1983

Upland soil conservation. Thailand and Philippines. David E. Harper. 1985

Vinegarweed *(Trichostema lanceolatum):* co-evolution with its pollinator, the bee fly *(Bombylius).* California. Neal L. Evenhuis. 1984

Water conservation in desert animals. Israel. Knut Schmidt-Nielsen. 1977, 1979

Web-spider resource partitioning. California and Costa Rica. Matthew H. Greenstone. 1979

Wildlife-habitat classification by satellite imagery. John J. Craighead. 1975

Wolf-elk and wolf-cattle relationships. Alberta, Canada. Robert R. Ream. 1982

Wood frogs: acid tolerance. Southern New England. Benjamin A. Pierce. 1984

ZOOLOGY

Actinians: symbiotic with pomacentrid fishes. Daphne F. Dunn. 1977

Amazonian amphibians, reptiles, and mammals: genetic differentiation. Peru. John E. Cadle. 1984

Animals with algal endosymbionts: defense against photosynthetic oxygen toxicity. Australia. J. Malcolm Shick. 1983

Antillean biogeography: biochemical approach. West Indies. Jay M. Savage. 1987

Cave fauna. Yucatán Peninsula. Robert W. Mitchell. 1974-75

Cetacean fauna and former dolphin fishery of St. Helena: taxonomy investigation. William F. Perrin. 1982

Madeira and Deserta Islands: fauna evolution. Laurence M. Cook. 1980

Marine-cave fauna. Indo-South Pacific. Thomas M. Iliffe. 1986

Marine fish eggs: chorion microstructure and sculpturing. George W. Boehlert. 1982

Marine organisms, complex: sensory information processing and visual behavior. Talbot H. Waterman. 1968-69, 1973-77

Moths and bats: behavioral ecology. Tanzania and Hawaii. James H. Fullard. 1979, 1982

Parthenogenetic organisms in the arid zone of Western Australia. Michael J. D. White. 1982

Reptiles, amphibians, and insects. Ethiopia. Thomas P. Monath. 1964

Vertebrate genetic systems: comparative population cytogenetics and evolutionary roles. William P. Hall, 3d. 1971

Vertebrates: locomotion. East Africa. Charles R. Taylor. 1976

—— Neotropical: seasonal patterns. Sinaloa, Mexico. Terry A. Vaughan. 1970

—— populations in strip-mine areas. Frederick J. Brenner. 1971, 1973-74

Wildlife survey. Sarpo National Park, Liberia. Phillip T. Robinson. 1981

—— and collection of specimens. Nepal. S. Dillon Ripley. 1948-49

Vertebrate Zoology
Herpetology

Alligators, American: thermoregulation and ecology. Frederick R. Gehlbach. 1971

—— chemical ecology. Louisiana. Paul J. Weldon. 1988

—— Chinese *(Alligator sinensis).* Myrna E. Watanabe. 1981

—— thermoregulation. Clifford Ray Johnson. 1974

Amphibians: ecology. Chaco Boreal, Paraguay. Lon L. McClanahan. 1983

—— Seychelles Islands, Indian Ocean. Ronald A. Nussbaum. 1976-77

—— West Africa. Victor H. Hutchison. 1980

—— and reptiles. Andes and Amazon Basin of Peru. William E. Duellman. 1974, 1985-86

—— and reptiles. Colombia. Victor H. Hutchison. 1965

—— and reptiles: systematics and ecology. Cerro Fabrega, Panama. Charles W. Myers. 1984

—— and reptiles. Yunnan Province, China. Robert F. Inger. 1986

Chameleons: distribution. Kenya. James J. Hebrard. 1980

Crocodiles, American: ecology. Jamaica. Leslie D. Garrick. 1983

—— mugger: reproductive biology and conservation. India. Jeffrey W. Lang. 1984-85

—— Northern Australia. Grahame J. W. Webb. 1979

Frogs, *Eleutherodactylus:* habitat and behavior of two species. Blue Mountains, Jamaica. Daniel S. Townsend. 1984

—— Neotropical. Kentwood D. Wells. 1978

—— Palearctic water: genetic variation and hybridization. Balkan Peninsula and Turkey. Thomas Uzzell. 1984

—— relation of activity periods to phototactic behavior. Robert G. Jaeger. 1972

—— sibling recognition. Cascades, Oregon. Andrew R. Blaustein. 1982

—— telmatobiid: physiological ecology. Lake Titicaca, Peru-Bolivia. Victor H. Hutchison. 1973

—— tree *(Hyla meridionalis* and *H. arborea):* mating calls. Canary Islands. H. Carl Gerhardt. 1978

—— tree *(Litoria):* communication. Australia. H. Carl Gerhardt. 1983

—— vocalizations. Panama. Michael J. Ryan. 1983

—— and reptiles. New Guinea. Richard G. Zweifel. 1968

Geckos, mourning: behavioral ecology. Hawaii. David P. Crews. 1983

Herpetofauna. Argentina. Raymond F. Laurent. 1977

Iguanas, land *(Conolophus pallidus* and *C. subcristatus):* conservation survey. Galápagos Islands. Dagmar I. Werner. 1975-78, 1980.

Live-bearing in reptiles: evolutionary changes. New South Wales, Australia. Owen J. Sexton. 1984

Lizards, *(Anolis).* Bahamas and West Indies. Thomas W. Schoener. 1968-70

—— *(Anolis):* island ecology. Caribbean. George C. Gorman. 1971

—— *(Anolis limifrons):* functions and social displays. Thomas A. Jenssen. 1971

—— collared: hybridization. Richard R. Montanucci. 1979

—— desert. Western Australia. Eric R. Pianka. 1977, 1979

—— giant *(Sauromalus):* behavioral ecology. Gulf of California. Ted J. Case. 1977, 1979, 1988

—— *(Heterontia):* origin and evolution of all-female species. Australia. Craig C. Moritz. 1987

—— iguanid *(Sceloporus aeneus):* genetic relationships. Mexico. Louis J. Guillette, Jr., and Karen L. Brown. 1984

—— iguanid *(Sceloporus graciosus):* genetic structure. Great Basin, United States. Jack W. Sites, Jr. 1984

—— iguanid *(Sceloporus grammicus):* biogeography of karyotype variation. William P. Hall, III. 1970

—— iguanid *(Sceloporus grammicus):* chromosomal variation. Mexico. Jack W. Sites, Jr. 1985

—— iguanid *(Sceloporus merriami):* range quality and life history variation. Big Bend National Park, Texas. Arthur E. Dunham. 1984

—— iguanid. South America. Richard E. Etheridge. 1982

—— Kalahari Desert, Africa. Raymond B. Huey. 1975

—— shiny: unisexual clones. Suriname and West Indies. Charles J. Cole. 1980, 1983, 1985

—— *Varanus gouldii:* behavioral ecology. South Australia. Ted J. Case. 1984

Rattlesnakes, eastern diamondback. D. Bruce Means. 1977

—— prairie *(Crotalus viridis):* ethology and movement. Wyoming. David J. Duvall. 1982-83

—— timber: population ecology. New York. William S. Brown. 1982-85

Reptiles. Gunong Mulu National Park, Sarawak. Ian R. Swingland. 1977
—— desert: orientation and navigation. Arizona. Kraig Adler. 1979
Salamanders, Chinese: antipredator mechanisms. Yunnan Province. Edmund D. Brodie, Jr. 1988
—— tropical: behavioral defense mechanisms. Edmund D. Brodie, Jr. 1973, 1975
Sea snakes. Philippines. George C. Gorman. 1977-78
Snakes and amphibians. French Guiana. Thomas P. Monath. 1963
Toads, *(Bufo canorus):* energetics and natural history. Yosemite National Park, United States. Martin L. Morton. 1973
—— *(Bufo marinus):* evolutionary genetics. Latin America and Caribbean. Simon Easteal. 1982
—— *(Bufo marinus):* evolutionary response. Michael D. Sabath. 1980
—— golden: mating behavior and larval biology. Costa Rica. Martha L. Crump. 1988
Tortoises. Galápagos. James L. Patton. 1976
—— population ecology. Galápagos. William G. Reeder and Craig G. MacFarland. 1968-69
Tuatara *(Sphenodon punctatum):* reproductive behavior. New Zealand. James C. Gillingham. 1987
Turtles. Africa. Roger C. Wood. 1967
—— freshwater chelid: taxonomy, distribution, and ecology. Australia. John M. Legler. 1972, 1974, 1976
—— giant leatherback: taxonomic study. Suriname. Wayne F. Frair. 1968-69
—— green. Ascension Island. Archie F. Carr. 1976
—— green *(Chelonia mydas).* Caribbean. John C. Ogden. 1981, 1983
—— green. Galápagos. William G. Reeder. 1981
—— Hawaiian basking green sea. G. Causey Whittow. 1977
—— marine: population structure and evolutionary genetics. Caribbean. John C. Avise. 1987
—— Pacific green. Galápagos. Craig G. MacFarland. 1975-77
—— Pacific ridley: nesting biology. David A. Hughes. 1971
—— pleurodiran: systematics, evolution, and ecology. South America. Roger C. Wood. 1970
—— sea, hawksbill: exploitation and ecology. Bernard Nietschmann. 1972
—— sea, olive ridley: population ecology. Mexico. John G. Frazier. 1980-81
—— side-necked: ploidy mosaicism. Suriname. John W. Bickham. 1986
—— slider *(Pseudemys scripta).* Panama. John M. Legler. 1966

Ichthyology

Anglerfishes: feeding mechanisms. Theodore W. Pietsch. 1977
Blenny, introduced *(Omobranchus punctatus):* reproductive ecology. Tropical western Atlantic and Fiji. Ronald E. Thresher. 1987

Characid, splashing *(Copeina arnoldi):* reproductive and parental behavior. Guyana. Charles O. Krekorian. 1973
Chubs (subgenus *Siphateles*): systematics and biogeography. Western U. S. Robert R. Miller. 1984
Coelacanth *(Latimeria chalumnae).* Indian Ocean. Keith Stewart Thomson. 1972
Damselfish, Caribbean juveniles: recruitment and habitat selection. Smithsonian Marine Laboratory, Belize. Gerard M. Wellington. 1987
—— domino *(Dascyllus albisella):* group living and population dynamics. Hawaii. Mark A. Hixon. 1988
—— effects of El Niño on population. Panama. Gerard M. Wellington. 1985
Eels, American: breeding area. James D. McCleave. 1980
—— American and European: migratory mechanisms in larvae and adults. James D. McCleave. 1977
—— American and European: spawning relative to a front in the Sargasso Sea. James D. McCleave. 1984
—— garden: ecological and behavioral study. Red Sea. Eugenie Clark. 1971.
Fish temperatures: thermal imaging. Northeast coast, U. S. Francis G. Carey. 1985
Fishes: Beebe Project: behavior of deep-sea fish, especially sharks. Bermuda. Eugenie Clark. 1986-87
—— benthic: recruitment. Chesapeake Bay. Denise L. Breitburg. 1987
—— cichlid: sexual selection and speciation. Lake Barombi Mbo, Cameroon. Wallace J. Dominey. 1984
—— collection. Río Nichare, Venezuela. James E. Böhlke. 1976
—— coral-reef: Bahamas. Raymond D. Clarke. 1974
—— coral-reef: deepwater community. Jamaica. Murray Itzkowitz. 1984
—— coral-reef: dispersal and life history strategies. Caribbean. Myra J. Shulman. 1985
—— coral-reef: genetic variability and kin groups. Elat, Gulf of Aqaba. Douglas Y. Shapiro. 1984
—— coral-reef. Moluccas, Indonesia. Victor G. Springer. 1973
—— coral-reef: Solomon Islands. John E. Randall. 1973
—— deep-sea, and shallow-water predators. California. Eugenie Clark and William Hamner. 1988
—— electric. Walter F. Heiligenberg. 1976, 1981-82
—— electric, mormyriform. Peter Moller. 1975, 1977
—— electric, mormyriform. Gabon. Carl D. Hopkins. 1976, 1979, 1981
—— electric, mormyriform. Sierra Leone. Peter Moller. 1985
—— freshwater: collection. Tropical Africa. Tyson R. Roberts. 1986
—— genetics. Atlantic and Pacific Oceans. Dennis A. Powers. 1975
—— glandulocaudin: zoogeography. South America. Stanley H. Weitzman. 1977

Bagging for tagging, biologist William S. Brown has studied the timber rattlesnake for nearly a decade. BIANCA LAVIES

Unwilling to mate, a female Galápagos tortoise gives a male the slip by fleeing to mud. CRAIG AND JAN MacFARLAND

A young brown bear feasts on salmon in Alaska. Research grants have funded nine bear studies. ALLAN L. EGBERT

The guanaco's wild relatives roam Tierra del Fuego as one of South America's cameloid species. WILLIAM L. FRANKLIN

—— hermaphroditic: mating success. Panama. Eric A. Fischer. 1986
—— kelp forest: biogeography and genetic divergence. Viña del Mar, Chile. Carol A. Stepien. 1987
—— labrid. David R. Robertson. 1975
—— Lord Howe Island. New South Wales, Australia. Frank H. Talbot. 1972
—— marine invertebrates and algae. Southeast Oceania. John E. Randall. 1969.
—— Neotropical stream: community structure and convergent ecomorphological trends. Venezuela. Kirk O. Winemiller. 1983
—— osteoglossid. South America. Joan Dorothy Fuller. 1972
—— pelagic. F. G. Walton Smith and Hilary B. Moore. 1953-60
—— pelagic. North Atlantic. Frank J. Mather 3d. 1962
—— St. Helena Island, South Atlantic. Alasdair J. Edwards. 1983
—— survey. Congo River's lower rapids. Tyson R. Roberts. 1972
—— temperate-zone herbivorous: feeding behavior. British Isles and western Europe. Michael H. Horn. 1985
—— tide-pool: seasonality and habitat constraints. Gulf of Maine. John R. Moring. 1985
—— toxic-repellent effect of certain species on sharks. Red Sea. Eugenie Clark. 1972.
—— *(Trichonotus nikii):* massive swarming and lek behavior. Red Sea. Eugenie Clark. 1982
—— tropical reef. Caribbean. Robert R. Warner. 1976
—— tropical sand-diving. Red Sea. Eugenie Clark. 1977
Guppies: sexual behavior. Trinidad. James A. Farr. 1984
Ichthyofauna: survey. Easter Island. John E. Randall. 1984
Killifish, annual: systematics, ecology, and distribution. Northern South America. Jamie E. Thomerson. 1971
Lungfish *(Clarias)* and *Tilapia.* East Africa. Geoffrey Moriaso Ole Maloiy. 1974-75
Piranhas. Venezuela. Leo G. Nico. 1988
Platyfish *(Xiphophorus aculatus):* selection on color patterns. Belize. John A. Endler and Alexandra L. Basolo. 1988
Poecilia: color-pattern convergences. Trinidad and Venezuela. John A. Endler. 1979
—— ethology. Mexico. Joseph S. Balsano and Ellen M. Rasch. 1976
—— *(Poecilia formosa):* evolutionary genetics. Mexico. Bruce J. Turner. 1980
Pollution: effects on fish gill structure, growth, and survival. Kenya. Geoffrey M. O. Maloiy. 1985
Rays, Pacific electric: movements and electrical behavior. California. Richard N. Bray. 1988
River fishes. Australia. Tim M. Berra. 1968-69

Salmon, Atlantic: male mating systems. Newfoundland. W. Linn Montgomery. 1984
Sculpins (Cottidae): genetic evolution. Lake Baikal, U.S.S.R. Irving L. Kornfield. 1984
Sharks, bull: speciation. Lake Nicaragua. Jack D. Burke. 1970
—— gray reef: social behavior and aggression. Donald R. Nelson. 1971-72
—— reef. Rangiroa, French Polynesia. Donald R. Nelson. 1973
—— scalloped hammerhead. Gulf of California. Peter Klimley and Donald R. Nelson. 1980
—— "sleeping." Mexican caves. Eugenie Clark. 1973-74.
—— teleost symbionts. Japan. Eugenie Clark. 1975
—— white: behavioral ecology. Point Reyes/Farallon Marine Sanctuary, California. A. Peter Klimley. 1984-85
Shore fishes. Easter Island. John E. Randall. 1968-69
Stingrays: freshwater adaptation. Thomas B. Thorson. 1974, 1976-79
Surgeonfishes, brown: migration and spawning. Red Sea. W. Linn Montgomery. 1987
—— spawning. Atlantic Ocean. Patrick L. Colin. 1977-78
Trout, cutthroat *(Salmo clarkii):* geographic variation and evolution. Yellowstone National Park and environs, U. S. Richard N. Williams. 1987
Tuna. Francis G. Carey. 1967-69

Mammalogy

Animal tracking by satellite. Frank C. Craighead, Jr. 1970
Anteaters, giant. Brazil. Kent H. Redford. 1980
Antelopes. East Africa. Richard Despard Estes. 1974
—— bongo: search for. Kenya. Theodore H. Reed. 1968
—— sable. Angola and Kenya. Richard Despard Estes. 1968-70, 1975
—— topi. Mara Game Preserve, Tanzania. Geoffrey Moriaso Ole Maloiy. 1972
Armadillos: habitat utilization. Brazil. Tracy S. Carter. 1979
—— long-nosed: ranging behavior and reproduction in females. Florida. Kent H. Redford. 1988
Baboons: energetics, ecology, and behavior. Amboseli National Park, Kenya. Stuart and Jeanne Altmann. 1986
—— olive: ecology and behavior. Kenya. Robert S. O. Harding. 1974
—— olive: social strategies of translocated troops. Kenya. Shirley C. Strum. 1984, 1986
—— olive: updating demographic records. Gombe National Park, Tanzania. David A. Collins. 1987
Bats, African megadermatid: communication. Kenya. Terry A. Vaughan. 1982
—— false vampire: social, foraging, and roosting behavior. Terry A. Vaughan. 1972

—— frog-eating. Panama and Kenya. Merlin D. Tuttle. 1979-80, 1983-84
—— fruit: cooperative foraging and harem evolution. Douglas W. Morrison. 1979
—— fruit. Ivory Coast. Donald W. Thomas. 1980
—— mouse-tailed: echolocation. James A. Simmons. 1979
—— mustache: acoustic basis of prey selection. Jamaica. O'Dell W. Henson, Jr. 1982
—— Neotropical: echolocation. Trinidad. Patricia E. Brown. 1979
—— Neotropical: mating and kinship. Trinidad. Gary F. McCracken. 1980
—— tent-making: cooperative behavior. Trinidad. Thomas H. Kunz. 1984
—— West African: energetics. Roger E. Carpenter. 1977
Bears, black: satellite monitoring during winter sleep. John J. Craighead. 1971
—— black: territoriality and habitat productivity. Pisgah National Forest, North Carolina. Roger A. Powell. 1984-85
—— brown. Alaska Peninsula. Allen W. Stokes. 1972-73
—— brown: radiotracking. Yugoslavia. Djuro Huber. 1985-86, 1988
—— grizzly. Yellowstone National Park, Wyoming. Frank C. Craighead, Jr., and John J. Craighead. 1959-67
—— grizzly: habitat survey by Landsat. John J. Craighead. 1976, 1979
—— grizzly: habitat use determined by satellite imagery. Alaska. John J. Craighead. 1987
—— polar: behavior and ecology. Northwest Territories, Canada. Brian M. Knudsen. 1970-71
—— polar: survey of dens. Svalbard, Arctic Ocean. Thor Larsen. 1971
Biotelemetry systems for wildlife research. Frank C. Craighead, Jr., and John J. Craighead. 1968-69
Bison, American: genetics and inbreeding. Badlands National Park, South Dakota. Joel Berger. 1986-87
—— social and sexual behavior. Montana. Dale F. Lott. 1967-71
Bobcats: ecology. Idaho. Maurice G. Hornocker. 1983
Burros, wild: social organization and communication behavior. Patricia D. Moehlman. 1970, 1972
Bushbaby, thick-tailed: ecology and behavior. South Africa. Gerald A. Doyle. 1968, 1970
Camels, one-humped: locomotion. Kenya. Geoffrey Moriaso Ole Maloiy. 1982
—— temperature regulation and dehydration. Australia. Knut Schmidt-Nielsen. 1982
Caribou. Labrador. Dietland Muller-Schwarze. 1980
—— satellite tracking. Alaska. John J. Craighead. 1986
—— telemetry tracking. Idaho. Donald R. Johnson. 1974
Cats, farm: nursing coalitions and infanticide. David W. MacDonald. 1979
—— Iriomote *(Mayailurus iriomotensis):* ecology and conservation. Ja-

pan. Paul Leyhausen. 1973
Cattle, native and crossbred: comparative productivity. India. Stewart Odend'hal. 1987
Cetacea: neurologic disease. Nicholas R. Hall. 1978
—— southern South American. Argentina. Rae Natalie P. Goodall. 1983, 1988
Cheetahs. Botswana. Mark J. Owens and Delia Owens. 1974
—— Serengeti: decline. Tanzania. Timothy M. Caro. 1987
—— East African. Kenya and Tanzania. Stephen J. O'Brien. 1985
—— male coalitions. Tanzania. Timothy M. Caro. 1982-83
Chimpanzees: communicative capacity. R. Allen Gardner and Beatrice T. Gardner. 1968-69
—— food calls. Kibale Forest Reserve, Uganda. Richard W. Wrangham. 1987
—— Gombe National Park. Tanzania. Jane Goodall. 1961-71, 1976, 1978
—— intrapersonal signing. Roger S. Fouts. 1986, 1988
—— pygmy *(Pan paniscus):* comparison with common chimpanzee. San Diego Zoo, California. Frans B. M. de Waal. 1983
—— pygmy: feeding ecology. Zaire. Randall L. Susman. 1979
Deer, Key. Florida. Willard D. Klimstra. 1968-71
Dolphins, bottlenose, Indian Ocean: behavior of wild dolphins habituated to humans. Shark Bay, Western Australia. Bernd G. Wursig. 1984
—— bottlenose: social relationships. Shark Bay, Western Australia. Richard W. Wrangham. 1986, 1988
—— dusky. Argentina. Roger S. Payne. 1974
—— dusky: foraging, group structure, and behavior. New Zealand. Bernd G. Wursig. 1987
—— dusky and southern common. Argentina. Charles Walcott. 1975-76
—— Franciscana: life history, behavior, and acoustics. Uruguay. Robert L. Brownell, Jr. 1972-73
—— Uruguay. Ricardo Praderi. 1980-82
Dugongs. Australia. Paul K. Anderson. 1975, 1980, 1987
Elephants, African. Iain Douglas-Hamilton. 1981
—— African. Phyllis C. Lee. 1982-83
—— African: acoustic communication. Etosha Park, Namibia and Zimbabwe. Katherine B. Payne and William R. Langbauer. 1986-87
—— African: resource competition. Amboseli National Park, Kenya. Sandy J. Andelman. 1984-85
—— African: taphonomic studies. Zimbabwe. Gary A. Haynes. 1983-85
—— African: vocal communication. Kenya. Joyce H. Poole. 1988
Ferrets, black-footed: conservation. Wyoming. Timothy W. Clark. 1977, 1982-83, 1985
—— black-footed, and prairie dogs. Wyoming. Timothy W. Clark. 1973

Gazelles, desert. Charles R. Taylor. 1971
—— Thompson's and wildebeest: ranging patterns. Amboseli National Park, Kenya. Jack W. Bradbury and Sandra L. Vehrencamp. 1985
Gibbons: vocal behavior. Indonesia. John C. Mitani. 1985
Giraffes: orthostatic adaptation. South Africa. Alan R. Hargens. 1985
Goats, wild: endangered. Thailand. Sandro Lovari. 1984
Gophers, pocket: zoogeography and systematics. Florida. S. David Webb. 1979
Gorillas, lowland: comparative ecological study. Central African Republic. J. Michael Fay. 1986
—— lowland: ecology. West Africa. Julie C. Webb. 1974-75
—— lowland: feeding ecology. Gabon. Mary E. Rogers. 1985, 1987
—— lowland: interrelationships with chimpanzees. Río Muni, West Africa. Arthur J. Riopelle. 1966-69
—— lowland: linguistic and cognitive capacities. Francine G. Patterson. 1976-82, 1985
—— mountain: behavior and ecology. Virunga Mountains, Rwanda. Dian Fossey. 1967-78, 1981, 1983
—— mountain. Rwanda and Zaire. Alexander H. Harcourt. 1979
—— white ("Snowflake"): adolescent development. Barcelona, Spain. Arthur J. Riopelle. 1970
Guanacos. South America. William L. Franklin. 1976, 1978
Horses, wild: social biology. Nevada. Joel Berger. 1982-83
—— and camels, wild: taphonomic studies. Australia. Gary A. Haynes. 1987
Hutia. Haiti. Charles A. Woods. 1974-75
Hyenas, spotted *(Crocuta crocuta):* social behavior. Kenya. Laurence G. Frank. 1980, 1982, 1985
Ibex, Nubian: nutrition ecology and behavior. Negev Desert, Israel. Montague W. Demment. 1986
Jackals. Serengeti Plain, Tanzania. Patricia D. Moehlman. 1975-76
—— Simien: population recensus. Bale Mountains, Ethiopia. James R. Malcolm. 1987
Jaguars. Brazil. George B. Schaller. 1976, 1980
—— Pantanal region, Brazil. Howard B. Quigley and George B. Schaller. 1983
Kangaroos, bettongs, Tasmanian *(Bettongia gaimardi):* ecology. Robert J. Taylor. 1986
—— rat: nutritional physiology. Australia. Ian D. Hume. 1983
Kobs: conventionality of territorial leks. Uganda. Helmut K. Buechner. 1971
—— white-eared, migratory: ecology. Boma region, Sudan. Anthony R. E. Sinclair. 1982
Lemmings, Norwegian: social organization. Edward J. Heske. 1985-86
—— wood: evolutionary ecology. Norway. Soren Bondrup-Nielsen. 1986

Lemurs, bamboo-eating: ecological niche separation. Madagascar. Patricia C. Wright. 1988

—— ecology, conservation, and management. Madagascar. Sheila M. O'Connor. 1983

—— black-and-white ruffed *(Varecia variegata):* behavior and ecology. Madagascar. Hilary J. Simons. 1986

—— black-and-white ruffed *(Varecia variegata):* Madagascar and Comoro Archipelago, Indian Ocean. Ian Tattersall. 1974, 1976,

—— ring-tailed *(Lemur catta):* feeding behavior. Madagascar. Michelle L. Sauther. 1987

Leopards, snow: radiotracking. Himalaya, Nepal. Rodney M. Jackson. 1981, 1983-84

Lions: communal suckling. Serengeti National Park, Tanzania. Anne E. Pusey. 1988

—— ecology. Kitengela Conservation Area, Kenya. Judith Ann Rudnai. 1974

—— male coalitions. Tanzania. Craig Packer. 1981

—— reproductive-genetic analysis. Serengeti ecosystem. Tanzania. Stephen J. O'Brien. 1987

Lynx: behavior and ecology. Washington. Maurice Hornocker. 1984

Macaques, Barbary: population dynamics and genetics. Algeria. Nelly Menard. 1988

—— biogeography and behavior. Sulawesi. Joseph M. Erwin. 1987

—— lion-tailed and sympatric species: communication. India. Detlev W. Ploog. 1986

—— Sri Lanka. Wolfgang P. J. Dittus. 1975

—— toque: factors affecting fitness. Sri Lanka. Wolfgang P. J. Dittus. 1985

—— wild bonnet. South India. Paul E. Simonds. 1975

Mammals: distribution and taxonomy. Chilean coastal islands. Bruce D. Patterson. 1982

—— effects of kinship on social behavior. Paul W. Sherman. 1979

—— evolution of extinct species. Madagascar. Ross D. E. MacPhee. 1984

—— highland. Papua New Guinea. Michael Archer. 1983

—— large, high-altitude. Pakistan and Nepal. George B. Schaller. 1971-73.

—— Neotropical. Ralph M. Wetzel. 1968-69

—— nocturnal. Botswana. Reay H. N. Smithers. 1969

—— Paraguay. Ralph M. Wetzel. 1973-75, 1977, 1981

—— particularly bats and murid rodents. Lesser Sunda Islands. Darrell J. Kitchener. 1987

—— small arboreal: community structure. John F. Eisenberg. Brazil. 1987

—— small. Cameroon. Duane A. Schlitter. 1978

—— small: microdistribution at the coniferous-deciduous interface. Gordon L. Kirkland, Jr. 1972

—— small: moist tropical forest communities. India. Melvin E. Sunquist. 1988

—— small: open-pit mine waste dumps. Gordon L. Kirkland, Jr. 1973

—— small: speciation. Apostle Islands, Lake Superior. Richard R. Meierotto. 1970-71, 1973

—— Uinta Mountains, Utah. Gordon L. Kirkland, Jr. 1976-77

—— and birds: collecting. Central Africa. Carnes Weeks and Gertrude S. Weeks. 1952

Manatees: behavior and ecology. Florida. Daniel S. Hartman. 1968

Margay, jaguarundi, and tayra: small feline behavioral ecology. Belize. Michael J. Konecny. 1984-85

Marine mammals. Guadalupe and Cedros Islands, Baja California. G. Dallas Hanna and A. W. Anthony. 1922

Marsupials, arboreal: utilization of eucalyptus foliage. Australia. Ian D. Hume. 1980, 1982

—— evolution. South America. Larry G. Marshall. 1974

—— reproductive biology. South America. C. H. Tyndale-Biscoe. 1971

Martens, American: thermoregulation. Wyoming. Steven W. Buskirk. 1985-86

—— ecology. Grand Teton National Park, Wyoming. Timothy W. Clark. 1975

Mice, pocket: competition and predation. Islands in the Sea of Cortés, Mexico. O. J. Reichman. 1986

Moles. North America. Robert J. Baker. 1977

Mongoose, dwarf: reproductive physiology. Serengeti National Park, Tanzania. Peter M. Waser. 1987

—— dwarf *(Helogale parvula)* and banded *(Mungos mungo):* ecology and social organization. Uganda and Tanzania. Jonathan P. Rood. 1973, 1985

Monkeys: biogeography and ecology. Mwanihana Forest, Tanzania. Samuel K. Wasser. 1985

—— capuchin *(Cebus nigrivittatus):* demography, genealogy, and social structure. Venezuela. John G. Robinson. 1980, 1987

—— howling: vocal communication and spacing. Costa Rica. James M. Whitehead. 1986

—— red colobus and agile mangabey. Kenya. Colin P. Groves. 1972

—— red howler *(Alouatta seniculus):* population. Venezuela. Carolyn M. Crockett. 1982

—— redtail: socioecology. Kibale Forest, Uganda. Thomas T. Struhsaker. 1984

—— rhesus: ecology and behavior. Nepal. Charles H. Southwick. 1973, 1975

—— rhesus: semantics of vocalizations. Puerto Rico. Peter Marler. 1988

—— spider: vocal communication. Peru. Margaret M. Symington. 1988

—— talapoin: mating behavior. Reserved Forest of Maolmayo, Cameroon. Thelma E. Rowell. 1973

—— tamarin, cotton-top: behavior and ecology. Colombia. Charles T. Snowdon. 1988

—— tamarin, golden lion: behavioral ecology and reintroduction studies. Brazil. Devra G. Kleiman. 1982

—— tamarin: mating system and social organization. Peruvian Amazon. Barbara F. Ruth. 1988

—— and lesser primates. Tigoni Primate Research Centre, Limuru, Kenya. Cynthia P. Booth. 1963

—— and loris. Sri Lanka. John F. Eisenberg. 1968

Mountain lion: ecology. Yellowstone National Park and environs, U. S. Maurice G. Hornocker. 1986, 1988

Ngorongoro Crater: aerial census of ungulates. Tanzania. Richard Despard Estes. 1977-78

Nyala, mountain. Ethiopia. Leslie H. Brown. 1965

Ocelots: ecology and behavior. Venezuela. Melvin E. Sunquist. 1983

Opossum, brush-tailed *(Trichosurus vulpecula).* Ian D. Hume. 1975

Orangutans. Mount Looser Reserve, Sumatra, and Tanjung Puting Reserve, Borneo. Biruté M. F. Galdikas. 1971, 1973-77, 1979, 1981, 1983

Otters, giant Brazilian. Suriname. Nicole Duplaix-Hall. 1976-77

—— South American marine *(Lutra felina):* behavioral ecology. Chile. Richard S. Ostfeld. 1987

—— southern river: ecology. Argentina. Claudio E. Chehebar. 1986

Pandas, giant: behavioral ecology. China. John F. Eisenberg. 1981

Peccaries *(Catagonus wagneri).* Lyle K. Sowls. 1980

—— Peru. John W. Terborgh. 1976

—— white-lipped: range and habitat use. Ecuador. Lynn E. Fowler de Neira. 1987-88

Pigs, domestic and wild: cultural and ecological aspects. New Guinea. James A. Baldwin. 1973, 1976

Pikas, Asian black-lipped *(Ochotona curzoniae):* behavioral ecology. China. Andrew T. Smith. 1983, 1985-86

—— ecological study. Western United States. Richard D. Bates. 1970-71

Prairie dogs, black-tailed: dispersal. Kansas. Zuleyma T. Halpin. 1980

—— black-tailed: sociobiology. John L. Hoogland. Wyoming. 1978-79, 1984

Primates: biogeography. China. Yongzu Zhang. 1986

—— great apes: vocal behavior. Indonesia. John C. Mitani. 1988

—— Neotropical. Manu National Park, Peru. John W. Terborgh. 1974-75

—— nonhuman. East Borneo. Peter S. Rodman. 1974

—— rain-forest. Niger and Cross Rivers, Nigeria. John F. Oates. 1987

—— vocal communication. Kenya. Peter R. Marler. 1977

Prosimians, nocturnal: competition and adaptation. Kenya. Caroline S. Harcourt. 1981

Pumas, Patagonian: ecology. Chile. William L. Franklin. 1987-88

Rabbit, volcano: ecology. Mexico. John E. Fa. 1987

Raccoon dogs: chromosome change and relationship to race-species formation. Japan. Oscar G. Ward. 1984

Raccoons, tropical: ecology and relationships. James D. Lazell, Jr. 1972

Rats, black: feeding behavior. Israel. Joseph Terkel. 1985

———— giant: conservation and zoogeography. Solomon Islands. Timothy F. Flannery. 1986

———— kangaroo: comparison of social structure and communication. Arizona. Janet A. Randall. 1982, 1986

———— kangaroo: radiotelemetry study. California. Martin Daly. 1983

———— naked mole: behavior and ecology. Africa. Paul W. Sherman. 1979

———— naked mole: influence of ecological factors on sociality. Kenya. Jennifer U. M. Jarvis. 1979

Rhinoceros, black: calf survival. Kenya. Vaughan A. Langman. 1982

———— black: conservation strategy. Zimbabwe. Raoul F. du Toit. 1988

Sea lions, Australian *(Neophoca cinerea):* foraging ecology. Daniel P. Costa. 1988

———— Galápagos: biology. Burney J. Le Boeuf. 1988

———— Hooker's: diving and attendance behavior. Enderby Island, New Zealand. Roger L. Gentry. 1985-86

———— sonar. Thomas C. Poulter. 1970

———— Steller. H. Dean Fisher. 1972

Seals, fur: feeding behavior. South America. Gerald L. Kooyman. 1982

———— fur, northern: PCB contamination. Pribilof Islands, Alaska. David A. Kurtz. 1984

———— fur, and sea lions. Galápagos. Gerald L. Kooyman. 1980

———— harbor and gray: feeding habits and population dynamics. Maine. David T. Richardson. 1972

———— Hawaiian monk *(Monachus schauinslandi).* Hawaii. G. Causey Whittow. 1976

———— Juan Fernandez fur. Daniel N. Torres. 1977

———— Juan Fernandez fur: diving and attendance behavior. Chile. John M. Francis. 1987

———— southern elephant: diving behavior and foraging strategy. Peninsula Valdes, Argentina. Burney J. Le Boeuf. 1986

Sheep, bighorn. Nez Perce Creek, Wyoming. E. Earl Willard. 1974-75

———— bighorn: conservation of genetic resources. Oregon. John T. Hogg. 1987

———— desert bighorn: environmental and physiological biology. Jack Chardon Turner. 1972

———— feral: longevity and survival. St. Kilda, Scotland. Peter A. Jewell. 1984

———— urial, and markhor goats. Pakistan. George B. Schaller. 1970

Shrews, golden-rumped elephant. Kenya. Galen B. Rathbun. 1971, 1974, 1976

———— giant African otter: thermoregulatory biology. Martin E. Nicoll. 1982

———— tree. Borneo. Louise H. Emmons. 1988

Squirrels, Idaho ground: behavior, ecology, and evolution. Paul W. Sherman. 1986

———— Kaibab. Joseph G. Hall. 1970-71

Tenrecs, biological energetics and reproduction. Madagascar. Martin E. Nicoll. 1984

———— Madagascar. Edwin Gould. 1963

Topi. East Africa. Richard Despard Estes. 1977

Walrus: female-calf bond. Edward H. Miller. 1980

———— and whale studies: observation cruise of the U. S. Coast Guard Cutter *Glacier.* G. Carleton Ray. 1977

Whales, bowhead: population. Arctic. John R. Bockstoce. 1976

———— California gray: tracking. John E. Schultz. 1968-69

———— gray. San Ignacio Lagoon, Baja California. Steven L. Swartz. 1978-81

———— gray. Scammon Lagoon, Baja California. Merrill P. Spencer. 1966

———— heartbeat. Scammon Lagoon, Baja California. Paul Dudley White. 1956

———— humpback. Roger S. Payne. 1976, 1979-80

———— humpback: behavior and migration patterns. Bermuda. Steven K. Katona. 1984-85

———— humpback: population genetics. Alaska. Charles S. Baker. 1987

———— humpback, minke, and right: publication of field study. Roger S. Payne. 1985

———— minke: field study. San Juan Islands, Washington. Eleanor M. Dorsey and Deborah A. Duffield. 1984

———— right: vocalizations and behavior. Argentina. Roger S. Payne. 1971-73

———— right. Charles Walcott. 1976-77

———— sperm: bioacoustic research. Kenneth S. Norris. 1970

———— sperm: identification and sonar tracking. Caribbean. William A. Watkins. 1983, 1986, 1988

———— tracking with new sonar system. Massachusetts. Harold E. Edgerton. 1984

Wildebeests. Ngorongoro Crater, Tanzania. Richard Despard Estes. 1963-66, 1972

Wolves: arctic. Ellesmere Island, Canada. L. David Mech. 1988

———— red, and coyotes: comparative study of vocalization. Howard McCarley. 1973

Wolverines: ecology. Northwestern Montana. Maurice G. Hornocker. 1973-75

———— ecology in an Arctic ecosystem. Brooks Range, Alaska. Philip S. Gipson. 1979

Yaks. Richard P. Palmieri. 1971, 1973

Zebras, Grevy's: behavioral ecology. Kenya. Joshua R. Ginsberg. 1983, 1985

Ornithology

Accipiters. North America. Noel F. R. Snyder. 1970-71

Albatrosses, Laysan: longevity, survival, and turnover in breeding populations. Harvey I. Fisher. 1971

Scarred humpback whale hangs head down to sing his complex song, probably related to courtship. FLIP NICKLIN

Japan's long-tailed fowl, or onagadori, *must live nearly a decade to grow 30-foot tail feathers.* EIJI MIYAZAWA, BLACK STAR

Hunger threatens a Philippine eagle chick, its parents' hunting curtailed by slash-and-burn farming. NEIL RETTIG

Anis: male incubation and communal nesting. Sandra L. Vehrencamp. 1978

Auklets, *(Aethia alcidea):* social signals. Aleutian Islands, Alaska. Ian L. Jones. 1988

Avian ecology expedition. Falkland Islands. Robin W. Woods. 1983

Bananaquits: foraging behavior on artificial flowers. Grenada. Joseph M. Wunderle, Jr. 1981

Bee-eaters, African: cooperative breeding and behavior. Kenya. Stephen T. Emlen. 1973-74, 1984-85

—— European. Fred N. White. 1975

Bird eggs: adaptation to high altitudes. Andes, Peru. Cynthia Carey. 1984, 1986, 1988

Bird-fossil comparative study. Trindade Island, South Atlantic Ocean. Storrs L. Olson. 1974

Birds: adaptations for tropical survival. North America. Eugene S. Morton. 1973

—— ant-following. South America and Africa. Edwin O. Willis. 1974, 1979, 1981-82

—— behavior. Bahama Islands. John T. Emlen. 1979

—— biogeography. Bermejo and Pilcomayo Rivers, northwestern Argentina. Manuel Nores. 1986

—— Chinese: museum study. Zheng Bao-Lai. 1983

—— collection. New Britain. E. Thomas Gilliard. 1958-59

—— communities: Australian shrub deserts. New South Wales. John A. Wiens. 1984

—— communities: Mediterranean-type habitat comparison. Southwestern Australia. Martin L. Cody. 1984

—— community structure, lowland forest. David L. Pearson. 1974, 1976

—— diversity patterns and components. Northeast Australia. Martin L. Cody. 1988

—— Dominican rain-forest: conservation. Peter G. H. Evans. 1983

—— ecological studies. Amazon forest. Thomas E. Lovejoy III. 1971

—— Ethiopian: library study. Emil K. Urban. 1966, 1968

—— field studies and collecting specimens. New Guinea. Jared M. Diamond. 1965-68

—— high-Andean. François Vuilleumier. 1975

—— marine: significance of feeding in mixed-species flocks. Spencer G. Sealy. 1978

—— migratory: en route behavioral ecology. North coast, Gulf of Mexico. Frank R. Moore. 1986

—— montane forest communities: ecology and conservation. Rwanda and Burundi. John G. Blake. 1985

—— montane forest. Nyika Plateau, Malawi. Françoise B. Dowsett-Lemaire. 1979

—— New Guinea. E. Thomas Gilliard. 1953-54

—— New Guinea, West Irian mountain ranges. Jared M. Diamond. 1980, 1982

—— New Zealand. Charles G. Sibley. 1982

—— North American. Hudson Bay,

Gulf of St. Lawrence, southern United States, Mexico, Georgia, Florida, North Dakota, New York. Arthur A. Allen. 1944-49

—— ornithological exploration. Cordillera divisor, Peru-Brazil border. John P. O'Neill. 1986

—— ornithological exploration. Pando region, Bolivian Amazon. James V. Remsen, Jr. 1986

—— Patagonian: speciation. Chile. François Vuilleumier. 1983

—— piscivorous: effects of human disturbance on breeding success. Eagle Lake, California. James R. Koplin. 1971

—— Polynesian: habitat mapping and conservation. David S. Simonett. 1987

—— post-fire competition among hole nesters. Dale L. Taylor. 1973

—— Procellariiformes: olfactory behavior and neurophysiology. Bernice M. Wenzel. 1977, 1980-81

—— radar study of transpacific migration. Timothy C. and Janet M. Williams. 1979

—— recolonization of exploded volcanic islands. New Guinea. Jared M. Diamond. 1972

—— Red Sea islands: reproductive biology and ecology. Egypt. Robert W. Storer. 1984

—— Rift Valley lakes, Ethiopia. Emil K. Urban. 1970

—— Rio Grande do Sul, Brazil. William Belton. 1976

—— São Paulo, Brazil. Yoshika Oniki Willis. 1978

—— Simien Mountains, Ethiopia. Michel Desfayes. 1970

—— small mammals, and bat distribution. Peru. Asa C. Thoresen. 1964-65

—— social systems. Africa. J. David Ligon. 1975

—— songs. John R. Krebs. 1977

—— songs. John R. Krebs and Malcolm L. Hunter, Jr. 1976

—— stranded on land-bridge islands. Jared M. Diamond. 1974

—— Sudan: Dinder Park and Lake Kundi expedition. Stewart M. Evans. 1980

—— survey. Brazil and Venezuela. Ernest G. Holt. 1929-30

—— systematics. South America. Ned K. Johnson. 1974

—— tropical-forest communities. James Richard Karr. 1975-76

—— tropical-forest communities. Costa Rica. John G. Blake. 1986, 1988

—— tropical Pacific islands. Jared M. Diamond. 1976

—— UHF radiolocation system. Frank C. Craighead, Jr. 1973

—— visual mimicry. New Guinea and Australia. Jared M. Diamond. 1979

—— wading: competition and migration schedule. Banc d'Arguin, Mauritania. Willem J. Wolff. 1985

—— wetland: distribution. West Africa. Patrick J. Dugan. 1983

—— wetland: migration and ecology. Khawr Bhawr al Hikman, Oman. John D. Uttley. 1988

——— wintering migrants: effect of habitat fragmentation. St. Thomas and St. John, Virgin Islands. Robert A. Askins. 1987

Birds of paradise: Lawes's six-wired: social organization and ecology. Papua New Guinea. Frank A. Pitelka. 1981-82

——— Little Tobago, West Indies. E. Thomas Gilliard. 1958

——— Macgregor's: ecology and behavior. Papua New Guinea. Bruce M. Beehler. 1980, 1986

Birds of prey: survey. South Africa. C.W.R. Knight. 1937

Blackbirds, red-winged: communication by call switching. Washington. Leslie D. Beletsky. 1985, 1987

——— red-winged: transplant experiments. Mexico. Frances C. James. 1983-87

Bluebirds, eastern *(Sialia sialis):* resource distribution, monogamy, and male parental care. South Carolina, New York, and Canada. Patricia A. Gowaty. 1984, 1987

Boobies, blue-footed and brown: infanticide. Isla Isabel, Mexico. Hugh Drummond. 1985

——— pelagic ecology, reproduction, and satellite tracking. Galápagos. Robert E. Ricklefs. 1985-86

Bowerbirds: comparative socioecology. Australia. Alan Lill. 1977-79

——— golden-fronted *(Amblyornis flavifrons):* search for. New Guinea. E. Thomas Gilliard. 1963

Brazil and Venezuela jungles: specimen collection. Orinoco headwaters. Ernest G. Holt. 1929-31

Caciques, yellow-rumped: communication. Peru. Jill M. Trainer. 1986

Canaries, wild *(Serinus canaria):* geographic variations in songs. Canary Islands. Paul C. Mundinger. 1984

Caracaras, striated. Falkland Islands. Ian J. Strange. 1984

Cock-of-the-rock: dancing courtship. British Guiana. E. Thomas Gilliard. 1961

——— *(Rupicola rupicola):* lek mating system. Suriname. Kurt M. Fristrup. 1980

——— *(Rupicola rupicola):* lek mating system. Suriname. Pepper W. Trail. 1979, 1981

Condors, Andean: effects of El Niño on population dynamics. Peru. Stanley A. Temple. 1984

——— number and range: preservation. California. National Audubon Society. 1961-64

Cotingas, cock-of-the-rock, and calfbird: lek behavior. Suriname. Pepper W. Trail. 1984

Cracticidae: comparative ecoethology. Australia. Eleanor D. Brown. 1987

Cranes: coiled tracheae. Wisconsin. Abbot S. Gaunt. 1983

Cuckoos, parasitic: social organization and mating. Robert B. Payne. 1982

Ducks, dabbling. Australia and New Zealand. Frank McKinney. 1980

——— torrent: reproduction dynamics and behavior. South America. Marvin C. Cecil. 1968-70

Eagles, bald: post-fledgling activities.

Thomas C. Dunstan. 1971.

——— bald, and crows and gulls: salmon scavenging. Pacific Northwest. Richard L. Knight. 1985

——— golden. Montana. John J. Craighead. 1973

——— golden: nesting behavior. Texas. W. Grainger Hunt. 1975

——— Philippine: population and breeding. Robert S. Kennedy. 1977, 1979-80

——— satellite tracking. Alaska. Frank C. Craighead, Jr. 1981

Falcons, Eleanora's: territory and aggression. Morocco. Hartmut Walter. 1968-69

——— gregarious: sociobiological studies. Hartmut Walter. 1977

——— gyrfalcons: population ecology. Iceland. Thomas J. Cade. 1981-85

——— laughing. Venezuela. William J. Mader. 1977

——— Patagonian. David H. Ellis. 1981

——— peregrine. Chihuahuan Desert, Mexico. Wilmer G. Hunt. 1977

——— peregrine: migration. North and South America. William W. Cochran. 1975

Finches, African *(Pyrenestes):* bill polymorphism. Cameroon. Thomas B. Smith. 1984-85

——— African parasitic. Kenya and Uganda. Robert B. Payne. 1988

——— alpine rosy: dispersion and evolution. Siberia to Alaska. Norman R. French. 1984, 1987

——— courtship behavior. Africa. Robert B. Payne. 1971

——— foraging behavior. Cocos Island, Costa Rica. Thomas W. Sherry and Tracey K. Warner. 1983-84

——— Galápagos: genetic analysis of evolution patterns. Robert I. Bowman. 1973

——— introduced: habitat selection. Hawaii. Michael P. Moulton. 1988

——— Mexican. John W. Hardy and Bertram G. Murray, Jr. 1977

——— St. Lucia black: behavior and taxonomy. St. Lucia Island, Caribbean. Pepper W. Trail. 1987

——— song mimicry. Cameroon. Robert B. Payne. 1980

Flamingos: ecology and reproductive biology. Florida. M. Philip Kahl. 1972

——— limnological studies of diets and distributions. Chile and Bolivia. Stuart H. Hurlbert. 1973, 1975

——— New World: population ecology. M. Philip Kahl. 1971

——— photographic study. Andros Island, Bahama Islands. John Oliver La Gorce and Louis Agassiz Fuertes. 1920

——— salt lakes of the Andean puna. Stuart H. Hurlbert. 1978-79, 1981-82

——— worldwide survey of population dynamics. M. Philip Kahl. 1974

Fowl, long-tailed. Japan. Frank X. Ogasawara. 1969

——— mallee (Galliformes): energetics and incubation ecology. Southern Australia. Wesley W. Weathers. 1986

Frigate bird, magnificent: behavioral ecology. Barbuda, West Indies. Wayne Z. Trivelpiece. 1986-87

Geese, cackling: breeding ecology. Yukon and Kuskokwim River Deltas, Alaska. Peter G. Mickelson. 1970-72

Grassquits, blue-black: thermal consequences of territorial displays. Panama. Wesley W. Weathers. 1982

Grebes, Clarke's western. California and Oregon. Gary L. Nuechterlein. 1975-78, 1984-85

——— eared. Minnesota. Gary L. Nuechterlein. 1987-88

——— hooded. Gary L. Nuechterlein. Argentina. 1980-81

——— hooded. Argentina. Gary L. Nuechterlein and Robert W. Storer. 1982

——— hooded. Patagonia. Robert W. Storer. 1975

——— pied-billed. Lake Atitlán, Guatemala. Anne LaBastille. 1967-68

Grosbeaks, evening. Colorado. Marc Bekoff. 1983

Grouse, spruce *(Canachites canadensis).* Montana. Stanley S. Frissell. 1975

Gulls, Ross': population. Point Barrow, Alaska. George J. Divoky. 1984-85

Hawks, savanna. Venezuela. William J. Mader. 1979

Hemipode *(Turnix sylvatica):* ecological relations, reproduction, and distribution. Andalusia, Spain. Gerald Collier. 1973

Herons, goliath. South Africa. Douglas W. Mock. 1977

History of ornithology in the Western Hemisphere. Keir B. Sterling. 1977

Hoatzin. British Guiana. J. Lear Grimmer. 1959-60

Honeycreepers: reproductive isolation and genetic variation in two taxa. Hawaii. Robert C. Fleischer. 1988

Honeyeaters (Meliphagidae). Australia. Richard E. MacMillen. 1983

Hoopoes, green wood. Kenya. J. David Ligon. 1976-77, 1984

Hornbills, African. Fred N. White. 1976

Hummingbirds: behavior and biology. Rocky Mountains. William A. Calder III. 1972, 1983-85, 1987

——— ecology. Mexico, Central America, and South America. Augusto Ruschi. 1974

——— migrants on Mexican wintering grounds. William A. Calder III. 1987

——— rufous: utilization of time and microhabitat. William A. Calder III. 1973, 1975

——— South America. Augusto Ruschi. 1962

Ibises, scarlet: search for rookery. Venezuela. Paul A. Zahl. 1949

Jays, Florida scrub. Glen E. Woolfenden and John W. Fitzpatrick. 1978

——— green: ecology. Colombia. Humberto Alvarez. 1974

——— social and reproductive biology. Yucatán. John William Hardy. 1973

Kakapos. Stewart Island, New Zealand. Margaret B. Shepard. 1979-80

Kites, hook-billed. Stanley A. Temple. 1979-80

Kiwi: olfactory sense. Bernice M. Wenzel. 1967

Loons, common. Saskatchewan, Canada. Judith W. McIntyre. 1980

Magpies, Australian: vocal and social behavior. Eleanor D. Brown and

Susan M. Farabaugh. 1984

Manakins: lek formation. Manu National Park, Peru. Mercedes S. Foster. 1985-86, 1988

—— long-tailed: male-male cooperation. Costa Rica. David B. McDonald. 1987

—— swallow-tailed. Paraguay. Mercedes S. Foster. 1977

Nightjars. Peru. John W. Hardy. 1981

Oilbirds. Colombia. Masakazu Konishi. 1975-76

—— Venezuela. Bernice Tannenbaum. 1976

Ospreys: ecology. Connecticut River. Roger Tory Peterson and Peter Ames. 1962

—— pesticide influence on reproductive function. Flathead Lake, Montana, and northwestern California. James R. Koplin. 1968-70, 1972

—— West Africa. Yves A. Prevost. 1978

Palila. Hawaii. Charles van Riper III. 1979

Parrots, kea: social foraging. New Zealand. Judy Diamond and Alan Bond. 1988

Pelicans, brown: embryos and chicks. Panama. George A. Bartholomew. 1982

—— great white *(Pelecanus onocrotalus):* breeding behavior. Ralph W. Schreiber. 1977

Penguins, gentoo and macaroni. South Georgia Island. Randall W. Davis. 1983

—— jackass *(Spheniscus demersus):* competition with commercial fishing. South African coast. David C. Duffy. 1984

—— jackass *(Spheniscus demersus):* Southern Africa. Walter R. Siegfried. 1973, 1976, 1979

Petrels, Leach's storm: adaptations to marine environment. Bay of Fundy. Robert E. Ricklefs. 1988

—— Leach's storm and ashy: nocturnal orientation. Robert I. Bowman. 1971

Phalaropes, Wilson's. Mono Lake, California. Joseph R. Jehl, Jr. 1980

—— Wilson's: opportunistic behavior. Saskatchewan, Canada. Lewis W. Oring. 1986

Pheasants, mikado and Swinhoe's. Taiwan. Sheldon R. Severinghaus. 1971

Pigeons, homing: navigation analysis. Charles Walcott. 1968-69

—— homing: role of gravity in navigation. Charles Walcott. 1982

—— pink. Mauritius. Anthony S. Cheke. 1973

Plovers, Egyptian. Thomas R. Howell. 1976

—— lesser golden: breeding behavior and ecology. Alaska. Peter G. Connors. 1987-88

—— lesser golden: wintering behavior. Hawaii. Oscar W. Johnson. 1982, 1984, 1986, 1988

Prairie chickens and sharp-tailed grouse. North Dakota. Donald W. Sparling, Jr. 1976

Ptarmigan, willow: aggression and territoriality of females. British Colum-

bia. Susan J. Hannon. 1986

Quails *(Coturnix):* calling behavior patterns. Wolfgang M. Schleidt. 1974

Raptors: tracking by satellite. Frank C. Craighead, Jr. 1976

Robin chats: brain anatomy and song-duetting. Kenya. Eliot A. Brenowitz. 1984

Ruffs, male *(Philomachus pugnax).* Julia Marian Wentworth-Shepard. 1974-75

—— male: variability of mating plumage and lek behavior. Finland and laboratory. David B. Lank. 1985, 1987-88

Seabirds: distribution of communities. Equatorial Pacific. David G. Ainley. 1986

—— ecology and reproductive behavior. Thomas R. Howell. 1969

—— ecology and tick distribution. Indian Ocean. Christopher J. Feare. 1976

—— ecology, numbers, and distribution. Aegean Sea. George E. Watson. 1966

—— foraging activity. Galápagos and central Pacific islands. Robert E. Ricklefs. 1988

—— population biology. Midway Island. Robert E. Ricklefs. 1981-83

—— population ecology. Christmas Island. Robert E. Ricklefs. 1980

—— recovery from population failure, 1982. Christmas Island. Ralph W. Schreiber. 1983

—— tropical: thermoregulation. Hawaii. George C. Whittow. 1987

Shorebirds, desert *(Peltohyas* and *Stiltia).* Australia. Gordon Lindsay Maclean. 1973

Sparrows, rufous-collared *(Zonotrichia capensis).* Bolivia. Kendall W. Corbin. 1979-80

Spoonbills, African: reproductive biology. M. Philip Kahl. 1980

—— Australian: reproductive biology and behavior. Lake Cowal, New South Wales. M. Philip Kahl. 1984

Starlings: fumigant effects of chemicals in plants used in nest construction. Pennsylvania. Larry Clark. 1984

Stilts, banded: ecology and behavior. Australia. Lindsay B. Scott. 1984

Storks: worldwide study of the 17 species. Asia and Africa. M. Philip Kahl. 1966-69.

Swallows, cave. Texas. Charles F. Martin. 1974, 1977

—— cliff: "sneaky" reproductive strategies. Nebraska. Charles R. Brown. 1985

—— wood (Artamidae): biology, phylogeny, and historical geography. Southwest Pacific. Thomas R. Howell. 1984

Swans, mute. Chesapeake Bay. Jan G. Reese. 1976-78

—— whistling: migrations. Alaska breeding grounds. William J. L. Sladen. 1972-74.

Taiko: search for. Chatham Island, New Zealand. David E. Crockett. 1980.

Terns, river-nesting: breeding biology under threat of floods. Nepal. Francesca J. Cuthbert. 1984

Tinamous, crested. Argentina. Hannon

B. Graves. 1979-80

Tody, Puerto Rican: cooperative breeding. Robert B. Waide. 1985

Vultures, Cape. Africa. Joan C. Dobbs. 1980

—— cathartid: competition for food. Venezuela. David C. Houston. 1984

Warblers, leaf: breeding biology. Kashmir, India. Trevor D. Price. 1985

Weaverbirds, northern masked: nonspecific nest parasitism. Kenya. Wendy M. Jackson. 1987-88

—— sociable: ecological role of the nest. George A. Bartholomew. 1972-73

—— white-browed sparrow: determinants of population structure. Zambia. Dale M. Lewis. 1979

—— white-browed sparrow: endocrinology of cooperative breeding. Zambia. Robert E. Hegner. 1985

Woodcreepers *(Dendrocincla tyrannina):* behavior. Colombia. Edwin O. Willis. 1988

Woodpeckers: behavior, ecology, and taxonomy. Asia. Lester L. Short. 1971

—— ivory-billed: search for. Louisiana and east Texas. John V. Dennis. 1967

Wrens, tropical house: demographic study. Panama. Leonard A. Freed. 1984-85

—— variation in communication. Panama. Eugene S. Morton. 1978

Invertebrate Zoology
Entomology

Ants, arboreal: cultivation and chemical ecology. Peru. Diane W. Davidson. 1986

—— African weaver. Berthold Hölldobler. 1977

—— Australian: social behavior and communication. Berthold Hölldobler. 1979

—— *(crematogaster):* nesting habits. Costa Rica. John T. Longino. 1984

—— division of labor. Florida. Prassede Calabi. 1982

—— giant Amazon. Brazil. Paul A. Zahl. 1957

—— giant tropical *(Peraponera clavata):* nest mate recognition and population structure. Costa Rica. Michael D. Breed. 1984, 1987

—— harvester: colony response to environmental change. Arizona. Deborah M. Gordon. 1988

—— Neotropical *(Leptothorax* and *Thaumatomyrmex).* Venezuela. Mark W. Moffett. 1988

—— parasitism. Europe. Berthold K. Hölldobler. 1986

—— *(Pheidologeton).* Asia. Mark W. Moffett. 1981-82, 1985

—— *(Polyergus breviceps):* slave-making behavior. Arizona. Howard Topoff. 1983-84

—— thatch *(Formica obscuripes):* foraging and predator strategies. Oregon. James D. McIver. 1987

—— and termites: inquilines and ecology. Northern Australia. David H. Kistner. 1987

Army ant mites and leafhoppers. Paraguay. Richard J. Elzinga. 1975
Arthropods: predator response to an ant-mimetic system. Oregon. James D. McIver. 1986
────── specialization and biological diversity on lava flows and in caves. Azores. N. Philip Ashmole. 1987
Bagworms: distribution and host-tree orientation of the eggs and parasites. Herbert M. Kulman. 1970
Bees, African "killer": genetic changes. Mexico. Orley R. Taylor, Jr. 1987
────── (Anthophoridae): territorial and mating behavior, population biology. Costa Rica. Gordon W. Frankie. 1979, 1981, 1984-85
────── euglossine: thermoregulation and flight energetics. Panama. Michael L. Lay. 1980
────── halictine *(Lasioglossum zephyrum):* mating system and social structure. Australia. Penelope F. Kukuk. 1988
────── honey *(Apis laboriosa):* thermal properties and cold-temperature adaptations. Nepal. Benjamin A. Underwood. 1987
────── honey: group decision making. Maine. Thomas D. Seeley. 1987
────── honey. Thailand. Thomas D. Seeley. 1978
────── honey: use of the earth's magnetic field. New Jersey. James L. Gould. 1983
────── Madagascan. Charles D. Michener. 1984
────── Neotropical (Panurginae). South America. Jerome G. Rozen, Jr. 1978, 1988
Beetles, dung. Bernd Heinrich and George A. Bartholomew. 1977
────── ground: inventory. British Columbia. David H. Kavanaugh. 1986
────── *(Leistotrophus versicolor):* foraging ecology and sexual selection. Costa Rica. John Alcock. 1987
────── (Staphylinidae): collection. Australia and New Zealand. Alfred F. Newton. 1984, 1986
────── scarab, "flower beetle": thermoregulation and energetics. Namibia. Bernd Heinrich. 1984
────── subarctic ground: paleoenvironmental significance. Manitoba. Clarke E. Garry. 1987
────── tropical rove: deception. Costa Rica. John Alcock. 1988
Butterflies, Alaskan: survey. Victoria Island, Canada. Kenelm W. Philip. 1974-75
────── *Boloria improba/acrocnema* complex: genetic variation. Rocky Mountains. Peter F. Brussard. 1988
────── cabbage. Morocco. Frances S. Chew. 1981
────── ecology and specimen collection. Aldabra Atoll, Indian Ocean. Jay C. Shaffer. 1967
────── equatorial alpine. Colombia. Arthur M. Shapiro. 1976
────── *(Heliconius).* Costa Rica. James L. B. Mallet. 1980
────── (Hesperiidae): systematic and distributional study. Mexico. Hugh A. Freeman. 1973-75
────── madrone *(Eucheira socialis):*

population biology. Mexico. Arthur M. Shapiro. 1987
────── monarch: migration. Texas, Florida, California, Australia, Mexico. Fred A. Urquhart. 1968-71, 1975-76, 1978
────── monarch: soaring flight and navigation. David L. Gibo. 1982
────── Neotropical: life history. Panama. Annette Aiello. 1982
────── Neotropical: seasonal migration. Monteverde, Costa Rica. William A. Haber. 1984
────── Neotropical. Trinidad. William Beebe and Jocelyn Crane. 1957
────── pierid: population ecology. Ward B. Watt. 1972
────── species diversity. Sulawesi, Indonesia. John B. Heppner. 1985
────── swallowtail, Brazilian *(Eurytides lysithous).* David A. West. 1981
────── *(Tatochila sterodice).* Argentina. Arthur M. Shapiro. 1980
────── viceroy: geographic variation, palatability, and mimicry. Georgia and Florida. Lincoln P. Brower. 1986
────── visual color signals in behavior. Colorado. Gary D. Bernard. 1988
Crickets: behavior subject to fly parasites. Texas. William H. Cade. 1986
────── East African (Grillidae). Kenya. Daniel Otte. 1987
────── Hawaiian: song evolution in relation to species formation. Daniel Otte. 1978
Diplopoda, Nearctic. Western U.S. and Canada. Rowland M. Shelly. 1985, 1988
Ectoparasites: biology and host associations. Sulawesi. Lance A. Durden. 1984
Fireflies: luminescence. Far East. John B. Buck. 1965-68
────── *(Pteroptyx).* Asia. Ivan Polunin. 1971
────── *(Pteroptyx).* Thailand. James E. Lloyd. 1980
Flies, acalyptrate: coastal habitats. Florida to Nova Scotia. Benjamin A. Foote. 1984, 1988
────── *(Drosophila conformis):* lek determinants of male mating success. Hawaii. Todd E. Shelly. 1985
────── *(Drosophila):* radiation. Hawaii. Wallace J. Dominey. 1987
────── snail-killing: Pacific Northwest. Benjamin A. Foote. 1971
────── stone flies *(Plecoptera):* fauna relationships. Mexico. Boris C. Kondratieff. 1987.
────── (Tabanidae). Thailand. John J. S. Burton. 1968-69
Grasshoppers, desert: reproductive behavior. California. Michael D. Greenfield. 1983
────── katydids (Tettagoniidae): systematics. Hawaii. Todd E. Shelly. 1987
Halobates. Lanna Cheng. 1977.
Hymenoptera, Neotropical Ichneumonidae. Charles C. Porter. 1974-75, 1979
────── stinging: phenology, mimics, and insectivorous birds. Gilbert P. Waldbauer. 1972
────── systematics and zoogeography. Charles C. Porter. 1973-75

Millions of migrating monarch butterflies spend the winter on a remote mountainside in Mexico. ALBERT MOLDVAY

A centipede is crushed by a marauder ant, **Pheidologeton diversus,** *on the island of Celebes in Indonesia.* MARK W. MOFFETT

While surveying the China-Tibet frontier in 1924, Joseph F. Rock lived in the lamasery of the Prince of Choni. JOSEPH F. ROCK

A cascade of pink shrimp harvested off southern Florida were nurtured in tidal estuaries. ROBERT F. SISSON, NGS

—— tropical and spiders, salticid: visual adaptations. Panama. Andrew D. Blest. 1982

Insects, flying: mechanics, energetics, and muscle physiology. Smithsonian Tropical Research Institute, Panama. Timothy M. Casey. 1985

—— glacial stream. Washington. Stamford D. Smith. 1982

—— marine. Seychelles. Lanna Cheng. 1985

—— water balance. Namib Desert, Namibia. Eric B. Edney. 1973

Millipedes *(Dolichoiulus).* Canary Islands. Henrik Enghoff. 1988

Mosquitoes, Holarctic *(Aedes).* Lewis T. Nielsen. Newfoundland, Canada. 1979, 1981

—— Holarctic *(Aedes).* Sweden and Norway. Lewis T. Nielsen. 1984

—— tree-hole: competition, predation, and evolution. France and England. William E. Bradshaw. 1984-85

Moths. Balkans. John B. Heppner. 1980

—— *(Microlepidoptera).* Chile. Don R. Davis. 1981

—— *(Microlepidoptera).* South America. John B. Heppner. 1977, 1979

—— (Micropterygidae): taphonomy. Southern Hemisphere. South Africa. George W. Gibbs. 1985

—— yucca: diversity and oviposition behavior. Western U.S. John F. Addicott. 1985

Neuroptera. South America. Lionel A. Stange. 1974-76

—— aquatic. Ecuador. Paul J. Spangler. 1975

—— aquatic: zoogeographical connections. New Caledonia. William L. Peters. 1972

—— collection. Africa. Edward S. Ross. 1957-58

—— collection. Southern Asia and Australia. Edward S. Ross. 1961-62

—— dispersal. Ethiopia. Jørgen Birket-Smith. 1966

Orthoptera: collection. Gulf of California, Mexico. David B. Weissman. 1983-84

—— Madeira. S. K. Gangwere. 1975

Saldidae: zoogeographical studies. Southern Hemisphere. John T. Polhemus. 1979, 1985-86

Spiders, aerial web: adaptation for flooding survival. Costa Rica. Jerome S. Rovner. 1987

—— cooperative *(Anelosimus eximius):* population genetics. Panama, Trinidad, Suriname, and Ecuador. Deborah R. Smith. 1985

—— funnel-web builders: niche analysis. Carrizozo Malpais, New Mexico. Susan E. Riechert. 1972, 1974

—— jumping: evolution. Kenya, Portugal, and New Zealand. Robert R. Jackson. 1985

—— jumping web-building. Asia and Africa. Robert R. Jackson. 1981

—— moth-attracting. United States. Mark K. Stowe. 1982

—— Neotropical *(Anelosimus eximius):* population genetics. Panama and Suriname. Deborah R. Smith. 1983

—— Neotropical jumping: visual acuity and ecology. Barrio Colorado Island, Panama. Andrew D. Blest. 1986

—— *(Nephila clavipes):* foraging behavior. Peru. Ann L. Rypstra. 1983

—— social: female-biased sex ratios. Ecuador. Laticia Aviles. 1988

—— web-building. Mexico. George W. Uetz. 1978, 1985

Spider webs: insect perception. Panama. Catherine L. Craig. 1988

Treehopper, membracid *(Umbonia crassicornis).* Florida. Thomas K. Wood. 1974

Triatominae. Central and South America. Pedro W. Wygodzinsky. 1963

Wasps, eumenid: biosystematic studies. Argentina and Chile. Abraham Willink. 1978

—— horned *(Synagris):* sexual selection and male dimorphism. West Africa. Robert W. Longair. 1988

—— solitary: biosystematics. Australia. Howard E. Evans. 1979, 1986

—— spider *(Trypoxylon):* behavioral ecology. Costa Rica. Rollin E. Coville. 1981

—— (Thyreodon): biosystematics and zoogeography. Mexico. Charles C. Porter. 1981

—— tropical: relatedness and sociality. Venezuela. David C. Queller. 1988

Water striders (Gerridae): habitat diversity. Sulawesi. Diane M. Calabrese. 1985

Weevils (Anthribidae): behavior and biology. Shimba Hills, Kenya, and Seychelles Islands. Barry D. Valentine. 1986

Malacology

Clams, giant: ecology. Samoa. Richard L. Radtke. 1983

—— giant: zooxanthellae influence on metamorphosis. Robert K. Trench. 1979

Conchs, queen: overfishing and larval recruitment. Eastern Caribbean. Carl J. Berg, Jr. 1984

Limpet, freshwater *(Latia neritoides):* luminescence. New Zealand. V. B. Meyer-Rochow. 1985

Marine invertebrates: biogeography and history. Moluccas. Joseph Rosewater and Barry R. Wilson. 1969

Marine mollusks: ecology and distribution. South Pacific. Harald A. Rehder. 1965, 1967, 1973, 1976

—— shallow-water. Yucatán Peninsula, Mexico. Walter E. Vokes. 1974

Mollusks. Maumee River Valley, Ohio and Indiana. Mark J. Camp. 1982

—— Peruvian: effect of 1982-83 El Niño. Harold B. Rollins. 1985

Nautilus, chambered: growth rate determined using natural radionuclides. James K. Cochran. 1982

—— long-term growth and movement. Palau. William B. Saunders. 1977-79

—— morphologic and genetic variation. Ambon, Indonesia. William B. Saunders. 1987

Snails *(Dyakia striata):* bioluminescence. Singapore. Jonathan Cope-
land. 1983
—— heat, desiccation, and starvation. Middle East. Knut Schmidt-
Nielsen. 1968-69
—— high-intertidal: crab predation
and shell architecture. Geerat J. Ver-
meij. 1974
—— land: Hispaniolan urocoptid.
Fred G. Thompson. 1975, 1978
—— land: marine and terrestrial survey. Kimberley region, Western Australia. Fred E. Wells. 1988
—— littorine: geographic variation.
Oregon. Sylvia B. Yamada. 1986
—— marine: natural selection and
development. Maine and Newfoundland. Robin H. Seeley. 1986
—— polymorphic: population survey. North Africa. Geoffrey Lewis.
1977

Other Invertebrates

Amphipods, coral reef: collection. Australasia. James D. Thomas. 1987
Brachiopods: marine environment.
Joyce R. Richardson. 1976, 1978,
1981
Brine shrimp *(Artemia).* France, Spain,
and North Africa. Robert A. Brown.
1985-86
Bryozoans. Florida. Judith E. Winston.
1983
—— and avicularia: biology. Puget
Sound, Washington. Judith E. Winston. 1987
Cephalopods, deep-sea: photographic
record. Noel Peter Dilly. 1971, 1973
Corals, blue *(Heliopora coerula).*
Branko Velimirov. 1978
—— gorgonian: predators and defenses. San Blas Islands, Panama.
Howard R. Lasker. 1985
—— non-symbiotic. Gerard Wellington and Robert K. Trench. 1982
Coral reefs. Lizard Island, Australia.
Michel Pichon. 1976
—— deep: community patterns. Jamaica. W. David Liddell. 1986
—— destruction and later recolonization. American Samoa. Austin E.
Lamberts. 1974, 1978
—— Florida. Gilbert L. Voss.
1961-63
—— Jamaica. Judith C. Lang. 1975
—— reef dynamics: anatomy and
growth. Antigua. H. Gray Multer.
1982
—— symbiotic invertebrates: adaptation to ultraviolet. Great Barrier
Reef, Australia. J. Malcolm Shick.
1988
Crabs, brachyuran. Gulf of Guinea.
Raymond B. Manning. 1972
—— fiddler. Europe. Jocelyn Crane.
1959
—— hermit: ethology. Alex Henderson and Syd Radinovsky. 1971
—— *(Ocypode):* acoustic-signal
processing. Kenneth W. Horah. 1977
—— tropical land. Charles L. Hogue
and Donald B. Bright. 1970
Crinoids, stalked: ecology and functional morphology. Jamaica. Michael C.
LaBarbera. 1987

Crustaceans, deep-sea: live retrieval.
James J. Childress. 1980
—— deep-sea: live retrieval for phys-
iological study. U.S.S.R. Ralph W.
Brauer. 1983
Diatoms: salt lake communities. North
America. Dean W. Blinn. 1988
Echinoderms, crinoid. Great Barrier
Reef, Australia. David L. Meyer.
1982
Foraminifera, large calcareous: ecolo-
gy. Queensland Shelf and Great Bar-
rier Reef, Australia. Charles A.
Ross. 1970
Invertebrate predation and crustacean
zooplankton. English Lake District.
W. Gary Sprules. 1976
Jellyfish. Palau. Leonard Muscatine.
1981
—— mangrove: zooxanthellae con-
tribution to respiration. Richard S.
Blanquet. 1979
Lobster, spiny: mass migrations. Wil-
liam F. Herrnkind. 1973
Marine invertebrates: biogeography.
Pacific Ocean. Richard C. Brusca.
1988
Ostracods, Caribbean *(Vargula):* bio-
luminescence, systematics, and bio-
geography. James G. Morin. 1983,
1985
Plankton: Florida Current. University
of Miami Institute of Marine Sci-
ences. 1950-52
Rotifers. Patagonia. David Kuczynski.
1983
Sandy beach fauna. Gulf of Suez,
Egypt. Deborah M. Dexter. 1984
Sea anemones (Actiniidae). Lisbeth
Francis. 1980
—— cloning and population. Mount
Desert Island, Maine. Richard J.
Hoffmann. 1987
Sea urchins *(Didema antillarum):* effect
of mass mortalities on coral reef dynamics. Caribbean. Terence P.
Hughes. 1986, 1988
Shrimp. Bermuda. Raymond B. Man-
ning. 1982
—— Florida. Clarence P. Idyll and
David A. Hughes. 1982
—— *(Macrobrachium):* migration
mechanisms. David A. Hughes.
1970
—— mantis: predation on prawns.
Gulf of California. Marea E. Hatzio-
los. 1979
—— symbiotic: local and long-
distance dispersal of larvae. Jamaica.
Nancy Knowlton. 1982
Sponges: antipredator and antifouling
agents on coral reefs. Fiji. Gerald J.
Bakus. 1986
—— morphological and ecological
studies. Pacific reef caves. Willard D.
Hartman. 1971
Squid: observations of activities by
acoustic telemetry. Azores. Francis
G. Carey. 1988
—— fisheries. North Atlantic. Gilbert L. Voss. 1965
Starfish, brittle stars: ecology and
paleoecology. Caribbean islands.
Richard B. Aronson. 1986
—— brittle stars: fission and sexual
reproduction. West Indies. Philip V.
Mladenov. 1984

—— coral-reef. Guam. Masashi Yamaguchi. 1974
—— crown-of-thorns *(Acenthaster
planci):* biology and epidemiology.
Walter A. Starck II. 1971.
Worms, gutless polychaetes: physiology
and metabolism. Bermuda. Horst
Felbeck. 1984
—— railroad *(Phrixothrix):* life history. Brazil. Darwin L. Tiemann.
1968-69
Zooplankton, demersal: distribution on
coral reefs. Alice L. Alldredge. 1978
—— freshwater. Indonesia. Con-
stantine H. Fernando. 1977
—— freshwater. Nigeria. Cecilia Y.
Jeje. 1988
—— nocturnal study. Laurence P.
Madin. 1981

Geography

Aerial survey: Washington to Buenos
Aires. Albert W. Stevens, Frederick
Simpich, and Jacob Gayer. 1930
Africa: a history of exploration by
Americans. James A. Casada. 1976
Antarctica: air exploration. Lincoln
Ellsworth. 1934
—— first expedition, 1928-30; sec-
ond expedition, 1933-35. Richard E.
Byrd, Jr.
Arctic: Franz Josef Land islands. Walter
Wellman. 1898, 1906
—— MacMillan expedition. Donald
B. MacMillan and Richard E. Byrd,
Jr. 1925
—— survey, area north of Alaska.
Robert A. Bartlett. 1924
Arizona: human disturbance and hy-
drology of Santa Rosa and Santa Cruz
Rivers. Bruce L. Rhoads. 1987
Cape Horn region, South America.
Amos Burg. 1934
Carlsbad Caverns: exploration, map-
ping, and photographing. New Mexi-
co. Willis T. Lee. 1924
China-Tibet frontier. Joseph F. Rock.
1923-30
Citröen-Haardt Trans-Asiatic Expedi-
tion. Beirut to Peking. Georges-
Marie Haardt. 1931
Delaware Bay: baseline study. William
S. Gaither. 1970
Everest, Mount: first American ascent.
Nepal. Norman G. Dyhrenfurth and
Barry C. Bishop. 1962-63
Geographic education assistance. Asso-
ciation of American Geographers.
1962
Himalaya. Bhutan. Pradyumna P.
Karan. 1964-65
International Geographical Congresses,
1871-1976: bibliography of papers.
George Kish. 1977
Italy, coastal: man-induced change. H.
Jesse Walker and Paolo Fabbri. 1986
Katmai, Mount: Valley of Ten
Thousand Smokes. Alaska. Robert F.
Griggs. 1915-20, 1930
McKinley, Mount: aerial photo survey.
Bradford Washburn. 1936
Nepal: land use changes in the Kath-
mandu Valley. Barry N. Haack. 1988

—— Tilicho Lake alpine-zone research project. Barry C. Bishop. 1983

New Guinea: eastern mountains. J. Linsley Gressitt. 1968-69

North Pole: attempt to reach. Walter Wellman. 1898

—— attempt to reach. William Ziegler, Anthony Fiala, and William J. Peters. 1903

—— attempt to reach, by dirigible balloon. Walter Wellman and Henry E. Hersey. 1906-07

—— attempt to reach, on skis. Bjørn O. Staib. 1964

—— first successful effort to reach. Robert E. Peary. 1908-09

Rock, Joseph F.: biography. Stephanne B. Sutton. 1971

St. Elias, Mount: first National Geographic Society expedition. Alaska-Canada. Israel C. Russell. 1890-91

St. Elias Mountains: Mount St. Elias-Mount Logan aerial photography. Alaska and Canada. Bradford Washburn. 1938

—— Yukon Territory, Canada. Bradford Washburn. 1935

Santa Inés. Tierra del Fuego, Chile. E. Jack Miller and Paul H. Dix. 1964

Skaftafell: physical and cultural change. Southeast Iceland. Jack D. Ives. 1986

Theodore Roosevelt National Memorial Park: feasibility study for expansion. North Dakota. Paul B. Kannowski. 1972

Vilcabamba Range: plateau between the Apurímac and Urubamba Rivers. Peru. G. Brooks Baekeland and Peter R. Gimbel. 1963

Vinson Massif ascent. Sentinel Range, Ellsworth Mountains, Antarctica. Nicholas B. Clinch. 1966

Yunnan-Sichuan: mountains and gorges. China. Joseph R. Rock. 1923, 1927, 1929

Zhujiang Delta: man-environment interactions. China. Chor-Pang Lo. 1987

PHYSICAL

Africa, tropical: Quaternary paleo-environmental data from cave sediments. George A. Brook. 1986

Alaska: ancient environments and age of nonglaciated terrain. Ian A. Worley. 1971

Alaska Peninsula and Aleutian Islands. Bernard R. Hubbard. 1934

Andes: climatic and vegetational changes. Peru. Herbert E. Wright, Jr. 1978, 1985-86

—— southern: Quaternary vegetation changes. Vera Markgraf. 1986

Australia, Western: geomorphology of the Limestone Ranges. Andrew S. Goudie. 1988

Belize: riparian woodland refuges within a savanna landscape. Martyn C. Kellman. 1987

China, east: environmental change. Yangtze River Delta. Kam-biu Liu. 1986

Chiquibul Caverns: geology, archaeology, and biology. Belize. Thomas E. Miller. 1984-85

Cocos Island: geologic, geophysical, and biologic study. Costa Rica. Rodey Batiza. 1983

Cocos Islands: subsurface geomorphology and Holocene development. Australia. Colin D. Woodroffe. 1987

Erosion, coastal. Puerto Rico. Jack Morelock. 1985

Green River: landscape change. Utah-Colorado. William L. Graf. 1976

Himalaya. Sir Edmund Hillary and Barry C. Bishop. 1960, 1962

Hudson Bay lowlands: potential climatic modifications. Canada. Wayne R. Rouse. 1977

Ice caves. Canadian Cordillera. Derek C. Ford. 1973

Late Quaternary environmental history of a glaciated tropical highland. Costa Rica. Sally P. Horn. 1988

Montana: Woody debris and sedimentation. Flathead River. David R. Butler. 1988

New Mexico, Zuni area: past environments. Stephen A. Hall. 1987

Norway: Jotunheimen research expedition. John A. Matthews. 1982

Reventazon and General Valleys: river terraces. Costa Rica. Richard H. Kesel. 1974, 1977

Saharan expansion. Southern Tunisia. Ian A. Campbell. 1970

Sediment transport and beach cusps: Northern Ireland. Douglas J. Sherman. 1986

Southern Colorado Plateau: transport and storage of natural mercury in stream sediments. William L. Graf. 1980, 1982

Stream terraces: geochronology. Pedregal Valley, Venezuela. Charles S. Alexander. 1984

HUMAN

Aborigines, Australian: health status. Gerald F. Pyle. 1988

Ankara: population changes since 1969. Turkey. John R. Clark. 1978

Bali: tourism and small-scale indigenous enterprise. Antonio Hussey. 1983

Bangladesh: change in agro-ecosystems. B. L. Turner and Abu Muhammad Shajaat Ali. 1984

Barbadian Londoners: social geography and ethnic identity. John C. Western. 1987

Beach erosion: economic impact on property values. Cape Shoalwater, Washington. Thomas A. Terich. 1984

Bolivia: access to the sea. Martin I. Glassner. 1981

Botswana: population pressure. Alan C. G. Best. 1986

China: changing agricultural geography. Jiangsu Province. Clifton W. Pannell. 1986

—— rural housing transformation. Ronald G. Knapp. 1986

Deforestation and desertification in the Sahel: the fuelwood crisis. Niamey, Niger. Hans-Joachim W. Spaeth. 1988

Estonia: urban transportation and structure in a planned society. Siim Sööt. 1983

France: nuclear energy development and implications. James R. McDonald. 1981

Franco-Italian borderland: impact of two decades of integration. Julian V. Minghi. 1979

Geographic factors in the occupational segregation of women. Worcester, Massachusetts. Susan Hanson. 1986, 1988

Georgia: farm survival and agrarian ideology. Dodge County. Peggy F. Barlett. 1987

Guatemala, eastern: social geography of the Black Christ of Esquipulas. John M. Hunter. 1986

Himalaya: mountain hazards and human response. Sikkim and Bhutan. P. F. Karan. 1984

Hungary: planning and ideology in "socialist cities." Darrick R. Danta. 1987

Indira Gandhi Nahar (Canal): evaluation of transformed ecosystem. India. Bheru L. Sukhwal. 1988

Indonesia and the Philippines: mobility behavior and employment characteristics. Richard Ulack and Thomas R. Leinbach. 1982

Irrigation, society, and change in an oasis. Fifuig, Morocco. Abdellatif Bencherifa. 1988

Ivory Coast: land-use competition. Thomas J. Bassett. 1987

Japan: three decades of change in two rural townships. Forrest R. Pitts. 1983

Karakoram Mountains and Tian Shan: irrigated mountain agropastoral systems. Pakistan and China. Nigel J. R. Allan. 1986

Kenya, western: contract farming, diet, and nutrition. Lawrence S. Grossman. 1987

—— land-use competition and wildlife conservation. Donald L. Capone. 1986

—— population pressure and environment. Derrick J. Thom. 1986

—— tropical agriculture and socioeconomic and physical factors. Ernestine Cary. 1982

Leeward Islands: land-use intensity and labor migration. St. Kitts and Nevis. Bonham C. Richardson. 1975

—— response to economic depression. Public Records Office, London. Bonham C. Richardson. 1986

Mexican undocumented migration: origin patterns. U. S. and Mexico. Richard C. Jones. 1984

Mexico: prehispanic wetland agriculture. Alfred H. Siemens. 1983-84

—— northwest: traditional water-harvesting systems. Gerald Fish. 1980

Micronesia: role of urban growth centers in economic development. John D. Eyre. 1983

North America: history of geography. Geoffrey J. Martin. 1981

Pakistan: northern mountain agro-ecosystems. Nigel J. R. Allan. 1982

Peru, eastern: food production in dooryard gardens. Martha A. Works. 1987

—— labor intensification and productivity. Lake Titicaca Basin. Roland W. Bergman and John S. Kusner. 1984-88

River blindness: settlement response to control of the disease. West Africa. John M. Hunter. 1988

Stoneybatter: historical geography of Dublin's oldest neighborhood. Ireland. Kevin C. Kearns. 1988

Thailand: highland-lowland economic integration and replacement of opium crops. Richard A. Crooker. 1986, 1988

Taiwan: impact of industrial estates on rural areas. Roger M. Selya. 1981

Tanzania: semiarid drainage basin potential. John W. Pawling. 1973

Torres Strait: traditional knowledge of marine environments and biota. Australia. Bernard Q. Nietschmann. 1980

United States: landscapes of the western interior. Thomas R. Vale. 1983

────── semiconductor industry: labor markets, organization, and geography. Santa Clara County, California, and elsewhere. David P. Angel. 1987

────── toxic riskscapes, the geography of airborne pollution. Susan L. Cutter. 1988

United States and Europe: emergency evacuation of cities. Wilbur Zelinsky. 1983

Venezuela: cultural and land-use effects of cocaine production. Tim W. Hudson. 1985

West African grain coast: ports. William R. Stanley. 1974

CARTOGRAPHY

American Revolution: military map sources. Douglas W. Marshall. 1976

Antarctica: mapping. Lincoln Ellsworth. 1934

Chan Chan-Moche Valley site: maps published. Peru. Carol J. Mackey and Michael E. Moseley. 1973

Cognitive world maps: parochial views and collection. Thomas F. Saarinen. 1985, 1987

Everest, Mount: photographic flights. Bradford Washburn. 1984

Grand Canyon of the Colorado: South Rim mapping. Bradford Washburn. 1971-72, 1974

Grand Canyon map: final revision. Bradford Washburn. 1979

Historical map testing. Roland E. Chardon. 1976

Kennedy, Mount, and Mount Hubbard: mapping. Canada. Bradford Washburn. 1965

────── mapping. Canada. Paul Ulmer. 1966

Roads Through History: map catalog publication. Peabody Institute Library. 1965

Sikkim: physical-cultural map. Pradyumna P. Karan. 1968

Geology

Ai (Et Tell), Israel: soils, construction, and geologic materials. George R. Glenn. 1970

Alaska: Ordovician and Devonian stratigraphic measurement and fossil collection. Alaska. Robert B. Blodgett. 1988

Alaska Range Quaternary Mapping Program. United States. Norman W. Ten Brink. 1981

Alluvial fans. Death Valley, California. Ronald I. Dorn. 1984

────── and other geomorphic features: response to climatic perturbation. California. Dale F. Ritter. 1988

Alpine chain: geological exploration. Southern Italy. Walter Alvarez. 1975

Aluminous laterite and bauxite: origin. Palau, western Pacific Ocean. Samuel S. Goldich. 1978

Andes: mapping of eastern slope. Quito region, Ecuador. Tomas Feininger. 1979

────── metamorphic rocks. Colombia and Ecuador. Tomas Feininger. 1971

────── terrane accretion, subduction, and orogenesis. Chile. Myrl E. Beck, Jr. 1988

Archaean rocks: tectonic and thermal history. West Greenland. Robert F. Dymek. 1979

Artificial acidification and deacidification: soluble aluminum. Norway. Roderick A. Parnell, Jr. 1987

Avalon Peninsula: biostratigraphy and depositional tectonics, Lower Cambrian. Newfoundland, Canada. Ed Landing. 1982-83

Basalts: petrology and geochemistry. Snake River Plain, Idaho. William P. Leeman. 1969

Bechan Cave: geochronology of adjacent canyon. Utah. Larry Agenbroad. 1985

Bentonite dating: Lower Paleozoic. Britain. Reuben J. Ross, Jr. 1976

Calcalkaline rocks: isotopic tracer studies. Mitsunobu Tatsumoto. 1979

Caledonites. Norway. William B. Size. 1976

Cambrian-Ordovician boundary: geochemical study. Jilin, China. Judith Wright. 1986

Carboniferous deposits: statistical analysis. Fife, Scotland. Edward S. Belt. 1972

Caribbean-Nazca plate boundary: geologic study. Panama. William P. Mann. 1985

Cenozoic tectonism. Apennines, Italy. Ivo Lucchitta. 1984

Chubb Crater. Quebec. V. Ben Meen. 1951.

Clay sediments: mineralogy and distribution. Turnagain Arm region, Alaska. Neal R. O'Brien. 1973

Climatic change at the fringe of the Sahara. Sudan. C. Vance Haynes. 1988

Colluvium-mantled hollows: deposits. Oregon and Washington. William E. Dietrich. 1987

Cretaceous-Tertiary boundary event. Texas, Tunisia, and Israel. Gerta Keller. 1987

Cumberland Peninsula, Baffin Island: south-coast reconnaissance, late Quaternary. Canada. William W. Locke III. 1982

Dolomite formation. Laguna Mormona, Baja California, Mexico. Kathe L. Bertine. 1985

Fine-tuning a Grand Canyon map, artist Tibor G. Toth, left, consults with surveyor Bradford Washburn.   JIM MENDENHALL

Discoverer of the Valley of Ten Thousand Smokes, Robert F. Griggs wades Alaska's ash-choked Katmai River.   B. B. FULTON

Forty feet from head to toe, a Brachiosaurus dwarfs a forelimb's upper bone and a man. ROY ANDERSEN

Lichens, here studied by geobotanist James Anderson, help track the retreat of Alaska's glaciers. CHRISTOPHER G. KNIGHT

Española Island: volcanic and biologic study. Galápagos. Minard L. Hall. 1979

Evaporites, Triassic: first deposits of the rifting Atlantic. Morocco. William T. Holser. 1982

Gem study. Asia. V. Ben Meen. 1964-65

Geomorphology: Baltit area. Karakoram Mountains, Pakistan. Andrew S. Goudie. 1980

Geothermal activity: remote sensing. East African Rift. Kathleen Crane. 1980

Glacial and floral changes: climatic history, last 140 centuries. Argentina. John H. Mercer. 1974

Glacial indicator fan: from Reindeer Lake Cretaceous shale. Saskatchewan, Canada. William G. Johnston. 1983

Glacial sediments: Precambrian. Sierra Leone and Senegal. Stephen J. Culver. 1983

Glaciation and climatic fluctuation: dating the pre-Wisconsin. Wrangell Mountains, Alaska. Edward Evenson. 1988

Gondwana: Paleozoic reconstruction of Asian-Australian terranes. Vietnam and India. Clive F. Burrett. 1988

Great Rift Valley: structural origin of the Ethiopian section. George H. Megrue and Paul A. Mohr. 1968-69

Himalaya and Eastern Zanskar ranges: stratigraphy and sedimentology. Michael E. Brookfield. 1986

Hydrographic evolution: late Glacial to Recent. Western Mediterranean. Daniel J. Stanley. 1970

Indus suture zone and Karakoram Mountains: radiometric dating of rocks. Michael E. Brookfield. 1979-80, 1983

Iron formation. Disko Island, western Greenland. John M. Bird. 1977, 1980-81

Italy: Plio-Pleistocene boundary. Charles W. Naeser. 1979

Karsts: development and archaeology. Belize. Thomas E. Miller. 1983

—— Permian topography. Slick Hills, Oklahoma. Raymond N. Donovan. 1988

—— Teng Long system. Hubei Province, China. Michael Dusar. 1988

Kenya, Mount: Quaternary history. East Africa. William C. Mahaney. 1976, 1981, 1983, 1986

Labrador Crater. Canada. V. Ben Meen. 1953-54

Laetoli Beds and footprint tuffs: geologic history. Tanzania. Richard L. Hay. 1976, 1978-82

Lake Erie: late Pleistocene coastal deposits. Charles H. Carter. 1986

Landslide history. Gros Ventre mountains, Wyoming. Robert C. Palmquist. 1980, 1982

Loess deposition: thermoluminescence chronology. Lanzhou, Gansu Province, China. Steven L. Forman. 1988

Magma intrusion: geochemical monitoring. Long Valley caldera, California. Stanley N. Williams. 1983

Marble Canyon quadrangle. Death Valley, California. Edward A. Johnson. 1973

Mauna Kea: glacial deposits. Hawaii. Ronald I. Dorn. 1987

Metamorphic rocks: petrographic mapping. New Caledonia. Philippa M. Black. 1970

Meteorite and tektite collection. Australia. Brian H. Mason and E. P. Henderson. 1963-67

Meteorite craters. Mauritania. Robert F. Fudali. 1969-70

—— possible impact site. Bolivia. Kenneth E. Campbell. 1986

Messina earthquake study. Sicily. Charles Will Wright. 1909

Mineralogical research. Prince of Wales Island, Alaska. George S. Switzer. 1967

Miocene rocks: stratigraphy and faunas. Northwestern Nebraska. Robert M. Hunt, Jr. 1972

Mirror Lake: magnetic studies of lake sediments and sources. New Hampshire. Frank Oldfield. 1981-82

Molokai, windward coast: geology and botany. Hawaii. Robert R. Compton. 1980

Morrison and Cloverly formations: study of sediments. Big Horn Basin, Wyoming. Carl F. Vondra. 1983

Nile Delta: Holocene evolution. Egypt. Daniel J. Stanley. 1986, 1988

Olduvai Gorge: geologic history. Tanzania. Richard L. Hay. 1962, 1968-70, 1972.

Paleoclimatic and geologic studies. Nubian and Western Deserts, Sudan and Egypt. C. Vance Haynes. 1977-80, 1984

Paleoenvironments: late Precambrian strata. Baffin Island. Keene Swett. 1987

—— origin of Precambrian iron formations. Hamersley Basin, Western Australia. Bruce M. Simonson. 1986-87

Paleohydrology. Lake Pagahrit, Utah. William L. Graf. 1985

Pleistocene alluvial sediments: paleoecological changes. Río General Valley, Costa Rica. Richard H. Kesel. 1985

Palsa development in permafrost. Yukon Territory, Canada. Ann M. Tallman. 1977

Patrick Buttes: Miocene rocks and fauna. Wyoming. Robert M. Hunt, Jr. 1979

Pegmatite mineral studies. Black Hills, South Dakota. George Rapp, Jr. 1964

Recent Nile cone history: based on sediment-core analysis. Daniel J. Stanley. 1974

Rukwa-Malawi Rift: tectonic study. Tanzania. Jeffrey A. Karson. 1985

Salmon River: batholith. Idaho. Philip J. Shenon and John C. Reed. 1935

Saltpeter conversion and cave nitrate origins. Carol A. Hill. 1974

Seamount interiors: magnetic properties. La Palma, Canary Islands. Hubert Staudigel. 1988

Sedimentation patterns: submarine. Wilmington Canyon, Atlantic Ocean. Daniel J. Stanley. 1966

—— late Cretaceous and early Tertiary fauna. Bolivia. Larry G. Marshall. 1982

—— Miocene and Pliocene. South Dakota. Morton Green. 1973

Mollusks, late Pleistocene: dating and climatic significance. Ohio and Indiana. Barry B. Miller. 1982, 1984-85

Natural Trap Cave: Pleistocene and Recent flora and fauna. Wyoming. B. Miles Gilbert. 1978

Nearctylodon: taxonomy of mammal-like reptiles. G. Edward Lewis. 1982

Old World monkey fossils *(Cercopithecoidea).* Mediterranean region. Eric Delson. 1971

Oldman formation: Cretaceous paleoecology. Dinosaur Provincial Park, Alberta, Canada. Peter Dodson. 1981-83

Ostrocods, marine: response to Cenozoic climatic change. Japan. Thomas M. Cronin. 1984

Paleoecology: late Quaternary. Saltville Valley, Virginia. Jerry N. McDonald. 1984

Paleofauna from caves in the Dominican Republic. Renato O. Rimoli M. 1977, 1979

Paleontology and archaeology: Lubbock Lake site. Texas. Craig C. Black. 1973-74

Papago Springs Cave: Sangamonian paleoecology. Arizona. Nicholas J. Czaplewski. 1988

Paraguay: stratigraphy and paleontological exploration. Rafael Herbst. 1979

—— and Uruguay: paleobotanical research. Rafael Herbst. 1982

Permo-Triassic boundary: paleobotany and paleoenvironment. Argentina and Uruguay. Rafael Herbst. 1985, 1988

Pinnipeds: late Tertiary evolution. Chile. Andre R. Wyss. 1988

Pliocene fossil localities. Rift Valley, Kenya. Vincent J. Maglio. 1972

Plio-Pleistocene fossils. Iran. Douglas M. Lay. 1976

Pollen: Mesozoic ultrastructure. Madagascar and South Africa. Michael S. Zavada. 1985, 1988

Precambrian eon: early history of life. U. S. and Canada. James W. Schopf. 1985-86

Pre-Carboniferous coal swamps: paleoecology. Southern Appalachia. Stephen E. Scheckler. 1981

Predynastic faunal and floral remains. Red Sea mountains, Egypt. Steven M. Goodman. 1986

Primates: early Miocene and late Oligocene. Argentina. John G. Fleagle. 1982, 1987-88

Pterosaurs, giant. Texas. Douglas A. Lawson. 1975

Rhinoceros herd: Miocene, buried in volcanic ash. Nebraska. Michael R. Voorhies. 1978-79

Rhinoceros and pig bones. South Dakota. Joseph P. Connolly and James D. Bump. 1940

Rocks, minerals, and fossils: collecting for conservation. Badlands, South Dakota. Robert W. Wilson. 1965, 1968-69

Salamander and frog fossils: paleogeography. Richard Dean Estes. 1973

Sangamon interglacial deposits. Natural Trap Cave, Wyoming. Larry D. Martin. 1983

Scaphites: late Cretaceous evolution and systematics. Wyoming. Neil H. Landman. 1988

Semionotus: adaptive radiations. Mesozoic lakes. Amy R. McCune. 1981

Siwalik Group: Neogene vertebrate paleontology and geology. Western Nepal. Robert M. West. 1981

Sponge reefs: Jurassic paleobiogeography, paleoecology, and evolution. Eastern and western Europe. Joseph A. Ghiold. 1985

Stanton's Cave: Pleistocene paleoclimatology. Grand Canyon, Arizona. Robert C. Euler. 1969-70

Sticklebacks: measuring tempo of evolution. Nevada. Michael A. Bell. 1984

Taphonomy: Cretaceous. Ellisdale Dinosaur Site, New Jersey. David C. Parris. 1986, 1988

—— Miocene. Flint Hill, South Dakota. James E. Martin. 1983-84

Tarija Basin: Pleistocene vertebrates and chronology. Bolivia. Bruce J. MacFadden. 1983

Tetrapods: early Jurassic. Nova Scotia. Paul E. Olsen. 1985

—— Middle Mississippian. Iowa. John R. Bolt. 1986

—— Triassic: South American faunal assemblage in Northern Hemisphere. Virginia. Hans-Dieter Sues. 1988

—— Upper Devonian. Australia. Richard C. Fox. 1983

—— Upper Permian and Triassic. Southern Brazil. Mario C. Barberena. 1978, 1980

Tobago: zoogeographical implications of Recent and fossil vertebrates. West Indies. Ralph E. Eshelman. 1980

Trace fossils: Proterozoic. Godavari Valley, India. James D. Howard. 1981

Turtles, African and South American: paleoecology and plate tectonics. Roger C. Wood. 1978

U-Bar Cave: late Pleistocene paleontology and paleoecology. Hidalgo County, New Mexico. Arthur H. Harris. 1984-85

Underwater paleontology. Florida. S. David Webb. 1968-69

Vertebrate biostratigraphy: Miocene sediments. Western Nebraska. John A. Breyer. 1977

Vertebrates. Australia. Thomas H. Rich. 1975

—— Baja California. Theodore Downs. 1974

—— Baja California. William J. Morris. 1965-71

—— Carboniferous: marine faunas and paleogeography. Chubut Province, Argentina. Carlos R. Gonzalez. 1987-88

—— Cenozoic. Pilbara and Canning

Entombed by an ashfall ten million years ago, the remains of a rhinoceros herd lie in a Nebraska ravine. ANNIE GRIFFITHS BELT

Scientists in 1940 unearth bones of the antelope-like Protoceras *in the Badlands of South Dakota.* JOSEPH P. CONNOLLY

From **Calypso,** *Capt. Jacques-Yves Cousteau prepares to test* **Denise,** *a two-man submersible.* THOMAS J. ABERCROMBIE, NGS

Harold E. Edgerton's cameras, strobo-scopic lights, and side-scan sonar have examined the seafloor. DAVID DOUBILET

Geophysics

OCEANOGRAPHY

Marine aerosols: chemical composition sampled worldwide from a sailing boat. Rene E. Van Grieken. 1979

Mid-Atlantic Ridge: topography, geology, and sea life. Maurice Ewing. 1947-48

Mid-Atlantic Ridge Rift Valley: sonar exploration. Harold E. Edgerton. 1969

Ocean floors: global physiographical study. Bruce C. Heezen. 1970

Photographic and echo-sounding research and equipment. Harold E. Edgerton. 1950, 1952-62, 1966, 1974

Photographic equipment. Walter A. Starck II. 1964

—— for study of living plankton in the sea. Harold E. Edgerton. 1978

Sediments: bioturbation. Puerto Rico. Jack Morelock. 1973

Underwater instrumentation: for geology, archaeology, and biology. Harold E. Edgerton. 1980

—— microorganisms studied with new optical instrument. Virgin Islands. J. Rudi Strickler. 1988

VOLCANOLOGY

Arenal volcano: eruption dynamics and petrology. Costa Rica. William G. Melson. 1969

Basement rock and volcanic correlations: Tertiary. Gulf of California. R. Gordon Gastil. 1972

Caldera beneath Yellowstone Lake. Wyoming. Paul Morgan. 1988

Campanian ignimbrite. Italy. Richard V. Fisher. 1987

Cerro Bravo volcano: recent volcanology. Colombia. Stanley N. Williams. 1987

Debris avalanches: Augustine volcano, Alaska. Lee Siebert. 1985-86

Fuji and Hakone volcanoes: evolution. Honshu, Japan. Richard J. Arculus. 1985

Katmai, Mount: examination following eruption. Alaska. George C. Martin. 1912

Lamongan volcano: 19th-century lava flows. Indonesia. Katherine V. Cashman. 1987

Melt lubrication and rapid uplift. Clearwater Mountains, Alaska. Lincoln S. Hollister. 1987

Nunivak Island: volcanic ejecta. Alaska. John Sloan Dickey, Jr. 1974

Panama: volcanic arc reconnaissance. Marc J. Defant. 1988

Pavlof volcano. Alaska Peninsula. Thomas A. Jaggar. 1928

Pelée, Mount: eruption. Martinique. Robert T. Hill, Israel C. Russell, and Thomas A. Jaggar. 1902

Poas volcano. Costa Rica. Susan L. Brantley. 1987

Rainier, Mount: summit crater geophysical and volcanological investigation. Washington. Barry W. Prather and Maynard M. Miller. 1970-71

Tenorio volcanic complex: evolution. Costa Rica. Jorge H. Barquero. 1987

Tephrachronology: southern Andes. Chile and Argentina. Charles R. Stern. 1986

Thera: before eruption of 1450 B.C. Greece. Grant H. Heiken. 1981

—— Bronze Age eruption date.

Aegean Sea. Charles J. Vitaliano. 1974

—— Minoan ash, downwind island distribution and relation to caldera size. Greece. Floyd W. McCoy. 1982

Tonga Islands volcanoes: survey of recent activity. William G. Melson and W. B. Bryan. 1968

Vesuvius, El Chichón, Tambora. Haraldur Sigursson. 1982, 1984-87

Volcanic flames and fumes: spectroscopy. Hawaii. Dale P. Cruikshank. 1971

Volcanic gas and fumes: spectroscopy. Hawaii. Dale P. Cruikshank and Jay M. Pasachoff. 1981

—— and petrology. Galápagos. Bert E. Nordlie. 1971

Volcanic rocks. Micronesia. Fred Barker. 1976

Volcanism. Austral Islands. Rockne H. Johnson. 1971

—— Zuni Centers volcanic field, late Cenozoic. New Mexico. A. William Laughlin. 1973

Volcanoes, submarine. Near Samoa. Rockne H. Johnson. 1975

Volcanologic studies: evidence for mantle upwelling. Azores. Martin F. J. Flower. 1983

History

Falkland Islands: Charles Darwin's expedition. Archives and Falklands. Patrick H. Armstrong. 1988

Hydraulic cement, early. Greece and Cyprus. Theodore A. Wertime. 1980

Llanos: tropical plains frontier. Northern South America. Jane M. Loy. 1973

Manuscript collections: survey. Nepal, Sikkim, and Bhutan monasteries. John F. Staal and Lewis R. Lancaster. 1973

Manuscripts: St. Mpatsis Monastery. Andros Island, Aegean Sea. Antonia Tripolitis. 1968-69

Metallurgic zones: descriptions by Homer and Strabo. Northern Turkey. Theodore A. Wertime. 1970

Naval documents: cataloging and indexing. Naval Historical Foundation. 1965

Nepala-mahatmya: translation of Sanskrit. Kathmandu Valley. Jayaraj Acharya. 1988

Plantation slaves: historical anthropology. Barbados. Jerome S. Handler. 1987

Persian Royal Road Survey. Anatolia, Turkey. S. Frederick Starr. 1961

Population dynamics: protohistoric aboriginal. Louisiana. Stephen Williams. 1985

Russians in Alaska, 18th- and 19th-century penetration: archival and on-site studies. Lydia T. Black. 1984

Aboard **Alvin**, *the submersible used for deep-sea exploration—including discovery of hydrothermal vents in the Galápagos Rift and the* Titanic *in 1985—pilot Dudley Foster, left, and Robert D. Ballard communicate with their mother ship.* MARTIN BOWEN

Sociology

City street life. New York City. William H. Whyte. 1972-73

Medals and Awards of the Society

A freestanding crystal globe and pedestal by Steuben Glass along with $10,000 for the pursuit of additional research was awarded to each of 15 outstanding contributors to geography and other fields of scientific study and exploration on November 17, 1988. The National Geographic Society Centennial Awards were presented at a banquet in Washington, D.C. There Society staff members and guests ranged along the head table to talk with the honorees.

EXTENDING ITS LONG TRADITION of recognizing distinguished achievement in discovery and research, the National Geographic Society in November 1988 presented to 15 illustrious explorers, scholars, and scientists Centennial Awards for major contributions to knowledge of the earth, its inhabitants, and the encompassing natural environment. The honorees' names were added to the roster of eminent men and women who from 1906 have received from the Society medals and other awards for outstanding service to geography.

The recipients, each presented with a crystal globe, exemplify high and continuing achievement in a wide range of disciplines and epitomize the Society's century of commitment to and support of research and exploration. Each honoree also received $10,000 for research. The recipients:

Robert D. Ballard was a principal discoverer of *Titanic* and has explored deep-ocean geology and hydrothermal vents. George F. Bass has applied the painstaking methods of land archaeology to the seafloor, thereby uncovering artifacts of great beauty and cultural significance. Jacques-Yves Cousteau, who codesigned the Aqua-Lung and developed vessels for oceanic exploration, has investigated the world's seas and brought their wonders to millions.

Frank C. Craighead, Jr., and John J. Craighead pioneered radio-tracking and satellite biotelemetry for the study of wildlife. Harold E. Edgerton invented the stroboscopic high-speed flash and developed side-scan sonar and underwater cameras.

Archaeologist Kenan T. Erim excavated a great Greco-Roman urban complex at Aphrodisias, Turkey. Senator John H. Glenn, Jr., first American to orbit the earth, opened a spectacular new vision of the "blue planet." The work of Jane Goodall with chimpanzees in Tanzania has helped humans gain a better understanding of their own place in nature.

Sir Edmund Hillary was first, with Sherpa Tenzing Norgay, to stand on the summit of Mount Everest. Mary D. Leakey and Richard E. Leakey have greatly advanced knowledge of the evolution of humans through their investigations of hominid remains in East Africa. For decades lecturer Thayer Soule has brought the world in all its diversity to Geographic audiences in Washington, D.C.

Barbara Washburn and Bradford Washburn have been leaders in aerial photography and mapping in the mountains of Alaska, the Himalaya, and the Grand Canyon.

HUBBARD MEDAL

The Hubbard Medal, named for Gardiner Greene Hubbard, first President of the Society, is awarded for distinction in exploration, discovery, and research.

JOHN W. YOUNG AND CAPT. ROBERT L. CRIPPEN, USN, 1981: For contributions to space science as crew of the space shuttle *Columbia*.

JAMES E. WEBB, 1978: Outstanding contribution to manned lunar landings.

BRUCE CHARLES HEEZEN AND MARIE THARP, 1978: Contributions to knowledge of the ocean floor.

ALEXANDER WETMORE, 1975: Contributions to ornithology.

NEIL A. ARMSTRONG, COL. EDWIN E. ALDRIN, JR., USAF, AND LT. COL. MICHAEL COLLINS, USAF, 1970: Space exploration; first moon landing as the crew of Apollo 11.

COL. FRANK BORMAN, USAF, CAPT. JAMES A. LOVELL, JR., USN, AND LT. COL. WILLIAM A. ANDERS, USAF, 1969: Space exploration; first to orbit the moon as crew of Apollo 8.

JUAN T. TRIPPE, 1967: Contributions to aviation.

AMERICAN MOUNT EVEREST EXPEDITION, 1963: Contributions to geography and high-altitude research through conquest of earth's highest mountain.

LT. COL. JOHN H. GLENN, JR., 1962: Space exploration.

LOUIS S. B. AND MARY D. LEAKEY, 1962: Anthropological discoveries in East Africa.

SIR VIVIAN FUCHS, 1959: Leadership of British trans-Antarctic expedition.

U.S. NAVY ANTARCTIC EXPEDITIONS, 1959: Antarctic research and exploration, 1955-59.

PAUL A. SIPLE, 1958: For 30 years of Antarctic explorations, including leadership of first group to winter at the South Pole.

BRITISH EVEREST EXPEDITION, 1954: First ascent of Mount Everest.

ROBERT S. OAKES, NGS

COMDR. DONALD B. MACMILLAN, 1953: Arctic explorations, 1908-52.

GEN. H. H. ARNOLD, 1945: Contributions to aviation.

LINCOLN ELLSWORTH, 1936: Extraordinary achievements in polar exploration.

CAPTS. ALBERT W. STEVENS AND ORVIL A. ANDERSON, 1935: World altitude record of 72,395 feet in balloon *Explorer II*.

ANNE MORROW LINDBERGH, 1934: Notable flights, as copilot, on Charles Lindbergh's aerial surveys.

ROY CHAPMAN ANDREWS, 1931: Geographic discoveries in Central Asia.

COL. CHARLES A. LINDBERGH, 1927: New York-Paris solo flight.

LT. COMDR. RICHARD E. BYRD, JR., 1926: First to reach North Pole by airplane. 1930, Special Medal of Honor: First to attain South Pole by air.

VILHJALMUR STEFANSSON, 1919: Discoveries in Canadian Arctic.

SIR ERNEST H. SHACKLETON, 1910: Antarctic explorations and farthest south, 88° 23'.

GROVE KARL GILBERT, 1909: Thirty years of achievements in physical geography.

CAPT. ROBERT A. BARTLETT, 1909: Far-north explorations with Peary's 1909 expedition.

CAPT. ROALD AMUNDSEN, 1907: Traverse of Northwest Passage. 1913, Special Gold Medal: Discovery of South Pole.

COMDR. ROBERT E. PEARY, 1906: Arctic explorations. 1909, Special Medal of Honor: Discovery of North Pole.

ALEXANDER GRAHAM BELL MEDAL

The Alexander Graham Bell Medal, named for the inventor and second Society President, is given for extraordinary achievement in geographic research, broadly construed.

BARBARA AND BRADFORD WASHBURN, 1980: For unique and notable contributions to geography and cartography.

GROSVENOR MEDAL

The Grosvenor Medal, named for Gilbert Hovey Grosvenor, Society President and Editor for 55 years, is awarded for exceptional service to geography by a Society officer or employee.

MELVIN MONROE PAYNE, 1982: For 50 years of dedicated service to the Society.

THOMAS WILLSON MCKNEW, 1980: For 48 years of dedicated service to the Society.

MELVILLE BELL GROSVENOR, 1974: Outstanding service to geography.

JOHN OLIVER LA GORCE, 1955: Outstanding service to the increase and diffusion of geographic knowledge, 1905-55.

GILBERT H. GROSVENOR, 1949: Outstanding service to geography as Editor of NATIONAL GEOGRAPHIC.

JOHN OLIVER LA GORCE MEDAL

The John Oliver La Gorce Medal, named for a former Society President and Editor, is presented for accomplishment in geographic exploration or in the sciences, or for public service to advance international understanding (formerly the Special Gold Medal).

ARTHUR H. ROBINSON, 1988: For outstanding achievements in cartography.

KAMOYA KIMEU, 1985: For contributions to the search for man's origins in Africa.

GEORGE F. BASS, 1979: For advancing the science of nautical archaeology.

Recipients of the 1988 National Geographic Centennial Awards join Society President and Chairman Gilbert M. Grosvenor. Standing from left: John H. Glenn, Jr., Robert D. Ballard, Kenan T. Erim, Bradford Washburn, Jane Goodall, Mr. Grosvenor, Richard E. Leakey, Thayer Soule, Sir Edmund Hillary; seated from left: George F. Bass, Harold E. Edgerton, Jacques-Yves Cousteau, Barbara Washburn, Mary D. Leakey, John J. Craighead, Frank C. Craighead, Jr. SISSE BRIMBERG

JOHN J. CRAIGHEAD AND FRANK C. CRAIGHEAD, JR.,1979: For pioneer use of biotelemetry to extend knowledge of wildlife behavior, life history, and ecology.

BEN L. ABRUZZO, MAXIE L. ANDERSON, AND LARRY NEWMAN, 1979: In recognition of the first manned transatlantic balloon flight.

PHILIP VAN HORN WEEMS, 1968: Contributions to marine, air, and space navigation.

HAROLD E. EDGERTON, 1968: Contributions to photographic and geophysical technology.

AMERICAN ANTARCTIC MOUNTAINEERING EXPEDITION, 1967: First ascent of Antarctica's highest peak, 1966-67.

CAPT. JACQUES-YVES COUSTEAU, 1961: Undersea exploration.

PRINCE PHILIP, DUKE OF EDINBURGH, 1957: Promoting science and better understanding among the world's peoples.

MRS. ROBERT E. PEARY, 1955: Contributions to husband's polar explorations.

THOMAS C. POULTER, 1937: Achievements, Byrd Antarctic expedition.

AMELIA EARHART, 1932: First solo Atlantic flight by a woman.

HUGO ECKENER, 1930: First global navigation by an airship.

FLOYD BENNETT, 1926: Flight to North Pole with Richard E. Byrd.

COL. GEORGE W. GOETHALS, 1914: Directing completion of Panama Canal.

AWARDS

CENTENNIAL AWARD, 1988

ROBERT D. BALLARD. Deep-sea explorer, marine geologist

GEORGE F. BASS. Undersea archaeologist

JACQUES-YVES COUSTEAU. Undersea explorer, inventor

FRANK C. CRAIGHEAD, JR. Bioecologist

JOHN J. CRAIGHEAD. Bioecologist

HAROLD E. EDGERTON. Electrical engineer

KENAN T. ERIM. Classical archaeologist

JOHN H. GLENN, JR. Senator, astronaut

JANE GOODALL. Zoologist

SIR EDMUND HILLARY. Mountaineer, diplomat

MARY D. LEAKEY. Archaeologist

RICHARD E. LEAKEY. Paleoanthropologist

THAYER SOULE. Lecturer

BRADFORD WASHBURN. Cartographer, photographer

BARBARA WASHBURN. Cartographer, mountaineer

JANE M. SMITH AWARD
Jane McGrew Smith directed that her bequest to the Society be used to establish an award in recognition of notable contributions to geography. The award was discontinued in 1977.

DR. CALVIN H. PLIMPTON, 1964. President, Amherst College

LYNDON B. JOHNSON, 1962. Vice President of the United States

ARLEIGH A. BURKE, 1960. Admiral, USN, Chief of Naval Operations

SIR BRUCE INGRAM, 1959. Editor, *Illustrated London News*

EDWIN A. LINK, 1959. Inventor and undersea pioneer

PHILIP VAN HORN WEEMS, 1959. Captain, USN (Ret.)

ALBERT A. STANLEY, 1959. U.S. Coast and Geodetic Survey

SIR VIVIAN FUCHS, 1959. British geologist, explorer

CHARLES P. MOUNTFORD, 1956. Australian anthropologist

ARDITO DESIO, 1955. Leader, K-2 expedition

IRA S. BOWEN, 1955. Astronomer

KENNETH H. GIBSON, 1953. Colonel, USAF

MRS. FRANKLIN L. FISHER, 1953. Widow of Illustrations Editor, NATIONAL GEOGRAPHIC

ROBERT B. ANDERSON, 1953. Secretary of the Navy

MAYNARD OWEN WILLIAMS, 1953. Chief of Foreign Staff, NATIONAL GEOGRAPHIC

ANDREW GEORGE LATTA MCNAUGHTON, 1952. General, Canadian Army (Ret.)

MRS. RUTH B. SHIPLEY, 1951. Passport Office, Department of State

MRS. J. R. HILDEBRAND, 1951. Widow of Assistant Editor, NATIONAL GEOGRAPHIC

HERBERT FRIEDMANN, 1951. Curator of Birds, U.S. National Museum

HUGH L. DRYDEN, 1951. Director, National Advisory Committee for Aeronautics

ALBERT E. GIESECKE, 1951. Government adviser, Peru

MRS. HENRY H. ARNOLD, 1950. Smith life member

MRS. ALBERT W. STEVENS, 1950. Smith life member

EARL B. SHAW, 1949. President, Council of Geography Teachers

GEORGE J. MILLER, 1949. Editor, *Journal of Geography*

JOHN O'KEEFE, 1949. U.S. Army Map Service

BENJAMIN R. HOFFMAN, 1948. Geographical Society of Philadelphia

NICHOLAS H. DARTON, 1948. Geologist

MAURICE EWING, 1947. Geologist

GEOFFREY T. HELLMAN, 1947. Essayist

MALCOLM J. PROUDFOOT, 1947. Geographer

CHESTER W. NIMITZ, 1946. Fleet Admiral, USN, Chief of Naval Operations

SALVADOR MASSIP, 1946. Geographer

S. S. VISHER, 1945. Geographer

FRANK M. MACFARLAND, 1945. President, California Academy of Sciences

FRANK B. JEWETT, 1945. President, National Academy of Sciences

CHRISTOVA LEITE DE CASTRO, 1944. Brazilian geographer

MRS. WILLIAM G. PADEN, 1943. Author

EDMUND W. STARLING, 1943. U.S. Secret Service

HARRY WARNER FRANTZ, 1943. Journalist

ELI HELMICK, 1943. Major General, USA (Ret.)

ALEXANDER M. PATCH, 1943. Major General, USA

SAMUEL WHITTEMORE BOGGS, 1943. Department of State geographer

CHARLES H. DEETZ, 1942. Cartographer, U.S. Coast and Geodetic Survey

J. FRED ESSARY, 1941. Journalist

GEORGE W. GODDARD, 1940. Major, USAF, aerial photographer

FRANKLIN ADAMS, 1938. Authority on Latin America

STEPHEN R. CAPPS, 1938. Geologist

WEB HILL, 1937. Merchant

PRINCE IESATO TOKUGAWA, 1937. Japan

W. J. PETERS, 1936. U.S. Geological Survey, retired

ROBERT MULDROW, 1936. U.S. Geological Survey, retired

H. L. BALDWIN, 1936. U.S. Geological Survey, retired

A. E. MURLIN, 1936. U.S. Geological Survey, retired

HIS MAJESTY KING LEOPOLD, 1936. Belgium

HERBERT HOLLICK-KENYON, 1936. Pilot, Canadian Airways

SAMUEL S. GANNETT, 1936. Geographer

ROGERS BIRNIE, JR., 1936. USA (Ret.)

RANDOLPH P. WILLIAMS, 1936. Captain, U.S. Army Air Corps

LAWRENCE J. BURPEE, 1936. Canadian commissioner

WILLIAM R. POPE, 1935. Colonel, USA

JOSEPH P. CONNOLLY, 1935. Geologist, college president

LEONHARD STEJNEGER, 1935. Biologist

CLIFFORD K. BERRYMAN, 1934. Political cartoonist

W. COLEMAN NEVILS, S. J., 1934. Classicist, President, Georgetown University

CHARLES F. MARVIN, 1934. Meteorologist

JAMES P. THOMSON, 1934. Royal Geographical Society of Australia

VERNON BAILEY, 1934. Naturalist

EUGENE EDWARD BUCK, 1934. President, American Society of Composers, Authors and Publishers

WILLIAM H. HOBBS, 1933. Geologist

LAURENCE M. GOULD, 1931. Biologist

ALBERT W. STEVENS, 1931. Captain, USA, aerial photographer

ANDRÉ CITROËN, 1931. French industrialist

DOUGLAS W. JOHNSON, 1931. Physiographer

ASHLEY C. MCKINLEY, 1931. Captain, USA, aerial photographer

SIR WILFRED GRENFELL, 1930. Surgeon, missionary, author

CORNELIUS A. PUGSLEY, 1929. Banker, conservationist

Herbert Putnam, 1929. Librarian of Congress

Andrew E. Douglass, 1929. Astronomer, dendrochronologist

Curtis D. Wilbur, 1929. Secretary of the Navy, retired

Charles A. Lindbergh, 1927. Transatlantic flight pioneer

Knud Rasmussen, 1926. Greenland explorer

William Brooks Cabot, 1925. Author, engineer

Philip Sidney Smith, 1925. Geologist

Joseph F. Rock, 1925. Explorer

Neil M. Judd, 1925. Archaeologist

Robert A. Bartlett, 1925. Far-north explorer

Charles Sheldon, 1925. Alaska explorer

Donald B. MacMillan, 1921. Explorer, Lieutenant, USNR

R. G. McConnell, 1921. Canadian explorer

Frank M. Chapman, 1921. Ornithologist

Herbert E. Gregory, 1921. Geologist

J. B. Tyrrell, 1921. Explorer

Joseph Strauss, 1919. Rear Admiral, USN

O. F. Cook, 1919. Plant explorer

Robert F. Griggs, 1919. Geographer

Walter T. Swingle, 1919. Plant explorer

Edward W. Nelson, 1919. Biologist

Stephen T. Mather, 1919. National Park Service Director

William H. Holmes, 1919. Curator

William H. Dall, 1919. Naturalist

Frank G. Carpenter, 1919. Journalist

George Kennan, 1917. Authority on Russia

Henry Pittier, 1917. Agriculturist

Hiram Bingham, 1917. Historian, explorer

Alfred H. Brooks, 1917. Geologist

FRANKLIN L. BURR AWARD

Mary C. Burr bequeathed a fund to the Society in memory of her father. Income is used to award cash prizes to leaders of the Society's expeditions and research projects for especially meritorious work in the field of geographic science.

Biruté M. F. Galdikas, 1981. Anthropologist

Fred A. Urquhart and Norah R. Urquhart, 1979. Entomologists

Jared M. Diamond, 1979. Ornithologist

Kenan T. Erim, 1973. Classical archaeologist

Dian J. Fossey, 1973. Zoologist

Maynard M. Miller, 1967. Glaciologist

Norman G. Dyhrenfurth, 1965. Mountaineer

Richard E. Leakey, 1965, 1973. Anthropologist

Helge Ingstad and Anne Stine Ingstad, 1964. Archaeologists

Barry C. Bishop, 1963. Mountaineer and glaciologist

Rear Adm. Donald B. MacMillan, 1963. Polar explorer

Jane Goodall, 1962, 1964. Zoologist

Louis S. B. Leakey and Mary D. Leakey, 1961. Anthropologists

Carl F. Miller, 1959. Archaeologist

Robert F. Griggs, 1956. Geographer

Mrs. Marie Peary Stafford, 1955. Scientific collaborator

Mrs. Robert E. Peary, 1955. Scientific collaborator

Neil M. Judd, 1955, 1963. Archaeologist

Harold E. Edgerton, 1952. Electrical engineer

Frank M. Setzler, 1950. Anthropologist

Charles P. Mountford, 1950. Anthropologist

Arthur A. Allen, 1948. Ornithologist

Edward A. Halbach, Francis J. Heyden, S. J., Carl W. Miller, and Charles H. Smiley, 1948. Astronomers

George Van Biesbroeck, 1947, 1948, 1953. Astronomer

Lyman J. Briggs, 1945, 1954, 1962. Chairman, Committee for Research and Exploration, National Geographic Society

Thomas A. Jagger, 1945. Engineer

Alexander Wetmore, 1944. Ornithologist

Mrs. Matthew W. Stirling, 1941. Archaeologist

Matthew W. Stirling, 1939, 1941, 1957. Archaeologist

Bradford Washburn, 1939, 1965. Geographer

Dr. and Mrs. William M. Mann, 1938. Zoologists

Capt. Randolph P. Williams, 1936. Aeronaut

Capt. Orvil A. Anderson, 1936. Aeronaut

Capt. Albert W. Stevens, 1933, 1936. Aeronaut

ARNOLD GUYOT MEMORIAL AWARD

This award, named for a distinguished professor of geology at Princeton University, was established from a bequest to recognize outstanding accomplishments in geology and paleontology.

Mary R. Dawson and Robert M. West, 1981. Vertebrate paleontologists

Richard L. Hay, 1978. Geologist

Robert W. Wilson, 1974. Paleontologist

Herbert Friedmann and William J. Morris, 1968. Paleontologists

SPECIAL NATIONAL GEOGRAPHIC SOCIETY AWARD

Heslon Mukiri Githua, 1968. Scientific collaborator

Library of Congress CIP Data

National geographic index, 1888-1988

  1. National geographic-Indexes. 2. Geography—Periodicals—Indexes. I. National Geographic Society (U.S.)
G1.N27 Suppl. 2   910'.5   88-33086
ISBN 0-87044-764-5
ISBN 0-87044-765-3 (deluxe ed.)

ARCTI

NORTH

NORTH AMERICA

ATLANTIC

PACIFIC

OCEAN

TROPIC OF CANCER

OCEAN

OCEAN

EQUATOR

SOUTH AMERICA

SOUT

TROPIC OF CAPRICORN

ATLAN

SOUTH PACIFIC OCEAN

OCE

Robinson Projection, Standard Parallels 38°N and 38°S
SCALE 1:37,250,000
1 CENTIMETER = 373 KILOMETERS OR 1 INCH = 588 MILES

STATUTE MILES

KILOMETERS

METRIC CONVERSIONS: 1 centimeter = 0.393701 = inches.
1 meter = 3.280840 = feet, 1 kilometer = 0.621371 = miles

ANTARCTIC CIRCLE